# Handbook of
# U.S. Labor
# Statistics

# HANDBOOK OF U.S. LABOR STATISTICS

## Employment, Earnings, Prices, Productivity, and Other Labor Data

**20th Edition**
2017

**Edited by Mary Meghan Ryan**

Bernan Press

Lanham, MD

Published in the United States of America
by Bernan Press, a wholly owned subsidiary of
The Rowman & Littlefield Publishing Group, Inc.
4501 Forbes Boulevard, Suite 200
Lanham, Maryland 20706

Bernan Press
800-462-6420
www.rowman.com

ISBN-13:   978-1-59888-901-7
eISBN-13:  978-1-59888-902-4

ISSN: 1526-2553

∞™ The paper used in this publication meets the minimum requirements of
American National Standard for Information Sciences—Permanence of
Paper for Printed Library Materials, ANSI/NISO Z39.48-1992.

Manufactured in the United States of America.

# CONTENTS

# LIST OF TABLES

## CHAPTER 1: POPULATION, LABOR FORCE, AND EMPLOYMENT STATUS

### *Population, Labor Force, and Employment Status*

## Employee Tenure

## Labor Force and Employment Characteristics of Selected Family Types

## Labor Force and Employment Characteristics of Foreign-Born Workers

## Labor Force and Employment Characteristics by Education

*Persons with a Disability: Labor Force Characteristics*

*Employment Situation of Veterans*

*Worker Displacement*

## CHAPTER 2: EMPLOYMENT, HOURS, AND EARNINGS

*Employment and Hours*

**CHAPTER 3: OCCUPATIONAL EMPLOYMENT AND WAGES**

**CHAPTER 4: LABOR FORCE AND EMPLOYMENT PROJECTIONS BY INDUSTRY AND OCCUPATION**

## CHAPTER 5: PRODUCTIVITY AND COSTS

## CHAPTER 6: COMPENSATION OF EMPLOYEES

### Employment Cost Index (ECI)

### Employer Costs for Employee Compensation (ECEC)

### Employee Benefits Survey

## CHAPTER 7: RECENT TRENDS IN THE LABOR MARKET

### Local Area Unemployment Statistics

# LIST OF FIGURES

# PREFACE

Bernan Press is pleased to present a compilation of Bureau of Labor Statistics (BLS) data in this 20th edition of its award-winning *Handbook of U.S Labor Statistics: Employment, Earnings, Prices, Productivity, and Other Labor Data.* BLS and the U.S. Census Bureau provide a treasure trove of historical information about all aspects of labor and employment in the United States. The current edition maintains the content of previous editions and updates the text with additional data and new features. The data in this *Handbook* are excellent sources of information for analysts in both government and the private sector.

The *Handbook* addresses many of the issues that are being discussed across the United States, such as high unemployment, employment projections for the future, the decline in income, the rapidly increasing costs of health care services, and the dramatic aging of the labor force. In addition, this publication provides an abundance of data on topics such as prices, productivity, consumer expenditures, occupational safety and health, volunteering, and much more.

The comprehensive and historical data presented in the *Handbook* allow the user to understand the background of current events and compare today's economy with previous years. Select data in this publication go back to 1913 and several tables have data going back to the 1940s.

## FEATURES OF THIS PUBLICATION

• Over 215 tables that present authoritative data on labor market statistics, including employment and unemployment, mass layoffs, prices, productivity, and data from the American Time Use Survey (ATUS).

• Each chapter is preceded by a figure that calls attention to noteworthy trends in the data.

• In addition to the figures, the introductory material for to each chapter also contains highlights of other salient data.

• The tables in each section are also preceded by notes and definitions, which contain concise descriptions of the data sources, concepts, definitions, and methodology from which the data are derived.

• The introductory notes also include references to more comprehensive reports. These reports provide additional data and more extensive descriptions of estimation methods, sampling, and reliability measures.

## NEW IN THIS EDITION

The 20th edition includes a new chapter titled "Volunteering in the United States". It includes information on who volunteered, where they volunteered, how often they volunteered, and how they got involved in volunteering. In addition, there are several new tables on occupational safety, work related injuries, and consumer expenditures.

## SOURCES OF ADDITIONAL INFORMATION

BLS data are primarily derived from surveys conducted by the federal government or through federal-state cooperative arrangements. The comparability of data over time can be affected by changes in the surveys, which are essential for keeping pace with the current structure of economic institutions and for taking advantage of improved survey techniques. Revisions of current data are also periodically made as a result of the availability of new information. In addition, some tables in this *Handbook* were dropped due to the data being from a one-time survey that is now outdated or due to the survey being entirely restructured. Introductory notes to each chapter summarize specific factors that may affect the data. In the tables, the ellipsis character ("…") indicates that data are not available.

More extensive methodological information, including further discussion of the sampling and estimation procedures used for each BLS program, is contained in the *BLS Handbook of Methods*. This publication is in the process of being updated, and completed chapters are available on the BLS Web site at <http://www.bls.gov>. Other sources of current data and analytical include the *Monthly Labor Review* and a daily Internet publication, *The Editor's Desk* (TED). All of these publications can be found on the BLS Web site as well. Other relevant publications, including those from the Census Bureau, are noted in the notes and definitions in each chapter.

## OTHER PUBLICATIONS BY BERNAN PRESS

The *Handbook of U.S. Labor Statistics: Employment, Earnings, Prices, Productivity, and Other Labor Data* is just one of a number of publications in Bernan Press's award-winning U.S. DataBook Series. Other titles include *The Almanac of American Education*; *Business Statistics of the United States: Patterns of Economic Change*; *Crime in the United States;* *Housing Statistics of the United States; States Profiles: The Population and Economy of Each U.S. State;* and *Vital Statistics of the United States: Births, Life Expectancy, Deaths, and Selected Health Data.* In addition, Bernan Press publishes *Employment, Hours, and Earnings: States and Areas* as a special edition of this *Handbook.* Each of these titles provides statistical information from official government sources.

# CHAPTER 1: POPULATION, LABOR FORCE, AND EMPLOYMENT STATUS

## HIGHLIGHTS

This chapter presents the detailed historical information collected in the Current Population Survey (CPS), a monthly survey of households that gathers data on the employment status of the population. Basic data on labor force, employment, and unemployment are shown for various characteristics of the population, including age, sex, race, Hispanic origin, and marital status.

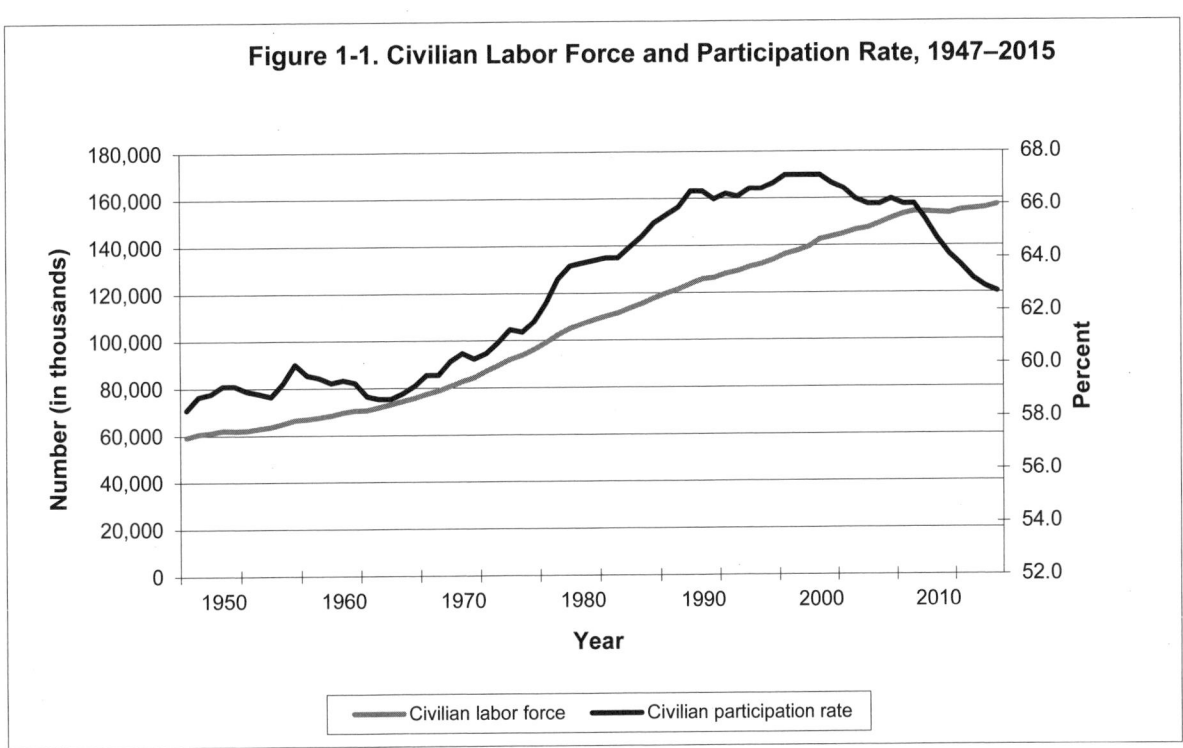

Over 157 million people were in the labor force in 2015 compared with less than 60 million people in 1947. While the labor force has grown considerably, the labor force participation rate has grown much slower increasing from 58.3 percent in 1947 to 62.7 percent in 2015. In fact, the labor force participation rate declined in 2015 for the seventh consecutive year. (See Table 1-1.)

## OTHER HIGHLIGHTS

- In 2015, employment increased 1.7 percent—slightly more than it did in 2014 or 2013. From 2008 through 2010, employment declined each year. The drop in employment was the steepest between 2008 and 2009 when it fell 3.8 percent. (See Table 1-1.)

- While the proportion of white men in the labor force declined from 1980 to 2015, the proportion of black women in the labor force increased from 4.9 percent to 6.5 percent. Hispanic representation in the labor force rose significantly increasing from 5.7 percent in 1980 to 16.6 percent in 2015. (See Table 1-7.)

- The labor force population rate remained stable or declined for each age group in 2015 except for those in the youngest and oldest age groups. The labor force participation rate for those 65 years increased again in 2015 after declining slightly in 2014. From 1999 to 2013, the labor force participation of those 65 years and older increased for fifteen consecutive years. In 2015, the labor force participation rate also increased for 16 to 19 year olds after declining in 2014. (See Table 1-8.)

## NOTES AND DEFINITIONS

### CURRENT POPULATION SURVEY OF HOUSEHOLDS

### Collection and Coverage

The Current Population Survey (CPS) is a monthly survey that analyzes and publishes statistics on the labor force, employment, and unemployment, classified by a variety of demographic, social, and economic characteristics. This survey is conducted by the Census Bureau for the Bureau of Labor Statistics (BLS). The information is collected from a probability sample of approximately 60,000 households. Respondents are interviewed to obtain information about the employment status of each household member age 16 years and over. Persons under 16 years of age are excluded from the official estimates because child labor laws, compulsory school attendance, and general social custom in the United States severely limit the types and amount of work that these children can do.

The inquiry relates to the household member's employment status during the calendar week, Sunday through Saturday that includes the 12th day of the month. This is known as the "reference week." Actual field interviewing is conducted during the following week (the week that contains the 19th day of the month).

### Concepts and Definitions

The concepts and definitions underlying the labor force data have been modified—but not substantially altered—since the inception of the survey in 1940 when it began as a Work Projects Administration program. Current definitions of some of the major concepts used in the CPS are described below.

*The civilian noninstitutional population* includes persons 16 years of age and over who reside in the 50 states and the District of Columbia who are not inmates of institutions (such as penal and mental facilities and homes for the aged) and who are not on active duty in the armed forces.

An *employed person* is any person who, during the reference week: (1) did any work at all (at least one hour) as a paid employees in their own business, profession, or on their own farm, or who worked 15 hours or more as an unpaid worker in an enterprise operated by a member of the family; and (2) any person who was not working but who had a job or business from which he or she was temporarily absent due to vacation, illness, bad weather, childcare problems, maternity or paternity leave, labor-management disputes, job training, or other family or personal reasons, despite whether the employee was being paid for the time off or was seeking other jobs.

Each employed person is counted only once, even if he or she holds more than one job. For purposes of occupation and industry classification, multiple jobholders are counted as being in the job at which they worked the greatest number of hours during the reference week.

Included in the total are employed citizens of foreign countries who were temporarily in the United States but not living on the premises of an embassy. Excluded are persons whose only activity during the reference week consisted of work around their own house (painting, repairing, or own home housework) or volunteer work for religious, charitable, and similar organizations.

*Unemployed persons* are all persons who had no employment during the reference week, but who were available for work (except for temporary illness) and had made specific efforts to find employment some time during the four-week period ending with the reference week. Persons who were waiting to be recalled to a job from which they had been laid off need not have been looking for work to be classified as unemployed.

*Reasons for unemployment* are divided into four major groups: (1) job losers, defined as (a) persons on temporary layoff, who have been given a date to return to work or who expect to return to work within six months; (b) permanent job losers, whose employment ended involuntarily and who began looking for work; and (c) persons who completed a temporary job and began looking for work after the job ended; (2) job leavers, defined as persons who quit or otherwise terminated their employment voluntarily and immediately began looking for work; (3) reentrants, defined as persons who previously worked but were out of the labor force prior to beginning their job search; and (4) new entrants, defined as persons who had never worked but were currently searching for work.

*Duration of unemployment* represents the length of time (through the current reference week) that persons classified as unemployed had been looking for work. For persons on layoff, duration of unemployment represents the number of full weeks they had been on layoff. Mean duration of unemployment is the arithmetic average computed from single weeks of unemployment; median duration of unemployment is the midpoint of a distribution of weeks of unemployment.

A *spell of unemployment* is a continuous period of unemployment of at least one week's duration and is terminated by either employment or withdrawal from the labor force.

*Extent of unemployment* refers to the number of workers and proportion of the labor force that were unemployed at some time during the year. The number of weeks unemployed is the total number of weeks accumulated during the entire calendar year.

The *unemployment rate* is the number of unemployed persons as a percentage of the civilian labor force.

The *civilian labor force* comprises all civilians classified as employed or unemployed.

The *participation rate* represents the proportion of the civilian noninstitutional population currently in the labor force.

The *employment-population ratio* represents the proportion of the population that is currently employed.

*Persons not in the labor force* are all persons in the civilian noninstitutional population who are neither employed nor unemployed. Information is collected about their desire for and availability to take a job at the time of the CPS interview, job search activity during the prior year, and reason for not looking for work during the four-week period ending with the reference week. Persons not in the labor force who want and are available for a job and who have looked for work within the past 12 months (or since the end of their last job, if they had held one within the past 12 months), but who are not currently looking, are designated as *marginally attached to the labor force*. The marginally attached are divided into those not currently looking because they believe their search would be futile—so-called *discouraged workers*—and those not currently looking for other reasons, such as family responsibilities, ill health, or lack of transportation.

*Discouraged workers* are defined as persons not in the labor force who want and are available for a job and who have looked for work sometime in the past 12 months (or since the end of their last job, if they held one within the past 12 months), but who are not currently looking because they believe that there are no jobs available or there are none for which they would qualify. The reasons for not currently looking for work include a person's belief that no work is available in his or her line of work or area; he or she could not find any work; he or she lacks necessary schooling, training, skills, or experience; employers would think he or she is too young or too old; or he or she would encounter hiring discrimination.

*Usual full- or part-time status* refers to hours usually worked per week. Full-time workers are those who usually work 35 hours or more (at all jobs). This group includes some individuals who worked less than 35 hours during the reference week for economic or noneconomic reasons. Part-time workers are those who usually work less than 35 hours per week (at all jobs), regardless of the number of hours worked during the reference week. These concepts are used to differentiate a person's normal schedule from his or her specific activity during the reference week. Unemployed persons who are looking for full-time work or who are on layoff from full-time jobs are counted as part of the full-time labor force; unemployed persons who are seeking part-time work or who are on layoff from part-time jobs are counted as part of the part-time labor force.

*Year-round, full-time workers* are workers who primarily worked at full-time jobs for 50 weeks or more during the preceding calendar year. Part-year workers worked either full- or part-time for 1 to 49 weeks.

*At work part-time for economic reasons*, sometimes called involuntary part-time, refers to individuals who gave an economic reason for working 1 to 34 hours during the reference week. Economic reasons include slack work or unfavorable business conditions, inability to find full-time work, and seasonal declines in demand. Those who usually work part-time must also indicate that they want and are available to work full-time to be classified as working part-time for economic reasons.

*At work part-time for noneconomic reasons* refers to persons who usually work part-time and were at work 1 to 34 hours during the reference week for a noneconomic reason. Noneconomic reasons include illness or other medical limitations, childcare problems or other family or personal obligations, school or training, retirement or Social Security limits on earnings, and being in a job where full-time work is less than 35 hours. This also includes workers who gave an economic reason for usually working 1 to 34 hours but said they do not want to work full-time or were unavailable for full-time work.

*Absences* are defined as instances in which persons who usually work 35 or more hours a week worked less than that during the reference period for reasons of illness or family obligations. Excluded are situations in which work was missed for vacation, holidays, or other reasons. The estimates are based on one-fourth of the sample only.

*Earnings* are a remuneration of a worker or group of workers for services performed during a specific period of time.

*Usual weekly earnings for wage and salary workers* include any overtime pay, commissions, or tips usually received (at the main job in the case of multiple jobholders). Earnings reported on a basis other than weekly (such as annual, monthly, or hourly) are converted to weekly. The term "usual" is as perceived by the respondent. If the respondent asks for a definition of usual, interviewers are instructed to define the term as more than half the weeks worked during the past 4 or 5 months.

*Minimum wage* refers to the prevailing federal minimum wage which was $7.25 in 2015. It increased from $6.55 per hour to $7.25 per hour on July 24, 2009 and has remained at that level since. Data are for wage and salary workers who were paid hourly rates and refer to a person's earnings at the sole or principal job.

A *multiple jobholder* is an employed person who, during the reference week, had two or more jobs as a wage and salary worker, was self-employed and also held a wage and salary job, or worked as an unpaid family worker and also held a wage and salary job.

Self-employed persons with multiple businesses and persons with multiple jobs as unpaid family workers are excluded.

*Occupation, industry, and class of worker* for members of the employed population are determined by the job held during the reference week. Persons with two or more jobs are classified as being in the job at which they worked the greatest number of hours. The unemployed are classified according to their last job. Beginning with data published in 2003, the systems used to classify occupational and industry data changed. They are currently based on the Standard Occupational Classification (SOC) system and the North American Industry Classification System (NAICS). (See the following section on historical comparability for a discussion of previous classification systems used in the CPS.) The class-of-worker breakdown assigns workers to one of the following categories: private and government wage and salary workers, self-employed workers, and unpaid family workers. Wage and salary workers receive wages, salaries, commissions, tips, or pay in kind from a private employer or from a government unit. Self-employed workers are those who work for profit or fees in their own businesses, professions, trades, or on their own farms. Only the unincorporated self-employed are included in the self-employed category in the class-of-worker typology. Self-employed workers who respond that their businesses are incorporated are included among wage and salary workers, because they are technically paid employees of a corporation. An unpaid family worker is a person working without pay for 15 hours or more per week on a farm or in a business operated by a member of the household to whom he or she is related by birth or marriage.

*Educational attainment* refers to years of school completed in regular schools, which include graded public, private, and parochial elementary, and high schools, whether day or night school. Colleges, universities, and professional schools are also included.

*Tenure* refers to length of time a worker has been continuously employed by his or her current employer. These data are collected through a supplement to the CPS. All employed persons were asked how long they had been working continuously for their present employer and, if the length of time was one or two years, a follow-up question was asked about the exact number of months. The follow-up question was included for the first time in the February 1996 supplement to the CPS. CPS supplements that obtained information on tenure in the January of 1983, 1987, and 1991 did not include the follow-up question. Prior to 1983, the question on tenure was asked differently. Data prior to 1983 are thus not strictly comparable to data for subsequent years.

*White, Black, and Asian* are terms used to describe the race of persons. Persons in these categories are those who selected that race only. Persons in the remaining race categories—American Indian or Alaskan Native, Native Hawaiian or Other Pacific Islander, and persons who selected more than one race category—are included in the estimates of total employment and unemployment but are not shown separately because the number

of survey respondents is too small to develop estimates of sufficient quality for monthly publication.

*Hispanic origin* refers to persons who identified themselves in the enumeration process as being Spanish, Hispanic, or Latino. Persons of Hispanic or Latino origin may be of any race.

*Single, never married; married, spouse present; and other marital status* are the terms used to define the marital status of individuals at the time of the CPS interview. Married, spouse present, applies to a husband and wife if both were living in the same household, even though one may be temporarily absent on business, vacation, in a hospital, etc. Other marital status applies to persons who are married, spouse absent; widowed; or divorced. Married, spouse absent relates to persons who are separated due to marital problems, as well as husbands and wives living apart because one was employed elsewhere, on duty with the armed forces, or any other reason.

A *household* consists of all persons—related family members and all unrelated persons—who occupy a housing unit and have no other usual address. A house, an apartment, a group of rooms, or a single room is regarded as a housing unit when occupied or intended for occupancy as separate living quarters.

A *householder* is the person (or one of the persons) in whose name the housing unit is owned or rented. The term is not applied to either husbands or wives in married-couple families; it refers only to persons in families maintained by either men or women without a spouse.

A *family* is defined as a group of two or more persons residing together who are related by birth, marriage, or adoption. All such persons are considered as members of one family. Families are classified as either married-couple families or families maintained by women or men without spouses.

*Children* refer to "own" children of the husband, wife, or person maintaining the family, including sons and daughters, stepchildren, and adopted children. Excluded are other related children, such as grandchildren, nieces, nephews, cousins, and unrelated children.

Persons are referred to as *disabled* if they answer yes to the following questions: 1.) Are you deaf or do you have serious difficulty hearing? 2.) Are you blind or do you serious difficulty seeing even when wearing glasses? 3.) Because of a physical, mental, or emotional condition, do you have serious difficulty concentrating, remembering, or making decisions? 4.) Do you have serious difficulty walking or climbing stairs? 5.) Do you have difficulty dressing or bathing? 6.) Because of a physical, mental, or emotional condition, do you have difficulty doing errands alone such as visiting a doctor's office or shopping? Labor force measures are only tabulated for persons 16 years and over.

*Veterans* are men and women who previously served on active duty in the U.S. Armed Forces and who were civilians at the time they were surveyed.

*Nonveterans* are men and women who never served on active duty in the U.S. Armed Forces.

*World War II, Korean War, Vietnam-era, and Gulf War-era veterans* are men and women who served in the Armed Forces during these periods, regardless of where they served.

*Veterans of other service periods* are men and women who served in the Armed Forces at any time other than World War II, the Korean War, the Vietnam era, or the Gulf War era.

*Veteran status* is obtained from responses to the question, "Did you ever serve on active duty in the U.S. Armed Forces?"

*Period of service* is obtained from answers to the question asked of veterans, "When did you serve on active duty in the U.S. Armed Forces?" The following service periods are identified:

Gulf War era II — September 2001–present

Gulf War era I — August 1990–August 2001

Vietnam era — August 1964–April 1975

Korean War — July 1950–January 1955

World War II — December 1941–December 1946

Other service periods — All other time periods

*Veterans who served in Iraq, Afghanistan, or both* are individuals who served in Iraq at any time since March 2003, in Afghanistan at any time since October 2001, or in both locations.

*Presence of service-connected disability* is determined by answers to the question, "Has the Department of Veterans Affairs (VA) or Department of Defense (DoD) determined that you have a service-connected disability, that is, a health condition or impairment caused or made worse by any of your military service?"

*Service-connected disability rating* is based on answers to the question, "What is your current service connected disability rating?" Answers can range from 0 to 100 percent, in increments of 10 percentage points.

*Displaced workers* are wage and salary workers 20 years of age and older who lost or left jobs because their plant or company closed or moved, there was insufficient work for them to do, or their position or shift was abolished. Data are often presented for long-tenured displaced workers—those who had worked for their employer for 3 or more years at the time of displacement.

## Historical Comparability

While the concepts and methods are very similar to those used for the inaugural survey in 1940, a number of changes have been made over the years to improve the accuracy and usefulness of the data. Only recent major changes are described here.

Major changes to the CPS, such as the complete redesign of the questionnaire and the use of computer-assisted interviewing for the entire survey, were introduced in 1994. In addition, there were revisions to some of the labor force concepts and definitions, including the implementation of changes recommended in 1979 by the National Commission on Employment and Unemployment Statistics (NCEUS, also known as the Levitan Commission). Some of the major changes to the survey at this time were:

1. The introduction of a redesigned and automated questionnaire. The CPS questionnaire was totally redesigned in order to obtain more accurate, comprehensive, and relevant information, and to take advantage of state-of-the-art computer interviewing techniques. Computer-assisted interviewing has important benefits most notably that it facilitates the use of a relatively complex questionnaire that incorporates complicated skip patterns and standardized follow-up questions. Additionally, certain questions are automatically tailored to the individual's situation to make them more understandable.

2. Official labor force measures were defined more precisely. While the labor force status of most people is straightforward, some persons are more difficult to classify correctly, especially if they are engaged in activities that are relatively informal or intermittent. Many of the changes to the questionnaire were made to deal with such cases. This was accomplished by rewording and adding questions to conform more precisely to the official definitions, making the questions easier to understand and answer, minimizing reliance on volunteered responses, revising response categories, and taking advantage of the benefits of an automated interview.

3. The amount of data available was expanded. The questionnaire redesign also made it possible to collect several types of data on topics such as multiple job holding and usual hours regularly for the first time.

4. Several labor definitions were modified. The most important definitional changes concerned discouraged workers. The Levitan Commission had criticized the former definition because it was based on a subjective desire for work and on somewhat arbitrary assumptions about an individual's availability to take a job. As a result of the redesign, two requirements were added: For persons to qualify as discouraged they must have engaged in some job search within the past year (or since they last worked, if they worked within the past year), and they must be currently available to take a job. (Formerly, availability was inferred from responses to other questions;

now, there is a direct question.) Also, beginning in January 1994, questions on this subject are asked of the full CPS sample, permitting estimates of the number of discouraged workers to be published monthly (rather than quarterly).

Beginning in January 2003, several other changes were introduced into the CPS. These changes included the following:

1. Population controls that reflected the results of the 2000 census were introduced into the monthly CPS estimation process. The new controls increased the size of the civilian noninstitutional population by about 3.5 million in May 2002. As a result, they also increased the estimated numbers of people unemployed and employed. Because the increases were roughly proportional, however, the overall unemployment rate did not change significantly. Data from January 2000 through December 2002 were revised to reflect these new controls. Over and above these revisions, the U.S. Census Bureau introduced another large upward adjustment to the controls as part of its annual update of population estimates for 2003. These updated population estimates were not available in time to incorporate them into the revised population controls for January 2000 to December 2002. Thus, the data on employment and unemployment levels for January 2003 (and beyond) are not strictly comparable with those for earlier months. The unemployment rate and other ratios, however, were not substantially affected by the 2003 population control revisions.

2. Questions on race and Hispanic origin were modified to comply with the new standards for maintaining, collecting, and presenting federal data on race and ethnicity for federal statistical agencies. The questions were reworded to indicate that individuals could select more than once race category and to convey more clearly that individuals should report their own perception of what race is. These changes had no impact on the overall civilian noninstitutional population and civilian labor force. However, they did reduce the population and labor force levels of Whites, Blacks, and Asians beginning in January 2003.

3. Improvements were introduced to both the second stage and composite weighting procedures. These changes adapted the weighting procedures to the new race/ethnic classification system and enhanced the stability over time for demographic groups. The second-stage weighting procedure substantially reduced the variability of estimates and corrected, to some extent, for CPS underreporting.

## Changes in the Occupational and Industrial Classification System

In January 2003, the CPS adopted the 2002 census industry and occupational classification systems, which were derived, respectively, from the 2002 North American Industry Classification System (NAICS) and the 2000 Standard Occupational Classification (SOC) system. The 1990 Census occupational and industry classifications were replaced. The introduction of the new industry and occupational classification systems in 2003 created a complete break in comparability at all levels of industry and occupation aggregation. The composition of detailed occupations and industries changed substantially in the 2002 systems compared with the 1990 systems, as did the structure for aggregating them into major groups. Therefore, any comparisons of data on the different classifications are not possible without major adjustments.

Historical employment series on the 2002 Census classifications are available at broad levels of occupational and industry aggregation back to 1983. However, historical employment series at the detailed occupational and industry levels on the 2002 classifications are available back to 2000 only.

In 2009, BLS began using the 2007 Census industry classification system, which was derived from the 2007 NAICS series, and still uses it currently. The 2010 Census occupational classification was introduced with data for January 2011 and replaced an earlier version that was based on the 2000 SOC. As a result of the classification change, occupational data beginning with January 2011 are not strictly comparable with earlier years. Although the names of the broad- and intermediate-level occupational groups in the 2010 Census occupational classification remained the same, some detailed occupations were re-classified between broader groups, affecting comparability over time.

The Current Population Survey currently uses the 2010 Census occupational classification and, beginning with data for January 2014, the 2012 Census industry classification. These classifications were derived from the 2010 Standard Occupational Classification (SOC) and the 2012 North American Industry Classification System (NAICS), respectively, to meet the special classification needs of demographic household surveys.

### Sources of Additional Information

A complete description of sampling and estimation procedures and further information on the impact of historical changes in the surveys can be found in the updated version of Chapter 1 of the *BLS Handbook of Methods*. This can be found on the BLS Web site at <http://www.bls.gov/opub/hom/>.

## Table 1-1.  Employment Status of the Civilian Noninstitutional Population, 1947–2015

(Thousands of people, percent.)

| Year | Civilian noninstitutional population | Civilian labor force | | | | | | | | Not in labor force |
|---|---|---|---|---|---|---|---|---|---|---|
| | | Total | Participation rate | Employed | | | | Unemployed | | |
| | | | | Total | Percent of population | Agriculture | Nonagricultural industries | Number | Unemploy-ment rate | |
| 1947 | 101 827 | 59 350 | 58.3 | 57 038 | 56.0 | 7 890 | 49 148 | 2 311 | 3.9 | 42 477 |
| 1948 | 103 068 | 60 621 | 58.8 | 58 343 | 56.6 | 7 629 | 50 714 | 2 276 | 3.8 | 42 447 |
| 1949 | 103 994 | 61 286 | 58.9 | 57 651 | 55.4 | 7 658 | 49 993 | 3 637 | 5.9 | 42 708 |
| 1950 | 104 995 | 62 208 | 59.2 | 58 918 | 56.1 | 7 160 | 51 758 | 3 288 | 5.3 | 42 787 |
| 1951 | 104 621 | 62 017 | 59.2 | 59 961 | 57.3 | 6 726 | 53 235 | 2 055 | 3.3 | 42 604 |
| 1952 | 105 231 | 62 138 | 59.0 | 60 250 | 57.3 | 6 500 | 53 749 | 1 883 | 3.0 | 43 093 |
| 1953 | 107 056 | 63 015 | 58.9 | 61 179 | 57.1 | 6 260 | 54 919 | 1 834 | 2.9 | 44 041 |
| 1954 | 108 321 | 63 643 | 58.8 | 60 109 | 55.5 | 6 205 | 53 904 | 3 532 | 5.5 | 44 678 |
| 1955 | 109 683 | 65 023 | 59.3 | 62 170 | 56.7 | 6 450 | 55 722 | 2 852 | 4.4 | 44 660 |
| 1956 | 110 954 | 66 552 | 60.0 | 63 799 | 57.5 | 6 283 | 57 514 | 2 750 | 4.1 | 44 402 |
| 1957 | 112 265 | 66 929 | 59.6 | 64 071 | 57.1 | 5 947 | 58 123 | 2 859 | 4.3 | 45 336 |
| 1958 | 113 727 | 67 639 | 59.5 | 63 036 | 55.4 | 5 586 | 57 450 | 4 602 | 6.8 | 46 088 |
| 1959 | 115 329 | 68 369 | 59.3 | 64 630 | 56.0 | 5 565 | 59 065 | 3 740 | 5.5 | 46 960 |
| 1960 | 117 245 | 69 628 | 59.4 | 65 778 | 56.1 | 5 458 | 60 318 | 3 852 | 5.5 | 47 617 |
| 1961 | 118 771 | 70 459 | 59.3 | 65 746 | 55.4 | 5 200 | 60 546 | 4 714 | 6.7 | 48 312 |
| 1962 | 120 153 | 70 614 | 58.8 | 66 702 | 55.5 | 4 944 | 61 759 | 3 911 | 5.5 | 49 539 |
| 1963 | 122 416 | 71 833 | 58.7 | 67 762 | 55.4 | 4 687 | 63 076 | 4 070 | 5.7 | 50 583 |
| 1964 | 124 485 | 73 091 | 58.7 | 69 305 | 55.7 | 4 523 | 64 782 | 3 786 | 5.2 | 51 394 |
| 1965 | 126 513 | 74 455 | 58.9 | 71 088 | 56.2 | 4 361 | 66 726 | 3 366 | 4.5 | 52 058 |
| 1966 | 128 058 | 75 770 | 59.2 | 72 895 | 56.9 | 3 979 | 68 915 | 2 875 | 3.8 | 52 288 |
| 1967 | 129 874 | 77 347 | 59.6 | 74 372 | 57.3 | 3 844 | 70 527 | 2 975 | 3.8 | 52 527 |
| 1968 | 132 028 | 78 737 | 59.6 | 75 920 | 57.5 | 3 817 | 72 103 | 2 817 | 3.6 | 53 291 |
| 1969 | 134 335 | 80 734 | 60.1 | 77 902 | 58.0 | 3 606 | 74 296 | 2 832 | 3.5 | 53 602 |
| 1970 | 137 085 | 82 771 | 60.4 | 78 678 | 57.4 | 3 463 | 75 215 | 4 093 | 4.9 | 54 315 |
| 1971 | 140 216 | 84 382 | 60.2 | 79 367 | 56.6 | 3 394 | 75 972 | 5 016 | 5.9 | 55 834 |
| 1972 | 144 126 | 87 034 | 60.4 | 82 153 | 57.0 | 3 484 | 78 669 | 4 882 | 5.6 | 57 091 |
| 1973 | 147 096 | 89 429 | 60.8 | 85 064 | 57.8 | 3 470 | 81 594 | 4 365 | 4.9 | 57 667 |
| 1974 | 150 120 | 91 949 | 61.3 | 86 794 | 57.8 | 3 515 | 83 279 | 5 156 | 5.6 | 58 171 |
| 1975 | 153 153 | 93 775 | 61.2 | 85 846 | 56.1 | 3 408 | 82 438 | 7 929 | 8.5 | 59 377 |
| 1976 | 156 150 | 96 158 | 61.6 | 88 752 | 56.8 | 3 331 | 85 421 | 7 406 | 7.7 | 59 991 |
| 1977 | 159 033 | 99 009 | 62.3 | 92 017 | 57.9 | 3 283 | 88 734 | 6 991 | 7.1 | 60 025 |
| 1978 | 161 910 | 102 251 | 63.2 | 96 048 | 59.3 | 3 387 | 92 661 | 6 202 | 6.1 | 59 659 |
| 1979 | 164 863 | 104 962 | 63.7 | 98 824 | 59.9 | 3 347 | 95 477 | 6 137 | 5.8 | 59 900 |
| 1980 | 167 745 | 106 940 | 63.8 | 99 303 | 59.2 | 3 364 | 95 938 | 7 637 | 7.1 | 60 806 |
| 1981 | 170 130 | 108 670 | 63.9 | 100 397 | 59.0 | 3 368 | 97 030 | 8 273 | 7.6 | 61 460 |
| 1982 | 172 271 | 110 204 | 64.0 | 99 526 | 57.8 | 3 401 | 96 125 | 10 678 | 9.7 | 62 067 |
| 1983 | 174 215 | 111 550 | 64.0 | 100 834 | 57.9 | 3 383 | 97 450 | 10 717 | 9.6 | 62 665 |
| 1984 | 176 383 | 113 544 | 64.4 | 105 005 | 59.5 | 3 321 | 101 685 | 8 539 | 7.5 | 62 839 |
| 1985 | 178 206 | 115 461 | 64.8 | 107 150 | 60.1 | 3 179 | 103 971 | 8 312 | 7.2 | 62 744 |
| 1986 | 180 587 | 117 834 | 65.3 | 109 597 | 60.7 | 3 163 | 106 434 | 8 237 | 7.0 | 62 752 |
| 1987 | 182 753 | 119 865 | 65.6 | 112 440 | 61.5 | 3 208 | 109 232 | 7 425 | 6.2 | 62 888 |
| 1988 | 184 613 | 121 669 | 65.9 | 114 968 | 62.3 | 3 169 | 111 800 | 6 701 | 5.5 | 62 944 |
| 1989 | 186 393 | 123 869 | 66.5 | 117 342 | 63.0 | 3 199 | 114 142 | 6 528 | 5.3 | 62 523 |
| 1990 | 189 164 | 125 840 | 66.5 | 118 793 | 62.8 | 3 223 | 115 570 | 7 047 | 5.6 | 63 324 |
| 1991 | 190 925 | 126 346 | 66.2 | 117 718 | 61.7 | 3 269 | 114 449 | 8 628 | 6.8 | 64 578 |
| 1992 | 192 805 | 128 105 | 66.4 | 118 492 | 61.5 | 3 247 | 115 245 | 9 613 | 7.5 | 64 700 |
| 1993 | 194 838 | 129 200 | 66.3 | 120 259 | 61.7 | 3 115 | 117 144 | 8 940 | 6.9 | 65 638 |
| 1994 | 196 814 | 131 056 | 66.6 | 123 060 | 62.5 | 3 409 | 119 651 | 7 996 | 6.1 | 65 758 |
| 1995 | 198 584 | 132 304 | 66.6 | 124 900 | 62.9 | 3 440 | 121 460 | 7 404 | 5.6 | 66 280 |
| 1996 | 200 591 | 133 943 | 66.8 | 126 708 | 63.2 | 3 443 | 123 264 | 7 236 | 5.4 | 66 647 |
| 1997 | 203 133 | 136 297 | 67.1 | 129 558 | 63.8 | 3 399 | 126 159 | 6 739 | 4.9 | 66 837 |
| 1998 | 205 220 | 137 673 | 67.1 | 131 463 | 64.1 | 3 378 | 128 085 | 6 210 | 4.5 | 67 547 |
| 1999 | 207 753 | 139 368 | 67.1 | 133 488 | 64.3 | 3 281 | 130 207 | 5 880 | 4.2 | 68 385 |
| 2000 | 212 577 | 142 583 | 67.1 | 136 891 | 64.4 | 2 464 | 134 427 | 5 692 | 4.0 | 69 994 |
| 2001 | 215 092 | 143 734 | 66.8 | 136 933 | 63.7 | 2 299 | 134 635 | 6 801 | 4.7 | 71 359 |
| 2002 | 217 570 | 144 863 | 66.6 | 136 485 | 62.7 | 2 311 | 134 174 | 8 378 | 5.8 | 72 707 |
| 2003 | 221 168 | 146 510 | 66.2 | 137 736 | 62.3 | 2 275 | 135 461 | 8 774 | 6.0 | 74 658 |
| 2004 | 223 357 | 147 401 | 66.0 | 139 252 | 62.3 | 2 232 | 137 020 | 8 149 | 5.5 | 75 956 |
| 2005 | 226 082 | 149 320 | 66.0 | 141 730 | 62.7 | 2 197 | 139 532 | 7 591 | 5.1 | 76 762 |
| 2006 | 228 815 | 151 428 | 66.2 | 144 427 | 63.1 | 2 206 | 142 221 | 7 001 | 4.6 | 77 387 |
| 2007 | 231 867 | 153 124 | 66.0 | 146 047 | 63.0 | 2 095 | 143 952 | 7 078 | 4.6 | 78 743 |
| 2008 | 233 788 | 154 287 | 66.0 | 145 362 | 62.2 | 2 168 | 143 194 | 8 924 | 5.8 | 79 501 |
| 2009 | 235 801 | 154 142 | 65.4 | 139 877 | 59.3 | 2 103 | 137 775 | 14 265 | 9.3 | 81 659 |
| 2010 | 237 830 | 153 889 | 64.7 | 139 064 | 58.5 | 2 206 | 136 858 | 14 825 | 9.6 | 83 941 |
| 2011 | 239 618 | 153 617 | 64.1 | 139 869 | 58.4 | 2 254 | 137 615 | 13 747 | 8.9 | 86 001 |
| 2012 | 243 284 | 154 975 | 63.7 | 142 469 | 58.6 | 2 186 | 140 283 | 12 506 | 8.1 | 88 310 |
| 2013 | 245 679 | 155 389 | 63.2 | 143 929 | 58.6 | 2 130 | 141 799 | 11 460 | 7.4 | 90 290 |
| 2014 | 247 947 | 155 922 | 62.9 | 146 305 | 59.0 | 2 237 | 144 068 | 9 617 | 6.2 | 92 025 |
| 2015 | 250 801 | 157 130 | 62.7 | 148 834 | 59.3 | 2 422 | 146 411 | 8 296 | 5.3 | 93 671 |

## Table 1-2. Employment Status of the Civilian Noninstitutional Population, by Sex, 1975–2015

(Thousands of people, percent.)

| Sex and year | Civilian noninstitutional population | Civilian labor force | | Employed | | | | Unemployed | | Not in labor force |
|---|---|---|---|---|---|---|---|---|---|---|
| | | Total | Participation rate | Total | Percent of population | Agriculture | Non-agricultural industries | Number | Unemployment rate | |
| **Men** | | | | | | | | | | |
| 1975 | 72 291 | 56 299 | 77.9 | 51 857 | 71.7 | 2 824 | 49 032 | 4 442 | 7.9 | 15 993 |
| 1976 | 73 759 | 57 174 | 77.5 | 53 138 | 72.0 | 2 744 | 50 394 | 4 036 | 7.1 | 16 585 |
| 1977 | 75 193 | 58 396 | 77.7 | 54 728 | 72.8 | 2 671 | 52 057 | 3 667 | 6.3 | 16 797 |
| 1978 | 76 576 | 59 620 | 77.9 | 56 479 | 73.8 | 2 718 | 53 761 | 3 142 | 5.3 | 16 956 |
| 1979 | 78 020 | 60 726 | 77.8 | 57 607 | 73.8 | 2 686 | 54 921 | 3 120 | 5.1 | 17 293 |
| 1980 | 79 398 | 61 453 | 77.4 | 57 186 | 72.0 | 2 709 | 54 477 | 4 267 | 6.9 | 17 945 |
| 1981 | 80 511 | 61 974 | 77.0 | 57 397 | 71.3 | 2 700 | 54 697 | 4 577 | 7.4 | 18 537 |
| 1982 | 81 523 | 62 450 | 76.6 | 56 271 | 69.0 | 2 736 | 53 534 | 6 179 | 9.9 | 19 073 |
| 1983 | 82 531 | 63 047 | 76.4 | 56 787 | 68.8 | 2 704 | 54 083 | 6 260 | 9.9 | 19 484 |
| 1984 | 83 605 | 63 835 | 76.4 | 59 091 | 70.7 | 2 668 | 56 423 | 4 744 | 7.4 | 19 771 |
| 1985 | 84 469 | 64 411 | 76.3 | 59 891 | 70.9 | 2 535 | 57 356 | 4 521 | 7.0 | 20 058 |
| 1986 | 85 798 | 65 422 | 76.3 | 60 892 | 71.0 | 2 511 | 58 381 | 4 530 | 6.9 | 20 376 |
| 1987 | 86 899 | 66 207 | 76.2 | 62 107 | 71.5 | 2 543 | 59 564 | 4 101 | 6.2 | 20 692 |
| 1988 | 87 857 | 66 927 | 76.2 | 63 273 | 72.0 | 2 493 | 60 780 | 3 655 | 5.5 | 20 930 |
| 1989 | 88 762 | 67 840 | 76.4 | 64 315 | 72.5 | 2 513 | 61 802 | 3 525 | 5.2 | 20 923 |
| 1990 | 90 377 | 69 011 | 76.4 | 65 104 | 72.0 | 2 546 | 62 559 | 3 906 | 5.7 | 21 367 |
| 1991 | 91 278 | 69 168 | 75.8 | 64 223 | 70.4 | 2 589 | 61 634 | 4 946 | 7.2 | 22 110 |
| 1992 | 92 270 | 69 964 | 75.8 | 64 440 | 69.8 | 2 575 | 61 866 | 5 523 | 7.9 | 22 306 |
| 1993 | 93 332 | 70 404 | 75.4 | 65 349 | 70.0 | 2 478 | 62 871 | 5 055 | 7.2 | 22 927 |
| 1994 | 94 355 | 70 817 | 75.1 | 66 450 | 70.4 | 2 554 | 63 896 | 4 367 | 6.2 | 23 538 |
| 1995 | 95 178 | 71 360 | 75.0 | 67 377 | 70.8 | 2 559 | 64 818 | 3 983 | 5.6 | 23 818 |
| 1996 | 96 206 | 72 087 | 74.9 | 68 207 | 70.9 | 2 573 | 65 634 | 3 880 | 5.4 | 24 119 |
| 1997 | 97 715 | 73 261 | 75.0 | 69 685 | 71.3 | 2 552 | 67 133 | 3 577 | 4.9 | 24 454 |
| 1998 | 98 758 | 73 959 | 74.9 | 70 693 | 71.6 | 2 553 | 68 140 | 3 266 | 4.4 | 24 799 |
| 1999 | 99 722 | 74 512 | 74.7 | 71 446 | 71.6 | 2 432 | 69 014 | 3 066 | 4.1 | 25 210 |
| 2000 | 101 964 | 76 280 | 74.8 | 73 305 | 71.9 | 1 861 | 71 444 | 2 975 | 3.9 | 25 684 |
| 2001 | 103 282 | 76 886 | 74.4 | 73 196 | 70.9 | 1 708 | 71 488 | 3 690 | 4.8 | 26 396 |
| 2002 | 104 585 | 77 500 | 74.1 | 72 903 | 69.7 | 1 724 | 71 179 | 4 597 | 5.9 | 27 085 |
| 2003 | 106 435 | 78 238 | 73.5 | 73 332 | 68.9 | 1 695 | 71 636 | 4 906 | 6.3 | 28 197 |
| 2004 | 107 710 | 78 980 | 73.3 | 74 524 | 69.2 | 1 687 | 72 838 | 4 456 | 5.6 | 28 730 |
| 2005 | 109 151 | 80 033 | 73.3 | 75 973 | 69.6 | 1 654 | 74 319 | 4 059 | 5.1 | 29 119 |
| 2006 | 110 605 | 81 255 | 73.5 | 77 502 | 70.1 | 1 663 | 75 838 | 3 753 | 4.6 | 29 350 |
| 2007 | 112 173 | 82 136 | 73.2 | 78 254 | 69.8 | 1 604 | 76 650 | 3 882 | 4.7 | 30 036 |
| 2008 | 113 113 | 82 520 | 73.0 | 77 486 | 68.5 | 1 650 | 75 836 | 5 033 | 6.1 | 30 593 |
| 2009 | 114 136 | 82 123 | 72.0 | 73 670 | 64.5 | 1 607 | 72 062 | 8 453 | 10.3 | 32 013 |
| 2010 | 115 174 | 81 985 | 71.2 | 73 359 | 63.7 | 1 665 | 71 694 | 8 626 | 10.5 | 33 189 |
| 2011 | 116 317 | 81 975 | 70.5 | 74 290 | 63.9 | 1 698 | 72 592 | 7 684 | 9.4 | 34 343 |
| 2012 | 117 343 | 82 327 | 70.2 | 75 555 | 64.4 | 1 626 | 73 930 | 6 771 | 8.2 | 35 017 |
| 2013 | 118 555 | 82 667 | 69.7 | 76 353 | 64.4 | 1 611 | 74 742 | 6 314 | 7.6 | 35 889 |
| 2014 | 119 748 | 82 882 | 69.2 | 77 692 | 64.9 | 1 685 | 76 007 | 5 190 | 6.3 | 36 865 |
| 2015 | 121 101 | 83 620 | 69.1 | 79 131 | 65.3 | 1 826 | 77 305 | 4 490 | 5.4 | 37 481 |
| **Women** | | | | | | | | | | |
| 1975 | 80 860 | 37 475 | 46.3 | 33 989 | 42.0 | 584 | 33 404 | 3 486 | 9.3 | 43 386 |
| 1976 | 82 390 | 38 983 | 47.3 | 35 615 | 43.2 | 588 | 35 027 | 3 369 | 8.6 | 43 406 |
| 1977 | 83 840 | 40 613 | 48.4 | 37 289 | 44.5 | 612 | 36 677 | 3 324 | 8.2 | 43 227 |
| 1978 | 85 334 | 42 631 | 50.0 | 39 569 | 46.4 | 669 | 38 900 | 3 061 | 7.2 | 42 703 |
| 1979 | 86 843 | 44 235 | 50.9 | 41 217 | 47.5 | 661 | 40 556 | 3 018 | 6.8 | 42 608 |
| 1980 | 88 348 | 45 487 | 51.5 | 42 117 | 47.7 | 656 | 41 461 | 3 370 | 7.4 | 42 861 |
| 1981 | 89 618 | 46 696 | 52.1 | 43 000 | 48.0 | 667 | 42 333 | 3 696 | 7.9 | 42 922 |
| 1982 | 90 748 | 47 755 | 52.6 | 43 256 | 47.7 | 665 | 42 591 | 4 499 | 9.4 | 42 993 |
| 1983 | 91 684 | 48 503 | 52.9 | 44 047 | 48.0 | 680 | 43 367 | 4 457 | 9.2 | 43 181 |
| 1984 | 92 778 | 49 709 | 53.6 | 45 915 | 49.5 | 653 | 45 262 | 3 794 | 7.6 | 43 068 |
| 1985 | 93 736 | 51 050 | 54.5 | 47 259 | 50.4 | 644 | 46 615 | 3 791 | 7.4 | 42 686 |
| 1986 | 94 789 | 52 413 | 55.3 | 48 706 | 51.4 | 652 | 48 054 | 3 707 | 7.1 | 42 376 |
| 1987 | 95 853 | 53 658 | 56.0 | 50 334 | 52.5 | 666 | 49 668 | 3 324 | 6.2 | 42 195 |
| 1988 | 96 756 | 54 742 | 56.6 | 51 696 | 53.4 | 676 | 51 020 | 3 046 | 5.6 | 42 014 |
| 1989 | 97 630 | 56 030 | 57.4 | 53 027 | 54.3 | 687 | 52 341 | 3 003 | 5.4 | 41 601 |
| 1990 | 98 787 | 56 829 | 57.5 | 53 689 | 54.3 | 678 | 53 011 | 3 140 | 5.5 | 41 957 |
| 1991 | 99 646 | 57 178 | 57.4 | 53 496 | 53.7 | 680 | 52 815 | 3 683 | 6.4 | 42 468 |
| 1992 | 100 535 | 58 141 | 57.8 | 54 052 | 53.8 | 672 | 53 380 | 4 090 | 7.0 | 42 394 |
| 1993 | 101 506 | 58 795 | 57.9 | 54 910 | 54.1 | 637 | 54 273 | 3 885 | 6.6 | 42 711 |
| 1994 | 102 460 | 60 239 | 58.8 | 56 610 | 55.3 | 855 | 55 755 | 3 629 | 6.0 | 42 221 |
| 1995 | 103 406 | 60 944 | 58.9 | 57 523 | 55.6 | 881 | 56 642 | 3 421 | 5.6 | 42 462 |
| 1996 | 104 385 | 61 857 | 59.3 | 58 501 | 56.0 | 871 | 57 630 | 3 356 | 5.4 | 42 528 |
| 1997 | 105 418 | 63 036 | 59.8 | 59 873 | 56.8 | 847 | 59 026 | 3 162 | 5.0 | 42 382 |
| 1998 | 106 462 | 63 714 | 59.8 | 60 771 | 57.1 | 825 | 59 945 | 2 944 | 4.6 | 42 748 |
| 1999 | 108 031 | 64 855 | 60.0 | 62 042 | 57.4 | 849 | 61 193 | 2 814 | 4.3 | 43 175 |
| 2000 | 110 613 | 66 303 | 59.9 | 63 586 | 57.5 | 602 | 62 983 | 2 717 | 4.1 | 44 310 |
| 2001 | 111 811 | 66 848 | 59.8 | 63 737 | 57.0 | 591 | 63 147 | 3 111 | 4.7 | 44 962 |
| 2002 | 112 985 | 67 363 | 59.6 | 63 582 | 56.3 | 587 | 62 995 | 3 781 | 5.6 | 45 621 |
| 2003 | 114 733 | 68 272 | 59.5 | 64 404 | 56.1 | 580 | 63 824 | 3 868 | 5.7 | 46 461 |
| 2004 | 115 647 | 68 421 | 59.2 | 64 728 | 56.0 | 546 | 64 182 | 3 694 | 5.4 | 47 225 |
| 2005 | 116 931 | 69 288 | 59.3 | 65 757 | 56.2 | 544 | 65 213 | 3 531 | 5.1 | 47 643 |
| 2006 | 118 210 | 70 173 | 59.4 | 66 925 | 56.6 | 543 | 66 382 | 3 247 | 4.6 | 48 037 |
| 2007 | 119 694 | 70 988 | 59.3 | 67 792 | 56.6 | 490 | 67 302 | 3 196 | 4.5 | 48 707 |
| 2008 | 120 675 | 71 767 | 59.5 | 67 876 | 56.2 | 518 | 67 358 | 3 891 | 5.4 | 48 908 |
| 2009 | 121 665 | 72 019 | 59.2 | 66 208 | 54.4 | 496 | 65 712 | 5 811 | 8.1 | 49 646 |
| 2010 | 122 656 | 71 904 | 58.6 | 65 705 | 53.6 | 541 | 65 164 | 6 199 | 8.6 | 50 752 |
| 2011 | 123 300 | 71 642 | 58.1 | 65 579 | 53.2 | 556 | 65 023 | 6 063 | 8.5 | 51 658 |
| 2012 | 125 941 | 72 648 | 57.7 | 66 914 | 53.1 | 560 | 66 353 | 5 734 | 7.9 | 53 293 |
| 2013 | 127 124 | 72 722 | 57.2 | 67 577 | 53.2 | 519 | 67 058 | 5 146 | 7.1 | 54 401 |
| 2014 | 128 199 | 73 039 | 57.0 | 68 613 | 53.5 | 552 | 68 061 | 4 426 | 6.1 | 55 159 |
| 2015 | 129 700 | 73 510 | 56.7 | 69 703 | 53.7 | 597 | 69 106 | 3 807 | 5.2 | 56 190 |

## Table 1-3.  Employment Status of the Civilian Noninstitutional Population, by Sex, Age, Race, and Hispanic Origin, 1995–2015

(Thousands of people.)

| Characteristic | 1995 | 1996 | 1997 | 1998 | 1999 | 2000 | 2001 | 2002 | 2003 | 2004 |
|---|---|---|---|---|---|---|---|---|---|---|
| **ALL RACES** | | | | | | | | | | |
| **Both Sexes** | | | | | | | | | | |
| Civilian noninstitutional population ... | 198 584 | 200 591 | 203 133 | 205 220 | 207 753 | 212 577 | 215 092 | 217 570 | 221 168 | 223 357 |
| Civilian labor force ............... | 132 304 | 133 943 | 136 297 | 137 673 | 139 368 | 142 583 | 143 734 | 144 863 | 146 510 | 147 401 |
| Employed .......................... | 124 900 | 126 708 | 129 558 | 131 463 | 133 488 | 136 891 | 136 933 | 136 485 | 137 736 | 139 252 |
| Agriculture ...................... | 3 440 | 3 443 | 3 399 | 3 378 | 3 281 | 2 464 | 2 299 | 2 311 | 2 275 | 2 232 |
| Nonagricultural industries ........... | 121 460 | 123 264 | 126 159 | 128 085 | 130 207 | 134 427 | 134 635 | 134 174 | 135 461 | 137 020 |
| Unemployed ........................ | 7 404 | 7 236 | 6 739 | 6 210 | 5 880 | 5 692 | 6 801 | 8 378 | 8 774 | 8 149 |
| Not in labor force .................... | 66 280 | 66 647 | 66 837 | 67 547 | 68 385 | 69 994 | 71 359 | 72 707 | 74 658 | 75 956 |
| **Men, 16 Years and Over** | | | | | | | | | | |
| Civilian noninstitutional population ... | 95 178 | 96 206 | 97 715 | 98 758 | 99 722 | 101 964 | 103 282 | 104 585 | 106 435 | 107 710 |
| Civilian labor force ............... | 71 360 | 72 087 | 73 261 | 73 959 | 74 512 | 76 280 | 76 886 | 77 500 | 78 238 | 78 980 |
| Employed .......................... | 67 377 | 68 207 | 69 685 | 70 693 | 71 446 | 73 305 | 73 196 | 72 903 | 73 332 | 74 524 |
| Agriculture ...................... | 2 559 | 2 573 | 2 552 | 2 553 | 2 432 | 1 861 | 1 708 | 1 724 | 1 695 | 1 688 |
| Nonagricultural industries ........... | 64 818 | 65 634 | 67 133 | 68 140 | 69 014 | 71 444 | 71 488 | 71 179 | 71 636 | 72 836 |
| Unemployed ........................ | 3 983 | 3 880 | 3 577 | 3 266 | 3 066 | 2 975 | 3 690 | 4 597 | 4 906 | 4 456 |
| Not in labor force .................... | 23 818 | 24 119 | 24 454 | 24 799 | 25 210 | 25 684 | 26 396 | 27 085 | 28 197 | 28 730 |
| **Men, 20 Years and Over** | | | | | | | | | | |
| Civilian noninstitutional population ... | 87 811 | 88 606 | 89 879 | 90 790 | 91 555 | 93 875 | 95 181 | 96 439 | 98 272 | 99 476 |
| Civilian labor force ............... | 67 324 | 68 044 | 69 166 | 69 715 | 70 194 | 72 010 | 72 816 | 73 630 | 74 623 | 75 364 |
| Employed .......................... | 64 085 | 64 897 | 66 284 | 67 135 | 67 761 | 69 634 | 69 776 | 69 734 | 70 415 | 71 572 |
| Agriculture ...................... | 2 335 | 2 356 | 2 356 | 2 350 | 2 244 | 1 756 | 1 613 | 1 629 | 1 614 | 1 596 |
| Nonagricultural industries ........... | 61 750 | 62 541 | 63 927 | 64 785 | 65 517 | 67 878 | 68 163 | 68 104 | 68 801 | 69 976 |
| Unemployed ........................ | 3 239 | 3 146 | 2 882 | 2 580 | 2 433 | 2 376 | 3 040 | 3 896 | 4 209 | 3 791 |
| Not in labor force .................... | 20 487 | 20 563 | 20 713 | 21 075 | 21 362 | 21 864 | 22 365 | 22 809 | 23 649 | 24 113 |
| **Women, 16 Years and Over** | | | | | | | | | | |
| Civilian noninstitutional population ... | 103 406 | 104 385 | 105 418 | 106 462 | 108 031 | 110 613 | 111 811 | 112 985 | 114 733 | 115 647 |
| Civilian labor force ............... | 60 944 | 61 857 | 63 036 | 63 714 | 64 855 | 66 303 | 66 848 | 67 363 | 68 272 | 68 421 |
| Employed .......................... | 57 523 | 58 501 | 59 873 | 60 771 | 62 042 | 63 586 | 63 737 | 63 582 | 64 404 | 64 728 |
| Agriculture ...................... | 881 | 871 | 847 | 825 | 849 | 602 | 591 | 587 | 580 | 547 |
| Nonagricultural industries ........... | 56 642 | 57 630 | 59 026 | 59 945 | 61 193 | 62 983 | 63 147 | 62 995 | 63 824 | 64 181 |
| Unemployed ........................ | 3 421 | 3 356 | 3 162 | 2 944 | 2 814 | 2 717 | 3 111 | 3 781 | 3 868 | 3 694 |
| Not in labor force .................... | 42 462 | 42 528 | 42 382 | 42 748 | 43 175 | 44 310 | 44 962 | 45 621 | 46 461 | 47 225 |
| **Women, 20 Years and Over** | | | | | | | | | | |
| Civilian noninstitutional population ... | 96 262 | 97 050 | 97 889 | 98 786 | 100 158 | 102 790 | 103 983 | 105 136 | 106 800 | 107 658 |
| Civilian labor force ............... | 57 215 | 58 094 | 59 198 | 59 702 | 60 840 | 62 301 | 63 016 | 63 648 | 64 716 | 64 923 |
| Employed .......................... | 54 396 | 55 311 | 56 613 | 57 278 | 58 555 | 60 067 | 60 417 | 60 420 | 61 402 | 61 773 |
| Agriculture ...................... | 830 | 827 | 798 | 768 | 803 | 567 | 558 | 557 | 550 | 515 |
| Nonagricultural industries ........... | 53 566 | 54 484 | 55 815 | 56 510 | 57 752 | 59 500 | 59 860 | 59 863 | 60 852 | 61 258 |
| Unemployed ........................ | 2 819 | 2 783 | 2 585 | 2 424 | 2 285 | 2 235 | 2 599 | 3 228 | 3 314 | 3 150 |
| Not in labor force .................... | 39 047 | 38 956 | 38 691 | 39 084 | 39 318 | 40 488 | 40 967 | 41 488 | 42 083 | 42 735 |
| **Both Sexes, 16 to 19 Years** | | | | | | | | | | |
| Civilian noninstitutional population ... | 14 511 | 14 934 | 15 365 | 15 644 | 16 040 | 15 912 | 15 929 | 15 994 | 16 096 | 16 222 |
| Civilian labor force ............... | 7 765 | 7 806 | 7 932 | 8 256 | 8 333 | 8 271 | 7 902 | 7 585 | 7 170 | 7 114 |
| Employed .......................... | 6 419 | 6 500 | 6 661 | 7 051 | 7 172 | 7 189 | 6 740 | 6 332 | 5 919 | 5 907 |
| Agriculture ...................... | 275 | 261 | 244 | 261 | 234 | 141 | 128 | 124 | 111 | 121 |
| Nonagricultural industries ........... | 6 144 | 6 239 | 6 417 | 6 790 | 6 938 | 7 049 | 6 611 | 6 207 | 5 808 | 5 786 |
| Unemployed ........................ | 1 346 | 1 306 | 1 271 | 1 205 | 1 162 | 1 081 | 1 162 | 1 253 | 1 251 | 1 208 |
| Not in labor force .................... | 6 746 | 7 128 | 7 433 | 7 388 | 7 706 | 7 642 | 8 027 | 8 409 | 8 926 | 9 108 |
| **WHITE**[1] | | | | | | | | | | |
| **Both Sexes** | | | | | | | | | | |
| Civilian noninstitutional population ... | 166 914 | 168 317 | 169 993 | 171 478 | 173 085 | 176 220 | 178 111 | 179 783 | 181 292 | 182 643 |
| Civilian labor force ............... | 111 950 | 113 108 | 114 693 | 115 415 | 116 509 | 118 545 | 119 399 | 120 150 | 120 546 | 121 086 |
| Employed .......................... | 106 490 | 107 808 | 109 856 | 110 931 | 112 235 | 114 424 | 114 430 | 114 013 | 114 235 | 115 239 |
| Agriculture ...................... | 3 194 | 3 276 | 3 208 | 3 160 | 3 083 | 2 320 | 2 174 | 2 171 | 2 148 | 2 103 |
| Nonagricultural industries ........... | 103 296 | 104 532 | 106 648 | 107 770 | 109 152 | 112 104 | 112 256 | 111 841 | 112 087 | 113 136 |
| Unemployed ........................ | 5 459 | 5 300 | 4 836 | 4 484 | 4 273 | 4 121 | 4 969 | 6 137 | 6 311 | 5 847 |
| Not in labor force .................... | 54 965 | 55 209 | 55 301 | 56 064 | 56 577 | 57 675 | 58 713 | 59 633 | 60 746 | 61 558 |
| **Men, 16 Years and Over** | | | | | | | | | | |
| Civilian noninstitutional population ... | 80 733 | 81 489 | 82 577 | 83 352 | 83 930 | 85 370 | 86 452 | 87 361 | 88 249 | 89 044 |
| Civilian labor force ............... | 61 146 | 61 783 | 62 639 | 63 034 | 63 413 | 64 466 | 64 966 | 65 308 | 65 509 | 65 994 |
| Employed .......................... | 58 146 | 58 888 | 59 998 | 60 604 | 61 139 | 62 289 | 62 212 | 61 849 | 61 866 | 62 712 |
| Agriculture ...................... | 2 347 | 2 436 | 2 389 | 2 376 | 2 273 | 1 743 | 1 606 | 1 611 | 1 597 | 1 583 |
| Nonagricultural industries ........... | 55 800 | 56 452 | 57 608 | 58 228 | 58 866 | 60 546 | 60 606 | 60 238 | 60 269 | 61 129 |
| Unemployed ........................ | 2 999 | 2 896 | 2 641 | 2 431 | 2 274 | 2 177 | 2 754 | 3 459 | 3 643 | 3 282 |
| Not in labor force .................... | 19 587 | 19 706 | 19 938 | 20 317 | 20 517 | 20 905 | 21 486 | 22 053 | 22 740 | 23 050 |
| **Men, 20 Years and Over** | | | | | | | | | | |
| Civilian noninstitutional population ... | 74 879 | 75 454 | 76 320 | 76 966 | 77 432 | 78 966 | 80 029 | 80 922 | 81 860 | 82 615 |
| Civilian labor force ............... | 57 719 | 58 340 | 59 126 | 59 421 | 59 747 | 60 850 | 61 519 | 62 067 | 62 473 | 62 944 |
| Employed .......................... | 55 254 | 55 977 | 56 986 | 57 500 | 57 934 | 59 119 | 59 245 | 59 124 | 59 348 | 60 159 |
| Agriculture ...................... | 2 132 | 2 224 | 2 201 | 2 182 | 2 094 | 1 640 | 1 512 | 1 519 | 1 517 | 1 495 |
| Nonagricultural industries ........... | 53 122 | 53 753 | 54 785 | 55 319 | 55 839 | 57 479 | 57 733 | 57 605 | 57 831 | 58 664 |
| Unemployed ........................ | 2 465 | 2 363 | 2 140 | 1 920 | 1 813 | 1 731 | 2 275 | 2 943 | 3 125 | 2 785 |
| Not in labor force .................... | 17 161 | 17 114 | 17 194 | 17 545 | 17 685 | 18 116 | 18 510 | 18 855 | 19 386 | 19 671 |

[1]Beginning in 2003, persons who selected this race group only; persons who selected more than one race group are not included. Prior to 2003, persons who reported more than one race group were included in the group they identified as the main race.

## Table 1-3. Employment Status of the Civilian Noninstitutional Population, by Sex, Age, Race, and Hispanic Origin, 1995–2015—Continued

(Thousands of people.)

| Characteristic | 2005 | 2006 | 2007 | 2008 | 2009 | 2010 | 2011 | 2012 | 2013 | 2014 | 2015 |
|---|---|---|---|---|---|---|---|---|---|---|---|
| **ALL RACES** | | | | | | | | | | | |
| **Both Sexes** | | | | | | | | | | | |
| Civilian noninstitutional population ... | 226 082 | 228 815 | 231 867 | 233 788 | 235 801 | 237 830 | 239 618 | 243 284 | 245 679 | 247 947 | 250 801 |
| Civilian labor force ......................... | 149 320 | 151 428 | 153 124 | 154 287 | 154 142 | 153 889 | 153 617 | 154 975 | 155 389 | 155 922 | 157 130 |
| Employed ....................................... | 141 730 | 144 427 | 146 047 | 145 362 | 139 877 | 139 064 | 139 869 | 142 469 | 143 929 | 146 305 | 148 834 |
| Agriculture ................................ | 2 197 | 2 206 | 2 095 | 2 168 | 2 103 | 2 206 | 2 254 | 2 186 | 2 130 | 2 237 | 2 422 |
| Nonagricultural industries ........... | 139 532 | 142 221 | 143 952 | 143 194 | 137 775 | 136 858 | 137 615 | 140 283 | 141 799 | 144 068 | 146 411 |
| Unemployed .................................. | 7 591 | 7 001 | 7 078 | 8 924 | 14 265 | 14 825 | 13 747 | 12 506 | 11 460 | 9 617 | 8 296 |
| Not in labor force .......................... | 76 762 | 77 387 | 78 743 | 79 501 | 81 659 | 83 941 | 86 001 | 88 310 | 90 290 | 92 025 | 93 671 |
| **Men, 16 Years and Over** | | | | | | | | | | | |
| Civilian noninstitutional population ... | 109 151 | 110 605 | 112 173 | 113 113 | 114 136 | 115 174 | 116 317 | 117 343 | 118 555 | 119 748 | 121 101 |
| Civilian labor force ......................... | 80 033 | 81 255 | 82 136 | 82 520 | 82 123 | 81 985 | 81 975 | 82 327 | 82 667 | 82 882 | 83 620 |
| Employed ....................................... | 75 973 | 77 502 | 78 254 | 77 486 | 73 670 | 73 359 | 74 290 | 75 555 | 76 353 | 77 692 | 79 131 |
| Agriculture ................................ | 1 654 | 1 663 | 1 604 | 1 650 | 1 607 | 1 665 | 1 698 | 1 626 | 1 611 | 1 685 | 1 826 |
| Nonagricultural industries ........... | 74 319 | 75 838 | 76 650 | 75 836 | 72 062 | 71 694 | 72 592 | 73 930 | 74 742 | 76 007 | 77 305 |
| Unemployed .................................. | 4 059 | 3 753 | 3 882 | 5 033 | 8 453 | 8 626 | 7 684 | 6 771 | 6 314 | 5 190 | 4 490 |
| Not in labor force .......................... | 29 119 | 29 350 | 30 036 | 30 593 | 32 013 | 33 189 | 34 343 | 35 017 | 35 889 | 36 865 | 37 481 |
| **Men, 20 Years and Over** | | | | | | | | | | | |
| Civilian noninstitutional population ... | 100 835 | 102 145 | 103 555 | 104 453 | 105 493 | 106 596 | 107 736 | 108 686 | 110 017 | 111 299 | 112 671 |
| Civilian labor force ......................... | 76 443 | 77 562 | 78 596 | 79 047 | 78 897 | 78 994 | 79 080 | 79 387 | 79 744 | 80 056 | 80 735 |
| Employed ....................................... | 73 050 | 74 431 | 75 337 | 74 750 | 71 341 | 71 230 | 72 182 | 73 403 | 74 176 | 75 471 | 76 776 |
| Agriculture ................................ | 1 577 | 1 579 | 1 514 | 1 552 | 1 514 | 1 589 | 1 611 | 1 547 | 1 532 | 1 614 | 1 757 |
| Nonagricultural industries ........... | 71 473 | 72 852 | 73 823 | 73 198 | 69 828 | 69 641 | 70 571 | 71 856 | 72 644 | 73 857 | 75 019 |
| Unemployed .................................. | 3 392 | 3 131 | 3 259 | 4 297 | 7 555 | 7 763 | 6 898 | 5 984 | 5 568 | 4 585 | 3 959 |
| Not in labor force .......................... | 24 392 | 24 584 | 24 959 | 25 406 | 26 596 | 27 603 | 28 656 | 29 299 | 30 273 | 31 243 | 31 936 |
| **Women, 16 Years and Over** | | | | | | | | | | | |
| Civilian noninstitutional population ... | 116 931 | 118 210 | 119 694 | 120 675 | 121 665 | 122 656 | 123 300 | 125 941 | 127 124 | 128 199 | 129 700 |
| Civilian labor force ......................... | 69 288 | 70 173 | 70 988 | 71 767 | 72 019 | 71 904 | 71 642 | 72 648 | 72 722 | 73 039 | 73 510 |
| Employed ....................................... | 65 757 | 66 925 | 67 792 | 67 876 | 66 208 | 65 705 | 65 579 | 66 914 | 67 577 | 68 613 | 69 703 |
| Agriculture ................................ | 544 | 543 | 490 | 518 | 496 | 541 | 556 | 560 | 519 | 552 | 597 |
| Nonagricultural industries ........... | 65 213 | 66 382 | 67 302 | 67 358 | 65 712 | 65 164 | 65 023 | 66 353 | 67 058 | 68 061 | 69 106 |
| Unemployed .................................. | 3 531 | 3 247 | 3 196 | 3 891 | 5 811 | 6 199 | 6 063 | 5 734 | 5 146 | 4 426 | 3 807 |
| Not in labor force .......................... | 47 643 | 48 037 | 48 707 | 48 908 | 49 646 | 50 752 | 51 658 | 53 293 | 54 401 | 55 159 | 56 190 |
| **Women, 20 Years and Over** | | | | | | | | | | | |
| Civilian noninstitutional population ... | 108 850 | 109 992 | 111 330 | 112 260 | 113 265 | 114 333 | 115 107 | 117 614 | 118 875 | 120 014 | 121 511 |
| Civilian labor force ......................... | 65 714 | 66 585 | 67 516 | 68 382 | 68 856 | 68 990 | 68 810 | 69 765 | 69 860 | 70 212 | 70 695 |
| Employed ....................................... | 62 702 | 63 834 | 64 799 | 65 039 | 63 699 | 63 456 | 63 360 | 64 640 | 65 295 | 66 287 | 67 323 |
| Agriculture ................................ | 519 | 520 | 460 | 491 | 471 | 519 | 534 | 534 | 498 | 536 | 574 |
| Nonagricultural industries ........... | 62 182 | 63 315 | 64 339 | 64 548 | 63 228 | 62 936 | 62 826 | 64 106 | 64 798 | 65 750 | 66 749 |
| Unemployed .................................. | 3 013 | 2 751 | 2 718 | 3 342 | 5 157 | 5 534 | 5 450 | 5 125 | 4 565 | 3 926 | 3 371 |
| Not in labor force .......................... | 43 136 | 43 407 | 43 814 | 43 878 | 44 409 | 45 343 | 46 297 | 47 849 | 49 015 | 49 802 | 50 816 |
| **Both Sexes, 16 to 19 Years** | | | | | | | | | | | |
| Civilian noninstitutional population ... | 16 398 | 16 678 | 16 982 | 17 075 | 17 043 | 16 901 | 16 774 | 16 984 | 16 787 | 16 633 | 16 619 |
| Civilian labor force ......................... | 7 164 | 7 281 | 7 012 | 6 858 | 6 390 | 5 906 | 5 727 | 5 823 | 5 785 | 5 654 | 5 700 |
| Employed ....................................... | 5 978 | 6 162 | 5 911 | 5 573 | 4 837 | 4 378 | 4 327 | 4 426 | 4 458 | 4 548 | 4 734 |
| Agriculture ................................ | 100 | 108 | 121 | 125 | 119 | 98 | 109 | 105 | 100 | 86 | 91 |
| Nonagricultural industries ........... | 5 877 | 6 054 | 5 790 | 5 448 | 4 719 | 4 281 | 4 218 | 4 321 | 4 358 | 4 462 | 4 643 |
| Unemployed .................................. | 1 186 | 1 119 | 1 101 | 1 285 | 1 552 | 1 528 | 1 400 | 1 397 | 1 327 | 1 106 | 966 |
| Not in labor force .......................... | 9 234 | 9 397 | 9 970 | 10 218 | 10 654 | 10 995 | 11 048 | 11 162 | 11 002 | 10 979 | 10 919 |
| **WHITE[1]** | | | | | | | | | | | |
| **Both Sexes** | | | | | | | | | | | |
| Civilian noninstitutional population ... | 184 446 | 186 264 | 188 253 | 189 540 | 190 902 | 192 075 | 193 077 | 193 204 | 194 333 | 195 498 | 196 868 |
| Civilian labor force ......................... | 122 299 | 123 834 | 124 935 | 125 635 | 125 644 | 125 084 | 124 579 | 123 684 | 123 412 | 123 327 | 123 607 |
| Employed ....................................... | 116 949 | 118 833 | 119 792 | 119 126 | 114 996 | 114 168 | 114 690 | 114 769 | 115 379 | 116 788 | 117 944 |
| Agriculture ................................ | 2 077 | 2 063 | 1 953 | 2 021 | 1 968 | 2 071 | 2 134 | 2 033 | 1 975 | 2 093 | 2 262 |
| Nonagricultural industries ........... | 114 872 | 116 769 | 117 839 | 117 104 | 113 028 | 112 098 | 112 556 | 112 735 | 113 404 | 114 695 | 115 682 |
| Unemployed .................................. | 5 350 | 5 002 | 5 143 | 6 509 | 10 648 | 10 916 | 9 889 | 8 915 | 8 033 | 6 540 | 5 662 |
| Not in labor force .......................... | 62 148 | 62 429 | 63 319 | 63 905 | 65 258 | 66 991 | 68 498 | 69 520 | 70 920 | 72 170 | 73 261 |
| **Men, 16 Years and Over** | | | | | | | | | | | |
| Civilian noninstitutional population ... | 90 027 | 91 021 | 92 073 | 92 725 | 93 433 | 94 082 | 94 801 | 94 266 | 94 865 | 95 513 | 96 147 |
| Civilian labor force ......................... | 66 694 | 67 613 | 68 158 | 68 351 | 68 051 | 67 728 | 67 551 | 66 921 | 66 842 | 66 680 | 67 018 |
| Employed ....................................... | 63 763 | 64 883 | 65 289 | 64 624 | 61 630 | 61 252 | 71 | 61 990 | 62 322 | 63 108 | 63 892 |
| Agriculture ................................ | 1 562 | 1 554 | 1 501 | 1 539 | 1 499 | 1 557 | 1 602 | 1 515 | 1 495 | 1 571 | 1 701 |
| Nonagricultural industries ........... | 62 201 | 63 330 | 63 788 | 63 085 | 60 131 | 59 695 | 60 318 | 60 476 | 60 827 | 61 537 | 62 192 |
| Unemployed .................................. | 2 931 | 2 730 | 2 869 | 3 727 | 6 421 | 6 476 | 5 631 | 4 931 | 4 520 | 3 572 | 3 126 |
| Not in labor force .......................... | 23 334 | 23 408 | 23 915 | 24 374 | 25 382 | 26 353 | 27 249 | 27 345 | 28 024 | 28 834 | 29 129 |
| **Men, 20 Years and Over** | | | | | | | | | | | |
| Civilian noninstitutional population ... | 83 556 | 84 466 | 85 420 | 86 056 | 86 789 | 87 502 | 88 191 | 87 780 | 88 474 | 89 193 | 89 865 |
| Civilian labor force ......................... | 63 705 | 64 540 | 65 214 | 65 483 | 65 372 | 65 265 | 65 165 | 64 540 | 64 505 | 64 430 | 64 710 |
| Employed ....................................... | 61 255 | 62 259 | 62 806 | 62 304 | 59 626 | 59 438 | 60 118 | 60 193 | 60 511 | 61 289 | 61 959 |
| Agriculture ................................ | 1 488 | 1 473 | 1 417 | 1 447 | 1 410 | 1 483 | 1 518 | 1 438 | 1 418 | 1 504 | 1 638 |
| Nonagricultural industries ........... | 59 767 | 60 785 | 61 389 | 60 857 | 58 216 | 57 955 | 58 600 | 58 755 | 59 093 | 59 785 | 60 321 |
| Unemployed .................................. | 2 450 | 2 281 | 2 408 | 3 179 | 5 746 | 5 828 | 5 046 | 4 347 | 3 994 | 3 141 | 2 751 |
| Not in labor force .......................... | 19 851 | 19 927 | 20 206 | 20 573 | 21 417 | 22 236 | 23 026 | 23 241 | 23 969 | 24 763 | 25 155 |

[1]Beginning in 2003, persons who selected this race group only; persons who selected more than one race group are not included. Prior to 2003, persons who reported more than one race group were included in the group they identified as the main race.

## Table 1-3. Employment Status of the Civilian Noninstitutional Population, by Sex, Age, Race, and Hispanic Origin, 1995–2015—*Continued*

(Thousands of people.)

| Characteristic | 1995 | 1996 | 1997 | 1998 | 1999 | 2000 | 2001 | 2002 | 2003 | 2004 |
|---|---|---|---|---|---|---|---|---|---|---|
| **WHITE**[1] | | | | | | | | | | |
| **Women, 16 Years and Over** | | | | | | | | | | |
| Civilian noninstitutional population ... | 86 181 | 86 828 | 87 417 | 88 126 | 89 156 | 90 850 | 91 660 | 92 422 | 93 043 | 93 599 |
| Civilian labor force | 50 804 | 51 325 | 52 054 | 52 380 | 53 096 | 54 079 | 54 433 | 54 842 | 55 037 | 55 092 |
| Employed | 48 344 | 48 920 | 49 859 | 50 327 | 51 096 | 52 136 | 52 218 | 52 164 | 52 369 | 52 527 |
| Agriculture | 847 | 840 | 819 | 784 | 810 | 578 | 568 | 560 | 551 | 520 |
| Nonagricultural industries | 47 497 | 48 080 | 49 040 | 49 543 | 50 286 | 51 558 | 51 650 | 51 604 | 51 818 | 52 007 |
| Unemployed | 2 460 | 2 404 | 2 195 | 2 053 | 1 999 | 1 944 | 2 215 | 2 678 | 2 668 | 2 565 |
| Not in labor force | 35 377 | 35 503 | 35 363 | 35 746 | 36 060 | 36 770 | 37 227 | 37 581 | 38 006 | 38 508 |
| **Women, 20 Years and Over** | | | | | | | | | | |
| Civilian noninstitutional population ... | 80 567 | 81 041 | 81 492 | 82 073 | 82 953 | 84 718 | 85 526 | 86 266 | 86 905 | 87 430 |
| Civilian labor force | 47 686 | 48 162 | 48 847 | 49 029 | 49 714 | 50 740 | 51 218 | 51 717 | 52 099 | 52 212 |
| Employed | 45 643 | 46 164 | 47 063 | 47 342 | 48 098 | 49 145 | 49 369 | 49 448 | 49 823 | 50 040 |
| Agriculture | 799 | 798 | 771 | 729 | 765 | 546 | 537 | 532 | 522 | 488 |
| Nonagricultural industries | 44 844 | 45 366 | 46 292 | 46 612 | 47 333 | 48 599 | 48 831 | 48 916 | 49 301 | 49 552 |
| Unemployed | 2 042 | 1 998 | 1 784 | 1 688 | 1 616 | 1 595 | 1 849 | 2 269 | 2 276 | 2 172 |
| Not in labor force | 32 881 | 32 879 | 32 645 | 33 044 | 33 239 | 33 978 | 34 308 | 34 548 | 34 806 | 35 218 |
| **Both Sexes, 16 to 19 Years** | | | | | | | | | | |
| Civilian noninstitutional population ... | 11 468 | 11 822 | 12 181 | 12 439 | 12 700 | 12 535 | 12 556 | 12 596 | 12 527 | 12 599 |
| Civilian labor force | 6 545 | 6 607 | 6 720 | 6 965 | 7 048 | 6 955 | 6 661 | 6 366 | 5 973 | 5 929 |
| Employed | 5 593 | 5 667 | 5 807 | 6 089 | 6 204 | 6 160 | 5 817 | 5 441 | 5 064 | 5 039 |
| Agriculture | 262 | 254 | 236 | 250 | 224 | 135 | 125 | 121 | 109 | 116 |
| Nonagricultural industries | 5 331 | 5 413 | 5 571 | 5 839 | 5 980 | 6 025 | 5 692 | 5 320 | 4 955 | 4 923 |
| Unemployed | 952 | 939 | 912 | 876 | 844 | 795 | 845 | 925 | 909 | 890 |
| Not in labor force | 4 923 | 5 215 | 5 462 | 5 475 | 5 652 | 5 581 | 5 894 | 6 230 | 6 554 | 6 669 |
| **BLACK**[1] | | | | | | | | | | |
| **Both Sexes** | | | | | | | | | | |
| Civilian noninstitutional population ... | 23 246 | 23 604 | 24 003 | 24 373 | 24 855 | 24 902 | 25 138 | 25 578 | 25 686 | 26 065 |
| Civilian labor force | 14 817 | 15 134 | 15 529 | 15 982 | 16 365 | 16 397 | 16 421 | 16 565 | 16 526 | 16 638 |
| Employed | 13 279 | 13 542 | 13 969 | 14 556 | 15 056 | 15 156 | 15 006 | 14 872 | 14 739 | 14 909 |
| Agriculture | 101 | 98 | 117 | 138 | 117 | 77 | 62 | 69 | 63 | 50 |
| Nonagricultural industries | 13 178 | 13 444 | 13 852 | 14 417 | 14 939 | 15 079 | 14 944 | 14 804 | 14 676 | 14 859 |
| Unemployed | 1 538 | 1 592 | 1 560 | 1 426 | 1 309 | 1 241 | 1 416 | 1 693 | 1 787 | 1 729 |
| Not in labor force | 8 429 | 8 470 | 8 474 | 8 391 | 8 490 | 8 505 | 8 717 | 9 013 | 9 161 | 9 428 |
| **Men, 16 Years and Over** | | | | | | | | | | |
| Civilian noninstitutional population ... | 10 411 | 10 575 | 10 763 | 10 927 | 11 143 | 11 129 | 11 172 | 11 391 | 11 454 | 11 656 |
| Civilian labor force | 7 183 | 7 264 | 7 354 | 7 542 | 7 652 | 7 702 | 7 647 | 7 794 | 7 711 | 7 773 |
| Employed | 6 422 | 6 456 | 6 607 | 6 871 | 7 027 | 7 082 | 6 938 | 6 959 | 6 820 | 6 912 |
| Agriculture | 93 | 86 | 103 | 118 | 99 | 67 | 56 | 63 | 52 | 43 |
| Nonagricultural industries | 6 329 | 6 371 | 6 504 | 6 752 | 6 952 | 7 015 | 6 882 | 6 896 | 6 768 | 6 869 |
| Unemployed | 762 | 808 | 747 | 671 | 671 | 620 | 709 | 835 | 891 | 860 |
| Not in labor force | 3 228 | 3 311 | 3 409 | 3 386 | 3 386 | 3 427 | 3 525 | 3 597 | 3 743 | 3 884 |
| **Men, 20 Years and Over** | | | | | | | | | | |
| Civilian noninstitutional population ... | 9 280 | 9 414 | 9 575 | 9 727 | 9 926 | 9 952 | 9 993 | 10 196 | 10 278 | 11 656 |
| Civilian labor force | 6 730 | 6 806 | 6 910 | 7 053 | 7 182 | 7 240 | 7 200 | 7 347 | 7 346 | 7 773 |
| Employed | 6 137 | 6 167 | 6 325 | 6 530 | 6 702 | 6 741 | 6 627 | 6 652 | 6 586 | 6 912 |
| Agriculture | 89 | 83 | 101 | 112 | 96 | 67 | 55 | 62 | 51 | 274 |
| Nonagricultural industries | 6 048 | 6 084 | 6 224 | 6 418 | 6 606 | 6 675 | 55 | 6 591 | 6 535 | 6 638 |
| Unemployed | 593 | 639 | 585 | 524 | 480 | 499 | 573 | 695 | 760 | 860 |
| Not in labor force | 2 550 | 2 608 | 2 665 | 2 673 | 2 743 | 2 711 | 2 792 | 2 848 | 2 932 | 3 884 |
| **Women, 16 Years and Over** | | | | | | | | | | |
| Civilian noninstitutional population ... | 12 835 | 13 029 | 13 241 | 13 446 | 13 711 | 13 772 | 13 966 | 14 187 | 14 232 | 14 409 |
| Civilian labor force | 7 634 | 7 869 | 8 175 | 8 441 | 8 713 | 8 695 | 8 774 | 8 772 | 8 815 | 8 865 |
| Employed | 6 857 | 7 086 | 7 362 | 7 685 | 8 029 | 8 073 | 8 068 | 7 914 | 7 919 | 7 997 |
| Agriculture | 8 | 13 | 14 | 20 | 18 | 10 | 6 | 6 | 11 | 7 |
| Nonagricultural industries | 6 849 | 7 073 | 7 348 | 7 665 | 8 011 | 8 064 | 8 062 | 7 907 | 7 908 | 7 990 |
| Unemployed | 777 | 784 | 813 | 756 | 684 | 621 | 706 | 858 | 895 | 868 |
| Not in labor force | 5 201 | 5 159 | 5 066 | 5 005 | 4 999 | 5 078 | 5 192 | 5 415 | 5 418 | 5 544 |
| **Women, 20 Years and Over** | | | | | | | | | | |
| Civilian noninstitutional population ... | 11 682 | 11 833 | 12 016 | 12 023 | 12 451 | 12 561 | 12 758 | 12 966 | 13 026 | 14 409 |
| Civilian labor force | 7 175 | 7 405 | 7 686 | 7 912 | 8 224 | 8 215 | 8 323 | 8 348 | 8 409 | 8 865 |
| Employed | 6 556 | 6 762 | 7 013 | 7 290 | 7 663 | 7 703 | 7 741 | 7 610 | 7 636 | 7 997 |
| Agriculture | 7 | 12 | 13 | 19 | 17 | 9 | 6 | 5 | 10 | 7 |
| Nonagricultural industries | 6 548 | 6 749 | 7 000 | 7 272 | 7 646 | 7 694 | 7 735 | 7 604 | 7 626 | 7 701 |
| Unemployed | 620 | 643 | 673 | 622 | 561 | 512 | 582 | 738 | 772 | 868 |
| Not in labor force | 4 507 | 4 428 | 4 330 | 4 291 | 4 226 | 4 346 | 4 434 | 4 618 | 4 618 | 5 544 |
| **Both Sexes, 16 to 19 Years** | | | | | | | | | | |
| Civilian noninstitutional population ... | 2 284 | 2 356 | 2 412 | 2 443 | 2 479 | 2 389 | 2 388 | 2 416 | 2 382 | 2 423 |
| Civilian labor force | 911 | 923 | 933 | 1 017 | 959 | 941 | 898 | 870 | 771 | 762 |
| Employed | 586 | 613 | 631 | 736 | 691 | 711 | 637 | 611 | 516 | 520 |
| Agriculture | 5 | 3 | 3 | 8 | 4 | 1 | 1 | 2 | 1 | 0 |
| Nonagricultural industries | 581 | 611 | 611 | 728 | 687 | 710 | 637 | 609 | 515 | 520 |
| Unemployed | 325 | 310 | 310 | 281 | 268 | 230 | 260 | 260 | 255 | 241 |
| Not in labor force | 1 372 | 1 434 | 1 434 | 1 427 | 1 520 | 1 448 | 1 490 | 1 546 | 1 611 | 1 661 |

[1]Beginning in 2003, persons who selected this race group only; persons who selected more than one race group are not included. Prior to 2003, persons who reported more than one race group were included in the group they identified as the main race.

## Table 1-3. Employment Status of the Civilian Noninstitutional Population, by Sex, Age, Race, and Hispanic Origin, 1995–2015—Continued

(Thousands of people.)

| Characteristic | 2005 | 2006 | 2007 | 2008 | 2009 | 2010 | 2011 | 2012 | 2013 | 2014 | 2015 |
|---|---|---|---|---|---|---|---|---|---|---|---|
| **WHITE[1]** | | | | | | | | | | | |
| **Women, 16 Years and Over** | | | | | | | | | | | |
| Civilian noninstitutional population ... | 94 419 | 95 242 | 96 180 | 96 814 | 97 469 | 97 993 | 98 276 | 98 938 | 99 467 | 99 984 | 100 720 |
| Civilian labor force ......................... | 55 605 | 56 221 | 56 777 | 57 284 | 57 593 | 57 356 | 57 028 | 56 763 | 56 571 | 56 648 | 56 589 |
| Employed ...................................... | 53 186 | 53 950 | 54 503 | 54 501 | 53 366 | 52 916 | 52 770 | 52 779 | 53 057 | 53 680 | 54 052 |
| Agriculture .............................. | 515 | 510 | 452 | 482 | 469 | 513 | 532 | 519 | 480 | 522 | 562 |
| Nonagricultural industries ........... | 52 672 | 53 440 | 54 050 | 54 019 | 52 897 | 52 402 | 52 238 | 52 260 | 52 577 | 53 158 | 53 490 |
| Unemployed .................................. | 2 419 | 2 271 | 2 274 | 2 782 | 4 227 | 4 440 | 4 257 | 3 985 | 3 513 | 2 968 | 2 537 |
| Not in labor force .......................... | 38 814 | 39 021 | 39 403 | 39 531 | 39 876 | 40 638 | 41 248 | 42 175 | 42 897 | 43 337 | 44 132 |
| **Women, 20 Years and Over** | | | | | | | | | | | |
| Civilian noninstitutional population ... | 88 200 | 88 942 | 89 790 | 90 400 | 91 078 | 91 683 | 92 068 | 92 766 | 93 360 | 93 928 | 94 680 |
| Civilian labor force ......................... | 52 643 | 53 286 | 53 925 | 54 508 | 54 976 | 54 957 | 54 700 | 54 475 | 54 299 | 54 421 | 54 410 |
| Employed ...................................... | 50 589 | 51 359 | 51 996 | 52 124 | 51 231 | 50 997 | 50 881 | 50 911 | 51 198 | 51 798 | 52 161 |
| Agriculture .............................. | 492 | 488 | 423 | 457 | 444 | 492 | 511 | 493 | 460 | 507 | 540 |
| Nonagricultural industries ........... | 50 097 | 50 871 | 51 572 | 51 667 | 50 787 | 50 505 | 50 371 | 50 418 | 50 737 | 51 291 | 51 621 |
| Unemployed .................................. | 2 054 | 1 927 | 1 930 | 2 384 | 3 745 | 3 960 | 3 818 | 3 564 | 3 102 | 2 623 | 2 249 |
| Not in labor force .......................... | 35 557 | 35 656 | 35 864 | 35 892 | 36 101 | 36 725 | 37 368 | 38 291 | 39 060 | 39 507 | 40 270 |
| **Both Sexes, 16 to 19 Years** | | | | | | | | | | | |
| Civilian noninstitutional population ... | 12 690 | 12 856 | 13 043 | 13 084 | 13 035 | 12 891 | 12 818 | 12 658 | 12 499 | 12 377 | 12 323 |
| Civilian labor force ......................... | 5 950 | 6 009 | 5 795 | 5 644 | 5 295 | 4 861 | 4 714 | 4 669 | 4 608 | 4 476 | 4 487 |
| Employed ...................................... | 5 105 | 5 215 | 4 990 | 4 697 | 4 138 | 3 733 | 3 691 | 3 665 | 3 671 | 3 701 | 3 824 |
| Agriculture .............................. | 97 | 102 | 113 | 118 | 114 | 96 | 105 | 103 | 97 | 82 | 84 |
| Nonagricultural industries ........... | 5 008 | 5 113 | 4 877 | 4 580 | 4 025 | 3 637 | 3 585 | 3 563 | 3 574 | 3 619 | 3 740 |
| Unemployed .................................. | 845 | 794 | 805 | 947 | 1 157 | 1 128 | 1 024 | 1 004 | 937 | 775 | 662 |
| Not in labor force .......................... | 6 739 | 6 847 | 7 248 | 7 440 | 7 740 | 8 030 | 8 103 | 7 988 | 7 891 | 7 901 | 7 836 |
| **BLACK[1]** | | | | | | | | | | | |
| **Both Sexes** | | | | | | | | | | | |
| Civilian noninstitutional population ... | 26 517 | 27 007 | 27 485 | 27 843 | 28 241 | 28 708 | 29 114 | 29 907 | 30 376 | 30 843 | 31 386 |
| Civilian labor force ......................... | 17 013 | 17 314 | 17 496 | 17 740 | 17 632 | 17 862 | 17 881 | 18 400 | 18 580 | 18 873 | 19 318 |
| Employed ...................................... | 15 313 | 15 765 | 16 051 | 15 953 | 15 025 | 15 010 | 15 051 | 15 856 | 16 151 | 16 732 | 17 472 |
| Agriculture .............................. | 51 | 60 | 53 | 55 | 66 | 59 | 52 | 61 | 58 | 62 | 66 |
| Nonagricultural industries ........... | 15 261 | 15 705 | 15 998 | 15 898 | 14 959 | 14 951 | 14 999 | 15 795 | 16 093 | 16 670 | 17 406 |
| Unemployed .................................. | 1 700 | 1 549 | 1 445 | 1 788 | 2 606 | 2 852 | 2 831 | 2 544 | 2 429 | 2 141 | 1 846 |
| Not in labor force .......................... | 9 504 | 9 693 | 9 989 | 10 103 | 10 609 | 10 846 | 11 233 | 11 508 | 11 797 | 11 970 | 12 068 |
| **Men, 16 Years and Over** | | | | | | | | | | | |
| Civilian noninstitutional population ... | 11 882 | 12 130 | 12 361 | 12 516 | 12 705 | 12 939 | 13 164 | 13 508 | 13 747 | 13 997 | 14 268 |
| Civilian labor force ......................... | 7 998 | 8 128 | 8 252 | 8 347 | 8 265 | 8 415 | 8 454 | 8 594 | 8 733 | 8 909 | 9 099 |
| Employed ...................................... | 7 155 | 7 354 | 7 500 | 7 398 | 6 817 | 6 865 | 6 953 | 7 302 | 7 497 | 7 818 | 8 164 |
| Agriculture .............................. | 43 | 51 | 46 | 49 | 56 | 53 | 47 | 51 | 48 | 54 | 57 |
| Nonagricultural industries ........... | 7 111 | 7 303 | 7 454 | 7 350 | 6 761 | 6 812 | 6 905 | 7 252 | 7 448 | 7 764 | 8 107 |
| Unemployed .................................. | 844 | 774 | 752 | 949 | 1 448 | 1 550 | 1 502 | 1 292 | 1 236 | 1 091 | 935 |
| Not in labor force .......................... | 3 884 | 4 002 | 4 110 | 4 169 | 4 441 | 4 524 | 4 710 | 4 913 | 5 014 | 5 089 | 5 169 |
| **Men, 20 Years and Over** | | | | | | | | | | | |
| Civilian noninstitutional population ... | 10 659 | 10 864 | 11 057 | 11 194 | 11 379 | 11 626 | 11 882 | 12 189 | 12 471 | 12 751 | 13 031 |
| Civilian labor force ......................... | 7 600 | 7 720 | 7 867 | 7 962 | 7 914 | 8 076 | 8 125 | 8 256 | 8 386 | 8 586 | 8 773 |
| Employed ...................................... | 6 901 | 7 079 | 7 245 | 7 151 | 6 628 | 6 680 | 6 765 | 7 104 | 7 304 | 7 613 | 7 938 |
| Agriculture .............................. | 43 | 49 | 45 | 47 | 55 | 52 | 46 | 50 | 48 | 54 | 55 |
| Nonagricultural industries ........... | 6 858 | 7 030 | 7 201 | 7 104 | 6 573 | 6 628 | 6 719 | 7 053 | 7 256 | 7 559 | 7 883 |
| Unemployed .................................. | 699 | 640 | 622 | 811 | 1 286 | 1 396 | 1 360 | 1 152 | 1 082 | 973 | 835 |
| Not in labor force .......................... | 3 060 | 3 144 | 3 189 | 3 232 | 3 465 | 3 550 | 17 | 3 932 | 4 084 | 4 165 | 4 258 |
| **Women, 16 Years and Over** | | | | | | | | | | | |
| Civilian noninstitutional population ... | 14 635 | 14 877 | 15 124 | 15 328 | 15 536 | 15 769 | 15 950 | 16 400 | 16 629 | 16 846 | 17 118 |
| Civilian labor force ......................... | 9 014 | 9 186 | 9 244 | 9 393 | 9 367 | 9 447 | 9 427 | 9 805 | 9 846 | 9 964 | 10 218 |
| Employed ...................................... | 8 158 | 8 410 | 8 551 | 8 554 | 8 208 | 8 145 | 8 098 | 8 553 | 8 654 | 8 915 | 9 308 |
| Agriculture .............................. | 8 | 9 | 7 | 6 | 10 | 6 | 5 | 10 | 9 | 8 | 10 |
| Nonagricultural industries ........... | 8 150 | 8 402 | 8 544 | 8 548 | 8 198 | 8 139 | 8 093 | 8 543 | 8 645 | 8 906 | 9 298 |
| Unemployed .................................. | 856 | 775 | 693 | 839 | 1 159 | 1 302 | 1 329 | 1 252 | 1 192 | 1 050 | 911 |
| Not in labor force .......................... | 5 621 | 5 691 | 5 879 | 5 934 | 6 169 | 6 322 | 6 523 | 6 595 | 6 783 | 6 881 | 6 899 |
| **Women, 20 Years and Over** | | | | | | | | | | | |
| Civilian noninstitutional population ... | 13 377 | 13 578 | 13 788 | 13 974 | 14 178 | 14 425 | 14 638 | 15 076 | 15 340 | 15 584 | 15 863 |
| Civilian labor force ......................... | 8 610 | 8 723 | 8 828 | 8 991 | 8 988 | 9 110 | 9 110 | 9 433 | 9 476 | 9 606 | 9 843 |
| Employed ...................................... | 7 876 | 8 068 | 8 240 | 8 260 | 7 956 | 7 944 | 7 906 | 8 313 | 8 408 | 8 663 | 9 032 |
| Agriculture .............................. | 7 | 7 | 7 | 6 | 10 | 6 | 5 | 10 | 9 | 8 | 10 |
| Nonagricultural industries ........... | 7 868 | 8 060 | 8 233 | 8 254 | 7 946 | 7 938 | 7 901 | 8 303 | 8 399 | 8 655 | 9 022 |
| Unemployed .................................. | 734 | 656 | 588 | 732 | 1 032 | 1 165 | 1 204 | 1 119 | 1 069 | 943 | 811 |
| Not in labor force .......................... | 4 768 | 4 854 | 4 960 | 4 982 | 5 190 | 5 315 | 5 529 | 5 643 | 5 864 | 5 978 | 6 021 |
| **Both Sexes, 16 to 19 Years** | | | | | | | | | | | |
| Civilian noninstitutional population ... | 2 481 | 2 565 | 2 640 | 2 676 | 2 684 | 2 657 | 2 594 | 2 643 | 2 565 | 2 508 | 2 491 |
| Civilian labor force ......................... | 803 | 871 | 801 | 787 | 729 | 677 | 647 | 711 | 717 | 681 | 701 |
| Employed ...................................... | 536 | 618 | 566 | 541 | 442 | 386 | 380 | 438 | 439 | 456 | 502 |
| Agriculture .............................. | 1 | 3 | 1 | 1 | 1 | 1 | 1 | 0 | 1 | 0 | 2 |
| Nonagricultural industries ........... | 535 | 614 | 564 | 540 | 440 | 385 | 379 | 438 | 438 | 456 | 500 |
| Unemployed .................................. | 267 | 253 | 235 | 246 | 288 | 291 | 267 | 272 | 278 | 225 | 199 |
| Not in labor force .......................... | 1 677 | 1 694 | 1 839 | 1 889 | 1 954 | 1 980 | 1 947 | 1 932 | 1 848 | 1 827 | 1 790 |

[1]Beginning in 2003, persons who selected this race group only; persons who selected more than one race group are not included. Prior to 2003, persons who reported more than one race group were included in the group they identified as the main race.

## Table 1-3. Employment Status of the Civilian Noninstitutional Population, by Sex, Age, Race, and Hispanic Origin, 1995–2015—*Continued*

(Thousands of people.)

| Characteristic | 1995 | 1996 | 1997 | 1998 | 1999 | 2000 | 2001 | 2002 | 2003 | 2004 |
|---|---|---|---|---|---|---|---|---|---|---|
| **HISPANIC**[2] | | | | | | | | | | |
| **Both Sexes** | | | | | | | | | | |
| Civilian noninstitutional population ... | 18 629 | 19 213 | 20 321 | 21 070 | 21 650 | 23 938 | 24 942 | 25 963 | 27 551 | 28 109 |
| Civilian labor force ......................... | 12 267 | 12 774 | 13 796 | 14 317 | 14 665 | 16 689 | 17 328 | 17 943 | 18 813 | 19 272 |
| Employed ...................................... | 11 127 | 11 642 | 12 726 | 13 291 | 13 720 | 15 735 | 16 190 | 16 590 | 17 372 | 17 930 |
| Agriculture ............................... | 604 | 609 | 660 | 742 | 734 | 536 | 423 | 448 | 446 | 441 |
| Nonagricultural industries ........... | 10 524 | 11 033 | 12 067 | 12 549 | 12 986 | 15 199 | 15 767 | 16 141 | 16 927 | 17 489 |
| Unemployed ................................... | 1 140 | 1 132 | 1 069 | 1 026 | 945 | 954 | 1 138 | 1 353 | 1 441 | 1 342 |
| Not in labor force ........................... | 6 362 | 6 439 | 6 526 | 6 753 | 6 985 | 7 249 | 7 614 | 8 020 | 8 738 | 8 837 |
| **Men, 16 Years and Over** | | | | | | | | | | |
| Civilian noninstitutional population ... | 9 329 | 9 604 | 10 368 | 10 734 | 10 713 | 12 174 | 12 695 | 13 221 | 14 098 | 14 417 |
| Civilian labor force ......................... | 7 376 | 7 646 | 8 309 | 8 571 | 8 546 | 9 923 | 10 279 | 10 609 | 11 288 | 11 587 |
| Employed ...................................... | 6 725 | 7 039 | 7 728 | 8 018 | 8 067 | 9 428 | 9 668 | 9 845 | 10 479 | 10 832 |
| Agriculture ............................... | 527 | 537 | 571 | 651 | 642 | 449 | 345 | 361 | 350 | 356 |
| Nonagricultural industries ........... | 6 198 | 6 502 | 7 157 | 7 367 | 7 425 | 8 979 | 9 323 | 9 484 | 10 129 | 10 476 |
| Unemployed ................................... | 651 | 607 | 582 | 552 | 480 | 494 | 611 | 764 | 809 | 755 |
| Not in labor force ........................... | 1 952 | 1 957 | 2 059 | 2 164 | 2 167 | 2 252 | 2 416 | 2 613 | 2 810 | 2 831 |
| **Men, 20 Years and Over** | | | | | | | | | | |
| Civilian noninstitutional population ... | 8 375 | 8 611 | 9 250 | 9 573 | 9 523 | 10 841 | 11 386 | 11 928 | 12 797 | 13 082 |
| Civilian labor force ......................... | 6 898 | 7 150 | 7 779 | 8 005 | 7 950 | 9 247 | 9 595 | 9 977 | 10 756 | 11 020 |
| Employed ...................................... | 6 367 | 6 655 | 7 307 | 7 570 | 7 576 | 8 859 | 9 100 | 9 341 | 10 063 | 10 385 |
| Agriculture ............................... | 501 | 510 | 544 | 621 | 602 | 423 | 328 | 345 | 336 | 335 |
| Nonagricultural industries ........... | 5 866 | 6 145 | 6 763 | 6 949 | 6 974 | 8 435 | 8 773 | 8 996 | 9 727 | 10 050 |
| Unemployed ................................... | 530 | 495 | 471 | 436 | 374 | 388 | 495 | 636 | 693 | 635 |
| Not in labor force ........................... | 1 477 | 1 461 | 1 471 | 1 568 | 1 573 | 1 595 | 1 791 | 1 951 | 2 041 | 2 061 |
| **Women, 16 Years and Over** | | | | | | | | | | |
| Civilian noninstitutional population ... | 9 300 | 9 610 | 9 953 | 10 335 | 10 937 | 11 764 | 12 247 | 12 742 | 13 452 | 13 692 |
| Civilian labor force ......................... | 4 891 | 5 128 | 5 486 | 5 746 | 6 119 | 6 767 | 7 049 | 7 334 | 7 525 | 7 685 |
| Employed ...................................... | 4 403 | 4 602 | 4 999 | 5 273 | 5 653 | 6 307 | 6 522 | 6 744 | 6 894 | 7 098 |
| Agriculture ............................... | 76 | 72 | 89 | 91 | 92 | 87 | 77 | 87 | 96 | 85 |
| Nonagricultural industries ........... | 4 326 | 4 531 | 4 910 | 5 182 | 5 561 | 6 220 | 6 445 | 6 657 | 6 798 | 7 013 |
| Unemployed ................................... | 488 | 525 | 488 | 473 | 466 | 460 | 527 | 590 | 631 | 587 |
| Not in labor force ........................... | 4 409 | 4 482 | 4 466 | 4 589 | 4 819 | 4 997 | 5 198 | 5 408 | 5 928 | 6 007 |
| **Women, 20 Years and Over** | | | | | | | | | | |
| Civilian noninstitutional population ... | 8 382 | 8 654 | 8 950 | 9 292 | 9 821 | 10 574 | 11 049 | 11 528 | 12 211 | 12 420 |
| Civilian labor force ......................... | 4 779 | 5 106 | 5 304 | 5 666 | 6 275 | 6 557 | 6 863 | 7 096 | 7 096 | 7 257 |
| Employed ...................................... | 4 116 | 4 341 | 4 705 | 4 928 | 5 290 | 5 903 | 6 121 | 6 367 | 6 541 | 6 752 |
| Agriculture ............................... | 72 | 69 | 83 | 85 | 88 | 81 | 73 | 84 | 91 | 78 |
| Nonagricultural industries ........... | 4 044 | 4 272 | 4 622 | 4 843 | 5 202 | 5 822 | 6 048 | 6 283 | 6 450 | 6 674 |
| Unemployed ................................... | 404 | 438 | 401 | 376 | 376 | 371 | 436 | 496 | 555 | 504 |
| Not in labor force ........................... | 3 863 | 3 875 | 3 845 | 3 988 | 4 155 | 4 299 | 4 492 | 4 666 | 5 114 | 5 163 |
| **Both Sexes, 16 to 19 Years** | | | | | | | | | | |
| Civilian noninstitutional population ... | 1 872 | 1 948 | 2 121 | 2 204 | 2 307 | 2 523 | 2 508 | 2 507 | 2 543 | 2 608 |
| Civilian labor force ......................... | 850 | 845 | 911 | 1 007 | 1 049 | 1 168 | 1 176 | 1 103 | 960 | 995 |
| Employed ...................................... | 645 | 646 | 714 | 793 | 854 | 973 | 969 | 882 | 768 | 792 |
| Agriculture ............................... | 31 | 29 | 33 | 36 | 45 | 31 | 22 | 19 | 19 | 25 |
| Nonagricultural industries ........... | 614 | 617 | 682 | 757 | 809 | 942 | 947 | 863 | 749 | 767 |
| Unemployed ................................... | 205 | 199 | 197 | 214 | 196 | 194 | 208 | 221 | 192 | 203 |
| Not in labor force ........................... | 1 022 | 1 103 | 1 210 | 1 197 | 1 257 | 1 355 | 1 331 | 1 404 | 1 583 | 1 612 |

[2]May be of any race.

## Table 1-3.  Employment Status of the Civilian Noninstitutional Population, by Sex, Age, Race, and Hispanic Origin, 1995–2015—Continued

(Thousands of people.)

| Characteristic | 2005 | 2006 | 2007 | 2008 | 2009 | 2010 | 2011 | 2012 | 2013 | 2014 | 2015 |
|---|---|---|---|---|---|---|---|---|---|---|---|
| **HISPANIC**[2] | | | | | | | | | | | |
| **Both Sexes** | | | | | | | | | | | |
| Civilian noninstitutional population ... | 29 133 | 30 103 | 31 383 | 32 141 | 32 891 | 33 713 | 34 438 | 36 759 | 37 517 | 38 400 | 39 617 |
| Civilian labor force | 19 824 | 20 694 | 21 602 | 22 024 | 22 352 | 22 748 | 22 898 | 24 391 | 24 771 | 25 370 | 26 126 |
| Employed | 18 632 | 19 613 | 20 382 | 20 346 | 19 647 | 19 906 | 20 269 | 21 878 | 22 514 | 23 492 | 24 400 |
| Agriculture | 423 | 428 | 426 | 441 | 426 | 480 | 523 | 491 | 495 | 517 | 580 |
| Nonagricultural industries | 18 209 | 19 185 | 19 956 | 19 904 | 19 221 | 19 426 | 19 746 | 21 387 | 22 019 | 22 975 | 23 820 |
| Unemployed | 1 191 | 1 081 | 1 220 | 1 678 | 2 706 | 2 843 | 2 629 | 2 514 | 2 257 | 1 878 | 1 726 |
| Not in labor force | 9 310 | 9 409 | 9 781 | 10 116 | 10 539 | 10 964 | 11 540 | 12 368 | 12 746 | 13 030 | 13 491 |
| **Men, 16 Years and Over** | | | | | | | | | | | |
| Civilian noninstitutional population ... | 14 962 | 15 473 | 16 154 | 16 524 | 16 897 | 17 359 | 17 753 | 18 434 | 18 798 | 19 244 | 19 745 |
| Civilian labor force | 11 985 | 12 488 | 13 005 | 13 255 | 13 310 | 13 511 | 13 576 | 14 026 | 14 341 | 14 651 | 15 054 |
| Employed | 11 337 | 11 887 | 12 310 | 12 248 | 11 640 | 11 800 | 12 049 | 12 643 | 13 078 | 13 655 | 14 111 |
| Agriculture | 350 | 347 | 352 | 364 | 344 | 377 | 418 | 388 | 392 | 403 | 454 |
| Nonagricultural industries | 10 987 | 11 540 | 11 958 | 11 884 | 11 296 | 11 423 | 11 631 | 12 255 | 12 686 | 13 251 | 13 657 |
| Unemployed | 647 | 601 | 695 | 1 007 | 1 670 | 1 711 | 1 527 | 1 383 | 1 263 | 996 | 943 |
| Not in labor force | 2 977 | 2 985 | 3 149 | 3 270 | 3 588 | 3 849 | 4 177 | 4 408 | 4 457 | 4 593 | 4 691 |
| **Men, 20 Years and Over** | | | | | | | | | | | |
| Civilian noninstitutional population ... | 13 586 | 14 046 | 14 649 | 14 971 | 15 305 | 15 693 | 15 941 | 16 555 | 16 928 | 17 371 | 17 860 |
| Civilian labor force | 11 408 | 11 888 | 12 403 | 12 629 | 12 730 | 12 958 | 13 030 | 13 407 | 13 728 | 14 066 | 14 444 |
| Employed | 10 872 | 11 391 | 11 827 | 11 769 | 11 256 | 11 438 | 11 685 | 12 212 | 12 638 | 13 202 | 13 624 |
| Agriculture | 341 | 337 | 337 | 351 | 332 | 367 | 405 | 374 | 378 | 391 | 440 |
| Nonagricultural industries | 10 532 | 11 054 | 11 490 | 11 418 | 10 924 | 11 071 | 11 281 | 11 838 | 12 259 | 12 811 | 13 184 |
| Unemployed | 536 | 497 | 576 | 860 | 1 474 | 1 519 | 1 345 | 1 195 | 1 090 | 864 | 820 |
| Not in labor force | 2 177 | 2 157 | 2 246 | 2 342 | 2 575 | 2 735 | 2 911 | 3 149 | 3 200 | 3 305 | 3 416 |
| **Women, 16 Years and Over** | | | | | | | | | | | |
| Civilian noninstitutional population ... | 14 172 | 14 630 | 15 229 | 15 616 | 15 993 | 16 353 | 16 685 | 18 324 | 18 719 | 19 156 | 19 872 |
| Civilian labor force | 7 839 | 8 206 | 8 597 | 8 769 | 9 043 | 9 238 | 9 322 | 10 365 | 10 430 | 10 720 | 11 072 |
| Employed | 7 295 | 7 725 | 8 072 | 8 098 | 8 007 | 8 106 | 8 220 | 9 235 | 9 437 | 9 838 | 10 289 |
| Agriculture | 73 | 80 | 74 | 77 | 82 | 103 | 105 | 103 | 103 | 114 | 126 |
| Nonagricultural industries | 7 222 | 7 645 | 7 999 | 8 021 | 7 925 | 8 003 | 8 115 | 9 131 | 9 334 | 9 724 | 10 163 |
| Unemployed | 544 | 480 | 525 | 672 | 1 036 | 1 132 | 1 102 | 1 130 | 994 | 882 | 783 |
| Not in labor force | 6 333 | 6 424 | 6 632 | 6 847 | 6 951 | 7 116 | 7 363 | 7 959 | 8 289 | 8 437 | 8 800 |
| **Women, 20 Years and Over** | | | | | | | | | | | |
| Civilian noninstitutional population ... | 12 858 | 13 262 | 13 791 | 14 127 | 14 463 | 14 776 | 15 090 | 16 548 | 16 938 | 17 367 | 18 052 |
| Civilian labor force | 7 377 | 7 735 | 8 108 | 8 274 | 8 560 | 8 789 | 8 902 | 9 853 | 9 911 | 10 195 | 10 539 |
| Employed | 6 913 | 7 321 | 7 662 | 7 707 | 59 | 7 788 | 8 902 | 8 858 | 9 056 | 9 431 | 9 853 |
| Agriculture | 70 | 77 | 69 | 75 | 78 | 101 | 104 | 100 | 99 | 111 | 123 |
| Nonagricultural industries | 6 843 | 7 244 | 7 593 | 7 632 | 7 570 | 7 687 | 7 814 | 8 758 | 8 957 | 9 320 | 9 730 |
| Unemployed | 464 | 414 | 446 | 567 | 911 | 1 001 | 984 | 995 | 855 | 764 | 686 |
| Not in labor force | 5 481 | 5 527 | 5 682 | 5 853 | 5 903 | 5 987 | 6 187 | 6 695 | 7 028 | 7 172 | 7 513 |
| **Both Sexes, 16 to 19 Years** | | | | | | | | | | | |
| Civilian noninstitutional population ... | 2 689 | 2 796 | 2 944 | 3 042 | 3 123 | 3 243 | 3 407 | 3 656 | 3 651 | 3 662 | 3 705 |
| Civilian labor force | 1 038 | 1 071 | 1 091 | 1 121 | 1 063 | 1 002 | 965 | 1 131 | 1 133 | 1 109 | 1 144 |
| Employed | 847 | 900 | 894 | 870 | 742 | 680 | 665 | 808 | 821 | 859 | 922 |
| Agriculture | 13 | 14 | 20 | 15 | 16 | 12 | 14 | 17 | 18 | 15 | 17 |
| Nonagricultural industries | 834 | 887 | 874 | 855 | 726 | 668 | 651 | 791 | 803 | 844 | 906 |
| Unemployed | 191 | 170 | 197 | 251 | 321 | 322 | 300 | 324 | 312 | 250 | 221 |
| Not in labor force | 1 651 | 1 725 | 1 853 | 1 921 | 2 061 | 2 242 | 2 442 | 2 524 | 2 518 | 2 553 | 2 562 |

[2]May be of any race.

## Table 1-4.  Employment Status of the Civilian Noninstitutional Population, by Sex and Marital Status, 1990–2015

(Thousands of people.)

| Race, marital status, and year | Men — Civilian noninstitutional population | Men — Civilian labor force Total | Men — Employed | Men — Unemployed | Women — Civilian noninstitutional population | Women — Civilian labor force Total | Women — Employed | Women — Unemployed |
|---|---|---|---|---|---|---|---|---|
| **ALL RACES** | | | | | | | | |
| **Single** | | | | | | | | |
| 1990 | 25 870 | 19 357 | 17 405 | 1 952 | 21 901 | 14 612 | 13 336 | 1 276 |
| 1991 | 26 197 | 19 411 | 17 011 | 2 400 | 22 173 | 14 681 | 13 198 | 1 482 |
| 1992 | 26 436 | 19 709 | 17 098 | 2 611 | 22 475 | 14 872 | 13 263 | 1 609 |
| 1993 | 26 570 | 19 706 | 17 261 | 2 445 | 22 713 | 15 031 | 13 484 | 1 547 |
| 1994 | 26 786 | 19 786 | 17 604 | 2 181 | 23 000 | 15 333 | 13 847 | 1 486 |
| 1995 | 26 918 | 19 841 | 17 833 | 2 007 | 23 151 | 15 467 | 14 053 | 1 413 |
| 1996 | 27 387 | 20 071 | 18 055 | 2 016 | 23 623 | 15 842 | 14 403 | 1 439 |
| 1997 | 28 311 | 20 689 | 18 783 | 1 906 | 24 285 | 16 492 | 15 037 | 1 455 |
| 1998 | 28 693 | 21 037 | 19 240 | 1 798 | 24 941 | 17 087 | 15 755 | 1 332 |
| 1999 | 29 104 | 21 351 | 19 686 | 1 665 | 25 576 | 17 575 | 16 267 | 1 308 |
| 2000 | 29 887 | 22 002 | 20 339 | 1 663 | 25 920 | 17 849 | 16 628 | 1 221 |
| 2001 | 30 646 | 22 285 | 20 298 | 1 988 | 26 462 | 18 021 | 16 635 | 1 386 |
| 2002 | 31 072 | 22 289 | 19 983 | 2 306 | 26 999 | 18 203 | 16 583 | 1 621 |
| 2003 | 31 691 | 22 297 | 19 841 | 2 457 | 27 802 | 18 397 | 16 723 | 1 674 |
| 2004 | 32 422 | 22 776 | 20 395 | 2 381 | 28 228 | 18 616 | 16 995 | 1 621 |
| 2005 | 33 125 | 23 214 | 21 006 | 2 209 | 29 046 | 19 183 | 17 588 | 1 595 |
| 2006 | 33 931 | 23 974 | 21 907 | 2 067 | 29 624 | 19 474 | 17 978 | 1 496 |
| 2007 | 34 650 | 24 276 | 22 143 | 2 132 | 30 219 | 19 745 | 18 322 | 1 422 |
| 2008 | 35 274 | 24 643 | 21 938 | 2 705 | 30 980 | 20 231 | 18 513 | 1 717 |
| 2009 | 36 087 | 24 640 | 20 628 | 4 011 | 31 500 | 20 224 | 17 800 | 2 424 |
| 2010 | 37 137 | 24 985 | 20 850 | 4 135 | 32 548 | 20 592 | 17 950 | 2 642 |
| 2011 | 37 782 | 25 301 | 21 474 | 3 827 | 33 266 | 20 878 | 18 266 | 2 612 |
| 2012 | 38 180 | 25 494 | 22 002 | 3 492 | 34 267 | 21 506 | 18 973 | 2 533 |
| 2013 | 38 930 | 26 046 | 22 648 | 3 398 | 35 047 | 22 070 | 19 690 | 2 381 |
| 2014 | 39 676 | 26 456 | 23 535 | 2 921 | 35 506 | 22 320 | 20 222 | 2 098 |
| 2015 | 40 151 | 26 803 | 24 267 | 2 537 | 36 145 | 22 738 | 20 881 | 1 857 |
| **Married, Spouse Present** | | | | | | | | |
| 1990 | 53 793 | 42 275 | 40 829 | 1 446 | 52 917 | 30 901 | 29 714 | 1 188 |
| 1991 | 54 158 | 42 303 | 40 429 | 1 875 | 53 169 | 31 112 | 29 698 | 1 415 |
| 1992 | 54 509 | 42 491 | 40 341 | 2 150 | 53 501 | 31 700 | 30 100 | 1 600 |
| 1993 | 55 178 | 42 834 | 40 935 | 1 899 | 53 838 | 31 980 | 30 499 | 1 482 |
| 1994 | 55 560 | 43 005 | 41 414 | 1 592 | 54 155 | 32 888 | 31 536 | 1 352 |
| 1995 | 56 100 | 43 472 | 42 048 | 1 424 | 54 716 | 33 359 | 32 063 | 1 296 |
| 1996 | 56 363 | 43 739 | 42 417 | 1 322 | 54 970 | 33 618 | 32 406 | 1 211 |
| 1997 | 56 396 | 43 808 | 42 642 | 1 167 | 54 915 | 33 802 | 32 755 | 1 047 |
| 1998 | 56 670 | 43 957 | 42 923 | 1 034 | 55 331 | 33 857 | 32 872 | 985 |
| 1999 | 57 089 | 44 244 | 43 254 | 990 | 56 178 | 34 372 | 33 450 | 921 |
| 2000 | 58 167 | 44 987 | 44 078 | 908 | 57 557 | 35 146 | 34 209 | 937 |
| 2001 | 58 448 | 45 233 | 44 007 | 1 226 | 57 610 | 35 236 | 34 153 | 1 083 |
| 2002 | 59 102 | 45 766 | 44 116 | 1 650 | 58 165 | 35 477 | 34 153 | 1 323 |
| 2003 | 60 063 | 46 404 | 44 653 | 1 751 | 59 069 | 36 046 | 34 695 | 1 352 |
| 2004 | 60 412 | 46 550 | 45 084 | 1 466 | 59 278 | 35 845 | 34 600 | 1 244 |
| 2005 | 60 545 | 46 771 | 45 483 | 1 287 | 59 205 | 35 941 | 34 773 | 1 168 |
| 2006 | 60 751 | 46 842 | 45 700 | 1 142 | 59 576 | 36 314 | 35 272 | 1 042 |
| 2007 | 61 760 | 47 520 | 46 314 | 1 206 | 60 474 | 36 881 | 35 832 | 1 049 |
| 2008 | 61 794 | 47 450 | 45 860 | 1 590 | 60 554 | 37 194 | 35 869 | 1 325 |
| 2009 | 61 773 | 47 114 | 43 998 | 3 115 | 60 675 | 37 264 | 35 207 | 2 057 |
| 2010 | 61 254 | 46 430 | 43 292 | 3 138 | 60 257 | 36 742 | 34 582 | 2 160 |
| 2011 | 61 358 | 45 954 | 43 283 | 2 671 | 60 061 | 36 141 | 34 110 | 2 031 |
| 2012 | 61 757 | 46 094 | 43 820 | 2 274 | 61 219 | 36 436 | 34 521 | 1 915 |
| 2013 | 61 932 | 45 971 | 43 978 | 1 993 | 61 386 | 36 137 | 34 484 | 1 653 |
| 2014 | 62 432 | 45 919 | 44 377 | 1 542 | 61 754 | 36 082 | 34 720 | 1 363 |
| 2015 | 62 975 | 46 248 | 44 938 | 1 310 | 62 203 | 36 135 | 34 997 | 1 138 |
| **Divorced, Widowed, or Separated** | | | | | | | | |
| 1990 | 10 714 | 7 378 | 6 871 | 508 | 23 968 | 11 315 | 10 639 | 676 |
| 1991 | 10 924 | 7 454 | 6 783 | 671 | 24 304 | 11 385 | 10 600 | 786 |
| 1992 | 11 325 | 7 763 | 7 001 | 762 | 24 559 | 11 570 | 10 689 | 881 |
| 1993 | 11 584 | 7 864 | 7 153 | 711 | 24 955 | 11 784 | 10 927 | 856 |
| 1994 | 12 008 | 8 026 | 7 432 | 594 | 25 304 | 12 018 | 11 227 | 791 |
| 1995 | 12 160 | 8 048 | 7 496 | 551 | 25 539 | 12 118 | 11 407 | 712 |
| 1996 | 12 456 | 8 276 | 7 735 | 541 | 25 791 | 12 397 | 11 691 | 706 |
| 1997 | 13 009 | 8 764 | 8 260 | 504 | 26 218 | 12 742 | 12 082 | 660 |
| 1998 | 13 394 | 8 965 | 8 530 | 435 | 26 190 | 12 771 | 12 143 | 628 |
| 1999 | 13 528 | 8 918 | 8 507 | 411 | 26 276 | 12 909 | 12 324 | 585 |
| 2000 | 13 910 | 9 291 | 8 888 | 403 | 27 135 | 13 308 | 12 748 | 559 |
| 2001 | 14 188 | 9 367 | 8 892 | 476 | 27 738 | 13 592 | 12 949 | 642 |
| 2002 | 14 411 | 9 445 | 8 804 | 641 | 27 821 | 13 683 | 12 846 | 837 |
| 2003 | 14 680 | 9 537 | 8 838 | 699 | 27 862 | 13 828 | 12 986 | 842 |
| 2004 | 14 875 | 9 654 | 9 045 | 608 | 28 141 | 13 961 | 13 133 | 828 |
| 2005 | 15 481 | 10 048 | 9 484 | 563 | 28 680 | 14 163 | 13 396 | 768 |
| 2006 | 15 923 | 10 440 | 9 895 | 545 | 29 010 | 14 385 | 13 675 | 709 |
| 2007 | 15 763 | 10 341 | 9 797 | 544 | 29 001 | 14 362 | 13 638 | 724 |
| 2008 | 16 044 | 10 427 | 9 688 | 739 | 29 141 | 14 342 | 13 494 | 849 |
| 2009 | 16 275 | 10 370 | 9 043 | 1 326 | 29 490 | 14 531 | 13 201 | 1 330 |
| 2010 | 16 783 | 10 570 | 9 217 | 1 352 | 29 851 | 14 570 | 13 173 | 1 397 |
| 2011 | 17 177 | 10 719 | 9 533 | 1 186 | 29 974 | 14 623 | 13 203 | 1 420 |
| 2012 | 17 406 | 10 738 | 9 734 | 1 005 | 30 454 | 14 706 | 13 420 | 1 286 |
| 2013 | 17 694 | 10 649 | 9 726 | 923 | 30 691 | 14 515 | 13 403 | 1 112 |
| 2014 | 17 639 | 10 508 | 9 780 | 727 | 30 938 | 14 637 | 13 672 | 965 |
| 2015 | 17 975 | 10 569 | 9 926 | 643 | 31 352 | 14 637 | 13 825 | 812 |

*Note:* See notes and definitions for information on historical comparability.

## Table 1-5. Employment Status of the Civilian Noninstitutional Population, by Region, Division, State, and Selected Territory, 2014–2015

(Thousands of people, percent.)

| Region, division, and state | 2014 | | | | | 2015 | | | | | |
|---|---|---|---|---|---|---|---|---|---|---|---|
| | Civilian noninstitutional population | Civilian labor force | | | | Civilian noninstitutional population | Civilian labor force | | | | |
| | | Total | Participation rate | Unemployed | Unemployment rate | | Total | Participation rate | Employed | Unemployed | Unemployment rate |
| UNITED STATES[1] | 247 947 | 155 922 | 62.9 | 9 617 | 6.2 | 250 801 | 157 130 | 62.7 | 148 834 | 8 296 | 5.3 |
| Northeast | 44 890 | 28 285 | 63.0 | 1 742 | 6.2 | 45 078 | 28 425 | 63.1 | 26 941 | 1 483 | 5.2 |
| New England | 11 854 | 7 785 | 65.7 | 457 | 5.9 | 11 918 | 7 778 | 65.3 | 7 392 | 385 | 5.0 |
| Connecticut | 2 866 | 1 886 | 65.8 | 125 | 6.6 | 2 873 | 1 888 | 65.7 | 1 782 | 106 | 5.6 |
| Maine | 1 089 | 697 | 64.0 | 39 | 5.6 | 1 092 | 680 | 62.3 | 650 | 30 | 4.4 |
| Massachusetts | 5 454 | 3 557 | 65.2 | 204 | 5.7 | 5 499 | 3 570 | 64.9 | 3 392 | 178 | 5.0 |
| New Hampshire | 1 079 | 741 | 68.7 | 32 | 4.3 | 1 084 | 741 | 68.4 | 716 | 25 | 3.4 |
| Rhode Island | 852 | 556 | 65.3 | 43 | 7.7 | 855 | 555 | 64.9 | 521 | 33 | 6.0 |
| Vermont | 515 | 348 | 67.6 | 14 | 4.0 | 515 | 344 | 66.8 | 332 | 13 | 3.7 |
| Middle Atlantic | 33 036 | 20 500 | 62.1 | 1 286 | 6.3 | 33 160 | 20 647 | 62.3 | 19 549 | 1 098 | 5.3 |
| New Jersey | 7 055 | 4 514 | 64.0 | 304 | 6.7 | 7 090 | 4 544 | 64.1 | 4 289 | 255 | 5.6 |
| New York | 15 771 | 9 595 | 60.8 | 606 | 6.3 | 15 837 | 9 679 | 61.1 | 9 166 | 513 | 5.3 |
| Pennsylvania | 10 209 | 6 391 | 62.6 | 376 | 5.9 | 10 232 | 6 424 | 62.8 | 6 094 | 330 | 5.1 |
| Midwest | 52 865 | 34 391 | 65.1 | 2 008 | 5.8 | 53 093 | 34 529 | 65.0 | 32 860 | 1 669 | 4.8 |
| East North Central | 36 619 | 23 287 | 63.6 | 1 497 | 6.4 | 36 737 | 23 324 | 63.5 | 22 104 | 1 220 | 5.2 |
| Illinois | 10 049 | 6 515 | 64.8 | 461 | 7.1 | 10 059 | 6 512 | 64.7 | 6 126 | 386 | 5.9 |
| Indiana | 5 097 | 3 228 | 63.3 | 192 | 5.9 | 5 125 | 3 266 | 63.7 | 3 109 | 157 | 4.8 |
| Michigan | 7 848 | 4 754 | 60.6 | 346 | 7.3 | 7 874 | 4 751 | 60.3 | 4 493 | 258 | 5.4 |
| Ohio | 9 092 | 5 703 | 62.7 | 330 | 5.8 | 9 124 | 5 700 | 62.5 | 5 423 | 277 | 4.9 |
| Wisconsin | 4 534 | 3 086 | 68.1 | 167 | 5.4 | 4 554 | 3 095 | 68.0 | 2 953 | 143 | 4.6 |
| West North Central | 16 246 | 11 104 | 68.3 | 511 | 4.6 | 16 356 | 11 204 | 68.5 | 10 756 | 448 | 4.0 |
| Iowa | 2 421 | 1 698 | 70.1 | 71 | 4.2 | 2 435 | 1 701 | 69.9 | 1 639 | 62 | 3.7 |
| Kansas | 2 196 | 1 494 | 68.0 | 68 | 4.6 | 2 208 | 1 499 | 67.9 | 1 436 | 63 | 4.2 |
| Minnesota | 4 258 | 2 983 | 70.1 | 124 | 4.2 | 4 289 | 3 010 | 70.2 | 2 899 | 112 | 3.7 |
| Missouri | 4 718 | 3 052 | 64.7 | 188 | 6.2 | 4 744 | 3 114 | 65.6 | 2 958 | 156 | 5.0 |
| Nebraska | 1 435 | 1 014 | 70.7 | 33 | 3.3 | 1 446 | 1 013 | 70.1 | 983 | 30 | 3.0 |
| North Dakota | 572 | 415 | 72.6 | 11 | 2.7 | 584 | 414 | 70.9 | 403 | 11 | 2.7 |
| South Dakota | 647 | 449 | 69.4 | 15 | 3.4 | 652 | 452 | 69.3 | 438 | 14 | 3.1 |
| South | 92 514 | 57 020 | 61.6 | 3 425 | 6.0 | 93 789 | 57 351 | 61.1 | 54 323 | 3 028 | 5.3 |
| South Atlantic | 49 022 | 30 276 | 61.8 | 1 892 | 6.3 | 49 719 | 30 506 | 61.4 | 28 841 | 1 665 | 5.5 |
| Delaware | 739 | 454 | 61.4 | 26 | 5.7 | 749 | 467 | 62.3 | 445 | 23 | 4.9 |
| District of Columbia | 545 | 378 | 69.4 | 29 | 7.8 | 554 | 388 | 70.0 | 362 | 27 | 6.9 |
| Florida | 15 995 | 9 607 | 60.1 | 607 | 6.3 | 16 313 | 9 675 | 59.3 | 9 153 | 522 | 5.4 |
| Georgia | 7 673 | 4 754 | 62.0 | 337 | 7.1 | 7 783 | 4 771 | 61.3 | 4 491 | 280 | 5.9 |
| Maryland | 4 683 | 3 128 | 66.8 | 182 | 5.8 | 4 716 | 3 152 | 66.8 | 2 988 | 164 | 5.2 |
| North Carolina | 7 689 | 4 691 | 61.0 | 294 | 6.3 | 7 792 | 4 769 | 61.2 | 4 495 | 274 | 5.7 |
| South Carolina | 3 761 | 2 217 | 58.9 | 143 | 6.4 | 3 823 | 2 257 | 59.0 | 2 123 | 135 | 6.0 |
| Virginia | 6 453 | 4 258 | 66.0 | 222 | 5.2 | 6 509 | 4 240 | 65.1 | 4 052 | 189 | 4.4 |
| West Virginia | 1 483 | 790 | 53.3 | 52 | 6.6 | 1 481 | 785 | 53.0 | 732 | 53 | 6.7 |
| East South Central | 14 598 | 8 463 | 58.0 | 570 | 6.7 | 14 692 | 8 435 | 57.4 | 7 939 | 496 | 5.9 |
| Alabama | 3 785 | 2 161 | 57.1 | 147 | 6.8 | 3 803 | 2 146 | 56.4 | 2 015 | 131 | 6.1 |
| Kentucky | 3 424 | 2 006 | 58.6 | 130 | 6.5 | 3 441 | 1 953 | 56.8 | 1 848 | 105 | 5.4 |
| Mississippi | 2 274 | 1 249 | 54.9 | 94 | 7.6 | 2 281 | 1 273 | 55.8 | 1 190 | 83 | 6.5 |
| Tennessee | 5 115 | 3 047 | 59.6 | 199 | 6.5 | 5 167 | 3 063 | 59.3 | 2 886 | 177 | 5.8 |
| West South Central | 28 895 | 18 282 | 63.3 | 963 | 5.3 | 29 379 | 18 411 | 62.7 | 17 544 | 867 | 4.7 |
| Arkansas | 2 286 | 1 304 | 57.0 | 80 | 6.1 | 2 299 | 1 330 | 57.9 | 1 261 | 69 | 5.2 |
| Louisiana | 3 550 | 2 157 | 60.8 | 138 | 6.4 | 3 573 | 2 160 | 60.5 | 2 025 | 135 | 6.3 |
| Oklahoma | 2 946 | 1 798 | 61.0 | 81 | 4.5 | 2 975 | 1 842 | 61.9 | 1 764 | 78 | 4.2 |
| Texas | 20 113 | 13 023 | 64.7 | 664 | 5.1 | 20 531 | 13 078 | 63.7 | 12 494 | 584 | 4.5 |
| West | 58 221 | 36 566 | 62.8 | 2 463 | 6.7 | 59 050 | 36 954 | 62.6 | 34 831 | 2 123 | 5.7 |
| Mountain | 17 733 | 11 271 | 63.6 | 653 | 5.8 | 18 045 | 11 417 | 63.3 | 10 838 | 579 | 5.1 |
| Arizona | 5 179 | 3 097 | 59.8 | 211 | 6.8 | 5 275 | 3 153 | 59.8 | 2 960 | 193 | 6.1 |
| Colorado | 4 148 | 2 815 | 67.9 | 141 | 5.0 | 4 240 | 2 829 | 66.7 | 2 719 | 110 | 3.9 |
| Idaho | 1 229 | 781 | 63.5 | 38 | 4.8 | 1 248 | 797 | 63.9 | 764 | 33 | 4.1 |
| Montana | 808 | 516 | 63.9 | 24 | 4.7 | 816 | 523 | 64.1 | 501 | 22 | 4.1 |
| Nevada | 2 210 | 1 402 | 63.4 | 111 | 7.9 | 2 256 | 1 426 | 63.2 | 1 330 | 96 | 6.7 |
| New Mexico | 1 602 | 921 | 57.5 | 62 | 6.7 | 1 607 | 920 | 57.2 | 859 | 61 | 6.6 |
| Utah | 2 106 | 1 432 | 68.0 | 55 | 3.8 | 2 151 | 1 464 | 68.1 | 1 412 | 52 | 3.5 |
| Wyoming | 451 | 307 | 68.1 | 13 | 4.1 | 452 | 306 | 67.7 | 293 | 13 | 4.2 |
| Pacific | 40 488 | 25 294 | 62.5 | 1 810 | 7.2 | 41 005 | 25 537 | 62.3 | 23 993 | 1 544 | 6.0 |
| Alaska | 540 | 366 | 67.8 | 25 | 6.9 | 542 | 364 | 67.2 | 340 | 24 | 6.5 |
| California | 30 163 | 18 828 | 62.4 | 1 410 | 7.5 | 30 523 | 18 982 | 62.2 | 17 799 | 1 183 | 6.2 |
| Hawaii | 1 084 | 668 | 61.6 | 29 | 4.4 | 1 093 | 677 | 61.9 | 653 | 25 | 3.6 |
| Oregon | 3 173 | 1 939 | 61.1 | 132 | 6.8 | 3 225 | 1 969 | 61.1 | 1 857 | 112 | 5.7 |
| Washington | 5 529 | 3 493 | 63.2 | 214 | 6.1 | 5 622 | 3 544 | 63.0 | 3 344 | 200 | 5.7 |

Note: Data refer to place of residence. Region and division data are derived from summing the component states. Sub-national data reflect revised population controls and model reestimation.

[1]Due to separate processing and weighing procedures, totals for the United States differ from the results obtained by aggregating data for regions, divisions, or states.

## Table 1-6.  Civilian Noninstitutional Population, by Age, Race, Sex, and Hispanic Origin, 1948–2015

(Thousands of people.)

| Race, Hispanic origin, sex, and year | 16 years and over | 16 to 19 years | | | 20 years and over | | | | | | |
|---|---|---|---|---|---|---|---|---|---|---|---|
| | | Total | 16 to 17 years | 18 to 19 years | Total | 20 to 24 years | 25 to 34 years | 35 to 44 years | 45 to 54 years | 55 to 64 years | 65 years and over |
| **ALL RACES** | | | | | | | | | | | |
| **Both Sexes** | | | | | | | | | | | |
| 1948 | 103 068 | 8 449 | 4 265 | 4 185 | 94 618 | 11 530 | 22 610 | 20 097 | 16 771 | 12 885 | 10 720 |
| 1949 | 103 994 | 8 215 | 4 139 | 4 079 | 95 778 | 11 312 | 22 822 | 20 401 | 17 002 | 13 201 | 11 035 |
| 1950 | 104 995 | 8 143 | 4 076 | 4 068 | 96 851 | 11 080 | 23 013 | 20 681 | 17 240 | 13 469 | 11 363 |
| 1951 | 104 621 | 7 865 | 4 096 | 3 771 | 96 755 | 10 167 | 22 843 | 20 863 | 17 464 | 13 692 | 11 724 |
| 1952 | 105 231 | 7 922 | 4 234 | 3 689 | 97 305 | 9 389 | 23 044 | 21 137 | 17 716 | 13 889 | 12 126 |
| 1953 | 107 056 | 8 014 | 4 241 | 3 773 | 99 041 | 8 960 | 23 266 | 21 922 | 17 991 | 13 830 | 13 075 |
| 1954 | 108 321 | 8 224 | 4 336 | 3 889 | 100 095 | 8 885 | 23 304 | 22 135 | 18 305 | 14 085 | 13 375 |
| 1955 | 109 683 | 8 364 | 4 440 | 3 925 | 101 318 | 9 036 | 23 249 | 22 348 | 18 643 | 14 309 | 13 728 |
| 1956 | 110 954 | 8 434 | 4 482 | 3 953 | 102 518 | 9 271 | 23 072 | 22 567 | 19 012 | 14 516 | 14 075 |
| 1957 | 112 265 | 8 612 | 4 587 | 4 026 | 103 653 | 9 486 | 22 849 | 22 786 | 19 424 | 14 727 | 14 376 |
| 1958 | 113 727 | 8 986 | 4 872 | 4 114 | 104 737 | 9 733 | 22 563 | 23 025 | 19 832 | 14 923 | 14 657 |
| 1959 | 115 329 | 9 618 | 5 337 | 4 282 | 105 711 | 9 975 | 22 201 | 23 207 | 20 203 | 15 134 | 14 985 |
| 1960 | 117 245 | 10 187 | 5 573 | 4 615 | 107 056 | 10 273 | 21 998 | 23 437 | 20 601 | 15 409 | 15 336 |
| 1961 | 118 771 | 10 513 | 5 462 | 5 052 | 108 255 | 10 583 | 21 829 | 23 585 | 20 893 | 15 675 | 15 685 |
| 1962 | 120 153 | 10 652 | 5 503 | 5 150 | 109 500 | 10 852 | 21 503 | 23 797 | 20 916 | 15 874 | 16 554 |
| 1963 | 122 416 | 11 370 | 6 301 | 5 070 | 111 045 | 11 464 | 21 400 | 23 948 | 21 144 | 16 138 | 16 945 |
| 1964 | 124 485 | 12 111 | 6 974 | 5 139 | 112 372 | 12 017 | 21 367 | 23 940 | 21 452 | 16 442 | 17 150 |
| 1965 | 126 513 | 12 930 | 6 936 | 5 995 | 113 582 | 12 442 | 21 417 | 23 832 | 21 728 | 16 727 | 17 432 |
| 1966 | 128 058 | 13 592 | 6 914 | 6 679 | 114 463 | 12 638 | 21 543 | 23 579 | 21 977 | 17 007 | 17 715 |
| 1967 | 129 874 | 13 480 | 7 003 | 6 480 | 116 391 | 13 421 | 22 057 | 23 313 | 22 256 | 17 310 | 18 029 |
| 1968 | 132 028 | 13 698 | 7 200 | 6 499 | 118 328 | 13 891 | 22 912 | 23 036 | 22 534 | 17 614 | 18 338 |
| 1969 | 134 335 | 14 095 | 7 422 | 6 673 | 120 238 | 14 488 | 23 645 | 22 709 | 22 806 | 17 930 | 18 657 |
| 1970 | 137 085 | 14 519 | 7 643 | 6 876 | 122 566 | 15 323 | 24 435 | 22 489 | 23 059 | 18 250 | 19 007 |
| 1971 | 140 216 | 15 022 | 7 849 | 7 173 | 125 193 | 16 345 | 25 337 | 22 274 | 23 244 | 18 581 | 19 406 |
| 1972 | 144 126 | 15 510 | 8 076 | 7 435 | 128 614 | 17 143 | 26 740 | 22 358 | 23 338 | 19 007 | 20 023 |
| 1973 | 147 096 | 15 840 | 8 227 | 7 613 | 131 253 | 17 692 | 28 172 | 22 287 | 23 431 | 19 281 | 20 389 |
| 1974 | 150 120 | 16 180 | 8 373 | 7 809 | 133 938 | 17 994 | 29 439 | 22 461 | 23 578 | 19 517 | 20 945 |
| 1975 | 153 153 | 16 418 | 8 419 | 7 999 | 136 733 | 18 595 | 30 710 | 22 526 | 23 535 | 19 844 | 21 525 |
| 1976 | 156 150 | 16 614 | 8 442 | 8 171 | 139 536 | 19 109 | 31 953 | 22 796 | 23 409 | 20 185 | 22 083 |
| 1977 | 159 033 | 16 688 | 8 482 | 8 206 | 142 345 | 19 582 | 33 117 | 23 296 | 23 197 | 20 557 | 22 597 |
| 1978 | 161 910 | 16 695 | 8 484 | 8 211 | 145 216 | 20 007 | 34 091 | 24 099 | 22 977 | 20 875 | 23 166 |
| 1979 | 164 863 | 16 657 | 8 389 | 8 268 | 148 205 | 20 353 | 35 261 | 24 861 | 22 752 | 21 210 | 23 767 |
| 1980 | 167 745 | 16 543 | 8 279 | 8 264 | 151 202 | 20 635 | 36 558 | 25 578 | 22 563 | 21 520 | 24 350 |
| 1981 | 170 130 | 16 214 | 8 068 | 8 145 | 153 916 | 20 820 | 37 777 | 26 291 | 22 422 | 21 756 | 24 850 |
| 1982 | 172 271 | 15 763 | 7 714 | 8 049 | 156 508 | 20 845 | 38 492 | 27 611 | 22 264 | 21 909 | 25 387 |
| 1983 | 174 215 | 15 274 | 7 385 | 7 889 | 158 941 | 20 799 | 39 147 | 28 932 | 22 167 | 22 003 | 25 892 |
| 1984 | 176 383 | 14 735 | 7 196 | 7 538 | 161 648 | 20 688 | 39 999 | 30 251 | 22 226 | 22 052 | 26 433 |
| 1985 | 178 206 | 14 506 | 7 232 | 7 274 | 163 700 | 20 097 | 40 670 | 31 379 | 22 418 | 22 140 | 26 997 |
| 1986 | 180 587 | 14 496 | 7 386 | 7 110 | 166 091 | 19 569 | 41 731 | 32 550 | 22 732 | 22 011 | 27 497 |
| 1987 | 182 753 | 14 606 | 7 501 | 7 104 | 168 147 | 18 970 | 42 297 | 33 755 | 23 183 | 21 835 | 28 108 |
| 1988 | 184 613 | 14 527 | 7 284 | 7 243 | 170 085 | 18 434 | 42 611 | 34 784 | 24 004 | 21 641 | 28 612 |
| 1989 | 186 393 | 14 223 | 6 886 | 7 338 | 172 169 | 18 025 | 42 845 | 35 977 | 24 744 | 21 406 | 29 173 |
| 1990 | 189 164 | 14 520 | 6 893 | 7 626 | 174 644 | 18 902 | 42 976 | 37 719 | 25 081 | 20 719 | 29 247 |
| 1991 | 190 925 | 14 073 | 6 901 | 7 173 | 176 852 | 18 963 | 42 688 | 39 116 | 25 709 | 20 675 | 29 700 |
| 1992 | 192 805 | 13 840 | 6 907 | 6 933 | 178 965 | 18 846 | 42 278 | 39 852 | 27 206 | 20 604 | 30 179 |
| 1993 | 194 838 | 13 935 | 7 010 | 6 925 | 180 903 | 18 642 | 41 771 | 40 733 | 28 549 | 20 574 | 30 634 |
| 1994 | 196 814 | 14 196 | 7 245 | 6 951 | 182 619 | 18 353 | 41 306 | 41 534 | 29 778 | 20 635 | 31 012 |
| 1995 | 198 584 | 14 511 | 7 407 | 7 104 | 184 073 | 17 864 | 40 798 | 42 254 | 30 974 | 20 735 | 31 448 |
| 1996 | 200 591 | 14 934 | 7 678 | 7 256 | 185 656 | 17 409 | 40 252 | 43 086 | 32 167 | 20 990 | 31 751 |
| 1997 | 203 133 | 15 365 | 7 861 | 7 504 | 187 769 | 17 442 | 39 559 | 43 883 | 33 391 | 21 505 | 31 989 |
| 1998 | 205 220 | 15 644 | 7 895 | 7 749 | 189 576 | 17 593 | 38 778 | 44 299 | 34 373 | 22 296 | 32 237 |
| 1999 | 207 753 | 16 040 | 8 060 | 7 979 | 191 713 | 17 968 | 37 976 | 44 635 | 35 587 | 23 064 | 32 484 |
| 2000 | 212 577 | 15 912 | 7 978 | 7 934 | 196 664 | 18 311 | 38 703 | 44 312 | 37 642 | 24 230 | 33 466 |
| 2001 | 215 092 | 15 929 | 8 020 | 7 909 | 199 164 | 18 877 | 38 505 | 44 195 | 38 904 | 25 011 | 33 672 |
| 2002 | 217 570 | 15 994 | 8 099 | 7 895 | 201 576 | 19 348 | 38 472 | 43 894 | 39 711 | 26 343 | 33 808 |
| 2003 | 221 168 | 16 096 | 8 561 | 7 535 | 205 072 | 19 801 | 39 021 | 43 746 | 40 522 | 27 728 | 34 253 |
| 2004 | 223 357 | 16 222 | 8 574 | 7 648 | 207 134 | 20 197 | 38 939 | 43 226 | 41 245 | 28 919 | 34 609 |
| 2005 | 226 082 | 16 398 | 8 778 | 7 619 | 209 685 | 20 276 | 39 064 | 43 005 | 42 107 | 30 165 | 35 068 |
| 2006 | 228 815 | 16 678 | 9 089 | 7 589 | 212 137 | 20 265 | 39 230 | 42 753 | 42 901 | 31 375 | 35 613 |
| 2007 | 231 867 | 16 982 | 9 222 | 7 760 | 214 885 | 20 427 | 39 751 | 42 401 | 43 544 | 32 533 | 36 228 |
| 2008 | 233 788 | 17 075 | 9 133 | 7 942 | 216 713 | 20 409 | 39 993 | 41 699 | 43 960 | 33 491 | 37 161 |
| 2009 | 235 801 | 17 043 | 8 944 | 8 100 | 218 757 | 20 524 | 40 280 | 40 919 | 44 365 | 34 671 | 37 998 |
| 2010 | 237 830 | 16 901 | 8 943 | 7 957 | 220 929 | 21 047 | 40 903 | 40 090 | 44 297 | 35 885 | 38 706 |
| 2011 | 239 618 | 16 774 | 8 727 | 8 048 | 222 843 | 21 423 | 41 364 | 39 499 | 43 842 | 36 987 | 39 729 |
| 2012 | 243 284 | 16 984 | 8 891 | 8 093 | 226 300 | 21 799 | 40 975 | 39 642 | 43 697 | 38 318 | 41 869 |
| 2013 | 245 679 | 16 787 | 8 943 | 7 845 | 228 892 | 22 052 | 41 548 | 39 613 | 43 246 | 39 022 | 43 412 |
| 2014 | 247 947 | 16 633 | 8 898 | 7 735 | 231 314 | 22 079 | 42 131 | 39 565 | 42 815 | 39 764 | 44 959 |
| 2015 | 250 801 | 16 619 | 8 852 | 7 767 | 234 182 | 21 971 | 42 771 | 39 701 | 42 637 | 40 594 | 46 509 |

## Table 1-6.  Civilian Noninstitutional Population, by Age, Race, Sex, and Hispanic Origin, 1948–2015
*—Continued*

(Thousands of people.)

| Race, Hispanic origin, sex, and year | 16 years and over | 16 to 19 years | | | 20 years and over | | | | | | |
|---|---|---|---|---|---|---|---|---|---|---|---|
| | | Total | 16 to 17 years | 18 to 19 years | Total | 20 to 24 years | 25 to 34 years | 35 to 44 years | 45 to 54 years | 55 to 64 years | 65 years and over |
| **ALL RACES** | | | | | | | | | | | |
| **Men** | | | | | | | | | | | |
| 1948 | 49 996 | 4 078 | 2 128 | 1 951 | 45 918 | 5 527 | 10 767 | 9 798 | 8 290 | 6 441 | 5 093 |
| 1949 | 50 321 | 3 946 | 2 062 | 1 884 | 46 378 | 5 405 | 10 871 | 9 926 | 8 379 | 6 568 | 5 226 |
| 1950 | 50 725 | 3 962 | 2 043 | 1 920 | 46 763 | 5 270 | 10 963 | 10 034 | 8 472 | 6 664 | 5 357 |
| 1951 | 49 727 | 3 725 | 2 039 | 1 687 | 46 001 | 4 451 | 10 709 | 10 049 | 8 551 | 6 737 | 5 503 |
| 1952 | 49 700 | 3 767 | 2 121 | 1 647 | 45 932 | 3 788 | 10 855 | 10 164 | 8 655 | 6 798 | 5 670 |
| 1953 | 50 750 | 3 823 | 2 122 | 1 701 | 46 927 | 3 482 | 11 020 | 10 632 | 8 878 | 6 798 | 6 119 |
| 1954 | 51 395 | 3 953 | 2 174 | 1 780 | 47 441 | 3 509 | 11 067 | 10 718 | 9 018 | 6 885 | 6 241 |
| 1955 | 52 109 | 4 022 | 2 225 | 1 798 | 48 086 | 3 708 | 11 068 | 10 804 | 9 164 | 6 960 | 6 380 |
| 1956 | 52 723 | 4 020 | 2 238 | 1 783 | 48 704 | 3 970 | 10 983 | 10 889 | 9 322 | 7 032 | 6 505 |
| 1957 | 53 315 | 4 083 | 2 284 | 1 800 | 49 231 | 4 166 | 10 889 | 10 965 | 9 499 | 7 109 | 6 602 |
| 1958 | 54 033 | 4 293 | 2 435 | 1 858 | 49 740 | 4 339 | 10 787 | 11 076 | 9 675 | 7 179 | 6 683 |
| 1959 | 54 793 | 4 652 | 2 681 | 1 971 | 50 140 | 4 488 | 10 625 | 11 149 | 9 832 | 7 259 | 6 785 |
| 1960 | 55 662 | 4 963 | 2 805 | 2 159 | 50 698 | 4 679 | 10 514 | 11 230 | 10 000 | 7 373 | 6 901 |
| 1961 | 56 286 | 5 112 | 2 742 | 2 371 | 51 173 | 4 844 | 10 440 | 11 286 | 10 112 | 7 483 | 7 006 |
| 1962 | 56 831 | 5 150 | 2 764 | 2 386 | 51 681 | 4 925 | 10 207 | 11 389 | 10 162 | 7 610 | 7 386 |
| 1963 | 57 921 | 5 496 | 3 162 | 2 334 | 52 425 | 5 240 | 10 165 | 11 476 | 10 274 | 7 740 | 7 526 |
| 1964 | 58 847 | 5 866 | 3 503 | 2 364 | 52 981 | 5 520 | 10 144 | 11 466 | 10 402 | 7 873 | 7 574 |
| 1965 | 59 782 | 6 318 | 3 488 | 2 831 | 53 463 | 5 701 | 10 182 | 11 427 | 10 512 | 7 990 | 7 649 |
| 1966 | 60 262 | 6 658 | 3 478 | 3 180 | 53 603 | 5 663 | 10 224 | 11 294 | 10 598 | 8 099 | 7 723 |
| 1967 | 60 905 | 6 537 | 3 528 | 3 010 | 54 367 | 5 977 | 10 495 | 11 161 | 10 705 | 8 218 | 7 809 |
| 1968 | 61 847 | 6 683 | 3 634 | 3 049 | 55 165 | 6 127 | 10 944 | 11 040 | 10 819 | 8 336 | 7 897 |
| 1969 | 62 898 | 6 928 | 3 741 | 3 187 | 55 969 | 6 379 | 11 309 | 10 890 | 10 935 | 8 464 | 7 990 |
| 1970 | 64 304 | 7 145 | 3 848 | 3 299 | 57 157 | 6 861 | 11 750 | 10 810 | 11 052 | 8 590 | 8 093 |
| 1971 | 65 942 | 7 430 | 3 954 | 3 477 | 58 511 | 7 511 | 12 227 | 10 721 | 11 129 | 8 711 | 8 208 |
| 1972 | 67 835 | 7 705 | 4 081 | 3 624 | 60 130 | 8 061 | 12 911 | 10 762 | 11 167 | 8 895 | 8 330 |
| 1973 | 69 292 | 7 855 | 4 152 | 3 703 | 61 436 | 8 429 | 13 641 | 10 746 | 11 202 | 8 990 | 8 426 |
| 1974 | 70 808 | 8 012 | 4 231 | 3 781 | 62 796 | 8 600 | 14 262 | 10 834 | 11 315 | 9 140 | 8 641 |
| 1975 | 72 291 | 8 134 | 4 252 | 3 882 | 64 158 | 8 950 | 14 899 | 10 874 | 11 298 | 9 286 | 8 852 |
| 1976 | 73 759 | 8 244 | 4 266 | 3 978 | 65 515 | 9 237 | 15 528 | 11 010 | 11 243 | 9 444 | 9 053 |
| 1977 | 75 193 | 8 288 | 4 290 | 4 000 | 66 904 | 9 477 | 16 108 | 11 260 | 11 144 | 9 616 | 9 297 |
| 1978 | 76 576 | 8 309 | 4 295 | 4 014 | 68 268 | 9 693 | 16 598 | 11 665 | 11 045 | 9 758 | 9 509 |
| 1979 | 78 020 | 8 310 | 4 251 | 4 060 | 69 709 | 9 873 | 17 193 | 12 046 | 10 944 | 9 907 | 9 746 |
| 1980 | 79 398 | 8 260 | 4 195 | 4 064 | 71 138 | 10 023 | 17 833 | 12 400 | 10 861 | 10 042 | 9 979 |
| 1981 | 80 511 | 8 092 | 4 087 | 4 005 | 72 419 | 10 116 | 18 427 | 12 758 | 10 797 | 10 151 | 10 170 |
| 1982 | 81 523 | 7 879 | 3 911 | 3 968 | 73 644 | 10 136 | 18 787 | 13 410 | 10 726 | 10 215 | 10 371 |
| 1983 | 82 531 | 7 659 | 3 750 | 3 908 | 74 872 | 10 140 | 19 143 | 14 067 | 10 689 | 10 261 | 10 573 |
| 1984 | 83 605 | 7 386 | 3 655 | 3 731 | 76 219 | 10 108 | 19 596 | 14 719 | 10 724 | 10 285 | 10 788 |
| 1985 | 84 469 | 7 275 | 3 689 | 3 586 | 77 195 | 9 746 | 19 864 | 15 265 | 10 844 | 10 392 | 11 084 |
| 1986 | 85 798 | 7 275 | 3 768 | 3 507 | 78 523 | 9 498 | 20 498 | 15 858 | 10 986 | 10 336 | 11 347 |
| 1987 | 86 899 | 7 335 | 3 824 | 3 510 | 79 565 | 9 195 | 20 781 | 16 475 | 11 215 | 10 267 | 11 632 |
| 1988 | 87 857 | 7 304 | 3 715 | 3 588 | 80 553 | 8 931 | 20 937 | 17 008 | 11 625 | 10 193 | 11 859 |
| 1989 | 88 762 | 7 143 | 3 524 | 3 619 | 81 619 | 8 743 | 21 080 | 17 590 | 11 981 | 10 092 | 12 134 |
| 1990 | 90 377 | 7 347 | 3 534 | 3 813 | 83 030 | 9 320 | 21 117 | 18 529 | 12 238 | 9 778 | 12 049 |
| 1991 | 91 278 | 7 134 | 3 548 | 3 586 | 84 144 | 9 367 | 20 977 | 19 213 | 12 554 | 9 780 | 12 254 |
| 1992 | 92 270 | 7 023 | 3 542 | 3 481 | 85 247 | 9 326 | 20 792 | 19 585 | 13 271 | 9 776 | 12 496 |
| 1993 | 93 332 | 7 076 | 3 595 | 3 481 | 86 256 | 9 216 | 20 569 | 20 037 | 13 944 | 9 773 | 12 717 |
| 1994 | 94 355 | 7 203 | 3 718 | 3 486 | 87 151 | 9 074 | 20 361 | 20 443 | 14 545 | 9 810 | 12 918 |
| 1995 | 95 178 | 7 367 | 3 794 | 3 573 | 87 811 | 8 835 | 20 079 | 20 800 | 15 111 | 9 856 | 13 130 |
| 1996 | 96 206 | 7 600 | 3 955 | 3 645 | 88 606 | 8 611 | 19 775 | 21 222 | 15 674 | 9 997 | 13 327 |
| 1997 | 97 715 | 7 836 | 4 053 | 3 783 | 89 879 | 8 706 | 19 478 | 21 669 | 16 276 | 10 282 | 13 469 |
| 1998 | 98 758 | 7 968 | 4 059 | 3 909 | 90 790 | 8 804 | 19 094 | 21 857 | 16 773 | 10 649 | 13 613 |
| 1999 | 99 722 | 8 167 | 4 143 | 4 024 | 91 555 | 8 899 | 18 565 | 21 969 | 17 335 | 11 008 | 13 779 |
| 2000 | 101 964 | 8 089 | 4 096 | 3 993 | 93 875 | 9 101 | 19 106 | 21 683 | 18 365 | 11 583 | 14 037 |
| 2001 | 103 282 | 8 101 | 4 102 | 3 999 | 95 181 | 9 368 | 19 056 | 21 643 | 18 987 | 11 972 | 14 155 |
| 2002 | 104 585 | 8 146 | 4 140 | 4 006 | 96 439 | 9 627 | 19 037 | 21 523 | 19 379 | 12 641 | 14 233 |
| 2003 | 106 435 | 8 163 | 4 365 | 3 797 | 98 272 | 9 878 | 19 347 | 21 463 | 19 784 | 13 305 | 14 496 |
| 2004 | 107 710 | 8 234 | 4 318 | 3 916 | 99 476 | 10 125 | 19 358 | 21 255 | 20 160 | 13 894 | 14 684 |
| 2005 | 109 151 | 8 317 | 4 481 | 3 836 | 100 835 | 10 181 | 19 446 | 21 177 | 20 585 | 14 502 | 14 944 |
| 2006 | 110 605 | 8 459 | 4 613 | 3 846 | 102 145 | 10 191 | 19 568 | 21 082 | 20 991 | 15 095 | 15 219 |
| 2007 | 112 173 | 8 618 | 4 658 | 3 960 | 103 555 | 10 291 | 19 858 | 20 910 | 21 313 | 15 658 | 15 525 |
| 2008 | 113 113 | 8 660 | 4 625 | 4 035 | 104 453 | 10 249 | 19 999 | 20 567 | 21 512 | 16 123 | 16 002 |
| 2009 | 114 136 | 8 643 | 4 548 | 4 095 | 105 493 | 10 284 | 20 167 | 20 199 | 21 731 | 16 698 | 16 414 |
| 2010 | 115 174 | 8 578 | 4 540 | 4 038 | 106 596 | 10 550 | 20 465 | 19 807 | 21 713 | 17 291 | 16 769 |
| 2011 | 116 317 | 8 582 | 4 486 | 4 095 | 107 736 | 10 844 | 20 711 | 19 446 | 21 451 | 17 810 | 17 474 |
| 2012 | 117 343 | 8 657 | 4 550 | 4 107 | 108 686 | 10 889 | 20 205 | 19 416 | 21 339 | 18 416 | 18 422 |
| 2013 | 118 555 | 8 539 | 4 532 | 4 006 | 110 017 | 11 038 | 20 511 | 19 404 | 21 125 | 18 751 | 19 189 |
| 2014 | 119 748 | 8 449 | 4 513 | 3 936 | 111 299 | 11 067 | 20 841 | 19 388 | 20 920 | 19 116 | 19 967 |
| 2015 | 121 101 | 8 430 | 4 509 | 3 920 | 112 671 | 11 012 | 21 142 | 19 444 | 20 839 | 19 518 | 20 717 |

## Table 1-6. Civilian Noninstitutional Population, by Age, Race, Sex, and Hispanic Origin, 1948–2015
### —Continued

(Thousands of people.)

| Race, Hispanic origin, sex, and year | 16 years and over | 16 to 19 years | | | 20 years and over | | | | | | |
|---|---|---|---|---|---|---|---|---|---|---|---|
| | | Total | 16 to 17 years | 18 to 19 years | Total | 20 to 24 years | 25 to 34 years | 35 to 44 years | 45 to 54 years | 55 to 64 years | 65 years and over |
| **ALL RACES** | | | | | | | | | | | |
| **Women** | | | | | | | | | | | |
| 1948 | 53 071 | 4 371 | 2 137 | 2 234 | 48 700 | 6 003 | 11 843 | 10 299 | 8 481 | 6 444 | 5 627 |
| 1949 | 53 670 | 4 269 | 2 077 | 2 195 | 49 400 | 5 907 | 11 951 | 10 475 | 8 623 | 6 633 | 5 809 |
| 1950 | 54 270 | 4 181 | 2 033 | 2 148 | 50 088 | 5 810 | 12 050 | 10 647 | 8 768 | 6 805 | 6 006 |
| 1951 | 54 895 | 4 140 | 2 057 | 2 084 | 50 754 | 5 716 | 12 134 | 10 814 | 8 913 | 6 955 | 6 221 |
| 1952 | 55 529 | 4 155 | 2 113 | 2 042 | 51 373 | 5 601 | 12 189 | 10 973 | 9 061 | 7 091 | 6 456 |
| 1953 | 56 305 | 4 191 | 2 119 | 2 072 | 52 114 | 5 478 | 12 246 | 11 290 | 9 113 | 7 032 | 6 956 |
| 1954 | 56 925 | 4 271 | 2 162 | 2 109 | 52 654 | 5 376 | 12 237 | 11 417 | 9 287 | 7 200 | 7 134 |
| 1955 | 57 574 | 4 342 | 2 215 | 2 127 | 53 232 | 5 328 | 12 181 | 11 544 | 9 479 | 7 349 | 7 348 |
| 1956 | 58 228 | 4 414 | 2 244 | 2 170 | 53 814 | 5 301 | 12 089 | 11 678 | 9 690 | 7 484 | 7 570 |
| 1957 | 58 951 | 4 529 | 2 303 | 2 226 | 54 421 | 5 320 | 11 960 | 11 821 | 9 925 | 7 618 | 7 774 |
| 1958 | 59 690 | 4 693 | 2 437 | 2 256 | 54 997 | 5 394 | 11 776 | 11 949 | 10 157 | 7 744 | 7 974 |
| 1959 | 60 534 | 4 966 | 2 656 | 2 311 | 55 570 | 5 487 | 11 576 | 12 058 | 10 371 | 7 875 | 8 200 |
| 1960 | 61 582 | 5 224 | 2 768 | 2 456 | 56 358 | 5 594 | 11 484 | 12 207 | 10 601 | 8 036 | 8 435 |
| 1961 | 62 484 | 5 401 | 2 720 | 2 681 | 57 082 | 5 739 | 11 389 | 12 299 | 10 781 | 8 192 | 8 679 |
| 1962 | 63 321 | 5 502 | 2 739 | 2 764 | 57 819 | 5 927 | 11 296 | 12 408 | 10 754 | 8 264 | 9 168 |
| 1963 | 64 494 | 5 874 | 3 139 | 2 736 | 58 620 | 6 224 | 11 235 | 12 472 | 10 870 | 8 398 | 9 419 |
| 1964 | 65 637 | 6 245 | 3 471 | 2 775 | 59 391 | 6 497 | 11 223 | 12 474 | 11 050 | 8 569 | 9 576 |
| 1965 | 66 731 | 6 612 | 3 448 | 3 164 | 60 119 | 6 741 | 11 235 | 12 405 | 11 216 | 8 737 | 9 783 |
| 1966 | 67 795 | 6 934 | 3 436 | 3 499 | 60 860 | 6 975 | 11 319 | 12 285 | 11 379 | 8 908 | 9 992 |
| 1967 | 68 968 | 6 943 | 3 475 | 3 470 | 62 026 | 7 445 | 11 562 | 12 152 | 11 551 | 9 092 | 10 220 |
| 1968 | 70 179 | 7 015 | 3 566 | 3 450 | 63 164 | 7 764 | 11 968 | 11 996 | 11 715 | 9 278 | 10 441 |
| 1969 | 71 436 | 7 167 | 3 681 | 3 486 | 64 269 | 8 109 | 12 336 | 11 819 | 11 871 | 9 466 | 10 667 |
| 1970 | 72 782 | 7 373 | 3 796 | 3 578 | 65 408 | 8 462 | 12 684 | 11 679 | 12 008 | 9 659 | 10 914 |
| 1971 | 74 274 | 7 591 | 3 895 | 3 697 | 66 682 | 8 834 | 13 110 | 11 553 | 12 115 | 9 870 | 11 198 |
| 1972 | 76 290 | 7 805 | 3 994 | 3 811 | 68 484 | 9 082 | 13 829 | 11 597 | 12 171 | 10 113 | 11 693 |
| 1973 | 77 804 | 7 985 | 4 076 | 3 909 | 69 819 | 9 263 | 14 531 | 11 541 | 12 229 | 10 290 | 11 963 |
| 1974 | 79 312 | 8 168 | 4 142 | 4 028 | 71 144 | 9 393 | 15 177 | 11 627 | 12 263 | 10 377 | 12 304 |
| 1975 | 80 860 | 8 285 | 4 168 | 4 117 | 72 576 | 9 645 | 15 811 | 11 652 | 12 237 | 10 558 | 12 673 |
| 1976 | 82 390 | 8 370 | 4 176 | 4 194 | 74 020 | 9 872 | 16 425 | 11 786 | 12 166 | 10 742 | 13 030 |
| 1977 | 83 840 | 8 400 | 4 193 | 4 206 | 75 441 | 10 103 | 17 008 | 12 036 | 12 053 | 10 940 | 13 300 |
| 1978 | 85 334 | 8 386 | 4 189 | 4 197 | 76 948 | 10 315 | 17 493 | 12 435 | 11 932 | 11 118 | 13 658 |
| 1979 | 86 843 | 8 347 | 4 139 | 4 208 | 78 496 | 10 480 | 18 070 | 12 815 | 11 808 | 11 303 | 14 021 |
| 1980 | 88 348 | 8 283 | 4 083 | 4 200 | 80 065 | 10 612 | 18 725 | 13 177 | 11 701 | 11 478 | 14 372 |
| 1981 | 89 618 | 8 121 | 3 981 | 4 140 | 81 497 | 10 705 | 19 350 | 13 533 | 11 625 | 11 605 | 14 680 |
| 1982 | 90 748 | 7 884 | 3 804 | 4 081 | 82 864 | 10 709 | 19 705 | 14 201 | 11 538 | 11 694 | 15 017 |
| 1983 | 91 684 | 7 616 | 3 635 | 3 981 | 84 069 | 10 660 | 20 004 | 14 865 | 11 478 | 11 742 | 15 319 |
| 1984 | 92 778 | 7 349 | 3 542 | 3 807 | 85 429 | 10 580 | 20 403 | 15 532 | 11 501 | 11 768 | 15 645 |
| 1985 | 93 736 | 7 231 | 3 543 | 3 688 | 86 506 | 10 351 | 20 805 | 16 114 | 11 574 | 11 748 | 15 913 |
| 1986 | 94 789 | 7 221 | 3 618 | 3 603 | 87 567 | 10 072 | 21 233 | 16 692 | 11 746 | 11 675 | 16 150 |
| 1987 | 95 853 | 7 271 | 3 677 | 3 594 | 88 583 | 9 776 | 21 516 | 17 279 | 11 968 | 11 567 | 16 476 |
| 1988 | 96 756 | 7 224 | 3 569 | 3 655 | 89 532 | 9 503 | 21 674 | 17 776 | 12 378 | 11 448 | 16 753 |
| 1989 | 97 630 | 7 080 | 3 361 | 3 719 | 90 550 | 9 282 | 21 765 | 18 387 | 12 763 | 11 314 | 17 039 |
| 1990 | 98 787 | 7 173 | 3 359 | 3 813 | 91 614 | 9 582 | 21 859 | 19 190 | 12 843 | 10 941 | 17 198 |
| 1991 | 99 646 | 6 939 | 3 353 | 3 586 | 92 708 | 9 597 | 21 711 | 19 903 | 13 155 | 10 895 | 17 446 |
| 1992 | 100 535 | 6 818 | 3 366 | 3 452 | 93 718 | 9 520 | 21 486 | 20 267 | 13 935 | 10 828 | 17 682 |
| 1993 | 101 506 | 6 859 | 3 415 | 3 444 | 94 647 | 9 426 | 21 202 | 20 696 | 14 605 | 10 801 | 17 917 |
| 1994 | 102 460 | 6 993 | 3 528 | 3 465 | 95 467 | 9 279 | 20 945 | 21 091 | 15 233 | 10 825 | 18 094 |
| 1995 | 103 406 | 7 144 | 3 613 | 3 531 | 96 262 | 9 029 | 20 719 | 21 454 | 15 862 | 10 879 | 18 318 |
| 1996 | 104 385 | 7 335 | 3 723 | 3 612 | 97 050 | 8 798 | 20 477 | 21 865 | 16 493 | 10 993 | 18 424 |
| 1997 | 105 418 | 7 528 | 3 808 | 3 721 | 97 889 | 8 736 | 20 081 | 22 214 | 17 115 | 11 224 | 18 520 |
| 1998 | 106 462 | 7 676 | 3 835 | 3 840 | 98 786 | 8 790 | 19 683 | 22 442 | 17 600 | 11 646 | 18 625 |
| 1999 | 108 031 | 7 873 | 3 917 | 3 955 | 100 158 | 9 069 | 19 411 | 22 666 | 18 251 | 12 056 | 18 705 |
| 2000 | 110 613 | 7 823 | 3 882 | 3 941 | 102 790 | 9 211 | 19 597 | 22 628 | 19 276 | 12 647 | 19 430 |
| 2001 | 111 811 | 7 828 | 3 917 | 3 910 | 103 983 | 9 509 | 19 449 | 22 552 | 19 917 | 13 039 | 19 517 |
| 2002 | 112 985 | 7 848 | 3 959 | 3 889 | 105 136 | 9 721 | 19 435 | 22 371 | 20 332 | 13 703 | 19 575 |
| 2003 | 114 733 | 7 934 | 4 195 | 3 738 | 106 800 | 9 924 | 19 674 | 22 283 | 20 738 | 14 423 | 19 758 |
| 2004 | 115 647 | 7 989 | 4 257 | 3 732 | 107 658 | 10 072 | 19 581 | 21 970 | 21 085 | 15 025 | 19 925 |
| 2005 | 116 931 | 8 081 | 4 297 | 3 784 | 108 850 | 10 095 | 19 618 | 21 828 | 21 521 | 15 663 | 20 125 |
| 2006 | 118 210 | 8 218 | 4 476 | 3 742 | 109 992 | 10 074 | 19 662 | 21 671 | 21 910 | 16 280 | 20 394 |
| 2007 | 119 694 | 8 364 | 4 564 | 3 800 | 111 330 | 10 137 | 19 893 | 21 491 | 22 231 | 16 876 | 20 703 |
| 2008 | 120 675 | 8 415 | 4 508 | 3 907 | 112 260 | 10 160 | 19 994 | 21 132 | 22 448 | 17 367 | 21 160 |
| 2009 | 121 665 | 8 401 | 4 396 | 4 004 | 113 265 | 10 240 | 20 113 | 20 721 | 22 633 | 17 973 | 21 584 |
| 2010 | 122 656 | 8 323 | 4 403 | 3 919 | 114 333 | 10 497 | 20 438 | 20 283 | 22 584 | 18 594 | 21 937 |
| 2011 | 123 300 | 8 193 | 4 241 | 3 952 | 115 107 | 10 579 | 20 653 | 20 053 | 22 391 | 19 177 | 22 255 |
| 2012 | 125 941 | 8 327 | 4 341 | 3 986 | 117 614 | 10 910 | 20 770 | 20 226 | 22 358 | 19 902 | 23 447 |
| 2013 | 127 124 | 8 249 | 4 410 | 3 838 | 118 875 | 11 014 | 21 037 | 20 209 | 22 121 | 20 271 | 24 222 |
| 2014 | 128 199 | 8 184 | 4 385 | 3 799 | 120 014 | 11 012 | 21 290 | 20 178 | 21 894 | 20 648 | 24 992 |
| 2015 | 129 700 | 8 189 | 4 342 | 3 847 | 121 511 | 10 959 | 21 629 | 20 257 | 21 798 | 21 076 | 25 792 |

## Table 1-6.  Civilian Noninstitutional Population, by Age, Race, Sex, and Hispanic Origin, 1948–2015
### —Continued

(Thousands of people.)

| Race, Hispanic origin, sex, and year | 16 years and over | 16 to 19 years | | | 20 years and over | | | | | | |
|---|---|---|---|---|---|---|---|---|---|---|---|
| | | Total | 16 to 17 years | 18 to 19 years | Total | 20 to 24 years | 25 to 34 years | 35 to 44 years | 45 to 54 years | 55 to 64 years | 65 years and over |
| **WHITE** | | | | | | | | | | | |
| **Both Sexes** | | | | | | | | | | | |
| 1954 | 97 705 | 7 180 | 3 786 | 3 394 | 90 524 | 7 794 | 20 818 | 19 915 | 16 569 | 12 993 | 12 438 |
| 1955 | 98 880 | 7 292 | 3 874 | 3 419 | 91 586 | 7 912 | 20 742 | 20 110 | 16 869 | 13 169 | 12 785 |
| 1956 | 99 976 | 7 346 | 3 908 | 3 438 | 92 629 | 8 106 | 20 564 | 20 314 | 17 198 | 13 341 | 13 105 |
| 1957 | 101 119 | 7 505 | 4 007 | 3 498 | 93 612 | 8 293 | 20 342 | 20 514 | 17 562 | 13 518 | 13 383 |
| 1958 | 102 392 | 7 843 | 4 271 | 3 573 | 94 547 | 8 498 | 20 063 | 20 734 | 17 924 | 13 681 | 13 645 |
| 1959 | 103 803 | 8 430 | 4 707 | 3 725 | 95 370 | 8 697 | 19 715 | 20 893 | 18 257 | 13 858 | 13 951 |
| 1960 | 105 282 | 8 924 | 4 909 | 4 016 | 96 355 | 8 927 | 19 470 | 21 049 | 18 578 | 14 070 | 14 260 |
| 1961 | 106 604 | 9 211 | 4 785 | 4 427 | 97 390 | 9 203 | 19 289 | 21 169 | 18 845 | 14 304 | 14 581 |
| 1962 | 107 715 | 9 343 | 4 818 | 4 526 | 98 371 | 9 484 | 18 974 | 21 293 | 18 872 | 14 450 | 15 297 |
| 1963 | 109 705 | 9 978 | 5 549 | 4 430 | 99 725 | 10 069 | 18 867 | 21 398 | 19 082 | 14 681 | 15 629 |
| 1964 | 111 534 | 10 616 | 6 137 | 4 481 | 100 916 | 10 568 | 18 838 | 21 375 | 19 360 | 14 957 | 15 816 |
| 1965 | 113 284 | 11 319 | 6 049 | 5 271 | 101 963 | 10 935 | 18 882 | 21 258 | 19 604 | 15 215 | 16 070 |
| 1966 | 114 566 | 11 862 | 5 993 | 5 870 | 102 702 | 11 094 | 18 989 | 21 005 | 19 822 | 15 469 | 16 322 |
| 1967 | 116 100 | 11 682 | 6 051 | 5 632 | 104 417 | 11 797 | 19 464 | 20 745 | 20 067 | 15 745 | 16 602 |
| 1968 | 117 948 | 11 840 | 6 225 | 5 616 | 106 107 | 12 184 | 20 245 | 20 474 | 20 310 | 16 018 | 16 875 |
| 1969 | 119 913 | 12 179 | 6 418 | 5 761 | 107 733 | 12 677 | 20 892 | 20 156 | 20 546 | 16 305 | 17 156 |
| 1970 | 122 174 | 12 521 | 6 591 | 5 931 | 109 652 | 13 359 | 21 546 | 19 929 | 20 760 | 16 591 | 17 469 |
| 1971 | 124 758 | 12 937 | 6 750 | 6 189 | 111 821 | 14 208 | 22 295 | 19 694 | 20 907 | 16 884 | 17 833 |
| 1972 | 127 906 | 13 301 | 6 910 | 6 392 | 114 603 | 14 897 | 23 555 | 19 673 | 20 950 | 17 250 | 18 278 |
| 1973 | 130 097 | 13 533 | 7 021 | 6 512 | 116 563 | 15 264 | 24 685 | 19 532 | 20 991 | 17 484 | 18 607 |
| 1974 | 132 417 | 13 784 | 7 114 | 6 671 | 118 632 | 15 502 | 25 711 | 19 628 | 21 061 | 17 645 | 19 085 |
| 1975 | 134 790 | 13 941 | 7 132 | 6 808 | 120 849 | 15 980 | 26 746 | 19 641 | 20 981 | 17 918 | 19 587 |
| 1976 | 137 106 | 14 055 | 7 125 | 6 930 | 123 050 | 16 368 | 27 757 | 19 827 | 20 816 | 18 220 | 20 064 |
| 1977 | 139 380 | 14 095 | 7 150 | 6 944 | 125 285 | 16 728 | 28 703 | 20 231 | 20 575 | 18 540 | 20 508 |
| 1978 | 141 612 | 14 060 | 7 132 | 6 928 | 127 552 | 17 038 | 29 453 | 20 932 | 20 322 | 18 799 | 21 007 |
| 1979 | 143 894 | 13 994 | 7 029 | 6 964 | 129 900 | 17 284 | 30 371 | 21 579 | 20 058 | 19 071 | 21 538 |
| 1980 | 146 122 | 13 854 | 6 912 | 6 943 | 132 268 | 17 484 | 31 407 | 22 174 | 19 837 | 19 316 | 22 050 |
| 1981 | 147 908 | 13 516 | 6 704 | 6 813 | 134 392 | 17 609 | 32 367 | 22 778 | 19 666 | 19 485 | 22 487 |
| 1982 | 149 441 | 13 076 | 6 383 | 6 693 | 136 366 | 17 579 | 32 863 | 23 910 | 19 478 | 19 591 | 22 945 |
| 1983 | 150 805 | 12 623 | 6 089 | 6 534 | 138 183 | 17 492 | 33 286 | 25 027 | 19 349 | 19 625 | 23 403 |
| 1984 | 152 347 | 12 147 | 5 918 | 6 228 | 140 200 | 17 304 | 33 889 | 26 124 | 19 348 | 19 629 | 23 906 |
| 1985 | 153 679 | 11 900 | 5 922 | 5 978 | 141 780 | 16 853 | 34 450 | 27 100 | 19 405 | 19 620 | 24 352 |
| 1986 | 155 432 | 11 879 | 6 036 | 5 843 | 143 553 | 16 353 | 35 293 | 28 062 | 19 587 | 19 477 | 24 780 |
| 1987 | 156 958 | 11 939 | 6 110 | 5 829 | 145 020 | 15 808 | 35 667 | 29 036 | 19 965 | 19 242 | 25 301 |
| 1988 | 158 194 | 11 838 | 5 893 | 5 945 | 146 357 | 15 276 | 35 876 | 29 818 | 20 652 | 18 996 | 25 739 |
| 1989 | 159 338 | 11 530 | 5 506 | 6 023 | 147 809 | 14 879 | 35 951 | 30 774 | 21 287 | 18 743 | 26 175 |
| 1990 | 160 625 | 11 630 | 5 464 | 6 166 | 148 996 | 15 538 | 35 661 | 31 739 | 21 535 | 18 204 | 26 319 |
| 1991 | 161 759 | 11 200 | 5 451 | 5 749 | 150 558 | 15 516 | 35 342 | 32 854 | 22 052 | 18 074 | 26 721 |
| 1992 | 162 972 | 11 004 | 5 478 | 5 526 | 151 968 | 15 354 | 34 885 | 33 305 | 23 364 | 17 951 | 27 108 |
| 1993 | 164 289 | 11 078 | 5 562 | 5 516 | 153 210 | 15 087 | 34 365 | 33 919 | 24 456 | 17 892 | 27 493 |
| 1994 | 165 555 | 11 264 | 5 710 | 5 554 | 154 291 | 14 708 | 33 865 | 34 582 | 25 435 | 17 924 | 27 776 |
| 1995 | 166 914 | 11 468 | 5 822 | 5 646 | 155 446 | 14 313 | 33 355 | 35 222 | 26 418 | 17 986 | 28 153 |
| 1996 | 168 317 | 11 822 | 6 026 | 5 796 | 156 495 | 13 907 | 32 852 | 35 810 | 27 403 | 18 136 | 28 387 |
| 1997 | 169 993 | 12 181 | 6 213 | 5 968 | 157 812 | 13 983 | 32 091 | 36 325 | 28 388 | 18 511 | 28 514 |
| 1998 | 171 478 | 12 439 | 6 264 | 6 176 | 159 039 | 14 138 | 31 286 | 36 610 | 29 132 | 19 231 | 28 642 |
| 1999 | 173 085 | 12 700 | 6 342 | 6 358 | 160 385 | 14 394 | 30 516 | 36 755 | 30 048 | 19 855 | 28 818 |
| 2000 | 176 220 | 12 535 | 6 264 | 6 271 | 163 685 | 14 552 | 30 948 | 36 261 | 31 550 | 20 757 | 29 617 |
| 2001 | 178 111 | 12 556 | 6 291 | 6 265 | 165 556 | 15 001 | 30 770 | 36 113 | 32 475 | 21 434 | 29 762 |
| 2002 | 179 783 | 12 596 | 6 346 | 6 250 | 167 187 | 15 360 | 30 676 | 35 750 | 33 012 | 22 540 | 29 849 |
| 2003 | 181 292 | 12 527 | 6 629 | 5 898 | 168 765 | 15 536 | 30 789 | 35 352 | 33 466 | 23 589 | 30 033 |
| 2004 | 182 643 | 12 599 | 6 561 | 6 038 | 170 045 | 15 817 | 30 585 | 34 845 | 34 005 | 24 549 | 30 245 |
| 2005 | 184 446 | 12 690 | 6 768 | 5 921 | 171 757 | 15 871 | 30 592 | 34 554 | 34 649 | 25 534 | 30 556 |
| 2006 | 186 264 | 12 856 | 6 981 | 5 875 | 173 408 | 15 848 | 30 661 | 34 217 | 35 228 | 26 486 | 30 968 |
| 2007 | 188 253 | 13 043 | 7 026 | 6 018 | 175 210 | 15 945 | 31 011 | 33 770 | 35 665 | 27 392 | 31 426 |
| 2008 | 189 540 | 13 084 | 6 962 | 6 122 | 176 456 | 15 914 | 31 234 | 33 093 | 35 941 | 28 109 | 32 165 |
| 2009 | 190 902 | 13 035 | 6 775 | 6 261 | 177 867 | 15 963 | 31 471 | 32 378 | 36 166 | 29 022 | 32 867 |
| 2010 | 192 075 | 12 891 | 6 799 | 6 091 | 179 184 | 16 280 | 31 813 | 31 647 | 36 064 | 29 983 | 33 396 |
| 2011 | 193 077 | 12 818 | 6 673 | 6 145 | 180 259 | 16 562 | 32 136 | 31 030 | 35 526 | 30 799 | 34 206 |
| 2012 | 193 204 | 12 658 | 6 617 | 6 040 | 180 547 | 16 289 | 31 242 | 30 597 | 34 935 | 31 511 | 35 973 |
| 2013 | 194 333 | 12 499 | 6 690 | 5 809 | 181 834 | 16 357 | 31 488 | 30 427 | 34 413 | 31 954 | 37 194 |
| 2014 | 195 498 | 12 377 | 6 650 | 5 727 | 183 121 | 16 329 | 31 782 | 30 254 | 33 948 | 32 450 | 38 358 |
| 2015 | 196 868 | 12 323 | 6 538 | 5 784 | 184 545 | 16 171 | 32 036 | 30 186 | 33 633 | 33 005 | 39 513 |

## Table 1-6.  Civilian Noninstitutional Population, by Age, Race, Sex, and Hispanic Origin, 1948–2015
### —Continued

(Thousands of people.)

| Race, Hispanic origin, sex, and year | 16 years and over | 16 to 19 years | | | 20 years and over | | | | | | |
|---|---|---|---|---|---|---|---|---|---|---|---|
| | | Total | 16 to 17 years | 18 to 19 years | Total | 20 to 24 years | 25 to 34 years | 35 to 44 years | 45 to 54 years | 55 to 64 years | 65 years and over |
| **WHITE** | | | | | | | | | | | |
| **Men** | | | | | | | | | | | |
| 1954 | 46 462 | 3 455 | 1 902 | 1 553 | 43 007 | 3 074 | 9 948 | 9 688 | 8 172 | 6 341 | 5 787 |
| 1955 | 47 076 | 3 507 | 1 945 | 1 563 | 43 569 | 3 241 | 9 936 | 9 768 | 8 303 | 6 398 | 5 923 |
| 1956 | 47 602 | 3 500 | 1 955 | 1 546 | 44 102 | 3 464 | 9 851 | 9 848 | 8 446 | 6 455 | 6 038 |
| 1957 | 48 119 | 3 556 | 2 000 | 1 557 | 44 563 | 3 638 | 9 758 | 9 917 | 8 605 | 6 518 | 6 127 |
| 1958 | 48 745 | 3 747 | 2 140 | 1 607 | 44 998 | 3 783 | 9 656 | 10 018 | 8 765 | 6 574 | 6 203 |
| 1959 | 49 408 | 4 079 | 2 370 | 1 710 | 45 329 | 3 903 | 9 499 | 10 081 | 8 909 | 6 639 | 6 298 |
| 1960 | 50 065 | 4 349 | 2 476 | 1 874 | 45 716 | 4 054 | 9 373 | 10 131 | 9 042 | 6 721 | 6 395 |
| 1961 | 50 608 | 4 479 | 2 407 | 2 073 | 46 129 | 4 204 | 9 290 | 10 178 | 9 148 | 6 819 | 6 490 |
| 1962 | 51 054 | 4 520 | 2 426 | 2 094 | 46 534 | 4 306 | 9 080 | 10 239 | 9 191 | 6 917 | 6 801 |
| 1963 | 52 031 | 4 827 | 2 792 | 2 036 | 47 204 | 4 610 | 9 039 | 10 309 | 9 297 | 7 031 | 6 919 |
| 1964 | 52 869 | 5 148 | 3 090 | 2 059 | 47 721 | 4 862 | 9 024 | 10 301 | 9 417 | 7 153 | 6 963 |
| 1965 | 53 681 | 5 541 | 3 050 | 2 492 | 48 140 | 5 017 | 9 056 | 10 262 | 9 516 | 7 261 | 7 028 |
| 1966 | 54 061 | 5 820 | 3 023 | 2 798 | 48 241 | 4 974 | 9 085 | 10 136 | 9 592 | 7 362 | 7 092 |
| 1967 | 54 608 | 5 671 | 3 058 | 2 613 | 48 937 | 5 257 | 9 339 | 10 013 | 9 688 | 7 474 | 7 167 |
| 1968 | 55 434 | 5 787 | 3 153 | 2 635 | 49 647 | 5 376 | 9 752 | 9 902 | 9 790 | 7 585 | 7 242 |
| 1969 | 56 348 | 6 005 | 3 246 | 2 759 | 50 343 | 5 589 | 10 074 | 9 760 | 9 895 | 7 705 | 7 320 |
| 1970 | 57 516 | 6 179 | 3 329 | 2 851 | 51 336 | 5 988 | 10 441 | 9 678 | 9 999 | 7 822 | 7 409 |
| 1971 | 58 900 | 6 420 | 3 412 | 3 008 | 52 481 | 6 546 | 10 841 | 9 578 | 10 066 | 7 933 | 7 517 |
| 1972 | 60 473 | 6 627 | 3 503 | 3 125 | 53 845 | 7 042 | 11 495 | 9 568 | 10 078 | 8 089 | 7 573 |
| 1973 | 61 577 | 6 737 | 3 555 | 3 182 | 54 842 | 7 312 | 12 075 | 9 514 | 10 099 | 8 178 | 7 664 |
| 1974 | 62 791 | 6 851 | 3 604 | 3 247 | 55 942 | 7 476 | 12 599 | 9 564 | 10 165 | 8 288 | 7 849 |
| 1975 | 63 981 | 6 929 | 3 609 | 3 320 | 57 052 | 7 766 | 13 131 | 9 578 | 10 134 | 8 413 | 8 031 |
| 1976 | 65 132 | 6 993 | 3 609 | 3 384 | 58 138 | 7 987 | 13 655 | 9 674 | 10 063 | 8 556 | 8 203 |
| 1977 | 66 301 | 7 024 | 3 625 | 3 399 | 59 278 | 8 175 | 14 139 | 9 880 | 9 957 | 8 708 | 8 420 |
| 1978 | 67 401 | 7 022 | 3 619 | 3 404 | 60 378 | 8 335 | 14 528 | 10 236 | 9 845 | 8 826 | 8 608 |
| 1979 | 68 547 | 7 007 | 3 568 | 3 439 | 61 540 | 8 470 | 15 008 | 10 563 | 9 730 | 8 949 | 8 820 |
| 1980 | 69 634 | 6 941 | 3 508 | 3 433 | 62 694 | 8 581 | 15 529 | 10 863 | 9 636 | 9 059 | 9 027 |
| 1981 | 70 480 | 6 764 | 3 401 | 3 363 | 63 715 | 8 644 | 16 005 | 11 171 | 9 560 | 9 139 | 9 195 |
| 1982 | 71 211 | 6 556 | 3 249 | 3 307 | 64 655 | 8 621 | 16 260 | 11 756 | 9 463 | 9 188 | 9 367 |
| 1983 | 71 922 | 6 340 | 3 098 | 3 242 | 65 581 | 8 597 | 16 499 | 12 314 | 9 408 | 9 208 | 9 556 |
| 1984 | 72 723 | 6 113 | 3 019 | 3 094 | 66 610 | 8 522 | 16 816 | 12 853 | 9 434 | 9 217 | 9 768 |
| 1985 | 73 373 | 5 987 | 3 026 | 2 961 | 67 386 | 8 246 | 17 042 | 13 337 | 9 488 | 9 262 | 10 010 |
| 1986 | 74 390 | 5 977 | 3 084 | 2 894 | 68 413 | 8 002 | 17 564 | 13 840 | 9 578 | 9 201 | 10 229 |
| 1987 | 75 189 | 6 015 | 3 125 | 2 890 | 69 175 | 7 729 | 17 754 | 14 338 | 9 771 | 9 101 | 10 481 |
| 1988 | 75 855 | 5 968 | 3 015 | 2 953 | 69 887 | 7 473 | 17 867 | 14 743 | 10 114 | 9 001 | 10 688 |
| 1989 | 76 468 | 5 813 | 2 817 | 2 996 | 70 654 | 7 279 | 17 908 | 15 237 | 10 434 | 8 900 | 10 897 |
| 1990 | 77 369 | 5 913 | 2 809 | 3 103 | 71 457 | 7 764 | 17 766 | 15 770 | 10 598 | 8 680 | 10 879 |
| 1991 | 77 977 | 5 704 | 2 805 | 2 899 | 72 274 | 7 748 | 17 615 | 16 340 | 10 856 | 8 640 | 11 074 |
| 1992 | 78 651 | 5 611 | 2 819 | 2 792 | 73 040 | 7 676 | 17 403 | 16 579 | 11 513 | 8 602 | 11 268 |
| 1993 | 79 371 | 5 650 | 2 862 | 2 788 | 73 721 | 7 545 | 17 158 | 16 900 | 12 058 | 8 590 | 11 470 |
| 1994 | 80 059 | 5 748 | 2 938 | 2 810 | 74 311 | 7 357 | 16 915 | 17 247 | 12 545 | 8 618 | 11 629 |
| 1995 | 80 733 | 5 854 | 2 995 | 2 859 | 74 879 | 7 163 | 16 653 | 17 567 | 13 028 | 8 653 | 11 815 |
| 1996 | 81 489 | 6 035 | 3 099 | 2 936 | 75 454 | 6 971 | 16 395 | 17 868 | 13 518 | 8 734 | 11 968 |
| 1997 | 82 577 | 6 257 | 3 209 | 3 048 | 76 320 | 7 087 | 16 043 | 18 163 | 14 030 | 8 929 | 12 067 |
| 1998 | 83 352 | 6 386 | 3 233 | 3 153 | 76 966 | 7 170 | 15 644 | 18 310 | 14 400 | 9 286 | 12 155 |
| 1999 | 83 930 | 6 498 | 3 266 | 3 232 | 77 432 | 7 244 | 15 150 | 18 340 | 14 834 | 9 581 | 12 283 |
| 2000 | 85 370 | 6 404 | 3 224 | 3 181 | 78 966 | 7 329 | 15 528 | 18 003 | 15 578 | 10 028 | 12 501 |
| 2001 | 86 452 | 6 422 | 3 229 | 3 194 | 80 029 | 7 564 | 15 486 | 17 960 | 16 047 | 10 369 | 12 604 |
| 2002 | 87 361 | 6 439 | 3 251 | 3 189 | 80 922 | 7 750 | 15 470 | 17 792 | 16 317 | 10 918 | 12 676 |
| 2003 | 88 249 | 6 390 | 3 378 | 3 012 | 81 860 | 7 856 | 15 569 | 17 620 | 16 555 | 11 442 | 12 818 |
| 2004 | 89 044 | 6 429 | 3 301 | 3 129 | 82 615 | 8 024 | 15 486 | 17 404 | 16 834 | 11 922 | 12 946 |
| 2005 | 90 027 | 6 471 | 3 464 | 3 006 | 83 556 | 8 057 | 15 507 | 17 286 | 17 169 | 12 415 | 13 123 |
| 2006 | 91 021 | 6 555 | 3 551 | 3 004 | 84 466 | 8 052 | 15 567 | 17 143 | 17 467 | 12 891 | 13 346 |
| 2007 | 92 073 | 6 653 | 3 567 | 3 086 | 85 420 | 8 113 | 15 762 | 16 927 | 17 686 | 13 341 | 13 591 |
| 2008 | 92 725 | 6 669 | 3 550 | 3 120 | 86 056 | 8 072 | 15 884 | 16 599 | 17 830 | 13 698 | 13 972 |
| 2009 | 93 433 | 6 644 | 3 469 | 3 175 | 86 789 | 8 076 | 16 011 | 16 260 | 17 956 | 14 154 | 14 332 |
| 2010 | 94 082 | 6 580 | 3 473 | 3 107 | 87 502 | 8 240 | 16 174 | 15 920 | 17 919 | 14 634 | 14 615 |
| 2011 | 94 801 | 6 610 | 3 496 | 3 114 | 88 191 | 8 485 | 16 332 | 15 540 | 17 602 | 15 018 | 15 213 |
| 2012 | 94 266 | 6 486 | 3 387 | 3 099 | 87 780 | 8 211 | 15 691 | 15 263 | 17 287 | 15 333 | 15 995 |
| 2013 | 94 865 | 6 391 | 3 413 | 2 978 | 88 474 | 8 256 | 15 824 | 15 185 | 17 043 | 15 547 | 16 619 |
| 2014 | 95 513 | 6 321 | 3 370 | 2 950 | 89 193 | 8 250 | 15 992 | 15 110 | 16 823 | 15 794 | 17 224 |
| 2015 | 96 147 | 6 282 | 3 328 | 2 955 | 89 865 | 8 164 | 16 087 | 15 067 | 16 677 | 16 067 | 17 802 |

## Table 1-6. Civilian Noninstitutional Population, by Age, Race, Sex, and Hispanic Origin, 1948–2015 —Continued

(Thousands of people.)

| Race, Hispanic origin, sex, and year | 16 years and over | 16 to 19 years | | | 20 years and over | | | | | | |
|---|---|---|---|---|---|---|---|---|---|---|---|
| | | Total | 16 to 17 years | 18 to 19 years | Total | 20 to 24 years | 25 to 34 years | 35 to 44 years | 45 to 54 years | 55 to 64 years | 65 years and over |
| **WHITE** | | | | | | | | | | | |
| **Women** | | | | | | | | | | | |
| 1954 | 51 242 | 3 725 | 1 884 | 1 841 | 47 517 | 4 720 | 10 870 | 10 227 | 8 397 | 6 652 | 6 651 |
| 1955 | 51 802 | 3 785 | 1 929 | 1 856 | 48 017 | 4 671 | 10 806 | 10 342 | 8 566 | 6 771 | 6 862 |
| 1956 | 52 373 | 3 846 | 1 953 | 1 892 | 48 527 | 4 642 | 10 713 | 10 466 | 8 752 | 6 886 | 7 067 |
| 1957 | 52 998 | 3 949 | 2 007 | 1 941 | 49 049 | 4 655 | 10 584 | 10 597 | 8 957 | 7 000 | 7 256 |
| 1958 | 53 645 | 4 096 | 2 131 | 1 966 | 49 549 | 4 715 | 10 407 | 10 716 | 9 159 | 7 107 | 7 442 |
| 1959 | 54 392 | 4 351 | 2 337 | 2 015 | 50 041 | 4 794 | 10 216 | 10 812 | 9 348 | 7 219 | 7 653 |
| 1960 | 55 214 | 4 575 | 2 433 | 2 142 | 50 639 | 4 873 | 10 097 | 10 918 | 9 536 | 7 349 | 7 865 |
| 1961 | 55 993 | 4 732 | 2 378 | 2 354 | 51 261 | 4 999 | 9 999 | 10 991 | 9 697 | 7 485 | 8 091 |
| 1962 | 56 660 | 4 823 | 2 392 | 2 432 | 51 837 | 5 178 | 9 894 | 11 054 | 9 681 | 7 533 | 8 496 |
| 1963 | 57 672 | 5 151 | 2 757 | 2 394 | 52 521 | 5 459 | 9 828 | 11 089 | 9 785 | 7 650 | 8 710 |
| 1964 | 58 663 | 5 468 | 3 047 | 2 422 | 53 195 | 5 706 | 9 814 | 11 074 | 9 943 | 7 804 | 8 853 |
| 1965 | 59 601 | 5 778 | 2 999 | 2 779 | 53 823 | 5 918 | 9 826 | 10 996 | 10 088 | 7 954 | 9 042 |
| 1966 | 60 503 | 6 042 | 2 970 | 3 072 | 54 461 | 6 120 | 9 904 | 10 869 | 10 230 | 8 107 | 9 230 |
| 1967 | 61 491 | 6 011 | 2 993 | 3 019 | 55 480 | 6 540 | 10 125 | 10 732 | 10 379 | 8 271 | 9 435 |
| 1968 | 62 512 | 6 053 | 3 072 | 2 981 | 56 460 | 6 809 | 10 493 | 10 572 | 10 520 | 8 433 | 9 633 |
| 1969 | 63 563 | 6 174 | 3 172 | 3 002 | 57 390 | 7 089 | 10 818 | 10 396 | 10 651 | 8 600 | 9 836 |
| 1970 | 64 656 | 6 342 | 3 262 | 3 080 | 58 315 | 7 370 | 11 105 | 10 251 | 10 761 | 8 769 | 10 060 |
| 1971 | 65 857 | 6 518 | 3 338 | 3 180 | 59 340 | 7 662 | 11 454 | 10 117 | 10 841 | 8 951 | 10 315 |
| 1972 | 67 431 | 6 673 | 3 407 | 3 267 | 60 758 | 7 855 | 12 060 | 10 105 | 10 872 | 9 161 | 10 705 |
| 1973 | 68 517 | 6 796 | 3 466 | 3 331 | 61 721 | 7 951 | 12 610 | 10 018 | 10 891 | 9 306 | 10 943 |
| 1974 | 69 623 | 6 933 | 3 510 | 3 424 | 62 690 | 8 026 | 13 112 | 10 064 | 10 896 | 9 356 | 11 236 |
| 1975 | 70 810 | 7 011 | 3 523 | 3 488 | 63 798 | 8 214 | 13 615 | 10 063 | 10 847 | 9 505 | 11 556 |
| 1976 | 71 974 | 7 062 | 3 516 | 3 546 | 64 912 | 8 381 | 14 102 | 10 153 | 10 752 | 9 664 | 11 860 |
| 1977 | 73 077 | 7 071 | 3 525 | 3 545 | 66 007 | 8 553 | 14 564 | 10 351 | 10 618 | 9 832 | 12 088 |
| 1978 | 74 213 | 7 038 | 3 513 | 3 524 | 67 174 | 8 704 | 14 926 | 10 696 | 10 476 | 9 974 | 12 399 |
| 1979 | 75 347 | 6 987 | 3 460 | 3 527 | 68 360 | 8 815 | 15 363 | 11 017 | 10 327 | 10 122 | 12 717 |
| 1980 | 76 489 | 6 914 | 3 403 | 3 511 | 69 575 | 8 904 | 15 878 | 11 313 | 10 201 | 10 256 | 13 022 |
| 1981 | 77 428 | 6 752 | 3 303 | 3 449 | 70 677 | 8 965 | 16 362 | 11 606 | 10 106 | 10 346 | 13 292 |
| 1982 | 78 230 | 6 519 | 3 134 | 3 385 | 71 711 | 8 959 | 16 603 | 12 154 | 10 015 | 10 402 | 13 579 |
| 1983 | 78 884 | 6 282 | 2 991 | 3 292 | 72 601 | 8 895 | 16 788 | 12 714 | 9 941 | 10 418 | 13 847 |
| 1984 | 79 624 | 6 034 | 2 899 | 3 135 | 73 590 | 8 782 | 17 073 | 13 271 | 9 914 | 10 412 | 14 138 |
| 1985 | 80 306 | 5 912 | 2 895 | 3 017 | 74 394 | 8 607 | 17 409 | 13 762 | 9 917 | 10 358 | 14 342 |
| 1986 | 81 042 | 5 902 | 2 953 | 2 949 | 75 140 | 8 351 | 17 728 | 14 223 | 10 009 | 10 277 | 14 551 |
| 1987 | 81 769 | 5 924 | 2 985 | 2 939 | 75 845 | 8 079 | 17 913 | 14 698 | 10 194 | 10 141 | 14 820 |
| 1988 | 82 340 | 5 869 | 2 878 | 2 991 | 76 470 | 7 804 | 18 009 | 15 074 | 10 537 | 9 994 | 15 052 |
| 1989 | 82 871 | 5 716 | 2 690 | 3 027 | 77 154 | 7 600 | 18 043 | 15 537 | 10 853 | 9 843 | 15 278 |
| 1990 | 83 256 | 5 717 | 2 654 | 3 063 | 77 539 | 7 774 | 17 895 | 15 969 | 10 937 | 9 524 | 15 440 |
| 1991 | 83 781 | 5 497 | 2 646 | 2 850 | 78 285 | 7 768 | 17 726 | 16 514 | 11 196 | 9 435 | 15 647 |
| 1992 | 84 321 | 5 393 | 2 659 | 2 734 | 78 928 | 7 678 | 17 482 | 16 727 | 11 851 | 9 350 | 15 841 |
| 1993 | 84 918 | 5 428 | 2 700 | 2 728 | 79 490 | 7 542 | 17 206 | 17 019 | 12 398 | 9 302 | 16 023 |
| 1994 | 85 496 | 5 516 | 2 772 | 2 744 | 79 980 | 7 351 | 16 950 | 17 335 | 12 890 | 9 306 | 16 148 |
| 1995 | 86 181 | 5 614 | 2 827 | 2 787 | 80 567 | 7 150 | 16 702 | 17 654 | 13 390 | 9 333 | 16 337 |
| 1996 | 86 828 | 5 787 | 2 927 | 2 860 | 81 041 | 6 936 | 16 457 | 17 943 | 13 884 | 9 402 | 16 419 |
| 1997 | 87 417 | 5 924 | 3 004 | 2 920 | 81 492 | 6 896 | 16 047 | 18 162 | 14 357 | 9 582 | 16 447 |
| 1998 | 88 126 | 6 053 | 3 031 | 3 023 | 82 073 | 6 969 | 15 642 | 18 300 | 14 732 | 9 944 | 16 486 |
| 1999 | 89 156 | 6 202 | 3 076 | 3 127 | 82 953 | 7 150 | 15 366 | 18 415 | 15 214 | 10 274 | 16 536 |
| 2000 | 90 850 | 6 131 | 3 041 | 3 090 | 84 718 | 7 223 | 15 420 | 18 258 | 15 972 | 10 729 | 17 116 |
| 2001 | 91 660 | 6 134 | 3 062 | 3 071 | 85 526 | 7 438 | 15 284 | 18 153 | 16 428 | 11 065 | 17 158 |
| 2002 | 92 422 | 6 157 | 3 096 | 3 061 | 86 266 | 7 611 | 15 207 | 17 958 | 16 695 | 11 622 | 17 173 |
| 2003 | 93 043 | 6 137 | 3 251 | 2 886 | 86 905 | 7 680 | 15 220 | 17 731 | 16 911 | 12 147 | 17 216 |
| 2004 | 93 599 | 6 169 | 3 260 | 2 909 | 87 430 | 7 794 | 15 099 | 17 441 | 17 170 | 12 627 | 17 299 |
| 2005 | 94 419 | 6 219 | 3 304 | 2 915 | 88 200 | 7 814 | 15 086 | 17 268 | 17 480 | 13 119 | 17 433 |
| 2006 | 95 242 | 6 301 | 3 429 | 2 871 | 88 942 | 7 796 | 15 094 | 17 074 | 17 760 | 13 596 | 17 623 |
| 2007 | 96 180 | 6 390 | 3 458 | 2 932 | 89 790 | 7 832 | 15 249 | 16 843 | 17 979 | 14 051 | 17 835 |
| 2008 | 96 814 | 6 414 | 3 412 | 3 003 | 90 400 | 7 842 | 15 349 | 16 493 | 18 111 | 14 411 | 18 193 |
| 2009 | 97 469 | 6 391 | 3 306 | 3 086 | 91 078 | 7 887 | 15 460 | 16 118 | 18 210 | 14 868 | 18 535 |
| 2010 | 97 993 | 6 311 | 3 327 | 2 984 | 91 683 | 8 040 | 15 640 | 15 727 | 18 146 | 15 349 | 18 781 |
| 2011 | 98 276 | 6 208 | 3 177 | 3 031 | 92 068 | 8 077 | 15 803 | 15 490 | 17 925 | 15 781 | 18 992 |
| 2012 | 98 938 | 6 172 | 3 230 | 2 942 | 92 766 | 8 078 | 15 550 | 15 334 | 17 648 | 16 179 | 19 978 |
| 2013 | 99 467 | 6 107 | 3 277 | 2 830 | 93 360 | 8 101 | 15 664 | 15 242 | 17 370 | 16 408 | 20 575 |
| 2014 | 99 984 | 6 056 | 3 280 | 2 777 | 93 928 | 8 079 | 15 790 | 15 144 | 17 125 | 16 656 | 21 134 |
| 2015 | 100 720 | 6 040 | 3 211 | 2 829 | 94 680 | 8 007 | 15 950 | 15 119 | 16 956 | 16 938 | 21 711 |

## Table 1-6.  Civilian Noninstitutional Population, by Age, Race, Sex, and Hispanic Origin, 1948–2015
### —Continued

(Thousands of people.)

| Race, Hispanic origin, sex, and year | 16 years and over | 16 to 19 years | | | 20 years and over | | | | | | |
|---|---|---|---|---|---|---|---|---|---|---|---|
| | | Total | 16 to 17 years | 18 to 19 years | Total | 20 to 24 years | 25 to 34 years | 35 to 44 years | 45 to 54 years | 55 to 64 years | 65 years and over |
| **BLACK** | | | | | | | | | | | |
| **Both Sexes** | | | | | | | | | | | |
| 1980 | 17 824 | 2 289 | 1 171 | 1 119 | 15 535 | 2 606 | 4 095 | 2 687 | 2 249 | 1 870 | 2 030 |
| 1981 | 18 219 | 2 288 | 1 161 | 1 127 | 15 931 | 2 642 | 4 290 | 2 758 | 2 260 | 1 913 | 2 069 |
| 1982 | 18 584 | 2 252 | 1 119 | 1 134 | 16 332 | 2 697 | 4 438 | 2 887 | 2 263 | 1 935 | 2 113 |
| 1983 | 18 925 | 2 225 | 1 092 | 1 133 | 16 700 | 2 734 | 4 607 | 2 999 | 2 260 | 1 964 | 2 135 |
| 1984 | 19 348 | 2 161 | 1 056 | 1 105 | 17 187 | 2 783 | 4 789 | 3 167 | 2 288 | 1 977 | 2 183 |
| 1985 | 19 664 | 2 160 | 1 083 | 1 077 | 17 504 | 2 649 | 4 873 | 3 290 | 2 372 | 2 060 | 2 259 |
| 1986 | 19 989 | 2 137 | 1 090 | 1 048 | 17 852 | 2 625 | 5 026 | 3 410 | 2 413 | 2 079 | 2 298 |
| 1987 | 20 352 | 2 163 | 1 123 | 1 040 | 18 189 | 2 578 | 5 139 | 3 563 | 2 460 | 2 097 | 2 352 |
| 1988 | 20 692 | 2 179 | 1 130 | 1 049 | 18 513 | 2 527 | 5 234 | 3 716 | 2 524 | 2 110 | 2 402 |
| 1989 | 21 021 | 2 176 | 1 116 | 1 060 | 18 846 | 2 479 | 5 308 | 3 900 | 2 587 | 2 118 | 2 454 |
| 1990 | 21 477 | 2 238 | 1 101 | 1 138 | 19 239 | 2 554 | 5 407 | 4 328 | 2 618 | 1 970 | 2 362 |
| 1991 | 21 799 | 2 187 | 1 085 | 1 102 | 19 612 | 2 585 | 5 419 | 4 538 | 2 682 | 1 985 | 2 403 |
| 1992 | 22 147 | 2 155 | 1 086 | 1 069 | 19 992 | 2 615 | 5 404 | 4 722 | 2 809 | 1 996 | 2 446 |
| 1993 | 22 521 | 2 181 | 1 113 | 1 069 | 20 339 | 2 600 | 5 409 | 4 886 | 2 941 | 2 016 | 2 487 |
| 1994 | 22 879 | 2 211 | 1 168 | 1 044 | 20 668 | 2 616 | 5 362 | 5 038 | 3 084 | 2 045 | 2 524 |
| 1995 | 23 246 | 2 284 | 1 198 | 1 086 | 20 962 | 2 554 | 5 337 | 5 178 | 3 244 | 2 079 | 2 571 |
| 1996 | 23 604 | 2 356 | 1 238 | 1 118 | 21 248 | 2 519 | 5 311 | 5 290 | 3 408 | 2 110 | 2 609 |
| 1997 | 24 003 | 2 412 | 1 255 | 1 158 | 21 591 | 2 515 | 5 279 | 5 410 | 3 571 | 2 164 | 2 653 |
| 1998 | 24 373 | 2 443 | 1 241 | 1 202 | 21 930 | 2 546 | 5 221 | 5 510 | 3 735 | 2 224 | 2 695 |
| 1999 | 24 855 | 2 479 | 1 250 | 1 229 | 22 376 | 2 615 | 5 197 | 5 609 | 3 919 | 2 295 | 2 741 |
| 2000 | 24 902 | 2 389 | 1 205 | 1 183 | 22 513 | 2 611 | 5 089 | 5 488 | 4 168 | 2 407 | 2 750 |
| 2001 | 25 138 | 2 388 | 1 212 | 1 176 | 22 750 | 2 686 | 5 003 | 5 467 | 4 343 | 2 478 | 2 775 |
| 2002 | 25 578 | 2 416 | 1 235 | 1 181 | 23 162 | 2 779 | 5 015 | 5 460 | 4 513 | 2 571 | 2 823 |
| 2003 | 25 686 | 2 382 | 1 309 | 1 074 | 23 304 | 2 773 | 4 978 | 5 387 | 4 628 | 2 692 | 2 846 |
| 2004 | 26 065 | 2 423 | 1 350 | 1 072 | 23 643 | 2 821 | 5 020 | 5 335 | 4 739 | 2 827 | 2 899 |
| 2005 | 26 517 | 2 481 | 1 341 | 1 140 | 24 036 | 2 835 | 5 075 | 5 311 | 4 869 | 2 980 | 2 967 |
| 2006 | 27 007 | 2 565 | 1 408 | 1 157 | 24 442 | 2 851 | 5 133 | 5 302 | 4 992 | 3 137 | 3 027 |
| 2007 | 27 485 | 2 640 | 1 497 | 1 143 | 24 845 | 2 891 | 5 210 | 5 271 | 5 110 | 3 284 | 3 080 |
| 2008 | 27 843 | 2 676 | 1 459 | 1 217 | 25 168 | 2 914 | 5 262 | 5 198 | 5 183 | 3 429 | 3 182 |
| 2009 | 28 241 | 2 684 | 1 462 | 1 221 | 25 557 | 2 973 | 5 349 | 5 109 | 5 290 | 3 596 | 3 239 |
| 2010 | 28 708 | 2 657 | 1 438 | 1 219 | 26 051 | 3 097 | 5 491 | 5 031 | 5 322 | 3 773 | 3 337 |
| 2011 | 29 114 | 2 594 | 1 353 | 1 240 | 26 520 | 3 168 | 5 606 | 4 995 | 5 357 | 3 955 | 3 440 |
| 2012 | 29 907 | 2 643 | 1 381 | 1 262 | 27 265 | 3 326 | 5 455 | 5 107 | 5 446 | 4 281 | 3 650 |
| 2013 | 30 376 | 2 565 | 1 344 | 1 221 | 27 811 | 3 425 | 5 585 | 5 131 | 5 429 | 4 430 | 3 811 |
| 2014 | 30 843 | 2 508 | 1 345 | 1 163 | 28 335 | 3 460 | 5 742 | 5 168 | 5 377 | 4 573 | 4 015 |
| 2015 | 31 386 | 2 491 | 1 343 | 1 148 | 28 895 | 3 425 | 5 929 | 5 232 | 5 383 | 4 718 | 4 207 |
| **Men** | | | | | | | | | | | |
| 1980 | 7 944 | 1 110 | 583 | 526 | 6 834 | 1 171 | 1 828 | 1 191 | 999 | 825 | 822 |
| 1981 | 8 117 | 1 110 | 577 | 534 | 7 007 | 1 189 | 1 914 | 1 224 | 1 003 | 844 | 835 |
| 1982 | 8 283 | 1 097 | 556 | 542 | 7 186 | 1 225 | 1 983 | 1 282 | 1 003 | 848 | 846 |
| 1983 | 8 447 | 1 087 | 542 | 545 | 7 360 | 1 254 | 2 068 | 1 333 | 1 000 | 857 | 847 |
| 1984 | 8 654 | 1 055 | 524 | 531 | 7 599 | 1 292 | 2 164 | 1 411 | 1 012 | 858 | 861 |
| 1985 | 8 790 | 1 059 | 543 | 517 | 7 731 | 1 202 | 2 180 | 1 462 | 1 060 | 924 | 902 |
| 1986 | 8 956 | 1 049 | 548 | 503 | 7 907 | 1 195 | 2 264 | 1 517 | 1 072 | 934 | 924 |
| 1987 | 9 128 | 1 065 | 566 | 499 | 8 063 | 1 173 | 2 320 | 1 587 | 1 092 | 944 | 947 |
| 1988 | 9 289 | 1 074 | 569 | 505 | 8 215 | 1 151 | 2 367 | 1 656 | 1 121 | 951 | 970 |
| 1989 | 9 439 | 1 075 | 575 | 501 | 8 364 | 1 128 | 2 403 | 1 741 | 1 145 | 956 | 989 |
| 1990 | 9 573 | 1 094 | 555 | 540 | 8 479 | 1 144 | 2 412 | 1 968 | 1 183 | 855 | 917 |
| 1991 | 9 725 | 1 072 | 546 | 526 | 8 652 | 1 168 | 2 417 | 2 060 | 1 211 | 864 | 933 |
| 1992 | 9 896 | 1 056 | 544 | 512 | 8 840 | 1 194 | 2 409 | 2 150 | 1 268 | 868 | 951 |
| 1993 | 10 083 | 1 075 | 559 | 516 | 9 008 | 1 181 | 2 425 | 2 228 | 1 330 | 874 | 969 |
| 1994 | 10 258 | 1 087 | 586 | 501 | 9 171 | 1 207 | 2 399 | 2 300 | 1 392 | 889 | 985 |
| 1995 | 10 411 | 1 131 | 601 | 530 | 9 280 | 1 161 | 2 388 | 2 362 | 1 462 | 901 | 1 006 |
| 1996 | 10 575 | 1 161 | 623 | 538 | 9 414 | 1 154 | 2 373 | 2 413 | 1 534 | 914 | 1 025 |
| 1997 | 10 763 | 1 188 | 634 | 553 | 9 575 | 1 153 | 2 363 | 2 471 | 1 607 | 936 | 1 045 |
| 1998 | 10 927 | 1 201 | 623 | 578 | 9 727 | 1 166 | 2 335 | 2 520 | 1 682 | 956 | 1 068 |
| 1999 | 11 143 | 1 218 | 628 | 589 | 9 926 | 1 197 | 2 321 | 2 566 | 1 765 | 986 | 1 091 |
| 2000 | 11 129 | 1 178 | 605 | 572 | 9 952 | 1 195 | 2 277 | 2 471 | 1 889 | 1 067 | 1 053 |
| 2001 | 11 172 | 1 179 | 606 | 573 | 9 993 | 1 224 | 2 212 | 2 440 | 1 960 | 1 096 | 1 060 |
| 2002 | 11 391 | 1 195 | 615 | 580 | 10 196 | 1 281 | 2 223 | 2 437 | 2 042 | 1 137 | 1 075 |
| 2003 | 11 454 | 1 176 | 661 | 515 | 10 278 | 1 291 | 2 210 | 2 401 | 2 094 | 1 189 | 1 093 |
| 2004 | 11 656 | 1 195 | 680 | 516 | 10 461 | 1 326 | 2 242 | 2 382 | 2 150 | 1 250 | 1 111 |
| 2005 | 11 882 | 1 223 | 682 | 541 | 10 659 | 1 341 | 2 277 | 2 372 | 2 202 | 1 319 | 1 148 |
| 2006 | 12 130 | 1 266 | 713 | 552 | 10 864 | 1 355 | 2 318 | 2 369 | 2 261 | 1 390 | 1 170 |
| 2007 | 12 361 | 1 305 | 742 | 563 | 11 057 | 1 380 | 2 366 | 2 352 | 2 318 | 1 454 | 1 186 |
| 2008 | 12 516 | 1 322 | 718 | 604 | 11 194 | 1 384 | 2 398 | 2 313 | 2 335 | 1 519 | 1 245 |
| 2009 | 12 705 | 1 326 | 736 | 590 | 11 379 | 1 410 | 2 454 | 2 271 | 2 392 | 1 592 | 1 260 |
| 2010 | 12 939 | 1 313 | 715 | 598 | 11 626 | 1 474 | 2 540 | 2 234 | 2 406 | 1 673 | 1 299 |
| 2011 | 13 164 | 1 282 | 642 | 640 | 11 882 | 1 510 | 2 612 | 2 222 | 2 435 | 1 759 | 1 344 |
| 2012 | 13 508 | 1 319 | 707 | 612 | 12 189 | 1 586 | 2 461 | 2 286 | 2 484 | 1 923 | 1 449 |
| 2013 | 13 747 | 1 276 | 685 | 591 | 12 471 | 1 647 | 2 536 | 2 299 | 2 474 | 1 992 | 1 522 |
| 2014 | 13 997 | 1 246 | 688 | 558 | 12 751 | 1 675 | 2 634 | 2 319 | 2 448 | 2 062 | 1 613 |
| 2015 | 14 268 | 1 237 | 697 | 540 | 13 031 | 1 662 | 2 740 | 2 353 | 2 454 | 2 130 | 1 692 |

## Table 1-6. Civilian Noninstitutional Population, by Age, Race, Sex, and Hispanic Origin, 1948–2015
—Continued

(Thousands of people.)

| Race, Hispanic origin, sex, and year | 16 years and over | 16 to 19 years | | | 20 years and over | | | | | | |
|---|---|---|---|---|---|---|---|---|---|---|---|
| | | Total | 16 to 17 years | 18 to 19 years | Total | 20 to 24 years | 25 to 34 years | 35 to 44 years | 45 to 54 years | 55 to 64 years | 65 years and over |
| **BLACK** | | | | | | | | | | | |
| **Women** | | | | | | | | | | | |
| 1980 | 9 880 | 1 180 | 586 | 593 | 8 700 | 1 435 | 2 267 | 1 496 | 1 250 | 1 045 | 1 208 |
| 1981 | 10 102 | 1 178 | 587 | 593 | 8 924 | 1 453 | 2 376 | 1 534 | 1 257 | 1 069 | 1 234 |
| 1982 | 10 300 | 1 155 | 584 | 592 | 9 146 | 1 472 | 2 455 | 1 605 | 1 260 | 1 087 | 1 267 |
| 1983 | 10 477 | 1 138 | 563 | 588 | 9 340 | 1 480 | 2 539 | 1 666 | 1 260 | 1 107 | 1 288 |
| 1984 | 10 694 | 1 106 | 550 | 574 | 9 588 | 1 491 | 2 625 | 1 756 | 1 276 | 1 119 | 1 322 |
| 1985 | 10 873 | 1 101 | 532 | 560 | 9 773 | 1 447 | 2 693 | 1 828 | 1 312 | 1 136 | 1 357 |
| 1986 | 11 033 | 1 088 | 540 | 545 | 9 945 | 1 430 | 2 762 | 1 893 | 1 341 | 1 145 | 1 374 |
| 1987 | 11 224 | 1 098 | 542 | 541 | 10 126 | 1 405 | 2 819 | 1 976 | 1 368 | 1 153 | 1 405 |
| 1988 | 11 402 | 1 105 | 557 | 544 | 10 298 | 1 376 | 2 867 | 2 060 | 1 403 | 1 159 | 1 432 |
| 1989 | 11 582 | 1 100 | 561 | 559 | 10 482 | 1 351 | 2 905 | 2 159 | 1 441 | 1 162 | 1 464 |
| 1990 | 11 904 | 1 144 | 541 | 598 | 10 760 | 1 410 | 2 995 | 2 360 | 1 435 | 1 114 | 1 446 |
| 1991 | 12 074 | 1 115 | 546 | 576 | 10 959 | 1 417 | 3 003 | 2 478 | 1 471 | 1 121 | 1 470 |
| 1992 | 12 251 | 1 099 | 539 | 557 | 11 152 | 1 421 | 2 995 | 2 573 | 1 542 | 1 127 | 1 495 |
| 1993 | 12 438 | 1 106 | 542 | 552 | 11 332 | 1 419 | 2 983 | 2 659 | 1 611 | 1 142 | 1 518 |
| 1994 | 12 621 | 1 125 | 554 | 543 | 11 496 | 1 410 | 2 963 | 2 738 | 1 692 | 1 156 | 1 538 |
| 1995 | 12 835 | 1 153 | 582 | 556 | 11 682 | 1 392 | 2 948 | 2 816 | 1 782 | 1 178 | 1 565 |
| 1996 | 13 029 | 1 195 | 597 | 580 | 11 833 | 1 364 | 2 938 | 2 877 | 1 874 | 1 196 | 1 584 |
| 1997 | 13 241 | 1 225 | 615 | 604 | 12 016 | 1 362 | 2 916 | 2 939 | 1 964 | 1 228 | 1 608 |
| 1998 | 13 446 | 1 243 | 620 | 624 | 12 203 | 1 380 | 2 886 | 2 991 | 2 053 | 1 268 | 1 626 |
| 1999 | 13 711 | 1 261 | 618 | 640 | 12 451 | 1 418 | 2 876 | 3 043 | 2 153 | 1 310 | 1 650 |
| 2000 | 13 772 | 1 211 | 621 | 611 | 12 561 | 1 416 | 2 812 | 3 017 | 2 279 | 1 340 | 1 697 |
| 2001 | 13 966 | 1 209 | 600 | 603 | 12 758 | 1 462 | 2 790 | 3 026 | 2 383 | 1 382 | 1 714 |
| 2002 | 14 187 | 1 221 | 606 | 601 | 12 966 | 1 498 | 2 792 | 3 023 | 2 471 | 1 434 | 1 747 |
| 2003 | 14 232 | 1 206 | 620 | 558 | 13 026 | 1 482 | 2 768 | 2 986 | 2 534 | 1 504 | 1 753 |
| 2004 | 14 409 | 1 227 | 648 | 557 | 13 182 | 1 495 | 2 778 | 2 954 | 2 590 | 1 577 | 1 789 |
| 2005 | 14 635 | 1 258 | 670 | 598 | 13 377 | 1 494 | 2 797 | 2 939 | 2 666 | 1 661 | 1 819 |
| 2006 | 14 877 | 1 299 | 659 | 605 | 13 578 | 1 495 | 2 815 | 2 933 | 2 731 | 1 747 | 1 857 |
| 2007 | 15 124 | 1 336 | 694 | 581 | 13 788 | 1 511 | 2 844 | 2 918 | 2 792 | 1 830 | 1 893 |
| 2008 | 15 328 | 1 354 | 755 | 613 | 13 974 | 1 530 | 2 864 | 2 885 | 2 848 | 1 910 | 1 937 |
| 2009 | 15 536 | 1 357 | 741 | 631 | 14 178 | 1 563 | 2 895 | 2 839 | 2 898 | 2 004 | 1 979 |
| 2010 | 15 769 | 1 344 | 726 | 621 | 14 425 | 1 623 | 2 951 | 2 796 | 2 916 | 2 101 | 2 038 |
| 2011 | 15 950 | 1 312 | 723 | 600 | 14 638 | 1 657 | 2 994 | 2 773 | 2 922 | 2 196 | 2 096 |
| 2012 | 16 400 | 1 324 | 712 | 650 | 15 076 | 1 740 | 2 994 | 2 821 | 2 963 | 2 358 | 2 201 |
| 2013 | 16 629 | 1 289 | 674 | 630 | 15 340 | 1 778 | 3 048 | 2 832 | 2 955 | 2 437 | 2 289 |
| 2014 | 16 846 | 1 262 | 659 | 605 | 15 584 | 1 785 | 3 108 | 2 849 | 2 929 | 2 511 | 2 402 |
| 2015 | 17 118 | 1 254 | 646 | 609 | 15 863 | 1 764 | 3 190 | 2 879 | 2 929 | 2 588 | 2 515 |
| **HISPANIC** | | | | | | | | | | | |
| **Both Sexes** | | | | | | | | | | | |
| 1980 | 9 598 | 1 281 | 638 | 643 | 8 317 | 1 564 | 2 508 | 1 575 | 1 190 | 782 | 698 |
| 1981 | 10 120 | 1 301 | 641 | 660 | 8 819 | 1 650 | 2 698 | 1 680 | 1 231 | 832 | 728 |
| 1982 | 10 580 | 1 307 | 639 | 668 | 9 273 | 1 724 | 2 871 | 1 779 | 1 264 | 880 | 755 |
| 1983 | 11 029 | 1 304 | 635 | 670 | 9 725 | 1 790 | 3 045 | 1 883 | 1 298 | 928 | 781 |
| 1984 | 11 478 | 1 300 | 633 | 667 | 10 178 | 1 839 | 3 224 | 1 996 | 1 336 | 973 | 810 |
| 1985 | 11 915 | 1 298 | 638 | 661 | 10 617 | 1 864 | 3 401 | 2 117 | 1 377 | 1 015 | 843 |
| 1986 | 12 344 | 1 302 | 658 | 644 | 11 042 | 1 899 | 3 510 | 2 239 | 1 496 | 1 023 | 875 |
| 1987 | 12 867 | 1 332 | 651 | 681 | 11 536 | 1 910 | 3 714 | 2 464 | 1 492 | 1 061 | 895 |
| 1988 | 13 325 | 1 354 | 662 | 692 | 11 970 | 1 948 | 3 807 | 2 565 | 1 571 | 1 159 | 920 |
| 1989 | 13 791 | 1 399 | 672 | 727 | 12 392 | 1 950 | 3 953 | 2 658 | 1 649 | 1 182 | 1 001 |
| 1990 | 15 904 | 1 737 | 821 | 915 | 14 167 | 2 428 | 4 589 | 3 001 | 1 817 | 1 247 | 1 084 |
| 1991 | 16 425 | 1 732 | 819 | 913 | 14 693 | 2 481 | 4 674 | 3 243 | 1 879 | 1 283 | 1 134 |
| 1992 | 16 961 | 1 737 | 836 | 901 | 15 224 | 2 444 | 4 806 | 3 458 | 1 980 | 1 321 | 1 216 |
| 1993 | 17 532 | 1 756 | 855 | 901 | 15 776 | 2 487 | 4 887 | 3 632 | 2 094 | 1 324 | 1 353 |
| 1994 | 18 117 | 1 818 | 902 | 916 | 16 300 | 2 518 | 5 000 | 3 756 | 2 223 | 1 401 | 1 401 |
| 1995 | 18 629 | 1 872 | 903 | 969 | 16 757 | 2 528 | 5 050 | 3 965 | 2 294 | 1 483 | 1 437 |
| 1996 | 19 213 | 1 948 | 962 | 986 | 17 265 | 2 524 | 5 181 | 4 227 | 2 275 | 1 546 | 1 512 |
| 1997 | 20 321 | 2 121 | 1 088 | 1 033 | 18 200 | 2 623 | 5 405 | 4 453 | 2 581 | 1 580 | 1 558 |
| 1998 | 21 070 | 2 204 | 1 070 | 1 135 | 18 865 | 2 731 | 5 447 | 4 636 | 2 775 | 1 615 | 1 662 |
| 1999 | 21 650 | 2 307 | 1 113 | 1 194 | 19 344 | 2 700 | 5 512 | 4 833 | 2 868 | 1 713 | 1 718 |
| 2000 | 23 938 | 2 523 | 1 214 | 1 309 | 21 415 | 3 255 | 6 466 | 5 189 | 3 061 | 1 736 | 1 708 |
| 2001 | 24 942 | 2 508 | 1 173 | 1 334 | 22 435 | 3 417 | 6 726 | 5 346 | 3 339 | 1 816 | 1 792 |
| 2002 | 25 963 | 2 507 | 1 216 | 1 291 | 23 456 | 3 508 | 7 010 | 5 606 | 3 494 | 1 953 | 1 885 |
| 2003 | 27 551 | 2 543 | 1 346 | 1 197 | 25 008 | 3 533 | 7 506 | 6 003 | 3 845 | 2 093 | 2 027 |
| 2004 | 28 109 | 2 608 | 1 337 | 1 270 | 25 502 | 3 666 | 7 470 | 6 055 | 3 987 | 2 208 | 2 115 |
| 2005 | 29 133 | 2 689 | 1 415 | 1 274 | 26 444 | 3 647 | 7 684 | 6 293 | 4 217 | 2 361 | 2 242 |
| 2006 | 30 103 | 2 796 | 1 518 | 1 277 | 27 307 | 3 603 | 7 856 | 6 519 | 4 466 | 2 516 | 2 347 |
| 2007 | 31 383 | 2 944 | 1 559 | 1 385 | 28 440 | 3 648 | 8 129 | 6 785 | 4 720 | 2 685 | 2 473 |
| 2008 | 32 141 | 3 042 | 1 620 | 1 422 | 29 098 | 3 620 | 8 147 | 6 946 | 4 937 | 2 840 | 2 609 |
| 2009 | 32 891 | 3 123 | 1 602 | 1 522 | 29 768 | 3 623 | 8 099 | 7 078 | 5 192 | 3 017 | 2 759 |
| 2010 | 33 713 | 3 243 | 1 673 | 1 570 | 30 469 | 3 880 | 8 084 | 7 123 | 5 351 | 3 167 | 2 864 |
| 2011 | 34 438 | 3 407 | 1 808 | 1 598 | 31 031 | 4 193 | 8 107 | 7 103 | 5 414 | 3 311 | 2 903 |
| 2012 | 36 759 | 3 656 | 1 906 | 1 750 | 33 103 | 4 502 | 8 512 | 7 551 | 5 831 | 3 613 | 3 094 |
| 2013 | 37 517 | 3 651 | 1 911 | 1 740 | 33 867 | 4 572 | 8 564 | 7 663 | 6 010 | 3 791 | 3 267 |
| 2014 | 38 400 | 3 662 | 1 949 | 1 713 | 34 738 | 4 642 | 8 656 | 7 792 | 6 192 | 3 989 | 3 467 |
| 2015 | 39 617 | 3 705 | 1 970 | 1 736 | 35 912 | 4 697 | 8 762 | 8 026 | 6 474 | 4 255 | 3 698 |

## Table 1-6.  Civilian Noninstitutional Population, by Age, Race, Sex, and Hispanic Origin, 1948–2015
### —Continued

(Thousands of people.)

| Race, Hispanic origin, sex, and year | 16 years and over | 16 to 19 years | | | 20 years and over | | | | | | |
|---|---|---|---|---|---|---|---|---|---|---|---|
| | | Total | 16 to 17 years | 18 to 19 years | Total | 20 to 24 years | 25 to 34 years | 35 to 44 years | 45 to 54 years | 55 to 64 years | 65 years and over |
| **HISPANIC** | | | | | | | | | | | |
| **Men** | | | | | | | | | | | |
| 1980 | 4 689 | . . . | . . . | . . . | 4 036 | . . . | . . . | . . . | . . . | . . . | . . . |
| 1981 | 4 968 | . . . | . . . | . . . | 4 306 | . . . | . . . | . . . | . . . | . . . | . . . |
| 1982 | 5 203 | . . . | . . . | . . . | 4 539 | . . . | . . . | . . . | . . . | . . . | . . . |
| 1983 | 5 432 | . . . | . . . | . . . | 4 771 | . . . | . . . | . . . | . . . | . . . | . . . |
| 1984 | 5 661 | . . . | . . . | . . . | 5 005 | . . . | . . . | . . . | . . . | . . . | . . . |
| 1985 | 5 885 | . . . | . . . | . . . | 5 232 | . . . | . . . | . . . | . . . | . . . | . . . |
| 1986 | 6 106 | . . . | . . . | . . . | 5 451 | . . . | . . . | . . . | . . . | . . . | . . . |
| 1987 | 6 371 | . . . | . . . | . . . | 5 700 | . . . | . . . | . . . | . . . | . . . | . . . |
| 1988 | 6 604 | . . . | . . . | . . . | 5 921 | . . . | . . . | . . . | . . . | . . . | . . . |
| 1989 | 6 825 | . . . | . . . | . . . | 6 114 | . . . | . . . | . . . | . . . | . . . | . . . |
| 1990 | 8 041 | . . . | . . . | . . . | 7 126 | . . . | . . . | . . . | . . . | . . . | . . . |
| 1991 | 8 296 | . . . | . . . | . . . | 7 392 | . . . | . . . | . . . | . . . | . . . | . . . |
| 1992 | 8 553 | . . . | . . . | . . . | 7 655 | . . . | . . . | . . . | . . . | . . . | . . . |
| 1993 | 8 824 | . . . | . . . | . . . | 7 930 | . . . | . . . | . . . | . . . | . . . | . . . |
| 1994 | 9 104 | 926 | 472 | 454 | 8 178 | 1 346 | 2 627 | 1 871 | 1 076 | 644 | 614 |
| 1995 | 9 329 | 954 | 481 | 473 | 8 375 | 1 337 | 2 657 | 1 966 | 1 127 | 668 | 619 |
| 1996 | 9 604 | 992 | 485 | 507 | 8 611 | 1 321 | 2 692 | 2 144 | 1 111 | 712 | 630 |
| 1997 | 10 368 | 1 119 | 585 | 534 | 9 250 | 1 439 | 2 872 | 2 275 | 1 266 | 747 | 651 |
| 1998 | 10 734 | 1 161 | 586 | 575 | 9 573 | 1 462 | 2 907 | 2 377 | 1 342 | 771 | 714 |
| 1999 | 10 713 | 1 190 | 571 | 619 | 9 523 | 1 398 | 2 805 | 2 407 | 1 397 | 767 | 749 |
| 2000 | 12 174 | 1 333 | 640 | 693 | 10 841 | 1 784 | 3 380 | 2 626 | 1 527 | 799 | 725 |
| 2001 | 12 695 | 1 310 | 619 | 690 | 11 386 | 1 846 | 3 529 | 2 765 | 1 650 | 848 | 749 |
| 2002 | 13 221 | 1 293 | 615 | 678 | 11 928 | 1 890 | 3 727 | 2 875 | 1 716 | 902 | 817 |
| 2003 | 14 098 | 1 301 | 674 | 627 | 12 797 | 1 905 | 4 033 | 3 098 | 1 910 | 989 | 862 |
| 2004 | 14 417 | 1 336 | 664 | 672 | 13 082 | 1 981 | 4 024 | 3 147 | 1 990 | 1 046 | 894 |
| 2005 | 14 962 | 1 376 | 730 | 646 | 13 586 | 1 956 | 4 155 | 3 284 | 2 114 | 1 123 | 953 |
| 2006 | 15 473 | 1 428 | 763 | 664 | 14 046 | 1 916 | 4 266 | 3 414 | 2 251 | 1 204 | 996 |
| 2007 | 16 154 | 1 505 | 790 | 714 | 14 649 | 1 928 | 4 430 | 3 563 | 2 384 | 1 287 | 1 058 |
| 2008 | 16 524 | 1 553 | 838 | 716 | 14 971 | 1 890 | 4 438 | 3 655 | 2 502 | 1 365 | 1 121 |
| 2009 | 16 897 | 1 593 | 818 | 774 | 15 305 | 1 875 | 4 405 | 3 735 | 2 647 | 1 459 | 1 184 |
| 2010 | 17 359 | 1 666 | 847 | 819 | 15 693 | 2 016 | 4 381 | 3 783 | 2 741 | 1 538 | 1 234 |
| 2011 | 17 753 | 1 812 | 951 | 861 | 15 941 | 2 278 | 4 379 | 3 702 | 2 717 | 1 604 | 1 260 |
| 2012 | 18 434 | 1 879 | 970 | 909 | 16 555 | 2 341 | 4 424 | 3 822 | 2 911 | 1 729 | 1 329 |
| 2013 | 18 798 | 1 870 | 988 | 882 | 16 928 | 2 364 | 4 453 | 3 880 | 3 012 | 1 818 | 1 402 |
| 2014 | 19 244 | 1 873 | 1 006 | 867 | 17 371 | 2 389 | 4 509 | 3 951 | 3 104 | 1 920 | 1 499 |
| 2015 | 19 745 | 1 886 | 1 014 | 872 | 17 860 | 2 396 | 4 516 | 4 053 | 3 241 | 2 050 | 1 604 |
| **HISPANIC** | | | | | | | | | | | |
| **Women** | | | | | | | | | | | |
| 1980 | 4 909 | . . . | . . . | . . . | 4 281 | . . . | . . . | . . . | . . . | . . . | . . . |
| 1981 | 5 151 | . . . | . . . | . . . | 4 513 | . . . | . . . | . . . | . . . | . . . | . . . |
| 1982 | 5 377 | . . . | . . . | . . . | 4 734 | . . . | . . . | . . . | . . . | . . . | . . . |
| 1983 | 5 597 | . . . | . . . | . . . | 4 954 | . . . | . . . | . . . | . . . | . . . | . . . |
| 1984 | 5 816 | . . . | . . . | . . . | 5 173 | . . . | . . . | . . . | . . . | . . . | . . . |
| 1985 | 6 029 | . . . | . . . | . . . | 5 385 | . . . | . . . | . . . | . . . | . . . | . . . |
| 1986 | 6 238 | . . . | . . . | . . . | 5 591 | . . . | . . . | . . . | . . . | . . . | . . . |
| 1987 | 6 496 | . . . | . . . | . . . | 5 835 | . . . | . . . | . . . | . . . | . . . | . . . |
| 1988 | 6 721 | . . . | . . . | . . . | 6 050 | . . . | . . . | . . . | . . . | . . . | . . . |
| 1989 | 6 965 | . . . | . . . | . . . | 6 278 | . . . | . . . | . . . | . . . | . . . | . . . |
| 1990 | 7 863 | . . . | . . . | . . . | 7 041 | . . . | . . . | . . . | . . . | . . . | . . . |
| 1991 | 8 130 | . . . | . . . | . . . | 7 301 | . . . | . . . | . . . | . . . | . . . | . . . |
| 1992 | 8 408 | . . . | . . . | . . . | 7 569 | . . . | . . . | . . . | . . . | . . . | . . . |
| 1993 | 8 708 | . . . | . . . | . . . | 7 846 | . . . | . . . | . . . | . . . | . . . | . . . |
| 1994 | 9 014 | 892 | 430 | 462 | 8 122 | 1 173 | 2 373 | 1 885 | 1 147 | 757 | 787 |
| 1995 | 9 300 | 918 | 422 | 496 | 8 382 | 1 191 | 2 393 | 1 999 | 1 167 | 815 | 818 |
| 1996 | 9 610 | 956 | 477 | 479 | 8 654 | 1 203 | 2 489 | 2 082 | 1 164 | 834 | 882 |
| 1997 | 9 953 | 1 003 | 503 | 500 | 8 950 | 1 184 | 2 533 | 2 178 | 1 315 | 833 | 907 |
| 1998 | 10 335 | 1 044 | 483 | 560 | 9 292 | 1 269 | 2 539 | 2 259 | 1 433 | 844 | 948 |
| 1999 | 10 937 | 1 116 | 542 | 575 | 9 821 | 1 302 | 2 707 | 2 425 | 1 470 | 947 | 969 |
| 2000 | 11 764 | 1 190 | 574 | 616 | 10 574 | 1 471 | 3 086 | 2 564 | 1 534 | 937 | 982 |
| 2001 | 12 247 | 1 198 | 554 | 644 | 11 049 | 1 571 | 3 198 | 2 581 | 1 689 | 968 | 1 043 |
| 2002 | 12 742 | 1 214 | 601 | 613 | 11 528 | 1 617 | 3 283 | 2 732 | 1 777 | 1 051 | 1 068 |
| 2003 | 13 452 | 1 242 | 672 | 570 | 12 211 | 1 628 | 3 473 | 2 905 | 1 935 | 1 105 | 1 166 |
| 2004 | 13 692 | 1 272 | 674 | 598 | 12 420 | 1 685 | 3 447 | 2 908 | 1 997 | 1 162 | 1 221 |
| 2005 | 14 172 | 1 313 | 685 | 628 | 12 858 | 1 692 | 3 529 | 3 009 | 2 103 | 1 237 | 1 289 |
| 2006 | 14 630 | 1 368 | 755 | 613 | 13 262 | 1 688 | 3 590 | 3 105 | 2 215 | 1 313 | 1 351 |
| 2007 | 15 229 | 1 439 | 769 | 670 | 13 791 | 1 720 | 3 698 | 3 222 | 2 336 | 1 398 | 1 416 |
| 2008 | 15 616 | 1 489 | 782 | 706 | 14 127 | 1 730 | 3 710 | 3 291 | 2 435 | 1 475 | 1 488 |
| 2009 | 15 993 | 1 531 | 783 | 748 | 14 463 | 1 748 | 3 694 | 3 343 | 2 545 | 1 558 | 1 576 |
| 2010 | 16 354 | 1 578 | 826 | 752 | 14 776 | 1 864 | 3 703 | 3 340 | 2 610 | 1 628 | 1 630 |
| 2011 | 16 685 | 1 595 | 857 | 738 | 15 090 | 1 915 | 3 727 | 3 401 | 2 696 | 1 707 | 1 643 |
| 2012 | 18 324 | 1 776 | 936 | 841 | 16 548 | 2 161 | 4 088 | 3 729 | 2 920 | 1 884 | 1 765 |
| 2013 | 18 719 | 1 781 | 923 | 858 | 16 938 | 2 208 | 4 110 | 3 783 | 2 998 | 1 973 | 1 866 |
| 2014 | 19 156 | 1 790 | 944 | 846 | 17 367 | 2 253 | 4 147 | 3 841 | 3 088 | 2 070 | 1 968 |
| 2015 | 19 872 | 1 820 | 956 | 864 | 18 052 | 2 301 | 4 247 | 3 973 | 3 233 | 2 205 | 2 094 |

. . . = Not available.

## Table 1-7. Civilian Labor Force, by Age, Sex, Race, and Hispanic Origin, 1948–2015

(Thousands of people.)

| Race, Hispanic origin, sex, and year | 16 years and over | 16 to 19 years | | | 20 years and over | | | | | | |
|---|---|---|---|---|---|---|---|---|---|---|---|
| | | Total | 16 to 17 years | 18 to 19 years | Total | 20 to 24 years | 25 to 34 years | 35 to 44 years | 45 to 54 years | 55 to 64 years | 65 years and over |
| **ALL RACES** | | | | | | | | | | | |
| **Both Sexes** | | | | | | | | | | | |
| 1948 | 60 621 | 4 435 | 1 780 | 2 654 | 56 187 | 7 392 | 14 258 | 13 397 | 10 914 | 7 329 | 2 897 |
| 1949 | 61 286 | 4 288 | 1 704 | 2 583 | 57 000 | 7 340 | 14 415 | 13 711 | 11 107 | 7 426 | 3 010 |
| 1950 | 62 208 | 4 216 | 1 659 | 2 557 | 57 994 | 7 307 | 14 619 | 13 954 | 11 444 | 7 633 | 3 036 |
| 1951 | 62 017 | 4 103 | 1 743 | 2 360 | 57 914 | 6 594 | 14 668 | 14 100 | 11 739 | 7 796 | 3 020 |
| 1952 | 62 138 | 4 064 | 1 806 | 2 257 | 58 075 | 5 840 | 14 904 | 14 383 | 11 961 | 7 980 | 3 005 |
| 1953 | 63 015 | 4 027 | 1 727 | 2 299 | 58 989 | 5 481 | 14 898 | 15 099 | 12 249 | 8 024 | 3 236 |
| 1954 | 63 643 | 3 976 | 1 643 | 2 300 | 59 666 | 5 475 | 14 983 | 15 221 | 12 524 | 8 269 | 3 192 |
| 1955 | 65 023 | 4 092 | 1 711 | 2 382 | 60 931 | 5 666 | 15 058 | 15 400 | 12 992 | 8 513 | 3 305 |
| 1956 | 66 552 | 4 296 | 1 878 | 2 418 | 62 257 | 5 940 | 14 961 | 15 694 | 13 407 | 8 830 | 3 423 |
| 1957 | 66 929 | 4 275 | 1 843 | 2 433 | 62 653 | 6 071 | 14 826 | 15 847 | 13 768 | 8 853 | 3 290 |
| 1958 | 67 639 | 4 260 | 1 818 | 2 442 | 63 377 | 6 272 | 14 668 | 16 028 | 14 179 | 9 031 | 3 199 |
| 1959 | 68 369 | 4 492 | 1 971 | 2 522 | 63 876 | 6 413 | 14 435 | 16 127 | 14 518 | 9 227 | 3 158 |
| 1960 | 69 628 | 4 841 | 2 095 | 2 747 | 64 788 | 6 702 | 14 382 | 16 269 | 14 852 | 9 385 | 3 195 |
| 1961 | 70 459 | 4 936 | 1 984 | 2 951 | 65 524 | 6 950 | 14 319 | 16 402 | 15 071 | 9 636 | 3 146 |
| 1962 | 70 614 | 4 916 | 1 919 | 2 997 | 65 699 | 7 082 | 14 023 | 16 589 | 15 096 | 9 757 | 3 154 |
| 1963 | 71 833 | 5 139 | 2 171 | 2 966 | 66 695 | 7 473 | 14 050 | 16 788 | 15 338 | 10 006 | 3 041 |
| 1964 | 73 091 | 5 388 | 2 449 | 2 940 | 67 702 | 7 963 | 14 056 | 16 771 | 15 637 | 10 182 | 3 090 |
| 1965 | 74 455 | 5 910 | 2 486 | 3 425 | 68 543 | 8 259 | 14 233 | 16 840 | 15 756 | 10 350 | 3 108 |
| 1966 | 75 770 | 6 558 | 2 664 | 3 893 | 69 219 | 8 410 | 14 458 | 16 738 | 15 984 | 10 575 | 3 053 |
| 1967 | 77 347 | 6 521 | 2 734 | 3 786 | 70 825 | 9 010 | 15 055 | 16 703 | 16 172 | 10 792 | 3 097 |
| 1968 | 78 737 | 6 619 | 2 817 | 3 803 | 72 118 | 9 305 | 15 708 | 16 591 | 16 397 | 10 964 | 3 153 |
| 1969 | 80 734 | 6 970 | 3 009 | 3 959 | 73 763 | 9 879 | 16 336 | 16 458 | 16 730 | 11 135 | 3 227 |
| 1970 | 82 771 | 7 249 | 3 135 | 4 115 | 75 521 | 10 597 | 17 036 | 16 437 | 16 949 | 11 283 | 3 222 |
| 1971 | 84 382 | 7 470 | 3 192 | 4 278 | 76 913 | 11 331 | 17 714 | 16 305 | 17 024 | 11 390 | 3 149 |
| 1972 | 87 034 | 8 054 | 3 420 | 4 636 | 78 980 | 12 130 | 18 960 | 16 398 | 16 967 | 11 412 | 3 114 |
| 1973 | 89 429 | 8 507 | 3 665 | 4 839 | 80 924 | 12 846 | 20 376 | 16 492 | 16 983 | 11 256 | 2 974 |
| 1974 | 91 949 | 8 871 | 3 810 | 5 059 | 83 080 | 13 314 | 21 654 | 16 763 | 17 131 | 11 284 | 2 934 |
| 1975 | 93 775 | 8 870 | 3 740 | 5 131 | 84 904 | 13 750 | 22 864 | 16 903 | 17 084 | 11 346 | 2 956 |
| 1976 | 96 158 | 9 056 | 3 767 | 5 288 | 87 103 | 14 284 | 24 203 | 17 317 | 16 982 | 11 422 | 2 895 |
| 1977 | 99 009 | 9 351 | 3 919 | 5 431 | 89 658 | 14 825 | 25 500 | 17 943 | 16 878 | 11 577 | 2 934 |
| 1978 | 102 251 | 9 652 | 4 127 | 5 526 | 92 598 | 15 370 | 26 703 | 18 821 | 16 891 | 11 744 | 3 070 |
| 1979 | 104 962 | 9 638 | 4 079 | 5 559 | 95 325 | 15 769 | 27 938 | 19 685 | 16 897 | 11 931 | 3 104 |
| 1980 | 106 940 | 9 378 | 3 883 | 5 496 | 97 561 | 15 922 | 29 227 | 20 463 | 16 910 | 11 985 | 3 054 |
| 1981 | 108 670 | 8 988 | 3 647 | 5 340 | 99 682 | 16 099 | 30 392 | 21 211 | 16 970 | 11 969 | 3 042 |
| 1982 | 110 204 | 8 526 | 3 336 | 5 189 | 101 679 | 16 082 | 31 186 | 22 431 | 16 889 | 12 062 | 3 030 |
| 1983 | 111 550 | 8 171 | 3 073 | 5 098 | 103 379 | 16 052 | 31 834 | 23 611 | 16 851 | 11 992 | 3 040 |
| 1984 | 113 544 | 7 943 | 3 050 | 4 894 | 105 601 | 16 046 | 32 723 | 24 933 | 17 006 | 11 961 | 2 933 |
| 1985 | 115 461 | 7 901 | 3 154 | 4 747 | 107 560 | 15 718 | 33 550 | 26 073 | 17 322 | 11 991 | 2 907 |
| 1986 | 117 834 | 7 926 | 3 287 | 4 639 | 109 908 | 15 441 | 34 591 | 27 232 | 17 739 | 11 894 | 3 010 |
| 1987 | 119 865 | 7 988 | 3 384 | 4 604 | 111 878 | 14 977 | 35 233 | 28 460 | 18 210 | 11 877 | 3 119 |
| 1988 | 121 669 | 8 031 | 3 286 | 4 745 | 113 638 | 14 505 | 35 503 | 29 435 | 19 104 | 11 808 | 3 284 |
| 1989 | 123 869 | 7 954 | 3 125 | 4 828 | 115 916 | 14 180 | 35 896 | 30 601 | 19 916 | 11 877 | 3 446 |
| 1990 | 125 840 | 7 792 | 2 937 | 4 856 | 118 047 | 14 700 | 35 929 | 32 145 | 20 248 | 11 575 | 3 451 |
| 1991 | 126 346 | 7 265 | 2 789 | 4 476 | 119 082 | 14 548 | 35 507 | 33 312 | 20 828 | 11 473 | 3 413 |
| 1992 | 128 105 | 7 096 | 2 769 | 4 327 | 121 009 | 14 521 | 35 369 | 33 899 | 22 160 | 11 587 | 3 473 |
| 1993 | 129 200 | 7 170 | 2 831 | 4 338 | 122 030 | 14 354 | 34 780 | 34 562 | 23 296 | 11 599 | 3 439 |
| 1994 | 131 056 | 7 481 | 3 134 | 4 347 | 123 576 | 14 131 | 34 353 | 35 226 | 24 318 | 11 713 | 3 834 |
| 1995 | 132 304 | 7 765 | 3 225 | 4 540 | 124 539 | 13 688 | 34 198 | 35 751 | 25 223 | 11 860 | 3 819 |
| 1996 | 133 943 | 7 806 | 3 263 | 4 543 | 126 137 | 13 377 | 33 833 | 36 556 | 26 397 | 12 146 | 3 828 |
| 1997 | 136 297 | 7 932 | 3 237 | 4 695 | 128 365 | 13 532 | 33 380 | 37 326 | 27 574 | 12 665 | 3 887 |
| 1998 | 137 673 | 8 256 | 3 335 | 4 921 | 129 417 | 13 638 | 32 813 | 37 536 | 28 368 | 13 215 | 3 847 |
| 1999 | 139 368 | 8 333 | 3 337 | 4 996 | 131 034 | 13 933 | 32 143 | 37 882 | 29 388 | 13 682 | 4 005 |
| 2000 | 142 583 | 8 271 | 3 261 | 5 010 | 134 312 | 14 250 | 32 755 | 37 567 | 31 071 | 14 356 | 4 312 |
| 2001 | 143 734 | 7 902 | 3 088 | 4 814 | 135 832 | 14 557 | 32 361 | 37 404 | 32 025 | 15 104 | 4 382 |
| 2002 | 144 863 | 7 585 | 2 870 | 4 715 | 137 278 | 14 781 | 32 196 | 36 926 | 32 597 | 16 309 | 4 469 |
| 2003 | 146 510 | 7 170 | 2 857 | 4 313 | 139 340 | 14 928 | 32 343 | 36 695 | 33 270 | 17 312 | 4 792 |
| 2004 | 147 401 | 7 114 | 2 747 | 4 367 | 140 287 | 15 154 | 32 207 | 36 158 | 33 758 | 18 013 | 4 998 |
| 2005 | 149 320 | 7 164 | 2 825 | 4 339 | 142 157 | 15 127 | 32 341 | 36 030 | 34 402 | 18 979 | 5 278 |
| 2006 | 151 428 | 7 281 | 2 952 | 4 329 | 144 147 | 15 113 | 32 573 | 35 848 | 35 146 | 19 984 | 5 484 |
| 2007 | 153 124 | 7 012 | 2 771 | 4 242 | 146 112 | 15 205 | 33 130 | 35 527 | 35 697 | 20 750 | 5 804 |
| 2008 | 154 287 | 6 858 | 2 552 | 4 306 | 147 429 | 15 174 | 33 332 | 35 061 | 36 003 | 21 615 | 6 243 |
| 2009 | 154 142 | 6 390 | 2 227 | 4 163 | 147 752 | 14 971 | 33 298 | 34 239 | 36 205 | 22 505 | 6 534 |
| 2010 | 153 889 | 5 906 | 2 000 | 3 905 | 147 983 | 15 028 | 33 614 | 33 366 | 35 960 | 23 297 | 6 718 |
| 2011 | 153 617 | 5 727 | 1 873 | 3 853 | 147 890 | 15 270 | 33 724 | 32 660 | 35 360 | 23 765 | 7 112 |
| 2012 | 154 975 | 5 823 | 1 952 | 3 870 | 149 152 | 15 462 | 33 465 | 32 734 | 35 054 | 24 710 | 7 727 |
| 2013 | 155 389 | 5 785 | 2 023 | 3 762 | 149 604 | 15 595 | 33 746 | 32 563 | 34 467 | 25 116 | 8 116 |
| 2014 | 155 922 | 5 654 | 1 971 | 3 683 | 150 268 | 15 641 | 34 199 | 32 506 | 34 062 | 25 502 | 8 358 |
| 2015 | 157 130 | 5 700 | 1 987 | 3 713 | 151 430 | 15 523 | 34 647 | 32 603 | 33 902 | 25 954 | 8 801 |

## Table 1-7.  Civilian Labor Force, by Age, Sex, Race, and Hispanic Origin, 1948–2015—*Continued*

(Thousands of people.)

| Race, Hispanic origin, sex, and year | 16 years and over | 16 to 19 years | | | 20 years and over | | | | | | |
|---|---|---|---|---|---|---|---|---|---|---|---|
| | | Total | 16 to 17 years | 18 to 19 years | Total | 20 to 24 years | 25 to 34 years | 35 to 44 years | 45 to 54 years | 55 to 64 years | 65 years and over |
| **ALL RACES** | | | | | | | | | | | |
| **Men** | | | | | | | | | | | |
| 1948 | 43 286 | 2 600 | 1 109 | 1 490 | 40 687 | 4 673 | 10 327 | 9 596 | 7 943 | 5 764 | 2 384 |
| 1949 | 43 498 | 2 477 | 1 056 | 1 420 | 41 022 | 4 682 | 10 418 | 9 722 | 8 008 | 5 748 | 2 454 |
| 1950 | 43 819 | 2 504 | 1 048 | 1 456 | 41 316 | 4 632 | 10 527 | 9 793 | 8 117 | 5 794 | 2 453 |
| 1951 | 43 001 | 2 347 | 1 081 | 1 266 | 40 655 | 3 935 | 10 375 | 9 799 | 8 205 | 5 873 | 2 469 |
| 1952 | 42 869 | 2 312 | 1 101 | 1 210 | 40 558 | 3 338 | 10 585 | 9 945 | 8 326 | 5 949 | 2 416 |
| 1953 | 43 633 | 2 320 | 1 070 | 1 249 | 41 315 | 3 053 | 10 736 | 10 437 | 8 570 | 5 975 | 2 543 |
| 1954 | 43 965 | 2 295 | 1 023 | 1 272 | 41 669 | 3 051 | 10 771 | 10 513 | 8 702 | 6 105 | 2 526 |
| 1955 | 44 475 | 2 369 | 1 070 | 1 299 | 42 106 | 3 221 | 10 806 | 10 595 | 8 838 | 6 122 | 2 526 |
| 1956 | 45 091 | 2 433 | 1 142 | 1 291 | 42 658 | 3 485 | 10 685 | 10 663 | 9 002 | 6 220 | 2 602 |
| 1957 | 45 197 | 2 415 | 1 127 | 1 289 | 42 780 | 3 629 | 10 571 | 10 731 | 9 153 | 6 222 | 2 477 |
| 1958 | 45 521 | 2 428 | 1 133 | 1 295 | 43 092 | 3 771 | 10 475 | 10 843 | 9 320 | 6 304 | 2 378 |
| 1959 | 45 886 | 2 596 | 1 206 | 1 390 | 43 289 | 3 940 | 10 346 | 10 899 | 9 438 | 6 345 | 2 322 |
| 1960 | 46 388 | 2 787 | 1 290 | 1 496 | 43 603 | 4 123 | 10 251 | 10 967 | 9 574 | 6 399 | 2 287 |
| 1961 | 46 653 | 2 794 | 1 210 | 1 583 | 43 860 | 4 253 | 10 176 | 11 012 | 9 668 | 6 530 | 2 220 |
| 1962 | 46 600 | 2 770 | 1 178 | 1 592 | 43 831 | 4 279 | 9 920 | 11 115 | 9 715 | 6 560 | 2 241 |
| 1963 | 47 129 | 2 907 | 1 321 | 1 586 | 44 222 | 4 514 | 9 876 | 11 187 | 9 836 | 6 675 | 2 135 |
| 1964 | 47 679 | 3 074 | 1 499 | 1 575 | 44 604 | 4 754 | 9 876 | 11 156 | 9 956 | 6 741 | 2 124 |
| 1965 | 48 255 | 3 397 | 1 532 | 1 866 | 44 857 | 4 894 | 9 903 | 11 120 | 10 045 | 6 763 | 2 132 |
| 1966 | 48 471 | 3 685 | 1 609 | 2 075 | 44 788 | 4 820 | 9 948 | 10 983 | 10 100 | 6 847 | 2 089 |
| 1967 | 48 987 | 3 634 | 1 658 | 1 976 | 45 354 | 5 043 | 10 207 | 10 859 | 10 189 | 6 937 | 2 118 |
| 1968 | 49 533 | 3 681 | 1 687 | 1 995 | 45 852 | 5 070 | 10 610 | 10 725 | 10 267 | 7 025 | 2 154 |
| 1969 | 50 221 | 3 870 | 1 770 | 2 100 | 46 351 | 5 282 | 10 941 | 10 556 | 10 344 | 7 058 | 2 170 |
| 1970 | 51 228 | 4 008 | 1 810 | 2 199 | 47 220 | 5 717 | 11 327 | 10 469 | 10 417 | 7 126 | 2 165 |
| 1971 | 52 180 | 4 172 | 1 856 | 2 315 | 48 009 | 6 233 | 11 731 | 10 347 | 10 451 | 7 155 | 2 090 |
| 1972 | 53 555 | 4 476 | 1 955 | 2 522 | 49 079 | 6 766 | 12 350 | 10 372 | 10 412 | 7 155 | 2 026 |
| 1973 | 54 624 | 4 693 | 2 073 | 2 618 | 49 932 | 7 183 | 13 056 | 10 338 | 10 416 | 7 028 | 1 913 |
| 1974 | 55 739 | 4 861 | 2 138 | 2 721 | 50 879 | 7 387 | 13 665 | 10 401 | 10 431 | 7 063 | 1 932 |
| 1975 | 56 299 | 4 805 | 2 065 | 2 740 | 51 494 | 7 565 | 14 192 | 10 398 | 10 401 | 7 023 | 1 914 |
| 1976 | 57 174 | 4 886 | 2 069 | 2 817 | 52 288 | 7 866 | 14 784 | 10 500 | 10 293 | 7 020 | 1 826 |
| 1977 | 58 396 | 5 048 | 2 155 | 2 893 | 53 348 | 8 109 | 15 353 | 10 771 | 10 158 | 7 100 | 1 857 |
| 1978 | 59 620 | 5 149 | 2 227 | 2 923 | 54 471 | 8 327 | 15 814 | 11 159 | 10 083 | 7 151 | 1 936 |
| 1979 | 60 726 | 5 111 | 2 192 | 2 919 | 55 615 | 8 535 | 16 387 | 11 531 | 10 008 | 7 212 | 1 943 |
| 1980 | 61 453 | 4 999 | 2 102 | 2 897 | 56 455 | 8 607 | 16 971 | 11 836 | 9 905 | 7 242 | 1 893 |
| 1981 | 61 974 | 4 777 | 1 957 | 2 820 | 57 197 | 8 648 | 17 479 | 12 166 | 9 868 | 7 170 | 1 866 |
| 1982 | 62 450 | 4 470 | 1 776 | 2 694 | 57 980 | 8 604 | 17 793 | 12 781 | 9 784 | 7 174 | 1 845 |
| 1983 | 63 047 | 4 303 | 1 621 | 2 682 | 58 744 | 8 601 | 18 038 | 13 398 | 9 746 | 7 119 | 1 842 |
| 1984 | 63 835 | 4 134 | 1 591 | 2 542 | 59 701 | 8 594 | 18 488 | 14 037 | 9 776 | 7 050 | 1 755 |
| 1985 | 64 411 | 4 134 | 1 663 | 2 471 | 60 277 | 8 283 | 18 808 | 14 506 | 9 870 | 7 060 | 1 750 |
| 1986 | 65 422 | 4 102 | 1 707 | 2 395 | 61 320 | 8 148 | 19 383 | 15 029 | 9 994 | 6 954 | 1 811 |
| 1987 | 66 207 | 4 112 | 1 745 | 2 367 | 62 095 | 7 837 | 19 656 | 15 587 | 10 176 | 6 940 | 1 899 |
| 1988 | 66 927 | 4 159 | 1 714 | 2 445 | 62 768 | 7 594 | 19 742 | 16 074 | 10 566 | 6 831 | 1 960 |
| 1989 | 67 840 | 4 136 | 1 630 | 2 505 | 63 704 | 7 458 | 19 905 | 16 622 | 10 919 | 6 783 | 2 017 |
| 1990 | 69 011 | 4 094 | 1 537 | 2 557 | 64 916 | 7 866 | 19 872 | 17 481 | 11 103 | 6 627 | 1 967 |
| 1991 | 69 168 | 3 795 | 1 452 | 2 343 | 65 374 | 7 820 | 19 641 | 18 077 | 11 362 | 6 550 | 1 924 |
| 1992 | 69 964 | 3 751 | 1 453 | 2 297 | 66 213 | 7 770 | 19 495 | 18 347 | 12 040 | 6 551 | 2 010 |
| 1993 | 70 404 | 3 762 | 1 497 | 2 265 | 66 642 | 7 671 | 19 214 | 18 713 | 12 562 | 6 502 | 1 980 |
| 1994 | 70 817 | 3 896 | 1 630 | 2 266 | 66 921 | 7 540 | 18 854 | 18 966 | 12 962 | 6 423 | 2 176 |
| 1995 | 71 360 | 4 036 | 1 668 | 2 368 | 67 324 | 7 338 | 18 670 | 19 189 | 13 421 | 6 504 | 2 201 |
| 1996 | 72 087 | 4 043 | 1 665 | 2 378 | 68 044 | 7 104 | 18 430 | 19 602 | 13 967 | 6 693 | 2 247 |
| 1997 | 73 261 | 4 095 | 1 676 | 2 419 | 69 166 | 7 184 | 18 110 | 20 058 | 14 564 | 6 952 | 2 298 |
| 1998 | 73 959 | 4 244 | 1 728 | 2 516 | 69 715 | 7 221 | 17 796 | 20 242 | 14 963 | 7 253 | 2 240 |
| 1999 | 74 512 | 4 318 | 1 732 | 2 587 | 70 194 | 7 291 | 17 318 | 20 382 | 15 394 | 7 477 | 2 333 |
| 2000 | 76 280 | 4 269 | 1 676 | 2 594 | 72 010 | 7 521 | 17 844 | 20 093 | 16 269 | 7 795 | 2 488 |
| 2001 | 76 886 | 4 070 | 1 568 | 2 501 | 72 816 | 7 640 | 17 671 | 20 018 | 16 804 | 8 171 | 2 511 |
| 2002 | 77 500 | 3 870 | 1 431 | 2 439 | 73 630 | 7 769 | 17 596 | 19 828 | 17 143 | 8 751 | 2 542 |
| 2003 | 78 238 | 3 614 | 1 405 | 2 209 | 74 623 | 7 906 | 17 767 | 19 762 | 17 352 | 9 144 | 2 692 |
| 2004 | 78 980 | 3 616 | 1 329 | 2 288 | 75 364 | 8 057 | 17 798 | 19 539 | 17 635 | 9 547 | 2 787 |
| 2005 | 80 033 | 3 590 | 1 368 | 2 222 | 76 443 | 8 054 | 17 837 | 19 495 | 18 053 | 10 045 | 2 959 |
| 2006 | 81 255 | 3 693 | 1 453 | 2 240 | 77 562 | 8 116 | 17 944 | 19 407 | 18 489 | 10 509 | 3 096 |
| 2007 | 82 136 | 3 541 | 1 354 | 2 187 | 78 596 | 8 095 | 18 308 | 19 299 | 18 801 | 10 904 | 3 188 |
| 2008 | 82 520 | 3 472 | 1 238 | 2 235 | 79 047 | 8 065 | 18 302 | 18 972 | 18 928 | 11 345 | 3 436 |
| 2009 | 82 123 | 3 226 | 1 103 | 2 123 | 78 897 | 7 839 | 18 211 | 18 518 | 19 001 | 11 730 | 3 598 |
| 2010 | 81 985 | 2 991 | 990 | 2 002 | 78 994 | 7 864 | 18 352 | 18 119 | 18 856 | 12 103 | 3 701 |
| 2011 | 81 975 | 2 895 | 917 | 1 978 | 79 080 | 8 101 | 18 469 | 17 686 | 18 483 | 12 350 | 3 990 |
| 2012 | 82 327 | 2 940 | 950 | 1 990 | 79 387 | 8 110 | 18 083 | 17 607 | 18 363 | 12 879 | 4 345 |
| 2013 | 82 667 | 2 923 | 987 | 1 936 | 79 744 | 8 156 | 18 287 | 17 605 | 18 071 | 13 117 | 4 507 |
| 2014 | 82 882 | 2 827 | 959 | 1 868 | 80 056 | 8 182 | 18 478 | 17 547 | 17 900 | 13 361 | 4 587 |
| 2015 | 83 620 | 2 885 | 997 | 1 888 | 80 735 | 8 038 | 18 776 | 17 556 | 17 893 | 13 627 | 4 845 |

**Table 1-7. Civilian Labor Force, by Age, Sex, Race, and Hispanic Origin, 1948–2015**—*Continued*

(Thousands of people.)

| Race, Hispanic origin, sex, and year | 16 years and over | 16 to 19 years | | | 20 years and over | | | | | | |
|---|---|---|---|---|---|---|---|---|---|---|---|
| | | Total | 16 to 17 years | 18 to 19 years | Total | 20 to 24 years | 25 to 34 years | 35 to 44 years | 45 to 54 years | 55 to 64 years | 65 years and over |
| **ALL RACES** | | | | | | | | | | | |
| **Women** | | | | | | | | | | | |
| 1948 | 17 335 | 1 835 | 671 | 671 | 15 500 | 2 719 | 3 931 | 3 801 | 2 971 | 1 565 | 513 |
| 1949 | 17 788 | 1 811 | 648 | 648 | 15 978 | 2 658 | 3 997 | 3 989 | 3 099 | 1 678 | 556 |
| 1950 | 18 389 | 1 712 | 611 | 611 | 16 678 | 2 675 | 4 092 | 4 161 | 3 327 | 1 839 | 583 |
| 1951 | 19 016 | 1 756 | 662 | 662 | 17 259 | 2 659 | 4 293 | 4 301 | 3 534 | 1 923 | 551 |
| 1952 | 19 269 | 1 752 | 705 | 705 | 17 517 | 2 502 | 4 319 | 4 438 | 3 635 | 2 031 | 589 |
| 1953 | 19 382 | 1 707 | 657 | 657 | 17 674 | 2 428 | 4 162 | 4 662 | 3 679 | 2 049 | 693 |
| 1954 | 19 678 | 1 681 | 620 | 620 | 17 997 | 2 424 | 4 212 | 4 708 | 3 822 | 2 164 | 666 |
| 1955 | 20 548 | 1 723 | 641 | 641 | 18 825 | 2 445 | 4 252 | 4 805 | 4 154 | 2 391 | 779 |
| 1956 | 21 461 | 1 863 | 736 | 736 | 19 599 | 2 455 | 4 276 | 5 031 | 4 405 | 2 610 | 821 |
| 1957 | 21 732 | 1 860 | 716 | 716 | 19 873 | 2 442 | 4 255 | 5 116 | 4 615 | 2 631 | 813 |
| 1958 | 22 118 | 1 832 | 685 | 685 | 20 285 | 2 501 | 4 193 | 5 185 | 4 859 | 2 727 | 821 |
| 1959 | 22 483 | 1 896 | 765 | 765 | 20 587 | 2 473 | 4 089 | 5 228 | 5 080 | 2 882 | 836 |
| 1960 | 23 240 | 2 054 | 805 | 805 | 21 185 | 2 579 | 4 131 | 5 302 | 5 278 | 2 986 | 908 |
| 1961 | 23 806 | 2 142 | 774 | 774 | 21 664 | 2 697 | 4 143 | 5 390 | 5 403 | 3 106 | 926 |
| 1962 | 24 014 | 2 146 | 741 | 741 | 21 868 | 2 803 | 4 103 | 5 474 | 5 381 | 3 197 | 913 |
| 1963 | 24 704 | 2 232 | 850 | 850 | 22 473 | 2 959 | 4 174 | 5 601 | 5 502 | 3 331 | 906 |
| 1964 | 25 412 | 2 314 | 950 | 950 | 23 098 | 3 209 | 4 180 | 5 615 | 5 681 | 3 441 | 966 |
| 1965 | 26 200 | 2 513 | 954 | 954 | 23 686 | 3 365 | 4 330 | 5 720 | 5 711 | 3 587 | 976 |
| 1966 | 27 299 | 2 873 | 1 055 | 1 055 | 24 431 | 3 590 | 4 510 | 5 755 | 5 884 | 3 728 | 964 |
| 1967 | 28 360 | 2 887 | 1 076 | 1 076 | 25 475 | 3 966 | 4 848 | 5 844 | 5 983 | 3 855 | 979 |
| 1968 | 29 204 | 2 938 | 1 130 | 1 130 | 26 266 | 4 235 | 5 098 | 5 866 | 6 130 | 3 939 | 999 |
| 1969 | 30 513 | 3 100 | 1 239 | 1 239 | 27 413 | 4 597 | 5 395 | 5 902 | 6 386 | 4 077 | 1 057 |
| 1970 | 31 543 | 3 241 | 1 325 | 1 325 | 28 301 | 4 880 | 5 708 | 5 968 | 6 532 | 4 157 | 1 056 |
| 1971 | 32 202 | 3 298 | 1 336 | 1 336 | 28 904 | 5 098 | 5 983 | 5 957 | 6 573 | 4 234 | 1 059 |
| 1972 | 33 479 | 3 578 | 1 464 | 1 464 | 29 901 | 5 364 | 6 610 | 6 027 | 6 555 | 4 257 | 1 089 |
| 1973 | 34 804 | 3 814 | 1 592 | 1 592 | 30 991 | 5 663 | 7 320 | 6 154 | 6 567 | 4 228 | 1 061 |
| 1974 | 36 211 | 4 010 | 1 672 | 1 672 | 32 201 | 5 926 | 7 989 | 6 362 | 6 699 | 4 221 | 1 002 |
| 1975 | 37 475 | 4 065 | 1 674 | 1 674 | 33 410 | 6 185 | 8 673 | 6 505 | 6 683 | 4 323 | 1 042 |
| 1976 | 38 983 | 4 170 | 1 698 | 1 698 | 34 814 | 6 418 | 9 419 | 6 817 | 6 689 | 4 402 | 1 069 |
| 1977 | 40 613 | 4 303 | 1 765 | 1 765 | 36 310 | 6 717 | 10 149 | 7 171 | 6 720 | 4 477 | 1 078 |
| 1978 | 42 631 | 4 503 | 1 900 | 1 900 | 38 128 | 7 043 | 10 888 | 7 662 | 6 807 | 4 593 | 1 134 |
| 1979 | 44 235 | 4 527 | 1 887 | 1 887 | 39 708 | 7 234 | 11 551 | 8 154 | 6 889 | 4 719 | 1 161 |
| 1980 | 45 487 | 4 381 | 1 781 | 1 781 | 41 106 | 7 315 | 12 257 | 8 627 | 7 004 | 4 742 | 1 161 |
| 1981 | 46 696 | 4 211 | 1 691 | 1 691 | 42 485 | 7 451 | 12 912 | 9 045 | 7 101 | 4 799 | 1 176 |
| 1982 | 47 755 | 4 056 | 1 561 | 1 561 | 43 699 | 7 477 | 13 393 | 9 651 | 7 105 | 4 888 | 1 185 |
| 1983 | 48 503 | 3 868 | 1 452 | 1 452 | 44 636 | 7 451 | 13 796 | 10 213 | 7 105 | 4 873 | 1 198 |
| 1984 | 49 709 | 3 810 | 1 458 | 1 458 | 45 900 | 7 451 | 14 234 | 10 886 | 7 230 | 4 911 | 1 177 |
| 1985 | 51 050 | 3 767 | 1 491 | 1 491 | 47 283 | 7 434 | 14 742 | 11 567 | 7 452 | 4 932 | 1 156 |
| 1986 | 52 413 | 3 824 | 1 580 | 1 580 | 48 589 | 7 293 | 15 208 | 12 204 | 7 746 | 4 940 | 1 199 |
| 1987 | 53 658 | 3 875 | 1 638 | 1 638 | 49 783 | 7 140 | 15 577 | 12 873 | 8 034 | 4 937 | 1 221 |
| 1988 | 54 742 | 3 872 | 1 572 | 1 572 | 50 870 | 6 910 | 15 761 | 13 361 | 8 537 | 4 977 | 1 324 |
| 1989 | 56 030 | 3 818 | 1 495 | 1 495 | 52 212 | 6 721 | 15 990 | 13 980 | 8 997 | 5 095 | 1 429 |
| 1990 | 56 829 | 3 698 | 1 400 | 1 400 | 53 131 | 6 834 | 16 058 | 14 663 | 9 145 | 4 948 | 1 483 |
| 1991 | 57 178 | 3 470 | 1 337 | 1 337 | 53 708 | 6 728 | 15 867 | 15 235 | 9 465 | 4 924 | 1 489 |
| 1992 | 58 141 | 3 345 | 1 316 | 1 316 | 54 796 | 6 750 | 15 875 | 15 552 | 10 120 | 5 035 | 1 464 |
| 1993 | 58 795 | 3 408 | 1 335 | 1 335 | 55 388 | 6 683 | 15 566 | 15 849 | 10 733 | 5 097 | 1 459 |
| 1994 | 60 239 | 3 585 | 1 504 | 1 504 | 56 655 | 6 592 | 15 499 | 16 259 | 11 357 | 5 289 | 1 658 |
| 1995 | 60 944 | 3 729 | 1 557 | 1 557 | 57 215 | 6 349 | 15 528 | 16 562 | 11 801 | 5 356 | 1 618 |
| 1996 | 61 857 | 3 763 | 1 599 | 1 599 | 58 094 | 6 273 | 15 403 | 16 954 | 12 430 | 5 452 | 1 581 |
| 1997 | 63 036 | 3 837 | 1 561 | 1 561 | 59 198 | 6 348 | 15 271 | 17 268 | 13 010 | 5 713 | 1 590 |
| 1998 | 63 714 | 4 012 | 1 607 | 1 607 | 59 702 | 6 418 | 15 017 | 17 294 | 13 405 | 5 962 | 1 607 |
| 1999 | 64 855 | 4 015 | 1 606 | 1 606 | 60 840 | 6 643 | 14 826 | 17 501 | 13 994 | 6 204 | 1 673 |
| 2000 | 66 303 | 4 002 | 1 585 | 1 585 | 62 301 | 6 730 | 14 912 | 17 473 | 14 802 | 6 561 | 1 823 |
| 2001 | 66 848 | 3 832 | 1 520 | 1 520 | 63 016 | 6 917 | 14 690 | 17 386 | 15 221 | 6 932 | 1 870 |
| 2002 | 67 363 | 3 715 | 1 439 | 1 439 | 63 648 | 7 012 | 14 600 | 17 098 | 15 454 | 7 559 | 1 926 |
| 2003 | 68 272 | 3 556 | 1 452 | 1 452 | 64 716 | 7 021 | 14 576 | 16 933 | 15 919 | 8 168 | 2 099 |
| 2004 | 68 421 | 3 498 | 1 418 | 1 418 | 64 923 | 7 097 | 14 409 | 16 619 | 16 123 | 8 466 | 2 211 |
| 2005 | 69 288 | 3 574 | 1 457 | 1 457 | 65 714 | 7 073 | 14 503 | 16 535 | 16 349 | 8 934 | 2 319 |
| 2006 | 70 173 | 3 588 | 1 499 | 1 499 | 66 585 | 6 997 | 14 628 | 16 441 | 16 656 | 9 475 | 2 388 |
| 2007 | 70 988 | 3 471 | 1 417 | 1 417 | 67 516 | 7 110 | 14 822 | 16 227 | 16 896 | 9 846 | 2 615 |
| 2008 | 71 767 | 3 385 | 1 314 | 1 314 | 68 382 | 7 109 | 15 030 | 16 089 | 17 075 | 10 270 | 2 808 |
| 2009 | 72 019 | 3 163 | 1 124 | 1 124 | 68 856 | 7 132 | 15 087 | 15 720 | 17 204 | 10 776 | 2 937 |
| 2010 | 71 904 | 2 914 | 1 011 | 1 011 | 68 990 | 7 164 | 15 263 | 15 247 | 17 104 | 11 194 | 3 017 |
| 2011 | 71 642 | 2 832 | 957 | 957 | 68 810 | 7 169 | 15 255 | 14 973 | 16 876 | 11 414 | 3 121 |
| 2012 | 72 648 | 2 883 | 1 003 | 1 003 | 69 765 | 7 352 | 15 382 | 15 127 | 16 692 | 11 830 | 3 383 |
| 2013 | 72 722 | 2 862 | 1 036 | 1 036 | 69 860 | 7 440 | 15 459 | 14 957 | 16 396 | 12 000 | 3 609 |
| 2014 | 73 039 | 2 827 | 1 012 | 1 815 | 70 212 | 7 459 | 15 721 | 14 958 | 16 163 | 12 141 | 3 771 |
| 2015 | 73 510 | 2 815 | 991 | 1 824 | 70 695 | 7 485 | 15 871 | 15 047 | 16 009 | 12 326 | 3 957 |

## Table 1-7.  Civilian Labor Force, by Age, Sex, Race, and Hispanic Origin, 1948–2015—*Continued*

(Thousands of people.)

| Race, Hispanic origin, sex, and year | 16 years and over | 16 to 19 years | | | 20 years and over | | | | | | |
|---|---|---|---|---|---|---|---|---|---|---|---|
| | | Total | 16 to 17 years | 18 to 19 years | Total | 20 to 24 years | 25 to 34 years | 35 to 44 years | 45 to 54 years | 55 to 64 years | 65 years and over |
| **WHITE** | | | | | | | | | | | |
| **Both Sexes** | | | | | | | | | | | |
| 1954 | 56 816 | 3 501 | 1 448 | 2 054 | 53 315 | 4 752 | 13 226 | 13 540 | 11 258 | 7 591 | 2 946 |
| 1955 | 58 085 | 3 598 | 1 511 | 2 087 | 54 487 | 4 941 | 13 267 | 13 729 | 11 680 | 7 810 | 3 062 |
| 1956 | 59 428 | 3 771 | 1 656 | 2 113 | 55 657 | 5 194 | 13 154 | 14 000 | 12 061 | 8 080 | 3 166 |
| 1957 | 59 754 | 3 775 | 1 637 | 2 135 | 55 979 | 5 283 | 13 044 | 14 117 | 12 382 | 8 091 | 3 049 |
| 1958 | 60 293 | 3 757 | 1 615 | 2 144 | 56 536 | 5 449 | 12 884 | 14 257 | 12 727 | 8 254 | 2 964 |
| 1959 | 60 952 | 4 000 | 1 775 | 2 225 | 56 952 | 5 544 | 12 670 | 14 355 | 13 048 | 8 411 | 2 925 |
| 1960 | 61 915 | 4 275 | 1 871 | 2 405 | 57 640 | 5 787 | 12 594 | 14 450 | 13 322 | 8 522 | 2 964 |
| 1961 | 62 656 | 4 362 | 1 767 | 2 594 | 58 294 | 6 026 | 12 503 | 14 557 | 13 517 | 8 773 | 2 917 |
| 1962 | 62 750 | 4 354 | 1 709 | 2 645 | 58 396 | 6 164 | 12 218 | 14 695 | 13 551 | 8 856 | 2 912 |
| 1963 | 63 830 | 4 559 | 1 950 | 2 608 | 59 271 | 6 537 | 12 229 | 14 859 | 13 789 | 9 067 | 2 790 |
| 1964 | 64 921 | 4 784 | 2 211 | 2 572 | 60 137 | 6 952 | 12 235 | 14 852 | 14 043 | 9 239 | 2 817 |
| 1965 | 66 137 | 5 267 | 2 221 | 3 044 | 60 870 | 7 189 | 12 391 | 14 900 | 14 162 | 9 392 | 2 839 |
| 1966 | 67 276 | 5 827 | 2 367 | 3 460 | 61 449 | 7 324 | 12 591 | 14 785 | 14 370 | 9 583 | 2 793 |
| 1967 | 68 699 | 5 749 | 2 432 | 3 318 | 62 950 | 7 886 | 13 123 | 14 765 | 14 545 | 9 817 | 2 821 |
| 1968 | 69 976 | 5 839 | 2 519 | 3 320 | 64 137 | 8 109 | 13 740 | 14 683 | 14 756 | 9 968 | 2 884 |
| 1969 | 71 778 | 6 168 | 2 698 | 3 470 | 65 611 | 8 614 | 14 289 | 14 564 | 15 057 | 10 132 | 2 954 |
| 1970 | 73 556 | 6 442 | 2 824 | 3 617 | 67 113 | 9 238 | 14 896 | 14 525 | 15 269 | 10 255 | 2 930 |
| 1971 | 74 963 | 6 681 | 2 894 | 3 787 | 68 282 | 9 889 | 15 445 | 14 374 | 15 343 | 10 351 | 2 880 |
| 1972 | 77 275 | 7 193 | 3 096 | 4 098 | 70 082 | 10 605 | 16 584 | 14 399 | 15 283 | 10 402 | 2 809 |
| 1973 | 79 151 | 7 579 | 3 320 | 4 260 | 71 572 | 11 182 | 17 764 | 14 440 | 15 256 | 10 240 | 2 687 |
| 1974 | 81 281 | 7 899 | 3 441 | 4 459 | 73 381 | 11 600 | 18 862 | 14 644 | 15 375 | 10 241 | 2 656 |
| 1975 | 82 831 | 7 899 | 3 375 | 4 525 | 74 932 | 12 019 | 19 897 | 14 753 | 15 308 | 10 287 | 2 668 |
| 1976 | 84 767 | 8 088 | 3 410 | 4 679 | 76 678 | 12 444 | 20 990 | 15 088 | 15 187 | 10 371 | 2 599 |
| 1977 | 87 141 | 8 352 | 3 562 | 4 790 | 78 789 | 12 892 | 22 099 | 15 604 | 15 053 | 10 495 | 2 647 |
| 1978 | 89 634 | 8 555 | 3 715 | 4 839 | 81 079 | 13 309 | 23 067 | 16 353 | 15 004 | 10 602 | 2 745 |
| 1979 | 91 923 | 8 548 | 3 668 | 4 881 | 83 375 | 13 632 | 24 101 | 17 123 | 14 965 | 10 767 | 2 787 |
| 1980 | 93 600 | 8 312 | 3 485 | 4 827 | 85 286 | 13 769 | 25 181 | 17 811 | 14 956 | 10 812 | 2 759 |
| 1981 | 95 052 | 7 962 | 3 274 | 4 688 | 87 089 | 13 926 | 26 208 | 18 445 | 14 993 | 10 764 | 2 753 |
| 1982 | 96 143 | 7 518 | 3 001 | 4 518 | 88 625 | 13 866 | 26 814 | 19 491 | 14 879 | 10 832 | 2 742 |
| 1983 | 97 021 | 7 186 | 2 765 | 4 421 | 89 835 | 13 816 | 27 237 | 20 488 | 14 798 | 10 732 | 2 766 |
| 1984 | 98 492 | 6 952 | 2 720 | 4 232 | 91 540 | 13 733 | 27 958 | 21 588 | 14 899 | 10 701 | 2 660 |
| 1985 | 99 926 | 6 841 | 2 777 | 4 065 | 93 085 | 13 469 | 28 640 | 22 591 | 15 101 | 10 679 | 2 605 |
| 1986 | 101 801 | 6 862 | 2 895 | 3 967 | 94 939 | 13 176 | 29 497 | 23 571 | 15 379 | 10 583 | 2 732 |
| 1987 | 103 290 | 6 893 | 2 963 | 3 931 | 96 396 | 12 764 | 29 956 | 24 581 | 15 792 | 10 497 | 2 806 |
| 1988 | 104 756 | 6 940 | 2 861 | 4 079 | 97 815 | 12 311 | 30 167 | 25 358 | 16 573 | 10 462 | 2 943 |
| 1989 | 106 355 | 6 809 | 2 685 | 4 124 | 99 546 | 11 940 | 30 388 | 26 312 | 17 278 | 10 533 | 3 094 |
| 1990 | 107 447 | 6 683 | 2 543 | 4 140 | 100 764 | 12 397 | 30 174 | 27 265 | 17 515 | 10 290 | 3 123 |
| 1991 | 107 743 | 6 245 | 2 432 | 3 813 | 101 498 | 12 248 | 29 794 | 28 213 | 18 028 | 10 129 | 3 086 |
| 1992 | 108 837 | 6 022 | 2 388 | 3 633 | 102 815 | 12 187 | 29 518 | 28 580 | 19 200 | 10 196 | 3 135 |
| 1993 | 109 700 | 6 105 | 2 458 | 3 647 | 103 595 | 11 987 | 29 027 | 29 056 | 20 181 | 10 215 | 3 129 |
| 1994 | 111 082 | 6 357 | 2 681 | 3 677 | 104 725 | 11 688 | 28 580 | 29 626 | 21 026 | 10 319 | 3 486 |
| 1995 | 111 950 | 6 545 | 2 749 | 3 796 | 105 404 | 11 266 | 28 325 | 30 112 | 21 804 | 10 432 | 3 466 |
| 1996 | 113 108 | 6 607 | 2 780 | 3 826 | 106 502 | 11 003 | 27 901 | 30 683 | 22 781 | 10 648 | 3 485 |
| 1997 | 114 693 | 6 720 | 2 779 | 3 941 | 107 973 | 11 127 | 27 362 | 31 171 | 23 709 | 11 086 | 3 517 |
| 1998 | 115 415 | 6 965 | 2 860 | 4 105 | 108 450 | 11 244 | 26 707 | 31 221 | 24 282 | 11 548 | 3 448 |
| 1999 | 116 509 | 7 048 | 2 849 | 4 199 | 109 461 | 11 436 | 25 978 | 31 391 | 25 102 | 11 960 | 3 595 |
| 2000 | 118 545 | 6 955 | 2 768 | 4 186 | 111 590 | 11 626 | 26 336 | 30 968 | 26 353 | 12 463 | 3 846 |
| 2001 | 119 399 | 6 661 | 2 626 | 4 035 | 112 737 | 11 883 | 26 010 | 30 778 | 27 062 | 13 121 | 3 883 |
| 2002 | 120 150 | 6 366 | 2 445 | 3 921 | 113 784 | 12 073 | 25 908 | 30 286 | 27 405 | 14 148 | 3 965 |
| 2003 | 120 546 | 5 973 | 2 414 | 3 560 | 114 572 | 12 064 | 25 752 | 29 788 | 27 786 | 14 944 | 4 238 |
| 2004 | 121 086 | 5 929 | 2 309 | 3 620 | 115 156 | 12 192 | 25 548 | 29 305 | 28 181 | 15 522 | 4 408 |
| 2005 | 122 299 | 5 950 | 2 390 | 3 560 | 116 349 | 12 109 | 25 548 | 29 107 | 28 685 | 16 275 | 4 624 |
| 2006 | 123 834 | 6 009 | 2 473 | 3 536 | 117 825 | 12 128 | 25 681 | 28 849 | 29 231 | 17 132 | 4 805 |
| 2007 | 124 935 | 5 795 | 2 326 | 3 470 | 119 139 | 12 176 | 26 076 | 28 394 | 29 627 | 17 782 | 5 085 |
| 2008 | 125 635 | 5 644 | 2 126 | 3 518 | 119 990 | 12 142 | 26 210 | 27 932 | 29 780 | 18 464 | 5 463 |
| 2009 | 125 644 | 5 295 | 1 883 | 3 413 | 120 349 | 11 995 | 26 277 | 27 263 | 29 903 | 19 199 | 5 711 |
| 2010 | 125 084 | 4 861 | 1 693 | 3 168 | 120 223 | 11 948 | 26 455 | 26 510 | 29 632 | 19 808 | 5 869 |
| 2011 | 124 579 | 4 714 | 1 581 | 3 134 | 119 865 | 12 120 | 26 511 | 25 834 | 29 036 | 20 188 | 6 175 |
| 2012 | 123 684 | 4 669 | 1 605 | 3 065 | 119 015 | 11 914 | 25 806 | 25 445 | 28 384 | 20 752 | 6 714 |
| 2013 | 123 412 | 4 608 | 1 669 | 2 939 | 118 804 | 11 962 | 25 898 | 25 167 | 27 776 | 20 945 | 7 056 |
| 2014 | 123 327 | 4 476 | 1 591 | 2 885 | 118 851 | 11 927 | 26 172 | 25 029 | 27 336 | 21 181 | 7 207 |
| 2015 | 123 607 | 4 487 | 1 579 | 2 908 | 119 120 | 11 755 | 26 305 | 24 929 | 27 066 | 21 534 | 7 531 |

## Table 1-7. Civilian Labor Force, by Age, Sex, Race, and Hispanic Origin, 1948–2015—*Continued*

(Thousands of people.)

| Race, Hispanic origin, sex, and year | 16 years and over | 16 to 19 years | | | 20 years and over | | | | | | |
| --- | --- | --- | --- | --- | --- | --- | --- | --- | --- | --- | --- |
| | | Total | 16 to 17 years | 18 to 19 years | Total | 20 to 24 years | 25 to 34 years | 35 to 44 years | 45 to 54 years | 55 to 64 years | 65 years and over |
| **WHITE** | | | | | | | | | | | |
| **Men** | | | | | | | | | | | |
| 1954 | 39 759 | 1 989 | 896 | 1 095 | 37 770 | 2 654 | 9 695 | 9 516 | 7 913 | 5 653 | 2 339 |
| 1955 | 40 197 | 2 056 | 935 | 1 121 | 38 141 | 2 803 | 9 721 | 9 597 | 8 025 | 5 654 | 2 343 |
| 1956 | 40 734 | 2 114 | 1 002 | 1 110 | 38 620 | 3 036 | 9 595 | 9 661 | 8 175 | 5 736 | 2 417 |
| 1957 | 40 826 | 2 108 | 992 | 1 114 | 38 718 | 3 152 | 9 483 | 9 719 | 8 317 | 5 735 | 2 307 |
| 1958 | 41 080 | 2 116 | 1 001 | 1 116 | 38 964 | 3 278 | 9 386 | 9 822 | 8 465 | 5 800 | 2 213 |
| 1959 | 41 397 | 2 279 | 1 077 | 1 202 | 39 118 | 3 409 | 9 261 | 9 876 | 8 581 | 5 833 | 2 158 |
| 1960 | 41 743 | 2 433 | 1 140 | 1 293 | 39 310 | 3 559 | 9 153 | 9 919 | 8 689 | 5 861 | 2 129 |
| 1961 | 41 986 | 2 439 | 1 067 | 1 372 | 39 547 | 3 681 | 9 072 | 9 961 | 8 776 | 5 988 | 2 068 |
| 1962 | 41 931 | 2 432 | 1 041 | 1 391 | 39 499 | 3 726 | 8 846 | 10 029 | 8 820 | 5 995 | 2 082 |
| 1963 | 42 404 | 2 563 | 1 183 | 1 380 | 39 841 | 3 955 | 8 805 | 10 079 | 8 944 | 6 090 | 1 967 |
| 1964 | 42 894 | 2 716 | 1 345 | 1 371 | 40 178 | 4 166 | 8 800 | 10 055 | 9 053 | 6 161 | 1 942 |
| 1965 | 43 400 | 2 999 | 1 359 | 1 639 | 40 401 | 4 279 | 8 824 | 10 023 | 9 130 | 6 188 | 1 959 |
| 1966 | 43 572 | 3 253 | 1 423 | 1 830 | 40 319 | 4 200 | 8 859 | 9 892 | 9 189 | 6 250 | 1 928 |
| 1967 | 44 041 | 3 191 | 1 464 | 1 727 | 40 851 | 4 416 | 9 102 | 9 785 | 9 260 | 6 348 | 1 944 |
| 1968 | 44 553 | 3 236 | 1 504 | 1 732 | 41 318 | 4 432 | 9 477 | 9 662 | 9 340 | 6 427 | 1 981 |
| 1969 | 45 185 | 3 413 | 1 583 | 1 830 | 41 772 | 4 615 | 9 773 | 9 509 | 9 413 | 6 467 | 1 996 |
| 1970 | 46 035 | 3 551 | 1 629 | 1 922 | 42 483 | 4 988 | 10 099 | 9 414 | 9 487 | 6 517 | 1 978 |
| 1971 | 46 904 | 3 719 | 1 681 | 2 039 | 43 185 | 5 448 | 10 444 | 9 294 | 9 528 | 6 550 | 1 922 |
| 1972 | 48 118 | 3 980 | 1 758 | 2 223 | 44 138 | 5 937 | 11 039 | 9 278 | 9 473 | 6 562 | 1 846 |
| 1973 | 48 920 | 4 174 | 1 875 | 2 300 | 44 747 | 6 274 | 11 621 | 9 212 | 9 445 | 6 452 | 1 740 |
| 1974 | 49 843 | 4 312 | 1 922 | 2 391 | 45 532 | 6 470 | 12 135 | 9 246 | 9 455 | 6 464 | 1 759 |
| 1975 | 50 324 | 4 290 | 1 871 | 2 418 | 46 034 | 6 642 | 12 579 | 9 231 | 9 415 | 6 425 | 1 742 |
| 1976 | 51 033 | 4 357 | 1 869 | 2 489 | 46 675 | 6 890 | 13 092 | 9 289 | 9 310 | 6 437 | 1 657 |
| 1977 | 52 033 | 4 496 | 1 949 | 2 548 | 47 537 | 7 097 | 13 575 | 9 509 | 9 175 | 6 492 | 1 688 |
| 1978 | 52 955 | 4 565 | 2 002 | 2 563 | 48 390 | 7 274 | 13 939 | 9 858 | 9 068 | 6 508 | 1 744 |
| 1979 | 53 856 | 4 537 | 1 974 | 2 563 | 49 320 | 7 421 | 14 415 | 10 183 | 8 968 | 6 571 | 1 761 |
| 1980 | 54 473 | 4 424 | 1 881 | 2 543 | 50 049 | 7 479 | 14 893 | 10 455 | 8 877 | 6 618 | 1 727 |
| 1981 | 54 895 | 4 224 | 1 751 | 2 473 | 50 671 | 7 521 | 15 340 | 10 740 | 8 836 | 6 530 | 1 704 |
| 1982 | 55 133 | 3 933 | 1 602 | 2 331 | 51 200 | 7 438 | 15 549 | 11 289 | 8 727 | 6 520 | 1 677 |
| 1983 | 55 480 | 3 764 | 1 452 | 2 312 | 51 716 | 7 406 | 15 707 | 11 817 | 8 649 | 6 446 | 1 691 |
| 1984 | 56 062 | 3 609 | 1 420 | 2 189 | 52 453 | 7 370 | 16 037 | 12 348 | 8 683 | 6 410 | 1 606 |
| 1985 | 56 472 | 3 576 | 1 467 | 2 109 | 52 895 | 7 122 | 16 306 | 12 767 | 8 730 | 6 376 | 1 595 |
| 1986 | 57 217 | 3 542 | 1 502 | 2 040 | 53 675 | 6 986 | 16 769 | 13 207 | 8 791 | 6 260 | 1 663 |
| 1987 | 57 779 | 3 547 | 1 524 | 2 023 | 54 232 | 6 717 | 16 963 | 13 674 | 8 945 | 6 200 | 1 733 |
| 1988 | 58 317 | 3 583 | 1 487 | 2 095 | 54 734 | 6 468 | 17 018 | 14 068 | 9 285 | 6 108 | 1 787 |
| 1989 | 58 988 | 3 546 | 1 401 | 2 146 | 55 441 | 6 316 | 17 077 | 14 516 | 9 615 | 6 082 | 1 835 |
| 1990 | 59 638 | 3 522 | 1 333 | 2 189 | 56 116 | 6 688 | 16 920 | 15 026 | 9 713 | 5 957 | 1 811 |
| 1991 | 59 656 | 3 269 | 1 266 | 2 003 | 56 387 | 6 619 | 16 709 | 15 523 | 9 926 | 5 847 | 1 763 |
| 1992 | 60 168 | 3 192 | 1 260 | 1 932 | 56 976 | 6 542 | 16 512 | 15 701 | 10 570 | 5 821 | 1 830 |
| 1993 | 60 484 | 3 200 | 1 292 | 1 908 | 57 284 | 6 449 | 16 244 | 15 971 | 11 010 | 5 784 | 1 825 |
| 1994 | 60 727 | 3 315 | 1 403 | 1 912 | 57 411 | 6 294 | 15 879 | 16 188 | 11 327 | 5 726 | 1 998 |
| 1995 | 61 146 | 3 427 | 1 429 | 1 998 | 57 719 | 6 096 | 15 669 | 16 414 | 11 730 | 5 809 | 2 000 |
| 1996 | 61 783 | 3 444 | 1 421 | 2 023 | 58 340 | 5 922 | 15 475 | 16 728 | 12 217 | 5 943 | 2 054 |
| 1997 | 62 639 | 3 513 | 1 440 | 2 073 | 59 126 | 6 029 | 15 120 | 17 019 | 12 710 | 6 154 | 2 094 |
| 1998 | 63 034 | 3 614 | 1 487 | 2 127 | 59 421 | 6 063 | 14 770 | 17 157 | 13 003 | 6 415 | 2 013 |
| 1999 | 63 413 | 3 666 | 1 478 | 2 188 | 59 747 | 6 151 | 14 292 | 17 201 | 13 368 | 6 618 | 2 117 |
| 2000 | 64 466 | 3 615 | 1 422 | 2 193 | 60 850 | 6 244 | 14 666 | 16 880 | 13 977 | 6 840 | 2 243 |
| 2001 | 64 966 | 3 446 | 1 334 | 2 112 | 61 519 | 6 363 | 14 536 | 16 809 | 14 400 | 7 169 | 2 241 |
| 2002 | 65 308 | 3 241 | 1 215 | 2 026 | 62 067 | 6 444 | 14 499 | 16 583 | 14 615 | 7 665 | 2 261 |
| 2003 | 65 509 | 3 036 | 1 193 | 1 843 | 62 473 | 6 479 | 14 529 | 16 398 | 14 708 | 7 973 | 2 386 |
| 2004 | 65 994 | 3 050 | 1 127 | 1 923 | 62 944 | 6 586 | 14 429 | 16 192 | 14 934 | 8 326 | 2 478 |
| 2005 | 66 694 | 2 988 | 1 162 | 1 826 | 63 705 | 6 562 | 14 426 | 16 080 | 15 273 | 8 734 | 2 631 |
| 2006 | 67 613 | 3 074 | 1 222 | 1 852 | 64 540 | 6 597 | 14 469 | 15 962 | 15 606 | 9 152 | 2 753 |
| 2007 | 68 158 | 2 944 | 1 147 | 1 798 | 65 214 | 6 567 | 14 715 | 15 765 | 15 846 | 9 500 | 2 821 |
| 2008 | 68 351 | 2 868 | 1 040 | 1 829 | 65 483 | 6 526 | 14 715 | 15 436 | 15 905 | 9 855 | 3 046 |
| 2009 | 68 051 | 2 679 | 933 | 1 746 | 65 372 | 6 348 | 14 669 | 15 066 | 15 943 | 10 160 | 3 186 |
| 2010 | 67 728 | 2 463 | 844 | 1 619 | 65 265 | 6 342 | 14 734 | 14 713 | 15 791 | 10 422 | 3 263 |
| 2011 | 67 551 | 2 386 | 780 | 1 606 | 65 165 | 6 539 | 14 785 | 14 317 | 15 400 | 10 629 | 3 494 |
| 2012 | 66 921 | 2 382 | 785 | 1 596 | 64 540 | 6 339 | 14 256 | 14 018 | 15 121 | 10 970 | 3 835 |
| 2013 | 66 842 | 2 337 | 821 | 1 516 | 64 505 | 6 353 | 14 325 | 13 909 | 14 804 | 11 125 | 3 990 |
| 2014 | 66 680 | 2 250 | 764 | 1 486 | 64 430 | 6 309 | 14 401 | 13 827 | 14 617 | 11 266 | 4 011 |
| 2015 | 67 018 | 2 308 | 798 | 1 511 | 64 710 | 6 165 | 14 533 | 13 757 | 14 539 | 11 489 | 4 227 |

## Table 1-7.  Civilian Labor Force, by Age, Sex, Race, and Hispanic Origin, 1948–2015—*Continued*

(Thousands of people.)

| Race, Hispanic origin, sex, and year | 16 years and over | 16 to 19 years | | | 20 years and over | | | | | | |
|---|---|---|---|---|---|---|---|---|---|---|---|
| | | Total | 16 to 17 years | 18 to 19 years | Total | 20 to 24 years | 25 to 34 years | 35 to 44 years | 45 to 54 years | 55 to 64 years | 65 years and over |
| **WHITE** | | | | | | | | | | | |
| **Women** | | | | | | | | | | | |
| 1954 | 17 057 | 1 512 | 552 | 959 | 15 545 | 2 098 | 3 531 | 4 024 | 3 345 | 1 938 | 607 |
| 1955 | 17 888 | 1 542 | 576 | 966 | 16 346 | 2 138 | 3 546 | 4 132 | 3 655 | 2 156 | 719 |
| 1956 | 18 694 | 1 657 | 654 | 1 003 | 17 037 | 2 158 | 3 559 | 4 339 | 3 886 | 2 344 | 749 |
| 1957 | 18 928 | 1 667 | 645 | 1 021 | 17 261 | 2 131 | 3 561 | 4 398 | 4 065 | 2 356 | 742 |
| 1958 | 19 213 | 1 641 | 614 | 1 028 | 17 572 | 2 171 | 3 498 | 4 435 | 4 262 | 2 454 | 751 |
| 1959 | 19 555 | 1 721 | 698 | 1 023 | 17 834 | 2 135 | 3 409 | 4 479 | 4 467 | 2 578 | 767 |
| 1960 | 20 172 | 1 842 | 731 | 1 112 | 18 330 | 2 228 | 3 441 | 4 531 | 4 633 | 2 661 | 835 |
| 1961 | 20 670 | 1 923 | 700 | 1 222 | 18 747 | 2 345 | 3 431 | 4 596 | 4 741 | 2 785 | 849 |
| 1962 | 20 819 | 1 922 | 668 | 1 254 | 18 897 | 2 438 | 3 372 | 4 666 | 4 731 | 2 861 | 830 |
| 1963 | 21 426 | 1 996 | 767 | 1 228 | 19 430 | 2 582 | 3 424 | 4 780 | 4 845 | 2 977 | 823 |
| 1964 | 22 027 | 2 068 | 866 | 1 201 | 19 959 | 2 786 | 3 435 | 4 797 | 4 990 | 3 078 | 875 |
| 1965 | 22 737 | 2 268 | 862 | 1 405 | 20 469 | 2 910 | 3 567 | 4 877 | 5 032 | 3 204 | 880 |
| 1966 | 23 704 | 2 574 | 944 | 1 630 | 21 130 | 3 124 | 3 732 | 4 893 | 5 181 | 3 333 | 865 |
| 1967 | 24 658 | 2 558 | 968 | 1 591 | 22 100 | 3 471 | 4 021 | 4 980 | 5 285 | 3 469 | 877 |
| 1968 | 25 423 | 2 603 | 1 015 | 1 588 | 22 821 | 3 677 | 4 263 | 5 021 | 5 416 | 3 541 | 903 |
| 1969 | 26 593 | 2 755 | 1 115 | 1 640 | 23 839 | 3 999 | 4 516 | 5 055 | 5 644 | 3 665 | 958 |
| 1970 | 27 521 | 2 891 | 1 195 | 1 695 | 24 630 | 4 250 | 4 797 | 5 111 | 5 781 | 3 738 | 952 |
| 1971 | 28 060 | 2 962 | 1 213 | 1 748 | 25 097 | 4 441 | 5 001 | 5 080 | 5 816 | 3 801 | 958 |
| 1972 | 29 157 | 3 213 | 1 338 | 1 875 | 25 945 | 4 668 | 5 544 | 5 121 | 5 810 | 3 839 | 963 |
| 1973 | 30 231 | 3 405 | 1 445 | 1 960 | 26 825 | 4 908 | 6 143 | 5 228 | 5 811 | 3 788 | 947 |
| 1974 | 31 437 | 3 588 | 1 520 | 2 068 | 27 850 | 5 131 | 6 727 | 5 399 | 5 920 | 3 777 | 897 |
| 1975 | 32 508 | 3 610 | 1 504 | 2 107 | 28 898 | 5 378 | 7 318 | 5 522 | 5 892 | 3 862 | 926 |
| 1976 | 33 735 | 3 731 | 1 541 | 2 189 | 30 004 | 5 554 | 7 898 | 5 799 | 5 877 | 3 935 | 940 |
| 1977 | 35 108 | 3 856 | 1 614 | 2 243 | 31 253 | 5 795 | 8 523 | 6 095 | 5 877 | 4 003 | 959 |
| 1978 | 36 679 | 3 990 | 1 713 | 2 276 | 32 689 | 6 035 | 9 128 | 6 495 | 5 936 | 4 094 | 1 001 |
| 1979 | 38 067 | 4 011 | 1 694 | 2 318 | 34 056 | 6 211 | 9 687 | 6 940 | 5 997 | 4 196 | 1 024 |
| 1980 | 39 127 | 3 888 | 1 605 | 2 284 | 35 239 | 6 290 | 10 289 | 7 356 | 6 079 | 4 194 | 1 032 |
| 1981 | 40 157 | 3 739 | 1 523 | 2 216 | 36 418 | 6 406 | 10 868 | 7 704 | 6 157 | 4 235 | 1 049 |
| 1982 | 41 010 | 3 585 | 1 399 | 2 186 | 37 425 | 6 428 | 11 264 | 8 202 | 6 152 | 4 313 | 1 065 |
| 1983 | 41 541 | 3 422 | 1 314 | 2 109 | 38 119 | 6 410 | 11 530 | 8 670 | 6 149 | 4 285 | 1 074 |
| 1984 | 42 431 | 3 343 | 1 300 | 2 043 | 39 087 | 6 363 | 11 922 | 9 240 | 6 217 | 4 292 | 1 054 |
| 1985 | 43 455 | 3 265 | 1 310 | 1 955 | 40 190 | 6 348 | 12 334 | 9 824 | 6 371 | 4 303 | 1 010 |
| 1986 | 44 584 | 3 320 | 1 393 | 1 927 | 41 264 | 6 191 | 12 729 | 10 364 | 6 588 | 4 323 | 1 069 |
| 1987 | 45 510 | 3 347 | 1 439 | 1 908 | 42 164 | 6 047 | 12 993 | 10 907 | 6 847 | 4 297 | 1 073 |
| 1988 | 46 439 | 3 358 | 1 374 | 1 984 | 43 081 | 5 844 | 13 149 | 11 291 | 7 288 | 4 354 | 1 156 |
| 1989 | 47 367 | 3 262 | 1 284 | 1 978 | 44 105 | 5 625 | 13 311 | 11 796 | 7 663 | 4 451 | 1 259 |
| 1990 | 47 809 | 3 161 | 1 210 | 1 951 | 44 648 | 5 709 | 13 254 | 12 239 | 7 802 | 4 333 | 1 312 |
| 1991 | 48 087 | 2 976 | 1 166 | 1 810 | 45 111 | 5 629 | 13 085 | 12 689 | 8 101 | 4 282 | 1 324 |
| 1992 | 48 669 | 2 830 | 1 128 | 1 702 | 45 839 | 5 645 | 13 006 | 12 879 | 8 630 | 4 375 | 1 305 |
| 1993 | 49 216 | 2 905 | 1 167 | 1 739 | 46 311 | 5 539 | 12 783 | 13 085 | 9 171 | 4 430 | 1 304 |
| 1994 | 50 356 | 3 042 | 1 278 | 1 764 | 47 314 | 5 394 | 12 702 | 13 439 | 9 699 | 4 593 | 1 487 |
| 1995 | 50 804 | 3 118 | 1 320 | 1 798 | 47 686 | 5 170 | 12 656 | 13 697 | 10 074 | 4 622 | 1 466 |
| 1996 | 51 325 | 3 163 | 1 360 | 1 803 | 48 162 | 5 081 | 12 426 | 13 955 | 10 563 | 4 706 | 1 431 |
| 1997 | 52 054 | 3 207 | 1 339 | 1 867 | 48 847 | 5 099 | 12 242 | 14 153 | 10 999 | 4 932 | 1 422 |
| 1998 | 52 380 | 3 351 | 1 373 | 1 977 | 49 029 | 5 180 | 11 937 | 14 064 | 11 279 | 5 133 | 1 435 |
| 1999 | 53 096 | 3 382 | 1 371 | 2 010 | 49 714 | 5 285 | 11 685 | 14 190 | 11 734 | 5 342 | 1 478 |
| 2000 | 54 079 | 3 339 | 1 346 | 1 993 | 50 740 | 5 381 | 11 669 | 14 088 | 12 376 | 5 623 | 1 602 |
| 2001 | 54 433 | 3 215 | 1 292 | 1 923 | 51 218 | 5 519 | 11 474 | 13 969 | 12 662 | 5 952 | 1 642 |
| 2002 | 54 842 | 3 125 | 1 229 | 1 895 | 51 717 | 5 628 | 11 409 | 13 703 | 12 790 | 6 482 | 1 704 |
| 2003 | 55 037 | 2 937 | 1 221 | 1 716 | 52 099 | 5 584 | 11 223 | 13 390 | 13 078 | 6 970 | 1 852 |
| 2004 | 55 092 | 2 879 | 1 182 | 1 697 | 52 212 | 5 606 | 11 119 | 13 114 | 13 247 | 7 197 | 1 930 |
| 2005 | 55 605 | 2 962 | 1 228 | 1 733 | 52 643 | 5 546 | 11 123 | 13 027 | 13 413 | 7 542 | 1 993 |
| 2006 | 56 221 | 2 935 | 1 251 | 1 684 | 53 286 | 5 530 | 11 212 | 12 886 | 13 625 | 7 980 | 2 052 |
| 2007 | 56 777 | 2 851 | 1 179 | 1 672 | 53 925 | 5 609 | 11 360 | 12 629 | 13 781 | 8 282 | 2 264 |
| 2008 | 57 284 | 2 776 | 1 086 | 1 690 | 54 508 | 5 616 | 11 495 | 12 495 | 13 875 | 8 609 | 2 417 |
| 2009 | 57 593 | 2 616 | 950 | 1 667 | 54 976 | 5 647 | 11 608 | 12 197 | 13 960 | 9 039 | 2 525 |
| 2010 | 57 356 | 2 398 | 849 | 1 549 | 54 957 | 5 607 | 11 721 | 11 796 | 13 841 | 9 386 | 2 607 |
| 2011 | 57 028 | 2 328 | 800 | 1 528 | 54 700 | 5 581 | 11 726 | 11 517 | 13 636 | 9 559 | 2 681 |
| 2012 | 56 763 | 2 288 | 819 | 1 469 | 54 475 | 5 575 | 11 550 | 11 428 | 13 263 | 9 782 | 2 879 |
| 2013 | 56 571 | 2 271 | 848 | 1 423 | 54 299 | 5 609 | 11 573 | 11 258 | 12 973 | 9 820 | 3 066 |
| 2014 | 56 648 | 2 226 | 827 | 1 399 | 54 421 | 5 618 | 11 771 | 11 202 | 12 719 | 9 915 | 3 196 |
| 2015 | 56 589 | 2 178 | 782 | 1 397 | 54 410 | 5 589 | 11 772 | 11 172 | 12 527 | 10 045 | 3 304 |

## Table 1-7. Civilian Labor Force, by Age, Sex, Race, and Hispanic Origin, 1948–2015—*Continued*

(Thousands of people.)

| Race, Hispanic origin, sex, and year | 16 years and over | 16 to 19 years | | | 20 years and over | | | | | | |
|---|---|---|---|---|---|---|---|---|---|---|---|
| | | Total | 16 to 17 years | 18 to 19 years | Total | 20 to 24 years | 25 to 34 years | 35 to 44 years | 45 to 54 years | 55 to 64 years | 65 years and over |
| **BLACK** | | | | | | | | | | | |
| **Both Sexes** | | | | | | | | | | | |
| 1980 | 10 865 | 891 | 326 | 565 | 9 975 | 1 802 | 3 259 | 2 081 | 1 596 | 978 | 257 |
| 1981 | 11 086 | 862 | 308 | 554 | 10 224 | 1 828 | 3 365 | 2 164 | 1 608 | 1 009 | 249 |
| 1982 | 11 331 | 824 | 268 | 556 | 10 507 | 1 849 | 3 492 | 2 303 | 1 610 | 1 012 | 243 |
| 1983 | 11 647 | 809 | 248 | 561 | 10 838 | 1 871 | 3 675 | 2 406 | 1 630 | 1 032 | 224 |
| 1984 | 12 033 | 827 | 268 | 558 | 11 206 | 1 926 | 3 800 | 2 565 | 1 671 | 1 020 | 224 |
| 1985 | 12 364 | 889 | 311 | 578 | 11 476 | 1 854 | 3 888 | 2 681 | 1 742 | 1 059 | 252 |
| 1986 | 12 654 | 883 | 322 | 562 | 11 770 | 1 881 | 4 028 | 2 793 | 1 793 | 1 051 | 224 |
| 1987 | 12 993 | 899 | 336 | 563 | 12 094 | 1 818 | 4 147 | 2 942 | 1 838 | 1 098 | 251 |
| 1988 | 13 205 | 889 | 344 | 545 | 12 316 | 1 782 | 4 226 | 3 069 | 1 894 | 1 069 | 276 |
| 1989 | 13 497 | 925 | 353 | 572 | 12 573 | 1 789 | 4 295 | 3 227 | 1 954 | 1 023 | 285 |
| 1990 | 13 740 | 866 | 306 | 560 | 12 874 | 1 758 | 4 307 | 3 566 | 2 003 | 977 | 262 |
| 1991 | 13 797 | 774 | 266 | 508 | 13 023 | 1 750 | 4 254 | 3 719 | 2 042 | 1 001 | 256 |
| 1992 | 14 162 | 816 | 285 | 532 | 13 346 | 1 763 | 4 309 | 3 843 | 2 142 | 1 029 | 259 |
| 1993 | 14 225 | 807 | 283 | 524 | 13 418 | 1 764 | 4 232 | 3 960 | 2 212 | 1 013 | 237 |
| 1994 | 14 502 | 852 | 351 | 501 | 13 650 | 1 800 | 4 199 | 4 068 | 2 308 | 1 007 | 267 |
| 1995 | 14 817 | 911 | 366 | 545 | 13 906 | 1 754 | 4 267 | 4 165 | 2 404 | 1 046 | 271 |
| 1996 | 15 134 | 923 | 366 | 556 | 14 211 | 1 738 | 4 305 | 4 287 | 2 553 | 1 073 | 255 |
| 1997 | 15 529 | 933 | 352 | 580 | 14 596 | 1 783 | 4 329 | 4 401 | 2 724 | 1 093 | 265 |
| 1998 | 15 982 | 1 017 | 370 | 646 | 14 966 | 1 797 | 4 332 | 4 531 | 2 863 | 1 163 | 278 |
| 1999 | 16 365 | 959 | 352 | 607 | 15 406 | 1 866 | 4 430 | 4 653 | 2 992 | 1 180 | 285 |
| 2000 | 16 397 | 941 | 356 | 585 | 15 456 | 1 873 | 4 281 | 4 515 | 3 203 | 1 264 | 320 |
| 2001 | 16 421 | 898 | 332 | 565 | 15 524 | 1 878 | 4 180 | 4 483 | 3 298 | 1 335 | 350 |
| 2002 | 16 565 | 870 | 297 | 574 | 15 695 | 1 908 | 4 134 | 4 458 | 3 435 | 1 407 | 353 |
| 2003 | 16 526 | 771 | 289 | 482 | 15 755 | 1 892 | 4 060 | 4 465 | 3 506 | 1 466 | 366 |
| 2004 | 16 638 | 762 | 272 | 489 | 15 876 | 1 926 | 4 076 | 4 380 | 3 578 | 1 538 | 380 |
| 2005 | 17 013 | 803 | 279 | 525 | 16 209 | 1 957 | 4 145 | 4 370 | 3 686 | 1 647 | 403 |
| 2006 | 17 314 | 871 | 318 | 553 | 16 443 | 1 960 | 4 197 | 4 348 | 3 785 | 1 739 | 414 |
| 2007 | 17 496 | 801 | 300 | 501 | 16 695 | 1 974 | 4 254 | 4 357 | 3 866 | 1 811 | 432 |
| 2008 | 17 740 | 787 | 270 | 517 | 16 953 | 1 981 | 4 328 | 4 316 | 3 945 | 1 908 | 476 |
| 2009 | 17 632 | 729 | 231 | 499 | 16 902 | 1 961 | 4 300 | 4 175 | 3 976 | 1 995 | 495 |
| 2010 | 17 862 | 677 | 203 | 473 | 17 186 | 2 072 | 4 418 | 4 095 | 3 991 | 2 104 | 506 |
| 2011 | 17 881 | 647 | 188 | 459 | 17 234 | 2 105 | 4 434 | 4 029 | 3 957 | 2 155 | 555 |
| 2012 | 18 400 | 711 | 213 | 498 | 17 689 | 2 210 | 4 333 | 4 120 | 4 057 | 2 369 | 599 |
| 2013 | 18 580 | 717 | 218 | 499 | 17 863 | 2 236 | 4 383 | 4 144 | 4 021 | 2 462 | 617 |
| 2014 | 18 873 | 681 | 227 | 454 | 18 192 | 2 305 | 4 541 | 4 159 | 4 013 | 2 528 | 648 |
| 2015 | 19 318 | 701 | 233 | 469 | 18 616 | 2 337 | 4 707 | 4 226 | 4 051 | 2 584 | 711 |
| **Men** | | | | | | | | | | | |
| 1980 | 5 612 | 479 | 181 | 298 | 5 134 | 935 | 1 659 | 1 061 | 830 | 509 | 138 |
| 1981 | 5 685 | 462 | 169 | 293 | 5 223 | 940 | 1 702 | 1 093 | 829 | 524 | 134 |
| 1982 | 5 804 | 436 | 137 | 300 | 5 368 | 964 | 1 769 | 1 152 | 824 | 525 | 135 |
| 1983 | 5 966 | 433 | 134 | 300 | 5 533 | 997 | 1 840 | 1 196 | 845 | 536 | 119 |
| 1984 | 6 126 | 440 | 141 | 299 | 5 686 | 1 022 | 1 924 | 1 270 | 847 | 505 | 118 |
| 1985 | 6 220 | 471 | 162 | 310 | 5 749 | 950 | 1 937 | 1 313 | 879 | 544 | 125 |
| 1986 | 6 373 | 458 | 164 | 294 | 5 915 | 957 | 2 029 | 1 359 | 901 | 552 | 116 |
| 1987 | 6 486 | 463 | 179 | 284 | 6 023 | 914 | 2 074 | 1 406 | 915 | 586 | 130 |
| 1988 | 6 596 | 469 | 186 | 283 | 6 127 | 913 | 2 114 | 1 459 | 936 | 565 | 139 |
| 1989 | 6 701 | 480 | 190 | 291 | 6 221 | 904 | 2 157 | 1 544 | 945 | 530 | 141 |
| 1990 | 6 802 | 445 | 161 | 284 | 6 357 | 879 | 2 142 | 1 733 | 988 | 496 | 119 |
| 1991 | 6 851 | 400 | 140 | 260 | 6 451 | 896 | 2 111 | 1 806 | 1 010 | 507 | 122 |
| 1992 | 6 997 | 429 | 149 | 280 | 6 568 | 900 | 2 121 | 1 859 | 1 037 | 521 | 130 |
| 1993 | 7 019 | 425 | 154 | 270 | 6 594 | 875 | 2 118 | 1 918 | 1 065 | 506 | 112 |
| 1994 | 7 089 | 443 | 176 | 266 | 6 646 | 891 | 2 068 | 1 975 | 1 102 | 484 | 125 |
| 1995 | 7 183 | 453 | 184 | 269 | 6 730 | 866 | 2 089 | 1 987 | 1 148 | 490 | 150 |
| 1996 | 7 264 | 458 | 182 | 276 | 6 806 | 848 | 2 077 | 2 036 | 1 204 | 509 | 132 |
| 1997 | 7 354 | 444 | 178 | 266 | 6 910 | 832 | 2 052 | 2 096 | 1 287 | 508 | 134 |
| 1998 | 7 542 | 488 | 181 | 307 | 7 053 | 837 | 2 034 | 2 142 | 1 343 | 548 | 150 |
| 1999 | 7 652 | 470 | 180 | 291 | 7 182 | 835 | 2 069 | 2 206 | 1 387 | 547 | 138 |
| 2000 | 7 702 | 462 | 181 | 281 | 7 240 | 875 | 1 999 | 2 105 | 1 497 | 612 | 151 |
| 2001 | 7 647 | 447 | 166 | 281 | 7 200 | 853 | 1 915 | 2 073 | 1 537 | 645 | 177 |
| 2002 | 7 794 | 446 | 149 | 297 | 7 347 | 906 | 1 909 | 2 064 | 1 623 | 664 | 181 |
| 2003 | 7 711 | 365 | 138 | 228 | 7 346 | 918 | 1 872 | 2 058 | 1 627 | 685 | 186 |
| 2004 | 7 773 | 359 | 128 | 231 | 7 414 | 927 | 1 931 | 2 000 | 1 654 | 714 | 188 |
| 2005 | 7 998 | 399 | 139 | 260 | 7 600 | 940 | 1 948 | 2 028 | 1 732 | 756 | 196 |
| 2006 | 8 128 | 409 | 152 | 256 | 7 720 | 971 | 1 986 | 1 999 | 1 792 | 777 | 195 |
| 2007 | 8 252 | 384 | 137 | 247 | 7 867 | 981 | 2 037 | 2 030 | 1 822 | 791 | 206 |
| 2008 | 8 347 | 385 | 124 | 261 | 7 962 | 984 | 2 047 | 2 008 | 1 846 | 852 | 225 |
| 2009 | 8 265 | 350 | 111 | 239 | 7 914 | 954 | 2 041 | 1 932 | 1 852 | 904 | 231 |
| 2010 | 8 415 | 339 | 96 | 244 | 8 076 | 986 | 2 118 | 1 924 | 1 862 | 950 | 236 |
| 2011 | 8 454 | 329 | 89 | 241 | 8 125 | 1 012 | 2 159 | 1 860 | 1 854 | 983 | 257 |
| 2012 | 8 594 | 338 | 99 | 239 | 8 256 | 1 054 | 2 030 | 1 908 | 1 884 | 1 099 | 281 |
| 2013 | 8 733 | 347 | 105 | 242 | 8 386 | 1 091 | 2 081 | 1 934 | 1 867 | 1 132 | 281 |
| 2014 | 8 909 | 323 | 115 | 208 | 8 586 | 1 138 | 2 174 | 1 931 | 1 870 | 1 176 | 297 |
| 2015 | 9 099 | 326 | 112 | 213 | 8 773 | 1 145 | 2 250 | 1 956 | 1 899 | 1 204 | 320 |

## Table 1-7.  Civilian Labor Force, by Age, Sex, Race, and Hispanic Origin, 1948–2015—*Continued*

(Thousands of people.)

| Race, Hispanic origin, sex, and year | 16 years and over | 16 to 19 years | | | 20 years and over | | | | | | |
|---|---|---|---|---|---|---|---|---|---|---|---|
| | | Total | 16 to 17 years | 18 to 19 years | Total | 20 to 24 years | 25 to 34 years | 35 to 44 years | 45 to 54 years | 55 to 64 years | 65 years and over |
| **BLACK** | | | | | | | | | | | |
| **Women** | | | | | | | | | | | |
| 1980 | 5 253 | 412 | 144 | 267 | 4 841 | 867 | 1 600 | 1 020 | 767 | 469 | 119 |
| 1981 | 5 401 | 400 | 139 | 261 | 5 001 | 888 | 1 663 | 1 071 | 779 | 485 | 115 |
| 1982 | 5 527 | 387 | 131 | 256 | 5 140 | 885 | 1 723 | 1 151 | 786 | 487 | 108 |
| 1983 | 5 681 | 375 | 114 | 261 | 5 306 | 874 | 1 835 | 1 210 | 785 | 496 | 105 |
| 1984 | 5 907 | 387 | 127 | 260 | 5 520 | 904 | 1 876 | 1 294 | 823 | 515 | 106 |
| 1985 | 6 144 | 417 | 149 | 268 | 5 727 | 904 | 1 951 | 1 368 | 862 | 515 | 127 |
| 1986 | 6 281 | 425 | 157 | 268 | 5 855 | 924 | 1 999 | 1 434 | 892 | 499 | 107 |
| 1987 | 6 507 | 435 | 157 | 278 | 6 071 | 904 | 2 073 | 1 537 | 924 | 512 | 121 |
| 1988 | 6 609 | 419 | 158 | 262 | 6 190 | 869 | 2 112 | 1 610 | 958 | 504 | 137 |
| 1989 | 6 796 | 445 | 163 | 281 | 6 352 | 885 | 2 138 | 1 683 | 1 009 | 493 | 144 |
| 1990 | 6 938 | 421 | 145 | 276 | 6 517 | 879 | 2 165 | 1 833 | 1 015 | 481 | 143 |
| 1991 | 6 946 | 374 | 126 | 248 | 6 572 | 854 | 2 143 | 1 913 | 1 032 | 494 | 135 |
| 1992 | 7 166 | 387 | 135 | 252 | 6 778 | 863 | 2 188 | 1 985 | 1 105 | 508 | 129 |
| 1993 | 7 206 | 383 | 129 | 254 | 6 824 | 889 | 2 115 | 2 042 | 1 147 | 506 | 125 |
| 1994 | 7 413 | 409 | 174 | 235 | 7 004 | 909 | 2 131 | 2 093 | 1 206 | 523 | 142 |
| 1995 | 7 634 | 458 | 182 | 276 | 7 175 | 887 | 2 177 | 2 178 | 1 256 | 556 | 121 |
| 1996 | 7 869 | 464 | 184 | 280 | 7 405 | 890 | 2 228 | 2 251 | 1 349 | 565 | 122 |
| 1997 | 8 175 | 489 | 175 | 314 | 7 686 | 951 | 2 277 | 2 305 | 1 437 | 585 | 131 |
| 1998 | 8 441 | 528 | 189 | 339 | 7 912 | 960 | 2 298 | 2 390 | 1 520 | 615 | 128 |
| 1999 | 8 713 | 489 | 172 | 316 | 8 224 | 1 031 | 2 360 | 2 447 | 1 606 | 633 | 147 |
| 2000 | 8 695 | 479 | 175 | 305 | 8 215 | 998 | 2 282 | 2 409 | 1 706 | 652 | 168 |
| 2001 | 8 774 | 451 | 166 | 284 | 8 323 | 1 025 | 2 265 | 2 410 | 1 762 | 690 | 173 |
| 2002 | 8 772 | 424 | 148 | 276 | 8 348 | 1 002 | 2 225 | 2 394 | 1 812 | 743 | 171 |
| 2003 | 8 815 | 406 | 151 | 255 | 8 409 | 973 | 2 188 | 2 407 | 1 879 | 781 | 180 |
| 2004 | 8 865 | 403 | 144 | 259 | 8 462 | 999 | 2 144 | 2 380 | 1 924 | 824 | 192 |
| 2005 | 9 014 | 405 | 140 | 265 | 8 610 | 1 017 | 2 197 | 2 342 | 1 954 | 891 | 207 |
| 2006 | 9 186 | 462 | 166 | 297 | 8 723 | 989 | 2 211 | 2 349 | 1 993 | 963 | 218 |
| 2007 | 9 244 | 417 | 163 | 254 | 8 828 | 993 | 2 218 | 2 328 | 2 044 | 1 019 | 227 |
| 2008 | 9 393 | 402 | 146 | 256 | 8 991 | 997 | 2 281 | 2 308 | 2 099 | 1 056 | 251 |
| 2009 | 9 367 | 379 | 119 | 260 | 8 988 | 1 008 | 2 258 | 2 243 | 2 124 | 1 091 | 264 |
| 2010 | 9 447 | 337 | 108 | 230 | 9 110 | 1 086 | 2 299 | 2 171 | 2 129 | 1 153 | 270 |
| 2011 | 9 427 | 318 | 99 | 219 | 9 110 | 1 093 | 2 275 | 2 168 | 2 104 | 1 172 | 298 |
| 2012 | 9 805 | 373 | 114 | 258 | 9 433 | 1 157 | 2 303 | 2 212 | 2 173 | 1 271 | 317 |
| 2013 | 9 846 | 370 | 113 | 257 | 9 476 | 1 145 | 2 303 | 2 210 | 2 153 | 1 330 | 336 |
| 2014 | 9 964 | 358 | 112 | 246 | 9 606 | 1 167 | 2 367 | 2 227 | 2 142 | 1 352 | 351 |
| 2015 | 10 218 | 376 | 120 | 255 | 9 843 | 1 192 | 2 457 | 2 270 | 2 152 | 1 381 | 391 |
| **HISPANIC** | | | | | | | | | | | |
| **Both Sexes** | | | | | | | | | | | |
| 1980 | 6 146 | 645 | 241 | 404 | 5 502 | 1 136 | 1 843 | 1 163 | 860 | 414 | 85 |
| 1981 | 6 492 | 603 | 215 | 388 | 5 888 | 1 231 | 2 015 | 1 239 | 886 | 430 | 87 |
| 1982 | 6 734 | 585 | 192 | 393 | 6 148 | 1 251 | 2 163 | 1 313 | 891 | 444 | 85 |
| 1983 | 7 033 | 590 | 189 | 401 | 6 442 | 1 282 | 2 267 | 1 380 | 931 | 495 | 86 |
| 1984 | 7 451 | 618 | 209 | 409 | 6 833 | 1 325 | 2 436 | 1 509 | 954 | 524 | 84 |
| 1985 | 7 698 | 579 | 199 | 379 | 7 119 | 1 358 | 2 571 | 1 595 | 985 | 527 | 82 |
| 1986 | 8 076 | 571 | 203 | 368 | 7 505 | 1 414 | 2 685 | 1 713 | 1 097 | 511 | 84 |
| 1987 | 8 541 | 610 | 206 | 404 | 7 931 | 1 425 | 2 890 | 1 904 | 1 086 | 545 | 81 |
| 1988 | 8 982 | 671 | 234 | 437 | 8 311 | 1 486 | 2 957 | 1 996 | 1 147 | 621 | 103 |
| 1989 | 9 323 | 680 | 224 | 456 | 8 643 | 1 483 | 3 118 | 2 092 | 1 205 | 625 | 120 |
| 1990 | 10 720 | 829 | 276 | 554 | 9 891 | 1 839 | 3 590 | 2 386 | 1 320 | 647 | 110 |
| 1991 | 10 920 | 781 | 249 | 532 | 10 139 | 1 835 | 3 596 | 2 539 | 1 376 | 681 | 111 |
| 1992 | 11 338 | 796 | 263 | 533 | 10 542 | 1 815 | 3 740 | 2 735 | 1 442 | 687 | 122 |
| 1993 | 11 610 | 771 | 246 | 525 | 10 839 | 1 811 | 3 800 | 2 865 | 1 534 | 684 | 145 |
| 1994 | 11 975 | 807 | 285 | 522 | 11 168 | 1 863 | 3 865 | 2 965 | 1 626 | 698 | 151 |
| 1995 | 12 267 | 850 | 291 | 559 | 11 417 | 1 818 | 3 943 | 3 113 | 1 671 | 720 | 152 |
| 1996 | 12 774 | 845 | 284 | 561 | 11 929 | 1 845 | 4 054 | 3 361 | 1 697 | 806 | 166 |
| 1997 | 13 796 | 911 | 315 | 596 | 12 884 | 2 004 | 4 298 | 3 601 | 1 945 | 850 | 186 |
| 1998 | 14 317 | 1 007 | 320 | 688 | 13 310 | 2 077 | 4 372 | 3 707 | 2 090 | 894 | 169 |
| 1999 | 14 665 | 1 049 | 333 | 717 | 13 616 | 2 052 | 4 330 | 3 929 | 2 178 | 927 | 199 |
| 2000 | 16 689 | 1 168 | 368 | 800 | 15 521 | 2 546 | 5 197 | 4 241 | 2 387 | 940 | 209 |
| 2001 | 17 328 | 1 176 | 352 | 824 | 16 152 | 2 616 | 5 380 | 4 377 | 2 583 | 1 000 | 195 |
| 2002 | 17 943 | 1 103 | 335 | 769 | 16 840 | 2 678 | 5 645 | 4 545 | 2 657 | 1 091 | 224 |
| 2003 | 18 813 | 960 | 322 | 638 | 17 853 | 2 672 | 5 960 | 4 867 | 2 894 | 1 201 | 259 |
| 2004 | 19 272 | 995 | 297 | 698 | 18 277 | 2 732 | 5 931 | 4 931 | 3 093 | 1 284 | 306 |
| 2005 | 19 824 | 1 038 | 331 | 708 | 18 785 | 2 651 | 6 080 | 5 110 | 3 256 | 1 378 | 311 |
| 2006 | 20 694 | 1 071 | 360 | 710 | 19 623 | 2 681 | 6 295 | 5 337 | 3 452 | 1 490 | 369 |
| 2007 | 21 602 | 1 091 | 347 | 744 | 20 511 | 2 728 | 6 559 | 5 552 | 3 707 | 1 569 | 395 |
| 2008 | 22 024 | 1 121 | 353 | 768 | 20 903 | 2 668 | 6 557 | 5 698 | 3 862 | 1 701 | 417 |
| 2009 | 22 352 | 1 063 | 301 | 762 | 21 290 | 2 647 | 6 435 | 5 752 | 4 116 | 1 866 | 472 |
| 2010 | 22 748 | 1 002 | 264 | 738 | 21 747 | 2 760 | 6 517 | 5 783 | 4 238 | 1 936 | 513 |
| 2011 | 22 898 | 965 | 251 | 713 | 21 933 | 3 017 | 6 416 | 5 702 | 4 272 | 2 015 | 511 |
| 2012 | 24 391 | 1 131 | 315 | 817 | 23 260 | 3 205 | 6 736 | 6 053 | 4 569 | 2 185 | 512 |
| 2013 | 24 771 | 1 133 | 328 | 805 | 23 639 | 3 276 | 6 705 | 6 094 | 4 695 | 2 311 | 557 |
| 2014 | 25 370 | 1 109 | 314 | 795 | 24 261 | 3 315 | 6 822 | 6 224 | 4 849 | 2 460 | 591 |
| 2015 | 26 126 | 1 144 | 327 | 817 | 24 983 | 3 365 | 6 863 | 6 383 | 5 070 | 2 666 | 637 |

## Table 1-7.  Civilian Labor Force, by Age, Sex, Race, and Hispanic Origin, 1948–2015—*Continued*

(Thousands of people.)

| Race, Hispanic origin, sex, and year | 16 years and over | 16 to 19 years | | | 20 years and over | | | | | | |
|---|---|---|---|---|---|---|---|---|---|---|---|
| | | Total | 16 to 17 years | 18 to 19 years | Total | 20 to 24 years | 25 to 34 years | 35 to 44 years | 45 to 54 years | 55 to 64 years | 65 years and over |
| **HISPANIC** | | | | | | | | | | | |
| **Men** | | | | | | | | | | | |
| 1980 | 3 818 | 392 | 147 | 245 | 3 426 | 697 | 1 161 | 713 | 522 | 270 | 62 |
| 1981 | 4 005 | 359 | 130 | 229 | 3 647 | 747 | 1 269 | 756 | 535 | 278 | 61 |
| 1982 | 4 148 | 333 | 111 | 221 | 3 815 | 759 | 1 361 | 808 | 539 | 290 | 58 |
| 1983 | 4 362 | 348 | 109 | 239 | 4 014 | 789 | 1 447 | 852 | 557 | 311 | 58 |
| 1984 | 4 563 | 345 | 113 | 232 | 4 218 | 822 | 1 540 | 910 | 570 | 325 | 51 |
| 1985 | 4 729 | 334 | 116 | 218 | 4 395 | 835 | 1 629 | 957 | 591 | 331 | 53 |
| 1986 | 4 948 | 336 | 114 | 222 | 4 612 | 888 | 1 669 | 1 015 | 661 | 323 | 56 |
| 1987 | 5 163 | 345 | 112 | 233 | 4 818 | 865 | 1 801 | 1 121 | 652 | 325 | 55 |
| 1988 | 5 409 | 378 | 123 | 255 | 5 031 | 897 | 1 834 | 1 189 | 686 | 355 | 69 |
| 1989 | 5 595 | 400 | 129 | 271 | 5 195 | 909 | 1 899 | 1 221 | 719 | 375 | 71 |
| 1990 | 6 546 | 512 | 165 | 346 | 6 034 | 1 182 | 2 230 | 1 403 | 775 | 380 | 65 |
| 1991 | 6 664 | 466 | 141 | 325 | 6 198 | 1 202 | 2 260 | 1 487 | 780 | 401 | 67 |
| 1992 | 6 900 | 468 | 154 | 314 | 6 432 | 1 141 | 2 366 | 1 593 | 844 | 414 | 74 |
| 1993 | 7 076 | 455 | 145 | 310 | 6 621 | 1 147 | 2 417 | 1 675 | 900 | 394 | 88 |
| 1994 | 7 210 | 463 | 163 | 300 | 6 747 | 1 184 | 2 430 | 1 713 | 922 | 410 | 89 |
| 1995 | 7 376 | 479 | 168 | 311 | 6 898 | 1 153 | 2 469 | 1 795 | 965 | 417 | 98 |
| 1996 | 7 646 | 496 | 156 | 340 | 7 150 | 1 132 | 2 510 | 1 966 | 967 | 469 | 105 |
| 1997 | 8 309 | 531 | 177 | 354 | 7 779 | 1 267 | 2 684 | 2 091 | 1 112 | 511 | 113 |
| 1998 | 8 571 | 565 | 188 | 377 | 8 005 | 1 288 | 2 733 | 2 173 | 1 164 | 541 | 106 |
| 1999 | 8 546 | 596 | 181 | 415 | 7 950 | 1 231 | 2 633 | 2 219 | 1 205 | 526 | 136 |
| 2000 | 9 923 | 676 | 204 | 471 | 9 247 | 1 590 | 3 181 | 2 451 | 1 337 | 555 | 134 |
| 2001 | 10 279 | 684 | 200 | 484 | 9 595 | 1 602 | 3 294 | 2 562 | 1 430 | 582 | 125 |
| 2002 | 10 609 | 632 | 183 | 449 | 9 977 | 1 627 | 3 484 | 2 647 | 1 478 | 607 | 134 |
| 2003 | 11 288 | 532 | 164 | 368 | 10 756 | 1 642 | 3 776 | 2 877 | 1 630 | 680 | 150 |
| 2004 | 11 587 | 567 | 156 | 410 | 11 020 | 1 671 | 3 765 | 2 934 | 1 736 | 728 | 186 |
| 2005 | 11 985 | 577 | 179 | 398 | 11 408 | 1 645 | 3 879 | 3 058 | 1 855 | 779 | 192 |
| 2006 | 12 488 | 600 | 189 | 411 | 11 888 | 1 646 | 4 014 | 3 203 | 1 960 | 838 | 228 |
| 2007 | 13 005 | 602 | 189 | 412 | 12 403 | 1 645 | 4 170 | 3 346 | 2 104 | 904 | 233 |
| 2008 | 13 255 | 626 | 202 | 424 | 12 629 | 1 594 | 4 172 | 3 425 | 2 216 | 979 | 243 |
| 2009 | 13 310 | 580 | 160 | 420 | 12 730 | 1 542 | 4 046 | 3 472 | 2 350 | 1 046 | 273 |
| 2010 | 13 511 | 553 | 132 | 420 | 12 958 | 1 612 | 4 061 | 3 515 | 2 407 | 1 061 | 302 |
| 2011 | 13 576 | 545 | 129 | 416 | 13 030 | 1 811 | 4 011 | 3 421 | 2 372 | 1 122 | 293 |
| 2012 | 14 026 | 620 | 162 | 457 | 13 407 | 1 837 | 4 053 | 3 480 | 2 542 | 1 215 | 280 |
| 2013 | 14 341 | 613 | 169 | 444 | 13 728 | 1 857 | 4 053 | 3 564 | 2 644 | 1 286 | 324 |
| 2014 | 14 651 | 584 | 157 | 428 | 14 066 | 1 862 | 4 081 | 3 671 | 2 724 | 1 399 | 329 |
| 2015 | 15 054 | 610 | 167 | 443 | 14 444 | 1 851 | 4 105 | 3 754 | 2 862 | 1 515 | 356 |
| **HISPANIC** | | | | | | | | | | | |
| **Women** | | | | | | | | | | | |
| 1980 | 2 328 | 252 | 93 | 159 | 2 076 | 439 | 682 | 450 | 337 | 144 | 22 |
| 1981 | 2 486 | 244 | 85 | 159 | 2 242 | 484 | 745 | 483 | 351 | 152 | 27 |
| 1982 | 2 586 | 252 | 81 | 172 | 2 333 | 492 | 802 | 504 | 352 | 155 | 28 |
| 1983 | 2 671 | 242 | 80 | 162 | 2 429 | 493 | 820 | 529 | 374 | 184 | 29 |
| 1984 | 2 888 | 273 | 96 | 177 | 2 615 | 503 | 896 | 599 | 384 | 199 | 34 |
| 1985 | 2 970 | 245 | 84 | 161 | 2 725 | 524 | 943 | 639 | 394 | 196 | 29 |
| 1986 | 3 128 | 236 | 89 | 147 | 2 893 | 526 | 1 016 | 698 | 436 | 189 | 28 |
| 1987 | 3 377 | 265 | 94 | 171 | 3 112 | 559 | 1 090 | 783 | 434 | 220 | 27 |
| 1988 | 3 573 | 293 | 111 | 182 | 3 281 | 589 | 1 123 | 806 | 461 | 267 | 34 |
| 1989 | 3 728 | 280 | 95 | 185 | 3 448 | 574 | 1 219 | 871 | 486 | 251 | 49 |
| 1990 | 4 174 | 318 | 110 | 207 | 3 857 | 657 | 1 360 | 983 | 545 | 268 | 45 |
| 1991 | 4 256 | 315 | 107 | 207 | 3 941 | 633 | 1 336 | 1 052 | 596 | 279 | 44 |
| 1992 | 4 439 | 328 | 110 | 219 | 4 110 | 674 | 1 374 | 1 142 | 599 | 273 | 48 |
| 1993 | 4 534 | 316 | 101 | 215 | 4 218 | 664 | 1 383 | 1 190 | 633 | 290 | 57 |
| 1994 | 4 765 | 345 | 122 | 222 | 4 421 | 679 | 1 435 | 1 252 | 704 | 288 | 62 |
| 1995 | 4 891 | 371 | 123 | 249 | 4 520 | 666 | 1 473 | 1 318 | 706 | 303 | 54 |
| 1996 | 5 128 | 349 | 128 | 221 | 4 779 | 713 | 1 544 | 1 395 | 729 | 338 | 61 |
| 1997 | 5 486 | 381 | 138 | 242 | 5 106 | 737 | 1 614 | 1 510 | 833 | 338 | 73 |
| 1998 | 5 746 | 442 | 132 | 310 | 5 304 | 789 | 1 639 | 1 533 | 927 | 353 | 62 |
| 1999 | 6 119 | 453 | 151 | 302 | 5 666 | 821 | 1 698 | 1 710 | 973 | 401 | 63 |
| 2000 | 6 767 | 492 | 164 | 328 | 6 275 | 956 | 2 016 | 1 791 | 1 051 | 386 | 75 |
| 2001 | 7 049 | 492 | 152 | 340 | 6 557 | 1 014 | 2 086 | 1 815 | 1 153 | 418 | 70 |
| 2002 | 7 334 | 471 | 152 | 320 | 6 863 | 1 051 | 2 161 | 1 897 | 1 179 | 484 | 90 |
| 2003 | 7 525 | 428 | 158 | 271 | 7 096 | 1 030 | 2 183 | 1 990 | 1 264 | 520 | 109 |
| 2004 | 7 685 | 429 | 141 | 288 | 7 257 | 1 060 | 2 166 | 1 998 | 1 357 | 556 | 119 |
| 2005 | 7 839 | 462 | 152 | 310 | 7 377 | 1 005 | 2 201 | 2 052 | 1 401 | 599 | 119 |
| 2006 | 8 206 | 471 | 171 | 300 | 7 735 | 1 035 | 2 280 | 2 134 | 1 492 | 652 | 141 |
| 2007 | 8 597 | 489 | 158 | 332 | 8 108 | 1 083 | 2 389 | 2 205 | 1 604 | 665 | 162 |
| 2008 | 8 769 | 495 | 151 | 344 | 8 274 | 1 074 | 2 384 | 2 274 | 1 646 | 722 | 174 |
| 2009 | 9 043 | 483 | 141 | 342 | 8 560 | 1 105 | 2 388 | 2 280 | 1 767 | 820 | 200 |
| 2010 | 9 238 | 449 | 132 | 317 | 8 789 | 1 147 | 2 456 | 2 268 | 1 831 | 875 | 211 |
| 2011 | 9 322 | 419 | 122 | 297 | 8 902 | 1 206 | 2 406 | 2 282 | 1 899 | 893 | 217 |
| 2012 | 10 365 | 512 | 152 | 360 | 9 853 | 1 368 | 2 683 | 2 574 | 2 027 | 969 | 232 |
| 2013 | 10 430 | 520 | 159 | 361 | 9 911 | 1 419 | 2 653 | 2 530 | 2 051 | 1 025 | 233 |
| 2014 | 10 720 | 525 | 158 | 367 | 10 195 | 1 453 | 2 741 | 2 552 | 2 125 | 1 061 | 262 |
| 2015 | 11 072 | 533 | 160 | 373 | 10 539 | 1 514 | 2 758 | 2 628 | 2 207 | 1 151 | 280 |

## Table 1-8.  Civilian Labor Force Participation Rates, by Age, Sex, Race, and Hispanic Origin, 1948–2015

(Percent.)

| Race, Hispanic origin, sex, and year | 16 years and over | 16 to 19 years | 20 years and over | | | | | | |
|---|---|---|---|---|---|---|---|---|---|
| | | | Total | 20 to 24 years | 25 to 34 years | 35 to 44 years | 45 to 54 years | 55 to 64 years | 65 years and over |
| **ALL RACES** | | | | | | | | | |
| **Both Sexes** | | | | | | | | | |
| 1948 | 58.8 | 52.5 | 59.4 | 64.1 | 63.1 | 66.7 | 65.1 | 56.9 | 27.0 |
| 1949 | 58.9 | 52.2 | 59.5 | 64.9 | 63.2 | 67.2 | 65.3 | 56.2 | 27.3 |
| 1950 | 59.2 | 51.8 | 59.9 | 65.9 | 63.5 | 67.5 | 66.4 | 56.7 | 26.7 |
| 1951 | 59.2 | 52.2 | 59.8 | 64.8 | 64.2 | 67.6 | 67.2 | 56.9 | 25.8 |
| 1952 | 59.0 | 51.3 | 59.7 | 62.2 | 64.7 | 68.0 | 67.5 | 57.5 | 24.8 |
| 1953 | 58.9 | 50.2 | 59.6 | 61.2 | 64.0 | 68.9 | 68.1 | 58.0 | 24.8 |
| 1954 | 58.8 | 48.3 | 59.6 | 61.6 | 64.3 | 68.8 | 68.4 | 58.7 | 23.9 |
| 1955 | 59.3 | 48.9 | 60.1 | 62.7 | 64.8 | 68.9 | 69.7 | 59.5 | 24.1 |
| 1956 | 60.0 | 50.9 | 60.7 | 64.1 | 64.8 | 69.5 | 70.5 | 60.8 | 24.3 |
| 1957 | 59.6 | 49.6 | 60.4 | 64.0 | 64.9 | 69.5 | 70.9 | 60.1 | 22.9 |
| 1958 | 59.5 | 47.4 | 60.5 | 64.4 | 65.0 | 69.6 | 71.5 | 60.5 | 21.8 |
| 1959 | 59.3 | 46.7 | 60.4 | 64.3 | 65.0 | 69.5 | 71.9 | 61.0 | 21.1 |
| 1960 | 59.4 | 47.5 | 60.5 | 65.2 | 65.4 | 69.4 | 72.2 | 60.9 | 20.8 |
| 1961 | 59.3 | 46.9 | 60.5 | 65.7 | 65.6 | 69.5 | 72.1 | 61.5 | 20.1 |
| 1962 | 58.8 | 46.1 | 60.0 | 65.3 | 65.2 | 69.7 | 72.2 | 61.5 | 19.1 |
| 1963 | 58.7 | 45.2 | 60.1 | 65.1 | 65.6 | 70.1 | 72.5 | 62.0 | 17.9 |
| 1964 | 58.7 | 44.5 | 60.2 | 66.3 | 65.8 | 70.0 | 72.9 | 61.9 | 18.0 |
| 1965 | 58.9 | 45.7 | 60.3 | 66.4 | 66.4 | 70.7 | 72.5 | 61.9 | 17.8 |
| 1966 | 59.2 | 48.2 | 60.5 | 66.5 | 67.1 | 71.0 | 72.7 | 62.2 | 17.2 |
| 1967 | 59.6 | 48.4 | 60.9 | 67.1 | 68.2 | 71.6 | 72.7 | 62.3 | 17.2 |
| 1968 | 59.6 | 48.3 | 60.9 | 67.0 | 68.6 | 72.0 | 72.8 | 62.2 | 17.2 |
| 1969 | 60.1 | 49.4 | 61.3 | 68.2 | 69.1 | 72.5 | 73.4 | 62.1 | 17.3 |
| 1970 | 60.4 | 49.9 | 61.6 | 69.2 | 69.7 | 73.1 | 73.5 | 61.8 | 17.0 |
| 1971 | 60.2 | 49.7 | 61.4 | 69.3 | 69.9 | 73.2 | 73.2 | 61.3 | 16.2 |
| 1972 | 60.4 | 51.9 | 61.4 | 70.8 | 70.9 | 73.3 | 72.7 | 60.0 | 15.6 |
| 1973 | 60.8 | 53.7 | 61.7 | 72.6 | 72.3 | 74.0 | 72.5 | 58.4 | 14.6 |
| 1974 | 61.3 | 54.8 | 62.0 | 74.0 | 73.6 | 74.6 | 72.7 | 57.8 | 14.0 |
| 1975 | 61.2 | 54.0 | 62.1 | 73.9 | 74.4 | 75.0 | 72.6 | 57.2 | 13.7 |
| 1976 | 61.6 | 54.5 | 62.4 | 74.7 | 75.7 | 76.0 | 72.5 | 56.6 | 13.1 |
| 1977 | 62.3 | 56.0 | 63.0 | 75.7 | 77.0 | 77.0 | 72.8 | 56.3 | 13.0 |
| 1978 | 63.2 | 57.8 | 63.8 | 76.8 | 78.3 | 78.1 | 73.5 | 56.3 | 13.3 |
| 1979 | 63.7 | 57.9 | 64.3 | 77.5 | 79.2 | 79.2 | 74.3 | 56.2 | 13.1 |
| 1980 | 63.8 | 56.7 | 64.5 | 77.2 | 79.9 | 80.0 | 74.9 | 55.7 | 12.5 |
| 1981 | 63.9 | 55.4 | 64.8 | 77.3 | 80.5 | 80.7 | 75.7 | 55.0 | 12.2 |
| 1982 | 64.0 | 54.1 | 65.0 | 77.1 | 81.0 | 81.2 | 75.9 | 55.1 | 11.9 |
| 1983 | 64.0 | 53.5 | 65.0 | 77.2 | 81.3 | 81.6 | 76.0 | 54.5 | 11.7 |
| 1984 | 64.4 | 53.9 | 65.3 | 77.6 | 81.8 | 82.4 | 76.5 | 54.2 | 11.1 |
| 1985 | 64.8 | 54.5 | 65.7 | 78.2 | 82.5 | 83.1 | 77.3 | 54.2 | 10.8 |
| 1986 | 65.3 | 54.7 | 66.2 | 78.9 | 82.9 | 83.7 | 78.0 | 54.0 | 10.9 |
| 1987 | 65.6 | 54.7 | 66.5 | 78.9 | 83.3 | 84.3 | 78.6 | 54.4 | 11.1 |
| 1988 | 65.9 | 55.3 | 66.8 | 78.7 | 83.3 | 84.6 | 79.6 | 54.6 | 11.5 |
| 1989 | 66.5 | 55.9 | 67.3 | 78.7 | 83.8 | 85.1 | 80.5 | 55.5 | 11.8 |
| 1990 | 66.5 | 53.7 | 67.6 | 77.8 | 83.6 | 85.2 | 80.7 | 55.9 | 11.8 |
| 1991 | 66.2 | 51.6 | 67.3 | 76.7 | 83.2 | 85.2 | 81.0 | 55.5 | 11.5 |
| 1992 | 66.4 | 51.3 | 67.6 | 77.0 | 83.7 | 85.1 | 81.5 | 56.2 | 11.5 |
| 1993 | 66.3 | 51.5 | 67.5 | 77.0 | 83.3 | 84.9 | 81.6 | 56.4 | 11.2 |
| 1994 | 66.6 | 52.7 | 67.7 | 77.0 | 83.2 | 84.8 | 81.7 | 56.8 | 12.4 |
| 1995 | 66.6 | 53.5 | 67.7 | 76.6 | 83.8 | 84.6 | 81.4 | 57.2 | 12.1 |
| 1996 | 66.8 | 52.3 | 67.9 | 76.8 | 84.1 | 84.8 | 82.1 | 57.9 | 12.1 |
| 1997 | 67.1 | 51.6 | 68.4 | 77.6 | 84.4 | 85.1 | 82.6 | 58.9 | 12.2 |
| 1998 | 67.1 | 52.8 | 68.3 | 77.5 | 84.6 | 84.7 | 82.5 | 59.3 | 11.9 |
| 1999 | 67.1 | 52.0 | 68.3 | 77.5 | 84.6 | 84.9 | 82.6 | 59.3 | 12.3 |
| 2000 | 67.1 | 52.0 | 68.3 | 77.8 | 84.6 | 84.8 | 82.5 | 59.2 | 12.9 |
| 2001 | 66.8 | 49.6 | 68.2 | 77.1 | 84.0 | 84.6 | 82.3 | 60.4 | 13.0 |
| 2002 | 66.6 | 47.4 | 68.1 | 76.4 | 83.7 | 84.1 | 82.1 | 61.9 | 13.2 |
| 2003 | 66.2 | 44.5 | 67.9 | 75.4 | 82.9 | 83.9 | 82.1 | 62.4 | 14.0 |
| 2004 | 66.0 | 43.9 | 67.7 | 75.0 | 82.7 | 83.6 | 81.8 | 62.3 | 14.4 |
| 2005 | 66.0 | 43.7 | 67.8 | 74.6 | 82.8 | 83.8 | 81.7 | 62.9 | 15.1 |
| 2006 | 66.2 | 43.7 | 67.9 | 74.6 | 83.0 | 83.8 | 81.9 | 63.7 | 15.4 |
| 2007 | 66.0 | 41.3 | 68.0 | 74.4 | 83.3 | 83.8 | 82.0 | 63.8 | 16.0 |
| 2008 | 66.0 | 40.2 | 68.0 | 74.4 | 83.3 | 84.1 | 81.9 | 64.5 | 16.8 |
| 2009 | 65.4 | 37.5 | 67.5 | 72.9 | 82.7 | 83.7 | 81.6 | 64.9 | 17.2 |
| 2010 | 64.7 | 34.9 | 67.0 | 71.4 | 82.2 | 83.2 | 81.2 | 64.9 | 17.4 |
| 2011 | 64.1 | 34.1 | 66.4 | 71.3 | 81.5 | 82.7 | 80.7 | 64.3 | 17.9 |
| 2012 | 63.7 | 34.3 | 65.9 | 70.9 | 81.7 | 82.6 | 80.2 | 64.5 | 18.5 |
| 2013 | 63.2 | 34.5 | 65.4 | 70.7 | 81.2 | 82.2 | 79.7 | 64.4 | 18.7 |
| 2014 | 62.9 | 34.0 | 65.0 | 70.8 | 81.2 | 82.2 | 79.6 | 64.1 | 18.6 |
| 2015 | 62.7 | 34.3 | 64.7 | 70.7 | 81.0 | 82.1 | 79.5 | 63.9 | 18.9 |

## Table 1-8.  Civilian Labor Force Participation Rates, by Age, Sex, Race, and Hispanic Origin, 1948–2015 —Continued

(Percent.)

| Race, Hispanic origin, sex, and year | 16 years and over | 16 to 19 years | 20 years and over | | | | | | |
|---|---|---|---|---|---|---|---|---|---|
| | | | Total | 20 to 24 years | 25 to 34 years | 35 to 44 years | 45 to 54 years | 55 to 64 years | 65 years and over |
| **ALL RACES** | | | | | | | | | |
| **Men** | | | | | | | | | |
| 1948 | 86.6 | 63.7 | 88.6 | 84.6 | 95.9 | 97.9 | 95.8 | 89.5 | 46.8 |
| 1949 | 86.4 | 62.8 | 88.5 | 86.6 | 95.8 | 97.9 | 95.6 | 87.5 | 47.0 |
| 1950 | 86.4 | 63.2 | 88.4 | 87.9 | 96.0 | 97.6 | 95.8 | 86.9 | 45.8 |
| 1951 | 86.3 | 63.0 | 88.2 | 88.4 | 96.9 | 97.5 | 95.9 | 87.2 | 44.9 |
| 1952 | 86.3 | 61.3 | 88.3 | 88.1 | 97.5 | 97.8 | 96.2 | 87.5 | 42.6 |
| 1953 | 86.0 | 60.7 | 88.0 | 87.7 | 97.4 | 98.2 | 96.5 | 87.9 | 41.6 |
| 1954 | 85.5 | 58.0 | 87.8 | 86.9 | 97.3 | 98.1 | 96.5 | 88.7 | 40.5 |
| 1955 | 85.4 | 58.9 | 87.6 | 86.9 | 97.6 | 98.1 | 96.4 | 87.9 | 39.6 |
| 1956 | 85.5 | 60.5 | 87.6 | 87.8 | 97.3 | 97.9 | 96.6 | 88.5 | 40.0 |
| 1957 | 84.8 | 59.1 | 86.9 | 87.1 | 97.1 | 97.9 | 96.3 | 87.5 | 37.5 |
| 1958 | 84.2 | 56.6 | 86.6 | 86.9 | 97.1 | 97.9 | 96.3 | 87.8 | 35.6 |
| 1959 | 83.7 | 55.8 | 86.3 | 87.8 | 97.4 | 97.8 | 96.0 | 87.4 | 34.2 |
| 1960 | 83.3 | 56.1 | 86.0 | 88.1 | 97.5 | 97.7 | 95.7 | 86.8 | 33.1 |
| 1961 | 82.9 | 54.6 | 85.7 | 87.8 | 97.5 | 97.6 | 95.6 | 87.3 | 31.7 |
| 1962 | 82.0 | 53.8 | 84.8 | 86.9 | 97.2 | 97.6 | 95.6 | 86.2 | 30.3 |
| 1963 | 81.4 | 52.9 | 84.4 | 86.1 | 97.1 | 97.5 | 95.7 | 86.2 | 28.4 |
| 1964 | 81.0 | 52.4 | 84.2 | 86.1 | 97.3 | 97.3 | 95.7 | 85.6 | 28.0 |
| 1965 | 80.7 | 53.8 | 83.9 | 85.8 | 97.2 | 97.3 | 95.6 | 84.6 | 27.9 |
| 1966 | 80.4 | 55.3 | 83.6 | 85.1 | 97.3 | 97.2 | 95.3 | 84.5 | 27.1 |
| 1967 | 80.4 | 55.6 | 83.4 | 84.4 | 97.2 | 97.3 | 95.2 | 84.4 | 27.1 |
| 1968 | 80.1 | 55.1 | 83.1 | 82.8 | 96.9 | 97.1 | 94.9 | 84.3 | 27.3 |
| 1969 | 79.8 | 55.9 | 82.8 | 82.8 | 96.7 | 96.9 | 94.6 | 83.4 | 27.2 |
| 1970 | 79.7 | 56.1 | 82.6 | 83.3 | 96.4 | 96.9 | 94.3 | 83.0 | 26.8 |
| 1971 | 79.1 | 56.1 | 82.1 | 83.0 | 95.9 | 96.5 | 93.9 | 82.1 | 25.5 |
| 1972 | 78.9 | 58.1 | 81.6 | 83.9 | 95.7 | 96.4 | 93.2 | 80.4 | 24.3 |
| 1973 | 78.8 | 59.7 | 81.3 | 85.2 | 95.7 | 96.2 | 93.0 | 78.2 | 22.7 |
| 1974 | 78.7 | 60.7 | 81.0 | 85.9 | 95.8 | 96.0 | 92.2 | 77.3 | 22.4 |
| 1975 | 77.9 | 59.1 | 80.3 | 84.5 | 95.2 | 95.6 | 92.1 | 75.6 | 21.6 |
| 1976 | 77.5 | 59.3 | 79.8 | 85.2 | 95.2 | 95.4 | 91.6 | 74.3 | 20.2 |
| 1977 | 77.7 | 60.9 | 79.7 | 85.6 | 95.3 | 95.7 | 91.1 | 73.8 | 20.0 |
| 1978 | 77.9 | 62.0 | 79.8 | 85.9 | 95.3 | 95.7 | 91.3 | 73.3 | 20.4 |
| 1979 | 77.8 | 61.5 | 79.8 | 86.4 | 95.3 | 95.7 | 91.4 | 72.8 | 19.9 |
| 1980 | 77.4 | 60.5 | 79.4 | 85.9 | 95.2 | 95.5 | 91.2 | 72.1 | 19.0 |
| 1981 | 77.0 | 59.0 | 79.0 | 85.5 | 94.9 | 95.4 | 91.4 | 70.6 | 18.4 |
| 1982 | 76.6 | 56.7 | 78.7 | 84.9 | 94.7 | 95.3 | 91.2 | 70.2 | 17.8 |
| 1983 | 76.4 | 56.2 | 78.5 | 84.8 | 94.2 | 95.2 | 91.2 | 69.4 | 17.4 |
| 1984 | 76.4 | 56.0 | 78.3 | 85.0 | 94.4 | 95.4 | 91.2 | 68.5 | 16.3 |
| 1985 | 76.3 | 56.8 | 78.1 | 85.0 | 94.7 | 95.0 | 91.0 | 67.9 | 15.8 |
| 1986 | 76.3 | 56.4 | 78.1 | 85.8 | 94.6 | 94.8 | 91.0 | 67.3 | 16.0 |
| 1987 | 76.2 | 56.1 | 78.0 | 85.2 | 94.6 | 94.6 | 90.7 | 67.6 | 16.3 |
| 1988 | 76.2 | 56.9 | 77.9 | 85.0 | 94.3 | 94.5 | 90.9 | 67.0 | 16.5 |
| 1989 | 76.4 | 57.9 | 78.1 | 85.3 | 94.4 | 94.5 | 91.1 | 67.2 | 16.6 |
| 1990 | 76.4 | 55.7 | 78.2 | 84.4 | 94.1 | 94.3 | 90.7 | 67.8 | 16.3 |
| 1991 | 75.8 | 53.2 | 77.7 | 83.5 | 93.6 | 94.1 | 90.5 | 67.0 | 15.7 |
| 1992 | 75.8 | 53.4 | 77.7 | 83.3 | 93.8 | 93.7 | 90.7 | 67.0 | 16.1 |
| 1993 | 75.4 | 53.2 | 77.3 | 83.2 | 93.4 | 93.4 | 90.1 | 66.5 | 15.6 |
| 1994 | 75.1 | 54.1 | 76.8 | 83.1 | 92.6 | 92.8 | 89.1 | 65.5 | 16.8 |
| 1995 | 75.0 | 54.8 | 76.7 | 83.1 | 93.0 | 92.3 | 88.8 | 66.0 | 16.8 |
| 1996 | 74.9 | 53.2 | 76.8 | 82.5 | 93.2 | 92.4 | 89.1 | 67.0 | 16.9 |
| 1997 | 75.0 | 52.3 | 77.0 | 82.5 | 93.0 | 92.6 | 89.5 | 67.6 | 17.1 |
| 1998 | 74.9 | 53.3 | 76.8 | 82.0 | 93.2 | 92.6 | 89.2 | 68.1 | 16.5 |
| 1999 | 74.7 | 52.9 | 76.7 | 81.9 | 93.3 | 92.8 | 88.8 | 67.9 | 16.9 |
| 2000 | 74.8 | 52.8 | 76.7 | 82.6 | 93.4 | 92.7 | 88.6 | 67.3 | 17.7 |
| 2001 | 74.4 | 50.2 | 76.5 | 81.6 | 92.7 | 92.5 | 88.5 | 68.3 | 17.7 |
| 2002 | 74.1 | 47.5 | 76.3 | 80.7 | 92.4 | 92.1 | 88.5 | 69.2 | 17.9 |
| 2003 | 73.5 | 44.3 | 75.9 | 80.0 | 91.8 | 92.1 | 87.7 | 68.7 | 18.6 |
| 2004 | 73.3 | 43.9 | 75.8 | 79.6 | 91.9 | 91.9 | 87.5 | 68.7 | 19.0 |
| 2005 | 73.3 | 43.2 | 75.8 | 79.1 | 91.7 | 92.1 | 87.7 | 69.3 | 19.8 |
| 2006 | 73.5 | 43.7 | 75.9 | 79.6 | 91.7 | 92.1 | 88.1 | 69.6 | 20.3 |
| 2007 | 73.2 | 41.1 | 75.9 | 78.7 | 92.2 | 92.3 | 88.2 | 69.6 | 20.5 |
| 2008 | 73.0 | 40.1 | 75.7 | 78.7 | 91.5 | 92.2 | 88.0 | 70.4 | 21.5 |
| 2009 | 72.0 | 37.3 | 74.8 | 76.2 | 90.3 | 91.7 | 87.4 | 70.2 | 21.9 |
| 2010 | 71.2 | 34.9 | 74.1 | 74.5 | 89.7 | 91.5 | 86.8 | 70.0 | 22.1 |
| 2011 | 70.5 | 33.7 | 73.4 | 74.7 | 89.2 | 90.9 | 86.2 | 69.3 | 22.8 |
| 2012 | 70.2 | 34.0 | 73.0 | 74.5 | 89.5 | 90.7 | 86.1 | 69.9 | 23.6 |
| 2013 | 69.7 | 34.2 | 72.5 | 73.9 | 89.2 | 90.7 | 85.5 | 70.0 | 23.5 |
| 2014 | 69.2 | 33.5 | 71.9 | 73.9 | 88.7 | 90.5 | 85.6 | 69.9 | 23.0 |
| 2015 | 69.1 | 34.2 | 71.7 | 73.0 | 88.8 | 90.3 | 85.9 | 69.8 | 23.4 |

**Table 1-8. Civilian Labor Force Participation Rates, by Age, Sex, Race, and Hispanic Origin, 1948–2015**
—*Continued*

(Percent.)

| Race, Hispanic origin, sex, and year | 16 years and over | 16 to 19 years | 20 years and over | | | | | | |
|---|---|---|---|---|---|---|---|---|---|
| | | | Total | 20 to 24 years | 25 to 34 years | 35 to 44 years | 45 to 54 years | 55 to 64 years | 65 years and over |
| **ALL RACES** | | | | | | | | | |
| **Women** | | | | | | | | | |
| 1948 | 32.7 | 42.0 | 31.8 | 45.3 | 33.2 | 36.9 | 35.0 | 24.3 | 9.1 |
| 1949 | 33.1 | 42.4 | 32.3 | 45.0 | 33.4 | 38.1 | 35.9 | 25.3 | 9.6 |
| 1950 | 33.9 | 41.0 | 33.3 | 46.0 | 34.0 | 39.1 | 37.9 | 27.0 | 9.7 |
| 1951 | 34.6 | 42.4 | 34.0 | 46.5 | 35.4 | 39.8 | 39.7 | 27.6 | 8.9 |
| 1952 | 34.7 | 42.2 | 34.1 | 44.7 | 35.4 | 40.4 | 40.1 | 28.7 | 9.1 |
| 1953 | 34.4 | 40.7 | 33.9 | 44.3 | 34.0 | 41.3 | 40.4 | 29.1 | 10.0 |
| 1954 | 34.6 | 39.4 | 34.2 | 45.1 | 34.4 | 41.2 | 41.2 | 30.0 | 9.3 |
| 1955 | 35.7 | 39.7 | 35.4 | 45.9 | 34.9 | 41.6 | 43.8 | 32.5 | 10.6 |
| 1956 | 36.9 | 42.2 | 36.4 | 46.3 | 35.4 | 43.1 | 45.5 | 34.9 | 10.8 |
| 1957 | 36.9 | 41.1 | 36.5 | 45.9 | 35.6 | 43.3 | 46.5 | 34.5 | 10.5 |
| 1958 | 37.1 | 39.0 | 36.9 | 46.3 | 35.6 | 43.4 | 47.8 | 35.2 | 10.3 |
| 1959 | 37.1 | 38.2 | 37.1 | 45.1 | 35.3 | 43.4 | 49.0 | 36.6 | 10.2 |
| 1960 | 37.7 | 39.3 | 37.6 | 46.1 | 36.0 | 43.4 | 49.9 | 37.2 | 10.8 |
| 1961 | 38.1 | 39.7 | 38.0 | 47.0 | 36.4 | 43.8 | 50.1 | 37.9 | 10.7 |
| 1962 | 37.9 | 39.0 | 37.8 | 47.3 | 36.3 | 44.1 | 50.0 | 38.7 | 10.0 |
| 1963 | 38.3 | 38.0 | 38.3 | 47.5 | 37.2 | 44.9 | 50.6 | 39.7 | 9.6 |
| 1964 | 38.7 | 37.0 | 38.9 | 49.4 | 37.2 | 45.0 | 51.4 | 40.2 | 10.1 |
| 1965 | 39.3 | 38.0 | 39.4 | 49.9 | 38.5 | 46.1 | 50.9 | 41.1 | 10.0 |
| 1966 | 40.3 | 41.4 | 40.1 | 51.5 | 39.8 | 46.8 | 51.7 | 41.8 | 9.6 |
| 1967 | 41.1 | 41.6 | 41.1 | 53.3 | 41.9 | 48.1 | 51.8 | 42.4 | 9.6 |
| 1968 | 41.6 | 41.9 | 41.6 | 54.5 | 42.6 | 48.9 | 52.3 | 42.4 | 9.6 |
| 1969 | 42.7 | 43.2 | 42.7 | 56.7 | 43.7 | 49.9 | 53.8 | 43.1 | 9.9 |
| 1970 | 43.3 | 44.0 | 43.3 | 57.7 | 45.0 | 51.1 | 54.4 | 43.0 | 9.7 |
| 1971 | 43.4 | 43.4 | 43.3 | 57.7 | 45.6 | 51.6 | 54.3 | 42.9 | 9.5 |
| 1972 | 43.9 | 45.8 | 43.7 | 59.1 | 47.8 | 52.0 | 53.9 | 42.1 | 9.3 |
| 1973 | 44.7 | 47.8 | 44.4 | 61.1 | 50.4 | 53.3 | 53.7 | 41.1 | 8.9 |
| 1974 | 45.7 | 49.1 | 45.3 | 63.1 | 52.6 | 54.7 | 54.6 | 40.7 | 8.1 |
| 1975 | 46.3 | 49.1 | 46.0 | 64.1 | 54.9 | 55.8 | 54.6 | 40.9 | 8.2 |
| 1976 | 47.3 | 49.8 | 47.0 | 65.0 | 57.3 | 57.8 | 55.0 | 41.0 | 8.2 |
| 1977 | 48.4 | 51.2 | 48.1 | 66.5 | 59.7 | 59.6 | 55.8 | 40.9 | 8.1 |
| 1978 | 50.0 | 53.7 | 49.6 | 68.3 | 62.2 | 61.6 | 57.1 | 41.3 | 8.3 |
| 1979 | 50.9 | 54.2 | 50.6 | 69.0 | 63.9 | 63.6 | 58.3 | 41.7 | 8.3 |
| 1980 | 51.5 | 52.9 | 51.3 | 68.9 | 65.5 | 65.5 | 59.9 | 41.3 | 8.1 |
| 1981 | 52.1 | 51.8 | 52.1 | 69.6 | 66.7 | 66.8 | 61.1 | 41.4 | 8.0 |
| 1982 | 52.6 | 51.4 | 52.7 | 69.8 | 68.0 | 68.0 | 61.6 | 41.8 | 7.9 |
| 1983 | 52.9 | 50.8 | 53.1 | 69.9 | 69.0 | 68.7 | 61.9 | 41.5 | 7.8 |
| 1984 | 53.6 | 51.8 | 53.7 | 70.4 | 69.8 | 70.1 | 62.9 | 41.7 | 7.5 |
| 1985 | 54.5 | 52.1 | 54.7 | 71.8 | 70.9 | 71.8 | 64.4 | 42.0 | 7.3 |
| 1986 | 55.3 | 53.0 | 55.5 | 72.4 | 71.6 | 73.1 | 65.9 | 42.3 | 7.4 |
| 1987 | 56.0 | 53.3 | 56.2 | 73.0 | 72.4 | 74.5 | 67.1 | 42.7 | 7.4 |
| 1988 | 56.6 | 53.6 | 56.8 | 72.7 | 72.7 | 75.2 | 69.0 | 43.5 | 7.9 |
| 1989 | 57.4 | 53.9 | 57.7 | 72.4 | 73.5 | 76.0 | 70.5 | 45.0 | 8.4 |
| 1990 | 57.5 | 51.6 | 58.0 | 71.3 | 73.5 | 76.4 | 71.2 | 45.2 | 8.6 |
| 1991 | 57.4 | 50.0 | 57.9 | 70.1 | 73.1 | 76.5 | 72.0 | 45.2 | 8.5 |
| 1992 | 57.8 | 49.1 | 58.5 | 70.9 | 73.9 | 76.7 | 72.6 | 46.5 | 8.3 |
| 1993 | 57.9 | 49.7 | 58.5 | 70.9 | 73.4 | 76.6 | 73.5 | 47.2 | 8.1 |
| 1994 | 58.8 | 51.3 | 59.3 | 71.0 | 74.0 | 77.1 | 74.6 | 48.9 | 9.2 |
| 1995 | 58.9 | 52.2 | 59.4 | 70.3 | 74.9 | 77.2 | 74.4 | 49.2 | 8.8 |
| 1996 | 59.3 | 51.3 | 59.9 | 71.3 | 75.2 | 77.5 | 75.4 | 49.6 | 8.6 |
| 1997 | 59.8 | 51.0 | 60.5 | 72.7 | 76.0 | 77.7 | 76.0 | 50.9 | 8.6 |
| 1998 | 59.8 | 52.3 | 60.4 | 73.0 | 76.3 | 77.1 | 76.2 | 51.2 | 8.6 |
| 1999 | 60.0 | 51.0 | 60.7 | 73.2 | 76.4 | 77.2 | 76.7 | 51.5 | 8.9 |
| 2000 | 59.9 | 51.2 | 60.6 | 73.1 | 76.1 | 77.2 | 76.8 | 51.9 | 9.4 |
| 2001 | 59.8 | 49.0 | 60.6 | 72.7 | 75.5 | 77.1 | 76.4 | 53.2 | 9.6 |
| 2002 | 59.6 | 47.3 | 60.5 | 72.1 | 75.1 | 76.4 | 76.0 | 55.2 | 9.8 |
| 2003 | 59.5 | 44.8 | 60.6 | 70.8 | 74.1 | 76.0 | 76.8 | 56.6 | 10.6 |
| 2004 | 59.2 | 43.8 | 60.3 | 70.5 | 73.6 | 75.6 | 76.5 | 56.3 | 11.1 |
| 2005 | 59.3 | 44.2 | 60.4 | 70.1 | 73.9 | 75.8 | 76.0 | 57.0 | 11.5 |
| 2006 | 59.4 | 43.7 | 60.5 | 69.5 | 74.4 | 75.9 | 76.0 | 58.2 | 11.7 |
| 2007 | 59.3 | 41.5 | 60.6 | 70.1 | 74.5 | 75.5 | 76.0 | 58.3 | 12.6 |
| 2008 | 59.5 | 40.2 | 60.9 | 70.0 | 75.2 | 76.1 | 76.1 | 59.1 | 13.3 |
| 2009 | 59.2 | 37.7 | 60.8 | 69.6 | 75.0 | 75.9 | 76.0 | 60.0 | 13.6 |
| 2010 | 58.6 | 35.0 | 60.3 | 68.3 | 74.7 | 75.2 | 75.7 | 60.2 | 13.8 |
| 2011 | 58.1 | 34.6 | 59.8 | 67.8 | 73.9 | 74.7 | 75.4 | 59.5 | 14.0 |
| 2012 | 57.7 | 34.6 | 59.3 | 67.4 | 74.1 | 74.8 | 74.7 | 59.4 | 14.4 |
| 2013 | 57.2 | 34.7 | 58.8 | 67.5 | 73.5 | 74.0 | 74.1 | 59.2 | 14.9 |
| 2014 | 57.0 | 34.5 | 58.5 | 67.7 | 73.8 | 74.1 | 73.8 | 58.8 | 15.1 |
| 2015 | 56.7 | 34.4 | 58.2 | 68.3 | 73.4 | 74.3 | 73.4 | 58.5 | 15.3 |

## Table 1-8.  Civilian Labor Force Participation Rates, by Age, Sex, Race, and Hispanic Origin, 1948–2015
### —Continued

(Percent.)

| Race, Hispanic origin, sex, and year | 16 years and over | 16 to 19 years | 20 years and over | | | | | | |
|---|---|---|---|---|---|---|---|---|---|
| | | | Total | 20 to 24 years | 25 to 34 years | 35 to 44 years | 45 to 54 years | 55 to 64 years | 65 years and over |
| **WHITE** | | | | | | | | | |
| **Both Sexes** | | | | | | | | | |
| 1954 | 58.2 | 48.8 | 58.9 | 61.0 | 63.5 | 68.0 | 67.9 | 58.4 | 23.7 |
| 1955 | 58.7 | 49.3 | 59.5 | 62.4 | 64.0 | 68.3 | 69.2 | 59.3 | 23.9 |
| 1956 | 59.4 | 51.3 | 60.1 | 64.1 | 64.0 | 68.9 | 70.1 | 60.6 | 24.2 |
| 1957 | 59.1 | 50.3 | 59.8 | 63.7 | 64.1 | 68.8 | 70.5 | 59.9 | 22.8 |
| 1958 | 58.9 | 47.9 | 59.8 | 64.1 | 64.2 | 68.8 | 71.0 | 60.3 | 21.7 |
| 1959 | 58.7 | 47.4 | 59.7 | 63.7 | 64.3 | 68.7 | 71.5 | 60.7 | 21.0 |
| 1960 | 58.8 | 47.9 | 59.8 | 64.8 | 64.7 | 68.6 | 71.7 | 60.6 | 20.8 |
| 1961 | 58.8 | 47.4 | 59.9 | 65.5 | 64.8 | 68.8 | 71.7 | 61.3 | 20.0 |
| 1962 | 58.3 | 46.6 | 59.4 | 65.0 | 64.4 | 69.0 | 71.8 | 61.3 | 19.0 |
| 1963 | 58.2 | 45.7 | 59.4 | 64.9 | 64.8 | 69.4 | 72.3 | 61.8 | 17.9 |
| 1964 | 58.2 | 45.1 | 59.6 | 65.8 | 64.9 | 69.5 | 72.5 | 61.8 | 17.8 |
| 1965 | 58.4 | 46.5 | 59.7 | 65.7 | 65.6 | 70.1 | 72.2 | 61.7 | 17.7 |
| 1966 | 58.7 | 49.1 | 59.8 | 66.0 | 66.3 | 70.4 | 72.5 | 61.9 | 17.1 |
| 1967 | 59.2 | 49.2 | 60.3 | 66.8 | 67.4 | 71.2 | 72.5 | 62.3 | 17.0 |
| 1968 | 59.3 | 49.3 | 60.4 | 66.6 | 67.9 | 71.7 | 72.7 | 62.2 | 17.1 |
| 1969 | 59.9 | 50.6 | 60.9 | 67.9 | 68.4 | 72.3 | 73.3 | 62.1 | 17.2 |
| 1970 | 60.2 | 51.4 | 61.2 | 69.2 | 69.1 | 72.9 | 73.5 | 61.8 | 16.8 |
| 1971 | 60.1 | 51.6 | 61.1 | 69.6 | 69.3 | 73.0 | 73.4 | 61.3 | 16.1 |
| 1972 | 60.4 | 54.1 | 61.2 | 71.2 | 70.4 | 73.2 | 72.9 | 60.3 | 15.4 |
| 1973 | 60.8 | 56.0 | 61.4 | 73.3 | 72.0 | 73.9 | 72.7 | 58.6 | 14.4 |
| 1974 | 61.4 | 57.3 | 61.9 | 74.8 | 73.4 | 74.6 | 73.0 | 58.0 | 13.9 |
| 1975 | 61.5 | 56.7 | 62.0 | 75.2 | 74.4 | 75.1 | 73.0 | 57.4 | 13.6 |
| 1976 | 61.8 | 57.5 | 62.3 | 76.0 | 75.6 | 76.1 | 73.0 | 56.9 | 13.0 |
| 1977 | 62.5 | 59.3 | 62.9 | 77.1 | 77.0 | 77.1 | 73.2 | 56.6 | 12.9 |
| 1978 | 63.3 | 60.8 | 63.6 | 78.1 | 78.3 | 78.1 | 73.8 | 56.4 | 13.1 |
| 1979 | 63.9 | 61.1 | 64.2 | 78.9 | 79.4 | 79.3 | 74.6 | 56.5 | 12.9 |
| 1980 | 64.1 | 60.0 | 64.5 | 78.7 | 80.2 | 80.3 | 75.4 | 56.0 | 12.5 |
| 1981 | 64.3 | 58.9 | 64.8 | 79.1 | 81.0 | 81.0 | 76.2 | 55.2 | 12.2 |
| 1982 | 64.3 | 57.5 | 65.0 | 78.9 | 81.6 | 81.5 | 76.4 | 55.3 | 12.0 |
| 1983 | 64.3 | 56.9 | 65.0 | 79.0 | 81.8 | 81.9 | 76.5 | 54.7 | 11.8 |
| 1984 | 64.6 | 57.2 | 65.3 | 79.4 | 82.5 | 82.6 | 77.0 | 54.5 | 11.1 |
| 1985 | 65.0 | 57.5 | 65.7 | 79.9 | 83.1 | 83.4 | 77.8 | 54.4 | 10.7 |
| 1986 | 65.5 | 57.8 | 66.1 | 80.6 | 83.6 | 84.0 | 78.5 | 54.3 | 11.0 |
| 1987 | 65.8 | 57.7 | 66.5 | 80.7 | 84.0 | 84.7 | 79.1 | 54.6 | 11.1 |
| 1988 | 66.2 | 58.6 | 66.8 | 80.6 | 84.1 | 85.0 | 80.3 | 55.1 | 11.4 |
| 1989 | 66.7 | 59.1 | 67.3 | 80.2 | 84.5 | 85.5 | 81.2 | 56.2 | 11.8 |
| 1990 | 66.9 | 57.5 | 67.6 | 79.8 | 84.6 | 85.9 | 81.3 | 56.5 | 11.9 |
| 1991 | 66.6 | 55.8 | 67.4 | 78.9 | 84.3 | 85.9 | 81.8 | 56.0 | 11.6 |
| 1992 | 66.8 | 54.7 | 67.7 | 79.4 | 84.6 | 85.8 | 82.2 | 56.8 | 11.6 |
| 1993 | 66.8 | 55.1 | 67.6 | 79.5 | 84.5 | 85.7 | 82.5 | 57.1 | 11.4 |
| 1994 | 67.1 | 56.4 | 67.9 | 79.5 | 84.4 | 85.7 | 82.7 | 57.6 | 12.5 |
| 1995 | 67.1 | 57.1 | 67.8 | 78.7 | 84.9 | 85.5 | 82.5 | 58.0 | 12.3 |
| 1996 | 67.2 | 55.9 | 68.1 | 79.1 | 84.9 | 85.7 | 83.1 | 58.7 | 12.3 |
| 1997 | 67.5 | 55.2 | 68.4 | 79.6 | 85.3 | 85.8 | 83.5 | 59.9 | 12.3 |
| 1998 | 67.3 | 56.0 | 68.2 | 79.5 | 85.4 | 85.3 | 83.4 | 60.1 | 12.0 |
| 1999 | 67.3 | 55.5 | 68.2 | 79.5 | 85.1 | 85.4 | 83.5 | 60.2 | 12.5 |
| 2000 | 67.3 | 55.5 | 68.2 | 79.9 | 85.1 | 85.4 | 83.5 | 60.0 | 13.0 |
| 2001 | 67.0 | 53.1 | 68.1 | 79.2 | 84.5 | 85.2 | 83.3 | 61.2 | 13.0 |
| 2002 | 66.8 | 50.5 | 68.1 | 78.6 | 84.5 | 84.7 | 83.0 | 62.8 | 13.3 |
| 2003 | 66.5 | 47.7 | 67.9 | 77.7 | 83.6 | 84.3 | 83.0 | 63.3 | 14.1 |
| 2004 | 66.3 | 47.1 | 67.7 | 77.1 | 83.5 | 84.1 | 82.9 | 63.2 | 14.6 |
| 2005 | 66.3 | 46.9 | 67.7 | 76.3 | 83.5 | 84.2 | 82.8 | 63.7 | 15.1 |
| 2006 | 66.5 | 46.7 | 67.9 | 76.5 | 83.8 | 84.3 | 83.0 | 64.7 | 15.5 |
| 2007 | 66.4 | 44.4 | 68.0 | 76.4 | 84.1 | 84.1 | 83.1 | 64.9 | 16.2 |
| 2008 | 66.3 | 43.1 | 68.0 | 76.3 | 83.9 | 84.4 | 82.9 | 65.7 | 17.0 |
| 2009 | 65.8 | 40.6 | 67.7 | 75.1 | 83.5 | 84.2 | 82.7 | 66.2 | 17.4 |
| 2010 | 65.1 | 37.7 | 67.1 | 73.4 | 83.2 | 83.8 | 82.2 | 66.1 | 17.6 |
| 2011 | 64.5 | 36.8 | 66.5 | 73.2 | 82.5 | 83.3 | 81.7 | 65.5 | 18.1 |
| 2012 | 64.0 | 36.9 | 65.9 | 73.1 | 82.6 | 83.2 | 81.2 | 65.9 | 18.7 |
| 2013 | 63.5 | 36.9 | 65.3 | 73.1 | 82.2 | 82.7 | 80.7 | 65.5 | 19.0 |
| 2014 | 63.1 | 36.2 | 64.9 | 73.0 | 82.3 | 82.7 | 80.5 | 65.3 | 18.8 |
| 2015 | 62.8 | 36.4 | 64.5 | 72.7 | 82.1 | 82.6 | 80.5 | 65.2 | 19.1 |

**Table 1-8.  Civilian Labor Force Participation Rates, by Age, Sex, Race, and Hispanic Origin, 1948–2015**
  —*Continued*

(Percent.)

| Race, Hispanic origin, sex, and year | 16 years and over | 16 to 19 years | 20 years and over | | | | | | |
|---|---|---|---|---|---|---|---|---|---|
| | | | Total | 20 to 24 years | 25 to 34 years | 35 to 44 years | 45 to 54 years | 55 to 64 years | 65 years and over |
| **WHITE** | | | | | | | | | |
| **Men** | | | | | | | | | |
| 1954 | 85.6 | 57.6 | 87.8 | 86.3 | 97.5 | 98.2 | 96.8 | 89.1 | 40.4 |
| 1955 | 85.4 | 58.6 | 87.5 | 86.5 | 97.8 | 98.2 | 96.7 | 88.4 | 39.6 |
| 1956 | 85.6 | 60.4 | 87.6 | 87.6 | 97.4 | 98.1 | 96.8 | 88.9 | 40.0 |
| 1957 | 84.8 | 59.2 | 86.9 | 86.6 | 97.2 | 98.0 | 96.7 | 88.0 | 37.7 |
| 1958 | 84.3 | 56.5 | 86.6 | 86.7 | 97.2 | 98.0 | 96.6 | 88.2 | 35.7 |
| 1959 | 83.8 | 55.9 | 86.3 | 87.3 | 97.5 | 98.0 | 96.3 | 87.9 | 34.3 |
| 1960 | 83.4 | 55.9 | 86.0 | 87.8 | 97.7 | 97.9 | 96.1 | 87.2 | 33.3 |
| 1961 | 83.0 | 54.5 | 85.7 | 87.6 | 97.7 | 97.9 | 95.9 | 87.8 | 31.9 |
| 1962 | 82.1 | 53.8 | 84.9 | 86.5 | 97.4 | 97.9 | 96.0 | 86.7 | 30.6 |
| 1963 | 81.5 | 53.1 | 84.4 | 85.8 | 97.4 | 97.8 | 96.2 | 86.6 | 28.4 |
| 1964 | 81.1 | 52.7 | 84.2 | 85.7 | 97.5 | 97.6 | 96.1 | 86.1 | 27.9 |
| 1965 | 80.8 | 54.1 | 83.9 | 85.3 | 97.4 | 97.7 | 95.9 | 85.2 | 27.9 |
| 1966 | 80.6 | 55.9 | 83.6 | 84.4 | 97.5 | 97.6 | 95.8 | 84.9 | 27.2 |
| 1967 | 80.6 | 56.3 | 83.5 | 84.0 | 97.5 | 97.7 | 95.6 | 84.9 | 27.1 |
| 1968 | 80.4 | 55.9 | 83.2 | 82.4 | 97.2 | 97.6 | 95.4 | 84.7 | 27.4 |
| 1969 | 80.2 | 56.8 | 83.0 | 82.6 | 97.0 | 97.4 | 95.1 | 83.9 | 27.3 |
| 1970 | 80.0 | 57.5 | 82.8 | 83.3 | 96.7 | 97.3 | 94.9 | 83.3 | 26.7 |
| 1971 | 79.6 | 57.9 | 82.3 | 83.2 | 96.3 | 97.0 | 94.7 | 82.6 | 25.6 |
| 1972 | 79.6 | 60.1 | 82.0 | 84.3 | 96.0 | 97.0 | 94.0 | 81.1 | 24.4 |
| 1973 | 79.4 | 62.0 | 81.6 | 85.8 | 96.2 | 96.8 | 93.5 | 78.9 | 22.7 |
| 1974 | 79.4 | 62.9 | 81.4 | 86.6 | 96.3 | 96.7 | 93.0 | 78.0 | 22.4 |
| 1975 | 78.7 | 61.9 | 80.7 | 85.5 | 95.8 | 96.4 | 92.9 | 76.4 | 21.7 |
| 1976 | 78.4 | 62.3 | 80.3 | 86.3 | 95.9 | 96.0 | 92.5 | 75.2 | 20.2 |
| 1977 | 78.5 | 64.0 | 80.2 | 86.8 | 96.0 | 96.2 | 92.1 | 74.6 | 20.0 |
| 1978 | 78.6 | 65.0 | 80.1 | 87.3 | 95.9 | 96.3 | 92.1 | 73.7 | 20.3 |
| 1979 | 78.6 | 64.8 | 80.1 | 87.6 | 96.0 | 96.4 | 92.2 | 73.4 | 20.0 |
| 1980 | 78.2 | 63.7 | 79.8 | 87.2 | 95.9 | 96.2 | 92.1 | 73.1 | 19.1 |
| 1981 | 77.9 | 62.4 | 79.5 | 87.0 | 95.8 | 96.1 | 92.4 | 71.5 | 18.5 |
| 1982 | 77.4 | 60.0 | 79.2 | 86.3 | 95.6 | 96.0 | 92.2 | 71.0 | 17.9 |
| 1983 | 77.1 | 59.4 | 78.9 | 86.1 | 95.2 | 96.0 | 91.9 | 70.0 | 17.7 |
| 1984 | 77.1 | 59.0 | 78.7 | 86.5 | 95.4 | 96.1 | 92.0 | 69.5 | 16.4 |
| 1985 | 77.0 | 59.7 | 78.5 | 86.4 | 95.7 | 95.7 | 92.0 | 68.8 | 15.9 |
| 1986 | 76.9 | 59.3 | 78.5 | 87.3 | 95.5 | 95.4 | 91.8 | 68.0 | 16.3 |
| 1987 | 76.8 | 59.0 | 78.4 | 86.9 | 95.5 | 95.4 | 91.6 | 68.1 | 16.5 |
| 1988 | 76.9 | 60.0 | 78.3 | 86.6 | 95.2 | 95.4 | 91.8 | 67.9 | 16.7 |
| 1989 | 77.1 | 61.0 | 78.5 | 86.8 | 95.4 | 95.3 | 92.2 | 68.3 | 16.8 |
| 1990 | 77.1 | 59.6 | 78.5 | 86.2 | 95.2 | 95.3 | 91.7 | 68.6 | 16.6 |
| 1991 | 76.5 | 57.3 | 78.0 | 85.4 | 94.9 | 95.0 | 91.4 | 67.7 | 15.9 |
| 1992 | 76.5 | 56.9 | 78.0 | 85.2 | 94.9 | 94.7 | 91.8 | 67.7 | 16.2 |
| 1993 | 76.2 | 56.6 | 77.7 | 85.5 | 94.7 | 94.5 | 91.3 | 67.3 | 15.9 |
| 1994 | 75.9 | 57.7 | 77.3 | 85.5 | 93.9 | 93.9 | 90.3 | 66.4 | 17.2 |
| 1995 | 75.7 | 58.5 | 77.1 | 85.1 | 94.1 | 93.4 | 90.0 | 67.1 | 16.9 |
| 1996 | 75.8 | 57.1 | 77.3 | 85.0 | 94.4 | 93.6 | 90.4 | 68.0 | 17.2 |
| 1997 | 75.9 | 56.1 | 77.5 | 85.1 | 94.2 | 93.7 | 90.6 | 68.9 | 17.4 |
| 1998 | 75.6 | 56.6 | 77.2 | 84.6 | 94.4 | 93.7 | 90.3 | 69.1 | 16.6 |
| 1999 | 75.6 | 56.4 | 77.2 | 84.9 | 94.3 | 93.8 | 90.1 | 69.1 | 17.2 |
| 2000 | 75.5 | 56.5 | 77.1 | 85.2 | 94.5 | 93.8 | 89.7 | 68.2 | 17.9 |
| 2001 | 75.1 | 53.7 | 76.9 | 84.1 | 93.9 | 93.6 | 89.7 | 69.1 | 17.8 |
| 2002 | 74.8 | 50.3 | 76.7 | 83.2 | 93.7 | 93.2 | 89.6 | 70.2 | 17.8 |
| 2003 | 74.2 | 47.5 | 76.3 | 82.5 | 93.3 | 93.1 | 88.8 | 69.7 | 18.6 |
| 2004 | 74.1 | 47.4 | 76.2 | 82.1 | 93.2 | 93.0 | 88.7 | 69.8 | 19.1 |
| 2005 | 74.1 | 46.2 | 76.2 | 81.4 | 93.0 | 93.0 | 89.0 | 70.4 | 20.0 |
| 2006 | 74.3 | 46.9 | 76.4 | 81.9 | 92.9 | 93.1 | 89.3 | 71.0 | 20.6 |
| 2007 | 74.0 | 44.3 | 76.3 | 80.9 | 93.4 | 93.1 | 89.6 | 71.2 | 20.8 |
| 2008 | 73.7 | 43.0 | 76.1 | 80.8 | 92.6 | 93.0 | 89.2 | 71.9 | 21.8 |
| 2009 | 72.8 | 40.3 | 75.3 | 78.6 | 91.6 | 92.7 | 88.8 | 71.8 | 22.2 |
| 2010 | 72.0 | 37.4 | 74.6 | 77.0 | 91.1 | 92.4 | 88.1 | 71.2 | 22.3 |
| 2011 | 71.3 | 36.1 | 73.9 | 77.1 | 90.5 | 92.1 | 87.5 | 70.8 | 23.0 |
| 2012 | 71.0 | 36.7 | 73.5 | 77.2 | 90.9 | 91.8 | 87.5 | 71.6 | 24.0 |
| 2013 | 70.5 | 36.6 | 72.9 | 76.9 | 90.5 | 91.6 | 86.9 | 71.6 | 24.0 |
| 2014 | 69.8 | 35.6 | 72.2 | 76.5 | 90.0 | 91.5 | 86.9 | 71.3 | 23.3 |
| 2015 | 69.7 | 36.7 | 72.0 | 75.5 | 90.3 | 91.3 | 87.2 | 71.5 | 23.7 |

**Table 1-8. Civilian Labor Force Participation Rates, by Age, Sex, Race, and Hispanic Origin, 1948–2015**
— *Continued*

(Percent.)

| Race, Hispanic origin, sex, and year | 16 years and over | 16 to 19 years | 20 years and over | | | | | | |
|---|---|---|---|---|---|---|---|---|---|
| | | | Total | 20 to 24 years | 25 to 34 years | 35 to 44 years | 45 to 54 years | 55 to 64 years | 65 years and over |
| **WHITE** | | | | | | | | | |
| **Women** | | | | | | | | | |
| 1954 | 33.3 | 40.6 | 32.7 | 44.4 | 32.5 | 39.3 | 39.8 | 29.1 | 9.1 |
| 1955 | 34.5 | 40.7 | 34.0 | 45.8 | 32.8 | 40.0 | 42.7 | 31.8 | 10.5 |
| 1956 | 35.7 | 43.1 | 35.1 | 46.5 | 33.2 | 41.5 | 44.4 | 34.0 | 10.6 |
| 1957 | 35.7 | 42.2 | 35.2 | 45.8 | 33.6 | 41.5 | 45.4 | 33.7 | 10.2 |
| 1958 | 35.8 | 40.1 | 35.5 | 46.0 | 33.6 | 41.4 | 46.5 | 34.5 | 10.1 |
| 1959 | 36.0 | 39.6 | 35.6 | 44.5 | 33.4 | 41.4 | 47.8 | 35.7 | 10.0 |
| 1960 | 36.5 | 40.3 | 36.2 | 45.7 | 34.1 | 41.5 | 48.6 | 36.2 | 10.6 |
| 1961 | 36.9 | 40.6 | 36.6 | 46.9 | 34.3 | 41.8 | 48.9 | 37.2 | 10.5 |
| 1962 | 36.7 | 39.8 | 36.5 | 47.1 | 34.1 | 42.2 | 48.9 | 38.0 | 9.8 |
| 1963 | 37.2 | 38.7 | 37.0 | 47.3 | 34.8 | 43.1 | 49.5 | 38.9 | 9.4 |
| 1964 | 37.5 | 37.8 | 37.5 | 48.8 | 35.0 | 43.3 | 50.2 | 39.4 | 9.9 |
| 1965 | 38.1 | 39.2 | 38.0 | 49.2 | 36.3 | 44.4 | 49.9 | 40.3 | 9.7 |
| 1966 | 39.2 | 42.6 | 38.8 | 51.0 | 37.7 | 45.0 | 50.6 | 41.1 | 9.4 |
| 1967 | 40.1 | 42.5 | 39.8 | 53.1 | 39.7 | 46.4 | 50.9 | 41.9 | 9.3 |
| 1968 | 40.7 | 43.0 | 40.4 | 54.0 | 40.6 | 47.5 | 51.5 | 42.0 | 9.4 |
| 1969 | 41.8 | 44.6 | 41.5 | 56.4 | 41.7 | 48.6 | 53.0 | 42.6 | 9.7 |
| 1970 | 42.6 | 45.6 | 42.2 | 57.7 | 43.2 | 49.9 | 53.7 | 42.6 | 9.5 |
| 1971 | 42.6 | 45.4 | 42.3 | 58.0 | 43.7 | 50.2 | 53.6 | 42.5 | 9.3 |
| 1972 | 43.2 | 48.1 | 42.7 | 59.4 | 46.0 | 50.7 | 53.4 | 41.9 | 9.0 |
| 1973 | 44.1 | 50.1 | 43.5 | 61.7 | 48.7 | 52.2 | 53.4 | 40.7 | 8.7 |
| 1974 | 45.2 | 51.7 | 44.4 | 63.9 | 51.3 | 53.6 | 54.3 | 40.4 | 8.0 |
| 1975 | 45.9 | 51.5 | 45.3 | 65.5 | 53.8 | 54.9 | 54.3 | 40.6 | 8.0 |
| 1976 | 46.9 | 52.8 | 46.2 | 66.3 | 56.0 | 57.1 | 54.7 | 40.7 | 7.9 |
| 1977 | 48.0 | 54.5 | 47.3 | 67.8 | 58.5 | 58.9 | 55.3 | 40.7 | 7.9 |
| 1978 | 49.4 | 56.7 | 48.7 | 69.3 | 61.2 | 60.7 | 56.7 | 41.1 | 8.1 |
| 1979 | 50.5 | 57.4 | 49.8 | 70.5 | 63.1 | 63.0 | 58.1 | 41.5 | 8.1 |
| 1980 | 51.2 | 56.2 | 50.6 | 70.6 | 64.8 | 65.0 | 59.6 | 40.9 | 7.9 |
| 1981 | 51.9 | 55.4 | 51.5 | 71.5 | 66.4 | 66.4 | 60.9 | 40.9 | 7.9 |
| 1982 | 52.4 | 55.0 | 52.2 | 71.8 | 67.8 | 67.5 | 61.4 | 41.5 | 7.8 |
| 1983 | 52.7 | 54.5 | 52.5 | 72.1 | 68.7 | 68.2 | 61.9 | 41.1 | 7.8 |
| 1984 | 53.3 | 55.4 | 53.1 | 72.5 | 69.8 | 69.6 | 62.7 | 41.2 | 7.5 |
| 1985 | 54.1 | 55.2 | 54.0 | 73.8 | 70.9 | 71.4 | 64.2 | 41.5 | 7.0 |
| 1986 | 55.0 | 56.3 | 54.9 | 74.1 | 71.8 | 72.9 | 65.8 | 42.1 | 7.3 |
| 1987 | 55.7 | 56.5 | 55.6 | 74.8 | 72.5 | 74.2 | 67.2 | 42.4 | 7.2 |
| 1988 | 56.4 | 57.2 | 56.3 | 74.9 | 73.0 | 74.9 | 69.2 | 43.6 | 7.7 |
| 1989 | 57.2 | 57.1 | 57.2 | 74.0 | 73.8 | 75.9 | 70.6 | 45.2 | 8.2 |
| 1990 | 57.4 | 55.3 | 57.6 | 73.4 | 74.1 | 76.6 | 71.3 | 45.5 | 8.5 |
| 1991 | 57.4 | 54.1 | 57.6 | 72.5 | 73.8 | 76.8 | 72.4 | 45.4 | 8.5 |
| 1992 | 57.7 | 52.5 | 58.1 | 73.5 | 74.4 | 77.0 | 72.8 | 46.8 | 8.2 |
| 1993 | 58.0 | 53.5 | 58.3 | 73.4 | 74.3 | 76.9 | 74.0 | 47.6 | 8.1 |
| 1994 | 58.9 | 55.1 | 59.2 | 73.4 | 74.9 | 77.5 | 75.2 | 49.4 | 9.2 |
| 1995 | 59.0 | 55.5 | 59.2 | 72.3 | 75.8 | 77.6 | 75.2 | 49.5 | 9.0 |
| 1996 | 59.1 | 54.7 | 59.4 | 73.3 | 75.5 | 77.8 | 76.1 | 50.1 | 8.7 |
| 1997 | 59.5 | 54.1 | 59.9 | 73.9 | 76.3 | 77.9 | 76.6 | 51.5 | 8.6 |
| 1998 | 59.4 | 55.4 | 59.7 | 74.3 | 76.3 | 76.9 | 76.6 | 51.6 | 8.7 |
| 1999 | 59.6 | 54.5 | 59.9 | 73.9 | 76.0 | 77.1 | 77.1 | 52.0 | 8.9 |
| 2000 | 59.5 | 54.5 | 59.9 | 74.5 | 75.7 | 77.2 | 77.5 | 52.4 | 9.4 |
| 2001 | 59.4 | 52.4 | 59.9 | 74.2 | 75.1 | 77.0 | 77.1 | 53.8 | 9.6 |
| 2002 | 59.3 | 50.8 | 60.0 | 74.0 | 75.0 | 76.3 | 76.6 | 55.8 | 9.9 |
| 2003 | 59.2 | 47.9 | 59.9 | 72.7 | 73.7 | 75.5 | 77.3 | 57.4 | 10.8 |
| 2004 | 58.9 | 46.7 | 59.7 | 71.9 | 73.6 | 75.2 | 77.1 | 57.0 | 11.2 |
| 2005 | 58.9 | 47.6 | 59.7 | 71.0 | 73.7 | 75.4 | 76.7 | 57.5 | 11.4 |
| 2006 | 59.0 | 46.6 | 59.9 | 70.9 | 74.3 | 75.5 | 76.7 | 58.7 | 11.6 |
| 2007 | 59.0 | 44.6 | 60.1 | 71.6 | 74.5 | 75.0 | 76.6 | 58.9 | 12.7 |
| 2008 | 59.2 | 43.3 | 60.3 | 71.6 | 74.9 | 75.8 | 76.6 | 59.7 | 13.3 |
| 2009 | 59.1 | 40.9 | 60.4 | 71.6 | 75.1 | 75.7 | 76.7 | 60.8 | 13.6 |
| 2010 | 58.5 | 38.0 | 59.9 | 69.7 | 74.9 | 75.0 | 76.3 | 61.1 | 13.9 |
| 2011 | 58.0 | 37.5 | 59.4 | 69.1 | 74.2 | 74.4 | 76.1 | 60.6 | 14.1 |
| 2012 | 57.4 | 37.1 | 58.7 | 69.0 | 74.3 | 74.5 | 75.2 | 60.5 | 14.4 |
| 2013 | 56.9 | 37.2 | 58.2 | 69.2 | 73.9 | 73.9 | 74.7 | 59.9 | 14.9 |
| 2014 | 56.7 | 36.8 | 57.9 | 69.5 | 74.5 | 74.0 | 74.3 | 57.2 | 14.5 |
| 2015 | 56.2 | 36.1 | 57.5 | 69.8 | 73.8 | 73.9 | 73.9 | 59.3 | 15.2 |

**Table 1-8.  Civilian Labor Force Participation Rates, by Age, Sex, Race, and Hispanic Origin, 1948–2015**
—*Continued*

(Percent.)

| Race, Hispanic origin, sex, and year | 16 years and over | 16 to 19 years | 20 years and over | | | | | | |
|---|---|---|---|---|---|---|---|---|---|
| | | | Total | 20 to 24 years | 25 to 34 years | 35 to 44 years | 45 to 54 years | 55 to 64 years | 65 years and over |
| **BLACK** | | | | | | | | | |
| **Both Sexes** | | | | | | | | | |
| 1980 | 61.0 | 38.9 | 64.1 | 69.0 | 79.5 | 77.4 | 71.4 | 52.6 | 13.0 |
| 1981 | 60.8 | 37.7 | 64.2 | 69.2 | 78.5 | 78.4 | 71.2 | 52.8 | 12.0 |
| 1982 | 61.0 | 36.6 | 64.3 | 68.6 | 78.7 | 79.8 | 71.1 | 52.3 | 11.5 |
| 1983 | 61.5 | 36.4 | 64.9 | 68.4 | 79.8 | 80.2 | 72.1 | 52.5 | 10.5 |
| 1984 | 62.2 | 38.3 | 65.2 | 69.2 | 79.3 | 81.0 | 73.0 | 51.6 | 10.3 |
| 1985 | 62.9 | 41.2 | 65.6 | 70.0 | 79.8 | 81.5 | 73.4 | 51.4 | 11.2 |
| 1986 | 63.3 | 41.3 | 65.9 | 71.7 | 80.1 | 81.9 | 74.3 | 50.6 | 9.7 |
| 1987 | 63.8 | 41.6 | 66.5 | 70.5 | 80.7 | 82.6 | 74.7 | 52.4 | 10.7 |
| 1988 | 63.8 | 40.8 | 66.5 | 70.5 | 80.8 | 82.6 | 75.0 | 50.6 | 11.5 |
| 1989 | 64.2 | 42.5 | 66.7 | 72.2 | 80.9 | 82.7 | 75.5 | 48.3 | 11.6 |
| 1990 | 64.0 | 38.7 | 66.9 | 68.8 | 79.7 | 82.4 | 76.5 | 49.6 | 11.1 |
| 1991 | 63.3 | 35.4 | 66.4 | 67.7 | 78.5 | 82.0 | 76.2 | 50.4 | 10.7 |
| 1992 | 63.9 | 37.9 | 66.8 | 67.4 | 79.7 | 81.4 | 76.2 | 51.6 | 10.6 |
| 1993 | 63.2 | 37.0 | 66.0 | 67.8 | 78.3 | 81.0 | 75.2 | 50.2 | 9.5 |
| 1994 | 63.4 | 38.5 | 66.0 | 68.8 | 78.3 | 80.8 | 74.8 | 49.3 | 10.6 |
| 1995 | 63.7 | 39.9 | 66.3 | 68.7 | 80.0 | 80.4 | 74.1 | 50.3 | 10.5 |
| 1996 | 64.1 | 39.2 | 66.9 | 69.0 | 81.1 | 81.0 | 74.9 | 50.9 | 9.8 |
| 1997 | 64.7 | 38.7 | 67.6 | 70.9 | 82.0 | 81.4 | 76.3 | 50.5 | 10.0 |
| 1998 | 65.6 | 41.6 | 68.2 | 70.6 | 83.0 | 82.2 | 76.7 | 52.3 | 10.3 |
| 1999 | 65.8 | 38.7 | 68.9 | 71.4 | 85.2 | 83.0 | 76.4 | 51.4 | 10.4 |
| 2000 | 65.8 | 39.4 | 68.7 | 71.8 | 84.1 | 82.3 | 76.9 | 52.5 | 11.6 |
| 2001 | 65.3 | 37.6 | 68.2 | 69.9 | 83.6 | 82.0 | 75.9 | 53.9 | 12.6 |
| 2002 | 64.8 | 36.0 | 67.8 | 68.6 | 82.4 | 81.6 | 76.1 | 54.7 | 12.5 |
| 2003 | 64.3 | 32.4 | 67.6 | 68.2 | 81.6 | 82.9 | 75.8 | 54.4 | 12.9 |
| 2004 | 63.8 | 31.4 | 67.2 | 68.3 | 81.2 | 82.1 | 75.5 | 54.4 | 13.1 |
| 2005 | 64.2 | 32.4 | 67.4 | 69.0 | 81.7 | 82.3 | 75.7 | 55.3 | 13.6 |
| 2006 | 64.1 | 34.0 | 67.3 | 68.8 | 81.8 | 82.0 | 75.8 | 55.4 | 13.7 |
| 2007 | 63.7 | 30.3 | 67.2 | 68.3 | 81.7 | 82.7 | 75.7 | 55.1 | 14.0 |
| 2008 | 63.7 | 29.4 | 67.4 | 68.0 | 82.2 | 83.0 | 76.1 | 55.6 | 15.0 |
| 2009 | 62.4 | 27.2 | 66.1 | 66.0 | 80.4 | 81.7 | 75.2 | 55.5 | 15.3 |
| 2010 | 62.2 | 25.5 | 66.0 | 66.9 | 80.5 | 81.4 | 75.0 | 55.7 | 15.2 |
| 2011 | 61.4 | 24.9 | 65.0 | 66.5 | 79.1 | 80.6 | 73.9 | 54.5 | 16.1 |
| 2012 | 61.5 | 26.9 | 64.9 | 66.5 | 79.4 | 80.7 | 74.5 | 55.3 | 16.4 |
| 2013 | 61.2 | 28.0 | 64.2 | 65.3 | 78.5 | 80.7 | 74.1 | 55.6 | 16.2 |
| 2014 | 61.2 | 27.2 | 64.2 | 66.6 | 79.1 | 80.5 | 74.6 | 55.3 | 16.1 |
| 2015 | 61.5 | 28.1 | 64.4 | 68.2 | 79.4 | 80.8 | 75.3 | 54.8 | 16.9 |
| **Men** | | | | | | | | | |
| 1980 | 70.3 | 43.2 | 75.1 | 79.9 | 90.9 | 89.1 | 83.0 | 61.9 | 16.9 |
| 1981 | 70.0 | 41.6 | 74.5 | 79.2 | 88.9 | 89.3 | 82.7 | 62.1 | 16.0 |
| 1982 | 70.1 | 39.8 | 74.7 | 78.7 | 89.2 | 89.8 | 82.2 | 61.9 | 15.9 |
| 1983 | 70.6 | 39.9 | 75.2 | 79.4 | 89.0 | 89.7 | 84.5 | 62.6 | 14.0 |
| 1984 | 70.8 | 41.7 | 74.8 | 79.1 | 88.9 | 90.0 | 83.7 | 58.9 | 13.7 |
| 1985 | 70.8 | 44.6 | 74.4 | 79.0 | 88.8 | 89.8 | 83.0 | 58.9 | 13.9 |
| 1986 | 71.2 | 43.7 | 74.8 | 80.1 | 89.6 | 89.6 | 84.1 | 59.1 | 12.6 |
| 1987 | 71.1 | 43.6 | 74.7 | 77.8 | 89.4 | 88.6 | 83.7 | 62.1 | 13.7 |
| 1988 | 71.0 | 43.8 | 74.6 | 79.3 | 89.3 | 88.2 | 83.5 | 59.4 | 14.3 |
| 1989 | 71.0 | 44.6 | 74.4 | 80.2 | 89.7 | 88.7 | 82.5 | 55.5 | 14.3 |
| 1990 | 71.0 | 40.7 | 75.0 | 76.8 | 88.8 | 88.1 | 83.5 | 58.0 | 13.0 |
| 1991 | 70.4 | 37.3 | 74.6 | 76.7 | 87.3 | 87.7 | 83.4 | 58.7 | 13.0 |
| 1992 | 70.7 | 40.6 | 74.3 | 75.4 | 88.0 | 86.5 | 81.8 | 60.0 | 13.7 |
| 1993 | 69.6 | 39.5 | 73.2 | 74.1 | 87.3 | 86.1 | 80.0 | 57.9 | 11.6 |
| 1994 | 69.1 | 40.8 | 72.5 | 73.9 | 86.2 | 85.9 | 79.1 | 54.5 | 12.7 |
| 1995 | 69.0 | 40.1 | 72.5 | 74.6 | 87.5 | 84.1 | 78.5 | 54.4 | 14.9 |
| 1996 | 68.7 | 39.5 | 72.3 | 73.4 | 87.5 | 84.4 | 78.5 | 55.6 | 12.9 |
| 1997 | 68.3 | 37.4 | 72.2 | 72.1 | 86.8 | 84.8 | 80.1 | 54.3 | 12.9 |
| 1998 | 69.0 | 40.7 | 72.5 | 71.8 | 87.1 | 85.0 | 79.9 | 57.3 | 14.0 |
| 1999 | 68.7 | 38.6 | 72.4 | 69.8 | 89.2 | 86.0 | 78.5 | 55.5 | 12.7 |
| 2000 | 69.2 | 39.2 | 72.8 | 73.3 | 87.8 | 85.2 | 79.2 | 57.4 | 14.4 |
| 2001 | 68.4 | 37.9 | 72.1 | 69.7 | 86.6 | 84.9 | 78.4 | 58.9 | 16.7 |
| 2002 | 68.4 | 37.3 | 72.1 | 70.7 | 85.9 | 84.7 | 79.5 | 58.4 | 16.9 |
| 2003 | 67.3 | 31.1 | 71.5 | 71.1 | 84.7 | 85.7 | 77.7 | 57.6 | 17.0 |
| 2004 | 66.7 | 30.0 | 70.9 | 69.9 | 86.1 | 84.0 | 76.9 | 57.1 | 17.0 |
| 2005 | 67.3 | 32.6 | 71.3 | 70.1 | 85.5 | 85.5 | 78.6 | 57.3 | 17.1 |
| 2006 | 67.0 | 32.3 | 71.1 | 71.6 | 85.7 | 84.4 | 79.2 | 55.9 | 16.7 |
| 2007 | 66.8 | 29.4 | 71.2 | 71.1 | 86.1 | 86.3 | 78.6 | 54.4 | 17.3 |
| 2008 | 66.7 | 29.1 | 71.1 | 71.1 | 85.3 | 86.8 | 79.1 | 56.1 | 18.1 |
| 2009 | 65.0 | 26.4 | 69.6 | 67.6 | 83.2 | 85.1 | 77.4 | 56.8 | 18.3 |
| 2010 | 65.0 | 25.8 | 69.5 | 66.9 | 83.4 | 86.1 | 77.4 | 56.8 | 18.1 |
| 2011 | 64.2 | 25.7 | 68.4 | 67.0 | 82.6 | 83.7 | 76.1 | 55.9 | 19.1 |
| 2012 | 63.6 | 25.6 | 67.7 | 66.4 | 82.5 | 83.5 | 75.9 | 57.1 | 19.4 |
| 2013 | 63.5 | 27.2 | 67.2 | 66.2 | 82.0 | 84.1 | 75.5 | 56.8 | 18.5 |
| 2014 | 63.6 | 25.9 | 67.3 | 67.9 | 82.5 | 83.3 | 76.4 | 57.0 | 18.4 |
| 2015 | 63.8 | 26.3 | 67.3 | 68.9 | 82.1 | 83.1 | 77.4 | 56.5 | 18.9 |

## Table 1-8. Civilian Labor Force Participation Rates, by Age, Sex, Race, and Hispanic Origin, 1948–2015
### —Continued

(Percent.)

| Race, Hispanic origin, sex, and year | 16 years and over | 16 to 19 years | 20 years and over | | | | | | |
|---|---|---|---|---|---|---|---|---|---|
| | | | Total | 20 to 24 years | 25 to 34 years | 35 to 44 years | 45 to 54 years | 55 to 64 years | 65 years and over |
| **BLACK** | | | | | | | | | |
| **Women** | | | | | | | | | |
| 1980 | 53.1 | 34.9 | 55.6 | 60.2 | 70.5 | 68.1 | 61.4 | 44.8 | 10.2 |
| 1981 | 53.5 | 34.0 | 56.0 | 61.1 | 70.0 | 69.8 | 62.0 | 45.4 | 9.3 |
| 1982 | 53.7 | 33.5 | 56.2 | 60.1 | 70.2 | 71.7 | 62.4 | 44.8 | 8.5 |
| 1983 | 54.2 | 33.0 | 56.8 | 59.1 | 72.3 | 72.6 | 62.3 | 44.8 | 8.2 |
| 1984 | 55.2 | 35.0 | 57.6 | 60.7 | 71.5 | 73.7 | 64.5 | 46.1 | 8.0 |
| 1985 | 56.5 | 37.9 | 58.6 | 62.5 | 72.4 | 74.8 | 65.7 | 45.3 | 9.4 |
| 1986 | 56.9 | 39.1 | 58.9 | 64.6 | 72.4 | 75.8 | 66.5 | 43.6 | 7.8 |
| 1987 | 58.0 | 39.6 | 60.0 | 64.4 | 73.5 | 77.8 | 67.5 | 44.4 | 8.6 |
| 1988 | 58.0 | 37.9 | 60.1 | 63.2 | 73.7 | 78.1 | 68.3 | 43.4 | 9.6 |
| 1989 | 58.7 | 40.4 | 60.6 | 65.5 | 73.6 | 78.0 | 70.0 | 42.4 | 9.8 |
| 1990 | 58.3 | 36.8 | 60.6 | 62.4 | 72.3 | 77.7 | 70.7 | 43.2 | 9.9 |
| 1991 | 57.5 | 33.5 | 60.0 | 60.3 | 71.4 | 77.2 | 70.2 | 44.1 | 9.2 |
| 1992 | 58.5 | 35.2 | 60.8 | 60.8 | 73.1 | 77.1 | 71.7 | 45.1 | 8.6 |
| 1993 | 57.9 | 34.6 | 60.2 | 62.6 | 70.9 | 76.8 | 71.2 | 44.4 | 8.3 |
| 1994 | 58.7 | 36.3 | 60.9 | 64.5 | 71.9 | 76.4 | 71.3 | 45.3 | 9.2 |
| 1995 | 59.5 | 39.8 | 61.4 | 63.7 | 73.9 | 77.3 | 70.5 | 47.2 | 7.7 |
| 1996 | 60.4 | 38.9 | 62.6 | 65.2 | 75.9 | 78.2 | 72.0 | 47.2 | 7.7 |
| 1997 | 61.7 | 39.9 | 64.0 | 69.9 | 78.1 | 78.4 | 73.2 | 47.6 | 8.2 |
| 1998 | 62.8 | 42.5 | 64.8 | 69.6 | 79.6 | 79.9 | 74.0 | 48.5 | 7.9 |
| 1999 | 63.5 | 38.8 | 66.1 | 72.7 | 82.1 | 80.4 | 74.6 | 48.4 | 8.9 |
| 2000 | 63.1 | 39.6 | 65.4 | 70.5 | 81.1 | 79.9 | 74.9 | 48.6 | 9.9 |
| 2001 | 62.8 | 37.3 | 65.2 | 70.1 | 81.2 | 79.6 | 73.9 | 49.9 | 10.1 |
| 2002 | 61.8 | 34.7 | 64.4 | 66.9 | 79.7 | 79.2 | 73.3 | 51.8 | 9.8 |
| 2003 | 61.9 | 33.7 | 64.6 | 65.7 | 79.1 | 80.6 | 74.2 | 51.9 | 10.3 |
| 2004 | 61.5 | 32.8 | 64.2 | 66.8 | 77.2 | 80.6 | 74.3 | 52.3 | 10.7 |
| 2005 | 61.6 | 32.2 | 64.4 | 68.1 | 78.5 | 79.7 | 73.3 | 53.7 | 11.4 |
| 2006 | 61.7 | 35.6 | 64.2 | 66.2 | 78.6 | 80.1 | 73.0 | 55.1 | 11.8 |
| 2007 | 61.1 | 31.2 | 64.0 | 65.7 | 78.0 | 79.8 | 73.2 | 55.7 | 12.0 |
| 2008 | 61.3 | 29.7 | 64.3 | 65.2 | 79.6 | 80.0 | 73.7 | 55.3 | 13.0 |
| 2009 | 60.3 | 27.9 | 63.4 | 64.5 | 78.0 | 79.0 | 73.3 | 54.4 | 13.3 |
| 2010 | 59.9 | 25.1 | 63.2 | 66.9 | 77.9 | 77.7 | 73.0 | 54.9 | 13.3 |
| 2011 | 59.1 | 24.2 | 62.2 | 65.9 | 76.0 | 78.2 | 72.0 | 53.4 | 14.2 |
| 2012 | 59.8 | 28.2 | 62.6 | 66.5 | 76.9 | 78.4 | 73.3 | 53.9 | 14.4 |
| 2013 | 59.2 | 28.7 | 61.8 | 64.4 | 75.5 | 78.0 | 72.9 | 54.6 | 14.7 |
| 2014 | 59.2 | 28.4 | 61.6 | 65.4 | 76.2 | 78.2 | 73.2 | 53.8 | 14.6 |
| 2015 | 59.7 | 29.9 | 62.0 | 67.6 | 77.0 | 78.9 | 73.5 | 53.4 | 15.6 |
| **HISPANIC** | | | | | | | | | |
| **Both Sexes** | | | | | | | | | |
| 1980 | 64.0 | 50.3 | 78.6 | ... | ... | ... | ... | ... | ... |
| 1981 | 64.1 | 46.4 | 72.4 | ... | ... | ... | ... | ... | ... |
| 1982 | 63.6 | 44.8 | 70.4 | ... | ... | ... | ... | ... | ... |
| 1983 | 63.8 | 45.3 | 71.0 | ... | ... | ... | ... | ... | ... |
| 1984 | 64.9 | 47.5 | 73.2 | ... | ... | ... | ... | ... | ... |
| 1985 | 64.6 | 44.6 | 69.0 | ... | ... | ... | ... | ... | ... |
| 1986 | 65.4 | 43.9 | 67.1 | ... | ... | ... | ... | ... | ... |
| 1987 | 66.4 | 45.8 | 69.0 | ... | ... | ... | ... | ... | ... |
| 1988 | 67.4 | 49.6 | 73.6 | ... | ... | ... | ... | ... | ... |
| 1989 | 67.6 | 48.6 | 71.9 | ... | ... | ... | ... | ... | ... |
| 1990 | 67.4 | 47.8 | 70.9 | ... | ... | ... | ... | ... | ... |
| 1991 | 66.5 | 45.1 | 67.8 | ... | ... | ... | ... | ... | ... |
| 1992 | 66.8 | 45.8 | 68.6 | ... | ... | ... | ... | ... | ... |
| 1993 | 66.2 | 43.9 | 66.3 | ... | ... | ... | ... | ... | ... |
| 1994 | 66.1 | 44.4 | 67.2 | 74.0 | 77.3 | 78.9 | 73.1 | 49.8 | 10.7 |
| 1995 | 65.8 | 45.4 | 69.0 | 71.9 | 78.1 | 78.5 | 72.8 | 48.6 | 10.5 |
| 1996 | 66.5 | 43.4 | 65.3 | 73.1 | 78.2 | 79.5 | 74.6 | 52.2 | 11.0 |
| 1997 | 67.9 | 43.0 | 63.3 | 76.4 | 79.5 | 80.9 | 75.4 | 53.8 | 11.9 |
| 1998 | 67.9 | 45.7 | 67.3 | 76.1 | 80.3 | 80.0 | 75.3 | 55.4 | 10.1 |
| 1999 | 67.7 | 45.5 | 67.2 | 76.0 | 78.6 | 81.3 | 75.9 | 54.1 | 11.6 |
| 2000 | 69.7 | 46.3 | 66.4 | 78.2 | 80.4 | 81.7 | 78.0 | 54.2 | 12.3 |
| 2001 | 69.5 | 46.9 | 67.5 | 76.6 | 80.0 | 81.9 | 77.4 | 55.1 | 10.9 |
| 2002 | 69.1 | 44.0 | 63.7 | 76.3 | 80.5 | 81.1 | 76.1 | 55.8 | 11.9 |
| 2003 | 68.3 | 37.7 | 55.2 | 75.6 | 79.4 | 81.1 | 75.3 | 57.4 | 12.8 |
| 2004 | 68.6 | 38.2 | 55.7 | 74.5 | 79.4 | 81.4 | 77.6 | 58.1 | 14.5 |
| 2005 | 68.0 | 38.6 | 56.8 | 72.7 | 79.1 | 81.2 | 77.2 | 58.4 | 13.9 |
| 2006 | 68.7 | 38.3 | 55.7 | 74.4 | 80.1 | 81.9 | 77.3 | 59.2 | 15.7 |
| 2007 | 68.8 | 37.1 | 53.9 | 74.8 | 80.7 | 81.8 | 78.6 | 58.5 | 16.0 |
| 2008 | 68.5 | 36.9 | 53.9 | 73.7 | 80.5 | 82.0 | 78.2 | 59.9 | 16.0 |
| 2009 | 68.0 | 34.0 | 50.0 | 73.1 | 79.5 | 81.3 | 79.3 | 61.9 | 17.1 |
| 2010 | 67.5 | 30.9 | 45.8 | 71.1 | 80.6 | 81.2 | 79.2 | 61.1 | 17.9 |
| 2011 | 66.5 | 28.3 | 42.6 | 72.0 | 79.1 | 80.3 | 78.9 | 60.8 | 17.6 |
| 2012 | 66.4 | 30.9 | 46.5 | 71.2 | 79.1 | 80.2 | 78.4 | 60.5 | 16.5 |
| 2013 | 66.0 | 31.0 | 47.0 | 71.7 | 78.3 | 79.5 | 78.1 | 61.0 | 17.0 |
| 2014 | 66.1 | 30.3 | 69.8 | 71.4 | 78.8 | 79.9 | 78.3 | 61.7 | 17.0 |
| 2015 | 65.9 | 30.9 | 69.6 | 71.6 | 78.3 | 79.5 | 78.3 | 62.7 | 17.2 |

. . . = Not available.

**Table 1-8.  Civilian Labor Force Participation Rates, by Age, Sex, Race, and Hispanic Origin, 1948–2015**
—*Continued*

(Percent.)

| Race, Hispanic origin, sex, and year | 16 years and over | 16 to 19 years | 20 years and over | | | | | | |
|---|---|---|---|---|---|---|---|---|---|
| | | | Total | 20 to 24 years | 25 to 34 years | 35 to 44 years | 45 to 54 years | 55 to 64 years | 65 years and over |
| **HISPANIC** | | | | | | | | | |
| **Men** | | | | | | | | | |
| 1980 | 81.4 | . . . | 84.9 | . . . | . . . | . . . | . . . | . . . | . . . |
| 1981 | 80.6 | . . . | 84.7 | . . . | . . . | . . . | . . . | . . . | . . . |
| 1982 | 79.7 | . . . | 84.0 | . . . | . . . | . . . | . . . | . . . | . . . |
| 1983 | 80.3 | . . . | 84.1 | . . . | . . . | . . . | . . . | . . . | . . . |
| 1984 | 80.6 | . . . | 84.3 | . . . | . . . | . . . | . . . | . . . | . . . |
| 1985 | 80.3 | . . . | 84.0 | . . . | . . . | . . . | . . . | . . . | . . . |
| 1986 | 81.0 | . . . | 84.6 | . . . | . . . | . . . | . . . | . . . | . . . |
| 1987 | 81.0 | . . . | 84.5 | . . . | . . . | . . . | . . . | . . . | . . . |
| 1988 | 81.9 | . . . | 85.0 | . . . | . . . | . . . | . . . | . . . | . . . |
| 1989 | 82.0 | . . . | 85.0 | . . . | . . . | . . . | . . . | . . . | . . . |
| 1990 | 81.4 | . . . | 84.7 | . . . | . . . | . . . | . . . | . . . | . . . |
| 1991 | 80.3 | . . . | 83.8 | . . . | . . . | . . . | . . . | . . . | . . . |
| 1992 | 80.7 | . . . | 84.0 | . . . | . . . | . . . | . . . | . . . | . . . |
| 1993 | 80.2 | . . . | 83.5 | . . . | . . . | . . . | . . . | . . . | . . . |
| 1994 | 79.2 | 50.0 | 82.5 | 88.0 | 92.5 | 91.5 | 85.7 | 63.6 | 14.4 |
| 1995 | 79.1 | 50.2 | 82.4 | 86.2 | 92.9 | 91.3 | 85.6 | 62.4 | 15.8 |
| 1996 | 79.6 | 50.0 | 83.0 | 85.7 | 93.2 | 91.7 | 87.0 | 65.9 | 16.7 |
| 1997 | 80.1 | 47.4 | 84.1 | 88.1 | 93.5 | 91.9 | 87.8 | 68.4 | 17.3 |
| 1998 | 79.8 | 48.7 | 83.6 | 88.1 | 94.0 | 91.4 | 86.7 | 70.2 | 14.9 |
| 1999 | 79.8 | 50.1 | 83.5 | 88.1 | 93.9 | 92.2 | 86.2 | 68.6 | 18.2 |
| 2000 | 81.5 | 50.7 | 85.3 | 89.1 | 94.1 | 93.3 | 87.6 | 69.4 | 18.5 |
| 2001 | 81.0 | 52.2 | 84.3 | 86.8 | 93.4 | 92.7 | 86.7 | 68.6 | 16.8 |
| 2002 | 80.2 | 48.8 | 83.6 | 86.1 | 93.5 | 92.1 | 86.1 | 67.3 | 16.3 |
| 2003 | 80.1 | 40.9 | 84.1 | 86.2 | 3.6 | 92.9 | 85.4 | 68.8 | 17.4 |
| 2004 | 80.4 | 42.4 | 84.2 | 84.4 | 3.6 | 93.2 | 87.2 | 69.6 | 20.8 |
| 2005 | 80.1 | 41.9 | 84.0 | 84.1 | 3.3 | 93.1 | 87.7 | 69.3 | 20.1 |
| 2006 | 80.7 | 42.0 | 84.6 | 85.9 | 4.1 | 93.8 | 87.1 | 69.6 | 22.9 |
| 2007 | 80.5 | 40.0 | 84.7 | 85.3 | 4.1 | 93.9 | 88.3 | 70.3 | 22.0 |
| 2008 | 80.2 | 40.3 | 84.4 | 84.3 | 4.0 | 93.7 | 88.6 | 71.7 | 21.7 |
| 2009 | 78.8 | 36.4 | 83.2 | 82.3 | 1.9 | 93.0 | 88.8 | 71.7 | 23.0 |
| 2010 | 77.8 | 33.2 | 82.6 | 80.0 | 2.7 | 92.9 | 87.8 | 69.0 | 24.5 |
| 2011 | 76.5 | 30.1 | 81.7 | 79.5 | 1.6 | 92.4 | 87.3 | 69.9 | 23.3 |
| 2012 | 76.1 | 33.0 | 81.0 | 78.5 | 1.6 | 91.1 | 87.3 | 70.3 | 21.1 |
| 2013 | 76.3 | 32.8 | 81.1 | 78.6 | 1.0 | 91.9 | 87.8 | 70.7 | 23.1 |
| 2014 | 76.1 | 31.2 | 81.0 | 77.9 | 90.5 | 92.9 | 87.8 | 72.9 | 21.9 |
| 2015 | 76.2 | 32.4 | 80.9 | 77.3 | 90.9 | 92.6 | 88.3 | 73.9 | 22.2 |
| **HISPANIC** | | | | | | | | | |
| **Women** | | | | | | | | | |
| 1980 | 47.4 | 48.5 | 48.5 | . . . | . . . | . . . | . . . | . . . | . . . |
| 1981 | 48.3 | 49.7 | 49.7 | . . . | . . . | . . . | . . . | . . . | . . . |
| 1982 | 48.1 | 49.3 | 49.3 | . . . | . . . | . . . | . . . | . . . | . . . |
| 1983 | 47.7 | 49.0 | 49.0 | . . . | . . . | . . . | . . . | . . . | . . . |
| 1984 | 49.6 | 50.5 | 50.5 | . . . | . . . | . . . | . . . | . . . | . . . |
| 1985 | 49.3 | 50.6 | 50.6 | . . . | . . . | . . . | . . . | . . . | . . . |
| 1986 | 50.1 | 51.7 | 51.7 | . . . | . . . | . . . | . . . | . . . | . . . |
| 1987 | 52.0 | 53.3 | 53.3 | . . . | . . . | . . . | . . . | . . . | . . . |
| 1988 | 53.2 | 54.2 | 54.2 | . . . | . . . | . . . | . . . | . . . | . . . |
| 1989 | 53.5 | 54.9 | 54.9 | . . . | . . . | . . . | . . . | . . . | . . . |
| 1990 | 53.1 | 54.8 | 54.8 | . . . | . . . | . . . | . . . | . . . | . . . |
| 1991 | 52.4 | 54.0 | 54.0 | . . . | . . . | . . . | . . . | . . . | . . . |
| 1992 | 52.8 | 54.3 | 54.3 | . . . | . . . | . . . | . . . | . . . | . . . |
| 1993 | 52.1 | 53.8 | 53.8 | . . . | . . . | . . . | . . . | . . . | . . . |
| 1994 | 52.9 | 54.4 | 54.4 | 57.9 | 60.5 | 66.4 | 61.4 | 38.1 | 7.9 |
| 1995 | 52.6 | 53.9 | 53.9 | 55.9 | 61.6 | 65.9 | 60.5 | 37.2 | 6.6 |
| 1996 | 53.4 | 55.2 | 55.2 | 59.2 | 62.0 | 67.0 | 62.7 | 40.5 | 6.9 |
| 1997 | 55.1 | 57.0 | 57.0 | 62.3 | 63.7 | 69.3 | 63.3 | 40.6 | 8.1 |
| 1998 | 55.6 | 57.1 | 57.1 | 62.2 | 64.5 | 67.9 | 64.7 | 41.9 | 6.6 |
| 1999 | 55.9 | 57.7 | 57.7 | 63.0 | 62.7 | 70.5 | 66.2 | 42.4 | 6.5 |
| 2000 | 57.5 | 59.3 | 59.3 | 65.0 | 65.3 | 69.9 | 68.5 | 41.2 | 7.7 |
| 2001 | 57.6 | 59.3 | 59.3 | 64.6 | 65.2 | 70.3 | 68.3 | 43.2 | 6.7 |
| 2002 | 57.6 | 59.5 | 59.5 | 65.0 | 65.8 | 69.5 | 66.3 | 46.1 | 8.5 |
| 2003 | 55.9 | 58.1 | 58.1 | 63.3 | 62.9 | 68.5 | 65.3 | 47.1 | 9.4 |
| 2004 | 56.1 | 58.4 | 58.4 | 62.9 | 62.9 | 68.7 | 67.9 | 47.8 | 9.8 |
| 2005 | 55.3 | 57.4 | 57.4 | 59.4 | 62.4 | 68.2 | 66.6 | 48.4 | 9.3 |
| 2006 | 56.1 | 58.3 | 58.3 | 61.3 | 63.5 | 68.7 | 67.4 | 49.7 | 10.4 |
| 2007 | 56.5 | 58.8 | 58.8 | 62.9 | 64.6 | 68.4 | 68.7 | 47.6 | 11.4 |
| 2008 | 56.2 | 58.6 | 58.6 | 62.1 | 64.3 | 69.1 | 67.6 | 48.9 | 11.7 |
| 2009 | 56.5 | 59.2 | 59.2 | 63.2 | 64.7 | 68.2 | 69.4 | 52.6 | 12.7 |
| 2010 | 56.5 | 59.5 | 59.5 | 61.6 | 66.3 | 67.9 | 70.2 | 53.7 | 13.0 |
| 2011 | 55.9 | 59.0 | 59.0 | 63.0 | 64.5 | 67.1 | 70.4 | 52.3 | 13.2 |
| 2012 | 56.6 | 59.5 | 59.5 | 63.3 | 65.6 | 69.0 | 69.4 | 51.4 | 13.2 |
| 2013 | 55.7 | 58.5 | 58.5 | 64.3 | 64.5 | 66.9 | 68.4 | 52.0 | 12.5 |
| 2014 | 56.0 | 29.3 | 58.7 | 64.5 | 66.1 | 66.4 | 68.8 | 51.3 | 13.3 |
| 2015 | 55.7 | 29.3 | 58.4 | 65.8 | 64.9 | 66.2 | 68.3 | 52.2 | 13.4 |

. . . = Not available.

## Table 1-9. Employed and Unemployed Full- and Part-Time Workers, by Age, Sex, and Race, 2000–2015

(Thousands of people.)

| Race, sex, age, and year | Employed[1] | | | | | | | | Unemployed | |
| --- | --- | --- | --- | --- | --- | --- | --- | --- | --- | --- |
| | Full-time workers | | | | Part-time workers | | | | | |
| | | At work | | | | At work[2] | | | | |
| | Total | 35 hours or more | 1 to 34 hours for economic or noneconomic reasons | Not at work | Total | For economic reasons | For noneconomic reasons | Not at work | Looking for full-time work | Looking for part-time work |

**ALL RACES**

**Both Sexes, 16 Years and Over**

| | | | | | | | | | | |
| --- | --- | --- | --- | --- | --- | --- | --- | --- | --- | --- |
| 2000 | 113 846 | 100 533 | 9 125 | 4 188 | 23 044 | 2 003 | 19 548 | 1 493 | 4 538 | 1 154 |
| 2001 | 113 573 | 99 047 | 10 464 | 4 061 | 23 361 | 2 297 | 19 494 | 1 570 | 5 546 | 1 254 |
| 2002 | 112 700 | 99 042 | 9 746 | 3 912 | 23 785 | 2 755 | 19 549 | 1 481 | 7 063 | 1 314 |
| 2003 | 113 324 | 99 539 | 9 841 | 3 944 | 24 412 | 3 184 | 19 702 | 1 525 | 7 361 | 1 413 |
| 2004 | 114 518 | 100 496 | 10 053 | 3 969 | 24 734 | 3 113 | 20 109 | 1 513 | 6 762 | 1 388 |
| 2005 | 117 016 | 103 044 | 9 983 | 3 990 | 24 714 | 2 963 | 20 229 | 1 522 | 6 175 | 1 415 |
| 2006 | 119 688 | 105 328 | 10 223 | 4 137 | 24 739 | 2 774 | 20 356 | 1 609 | 5 675 | 1 326 |
| 2007 | 121 091 | 106 990 | 9 976 | 4 125 | 24 956 | 2 851 | 20 511 | 1 594 | 5 789 | 1 289 |
| 2008 | 120 030 | 105 575 | 10 426 | 4 030 | 25 332 | 3 814 | 20 009 | 1 509 | 7 446 | 1 478 |
| 2009 | 112 634 | 95 911 | 12 853 | 3 870 | 27 244 | 6 353 | 19 327 | 1 563 | 12 523 | 1 741 |
| 2010 | 111 714 | 97 946 | 10 217 | 3 551 | 27 350 | 6 965 | 18 876 | 1 509 | 12 970 | 1 854 |
| 2011 | 112 556 | 98 976 | 10 047 | 3 534 | 27 313 | 6 872 | 18 984 | 1 525 | 11 914 | 1 833 |
| 2012 | 114 809 | 101 877 | 9 324 | 3 607 | 27 661 | 6 626 | 19 509 | 1 525 | 10 699 | 1 807 |
| 2013 | 116 314 | 104 069 | 8 756 | 3 489 | 27 615 | 6 479 | 19 621 | 1 514 | 9 726 | 1 733 |
| 2014 | 118 718 | 105 416 | 9 772 | 3 531 | 27 587 | 5 904 | 20 185 | 1 498 | 8 055 | 1 561 |
| 2015 | 121 492 | 106 611 | 11 263 | 3 618 | 27 341 | 5 143 | 20 750 | 1 448 | 6 888 | 1 409 |

**Both Sexes, 20 Years and Over**

| | | | | | | | | | | |
| --- | --- | --- | --- | --- | --- | --- | --- | --- | --- | --- |
| 2000 | 111 353 | 98 439 | 8 787 | 4 127 | 18 348 | 1 747 | 15 297 | 1 304 | 3 978 | 632 |
| 2001 | 111 323 | 97 161 | 10 156 | 4 006 | 18 870 | 2 013 | 15 486 | 1 371 | 4 956 | 682 |
| 2002 | 110 679 | 97 342 | 9 474 | 3 862 | 19 475 | 2 448 | 15 704 | 1 322 | 6 395 | 730 |
| 2003 | 111 578 | 98 087 | 9 587 | 3 904 | 20 239 | 2 875 | 16 001 | 1 363 | 6 705 | 818 |
| 2004 | 112 747 | 99 034 | 9 789 | 3 924 | 20 598 | 2 817 | 16 436 | 1 345 | 6 178 | 764 |
| 2005 | 115 206 | 101 534 | 9 729 | 3 942 | 20 546 | 2 698 | 16 489 | 1 359 | 5 619 | 786 |
| 2006 | 117 844 | 103 779 | 9 974 | 4 090 | 20 421 | 2 510 | 16 478 | 1 433 | 5 117 | 765 |
| 2007 | 119 317 | 105 499 | 9 738 | 4 080 | 20 819 | 2 587 | 16 819 | 1 413 | 5 234 | 742 |
| 2008 | 118 404 | 104 212 | 10 204 | 3 989 | 21 385 | 3 492 | 16 543 | 1 350 | 6 790 | 849 |
| 2009 | 111 414 | 94 928 | 12 647 | 3 839 | 23 626 | 5 934 | 16 286 | 1 406 | 11 651 | 1 061 |
| 2010 | 110 622 | 97 037 | 10 057 | 3 528 | 24 064 | 6 552 | 16 138 | 1 373 | 12 155 | 1 142 |
| 2011 | 111 500 | 98 103 | 9 888 | 3 508 | 24 043 | 6 457 | 16 259 | 1 327 | 11 180 | 1 167 |
| 2012 | 113 667 | 100 919 | 9 167 | 3 582 | 24 376 | 6 240 | 16 750 | 1 385 | 9 968 | 1 141 |
| 2013 | 115 106 | 103 041 | 8 601 | 3 464 | 24 365 | 6 103 | 16 877 | 1 386 | 9 043 | 1 090 |
| 2014 | 117 514 | 104 403 | 9 604 | 3 506 | 24 244 | 5 551 | 17 334 | 1 358 | 7 503 | 1 008 |
| 2015 | 120 199 | 105 523 | 11 088 | 3 588 | 23 901 | 4 822 | 17 771 | 1 308 | 6 378 | 953 |

**Men, 16 Years and Over**

| | | | | | | | | | | |
| --- | --- | --- | --- | --- | --- | --- | --- | --- | --- | --- |
| 2000 | 65 930 | 59 345 | 4 555 | 2 030 | 7 375 | 856 | 6 105 | 414 | 2 486 | 488 |
| 2001 | 65 623 | 58 386 | 5 241 | 1 996 | 7 573 | 1 021 | 6 129 | 424 | 3 144 | 546 |
| 2002 | 65 205 | 58 318 | 4 971 | 1 916 | 7 697 | 1 246 | 6 050 | 401 | 4 029 | 568 |
| 2003 | 65 379 | 58 428 | 5 023 | 1 927 | 7 953 | 1 473 | 6 056 | 423 | 4 291 | 615 |
| 2004 | 66 444 | 59 363 | 5 148 | 1 933 | 8 080 | 1 405 | 6 258 | 417 | 3 843 | 613 |
| 2005 | 67 858 | 60 825 | 5 096 | 1 937 | 8 115 | 1 316 | 6 370 | 429 | 3 444 | 616 |
| 2006 | 69 307 | 62 087 | 5 237 | 1 984 | 8 194 | 1 232 | 6 510 | 452 | 3 192 | 561 |
| 2007 | 70 035 | 62 965 | 5 095 | 1 975 | 8 220 | 1 319 | 6 424 | 477 | 3 326 | 556 |
| 2008 | 68 853 | 61 436 | 5 443 | 1 974 | 8 634 | 1 842 | 6 349 | 442 | 4 396 | 637 |
| 2009 | 63 951 | 55 317 | 6 772 | 1 862 | 9 719 | 3 035 | 6 170 | 514 | 7 696 | 757 |
| 2010 | 63 501 | 56 425 | 5 352 | 1 723 | 9 858 | 3 316 | 6 066 | 476 | 7 827 | 799 |
| 2011 | 64 333 | 57 413 | 5 189 | 1 731 | 9 957 | 3 262 | 6 216 | 479 | 6 903 | 781 |
| 2012 | 65 477 | 58 956 | 4 803 | 1 719 | 10 078 | 3 089 | 6 491 | 498 | 5 988 | 784 |
| 2013 | 66 335 | 60 112 | 4 531 | 1 692 | 10 017 | 2 985 | 6 526 | 507 | 5 563 | 752 |
| 2014 | 67 829 | 61 128 | 5 004 | 1 697 | 9 863 | 2 712 | 6 663 | 487 | 4 516 | 674 |
| 2015 | 69 351 | 61 892 | 5 737 | 1 722 | 9 780 | 2 368 | 6 927 | 485 | 3 888 | 602 |

**Men, 20 Years and Over**

| | | | | | | | | | | |
| --- | --- | --- | --- | --- | --- | --- | --- | --- | --- | --- |
| 2000 | 64 464 | 58 095 | 4 370 | 2 000 | 5 170 | 733 | 4 109 | 328 | 2 162 | 214 |
| 2001 | 64 311 | 57 273 | 5 072 | 1 966 | 5 465 | 881 | 4 253 | 331 | 2 801 | 239 |
| 2002 | 64 006 | 57 302 | 4 815 | 1 889 | 5 728 | 1 093 | 4 299 | 336 | 3 642 | 254 |
| 2003 | 64 364 | 57 580 | 4 879 | 1 905 | 6 051 | 1 314 | 4 388 | 348 | 3 906 | 302 |
| 2004 | 65 377 | 58 471 | 5 000 | 1 906 | 6 196 | 1 251 | 4 600 | 345 | 3 511 | 281 |
| 2005 | 66 803 | 59 934 | 4 955 | 1 914 | 6 247 | 1 182 | 4 705 | 360 | 3 118 | 274 |
| 2006 | 68 193 | 61 140 | 5 095 | 1 958 | 6 238 | 1 100 | 4 762 | 376 | 2 861 | 270 |
| 2007 | 68 968 | 62 057 | 4 959 | 1 952 | 6 369 | 1 190 | 4 782 | 397 | 2 990 | 268 |
| 2008 | 67 895 | 60 625 | 5 315 | 1 955 | 6 855 | 1 675 | 4 802 | 378 | 3 994 | 303 |
| 2009 | 63 242 | 54 738 | 6 659 | 1 845 | 8 099 | 2 827 | 4 828 | 445 | 7 151 | 404 |
| 2010 | 62 854 | 55 887 | 5 258 | 1 710 | 8 376 | 3 102 | 4 857 | 417 | 7 336 | 427 |
| 2011 | 63 690 | 56 870 | 5 104 | 1 715 | 8 492 | 3 059 | 5 010 | 423 | 6 461 | 437 |
| 2012 | 64 810 | 58 386 | 4 719 | 1 705 | 8 593 | 2 883 | 5 271 | 439 | 5 547 | 437 |
| 2013 | 65 631 | 59 504 | 4 448 | 1 679 | 8 545 | 2 797 | 5 301 | 447 | 5 144 | 424 |
| 2014 | 67 093 | 60 498 | 4 911 | 1 684 | 8 378 | 2 532 | 5 422 | 424 | 4 192 | 393 |
| 2015 | 68 588 | 61 240 | 5 642 | 1 706 | 8 189 | 2 200 | 5 570 | 419 | 3 594 | 365 |

[1] Employed persons are classified as full- or part-time workers based on their usual weekly hours at all jobs, regardless of the number of hours they were at work during the reference week. Persons absent from work are also classified according to their usual status.
[2] Includes some persons at work 35 hours or more classified by their reason for working part time.

## Table 1-9. Employed and Unemployed Full- and Part-Time Workers, by Age, Sex, and Race, 2000–2015
### —Continued

(Thousands of people.)

| Race, sex, age, and year | Employed[1] | | | | | | | | Unemployed | |
|---|---|---|---|---|---|---|---|---|---|---|
| | Full-time workers | | | | Part-time workers | | | | | |
| | | At work | | | | At work[2] | | | | |
| | Total | 35 hours or more | 1 to 34 hours for economic or noneconomic reasons | Not at work | Total | For economic reasons | For noneconomic reasons | Not at work | Looking for full-time work | Looking for part-time work |
| **ALL RACES**—Continued | | | | | | | | | | |
| **Women, 16 Years and Over** | | | | | | | | | | |
| 2000 | 47 916 | 41 188 | 4 570 | 2 158 | 15 670 | 1 147 | 13 443 | 1 080 | 2 052 | 666 |
| 2001 | 47 950 | 40 661 | 5 223 | 2 065 | 15 788 | 1 276 | 13 365 | 1 146 | 2 402 | 709 |
| 2002 | 47 494 | 40 723 | 4 775 | 1 996 | 16 088 | 1 509 | 13 498 | 1 080 | 3 034 | 747 |
| 2003 | 47 946 | 41 111 | 4 818 | 2 017 | 16 459 | 1 711 | 13 646 | 1 102 | 3 070 | 798 |
| 2004 | 48 073 | 41 133 | 4 905 | 2 036 | 16 654 | 1 708 | 13 851 | 1 096 | 2 919 | 775 |
| 2005 | 49 158 | 42 219 | 4 887 | 2 052 | 16 598 | 1 647 | 13 859 | 1 092 | 2 732 | 799 |
| 2006 | 50 380 | 43 241 | 4 986 | 2 153 | 16 545 | 1 542 | 13 846 | 1 157 | 2 483 | 764 |
| 2007 | 51 056 | 44 025 | 4 881 | 2 150 | 16 736 | 1 532 | 14 087 | 1 117 | 2 463 | 732 |
| 2008 | 51 178 | 44 139 | 4 983 | 2 056 | 16 698 | 1 972 | 13 660 | 1 067 | 3 050 | 841 |
| 2009 | 48 683 | 40 594 | 6 080 | 2 009 | 17 525 | 3 318 | 13 157 | 1 050 | 4 827 | 984 |
| 2010 | 48 214 | 41 521 | 4 865 | 1 828 | 17 491 | 3 648 | 12 810 | 1 033 | 5 144 | 1 055 |
| 2011 | 48 224 | 41 563 | 4 858 | 1 802 | 17 355 | 3 610 | 12 767 | 977 | 5 011 | 1 052 |
| 2012 | 49 331 | 42 921 | 4 521 | 1 888 | 17 583 | 3 538 | 13 018 | 1 026 | 4 711 | 1 023 |
| 2013 | 49 979 | 43 957 | 4 225 | 1 797 | 17 598 | 3 495 | 13 095 | 1 008 | 4 164 | 982 |
| 2014 | 50 889 | 44 287 | 4 768 | 1 834 | 17 724 | 3 192 | 13 521 | 1 011 | 3 539 | 887 |
| 2015 | 52 142 | 44 719 | 5 527 | 1 896 | 17 561 | 2 775 | 13 823 | 963 | 3 000 | 807 |
| **Women, 20 Years and Over** | | | | | | | | | | |
| 2000 | 46 889 | 40 344 | 4 417 | 2 128 | 13 178 | 1 013 | 11 188 | 976 | 1 816 | 419 |
| 2001 | 47 012 | 39 889 | 5 083 | 2 040 | 13 405 | 1 132 | 11 233 | 1 040 | 2 155 | 444 |
| 2002 | 46 673 | 40 040 | 4 660 | 1 973 | 13 747 | 1 355 | 11 406 | 986 | 2 752 | 476 |
| 2003 | 47 215 | 40 507 | 4 708 | 2 000 | 14 188 | 1 560 | 11 613 | 1 015 | 2 799 | 515 |
| 2004 | 47 371 | 40 563 | 4 790 | 2 017 | 14 402 | 1 567 | 11 836 | 1 000 | 2 667 | 483 |
| 2005 | 48 403 | 41 600 | 4 774 | 2 028 | 14 299 | 1 516 | 11 784 | 999 | 2 501 | 512 |
| 2006 | 49 651 | 42 639 | 4 880 | 2 132 | 14 183 | 1 410 | 11 716 | 1 057 | 2 256 | 495 |
| 2007 | 50 349 | 43 442 | 4 779 | 2 128 | 14 450 | 1 397 | 12 037 | 1 016 | 2 244 | 474 |
| 2008 | 50 509 | 43 587 | 4 888 | 2 034 | 14 530 | 1 817 | 11 740 | 973 | 2 796 | 546 |
| 2009 | 48 171 | 40 190 | 5 988 | 1 994 | 15 527 | 3 107 | 11 459 | 961 | 4 500 | 657 |
| 2010 | 47 767 | 41 150 | 4 799 | 1 818 | 15 688 | 3 450 | 11 282 | 956 | 4 819 | 715 |
| 2011 | 47 810 | 41 233 | 4 784 | 1 792 | 15 551 | 3 398 | 11 249 | 904 | 4 719 | 730 |
| 2012 | 48 857 | 42 533 | 4 448 | 1 877 | 15 783 | 3 358 | 11 480 | 946 | 4 420 | 704 |
| 2013 | 49 475 | 43 537 | 4 153 | 1 785 | 15 820 | 3 306 | 11 575 | 939 | 3 900 | 665 |
| 2014 | 50 421 | 43 905 | 4 693 | 1 823 | 15 865 | 3 019 | 11 912 | 934 | 3 311 | 615 |
| 2015 | 51 611 | 44 284 | 5 446 | 1 881 | 15 712 | 2 622 | 12 201 | 889 | 2 784 | 588 |
| **WHITE**[3] | | | | | | | | | | |
| **Men, 16 Years and Over** | | | | | | | | | | |
| 2000 | 56 068 | 50 434 | 3 896 | 1 738 | 6 221 | 656 | 5 213 | 351 | 1 798 | 379 |
| 2001 | 55 830 | 49 625 | 4 504 | 1 701 | 6 381 | 793 | 5 225 | 364 | 2 323 | 431 |
| 2002 | 55 369 | 49 459 | 4 267 | 1 644 | 6 480 | 980 | 5 150 | 350 | 3 017 | 443 |
| 2003 | 55 216 | 49 323 | 4 266 | 1 628 | 6 650 | 1 146 | 5 148 | 357 | 3 164 | 479 |
| 2004 | 55 926 | 49 891 | 4 396 | 1 638 | 6 786 | 1 092 | 5 331 | 363 | 2 805 | 477 |
| 2005 | 56 955 | 50 965 | 4 334 | 1 656 | 6 808 | 1 014 | 5 424 | 370 | 2 459 | 471 |
| 2006 | 58 063 | 51 894 | 4 484 | 1 685 | 6 820 | 947 | 5 481 | 393 | 2 299 | 432 |
| 2007 | 58 494 | 52 460 | 4 359 | 1 676 | 6 795 | 1 022 | 5 368 | 406 | 2 444 | 425 |
| 2008 | 57 432 | 51 104 | 4 653 | 1 675 | 7 192 | 1 433 | 5 379 | 379 | 3 235 | 492 |
| 2009 | 53 506 | 46 153 | 5 770 | 1 583 | 8 124 | 2 438 | 5 240 | 446 | 5 819 | 602 |
| 2010 | 53 086 | 47 055 | 4 554 | 1 477 | 8 166 | 2 662 | 5 102 | 402 | 5 832 | 644 |
| 2011 | 53 727 | 47 865 | 4 397 | 1 465 | 8 193 | 2 560 | 5 227 | 405 | 5 020 | 611 |
| 2012 | 53 857 | 48 409 | 4 009 | 1 439 | 8 133 | 2 383 | 5 334 | 416 | 4 330 | 600 |
| 2013 | 54 263 | 49 091 | 3 775 | 1 397 | 8 059 | 2 281 | 5 357 | 421 | 3 941 | 579 |
| 2014 | 55 281 | 49 766 | 4 107 | 1 408 | 7 827 | 2 027 | 5 402 | 399 | 3 086 | 486 |
| 2015 | 56 176 | 50 088 | 4 673 | 1 415 | 7 716 | 1 752 | 5 567 | 397 | 2 678 | 448 |
| **Men, 20 Years and Over** | | | | | | | | | | |
| 2000 | 54 778 | 49 335 | 3 733 | 1 710 | 4 341 | 558 | 3 505 | 278 | 1 566 | 165 |
| 2001 | 54 666 | 48 636 | 4 354 | 1 676 | 4 579 | 677 | 3 616 | 285 | 2 080 | 195 |
| 2002 | 54 333 | 48 581 | 4 133 | 1 619 | 4 790 | 857 | 3 640 | 293 | 2 743 | 200 |
| 2003 | 54 339 | 48 585 | 4 145 | 1 609 | 5 010 | 1 016 | 3 703 | 291 | 2 893 | 231 |
| 2004 | 55 005 | 49 124 | 4 267 | 1 614 | 5 154 | 961 | 3 895 | 299 | 2 567 | 217 |
| 2005 | 56 050 | 50 203 | 4 213 | 1 634 | 5 205 | 905 | 3 990 | 310 | 2 242 | 209 |
| 2006 | 57 108 | 51 081 | 4 365 | 1 662 | 5 150 | 840 | 3 987 | 324 | 2 074 | 208 |
| 2007 | 57 591 | 51 691 | 4 243 | 1 656 | 5 216 | 915 | 3 967 | 334 | 2 204 | 204 |
| 2008 | 56 623 | 50 421 | 4 542 | 1 660 | 5 681 | 1 302 | 4 055 | 324 | 2 944 | 235 |
| 2009 | 52 899 | 45 654 | 5 676 | 1 569 | 6 728 | 2 269 | 4 075 | 384 | 5 421 | 325 |
| 2010 | 52 530 | 46 592 | 4 472 | 1 466 | 6 907 | 2 484 | 4 071 | 352 | 5 481 | 347 |
| 2011 | 53 186 | 47 406 | 4 328 | 1 451 | 6 933 | 2 392 | 4 184 | 357 | 4 702 | 344 |
| 2012 | 53 302 | 47 934 | 3 941 | 1 427 | 6 891 | 2 218 | 4 306 | 367 | 4 014 | 333 |
| 2013 | 53 660 | 48 569 | 3 706 | 1 386 | 6 850 | 2 132 | 4 349 | 370 | 3 657 | 337 |
| 2014 | 54 671 | 49 249 | 4 026 | 1 395 | 6 619 | 1 889 | 4 382 | 348 | 2 855 | 286 |
| 2015 | 55 533 | 49 536 | 4 593 | 1 403 | 6 426 | 1 622 | 4 460 | 345 | 2 480 | 271 |

[1]Employed persons are classified as full- or part-time workers based on their usual weekly hours at all jobs, regardless of the number of hours they were at work during the reference week. Persons absent from work are also classified according to their usual status.
[2]Includes some persons at work 35 hours or more classified by their reason for working part time.
[3]Beginning in 2003, persons who selected this race group only; persons who selected more than one race group are not included. Prior to 2003, persons who reported more than one race group were included in the group they identified as their main race.

## Table 1-9. Employed and Unemployed Full- and Part-Time Workers, by Age, Sex, and Race, 2000–2015 —*Continued*

(Thousands of people.)

| Race, sex, age, and year | Employed[1] Full-time workers Total | At work 35 hours or more | 1 to 34 hours for economic or noneconomic reasons | Not at work | Part-time workers Total | At work[2] For economic reasons | For noneconomic reasons | Not at work | Unemployed Looking for full-time work | Looking for part-time work |
|---|---|---|---|---|---|---|---|---|---|---|
| **WHITE[3]**—*Continued* | | | | | | | | | | |
| **Women, 16 Years and Over** | | | | | | | | | | |
| 2000 | 38 438 | 32 942 | 3 729 | 1 767 | 13 698 | 867 | 11 870 | 961 | 1 422 | 521 |
| 2001 | 38 445 | 32 491 | 4 252 | 1 702 | 13 773 | 971 | 11 787 | 1 015 | 1 664 | 551 |
| 2002 | 38 152 | 32 623 | 3 896 | 1 633 | 14 011 | 1 152 | 11 903 | 956 | 2 084 | 595 |
| 2003 | 38 249 | 32 659 | 3 939 | 1 652 | 14 120 | 1 304 | 11 860 | 956 | 2 038 | 629 |
| 2004 | 38 240 | 32 555 | 4 018 | 1 667 | 14 287 | 1 280 | 12 038 | 969 | 1 968 | 597 |
| 2005 | 38 973 | 33 325 | 3 976 | 1 672 | 14 213 | 1 207 | 12 043 | 963 | 1 807 | 612 |
| 2006 | 39 813 | 33 980 | 4 082 | 1 751 | 14 137 | 1 157 | 11 967 | 1 013 | 1 670 | 601 |
| 2007 | 40 238 | 34 486 | 4 014 | 1 738 | 14 265 | 1 143 | 12 148 | 973 | 1 694 | 579 |
| 2008 | 40 292 | 34 569 | 4 076 | 1 647 | 14 209 | 1 518 | 11 761 | 931 | 2 119 | 664 |
| 2009 | 38 456 | 31 885 | 4 946 | 1 626 | 14 910 | 2 579 | 11 418 | 913 | 3 442 | 785 |
| 2010 | 38 158 | 32 710 | 3 958 | 1 490 | 14 758 | 2 846 | 11 029 | 883 | 3 612 | 828 |
| 2011 | 38 152 | 32 731 | 3 944 | 1 477 | 14 618 | 2 775 | 10 994 | 850 | 3 450 | 807 |
| 2012 | 38 362 | 33 244 | 3 614 | 1 504 | 14 416 | 2 674 | 10 875 | 867 | 3 191 | 794 |
| 2013 | 38 629 | 33 870 | 3 329 | 1 430 | 14 428 | 2 605 | 10 986 | 837 | 2 756 | 757 |
| 2014 | 39 241 | 22 994 | 3 770 | 1 477 | 14 439 | 2 345 | 11 242 | 852 | 2 304 | 664 |
| 2015 | 39 823 | 34 038 | 4 311 | 1 474 | 14 228 | 2 035 | 11 395 | 798 | 1 945 | 592 |
| **Women, 20 Years and Over** | | | | | | | | | | |
| 2000 | 37 585 | 32 242 | 3 600 | 1 743 | 11 560 | 754 | 9 935 | 872 | 1 256 | 339 |
| 2001 | 37 658 | 31 839 | 4 139 | 1 680 | 11 711 | 853 | 9 933 | 924 | 1 492 | 357 |
| 2002 | 37 467 | 32 049 | 3 803 | 1 615 | 11 981 | 1 029 | 10 079 | 873 | 1 888 | 381 |
| 2003 | 37 640 | 32 158 | 3 845 | 1 637 | 12 183 | 1 180 | 10 124 | 879 | 1 866 | 411 |
| 2004 | 37 663 | 32 085 | 3 927 | 1 652 | 12 377 | 1 166 | 10 326 | 885 | 1 795 | 377 |
| 2005 | 38 354 | 32 820 | 3 882 | 1 652 | 12 235 | 1 108 | 10 248 | 879 | 1 653 | 401 |
| 2006 | 39 232 | 33 500 | 3 998 | 1 733 | 12 128 | 1 050 | 10 151 | 927 | 1 524 | 402 |
| 2007 | 39 670 | 34 015 | 3 932 | 1 722 | 12 326 | 1 037 | 10 402 | 887 | 1 547 | 383 |
| 2008 | 39 765 | 34 128 | 4 005 | 1 632 | 12 359 | 1 392 | 10 116 | 851 | 1 949 | 435 |
| 2009 | 38 033 | 31 547 | 4 872 | 1 614 | 13 198 | 2 411 | 9 952 | 835 | 3 216 | 529 |
| 2010 | 37 789 | 32 404 | 3 904 | 1 481 | 13 208 | 2 684 | 9 705 | 818 | 3 389 | 571 |
| 2011 | 37 816 | 32 466 | 3 882 | 1 468 | 13 065 | 2 597 | 9 683 | 785 | 3 255 | 563 |
| 2012 | 38 362 | 32 936 | 3 556 | 1 497 | 12 923 | 2 533 | 9 591 | 799 | 3 009 | 555 |
| 2013 | 38 233 | 33 544 | 3 269 | 1 420 | 12 964 | 2 462 | 9 719 | 783 | 2 586 | 516 |
| 2014 | 39 241 | 33 994 | 3 770 | 1 477 | 14 439 | 2 345 | 11 242 | 852 | 2 304 | 664 |
| 2015 | 39 418 | 33 707 | 4 249 | 1 462 | 12 743 | 1 915 | 10 091 | 736 | 1 812 | 437 |
| **BLACK[3]** | | | | | | | | | | |
| **Men, 16 Years and Over** | | | | | | | | | | |
| 2000 | 6 350 | 5 704 | 445 | 202 | 732 | 144 | 548 | 41 | 542 | 78 |
| 2001 | 6 178 | 5 509 | 468 | 200 | 761 | 165 | 557 | 39 | 626 | 83 |
| 2002 | 6 194 | 5 541 | 480 | 173 | 765 | 188 | 546 | 30 | 749 | 86 |
| 2003 | 6 055 | 5 414 | 453 | 188 | 765 | 221 | 505 | 39 | 804 | 87 |
| 2004 | 6 177 | 5 538 | 460 | 179 | 736 | 205 | 499 | 32 | 763 | 98 |
| 2005 | 6 381 | 5 745 | 463 | 174 | 773 | 207 | 533 | 33 | 742 | 102 |
| 2006 | 6 529 | 5 907 | 446 | 176 | 825 | 201 | 590 | 34 | 681 | 93 |
| 2007 | 6 673 | 6 068 | 429 | 176 | 826 | 195 | 589 | 42 | 660 | 92 |
| 2008 | 6 548 | 5 935 | 440 | 173 | 850 | 276 | 542 | 32 | 849 | 100 |
| 2009 | 5 871 | 5 166 | 556 | 150 | 946 | 379 | 530 | 36 | 1 348 | 100 |
| 2010 | 5 856 | 5 279 | 446 | 130 | 1 009 | 419 | 550 | 41 | 1 448 | 102 |
| 2011 | 5 892 | 5 293 | 445 | 154 | 1 060 | 452 | 566 | 43 | 1 393 | 108 |
| 2012 | 6 185 | 5 579 | 453 | 153 | 1 117 | 442 | 629 | 46 | 1 169 | 123 |
| 2013 | 6 331 | 5 752 | 423 | 156 | 1 166 | 471 | 651 | 44 | 1 124 | 112 |
| 2014 | 6 678 | 6 032 | 488 | 158 | 1 140 | 442 | 651 | 47 | 973 | 118 |
| 2015 | 6 974 | 6 258 | 553 | 164 | 1 190 | 400 | 740 | 50 | 839 | 96 |
| **Men, 20 Years and Over** | | | | | | | | | | |
| 2000 | 6 222 | 5 594 | 429 | 199 | 520 | 125 | 363 | 32 | 468 | 31 |
| 2001 | 6 069 | 5 417 | 455 | 197 | 558 | 145 | 382 | 31 | 542 | 31 |
| 2002 | 6 073 | 5 437 | 465 | 171 | 579 | 166 | 387 | 26 | 660 | 35 |
| 2003 | 5 980 | 5 355 | 439 | 185 | 607 | 201 | 372 | 34 | 717 | 43 |
| 2004 | 6 089 | 5 463 | 449 | 177 | 592 | 189 | 376 | 27 | 689 | 44 |
| 2005 | 6 287 | 5 662 | 452 | 174 | 614 | 189 | 397 | 28 | 655 | 44 |
| 2006 | 6 424 | 5 816 | 433 | 175 | 655 | 185 | 441 | 30 | 596 | 44 |
| 2007 | 6 574 | 5 983 | 417 | 174 | 671 | 181 | 452 | 37 | 580 | 43 |
| 2008 | 6 461 | 5 860 | 430 | 171 | 690 | 252 | 409 | 29 | 764 | 46 |
| 2009 | 5 811 | 5 119 | 544 | 148 | 817 | 355 | 428 | 34 | 1 238 | 49 |
| 2010 | 5 803 | 5 235 | 439 | 129 | 877 | 392 | 447 | 37 | 1 344 | 52 |
| 2011 | 5 830 | 5 242 | 435 | 153 | 935 | 428 | 470 | 38 | 1 299 | 61 |
| 2012 | 6 117 | 5 522 | 443 | 152 | 987 | 421 | 526 | 40 | 1 081 | 71 |
| 2013 | 6 279 | 5 707 | 416 | 156 | 1 025 | 450 | 534 | 41 | 1 026 | 56 |
| 2014 | 6 614 | 5 975 | 482 | 158 | 998 | 418 | 539 | 41 | 909 | 64 |
| 2015 | 6 910 | 6 203 | 545 | 162 | 1 028 | 375 | 610 | 43 | 775 | 60 |

[1]Employed persons are classified as full- or part-time workers based on their usual weekly hours at all jobs, regardless of the number of hours they were at work during the reference week. Persons absent from work are also classified according to their usual status.

[2]Includes some persons at work 35 hours or more classified by their reason for working part time.

[3]Beginning in 2003, persons who selected this race group only; persons who selected more than one race group are not included. Prior to 2003, persons who reported more than one race group were included in the group they identified as their main race.

## Table 1-9. Employed and Unemployed Full- and Part-Time Workers, by Age, Sex, and Race, 2000–2015
### —Continued

(Thousands of people.)

| Race, sex, age, and year | Employed[1] | | | | | | | | Unemployed | |
| | Full-time workers | | | | Part-time workers | | | | | |
| | | At work | | | | At work[2] | | | | |
| | Total | 35 hours or more | 1 to 34 hours for economic or noneconomic reasons | Not at work | Total | For economic reasons | For noneconomic reasons | Not at work | Looking for full-time work | Looking for part-time work |
|---|---|---|---|---|---|---|---|---|---|---|
| **BLACK**[3]—*Continued* | | | | | | | | | | |
| **Women, 16 Years and Over** | | | | | | | | | | |
| 2000 | 6 780 | 5 862 | 632 | 287 | 1 293 | 211 | 1 005 | 77 | 515 | 106 |
| 2001 | 6 761 | 5 777 | 715 | 270 | 1 307 | 223 | 998 | 85 | 584 | 122 |
| 2002 | 6 588 | 5 685 | 640 | 263 | 1 326 | 259 | 991 | 76 | 744 | 114 |
| 2003 | 6 552 | 5 709 | 595 | 247 | 1 367 | 274 | 1 017 | 76 | 774 | 121 |
| 2004 | 6 597 | 5 740 | 611 | 246 | 1 399 | 306 | 1 022 | 71 | 744 | 124 |
| 2005 | 6 750 | 5 871 | 619 | 260 | 1 407 | 320 | 1 018 | 70 | 723 | 133 |
| 2006 | 7 001 | 6 131 | 605 | 265 | 1 410 | 274 | 1 054 | 82 | 655 | 120 |
| 2007 | 7 119 | 6 272 | 584 | 263 | 1 432 | 273 | 1 085 | 75 | 589 | 104 |
| 2008 | 7 105 | 6 238 | 596 | 272 | 1 449 | 302 | 1 070 | 77 | 717 | 122 |
| 2009 | 6 666 | 5 696 | 718 | 252 | 1 542 | 480 | 984 | 78 | 1 027 | 132 |
| 2010 | 6 525 | 5 727 | 582 | 215 | 1 621 | 528 | 1 010 | 82 | 1 142 | 160 |
| 2011 | 6 450 | 5 651 | 592 | 207 | 1 648 | 573 | 1 004 | 72 | 1 165 | 164 |
| 2012 | 6 750 | 5 956 | 557 | 236 | 1 803 | 559 | 1 157 | 88 | 1 099 | 153 |
| 2013 | 6 868 | 6 097 | 553 | 218 | 1 786 | 572 | 1 128 | 86 | 1 043 | 150 |
| 2014 | 7 063 | 6 213 | 626 | 224 | 1 852 | 538 | 1 229 | 85 | 899 | 151 |
| 2015 | 7 424 | 6 457 | 715 | 252 | 1 884 | 504 | 1 298 | 82 | 777 | 134 |
| **Women, 20 Years and Over** | | | | | | | | | | |
| 2000 | 6 651 | 5 753 | 615 | 283 | 1 052 | 197 | 788 | 67 | 456 | 56 |
| 2001 | 6 647 | 5 684 | 695 | 268 | 1 094 | 203 | 816 | 75 | 521 | 61 |
| 2002 | 6 492 | 5 605 | 626 | 261 | 1 117 | 234 | 816 | 68 | 671 | 67 |
| 2003 | 6 468 | 5 639 | 583 | 246 | 1 195 | 257 | 842 | 69 | 698 | 75 |
| 2004 | 6 512 | 5 674 | 595 | 243 | 1 195 | 287 | 844 | 64 | 679 | 76 |
| 2005 | 6 653 | 5 789 | 606 | 258 | 1 222 | 298 | 861 | 63 | 660 | 74 |
| 2006 | 6 893 | 6 042 | 588 | 263 | 1 175 | 255 | 848 | 72 | 588 | 67 |
| 2007 | 7 024 | 6 194 | 570 | 260 | 1 216 | 254 | 897 | 65 | 527 | 61 |
| 2008 | 7 006 | 6 160 | 580 | 267 | 1 254 | 283 | 902 | 68 | 654 | 78 |
| 2009 | 6 600 | 5 644 | 705 | 250 | 1 356 | 449 | 837 | 71 | 951 | 82 |
| 2010 | 6 471 | 5 681 | 575 | 215 | 1 473 | 504 | 894 | 75 | 1 063 | 103 |
| 2011 | 6 402 | 5 610 | 586 | 207 | 1 504 | 549 | 888 | 67 | 1 095 | 108 |
| 2012 | 6 682 | 5 901 | 547 | 235 | 1 631 | 531 | 1 021 | 79 | 1 021 | 98 |
| 2013 | 6 802 | 6 039 | 546 | 216 | 1 606 | 541 | 986 | 79 | 969 | 100 |
| 2014 | 7 063 | 6 213 | 626 | 224 | 1 852 | 538 | 1 229 | 85 | 899 | 151 |
| 2015 | 7 345 | 6 389 | 705 | 250 | 1 687 | 482 | 1 130 | 74 | 714 | 97 |

[1]Employed persons are classified as full- or part-time workers based on their usual weekly hours at all jobs, regardless of the number of hours they were at work during the reference week. Persons absent from work are also classified according to their usual status.
[2]Includes some persons at work 35 hours or more classified by their reason for working part time.
[3]Beginning in 2003, persons who selected this race group only; persons who selected more than one race group are not included. Prior to 2003, persons who reported more than one race group were included in the group they identified as their main race.

## Table 1-10.  Persons Not in the Labor Force, by Age, Sex, and Desire and Availability for Work, 2012–2015

(Thousands of people.)

| Category | Total | | Age | | | | | | Sex | | | |
|---|---|---|---|---|---|---|---|---|---|---|---|---|
| | | | 16 to 24 years | | 25 to 54 years | | 55 years and over | | Men | | Women | |
| | 2012 | 2013 | 2012 | 2013 | 2012 | 2013 | 2012 | 2013 | 2012 | 2013 | 2012 | 2013 |
| **TOTAL, NOT IN THE LABOR FORCE** ................................... | 88 310 | 90 290 | 17 499 | 17 458 | 23 061 | 23 630 | 47 750 | 49 201 | 35 017 | 35 889 | 53 293 | 54 401 |
| **Do Not Want a Job Now**[1] .............................................. | 81 752 | 83 901 | 15 383 | 15 362 | 20 248 | 20 898 | 46 120 | 47 641 | 31 989 | 32 947 | 49 763 | 50 953 |
| **Want a Job**[1] ................................................................. | 6 558 | 6 390 | 2 115 | 2 096 | 2 813 | 2 733 | 1 630 | 1 561 | 3 028 | 2 941 | 3 530 | 3 448 |
| Did not search for work in the previous year ............................ | 3 390 | 3 402 | 1 064 | 1 079 | 1 328 | 1 327 | 998 | 996 | 1 490 | 1 479 | 1 900 | 1 923 |
| Searched for work in the previous year[2] ............................... | 3 168 | 2 988 | 1 052 | 1 017 | 1 484 | 1 406 | 632 | 565 | 1 537 | 1 463 | 1 630 | 1 525 |
| Not available to work now .................................................. | 651 | 628 | 282 | 286 | 288 | 272 | 82 | 70 | 253 | 239 | 399 | 390 |
| Available to work now ....................................................... | 2 516 | 2 360 | 770 | 731 | 1 196 | 1 134 | 550 | 495 | 1 285 | 1 224 | 1 232 | 1 135 |
| Reason not currently looking: | | | | | | | | | | | | |
| Discouragement over job prospects[3] ............................ | 909 | 861 | 217 | 213 | 451 | 431 | 241 | 218 | 541 | 510 | 368 | 351 |
| Reasons other than discouragement ........................... | 1 608 | 1 498 | 553 | 518 | 746 | 703 | 309 | 277 | 743 | 714 | 864 | 784 |
| Family responsibilities ............................................... | 229 | 229 | 33 | 33 | 147 | 148 | 49 | 48 | 61 | 61 | 168 | 169 |
| In school or training ................................................. | 339 | 294 | 257 | 234 | 73 | 56 | 9 | 4 | 175 | 159 | 164 | 135 |
| Ill health or disability ............................................... | 168 | 151 | 18 | 18 | 83 | 74 | 66 | 58 | 80 | 74 | 87 | 77 |
| Other[4] ................................................................... | 871 | 823 | 245 | 232 | 442 | 425 | 185 | 166 | 427 | 420 | 444 | 403 |

| Category | Total | | Age | | | | | | Sex | | | |
|---|---|---|---|---|---|---|---|---|---|---|---|---|
| | | | 16 to 24 years | | 25 to 54 years | | 55 years and over | | Men | | Women | |
| | 2014 | 2015 | 2014 | 2015 | 2014 | 2015 | 2014 | 2015 | 2014 | 2015 | 2014 | 2015 |
| **TOTAL, NOT IN THE LABOR FORCE** ................................... | 92 025 | 93 671 | 17 418 | 17 367 | 23 744 | 23 957 | 50 863 | 52 347 | 36 865 | 37 481 | 55 159 | 56 190 |
| **Do Not Want a Job Now**[1] .............................................. | 85 702 | 87 589 | 15 377 | 15 525 | 21 075 | 21 344 | 49 250 | 50 719 | 33 932 | 34 681 | 51 770 | 52 907 |
| **Want a Job**[1] ................................................................. | 6 323 | 6 082 | 2 041 | 1 842 | 2 669 | 2 612 | 1 614 | 1 628 | 2 934 | 2 799 | 3 389 | 3 283 |
| Did not search for work in the previous year ............................ | 3 448 | 3 454 | 1 072 | 1 030 | 1 337 | 1 357 | 1 039 | 1 067 | 1 524 | 1 507 | 1 924 | 1 947 |
| Searched for work in the previous year[2] ............................... | 2 875 | 2 628 | 969 | 812 | 1 332 | 1 256 | 574 | 561 | 1 409 | 1 292 | 1 465 | 1 336 |
| Not available to work now .................................................. | 667 | 673 | 303 | 287 | 284 | 307 | 81 | 79 | 270 | 277 | 397 | 395 |
| Available to work now ....................................................... | 2 207 | 1 956 | 666 | 525 | 1 048 | 949 | 493 | 482 | 1 139 | 1 015 | 1 068 | 941 |
| Reason not currently looking: | | | | | | | | | | | | |
| Discouragement over job prospects[3] ............................ | 739 | 664 | 184 | 159 | 350 | 316 | 205 | 189 | 443 | 404 | 1 068 | 261 |
| Reasons other than discouragement ........................... | 1 468 | 1 291 | 482 | 366 | 697 | 632 | 289 | 293 | 696 | 611 | 772 | 680 |
| Family responsibilities ............................................... | 239 | 216 | 34 | 23 | 160 | 138 | 45 | 55 | 65 | 64 | 174 | 153 |
| In school or training ................................................. | 267 | 212 | 208 | 154 | 54 | 51 | 4 | 7 | 149 | 106 | 118 | 107 |
| Ill health or disability ............................................... | 161 | 168 | 16 | 16 | 84 | 77 | 61 | 75 | 82 | 84 | 80 | 84 |
| Other[4] ................................................................... | 801 | 695 | 224 | 174 | 398 | 366 | 179 | 155 | 400 | 358 | 401 | 337 |

[1]Includes some persons who were not asked if they wanted a job.
[2]Persons who had a job during the prior 12 months must have searched since the end of that job.
[3]Includes believes no work available, could not find work, lacks necessary schooling or training, employer thinks too young or old, and other types of discrimination.
[4]Includes those who did not actively look for work in the prior four weeks for reasons such as childcare and transportation problems, as well as a small number for whom reason for nonparticipation was not ascertained.

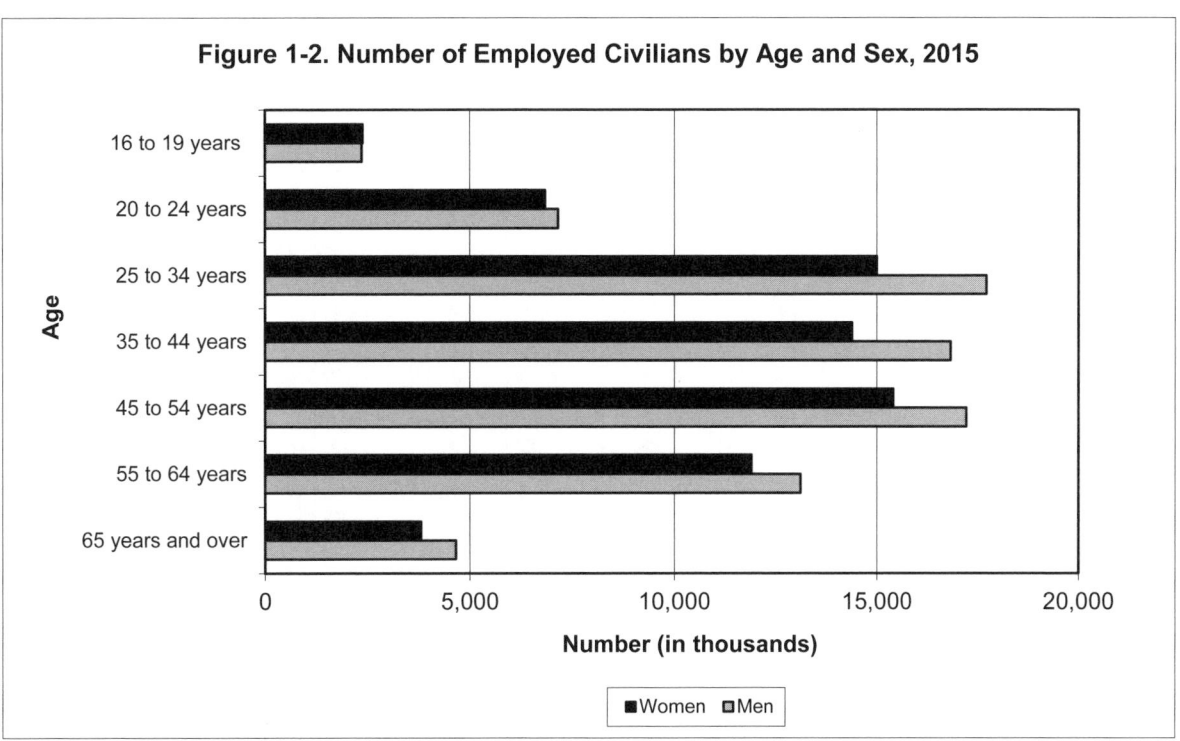

Figure 1-2. Number of Employed Civilians by Age and Sex, 2015

There were over 148.8 million employed civilians in the labor force in 2015—the highest amount ever. This represented an increase of 1.7 percent from 2014. From 2007 to 2011, the number of employed civilians declined 4.2 percent. (See Table 1-11.)

## OTHER HIGHLIGHTS

- While men made up 53.2 percent of employed civilians in 2015, they only made up 12.4 percent of employees in healthcare support occupations; 26.6 percent of employees in education, training, and library occupations; and 27.8 percent of employees in office and administrative support occupations. (See Table 1-13.)

- In 2015, employment increased for all groups regardless of educational attainment. It increased 0.5 for those with an associate's degree, 3.2 percent for those with a bachelor's degree only and 4.0 percent for those that are college graduates or higher. (See Table 1-16.)

- The multiple jobholding rate increased in May 2016 after decreasing in 2015. It was significantly higher for women (5.4 percent) than for men (4.6 percent). (See Table 1-17.)

- In 2015, slightly more than 5.6 million families had an unemployed member—a decline from nearly 6.5 million in 2014, 7.7 million in 2013, and 8.4 million in 2012. (See Table 1-20.)

## Table 1-11. Employed Civilians, by Age, Sex, Race, and Hispanic Origin, 1948–2015

(Thousands of people.)

| Race, Hispanic origin, sex, and year | 16 years and over | 16 to 19 years | | | 20 years and over | | | | | | |
|---|---|---|---|---|---|---|---|---|---|---|---|
| | | Total | 16 to 17 years | 18 to 19 years | Total | 20 to 24 years | 25 to 34 years | 35 to 44 years | 45 to 54 years | 55 to 64 years | 65 years and over |
| **ALL RACES** | | | | | | | | | | | |
| **Both Sexes** | | | | | | | | | | | |
| 1948 | 58 343 | 4 026 | 1 600 | 2 426 | 54 318 | 6 937 | 13 801 | 13 050 | 10 624 | 7 103 | 2 804 |
| 1949 | 57 651 | 3 712 | 1 466 | 2 246 | 53 940 | 6 660 | 13 639 | 13 108 | 10 636 | 7 042 | 2 864 |
| 1950 | 58 918 | 3 703 | 1 433 | 2 270 | 55 218 | 6 746 | 13 917 | 13 424 | 10 966 | 7 265 | 2 899 |
| 1951 | 59 961 | 3 767 | 1 575 | 2 192 | 56 196 | 6 321 | 14 233 | 13 746 | 11 421 | 7 558 | 2 917 |
| 1952 | 60 250 | 3 719 | 1 626 | 2 092 | 56 536 | 5 572 | 14 515 | 14 058 | 11 687 | 7 785 | 2 919 |
| 1953 | 61 179 | 3 720 | 1 577 | 2 142 | 57 460 | 5 225 | 14 519 | 14 774 | 11 969 | 7 806 | 3 166 |
| 1954 | 60 109 | 3 475 | 1 422 | 2 053 | 56 634 | 4 971 | 14 190 | 14 541 | 11 976 | 7 895 | 3 060 |
| 1955 | 62 170 | 3 642 | 1 500 | 2 143 | 58 528 | 5 270 | 14 481 | 14 879 | 12 556 | 8 158 | 3 185 |
| 1956 | 63 799 | 3 818 | 1 647 | 2 171 | 59 983 | 5 545 | 14 407 | 15 218 | 12 978 | 8 519 | 3 314 |
| 1957 | 64 071 | 3 778 | 1 613 | 2 167 | 60 291 | 5 641 | 14 253 | 15 348 | 13 320 | 8 553 | 3 179 |
| 1958 | 63 036 | 3 582 | 1 519 | 2 063 | 59 454 | 5 571 | 13 675 | 15 157 | 13 448 | 8 559 | 3 045 |
| 1959 | 64 630 | 3 838 | 1 670 | 2 168 | 60 791 | 5 870 | 13 709 | 15 454 | 13 915 | 8 822 | 3 023 |
| 1960 | 65 778 | 4 129 | 1 770 | 2 360 | 61 648 | 6 119 | 13 630 | 15 598 | 14 238 | 8 989 | 3 073 |
| 1961 | 65 746 | 4 108 | 1 621 | 2 486 | 61 638 | 6 227 | 13 429 | 15 552 | 14 320 | 9 120 | 2 987 |
| 1962 | 66 702 | 4 195 | 1 607 | 2 588 | 62 508 | 6 446 | 13 311 | 15 901 | 14 491 | 9 346 | 3 013 |
| 1963 | 67 762 | 4 255 | 1 751 | 2 504 | 63 508 | 6 815 | 13 318 | 16 114 | 14 749 | 9 596 | 2 915 |
| 1964 | 69 305 | 4 516 | 2 013 | 2 503 | 64 789 | 7 303 | 13 449 | 16 166 | 15 094 | 9 804 | 2 973 |
| 1965 | 71 088 | 5 036 | 2 075 | 2 962 | 66 052 | 7 702 | 13 704 | 16 294 | 15 320 | 10 028 | 3 005 |
| 1966 | 72 895 | 5 721 | 2 269 | 3 452 | 67 178 | 7 964 | 14 017 | 16 312 | 15 615 | 10 310 | 2 961 |
| 1967 | 74 372 | 5 682 | 2 334 | 3 348 | 68 690 | 8 499 | 14 575 | 16 281 | 15 789 | 10 536 | 3 011 |
| 1968 | 75 920 | 5 781 | 2 403 | 3 377 | 70 141 | 8 762 | 15 265 | 16 220 | 16 083 | 10 745 | 3 065 |
| 1969 | 77 902 | 6 117 | 2 573 | 3 543 | 71 785 | 9 319 | 15 883 | 16 100 | 16 410 | 10 919 | 3 155 |
| 1970 | 78 678 | 6 144 | 2 598 | 3 546 | 72 534 | 9 731 | 16 318 | 15 922 | 16 473 | 10 974 | 3 118 |
| 1971 | 79 367 | 6 208 | 2 596 | 3 613 | 73 158 | 10 201 | 16 781 | 15 675 | 16 451 | 11 009 | 3 040 |
| 1972 | 82 153 | 6 746 | 2 787 | 3 959 | 75 407 | 10 999 | 18 082 | 15 822 | 16 457 | 11 044 | 3 003 |
| 1973 | 85 064 | 7 271 | 3 032 | 4 239 | 77 793 | 11 839 | 19 509 | 16 041 | 16 553 | 10 966 | 2 886 |
| 1974 | 86 794 | 7 448 | 3 111 | 4 338 | 79 347 | 12 101 | 20 610 | 16 203 | 16 633 | 10 964 | 2 835 |
| 1975 | 85 846 | 7 104 | 2 941 | 4 162 | 78 744 | 11 885 | 21 087 | 15 953 | 16 190 | 10 827 | 2 801 |
| 1976 | 88 752 | 7 336 | 2 972 | 4 363 | 81 416 | 12 570 | 22 493 | 16 468 | 16 224 | 10 912 | 2 747 |
| 1977 | 92 017 | 7 688 | 3 138 | 4 550 | 84 329 | 13 196 | 23 850 | 17 157 | 16 212 | 11 126 | 2 787 |
| 1978 | 96 048 | 8 070 | 3 330 | 4 739 | 87 979 | 13 887 | 25 281 | 18 128 | 16 338 | 11 400 | 2 946 |
| 1979 | 98 824 | 8 083 | 3 340 | 4 743 | 90 741 | 14 327 | 26 492 | 18 981 | 16 357 | 11 585 | 2 999 |
| 1980 | 99 303 | 7 710 | 3 106 | 4 605 | 91 593 | 14 087 | 27 204 | 19 523 | 16 234 | 11 586 | 2 960 |
| 1981 | 100 397 | 7 225 | 2 866 | 4 359 | 93 172 | 14 122 | 28 180 | 20 145 | 16 255 | 11 525 | 2 945 |
| 1982 | 99 526 | 6 549 | 2 505 | 4 044 | 92 978 | 13 690 | 28 149 | 20 879 | 15 923 | 11 414 | 2 923 |
| 1983 | 100 834 | 6 342 | 2 320 | 4 022 | 94 491 | 13 722 | 28 756 | 21 960 | 15 812 | 11 315 | 2 927 |
| 1984 | 105 005 | 6 444 | 2 404 | 4 040 | 98 562 | 14 207 | 30 348 | 23 598 | 16 178 | 11 395 | 2 835 |
| 1985 | 107 150 | 6 434 | 2 492 | 3 941 | 100 716 | 13 980 | 31 208 | 24 732 | 16 509 | 11 474 | 2 813 |
| 1986 | 109 597 | 6 472 | 2 622 | 3 850 | 103 125 | 13 790 | 32 201 | 25 861 | 16 949 | 11 405 | 2 919 |
| 1987 | 112 440 | 6 640 | 2 736 | 3 905 | 105 800 | 13 524 | 33 105 | 27 179 | 17 487 | 11 465 | 3 041 |
| 1988 | 114 968 | 6 805 | 2 713 | 4 092 | 108 164 | 13 244 | 33 574 | 28 269 | 18 447 | 11 433 | 3 197 |
| 1989 | 117 342 | 6 759 | 2 588 | 4 172 | 110 582 | 12 962 | 34 045 | 29 443 | 19 279 | 11 499 | 3 355 |
| 1990 | 118 793 | 6 581 | 2 410 | 4 171 | 112 213 | 13 401 | 33 935 | 30 817 | 19 525 | 11 189 | 3 346 |
| 1991 | 117 718 | 5 906 | 2 202 | 3 704 | 111 812 | 12 975 | 33 061 | 31 593 | 19 882 | 11 001 | 3 300 |
| 1992 | 118 492 | 5 669 | 2 128 | 3 540 | 112 824 | 12 872 | 32 667 | 31 923 | 21 022 | 10 998 | 3 341 |
| 1993 | 120 259 | 5 805 | 2 226 | 3 579 | 114 455 | 12 840 | 32 385 | 32 666 | 22 175 | 11 058 | 3 331 |
| 1994 | 123 060 | 6 161 | 2 510 | 3 651 | 116 899 | 12 758 | 32 286 | 33 599 | 23 348 | 11 228 | 3 681 |
| 1995 | 124 900 | 6 419 | 2 573 | 3 846 | 118 481 | 12 443 | 32 356 | 34 202 | 24 378 | 11 435 | 3 666 |
| 1996 | 126 708 | 6 500 | 2 646 | 3 853 | 120 208 | 12 138 | 32 077 | 35 051 | 25 514 | 11 739 | 3 690 |
| 1997 | 129 558 | 6 661 | 2 648 | 4 012 | 122 897 | 12 380 | 31 809 | 35 908 | 26 744 | 12 296 | 3 761 |
| 1998 | 131 463 | 7 051 | 2 762 | 4 289 | 124 413 | 12 557 | 31 394 | 36 278 | 27 587 | 12 872 | 3 725 |
| 1999 | 133 488 | 7 172 | 2 793 | 4 379 | 126 316 | 12 891 | 30 865 | 36 728 | 28 635 | 13 315 | 3 882 |
| 2000 | 136 891 | 7 189 | 2 759 | 4 431 | 129 701 | 13 229 | 31 549 | 36 433 | 30 310 | 14 002 | 4 179 |
| 2001 | 136 933 | 6 740 | 2 558 | 4 182 | 130 194 | 13 348 | 30 863 | 36 049 | 31 036 | 14 645 | 4 253 |
| 2002 | 136 485 | 6 332 | 2 330 | 4 002 | 130 154 | 13 351 | 30 306 | 35 235 | 31 281 | 15 674 | 4 306 |
| 2003 | 137 736 | 5 919 | 2 312 | 3 607 | 131 817 | 13 433 | 30 383 | 34 881 | 31 914 | 16 598 | 4 608 |
| 2004 | 139 252 | 5 907 | 2 193 | 3 714 | 133 345 | 13 723 | 30 423 | 34 580 | 32 469 | 17 331 | 4 819 |
| 2005 | 141 730 | 5 978 | 2 284 | 3 694 | 135 752 | 13 792 | 30 680 | 34 630 | 33 207 | 18 349 | 5 094 |
| 2006 | 144 427 | 6 162 | 2 444 | 3 719 | 138 265 | 13 878 | 31 051 | 34 569 | 34 052 | 19 389 | 5 325 |
| 2007 | 146 047 | 5 911 | 2 286 | 3 625 | 140 136 | 13 964 | 31 586 | 34 302 | 34 563 | 20 108 | 5 614 |
| 2008 | 145 362 | 5 573 | 1 989 | 3 584 | 139 790 | 13 629 | 31 383 | 33 457 | 34 529 | 20 812 | 5 979 |
| 2009 | 139 877 | 4 837 | 1 651 | 3 187 | 135 040 | 12 764 | 30 014 | 31 517 | 33 613 | 21 019 | 6 114 |
| 2010 | 139 064 | 4 378 | 1 418 | 2 960 | 134 686 | 12 699 | 30 229 | 30 663 | 33 191 | 21 636 | 6 268 |
| 2011 | 139 869 | 4 327 | 1 355 | 2 972 | 135 542 | 13 036 | 30 537 | 30 270 | 32 867 | 22 186 | 6 647 |
| 2012 | 142 469 | 4 426 | 1 419 | 3 007 | 138 043 | 13 408 | 30 701 | 30 576 | 32 874 | 23 239 | 7 245 |
| 2013 | 143 929 | 4 458 | 1 487 | 2 971 | 139 471 | 13 599 | 31 242 | 30 650 | 32 523 | 23 776 | 7 681 |
| 2014 | 146 305 | 4 548 | 1 545 | 3 003 | 141 757 | 13 894 | 31 975 | 30 966 | 32 556 | 24 395 | 7 971 |
| 2015 | 148 834 | 4 734 | 1 624 | 3 110 | 144 099 | 14 022 | 32 742 | 31 252 | 32 643 | 24 975 | 8 465 |

## Table 1-11. Employed Civilians, by Age, Sex, Race, and Hispanic Origin, 1948–2015—*Continued*

(Thousands of people.)

| Race, Hispanic origin, sex, and year | 16 years and over | 16 to 19 years | | | 20 years and over | | | | | | |
|---|---|---|---|---|---|---|---|---|---|---|---|
| | | Total | 16 to 17 years | 18 to 19 years | Total | 20 to 24 years | 25 to 34 years | 35 to 44 years | 45 to 54 years | 55 to 64 years | 65 years and over |
| **ALL RACES** | | | | | | | | | | | |
| **Men** | | | | | | | | | | | |
| 1948 | 41 725 | 2 344 | 996 | 1 348 | 39 382 | 4 349 | 10 038 | 9 363 | 7 742 | 5 587 | 2 303 |
| 1949 | 40 925 | 2 124 | 911 | 1 213 | 38 803 | 4 197 | 9 879 | 9 308 | 7 661 | 5 438 | 2 329 |
| 1950 | 41 578 | 2 186 | 909 | 1 277 | 39 394 | 4 255 | 10 060 | 9 445 | 7 790 | 5 508 | 2 336 |
| 1951 | 41 780 | 2 156 | 979 | 1 177 | 39 626 | 3 780 | 10 134 | 9 607 | 8 012 | 5 711 | 2 382 |
| 1952 | 41 682 | 2 107 | 985 | 1 121 | 39 578 | 3 183 | 10 352 | 9 753 | 8 144 | 5 804 | 2 343 |
| 1953 | 42 430 | 2 136 | 976 | 1 159 | 40 296 | 2 901 | 10 500 | 10 229 | 8 374 | 5 808 | 2 483 |
| 1954 | 41 619 | 1 985 | 881 | 1 104 | 39 634 | 2 724 | 10 254 | 10 082 | 8 330 | 5 830 | 2 414 |
| 1955 | 42 621 | 2 095 | 936 | 1 159 | 40 526 | 2 973 | 10 453 | 10 267 | 8 553 | 5 857 | 2 424 |
| 1956 | 43 379 | 2 164 | 1 008 | 1 156 | 41 216 | 3 245 | 10 337 | 10 385 | 8 732 | 6 004 | 2 512 |
| 1957 | 43 357 | 2 115 | 987 | 1 130 | 41 239 | 3 346 | 10 222 | 10 427 | 8 851 | 6 002 | 2 394 |
| 1958 | 42 423 | 2 012 | 948 | 1 064 | 40 411 | 3 293 | 9 790 | 10 291 | 8 828 | 5 955 | 2 254 |
| 1959 | 43 466 | 2 198 | 1 015 | 1 183 | 41 267 | 3 597 | 9 862 | 10 492 | 9 048 | 6 058 | 2 210 |
| 1960 | 43 904 | 2 361 | 1 090 | 1 271 | 41 543 | 3 754 | 9 759 | 10 552 | 9 182 | 6 105 | 2 191 |
| 1961 | 43 656 | 2 315 | 989 | 1 325 | 41 342 | 3 795 | 9 591 | 10 505 | 9 195 | 6 155 | 2 098 |
| 1962 | 44 177 | 2 362 | 990 | 1 372 | 41 815 | 3 898 | 9 475 | 10 711 | 9 333 | 6 260 | 2 138 |
| 1963 | 44 657 | 2 406 | 1 073 | 1 334 | 42 251 | 4 118 | 9 431 | 10 801 | 9 478 | 6 385 | 2 038 |
| 1964 | 45 474 | 2 587 | 1 242 | 1 345 | 42 886 | 4 370 | 9 531 | 10 832 | 9 637 | 6 478 | 2 039 |
| 1965 | 46 340 | 2 918 | 1 285 | 1 634 | 43 422 | 4 583 | 9 611 | 10 837 | 9 792 | 6 542 | 2 057 |
| 1966 | 46 919 | 3 253 | 1 389 | 1 863 | 43 668 | 4 599 | 9 709 | 10 764 | 9 904 | 6 668 | 2 024 |
| 1967 | 47 479 | 3 186 | 1 417 | 1 769 | 44 294 | 4 809 | 9 988 | 10 674 | 9 990 | 6 774 | 2 058 |
| 1968 | 48 114 | 3 255 | 1 453 | 1 802 | 44 859 | 4 812 | 10 405 | 10 554 | 10 102 | 6 893 | 2 093 |
| 1969 | 48 818 | 3 430 | 1 526 | 1 904 | 45 388 | 5 012 | 10 736 | 10 401 | 10 187 | 6 931 | 2 122 |
| 1970 | 48 990 | 3 409 | 1 504 | 1 905 | 45 581 | 5 237 | 10 936 | 10 216 | 10 170 | 6 928 | 2 094 |
| 1971 | 49 390 | 3 478 | 1 510 | 1 968 | 45 912 | 5 593 | 11 218 | 10 028 | 10 139 | 6 916 | 2 019 |
| 1972 | 50 896 | 3 765 | 1 598 | 2 167 | 47 130 | 6 138 | 11 884 | 10 088 | 10 139 | 6 929 | 1 953 |
| 1973 | 52 349 | 4 039 | 1 721 | 2 318 | 48 310 | 6 655 | 12 617 | 10 126 | 10 197 | 6 857 | 1 856 |
| 1974 | 53 024 | 4 103 | 1 744 | 2 359 | 48 922 | 6 739 | 13 119 | 10 135 | 10 181 | 6 880 | 1 869 |
| 1975 | 51 857 | 3 839 | 1 621 | 2 219 | 48 018 | 6 484 | 13 205 | 9 891 | 9 902 | 6 722 | 1 811 |
| 1976 | 53 138 | 3 947 | 1 626 | 2 321 | 49 190 | 6 915 | 13 869 | 10 069 | 9 881 | 6 724 | 1 732 |
| 1977 | 54 728 | 4 174 | 1 733 | 2 441 | 50 555 | 7 232 | 14 483 | 10 399 | 9 832 | 6 848 | 1 761 |
| 1978 | 56 479 | 4 336 | 1 800 | 2 535 | 52 143 | 7 559 | 15 124 | 10 845 | 9 806 | 6 954 | 1 855 |
| 1979 | 57 607 | 4 300 | 1 799 | 2 501 | 53 308 | 7 791 | 15 688 | 11 202 | 9 735 | 7 015 | 1 876 |
| 1980 | 57 186 | 4 085 | 1 672 | 2 412 | 53 101 | 7 532 | 15 832 | 11 355 | 9 548 | 6 999 | 1 835 |
| 1981 | 57 397 | 3 815 | 1 526 | 2 289 | 53 582 | 7 504 | 16 266 | 11 613 | 9 478 | 6 909 | 1 812 |
| 1982 | 56 271 | 3 379 | 1 307 | 2 072 | 52 891 | 7 197 | 16 002 | 11 902 | 9 234 | 6 781 | 1 776 |
| 1983 | 56 787 | 3 300 | 1 213 | 2 087 | 53 487 | 7 232 | 16 216 | 12 450 | 9 133 | 6 686 | 1 770 |
| 1984 | 59 091 | 3 322 | 1 244 | 2 078 | 55 769 | 7 571 | 17 166 | 13 309 | 9 326 | 6 694 | 1 703 |
| 1985 | 59 891 | 3 328 | 1 300 | 2 029 | 56 562 | 7 339 | 17 564 | 13 800 | 9 411 | 6 753 | 1 695 |
| 1986 | 60 892 | 3 323 | 1 352 | 1 971 | 57 569 | 7 250 | 18 092 | 14 266 | 9 554 | 6 654 | 1 753 |
| 1987 | 62 107 | 3 381 | 1 393 | 1 988 | 58 726 | 7 058 | 18 487 | 14 898 | 9 750 | 6 682 | 1 850 |
| 1988 | 63 273 | 3 492 | 1 403 | 2 089 | 59 781 | 6 918 | 18 702 | 15 457 | 10 201 | 6 591 | 1 911 |
| 1989 | 64 315 | 3 477 | 1 327 | 2 150 | 60 837 | 6 799 | 18 952 | 16 002 | 10 569 | 6 548 | 1 968 |
| 1990 | 65 104 | 3 427 | 1 254 | 2 173 | 61 678 | 7 151 | 18 779 | 16 771 | 10 690 | 6 378 | 1 909 |
| 1991 | 64 223 | 3 044 | 1 135 | 1 909 | 61 178 | 6 909 | 18 265 | 17 086 | 10 813 | 6 245 | 1 860 |
| 1992 | 64 440 | 2 944 | 1 096 | 1 848 | 61 496 | 6 819 | 17 966 | 17 230 | 11 365 | 6 173 | 1 943 |
| 1993 | 65 349 | 2 994 | 1 155 | 1 839 | 62 355 | 6 805 | 17 877 | 17 665 | 11 927 | 6 166 | 1 916 |
| 1994 | 66 450 | 3 156 | 1 288 | 1 868 | 63 294 | 6 771 | 17 741 | 18 111 | 12 439 | 6 142 | 2 089 |
| 1995 | 67 377 | 3 292 | 1 316 | 1 977 | 64 085 | 6 665 | 17 709 | 18 374 | 12 958 | 6 272 | 2 108 |
| 1996 | 68 207 | 3 310 | 1 318 | 1 992 | 64 897 | 6 429 | 17 527 | 18 816 | 13 483 | 6 470 | 2 172 |
| 1997 | 69 685 | 3 401 | 1 355 | 2 045 | 66 284 | 6 548 | 17 338 | 19 327 | 14 107 | 6 735 | 2 229 |
| 1998 | 70 693 | 3 558 | 1 398 | 2 161 | 67 135 | 6 638 | 17 097 | 19 634 | 14 544 | 7 052 | 2 171 |
| 1999 | 71 446 | 3 685 | 1 437 | 2 249 | 67 761 | 6 729 | 16 694 | 19 811 | 14 991 | 7 274 | 2 263 |
| 2000 | 73 305 | 3 671 | 1 394 | 2 276 | 69 634 | 6 974 | 17 241 | 19 537 | 15 871 | 7 606 | 2 406 |
| 2001 | 73 196 | 3 420 | 1 268 | 2 151 | 69 776 | 6 952 | 16 915 | 19 305 | 16 268 | 7 900 | 2 437 |
| 2002 | 72 903 | 3 169 | 1 130 | 2 040 | 69 734 | 6 978 | 16 573 | 18 932 | 16 419 | 8 378 | 2 455 |
| 2003 | 73 332 | 2 917 | 1 115 | 1 802 | 70 415 | 7 065 | 16 670 | 18 774 | 16 588 | 8 733 | 2 585 |
| 2004 | 74 524 | 2 952 | 1 037 | 1 915 | 71 572 | 7 246 | 16 818 | 18 700 | 16 951 | 9 174 | 2 683 |
| 2005 | 75 973 | 2 923 | 1 067 | 1 855 | 73 050 | 7 279 | 16 993 | 18 780 | 17 429 | 9 714 | 2 857 |
| 2006 | 77 502 | 3 071 | 1 182 | 1 888 | 74 431 | 7 412 | 17 134 | 18 765 | 17 920 | 10 192 | 3 008 |
| 2007 | 78 254 | 2 917 | 1 091 | 1 827 | 75 337 | 7 374 | 17 452 | 18 666 | 18 210 | 10 556 | 3 080 |
| 2008 | 77 486 | 2 736 | 926 | 1 810 | 74 750 | 7 145 | 17 183 | 18 097 | 18 124 | 10 919 | 3 282 |
| 2009 | 73 670 | 2 328 | 786 | 1 543 | 71 341 | 6 510 | 16 223 | 16 918 | 17 443 | 10 890 | 3 357 |
| 2010 | 73 359 | 2 129 | 675 | 1 454 | 71 230 | 6 466 | 16 358 | 16 585 | 17 242 | 11 140 | 3 439 |
| 2011 | 74 290 | 2 108 | 650 | 1 459 | 72 182 | 6 826 | 16 674 | 16 370 | 17 113 | 11 469 | 3 730 |
| 2012 | 75 555 | 2 152 | 659 | 1 493 | 73 403 | 6 948 | 16 607 | 16 483 | 17 221 | 12 068 | 4 077 |
| 2013 | 76 353 | 2 177 | 700 | 1 477 | 74 176 | 7 013 | 16 907 | 16 590 | 17 033 | 12 276 | 4 257 |
| 2014 | 77 692 | 2 222 | 729 | 1 493 | 75 471 | 7 187 | 17 293 | 16 735 | 17 118 | 12 762 | 4 377 |
| 2015 | 79 131 | 2 354 | 799 | 1 555 | 76 776 | 7 173 | 17 746 | 16 861 | 17 245 | 13 092 | 4 661 |

## Table 1-11. Employed Civilians, by Age, Sex, Race, and Hispanic Origin, 1948–2015—*Continued*

(Thousands of people.)

| Race, Hispanic origin, sex, and year | 16 years and over | 16 to 19 years | | | 20 years and over | | | | | | |
|---|---|---|---|---|---|---|---|---|---|---|---|
| | | Total | 16 to 17 years | 18 to 19 years | Total | 20 to 24 years | 25 to 34 years | 35 to 44 years | 45 to 54 years | 55 to 64 years | 65 years and over |
| **ALL RACES** | | | | | | | | | | | |
| **Women** | | | | | | | | | | | |
| 1948 | 16 617 | 1 682 | 604 | 1 078 | 14 936 | 2 588 | 3 763 | 3 687 | 2 882 | 1 516 | 501 |
| 1949 | 16 723 | 1 588 | 555 | 1 033 | 15 137 | 2 463 | 3 760 | 3 800 | 2 975 | 1 604 | 535 |
| 1950 | 17 340 | 1 517 | 524 | 993 | 15 824 | 2 491 | 3 857 | 3 979 | 3 176 | 1 757 | 563 |
| 1951 | 18 181 | 1 611 | 596 | 1 015 | 16 570 | 2 541 | 4 099 | 4 139 | 3 409 | 1 847 | 535 |
| 1952 | 18 568 | 1 612 | 641 | 971 | 16 958 | 2 389 | 4 163 | 4 305 | 3 543 | 1 981 | 576 |
| 1953 | 18 749 | 1 584 | 601 | 983 | 17 164 | 2 324 | 4 019 | 4 545 | 3 595 | 1 998 | 683 |
| 1954 | 18 490 | 1 490 | 541 | 949 | 17 000 | 2 247 | 3 936 | 4 459 | 3 646 | 2 065 | 646 |
| 1955 | 19 551 | 1 547 | 564 | 984 | 18 002 | 2 297 | 4 028 | 4 612 | 4 003 | 2 301 | 761 |
| 1956 | 20 419 | 1 654 | 639 | 1 015 | 18 767 | 2 300 | 4 070 | 4 833 | 4 246 | 2 515 | 802 |
| 1957 | 20 714 | 1 663 | 626 | 1 037 | 19 052 | 2 295 | 4 031 | 4 921 | 4 469 | 2 551 | 785 |
| 1958 | 20 613 | 1 570 | 571 | 999 | 19 043 | 2 278 | 3 885 | 4 866 | 4 620 | 2 604 | 791 |
| 1959 | 21 164 | 1 640 | 655 | 985 | 19 524 | 2 273 | 3 847 | 4 962 | 4 867 | 2 764 | 813 |
| 1960 | 21 874 | 1 768 | 680 | 1 089 | 20 105 | 2 365 | 3 871 | 5 046 | 5 056 | 2 884 | 882 |
| 1961 | 22 090 | 1 793 | 632 | 1 161 | 20 296 | 2 432 | 3 838 | 5 047 | 5 125 | 2 965 | 889 |
| 1962 | 22 525 | 1 833 | 617 | 1 216 | 20 693 | 2 548 | 3 836 | 5 190 | 5 158 | 3 086 | 875 |
| 1963 | 23 105 | 1 849 | 678 | 1 170 | 21 257 | 2 697 | 3 887 | 5 313 | 5 271 | 3 211 | 877 |
| 1964 | 23 831 | 1 929 | 771 | 1 158 | 21 903 | 2 933 | 3 918 | 5 334 | 5 457 | 3 326 | 934 |
| 1965 | 24 748 | 2 118 | 790 | 1 328 | 22 630 | 3 119 | 4 093 | 5 457 | 5 528 | 3 486 | 948 |
| 1966 | 25 976 | 2 468 | 880 | 1 589 | 23 510 | 3 365 | 4 308 | 5 548 | 5 711 | 3 642 | 937 |
| 1967 | 26 893 | 2 496 | 917 | 1 579 | 24 397 | 3 690 | 4 587 | 5 607 | 5 799 | 3 762 | 953 |
| 1968 | 27 807 | 2 526 | 950 | 1 575 | 25 281 | 3 950 | 4 860 | 5 666 | 5 981 | 3 852 | 972 |
| 1969 | 29 084 | 2 687 | 1 047 | 1 639 | 26 397 | 4 307 | 5 147 | 5 699 | 6 223 | 3 988 | 1 033 |
| 1970 | 29 688 | 2 735 | 1 094 | 1 641 | 26 952 | 4 494 | 5 382 | 5 706 | 6 303 | 4 046 | 1 023 |
| 1971 | 29 976 | 2 730 | 1 086 | 1 645 | 27 246 | 4 609 | 5 563 | 5 647 | 6 313 | 4 093 | 1 021 |
| 1972 | 31 257 | 2 980 | 1 188 | 1 792 | 28 276 | 4 861 | 6 197 | 5 734 | 6 318 | 4 115 | 1 051 |
| 1973 | 32 715 | 3 231 | 1 310 | 1 920 | 29 484 | 5 184 | 6 893 | 5 915 | 6 356 | 4 109 | 1 029 |
| 1974 | 33 769 | 3 345 | 1 367 | 1 978 | 30 424 | 5 363 | 7 492 | 6 068 | 6 451 | 4 084 | 966 |
| 1975 | 33 989 | 3 263 | 1 320 | 1 943 | 30 726 | 5 401 | 7 882 | 6 061 | 6 288 | 4 105 | 989 |
| 1976 | 35 615 | 3 389 | 1 346 | 2 043 | 32 226 | 5 655 | 8 624 | 6 400 | 6 343 | 4 188 | 1 017 |
| 1977 | 37 289 | 3 514 | 1 403 | 2 110 | 33 775 | 5 965 | 9 367 | 6 758 | 6 380 | 4 279 | 1 027 |
| 1978 | 39 569 | 3 734 | 1 530 | 2 204 | 35 836 | 6 328 | 10 157 | 7 282 | 6 532 | 4 446 | 1 091 |
| 1979 | 41 217 | 3 783 | 1 541 | 2 242 | 37 434 | 6 538 | 10 802 | 7 779 | 6 622 | 4 569 | 1 124 |
| 1980 | 42 117 | 3 625 | 1 433 | 2 192 | 38 492 | 6 555 | 11 370 | 8 168 | 6 686 | 4 587 | 1 125 |
| 1981 | 43 000 | 3 411 | 1 340 | 2 070 | 39 590 | 6 618 | 11 914 | 8 532 | 6 777 | 4 616 | 1 133 |
| 1982 | 43 256 | 3 170 | 1 198 | 1 972 | 40 086 | 6 492 | 12 147 | 8 977 | 6 689 | 4 634 | 1 147 |
| 1983 | 44 047 | 3 043 | 1 107 | 1 935 | 41 004 | 6 490 | 12 540 | 9 510 | 6 678 | 4 629 | 1 157 |
| 1984 | 45 915 | 3 122 | 1 161 | 1 962 | 42 793 | 6 636 | 13 182 | 10 289 | 6 852 | 4 700 | 1 133 |
| 1985 | 47 259 | 3 105 | 1 193 | 1 913 | 44 154 | 6 640 | 13 644 | 10 933 | 7 097 | 4 721 | 1 118 |
| 1986 | 48 706 | 3 149 | 1 270 | 1 879 | 45 556 | 6 540 | 14 109 | 11 595 | 7 395 | 4 751 | 1 165 |
| 1987 | 50 334 | 3 260 | 1 343 | 1 917 | 47 074 | 6 466 | 14 617 | 12 281 | 7 737 | 4 783 | 1 191 |
| 1988 | 51 696 | 3 313 | 1 310 | 2 003 | 48 383 | 6 326 | 14 872 | 12 811 | 8 246 | 4 841 | 1 286 |
| 1989 | 53 027 | 3 282 | 1 261 | 2 021 | 49 745 | 6 163 | 15 093 | 13 440 | 8 711 | 4 950 | 1 388 |
| 1990 | 53 689 | 3 154 | 1 156 | 1 998 | 50 535 | 6 250 | 15 155 | 14 046 | 8 835 | 4 811 | 1 437 |
| 1991 | 53 496 | 2 862 | 1 067 | 1 794 | 50 634 | 6 066 | 14 796 | 14 507 | 9 069 | 4 756 | 1 440 |
| 1992 | 54 052 | 2 724 | 1 032 | 1 692 | 51 328 | 6 053 | 14 701 | 14 693 | 9 657 | 4 825 | 1 398 |
| 1993 | 54 910 | 2 811 | 1 071 | 1 740 | 52 099 | 6 035 | 14 508 | 15 002 | 10 248 | 4 892 | 1 414 |
| 1994 | 56 610 | 3 005 | 1 222 | 1 783 | 53 606 | 5 987 | 14 545 | 15 488 | 10 908 | 5 085 | 1 592 |
| 1995 | 57 523 | 3 127 | 1 258 | 1 869 | 54 396 | 5 779 | 14 647 | 15 828 | 11 421 | 5 163 | 1 558 |
| 1996 | 58 501 | 3 190 | 1 328 | 1 862 | 55 311 | 5 709 | 14 549 | 16 235 | 12 031 | 5 269 | 1 518 |
| 1997 | 59 873 | 3 260 | 1 293 | 1 967 | 56 613 | 5 831 | 14 471 | 16 581 | 12 637 | 5 561 | 1 532 |
| 1998 | 60 771 | 3 493 | 1 364 | 2 128 | 57 278 | 5 919 | 14 298 | 16 644 | 13 043 | 5 820 | 1 554 |
| 1999 | 62 042 | 3 487 | 1 357 | 2 130 | 58 555 | 6 163 | 14 171 | 16 917 | 13 644 | 6 041 | 1 619 |
| 2000 | 63 586 | 3 519 | 1 364 | 2 154 | 60 067 | 6 255 | 14 308 | 16 897 | 14 438 | 6 396 | 1 773 |
| 2001 | 63 737 | 3 320 | 1 289 | 2 031 | 60 417 | 6 396 | 13 948 | 16 744 | 14 768 | 6 745 | 1 815 |
| 2002 | 63 582 | 3 162 | 1 200 | 1 962 | 60 420 | 6 374 | 13 733 | 16 303 | 14 863 | 7 296 | 1 851 |
| 2003 | 64 404 | 3 002 | 1 197 | 1 805 | 61 402 | 6 367 | 13 714 | 16 106 | 15 326 | 7 866 | 2 023 |
| 2004 | 64 728 | 2 955 | 1 156 | 1 799 | 61 773 | 6 477 | 13 605 | 15 880 | 15 518 | 8 157 | 2 135 |
| 2005 | 65 757 | 3 055 | 1 217 | 1 838 | 62 702 | 6 513 | 13 687 | 15 850 | 15 779 | 8 635 | 2 238 |
| 2006 | 66 925 | 3 091 | 1 261 | 1 830 | 63 834 | 6 467 | 13 917 | 15 804 | 16 132 | 9 198 | 2 316 |
| 2007 | 67 792 | 2 994 | 1 195 | 1 798 | 64 799 | 6 590 | 14 133 | 15 636 | 16 353 | 9 553 | 2 534 |
| 2008 | 67 876 | 2 837 | 1 063 | 1 774 | 65 039 | 6 484 | 14 200 | 15 360 | 16 406 | 9 893 | 2 697 |
| 2009 | 66 208 | 2 509 | 865 | 1 644 | 63 699 | 6 254 | 13 791 | 14 599 | 16 170 | 10 128 | 2 757 |
| 2010 | 65 705 | 2 249 | 743 | 1 506 | 63 456 | 6 233 | 13 870 | 14 078 | 15 949 | 10 496 | 2 830 |
| 2011 | 65 579 | 2 219 | 705 | 1 514 | 63 360 | 6 209 | 13 863 | 13 900 | 15 753 | 10 717 | 2 917 |
| 2012 | 66 914 | 2 274 | 760 | 1 514 | 64 640 | 6 460 | 14 094 | 14 093 | 15 653 | 11 171 | 3 168 |
| 2013 | 67 577 | 2 281 | 787 | 1 494 | 65 295 | 6 586 | 14 336 | 14 060 | 15 490 | 11 400 | 3 424 |
| 2014 | 68 613 | 2 326 | 817 | 1 510 | 66 287 | 6 707 | 14 682 | 14 232 | 15 438 | 11 634 | 3 594 |
| 2015 | 69 703 | 2 380 | 825 | 1 555 | 67 323 | 6 849 | 14 996 | 14 391 | 15 399 | 11 884 | 3 804 |

## Table 1-11. Employed Civilians, by Age, Sex, Race, and Hispanic Origin, 1948–2015—*Continued*

(Thousands of people.)

| Race, Hispanic origin, sex, and year | 16 years and over | 16 to 19 years | | | 20 years and over | | | | | | |
|---|---|---|---|---|---|---|---|---|---|---|---|
| | | Total | 16 to 17 years | 18 to 19 years | Total | 20 to 24 years | 25 to 34 years | 35 to 44 years | 45 to 54 years | 55 to 64 years | 65 years and over |
| **WHITE** | | | | | | | | | | | |
| **Both Sexes** | | | | | | | | | | | |
| 1954 | 53 957 | 3 078 | 1 257 | 1 822 | 50 879 | 4 358 | 12 616 | 13 000 | 10 811 | 7 262 | 2 831 |
| 1955 | 55 833 | 3 225 | 1 330 | 1 896 | 52 608 | 4 637 | 12 855 | 13 327 | 11 322 | 7 510 | 2 957 |
| 1956 | 57 269 | 3 389 | 1 465 | 1 922 | 53 880 | 4 897 | 12 748 | 13 637 | 11 706 | 7 822 | 3 068 |
| 1957 | 57 465 | 3 374 | 1 442 | 1 931 | 54 091 | 4 952 | 12 619 | 13 716 | 12 009 | 7 829 | 2 951 |
| 1958 | 56 613 | 3 216 | 1 370 | 1 847 | 53 397 | 4 908 | 12 128 | 13 571 | 12 113 | 7 849 | 2 828 |
| 1959 | 58 006 | 3 475 | 1 520 | 1 955 | 54 531 | 5 138 | 12 144 | 13 830 | 12 552 | 8 063 | 2 805 |
| 1960 | 58 850 | 3 700 | 1 598 | 2 103 | 55 150 | 5 331 | 12 021 | 13 930 | 12 820 | 8 192 | 2 855 |
| 1961 | 58 913 | 3 693 | 1 472 | 2 220 | 55 220 | 5 460 | 11 835 | 13 905 | 12 906 | 8 335 | 2 778 |
| 1962 | 59 698 | 3 774 | 1 447 | 2 327 | 55 924 | 5 676 | 11 703 | 14 173 | 13 066 | 8 511 | 2 795 |
| 1963 | 60 622 | 3 851 | 1 600 | 2 250 | 56 771 | 6 036 | 11 689 | 14 341 | 13 304 | 8 718 | 2 683 |
| 1964 | 61 922 | 4 076 | 1 846 | 2 230 | 57 846 | 6 444 | 11 794 | 14 380 | 13 596 | 8 916 | 2 717 |
| 1965 | 63 446 | 4 562 | 1 892 | 2 670 | 58 884 | 6 752 | 11 992 | 14 473 | 13 804 | 9 116 | 2 748 |
| 1966 | 65 021 | 5 176 | 2 052 | 3 124 | 59 845 | 6 986 | 12 268 | 14 449 | 14 072 | 9 356 | 2 713 |
| 1967 | 66 361 | 5 114 | 2 121 | 2 993 | 61 247 | 7 493 | 12 763 | 14 429 | 14 224 | 9 596 | 2 746 |
| 1968 | 67 750 | 5 195 | 2 193 | 3 002 | 62 555 | 7 687 | 13 410 | 14 386 | 14 487 | 9 781 | 2 804 |
| 1969 | 69 518 | 5 508 | 2 347 | 3 161 | 64 010 | 8 182 | 13 935 | 14 270 | 14 788 | 9 947 | 2 888 |
| 1970 | 70 217 | 5 571 | 2 386 | 3 185 | 64 645 | 8 559 | 14 326 | 14 092 | 14 854 | 9 979 | 2 835 |
| 1971 | 70 878 | 5 670 | 2 404 | 3 266 | 65 208 | 9 000 | 14 713 | 13 858 | 14 843 | 10 014 | 2 780 |
| 1972 | 73 370 | 6 173 | 2 581 | 3 592 | 67 197 | 9 718 | 15 904 | 13 940 | 14 845 | 10 077 | 2 714 |
| 1973 | 75 708 | 6 623 | 2 806 | 3 816 | 69 086 | 10 424 | 17 099 | 14 083 | 14 886 | 9 983 | 2 610 |
| 1974 | 77 184 | 6 796 | 2 881 | 3 916 | 70 388 | 10 676 | 18 040 | 14 196 | 14 948 | 9 958 | 2 568 |
| 1975 | 76 411 | 6 487 | 2 721 | 3 770 | 69 924 | 10 546 | 18 485 | 13 979 | 14 555 | 9 827 | 2 533 |
| 1976 | 78 853 | 6 724 | 2 762 | 3 962 | 72 129 | 11 119 | 19 662 | 14 407 | 14 549 | 9 923 | 2 470 |
| 1977 | 81 700 | 7 068 | 2 926 | 4 142 | 74 632 | 11 696 | 20 844 | 14 984 | 14 483 | 10 107 | 2 518 |
| 1978 | 84 936 | 7 367 | 3 085 | 4 282 | 77 569 | 12 251 | 22 008 | 15 809 | 14 550 | 10 311 | 2 642 |
| 1979 | 87 259 | 7 356 | 3 079 | 4 278 | 79 904 | 12 594 | 23 033 | 16 578 | 14 522 | 10 477 | 2 699 |
| 1980 | 87 715 | 7 021 | 2 861 | 4 161 | 80 694 | 12 405 | 23 653 | 17 071 | 14 405 | 10 475 | 2 684 |
| 1981 | 88 709 | 6 588 | 2 645 | 3 943 | 82 121 | 12 477 | 24 551 | 17 617 | 14 414 | 10 386 | 2 676 |
| 1982 | 87 903 | 5 984 | 2 317 | 3 667 | 81 918 | 12 097 | 24 531 | 18 268 | 14 083 | 10 283 | 2 656 |
| 1983 | 88 893 | 5 799 | 2 156 | 3 643 | 83 094 | 12 138 | 24 955 | 19 194 | 13 961 | 10 169 | 2 678 |
| 1984 | 92 120 | 5 836 | 2 209 | 3 627 | 86 284 | 12 451 | 26 235 | 20 552 | 14 239 | 10 227 | 2 580 |
| 1985 | 93 736 | 5 768 | 2 270 | 3 498 | 87 968 | 12 235 | 26 945 | 21 552 | 14 459 | 10 247 | 2 530 |
| 1986 | 95 660 | 5 792 | 2 386 | 3 406 | 89 869 | 12 027 | 27 746 | 22 515 | 14 750 | 10 176 | 2 654 |
| 1987 | 97 789 | 5 898 | 2 468 | 3 431 | 91 890 | 11 748 | 28 429 | 23 596 | 15 216 | 10 164 | 2 738 |
| 1988 | 99 812 | 6 030 | 2 424 | 3 606 | 93 782 | 11 438 | 28 796 | 24 468 | 16 054 | 10 153 | 2 874 |
| 1989 | 101 584 | 5 946 | 2 278 | 3 668 | 95 638 | 11 084 | 29 091 | 25 442 | 16 775 | 10 223 | 3 024 |
| 1990 | 102 261 | 5 779 | 2 141 | 3 638 | 96 481 | 11 498 | 28 773 | 26 282 | 16 933 | 9 960 | 3 035 |
| 1991 | 101 182 | 5 216 | 1 971 | 3 246 | 95 966 | 11 116 | 27 989 | 26 883 | 17 269 | 9 719 | 2 990 |
| 1992 | 101 669 | 4 985 | 1 904 | 3 081 | 96 684 | 11 031 | 27 552 | 27 097 | 18 285 | 9 701 | 3 019 |
| 1993 | 103 045 | 5 113 | 1 990 | 3 123 | 97 932 | 10 931 | 27 274 | 27 645 | 19 273 | 9 772 | 3 037 |
| 1994 | 105 190 | 5 398 | 2 210 | 3 188 | 99 792 | 10 736 | 27 101 | 28 442 | 20 247 | 9 912 | 3 354 |
| 1995 | 106 490 | 5 593 | 2 273 | 3 320 | 100 897 | 10 400 | 27 014 | 28 951 | 21 127 | 10 070 | 3 335 |
| 1996 | 107 808 | 5 667 | 2 325 | 3 343 | 102 141 | 10 149 | 26 678 | 29 566 | 22 071 | 10 313 | 3 364 |
| 1997 | 109 856 | 5 807 | 2 341 | 3 466 | 104 049 | 10 362 | 26 294 | 30 137 | 23 061 | 10 785 | 3 411 |
| 1998 | 110 931 | 6 089 | 2 436 | 3 653 | 104 842 | 10 512 | 25 729 | 30 320 | 23 662 | 11 272 | 3 347 |
| 1999 | 112 235 | 6 204 | 2 435 | 3 769 | 106 032 | 10 716 | 25 113 | 30 548 | 24 507 | 11 657 | 3 491 |
| 2000 | 114 424 | 6 160 | 2 383 | 3 777 | 108 264 | 10 944 | 25 500 | 30 151 | 25 762 | 12 169 | 3 738 |
| 2001 | 114 430 | 5 817 | 2 224 | 3 593 | 108 613 | 11 054 | 24 948 | 29 793 | 26 301 | 12 743 | 3 774 |
| 2002 | 114 013 | 5 441 | 2 037 | 3 404 | 108 572 | 11 096 | 24 568 | 29 049 | 26 401 | 13 630 | 3 828 |
| 2003 | 114 235 | 5 064 | 1 999 | 3 065 | 109 171 | 11 052 | 24 399 | 28 501 | 26 762 | 14 375 | 4 083 |
| 2004 | 115 239 | 5 039 | 1 895 | 3 145 | 110 199 | 11 233 | 24 337 | 28 176 | 27 228 | 14 965 | 4 260 |
| 2005 | 116 949 | 5 105 | 1 999 | 3 106 | 111 844 | 11 231 | 24 443 | 28 102 | 27 801 | 15 788 | 4 480 |
| 2006 | 118 833 | 5 215 | 2 099 | 3 117 | 113 618 | 11 296 | 24 652 | 27 929 | 28 419 | 16 652 | 4 670 |
| 2007 | 119 792 | 4 990 | 1 965 | 3 026 | 114 802 | 11 325 | 25 024 | 27 492 | 28 779 | 17 262 | 4 921 |
| 2008 | 119 126 | 4 697 | 1 703 | 2 994 | 114 428 | 11 055 | 24 875 | 26 736 | 28 686 | 17 829 | 5 247 |
| 2009 | 114 996 | 4 138 | 1 443 | 2 696 | 110 858 | 10 438 | 23 957 | 25 237 | 27 891 | 17 978 | 5 357 |
| 2010 | 114 168 | 3 733 | 1 248 | 2 485 | 110 435 | 10 334 | 24 097 | 24 540 | 27 502 | 18 464 | 5 496 |
| 2011 | 114 690 | 3 691 | 1 189 | 2 501 | 111 000 | 10 574 | 24 376 | 24 156 | 27 176 | 18 937 | 5 780 |
| 2012 | 114 769 | 3 665 | 1 207 | 2 458 | 111 104 | 10 561 | 23 925 | 23 931 | 26 769 | 19 608 | 6 309 |
| 2013 | 115 379 | 3 671 | 1 274 | 2 397 | 111 708 | 10 662 | 24 247 | 23 833 | 26 363 | 19 913 | 6 690 |
| 2014 | 116 788 | 3 701 | 1 289 | 2 412 | 113 087 | 10 842 | 24 771 | 23 970 | 26 251 | 20 351 | 6 902 |
| 2015 | 117 944 | 3 824 | 1 319 | 2 505 | 114 120 | 10 784 | 25 111 | 24 012 | 26 154 | 20 783 | 7 276 |

## Table 1-11. Employed Civilians, by Age, Sex, Race, and Hispanic Origin, 1948–2015—*Continued*

(Thousands of people.)

| Race, Hispanic origin, sex, and year | 16 years and over | 16 to 19 years | | | 20 years and over | | | | | | |
|---|---|---|---|---|---|---|---|---|---|---|---|
| | | Total | 16 to 17 years | 18 to 19 years | Total | 20 to 24 years | 25 to 34 years | 35 to 44 years | 45 to 54 years | 55 to 64 years | 65 years and over |
| **WHITE** | | | | | | | | | | | |
| **Men** | | | | | | | | | | | |
| 1954 | 37 846 | 1 723 | 771 | 953 | 36 123 | 2 394 | 9 287 | 9 175 | 7 614 | 5 412 | 2 241 |
| 1955 | 38 719 | 1 824 | 821 | 1 004 | 36 895 | 2 607 | 9 461 | 9 351 | 7 792 | 5 431 | 2 254 |
| 1956 | 39 368 | 1 893 | 890 | 1 002 | 37 475 | 2 850 | 9 330 | 9 449 | 7 950 | 5 559 | 2 336 |
| 1957 | 39 349 | 1 865 | 874 | 990 | 37 484 | 2 930 | 9 226 | 9 480 | 8 067 | 5 542 | 2 234 |
| 1958 | 38 591 | 1 783 | 852 | 932 | 36 808 | 2 896 | 8 861 | 9 386 | 8 061 | 5 501 | 2 103 |
| 1959 | 39 494 | 1 961 | 915 | 1 046 | 37 533 | 3 153 | 8 911 | 9 560 | 8 261 | 5 588 | 2 060 |
| 1960 | 39 755 | 2 092 | 973 | 1 119 | 37 663 | 3 264 | 8 777 | 9 589 | 8 372 | 5 618 | 2 043 |
| 1961 | 39 588 | 2 055 | 891 | 1 164 | 37 533 | 3 311 | 8 630 | 9 566 | 8 394 | 5 670 | 1 961 |
| 1962 | 40 016 | 2 098 | 883 | 1 215 | 37 918 | 3 426 | 8 514 | 9 718 | 8 512 | 5 749 | 1 998 |
| 1963 | 40 428 | 2 156 | 972 | 1 184 | 38 272 | 3 646 | 8 463 | 9 782 | 8 650 | 5 844 | 1 887 |
| 1964 | 41 115 | 2 316 | 1 128 | 1 188 | 38 799 | 3 856 | 8 538 | 9 800 | 8 787 | 5 945 | 1 872 |
| 1965 | 41 844 | 2 612 | 1 159 | 1 453 | 39 232 | 4 025 | 8 598 | 9 795 | 8 924 | 5 998 | 1 892 |
| 1966 | 42 331 | 2 913 | 1 245 | 1 668 | 39 418 | 4 028 | 8 674 | 9 719 | 9 029 | 6 096 | 1 871 |
| 1967 | 42 833 | 2 849 | 1 278 | 1 571 | 39 985 | 4 231 | 8 931 | 9 632 | 9 093 | 6 208 | 1 892 |
| 1968 | 43 411 | 2 908 | 1 319 | 1 589 | 40 503 | 4 226 | 9 315 | 9 522 | 9 198 | 6 316 | 1 926 |
| 1969 | 44 048 | 3 070 | 1 385 | 1 685 | 40 978 | 4 401 | 9 608 | 9 379 | 9 279 | 6 359 | 1 953 |
| 1970 | 44 178 | 3 066 | 1 374 | 1 692 | 41 112 | 4 601 | 9 784 | 9 202 | 9 271 | 6 340 | 1 914 |
| 1971 | 44 595 | 3 157 | 1 393 | 1 764 | 41 438 | 4 935 | 10 026 | 9 026 | 9 256 | 6 339 | 1 856 |
| 1972 | 45 944 | 3 416 | 1 470 | 1 947 | 42 528 | 5 431 | 10 664 | 9 047 | 9 236 | 6 363 | 1 786 |
| 1973 | 47 085 | 3 660 | 1 590 | 2 071 | 43 424 | 5 863 | 11 268 | 9 046 | 9 257 | 6 299 | 1 689 |
| 1974 | 47 674 | 3 728 | 1 611 | 2 117 | 43 946 | 5 965 | 11 701 | 9 027 | 9 242 | 6 304 | 1 706 |
| 1975 | 46 697 | 3 505 | 1 502 | 2 002 | 43 192 | 5 770 | 11 783 | 8 818 | 9 005 | 6 160 | 1 656 |
| 1976 | 47 775 | 3 604 | 1 501 | 2 103 | 44 171 | 6 140 | 12 362 | 8 944 | 8 968 | 6 176 | 1 579 |
| 1977 | 49 150 | 3 824 | 1 607 | 2 217 | 45 326 | 6 437 | 12 893 | 9 212 | 8 898 | 6 279 | 1 605 |
| 1978 | 50 544 | 3 950 | 1 664 | 2 286 | 46 594 | 6 717 | 13 413 | 9 608 | 8 840 | 6 339 | 1 677 |
| 1979 | 51 452 | 3 904 | 1 654 | 2 250 | 47 546 | 6 868 | 13 888 | 9 930 | 8 748 | 6 406 | 1 707 |
| 1980 | 51 127 | 3 708 | 1 534 | 2 174 | 47 419 | 6 652 | 14 009 | 10 077 | 8 586 | 6 412 | 1 684 |
| 1981 | 51 315 | 3 469 | 1 402 | 2 066 | 47 846 | 6 652 | 14 398 | 10 307 | 8 518 | 6 309 | 1 662 |
| 1982 | 50 287 | 3 079 | 1 214 | 1 865 | 47 209 | 6 372 | 14 164 | 10 593 | 8 267 | 6 188 | 1 624 |
| 1983 | 50 621 | 3 003 | 1 124 | 1 879 | 47 618 | 6 386 | 14 297 | 11 062 | 8 152 | 6 084 | 1 637 |
| 1984 | 52 462 | 3 001 | 1 140 | 1 861 | 49 461 | 6 647 | 15 045 | 11 776 | 8 320 | 6 108 | 1 564 |
| 1985 | 53 046 | 2 985 | 1 185 | 1 800 | 50 061 | 6 428 | 15 374 | 12 214 | 8 374 | 6 118 | 1 552 |
| 1986 | 53 785 | 2 966 | 1 225 | 1 741 | 50 818 | 6 340 | 15 790 | 12 620 | 8 442 | 6 012 | 1 612 |
| 1987 | 54 647 | 2 999 | 1 252 | 1 747 | 51 649 | 6 150 | 16 084 | 13 138 | 8 596 | 5 991 | 1 690 |
| 1988 | 55 550 | 3 084 | 1 248 | 1 836 | 52 466 | 5 987 | 16 241 | 13 590 | 8 992 | 5 909 | 1 748 |
| 1989 | 56 352 | 3 060 | 1 171 | 1 889 | 53 292 | 5 839 | 16 383 | 14 046 | 9 335 | 5 891 | 1 797 |
| 1990 | 56 703 | 3 018 | 1 119 | 1 899 | 53 685 | 6 179 | 16 124 | 14 496 | 9 383 | 5 744 | 1 760 |
| 1991 | 55 797 | 2 694 | 1 017 | 1 677 | 53 103 | 5 942 | 15 644 | 14 743 | 9 488 | 5 578 | 1 707 |
| 1992 | 55 959 | 2 602 | 990 | 1 612 | 53 357 | 5 855 | 15 357 | 14 842 | 10 027 | 5 503 | 1 772 |
| 1993 | 56 656 | 2 634 | 1 031 | 1 603 | 54 021 | 5 830 | 15 230 | 15 178 | 10 497 | 5 514 | 1 772 |
| 1994 | 57 452 | 2 776 | 1 144 | 1 632 | 54 676 | 5 738 | 15 052 | 15 562 | 10 910 | 5 490 | 1 925 |
| 1995 | 58 146 | 2 892 | 1 169 | 1 723 | 55 254 | 5 613 | 14 958 | 15 793 | 11 359 | 5 609 | 1 921 |
| 1996 | 58 888 | 2 911 | 1 161 | 1 750 | 55 977 | 5 444 | 14 820 | 16 136 | 11 834 | 5 755 | 1 987 |
| 1997 | 59 998 | 3 011 | 1 206 | 1 806 | 56 986 | 5 590 | 14 567 | 16 470 | 12 352 | 5 972 | 2 037 |
| 1998 | 60 604 | 3 103 | 1 233 | 1 870 | 57 500 | 5 659 | 14 259 | 16 715 | 12 661 | 6 251 | 1 955 |
| 1999 | 61 139 | 3 205 | 1 254 | 1 951 | 57 934 | 5 753 | 13 851 | 16 781 | 13 046 | 6 447 | 2 056 |
| 2000 | 62 289 | 3 169 | 1 205 | 1 965 | 59 119 | 5 876 | 14 238 | 16 477 | 13 675 | 6 678 | 2 175 |
| 2001 | 62 212 | 2 967 | 1 102 | 1 865 | 59 245 | 5 870 | 13 989 | 16 280 | 13 987 | 6 941 | 2 178 |
| 2002 | 61 849 | 2 725 | 987 | 1 738 | 59 124 | 5 882 | 13 727 | 15 910 | 14 060 | 7 360 | 2 184 |
| 2003 | 61 866 | 2 518 | 972 | 1 546 | 59 348 | 5 890 | 13 731 | 15 675 | 14 117 | 7 640 | 2 295 |
| 2004 | 62 712 | 2 553 | 903 | 1 650 | 60 159 | 6 026 | 13 735 | 15 572 | 14 418 | 8 018 | 2 390 |
| 2005 | 63 763 | 2 508 | 942 | 1 566 | 61 255 | 6 041 | 13 840 | 15 544 | 14 810 | 8 471 | 2 550 |
| 2006 | 64 883 | 2 625 | 1 020 | 1 605 | 62 259 | 6 114 | 13 903 | 15 480 | 15 189 | 8 893 | 2 680 |
| 2007 | 65 289 | 2 483 | 951 | 1 531 | 62 806 | 6 066 | 14 112 | 15 287 | 15 399 | 9 215 | 2 727 |
| 2008 | 64 624 | 2 320 | 808 | 1 512 | 62 304 | 5 858 | 13 931 | 14 775 | 15 300 | 9 518 | 2 922 |
| 2009 | 61 630 | 2 004 | 692 | 1 312 | 59 626 | 5 379 | 13 230 | 13 858 | 14 710 | 9 465 | 2 984 |
| 2010 | 61 252 | 1 815 | 598 | 1 217 | 59 438 | 5 347 | 13 282 | 13 583 | 14 542 | 9 637 | 3 047 |
| 2011 | 61 920 | 1 802 | 573 | 1 229 | 60 118 | 5 630 | 13 548 | 13 366 | 14 370 | 9 932 | 3 271 |
| 2012 | 61 990 | 1 797 | 563 | 1 234 | 60 193 | 5 547 | 13 212 | 13 224 | 14 264 | 10 334 | 3 611 |
| 2013 | 62 322 | 1 811 | 608 | 1 203 | 60 511 | 5 597 | 13 381 | 13 182 | 14 035 | 10 541 | 3 775 |
| 2014 | 63 108 | 1 819 | 599 | 1 219 | 61 289 | 5 681 | 13 627 | 13 258 | 14 060 | 10 817 | 3 847 |
| 2015 | 63 892 | 1 934 | 653 | 1 280 | 61 959 | 5 585 | 13 866 | 13 273 | 14 059 | 11 088 | 4 088 |

## Table 1-11. Employed Civilians, by Age, Sex, Race, and Hispanic Origin, 1948–2015—*Continued*

(Thousands of people.)

| Race, Hispanic origin, sex, and year | 16 years and over | 16 to 19 years | | | 20 years and over | | | | | | |
|---|---|---|---|---|---|---|---|---|---|---|---|
| | | Total | 16 to 17 years | 18 to 19 years | Total | 20 to 24 years | 25 to 34 years | 35 to 44 years | 45 to 54 years | 55 to 64 years | 65 years and over |
| **WHITE** | | | | | | | | | | | |
| **Women** | | | | | | | | | | | |
| 1954 | 16 111 | 1 355 | 486 | 869 | 14 756 | 1 964 | 3 329 | 3 825 | 3 197 | 1 850 | 590 |
| 1955 | 17 114 | 1 401 | 509 | 892 | 15 713 | 2 030 | 3 394 | 3 976 | 3 530 | 2 079 | 703 |
| 1956 | 17 901 | 1 496 | 575 | 920 | 16 405 | 2 047 | 3 418 | 4 188 | 3 756 | 2 263 | 732 |
| 1957 | 18 116 | 1 509 | 568 | 941 | 16 607 | 2 022 | 3 393 | 4 236 | 3 942 | 2 287 | 717 |
| 1958 | 18 022 | 1 433 | 518 | 915 | 16 589 | 2 012 | 3 267 | 4 185 | 4 052 | 2 348 | 725 |
| 1959 | 18 512 | 1 514 | 605 | 909 | 16 998 | 1 985 | 3 233 | 4 270 | 4 291 | 2 475 | 745 |
| 1960 | 19 095 | 1 608 | 625 | 984 | 17 487 | 2 067 | 3 244 | 4 341 | 4 448 | 2 574 | 812 |
| 1961 | 19 325 | 1 638 | 581 | 1 056 | 17 687 | 2 149 | 3 205 | 4 339 | 4 512 | 2 665 | 817 |
| 1962 | 19 682 | 1 676 | 564 | 1 112 | 18 006 | 2 250 | 3 189 | 4 455 | 4 554 | 2 762 | 797 |
| 1963 | 20 194 | 1 695 | 628 | 1 066 | 18 499 | 2 390 | 3 226 | 4 559 | 4 654 | 2 874 | 796 |
| 1964 | 20 807 | 1 760 | 718 | 1 042 | 19 047 | 2 588 | 3 256 | 4 580 | 4 809 | 2 971 | 845 |
| 1965 | 21 602 | 1 950 | 733 | 1 217 | 19 652 | 2 727 | 3 394 | 4 678 | 4 880 | 3 118 | 856 |
| 1966 | 22 690 | 2 263 | 807 | 1 456 | 20 427 | 2 958 | 3 594 | 4 730 | 5 043 | 3 260 | 842 |
| 1967 | 23 528 | 2 265 | 843 | 1 422 | 21 263 | 3 262 | 3 832 | 4 797 | 5 131 | 3 388 | 854 |
| 1968 | 24 339 | 2 287 | 874 | 1 413 | 22 052 | 3 461 | 4 095 | 4 864 | 5 289 | 3 465 | 878 |
| 1969 | 25 470 | 2 438 | 962 | 1 476 | 23 032 | 3 781 | 4 327 | 4 891 | 5 509 | 3 588 | 935 |
| 1970 | 26 039 | 2 505 | 1 012 | 1 493 | 23 534 | 3 959 | 4 542 | 4 890 | 5 582 | 3 640 | 921 |
| 1971 | 26 283 | 2 513 | 1 011 | 1 502 | 23 770 | 4 065 | 4 687 | 4 831 | 5 588 | 3 675 | 924 |
| 1972 | 27 426 | 2 755 | 1 111 | 1 645 | 24 669 | 4 286 | 5 240 | 4 893 | 5 608 | 3 714 | 928 |
| 1973 | 28 623 | 2 962 | 1 217 | 1 746 | 25 661 | 4 562 | 5 831 | 5 036 | 5 628 | 3 684 | 920 |
| 1974 | 29 511 | 3 069 | 1 269 | 1 799 | 26 442 | 4 711 | 6 340 | 5 169 | 5 706 | 3 654 | 862 |
| 1975 | 29 714 | 2 983 | 1 215 | 1 767 | 26 731 | 4 775 | 6 701 | 5 161 | 5 550 | 3 667 | 877 |
| 1976 | 31 078 | 3 120 | 1 260 | 1 860 | 27 958 | 4 978 | 7 300 | 5 462 | 5 580 | 3 746 | 891 |
| 1977 | 32 550 | 3 244 | 1 319 | 1 923 | 29 306 | 5 259 | 7 950 | 5 772 | 5 585 | 3 829 | 912 |
| 1978 | 34 392 | 3 416 | 1 420 | 1 996 | 30 975 | 5 535 | 8 595 | 6 201 | 5 710 | 3 972 | 964 |
| 1979 | 35 807 | 3 451 | 1 423 | 2 027 | 32 357 | 5 726 | 9 145 | 6 648 | 5 773 | 4 071 | 993 |
| 1980 | 36 587 | 3 314 | 1 327 | 1 986 | 33 275 | 5 753 | 9 644 | 6 994 | 5 818 | 4 064 | 1 001 |
| 1981 | 37 394 | 3 119 | 1 242 | 1 877 | 34 275 | 5 826 | 10 153 | 7 311 | 5 896 | 4 077 | 1 013 |
| 1982 | 37 615 | 2 905 | 1 103 | 1 802 | 34 710 | 5 724 | 10 367 | 7 675 | 5 816 | 4 095 | 1 032 |
| 1983 | 38 272 | 2 796 | 1 032 | 1 764 | 35 476 | 5 751 | 10 659 | 8 132 | 5 809 | 4 084 | 1 041 |
| 1984 | 39 659 | 2 835 | 1 069 | 1 766 | 36 823 | 5 804 | 11 190 | 8 776 | 5 920 | 4 118 | 1 015 |
| 1985 | 40 690 | 2 783 | 1 085 | 1 698 | 37 907 | 5 807 | 11 571 | 9 338 | 6 084 | 4 128 | 978 |
| 1986 | 41 876 | 2 825 | 1 160 | 1 665 | 39 050 | 5 687 | 11 956 | 9 895 | 6 307 | 4 164 | 1 042 |
| 1987 | 43 142 | 2 900 | 1 216 | 1 684 | 40 242 | 5 598 | 12 345 | 10 459 | 6 620 | 4 172 | 1 047 |
| 1988 | 44 262 | 2 946 | 1 176 | 1 770 | 41 316 | 5 450 | 12 555 | 10 878 | 7 062 | 4 244 | 1 126 |
| 1989 | 45 232 | 2 886 | 1 107 | 1 779 | 42 346 | 5 245 | 12 708 | 11 395 | 7 440 | 4 332 | 1 227 |
| 1990 | 45 558 | 2 762 | 1 023 | 1 739 | 42 796 | 5 319 | 12 649 | 11 785 | 7 551 | 4 217 | 1 275 |
| 1991 | 45 385 | 2 523 | 954 | 1 569 | 42 862 | 5 174 | 12 344 | 12 139 | 7 781 | 4 141 | 1 283 |
| 1992 | 45 710 | 2 383 | 915 | 1 468 | 43 327 | 5 176 | 12 195 | 12 254 | 8 258 | 4 198 | 1 246 |
| 1993 | 46 390 | 2 479 | 959 | 1 520 | 43 910 | 5 101 | 12 044 | 12 467 | 8 776 | 4 258 | 1 265 |
| 1994 | 47 738 | 2 622 | 1 066 | 1 556 | 45 116 | 4 997 | 12 049 | 12 880 | 9 338 | 4 423 | 1 429 |
| 1995 | 48 344 | 2 701 | 1 104 | 1 597 | 45 643 | 4 787 | 12 056 | 13 157 | 9 768 | 4 461 | 1 415 |
| 1996 | 48 920 | 2 756 | 1 164 | 1 592 | 46 164 | 4 705 | 11 858 | 13 430 | 10 237 | 4 558 | 1 376 |
| 1997 | 49 859 | 2 796 | 1 136 | 1 660 | 47 063 | 4 773 | 11 727 | 13 667 | 10 709 | 4 813 | 1 374 |
| 1998 | 50 327 | 2 986 | 1 203 | 1 783 | 47 342 | 4 853 | 11 470 | 13 604 | 11 001 | 5 021 | 1 392 |
| 1999 | 51 096 | 2 999 | 1 181 | 1 817 | 48 098 | 4 963 | 11 262 | 13 767 | 11 461 | 5 211 | 1 435 |
| 2000 | 52 136 | 2 991 | 1 178 | 1 813 | 49 145 | 5 068 | 11 262 | 13 674 | 12 087 | 5 490 | 1 564 |
| 2001 | 52 218 | 2 850 | 1 122 | 1 727 | 49 369 | 5 184 | 10 959 | 13 513 | 12 314 | 5 802 | 1 597 |
| 2002 | 52 164 | 2 716 | 1 050 | 1 665 | 49 448 | 5 214 | 10 842 | 13 138 | 12 341 | 6 269 | 1 644 |
| 2003 | 52 369 | 2 546 | 1 027 | 1 519 | 49 823 | 5 161 | 10 668 | 12 826 | 12 645 | 6 735 | 1 788 |
| 2004 | 52 527 | 2 486 | 991 | 1 495 | 50 040 | 5 207 | 10 602 | 12 604 | 12 810 | 6 947 | 1 870 |
| 2005 | 53 186 | 2 597 | 1 057 | 1 540 | 50 589 | 5 190 | 10 603 | 12 558 | 12 991 | 7 317 | 1 930 |
| 2006 | 53 950 | 2 590 | 1 079 | 1 512 | 51 359 | 5 182 | 10 750 | 12 449 | 13 230 | 7 758 | 1 991 |
| 2007 | 54 503 | 2 507 | 1 013 | 1 494 | 51 996 | 5 259 | 10 912 | 12 205 | 13 380 | 8 047 | 2 193 |
| 2008 | 54 501 | 2 377 | 895 | 1 482 | 52 124 | 5 197 | 10 943 | 11 961 | 13 386 | 8 312 | 2 325 |
| 2009 | 53 366 | 2 134 | 751 | 1 383 | 51 231 | 5 060 | 10 727 | 11 379 | 13 181 | 8 513 | 2 373 |
| 2010 | 52 916 | 1 918 | 650 | 1 268 | 50 997 | 4 988 | 10 815 | 10 958 | 12 960 | 8 827 | 2 450 |
| 2011 | 52 770 | 1 889 | 617 | 1 272 | 50 881 | 4 943 | 10 828 | 10 789 | 12 806 | 9 005 | 2 509 |
| 2012 | 52 779 | 1 868 | 644 | 1 224 | 50 911 | 5 014 | 10 713 | 10 708 | 12 505 | 9 274 | 2 698 |
| 2013 | 53 057 | 1 860 | 665 | 1 195 | 51 198 | 5 066 | 10 866 | 10 651 | 12 328 | 9 371 | 2 915 |
| 2014 | 53 680 | 1 882 | 690 | 1 192 | 51 798 | 5 161 | 11 143 | 10 712 | 12 192 | 9 535 | 3 055 |
| 2015 | 54 052 | 1 891 | 666 | 1 225 | 52 161 | 5 200 | 11 245 | 10 739 | 12 094 | 9 695 | 3 188 |

## Table 1-11. Employed Civilians, by Age, Sex, Race, and Hispanic Origin, 1948–2015—*Continued*

(Thousands of people.)

| Race, Hispanic origin, sex, and year | 16 years and over | 16 to 19 years | | | 20 years and over | | | | | | |
|---|---|---|---|---|---|---|---|---|---|---|---|
| | | Total | 16 to 17 years | 18 to 19 years | Total | 20 to 24 years | 25 to 34 years | 35 to 44 years | 45 to 54 years | 55 to 64 years | 65 years and over |
| **BLACK** | | | | | | | | | | | |
| **Both Sexes** | | | | | | | | | | | |
| 1980 | 9 313 | 547 | 192 | 356 | 8 765 | 1 376 | 2 827 | 1 910 | 1 487 | 925 | 239 |
| 1981 | 9 355 | 505 | 170 | 335 | 8 849 | 1 346 | 2 872 | 1 957 | 1 489 | 954 | 231 |
| 1982 | 9 189 | 428 | 138 | 290 | 8 761 | 1 283 | 2 830 | 2 025 | 1 469 | 928 | 225 |
| 1983 | 9 375 | 416 | 123 | 294 | 8 959 | 1 280 | 2 976 | 2 107 | 1 456 | 937 | 204 |
| 1984 | 10 119 | 474 | 146 | 328 | 9 645 | 1 423 | 3 223 | 2 311 | 1 533 | 945 | 209 |
| 1985 | 10 501 | 532 | 175 | 356 | 9 969 | 1 399 | 3 325 | 2 427 | 1 598 | 985 | 235 |
| 1986 | 10 814 | 536 | 183 | 353 | 10 278 | 1 429 | 3 464 | 2 524 | 1 666 | 982 | 214 |
| 1987 | 11 309 | 587 | 203 | 385 | 10 722 | 1 421 | 3 614 | 2 695 | 1 714 | 1 036 | 241 |
| 1988 | 11 658 | 601 | 223 | 378 | 11 057 | 1 433 | 3 725 | 2 839 | 1 783 | 1 018 | 261 |
| 1989 | 11 953 | 625 | 237 | 388 | 11 328 | 1 467 | 3 801 | 2 981 | 1 844 | 970 | 265 |
| 1990 | 12 175 | 598 | 194 | 404 | 11 577 | 1 409 | 3 803 | 3 287 | 1 897 | 933 | 248 |
| 1991 | 12 074 | 494 | 161 | 334 | 11 580 | 1 373 | 3 714 | 3 401 | 1 892 | 957 | 243 |
| 1992 | 12 151 | 492 | 157 | 335 | 11 659 | 1 343 | 3 699 | 3 441 | 1 964 | 965 | 246 |
| 1993 | 12 382 | 494 | 171 | 323 | 11 888 | 1 377 | 3 700 | 3 584 | 2 059 | 941 | 226 |
| 1994 | 12 835 | 552 | 224 | 328 | 12 284 | 1 449 | 3 732 | 3 722 | 2 178 | 953 | 251 |
| 1995 | 13 279 | 586 | 223 | 363 | 12 693 | 1 443 | 3 844 | 3 861 | 2 288 | 1 004 | 253 |
| 1996 | 13 542 | 613 | 233 | 380 | 12 929 | 1 411 | 3 851 | 3 974 | 2 426 | 1 025 | 241 |
| 1997 | 13 969 | 631 | 229 | 401 | 13 339 | 1 456 | 3 903 | 4 094 | 2 588 | 1 048 | 249 |
| 1998 | 14 556 | 736 | 246 | 490 | 13 820 | 1 496 | 3 967 | 4 238 | 2 739 | 1 118 | 262 |
| 1999 | 15 056 | 691 | 243 | 448 | 14 365 | 1 594 | 4 091 | 4 404 | 2 872 | 1 134 | 271 |
| 2000 | 15 156 | 711 | 260 | 451 | 14 444 | 1 593 | 3 993 | 4 261 | 3 073 | 1 226 | 300 |
| 2001 | 15 006 | 637 | 230 | 408 | 14 368 | 1 571 | 3 840 | 4 200 | 3 139 | 1 283 | 335 |
| 2002 | 14 872 | 611 | 193 | 417 | 14 262 | 1 543 | 3 726 | 4 109 | 3 220 | 1 332 | 332 |
| 2003 | 14 739 | 516 | 196 | 320 | 14 222 | 1 516 | 3 618 | 4 080 | 3 289 | 1 373 | 346 |
| 2004 | 14 909 | 520 | 169 | 351 | 14 389 | 1 572 | 3 635 | 4 039 | 3 332 | 1 452 | 359 |
| 2005 | 15 313 | 536 | 164 | 372 | 14 776 | 1 599 | 3 722 | 4 060 | 3 464 | 1 555 | 375 |
| 2006 | 15 765 | 618 | 215 | 402 | 15 147 | 1 643 | 3 809 | 4 072 | 3 570 | 1 659 | 394 |
| 2007 | 16 051 | 566 | 202 | 364 | 15 485 | 1 674 | 3 888 | 4 120 | 3 658 | 1 732 | 413 |
| 2008 | 15 953 | 541 | 172 | 369 | 15 411 | 1 625 | 3 870 | 4 015 | 3 670 | 1 791 | 440 |
| 2009 | 15 025 | 442 | 131 | 310 | 14 584 | 1 474 | 3 582 | 3 686 | 3 562 | 1 827 | 453 |
| 2010 | 15 010 | 386 | 106 | 280 | 14 624 | 1 532 | 3 641 | 3 561 | 3 531 | 1 899 | 460 |
| 2011 | 15 051 | 380 | 99 | 281 | 14 671 | 1 574 | 3 632 | 3 499 | 3 513 | 1 943 | 508 |
| 2012 | 15 856 | 438 | 119 | 319 | 15 417 | 1 700 | 3 693 | 3 662 | 3 660 | 2 161 | 540 |
| 2013 | 16 151 | 439 | 117 | 322 | 15 712 | 1 727 | 3 780 | 3 730 | 3 644 | 2 263 | 567 |
| 2014 | 16 732 | 456 | 142 | 315 | 16 276 | 1 839 | 3 936 | 3 834 | 3 728 | 2 342 | 596 |
| 2015 | 17 472 | 502 | 164 | 338 | 16 970 | 1 953 | 4 190 | 3 928 | 3 806 | 2 433 | 660 |
| **Men** | | | | | | | | | | | |
| 1980 | 4 798 | 299 | 109 | 191 | 4 498 | 713 | 1 438 | 975 | 770 | 478 | 126 |
| 1981 | 4 794 | 273 | 95 | 178 | 4 520 | 693 | 1 457 | 991 | 764 | 492 | 123 |
| 1982 | 4 637 | 223 | 65 | 158 | 4 414 | 660 | 1 414 | 997 | 750 | 471 | 122 |
| 1983 | 4 753 | 222 | 64 | 158 | 4 531 | 684 | 1 483 | 1 034 | 749 | 477 | 105 |
| 1984 | 5 124 | 252 | 79 | 173 | 4 871 | 750 | 1 635 | 1 138 | 780 | 460 | 108 |
| 1985 | 5 270 | 278 | 92 | 186 | 4 992 | 726 | 1 669 | 1 187 | 795 | 501 | 114 |
| 1986 | 5 428 | 278 | 96 | 182 | 5 150 | 732 | 1 756 | 1 211 | 831 | 507 | 112 |
| 1987 | 5 661 | 304 | 109 | 195 | 5 357 | 728 | 1 821 | 1 283 | 853 | 547 | 124 |
| 1988 | 5 824 | 316 | 122 | 193 | 5 509 | 736 | 1 881 | 1 348 | 878 | 536 | 131 |
| 1989 | 5 928 | 327 | 124 | 202 | 5 602 | 742 | 1 931 | 1 415 | 886 | 498 | 131 |
| 1990 | 5 995 | 303 | 99 | 204 | 5 692 | 702 | 1 895 | 1 586 | 926 | 469 | 114 |
| 1991 | 5 961 | 255 | 85 | 170 | 5 706 | 695 | 1 859 | 1 634 | 923 | 481 | 114 |
| 1992 | 5 930 | 249 | 78 | 170 | 5 681 | 679 | 1 819 | 1 650 | 930 | 478 | 124 |
| 1993 | 6 047 | 254 | 88 | 166 | 5 793 | 674 | 1 858 | 1 717 | 978 | 461 | 106 |
| 1994 | 6 241 | 276 | 107 | 169 | 5 964 | 718 | 1 850 | 1 795 | 1 030 | 455 | 115 |
| 1995 | 6 422 | 285 | 111 | 174 | 6 137 | 714 | 1 895 | 1 836 | 1 085 | 468 | 138 |
| 1996 | 6 456 | 289 | 109 | 180 | 6 167 | 685 | 1 867 | 1 878 | 1 129 | 482 | 126 |
| 1997 | 6 607 | 282 | 108 | 174 | 6 325 | 668 | 1 874 | 1 955 | 1 215 | 487 | 127 |
| 1998 | 6 871 | 341 | 120 | 221 | 6 530 | 686 | 1 886 | 2 008 | 1 284 | 524 | 142 |
| 1999 | 7 027 | 325 | 120 | 205 | 6 702 | 700 | 1 926 | 2 092 | 1 327 | 525 | 131 |
| 2000 | 7 082 | 341 | 129 | 211 | 6 741 | 730 | 1 865 | 1 984 | 1 425 | 596 | 142 |
| 2001 | 6 938 | 311 | 115 | 196 | 6 627 | 703 | 1 757 | 1 931 | 1 452 | 614 | 170 |
| 2002 | 6 959 | 306 | 95 | 212 | 6 652 | 725 | 1 729 | 1 899 | 1 503 | 624 | 172 |
| 2003 | 6 820 | 234 | 89 | 145 | 6 586 | 726 | 1 660 | 1 868 | 1 518 | 638 | 176 |
| 2004 | 6 912 | 231 | 76 | 155 | 6 681 | 739 | 1 720 | 1 840 | 1 534 | 668 | 180 |
| 2005 | 7 155 | 254 | 76 | 178 | 6 901 | 748 | 1 759 | 1 886 | 1 616 | 711 | 182 |
| 2006 | 7 354 | 275 | 99 | 175 | 7 079 | 804 | 1 797 | 1 882 | 1 680 | 734 | 184 |
| 2007 | 7 500 | 254 | 82 | 172 | 7 245 | 816 | 1 851 | 1 916 | 1 717 | 750 | 195 |
| 2008 | 7 398 | 247 | 70 | 177 | 7 151 | 794 | 1 805 | 1 854 | 1 703 | 792 | 204 |
| 2009 | 6 817 | 189 | 56 | 133 | 6 628 | 689 | 1 635 | 1 662 | 1 622 | 813 | 206 |
| 2010 | 6 865 | 185 | 48 | 137 | 6 680 | 692 | 1 710 | 1 638 | 1 594 | 834 | 211 |
| 2011 | 6 953 | 187 | 49 | 138 | 6 765 | 734 | 1 733 | 1 583 | 1 621 | 858 | 236 |
| 2012 | 7 302 | 198 | 52 | 146 | 7 104 | 784 | 1 723 | 1 667 | 1 693 | 988 | 249 |
| 2013 | 7 497 | 192 | 51 | 141 | 7 304 | 818 | 1 782 | 1 738 | 1 675 | 1 036 | 256 |
| 2014 | 7 818 | 205 | 70 | 134 | 7 613 | 887 | 1 879 | 1 772 | 1 721 | 1 081 | 272 |
| 2015 | 8 164 | 226 | 75 | 150 | 7 938 | 936 | 1 995 | 1 816 | 1 780 | 1 115 | 297 |

## Table 1-11. Employed Civilians, by Age, Sex, Race, and Hispanic Origin, 1948–2015—*Continued*

(Thousands of people.)

| Race, Hispanic origin, sex, and year | 16 years and over | 16 to 19 years | | | 20 years and over | | | | | | |
|---|---|---|---|---|---|---|---|---|---|---|---|
| | | Total | 16 to 17 years | 18 to 19 years | Total | 20 to 24 years | 25 to 34 years | 35 to 44 years | 45 to 54 years | 55 to 64 years | 65 years and over |
| **BLACK** | | | | | | | | | | | |
| **Women** | | | | | | | | | | | |
| 1980 | 4 515 | 248 | 82 | 165 | 4 267 | 663 | 1 389 | 936 | 717 | 448 | 113 |
| 1981 | 4 561 | 232 | 75 | 157 | 4 329 | 653 | 1 415 | 966 | 725 | 462 | 108 |
| 1982 | 4 552 | 205 | 73 | 132 | 4 347 | 623 | 1 416 | 1 028 | 719 | 457 | 103 |
| 1983 | 4 622 | 194 | 59 | 136 | 4 428 | 596 | 1 493 | 1 073 | 707 | 460 | 99 |
| 1984 | 4 995 | 222 | 67 | 155 | 4 773 | 673 | 1 588 | 1 173 | 753 | 485 | 101 |
| 1985 | 5 231 | 254 | 83 | 171 | 4 977 | 673 | 1 656 | 1 240 | 804 | 484 | 121 |
| 1986 | 5 386 | 259 | 87 | 171 | 5 128 | 696 | 1 708 | 1 313 | 835 | 475 | 102 |
| 1987 | 5 648 | 283 | 93 | 190 | 5 365 | 693 | 1 793 | 1 412 | 860 | 489 | 117 |
| 1988 | 5 834 | 285 | 101 | 184 | 5 548 | 697 | 1 844 | 1 491 | 905 | 482 | 129 |
| 1989 | 6 025 | 298 | 113 | 185 | 5 727 | 725 | 1 870 | 1 566 | 959 | 472 | 134 |
| 1990 | 6 180 | 296 | 96 | 200 | 5 884 | 707 | 1 907 | 1 701 | 971 | 464 | 135 |
| 1991 | 6 113 | 239 | 76 | 164 | 5 874 | 677 | 1 855 | 1 768 | 969 | 476 | 129 |
| 1992 | 6 221 | 243 | 79 | 164 | 5 978 | 664 | 1 880 | 1 791 | 1 034 | 487 | 123 |
| 1993 | 6 334 | 239 | 82 | 157 | 6 095 | 703 | 1 842 | 1 867 | 1 081 | 480 | 121 |
| 1994 | 6 595 | 275 | 117 | 158 | 6 320 | 731 | 1 882 | 1 926 | 1 147 | 497 | 136 |
| 1995 | 6 857 | 301 | 112 | 189 | 6 556 | 729 | 1 949 | 2 025 | 1 202 | 536 | 114 |
| 1996 | 7 086 | 324 | 124 | 200 | 6 762 | 726 | 1 984 | 2 096 | 1 297 | 543 | 115 |
| 1997 | 7 362 | 349 | 122 | 227 | 7 013 | 789 | 2 029 | 2 139 | 1 373 | 561 | 122 |
| 1998 | 7 685 | 395 | 126 | 268 | 7 290 | 810 | 2 081 | 2 230 | 1 455 | 594 | 120 |
| 1999 | 8 029 | 366 | 123 | 243 | 7 663 | 893 | 2 165 | 2 312 | 1 545 | 609 | 139 |
| 2000 | 8 073 | 370 | 131 | 240 | 7 703 | 862 | 2 128 | 2 277 | 1 647 | 630 | 158 |
| 2001 | 8 068 | 327 | 115 | 212 | 7 741 | 868 | 2 084 | 2 269 | 1 686 | 668 | 165 |
| 2002 | 7 914 | 304 | 99 | 205 | 7 610 | 819 | 1 997 | 2 209 | 1 717 | 708 | 160 |
| 2003 | 7 919 | 283 | 107 | 175 | 7 636 | 790 | 1 959 | 2 211 | 1 770 | 735 | 171 |
| 2004 | 7 997 | 289 | 93 | 196 | 7 707 | 833 | 1 914 | 2 199 | 1 798 | 784 | 179 |
| 2005 | 8 158 | 282 | 88 | 194 | 7 876 | 852 | 1 964 | 2 175 | 1 848 | 844 | 193 |
| 2006 | 8 410 | 343 | 116 | 227 | 8 068 | 839 | 2 012 | 2 191 | 1 890 | 925 | 210 |
| 2007 | 8 551 | 311 | 120 | 191 | 8 240 | 858 | 2 037 | 2 205 | 1 941 | 982 | 218 |
| 2008 | 8 554 | 294 | 102 | 192 | 8 260 | 831 | 2 065 | 2 161 | 1 967 | 1 000 | 236 |
| 2009 | 8 208 | 252 | 75 | 178 | 7 956 | 784 | 1 947 | 2 024 | 1 939 | 1 014 | 246 |
| 2010 | 8 145 | 201 | 58 | 143 | 7 944 | 841 | 1 931 | 1 923 | 1 936 | 1 065 | 248 |
| 2011 | 8 098 | 193 | 50 | 142 | 7 906 | 840 | 1 899 | 1 916 | 1 892 | 1 086 | 272 |
| 2012 | 8 553 | 240 | 67 | 173 | 8 313 | 916 | 1 970 | 1 995 | 1 968 | 1 173 | 291 |
| 2013 | 8 654 | 246 | 66 | 180 | 8 408 | 909 | 1 998 | 1 992 | 1 970 | 1 228 | 311 |
| 2014 | 8 915 | 252 | 71 | 180 | 8 663 | 952 | 2 057 | 2 061 | 2 007 | 1 261 | 325 |
| 2015 | 9 308 | 276 | 89 | 188 | 9 032 | 1 017 | 2 195 | 2 112 | 2 026 | 1 319 | 363 |
| **HISPANIC** | | | | | | | | | | | |
| **Both Sexes** | | | | | | | | | | | |
| 1980 | 5 527 | 500 | 174 | 325 | 5 028 | 998 | 1 675 | 1 074 | 811 | 389 | 80 |
| 1981 | 5 813 | 459 | 155 | 304 | 5 354 | 1 060 | 1 837 | 1 147 | 829 | 399 | 82 |
| 1982 | 5 805 | 410 | 119 | 291 | 5 394 | 1 030 | 1 896 | 1 173 | 816 | 399 | 80 |
| 1983 | 6 072 | 423 | 125 | 297 | 5 649 | 1 068 | 1 997 | 1 224 | 837 | 441 | 81 |
| 1984 | 6 651 | 468 | 148 | 320 | 6 182 | 1 160 | 2 201 | 1 385 | 883 | 474 | 79 |
| 1985 | 6 888 | 438 | 144 | 294 | 6 449 | 1 187 | 2 316 | 1 473 | 913 | 486 | 75 |
| 1986 | 7 219 | 430 | 146 | 284 | 6 789 | 1 231 | 2 427 | 1 570 | 1 011 | 474 | 76 |
| 1987 | 7 790 | 474 | 149 | 325 | 7 316 | 1 273 | 2 668 | 1 775 | 1 010 | 512 | 76 |
| 1988 | 8 250 | 523 | 171 | 353 | 7 727 | 1 341 | 2 749 | 1 876 | 1 078 | 585 | 97 |
| 1989 | 8 573 | 548 | 165 | 383 | 8 025 | 1 325 | 2 900 | 1 968 | 1 129 | 589 | 114 |
| 1990 | 9 845 | 668 | 208 | 460 | 9 177 | 1 672 | 3 327 | 2 229 | 1 235 | 611 | 103 |
| 1991 | 9 828 | 602 | 169 | 433 | 9 225 | 1 622 | 3 264 | 2 333 | 1 266 | 637 | 103 |
| 1992 | 10 027 | 577 | 169 | 408 | 9 450 | 1 575 | 3 350 | 2 468 | 1 316 | 628 | 112 |
| 1993 | 10 361 | 570 | 160 | 410 | 9 792 | 1 574 | 3 446 | 2 605 | 1 402 | 630 | 135 |
| 1994 | 10 788 | 609 | 195 | 415 | 10 178 | 1 643 | 3 517 | 2 737 | 1 495 | 647 | 139 |
| 1995 | 11 127 | 645 | 194 | 450 | 10 483 | 1 609 | 3 618 | 2 889 | 1 565 | 666 | 135 |
| 1996 | 11 642 | 646 | 199 | 447 | 10 996 | 1 628 | 3 758 | 3 115 | 1 595 | 748 | 152 |
| 1997 | 12 726 | 714 | 228 | 487 | 12 012 | 1 798 | 4 029 | 3 371 | 1 846 | 794 | 173 |
| 1998 | 13 291 | 793 | 230 | 563 | 12 498 | 1 883 | 4 113 | 3 504 | 1 994 | 846 | 158 |
| 1999 | 13 720 | 854 | 254 | 600 | 12 866 | 1 881 | 4 097 | 3 738 | 2 074 | 886 | 190 |
| 2000 | 15 735 | 973 | 285 | 688 | 14 762 | 2 356 | 4 950 | 4 052 | 2 308 | 898 | 197 |
| 2001 | 16 190 | 969 | 268 | 701 | 15 221 | 2 404 | 5 065 | 4 149 | 2 472 | 944 | 187 |
| 2002 | 16 590 | 882 | 254 | 628 | 15 708 | 2 413 | 5 272 | 4 273 | 2 511 | 1 029 | 209 |
| 2003 | 17 372 | 768 | 242 | 525 | 16 604 | 2 399 | 5 541 | 4 573 | 2 711 | 1 132 | 249 |
| 2004 | 17 930 | 792 | 211 | 581 | 17 138 | 2 477 | 5 560 | 4 671 | 2 932 | 1 210 | 288 |
| 2005 | 18 632 | 847 | 253 | 595 | 17 785 | 2 423 | 5 756 | 4 879 | 3 114 | 1 317 | 296 |
| 2006 | 19 613 | 900 | 287 | 614 | 18 712 | 2 487 | 6 001 | 5 106 | 3 324 | 1 441 | 354 |
| 2007 | 20 382 | 894 | 269 | 625 | 19 488 | 2 516 | 6 237 | 5 314 | 3 547 | 1 499 | 376 |
| 2008 | 20 346 | 870 | 248 | 622 | 19 476 | 2 361 | 6 119 | 5 371 | 3 620 | 1 619 | 385 |
| 2009 | 19 647 | 742 | 192 | 550 | 18 905 | 2 218 | 5 704 | 5 168 | 3 700 | 1 680 | 435 |
| 2010 | 19 906 | 680 | 165 | 515 | 19 226 | 2 281 | 5 781 | 5 185 | 3 779 | 1 737 | 464 |
| 2011 | 20 269 | 665 | 155 | 510 | 19 604 | 2 544 | 5 747 | 5 179 | 3 848 | 1 820 | 465 |
| 2012 | 21 878 | 808 | 204 | 604 | 21 070 | 2 761 | 6 119 | 5 552 | 4 188 | 1 983 | 467 |
| 2013 | 22 514 | 821 | 217 | 604 | 21 693 | 2 857 | 6 157 | 5 652 | 4 374 | 2 140 | 514 |
| 2014 | 23 492 | 859 | 225 | 634 | 22 633 | 2 947 | 6 354 | 5 869 | 4 593 | 2 313 | 557 |
| 2015 | 24 400 | 922 | 253 | 669 | 23 477 | 3 027 | 6 432 | 6 063 | 4 831 | 2 523 | 601 |

## Table 1-11.  Employed Civilians, by Age, Sex, Race, and Hispanic Origin, 1948–2015—*Continued*

(Thousands of people.)

| Race, Hispanic origin, sex, and year | 16 years and over | 16 to 19 years | | | 20 years and over | | | | | | |
|---|---|---|---|---|---|---|---|---|---|---|---|
| | | Total | 16 to 17 years | 18 to 19 years | Total | 20 to 24 years | 25 to 34 years | 35 to 44 years | 45 to 54 years | 55 to 64 years | 65 years and over |
| **HISPANIC** | | | | | | | | | | | |
| **Men** | | | | | | | | | | | |
| 1980 | 3 448 | 306 | 109 | 198 | 3 142 | 611 | 1 065 | 662 | 491 | 254 | . . . |
| 1981 | 3 597 | 272 | 90 | 182 | 3 325 | 642 | 1 157 | 707 | 504 | 259 | . . . |
| 1982 | 3 583 | 229 | 66 | 162 | 3 354 | 621 | 1 192 | 729 | 498 | 261 | . . . |
| 1983 | 3 771 | 248 | 71 | 177 | 3 523 | 655 | 1 280 | 760 | 499 | 275 | . . . |
| 1984 | 4 083 | 258 | 78 | 180 | 3 825 | 718 | 1 398 | 841 | 530 | 292 | . . . |
| 1985 | 4 245 | 251 | 82 | 169 | 3 994 | 727 | 1 473 | 888 | 550 | 308 | . . . |
| 1986 | 4 428 | 254 | 82 | 172 | 4 174 | 773 | 1 510 | 929 | 614 | 297 | . . . |
| 1987 | 4 713 | 268 | 81 | 188 | 4 444 | 777 | 1 664 | 1 044 | 606 | 303 | . . . |
| 1988 | 4 972 | 292 | 87 | 205 | 4 680 | 815 | 1 706 | 1 120 | 645 | 331 | . . . |
| 1989 | 5 172 | 319 | 94 | 225 | 4 853 | 821 | 1 787 | 1 152 | 676 | 350 | . . . |
| 1990 | 6 021 | 412 | 126 | 286 | 5 609 | 1 083 | 2 076 | 1 312 | 722 | 355 | . . . |
| 1991 | 5 979 | 356 | 94 | 263 | 5 623 | 1 063 | 2 050 | 1 360 | 719 | 369 | . . . |
| 1992 | 6 093 | 336 | 97 | 238 | 5 757 | 985 | 2 127 | 1 437 | 768 | 372 | . . . |
| 1993 | 6 328 | 337 | 95 | 242 | 5 992 | 1 003 | 2 200 | 1 527 | 822 | 360 | . . . |
| 1994 | 6 530 | 341 | 109 | 233 | 6 189 | 1 056 | 2 227 | 1 600 | 847 | 379 | 79 |
| 1995 | 6 725 | 358 | 110 | 248 | 6 367 | 1 030 | 2 284 | 1 675 | 908 | 384 | 85 |
| 1996 | 7 039 | 384 | 107 | 277 | 6 655 | 1 015 | 2 345 | 1 842 | 918 | 438 | 96 |
| 1997 | 7 728 | 420 | 130 | 290 | 7 307 | 1 142 | 2 547 | 1 978 | 1 059 | 477 | 105 |
| 1998 | 8 018 | 449 | 133 | 315 | 7 570 | 1 173 | 2 592 | 2 077 | 1 115 | 512 | 101 |
| 1999 | 8 067 | 491 | 139 | 352 | 7 576 | 1 135 | 2 524 | 2 135 | 1 151 | 502 | 130 |
| 2000 | 9 428 | 570 | 159 | 411 | 8 859 | 1 486 | 3 063 | 2 358 | 1 295 | 532 | 126 |
| 2001 | 9 668 | 568 | 149 | 419 | 9 100 | 1 473 | 3 142 | 2 446 | 1 375 | 545 | 119 |
| 2002 | 9 845 | 504 | 141 | 363 | 9 341 | 1 476 | 3 271 | 2 503 | 1 396 | 569 | 125 |
| 2003 | 10 479 | 415 | 121 | 294 | 10 063 | 1 485 | 3 537 | 2 724 | 1 533 | 639 | 144 |
| 2004 | 10 832 | 446 | 108 | 338 | 10 385 | 1 514 | 3 557 | 2 801 | 1 654 | 687 | 174 |
| 2005 | 11 337 | 465 | 137 | 328 | 10 872 | 1 511 | 3 711 | 2 939 | 1 781 | 748 | 183 |
| 2006 | 11 887 | 496 | 146 | 350 | 11 391 | 1 535 | 3 845 | 3 088 | 1 894 | 809 | 220 |
| 2007 | 12 310 | 483 | 145 | 338 | 11 827 | 1 524 | 3 982 | 3 220 | 2 012 | 869 | 220 |
| 2008 | 12 248 | 479 | 140 | 340 | 11 769 | 1 406 | 3 897 | 3 233 | 2 080 | 929 | 224 |
| 2009 | 11 640 | 383 | 94 | 289 | 11 256 | 1 287 | 3 576 | 3 108 | 2 104 | 930 | 251 |
| 2010 | 11 800 | 361 | 78 | 283 | 11 438 | 1 319 | 3 591 | 3 169 | 2 137 | 949 | 273 |
| 2011 | 12 049 | 364 | 76 | 287 | 11 685 | 1 535 | 3 615 | 3 124 | 2 141 | 1 006 | 266 |
| 2012 | 12 643 | 431 | 97 | 334 | 12 212 | 1 584 | 3 714 | 3 229 | 2 334 | 1 097 | 256 |
| 2013 | 13 078 | 440 | 111 | 329 | 12 638 | 1 609 | 3 748 | 3 332 | 2 471 | 1 181 | 296 |
| 2014 | 13 655 | 453 | 108 | 344 | 13 202 | 1 655 | 3 830 | 1 949 | 2 600 | 1 317 | 307 |
| 2015 | 14 111 | 487 | 127 | 359 | 13 624 | 1 655 | 3 873 | 3 604 | 2 730 | 1 432 | 331 |
| **HISPANIC** | | | | | | | | | | | |
| **Women** | | | | | | | | | | | |
| 1980 | 2 079 | 193 | 65 | 128 | 1 886 | 387 | 610 | 412 | 320 | 136 | . . . |
| 1981 | 2 216 | 187 | 65 | 122 | 2 029 | 418 | 680 | 440 | 326 | 139 | . . . |
| 1982 | 2 222 | 181 | 52 | 129 | 2 040 | 409 | 704 | 444 | 318 | 139 | . . . |
| 1983 | 2 301 | 175 | 54 | 120 | 2 127 | 413 | 717 | 464 | 338 | 166 | . . . |
| 1984 | 2 568 | 211 | 71 | 140 | 2 357 | 442 | 804 | 544 | 354 | 181 | . . . |
| 1985 | 2 642 | 187 | 62 | 125 | 2 456 | 460 | 843 | 585 | 362 | 178 | . . . |
| 1986 | 2 791 | 176 | 64 | 112 | 2 615 | 458 | 917 | 641 | 397 | 177 | . . . |
| 1987 | 3 077 | 206 | 69 | 137 | 2 872 | 496 | 1 004 | 732 | 405 | 209 | . . . |
| 1988 | 3 278 | 231 | 84 | 147 | 3 047 | 526 | 1 042 | 756 | 434 | 254 | . . . |
| 1989 | 3 401 | 229 | 71 | 158 | 3 172 | 504 | 1 114 | 816 | 453 | 239 | . . . |
| 1990 | 3 823 | 256 | 82 | 174 | 3 567 | 588 | 1 251 | 917 | 513 | 256 | . . . |
| 1991 | 3 848 | 246 | 76 | 170 | 3 603 | 559 | 1 214 | 972 | 548 | 268 | . . . |
| 1992 | 3 934 | 242 | 72 | 170 | 3 693 | 591 | 1 223 | 1 031 | 548 | 256 | . . . |
| 1993 | 4 033 | 233 | 65 | 168 | 3 800 | 571 | 1 246 | 1 077 | 581 | 269 | . . . |
| 1994 | 4 258 | 268 | 86 | 182 | 3 989 | 587 | 1 290 | 1 137 | 648 | 268 | 59 |
| 1995 | 4 403 | 287 | 85 | 202 | 4 116 | 579 | 1 334 | 1 213 | 657 | 282 | 50 |
| 1996 | 4 602 | 261 | 92 | 169 | 4 341 | 612 | 1 412 | 1 273 | 677 | 310 | 56 |
| 1997 | 4 999 | 294 | 98 | 196 | 4 705 | 656 | 1 482 | 1 393 | 787 | 318 | 69 |
| 1998 | 5 273 | 345 | 97 | 247 | 4 928 | 710 | 1 521 | 1 428 | 879 | 334 | 57 |
| 1999 | 5 653 | 363 | 115 | 248 | 5 290 | 746 | 1 574 | 1 603 | 923 | 384 | 60 |
| 2000 | 6 307 | 404 | 127 | 277 | 5 903 | 870 | 1 887 | 1 695 | 1 013 | 366 | 72 |
| 2001 | 6 522 | 401 | 119 | 282 | 6 121 | 931 | 1 923 | 1 703 | 1 097 | 398 | 67 |
| 2002 | 6 744 | 378 | 113 | 265 | 6 367 | 937 | 2 001 | 1 770 | 1 114 | 460 | 84 |
| 2003 | 6 894 | 353 | 121 | 231 | 6 541 | 914 | 2 004 | 1 849 | 1 178 | 493 | 105 |
| 2004 | 7 098 | 346 | 103 | 243 | 6 752 | 964 | 2 003 | 1 870 | 1 279 | 523 | 114 |
| 2005 | 7 295 | 382 | 116 | 266 | 6 913 | 912 | 2 045 | 1 940 | 1 333 | 569 | 113 |
| 2006 | 7 725 | 404 | 140 | 264 | 7 321 | 951 | 2 155 | 2 018 | 1 430 | 632 | 135 |
| 2007 | 8 072 | 410 | 124 | 287 | 7 662 | 991 | 2 255 | 2 094 | 1 535 | 631 | 155 |
| 2008 | 8 098 | 391 | 108 | 282 | 7 707 | 955 | 2 222 | 2 138 | 1 541 | 690 | 161 |
| 2009 | 8 007 | 358 | 98 | 261 | 7 649 | 931 | 2 128 | 2 060 | 1 596 | 751 | 183 |
| 2010 | 8 106 | 318 | 87 | 231 | 7 788 | 962 | 2 189 | 2 016 | 1 642 | 788 | 191 |
| 2011 | 8 220 | 301 | 79 | 223 | 7 918 | 1 010 | 2 132 | 2 055 | 1 707 | 814 | 200 |
| 2012 | 9 235 | 377 | 107 | 269 | 8 858 | 1 178 | 2 405 | 2 323 | 1 854 | 887 | 212 |
| 2013 | 9 437 | 381 | 107 | 274 | 9 056 | 1 249 | 2 409 | 2 320 | 1 902 | 959 | 217 |
| 2014 | 9 838 | 407 | 117 | 290 | 9 431 | 1 291 | 2 524 | 2 376 | 1 993 | 997 | 250 |
| 2015 | 10 289 | 436 | 126 | 310 | 9 853 | 1 372 | 2 560 | 2 460 | 2 101 | 1 091 | 270 |

. . . = Not available.

## Table 1-12.  Civilian Employment-Population Ratios, by Sex, Age, Race, and Hispanic Origin, 1948–2015

(Percent.)

| Race, Hispanic origin, and year | Both sexes | | | Men | | | Women | | |
|---|---|---|---|---|---|---|---|---|---|
| | 16 years and over | 16 to 19 years | 20 years and over | 16 years and over | 16 to 19 years | 20 years and over | 16 years and over | 16 to 19 years | 20 years and over |
| **ALL RACES** | | | | | | | | | |
| 1948 | 56.6 | 47.7 | 57.4 | 83.5 | 57.5 | 85.8 | 31.3 | 38.5 | 30.7 |
| 1949 | 55.4 | 45.2 | 56.3 | 81.3 | 53.8 | 83.7 | 31.2 | 37.2 | 30.6 |
| 1950 | 56.1 | 45.5 | 57.0 | 82.0 | 55.2 | 84.2 | 32.0 | 36.3 | 31.6 |
| 1951 | 57.3 | 47.9 | 58.1 | 84.0 | 57.9 | 86.1 | 33.1 | 38.9 | 32.6 |
| 1952 | 57.3 | 46.9 | 58.1 | 83.9 | 55.9 | 86.2 | 33.4 | 38.8 | 33.0 |
| 1953 | 57.1 | 46.4 | 58.0 | 83.6 | 55.9 | 85.9 | 33.3 | 37.8 | 32.9 |
| 1954 | 55.5 | 42.3 | 56.6 | 81.0 | 50.2 | 83.5 | 32.5 | 34.9 | 32.3 |
| 1955 | 56.7 | 43.5 | 57.8 | 81.8 | 52.1 | 84.3 | 34.0 | 35.6 | 33.8 |
| 1956 | 57.5 | 45.3 | 58.5 | 82.3 | 53.8 | 84.6 | 35.1 | 37.5 | 34.9 |
| 1957 | 57.1 | 43.9 | 58.2 | 81.3 | 51.8 | 83.8 | 35.1 | 36.7 | 35.0 |
| 1958 | 55.4 | 39.9 | 56.8 | 78.5 | 46.9 | 81.2 | 34.5 | 33.5 | 34.6 |
| 1959 | 56.0 | 39.9 | 57.5 | 79.3 | 47.2 | 82.3 | 35.0 | 33.0 | 35.1 |
| 1960 | 56.1 | 40.5 | 57.6 | 78.9 | 47.6 | 81.9 | 35.5 | 33.8 | 35.7 |
| 1961 | 55.4 | 39.1 | 56.9 | 77.6 | 45.3 | 80.8 | 35.4 | 33.2 | 35.6 |
| 1962 | 55.5 | 39.4 | 57.1 | 77.7 | 45.9 | 80.9 | 35.6 | 33.3 | 35.8 |
| 1963 | 55.4 | 37.4 | 57.2 | 77.1 | 43.8 | 80.6 | 35.8 | 31.5 | 36.3 |
| 1964 | 55.7 | 37.3 | 57.7 | 77.3 | 44.1 | 80.9 | 36.3 | 30.9 | 36.9 |
| 1965 | 56.2 | 38.9 | 58.2 | 77.5 | 46.2 | 81.2 | 37.1 | 32.0 | 37.6 |
| 1966 | 56.9 | 42.1 | 58.7 | 77.9 | 48.9 | 81.5 | 38.3 | 35.6 | 38.6 |
| 1967 | 57.3 | 42.2 | 59.0 | 78.0 | 48.7 | 81.5 | 39.0 | 35.9 | 39.3 |
| 1968 | 57.5 | 42.2 | 59.3 | 77.8 | 48.7 | 81.3 | 39.6 | 36.0 | 40.0 |
| 1969 | 58.0 | 43.4 | 59.7 | 77.6 | 49.5 | 81.1 | 40.7 | 37.5 | 41.1 |
| 1970 | 57.4 | 42.3 | 59.2 | 76.2 | 47.7 | 79.7 | 40.8 | 37.1 | 41.2 |
| 1971 | 56.6 | 41.3 | 58.4 | 74.9 | 46.8 | 78.5 | 40.4 | 36.0 | 40.9 |
| 1972 | 57.0 | 43.5 | 58.6 | 75.0 | 48.9 | 78.4 | 41.0 | 38.2 | 41.3 |
| 1973 | 57.8 | 45.9 | 59.3 | 75.5 | 51.4 | 78.6 | 42.0 | 40.5 | 42.2 |
| 1974 | 57.8 | 46.0 | 59.2 | 74.9 | 51.2 | 77.9 | 42.6 | 41.0 | 42.8 |
| 1975 | 56.1 | 43.3 | 57.6 | 71.7 | 47.2 | 74.8 | 42.0 | 39.4 | 42.3 |
| 1976 | 56.8 | 44.2 | 58.3 | 72.0 | 47.9 | 75.1 | 43.2 | 40.5 | 43.5 |
| 1977 | 57.9 | 46.1 | 59.2 | 72.8 | 50.4 | 75.6 | 44.5 | 41.8 | 44.8 |
| 1978 | 59.3 | 48.3 | 60.6 | 73.8 | 52.2 | 76.4 | 46.4 | 44.5 | 46.6 |
| 1979 | 59.9 | 48.5 | 61.2 | 73.8 | 51.7 | 76.5 | 47.5 | 45.3 | 47.7 |
| 1980 | 59.2 | 46.6 | 60.6 | 72.0 | 49.5 | 74.6 | 47.7 | 43.8 | 48.1 |
| 1981 | 59.0 | 44.6 | 60.5 | 71.3 | 47.1 | 74.0 | 48.0 | 42.0 | 48.6 |
| 1982 | 57.8 | 41.5 | 59.4 | 69.0 | 42.9 | 71.8 | 47.7 | 40.2 | 48.4 |
| 1983 | 57.9 | 41.5 | 59.5 | 68.8 | 43.1 | 71.4 | 48.0 | 40.0 | 48.8 |
| 1984 | 59.5 | 43.7 | 61.0 | 70.7 | 45.0 | 73.2 | 49.5 | 42.5 | 50.1 |
| 1985 | 60.1 | 44.4 | 61.5 | 70.9 | 45.7 | 73.3 | 50.4 | 42.9 | 51.0 |
| 1986 | 60.7 | 44.6 | 62.1 | 71.0 | 45.7 | 73.3 | 51.4 | 43.6 | 52.0 |
| 1987 | 61.5 | 45.5 | 62.9 | 71.5 | 46.1 | 73.8 | 52.5 | 44.8 | 53.1 |
| 1988 | 62.3 | 46.8 | 63.6 | 72.0 | 47.8 | 74.2 | 53.4 | 45.9 | 54.0 |
| 1989 | 63.0 | 47.5 | 64.2 | 72.5 | 48.7 | 74.5 | 54.3 | 46.4 | 54.9 |
| 1990 | 62.8 | 45.3 | 64.3 | 72.0 | 46.6 | 74.3 | 54.3 | 44.0 | 55.2 |
| 1991 | 61.7 | 42.0 | 63.2 | 70.4 | 42.7 | 72.7 | 53.7 | 41.2 | 54.6 |
| 1992 | 61.5 | 41.0 | 63.0 | 69.8 | 41.9 | 72.1 | 53.8 | 40.0 | 54.8 |
| 1993 | 61.7 | 41.7 | 63.3 | 70.0 | 42.3 | 72.3 | 54.1 | 41.0 | 55.0 |
| 1994 | 62.5 | 43.4 | 64.0 | 70.4 | 43.8 | 72.6 | 55.3 | 43.0 | 56.2 |
| 1995 | 62.9 | 44.2 | 64.4 | 70.8 | 44.7 | 73.0 | 55.6 | 43.8 | 56.5 |
| 1996 | 63.2 | 43.5 | 64.7 | 70.9 | 43.6 | 73.2 | 56.0 | 43.5 | 57.0 |
| 1997 | 63.8 | 43.4 | 65.5 | 71.3 | 43.4 | 73.7 | 56.8 | 43.3 | 57.8 |
| 1998 | 64.1 | 45.1 | 65.6 | 71.6 | 44.7 | 73.9 | 57.1 | 45.5 | 58.0 |
| 1999 | 64.3 | 44.7 | 65.9 | 71.6 | 45.1 | 74.0 | 57.4 | 44.3 | 58.5 |
| 2000 | 64.4 | 45.2 | 66.0 | 71.9 | 45.4 | 74.2 | 57.5 | 45.0 | 58.4 |
| 2001 | 63.7 | 42.3 | 65.4 | 70.9 | 42.2 | 73.3 | 57.0 | 42.4 | 58.1 |
| 2002 | 62.7 | 39.6 | 64.6 | 69.7 | 38.9 | 72.3 | 56.3 | 40.3 | 57.5 |
| 2003 | 62.3 | 36.8 | 64.3 | 68.9 | 35.7 | 71.7 | 56.1 | 37.8 | 57.5 |
| 2004 | 62.3 | 36.4 | 64.4 | 69.2 | 35.9 | 71.9 | 56.0 | 37.0 | 57.4 |
| 2005 | 62.7 | 36.5 | 64.7 | 69.6 | 35.1 | 72.4 | 56.2 | 37.8 | 57.6 |
| 2006 | 63.1 | 36.9 | 65.2 | 70.1 | 36.3 | 72.9 | 56.6 | 37.6 | 58.0 |
| 2007 | 63.0 | 34.8 | 65.2 | 69.8 | 33.8 | 72.8 | 56.6 | 35.8 | 58.2 |
| 2008 | 62.2 | 32.6 | 64.5 | 68.5 | 31.6 | 71.6 | 56.2 | 33.7 | 57.9 |
| 2009 | 59.3 | 28.4 | 61.7 | 64.5 | 26.9 | 67.6 | 54.4 | 29.9 | 56.2 |
| 2010 | 58.5 | 25.9 | 61.0 | 63.7 | 24.8 | 66.8 | 53.6 | 27.0 | 55.5 |
| 2011 | 58.4 | 25.8 | 60.8 | 63.9 | 24.6 | 67.0 | 53.2 | 27.1 | 55.0 |
| 2012 | 58.6 | 26.1 | 61.0 | 64.4 | 24.9 | 67.5 | 53.1 | 27.3 | 55.0 |
| 2013 | 58.6 | 26.6 | 60.9 | 64.4 | 25.5 | 67.4 | 53.2 | 27.7 | 54.9 |
| 2014 | 59.0 | 27.3 | 61.3 | 64.9 | 26.3 | 67.8 | 53.5 | 28.4 | 55.2 |
| 2015 | 59.3 | 28.5 | 61.5 | 65.3 | 27.9 | 68.1 | 53.7 | 29.1 | 55.4 |

**Table 1-12.  Civilian Employment-Population Ratios, by Sex, Age, Race, and Hispanic Origin, 1948–2015** —*Continued*

(Percent.)

| Race, Hispanic origin, and year | Both sexes | | | Men | | | Women | | |
|---|---|---|---|---|---|---|---|---|---|
| | 16 years and over | 16 to 19 years | 20 years and over | 16 years and over | 16 to 19 years | 20 years and over | 16 years and over | 16 to 19 years | 20 years and over |
| **WHITE** | | | | | | | | | |
| 1954 | 55.2 | 42.9 | 56.2 | 81.5 | 49.9 | 84.0 | 31.4 | 36.4 | 31.1 |
| 1955 | 56.5 | 44.2 | 57.4 | 82.2 | 52.0 | 84.7 | 33.0 | 37.0 | 32.7 |
| 1956 | 57.3 | 46.1 | 58.2 | 82.7 | 54.1 | 85.0 | 34.2 | 38.9 | 33.8 |
| 1957 | 56.8 | 45.0 | 57.8 | 81.8 | 52.4 | 84.1 | 34.2 | 38.2 | 33.9 |
| 1958 | 55.3 | 41.0 | 56.5 | 79.2 | 47.6 | 81.8 | 33.6 | 35.0 | 33.5 |
| 1959 | 55.9 | 41.2 | 57.2 | 79.9 | 48.1 | 82.8 | 34.0 | 34.8 | 34.0 |
| 1960 | 55.9 | 41.5 | 57.2 | 79.4 | 48.1 | 82.4 | 34.6 | 35.1 | 34.5 |
| 1961 | 55.3 | 40.1 | 56.7 | 78.2 | 45.9 | 81.4 | 34.5 | 34.6 | 34.5 |
| 1962 | 55.4 | 40.4 | 56.9 | 78.4 | 46.4 | 81.5 | 34.7 | 34.8 | 34.7 |
| 1963 | 55.3 | 38.6 | 56.9 | 77.7 | 44.7 | 81.1 | 35.0 | 32.9 | 35.2 |
| 1964 | 55.5 | 38.4 | 57.3 | 77.8 | 45.0 | 81.3 | 35.5 | 32.2 | 35.8 |
| 1965 | 56.0 | 40.3 | 57.8 | 77.9 | 47.1 | 81.5 | 36.2 | 33.7 | 36.5 |
| 1966 | 56.8 | 43.6 | 58.3 | 78.3 | 50.1 | 81.7 | 37.5 | 37.5 | 37.5 |
| 1967 | 57.2 | 43.8 | 58.7 | 78.4 | 50.2 | 81.7 | 38.3 | 37.7 | 38.3 |
| 1968 | 57.4 | 43.9 | 59.0 | 78.3 | 50.3 | 81.6 | 38.9 | 37.8 | 39.1 |
| 1969 | 58.0 | 45.2 | 59.4 | 78.2 | 51.1 | 81.4 | 40.1 | 39.5 | 40.1 |
| 1970 | 57.5 | 44.5 | 59.0 | 76.8 | 49.6 | 80.1 | 40.3 | 39.5 | 40.4 |
| 1971 | 56.8 | 43.8 | 58.3 | 75.7 | 49.2 | 79.0 | 39.9 | 38.6 | 40.1 |
| 1972 | 57.4 | 46.4 | 58.6 | 76.0 | 51.5 | 79.0 | 40.7 | 41.3 | 40.6 |
| 1973 | 58.2 | 48.9 | 59.3 | 76.5 | 54.3 | 79.2 | 41.8 | 43.6 | 41.6 |
| 1974 | 58.3 | 49.3 | 59.3 | 75.9 | 54.4 | 78.6 | 42.4 | 44.3 | 42.2 |
| 1975 | 56.7 | 46.5 | 57.9 | 73.0 | 50.6 | 75.7 | 42.0 | 42.5 | 41.9 |
| 1976 | 57.5 | 47.8 | 58.6 | 73.4 | 51.5 | 76.0 | 43.2 | 44.2 | 43.1 |
| 1977 | 58.6 | 50.1 | 59.6 | 74.1 | 54.4 | 76.5 | 44.5 | 45.9 | 44.4 |
| 1978 | 60.0 | 52.4 | 60.8 | 75.0 | 56.3 | 77.2 | 46.3 | 48.5 | 46.1 |
| 1979 | 60.6 | 52.6 | 61.5 | 75.1 | 55.7 | 77.3 | 47.5 | 49.4 | 47.3 |
| 1980 | 60.0 | 50.7 | 61.0 | 73.4 | 53.4 | 75.6 | 47.8 | 47.9 | 47.8 |
| 1981 | 60.0 | 48.7 | 61.1 | 72.8 | 51.3 | 75.1 | 48.3 | 46.2 | 48.5 |
| 1982 | 58.8 | 45.8 | 60.1 | 70.6 | 47.0 | 73.0 | 48.1 | 44.6 | 48.4 |
| 1983 | 58.9 | 45.9 | 60.1 | 70.4 | 47.4 | 72.6 | 48.5 | 44.5 | 48.9 |
| 1984 | 60.5 | 48.0 | 61.5 | 72.1 | 49.1 | 74.3 | 49.8 | 47.0 | 50.0 |
| 1985 | 61.0 | 48.5 | 62.0 | 72.3 | 49.9 | 74.3 | 50.7 | 47.1 | 51.0 |
| 1986 | 61.5 | 48.8 | 62.6 | 72.3 | 49.6 | 74.3 | 51.7 | 47.9 | 52.0 |
| 1987 | 62.3 | 49.4 | 63.4 | 72.7 | 49.9 | 74.7 | 52.8 | 49.0 | 53.1 |
| 1988 | 63.1 | 50.9 | 64.1 | 73.2 | 51.7 | 75.1 | 53.8 | 50.2 | 54.0 |
| 1989 | 63.8 | 51.6 | 64.7 | 73.7 | 52.6 | 75.4 | 54.6 | 50.5 | 54.9 |
| 1990 | 63.7 | 49.7 | 64.8 | 73.3 | 51.0 | 75.1 | 54.7 | 48.3 | 55.2 |
| 1991 | 62.6 | 46.6 | 63.7 | 71.6 | 47.2 | 73.5 | 54.2 | 45.9 | 54.8 |
| 1992 | 62.4 | 45.3 | 63.6 | 71.1 | 46.4 | 73.1 | 54.2 | 44.2 | 54.9 |
| 1993 | 62.7 | 46.2 | 63.9 | 71.4 | 46.6 | 73.3 | 54.6 | 45.7 | 55.2 |
| 1994 | 63.5 | 47.9 | 64.7 | 71.8 | 48.3 | 73.6 | 55.8 | 47.5 | 56.4 |
| 1995 | 63.8 | 48.8 | 64.9 | 72.0 | 49.4 | 73.8 | 56.1 | 48.1 | 56.7 |
| 1996 | 64.1 | 47.9 | 65.3 | 72.3 | 48.2 | 74.2 | 56.3 | 47.6 | 57.0 |
| 1997 | 64.6 | 47.7 | 65.9 | 72.7 | 48.1 | 74.7 | 57.0 | 47.2 | 57.8 |
| 1998 | 64.7 | 49.0 | 65.9 | 72.7 | 48.6 | 74.7 | 57.1 | 49.3 | 57.7 |
| 1999 | 64.8 | 48.9 | 66.1 | 72.8 | 49.3 | 74.8 | 57.3 | 48.4 | 58.0 |
| 2000 | 64.9 | 49.1 | 66.1 | 73.0 | 49.5 | 74.9 | 57.4 | 48.8 | 58.0 |
| 2001 | 64.2 | 46.3 | 65.6 | 72.0 | 46.2 | 74.0 | 57.0 | 46.5 | 57.7 |
| 2002 | 63.4 | 43.2 | 64.9 | 70.8 | 42.3 | 73.1 | 56.4 | 44.1 | 57.3 |
| 2003 | 63.0 | 40.4 | 64.7 | 70.1 | 39.4 | 72.5 | 56.3 | 41.5 | 57.3 |
| 2004 | 63.1 | 40.0 | 64.8 | 70.4 | 39.7 | 72.8 | 56.1 | 40.3 | 57.2 |
| 2005 | 63.4 | 40.2 | 65.1 | 70.8 | 38.8 | 73.3 | 56.3 | 41.8 | 57.4 |
| 2006 | 63.8 | 40.6 | 65.5 | 71.3 | 40.0 | 73.7 | 56.6 | 41.1 | 57.7 |
| 2007 | 63.6 | 38.3 | 65.5 | 70.9 | 37.3 | 73.5 | 56.7 | 39.2 | 57.9 |
| 2008 | 62.9 | 35.9 | 64.8 | 69.7 | 34.8 | 72.4 | 56.3 | 37.1 | 57.7 |
| 2009 | 60.2 | 31.7 | 62.3 | 66.0 | 30.2 | 68.7 | 54.8 | 33.4 | 56.2 |
| 2010 | 59.4 | 29.0 | 61.6 | 65.1 | 27.6 | 67.9 | 54.0 | 30.4 | 55.6 |
| 2011 | 59.4 | 28.8 | 61.6 | 65.3 | 27.3 | 68.2 | 53.7 | 30.4 | 55.3 |
| 2012 | 59.4 | 29.0 | 61.5 | 65.8 | 27.7 | 68.6 | 53.3 | 30.3 | 54.9 |
| 2013 | 59.4 | 29.4 | 61.4 | 65.7 | 28.3 | 68.4 | 53.3 | 30.5 | 54.8 |
| 2014 | 59.7 | 29.9 | 61.8 | 66.1 | 28.8 | 68.7 | 56.7 | 36.8 | 57.9 |
| 2015 | 59.9 | 31.0 | 61.8 | 66.5 | 30.8 | 68.9 | 53.7 | 31.3 | 55.1 |

**Table 1-12.  Civilian Employment-Population Ratios, by Sex, Age, Race, and Hispanic Origin, 1948–2015**
—*Continued*

(Percent.)

| Race, Hispanic origin, and year | Both sexes | | | Men | | | Women | | |
|---|---|---|---|---|---|---|---|---|---|
| | 16 years and over | 16 to 19 years | 20 years and over | 16 years and over | 16 to 19 years | 20 years and over | 16 years and over | 16 to 19 years | 20 years and over |
| **BLACK** | | | | | | | | | |
| 1980 | 52.2 | 23.9 | 56.4 | 60.4 | 26.9 | 65.8 | 45.7 | 21.0 | 49.0 |
| 1981 | 51.3 | 22.1 | 55.5 | 59.1 | 24.6 | 64.5 | 45.1 | 19.7 | 48.5 |
| 1982 | 49.4 | 19.0 | 53.6 | 56.0 | 20.3 | 61.4 | 44.2 | 17.7 | 47.5 |
| 1983 | 49.5 | 18.7 | 53.6 | 56.3 | 20.4 | 61.6 | 44.1 | 17.0 | 47.4 |
| 1984 | 52.3 | 21.9 | 56.1 | 59.2 | 23.9 | 64.1 | 46.7 | 20.1 | 49.8 |
| 1985 | 53.4 | 24.6 | 57.0 | 60.0 | 26.3 | 64.6 | 48.1 | 23.1 | 50.9 |
| 1986 | 54.1 | 25.1 | 57.6 | 60.6 | 26.5 | 65.1 | 48.8 | 23.8 | 51.6 |
| 1987 | 55.6 | 27.1 | 58.9 | 62.0 | 28.5 | 66.4 | 50.3 | 25.8 | 53.0 |
| 1988 | 56.3 | 27.6 | 59.7 | 62.7 | 29.4 | 67.1 | 51.2 | 25.8 | 53.9 |
| 1989 | 56.9 | 28.7 | 60.1 | 62.8 | 30.4 | 67.0 | 52.0 | 27.1 | 54.6 |
| 1990 | 56.7 | 26.7 | 60.2 | 62.6 | 27.7 | 67.1 | 51.9 | 25.9 | 54.7 |
| 1991 | 55.4 | 22.6 | 59.0 | 61.3 | 23.8 | 66.0 | 50.6 | 21.4 | 53.6 |
| 1992 | 54.9 | 22.8 | 58.3 | 59.9 | 23.6 | 64.3 | 50.8 | 22.1 | 53.6 |
| 1993 | 55.0 | 22.7 | 58.4 | 60.0 | 23.6 | 64.3 | 50.9 | 21.6 | 53.8 |
| 1994 | 56.1 | 25.0 | 59.4 | 60.8 | 25.4 | 65.0 | 52.3 | 24.4 | 55.0 |
| 1995 | 57.1 | 25.7 | 60.6 | 61.7 | 25.2 | 66.1 | 53.4 | 26.1 | 56.1 |
| 1996 | 57.4 | 26.0 | 60.8 | 61.0 | 24.9 | 65.5 | 54.4 | 27.1 | 57.1 |
| 1997 | 58.2 | 26.2 | 61.8 | 61.4 | 23.7 | 66.1 | 55.6 | 28.5 | 58.4 |
| 1998 | 59.7 | 30.1 | 63.0 | 62.9 | 28.4 | 67.1 | 57.2 | 31.8 | 59.7 |
| 1999 | 60.6 | 27.9 | 64.2 | 63.1 | 26.7 | 67.5 | 58.6 | 29.0 | 61.5 |
| 2000 | 60.9 | 29.8 | 64.2 | 63.6 | 28.9 | 67.7 | 58.6 | 30.6 | 61.3 |
| 2001 | 59.7 | 26.7 | 63.2 | 62.1 | 26.4 | 66.3 | 57.8 | 27.0 | 60.7 |
| 2002 | 58.1 | 25.3 | 61.6 | 61.1 | 25.6 | 65.2 | 55.8 | 24.9 | 58.7 |
| 2003 | 57.4 | 21.7 | 61.0 | 59.5 | 19.9 | 64.1 | 55.6 | 23.5 | 58.6 |
| 2004 | 57.2 | 21.5 | 60.9 | 59.3 | 19.3 | 63.9 | 55.5 | 23.6 | 58.5 |
| 2005 | 57.7 | 21.6 | 61.5 | 60.2 | 20.8 | 64.7 | 55.7 | 22.4 | 58.9 |
| 2006 | 58.4 | 24.1 | 62.0 | 60.6 | 21.7 | 65.2 | 56.5 | 26.4 | 59.4 |
| 2007 | 58.4 | 21.4 | 62.3 | 60.7 | 19.5 | 65.5 | 56.5 | 23.3 | 59.8 |
| 2008 | 57.3 | 20.2 | 61.2 | 59.1 | 18.7 | 63.9 | 55.8 | 21.7 | 59.1 |
| 2009 | 53.2 | 16.5 | 57.1 | 53.7 | 14.3 | 58.2 | 52.8 | 18.6 | 56.1 |
| 2010 | 52.3 | 14.5 | 56.1 | 53.1 | 14.1 | 57.5 | 51.7 | 15.0 | 55.1 |
| 2011 | 51.7 | 14.6 | 55.3 | 52.8 | 14.6 | 56.9 | 50.8 | 14.7 | 54.0 |
| 2012 | 53.0 | 16.6 | 56.5 | 54.1 | 15.0 | 58.3 | 52.2 | 18.1 | 55.1 |
| 2013 | 53.2 | 17.1 | 56.5 | 54.5 | 15.0 | 58.6 | 52.0 | 19.1 | 54.8 |
| 2014 | 54.3 | 18.2 | 57.4 | 55.9 | 16.4 | 59.7 | 52.9 | 19.9 | 55.6 |
| 2015 | 55.7 | 20.1 | 58.7 | 57.2 | 18.2 | 60.9 | 54.4 | 22.0 | 56.9 |
| **HISPANIC** | | | | | | | | | |
| 1980 | 57.6 | 39.0 | 60.5 | ... | ... | ... | ... | ... | ... |
| 1981 | 57.4 | 35.3 | 60.7 | ... | ... | ... | ... | ... | ... |
| 1982 | 54.9 | 31.4 | 58.2 | ... | ... | ... | ... | ... | ... |
| 1983 | 55.1 | 32.4 | 58.1 | ... | ... | ... | ... | ... | ... |
| 1984 | 57.9 | 36.0 | 60.7 | ... | ... | ... | ... | ... | ... |
| 1985 | 57.8 | 33.7 | 60.7 | ... | ... | ... | ... | ... | ... |
| 1986 | 58.5 | 33.0 | 61.5 | ... | ... | ... | ... | ... | ... |
| 1987 | 60.5 | 35.6 | 63.4 | ... | ... | ... | ... | ... | ... |
| 1988 | 61.9 | 38.6 | 64.6 | ... | ... | ... | ... | ... | ... |
| 1989 | 62.2 | 39.2 | 64.8 | ... | ... | ... | ... | ... | ... |
| 1990 | 61.9 | 38.5 | 64.8 | ... | ... | ... | ... | ... | ... |
| 1991 | 59.8 | 34.8 | 62.8 | ... | ... | ... | ... | ... | ... |
| 1992 | 59.1 | 33.2 | 62.1 | ... | ... | ... | ... | ... | ... |
| 1993 | 59.1 | 32.5 | 62.1 | ... | ... | ... | ... | ... | ... |
| 1994 | 59.5 | 33.5 | 62.4 | 71.7 | 36.8 | ... | 47.2 | 30.1 | ... |
| 1995 | 59.7 | 34.5 | 62.6 | 72.1 | 37.5 | ... | 47.3 | 31.3 | ... |
| 1996 | 60.6 | 33.2 | 63.7 | 73.3 | 38.8 | ... | 47.9 | 27.3 | ... |
| 1997 | 62.6 | 33.7 | 66.0 | 74.5 | 37.6 | ... | 50.2 | 29.3 | ... |
| 1998 | 63.1 | 36.0 | 66.2 | 74.7 | 38.6 | ... | 51.0 | 33.0 | ... |
| 1999 | 63.4 | 37.0 | 66.5 | 75.3 | 41.2 | ... | 51.7 | 32.5 | ... |
| 2000 | 65.7 | 38.6 | 68.9 | 77.4 | 42.8 | 81.7 | 53.6 | 33.9 | 55.8 |
| 2001 | 64.9 | 38.6 | 67.8 | 76.2 | 43.3 | 79.9 | 53.3 | 33.5 | 55.4 |
| 2002 | 63.9 | 35.2 | 67.0 | 74.5 | 39.0 | 78.3 | 52.9 | 31.1 | 55.2 |
| 2003 | 63.1 | 30.2 | 66.4 | 74.3 | 31.9 | 78.6 | 51.2 | 28.4 | 53.6 |
| 2004 | 63.8 | 30.4 | 67.2 | 75.1 | 33.4 | 79.4 | 51.8 | 27.2 | 54.4 |
| 2005 | 64.0 | 31.5 | 67.3 | 75.8 | 33.8 | 80.0 | 51.5 | 29.1 | 53.8 |
| 2006 | 65.2 | 32.2 | 68.5 | 76.8 | 34.8 | 81.1 | 52.8 | 29.5 | 55.2 |
| 2007 | 64.9 | 30.4 | 68.5 | 76.2 | 32.1 | 80.7 | 53.0 | 28.5 | 55.6 |
| 2008 | 63.3 | 28.6 | 66.9 | 74.1 | 30.9 | 78.6 | 51.9 | 26.2 | 54.6 |
| 2009 | 59.7 | 23.8 | 63.5 | 68.9 | 24.1 | 73.5 | 50.1 | 23.4 | 52.9 |
| 2010 | 59.0 | 21.0 | 63.1 | 68.0 | 21.7 | 72.9 | 49.6 | 20.2 | 52.7 |
| 2011 | 58.9 | 19.5 | 63.2 | 67.9 | 20.1 | 73.3 | 49.3 | 18.9 | 52.5 |
| 2012 | 59.5 | 22.1 | 63.6 | 68.6 | 22.9 | 73.8 | 50.4 | 21.2 | 53.5 |
| 2013 | 60.0 | 22.5 | 64.1 | 69.6 | 23.5 | 74.7 | 50.4 | 21.4 | 53.5 |
| 2014 | 61.2 | 23.5 | 65.2 | 71.0 | 24.2 | 76.0 | 51.4 | 22.7 | 54.3 |
| 2015 | 61.6 | 24.9 | 65.4 | 71.5 | 25.8 | 76.3 | 51.8 | 23.9 | 54.6 |

. . . = Not available.

## Table 1-13. Employed Civilians, by Sex, Race, Hispanic Origin, and Occupation, 2013–2015

(Thousands of people.)

| Year and occupation | Total | Men | Women | White | Black | Hispanic[1] |
|---|---|---|---|---|---|---|
| **2013** | | | | | | |
| **All Occupations** | 143 929 | 76 353 | 67 577 | 115 379 | 16 151 | 22 514 |
| Management, professional, and related occupations | 54 712 | 26 597 | 28 114 | 44 744 | 4 641 | 4 546 |
| Management, business, and financial operations occupations | 22 794 | 12 898 | 9 896 | 19 218 | 1 683 | 1 924 |
| Computer and mathematical occupations | 3 980 | 2 941 | 1 039 | 2 821 | 329 | 251 |
| Architecture and engineering occupations | 2 806 | 2 410 | 396 | 2 280 | 153 | 209 |
| Life, physical and social science occupations | 1 307 | 705 | 602 | 1 040 | 74 | 103 |
| Community and social service occupations | 2 332 | 879 | 1 453 | 1 758 | 433 | 232 |
| Legal occupations | 1 809 | 891 | 918 | 1 571 | 111 | 148 |
| Education, training, and library occupations | 8 623 | 2 261 | 6 362 | 7 221 | 810 | 826 |
| Arts, design, entertainment, sports, and media occupations | 2 879 | 1 520 | 1 359 | 2 451 | 186 | 242 |
| Healthcare practitioner and technical occupations | 8 182 | 2 092 | 6 090 | 6 385 | 863 | 609 |
| Healthcare support occupations | 3 537 | 393 | 3 145 | 2 300 | 935 | 564 |
| Protective service occupations | 3 130 | 2 469 | 661 | 2 338 | 584 | 471 |
| Food preparation and serving related occupations | 8 209 | 3 721 | 4 488 | 6 370 | 1 002 | 2 002 |
| Building and grounds cleaning and maintenance occupations | 5 661 | 3 473 | 2 188 | 4 435 | 827 | 2 034 |
| Personal care and service occupations | 5 392 | 1 205 | 4 187 | 3 921 | 786 | 909 |
| Sales and related occupations | 15 444 | 7 935 | 7 509 | 12 542 | 1 599 | 2 234 |
| Office and administrative support occupations | 17 802 | 4 745 | 13 057 | 14 177 | 2 333 | 17 802 |
| Farming, fishing, and forestry occupations | 964 | 755 | 209 | 854 | 54 | 412 |
| Construction and extraction occupations | 7 130 | 6 948 | 182 | 6 307 | 439 | 2 214 |
| Installation, maintenance, and repair occupations | 4 964 | 4 757 | 207 | 4 259 | 424 | 844 |
| Production occupations | 8 275 | 5 991 | 2 284 | 6 474 | 1 016 | 1 860 |
| Transportation and material moving occupations | 8 709 | 7 363 | 1 346 | 6 658 | 1 512 | 8 709 |
| **2014** | | | | | | |
| **All Occupations** | 0 | 77 692 | 68 613 | 116 788 | 16 732 | 23 492 |
| Management, professional, and related occupations | 56 050 | 27 119 | 28 931 | 45 588 | 4 939 | 4 888 |
| Management, business, and financial operations occupations | 23 171 | 13 041 | 10 129 | 19 518 | 1 745 | 2 066 |
| Computer and mathematical occupations | 4 303 | 3 204 | 1 100 | 3 013 | 355 | 286 |
| Architecture and engineering occupations | 2 798 | 2 369 | 430 | 2 261 | 146 | 2 798 |
| Life, physical and social science occupations | 1 355 | 737 | 618 | 1 066 | 86 | 1 355 |
| Community and social service occupations | 2 495 | 890 | 1 605 | 1 885 | 436 | 2 495 |
| Legal occupations | 1 814 | 893 | 921 | 1 558 | 136 | 1 814 |
| Education, training, and library occupations | 8 686 | 2 252 | 6 434 | 7 214 | 897 | 827 |
| Arts, design, entertainment, sports, and media occupations | 2 935 | 1 544 | 1 391 | 2 510 | 186 | 2 935 |
| Healthcare practitioner and technical occupations | 8 493 | 2 189 | 6 304 | 6 564 | 953 | 8 493 |
| Healthcare support occupations | 3 461 | 430 | 3 031 | 2 276 | 888 | 3 461 |
| Protective service occupations | 3 140 | 2 456 | 684 | 2 333 | 619 | 3 140 |
| Food preparation and serving related occupations | 8 112 | 3 641 | 4 471 | 6 237 | 1 026 | 8 112 |
| Building and grounds cleaning and maintenance occupations | 5 803 | 3 469 | 2 335 | 4 530 | 845 | 2 132 |
| Personal care and service occupations | 5 337 | 1 207 | 4 130 | 3 880 | 801 | 883 |
| Sales and related occupations | 15 646 | 7 948 | 7 697 | 12 682 | 1 670 | 2 298 |
| Office and administrative support occupations | 17 771 | 4 813 | 12 958 | 14 065 | 2 333 | 17 771 |
| Farming, fishing, and forestry occupations | 1 022 | 792 | 229 | 912 | 61 | 1 022 |
| Construction and extraction occupations | 7 637 | 7 440 | 197 | 6 707 | 523 | 7 637 |
| Installation, maintenance, and repair occupations | 4 879 | 4 707 | 172 | 4 174 | 408 | 820 |
| Production occupations | 8 438 | 6 074 | 2 364 | 6 579 | 2 619 | 1 846 |
| Transportation and material moving occupations | 9 010 | 7 596 | 1 414 | 6 826 | 1 561 | 9 010 |
| **2015** | | | | | | |
| **All Occupations** | 148 834 | 79 131 | 69 703 | 117 944 | 17 472 | 24 400 |
| Management, professional, and related occupations | 57 960 | 28 090 | 29 871 | 46 757 | 5 308 | 5 249 |
| Management, business, and financial operations occupations | 24 108 | 13 589 | 10 519 | 20 039 | 1 975 | 2 278 |
| Computer and mathematical occupations | 4 369 | 3 291 | 1 078 | 2 989 | 374 | 297 |
| Architecture and engineering occupations | 2 954 | 2 508 | 446 | 2 377 | 176 | 241 |
| Life, physical and social science occupations | 1 404 | 750 | 654 | 1 081 | 85 | 98 |
| Community and social service occupations | 2 596 | 900 | 1 696 | 1 965 | 452 | 277 |
| Legal occupations | 1 803 | 897 | 905 | 1 566 | 122 | 135 |
| Education, training, and library occupations | 8 908 | 2 368 | 6 540 | 7 383 | 925 | 884 |
| Arts, design, entertainment, sports, and media occupations | 3 051 | 1 599 | 1 452 | 2 615 | 193 | 328 |
| Healthcare practitioner and technical occupations | 8 766 | 2 186 | 6 580 | 6 742 | 1 006 | 710 |
| Healthcare support occupations | 3 514 | 436 | 3 079 | 2 206 | 951 | 580 |
| Protective service occupations | 3 109 | 2 447 | 662 | 2 320 | 596 | 433 |
| Food preparation and serving related occupations | 8 142 | 3 702 | 4 440 | 6 174 | 1 121 | 2 057 |
| Building and grounds cleaning and maintenance occupations | 5 716 | 3 368 | 2 348 | 4 475 | 826 | 2 171 |
| Personal care and service occupations | 5 415 | 1 257 | 4 157 | 3 884 | 843 | 842 |
| Sales and related occupations | 33 598 | 7 960 | 7 741 | 12 694 | 4 138 | 2 363 |
| Office and administrative support occupations | 17 897 | 4 980 | 12 918 | 13 953 | 2 480 | 2 787 |
| Farming, fishing, and forestry occupations | 1 073 | 813 | 260 | 958 | 55 | 490 |
| Construction and extraction occupations | 7 652 | 7 445 | 207 | 6 752 | 527 | 2 546 |
| Installation, maintenance, and repair occupations | 5 008 | 4 833 | 175 | 4 278 | 413 | 944 |
| Production occupations | 8 522 | 6 070 | 2 452 | 6 630 | 1 067 | 1 898 |
| Transportation and material moving occupations | 9 125 | 7 731 | 1 394 | 6 863 | 1 625 | 2 039 |

[1] May be of any race.

## Table 1-14.  Employed Civilians, by Selected Occupation and Industry, 2013–2015

(Thousands of people.)

| Year and occupation | Total employed | Agriculture, forestry, fishing, and hunting | Mining | Construction | Manufacturing | | | Wholesale trade |
|---|---|---|---|---|---|---|---|---|
| | | | | | Total | Durable goods | Nondurable goods | |
| **2013** | | | | | | | | |
| **All Occupations** | 143 929 | 2 130 | 1 065 | 9 271 | 14 869 | 9 391 | 5 478 | 3 646 |
| Management, professional, and related occupations | 54 712 | 1 011 | 313 | 1 988 | 4 560 | 3 144 | 1 415 | 676 |
| Management, business, and financial operations occupations | 22 794 | 961 | 172 | 1 765 | 2 435 | 1 601 | 834 | 531 |
| Computer and mathematical occupations | 3 980 | 1 | 14 | 12 | 453 | 358 | 95 | 67 |
| Architecture and engineering occupations | 2 806 | 2 | 63 | 171 | 1 128 | 964 | 164 | 23 |
| Life, physical and social science occupations | 1 307 | 35 | 41 | 7 | 222 | 36 | 186 | 10 |
| Community and social service occupations | 2 332 | 3 | 0 | 2 | 4 | 3 | 1 | 0 |
| Legal occupations | 1 809 | 0 | 13 | 4 | 34 | 16 | 19 | 5 |
| Education, training, and library occupations | 8 623 | 4 | 3 | 4 | 28 | 17 | 11 | 5 |
| Arts, design, entertainment, sports, and media occupations | 2 879 | 2 | 3 | 19 | 207 | 126 | 81 | 24 |
| Healthcare practitioner and technical occupations | 8 182 | 3 | 4 | 4 | 49 | 24 | 25 | 9 |
| Healthcare support occupations | 3 537 | X | 0 | 1 | 6 | 3 | 2 | 1 |
| Protective service occupations | 3 130 | 15 | 3 | 14 | 25 | 16 | 9 | 5 |
| Food preparation and serving related occupations | 8 209 | 3 | 4 | 4 | 54 | 10 | 44 | 8 |
| Building and grounds cleaning and maintenance occupations | 5 661 | 29 | 13 | 39 | 136 | 68 | 68 | 26 |
| Personal care and service occupations | 5 392 | 29 | 2 | 3 | 7 | 6 | 2 | 3 |
| Sales and related occupations | 33 246 | 94 | 97 | 564 | 2 006 | 1 213 | 793 | 1 905 |
| Office and administrative support occupations | 17 802 | 84 | 76 | 488 | 1 328 | 841 | 488 | 587 |
| Farming, fishing, and forestry occupations | 964 | 808 | 1 | 2 | 58 | 8 | 50 | 37 |
| Construction and extraction occupations | 7 130 | 8 | 338 | 5 780 | 296 | 231 | 6 | 23 |
| Installation, maintenance, and repair occupations | 4 964 | 33 | 85 | 507 | 721 | 472 | 249 | 123 |
| Production occupations | 8 275 | 23 | 77 | 140 | 5 891 | 3 654 | 2 237 | 126 |
| Transportation and material moving occupations | 8 709 | 78 | 132 | 229 | 1 108 | 566 | 542 | 713 |
| **2014** | | | | | | | | |
| **All Occupations** | 146 305 | 2 237 | 1 088 | 9 813 | 15 100 | 9 542 | 5 559 | 3 642 |
| Management, professional, and related occupations | 56 050 | 1 029 | 332 | 1 910 | 4 636 | 3 148 | 1 488 | 676 |
| Management, business, and financial operations occupations | 23 171 | 971 | 183 | 1 708 | 2 536 | 1 643 | 893 | 529 |
| Computer and mathematical occupations | 4 303 | 2 | 11 | 21 | 466 | 361 | 105 | 77 |
| Architecture and engineering occupations | 2 798 | 5 | 76 | 141 | 1 086 | 920 | 165 | 21 |
| Life, physical and social science occupations | 1 355 | 39 | 42 | 4 | 235 | 42 | 192 | 5 |
| Community and social service occupations | 2 495 | 1 | 1 | 0 | 4 | 2 | 2 | 0 |
| Legal occupations | 1 814 | 0 | 11 | 4 | 27 | 16 | 11 | 9 |
| Education, training, and library occupations | 8 686 | 3 | 2 | 6 | 27 | 14 | 13 | 6 |
| Arts, design, entertainment, sports, and media occupations | 2 935 | 3 | 2 | 23 | 210 | 123 | 87 | 21 |
| Healthcare practitioner and technical occupations | 8 493 | 4 | 6 | 3 | 44 | 25 | 19 | 8 |
| Healthcare support occupations | 3 461 | 1 | 0 | 0 | 12 | 7 | 5 | 4 |
| Protective service occupations | 3 140 | 15 | 3 | 11 | 29 | 17 | 13 | 5 |
| Food preparation and serving related occupations | 8 112 | 4 | 2 | 3 | 52 | 12 | 41 | 11 |
| Building and grounds cleaning and maintenance occupations | 5 803 | 28 | 3 | 41 | 141 | 72 | 70 | 27 |
| Personal care and service occupations | 5 337 | 42 | 1 | 2 | 10 | 6 | 4 | 3 |
| Sales and related occupations | 15 646 | 17 | 14 | 112 | 640 | 337 | 303 | 1 322 |
| Office and administrative support occupations | 17 771 | 93 | 82 | 481 | 1 329 | 821 | 508 | 619 |
| Farming, fishing, and forestry occupations | 1 022 | 862 | 1 | 3 | 49 | 8 | 40 | 41 |
| Construction and extraction occupations | 7 637 | 13 | 371 | 6 319 | 267 | 208 | 59 | 25 |
| Installation, maintenance, and repair occupations | 4 879 | 33 | 90 | 528 | 675 | 417 | 258 | 112 |
| Production occupations | 8 438 | 17 | 70 | 162 | 6 045 | 3 827 | 2 218 | 125 |
| Transportation and material moving occupations | 9 010 | 84 | 118 | 241 | 1 215 | 664 | 551 | 673 |
| **2015** | | | | | | | | |
| **All Occupations** | 148 834 | 2 422 | 917 | 9 935 | 15 338 | 9 709 | 5 629 | 3 635 |
| Management, professional, and related occupations | 57 960 | 1 135 | 297 | 1 998 | 4 799 | 3 239 | 1 559 | 699 |
| Management, business, and financial operations occupations | 24 108 | 1 085 | 150 | 1 762 | 2 619 | 1 673 | 946 | 531 |
| Computer and mathematical occupations | 4 369 | 5 | 12 | 33 | 442 | 355 | 87 | 79 |
| Architecture and engineering occupations | 2 954 | 6 | 81 | 153 | 1 140 | 963 | 178 | 22 |
| Life, physical and social science occupations | 1 404 | 26 | 42 | 2 | 251 | 37 | 213 | 8 |
| Community and social service occupations | 2 596 | 3 | X | X | 5 | 5 | 1 | X |
| Legal occupations | 1 803 | 0 | 6 | 8 | 36 | 22 | 13 | 7 |
| Education, training, and library occupations | 8 908 | 7 | 2 | 3 | 33 | 22 | 12 | 11 |
| Arts, design, entertainment, sports, and media occupations | 3 051 | 1 | 1 | 35 | 233 | 141 | 92 | 31 |
| Healthcare practitioner and technical occupations | 8 766 | 1 | 5 | 3 | 39 | 22 | 17 | 10 |
| Healthcare support occupations | 3 514 | X | 0 | X | 12 | 9 | 3 | 1 |
| Protective service occupations | 3 109 | 18 | 2 | 10 | 30 | 16 | 14 | 6 |
| Food preparation and serving related occupations | 8 142 | 2 | 1 | 2 | 45 | 7 | 37 | 12 |
| Building and grounds cleaning and maintenance occupations | 5 716 | 37 | 4 | 36 | 129 | 69 | 60 | 28 |
| Personal care and service occupations | 5 415 | 52 | 0 | 1 | 8 | 4 | 5 | 3 |
| Sales and related occupations | 15 700 | 17 | 12 | 98 | 663 | 357 | 306 | 1 895 |
| Office and administrative support occupations | 17 897 | 87 | 73 | 509 | 1 281 | 777 | 504 | 591 |
| Farming, fishing, and forestry occupations | 1 073 | 903 | 1 | 4 | 55 | 4 | 51 | 52 |
| Construction and extraction occupations | 7 652 | 14 | 292 | 6 347 | 294 | 239 | 55 | 30 |
| Installation, maintenance, and repair occupations | 5 008 | 31 | 73 | 534 | 680 | 436 | 244 | 129 |
| Production occupations | 8 522 | 30 | 62 | 153 | 6 072 | 3 854 | 2 218 | 108 |
| Transportation and material moving occupations | 9 125 | 95 | 100 | 244 | 1 271 | 698 | 573 | 672 |

X = Not applicable.

## Table 1-14. Employed Civilians, by Selected Occupation and Industry, 2013–2015—*Continued*

(Thousands of people.)

| Year and occupation | Retail trade | Transportation and warehousing | Utilities | Information | Finance and insurance | Real estate and rental and leasing | Professional and technical services |
|---|---|---|---|---|---|---|---|
| **2013** | | | | | | | |
| **All Occupations** | 16 007 | 6 228 | 1 187 | 2 960 | 6 984 | 2 865 | 10 110 |
| Management, professional, and related occupations | 1 706 | 717 | 375 | 1 641 | 3 791 | 1 020 | 8 088 |
| Management, business, and financial operations occupations | 854 | 568 | 195 | 627 | 3 142 | 925 | 3 216 |
| Computer and mathematical occupations | 141 | 56 | 45 | 279 | 429 | 18 | 1 559 |
| Architecture and engineering occupations | 22 | 47 | 92 | 77 | 16 | 7 | 857 |
| Life, physical and social science occupations | 7 | 1 | 21 | 9 | 8 | 1 | 297 |
| Community and social service occupations | 2 | 1 | X | 4 | 21 | 6 | 13 |
| Legal occupations | 18 | 8 | 6 | 14 | 76 | 32 | 1 196 |
| Education, training, and library occupations | 18 | 23 | 4 | 110 | 18 | 5 | 51 |
| Arts, design, entertainment, sports, and media occupations | 184 | 9 | 7 | 517 | 30 | 19 | 682 |
| Healthcare practitioner and technical occupations | 460 | 5 | 4 | 3 | 51 | 6 | 217 |
| Healthcare support occupations | 38 | 2 | 0 | 0 | 6 | 5 | 43 |
| Protective service occupations | 64 | 38 | 11 | 7 | 26 | 20 | 24 |
| Food preparation and serving related occupations | 378 | 12 | 1 | 20 | 8 | 27 | 5 |
| Building and grounds cleaning and maintenance occupations | 155 | 56 | 12 | 18 | 18 | 220 | 23 |
| Personal care and service occupations | 49 | 53 | 0 | 24 | 8 | 36 | 27 |
| Sales and related occupations | 11 293 | 1 504 | 239 | 838 | 3 069 | 1 223 | 312 |
| Office and administrative support occupations | 2 566 | 1 390 | 215 | 502 | 1 926 | 342 | 1 252 |
| Farming, fishing, and forestry occupations | 14 | 6 | 0 | 0 | 1 | 0 | 4 |
| Construction and extraction occupations | 75 | 63 | 110 | 18 | 4 | 47 | 56 |
| Installation, maintenance, and repair occupations | 627 | 342 | 194 | 284 | 26 | 139 | 85 |
| Production occupations | 448 | 99 | 194 | 60 | 23 | 19 | 129 |
| Transportation and material moving occupations | 1 162 | 3 336 | 50 | 50 | 4 | 109 | 62 |
| **2014** | | | | | | | |
| **All Occupations** | 16 609 | 6 377 | 1 204 | 3 115 | 6 956 | 2 915 | 10 327 |
| Management, professional, and related occupations | 1 839 | 742 | 389 | 1 773 | 3 860 | 1 021 | 8 311 |
| Management, business, and financial operations occupations | 891 | 588 | 207 | 631 | 3 120 | 927 | 3 268 |
| Computer and mathematical occupations | 174 | 62 | 41 | 339 | 497 | 25 | 5 043 |
| Architecture and engineering occupations | 23 | 45 | 97 | 88 | 20 | 7 | 880 |
| Life, physical and social science occupations | 5 | 3 | 32 | 8 | 13 | 4 | 303 |
| Community and social service occupations | 1 | 5 | X | 0 | 17 | 3 | 14 |
| Legal occupations | 15 | 8 | 3 | 15 | 87 | 30 | 1 224 |
| Education, training, and library occupations | 25 | 11 | 4 | 116 | 19 | 2 | 46 |
| Arts, design, entertainment, sports, and media occupations | 207 | 13 | 4 | 570 | 28 | 18 | 709 |
| Healthcare practitioner and technical occupations | 497 | 6 | 0 | 4 | 58 | 5 | 220 |
| Healthcare support occupations | 46 | 1 | 2 | 1 | 7 | 5 | 49 |
| Protective service occupations | 72 | 38 | 11 | 10 | 37 | 21 | 30 |
| Food preparation and serving related occupations | 408 | 16 | 2 | 27 | 8 | 18 | 3 |
| Building and grounds cleaning and maintenance occupations | 184 | 59 | 11 | 19 | 18 | 221 | 18 |
| Personal care and service occupations | 59 | 42 | X | 33 | 9 | 34 | 41 |
| Sales and related occupations | 8 911 | 95 | 23 | 354 | 1 098 | 972 | 311 |
| Office and administrative support occupations | 2 617 | 1 403 | 207 | 482 | 1 873 | 313 | 1 227 |
| Farming, fishing, and forestry occupations | 11 | 7 | 3 | X | X | X | 2 |
| Construction and extraction occupations | 86 | 57 | 107 | 10 | 5 | 36 | 57 |
| Installation, maintenance, and repair occupations | 629 | 305 | 190 | 294 | 15 | 149 | 104 |
| Production occupations | 496 | 116 | 211 | 59 | 17 | 18 | 123 |
| Transportation and material moving occupations | 1 250 | 3 497 | 48 | 52 | 10 | 106 | 52 |
| **2015** | | | | | | | |
| **All Occupations** | 16 686 | 6 459 | 1 267 | 2 988 | 7 081 | 3 005 | 10 625 |
| Management, professional, and related occupations | 1 853 | 715 | 438 | 1 743 | 3 950 | 1 029 | 8 559 |
| Management, business, and financial operations occupations | 913 | 565 | 225 | 619 | 3 201 | 952 | 3 359 |
| Computer and mathematical occupations | 166 | 59 | 43 | 330 | 468 | 24 | 1 745 |
| Architecture and engineering occupations | 25 | 46 | 115 | 106 | 19 | 7 | 911 |
| Life, physical and social science occupations | 5 | 1 | 32 | 8 | 14 | 1 | 300 |
| Community and social service occupations | 3 | 1 | 1 | 2 | 27 | 5 | 23 |
| Legal occupations | 18 | 5 | 7 | 16 | 96 | 21 | 1 191 |
| Education, training, and library occupations | 21 | 23 | 2 | 107 | 34 | 2 | 34 |
| Arts, design, entertainment, sports, and media occupations | 195 | 10 | 10 | 552 | 43 | 9 | 722 |
| Healthcare practitioner and technical occupations | 507 | 5 | 4 | 4 | 47 | 8 | 274 |
| Healthcare support occupations | 41 | 3 | 0 | 1 | 6 | 3 | 37 |
| Protective service occupations | 72 | 27 | 8 | 13 | 30 | 22 | 23 |
| Food preparation and serving related occupations | 382 | 15 | 1 | 25 | 5 | 16 | 5 |
| Building and grounds cleaning and maintenance occupations | 160 | 54 | 16 | 17 | 22 | 226 | 30 |
| Personal care and service occupations | 68 | 35 | 0 | 32 | 9 | 29 | 36 |
| Sales and related occupations | 11 601 | 1 525 | 228 | 771 | 3 011 | 1 332 | 1 566 |
| Office and administrative support occupations | 2 729 | 1 438 | 210 | 442 | 1 864 | 308 | 1 242 |
| Farming, fishing, and forestry occupations | 11 | 3 | 2 | 0 | 1 | X | 2 |
| Construction and extraction occupations | 77 | 68 | 95 | 5 | 4 | 30 | 60 |
| Installation, maintenance, and repair occupations | 641 | 296 | 201 | 296 | 20 | 200 | 92 |
| Production occupations | 516 | 92 | 231 | 46 | 12 | 23 | 150 |
| Transportation and material moving occupations | 1 264 | 3 627 | 46 | 39 | 12 | 95 | 65 |

X = Not applicable.

## Table 1-14. Employed Civilians, by Selected Occupation and Industry, 2013–2015—*Continued*

(Thousands of people.)

| Year and occupation | Management, administrative, and waste services | Educational services | Health care and social assistance | Arts, entertainment, and recreation | Accommodation and food services | Other services (except public administration) | Public administration |
|---|---|---|---|---|---|---|---|
| **2013** | | | | | | | |
| **All Occupations** | 6 682 | 12 974 | 19 562 | 3 205 | 10 349 | 7 127 | 6 708 |
| Management, professional, and related occupations | 1 246 | 10 079 | 10 493 | 1 094 | 1 554 | 1 563 | 2 798 |
| Management, business, and financial operations occupations | 893 | 1 224 | 1 633 | 312 | 1 472 | 650 | 1 222 |
| Computer and mathematical occupations | 97 | 225 | 215 | 26 | 11 | 61 | 269 |
| Architecture and engineering occupations | 43 | 32 | 25 | 8 | 5 | 21 | 167 |
| Life, physical and social science occupations | 24 | 201 | 215 | 12 | 1 | 10 | 185 |
| Community and social service occupations | 15 | 337 | 985 | 6 | 5 | 598 | 331 |
| Legal occupations | 42 | 10 | 42 | 3 | 2 | 12 | 292 |
| Education, training, and library occupations | 22 | 7 502 | 610 | 62 | 28 | 64 | 61 |
| Arts, design, entertainment, sports, and media occupations | 50 | 233 | 56 | 654 | 19 | 116 | 48 |
| Healthcare practitioner and technical occupations | 60 | 317 | 6 714 | 10 | 12 | 32 | 223 |
| Healthcare support occupations | 52 | 36 | 3 132 | 21 | 14 | 139 | 41 |
| Protective service occupations | 505 | 119 | 65 | 185 | 37 | 25 | 1 940 |
| Food preparation and serving related occupations | 37 | 418 | 414 | 260 | 6 476 | 46 | 34 |
| Building and grounds cleaning and maintenance occupations | 2 505 | 574 | 488 | 264 | 517 | 448 | 120 |
| Personal care and service occupations | 25 | 201 | 1 879 | 798 | 104 | 2 033 | 111 |
| Sales and related occupations | 263 | 53 | 66 | 158 | 843 | 393 | 30 |
| Office and administrative support occupations | 985 | 1 017 | 2 582 | 229 | 397 | 610 | 1 227 |
| Farming, fishing, and forestry occupations | 4 | 3 | 2 | 4 | 4 | 0 | 16 |
| Construction and extraction occupations | 81 | 54 | 31 | 18 | 9 | 30 | 89 |
| Installation, maintenance, and repair occupations | 209 | 111 | 114 | 78 | 55 | 1 084 | 147 |
| Production occupations | 244 | 30 | 138 | 28 | 103 | 441 | 61 |
| Transportation and material moving occupations | 526 | 280 | 158 | 69 | 236 | 315 | 94 |
| **2014** | | | | | | | |
| **All Occupations** | 6 677 | 13 253 | 19 577 | 3 082 | 10 407 | 7 169 | 6 757 |
| Management, professional, and related occupations | 1 288 | 10 319 | 10 803 | 1 088 | 1 582 | 1 589 | 2 864 |
| Management, business, and financial operations occupations | 955 | 1 331 | 1 651 | 322 | 1 500 | 658 | 1 195 |
| Computer and mathematical occupations | 333 | 8 987 | 9 151 | 766 | 83 | 931 | 1 669 |
| Architecture and engineering occupations | 40 | 51 | 18 | 6 | 10 | 11 | 171 |
| Life, physical and social science occupations | 18 | 210 | 224 | 11 | 1 | 12 | 186 |
| Community and social service occupations | 11 | 351 | 1 072 | 12 | 4 | 633 | 365 |
| Legal occupations | 38 | 5 | 29 | 3 | 3 | 10 | 292 |
| Education, training, and library occupations | 23 | 7 571 | 586 | 67 | 29 | 77 | 67 |
| Arts, design, entertainment, sports, and media occupations | 46 | 243 | 42 | 627 | 13 | 103 | 55 |
| Healthcare practitioner and technical occupations | 69 | 303 | 6 973 | 14 | 9 | 31 | 237 |
| Healthcare support occupations | 50 | 35 | 3 028 | 21 | 9 | 145 | 47 |
| Protective service occupations | 527 | 126 | 73 | 151 | 30 | 29 | 1 922 |
| Food preparation and serving related occupations | 30 | 395 | 358 | 244 | 6 447 | 52 | 30 |
| Building and grounds cleaning and maintenance occupations | 2 489 | 594 | 489 | 249 | 572 | 518 | 121 |
| Personal care and service occupations | 31 | 235 | 1 824 | 772 | 104 | 1 958 | 139 |
| Sales and related occupations | 266 | 61 | 73 | 160 | 810 | 379 | 29 |
| Office and administrative support occupations | 1 000 | 1 024 | 2 509 | 228 | 441 | 626 | 1 215 |
| Farming, fishing, and forestry occupations | 9 | 1 | 1 | 3 | 3 | 4 | 21 |
| Construction and extraction occupations | 75 | 49 | 30 | 24 | 9 | 18 | 79 |
| Installation, maintenance, and repair occupations | 185 | 116 | 121 | 62 | 50 | 1 091 | 132 |
| Production occupations | 226 | 27 | 131 | 18 | 102 | 415 | 61 |
| Transportation and material moving occupations | 502 | 271 | 139 | 64 | 246 | 346 | 97 |
| **2015** | | | | | | | |
| **All Occupations** | 6 784 | 13 601 | 20 077 | 3 184 | 10 637 | 7 264 | 6 928 |
| Management, professional, and related occupations | 1 337 | 10 633 | 11 281 | 1 116 | 1 722 | 1 649 | 3 008 |
| Management, business, and financial operations occupations | 984 | 1 471 | 1 789 | 303 | 1 628 | 651 | 1 300 |
| Computer and mathematical occupations | 97 | 272 | 198 | 29 | 12 | 53 | 301 |
| Architecture and engineering occupations | 44 | 41 | 31 | 8 | 7 | 11 | 180 |
| Life, physical and social science occupations | 12 | 244 | 246 | 9 | 2 | 17 | 186 |
| Community and social service occupations | 7 | 364 | 1 097 | 5 | 7 | 692 | 353 |
| Legal occupations | 29 | 8 | 20 | 3 | 2 | 15 | 316 |
| Education, training, and library occupations | 24 | 7 685 | 673 | 78 | 35 | 74 | 62 |
| Arts, design, entertainment, sports, and media occupations | 58 | 237 | 54 | 670 | 20 | 109 | 62 |
| Healthcare practitioner and technical occupations | 82 | 310 | 7 173 | 11 | 9 | 27 | 247 |
| Healthcare support occupations | 49 | 28 | 3 088 | 19 | 5 | 167 | 54 |
| Protective service occupations | 511 | 112 | 80 | 148 | 34 | 15 | 1 949 |
| Food preparation and serving related occupations | 16 | 401 | 366 | 251 | 6 510 | 60 | 28 |
| Building and grounds cleaning and maintenance occupations | 2 495 | 565 | 484 | 240 | 534 | 503 | 137 |
| Personal care and service occupations | 26 | 249 | 1 836 | 827 | 100 | 1 966 | 137 |
| Sales and related occupations | 1 292 | 1 167 | 2 510 | 416 | 1 301 | 999 | 1 243 |
| Office and administrative support occupations | 1 012 | 1 124 | 2 436 | 238 | 464 | 633 | 1 216 |
| Farming, fishing, and forestry occupations | 10 | 1 | 0 | 2 | 2 | 4 | 21 |
| Construction and extraction occupations | 101 | 55 | 34 | 22 | 16 | 25 | 82 |
| Installation, maintenance, and repair occupations | 200 | 114 | 118 | 55 | 57 | 1 148 | 123 |
| Production occupations | 227 | 27 | 145 | 29 | 117 | 425 | 57 |
| Transportation and material moving occupations | 520 | 249 | 134 | 59 | 240 | 306 | 87 |

## Table 1-15.  Employed Civilians in Agriculture and Nonagricultural Industries, by Class of Worker and Sex, 1995–2015

(Thousands of people.)

| Sex and year | Total employed | Agriculture | | | | Nonagricultural industries | | | | | | |
| --- | --- | --- | --- | --- | --- | --- | --- | --- | --- | --- | --- | --- |
| | | | | | | | Wage and salary workers | | | | | |
| | | Total | Wage and salary workers | Self-employed workers | Unpaid family workers | Total employed | Total | Government | Private household | Other industries except private households | Self-employed workers | Unpaid family workers |
| **Both Sexes** | | | | | | | | | | | | |
| 1995 | 124 900 | 3 440 | 1 814 | 1 580 | 45 | 121 460 | 112 448 | 18 362 | 963 | 93 123 | 8 902 | 110 |
| 1996 | 126 707 | 3 443 | 1 869 | 1 518 | 56 | 123 264 | 114 171 | 18 217 | 928 | 95 026 | 8 971 | 122 |
| 1997 | 129 558 | 3 399 | 1 890 | 1 457 | 51 | 126 159 | 116 983 | 18 131 | 915 | 97 937 | 9 056 | 120 |
| 1998 | 131 463 | 3 378 | 2 000 | 1 341 | 38 | 128 085 | 119 019 | 18 383 | 962 | 99 674 | 8 962 | 103 |
| 1999 | 133 488 | 3 281 | 1 944 | 1 297 | 40 | 130 207 | 121 323 | 18 903 | 933 | 101 487 | 8 790 | 95 |
| 2000 | 136 891 | 2 464 | 1 421 | 1 010 | 33 | 134 427 | 125 114 | 19 248 | 718 | 105 148 | 9 205 | 108 |
| 2001 | 136 933 | 2 299 | 1 283 | 988 | 28 | 134 635 | 125 407 | 19 335 | 694 | 105 378 | 9 121 | 107 |
| 2002 | 136 485 | 2 311 | 1 282 | 1 003 | 26 | 134 174 | 125 156 | 19 636 | 757 | 104 764 | 8 923 | 95 |
| 2003 | 137 736 | 2 275 | 1 299 | 951 | 25 | 135 461 | 126 015 | 19 634 | 764 | 105 616 | 9 344 | 101 |
| 2004 | 139 252 | 2 232 | 1 242 | 964 | 27 | 137 020 | 127 463 | 19 983 | 779 | 106 701 | 9 467 | 90 |
| 2005 | 141 730 | 2 197 | 1 212 | 955 | 30 | 139 532 | 129 931 | 20 357 | 812 | 108 761 | 9 509 | 93 |
| 2006 | 144 427 | 2 206 | 1 287 | 901 | 18 | 142 221 | 132 449 | 20 337 | 803 | 111 309 | 9 685 | 87 |
| 2007 | 146 047 | 2 095 | 1 220 | 856 | 19 | 143 952 | 134 283 | 21 003 | 813 | 112 467 | 9 557 | 112 |
| 2008 | 145 362 | 2 168 | 1 279 | 860 | 28 | 143 194 | 133 882 | 21 258 | 805 | 111 819 | 9 219 | 93 |
| 2009 | 139 877 | 2 103 | 1 242 | 836 | 25 | 137 775 | 128 713 | 21 178 | 783 | 106 752 | 836 | 25 |
| 2010 | 139 064 | 2 206 | 1 353 | 821 | 33 | 136 858 | 127 914 | 21 003 | 667 | 106 244 | 8 860 | 84 |
| 2011 | 139 869 | 2 254 | 1 380 | 846 | 28 | 137 615 | 128 934 | 20 536 | 722 | 107 676 | 8 603 | 78 |
| 2012 | 142 469 | 2 186 | 1 377 | 780 | 29 | 140 283 | 131 452 | 20 360 | 738 | 110 355 | 8 749 | 81 |
| 2013 | 143 929 | 2 130 | 1 310 | 789 | 31 | 141 799 | 133 111 | 20 247 | 723 | 112 141 | 8 619 | 70 |
| 2014 | 146 305 | 2 237 | 1 459 | 756 | 22 | 144 068 | 135 402 | 20 135 | 820 | 114 446 | 8 602 | 64 |
| 2015 | 148 834 | 2 422 | 1 547 | 844 | 32 | 146 411 | 137 678 | 20 601 | 798 | 116 279 | 8 665 | 68 |
| **Men** | | | | | | | | | | | | |
| 1995 | 67 377 | 2 559 | 1 395 | 1 138 | 26 | 64 818 | 59 332 | 8 267 | 96 | 50 969 | 5 461 | 25 |
| 1996 | 68 207 | 2 573 | 1 418 | 1 124 | 31 | 65 634 | 60 133 | 8 110 | 99 | 51 924 | 5 465 | 36 |
| 1997 | 69 685 | 2 552 | 1 439 | 1 084 | 29 | 67 133 | 61 595 | 8 015 | 81 | 53 499 | 5 506 | 31 |
| 1998 | 70 693 | 2 553 | 1 526 | 1 005 | 23 | 68 140 | 62 630 | 8 178 | 86 | 54 366 | 5 480 | 29 |
| 1999 | 71 446 | 2 432 | 1 450 | 962 | 20 | 69 014 | 63 624 | 8 278 | 74 | 55 272 | 5 366 | 25 |
| 2000 | 73 305 | 1 861 | 1 116 | 725 | 20 | 71 444 | 65 838 | 8 309 | 71 | 57 458 | 5 573 | 33 |
| 2001 | 73 196 | 1 708 | 990 | 703 | 15 | 71 488 | 65 930 | 8 342 | 63 | 57 524 | 5 527 | 31 |
| 2002 | 72 903 | 1 724 | 979 | 731 | 14 | 71 179 | 65 726 | 8 437 | 76 | 57 212 | 5 425 | 29 |
| 2003 | 73 332 | 1 695 | 991 | 694 | 11 | 71 636 | 65 871 | 8 368 | 59 | 57 444 | 5 736 | 30 |
| 2004 | 74 525 | 1 687 | 970 | 702 | 15 | 72 838 | 66 951 | 8 616 | 60 | 58 275 | 5 860 | 27 |
| 2005 | 75 973 | 1 654 | 949 | 688 | 17 | 74 319 | 68 345 | 8 760 | 67 | 59 518 | 5 944 | 30 |
| 2006 | 77 502 | 1 663 | 989 | 664 | 10 | 75 838 | 69 811 | 8 696 | 60 | 61 055 | 6 004 | 23 |
| 2007 | 78 254 | 1 604 | 973 | 623 | 8 | 76 650 | 70 697 | 9 022 | 76 | 61 599 | 5 920 | 32 |
| 2008 | 77 486 | 1 650 | 997 | 637 | 16 | 75 836 | 70 072 | 9 089 | 70 | 60 912 | 5 736 | 29 |
| 2009 | 73 670 | 1 607 | 977 | 613 | 17 | 72 062 | 66 517 | 9 013 | 74 | 57 430 | 5 527 | 19 |
| 2010 | 73 359 | 1 665 | 1 051 | 598 | 17 | 71 694 | 66 189 | 9 059 | 60 | 57 070 | 5 472 | 33 |
| 2011 | 74 290 | 1 698 | 1 050 | 632 | 16 | 72 592 | 67 306 | 8 922 | 78 | 58 307 | 5 262 | 24 |
| 2012 | 75 555 | 1 626 | 1 048 | 562 | 16 | 73 930 | 68 629 | 8 760 | 82 | 59 786 | 5 266 | 34 |
| 2013 | 76 353 | 1 611 | 1 020 | 571 | 20 | 74 742 | 69 606 | 8 799 | 62 | 60 744 | 5 111 | 25 |
| 2014 | 77 692 | 1 685 | 1 119 | 554 | 12 | 76 007 | 70 828 | 8 633 | 64 | 62 131 | 5 158 | 22 |
| 2015 | 79 131 | 1 826 | 1 194 | 615 | 17 | 77 305 | 72 016 | 8 870 | 58 | 63 088 | 5 269 | 21 |
| **Women** | | | | | | | | | | | | |
| 1995 | 57 523 | 881 | 419 | 442 | 20 | 56 642 | 53 115 | 10 095 | 867 | 42 153 | 3 440 | 86 |
| 1996 | 58 501 | 871 | 452 | 394 | 25 | 57 630 | 54 037 | 10 107 | 830 | 43 100 | 3 506 | 87 |
| 1997 | 59 873 | 847 | 451 | 373 | 23 | 59 026 | 55 388 | 10 116 | 834 | 44 438 | 3 550 | 89 |
| 1998 | 60 770 | 825 | 474 | 336 | 15 | 59 945 | 56 389 | 10 205 | 876 | 45 308 | 3 482 | 74 |
| 1999 | 62 042 | 849 | 494 | 335 | 20 | 61 193 | 57 699 | 10 625 | 859 | 46 215 | 3 424 | 70 |
| 2000 | 63 586 | 602 | 305 | 285 | 12 | 62 983 | 59 277 | 10 939 | 647 | 47 690 | 3 631 | 76 |
| 2001 | 63 737 | 591 | 293 | 284 | 13 | 63 147 | 59 477 | 10 993 | 630 | 47 853 | 3 594 | 75 |
| 2002 | 63 582 | 587 | 303 | 272 | 12 | 62 995 | 59 431 | 11 199 | 680 | 47 552 | 3 499 | 66 |
| 2003 | 64 404 | 580 | 309 | 257 | 14 | 63 824 | 60 144 | 11 267 | 705 | 48 172 | 3 609 | 72 |
| 2004 | 64 728 | 546 | 271 | 262 | 12 | 64 182 | 60 512 | 11 367 | 719 | 48 426 | 3 607 | 63 |
| 2005 | 65 757 | 544 | 263 | 267 | 13 | 65 213 | 61 586 | 11 598 | 745 | 49 243 | 3 565 | 63 |
| 2006 | 66 925 | 543 | 298 | 237 | 8 | 66 382 | 62 638 | 11 641 | 742 | 50 254 | 3 681 | 64 |
| 2007 | 67 792 | 490 | 247 | 233 | 11 | 67 302 | 63 586 | 11 981 | 737 | 50 868 | 3 637 | 80 |
| 2008 | 67 876 | 518 | 282 | 224 | 12 | 67 358 | 63 810 | 12 169 | 735 | 50 907 | 3 483 | 65 |
| 2009 | 66 208 | 496 | 265 | 223 | 8 | 65 712 | 62 197 | 12 165 | 709 | 49 322 | 3 468 | 47 |
| 2010 | 65 705 | 541 | 302 | 223 | 16 | 65 164 | 61 725 | 11 944 | 607 | 49 174 | 3 388 | 51 |
| 2011 | 65 579 | 556 | 330 | 214 | 12 | 65 023 | 61 628 | 11 614 | 644 | 49 370 | 3 341 | 54 |
| 2012 | 66 914 | 560 | 329 | 218 | 13 | 66 353 | 62 824 | 11 600 | 656 | 50 568 | 3 483 | 47 |
| 2013 | 67 577 | 519 | 290 | 218 | 11 | 67 058 | 63 505 | 11 447 | 661 | 51 396 | 3 508 | 45 |
| 2014 | 68 613 | 552 | 340 | 202 | 10 | 68 061 | 64 574 | 11 502 | 757 | 52 316 | 3 444 | 43 |
| 2015 | 69 703 | 597 | 353 | 229 | 14 | 69 106 | 65 663 | 11 731 | 741 | 53 191 | 3 396 | 48 |

## Table 1-16. Number of Employed Persons Age 25 Years and Over, by Educational Attainment, Sex, Race, and Hispanic Origin, 2005–2015

(Thousands of people.)

| Race, Hispanic origin, sex, and year | Total | Less than a high school diploma | High school graduate, no college | Some college, no degree | Associate's degree | College graduate or higher | |
|---|---|---|---|---|---|---|---|
| | | | | | | Total | Bachelor's degree only |
| **Both Sexes** | | | | | | | |
| 2005 | 121 960 | 11 712 | 36 398 | 21 380 | 12 245 | 40 225 | 26 027 |
| 2006 | 124 386 | 11 892 | 36 702 | 21 630 | 12 514 | 41 649 | 26 960 |
| 2007 | 126 172 | 11 521 | 36 857 | 22 076 | 12 535 | 43 182 | 28 055 |
| 2008 | 126 161 | 11 073 | 36 097 | 22 092 | 12 948 | 43 951 | 28 460 |
| 2009 | 122 277 | 10 371 | 34 487 | 21 016 | 12 872 | 43 531 | 27 964 |
| 2010 | 121 987 | 10 115 | 34 293 | 20 838 | 12 910 | 43 832 | 27 977 |
| 2011 | 122 507 | 9 967 | 33 823 | 20 712 | 13 182 | 44 822 | 28 333 |
| 2012 | 124 635 | 9 923 | 33 718 | 20 936 | 13 770 | 46 288 | 29 371 |
| 2013 | 125 872 | 9 798 | 33 619 | 20 914 | 14 011 | 47 531 | 30 140 |
| 2014 | 127 863 | 9 852 | 33 865 | 21 159 | 14 139 | 48 848 | 30 789 |
| 2015 | 130 077 | 10 098 | 33 402 | 21 573 | 14 213 | 50 792 | 31 772 |
| **Men** | | | | | | | |
| 2005 | 65 772 | 7 487 | 20 127 | 10 993 | 5 739 | 21 427 | 13 687 |
| 2006 | 67 019 | 7 614 | 20 345 | 11 110 | 5 835 | 22 114 | 14 138 |
| 2007 | 67 963 | 7 450 | 20 434 | 11 382 | 5 862 | 22 835 | 14 680 |
| 2008 | 67 605 | 7 108 | 20 093 | 11 356 | 6 021 | 23 027 | 14 845 |
| 2009 | 64 831 | 6 569 | 19 085 | 10 772 | 5 864 | 22 541 | 14 368 |
| 2010 | 64 765 | 6 434 | 19 159 | 10 737 | 5 829 | 22 606 | 14 359 |
| 2011 | 65 356 | 6 388 | 19 059 | 10 741 | 6 029 | 23 138 | 14 637 |
| 2012 | 66 455 | 6 309 | 19 192 | 10 862 | 6 364 | 23 729 | 15 024 |
| 2013 | 67 163 | 6 335 | 19 103 | 10 946 | 6 446 | 24 333 | 15 487 |
| 2014 | 68 284 | 6 410 | 19 403 | 11 151 | 6 531 | 24 791 | 15 706 |
| 2015 | 69 604 | 6 573 | 19 302 | 11 293 | 6 660 | 25 776 | 16 323 |
| **Women** | | | | | | | |
| 2005 | 56 188 | 4 226 | 16 271 | 10 388 | 6 506 | 18 798 | 12 340 |
| 2006 | 57 367 | 4 278 | 16 357 | 10 520 | 6 678 | 19 535 | 12 822 |
| 2007 | 58 209 | 4 071 | 16 423 | 10 695 | 6 674 | 20 346 | 13 375 |
| 2008 | 58 555 | 3 965 | 16 004 | 10 737 | 6 926 | 20 924 | 13 614 |
| 2009 | 57 445 | 3 802 | 15 402 | 10 244 | 7 008 | 20 990 | 13 597 |
| 2010 | 57 222 | 3 681 | 15 134 | 10 101 | 7 080 | 21 226 | 13 618 |
| 2011 | 57 151 | 3 579 | 14 764 | 9 971 | 7 153 | 21 684 | 13 697 |
| 2012 | 58 180 | 3 614 | 14 527 | 10 074 | 7 405 | 22 559 | 14 347 |
| 2013 | 58 710 | 3 463 | 14 516 | 9 968 | 7 565 | 23 198 | 14 653 |
| 2014 | 59 579 | 3 442 | 14 462 | 10 009 | 7 609 | 24 057 | 15 083 |
| 2015 | 60 474 | 3 525 | 14 100 | 10 280 | 7 553 | 25 016 | 15 449 |
| **White[1]** | | | | | | | |
| 2005 | 100 613 | 9 579 | 29 911 | 17 515 | 10 256 | 33 352 | 21 550 |
| 2006 | 102 322 | 9 720 | 30 188 | 17 632 | 10 424 | 34 357 | 22 272 |
| 2007 | 103 477 | 9 446 | 30 140 | 17 936 | 10 419 | 35 535 | 23 138 |
| 2008 | 103 373 | 9 036 | 29 495 | 17 873 | 10 742 | 36 228 | 23 511 |
| 2009 | 100 419 | 8 497 | 28 372 | 16 983 | 10 714 | 35 854 | 23 109 |
| 2010 | 100 100 | 8 290 | 28 128 | 16 800 | 10 707 | 36 176 | 23 179 |
| 2011 | 100 426 | 8 248 | 27 568 | 16 713 | 10 922 | 36 975 | 23 533 |
| 2012 | 100 543 | 8 100 | 27 112 | 16 594 | 11 260 | 37 476 | 23 942 |
| 2013 | 101 046 | 7 885 | 27 049 | 16 425 | 11 460 | 38 228 | 24 419 |
| 2014 | 102 245 | 7 895 | 27 132 | 16 556 | 11 556 | 39 106 | 24 879 |
| 2015 | 103 336 | 8 128 | 26 508 | 16 820 | 11 501 | 40 380 | 25 395 |
| **Black[1]** | | | | | | | |
| 2005 | 13 177 | 1 369 | 4 742 | 2 720 | 1 288 | 3 057 | 2 106 |
| 2006 | 13 504 | 1 389 | 4 697 | 2 816 | 1 338 | 3 263 | 2 243 |
| 2007 | 13 811 | 1 293 | 4 783 | 2 912 | 1 389 | 3 435 | 2 362 |
| 2008 | 13 786 | 1 234 | 4 719 | 2 972 | 1 439 | 3 423 | 2 354 |
| 2009 | 13 110 | 1 096 | 4 375 | 2 855 | 1 422 | 3 363 | 2 253 |
| 2010 | 13 092 | 1 103 | 4 234 | 2 864 | 1 482 | 3 409 | 2 260 |
| 2011 | 13 097 | 1 013 | 4 298 | 2 792 | 1 519 | 3 474 | 2 257 |
| 2012 | 13 717 | 1 016 | 4 397 | 2 919 | 1 584 | 3 801 | 2 479 |
| 2013 | 13 985 | 1 064 | 4 343 | 3 034 | 1 583 | 3 961 | 2 582 |
| 2014 | 14 437 | 1 084 | 4 442 | 3 119 | 1 674 | 4 117 | 2 623 |
| 2015 | 15 017 | 1 033 | 4 549 | 5 017 | 1 775 | 4 418 | 2 850 |
| **Hispanic[2]** | | | | | | | |
| 2005 | 15 362 | 5 367 | 4 535 | 2 230 | 997 | 2 232 | 1 595 |
| 2006 | 16 225 | 5 620 | 4 801 | 2 282 | 1 095 | 2 428 | 1 698 |
| 2007 | 16 973 | 5 677 | 5 110 | 2 382 | 1 160 | 2 644 | 1 898 |
| 2008 | 17 115 | 5 426 | 5 232 | 2 484 | 1 236 | 2 736 | 1 930 |
| 2009 | 18 642 | 6 064 | 5 658 | 2 670 | 1 357 | 2 894 | 2 063 |
| 2010 | 16 946 | 5 183 | 5 175 | 2 474 | 1 252 | 2 862 | 2 025 |
| 2011 | 17 059 | 5 156 | 5 216 | 2 513 | 1 317 | 2 857 | 1 982 |
| 2012 | 18 309 | 5 269 | 5 613 | 2 734 | 1 482 | 3 210 | 2 221 |
| 2013 | 18 836 | 5 297 | 5 754 | 2 781 | 1 543 | 3 460 | 2 428 |
| 2014 | 19 686 | 5 365 | 5 954 | 2 990 | 1 636 | 3 741 | 2 648 |
| 2015 | 20 450 | 5 592 | 6 064 | 3 119 | 1 739 | 3 936 | 2 694 |

[1]Beginning in 2003, persons who selected this race group only; persons who selected more than one race group are not included. Prior to 2003, persons who reported more than one race group were included in the group they identified as their main race.
[2]May be of any race.

## Table 1-16. Number of Employed Persons Age 25 Years and Over, by Educational Attainment, Sex, Race, and Hispanic Origin, 2005–2015—*Continued*

(Thousands of people.)

| Race, Hispanic origin, sex, and year | Total | Less than a high school diploma | High school graduate, no college | Some college, no degree | Associate's degree | College graduate or higher — Total | College graduate or higher — Bachelor's degree only |
|---|---|---|---|---|---|---|---|
| **White Men[1]** | | | | | | | |
| 2005 | 55 214 | 6 368 | 16 750 | 9 225 | 4 851 | 18 021 | 11 551 |
| 2006 | 56 145 | 6 448 | 17 018 | 9 244 | 4 952 | 18 483 | 11 881 |
| 2007 | 56 740 | 6 364 | 17 039 | 9 409 | 4 964 | 18 964 | 12 260 |
| 2008 | 56 446 | 6 066 | 16 741 | 9 397 | 5 070 | 19 171 | 12 482 |
| 2009 | 54 248 | 5 583 | 15 966 | 8 937 | 4 948 | 18 813 | 12 112 |
| 2010 | 54 091 | 5 461 | 15 952 | 8 846 | 4 922 | 18 910 | 12 128 |
| 2011 | 54 488 | 5 450 | 15 776 | 8 878 | 5 082 | 19 303 | 12 344 |
| 2012 | 54 646 | 5 339 | 15 711 | 8 809 | 5 273 | 19 513 | 12 495 |
| 2013 | 54 914 | 5 286 | 15 672 | 9 356 | 5 611 | 20 542 | 13 287 |
| 2014 | 55 608 | 5 299 | 15 830 | 8 942 | 5 424 | 20 113 | 12 957 |
| 2015 | 56 374 | 5 484 | 15 617 | 9 037 | 5 533 | 20 702 | 13 265 |
| **White Women[1]** | | | | | | | |
| 2005 | 45 399 | 3 211 | 13 162 | 8 290 | 5 405 | 15 331 | 9 999 |
| 2006 | 46 177 | 3 272 | 13 171 | 8 388 | 5 473 | 15 874 | 10 391 |
| 2007 | 46 737 | 3 082 | 13 102 | 8 527 | 5 455 | 16 571 | 10 878 |
| 2008 | 46 928 | 2 970 | 12 753 | 8 477 | 5 672 | 17 056 | 11 029 |
| 2009 | 46 172 | 2 913 | 12 406 | 8 046 | 5 766 | 17 040 | 10 997 |
| 2010 | 46 010 | 2 829 | 12 176 | 7 953 | 5 785 | 17 266 | 11 051 |
| 2011 | 45 938 | 2 798 | 11 792 | 7 835 | 5 840 | 17 672 | 11 189 |
| 2012 | 45 897 | 2 761 | 11 402 | 7 784 | 5 987 | 17 963 | 11 447 |
| 2013 | 46 132 | 2 598 | 11 377 | 7 649 | 6 111 | 18 396 | 11 637 |
| 2014 | 46 637 | 2 596 | 11 302 | 7 614 | 6 132 | 18 993 | 11 923 |
| 2015 | 46 962 | 2 643 | 10 891 | 7 782 | 5 968 | 19 677 | 12 131 |
| **Black Men[1]** | | | | | | | |
| 2005 | 6 153 | 697 | 2 417 | 1 171 | 558 | 1 310 | 938 |
| 2006 | 6 276 | 720 | 2 338 | 1 249 | 535 | 1 433 | 1 002 |
| 2007 | 6 429 | 653 | 2 340 | 1 320 | 570 | 1 547 | 1 076 |
| 2008 | 6 357 | 616 | 2 358 | 1 296 | 579 | 1 508 | 1 036 |
| 2009 | 5 939 | 551 | 2 199 | 1 225 | 544 | 1 419 | 958 |
| 2010 | 5 988 | 561 | 2 164 | 1 270 | 567 | 1 426 | 960 |
| 2011 | 6 031 | 532 | 2 225 | 1 235 | 591 | 1 449 | 968 |
| 2012 | 6 320 | 530 | 2 281 | 1 328 | 639 | 1 541 | 1 024 |
| 2013 | 6 487 | 569 | 2 222 | 1 400 | 623 | 1 673 | 1 134 |
| 2014 | 6 726 | 592 | 2 319 | 1 433 | 662 | 1 720 | 1 136 |
| 2015 | 7 003 | 545 | 2 407 | 1 477 | 679 | 1 895 | 1 283 |
| **Black Women[1]** | | | | | | | |
| 2005 | 7 024 | 672 | 2 325 | 1 549 | 730 | 1 748 | 1 169 |
| 2006 | 7 228 | 669 | 2 359 | 1 567 | 803 | 1 830 | 1 241 |
| 2007 | 7 382 | 641 | 2 443 | 1 592 | 819 | 1 888 | 1 286 |
| 2008 | 7 429 | 617 | 2 361 | 1 676 | 859 | 1 915 | 1 318 |
| 2009 | 7 171 | 544 | 2 176 | 1 631 | 877 | 1 943 | 1 295 |
| 2010 | 7 104 | 542 | 2 070 | 1 594 | 915 | 1 983 | 1 300 |
| 2011 | 7 066 | 481 | 2 073 | 1 558 | 928 | 2 026 | 1 289 |
| 2012 | 7 397 | 487 | 2 115 | 1 591 | 945 | 2 260 | 1 455 |
| 2013 | 7 498 | 495 | 2 121 | 1 634 | 961 | 2 288 | 1 448 |
| 2014 | 7 711 | 492 | 2 123 | 1 686 | 1 012 | 2 398 | 1 487 |
| 2015 | 8 014 | 488 | 2 142 | 1 765 | 1 096 | 2 523 | 1 567 |
| **Hispanic Men[2]** | | | | | | | |
| 2005 | 9 361 | 3 639 | 2 775 | 1 251 | 503 | 1 193 | 847 |
| 2006 | 9 856 | 3 823 | 2 932 | 1 260 | 547 | 1 293 | 891 |
| 2007 | 10 303 | 3 947 | 3 100 | 1 285 | 567 | 1 403 | 1 000 |
| 2008 | 10 363 | 3 714 | 3 231 | 1 371 | 607 | 1 439 | 1 008 |
| 2009 | 9 969 | 3 508 | 3 114 | 1 321 | 595 | 1 431 | 992 |
| 2010 | 10 120 | 3 517 | 3 176 | 1 341 | 595 | 1 491 | 1 045 |
| 2011 | 10 151 | 3 487 | 3 158 | 1 377 | 636 | 1 492 | 1 044 |
| 2012 | 10 629 | 3 512 | 3 391 | 1 420 | 693 | 1 612 | 1 115 |
| 2013 | 11 029 | 3 599 | 3 475 | 1 486 | 718 | 1 751 | 1 236 |
| 2014 | 11 546 | 3 651 | 3 584 | 1 637 | 791 | 1 883 | 1 362 |
| 2015 | 11 969 | 3 787 | 3 664 | 1 642 | 875 | 2 001 | 1 402 |
| **Hispanic Women[2]** | | | | | | | |
| 2005 | 6 000 | 1 728 | 1 759 | 979 | 495 | 1 039 | 748 |
| 2006 | 6 370 | 1 797 | 1 868 | 1 021 | 548 | 1 135 | 807 |
| 2007 | 6 670 | 1 730 | 2 010 | 1 097 | 593 | 1 241 | 898 |
| 2008 | 6 752 | 1 712 | 2 001 | 1 113 | 629 | 1 297 | 922 |
| 2009 | 6 718 | 1 724 | 1 955 | 1 093 | 647 | 1 298 | 941 |
| 2010 | 6 826 | 1 666 | 1 999 | 1 133 | 656 | 1 371 | 979 |
| 2011 | 6 908 | 1 669 | 2 058 | 1 136 | 681 | 1 365 | 938 |
| 2012 | 7 680 | 1 757 | 2 222 | 1 315 | 788 | 1 598 | 1 106 |
| 2013 | 7 807 | 1 698 | 2 280 | 1 295 | 826 | 1 709 | 1 192 |
| 2014 | 8 140 | 1 713 | 2 370 | 1 353 | 845 | 1 859 | 1 287 |
| 2015 | 8 481 | 1 805 | 2 401 | 1 477 | 864 | 1 935 | 1 292 |

[1]Beginning in 2003, persons who selected this race group only; persons who selected more than one race group are not included. Prior to 2003, persons who reported more than one race group were included in the group they identified as their main race.

[2]May be of any race.

## Table 1-17.  Multiple Jobholders and Multiple Jobholding Rates, by Selected Characteristics, May of Selected Years, 1970–2016

(Thousands of people, percent, not seasonally adjusted.)

| Year | Total employed | Multiple jobholders | | | | Multiple jobholding rate[1] | | | | | | |
|---|---|---|---|---|---|---|---|---|---|---|---|---|
| | | Total | Men | Women | | Total | Men | Women | White | Black[2] | Asian | Hispanic[3] |
| | | | | Number | Percent of all multiple jobholders | | | | | | | |
| 1970 | 78 358 | 4 048 | 3 412 | 636 | 15.7 | 5.2 | 7.0 | 2.2 | 5.3 | 4.4 | ... | ... |
| 1971 | 78 708 | 4 035 | 3 270 | 765 | 19.0 | 5.1 | 6.7 | 2.6 | 5.3 | 3.8 | ... | ... |
| 1972 | 81 224 | 3 770 | 3 035 | 735 | 19.5 | 4.6 | 6.0 | 2.4 | 4.8 | 3.7 | ... | ... |
| 1973 | 83 758 | 4 262 | 3 393 | 869 | 20.4 | 5.1 | 6.6 | 2.7 | 5.1 | 4.7 | ... | ... |
| 1974 | 85 786 | 3 889 | 3 022 | 867 | 22.3 | 4.5 | 5.8 | 2.6 | 4.6 | 3.8 | ... | ... |
| 1975 | 84 146 | 3 918 | 2 962 | 956 | 24.4 | 4.7 | 5.8 | 2.9 | 4.8 | 3.7 | ... | ... |
| 1976 | 87 278 | 3 948 | 3 037 | 911 | 23.1 | 4.5 | 5.8 | 2.6 | 4.7 | 2.8 | ... | ... |
| 1977 | 90 482 | 4 558 | 3 317 | 1 241 | 27.2 | 5.0 | 6.2 | 3.4 | 5.3 | 2.6 | ... | ... |
| 1978 | 93 904 | 4 493 | 3 212 | 1 281 | 28.5 | 4.8 | 5.8 | 3.3 | 5.0 | 3.1 | ... | ... |
| 1979 | 96 327 | 4 724 | 3 317 | 1 407 | 29.8 | 4.9 | 5.9 | 3.5 | 5.1 | 3.0 | ... | ... |
| 1980 | 96 809 | 4 759 | 3 210 | 1 549 | 32.5 | 4.9 | 5.8 | 3.8 | 5.1 | 3.2 | ... | ... |
| 1985 | 106 878 | 5 730 | 3 537 | 2 192 | 38.3 | 5.4 | 5.9 | 4.7 | 5.7 | 3.2 | ... | ... |
| 1989 | 117 084 | 7 225 | 4 115 | 3 109 | 43.0 | 6.2 | 6.4 | 5.9 | 6.5 | 4.3 | ... | ... |
| 1991 | 116 626 | 7 183 | 4 054 | 3 129 | 43.6 | 6.2 | 6.4 | 5.9 | 6.4 | 4.9 | ... | ... |
| 1994 | 122 946 | 7 316 | 3 973 | 3 343 | 45.7 | 6.0 | 6.0 | 5.9 | 6.1 | 4.9 | ... | 3.8 |
| 1995 | 124 554 | 7 952 | 4 225 | 3 727 | 46.9 | 6.4 | 6.3 | 6.5 | 6.6 | 5.2 | ... | 3.6 |
| 1996 | 126 391 | 7 846 | 4 352 | 3 494 | 44.5 | 6.2 | 6.4 | 6.0 | 6.4 | 5.1 | ... | 4.0 |
| 1997 | 129 565 | 8 197 | 4 398 | 3 800 | 46.4 | 6.3 | 6.3 | 6.4 | 6.5 | 5.7 | ... | 4.1 |
| 1998 | 131 476 | 8 126 | 4 438 | 3 688 | 45.4 | 6.2 | 6.3 | 6.1 | 6.3 | 5.5 | ... | 4.4 |
| 1999 | 133 411 | 7 895 | 4 117 | 3 778 | 47.9 | 5.9 | 5.8 | 6.1 | 6.0 | 5.5 | ... | 3.6 |
| 2000 | 136 685 | 7 751 | 4 084 | 3 667 | 47.3 | 5.7 | 5.6 | 5.8 | 5.9 | 4.9 | 3.4 | 3.2 |
| 2001 | 137 121 | 7 540 | 3 914 | 3 626 | 48.1 | 5.5 | 5.3 | 5.7 | 5.6 | 5.3 | 3.7 | 3.4 |
| 2002 | 136 559 | 7 247 | 3 736 | 3 511 | 48.4 | 5.3 | 5.1 | 5.5 | 5.5 | 4.7 | 4.0 | 3.8 |
| 2003 | 137 567 | 7 338 | 3 841 | 3 498 | 47.7 | 5.3 | 5.3 | 5.4 | 5.5 | 4.3 | 4.2 | 3.4 |
| 2004 | 138 867 | 7 258 | 3 653 | 3 605 | 49.7 | 5.2 | 4.9 | 5.6 | 5.3 | 5.1 | 3.7 | 3.4 |
| 2005 | 141 591 | 7 348 | 3 741 | 3 607 | 49.1 | 5.2 | 4.9 | 5.5 | 5.4 | 4.4 | 3.5 | 2.8 |
| 2006 | 144 041 | 7 641 | 3 863 | 3 778 | 49.4 | 5.3 | 5.0 | 5.7 | 5.3 | 5.4 | 3.7 | 3.1 |
| 2007 | 145 864 | 7 693 | 3 835 | 3 858 | 50.1 | 5.3 | 4.9 | 5.7 | 5.5 | 4.4 | 3.7 | 3.0 |
| 2008 | 145 927 | 7 653 | 3 842 | 3 812 | 49.8 | 5.2 | 4.9 | 5.6 | 5.4 | 4.9 | 3.8 | 2.9 |
| 2009 | 140 363 | 7 265 | 3 540 | 3 725 | 51.3 | 5.2 | 4.8 | 5.6 | 5.3 | 4.8 | 3.9 | 3.0 |
| 2010 | 139 497 | 7 261 | 3 559 | 3 702 | 51.0 | 5.2 | 4.8 | 5.6 | 5.4 | 4.6 | 3.1 | 3.1 |
| 2011 | 140 028 | 7 084 | 3 491 | 3 593 | 50.7 | 5.1 | 4.7 | 5.5 | 5.3 | 4.5 | 3.1 | 3.3 |
| 2012 | 142 727 | 7 174 | 3 605 | 3 569 | 49.7 | 5.0 | 4.8 | 5.3 | 5.2 | 4.9 | 3.3 | 3.1 |
| 2013 | 144 432 | 7 123 | 3 570 | 3 553 | 49.9 | 4.9 | 4.7 | 5.2 | 5.1 | 4.4 | 3.7 | 3.7 |
| 2014 | 146 398 | 7 305 | 3 647 | 3 658 | 50.1 | 5.0 | 4.7 | 5.3 | 5.0 | 4.9 | 4.0 | 3.7 |
| 2015 | 149 349 | 7 081 | 3 441 | 3 641 | 51.4 | 4.7 | 4.3 | 5.2 | 4.8 | 5.1 | 2.9 | 3.1 |
| 2016 | 151 594 | 7 472 | 3 677 | 3 796 | 50.8 | 4.9 | 4.6 | 5.4 | 5.0 | 5.4 | 3.0 | 2.7 |

*Note:* Data prior to 1985 reflect 1970 census–based population controls; years 1985–1991 reflect 1980 census–based controls; years 1994–1999 reflect 1990 census–based controls adjusted for the estimated undercount; and data for years 2000–2002 have been revised to incorporate population controls from the 2000 census. Prior to 1994, data on multiple jobholders were collected only through special periodic supplements to the Current Population Survey (CPS) in May of various years; these supplemental surveys were not conducted in 1981–1984, 1986–1988, 1990, or 1992–1993. Beginning in 1994, data reflect the introduction of a major redesign of the CPS, including the collection of monthly data on multiple jobholders.

[1]Multiple jobholders as a percent of all employed persons in specified group.
[2]Data for years prior to 1977 refer to the Black-and-Other population group.
[3]May be of any race.
. . . = Not available.

## Table 1-18. Multiple Jobholders, by Sex, Age, Marital Status, Race, Hispanic Origin, and Job Status, 2012–2015

(Thousands of people, percent.)

| Characteristic | Both sexes | | | | Men | | | | Women | | | |
|---|---|---|---|---|---|---|---|---|---|---|---|---|
| | Number | | Rate[1] | | Number | | Rate[1] | | Number | | Rate[1] | |
| | 2012 | 2013 | 2012 | 2013 | 2012 | 2013 | 2012 | 2013 | 2012 | 2013 | 2012 | 2013 |
| **Age** | | | | | | | | | | | | |
| Total, 16 years and over[2] | 6 943 | 7 002 | 4.9 | 4.9 | 3 448 | 3 486 | 4.6 | 4.6 | 3 495 | 3 517 | 5.2 | 5.2 |
| 16 to 19 years | 178 | 198 | 4.0 | 4.4 | 73 | 84 | 3.4 | 3.9 | 105 | 114 | 4.6 | 5.0 |
| 20 to 24 years | 725 | 789 | 5.4 | 5.8 | 298 | 330 | 4.3 | 4.7 | 427 | 459 | 6.6 | 7.0 |
| 25 to 34 years | 1 488 | 1 509 | 4.8 | 4.8 | 772 | 774 | 4.6 | 4.6 | 716 | 735 | 5.1 | 5.1 |
| 35 to 44 years | 1 474 | 1 491 | 4.8 | 4.9 | 786 | 794 | 4.8 | 4.8 | 688 | 698 | 4.9 | 5.0 |
| 45 to 54 years | 1 678 | 1 639 | 5.1 | 5.0 | 802 | 794 | 4.7 | 4.7 | 875 | 845 | 5.6 | 5.5 |
| 55 to 64 years | 1 136 | 1 108 | 4.9 | 4.7 | 550 | 551 | 4.6 | 4.5 | 586 | 557 | 5.2 | 4.9 |
| 65 years and over | 264 | 269 | 3.6 | 3.5 | 168 | 159 | 4.1 | 3.7 | 96 | 110 | 3.0 | 3.2 |
| **Marital Status** | | | | | | | | | | | | |
| Single | 2 031 | 2 197 | 5.0 | 5.2 | 917 | 995 | 4.2 | 4.4 | 1 114 | 1 203 | 5.9 | 6.1 |
| Married, spouse present | 3 683 | 3 607 | 4.7 | 4.6 | 2 108 | 2 060 | 4.8 | 4.7 | 1 575 | 1 548 | 4.6 | 4.5 |
| Widowed, divorced, or separated | 1 229 | 1 198 | 5.3 | 5.2 | 422 | 431 | 4.3 | 4.4 | 806 | 766 | 6.0 | 5.7 |
| **Race and Hispanic Origin** | | | | | | | | | | | | |
| White | 5 756 | 5 751 | 5.0 | 5.0 | 2 879 | 2 895 | 4.6 | 4.6 | 2 877 | 2 856 | 5.0 | 5.4 |
| Black | 709 | 755 | 4.5 | 4.7 | 337 | 755 | 4.6 | 4.7 | 709 | 401 | 4.5 | 4.6 |
| Hispanic[3] | 668 | 717 | 3.1 | 3.2 | 373 | 717 | 3.0 | 3.0 | 295 | 324 | 3.2 | 3.4 |
| **Full- or Part-Time Status** | | | | | | | | | | | | |
| Primary job full time, secondary job part time | 3 590 | 3 716 | ... | ... | 223 | 2 072 | ... | ... | 134 | 1 644 | ... | ... |
| Primary and secondary jobs, both part time | 1 906 | 1 910 | ... | ... | 73 | 20 | ... | ... | 110 | 1 253 | ... | ... |
| Primary and secondary jobs, both full time | 252 | 231 | ... | ... | 22 | 140 | ... | ... | 14 | 92 | ... | ... |
| Hours vary on primary or secondary job | 1 146 | 1 102 | ... | ... | 51 | 598 | ... | ... | 34 | 504 | ... | ... |

| Characteristic | Both sexes | | | | Men | | | | Women | | | |
|---|---|---|---|---|---|---|---|---|---|---|---|---|
| | Number | | Rate[1] | | Number | | Rate[1] | | Number | | Rate[1] | |
| | 2014 | 2015 | 2014 | 2015 | 2014 | 2015 | 2014 | 2015 | 2014 | 2015 | 2014 | 2015 |
| **Age** | | | | | | | | | | | | |
| Total, 16 years and over[2] | 7 146 | 7 262 | 4.9 | 4.9 | 3 511 | 3 571 | 4.5 | 4.5 | 3 636 | 3 692 | 5.3 | 5.3 |
| 16 to 19 years | 194 | 199 | 4.3 | 4.2 | 80 | 73 | 3.6 | 3.1 | 113 | 126 | 4.9 | 5.3 |
| 20 to 24 years | 811 | 799 | 5.8 | 5.7 | 346 | 329 | 4.8 | 4.6 | 465 | 470 | 6.9 | 6.9 |
| 25 to 34 years | 1 581 | 1 616 | 4.9 | 4.9 | 810 | 810 | 4.7 | 4.6 | 771 | 806 | 5.2 | 5.4 |
| 35 to 44 years | 1 486 | 1 530 | 4.8 | 4.9 | 767 | 796 | 4.6 | 4.7 | 718 | 734 | 5.0 | 5.1 |
| 45 to 54 years | 1 646 | 1 637 | 5.1 | 5.0 | 785 | 803 | 4.6 | 4.7 | 861 | 834 | 5.6 | 5.4 |
| 55 to 64 years | 1 146 | 1 162 | 4.7 | 4.7 | 557 | 587 | 4.4 | 4.5 | 588 | 575 | 5.1 | 4.8 |
| 65 years and over | 284 | 319 | 3.6 | 3.8 | 165 | 174 | 3.8 | 3.7 | 119 | 145 | 3.3 | 3.8 |
| **Marital Status** | | | | | | | | | | | | |
| Single | 2 277 | 2 318 | 5.2 | 5.1 | 1 038 | 1 027 | 4.4 | 4.2 | 1 239 | 1 291 | 6.1 | 6.2 |
| Married, spouse present | 3 651 | 3 702 | 4.6 | 4.6 | 2 084 | 2 121 | 4.7 | 4.7 | 1 567 | 1 581 | 4.5 | 4.5 |
| Widowed, divorced, or separated | 1 218 | 2 318 | 5.2 | 5.2 | 389 | 423 | 4.0 | 4.3 | 829 | 1 291 | 6.1 | 6.2 |
| **Race and Hispanic Origin** | | | | | | | | | | | | |
| White | 5 817 | 5 881 | 5.0 | 5.0 | 2 877 | 2 917 | 4.6 | 5.0 | 2 940 | 2 964 | 5.5 | 5.5 |
| Black | 822 | 869 | 4.9 | 5.0 | 392 | 410 | 5.0 | 5.0 | 430 | 459 | 4.8 | 4.9 |
| Hispanic[3] | 779 | 782 | 3.3 | 3.2 | 426 | 782 | 3.1 | 3.2 | 779 | 352 | 3.6 | 3.4 |
| **Full- or Part-Time Status** | | | | | | | | | | | | |
| Primary job full time, secondary job part time | 3 768 | 3 909 | ... | ... | 2 081 | 2 128 | ... | ... | 1 686 | 1 781 | ... | ... |
| Primary and secondary jobs, both part time | 1 955 | 1 951 | ... | ... | 665 | 662 | ... | ... | 1 291 | 1 288 | ... | ... |
| Primary and secondary jobs, both full time | 254 | 242 | ... | ... | 159 | 156 | ... | ... | 95 | 86 | ... | ... |
| Hours vary on primary or secondary job | 1 120 | 1 114 | ... | ... | 583 | 600 | ... | ... | 538 | 514 | ... | ... |

Note: Estimates for the above race groups (White or Black) do not sum to totals because data are not presented for all races. Beginning in January 2003, data reflect the revised population controls used in the household survey.

[1]Multiple jobholders as a percent of all employed persons in specified group.
[2]Includes a small number of persons who work part time at their primary job and full time at their secondary job(s), not shown separately.
[3]May be of any race.
. . . = Not available.

## Table 1-19. Multiple Jobholders, by Sex and Industry of Principal Secondary Job, Annual Averages, 2013–2015

(Thousands of people.)

| Year and industry of secondary job | Both sexes | Men | Women |
|---|---|---|---|
| **2013** | | | |
| **All Nonagricultural Industries, Wage and Salary Workers** | 5 138 | 2 417 | 2 721 |
| Mining, quarrying, and oil and gas extraction | 16 | 9 | 8 |
| Construction | 182 | 137 | 45 |
| Manufacturing | 167 | 93 | 74 |
| Durable goods | 77 | 48 | 29 |
| Nondurable goods | 90 | 45 | 45 |
| Wholesale and retail trade | 939 | 389 | 550 |
| Wholesale trade | 71 | 50 | 21 |
| Retail trade | 867 | 339 | 529 |
| Transportation and utilities | 175 | 143 | 32 |
| Transportation and warehousing | 162 | 133 | 29 |
| Utilities | 13 | 10 | 3 |
| Information | 115 | 68 | 47 |
| Financial activities | 268 | 158 | 110 |
| Professional and business services | 702 | 415 | 287 |
| Education and health services | 1 713 | 609 | 1 104 |
| Leisure and hospitality | 1 172 | 597 | 575 |
| Other services | 523 | 237 | 286 |
| Other services, except private households | 457 | 232 | 225 |
| Other services, private households | 66 | 5 | 61 |
| Public administration | 187 | 132 | 55 |
| **2014** | | | |
| **All Nonagricultural Industries, Wage and Salary Workers** | 5 049 | 2 368 | 2 681 |
| Mining, quarrying, and oil and gas extraction | 13 | 11 | 2 |
| Construction | 172 | 133 | 39 |
| Manufacturing | 153 | 87 | 66 |
| Durable goods | 76 | 50 | 26 |
| Nondurable goods | 77 | 37 | 40 |
| Wholesale and retail trade | 973 | 429 | 544 |
| Wholesale trade | 66 | 42 | 24 |
| Retail trade | 907 | 387 | 520 |
| Transportation and utilities | 171 | 122 | 49 |
| Transportation and warehousing | 163 | 114 | 49 |
| Utilities | 8 | 8 | 0 |
| Information | 112 | 74 | 38 |
| Financial activities | 274 | 163 | 111 |
| Professional and business services | 747 | 432 | 315 |
| Education and health services | 1 625 | 544 | 1 082 |
| Leisure and hospitality | 1 110 | 554 | 556 |
| Other services | 522 | 230 | 293 |
| Other services, except private households | 447 | 224 | 223 |
| Other services, private households | 76 | 6 | 70 |
| Public administration | 164 | 110 | 55 |
| **2015** | | | |
| **All Nonagricultural Industries, Wage and Salary Workers** | 5 299 | 2 412 | 2 887 |
| Mining, quarrying, and oil and gas extraction | 10 | 6 | 4 |
| Construction | 104 | 83 | 21 |
| Manufacturing | 130 | 73 | 56 |
| Durable goods | 67 | 43 | 24 |
| Nondurable goods | 63 | 30 | 33 |
| Wholesale and retail trade | 877 | 369 | 508 |
| Wholesale trade | 64 | 36 | 28 |
| Retail trade | 813 | 333 | 480 |
| Transportation and utilities | 183 | 133 | 50 |
| Transportation and warehousing | 172 | 126 | 47 |
| Utilities | 11 | 8 | 3 |
| Information | 42 | 23 | 19 |
| Financial activities | 199 | 120 | 79 |
| Professional and business services | 523 | 289 | 234 |
| Education and health services | 1 520 | 500 | 1 021 |
| Leisure and hospitality | 1 058 | 495 | 563 |
| Other services | 417 | 170 | 246 |
| Other services, except private households | 336 | 164 | 172 |
| Other services, private households | 80 | 6 | 74 |
| Public administration | 176 | 117 | 59 |

## Table 1-20. Employment and Unemployment in Families, by Race and Hispanic Origin, Annual Averages, 2005–2015

(Thousands of people, percent.)

| Characteristic | 2005 | 2006 | 2007 | 2008 | 2009 | 2010 | 2011 | 2012 | 2013 | 2014 | 2015 |
|---|---|---|---|---|---|---|---|---|---|---|---|
| **ALL RACES** | | | | | | | | | | | |
| **Total Families** | 76 443 | 77 017 | 77 894 | 77 943 | 78 361 | 78 246 | 78 362 | 80 141 | 80 445 | 80 889 | 81 410 |
| With employed member(s) | 62 933 | 63 492 | 64 330 | 64 058 | 63 010 | 62 560 | 62 529 | 64 091 | 64 318 | 64 832 | 65 360 |
| As percent of total families | 82.3 | 82.4 | 82.6 | 82.2 | 80.4 | 80.0 | 79.8 | 80.0 | 80.0 | 80.1 | 80.3 |
| Some usually work full time[1] | 58 276 | 58 918 | 59 616 | 59 116 | 57 037 | 56 471 | 56 498 | 58 007 | 58 113 | 58 762 | 59 520 |
| With no employed member | 13 509 | 13 525 | 13 564 | 13 884 | 15 351 | 15 686 | 15 833 | 16 050 | 16 127 | 16 057 | 16 050 |
| As percent of total families | 17.7 | 17.6 | 17.4 | 17.8 | 19.6 | 20.0 | 20.2 | 20.0 | 20.0 | 19.9 | 19.7 |
| With unemployed member(s) | 5 318 | 4 913 | 4 914 | 6 104 | 9 381 | 9 695 | 9 043 | 8 444 | 7 685 | 6 486 | 5 615 |
| As percent of total families | 7.0 | 6.4 | 6.3 | 7.8 | 12.0 | 12.4 | 11.5 | 10.5 | 9.6 | 8.0 | 6.9 |
| Some member(s) employed | 3 717 | 3 419 | 3 497 | 4 319 | 6 438 | 6 566 | 6 079 | 5 702 | 5 192 | 4 419 | 3 831 |
| As percent of families with unemployed member(s) | 69.9 | 69.6 | 71.2 | 70.8 | 68.6 | 67.7 | 67.2 | 67.5 | 67.6 | 68.1 | 68.2 |
| Some usually work full time[1] | 3 310 | 3 049 | 3 096 | 3 830 | 5 460 | 5 572 | 5 211 | 4 902 | 4 453 | 3 819 | 3 302 |
| As percent of families with unemployed member(s) | 62.2 | 62.1 | 63.0 | 62.7 | 58.2 | 57.5 | 57.6 | 58.1 | 58.0 | 58.9 | 58.8 |
| **WHITE[2]** | | | | | | | | | | | |
| **Total Families** | 62 567 | 62 977 | 63 667 | 63 490 | 63 774 | 63 551 | 63 635 | 64 246 | 64 294 | 64 476 | 64 663 |
| With employed member(s) | 51 645 | 52 054 | 52 669 | 52 273 | 51 494 | 51 048 | 51 030 | 51 491 | 51 471 | 51 661 | 51 769 |
| As percent of total families | 82.5 | 83.0 | 82.7 | 82.3 | 80.7 | 80.3 | 80.2 | 80.1 | 80.1 | 80.1 | 80.1 |
| Some usually work full time[1] | 47 883 | 48 395 | 48 879 | 48 271 | 46 629 | 46 150 | 46 203 | 46 710 | 46 636 | 46 937 | 47 225 |
| With no employed member | 10 922 | 10 923 | 10 997 | 11 217 | 12 280 | 12 502 | 12 605 | 12 755 | 12 822 | 12 815 | 12 894 |
| As percent of total families | 17.5 | 17.0 | 17.3 | 17.7 | 19.3 | 19.7 | 19.8 | 19.9 | 19.9 | 19.9 | 19.9 |
| With unemployed member(s) | 3 801 | 3 556 | 3 587 | 4 506 | 7 089 | 7 202 | 6 608 | 6 133 | 5 471 | 4 499 | 3 908 |
| As percent of total families | 6.1 | 5.6 | 5.6 | 7.1 | 11.1 | 11.3 | 10.4 | 9.5 | 8.5 | 7.0 | 6.0 |
| Some member(s) employed | 2 782 | 2 582 | 2 653 | 3 332 | 5 072 | 5 069 | 4 627 | 4 321 | 3 845 | 3 195 | 2 784 |
| As percent of families with unemployed member(s) | 73.2 | 72.6 | 73.9 | 74.0 | 71.5 | 70.4 | 70.0 | 70.5 | 70.3 | 71.0 | 71.2 |
| Some usually work full time[1] | 2 477 | 2 306 | 2 350 | 2 955 | 4 294 | 4 289 | 3 964 | 3 719 | 3 310 | 2 767 | 2 408 |
| As percent of families with unemployed member(s) | 65.2 | 64.8 | 65.5 | 65.6 | 60.6 | 59.6 | 60.0 | 60.6 | 60.5 | 61.5 | 61.6 |
| **BLACK[2]** | | | | | | | | | | | |
| **Total Families** | 8 952 | 9 058 | 9 184 | 9 297 | 9 318 | 9 404 | 9 370 | 9 671 | 9 737 | 9 793 | 9 854 |
| With employed member(s) | 6 986 | 7 078 | 7 249 | 7 290 | 7 022 | 7 030 | 6 954 | 7 290 | 7 373 | 7 481 | 7 652 |
| As percent of total families | 78.0 | 78.0 | 78.9 | 78.4 | 75.4 | 74.8 | 74.2 | 75.4 | 75.7 | 76.4 | 77.7 |
| Some usually work full time[1] | 6 353 | 6 437 | 6 608 | 6 622 | 6 265 | 6 222 | 6 105 | 6 419 | 6 451 | 6 596 | 6 792 |
| With no employed member | 1 966 | 1 980 | 1 935 | 2 006 | 2 296 | 2 374 | 2 416 | 2 380 | 2 363 | 2 312 | 2 202 |
| As percent of total families | 22.0 | 21.9 | 21.1 | 21.6 | 24.6 | 25.2 | 25.8 | 24.6 | 24.3 | 23.6 | 22.3 |
| With unemployed member(s) | 1 140 | 1 036 | 990 | 1 188 | 1 624 | 1 807 | 1 767 | 1 629 | 1 555 | 1 376 | 1 184 |
| As percent of total families | 12.7 | 11.4 | 10.8 | 12.8 | 17.4 | 19.2 | 18.9 | 16.8 | 16.0 | 14.1 | 12.0 |
| Some member(s) employed | 657 | 596 | 591 | 686 | 886 | 1 009 | 985 | 885 | 880 | 780 | 666 |
| As percent of families with unemployed member(s) | 57.7 | 57.6 | 59.7 | 57.8 | 54.5 | 55.8 | 55.7 | 54.3 | 56.6 | 56.7 | 56.3 |
| Some usually work full time[1] | 583 | 526 | 519 | 605 | 748 | 862 | 835 | 752 | 733 | 666 | 558 |
| As percent of families with unemployed member(s) | 51.1 | 50.8 | 52.4 | 50.9 | 46.0 | 47.7 | 47.3 | 46.1 | 47.1 | 48.4 | 47.2 |
| **HISPANIC[3]** | | | | | | | | | | | |
| **Total Families** | 9 603 | 9 905 | 10 332 | 10 500 | 10 489 | 10 561 | 10 902 | 11 769 | 12 023 | 12 178 | 12 602 |
| With employed member(s) | 8 312 | 8 641 | 9 048 | 9 135 | 8 852 | 8 897 | 9 178 | 9 962 | 10 231 | 10 456 | 10 883 |
| As percent of total families | 86.6 | 87.2 | 87.6 | 87.0 | 84.4 | 84.2 | 84.2 | 84.6 | 85.1 | 85.9 | 86.4 |
| Some usually work full time[1] | 7 786 | 8 129 | 8 492 | 8 466 | 7 923 | 7 934 | 8 201 | 8 978 | 9 242 | 9 429 | 9 914 |
| With no employed member | 1 291 | 1 264 | 1 285 | 1 365 | 1 637 | 1 664 | 1 724 | 1 808 | 1 792 | 1 722 | 1 719 |
| As percent of total families | 13.4 | 12.8 | 12.4 | 13.0 | 15.6 | 15.8 | 15.8 | 15.4 | 14.9 | 14.1 | 13.6 |
| With unemployed member(s) | 860 | 793 | 876 | 1 159 | 1 770 | 1 841 | 1 781 | 1 707 | 1 547 | 1 311 | 1 220 |
| As percent of total families | 9.0 | 8.0 | 8.5 | 11.0 | 16.9 | 17.4 | 16.3 | 14.5 | 12.9 | 10.8 | 9.7 |
| Some member(s) employed | 606 | 544 | 619 | 846 | 1 228 | 1 262 | 1 226 | 1 197 | 1 078 | 933 | 864 |
| As percent of families with unemployed member(s) | 70.5 | 68.6 | 70.6 | 73.0 | 69.3 | 68.6 | 68.8 | 70.1 | 69.7 | 71.1 | 70.8 |
| Some usually work full time[1] | 544 | 491 | 554 | 743 | 1 021 | 1 060 | 1 030 | 1 020 | 919 | 798 | 740 |
| As percent of families with unemployed member(s) | 63.2 | 61.9 | 63.2 | 64.1 | 57.7 | 57.6 | 57.8 | 59.7 | 59.4 | 60.9 | 60.7 |

*Note:* The race or ethnicity of the family is determined by the race of the householder. Estimates for the above race groups (White or Black) do not sum to totals because data are not presented for all races.

[1] Usually work 35 hours or more a week at all jobs.
[2] Beginning in 2003, families where the householder selected this race group only; families where the householder selected more than one race group are excluded. Prior to 2003, families where the householder selected more than one race group were included in the group that the householder identified as the main race.
[3] May be of any race.

## Table 1-21.  Families, by Presence and Relationship of Employed Members and Family Type, Annual Averages, 2005–2015

(Thousands of people, percent.)

| Characteristic | Number of families | | | | | | | | | | |
|---|---|---|---|---|---|---|---|---|---|---|---|
| | 2005 | 2006 | 2007 | 2008 | 2009 | 2010 | 2011 | 2012 | 2013 | 2014 | 2015 |
| **MARRIED-COUPLE FAMILIES** | | | | | | | | | | | |
| Total .................................................................. | 57 167 | 57 509 | 58 145 | 58 125 | 58 124 | 57 524 | 57 290 | 58 431 | 58 529 | 58 806 | 59 217 |
| Member(s) employed, total ................................ | 47 895 | 48 196 | 48 676 | 48 541 | 47 876 | 47 238 | 46 910 | 47 830 | 47 722 | 47 852 | 48 205 |
| Husband only ................................................ | 11 562 | 11 399 | 11 509 | 11 351 | 11 371 | 11 311 | 11 426 | 11 815 | 11 755 | 11 713 | 11 726 |
| Wife only ....................................................... | 3 715 | 3 754 | 3 858 | 4 036 | 4 909 | 4 937 | 4 764 | 4 696 | 4 578 | 4 422 | 4 209 |
| Husband and wife ......................................... | 29 330 | 29 799 | 30 055 | 29 854 | 28 211 | 27 501 | 27 229 | 27 708 | 27 748 | 28 042 | 28 434 |
| Other employment combinations ................... | 3 288 | 3 244 | 3 254 | 3 300 | 3 384 | 3 489 | 3 491 | 3 612 | 3 640 | 3 676 | 3 837 |
| No member(s) employed ..................................... | 9 272 | 9 313 | 9 469 | 9 585 | 10 248 | 10 286 | 10 379 | 10 601 | 10 807 | 10 954 | 11 012 |
| **FAMILIES MAINTAINED BY WOMEN**[1] | | | | | | | | | | | |
| Total .................................................................. | 14 035 | 14 208 | 14 423 | 14 383 | 14 610 | 14 913 | 15 147 | 15 517 | 15 507 | 15 581 | 15 693 |
| Member(s) employed, total ................................ | 10 609 | 10 796 | 11 087 | 10 929 | 10 642 | 10 715 | 10 867 | 11 236 | 11 360 | 11 585 | 11 765 |
| Householder only .......................................... | 6 052 | 6 103 | 6 307 | 6 250 | 6 135 | 6 189 | 6 248 | 6 403 | 6 359 | 6 368 | 6 451 |
| Householder and other member(s) ............... | 2 830 | 2 955 | 2 994 | 2 870 | 2 642 | 2 603 | 2 683 | 2 896 | 2 933 | 3 059 | 3 181 |
| Other member(s), not householder .............. | 1 727 | 1 738 | 1 785 | 1 809 | 1 866 | 1 923 | 1 937 | 1 937 | 2 069 | 2 159 | 2 133 |
| No member(s) employed ..................................... | 3 426 | 3 412 | 3 336 | 3 454 | 3 968 | 4 198 | 4 280 | 4 281 | 4 147 | 3 995 | 3 928 |
| **FAMILIES MAINTAINED BY MEN**[1] | | | | | | | | | | | |
| Total .................................................................. | 5 242 | 5 300 | 5 327 | 5 435 | 5 627 | 5 809 | 5 926 | 6 192 | 6 410 | 6 502 | 6 499 |
| Member(s) employed, total ................................ | 4 430 | 4 500 | 4 568 | 4 589 | 4 492 | 4 607 | 4 752 | 5 025 | 5 236 | 5 394 | 5 389 |
| Householder only .......................................... | 2 093 | 2 089 | 2 170 | 2 178 | 2 104 | 2 215 | 2 399 | 2 514 | 2 529 | 2 568 | 2 517 |
| Householder and other member(s) ............... | 1 639 | 1 715 | 1 696 | 1 659 | 1 557 | 1 525 | 1 506 | 1 622 | 1 736 | 1 891 | 1 932 |
| Other member(s), not householder .............. | 698 | 696 | 701 | 752 | 831 | 867 | 847 | 889 | 971 | 935 | 940 |
| No member(s) employed ..................................... | 812 | 800 | 759 | 845 | 1 135 | 1 202 | 1 174 | 1 168 | 1 174 | 1 108 | 1 110 |

| Characteristic | Percent distribution | | | | | | | | | | |
|---|---|---|---|---|---|---|---|---|---|---|---|
| | 2005 | 2006 | 2007 | 2008 | 2009 | 2010 | 2011 | 2012 | 2013 | 2014 | 2015 |
| **MARRIED-COUPLE FAMILIES** | | | | | | | | | | | |
| Total .................................................................. | 100.0 | 100.0 | 100.0 | 100.0 | 100.0 | 100.0 | 100.0 | 100.0 | 100.0 | 100.0 | 100.0 |
| Member(s) employed, total ................................ | 84.0 | 84.0 | 83.7 | 83.5 | 82.4 | 82.1 | 81.9 | 81.9 | 81.5 | 81.4 | 81.4 |
| Husband only ................................................ | 20.0 | 20.0 | 19.8 | 19.5 | 19.6 | 19.7 | 19.9 | 20.2 | 20.1 | 19.9 | 19.8 |
| Wife only ....................................................... | 7.0 | 7.0 | 6.6 | 6.9 | 8.4 | 8.6 | 8.3 | 8.0 | 7.8 | 7.5 | 7.1 |
| Husband and wife ......................................... | 51.0 | 52.0 | 51.7 | 51.4 | 48.5 | 47.8 | 47.5 | 47.4 | 47.4 | 47.7 | 48.0 |
| Other employment combinations ................... | 6.0 | 6.0 | 5.6 | 5.7 | 5.8 | 6.1 | 6.1 | 6.2 | 6.2 | 6.3 | 6.5 |
| No member(s) employed ..................................... | 16.0 | 16.0 | 16.3 | 16.5 | 17.6 | 17.9 | 18.1 | 18.1 | 18.5 | 18.6 | 18.6 |
| **FAMILIES MAINTAINED BY WOMEN**[1] | | | | | | | | | | | |
| Total .................................................................. | 100.0 | 100.0 | 100.0 | 100.0 | 100.0 | 100.0 | 100.0 | 100.0 | 100.0 | 100.0 | 100.0 |
| Member(s) employed, total ................................ | 76.0 | 76.0 | 76.9 | 76.0 | 72.8 | 71.9 | 71.7 | 72.4 | 73.3 | 74.4 | 75.0 |
| Householder only .......................................... | 43.0 | 43.0 | 43.7 | 43.5 | 42.0 | 41.5 | 41.2 | 41.3 | 41.0 | 40.9 | 41.1 |
| Householder and other member(s) ............... | 20.0 | 21.0 | 20.8 | 20.0 | 18.1 | 17.5 | 17.7 | 18.7 | 18.9 | 19.6 | 20.3 |
| Other member(s), not householder .............. | 12.0 | 12.0 | 12.4 | 12.6 | 12.8 | 12.9 | 12.8 | 12.5 | 13.3 | 13.9 | 13.6 |
| No member(s) employed ..................................... | 24.0 | 24.0 | 23.1 | 24.0 | 27.2 | 28.1 | 28.3 | 27.6 | 26.7 | 25.6 | 25.0 |
| **FAMILIES MAINTAINED BY MEN**[1] | | | | | | | | | | | |
| Total .................................................................. | 100.0 | 100.0 | 100.0 | 100.0 | 100.0 | 100.0 | 100.0 | 100.0 | 100.0 | 100.0 | 100.0 |
| Member(s) employed, total ................................ | 85.0 | 85.0 | 85.7 | 84.4 | 79.8 | 79.3 | 80.2 | 81.1 | 81.7 | 83.0 | 82.9 |
| Householder only .......................................... | 40.0 | 39.0 | 40.7 | 40.1 | 37.4 | 38.1 | 40.5 | 40.6 | 39.5 | 39.5 | 38.7 |
| Householder and other member(s) ............... | 31.0 | 32.0 | 31.8 | 30.5 | 27.7 | 26.2 | 25.4 | 26.2 | 27.1 | 29.1 | 29.7 |
| Other member(s), not householder .............. | 13.3 | 13.1 | 13.2 | 13.8 | 14.8 | 14.9 | 14.3 | 14.4 | 15.1 | 14.4 | 14.5 |
| No member(s) employed ..................................... | 16.0 | 15.0 | 14.3 | 15.6 | 20.2 | 20.7 | 19.8 | 18.9 | 18.3 | 17.0 | 17.1 |

*Note:* Detail may not sum to total due to rounding.

[1]No spouse present.

## Table 1-22. Unemployment in Families, by Presence and Relationship of Employed Members and Family Type, Annual Averages, 2005–2015

(Thousands of people, percent.)

| Characteristic | Number | | | | | | | | | | |
|---|---|---|---|---|---|---|---|---|---|---|---|
| | 2005 | 2006 | 2007 | 2008 | 2009 | 2010 | 2011 | 2012 | 2013 | 2014 | 2015 |
| **MARRIED-COUPLE FAMILIES** | | | | | | | | | | | |
| With Unemployed Member(s), Total | 3 243 | 2 968 | 2 978 | 3 796 | 6 056 | 6 147 | 5 576 | 5 140 | 4 586 | 3 765 | 3 292 |
| No member employed | 580 | 526 | 512 | 663 | 1 218 | 4 884 | 4 413 | 4 123 | 3 639 | 3 028 | 2 653 |
| Some member(s) employed | 2 664 | 2 442 | 2 467 | 3 133 | 4 838 | 1 263 | 1 162 | 1 017 | 946 | 737 | 639 |
| Husband unemployed | 1 190 | 1 061 | 1 110 | 1 439 | 2 808 | 2 813 | 2 387 | 2 066 | 1 824 | 1 398 | 1 194 |
| Wife employed | 753 | 679 | 725 | 927 | 1 799 | 1 783 | 1 497 | 1 307 | 1 134 | 872 | 739 |
| Wife unemployed | 1 004 | 898 | 902 | 1 114 | 1 630 | 1 697 | 1 610 | 1 567 | 1 346 | 1 121 | 947 |
| Husband employed | 873 | 772 | 783 | 975 | 1 397 | 1 455 | 1 350 | 1 328 | 1 129 | 943 | 786 |
| Other family member unemployed | 1 049 | 1 010 | 966 | 1 243 | 1 618 | 1 637 | 1 579 | 1 507 | 1 416 | 1 246 | 1 151 |
| **FAMILIES MAINTAINED BY WOMEN[1]** | | | | | | | | | | | |
| With Unemployed Member(s), Total | 1 539 | 1 429 | 1 416 | 1 666 | 2 309 | 2 446 | 2 498 | 2 372 | 2 165 | 1 933 | 1 666 |
| No member employed | 797 | 753 | 701 | 849 | 1 244 | 1 094 | 1 146 | 1 081 | 1 026 | 936 | 804 |
| Some member(s) employed | 743 | 675 | 714 | 817 | 1 065 | 1 351 | 1 352 | 1 290 | 1 139 | 997 | 862 |
| Householder unemployed | 746 | 688 | 650 | 796 | 1 141 | 1 227 | 1 268 | 1 191 | 1 053 | 892 | 770 |
| Other member(s) employed | 161 | 132 | 144 | 181 | 225 | 254 | 275 | 250 | 251 | 216 | 181 |
| Other member(s) unemployed | 793 | 740 | 766 | 870 | 1 168 | 1 218 | 1 229 | 1 180 | 1 112 | 1 040 | 896 |
| **FAMILIES MAINTAINED BY MEN[1]** | | | | | | | | | | | |
| With Unemployed Member(s), Total | 536 | 516 | 520 | 642 | 1 016 | 1 102 | 970 | 932 | 934 | 789 | 657 |
| No member employed | 225 | 215 | 205 | 274 | 482 | 587 | 520 | 497 | 527 | 455 | 375 |
| Some member(s) employed | 310 | 301 | 316 | 368 | 535 | 515 | 450 | 435 | 408 | 333 | 282 |
| Householder unemployed | 301 | 284 | 294 | 385 | 626 | 680 | 575 | 535 | 550 | 446 | 378 |
| Other member(s) employed | 122 | 118 | 137 | 164 | 239 | 259 | 231 | 209 | 238 | 200 | 158 |
| Other member(s) unemployed | 235 | 232 | 226 | 257 | 391 | 422 | 394 | 397 | 385 | 343 | 280 |

| Characteristic | Number | Percent distribution | | | | | | | | | |
|---|---|---|---|---|---|---|---|---|---|---|---|
| | 2005 | 2006 | 2007 | 2008 | 2009 | 2010 | 2011 | 2012 | 2013 | 2014 | 2015 |
| **MARRIED-COUPLE FAMILIES** | | | | | | | | | | | |
| With Unemployed Member(s), Total | 100.0 | 100.0 | 100.0 | 100.0 | 100.0 | 100.0 | 100.0 | 100.0 | 100.0 | 100.0 | 100.0 |
| No member employed | 17.9 | 17.7 | 17.2 | 17.5 | 20.1 | 79.4 | 79.2 | 80.2 | 79.4 | 80.4 | 80.6 |
| Some member(s) employed | 82.1 | 82.3 | 82.8 | 82.5 | 79.9 | 20.6 | 20.8 | 19.8 | 20.6 | 19.6 | 19.4 |
| Husband unemployed | 36.7 | 35.7 | 37.3 | 37.9 | 46.4 | 45.8 | 42.8 | 40.2 | 39.8 | 37.1 | 36.3 |
| Wife employed | 23.2 | 22.9 | 24.3 | 24.4 | 29.7 | 29.0 | 26.9 | 25.4 | 24.7 | 23.2 | 22.5 |
| Wife unemployed | 31.0 | 30.3 | 30.3 | 29.3 | 26.9 | 27.6 | 28.9 | 30.5 | 29.4 | 29.8 | 28.8 |
| Husband employed | 26.9 | 26.0 | 26.3 | 25.7 | 23.1 | 23.7 | 24.2 | 25.8 | 24.6 | 25.1 | 23.9 |
| Other family member unemployed | 32.4 | 34.0 | 32.4 | 32.7 | 26.7 | 26.6 | 28.3 | 29.3 | 30.9 | 33.1 | 35.0 |
| **FAMILIES MAINTAINED BY WOMEN[1]** | | | | | | | | | | | |
| With Unemployed Member(s), Total | 100.0 | 100.0 | 100.0 | 100.0 | 100.0 | 100.0 | 100.0 | 100.0 | 100.0 | 100.0 | 100.0 |
| No member employed | 51.8 | 52.7 | 49.5 | 50.9 | 53.9 | 44.7 | 45.9 | 45.6 | 47.4 | 48.4 | 48.2 |
| Some member(s) employed | 48.2 | 47.3 | 50.5 | 49.1 | 46.1 | 55.3 | 54.1 | 54.4 | 52.6 | 51.6 | 51.8 |
| Householder unemployed | 48.5 | 48.2 | 45.9 | 47.8 | 49.4 | 50.2 | 50.8 | 50.2 | 48.6 | 46.2 | 46.2 |
| Other member(s) employed | 10.5 | 9.3 | 10.2 | 10.9 | 9.7 | 10.4 | 11.0 | 10.6 | 11.6 | 11.2 | 10.8 |
| Other member(s) unemployed | 51.5 | 51.8 | 54.1 | 52.2 | 50.6 | 49.8 | 49.2 | 49.8 | 51.4 | 53.8 | 53.8 |
| **FAMILIES MAINTAINED BY MEN[1]** | | | | | | | | | | | |
| With Unemployed Member(s), Total | 100.0 | 100.0 | 100.0 | 100.0 | 100.0 | 100.0 | 100.0 | 100.0 | 100.0 | 100.0 | 100.0 |
| No member employed | 42.1 | 41.7 | 39.3 | 42.7 | 47.4 | 53.3 | 53.6 | 53.3 | 56.4 | 57.7 | 57.0 |
| Some member(s) employed | 57.9 | 58.3 | 60.7 | 57.3 | 52.6 | 46.7 | 46.4 | 46.7 | 43.6 | 42.3 | 43.0 |
| Householder unemployed | 56.1 | 55.0 | 56.6 | 60.0 | 61.6 | 61.7 | 59.4 | 57.4 | 58.8 | 56.5 | 57.5 |
| Other member(s) employed | 22.8 | 22.8 | 26.3 | 25.6 | 23.5 | 23.5 | 23.8 | 22.5 | 25.5 | 25.4 | 24.1 |
| Other member(s) unemployed | 43.9 | 45.0 | 43.4 | 40.0 | 38.4 | 38.3 | 40.6 | 42.6 | 41.2 | 43.5 | 42.5 |

*Note:* Detail may not sum to total due to rounding.

[1]No spouse present.

## Table 1-23. Employment Status of the Population, by Sex, Marital Status, and Presence and Age of Own Children Under 18 Years, Annual Averages, 2008–2015

(Thousands of people, percent.)

| Characteristic | 2008 Both sexes | 2008 Men | 2008 Women | 2009 Both sexes | 2009 Men | 2009 Women | 2010 Both sexes | 2010 Men | 2010 Women | 2011 Both sexes | 2011 Men | 2011 Women |
|---|---|---|---|---|---|---|---|---|---|---|---|---|
| **With Own Children Under 18 Years, Total** | | | | | | | | | | | | |
| Civilian noninstitutional population | 65 655 | 29 142 | 36 513 | 64 854 | 28 778 | 36 076 | 64 488 | 28 463 | 36 025 | 63 885 | 28 143 | 35 743 |
| Civilian labor force | 53 506 | 27 422 | 26 085 | 52 748 | 26 985 | 25 763 | 52 159 | 26 661 | 25 499 | 51 521 | 26 302 | 25 219 |
| Participation rate | 81.5 | 94.1 | 71.4 | 81.3 | 93.8 | 71.4 | 80.9 | 93.7 | 70.8 | 80.6 | 93.5 | 70.6 |
| Employed | 51 017 | 26 380 | 24 637 | 48 621 | 24 989 | 23 632 | 47 863 | 24 653 | 23 210 | 47 578 | 24 619 | 22 959 |
| Employment-population ratio | 77.7 | 90.5 | 67.5 | 75.0 | 86.8 | 65.5 | 74.2 | 86.6 | 64.4 | 74.5 | 87.5 | 64.2 |
| Full-time workers[1] | 43 967 | 25 338 | 18 629 | 41 003 | 23 583 | 17 419 | 7 581 | 1 477 | 6 104 | 7 303 | 1 374 | 5 930 |
| Part-time workers[2] | 7 050 | 1 042 | 6 008 | 7 618 | 1 406 | 6 212 | 74 | 87 | 64 | 74 | 88 | 64 |
| Unemployed | 2 490 | 1 041 | 1 448 | 4 128 | 1 996 | 2 132 | 4 296 | 2 008 | 2 289 | 3 943 | 1 683 | 2 260 |
| Unemployment rate | 4.7 | 3.8 | 5.6 | 7.8 | 7.4 | 8.3 | 8.2 | 7.5 | 9.0 | 7.7 | 6.4 | 9.0 |
| **Married, Spouse Present** | | | | | | | | | | | | |
| Civilian noninstitutional population | 52 433 | 26 647 | 25 786 | 51 634 | 26 249 | 25 385 | 50 868 | 25 820 | 25 049 | 49 999 | 25 392 | 24 607 |
| Civilian labor force | 43 137 | 25 205 | 17 933 | 42 424 | 24 763 | 17 661 | 41 600 | 24 332 | 17 268 | 40 783 | 23 873 | 16 911 |
| Participation rate | 82.3 | 94.6 | 69.5 | 82.2 | 94.3 | 69.6 | 81.8 | 94.2 | 68.9 | 81.6 | 94.0 | 68.7 |
| Employed | 41 611 | 24 353 | 17 258 | 39 732 | 23 100 | 16 632 | 38 870 | 22 689 | 16 181 | 38 379 | 22 480 | 15 900 |
| Employment-population ratio | 79.4 | 91.4 | 66.9 | 76.9 | 88.0 | 65.5 | 76.4 | 87.9 | 64.6 | 76.8 | 88.5 | 64.6 |
| Full-time workers[1] | 36 128 | 23 444 | 12 685 | 33 846 | 21 871 | 11 975 | 5 728 | 1 245 | 4 482 | 5 440 | 1 158 | 4 282 |
| Part-time workers[2] | 5 482 | 909 | 4 573 | 5 886 | 1 229 | 4 657 | 76 | 88 | 65 | 77 | 88 | 65 |
| Unemployed | 1 527 | 852 | 675 | 2 692 | 1 663 | 1 029 | 2 730 | 1 643 | 1 087 | 2 404 | 1 393 | 1 011 |
| Unemployment rate | 3.5 | 3.4 | 3.8 | 6.3 | 6.7 | 5.8 | 6.6 | 6.8 | 6.3 | 5.9 | 5.8 | 6.0 |
| **Other Marital Status[3]** | | | | | | | | | | | | |
| Civilian noninstitutional population | 13 222 | 2 495 | 10 727 | 13 221 | 2 529 | 10 691 | 13 620 | 2 643 | 10 977 | 13 886 | 2 751 | 11 135 |
| Civilian labor force | 10 369 | 2 217 | 8 152 | 10 325 | 2 223 | 8 102 | 10 559 | 2 329 | 8 230 | 10 737 | 2 429 | 8 308 |
| Participation rate | 78.4 | 88.9 | 76.0 | 78.1 | 87.9 | 75.8 | 77.5 | 88.1 | 75.0 | 77.3 | 88.3 | 74.6 |
| Employed | 9 406 | 2 027 | 7 379 | 8 889 | 1 889 | 7 000 | 8 994 | 1 964 | 7 029 | 9 198 | 2 139 | 7 059 |
| Employment-population ratio | 71.1 | 81.3 | 68.8 | 67.2 | 74.7 | 65.5 | 66.0 | 74.3 | 64.0 | 66.2 | 77.8 | 63.4 |
| Full-time workers[1] | 7 838 | 1 894 | 5 944 | 7 157 | 1 712 | 5 445 | 1 853 | 232 | 1 621 | 1 864 | 216 | 1 647 |
| Part-time workers[2] | 1 568 | 133 | 1 435 | 1 732 | 177 | 1 555 | 66 | 74 | 64 | 66 | 78 | 63 |
| Unemployed | 963 | 190 | 773 | 1 436 | 334 | 1 103 | 1 566 | 365 | 1 201 | 1 539 | 290 | 1 249 |
| Unemployment rate | 9.3 | 8.6 | 9.5 | 13.9 | 15.0 | 13.6 | 14.8 | 15.7 | 14.6 | 14.3 | 11.9 | 15.0 |
| **With Own Children 6 to 17 Years, None Younger** | | | | | | | | | | | | |
| Civilian noninstitutional population | 36 581 | 16 256 | 20 325 | 35 885 | 15 982 | 19 903 | 35 402 | 15 639 | 19 763 | 35 027 | 15 431 | 19 596 |
| Civilian labor force | 30 846 | 15 128 | 15 718 | 30 200 | 14 821 | 15 379 | 29 625 | 14 515 | 15 110 | 29 193 | 14 289 | 14 904 |
| Participation rate | 84.3 | 93.1 | 77.3 | 84.2 | 92.7 | 77.3 | 83.7 | 92.8 | 76.5 | 77.6 | 87.0 | 70.2 |
| Employed | 29 590 | 14 588 | 15 003 | 28 059 | 13 775 | 14 284 | 27 421 | 13 482 | 13 939 | 27 178 | 13 422 | 13 756 |
| Employment-population ratio | 80.9 | 89.7 | 73.8 | 78.2 | 86.2 | 71.8 | 77.5 | 86.2 | 70.5 | 77.6 | 87.0 | 70.2 |
| Full-time workers[1] | 25 733 | 14 054 | 11 679 | 23 864 | 13 067 | 10 798 | 4 182 | 757 | 3 425 | 3 992 | 686 | 3 306 |
| Part-time workers[2] | 3 858 | 534 | 3 324 | 4 194 | 708 | 3 486 | 78 | 86 | 71 | 78 | 87 | 70 |
| Unemployed | 1 255 | 541 | 715 | 2 141 | 1 046 | 1 095 | 2 204 | 1 032 | 1 172 | 2 015 | 867 | 1 148 |
| Unemployment rate | 4.1 | 3.6 | 4.5 | 7.1 | 7.1 | 7.1 | 7.4 | 7.1 | 7.8 | 6.9 | 6.1 | 7.7 |
| **With Own Children Under 6 Years** | | | | | | | | | | | | |
| Civilian noninstitutional population | 29 074 | 12 886 | 16 188 | 28 969 | 12 796 | 16 173 | 29 086 | 12 824 | 16 262 | 28 858 | 12 712 | 16 146 |
| Civilian labor force | 22 661 | 12 293 | 10 367 | 22 549 | 12 164 | 10 384 | 22 534 | 12 146 | 10 388 | 22 328 | 12 013 | 10 315 |
| Participation rate | 77.9 | 95.4 | 64.0 | 77.8 | 95.1 | 64.2 | 77.5 | 94.7 | 63.9 | 77.4 | 94.5 | 63.9 |
| Employed | 21 426 | 11 792 | 9 634 | 20 562 | 11 214 | 9 348 | 20 442 | 11 171 | 9 271 | 20 400 | 11 197 | 9 203 |
| Employment-population ratio | 73.7 | 91.5 | 59.5 | 71.0 | 87.6 | 57.8 | 70.3 | 87.1 | 57.0 | 70.7 | 88.1 | 57.0 |
| Full-time workers[1] | 18 234 | 11 284 | 6 950 | 17 138 | 10 517 | 6 622 | 3 399 | 720 | 2 679 | 3 311 | 687 | 2 624 |
| Part-time workers[2] | 3 193 | 508 | 2 684 | 3 424 | 697 | 2 726 | 70 | 87 | 57 | 71 | 88 | 57 |
| Unemployed | 1 234 | 501 | 733 | 1 987 | 950 | 1 036 | 2 092 | 975 | 1 117 | 1 928 | 816 | 1 112 |
| Unemployment rate | 5.4 | 4.1 | 7.1 | 8.8 | 7.8 | 10.0 | 9.3 | 8.0 | 10.8 | 8.6 | 6.8 | 10.8 |
| **With No Own Children Under 18 Years** | | | | | | | | | | | | |
| Civilian noninstitutional population | 168 133 | 83 971 | 84 162 | 170 947 | 85 358 | 85 589 | 173 342 | 86 711 | 86 631 | 175 732 | 88 175 | 87 558 |
| Civilian labor force | 100 780 | 55 098 | 45 682 | 101 394 | 55 138 | 46 256 | 101 729 | 55 324 | 46 405 | 102 096 | 55 673 | 46 423 |
| Participation rate | 59.9 | 65.6 | 54.3 | 59.3 | 64.6 | 54.0 | 58.7 | 63.8 | 53.6 | 58.1 | 63.1 | 53.0 |
| Employed | 94 346 | 51 106 | 43 239 | 91 257 | 48 681 | 42 576 | 91 201 | 48 706 | 42 495 | 92 291 | 49 671 | 42 620 |
| Employment-population ratio | 56.1 | 60.9 | 51.4 | 53.4 | 57.0 | 49.7 | 52.6 | 56.2 | 49.1 | 52.5 | 56.3 | 48.7 |
| Full-time workers[1] | 76 064 | 43 515 | 32 549 | 71 631 | 40 368 | 31 263 | 19 769 | 8 381 | 11 387 | 20 010 | 8 584 | 11 426 |
| Part-time workers[2] | 18 282 | 7 592 | 10 690 | 19 626 | 8 313 | 11 313 | 53 | 56 | 49 | 52 | 56 | 49 |
| Unemployed | 6 435 | 3 992 | 2 443 | 10 137 | 6 457 | 3 680 | 10 528 | 6 618 | 3 910 | 9 805 | 6 002 | 3 803 |
| Unemployment rate | 6.4 | 7.2 | 5.3 | 10.0 | 11.7 | 8.0 | 10.3 | 12.0 | 8.4 | 9.6 | 10.8 | 8.2 |

*Note:* Own children include sons, daughters, stepchildren, and adopted children. Not included are nieces, nephews, grandchildren, and other related and unrelated children. Detail may not sum to total due to rounding.

[1]Usually work 35 hours or more a week at all jobs.
[2]Usually work less than 35 hours a week at all jobs.
[3]Includes never-married, divorced, separated, and widowed persons.

## Table 1-23. Employment Status of the Population, by Sex, Marital Status, and Presence and Age of Own Children Under 18 Years, Annual Averages, 2008–2015—Continued

(Thousands of people, percent.)

| Characteristic | 2012 Both sexes | 2012 Men | 2012 Women | 2013 Both sexes | 2013 Men | 2013 Women | 2014 Both sexes | 2014 Men | 2014 Women | 2015 Both sexes | 2015 Men | 2015 Women |
|---|---|---|---|---|---|---|---|---|---|---|---|---|
| **With Own Children Under 18 Years, Total** | | | | | | | | | | | | |
| Civilian noninstitutional population | 65 620 | 28 943 | 36 676 | 65 385 | 28 947 | 36 438 | 65 643 | 29 040 | 36 602 | 65 564 | 29 095 | 36 469 |
| Civilian labor force | 52 754 | 26 954 | 25 800 | 52 335 | 26 869 | 25 466 | 52 580 | 26 939 | 25 641 | 52 476 | 26 978 | 25 498 |
| Participation rate | 80.4 | 93.1 | 70.3 | 80.0 | 92.8 | 69.9 | 80.1 | 92.8 | 70.1 | 80.0 | 92.7 | 69.9 |
| Employed | 49 101 | 25 460 | 23 641 | 49 146 | 25 540 | 23 606 | 49 948 | 25 899 | 24 049 | 50 238 | 26 079 | 24 159 |
| Employment-population ratio | 74.8 | 88.0 | 64.5 | 75.2 | 88.2 | 64.8 | 76.1 | 89.2 | 65.7 | 76.6 | 89.6 | 66.2 |
| Full-time workers[1] | 41 698 | 24 055 | 17 643 | 7 302 | 1 333 | 5 969 | 66 | 1 284 | 5 937 | 6 989 | 1 199 | 5 790 |
| Part-time workers[2] | 7 403 | 1 405 | 5 999 | 75 | 88 | 65 | 76 | 89 | 66 | 77 | 90 | 66 |
| Unemployed | 3 653 | 1 494 | 2 159 | 3 189 | 1 329 | 1 860 | 2 632 | 1 040 | 1 592 | 2 238 | 899 | 1 339 |
| Unemployment rate | 6.9 | 5.5 | 8.4 | 6.1 | 4.9 | 7.3 | 5.0 | 3.9 | 6.2 | 4.3 | 3.3 | 5.3 |
| **Married, Spouse Present** | | | | | | | | | | | | |
| Civilian noninstitutional population | 49 595 | 25 013 | 24 582 | 49 595 | 25 035 | 24 560 | 49 739 | 25 098 | 24 641 | 49 822 | 25 122 | 24 700 |
| Civilian labor force | 40 277 | 23 481 | 16 796 | 40 096 | 23 447 | 16 650 | 40 220 | 23 505 | 16 715 | 40 226 | 23 532 | 16 694 |
| Participation rate | 81.2 | 93.9 | 68.3 | 80.8 | 93.7 | 67.8 | 80.9 | 93.7 | 67.8 | 80.7 | 93.7 | 67.6 |
| Employed | 38 261 | 22 374 | 15 886 | 38 325 | 22 478 | 15 847 | 38 804 | 22 762 | 16 042 | 39 026 | 22 889 | 16 137 |
| Employment-population ratio | 77.1 | 89.5 | 64.6 | 77.3 | 89.8 | 64.5 | 78.0 | 90.7 | 65.1 | 78.3 | 91.1 | 65.3 |
| Full-time workers[1] | 32 961 | 21 277 | 11 684 | 5 130 | 1 042 | 4 088 | 5 032 | 1 012 | 4 020 | 4 877 | 931 | 3 947 |
| Part-time workers[2] | 5 299 | 1 097 | 4 202 | 77 | 90 | 64 | 78 | 91 | 65 | 78 | 91 | 65 |
| Unemployed | 2 017 | 1 106 | 910 | 1 771 | 969 | 802 | 1 415 | 742 | 673 | 1 200 | 643 | 557 |
| Unemployment rate | 5.0 | 4.7 | 5.4 | 4.4 | 4.1 | 4.8 | 3.5 | 3.2 | 4.0 | 3.0 | 2.7 | 3.3 |
| **Other Marital Status[3]** | | | | | | | | | | | | |
| Civilian noninstitutional population | 16 025 | 3 930 | 12 095 | 15 789 | 3 912 | 11 878 | 15 904 | 3 943 | 11 961 | 15 742 | 3 973 | 11 769 |
| Civilian labor force | 12 477 | 3 473 | 9 004 | 12 238 | 3 422 | 8 817 | 12 360 | 3 434 | 8 926 | 12 250 | 3 446 | 8 804 |
| Participation rate | 77.9 | 88.4 | 74.4 | 77.5 | 87.5 | 74.2 | 77.7 | 87.1 | 74.6 | 77.8 | 86.7 | 74.8 |
| Employed | 10 840 | 3 085 | 7 755 | 10 820 | 3 062 | 7 759 | 11 143 | 3 137 | 8 007 | 11 213 | 3 190 | 8 022 |
| Employment-population ratio | 67.6 | 78.5 | 64.1 | 68.5 | 78.3 | 65.3 | 70.1 | 79.6 | 66.9 | 71.2 | 80.3 | 68.2 |
| Full-time workers[1] | 8 736 | 2 777 | 5 959 | 2 172 | 291 | 1 881 | 2 189 | 272 | 1 917 | 2 111 | 268 | 1 843 |
| Part-time workers[2] | 2 104 | 308 | 1 796 | 68 | 78 | 65 | 70 | 80 | 67 | 71 | 80 | 68 |
| Unemployed | 1 636 | 388 | 1 249 | 1 418 | 360 | 1 058 | 1 217 | 298 | 919 | 1 038 | 256 | 782 |
| Unemployment rate | 13.1 | 11.2 | 13.9 | 11.6 | 10.5 | 12.0 | 9.8 | 8.7 | 10.3 | 8.5 | 7.4 | 8.9 |
| **With Own Children 6 to 17 Years, None Younger** | | | | | | | | | | | | |
| Civilian noninstitutional population | 35 786 | 15 777 | 20 009 | 36 218 | 16 007 | 20 212 | 36 486 | 16 114 | 20 372 | 36 616 | 16 171 | 20 445 |
| Civilian labor force | 29 573 | 14 545 | 15 028 | 29 815 | 14 714 | 15 101 | 29 989 | 14 768 | 15 221 | 30 057 | 14 840 | 15 218 |
| Participation rate | 82.6 | 92.2 | 75.1 | 82.3 | 91.9 | 74.7 | 82.2 | 91.6 | 74.7 | 82.1 | 91.8 | 74.4 |
| Employed | 27 722 | 13 791 | 13 931 | 28 216 | 14 047 | 14 169 | 28 689 | 14 244 | 14 445 | 28 923 | 14 392 | 14 531 |
| Employment-population ratio | 77.5 | 87.4 | 69.6 | 77.9 | 87.8 | 70.1 | 78.6 | 88.4 | 70.9 | 79.0 | 89.0 | 71.1 |
| Full-time workers[1] | 23 783 | 13 074 | 10 709 | 4 035 | 686 | 3 349 | 3 943 | 650 | 3 292 | 3 850 | 607 | 3 243 |
| Part-time workers[2] | 3 939 | 717 | 3 222 | 78 | 88 | 70 | 79 | 88 | 71 | 79 | 89 | 71 |
| Unemployed | 1 851 | 754 | 1 097 | 1 599 | 667 | 933 | 1 300 | 524 | 775 | 1 134 | 448 | 687 |
| Unemployment rate | 6.3 | 5.2 | 7.3 | 5.4 | 4.5 | 6.2 | 4.3 | 3.6 | 5.1 | 3.8 | 3.0 | 4.5 |
| **With Own Children Under 6 Years** | | | | | | | | | | | | |
| Civilian noninstitutional population | 29 834 | 13 167 | 16 667 | 29 166 | 12 940 | 16 226 | 29 157 | 12 927 | 16 230 | 28 948 | 12 924 | 16 024 |
| Civilian labor force | 23 181 | 12 409 | 10 772 | 22 519 | 12 155 | 10 365 | 22 591 | 12 171 | 10 420 | 22 419 | 12 138 | 10 281 |
| Participation rate | 77.7 | 94.2 | 64.6 | 77.2 | 93.9 | 63.9 | 77.5 | 94.2 | 64.2 | 77.4 | 93.9 | 64.2 |
| Employed | 21 379 | 11 669 | 9 710 | 20 930 | 11 493 | 9 437 | 21 259 | 11 655 | 9 604 | 21 315 | 11 687 | 9 628 |
| Employment-population ratio | 71.7 | 88.6 | 58.3 | 77.2 | 93.9 | 63.9 | 72.9 | 90.2 | 59.2 | 73.6 | 90.4 | 60.1 |
| Full-time workers[1] | 17 915 | 10 981 | 6 934 | 3 267 | 647 | 2 620 | 3 278 | 634 | 2 644 | 3 139 | 592 | 2 547 |
| Part-time workers[2] | 3 464 | 688 | 2 776 | 72 | 89 | 58 | 73 | 90 | 59 | 74 | 90 | 60 |
| Unemployed | 1 802 | 740 | 1 062 | 1 589 | 662 | 928 | 1 332 | 516 | 816 | 1 104 | 451 | 652 |
| Unemployment rate | 7.8 | 6.0 | 9.9 | 7.1 | 5.4 | 8.9 | 5.9 | 4.2 | 7.8 | 4.9 | 3.7 | 6.3 |
| **With No Own Children Under 18 Years** | | | | | | | | | | | | |
| Civilian noninstitutional population | 177 665 | 88 400 | 89 264 | 180 295 | 89 609 | 90 686 | 182 304 | 90 707 | 91 596 | 185 237 | 92 006 | 93 231 |
| Civilian labor force | 102 221 | 55 373 | 46 848 | 103 055 | 55 798 | 47 256 | 103 342 | 55 943 | 47 399 | 104 654 | 56 643 | 48 011 |
| Participation rate | 57.5 | 62.6 | 52.5 | 57.2 | 62.3 | 52.1 | 56.7 | 61.7 | 51.7 | 56.5 | 61.6 | 51.5 |
| Employed | 93 368 | 50 096 | 43 272 | 94 783 | 50 813 | 43 971 | 96 357 | 51 793 | 44 564 | 98 595 | 53 052 | 45 544 |
| Employment-population ratio | 52.6 | 56.7 | 48.5 | 57.2 | 62.3 | 52.1 | 52.9 | 57.1 | 48.7 | 53.2 | 57.7 | 48.9 |
| Full-time workers[1] | 73 111 | 41 423 | 31 688 | 20 313 | 8 685 | 11 629 | 20 366 | 8 579 | 11 787 | 20 353 | 8 581 | 11 772 |
| Part-time workers[2] | 20 257 | 8 673 | 11 584 | 53 | 57 | 49 | 53 | 57 | 49 | 53 | 58 | 49 |
| Unemployed | 8 853 | 5 277 | 3 575 | 8 271 | 4 986 | 3 285 | 6 985 | 4 150 | 2 835 | 6 058 | 3 591 | 2 468 |
| Unemployment rate | 8.7 | 9.5 | 7.6 | 8.0 | 8.9 | 7.0 | 6.8 | 7.4 | 6.0 | 5.8 | 6.3 | 5.1 |

*Note:* Own children include sons, daughters, stepchildren, and adopted children. Not included are nieces, nephews, grandchildren, and other related and unrelated children. Detail may not sum to total due to rounding.

[1] Usually work 35 hours or more a week at all jobs.
[2] Usually work less than 35 hours a week at all jobs.
[3] Includes never-married, divorced, separated, and widowed persons.

## Table 1-24. Employment Status of Mothers with Own Children Under 3 Years of Age, by Age of Youngest Child and Marital Status, Annual Averages, 2006–2015

(Thousands of people, percent.)

| Year and characteristic | Civilian noninsti-tutional population | Civilian labor force | | | | | | Unemployed | |
|---|---|---|---|---|---|---|---|---|---|
| | | Total | Percent of population | Employed | | | | Number | Percent of labor force |
| | | | | Total | Percent of population | Full-time workers[1] | Part-time workers[2] | | |
| **2006** | | | | | | | | | |
| **Total Mothers with Own Children Under 3 Years** | 9 431 | 5 675 | 60.2 | 5 315 | 56.4 | 3 751 | 1 564 | 360 | 6.3 |
| 2 years | 2 864 | 1 847 | 64.5 | 1 746 | 61.0 | 1 280 | 466 | 101 | 5.5 |
| 1 year | 3 318 | 2 006 | 60.5 | 1 883 | 56.7 | 1 305 | 577 | 123 | 6.1 |
| Under 1 year | 3 248 | 1 822 | 56.1 | 1 686 | 51.9 | 1 166 | 520 | 136 | 7.4 |
| **Married, Spouse Present with Own Children Under 3 Years** | 6 998 | 4 076 | 58.2 | 3 933 | 56.2 | 2 756 | 1 177 | 143 | 3.5 |
| 2 years | 2 114 | 1 305 | 61.7 | 1 265 | 59.8 | 910 | 354 | 40 | 3.1 |
| 1 year | 2 494 | 1 456 | 58.4 | 1 404 | 56.3 | 962 | 442 | 52 | 3.6 |
| Under 1 year | 2 390 | 1 315 | 55.0 | 1 264 | 52.9 | 883 | 381 | 51 | 3.9 |
| **Other Marital Status with Own Children Under 3 Years**[3] | 2 433 | 1 600 | 65.7 | 1 382 | 56.8 | 996 | 386 | 217 | 13.6 |
| 2 years | 750 | 543 | 72.3 | 481 | 64.2 | 369 | 112 | 61 | 11.3 |
| 1 year | 824 | 550 | 66.7 | 479 | 58.1 | 344 | 135 | 71 | 13.0 |
| Under 1 year | 859 | 507 | 59.0 | 422 | 49.2 | 283 | 139 | 85 | 16.7 |
| **2007** | | | | | | | | | |
| **Total Mothers with Own Children Under 3 Years** | 9 659 | 5 721 | 59.2 | 5 354 | 55.4 | 3 783 | 1 571 | 367 | 6.4 |
| 2 years | 2 812 | 1 808 | 64.3 | 1 694 | 60.2 | 1 225 | 469 | 114 | 6.3 |
| 1 year | 3 501 | 2 068 | 59.1 | 1 938 | 55.4 | 1 350 | 589 | 130 | 6.3 |
| Under 1 year | 3 346 | 1 845 | 55.1 | 1 721 | 51.4 | 1 208 | 513 | 123 | 6.7 |
| **Married, Spouse Present with Own Children Under 3 Years** | 7 018 | 4 027 | 57.4 | 3 888 | 55.4 | 2 730 | 1 157 | 140 | 3.5 |
| 2 years | 2 076 | 1 281 | 61.7 | 1 230 | 59.2 | 881 | 349 | 51 | 4.0 |
| 1 year | 2 536 | 1 433 | 56.5 | 1 388 | 54.7 | 954 | 434 | 46 | 3.2 |
| Under 1 year | 2 406 | 1 313 | 54.6 | 1 270 | 52.8 | 896 | 374 | 43 | 3.3 |
| **Other Marital Status with Own Children Under 3 Years**[3] | 2 641 | 1 694 | 64.1 | 1 466 | 55.5 | 1 052 | 414 | 227 | 13.4 |
| 2 years | 736 | 528 | 71.6 | 464 | 63.1 | 344 | 120 | 63 | 12.0 |
| 1 year | 965 | 635 | 65.8 | 551 | 57.1 | 396 | 155 | 84 | 13.2 |
| Under 1 year | 940 | 531 | 56.5 | 451 | 48.0 | 312 | 139 | 80 | 15.1 |
| **2008** | | | | | | | | | |
| **Total Mothers with Own Children Under 3 Years** | 9 595 | 5 792 | 60.4 | 5 354 | 55.8 | 3 782 | 1 573 | 438 | 7.6 |
| 2 years | 2 934 | 1 852 | 63.1 | 1 734 | 59.1 | 1 264 | 470 | 118 | 6.4 |
| 1 year | 3 342 | 2 069 | 61.9 | 1 905 | 57.0 | 1 337 | 568 | 164 | 7.9 |
| Under 1 year | 3 319 | 1 871 | 56.4 | 1 715 | 51.7 | 1 180 | 535 | 156 | 8.4 |
| **Married, Spouse Present with Own Children Under 3 Years** | 6 868 | 4 035 | 58.7 | 3 848 | 56.0 | 2 717 | 1 132 | 186 | 4.6 |
| 2 years | 2 088 | 1 255 | 60.1 | 1 206 | 57.8 | 871 | 335 | 49 | 3.9 |
| 1 year | 2 414 | 1 450 | 60.1 | 1 380 | 57.2 | 970 | 410 | 70 | 4.8 |
| Under 1 year | 2 366 | 1 330 | 56.2 | 1 263 | 53.4 | 875 | 388 | 67 | 5.0 |
| **Other Marital Status with Own Children Under 3 Years**[3] | 2 727 | 1 758 | 64.4 | 1 506 | 55.2 | 1 065 | 441 | 252 | 14.3 |
| 2 years | 847 | 597 | 70.5 | 528 | 62.4 | 393 | 135 | 69 | 11.5 |
| 1 year | 928 | 619 | 66.7 | 525 | 56.6 | 367 | 159 | 94 | 15.1 |
| Under 1 year | 953 | 542 | 56.8 | 452 | 47.5 | 305 | 147 | 89 | 16.5 |
| **2009** | | | | | | | | | |
| **Total Mothers with Own Children Under 3 Years** | 9 476 | 5 787 | 61.1 | 5 191 | 54.8 | 3 626 | 1 565 | 595 | 10.3 |
| 2 years | 2 848 | 1 855 | 65.1 | 1 693 | 59.4 | 1 195 | 498 | 162 | 8.7 |
| 1 year | 3 398 | 2 104 | 61.9 | 1 880 | 55.3 | 1 314 | 566 | 224 | 10.6 |
| Under 1 year | 3 231 | 1 828 | 56.6 | 1 619 | 50.1 | 1 117 | 502 | 209 | 11.4 |
| **Married, Spouse Present with Own Children Under 3 Years** | 6 784 | 4 047 | 59.7 | 3 780 | 55.7 | 2 657 | 1 123 | 267 | 6.6 |
| 2 years | 2 053 | 1 288 | 62.7 | 1 208 | 58.8 | 858 | 350 | 80 | 6.2 |
| 1 year | 2 425 | 1 465 | 60.4 | 1 369 | 56.4 | 963 | 406 | 96 | 6.6 |
| Under 1 year | 2 306 | 1 293 | 56.1 | 1 204 | 52.2 | 836 | 368 | 90 | 7.0 |
| **Other Marital Status with Own Children Under 3 Years**[3] | 2 693 | 1 740 | 64.6 | 1 411 | 52.4 | 969 | 442 | 328 | 18.9 |
| 2 years | 795 | 567 | 71.3 | 485 | 61.0 | 337 | 148 | 82 | 14.4 |
| 1 year | 973 | 639 | 65.6 | 511 | 52.5 | 351 | 160 | 127 | 20.0 |
| Under 1 year | 925 | 534 | 57.8 | 415 | 44.9 | 281 | 134 | 119 | 22.3 |
| **2010** | | | | | | | | | |
| **Total Mothers with Own Children Under 3 Years** | 9 503 | 5 770 | 60.7 | 5 114 | 53.8 | 3 570 | 1 543 | 656 | 11.4 |
| 2 years | 2 968 | 1 908 | 64.3 | 1 708 | 57.5 | 1 200 | 509 | 199 | 10.5 |
| 1 year | 3 351 | 2 062 | 61.5 | 1 815 | 54.2 | 1 243 | 572 | 246 | 12.0 |
| Under 1 year | 3 184 | 1 800 | 56.5 | 1 590 | 49.9 | 1 128 | 462 | 210 | 11.7 |
| **Married, Spouse Present with Own Children Under 3 Years** | 6 642 | 3 941 | 59.3 | 3 670 | 55.3 | 2 596 | 1 074 | 271 | 6.9 |
| 2 years | 2 055 | 1 275 | 62.1 | 1 195 | 58.2 | 841 | 354 | 80 | 6.3 |
| 1 year | 2 344 | 1 403 | 59.8 | 1 301 | 55.5 | 896 | 405 | 101 | 7.2 |
| Under 1 year | 3 184 | 1 800 | 56.5 | 1 590 | 49.9 | 1 128 | 462 | 210 | 11.7 |
| **Other Marital Status with Own Children Under 3 Years**[3] | 2 862 | 1 828 | 63.9 | 1 444 | 50.5 | 974 | 470 | 385 | 21.0 |
| 2 years | 914 | 633 | 69.2 | 514 | 56.2 | 359 | 155 | 119 | 18.8 |
| 1 year | 1 007 | 659 | 65.5 | 514 | 51.0 | 346 | 168 | 145 | 22.0 |
| Under 1 year | 941 | 537 | 57.0 | 416 | 44.2 | 269 | 147 | 121 | 22.5 |

*Note:* Own children include sons, daughters, stepchildren, and adopted children. Not included are nieces, nephews, grandchildren, and other related and unrelated children. Detail may not sum to total due to rounding. Updated population controls are introduced annually with the release of January data.

[1]Usually work 35 hours or more a week at all jobs.
[2]Usually work less than 35 hours a week at all jobs.
[3]Includes never-married, divorced, separated, and widowed persons.

## Table 1-24. Employment Status of Mothers with Own Children Under 3 Years of Age, by Age of Youngest Child and Marital Status, Annual Averages, 2006–2015—*Continued*

(Thousands of people, percent.)

| Year and characteristic | Civilian noninsti-tutional population | Civilian labor force | | | | | | Unemployed | |
|---|---|---|---|---|---|---|---|---|---|
| | | Total | Percent of population | Employed | | | | Number | Percent of labor force |
| | | | | Total | Percent of population | Full-time workers[1] | Part-time workers[2] | | |
| **2011** | | | | | | | | | |
| Total Mothers with Own Children Under 3 Years | 9 259 | 5 613 | 60.6 | 4 977 | 53.8 | 3 486 | 1 492 | 635 | 11.3 |
| 2 years | 2 893 | 1 848 | 63.9 | 1 645 | 56.9 | 1 169 | 476 | 202 | 11.0 |
| 1 year | 3 353 | 2 083 | 62.1 | 1 844 | 55.0 | 1 296 | 548 | 239 | 11.5 |
| Under 1 year | 3 013 | 1 682 | 55.8 | 1 488 | 49.4 | 1 021 | 467 | 194 | 11.5 |
| Married, Spouse Present with Own Children Under 3 Years | 6 488 | 3 854 | 59.4 | 3 603 | 55.5 | 2 594 | 1 009 | 251 | 6.5 |
| 2 years | 1 999 | 1 220 | 61.0 | 1 138 | 56.9 | 822 | 316 | 82 | 6.7 |
| 1 year | 2 381 | 1 434 | 60.2 | 1 342 | 56.4 | 967 | 375 | 92 | 6.4 |
| Under 1 year | 2 109 | 1 200 | 56.9 | 1 123 | 53.3 | 805 | 318 | 77 | 6.4 |
| Other Marital Status with Own Children Under 3 Years[3] | 2 771 | 1 759 | 63.5 | 1 375 | 49.6 | 892 | 483 | 384 | 21.8 |
| 2 years | 894 | 628 | 70.3 | 508 | 56.8 | 347 | 161 | 120 | 19.2 |
| 1 year | 973 | 649 | 66.8 | 502 | 51.6 | 329 | 173 | 147 | 22.6 |
| Under 1 year | 905 | 482 | 53.2 | 365 | 40.3 | 216 | 149 | 117 | 24.2 |
| **2012** | | | | | | | | | |
| Total Mothers with Own Children Under 3 Years | 9 540 | 5 839 | 61.2 | 5 245 | 55.0 | 3 690 | 1 555 | 594 | 10.2 |
| 2 years | 2 922 | 1 890 | 64.7 | 1 708 | 58.5 | 1 215 | 493 | 181 | 9.6 |
| 1 year | 3 393 | 2 119 | 62.5 | 1 909 | 56.3 | 1 314 | 595 | 210 | 9.9 |
| Under 1 year | 3 224 | 1 830 | 56.7 | 1 628 | 50.5 | 1 161 | 467 | 202 | 11.0 |
| Married, Spouse Present with Own Children Under 3 Years | 6 334 | 3 808 | 60.1 | 3 600 | 56.8 | 2 595 | 1 005 | 208 | 5.5 |
| 2 years | 1 940 | 1 198 | 61.8 | 1 134 | 58.5 | 816 | 318 | 64 | 5.4 |
| 1 year | 2 288 | 1 409 | 61.6 | 1 332 | 58.2 | 928 | 405 | 77 | 5.5 |
| Under 1 year | 2 106 | 1 200 | 57.0 | 1 134 | 53.8 | 852 | 282 | 66 | 5.5 |
| Other Marital Status with Own Children Under 3 Years[3] | 3 206 | 2 031 | 63.4 | 1 645 | 51.3 | 1 095 | 550 | 386 | 19.0 |
| 2 years | 982 | 691 | 70.4 | 574 | 58.5 | 399 | 175 | 117 | 17.0 |
| 1 year | 1 105 | 710 | 64.2 | 577 | 52.2 | 386 | 191 | 133 | 18.8 |
| Under 1 year | 1 119 | 630 | 56.3 | 494 | 44.2 | 309 | 185 | 136 | 21.6 |
| **2013** | | | | | | | | | |
| Total Mothers with Own Children Under 3 Years | 9 211 | 5 626 | 61.1 | 5 113 | 55.5 | 3 615 | 1 497 | 514 | 9.1 |
| 2 years | 2 877 | 1 875 | 65.2 | 1 723 | 59.9 | 1 240 | 482 | 152 | 8.1 |
| 1 year | 3 266 | 1 995 | 61.1 | 1 798 | 55.0 | 1 251 | 547 | 197 | 9.9 |
| Under 1 year | 3 069 | 1 757 | 57.3 | 1 593 | 51.9 | 1 124 | 469 | 164 | 9.3 |
| Married, Spouse Present with Own Children Under 3 Years | 6 224 | 3 689 | 59.3 | 3 503 | 56.3 | 2 541 | 962 | 186 | 5.0 |
| 2 years | 1 913 | 1 194 | 62.4 | 1 141 | 59.6 | 835 | 305 | 54 | 4.5 |
| 1 year | 2 232 | 1 299 | 58.2 | 1 224 | 54.9 | 867 | 357 | 75 | 5.8 |
| Under 1 year | 2 080 | 1 196 | 57.5 | 1 138 | 54.7 | 839 | 299 | 58 | 4.8 |
| Other Marital Status with Own Children Under 3 Years[3] | 2 987 | 1 937 | 64.9 | 1 610 | 53.9 | 1 075 | 535 | 327 | 16.9 |
| 2 years | 964 | 681 | 70.6 | 582 | 60.3 | 405 | 177 | 99 | 14.5 |
| 1 year | 1 034 | 695 | 67.3 | 573 | 55.5 | 384 | 189 | 122 | 17.5 |
| Under 1 year | 989 | 561 | 56.7 | 455 | 46.0 | 285 | 169 | 107 | 19.0 |
| **2014** | | | | | | | | | |
| Total Mothers with Own Children Under 3 Years | 9 224 | 5 624 | 61.0 | 5 169 | 56.0 | 3 685 | 1 484 | 456 | 8.1 |
| 2 years | 2 834 | 1 799 | 63.5 | 1 661 | 58.6 | 1 185 | 477 | 137 | 7.6 |
| 1 year | 3 293 | 2 056 | 62.4 | 1 880 | 57.1 | 1 325 | 555 | 176 | 8.6 |
| Under 1 year | 3 097 | 1 770 | 57.1 | 1 628 | 52.6 | 1 175 | 453 | 142 | 8.0 |
| Married, Spouse Present with Own Children Under 3 Years | 6 243 | 3 691 | 59.1 | 3 526 | 56.5 | 2 602 | 925 | 165 | 4.5 |
| 2 years | 1 934 | 1 153 | 59.6 | 1 104 | 57.1 | 807 | 296 | 49 | 4.3 |
| 1 year | 2 300 | 1 376 | 59.8 | 1 307 | 56.8 | 950 | 357 | 68 | 5.0 |
| Under 1 year | 2 009 | 1 163 | 57.9 | 1 116 | 55.5 | 844 | 271 | 47 | 4.1 |
| Other Marital Status with Own Children Under 3 Years[3] | 2 981 | 1 933 | 64.9 | 1 642 | 55.1 | 1 083 | 559 | 291 | 15.0 |
| 2 years | 900 | 646 | 71.8 | 558 | 62.0 | 377 | 180 | 88 | 13.6 |
| 1 year | 993 | 681 | 68.6 | 573 | 57.7 | 375 | 197 | 108 | 15.8 |
| Under 1 year | 1 088 | 607 | 55.8 | 512 | 47.0 | 330 | 182 | 95 | 15.6 |
| **2015** | | | | | | | | | |
| Total Mothers with Own Children Under 3 Years | 9 308 | 5 714 | 61.4 | 5 336 | 57.3 | 3 882 | 1 455 | 377 | 6.6 |
| 2 years | 2 920 | 1 869 | 64.0 | 1 741 | 59.6 | 1 280 | 462 | 127 | 6.8 |
| 1 year | 3 254 | 2 024 | 62.2 | 1 897 | 58.3 | 1 370 | 526 | 128 | 6.3 |
| Under 1 year | 3 134 | 1 821 | 58.1 | 1 698 | 54.2 | 1 232 | 466 | 123 | 6.7 |
| Married, Spouse Present with Own Children Under 3 Years | 6 341 | 3 772 | 59.5 | 3 628 | 57.2 | 2 698 | 931 | 144 | 3.8 |
| 2 years | 1 974 | 1 198 | 60.7 | 1 149 | 58.2 | 864 | 285 | 49 | 4.1 |
| 1 year | 2 252 | 1 356 | 60.2 | 1 300 | 57.7 | 961 | 339 | 55 | 4.1 |
| Under 1 year | 2 114 | 1 218 | 57.6 | 1 179 | 55.8 | 873 | 306 | 39 | 3.2 |
| Other Marital Status with Own Children Under 3 Years[3] | 2 967 | 1 942 | 65.4 | 1 708 | 57.6 | 1 184 | 524 | 234 | 12.0 |
| 2 years | 946 | 670 | 70.9 | 592 | 62.6 | 415 | 177 | 78 | 11.6 |
| 1 year | 1 001 | 669 | 66.8 | 596 | 59.5 | 409 | 187 | 72 | 10.8 |
| Under 1 year | 1 020 | 603 | 59.1 | 519 | 50.9 | 359 | 160 | 84 | 13.9 |

*Note:* Own children include sons, daughters, stepchildren, and adopted children. Not included are nieces, nephews, grandchildren, and other related and unrelated children. Detail may not sum to total due to rounding. Updated population controls are introduced annually with the release of January data.

[1]Usually work 35 hours or more a week at all jobs.
[2]Usually work less than 35 hours a week at all jobs.
[3]Includes never-married, divorced, separated, and widowed persons.

## UNEMPLOYMENT

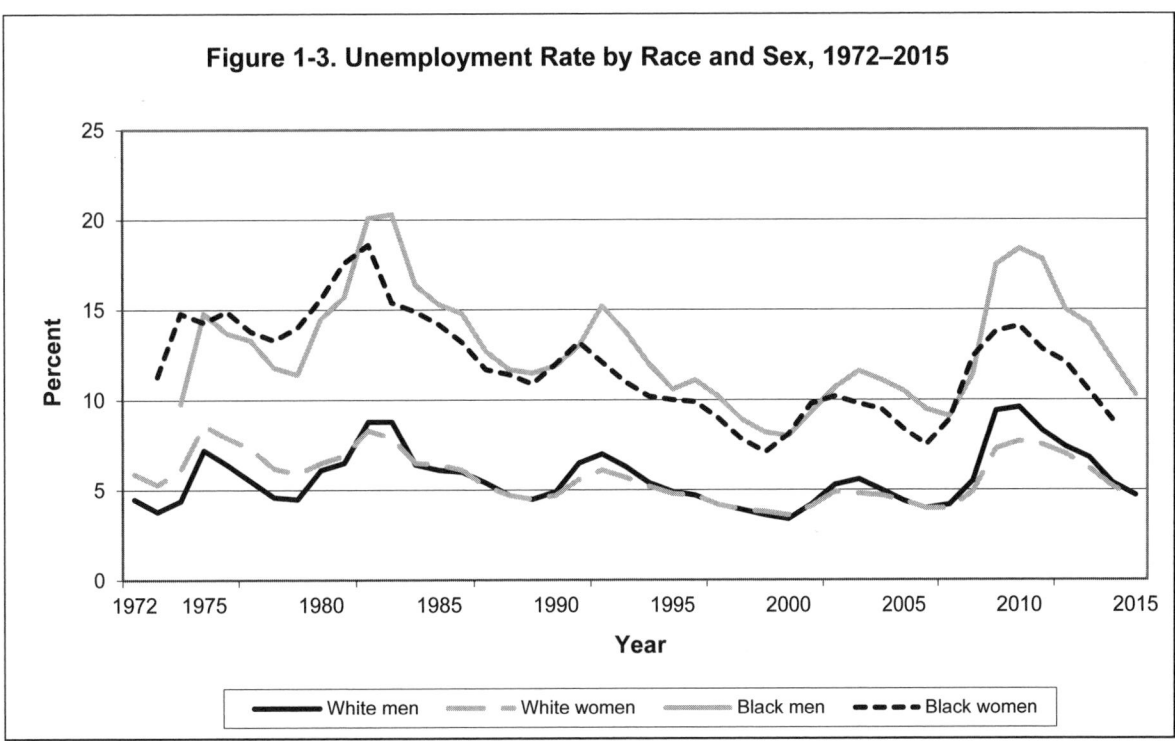

The unemployment rate declined for the fifth consecutive year in 2015 from 6.2 percent in 2014 to 5.3 percent in 2015. Although the unemployment rate continued to be higher for men (5.4 percent) than for women (5.2 percent), the gap was closing. In 2010, men had an unemployment rate of 10.5 percent compared with an unemployment rate of 8.6 percent for women. In 2015, Black men had the highest unemployment rate at 10.3 percent followed by Black women with an unemployment rate of 8.9 percent. From 2014 to 2015, the unemployment rate decreased by 1.7 percent for both Blacks and 0.7 percent for Whites. (See Table 1-27.)

## OTHER HIGHLIGHTS

- While the unemployment rate decreased for every age group again in 2015, the disparity in unemployment rates among age groups continued to be substantial as younger workers experienced much higher levels of unemployment. In 2015, the unemployment rate for those age 16 to 19 years was 16.9 percent, while it was only 3.7 percent for those age 45 to 54 years and 3.8 percent for those 55 years and over. (See Table 1-27.)

- Among the major industries, agriculture and private wage salary workers continued to have the highest unemployment rate at 9.4 percent, followed by and leisure and hospitality workers (7.9 percent). Government had the lowest unemployment rate at 2.7 percent. (See Table 1-29.)

- The number of persons unemployed 27 weeks and over declined again in 2015 to 2.3 million. Although this was a 64 percent decline from 2010, it was still much higher than the number of unemployed people in 2007 (1.2 million). (See Table 1-31.)

- In 2015, unemployment declined in 47 states and the District of Columbia. It increased in two states (West Virginia and Wyoming) and remained unchanged in one state (North Dakota). (See Table 1-5.)

## Table 1-25.  Unemployment Rate, by Selected Characteristics, 1948–2015

(Unemployment as a percent of civilian labor force.)

| Year | All civilian workers | Both sexes, 16 to 19 years | Men, 20 years and over | Women, 20 years and over | White[1] | Black[1] | Asian[1] | Hispanic[2] | Men Single, never married | Men Married, spouse present | Men Widowed, divorced, or separated | Women Single, never married | Women Married, spouse present | Women Widowed, divorced, or separated |
|---|---|---|---|---|---|---|---|---|---|---|---|---|---|---|
| 1948 | 3.8 | 9.2 | 3.2 | 3.6 | ... | ... | ... | ... | ... | ... | ... | ... | ... | ... |
| 1949 | 5.9 | 13.4 | 5.4 | 5.3 | ... | ... | ... | ... | ... | ... | ... | ... | ... | ... |
| 1950 | 5.3 | 12.2 | 4.7 | 5.1 | ... | ... | ... | ... | ... | ... | ... | ... | ... | ... |
| 1951 | 3.3 | 8.2 | 2.5 | 4.0 | ... | ... | ... | ... | ... | ... | ... | ... | ... | ... |
| 1952 | 3.0 | 8.5 | 2.4 | 3.2 | ... | ... | ... | ... | ... | ... | ... | ... | ... | ... |
| 1953 | 2.9 | 7.6 | 2.5 | 2.9 | ... | ... | ... | ... | ... | ... | ... | ... | ... | ... |
| 1954 | 5.5 | 12.6 | 4.9 | 5.5 | 5.0 | ... | ... | ... | ... | ... | ... | ... | ... | ... |
| 1955 | 4.4 | 11.0 | 3.8 | 4.4 | 3.9 | ... | ... | ... | 8.6 | 2.6 | 7.1 | 5.0 | 3.7 | ... |
| 1956 | 4.1 | 11.1 | 3.4 | 4.2 | 3.6 | ... | ... | ... | 7.7 | 2.3 | 6.2 | 5.3 | 3.6 | ... |
| 1957 | 4.3 | 11.6 | 3.6 | 4.1 | 3.8 | ... | ... | ... | 9.2 | 2.8 | 6.8 | 5.6 | 4.3 | 4.7 |
| 1958 | 6.8 | 15.9 | 6.2 | 6.1 | 6.1 | ... | ... | ... | 13.3 | 5.1 | 11.2 | 7.4 | 6.5 | 6.7 |
| 1959 | 5.5 | 14.6 | 4.7 | 5.2 | 4.8 | ... | ... | ... | 11.6 | 3.6 | 8.6 | 7.1 | 5.2 | 6.2 |
| 1960 | 5.5 | 14.7 | 4.7 | 5.1 | 5.0 | ... | ... | ... | 11.7 | 3.7 | 8.4 | 7.5 | 5.2 | 5.9 |
| 1961 | 6.7 | 16.8 | 5.7 | 6.3 | 6.0 | ... | ... | ... | 13.1 | 4.6 | 10.3 | 8.7 | 6.4 | 7.4 |
| 1962 | 5.5 | 14.7 | 4.6 | 5.4 | 4.9 | ... | ... | ... | 11.2 | 3.6 | 9.9 | 7.9 | 5.4 | 6.4 |
| 1963 | 5.7 | 17.2 | 4.5 | 5.4 | 5.0 | ... | ... | ... | 12.4 | 3.4 | 9.6 | 8.9 | 5.4 | 6.7 |
| 1964 | 5.2 | 16.2 | 3.9 | 5.2 | 4.6 | ... | ... | ... | 11.5 | 2.8 | 8.9 | 8.7 | 5.1 | 6.4 |
| 1965 | 4.5 | 14.8 | 3.2 | 4.5 | 4.1 | ... | ... | ... | 10.1 | 2.4 | 7.2 | 8.2 | 4.5 | 5.4 |
| 1966 | 3.8 | 12.8 | 2.5 | 3.8 | 3.4 | ... | ... | ... | 8.6 | 1.9 | 5.5 | 7.9 | 3.7 | 4.7 |
| 1967 | 3.8 | 12.9 | 2.3 | 4.2 | 3.4 | ... | ... | ... | 8.3 | 1.8 | 4.9 | 7.5 | 4.5 | 4.6 |
| 1968 | 3.6 | 12.7 | 2.2 | 3.8 | 3.2 | ... | ... | ... | 8.0 | 1.6 | 4.2 | 7.6 | 3.9 | 4.2 |
| 1969 | 3.5 | 12.2 | 2.1 | 3.7 | 3.1 | ... | ... | ... | 8.0 | 1.5 | 4.0 | 7.3 | 3.9 | 4.0 |
| 1970 | 4.9 | 15.3 | 3.5 | 4.8 | 4.5 | ... | ... | ... | 11.2 | 2.6 | 6.4 | 9.0 | 4.9 | 5.2 |
| 1971 | 5.9 | 16.9 | 4.4 | 5.7 | 5.4 | ... | ... | ... | 13.2 | 3.2 | 7.4 | 10.5 | 5.7 | 6.3 |
| 1972 | 5.6 | 16.2 | 4.0 | 5.4 | 5.1 | 10.4 | ... | ... | 12.4 | 2.8 | 7.0 | 10.1 | 5.4 | 6.1 |
| 1973 | 4.9 | 14.5 | 3.3 | 4.9 | 4.3 | 9.4 | ... | 7.5 | 10.4 | 2.3 | 5.4 | 9.4 | 4.7 | 5.8 |
| 1974 | 5.6 | 16.0 | 3.8 | 5.5 | 5.0 | 10.5 | ... | 8.1 | 11.8 | 2.7 | 6.2 | 10.5 | 5.3 | 6.3 |
| 1975 | 8.5 | 19.9 | 6.8 | 8.0 | 7.8 | 14.8 | ... | 12.2 | 16.1 | 5.1 | 11.0 | 13.0 | 7.9 | 8.9 |
| 1976 | 7.7 | 19.0 | 5.9 | 7.4 | 7.0 | 14.0 | ... | 11.5 | 14.9 | 4.2 | 9.8 | 12.1 | 7.1 | 8.7 |
| 1977 | 7.1 | 17.8 | 5.2 | 7.0 | 6.2 | 14.0 | ... | 10.1 | 13.5 | 3.6 | 8.2 | 12.1 | 6.5 | 7.9 |
| 1978 | 6.1 | 16.4 | 4.3 | 6.0 | 5.2 | 12.8 | ... | 9.1 | 11.7 | 2.8 | 6.6 | 10.9 | 5.5 | 6.9 |
| 1979 | 5.8 | 16.1 | 4.2 | 5.7 | 5.1 | 12.3 | ... | 8.3 | 11.1 | 2.8 | 6.5 | 10.4 | 5.1 | 6.7 |
| 1980 | 7.1 | 17.8 | 5.9 | 6.4 | 6.3 | 14.3 | ... | 10.1 | 13.6 | 4.2 | 8.6 | 10.9 | 5.8 | 7.2 |
| 1981 | 7.6 | 19.6 | 6.3 | 6.8 | 6.7 | 15.6 | ... | 10.4 | 14.6 | 4.3 | 9.1 | 11.9 | 6.0 | 8.1 |
| 1982 | 9.7 | 23.2 | 8.8 | 8.3 | 8.6 | 18.9 | ... | 13.8 | 17.7 | 6.5 | 12.4 | 13.6 | 7.4 | 9.5 |
| 1983 | 9.6 | 22.4 | 8.9 | 8.1 | 8.4 | 19.5 | ... | 13.7 | 17.3 | 6.5 | 13.0 | 13.1 | 7.0 | 9.9 |
| 1984 | 7.5 | 18.9 | 6.6 | 6.8 | 6.5 | 15.9 | ... | 10.7 | 13.5 | 4.6 | 9.4 | 11.1 | 5.7 | 8.4 |
| 1985 | 7.2 | 18.6 | 6.2 | 6.6 | 6.2 | 15.1 | ... | 10.5 | 12.7 | 4.3 | 9.2 | 10.7 | 5.6 | 8.3 |
| 1986 | 7.0 | 18.3 | 6.1 | 6.2 | 6.0 | 14.5 | ... | 10.6 | 12.2 | 4.4 | 8.8 | 10.7 | 5.2 | 7.7 |
| 1987 | 6.2 | 16.9 | 5.4 | 5.4 | 5.3 | 13.0 | ... | 8.8 | 11.1 | 3.9 | 7.6 | 9.5 | 4.3 | 7.0 |
| 1988 | 5.5 | 15.3 | 4.8 | 4.9 | 4.7 | 11.7 | ... | 8.2 | 9.9 | 3.3 | 7.0 | 8.6 | 3.9 | 6.3 |
| 1989 | 5.3 | 15.0 | 4.5 | 4.7 | 4.5 | 11.4 | ... | 8.0 | 9.6 | 3.0 | 6.3 | 8.4 | 3.7 | 5.9 |
| 1990 | 5.6 | 15.5 | 5.0 | 4.9 | 4.8 | 11.4 | ... | 8.2 | 10.1 | 3.4 | 6.9 | 8.7 | 3.8 | 6.0 |
| 1991 | 6.8 | 18.7 | 6.4 | 5.7 | 6.1 | 12.5 | ... | 10.0 | 12.4 | 4.4 | 9.0 | 10.1 | 4.5 | 6.9 |
| 1992 | 7.5 | 20.1 | 7.1 | 6.3 | 6.6 | 14.2 | ... | 11.6 | 13.2 | 5.1 | 9.8 | 10.8 | 5.0 | 7.6 |
| 1993 | 6.9 | 19.0 | 6.4 | 5.9 | 6.1 | 13.0 | ... | 10.8 | 12.4 | 4.4 | 9.0 | 10.3 | 4.6 | 7.3 |
| 1994 | 6.1 | 17.6 | 5.4 | 5.4 | 5.3 | 11.5 | ... | 9.9 | 11.0 | 3.7 | 7.4 | 9.7 | 4.1 | 6.6 |
| 1995 | 5.6 | 17.3 | 4.8 | 4.9 | 4.9 | 10.4 | ... | 9.3 | 10.1 | 3.3 | 6.9 | 9.1 | 3.9 | 5.9 |
| 1996 | 5.4 | 16.7 | 4.6 | 4.8 | 4.7 | 10.5 | ... | 8.9 | 10.0 | 3.0 | 6.5 | 9.1 | 3.6 | 5.7 |
| 1997 | 4.9 | 16.0 | 4.2 | 4.4 | 4.2 | 10.0 | ... | 7.7 | 9.2 | 2.7 | 5.8 | 8.8 | 3.1 | 5.2 |
| 1998 | 4.5 | 14.6 | 3.7 | 4.1 | 3.9 | 8.9 | ... | 7.2 | 8.5 | 2.4 | 4.8 | 7.8 | 2.9 | 4.9 |
| 1999 | 4.2 | 13.9 | 3.5 | 3.8 | 3.7 | 8.0 | ... | 6.4 | 7.8 | 2.2 | 4.6 | 7.4 | 2.7 | 4.5 |
| 2000 | 4.0 | 13.1 | 3.3 | 3.6 | 3.5 | 7.6 | 3.6 | 5.7 | 7.6 | 2.0 | 4.3 | 6.8 | 2.7 | 4.2 |
| 2001 | 4.7 | 14.7 | 4.2 | 4.1 | 4.2 | 8.6 | 4.5 | 6.6 | 8.9 | 2.7 | 5.1 | 7.7 | 3.1 | 4.7 |
| 2002 | 5.8 | 16.5 | 5.3 | 5.1 | 5.1 | 10.2 | 5.9 | 7.5 | 10.3 | 3.6 | 6.8 | 8.9 | 3.7 | 6.1 |
| 2003 | 6.0 | 17.5 | 5.6 | 5.1 | 5.2 | 10.8 | 6.0 | 7.7 | 11.0 | 3.8 | 7.3 | 9.1 | 3.7 | 6.1 |
| 2004 | 5.5 | 17.0 | 5.0 | 4.9 | 4.8 | 10.4 | 4.4 | 7.0 | 10.5 | 3.1 | 6.3 | 8.7 | 3.5 | 5.9 |
| 2005 | 5.1 | 16.6 | 4.4 | 4.6 | 4.4 | 10.0 | 4.0 | 6.0 | 9.5 | 2.8 | 5.6 | 8.3 | 3.3 | 5.4 |
| 2006 | 4.6 | 15.4 | 4.0 | 4.1 | 4.0 | 8.9 | 3.0 | 5.2 | 8.6 | 2.4 | 5.2 | 7.7 | 2.9 | 4.9 |
| 2007 | 4.6 | 15.7 | 4.1 | 4.0 | 4.1 | 8.3 | 3.2 | 5.6 | 8.8 | 2.5 | 5.3 | 7.2 | 2.8 | 5.0 |
| 2008 | 5.8 | 18.7 | 5.4 | 4.9 | 5.2 | 10.1 | 4.0 | 7.6 | 11.0 | 3.4 | 7.1 | 8.5 | 3.6 | 5.9 |
| 2009 | 9.3 | 24.3 | 9.6 | 7.5 | 8.5 | 14.8 | 7.3 | 12.1 | 16.3 | 6.6 | 12.8 | 12.0 | 5.5 | 9.2 |
| 2010 | 9.6 | 25.9 | 9.8 | 8.0 | 8.7 | 16.0 | 7.5 | 12.5 | 16.5 | 6.8 | 12.8 | 12.8 | 5.9 | 9.6 |
| 2011 | 8.9 | 24.4 | 8.7 | 7.9 | 7.9 | 15.8 | 7.0 | 11.5 | 15.1 | 5.8 | 11.1 | 12.5 | 5.6 | 9.7 |
| 2012 | 8.1 | 24.0 | 7.5 | 7.3 | 7.2 | 13.8 | 5.9 | 10.3 | 13.7 | 4.9 | 9.4 | 11.8 | 5.3 | 8.7 |
| 2013 | 7.4 | 22.9 | 7.0 | 6.5 | 6.5 | 13.1 | 5.2 | 9.1 | 13.0 | 4.3 | 8.7 | 10.8 | 4.6 | 7.7 |
| 2014 | 6.2 | 19.6 | 5.7 | 5.6 | 5.3 | 11.3 | 5.0 | 7.4 | 11.0 | 3.4 | 6.9 | 9.4 | 3.8 | 6.6 |
| 2015 | 5.3 | 16.9 | 4.9 | 4.8 | 4.6 | 9.6 | 3.8 | 6.6 | 9.5 | 2.8 | 6.1 | 8.2 | 3.1 | 5.5 |

*Note:* See notes and definitions for information on historical comparability.

[1]Beginning in 2003, persons who selected this race group only; persons who selected more than one race group are not included. Prior to 2003, persons who reported more than one race group were included in the group they identified as their main race.
[2]May be of any race.
. . . = Not available.

## Table 1-26. Unemployed Persons, by Age, Sex, Race, and Hispanic Origin, 1948–2015

(Thousands of people.)

| Race, Hispanic origin, sex, and year | 16 years and over | 16 to 19 years | | | 20 years and over | | | | | | |
|---|---|---|---|---|---|---|---|---|---|---|---|
| | | Total | 16 to 17 years | 18 to 19 years | Total | 20 to 24 years | 25 to 34 years | 35 to 44 years | 45 to 54 years | 55 to 64 years | 65 years and over |
| **ALL RACES** | | | | | | | | | | | |
| **Both Sexes** | | | | | | | | | | | |
| 1948 | 2 276 | 409 | 180 | 228 | 1 869 | 455 | 457 | 347 | 290 | 226 | 93 |
| 1949 | 3 637 | 576 | 238 | 337 | 3 060 | 680 | 776 | 603 | 471 | 384 | 146 |
| 1950 | 3 288 | 513 | 226 | 287 | 2 776 | 561 | 702 | 530 | 478 | 368 | 137 |
| 1951 | 2 055 | 336 | 168 | 168 | 1 718 | 273 | 435 | 354 | 318 | 238 | 103 |
| 1952 | 1 883 | 345 | 180 | 165 | 1 539 | 268 | 389 | 325 | 274 | 195 | 86 |
| 1953 | 1 834 | 307 | 150 | 157 | 1 529 | 256 | 379 | 325 | 280 | 218 | 70 |
| 1954 | 3 532 | 501 | 221 | 247 | 3 032 | 504 | 793 | 680 | 548 | 374 | 132 |
| 1955 | 2 852 | 450 | 211 | 239 | 2 403 | 396 | 577 | 521 | 436 | 355 | 120 |
| 1956 | 2 750 | 478 | 231 | 247 | 2 274 | 395 | 554 | 476 | 429 | 311 | 109 |
| 1957 | 2 859 | 497 | 230 | 266 | 2 362 | 430 | 573 | 499 | 448 | 300 | 111 |
| 1958 | 4 602 | 678 | 299 | 379 | 3 923 | 701 | 993 | 871 | 731 | 472 | 154 |
| 1959 | 3 740 | 654 | 301 | 354 | 3 085 | 543 | 726 | 673 | 603 | 405 | 135 |
| 1960 | 3 852 | 712 | 325 | 387 | 3 140 | 583 | 752 | 671 | 614 | 396 | 122 |
| 1961 | 4 714 | 828 | 363 | 465 | 3 886 | 723 | 890 | 850 | 751 | 516 | 159 |
| 1962 | 3 911 | 721 | 312 | 409 | 3 191 | 636 | 712 | 688 | 605 | 411 | 141 |
| 1963 | 4 070 | 884 | 420 | 462 | 3 187 | 658 | 732 | 674 | 589 | 410 | 126 |
| 1964 | 3 786 | 872 | 436 | 437 | 2 913 | 660 | 607 | 605 | 543 | 378 | 117 |
| 1965 | 3 366 | 874 | 411 | 463 | 2 491 | 557 | 529 | 546 | 436 | 322 | 103 |
| 1966 | 2 875 | 837 | 395 | 441 | 2 041 | 446 | 441 | 426 | 369 | 265 | 92 |
| 1967 | 2 975 | 839 | 400 | 438 | 2 140 | 511 | 480 | 422 | 383 | 256 | 86 |
| 1968 | 2 817 | 838 | 414 | 426 | 1 978 | 543 | 443 | 371 | 314 | 219 | 88 |
| 1969 | 2 832 | 853 | 436 | 416 | 1 978 | 560 | 453 | 358 | 320 | 216 | 72 |
| 1970 | 4 093 | 1 106 | 537 | 569 | 2 987 | 866 | 718 | 515 | 476 | 309 | 104 |
| 1971 | 5 016 | 1 262 | 596 | 665 | 3 755 | 1 130 | 933 | 630 | 573 | 381 | 109 |
| 1972 | 4 882 | 1 308 | 633 | 676 | 3 573 | 1 132 | 878 | 576 | 510 | 368 | 111 |
| 1973 | 4 365 | 1 235 | 634 | 600 | 3 130 | 1 008 | 866 | 451 | 430 | 290 | 88 |
| 1974 | 5 156 | 1 422 | 699 | 722 | 3 733 | 1 212 | 1 044 | 559 | 498 | 321 | 99 |
| 1975 | 7 929 | 1 767 | 799 | 968 | 6 161 | 1 865 | 1 776 | 951 | 893 | 520 | 155 |
| 1976 | 7 406 | 1 719 | 796 | 924 | 5 687 | 1 714 | 1 710 | 849 | 758 | 510 | 147 |
| 1977 | 6 991 | 1 663 | 781 | 881 | 5 330 | 1 629 | 1 650 | 785 | 666 | 450 | 147 |
| 1978 | 6 202 | 1 583 | 796 | 787 | 4 620 | 1 483 | 1 422 | 694 | 552 | 345 | 123 |
| 1979 | 6 137 | 1 555 | 739 | 816 | 4 583 | 1 442 | 1 446 | 705 | 540 | 346 | 104 |
| 1980 | 7 637 | 1 669 | 778 | 890 | 5 969 | 1 835 | 2 024 | 940 | 676 | 399 | 94 |
| 1981 | 8 273 | 1 763 | 781 | 981 | 6 510 | 1 976 | 2 211 | 1 065 | 715 | 444 | 98 |
| 1982 | 10 678 | 1 977 | 831 | 1 145 | 8 701 | 2 392 | 3 037 | 1 552 | 966 | 647 | 107 |
| 1983 | 10 717 | 1 829 | 753 | 1 076 | 8 888 | 2 330 | 3 078 | 1 650 | 1 039 | 677 | 114 |
| 1984 | 8 539 | 1 499 | 646 | 854 | 7 039 | 1 838 | 2 374 | 1 335 | 828 | 566 | 97 |
| 1985 | 8 312 | 1 468 | 662 | 806 | 6 844 | 1 738 | 2 341 | 1 340 | 813 | 518 | 93 |
| 1986 | 8 237 | 1 454 | 665 | 789 | 6 783 | 1 651 | 2 390 | 1 371 | 790 | 489 | 91 |
| 1987 | 7 425 | 1 347 | 648 | 700 | 6 077 | 1 453 | 2 129 | 1 281 | 723 | 412 | 78 |
| 1988 | 6 701 | 1 226 | 573 | 653 | 5 475 | 1 261 | 1 929 | 1 166 | 657 | 375 | 87 |
| 1989 | 6 528 | 1 194 | 537 | 657 | 5 333 | 1 218 | 1 851 | 1 159 | 637 | 379 | 91 |
| 1990 | 7 047 | 1 212 | 527 | 685 | 5 835 | 1 299 | 1 995 | 1 328 | 723 | 386 | 105 |
| 1991 | 8 628 | 1 359 | 587 | 772 | 7 269 | 1 573 | 2 447 | 1 719 | 946 | 473 | 113 |
| 1992 | 9 613 | 1 427 | 641 | 787 | 8 186 | 1 649 | 2 702 | 1 976 | 1 138 | 589 | 132 |
| 1993 | 8 940 | 1 365 | 606 | 759 | 7 575 | 1 514 | 2 395 | 1 896 | 1 121 | 541 | 108 |
| 1994 | 7 996 | 1 320 | 624 | 696 | 6 676 | 1 373 | 2 067 | 1 627 | 971 | 485 | 153 |
| 1995 | 7 404 | 1 346 | 652 | 695 | 6 058 | 1 244 | 1 841 | 1 549 | 844 | 425 | 153 |
| 1996 | 7 236 | 1 306 | 617 | 689 | 5 929 | 1 239 | 1 757 | 1 505 | 883 | 406 | 139 |
| 1997 | 6 739 | 1 271 | 589 | 683 | 5 467 | 1 152 | 1 571 | 1 418 | 830 | 369 | 127 |
| 1998 | 6 210 | 1 205 | 573 | 632 | 5 005 | 1 081 | 1 419 | 1 258 | 782 | 343 | 122 |
| 1999 | 5 880 | 1 162 | 544 | 618 | 4 718 | 1 042 | 1 278 | 1 154 | 753 | 367 | 124 |
| 2000 | 5 692 | 1 081 | 502 | 579 | 4 611 | 1 022 | 1 207 | 1 133 | 762 | 355 | 132 |
| 2001 | 6 801 | 1 162 | 531 | 632 | 5 638 | 1 209 | 1 498 | 1 355 | 989 | 458 | 129 |
| 2002 | 8 378 | 1 253 | 540 | 714 | 7 124 | 1 430 | 1 890 | 1 691 | 1 315 | 635 | 163 |
| 2003 | 8 774 | 1 251 | 545 | 706 | 7 523 | 1 495 | 1 960 | 1 815 | 1 356 | 713 | 183 |
| 2004 | 8 149 | 1 208 | 554 | 653 | 6 942 | 1 431 | 1 784 | 1 578 | 1 288 | 682 | 179 |
| 2005 | 7 591 | 1 186 | 541 | 645 | 6 405 | 1 335 | 1 661 | 1 400 | 1 195 | 630 | 184 |
| 2006 | 7 001 | 1 119 | 509 | 610 | 5 882 | 1 234 | 1 521 | 1 279 | 1 094 | 595 | 159 |
| 2007 | 7 078 | 1 101 | 485 | 616 | 5 976 | 1 241 | 1 544 | 1 225 | 1 135 | 642 | 190 |
| 2008 | 8 924 | 1 285 | 563 | 722 | 7 639 | 1 545 | 1 949 | 1 604 | 1 473 | 803 | 264 |
| 2009 | 14 265 | 1 552 | 576 | 976 | 12 712 | 2 207 | 3 284 | 2 722 | 2 592 | 1 487 | 421 |
| 2010 | 14 825 | 1 528 | 582 | 945 | 13 297 | 2 329 | 3 386 | 2 703 | 2 769 | 1 660 | 449 |
| 2011 | 13 747 | 1 400 | 519 | 881 | 12 348 | 2 234 | 3 187 | 2 389 | 2 493 | 1 579 | 465 |
| 2012 | 12 506 | 1 397 | 533 | 863 | 11 109 | 2 054 | 2 764 | 2 158 | 2 181 | 1 470 | 482 |
| 2013 | 11 460 | 1 327 | 536 | 791 | 10 133 | 1 997 | 2 504 | 1 913 | 1 945 | 1 340 | 435 |
| 2014 | 9 617 | 680 | 426 | 1 106 | 8 511 | 1 747 | 2 224 | 1 539 | 1 507 | 1 107 | 387 |
| 2015 | 8 296 | 966 | 363 | 603 | 7 330 | 1 501 | 1 905 | 1 351 | 1 259 | 978 | 337 |

## Table 1-26. Unemployed Persons, by Age, Sex, Race, and Hispanic Origin, 1948–2015—*Continued*

(Thousands of people.)

| Race, Hispanic origin, sex, and year | 16 years and over | 16 to 19 years | | | 20 years and over | | | | | | |
|---|---|---|---|---|---|---|---|---|---|---|---|
| | | Total | 16 to 17 years | 18 to 19 years | Total | 20 to 24 years | 25 to 34 years | 35 to 44 years | 45 to 54 years | 55 to 64 years | 65 years and over |
| **ALL RACES** | | | | | | | | | | | |
| **Men** | | | | | | | | | | | |
| 1948 | 1 559 | 256 | 113 | 142 | 1 305 | 324 | 289 | 233 | 201 | 177 | 81 |
| 1949 | 2 572 | 353 | 145 | 207 | 2 219 | 485 | 539 | 414 | 347 | 310 | 125 |
| 1950 | 2 239 | 318 | 139 | 179 | 1 922 | 377 | 467 | 348 | 327 | 286 | 117 |
| 1951 | 1 221 | 191 | 102 | 89 | 1 029 | 155 | 241 | 192 | 193 | 162 | 87 |
| 1952 | 1 185 | 205 | 116 | 89 | 980 | 155 | 233 | 192 | 182 | 145 | 73 |
| 1953 | 1 202 | 184 | 94 | 90 | 1 019 | 152 | 236 | 208 | 196 | 167 | 60 |
| 1954 | 2 344 | 310 | 142 | 168 | 2 035 | 327 | 517 | 431 | 372 | 275 | 112 |
| 1955 | 1 854 | 274 | 134 | 140 | 1 580 | 248 | 353 | 328 | 285 | 265 | 102 |
| 1956 | 1 711 | 269 | 134 | 135 | 1 442 | 240 | 348 | 278 | 270 | 216 | 90 |
| 1957 | 1 841 | 300 | 140 | 159 | 1 541 | 283 | 349 | 304 | 302 | 220 | 83 |
| 1958 | 3 098 | 416 | 185 | 231 | 2 681 | 478 | 685 | 552 | 492 | 349 | 124 |
| 1959 | 2 420 | 398 | 191 | 207 | 2 022 | 343 | 484 | 407 | 390 | 287 | 112 |
| 1960 | 2 486 | 426 | 200 | 225 | 2 060 | 369 | 492 | 415 | 392 | 294 | 96 |
| 1961 | 2 997 | 479 | 221 | 258 | 2 518 | 458 | 585 | 507 | 473 | 375 | 122 |
| 1962 | 2 423 | 408 | 188 | 220 | 2 016 | 381 | 445 | 404 | 382 | 300 | 103 |
| 1963 | 2 472 | 501 | 248 | 252 | 1 971 | 396 | 445 | 386 | 358 | 290 | 97 |
| 1964 | 2 205 | 487 | 257 | 230 | 1 718 | 384 | 345 | 324 | 319 | 263 | 85 |
| 1965 | 1 914 | 479 | 247 | 232 | 1 435 | 311 | 292 | 283 | 253 | 221 | 75 |
| 1966 | 1 551 | 432 | 220 | 212 | 1 120 | 221 | 239 | 219 | 196 | 179 | 65 |
| 1967 | 1 508 | 448 | 241 | 207 | 1 060 | 235 | 219 | 185 | 199 | 163 | 60 |
| 1968 | 1 419 | 426 | 234 | 193 | 993 | 258 | 205 | 171 | 165 | 132 | 61 |
| 1969 | 1 403 | 440 | 244 | 196 | 963 | 270 | 205 | 155 | 157 | 127 | 48 |
| 1970 | 2 238 | 599 | 306 | 294 | 1 638 | 479 | 391 | 253 | 247 | 198 | 71 |
| 1971 | 2 789 | 693 | 346 | 347 | 2 097 | 640 | 513 | 320 | 313 | 239 | 71 |
| 1972 | 2 659 | 711 | 357 | 355 | 1 948 | 628 | 466 | 284 | 272 | 227 | 73 |
| 1973 | 2 275 | 653 | 352 | 300 | 1 624 | 528 | 439 | 211 | 219 | 171 | 57 |
| 1974 | 2 714 | 757 | 394 | 362 | 1 957 | 649 | 546 | 266 | 250 | 183 | 63 |
| 1975 | 4 442 | 966 | 445 | 521 | 3 476 | 1 081 | 986 | 507 | 499 | 302 | 103 |
| 1976 | 4 036 | 939 | 443 | 496 | 3 098 | 951 | 914 | 431 | 411 | 296 | 94 |
| 1977 | 3 667 | 874 | 421 | 453 | 2 794 | 877 | 869 | 373 | 326 | 252 | 97 |
| 1978 | 3 142 | 813 | 426 | 388 | 2 328 | 768 | 691 | 314 | 277 | 198 | 81 |
| 1979 | 3 120 | 811 | 393 | 418 | 2 308 | 744 | 699 | 329 | 272 | 196 | 67 |
| 1980 | 4 267 | 913 | 429 | 485 | 3 353 | 1 076 | 1 137 | 482 | 357 | 243 | 58 |
| 1981 | 4 577 | 962 | 431 | 531 | 3 615 | 1 144 | 1 213 | 552 | 390 | 261 | 55 |
| 1982 | 6 179 | 1 090 | 469 | 621 | 5 089 | 1 407 | 1 791 | 879 | 550 | 393 | 69 |
| 1983 | 6 260 | 1 003 | 408 | 595 | 5 257 | 1 369 | 1 822 | 947 | 613 | 433 | 73 |
| 1984 | 4 744 | 812 | 348 | 464 | 3 932 | 1 023 | 1 322 | 728 | 450 | 356 | 53 |
| 1985 | 4 521 | 806 | 363 | 443 | 3 715 | 944 | 1 244 | 706 | 459 | 307 | 55 |
| 1986 | 4 530 | 779 | 355 | 424 | 3 751 | 899 | 1 291 | 763 | 440 | 301 | 58 |
| 1987 | 4 101 | 732 | 353 | 379 | 3 369 | 779 | 1 169 | 689 | 426 | 258 | 49 |
| 1988 | 3 655 | 667 | 311 | 356 | 2 987 | 676 | 1 040 | 617 | 366 | 240 | 49 |
| 1989 | 3 525 | 658 | 303 | 355 | 2 867 | 660 | 953 | 619 | 351 | 234 | 49 |
| 1990 | 3 906 | 667 | 283 | 384 | 3 239 | 715 | 1 092 | 711 | 413 | 249 | 59 |
| 1991 | 4 946 | 751 | 317 | 433 | 4 195 | 911 | 1 375 | 990 | 550 | 305 | 64 |
| 1992 | 5 523 | 806 | 357 | 449 | 4 717 | 951 | 1 529 | 1 118 | 675 | 378 | 67 |
| 1993 | 5 055 | 768 | 342 | 426 | 4 287 | 865 | 1 338 | 1 049 | 636 | 336 | 64 |
| 1994 | 4 367 | 740 | 342 | 398 | 3 627 | 768 | 1 113 | 855 | 522 | 281 | 88 |
| 1995 | 3 983 | 744 | 352 | 391 | 3 239 | 673 | 961 | 815 | 464 | 233 | 94 |
| 1996 | 3 880 | 733 | 347 | 387 | 3 146 | 675 | 903 | 786 | 484 | 223 | 76 |
| 1997 | 3 577 | 694 | 321 | 373 | 2 882 | 636 | 772 | 732 | 457 | 217 | 69 |
| 1998 | 3 266 | 686 | 330 | 355 | 2 580 | 583 | 699 | 609 | 420 | 201 | 69 |
| 1999 | 3 066 | 633 | 295 | 338 | 2 433 | 562 | 624 | 571 | 403 | 203 | 70 |
| 2000 | 2 975 | 599 | 281 | 317 | 2 376 | 547 | 602 | 557 | 398 | 189 | 83 |
| 2001 | 3 690 | 650 | 300 | 350 | 3 040 | 688 | 756 | 714 | 536 | 272 | 74 |
| 2002 | 4 597 | 700 | 301 | 399 | 3 896 | 792 | 1 023 | 897 | 725 | 373 | 87 |
| 2003 | 4 906 | 697 | 291 | 407 | 4 209 | 841 | 1 097 | 988 | 764 | 412 | 107 |
| 2004 | 4 456 | 664 | 292 | 372 | 3 791 | 811 | 980 | 839 | 684 | 373 | 104 |
| 2005 | 4 059 | 667 | 300 | 367 | 3 392 | 775 | 844 | 715 | 624 | 331 | 102 |
| 2006 | 3 753 | 622 | 271 | 352 | 3 131 | 705 | 810 | 642 | 569 | 318 | 88 |
| 2007 | 3 882 | 623 | 263 | 360 | 3 259 | 721 | 856 | 634 | 591 | 349 | 108 |
| 2008 | 5 033 | 736 | 312 | 425 | 4 297 | 920 | 1 119 | 875 | 804 | 425 | 153 |
| 2009 | 8 453 | 898 | 317 | 581 | 7 555 | 1 329 | 1 988 | 1 600 | 1 558 | 840 | 241 |
| 2010 | 8 626 | 863 | 315 | 548 | 7 763 | 1 398 | 1 993 | 1 534 | 1 614 | 962 | 262 |
| 2011 | 7 684 | 786 | 267 | 520 | 6 898 | 1 275 | 1 795 | 1 316 | 1 370 | 882 | 261 |
| 2012 | 6 771 | 787 | 291 | 497 | 5 984 | 1 163 | 1 476 | 1 124 | 1 142 | 811 | 268 |
| 2013 | 6 314 | 746 | 287 | 459 | 5 568 | 1 143 | 1 381 | 1 015 | 1 039 | 741 | 250 |
| 2014 | 5 190 | 605 | 230 | 375 | 4 585 | 996 | 1 185 | 813 | 782 | 600 | 210 |
| 2015 | 4 490 | 531 | 197 | 333 | 3 959 | 865 | 1 030 | 695 | 649 | 536 | 184 |

## Table 1-26. Unemployed Persons, by Age, Sex, Race, and Hispanic Origin, 1948–2015—*Continued*

(Thousands of people.)

| Race, Hispanic origin, sex, and year | 16 years and over | 16 to 19 years | | | 20 years and over | | | | | | |
|---|---|---|---|---|---|---|---|---|---|---|---|
| | | Total | 16 to 17 years | 18 to 19 years | Total | 20 to 24 years | 25 to 34 years | 35 to 44 years | 45 to 54 years | 55 to 64 years | 65 years and over |
| **ALL RACES** | | | | | | | | | | | |
| **Women** | | | | | | | | | | | |
| 1948 | 717 | 153 | 67 | 86 | 564 | 131 | 168 | 114 | 89 | 49 | 12 |
| 1949 | 1 065 | 223 | 93 | 130 | 841 | 195 | 237 | 189 | 124 | 74 | 21 |
| 1950 | 1 049 | 195 | 87 | 108 | 854 | 184 | 235 | 182 | 151 | 82 | 20 |
| 1951 | 834 | 145 | 66 | 79 | 689 | 118 | 194 | 162 | 125 | 76 | 16 |
| 1952 | 698 | 140 | 64 | 76 | 559 | 113 | 156 | 133 | 92 | 50 | 13 |
| 1953 | 632 | 123 | 56 | 67 | 510 | 104 | 143 | 117 | 84 | 51 | 10 |
| 1954 | 1 188 | 191 | 79 | 79 | 997 | 177 | 276 | 249 | 176 | 99 | 20 |
| 1955 | 998 | 176 | 77 | 99 | 823 | 148 | 224 | 193 | 151 | 90 | 18 |
| 1956 | 1 039 | 209 | 97 | 112 | 832 | 155 | 206 | 198 | 159 | 95 | 19 |
| 1957 | 1 018 | 197 | 90 | 107 | 821 | 147 | 224 | 195 | 146 | 80 | 28 |
| 1958 | 1 504 | 262 | 114 | 148 | 1 242 | 223 | 308 | 319 | 239 | 123 | 30 |
| 1959 | 1 320 | 256 | 110 | 147 | 1 063 | 200 | 242 | 266 | 213 | 118 | 23 |
| 1960 | 1 366 | 286 | 125 | 162 | 1 080 | 214 | 260 | 256 | 222 | 102 | 26 |
| 1961 | 1 717 | 349 | 142 | 207 | 1 368 | 265 | 305 | 343 | 278 | 141 | 37 |
| 1962 | 1 488 | 313 | 124 | 189 | 1 175 | 255 | 267 | 284 | 223 | 111 | 38 |
| 1963 | 1 598 | 383 | 172 | 210 | 1 216 | 262 | 287 | 288 | 231 | 120 | 29 |
| 1964 | 1 581 | 385 | 179 | 207 | 1 195 | 276 | 262 | 281 | 224 | 115 | 32 |
| 1965 | 1 452 | 395 | 164 | 231 | 1 056 | 246 | 237 | 263 | 183 | 101 | 28 |
| 1966 | 1 324 | 405 | 175 | 229 | 921 | 225 | 202 | 207 | 173 | 86 | 27 |
| 1967 | 1 468 | 391 | 159 | 231 | 1 078 | 277 | 261 | 237 | 184 | 93 | 26 |
| 1968 | 1 397 | 412 | 180 | 233 | 985 | 285 | 238 | 200 | 149 | 87 | 27 |
| 1969 | 1 429 | 413 | 192 | 220 | 1 015 | 290 | 248 | 203 | 163 | 89 | 24 |
| 1970 | 1 855 | 506 | 231 | 275 | 1 349 | 387 | 327 | 262 | 229 | 111 | 33 |
| 1971 | 2 227 | 568 | 250 | 318 | 1 658 | 489 | 420 | 310 | 260 | 142 | 38 |
| 1972 | 2 222 | 598 | 276 | 322 | 1 625 | 503 | 413 | 293 | 237 | 141 | 38 |
| 1973 | 2 089 | 583 | 282 | 301 | 1 507 | 480 | 427 | 240 | 212 | 119 | 31 |
| 1974 | 2 441 | 665 | 305 | 360 | 1 777 | 564 | 497 | 294 | 248 | 137 | 36 |
| 1975 | 3 486 | 802 | 355 | 447 | 2 684 | 783 | 791 | 444 | 395 | 219 | 52 |
| 1976 | 3 369 | 780 | 352 | 429 | 2 588 | 763 | 795 | 417 | 346 | 214 | 53 |
| 1977 | 3 324 | 789 | 361 | 428 | 2 535 | 752 | 782 | 412 | 340 | 198 | 50 |
| 1978 | 3 061 | 769 | 370 | 399 | 2 292 | 714 | 731 | 381 | 275 | 148 | 43 |
| 1979 | 3 018 | 743 | 346 | 396 | 2 276 | 697 | 748 | 375 | 268 | 150 | 38 |
| 1980 | 3 370 | 755 | 349 | 407 | 2 615 | 760 | 886 | 459 | 318 | 155 | 36 |
| 1981 | 3 696 | 800 | 350 | 450 | 2 895 | 833 | 998 | 513 | 325 | 184 | 43 |
| 1982 | 4 499 | 886 | 362 | 524 | 3 613 | 985 | 1 246 | 673 | 416 | 254 | 38 |
| 1983 | 4 457 | 825 | 344 | 481 | 3 632 | 961 | 1 255 | 703 | 427 | 244 | 41 |
| 1984 | 3 794 | 687 | 298 | 390 | 3 107 | 815 | 1 052 | 607 | 378 | 211 | 45 |
| 1985 | 3 791 | 661 | 298 | 363 | 3 129 | 794 | 1 098 | 634 | 355 | 211 | 39 |
| 1986 | 3 707 | 675 | 310 | 365 | 3 032 | 752 | 1 099 | 609 | 350 | 189 | 33 |
| 1987 | 3 324 | 616 | 295 | 321 | 2 709 | 674 | 960 | 592 | 298 | 155 | 30 |
| 1988 | 3 046 | 558 | 262 | 297 | 2 487 | 585 | 889 | 550 | 291 | 136 | 38 |
| 1989 | 3 003 | 536 | 234 | 302 | 2 467 | 558 | 897 | 540 | 286 | 144 | 41 |
| 1990 | 3 140 | 544 | 243 | 301 | 2 596 | 584 | 902 | 617 | 310 | 137 | 46 |
| 1991 | 3 683 | 608 | 270 | 338 | 3 074 | 662 | 1 071 | 728 | 396 | 168 | 49 |
| 1992 | 4 090 | 621 | 283 | 338 | 3 469 | 698 | 1 173 | 858 | 463 | 210 | 66 |
| 1993 | 3 885 | 597 | 264 | 333 | 3 288 | 648 | 1 058 | 847 | 485 | 205 | 45 |
| 1994 | 3 629 | 580 | 282 | 298 | 3 049 | 605 | 954 | 772 | 449 | 204 | 66 |
| 1995 | 3 421 | 602 | 299 | 303 | 2 819 | 571 | 880 | 735 | 381 | 193 | 60 |
| 1996 | 3 356 | 573 | 270 | 303 | 2 783 | 564 | 854 | 720 | 399 | 183 | 63 |
| 1997 | 3 162 | 577 | 268 | 310 | 2 585 | 516 | 800 | 686 | 373 | 152 | 58 |
| 1998 | 2 944 | 519 | 242 | 277 | 2 424 | 498 | 720 | 650 | 362 | 141 | 53 |
| 1999 | 2 814 | 529 | 249 | 280 | 2 285 | 480 | 654 | 584 | 350 | 163 | 54 |
| 2000 | 2 717 | 483 | 221 | 262 | 2 235 | 475 | 604 | 577 | 364 | 165 | 50 |
| 2001 | 3 111 | 512 | 230 | 282 | 2 599 | 521 | 742 | 641 | 453 | 187 | 55 |
| 2002 | 3 781 | 553 | 238 | 315 | 3 228 | 638 | 866 | 795 | 591 | 263 | 76 |
| 2003 | 3 868 | 554 | 255 | 299 | 3 314 | 654 | 863 | 827 | 592 | 302 | 76 |
| 2004 | 3 694 | 543 | 262 | 281 | 3 150 | 619 | 804 | 739 | 605 | 309 | 75 |
| 2005 | 3 531 | 519 | 240 | 278 | 3 013 | 560 | 817 | 685 | 571 | 299 | 82 |
| 2006 | 3 247 | 496 | 238 | 258 | 2 751 | 530 | 711 | 637 | 524 | 277 | 71 |
| 2007 | 3 196 | 478 | 222 | 256 | 2 718 | 520 | 688 | 591 | 544 | 293 | 81 |
| 2008 | 3 891 | 549 | 251 | 297 | 3 342 | 625 | 830 | 730 | 669 | 377 | 111 |
| 2009 | 5 811 | 654 | 259 | 395 | 5 157 | 878 | 1 296 | 1 121 | 1 034 | 647 | 180 |
| 2010 | 6 199 | 665 | 268 | 397 | 5 534 | 931 | 1 392 | 1 169 | 1 156 | 698 | 187 |
| 2011 | 6 063 | 613 | 252 | 362 | 5 450 | 960 | 1 392 | 1 073 | 1 123 | 697 | 204 |
| 2012 | 5 734 | 609 | 242 | 367 | 5 125 | 891 | 1 288 | 1 034 | 1 039 | 659 | 214 |
| 2013 | 5 146 | 581 | 249 | 332 | 4 565 | 854 | 1 123 | 898 | 906 | 600 | 185 |
| 2014 | 4 426 | 501 | 196 | 305 | 3 926 | 751 | 1 039 | 726 | 725 | 507 | 177 |
| 2015 | 3 807 | 435 | 166 | 269 | 3 371 | 636 | 874 | 656 | 610 | 442 | 153 |

## Table 1-26.  Unemployed Persons, by Age, Sex, Race, and Hispanic Origin, 1948–2015—*Continued*

(Thousands of people.)

| Race, Hispanic origin, sex, and year | 16 years and over | 16 to 19 years | | | 20 years and over | | | | | | |
|---|---|---|---|---|---|---|---|---|---|---|---|
| | | Total | 16 to 17 years | 18 to 19 years | Total | 20 to 24 years | 25 to 34 years | 35 to 44 years | 45 to 54 years | 55 to 64 years | 65 years and over |
| **WHITE** | | | | | | | | | | | |
| **Both Sexes** | | | | | | | | | | | |
| 1954 | 2 859 | 423 | 191 | 232 | 2 436 | 394 | 610 | 540 | 447 | 329 | 115 |
| 1955 | 2 252 | 373 | 181 | 191 | 1 879 | 304 | 412 | 402 | 358 | 300 | 105 |
| 1956 | 2 159 | 382 | 191 | 191 | 1 777 | 297 | 406 | 363 | 355 | 258 | 98 |
| 1957 | 2 289 | 401 | 195 | 204 | 1 888 | 331 | 425 | 401 | 373 | 262 | 98 |
| 1958 | 3 680 | 541 | 245 | 297 | 3 139 | 541 | 756 | 686 | 614 | 405 | 136 |
| 1959 | 2 946 | 525 | 255 | 270 | 2 421 | 406 | 526 | 525 | 496 | 348 | 120 |
| 1960 | 3 065 | 575 | 273 | 302 | 2 490 | 456 | 573 | 520 | 502 | 330 | 109 |
| 1961 | 3 743 | 669 | 295 | 374 | 3 074 | 566 | 668 | 652 | 611 | 438 | 139 |
| 1962 | 3 052 | 580 | 262 | 318 | 2 472 | 488 | 515 | 522 | 485 | 345 | 117 |
| 1963 | 3 208 | 708 | 350 | 358 | 2 500 | 501 | 540 | 518 | 485 | 349 | 107 |
| 1964 | 2 999 | 708 | 365 | 342 | 2 291 | 508 | 441 | 472 | 447 | 323 | 100 |
| 1965 | 2 691 | 705 | 329 | 374 | 1 986 | 437 | 399 | 427 | 358 | 276 | 91 |
| 1966 | 2 255 | 651 | 315 | 336 | 1 604 | 338 | 323 | 336 | 298 | 227 | 80 |
| 1967 | 2 338 | 635 | 311 | 325 | 1 703 | 393 | 360 | 336 | 321 | 221 | 75 |
| 1968 | 2 226 | 644 | 326 | 318 | 1 582 | 422 | 330 | 297 | 269 | 187 | 80 |
| 1969 | 2 260 | 660 | 351 | 309 | 1 601 | 432 | 354 | 294 | 269 | 185 | 66 |
| 1970 | 3 339 | 871 | 438 | 432 | 2 468 | 679 | 570 | 433 | 415 | 275 | 95 |
| 1971 | 4 085 | 1 011 | 491 | 521 | 3 074 | 887 | 732 | 517 | 500 | 338 | 100 |
| 1972 | 3 906 | 1 021 | 515 | 506 | 2 885 | 887 | 679 | 459 | 439 | 324 | 95 |
| 1973 | 3 442 | 955 | 513 | 443 | 2 486 | 758 | 664 | 358 | 371 | 257 | 77 |
| 1974 | 4 097 | 1 104 | 561 | 544 | 2 993 | 925 | 821 | 448 | 427 | 283 | 88 |
| 1975 | 6 421 | 1 413 | 657 | 755 | 5 007 | 1 474 | 1 413 | 774 | 753 | 460 | 136 |
| 1976 | 5 914 | 1 364 | 649 | 715 | 4 550 | 1 326 | 1 329 | 682 | 637 | 448 | 128 |
| 1977 | 5 441 | 1 284 | 636 | 648 | 4 157 | 1 195 | 1 255 | 621 | 569 | 388 | 129 |
| 1978 | 4 698 | 1 189 | 631 | 558 | 3 509 | 1 059 | 1 059 | 543 | 453 | 290 | 104 |
| 1979 | 4 664 | 1 193 | 589 | 603 | 3 472 | 1 038 | 1 068 | 545 | 443 | 290 | 87 |
| 1980 | 5 884 | 1 291 | 625 | 666 | 4 593 | 1 364 | 1 528 | 740 | 550 | 335 | 74 |
| 1981 | 6 343 | 1 374 | 629 | 745 | 4 968 | 1 449 | 1 658 | 827 | 578 | 379 | 77 |
| 1982 | 8 241 | 1 534 | 683 | 851 | 6 707 | 1 770 | 2 283 | 1 223 | 796 | 549 | 86 |
| 1983 | 8 128 | 1 387 | 609 | 778 | 6 741 | 1 678 | 2 282 | 1 294 | 837 | 563 | 88 |
| 1984 | 6 372 | 1 116 | 510 | 605 | 5 256 | 1 282 | 1 723 | 1 036 | 660 | 475 | 81 |
| 1985 | 6 191 | 1 074 | 507 | 567 | 5 117 | 1 235 | 1 695 | 1 039 | 642 | 432 | 75 |
| 1986 | 6 140 | 1 070 | 509 | 561 | 5 070 | 1 149 | 1 751 | 1 056 | 629 | 407 | 78 |
| 1987 | 5 501 | 995 | 495 | 500 | 4 506 | 1 017 | 1 527 | 984 | 576 | 333 | 68 |
| 1988 | 4 944 | 910 | 437 | 473 | 4 033 | 874 | 1 371 | 890 | 520 | 309 | 69 |
| 1989 | 4 770 | 863 | 407 | 456 | 3 908 | 856 | 1 297 | 871 | 503 | 311 | 70 |
| 1990 | 5 186 | 903 | 401 | 502 | 4 283 | 899 | 1 401 | 983 | 582 | 330 | 88 |
| 1991 | 6 560 | 1 029 | 461 | 568 | 5 532 | 1 132 | 1 805 | 1 330 | 759 | 410 | 96 |
| 1992 | 7 169 | 1 037 | 484 | 553 | 6 132 | 1 156 | 1 967 | 1 483 | 915 | 495 | 116 |
| 1993 | 6 655 | 992 | 468 | 523 | 5 663 | 1 057 | 1 754 | 1 411 | 907 | 442 | 92 |
| 1994 | 5 892 | 960 | 471 | 489 | 4 933 | 952 | 1 479 | 1 184 | 779 | 407 | 132 |
| 1995 | 5 459 | 952 | 476 | 476 | 4 507 | 866 | 1 311 | 1 161 | 676 | 362 | 131 |
| 1996 | 5 300 | 939 | 456 | 484 | 4 361 | 854 | 1 223 | 1 117 | 709 | 336 | 122 |
| 1997 | 4 836 | 912 | 438 | 475 | 3 924 | 765 | 1 068 | 1 035 | 648 | 302 | 106 |
| 1998 | 4 484 | 876 | 424 | 451 | 3 608 | 731 | 978 | 901 | 620 | 276 | 101 |
| 1999 | 4 273 | 844 | 414 | 430 | 3 429 | 720 | 865 | 843 | 595 | 303 | 104 |
| 2000 | 4 121 | 795 | 386 | 409 | 3 326 | 682 | 835 | 817 | 591 | 294 | 107 |
| 2001 | 4 969 | 845 | 402 | 443 | 4 124 | 829 | 1 062 | 985 | 761 | 378 | 109 |
| 2002 | 6 137 | 925 | 407 | 518 | 5 212 | 977 | 1 340 | 1 237 | 1 004 | 518 | 137 |
| 2003 | 6 311 | 909 | 414 | 495 | 5 401 | 1 012 | 1 354 | 1 287 | 1 025 | 569 | 155 |
| 2004 | 5 847 | 890 | 414 | 476 | 4 957 | 959 | 1 211 | 1 130 | 953 | 557 | 148 |
| 2005 | 5 350 | 845 | 391 | 454 | 4 505 | 878 | 1 106 | 1 006 | 884 | 488 | 144 |
| 2006 | 5 002 | 794 | 375 | 419 | 4 208 | 832 | 1 029 | 920 | 813 | 480 | 135 |
| 2007 | 5 143 | 805 | 361 | 444 | 4 338 | 851 | 1 052 | 902 | 848 | 520 | 164 |
| 2008 | 6 509 | 947 | 422 | 524 | 5 562 | 1 087 | 1 336 | 1 196 | 1 094 | 634 | 216 |
| 2009 | 10 648 | 1 157 | 440 | 717 | 9 491 | 1 556 | 2 320 | 2 026 | 2 012 | 1 221 | 355 |
| 2010 | 10 916 | 1 128 | 445 | 683 | 9 788 | 1 614 | 2 358 | 1 969 | 2 130 | 1 344 | 373 |
| 2011 | 9 889 | 1 024 | 391 | 633 | 8 865 | 1 546 | 2 135 | 1 678 | 1 859 | 1 251 | 395 |
| 2012 | 8 915 | 1 004 | 397 | 607 | 7 911 | 1 353 | 1 881 | 1 514 | 1 614 | 1 144 | 405 |
| 2013 | 8 033 | 937 | 395 | 542 | 7 096 | 1 299 | 1 651 | 1 334 | 1 414 | 1 032 | 366 |
| 2014 | 6 540 | 775 | 302 | 473 | 5 764 | 1 084 | 1 402 | 1 059 | 1 085 | 829 | 305 |
| 2015 | 5 662 | 662 | 260 | 402 | 5 000 | 970 | 1 194 | 917 | 913 | 751 | 255 |

## Table 1-26. Unemployed Persons, by Age, Sex, Race, and Hispanic Origin, 1948–2015—*Continued*

(Thousands of people.)

| Race, Hispanic origin, sex, and year | 16 years and over | 16 to 19 years | | | 20 years and over | | | | | | |
|---|---|---|---|---|---|---|---|---|---|---|---|
| | | Total | 16 to 17 years | 18 to 19 years | Total | 20 to 24 years | 25 to 34 years | 35 to 44 years | 45 to 54 years | 55 to 64 years | 65 years and over |
| **WHITE** | | | | | | | | | | | |
| **Men** | | | | | | | | | | | |
| 1954 | 1 913 | 266 | 125 | 142 | 1 647 | 260 | 408 | 341 | 299 | 241 | 98 |
| 1955 | 1 478 | 232 | 114 | 117 | 1 246 | 196 | 260 | 246 | 233 | 223 | 89 |
| 1956 | 1 366 | 221 | 112 | 108 | 1 145 | 186 | 265 | 212 | 225 | 177 | 81 |
| 1957 | 1 477 | 243 | 118 | 124 | 1 234 | 222 | 257 | 239 | 250 | 193 | 73 |
| 1958 | 2 489 | 333 | 149 | 184 | 2 156 | 382 | 525 | 436 | 404 | 299 | 110 |
| 1959 | 1 903 | 318 | 162 | 156 | 1 585 | 256 | 350 | 316 | 320 | 245 | 98 |
| 1960 | 1 988 | 341 | 167 | 174 | 1 647 | 295 | 376 | 330 | 317 | 243 | 86 |
| 1961 | 2 398 | 384 | 176 | 208 | 2 014 | 370 | 442 | 395 | 382 | 318 | 107 |
| 1962 | 1 915 | 334 | 158 | 176 | 1 581 | 300 | 332 | 311 | 308 | 246 | 84 |
| 1963 | 1 976 | 407 | 211 | 196 | 1 569 | 309 | 342 | 297 | 294 | 246 | 80 |
| 1964 | 1 779 | 400 | 217 | 183 | 1 379 | 310 | 262 | 255 | 266 | 216 | 70 |
| 1965 | 1 556 | 387 | 200 | 186 | 1 169 | 254 | 226 | 228 | 206 | 190 | 67 |
| 1966 | 1 241 | 340 | 178 | 162 | 901 | 172 | 185 | 173 | 160 | 154 | 57 |
| 1967 | 1 208 | 342 | 186 | 156 | 866 | 185 | 171 | 153 | 167 | 140 | 52 |
| 1968 | 1 142 | 328 | 185 | 143 | 814 | 206 | 162 | 140 | 142 | 111 | 55 |
| 1969 | 1 137 | 343 | 198 | 145 | 794 | 214 | 165 | 130 | 134 | 108 | 43 |
| 1970 | 1 857 | 485 | 255 | 230 | 1 372 | 388 | 316 | 212 | 216 | 177 | 64 |
| 1971 | 2 309 | 562 | 288 | 275 | 1 747 | 513 | 418 | 268 | 272 | 211 | 66 |
| 1972 | 2 173 | 564 | 288 | 276 | 1 610 | 506 | 375 | 231 | 237 | 199 | 60 |
| 1973 | 1 836 | 513 | 284 | 229 | 1 323 | 411 | 353 | 166 | 188 | 153 | 51 |
| 1974 | 2 169 | 584 | 311 | 274 | 1 585 | 505 | 434 | 218 | 213 | 161 | 53 |
| 1975 | 3 627 | 785 | 369 | 416 | 2 841 | 871 | 796 | 412 | 411 | 265 | 86 |
| 1976 | 3 258 | 754 | 368 | 385 | 2 504 | 750 | 730 | 346 | 341 | 259 | 78 |
| 1977 | 2 883 | 672 | 342 | 330 | 2 211 | 660 | 682 | 297 | 276 | 213 | 82 |
| 1978 | 2 411 | 615 | 338 | 277 | 1 797 | 558 | 525 | 250 | 227 | 169 | 68 |
| 1979 | 2 405 | 633 | 319 | 313 | 1 773 | 553 | 526 | 253 | 220 | 165 | 56 |
| 1980 | 3 345 | 716 | 347 | 369 | 2 629 | 827 | 884 | 378 | 291 | 206 | 44 |
| 1981 | 3 580 | 755 | 349 | 406 | 2 825 | 869 | 943 | 433 | 317 | 221 | 42 |
| 1982 | 4 846 | 854 | 387 | 467 | 3 991 | 1 066 | 1 385 | 696 | 460 | 331 | 53 |
| 1983 | 4 859 | 761 | 328 | 433 | 4 098 | 1 019 | 1 410 | 755 | 497 | 362 | 54 |
| 1984 | 3 600 | 608 | 280 | 328 | 2 992 | 722 | 991 | 572 | 363 | 302 | 42 |
| 1985 | 3 426 | 592 | 282 | 310 | 2 834 | 694 | 931 | 553 | 356 | 257 | 43 |
| 1986 | 3 433 | 576 | 276 | 299 | 2 857 | 645 | 978 | 586 | 349 | 248 | 51 |
| 1987 | 3 132 | 548 | 272 | 276 | 2 584 | 568 | 879 | 536 | 350 | 209 | 43 |
| 1988 | 2 766 | 499 | 239 | 260 | 2 268 | 480 | 777 | 477 | 293 | 200 | 40 |
| 1989 | 2 636 | 487 | 230 | 257 | 2 149 | 476 | 694 | 470 | 280 | 191 | 38 |
| 1990 | 2 935 | 504 | 214 | 290 | 2 431 | 510 | 796 | 530 | 330 | 214 | 51 |
| 1991 | 3 859 | 575 | 249 | 327 | 3 284 | 677 | 1 064 | 780 | 438 | 269 | 55 |
| 1992 | 4 209 | 590 | 270 | 319 | 3 620 | 686 | 1 155 | 858 | 543 | 318 | 58 |
| 1993 | 3 828 | 565 | 261 | 305 | 3 263 | 619 | 1 015 | 793 | 512 | 270 | 53 |
| 1994 | 3 275 | 540 | 259 | 280 | 2 735 | 555 | 827 | 626 | 417 | 236 | 74 |
| 1995 | 2 999 | 535 | 260 | 275 | 2 465 | 483 | 711 | 621 | 371 | 200 | 79 |
| 1996 | 2 896 | 532 | 260 | 273 | 2 363 | 478 | 655 | 592 | 383 | 188 | 67 |
| 1997 | 2 641 | 502 | 234 | 268 | 2 140 | 439 | 553 | 549 | 358 | 182 | 58 |
| 1998 | 2 431 | 510 | 254 | 257 | 1 920 | 405 | 512 | 441 | 342 | 164 | 58 |
| 1999 | 2 274 | 461 | 223 | 237 | 1 813 | 398 | 441 | 419 | 322 | 172 | 61 |
| 2000 | 2 177 | 446 | 217 | 229 | 1 731 | 368 | 428 | 403 | 302 | 162 | 68 |
| 2001 | 2 754 | 479 | 232 | 247 | 2 275 | 494 | 547 | 529 | 413 | 229 | 64 |
| 2002 | 3 459 | 516 | 228 | 288 | 2 943 | 562 | 772 | 672 | 554 | 305 | 77 |
| 2003 | 3 643 | 518 | 221 | 298 | 3 125 | 589 | 798 | 723 | 591 | 333 | 91 |
| 2004 | 3 282 | 497 | 224 | 274 | 2 785 | 560 | 694 | 620 | 516 | 307 | 88 |
| 2005 | 2 931 | 480 | 220 | 260 | 2 450 | 522 | 586 | 536 | 463 | 263 | 81 |
| 2006 | 2 730 | 449 | 202 | 247 | 2 281 | 483 | 567 | 482 | 417 | 259 | 73 |
| 2007 | 2 869 | 461 | 195 | 266 | 2 408 | 501 | 604 | 478 | 447 | 285 | 93 |
| 2008 | 3 727 | 548 | 231 | 317 | 3 179 | 668 | 784 | 662 | 604 | 337 | 124 |
| 2009 | 6 421 | 675 | 241 | 434 | 5 746 | 969 | 1 439 | 1 208 | 1 233 | 695 | 202 |
| 2010 | 6 476 | 648 | 246 | 402 | 5 828 | 995 | 1 452 | 1 131 | 1 249 | 785 | 216 |
| 2011 | 5 631 | 585 | 208 | 377 | 5 046 | 909 | 1 237 | 951 | 1 030 | 697 | 223 |
| 2012 | 4 931 | 584 | 222 | 362 | 4 347 | 792 | 1 044 | 794 | 856 | 637 | 224 |
| 2013 | 4 520 | 526 | 213 | 313 | 3 994 | 756 | 944 | 727 | 769 | 583 | 215 |
| 2014 | 3 572 | 431 | 165 | 266 | 3 141 | 628 | 774 | 568 | 558 | 449 | 164 |
| 2015 | 3 126 | 375 | 144 | 231 | 2 751 | 581 | 667 | 484 | 480 | 400 | 139 |

## Table 1-26.  Unemployed Persons, by Age, Sex, Race, and Hispanic Origin, 1948–2015—*Continued*

(Thousands of people.)

| Race, Hispanic origin, sex, and year | 16 years and over | 16 to 19 years | | | 20 years and over | | | | | | |
| --- | --- | --- | --- | --- | --- | --- | --- | --- | --- | --- | --- |
| | | Total | 16 to 17 years | 18 to 19 years | Total | 20 to 24 years | 25 to 34 years | 35 to 44 years | 45 to 54 years | 55 to 64 years | 65 years and over |
| **WHITE** | | | | | | | | | | | |
| **Women** | | | | | | | | | | | |
| 1954 | 946 | 157 | 66 | 90 | 789 | 134 | 202 | 199 | 148 | 88 | 17 |
| 1955 | 774 | 141 | 67 | 74 | 633 | 108 | 152 | 156 | 125 | 77 | 16 |
| 1956 | 793 | 161 | 79 | 83 | 632 | 111 | 141 | 151 | 130 | 81 | 17 |
| 1957 | 812 | 158 | 77 | 80 | 654 | 109 | 168 | 162 | 123 | 69 | 25 |
| 1958 | 1 191 | 208 | 96 | 113 | 983 | 159 | 231 | 250 | 210 | 106 | 26 |
| 1959 | 1 043 | 207 | 93 | 114 | 836 | 150 | 176 | 209 | 176 | 103 | 22 |
| 1960 | 1 077 | 234 | 106 | 128 | 843 | 161 | 197 | 190 | 185 | 87 | 23 |
| 1961 | 1 345 | 285 | 119 | 166 | 1 060 | 196 | 226 | 257 | 229 | 120 | 32 |
| 1962 | 1 137 | 246 | 104 | 142 | 891 | 188 | 183 | 211 | 177 | 99 | 33 |
| 1963 | 1 232 | 301 | 139 | 162 | 931 | 192 | 198 | 221 | 191 | 103 | 27 |
| 1964 | 1 220 | 308 | 148 | 159 | 912 | 198 | 179 | 217 | 181 | 107 | 30 |
| 1965 | 1 135 | 318 | 129 | 188 | 817 | 183 | 173 | 199 | 152 | 86 | 24 |
| 1966 | 1 014 | 311 | 137 | 174 | 703 | 166 | 138 | 163 | 138 | 73 | 23 |
| 1967 | 1 130 | 293 | 125 | 169 | 837 | 209 | 189 | 183 | 154 | 81 | 23 |
| 1968 | 1 084 | 316 | 141 | 175 | 768 | 216 | 168 | 157 | 127 | 76 | 25 |
| 1969 | 1 123 | 317 | 153 | 164 | 806 | 218 | 189 | 164 | 135 | 77 | 23 |
| 1970 | 1 482 | 386 | 183 | 202 | 1 096 | 291 | 254 | 221 | 199 | 98 | 31 |
| 1971 | 1 777 | 449 | 203 | 246 | 1 328 | 376 | 314 | 249 | 228 | 126 | 34 |
| 1972 | 1 733 | 457 | 227 | 230 | 1 275 | 381 | 304 | 227 | 202 | 125 | 35 |
| 1973 | 1 606 | 442 | 228 | 214 | 1 164 | 347 | 311 | 192 | 183 | 104 | 26 |
| 1974 | 1 927 | 519 | 250 | 270 | 1 408 | 420 | 387 | 230 | 214 | 122 | 35 |
| 1975 | 2 794 | 628 | 288 | 340 | 2 166 | 602 | 617 | 362 | 342 | 195 | 49 |
| 1976 | 2 656 | 611 | 280 | 330 | 2 045 | 577 | 598 | 336 | 296 | 188 | 49 |
| 1977 | 2 558 | 612 | 294 | 318 | 1 946 | 536 | 573 | 323 | 293 | 175 | 47 |
| 1978 | 2 287 | 574 | 292 | 281 | 1 713 | 500 | 533 | 294 | 226 | 122 | 37 |
| 1979 | 2 260 | 560 | 270 | 290 | 1 699 | 485 | 542 | 293 | 223 | 125 | 32 |
| 1980 | 2 540 | 576 | 278 | 298 | 1 964 | 537 | 645 | 362 | 259 | 129 | 31 |
| 1981 | 2 762 | 620 | 281 | 339 | 2 143 | 580 | 715 | 394 | 261 | 158 | 36 |
| 1982 | 3 395 | 680 | 296 | 384 | 2 715 | 704 | 898 | 527 | 337 | 217 | 33 |
| 1983 | 3 270 | 626 | 282 | 345 | 2 643 | 659 | 872 | 539 | 340 | 201 | 33 |
| 1984 | 2 772 | 508 | 231 | 277 | 2 264 | 559 | 731 | 464 | 297 | 173 | 39 |
| 1985 | 2 765 | 482 | 225 | 257 | 2 283 | 541 | 763 | 486 | 286 | 175 | 32 |
| 1986 | 2 708 | 495 | 233 | 262 | 2 213 | 504 | 773 | 470 | 281 | 159 | 27 |
| 1987 | 2 369 | 447 | 223 | 224 | 1 922 | 449 | 648 | 448 | 227 | 124 | 25 |
| 1988 | 2 177 | 412 | 198 | 214 | 1 766 | 393 | 594 | 413 | 227 | 110 | 30 |
| 1989 | 2 135 | 376 | 177 | 199 | 1 758 | 380 | 603 | 401 | 223 | 120 | 32 |
| 1990 | 2 251 | 399 | 187 | 212 | 1 852 | 389 | 605 | 453 | 251 | 116 | 37 |
| 1991 | 2 701 | 453 | 212 | 241 | 2 248 | 455 | 741 | 550 | 320 | 141 | 41 |
| 1992 | 2 959 | 447 | 214 | 233 | 2 512 | 469 | 811 | 625 | 372 | 177 | 58 |
| 1993 | 2 827 | 426 | 208 | 219 | 2 400 | 438 | 739 | 618 | 395 | 172 | 39 |
| 1994 | 2 617 | 420 | 211 | 208 | 2 197 | 397 | 652 | 558 | 361 | 170 | 58 |
| 1995 | 2 460 | 418 | 216 | 201 | 2 042 | 384 | 600 | 540 | 306 | 162 | 52 |
| 1996 | 2 404 | 407 | 196 | 211 | 1 998 | 376 | 568 | 525 | 326 | 148 | 55 |
| 1997 | 2 195 | 411 | 204 | 207 | 1 784 | 326 | 515 | 486 | 290 | 119 | 49 |
| 1998 | 2 053 | 365 | 171 | 195 | 1 688 | 327 | 467 | 460 | 279 | 112 | 43 |
| 1999 | 1 999 | 383 | 190 | 193 | 1 616 | 322 | 423 | 423 | 273 | 131 | 43 |
| 2000 | 1 944 | 349 | 168 | 180 | 1 595 | 314 | 407 | 414 | 289 | 133 | 39 |
| 2001 | 2 215 | 366 | 170 | 196 | 1 849 | 335 | 515 | 456 | 348 | 150 | 45 |
| 2002 | 2 678 | 409 | 179 | 230 | 2 269 | 415 | 567 | 565 | 449 | 213 | 60 |
| 2003 | 2 668 | 391 | 194 | 197 | 2 276 | 423 | 555 | 564 | 434 | 235 | 64 |
| 2004 | 2 565 | 393 | 191 | 202 | 2 172 | 399 | 516 | 510 | 437 | 250 | 60 |
| 2005 | 2 419 | 365 | 172 | 193 | 2 054 | 356 | 520 | 469 | 421 | 225 | 63 |
| 2006 | 2 271 | 345 | 173 | 172 | 1 927 | 349 | 462 | 437 | 395 | 222 | 62 |
| 2007 | 2 274 | 344 | 166 | 178 | 1 930 | 350 | 448 | 425 | 401 | 235 | 71 |
| 2008 | 2 782 | 399 | 191 | 207 | 2 384 | 419 | 552 | 534 | 489 | 298 | 92 |
| 2009 | 4 227 | 482 | 199 | 283 | 3 745 | 587 | 881 | 818 | 780 | 526 | 153 |
| 2010 | 4 440 | 480 | 199 | 281 | 3 960 | 619 | 906 | 839 | 881 | 559 | 157 |
| 2011 | 4 257 | 439 | 184 | 255 | 3 818 | 637 | 899 | 728 | 829 | 554 | 171 |
| 2012 | 3 985 | 420 | 176 | 245 | 3 564 | 561 | 837 | 720 | 758 | 508 | 181 |
| 2013 | 3 513 | 411 | 183 | 228 | 3 102 | 543 | 707 | 607 | 645 | 449 | 151 |
| 2014 | 2 968 | 344 | 138 | 207 | 2 623 | 457 | 628 | 490 | 527 | 380 | 141 |
| 2015 | 2 537 | 288 | 116 | 172 | 2 249 | 390 | 527 | 433 | 433 | 351 | 116 |

## Table 1-26. Unemployed Persons, by Age, Sex, Race, and Hispanic Origin, 1948–2015—*Continued*

(Thousands of people.)

| Race, Hispanic origin, sex, and year | 16 years and over | 16 to 19 years | | | 20 years and over | | | | | | |
|---|---|---|---|---|---|---|---|---|---|---|---|
| | | Total | 16 to 17 years | 18 to 19 years | Total | 20 to 24 years | 25 to 34 years | 35 to 44 years | 45 to 54 years | 55 to 64 years | 65 years and over |
| **BLACK** | | | | | | | | | | | |
| **Both Sexes** | | | | | | | | | | | |
| 1980 | 1 553 | 343 | 134 | 210 | 1 209 | 426 | 433 | 171 | 109 | 53 | 18 |
| 1981 | 1 731 | 357 | 138 | 219 | 1 374 | 483 | 493 | 207 | 119 | 55 | 17 |
| 1982 | 2 142 | 396 | 130 | 266 | 1 747 | 565 | 662 | 278 | 141 | 84 | 17 |
| 1983 | 2 272 | 392 | 125 | 267 | 1 879 | 591 | 700 | 299 | 174 | 95 | 21 |
| 1984 | 1 914 | 353 | 122 | 230 | 1 561 | 504 | 577 | 253 | 138 | 75 | 15 |
| 1985 | 1 864 | 357 | 135 | 221 | 1 507 | 455 | 562 | 254 | 143 | 74 | 18 |
| 1986 | 1 840 | 347 | 138 | 209 | 1 493 | 453 | 564 | 269 | 127 | 69 | 10 |
| 1987 | 1 684 | 312 | 134 | 178 | 1 373 | 397 | 533 | 247 | 124 | 62 | 10 |
| 1988 | 1 547 | 288 | 121 | 167 | 1 259 | 349 | 502 | 230 | 111 | 51 | 15 |
| 1989 | 1 544 | 300 | 116 | 184 | 1 245 | 322 | 494 | 246 | 109 | 53 | 20 |
| 1990 | 1 565 | 268 | 112 | 156 | 1 297 | 349 | 505 | 278 | 106 | 44 | 14 |
| 1991 | 1 723 | 280 | 105 | 175 | 1 443 | 378 | 539 | 318 | 151 | 44 | 13 |
| 1992 | 2 011 | 324 | 127 | 197 | 1 687 | 421 | 610 | 402 | 178 | 64 | 13 |
| 1993 | 1 844 | 313 | 112 | 201 | 1 530 | 387 | 532 | 376 | 153 | 72 | 11 |
| 1994 | 1 666 | 300 | 127 | 173 | 1 366 | 351 | 468 | 346 | 130 | 55 | 16 |
| 1995 | 1 538 | 325 | 143 | 182 | 1 213 | 311 | 423 | 303 | 116 | 42 | 18 |
| 1996 | 1 592 | 310 | 133 | 177 | 1 282 | 327 | 454 | 313 | 127 | 48 | 13 |
| 1997 | 1 560 | 302 | 123 | 179 | 1 258 | 327 | 426 | 307 | 136 | 45 | 16 |
| 1998 | 1 426 | 281 | 124 | 156 | 1 146 | 301 | 366 | 294 | 125 | 45 | 16 |
| 1999 | 1 309 | 268 | 109 | 159 | 1 041 | 273 | 339 | 249 | 121 | 46 | 14 |
| 2000 | 1 241 | 230 | 96 | 134 | 1 011 | 281 | 289 | 254 | 131 | 38 | 20 |
| 2001 | 1 416 | 260 | 102 | 158 | 1 155 | 307 | 340 | 283 | 159 | 52 | 15 |
| 2002 | 1 693 | 260 | 103 | 156 | 1 433 | 365 | 407 | 349 | 215 | 76 | 21 |
| 2003 | 1 787 | 255 | 93 | 162 | 1 532 | 375 | 442 | 385 | 217 | 93 | 20 |
| 2004 | 1 729 | 241 | 103 | 138 | 1 487 | 353 | 441 | 341 | 245 | 86 | 21 |
| 2005 | 1 700 | 267 | 115 | 152 | 1 433 | 358 | 423 | 310 | 222 | 92 | 28 |
| 2006 | 1 549 | 253 | 102 | 151 | 1 296 | 318 | 388 | 276 | 214 | 81 | 19 |
| 2007 | 1 445 | 235 | 98 | 138 | 1 210 | 300 | 367 | 237 | 208 | 79 | 19 |
| 2008 | 1 788 | 246 | 98 | 148 | 1 542 | 355 | 458 | 301 | 275 | 117 | 36 |
| 2009 | 2 606 | 288 | 99 | 189 | 2 319 | 488 | 717 | 489 | 415 | 168 | 42 |
| 2010 | 2 852 | 291 | 97 | 194 | 2 562 | 539 | 776 | 534 | 461 | 204 | 47 |
| 2011 | 2 831 | 267 | 88 | 179 | 2 564 | 531 | 801 | 529 | 444 | 212 | 47 |
| 2012 | 2 544 | 272 | 94 | 179 | 2 272 | 510 | 640 | 457 | 397 | 209 | 59 |
| 2013 | 2 429 | 278 | 101 | 177 | 2 151 | 509 | 603 | 414 | 376 | 199 | 50 |
| 2014 | 2 141 | 225 | 85 | 139 | 1 916 | 466 | 605 | 325 | 284 | 186 | 51 |
| 2015 | 1 846 | 199 | 69 | 131 | 1 646 | 384 | 517 | 298 | 245 | 151 | 51 |
| **Men** | | | | | | | | | | | |
| 1980 | 815 | 179 | 72 | 108 | 636 | 222 | 222 | 88 | 60 | 32 | 12 |
| 1981 | 891 | 188 | 73 | 115 | 703 | 248 | 245 | 102 | 65 | 32 | 10 |
| 1982 | 1 167 | 213 | 72 | 141 | 954 | 304 | 355 | 154 | 74 | 54 | 12 |
| 1983 | 1 213 | 211 | 70 | 142 | 1 002 | 313 | 358 | 162 | 96 | 59 | 14 |
| 1984 | 1 003 | 188 | 62 | 126 | 815 | 272 | 289 | 132 | 67 | 45 | 9 |
| 1985 | 951 | 193 | 69 | 124 | 757 | 224 | 268 | 127 | 85 | 43 | 11 |
| 1986 | 946 | 180 | 68 | 112 | 765 | 225 | 273 | 148 | 70 | 44 | 5 |
| 1987 | 826 | 160 | 70 | 90 | 666 | 186 | 253 | 122 | 61 | 39 | 6 |
| 1988 | 771 | 154 | 64 | 90 | 617 | 177 | 233 | 111 | 58 | 30 | 8 |
| 1989 | 773 | 153 | 65 | 88 | 619 | 162 | 226 | 129 | 59 | 33 | 10 |
| 1990 | 806 | 142 | 62 | 80 | 664 | 177 | 247 | 146 | 62 | 27 | 6 |
| 1991 | 890 | 145 | 54 | 91 | 745 | 201 | 252 | 172 | 87 | 25 | 7 |
| 1992 | 1 067 | 180 | 71 | 109 | 886 | 221 | 301 | 208 | 107 | 42 | 6 |
| 1993 | 971 | 170 | 66 | 104 | 801 | 201 | 260 | 201 | 87 | 46 | 7 |
| 1994 | 848 | 167 | 69 | 97 | 682 | 173 | 218 | 180 | 72 | 29 | 10 |
| 1995 | 762 | 168 | 73 | 95 | 593 | 153 | 195 | 150 | 63 | 21 | 11 |
| 1996 | 808 | 169 | 73 | 96 | 639 | 163 | 210 | 158 | 75 | 26 | 7 |
| 1997 | 747 | 162 | 70 | 92 | 585 | 165 | 178 | 141 | 72 | 22 | 7 |
| 1998 | 671 | 147 | 61 | 86 | 524 | 151 | 148 | 133 | 60 | 24 | 8 |
| 1999 | 626 | 145 | 60 | 85 | 480 | 135 | 143 | 114 | 60 | 22 | 7 |
| 2000 | 620 | 121 | 52 | 70 | 499 | 145 | 134 | 121 | 72 | 17 | 9 |
| 2001 | 709 | 136 | 51 | 85 | 573 | 150 | 159 | 142 | 84 | 31 | 7 |
| 2002 | 835 | 140 | 54 | 85 | 695 | 181 | 180 | 165 | 120 | 40 | 9 |
| 2003 | 891 | 132 | 49 | 83 | 760 | 192 | 212 | 189 | 109 | 47 | 10 |
| 2004 | 860 | 128 | 52 | 75 | 733 | 188 | 211 | 160 | 120 | 46 | 8 |
| 2005 | 844 | 145 | 63 | 82 | 699 | 192 | 189 | 143 | 116 | 45 | 14 |
| 2006 | 774 | 134 | 53 | 81 | 640 | 167 | 189 | 118 | 112 | 43 | 11 |
| 2007 | 752 | 130 | 55 | 75 | 622 | 166 | 186 | 114 | 106 | 41 | 10 |
| 2008 | 949 | 138 | 54 | 84 | 811 | 190 | 242 | 154 | 143 | 61 | 21 |
| 2009 | 1 448 | 161 | 55 | 106 | 1 286 | 264 | 406 | 270 | 230 | 91 | 24 |
| 2010 | 1 550 | 154 | 47 | 107 | 1 396 | 294 | 408 | 286 | 268 | 116 | 24 |
| 2011 | 1 502 | 142 | 39 | 102 | 1 360 | 278 | 426 | 277 | 233 | 125 | 21 |
| 2012 | 1 292 | 140 | 47 | 93 | 1 152 | 269 | 308 | 241 | 191 | 110 | 32 |
| 2013 | 1 236 | 154 | 54 | 101 | 1 082 | 273 | 298 | 196 | 193 | 96 | 26 |
| 2014 | 1 091 | 118 | 44 | 74 | 973 | 251 | 295 | 159 | 149 | 95 | 25 |
| 2015 | 935 | 100 | 37 | 63 | 835 | 209 | 254 | 140 | 119 | 89 | 23 |

## Table 1-26. Unemployed Persons, by Age, Sex, Race, and Hispanic Origin, 1948–2015—*Continued*

(Thousands of people.)

| Race, Hispanic origin, sex, and year | 16 years and over | 16 to 19 years | | | 20 years and over | | | | | | |
|---|---|---|---|---|---|---|---|---|---|---|---|
| | | Total | 16 to 17 years | 18 to 19 years | Total | 20 to 24 years | 25 to 34 years | 35 to 44 years | 45 to 54 years | 55 to 64 years | 65 years and over |
| **BLACK** | | | | | | | | | | | |
| **Women** | | | | | | | | | | | |
| 1980 | 738 | 164 | 62 | 102 | 574 | 204 | 211 | 738 | 49 | 21 | 6 |
| 1981 | 840 | 169 | 65 | 104 | 671 | 235 | 248 | 840 | 54 | 23 | 7 |
| 1982 | 975 | 182 | 58 | 124 | 793 | 261 | 307 | 975 | 67 | 29 | 5 |
| 1983 | 1 059 | 181 | 56 | 125 | 878 | 278 | 342 | 1 059 | 77 | 36 | 7 |
| 1984 | 911 | 165 | 60 | 104 | 747 | 231 | 288 | 911 | 71 | 30 | 5 |
| 1985 | 913 | 164 | 66 | 98 | 750 | 231 | 295 | 913 | 58 | 31 | 7 |
| 1986 | 894 | 167 | 70 | 97 | 728 | 228 | 291 | 894 | 57 | 25 | 5 |
| 1987 | 858 | 152 | 64 | 88 | 706 | 211 | 280 | 858 | 63 | 23 | 4 |
| 1988 | 776 | 134 | 57 | 78 | 642 | 172 | 269 | 776 | 53 | 22 | 7 |
| 1989 | 772 | 147 | 51 | 96 | 625 | 160 | 267 | 772 | 50 | 21 | 9 |
| 1990 | 758 | 126 | 49 | 76 | 633 | 172 | 258 | 758 | 44 | 17 | 8 |
| 1991 | 833 | 135 | 51 | 84 | 698 | 177 | 288 | 833 | 64 | 19 | 6 |
| 1992 | 944 | 144 | 56 | 88 | 800 | 200 | 308 | 944 | 71 | 22 | 6 |
| 1993 | 872 | 143 | 46 | 97 | 729 | 186 | 272 | 872 | 66 | 26 | 5 |
| 1994 | 818 | 133 | 57 | 76 | 685 | 178 | 249 | 818 | 59 | 26 | 6 |
| 1995 | 777 | 157 | . . . | 87 | 620 | 158 | 228 | 777 | 53 | 20 | 7 |
| 1996 | 784 | 141 | 60 | 80 | 643 | 164 | 244 | 784 | 52 | 21 | 7 |
| 1997 | 813 | 140 | 53 | 87 | 673 | 163 | 248 | 813 | 64 | 24 | 9 |
| 1998 | 756 | 134 | 63 | 71 | 622 | 150 | 218 | 756 | 65 | 21 | 8 |
| 1999 | 684 | 123 | 49 | 74 | 561 | 138 | 196 | 684 | 61 | 25 | 7 |
| 2000 | 621 | 109 | 44 | 65 | 512 | 136 | 154 | 621 | 59 | 22 | 10 |
| 2001 | 706 | 124 | 52 | 72 | 582 | 157 | 181 | 706 | 75 | 21 | 8 |
| 2002 | 858 | 120 | 49 | 71 | 738 | 183 | 228 | 858 | 95 | 35 | 12 |
| 2003 | 895 | 123 | 44 | 79 | 772 | 183 | 230 | 895 | 109 | 46 | 10 |
| 2004 | 868 | 114 | 51 | 63 | 755 | 166 | 230 | 868 | 126 | 40 | 13 |
| 2005 | 856 | 123 | 52 | 70 | 734 | 166 | 233 | 856 | 106 | 47 | 14 |
| 2006 | 775 | 120 | 50 | 70 | 656 | 150 | 199 | 775 | 102 | 38 | 8 |
| 2007 | 693 | 106 | 43 | 63 | 588 | 135 | 181 | 693 | 103 | 38 | 9 |
| 2008 | 839 | 108 | 44 | 64 | 732 | 166 | 216 | 839 | 132 | 56 | 15 |
| 2009 | 1 159 | 127 | 44 | 82 | 1 032 | 223 | 311 | 1 159 | 185 | 77 | 17 |
| 2010 | 1 302 | 137 | 50 | 87 | 1 165 | 245 | 369 | 1 302 | 193 | 88 | 22 |
| 2011 | 1 329 | 125 | 49 | 76 | 1 204 | 253 | 376 | 1 329 | 211 | 86 | 25 |
| 2012 | 1 252 | 133 | 47 | 85 | 1 119 | 241 | 333 | 1 252 | 205 | 98 | 26 |
| 2013 | 1 192 | 124 | 47 | 77 | 1 069 | 235 | 305 | 1 192 | 184 | 103 | 24 |
| 2014 | 1 050 | 106 | 41 | 65 | 943 | 215 | 310 | 166 | 136 | 91 | 26 |
| 2015 | 911 | 99 | 32 | 68 | 811 | 174 | 263 | 158 | 126 | 62 | 28 |
| **HISPANIC** | | | | | | | | | | | |
| **Both Sexes** | | | | | | | | | | | |
| 1980 | 620 | 145 | 66 | 79 | 474 | 138 | 168 | 90 | 49 | 24 | 5 |
| 1981 | 678 | 144 | 60 | 84 | 533 | 171 | 178 | 92 | 57 | 31 | 5 |
| 1982 | 929 | 175 | 73 | 102 | 754 | 221 | 267 | 140 | 75 | 45 | 6 |
| 1983 | 961 | 167 | 64 | 104 | 793 | 214 | 270 | 156 | 93 | 54 | 5 |
| 1984 | 800 | 149 | 60 | 88 | 651 | 164 | 235 | 124 | 71 | 51 | 5 |
| 1985 | 811 | 141 | 55 | 85 | 670 | 171 | 256 | 123 | 73 | 41 | 7 |
| 1986 | 857 | 141 | 57 | 84 | 716 | 183 | 258 | 143 | 85 | 38 | 9 |
| 1987 | 751 | 136 | 57 | 79 | 615 | 152 | 222 | 128 | 75 | 33 | 5 |
| 1988 | 732 | 148 | 63 | 84 | 585 | 145 | 209 | 120 | 69 | 36 | 6 |
| 1989 | 750 | 132 | 59 | 73 | 618 | 158 | 218 | 124 | 76 | 36 | 6 |
| 1990 | 876 | 161 | 68 | 94 | 714 | 167 | 263 | 156 | 85 | 36 | 7 |
| 1991 | 1 092 | 179 | 79 | 99 | 913 | 214 | 332 | 206 | 110 | 44 | 8 |
| 1992 | 1 311 | 219 | 94 | 124 | 1 093 | 240 | 390 | 267 | 126 | 59 | 10 |
| 1993 | 1 248 | 201 | 86 | 115 | 1 047 | 237 | 354 | 261 | 132 | 54 | 10 |
| 1994 | 1 187 | 198 | 90 | 108 | 989 | 220 | 348 | 227 | 132 | 51 | 12 |
| 1995 | 1 140 | 205 | 96 | 109 | 934 | 209 | 325 | 224 | 106 | 54 | 16 |
| 1996 | 1 132 | 199 | 85 | 114 | 933 | 217 | 296 | 246 | 101 | 59 | 14 |
| 1997 | 1 069 | 197 | 87 | 110 | 872 | 206 | 269 | 229 | 99 | 56 | 13 |
| 1998 | 1 026 | 214 | 89 | 125 | 812 | 194 | 260 | 203 | 96 | 48 | 11 |
| 1999 | 945 | 196 | 79 | 117 | 750 | 171 | 233 | 190 | 104 | 42 | 10 |
| 2000 | 954 | 194 | 83 | 112 | 759 | 190 | 247 | 189 | 79 | 42 | 12 |
| 2001 | 1 138 | 208 | 84 | 123 | 931 | 212 | 315 | 228 | 111 | 56 | 9 |
| 2002 | 1 353 | 221 | 81 | 140 | 1 132 | 265 | 373 | 271 | 146 | 62 | 15 |
| 2003 | 1 441 | 192 | 79 | 113 | 1 249 | 273 | 419 | 294 | 183 | 69 | 10 |
| 2004 | 1 342 | 203 | 86 | 117 | 1 139 | 255 | 371 | 261 | 161 | 74 | 18 |
| 2005 | 1 191 | 191 | 78 | 113 | 1 000 | 227 | 324 | 231 | 142 | 61 | 15 |
| 2006 | 1 081 | 170 | 74 | 97 | 911 | 194 | 294 | 231 | 128 | 49 | 14 |
| 2007 | 1 220 | 197 | 78 | 119 | 1 023 | 213 | 322 | 238 | 161 | 70 | 19 |
| 2008 | 1 678 | 251 | 105 | 146 | 1 427 | 307 | 437 | 328 | 242 | 81 | 32 |
| 2009 | 2 706 | 321 | 109 | 212 | 2 385 | 429 | 731 | 584 | 416 | 186 | 38 |
| 2010 | 2 843 | 322 | 99 | 223 | 2 520 | 479 | 736 | 598 | 459 | 199 | 49 |
| 2011 | 2 629 | 300 | 96 | 203 | 2 329 | 473 | 669 | 524 | 424 | 195 | 45 |
| 2012 | 2 514 | 324 | 111 | 213 | 2 190 | 444 | 618 | 502 | 381 | 201 | 44 |
| 2013 | 2 257 | 312 | 111 | 201 | 1 945 | 418 | 549 | 442 | 321 | 172 | 43 |
| 2014 | 1 878 | 250 | 89 | 160 | 1 628 | 368 | 469 | 355 | 255 | 147 | 33 |
| 2015 | 1 726 | 221 | 74 | 147 | 1 505 | 338 | 430 | 319 | 239 | 143 | 36 |

. . . = Not available.

## Table 1-26. Unemployed Persons, by Age, Sex, Race, and Hispanic Origin, 1948–2015—*Continued*

(Thousands of people.)

| Race, Hispanic origin, sex, and year | 16 years and over | 16 to 19 years | | | 20 years and over | | | | | | |
|---|---|---|---|---|---|---|---|---|---|---|---|
| | | Total | 16 to 17 years | 18 to 19 years | Total | 20 to 24 years | 25 to 34 years | 35 to 44 years | 45 to 54 years | 55 to 64 years | 65 years and over |
| **HISPANIC** | | | | | | | | | | | |
| **Men** | | | | | | | | | | | |
| 1980 | 370 | 86 | 39 | 47 | 284 | 85 | 96 | 51 | 31 | 16 | . . . |
| 1981 | 408 | 87 | 40 | 47 | 321 | 105 | 113 | 49 | 31 | 19 | . . . |
| 1982 | 565 | 104 | 45 | 59 | 461 | 138 | 169 | 80 | 40 | 29 | . . . |
| 1983 | 591 | 100 | 38 | 62 | 491 | 134 | 168 | 92 | 57 | 36 | . . . |
| 1984 | 480 | 87 | 36 | 51 | 393 | 103 | 142 | 69 | 41 | 33 | . . . |
| 1985 | 483 | 82 | 34 | 49 | 401 | 108 | 156 | 69 | 40 | 23 | . . . |
| 1986 | 520 | 82 | 33 | 50 | 438 | 115 | 159 | 86 | 46 | 26 | . . . |
| 1987 | 451 | 77 | 32 | 45 | 374 | 88 | 137 | 77 | 46 | 22 | . . . |
| 1988 | 437 | 86 | 36 | 50 | 351 | 83 | 128 | 70 | 42 | 24 | . . . |
| 1989 | 423 | 81 | 36 | 45 | 342 | 88 | 113 | 69 | 43 | 25 | . . . |
| 1990 | 524 | 100 | 40 | 60 | 425 | 99 | 154 | 91 | 53 | 25 | . . . |
| 1991 | 685 | 110 | 47 | 62 | 575 | 139 | 210 | 126 | 62 | 33 | . . . |
| 1992 | 807 | 132 | 56 | 75 | 675 | 156 | 239 | 156 | 75 | 42 | . . . |
| 1993 | 747 | 118 | 50 | 68 | 629 | 144 | 217 | 148 | 79 | 33 | . . . |
| 1994 | 680 | 121 | 54 | 67 | 558 | 128 | 203 | 113 | 75 | 30 | 9 |
| 1995 | 651 | 121 | 59 | 63 | 530 | 123 | 185 | 120 | 57 | 33 | 13 |
| 1996 | 607 | 112 | 49 | 63 | 495 | 117 | 165 | 124 | 49 | 31 | 9 |
| 1997 | 582 | 110 | 47 | 63 | 471 | 125 | 137 | 113 | 54 | 35 | 8 |
| 1998 | 552 | 117 | 54 | 62 | 436 | 115 | 142 | 97 | 49 | 29 | 5 |
| 1999 | 480 | 106 | 42 | 63 | 374 | 96 | 109 | 83 | 54 | 24 | 7 |
| 2000 | 494 | 106 | 46 | 60 | 388 | 105 | 118 | 93 | 42 | 23 | 8 |
| 2001 | 611 | 117 | 52 | 65 | 495 | 129 | 152 | 116 | 55 | 36 | 6 |
| 2002 | 764 | 127 | 42 | 86 | 636 | 151 | 213 | 144 | 82 | 38 | 8 |
| 2003 | 809 | 116 | 42 | 74 | 693 | 157 | 239 | 153 | 98 | 41 | 5 |
| 2004 | 755 | 120 | 48 | 72 | 635 | 158 | 207 | 133 | 82 | 41 | 13 |
| 2005 | 647 | 112 | 42 | 70 | 536 | 134 | 168 | 119 | 74 | 31 | 9 |
| 2006 | 601 | 104 | 43 | 61 | 497 | 110 | 169 | 114 | 66 | 29 | 8 |
| 2007 | 695 | 119 | 44 | 74 | 576 | 121 | 189 | 126 | 92 | 35 | 13 |
| 2008 | 1 007 | 147 | 63 | 84 | 860 | 188 | 275 | 192 | 136 | 50 | 19 |
| 2009 | 1 670 | 196 | 66 | 131 | 1 474 | 255 | 470 | 364 | 246 | 117 | 21 |
| 2010 | 1 711 | 191 | 54 | 137 | 1 519 | 294 | 470 | 346 | 269 | 112 | 28 |
| 2011 | 1 527 | 182 | 53 | 129 | 1 345 | 277 | 395 | 297 | 231 | 116 | 28 |
| 2012 | 1 383 | 189 | 66 | 123 | 1 195 | 254 | 339 | 251 | 208 | 119 | 24 |
| 2013 | 1 263 | 173 | 58 | 115 | 1 090 | 248 | 305 | 232 | 173 | 105 | 28 |
| 2014 | 996 | 132 | 48 | 83 | 864 | 207 | 251 | 179 | 124 | 82 | 22 |
| 2015 | 943 | 124 | 40 | 84 | 820 | 196 | 232 | 151 | 133 | 83 | 25 |
| **HISPANIC** | | | | | | | | | | | |
| **Women** | | | | | | | | | | | |
| 1980 | 249 | 59 | 28 | 31 | 190 | 53 | 72 | 39 | 18 | 8 | . . . |
| 1981 | 269 | 57 | 20 | 37 | 212 | 65 | 65 | 43 | 25 | 13 | . . . |
| 1982 | 364 | 71 | 28 | 43 | 293 | 83 | 98 | 60 | 35 | 16 | . . . |
| 1983 | 369 | 68 | 26 | 42 | 302 | 80 | 102 | 65 | 36 | 18 | . . . |
| 1984 | 320 | 62 | 25 | 37 | 258 | 61 | 93 | 55 | 30 | 17 | . . . |
| 1985 | 327 | 58 | 22 | 37 | 269 | 63 | 100 | 54 | 32 | 18 | . . . |
| 1986 | 337 | 59 | 25 | 35 | 278 | 68 | 99 | 57 | 39 | 12 | . . . |
| 1987 | 300 | 59 | 25 | 34 | 241 | 64 | 85 | 51 | 29 | 11 | . . . |
| 1988 | 296 | 62 | 27 | 34 | 234 | 63 | 81 | 50 | 27 | 12 | . . . |
| 1989 | 327 | 51 | 23 | 28 | 276 | 70 | 105 | 55 | 33 | 11 | . . . |
| 1990 | 351 | 62 | 28 | 34 | 289 | 68 | 109 | 65 | 32 | 11 | . . . |
| 1991 | 407 | 69 | 32 | 37 | 339 | 74 | 122 | 80 | 48 | 12 | . . . |
| 1992 | 504 | 87 | 38 | 49 | 418 | 84 | 151 | 111 | 51 | 17 | . . . |
| 1993 | 501 | 83 | 36 | 47 | 418 | 93 | 136 | 113 | 53 | 21 | . . . |
| 1994 | 508 | 77 | 36 | 40 | 431 | 92 | 145 | 115 | 57 | 21 | 2 |
| 1995 | 488 | 84 | 38 | 46 | 404 | 86 | 140 | 104 | 50 | 21 | 3 |
| 1996 | 525 | 88 | 36 | 52 | 438 | 100 | 131 | 122 | 52 | 27 | 5 |
| 1997 | 488 | 87 | 40 | 46 | 401 | 81 | 132 | 117 | 46 | 21 | 4 |
| 1998 | 473 | 98 | 35 | 63 | 376 | 80 | 118 | 106 | 48 | 19 | 5 |
| 1999 | 466 | 90 | 36 | 54 | 376 | 75 | 124 | 107 | 50 | 17 | 3 |
| 2000 | 460 | 88 | 37 | 51 | 371 | 86 | 129 | 96 | 38 | 19 | 4 |
| 2001 | 527 | 91 | 33 | 58 | 436 | 83 | 163 | 112 | 56 | 20 | 3 |
| 2002 | 590 | 94 | 39 | 54 | 496 | 113 | 160 | 127 | 65 | 24 | 7 |
| 2003 | 631 | 76 | 37 | 39 | 555 | 116 | 180 | 141 | 86 | 28 | 5 |
| 2004 | 587 | 83 | 38 | 45 | 504 | 97 | 164 | 128 | 78 | 32 | 5 |
| 2005 | 544 | 80 | 36 | 43 | 464 | 93 | 156 | 112 | 68 | 30 | 6 |
| 2006 | 480 | 67 | 31 | 36 | 414 | 84 | 125 | 116 | 62 | 20 | 6 |
| 2007 | 525 | 79 | 34 | 45 | 446 | 92 | 134 | 111 | 69 | 35 | 6 |
| 2008 | 672 | 104 | 42 | 62 | 567 | 119 | 162 | 136 | 105 | 32 | 13 |
| 2009 | 1 036 | 125 | 44 | 81 | 911 | 174 | 260 | 220 | 170 | 70 | 17 |
| 2010 | 1 132 | 131 | 45 | 86 | 1 001 | 186 | 267 | 252 | 190 | 87 | 20 |
| 2011 | 1 102 | 118 | 44 | 74 | 984 | 196 | 274 | 227 | 192 | 78 | 17 |
| 2012 | 1 130 | 135 | 45 | 90 | 995 | 190 | 278 | 251 | 173 | 83 | 20 |
| 2013 | 994 | 139 | 52 | 86 | 855 | 170 | 244 | 210 | 148 | 67 | 15 |
| 2014 | 882 | 118 | 41 | 77 | 764 | 162 | 218 | 176 | 131 | 65 | 11 |
| 2015 | 783 | 98 | 34 | 63 | 686 | 142 | 198 | 168 | 107 | 60 | 11 |

. . . = Not available.

**Table 1-27. Unemployment Rates of Civilian Workers, by Age, Sex, Race, and Hispanic Origin, 1948–2015**

(Percent of labor force.)

| Race, Hispanic origin, sex, and year | 16 years and over | 16 to 19 years | | | 20 years and over | | | | | | |
|---|---|---|---|---|---|---|---|---|---|---|---|
| | | Total | 16 to 17 years | 18 to 19 years | Total | 20 to 24 years | 25 to 34 years | 35 to 44 years | 45 to 54 years | 55 to 64 years | 65 years and over |
| **ALL RACES** | | | | | | | | | | | |
| **Both Sexes** | | | | | | | | | | | |
| 1948 | 3.8 | 9.2 | 10.1 | 8.6 | 3.3 | 6.2 | 3.2 | 2.6 | 2.7 | 3.1 | 3.2 |
| 1949 | 5.9 | 13.4 | 14.0 | 13.0 | 5.4 | 9.3 | 5.4 | 4.4 | 4.2 | 5.2 | 4.9 |
| 1950 | 5.3 | 12.2 | 13.6 | 11.2 | 4.8 | 7.7 | 4.8 | 3.8 | 4.2 | 4.8 | 4.5 |
| 1951 | 3.3 | 8.2 | 9.6 | 7.1 | 3.0 | 4.1 | 3.0 | 2.5 | 2.7 | 3.1 | 3.4 |
| 1952 | 3.0 | 8.5 | 10.0 | 7.3 | 2.7 | 4.6 | 2.6 | 2.3 | 2.3 | 2.4 | 2.9 |
| 1953 | 2.9 | 7.6 | 8.7 | 6.8 | 2.6 | 4.7 | 2.5 | 2.2 | 2.3 | 2.7 | 2.2 |
| 1954 | 5.5 | 12.6 | 13.5 | 10.7 | 5.1 | 9.2 | 5.3 | 4.5 | 4.4 | 4.5 | 4.1 |
| 1955 | 4.4 | 11.0 | 12.3 | 10.0 | 3.9 | 7.0 | 3.8 | 3.4 | 3.4 | 4.2 | 3.6 |
| 1956 | 4.1 | 11.1 | 12.3 | 10.2 | 3.7 | 6.6 | 3.7 | 3.0 | 3.2 | 3.5 | 3.2 |
| 1957 | 4.3 | 11.6 | 12.5 | 10.9 | 3.8 | 7.1 | 3.9 | 3.1 | 3.3 | 3.4 | 3.4 |
| 1958 | 6.8 | 15.9 | 16.4 | 15.5 | 6.2 | 11.2 | 6.8 | 5.4 | 5.2 | 5.2 | 4.8 |
| 1959 | 5.5 | 14.6 | 15.3 | 14.0 | 4.8 | 8.5 | 5.0 | 4.2 | 4.2 | 4.4 | 4.3 |
| 1960 | 5.5 | 14.7 | 15.5 | 14.1 | 4.8 | 8.7 | 5.2 | 4.1 | 4.1 | 4.2 | 3.8 |
| 1961 | 6.7 | 16.8 | 18.3 | 15.8 | 5.9 | 10.4 | 6.2 | 5.2 | 5.0 | 5.4 | 5.1 |
| 1962 | 5.5 | 14.7 | 16.3 | 13.6 | 4.9 | 9.0 | 5.1 | 4.1 | 4.0 | 4.2 | 4.5 |
| 1963 | 5.7 | 17.2 | 19.3 | 15.6 | 4.8 | 8.8 | 5.2 | 4.0 | 3.8 | 4.1 | 4.1 |
| 1964 | 5.2 | 16.2 | 17.8 | 14.9 | 4.3 | 8.3 | 4.3 | 3.6 | 3.5 | 3.7 | 3.8 |
| 1965 | 4.5 | 14.8 | 16.5 | 13.5 | 3.6 | 6.7 | 3.7 | 3.2 | 2.8 | 3.1 | 3.3 |
| 1966 | 3.8 | 12.8 | 14.8 | 11.3 | 2.9 | 5.3 | 3.1 | 2.5 | 2.3 | 2.5 | 3.0 |
| 1967 | 3.8 | 12.9 | 14.6 | 11.6 | 3.0 | 5.7 | 3.2 | 2.5 | 2.4 | 2.4 | 2.8 |
| 1968 | 3.6 | 12.7 | 14.7 | 11.2 | 2.7 | 5.8 | 2.8 | 2.2 | 1.9 | 2.0 | 2.8 |
| 1969 | 3.5 | 12.2 | 14.5 | 10.5 | 2.7 | 5.7 | 2.8 | 2.2 | 1.9 | 1.9 | 2.2 |
| 1970 | 4.9 | 15.3 | 17.1 | 13.8 | 4.0 | 8.2 | 4.2 | 3.1 | 2.8 | 2.7 | 3.2 |
| 1971 | 5.9 | 16.9 | 18.7 | 15.5 | 4.9 | 10.0 | 5.3 | 3.9 | 3.4 | 3.3 | 3.5 |
| 1972 | 5.6 | 16.2 | 18.5 | 14.6 | 4.5 | 9.3 | 4.6 | 3.5 | 3.0 | 3.2 | 3.6 |
| 1973 | 4.9 | 14.5 | 17.3 | 12.4 | 3.9 | 7.8 | 4.2 | 2.7 | 2.5 | 2.6 | 3.0 |
| 1974 | 5.6 | 16.0 | 18.3 | 14.3 | 4.5 | 9.1 | 4.8 | 3.3 | 2.9 | 2.8 | 3.4 |
| 1975 | 8.5 | 19.9 | 21.4 | 18.9 | 7.3 | 13.6 | 7.8 | 5.6 | 5.2 | 4.6 | 5.2 |
| 1976 | 7.7 | 19.0 | 21.1 | 17.5 | 6.5 | 12.0 | 7.1 | 4.9 | 4.5 | 4.5 | 5.1 |
| 1977 | 7.1 | 17.8 | 19.9 | 16.2 | 5.9 | 11.0 | 6.5 | 4.4 | 3.9 | 3.9 | 5.0 |
| 1978 | 6.1 | 16.4 | 19.3 | 14.2 | 5.0 | 9.6 | 5.3 | 3.7 | 3.3 | 2.9 | 4.0 |
| 1979 | 5.8 | 16.1 | 18.1 | 14.7 | 4.8 | 9.1 | 5.2 | 3.6 | 3.2 | 2.9 | 3.4 |
| 1980 | 7.1 | 17.8 | 20.0 | 16.2 | 6.1 | 11.5 | 6.9 | 4.6 | 4.0 | 3.3 | 3.1 |
| 1981 | 7.6 | 19.6 | 21.4 | 18.4 | 6.5 | 12.3 | 7.3 | 5.0 | 4.2 | 3.7 | 3.2 |
| 1982 | 9.7 | 23.2 | 24.9 | 22.1 | 8.6 | 14.9 | 9.7 | 6.9 | 5.7 | 5.4 | 3.5 |
| 1983 | 9.6 | 22.4 | 24.5 | 21.1 | 8.6 | 14.5 | 9.7 | 7.0 | 6.2 | 5.6 | 3.7 |
| 1984 | 7.5 | 18.9 | 21.2 | 17.4 | 6.7 | 11.5 | 7.3 | 5.4 | 4.9 | 4.7 | 3.3 |
| 1985 | 7.2 | 18.6 | 21.0 | 17.0 | 6.4 | 11.1 | 7.0 | 5.1 | 4.7 | 4.3 | 3.2 |
| 1986 | 7.0 | 18.3 | 20.2 | 17.0 | 6.2 | 10.7 | 6.9 | 5.0 | 4.5 | 4.1 | 3.0 |
| 1987 | 6.2 | 16.9 | 19.1 | 15.2 | 5.4 | 9.7 | 6.0 | 4.5 | 4.0 | 3.5 | 2.5 |
| 1988 | 5.5 | 15.3 | 17.4 | 13.8 | 4.8 | 8.7 | 5.4 | 4.0 | 3.4 | 3.2 | 2.7 |
| 1989 | 5.3 | 15.0 | 17.2 | 13.6 | 4.6 | 8.6 | 5.2 | 3.8 | 3.2 | 3.2 | 2.6 |
| 1990 | 5.6 | 15.5 | 17.9 | 14.1 | 4.9 | 8.8 | 5.6 | 4.1 | 3.6 | 3.3 | 3.0 |
| 1991 | 6.8 | 18.7 | 21.0 | 17.2 | 6.1 | 10.8 | 6.9 | 5.2 | 4.5 | 4.1 | 3.3 |
| 1992 | 7.5 | 20.1 | 23.1 | 18.2 | 6.8 | 11.4 | 7.6 | 5.8 | 5.1 | 5.1 | 3.8 |
| 1993 | 6.9 | 19.0 | 21.4 | 17.5 | 6.2 | 10.5 | 6.9 | 5.5 | 4.8 | 4.7 | 3.2 |
| 1994 | 6.1 | 17.6 | 19.9 | 16.0 | 5.4 | 9.7 | 6.0 | 4.6 | 4.0 | 4.1 | 4.0 |
| 1995 | 5.6 | 17.3 | 20.2 | 15.3 | 4.9 | 9.1 | 5.4 | 4.3 | 3.3 | 3.6 | 4.0 |
| 1996 | 5.4 | 16.7 | 18.9 | 15.2 | 4.7 | 9.3 | 5.2 | 4.1 | 3.3 | 3.3 | 3.6 |
| 1997 | 4.9 | 16.0 | 18.2 | 14.5 | 4.3 | 8.5 | 4.7 | 3.8 | 3.0 | 2.9 | 3.3 |
| 1998 | 4.5 | 14.6 | 17.2 | 12.8 | 3.9 | 7.9 | 4.3 | 3.4 | 2.8 | 2.6 | 3.2 |
| 1999 | 4.2 | 13.9 | 16.3 | 12.4 | 3.6 | 7.5 | 4.0 | 3.0 | 2.6 | 2.7 | 3.1 |
| 2000 | 4.0 | 13.1 | 15.4 | 11.6 | 3.4 | 7.2 | 3.7 | 3.0 | 2.5 | 2.5 | 3.1 |
| 2001 | 4.7 | 14.7 | 17.2 | 13.1 | 4.2 | 8.3 | 4.6 | 3.6 | 3.1 | 3.0 | 2.9 |
| 2002 | 5.8 | 16.5 | 18.8 | 15.1 | 5.2 | 9.7 | 5.9 | 4.6 | 4.0 | 3.9 | 3.6 |
| 2003 | 6.0 | 17.5 | 19.1 | 16.4 | 5.4 | 10.0 | 6.1 | 4.9 | 4.1 | 4.1 | 3.8 |
| 2004 | 5.5 | 17.0 | 20.2 | 15.0 | 4.9 | 9.4 | 5.5 | 4.4 | 3.8 | 3.8 | 3.6 |
| 2005 | 5.1 | 16.6 | 19.1 | 14.9 | 4.5 | 8.8 | 5.1 | 3.9 | 3.5 | 3.3 | 3.5 |
| 2006 | 4.6 | 15.4 | 17.2 | 14.1 | 4.1 | 8.2 | 4.7 | 3.6 | 3.1 | 3.0 | 2.9 |
| 2007 | 4.6 | 15.7 | 17.5 | 14.5 | 4.1 | 8.2 | 4.7 | 3.4 | 3.2 | 3.1 | 3.3 |
| 2008 | 5.8 | 18.7 | 22.1 | 16.8 | 5.2 | 10.2 | 5.8 | 4.6 | 4.1 | 3.7 | 4.2 |
| 2009 | 9.3 | 24.3 | 25.9 | 23.4 | 8.6 | 14.7 | 9.9 | 7.9 | 7.2 | 6.6 | 6.4 |
| 2010 | 9.6 | 25.9 | 29.1 | 24.2 | 9.0 | 15.5 | 10.1 | 8.1 | 7.7 | 7.1 | 6.7 |
| 2011 | 8.9 | 24.4 | 27.7 | 22.9 | 8.3 | 14.6 | 9.5 | 7.3 | 7.1 | 6.6 | 6.5 |
| 2012 | 8.1 | 24.0 | 27.3 | 22.3 | 7.4 | 13.3 | 8.3 | 6.6 | 6.2 | 5.9 | 6.2 |
| 2013 | 7.4 | 22.9 | 26.5 | 21.0 | 6.8 | 12.8 | 7.4 | 5.9 | 5.6 | 5.3 | 5.4 |
| 2014 | 6.2 | 19.6 | 21.6 | 18.5 | 5.7 | 11.2 | 6.5 | 4.7 | 4.4 | 4.3 | 4.1 |
| 2015 | 5.3 | 16.9 | 18.3 | 16.2 | 4.8 | 9.7 | 5.5 | 4.1 | 3.7 | 3.8 | 3.8 |

## Table 1-27. Unemployment Rates of Civilian Workers, by Age, Sex, Race, and Hispanic Origin, 1948–2015
### —Continued

(Percent of labor force.)

| Race, Hispanic origin, sex, and year | 16 years and over | 16 to 19 years | | | 20 years and over | | | | | | |
|---|---|---|---|---|---|---|---|---|---|---|---|
| | | Total | 16 to 17 years | 18 to 19 years | Total | 20 to 24 years | 25 to 34 years | 35 to 44 years | 45 to 54 years | 55 to 64 years | 65 years and over |
| **ALL RACES** | | | | | | | | | | | |
| **Men** | | | | | | | | | | | |
| 1948 | 3.6 | 9.8 | 10.2 | 9.5 | 3.2 | 6.9 | 2.8 | 2.4 | 2.5 | 3.1 | 3.4 |
| 1949 | 5.9 | 14.3 | 13.7 | 14.6 | 5.4 | 10.4 | 5.2 | 4.3 | 4.3 | 5.4 | 5.1 |
| 1950 | 5.1 | 12.7 | 13.3 | 12.3 | 4.7 | 8.1 | 4.4 | 3.6 | 4.0 | 4.9 | 4.8 |
| 1951 | 2.8 | 8.1 | 9.4 | 7.0 | 2.5 | 3.9 | 2.3 | 2.0 | 2.4 | 2.8 | 3.5 |
| 1952 | 2.8 | 8.9 | 10.5 | 7.4 | 2.4 | 4.6 | 2.2 | 1.9 | 2.2 | 2.4 | 3.0 |
| 1953 | 2.8 | 7.9 | 8.8 | 7.2 | 2.5 | 5.0 | 2.2 | 2.0 | 2.3 | 2.8 | 2.4 |
| 1954 | 5.3 | 13.5 | 13.9 | 13.2 | 4.9 | 10.7 | 4.8 | 4.1 | 4.3 | 4.5 | 4.4 |
| 1955 | 4.2 | 11.6 | 12.5 | 10.8 | 3.8 | 7.7 | 3.3 | 3.1 | 3.2 | 4.3 | 4.0 |
| 1956 | 3.8 | 11.1 | 11.7 | 10.5 | 3.4 | 6.9 | 3.3 | 2.6 | 3.0 | 3.5 | 3.5 |
| 1957 | 4.1 | 12.4 | 12.4 | 12.3 | 3.6 | 7.8 | 3.3 | 2.8 | 3.3 | 3.5 | 3.4 |
| 1958 | 6.8 | 17.1 | 16.3 | 17.8 | 6.2 | 12.7 | 6.5 | 5.1 | 5.3 | 5.5 | 5.2 |
| 1959 | 5.2 | 15.3 | 15.8 | 14.9 | 4.7 | 8.7 | 4.7 | 3.7 | 4.1 | 4.5 | 4.8 |
| 1960 | 5.4 | 15.3 | 15.5 | 15.0 | 4.7 | 8.9 | 4.8 | 3.8 | 4.1 | 4.6 | 4.2 |
| 1961 | 6.4 | 17.1 | 18.3 | 16.3 | 5.7 | 10.8 | 5.7 | 4.6 | 4.9 | 5.7 | 5.5 |
| 1962 | 5.2 | 14.7 | 16.0 | 13.8 | 4.6 | 8.9 | 4.5 | 3.6 | 3.9 | 4.6 | 4.6 |
| 1963 | 5.2 | 17.2 | 18.8 | 15.9 | 4.5 | 8.8 | 4.5 | 3.5 | 3.6 | 4.3 | 4.5 |
| 1964 | 4.6 | 15.8 | 17.1 | 14.6 | 3.9 | 8.1 | 3.5 | 2.9 | 3.2 | 3.9 | 4.0 |
| 1965 | 4.0 | 14.1 | 16.1 | 12.4 | 3.2 | 6.4 | 2.9 | 2.5 | 2.5 | 3.3 | 3.5 |
| 1966 | 3.2 | 11.7 | 13.7 | 10.2 | 2.5 | 4.6 | 2.4 | 2.0 | 1.9 | 2.6 | 3.1 |
| 1967 | 3.1 | 12.3 | 14.5 | 10.5 | 2.3 | 4.7 | 2.1 | 1.7 | 2.0 | 2.3 | 2.8 |
| 1968 | 2.9 | 11.6 | 13.9 | 9.7 | 2.2 | 5.1 | 1.9 | 1.6 | 1.6 | 1.9 | 2.8 |
| 1969 | 2.8 | 11.4 | 13.8 | 9.3 | 2.1 | 5.1 | 1.9 | 1.5 | 1.5 | 1.8 | 2.2 |
| 1970 | 4.4 | 15.0 | 16.9 | 13.4 | 3.5 | 8.4 | 3.5 | 2.4 | 2.4 | 2.8 | 3.3 |
| 1971 | 5.3 | 16.6 | 18.7 | 15.0 | 4.4 | 10.3 | 4.4 | 3.1 | 3.0 | 3.3 | 3.4 |
| 1972 | 5.0 | 15.9 | 18.3 | 14.1 | 4.0 | 9.3 | 3.8 | 2.7 | 2.6 | 3.2 | 3.6 |
| 1973 | 4.2 | 13.9 | 17.0 | 11.4 | 3.3 | 7.3 | 3.4 | 2.0 | 2.1 | 2.4 | 3.0 |
| 1974 | 4.9 | 15.6 | 18.4 | 13.3 | 3.8 | 8.8 | 4.0 | 2.6 | 2.4 | 2.6 | 3.3 |
| 1975 | 7.9 | 20.1 | 21.6 | 19.0 | 6.8 | 14.3 | 6.9 | 4.9 | 4.8 | 4.3 | 5.4 |
| 1976 | 7.1 | 19.2 | 21.4 | 17.6 | 5.9 | 12.1 | 6.2 | 4.1 | 4.0 | 4.2 | 5.1 |
| 1977 | 6.3 | 17.3 | 19.5 | 15.6 | 5.2 | 10.8 | 5.7 | 3.5 | 3.2 | 3.6 | 5.2 |
| 1978 | 5.3 | 15.8 | 19.1 | 13.3 | 4.3 | 9.2 | 4.4 | 2.8 | 2.7 | 2.8 | 4.2 |
| 1979 | 5.1 | 15.9 | 17.9 | 14.3 | 4.2 | 8.7 | 4.3 | 2.9 | 2.7 | 2.7 | 3.4 |
| 1980 | 6.9 | 18.3 | 20.4 | 16.7 | 5.9 | 12.5 | 6.7 | 4.1 | 3.6 | 3.4 | 3.1 |
| 1981 | 7.4 | 20.1 | 22.0 | 18.8 | 6.3 | 13.2 | 6.9 | 4.5 | 4.0 | 3.6 | 2.9 |
| 1982 | 9.9 | 24.4 | 26.4 | 23.1 | 8.8 | 16.4 | 10.1 | 6.9 | 5.6 | 5.5 | 3.7 |
| 1983 | 9.9 | 23.3 | 25.2 | 22.2 | 8.9 | 15.9 | 10.1 | 7.1 | 6.3 | 6.1 | 3.9 |
| 1984 | 7.4 | 19.6 | 21.9 | 18.3 | 6.6 | 11.9 | 7.2 | 5.2 | 4.6 | 5.0 | 3.0 |
| 1985 | 7.0 | 19.5 | 21.9 | 17.9 | 6.2 | 11.4 | 6.6 | 4.9 | 4.6 | 4.3 | 3.1 |
| 1986 | 6.9 | 19.0 | 20.8 | 17.7 | 6.1 | 11.0 | 6.7 | 5.1 | 4.4 | 4.3 | 3.2 |
| 1987 | 6.2 | 17.8 | 20.2 | 16.0 | 5.4 | 9.9 | 5.9 | 4.4 | 4.2 | 3.7 | 2.6 |
| 1988 | 5.5 | 16.0 | 18.2 | 14.6 | 4.8 | 8.9 | 5.3 | 3.8 | 3.5 | 3.5 | 2.5 |
| 1989 | 5.2 | 15.9 | 18.6 | 14.2 | 4.5 | 8.8 | 4.8 | 3.7 | 3.2 | 3.5 | 2.4 |
| 1990 | 5.7 | 16.3 | 18.4 | 15.0 | 5.0 | 9.1 | 5.5 | 4.1 | 3.7 | 3.8 | 3.0 |
| 1991 | 7.2 | 19.8 | 21.8 | 18.5 | 6.4 | 11.6 | 7.0 | 5.5 | 4.8 | 4.6 | 3.3 |
| 1992 | 7.9 | 21.5 | 24.6 | 19.5 | 7.1 | 12.2 | 7.8 | 6.1 | 5.6 | 5.8 | 3.3 |
| 1993 | 7.2 | 20.4 | 22.9 | 18.8 | 6.4 | 11.3 | 7.0 | 5.6 | 5.1 | 5.2 | 3.2 |
| 1994 | 6.2 | 19.0 | 21.0 | 17.6 | 5.4 | 10.2 | 5.9 | 4.5 | 4.0 | 4.4 | 4.0 |
| 1995 | 5.6 | 18.4 | 21.1 | 16.5 | 4.8 | 9.2 | 5.1 | 4.2 | 3.5 | 3.6 | 4.3 |
| 1996 | 5.4 | 18.1 | 20.8 | 16.3 | 4.6 | 9.5 | 4.9 | 4.0 | 3.5 | 3.3 | 3.4 |
| 1997 | 4.9 | 16.9 | 19.1 | 15.4 | 4.2 | 8.9 | 4.3 | 3.6 | 3.1 | 3.1 | 3.0 |
| 1998 | 4.4 | 16.2 | 19.1 | 14.1 | 3.7 | 8.1 | 3.9 | 3.0 | 2.8 | 2.8 | 3.1 |
| 1999 | 4.1 | 14.7 | 17.0 | 13.1 | 3.5 | 7.7 | 3.6 | 2.8 | 2.6 | 2.7 | 3.0 |
| 2000 | 3.9 | 14.0 | 16.8 | 12.2 | 3.3 | 7.3 | 3.4 | 2.8 | 2.4 | 2.4 | 3.3 |
| 2001 | 4.8 | 16.0 | 19.1 | 14.0 | 4.2 | 9.0 | 4.3 | 3.6 | 3.2 | 3.3 | 3.0 |
| 2002 | 5.9 | 18.1 | 21.1 | 16.4 | 5.3 | 10.2 | 5.8 | 4.5 | 4.2 | 4.3 | 3.4 |
| 2003 | 6.3 | 19.3 | 20.7 | 18.4 | 5.6 | 10.6 | 6.2 | 5.0 | 4.4 | 4.5 | 4.0 |
| 2004 | 5.6 | 18.4 | 22.0 | 16.3 | 5.0 | 10.1 | 5.5 | 4.3 | 3.9 | 3.9 | 3.7 |
| 2005 | 5.1 | 18.6 | 22.0 | 16.5 | 4.4 | 9.6 | 4.7 | 3.7 | 3.5 | 3.3 | 3.4 |
| 2006 | 4.6 | 16.9 | 18.6 | 15.7 | 4.0 | 8.7 | 4.5 | 3.3 | 3.1 | 3.0 | 2.8 |
| 2007 | 4.7 | 17.6 | 19.4 | 16.5 | 4.1 | 8.9 | 4.7 | 3.3 | 3.1 | 3.2 | 3.4 |
| 2008 | 6.1 | 21.2 | 25.2 | 19.0 | 5.4 | 11.4 | 6.1 | 4.6 | 4.2 | 3.8 | 4.5 |
| 2009 | 10.3 | 27.8 | 28.7 | 27.4 | 9.6 | 17.0 | 10.9 | 8.6 | 8.2 | 7.2 | 6.7 |
| 2010 | 10.5 | 28.8 | 31.8 | 27.4 | 9.8 | 17.8 | 10.9 | 8.5 | 8.6 | 8.0 | 7.1 |
| 2011 | 9.4 | 27.2 | 29.1 | 26.3 | 8.7 | 15.7 | 9.7 | 7.4 | 7.4 | 7.1 | 6.5 |
| 2012 | 8.2 | 26.8 | 30.6 | 25.0 | 7.5 | 14.3 | 8.2 | 6.4 | 6.2 | 6.3 | 6.2 |
| 2013 | 7.6 | 25.5 | 29.1 | 23.7 | 7.0 | 14.0 | 7.6 | 5.8 | 5.7 | 5.6 | 5.5 |
| 2014 | 6.3 | 21.4 | 24.0 | 20.1 | 5.7 | 12.2 | 6.4 | 4.6 | 4.4 | 4.5 | 4.6 |
| 2015 | 5.4 | 18.4 | 19.8 | 17.6 | 4.9 | 10.8 | 5.5 | 4.0 | 3.6 | 3.9 | 3.8 |

## Table 1-27. Unemployment Rates of Civilian Workers, by Age, Sex, Race, and Hispanic Origin, 1948–2015
### —Continued

(Percent of labor force.)

| Race, Hispanic origin, sex, and year | 16 years and over | 16 to 19 years | | | 20 years and over | | | | | | |
|---|---|---|---|---|---|---|---|---|---|---|---|
| | | Total | 16 to 17 years | 18 to 19 years | Total | 20 to 24 years | 25 to 34 years | 35 to 44 years | 45 to 54 years | 55 to 64 years | 65 years and over |
| **ALL RACES** | | | | | | | | | | | |
| **Women** | | | | | | | | | | | |
| 1948 | 4.1 | 8.3 | 10.0 | 7.4 | 3.6 | 4.8 | 4.3 | 3.0 | 3.0 | 3.1 | 2.3 |
| 1949 | 6.0 | 12.3 | 14.4 | 11.2 | 5.3 | 7.3 | 5.9 | 4.7 | 4.0 | 4.4 | 3.8 |
| 1950 | 5.7 | 11.4 | 14.2 | 9.8 | 5.1 | 6.9 | 5.7 | 4.4 | 4.5 | 4.5 | 3.4 |
| 1951 | 4.4 | 8.3 | 10.0 | 7.2 | 4.0 | 4.4 | 4.5 | 3.8 | 3.5 | 4.0 | 2.9 |
| 1952 | 3.6 | 8.0 | 9.1 | 7.3 | 3.2 | 4.5 | 3.6 | 3.0 | 2.5 | 2.5 | 2.2 |
| 1953 | 3.3 | 7.2 | 8.5 | 6.4 | 2.9 | 4.3 | 3.4 | 2.5 | 2.3 | 2.5 | 1.4 |
| 1954 | 6.0 | 11.4 | 12.7 | 7.7 | 5.5 | 7.3 | 6.6 | 5.3 | 4.6 | 4.6 | 3.0 |
| 1955 | 4.9 | 10.2 | 12.0 | 9.1 | 4.4 | 6.1 | 5.3 | 4.0 | 3.6 | 3.8 | 2.3 |
| 1956 | 4.8 | 11.2 | 13.2 | 9.9 | 4.2 | 6.3 | 4.8 | 3.9 | 3.6 | 3.6 | 2.3 |
| 1957 | 4.7 | 10.6 | 12.6 | 9.4 | 4.1 | 6.0 | 5.3 | 3.8 | 3.2 | 3.0 | 3.4 |
| 1958 | 6.8 | 14.3 | 16.6 | 12.9 | 6.1 | 8.9 | 7.3 | 6.2 | 4.9 | 4.5 | 3.7 |
| 1959 | 5.9 | 13.5 | 14.4 | 13.0 | 5.2 | 8.1 | 5.9 | 5.1 | 4.2 | 4.1 | 2.8 |
| 1960 | 5.9 | 13.9 | 15.5 | 12.9 | 5.1 | 8.3 | 6.3 | 4.8 | 4.2 | 3.4 | 2.9 |
| 1961 | 7.2 | 16.3 | 18.3 | 15.1 | 6.3 | 9.8 | 7.4 | 6.4 | 5.1 | 4.5 | 4.0 |
| 1962 | 6.2 | 14.6 | 16.7 | 13.5 | 5.4 | 9.1 | 6.5 | 5.2 | 4.1 | 3.5 | 4.2 |
| 1963 | 6.5 | 17.2 | 20.2 | 15.2 | 5.4 | 8.9 | 6.9 | 5.1 | 4.2 | 3.6 | 3.2 |
| 1964 | 6.2 | 16.6 | 18.8 | 15.2 | 5.2 | 8.6 | 6.3 | 5.0 | 3.9 | 3.3 | 3.3 |
| 1965 | 5.5 | 15.7 | 17.2 | 14.8 | 4.5 | 7.3 | 5.5 | 4.6 | 3.2 | 2.8 | 2.9 |
| 1966 | 4.8 | 14.1 | 16.6 | 12.6 | 3.8 | 6.3 | 4.5 | 3.6 | 2.9 | 2.3 | 2.8 |
| 1967 | 5.2 | 13.5 | 14.8 | 12.8 | 4.2 | 7.0 | 5.4 | 4.1 | 3.1 | 2.4 | 2.7 |
| 1968 | 4.8 | 14.0 | 15.9 | 12.9 | 3.8 | 6.7 | 4.7 | 3.4 | 2.4 | 2.2 | 2.7 |
| 1969 | 4.7 | 13.3 | 15.5 | 11.8 | 3.7 | 6.3 | 4.6 | 3.4 | 2.6 | 2.2 | 2.3 |
| 1970 | 5.9 | 15.6 | 17.4 | 14.4 | 4.8 | 7.9 | 5.7 | 4.4 | 3.5 | 2.7 | 3.1 |
| 1971 | 6.9 | 17.2 | 18.7 | 16.2 | 5.7 | 9.6 | 7.0 | 5.2 | 4.0 | 3.3 | 3.6 |
| 1972 | 6.6 | 16.7 | 18.8 | 15.2 | 5.4 | 9.4 | 6.2 | 4.9 | 3.6 | 3.3 | 3.5 |
| 1973 | 6.0 | 15.3 | 17.7 | 13.5 | 4.9 | 8.5 | 5.8 | 3.9 | 3.2 | 2.8 | 2.9 |
| 1974 | 6.7 | 16.6 | 18.2 | 15.4 | 5.5 | 9.5 | 6.2 | 4.6 | 3.7 | 3.2 | 3.6 |
| 1975 | 9.3 | 19.7 | 21.2 | 18.7 | 8.0 | 12.7 | 9.1 | 6.8 | 5.9 | 5.1 | 5.0 |
| 1976 | 8.6 | 18.7 | 20.8 | 17.4 | 7.4 | 11.9 | 8.4 | 6.1 | 5.2 | 4.9 | 5.0 |
| 1977 | 8.2 | 18.3 | 20.5 | 16.9 | 7.0 | 11.2 | 7.7 | 5.7 | 5.1 | 4.4 | 4.7 |
| 1978 | 7.2 | 17.1 | 19.5 | 15.3 | 6.0 | 10.1 | 6.7 | 5.0 | 4.0 | 3.2 | 3.8 |
| 1979 | 6.8 | 16.4 | 18.3 | 15.0 | 5.7 | 9.6 | 6.5 | 4.6 | 3.9 | 3.2 | 3.3 |
| 1980 | 7.4 | 17.2 | 19.6 | 15.6 | 6.4 | 10.4 | 7.2 | 5.3 | 4.5 | 3.3 | 3.1 |
| 1981 | 7.9 | 19.0 | 20.7 | 17.9 | 6.8 | 11.2 | 7.7 | 5.7 | 4.6 | 3.8 | 3.6 |
| 1982 | 9.4 | 21.9 | 23.2 | 21.0 | 8.3 | 13.2 | 9.3 | 7.0 | 5.9 | 5.2 | 3.2 |
| 1983 | 9.2 | 21.3 | 23.7 | 19.9 | 8.1 | 12.9 | 9.1 | 6.9 | 6.0 | 5.0 | 3.4 |
| 1984 | 7.6 | 18.0 | 20.4 | 16.6 | 6.8 | 10.9 | 7.4 | 5.6 | 5.2 | 4.3 | 3.8 |
| 1985 | 7.4 | 17.6 | 20.0 | 16.0 | 6.6 | 10.7 | 7.4 | 5.5 | 4.8 | 4.3 | 3.3 |
| 1986 | 7.1 | 17.6 | 19.6 | 16.3 | 6.2 | 10.3 | 7.2 | 5.0 | 4.5 | 3.8 | 2.8 |
| 1987 | 6.2 | 15.9 | 18.0 | 14.3 | 5.4 | 9.4 | 6.2 | 4.6 | 3.7 | 3.1 | 2.4 |
| 1988 | 5.6 | 14.4 | 16.6 | 12.9 | 4.9 | 8.5 | 5.6 | 4.1 | 3.4 | 2.7 | 2.9 |
| 1989 | 5.4 | 14.0 | 15.7 | 13.0 | 4.7 | 8.3 | 5.6 | 3.9 | 3.2 | 2.8 | 2.9 |
| 1990 | 5.5 | 14.7 | 17.4 | 13.1 | 4.9 | 8.5 | 5.6 | 4.2 | 3.4 | 2.8 | 3.1 |
| 1991 | 6.4 | 17.5 | 20.2 | 15.9 | 5.7 | 9.8 | 6.8 | 4.8 | 4.2 | 3.4 | 3.3 |
| 1992 | 7.0 | 18.6 | 21.5 | 16.6 | 6.3 | 10.3 | 7.4 | 5.5 | 4.6 | 4.2 | 4.5 |
| 1993 | 6.6 | 17.5 | 19.8 | 16.1 | 5.9 | 9.7 | 6.8 | 5.3 | 4.5 | 4.0 | 3.1 |
| 1994 | 6.0 | 16.2 | 18.7 | 14.3 | 5.4 | 9.2 | 6.2 | 4.7 | 4.0 | 3.9 | 4.0 |
| 1995 | 5.6 | 16.1 | 19.2 | 14.0 | 4.9 | 9.0 | 5.7 | 4.4 | 3.2 | 3.6 | 3.7 |
| 1996 | 5.4 | 15.2 | 16.9 | 14.0 | 4.8 | 9.0 | 5.5 | 4.2 | 3.2 | 3.4 | 4.0 |
| 1997 | 5.0 | 15.0 | 17.2 | 13.6 | 4.4 | 8.1 | 5.2 | 4.0 | 2.9 | 2.7 | 3.6 |
| 1998 | 4.6 | 12.9 | 15.1 | 11.5 | 4.1 | 7.8 | 4.8 | 3.8 | 2.7 | 2.4 | 3.3 |
| 1999 | 4.3 | 13.2 | 15.5 | 11.6 | 3.8 | 7.2 | 4.4 | 3.3 | 2.5 | 2.6 | 3.2 |
| 2000 | 4.1 | 12.1 | 13.9 | 10.8 | 3.6 | 7.1 | 4.1 | 3.3 | 2.5 | 2.5 | 2.7 |
| 2001 | 4.7 | 13.4 | 15.2 | 12.2 | 4.1 | 7.5 | 5.1 | 3.7 | 3.0 | 2.7 | 2.9 |
| 2002 | 5.6 | 14.9 | 16.6 | 13.8 | 5.1 | 9.1 | 5.9 | 4.6 | 3.8 | 3.5 | 3.9 |
| 2003 | 5.7 | 15.6 | 17.5 | 14.2 | 5.1 | 9.3 | 5.9 | 4.9 | 3.7 | 3.7 | 3.6 |
| 2004 | 5.4 | 15.5 | 18.5 | 13.5 | 4.9 | 8.7 | 5.6 | 4.4 | 3.7 | 3.6 | 3.4 |
| 2005 | 5.1 | 14.5 | 16.5 | 13.1 | 4.6 | 7.9 | 5.6 | 4.1 | 3.5 | 3.3 | 3.5 |
| 2006 | 4.6 | 13.8 | 15.9 | 12.4 | 4.1 | 7.6 | 4.9 | 3.9 | 3.1 | 2.9 | 3.0 |
| 2007 | 4.5 | 13.8 | 15.7 | 12.5 | 4.0 | 7.3 | 4.6 | 3.6 | 3.2 | 3.0 | 3.1 |
| 2008 | 5.4 | 16.2 | 19.1 | 14.3 | 4.9 | 8.8 | 5.5 | 4.5 | 3.9 | 3.7 | 3.9 |
| 2009 | 8.1 | 20.7 | 23.1 | 19.4 | 7.5 | 12.3 | 8.6 | 7.1 | 6.0 | 6.0 | 6.1 |
| 2010 | 8.6 | 22.8 | 26.5 | 20.9 | 8.0 | 13.0 | 9.1 | 7.7 | 6.8 | 6.2 | 6.2 |
| 2011 | 8.5 | 21.7 | 26.3 | 19.3 | 7.9 | 13.4 | 9.1 | 7.2 | 6.7 | 6.1 | 6.5 |
| 2012 | 7.9 | 21.1 | 24.2 | 19.5 | 7.3 | 12.1 | 8.4 | 6.8 | 6.2 | 5.6 | 6.3 |
| 2013 | 7.1 | 20.3 | 24.0 | 18.2 | 6.5 | 11.5 | 7.3 | 6.0 | 5.5 | 5.0 | 5.1 |
| 2014 | 6.1 | 17.7 | 19.3 | 16.8 | 5.6 | 10.1 | 6.6 | 4.9 | 4.5 | 4.2 | 4.7 |
| 2015 | 5.2 | 15.5 | 16.7 | 14.8 | 4.8 | 8.5 | 5.5 | 4.4 | 3.8 | 3.6 | 3.9 |

**Table 1-27.  Unemployment Rates of Civilian Workers, by Age, Sex, Race, and Hispanic Origin, 1948–2015**
—*Continued*

(Percent of labor force.)

| Race, Hispanic origin, sex, and year | 16 years and over | 16 to 19 years | | | 20 years and over | | | | | | |
|---|---|---|---|---|---|---|---|---|---|---|---|
| | | Total | 16 to 17 years | 18 to 19 years | Total | 20 to 24 years | 25 to 34 years | 35 to 44 years | 45 to 54 years | 55 to 64 years | 65 years and over |
| **WHITE** | | | | | | | | | | | |
| **Both Sexes** | | | | | | | | | | | |
| 1954 | 5.0 | 12.1 | 13.2 | 11.3 | 4.6 | 8.3 | 4.6 | 4.0 | 4.0 | 4.3 | 3.9 |
| 1955 | 3.9 | 10.4 | 12.0 | 9.2 | 3.4 | 6.2 | 3.1 | 2.9 | 3.1 | 3.8 | 3.4 |
| 1956 | 3.6 | 10.1 | 11.5 | 9.0 | 3.2 | 5.7 | 3.1 | 2.6 | 2.9 | 3.2 | 3.1 |
| 1957 | 3.8 | 10.6 | 11.9 | 9.6 | 3.4 | 6.3 | 3.3 | 2.8 | 3.0 | 3.2 | 3.2 |
| 1958 | 6.1 | 14.4 | 15.2 | 13.9 | 5.6 | 9.9 | 5.9 | 4.8 | 4.8 | 4.9 | 4.6 |
| 1959 | 4.8 | 13.1 | 14.4 | 12.1 | 4.3 | 7.3 | 4.2 | 3.7 | 3.8 | 4.1 | 4.1 |
| 1960 | 5.0 | 13.5 | 14.6 | 12.6 | 4.3 | 7.9 | 4.5 | 3.6 | 3.8 | 3.9 | 3.7 |
| 1961 | 6.0 | 15.3 | 16.7 | 14.4 | 5.3 | 9.4 | 5.3 | 4.5 | 4.5 | 5.0 | 4.8 |
| 1962 | 4.9 | 13.3 | 15.3 | 12.0 | 4.2 | 7.9 | 4.2 | 3.6 | 3.6 | 3.9 | 4.0 |
| 1963 | 5.0 | 15.5 | 17.9 | 13.7 | 4.2 | 7.7 | 4.4 | 3.5 | 3.5 | 3.8 | 3.8 |
| 1964 | 4.6 | 14.8 | 16.5 | 13.3 | 3.8 | 7.3 | 3.6 | 3.2 | 3.2 | 3.5 | 3.5 |
| 1965 | 4.1 | 13.4 | 14.8 | 12.3 | 3.3 | 6.1 | 3.2 | 2.9 | 2.5 | 2.9 | 3.2 |
| 1966 | 3.4 | 11.2 | 13.3 | 9.7 | 2.6 | 4.6 | 2.6 | 2.3 | 2.1 | 2.4 | 2.9 |
| 1967 | 3.4 | 11.0 | 12.8 | 9.8 | 2.7 | 5.0 | 2.7 | 2.3 | 2.2 | 2.3 | 2.7 |
| 1968 | 3.2 | 11.0 | 12.9 | 9.6 | 2.5 | 5.2 | 2.4 | 2.0 | 1.8 | 1.9 | 2.8 |
| 1969 | 3.1 | 10.7 | 13.0 | 8.9 | 2.4 | 5.0 | 2.5 | 2.0 | 1.8 | 1.8 | 2.2 |
| 1970 | 4.5 | 13.5 | 15.5 | 11.9 | 3.7 | 7.3 | 3.8 | 3.0 | 2.7 | 2.7 | 3.2 |
| 1971 | 5.4 | 15.1 | 17.0 | 13.8 | 4.5 | 9.0 | 4.7 | 3.6 | 3.3 | 3.3 | 3.5 |
| 1972 | 5.1 | 14.2 | 16.6 | 12.3 | 4.1 | 8.4 | 4.1 | 3.2 | 2.9 | 3.1 | 3.4 |
| 1973 | 4.3 | 12.6 | 15.4 | 10.4 | 3.5 | 6.8 | 3.7 | 2.5 | 2.4 | 2.5 | 2.9 |
| 1974 | 5.0 | 14.0 | 16.3 | 12.2 | 4.1 | 8.0 | 4.4 | 3.1 | 2.8 | 2.8 | 3.3 |
| 1975 | 7.8 | 17.9 | 19.5 | 16.7 | 6.7 | 12.3 | 7.1 | 5.2 | 4.9 | 4.5 | 5.1 |
| 1976 | 7.0 | 16.9 | 19.0 | 15.3 | 5.9 | 10.7 | 6.3 | 4.5 | 4.2 | 4.3 | 4.9 |
| 1977 | 6.2 | 15.4 | 17.9 | 13.5 | 5.3 | 9.3 | 5.7 | 4.0 | 3.8 | 3.7 | 4.9 |
| 1978 | 5.2 | 13.9 | 17.0 | 11.5 | 4.3 | 8.0 | 4.6 | 3.3 | 3.0 | 2.7 | 3.8 |
| 1979 | 5.1 | 14.0 | 16.1 | 12.4 | 4.2 | 7.6 | 4.4 | 3.2 | 3.0 | 2.7 | 3.1 |
| 1980 | 6.3 | 15.5 | 17.9 | 13.8 | 5.4 | 9.9 | 6.1 | 4.2 | 3.7 | 3.1 | 2.7 |
| 1981 | 6.7 | 17.3 | 19.2 | 15.9 | 5.7 | 10.4 | 6.3 | 4.5 | 3.9 | 3.5 | 2.8 |
| 1982 | 8.6 | 20.4 | 22.8 | 18.8 | 7.6 | 12.8 | 8.5 | 6.3 | 5.4 | 5.1 | 3.1 |
| 1983 | 8.4 | 19.3 | 22.0 | 17.6 | 7.5 | 12.1 | 8.4 | 6.3 | 5.7 | 5.2 | 3.2 |
| 1984 | 6.5 | 16.0 | 18.8 | 14.3 | 5.7 | 9.3 | 6.2 | 4.8 | 4.4 | 4.4 | 3.0 |
| 1985 | 6.2 | 15.7 | 18.3 | 13.9 | 5.5 | 9.2 | 5.9 | 4.6 | 4.3 | 4.0 | 2.9 |
| 1986 | 6.0 | 15.6 | 17.6 | 14.1 | 5.3 | 8.7 | 5.9 | 4.5 | 4.1 | 3.8 | 2.9 |
| 1987 | 5.3 | 14.4 | 16.7 | 12.7 | 4.7 | 8.0 | 5.1 | 4.0 | 3.7 | 3.2 | 2.4 |
| 1988 | 4.7 | 13.1 | 15.3 | 11.6 | 4.1 | 7.1 | 4.5 | 3.5 | 3.1 | 3.0 | 2.4 |
| 1989 | 4.5 | 12.7 | 15.2 | 11.1 | 3.9 | 7.2 | 4.3 | 3.3 | 2.9 | 3.0 | 2.3 |
| 1990 | 4.8 | 13.5 | 15.8 | 12.1 | 4.3 | 7.3 | 4.6 | 3.6 | 3.3 | 3.2 | 2.8 |
| 1991 | 6.1 | 16.5 | 19.0 | 14.9 | 5.5 | 9.2 | 6.1 | 4.7 | 4.2 | 4.0 | 3.1 |
| 1992 | 6.6 | 17.2 | 20.3 | 15.2 | 6.0 | 9.5 | 6.7 | 5.2 | 4.8 | 4.9 | 3.7 |
| 1993 | 6.1 | 16.2 | 19.0 | 14.4 | 5.5 | 8.8 | 6.0 | 4.9 | 4.5 | 4.3 | 3.0 |
| 1994 | 5.3 | 15.1 | 17.6 | 13.3 | 4.7 | 8.1 | 5.2 | 4.0 | 3.7 | 3.9 | 3.8 |
| 1995 | 4.9 | 14.5 | 17.3 | 12.5 | 4.3 | 7.7 | 4.6 | 3.9 | 3.1 | 3.5 | 3.8 |
| 1996 | 4.7 | 14.2 | 16.4 | 12.6 | 4.1 | 7.8 | 4.4 | 3.6 | 3.1 | 3.2 | 3.5 |
| 1997 | 4.2 | 13.6 | 15.8 | 12.0 | 3.6 | 6.9 | 3.9 | 3.3 | 2.7 | 2.7 | 3.0 |
| 1998 | 3.9 | 12.6 | 14.8 | 11.0 | 3.3 | 6.5 | 3.7 | 2.9 | 2.6 | 2.4 | 2.9 |
| 1999 | 3.7 | 12.0 | 14.5 | 10.2 | 3.1 | 6.3 | 3.3 | 2.7 | 2.4 | 2.5 | 2.9 |
| 2000 | 3.5 | 11.4 | 13.9 | 9.8 | 3.0 | 5.9 | 3.2 | 2.6 | 2.2 | 2.4 | 2.8 |
| 2001 | 4.2 | 12.7 | 15.3 | 11.0 | 3.7 | 7.0 | 4.1 | 3.2 | 2.8 | 2.9 | 2.8 |
| 2002 | 5.1 | 14.5 | 16.7 | 13.2 | 4.6 | 8.1 | 5.2 | 4.1 | 3.7 | 3.7 | 3.5 |
| 2003 | 5.2 | 15.2 | 17.2 | 13.9 | 4.7 | 8.4 | 5.3 | 4.3 | 3.7 | 3.8 | 3.7 |
| 2004 | 4.8 | 15.0 | 17.9 | 13.1 | 4.3 | 7.9 | 4.7 | 3.9 | 3.4 | 3.6 | 3.3 |
| 2005 | 4.4 | 14.2 | 16.4 | 12.7 | 3.9 | 7.2 | 4.3 | 3.5 | 3.1 | 3.0 | 3.1 |
| 2006 | 4.0 | 13.2 | 15.1 | 11.9 | 3.6 | 6.9 | 4.0 | 3.2 | 2.8 | 2.8 | 2.8 |
| 2007 | 4.1 | 13.9 | 15.5 | 12.8 | 3.6 | 7.0 | 4.0 | 3.2 | 2.9 | 2.9 | 3.2 |
| 2008 | 5.2 | 16.8 | 19.9 | 14.9 | 4.6 | 9.0 | 5.1 | 4.3 | 3.7 | 3.4 | 4.0 |
| 2009 | 8.5 | 21.8 | 23.4 | 21.0 | 7.9 | 13.0 | 8.8 | 7.4 | 6.7 | 6.4 | 6.2 |
| 2010 | 8.7 | 23.2 | 26.3 | 21.6 | 8.1 | 13.5 | 8.9 | 7.4 | 7.2 | 6.8 | 6.4 |
| 2011 | 7.9 | 21.7 | 24.7 | 20.2 | 7.4 | 12.8 | 8.1 | 6.5 | 6.4 | 6.2 | 6.4 |
| 2012 | 7.2 | 21.5 | 24.8 | 19.8 | 6.6 | 11.4 | 7.3 | 5.9 | 5.7 | 5.5 | 6.0 |
| 2013 | 6.5 | 20.3 | 23.7 | 18.4 | 6.0 | 10.9 | 6.4 | 5.3 | 5.1 | 4.9 | 5.2 |
| 2014 | 5.3 | 17.3 | 19.0 | 16.4 | 4.9 | 9.1 | 5.4 | 4.2 | 4.0 | 3.9 | 4.2 |
| 2015 | 4.6 | 14.8 | 16.5 | 13.8 | 4.2 | 8.3 | 4.5 | 3.7 | 3.4 | 3.5 | 3.4 |

**Table 1-27. Unemployment Rates of Civilian Workers, by Age, Sex, Race, and Hispanic Origin, 1948–2015**
—*Continued*

(Percent of labor force.)

| Race, Hispanic origin, sex, and year | 16 years and over | 16 to 19 years | | | 20 years and over | | | | | | |
| --- | --- | --- | --- | --- | --- | --- | --- | --- | --- | --- | --- |
| | | Total | 16 to 17 years | 18 to 19 years | Total | 20 to 24 years | 25 to 34 years | 35 to 44 years | 45 to 54 years | 55 to 64 years | 65 years and over |
| **WHITE** | | | | | | | | | | | |
| **Men** | | | | | | | | | | | |
| 1954 | 4.8 | 13.4 | 14.0 | 13.0 | 4.4 | 9.8 | 4.2 | 3.6 | 3.8 | 4.3 | 4.2 |
| 1955 | 3.7 | 11.3 | 12.2 | 10.4 | 3.3 | 7.0 | 2.7 | 2.6 | 2.9 | 3.9 | 3.8 |
| 1956 | 3.4 | 10.5 | 11.2 | 9.7 | 3.0 | 6.1 | 2.8 | 2.2 | 2.8 | 3.1 | 3.4 |
| 1957 | 3.6 | 11.5 | 11.9 | 11.1 | 3.2 | 7.0 | 2.7 | 2.5 | 3.0 | 3.4 | 3.2 |
| 1958 | 6.1 | 15.7 | 14.9 | 16.5 | 5.5 | 11.7 | 5.6 | 4.4 | 4.8 | 5.2 | 5.0 |
| 1959 | 4.6 | 14.0 | 15.0 | 13.0 | 4.1 | 7.5 | 3.8 | 3.2 | 3.7 | 4.2 | 4.5 |
| 1960 | 4.8 | 14.0 | 14.6 | 13.5 | 4.2 | 8.3 | 4.1 | 3.3 | 3.6 | 4.1 | 4.0 |
| 1961 | 5.7 | 15.7 | 16.5 | 15.2 | 5.1 | 10.1 | 4.9 | 4.0 | 4.4 | 5.3 | 5.2 |
| 1962 | 4.6 | 13.7 | 15.2 | 12.7 | 4.0 | 8.1 | 3.8 | 3.1 | 3.5 | 4.1 | 4.0 |
| 1963 | 4.7 | 15.9 | 17.8 | 14.2 | 3.9 | 7.8 | 3.9 | 2.9 | 3.3 | 4.0 | 4.1 |
| 1964 | 4.1 | 14.7 | 16.1 | 13.3 | 3.4 | 7.4 | 3.0 | 2.5 | 2.9 | 3.5 | 3.6 |
| 1965 | 3.6 | 12.9 | 14.7 | 11.3 | 2.9 | 5.9 | 2.6 | 2.3 | 2.3 | 3.1 | 3.4 |
| 1966 | 2.8 | 10.5 | 12.5 | 8.9 | 2.2 | 4.1 | 2.1 | 1.7 | 1.7 | 2.5 | 3.0 |
| 1967 | 2.7 | 10.7 | 12.7 | 9.0 | 2.1 | 4.2 | 1.9 | 1.6 | 1.8 | 2.2 | 2.7 |
| 1968 | 2.6 | 10.1 | 12.3 | 8.3 | 2.0 | 4.6 | 1.7 | 1.4 | 1.5 | 1.7 | 2.8 |
| 1969 | 2.5 | 10.0 | 12.5 | 7.9 | 1.9 | 4.6 | 1.7 | 1.4 | 1.4 | 1.7 | 2.2 |
| 1970 | 4.0 | 13.7 | 15.7 | 12.0 | 3.2 | 7.8 | 3.1 | 2.3 | 2.3 | 2.7 | 3.2 |
| 1971 | 4.9 | 15.1 | 17.1 | 13.5 | 4.0 | 9.4 | 4.0 | 2.9 | 2.9 | 3.2 | 3.4 |
| 1972 | 4.5 | 14.2 | 16.4 | 12.4 | 3.6 | 8.5 | 3.4 | 2.5 | 2.5 | 3.0 | 3.3 |
| 1973 | 3.8 | 12.3 | 15.2 | 10.0 | 3.0 | 6.6 | 3.0 | 1.8 | 2.0 | 2.4 | 2.9 |
| 1974 | 4.4 | 13.5 | 16.2 | 11.5 | 3.5 | 7.8 | 3.6 | 2.4 | 2.2 | 2.5 | 3.0 |
| 1975 | 7.2 | 18.3 | 19.7 | 17.2 | 6.2 | 13.1 | 6.3 | 4.5 | 4.4 | 4.1 | 5.0 |
| 1976 | 6.4 | 17.3 | 19.7 | 15.5 | 5.4 | 10.9 | 5.6 | 3.7 | 3.7 | 4.0 | 4.7 |
| 1977 | 5.5 | 15.0 | 17.6 | 13.0 | 4.7 | 9.3 | 5.0 | 3.1 | 3.0 | 3.3 | 4.9 |
| 1978 | 4.6 | 13.5 | 16.9 | 10.8 | 3.7 | 7.7 | 3.8 | 2.5 | 2.5 | 2.6 | 3.9 |
| 1979 | 4.5 | 13.9 | 16.1 | 12.2 | 3.6 | 7.5 | 3.7 | 2.5 | 2.5 | 2.5 | 3.2 |
| 1980 | 6.1 | 16.2 | 18.5 | 14.5 | 5.3 | 11.1 | 5.9 | 3.6 | 3.3 | 3.1 | 2.5 |
| 1981 | 6.5 | 17.9 | 19.9 | 16.4 | 5.6 | 11.6 | 6.1 | 4.0 | 3.6 | 3.4 | 2.4 |
| 1982 | 8.8 | 21.7 | 24.2 | 20.0 | 7.8 | 14.3 | 8.9 | 6.2 | 5.3 | 5.1 | 3.2 |
| 1983 | 8.8 | 20.2 | 22.6 | 18.7 | 7.9 | 13.8 | 9.0 | 6.4 | 5.7 | 5.6 | 3.2 |
| 1984 | 6.4 | 16.8 | 19.7 | 15.0 | 5.7 | 9.8 | 6.2 | 4.6 | 4.2 | 4.7 | 2.6 |
| 1985 | 6.1 | 16.5 | 19.2 | 14.7 | 5.4 | 9.7 | 5.7 | 4.3 | 4.1 | 4.0 | 2.7 |
| 1986 | 6.0 | 16.3 | 18.4 | 14.7 | 5.3 | 9.2 | 5.8 | 4.4 | 4.0 | 4.0 | 3.0 |
| 1987 | 5.4 | 15.5 | 17.9 | 13.7 | 4.8 | 8.4 | 5.2 | 3.9 | 3.9 | 3.4 | 2.5 |
| 1988 | 4.7 | 13.9 | 16.1 | 12.4 | 4.1 | 7.4 | 4.6 | 3.4 | 3.2 | 3.3 | 2.2 |
| 1989 | 4.5 | 13.7 | 16.4 | 12.0 | 3.9 | 7.5 | 4.1 | 3.2 | 2.9 | 3.1 | 2.1 |
| 1990 | 4.9 | 14.3 | 16.1 | 13.2 | 4.3 | 7.6 | 4.7 | 3.5 | 3.4 | 3.6 | 2.8 |
| 1991 | 6.5 | 17.6 | 19.7 | 16.3 | 5.8 | 10.2 | 6.4 | 5.0 | 4.4 | 4.6 | 3.1 |
| 1992 | 7.0 | 18.5 | 21.5 | 16.5 | 6.4 | 10.5 | 7.0 | 5.5 | 5.1 | 5.5 | 3.2 |
| 1993 | 6.3 | 17.7 | 20.2 | 16.0 | 5.7 | 9.6 | 6.2 | 5.0 | 4.7 | 4.7 | 2.9 |
| 1994 | 5.4 | 16.3 | 18.5 | 14.7 | 4.8 | 8.8 | 5.2 | 3.9 | 3.7 | 4.1 | 3.7 |
| 1995 | 4.9 | 15.6 | 18.2 | 13.8 | 4.3 | 7.9 | 4.5 | 3.8 | 3.2 | 3.4 | 4.0 |
| 1996 | 4.7 | 15.5 | 18.3 | 13.5 | 4.1 | 8.1 | 4.2 | 3.5 | 3.1 | 3.2 | 3.2 |
| 1997 | 4.2 | 14.3 | 16.3 | 12.9 | 3.6 | 7.3 | 3.7 | 3.2 | 2.8 | 3.0 | 2.7 |
| 1998 | 3.9 | 14.1 | 17.1 | 12.1 | 3.2 | 6.7 | 3.5 | 2.6 | 2.6 | 2.6 | 2.9 |
| 1999 | 3.6 | 12.6 | 15.1 | 10.8 | 3.0 | 6.5 | 3.1 | 2.4 | 2.4 | 2.6 | 2.9 |
| 2000 | 3.4 | 12.3 | 15.3 | 10.4 | 2.8 | 5.9 | 2.9 | 2.4 | 2.2 | 2.4 | 3.0 |
| 2001 | 4.2 | 13.9 | 17.4 | 11.7 | 3.7 | 7.8 | 3.8 | 3.1 | 2.9 | 3.2 | 2.8 |
| 2002 | 5.3 | 15.9 | 18.8 | 14.2 | 4.7 | 8.7 | 5.3 | 4.1 | 3.8 | 4.0 | 3.4 |
| 2003 | 5.6 | 17.1 | 18.5 | 16.1 | 5.0 | 9.1 | 5.5 | 4.4 | 4.0 | 4.2 | 3.8 |
| 2004 | 5.0 | 16.3 | 19.8 | 14.2 | 4.4 | 8.5 | 4.8 | 3.8 | 3.5 | 3.7 | 3.5 |
| 2005 | 4.4 | 16.1 | 18.9 | 14.3 | 3.8 | 7.9 | 4.1 | 3.3 | 3.0 | 3.0 | 3.1 |
| 2006 | 4.0 | 14.6 | 16.5 | 13.4 | 3.5 | 7.3 | 3.9 | 3.0 | 2.7 | 2.8 | 2.7 |
| 2007 | 4.2 | 15.7 | 17.0 | 14.8 | 3.7 | 7.6 | 4.1 | 3.0 | 2.8 | 3.0 | 3.3 |
| 2008 | 5.5 | 19.1 | 22.2 | 17.3 | 4.9 | 10.2 | 5.3 | 4.3 | 3.8 | 3.4 | 4.1 |
| 2009 | 9.4 | 25.2 | 25.9 | 24.8 | 8.8 | 15.3 | 9.8 | 8.0 | 7.7 | 6.8 | 6.3 |
| 2010 | 9.6 | 26.3 | 29.2 | 24.8 | 8.9 | 15.7 | 9.9 | 7.7 | 7.9 | 7.5 | 6.6 |
| 2011 | 8.3 | 24.5 | 26.6 | 23.5 | 7.7 | 13.9 | 8.4 | 6.6 | 6.7 | 6.6 | 6.4 |
| 2012 | 7.4 | 24.5 | 28.3 | 22.7 | 6.7 | 12.5 | 7.3 | 5.7 | 5.7 | 5.8 | 5.8 |
| 2013 | 6.8 | 22.5 | 25.9 | 20.7 | 6.2 | 11.9 | 6.6 | 5.2 | 5.2 | 5.2 | 5.4 |
| 2014 | 5.4 | 19.2 | 21.6 | 17.9 | 4.9 | 9.9 | 5.4 | 4.1 | 3.8 | 4.0 | 4.1 |
| 2015 | 4.7 | 16.2 | 18.1 | 15.3 | 4.3 | 9.4 | 4.6 | 3.5 | 3.3 | 3.5 | 3.3 |

**Table 1-27.  Unemployment Rates of Civilian Workers, by Age, Sex, Race, and Hispanic Origin, 1948–2015**
—*Continued*

(Percent of labor force.)

| Race, Hispanic origin, sex, and year | 16 years and over | 16 to 19 years | | | 20 years and over | | | | | | |
|---|---|---|---|---|---|---|---|---|---|---|---|
| | | Total | 16 to 17 years | 18 to 19 years | Total | 20 to 24 years | 25 to 34 years | 35 to 44 years | 45 to 54 years | 55 to 64 years | 65 years and over |
| **WHITE** | | | | | | | | | | | |
| **Women** | | | | | | | | | | | |
| 1954 | 5.5 | 10.4 | 12.0 | 9.4 | 5.1 | 6.4 | 5.7 | 4.9 | 4.4 | 4.5 | 2.8 |
| 1955 | 4.3 | 9.1 | 11.6 | 7.7 | 3.9 | 5.1 | 4.3 | 3.8 | 3.4 | 3.6 | 2.2 |
| 1956 | 4.2 | 9.7 | 12.1 | 8.3 | 3.7 | 5.1 | 4.0 | 3.5 | 3.3 | 3.5 | 2.3 |
| 1957 | 4.3 | 9.5 | 11.9 | 7.8 | 3.8 | 5.1 | 4.7 | 3.7 | 3.0 | 2.9 | 3.4 |
| 1958 | 6.2 | 12.7 | 15.6 | 11.0 | 5.6 | 7.3 | 6.6 | 5.6 | 4.9 | 4.3 | 3.5 |
| 1959 | 5.3 | 12.0 | 13.3 | 11.1 | 4.7 | 7.0 | 5.2 | 4.7 | 3.9 | 4.0 | 2.9 |
| 1960 | 5.3 | 12.7 | 14.5 | 11.5 | 4.6 | 7.2 | 5.7 | 4.2 | 4.0 | 3.3 | 2.8 |
| 1961 | 6.5 | 14.8 | 17.0 | 13.6 | 5.7 | 8.4 | 6.6 | 5.6 | 4.8 | 4.3 | 3.8 |
| 1962 | 5.5 | 12.8 | 15.6 | 11.3 | 4.7 | 7.7 | 5.4 | 4.5 | 3.7 | 3.5 | 4.0 |
| 1963 | 5.8 | 15.1 | 18.1 | 13.2 | 4.8 | 7.4 | 5.8 | 4.6 | 3.9 | 3.5 | 3.3 |
| 1964 | 5.5 | 14.9 | 17.1 | 13.2 | 4.6 | 7.1 | 5.2 | 4.5 | 3.6 | 3.5 | 3.4 |
| 1965 | 5.0 | 14.0 | 15.0 | 13.4 | 4.0 | 6.3 | 4.9 | 4.1 | 3.0 | 2.7 | 2.7 |
| 1966 | 4.3 | 12.1 | 14.5 | 10.7 | 3.3 | 5.3 | 3.7 | 3.3 | 2.7 | 2.2 | 2.7 |
| 1967 | 4.6 | 11.5 | 12.9 | 10.6 | 3.8 | 6.0 | 4.7 | 3.7 | 2.9 | 2.3 | 2.6 |
| 1968 | 4.3 | 12.1 | 13.9 | 11.0 | 3.4 | 5.9 | 3.9 | 3.1 | 2.3 | 2.1 | 2.8 |
| 1969 | 4.2 | 11.5 | 13.7 | 10.0 | 3.4 | 5.5 | 4.2 | 3.2 | 2.4 | 2.1 | 2.4 |
| 1970 | 5.4 | 13.4 | 15.3 | 11.9 | 4.4 | 6.9 | 5.3 | 4.3 | 3.4 | 2.6 | 3.3 |
| 1971 | 6.3 | 15.1 | 16.7 | 14.1 | 5.3 | 8.5 | 6.3 | 4.9 | 3.9 | 3.3 | 3.6 |
| 1972 | 5.9 | 14.2 | 17.0 | 12.3 | 4.9 | 8.2 | 5.5 | 4.4 | 3.5 | 3.3 | 3.7 |
| 1973 | 5.3 | 13.0 | 15.8 | 10.9 | 4.3 | 7.1 | 5.1 | 3.7 | 3.2 | 2.7 | 2.8 |
| 1974 | 6.1 | 14.5 | 16.4 | 13.0 | 5.1 | 8.2 | 5.8 | 4.3 | 3.6 | 3.2 | 3.9 |
| 1975 | 8.6 | 17.4 | 19.2 | 16.1 | 7.5 | 11.2 | 8.4 | 6.5 | 5.8 | 5.0 | 5.3 |
| 1976 | 7.9 | 16.4 | 18.2 | 15.1 | 6.8 | 10.4 | 7.6 | 5.8 | 5.0 | 4.8 | 5.3 |
| 1977 | 7.3 | 15.9 | 18.2 | 14.2 | 6.2 | 9.3 | 6.7 | 5.3 | 5.0 | 4.4 | 4.9 |
| 1978 | 6.2 | 14.4 | 17.1 | 12.4 | 5.2 | 8.3 | 5.8 | 4.5 | 3.8 | 3.0 | 3.7 |
| 1979 | 5.9 | 14.0 | 15.9 | 12.5 | 5.0 | 7.8 | 5.6 | 4.2 | 3.7 | 3.0 | 3.1 |
| 1980 | 6.5 | 14.8 | 17.3 | 13.1 | 5.6 | 8.5 | 6.3 | 4.9 | 4.3 | 3.1 | 3.0 |
| 1981 | 6.9 | 16.6 | 18.4 | 15.3 | 5.9 | 9.1 | 6.6 | 5.1 | 4.2 | 3.7 | 3.4 |
| 1982 | 8.3 | 19.0 | 21.2 | 17.6 | 7.3 | 10.9 | 8.0 | 6.4 | 5.5 | 5.0 | 3.1 |
| 1983 | 7.9 | 18.3 | 21.4 | 16.4 | 6.9 | 10.3 | 7.6 | 6.2 | 5.5 | 4.7 | 3.1 |
| 1984 | 6.5 | 15.2 | 17.8 | 13.6 | 5.8 | 8.8 | 6.1 | 5.0 | 4.8 | 4.0 | 3.7 |
| 1985 | 6.4 | 14.8 | 17.2 | 13.1 | 5.7 | 8.5 | 6.2 | 4.9 | 4.5 | 4.1 | 3.1 |
| 1986 | 6.1 | 14.9 | 16.7 | 13.6 | 5.4 | 8.1 | 6.1 | 4.5 | 4.3 | 3.7 | 2.6 |
| 1987 | 5.2 | 13.4 | 15.5 | 11.7 | 4.6 | 7.4 | 5.0 | 4.1 | 3.3 | 2.9 | 2.4 |
| 1988 | 4.7 | 12.3 | 14.4 | 10.8 | 4.1 | 6.7 | 4.5 | 3.7 | 3.1 | 2.5 | 2.6 |
| 1989 | 4.5 | 11.5 | 13.8 | 10.1 | 4.0 | 6.8 | 4.5 | 3.4 | 2.9 | 2.7 | 2.5 |
| 1990 | 4.7 | 12.6 | 15.5 | 10.9 | 4.1 | 6.8 | 4.6 | 3.7 | 3.2 | 2.7 | 2.8 |
| 1991 | 5.6 | 15.2 | 18.2 | 13.3 | 5.0 | 8.1 | 5.7 | 4.3 | 4.0 | 3.3 | 3.1 |
| 1992 | 6.1 | 15.8 | 18.9 | 13.7 | 5.5 | 8.3 | 6.2 | 4.9 | 4.3 | 4.0 | 4.5 |
| 1993 | 5.7 | 14.7 | 17.8 | 12.6 | 5.2 | 7.9 | 5.8 | 4.7 | 4.3 | 3.9 | 3.0 |
| 1994 | 5.2 | 13.8 | 16.6 | 11.8 | 4.6 | 7.4 | 5.1 | 4.2 | 3.7 | 3.7 | 3.9 |
| 1995 | 4.8 | 13.4 | 16.4 | 11.2 | 4.3 | 7.4 | 4.7 | 3.9 | 3.0 | 3.5 | 3.5 |
| 1996 | 4.7 | 12.9 | 14.4 | 11.7 | 4.1 | 7.4 | 4.6 | 3.8 | 3.1 | 3.1 | 3.8 |
| 1997 | 4.2 | 12.8 | 15.2 | 11.1 | 3.7 | 6.4 | 4.2 | 3.4 | 2.6 | 2.4 | 3.4 |
| 1998 | 3.9 | 10.9 | 12.4 | 9.8 | 3.4 | 6.3 | 3.9 | 3.3 | 2.5 | 2.2 | 3.0 |
| 1999 | 3.8 | 11.3 | 13.9 | 9.6 | 3.3 | 6.1 | 3.6 | 3.0 | 2.3 | 2.5 | 2.9 |
| 2000 | 3.6 | 10.4 | 12.5 | 9.0 | 3.1 | 5.8 | 3.5 | 2.9 | 2.3 | 2.4 | 2.4 |
| 2001 | 4.1 | 11.4 | 13.1 | 10.2 | 3.6 | 6.1 | 4.5 | 3.3 | 2.7 | 2.5 | 2.7 |
| 2002 | 4.9 | 13.1 | 14.6 | 12.1 | 4.4 | 7.4 | 5.0 | 4.1 | 3.5 | 3.3 | 3.5 |
| 2003 | 4.8 | 13.3 | 15.9 | 11.5 | 4.4 | 7.6 | 4.9 | 4.2 | 3.3 | 3.4 | 3.5 |
| 2004 | 4.7 | 13.6 | 16.1 | 11.9 | 4.2 | 7.1 | 4.6 | 3.9 | 3.3 | 3.5 | 3.1 |
| 2005 | 4.4 | 12.3 | 14.0 | 11.1 | 3.9 | 6.4 | 4.7 | 3.6 | 3.1 | 3.0 | 3.2 |
| 2006 | 4.0 | 11.7 | 13.8 | 10.2 | 3.6 | 6.3 | 4.1 | 3.4 | 2.9 | 2.8 | 3.0 |
| 2007 | 4.0 | 12.1 | 14.1 | 10.6 | 3.6 | 6.2 | 3.9 | 3.4 | 2.9 | 2.8 | 3.1 |
| 2008 | 4.9 | 14.4 | 17.6 | 12.3 | 4.4 | 7.5 | 4.8 | 4.3 | 3.5 | 3.5 | 3.8 |
| 2009 | 7.3 | 18.4 | 20.9 | 17.0 | 6.8 | 10.4 | 7.6 | 6.7 | 5.6 | 5.8 | 6.0 |
| 2010 | 7.7 | 20.0 | 23.4 | 18.1 | 7.2 | 11.0 | 7.7 | 7.1 | 6.4 | 6.0 | 6.0 |
| 2011 | 7.5 | 18.9 | 22.9 | 16.7 | 7.0 | 11.4 | 7.7 | 6.3 | 6.1 | 5.8 | 6.4 |
| 2012 | 7.0 | 18.4 | 21.4 | 16.7 | 6.5 | 10.1 | 7.2 | 6.3 | 5.7 | 5.2 | 6.3 |
| 2013 | 6.2 | 18.1 | 21.5 | 16.0 | 5.7 | 9.7 | 6.1 | 5.4 | 5.0 | 4.6 | 4.9 |
| 2014 | 5.2 | 15.5 | 16.6 | 14.8 | 4.8 | 8.1 | 5.3 | 4.4 | 4.1 | 3.8 | 4.4 |
| 2015 | 4.5 | 13.2 | 14.8 | 12.3 | 4.1 | 7.0 | 4.5 | 3.9 | 3.5 | 3.5 | 3.5 |

## Table 1-27.  Unemployment Rates of Civilian Workers, by Age, Sex, Race, and Hispanic Origin, 1948–2015
### —Continued

(Percent of labor force.)

| Race, Hispanic origin, sex, and year | 16 years and over | 16 to 19 years | | | 20 years and over | | | | | | |
|---|---|---|---|---|---|---|---|---|---|---|---|
| | | Total | 16 to 17 years | 18 to 19 years | Total | 20 to 24 years | 25 to 34 years | 35 to 44 years | 45 to 54 years | 55 to 64 years | 65 years and over |
| **BLACK** | | | | | | | | | | | |
| **Both Sexes** | | | | | | | | | | | |
| 1980 | 14.3 | 38.5 | 41.1 | 37.1 | 12.1 | 23.6 | 13.3 | 8.2 | 6.8 | 5.4 | 6.9 |
| 1981 | 15.6 | 41.4 | 44.8 | 39.5 | 13.4 | 26.4 | 14.7 | 9.5 | 7.4 | 5.5 | 7.0 |
| 1982 | 18.9 | 48.0 | 48.6 | 47.8 | 16.6 | 30.6 | 19.0 | 12.1 | 8.7 | 8.3 | 7.1 |
| 1983 | 19.5 | 48.5 | 50.5 | 47.6 | 17.3 | 31.6 | 19.0 | 12.4 | 10.7 | 9.2 | 9.2 |
| 1984 | 15.9 | 42.7 | 45.7 | 41.2 | 13.9 | 26.1 | 15.2 | 9.9 | 8.2 | 7.4 | 6.5 |
| 1985 | 15.1 | 40.2 | 43.6 | 38.3 | 13.1 | 24.5 | 14.5 | 9.5 | 8.2 | 7.0 | 7.0 |
| 1986 | 14.5 | 39.3 | 43.0 | 37.2 | 12.7 | 24.1 | 14.0 | 9.6 | 7.1 | 6.6 | 4.5 |
| 1987 | 13.0 | 34.7 | 39.7 | 31.6 | 11.3 | 21.8 | 12.8 | 8.4 | 6.8 | 5.6 | 3.9 |
| 1988 | 11.7 | 32.4 | 35.1 | 30.7 | 10.2 | 19.6 | 11.9 | 7.5 | 5.9 | 4.8 | 5.5 |
| 1989 | 11.4 | 32.4 | 32.9 | 32.2 | 9.9 | 18.0 | 11.5 | 7.6 | 5.6 | 5.2 | 6.9 |
| 1990 | 11.4 | 30.9 | 36.5 | 27.8 | 10.1 | 19.9 | 11.7 | 7.8 | 5.3 | 4.6 | 5.3 |
| 1991 | 12.5 | 36.1 | 39.5 | 34.4 | 11.1 | 21.6 | 12.7 | 8.5 | 7.4 | 4.4 | 5.2 |
| 1992 | 14.2 | 39.7 | 44.7 | 37.1 | 12.6 | 23.8 | 14.2 | 10.5 | 8.3 | 6.2 | 4.9 |
| 1993 | 13.0 | 38.8 | 39.7 | 38.4 | 11.4 | 21.9 | 12.6 | 9.5 | 6.9 | 7.1 | 4.7 |
| 1994 | 11.5 | 35.2 | 36.1 | 34.6 | 10.0 | 19.5 | 11.1 | 8.5 | 5.6 | 5.4 | 6.2 |
| 1995 | 10.4 | 35.7 | 39.1 | 33.4 | 8.7 | 17.7 | 9.9 | 7.3 | 4.8 | 4.0 | 6.7 |
| 1996 | 10.5 | 33.6 | 36.3 | 31.7 | 9.0 | 18.8 | 10.5 | 7.3 | 5.0 | 4.4 | 5.3 |
| 1997 | 10.0 | 32.4 | 35.0 | 30.8 | 8.6 | 18.3 | 9.9 | 7.0 | 5.0 | 4.2 | 6.1 |
| 1998 | 8.9 | 27.6 | 33.6 | 24.2 | 7.7 | 16.8 | 8.4 | 6.5 | 4.4 | 3.9 | 5.6 |
| 1999 | 8.0 | 27.9 | 31.0 | 26.2 | 6.8 | 14.6 | 7.6 | 5.3 | 4.0 | 3.9 | 5.0 |
| 2000 | 7.6 | 24.5 | 26.9 | 22.9 | 6.5 | 15.0 | 6.7 | 5.6 | 4.1 | 3.0 | 6.1 |
| 2001 | 8.6 | 29.0 | 30.8 | 27.9 | 7.4 | 16.3 | 8.1 | 6.3 | 4.8 | 3.9 | 4.3 |
| 2002 | 10.2 | 29.8 | 34.9 | 27.2 | 9.1 | 19.1 | 9.9 | 7.8 | 6.3 | 5.4 | 5.9 |
| 2003 | 10.8 | 33.0 | 32.2 | 33.5 | 9.7 | 19.8 | 10.9 | 8.6 | 6.2 | 6.3 | 5.4 |
| 2004 | 10.4 | 31.7 | 37.8 | 28.3 | 9.4 | 18.4 | 10.8 | 7.8 | 6.9 | 5.6 | 5.5 |
| 2005 | 10.0 | 33.3 | 41.2 | 29.0 | 8.8 | 18.3 | 10.2 | 7.1 | 6.0 | 5.6 | 6.9 |
| 2006 | 8.9 | 29.1 | 32.2 | 27.3 | 7.9 | 16.2 | 9.3 | 6.3 | 5.7 | 4.6 | 4.7 |
| 2007 | 8.3 | 29.4 | 32.6 | 27.4 | 7.2 | 15.2 | 8.6 | 5.4 | 5.4 | 4.3 | 4.5 |
| 2008 | 10.1 | 31.2 | 36.3 | 28.5 | 9.1 | 17.9 | 10.6 | 7.0 | 7.0 | 6.1 | 7.5 |
| 2009 | 14.8 | 39.5 | 43.1 | 37.8 | 13.7 | 24.9 | 16.7 | 11.7 | 10.4 | 8.4 | 8.5 |
| 2010 | 16.0 | 43.0 | 47.8 | 40.9 | 14.9 | 26.0 | 17.6 | 13.0 | 11.5 | 9.7 | 9.2 |
| 2011 | 15.8 | 41.3 | 47.1 | 38.9 | 14.9 | 25.2 | 18.1 | 13.1 | 11.2 | 9.8 | 8.4 |
| 2012 | 13.8 | 38.3 | 44.0 | 35.9 | 12.8 | 23.1 | 14.8 | 11.1 | 9.8 | 8.8 | 9.8 |
| 2013 | 13.1 | 38.8 | 46.2 | 35.5 | 12.0 | 22.8 | 13.8 | 10.0 | 9.4 | 8.1 | 8.1 |
| 2014 | 11.3 | 33.0 | 37.6 | 30.7 | 10.5 | 20.2 | 13.3 | 7.8 | 7.1 | 7.3 | 6.7 |
| 2015 | 9.6 | 28.4 | 29.6 | 27.9 | 8.8 | 16.4 | 11.0 | 7.1 | 6.1 | 5.8 | 7.2 |
| **Men** | | | | | | | | | | | |
| 1980 | 14.5 | 37.5 | 39.7 | 36.2 | 12.4 | 23.7 | 13.4 | 8.2 | 7.2 | 6.2 | 8.7 |
| 1981 | 15.7 | 40.7 | 43.2 | 39.2 | 13.5 | 26.4 | 14.4 | 9.3 | 7.8 | 6.1 | 7.5 |
| 1982 | 20.1 | 48.9 | 52.7 | 47.1 | 17.8 | 31.5 | 20.1 | 13.4 | 9.0 | 10.3 | 9.3 |
| 1983 | 20.3 | 48.8 | 52.2 | 47.3 | 18.1 | 31.4 | 19.4 | 13.5 | 11.4 | 11.0 | 11.8 |
| 1984 | 16.4 | 42.7 | 44.0 | 42.2 | 14.3 | 26.6 | 15.0 | 10.4 | 7.9 | 8.9 | 7.9 |
| 1985 | 15.3 | 41.0 | 42.9 | 40.0 | 13.2 | 23.5 | 13.8 | 9.6 | 9.7 | 7.9 | 8.9 |
| 1986 | 14.8 | 39.3 | 41.4 | 38.2 | 12.9 | 23.5 | 13.5 | 10.9 | 7.8 | 8.0 | 4.3 |
| 1987 | 12.7 | 34.4 | 39.0 | 31.6 | 11.1 | 20.3 | 12.2 | 8.7 | 6.7 | 6.6 | 4.3 |
| 1988 | 11.7 | 32.7 | 34.4 | 31.7 | 10.1 | 19.4 | 11.0 | 7.6 | 6.2 | 5.2 | 5.6 |
| 1989 | 11.5 | 31.9 | 34.4 | 30.3 | 10.0 | 17.9 | 10.5 | 8.4 | 6.2 | 6.2 | 7.4 |
| 1990 | 11.9 | 31.9 | 38.8 | 28.0 | 10.4 | 20.1 | 11.5 | 8.4 | 6.3 | 5.4 | 4.6 |
| 1991 | 13.0 | 36.3 | 39.0 | 34.8 | 11.5 | 22.4 | 11.9 | 9.5 | 8.6 | 5.0 | 6.1 |
| 1992 | 15.2 | 42.0 | 47.5 | 39.1 | 13.5 | 24.6 | 14.2 | 11.2 | 10.3 | 8.1 | 4.9 |
| 1993 | 13.8 | 40.1 | 42.7 | 38.6 | 12.1 | 23.0 | 12.3 | 10.5 | 8.1 | 9.0 | 5.8 |
| 1994 | 12.0 | 37.6 | 39.3 | 36.5 | 10.3 | 19.4 | 10.6 | 9.1 | 6.5 | 6.0 | 8.2 |
| 1995 | 10.6 | 37.1 | 39.7 | 35.4 | 8.8 | 17.6 | 9.3 | 7.6 | 5.5 | 4.4 | 7.6 |
| 1996 | 11.1 | 36.9 | 39.9 | 34.9 | 9.4 | 19.2 | 10.1 | 7.8 | 6.3 | 5.2 | 5.0 |
| 1997 | 10.2 | 36.5 | 39.5 | 34.4 | 8.5 | 19.8 | 8.7 | 6.7 | 5.6 | 4.2 | 5.5 |
| 1998 | 8.9 | 30.1 | 33.9 | 27.9 | 7.4 | 18.0 | 7.3 | 6.2 | 4.4 | 4.5 | 5.2 |
| 1999 | 8.2 | 30.9 | 33.3 | 29.4 | 6.7 | 16.2 | 6.9 | 5.2 | 4.3 | 3.9 | 5.0 |
| 2000 | 8.0 | 26.2 | 28.5 | 24.7 | 6.9 | 16.6 | 6.7 | 5.8 | 4.8 | 2.7 | 6.3 |
| 2001 | 9.3 | 30.4 | 30.5 | 30.4 | 8.0 | 17.6 | 8.3 | 6.9 | 5.5 | 4.8 | 4.0 |
| 2002 | 10.7 | 31.3 | 36.6 | 28.7 | 9.5 | 20.0 | 9.4 | 8.0 | 7.4 | 6.1 | 5.0 |
| 2003 | 11.6 | 36.0 | 35.6 | 36.3 | 10.3 | 20.9 | 11.3 | 9.2 | 6.7 | 6.8 | 5.6 |
| 2004 | 11.1 | 35.6 | 40.8 | 32.7 | 9.9 | 20.3 | 10.9 | 8.0 | 7.2 | 6.4 | 4.2 |
| 2005 | 10.5 | 36.3 | 45.1 | 31.5 | 9.2 | 20.5 | 9.7 | 7.0 | 6.7 | 5.9 | 7.1 |
| 2006 | 9.5 | 32.7 | 34.8 | 31.5 | 8.3 | 17.2 | 9.5 | 5.9 | 6.3 | 5.5 | 5.8 |
| 2007 | 9.1 | 33.8 | 40.1 | 30.2 | 7.9 | 16.9 | 9.1 | 5.6 | 5.8 | 5.2 | 5.0 |
| 2008 | 11.4 | 35.9 | 43.9 | 32.0 | 10.2 | 19.3 | 11.8 | 7.7 | 7.7 | 7.1 | 9.5 |
| 2009 | 17.5 | 46.0 | 49.3 | 44.5 | 16.3 | 27.7 | 19.9 | 14.0 | 12.4 | 10.1 | 10.6 |
| 2010 | 18.4 | 45.4 | 49.4 | 43.9 | 17.3 | 29.8 | 19.3 | 14.9 | 14.4 | 12.2 | 10.4 |
| 2011 | 17.8 | 43.1 | 44.5 | 42.5 | 16.7 | 27.4 | 19.7 | 14.9 | 12.5 | 12.7 | 8.2 |
| 2012 | 15.0 | 41.3 | 47.2 | 38.9 | 14.0 | 25.6 | 15.2 | 12.6 | 10.2 | 10.1 | 11.5 |
| 2013 | 14.2 | 44.5 | 51.2 | 41.6 | 12.9 | 25.1 | 14.3 | 10.1 | 10.3 | 8.5 | 9.1 |
| 2014 | 12.2 | 36.5 | 38.5 | 35.5 | 11.3 | 22.1 | 13.6 | 8.2 | 7.9 | 8.0 | 8.5 |
| 2015 | 10.3 | 30.8 | 33.1 | 29.5 | 9.5 | 18.3 | 11.3 | 7.2 | 6.3 | 7.4 | 7.2 |

**Table 1-27.  Unemployment Rates of Civilian Workers, by Age, Sex, Race, and Hispanic Origin, 1948–2015**
*—Continued*

(Percent of labor force.)

| Race, Hispanic origin, sex, and year | 16 years and over | 16 to 19 years | | | 20 years and over | | | | | | |
|---|---|---|---|---|---|---|---|---|---|---|---|
| | | Total | 16 to 17 years | 18 to 19 years | Total | 20 to 24 years | 25 to 34 years | 35 to 44 years | 45 to 54 years | 55 to 64 years | 65 years and over |
| **BLACK** | | | | | | | | | | | |
| **Women** | | | | | | | | | | | |
| 1980 | 14.0 | 39.8 | 42.9 | 38.2 | 11.9 | 23.5 | 13.2 | 8.2 | 6.4 | 5.2 | 4.9 |
| 1981 | 15.6 | 42.2 | 46.5 | 39.8 | 13.4 | 26.4 | 14.9 | 9.8 | 6.9 | 4.7 | 6.0 |
| 1982 | 17.6 | 47.1 | 44.2 | 48.6 | 15.4 | 29.6 | 17.8 | 10.7 | 8.5 | 4.5 | 4.5 |
| 1983 | 18.6 | 48.2 | 48.6 | 48.0 | 16.5 | 31.8 | 18.6 | 11.4 | 9.9 | 4.7 | 6.3 |
| 1984 | 15.4 | 42.6 | 47.5 | 40.2 | 13.5 | 25.6 | 15.4 | 9.4 | 8.6 | 6.1 | 4.9 |
| 1985 | 14.9 | 39.2 | 44.3 | 36.4 | 13.1 | 25.6 | 15.1 | 9.3 | 6.8 | 7.3 | 5.2 |
| 1986 | 14.2 | 39.2 | 44.6 | 36.1 | 12.4 | 24.7 | 14.6 | 8.5 | 6.4 | 5.9 | 4.9 |
| 1987 | 13.2 | 34.9 | 40.5 | 31.7 | 11.6 | 23.3 | 13.5 | 8.1 | 6.9 | 6.0 | 3.4 |
| 1988 | 11.7 | 32.0 | 35.9 | 29.6 | 10.4 | 19.8 | 12.7 | 7.4 | 5.6 | 5.0 | 5.4 |
| 1989 | 11.4 | 33.0 | 31.1 | 34.0 | 9.8 | 18.1 | 12.5 | 7.0 | 5.0 | 4.5 | 6.4 |
| 1990 | 10.9 | 29.9 | 34.1 | 27.6 | 9.7 | 19.6 | 11.9 | 7.2 | 4.3 | 4.3 | 5.9 |
| 1991 | 12.0 | 36.0 | 40.1 | 33.9 | 10.6 | 20.7 | 13.4 | 7.6 | 6.2 | 4.2 | 4.4 |
| 1992 | 13.2 | 37.2 | 41.7 | 34.8 | 11.8 | 23.1 | 14.1 | 9.8 | 6.4 | 3.6 | 5.0 |
| 1993 | 12.1 | 37.4 | 36.1 | 38.1 | 10.7 | 20.9 | 12.9 | 8.6 | 5.8 | 3.8 | 3.6 |
| 1994 | 11.0 | 32.6 | 32.9 | 32.5 | 9.8 | 19.6 | 11.7 | 8.0 | 4.9 | 4.2 | 4.4 |
| 1995 | 10.2 | 34.3 | 38.5 | 31.5 | 8.6 | 17.8 | 10.5 | 7.0 | 4.2 | 5.1 | 5.6 |
| 1996 | 10.0 | 30.3 | 32.8 | 28.6 | 8.7 | 18.4 | 11.0 | 6.9 | 3.8 | 4.9 | 6.6 |
| 1997 | 9.9 | 28.7 | 30.3 | 27.8 | 8.8 | 17.1 | 10.9 | 7.2 | 4.4 | 3.6 | 6.1 |
| 1998 | 9.0 | 25.3 | 33.2 | 20.9 | 7.9 | 15.7 | 9.5 | 6.7 | 4.3 | 3.8 | 5.0 |
| 1999 | 7.8 | 25.1 | 28.5 | 23.3 | 6.8 | 13.4 | 8.3 | 5.5 | 3.8 | 4.1 | 6.0 |
| 2000 | 7.1 | 22.8 | 25.3 | 21.3 | 6.2 | 13.6 | 6.8 | 5.5 | 3.4 | 3.4 | 4.6 |
| 2001 | 8.1 | 27.5 | 31.2 | 25.4 | 7.0 | 15.3 | 8.0 | 5.8 | 4.3 | 3.9 | 6.9 |
| 2002 | 9.8 | 28.3 | 33.2 | 25.6 | 8.8 | 18.3 | 10.2 | 7.7 | 5.3 | 3.3 | 5.3 |
| 2003 | 10.2 | 30.3 | 29.1 | 31.1 | 9.2 | 18.8 | 10.5 | 8.1 | 5.8 | 3.1 | 6.8 |
| 2004 | 9.8 | 28.2 | 35.2 | 24.3 | 8.9 | 16.6 | 10.7 | 7.6 | 6.5 | 4.7 | 6.6 |
| 2005 | 9.5 | 30.3 | 37.3 | 26.6 | 8.5 | 16.3 | 10.6 | 7.2 | 5.4 | 5.9 | 3.7 |
| 2006 | 8.4 | 25.9 | 29.9 | 23.6 | 7.5 | 15.2 | 9.0 | 6.7 | 5.1 | 4.8 | 4.0 |
| 2007 | 7.5 | 25.3 | 26.4 | 24.7 | 6.7 | 13.6 | 8.1 | 5.3 | 5.0 | 5.3 | 5.8 |
| 2008 | 8.9 | 26.8 | 29.9 | 25.0 | 8.1 | 16.6 | 9.5 | 6.4 | 6.3 | 3.9 | 6.6 |
| 2009 | 12.4 | 33.4 | 37.2 | 31.7 | 11.5 | 22.2 | 13.8 | 9.7 | 8.7 | 3.7 | 8.2 |
| 2010 | 13.8 | 40.5 | 46.4 | 37.7 | 12.8 | 22.6 | 16.0 | 11.4 | 9.1 | 5.3 | 8.5 |
| 2011 | 14.1 | 39.4 | 49.5 | 34.8 | 13.2 | 23.1 | 16.5 | 11.6 | 10.0 | 7.1 | 8.2 |
| 2012 | 12.8 | 35.6 | 41.3 | 33.1 | 11.9 | 20.8 | 14.4 | 9.8 | 9.4 | 7.6 | 7.2 |
| 2013 | 12.1 | 33.4 | 41.6 | 29.8 | 11.3 | 20.6 | 13.2 | 9.8 | 8.5 | 7.4 | 7.2 |
| 2014 | 10.5 | 29.7 | 36.7 | 26.6 | 9.8 | 18.4 | 13.1 | 7.4 | 7.9 | 6.7 | 7.4 |
| 2015 | 8.9 | 26.4 | 26.3 | 26.5 | 8.2 | 14.6 | 10.7 | 7.0 | 5.9 | 4.5 | 7.2 |
| **HISPANIC** | | | | | | | | | | | |
| **Both Sexes** | | | | | | | | | | | |
| 1980 | 10.1 | 22.5 | 27.6 | 19.5 | 8.6 | 12.1 | 9.1 | 7.7 | 5.7 | 5.9 | 6.0 |
| 1981 | 10.4 | 23.9 | 28.0 | 21.7 | 9.1 | 13.9 | 8.8 | 7.4 | 6.4 | 7.3 | 5.4 |
| 1982 | 13.8 | 29.9 | 38.1 | 25.9 | 12.3 | 17.7 | 12.3 | 10.7 | 8.4 | 10.1 | 6.5 |
| 1983 | 13.7 | 28.4 | 33.8 | 25.8 | 12.3 | 16.7 | 11.9 | 11.3 | 10.0 | 10.9 | 5.8 |
| 1984 | 10.7 | 24.1 | 28.9 | 21.6 | 9.5 | 12.4 | 9.7 | 8.2 | 7.5 | 9.7 | 6.1 |
| 1985 | 10.5 | 24.3 | 27.8 | 22.5 | 9.4 | 12.6 | 9.9 | 7.7 | 7.4 | 7.8 | 8.1 |
| 1986 | 10.6 | 24.7 | 28.1 | 22.9 | 9.5 | 12.9 | 9.6 | 8.4 | 7.8 | 7.3 | 10.1 |
| 1987 | 8.8 | 22.3 | 27.7 | 19.5 | 7.8 | 10.6 | 7.7 | 6.7 | 6.9 | 6.0 | 6.5 |
| 1988 | 8.2 | 22.0 | 27.1 | 19.3 | 7.0 | 9.8 | 7.1 | 6.0 | 6.0 | 5.8 | 5.6 |
| 1989 | 8.0 | 19.4 | 26.4 | 16.0 | 7.2 | 10.7 | 7.0 | 5.9 | 6.3 | 5.8 | 5.3 |
| 1990 | 8.2 | 19.5 | 24.5 | 16.9 | 7.2 | 9.1 | 7.3 | 6.6 | 6.4 | 5.6 | 6.0 |
| 1991 | 10.0 | 22.9 | 31.9 | 18.7 | 9.0 | 11.6 | 9.2 | 8.1 | 8.0 | 6.5 | 7.0 |
| 1992 | 11.6 | 27.5 | 35.7 | 23.4 | 10.4 | 13.2 | 10.4 | 9.8 | 8.8 | 8.6 | 8.1 |
| 1993 | 10.8 | 26.1 | 35.1 | 21.8 | 9.7 | 13.1 | 9.3 | 9.1 | 8.6 | 8.0 | 6.6 |
| 1994 | 9.9 | 24.5 | 31.7 | 20.6 | 8.9 | 11.8 | 9.0 | 7.7 | 8.1 | 7.3 | 7.9 |
| 1995 | 9.3 | 24.1 | 33.1 | 19.5 | 8.2 | 11.5 | 8.2 | 7.2 | 6.4 | 7.5 | 10.6 |
| 1996 | 8.9 | 23.6 | 30.0 | 20.3 | 7.8 | 11.8 | 7.3 | 7.3 | 6.0 | 7.3 | 8.2 |
| 1997 | 7.7 | 21.6 | 27.7 | 18.4 | 6.8 | 10.3 | 6.3 | 6.4 | 5.1 | 6.5 | 6.8 |
| 1998 | 7.2 | 21.3 | 28.0 | 18.1 | 6.1 | 9.4 | 5.9 | 5.5 | 4.6 | 5.3 | 6.4 |
| 1999 | 6.4 | 18.6 | 23.7 | 16.3 | 5.5 | 8.3 | 5.4 | 4.8 | 4.8 | 4.5 | 5.0 |
| 2000 | 5.7 | 16.6 | 22.5 | 13.9 | 4.9 | 7.5 | 4.8 | 4.5 | 3.3 | 4.5 | 5.7 |
| 2001 | 6.6 | 17.7 | 24.0 | 15.0 | 5.8 | 8.1 | 5.9 | 5.2 | 4.3 | 5.6 | 4.5 |
| 2002 | 7.5 | 20.1 | 24.2 | 18.2 | 6.7 | 9.9 | 6.6 | 6.0 | 5.5 | 5.7 | 6.8 |
| 2003 | 7.7 | 20.0 | 24.6 | 17.7 | 7.0 | 10.2 | 7.0 | 6.0 | 6.3 | 5.7 | 3.9 |
| 2004 | 7.0 | 20.4 | 29.0 | 16.8 | 6.2 | 9.3 | 6.3 | 5.3 | 5.2 | 5.8 | 6.0 |
| 2005 | 6.0 | 18.4 | 23.6 | 16.0 | 5.3 | 8.6 | 5.3 | 4.5 | 4.4 | 4.4 | 4.9 |
| 2006 | 5.2 | 15.9 | 20.4 | 13.6 | 4.6 | 7.2 | 4.7 | 4.3 | 3.7 | 3.3 | 3.9 |
| 2007 | 5.6 | 18.1 | 22.5 | 16.0 | 5.0 | 7.8 | 4.9 | 4.3 | 4.3 | 4.5 | 4.9 |
| 2008 | 7.6 | 22.4 | 29.8 | 19.0 | 6.8 | 11.5 | 6.7 | 5.8 | 6.3 | 4.8 | 7.8 |
| 2009 | 12.1 | 30.2 | 36.3 | 27.8 | 11.2 | 16.2 | 11.4 | 10.2 | 10.1 | 10.0 | 8.0 |
| 2010 | 12.5 | 32.2 | 37.6 | 30.2 | 11.6 | 17.4 | 11.3 | 10.3 | 10.8 | 10.3 | 9.5 |
| 2011 | 11.5 | 31.1 | 38.3 | 28.5 | 10.6 | 15.7 | 10.4 | 9.2 | 9.9 | 9.7 | 8.8 |
| 2012 | 10.3 | 28.6 | 35.2 | 26.1 | 9.4 | 13.8 | 9.2 | 8.3 | 8.3 | 9.2 | 8.7 |
| 2013 | 9.1 | 27.5 | 33.7 | 25.0 | 8.2 | 12.8 | 8.2 | 7.3 | 6.8 | 7.4 | 7.7 |
| 2014 | 7.4 | 22.5 | 28.5 | 20.2 | 6.7 | 11.1 | 6.9 | 5.7 | 5.3 | 6.0 | 5.7 |
| 2015 | 6.6 | 19.3 | 22.6 | 18.0 | 6.0 | 10.0 | 6.3 | 5.0 | 4.7 | 5.4 | 5.6 |

## Table 1-27.  Unemployment Rates of Civilian Workers, by Age, Sex, Race, and Hispanic Origin, 1948–2015
### —Continued

(Percent of labor force.)

| Race, Hispanic origin, sex, and year | 16 years and over | 16 to 19 years | | | 20 years and over | | | | | | |
|---|---|---|---|---|---|---|---|---|---|---|---|
| | | Total | 16 to 17 years | 18 to 19 years | Total | 20 to 24 years | 25 to 34 years | 35 to 44 years | 45 to 54 years | 55 to 64 years | 65 years and over |
| **HISPANIC** | | | | | | | | | | | |
| **Men** | | | | | | | | | | | |
| 1980 | 9.7 | 21.9 | 26.2 | 19.3 | 8.3 | 12.2 | 8.3 | 7.1 | 6.0 | 5.9 | . . . |
| 1981 | 10.2 | 24.3 | 30.9 | 20.3 | 8.8 | 14.1 | 8.9 | 6.5 | 5.9 | 6.7 | . . . |
| 1982 | 13.6 | 31.3 | 40.2 | 26.8 | 12.1 | 18.2 | 12.4 | 9.9 | 7.5 | 10.0 | . . . |
| 1983 | 13.6 | 28.7 | 34.7 | 25.9 | 12.2 | 17.0 | 11.6 | 10.8 | 10.3 | 11.7 | . . . |
| 1984 | 10.5 | 25.2 | 31.5 | 22.2 | 9.3 | 12.5 | 9.2 | 7.6 | 7.2 | 10.2 | . . . |
| 1985 | 10.2 | 24.7 | 29.1 | 22.4 | 9.1 | 12.9 | 9.6 | 7.2 | 6.8 | 7.0 | . . . |
| 1986 | 10.5 | 24.5 | 28.5 | 22.4 | 9.5 | 13.0 | 9.5 | 8.5 | 7.0 | 8.0 | . . . |
| 1987 | 8.7 | 22.2 | 28.2 | 19.3 | 7.8 | 10.2 | 7.6 | 6.9 | 7.1 | 6.7 | . . . |
| 1988 | 8.1 | 22.7 | 29.5 | 19.5 | 7.0 | 9.2 | 7.0 | 5.9 | 6.1 | 6.7 | . . . |
| 1989 | 7.6 | 20.2 | 27.6 | 16.8 | 6.6 | 9.7 | 5.9 | 5.7 | 6.0 | 6.6 | . . . |
| 1990 | 8.0 | 19.5 | 24.0 | 17.4 | 7.0 | 8.4 | 6.9 | 6.5 | 6.8 | 6.5 | . . . |
| 1991 | 10.3 | 23.5 | 33.6 | 19.2 | 9.3 | 11.6 | 9.3 | 8.5 | 7.9 | 8.1 | . . . |
| 1992 | 11.7 | 28.2 | 36.6 | 24.0 | 10.5 | 13.7 | 10.1 | 9.8 | 8.9 | 10.2 | . . . |
| 1993 | 10.6 | 25.9 | 34.5 | 21.9 | 9.5 | 12.6 | 9.0 | 8.8 | 8.8 | 8.5 | . . . |
| 1994 | 9.4 | 26.3 | 33.3 | 22.5 | 8.3 | 10.8 | 8.4 | 6.6 | 8.1 | 7.4 | 10.5 |
| 1995 | 8.8 | 25.3 | 34.8 | 20.2 | 7.7 | 10.6 | 7.5 | 6.7 | 5.9 | 7.9 | 12.9 |
| 1996 | 7.9 | 22.5 | 31.5 | 18.4 | 6.9 | 10.3 | 6.6 | 6.3 | 5.1 | 6.7 | 8.3 |
| 1997 | 7.0 | 20.8 | 26.5 | 17.9 | 6.1 | 9.8 | 5.1 | 5.4 | 4.8 | 6.8 | 7.2 |
| 1998 | 6.4 | 20.6 | 29.0 | 16.4 | 5.4 | 8.9 | 5.2 | 4.5 | 4.2 | 5.3 | 5.0 |
| 1999 | 5.6 | 17.8 | 23.4 | 15.3 | 4.7 | 7.8 | 4.1 | 3.8 | 4.5 | 4.6 | 5.0 |
| 2000 | 5.0 | 15.7 | 22.3 | 12.8 | 4.2 | 6.6 | 3.7 | 3.8 | 3.1 | 4.1 | 6.2 |
| 2001 | 5.9 | 17.1 | 25.8 | 13.4 | 5.2 | 8.1 | 4.6 | 4.5 | 3.8 | 6.3 | 4.8 |
| 2002 | 7.2 | 20.2 | 22.9 | 19.1 | 6.4 | 9.3 | 6.1 | 5.4 | 5.5 | 6.2 | 6.3 |
| 2003 | 7.2 | 21.9 | 25.9 | 20.1 | 6.4 | 9.6 | 6.3 | 5.3 | 6.0 | 6.0 | 3.6 |
| 2004 | 6.5 | 21.2 | 30.7 | 17.6 | 5.8 | 9.4 | 5.5 | 4.5 | 4.7 | 5.7 | 6.9 |
| 2005 | 5.4 | 19.3 | 23.4 | 17.5 | 4.7 | 8.2 | 4.3 | 3.9 | 4.0 | 4.0 | 4.8 |
| 2006 | 4.8 | 17.3 | 22.6 | 14.8 | 4.2 | 6.7 | 4.2 | 3.6 | 3.4 | 3.5 | 3.7 |
| 2007 | 5.3 | 19.7 | 23.4 | 18.0 | 4.6 | 7.4 | 4.5 | 3.8 | 4.4 | 3.9 | 5.5 |
| 2008 | 7.6 | 23.4 | 30.9 | 19.9 | 6.8 | 11.8 | 6.6 | 5.6 | 6.2 | 5.1 | 7.8 |
| 2009 | 12.5 | 33.8 | 41.1 | 31.1 | 11.6 | 16.6 | 11.6 | 10.5 | 10.5 | 11.2 | 7.8 |
| 2010 | 12.7 | 34.6 | 41.0 | 32.6 | 11.7 | 18.2 | 11.6 | 9.8 | 11.2 | 10.6 | 9.4 |
| 2011 | 11.2 | 33.3 | 40.7 | 31.0 | 10.3 | 15.3 | 9.9 | 8.7 | 9.8 | 10.4 | 9.5 |
| 2012 | 9.9 | 30.5 | 40.6 | 26.9 | 8.9 | 13.8 | 8.4 | 7.2 | 8.2 | 9.8 | 8.6 |
| 2013 | 8.8 | 28.2 | 34.5 | 25.8 | 7.9 | 13.4 | 7.5 | 6.5 | 6.5 | 8.2 | 8.5 |
| 2014 | 6.8 | 22.5 | 30.8 | 19.5 | 6.1 | 11.1 | 6.1 | 4.9 | 4.6 | 5.9 | 6.6 |
| 2015 | 6.3 | 20.3 | 23.8 | 18.9 | 5.7 | 10.6 | 5.7 | 4.0 | 4.6 | 5.5 | 7.0 |
| **HISPANIC** | | | | | | | | | | | |
| **Women** | | | | | | | | | | | |
| 1980 | 10.7 | 23.4 | 29.7 | 19.8 | 9.2 | 12.0 | 10.6 | 8.6 | 5.3 | 5.8 | . . . |
| 1981 | 10.8 | 23.4 | 23.5 | 23.4 | 9.5 | 13.5 | 8.7 | 8.9 | 7.2 | 8.4 | . . . |
| 1982 | 14.1 | 28.2 | 35.1 | 25.0 | 12.5 | 16.8 | 12.2 | 11.9 | 9.9 | 10.4 | . . . |
| 1983 | 13.8 | 28.0 | 32.5 | 25.7 | 12.4 | 16.2 | 12.5 | 12.2 | 9.7 | 9.6 | . . . |
| 1984 | 11.1 | 22.8 | 26.1 | 21.0 | 9.9 | 12.2 | 10.3 | 9.1 | 7.9 | 8.8 | . . . |
| 1985 | 11.0 | 23.8 | 26.2 | 22.6 | 9.9 | 12.1 | 10.6 | 8.5 | 8.1 | 9.2 | . . . |
| 1986 | 10.8 | 25.1 | 27.6 | 23.6 | 9.6 | 12.9 | 9.8 | 8.2 | 8.9 | 6.2 | . . . |
| 1987 | 8.9 | 22.4 | 27.1 | 19.9 | 7.7 | 11.4 | 7.8 | 6.5 | 6.7 | 5.0 | . . . |
| 1988 | 8.3 | 21.0 | 24.5 | 18.9 | 7.1 | 10.7 | 7.2 | 6.2 | 5.9 | 4.6 | . . . |
| 1989 | 8.8 | 18.2 | 24.7 | 14.9 | 8.0 | 12.2 | 8.6 | 6.3 | 6.7 | 4.5 | . . . |
| 1990 | 8.4 | 19.4 | 25.4 | 16.2 | 7.5 | 10.4 | 8.0 | 6.7 | 6.0 | 4.3 | . . . |
| 1991 | 9.6 | 21.9 | 29.6 | 17.9 | 8.6 | 11.7 | 9.1 | 7.6 | 8.1 | 4.1 | . . . |
| 1992 | 11.4 | 26.4 | 34.5 | 22.4 | 10.2 | 12.4 | 11.0 | 9.7 | 8.5 | 6.2 | . . . |
| 1993 | 11.0 | 26.3 | 36.0 | 21.7 | 9.9 | 14.0 | 9.9 | 9.5 | 8.3 | 7.2 | . . . |
| 1994 | 10.7 | 22.2 | 29.7 | 18.1 | 9.8 | 13.5 | 10.1 | 9.2 | 8.0 | 7.1 | 3.6 |
| 1995 | 10.0 | 22.6 | 30.7 | 18.7 | 8.9 | 13.0 | 9.5 | 7.9 | 7.0 | 6.8 | 6.4 |
| 1996 | 10.2 | 25.1 | 28.2 | 23.3 | 9.2 | 14.1 | 8.5 | 8.7 | 7.2 | 8.1 | 8.0 |
| 1997 | 8.9 | 22.7 | 29.2 | 19.1 | 7.9 | 11.0 | 8.2 | 7.7 | 5.5 | 6.1 | 6.0 |
| 1998 | 8.2 | 22.1 | 26.4 | 20.2 | 7.1 | 10.1 | 7.2 | 6.9 | 5.1 | 5.4 | 8.8 |
| 1999 | 7.6 | 19.8 | 24.0 | 17.7 | 6.6 | 9.1 | 7.3 | 6.3 | 5.1 | 4.3 | 4.8 |
| 2000 | 6.8 | 18.0 | 22.7 | 15.6 | 5.9 | 9.0 | 6.4 | 5.4 | 3.6 | 5.0 | 4.8 |
| 2001 | 7.5 | 18.5 | 21.6 | 17.1 | 6.6 | 8.2 | 7.8 | 6.2 | 4.8 | 4.8 | 4.0 |
| 2002 | 8.0 | 19.9 | 25.8 | 17.0 | 7.2 | 10.8 | 7.4 | 6.7 | 5.5 | 5.0 | 7.5 |
| 2003 | 8.4 | 17.7 | 23.2 | 14.4 | 7.8 | 11.3 | 8.2 | 7.1 | 6.8 | 5.3 | 4.4 |
| 2004 | 7.6 | 19.3 | 27.0 | 15.5 | 7.0 | 9.1 | 7.6 | 6.4 | 5.8 | 5.8 | 4.6 |
| 2005 | 6.9 | 17.2 | 23.8 | 14.0 | 6.3 | 9.2 | 7.1 | 5.5 | 4.8 | 5.0 | 5.1 |
| 2006 | 5.9 | 14.1 | 18.1 | 11.9 | 5.3 | 8.1 | 5.5 | 5.5 | 4.2 | 3.1 | 4.2 |
| 2007 | 6.1 | 16.1 | 21.3 | 13.6 | 5.5 | 8.5 | 5.6 | 5.1 | 4.3 | 5.2 | 4.0 |
| 2008 | 7.7 | 21.1 | 28.1 | 18.0 | 6.9 | 11.1 | 6.8 | 6.0 | 6.4 | 4.4 | 7.7 |
| 2009 | 11.5 | 25.8 | 30.8 | 23.8 | 10.6 | 15.7 | 10.9 | 9.7 | 9.6 | 8.5 | 8.3 |
| 2010 | 12.3 | 29.1 | 34.2 | 27.0 | 11.4 | 16.2 | 10.9 | 11.1 | 10.4 | 9.9 | 9.6 |
| 2011 | 11.8 | 28.1 | 35.7 | 25.0 | 11.1 | 16.3 | 11.4 | 9.9 | 10.1 | 8.8 | 8.0 |
| 2012 | 10.9 | 26.4 | 29.4 | 25.1 | 10.1 | 13.9 | 10.4 | 9.7 | 8.5 | 8.5 | 8.8 |
| 2013 | 9.5 | 26.7 | 33.0 | 23.9 | 8.6 | 12.0 | 9.2 | 8.3 | 7.2 | 6.5 | 6.7 |
| 2014 | 8.2 | 22.5 | 26.1 | 21.0 | 7.5 | 11.1 | 7.9 | 6.9 | 6.2 | 6.1 | 4.5 |
| 2015 | 7.1 | 18.3 | 21.4 | 16.9 | 6.5 | 9.4 | 7.2 | 6.4 | 4.8 | 5.2 | 3.9 |

. . . = Not available.

## Table 1-28. Unemployed Persons and Unemployment Rates, by Selected Occupation, 2005–2015

(Thousands of people, percent of civilian labor force.)

| Occupation | 2005 | 2006 | 2007 | 2008 | 2009 | 2010 | 2011 | 2012 | 2013 | 2014 | 2015 |
|---|---|---|---|---|---|---|---|---|---|---|---|
| **Total Unemployed Persons, 16 Years and Over**[1] .. | 7 591 | 7 001 | 7 078 | 8 924 | 14 265 | 14 825 | 13 747 | 12 506 | 11 460 | 9 617 | 8 296 |
| Management, professional, and related .................... | 1 172 | 1 065 | 1 090 | 1 463 | 2 531 | 2 566 | 2 458 | 2 318 | 2 036 | 1 777 | 1 504 |
| Management, business, and financial operations .. | 464 | 427 | 429 | 619 | 1 105 | 1 117 | 1 067 | 935 | 831 | 704 | 602 |
| Professional and related ........................................ | 708 | 638 | 662 | 844 | 1 427 | 1 449 | 1 392 | 1 383 | 1 205 | 1 073 | 902 |
| Services ...................................................................... | 1 587 | 1 485 | 1 521 | 1 769 | 2 605 | 2 819 | 2 727 | 2 540 | 2 444 | 2 048 | 1 855 |
| Sales and office ........................................................ | 1 820 | 1 667 | 1 638 | 2 006 | 3 143 | 3 315 | 3 135 | 2 775 | 2 575 | 2 119 | 1 792 |
| Sales and related ................................................... | 874 | 812 | 835 | 980 | 1 501 | 1 596 | 1 481 | 1 318 | 1 212 | 1 022 | 909 |
| Office and administrative support .......................... | 946 | 856 | 804 | 1 026 | 1 642 | 1 719 | 1 653 | 1 457 | 1 363 | 1 096 | 883 |
| Natural resources, construction, and maintenance .... | 1 069 | 1 007 | 1 052 | 1 421 | 2 464 | 2 504 | 2 000 | 1 668 | 1 423 | 1 171 | 1 058 |
| Farming, fishing, and forestry .............................. | 103 | 101 | 89 | 112 | 179 | 193 | 181 | 167 | 124 | 134 | 132 |
| Construction and extraction ................................... | 751 | 699 | 781 | 1 067 | 1 825 | 1 809 | 1 414 | 1 181 | 1 016 | 813 | 701 |
| Installation, maintenance, and repair .................... | 214 | 207 | 182 | 243 | 459 | 503 | 406 | 320 | 284 | 224 | 225 |
| Production, transportation, and material moving ........ | 1 245 | 1 127 | 1 128 | 1 474 | 2 453 | 2 365 | 2 099 | 1 845 | 1 690 | 1 385 | 1 182 |
| Production ............................................................... | 677 | 544 | 564 | 746 | 1 322 | 1 206 | 1 025 | 865 | 792 | 632 | 513 |
| Transportation and material moving ...................... | 568 | 583 | 564 | 727 | 1 131 | 1 159 | 1 073 | 980 | 898 | 754 | 668 |
| **Total Unemployment Rate, 16 Years and Over**[1] .... | 5.1 | 4.6 | 4.6 | 5.8 | 9.3 | 9.6 | 8.9 | 8.1 | 7.4 | 6.2 | 5.3 |
| Management, professional, and related .................... | 2.3 | 2.1 | 2.1 | 2.7 | 4.6 | 4.7 | 4.5 | 4.1 | 3.6 | 3.1 | 2.5 |
| Management, business, and financial operations .. | 2.2 | 2.0 | 1.9 | 2.7 | 4.9 | 5.1 | 4.7 | 4.0 | 3.5 | 2.9 | 2.4 |
| Professional and related ........................................ | 2.4 | 2.1 | 2.1 | 2.7 | 4.4 | 4.5 | 4.3 | 4.2 | 3.6 | 3.2 | 2.6 |
| Services ...................................................................... | 6.4 | 5.9 | 5.9 | 6.7 | 9.6 | 10.3 | 9.9 | 9.1 | 8.6 | 7.3 | 6.7 |
| Sales and office ........................................................ | 4.8 | 4.4 | 4.3 | 5.3 | 8.5 | 9.0 | 8.7 | 7.7 | 7.2 | 6.0 | 5.1 |
| Sales and related ................................................... | 5.0 | 4.7 | 4.8 | 5.7 | 8.8 | 9.4 | 8.8 | 7.9 | 7.3 | 6.1 | 5.5 |
| Office and administrative support .......................... | 4.6 | 4.2 | 4.0 | 5.1 | 8.3 | 8.7 | 8.5 | 7.6 | 7.1 | 5.8 | 4.7 |
| Natural resources, construction, and maintenance .... | 6.5 | 6.0 | 6.3 | 8.8 | 15.6 | 16.1 | 13.3 | 11.5 | 9.8 | 8.0 | 7.2 |
| Farming, fishing, and forestry .............................. | 9.6 | 9.5 | 8.5 | 10.2 | 16.2 | 16.3 | 15.3 | 14.4 | 11.4 | 11.6 | 10.9 |
| Construction and extraction ................................... | 7.6 | 6.8 | 7.6 | 11.0 | 19.7 | 20.1 | 16.6 | 14.4 | 12.5 | 9.6 | 8.4 |
| Installation, maintenance, and repair .................... | 3.9 | 3.7 | 3.4 | 4.5 | 8.5 | 9.3 | 7.7 | 6.2 | 5.4 | 4.4 | 4.3 |
| Production, transportation, and material moving ........ | 6.5 | 5.8 | 5.8 | 7.6 | 13.3 | 12.8 | 11.3 | 9.8 | 9.1 | 7.4 | 6.3 |
| Production ............................................................... | 6.7 | 5.5 | 5.7 | 7.7 | 14.7 | 13.1 | 11.2 | 9.3 | 8.7 | 7.0 | 5.7 |
| Transportation and material moving ...................... | 6.2 | 6.2 | 6.0 | 7.6 | 12.0 | 12.4 | 11.4 | 10.3 | 9.4 | 7.7 | 6.8 |

[1]Includes persons with no work experience and persons whose last job was in the armed forces.

## Table 1-29.  Unemployed Persons and Unemployment Rates, by Class of Worker and Industry, 2005–2015

(Thousands of people, percent.)

| Class of worker and industry | 2005 | 2006 | 2007 | 2008 | 2009 | 2010 | 2011 | 2012 | 2013 | 2014 | 2015 |
|---|---|---|---|---|---|---|---|---|---|---|---|
| **Total Unemployed Persons, 16 Years and Over** | 7 591 | 7 001 | 7 078 | 8 924 | 14 265 | 14 825 | 13 747 | 12 506 | 11 460 | 9 617 | 8 296 |
| Nonagricultural private wage and salary workers | 5 989 | 5 523 | 5 559 | 7 118 | 11 654 | 11 808 | 10 655 | 9 531 | 8 693 | 7 267 | 6 299 |
| Mining, quarrying, and oil and gas extraction | 20 | 22 | 25 | 25 | 90 | 73 | 52 | 59 | 64 | 52 | 84 |
| Construction | 712 | 671 | 757 | 1 030 | 1 770 | 1 801 | 1 383 | 1 129 | 935 | 762 | 624 |
| Manufacturing | 812 | 699 | 706 | 945 | 1 890 | 1 622 | 1 373 | 1 122 | 1 019 | 754 | 677 |
| Durable goods | 485 | 410 | 436 | 597 | 1 279 | 1 074 | 887 | 693 | 612 | 454 | 410 |
| Nondurable goods | 326 | 289 | 270 | 348 | 611 | 548 | 485 | 430 | 407 | 300 | 267 |
| Wholesale trade and retail trade | 1 137 | 1 039 | 975 | 1 205 | 1 844 | 1 963 | 1 834 | 1 663 | 1 463 | 1 260 | 1 135 |
| Transportation and utilities | 232 | 229 | 233 | 312 | 525 | 492 | 484 | 410 | 406 | 357 | 275 |
| Information | 163 | 126 | 120 | 167 | 294 | 303 | 222 | 218 | 175 | 153 | 108 |
| Financial activities | 272 | 264 | 289 | 380 | 598 | 626 | 582 | 466 | 424 | 373 | 247 |
| Professional and business services | 792 | 746 | 740 | 921 | 1 522 | 1 561 | 1 430 | 1 358 | 1 284 | 1 083 | 894 |
| Education and health services | 627 | 568 | 575 | 698 | 1 100 | 1 243 | 1 217 | 1 232 | 1 098 | 935 | 823 |
| Leisure and hospitality | 921 | 865 | 896 | 1 102 | 1 543 | 1 592 | 1 527 | 1 403 | 1 379 | 1 168 | 1 092 |
| Other services | 301 | 293 | 241 | 332 | 477 | 533 | 551 | 470 | 445 | 368 | 340 |
| Agriculture and related private wage and salary workers | 104 | 95 | 78 | 123 | 200 | 211 | 190 | 188 | 141 | 146 | 155 |
| Government workers | 534 | 473 | 505 | 534 | 799 | 969 | 1 013 | 923 | 851 | 678 | 573 |
| Self-employed and unpaid family workers | 298 | 293 | 309 | 383 | 577 | 617 | 605 | 547 | 527 | 440 | 389 |
| **Total Unemployment Rate, 16 Years and Over**[1] | 5.1 | 4.6 | 4.6 | 5.8 | 9.3 | 9.6 | 8.9 | 8.1 | 7.4 | 6.2 | 5.3 |
| Nonagricultural private wage and salary workers | 5.2 | 4.7 | 4.7 | 5.9 | 9.8 | 9.9 | 9.0 | 7.9 | 7.2 | 5.9 | 5.1 |
| Mining | 3.1 | 3.2 | 3.4 | 3.1 | 11.6 | 9.4 | 6.1 | 6.0 | 5.8 | 4.7 | 8.6 |
| Construction | 7.4 | 6.7 | 7.4 | 10.6 | 19.0 | 20.6 | 16.4 | 13.9 | 11.3 | 8.9 | 7.3 |
| Manufacturing | 4.9 | 4.2 | 4.3 | 5.8 | 12.1 | 10.6 | 9.0 | 7.3 | 6.6 | 4.9 | 4.3 |
| Durable goods | 4.6 | 3.9 | 4.2 | 5.6 | 12.9 | 11.2 | 9.2 | 7.2 | 6.3 | 4.7 | 4.1 |
| Nondurable goods | 5.3 | 4.8 | 4.5 | 6.0 | 10.6 | 9.6 | 8.5 | 7.5 | 7.1 | 5.2 | 4.6 |
| Wholesale trade and retail trade | 5.4 | 4.9 | 4.7 | 5.9 | 9.0 | 9.5 | 8.9 | 8.1 | 7.3 | 6.1 | 5.5 |
| Transportation and utilities | 4.1 | 4.0 | 3.9 | 5.1 | 8.9 | 8.4 | 8.2 | 6.9 | 6.6 | 5.7 | 4.4 |
| Information | 5.0 | 3.7 | 3.6 | 5.0 | 9.2 | 9.7 | 7.3 | 7.6 | 6.2 | 5.2 | 3.9 |
| Financial activities | 2.9 | 2.7 | 3.0 | 3.9 | 6.4 | 6.9 | 6.4 | 5.1 | 4.5 | 4.0 | 2.6 |
| Professional and business services | 6.2 | 5.6 | 5.3 | 6.5 | 10.8 | 10.8 | 9.7 | 8.9 | 8.3 | 6.9 | 5.6 |
| Education and health services | 3.4 | 3.0 | 3.0 | 3.5 | 5.3 | 5.8 | 5.6 | 5.5 | 4.9 | 4.2 | 3.6 |
| Leisure and hospitality | 7.8 | 7.3 | 7.4 | 8.6 | 11.7 | 12.2 | 11.6 | 10.4 | 10.0 | 8.6 | 7.9 |
| Other services | 4.8 | 4.7 | 3.9 | 5.3 | 7.5 | 8.5 | 8.8 | 7.2 | 6.9 | 5.7 | 5.2 |
| Agriculture and related private wage and salary workers | 8.3 | 7.2 | 6.3 | 9.2 | 14.3 | 13.9 | 12.5 | 12.4 | 10.1 | 9.4 | 9.4 |
| Government workers | 2.6 | 2.3 | 2.3 | 2.4 | 3.6 | 4.4 | 4.7 | 4.3 | 4.0 | 3.2 | 2.7 |
| Self-employed and unpaid family workers | 2.7 | 2.7 | 2.8 | 3.6 | 5.5 | 5.9 | 6.0 | 5.4 | 5.3 | 4.4 | 3.9 |

Note: See notes and definitions for information on historical comparability.

[1]Includes persons with no work experience and persons whose last job was in the armed forces.

## Table 1-30. Unemployed Persons, by Duration of Unemployment, 1948–2015

(Thousands of people, number of weeks.)

| Year | Total unemployed | Duration of unemployment | | | | | | | | | | Average duration, in weeks | Median duration, in weeks |
|---|---|---|---|---|---|---|---|---|---|---|---|---|---|
| | | Less than 5 weeks | | 5 to 14 weeks | | 15 weeks and over | | | | | | | |
| | | | | | | | | 15 to 26 weeks | | 27 weeks and over | | | |
| | | Number | Percent | Number | Percent | Number | Percent | Number | Percent | Number | Percent | | |
| 1948 | 2 276 | 1 300 | 57.1 | 669 | 29.4 | 309 | 13.6 | 193 | 8.5 | 116 | 5.1 | 8.6 | ... |
| 1949 | 3 637 | 1 756 | 48.3 | 1 194 | 32.8 | 684 | 18.8 | 428 | 11.8 | 256 | 7.0 | 10.0 | ... |
| 1950 | 3 288 | 1 450 | 44.1 | 1 055 | 32.1 | 782 | 23.8 | 425 | 12.9 | 357 | 10.9 | 12.1 | ... |
| 1951 | 2 055 | 1 177 | 57.3 | 574 | 27.9 | 303 | 14.7 | 166 | 8.1 | 137 | 6.7 | 9.7 | ... |
| 1952 | 1 883 | 1 135 | 60.3 | 516 | 27.4 | 232 | 12.3 | 148 | 7.9 | 84 | 4.5 | 8.4 | ... |
| 1953 | 1 834 | 1 142 | 62.3 | 482 | 26.3 | 210 | 11.5 | 132 | 7.2 | 78 | 4.3 | 8.0 | ... |
| 1954 | 3 532 | 1 605 | 45.4 | 1 116 | 31.6 | 812 | 23.0 | 495 | 14.0 | 317 | 9.0 | 11.8 | ... |
| 1955 | 2 852 | 1 335 | 46.8 | 815 | 28.6 | 702 | 24.6 | 366 | 12.8 | 336 | 11.8 | 13.0 | ... |
| 1956 | 2 750 | 1 412 | 51.3 | 805 | 29.3 | 533 | 19.4 | 301 | 10.9 | 232 | 8.4 | 11.3 | ... |
| 1957 | 2 859 | 1 408 | 49.2 | 891 | 31.2 | 560 | 19.6 | 321 | 11.2 | 239 | 8.4 | 10.5 | ... |
| 1958 | 4 602 | 1 753 | 38.1 | 1 396 | 30.3 | 1 452 | 31.6 | 785 | 17.1 | 667 | 14.5 | 13.9 | ... |
| 1959 | 3 740 | 1 585 | 42.4 | 1 114 | 29.8 | 1 040 | 27.8 | 469 | 12.5 | 571 | 15.3 | 14.4 | ... |
| 1960 | 3 852 | 1 719 | 44.6 | 1 176 | 30.5 | 957 | 24.8 | 503 | 13.1 | 454 | 11.8 | 12.8 | ... |
| 1961 | 4 714 | 1 806 | 38.3 | 1 376 | 29.2 | 1 532 | 32.5 | 728 | 15.4 | 804 | 17.1 | 15.6 | ... |
| 1962 | 3 911 | 1 663 | 42.5 | 1 134 | 29.0 | 1 119 | 28.6 | 534 | 13.7 | 585 | 15.0 | 14.7 | ... |
| 1963 | 4 070 | 1 751 | 43.0 | 1 231 | 30.2 | 1 088 | 26.7 | 535 | 13.1 | 553 | 13.6 | 14.0 | ... |
| 1964 | 3 786 | 1 697 | 44.8 | 1 117 | 29.5 | 973 | 25.7 | 491 | 13.0 | 482 | 12.7 | 13.3 | ... |
| 1965 | 3 366 | 1 628 | 48.4 | 983 | 29.2 | 755 | 22.4 | 404 | 12.0 | 351 | 10.4 | 11.8 | ... |
| 1966 | 2 875 | 1 573 | 54.7 | 779 | 27.1 | 526 | 18.3 | 287 | 10.0 | 239 | 8.3 | 10.4 | ... |
| 1967 | 2 975 | 1 634 | 54.9 | 893 | 30.0 | 448 | 15.1 | 271 | 9.1 | 177 | 5.9 | 8.7 | 2.3 |
| 1968 | 2 817 | 1 594 | 56.6 | 810 | 28.8 | 412 | 14.6 | 256 | 9.1 | 156 | 5.5 | 8.4 | 4.5 |
| 1969 | 2 832 | 1 629 | 57.5 | 827 | 29.2 | 375 | 13.2 | 242 | 8.5 | 133 | 4.7 | 7.8 | 4.4 |
| 1970 | 4 093 | 2 139 | 52.3 | 1 290 | 31.5 | 663 | 16.2 | 428 | 10.4 | 235 | 5.8 | 8.6 | 4.9 |
| 1971 | 5 016 | 2 245 | 44.8 | 1 585 | 31.6 | 1 187 | 23.7 | 668 | 13.3 | 519 | 10.4 | 11.3 | 6.3 |
| 1972 | 4 882 | 2 242 | 45.9 | 1 472 | 30.2 | 1 167 | 23.9 | 601 | 12.3 | 566 | 11.6 | 12.0 | 6.2 |
| 1973 | 4 365 | 2 224 | 51.0 | 1 314 | 30.1 | 826 | 18.9 | 483 | 11.1 | 343 | 7.9 | 10.0 | 5.2 |
| 1974 | 5 156 | 2 604 | 50.5 | 1 597 | 31.0 | 955 | 18.5 | 574 | 11.1 | 381 | 7.4 | 9.8 | 5.2 |
| 1975 | 7 929 | 2 940 | 37.1 | 2 484 | 31.3 | 2 505 | 31.6 | 1 303 | 16.4 | 1 203 | 15.2 | 14.2 | 8.4 |
| 1976 | 7 406 | 2 844 | 38.4 | 2 196 | 29.6 | 2 366 | 32.0 | 1 018 | 13.8 | 1 348 | 18.2 | 15.8 | 8.2 |
| 1977 | 6 991 | 2 919 | 41.8 | 2 132 | 30.5 | 1 942 | 27.8 | 913 | 13.1 | 1 028 | 14.7 | 14.3 | 7.0 |
| 1978 | 6 202 | 2 865 | 46.2 | 1 923 | 31.0 | 1 414 | 22.8 | 766 | 12.3 | 648 | 10.5 | 11.9 | 5.9 |
| 1979 | 6 137 | 2 950 | 48.1 | 1 946 | 31.7 | 1 241 | 20.2 | 706 | 11.5 | 535 | 8.7 | 10.8 | 5.4 |
| 1980 | 7 637 | 3 295 | 43.2 | 2 470 | 32.3 | 1 871 | 24.5 | 1 052 | 13.8 | 820 | 10.7 | 11.9 | 6.5 |
| 1981 | 8 273 | 3 449 | 41.7 | 2 539 | 30.7 | 2 285 | 27.6 | 1 122 | 13.6 | 1 162 | 14.0 | 13.7 | 6.9 |
| 1982 | 10 678 | 3 883 | 36.4 | 3 311 | 31.0 | 3 485 | 32.6 | 1 708 | 16.0 | 1 776 | 16.6 | 15.6 | 8.7 |
| 1983 | 10 717 | 3 570 | 33.3 | 2 937 | 27.4 | 4 210 | 39.3 | 1 652 | 15.4 | 2 559 | 23.9 | 20.0 | 10.1 |
| 1984 | 8 539 | 3 350 | 39.2 | 2 451 | 28.7 | 2 737 | 32.1 | 1 104 | 12.9 | 1 634 | 19.1 | 18.2 | 7.9 |
| 1985 | 8 312 | 3 498 | 42.1 | 2 509 | 30.2 | 2 305 | 27.7 | 1 025 | 12.3 | 1 280 | 15.4 | 15.6 | 6.8 |
| 1986 | 8 237 | 3 448 | 41.9 | 2 557 | 31.0 | 2 232 | 27.1 | 1 045 | 12.7 | 1 187 | 14.4 | 15.0 | 6.9 |
| 1987 | 7 425 | 3 246 | 43.7 | 2 196 | 29.6 | 1 983 | 26.7 | 943 | 12.7 | 1 040 | 14.0 | 14.5 | 6.5 |
| 1988 | 6 701 | 3 084 | 46.0 | 2 007 | 30.0 | 1 610 | 24.0 | 801 | 12.0 | 809 | 12.1 | 13.5 | 5.9 |
| 1989 | 6 528 | 3 174 | 48.6 | 1 978 | 30.3 | 1 375 | 21.1 | 730 | 11.2 | 646 | 9.9 | 11.9 | 4.8 |
| 1990 | 7 047 | 3 265 | 46.3 | 2 257 | 32.0 | 1 525 | 21.6 | 822 | 11.7 | 703 | 10.0 | 12.0 | 5.3 |
| 1991 | 8 628 | 3 480 | 40.3 | 2 791 | 32.4 | 2 357 | 27.3 | 1 246 | 14.4 | 1 111 | 12.9 | 13.7 | 6.8 |
| 1992 | 9 613 | 3 376 | 35.1 | 2 830 | 29.4 | 3 408 | 35.4 | 1 453 | 15.1 | 1 954 | 20.3 | 17.7 | 8.7 |
| 1993 | 8 940 | 3 262 | 36.5 | 2 584 | 28.9 | 3 094 | 34.6 | 1 297 | 14.5 | 1 798 | 20.1 | 18.0 | 8.3 |
| 1994 | 7 996 | 2 728 | 34.1 | 2 408 | 30.1 | 2 860 | 35.8 | 1 237 | 15.5 | 1 623 | 20.3 | 18.8 | 9.2 |
| 1995 | 7 404 | 2 700 | 36.5 | 2 342 | 31.6 | 2 363 | 31.9 | 1 085 | 14.6 | 1 278 | 17.3 | 16.6 | 8.3 |
| 1996 | 7 236 | 2 633 | 36.4 | 2 287 | 31.6 | 2 316 | 32.0 | 1 053 | 14.6 | 1 262 | 17.4 | 16.7 | 8.3 |
| 1997 | 6 739 | 2 538 | 37.7 | 2 138 | 31.7 | 2 062 | 30.6 | 995 | 14.8 | 1 067 | 15.8 | 15.8 | 8.0 |
| 1998 | 6 210 | 2 622 | 42.2 | 1 950 | 31.4 | 1 637 | 26.4 | 763 | 12.3 | 875 | 14.1 | 14.5 | 6.7 |
| 1999 | 5 880 | 2 568 | 43.7 | 1 832 | 31.2 | 1 480 | 25.2 | 755 | 12.8 | 725 | 12.3 | 13.4 | 6.4 |
| 2000 | 5 692 | 2 558 | 44.9 | 1 815 | 31.9 | 1 318 | 23.2 | 669 | 11.8 | 649 | 11.4 | 12.6 | 5.9 |
| 2001 | 6 801 | 2 853 | 42.0 | 2 196 | 32.3 | 1 752 | 25.8 | 951 | 14.0 | 801 | 11.8 | 13.1 | 6.8 |
| 2002 | 8 378 | 2 893 | 34.5 | 2 580 | 30.8 | 2 904 | 34.7 | 1 369 | 16.3 | 1 535 | 18.3 | 16.6 | 9.1 |
| 2003 | 8 774 | 2 785 | 31.7 | 2 612 | 29.8 | 3 378 | 38.5 | 1 442 | 16.4 | 1 936 | 22.1 | 19.2 | 10.1 |
| 2004 | 8 149 | 2 696 | 33.1 | 2 382 | 29.2 | 3 072 | 37.7 | 1 293 | 15.9 | 1 779 | 21.8 | 19.6 | 9.8 |
| 2005 | 7 591 | 2 667 | 35.1 | 2 304 | 30.4 | 2 619 | 34.5 | 1 130 | 14.9 | 1 490 | 19.6 | 18.4 | 8.9 |
| 2006 | 7 001 | 2 614 | 37.3 | 2 121 | 30.3 | 2 266 | 32.4 | 1 031 | 14.7 | 1 235 | 17.6 | 16.8 | 8.3 |
| 2007 | 7 078 | 2 542 | 35.9 | 2 232 | 31.5 | 2 303 | 32.5 | 1 061 | 15.0 | 1 243 | 17.6 | 16.8 | 8.5 |
| 2008 | 8 924 | 2 932 | 32.8 | 2 804 | 31.4 | 3 188 | 35.7 | 1 427 | 16.0 | 1 761 | 19.7 | 17.9 | 9.4 |
| 2009 | 14 265 | 3 165 | 22.2 | 3 828 | 26.8 | 7 272 | 51.0 | 2 775 | 19.5 | 4 496 | 31.5 | 24.4 | 15.1 |
| 2010 | 14 825 | 2 771 | 18.7 | 3 267 | 22.0 | 8 786 | 59.3 | 2 371 | 16.0 | 6 415 | 43.3 | 33.0 | 21.4 |
| 2011 | 13 747 | 2 677 | 19.5 | 2 993 | 21.8 | 8 077 | 58.8 | 2 061 | 15.0 | 6 016 | 43.8 | 39.3 | 21.4 |
| 2012 | 12 506 | 2 644 | 21.1 | 2 866 | 22.9 | 6 996 | 55.9 | 1 859 | 14.9 | 5 136 | 41.1 | 39.4 | 19.3 |
| 2013 | 11 460 | 2 584 | 22.5 | 2 759 | 24.1 | 6 117 | 53.4 | 1 807 | 15.8 | 4 310 | 37.6 | 36.5 | 17.0 |
| 2014 | 9 617 | 2 471 | 25.7 | 2 432 | 25.3 | 4 714 | 49.0 | 1 497 | 15.6 | 3 218 | 33.5 | 33.7 | 14.0 |
| 2015 | 8 296 | 2 399 | 28.9 | 2 302 | 27.7 | 3 595 | 43.3 | 1 267 | 15.3 | 2 328 | 28.1 | 29.2 | 11.6 |

. . . = Not available.

## Table 1-31. Long-Term Unemployment, by Industry and Selected Occupation, 2005–2015

(Thousands of people.)

| Length of unemployment, industry, and occupation | 2005 | 2006 | 2007 | 2008 | 2009 | 2010 | 2011 | 2012 | 2013 | 2014 | 2015 |
|---|---|---|---|---|---|---|---|---|---|---|---|
| **UNEMPLOYED 15 WEEKS AND OVER** | | | | | | | | | | | |
| Total | 2 619 | 2 266 | 2 303 | 3 188 | 7 272 | 8 786 | 8 077 | 6 996 | 6 117 | 4 714 | 3 595 |
| **Wage and Salary Workers, by Industry** | | | | | | | | | | | |
| Agriculture and related | 29 | 30 | 28 | 42 | 96 | 100 | 99 | 92 | 71 | 71 | 62 |
| Mining [1] | 8 | 5 | 6 | 7 | 44 | 46 | 31 | 25 | 27 | 23 | 28 |
| Construction | 216 | 177 | 215 | 339 | 907 | 1 083 | 822 | 643 | 476 | 340 | 264 |
| Manufacturing | 326 | 257 | 259 | 385 | 1 059 | 1 122 | 922 | 702 | 611 | 410 | 311 |
| Durable goods | 199 | 140 | 162 | 246 | 702 | 773 | 611 | 443 | 367 | 246 | 189 |
| Nondurable goods | 127 | 116 | 97 | 139 | 357 | 350 | 311 | 259 | 244 | 165 | 122 |
| Wholesale and retail trade | 415 | 337 | 334 | 440 | 962 | 1 215 | 1 118 | 971 | 834 | 635 | 522 |
| Transportation and utilities | 91 | 87 | 95 | 142 | 290 | 343 | 343 | 262 | 249 | 212 | 135 |
| Information | 76 | 55 | 49 | 66 | 170 | 204 | 146 | 142 | 109 | 84 | 53 |
| Financial activities | 91 | 103 | 100 | 168 | 357 | 446 | 411 | 312 | 261 | 220 | 130 |
| Professional and business services | 299 | 266 | 247 | 346 | 810 | 985 | 878 | 793 | 739 | 541 | 429 |
| Education and health services | 271 | 263 | 253 | 320 | 691 | 898 | 910 | 907 | 772 | 588 | 443 |
| Leisure and hospitality | 277 | 259 | 274 | 356 | 755 | 898 | 830 | 740 | 682 | 562 | 441 |
| Other services | 117 | 97 | 80 | 132 | 245 | 310 | 336 | 261 | 236 | 179 | 295 |
| Public administration | 62 | 34 | 51 | 55 | 107 | 164 | 185 | 144 | 141 | 101 | 74 |
| **Experienced Workers, by Occupation** | | | | | | | | | | | |
| Management, professional, and related | 436 | 373 | 368 | 569 | 1 331 | 1 600 | 1 482 | 1 362 | 1 116 | 884 | 662 |
| Services | 511 | 464 | 482 | 595 | 1 243 | 1 557 | 1 500 | 1 356 | 1 261 | 984 | 788 |
| Sales and office | 641 | 561 | 560 | 741 | 1 675 | 2 048 | 1 949 | 1 622 | 1 446 | 1 099 | 809 |
| Natural resources, construction, and maintenance | 341 | 294 | 299 | 463 | 1 224 | 1 445 | 1 150 | 914 | 715 | 534 | 436 |
| Production, transportation, and material moving | 461 | 380 | 384 | 570 | 1 302 | 1 498 | 1 290 | 1 041 | 944 | 683 | 508 |
| **UNEMPLOYED 27 WEEKS AND OVER** | | | | | | | | | | | |
| Total | 1 490 | 1 235 | 1 243 | 1 761 | 4 496 | 6 415 | 6 016 | 5 136 | 4 310 | 3 218 | 2 328 |
| **Wage and Salary Workers, by Industry** | | | | | | | | | | | |
| Agriculture and related | 16 | 13 | 14 | 17 | 51 | 57 | 58 | 55 | 39 | 40 | 33 |
| Mining [1] | 4 | 3 | 3 | 4 | 23 | 37 | 22 | 17 | 15 | 13 | 15 |
| Construction | 108 | 92 | 107 | 168 | 530 | 773 | 617 | 464 | 324 | 218 | 161 |
| Manufacturing | 195 | 140 | 152 | 230 | 657 | 888 | 725 | 533 | 439 | 291 | 202 |
| Durable goods | 124 | 75 | 93 | 150 | 428 | 619 | 486 | 341 | 273 | 172 | 123 |
| Nondurable goods | 71 | 64 | 58 | 80 | 229 | 269 | 239 | 192 | 166 | 118 | 79 |
| Wholesale and retail trade | 230 | 183 | 171 | 237 | 607 | 904 | 833 | 731 | 604 | 427 | 336 |
| Transportation and utilities | 50 | 42 | 58 | 77 | 180 | 263 | 265 | 198 | 180 | 141 | 90 |
| Information | 41 | 30 | 29 | 38 | 115 | 159 | 116 | 107 | 77 | 60 | 40 |
| Financial activities | 56 | 56 | 50 | 97 | 232 | 332 | 315 | 245 | 185 | 156 | 130 |
| Professional and business services | 172 | 144 | 130 | 184 | 510 | 722 | 641 | 580 | 518 | 369 | 429 |
| Education and health services | 156 | 144 | 132 | 182 | 432 | 644 | 671 | 668 | 561 | 417 | 443 |
| Leisure and hospitality | 148 | 135 | 142 | 196 | 445 | 624 | 596 | 519 | 472 | 379 | 441 |
| Other services | 74 | 51 | 43 | 73 | 161 | 223 | 249 | 192 | 161 | 126 | 156 |
| Public administration | 38 | 21 | 29 | 29 | 66 | 121 | 140 | 112 | 101 | 74 | 74 |
| **Experienced Workers, by Occupation** | | | | | | | | | | | |
| Management, professional, and related | 269 | 206 | 207 | 569 | 840 | 6 415 | 1 121 | 1 022 | 801 | 625 | 442 |
| Services | 284 | 249 | 251 | 595 | 750 | 1 094 | 1 086 | 971 | 896 | 673 | 513 |
| Sales and office | 354 | 299 | 285 | 741 | 1 067 | 1 513 | 1 486 | 1 211 | 1 042 | 760 | 521 |
| Natural resources, construction, and maintenance | 186 | 158 | 157 | 463 | 724 | 1 042 | 855 | 676 | 487 | 346 | 265 |
| Production, transportation, and material moving | 261 | 206 | 219 | 570 | 814 | 1 142 | 973 | 773 | 656 | 461 | 331 |

[1] For 2009 through 2014, mining includes quarrying, and oil and gas extraction.

**Table 1-32.  Unemployed Persons and Unemployment Rates, by Reason for Unemployment, Sex, and Age, 1985–2015**

(Thousands of people, percent.)

| Sex, age, and year | Number of unemployed | | | | | Unemployed as a percent of the total civilian labor force | | | |
|---|---|---|---|---|---|---|---|---|---|
| | Total | Job losers and persons who completed temporary jobs | Job leavers | Entrants | | Job losers and persons who completed temporary jobs | Job leavers | Entrants | |
| | | | | Reentrants | New entrants | | | Reentrants | New entrants |
| **Both Sexes, 16 Years and Over** | | | | | | | | | |
| 1985 | 8 312 | 4 139 | 877 | 2 256 | 1 039 | 3.6 | 0.8 | 2.0 | 0.9 |
| 1986 | 8 237 | 4 033 | 1 015 | 2 160 | 1 029 | 3.4 | 0.9 | 1.8 | 0.9 |
| 1987 | 7 425 | 3 566 | 965 | 1 974 | 920 | 3.0 | 0.8 | 1.6 | 0.8 |
| 1988 | 6 701 | 3 092 | 983 | 1 809 | 816 | 2.5 | 0.8 | 1.5 | 0.7 |
| 1989 | 6 528 | 2 983 | 1 024 | 1 843 | 677 | 2.4 | 0.8 | 1.5 | 0.5 |
| 1990 | 7 047 | 3 387 | 1 041 | 1 930 | 688 | 2.7 | 0.8 | 1.5 | 0.5 |
| 1991 | 8 628 | 4 694 | 1 004 | 2 139 | 792 | 3.7 | 0.8 | 1.7 | 0.6 |
| 1992 | 9 613 | 5 389 | 1 002 | 2 285 | 937 | 4.2 | 0.8 | 1.8 | 0.7 |
| 1993 | 8 940 | 4 848 | 976 | 2 198 | 919 | 3.8 | 0.8 | 1.7 | 0.7 |
| 1994 | 7 996 | 3 815 | 791 | 2 786 | 604 | 2.9 | 0.6 | 2.1 | 0.5 |
| 1995 | 7 404 | 3 476 | 824 | 2 525 | 579 | 2.6 | 0.6 | 1.9 | 0.4 |
| 1996 | 7 236 | 3 370 | 774 | 2 512 | 580 | 2.5 | 0.6 | 1.9 | 0.4 |
| 1997 | 6 739 | 3 037 | 795 | 2 338 | 569 | 2.2 | 0.6 | 1.7 | 0.4 |
| 1998 | 6 210 | 2 822 | 734 | 2 132 | 520 | 2.1 | 0.5 | 1.5 | 0.4 |
| 1999 | 5 880 | 2 622 | 783 | 2 005 | 469 | 1.9 | 0.6 | 1.4 | 0.3 |
| 2000 | 5 692 | 2 517 | 780 | 1 961 | 434 | 1.8 | 0.5 | 1.4 | 0.3 |
| 2001 | 6 801 | 3 476 | 835 | 2 031 | 459 | 2.4 | 0.6 | 1.4 | 0.3 |
| 2002 | 8 378 | 4 607 | 866 | 2 368 | 536 | 3.2 | 0.6 | 1.6 | 0.4 |
| 2003 | 8 774 | 4 838 | 818 | 2 477 | 641 | 3.3 | 0.6 | 1.7 | 0.4 |
| 2004 | 8 149 | 4 197 | 858 | 2 408 | 686 | 2.8 | 0.6 | 1.6 | 0.5 |
| 2005 | 7 591 | 3 667 | 872 | 2 386 | 666 | 2.5 | 0.6 | 1.6 | 0.4 |
| 2006 | 7 001 | 3 321 | 827 | 2 237 | 616 | 2.2 | 0.5 | 1.5 | 0.4 |
| 2007 | 7 078 | 3 515 | 793 | 2 142 | 627 | 2.3 | 0.5 | 1.4 | 0.4 |
| 2008 | 8 924 | 4 789 | 896 | 2 472 | 766 | 3.1 | 0.6 | 1.6 | 0.5 |
| 2009 | 14 265 | 9 160 | 882 | 3 187 | 1 035 | 5.9 | 0.6 | 2.1 | 0.7 |
| 2010 | 14 825 | 9 250 | 889 | 3 466 | 1 220 | 6.0 | 0.6 | 2.3 | 0.8 |
| 2011 | 13 747 | 8 106 | 956 | 3 401 | 1 284 | 5.3 | 0.6 | 2.2 | 0.8 |
| 2012 | 12 506 | 6 877 | 967 | 3 345 | 1 316 | 4.4 | 0.6 | 2.2 | 0.8 |
| 2013 | 11 460 | 6 073 | 932 | 3 207 | 1 247 | 3.9 | 0.6 | 2.1 | 0.8 |
| 2014 | 9 617 | 4 878 | 824 | 2 829 | 1 086 | 3.1 | 0.5 | 1.8 | 0.7 |
| 2015 | 8 296 | 4 063 | 819 | 2 535 | 879 | 2.6 | 0.5 | 1.6 | 0.6 |
| **Both Sexes, 16 to 19 Years** | | | | | | | | | |
| 1985 | 1 468 | 275 | 113 | 390 | 689 | 3.5 | 1.4 | 4.9 | 8.7 |
| 1986 | 1 454 | 240 | 145 | 374 | 695 | 3.0 | 1.8 | 4.7 | 8.8 |
| 1987 | 1 347 | 210 | 146 | 375 | 617 | 2.7 | 1.8 | 4.7 | 7.7 |
| 1988 | 1 226 | 207 | 159 | 310 | 550 | 2.6 | 2.0 | 3.9 | 6.8 |
| 1989 | 1 194 | 198 | 200 | 345 | 452 | 2.5 | 2.5 | 4.3 | 5.7 |
| 1990 | 1 212 | 233 | 181 | 338 | 460 | 3.0 | 2.3 | 4.3 | 5.9 |
| 1991 | 1 359 | 289 | 180 | 365 | 524 | 4.0 | 2.5 | 5.0 | 7.2 |
| 1992 | 1 427 | 259 | 149 | 377 | 643 | 3.6 | 2.1 | 5.3 | 9.1 |
| 1993 | 1 365 | 233 | 151 | 353 | 628 | 3.3 | 2.1 | 4.9 | 8.8 |
| 1994 | 1 320 | 185 | 84 | 634 | 416 | 2.5 | 1.1 | 8.5 | 5.6 |
| 1995 | 1 346 | 214 | 102 | 615 | 415 | 2.8 | 1.3 | 7.9 | 5.3 |
| 1996 | 1 306 | 182 | 91 | 625 | 409 | 2.3 | 1.2 | 8.0 | 5.2 |
| 1997 | 1 271 | 174 | 104 | 606 | 388 | 2.2 | 1.3 | 7.6 | 4.9 |
| 1998 | 1 205 | 181 | 86 | 577 | 361 | 2.2 | 1.0 | 7.0 | 4.4 |
| 1999 | 1 162 | 173 | 114 | 547 | 328 | 2.1 | 1.4 | 6.6 | 3.9 |
| 2000 | 1 081 | 157 | 109 | 516 | 299 | 1.9 | 1.3 | 6.2 | 3.6 |
| 2001 | 1 162 | 185 | 98 | 568 | 311 | 2.3 | 1.2 | 7.2 | 3.9 |
| 2002 | 1 253 | 197 | 91 | 597 | 368 | 2.6 | 1.2 | 7.9 | 4.9 |
| 2003 | 1 251 | 188 | 85 | 554 | 424 | 2.6 | 1.2 | 7.7 | 5.9 |
| 2004 | 1 208 | 165 | 76 | 510 | 456 | 2.3 | 1.1 | 7.2 | 6.4 |
| 2005 | 1 186 | 155 | 76 | 489 | 466 | 2.2 | 1.1 | 6.8 | 6.5 |
| 2006 | 1 119 | 145 | 78 | 461 | 435 | 2.0 | 1.1 | 6.3 | 6.0 |
| 2007 | 1 101 | 176 | 71 | 435 | 419 | 2.5 | 1.0 | 6.2 | 6.0 |
| 2008 | 1 285 | 203 | 80 | 490 | 511 | 3.0 | 1.2 | 7.1 | 7.5 |
| 2009 | 1 552 | 271 | 56 | 548 | 677 | 4.2 | 0.9 | 8.6 | 10.6 |
| 2010 | 1 528 | 220 | 42 | 487 | 778 | 3.7 | 0.7 | 8.2 | 13.2 |
| 2011 | 1 400 | 181 | 52 | 429 | 739 | 3.2 | 0.9 | 7.5 | 12.9 |
| 2012 | 1 397 | 176 | 43 | 419 | 758 | 3.0 | 0.7 | 7.2 | 13.0 |
| 2013 | 1 327 | 170 | 53 | 386 | 718 | 2.9 | 0.9 | 6.7 | 12.4 |
| 2014 | 1 106 | 140 | 44 | 327 | 595 | 2.5 | 0.8 | 5.8 | 10.5 |
| 2015 | 966 | 132 | 51 | 301 | 481 | 2.6 | 0.5 | 1.6 | 0.6 |

*Note:* See notes and definitions for information on historical comparability.

## Table 1-32. Unemployed Persons and Unemployment Rates, by Reason for Unemployment, Sex, and Age, 1985–2015—*Continued*

(Thousands of people, percent.)

| Sex, age, and year | Number of unemployed | | | | | Unemployed as a percent of the total civilian labor force | | | |
|---|---|---|---|---|---|---|---|---|---|
| | Total | Job losers and persons who completed temporary jobs | Job leavers | Entrants | | Job losers and persons who completed temporary jobs | Job leavers | Entrants | |
| | | | | Reentrants | New entrants | | | Reentrants | New entrants |
| **Men, 20 Years and Over** | | | | | | | | | |
| 1985 | 3 715 | 2 568 | 352 | 671 | 124 | 4.3 | 0.6 | 1.1 | 0.2 |
| 1986 | 3 751 | 2 568 | 444 | 611 | 128 | 4.1 | 0.7 | 1.0 | 0.2 |
| 1987 | 3 369 | 2 289 | 413 | 558 | 108 | 3.7 | 0.7 | 0.9 | 0.2 |
| 1988 | 2 987 | 1 939 | 416 | 534 | 98 | 3.1 | 0.7 | 0.9 | 0.2 |
| 1989 | 2 867 | 1 843 | 394 | 541 | 88 | 2.9 | 0.6 | 0.8 | 0.1 |
| 1990 | 3 239 | 2 100 | 431 | 626 | 82 | 3.2 | 0.7 | 1.0 | 0.1 |
| 1991 | 4 195 | 2 982 | 411 | 698 | 105 | 4.6 | 0.6 | 1.1 | 0.2 |
| 1992 | 4 717 | 3 420 | 421 | 765 | 111 | 5.2 | 0.6 | 1.2 | 0.2 |
| 1993 | 4 287 | 2 996 | 429 | 747 | 114 | 4.5 | 0.6 | 1.1 | 0.2 |
| 1994 | 3 627 | 2 296 | 367 | 898 | 65 | 3.4 | 0.5 | 1.3 | 0.1 |
| 1995 | 3 239 | 2 051 | 356 | 775 | 57 | 3.0 | 0.5 | 1.2 | 0.1 |
| 1996 | 3 146 | 2 043 | 322 | 731 | 51 | 3.0 | 0.5 | 1.1 | 0.1 |
| 1997 | 2 882 | 1 795 | 358 | 675 | 55 | 2.6 | 0.5 | 1.0 | 0.1 |
| 1998 | 2 580 | 1 588 | 318 | 611 | 63 | 2.3 | 0.5 | 0.9 | 0.1 |
| 1999 | 2 433 | 1 459 | 336 | 592 | 46 | 2.1 | 0.5 | 0.8 | 0.1 |
| 2000 | 2 376 | 1 416 | 328 | 577 | 55 | 2.0 | 0.5 | 0.8 | 0.1 |
| 2001 | 3 040 | 1 999 | 372 | 612 | 56 | 2.7 | 0.5 | 0.8 | 0.1 |
| 2002 | 3 896 | 2 702 | 386 | 743 | 65 | 3.7 | 0.5 | 1.0 | 0.1 |
| 2003 | 4 209 | 2 899 | 376 | 846 | 88 | 3.9 | 0.5 | 1.1 | 0.1 |
| 2004 | 3 791 | 2 503 | 398 | 791 | 99 | 3.3 | 0.5 | 1.0 | 0.1 |
| 2005 | 4 059 | 2 188 | 445 | 1 067 | 359 | 2.7 | 0.5 | 1.0 | 0.1 |
| 2006 | 3 131 | 1 927 | 368 | 757 | 78 | 2.5 | 0.5 | 1.0 | 0.1 |
| 2007 | 3 259 | 2 064 | 371 | 723 | 101 | 2.6 | 0.5 | 0.9 | 0.1 |
| 2008 | 4 297 | 2 918 | 410 | 969 | 856 | 3.7 | 0.5 | 1.1 | 0.1 |
| 2009 | 7 555 | 5 796 | 407 | 1 190 | 162 | 7.3 | 0.5 | 1.5 | 0.2 |
| 2010 | 7 763 | 5 773 | 433 | 1 346 | 211 | 7.3 | 0.5 | 1.7 | 0.3 |
| 2011 | 6 898 | 4 856 | 464 | 1 312 | 267 | 6.1 | 0.6 | 1.7 | 0.3 |
| 2012 | 5 984 | 3 996 | 464 | 1 250 | 274 | 5.0 | 0.6 | 1.6 | 0.3 |
| 2013 | 5 568 | 3 582 | 440 | 1 285 | 261 | 4.5 | 0.6 | 1.6 | 0.3 |
| 2014 | 4 585 | 2 839 | 392 | 1 109 | 245 | 3.5 | 0.5 | 1.4 | 0.3 |
| 2015 | 3 959 | 2 361 | 379 | 1 014 | 206 | 2.9 | 0.5 | 1.3 | 0.3 |
| **Women, 20 Years and Over** | | | | | | | | | |
| 1985 | 3 129 | 1 296 | 412 | 1 195 | 227 | 2.7 | 0.9 | 2.5 | 0.5 |
| 1986 | 3 032 | 1 225 | 426 | 1 175 | 206 | 2.5 | 0.9 | 2.4 | 0.4 |
| 1987 | 2 709 | 1 067 | 406 | 1 041 | 194 | 2.2 | 0.8 | 2.1 | 0.4 |
| 1988 | 2 487 | 946 | 408 | 965 | 168 | 1.9 | 0.8 | 1.9 | 0.3 |
| 1989 | 2 467 | 942 | 430 | 958 | 137 | 1.8 | 0.8 | 1.8 | 0.3 |
| 1990 | 2 596 | 1 054 | 429 | 966 | 146 | 2.0 | 0.8 | 1.8 | 0.3 |
| 1991 | 3 074 | 1 423 | 413 | 1 075 | 163 | 2.6 | 0.8 | 2.0 | 0.3 |
| 1992 | 3 469 | 1 710 | 433 | 1 142 | 183 | 3.1 | 0.8 | 2.1 | 0.3 |
| 1993 | 3 288 | 1 619 | 395 | 1 098 | 176 | 2.9 | 0.7 | 2.0 | 0.3 |
| 1994 | 3 049 | 1 334 | 339 | 1 253 | 122 | 2.4 | 0.6 | 2.2 | 0.2 |
| 1995 | 2 819 | 1 211 | 366 | 1 135 | 107 | 2.1 | 0.6 | 2.0 | 0.2 |
| 1996 | 2 783 | 1 145 | 361 | 1 156 | 120 | 2.0 | 0.6 | 2.0 | 0.2 |
| 1997 | 2 585 | 1 069 | 333 | 1 057 | 126 | 1.8 | 0.6 | 1.8 | 0.2 |
| 1998 | 2 424 | 1 053 | 330 | 944 | 97 | 1.8 | 0.6 | 1.6 | 0.2 |
| 1999 | 2 285 | 990 | 333 | 866 | 96 | 1.6 | 0.5 | 1.4 | 0.2 |
| 2000 | 2 235 | 943 | 343 | 868 | 80 | 1.5 | 0.6 | 1.4 | 0.1 |
| 2001 | 2 599 | 1 291 | 365 | 850 | 92 | 2.0 | 0.6 | 1.3 | 0.1 |
| 2002 | 3 228 | 1 708 | 389 | 1 028 | 102 | 2.7 | 0.6 | 1.6 | 0.2 |
| 2003 | 3 314 | 1 751 | 357 | 1 076 | 130 | 2.7 | 0.6 | 1.7 | 0.2 |
| 2004 | 3 150 | 1 529 | 384 | 1 107 | 131 | 2.4 | 0.6 | 1.7 | 0.2 |
| 2005 | 3 013 | 1 417 | 391 | 1 103 | 101 | 2.2 | 0.6 | 1.7 | 0.2 |
| 2006 | 2 751 | 1 249 | 380 | 1 019 | 103 | 1.9 | 0.6 | 1.5 | 0.2 |
| 2007 | 2 718 | 1 276 | 351 | 984 | 107 | 1.9 | 0.5 | 1.7 | 0.4 |
| 2008 | 3 342 | 1 668 | 406 | 1 126 | 143 | 2.4 | 0.6 | 1.6 | 0.2 |
| 2009 | 5 157 | 3 093 | 419 | 1 449 | 196 | 4.5 | 0.6 | 2.1 | 0.3 |
| 2010 | 5 534 | 3 257 | 413 | 1 633 | 231 | 4.7 | 0.6 | 2.4 | 0.3 |
| 2011 | 5 450 | 3 070 | 441 | 1 661 | 279 | 4.5 | 0.6 | 2.4 | 0.4 |
| 2012 | 5 125 | 2 705 | 460 | 1 676 | 284 | 3.9 | 0.7 | 2.4 | 0.4 |
| 2013 | 4 565 | 2 322 | 439 | 1 536 | 269 | 3.3 | 0.6 | 2.2 | 0.4 |
| 2014 | 3 926 | 1 899 | 388 | 1 393 | 245 | 2.7 | 0.6 | 2.0 | 0.3 |
| 2015 | 3 371 | 1 570 | 389 | 1 220 | 192 | 2.2 | 0.6 | 1.7 | 0.3 |

*Note:* See notes and definitions for information on historical comparability.

## Table 1-33.  Percent of the Population with Work Experience During the Year, by Age and Sex, 1995–2015

(Percent.)

| Sex and year | Total | 16 to 17 years | 18 to 19 years | 20 to 24 years | 25 to 34 years | 35 to 44 years | 45 to 54 years | 55 to 59 years | 60 to 64 years | 65 to 69 years | 70 years and over |
|---|---|---|---|---|---|---|---|---|---|---|---|
| **Both Sexes** | | | | | | | | | | | |
| 1995 | 69.6 | 44.4 | 71.2 | 82.0 | 85.6 | 85.9 | 83.4 | 72.2 | 53.3 | 28.0 | 10.2 |
| 1996 | 69.9 | 43.3 | 70.5 | 83.1 | 86.1 | 85.7 | 84.3 | 73.3 | 54.3 | 27.8 | 10.4 |
| 1997 | 70.1 | 43.6 | 70.5 | 83.0 | 87.1 | 85.9 | 84.4 | 73.8 | 53.8 | 28.5 | 10.0 |
| 1998 | 70.1 | 42.1 | 69.9 | 82.9 | 86.7 | 86.3 | 84.2 | 73.7 | 54.5 | 29.2 | 10.6 |
| 1999 | 70.7 | 43.7 | 71.2 | 82.7 | 87.3 | 86.9 | 85.0 | 72.3 | 55.8 | 30.5 | 11.6 |
| 2000 | 70.5 | 42.2 | 69.6 | 82.6 | 87.1 | 87.0 | 84.6 | 72.9 | 55.1 | 30.8 | 11.4 |
| 2001 | 69.4 | 37.7 | 66.7 | 80.8 | 86.1 | 85.8 | 83.7 | 73.5 | 56.7 | 30.6 | 10.5 |
| 2002 | 68.5 | 34.5 | 62.8 | 78.5 | 84.4 | 85.0 | 83.7 | 74.7 | 56.8 | 33.1 | 10.4 |
| 2003 | 67.8 | 32.0 | 61.7 | 77.5 | 83.7 | 84.0 | 82.9 | 73.9 | 56.5 | 33.2 | 11.4 |
| 2004 | 67.7 | 32.6 | 59.8 | 76.9 | 83.3 | 84.2 | 82.6 | 73.9 | 57.0 | 32.7 | 12.2 |
| 2005 | 67.8 | 31.1 | 60.1 | 77.3 | 83.7 | 84.1 | 82.8 | 74.4 | 58.2 | 32.0 | 12.1 |
| 2006 | 67.9 | 30.9 | 58.3 | 76.9 | 84.4 | 84.3 | 82.8 | 74.5 | 58.2 | 33.6 | 12.6 |
| 2007 | 67.8 | 28.5 | 57.3 | 76.6 | 84.2 | 84.4 | 82.4 | 75.6 | 59.7 | 35.2 | 13.0 |
| 2008 | 67.1 | 24.6 | 55.3 | 76.0 | 84.1 | 83.9 | 81.8 | 74.6 | 60.3 | 34.9 | 13.5 |
| 2009 | 65.0 | 21.9 | 48.7 | 71.0 | 81.6 | 82.0 | 80.5 | 73.8 | 59.3 | 35.3 | 12.8 |
| 2010 | 63.8 | 17.8 | 43.9 | 69.1 | 80.2 | 81.3 | 79.2 | 73.8 | 58.4 | 37.1 | 13.0 |
| 2011 | 63.4 | 17.0 | 44.8 | 69.8 | 79.7 | 81.3 | 79.0 | 72.0 | 59.5 | 36.5 | 13.3 |
| 2012 | 63.9 | 19.9 | 47.1 | 70.1 | 80.6 | 81.3 | 79.4 | 74.5 | 59.2 | 37.5 | 14.0 |
| 2013 | 63.6 | 19.9 | 46.3 | 71.0 | 80.2 | 81.0 | 79.9 | 72.4 | 59.3 | 36.8 | 14.7 |
| 2014 | 63.7 | 20.4 | 46.7 | 70.0 | 80.5 | 82.0 | 79.5 | 73.0 | 60.4 | 37.7 | 14.7 |
| 2015 | 64.3 | 22.4 | 48.6 | 71.3 | 81.7 | 82.3 | 80.1 | 74.6 | 60.5 | 38.2 | 14.9 |
| **Men** | | | | | | | | | | | |
| 1995 | 77.0 | 43.7 | 73.6 | 86.4 | 92.6 | 92.2 | 89.7 | 81.5 | 62.1 | 34.5 | 14.9 |
| 1996 | 77.2 | 44.1 | 71.8 | 86.7 | 93.4 | 92.1 | 90.4 | 81.8 | 62.5 | 33.6 | 15.2 |
| 1997 | 77.1 | 43.4 | 70.3 | 86.6 | 94.1 | 92.3 | 90.7 | 81.4 | 62.9 | 33.8 | 13.9 |
| 1998 | 76.9 | 40.4 | 71.6 | 86.4 | 93.5 | 92.7 | 90.1 | 81.7 | 63.5 | 35.5 | 14.7 |
| 1999 | 77.3 | 44.7 | 72.3 | 85.5 | 93.9 | 93.2 | 89.9 | 79.2 | 65.1 | 37.4 | 16.5 |
| 2000 | 77.1 | 42.1 | 70.2 | 85.1 | 93.4 | 93.6 | 89.8 | 80.6 | 64.4 | 38.4 | 16.0 |
| 2001 | 76.3 | 37.4 | 67.7 | 84.8 | 93.2 | 92.2 | 89.1 | 80.4 | 64.3 | 37.8 | 14.5 |
| 2002 | 75.2 | 34.7 | 62.8 | 82.1 | 91.6 | 91.8 | 88.9 | 80.7 | 64.3 | 39.3 | 14.6 |
| 2003 | 74.3 | 32.8 | 61.7 | 80.2 | 90.8 | 90.9 | 87.7 | 80.9 | 63.1 | 37.3 | 15.8 |
| 2004 | 74.2 | 32.1 | 58.9 | 80.2 | 91.0 | 91.1 | 87.9 | 80.1 | 64.5 | 37.1 | 16.7 |
| 2005 | 74.6 | 31.1 | 60.7 | 80.8 | 91.3 | 91.6 | 88.2 | 80.1 | 64.3 | 37.6 | 17.0 |
| 2006 | 74.5 | 30.9 | 57.9 | 80.1 | 91.9 | 91.8 | 88.0 | 80.6 | 64.1 | 38.3 | 17.3 |
| 2007 | 74.3 | 28.5 | 59.0 | 80.5 | 90.5 | 91.5 | 88.2 | 80.3 | 66.2 | 39.3 | 17.9 |
| 2008 | 73.2 | 24.4 | 55.1 | 78.7 | 90.7 | 91.1 | 86.4 | 79.3 | 66.0 | 40.3 | 17.9 |
| 2009 | 70.8 | 22.2 | 48.0 | 73.3 | 87.7 | 89.1 | 85.0 | 78.3 | 64.8 | 39.8 | 17.2 |
| 2010 | 69.4 | 16.9 | 43.2 | 71.3 | 86.0 | 88.0 | 84.1 | 78.9 | 62.8 | 43.4 | 17.5 |
| 2011 | 69.0 | 16.1 | 43.2 | 71.6 | 86.2 | 88.1 | 84.3 | 76.7 | 64.0 | 42.6 | 18.2 |
| 2012 | 69.7 | 19.1 | 45.9 | 72.2 | 86.9 | 88.9 | 84.8 | 79.9 | 64.2 | 43.2 | 18.5 |
| 2013 | 69.3 | 18.4 | 46.6 | 72.5 | 86.5 | 88.0 | 85.8 | 77.0 | 64.6 | 42.0 | 19.4 |
| 2014 | 69.4 | 20.5 | 44.9 | 70.4 | 87.2 | 89.0 | 85.1 | 78.1 | 66.5 | 42.2 | 19.4 |
| 2015 | 70.2 | 22.2 | 48.2 | 72.9 | 87.8 | 89.4 | 86.2 | 79.4 | 66.1 | 43.5 | 19.8 |
| **Women** | | | | | | | | | | | |
| 1995 | 62.8 | 45.2 | 68.7 | 77.7 | 78.8 | 79.8 | 77.6 | 63.2 | 45.6 | 22.4 | 7.1 |
| 1996 | 63.2 | 42.5 | 69.2 | 79.5 | 78.9 | 79.5 | 78.4 | 65.4 | 46.9 | 23.0 | 7.1 |
| 1997 | 63.6 | 43.9 | 70.7 | 79.5 | 80.1 | 79.6 | 78.4 | 66.7 | 45.6 | 24.0 | 7.3 |
| 1998 | 63.7 | 44.1 | 68.2 | 79.4 | 80.1 | 80.0 | 78.6 | 66.3 | 46.2 | 23.8 | 7.8 |
| 1999 | 64.5 | 42.6 | 70.1 | 79.9 | 80.9 | 80.7 | 80.3 | 66.2 | 47.3 | 24.4 | 8.2 |
| 2000 | 64.3 | 42.3 | 69.0 | 80.2 | 80.9 | 80.5 | 79.5 | 65.7 | 47.0 | 23.9 | 8.2 |
| 2001 | 63.1 | 38.1 | 65.7 | 76.9 | 79.2 | 79.5 | 78.6 | 67.1 | 49.8 | 24.2 | 7.9 |
| 2002 | 62.3 | 34.3 | 62.8 | 74.9 | 77.2 | 78.4 | 78.7 | 69.1 | 50.0 | 27.8 | 7.4 |
| 2003 | 61.7 | 31.2 | 61.6 | 74.6 | 76.6 | 77.2 | 78.4 | 67.3 | 50.7 | 29.6 | 8.3 |
| 2004 | 61.5 | 33.1 | 60.7 | 73.7 | 75.6 | 77.4 | 77.5 | 68.2 | 50.3 | 28.7 | 9.0 |
| 2005 | 61.4 | 31.2 | 59.6 | 73.7 | 76.1 | 76.8 | 77.6 | 68.9 | 52.7 | 27.1 | 8.7 |
| 2006 | 61.6 | 30.9 | 58.7 | 73.7 | 76.9 | 76.9 | 77.9 | 68.8 | 53.0 | 29.5 | 9.3 |
| 2007 | 61.6 | 28.5 | 55.6 | 72.6 | 77.8 | 77.4 | 76.9 | 71.2 | 53.7 | 31.5 | 9.5 |
| 2008 | 61.3 | 24.8 | 55.4 | 73.2 | 77.3 | 76.7 | 77.3 | 70.1 | 55.0 | 30.1 | 10.3 |
| 2009 | 59.6 | 21.6 | 49.5 | 68.6 | 75.4 | 75.0 | 76.1 | 69.5 | 54.4 | 31.1 | 9.7 |
| 2010 | 58.5 | 18.7 | 44.5 | 66.9 | 74.3 | 74.7 | 74.4 | 69.1 | 54.2 | 31.6 | 9.6 |
| 2011 | 58.1 | 18.0 | 46.5 | 68.0 | 73.4 | 74.7 | 73.8 | 67.7 | 55.4 | 31.0 | 9.6 |
| 2012 | 58.4 | 20.7 | 48.3 | 68.1 | 74.3 | 73.8 | 74.3 | 69.4 | 54.8 | 32.2 | 10.6 |
| 2013 | 58.2 | 21.4 | 46.1 | 69.5 | 74.0 | 74.2 | 74.3 | 68.0 | 54.4 | 32.1 | 11.2 |
| 2014 | 58.3 | 20.2 | 48.5 | 69.6 | 73.8 | 75.1 | 74.1 | 68.3 | 54.7 | 33.7 | 11.2 |
| 2015 | 58.8 | 22.6 | 49.1 | 69.7 | 75.7 | 75.4 | 74.3 | 70.1 | 55.4 | 33.5 | 11.3 |

Note: See notes and definitions for information on historical comparability.

## Table 1-34. Persons with Work Experience During the Year, by Industry and Class of Worker of Job Held the Longest, 2005–2015

(Thousands of people.)

| Industry and class of worker | 2005 | 2006 | 2007 | 2008 | 2009 | 2010 | 2011 | 2012 | 2013 | 2014 | 2015 |
|---|---|---|---|---|---|---|---|---|---|---|---|
| TOTAL | 155 127 | 157 352 | 158 468 | 158 317 | 154 772 | 153 141 | 154 330 | 157 050 | 157 878 | 159 881 | 163 169 |
| Agriculture | 2 344 | 2 332 | 2 407 | 2 382 | 2 581 | 2 383 | 2 470 | 2 176 | 2 497 | 2 748 | 2 890 |
| Wage and salary workers | 1 501 | 1 495 | 1 525 | 1 522 | 1 733 | 1 578 | 1 679 | 1 504 | 1 769 | 1 918 | 2 041 |
| Self-employed workers | 829 | 812 | 846 | 824 | 813 | 788 | 750 | 649 | 706 | 794 | 831 |
| Unpaid family workers | 14 | 25 | 36 | 37 | 35 | 17 | 42 | 22 | 22 | 36 | 19 |
| Nonagricultural Industries | 152 783 | 155 021 | 156 061 | 155 934 | 152 191 | 150 759 | 151 859 | 154 874 | 155 381 | 157 133 | 160 279 |
| Wage and salary workers | 143 002 | 145 152 | 146 485 | 146 521 | 142 946 | 141 686 | 142 962 | 145 787 | 146 688 | 148 247 | 151 029 |
| Mining | 696 | 758 | 746 | 840 | 778 | 771 | 890 | 1 146 | 1 173 | 1 114 | 1 000 |
| Construction | 10 423 | 10 989 | 10 547 | 10 234 | 9 443 | 8 633 | 8 607 | 8 445 | 8 589 | 9 015 | 9 173 |
| Manufacturing | 17 243 | 17 112 | 16 641 | 16 332 | 14 956 | 14 865 | 15 139 | 15 139 | 15 688 | 15 445 | 15 748 |
| Durable goods | 10 930 | 10 995 | 10 687 | 10 477 | 9 342 | 9 288 | 9 586 | 9 585 | 9 916 | 9 981 | 9 897 |
| Nondurable goods | 6 313 | 6 116 | 5 954 | 5 855 | 5 613 | 5 577 | 5 552 | 5 554 | 5 773 | 5 465 | 5 851 |
| Wholesale and retail trade | 22 479 | 21 822 | 21 837 | 21 838 | 21 210 | 20 854 | 20 685 | 20 485 | 21 353 | 21 352 | 21 339 |
| Wholesale trade | 4 517 | 4 395 | 4 017 | 4 016 | 3 849 | 3 921 | 3 601 | 3 606 | 3 738 | 3 840 | 3 761 |
| Retail trade | 17 962 | 17 427 | 17 820 | 17 822 | 17 361 | 16 933 | 17 084 | 16 879 | 17 615 | 17 512 | 17 578 |
| Transportation and utilities | 7 248 | 7 413 | 8 023 | 7 675 | 7 309 | 6 993 | 7 173 | 7 573 | 7 493 | 7 504 | 8 128 |
| Transportation and warehousing | 6 095 | 6 197 | 6 750 | 6 365 | 6 025 | 5 701 | 5 944 | 6 336 | 6 318 | 6 215 | 6 737 |
| Utilities | 1 153 | 1 216 | 1 273 | 1 310 | 1 284 | 1 292 | 1 229 | 1 237 | 1 175 | 1 290 | 1 392 |
| Information | 3 495 | 3 710 | 3 687 | 3 455 | 3 375 | 3 380 | 3 137 | 3 144 | 3 384 | 3 010 | 3 005 |
| Financial activities | 9 748 | 10 101 | 10 013 | 9 671 | 9 409 | 9 239 | 9 443 | 9 889 | 9 987 | 9 835 | 9 993 |
| Finance and insurance | 7 011 | 7 190 | 7 347 | 6 994 | 6 792 | 6 726 | 6 909 | 7 293 | 7 231 | 7 073 | 7 101 |
| Real estate and rental and leasing | 2 737 | 2 912 | 2 666 | 2 677 | 2 617 | 2 512 | 2 534 | 2 595 | 2 756 | 2 762 | 2 892 |
| Professional and business services | 13 537 | 14 412 | 14 659 | 14 868 | 14 633 | 15 094 | 15 339 | 15 924 | 15 923 | 16 375 | 16 949 |
| Professional, scientific, and technical services | 7 768 | 8 294 | 8 676 | 8 742 | 8 475 | 8 841 | 9 054 | 9 370 | 9 401 | 10 077 | 10 485 |
| Management, administration, and waste management services | 5 769 | 6 118 | 5 982 | 6 127 | 6 159 | 6 253 | 6 285 | 6 553 | 6 522 | 6 297 | 6 464 |
| Education and health services | 30 552 | 31 314 | 31 921 | 32 828 | 33 465 | 33 596 | 33 424 | 34 156 | 33 943 | 34 724 | 35 682 |
| Education services | 13 282 | 13 659 | 13 989 | 14 396 | 14 457 | 14 157 | 13 917 | 14 256 | 14 394 | 14 770 | 14 899 |
| Health care and social assistance services | 17 270 | 17 655 | 17 932 | 18 432 | 19 008 | 19 439 | 19 507 | 19 900 | 19 549 | 19 953 | 20 783 |
| Leisure and hospitality | 13 405 | 13 455 | 13 959 | 14 242 | 13 917 | 13 718 | 14 293 | 15 103 | 14 688 | 14 998 | 15 291 |
| Arts, entertainment, and recreation | 2 877 | 2 797 | 3 124 | 3 047 | 3 284 | 2 993 | 3 116 | 3 332 | 3 232 | 3 022 | 3 120 |
| Accommodation and food services | 10 528 | 10 658 | 10 835 | 11 195 | 10 633 | 10 725 | 11 177 | 11 771 | 11 457 | 11 976 | 12 171 |
| Other services and private household | 6 490 | 6 341 | 6 603 | 6 590 | 6 233 | 6 111 | 6 717 | 6 643 | 6 571 | 6 818 | 6 558 |
| Private households | 866 | 912 | 888 | 912 | 757 | 816 | 773 | 833 | 942 | 929 | 769 |
| Public administration | 6 917 | 7 076 | 7 095 | 7 121 | 7 332 | 7 597 | 7 270 | 7 333 | 7 094 | 7 245 | 7 398 |
| Self-employed workers | 9 658 | 9 733 | 9 451 | 9 332 | 9 121 | 8 962 | 8 778 | 8 955 | 8 605 | 8 786 | 9 122 |
| Unpaid family workers | 123 | 135 | 126 | 82 | 124 | 111 | 120 | 132 | 87 | 101 | 129 |

Note: See notes and definitions for information on historical comparability.

**Table 1-35.  Number of Persons with Work Experience During the Year, by Extent of Employment and Sex, 1995–2015**

(Thousands of people.)

| Sex and year | Total | Full-time workers | | | | Part-time workers | | | |
|---|---|---|---|---|---|---|---|---|---|
| | | Total | 50 to 52 weeks | 27 to 49 weeks | 1 to 26 weeks | Total | 50 to 52 weeks | 27 to 49 weeks | 1 to 26 weeks |
| **Both Sexes** | | | | | | | | | |
| 1995 | 139 724 | 110 063 | 88 173 | 12 970 | 8 920 | 29 661 | 12 725 | 6 831 | 10 105 |
| 1996 | 142 201 | 112 313 | 90 252 | 12 997 | 9 064 | 29 888 | 13 382 | 6 643 | 9 863 |
| 1997 | 143 968 | 113 879 | 92 631 | 12 508 | 8 740 | 30 089 | 13 810 | 6 565 | 9 714 |
| 1998 | 145 566 | 116 412 | 95 772 | 12 156 | 8 484 | 29 155 | 13 538 | 6 480 | 9 137 |
| 1999 | 148 295 | 119 096 | 97 941 | 12 294 | 8 861 | 29 199 | 13 680 | 6 317 | 9 202 |
| 2000 | 149 361 | 120 591 | 100 349 | 12 071 | 8 171 | 28 770 | 13 865 | 6 161 | 8 744 |
| 2001 | 151 042 | 121 921 | 100 357 | 13 172 | 8 392 | 29 121 | 14 038 | 6 139 | 8 944 |
| 2002 | 151 546 | 121 726 | 100 659 | 12 544 | 8 523 | 29 819 | 14 635 | 6 184 | 9 000 |
| 2003 | 151 553 | 121 158 | 100 700 | 11 972 | 8 486 | 30 395 | 15 333 | 6 027 | 9 035 |
| 2004 | 153 024 | 122 404 | 102 427 | 11 862 | 8 115 | 30 621 | 15 552 | 6 077 | 8 992 |
| 2005 | 155 127 | 124 683 | 104 876 | 11 816 | 7 991 | 30 444 | 15 374 | 6 161 | 8 909 |
| 2006 | 157 352 | 127 340 | 107 734 | 11 736 | 7 870 | 30 012 | 15 131 | 6 223 | 8 657 |
| 2007 | 158 468 | 128 332 | 108 617 | 11 901 | 7 814 | 30 136 | 15 477 | 6 194 | 8 466 |
| 2008 | 158 317 | 125 937 | 104 023 | 13 421 | 8 493 | 32 380 | 16 562 | 6 630 | 9 188 |
| 2009 | 154 772 | 121 355 | 99 306 | 12 350 | 9 698 | 33 418 | 17 417 | 6 674 | 9 327 |
| 2010 | 153 141 | 119 940 | 99 250 | 11 705 | 8 985 | 33 201 | 17 122 | 6 582 | 9 497 |
| 2011 | 154 330 | 121 400 | 101 700 | 11 040 | 8 661 | 32 929 | 17 261 | 6 288 | 9 380 |
| 2012 | 157 050 | 123 229 | 103 078 | 11 708 | 8 442 | 33 821 | 17 494 | 6 681 | 9 646 |
| 2013 | 157 878 | 124 875 | 105 839 | 10 945 | 8 090 | 33 003 | 17 151 | 6 733 | 9 119 |
| 2014 | 159 881 | 127 353 | 108 687 | 11 297 | 7 369 | 32 528 | 17 144 | 6 539 | 8 845 |
| 2015 | 163 169 | 130 053 | 111 079 | 11 586 | 7 388 | 33 116 | 17 305 | 6 472 | 9 339 |
| **Men** | | | | | | | | | |
| 1995 | 74 381 | 64 145 | 52 671 | 6 973 | 4 501 | 10 236 | 4 034 | 2 257 | 3 945 |
| 1996 | 75 760 | 65 356 | 53 795 | 6 891 | 4 670 | 10 404 | 4 321 | 2 136 | 3 947 |
| 1997 | 76 408 | 66 089 | 54 918 | 6 638 | 4 533 | 10 319 | 4 246 | 2 274 | 3 799 |
| 1998 | 76 918 | 67 250 | 56 953 | 6 208 | 4 089 | 9 669 | 4 197 | 2 090 | 3 382 |
| 1999 | 78 145 | 68 347 | 57 520 | 6 401 | 4 426 | 9 797 | 4 297 | 2 062 | 3 438 |
| 2000 | 78 804 | 68 925 | 58 756 | 6 094 | 4 075 | 9 879 | 4 485 | 1 957 | 3 437 |
| 2001 | 79 971 | 70 074 | 58 715 | 7 087 | 4 272 | 9 897 | 4 306 | 1 989 | 3 602 |
| 2002 | 80 282 | 70 132 | 58 765 | 6 804 | 4 563 | 10 151 | 4 519 | 2 042 | 3 590 |
| 2003 | 80 317 | 69 766 | 58 778 | 6 479 | 4 509 | 10 551 | 5 042 | 1 872 | 3 637 |
| 2004 | 81 261 | 70 780 | 60 096 | 6 428 | 4 256 | 10 482 | 4 987 | 1 992 | 3 503 |
| 2005 | 82 735 | 72 056 | 61 510 | 6 299 | 4 247 | 10 679 | 5 153 | 2 074 | 3 452 |
| 2006 | 83 767 | 73 578 | 63 058 | 6 373 | 4 147 | 10 189 | 4 747 | 2 046 | 3 396 |
| 2007 | 84 292 | 73 734 | 62 994 | 6 583 | 4 157 | 10 558 | 4 933 | 2 165 | 3 460 |
| 2008 | 83 889 | 72 204 | 59 869 | 7 645 | 4 690 | 11 685 | 5 425 | 2 457 | 3 803 |
| 2009 | 81 835 | 69 178 | 56 058 | 7 339 | 5 780 | 12 658 | 5 911 | 2 526 | 4 221 |
| 2010 | 81 076 | 68 402 | 56 416 | 6 760 | 5 225 | 12 674 | 5 883 | 2 523 | 4 267 |
| 2011 | 81 272 | 69 029 | 58 004 | 6 183 | 4 842 | 12 243 | 5 797 | 2 408 | 4 037 |
| 2012 | 82 910 | 70 181 | 59 022 | 6 547 | 4 611 | 12 729 | 6 199 | 2 481 | 4 049 |
| 2013 | 83 420 | 71 388 | 60 769 | 6 024 | 4 595 | 12 032 | 5 863 | 2 306 | 3 863 |
| 2014 | 84 358 | 72 398 | 62 445 | 6 016 | 3 937 | 11 960 | 6 018 | 2 313 | 3 628 |
| 2015 | 86 270 | 73 900 | 63 869 | 6 027 | 4 003 | 12 371 | 6 050 | 2 414 | 3 907 |
| **Women** | | | | | | | | | |
| 1995 | 65 342 | 45 917 | 35 502 | 5 997 | 4 418 | 19 425 | 8 691 | 4 574 | 6 160 |
| 1996 | 66 439 | 46 955 | 36 457 | 6 105 | 4 393 | 19 484 | 9 061 | 4 507 | 5 916 |
| 1997 | 67 559 | 47 790 | 37 713 | 5 870 | 4 207 | 19 769 | 9 564 | 4 291 | 5 914 |
| 1998 | 68 648 | 49 162 | 38 819 | 5 948 | 4 395 | 19 486 | 9 341 | 4 390 | 5 755 |
| 1999 | 70 150 | 50 748 | 40 421 | 5 892 | 4 435 | 19 402 | 9 383 | 4 255 | 5 764 |
| 2000 | 70 556 | 51 665 | 41 593 | 5 977 | 4 095 | 18 891 | 9 380 | 4 204 | 5 307 |
| 2001 | 71 071 | 51 848 | 41 642 | 6 085 | 4 120 | 19 223 | 9 731 | 4 150 | 5 342 |
| 2002 | 71 263 | 51 593 | 41 893 | 5 741 | 3 959 | 19 671 | 10 117 | 4 143 | 5 411 |
| 2003 | 71 236 | 51 391 | 41 921 | 5 493 | 3 977 | 19 844 | 10 291 | 4 155 | 5 398 |
| 2004 | 71 763 | 51 624 | 42 331 | 5 434 | 3 859 | 20 139 | 10 565 | 4 085 | 5 489 |
| 2005 | 72 392 | 52 627 | 43 366 | 5 517 | 3 744 | 19 765 | 10 222 | 4 087 | 5 456 |
| 2006 | 73 585 | 53 762 | 44 676 | 5 364 | 3 723 | 19 823 | 10 384 | 4 178 | 5 261 |
| 2007 | 74 176 | 54 598 | 45 622 | 5 318 | 3 657 | 19 579 | 10 543 | 4 029 | 5 006 |
| 2008 | 74 428 | 53 733 | 44 154 | 5 776 | 3 803 | 20 695 | 11 137 | 4 172 | 5 385 |
| 2009 | 72 937 | 52 177 | 43 248 | 5 012 | 3 918 | 20 760 | 11 506 | 4 147 | 5 107 |
| 2010 | 72 066 | 51 538 | 42 834 | 4 944 | 3 760 | 20 528 | 11 239 | 4 058 | 5 230 |
| 2011 | 73 058 | 52 371 | 43 696 | 4 857 | 3 818 | 20 687 | 11 464 | 3 880 | 5 343 |
| 2012 | 74 140 | 53 048 | 44 055 | 5 161 | 3 831 | 21 092 | 11 295 | 4 200 | 5 597 |
| 2013 | 74 458 | 53 486 | 45 070 | 4 922 | 3 495 | 20 972 | 11 288 | 4 427 | 5 256 |
| 2014 | 75 523 | 54 955 | 46 241 | 5 281 | 3 432 | 20 568 | 11 125 | 4 226 | 5 217 |
| 2015 | 76 899 | 56 153 | 47 210 | 5 558 | 3 385 | 20 745 | 11 254 | 4 058 | 5 433 |

*Note:* See notes and definitions for information on historical comparability.

**Table 1-36. Percent Distribution of the Population with Work Experience During the Year, by Extent of Employment and Sex, 1995–2015**

(Percent of total people with work experience.)

| Sex and year | Total | Full-time workers | | | | Part-time workers | | | |
|---|---|---|---|---|---|---|---|---|---|
| | | Total | 50 to 52 weeks | 27 to 49 weeks | 1 to 26 weeks | Total | 50 to 52 weeks | 27 to 49 weeks | 1 to 26 weeks |
| **Both Sexes** | | | | | | | | | |
| 1995 | 100.0 | 78.8 | 63.1 | 9.3 | 6.4 | 21.2 | 9.1 | 4.9 | 7.2 |
| 1996 | 100.0 | 79.0 | 63.5 | 9.1 | 6.4 | 21.0 | 9.4 | 4.7 | 6.9 |
| 1997 | 100.0 | 79.1 | 64.3 | 8.7 | 6.1 | 20.9 | 9.6 | 4.6 | 6.7 |
| 1998 | 100.0 | 80.0 | 65.8 | 8.4 | 5.8 | 20.1 | 9.3 | 4.5 | 6.3 |
| 1999 | 100.0 | 80.3 | 66.0 | 8.3 | 6.0 | 19.7 | 9.2 | 4.3 | 6.2 |
| 2000 | 100.0 | 80.8 | 67.2 | 8.1 | 5.5 | 19.3 | 9.3 | 4.1 | 5.9 |
| 2001 | 100.0 | 80.7 | 66.4 | 8.7 | 5.6 | 19.3 | 9.3 | 4.1 | 5.9 |
| 2002 | 100.0 | 80.3 | 66.4 | 8.3 | 5.6 | 19.7 | 9.7 | 4.1 | 5.9 |
| 2003 | 100.0 | 79.9 | 66.4 | 7.9 | 5.6 | 20.1 | 10.1 | 4.0 | 6.0 |
| 2004 | 100.0 | 80.0 | 66.9 | 7.8 | 5.3 | 20.1 | 10.2 | 4.0 | 5.9 |
| 2005 | 100.0 | 80.4 | 67.6 | 7.6 | 5.2 | 19.6 | 9.9 | 4.0 | 5.7 |
| 2006 | 100.0 | 80.9 | 68.5 | 7.5 | 5.0 | 19.1 | 9.6 | 4.0 | 5.5 |
| 2007 | 100.0 | 81.0 | 68.5 | 7.5 | 4.9 | 19.0 | 9.8 | 3.9 | 5.3 |
| 2008 | 100.0 | 79.5 | 65.7 | 8.5 | 5.4 | 20.5 | 10.5 | 4.2 | 5.8 |
| 2009 | 100.0 | 78.4 | 64.2 | 8.0 | 6.3 | 21.6 | 11.3 | 4.3 | 6.0 |
| 2010 | 100.0 | 78.3 | 64.8 | 7.6 | 5.9 | 21.7 | 11.2 | 4.3 | 6.2 |
| 2011 | 100.0 | 78.7 | 65.9 | 7.2 | 5.6 | 21.3 | 11.2 | 4.1 | 6.1 |
| 2012 | 100.0 | 78.5 | 65.6 | 7.5 | 5.4 | 21.5 | 11.1 | 4.3 | 6.1 |
| 2013 | 100.0 | 79.1 | 67.0 | 6.9 | 5.1 | 20.9 | 10.9 | 4.3 | 5.8 |
| 2014 | 100.0 | 79.7 | 68.0 | 7.1 | 4.6 | 20.3 | 10.7 | 4.1 | 5.5 |
| 2015 | 100.0 | 79.7 | 68.1 | 7.1 | 4.5 | 20.3 | 10.6 | 4.0 | 5.7 |
| **Men** | | | | | | | | | |
| 1995 | 100.0 | 86.3 | 70.8 | 9.4 | 6.1 | 13.7 | 5.4 | 3.0 | 5.3 |
| 1996 | 100.0 | 86.3 | 71.0 | 9.1 | 6.2 | 13.7 | 5.7 | 2.8 | 5.2 |
| 1997 | 100.0 | 86.5 | 71.9 | 8.7 | 5.9 | 13.6 | 5.6 | 3.0 | 5.0 |
| 1998 | 100.0 | 87.4 | 74.0 | 8.1 | 5.3 | 12.6 | 5.5 | 2.7 | 4.4 |
| 1999 | 100.0 | 87.5 | 73.6 | 8.2 | 5.7 | 12.5 | 5.5 | 2.6 | 4.4 |
| 2000 | 100.0 | 87.5 | 74.6 | 7.7 | 5.2 | 12.6 | 5.7 | 2.5 | 4.4 |
| 2001 | 100.0 | 87.6 | 73.4 | 8.9 | 5.3 | 12.4 | 5.4 | 2.5 | 4.5 |
| 2002 | 100.0 | 87.4 | 73.2 | 8.5 | 5.7 | 12.6 | 5.6 | 2.5 | 4.5 |
| 2003 | 100.0 | 86.9 | 73.2 | 8.1 | 5.6 | 13.1 | 6.3 | 2.3 | 4.5 |
| 2004 | 100.0 | 87.1 | 74.0 | 7.9 | 5.2 | 12.9 | 6.1 | 2.5 | 4.3 |
| 2005 | 100.0 | 87.0 | 74.3 | 7.6 | 5.1 | 12.9 | 6.2 | 2.5 | 4.2 |
| 2006 | 100.0 | 87.8 | 75.3 | 7.6 | 5.0 | 12.2 | 5.7 | 2.4 | 4.1 |
| 2007 | 100.0 | 87.5 | 74.7 | 7.8 | 4.9 | 12.5 | 5.9 | 2.6 | 4.1 |
| 2008 | 100.0 | 86.1 | 71.4 | 9.1 | 5.6 | 13.9 | 6.5 | 2.9 | 4.5 |
| 2009 | 100.0 | 84.5 | 68.5 | 9.0 | 7.1 | 15.5 | 7.2 | 3.1 | 5.2 |
| 2010 | 100.0 | 84.4 | 69.6 | 8.3 | 6.4 | 15.6 | 7.3 | 3.1 | 5.3 |
| 2011 | 100.0 | 84.9 | 71.4 | 7.6 | 6.0 | 15.1 | 7.1 | 3.0 | 5.0 |
| 2012 | 100.0 | 84.6 | 71.2 | 7.9 | 5.6 | 15.4 | 7.5 | 3.0 | 4.9 |
| 2013 | 100.0 | 85.6 | 72.8 | 7.2 | 5.5 | 14.4 | 7.0 | 2.8 | 4.6 |
| 2014 | 100.0 | 85.8 | 74.0 | 7.1 | 4.7 | 14.2 | 7.1 | 2.7 | 4.3 |
| 2015 | 100.0 | 85.7 | 74.0 | 7.0 | 4.6 | 14.3 | 7.0 | 2.8 | 4.5 |
| **Women** | | | | | | | | | |
| 1995 | 100.0 | 70.3 | 54.3 | 9.2 | 6.8 | 29.7 | 13.3 | 7.0 | 9.4 |
| 1996 | 100.0 | 70.7 | 54.9 | 9.2 | 6.6 | 29.3 | 13.6 | 6.8 | 8.9 |
| 1997 | 100.0 | 70.7 | 55.8 | 8.7 | 6.2 | 29.4 | 14.2 | 6.4 | 8.8 |
| 1998 | 100.0 | 71.6 | 56.5 | 8.7 | 6.4 | 28.4 | 13.6 | 6.4 | 8.4 |
| 1999 | 100.0 | 72.3 | 57.6 | 8.4 | 6.3 | 27.7 | 13.4 | 6.1 | 8.2 |
| 2000 | 100.0 | 73.2 | 58.9 | 8.5 | 5.8 | 26.8 | 13.3 | 6.0 | 7.5 |
| 2001 | 100.0 | 73.0 | 58.6 | 8.6 | 5.8 | 27.0 | 13.7 | 5.8 | 7.5 |
| 2002 | 100.0 | 72.5 | 58.8 | 8.1 | 5.6 | 27.6 | 14.2 | 5.8 | 7.6 |
| 2003 | 100.0 | 72.1 | 58.8 | 7.7 | 5.6 | 27.8 | 14.4 | 5.8 | 7.6 |
| 2004 | 100.0 | 72.0 | 59.0 | 7.6 | 5.4 | 28.0 | 14.7 | 5.7 | 7.6 |
| 2005 | 100.0 | 72.7 | 59.9 | 7.6 | 5.2 | 27.2 | 14.1 | 5.6 | 7.5 |
| 2006 | 100.0 | 73.1 | 60.7 | 7.3 | 5.1 | 26.9 | 14.1 | 5.7 | 7.1 |
| 2007 | 100.0 | 73.6 | 61.5 | 7.2 | 4.9 | 26.4 | 14.2 | 5.4 | 6.7 |
| 2008 | 100.0 | 72.2 | 59.3 | 7.8 | 5.1 | 27.8 | 15.0 | 5.6 | 7.2 |
| 2009 | 100.0 | 71.5 | 59.3 | 6.9 | 5.4 | 28.5 | 15.8 | 5.7 | 7.0 |
| 2010 | 100.0 | 71.5 | 59.4 | 6.9 | 5.2 | 28.5 | 15.6 | 5.6 | 7.3 |
| 2011 | 100.0 | 71.7 | 59.8 | 6.6 | 5.2 | 28.3 | 15.7 | 5.3 | 7.3 |
| 2012 | 100.0 | 71.6 | 59.4 | 7.0 | 5.2 | 28.4 | 15.2 | 5.7 | 7.5 |
| 2013 | 100.0 | 71.8 | 60.5 | 6.6 | 4.7 | 28.2 | 15.2 | 5.9 | 7.1 |
| 2014 | 100.0 | 72.8 | 61.2 | 7.0 | 4.5 | 27.2 | 14.7 | 5.6 | 6.9 |
| 2015 | 100.0 | 73.0 | 61.4 | 7.2 | 4.4 | 27.0 | 14.6 | 5.3 | 7.1 |

*Note:* See notes and definitions for information on historical comparability.

## Table 1-37.  Extent of Unemployment During the Year, by Sex, 1990–2015

(Thousands of people, percent.)

| Sex and extent of unemployment | 1990 | 1991 | 1992 | 1993 | 1994 | 1995 | 1996 | 1997 | 1998 | 1999 | 2000 | 2001 | 2002 |
|---|---|---|---|---|---|---|---|---|---|---|---|---|---|
| **BOTH SEXES** | | | | | | | | | | | | | |
| **Total Who Worked or Looked for Work** | 135 408 | 135 826 | 136 654 | 139 786 | 141 325 | 142 413 | 144 528 | 146 096 | 147 295 | 149 798 | 150 786 | 153 056 | 154 205 |
| Percent with unemployment | 14.6 | 15.7 | 15.7 | 14.7 | 13.4 | 12.7 | 11.6 | 10.7 | 9.5 | 8.7 | 8.1 | 10.4 | 10.9 |
| **Total with Unemployment** | 19 809 | 21 276 | 21 455 | 20 527 | 18 966 | 18 067 | 16 789 | 15 637 | 14 044 | 13 068 | 12 269 | 15 843 | 16 824 |
| Did not work but looked for work | 1 874 | 2 415 | 2 742 | 3 432 | 2 857 | 2 690 | 2 329 | 2 129 | 1 729 | 1 503 | 1 425 | 2 014 | 2 660 |
| Worked during the year | 17 936 | 18 861 | 18 714 | 17 094 | 16 109 | 15 377 | 14 460 | 13 508 | 12 316 | 11 566 | 10 845 | 13 829 | 14 164 |
| Year-round workers with 1 or 2 weeks of unemployment | 1 056 | 966 | 871 | 688 | 746 | 715 | 589 | 611 | 630 | 562 | 573 | 602 | 584 |
| Part-year workers with unemployment | 16 880 | 17 895 | 17 843 | 16 406 | 15 363 | 14 662 | 13 871 | 12 897 | 11 686 | 11 004 | 10 272 | 13 227 | 13 580 |
| 1 to 4 weeks | 3 645 | 3 224 | 2 944 | 2 626 | 2 788 | 2 812 | 2 550 | 2 582 | 2 323 | 2 361 | 2 233 | 2 368 | 2 002 |
| 5 to 10 weeks | 3 669 | 3 655 | 3 496 | 2 898 | 2 983 | 2 725 | 2 671 | 2 601 | 2 495 | 2 218 | 2 014 | 2 557 | 2 373 |
| 11 to 14 weeks | 2 501 | 2 587 | 2 574 | 2 300 | 2 265 | 2 147 | 2 020 | 1 822 | 1 701 | 1 594 | 1 505 | 2 038 | 1 970 |
| 15 to 26 weeks | 4 316 | 4 927 | 4 877 | 4 549 | 4 158 | 4 013 | 3 662 | 3 378 | 3 019 | 2 803 | 2 641 | 3 683 | 3 848 |
| 27 weeks or more | 2 749 | 3 502 | 3 952 | 4 033 | 3 169 | 2 965 | 2 968 | 2 514 | 2 148 | 2 028 | 1 879 | 2 582 | 3 387 |
| With 2 or more spells of unemployment | 5 811 | 5 864 | 5 734 | 5 338 | 4 783 | 4 468 | 4 237 | 4 044 | 3 628 | 3 225 | 3 079 | 3 421 | 3 226 |
| 2 spells | 2 855 | 2 738 | 2 698 | 2 572 | 2 207 | 1 963 | 1 982 | 1 853 | 1 650 | 1 449 | 1 397 | 1 643 | 1 556 |
| 3 or more spells | 2 956 | 3 126 | 3 036 | 2 766 | 2 576 | 2 505 | 2 255 | 2 191 | 1 978 | 1 776 | 1 682 | 1 779 | 1 670 |
| **MEN** | | | | | | | | | | | | | |
| **Total Who Worked or Looked for Work** | 72 844 | 72 909 | 73 387 | 74 516 | 75 244 | 75 698 | 76 786 | 77 385 | 77 704 | 78 905 | 79 546 | 80 975 | 81 651 |
| Percent with unemployment | 15.5 | 17.3 | 17.5 | 15.7 | 14.1 | 13.2 | 11.9 | 11.1 | 9.4 | 9.0 | 8.6 | 11.0 | 11.8 |
| **Total with Unemployment** | 11 307 | 12 642 | 12 844 | 11 723 | 10 582 | 9 996 | 9 157 | 8 604 | 7 284 | 7 091 | 6 806 | 8 928 | 9 621 |
| Did not work but looked for work | 891 | 1 210 | 1 379 | 1 641 | 1 286 | 1 317 | 1 026 | 978 | 787 | 760 | 742 | 1 004 | 1 369 |
| Worked during the year | 10 415 | 11 432 | 11 466 | 10 082 | 9 296 | 8 679 | 8 130 | 7 626 | 6 497 | 6 332 | 6 064 | 7 924 | 8 252 |
| Year-round workers with 1 or 2 weeks of unemployment | 711 | 612 | 567 | 449 | 527 | 462 | 395 | 382 | 386 | 373 | 379 | 421 | 365 |
| Part-year workers with unemployment | 9 704 | 10 820 | 10 899 | 9 633 | 8 769 | 8 217 | 7 735 | 7 244 | 6 111 | 5 959 | 5 685 | 7 502 | 7 887 |
| 1 to 4 weeks | 1 819 | 1 591 | 1 563 | 1 343 | 1 365 | 1 398 | 1 272 | 1 275 | 1 085 | 1 166 | 1 070 | 1 247 | 1 075 |
| 5 to 10 weeks | 2 041 | 2 111 | 2 039 | 1 647 | 1 666 | 1 434 | 1 478 | 1 474 | 1 363 | 1 168 | 1 135 | 1 446 | 1 342 |
| 11 to 14 weeks | 1 462 | 1 659 | 1 615 | 1 354 | 1 370 | 1 253 | 1 258 | 1 068 | 980 | 937 | 880 | 1 207 | 1 186 |
| 15 to 26 weeks | 2 645 | 3 206 | 3 165 | 2 862 | 2 449 | 2 439 | 2 076 | 1 949 | 1 585 | 1 655 | 1 595 | 2 191 | 2 282 |
| 27 weeks or more | 1 737 | 2 253 | 2 517 | 2 427 | 1 919 | 1 693 | 1 651 | 1 478 | 1 098 | 1 033 | 1 005 | 1 412 | 2 002 |
| With 2 or more spells of unemployment | 3 689 | 3 886 | 3 889 | 3 451 | 2 940 | 2 793 | 2 554 | 2 437 | 2 014 | 1 845 | 1 809 | 2 100 | 1 920 |
| 2 spells | 1 676 | 1 742 | 1 781 | 1 580 | 1 266 | 1 110 | 1 109 | 1 078 | 880 | 787 | 804 | 1 002 | 914 |
| 3 or more spells | 2 013 | 2 144 | 2 108 | 1 871 | 1 674 | 1 683 | 1 445 | 1 359 | 1 134 | 1 058 | 1 005 | 1 099 | 1 006 |
| **WOMEN** | | | | | | | | | | | | | |
| **Total Who Worked or Looked for Work** | 62 564 | 62 917 | 63 267 | 65 270 | 66 081 | 66 716 | 67 742 | 68 710 | 69 591 | 70 893 | 71 240 | 72 081 | 72 554 |
| Percent with unemployment | 13.6 | 13.7 | 13.6 | 13.5 | 12.7 | 12.1 | 11.3 | 10.2 | 9.7 | 8.4 | 7.7 | 9.6 | 9.9 |
| **Total with Unemployment** | 8 502 | 8 634 | 8 611 | 8 804 | 8 383 | 8 070 | 7 632 | 7 033 | 6 760 | 5 976 | 5 463 | 6 915 | 7 203 |
| Did not work but looked for work | 982 | 1 205 | 1 363 | 1 791 | 1 570 | 1 373 | 1 303 | 1 151 | 942 | 743 | 683 | 1 010 | 1 291 |
| Worked during the year | 7 520 | 7 427 | 7 247 | 7 014 | 6 813 | 6 696 | 6 330 | 5 882 | 5 816 | 5 234 | 4 779 | 5 905 | 5 913 |
| Year-round workers with 1 or 2 weeks of unemployment | 344 | 354 | 304 | 239 | 219 | 253 | 194 | 229 | 243 | 189 | 193 | 180 | 220 |
| Part-year workers with unemployment | 7 176 | 7 073 | 6 943 | 6 775 | 6 594 | 6 443 | 6 136 | 5 653 | 5 573 | 5 045 | 4 586 | 5 725 | 5 693 |
| 1 to 4 weeks | 1 827 | 1 633 | 1 380 | 1 284 | 1 422 | 1 413 | 1 279 | 1 307 | 1 237 | 1 194 | 1 164 | 1 121 | 927 |
| 5 to 10 weeks | 1 627 | 1 544 | 1 457 | 1 252 | 1 317 | 1 291 | 1 192 | 1 127 | 1 131 | 1 050 | 878 | 1 111 | 1 031 |
| 11 to 14 weeks | 1 038 | 927 | 959 | 946 | 896 | 893 | 762 | 754 | 721 | 657 | 625 | 831 | 784 |
| 15 to 26 weeks | 1 671 | 1 720 | 1 712 | 1 687 | 1 708 | 1 574 | 1 586 | 1 429 | 1 434 | 1 148 | 1 045 | 1 492 | 1 566 |
| 27 weeks or more | 1 013 | 1 249 | 1 435 | 1 606 | 1 251 | 1 272 | 1 317 | 1 036 | 1 050 | 996 | 874 | 1 170 | 1 385 |
| With 2 or more spells of unemployment | 2 122 | 1 979 | 1 844 | 1 887 | 1 843 | 1 675 | 1 682 | 1 607 | 1 614 | 1 379 | 1 270 | 1 321 | 1 306 |
| 2 spells | 1 179 | 997 | 916 | 992 | 941 | 853 | 872 | 775 | 770 | 662 | 593 | 641 | 642 |
| 3 or more spells | 943 | 982 | 928 | 895 | 902 | 822 | 810 | 832 | 844 | 717 | 677 | 680 | 664 |

## Table 1-37.  Extent of Unemployment During the Year, by Sex, 1990–2015—*Continued*

(Thousands of people, percent.)

| Sex and extent of unemployment | 2003 | 2004 | 2005 | 2006 | 2007 | 2008 | 2009 | 2010 | 2011 | 2012 | 2013 | 2014 | 2015 |
|---|---|---|---|---|---|---|---|---|---|---|---|---|---|
| **BOTH SEXES** | | | | | | | | | | | | | |
| **Total Who Worked or Looked for Work** | 154 315 | 155 576 | 157 549 | 159 259 | 160 565 | 161 506 | 160 624 | 159 706 | 160 545 | 162 574 | 162 706 | 163 582 | 166 339 |
| Percent with unemployment | 10.7 | 9.7 | 9.2 | 9.1 | 9.4 | 13.1 | 16.3 | 15.8 | 14.8 | 13.8 | 12.9 | 10.8 | 10.2 |
| **Total with Unemployment** | 16 462 | 15 074 | 14 558 | 14 447 | 15 130 | 21 231 | 26 151 | 25 262 | 23 752 | 22 460 | 20 908 | 17 731 | 16 940 |
| Did not work but looked for work | 2 762 | 2 551 | 2 422 | 1 907 | 2 097 | 3 189 | 5 851 | 6 564 | 6 216 | 5 525 | 4 828 | 3 701 | 3 170 |
| Worked during the year | 13 699 | 12 522 | 12 136 | 12 540 | 13 033 | 18 042 | 20 300 | 18 698 | 17 537 | 16 936 | 16 080 | 14 030 | 13 770 |
| Year-round workers with 1 or 2 weeks of unemployment | 534 | 465 | 431 | 450 | 500 | 763 | 693 | 591 | 417 | 465 | 462 | 392 | 392 |
| Part-year workers with unemployment | 13 165 | 12 057 | 11 705 | 12 090 | 12 533 | 17 279 | 19 607 | 18 107 | 17 119 | 16 470 | 15 618 | 13 638 | 13 378 |
| 1 to 4 weeks | 1 839 | 1 985 | 1 941 | 2 601 | 2 593 | 2 794 | 2 528 | 2 267 | 2 211 | 2 252 | 2 395 | 2 372 | 2 621 |
| 5 to 10 weeks | 2 264 | 2 100 | 2 170 | 2 107 | 2 090 | 2 944 | 2 562 | 2 397 | 2 276 | 2 351 | 2 176 | 2 001 | 2 104 |
| 11 to 14 weeks | 1 749 | 1 773 | 1 698 | 1 615 | 1 888 | 2 438 | 2 414 | 2 302 | 2 064 | 2 176 | 2 032 | 1 889 | 1 917 |
| 15 to 26 weeks | 3 778 | 3 448 | 3 349 | 3 176 | 3 373 | 4 859 | 5 698 | 5 116 | 4 949 | 4 715 | 4 487 | 3 864 | 3 572 |
| 27 weeks or more | 3 535 | 2 751 | 2 547 | 2 592 | 2 589 | 4 244 | 6 405 | 6 025 | 5 619 | 4 976 | 4 528 | 3 512 | 3 164 |
| With 2 or more spells of unemployment | 3 093 | 2 896 | 3 095 | 3 076 | 3 108 | 3 991 | 4 152 | 3 875 | 3 527 | 3 763 | 3 325 | 2 873 | 2 975 |
| 2 spells | 1 585 | 1 344 | 1 477 | 1 564 | 1 427 | 1 987 | 1 918 | 1 789 | 1 745 | 1 730 | 1 612 | 1 472 | 1 376 |
| 3 or more spells | 1 508 | 1 552 | 1 618 | 1 513 | 1 681 | 2 004 | 2 234 | 2 086 | 1 782 | 2 033 | 1 713 | 1 401 | 1 599 |
| **MEN** | | | | | | | | | | | | | |
| **Total Who Worked or Looked for Work** | 81 804 | 82 478 | 83 951 | 84 736 | 85 368 | 85 563 | 85 161 | 84 738 | 84 486 | 85 778 | 85 863 | 86 320 | 87 904 |
| Percent with unemployment | 11.4 | 10.0 | 9.7 | 9.6 | 10.2 | 14.4 | 18.6 | 17.6 | 15.7 | 14.4 | 13.4 | 11.4 | 10.3 |
| **Total with Unemployment** | 9 339 | 8 256 | 8 116 | 8 115 | 8 698 | 12 331 | 15 877 | 14 900 | 13 273 | 12 388 | 11 548 | 9 807 | 9 076 |
| Did not work but looked for work | 1 487 | 1 217 | 1 216 | 969 | 1 076 | 1 674 | 3 325 | 3 662 | 3 214 | 2 868 | 2 443 | 1 962 | 1 634 |
| Worked during the year | 7 854 | 7 039 | 6 899 | 7 146 | 7 622 | 10 656 | 12 552 | 11 238 | 10 059 | 9 520 | 9 104 | 7 845 | 7 442 |
| Year-round workers with 1 or 2 weeks of unemployment | 359 | 289 | 296 | 295 | 365 | 484 | 458 | 379 | 271 | 310 | 259 | 286 | 245 |
| Part-year workers with unemployment | 7 495 | 6 750 | 6 603 | 6 850 | 7 257 | 10 172 | 12 093 | 10 859 | 9 788 | 9 210 | 8 845 | 7 559 | 7 197 |
| 1 to 4 weeks | 958 | 1 028 | 1 052 | 1 283 | 1 367 | 1 523 | 1 466 | 1 186 | 1 170 | 1 189 | 1 235 | 1 234 | 1 370 |
| 5 to 10 weeks | 1 314 | 1 170 | 1 209 | 1 267 | 1 214 | 1 701 | 1 594 | 1 423 | 1 240 | 1 364 | 1 238 | 1 170 | 1 162 |
| 11 to 14 weeks | 1 039 | 1 021 | 1 024 | 961 | 1 163 | 1 467 | 1 558 | 1 441 | 1 277 | 1 243 | 1 126 | 1 095 | 993 |
| 15 to 26 weeks | 2 178 | 2 065 | 1 923 | 1 868 | 2 058 | 3 035 | 3 564 | 3 233 | 2 941 | 2 719 | 2 607 | 2 133 | 2 000 |
| 27 weeks or more | 2 006 | 1 466 | 1 395 | 1 472 | 1 455 | 2 445 | 3 911 | 3 577 | 3 159 | 2 696 | 2 640 | 1 928 | 1 672 |
| With 2 or more spells of unemployment | 1 882 | 1 828 | 1 975 | 1 936 | 1 992 | 2 623 | 2 865 | 2 623 | 2 450 | 2 328 | 2 070 | 1 789 | 1 766 |
| 2 spells | 946 | 808 | 940 | 945 | 847 | 1 234 | 1 299 | 1 133 | 1 121 | 1 003 | 954 | 934 | 767 |
| 3 or more spells | 936 | 1 020 | 1 035 | 991 | 1 145 | 1 389 | 1 566 | 1 491 | 1 329 | 1 325 | 1 117 | 855 | 998 |
| **WOMEN** | | | | | | | | | | | | | |
| **Total Who Worked or Looked for Work** | 72 511 | 73 097 | 73 598 | 74 523 | 75 197 | 75 943 | 75 463 | 74 968 | 76 060 | 76 797 | 76 843 | 77 263 | 78 435 |
| Percent with unemployment | 9.8 | 9.3 | 8.8 | 8.5 | 8.6 | 11.7 | 13.6 | 13.8 | 13.8 | 13.1 | 12.2 | 10.3 | 10.0 |
| **Total with Unemployment** | 7 123 | 6 818 | 6 442 | 6 332 | 6 432 | 8 900 | 10 274 | 10 362 | 10 479 | 10 073 | 9 361 | 7 924 | 7 864 |
| Did not work but looked for work | 1 275 | 1 334 | 1 206 | 938 | 1 021 | 1 514 | 2 526 | 2 903 | 3 002 | 2 657 | 2 385 | 1 740 | 1 536 |
| Worked during the year | 5 848 | 5 484 | 5 236 | 5 394 | 5 411 | 7 385 | 7 748 | 7 459 | 7 478 | 7 416 | 6 975 | 6 185 | 6 328 |
| Year-round workers with 1 or 2 weeks of unemployment | 176 | 177 | 136 | 154 | 135 | 279 | 235 | 211 | 147 | 155 | 203 | 106 | 147 |
| Part-year workers with unemployment | 5 672 | 5 307 | 5 100 | 5 240 | 5 276 | 7 106 | 7 513 | 7 248 | 7 331 | 7 261 | 6 773 | 5 344 | 6 181 |
| 1 to 4 weeks | 882 | 957 | 888 | 1 317 | 1 226 | 1 270 | 1 061 | 1 081 | 1 041 | 1 064 | 1 160 | 1 138 | 1 251 |
| 5 to 10 weeks | 950 | 929 | 961 | 840 | 876 | 1 243 | 968 | 974 | 1 036 | 987 | 938 | 831 | 943 |
| 11 to 14 weeks | 710 | 752 | 674 | 655 | 725 | 971 | 857 | 861 | 787 | 933 | 907 | 794 | 924 |
| 15 to 26 weeks | 1 600 | 1 384 | 1 426 | 1 307 | 1 316 | 1 823 | 2 134 | 1 883 | 2 008 | 1 997 | 1 881 | 1 731 | 1 571 |
| 27 weeks or more | 1 530 | 1 285 | 1 151 | 1 120 | 1 134 | 1 800 | 2 494 | 2 448 | 2 459 | 2 280 | 1 887 | 849 | 1 492 |
| With 2 or more spells of unemployment | 1 211 | 1 069 | 1 120 | 1 140 | 1 116 | 1 368 | 1 287 | 1 252 | 1 077 | 1 435 | 1 254 | 1 084 | 1 210 |
| 2 spells | 639 | 537 | 537 | 619 | 580 | 753 | 619 | 657 | 624 | 727 | 658 | 539 | 609 |
| 3 or more spells | 572 | 532 | 583 | 521 | 536 | 616 | 668 | 595 | 453 | 707 | 596 | 546 | 601 |

**Table 1-38.  Percent Distribution of Persons with Unemployment During the Year, by Sex and Extent of Unemployment, 1990–2015**

(Percent.)

| Sex and extent of unemployment | 1990 | 1991 | 1992 | 1993 | 1994 | 1995 | 1996 | 1997 | 1998 | 1999 | 2000 | 2001 | 2002 |
|---|---|---|---|---|---|---|---|---|---|---|---|---|---|
| **BOTH SEXES** | | | | | | | | | | | | | |
| **Total with Unemployment Who Worked During the Year** | 100.0 | 100.0 | 100.0 | 100.0 | 100.0 | 100.0 | 100.0 | 100.0 | 100.0 | 100.0 | 100.0 | 100.0 | 100.0 |
| Year-round workers with 1 or 2 weeks of unemployment | 5.9 | 5.1 | 4.7 | 4.0 | 4.6 | 4.6 | 4.1 | 4.5 | 5.1 | 4.9 | 5.3 | 4.4 | 4.1 |
| Part-year workers with unemployment | 94.1 | 94.8 | 95.4 | 96.1 | 95.4 | 95.4 | 96.0 | 95.5 | 95.0 | 95.1 | 94.8 | 95.6 | 95.9 |
| 1 to 4 weeks | 20.3 | 17.1 | 15.7 | 15.4 | 17.3 | 18.3 | 17.6 | 19.1 | 18.9 | 20.4 | 20.6 | 17.1 | 14.1 |
| 5 to 10 weeks | 20.5 | 19.4 | 18.7 | 17.0 | 18.5 | 17.7 | 18.5 | 19.3 | 20.3 | 19.2 | 18.6 | 18.5 | 16.8 |
| 11 to 14 weeks | 13.9 | 13.7 | 13.8 | 13.5 | 14.1 | 14.0 | 14.0 | 13.5 | 13.8 | 13.8 | 13.9 | 14.7 | 13.9 |
| 15 to 26 weeks | 24.1 | 26.1 | 26.1 | 26.6 | 25.8 | 26.1 | 25.3 | 25.0 | 24.5 | 24.2 | 24.4 | 26.6 | 27.2 |
| 27 weeks or more | 15.3 | 18.5 | 21.1 | 23.6 | 19.7 | 19.3 | 20.6 | 18.6 | 17.5 | 17.5 | 17.3 | 18.7 | 23.9 |
| With 2 or more spells of unemployment | 32.4 | 31.1 | 30.6 | 31.2 | 29.7 | 29.1 | 29.3 | 29.9 | 29.5 | 27.9 | 28.4 | 24.8 | 22.8 |
| 2 spells | 15.9 | 14.5 | 14.4 | 15.0 | 13.7 | 12.8 | 13.7 | 13.7 | 13.4 | 12.5 | 12.9 | 11.9 | 11.0 |
| 3 or more spells | 16.5 | 16.6 | 16.2 | 16.2 | 16.0 | 16.3 | 15.6 | 16.2 | 16.1 | 15.4 | 15.5 | 12.9 | 11.8 |
| **MEN** | | | | | | | | | | | | | |
| **Total with Unemployment Who Worked During the Year** | 100.0 | 100.0 | 100.0 | 100.0 | 100.0 | 100.0 | 100.0 | 100.0 | 100.0 | 100.0 | 100.0 | 100.0 | 100.0 |
| Year-round workers with 1 or 2 weeks of unemployment | 6.8 | 5.4 | 4.9 | 4.4 | 5.7 | 5.3 | 4.9 | 5.0 | 5.9 | 5.9 | 6.3 | 5.3 | 4.4 |
| Part-year workers with unemployment | 93.2 | 94.6 | 95.0 | 95.5 | 94.3 | 94.7 | 95.1 | 95.1 | 94.1 | 94.0 | 93.6 | 94.7 | 95.6 |
| 1 to 4 weeks | 17.5 | 13.9 | 13.6 | 13.3 | 14.7 | 16.1 | 15.6 | 16.7 | 16.7 | 18.4 | 17.6 | 15.7 | 13.0 |
| 5 to 10 weeks | 19.6 | 18.5 | 17.8 | 16.3 | 17.9 | 16.5 | 18.2 | 19.3 | 21.0 | 18.4 | 18.7 | 18.2 | 16.3 |
| 11 to 14 weeks | 14.0 | 14.5 | 14.1 | 13.4 | 14.7 | 14.4 | 15.5 | 14.0 | 15.1 | 14.8 | 14.5 | 15.2 | 14.4 |
| 15 to 26 weeks | 25.4 | 28.0 | 27.6 | 28.4 | 26.4 | 28.1 | 25.5 | 25.6 | 24.4 | 26.1 | 26.3 | 27.6 | 27.7 |
| 27 weeks or more | 16.7 | 19.7 | 21.9 | 24.1 | 20.6 | 19.5 | 20.3 | 19.4 | 16.9 | 16.3 | 16.5 | 17.8 | 24.3 |
| With 2 or more spells of unemployment | 35.4 | 34.0 | 33.9 | 34.3 | 31.6 | 32.2 | 31.4 | 31.9 | 31.0 | 29.1 | 29.9 | 26.5 | 23.3 |
| 2 spells | 16.1 | 15.2 | 15.5 | 15.7 | 13.6 | 12.8 | 13.6 | 14.1 | 13.5 | 12.4 | 13.3 | 12.6 | 11.1 |
| 3 or more spells | 19.3 | 18.8 | 18.4 | 18.6 | 18.0 | 19.4 | 17.8 | 17.8 | 17.5 | 16.7 | 16.6 | 13.9 | 12.2 |
| **WOMEN** | | | | | | | | | | | | | |
| **Total With Unemployment Who Worked During the Year** | 100.0 | 100.0 | 100.0 | 100.0 | 100.0 | 100.0 | 100.0 | 100.0 | 100.0 | 100.0 | 100.0 | 100.0 | 100.0 |
| Year-round workers with 1 or 2 weeks of unemployment | 4.6 | 4.8 | 4.2 | 3.4 | 3.2 | 3.8 | 3.1 | 3.9 | 4.2 | 3.6 | 4.0 | 3.1 | 3.7 |
| Part-year workers with unemployment | 95.3 | 95.3 | 95.7 | 96.6 | 96.7 | 96.2 | 96.9 | 96.1 | 95.8 | 96.4 | 96.0 | 96.9 | 96.3 |
| 1 to 4 weeks | 24.3 | 22.0 | 19.0 | 18.3 | 20.9 | 21.1 | 20.2 | 22.2 | 21.3 | 22.8 | 24.3 | 19.0 | 15.7 |
| 5 to 10 weeks | 21.6 | 20.8 | 20.1 | 17.8 | 19.3 | 19.3 | 18.8 | 19.2 | 19.4 | 20.1 | 18.4 | 18.8 | 17.4 |
| 11 to 14 weeks | 13.8 | 12.5 | 13.2 | 13.5 | 13.1 | 13.3 | 12.0 | 12.8 | 12.4 | 12.6 | 13.1 | 14.1 | 13.3 |
| 15 to 26 weeks | 22.2 | 23.2 | 23.6 | 24.1 | 25.1 | 23.5 | 25.1 | 24.3 | 24.7 | 21.9 | 21.9 | 25.3 | 26.5 |
| 27 weeks or more | 13.4 | 16.8 | 19.8 | 22.9 | 18.3 | 19.0 | 20.8 | 17.6 | 18.0 | 19.0 | 18.3 | 19.8 | 23.4 |
| With 2 or more spells of unemployment | 28.2 | 26.6 | 25.4 | 26.9 | 27.0 | 25.0 | 26.6 | 27.3 | 27.7 | 26.3 | 26.6 | 22.4 | 22.1 |
| 2 spells | 15.7 | 13.4 | 12.6 | 14.1 | 13.8 | 12.7 | 13.8 | 13.2 | 13.2 | 12.6 | 12.4 | 10.9 | 10.9 |
| 3 or more spells | 12.5 | 13.2 | 12.8 | 12.8 | 13.2 | 12.3 | 12.8 | 14.1 | 14.5 | 13.7 | 14.2 | 11.5 | 11.2 |

**Table 1-38. Percent Distribution of Persons with Unemployment During the Year, by Sex and Extent of Unemployment, 1990–2015**—*Continued*

(Percent.)

| Sex and extent of unemployment | 2003 | 2004 | 2005 | 2006 | 2007 | 2008 | 2009 | 2010 | 2011 | 2012 | 2013 | 2014 | 2015 |
|---|---|---|---|---|---|---|---|---|---|---|---|---|---|
| **BOTH SEXES** | | | | | | | | | | | | | |
| **Total with Unemployment Who Worked During the Year** | 100.0 | 100.0 | 100.0 | 100.0 | 100.0 | 100.0 | 100.0 | 100.0 | 100.0 | 100.0 | 100.0 | 100.0 | 100.0 |
| Year-round workers with 1 or 2 weeks of unemployment | 3.9 | 3.7 | 3.6 | 3.6 | 3.8 | 4.2 | 3.4 | 3.2 | 2.4 | 2.7 | 2.9 | 2.8 | 2.8 |
| Part-year workers with unemployment | 96.1 | 96.3 | 96.4 | 96.4 | 96.1 | 95.8 | 96.5 | 96.8 | 97.6 | 97.3 | 97.1 | 97.2 | 97.2 |
| 1 to 4 weeks | 13.4 | 15.9 | 16.0 | 20.7 | 19.9 | 15.5 | 12.5 | 12.1 | 12.6 | 13.3 | 14.9 | 16.9 | 19.0 |
| 5 to 10 weeks | 16.5 | 16.8 | 17.9 | 16.8 | 16.0 | 16.3 | 12.6 | 12.8 | 13.0 | 13.9 | 13.5 | 14.3 | 15.3 |
| 11 to 14 weeks | 12.8 | 14.2 | 14.0 | 12.9 | 14.5 | 13.5 | 11.9 | 12.3 | 11.8 | 12.8 | 12.6 | 13.5 | 13.9 |
| 15 to 26 weeks | 27.6 | 27.5 | 27.6 | 25.3 | 25.9 | 26.9 | 28.1 | 27.4 | 28.2 | 27.8 | 27.9 | 27.5 | 25.9 |
| 27 weeks or more | 25.8 | 22.0 | 20.9 | 20.7 | 19.8 | 23.5 | 31.5 | 32.2 | 32.0 | 29.4 | 28.2 | 25.0 | 22.9 |
| With 2 or more spells of unemployment | 22.6 | 23.1 | 25.5 | 24.5 | 23.8 | 22.1 | 20.5 | 20.7 | 20.1 | 22.2 | 20.7 | 20.5 | 21.6 |
| 2 spells | 11.6 | 10.7 | 12.2 | 12.5 | 10.9 | 11.0 | 9.4 | 9.6 | 10.0 | 10.2 | 10.0 | 10.5 | 10.0 |
| 3 or more spells | 11.0 | 12.4 | 13.3 | 12.1 | 12.9 | 11.1 | 11.0 | 11.2 | 10.2 | 12.0 | 10.7 | 10.0 | 11.6 |
| **MEN** | | | | | | | | | | | | | |
| **Total with Unemployment Who Worked During the Year** | 100.0 | 100.0 | 100.0 | 100.0 | 100.0 | 100.0 | 100.0 | 100.0 | 100.0 | 100.0 | 100.0 | 100.0 | 100.0 |
| Year-round workers with 1 or 2 weeks of unemployment | 4.6 | 4.1 | 4.3 | 4.1 | 4.8 | 4.5 | 3.7 | 3.4 | 2.7 | 3.3 | 2.8 | 3.6 | 3.3 |
| Part-year workers with unemployment | 95.4 | 95.9 | 95.7 | 95.9 | 95.2 | 95.5 | 96.4 | 96.6 | 97.3 | 96.7 | 97.2 | 96.4 | 96.7 |
| 1 to 4 weeks | 12.2 | 14.6 | 15.3 | 18.0 | 17.9 | 14.3 | 11.7 | 10.5 | 11.6 | 12.5 | 13.6 | 15.7 | 18.4 |
| 5 to 10 weeks | 16.7 | 16.6 | 17.5 | 17.7 | 15.9 | 16.0 | 12.7 | 12.7 | 12.3 | 14.3 | 13.6 | 14.9 | 15.6 |
| 11 to 14 weeks | 13.2 | 14.5 | 14.8 | 13.4 | 15.3 | 13.8 | 12.4 | 12.8 | 12.7 | 13.1 | 12.4 | 14.0 | 13.3 |
| 15 to 26 weeks | 27.7 | 29.3 | 27.9 | 26.1 | 27.0 | 28.5 | 28.4 | 28.4 | 29.2 | 28.6 | 28.6 | 27.2 | 26.9 |
| 27 weeks or more | 25.5 | 20.8 | 20.2 | 20.6 | 19.1 | 22.9 | 31.2 | 31.8 | 31.4 | 28.3 | 29.0 | 24.6 | 22.5 |
| With 2 or more spells of unemployment | 24.0 | 26.0 | 28.6 | 27.1 | 26.1 | 24.6 | 22.8 | 23.3 | 24.4 | 24.5 | 22.7 | 22.8 | 23.7 |
| 2 spells | 12.1 | 11.5 | 13.6 | 13.2 | 11.1 | 11.6 | 10.3 | 10.1 | 11.1 | 10.5 | 10.5 | 11.9 | 10.3 |
| 3 or more spells | 11.9 | 14.5 | 15.0 | 13.9 | 15.0 | 13.0 | 12.5 | 13.3 | 13.2 | 13.9 | 12.3 | 10.9 | 13.4 |
| **WOMEN** | | | | | | | | | | | | | |
| **Total With Unemployment Who Worked During the Year** | 100.0 | 100.0 | 100.0 | 100.0 | 100.0 | 100.0 | 100.0 | 100.0 | 100.0 | 100.0 | 100.0 | 100.0 | 100.0 |
| Year-round workers with 1 or 2 weeks of unemployment | 3.0 | 3.2 | 2.6 | 2.9 | 2.5 | 3.8 | 3.0 | 2.8 | 2.0 | 2.1 | 2.9 | 1.7 | 2.3 |
| Part-year workers with unemployment | 97.0 | 96.8 | 97.4 | 97.1 | 97.4 | 96.2 | 96.9 | 97.2 | 98.0 | 97.9 | 97.1 | 98.3 | 97.7 |
| 1 to 4 weeks | 15.1 | 17.4 | 17.0 | 24.4 | 22.6 | 17.2 | 13.7 | 14.5 | 13.9 | 14.3 | 16.6 | 18.4 | 19.8 |
| 5 to 10 weeks | 16.2 | 16.9 | 18.4 | 15.6 | 16.2 | 16.8 | 12.5 | 13.1 | 13.9 | 13.3 | 13.4 | 13.4 | 14.9 |
| 11 to 14 weeks | 12.1 | 13.7 | 12.9 | 12.1 | 13.4 | 13.1 | 11.1 | 11.5 | 10.5 | 12.6 | 13.0 | 12.8 | 14.6 |
| 15 to 26 weeks | 27.4 | 25.2 | 27.2 | 24.2 | 24.3 | 24.7 | 27.5 | 25.2 | 26.8 | 26.9 | 27.0 | 28.0 | 24.8 |
| 27 weeks or more | 26.2 | 23.5 | 22.0 | 20.8 | 20.9 | 24.4 | 32.1 | 32.8 | 32.9 | 30.8 | 27.1 | 25.6 | 23.6 |
| With 2 or more spells of unemployment | 20.7 | 19.5 | 21.4 | 21.1 | 20.6 | 18.5 | 16.6 | 16.8 | 14.4 | 19.3 | 18.0 | 17.5 | 19.1 |
| 2 spells | 10.9 | 9.8 | 10.3 | 11.5 | 10.7 | 10.2 | 8.0 | 8.8 | 8.3 | 9.8 | 9.4 | 8.7 | 9.6 |
| 3 or more spells | 9.8 | 9.7 | 11.1 | 9.7 | 9.9 | 8.3 | 8.6 | 8.0 | 6.1 | 9.5 | 8.5 | 8.8 | 9.5 |

## Table 1-39.  Number and Median Annual Earnings of Year-Round, Full-Time Wage and Salary Workers, by Age, Sex, and Race, 1990–2015

(Thousands of people, dollars.)

| Sex, age, and race | 1990 | 1991 | 1992 | 1993 | 1994 | 1995 | 1996 | 1997 | 1998 | 1999 | 2000 | 2001 | 2002 |
|---|---|---|---|---|---|---|---|---|---|---|---|---|---|
| **NUMBER** | | | | | | | | | | | | | |
| **Both Sexes, 16 Years and Over** | 74 728 | 74 449 | 75 517 | 77 427 | 79 875 | 83 407 | 85 611 | 86 905 | 89 748 | 91 722 | 94 359 | 94 531 | 94 526 |
| 16 to 24 years | 6 978 | 6 571 | 6 224 | 6 685 | 6 684 | 6 892 | 6 809 | 7 063 | 7 618 | 7 631 | 8 384 | 7 989 | 7 903 |
| 25 to 44 years | 45 086 | 44 811 | 45 022 | 45 951 | 47 150 | 48 695 | 49 225 | 49 513 | 50 264 | 50 532 | 51 159 | 49 939 | 49 120 |
| 25 to 34 years | 23 201 | 22 541 | 22 469 | 22 637 | 23 193 | 23 310 | 23 071 | 23 186 | 23 048 | 22 952 | 23 044 | 22 744 | 22 657 |
| 35 to 44 years | 21 885 | 22 270 | 22 553 | 23 314 | 23 957 | 25 385 | 26 154 | 26 327 | 27 216 | 27 580 | 28 115 | 27 195 | 26 463 |
| 45 to 54 years | 14 070 | 14 718 | 15 652 | 16 424 | 17 366 | 18 436 | 19 714 | 20 109 | 21 274 | 22 375 | 23 307 | 23 855 | 23 999 |
| 55 to 64 years | 7 458 | 7 219 | 7 590 | 7 208 | 7 500 | 8 122 | 8 455 | 8 901 | 9 273 | 9 594 | 9 870 | 10 948 | 11 584 |
| 65 years and over | 1 137 | 1 130 | 1 029 | 1 159 | 1 174 | 1 263 | 1 408 | 1 318 | 1 318 | 1 590 | 1 639 | 1 800 | 1 921 |
| **Men, 16 Years and Over** | 44 574 | 43 523 | 43 894 | 45 494 | 47 255 | 49 334 | 50 407 | 50 772 | 52 509 | 53 132 | 54 477 | 54 630 | 54 420 |
| 16 to 24 years | 3 982 | 3 596 | 3 457 | 3 853 | 3 918 | 4 094 | 3 942 | 4 021 | 4 479 | 4 347 | 4 602 | 4 605 | 4 570 |
| 25 to 44 years | 27 069 | 26 353 | 26 335 | 27 161 | 28 000 | 28 940 | 29 282 | 29 453 | 29 763 | 29 738 | 30 080 | 29 271 | 28 855 |
| 25 to 34 years | 13 941 | 13 303 | 13 146 | 13 400 | 13 749 | 13 844 | 13 817 | 13 735 | 13 612 | 13 471 | 13 497 | 13 386 | 13 400 |
| 35 to 44 years | 13 128 | 13 050 | 13 189 | 13 761 | 14 251 | 15 096 | 15 465 | 15 718 | 16 151 | 16 267 | 16 583 | 15 885 | 15 455 |
| 45 to 54 years | 8 168 | 8 479 | 8 908 | 9 522 | 10 120 | 10 589 | 11 372 | 11 388 | 12 030 | 12 546 | 13 045 | 13 363 | 13 330 |
| 55 to 64 years | 4 650 | 4 403 | 4 588 | 4 238 | 4 460 | 4 884 | 4 908 | 5 133 | 5 438 | 5 498 | 5 693 | 6 253 | 6 502 |
| 65 years and over | 705 | 694 | 606 | 719 | 757 | 827 | 903 | 775 | 801 | 1 003 | 1 057 | 1 138 | 1 163 |
| **Women, 16 Years and Over** | 30 155 | 30 925 | 31 622 | 31 933 | 32 619 | 34 073 | 35 203 | 36 133 | 37 239 | 38 591 | 39 887 | 39 901 | 40 106 |
| 16 to 24 years | 2 995 | 2 976 | 2 767 | 2 832 | 2 767 | 2 798 | 2 867 | 3 041 | 3 140 | 3 285 | 3 782 | 3 384 | 3 333 |
| 25 to 44 years | 18 017 | 18 458 | 18 688 | 18 790 | 19 150 | 19 755 | 19 942 | 20 060 | 20 503 | 20 794 | 21 081 | 20 668 | 20 264 |
| 25 to 34 years | 9 260 | 9 238 | 9 323 | 9 237 | 9 444 | 9 467 | 9 254 | 9 451 | 9 437 | 9 481 | 9 548 | 9 358 | 9 257 |
| 35 to 44 years | 8 757 | 9 220 | 9 365 | 9 553 | 9 706 | 10 288 | 10 688 | 10 609 | 11 066 | 11 313 | 11 533 | 11 310 | 11 007 |
| 45 to 54 years | 5 902 | 6 239 | 6 744 | 6 902 | 7 246 | 7 847 | 8 343 | 8 721 | 9 244 | 9 829 | 10 263 | 10 493 | 10 669 |
| 55 to 64 years | 2 808 | 2 816 | 3 002 | 2 970 | 3 040 | 3 238 | 3 547 | 3 767 | 3 836 | 4 096 | 4 178 | 4 695 | 5 082 |
| 65 years and over | 433 | 436 | 423 | 439 | 417 | 436 | 505 | 543 | 517 | 586 | 583 | 662 | 758 |
| **White, 16 Years and Over** | 64 128 | 63 926 | 64 706 | 65 656 | 67 370 | 70 430 | 72 068 | 72 650 | 75 046 | 76 203 | 77 790 | 78 306 | 77 632 |
| Men | 38 915 | 38 018 | 38 267 | 39 347 | 40 589 | 42 608 | 43 554 | 43 429 | 44 901 | 45 211 | 46 105 | 46 373 | 45 823 |
| Women | 25 213 | 25 908 | 26 439 | 26 309 | 26 782 | 27 822 | 28 514 | 29 221 | 30 145 | 30 992 | 31 685 | 31 933 | 31 809 |
| **Black, 16 Years and Over** | 8 027 | 7 941 | 7 995 | 8 478 | 9 074 | 9 446 | 9 706 | 10 248 | 10 532 | 11 145 | 11 899 | 11 001 | 10 966 |
| Men | 4 162 | 4 001 | 4 011 | 4 259 | 4 598 | 4 686 | 4 682 | 5 026 | 5 202 | 5 411 | 5 636 | 5 281 | 5 150 |
| Women | 3 865 | 3 940 | 3 984 | 4 219 | 4 476 | 4 759 | 5 024 | 5 222 | 5 329 | 5 734 | 6 264 | 5 720 | 5 816 |
| **MEDIAN ANNUAL EARNINGS** | | | | | | | | | | | | | |
| **Both Sexes, 16 Years and Over** | 24 000 | 25 000 | 25 871 | 26 000 | 26 620 | 27 000 | 28 000 | 30 000 | 30 000 | 31 000 | 32 000 | 34 000 | 35 000 |
| 16 to 24 years | 14 400 | 14 100 | 15 000 | 15 000 | 15 000 | 15 500 | 15 600 | 16 000 | 18 000 | 18 000 | 19 000 | 20 000 | 20 000 |
| 25 to 34 years | 22 000 | 23 000 | 24 000 | 24 000 | 24 480 | 25 000 | 25 300 | 27 000 | 28 500 | 30 000 | 30 000 | 31 000 | 31 800 |
| 35 to 44 years | 27 970 | 28 000 | 29 483 | 30 000 | 30 000 | 30 000 | 31 000 | 32 000 | 33 000 | 34 992 | 35 000 | 36 000 | 37 000 |
| 45 to 54 years | 28 000 | 29 000 | 30 000 | 30 500 | 32 343 | 32 000 | 33 000 | 35 000 | 35 000 | 36 000 | 38 000 | 39 500 | 40 000 |
| 55 to 64 years | 26 000 | 27 000 | 27 430 | 28 000 | 30 000 | 30 000 | 30 000 | 32 000 | 34 000 | 35 000 | 35 000 | 36 400 | 39 145 |
| 65 years and over | 23 841 | 22 000 | 24 000 | 24 000 | 24 377 | 29 600 | 26 496 | 28 200 | 26 000 | 30 000 | 32 000 | 32 000 | 33 000 |
| **Men, 16 Years and Over** | 28 000 | 29 120 | 30 000 | 30 000 | 30 000 | 31 000 | 32 000 | 34 000 | 35 000 | 36 000 | 37 600 | 38 500 | 40 000 |
| 16 to 24 years | 15 000 | 15 000 | 15 000 | 15 000 | 15 000 | 16 000 | 17 000 | 17 000 | 18 720 | 19 000 | 20 000 | 20 000 | 20 000 |
| 25 to 34 years | 25 000 | 25 000 | 26 000 | 25 000 | 26 000 | 27 000 | 28 000 | 29 852 | 30 000 | 32 000 | 33 500 | 34 000 | 34 740 |
| 35 to 44 years | 32 000 | 33 000 | 34 000 | 35 000 | 35 000 | 35 000 | 36 000 | 37 000 | 38 000 | 40 000 | 40 000 | 42 000 | 43 000 |
| 45 to 54 years | 35 000 | 36 000 | 37 000 | 38 000 | 40 000 | 40 000 | 40 000 | 41 000 | 42 000 | 44 616 | 45 000 | 45 000 | 47 000 |
| 55 to 64 years | 31 875 | 33 000 | 33 000 | 34 000 | 36 000 | 36 000 | 36 000 | 39 000 | 40 000 | 40 853 | 44 000 | 45 000 | 47 000 |
| 65 years and over | 29 000 | 28 000 | 30 000 | 28 000 | 30 000 | 36 000 | 33 000 | 36 400 | 35 000 | 36 000 | 35 999 | 35 000 | 37 861 |
| **Women, 16 Years and Over** | 20 000 | 20 000 | 21 500 | 22 000 | 22 150 | 23 000 | 24 000 | 25 000 | 25 000 | 26 000 | 27 500 | 29 000 | 30 000 |
| 16 to 24 years | 13 392 | 13 800 | 14 000 | 14 872 | 14 560 | 15 000 | 15 000 | 15 000 | 17 000 | 17 000 | 18 000 | 19 000 | 19 000 |
| 25 to 34 years | 19 500 | 20 000 | 21 000 | 21 000 | 22 000 | 22 000 | 23 000 | 24 000 | 25 000 | 26 000 | 27 000 | 28 080 | 29 500 |
| 35 to 44 years | 22 000 | 22 510 | 23 397 | 24 000 | 25 000 | 25 000 | 25 000 | 26 000 | 27 200 | 28 000 | 29 000 | 30 000 | 30 400 |
| 45 to 54 years | 21 000 | 22 000 | 24 000 | 24 000 | 25 000 | 25 000 | 26 000 | 27 040 | 28 132 | 30 000 | 30 000 | 32 000 | 32 000 |
| 55 to 64 years | 19 000 | 20 000 | 22 000 | 21 500 | 22 000 | 22 500 | 24 000 | 24 800 | 25 775 | 27 000 | 28 000 | 30 000 | 31 410 |
| 65 years and over | 18 586 | 17 000 | 18 500 | 20 000 | 19 000 | 23 290 | 20 800 | 24 000 | 22 000 | 20 800 | 24 000 | 25 000 | 28 000 |
| **White, 16 Years and Over** | 25 000 | 25 000 | 26 200 | 27 000 | 28 000 | 28 000 | 29 000 | 30 000 | 31 000 | 32 000 | 34 000 | 35 000 | 35 000 |
| Men | 29 000 | 30 000 | 31 000 | 30 700 | 32 000 | 32 000 | 33 000 | 35 000 | 36 000 | 37 200 | 39 000 | 40 000 | 40 000 |
| Women | 20 000 | 20 500 | 22 000 | 22 000 | 23 000 | 23 000 | 24 000 | 25 000 | 26 000 | 27 000 | 28 000 | 30 000 | 30 000 |
| **Black, 16 Years and Over** | 19 350 | 20 000 | 21 000 | 20 800 | 21 000 | 22 000 | 23 784 | 24 000 | 25 000 | 25 760 | 26 000 | 28 500 | 29 000 |
| Men | 20 800 | 22 000 | 22 312 | 23 000 | 23 500 | 24 500 | 26 000 | 26 000 | 27 000 | 30 000 | 30 000 | 30 000 | 30 000 |
| Women | 18 000 | 18 500 | 20 000 | 19 843 | 20 000 | 20 000 | 21 000 | 22 000 | 23 000 | 24 000 | 25 000 | 26 000 | 26 000 |

**Table 1-39. Number and Median Annual Earnings of Year-Round, Full-Time Wage and Salary Workers, by Age, Sex, and Race, 1990–2015**—*Continued*

(Thousands of people, dollars.)

| Sex, age, and race | 2003 | 2004 | 2005 | 2006 | 2007 | 2008 | 2009 | 2010 | 2011 | 2012 | 2013 | 2014 | 2015 |
|---|---|---|---|---|---|---|---|---|---|---|---|---|---|
| **NUMBER** | | | | | | | | | | | | | |
| **Both Sexes, 16 Years and Over** | 94 731 | 96 098 | 98 632 | 101 353 | 102 441 | 98 493 | 94 012 | 94 110 | 96 562 | 97 879 | 100 711 | 103 308 | 105 520 |
| 16 to 24 years | 7 631 | 7 702 | 7 956 | 8 113 | 8 064 | 7 242 | 6 302 | 6 073 | 6 411 | 6 424 | 6 969 | 7 135 | 7 241 |
| 25 to 44 years | 48 343 | 48 421 | 49 149 | 50 056 | 49 725 | 47 364 | 44 579 | 44 441 | 45 166 | 45 812 | 46 478 | 48 188 | 49 130 |
| 25 to 34 years | 22 512 | 22 405 | 22 808 | 23 613 | 23 646 | 22 786 | 21 572 | 21 894 | 21 989 | 22 690 | 23 141 | 24 099 | 25 008 |
| 35 to 44 years | 25 831 | 26 016 | 26 341 | 26 443 | 26 080 | 24 578 | 23 007 | 22 546 | 23 177 | 23 122 | 23 337 | 24 090 | 24 123 |
| 45 to 54 years | 24 507 | 25 074 | 25 661 | 26 338 | 26 566 | 25 722 | 24 877 | 24 388 | 24 782 | 24 593 | 25 245 | 25 018 | 25 334 |
| 55 to 64 years | 12 207 | 12 812 | 13 605 | 14 340 | 15 248 | 15 286 | 15 274 | 16 073 | 16 622 | 17 255 | 17 721 | 18 416 | 19 152 |
| 65 years and over | 2 042 | 2 090 | 2 262 | 2 507 | 2 837 | 2 879 | 2 980 | 3 135 | 3 582 | 3 795 | 4 299 | 4 551 | 4 663 |
| **Men, 16 Years and Over** | 54 575 | 55 610 | 57 020 | 58 533 | 58 673 | 55 973 | 52 362 | 52 793 | 54 542 | 55 489 | 57 263 | 58 719 | 60 012 |
| 16 to 24 years | 4 421 | 4 493 | 4 663 | 4 812 | 4 719 | 4 112 | 3 494 | 3 462 | 3 649 | 3 730 | 3 952 | 3 914 | 4 107 |
| 25 to 44 years | 28 499 | 28 763 | 29 151 | 29 589 | 29 004 | 27 546 | 25 324 | 25 449 | 25 959 | 26 476 | 26 924 | 27 941 | 28 399 |
| 25 to 34 years | 13 288 | 13 430 | 13 629 | 13 933 | 13 706 | 13 208 | 12 085 | 12 475 | 12 616 | 13 043 | 13 370 | 14 123 | 14 406 |
| 35 to 44 years | 15 211 | 15 333 | 15 522 | 15 655 | 15 298 | 14 337 | 13 239 | 12 974 | 13 343 | 13 433 | 13 555 | 13 818 | 13 993 |
| 45 to 54 years | 13 616 | 13 975 | 14 382 | 14 758 | 14 810 | 14 199 | 13 521 | 13 373 | 13 723 | 13 690 | 14 094 | 14 026 | 14 278 |
| 55 to 64 years | 6 872 | 7 165 | 7 489 | 7 905 | 8 449 | 8 397 | 8 289 | 8 727 | 9 066 | 9 315 | 9 747 | 10 199 | 10 461 |
| 65 years and over | 1 165 | 1 213 | 1 334 | 1 469 | 1 692 | 1 720 | 1 733 | 1 782 | 2 146 | 2 278 | 2 546 | 2 640 | 2 767 |
| **Women, 16 Years and Over** | 40 156 | 40 488 | 41 613 | 42 820 | 43 768 | 42 520 | 41 650 | 41 318 | 42 020 | 42 390 | 43 448 | 44 589 | 45 508 |
| 16 to 24 years | 3 210 | 3 209 | 3 293 | 3 301 | 3 345 | 3 130 | 2 808 | 2 611 | 2 762 | 2 694 | 3 016 | 3 222 | 3 134 |
| 25 to 44 years | 19 844 | 19 656 | 19 997 | 20 467 | 20 721 | 19 819 | 19 255 | 18 992 | 19 207 | 19 336 | 19 554 | 20 248 | 20 731 |
| 25 to 34 years | 9 224 | 8 974 | 9 179 | 9 679 | 9 940 | 9 578 | 9 487 | 9 420 | 9 373 | 9 647 | 9 771 | 9 976 | 10 602 |
| 35 to 44 years | 10 620 | 10 682 | 10 818 | 10 788 | 10 782 | 10 240 | 9 768 | 9 572 | 9 834 | 9 689 | 9 782 | 10 272 | 10 130 |
| 45 to 54 years | 10 891 | 11 099 | 11 279 | 11 580 | 11 757 | 11 524 | 11 356 | 11 016 | 11 059 | 10 903 | 11 151 | 10 992 | 11 056 |
| 55 to 64 years | 5 335 | 5 647 | 6 116 | 6 434 | 6 799 | 6 889 | 6 984 | 7 346 | 7 556 | 7 940 | 7 974 | 8 217 | 8 691 |
| 65 years and over | 877 | 877 | 927 | 1 038 | 1 146 | 1 158 | 1 247 | 1 354 | 1 436 | 1 518 | 1 753 | 1 911 | 1 896 |
| **White, 16 Years and Over** | 77 545 | 78 236 | 80 546 | 82 411 | 83 139 | 79 980 | 76 470 | 76 557 | 77 669 | 78 266 | 80 188 | 81 557 | 82 879 |
| Men | 45 816 | 46 317 | 47 790 | 48 897 | 48 825 | 46 608 | 43 622 | 44 018 | 45 037 | 45 460 | 46 764 | 47 591 | 48 333 |
| Women | 31 729 | 31 919 | 32 756 | 33 513 | 34 314 | 33 372 | 32 848 | 32 540 | 32 632 | 32 806 | 33 424 | 33 966 | 34 546 |
| **Black, 16 Years and Over** | 10 979 | 11 301 | 11 417 | 11 988 | 11 987 | 11 424 | 10 716 | 10 676 | 11 009 | 11 193 | 11 865 | 12 370 | 12 754 |
| Men | 5 196 | 5 470 | 5 402 | 5 679 | 5 689 | 5 377 | 4 952 | 4 957 | 5 111 | 5 323 | 5 617 | 5 910 | 6 178 |
| Women | 5 783 | 5 832 | 6 015 | 6 309 | 6 299 | 6 046 | 5 764 | 5 719 | 5 898 | 5 870 | 6 248 | 6 460 | 6 577 |
| **MEDIAN ANNUAL EARNINGS** | | | | | | | | | | | | | |
| **Both Sexes, 16 Years and Over** | 35 000 | 35 672 | 36 400 | 38 000 | 40 000 | 40 000 | 41 000 | 42 000 | 42 000 | 44 000 | 44 000 | 45 000 | 45 000 |
| 16 to 24 years | 20 000 | 20 000 | 20 000 | 21 000 | 22 421 | 24 000 | 23 532 | 23 000 | 22 650 | 23 000 | 24 570 | 25 000 | 25 000 |
| 25 to 34 years | 32 000 | 33 000 | 33 000 | 35 000 | 35 000 | 36 500 | 38 000 | 37 815 | 38 000 | 39 000 | 40 000 | 40 000 | 40 000 |
| 35 to 44 years | 39 000 | 40 000 | 40 000 | 41 000 | 43 000 | 45 000 | 45 000 | 45 000 | 45 000 | 48 000 | 48 000 | 48 000 | 50 000 |
| 45 to 54 years | 40 000 | 40 000 | 42 000 | 44 000 | 45 000 | 45 000 | 46 000 | 48 000 | 48 000 | 50 000 | 49 920 | 50 000 | 50 000 |
| 55 to 64 years | 40 000 | 40 000 | 41 000 | 43 000 | 45 000 | 46 000 | 48 000 | 48 000 | 49 000 | 50 000 | 50 000 | 50 000 | 51 000 |
| 65 years and over | 32 000 | 35 000 | 35 000 | 35 001 | 40 000 | 42 000 | 42 000 | 45 000 | 44 200 | 48 000 | 48 000 | 50 000 | 50 000 |
| **Men, 16 Years and Over** | 40 000 | 40 000 | 40 051 | 42 000 | 45 000 | 46 000 | 48 000 | 48 000 | 48 000 | 50 000 | 50 000 | 50 000 | 50 000 |
| 16 to 24 years | 20 800 | 20 800 | 20 800 | 22 000 | 23 000 | 25 000 | 25 000 | 24 000 | 24 000 | 24 480 | 25 000 | 26 000 | 25 000 |
| 25 to 34 years | 35 000 | 35 000 | 35 000 | 36 000 | 38 000 | 40 000 | 40 000 | 40 000 | 40 000 | 40 000 | 40 000 | 42 000 | 43 000 |
| 35 to 44 years | 43 900 | 45 000 | 45 000 | 48 000 | 50 000 | 50 000 | 50 000 | 50 000 | 51 000 | 52 000 | 52 000 | 52 000 | 55 132 |
| 45 to 54 years | 48 000 | 48 000 | 50 000 | 50 000 | 50 000 | 52 000 | 53 004 | 55 000 | 55 000 | 57 000 | 56 000 | 60 000 | 60 000 |
| 55 to 64 years | 50 000 | 50 000 | 50 000 | 50 000 | 52 000 | 54 000 | 55 000 | 55 000 | 57 000 | 55 000 | 57 998 | 58 000 | 60 000 |
| 65 years and over | 42 000 | 40 000 | 41 000 | 44 000 | 44 000 | 50 000 | 49 000 | 50 002 | 50 000 | 53 700 | 55 000 | 60 000 | 60 000 |
| **Women, 16 Years and Over** | 30 000 | 30 001 | 32 000 | 33 000 | 35 000 | 35 000 | 36 000 | 37 000 | 37 000 | 38 000 | 39 000 | 40 000 | 40 000 |
| 16 to 24 years | 20 000 | 20 000 | 20 000 | 20 000 | 22 000 | 22 000 | 22 000 | 20 816 | 22 000 | 22 000 | 23 000 | 22 880 | 24 000 |
| 25 to 34 years | 30 000 | 30 000 | 30 000 | 31 000 | 33 000 | 34 000 | 35 000 | 35 000 | 35 000 | 35 002 | 37 000 | 36 000 | 38 000 |
| 35 to 44 years | 32 000 | 32 800 | 35 000 | 35 000 | 36 000 | 38 000 | 38 000 | 40 000 | 40 000 | 40 000 | 40 000 | 42 000 | 45 000 |
| 45 to 54 years | 33 466 | 34 771 | 35 000 | 36 000 | 37 163 | 38 000 | 40 000 | 40 000 | 40 000 | 40 000 | 40 000 | 42 000 | 43 000 |
| 55 to 64 years | 32 000 | 33 000 | 33 000 | 35 000 | 37 100 | 39 000 | 40 000 | 40 000 | 40 000 | 41 000 | 41 161 | 41 000 | 44 000 |
| 65 years and over | 26 000 | 27 000 | 28 768 | 27 878 | 31 000 | 34 193 | 36 000 | 40 000 | 37 000 | 38 000 | 40 000 | 40 000 | 42 500 |
| **White, 16 Years and Over** | 36 000 | 37 000 | 38 000 | 40 000 | 40 000 | 41 600 | 42 000 | 43 502 | 44 000 | 45 000 | 45 000 | 45 000 | 48 000 |
| Men | 40 000 | 42 000 | 42 000 | 44 707 | 45 000 | 48 000 | 49 000 | 50 000 | 50 000 | 50 000 | 50 000 | 50 000 | 52 000 |
| Women | 31 000 | 31 800 | 32 000 | 34 000 | 35 000 | 35 500 | 36 002 | 38 000 | 38 000 | 39 520 | 40 000 | 40 000 | 40 000 |
| **Black, 16 Years and Over** | 30 000 | 30 000 | 30 000 | 31 000 | 33 000 | 34 000 | 35 000 | 35 000 | 35 000 | 35 000 | 36 000 | 36 000 | 38 000 |
| Men | 32 000 | 30 000 | 33 000 | 34 000 | 35 000 | 37 500 | 38 000 | 38 000 | 36 000 | 39 000 | 38 000 | 40 000 | 40 000 |
| Women | 27 000 | 28 000 | 29 141 | 30 000 | 30 000 | 30 002 | 32 000 | 32 000 | 34 000 | 34 000 | 34 000 | 33 000 | 35 000 |

**Table 1-40.  Number and Median Annual Earnings of Year-Round, Full-Time Wage and Salary Workers, by Sex and Occupation of Job Held the Longest, 2005–2015**

(Thousands of people, dollars.)

| Sex and occupation | 2005 | 2006 | 2007 | 2008 | 2009 | 2010 | 2011 | 2012 | 2013 | 2014 | 2015 |
|---|---|---|---|---|---|---|---|---|---|---|---|
| **Both Sexes, Number of Workers** | | | | | | | | | | | |
| Management, business, and financial operations ..... | 16 299 | 16 806 | 17 115 | 17 259 | 16 491 | 16 889 | 17 396 | 17 799 | 18 241 | 19 020 | 19 937 |
| Management ................................................. | 11 685 | 11 866 | 12 191 | 12 256 | 11 733 | 11 804 | 12 140 | 12 548 | 12 646 | 13 240 | 13 928 |
| Business and financial operations ...................... | 4 613 | 4 941 | 4 924 | 5 003 | 4 758 | 5 085 | 5 256 | 5 251 | 5 595 | 5 780 | 6 009 |
| Professional and related ....................................... | 20 093 | 21 268 | 21 939 | 21 748 | 21 831 | 21 966 | 22 165 | 22 751 | 23 251 | 24 109 | 24 721 |
| Computer and mathematical ........................... | 2 779 | 2 888 | 3 180 | 3 089 | 3 100 | 2 993 | 3 171 | 3 524 | 3 439 | 3 690 | 4 044 |
| Architecture and engineering ......................... | 2 361 | 2 491 | 2 467 | 2 360 | 2 133 | 2 409 | 2 451 | 2 398 | 2 302 | 2 362 | 2 602 |
| Life, physical, and social sciences ................ | 1 096 | 1 142 | 1 026 | 1 044 | 1 054 | 993 | 991 | 1 050 | 1 075 | 1 090 | 1 085 |
| Community and social services ...................... | 1 728 | 1 835 | 1 791 | 1 754 | 1 827 | 1 905 | 1 784 | 1 846 | 1 982 | 1 947 | 2 002 |
| Legal ............................................................. | 1 093 | 1 168 | 1 159 | 1 228 | 1 230 | 1 255 | 1 226 | 1 350 | 1 350 | 1 360 | 1 271 |
| Education, training, and library ...................... | 4 894 | 5 195 | 5 482 | 5 478 | 5 500 | 5 510 | 5 390 | 5 285 | 5 588 | 5 683 | 5 546 |
| Arts, design, entertainment, sports, and media ..... | 1 362 | 1 633 | 1 554 | 1 415 | 1 404 | 1 380 | 1 449 | 1 445 | 1 582 | 1 658 | 1 660 |
| Health care practitioner and technical .................. | 4 780 | 4 916 | 5 278 | 5 380 | 5 583 | 5 521 | 5 703 | 5 852 | 5 932 | 6 319 | 6 512 |
| Services .............................................................. | 13 117 | 13 236 | 13 553 | 13 034 | 12 944 | 12 855 | 13 676 | 13 456 | 13 650 | 13 795 | 14 426 |
| Health care support ...................................... | 2 027 | 2 081 | 2 027 | 2 019 | 2 135 | 2 008 | 2 236 | 2 037 | 2 307 | 2 144 | 2 261 |
| Protective services ........................................ | 2 429 | 2 506 | 2 511 | 2 472 | 2 593 | 2 589 | 2 571 | 2 535 | 2 582 | 2 498 | 2 482 |
| Food preparation and serving related ................. | 3 586 | 3 646 | 3 769 | 3 504 | 3 307 | 3 408 | 3 797 | 3 631 | 3 508 | 3 641 | 4 130 |
| Building and grounds cleaning and maintenance .. | 3 285 | 3 120 | 3 198 | 3 027 | 2 870 | 2 942 | 3 098 | 3 056 | 3 190 | 3 243 | 3 205 |
| Personal care and services ........................... | 1 790 | 1 883 | 2 048 | 2 012 | 2 038 | 1 908 | 1 974 | 2 196 | 2 062 | 2 269 | 2 348 |
| Sales and office ................................................... | 24 010 | 24 467 | 24 472 | 23 058 | 22 320 | 21 859 | 21 949 | 22 121 | 22 841 | 22 843 | 22 520 |
| Sales and related .......................................... | 10 251 | 10 497 | 10 301 | 9 763 | 9 275 | 9 187 | 9 191 | 9 312 | 10 010 | 9 937 | 9 757 |
| Office and administrative support ....................... | 13 758 | 13 970 | 14 171 | 13 294 | 13 045 | 12 671 | 12 758 | 12 810 | 12 831 | 12 906 | 12 763 |
| Natural resources, construction, and maintenance ... | 10 864 | 11 295 | 10 745 | 10 002 | 8 599 | 8 298 | 8 584 | 8 897 | 9 317 | 9 715 | 9 846 |
| Farming, fishing, and forestry ........................ | 556 | 585 | 607 | 581 | 555 | 532 | 562 | 539 | 621 | 631 | 768 |
| Construction and extraction ........................... | 6 145 | 6 484 | 5 885 | 5 158 | 4 172 | 4 029 | 4 283 | 4 329 | 4 604 | 5 077 | 5 081 |
| Installation, maintenance, and repair .............. | 4 163 | 4 226 | 4 252 | 4 264 | 3 872 | 3 737 | 3 739 | 4 029 | 4 093 | 4 006 | 3 997 |
| Production, transportation, and material moving ....... | 13 586 | 13 704 | 13 907 | 12 649 | 11 062 | 11 518 | 12 041 | 12 166 | 12 724 | 13 129 | 13 388 |
| Production ..................................................... | 7 623 | 7 762 | 7 589 | 6 652 | 5 834 | 6 226 | 6 574 | 6 410 | 6 723 | 6 904 | 7 080 |
| Transportation and material moving .................... | 5 963 | 5 942 | 6 318 | 5 997 | 5 228 | 5 292 | 5 467 | 5 756 | 6 001 | 6 225 | 6 308 |
| Armed forces ....................................................... | 664 | 576 | 709 | 744 | 765 | 727 | 749 | 689 | 687 | 697 | 681 |
| **Both Sexes, Median Annual Earnings** | | | | | | | | | | | |
| Management, business, and financial operations ..... | 57 000 | 60 000 | 60 000 | 60 800 | 60 000 | 64 000 | 65 000 | 65 000 | 65 000 | 65 000 | 70 000 |
| Management ................................................. | 60 000 | 62 500 | 65 000 | 65 000 | 65 000 | 68 000 | 70 000 | 70 000 | 70 000 | 70 000 | 75 000 |
| Business and financial operations ...................... | 49 000 | 50 000 | 50 000 | 52 000 | 55 000 | 56 000 | 57 000 | 57 000 | 60 000 | 60 000 | 60 000 |
| Professional and related ....................................... | 50 000 | 50 000 | 51 000 | 54 000 | 55 000 | 55 000 | 56 000 | 58 705 | 58 000 | 59 000 | 60 000 |
| Computer and mathematical ........................... | 62 400 | 68 000 | 70 000 | 70 000 | 72 000 | 70 000 | 73 000 | 75 000 | 75 000 | 80 000 | 80 000 |
| Architecture and engineering ......................... | 65 000 | 69 000 | 70 000 | 70 000 | 70 000 | 75 000 | 75 000 | 75 000 | 80 000 | 76 000 | 80 000 |
| Life, physical, and social sciences ................ | 53 500 | 57 000 | 60 000 | 57 532 | 60 000 | 60 000 | 61 599 | 67 000 | 70 000 | 65 000 | 70 000 |
| Community and social services ...................... | 36 000 | 36 780 | 39 000 | 40 000 | 40 000 | 40 000 | 40 000 | 41 000 | 42 000 | 44 000 | 45 000 |
| Legal ............................................................. | 72 000 | 70 000 | 70 000 | 75 000 | 80 000 | 75 000 | 85 000 | 80 000 | 86 000 | 90 000 | 88 000 |
| Education, training, and library ...................... | 40 000 | 40 282 | 44 984 | 45 000 | 46 000 | 45 000 | 46 200 | 47 000 | 45 000 | 47 907 | 49 000 |
| Arts, design, entertainment, sports, and media ..... | 42 000 | 45 000 | 44 297 | 47 000 | 49 000 | 48 000 | 50 000 | 50 000 | 50 000 | 52 000 | 52 000 |
| Health care practitioner and technical .................. | 50 000 | 52 000 | 52 800 | 55 000 | 55 000 | 57 638 | 58 000 | 60 000 | 60 000 | 58 000 | 60 000 |
| Services .............................................................. | 23 000 | 24 000 | 25 000 | 25 000 | 26 000 | 26 000 | 26 000 | 27 000 | 26 255 | 27 040 | 29 044 |
| Health care support ...................................... | 22 000 | 23 000 | 24 500 | 26 000 | 26 000 | 26 270 | 26 000 | 26 000 | 28 000 | 26 922 | 28 000 |
| Protective services ........................................ | 42 000 | 45 000 | 45 000 | 45 000 | 46 000 | 48 000 | 50 000 | 50 000 | 50 000 | 50 000 | 50 000 |
| Food preparation and serving related ................. | 19 656 | 19 000 | 20 000 | 20 800 | 20 000 | 20 800 | 21 000 | 21 840 | 22 000 | 22 607 | 25 000 |
| Building and grounds cleaning and maintenance .. | 21 000 | 23 000 | 23 000 | 24 000 | 24 024 | 25 000 | 24 002 | 25 000 | 24 000 | 25 301 | 28 000 |
| Personal care and services ........................... | 23 000 | 23 000 | 25 000 | 25 000 | 25 000 | 25 000 | 25 000 | 25 000 | 24 000 | 25 500 | 30 000 |
| Sales and office ................................................... | 31 200 | 32 002 | 34 000 | 35 000 | 35 000 | 35 000 | 35 002 | 36 000 | 37 440 | 37 000 | 39 000 |
| Sales and related .......................................... | 35 000 | 37 000 | 38 000 | 38 500 | 38 000 | 40 000 | 40 000 | 40 000 | 40 000 | 40 000 | 43 000 |
| Office and administrative support ....................... | 30 000 | 30 000 | 32 000 | 32 500 | 34 000 | 34 000 | 35 000 | 35 000 | 35 000 | 35 000 | 36 000 |
| Natural resources, construction, and maintenance ... | 35 000 | 35 000 | 36 000 | 40 000 | 40 000 | 40 000 | 40 000 | 40 000 | 40 000 | 40 000 | 41 000 |
| Farming, fishing, and forestry ........................ | 21 000 | 20 000 | 24 000 | 24 000 | 24 000 | 23 000 | 24 000 | 24 000 | 25 600 | 27 300 | 26 443 |
| Construction and extraction ........................... | 32 000 | 35 000 | 35 000 | 39 000 | 40 000 | 40 000 | 39 500 | 38 000 | 40 000 | 40 000 | 40 000 |
| Installation, maintenance, and repair .............. | 40 000 | 40 000 | 40 000 | 42 000 | 44 192 | 43 981 | 44 018 | 44 000 | 45 000 | 45 000 | 46 000 |
| Production, transportation, and material moving ....... | 30 200 | 30 000 | 33 000 | 34 000 | 34 000 | 34 000 | 35 000 | 36 000 | 35 761 | 36 000 | 37 000 |
| Production ..................................................... | 30 000 | 30 000 | 33 000 | 34 000 | 32 006 | 34 000 | 35 000 | 36 000 | 36 000 | 36 000 | 36 000 |
| Transportation and material moving .................... | 30 800 | 30 000 | 33 800 | 34 000 | 35 000 | 33 000 | 35 000 | 36 000 | 35 000 | 35 000 | 38 000 |
| Armed forces ....................................................... | 39 000 | 40 000 | 42 000 | 45 000 | 47 000 | 47 000 | 45 000 | 45 000 | 47 000 | 48 000 | 50 000 |

**Table 1-40. Number and Median Annual Earnings of Year-Round, Full-Time Wage and Salary Workers, by Sex and Occupation of Job Held the Longest, 2005–2015**—*Continued*

(Thousands of people, dollars.)

| Sex and occupation | 2005 | 2006 | 2007 | 2008 | 2009 | 2010 | 2011 | 2012 | 2013 | 2014 | 2015 |
|---|---|---|---|---|---|---|---|---|---|---|---|
| **Men, Number of Workers** | | | | | | | | | | | |
| Management, business, and financial operations ..... | 9 496 | 9 519 | 9 784 | 9 836 | 9 418 | 9 569 | 9 886 | 9 917 | 10 137 | 10 773 | 11 084 |
| Management ............................................ | 7 477 | 7 361 | 7 619 | 7 714 | 7 300 | 7 249 | 7 497 | 7 666 | 7 742 | 8 103 | 8 344 |
| Business and financial operations ................. | 2 019 | 2 157 | 2 165 | 2 122 | 2 117 | 2 320 | 2 389 | 2 252 | 2 395 | 2 670 | 2 739 |
| Professional and related ................................. | 9 561 | 10 387 | 10 274 | 10 074 | 10 036 | 10 126 | 10 228 | 10 731 | 10 858 | 11 194 | 11 520 |
| Computer and mathematical ....................... | 2 060 | 2 159 | 2 378 | 2 348 | 2 227 | 2 244 | 2 329 | 2 564 | 2 636 | 2 821 | 3 100 |
| Architecture and engineering ..................... | 2 041 | 2 174 | 2 172 | 2 068 | 1 859 | 2 110 | 2 144 | 2 073 | 2 004 | 2 044 | 2 231 |
| Life, physical, and social sciences ............. | 668 | 748 | 611 | 581 | 575 | 562 | 605 | 615 | 589 | 622 | 656 |
| Community and social services ................... | 713 | 756 | 744 | 675 | 707 | 701 | 679 | 742 | 792 | 740 | 704 |
| Legal ....................................................... | 490 | 546 | 515 | 595 | 645 | 605 | 616 | 686 | 615 | 666 | 611 |
| Education, training, and library .................... | 1 421 | 1 587 | 1 651 | 1 535 | 1 650 | 1 601 | 1 522 | 1 504 | 1 586 | 1 653 | 1 577 |
| Arts, design, entertainment, sports, and media ..... | 789 | 953 | 790 | 782 | 829 | 839 | 860 | 824 | 989 | 937 | 940 |
| Health care practitioner and technical ........... | 1 378 | 1 464 | 1 413 | 1 490 | 1 544 | 1 464 | 1 473 | 1 724 | 1 645 | 1 711 | 1 701 |
| Services ....................................................... | 6 658 | 6 715 | 6 871 | 6 389 | 6 379 | 6 426 | 6 923 | 7 040 | 6 931 | 6 922 | 7 323 |
| Health care support ................................... | 240 | 252 | 261 | 204 | 247 | 242 | 268 | 269 | 277 | 284 | 280 |
| Protective services .................................... | 1 919 | 1 998 | 2 000 | 1 930 | 2 026 | 2 070 | 2 108 | 2 041 | 2 087 | 2 054 | 1 998 |
| Food preparation and serving related ........... | 1 873 | 1 991 | 1 985 | 1 816 | 1 744 | 1 743 | 2 050 | 2 068 | 1 880 | 1 896 | 2 309 |
| Building and grounds cleaning and maintenance .. | 2 153 | 1 939 | 2 048 | 1 911 | 1 832 | 1 862 | 1 974 | 2 055 | 2 069 | 2 057 | 2 050 |
| Personal care and services ........................ | 473 | 535 | 576 | 527 | 530 | 508 | 523 | 606 | 618 | 629 | 685 |
| Sales and office ............................................ | 9 464 | 9 747 | 9 694 | 9 128 | 8 680 | 8 872 | 8 971 | 8 874 | 9 386 | 9 395 | 9 234 |
| Sales and related ...................................... | 5 896 | 6 125 | 6 019 | 5 690 | 5 231 | 5 363 | 5 425 | 5 436 | 5 867 | 5 680 | 5 631 |
| Office and administrative support ................. | 3 568 | 3 622 | 3 675 | 3 438 | 3 449 | 3 509 | 3 545 | 3 439 | 3 519 | 3 715 | 3 603 |
| Natural resources, construction, and maintenance ... | 10 503 | 10 904 | 10 343 | 9 627 | 8 225 | 7 936 | 8 274 | 8 550 | 8 996 | 9 330 | 9 456 |
| Farming, fishing, and forestry ..................... | 469 | 482 | 516 | 489 | 425 | 430 | 474 | 445 | 501 | 521 | 617 |
| Construction and extraction ........................ | 6 026 | 6 344 | 5 753 | 5 056 | 4 068 | 3 909 | 4 192 | 4 245 | 4 534 | 4 948 | 4 959 |
| Installation, maintenance, and repair ........... | 4 008 | 4 078 | 4 074 | 4 081 | 3 732 | 3 597 | 3 608 | 3 860 | 3 961 | 3 861 | 3 880 |
| Production, transportation, and material moving ....... | 10 747 | 10 733 | 11 047 | 10 226 | 8 921 | 9 214 | 9 583 | 9 754 | 10 331 | 10 490 | 10 775 |
| Production ................................................ | 5 503 | 5 525 | 5 461 | 4 983 | 4 370 | 4 612 | 4 813 | 4 814 | 5 090 | 5 098 | 5 281 |
| Transportation and material moving ............. | 5 244 | 5 208 | 5 585 | 5 242 | 4 552 | 4 602 | 4 770 | 4 940 | 5 241 | 5 392 | 5 495 |
| Armed forces ............................................... | 591 | 528 | 660 | 696 | 703 | 649 | 677 | 622 | 625 | 616 | 620 |
| **Men, Median Annual Earnings** | | | | | | | | | | | |
| Management, business, and financial operations ..... | 69 000 | 68 000 | 70 000 | 72 000 | 72 000 | 75 000 | 75 000 | 75 000 | 75 000 | 75 000 | 80 000 |
| Management ............................................ | 70 000 | 70 000 | 75 000 | 75 000 | 75 000 | 78 000 | 80 000 | 75 056 | 77 975 | 78 000 | 82 000 |
| Business and financial operations ................. | 60 000 | 60 000 | 60 000 | 65 000 | 65 000 | 67 000 | 65 000 | 67 500 | 70 000 | 68 000 | 70 000 |
| Professional and related ................................. | 60 000 | 61 000 | 62 000 | 67 000 | 65 000 | 67 000 | 70 000 | 70 000 | 71 000 | 70 000 | 75 000 |
| Computer and mathematical ....................... | 65 000 | 70 000 | 70 000 | 74 000 | 75 000 | 75 000 | 79 000 | 80 000 | 78 000 | 81 000 | 85 000 |
| Architecture and engineering ..................... | 66 921 | 70 000 | 72 000 | 74 000 | 72 000 | 77 000 | 75 000 | 79 002 | 80 000 | 78 000 | 80 000 |
| Life, physical, and social sciences ............. | 62 000 | 61 000 | 65 000 | 65 000 | 65 000 | 64 000 | 65 000 | 72 000 | 76 000 | 70 000 | 75 000 |
| Community and social services ................... | 40 000 | 39 000 | 40 000 | 44 085 | 45 000 | 42 002 | 42 000 | 42 000 | 42 640 | 45 000 | 50 000 |
| Legal ....................................................... | 108 000 | 100 000 | 104 146 | 130 000 | 120 000 | 120 000 | 120 000 | 100 000 | 125 000 | 127 000 | 120 000 |
| Education, training, and library .................... | 50 000 | 50 000 | 50 000 | 54 000 | 52 000 | 53 000 | 55 000 | 55 000 | 56 000 | 55 000 | 56 000 |
| Arts, design, entertainment, sports, and media ..... | 50 000 | 50 000 | 50 000 | 52 000 | 50 000 | 50 000 | 55 000 | 55 000 | 55 000 | 58 000 | 51 000 |
| Health care practitioner and technical ........... | 70 000 | 72 000 | 75 000 | 75 000 | 74 000 | 75 000 | 75 000 | 75 000 | 78 000 | 75 000 | 85 000 |
| Services ....................................................... | 26 000 | 29 000 | 29 000 | 30 000 | 30 000 | 30 002 | 30 000 | 30 000 | 31 000 | 32 000 | 32 000 |
| Health care support ................................... | 22 880 | 25 000 | 25 000 | 28 000 | 30 000 | 34 000 | 29 904 | 30 000 | 35 000 | 30 000 | 30 000 |
| Protective services .................................... | 45 000 | 46 886 | 49 000 | 49 000 | 49 500 | 50 000 | 50 000 | 54 000 | 51 000 | 54 000 | 52 002 |
| Food preparation and serving related ........... | 20 000 | 20 000 | 21 000 | 21 500 | 21 000 | 23 000 | 23 400 | 24 000 | 22 709 | 24 000 | 25 000 |
| Building and grounds cleaning and maintenance .. | 24 000 | 25 000 | 25 000 | 27 012 | 26 000 | 28 600 | 27 000 | 28 000 | 28 000 | 29 000 | 30 000 |
| Personal care and services ........................ | 30 000 | 30 000 | 30 000 | 30 500 | 30 000 | 30 000 | 32 000 | 32 000 | 30 000 | 32 000 | 35 000 |
| Sales and office ............................................ | 40 000 | 40 000 | 42 000 | 40 000 | 42 002 | 42 000 | 43 000 | 45 000 | 44 400 | 45 000 | 48 000 |
| Sales and related ...................................... | 42 000 | 45 000 | 45 000 | 48 000 | 48 002 | 48 000 | 50 000 | 49 000 | 50 000 | 50 000 | 51 000 |
| Office and administrative support ................. | 34 000 | 35 000 | 36 000 | 35 000 | 37 400 | 37 000 | 37 000 | 40 000 | 40 000 | 40 000 | 40 000 |
| Natural resources, construction, and maintenance ... | 35 000 | 35 674 | 36 000 | 40 000 | 40 000 | 40 000 | 40 000 | 40 000 | 40 000 | 40 000 | 42 000 |
| Farming, fishing, and forestry ..................... | 22 500 | 20 000 | 24 000 | 24 000 | 25 000 | 23 400 | 25 000 | 25 000 | 28 705 | 29 900 | 28 000 |
| Construction and extraction ........................ | 32 000 | 35 000 | 35 000 | 40 000 | 40 000 | 40 000 | 40 000 | 39 000 | 40 000 | 40 000 | 40 000 |
| Installation, maintenance, and repair ........... | 40 000 | 40 000 | 40 000 | 42 685 | 45 000 | 44 000 | 45 000 | 44 000 | 45 000 | 45 000 | 47 000 |
| Production, transportation, and material moving ....... | 34 000 | 33 358 | 35 000 | 35 360 | 35 198 | 36 000 | 38 500 | 40 000 | 39 000 | 40 000 | 40 000 |
| Production ................................................ | 35 000 | 35 000 | 36 000 | 36 000 | 36 000 | 36 944 | 40 000 | 40 000 | 40 000 | 40 000 | 40 000 |
| Transportation and material moving ............. | 32 760 | 32 000 | 35 000 | 35 000 | 35 000 | 35 000 | 37 440 | 38 638 | 37 000 | 38 000 | 40 000 |
| Armed forces ............................................... | 40 000 | 40 000 | 42 000 | 45 000 | 47 000 | 47 000 | 45 000 | 45 000 | 49 999 | 48 000 | 50 000 |

**Table 1-40.  Number and Median Annual Earnings of Year-Round, Full-Time Wage and Salary Workers, by Sex and Occupation of Job Held the Longest, 2005–2015**—*Continued*

(Thousands of people, dollars.)

| Sex and occupation | 2005 | 2006 | 2007 | 2008 | 2009 | 2010 | 2011 | 2012 | 2013 | 2014 | 2015 |
|---|---|---|---|---|---|---|---|---|---|---|---|
| **Women, Number of Workers** | | | | | | | | | | | |
| Management, business, and financial operations ..... | 6 803 | 7 287 | 7 332 | 7 423 | 7 073 | 7 320 | 7 511 | 7 881 | 8 104 | 8 248 | 8 853 |
| Management ................................................ | 4 209 | 4 504 | 4 573 | 4 542 | 4 432 | 4 555 | 4 643 | 4 882 | 4 904 | 5 137 | 5 584 |
| Business and financial operations ......................... | 2 594 | 2 783 | 2 759 | 2 881 | 2 641 | 2 765 | 2 867 | 2 999 | 3 200 | 3 110 | 3 269 |
| Professional and related ........................................ | 10 532 | 10 881 | 11 664 | 11 675 | 11 795 | 11 840 | 11 937 | 12 020 | 12 394 | 12 915 | 13 202 |
| Computer and mathematical ................................ | 718 | 729 | 802 | 741 | 873 | 748 | 842 | 960 | 803 | 869 | 944 |
| Architecture and engineering ............................. | 320 | 317 | 295 | 293 | 274 | 299 | 307 | 325 | 298 | 318 | 371 |
| Life, physical, and social sciences ........................ | 428 | 394 | 415 | 462 | 479 | 431 | 386 | 435 | 486 | 468 | 429 |
| Community and social services ........................... | 1 015 | 1 079 | 1 047 | 1 079 | 1 119 | 1 204 | 1 105 | 1 104 | 1 190 | 1 208 | 1 298 |
| Legal .......................................................... | 603 | 622 | 645 | 633 | 585 | 650 | 610 | 664 | 735 | 694 | 660 |
| Education, training, and library ............................ | 3 473 | 3 608 | 3 831 | 3 944 | 3 850 | 3 909 | 3 868 | 3 781 | 4 001 | 4 030 | 3 969 |
| Arts, design, entertainment, sports, and media ..... | 573 | 681 | 764 | 633 | 575 | 541 | 589 | 622 | 593 | 721 | 720 |
| Health care practitioner and technical .................. | 3 403 | 3 452 | 3 865 | 3 890 | 4 039 | 4 057 | 4 230 | 4 129 | 4 287 | 4 608 | 4 811 |
| Services ........................................................... | 6 459 | 6 522 | 6 682 | 6 645 | 6 565 | 6 429 | 6 753 | 6 416 | 6 718 | 6 874 | 7 103 |
| Health care support ......................................... | 1 787 | 1 829 | 1 766 | 1 815 | 1 888 | 1 766 | 1 969 | 1 768 | 2 030 | 1 860 | 1 980 |
| Protective services .......................................... | 510 | 509 | 511 | 541 | 567 | 519 | 463 | 494 | 495 | 443 | 484 |
| Food preparation and serving related .................. | 1 713 | 1 655 | 1 784 | 1 688 | 1 563 | 1 665 | 1 747 | 1 562 | 1 628 | 1 745 | 1 821 |
| Building and grounds cleaning and maintenance .. | 1 132 | 1 181 | 1 150 | 1 116 | 1 038 | 1 079 | 1 125 | 1 001 | 1 121 | 1 186 | 1 155 |
| Personal care and services .............................. | 1 317 | 1 349 | 1 471 | 1 485 | 1 508 | 1 400 | 1 451 | 1 590 | 1 444 | 1 640 | 1 663 |
| Sales and office .................................................. | 14 546 | 14 720 | 14 778 | 13 930 | 13 640 | 12 986 | 12 979 | 13 247 | 13 455 | 13 448 | 13 285 |
| Sales and related ........................................... | 4 355 | 4 372 | 4 282 | 4 073 | 4 044 | 3 824 | 3 766 | 3 876 | 4 143 | 4 256 | 4 126 |
| Office and administrative support ......................... | 10 191 | 10 348 | 10 496 | 9 856 | 9 596 | 9 162 | 9 213 | 9 371 | 9 313 | 9 191 | 9 159 |
| Natural resources, construction, and maintenance ... | 360 | 391 | 402 | 376 | 374 | 361 | 310 | 347 | 321 | 385 | 390 |
| Farming, fishing, and forestry ............................. | 87 | 104 | 92 | 91 | 130 | 102 | 87 | 94 | 120 | 110 | 151 |
| Construction and extraction ............................... | 119 | 140 | 132 | 101 | 104 | 120 | 91 | 85 | 70 | 130 | 122 |
| Installation, maintenance, and repair .................... | 155 | 148 | 178 | 183 | 140 | 140 | 131 | 169 | 132 | 145 | 117 |
| Production, transportation, and material moving ....... | 2 839 | 2 971 | 2 861 | 2 423 | 2 141 | 2 304 | 2 458 | 2 412 | 2 393 | 2 639 | 2 613 |
| Production ..................................................... | 2 120 | 2 237 | 2 128 | 1 668 | 1 464 | 1 614 | 1 761 | 1 596 | 1 633 | 1 806 | 1 800 |
| Transportation and material moving .................... | 719 | 734 | 733 | 755 | 676 | 690 | 697 | 816 | 760 | 833 | 813 |
| Armed forces ...................................................... | 73 | 48 | 49 | 49 | 62 | 78 | 72 | 67 | 62 | 81 | 61 |
| | | | | | | | | | | | |
| **Women, Median Annual Earnings** | | | | | | | | | | | |
| Management, business, and financial operations ..... | 46 000 | 50 000 | 50 000 | 50 000 | 50 000 | 52 779 | 52 000 | 54 000 | 55 000 | 56 000 | 59 000 |
| Management ................................................ | 50 000 | 52 000 | 52 000 | 55 000 | 52 999 | 55 000 | 55 000 | 58 000 | 57 000 | 60 000 | 60 000 |
| Business and financial operations ......................... | 41 000 | 46 000 | 45 000 | 48 000 | 48 000 | 50 000 | 50 000 | 50 000 | 52 000 | 52 000 | 52 000 |
| Professional and related ........................................ | 42 000 | 43 000 | 45 000 | 46 000 | 48 002 | 49 000 | 50 000 | 50 000 | 50 000 | 50 000 | 51 500 |
| Computer and mathematical ................................ | 57 000 | 60 000 | 60 000 | 62 000 | 65 000 | 65 000 | 65 000 | 66 002 | 71 000 | 73 000 | 70 000 |
| Architecture and engineering ............................. | 55 000 | 52 000 | 55 000 | 50 000 | 61 000 | 60 000 | 62 400 | 65 000 | 64 000 | 65 000 | 65 000 |
| Life, physical, and social sciences ........................ | 50 000 | 48 000 | 48 000 | 49 000 | 54 651 | 56 000 | 55 000 | 61 008 | 63 000 | 56 627 | 65 465 |
| Community and social services ........................... | 35 000 | 36 000 | 37 000 | 37 700 | 39 000 | 39 000 | 40 000 | 40 000 | 40 000 | 42 720 | 43 000 |
| Legal .......................................................... | 47 500 | 50 000 | 47 500 | 52 001 | 60 000 | 57 257 | 51 875 | 55 000 | 57 075 | 60 000 | 66 000 |
| Education, training, and library ............................ | 38 000 | 38 632 | 41 000 | 42 000 | 43 000 | 42 000 | 45 000 | 44 000 | 43 000 | 45 000 | 45 040 |
| Arts, design, entertainment, sports, and media ..... | 35 000 | 38 000 | 40 000 | 40 000 | 45 000 | 42 000 | 43 000 | 45 000 | 48 000 | 49 000 | 53 000 |
| Health care practitioner and technical .................. | 46 000 | 48 000 | 50 000 | 50 000 | 52 000 | 53 000 | 53 000 | 55 000 | 55 000 | 55 000 | 56 000 |
| Services ........................................................... | 20 000 | 20 500 | 22 000 | 23 516 | 24 000 | 23 000 | 23 000 | 24 000 | 24 000 | 24 000 | 25 000 |
| Health care support ......................................... | 21 000 | 23 000 | 24 500 | 26 000 | 25 000 | 25 000 | 26 000 | 26 000 | 27 000 | 26 000 | 27 040 |
| Protective services .......................................... | 34 344 | 37 896 | 35 000 | 35 000 | 38 000 | 38 500 | 42 000 | 42 000 | 43 419 | 38 000 | 39 800 |
| Food preparation and serving related .................. | 18 000 | 18 000 | 19 000 | 20 000 | 19 000 | 19 000 | 20 000 | 20 000 | 22 000 | 20 000 | 24 000 |
| Building and grounds cleaning and maintenance .. | 18 000 | 19 000 | 19 500 | 20 000 | 20 000 | 20 000 | 20 020 | 20 000 | 20 000 | 21 000 | 22 000 |
| Personal care and services .............................. | 20 800 | 20 000 | 24 000 | 24 000 | 24 700 | 23 000 | 23 000 | 25 000 | 22 000 | 25 000 | 26 000 |
| Sales and office .................................................. | 29 000 | 30 000 | 30 000 | 30 600 | 31 400 | 32 000 | 33 000 | 33 000 | 35 000 | 34 000 | 35 000 |
| Sales and related ........................................... | 26 000 | 26 000 | 28 000 | 29 000 | 30 000 | 30 000 | 30 000 | 30 000 | 30 000 | 30 000 | 32 000 |
| Office and administrative support ......................... | 29 800 | 30 000 | 30 002 | 32 000 | 32 100 | 33 000 | 34 000 | 35 000 | 35 000 | 35 000 | 35 000 |
| Natural resources, construction, and maintenance .... | 30 200 | 27 000 | 37 025 | 30 000 | 30 000 | 30 000 | 30 000 | 32 000 | 30 000 | 30 000 | 30 000 |
| Farming, fishing, and forestry ............................. | 18 000 | 18 808 | 24 117 | 24 685 | 21 000 | 20 000 | 20 000 | 20 498 | 22 093 | 23 000 | 25 000 |
| Construction and extraction ............................... | 31 200 | 24 980 | 40 000 | 34 500 | 31 000 | 33 670 | 28 323 | 30 645 | 31 200 | 29 052 | 38 801 |
| Installation, maintenance, and repair .................... | 36 000 | 40 000 | 42 000 | 33 913 | 38 139 | 41 888 | 35 000 | 43 889 | 43 000 | 37 000 | 38 639 |
| Production, transportation, and material moving ....... | 23 000 | 23 000 | 25 000 | 25 000 | 25 000 | 25 000 | 25 000 | 27 560 | 28 000 | 27 000 | 29 000 |
| Production ..................................................... | 23 400 | 23 000 | 25 000 | 25 000 | 25 000 | 25 000 | 25 000 | 27 000 | 27 901 | 27 000 | 29 000 |
| Transportation and material moving .................... | 21 000 | 24 000 | 27 000 | 24 000 | 25 000 | 25 000 | 26 000 | 28 000 | 28 000 | 27 000 | 29 000 |
| Armed forces ...................................................... | 32 652 | 32 000 | 41 000 | 32 000 | 43 600 | 50 000 | 52 000 | 48 000 | 39 000 | 45 000 | 50 121 |

## Table 1-41. Distribution of Employed Wage and Salary Workers by Tenure with Current Employer, Age, Sex, Race, and Hispanic Origin, January 2016

(Thousands of people, percent.)

| Characteristic | Number employed/ (in thousands) | Percent distribution by tenure with current employer | | | | | | | | |
|---|---|---|---|---|---|---|---|---|---|---|
| | | Total | 12 months or less | 13 to 23 months | 2 years | 3 to 4 years | 5 to 9 years | 10 to 14 years | 15 to 19 years | 20 years or more |
| **Both Sexes** | | | | | | | | | | |
| 16 years and over | 134 167 | 100.0 | 22.6 | 7.0 | 5.5 | 17.1 | 19.0 | 11.5 | 7.1 | 10.3 |
| 16 to 19 years | 4 432 | 100.0 | 73.7 | 11.7 | 7.5 | 7.0 | 0.1 | - | - | - |
| 20 years and over | 129 735 | 100.0 | 20.9 | 6.9 | 5.4 | 17.4 | 19.6 | 11.9 | 7.3 | 10.6 |
| 20 to 24 years | 13 396 | 100.0 | 50.8 | 14.2 | 10.8 | 19.1 | 5.0 | 0.1 | - | - |
| 25 to 34 years | 31 304 | 100.0 | 28.9 | 9.4 | 7.8 | 24.9 | 21.7 | 6.7 | 0.7 | (2) |
| 35 to 44 years | 28 272 | 100.0 | 17.1 | 6.1 | 4.8 | 18.4 | 24.4 | 16.5 | 9.4 | 3.4 |
| 45 to 54 years | 28 737 | 100.0 | 12.4 | 5.0 | 3.4 | 13.7 | 20.6 | 15.7 | 11.9 | 17.3 |
| 55 to 64 years | 21 601 | 100.0 | 10.2 | 3.5 | 2.9 | 11.7 | 18.1 | 14.4 | 11.3 | 28.0 |
| 65 years and over | 6 425 | 100.0 | 9.9 | 2.9 | 2.3 | 9.8 | 19.9 | 15.6 | 11.6 | 28.1 |
| **Men** | | | | | | | | | | |
| 16 years and over | 69 068 | 100.0 | 22.0 | 7.0 | 5.3 | 17.0 | 19.3 | 11.4 | 7.0 | 11.0 |
| 16 to 19 years | 2 113 | 100.0 | 72.7 | 13.3 | 6.4 | 7.6 | 0.1 | - | - | - |
| 20 years and over | 66 955 | 100.0 | 20.4 | 6.8 | 5.3 | 17.3 | 19.9 | 11.7 | 7.3 | 11.4 |
| 20 to 24 years | 6 754 | 100.0 | 49.7 | 14.1 | 11.8 | 18.4 | 5.9 | 0.1 | - | - |
| 25 to 34 years | 16 665 | 100.0 | 27.5 | 9.1 | 7.6 | 24.9 | 22.7 | 7.3 | 0.9 | (2) |
| 35 to 44 years | 14 922 | 100.0 | 17.1 | 5.8 | 4.5 | 18.1 | 24.8 | 16.3 | 9.6 | 3.8 |
| 45 to 54 years | 14 626 | 100.0 | 11.7 | 5.1 | 3.2 | 13.0 | 19.6 | 15.4 | 12.5 | 19.4 |
| 55 to 64 years | 10 809 | 100.0 | 10.6 | 3.5 | 2.7 | 11.7 | 17.4 | 13.7 | 10.1 | 30.3 |
| 65 years and over | 3 179 | 100.0 | 9.3 | 2.7 | 2.0 | 9.1 | 22.3 | 14.2 | 11.0 | 29.4 |
| **Women** | | | | | | | | | | |
| 16 years and over | 65 099 | 100.0 | 23.3 | 7.1 | 5.6 | 17.2 | 18.6 | 11.6 | 7.1 | 9.5 |
| 16 to 19 years | 2 319 | 100.0 | 74.6 | 10.3 | 8.6 | 6.4 | 0.1 | - | - | - |
| 20 years and over | 62 780 | 100.0 | 21.4 | 7.0 | 5.4 | 17.6 | 19.3 | 12.0 | 7.3 | 9.8 |
| 20 to 24 years | 6 642 | 100.0 | 52.0 | 14.3 | 9.7 | 19.7 | 4.2 | 0.1 | - | - |
| 25 to 34 years | 14 640 | 100.0 | 30.4 | 9.8 | 7.9 | 24.8 | 20.5 | 6.0 | 0.6 | - |
| 35 to 44 years | 13 350 | 100.0 | 17.2 | 6.4 | 5.0 | 18.8 | 23.9 | 16.6 | 9.1 | 3.0 |
| 45 to 54 years | 14 111 | 100.0 | 13.0 | 4.8 | 3.7 | 14.5 | 21.6 | 16.1 | 11.2 | 15.1 |
| 55 to 64 years | 10 791 | 100.0 | 9.8 | 3.5 | 3.1 | 11.7 | 18.8 | 15.1 | 12.4 | 25.6 |
| 65 years and over | 3 246 | 100.0 | 10.5 | 3.0 | 2.7 | 10.4 | 17.5 | 17.0 | 12.1 | 26.8 |
| **White** | | | | | | | | | | |
| 16 years and over | 105 057 | 100.0 | 21.7 | 7.0 | 5.2 | 16.9 | 19.0 | 11.7 | 7.4 | 11.1 |
| Men | 54 917 | 100.0 | 21.1 | 6.9 | 5.2 | 16.4 | 19.6 | 11.5 | 7.4 | 12.0 |
| Women | 50 140 | 100.0 | 22.4 | 7.2 | 5.3 | 17.4 | 18.4 | 12.0 | 7.4 | 10.0 |
| **Black** | | | | | | | | | | |
| 16 years and over | 16 509 | 100.0 | 25.8 | 6.7 | 6.5 | 17.8 | 18.3 | 10.3 | 6.4 | 8.2 |
| Men | 7 522 | 100.0 | 26.8 | 6.7 | 6.0 | 18.3 | 17.2 | 10.2 | 6.6 | 8.2 |
| Women | 8 987 | 100.0 | 25.0 | 6.8 | 6.8 | 17.4 | 19.3 | 10.4 | 6.2 | 8.2 |
| **Asian** | | | | | | | | | | |
| 16 years and over | 7 843 | 100.0 | 21.4 | 7.5 | 6.4 | 18.1 | 21.5 | 12.4 | 5.7 | 7.0 |
| Men | 4 170 | 100.0 | 18.9 | 8.3 | 6.7 | 19.2 | 21.2 | 13.5 | 5.5 | 6.9 |
| Women | 3 673 | 100.0 | 24.3 | 6.7 | 6.1 | 16.8 | 21.8 | 11.2 | 5.9 | 7.2 |
| **Hispanic**[1] | | | | | | | | | | |
| 16 years and over | 22 637 | 100.0 | 25.1 | 6.4 | 7.8 | 19.2 | 19.6 | 11.0 | 5.3 | 5.6 |
| Men | 12 709 | 100.0 | 24.5 | 6.1 | 7.2 | 19.1 | 20.8 | 11.4 | 5.2 | 5.7 |
| Women | 9 928 | 100.0 | 25.9 | 6.9 | 8.6 | 19.4 | 18.1 | 10.5 | 5.3 | 5.3 |

[1]May be of any race.
[2]Less than 0.05 percent.
- = Data represents or rounds to zero.

**Table 1-42.  Median Years of Tenure with Current Employer for Employed Wage and Salary Workers, 25 Years and Over, by Educational Attainment, Sex, and Age, January 2016**

(Number of years.)

| Year, sex, and age | Total employed | 25 to 34 years | 35 to 44 years | 45 to 54 years | 55 to 64 years | 65 years and over |
|---|---|---|---|---|---|---|
| **Both Sexes** | 5.1 | 2.8 | 4.9 | 7.9 | 10.1 | 10.3 |
| Less than a high school diploma | 4.7 | 2.8 | 4.3 | 5.3 | 8.3 | 10.2 |
| High school graduates, no college | 5.2 | 2.8 | 4.7 | 7.8 | 10.1 | 10.4 |
| Some college, no degree | 5.0 | 2.7 | 5.0 | 8.0 | 9.9 | 9.8 |
| Associate degree | 5.2 | 2.8 | 4.6 | 7.7 | 10.2 | 10.6 |
| College graduates | 5.2 | 2.8 | 5.2 | 8.3 | 10.4 | 10.6 |
| Bachelor's degree | 4.9 | 2.7 | 5.1 | 8.2 | 10.0 | 10.2 |
| Master's degree | 5.9 | 3.0 | 5.6 | 8.5 | 11.6 | 10.3 |
| Doctoral or professional degree | 5.6 | 2.4 | 5.2 | 9.4 | 12.8 | 15.0 |
| **Men** | 5.2 | 2.9 | 5.0 | 8.4 | 10.2 | 10.2 |
| Less than a high school diploma | 4.8 | 3.1 | 4.4 | 5.7 | 9.1 | 10.4 |
| High school graduates, no college | 5.2 | 2.9 | 4.8 | 8.9 | 10.1 | 10.1 |
| Some college, no degree | 5.1 | 2.9 | 5.3 | 8.5 | 10.2 | 9.8 |
| Associate degree | 5.6 | 3.3 | 5.7 | 8.7 | 10.2 | 10.9 |
| College graduates | 5.2 | 2.7 | 5.1 | 8.7 | 10.8 | 10.7 |
| Bachelor's degree | 5.0 | 2.8 | 5.2 | 9.2 | 10.2 | 10.4 |
| Master's degree | 5.6 | 2.9 | 5.1 | 7.9 | 12.2 | 9.6 |
| Doctoral or professional degree | 6.0 | 2.3 | 4.8 | 9.3 | 14.2 | 18.0 |
| **Women** | 5.0 | 2.6 | 4.8 | 7.5 | 10.0 | 10.4 |
| Less than a high school diploma | 4.4 | 2.4 | 4.1 | 4.6 | 7.6 | 10.0 |
| High school graduates, no college | 5.3 | 2.6 | 4.6 | 6.5 | 10.1 | 11.0 |
| Some college, no degree | 4.9 | 2.5 | 4.7 | 7.5 | 9.6 | 9.8 |
| Associate degree | 4.8 | 2.4 | 4.0 | 7.3 | 10.3 | 10.6 |
| College graduates | 5.1 | 2.8 | 5.3 | 8.1 | 10.2 | 10.5 |
| Bachelor's degree | 4.8 | 2.7 | 5.0 | 7.5 | 9.8 | 10.1 |
| Master's degree | 6.1 | 3.0 | 6.2 | 9.2 | 11.3 | 11.7 |
| Doctoral or professional degree | 5.2 | 2.5 | 5.6 | 9.5 | 12.0 | 10.3 |

**Table 1-43.  Median Years of Tenure with Current Employer for Employed Wage and Salary Workers, by Age and Sex, Selected Years, February 1998–January 2016**

(Number of years.)

| Sex and age | February 1998 | February 2000 | January 2002 | January 2004 | January 2006 | January 2008 | January 2010 | January 2012 | January 2014 | January 2016 |
|---|---|---|---|---|---|---|---|---|---|---|
| **Both Sexes** | | | | | | | | | | |
| 16 years and over | 3.6 | 3.5 | 3.7 | 4.0 | 4.0 | 4.1 | 4.4 | 4.6 | 4.6 | 4.2 |
| 16 to 17 years | 0.6 | 0.6 | 0.7 | 0.7 | 0.6 | 0.7 | 0.7 | 0.7 | 0.7 | 0.6 |
| 18 to 19 years | 0.7 | 0.7 | 0.8 | 0.8 | 0.7 | 0.8 | 1.0 | 0.8 | 0.8 | 0.8 |
| 20 to 24 years | 1.1 | 1.1 | 1.2 | 1.3 | 1.3 | 1.3 | 1.5 | 1.3 | 1.3 | 1.3 |
| 25 years and over | 4.7 | 4.7 | 4.7 | 4.9 | 4.9 | 5.1 | 5.2 | 5.4 | 5.5 | 5.1 |
| 25 to 34 years | 2.7 | 2.6 | 2.7 | 2.9 | 2.9 | 2.7 | 3.1 | 3.2 | 3.0 | 2.8 |
| 35 to 44 years | 5.0 | 4.8 | 4.6 | 4.9 | 4.9 | 4.9 | 5.1 | 5.3 | 5.2 | 4.9 |
| 45 to 54 years | 8.1 | 8.2 | 7.6 | 7.7 | 7.3 | 7.6 | 7.8 | 7.8 | 7.9 | 7.9 |
| 55 to 64 years | 10.1 | 10.0 | 9.9 | 9.6 | 9.3 | 9.9 | 10.0 | 10.3 | 10.4 | 10.1 |
| 65 years and over | 7.8 | 9.4 | 8.6 | 9.0 | 8.8 | 10.2 | 9.9 | 10.3 | 10.3 | 10.3 |
| **Men** | | | | | | | | | | |
| 16 years and over | 3.8 | 3.8 | 3.9 | 4.1 | 4.1 | 4.2 | 4.6 | 4.7 | 4.7 | 4.3 |
| 16 to 17 years | 0.6 | 0.6 | 0.8 | 0.7 | 0.7 | 0.7 | 0.7 | 0.6 | 0.7 | 0.6 |
| 18 to 19 years | 0.7 | 0.7 | 0.8 | 0.8 | 0.7 | 0.8 | 1.0 | 0.8 | 0.9 | 0.8 |
| 20 to 24 years | 1.2 | 1.2 | 1.4 | 1.3 | 1.4 | 1.4 | 1.6 | 1.4 | 1.4 | 1.3 |
| 25 years and over | 4.9 | 4.9 | 4.9 | 5.1 | 5.0 | 5.2 | 5.3 | 5.5 | 5.5 | 5.2 |
| 25 to 34 years | 2.8 | 2.7 | 2.8 | 3.0 | 2.9 | 2.8 | 3.2 | 3.2 | 3.1 | 2.9 |
| 35 to 44 years | 5.5 | 5.3 | 5.0 | 5.2 | 5.1 | 5.2 | 5.3 | 5.4 | 5.4 | 5.0 |
| 45 to 54 years | 9.4 | 9.5 | 9.1 | 9.6 | 8.1 | 8.2 | 8.5 | 8.5 | 8.2 | 8.4 |
| 55 to 64 years | 11.2 | 10.2 | 10.2 | 9.8 | 9.5 | 10.1 | 10.4 | 10.7 | 10.7 | 10.2 |
| 65 years and over | 7.1 | 9.0 | 8.1 | 8.2 | 8.3 | 10.4 | 9.7 | 10.2 | 10.0 | 10.2 |
| **Women** | | | | | | | | | | |
| 16 years and over | 3.4 | 3.3 | 3.4 | 3.8 | 3.9 | 3.9 | 4.2 | 4.6 | 4.5 | 4.0 |
| 16 to 17 years | 0.6 | 0.6 | 0.7 | 0.6 | 0.6 | 0.6 | 0.7 | 0.7 | 0.7 | 0.6 |
| 18 to 19 years | 0.7 | 0.7 | 0.8 | 0.8 | 0.7 | 0.8 | 1.0 | 0.8 | 0.8 | 0.8 |
| 20 to 24 years | 1.1 | 1.0 | 1.1 | 1.3 | 1.2 | 1.3 | 1.5 | 1.3 | 1.3 | 1.2 |
| 25 years and over | 4.4 | 4.4 | 4.4 | 4.7 | 4.8 | 4.9 | 5.1 | 5.4 | 5.4 | 5.0 |
| 25 to 34 years | 2.5 | 2.5 | 2.5 | 2.8 | 2.8 | 2.6 | 3.0 | 3.1 | 2.9 | 2.6 |
| 35 to 44 years | 4.5 | 4.3 | 4.2 | 4.5 | 4.6 | 4.7 | 4.9 | 5.2 | 5.1 | 4.8 |
| 45 to 54 years | 7.2 | 7.3 | 6.5 | 6.4 | 6.7 | 7.0 | 7.1 | 7.3 | 7.6 | 7.5 |
| 55 to 64 years | 9.6 | 9.9 | 9.6 | 9.2 | 9.2 | 9.8 | 9.7 | 10.0 | 10.2 | 10.0 |
| 65 years and over | 8.7 | 9.7 | 9.4 | 9.6 | 9.5 | 9.9 | 10.1 | 10.5 | 10.5 | 10.4 |

## Table 1-44. Median Years of Tenure with Current Employer for Employed Wage and Salary Workers, by Industry, Selected Years, February 2000–January 2016

(Number of years.)

| Industry | February 2000 | January 2002 | January 2004 | January 2006 | January 2008 | January 2010 | January 2012 | January 2014 | January 2016 |
|---|---|---|---|---|---|---|---|---|---|
| TOTAL, 16 YEARS AND OVER | 3.5 | 3.7 | 4.0 | 4.0 | 4.1 | 4.4 | 4.6 | 4.6 | 4.2 |
| **Private Sector** | 3.2 | 3.3 | 3.5 | 3.6 | 3.6 | 4.0 | 4.2 | 4.1 | 3.7 |
| Agriculture and related industries | 3.7 | 4.2 | 3.7 | 3.8 | 4.3 | 4.8 | 4.1 | 3.6 | 4.5 |
| Nonagricultural industries | 3.2 | 3.3 | 3.5 | 3.6 | 3.6 | 4.0 | 4.2 | 4.1 | 3.7 |
| Mining | 4.8 | 4.5 | 5.2 | 3.8 | 4.1 | 4.8 | 3.5 | 4.0 | 4.6 |
| Construction | 2.7 | 3.0 | 3.0 | 3.0 | 3.5 | 4.2 | 4.3 | 3.9 | 4.0 |
| Manufacturing | 4.9 | 5.4 | 5.8 | 5.5 | 5.9 | 6.1 | 6.0 | 5.9 | 5.3 |
| Durable goods manufacturing | 4.8 | 5.5 | 6.0 | 5.6 | 6.1 | 6.6 | 6.1 | 6.0 | 5.4 |
| Nonmetallic mineral product | 5.5 | 5.3 | 4.8 | 5.0 | 4.8 | 7.7 | 7.0 | 7.6 | 5.1 |
| Primary metals and fabricated metal product | 5.0 | 6.3 | 6.4 | 6.2 | 5.2 | 7.2 | 5.6 | 6.1 | 6.0 |
| Machinery manufacturing | 5.3 | 6.8 | 6.4 | 6.6 | 6.0 | 8.3 | 5.4 | 6.2 | 5.5 |
| Computers and electronic product | 3.9 | 4.7 | 5.2 | 5.9 | 6.7 | 5.9 | 7.7 | 5.1 | 5.3 |
| Electrical equipment and appliances | 5.0 | 5.5 | 9.8 | 6.2 | 6.2 | 5.0 | 5.9 | 5.8 | 4.7 |
| Transportation equipment | 6.4 | 7.0 | 7.7 | 7.2 | 7.8 | 8.3 | 7.1 | 7.1 | 6.1 |
| Wood product | 3.7 | 4.3 | 5.0 | 4.7 | 6.2 | 4.7 | 5.3 | 4.6 | 4.7 |
| Furniture and fixtures | 4.4 | 4.7 | 4.7 | 4.2 | 5.2 | 5.0 | 6.5 | 5.9 | 4.8 |
| Miscellaneous manufacturing | 3.7 | 4.5 | 4.6 | 3.9 | 4.7 | 5.4 | 4.8 | 5.1 | 5.0 |
| Nondurable goods manufacturing | 5.0 | 5.3 | 5.5 | 5.4 | 5.4 | 5.5 | 5.8 | 5.9 | 5.1 |
| Food manufacturing | 4.6 | 5.0 | 4.9 | 5.2 | 4.3 | 4.7 | 4.9 | 4.7 | 4.5 |
| Beverage and tobacco product | 5.5 | 4.6 | 8.0 | 5.4 | 6.9 | 8.1 | 6.4 | 4.8 | 4.3 |
| Textiles, apparel, and leather | 4.7 | 5.0 | 5.0 | 4.4 | 4.6 | 4.7 | 4.3 | 5.3 | 5.6 |
| Paper and printing | 5.1 | 6.2 | 6.9 | 6.3 | 5.5 | 6.8 | 9.7 | 9.7 | 5.3 |
| Petroleum and coal product | 9.5 | 9.8 | 11.4 | 5.0 | 4.3 | 5.1 | 6.4 | 6.1 | 6.6 |
| Chemicals | 6.0 | 5.7 | 5.3 | 6.1 | 7.6 | 7.3 | 6.1 | 7.1 | 5.3 |
| Plastics and rubber product | 4.6 | 5.3 | 5.7 | 5.0 | 5.3 | 7.4 | 6.1 | 6.5 | 5.3 |
| Wholesale and retail trade | 2.7 | 2.8 | 3.1 | 3.1 | 3.2 | 3.6 | 3.7 | 3.6 | 3.3 |
| Wholesale trade | 3.9 | 3.9 | 4.3 | 4.6 | 5.0 | 5.2 | 5.5 | 5.8 | 5.2 |
| Retail trade | 2.5 | 2.6 | 2.8 | 2.8 | 2.9 | 3.3 | 3.3 | 3.3 | 3.0 |
| Transportation and utilities | 4.7 | 4.9 | 5.3 | 4.9 | 5.1 | 5.3 | 5.6 | 5.1 | 4.6 |
| Transportation and warehousing | 4.0 | 4.3 | 4.7 | 4.3 | 4.6 | 5.0 | 5.3 | 4.7 | 4.4 |
| Utilities | 11.5 | 13.4 | 13.3 | 10.4 | 10.1 | 9.1 | 9.5 | 9.2 | 7.4 |
| Information[1] | 3.4 | 3.3 | 4.3 | 4.8 | 4.7 | 5.0 | 5.4 | 4.8 | 4.3 |
| Publishing, except Internet | 4.2 | 4.8 | 4.7 | 5.3 | 4.7 | 5.6 | 6.6 | 5.3 | 5.7 |
| Motion picture and sound recording industries | 1.6 | 2.3 | 2.2 | 1.9 | 1.9 | 3.8 | 2.6 | 2.4 | 2.4 |
| Broadcasting, except Internet | 3.6 | 3.1 | 4.0 | 4.6 | 3.4 | 4.3 | 4.9 | 4.1 | 3.6 |
| Telecommunications | 4.3 | 3.4 | 4.6 | 5.3 | 6.9 | 6.6 | 7.4 | 7.8 | 6.0 |
| Financial activities | 3.5 | 3.6 | 3.9 | 4.0 | 4.5 | 4.6 | 4.9 | 5.0 | 4.8 |
| Finance and insurance | 3.6 | 3.9 | 4.1 | 4.1 | 4.7 | 4.8 | 5.0 | 5.3 | 5.0 |
| Finance | 3.3 | 3.6 | 4.0 | 3.9 | 4.4 | 4.5 | 4.7 | 5.0 | 5.0 |
| Insurance | 4.4 | 4.5 | 4.4 | 4.7 | 5.2 | 5.5 | 5.7 | 6.0 | 5.2 |
| Real estate and rental and leasing | 3.1 | 3.0 | 3.3 | 3.4 | 3.7 | 3.9 | 4.5 | 4.4 | 3.8 |
| Real estate | 3.1 | 3.2 | 3.5 | 3.5 | 3.9 | 4.1 | 4.5 | 4.6 | 3.9 |
| Rental and leasing services | 3.0 | 2.2 | 2.9 | 3.1 | 3.0 | 3.3 | 4.2 | 3.5 | 3.4 |
| Professional and business services | 2.4 | 2.7 | 3.2 | 3.2 | 3.1 | 3.4 | 3.8 | 3.6 | 3.4 |
| Professional and technical services | 2.6 | 3.1 | 3.6 | 3.8 | 3.3 | 4.0 | 4.4 | 4.2 | 3.9 |
| Management, administrative, and waste services[1] | 2.0 | 2.1 | 2.6 | 2.5 | 2.5 | 2.9 | 3.1 | 3.1 | 2.8 |
| Administrative and support services | 1.8 | 1.9 | 2.4 | 2.4 | 2.4 | 2.8 | 3.0 | 3.0 | 2.6 |
| Waste management and remediation services | 3.6 | 4.3 | 3.4 | 4.1 | 4.1 | 2.9 | 4.4 | 4.7 | 4.6 |
| Education and health services | 3.4 | 3.5 | 3.6 | 4.0 | 4.1 | 4.1 | 4.4 | 4.5 | 3.9 |
| Education services | 3.2 | 3.6 | 3.8 | 4.0 | 4.3 | 4.4 | 4.3 | 4.8 | 4.0 |
| Health care and social assistance | 3.5 | 3.5 | 3.6 | 4.1 | 4.1 | 4.1 | 4.4 | 4.4 | 3.9 |
| Hospitals | 5.1 | 4.9 | 4.7 | 5.2 | 5.4 | 5.3 | 6.0 | 5.7 | 5.6 |
| Health services, except hospitals | 3.2 | 3.1 | 3.3 | 3.6 | 3.6 | 3.6 | 3.8 | 3.9 | 3.4 |
| Social assistance | 2.4 | 2.5 | 2.8 | 3.1 | 3.0 | 3.1 | 3.1 | 3.2 | 2.6 |
| Leisure and hospitality | 1.7 | 1.8 | 2.0 | 1.9 | 2.1 | 2.5 | 2.4 | 2.3 | 2.2 |
| Arts, entertainment, and recreation | 2.6 | 2.3 | 2.8 | 3.1 | 2.8 | 3.3 | 3.1 | 3.0 | 3.2 |
| Accommodation and food services | 1.5 | 1.6 | 1.9 | 1.6 | 1.9 | 2.3 | 2.3 | 2.1 | 2.0 |
| Accommodation | 2.8 | 2.7 | 3.1 | 2.5 | 3.1 | 3.3 | 3.8 | 3.5 | 3.0 |
| Food services and drinking places | 1.4 | 1.4 | 1.6 | 1.4 | 1.6 | 2.2 | 2.1 | 2.0 | 1.8 |
| Other services | 3.1 | 3.3 | 3.3 | 3.2 | 3.3 | 4.0 | 3.8 | 4.0 | 3.9 |
| Other services, except private households | 3.2 | 3.3 | 3.5 | 3.3 | 3.4 | 4.1 | 3.8 | 4.2 | 4.1 |
| Repair and maintenance | 3.0 | 3.0 | 3.2 | 2.9 | 3.0 | 4.0 | 3.7 | 4.0 | 3.5 |
| Personal and laundry services | 2.7 | 2.8 | 3.4 | 2.8 | 3.2 | 3.5 | 3.5 | 3.7 | 3.8 |
| Membership associations and organizations | 4.0 | 4.1 | 3.9 | 4.2 | 4.4 | 4.5 | 4.3 | 4.9 | 4.9 |
| Other services, private households | 3.0 | 2.7 | 2.3 | 2.8 | 2.8 | 3.4 | 3.3 | 3.0 | 3.3 |
| **Public Sector** | 7.1 | 6.7 | 6.9 | 6.9 | 7.2 | 7.2 | 7.8 | 7.8 | 7.7 |
| Federal government | 11.5 | 11.3 | 10.4 | 9.9 | 9.9 | 7.9 | 9.5 | 8.5 | 8.8 |
| State government | 5.5 | 5.4 | 6.4 | 6.3 | 6.5 | 6.4 | 6.4 | 7.4 | 5.8 |
| Local government | 6.7 | 6.2 | 6.4 | 6.6 | 7.1 | 7.5 | 8.1 | 7.9 | 8.3 |

[1]Includes other industries not shown separately.

## Table 1-45.  Employment Status of the Population, by Sex and Marital Status, March 1995–March 2016

(Thousands of people, percent.)

| Marital status and year | Men | | | | | | Women | | | | | |
|---|---|---|---|---|---|---|---|---|---|---|---|---|
| | | Labor force | | | | | | Labor force | | | | |
| | | Total | | Employed | Unemployed | | | Total | | Employed | Unemployed | |
| | Population | Number | Percent of population | | Number | Percent of labor force | Population | Number | Percent of population | | Number | Percent of labor force |
| **Single** | | | | | | | | | | | | |
| 1995 | 28 318 | 20 449 | 72.2 | 18 286 | 2 163 | 10.6 | 22 853 | 14 974 | 65.5 | 13 673 | 1 301 | 8.7 |
| 1996 | 28 695 | 20 561 | 71.7 | 18 097 | 2 464 | 12.0 | 23 632 | 15 417 | 65.2 | 14 084 | 1 333 | 8.6 |
| 1997 | 29 294 | 20 942 | 71.5 | 18 683 | 2 259 | 10.8 | 24 215 | 16 178 | 66.8 | 14 747 | 1 431 | 8.8 |
| 1998 | 29 558 | 21 255 | 71.9 | 19 124 | 2 131 | 10.0 | 24 808 | 16 885 | 68.1 | 15 626 | 1 259 | 7.5 |
| 1999 | 29 883 | 21 329 | 71.4 | 19 465 | 1 864 | 8.7 | 25 674 | 17 486 | 68.1 | 16 185 | 1 301 | 7.4 |
| 2000 | 30 232 | 21 641 | 71.6 | 19 823 | 1 818 | 8.4 | 25 863 | 17 749 | 68.6 | 16 446 | 1 303 | 7.3 |
| 2001 | 30 968 | 22 232 | 71.8 | 20 239 | 1 993 | 9.0 | 26 180 | 17 900 | 68.4 | 16 631 | 1 269 | 7.1 |
| 2002 | 32 220 | 22 761 | 70.6 | 20 066 | 2 695 | 11.8 | 26 942 | 18 079 | 67.1 | 16 499 | 1 580 | 8.7 |
| 2003 | 32 852 | 22 821 | 69.5 | 20 194 | 2 627 | 11.5 | 27 527 | 17 901 | 65.0 | 16 219 | 1 682 | 9.4 |
| 2004 | 33 786 | 23 212 | 68.7 | 20 434 | 2 778 | 12.0 | 28 033 | 18 089 | 64.5 | 16 506 | 1 583 | 8.8 |
| 2005 | 34 069 | 23 335 | 68.5 | 20 831 | 2 504 | 10.7 | 28 508 | 18 554 | 65.1 | 16 902 | 1 652 | 8.9 |
| 2006 | 34 906 | 24 369 | 69.8 | 21 961 | 2 408 | 9.9 | 29 357 | 18 989 | 64.7 | 17 444 | 1 545 | 8.1 |
| 2007 | 35 359 | 24 506 | 69.3 | 22 224 | 2 281 | 9.3 | 29 695 | 19 218 | 64.7 | 17 935 | 1 284 | 6.7 |
| 2008 | 36 522 | 25 229 | 69.1 | 22 695 | 2 534 | 10.0 | 30 772 | 19 889 | 64.6 | 18 369 | 1 520 | 7.6 |
| 2009 | 36 907 | 24 930 | 67.5 | 20 645 | 4 284 | 17.2 | 31 038 | 19 785 | 63.7 | 17 714 | 2 071 | 10.5 |
| 2010 | 38 110 | 25 663 | 67.3 | 21 038 | 4 626 | 18.0 | 32 085 | 19 973 | 62.3 | 17 517 | 2 457 | 12.3 |
| 2011 | 38 766 | 25 646 | 66.2 | 21 389 | 4 256 | 16.6 | 33 041 | 20 581 | 62.3 | 18 117 | 2 463 | 12.0 |
| 2012 | 38 933 | 25 615 | 65.8 | 21 838 | 3 778 | 14.7 | 34 241 | 21 417 | 62.5 | 18 895 | 2 523 | 11.8 |
| 2013 | 39 482 | 25 881 | 65.6 | 22 306 | 3 575 | 13.8 | 34 889 | 21 739 | 62.3 | 19 319 | 2 419 | 11.1 |
| 2014 | 40 338 | 26 602 | 65.9 | 23 220 | 3 382 | 12.7 | 35 288 | 22 174 | 62.8 | 19 974 | 2 200 | 9.9 |
| 2015 | 40 893 | 26 949 | 65.9 | 24 094 | 2 855 | 10.6 | 36 036 | 22 385 | 62.1 | 20 530 | 1 855 | 8.3 |
| 2016 | 41 933 | 27 894 | 66.5 | 25 275 | 2 619 | 9.4 | 37 035 | 23 216 | 62.7 | 21 359 | 1 856 | 8.0 |
| **Married, Spouse Present** | | | | | | | | | | | | |
| 1995 | 54 166 | 41 806 | 77.2 | 40 262 | 1 544 | 3.7 | 54 902 | 33 563 | 61.1 | 32 267 | 1 296 | 3.9 |
| 1996 | 53 996 | 41 837 | 77.5 | 40 356 | 1 481 | 3.5 | 54 640 | 33 382 | 61.1 | 32 258 | 1 124 | 3.4 |
| 1997 | 53 981 | 41 967 | 77.7 | 40 628 | 1 339 | 3.2 | 54 611 | 33 907 | 62.1 | 32 836 | 1 071 | 3.2 |
| 1998 | 54 685 | 42 288 | 77.3 | 41 039 | 1 249 | 3.0 | 55 241 | 34 136 | 61.8 | 33 028 | 1 108 | 3.2 |
| 1999 | 55 256 | 42 557 | 77.0 | 41 476 | 1 081 | 2.5 | 55 801 | 34 349 | 61.6 | 33 403 | 946 | 2.8 |
| 2000 | 55 897 | 43 254 | 77.4 | 42 261 | 993 | 2.3 | 56 432 | 34 959 | 61.9 | 33 998 | 961 | 2.7 |
| 2001 | 56 152 | 43 463 | 77.4 | 42 245 | 1 218 | 2.8 | 56 740 | 35 234 | 62.1 | 34 273 | 961 | 2.7 |
| 2002 | 57 325 | 44 271 | 77.2 | 42 508 | 1 763 | 4.0 | 57 883 | 35 624 | 61.5 | 34 295 | 1 329 | 3.7 |
| 2003 | 57 940 | 44 700 | 77.1 | 42 797 | 1 903 | 4.3 | 58 545 | 36 185 | 61.8 | 34 806 | 1 379 | 3.8 |
| 2004 | 58 395 | 44 860 | 76.8 | 43 247 | 1 613 | 3.6 | 59 008 | 35 918 | 60.9 | 34 582 | 1 336 | 3.7 |
| 2005 | 58 854 | 45 263 | 76.9 | 43 763 | 1 500 | 3.3 | 59 449 | 35 809 | 60.2 | 34 738 | 1 071 | 3.0 |
| 2006 | 58 850 | 45 082 | 76.6 | 43 877 | 1 205 | 2.7 | 59 476 | 36 192 | 60.9 | 35 185 | 1 007 | 2.8 |
| 2007 | 60 126 | 46 129 | 76.7 | 44 813 | 1 317 | 2.9 | 60 656 | 37 335 | 61.6 | 36 370 | 965 | 2.6 |
| 2008 | 59 455 | 45 451 | 76.4 | 43 958 | 1 493 | 3.3 | 60 108 | 37 074 | 61.7 | 35 919 | 1 155 | 3.1 |
| 2009 | 60 132 | 45 741 | 76.1 | 42 667 | 3 074 | 6.7 | 60 818 | 37 536 | 61.7 | 35 540 | 1 996 | 5.3 |
| 2010 | 59 694 | 45 110 | 75.6 | 41 762 | 3 348 | 7.4 | 60 339 | 37 201 | 61.7 | 34 964 | 2 237 | 6.0 |
| 2011 | 59 477 | 44 553 | 74.9 | 41 667 | 2 886 | 6.5 | 60 095 | 36 383 | 60.5 | 34 340 | 2 043 | 5.6 |
| 2012 | 60 346 | 44 915 | 74.4 | 42 387 | 2 528 | 5.6 | 61 011 | 36 363 | 59.6 | 34 423 | 1 940 | 5.3 |
| 2013 | 60 630 | 44 904 | 74.1 | 42 760 | 2 145 | 4.8 | 61 269 | 36 292 | 59.2 | 34 601 | 1 691 | 4.7 |
| 2014 | 61 224 | 44 874 | 73.3 | 43 091 | 1 784 | 4.0 | 61 917 | 36 257 | 58.6 | 34 759 | 1 499 | 4.1 |
| 2015 | 61 568 | 45 185 | 73.4 | 43 783 | 1 403 | 3.1 | 62 171 | 36 388 | 58.5 | 35 314 | 1 074 | 3.0 |
| 2016 | 61 973 | 45 348 | 73.2 | 44 021 | 1 327 | 2.9 | 62 577 | 36 858 | 58.9 | 35 731 | 1 127 | 3.1 |
| **Widowed, Divorced, or Separated** | | | | | | | | | | | | |
| 1995 | 12 410 | 8 315 | 67.0 | 7 632 | 683 | 8.2 | 25 373 | 12 001 | 47.3 | 11 308 | 693 | 5.8 |
| 1996 | 13 176 | 8 697 | 66.0 | 7 976 | 721 | 8.3 | 25 786 | 12 430 | 48.2 | 11 742 | 688 | 5.5 |
| 1997 | 14 113 | 9 420 | 66.7 | 8 715 | 705 | 7.5 | 26 301 | 12 814 | 48.7 | 12 071 | 743 | 5.8 |
| 1998 | 14 166 | 9 482 | 66.9 | 8 954 | 528 | 5.6 | 26 092 | 12 880 | 49.4 | 12 235 | 645 | 5.0 |
| 1999 | 14 225 | 9 449 | 66.4 | 8 971 | 478 | 5.1 | 26 199 | 12 951 | 49.4 | 12 307 | 644 | 5.0 |
| 2000 | 14 289 | 9 623 | 67.3 | 9 152 | 471 | 4.9 | 26 354 | 13 228 | 50.2 | 12 657 | 571 | 4.3 |
| 2001 | 14 392 | 9 421 | 65.5 | 8 927 | 494 | 5.2 | 26 747 | 13 454 | 50.3 | 12 887 | 567 | 4.2 |
| 2002 | 14 617 | 9 650 | 66.0 | 8 931 | 719 | 7.5 | 27 802 | 13 716 | 49.3 | 12 855 | 861 | 6.3 |
| 2003 | 15 180 | 9 855 | 64.9 | 9 020 | 835 | 8.5 | 28 240 | 14 154 | 50.1 | 13 240 | 914 | 6.5 |
| 2004 | 15 059 | 9 789 | 65.0 | 9 059 | 730 | 7.5 | 28 228 | 14 194 | 50.3 | 13 324 | 870 | 6.1 |
| 2005 | 15 779 | 10 256 | 65.0 | 9 569 | 687 | 6.7 | 28 576 | 14 233 | 49.8 | 13 472 | 761 | 5.3 |
| 2006 | 16 405 | 10 815 | 65.9 | 10 141 | 674 | 6.2 | 28 981 | 14 220 | 49.1 | 13 539 | 681 | 4.8 |
| 2007 | 16 247 | 10 799 | 66.5 | 10 150 | 650 | 6.0 | 28 950 | 14 320 | 49.5 | 13 620 | 700 | 4.9 |
| 2008 | 16 718 | 10 896 | 65.2 | 10 083 | 812 | 7.5 | 29 419 | 14 553 | 49.5 | 13 765 | 787 | 5.4 |
| 2009 | 16 719 | 10 687 | 63.9 | 9 224 | 1 463 | 13.7 | 29 471 | 14 449 | 49.0 | 13 169 | 1 281 | 8.9 |
| 2010 | 17 016 | 10 863 | 63.8 | 9 188 | 1 675 | 15.4 | 29 915 | 14 707 | 49.2 | 13 285 | 1 422 | 9.7 |
| 2011 | 17 744 | 11 095 | 62.5 | 9 676 | 1 420 | 12.8 | 29 876 | 14 610 | 48.9 | 13 221 | 1 389 | 9.5 |
| 2012 | 17 704 | 11 076 | 62.6 | 9 884 | 1 192 | 10.8 | 30 367 | 14 825 | 48.8 | 13 543 | 1 283 | 8.7 |
| 2013 | 18 090 | 11 045 | 61.1 | 9 968 | 1 077 | 10.8 | 30 633 | 14 688 | 47.9 | 13 494 | 1 193 | 8.1 |
| 2014 | 17 833 | 10 681 | 59.9 | 9 842 | 839 | 7.9 | 30 657 | 14 853 | 48.4 | 13 789 | 1 064 | 7.2 |
| 2015 | 18 277 | 10 973 | 60.0 | 10 110 | 864 | 7.9 | 31 135 | 14 607 | 46.9 | 13 792 | 815 | 5.6 |
| 2016 | 18 205 | 10 901 | 59.9 | 10 210 | 691 | 6.3 | 31 044 | 14 659 | 47.2 | 13 966 | 693 | 4.7 |

*Note:* See notes and definitions for information on historical comparability.

## Table 1-45. Employment Status of the Population, by Sex and Marital Status, March 1995–March 2016
### —Continued

(Thousands of people, percent.)

| Marital status and year | Men | | | | | | Women | | | | | |
|---|---|---|---|---|---|---|---|---|---|---|---|---|
| | Population | Labor force | | | | | Population | Labor force | | | | |
| | | Total | | Employed | Unemployed | | | Total | | Employed | Unemployed | |
| | | Number | Percent of population | | Number | Percent of labor force | | | Number | Percent of population | | Number | Percent of labor force |
| **Widowed** | | | | | | | | | | | | |
| 1995 | 2 282 | 496 | 21.7 | 469 | 27 | 5.4 | 11 080 | 1 941 | 17.5 | 1 844 | 97 | 5.0 |
| 1996 | 2 476 | 487 | 19.7 | 466 | 21 | 4.3 | 11 070 | 1 916 | 17.3 | 1 820 | 96 | 5.0 |
| 1997 | 2 686 | 559 | 20.8 | 529 | 30 | 5.4 | 11 058 | 2 018 | 18.2 | 1 926 | 92 | 4.6 |
| 1998 | 2 567 | 563 | 21.9 | 551 | 12 | 2.1 | 11 027 | 2 157 | 19.6 | 2 071 | 86 | 4.0 |
| 1999 | 2 540 | 562 | 22.1 | 532 | 30 | 5.3 | 10 943 | 2 039 | 18.6 | 1 942 | 97 | 4.8 |
| 2000 | 2 601 | 583 | 22.4 | 547 | 36 | 6.2 | 11 061 | 2 011 | 18.2 | 1 911 | 100 | 5.0 |
| 2001 | 2 638 | 568 | 21.5 | 546 | 22 | 3.9 | 11 182 | 2 137 | 19.1 | 2 045 | 92 | 4.3 |
| 2002 | 2 635 | 629 | 23.9 | 581 | 48 | 7.6 | 11 411 | 2 001 | 17.5 | 1 887 | 114 | 5.7 |
| 2003 | 2 694 | 628 | 23.3 | 588 | 40 | 6.4 | 11 295 | 2 087 | 18.5 | 1 991 | 96 | 4.6 |
| 2004 | 2 651 | 581 | 21.9 | 558 | 23 | 4.0 | 11 159 | 2 157 | 19.3 | 2 048 | 109 | 5.1 |
| 2005 | 2 729 | 618 | 22.6 | 590 | 28 | 4.5 | 11 125 | 2 111 | 19.0 | 2 005 | 106 | 5.0 |
| 2006 | 2 626 | 610 | 23.2 | 563 | 47 | 7.7 | 11 305 | 2 164 | 19.1 | 2 094 | 70 | 3.2 |
| 2007 | 2 697 | 631 | 23.4 | 588 | 43 | 6.8 | 11 220 | 2 058 | 18.3 | 1 971 | 87 | 4.2 |
| 2008 | 2 911 | 656 | 22.5 | 611 | 44 | 6.8 | 11 399 | 2 218 | 19.5 | 2 101 | 117 | 5.3 |
| 2009 | 2 813 | 632 | 22.5 | 543 | 90 | 14.2 | 11 446 | 2 174 | 19.0 | 2 032 | 143 | 6.6 |
| 2010 | 2 969 | 776 | 26.1 | 684 | 92 | 11.8 | 11 379 | 2 214 | 19.5 | 2 036 | 178 | 8.0 |
| 2011 | 2 931 | 698 | 23.8 | 648 | 50 | 7.1 | 11 310 | 2 291 | 20.3 | 2 118 | 173 | 7.6 |
| 2012 | 2 864 | 639 | 22.3 | 595 | 43 | 6.8 | 11 197 | 2 179 | 19.5 | 2 044 | 135 | 6.2 |
| 2013 | 3 122 | 686 | 22.0 | 631 | 55 | 8.1 | 11 234 | 2 132 | 19.0 | 1 987 | 145 | 6.8 |
| 2014 | 3 068 | 722 | 23.5 | 668 | 54 | 7.5 | 11 132 | 2 079 | 18.7 | 1 922 | 157 | 7.6 |
| 2015 | 3 271 | 782 | 23.9 | 746 | 36 | 4.6 | 11 333 | 2 153 | 19.0 | 2 035 | 119 | 5.5 |
| 2016 | 3 471 | 904 | 26.1 | 862 | 42 | 4.7 | 11 423 | 2 224 | 19.5 | 2 139 | 85 | 3.8 |
| **Divorced** | | | | | | | | | | | | |
| 1995 | 7 343 | 5 739 | 78.2 | 5 266 | 473 | 8.2 | 10 262 | 7 559 | 73.7 | 7 206 | 353 | 4.7 |
| 1996 | 7 734 | 5 954 | 77.0 | 5 468 | 486 | 8.2 | 10 508 | 7 829 | 74.5 | 7 468 | 361 | 4.6 |
| 1997 | 8 191 | 6 298 | 76.9 | 5 851 | 447 | 7.1 | 11 102 | 8 092 | 72.9 | 7 666 | 426 | 5.3 |
| 1998 | 8 307 | 6 378 | 76.8 | 6 045 | 333 | 5.2 | 11 065 | 8 038 | 72.6 | 7 687 | 351 | 4.4 |
| 1999 | 8 529 | 6 481 | 76.0 | 6 151 | 330 | 5.1 | 11 130 | 8 171 | 73.4 | 7 841 | 330 | 4.0 |
| 2000 | 8 532 | 6 583 | 77.2 | 6 279 | 304 | 4.6 | 11 061 | 8 505 | 76.9 | 8 217 | 288 | 3.4 |
| 2001 | 8 580 | 6 403 | 74.6 | 6 074 | 329 | 5.1 | 11 719 | 8 662 | 73.9 | 8 335 | 327 | 3.8 |
| 2002 | 8 643 | 6 519 | 75.4 | 6 053 | 466 | 7.1 | 12 227 | 8 902 | 72.8 | 8 416 | 486 | 5.5 |
| 2003 | 8 938 | 6 621 | 74.1 | 6 052 | 569 | 8.6 | 12 653 | 9 191 | 72.6 | 8 673 | 518 | 5.6 |
| 2004 | 8 942 | 6 622 | 74.1 | 6 104 | 518 | 7.8 | 12 817 | 9 246 | 72.1 | 8 706 | 540 | 5.8 |
| 2005 | 9 196 | 6 754 | 73.4 | 6 281 | 473 | 7.0 | 12 950 | 9 253 | 71.5 | 8 836 | 417 | 4.5 |
| 2006 | 9 646 | 7 065 | 73.2 | 6 631 | 434 | 6.1 | 13 107 | 9 188 | 70.1 | 8 799 | 389 | 4.2 |
| 2007 | 9 608 | 7 110 | 74.0 | 6 679 | 431 | 6.1 | 13 214 | 9 334 | 70.6 | 8 896 | 439 | 4.7 |
| 2008 | 9 767 | 7 106 | 72.8 | 6 607 | 499 | 7.0 | 13 551 | 9 387 | 69.3 | 8 938 | 449 | 4.8 |
| 2009 | 9 938 | 7 052 | 71.0 | 6 064 | 988 | 14.0 | 13 301 | 9 176 | 69.0 | 8 402 | 774 | 8.4 |
| 2010 | 9 944 | 7 018 | 70.6 | 5 888 | 1 131 | 16.1 | 13 758 | 9 394 | 68.3 | 8 510 | 885 | 9.4 |
| 2011 | 10 635 | 7 394 | 69.5 | 6 430 | 965 | 13.0 | 13 757 | 9 230 | 67.1 | 8 407 | 823 | 8.9 |
| 2012 | 10 662 | 7 394 | 69.3 | 6 572 | 822 | 11.1 | 14 210 | 9 416 | 66.3 | 8 620 | 797 | 8.5 |
| 2013 | 10 923 | 7 420 | 67.9 | 6 718 | 702 | 9.5 | 14 428 | 9 416 | 65.3 | 8 704 | 713 | 7.6 |
| 2014 | 10 630 | 7 044 | 66.3 | 6 456 | 588 | 8.3 | 14 633 | 9 615 | 65.7 | 9 020 | 596 | 6.2 |
| 2015 | 10 928 | 7 197 | 65.9 | 6 598 | 600 | 8.3 | 14 855 | 9 365 | 63.0 | 8 901 | 464 | 5.0 |
| 2016 | 10 689 | 7 117 | 66.6 | 6 671 | 446 | 6.3 | 14 835 | 9 358 | 63.1 | 8 923 | 435 | 4.7 |
| **Separated** | | | | | | | | | | | | |
| 1995 | 2 784 | 2 081 | 74.7 | 1 898 | 183 | 8.8 | 4 031 | 2 501 | 62.0 | 2 258 | 243 | 9.7 |
| 1996 | 2 966 | 2 255 | 76.0 | 2 041 | 214 | 9.5 | 4 209 | 2 684 | 63.8 | 2 453 | 231 | 8.6 |
| 1997 | 3 236 | 2 563 | 79.2 | 2 335 | 228 | 8.9 | 4 141 | 2 705 | 65.3 | 2 480 | 225 | 8.3 |
| 1998 | 3 293 | 2 542 | 77.2 | 2 358 | 184 | 7.2 | 4 000 | 2 683 | 67.1 | 2 476 | 207 | 7.7 |
| 1999 | 3 156 | 2 405 | 76.2 | 2 287 | 118 | 4.9 | 4 126 | 2 740 | 66.4 | 2 523 | 217 | 7.9 |
| 2000 | 3 157 | 2 456 | 77.8 | 2 326 | 130 | 5.3 | 4 012 | 2 711 | 67.6 | 2 528 | 183 | 6.8 |
| 2001 | 3 174 | 2 450 | 77.2 | 2 307 | 143 | 5.8 | 3 846 | 2 654 | 69.0 | 2 507 | 147 | 5.5 |
| 2002 | 3 339 | 2 502 | 74.9 | 2 297 | 205 | 8.2 | 4 164 | 2 812 | 67.5 | 2 551 | 261 | 9.3 |
| 2003 | 3 548 | 2 606 | 73.4 | 2 380 | 226 | 8.7 | 4 293 | 2 877 | 67.0 | 2 576 | 301 | 10.5 |
| 2004 | 3 466 | 2 586 | 74.6 | 2 397 | 189 | 7.3 | 4 251 | 2 791 | 65.7 | 2 569 | 222 | 8.0 |
| 2005 | 3 855 | 2 884 | 74.8 | 2 698 | 186 | 6.4 | 4 501 | 2 870 | 63.8 | 2 632 | 238 | 8.3 |
| 2006 | 4 132 | 3 141 | 76.0 | 2 947 | 194 | 6.2 | 4 569 | 2 869 | 62.8 | 2 647 | 222 | 7.7 |
| 2007 | 3 943 | 3 058 | 77.6 | 2 883 | 176 | 5.7 | 4 516 | 2 927 | 64.8 | 2 753 | 174 | 6.0 |
| 2008 | 4 040 | 3 134 | 77.6 | 2 865 | 269 | 8.6 | 4 469 | 2 947 | 65.9 | 2 726 | 221 | 7.5 |
| 2009 | 3 968 | 3 002 | 75.7 | 2 617 | 386 | 12.8 | 4 725 | 3 099 | 65.6 | 2 734 | 364 | 11.8 |
| 2010 | 4 103 | 3 069 | 74.8 | 2 616 | 452 | 14.7 | 4 778 | 3 099 | 64.8 | 2 739 | 359 | 11.6 |
| 2011 | 4 178 | 3 004 | 71.9 | 2 598 | 406 | 13.5 | 4 809 | 3 089 | 64.2 | 2 696 | 393 | 12.7 |
| 2012 | 4 177 | 3 044 | 72.9 | 2 717 | 327 | 10.7 | 4 960 | 3 230 | 65.1 | 2 879 | 351 | 10.9 |
| 2013 | 4 045 | 2 939 | 72.7 | 2 619 | 320 | 10.9 | 4 970 | 3 139 | 63.2 | 2 803 | 336 | 10.7 |
| 2014 | 4 134 | 2 915 | 70.5 | 2 718 | 197 | 6.8 | 4 892 | 3 159 | 64.6 | 2 848 | 311 | 9.9 |
| 2015 | 4 078 | 2 994 | 73.4 | 2 766 | 228 | 7.6 | 4 946 | 3 089 | 62.5 | 2 856 | 233 | 7.5 |
| 2016 | 4 045 | 2 879 | 71.2 | 2 677 | 202 | 7.0 | 4 786 | 3 077 | 64.3 | 2 905 | 172 | 5.6 |

Note: See notes and definitions for information on historical comparability.

## Table 1-46.  Employment Status of All Women and Single Women, by Presence and Age of Children, March 1995–March 2016

(Thousands of women, percent.)

| Presence and age of children and year | All women | | | | | | | Single women | | | | | | |
|---|---|---|---|---|---|---|---|---|---|---|---|---|---|---|
| | Civilian labor force | Civilian labor force as percent of population | Employed | | | Unemployed | | Civilian labor force | Civilian labor force as percent of population | Employed | | | Unemployed | |
| | | | Number | Percent full time | Percent part time | Number | Percent of labor force | | | Number | Percent full time | Percent part time | Number | Percent of labor force |
| **Women with No Children Under 18 Years** | | | | | | | | | | | | | | |
| 1995 | 35 843 | 52.9 | 34 054 | 72.9 | 27.1 | 1 789 | 5.0 | 12 870 | 67.1 | 11 919 | 64.5 | 35.5 | 951 | 7.4 |
| 1996 | 36 509 | 53.0 | 34 698 | 73.3 | 26.7 | 1 811 | 5.0 | 13 172 | 66.1 | 12 255 | 64.6 | 35.4 | 918 | 7.0 |
| 1997 | 37 295 | 53.6 | 35 572 | 73.7 | 26.3 | 1 723 | 4.6 | 13 405 | 66.5 | 12 442 | 64.0 | 36.0 | 964 | 7.2 |
| 1998 | 38 253 | 54.1 | 36 680 | 74.1 | 25.9 | 1 573 | 4.1 | 13 888 | 67.2 | 13 082 | 64.8 | 35.2 | 806 | 5.8 |
| 1999 | 39 316 | 54.3 | 37 589 | 74.6 | 25.4 | 1 727 | 4.4 | 14 435 | 67.1 | 13 491 | 65.6 | 34.4 | 944 | 6.5 |
| 2000 | 40 142 | 54.8 | 38 408 | 75.4 | 24.6 | 1 733 | 4.3 | 14 677 | 67.6 | 13 713 | 66.6 | 33.4 | 964 | 6.6 |
| 2001 | 40 836 | 54.9 | 39 219 | 75.7 | 24.3 | 1 617 | 4.0 | 14 877 | 67.4 | 13 993 | 67.3 | 32.7 | 884 | 5.9 |
| 2002 | 41 278 | 54.0 | 39 038 | 75.1 | 24.9 | 2 241 | 5.4 | 14 855 | 65.6 | 13 682 | 65.9 | 34.1 | 1 173 | 7.9 |
| 2003 | 42 039 | 54.1 | 39 667 | 74.8 | 25.2 | 2 372 | 5.6 | 14 678 | 63.5 | 13 430 | 65.1 | 34.9 | 1 249 | 8.5 |
| 2004 | 42 289 | 53.8 | 40 000 | 74.6 | 25.4 | 2 289 | 5.4 | 14 828 | 63.0 | 13 670 | 65.5 | 34.5 | 1 157 | 7.8 |
| 2005 | 42 039 | 54.1 | 39 667 | 74.8 | 25.2 | 2 372 | 5.6 | 14 678 | 63.5 | 13 430 | 65.1 | 34.9 | 1 249 | 8.5 |
| 2006 | 43 392 | 53.6 | 41 440 | 75.3 | 24.7 | 1 952 | 4.5 | 15 673 | 63.4 | 14 547 | 66.5 | 33.5 | 1 125 | 7.2 |
| 2007 | 44 039 | 53.9 | 42 279 | 75.3 | 24.7 | 1 760 | 4.0 | 15 704 | 63.4 | 14 801 | 66.4 | 33.6 | 903 | 5.7 |
| 2008 | 45 585 | 54.3 | 43 417 | 75.7 | 24.3 | 2 168 | 4.8 | 16 378 | 63.4 | 15 261 | 67.4 | 32.6 | 1 116 | 6.8 |
| 2009 | 45 649 | 53.8 | 42 343 | 73.3 | 26.7 | 3 306 | 7.2 | 16 112 | 62.1 | 14 607 | 64.9 | 35.1 | 1 506 | 9.3 |
| 2010 | 46 098 | 53.5 | 42 256 | 73.5 | 26.5 | 3 842 | 8.3 | 16 331 | 60.7 | 14 533 | 65.6 | 34.4 | 1 798 | 11.0 |
| 2011 | 46 198 | 53.0 | 42 569 | 73.3 | 26.7 | 3 629 | 7.9 | 16 758 | 60.8 | 15 016 | 65.2 | 34.8 | 1 743 | 10.4 |
| 2012 | 47 222 | 52.6 | 43 494 | 74.0 | 26.0 | 3 728 | 7.9 | 17 310 | 60.7 | 15 473 | 66.3 | 33.7 | 1 837 | 10.6 |
| 2013 | 47 607 | 52.3 | 44 294 | 73.6 | 26.4 | 3 313 | 7.0 | 17 650 | 60.5 | 15 915 | 65.5 | 34.5 | 1 735 | 9.8 |
| 2014 | 48 076 | 52.1 | 44 980 | 73.3 | 26.7 | 3 096 | 6.4 | 18 168 | 61.2 | 16 552 | 65.1 | 34.9 | 1 616 | 8.9 |
| 2015 | 48 273 | 51.7 | 45 794 | 74.4 | 25.6 | 2 479 | 5.1 | 18 199 | 60.2 | 16 873 | 67.9 | 32.1 | 1 326 | 7.3 |
| 2016 | 49 663 | 52.1 | 47 180 | 74.5 | 25.5 | 2 484 | 5.0 | 19 130 | 60.9 | 17 699 | 68.0 | 32.0 | 1 430 | 7.5 |
| **Women with Children Under 18 Years** | | | | | | | | | | | | | | |
| 1995 | 24 695 | 69.7 | 23 195 | 71.7 | 28.3 | 1 500 | 6.1 | 2 104 | 57.5 | 1 754 | 73.6 | 26.4 | 350 | 16.6 |
| 1996 | 24 720 | 70.2 | 23 386 | 72.6 | 27.4 | 1 334 | 5.4 | 2 245 | 60.5 | 1 829 | 73.5 | 26.5 | 416 | 18.5 |
| 1997 | 25 604 | 72.1 | 24 082 | 74.1 | 25.9 | 1 522 | 5.9 | 2 772 | 68.1 | 2 305 | 76.6 | 23.4 | 467 | 16.8 |
| 1998 | 25 647 | 72.3 | 24 209 | 74.0 | 26.0 | 1 438 | 5.6 | 2 997 | 72.5 | 2 544 | 75.6 | 24.4 | 453 | 15.1 |
| 1999 | 25 469 | 72.1 | 24 305 | 74.1 | 25.9 | 1 165 | 4.6 | 3 051 | 73.4 | 2 694 | 75.8 | 24.2 | 357 | 11.7 |
| 2000 | 25 795 | 72.9 | 24 693 | 74.6 | 25.4 | 1 102 | 4.3 | 3 073 | 73.9 | 2 734 | 79.7 | 20.3 | 339 | 11.0 |
| 2001 | 25 751 | 73.1 | 24 572 | 75.6 | 24.4 | 1 179 | 4.6 | 3 022 | 73.8 | 2 638 | 81.8 | 18.2 | 385 | 12.7 |
| 2002 | 26 140 | 72.2 | 24 612 | 74.8 | 25.2 | 1 529 | 5.8 | 3 224 | 75.3 | 2 818 | 79.1 | 20.9 | 406 | 12.6 |
| 2003 | 26 202 | 71.7 | 24 598 | 74.3 | 25.7 | 1 603 | 6.1 | 3 222 | 73.1 | 2 789 | 79.5 | 20.5 | 433 | 13.4 |
| 2004 | 25 913 | 70.7 | 24 413 | 74.2 | 25.8 | 1 501 | 5.8 | 3 262 | 72.6 | 2 836 | 76.8 | 23.2 | 426 | 13.1 |
| 2005 | 26 202 | 71.7 | 24 598 | 74.3 | 25.7 | 1 603 | 6.1 | 3 222 | 73.1 | 2 789 | 79.5 | 20.5 | 433 | 13.4 |
| 2006 | 26 009 | 70.6 | 24 728 | 75.6 | 24.4 | 1 281 | 4.9 | 3 317 | 71.5 | 2 896 | 77.8 | 22.2 | 420 | 12.7 |
| 2007 | 26 834 | 71.3 | 25 646 | 75.2 | 24.8 | 1 188 | 4.4 | 3 514 | 71.4 | 3 133 | 76.4 | 23.6 | 381 | 10.8 |
| 2008 | 25 930 | 71.2 | 24 637 | 75.7 | 24.3 | 1 294 | 5.0 | 3 511 | 71.0 | 3 108 | 78.0 | 22.0 | 403 | 11.5 |
| 2009 | 26 122 | 71.6 | 24 079 | 74.6 | 25.4 | 2 043 | 7.8 | 3 673 | 72.0 | 3 108 | 75.8 | 24.2 | 566 | 18.2 |
| 2010 | 25 783 | 71.3 | 23 510 | 73.7 | 26.3 | 2 273 | 8.8 | 3 642 | 70.1 | 2 984 | 71.9 | 28.1 | 659 | 18.1 |
| 2011 | 25 376 | 70.9 | 23 109 | 74.2 | 25.8 | 2 266 | 8.9 | 3 822 | 70.0 | 3 102 | 71.9 | 28.1 | 721 | 18.9 |
| 2012 | 25 384 | 70.9 | 23 366 | 75.4 | 24.6 | 2 018 | 7.9 | 4 108 | 71.5 | 3 422 | 73.2 | 26.8 | 686 | 16.7 |
| 2013 | 25 112 | 70.3 | 23 121 | 74.8 | 25.2 | 1 991 | 7.9 | 4 088 | 71.3 | 3 404 | 71.9 | 28.1 | 684 | 16.7 |
| 2014 | 25 209 | 70.8 | 23 542 | 75.6 | 24.4 | 1 667 | 6.6 | 4 007 | 71.4 | 3 423 | 74.8 | 25.2 | 584 | 14.6 |
| 2015 | 25 107 | 69.9 | 23 841 | 76.3 | 23.7 | 1 265 | 5.0 | 4 186 | 72.2 | 3 657 | 74.5 | 25.5 | 529 | 12.6 |
| 2016 | 25 070 | 70.8 | 23 877 | 76.4 | 23.6 | 1 193 | 4.8 | 4 086 | 72.8 | 3 660 | 73.3 | 26.7 | 426 | 10.4 |
| **Women with Children Under 6 Years** | | | | | | | | | | | | | | |
| 1995 | 10 395 | 62.3 | 9 587 | 67.5 | 32.5 | 809 | 7.8 | 1 328 | 53.0 | 1 069 | 68.6 | 31.4 | 259 | 19.5 |
| 1996 | 10 293 | 62.3 | 9 592 | 68.4 | 31.6 | 701 | 6.8 | 1 378 | 55.1 | 1 099 | 67.3 | 32.7 | 279 | 20.2 |
| 1997 | 10 610 | 65.0 | 9 800 | 70.5 | 29.5 | 810 | 7.6 | 1 755 | 65.1 | 1 424 | 71.6 | 28.4 | 330 | 18.8 |
| 1998 | 10 619 | 65.2 | 9 839 | 69.8 | 30.2 | 780 | 7.3 | 1 755 | 67.3 | 1 448 | 71.7 | 28.3 | 307 | 17.5 |
| 1999 | 10 322 | 64.4 | 9 674 | 69.0 | 31.0 | 648 | 6.3 | 1 811 | 68.1 | 1 565 | 71.0 | 29.0 | 246 | 13.6 |
| 2000 | 10 316 | 65.3 | 9 763 | 70.5 | 29.5 | 553 | 5.4 | 1 835 | 70.5 | 1 603 | 75.3 | 24.7 | 232 | 12.6 |
| 2001 | 10 200 | 64.9 | 9 618 | 71.2 | 28.8 | 582 | 5.7 | 1 783 | 69.7 | 1 542 | 79.1 | 20.9 | 242 | 13.6 |
| 2002 | 10 193 | 64.1 | 9 441 | 70.4 | 29.6 | 752 | 7.4 | 1 819 | 71.0 | 1 568 | 74.5 | 25.5 | 251 | 13.8 |
| 2003 | 10 209 | 62.9 | 9 433 | 70.0 | 30.0 | 776 | 7.6 | 1 893 | 70.2 | 1 614 | 75.2 | 24.8 | 279 | 14.7 |
| 2004 | 10 131 | 62.2 | 9 407 | 69.4 | 30.6 | 724 | 7.1 | 1 885 | 68.4 | 1 605 | 70.1 | 29.9 | 279 | 14.8 |
| 2005 | 10 209 | 62.9 | 9 433 | 70.0 | 30.0 | 776 | 7.6 | 1 893 | 70.2 | 1 614 | 75.2 | 24.8 | 279 | 14.7 |
| 2006 | 10 430 | 63.0 | 9 779 | 72.0 | 28.0 | 651 | 6.2 | 1 934 | 68.6 | 1 659 | 72.8 | 27.2 | 276 | 14.3 |
| 2007 | 10 894 | 63.5 | 10 305 | 71.9 | 28.1 | 589 | 5.4 | 2 066 | 67.4 | 1 827 | 72.7 | 27.3 | 239 | 11.6 |
| 2008 | 10 452 | 63.6 | 9 794 | 72.1 | 27.9 | 657 | 6.3 | 1 982 | 66.0 | 1 705 | 72.2 | 27.8 | 277 | 14.0 |
| 2009 | 10 497 | 63.6 | 9 517 | 71.8 | 28.2 | 980 | 9.3 | 2 137 | 67.8 | 1 754 | 70.3 | 29.7 | 383 | 17.9 |
| 2010 | 10 536 | 64.2 | 9 452 | 70.9 | 29.1 | 1 085 | 10.3 | 2 076 | 65.6 | 1 643 | 67.0 | 33.0 | 433 | 20.9 |
| 2011 | 10 403 | 64.2 | 9 268 | 71.3 | 28.7 | 1 135 | 10.9 | 2 177 | 65.8 | 1 678 | 65.5 | 34.5 | 499 | 22.9 |
| 2012 | 10 462 | 64.7 | 9 458 | 72.6 | 27.4 | 1 004 | 9.6 | 2 408 | 68.1 | 1 958 | 69.0 | 31.0 | 450 | 18.7 |
| 2013 | 10 171 | 64.7 | 9 212 | 72.8 | 27.2 | 958 | 9.4 | 2 305 | 68.2 | 1 864 | 66.7 | 33.3 | 441 | 19.1 |
| 2014 | 9 982 | 64.3 | 9 153 | 73.5 | 26.5 | 829 | 8.3 | 2 221 | 67.6 | 1 836 | 71.7 | 28.3 | 385 | 17.3 |
| 2015 | 10 048 | 63.9 | 9 405 | 73.4 | 26.6 | 643 | 6.4 | 2 333 | 68.5 | 1 993 | 68.9 | 31.1 | 340 | 14.6 |
| 2016 | 9 934 | 65.3 | 9 358 | 73.9 | 26.1 | 576 | 5.8 | 2 161 | 68.6 | 1 903 | 69.4 | 30.6 | 258 | 11.9 |

*Note:* See notes and definitions for information on historical comparability.

### Table 1-47.  Employment Status of Ever-Married Women and Married Women, Spouse Present, by Presence and Age of Children, March 1995–March 2016

(Thousands of women, percent.)

| Presence and age of children and year | Ever-married women[1] | | | | | | | Married women, spouse present | | | | | | |
|---|---|---|---|---|---|---|---|---|---|---|---|---|---|---|
| | Civilian labor force | Civilian labor force as percent of population | Employed | | | Unemployed | | Civilian labor force | Civilian labor force as percent of population | Employed | | | Unemployed | |
| | | | Number | Percent full time | Percent part time | Number | Percent of labor force | | | Number | Percent full time | Percent part time | Number | Percent of labor force |
| **Women with No Children Under 18 Years** | | | | | | | | | | | | | | |
| 1995 | 22 973 | 47.3 | 22 134 | 77.4 | 22.6 | 839 | 3.7 | 15 594 | 53.2 | 15 072 | 76.3 | 23.7 | 522 | 3.3 |
| 1996 | 23 337 | 47.7 | 22 444 | 78.1 | 21.9 | 893 | 3.8 | 15 628 | 53.4 | 15 123 | 76.8 | 23.2 | 506 | 3.2 |
| 1997 | 23 890 | 48.3 | 23 130 | 78.9 | 21.1 | 760 | 3.2 | 15 750 | 54.2 | 15 315 | 77.7 | 22.3 | 435 | 2.8 |
| 1998 | 24 366 | 48.7 | 23 598 | 79.3 | 20.7 | 767 | 3.1 | 16 007 | 54.1 | 15 581 | 78.3 | 21.7 | 426 | 2.7 |
| 1999 | 24 881 | 48.9 | 24 098 | 79.7 | 20.3 | 783 | 3.1 | 16 484 | 54.4 | 16 061 | 78.2 | 21.8 | 423 | 2.6 |
| 2000 | 25 465 | 49.4 | 24 695 | 80.3 | 19.7 | 769 | 3.0 | 16 786 | 54.7 | 16 357 | 79.1 | 20.9 | 429 | 2.6 |
| 2001 | 25 959 | 49.6 | 25 226 | 80.4 | 19.6 | 733 | 2.8 | 16 909 | 54.8 | 16 528 | 78.7 | 21.3 | 381 | 2.3 |
| 2002 | 26 423 | 49.1 | 25 356 | 80.0 | 20.0 | 1 068 | 4.0 | 17 353 | 54.8 | 16 780 | 78.4 | 21.6 | 573 | 3.3 |
| 2003 | 27 361 | 50.1 | 26 238 | 79.7 | 20.3 | 1 123 | 4.1 | 17 901 | 55.7 | 17 273 | 78.6 | 21.4 | 628 | 3.5 |
| 2004 | 27 461 | 49.8 | 26 329 | 79.3 | 20.7 | 1 131 | 4.1 | 17 965 | 55.0 | 17 367 | 78.6 | 21.4 | 598 | 3.3 |
| 2005 | 27 361 | 50.1 | 26 238 | 79.7 | 20.3 | 1 123 | 4.1 | 17 901 | 55.7 | 17 273 | 78.6 | 21.4 | 628 | 3.5 |
| 2006 | 27 719 | 49.3 | 26 893 | 80.1 | 19.9 | 827 | 3.0 | 18 124 | 54.8 | 17 691 | 79.3 | 20.7 | 434 | 2.4 |
| 2007 | 28 335 | 49.8 | 27 477 | 80.1 | 19.9 | 858 | 3.0 | 18 766 | 55.4 | 18 326 | 79.6 | 20.4 | 441 | 2.3 |
| 2008 | 29 207 | 50.3 | 28 156 | 80.2 | 19.8 | 1 052 | 3.6 | 19 188 | 55.9 | 18 650 | 79.8 | 20.2 | 539 | 2.8 |
| 2009 | 29 536 | 50.2 | 27 737 | 77.8 | 22.2 | 1 800 | 6.1 | 19 541 | 55.8 | 18 521 | 77.3 | 22.7 | 1 019 | 5.2 |
| 2010 | 29 767 | 50.2 | 27 723 | 77.7 | 22.3 | 2 044 | 6.9 | 19 579 | 55.8 | 18 454 | 77.3 | 22.7 | 1 125 | 5.7 |
| 2011 | 29 440 | 49.4 | 27 553 | 77.7 | 22.3 | 1 886 | 6.4 | 19 316 | 54.6 | 18 285 | 77.4 | 22.6 | 1 031 | 5.3 |
| 2012 | 29 912 | 48.8 | 28 021 | 78.2 | 21.8 | 1 891 | 6.3 | 19 617 | 53.6 | 18 536 | 77.8 | 22.2 | 1 081 | 5.5 |
| 2013 | 29 956 | 48.4 | 28 379 | 78.1 | 21.9 | 1 578 | 5.3 | 19 507 | 53.3 | 18 706 | 77.5 | 22.5 | 801 | 4.1 |
| 2014 | 29 908 | 47.8 | 28 428 | 78.0 | 22.0 | 1 480 | 4.9 | 19 350 | 52.0 | 18 582 | 77.5 | 22.5 | 768 | 4.1 |
| 2015 | 30 074 | 47.6 | 28 921 | 78.2 | 21.8 | 1 153 | 3.8 | 19 609 | 52.5 | 19 009 | 77.6 | 22.4 | 600 | 3.1 |
| 2016 | 30 534 | 47.8 | 29 481 | 78.3 | 21.7 | 1 053 | 3.4 | 19 977 | 52.6 | 19 392 | 78.2 | 21.8 | 584 | 2.9 |
| **Women with Children Under 18 Years** | | | | | | | | | | | | | | |
| 1995 | 22 591 | 71.1 | 21 441 | 71.5 | 28.5 | 1 150 | 5.1 | 17 969 | 70.2 | 17 195 | 68.8 | 31.2 | 774 | 4.3 |
| 1996 | 22 475 | 71.4 | 21 556 | 72.5 | 27.5 | 919 | 4.1 | 17 754 | 70.0 | 17 136 | 69.6 | 30.4 | 618 | 3.5 |
| 1997 | 22 831 | 72.6 | 21 777 | 73.9 | 26.1 | 1 054 | 4.6 | 18 157 | 71.1 | 17 521 | 71.6 | 28.4 | 636 | 3.5 |
| 1998 | 22 650 | 72.3 | 21 665 | 73.8 | 26.2 | 985 | 4.3 | 18 129 | 70.6 | 17 447 | 71.5 | 28.5 | 682 | 3.8 |
| 1999 | 22 419 | 71.9 | 21 611 | 73.9 | 26.1 | 808 | 3.6 | 17 865 | 70.1 | 17 342 | 71.5 | 28.5 | 523 | 2.9 |
| 2000 | 22 722 | 72.7 | 21 960 | 74.0 | 26.0 | 763 | 3.4 | 18 174 | 70.6 | 17 641 | 71.7 | 28.3 | 533 | 2.9 |
| 2001 | 22 729 | 73.0 | 21 934 | 74.9 | 25.1 | 795 | 3.5 | 18 325 | 70.8 | 17 745 | 72.6 | 27.4 | 580 | 3.2 |
| 2002 | 22 917 | 71.8 | 21 794 | 74.3 | 25.7 | 1 122 | 4.9 | 18 271 | 69.6 | 17 515 | 71.7 | 28.3 | 756 | 4.1 |
| 2003 | 22 979 | 71.5 | 21 809 | 73.7 | 26.3 | 1 170 | 5.1 | 18 284 | 69.2 | 17 533 | 71.0 | 29.0 | 751 | 4.1 |
| 2004 | 22 651 | 70.5 | 21 576 | 73.8 | 26.2 | 1 075 | 4.7 | 17 953 | 68.2 | 17 215 | 71.3 | 28.7 | 738 | 4.1 |
| 2005 | 22 979 | 71.5 | 21 809 | 73.7 | 26.3 | 1 170 | 5.1 | 18 284 | 69.2 | 17 533 | 71.0 | 29.0 | 751 | 4.1 |
| 2006 | 22 692 | 70.5 | 21 831 | 75.3 | 24.7 | 861 | 3.8 | 18 067 | 68.4 | 17 494 | 73.0 | 27.0 | 574 | 3.2 |
| 2007 | 23 320 | 71.3 | 22 513 | 75.0 | 25.0 | 807 | 3.5 | 18 569 | 69.3 | 18 045 | 72.6 | 27.4 | 524 | 2.8 |
| 2008 | 22 419 | 71.2 | 21 529 | 75.4 | 24.6 | 890 | 4.0 | 17 886 | 69.4 | 17 269 | 73.6 | 26.4 | 616 | 3.4 |
| 2009 | 22 449 | 71.5 | 20 972 | 74.5 | 25.5 | 1 477 | 6.6 | 17 995 | 69.8 | 17 018 | 73.1 | 26.9 | 977 | 5.4 |
| 2010 | 22 141 | 71.5 | 20 526 | 74.0 | 26.0 | 1 615 | 7.3 | 17 622 | 69.7 | 16 510 | 72.6 | 27.4 | 1 112 | 6.3 |
| 2011 | 21 553 | 71.1 | 20 008 | 74.6 | 25.4 | 1 546 | 7.2 | 17 067 | 69.1 | 16 055 | 73.1 | 26.9 | 1 012 | 5.9 |
| 2012 | 21 276 | 70.7 | 19 944 | 75.8 | 24.2 | 1 332 | 6.3 | 16 746 | 68.5 | 15 887 | 74.1 | 25.9 | 859 | 5.1 |
| 2013 | 21 024 | 70.1 | 19 717 | 75.3 | 24.7 | 1 306 | 6.2 | 16 786 | 68.1 | 15 896 | 74.1 | 25.9 | 890 | 5.3 |
| 2014 | 21 202 | 70.6 | 20 120 | 75.8 | 24.2 | 1 083 | 5.1 | 16 907 | 68.4 | 16 176 | 74.7 | 25.3 | 730 | 4.3 |
| 2015 | 20 921 | 69.5 | 20 185 | 76.7 | 23.3 | 736 | 3.5 | 16 779 | 67.6 | 16 305 | 75.3 | 24.7 | 474 | 2.8 |
| 2016 | 20 984 | 70.5 | 20 217 | 77.0 | 23.0 | 767 | 3.7 | 16 882 | 68.6 | 16 339 | 76.3 | 23.7 | 543 | 3.2 |
| **Women with Children Under 6 Years** | | | | | | | | | | | | | | |
| 1995 | 9 067 | 63.9 | 8 517 | 67.4 | 32.6 | 550 | 6.1 | 7 759 | 63.5 | 7 349 | 66.1 | 33.9 | 409 | 5.3 |
| 1996 | 8 915 | 63.6 | 8 493 | 68.6 | 31.4 | 422 | 4.7 | 7 590 | 62.7 | 7 297 | 66.5 | 33.5 | 293 | 3.9 |
| 1997 | 8 856 | 64.9 | 8 376 | 70.3 | 29.7 | 480 | 5.4 | 7 582 | 63.6 | 7 252 | 69.1 | 30.9 | 330 | 4.4 |
| 1998 | 8 864 | 64.8 | 8 391 | 69.5 | 30.5 | 473 | 5.3 | 7 655 | 63.7 | 7 309 | 68.1 | 31.9 | 346 | 4.5 |
| 1999 | 8 511 | 63.7 | 8 109 | 68.6 | 31.4 | 402 | 4.7 | 7 246 | 61.8 | 6 979 | 67.1 | 32.9 | 267 | 3.7 |
| 2000 | 8 481 | 64.3 | 8 159 | 69.5 | 30.5 | 321 | 3.8 | 7 341 | 62.8 | 7 087 | 68.1 | 31.9 | 254 | 3.5 |
| 2001 | 8 417 | 64.0 | 8 077 | 69.7 | 30.3 | 340 | 4.0 | 7 319 | 62.5 | 7 062 | 68.5 | 31.5 | 257 | 3.5 |
| 2002 | 8 373 | 62.8 | 7 873 | 69.6 | 30.4 | 501 | 6.0 | 7 166 | 60.8 | 6 804 | 67.7 | 32.3 | 363 | 5.1 |
| 2003 | 8 315 | 61.4 | 7 818 | 68.9 | 31.1 | 497 | 6.0 | 7 175 | 59.8 | 6 826 | 67.1 | 32.9 | 349 | 4.9 |
| 2004 | 8 246 | 61.0 | 7 801 | 69.3 | 30.7 | 445 | 5.4 | 7 107 | 59.3 | 6 774 | 68.1 | 31.9 | 332 | 4.7 |
| 2005 | 8 315 | 61.4 | 7 818 | 68.9 | 31.1 | 497 | 6.0 | 7 175 | 59.8 | 6 826 | 67.1 | 32.9 | 349 | 4.9 |
| 2006 | 8 496 | 61.9 | 8 121 | 71.8 | 28.2 | 375 | 4.4 | 7 366 | 60.3 | 7 092 | 70.6 | 29.4 | 274 | 3.7 |
| 2007 | 8 829 | 62.7 | 8 479 | 71.7 | 28.3 | 350 | 4.0 | 7 664 | 61.5 | 7 407 | 70.8 | 29.2 | 257 | 3.4 |
| 2008 | 8 470 | 63.0 | 8 089 | 72.1 | 27.9 | 381 | 4.5 | 7 285 | 61.6 | 6 999 | 70.9 | 29.1 | 285 | 3.9 |
| 2009 | 8 360 | 62.6 | 7 763 | 72.1 | 27.9 | 597 | 7.1 | 7 231 | 61.6 | 6 805 | 71.4 | 28.6 | 426 | 5.9 |
| 2010 | 8 460 | 63.8 | 7 809 | 71.7 | 28.3 | 651 | 7.7 | 7 227 | 62.5 | 6 741 | 71.5 | 28.5 | 486 | 6.7 |
| 2011 | 8 226 | 63.7 | 7 590 | 72.5 | 27.5 | 636 | 7.7 | 7 061 | 62.3 | 6 608 | 71.9 | 28.1 | 453 | 6.4 |
| 2012 | 8 054 | 63.7 | 7 501 | 73.5 | 26.5 | 554 | 6.9 | 6 878 | 62.3 | 6 491 | 72.7 | 27.3 | 387 | 5.6 |
| 2013 | 7 866 | 63.7 | 7 349 | 74.3 | 25.7 | 517 | 6.6 | 6 737 | 62.0 | 6 384 | 74.1 | 25.9 | 352 | 5.2 |
| 2014 | 7 761 | 63.4 | 7 317 | 73.9 | 26.1 | 444 | 5.7 | 6 663 | 61.5 | 6 326 | 73.7 | 26.3 | 336 | 5.0 |
| 2015 | 7 714 | 62.7 | 7 411 | 74.6 | 25.4 | 303 | 3.9 | 6 653 | 61.3 | 6 454 | 74.4 | 25.6 | 198 | 3.0 |
| 2016 | 7 773 | 64.4 | 7 455 | 75.0 | 25.0 | 318 | 4.1 | 6 715 | 62.9 | 6 483 | 74.6 | 25.4 | 232 | 3.4 |

[1] Ever-married women are women who are, or have ever been, married.

## Table 1-48. Employment Status of Women Who Maintain Families, by Marital Status and Presence and Age of Children, March 2000–March 2016

(Thousands of women, percent.)

| Marital status, age of children, and year | Civilian noninstitutional population | Civilian labor force | | | | | Not in the labor force |
|---|---|---|---|---|---|---|---|
| | | Number | Percent of the population | Employed | Unemployed | | |
| | | | | | Number | Percent of the labor force | |
| **Total, Women Who Maintain Families** | | | | | | | |
| 2000 | 13 145 | 9 226 | 70.2 | 8 592 | 634 | 6.9 | 3 918 |
| 2001 | 12 930 | 9 034 | 69.9 | 8 453 | 581 | 6.4 | 3 897 |
| 2002 | 13 489 | 9 523 | 70.6 | 8 755 | 768 | 8.1 | 3 966 |
| 2003 | 14 000 | 9 759 | 69.7 | 8 898 | 861 | 8.8 | 4 241 |
| 2004 | 14 165 | 9 869 | 69.7 | 9 054 | 815 | 8.3 | 4 297 |
| 2005 | 14 391 | 9 941 | 69.1 | 9 140 | 801 | 8.1 | 4 450 |
| 2006 | 14 485 | 9 966 | 68.8 | 9 227 | 739 | 7.4 | 4 520 |
| 2007 | 14 833 | 10 172 | 68.6 | 9 510 | 661 | 6.5 | 4 662 |
| 2008 | 14 820 | 10 166 | 68.6 | 9 447 | 719 | 7.1 | 4 654 |
| 2009 | 14 813 | 10 140 | 68.5 | 9 034 | 1 106 | 10.9 | 4 673 |
| 2010 | 15 214 | 10 206 | 67.1 | 9 027 | 1 179 | 11.6 | 5 008 |
| 2011 | 15 461 | 10 462 | 67.7 | 9 141 | 1 321 | 12.6 | 5 000 |
| 2012 | 16 122 | 11 009 | 68.3 | 9 807 | 1 202 | 10.9 | 5 113 |
| 2013 | 15 914 | 10 793 | 67.8 | 9 589 | 1 204 | 11.2 | 5 121 |
| 2014 | 15 612 | 10 505 | 67.3 | 9 511 | 994 | 9.5 | 5 107 |
| 2015 | 16 017 | 10 691 | 66.7 | 9 848 | 843 | 7.9 | 5 326 |
| 2016 | 16 003 | 10 695 | 66.8 | 9 988 | 707 | 6.6 | 5 308 |
| **Women with No Children Under 18 Years** | | | | | | | |
| 2000 | 5 097 | 2 707 | 53.1 | 2 546 | 161 | 5.9 | 2 390 |
| 2001 | 5 185 | 2 772 | 53.5 | 2 668 | 104 | 3.8 | 2 413 |
| 2002 | 5 119 | 2 764 | 54.0 | 2 628 | 136 | 4.9 | 2 355 |
| 2003 | 5 457 | 2 934 | 53.8 | 2 728 | 206 | 7.0 | 2 522 |
| 2004 | 5 551 | 3 052 | 55.0 | 2 855 | 197 | 6.5 | 2 499 |
| 2005 | 5 692 | 3 095 | 54.4 | 2 961 | 134 | 4.3 | 2 597 |
| 2006 | 5 693 | 3 088 | 54.2 | 2 945 | 143 | 4.6 | 2 604 |
| 2007 | 5 823 | 3 124 | 53.7 | 2 990 | 134 | 4.3 | 2 699 |
| 2008 | 6 022 | 3 352 | 55.7 | 3 167 | 185 | 5.5 | 2 670 |
| 2009 | 6 068 | 3 332 | 54.9 | 3 075 | 258 | 7.7 | 2 735 |
| 2010 | 6 414 | 3 417 | 53.3 | 3 131 | 286 | 8.4 | 2 997 |
| 2011 | 6 403 | 3 455 | 54.0 | 3 131 | 324 | 9.4 | 2 948 |
| 2012 | 6 773 | 3 779 | 55.8 | 3 464 | 316 | 8.4 | 2 994 |
| 2013 | 6 822 | 3 790 | 55.5 | 3 466 | 324 | 8.5 | 3 032 |
| 2014 | 6 715 | 3 566 | 53.1 | 3 301 | 265 | 7.4 | 3 149 |
| 2015 | 6 977 | 3 732 | 53.5 | 3 521 | 211 | 5.7 | 3 246 |
| 2016 | 7 084 | 3 798 | 53.6 | 3 593 | 205 | 5.4 | 3 286 |
| **Women with Children Under 18 Years** | | | | | | | |
| 2000 | 8 048 | 6 520 | 81.0 | 6 046 | 474 | 7.3 | 1 528 |
| 2001 | 7 746 | 6 261 | 80.8 | 5 785 | 476 | 7.6 | 1 484 |
| 2002 | 8 370 | 6 759 | 80.8 | 6 127 | 632 | 9.4 | 1 611 |
| 2003 | 8 543 | 6 825 | 79.9 | 6 170 | 655 | 9.6 | 1 718 |
| 2004 | 8 614 | 6 817 | 79.1 | 6 199 | 618 | 9.1 | 1 798 |
| 2005 | 8 699 | 6 846 | 78.7 | 6 179 | 667 | 9.7 | 1 853 |
| 2006 | 8 793 | 6 878 | 78.2 | 6 282 | 596 | 8.7 | 1 915 |
| 2007 | 9 010 | 7 047 | 78.2 | 6 520 | 527 | 7.5 | 1 963 |
| 2008 | 8 798 | 6 814 | 77.4 | 6 280 | 535 | 7.8 | 1 984 |
| 2009 | 8 745 | 6 807 | 77.8 | 5 959 | 848 | 12.5 | 1 938 |
| 2010 | 8 800 | 6 789 | 77.1 | 5 896 | 893 | 13.2 | 2 011 |
| 2011 | 9 059 | 7 007 | 77.4 | 6 009 | 998 | 14.2 | 2 052 |
| 2012 | 9 349 | 7 230 | 77.3 | 6 343 | 887 | 12.3 | 2 119 |
| 2013 | 9 092 | 7 003 | 77.0 | 6 123 | 880 | 12.6 | 2 089 |
| 2014 | 8 896 | 6 939 | 78.0 | 6 210 | 729 | 10.5 | 1 957 |
| 2015 | 9 040 | 6 959 | 77.0 | 6 327 | 632 | 9.1 | 2 081 |
| 2016 | 8 920 | 6 897 | 77.3 | 6 396 | 502 | 7.3 | 2 022 |
| **Single Women with No Children Under 18 Years** | | | | | | | |
| 2000 | 1 004 | 720 | 71.7 | 642 | 78 | 10.8 | 284 |
| 2001 | 1 096 | 787 | 71.8 | 756 | 31 | 3.9 | 309 |
| 2002 | 1 154 | 796 | 69.0 | 747 | 49 | 6.2 | 358 |
| 2003 | 1 254 | 814 | 64.9 | 713 | 101 | 12.4 | 440 |
| 2004 | 1 381 | 977 | 70.7 | 887 | 90 | 9.2 | 404 |
| 2005 | 1 388 | 926 | 66.7 | 855 | 71 | 7.7 | 463 |
| 2006 | 1 370 | 933 | 68.1 | 861 | 72 | 7.7 | 437 |
| 2007 | 1 413 | 986 | 69.8 | 930 | 57 | 5.7 | 427 |
| 2008 | 1 515 | 1 057 | 69.8 | 989 | 68 | 6.5 | 458 |
| 2009 | 1 531 | 1 069 | 69.8 | 967 | 102 | 9.6 | 462 |
| 2010 | 1 718 | 1 166 | 67.9 | 1 041 | 125 | 10.7 | 552 |
| 2011 | 1 729 | 1 178 | 68.2 | 1 047 | 132 | 11.2 | 551 |
| 2012 | 1 836 | 1 241 | 67.6 | 1 099 | 143 | 11.5 | 595 |
| 2013 | 1 933 | 1 322 | 68.4 | 1 178 | 144 | 10.9 | 611 |
| 2014 | 1 840 | 1 224 | 66.5 | 1 105 | 119 | 9.7 | 616 |
| 2015 | 2 008 | 1 288 | 64.1 | 1 203 | 85 | 6.6 | 720 |
| 2016 | 2 097 | 1 412 | 67.3 | 1 320 | 92 | 6.5 | 685 |

*Note:* See notes and definitions for information on historical comparability.

## Table 1-48. Employment Status of Women Who Maintain Families, by Marital Status and Presence and Age of Children, March 2000–March 2016—*Continued*

(Thousands of women, percent.)

| Marital status, age of children, and year | Civilian noninstitutional population | Civilian labor force | | | | | Not in the labor force |
|---|---|---|---|---|---|---|---|
| | | Number | Percent of the population | Employed | Unemployed | | |
| | | | | | Number | Percent of the labor force | |
| **Single Women with Children Under 18 Years** | | | | | | | |
| 2000 | 3 167 | 2 413 | 76.2 | 2 151 | 262 | 10.9 | 754 |
| 2001 | 3 097 | 2 351 | 75.9 | 2 055 | 296 | 12.6 | 745 |
| 2002 | 3 315 | 2 566 | 77.4 | 2 241 | 325 | 12.7 | 749 |
| 2003 | 3 421 | 2 584 | 75.5 | 2 272 | 312 | 12.1 | 837 |
| 2004 | 3 414 | 2 568 | 75.2 | 2 233 | 335 | 13.0 | 846 |
| 2005 | 3 591 | 2 708 | 75.4 | 2 325 | 383 | 14.1 | 882 |
| 2006 | 3 671 | 2 710 | 73.8 | 2 370 | 340 | 12.5 | 961 |
| 2007 | 3 748 | 2 782 | 74.2 | 2 491 | 291 | 10.4 | 966 |
| 2008 | 3 721 | 2 743 | 73.7 | 2 448 | 295 | 10.8 | 978 |
| 2009 | 3 872 | 2 877 | 74.3 | 2 448 | 429 | 14.9 | 995 |
| 2010 | 3 948 | 2 868 | 72.6 | 2 379 | 488 | 17.0 | 1 081 |
| 2011 | 4 193 | 3 072 | 73.3 | 2 522 | 550 | 17.9 | 1 120 |
| 2012 | 4 442 | 3 263 | 73.5 | 2 746 | 517 | 15.8 | 1 179 |
| 2013 | 4 403 | 3 220 | 73.1 | 2 698 | 522 | 16.2 | 1 183 |
| 2014 | 4 297 | 3 137 | 73.0 | 2 698 | 439 | 14.0 | 1 161 |
| 2015 | 4 438 | 3 296 | 74.3 | 2 889 | 407 | 12.4 | 1 142 |
| 2016 | 4 362 | 3 252 | 74.5 | 2 941 | 310 | 9.5 | 1 110 |
| **Widowed, Divorced, or Separated Women with No Children Under 18 Years** | | | | | | | |
| 2000 | 4 093 | 1 987 | 48.5 | 1 904 | 83 | 4.2 | 2 106 |
| 2001 | 4 088 | 1 985 | 48.6 | 1 912 | 73 | 3.7 | 2 104 |
| 2002 | 3 964 | 1 968 | 49.6 | 1 882 | 86 | 4.4 | 1 997 |
| 2003 | 4 203 | 2 121 | 50.5 | 2 016 | 105 | 5.0 | 2 082 |
| 2004 | 4 170 | 2 075 | 49.8 | 1 968 | 107 | 5.2 | 2 095 |
| 2005 | 4 304 | 2 170 | 50.4 | 2 106 | 64 | 2.9 | 2 135 |
| 2006 | 4 323 | 2 156 | 49.9 | 2 084 | 72 | 3.3 | 2 168 |
| 2007 | 4 410 | 2 138 | 48.5 | 2 061 | 77 | 3.6 | 2 272 |
| 2008 | 4 507 | 2 295 | 50.9 | 2 178 | 117 | 5.1 | 2 213 |
| 2009 | 4 536 | 2 263 | 49.9 | 2 108 | 155 | 6.9 | 2 273 |
| 2010 | 4 696 | 2 251 | 47.9 | 2 090 | 161 | 7.1 | 2 445 |
| 2011 | 4 674 | 2 276 | 48.7 | 2 084 | 192 | 8.4 | 2 397 |
| 2012 | 4 937 | 2 538 | 51.4 | 2 365 | 173 | 6.8 | 2 399 |
| 2013 | 4 889 | 2 468 | 50.5 | 2 288 | 180 | 7.3 | 2 421 |
| 2014 | 4 875 | 2 342 | 48.0 | 2 196 | 146 | 6.2 | 2 533 |
| 2015 | 4 969 | 2 444 | 49.2 | 2 317 | 126 | 5.2 | 2 526 |
| 2016 | 4 987 | 2 386 | 47.8 | 2 273 | 113 | 4.7 | 2 601 |
| **Widowed, Divorced, or Separated Women with Children Under 18 Years** | | | | | | | |
| 2000 | 4 881 | 4 107 | 84.1 | 3 895 | 212 | 5.2 | 774 |
| 2001 | 4 649 | 3 910 | 84.1 | 3 730 | 180 | 4.6 | 739 |
| 2002 | 5 056 | 4 193 | 82.9 | 3 886 | 307 | 7.3 | 862 |
| 2003 | 5 122 | 4 241 | 82.8 | 3 898 | 343 | 8.1 | 881 |
| 2004 | 5 201 | 4 249 | 81.7 | 3 966 | 283 | 6.7 | 952 |
| 2005 | 5 108 | 4 137 | 81.0 | 3 854 | 283 | 6.8 | 971 |
| 2006 | 5 121 | 4 167 | 81.4 | 3 912 | 255 | 6.1 | 955 |
| 2007 | 5 262 | 4 266 | 81.1 | 4 029 | 237 | 5.5 | 997 |
| 2008 | 5 077 | 4 071 | 80.2 | 3 832 | 239 | 5.9 | 1 006 |
| 2009 | 4 873 | 3 930 | 80.7 | 3 511 | 420 | 10.7 | 943 |
| 2010 | 4 852 | 3 922 | 80.8 | 3 517 | 405 | 10.3 | 931 |
| 2011 | 4 866 | 3 935 | 80.9 | 3 487 | 448 | 11.4 | 931 |
| 2012 | 4 907 | 3 966 | 80.8 | 3 597 | 370 | 9.3 | 940 |
| 2013 | 4 689 | 3 783 | 80.7 | 3 425 | 358 | 9.5 | 906 |
| 2014 | 4 599 | 3 802 | 82.7 | 3 512 | 290 | 7.6 | 797 |
| 2015 | 4 602 | 3 663 | 79.6 | 3 438 | 225 | 6.1 | 939 |
| 2016 | 4 558 | 3 646 | 80.0 | 3 455 | 191 | 5.2 | 912 |

*Note:* See notes and definitions for information on historical comparability.

## Table 1-49. Number and Age of Children in Families, by Type of Family and Labor Force Status of Mother, March 1995–March 2016

(Thousands of children.)

| Age of children and year | Total children | Mother in labor force | Mother not in labor force | Married-couple families | | | Families maintained by women | | | Families maintained by men |
|---|---|---|---|---|---|---|---|---|---|---|
| | | | | Total | Mother in labor force | Mother not in labor force | Total | Mother in labor force | Mother not in labor force | |
| **Children Under 18 Years** | | | | | | | | | | |
| 1995 | 63 989 | 41 365 | 20 421 | 47 675 | 32 190 | 15 486 | 14 111 | 9 176 | 4 935 | 2 202 |
| 1996 | 64 506 | 41 573 | 20 449 | 47 484 | 31 764 | 15 720 | 14 538 | 9 809 | 4 729 | 2 484 |
| 1997 | 64 710 | 42 747 | 19 223 | 47 529 | 32 263 | 15 265 | 14 441 | 10 483 | 3 958 | 2 740 |
| 1998 | 65 043 | 43 156 | 19 069 | 47 909 | 32 533 | 15 376 | 14 317 | 10 623 | 3 694 | 2 818 |
| 1999 | 65 191 | 43 419 | 19 074 | 47 945 | 32 193 | 15 752 | 14 547 | 11 226 | 3 322 | 2 699 |
| 2000 | 65 601 | 44 188 | 18 674 | 48 902 | 33 149 | 15 753 | 13 960 | 11 039 | 2 921 | 2 739 |
| 2001 | 65 777 | 44 051 | 18 864 | 49 352 | 33 436 | 15 916 | 13 563 | 10 615 | 2 948 | 2 862 |
| 2002 | 65 978 | 43 821 | 19 243 | 48 836 | 32 673 | 16 163 | 14 228 | 11 149 | 3 079 | 2 914 |
| 2003 | 66 521 | 43 769 | 19 782 | 49 004 | 32 411 | 16 593 | 14 547 | 11 359 | 3 189 | 2 970 |
| 2004 | 66 386 | 43 144 | 20 229 | 48 656 | 31 892 | 16 764 | 14 717 | 11 252 | 3 465 | 3 014 |
| 2005 | 66 526 | 43 239 | 20 179 | 48 688 | 31 886 | 16 802 | 14 729 | 11 352 | 3 377 | 3 108 |
| 2006 | 66 883 | 43 278 | 20 440 | 48 853 | 31 946 | 16 908 | 14 865 | 11 332 | 3 532 | 3 165 |
| 2007 | 67 228 | 44 116 | 20 073 | 48 927 | 32 496 | 16 431 | 15 263 | 11 620 | 3 643 | 3 038 |
| 2008 | 67 153 | 43 798 | 19 966 | 48 303 | 32 110 | 16 193 | 15 461 | 11 688 | 3 773 | 3 388 |
| 2009 | 66 913 | 43 509 | 20 074 | 48 384 | 32 065 | 16 315 | 15 204 | 11 444 | 3 759 | 3 326 |
| 2010 | 66 811 | 43 335 | 19 913 | 47 730 | 31 686 | 16 044 | 15 518 | 11 649 | 3 869 | 3 563 |
| 2011 | 66 804 | 42 882 | 20 260 | 47 051 | 30 902 | 16 149 | 16 091 | 11 980 | 4 111 | 3 662 |
| 2012 | 66 472 | 42 643 | 19 885 | 45 989 | 30 228 | 15 761 | 16 539 | 12 414 | 4 125 | 3 944 |
| 2013 | 66 661 | 42 454 | 20 012 | 46 254 | 30 294 | 15 960 | 16 211 | 12 159 | 4 052 | 4 195 |
| 2014 | 66 137 | 42 447 | 19 718 | 46 428 | 30 471 | 15 958 | 15 737 | 11 977 | 3 760 | 3 972 |
| 2015 | 65 916 | 41 721 | 20 356 | 46 256 | 29 949 | 16 307 | 15 820 | 11 772 | 4 048 | 3 839 |
| 2016 | 66 124 | 42 427 | 19 675 | 46 198 | 30 450 | 15 748 | 15 903 | 11 976 | 3 927 | 4 022 |
| **Children 6 to 17 Years Years** | | | | | | | | | | |
| 1995 | 42 423 | 28 931 | 12 000 | 31 298 | 22 239 | 9 059 | 9 633 | 6 692 | 2 941 | 1 492 |
| 1996 | 42 964 | 29 381 | 11 897 | 31 231 | 22 092 | 9 139 | 10 047 | 7 289 | 2 758 | 1 685 |
| 1997 | 43 488 | 30 308 | 11 400 | 31 509 | 22 602 | 8 906 | 10 199 | 7 705 | 2 493 | 1 781 |
| 1998 | 43 771 | 30 579 | 11 367 | 31 707 | 22 706 | 9 001 | 10 238 | 7 873 | 2 365 | 1 826 |
| 1999 | 44 110 | 30 885 | 11 370 | 31 975 | 22 706 | 9 269 | 10 281 | 8 179 | 2 101 | 1 855 |
| 2000 | 44 562 | 31 531 | 11 198 | 32 732 | 23 393 | 9 339 | 9 997 | 8 138 | 1 859 | 1 833 |
| 2001 | 44 458 | 31 411 | 11 153 | 32 957 | 23 599 | 9 358 | 9 608 | 7 813 | 1 795 | 1 894 |
| 2002 | 44 865 | 31 437 | 11 510 | 32 799 | 23 296 | 9 504 | 10 148 | 8 142 | 2 006 | 1 918 |
| 2003 | 45 273 | 31 559 | 11 635 | 32 782 | 23 160 | 9 622 | 10 412 | 8 399 | 2 013 | 2 080 |
| 2004 | 45 066 | 31 040 | 11 968 | 32 506 | 22 736 | 9 769 | 10 502 | 8 304 | 2 199 | 2 058 |
| 2005 | 45 027 | 30 930 | 11 995 | 32 412 | 22 565 | 9 847 | 10 514 | 8 366 | 2 148 | 2 102 |
| 2006 | 45 039 | 30 591 | 12 250 | 32 311 | 22 315 | 9 996 | 10 530 | 8 276 | 2 254 | 2 198 |
| 2007 | 45 155 | 31 252 | 11 855 | 32 417 | 22 788 | 9 629 | 10 690 | 8 464 | 2 226 | 2 048 |
| 2008 | 44 909 | 30 853 | 11 874 | 31 990 | 22 413 | 9 577 | 10 737 | 8 440 | 2 297 | 2 182 |
| 2009 | 44 595 | 30 600 | 11 811 | 31 966 | 22 425 | 9 537 | 10 449 | 8 175 | 2 274 | 2 180 |
| 2010 | 44 456 | 30 209 | 11 922 | 31 468 | 21 957 | 9 510 | 10 663 | 8 251 | 2 412 | 2 325 |
| 2011 | 44 471 | 29 904 | 12 244 | 31 072 | 21 365 | 9 707 | 11 076 | 8 539 | 2 537 | 2 323 |
| 2012 | 45 049 | 30 143 | 12 315 | 30 923 | 21 163 | 9 760 | 11 535 | 8 980 | 2 556 | 2 591 |
| 2013 | 45 492 | 30 091 | 12 694 | 31 411 | 21 352 | 10 058 | 11 375 | 8 738 | 2 636 | 2 707 |
| 2014 | 45 059 | 30 205 | 12 233 | 31 471 | 21 540 | 9 931 | 10 968 | 8 665 | 2 302 | 2 621 |
| 2015 | 44 817 | 29 490 | 12 830 | 31 359 | 21 090 | 10 269 | 10 961 | 8 400 | 2 560 | 2 498 |
| 2016 | 45 131 | 29 929 | 12 553 | 31 251 | 21 243 | 10 008 | 11 230 | 8 685 | 2 545 | 2 649 |
| **Children Under 6 Years** | | | | | | | | | | |
| 1995 | 21 566 | 12 435 | 8 421 | 16 377 | 9 951 | 6 427 | 4 478 | 2 484 | 1 995 | 710 |
| 1996 | 21 542 | 12 192 | 8 552 | 16 253 | 9 672 | 6 581 | 4 491 | 2 520 | 1 971 | 799 |
| 1997 | 21 222 | 12 439 | 7 823 | 16 020 | 9 661 | 6 359 | 4 243 | 2 778 | 1 464 | 959 |
| 1998 | 21 272 | 12 577 | 7 703 | 16 201 | 9 827 | 6 375 | 4 079 | 2 751 | 1 328 | 992 |
| 1999 | 21 081 | 12 533 | 7 704 | 15 971 | 9 487 | 6 484 | 4 267 | 3 046 | 1 220 | 844 |
| 2000 | 21 039 | 12 657 | 7 476 | 16 170 | 9 757 | 6 413 | 3 963 | 2 901 | 1 062 | 906 |
| 2001 | 21 318 | 12 640 | 7 711 | 16 395 | 9 837 | 6 558 | 3 956 | 2 802 | 1 153 | 968 |
| 2002 | 21 113 | 12 384 | 7 733 | 16 037 | 9 377 | 6 660 | 4 080 | 3 007 | 1 073 | 996 |
| 2003 | 21 248 | 12 210 | 8 147 | 16 222 | 9 251 | 6 971 | 4 136 | 2 960 | 1 176 | 890 |
| 2004 | 21 321 | 12 104 | 8 261 | 16 151 | 9 156 | 6 995 | 4 214 | 2 948 | 1 266 | 956 |
| 2005 | 21 498 | 12 308 | 8 184 | 16 276 | 9 321 | 6 955 | 4 216 | 2 987 | 1 229 | 1 006 |
| 2006 | 21 844 | 12 687 | 8 190 | 16 542 | 9 631 | 6 911 | 4 335 | 3 057 | 1 278 | 968 |
| 2007 | 22 073 | 12 864 | 8 218 | 16 509 | 9 708 | 6 802 | 4 572 | 3 156 | 1 416 | 991 |
| 2008 | 22 244 | 12 946 | 8 092 | 16 313 | 9 697 | 6 616 | 4 724 | 3 248 | 1 476 | 1 207 |
| 2009 | 22 318 | 12 909 | 8 263 | 16 418 | 9 640 | 6 778 | 4 755 | 3 270 | 1 485 | 1 146 |
| 2010 | 22 355 | 13 127 | 7 991 | 16 262 | 9 729 | 6 533 | 4 855 | 3 398 | 1 457 | 1 237 |
| 2011 | 22 333 | 12 978 | 8 015 | 15 979 | 9 537 | 6 442 | 5 015 | 3 441 | 1 573 | 1 340 |
| 2012 | 21 423 | 12 500 | 7 570 | 15 066 | 9 065 | 6 001 | 5 004 | 3 435 | 1 569 | 1 353 |
| 2013 | 21 169 | 12 363 | 7 317 | 14 844 | 8 942 | 5 902 | 4 837 | 3 421 | 1 416 | 1 489 |
| 2014 | 21 078 | 12 242 | 7 484 | 14 958 | 8 931 | 6 027 | 4 769 | 3 312 | 1 457 | 1 351 |
| 2015 | 21 099 | 12 231 | 7 526 | 14 898 | 8 859 | 6 038 | 4 860 | 3 372 | 1 488 | 1 341 |
| 2016 | 20 993 | 12 498 | 7 121 | 14 947 | 9 207 | 5 739 | 4 673 | 3 291 | 1 382 | 1 373 |

*Note:* See notes and definitions for information on historical comparability.

## Table 1-50.  Number of Families and Median Family Income, by Type of Family and Earner Status of Members, 1995–2015

(Thousands of families, dollars.)

| Number and type of families and median family income | 1995 | 1996 | 1997 | 1998 | 1999 | 2000 | 2001 | 2002 | 2003 | 2004 |
|---|---|---|---|---|---|---|---|---|---|---|
| **NUMBER OF FAMILIES** | | | | | | | | | | |
| **Married-Couple Families, Total** | 53 621 | 53 654 | 54 362 | 54 829 | 55 352 | 55 650 | 56 798 | 57 362 | 57 767 | 58 180 |
| No earners | 7 276 | 7 145 | 7 286 | 7 257 | 7 160 | 7 297 | 7 662 | 7 803 | 8 043 | 7 998 |
| One earner | 11 708 | 11 493 | 11 700 | 12 246 | 12 290 | 12 450 | 12 852 | 13 503 | 14 061 | 14 385 |
| Husband | 8 792 | 8 611 | 8 770 | 9 173 | 9 062 | 9 319 | 9 573 | 10 121 | 10 478 | 10 853 |
| Wife | 2 251 | 2 207 | 2 298 | 2 411 | 2 585 | 2 545 | 2 689 | 2 821 | 3 027 | 2 993 |
| Other family member | 666 | 674 | 632 | 662 | 643 | 586 | 590 | 560 | 557 | 539 |
| Two earners | 27 180 | 27 260 | 27 712 | 27 593 | 28 010 | 28 329 | 28 779 | 28 891 | 28 693 | 28 806 |
| Husband and wife | 25 274 | 25 274 | 25 731 | 25 696 | 26 134 | 26 447 | 26 829 | 26 966 | 26 860 | 26 758 |
| Husband and other family member | 1 393 | 1 483 | 1 406 | 1 306 | 1 325 | 1 277 | 1 424 | 1 391 | 1 322 | 1 462 |
| Husband not an earner | 513 | 502 | 575 | 590 | 552 | 605 | 526 | 534 | 511 | 586 |
| Three earners or more | 7 456 | 7 756 | 7 664 | 7 733 | 7 892 | 7 575 | 7 504 | 7 165 | 6 970 | 6 991 |
| Husband and wife | 6 770 | 7 126 | 7 023 | 7 102 | 7 220 | 6 917 | 6 859 | 6 565 | 6 349 | 6 459 |
| Husband, not wife | 531 | 479 | 478 | 456 | 528 | 537 | 530 | 455 | 467 | 381 |
| Husband not an earner | 155 | 150 | 163 | 176 | 144 | 120 | 115 | 145 | 154 | 152 |
| **Families Maintained by Women, Total** | 13 007 | 13 277 | 13 115 | 13 206 | 13 164 | 12 950 | 13 517 | 14 033 | 14 196 | 14 404 |
| No earners | 2 664 | 2 574 | 2 332 | 2 143 | 1 883 | 1 786 | 2 076 | 2 228 | 2 451 | 2 610 |
| One earner | 6 815 | 7 027 | 7 091 | 7 351 | 7 441 | 7 462 | 7 693 | 8 153 | 8 012 | 8 074 |
| Householder | 5 590 | 5 817 | 5 841 | 6 167 | 6 127 | 6 132 | 6 436 | 6 832 | 6 725 | 6 788 |
| Other family member | 1 225 | 1 211 | 1 251 | 1 183 | 1 314 | 1 331 | 1 257 | 1 321 | 1 286 | 1 285 |
| Two earners or more | 3 527 | 3 675 | 3 692 | 3 712 | 3 840 | 3 702 | 3 748 | 3 652 | 3 733 | 3 720 |
| Householder and other family member(s) | 3 225 | 3 431 | 3 398 | 3 399 | 3 508 | 3 376 | 3 442 | 3 290 | 3 364 | 3 399 |
| Householder not an earner | 302 | 245 | 294 | 313 | 332 | 325 | 306 | 362 | 369 | 321 |
| **Families Maintained by Men, Total** | 3 557 | 3 924 | 3 982 | 4 041 | 4 086 | 4 316 | 4 499 | 4 747 | 4 778 | 4 953 |
| No earners | 357 | 359 | 344 | 381 | 376 | 380 | 461 | 466 | 530 | 492 |
| One earner | 1 800 | 1 972 | 2 104 | 2 027 | 2 044 | 2 223 | 2 319 | 2 434 | 2 466 | 2 573 |
| Householder | 1 548 | 1 667 | 1 791 | 1 725 | 1 721 | 1 879 | 1 911 | 2 026 | 2 053 | 2 152 |
| Other family member | 253 | 305 | 313 | 302 | 323 | 344 | 408 | 408 | 413 | 421 |
| Two earners or more | 1 400 | 1 593 | 1 534 | 1 634 | 1 666 | 1 713 | 1 719 | 1 847 | 1 782 | 1 888 |
| Householder and other family member(s) | 1 302 | 1 469 | 1 427 | 1 532 | 1 522 | 1 585 | 1 629 | 1 709 | 1 625 | 1 736 |
| Householder not an earner | 98 | 124 | 107 | 102 | 143 | 128 | 90 | 138 | 157 | 152 |
| **MEDIAN FAMILY INCOME** | | | | | | | | | | |
| **Married-Couple Families, Total** | 47 000 | 49 614 | 51 475 | 54 043 | 56 792 | 59 200 | 60 100 | 61 000 | 62 388 | 63 627 |
| No earners | 21 888 | 22 622 | 23 782 | 24 525 | 25 262 | 25 356 | 25 900 | 25 954 | 26 312 | 26 798 |
| One earner | 35 100 | 36 468 | 39 140 | 40 519 | 41 261 | 44 424 | 44 400 | 45 000 | 46 546 | 47 749 |
| Husband | 36 052 | 38 150 | 40 300 | 42 000 | 44 200 | 47 010 | 47 500 | 48 004 | 48 948 | 50 000 |
| Wife | 32 098 | 30 301 | 34 050 | 35 625 | 35 546 | 36 458 | 36 140 | 39 072 | 41 180 | 41 000 |
| Other family member | 37 784 | 39 644 | 40 317 | 42 414 | 41 120 | 45 492 | 44 270 | 40 927 | 45 936 | 46 324 |
| Two earners | 53 500 | 56 000 | 58 020 | 61 300 | 64 007 | 67 500 | 69 543 | 71 282 | 73 309 | 75 100 |
| Husband and wife | 53 626 | 56 392 | 58 564 | 61 900 | 64 950 | 68 132 | 70 000 | 72 150 | 74 500 | 76 000 |
| Husband and other family member | 52 530 | 49 610 | 53 854 | 57 680 | 53 541 | 56 503 | 65 240 | 62 848 | 60 100 | 66 120 |
| Husband not an earner | 47 121 | 46 990 | 47 979 | 50 955 | 52 466 | 53 430 | 58 725 | 54 840 | 58 000 | 63 050 |
| Three earners or more | 68 996 | 70 400 | 75 593 | 78 973 | 81 940 | 83 990 | 86 090 | 88 632 | 93 000 | 94 212 |
| Husband and wife | 69 371 | 71 148 | 76 105 | 79 907 | 83 000 | 84 634 | 87 000 | 89 962 | 94 353 | 95 524 |
| Husband, not wife | 60 360 | 61 824 | 68 890 | 71 001 | 69 561 | 79 050 | 76 230 | 82 180 | 77 316 | 87 000 |
| Husband not an earner | 61 196 | 55 495 | 62 684 | 63 205 | 69 275 | 68 050 | 80 661 | 68 400 | 91 771 | 73 137 |
| **Families Maintained by Women, Total** | 19 306 | 19 416 | 20 470 | 21 875 | 23 100 | 25 000 | 25 064 | 26 000 | 26 000 | 26 400 |
| No earners | 7 440 | 7 092 | 7 476 | 7 737 | 8 010 | 8 988 | 8 160 | 8 808 | 8 344 | 8 400 |
| One earner | 18 824 | 18 500 | 19 000 | 20 000 | 20 092 | 22 306 | 23 008 | 24 597 | 24 752 | 25 040 |
| Householder | 17 890 | 18 000 | 18 000 | 18 800 | 19 000 | 21 400 | 22 001 | 23 760 | 23 832 | 24 801 |
| Other family member | 23 166 | 21 000 | 22 870 | 25 981 | 26 800 | 27 524 | 28 476 | 29 524 | 28 857 | 29 700 |
| Two earners or more | 35 000 | 36 400 | 39 275 | 40 000 | 41 144 | 43 035 | 45 244 | 46 580 | 47 576 | 48 549 |
| Householder and other family member(s) | 34 674 | 36 400 | 39 000 | 39 713 | 40 855 | 43 000 | 44 842 | 46 000 | 46 701 | 47 974 |
| Householder not an earner | 39 444 | 38 249 | 47 471 | 43 725 | 48 004 | 45 600 | 51 000 | 51 248 | 57 267 | 56 799 |
| **Families Maintained by Men, Total** | 30 000 | 31 500 | 32 984 | 35 000 | 37 000 | 37 040 | 36 000 | 37 440 | 37 914 | 40 000 |
| No earners | 12 240 | 12 030 | 14 252 | 15 468 | 13 752 | 14 946 | 12 840 | 15 200 | 15 408 | 14 167 |
| One earner | 25 337 | 26 100 | 26 897 | 29 125 | 31 038 | 30 160 | 30 800 | 30 139 | 32 097 | 35 000 |
| Householder | 25 069 | 25 874 | 27 000 | 29 125 | 30 483 | 30 816 | 30 500 | 30 014 | 31 355 | 35 000 |
| Other family member | 27 291 | 28 584 | 25 486 | 28 241 | 34 756 | 29 118 | 31 052 | 32 000 | 35 525 | 35 438 |
| Two earners or more | 43 100 | 44 275 | 49 900 | 51 288 | 51 040 | 55 010 | 55 024 | 55 000 | 57 840 | 57 600 |
| Householder and other family member(s) | 43 000 | 43 065 | 50 000 | 50 954 | 50 960 | 55 400 | 54 850 | 55 220 | 57 400 | 57 058 |
| Householder not an earner | 55 133 | 47 001 | 44 786 | 68 257 | 57 407 | 51 945 | 61 824 | 49 852 | 64 658 | 65 400 |

*Note:* See notes and definitions for information on historical comparability.

**Table 1-50.  Number of Families and Median Family Income, by Type of Family and Earner Status of Members, 1995–2015**—*Continued*

(Thousands of families, dollars.)

| Number and type of families and median family income | 2005 | 2006 | 2007 | 2008 | 2009 | 2010 | 2011 | 2012 | 2013 | 2014 | 2015 |
|---|---|---|---|---|---|---|---|---|---|---|---|
| **NUMBER OF FAMILIES** | | | | | | | | | | | |
| **Married-Couple Families, Total** | 58 225 | 59 050 | 58 490 | 59 181 | 58 521 | 58 135 | 59 071 | 59 327 | 59 795 | 60 091 | 60 338 |
| No earners | 8 017 | 8 091 | 7 914 | 8 083 | 8 467 | 8 626 | 9 152 | 9 101 | 9 556 | 9 437 | 9 380 |
| One earner | 14 301 | 14 562 | 14 272 | 14 625 | 15 046 | 15 421 | 15 981 | 15 841 | 15 828 | 15 642 | 15 653 |
| Husband | 10 611 | 10 706 | 10 396 | 10 567 | 10 570 | 10 895 | 11 308 | 11 276 | 11 370 | 11 246 | 11 185 |
| Wife | 3 097 | 3 264 | 3 267 | 3 437 | 3 854 | 3 935 | 4 016 | 3 894 | 3 788 | 3 776 | 3 739 |
| Other family member | 593 | 591 | 608 | 620 | 621 | 591 | 658 | 671 | 669 | 620 | 729 |
| Two earners or more | 28 802 | 29 216 | 29 256 | 29 466 | 28 371 | 27 821 | 27 661 | 27 902 | 27 978 | 28 255 | 28 505 |
| Husband and wife | 26 833 | 27 241 | 27 264 | 27 531 | 26 298 | 25 801 | 25 581 | 25 718 | 25 846 | 25 978 | 26 251 |
| Husband and other family member | 1 376 | 1 358 | 1 393 | 1 308 | 1 363 | 1 317 | 1 370 | 1 447 | 1 457 | 1 561 | 1 520 |
| Husband not an earner | 594 | 616 | 599 | 627 | 710 | 703 | 710 | 738 | 675 | 716 | 735 |
| Three earners or more | 7 104 | 7 181 | 7 048 | 7 008 | 6 638 | 6 267 | 6 277 | 6 482 | 6 434 | 6 756 | 6 800 |
| Husband and wife | 6 535 | 6 620 | 6 452 | 6 393 | 6 024 | 5 609 | 5 621 | 5 865 | 5 839 | 6 002 | 6 061 |
| Husband, not wife | 445 | 397 | 452 | 432 | 425 | 466 | 462 | 435 | 389 | 521 | 514 |
| Husband not an earner | 124 | 165 | 144 | 182 | 189 | 192 | 193 | 182 | 206 | 233 | 224 |
| | | | | | | | | | | | |
| **Families Maintained by Women, Total** | 14 505 | 14 852 | 14 846 | 14 842 | 15 236 | 15 491 | 16 154 | 15 949 | 15 632 | 16 055 | 16 038 |
| No earners | 2 616 | 2 627 | 2 502 | 2 678 | 3 076 | 3 297 | 3 373 | 3 300 | 3 143 | 3 173 | 3 022 |
| One earner | 8 052 | 8 303 | 8 418 | 8 381 | 8 475 | 8 638 | 8 790 | 8 621 | 8 537 | 8 702 | 8 672 |
| Householder | 6 724 | 6 904 | 7 020 | 6 978 | 6 941 | 7 158 | 7 303 | 7 170 | 6 998 | 7 158 | 7 076 |
| Other family member | 1 329 | 1 398 | 1 398 | 1 404 | 1 533 | 1 480 | 1 487 | 1 451 | 1 538 | 1 544 | 1 596 |
| Two earners or more | 3 836 | 3 923 | 3 925 | 3 783 | 3 685 | 3 555 | 3 991 | 4 028 | 3 953 | 4 180 | 4 344 |
| Householder and other family member(s) | 3 468 | 3 547 | 3 572 | 3 467 | 3 281 | 3 149 | 3 552 | 3 623 | 3 438 | 3 700 | 3 880 |
| Householder not an earner | 368 | 376 | 353 | 316 | 405 | 406 | 439 | 405 | 515 | 480 | 465 |
| | | | | | | | | | | | |
| **Families Maintained by Men, Total** | 5 193 | 5 119 | 5 181 | 5 301 | 5 630 | 5 649 | 5 975 | 6 308 | 6 384 | 6 236 | 6 386 |
| No earners | 537 | 555 | 532 | 611 | 539 | 775 | 838 | 883 | 824 | 817 | 802 |
| One earner | 2 661 | 2 584 | 2 703 | 2 636 | 2 801 | 2 911 | 3 106 | 3 242 | 3 311 | 3 230 | 3 236 |
| Householder | 2 196 | 2 155 | 2 297 | 2 199 | 2 261 | 2 389 | 2 535 | 2 698 | 2 715 | 2 664 | 2 634 |
| Other family member | 464 | 429 | 406 | 437 | 539 | 521 | 571 | 544 | 595 | 566 | 601 |
| Two earners or more | 1 995 | 1 979 | 1 947 | 2 054 | 2 030 | 1 963 | 2 031 | 2 183 | 2 249 | 2 190 | 2 348 |
| Householder and other family member(s) | 1 848 | 1 828 | 1 812 | 1 889 | 1 822 | 1 751 | 1 811 | 1 951 | 2 029 | 1 981 | 2 156 |
| Householder not an earner | 147 | 152 | 134 | 165 | 208 | 212 | 220 | 232 | 220 | 208 | 193 |
| | | | | | | | | | | | |
| **MEDIAN FAMILY INCOME** | | | | | | | | | | | |
| **Married-Couple Families, Total** | 65 586 | 69 300 | 72 802 | 72 805 | 71 464 | 72 224 | 73 678 | 75 002 | 76 000 | 80 234 | 84 076 |
| No earners | 28 376 | 30 000 | 30 134 | 31 164 | 32 093 | 32 350 | 33 756 | 33 584 | 35 948 | 36 748 | 37 678 |
| One earner | 50 000 | 50 400 | 52 686 | 53 865 | 53 087 | 55 000 | 56 609 | 58 415 | 57 000 | 60 009 | 63 015 |
| Husband | 52 000 | 53 360 | 55 350 | 56 000 | 55 333 | 56 533 | 59 842 | 60 002 | 59 748 | 60 381 | 64 490 |
| Wife | 43 505 | 45 000 | 47 000 | 47 015 | 47 550 | 50 150 | 52 007 | 52 517 | 52 000 | 57 189 | 59 914 |
| Other family member | 50 263 | 49 352 | 48 922 | 55 114 | 55 166 | 57 264 | 56 949 | 53 195 | 56 949 | 59 818 | 62 842 |
| Two earners | 76 960 | 81 500 | 85 012 | 85 500 | 86 361 | 88 500 | 90 001 | 91 651 | 94 100 | 98 023 | 102 256 |
| Husband and wife | 77 539 | 82 762 | 86 000 | 86 842 | 87 939 | 90 000 | 90 976 | 93 125 | 95 200 | 100 000 | 104 113 |
| Husband and other family member | 67 350 | 68 828 | 71 573 | 68 755 | 73 720 | 74 973 | 77 888 | 76 408 | 75 099 | 78 161 | 82 000 |
| Husband not an earner | 65 622 | 63 657 | 68 032 | 66 445 | 70 017 | 72 317 | 72 644 | 73 906 | 74 198 | 80 716 | 81 897 |
| Three earners or more | 98 000 | 103 803 | 106 747 | 105 618 | 107 000 | 107 542 | 111 000 | 114 201 | 118 408 | 123 850 | 127 000 |
| Husband and wife | 99 800 | 104 045 | 107 630 | 106 493 | 108 703 | 108 714 | 112 943 | 115 800 | 119 184 | 126 250 | 128 420 |
| Husband, not wife | 79 417 | 91 965 | 101 771 | 99 731 | 85 574 | 93 000 | 96 756 | 90 956 | 105 360 | 109 076 | 108 423 |
| Husband not an earner | 84 638 | 97 510 | 92 428 | 93 961 | 95 251 | 100 105 | 97 491 | 96 968 | 120 913 | 110 120 | 121 350 |
| | | | | | | | | | | | |
| **Families Maintained by Women, Total** | 27 000 | 28 218 | 30 000 | 29 698 | 29 025 | 28 774 | 29 848 | 30 000 | 30 500 | 30 816 | 33 405 |
| No earners | 8 228 | 8 657 | 8 873 | 9 404 | 10 037 | 9 600 | 9 600 | 10 299 | 10 224 | 10 205 | 10 736 |
| One earner | 25 308 | 26 393 | 27 795 | 28 060 | 29 000 | 29 009 | 28 912 | 29 558 | 30 000 | 29 740 | 30 205 |
| Householder | 24 505 | 25 381 | 26 644 | 27 000 | 27 928 | 27 924 | 27 488 | 28 077 | 28 000 | 28 000 | 29 402 |
| Other family member | 31 700 | 31 462 | 31 950 | 34 814 | 34 421 | 33 957 | 35 161 | 35 000 | 38 003 | 38 446 | 37 334 |
| Two earners or more | 50 000 | 52 400 | 55 749 | 54 369 | 54 500 | 55 047 | 56 000 | 58 694 | 58 535 | 59 008 | 63 651 |
| Householder and other family member(s) | 48 989 | 51 479 | 55 010 | 54 306 | 54 448 | 54 000 | 55 500 | 57 561 | 58 004 | 58 016 | 62 405 |
| Householder not an earner | 64 805 | 61 699 | 64 094 | 54 978 | 56 203 | 61 781 | 60 015 | 71 367 | 63 773 | 62 676 | 75 555 |
| | | | | | | | | | | | |
| **Families Maintained by Men, Total** | 40 293 | 41 130 | 44 001 | 43 050 | 41 000 | 42 500 | 43 000 | 42 000 | 44 394 | 47 159 | 49 000 |
| No earners | 13 950 | 15 462 | 12 921 | 15 557 | 15 653 | 16 176 | 17 945 | 18 006 | 16 440 | 15 828 | 17 107 |
| One earner | 35 001 | 35 100 | 37 716 | 36 806 | 35 116 | 37 707 | 38 000 | 38 500 | 38 300 | 40 754 | 40 989 |
| Householder | 35 075 | 35 011 | 37 720 | 37 569 | 35 117 | 37 990 | 38 069 | 36 000 | 39 185 | 40 530 | 42 000 |
| Other family member | 35 000 | 37 840 | 37 522 | 34 404 | 35 086 | 37 041 | 36 983 | 34 892 | 35 600 | 41 426 | 39 457 |
| Two earners or more | 60 024 | 61 000 | 63 600 | 64 077 | 64 747 | 66 000 | 67 301 | 65 017 | 69 505 | 71 997 | 77 729 |
| Householder and other family member(s) | 60 000 | 61 000 | 64 000 | 63 416 | 64 743 | 65 200 | 66 708 | 65 024 | 68 029 | 72 000 | 78 088 |
| Householder not an earner | 70 879 | 62 000 | 60 498 | 69 794 | 65 618 | 71 962 | 73 242 | 64 799 | 79 466 | 70 000 | 73 516 |

*Note:* See notes and definitions for information on historical comparability.

## Table 1-51. Employment Status of the Foreign-Born and Native-Born Populations, by Selected Characteristics, 2014–2015

(Thousands of people, percent.)

| Year and characteristic | Civilian noninstitutional population | Civilian labor force | | | | |
| --- | --- | --- | --- | --- | --- | --- |
| | | Total | Participation rate | Employed | Unemployed | |
| | | | | | Number | Rate |
| **2014** | | | | | | |
| **TOTAL** | | | | | | |
| Both sexes, 16 years and over ........................................ | 247 947 | 155 922 | 62.9 | 146 305 | 9 617 | 6.2 |
| Men ......................................................................... | 119 748 | 82 882 | 69.2 | 77 692 | 5 190 | 6.3 |
| Women ...................................................................... | 128 199 | 73 039 | 57.0 | 68 613 | 4 426 | 6.1 |
| **FOREIGN BORN** | | | | | | |
| Both sexes, 16 years and over ........................................ | 38 997 | 25 735 | 66.0 | 24 282 | 1 453 | 5.6 |
| Men ......................................................................... | 18 997 | 14 957 | 78.7 | 14 204 | 753 | 5.0 |
| Women ...................................................................... | 20 000 | 10 779 | 53.9 | 10 078 | 700 | 6.5 |
| **Age** | | | | | | |
| 16 to 24 years ........................................................... | 3 543 | 1 852 | 52.3 | 1 645 | 207 | 11.2 |
| 25 to 34 years ........................................................... | 7 554 | 5 647 | 74.8 | 5 324 | 323 | 5.7 |
| 35 to 44 years ........................................................... | 8 897 | 7 032 | 79.0 | 6 697 | 336 | 4.8 |
| 45 to 54 years ........................................................... | 7 949 | 6 441 | 81.0 | 6 109 | 332 | 5.2 |
| 55 to 64 years ........................................................... | 5 534 | 3 715 | 67.1 | 3 515 | 200 | 5.4 |
| 65 years and over ...................................................... | 5 520 | 1 047 | 19.0 | 992 | 55 | 5.2 |
| **Race and Hispanic Origin** | | | | | | |
| White, non-Hispanic ................................................... | 7 564 | 4 500 | 59.5 | 4 290 | 211 | 4.7 |
| Black, non-Hispanic ................................................... | 3 243 | 2 305 | 71.1 | 2 106 | 199 | 8.6 |
| Asian, non-Hispanic ................................................... | 9 729 | 6 211 | 63.8 | 5 924 | 287 | 4.6 |
| Hispanic[1] ............................................................... | 18 053 | 12 431 | 68.9 | 11 692 | 739 | 5.9 |
| **Educational Attainment** | | | | | | |
| Total, 25 years and over ............................................. | 35 455 | 23 883 | 67.4 | 22 637 | 1 246 | 5.2 |
| Less than a high school diploma ................................. | 9 649 | 5 684 | 58.9 | 5 321 | 363 | 6.4 |
| High school graduate, no college[2] ............................ | 8 924 | 5 856 | 65.6 | 5 547 | 309 | 5.3 |
| Some college or associate's degree ............................ | 5 816 | 4 168 | 71.7 | 3 932 | 236 | 5.7 |
| Bachelor's degree or higher[3] ................................... | 11 065 | 8 176 | 73.9 | 7 838 | 338 | 4.1 |
| **NATIVE BORN** | | | | | | |
| Both sexes, 16 years and over ........................................ | 208 949 | 130 187 | 62.3 | 122 023 | 8 164 | 6.3 |
| Men ......................................................................... | 100 751 | 67 926 | 67.4 | 63 488 | 4 437 | 6.5 |
| Women ...................................................................... | 108 199 | 62 261 | 57.5 | 58 535 | 3 726 | 6.0 |
| **Age** | | | | | | |
| 16 to 24 years ........................................................... | 35 170 | 19 443 | 55.3 | 16 797 | 2 646 | 13.6 |
| 25 to 34 years ........................................................... | 34 577 | 28 551 | 82.6 | 26 651 | 1 901 | 6.7 |
| 35 to 44 years ........................................................... | 30 668 | 25 473 | 83.1 | 24 270 | 1 203 | 4.7 |
| 45 to 54 years ........................................................... | 34 866 | 27 621 | 79.2 | 26 446 | 1 175 | 4.3 |
| 55 to 64 years ........................................................... | 34 230 | 21 787 | 63.6 | 20 880 | 907 | 4.2 |
| 65 years and over ...................................................... | 39 439 | 7 311 | 18.5 | 6 979 | 332 | 4.5 |
| **Race and Hispanic Origin** | | | | | | |
| White, non-Hispanic ................................................... | 153 630 | 96 161 | 62.6 | 91 456 | 4 705 | 4.9 |
| Black, non-Hispanic ................................................... | 25 844 | 15 437 | 59.7 | 13 608 | 1 829 | 11.8 |
| Asian, non-Hispanic ................................................... | 3 738 | 2 325 | 62.2 | 2 195 | 130 | 5.6 |
| Hispanic[1] ............................................................... | 20 347 | 12 939 | 63.6 | 11 800 | 1 139 | 8.8 |
| **Educational Attainment** | | | | | | |
| Total, 25 years and over ............................................. | 173 780 | 110 744 | 63.7 | 105 226 | 5 518 | 5.0 |
| Less than a high school diploma ................................. | 14 493 | 5 144 | 35.5 | 4 531 | 613 | 11.9 |
| High school graduates, no college[2] .......................... | 53 136 | 30 177 | 56.8 | 28 319 | 1 858 | 6.2 |
| Some college or associate's degree ............................ | 49 878 | 33 153 | 66.5 | 31 367 | 1 786 | 5.4 |
| Bachelor's degree or higher[3] ................................... | 56 272 | 42 270 | 75.1 | 41 010 | 1 261 | 3.0 |

*Note:* Updated population controls are introduced annually with the release of January data.

[1]May be of any race.
[2]Includes persons with a high school diploma or equivalent.
[3]Includes persons with bachelor's, master's, professional, and doctoral degrees.

**Table 1-51.  Employment Status of the Foreign-Born and Native-Born Populations, by Selected Characteristics, 2014–2015**—*Continued*

(Thousands of people, percent.)

| Year and characteristic | Civilian noninstitutional population | Civilian labor force | | | | |
|---|---|---|---|---|---|---|
| | | Total | Participation rate | Employed | Unemployed | |
| | | | | | Number | Rate |
| **2015** | | | | | | |
| **TOTAL** | | | | | | |
| Both sexes, 16 years and over | 250 801 | 157 130 | 62.7 | 148 834 | 8 296 | 5.3 |
| Men | 121 101 | 83 620 | 69.1 | 79 131 | 4 490 | 5.4 |
| Women | 129 700 | 73 510 | 56.7 | 69 703 | 3 807 | 5.2 |
| **FOREIGN BORN** | | | | | | |
| Both sexes, 16 years and over | 40 257 | 26 258 | 65.2 | 24 963 | 1 295 | 4.9 |
| Men | 19 548 | 15 296 | 78.2 | 14 615 | 681 | 4.5 |
| Women | 20 709 | 10 961 | 52.9 | 10 348 | 613 | 5.6 |
| **Age** | | | | | | |
| 16 to 24 years | 3 625 | 1 861 | 51.3 | 1 674 | 187 | 10.0 |
| 25 to 34 years | 7 660 | 5 657 | 73.9 | 5 373 | 284 | 5.0 |
| 35 to 44 years | 9 153 | 7 183 | 78.5 | 6 880 | 303 | 4.2 |
| 45 to 54 years | 8 142 | 6 513 | 80.0 | 6 248 | 265 | 4.1 |
| 55 to 64 years | 5 798 | 3 891 | 67.1 | 3 698 | 193 | 5.0 |
| 65 years and over | 5 879 | 1 152 | 19.6 | 1 090 | 62 | 5.4 |
| **Race and Hispanic Origin** | | | | | | |
| White, non-Hispanic | 7 495 | 4 401 | 58.7 | 4 224 | 177 | 4.0 |
| Black, non-Hispanic | 3 411 | 2 415 | 70.8 | 2 237 | 179 | 7.4 |
| Asian, non-Hispanic | 10 123 | 6 335 | 62.6 | 6 101 | 234 | 3.7 |
| Hispanic[1] | 18 797 | 12 814 | 68.2 | 12 126 | 687 | 5.4 |
| **Educational Attainment** | | | | | | |
| Total, 25 years and over | 36 632 | 24 397 | 66.6 | 23 289 | 1 108 | 4.5 |
| Less than a high school diploma | 9 968 | 5 828 | 58.5 | 5 500 | 328 | 5.6 |
| High school graduates, no college[2] | 9 172 | 5 951 | 64.9 | 5 649 | 303 | 5.1 |
| Some college or associate degree | 5 896 | 4 111 | 69.7 | 3 917 | 193 | 4.7 |
| Bachelor's degree and higher[3] | 11 595 | 8 507 | 73.4 | 8 223 | 284 | 3.3 |
| **NATIVE BORN** | | | | | | |
| Both sexes, 16 years and over | 210 544 | 130 872 | 62.2 | 123 871 | 7 002 | 5.4 |
| Men | 101 553 | 68 324 | 67.3 | 64 516 | 3 808 | 5.6 |
| Women | 108 991 | 62 548 | 57.4 | 59 355 | 3 193 | 5.1 |
| **Age** | | | | | | |
| 16 to 24 years | 34 965 | 19 362 | 55.4 | 17 082 | 2 280 | 11.8 |
| 25 to 34 years | 35 111 | 28 989 | 82.6 | 27 369 | 1 620 | 5.6 |
| 35 to 44 years | 30 548 | 25 420 | 83.2 | 24 373 | 1 048 | 4.1 |
| 45 to 54 years | 34 495 | 27 389 | 79.4 | 26 395 | 994 | 3.6 |
| 55 to 64 years | 34 796 | 22 063 | 63.4 | 21 278 | 785 | 3.6 |
| 65 years and over | 40 630 | 7 649 | 18.8 | 7 374 | 275 | 3.6 |
| **Race and Hispanic Origin** | | | | | | |
| White, non-Hispanic | 154 058 | 96 007 | 62.3 | 92 010 | 3 997 | 4.2 |
| Black, non-Hispanic | 26 306 | 15 780 | 60.0 | 14 219 | 1 561 | 9.9 |
| Asian, non-Hispanic | 3 908 | 2 437 | 62.4 | 2 333 | 104 | 4.3 |
| Hispanic[1] | 20 821 | 13 313 | 63.9 | 12 273 | 1 039 | 7.8 |
| **Educational Attainment** | | | | | | |
| Total, 25 years and over | 175 579 | 111 510 | 63.5 | 106 788 | 4 722 | 4.2 |
| Less than a high school diploma | 14 206 | 5 143 | 36.2 | 4 598 | 545 | 10.6 |
| High school graduates, no college[2] | 52 540 | 29 371 | 55.9 | 27 753 | 1 617 | 5.5 |
| Some college or associate degree | 50 367 | 33 370 | 66.3 | 31 868 | 1 502 | 4.5 |
| Bachelor's degree or higher[3] | 58 466 | 43 626 | 74.6 | 42 569 | 1 057 | 2.4 |

*Note:* Updated population controls are introduced annually with the release of January data.

[1]May be of any race.
[2]Includes persons with a high school diploma or equivalent.
[3]Includes persons with bachelor's, master's, professional, and doctoral degrees.

## Table 1-52. Employment Status of the Foreign-Born and Native-Born Populations Age 16 Years and Over, by Sex and Presence and Age of Youngest Child, Annual Averages, 2014–2015

(Thousands of people, percent.)

| Characteristic | 2014 | | | 2015 | | |
|---|---|---|---|---|---|---|
| | Both sexes | Men | Women | Both sexes | Men | Women |
| **FOREIGN BORN** | | | | | | |
| **With Own Children Under 18 Years** | | | | | | |
| Civilian noninstitutional population .............................................. | 15 109 | 7 055 | 8 054 | 15 517 | 7 300 | 8 217 |
| Civilian labor force ......................................................... | 11 382 | 6 619 | 4 763 | 11 583 | 6 831 | 4 753 |
| Participation rate ........................................................ | 75.3 | 93.8 | 59.1 | 74.6 | 93.6 | 57.8 |
| Employed ................................................................. | 10 786 | 6 355 | 4 431 | 11 076 | 6 597 | 4 480 |
| Employment-population ratio ..................................... | 71.4 | 90.1 | 55.0 | 71.4 | 90.4 | 54.5 |
| Unemployed .......................................................... | 596 | 265 | 332 | 507 | 234 | 273 |
| Unemployment rate .......................................... | 5.2 | 4.0 | 7.0 | 4.4 | 3.4 | 5.7 |
| **With Own Children 6 to 17 Years, None Younger** | | | | | | |
| Civilian noninstitutional population .............................................. | 8 197 | 3 719 | 4 478 | 8 603 | 3 961 | 4 642 |
| Civilian labor force ......................................................... | 6 420 | 3 447 | 2 972 | 6 680 | 3 674 | 3 006 |
| Participation rate ........................................................ | 78.3 | 92.7 | 66.4 | 77.6 | 92.7 | 64.8 |
| Employed ................................................................. | 6 082 | 3 297 | 2 785 | 6 397 | 3 548 | 2 849 |
| Employment-population ratio ..................................... | 74.2 | 88.6 | 62.2 | 74.4 | 89.6 | 61.4 |
| Unemployed .......................................................... | 338 | 151 | 187 | 284 | 126 | 158 |
| Unemployment rate .......................................... | 5.3 | 4.4 | 6.3 | 4.2 | 3.4 | 5.3 |
| **With Own Children Under 6 Years** | | | | | | |
| Civilian noninstitutional population .............................................. | 6 912 | 3 336 | 3 577 | 6 914 | 3 338 | 3 575 |
| Civilian labor force ......................................................... | 4 963 | 3 172 | 1 791 | 4 903 | 3 157 | 1 746 |
| Participation rate ........................................................ | 71.8 | 95.1 | 50.1 | 70.9 | 94.6 | 48.8 |
| Employed ................................................................. | 4 704 | 3 058 | 1 646 | 4 680 | 3 049 | 1 631 |
| Employment-population ratio ..................................... | 68.1 | 91.7 | 46.0 | 67.7 | 91.3 | 45.6 |
| Unemployed .......................................................... | 259 | 114 | 145 | 223 | 108 | 115 |
| Unemployment rate .......................................... | 5.2 | 3.6 | 8.1 | 4.6 | 3.4 | 6.6 |
| **With Own Children Under 3 Years** | | | | | | |
| Civilian noninstitutional population .............................................. | 3 742 | 1 816 | 1 926 | 3 810 | 1 878 | 1 932 |
| Civilian labor force ......................................................... | 2 607 | 1 733 | 874 | 2 639 | 1 770 | 869 |
| Participation rate ........................................................ | 69.7 | 95.4 | 45.4 | 69.3 | 94.2 | 45.0 |
| Employed ................................................................. | 2 468 | 1 665 | 802 | 2 517 | 1 711 | 806 |
| Employment-population ratio ..................................... | 65.9 | 91.7 | 41.7 | 66.1 | 91.1 | 41.7 |
| Unemployed .......................................................... | 140 | 68 | 72 | 122 | 59 | 63 |
| Unemployment rate .......................................... | 5.4 | 3.9 | 8.2 | 4.6 | 3.3 | 7.3 |
| **With No Own Children Under 18 Years** | | | | | | |
| Civilian noninstitutional population .............................................. | 23 888 | 11 942 | 11 946 | 24 740 | 12 248 | 12 492 |
| Civilian labor force ......................................................... | 14 353 | 8 337 | 6 016 | 14 674 | 8 465 | 6 209 |
| Participation rate ........................................................ | 60.1 | 69.8 | 50.4 | 59.3 | 69.1 | 49.7 |
| Employed ................................................................. | 13 496 | 7 849 | 5 647 | 13 887 | 8 018 | 5 868 |
| Employment-population ratio ..................................... | 56.5 | 65.7 | 47.3 | 56.1 | 65.5 | 47.0 |
| Unemployed .......................................................... | 857 | 488 | 368 | 787 | 447 | 340 |
| Unemployment rate .......................................... | 6.0 | 5.9 | 6.1 | 5.4 | 5.3 | 5.5 |

*Note:* Updated population controls are introduced annually with the release of January data.

**Table 1-52.  Employment Status of the Foreign-Born and Native-Born Populations Age 16 Years and Over, by Sex and Presence and Age of Youngest Child, Annual Averages, 2014–2015**—*Continued*

(Thousands of people, percent.)

| Characteristic | 2014 | | | 2015 | | |
|---|---|---|---|---|---|---|
| | Both sexes | Men | Women | Both sexes | Men | Women |
| **NATIVE BORN** | | | | | | |
| **With Own Children Under 18 Years** | | | | | | |
| Civilian noninstitutional population ............................................. | 50 534 | 21 986 | 28 548 | 50 047 | 21 795 | 28 252 |
| Civilian labor force ................................................................. | 41 198 | 20 320 | 20 878 | 40 893 | 20 147 | 20 746 |
| Participation rate ............................................................. | 81.5 | 92.4 | 73.1 | 81.7 | 92.4 | 73.4 |
| Employed ........................................................................... | 39 162 | 19 544 | 19 618 | 39 162 | 19 482 | 19 680 |
| Employment-population ratio ......................................... | 77.5 | 88.9 | 68.7 | 78.3 | 89.4 | 69.7 |
| Unemployed ...................................................................... | 2 036 | 776 | 1 260 | 1 731 | 665 | 1 066 |
| Unemployment rate ......................................................... | 4.9 | 3.8 | 6.0 | 4.2 | 3.3 | 5.1 |
| **With Own Children 6 to 17 Years, None Younger** | | | | | | |
| Civilian noninstitutional population ............................................. | 28 289 | 12 395 | 15 895 | 28 013 | 12 209 | 15 803 |
| Civilian labor force ................................................................. | 23 569 | 11 321 | 12 248 | 23 377 | 11 166 | 12 211 |
| Participation rate ............................................................. | 83.3 | 91.3 | 77.1 | 83.5 | 91.5 | 77.3 |
| Employed ........................................................................... | 22 607 | 10 947 | 11 660 | 22 526 | 10 844 | 11 682 |
| Employment-population ratio ......................................... | 79.9 | 88.3 | 73.4 | 80.4 | 88.8 | 73.9 |
| Unemployed ...................................................................... | 962 | 374 | 588 | 851 | 322 | 529 |
| Unemployment rate ......................................................... | 4.1 | 3.3 | 4.8 | 3.6 | 2.9 | 4.3 |
| **With Own Children Under 6 Years** | | | | | | |
| Civilian noninstitutional population ............................................. | 22 244 | 9 591 | 12 653 | 22 034 | 9 586 | 12 449 |
| Civilian labor force ................................................................. | 17 628 | 8 999 | 8 629 | 17 516 | 8 981 | 8 535 |
| Participation rate ............................................................. | 79.2 | 93.8 | 68.2 | 79.5 | 93.7 | 68.6 |
| Employed ........................................................................... | 16 555 | 8 597 | 7 958 | 16 636 | 8 638 | 7 997 |
| Employment-population ratio ......................................... | 74.4 | 89.6 | 62.9 | 75.5 | 90.1 | 64.2 |
| Unemployed ...................................................................... | 1 074 | 402 | 672 | 880 | 343 | 537 |
| Unemployment rate ......................................................... | 6.1 | 4.5 | 7.8 | 5.0 | 3.8 | 6.3 |
| **With Own Children Under 3 Years** | | | | | | |
| Civilian noninstitutional population ............................................. | 12 986 | 5 688 | 7 298 | 13 144 | 5 769 | 7 375 |
| Civilian labor force ................................................................. | 10 102 | 5 352 | 4 750 | 10 255 | 5 411 | 4 845 |
| Participation rate ............................................................. | 77.8 | 94.1 | 65.1 | 78.0 | 93.8 | 65.7 |
| Employed ........................................................................... | 9 472 | 5 105 | 4 367 | 9 733 | 5 203 | 4 530 |
| Employment-population ratio ......................................... | 72.9 | 89.8 | 59.8 | 74.0 | 90.2 | 61.4 |
| Unemployed ...................................................................... | 631 | 247 | 384 | 522 | 208 | 314 |
| Unemployment rate ......................................................... | 6.2 | 4.6 | 8.1 | 5.1 | 3.8 | 6.5 |
| **With No Own Children Under 18 Years** | | | | | | |
| Civilian noninstitutional population ............................................. | 158 415 | 78 765 | 79 651 | 160 497 | 79 757 | 80 739 |
| Civilian labor force ................................................................. | 88 989 | 47 606 | 41 383 | 89 980 | 48 177 | 41 803 |
| Participation rate ............................................................. | 56.2 | 60.4 | 52.0 | 56.1 | 60.4 | 51.8 |
| Employed ........................................................................... | 82 861 | 43 944 | 38 917 | 84 709 | 45 034 | 39 675 |
| Employment-population ratio ......................................... | 52.3 | 55.8 | 48.9 | 52.8 | 56.5 | 49.1 |
| Unemployed ...................................................................... | 6 128 | 3 662 | 2 466 | 5 271 | 3 143 | 2 127 |
| Unemployment rate ......................................................... | 6.9 | 7.7 | 6.0 | 5.9 | 6.5 | 5.1 |

*Note:* Updated population controls are introduced annually with the release of January data.

## Table 1-53. Employment Status of the Foreign-Born and Native-Born Populations Age 25 Years and Over, by Educational Attainment, Race, and Hispanic Origin, Annual Averages, 2014–2015

(Thousands of people, percent.)

| Characteristic | 2014 | | | | 2015 | | | |
|---|---|---|---|---|---|---|---|---|
| | Less than a high school diploma | High school graduate, no college[1] | Some college or associate's degree | Bachelor's degree or higher[2] | Less than a high school diploma | High school graduate, no college[1] | Some college or associate's degree | Bachelor's degree or higher[2] |
| **FOREIGN BORN** | | | | | | | | |
| **White, Non-Hispanic** | | | | | | | | |
| Civilian noninstitutional population | 736 | 1 671 | 1 413 | 3 184 | 661 | 1 658 | 1 372 | 3 246 |
| Civilian labor force | 258 | 856 | 890 | 2 234 | 227 | 837 | 801 | 2 269 |
| Participation rate | 35.0 | 51.2 | 63.0 | 70.2 | 34.3 | 50.5 | 58.4 | 69.9 |
| Employed | 245 | 822 | 844 | 2 146 | 220 | 804 | 760 | 2 200 |
| Employment-population ratio | 33.2 | 49.2 | 59.7 | 67.4 | 33.3 | 48.5 | 55.4 | 67.8 |
| Unemployed | 13 | 34 | 46 | 88 | 7 | 32 | 41 | 69 |
| Unemployment rate | 5.0 | 4.0 | 5.2 | 3.9 | 2.9 | 3.9 | 5.1 | 3.0 |
| **Black, Non-Hispanic** | | | | | | | | |
| Civilian noninstitutional population | 410 | 810 | 749 | 899 | 388 | 837 | 772 | 992 |
| Civilian labor force | 216 | 576 | 597 | 733 | 210 | 575 | 609 | 823 |
| Participation rate | 53.0 | 71.0 | 80.0 | 82.0 | 54.0 | 69.0 | 78.9 | 83.0 |
| Employed | 193 | 528 | 546 | 689 | 188 | 529 | 572 | 782 |
| Employment-population ratio | 46.9 | 65.2 | 72.8 | 76.7 | 48.5 | 63.2 | 74.1 | 78.9 |
| Unemployed | 24 | 48 | 52 | 44 | 22 | 46 | 37 | 41 |
| Unemployment rate | 11.1 | 8.4 | 8.6 | 6.1 | 10.4 | 8.0 | 6.1 | 5.0 |
| **Asian, Non-Hispanic** | | | | | | | | |
| Civilian noninstitutional population | 1 041 | 1 758 | 1 296 | 4 825 | 1 036 | 1 854 | 1 277 | 5 135 |
| Civilian labor force | 407 | 1 043 | 877 | 3 568 | 409 | 1 065 | 854 | 3 702 |
| Participation rate | 39.1 | 59.3 | 67.7 | 74.0 | 39.5 | 57.4 | 66.9 | 72.0 |
| Employed | 379 | 1 001 | 835 | 3 435 | 389 | 1 023 | 825 | 3 591 |
| Employment-population ratio | 36.4 | 56.9 | 64.4 | 71.2 | 37.5 | 55.2 | 64.6 | 69.9 |
| Unemployed | 28 | 42 | 42 | 133 | 20 | 42 | 28 | 111 |
| Unemployment rate | 6.9 | 4.0 | 4.8 | 4.0 | 5.0 | 4.0 | 3.3 | 3.0 |
| **Hispanic[3]** | | | | | | | | |
| Civilian noninstitutional population | 7 392 | 4 593 | 2 272 | 2 040 | 7 816 | 4 724 | 2 381 | 2 089 |
| Civilian labor force | 4 765 | 3 314 | 1 740 | 1 544 | 4 955 | 3 406 | 1 779 | 1 603 |
| Participation rate | 64.5 | 72.0 | 77.0 | 76.0 | 63.4 | 72.0 | 74.7 | 76.7 |
| Employed | 4 470 | 3 134 | 1 649 | 1 473 | 4 677 | 3 230 | 1 696 | 1 543 |
| Employment-population ratio | 60.5 | 68.2 | 72.6 | 72.2 | 59.8 | 68.4 | 71.2 | 73.9 |
| Unemployed | 295 | 180 | 91 | 70 | 277 | 176 | 83 | 60 |
| Unemployment rate | 6.2 | 5.4 | 5.2 | 4.5 | 5.6 | 5.2 | 4.7 | 3.7 |
| **NATIVE BORN** | | | | | | | | |
| **White, Non-Hispanic** | | | | | | | | |
| Civilian noninstitutional population | 8 941 | 39 783 | 37 386 | 46 674 | 8 769 | 39 059 | 37 445 | 48 179 |
| Civilian labor force | 3 012 | 22 023 | 24 287 | 34 576 | 3 033 | 21 173 | 24 197 | 35 522 |
| Participation rate | 33.7 | 55.4 | 65.0 | 74.1 | 34.6 | 54.2 | 64.6 | 73.7 |
| Employed | 2 733 | 20 932 | 23 188 | 33 647 | 2 793 | 20 250 | 23 282 | 34 735 |
| Employment-population ratio | 30.6 | 52.6 | 62.0 | 72.1 | 31.9 | 51.8 | 62.2 | 72.1 |
| Unemployed | 278 | 1 090 | 1 099 | 929 | 240 | 923 | 915 | 787 |
| Unemployment rate | 9.2 | 5.0 | 4.5 | 2.7 | 7.9 | 4.4 | 3.8 | 2.2 |
| **Black, Non-Hispanic** | | | | | | | | |
| Civilian noninstitutional population | 2 715 | 7 163 | 6 399 | 4 404 | 2 591 | 7 344 | 6 583 | 4 700 |
| Civilian labor force | 906 | 4 134 | 4 397 | 3 432 | 857 | 4 196 | 4 528 | 3 586 |
| Participation rate | 33.4 | 57.7 | 68.7 | 77.9 | 33.1 | 57.1 | 68.8 | 76.3 |
| Employed | 733 | 3 669 | 3 998 | 3 258 | 701 | 3 780 | 4 188 | 3 449 |
| Employment-population ratio | 27.0 | 51.2 | 62.5 | 74.0 | 27.1 | 51.5 | 63.6 | 73.4 |
| Unemployed | 173 | 465 | 398 | 174 | 156 | 416 | 340 | 137 |
| Unemployment rate | 19.1 | 11.3 | 9.1 | 5.1 | 18.2 | 9.9 | 7.5 | 3.8 |
| **Asian, Non-Hispanic** | | | | | | | | |
| Civilian noninstitutional population | 141 | 449 | 566 | 1 416 | 138 | 443 | 576 | 1 541 |
| Civilian labor force | 61 | 253 | 392 | 1 135 | 57 | 273 | 402 | 1 213 |
| Participation rate | 43.0 | 56.4 | 69.3 | 80.2 | 41.4 | 61.7 | 69.8 | 78.7 |
| Employed | 56 | 236 | 373 | 1 097 | 52 | 260 | 388 | 1 187 |
| Employment-population ratio | 39.5 | 52.7 | 65.9 | 77.5 | 37.7 | 58.7 | 67.4 | 77.0 |
| Unemployed | 5 | 17 | 19 | 39 | 5 | 13 | 14 | 26 |
| Unemployment rate | 8.1 | 6.6 | 4.9 | 3.4 | 8.9 | 4.9 | 3.4 | 2.1 |
| **Hispanic[3]** | | | | | | | | |
| Civilian noninstitutional population | 2 291 | 4 505 | 4 190 | 2 811 | 2 278 | 4 536 | 4 393 | 2 997 |
| Civilian labor force | 1 027 | 3 034 | 3 172 | 2 349 | 1 031 | 3 037 | 3 333 | 2 473 |
| Participation rate | 44.8 | 67.4 | 75.7 | 83.6 | 45.3 | 67.0 | 75.9 | 82.5 |
| Employed | 895 | 2 820 | 2 977 | 2 268 | 915 | 2 834 | 3 163 | 2 392 |
| Employment-population ratio | 39.1 | 62.6 | 71.0 | 80.7 | 40.1 | 62.5 | 72.0 | 79.8 |
| Unemployed | 132 | 215 | 194 | 81 | 117 | 203 | 170 | 81 |
| Unemployment rate | 12.9 | 7.1 | 6.1 | 3.5 | 11.3 | 6.7 | 5.1 | 3.3 |

*Note:* Updated population controls are introduced annually with the release of January data.

[1]Includes persons with a high school diploma or equivalent.
[2]Includes persons with bachelor's, master's, professional, and doctoral degrees.
[3]May be of any race.

**Table 1-54.  Employed Foreign-Born and Native-Born Persons Age 16 Years and Over, by Occupation and Sex, Annual Averages, 2014–2015**

(Thousands of people, percent.)

| Occupation | 2014 | | | | | |
| | Foreign born | | | Native born | | |
| | Both sexes | Male | Female | Both sexes | Male | Female |
|---|---|---|---|---|---|---|
| TOTAL EMPLOYED | 24 282 | 14 204 | 10 078 | 122 023 | 63 488 | 58 535 |
| | | | | | | |
| Percent Employed | 100.0 | 100.0 | 100.0 | 100.0 | 100.0 | 100.0 |
| Management, professional, and related | 30.7 | 28.5 | 33.7 | 39.8 | 36.3 | 43.6 |
| Management, business, and financial operations | 11.5 | 11.5 | 11.6 | 16.7 | 18.0 | 15.3 |
| Management | 8.0 | 8.8 | 6.9 | 11.7 | 13.7 | 9.5 |
| Business and financial operations | 3.5 | 2.7 | 4.7 | 5.0 | 4.3 | 5.8 |
| Professional and related | 19.1 | 17.0 | 22.2 | 23.1 | 18.4 | 28.3 |
| Computer and mathematical | 4.3 | 5.6 | 2.5 | 2.7 | 3.8 | 1.4 |
| Architecture and engineering | 2.2 | 3.0 | 0.9 | 1.9 | 3.1 | 0.6 |
| Life, physical, and social sciences | 1.1 | 1.1 | 1.0 | 0.9 | 0.9 | 0.9 |
| Community and social services | 1.0 | 0.7 | 1.4 | 1.8 | 1.2 | 2.5 |
| Legal | 0.5 | 0.4 | 0.8 | 1.4 | 1.3 | 1.4 |
| Education, training, and library | 3.4 | 1.9 | 5.5 | 6.4 | 3.1 | 10.0 |
| Arts, design, entertainment, sports, and media | 1.4 | 1.3 | 1.4 | 2.1 | 2.1 | 2.1 |
| Health care practitioner and technical | 5.3 | 3.0 | 8.6 | 5.9 | 2.8 | 9.3 |
| Services | 24.1 | 18.1 | 32.4 | 16.4 | 13.6 | 19.5 |
| Health care support | 2.7 | 0.7 | 5.4 | 2.3 | 0.5 | 4.2 |
| Protective services | 1.0 | 1.4 | 0.5 | 2.4 | 3.6 | 1.1 |
| Food preparation and serving related | 7.3 | 6.9 | 7.7 | 5.2 | 4.2 | 6.3 |
| Building and grounds cleaning and maintenance | 8.7 | 7.5 | 10.2 | 3.0 | 3.8 | 2.2 |
| Personal care and services | 4.4 | 1.6 | 8.5 | 3.5 | 1.6 | 5.6 |
| Sales and office | 16.0 | 11.7 | 22.2 | 24.2 | 17.5 | 31.5 |
| Sales and related | 8.4 | 7.2 | 10.1 | 11.2 | 10.9 | 11.4 |
| Office and administrative support | 7.7 | 4.5 | 12.1 | 13.0 | 6.6 | 20.1 |
| Natural resources, construction, and maintenance | 13.7 | 22.2 | 1.7 | 8.4 | 15.4 | 0.7 |
| Farming, fishing, and forestry | 1.7 | 2.2 | 1.0 | 0.5 | 0.8 | 0.2 |
| Construction and extraction | 9.0 | 15.2 | 0.3 | 4.5 | 8.3 | 0.3 |
| Installation, maintenance, and repair | 2.9 | 4.8 | 0.3 | 3.4 | 6.3 | 0.2 |
| Production, transportation, and material moving | 15.6 | 19.5 | 10.0 | 11.2 | 17.2 | 4.7 |
| Production | 8.0 | 8.5 | 7.3 | 5.3 | 7.7 | 2.8 |
| Transportation and material moving | 7.6 | 11.0 | 2.8 | 5.9 | 9.5 | 1.9 |

| Occupation | 2015 | | | | | |
| | Foreign born | | | Native born | | |
| | Both sexes | Male | Female | Both sexes | Male | Female |
|---|---|---|---|---|---|---|
| TOTAL EMPLOYED | 24 963 | 14 615 | 10 348 | 123 871 | 64 516 | 59 355 |
| | | | | | | |
| Percent Employed | 100.0 | 100.0 | 100.0 | 100.0 | 100.0 | 100.0 |
| Management, professional, and related | 30.8 | 28.5 | 34.1 | 40.6 | 37.1 | 44.4 |
| Management, business, and financial operations | 11.7 | 11.5 | 11.9 | 17.1 | 18.4 | 15.7 |
| Management | 8.1 | 8.7 | 7.4 | 12.1 | 14.1 | 9.9 |
| Business and financial operations | 3.5 | 2.9 | 4.5 | 5.0 | 4.4 | 5.7 |
| Professional and related | 19.1 | 17.0 | 22.3 | 23.5 | 18.6 | 28.7 |
| Computer and mathematical | 4.3 | 5.6 | 2.6 | 2.7 | 3.8 | 1.4 |
| Architecture and engineering | 2.2 | 3.1 | 1.0 | 1.9 | 3.2 | 0.6 |
| Life, physical, and social sciences | 1.2 | 1.2 | 1.2 | 0.9 | 0.9 | 0.9 |
| Community and social services | 0.9 | 0.7 | 1.2 | 1.9 | 1.2 | 2.6 |
| Legal | 0.4 | 0.2 | 0.7 | 1.4 | 1.3 | 1.4 |
| Education, training, and library | 3.5 | 2.1 | 5.5 | 6.5 | 3.2 | 10.1 |
| Arts, design, entertainment, sports, and media | 1.4 | 1.3 | 1.6 | 2.2 | 2.2 | 2.2 |
| Health care practitioner and technical | 5.2 | 2.8 | 8.5 | 6.0 | 2.8 | 9.6 |
| Services | 23.4 | 17.3 | 32.1 | 16.2 | 13.5 | 19.2 |
| Health care support | 2.7 | 0.7 | 5.5 | 2.3 | 0.5 | 4.2 |
| Protective services | 0.9 | 1.3 | 0.4 | 2.3 | 3.5 | 1.0 |
| Food preparation and serving related | 7.1 | 6.6 | 7.8 | 5.1 | 4.2 | 6.1 |
| Building and grounds cleaning and maintenance | 8.4 | 7.1 | 10.3 | 2.9 | 3.6 | 2.2 |
| Personal care and services | 4.3 | 1.6 | 8.1 | 3.5 | 1.6 | 5.6 |
| Sales and office | 16.6 | 12.4 | 22.5 | 23.8 | 17.3 | 30.9 |
| Sales and related | 8.6 | 7.7 | 9.8 | 10.9 | 10.6 | 11.3 |
| Office and administrative support | 8.0 | 4.7 | 12.7 | 12.8 | 6.7 | 19.6 |
| Natural resources, construction, and maintenance | 13.8 | 22.4 | 1.8 | 8.3 | 15.2 | 0.8 |
| Farming, fishing, and forestry | 1.8 | 2.3 | 1.1 | 0.5 | 0.8 | 0.2 |
| Construction and extraction | 9.0 | 15.1 | 0.4 | 4.4 | 8.1 | 0.3 |
| Installation, maintenance, and repair | 3.0 | 5.0 | 0.2 | 3.4 | 6.4 | 0.3 |
| Production, transportation, and material moving | 15.4 | 19.5 | 9.6 | 11.1 | 17.0 | 4.8 |
| Production | 7.9 | 8.6 | 6.9 | 5.3 | 7.5 | 2.9 |
| Transportation and material moving | 7.5 | 10.9 | 2.7 | 5.9 | 9.5 | 1.9 |

*Note:* Updated population controls are introduced annually with the release of January data.

**Table 1-55.   Median Usual Weekly Earnings of Full-Time Wage and Salary Workers for the Foreign-Born and Native-Born Populations, by Selected Characteristics, Annual Averages, 2014–2015**

(Thousands of people, dollars, percent.)

| Year and characteristic | Foreign born | | Native born | | Earnings of foreign born as a percent of earnings of native born[1] |
| --- | --- | --- | --- | --- | --- |
| | Number | Median weekly earnings | Number | Median weekly earnings | |
| **2014** | | | | | |
| **Both Sexes, 16 Years and Over** ......................................... | 18 094 | 664 | 88 433 | 820 | 81.0 |
| Men ............................................................................................ | 11 143 | 695 | 48 307 | 912 | 76.2 |
| Women ........................................................................................ | 6 951 | 613 | 40 126 | 734 | 83.5 |
| **Age** | | | | | |
| 16 to 24 years ............................................................................ | 1 020 | 423 | 8 563 | 482 | 87.8 |
| 25 to 34 years ............................................................................ | 4 214 | 609 | 21 508 | 744 | 81.9 |
| 35 to 44 years ............................................................................ | 5 176 | 715 | 19 414 | 919 | 77.8 |
| 45 to 54 years ............................................................................ | 4 600 | 708 | 20 759 | 939 | 75.4 |
| 55 to 64 years ............................................................................ | 2 505 | 734 | 15 103 | 940 | 78.1 |
| 65 years and over ...................................................................... | 580 | 689 | 3 086 | 856 | 80.5 |
| **Race and Hispanic Origin** | | | | | |
| White, non-Hispanic .................................................................... | 2 906 | 931 | 65 572 | 880 | 105.8 |
| Black, non-Hispanic .................................................................... | 1 638 | 661 | 10 498 | 640 | 103.3 |
| Asian, non-Hispanic .................................................................... | 4 549 | 969 | 1 591 | 924 | 104.9 |
| Hispanic[2] .................................................................................... | 8 792 | 523 | 8 683 | 662 | 79.0 |
| **Educational Attainment** | | | | | |
| Total, 25 years and over ............................................................ | 17 074 | 687 | 79 869 | 871 | 78.9 |
| Less than a high school diploma ............................................... | 3 952 | 463 | 2 974 | 517 | 89.6 |
| High school graduate, no college[3] ........................................... | 4 105 | 581 | 21 425 | 689 | 84.3 |
| Some college ............................................................................. | 2 866 | 685 | 23 542 | 771 | 88.8 |
| Bachelor's degree or higher[4] ................................................... | 6 151 | 1 222 | 31 929 | 1 188 | 102.9 |
| **2015** | | | | | |
| **Both Sexes, 16 Years and Over** ......................................... | 18 792 | 681 | 90 289 | 837 | 81.4 |
| Men ............................................................................................ | 11 561 | 712 | 49 185 | 934 | 76.2 |
| Women ........................................................................................ | 7 231 | 626 | 41 103 | 740 | 84.6 |
| **Age** | | | | | |
| 16 to 24 years ............................................................................ | 995 | 464 | 8 795 | 490 | 94.7 |
| 25 to 34 years ............................................................................ | 4 247 | 622 | 22 364 | 751 | 82.8 |
| 35 to 44 years ............................................................................ | 5 378 | 721 | 19 538 | 940 | 76.7 |
| 45 to 54 years ............................................................................ | 4 745 | 724 | 20 832 | 965 | 75.0 |
| 55 to 64 years ............................................................................ | 2 744 | 731 | 15 364 | 961 | 76.1 |
| 65 years and over ...................................................................... | 683 | 731 | 3 395 | 895 | 81.7 |
| **Race and Hispanic Origin** | | | | | |
| White, non-Hispanic .................................................................... | 2 888 | 999 | 66 208 | 900 | 111.0 |
| Black, non-Hispanic .................................................................... | 1 734 | 674 | 11 055 | 643 | 104.8 |
| Asian, non-Hispanic .................................................................... | 4 706 | 1 010 | 1 755 | 973 | 103.8 |
| Hispanic[2] .................................................................................... | 9 246 | 548 | 9 065 | 679 | 80.7 |
| **Educational Attainment** | | | | | |
| Total, 25 years and over ............................................................ | 17 797 | 702 | 81 494 | 891 | 78.8 |
| Less than a high school diploma ............................................... | 4 217 | 476 | 3 073 | 519 | 91.7 |
| High school graduates, no college[3] ......................................... | 4 218 | 599 | 21 003 | 696 | 86.1 |
| Some college ............................................................................. | 2 845 | 699 | 23 956 | 770 | 90.8 |
| Bachelor's degree and higher[4] ................................................ | 6 517 | 1 259 | 33 462 | 1 225 | 102.8 |

*Note:* Updated population controls are introduced annually with the release of January data.

[1]These figures are computed using unrounded medians and may differ slightly from percentages computed using the rounded medians displayed in this table.
[2]May be of any race.
[3]Includes persons with a high school diploma or equivalent.
[4]Includes persons with bachelor's, master's, professional, and doctoral degrees.

**Table 1-56. Percent Distribution of the Civilian Labor Force Age 25 to 64 Years, by Educational Attainment, Sex, and Race, March 1990–March 2016**

(Thousands of people, percent.)

| Sex, race, and year | Civilian labor force | Percent distribution | | | | |
|---|---|---|---|---|---|---|
| | | Total | Less than a high school diploma | 4 years of high school only | 1 to 3 years of college | 4 or more years of college |
| **Both Sexes** | | | | | | |
| 1990 | 99 175 | 100.0 | 13.4 | 39.5 | 20.7 | 26.4 |
| 1991 | 100 480 | 100.0 | 13.0 | 39.4 | 21.1 | 26.5 |
| 1992 | 102 387 | 100.0 | 12.2 | 36.2 | 25.2 | 26.4 |
| 1993 | 103 504 | 100.0 | 11.5 | 35.2 | 26.3 | 27.0 |
| 1994 | 104 868 | 100.0 | 11.0 | 34.0 | 27.7 | 27.3 |
| 1995 | 106 519 | 100.0 | 10.8 | 33.1 | 27.8 | 28.3 |
| 1996 | 108 037 | 100.0 | 10.9 | 32.9 | 27.7 | 28.5 |
| 1997 | 110 514 | 100.0 | 10.9 | 33.0 | 27.4 | 28.6 |
| 1998 | 111 857 | 100.0 | 10.7 | 32.8 | 27.4 | 29.1 |
| 1999 | 112 542 | 100.0 | 10.3 | 32.3 | 27.4 | 30.0 |
| 2000 | 114 052 | 100.0 | 9.8 | 31.8 | 27.9 | 30.4 |
| 2001 | 115 073 | 100.0 | 9.8 | 31.4 | 28.1 | 30.7 |
| 2002 | 117 738 | 100.0 | 10.1 | 30.6 | 27.7 | 31.6 |
| 2003 | 119 261 | 100.0 | 10.1 | 30.1 | 27.8 | 31.9 |
| 2004 | 119 392 | 100.0 | 9.7 | 30.1 | 27.8 | 32.4 |
| 2005 | 120 461 | 100.0 | 9.8 | 30.1 | 27.8 | 32.3 |
| 2006 | 122 541 | 100.0 | 9.8 | 29.6 | 28.0 | 32.6 |
| 2007 | 124 581 | 100.0 | 9.8 | 29.3 | 27.3 | 33.6 |
| 2008 | 125 493 | 100.0 | 9.0 | 28.8 | 27.9 | 34.4 |
| 2009 | 125 655 | 100.0 | 9.0 | 28.7 | 27.9 | 34.3 |
| 2010 | 126 363 | 100.0 | 8.8 | 29.1 | 27.5 | 34.5 |
| 2011 | 125 385 | 100.0 | 8.5 | 28.2 | 28.0 | 35.4 |
| 2012 | 125 726 | 100.0 | 8.6 | 27.5 | 27.9 | 36.0 |
| 2013 | 125 744 | 100.0 | 8.2 | 27.0 | 28.1 | 36.7 |
| 2014 | 125 847 | 100.0 | 8.4 | 26.9 | 27.8 | 37.0 |
| 2015 | 126 863 | 100.0 | 8.2 | 26.3 | 27.7 | 37.7 |
| 2016 | 128 660 | 100.0 | 7.9 | 25.8 | 27.6 | 38.8 |
| **Men** | | | | | | |
| 1990 | 54 476 | 100.0 | 15.1 | 37.2 | 19.7 | 28.0 |
| 1991 | 55 165 | 100.0 | 14.7 | 37.5 | 20.2 | 27.6 |
| 1992 | 55 917 | 100.0 | 13.9 | 34.7 | 23.8 | 27.5 |
| 1993 | 56 544 | 100.0 | 13.2 | 33.9 | 24.7 | 28.1 |
| 1994 | 56 633 | 100.0 | 12.7 | 32.9 | 25.8 | 28.6 |
| 1995 | 57 454 | 100.0 | 12.2 | 32.3 | 25.7 | 29.7 |
| 1996 | 58 121 | 100.0 | 12.7 | 32.2 | 26.0 | 29.1 |
| 1997 | 59 268 | 100.0 | 12.8 | 32.2 | 25.8 | 29.2 |
| 1998 | 59 905 | 100.0 | 12.3 | 32.3 | 25.8 | 29.6 |
| 1999 | 60 030 | 100.0 | 11.7 | 32.0 | 25.8 | 30.5 |
| 2000 | 60 510 | 100.0 | 11.1 | 31.8 | 26.1 | 30.9 |
| 2001 | 61 091 | 100.0 | 11.0 | 31.6 | 26.3 | 31.1 |
| 2002 | 62 794 | 100.0 | 11.8 | 30.6 | 25.9 | 31.7 |
| 2003 | 63 466 | 100.0 | 12.0 | 30.1 | 25.8 | 32.1 |
| 2004 | 63 699 | 100.0 | 11.5 | 30.5 | 25.8 | 32.2 |
| 2005 | 64 562 | 100.0 | 11.6 | 31.4 | 25.4 | 31.6 |
| 2006 | 65 708 | 100.0 | 11.8 | 30.7 | 25.7 | 31.8 |
| 2007 | 66 742 | 100.0 | 11.7 | 30.6 | 25.1 | 32.7 |
| 2008 | 66 957 | 100.0 | 11.0 | 30.3 | 25.8 | 33.0 |
| 2009 | 66 843 | 100.0 | 10.8 | 30.4 | 26.0 | 32.8 |
| 2010 | 67 261 | 100.0 | 10.6 | 31.2 | 25.3 | 32.9 |
| 2011 | 66 801 | 100.0 | 10.2 | 30.4 | 25.5 | 33.9 |
| 2012 | 66 539 | 100.0 | 10.1 | 29.7 | 25.9 | 34.3 |
| 2013 | 66 594 | 100.0 | 9.9 | 29.1 | 26.2 | 34.8 |
| 2014 | 66 625 | 100.0 | 10.2 | 29.4 | 25.8 | 34.7 |
| 2015 | 67 578 | 100.0 | 10.0 | 29.1 | 25.8 | 35.1 |
| 2016 | 68 329 | 100.0 | 9.5 | 28.5 | 25.8 | 36.1 |
| **Women** | | | | | | |
| 1990 | 44 699 | 100.0 | 11.3 | 42.4 | 21.9 | 24.5 |
| 1991 | 45 315 | 100.0 | 10.9 | 41.6 | 22.2 | 25.2 |
| 1992 | 46 469 | 100.0 | 10.2 | 37.9 | 26.9 | 25.0 |
| 1993 | 46 961 | 100.0 | 9.3 | 36.7 | 28.2 | 25.8 |
| 1994 | 48 235 | 100.0 | 9.1 | 35.3 | 29.8 | 25.8 |
| 1995 | 49 065 | 100.0 | 9.1 | 34.1 | 30.2 | 26.6 |
| 1996 | 49 916 | 100.0 | 8.8 | 33.7 | 29.7 | 27.8 |
| 1997 | 51 246 | 100.0 | 8.7 | 34.0 | 29.3 | 28.0 |
| 1998 | 51 953 | 100.0 | 8.8 | 33.3 | 29.3 | 28.6 |
| 1999 | 52 512 | 100.0 | 8.7 | 32.7 | 29.2 | 29.5 |
| 2000 | 53 541 | 100.0 | 8.4 | 31.8 | 30.0 | 29.8 |
| 2001 | 53 982 | 100.0 | 8.5 | 31.1 | 30.1 | 30.2 |
| 2002 | 54 944 | 100.0 | 8.2 | 30.6 | 29.7 | 31.5 |
| 2003 | 55 795 | 100.0 | 8.0 | 30.1 | 30.1 | 31.8 |
| 2004 | 55 693 | 100.0 | 7.7 | 29.6 | 30.2 | 32.5 |
| 2005 | 55 899 | 100.0 | 7.8 | 28.6 | 30.5 | 33.1 |
| 2006 | 56 833 | 100.0 | 7.6 | 28.2 | 30.6 | 33.6 |
| 2007 | 57 839 | 100.0 | 7.5 | 27.9 | 29.9 | 34.6 |
| 2008 | 58 536 | 100.0 | 6.7 | 27.0 | 30.4 | 35.9 |
| 2009 | 58 811 | 100.0 | 7.0 | 26.9 | 30.2 | 35.9 |
| 2010 | 59 102 | 100.0 | 6.8 | 26.8 | 30.1 | 36.3 |
| 2011 | 58 584 | 100.0 | 6.5 | 25.7 | 30.7 | 37.1 |
| 2012 | 59 187 | 100.0 | 6.8 | 25.1 | 30.2 | 37.9 |
| 2013 | 59 150 | 100.0 | 6.3 | 24.6 | 30.2 | 38.9 |
| 2014 | 59 222 | 100.0 | 6.4 | 24.1 | 30.0 | 39.6 |
| 2015 | 59 285 | 100.0 | 6.2 | 23.2 | 29.9 | 40.7 |
| 2016 | 60 331 | 100.0 | 6.1 | 22.6 | 29.6 | 41.7 |

**Table 1-56. Percent Distribution of the Civilian Labor Force Age 25 to 64 Years, by Educational Attainment, Sex, and Race, March 1990–March 2016**—*Continued*

(Thousands of people, percent.)

| Sex, race, and year | Civilian labor force | Percent distribution | | | | |
|---|---|---|---|---|---|---|
| | | Total | Less than a high school diploma | 4 years of high school only | 1 to 3 years of college | 4 or more years of college |
| **White**[1] | | | | | | |
| 1990 | 85 238 | 100.0 | 12.6 | 39.6 | 20.6 | 27.1 |
| 1991 | 86 344 | 100.0 | 12.2 | 39.3 | 21.1 | 27.4 |
| 1992 | 87 656 | 100.0 | 11.3 | 36.1 | 25.5 | 27.1 |
| 1993 | 88 457 | 100.0 | 10.7 | 35.0 | 26.4 | 27.9 |
| 1994 | 89 009 | 100.0 | 10.5 | 33.7 | 27.7 | 28.1 |
| 1995 | 90 192 | 100.0 | 10.0 | 32.8 | 27.8 | 29.3 |
| 1996 | 91 506 | 100.0 | 10.4 | 32.8 | 27.5 | 29.3 |
| 1997 | 93 179 | 100.0 | 10.4 | 32.8 | 27.3 | 29.5 |
| 1998 | 93 527 | 100.0 | 10.2 | 32.7 | 27.4 | 29.8 |
| 1999 | 94 216 | 100.0 | 9.8 | 32.2 | 27.2 | 30.8 |
| 2000 | 95 073 | 100.0 | 9.5 | 31.8 | 27.7 | 31.0 |
| 2001 | 95 562 | 100.0 | 9.5 | 31.0 | 28.0 | 31.4 |
| 2002 | 97 699 | 100.0 | 9.8 | 30.6 | 27.6 | 32.0 |
| 2003 | 98 241 | 100.0 | 9.9 | 30.0 | 27.7 | 32.4 |
| 2004 | 98 030 | 100.0 | 9.5 | 29.8 | 27.8 | 32.9 |
| 2005 | 98 581 | 100.0 | 9.7 | 29.8 | 27.8 | 32.7 |
| 2006 | 100 205 | 100.0 | 9.7 | 29.3 | 28.1 | 32.9 |
| 2007 | 101 548 | 100.0 | 9.7 | 29.1 | 27.3 | 33.9 |
| 2008 | 102 077 | 100.0 | 8.9 | 28.7 | 27.8 | 34.6 |
| 2009 | 102 261 | 100.0 | 9.1 | 28.6 | 27.7 | 34.6 |
| 2010 | 102 634 | 100.0 | 8.8 | 29.0 | 27.4 | 34.8 |
| 2011 | 101 707 | 100.0 | 8.4 | 27.8 | 27.9 | 35.8 |
| 2012 | 100 382 | 100.0 | 8.6 | 27.4 | 27.7 | 36.4 |
| 2013 | 99 964 | 100.0 | 8.2 | 27.0 | 27.9 | 36.9 |
| 2014 | 99 664 | 100.0 | 8.3 | 26.8 | 27.8 | 37.2 |
| 2015 | 99 813 | 100.0 | 8.4 | 26.3 | 27.5 | 37.9 |
| 2016 | 100 886 | 100.0 | 8.0 | 25.7 | 27.4 | 38.9 |
| **Black**[1] | | | | | | |
| 1990 | 10 537 | 100.0 | 19.9 | 42.5 | 22.1 | 15.5 |
| 1991 | 10 650 | 100.0 | 19.5 | 42.9 | 22.1 | 15.4 |
| 1992 | 10 936 | 100.0 | 19.2 | 40.3 | 24.9 | 15.6 |
| 1993 | 11 051 | 100.0 | 16.8 | 39.5 | 27.6 | 16.1 |
| 1994 | 11 368 | 100.0 | 14.5 | 39.3 | 29.2 | 17.0 |
| 1995 | 11 695 | 100.0 | 14.1 | 38.6 | 29.6 | 17.7 |
| 1996 | 11 891 | 100.0 | 14.2 | 37.2 | 31.2 | 17.4 |
| 1997 | 12 253 | 100.0 | 14.3 | 37.8 | 31.3 | 16.6 |
| 1998 | 12 893 | 100.0 | 14.3 | 37.3 | 30.1 | 18.2 |
| 1999 | 12 945 | 100.0 | 13.0 | 37.2 | 30.4 | 19.5 |
| 2000 | 13 383 | 100.0 | 11.8 | 36.1 | 31.5 | 20.7 |
| 2001 | 13 617 | 100.0 | 12.0 | 37.1 | 31.1 | 19.8 |
| 2002 | 13 319 | 100.0 | 12.4 | 34.5 | 32.0 | 21.0 |
| 2003 | 13 315 | 100.0 | 11.3 | 35.6 | 31.5 | 21.6 |
| 2004 | 13 372 | 100.0 | 11.0 | 36.6 | 30.5 | 21.9 |
| 2005 | 13 635 | 100.0 | 11.2 | 37.3 | 29.9 | 21.6 |
| 2006 | 13 855 | 100.0 | 10.9 | 35.6 | 30.4 | 23.0 |
| 2007 | 14 186 | 100.0 | 10.1 | 35.4 | 31.4 | 23.1 |
| 2008 | 14 356 | 100.0 | 9.5 | 34.3 | 32.1 | 24.1 |
| 2009 | 14 325 | 100.0 | 8.5 | 35.1 | 33.0 | 23.5 |
| 2010 | 14 483 | 100.0 | 8.9 | 34.5 | 32.4 | 24.2 |
| 2011 | 14 377 | 100.0 | 8.5 | 33.8 | 33.1 | 24.6 |
| 2012 | 14 721 | 100.0 | 8.5 | 32.0 | 33.4 | 26.0 |
| 2013 | 14 869 | 100.0 | 8.5 | 31.4 | 33.4 | 26.7 |
| 2014 | 15 121 | 100.0 | 8.9 | 31.3 | 32.2 | 27.6 |
| 2015 | 15 415 | 100.0 | 7.1 | 31.2 | 34.1 | 27.5 |
| 2015 | 15 666 | 100.0 | 7.5 | 30.7 | 33.1 | 28.7 |

[1]Beginning in 2003, persons who selected this race group only; persons who selected more than one race group are not included. Prior to 2003, persons who reported more than one race group were included in the group they identified as their main race.

## Table 1-57. Labor Force Participation Rates of Persons Age 25 to 64 Years, by Educational Attainment, Sex, and Race, March 1990–March 2016

(Civilian labor force as a percent of the civilian noninstitutional population.)

| Sex, race, and year | Participation rates | | | | |
| --- | --- | --- | --- | --- | --- |
| | Total | Less than a high school diploma | 4 years of high school only | 1 to 3 years of college | 4 or more years of college |
| **Both Sexes** | | | | | |
| 1990 | 78.6 | 60.7 | 78.2 | 83.3 | 88.4 |
| 1991 | 78.6 | 60.7 | 78.1 | 83.2 | 88.4 |
| 1992 | 79.0 | 60.3 | 78.3 | 83.5 | 88.4 |
| 1993 | 78.9 | 59.6 | 77.7 | 82.9 | 88.3 |
| 1994 | 78.9 | 58.3 | 77.8 | 83.2 | 88.2 |
| 1995 | 79.3 | 59.8 | 77.3 | 83.2 | 88.7 |
| 1996 | 79.4 | 60.2 | 77.9 | 83.7 | 87.8 |
| 1997 | 80.1 | 61.7 | 78.5 | 83.7 | 88.5 |
| 1998 | 80.2 | 63.0 | 78.4 | 83.5 | 88.0 |
| 1999 | 80.0 | 62.7 | 78.1 | 83.0 | 87.6 |
| 2000 | 80.3 | 62.7 | 78.4 | 83.2 | 87.8 |
| 2001 | 80.2 | 63.5 | 78.4 | 83.0 | 87.0 |
| 2002 | 79.7 | 63.5 | 77.7 | 82.1 | 86.7 |
| 2003 | 79.4 | 64.1 | 76.9 | 81.9 | 86.2 |
| 2004 | 78.8 | 63.2 | 76.1 | 81.2 | 85.9 |
| 2005 | 78.5 | 62.9 | 75.7 | 81.1 | 85.7 |
| 2006 | 78.7 | 63.2 | 75.9 | 81.0 | 85.9 |
| 2007 | 79.0 | 63.7 | 76.3 | 81.1 | 85.9 |
| 2008 | 79.0 | 62.5 | 76.0 | 80.9 | 86.1 |
| 2009 | 78.6 | 62.3 | 75.7 | 80.3 | 85.9 |
| 2010 | 78.7 | 62.7 | 76.2 | 79.7 | 85.7 |
| 2011 | 77.6 | 61.0 | 74.3 | 78.6 | 85.3 |
| 2012 | 77.4 | 61.7 | 73.2 | 78.5 | 85.5 |
| 2013 | 77.2 | 60.9 | 73.0 | 78.1 | 85.1 |
| 2014 | 76.7 | 61.3 | 72.3 | 77.3 | 84.9 |
| 2015 | 76.7 | 60.2 | 71.8 | 77.9 | 84.8 |
| 2016 | 77.2 | 61.6 | 71.9 | 77.3 | 85.6 |
| **Men** | | | | | |
| 1990 | 88.8 | 75.1 | 89.9 | 91.5 | 94.5 |
| 1991 | 88.6 | 75.1 | 89.3 | 92.0 | 94.2 |
| 1992 | 88.6 | 75.1 | 89.0 | 91.8 | 93.7 |
| 1993 | 88.1 | 74.9 | 88.1 | 90.6 | 93.7 |
| 1994 | 87.0 | 71.5 | 86.8 | 90.3 | 93.2 |
| 1995 | 87.4 | 72.0 | 86.9 | 90.1 | 93.8 |
| 1996 | 87.5 | 74.3 | 86.9 | 90.0 | 92.9 |
| 1997 | 87.7 | 75.2 | 86.4 | 90.6 | 93.5 |
| 1998 | 87.8 | 75.3 | 86.7 | 90.0 | 93.4 |
| 1999 | 87.5 | 74.4 | 86.6 | 89.4 | 93.0 |
| 2000 | 87.5 | 74.9 | 86.2 | 88.9 | 93.3 |
| 2001 | 87.4 | 75.4 | 85.8 | 89.1 | 92.9 |
| 2002 | 87.0 | 75.5 | 85.3 | 88.8 | 92.4 |
| 2003 | 86.4 | 76.1 | 84.3 | 87.5 | 92.2 |
| 2004 | 85.9 | 75.2 | 83.8 | 87.0 | 91.9 |
| 2005 | 86.0 | 75.7 | 83.7 | 87.5 | 91.7 |
| 2006 | 86.0 | 76.3 | 83.4 | 87.8 | 91.7 |
| 2007 | 86.2 | 75.7 | 83.9 | 87.2 | 92.4 |
| 2008 | 85.8 | 74.8 | 83.6 | 86.5 | 91.9 |
| 2009 | 85.1 | 73.7 | 82.3 | 86.0 | 91.9 |
| 2010 | 85.3 | 74.5 | 83.2 | 85.3 | 91.5 |
| 2011 | 84.0 | 73.3 | 81.8 | 83.2 | 91.1 |
| 2012 | 84.1 | 72.9 | 80.7 | 84.3 | 91.4 |
| 2013 | 84.0 | 72.7 | 80.5 | 83.8 | 91.4 |
| 2014 | 83.2 | 73.1 | 79.8 | 82.4 | 90.8 |
| 2015 | 83.6 | 73.4 | 80.0 | 83.7 | 90.6 |
| 2016 | 83.8 | 74.0 | 79.7 | 83.0 | 91.4 |
| **Women** | | | | | |
| 1990 | 68.9 | 46.2 | 68.7 | 75.9 | 81.1 |
| 1991 | 69.1 | 46.2 | 68.6 | 75.2 | 81.8 |
| 1992 | 70.0 | 45.6 | 69.1 | 76.2 | 82.2 |
| 1993 | 70.0 | 44.2 | 68.8 | 76.1 | 82.2 |
| 1994 | 71.1 | 44.7 | 70.0 | 77.0 | 82.5 |
| 1995 | 71.5 | 47.2 | 68.9 | 77.3 | 82.8 |
| 1996 | 71.8 | 45.7 | 69.8 | 78.1 | 82.3 |
| 1997 | 72.8 | 47.1 | 71.4 | 77.6 | 83.2 |
| 1998 | 73.0 | 49.8 | 70.9 | 77.8 | 82.3 |
| 1999 | 72.8 | 50.5 | 70.4 | 77.4 | 81.9 |
| 2000 | 73.5 | 50.4 | 71.2 | 78.3 | 82.0 |
| 2001 | 73.4 | 51.7 | 71.3 | 77.7 | 80.9 |
| 2002 | 72.7 | 50.4 | 70.4 | 76.4 | 81.0 |
| 2003 | 72.6 | 50.5 | 69.8 | 77.1 | 80.1 |
| 2004 | 72.0 | 49.7 | 68.6 | 76.2 | 80.0 |
| 2005 | 71.4 | 48.7 | 67.4 | 75.8 | 79.8 |
| 2006 | 71.7 | 48.3 | 68.2 | 75.3 | 80.4 |
| 2007 | 72.1 | 49.6 | 68.4 | 76.0 | 79.7 |
| 2008 | 72.5 | 47.9 | 68.2 | 76.1 | 80.9 |
| 2009 | 72.4 | 49.0 | 68.7 | 75.4 | 80.5 |
| 2010 | 72.3 | 48.9 | 68.6 | 75.0 | 80.4 |
| 2011 | 71.3 | 46.8 | 66.1 | 74.7 | 80.0 |
| 2012 | 71.1 | 49.2 | 65.2 | 73.5 | 80.3 |
| 2013 | 70.8 | 47.3 | 65.1 | 73.3 | 79.6 |
| 2014 | 70.6 | 47.6 | 64.1 | 72.9 | 79.8 |
| 2015 | 70.1 | 45.3 | 62.6 | 72.9 | 79.9 |
| 2016 | 70.8 | 47.6 | 63.2 | 72.4 | 80.5 |

**Table 1-57. Labor Force Participation Rates of Persons Age 25 to 64 Years, by Educational Attainment, Sex, and Race, March 1990–March 2016**—*Continued*

(Civilian labor force as a percent of the civilian noninstitutional population.)

| Sex, race, and year | Participation rates | | | | |
|---|---|---|---|---|---|
| | Total | Less than a high school diploma | 4 years of high school only | 1 to 3 years of college | 4 or more years of college |
| **White[1]** | | | | | |
| 1990 | 79.2 | 62.5 | 78.4 | 83.3 | 88.3 |
| 1991 | 79.4 | 62.5 | 78.3 | 83.1 | 88.6 |
| 1992 | 79.8 | 61.5 | 78.7 | 83.8 | 88.7 |
| 1993 | 79.7 | 61.1 | 78.2 | 83.1 | 88.8 |
| 1994 | 79.8 | 60.3 | 78.3 | 83.5 | 88.5 |
| 1995 | 80.1 | 61.6 | 77.9 | 83.4 | 88.8 |
| 1996 | 80.4 | 62.5 | 78.6 | 83.9 | 88.2 |
| 1997 | 81.0 | 63.8 | 79.2 | 83.9 | 89.0 |
| 1998 | 80.6 | 63.8 | 78.6 | 83.5 | 88.3 |
| 1999 | 80.6 | 64.2 | 78.5 | 83.3 | 87.9 |
| 2000 | 80.8 | 64.2 | 78.7 | 83.1 | 87.9 |
| 2001 | 80.7 | 64.5 | 78.7 | 83.1 | 87.2 |
| 2002 | 80.3 | 65.0 | 78.2 | 82.4 | 87.0 |
| 2003 | 80.1 | 65.7 | 77.5 | 82.3 | 86.5 |
| 2004 | 79.5 | 64.6 | 76.7 | 81.6 | 86.2 |
| 2005 | 79.2 | 63.8 | 76.4 | 81.5 | 86.1 |
| 2006 | 79.5 | 65.1 | 76.5 | 81.4 | 86.2 |
| 2007 | 79.6 | 65.1 | 77.2 | 81.4 | 86.1 |
| 2008 | 79.6 | 63.8 | 76.8 | 81.2 | 86.3 |
| 2009 | 79.4 | 64.7 | 76.4 | 80.7 | 86.2 |
| 2010 | 79.5 | 64.5 | 77.1 | 80.4 | 86.0 |
| 2011 | 78.5 | 62.9 | 75.3 | 79.3 | 85.5 |
| 2012 | 78.3 | 63.8 | 74.2 | 78.8 | 86.0 |
| 2013 | 78.0 | 63.0 | 73.9 | 78.5 | 85.6 |
| 2014 | 77.6 | 62.9 | 73.4 | 77.8 | 85.4 |
| 2015 | 77.5 | 62.4 | 72.8 | 78.1 | 85.4 |
| 2016 | 78.0 | 63.6 | 73.1 | 77.7 | 86.2 |
| **Black[1]** | | | | | |
| 1990 | 74.6 | 54.5 | 78.2 | 84.2 | 92.0 |
| 1991 | 73.9 | 53.9 | 77.1 | 84.1 | 90.2 |
| 1992 | 74.4 | 55.4 | 76.9 | 83.4 | 89.1 |
| 1993 | 73.8 | 53.4 | 74.7 | 83.0 | 89.6 |
| 1994 | 73.5 | 49.4 | 75.2 | 82.4 | 89.5 |
| 1995 | 74.2 | 51.0 | 74.5 | 82.8 | 90.9 |
| 1996 | 73.7 | 50.1 | 74.3 | 83.0 | 87.9 |
| 1997 | 74.9 | 52.9 | 75.0 | 83.8 | 89.0 |
| 1998 | 77.7 | 59.3 | 77.0 | 85.0 | 88.8 |
| 1999 | 76.5 | 55.1 | 76.5 | 82.9 | 88.6 |
| 2000 | 77.9 | 55.5 | 77.0 | 84.2 | 90.3 |
| 2001 | 78.1 | 58.7 | 76.8 | 83.0 | 90.5 |
| 2002 | 76.4 | 56.6 | 75.0 | 81.7 | 88.9 |
| 2003 | 75.8 | 55.4 | 73.9 | 81.2 | 88.2 |
| 2004 | 75.0 | 55.2 | 73.4 | 79.0 | 87.9 |
| 2005 | 75.2 | 58.2 | 72.6 | 79.5 | 87.2 |
| 2006 | 75.0 | 54.0 | 73.3 | 79.6 | 87.7 |
| 2007 | 75.6 | 55.3 | 72.5 | 80.7 | 88.0 |
| 2008 | 75.6 | 54.3 | 72.8 | 80.0 | 87.5 |
| 2009 | 74.4 | 50.0 | 72.6 | 78.7 | 86.2 |
| 2010 | 74.2 | 52.2 | 71.7 | 77.5 | 87.0 |
| 2011 | 72.4 | 49.0 | 69.6 | 76.3 | 85.5 |
| 2012 | 72.9 | 50.8 | 68.6 | 77.2 | 85.7 |
| 2013 | 73.0 | 50.2 | 69.2 | 77.7 | 84.2 |
| 2014 | 72.8 | 54.4 | 67.9 | 75.4 | 86.0 |
| 2015 | 72.8 | 49.0 | 66.6 | 78.1 | 85.4 |
| 2016 | 72.7 | 50.9 | 66.9 | 76.2 | 85.8 |

[1]Beginning in 2003, persons who selected this race group only; persons who selected more than one race group are not included. Prior to 2003, persons who reported more than one race group were included in the group they identified as their main race.

**Table 1-58.  Unemployment Rates of Persons Age 25 to 64 Years, by Educational Attainment and Sex, March 1990–March 2016**

(Unemployment as a percent of the civilian labor force.)

| Sex, race, and year | Unemployment rates | | | | |
| --- | --- | --- | --- | --- | --- |
| | Total | Less than a high school diploma | 4 years of high school only | 1 to 3 years of college | 4 or more years of college |
| **Both Sexes** | | | | | |
| 1990 | 4.5 | 9.6 | 4.9 | 3.7 | 1.9 |
| 1991 | 6.1 | 12.3 | 6.7 | 5.0 | 2.9 |
| 1992 | 6.7 | 13.5 | 7.7 | 5.9 | 2.9 |
| 1993 | 6.4 | 13.0 | 7.3 | 5.5 | 3.2 |
| 1994 | 5.8 | 12.6 | 6.7 | 5.0 | 2.9 |
| 1995 | 4.8 | 10.0 | 5.2 | 4.5 | 2.5 |
| 1996 | 4.8 | 10.9 | 5.5 | 4.1 | 2.2 |
| 1997 | 4.4 | 10.4 | 5.1 | 3.8 | 2.0 |
| 1998 | 4.0 | 8.5 | 4.8 | 3.6 | 1.8 |
| 1999 | 3.5 | 7.7 | 4.0 | 3.1 | 1.9 |
| 2000 | 3.3 | 7.9 | 3.8 | 3.0 | 1.5 |
| 2001 | 3.5 | 8.1 | 4.2 | 2.9 | 2.0 |
| 2002 | 5.0 | 10.2 | 6.1 | 4.5 | 2.8 |
| 2003 | 5.3 | 9.9 | 6.4 | 5.2 | 3.0 |
| 2004 | 5.1 | 10.5 | 5.9 | 4.9 | 2.9 |
| 2005 | 4.4 | 9.0 | 5.5 | 4.1 | 2.3 |
| 2006 | 4.1 | 8.3 | 4.7 | 3.9 | 2.3 |
| 2007 | 3.9 | 8.5 | 4.7 | 3.7 | 1.8 |
| 2008 | 4.4 | 10.1 | 5.8 | 4.2 | 2.1 |
| 2009 | 8.1 | 15.8 | 10.4 | 8.0 | 4.3 |
| 2010 | 9.1 | 16.8 | 12.1 | 8.8 | 4.7 |
| 2011 | 8.3 | 16.2 | 10.9 | 8.1 | 4.4 |
| 2012 | 7.4 | 14.3 | 9.2 | 7.9 | 4.1 |
| 2013 | 6.6 | 12.7 | 8.7 | 6.5 | 3.8 |
| 2014 | 5.8 | 10.6 | 7.4 | 6.1 | 3.4 |
| 2015 | 4.7 | 9.2 | 6.2 | 4.9 | 2.4 |
| 2016 | 4.4 | 8.1 | 6.1 | 4.5 | 2.4 |
| **Men** | | | | | |
| 1990 | 4.8 | 9.6 | 5.3 | 3.9 | 2.1 |
| 1991 | 6.8 | 13.4 | 7.7 | 5.2 | 3.2 |
| 1992 | 7.5 | 14.8 | 8.8 | 6.4 | 3.2 |
| 1993 | 7.3 | 14.1 | 8.7 | 6.3 | 3.4 |
| 1994 | 6.2 | 12.8 | 7.2 | 5.3 | 2.9 |
| 1995 | 5.1 | 10.9 | 5.7 | 4.4 | 2.6 |
| 1996 | 5.3 | 11.0 | 6.4 | 4.5 | 2.3 |
| 1997 | 4.7 | 9.9 | 5.6 | 4.0 | 2.1 |
| 1998 | 4.1 | 8.0 | 5.1 | 3.7 | 1.7 |
| 1999 | 3.5 | 7.0 | 4.1 | 3.2 | 1.9 |
| 2000 | 3.3 | 7.1 | 3.9 | 3.1 | 1.6 |
| 2001 | 3.7 | 7.5 | 4.6 | 3.2 | 1.9 |
| 2002 | 5.5 | 9.9 | 6.7 | 4.9 | 3.0 |
| 2003 | 5.8 | 9.5 | 6.9 | 6.0 | 3.2 |
| 2004 | 5.4 | 9.4 | 6.6 | 5.4 | 3.0 |
| 2005 | 4.7 | 7.9 | 6.0 | 4.3 | 2.5 |
| 2006 | 4.3 | 7.6 | 5.0 | 4.2 | 2.4 |
| 2007 | 4.3 | 8.4 | 5.5 | 3.9 | 1.9 |
| 2008 | 4.9 | 10.9 | 6.3 | 4.2 | 2.0 |
| 2009 | 9.5 | 16.5 | 12.4 | 9.3 | 4.7 |
| 2010 | 10.5 | 17.8 | 13.8 | 10.2 | 5.1 |
| 2011 | 9.2 | 16.7 | 12.2 | 8.7 | 4.6 |
| 2012 | 8.0 | 13.6 | 10.1 | 8.2 | 4.3 |
| 2013 | 6.9 | 11.9 | 9.2 | 6.5 | 3.7 |
| 2014 | 5.9 | 9.4 | 7.8 | 5.9 | 3.4 |
| 2015 | 5.0 | 8.4 | 6.7 | 4.9 | 2.8 |
| 2016 | 4.5 | 7.5 | 6.3 | 4.7 | 2.3 |
| **Women** | | | | | |
| 1990 | 4.2 | 9.5 | 4.6 | 3.5 | 1.7 |
| 1991 | 5.2 | 10.7 | 5.5 | 4.8 | 2.5 |
| 1992 | 5.7 | 11.4 | 6.5 | 5.3 | 2.5 |
| 1993 | 5.2 | 11.2 | 5.8 | 4.6 | 2.9 |
| 1994 | 5.4 | 12.4 | 6.2 | 4.7 | 2.9 |
| 1995 | 4.4 | 8.6 | 4.6 | 4.5 | 2.4 |
| 1996 | 4.1 | 10.7 | 4.4 | 3.8 | 2.1 |
| 1997 | 4.1 | 11.3 | 4.5 | 3.6 | 2.0 |
| 1998 | 3.9 | 9.3 | 4.4 | 3.5 | 1.9 |
| 1999 | 3.5 | 8.8 | 3.9 | 3.0 | 1.9 |
| 2000 | 3.2 | 9.1 | 3.6 | 2.9 | 1.4 |
| 2001 | 3.3 | 8.9 | 3.8 | 2.6 | 2.0 |
| 2002 | 4.6 | 10.6 | 5.4 | 4.1 | 2.6 |
| 2003 | 4.8 | 10.6 | 5.9 | 4.4 | 2.8 |
| 2004 | 4.7 | 12.2 | 5.2 | 4.3 | 2.9 |
| 2005 | 4.2 | 10.9 | 4.8 | 4.0 | 2.2 |
| 2006 | 3.8 | 9.4 | 4.4 | 3.7 | 2.1 |
| 2007 | 3.4 | 8.5 | 3.8 | 3.6 | 1.8 |
| 2008 | 4.0 | 8.5 | 5.1 | 4.2 | 2.1 |
| 2009 | 6.6 | 14.5 | 7.9 | 6.7 | 4.0 |
| 2010 | 7.5 | 15.0 | 9.8 | 7.5 | 4.3 |
| 2011 | 7.2 | 15.2 | 9.1 | 7.5 | 4.3 |
| 2012 | 6.8 | 15.4 | 8.1 | 7.7 | 3.8 |
| 2013 | 6.3 | 14.1 | 8.1 | 6.4 | 3.8 |
| 2014 | 5.7 | 12.7 | 6.8 | 6.3 | 3.4 |
| 2015 | 4.3 | 10.6 | 5.6 | 5.0 | 2.1 |
| 2016 | 4.2 | 9.2 | 5.8 | 4.3 | 2.6 |

## Table 1-58. Unemployment Rates of Persons Age 25 to 64 Years, by Educational Attainment and Sex, March 1990–March 2016—*Continued*

(Unemployment as a percent of the civilian labor force.)

| Sex, race, and year | Unemployment rates | | | | |
|---|---|---|---|---|---|
| | Total | Less than a high school diploma | 4 years of high school only | 1 to 3 years of college | 4 or more years of college |
| **White[1]** | | | | | |
| 1990 | 4.0 | 8.3 | 4.4 | 3.3 | 1.8 |
| 1991 | 5.6 | 11.6 | 6.2 | 4.6 | 2.7 |
| 1992 | 6.0 | 12.9 | 6.8 | 5.3 | 2.7 |
| 1993 | 5.8 | 12.4 | 6.5 | 5.0 | 3.1 |
| 1994 | 5.2 | 11.7 | 5.8 | 4.5 | 2.6 |
| 1995 | 4.3 | 9.2 | 4.6 | 4.2 | 2.3 |
| 1996 | 4.2 | 10.2 | 4.6 | 3.7 | 2.1 |
| 1997 | 3.9 | 9.4 | 4.6 | 3.4 | 1.8 |
| 1998 | 3.5 | 7.5 | 4.2 | 3.2 | 1.7 |
| 1999 | 3.1 | 7.0 | 3.4 | 2.8 | 1.7 |
| 2000 | 3.0 | 7.5 | 3.3 | 2.7 | 1.4 |
| 2001 | 3.1 | 7.2 | 3.6 | 2.7 | 1.8 |
| 2002 | 4.6 | 9.1 | 5.5 | 4.1 | 2.6 |
| 2003 | 4.7 | 9.0 | 5.7 | 4.5 | 2.7 |
| 2004 | 4.6 | 9.6 | 5.4 | 4.4 | 2.8 |
| 2005 | 3.9 | 7.7 | 4.9 | 3.6 | 2.2 |
| 2006 | 3.5 | 7.1 | 4.0 | 3.5 | 2.1 |
| 2007 | 3.5 | 7.8 | 4.2 | 3.3 | 1.7 |
| 2008 | 4.0 | 9.2 | 5.1 | 3.7 | 1.9 |
| 2009 | 7.6 | 15.2 | 9.9 | 7.4 | 4.0 |
| 2010 | 8.4 | 16.3 | 11.3 | 8.1 | 4.3 |
| 2011 | 7.5 | 15.1 | 9.9 | 7.2 | 4.0 |
| 2012 | 6.7 | 13.5 | 8.3 | 6.9 | 3.7 |
| 2013 | 5.9 | 11.2 | 7.7 | 5.7 | 3.5 |
| 2014 | 5.1 | 9.2 | 6.3 | 5.4 | 3.1 |
| 2015 | 4.1 | 8.2 | 5.3 | 4.2 | 2.3 |
| 2016 | 3.8 | 6.7 | 5.2 | 3.8 | 2.3 |
| **Black[1]** | | | | | |
| 1990 | 8.6 | 15.9 | 8.6 | 6.5 | 1.9 |
| 1991 | 10.1 | 15.9 | 10.3 | 8.0 | 5.2 |
| 1992 | 12.4 | 17.2 | 14.1 | 10.7 | 4.8 |
| 1993 | 10.9 | 17.3 | 12.4 | 8.7 | 4.1 |
| 1994 | 10.6 | 17.4 | 12.2 | 8.3 | 4.9 |
| 1995 | 7.7 | 13.7 | 8.4 | 6.3 | 4.1 |
| 1996 | 8.9 | 15.3 | 10.8 | 6.9 | 3.3 |
| 1997 | 8.1 | 16.6 | 8.2 | 6.1 | 4.4 |
| 1998 | 7.3 | 13.4 | 8.4 | 6.4 | 2.1 |
| 1999 | 6.3 | 12.0 | 6.7 | 5.2 | 3.3 |
| 2000 | 5.4 | 10.4 | 6.3 | 4.3 | 2.5 |
| 2001 | 6.5 | 14.0 | 7.7 | 4.3 | 3.3 |
| 2002 | 8.1 | 15.4 | 9.7 | 6.0 | 4.1 |
| 2003 | 9.0 | 14.7 | 9.9 | 8.9 | 4.7 |
| 2004 | 8.4 | 15.8 | 9.3 | 7.9 | 3.7 |
| 2005 | 8.3 | 17.9 | 8.6 | 7.5 | 3.6 |
| 2006 | 7.8 | 16.4 | 9.0 | 6.5 | 3.6 |
| 2007 | 6.5 | 14.0 | 7.7 | 5.7 | 2.5 |
| 2008 | 7.6 | 16.7 | 9.3 | 6.5 | 3.3 |
| 2009 | 12.1 | 22.0 | 14.0 | 11.2 | 7.2 |
| 2010 | 14.1 | 22.4 | 17.5 | 12.9 | 7.9 |
| 2011 | 13.9 | 25.0 | 16.6 | 12.7 | 7.7 |
| 2012 | 12.3 | 21.4 | 14.2 | 12.7 | 6.3 |
| 2013 | 11.4 | 22.8 | 14.2 | 10.0 | 6.1 |
| 2014 | 10.7 | 19.7 | 13.8 | 10.0 | 5.0 |
| 2015 | 8.8 | 17.6 | 10.8 | 8.6 | 4.3 |
| 2016 | 7.9 | 17.3 | 10.5 | 7.4 | 3.3 |

[1]Beginning in 2003, persons who selected this race group only; persons who selected more than one race group are not included. Prior to 2003, persons who reported more than one race group were included in the group they identified as their main race.

**Table 1-59.  Workers Age 25 to 64 Years, by Educational Attainment, Occupation of Longest Job Held, and Sex, 2014–2015**

(Thousands of people with work experience during the year.)

| Year, sex, and occupation | Total | Less than a high school diploma | 4 years of high school only | 1 to 3 years of college | 4 or more years of college |
|---|---|---|---|---|---|
| **2014** | | | | | |
| **Both Sexes** | 128 460 | 10 333 | 33 593 | 35 852 | 48 682 |
| Management, business, and financial operations | 21 659 | 470 | 3 274 | 5 084 | 12 831 |
| Management | 15 205 | 420 | 2 655 | 3 698 | 8 432 |
| Business and financial operations | 6 454 | 50 | 619 | 1 386 | 4 399 |
| Professional and related | 30 342 | 152 | 2 053 | 6 159 | 21 978 |
| Computer and mathematical | 3 934 | 16 | 207 | 825 | 2 887 |
| Architecture and engineering | 2 447 | 7 | 230 | 505 | 1 704 |
| Life, physical, and social sciences | 1 311 | . . . | 64 | 118 | 1 129 |
| Community and social services | 2 249 | 17 | 190 | 369 | 1 674 |
| Legal | 1 506 | 6 | 64 | 212 | 1 223 |
| Education, training, and library | 8 294 | 26 | 488 | 1 007 | 6 773 |
| Arts, design, entertainment, sports, and media | 2 703 | 41 | 270 | 604 | 1 788 |
| Health care practitioner and technical | 7 899 | 39 | 540 | 2 520 | 4 800 |
| Services | 19 996 | 3 271 | 7 166 | 6 545 | 3 015 |
| Health care support | 2 998 | 283 | 871 | 1 408 | 436 |
| Protective services | 2 682 | 76 | 698 | 1 154 | 754 |
| Food preparation and serving related | 5 209 | 985 | 2 111 | 1 477 | 637 |
| Building and grounds cleaning and maintenance | 4 965 | 1 563 | 2 106 | 974 | 323 |
| Personal care and services | 4 142 | 364 | 1 381 | 1 533 | 865 |
| Sales and office | 27 575 | 1 145 | 8 515 | 9 887 | 8 027 |
| Sales and related | 12 255 | 628 | 3 519 | 3 857 | 4 250 |
| Office and administrative support | 15 320 | 517 | 4 996 | 6 030 | 3 777 |
| Natural resources, construction, and maintenance | 12 755 | 2 770 | 5 290 | 3 569 | 1 126 |
| Farming, fishing, and forestry | 1 011 | 445 | 327 | 135 | 105 |
| Construction and extraction | 7 257 | 1 821 | 3 162 | 1 728 | 545 |
| Installation, maintenance, and repair | 4 487 | 505 | 1 801 | 1 705 | 477 |
| Production, transportation, and material moving | 15 501 | 2 522 | 7 187 | 4 327 | 1 465 |
| Production | 7 686 | 1 261 | 3 484 | 2 196 | 745 |
| Transportation and material moving | 7 815 | 1 261 | 3 703 | 2 131 | 721 |
| Armed forces | 631 | 2 | 108 | 281 | 240 |
| | | | | | |
| **Men** | 68 115 | 6 664 | 19 562 | 17 827 | 24 061 |
| Management, business, and financial operations | 12 130 | 321 | 1 938 | 2 669 | 7 201 |
| Management | 9 189 | 306 | 1 723 | 2 152 | 5 008 |
| Business and financial operations | 2 941 | 15 | 216 | 517 | 2 194 |
| Professional and related | 12 430 | 67 | 786 | 2 150 | 9 426 |
| Computer and mathematical | 2 914 | 10 | 154 | 612 | 2 138 |
| Architecture and engineering | 2 070 | 4 | 196 | 445 | 1 425 |
| Life, physical, and social sciences | 705 | . . . | 48 | 61 | 596 |
| Community and social services | 772 | 10 | 62 | 117 | 584 |
| Legal | 693 | 3 | 6 | 13 | 671 |
| Education, training, and library | 1 988 | 5 | 64 | 151 | 1 769 |
| Arts, design, entertainment, sports, and media | 1 421 | 20 | 167 | 324 | 910 |
| Health care practitioner and technical | 1 867 | 16 | 90 | 427 | 1 334 |
| Services | 8 508 | 1 434 | 3 029 | 2 582 | 1 462 |
| Health care support | 347 | 15 | 98 | 131 | 103 |
| Protective services | 2 160 | 58 | 562 | 932 | 609 |
| Food preparation and serving related | 2 332 | 495 | 899 | 617 | 321 |
| Building and grounds cleaning and maintenance | 2 801 | 800 | 1 193 | 605 | 203 |
| Personal care and services | 867 | 67 | 277 | 296 | 227 |
| Sales and office | 10 391 | 411 | 2 958 | 3 370 | 3 651 |
| Sales and related | 6 361 | 244 | 1 622 | 1 933 | 2 562 |
| Office and administrative support | 4 030 | 167 | 1 336 | 1 437 | 1 089 |
| Natural resources, construction, and maintenance | 12 134 | 2 610 | 5 107 | 3 407 | 1 010 |
| Farming, fishing, and forestry | 756 | 334 | 257 | 109 | 56 |
| Construction and extraction | 7 063 | 1 791 | 3 089 | 1 666 | 517 |
| Installation, maintenance, and repair | 4 315 | 486 | 1 761 | 1 632 | 437 |
| Production, transportation, and material moving | 11 967 | 1 818 | 5 639 | 3 403 | 1 108 |
| Production | 5 440 | 790 | 2 492 | 1 645 | 514 |
| Transportation and material moving | 6 527 | 1 028 | 3 147 | 1 758 | 594 |
| Armed forces | 554 | 2 | 104 | 246 | 202 |
| | | | | | |
| **Women** | 60 345 | 3 668 | 14 031 | 18 024 | 24 622 |
| Management, business, and financial operations | 9 529 | 149 | 1 336 | 2 415 | 5 630 |
| Management | 6 017 | 114 | 932 | 1 546 | 3 425 |
| Business and financial operations | 3 513 | 35 | 404 | 869 | 2 205 |
| Professional and related | 17 912 | 85 | 1 267 | 4 009 | 12 552 |
| Computer and mathematical | 1 020 | 5 | 53 | 213 | 750 |
| Architecture and engineering | 378 | 4 | 34 | 61 | 280 |
| Life, physical, and social sciences | 606 | . . . | 17 | 57 | 532 |
| Community and social services | 1 477 | 7 | 128 | 252 | 1 090 |
| Legal | 813 | 3 | 59 | 199 | 552 |
| Education, training, and library | 6 305 | 21 | 424 | 856 | 5 004 |
| Arts, design, entertainment, sports, and media | 1 282 | 21 | 103 | 280 | 878 |
| Health care practitioner and technical | 6 032 | 23 | 451 | 2 093 | 3 466 |
| Services | 11 488 | 1 837 | 4 136 | 3 963 | 1 552 |
| Health care support | 2 651 | 269 | 772 | 1 277 | 333 |
| Protective services | 521 | 18 | 136 | 221 | 146 |
| Food preparation and serving related | 2 877 | 490 | 1 211 | 860 | 316 |
| Building and grounds cleaning and maintenance | 2 164 | 763 | 913 | 369 | 120 |
| Personal care and services | 3 275 | 297 | 1 103 | 1 236 | 638 |
| Sales and office | 17 184 | 734 | 5 557 | 6 517 | 4 376 |
| Sales and related | 5 894 | 384 | 1 896 | 1 924 | 1 689 |
| Office and administrative support | 11 290 | 349 | 3 661 | 4 593 | 2 688 |
| Natural resources, construction, and maintenance | 620 | 160 | 183 | 161 | 116 |
| Farming, fishing, and forestry | 255 | 111 | 70 | 26 | 48 |
| Construction and extraction | 193 | 30 | 73 | 62 | 27 |
| Installation, maintenance, and repair | 172 | 19 | 40 | 73 | 40 |
| Production, transportation, and material moving | 3 534 | 704 | 1 548 | 924 | 358 |
| Production | 2 246 | 471 | 992 | 551 | 231 |
| Transportation and material moving | 1 288 | 232 | 556 | 373 | 127 |
| Armed forces | 77 | . . . | 4 | 36 | 37 |

. . . = Not available.

**Table 1-59. Workers Age 25 to 64 Years, by Educational Attainment, Occupation of Longest Job Held, and Sex, 2014–2015**—*Continued*

(Thousands of people with work experience during the year.)

| Year, sex, and occupation | Total | Less than a high school diploma | 4 years of high school only | 1 to 3 years of college | 4 or more years of college |
|---|---|---|---|---|---|
| **2015** | | | | | |
| **Both Sexes** | 130 757 | 10 199 | 33 460 | 36 553 | 50 546 |
| Management, business, and financial operations | 22 707 | 462 | 3 270 | 5 326 | 13 649 |
| Management | 15 883 | 419 | 2 572 | 3 771 | 9 121 |
| Business and financial operations | 6 823 | 42 | 698 | 1 555 | 4 528 |
| Professional and related | 31 416 | 153 | 1 931 | 6 422 | 22 909 |
| Computer and mathematical | 4 355 | 9 | 208 | 964 | 3 174 |
| Architecture and engineering | 2 645 | 6 | 237 | 504 | 1 899 |
| Life, physical, and social sciences | 1 228 | 1 | 56 | 129 | 1 041 |
| Community and social services | 2 411 | 11 | 178 | 387 | 1 835 |
| Legal | 1 484 | 11 | 68 | 217 | 1 187 |
| Education, training, and library | 8 383 | 48 | 479 | 1 019 | 6 837 |
| Arts, design, entertainment, sports, and media | 2 708 | 44 | 273 | 617 | 1 774 |
| Health care practitioner and technical | 8 204 | 23 | 431 | 2 587 | 5 163 |
| Services | 20 352 | 3 374 | 7 358 | 6 637 | 2 982 |
| Health care support | 3 005 | 222 | 961 | 1 437 | 384 |
| Protective services | 2 588 | 65 | 663 | 1 068 | 791 |
| Food preparation and serving related | 5 416 | 1 080 | 2 214 | 1 481 | 641 |
| Building and grounds cleaning and maintenance | 5 092 | 1 549 | 2 086 | 1 073 | 384 |
| Personal care and services | 4 251 | 457 | 1 434 | 1 578 | 783 |
| Sales and office | 27 184 | 1 126 | 8 064 | 9 840 | 8 154 |
| Sales and related | 12 221 | 624 | 3 397 | 3 865 | 4 335 |
| Office and administrative support | 14 963 | 503 | 4 667 | 5 975 | 3 818 |
| Natural resources, construction, and maintenance | 12 802 | 2 585 | 5 417 | 3 692 | 1 108 |
| Farming, fishing, and forestry | 1 103 | 494 | 383 | 144 | 81 |
| Construction and extraction | 7 310 | 1 667 | 3 256 | 1 785 | 602 |
| Installation, maintenance, and repair | 4 390 | 424 | 1 778 | 1 763 | 424 |
| Production, transportation, and material moving | 15 661 | 2 498 | 7 306 | 4 333 | 1 525 |
| Production | 7 729 | 1 269 | 3 445 | 2 232 | 783 |
| Transportation and material moving | 7 932 | 1 228 | 3 861 | 2 101 | 742 |
| Armed forces | 636 | 1 | 113 | 302 | 219 |
| | | | | | |
| **Men** | 69 229 | 6 476 | 19 551 | 18 174 | 25 028 |
| Management, business, and financial operations | 12 312 | 325 | 1 864 | 2 677 | 7 446 |
| Management | 9 366 | 294 | 1 655 | 2 181 | 5 236 |
| Business and financial operations | 2 947 | 31 | 210 | 496 | 2 210 |
| Professional and related | 13 082 | 44 | 753 | 2 280 | 10 005 |
| Computer and mathematical | 3 343 | 3 | 154 | 716 | 2 470 |
| Architecture and engineering | 2 215 | 2 | 193 | 429 | 1 592 |
| Life, physical, and social sciences | 699 | 1 | 34 | 86 | 579 |
| Community and social services | 776 | 3 | 61 | 132 | 579 |
| Legal | 690 | 1 | 9 | 13 | 666 |
| Education, training, and library | 2 109 | 4 | 44 | 182 | 1 880 |
| Arts, design, entertainment, sports, and media | 1 402 | 28 | 169 | 358 | 847 |
| Health care practitioner and technical | 1 848 | 2 | 89 | 363 | 1 393 |
| Services | 8 778 | 1 491 | 3 107 | 2 676 | 1 503 |
| Health care support | 344 | 12 | 99 | 158 | 75 |
| Protective services | 2 068 | 40 | 515 | 890 | 623 |
| Food preparation and serving related | 2 581 | 540 | 1 029 | 669 | 344 |
| Building and grounds cleaning and maintenance | 2 869 | 812 | 1 168 | 684 | 205 |
| Personal care and services | 916 | 86 | 297 | 276 | 256 |
| Sales and office | 10 242 | 415 | 2 803 | 3 328 | 3 697 |
| Sales and related | 6 384 | 236 | 1 590 | 1 981 | 2 576 |
| Office and administrative support | 3 858 | 178 | 1 212 | 1 347 | 1 121 |
| Natural resources, construction, and maintenance | 12 112 | 2 383 | 5 204 | 3 518 | 1 007 |
| Farming, fishing, and forestry | 798 | 339 | 289 | 112 | 59 |
| Construction and extraction | 7 072 | 1 630 | 3 171 | 1 718 | 553 |
| Installation, maintenance, and repair | 4 242 | 414 | 1 743 | 1 688 | 396 |
| Production, transportation, and material moving | 12 134 | 1 817 | 5 716 | 3 423 | 1 178 |
| Production | 5 537 | 804 | 2 477 | 1 707 | 549 |
| Transportation and material moving | 6 598 | 1 013 | 3 239 | 1 716 | 630 |
| Armed forces | 569 | 1 | 104 | 271 | 193 |
| | | | | | |
| **Women** | 61 528 | 3 723 | 13 909 | 18 379 | 25 517 |
| Management, business, and financial operations | 10 394 | 137 | 1 406 | 2 648 | 6 203 |
| Management | 6 518 | 126 | 917 | 1 590 | 3 885 |
| Business and financial operations | 3 877 | 11 | 488 | 1 059 | 2 319 |
| Professional and related | 18 334 | 109 | 1 178 | 4 142 | 12 905 |
| Computer and mathematical | 1 012 | 7 | 54 | 247 | 704 |
| Architecture and engineering | 430 | 4 | 44 | 75 | 307 |
| Life, physical, and social sciences | 528 | . . . | 22 | 43 | 463 |
| Community and social services | 1 635 | 8 | 117 | 254 | 1 256 |
| Legal | 794 | 10 | 59 | 204 | 521 |
| Education, training, and library | 6 273 | 44 | 435 | 837 | 4 957 |
| Arts, design, entertainment, sports, and media | 1 306 | 16 | 105 | 258 | 927 |
| Health care practitioner and technical | 6 355 | 21 | 342 | 2 224 | 3 769 |
| Services | 11 574 | 1 883 | 4 251 | 3 961 | 1 479 |
| Health care support | 2 661 | 210 | 862 | 1 280 | 309 |
| Protective services | 519 | 25 | 148 | 178 | 169 |
| Food preparation and serving related | 2 835 | 540 | 1 185 | 812 | 297 |
| Building and grounds cleaning and maintenance | 2 223 | 737 | 918 | 390 | 179 |
| Personal care and services | 3 336 | 371 | 1 137 | 1 301 | 526 |
| Sales and office | 16 942 | 712 | 5 261 | 6 512 | 4 457 |
| Sales and related | 5 837 | 387 | 1 806 | 1 884 | 1 760 |
| Office and administrative support | 11 104 | 324 | 3 454 | 4 628 | 2 697 |
| Natural resources, construction, and maintenance | 690 | 202 | 214 | 174 | 100 |
| Farming, fishing, and forestry | 305 | 155 | 94 | 33 | 23 |
| Construction and extraction | 237 | 37 | 84 | 67 | 49 |
| Installation, maintenance, and repair | 148 | 10 | 35 | 75 | 28 |
| Production, transportation, and material moving | 3 527 | 681 | 1 590 | 909 | 346 |
| Production | 2 192 | 466 | 968 | 525 | 234 |
| Transportation and material moving | 1 334 | 215 | 622 | 384 | 112 |
| Armed forces | 67 | . . . | 9 | 32 | 27 |

. . . = Not available.

**Table 1-60.  Percent Distribution of Workers Age 25 to 64 Years, by Educational Attainment, Occupation of Longest Job Held, and Sex, 2014–2015**

(Percent of total workers in occupation.)

| Year, sex, and occupation | Total | Less than a high school diploma | 4 years of high school only | 1 to 3 years of college | 4 or more years of college |
|---|---|---|---|---|---|
| **2014** | | | | | |
| **Both Sexes** | 100.0 | 8.0 | 26.2 | 27.9 | 37.9 |
| Management, business, and financial operations | 100.0 | 2.2 | 15.1 | 23.5 | 59.2 |
| Management | 100.0 | 2.8 | 17.5 | 24.3 | 55.5 |
| Business and financial operations | 100.0 | 0.8 | 9.6 | 21.5 | 68.2 |
| Professional and related | 100.0 | 0.5 | 6.8 | 20.3 | 72.4 |
| Computer and mathematical | 100.0 | 0.4 | 5.3 | 21.0 | 73.4 |
| Architecture and engineering | 100.0 | 0.3 | 9.4 | 20.6 | 69.6 |
| Life, physical, and social sciences | 100.0 | . . . | 4.9 | 9.0 | 86.1 |
| Community and social services | 100.0 | 0.8 | 8.4 | 16.4 | 74.4 |
| Legal | 100.0 | 0.4 | 4.3 | 14.1 | 81.2 |
| Education, training, and library | 100.0 | 0.3 | 5.9 | 12.1 | 81.7 |
| Arts, design, entertainment, sports, and media | 100.0 | 1.5 | 10.0 | 22.3 | 66.2 |
| Health care practitioner and technical | 100.0 | 0.5 | 6.8 | 31.9 | 60.8 |
| Services | 100.0 | 16.4 | 35.8 | 32.7 | 15.1 |
| Health care support | 100.0 | 9.5 | 29.0 | 47.0 | 14.5 |
| Protective services | 100.0 | 2.8 | 26.0 | 43.0 | 28.1 |
| Food preparation and serving related | 100.0 | 18.9 | 40.5 | 28.3 | 12.2 |
| Building and grounds cleaning and maintenance | 100.0 | 31.5 | 42.4 | 19.6 | 6.5 |
| Personal care and services | 100.0 | 8.8 | 33.3 | 37.0 | 20.9 |
| Sales and office | 100.0 | 4.2 | 30.9 | 35.9 | 29.1 |
| Sales and related | 100.0 | 5.1 | 28.7 | 31.5 | 34.7 |
| Office and administrative support | 100.0 | 3.4 | 32.6 | 39.4 | 24.7 |
| Natural resources, construction, and maintenance | 100.0 | 21.7 | 41.5 | 28.0 | 8.8 |
| Farming, fishing, and forestry | 100.0 | 44.0 | 32.3 | 13.4 | 10.3 |
| Construction and extraction | 100.0 | 25.1 | 43.6 | 23.8 | 7.5 |
| Installation, maintenance, and repair | 100.0 | 11.2 | 40.1 | 38.0 | 10.6 |
| Production, transportation, and material moving | 100.0 | 16.3 | 46.4 | 27.9 | 9.5 |
| Production | 100.0 | 16.4 | 45.3 | 28.6 | 9.7 |
| Transportation and material moving | 100.0 | 16.1 | 47.4 | 27.3 | 9.2 |
| Armed forces | 100.0 | 0.3 | 17.2 | 44.6 | 37.9 |
| | | | | | |
| **Men** | 100.0 | 9.8 | 28.7 | 26.2 | 35.3 |
| Management, business, and financial operations | 100.0 | 2.6 | 16.0 | 22.0 | 59.4 |
| Management | 100.0 | 3.3 | 18.8 | 23.4 | 54.5 |
| Business and financial operations | 100.0 | 0.5 | 7.3 | 17.6 | 74.6 |
| Professional and related | 100.0 | 0.5 | 6.3 | 17.3 | 75.8 |
| Computer and mathematical | 100.0 | 0.4 | 5.3 | 21.0 | 73.4 |
| Architecture and engineering | 100.0 | 0.2 | 9.5 | 21.5 | 68.8 |
| Life, physical, and social sciences | 100.0 | . . . | 6.8 | 8.6 | 84.6 |
| Community and social services | 100.0 | 1.3 | 8.0 | 15.1 | 75.6 |
| Legal | 100.0 | 0.4 | 0.8 | 1.9 | 96.8 |
| Education, training, and library | 100.0 | 0.2 | 3.2 | 7.6 | 88.9 |
| Arts, design, entertainment, sports, and media | 100.0 | 1.4 | 11.8 | 22.8 | 64.0 |
| Health care practitioner and technical | 100.0 | 0.9 | 4.8 | 22.9 | 71.5 |
| Services | 100.0 | 16.9 | 35.6 | 30.4 | 17.2 |
| Health care support | 100.0 | 4.3 | 28.4 | 37.8 | 29.5 |
| Protective services | 100.0 | 2.7 | 26.0 | 43.2 | 28.2 |
| Food preparation and serving related | 100.0 | 21.2 | 38.5 | 26.5 | 13.8 |
| Building and grounds cleaning and maintenance | 100.0 | 28.6 | 42.6 | 21.6 | 7.2 |
| Personal care and services | 100.0 | 7.7 | 32.0 | 34.2 | 26.2 |
| Sales and office | 100.0 | 4.0 | 28.5 | 32.4 | 35.1 |
| Sales and related | 100.0 | 3.8 | 25.5 | 30.4 | 40.3 |
| Office and administrative support | 100.0 | 4.2 | 33.1 | 35.7 | 27.0 |
| Natural resources, construction, and maintenance | 100.0 | 21.5 | 42.1 | 28.1 | 8.3 |
| Farming, fishing, and forestry | 100.0 | 44.1 | 34.0 | 14.5 | 7.4 |
| Construction and extraction | 100.0 | 25.4 | 43.7 | 23.6 | 7.3 |
| Installation, maintenance, and repair | 100.0 | 11.3 | 40.8 | 37.8 | 10.1 |
| Production, transportation, and material moving | 100.0 | 15.2 | 47.1 | 28.4 | 9.3 |
| Production | 100.0 | 14.5 | 45.8 | 30.2 | 9.4 |
| Transportation and material moving | 100.0 | 15.8 | 48.2 | 26.9 | 9.1 |
| Armed forces | 100.0 | 0.4 | 18.8 | 44.3 | 36.5 |
| | | | | | |
| **Women** | 100.0 | 6.1 | 23.3 | 29.9 | 40.8 |
| Management, business, and financial operations | 100.0 | 1.6 | 14.0 | 25.3 | 59.1 |
| Management | 100.0 | 1.9 | 15.5 | 25.7 | 56.9 |
| Business and financial operations | 100.0 | 1.0 | 11.5 | 24.7 | 62.8 |
| Professional and related | 100.0 | 0.5 | 7.1 | 22.4 | 70.1 |
| Computer and mathematical | 100.0 | 0.5 | 5.2 | 20.9 | 73.5 |
| Architecture and engineering | 100.0 | 0.9 | 9.0 | 16.0 | 74.1 |
| Life, physical, and social sciences | 100.0 | . . . | 2.8 | 9.3 | 87.9 |
| Community and social services | 100.0 | 0.5 | 8.7 | 17.0 | 73.8 |
| Legal | 100.0 | 0.4 | 7.2 | 24.5 | 67.9 |
| Education, training, and library | 100.0 | 0.3 | 6.7 | 13.6 | 79.4 |
| Arts, design, entertainment, sports, and media | 100.0 | 1.7 | 8.0 | 21.8 | 68.5 |
| Health care practitioner and technical | 100.0 | 0.4 | 7.5 | 34.7 | 57.5 |
| Services | 100.0 | 16.0 | 36.0 | 34.5 | 13.5 |
| Health care support | 100.0 | 10.1 | 29.1 | 48.2 | 12.6 |
| Protective services | 100.0 | 3.4 | 26.1 | 42.5 | 28.0 |
| Food preparation and serving related | 100.0 | 17.0 | 42.1 | 29.9 | 11.0 |
| Building and grounds cleaning and maintenance | 100.0 | 35.2 | 42.2 | 17.0 | 5.5 |
| Personal care and services | 100.0 | 9.1 | 33.7 | 37.7 | 19.5 |
| Sales and office | 100.0 | 4.3 | 32.3 | 37.9 | 25.5 |
| Sales and related | 100.0 | 6.5 | 32.2 | 32.6 | 28.7 |
| Office and administrative support | 100.0 | 3.1 | 32.4 | 40.7 | 23.8 |
| Natural resources, construction, and maintenance | 100.0 | 25.8 | 29.5 | 26.0 | 18.7 |
| Farming, fishing, and forestry | 100.0 | 43.5 | 27.5 | 10.1 | 18.9 |
| Construction and extraction | 100.0 | 15.7 | 37.9 | 32.3 | 14.2 |
| Installation, maintenance, and repair | 100.0 | 11.0 | 23.1 | 42.6 | 23.2 |
| Production, transportation, and material moving | 100.0 | 19.9 | 43.8 | 26.1 | 10.1 |
| Production | 100.0 | 21.0 | 44.2 | 24.5 | 10.3 |
| Transportation and material moving | 100.0 | 18.1 | 43.2 | 28.9 | 9.8 |
| Armed forces | 100.0 | . . . | 5.0 | 46.4 | 48.6 |

. . . = Not available.

## Table 1-60.  Percent Distribution of Workers Age 25 to 64 Years, by Educational Attainment, Occupation of Longest Job Held, and Sex, 2014–2015—*Continued*

(Percent of total workers in occupation.)

| Year, sex, and occupation | Total | Less than a high school diploma | 4 years of high school only | 1 to 3 years of college | 4 or more years of college |
|---|---|---|---|---|---|
| **2015** | | | | | |
| **Both Sexes** | 100.0 | 7.8 | 25.6 | 28.0 | 38.7 |
| Management, business, and financial operations | 100.0 | 2.0 | 14.4 | 23.5 | 60.1 |
| Management | 100.0 | 2.6 | 16.2 | 23.7 | 57.4 |
| Business and financial operations | 100.0 | 0.6 | 10.2 | 22.8 | 66.4 |
| Professional and related | 100.0 | 0.5 | 6.1 | 20.4 | 72.9 |
| Computer and mathematical | 100.0 | 0.2 | 4.8 | 22.1 | 72.9 |
| Architecture and engineering | 100.0 | 0.2 | 8.9 | 19.0 | 71.8 |
| Life, physical, and social sciences | 100.0 | 0.1 | 4.6 | 10.5 | 84.8 |
| Community and social services | 100.0 | 0.5 | 7.4 | 16.0 | 76.1 |
| Legal | 100.0 | 0.7 | 4.6 | 14.6 | 80.0 |
| Education, training, and library | 100.0 | 0.6 | 5.7 | 12.2 | 81.6 |
| Arts, design, entertainment, sports, and media | 100.0 | 1.6 | 10.1 | 22.8 | 65.5 |
| Health care practitioner and technical | 100.0 | 0.3 | 5.3 | 31.5 | 62.9 |
| Services | 100.0 | 16.6 | 36.2 | 32.6 | 14.7 |
| Health care support | 100.0 | 7.4 | 32.0 | 47.8 | 12.8 |
| Protective services | 100.0 | 2.5 | 25.6 | 41.3 | 30.6 |
| Food preparation and serving related | 100.0 | 19.9 | 40.9 | 27.3 | 11.8 |
| Building and grounds cleaning and maintenance | 100.0 | 30.4 | 41.0 | 21.1 | 7.5 |
| Personal care and services | 100.0 | 10.8 | 33.7 | 37.1 | 18.4 |
| Sales and office | 100.0 | 4.1 | 29.7 | 36.2 | 30.0 |
| Sales and related | 100.0 | 5.1 | 27.8 | 31.6 | 35.5 |
| Office and administrative support | 100.0 | 3.4 | 31.2 | 39.9 | 25.5 |
| Natural resources, construction, and maintenance | 100.0 | 20.2 | 42.3 | 28.8 | 8.7 |
| Farming, fishing, and forestry | 100.0 | 44.8 | 34.7 | 13.1 | 7.4 |
| Construction and extraction | 100.0 | 22.8 | 44.5 | 24.4 | 8.2 |
| Installation, maintenance, and repair | 100.0 | 9.7 | 40.5 | 40.2 | 9.7 |
| Production, transportation, and material moving | 100.0 | 15.9 | 46.7 | 27.7 | 9.7 |
| Production | 100.0 | 16.4 | 44.6 | 28.9 | 10.1 |
| Transportation and material moving | 100.0 | 15.5 | 48.7 | 26.5 | 9.4 |
| Armed forces | 100.0 | 0.2 | 17.8 | 47.5 | 34.5 |
| **Men** | 100.0 | 9.4 | 28.2 | 26.3 | 36.2 |
| Management, business, and financial operations | 100.0 | 2.6 | 15.1 | 21.7 | 60.5 |
| Management | 100.0 | 3.1 | 17.7 | 23.3 | 55.9 |
| Business and financial operations | 100.0 | 1.1 | 7.1 | 16.8 | 75.0 |
| Professional and related | 100.0 | 0.3 | 5.8 | 17.4 | 76.5 |
| Computer and mathematical | 100.0 | 0.1 | 4.6 | 21.4 | 73.9 |
| Architecture and engineering | 100.0 | 0.1 | 8.7 | 19.4 | 71.8 |
| Life, physical, and social sciences | 100.0 | 0.1 | 4.9 | 12.3 | 82.7 |
| Community and social services | 100.0 | 0.4 | 7.9 | 17.1 | 74.6 |
| Legal | 100.0 | 0.1 | 1.3 | 1.9 | 96.6 |
| Education, training, and library | 100.0 | 0.2 | 2.1 | 8.6 | 89.1 |
| Arts, design, entertainment, sports, and media | 100.0 | 2.0 | 12.0 | 25.6 | 60.4 |
| Health care practitioner and technical | 100.0 | 0.1 | 4.8 | 19.7 | 75.4 |
| Services | 100.0 | 17.0 | 35.4 | 30.5 | 17.1 |
| Health care support | 100.0 | 3.6 | 28.7 | 45.8 | 21.9 |
| Protective services | 100.0 | 2.0 | 24.9 | 43.0 | 30.1 |
| Food preparation and serving related | 100.0 | 20.9 | 39.8 | 25.9 | 13.3 |
| Building and grounds cleaning and maintenance | 100.0 | 28.3 | 40.7 | 23.8 | 7.2 |
| Personal care and services | 100.0 | 9.4 | 32.4 | 30.2 | 28.0 |
| Sales and office | 100.0 | 4.0 | 27.4 | 32.5 | 36.1 |
| Sales and related | 100.0 | 3.7 | 24.9 | 31.0 | 40.3 |
| Office and administrative support | 100.0 | 4.6 | 31.4 | 34.9 | 29.1 |
| Natural resources, construction, and maintenance | 100.0 | 19.7 | 43.0 | 29.0 | 8.3 |
| Farming, fishing, and forestry | 100.0 | 42.5 | 36.2 | 14.0 | 7.4 |
| Construction and extraction | 100.0 | 23.1 | 44.8 | 24.3 | 7.8 |
| Installation, maintenance, and repair | 100.0 | 9.8 | 41.1 | 39.8 | 9.3 |
| Production, transportation, and material moving | 100.0 | 15.0 | 47.1 | 28.2 | 9.7 |
| Production | 100.0 | 14.5 | 44.7 | 30.8 | 9.9 |
| Transportation and material moving | 100.0 | 15.4 | 49.1 | 26.0 | 9.5 |
| Armed forces | 100.0 | 0.2 | 18.3 | 47.6 | 33.9 |
| **Women** | 100.0 | 6.1 | 22.6 | 29.9 | 41.5 |
| Management, business, and financial operations | 100.0 | 1.3 | 13.5 | 25.5 | 59.7 |
| Management | 100.0 | 1.9 | 14.1 | 24.4 | 59.6 |
| Business and financial operations | 100.0 | 0.3 | 12.6 | 27.3 | 59.8 |
| Professional and related | 100.0 | 0.6 | 6.4 | 22.6 | 70.4 |
| Computer and mathematical | 100.0 | 0.7 | 5.3 | 24.4 | 69.6 |
| Architecture and engineering | 100.0 | 0.9 | 10.1 | 17.4 | 71.6 |
| Life, physical, and social sciences | 100.0 | . . . | 4.2 | 8.2 | 87.6 |
| Community and social services | 100.0 | 0.5 | 7.2 | 15.5 | 76.8 |
| Legal | 100.0 | 1.3 | 7.5 | 25.6 | 65.6 |
| Education, training, and library | 100.0 | 0.7 | 6.9 | 13.3 | 79.0 |
| Arts, design, entertainment, sports, and media | 100.0 | 1.2 | 8.0 | 19.8 | 71.0 |
| Health care practitioner and technical | 100.0 | 0.3 | 5.4 | 35.0 | 59.3 |
| Services | 100.0 | 16.3 | 36.7 | 34.2 | 12.8 |
| Health care support | 100.0 | 7.9 | 32.4 | 48.1 | 11.6 |
| Protective services | 100.0 | 4.7 | 28.5 | 34.3 | 32.5 |
| Food preparation and serving related | 100.0 | 19.0 | 41.8 | 28.7 | 10.5 |
| Building and grounds cleaning and maintenance | 100.0 | 33.2 | 41.3 | 17.5 | 8.0 |
| Personal care and services | 100.0 | 11.1 | 34.1 | 39.0 | 15.8 |
| Sales and office | 100.0 | 4.2 | 31.1 | 38.4 | 26.3 |
| Sales and related | 100.0 | 6.6 | 30.9 | 32.3 | 30.1 |
| Office and administrative support | 100.0 | 2.9 | 31.1 | 41.7 | 24.3 |
| Natural resources, construction, and maintenance | 100.0 | 29.3 | 31.0 | 25.3 | 14.5 |
| Farming, fishing, and forestry | 100.0 | 50.9 | 30.9 | 10.7 | 7.5 |
| Construction and extraction | 100.0 | 15.5 | 35.6 | 28.3 | 20.7 |
| Installation, maintenance, and repair | 100.0 | 6.9 | 23.7 | 50.3 | 19.1 |
| Production, transportation, and material moving | 100.0 | 19.3 | 45.1 | 25.8 | 9.8 |
| Production | 100.0 | 21.2 | 44.2 | 23.9 | 10.7 |
| Transportation and material moving | 100.0 | 16.1 | 46.6 | 28.8 | 8.4 |
| Armed forces | 100.0 | . . . | 13.6 | 47.0 | 39.4 |

. . . = Not available.

**Table 1-61.  Median Annual Earnings of Year-Round, Full-Time Wage and Salary Workers Age 25 to 64 Years, by Educational Attainment and Sex, 2004–2015**

(Thousands of workers, dollars.)

| Year and sex | Total | Less than a high school diploma | 4 years of high school only | 1 to 3 years of college | 4 or more years of college |
|---|---|---|---|---|---|
| **2004** | | | | | |
| **Both Sexes** | | | | | |
| Number of workers | 86 306 | 7 648 | 25 786 | 23 897 | 28 976 |
| Median annual earnings | 38 000 | 21 840 | 30 000 | 37 000 | 55 000 |
| **Men** | | | | | |
| Number of workers | 49 904 | 5 178 | 15 263 | 12 822 | 16 642 |
| Median annual earnings | 42 900 | 24 000 | 35 000 | 43 000 | 65 000 |
| **Women** | | | | | |
| Number of workers | 36 402 | 2 470 | 10 523 | 11 074 | 12 334 |
| Median annual earnings | 32 000 | 18 000 | 25 280 | 31 200 | 45 000 |
| **2005** | | | | | |
| **Both Sexes** | | | | | |
| Number of workers | 88 415 | 7 758 | 26 023 | 24 623 | 30 012 |
| Median annual earnings | 39 768 | 22 880 | 31 000 | 38 000 | 55 000 |
| **Men** | | | | | |
| Number of workers | 51 022 | 5 376 | 15 451 | 13 199 | 16 996 |
| Median annual earnings | 44 000 | 25 000 | 35 360 | 45 000 | 65 000 |
| **Women** | | | | | |
| Number of workers | 37 393 | 2 381 | 10 571 | 11 424 | 13 016 |
| Median annual earnings | 33 644 | 18 200 | 26 000 | 32 000 | 46 700 |
| **2006** | | | | | |
| **Both Sexes** | | | | | |
| Number of workers | 90 733 | 7 951 | 26 233 | 24 737 | 31 812 |
| Median annual earnings | 40 000 | 23 000 | 32 000 | 39 482 | 57 588 |
| **Men** | | | | | |
| Number of workers | 52 252 | 5 485 | 15 525 | 13 204 | 18 038 |
| Median annual earnings | 45 000 | 25 000 | 36 665 | 45 000 | 68 000 |
| **Women** | | | | | |
| Number of workers | 38 481 | 2 466 | 10 708 | 11 533 | 13 774 |
| Median annual earnings | 35 000 | 19 000 | 26 800 | 33 000 | 49 000 |
| **2007** | | | | | |
| **Both Sexes** | | | | | |
| Number of workers | 91 540 | 7 123 | 25 925 | 25 574 | 32 918 |
| Median annual earnings | 41 000 | 24 000 | 33 000 | 40 000 | 60 000 |
| **Men** | | | | | |
| Number of workers | 52 262 | 4 902 | 15 390 | 13 655 | 18 316 |
| Median annual earnings | 47 000 | 25 000 | 38 000 | 45 188 | 70 000 |
| **Women** | | | | | |
| Number of workers | 39 277 | 2 221 | 10 535 | 11 919 | 14 603 |
| Median annual earnings | 35 000 | 19 200 | 27 120 | 35 000 | 50 000 |
| **2008** | | | | | |
| **Both Sexes** | | | | | |
| Number of workers | 88 373 | 6 600 | 24 531 | 24 887 | 32 355 |
| Median annual earnings | 42 000 | 24 000 | 34 000 | 40 000 | 60 000 |
| **Men** | | | | | |
| Number of workers | 50 141 | 4 503 | 14 480 | 13 283 | 17 876 |
| Median annual earnings | 49 564 | 27 000 | 39 040 | 47 000 | 72 000 |
| **Women** | | | | | |
| Number of workers | 38 231 | 2 097 | 10 051 | 11 604 | 14 479 |
| Median annual earnings | 36 000 | 19 567 | 28 000 | 35 000 | 50 000 |
| **2009** | | | | | |
| **Both Sexes** | | | | | |
| Number of workers | 84 730 | 5 847 | 23 277 | 23 515 | 32 091 |
| Median annual earnings | 43 000 | 24 000 | 34 320 | 40 000 | 60 000 |
| **Men** | | | | | |
| Number of workers | 47 135 | 3 809 | 13 620 | 12 283 | 17 424 |
| Median annual earnings | 50 000 | 26 000 | 40 000 | 49 000 | 71 000 |
| **Women** | | | | | |
| Number of workers | 37 595 | 2 037 | 9 657 | 11 233 | 14 667 |
| Median annual earnings | 38 000 | 20 000 | 29 000 | 35 000 | 52 000 |

## Table 1-61.  Median Annual Earnings of Year-Round, Full-Time Wage and Salary Workers Age 25 to 64 Years, by Educational Attainment and Sex, 2004–2015—*Continued*

(Thousands of workers, dollars.)

| Year and sex | Total | Less than a high school diploma | 4 years of high school only | 1 to 3 years of college | 4 or more years of college |
|---|---|---|---|---|---|
| **2010** | | | | | |
| **Both Sexes** | | | | | |
| Number of workers ............................... | 84 902 | 5 548 | 22 768 | 23 725 | 32 861 |
| Median annual earnings ........................ | 44 217 | 24 000 | 35 000 | 40 000 | 60 000 |
| **Men** | | | | | |
| Number of workers ............................... | 47 549 | 3 653 | 13 526 | 12 405 | 17 965 |
| Median annual earnings ........................ | 50 000 | 26 500 | 40 000 | 48 000 | 72 000 |
| **Women** | | | | | |
| Number of workers ............................... | 37 353 | 1 895 | 9 241 | 11 321 | 14 896 |
| Median annual earnings ........................ | 38 000 | 20 000 | 30 000 | 35 000 | 51 000 |
| **2011** | | | | | |
| **Both Sexes** | | | | | |
| Number of workers ............................... | 86 570 | 5 858 | 22 921 | 23 947 | 33 843 |
| Median annual earnings ........................ | 45 000 | 25 000 | 35 000 | 41 000 | 62 000 |
| **Men** | | | | | |
| Number of workers ............................... | 48 748 | 3 971 | 13 750 | 12 705 | 18 322 |
| Median annual earnings ........................ | 50 000 | 27 819 | 40 000 | 50 000 | 75 000 |
| **Women** | | | | | |
| Number of workers ............................... | 37 822 | 1 887 | 9 171 | 11 243 | 15 521 |
| Median annual earnings ........................ | 39 000 | 20 000 | 30 000 | 35 000 | 52 000 |
| **2012** | | | | | |
| **Both Sexes** | | | | | |
| Number of workers ............................... | 87 660 | 5 671 | 22 628 | 24 217 | 35 144 |
| Median annual earnings ........................ | 45 000 | 24 750 | 35 000 | 41 500 | 63 000 |
| **Men** | | | | | |
| Number of workers ............................... | 49 481 | 3 874 | 13 629 | 13 051 | 18 927 |
| Median annual earnings ........................ | 50 000 | 26 000 | 40 000 | 49 000 | 75 000 |
| **Women** | | | | | |
| Number of workers ............................... | 38 179 | 1 797 | 8 999 | 11 165 | 16 217 |
| Median annual earnings ........................ | 40 000 | 20 000 | 30 000 | 35 395 | 54 000 |
| **2013** | | | | | |
| **Both Sexes** | | | | | |
| Number of workers ............................... | 89 443 | 6 100 | 23 427 | 24 477 | 35 440 |
| Median annual earnings ........................ | 45 000 | 25 000 | 35 000 | 42 000 | 65 000 |
| **Men** | | | | | |
| Number of workers ............................... | 50 765 | 4 260 | 14 338 | 13 201 | 18 965 |
| Median annual earnings ........................ | 50 000 | 28 000 | 40 000 | 49 999 | 75 000 |
| **Women** | | | | | |
| Number of workers ............................... | 38 678 | 1 840 | 9 089 | 11 275 | 16 475 |
| Median annual earnings ........................ | 40 000 | 20 800 | 30 000 | 35 340 | 55 000 |
| **2014** | | | | | |
| **Both Sexes** | | | | | |
| Number of workers ............................... | 91 622 | 6 280 | 23 537 | 24 967 | 36 837 |
| Median annual earnings ........................ | 46 000 | 25 000 | 35 000 | 41 600 | 65 000 |
| **Men** | | | | | |
| Number of workers ............................... | 52 165 | 4 377 | 14 649 | 13 402 | 19 736 |
| Median annual earnings ........................ | 50 000 | 29 000 | 40 000 | 49 000 | 75 000 |
| **Women** | | | | | |
| Number of workers ............................... | 39 456 | 1 903 | 8 888 | 11 565 | 17 101 |
| Median annual earnings ........................ | 40 000 | 20 800 | 30 000 | 35 000 | 55 000 |
| **2015** | | | | | |
| **Both Sexes** | | | | | |
| Number of workers ............................... | 93 616 | 6 208 | 23 376 | 25 747 | 38 284 |
| Median annual earnings ........................ | 48 000 | 27 000 | 36 000 | 43 000 | 68 000 |
| **Men** | | | | | |
| Number of workers ............................... | 53 137 | 4 313 | 14 495 | 13 830 | 20 499 |
| Median annual earnings ........................ | 53 000 | 30 000 | 40 000 | 50 000 | 80 000 |
| **Women** | | | | | |
| Number of workers ............................... | 40 478 | 1 895 | 8 881 | 11 917 | 17 785 |
| Median annual earnings ........................ | 41 600 | 20 800 | 30 000 | 37 000 | 57 747 |

## Table 1-62.   Employment Status of the Civilian Noninstitutional Population by Disability Status and Selected Characteristics, 2015 Annual Averages

(Thousands of people, percent.)

| Characteristic | Civilian noninstitutional population | Civilian labor force | | | | | | Not in labor force |
|---|---|---|---|---|---|---|---|---|
| | | Total | Participation rate | Employed | | Unemployed | | |
| | | | | Total | Percent | Total | Rate | |
| **TOTAL** | | | | | | | | |
| Total, 16 Years and Over ...................................... | 250 801 | 157 130 | 62.7 | 148 834 | 59.3 | 8 296 | 5.3 | 93 671 |
| Men ...................................................................... | 121 101 | 83 620 | 69.1 | 79 131 | 65.3 | 4 490 | 5.4 | 37 481 |
| Women ................................................................. | 129 700 | 73 510 | 56.7 | 69 703 | 53.7 | 3 807 | 5.2 | 56 190 |
| **PERSONS WITH A DISABILITY** ........................... | 29 752 | 5 813 | 19.5 | 5 193 | 17.5 | 621 | 10.7 | 23 939 |
| **Sex** | | | | | | | | |
| Men ...................................................................... | 13 739 | 3 134 | 22.8 | 2 803 | 20.4 | 331 | 10.6 | 10 605 |
| Women ................................................................. | 16 014 | 2 679 | 16.7 | 2 389 | 14.9 | 290 | 10.8 | 13 334 |
| **Age** | | | | | | | | |
| 16 to 64 years ..................................................... | 15 771 | 4 812 | 30.5 | 4 250 | 26.9 | 562 | 11.7 | 10 959 |
| 16 to 19 years ................................................. | 620 | 137 | 22.2 | 95 | 15.4 | 42 | 30.7 | 482 |
| 20 to 24 years ................................................. | 902 | 397 | 44.0 | 316 | 35.0 | 81 | 20.3 | 505 |
| 25 to 34 years ................................................. | 1 805 | 762 | 42.2 | 639 | 35.4 | 123 | 16.1 | 1 043 |
| 35 to 44 years ................................................. | 2 198 | 809 | 36.8 | 713 | 32.4 | 96 | 11.8 | 1 389 |
| 45 to 54 years ................................................. | 4 023 | 1 199 | 29.8 | 1 094 | 27.2 | 105 | 8.8 | 2 824 |
| 55 to 64 years ................................................. | 6 224 | 1 508 | 24.2 | 1 393 | 22.4 | 115 | 7.7 | 4 715 |
| 65 years and over ............................................... | 13 981 | 1 001 | 7.2 | 942 | 6.7 | 59 | 5.9 | 12 980 |
| **Race and Hispanic Origin** | | | | | | | | |
| White .................................................................... | 23 812 | 4 693 | 19.7 | 4 242 | 17.8 | 451 | 9.6 | 19 119 |
| Black or African American ................................... | 4 057 | 704 | 17.4 | 582 | 14.3 | 122 | 17.4 | 3 353 |
| Asian ................................................................... | 828 | 136 | 16.4 | 126 | 15.2 | 10 | 7.4 | 691 |
| Hispanic[1] ........................................................... | 3 140 | 709 | 22.6 | 614 | 19.6 | 94 | 13.3 | 2 432 |
| **Educational Attainment** | | | | | | | | |
| Total, 25 years and over ...................................... | 28 230 | 5 279 | 18.7 | 4 781 | 16.9 | 498 | 9.4 | 22 951 |
| Less than a high school diploma ......................... | 5 909 | 578 | 9.8 | 505 | 8.5 | 73 | 12.6 | 5 331 |
| High school graduates, no college[2] ................... | 10 323 | 1 651 | 16.0 | 1 488 | 14.4 | 163 | 9.9 | 8 672 |
| Some college or associate degree ...................... | 7 234 | 1 757 | 24.3 | 1 583 | 21.9 | 175 | 9.9 | 5 476 |
| Bachelor's degree and higher[3] ......................... | 4 765 | 1 293 | 27.1 | 1 206 | 25.3 | 87 | 6.8 | 3 472 |

[1]May be of any race.
[2]Includes persons with a high school diploma or equivalent.
[3]Includes persons with bachelor's, master's, professional, and doctoral degrees.

## Table 1-63.   Employed Full- and Part-Time Workers by Disability Status and Age, 2015 Annual Averages

(Thousands of people.)

| Disability status and age | Employed | | | At work part-time for economic reasons[1] |
|---|---|---|---|---|
| | Total | Usually work full-time | Usually work part-time | |
| **TOTAL** | | | | |
| Total, 16 Years and Over ...................................... | 148 834 | 121 492 | 27 341 | 6 371 |
| 16 to 64 years ..................................................... | 140 369 | 116 240 | 24 129 | 6 141 |
| 65 years and over ................................................ | 8 465 | 5 252 | 3 213 | 231 |
| **Persons With a Disability** | | | | |
| 16 years and over ................................................ | 5 193 | 3 508 | 1 684 | 311 |
| 16 to 64 years ..................................................... | 4 250 | 3 025 | 1 225 | 290 |
| 65 years and over ................................................ | 942 | 483 | 459 | 21 |
| **Persons Without a Disability** | | | | |
| 16 years and over ................................................ | 143 641 | 117 984 | 25 657 | 6 060 |
| 16 to 64 years ..................................................... | 136 119 | 113 215 | 22 903 | 5 850 |
| 65 years and over ................................................ | 7 522 | 4 769 | 2 754 | 210 |

*Note:* Full time refers to persons who usually work 35 hours or more per week; part time refers to persons who usually work less than 35 hours per week.

[1]Refers to persons who, whether they usually work full or part time, worked 1 to 34 hours during the reference week for an economic reason such as slack work or unfavorable business conditions, inability to find full-time work, or seasonal declines in demand.

## Table 1-64.  Employed Persons by Disability Status, Occupation, and Sex, 2015 Annual Averages

(Number in thousands, percent.)

| Occupation | Persons with a disability | | | Persons with no disability | | |
|---|---|---|---|---|---|---|
| | Total | Men | Women | Total | Men | Women |
| **TOTAL EMPLOYED** ........................................................................... | 5 193 | 2 803 | 2 389 | 143 641 | 76 327 | 67 314 |
| **Occupation as a Percent of Total Employed** | | | | | | |
| Total ........................................................................................................ | 100.0 | 100.0 | 100.0 | 100.0 | 100.0 | 100.0 |
| Management, professional, and related ............................................... | 31.3 | 28.7 | 34.3 | 39.2 | 35.7 | 43.2 |
| Management, business, and financial operations ............................ | 14.1 | 15.4 | 12.7 | 16.3 | 17.2 | 15.2 |
| Management ................................................................................ | 10.7 | 12.6 | 8.4 | 11.4 | 13.1 | 9.6 |
| Business and financial operations ............................................. | 3.5 | 2.7 | 4.3 | 4.8 | 4.2 | 5.6 |
| Professional and related ................................................................... | 17.2 | 13.4 | 21.6 | 22.9 | 18.5 | 28.0 |
| Computer and mathematical ...................................................... | 1.9 | 2.3 | 1.6 | 3.0 | 4.2 | 1.5 |
| Architecture and engineering .................................................... | 1.5 | 2.4 | 0.4 | 2.0 | 3.2 | 0.6 |
| Life, physical, and social science ............................................. | 0.7 | 0.5 | 0.9 | 1.0 | 1.0 | 0.9 |
| Community and social services .................................................. | 1.7 | 1.2 | 2.4 | 1.7 | 1.1 | 2.4 |
| Legal ............................................................................................ | 0.8 | 0.9 | 0.7 | 1.2 | 1.1 | 1.3 |
| Education, training, and library .................................................. | 4.6 | 2.6 | 7.0 | 6.0 | 3.0 | 9.5 |
| Arts, design, entertainment, sports, and media ........................ | 1.9 | 1.6 | 2.3 | 2.1 | 2.0 | 2.1 |
| Healthcare practitioner and technical ........................................ | 4.0 | 1.9 | 6.4 | 6.0 | 2.8 | 9.5 |
| Service ............................................................................................... | 21.7 | 17.5 | 26.7 | 17.2 | 14.0 | 20.9 |
| Healthcare support .......................................................................... | 2.3 | 0.4 | 4.6 | 2.4 | 0.6 | 4.4 |
| Protective service ........................................................................... | 2.1 | 2.8 | 1.2 | 2.1 | 3.1 | 0.9 |
| Food preparation and serving related ............................................ | 6.1 | 5.0 | 7.4 | 5.4 | 4.7 | 6.3 |
| Building and grounds cleaning and maintenance ........................... | 6.3 | 7.1 | 5.4 | 3.8 | 4.2 | 3.3 |
| Personal care and service ............................................................... | 4.9 | 2.3 | 8.0 | 3.6 | 1.6 | 5.9 |
| Sales and office ................................................................................... | 22.9 | 16.3 | 30.6 | 22.6 | 16.4 | 29.6 |
| Sales and related ............................................................................ | 10.0 | 9.2 | 10.8 | 10.6 | 10.1 | 11.1 |
| Office and administrative support ................................................... | 12.9 | 7.1 | 19.7 | 12.0 | 6.3 | 18.5 |
| Natural resources, construction, and maintenance ........................... | 9.7 | 16.6 | 1.6 | 9.2 | 16.5 | 0.9 |
| Farming, fishing, and forestry ........................................................ | 1.0 | 1.4 | 0.6 | 0.7 | 1.0 | 0.4 |
| Construction and extraction ............................................................ | 5.0 | 8.8 | 0.4 | 5.1 | 9.4 | 0.3 |
| Installation, maintenance, and repair ............................................. | 3.7 | 6.3 | 0.5 | 3.4 | 6.1 | 0.2 |
| Production, transportation, and material moving ............................... | 14.4 | 20.8 | 6.9 | 11.8 | 17.3 | 5.5 |
| Production .................................................................................... | 6.9 | 9.2 | 4.3 | 5.7 | 7.6 | 3.5 |
| Transportation and material moving ............................................... | 7.5 | 11.7 | 2.6 | 6.1 | 9.7 | 2.0 |

## Table 1-65.  Persons Not in the Labor Force by Disability Status, Age, and Sex, 2015 Annual Averages

(Thousands of people, percent distribution.)

| Category | Total, 16 years and over | 16 to 64 years | | | Total, 65 years and over |
|---|---|---|---|---|---|
| | | Total | Men | Women | |
| **Persons With a Disability** | | | | | |
| Total not in the labor force .................................................. | 23 939 | 10 959 | 5 151 | 5 808 | 12 980 |
| Persons who currently want a job ...................................... | 744 | 523 | 252 | 271 | 221 |
| Marginally attached to the labor force[1] ........................ | 219 | 176 | 86 | 90 | 43 |
| Discouraged workers[2] ............................................. | 62 | 45 | 26 | 18 | 17 |
| Other persons marginally attached to the labor force[3] ..................................................................... | 157 | 131 | 59 | 72 | 26 |
| **Persons Without a Disability** | | | | | |
| Total not in the labor force .................................................. | 69 732 | 45 004 | 16 457 | 28 547 | 24 728 |
| Persons who currently want a job ...................................... | 5 338 | 4 755 | 2 152 | 2 603 | 583 |
| Marginally attached to the labor force[1] ........................ | 1 737 | 1 598 | 830 | 768 | 139 |
| Discouraged workers[2] ............................................. | 603 | 546 | 333 | 213 | 56 |
| Other persons marginally attached to the labor force[3] ..................................................................... | 1 134 | 1 051 | 497 | 555 | 83 |

[1]Data refer to persons who want a job, have searched for work during the prior 12 months, and were available to take a job during the reference week, but had not looked for work in the past 4 weeks.
[2]Includes those who did not actively look for work in the prior 4 weeks for reasons such as thinks no work available, could not find work, lacks schooling or training, employer thinks too young or old, and other types of discrimination.
[3]Includes those who did not actively look for work in the prior 4 weeks for such reasons as school or family responsibilities, ill health, and transportation problems, as well as a number for whom reason for nonparticipation was not determined.

**Table 1-66.   Employment Status of Persons 18 Years and Over by Veteran Status, Period of Service, Sex, Race, and Hispanic or Latino Ethnicity, 2015**

(Thousands of people, percent.)

| Characteristic | Civilian noninstitutional population | Civilian labor force | | Employed | | Unemployed | | Not in labor force |
|---|---|---|---|---|---|---|---|---|
| | | Total | Percent of population | Total | Percent of population | Total | Percent of labor force | |
| **TOTAL** | | | | | | | | |
| Total, 18 Years and Over ............................... | 241 949 | 155 143 | 64.1 | 147 209 | 60.8 | 7 933 | 5.1 | 86 807 |
| Veterans ............................................ | 21 209 | 10 757 | 50.7 | 10 263 | 48.4 | 495 | 4.6 | 10 452 |
| Gulf War era, total ......................... | 7 035 | 5 681 | 80.8 | 5 407 | 76.9 | 274 | 4.8 | 1 354 |
| Gulf War era II .......................... | 3 594 | 2 913 | 81.0 | 2 745 | 76.4 | 168 | 5.8 | 681 |
| Gulf War era I ........................... | 3 440 | 2 768 | 80.4 | 2 662 | 77.4 | 105 | 3.8 | 673 |
| WW II, Korean War, and Vietnam era ........ | 8 901 | 2 350 | 26.4 | 2 248 | 25.3 | 102 | 4.3 | 6 551 |
| Other service periods ...................... | 5 273 | 2 726 | 51.7 | 2 608 | 49.5 | 119 | 4.4 | 2 547 |
| Nonveterans ....................................... | 220 740 | 144 385 | 65.4 | 136 947 | 62.0 | 7 439 | 5.2 | 76 355 |
| **MEN** | | | | | | | | |
| Total, 18 Years and Over ............................... | 116 591 | 82 624 | 70.9 | 78 332 | 67.2 | 4 292 | 5.2 | 33 968 |
| Veterans ............................................ | 19 212 | 9 517 | 49.5 | 9 089 | 47.3 | 428 | 4.5 | 9 695 |
| Gulf War era, total ......................... | 5 870 | 4 840 | 82.5 | 4 617 | 78.6 | 224 | 4.6 | 1 030 |
| Gulf War era II .......................... | 2 959 | 2 462 | 83.2 | 2 322 | 78.5 | 140 | 5.7 | 497 |
| Gulf War era I ........................... | 2 911 | 2 378 | 81.7 | 2 294 | 78.8 | 84 | 3.5 | 533 |
| WW II, Korean War, and Vietnam era ........ | 8 585 | 2 264 | 26.4 | 2 168 | 25.3 | 96 | 4.2 | 6 320 |
| Other service periods ...................... | 4 756 | 2 412 | 50.7 | 2 303 | 48.4 | 108 | 4.5 | 2 345 |
| Nonveterans ....................................... | 97 380 | 73 107 | 75.1 | 69 243 | 71.1 | 3 864 | 5.3 | 24 273 |
| **WOMEN** | | | | | | | | |
| Total, 18 Years and Over ............................... | 125 358 | 72 519 | 57.8 | 68 878 | 54.9 | 3 641 | 5.0 | 52 839 |
| Veterans ............................................ | 1 997 | 1 241 | 62.1 | 1 174 | 58.8 | 67 | 5.4 | 757 |
| Gulf War era, total ......................... | 1 164 | 840 | 72.2 | 790 | 67.8 | 50 | 6.0 | 324 |
| Gulf War era II .......................... | 635 | 451 | 71.0 | 422 | 66.4 | 29 | 6.4 | 184 |
| Gulf War era I ........................... | 529 | 389 | 73.6 | 368 | 69.5 | 21 | 5.5 | 140 |
| WW II, Korean War, and Vietnam era ........ | 317 | 86 | 27.2 | 80 | 25.3 | 6 | 6.8 | 231 |
| Other service periods ...................... | 516 | 314 | 60.9 | 304 | 58.9 | 10 | 3.3 | 202 |
| Nonveterans ....................................... | 123 360 | 71 278 | 57.8 | 67 704 | 54.9 | 3 574 | 5.0 | 52 082 |
| **WHITE** | | | | | | | | |
| Total, 18 Years and Over ............................... | 190 329 | 122 028 | 64.1 | 116 625 | 61.3 | 5 402 | 4.4 | 68 302 |
| Veterans ............................................ | 17 822 | 8 770 | 49.2 | 8 416 | 47.2 | 353 | 4.0 | 9 053 |
| Gulf War era, total ......................... | 5 483 | 4 474 | 81.6 | 4 282 | 78.1 | 192 | 4.3 | 1 009 |
| Gulf War era II .......................... | 2 847 | 2 328 | 81.8 | 2 208 | 77.6 | 119 | 5.1 | 519 |
| Gulf War era I ........................... | 2 637 | 2 146 | 81.4 | 2 074 | 78.6 | 73 | 3.4 | 490 |
| WW II, Korean War, and Vietnam era ........ | 7 932 | 2 096 | 26.4 | 2 019 | 25.4 | 77 | 3.7 | 5 837 |
| Other service periods ...................... | 4 407 | 2 200 | 49.9 | 2 115 | 48.0 | 84 | 3.8 | 2 207 |
| Nonveterans ....................................... | 172 507 | 113 258 | 65.7 | 108 209 | 62.7 | 5 049 | 4.5 | 59 249 |
| **BLACK** | | | | | | | | |
| Total, 18 Years and Over ............................... | 30 112 | 19 144 | 63.6 | 17 365 | 57.7 | 1 779 | 9.3 | 10 969 |
| Veterans ............................................ | 2 475 | 1 437 | 58.1 | 1 328 | 53.7 | 110 | 7.6 | 1 038 |
| Gulf War era, total ......................... | 1 109 | 856 | 77.2 | 793 | 71.5 | 64 | 7.4 | 252 |
| Gulf War era II .......................... | 515 | 398 | 77.3 | 361 | 70.1 | 37 | 9.3 | 117 |
| Gulf War era I ........................... | 594 | 458 | 77.2 | 432 | 72.7 | 27 | 5.8 | 135 |
| WW II, Korean War, and Vietnam era ........ | 706 | 181 | 25.7 | 162 | 23.0 | 19 | 10.7 | 524 |
| Other service periods ...................... | 660 | 399 | 60.5 | 373 | 56.5 | 26 | 6.6 | 261 |
| Nonveterans ....................................... | 27 638 | 17 706 | 64.1 | 16 037 | 58.0 | 1 669 | 9.4 | 9 931 |
| **ASIAN** | | | | | | | | |
| Total, 18 Years and Over ............................... | 13 885 | 8 922 | 64.3 | 8 587 | 61.8 | 335 | 3.8 | 4 963 |
| Veterans ............................................ | 301 | 192 | 63.6 | 186 | 61.7 | 6 | 3.1 | 110 |
| Gulf War era, total ......................... | 150 | 123 | 81.7 | 120 | 79.9 | 3 | 2.2 | 28 |
| Gulf War era II .......................... | 85 | 66 | 78.3 | 65 | 76.6 | 1 | 2.1 | 18 |
| Gulf War era I ........................... | 66 | 57 | 86.1 | 55 | 84.2 | 1 | 2.3 | 9 |
| WW II, Korean War, and Vietnam era ........ | 89 | 31 | 34.5 | 29 | 33.2 | 1 | . . . | 58 |
| Other service periods ...................... | 62 | 38 | 61.6 | 36 | 58.0 | 2 | 5.8 | 24 |
| Nonveterans ....................................... | 13 583 | 8 730 | 64.3 | 8 401 | 61.8 | 329 | 3.8 | 4 853 |
| **HISPANIC[1]** | | | | | | | | |
| Total, 18 Years and Over ............................... | 37 504 | 25 678 | 68.5 | 24 031 | 64.1 | 1 647 | 6.4 | 11 826 |
| Veterans ............................................ | 1 468 | 958 | 65.3 | 899 | 61.2 | 60 | 6.2 | 509 |
| Gulf War era, total ......................... | 773 | 638 | 82.6 | 598 | 77.3 | 41 | 6.4 | 135 |
| Gulf War era II .......................... | 493 | 406 | 82.3 | 379 | 77.0 | 26 | 6.5 | 87 |
| Gulf War era I ........................... | 280 | 233 | 83.1 | 218 | 77.9 | 15 | 6.3 | 47 |
| WW II, Korean War, and Vietnam era ........ | 381 | 122 | 32.1 | 119 | 31.1 | 4 | 3.0 | 259 |
| Other service periods ...................... | 314 | 198 | 63.0 | 183 | 58.2 | 15 | 7.5 | 116 |
| Nonveterans ....................................... | 36 036 | 24 720 | 68.6 | 23 132 | 64.2 | 1 588 | 6.4 | 11 317 |

Note: Veterans are men and women who served in the U.S. Armed Forces during World War II, the Korean War, the Vietnam era, the Gulf War era, and all other service periods. Nonveterans are men and women who never served in the U.S. Armed Forces. Other service periods include the periods between World War II and the Korean War, between the Korean War and the Vietnam era, and between the Vietnam era and the Gulf War era. Estimates for the above race groups (White, Black, and Asian) do not sum to totals because data are not presented for all races.

[1]May be of any race.
. . . = Not available.

## Table 1-67. Employment Status of Persons 18 Years and Over by Veteran Status, Age, Period of Service, and Sex, 2015 Annual Averages

(Thousands of people, percent.)

| Veteran status, age, period of service, and sex | Civilian noninstitutional population | Civilian labor force Total | Percent of population | Employed Total | Employed Percent of population | Unemployed Total | Unemployed Percent of labor force | Not in labor force |
|---|---|---|---|---|---|---|---|---|
| **TOTAL VETERANS** | | | | | | | | |
| Total, 18 years and over | 21 209 | 10 757 | 50.7 | 10 263 | 48.4 | 495 | 4.6 | 10 452 |
| 18 to 24 years | 264 | 199 | 75.3 | 173 | 65.6 | 26 | 13.0 | 65 |
| 25 to 34 years | 1 764 | 1 457 | 82.6 | 1 356 | 76.9 | 101 | 6.9 | 307 |
| 35 to 44 years | 2 332 | 2 020 | 86.6 | 1 936 | 83.1 | 83 | 4.1 | 312 |
| 45 to 54 years | 3 334 | 2 779 | 83.4 | 2 684 | 80.5 | 95 | 3.4 | 554 |
| 55 to 64 years | 3 871 | 2 382 | 61.5 | 2 270 | 58.6 | 112 | 4.7 | 1 489 |
| 65 years and over | 9 645 | 1 921 | 19.9 | 1 843 | 19.1 | 77 | 4.0 | 7 724 |
| **Gulf War Era, Total** | | | | | | | | |
| Total, 18 years and over | 7 035 | 5 681 | 80.8 | 5 407 | 76.9 | 274 | 4.8 | 1 354 |
| 18 to 24 years | 264 | 199 | 75.3 | 173 | 65.6 | 26 | 13.0 | 65 |
| 25 to 34 years | 1 764 | 1 457 | 82.6 | 1 356 | 76.9 | 101 | 6.9 | 307 |
| 35 to 44 years | 2 274 | 1 970 | 86.6 | 1 888 | 83.0 | 83 | 4.2 | 304 |
| 45 to 54 years | 1 759 | 1 492 | 84.8 | 1 448 | 82.3 | 44 | 3.0 | 267 |
| 55 to 64 years | 740 | 502 | 67.8 | 484 | 65.5 | 17 | 3.4 | 238 |
| 65 years and over | 234 | 61 | 26.1 | 58 | 24.8 | 3 | 5.0 | 173 |
| **Gulf War Era II** | | | | | | | | |
| Total, 18 years and over | 3 594 | 2 913 | 81.0 | 2 745 | 76.4 | 168 | 5.8 | 681 |
| 18 to 24 years | 264 | 199 | 75.3 | 173 | 65.6 | 26 | 13.0 | 65 |
| 25 to 34 years | 1 669 | 1 381 | 82.7 | 1 287 | 77.1 | 94 | 6.8 | 288 |
| 35 to 44 years | 829 | 700 | 84.5 | 672 | 81.1 | 28 | 4.0 | 129 |
| 45 to 54 years | 565 | 469 | 83.1 | 456 | 80.7 | 14 | 2.9 | 95 |
| 55 to 64 years | 210 | 144 | 68.7 | 138 | 65.8 | 6 | 4.3 | 66 |
| 65 years and over | 58 | 19 | 33.9 | 19 | 32.3 | 1 | . . . | 38 |
| **Gulf War Era I** | | | | | | | | |
| Total, 25 years and over | 3 440 | 2 768 | 80.4 | 2 662 | 77.4 | 105 | 3.8 | 673 |
| 25 to 34 years | 95 | 76 | 80.4 | 69 | 72.4 | 8 | 9.9 | 19 |
| 35 to 44 years | 1 446 | 1 270 | 87.9 | 1 216 | 84.1 | 54 | 4.3 | 175 |
| 45 to 54 years | 1 194 | 1 023 | 85.6 | 992 | 83.1 | 30 | 3.0 | 171 |
| 55 to 64 years | 530 | 357 | 67.4 | 346 | 65.4 | 11 | 3.1 | 173 |
| 65 years and over | 176 | 41 | 23.5 | 39 | 22.3 | 2 | 5.2 | 135 |
| **World War II, Korean War, Vietnam War** | | | | | | | | |
| Total, 55 years and over | 8 901 | 2 350 | 26.4 | 2 248 | 25.3 | 102 | 4.3 | 6 551 |
| 55 to 64 years | 1 580 | 818 | 51.8 | 776 | 49.1 | 42 | 5.1 | 762 |
| 65 years and over | 7 321 | 1 532 | 20.9 | 1 472 | 20.1 | 60 | 3.9 | 5 789 |
| **Other Service Periods** | | | | | | | | |
| Total, 35 years and over | 5 273 | 2 726 | 51.7 | 2 608 | 49.5 | 119 | 4.4 | 2 547 |
| 35 to 44 years | 57 | 50 | 86.9 | 49 | 85.4 | 1 | 1.7 | 8 |
| 45 to 54 years | 1 575 | 1 287 | 81.7 | 1 236 | 78.5 | 51 | 4.0 | 288 |
| 55 to 64 years | 1 551 | 1 062 | 68.4 | 1 009 | 65.1 | 52 | 4.9 | 489 |
| 65 years and over | 2 090 | 328 | 15.7 | 313 | 15.0 | 14 | 4.4 | 1 762 |
| **TOTAL NONVETERANS** | | | | | | | | |
| Total, 18 years and over | 220 740 | 144 385 | 65.4 | 136 947 | 62.0 | 7 439 | 5.2 | 76 355 |
| 18 to 24 years | 29 474 | 19 037 | 64.6 | 16 959 | 57.5 | 2 078 | 10.9 | 10 438 |
| 25 to 34 years | 41 007 | 33 190 | 80.9 | 31 386 | 76.5 | 1 803 | 5.4 | 7 818 |
| 35 to 44 years | 37 369 | 30 583 | 81.8 | 29 316 | 78.4 | 1 267 | 4.1 | 6 786 |
| 45 to 54 years | 39 303 | 31 123 | 79.2 | 29 959 | 76.2 | 1 164 | 3.7 | 8 180 |
| 55 to 64 years | 36 725 | 23 574 | 64.2 | 22 706 | 61.8 | 869 | 3.7 | 13 151 |
| 65 years and over | 36 862 | 6 879 | 18.7 | 6 621 | 18.0 | 258 | 3.7 | 29 984 |

*Note:* Veterans are men and women who served in the U.S. Armed Forces during World War II, the Korean War, the Vietnam era, the Gulf War era, and all other service periods. Nonveterans are men and women who never served in the U.S. Armed Forces. Other service periods include the periods between World War II and the Korean War, between the Korean War and the Vietnam era, and between the Vietnam era and the Gulf War era.

. . . = Not available.

**Table 1-67.  Employment Status of Persons 18 Years and Over by Veteran Status, Age, Period of Service, and Sex, 2015 Annual Averages**—*Continued*

(Thousands of people, percent.)

| Veteran status, age, period of service, and sex | Civilian noninstitutional population | Civilian labor force | | | | | | Not in labor force |
|---|---|---|---|---|---|---|---|---|
| | | Total | Percent of population | Employed | | Unemployed | | |
| | | | | Total | Percent of population | Total | Percent of labor force | |
| **VETERANS, MEN** | | | | | | | | |
| Total, 18 years and over ........................................ | 19 212 | 9 517 | 49.5 | 9 089 | 47.3 | 428 | 4.5 | 9 695 |
| 18 to 24 years ........................................ | 209 | 159 | 75.7 | 137 | 65.5 | 21 | 13.6 | 51 |
| 25 to 34 years ........................................ | 1 440 | 1 231 | 85.5 | 1 146 | 79.6 | 85 | 6.9 | 209 |
| 35 to 44 years ........................................ | 1 923 | 1 701 | 88.4 | 1 637 | 85.1 | 64 | 3.8 | 223 |
| 45 to 54 years ........................................ | 2 858 | 2 418 | 84.6 | 2 335 | 81.7 | 83 | 3.4 | 440 |
| 55 to 64 years ........................................ | 3 472 | 2 144 | 61.8 | 2 043 | 58.8 | 102 | 4.7 | 1 328 |
| 65 years and over ........................................ | 9 309 | 1 864 | 20.0 | 1 791 | 19.2 | 74 | 4.0 | 7 444 |
| **Gulf War Era, Total** | | | | | | | | |
| Total, 18 years and over ........................................ | 5 870 | 4 840 | 82.5 | 4 617 | 78.6 | 224 | 4.6 | 1 030 |
| 18 to 24 years ........................................ | 209 | 159 | 75.7 | 137 | 65.5 | 21 | 13.6 | 51 |
| 25 to 34 years ........................................ | 1 440 | 1 231 | 85.5 | 1 146 | 79.6 | 85 | 6.9 | 209 |
| 35 to 44 years ........................................ | 1 880 | 1 664 | 88.5 | 1 600 | 85.1 | 64 | 3.8 | 216 |
| 45 to 54 years ........................................ | 1 498 | 1 291 | 86.2 | 1 255 | 83.8 | 35 | 2.7 | 207 |
| 55 to 64 years ........................................ | 642 | 445 | 69.3 | 429 | 66.8 | 16 | 3.6 | 197 |
| 65 years and over ........................................ | 201 | 51 | 25.4 | 49 | 24.3 | 2 | 4.4 | 150 |
| **Gulf War Era II** | | | | | | | | |
| Total, 18 years and over ........................................ | 2 959 | 2 462 | 83.2 | 2 322 | 78.5 | 140 | 5.7 | 497 |
| 18 to 24 years ........................................ | 209 | 159 | 75.7 | 137 | 65.5 | 21 | 13.6 | 51 |
| 25 to 34 years ........................................ | 1 367 | 1 169 | 85.6 | 1 090 | 79.8 | 79 | 6.8 | 197 |
| 35 to 44 years ........................................ | 685 | 593 | 86.6 | 571 | 83.3 | 22 | 3.8 | 92 |
| 45 to 54 years ........................................ | 476 | 402 | 84.4 | 391 | 82.2 | 11 | 2.6 | 74 |
| 55 to 64 years ........................................ | 177 | 126 | 70.8 | 120 | 67.8 | 5 | 4.3 | 52 |
| 65 years and over ........................................ | 44 | 13 | 29.6 | 13 | 28.3 | 1 | . . . | 31 |
| **Gulf War Era I** | | | | | | | | |
| Total, 25 years and over ........................................ | 2 911 | 2 378 | 81.7 | 2 294 | 78.8 | 84 | 3.5 | 533 |
| 25 to 34 years ........................................ | 73 | 61 | 84.3 | 56 | 76.8 | 5 | 8.9 | 11 |
| 35 to 44 years ........................................ | 1 195 | 1 071 | 89.6 | 1 029 | 86.2 | 41 | 3.9 | 124 |
| 45 to 54 years ........................................ | 1 022 | 889 | 87.0 | 864 | 84.6 | 25 | 2.8 | 133 |
| 55 to 64 years ........................................ | 465 | 319 | 68.7 | 309 | 66.4 | 11 | 3.4 | 146 |
| 65 years and over ........................................ | 157 | 38 | 24.2 | 36 | 23.1 | 2 | 4.4 | 119 |
| **World War II, Korean War, and Vietnam War** | | | | | | | | |
| Total, 55 years and over ........................................ | 8 585 | 2 264 | 26.4 | 2 168 | 25.3 | 96 | 4.2 | 6 320 |
| 55 to 64 years ........................................ | 1 484 | 770 | 51.9 | 732 | 49.3 | 39 | 5.0 | 714 |
| 65 years and over ........................................ | 7 100 | 1 494 | 21.0 | 1 437 | 20.2 | 57 | 3.8 | 5 606 |
| **Other Service Periods** | | | | | | | | |
| Total, 35 years and over ........................................ | 4 756 | 2 412 | 50.7 | 2 303 | 48.4 | 108 | 4.5 | 2 345 |
| 35 to 44 years ........................................ | 43 | 37 | 84.8 | 36 | 84.0 | 0 | 0.9 | 7 |
| 45 to 54 years ........................................ | 1 360 | 1 127 | 82.8 | 1 080 | 79.4 | 47 | 4.2 | 233 |
| 55 to 64 years ........................................ | 1 346 | 929 | 69.0 | 882 | 65.6 | 47 | 5.0 | 417 |
| 65 years and over ........................................ | 2 007 | 319 | 15.9 | 305 | 15.2 | 14 | 4.4 | 1 688 |
| **NONVETERANS, MEN** | | | | | | | | |
| Total, 18 years and over ........................................ | 97 380 | 73 107 | 75.1 | 69 243 | 71.1 | 3 864 | 5.3 | 24 273 |
| 18 to 24 years ........................................ | 14 723 | 9 767 | 66.3 | 8 591 | 58.4 | 1 177 | 12.0 | 4 955 |
| 25 to 34 years ........................................ | 19 703 | 17 545 | 89.1 | 16 600 | 84.3 | 946 | 5.4 | 2 157 |
| 35 to 44 years ........................................ | 17 520 | 15 856 | 90.5 | 15 225 | 86.9 | 631 | 4.0 | 1 665 |
| 45 to 54 years ........................................ | 17 980 | 15 475 | 86.1 | 14 909 | 82.9 | 566 | 3.7 | 2 505 |
| 55 to 64 years ........................................ | 16 048 | 11 486 | 71.6 | 11 049 | 68.8 | 437 | 3.8 | 4 563 |
| 65 years and over ........................................ | 11 406 | 2 978 | 26.1 | 2 870 | 25.2 | 108 | 3.6 | 8 428 |

*Note:* Veterans are men and women who served in the U.S. Armed Forces during World War II, the Korean War, the Vietnam era, the Gulf War era, and all other service periods. Nonveterans are men and women who never served in the U.S. Armed Forces. Other service periods include the periods between World War II and the Korean War, between the Korean War and the Vietnam era, and between the Vietnam era and the Gulf War era.

. . . = Not available.

## Table 1-67.  Employment Status of Persons 18 Years and Over by Veteran Status, Age, Period of Service, and Sex, 2015 Annual Averages—*Continued*

(Thousands of people, percent.)

| Veteran status, age, period of service, and sex | Civilian noninstitutional population | Civilian labor force | | Employed | | Unemployed | | Not in labor force |
|---|---|---|---|---|---|---|---|---|
| | | Total | Percent of population | Total | Percent of population | Total | Percent of labor force | |
| **VETERANS, WOMEN** | | | | | | | | |
| Total, 18 years and over ................................... | 1 997 | 1 241 | 62.1 | 1 174 | 58.8 | 67 | 5.4 | 757 |
| 18 to 24 years ............................................... | 55 | 40 | 73.9 | 36 | 66.0 | 4 | 10.7 | 14 |
| 25 to 34 years ............................................... | 324 | 226 | 69.7 | 210 | 64.6 | 17 | 7.3 | 98 |
| 35 to 44 years ............................................... | 408 | 319 | 78.2 | 300 | 73.4 | 19 | 6.1 | 89 |
| 45 to 54 years ............................................... | 476 | 361 | 76.0 | 349 | 73.4 | 12 | 3.5 | 114 |
| 55 to 64 years ............................................... | 398 | 237 | 59.5 | 227 | 57.0 | 10 | 4.2 | 161 |
| 65 years and over .......................................... | 336 | 57 | 16.8 | 53 | 15.7 | 4 | 6.6 | 280 |
| **Gulf Era, Total** | | | | | | | | |
| Total, 18 years and over ................................... | 1 164 | 840 | 72.2 | 790 | 67.8 | 50 | 6.0 | 324 |
| 18 to 24 years ............................................... | 55 | 40 | 73.9 | 36 | 66.0 | 4 | 10.7 | 14 |
| 25 to 34 years ............................................... | 324 | 226 | 69.7 | 210 | 64.6 | 17 | 7.3 | 98 |
| 35 to 44 years ............................................... | 394 | 306 | 77.6 | 287 | 72.9 | 19 | 6.2 | 88 |
| 45 to 54 years ............................................... | 261 | 201 | 77.1 | 192 | 73.7 | 9 | 4.4 | 60 |
| 55 to 64 years ............................................... | 97 | 57 | 58.0 | 55 | 56.9 | 1 | 1.8 | 41 |
| 65 years and over .......................................... | 32 | 10 | . . . | 9 | . . . | 1 | . . . | 23 |
| **Gulf Era II** | | | | | | | | |
| Total, 18 years and over ................................... | 635 | 451 | 71.0 | 422 | 66.4 | 29 | 6.4 | 184 |
| 18 to 24 years ............................................... | 55 | 40 | 73.9 | 36 | 66.0 | 4 | 10.7 | 14 |
| 25 to 34 years ............................................... | 302 | 212 | 69.9 | 197 | 65.1 | 14 | 6.8 | 91 |
| 35 to 44 years ............................................... | 143 | 106 | 74.3 | 101 | 70.2 | 6 | 5.4 | 37 |
| 45 to 54 years ............................................... | 89 | 67 | 76.1 | 64 | 72.6 | 3 | 4.6 | 21 |
| 55 to 64 years ............................................... | 33 | 19 | . . . | 18 | . . . | 1 | . . . | 14 |
| 65 years and over .......................................... | 13 | 6 | . . . | 6 | . . . | 0 | . . . | 7 |
| **Gulf Era I** | | | | | | | | |
| Total, 25 Years and over ................................... | 529 | 389 | 73.6 | 368 | 69.5 | 21 | 5.5 | 140 |
| 25 to 34 years ............................................... | 22 | 15 | . . . | 13 | . . . | 2 | . . . | 7 |
| 35 to 44 years ............................................... | 251 | 200 | 79.6 | 187 | 74.3 | 13 | 6.6 | 51 |
| 45 to 54 years ............................................... | 172 | 134 | 77.6 | 128 | 74.3 | 6 | 4.3 | 39 |
| 55 to 64 years ............................................... | 65 | 38 | 58.3 | 38 | 58.1 | 0 | 0.3 | 27 |
| 65 years and over .......................................... | 19 | 3 | . . . | 3 | . . . | 0 | . . . | 16 |
| **World War II, Korean War, and Vietnam Era** | | | | | | | | |
| Total, 55 years and over ................................... | 317 | 86 | 27.2 | 80 | 25.3 | 6 | 6.8 | 231 |
| 55 to 64 years ............................................... | 96 | 48 | 50.0 | 45 | 46.6 | 3 | 6.7 | 48 |
| 65 years and over .......................................... | 221 | 38 | 17.3 | 36 | 16.1 | 3 | 6.8 | 183 |
| **Other Service Periods** | | | | | | | | |
| Total, 35 years and over ................................... | 516 | 314 | 60.9 | 304 | 58.9 | 10 | 3.3 | 202 |
| 35 to 44 years ............................................... | 14 | 13 | . . . | 12 | . . . | 1 | . . . | 1 |
| 45 to 54 years ............................................... | 215 | 160 | 74.7 | 157 | 73.0 | 4 | 2.3 | 54 |
| 55 to 64 years ............................................... | 205 | 133 | 64.7 | 127 | 61.8 | 6 | 4.4 | 73 |
| 65 years and over .......................................... | 83 | 9 | 10.3 | 8 | 10.0 | 0 | . . . | 74 |
| **NONVETERANS, WOMEN** | | | | | | | | |
| Total, 18 years and over ................................... | 123 360 | 71 278 | 57.8 | 67 704 | 54.9 | 3 574 | 5.0 | 52 082 |
| 18 to 24 years ............................................... | 14 751 | 9 269 | 62.8 | 8 368 | 56.7 | 901 | 9.7 | 5 482 |
| 25 to 34 years ............................................... | 21 305 | 15 644 | 73.4 | 14 787 | 69.4 | 858 | 5.5 | 5 660 |
| 35 to 44 years ............................................... | 19 849 | 14 728 | 74.2 | 14 091 | 71.0 | 636 | 4.3 | 5 121 |
| 45 to 54 years ............................................... | 21 323 | 15 648 | 73.4 | 15 050 | 70.6 | 598 | 3.8 | 5 675 |
| 55 to 64 years ............................................... | 20 677 | 12 089 | 58.5 | 11 657 | 56.4 | 432 | 3.6 | 8 588 |
| 65 years and over .......................................... | 25 456 | 3 900 | 15.3 | 3 751 | 14.7 | 149 | 3.8 | 21 556 |

*Note:* Veterans are men and women who served in the U.S. Armed Forces during World War II, the Korean War, the Vietnam era, the Gulf War era, and all other service periods. Nonveterans are men and women who never served in the U.S. Armed Forces. Other service periods include the periods between World War II and the Korean War, between the Korean War and the Vietnam era, and between the Vietnam era and the Gulf War era.

. . . = Not available.

## Table 1-68.  Employment Status of Gulf War Era Veterans by Reserve or National Guard Status, August 2015, Not Seasonally Adjusted

(Thousands of people, percent.)

| Reserve or National Guard status | Civilian noninstitutional population | Civilian labor force | | | | | | | Not in labor force |
|---|---|---|---|---|---|---|---|---|---|
| | | Total | Percent of population | Employed | | Unemployed | | | |
| | | | | Total | Percent of population | Total | Percent of labor force | | |
| **GULF WAR ERA** | | | | | | | | | |
| Total ........................................................ | 7 059 | 5 804 | 82.2 | 5 536 | 78.4 | 268 | 4.6 | | 1 255 |
| Current or past member of Reserve or National Guard ....... | 2 470 | 2 052 | 83.1 | 1 969 | 79.7 | 83 | 4.1 | | 418 |
| Never a member of Reserve or National Guard ................ | 4 363 | 3 593 | 82.4 | 3 409 | 78.1 | 185 | 5.1 | | 769 |
| Reserve or National Guard membership not reported ......... | 226 | 158 | 69.9 | 158 | 69.9 | 0 | 0.0 | | 68 |
| **GULF WAR ERA II** | | | | | | | | | |
| Total ........................................................ | 3 609 | 2 959 | 82.0 | 2 812 | 77.9 | 148 | 5.0 | | 649 |
| Current or past member of Reserve or National Guard ....... | 1 393 | 1 160 | 83.3 | 1 119 | 80.3 | 41 | 3.5 | | 233 |
| Never a member of Reserve or National Guard ................ | 2 083 | 1 720 | 82.6 | 1 614 | 77.5 | 107 | 6.2 | | 363 |
| Reserve or National Guard membership not reported ......... | 132 | 79 | 59.6 | 79 | 59.6 | 0 | 0.0 | | 53 |
| **GULF WAR ERA I** | | | | | | | | | |
| Total ........................................................ | 3 450 | 2 845 | 82.4 | 2 724 | 79.0 | 120 | 4.2 | | 606 |
| Current or past member of Reserve or National Guard ....... | 1 077 | 892 | 82.9 | 850 | 78.9 | 42 | 4.7 | | 184 |
| Never a member of Reserve or National Guard ................ | 2 280 | 1 873 | 82.2 | 1 795 | 78.7 | 78 | 4.2 | | 407 |
| Reserve or National Guard membership not reported ......... | 94 | 79 | 84.3 | 79 | 84.3 | 0 | 0.0 | | 15 |

*Note:* Veterans are men and women who served in the U.S. Armed Forces during World War II, the Korean War, the Vietnam era, the Gulf War era, and all other service periods. The Gulf War era began in August 1990 and continues to the present day. It is divided into two periods of service: Gulf War era II (September 2001–present) and Gulf War era I (August 1990–August 2001).

## Table 1-69. Employed Persons 18 Years and Over by Occupation, Sex, Veteran Status, and Period of Service, 2015 Annual Averages

(Number in thousands, percent distribution.)

| Occupation | Total veterans | Gulf War era | | | WWII, Korean War, and Vietnam War | Other services periods | Non-veteran |
|---|---|---|---|---|---|---|---|
| | | Total | Gulf War era II | Gulf War era I | | | |
| **TOTAL** | | | | | | | |
| **Total, 18 Years and Over** ............................................................ | 10 263 | 5 407 | 2 745 | 2 662 | 2 248 | 2 608 | 136 947 |
| Percent ...................................................................................... | 100.0 | 100.0 | 100.0 | 100.0 | 100.0 | 100.0 | 100.0 |
| Management, professional, and related occupations ........................... | 38.5 | 39.3 | 37.5 | 41.1 | 39.2 | 36.4 | 39.4 |
| Management, business, and financial operations occupations ................. | 18.7 | 18.2 | 17.1 | 19.3 | 21.2 | 17.7 | 16.2 |
| Professional and related occupations .......................................... | 19.8 | 21.1 | 20.4 | 21.9 | 17.9 | 18.7 | 23.2 |
| Service occupations ...................................................................... | 14.2 | 15.3 | 16.9 | 13.6 | 12.9 | 13.2 | 17.3 |
| Sales and office occupations .......................................................... | 16.8 | 16.6 | 16.7 | 16.5 | 18.0 | 16.2 | 22.9 |
| Sales and related occupations .................................................. | 8.6 | 7.8 | 7.2 | 8.4 | 11.6 | 7.8 | 10.5 |
| Office and administrative support occupations ............................. | 8.2 | 8.8 | 9.5 | 8.1 | 6.4 | 8.5 | 12.4 |
| Natural resources, construction, and maintenance occupations ................. | 13.5 | 13.5 | 13.9 | 13.1 | 12.1 | 14.5 | 8.9 |
| Farming, fishing, and forestry occupations ................................... | 0.4 | 0.3 | 0.3 | 0.3 | 0.8 | 0.4 | 0.7 |
| Construction and extraction occupations ..................................... | 5.8 | 5.5 | 5.5 | 5.4 | 5.5 | 6.8 | 5.1 |
| Installation, maintenance, and repair occupations ......................... | 7.2 | 7.7 | 8.1 | 7.4 | 5.8 | 7.4 | 3.1 |
| Production, transportation, and material moving occupations ................... | 17.0 | 15.3 | 14.9 | 15.7 | 17.9 | 19.7 | 11.5 |
| Production occupations .............................................................. | 6.7 | 6.8 | 6.7 | 7.0 | 5.7 | 7.5 | 5.7 |
| Transportation and material moving occupations ........................... | 10.2 | 8.5 | 8.3 | 8.7 | 12.1 | 12.2 | 5.8 |
| **MEN** | | | | | | | |
| **Total, 18 Years and Over** ............................................................ | 9 089 | 4 617 | 2 322 | 2 294 | 2 168 | 2 303 | 69 243 |
| Percent ...................................................................................... | 100.0 | 100.0 | 100.0 | 100.0 | 100.0 | 100.0 | 100.0 |
| Management, professional, and related occupations ........................... | 36.9 | 37.3 | 35.8 | 38.8 | 38.7 | 34.3 | 35.6 |
| Management, business, and financial operations occupations ................. | 18.5 | 17.9 | 16.7 | 19.1 | 21.1 | 17.4 | 17.2 |
| Professional and related occupations .......................................... | 18.4 | 19.4 | 19.1 | 19.7 | 17.6 | 16.9 | 18.5 |
| Service occupations ...................................................................... | 14.0 | 15.0 | 16.4 | 13.5 | 12.8 | 13.0 | 13.8 |
| Sales and office occupations .......................................................... | 15.6 | 15.0 | 15.0 | 15.0 | 17.6 | 14.7 | 16.4 |
| Sales and related occupations .................................................. | 8.8 | 7.7 | 6.9 | 8.6 | 11.7 | 8.0 | 10.1 |
| Office and administrative support occupations ............................. | 6.8 | 7.3 | 8.1 | 6.5 | 5.9 | 6.8 | 6.2 |
| Natural resources, construction, and maintenance occupations ................. | 15.0 | 15.6 | 16.1 | 15.1 | 12.5 | 16.3 | 16.8 |
| Farming, fishing, and forestry occupations ................................... | 0.5 | 0.3 | 0.3 | 0.4 | 0.8 | 0.4 | 1.1 |
| Construction and extraction occupations ..................................... | 6.5 | 6.4 | 6.5 | 6.2 | 5.7 | 7.6 | 9.8 |
| Installation, maintenance, and repair occupations ......................... | 8.1 | 8.9 | 9.3 | 8.5 | 6.1 | 8.3 | 5.9 |
| Production, transportation, and material moving occupations ................... | 18.5 | 17.1 | 16.6 | 17.6 | 18.4 | 21.6 | 17.4 |
| Production occupations .............................................................. | 7.2 | 7.4 | 7.2 | 7.6 | 5.9 | 8.1 | 7.8 |
| Transportation and material moving occupations ........................... | 11.3 | 9.7 | 9.4 | 9.9 | 12.5 | 13.5 | 9.6 |
| **WOMEN** | | | | | | | |
| **Total, 18 Years and Over** ............................................................ | 1 174 | 790 | 422 | 368 | 80 | 304 | 67 704 |
| Percent ...................................................................................... | 100.0 | 100.0 | 100.0 | 100.0 | 100.0 | 100.0 | 100.0 |
| Management, professional, and related occupations ........................... | 51.4 | 51.1 | 47.1 | 55.7 | 51.4 | 51.9 | 43.2 |
| Management, business, and financial operations occupations ................. | 20.3 | 19.9 | 19.6 | 20.4 | 24.7 | 20.3 | 15.2 |
| Professional and related occupations .......................................... | 31.0 | 31.2 | 27.6 | 35.4 | 26.7 | 31.7 | 28.0 |
| Service occupations ...................................................................... | 16.2 | 17.0 | 19.7 | 13.9 | 16.3 | 14.0 | 20.8 |
| Sales and office occupations .......................................................... | 26.4 | 25.8 | 26.2 | 25.4 | 27.2 | 27.9 | 29.6 |
| Sales and related occupations .................................................. | 7.7 | 8.2 | 8.9 | 7.4 | 7.9 | 6.4 | 10.9 |
| Office and administrative support occupations ............................. | 18.7 | 17.6 | 17.3 | 18.0 | 19.3 | 21.5 | 18.7 |
| Natural resources, construction, and maintenance occupations ................. | 1.2 | 1.3 | 1.3 | 1.2 | 1.3 | 1.0 | 0.9 |
| Farming, fishing, and forestry occupations ................................... | 0.0 | 0.1 | 0.1 | 0.0 | 0.0 | 0.0 | 0.4 |
| Construction and extraction occupations ..................................... | 0.5 | 0.4 | 0.3 | 0.6 | 1.3 | 0.4 | 0.3 |
| Installation, maintenance, and repair occupations ......................... | 0.7 | 0.8 | 1.0 | 0.6 | 0.0 | 0.6 | 0.2 |
| Production, transportation, and material moving occupations ................... | 4.9 | 4.8 | 5.7 | 3.8 | 3.9 | 5.2 | 5.5 |
| Production occupations .............................................................. | 3.0 | 3.2 | 3.6 | 2.8 | 1.3 | 2.7 | 3.5 |
| Transportation and material moving occupations ........................... | 1.9 | 1.6 | 2.1 | 1.0 | 2.6 | 2.5 | 2.0 |

*Note:* Veterans are men and women who served in the U.S. Armed Forces during World War II, the Korean War, the Vietnam era, the Gulf War era, and all other service periods. Nonveterans are men and women who never served in the U.S. Armed Forces. Other service periods include the periods between World War II and the Korean War, between the Korean War and the Vietnam era, and between the Vietnam era and the Gulf War era.

## Table 1-70.  Employed Persons 18 Years and Over by Industry, Class of Worker, Sex, Veteran Status, and Period of Service, 2015 Annual Averages

(Number in thousands, percent distribution.)

| Industry and class of worker | Total veterans | Gulf War era | | | WWII, Korean War, and Vietnam War | Other services periods | Non-veteran |
|---|---|---|---|---|---|---|---|
| | | Total | Gulf War era II | Gulf War era I | | | |
| **TOTAL** | | | | | | | |
| **Total, 18 Years and Over** | 10 263 | 5 407 | 2 745 | 2 662 | 2 248 | 2 608 | 136 947 |
| Percent | 100.0 | 100.0 | 100.0 | 100.0 | 100.0 | 100.0 | 100.0 |
| Agriculture and related industries | 1.9 | 0.7 | 0.7 | 0.7 | 4.8 | 1.8 | 1.6 |
| Wage and salary workers | 0.9 | 0.5 | 0.5 | 0.5 | 1.7 | 0.9 | 1.0 |
| Self-employed workers | 1.0 | 0.2 | 0.2 | 0.1 | 3.0 | 0.8 | 0.5 |
| Nonagricultural industries | 98.1 | 99.3 | 99.3 | 99.3 | 95.2 | 98.2 | 98.4 |
| Wage and salary workers | 92.0 | 96.2 | 97.1 | 95.3 | 82.8 | 91.2 | 92.6 |
| Private industries | 70.6 | 70.7 | 70.8 | 70.6 | 68.6 | 72.0 | 79.0 |
| Mining | 1.0 | 1.2 | 1.2 | 1.1 | 0.7 | 0.8 | 0.6 |
| Construction | 5.8 | 5.5 | 5.8 | 5.1 | 5.4 | 6.6 | 5.3 |
| Manufacturing | 12.7 | 12.7 | 11.7 | 13.7 | 11.0 | 14.2 | 9.9 |
| Wholesale trade | 2.5 | 2.4 | 2.3 | 2.4 | 2.7 | 2.5 | 2.3 |
| Retail trade | 8.5 | 8.5 | 9.1 | 7.9 | 9.3 | 7.9 | 10.7 |
| Transportation and utilities | 7.5 | 7.1 | 6.9 | 7.3 | 6.4 | 9.1 | 3.8 |
| Information | 1.9 | 2.2 | 2.0 | 2.4 | 1.3 | 2.0 | 1.8 |
| Financial activities | 4.7 | 4.1 | 3.9 | 4.2 | 6.0 | 4.7 | 6.4 |
| Professional and business services | 10.9 | 11.6 | 11.7 | 11.4 | 10.5 | 9.7 | 10.1 |
| Education and health services | 8.2 | 8.5 | 8.9 | 8.1 | 7.9 | 8.0 | 15.5 |
| Leisure and hospitality | 3.8 | 4.1 | 4.5 | 3.7 | 3.5 | 3.2 | 8.4 |
| Other services | 3.2 | 3.0 | 2.7 | 3.2 | 3.9 | 3.0 | 4.3 |
| Government | 21.4 | 25.5 | 26.4 | 24.7 | 14.1 | 19.2 | 13.5 |
| Federal | 9.2 | 12.3 | 14.3 | 10.2 | 4.2 | 7.0 | 2.0 |
| State | 4.9 | 5.4 | 4.9 | 6.0 | 3.8 | 4.7 | 4.7 |
| Local | 7.4 | 7.8 | 7.2 | 8.5 | 6.1 | 7.6 | 6.8 |
| Self-employed workers | 6.1 | 3.1 | 2.2 | 4.0 | 12.3 | 7.0 | 5.8 |
| **MEN** | | | | | | | |
| **Total, 18 Years and Over** | 9 089 | 4 617 | 2 322 | 2 294 | 2 168 | 2 303 | 69 243 |
| Percent | 100.0 | 100.0 | 100.0 | 100.0 | 100.0 | 100.0 | 100.0 |
| Agriculture and related industries | 2.0 | 0.7 | 0.7 | 0.8 | 4.9 | 1.9 | 2.3 |
| Wage and salary workers | 1.0 | 0.6 | 0.6 | 0.6 | 1.8 | 0.9 | 1.5 |
| Self-employed workers | 1.1 | 0.2 | 0.2 | 0.2 | 3.1 | 0.9 | 0.7 |
| Nonagricultural industries | 98.0 | 99.3 | 99.3 | 99.2 | 95.1 | 98.1 | 97.7 |
| Wage and salary workers | 91.4 | 96.1 | 97.1 | 95.1 | 83.4 | 90.7 | 91.0 |
| Private industries | 71.0 | 71.2 | 70.8 | 71.7 | 68.5 | 72.9 | 80.7 |
| Mining | 1.1 | 1.3 | 1.5 | 1.2 | 0.7 | 0.9 | 1.0 |
| Construction | 6.4 | 6.3 | 6.7 | 5.8 | 5.6 | 7.3 | 9.4 |
| Manufacturing | 13.6 | 13.9 | 12.8 | 15.0 | 11.2 | 15.2 | 13.5 |
| Wholesale trade | 2.6 | 2.6 | 2.6 | 2.6 | 2.7 | 2.6 | 3.2 |
| Retail trade | 8.5 | 8.4 | 8.9 | 7.8 | 9.2 | 8.2 | 10.5 |
| Transportation and utilities | 8.1 | 7.8 | 7.4 | 8.2 | 6.6 | 10.0 | 5.8 |
| Information | 1.9 | 2.2 | 2.1 | 2.3 | 1.3 | 2.1 | 2.1 |
| Financial activities | 4.5 | 4.0 | 3.8 | 4.1 | 6.0 | 4.3 | 5.5 |
| Professional and business services | 11.0 | 11.9 | 11.9 | 11.9 | 10.6 | 9.7 | 11.2 |
| Education and health services | 6.4 | 6.0 | 6.2 | 5.8 | 7.3 | 6.4 | 6.7 |
| Leisure and hospitality | 3.6 | 3.8 | 4.0 | 3.6 | 3.3 | 3.3 | 7.9 |
| Other services | 3.2 | 3.1 | 2.7 | 3.4 | 4.0 | 2.9 | 3.9 |
| Government | 20.4 | 24.8 | 26.3 | 23.4 | 13.8 | 17.8 | 10.3 |
| Federal | 8.4 | 11.6 | 13.8 | 9.3 | 4.0 | 6.3 | 1.9 |
| State | 4.6 | 5.1 | 4.9 | 5.3 | 3.8 | 4.3 | 3.4 |
| Local | 7.4 | 8.2 | 7.6 | 8.7 | 6.0 | 7.2 | 5.0 |
| Self-employed workers | 6.5 | 3.2 | 2.2 | 4.2 | 12.5 | 7.5 | 6.7 |
| **WOMEN** | | | | | | | |
| **Total, 18 Years and Over** | 1 174 | 790 | 422 | 368 | 80 | 304 | 67 704 |
| Percent | 100.0 | 100.0 | 100.0 | 100.0 | 100.0 | 100.0 | 100.0 |
| Agriculture and related industries | 0.5 | 0.3 | 0.4 | 0.1 | 0.3 | 1.2 | 0.9 |
| Wage and salary workers | 0.3 | 0.1 | 0.1 | 0.1 | 0.3 | 0.8 | 0.5 |
| Self-employed workers | 0.2 | 0.2 | 0.2 | 0.0 | 0.0 | 0.4 | 0.3 |
| Nonagricultural industries | 99.5 | 99.7 | 99.6 | 99.9 | 99.7 | 98.8 | 99.1 |
| Wage and salary workers | 96.5 | 97.3 | 97.6 | 96.8 | 94.1 | 95.1 | 94.1 |
| Private industries | 67.2 | 67.7 | 70.8 | 64.2 | 71.5 | 64.9 | 77.3 |
| Mining | 0.1 | 0.1 | 0.1 | 0.1 | 0.0 | 0.1 | 0.2 |
| Construction | 1.0 | 0.7 | 0.8 | 0.6 | 0.0 | 1.9 | 1.2 |
| Manufacturing | 6.0 | 5.8 | 5.5 | 6.1 | 7.1 | 6.5 | 6.3 |
| Wholesale trade | 1.4 | 1.1 | 0.7 | 1.6 | 4.2 | 1.3 | 1.5 |
| Retail trade | 8.7 | 9.4 | 9.7 | 9.0 | 12.0 | 6.0 | 10.8 |
| Transportation and utilities | 2.5 | 2.7 | 3.7 | 1.6 | 0.5 | 2.4 | 1.9 |
| Information | 1.9 | 2.1 | 1.2 | 3.2 | 0.3 | 1.7 | 1.4 |
| Financial activities | 5.6 | 4.7 | 4.7 | 4.7 | 5.4 | 8.1 | 7.2 |
| Professional and business services | 9.6 | 9.8 | 11.0 | 8.3 | 7.8 | 9.8 | 8.9 |
| Education and health services | 22.3 | 22.9 | 23.4 | 22.2 | 24.4 | 20.3 | 24.4 |
| Leisure and hospitality | 5.2 | 5.9 | 7.0 | 4.7 | 6.7 | 2.9 | 8.9 |
| Other services | 3.0 | 2.6 | 3.1 | 2.0 | 3.1 | 3.9 | 4.6 |
| Government | 29.2 | 29.5 | 26.8 | 32.7 | 22.6 | 30.2 | 16.8 |
| Federal | 14.7 | 16.2 | 17.0 | 15.4 | 9.9 | 11.9 | 2.2 |
| State | 7.3 | 7.3 | 4.9 | 10.1 | 6.0 | 7.5 | 6.1 |
| Local | 7.3 | 6.0 | 4.9 | 7.2 | 6.6 | 10.8 | 8.5 |
| Self-employed workers | 3.0 | 2.5 | 1.9 | 3.0 | 5.1 | 3.7 | 4.9 |

Note: Veterans are men and women who served in the U.S. Armed Forces during World War II, the Korean War, the Vietnam era, the Gulf War era, and all other service periods. Nonveterans are men and women who never served in the U.S. Armed Forces. Other service periods include the periods between World War II and the Korean War, between the Korean War and the Vietnam era, and between the Vietnam era and the Gulf War era.

## Table 1-71.  Employed Persons 18 Years and Over by Veteran Status, Presence of Service-Connected Disability, Period of Service, and Class of Worker, August 2015, Not Seasonally Adjusted

(Numbers in thousands, percent distribution.)

| Veteran status, presence of disability, and period of service | Total employed (number) | Total employed (percent) | Agriculture and related industries | Nonagricultural industries | | | | | | Self-employed, unincorporated, and unpaid family workers |
|---|---|---|---|---|---|---|---|---|---|---|
| | | | | Wage and salary workers | | | | | | |
| | | | | Total | Private sector | Government | | | | |
| | | | | | | Total | Federal | State and local | | |
| **Veterans, Total**[1] | 10 121 | 100.0 | 1.7 | 98.3 | 70.2 | 22.5 | 10.2 | 12.4 | | 5.6 |
| With service-connected disability | 1 866 | 100.0 | 1.6 | 98.4 | 58.5 | 36.1 | 25.0 | 11.1 | | 3.8 |
| Without service-connected disability | 7 987 | 100.0 | 1.7 | 98.3 | 72.6 | 19.6 | 6.9 | 12.7 | | 6.1 |
| **Gulf War Era, Total**[1] | 5 536 | 100.0 | 0.7 | 99.3 | 70.0 | 26.6 | 13.3 | 13.3 | | 2.7 |
| With service-connected disability | 1 368 | 100.0 | 0.6 | 99.4 | 58.2 | 38.5 | 27.6 | 10.9 | | 2.6 |
| Without service-connected disability | 4 040 | 100.0 | 0.7 | 99.3 | 73.9 | 22.8 | 8.7 | 14.2 | | 2.6 |
| **Gulf War Era II**[1] | 2 812 | 100.0 | 0.8 | 99.2 | 70.3 | 27.2 | 15.1 | 12.2 | | 1.6 |
| With service-connected disability | 816 | 100.0 | 0.8 | 99.2 | 60.2 | 36.2 | 24.8 | 11.3 | | 2.9 |
| Without service-connected disability | 1 916 | 100.0 | 0.9 | 99.1 | 74.4 | 23.5 | 11.1 | 12.5 | | 1.2 |
| **Gulf War Era I**[1] | 2 724 | 100.0 | 0.5 | 99.5 | 69.7 | 26.0 | 11.5 | 14.5 | | 3.7 |
| With service-connected disability | 552 | 100.0 | 0.4 | 99.6 | 55.3 | 41.9 | 31.7 | 10.2 | | 2.3 |
| Without service-connected disability | 2 123 | 100.0 | 0.5 | 99.5 | 73.3 | 22.2 | 6.5 | 15.7 | | 3.9 |
| **WW II, Korean War, and Vietnam Era**[1] | 2 072 | 100.0 | 4.2 | 95.8 | 68.1 | 14.1 | 5.4 | 8.7 | | 13.6 |
| With service-connected disability | 207 | 100.0 | 8.9 | 91.1 | 58.3 | 18.6 | 10.9 | 7.7 | | 14.2 |
| Without service-connected disability | 1 779 | 100.0 | 3.5 | 96.5 | 68.5 | 13.7 | 5.0 | 8.8 | | 14.2 |
| **Other Service Periods**[1] | 2 513 | 100.0 | 1.8 | 98.2 | 72.4 | 20.4 | 7.1 | 13.2 | | 5.4 |
| With service-connected disability | 291 | 100.0 | 0.7 | 99.3 | 60.2 | 37.3 | 22.5 | 14.8 | | 1.7 |
| Without service-connected disability | 2 168 | 100.0 | 2.0 | 98.0 | 73.5 | 18.4 | 5.2 | 13.2 | | 6.0 |
| **Nonveterans** | 137 213 | 100.0 | 1.7 | 98.3 | 79.4 | 13.0 | 2.0 | 11.0 | | 5.9 |

*Note:* Veterans are men and women who served in the U.S. Armed Forces during World War II, the Korean War, the Vietnam era, the Gulf War era, and all other service periods. Nonveterans are men and women who never served in the U.S. Armed Forces. Other service periods include the periods between World War II and the Korean War, between the Korean War and the Vietnam era, and between the Vietnam era and the Gulf War era.

[1]Includes veterans who did not report presence of disability.

## Table 1-72. Long-Tenured Displaced Workers[1] by Age, Sex, Race, and Hispanic Origin, January 2016

(Numbers in thousands, percent.)

| Characteristic | Total | Percent distribution by employment status | | | |
| --- | --- | --- | --- | --- | --- |
| | | Total | Employed | Unemployed | Not in the labor force |
| **TOTAL** | | | | | |
| Total, 20 years and over | 3 191 | 100.0 | 65.5 | 15.9 | 18.6 |
| 20 to 24 years | 71 | 100.0 | ([2]) | ([2]) | ([2]) |
| 25 to 54 years | 2 023 | 100.0 | 72.5 | 17.1 | 10.4 |
| 55 to 64 years | 853 | 100.0 | 60.0 | 15.0 | 24.9 |
| 65 years and over | 245 | 100.0 | 26.5 | 10.7 | 62.8 |
| **Men** | | | | | |
| Total, 20 years and over | 1 773 | 100.0 | 66.5 | 15.7 | 17.8 |
| 20 to 24 years | 33 | 100.0 | ([2]) | ([2]) | ([2]) |
| 25 to 54 years | 1 151 | 100.0 | 72.7 | 17.2 | 10.1 |
| 55 to 64 years | 469 | 100.0 | 62.6 | 15.1 | 22.3 |
| 65 years and over | 119 | 100.0 | 24.0 | 7.9 | 68.1 |
| **Women** | | | | | |
| Total, 20 years and over | 1 419 | 100.0 | 64.1 | 16.3 | 19.6 |
| 20 to 24 years | 38 | 100.0 | ([2]) | ([2]) | ([2]) |
| 25 to 54 years | 872 | 100.0 | 72.3 | 17.0 | 10.7 |
| 55 to 64 years | 383 | 100.0 | 56.8 | 15.0 | 28.2 |
| 65 years and over | 125 | 100.0 | 28.9 | 13.3 | 57.8 |
| **White** | | | | | |
| Total, 20 years and over | 2 573 | 100.0 | 66.5 | 14.8 | 18.6 |
| Men | 1 450 | 100.0 | 67.7 | 14.8 | 17.5 |
| Women | 1 123 | 100.0 | 65.0 | 14.9 | 20.1 |
| **Black** | | | | | |
| Total, 20 years and over | 394 | 100.0 | 61.5 | 20.3 | 18.2 |
| Men | 170 | 100.0 | 60.1 | 19.6 | 20.3 |
| Women | 224 | 100.0 | 62.5 | 20.9 | 16.6 |
| **Asian** | | | | | |
| Total, 20 years and over | 145 | 100.0 | 54.9 | 24.7 | 20.3 |
| Men | 96 | 100.0 | 59.4 | 20.3 | 20.3 |
| Women | 49 | 100.0 | ([2]) | ([2]) | ([2]) |
| **Hispanic**[3] | | | | | |
| Total, 20 years and over | 423 | 100.0 | 69.4 | 14.3 | 16.3 |
| Men | 236 | 100.0 | 75.4 | 11.0 | 13.7 |
| Women | 187 | 100.0 | 61.9 | 18.4 | 19.6 |

[1]Data refer to persons who had three or more years of tenure on a job that they had lost between January 2013 and December 2015 because of plant or company closings or moves, insufficient work, or the abolishment of their positions or skills.
[2]Data not shown where the base is less than 75,000.
[3]Persons of Hispanic origin may be of any race.

## Table 1-73. Long-Tenured Displaced Workers[1] by Age, Sex, Race, and Hispanic Origin and Reason for Job Loss, January 2016

(Numbers in thousands, percent.)

| Characteristic | Total | Percent distribution by reasons for job loss | | | |
| --- | --- | --- | --- | --- | --- |
| | | Total | Plant or company closed down or moving | Insufficient work | Position or shift abolished |
| **TOTAL** | | | | | |
| Total, 20 years and over ...................... | 3 191 | 100.0 | 37.4 | 25.6 | 37.1 |
| 20 to 24 years ......................................... | 71 | 100.0 | ([2]) | ([2]) | ([2]) |
| 25 to 54 years ......................................... | 2 023 | 100.0 | 37.4 | 27.4 | 35.2 |
| 55 to 64 years ......................................... | 853 | 100.0 | 36.4 | 22.8 | 40.8 |
| 65 years and over .................................. | 245 | 100.0 | 33.9 | 23.7 | 42.4 |
| **Men** | | | | | |
| Total, 20 years and over ...................... | 1 773 | 100.0 | 37.2 | 29.0 | 33.8 |
| 20 to 24 years ......................................... | 33 | 100.0 | ([2]) | ([2]) | ([2]) |
| 25 to 54 years ......................................... | 1 151 | 100.0 | 36.9 | 31.3 | 31.8 |
| 55 to 64 years ......................................... | 469 | 100.0 | 38.4 | 24.3 | 37.3 |
| 65 years and over .................................. | 119 | 100.0 | 25.9 | 31.7 | 42.4 |
| **Women** | | | | | |
| Total, 20 years and over ...................... | 1 419 | 100.0 | 37.5 | 21.3 | 41.1 |
| 20 to 24 years ......................................... | 38 | 100.0 | ([2]) | ([2]) | ([2]) |
| 25 to 54 years ......................................... | 872 | 100.0 | 38.1 | 22.2 | 39.7 |
| 55 to 64 years ......................................... | 383 | 100.0 | 33.9 | 20.9 | 45.2 |
| 65 years and over .................................. | 125 | 100.0 | 41.6 | 16.0 | 42.4 |
| **White** | | | | | |
| Total, 20 years and over ...................... | 2 573 | 100.0 | 37.2 | 25.9 | 36.9 |
| Men ............................................................ | 1 450 | 100.0 | 37.1 | 30.6 | 32.3 |
| Women ...................................................... | 1 123 | 100.0 | 37.4 | 19.7 | 42.9 |
| **Black** | | | | | |
| Total, 20 years and over ...................... | 394 | 100.0 | 35.4 | 27.7 | 36.9 |
| Men ............................................................ | 170 | 100.0 | 33.4 | 23.7 | 42.9 |
| Women ...................................................... | 224 | 100.0 | 36.9 | 30.7 | 32.4 |
| **Asian** | | | | | |
| Total, 20 years and over ...................... | 145 | 100.0 | 45.9 | 21.3 | 32.8 |
| Men ............................................................ | 96 | 100.0 | 46.7 | 19.8 | 33.5 |
| Women ...................................................... | 49 | 100.0 | ([2]) | ([2]) | ([2]) |
| **Hispanic[3]** | | | | | |
| Total, 20 years and over ...................... | 423 | 100.0 | 45.3 | 24.4 | 30.3 |
| Men ............................................................ | 236 | 100.0 | 43.5 | 27.2 | 29.3 |
| Women ...................................................... | 187 | 100.0 | 47.4 | 20.9 | 31.7 |

[1]Data refer to persons who had three or more years of tenure on a job that they had lost between January 2013 and December 2015 because of plant or company closings or moves, insufficient work, or the abolishment of their positions or skills.
[2]Data not shown where the base is less than 75,000.
[3]Persons of Hispanic origin may be of any race.

## Table 1-74.  Long-Tenured Displaced Workers[1] by Whether they Received Written Advance Notice, Reason for Job Loss, and Employment Status, January 2016

(Numbers in thousands, percent.)

| Characteristic | Total | Percent distribution by employment status | | | |
| --- | --- | --- | --- | --- | --- |
| | | Total | Employed | Unemployed | Not in the labor force |
| **TOTAL** | | | | | |
| Total, 20 years and over[2] ....................................................... | 3 191 | 100.0 | 65.5 | 15.9 | 18.6 |
| Received written advance notice ...................................... | 1 424 | 100.0 | 63.3 | 16.9 | 19.8 |
| Did not receive written advance notice ............................. | 1 716 | 100.0 | 67.5 | 14.7 | 17.8 |
| **Plant or Company Closed Down or Moved** | | | | | |
| Total, 20 years and over[2] ....................................................... | 1 192 | 100.0 | 64.0 | 14.7 | 21.3 |
| Received written advance notice ...................................... | 712 | 100.0 | 63.7 | 15.9 | 20.4 |
| Did not receive written advance notice ............................. | 468 | 100.0 | 65.2 | 11.5 | 23.3 |
| **Insufficient Work** | | | | | |
| Total, 20 years and over[2] ....................................................... | 816 | 100.0 | 64.7 | 19.3 | 16.0 |
| Received written advance notice ...................................... | 231 | 100.0 | 56.8 | 24.2 | 19.0 |
| Did not receive written advance notice ............................. | 568 | 100.0 | 67.5 | 17.2 | 15.3 |
| **Position or Shift Abolished** | | | | | |
| Total, 20 years and over[2] ....................................................... | 1 183 | 100.0 | 67.5 | 14.9 | 17.6 |
| Received written advance notice ...................................... | 481 | 100.0 | 66.0 | 14.7 | 19.3 |
| Did not receive written advance notice ............................. | 681 | 100.0 | 69.1 | 14.9 | 16.0 |

[1]Data refer to persons who had three or more years of tenure on a job that they had lost between January 2013 and December 2015 because of plant or company closings or moves, insufficient work, or the abolishment of their positions or skills.
[2]Includes a small number who did not report information on advance notice.

## Table 1-75. Long-Tenured Displaced Workers[1] by Industry and Class of Worker of Lost Job and Employment Status, January 2016

(Numbers in thousands, percent.)

| Industry of class of worker of lost job | Total | Percent distribution by employment status | | | |
|---|---|---|---|---|---|
| | | Total | Employed | Unemployed | Not in the labor force |
| **TOTAL, 20 YEARS AND OVER**[2] | 3 191 | 100.0 | 65.5 | 15.9 | 18.6 |
| Agriculture and related industries wage and salary workers | 11 | 100.0 | ([3]) | ([3]) | ([3]) |
| Nonagricultural industries wage and salary workers | 3 125 | 100.0 | 65.4 | 16.0 | 18.6 |
| Private nonagricultural wage and salary workers | 2 960 | 100.0 | 65.9 | 15.9 | 18.3 |
| Mining, quarrying, and oil and gas extraction | 76 | 100.0 | 41.2 | 33.4 | 25.4 |
| Construction | 217 | 100.0 | 71.9 | 15.7 | 12.4 |
| Manufacturing | 553 | 100.0 | 63.2 | 15.0 | 21.7 |
| Durable goods manufacturing | 332 | 100.0 | 66.0 | 13.6 | 20.4 |
| Primary metals and fabricated metal products | 40 | 100.0 | ([3]) | ([3]) | ([3]) |
| Machinery manufacturing | 46 | 100.0 | ([3]) | ([3]) | ([3]) |
| Computers and electronic products | 59 | 100.0 | ([3]) | ([3]) | ([3]) |
| Electrical equipment and appliances | 28 | 100.0 | ([3]) | ([3]) | ([3]) |
| Transportation equipment | 75 | 100.0 | 52.0 | 10.3 | 37.7 |
| Miscellaneous manufacturing | 52 | 100.0 | ([3]) | ([3]) | ([3]) |
| Other durable goods industries | 32 | 100.0 | ([3]) | ([3]) | ([3]) |
| Nondurable goods manufacturing | 221 | 100.0 | 59.1 | 17.1 | 23.8 |
| Food manufacturing | 44 | 100.0 | ([3]) | ([3]) | ([3]) |
| Textiles, apparel, and leather | 35 | 100.0 | ([3]) | ([3]) | ([3]) |
| Paper and printing | 57 | 100.0 | ([3]) | ([3]) | ([3]) |
| Other nondurable goods industries | 85 | 100.0 | 50.8 | 21.0 | 28.1 |
| Wholesale and retail trade | 480 | 100.0 | 63.9 | 14.4 | 21.7 |
| Wholesale trade | 118 | 100.0 | 69.7 | 13.3 | 17.0 |
| Retail trade | 362 | 100.0 | 62.0 | 14.7 | 23.2 |
| Transportation and utilities | 112 | 100.0 | 62.5 | 8.6 | 28.8 |
| Transportation and warehousing | 96 | 100.0 | 59.5 | 10.0 | 30.4 |
| Information | 159 | 100.0 | 74.7 | 11.7 | 13.6 |
| Telecommunications | 63 | 100.0 | ([3]) | ([3]) | ([3]) |
| Financial activities | 279 | 100.0 | 64.8 | 20.7 | 14.5 |
| Finance and insurance | 197 | 100.0 | 66.7 | 20.4 | 12.8 |
| Finance | 151 | 100.0 | 66.5 | 21.5 | 12.0 |
| Insurance | 46 | 100.0 | ([3]) | ([3]) | ([3]) |
| Real estate and rental and leasing | 82 | 100.0 | 60.1 | 21.3 | 18.6 |
| Professional and business services | 383 | 100.0 | 68.9 | 11.0 | 20.2 |
| Professional and technical services | 265 | 100.0 | 67.8 | 8.4 | 23.9 |
| Management, administrative, and waste services | 118 | 100.0 | 71.4 | 16.8 | 11.8 |
| Education and health services | 384 | 100.0 | 69.9 | 16.9 | 13.2 |
| Educational services | 85 | 100.0 | 64.7 | 8.8 | 26.5 |
| Health care and social assistance | 298 | 100.0 | 71.4 | 19.2 | 9.4 |
| Hospitals | 81 | 100.0 | 76.6 | 9.5 | 14.0 |
| Health services, except hospitals | 160 | 100.0 | 71.1 | 23.5 | 5.4 |
| Leisure and hospitality | 207 | 100.0 | 66.2 | 21.1 | 12.7 |
| Accommodation and food services | 152 | 100.0 | 69.0 | 20.2 | 10.8 |
| Food services and drinking places | 143 | 100.0 | 70.0 | 21.4 | 8.5 |
| Other services | 109 | 100.0 | 59.5 | 20.3 | 20.2 |
| Government wage and salary workers | 165 | 100.0 | 56.5 | 18.9 | 24.6 |

[1]Data refer to persons who had three or more years of tenure on a job that they had lost between January 2013 and December 2015 because of plant or company closings or moves, insufficient work, or the abolishment of their positions or skills.
[2]Total includes a small number of unpaid family workers and persons who did not report industry or class of worker, not shown separately.
[3]Data not shown where base is less than 75,000.

## Table 1-76.  Long-Tenured Displaced Workers[1] by Occupation of Lost Job and Employment Status, January 2016

(Numbers in thousands, percent.)

| Occupation of lost job | Total | Percent distribution by employment status | | | |
|---|---|---|---|---|---|
| | | Total | Employed | Unemployed | Not in the labor force |
| **TOTAL, 20 YEARS AND OVER**[2] ...................................................... | 3 191 | 100.0 | 65.5 | 15.9 | 18.6 |
| Management, professional, and related occupations ...................... | 1 301 | 100.0 | 69.0 | 13.5 | 17.4 |
| Management, business, and financial operations occupations .... | 702 | 100.0 | 72.1 | 14.6 | 13.3 |
| Professional and related occupations ........................................... | 598 | 100.0 | 65.5 | 12.3 | 22.3 |
| Service occupations ..................................................................... | 313 | 100.0 | 63.4 | 19.0 | 17.6 |
| Sales and office occupations ....................................................... | 820 | 100.0 | 63.2 | 15.2 | 21.6 |
| Sales and related occupations ................................................... | 340 | 100.0 | 66.1 | 18.3 | 15.6 |
| Office and administrative support occupations ........................... | 479 | 100.0 | 61.1 | 13.0 | 25.9 |
| Natural resources, construction, and maintenance occupations ...... | 302 | 100.0 | 62.0 | 23.7 | 14.2 |
| Farming, fishing, and forestry occupations ................................. | 8 | 100.0 | (³) | (³) | (³) |
| Construction and extraction occupations .................................... | 193 | 100.0 | 61.1 | 28.5 | 10.4 |
| Installation, maintenance, and repair occupations ....................... | 102 | 100.0 | 62.3 | 16.4 | 21.3 |
| Production, transportation, and material moving occupations .......... | 418 | 100.0 | 65.0 | 16.2 | 18.8 |
| Production occupations ................................................................ | 246 | 100.0 | 55.3 | 21.1 | 23.6 |
| Transportation and material moving occupations ........................ | 171 | 100.0 | 78.9 | 9.1 | 12.0 |

[1]Data refer to persons who had three or more years of tenure on a job that they had lost between January 2013 and December 2015 because of plant or company closings or moves, insufficient work, or the abolishment of their positions or skills.
[2]Includes a small number who did not report occupation.
[3]Data not shown where base is 75,000.

## Table 1-77.  Long-Tenured Displaced Workers[1] by Selected Characteristics and Area of Residence, January 2016

(Numbers in thousands.)

| Characteristic | Total | New England | Middle Atlantic | East North Central | West North Central |
|---|---|---|---|---|---|
| **Workers who Lost Jobs** | | | | | |
| Total, 20 years and over ................................................................ | 3 191 | 154 | 392 | 519 | 267 |
| Men ..................................................................................................... | 1 773 | 94 | 202 | 284 | 139 |
| Women ................................................................................................ | 1 419 | 59 | 190 | 235 | 128 |
| **Reason for Loss** | | | | | |
| Plant or company closed down or moved ........................................ | 1 192 | 49 | 168 | 194 | 98 |
| Insufficient work ................................................................................ | 816 | 43 | 110 | 144 | 47 |
| Position or shift abolished ................................................................ | 1 183 | 63 | 114 | 181 | 121 |
| **Industry and Class of Worker who Lost Job[2]** | | | | | |
| Agriculture and related industries wage and salary workers ........... | 11 | - | - | - | 2 |
| Nonagricultural industries wage and salary workers ....................... | 3 125 | 149 | 385 | 512 | 262 |
| Private nonagricultural wage and salary ......................................... | 2 960 | 140 | 368 | 491 | 244 |
| Mining, quarrying, and oil and gas extraction ............................ | 76 | - | 3 | - | 3 |
| Construction ............................................................................... | 217 | 11 | 32 | 50 | 17 |
| Manufacturing ............................................................................. | 553 | 36 | 72 | 115 | 64 |
| Durable goods ....................................................................... | 332 | 25 | 40 | 81 | 34 |
| Nondurable goods ................................................................. | 221 | 12 | 31 | 33 | 30 |
| Wholesale and retail trade ......................................................... | 480 | 18 | 60 | 70 | 48 |
| Transportation and utilities ........................................................ | 112 | 10 | 14 | 10 | 2 |
| Information .................................................................................. | 159 | 3 | 18 | 18 | 19 |
| Financial activities ..................................................................... | 279 | 22 | 38 | 42 | 28 |
| Professional and business services .......................................... | 383 | 19 | 38 | 78 | 20 |
| Education and health services ................................................... | 384 | 14 | 62 | 60 | 19 |
| Leisure and hospitality .............................................................. | 207 | 2 | 13 | 33 | 14 |
| Other services ........................................................................... | 109 | 4 | 17 | 16 | 9 |
| Government wage and salary workers ............................................. | 165 | 9 | 17 | 22 | 18 |
| **Employment Status in January 2014** | | | | | |
| Employed ........................................................................................... | 2 089 | 84 | 221 | 319 | 191 |
| Unemployed ....................................................................................... | 509 | 26 | 81 | 92 | 29 |
| Not in the labor force ........................................................................ | 593 | 44 | 90 | 108 | 47 |

| Characteristic | South Atlantic | East South Central | West South Central | Mountain | Pacific |
|---|---|---|---|---|---|
| **Workers who Lost Jobs** | | | | | |
| Total, 20 years and over ................................................................ | 640 | 145 | 299 | 275 | 501 |
| Men ..................................................................................................... | 327 | 62 | 164 | 186 | 313 |
| Women ................................................................................................ | 313 | 83 | 135 | 88 | 188 |
| **Reason for Loss** | | | | | |
| Plant or company closed down or moved ........................................ | 248 | 53 | 111 | 88 | 182 |
| Insufficient work ................................................................................ | 154 | 36 | 99 | 62 | 121 |
| Position or shift abolished ................................................................ | 238 | 56 | 88 | 125 | 197 |
| **Industry and Class of Worker who Lost Job[2]** | | | | | |
| Agriculture and related industries wage and salary workers ........... | 3 | 1 | - | 1 | 4 |
| Nonagricultural industries wage and salary workers ....................... | 617 | 144 | 297 | 266 | 492 |
| Private nonagricultural wage and salary ......................................... | 588 | 130 | 278 | 257 | 463 |
| Mining, quarrying, and oil and gas extraction ............................ | 8 | 7 | 26 | 21 | 7 |
| Construction ............................................................................... | 35 | 7 | 5 | 16 | 43 |
| Manufacturing ............................................................................. | 75 | 23 | 69 | 44 | 56 |
| Durable goods ....................................................................... | 31 | 7 | 41 | 34 | 38 |
| Nondurable goods ................................................................. | 44 | 16 | 28 | 10 | 18 |
| Wholesale and retail trade ......................................................... | 103 | 33 | 50 | 33 | 65 |
| Transportation and utilities ........................................................ | 22 | 6 | 15 | 1 | 32 |
| Information .................................................................................. | 47 | 7 | 4 | 15 | 27 |
| Financial activities ..................................................................... | 52 | 11 | 33 | 24 | 29 |
| Professional and business services .......................................... | 97 | 10 | 22 | 40 | 59 |
| Education and health services ................................................... | 75 | 25 | 38 | 36 | 54 |
| Leisure and hospitality .............................................................. | 43 | 2 | 16 | 17 | 69 |
| Other services ........................................................................... | 31 | - | - | 8 | 22 |
| Government wage and salary workers ............................................. | 29 | 13 | 20 | 9 | 29 |
| **Employment Status in January 2014** | | | | | |
| Employed ........................................................................................... | 432 | 77 | 203 | 206 | 356 |
| Unemployed ....................................................................................... | 106 | 27 | 35 | 31 | 82 |
| Not in the labor force ........................................................................ | 102 | 41 | 61 | 38 | 62 |

[1]Data refer to persons who had three or more years of tenure on a job that they had lost between January 2013 and December 2015 because of plant or company closings or moves,  insufficient work, or the abolishment of their positions or skills.
[2]Total includes a small number of unpaid family workers and persons who did not report industry or class of worker, not shown separately.
- = Represents or rounds to zero.

**Table 1-78.  Long-Tenured Displaced Workers Who Lost Full-Time Wage and Salary Jobs and Were Reemployed in January 2016 by Industry of Lost Job and Characteristic of New Job**

(Numbers in thousands.)

| Industry and class of worker of lost job[1] | Total | Reemployed in January 2016 | | | | | | | Self-employed and unpaid family workers |
|---|---|---|---|---|---|---|---|---|---|
| | | Wage and salary workers | | | | | | | |
| | | Part-time | Full-time | | | | | | |
| | | | Total[2] | Earnings relative to those of lost job | | | | | |
| | | | | 20 percent or more below | Below, but within 20 percent | Equal or above, but within 20 percent | 20 percent or more above | | |
| **TOTAL WHO LOST FULL-TIME WAGE AND SALARY JOBS[3]** .... | 1 838 | 231 | 1 470 | 340 | 239 | 391 | 258 | | 137 |
| Agriculture and related industries wage and salary workers ............ | 10 | 3 | 1 | 1 | - | - | - | | 5 |
| Nonagricultural industries wage and salary workers ........................ | 1 799 | 221 | 1 447 | 339 | 239 | 387 | 252 | | 131 |
| Private nonagricultural wage and salary workers ........................... | 1 734 | 206 | 1 396 | 334 | 239 | 366 | 232 | | 131 |
| Mining, quarrying, and oil and gas extraction ............................. | 26 | - | 26 | 14 | 1 | - | 2 | | - |
| Construction ......................................................................... | 143 | 19 | 101 | 20 | 18 | 36 | 10 | | 24 |
| Manufacturing ...................................................................... | 332 | 35 | 273 | 59 | 57 | 86 | 35 | | 25 |
| Durable goods ................................................................ | 207 | 21 | 178 | 28 | 38 | 65 | 25 | | 8 |
| Nondurable goods ........................................................... | 125 | 14 | 95 | 31 | 19 | 21 | 10 | | 16 |
| Wholesale and retail trade .................................................... | 257 | 23 | 217 | 75 | 32 | 26 | 50 | | 16 |
| Transportation and utilities .................................................. | 64 | - | 59 | 11 | 11 | 23 | 8 | | 5 |
| Information ........................................................................... | 119 | 6 | 100 | 34 | 23 | 13 | 14 | | 13 |
| Financial activities ............................................................... | 170 | 14 | 145 | 26 | 38 | 20 | 28 | | 12 |
| Professional and business services ....................................... | 233 | 30 | 184 | 36 | 20 | 76 | 14 | | 19 |
| Education and health services .............................................. | 231 | 65 | 165 | 24 | 20 | 54 | 54 | | 2 |
| Leisure and hospitality ......................................................... | 104 | 10 | 83 | 23 | 11 | 20 | 15 | | 11 |
| Other services ..................................................................... | 52 | 4 | 43 | 12 | 8 | 12 | 1 | | 5 |
| Government wage and salary workers ........................................ | 66 | 15 | 50 | 5 | - | 21 | 20 | | - |

*Note:* Dash represents or rounds to zero.

[1]Data refer to persons who had three or more years of tenure on a job that they had lost between January 2013 and December 2015 because of plant or company closings or moves, insufficient work, or the abolishment of their positions or skills.
[2]Includes about 330,000 persons who did not report earnings on lost job.
[3]Includes a small number who did not report industry

## Table 1-79.  Total Displaced Workers by Selected Characteristics and Employment Status in January 2016

(Numbers in thousands, percent.)

| Characteristic[1] | Total | Percent Distribution by Employment Status | | | |
|---|---|---|---|---|---|
| | | Total | Employed | Unemployed | Not in the labor force |
| **WORKERS WHO LOST JOBS** | | | | | |
| **Sex and Age** | | | | | |
| Total, 20 years and over ............................................. | 7 440 | 100.0 | 66.5 | 16.9 | 16.5 |
| 20 to 24 years ............................................................. | 708 | 100.0 | 62.5 | 20.2 | 17.3 |
| 25 to 54 years ............................................................. | 4 972 | 100.0 | 71.3 | 17.1 | 11.5 |
| 55 to 64 years ............................................................. | 1 386 | 100.0 | 61.0 | 16.6 | 22.5 |
| 65 years and over ....................................................... | 374 | 100.0 | 30.8 | 9.7 | 59.4 |
| | | | | | |
| Men, 20 years and over ............................................. | 4 242 | 100.0 | 68.4 | 16.7 | 14.8 |
| 20 to 24 years ............................................................. | 441 | 100.0 | 62.4 | 20.5 | 17.1 |
| 25 to 54 years ............................................................. | 2 833 | 100.0 | 73.2 | 17.2 | 9.6 |
| 55 to 64 years ............................................................. | 761 | 100.0 | 64.6 | 14.7 | 20.6 |
| 65 years and over ....................................................... | 206 | 100.0 | 29.4 | 9.3 | 61.3 |
| | | | | | |
| Women, 20 years and over ......................................... | 3 199 | 100.0 | 64.0 | 17.2 | 18.7 |
| 20 to 24 years ............................................................. | 267 | 100.0 | 62.7 | 19.6 | 17.6 |
| 25 to 54 years ............................................................. | 2 139 | 100.0 | 68.9 | 17.0 | 14.1 |
| 55 to 64 years ............................................................. | 625 | 100.0 | 56.5 | 18.8 | 24.7 |
| 65 years and over ....................................................... | 168 | 100.0 | 32.5 | 10.3 | 57.2 |
| | | | | | |
| **Race and Hispanic Origin** | | | | | |
| White ......................................................................... | 5 673 | 100.0 | 68.1 | 15.3 | 16.6 |
| Black or African American ........................................... | 1 155 | 100.0 | 59.9 | 25.3 | 14.8 |
| Asian ......................................................................... | 309 | 100.0 | 63.4 | 19.6 | 17.0 |
| Hispanic[2] ................................................................. | 1 219 | 100.0 | 68.0 | 15.9 | 16.1 |
| | | | | | |
| **Reason for Job Loss** | | | | | |
| Plant or company closed down or moved ........................ | 2 350 | 100.0 | 67.0 | 15.5 | 17.5 |
| Insufficient work .......................................................... | 2 839 | 100.0 | 66.1 | 18.4 | 15.6 |
| Position or shift abolished ............................................ | 2 252 | 100.0 | 66.7 | 16.7 | 16.6 |
| | | | | | |
| **Occupation of Lost Job**[3] | | | | | |
| Management, professional, and related occupations ...... | 2 470 | 100.0 | 71.5 | 13.6 | 14.9 |
| Management, business, and financial operations occupations .... | 1 149 | 100.0 | 71.0 | 16.0 | 13.0 |
| Professional and related occupations ............................ | 1 320 | 100.0 | 71.9 | 11.6 | 16.6 |
| Service occupations ................................................... | 949 | 100.0 | 65.8 | 15.7 | 18.5 |
| Sales and office occupations ....................................... | 1 794 | 100.0 | 64.7 | 16.2 | 19.1 |
| Sales and related occupations ..................................... | 759 | 100.0 | 66.2 | 15.9 | 17.9 |
| Office and administrative support occupations ............... | 1 035 | 100.0 | 63.6 | 16.4 | 19.9 |
| Natural resources, construction, and maintenance occupations ...... | 878 | 100.0 | 67.3 | 21.3 | 11.4 |
| Farming, fishing, and forestry occupations .................... | 22 | 100.0 | ($^4$) | ($^4$) | ($^4$) |
| Construction and extraction occupations ....................... | 567 | 100.0 | 68.8 | 20.5 | 10.8 |
| Installation, maintenance, and repair occupations ......... | 289 | 100.0 | 66.3 | 22.7 | 11.1 |
| Production, transportation, and material moving occupations ......... | 1 082 | 100.0 | 63.1 | 20.0 | 16.9 |
| Production occupations ............................................... | 567 | 100.0 | 63.6 | 20.4 | 16.0 |
| Transportation and material moving occupations ........... | 515 | 100.0 | 62.5 | 19.7 | 17.8 |
| Agriculture and related industries wage and salary workers ........... | 26 | 100.0 | ($^4$) | ($^4$) | ($^4$) |
| Nonagricultural industries wage and salary workers ...... | 7 107 | 100.0 | 67.2 | 16.5 | 16.4 |
| Private nonagricultural wage and salary workers ........... | 6 771 | 100.0 | 67.1 | 16.5 | 16.4 |
| Mining, quarrying, and oil and gas extraction ............... | 190 | 100.0 | 62.5 | 24.4 | 13.0 |
| Construction ............................................................. | 605 | 100.0 | 72.7 | 16.4 | 10.9 |
| Manufacturing ........................................................... | 1 055 | 100.0 | 65.6 | 16.4 | 18.0 |
| Durable goods ...................................................... | 665 | 100.0 | 65.6 | 15.7 | 18.7 |
| Nondurable goods ................................................. | 390 | 100.0 | 65.6 | 17.6 | 16.8 |
| Wholesale and retail trade .......................................... | 1 081 | 100.0 | 62.7 | 17.1 | 20.2 |
| Transportation and utilities ......................................... | 292 | 100.0 | 62.7 | 14.7 | 22.6 |
| Information ............................................................... | 260 | 100.0 | 68.4 | 20.4 | 11.2 |
| Financial activities ..................................................... | 555 | 100.0 | 67.6 | 18.6 | 13.8 |
| Professional and business services ............................. | 1 005 | 100.0 | 73.0 | 12.2 | 14.9 |
| Education and health services ..................................... | 800 | 100.0 | 68.6 | 17.2 | 14.2 |
| Leisure and hospitality ............................................... | 614 | 100.0 | 62.5 | 17.9 | 19.6 |
| Other services .......................................................... | 308 | 100.0 | 66.9 | 15.4 | 17.7 |
| Government wage and salary workers ........................... | 337 | 100.0 | 68.5 | 14.8 | 16.6 |

*Note:* Dash represents or rounds to zero.

[1]Data refer to all persons (regardless of years of tenure on lost job) who had lost or left a job between January 2013 and December 2015 because of plant or company closings or moves, insufficient work, or the abolishment of their positions or shifts.
[2]Persons of Hispanic origin may be of any race.
[3]Total includes a small number of unpaid family workers and persons who did not report occupation, industry, or class of worker, not shown separately.
[4]Data not shown where base is less than 75,000.

# CHAPTER 2: EMPLOYMENT, HOURS, AND EARNINGS

## HIGHLIGHTS

The employment, hours, and earnings data in this section are presented by industry and state and are derived from the Current Employment Statistics (CES) survey, which covers approximately 634,000 individual worksites and 147,000 business and government agencies. The employment numbers differ from those presented in from the household survey in Chapter 1 because of dissimilarities in methodology, concepts, definitions, and coverage. As the CES survey data are obtained from payroll records, they are consistent for industry classifications.

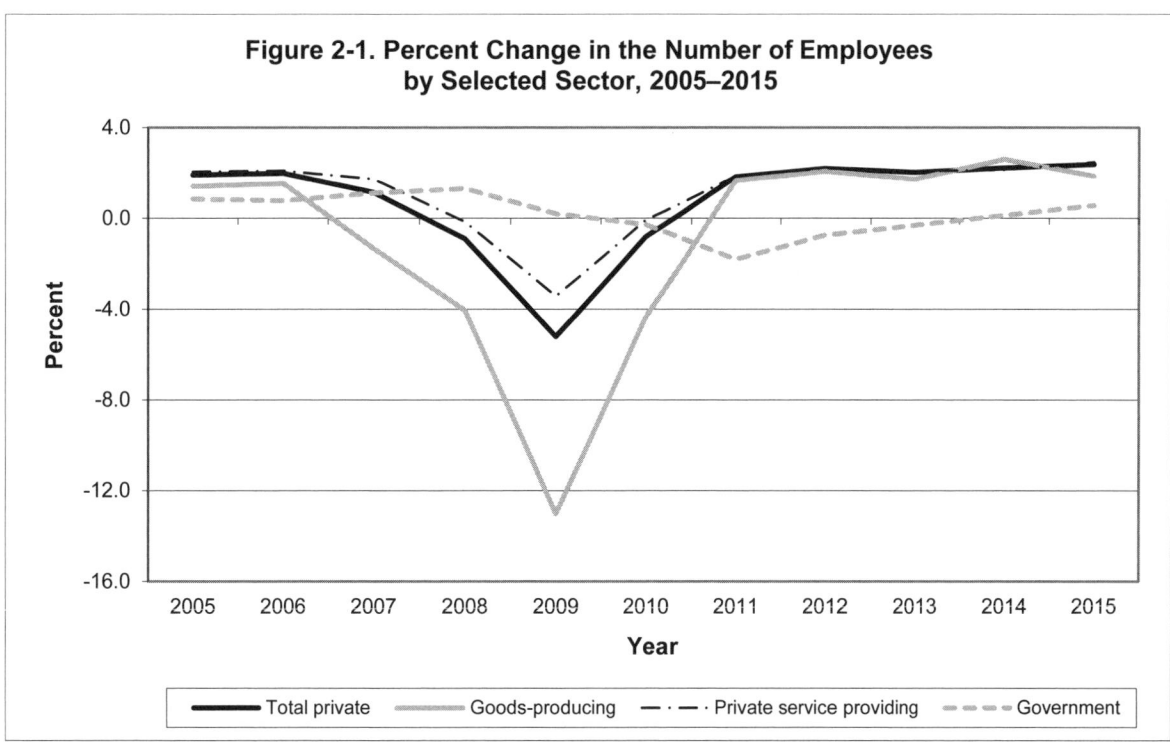

Figure 2-1. Percent Change in the Number of Employees by Selected Sector, 2005–2015

In 2015, total private employment increased for the fifth consecutive year after declining each year from 2008 to 2010. It increased 1.9 percent in the goods-producing sector and from 2014 to 2015 and 2.5 percent in the private service providing industry. (See Table 2-1.)

## OTHER HIGHLIGHTS

- In 2015, employment in construction increased for the fifth consecutive year in 2015 after declining each year from 2007 through 2010. Employment in mining and logging decreased in 2015 after increasing the previous five years. Manufacturing employment increased 1.1 percent. (See Table 2-1.)

- From 2005 to 2015, the number of women employees on nonfarm payrolls has increased 7.7 percent. (See Table 2-2.)

- Average weekly hours of all employees on private nonfarm payrolls remained steady at 34.5 hours. Employees in mining and logging worked the longest week (44.0 hours) followed by workers in utilities (42.5 hours) and manufacturing (40.8 hours). Workers in leisure and hospitality worked the shortest (26.3 hours). (See Table 2-6.)

## NOTES AND DEFINITIONS

### EMPLOYMENT, HOURS, AND EARNINGS

#### Collection and Coverage

The Bureau of Labor Statistics (BLS) conducts the Current Employment Statistics (CES), or establishment, survey. This survey collects monthly data on employment, hours, and earnings from a sample of nonfarm establishments (including government).

The CES sample includes about 147,000 businesses and government agencies and covers approximately 634,000 individual worksites. The reference period for the CES survey is the pay period which includes the 12th of the month.

The BLS publishes:

- About 2,200 not seasonally adjusted employment series for all employees, production and nonsupervisory employees, and women employees are published monthly. The series for all employees include over 900 industries at various levels of aggregation.

- Approximately 8,600 not seasonally adjusted special derivative series such as average weekly earnings, indexes, and constant dollar series for all employees and production and nonsupervisory employees are also published for over 600 industries.

- About 5,900 seasonally adjusted employment, hours, and earnings series for all employees, production and nonsupervisory employees, and women employees are published.

- Approximately 2,600 all employees and production and nonsupervisory employees series for average hourly earnings, average weekly hours, and, in manufacturing, average weekly overtime hours are published monthly on a not seasonally adjusted basis and cover over 600 industries.

#### Industry Classification

The CES survey completed a conversion from its original quota sample design to a probability-based sample survey design, and switched from the Standard Industrial Classification (SIC) system to the North American Industry Classification System (NAICS) in 2003. The industry-coding update included reconstruction of historical estimates in order to preserve time series for data users. The foundation of industrial classification with NAICS has changed how establishments are classified into industries and how businesses, as they exist today, are recognized. With the release of January 2008 data on February 1, 2008, the CES National Nonfarm Payroll series was updated to the 2007 North American Industry Classification System (NAICS) from the 2002 NAICS basis. In February 2012, the CES National Nonfarm Payroll series was updated again from the 2007 version to the 2012 version of NAICS with the release of January data.

### Industry Employment

Employment data refer to persons on establishment payrolls who received pay for any part of the pay period containing the 12th day of the month. The data exclude proprietors, the self-employed, unpaid volunteer or family workers, farm workers, and domestic workers. Salaried officers of corporations are included. Government employment covers only civilian employees; military personnel are excluded. Employees of the Central Intelligence Agency, the National Security Agency, the National Imagery and Mapping Agency, and the Defense Intelligence Agency are also excluded.

Persons on establishment payrolls who were on paid sick leave (for cases in which pay is received directly from the firm), paid holiday, or vacation leave, or who work during part of the pay period despite being unemployed or on strike during the rest of the period were counted as employed. Not counted as employed were persons on layoff, on leave without pay, on strike for the entire period, or who had been hired but had not yet reported during to their new jobs.

Beginning with the June 2003 publication of May 2003 data, the CES national federal government employment series has been estimated from a sample of federal establishments and benchmarked annually to counts from unemployment insurance tax records. It reflects employee counts as of the pay period containing the 12th day of the month, which is consistent with other CES industry series. Previously, the national series was an end-of-month count produced by the Office of Personnel Management.

The exclusion of farm employment, self-employment, and domestic service employment accounts from the payroll survey accounts for the differences in employment figures between the household and payroll surveys. The payroll survey also excludes workers on leave without pay. (These workers are counted as employed in the household survey.) Persons who worked in more than one establishment during the reporting period are counted each time their names appear on payrolls; these persons are only counted once in the household survey.

### Concepts and Definitions

*Production and related workers.* This category includes working supervisors and all nonsupervisory workers (including group leaders and trainees) engaged in fabricating, processing, assembling, inspecting, receiving, storing, handling, packing, warehousing, shipping, trucking, hauling, maintenance, repair, janitorial, guard services, product development, auxiliary production for plant's own use (such as a power plant), record-keeping, and other services closely associated with production operations.

*Construction workers.* This group includes the following employees in the construction division: working supervisors, qualified craft workers, mechanics, apprentices, helpers, and laborers engaged in new work, alterations, demolition, repair, maintenance, and the like, whether working at the site of construction or at jobs in shops or yards at jobs (such as precutting and pre-assembling) ordinarily performed by members of the construction trades.

*Nonsupervisory workers.* This category consists of employees such as office and clerical workers, repairers, salespersons, operators, drivers, physicians, lawyers, accountants, nurses, social workers, research aides, teachers, drafters, photographers, beauticians, musicians, restaurant workers, custodial workers, attendants, line installers and repairers, laborers, janitors, guards, and other employees at similar occupational levels whose services are closely associated with those of the employees listed. It excludes persons in executive, managerial, and supervisory positions.

*Payroll.* This refers to payments made to full- and part-time production, construction, or nonsupervisory workers who received pay for any part of the pay period containing the 12th day of the month. The payroll is reported before deductions of any kind, such as those for old age and unemployment insurance, group insurance, withholding tax, bonds, or union dues. Also included is pay for overtime, holidays, and vacation, as well as for sick leave paid directly by the firm. Bonuses (unless earned and paid regularly each pay period), other pay not earned in the pay period reported (such as retroactive pay), tips, and the value of free rent, fuel, meals, or other payment-in-kind are excluded. Employee benefits (such as health and other types of insurance and contributions to retirement, as paid by the employer) are also excluded.

*Total hours.* During the pay period, total hours include all hours worked (including overtime hours), hours paid for standby or reporting time, and equivalent hours for which employees received pay directly from the employer for sick leave, holidays, vacations, and other leave. Overtime and other premium pay hours are not converted to straight-time equivalent hours. The concept of total hours differs from those of scheduled hours and hours worked. The average weekly hours derived from paid total hours reflect the effects of such factors as unpaid absenteeism, labor turnover, part-time work, and work stoppages, as well as fluctuations in work schedules.

*Average weekly hours.* The workweek information relates to the average hours for which pay was received and is different from standard or scheduled hours. Such factors as unpaid absenteeism, labor turnover, part-time work, and work stoppages cause average weekly hours to be lower than scheduled hours of work for an establishment. Group averages further reflect changes in the workweeks of component industries.

*Overtime hours.* These are hours worked by production or related workers for which overtime premiums were paid because the hours were in excess of the number of hours of either the straight-time workday or the total workweek. Weekend and holiday hours are included only if overtime premiums were paid. Hours for which only shift differential, hazard, incentive, or other similar types of premiums were paid are excluded.

*Average overtime hours.* Overtime hours represent the portion of average weekly hours that exceeded regular hours and for which overtime premiums were paid. If an employee worked during a paid holiday at regular rates, receiving as total compensation his or her holiday pay plus straight-time pay for hours worked that day, no overtime hours would be reported.

Since overtime hours are premium hours by definition, weekly hours and overtime hours do not necessarily move in the same direction from month to month. Factors such as work stoppages, absenteeism, and labor turnover may not have the same influence on overtime hours as on average hours. Diverse trends at the industry group level may also be caused by a marked change in hours for a component industry in which little or no overtime was worked in both the previous and current months.

*Industry hours and earnings.* Average hours and earnings data are derived from reports of payrolls and hours for production and related workers in manufacturing and natural resources and mining, construction workers in construction, and nonsupervisory employees in private service-providing industries.

*Average hourly earnings.* Average hourly earnings are on a "gross" basis. They reflect not only changes in basic hourly and incentive wage rates, but also such variable factors as premium pay for overtime and late-shift work and changes in output of workers paid on an incentive plan. They also reflect shifts in the number of employees between relatively high-paid and low-paid work and changes in workers' earnings in individual establishments. Averages for groups and divisions further reflect changes in average hourly earnings for individual industries.

Averages of hourly earnings differ from wage rates. Earnings are the actual return to the worker for a stated period; rates are the amount stipulated for a given unit of work or time. The earnings series do not measure the level of total labor costs on the part of the employer because the following items are excluded: irregular bonuses, retroactive items, payroll taxes paid by employers, and earnings for those employees not covered under the definitions of production workers, construction workers, or nonsupervisory employees.

Average hourly earnings, excluding overtime-premium pay, are computed by dividing the total production worker payroll for the industry group by the sum of total production worker hours and one-half of total overtime hours. No adjustments are made for other premium payment provisions, such as holiday pay, late-shift premiums, and overtime rates other than time and one-half.

*Average weekly earnings.* These estimates are derived by multiplying average weekly hours estimates by average hourly earnings estimates. Therefore, weekly earnings are affected not only by changes in average hourly earnings but also by changes in the length of the workweek. Monthly variations in factors, such as the proportion of part-time workers, work stoppages, labor turnover during the survey period, and absenteeism for which employees are not paid may cause the average workweek to fluctuate.

Long-term trends of average weekly earnings can be affected by structural changes in the makeup of the workforce. For example, persistent long-term increases in the proportion of part-time workers in retail trade and many of the services industries have reduced average workweeks in these industries and have affected the average weekly earnings series.

These earnings are in constant dollars and are calculated from the earnings averages for the current month using a deflator derived from the Consumer Price Index for Urban Wage Earnings and Clerical Workers (CPI-W). The reference year for these series is 1982.

*Seasonal adjustment* removes the change in employment that is due to normal seasonal hiring or layoffs, thus leaving an over-the-month change that reflects only employment changes due to trend and irregular movements. Seasonally adjusted estimates of employment and other series are generated using the X-12 ARIMA program developed by the United States Census Bureau.

## Data Revisions

CES revises published estimates to improve its data series by incorporating additional information that was not available at the time of the initial publication of the estimates. Each year, the CES incorporates a benchmark revision that re-anchors estimates to nearly complete employment counts available from Quarterly Census of Employment and Wages (QCEW) data, County Business Pattern data, and other state collected data. The benchmark helps to control for sampling error in the estimates. See more about the QCEW later in this chapter.

It can be nearly 2 years before not seasonally adjusted CES estimates are considered final. The first preliminary CES estimates of employment, hours, and earnings are published each month approximately 3 weeks after the reference period. Estimates are then revised twice before being held constant until the annual benchmark release. Second preliminary estimates for a given month are published the month following the initial release, and final sample-based estimates are published 2 months after the initial release. The annual benchmark revisions affect nearly 2 years of data, so most months are subject to revisions during 2 separate benchmark periods.

## Sources of Additional Information

For further information on sampling, estimation methods, and data revisions for national data visit the Employment, Hours, and Earnings homepage on the BLS Web site at <http://www.bls.gov/ces>. For more information on state and area data, please visit the BLS Web site at <http://www.bls.gov/sae>.

## Table 2-1.  Employees on Nonfarm Payrolls, by Super Sector and Selected Component Groups, NAICS Basis, 2005–2015

(Thousands of people.)

| Industry | 2005 | 2006 | 2007 | 2008 | 2009 | 2010 | 2011 | 2012 | 2013 | 2014 | 2015 |
|---|---|---|---|---|---|---|---|---|---|---|---|
| **TOTAL** | 134 051 | 136 453 | 137 999 | 137 242 | 131 313 | 130 361 | 131 932 | 134 175 | 136 381 | 138 958 | 141 865 |
| **Total Private** | 112 247 | 114 479 | 115 781 | 114 732 | 108 758 | 107 871 | 109 845 | 112 255 | 114 529 | 117 076 | 119 859 |
| **Goods-Producing** | 22 190 | 22 530 | 22 233 | 21 335 | 18 558 | 17 751 | 18 047 | 18 420 | 18 738 | 19 226 | 19 584 |
| **Mining and Logging** | 628 | 684 | 724 | 767 | 694 | 705 | 788 | 848 | 863 | 891 | 820 |
| Mining | 562 | 620 | 664 | 710 | 643 | 655 | 739 | 797 | 811 | 839 | 768 |
| Logging | 65 | 64 | 60 | 57 | 50 | 50 | 49 | 51 | 52 | 52 | 52 |
| **Construction** | 7 336 | 7 691 | 7 630 | 7 162 | 6 016 | 5 518 | 5 533 | 5 646 | 5 856 | 6 151 | 6 446 |
| Construction of buildings | 1 712 | 1 805 | 1 774 | 1 642 | 1 357 | 1 230 | 1 222 | 1 240 | 1 286 | 1 358 | 1 416 |
| Heavy and civil engineering | 951 | 985 | 1 005 | 965 | 851 | 825 | 837 | 868 | 885 | 912 | 935 |
| Specialty trade contractors | 4 673 | 4 901 | 4 850 | 4 556 | 3 808 | 3 463 | 3 474 | 3 537 | 3 684 | 3 881 | 4 095 |
| **Manufacturing** | 14 227 | 14 155 | 13 879 | 13 406 | 11 847 | 11 528 | 11 726 | 11 927 | 12 020 | 12 185 | 12 318 |
| Durable goods | 8 956 | 8 981 | 8 808 | 8 463 | 7 284 | 7 064 | 7 273 | 7 470 | 7 548 | 7 674 | 7 756 |
| Wood product | 561 | 561 | 517 | 458 | 360 | 342 | 337 | 339 | 353 | 372 | 380 |
| Nonmetallic mineral product | 505 | 510 | 501 | 465 | 394 | 371 | 367 | 365 | 373 | 384 | 396 |
| Primary metals | 466 | 464 | 456 | 442 | 362 | 362 | 388 | 402 | 395 | 399 | 393 |
| Fabricated metal product | 1 522 | 1 553 | 1 563 | 1 528 | 1 312 | 1 282 | 1 347 | 1 410 | 1 432 | 1 454 | 1 459 |
| Machinery | 1 166 | 1 183 | 1 187 | 1 188 | 1 029 | 996 | 1 056 | 1 099 | 1 105 | 1 127 | 1 122 |
| Computer and electronic product | 1 316 | 1 308 | 1 273 | 1 244 | 1 137 | 1 095 | 1 104 | 1 089 | 1 066 | 1 049 | 1 050 |
| Electrical equipment and appliances | 434 | 433 | 429 | 424 | 374 | 360 | 366 | 373 | 374 | 378 | 384 |
| Transportation equipment | 1 772 | 1 769 | 1 712 | 1 608 | 1 348 | 1 333 | 1 382 | 1 461 | 1 509 | 1 559 | 1 599 |
| Furniture and related product | 566 | 558 | 529 | 478 | 384 | 357 | 353 | 351 | 360 | 370 | 381 |
| Miscellaneous manufacturing | 647 | 644 | 642 | 629 | 584 | 567 | 574 | 580 | 581 | 582 | 592 |
| Nondurable goods | 5 271 | 5 174 | 5 071 | 4 943 | 4 564 | 4 464 | 4 453 | 4 457 | 4 472 | 4 512 | 4 562 |
| Food manufacturing | 1 478 | 1 479 | 1 484 | 1 481 | 1 456 | 1 451 | 1 459 | 1 469 | 1 474 | 1 484 | 1 505 |
| Textile mills | 218 | 195 | 170 | 151 | 124 | 119 | 120 | 119 | 117 | 117 | 116 |
| Textile product mills | 176 | 167 | 158 | 147 | 126 | 119 | 118 | 116 | 114 | 115 | 116 |
| Apparel | 251 | 232 | 215 | 199 | 168 | 157 | 152 | 148 | 145 | 140 | 137 |
| Paper and paper product | 484 | 471 | 458 | 445 | 407 | 395 | 387 | 380 | 378 | 373 | 373 |
| Printing and related support activities | 646 | 634 | 622 | 594 | 522 | 488 | 472 | 462 | 452 | 454 | 449 |
| Petroleum and coal product | 112 | 113 | 115 | 117 | 115 | 114 | 112 | 112 | 110 | 112 | 114 |
| Chemicals | 872 | 866 | 861 | 847 | 804 | 787 | 784 | 783 | 793 | 803 | 810 |
| Plastics and rubber product | 802 | 786 | 757 | 729 | 625 | 625 | 635 | 645 | 659 | 674 | 687 |
| **Private Service-Providing** | 90 057 | 91 949 | 93 548 | 93 398 | 90 201 | 90 120 | 91 798 | 93 834 | 95 791 | 97 850 | 100 275 |
| **Trade, Transportation, and Utilities** | 25 959 | 26 276 | 26 630 | 26 293 | 24 906 | 24 636 | 25 065 | 25 476 | 25 862 | 26 383 | 26 920 |
| **Wholesale Trade** | 5 764 | 5 905 | 6 015 | 5 943 | 5 587 | 5 452 | 5 543 | 5 667 | 5 733 | 5 813 | 5 875 |
| Durable goods | 2 999 | 3 075 | 3 122 | 3 052 | 2 810 | 2 714 | 2 765 | 2 832 | 2 864 | 2 905 | 2 935 |
| Nondurable goods | 2 022 | 2 041 | 2 062 | 2 048 | 1 966 | 1 928 | 1 939 | 1 965 | 1 985 | 2 012 | 2 036 |
| Electronic markets, agents, and brokers | 743 | 789 | 832 | 843 | 811 | 811 | 839 | 869 | 884 | 896 | 904 |
| **Retail Trade** | 15 280 | 15 353 | 15 520 | 15 283 | 14 522 | 14 440 | 14 668 | 14 841 | 15 079 | 15 357 | 15 641 |
| Motor vehicle and parts dealers | 1 919 | 1 910 | 1 908 | 1 831 | 1 638 | 1 629 | 1 691 | 1 737 | 1 793 | 1 862 | 1 934 |
| Furniture and home furnishing stores | 576 | 587 | 575 | 531 | 449 | 438 | 439 | 439 | 446 | 456 | 469 |
| Electronic and appliance stores | 585 | 581 | 583 | 570 | 516 | 522 | 527 | 507 | 497 | 497 | 523 |
| Building material and garden supply stores | 1 276 | 1 324 | 1 309 | 1 248 | 1 156 | 1 132 | 1 146 | 1 174 | 1 208 | 1 228 | 1 238 |
| Food and beverage stores | 2 818 | 2 821 | 2 844 | 2 862 | 2 830 | 2 808 | 2 823 | 2 861 | 2 930 | 3 004 | 3 066 |
| Health and personal care stores | 954 | 961 | 993 | 1 003 | 986 | 981 | 981 | 998 | 1 016 | 1 023 | 1 033 |
| Gasoline stations | 871 | 864 | 862 | 842 | 826 | 819 | 831 | 844 | 866 | 881 | 905 |
| Clothing and clothing accessories stores | 1 415 | 1 451 | 1 500 | 1 468 | 1 364 | 1 353 | 1 361 | 1 391 | 1 391 | 1 370 | 1 363 |
| Sporting goods, hobby, and music stores | 598 | 606 | 623 | 622 | 589 | 579 | 578 | 582 | 603 | 619 | 625 |
| General merchandise stores | 2 934 | 2 935 | 3 021 | 3 026 | 2 966 | 2 998 | 3 085 | 3 065 | 3 060 | 3 102 | 3 140 |
| Miscellaneous store retailers | 900 | 881 | 865 | 843 | 782 | 762 | 772 | 794 | 803 | 818 | 830 |
| Nonstore retailers | 435 | 433 | 438 | 438 | 421 | 421 | 434 | 447 | 467 | 497 | 514 |
| **Transportation and Warehousing** | 4 361 | 4 470 | 4 541 | 4 508 | 4 236 | 4 191 | 4 302 | 4 416 | 4 498 | 4 661 | 4 845 |
| Air transportation | 501 | 487 | 492 | 491 | 463 | 458 | 457 | 459 | 444 | 444 | 456 |
| Rail transportation | 228 | 228 | 234 | 231 | 218 | 216 | 228 | 231 | 231 | 236 | 242 |
| Water transportation | 61 | 63 | 66 | 67 | 63 | 62 | 61 | 64 | 65 | 67 | 65 |
| Truck transportation | 1 398 | 1 436 | 1 439 | 1 389 | 1 268 | 1 250 | 1 301 | 1 349 | 1 382 | 1 417 | 1 455 |
| Transit and ground passenger transportation | 389 | 399 | 412 | 423 | 422 | 430 | 440 | 440 | 449 | 467 | 475 |
| Pipeline transportation | 38 | 39 | 40 | 42 | 43 | 42 | 43 | 44 | 45 | 47 | 49 |
| Scenic and sightseeing transportation | 29 | 28 | 29 | 28 | 28 | 27 | 28 | 28 | 29 | 31 | 32 |
| Support activities for transportation | 552 | 571 | 584 | 592 | 549 | 543 | 562 | 580 | 598 | 626 | 649 |
| Couriers and messengers | 571 | 582 | 581 | 573 | 546 | 528 | 529 | 534 | 544 | 577 | 608 |
| Warehousing and storage | 595 | 638 | 665 | 672 | 637 | 633 | 653 | 687 | 711 | 750 | 813 |
| **Utilities** | 554 | 549 | 553 | 559 | 560 | 553 | 553 | 553 | 552 | 552 | 559 |
| **Information** | 3 061 | 3 038 | 3 032 | 2 984 | 2 804 | 2 707 | 2 674 | 2 676 | 2 706 | 2 726 | 2 750 |
| Publishing industries, except Internet | 904 | 902 | 901 | 880 | 796 | 759 | 749 | 740 | 733 | 727 | 725 |
| Motion picture and sound recording industry | 378 | 376 | 381 | 371 | 358 | 370 | 362 | 362 | 371 | 379 | 398 |
| Broadcasting, except Internet | 328 | 328 | 325 | 319 | 301 | 290 | 283 | 285 | 284 | 283 | 279 |
| Internet publishing and broadcasting and web search portals | 67 | 69 | 73 | 81 | 83 | 92 | 110 | 125 | 142 | 163 | 185 |
| Telecommunications | 1 071 | 1 048 | 1 031 | 1 019 | 966 | 903 | 874 | 857 | 853 | 839 | 810 |
| Other information services | 118 | 121 | 126 | 134 | 135 | 142 | 160 | 177 | 196 | 219 | 242 |
| **Financial Activities** | 8 197 | 8 367 | 8 348 | 8 206 | 7 838 | 7 695 | 7 697 | 7 784 | 7 886 | 7 977 | 8 124 |
| Finance and insurance | 6 063 | 6 194 | 6 179 | 6 076 | 5 844 | 5 761 | 5 769 | 5 828 | 5 886 | 5 931 | 6 038 |
| Monetary authorities, central bank | 21 | 21 | 22 | 22 | 21 | 20 | 18 | 18 | 18 | 18 | 18 |
| Credit intermediation | 2 869 | 2 925 | 2 866 | 2 733 | 2 590 | 2 550 | 2 554 | 2 583 | 2 614 | 2 564 | 2 568 |

## Table 2-1.  Employees on Nonfarm Payrolls, by Super Sector and Selected Component Groups, NAICS Basis, 2005–2015—Continued

(Thousands of people.)

| Industry | 2005 | 2006 | 2007 | 2008 | 2009 | 2010 | 2011 | 2012 | 2013 | 2014 | 2015 |
|---|---|---|---|---|---|---|---|---|---|---|---|
| Securities, commodity contracts, investments, and funds and trusts | 834 | 869 | 900 | 916 | 862 | 850 | 860 | 859 | 865 | 883 | 908 |
| Insurance carriers and related activities | 2 339 | 2 379 | 2 392 | 2 405 | 2 371 | 2 341 | 2 336 | 2 368 | 2 389 | 2 466 | 2 545 |
| Real estate and rental and leasing | 2 134 | 2 173 | 2 169 | 2 130 | 1 994 | 1 934 | 1 927 | 1 955 | 2 000 | 2 046 | 2 086 |
| Real estate | 1 461 | 1 499 | 1 500 | 1 485 | 1 420 | 1 396 | 1 401 | 1 420 | 1 459 | 1 487 | 1 518 |
| Rental and leasing services | 646 | 646 | 640 | 617 | 547 | 514 | 502 | 511 | 518 | 535 | 544 |
| Lessors of nonfinancial intangible assets | 27 | 28 | 28 | 28 | 27 | 25 | 24 | 24 | 24 | 24 | 24 |
| **Professional and Business Services** | 16 954 | 17 566 | 17 942 | 17 735 | 16 579 | 16 728 | 17 332 | 17 932 | 18 515 | 19 062 | 19 672 |
| Professional and technical services | 7 025 | 7 357 | 7 660 | 7 799 | 7 509 | 7 441 | 7 666 | 7 892 | 8 121 | 8 336 | 8 624 |
| Management and technical consulting services | 824 | 886 | 953 | 1 002 | 995 | 999 | 1 065 | 1 118 | 1 180 | 1 232 | 1 273 |
| Administrative and management consulting services | 308 | 331 | 357 | 374 | 368 | 375 | 398 | 415 | 444 | 474 | 492 |
| Waste management and remediation services | 338 | 348 | 355 | 357 | 352 | 357 | 365 | 372 | 378 | 386 | 398 |
| **Education and Health Services** | 17 676 | 18 154 | 18 676 | 19 228 | 19 630 | 19 975 | 20 318 | 20 769 | 21 086 | 21 439 | 22 055 |
| Education services | 2 836 | 2 901 | 2 941 | 3 040 | 3 090 | 3 155 | 3 250 | 3 341 | 3 354 | 3 417 | 3 465 |
| Health care and social assistance | 14 840 | 15 253 | 15 735 | 16 188 | 16 540 | 16 820 | 17 069 | 17 428 | 17 731 | 18 022 | 18 590 |
| Ambulatory health care services | 5 114 | 5 286 | 5 474 | 5 647 | 5 793 | 5 975 | 6 136 | 6 307 | 6 477 | 6 632 | 6 872 |
| Hospitals | 4 345 | 4 423 | 4 515 | 4 627 | 4 667 | 4 679 | 4 722 | 4 779 | 4 786 | 4 787 | 4 913 |
| Nursing and residential health facilities | 2 855 | 2 893 | 2 958 | 3 016 | 3 082 | 3 124 | 3 168 | 3 196 | 3 229 | 3 258 | 3 295 |
| Social assistance | 2 527 | 2 651 | 2 788 | 2 898 | 2 997 | 3 043 | 3 043 | 3 147 | 3 240 | 3 346 | 3 510 |
| **Leisure and Hospitality** | 12 816 | 13 110 | 13 427 | 13 436 | 13 077 | 13 049 | 13 353 | 13 768 | 14 254 | 14 696 | 15 128 |
| Arts, entertainment, and recreation | 1 892 | 1 929 | 1 969 | 1 970 | 1 916 | 1 913 | 1 919 | 1 969 | 2 030 | 2 103 | 2 166 |
| Performing arts and spectator sports | 376 | 399 | 405 | 406 | 397 | 406 | 394 | 402 | 419 | 443 | 455 |
| Museums, historical sites | 121 | 124 | 130 | 132 | 129 | 128 | 133 | 136 | 140 | 147 | 152 |
| Amusements, gambling, and recreation | 1 395 | 1 406 | 1 434 | 1 433 | 1 389 | 1 379 | 1 392 | 1 430 | 1 470 | 1 513 | 1 559 |
| Accommodation and food services | 10 923 | 11 181 | 11 457 | 11 466 | 11 162 | 11 135 | 11 434 | 11 800 | 12 224 | 12 593 | 12 962 |
| Accommodation | 1 819 | 1 832 | 1 867 | 1 869 | 1 763 | 1 760 | 1 801 | 1 825 | 1 865 | 1 895 | 1 918 |
| Food services and drinking places | 9 104 | 9 349 | 9 590 | 9 598 | 9 399 | 9 376 | 9 633 | 9 975 | 10 359 | 10 698 | 11 044 |
| **Other Services** | 5 395 | 5 438 | 5 494 | 5 515 | 5 367 | 5 331 | 5 360 | 5 430 | 5 483 | 5 567 | 5 625 |
| Repair and maintenance | 1 236 | 1 249 | 1 253 | 1 227 | 1 150 | 1 139 | 1 169 | 1 194 | 1 217 | 1 242 | 1 277 |
| Personal and laundry services | 1 277 | 1 288 | 1 310 | 1 323 | 1 281 | 1 265 | 1 289 | 1 314 | 1 342 | 1 371 | 1 402 |
| Membership associations and organizations | 2 882 | 2 901 | 2 931 | 2 966 | 2 936 | 2 926 | 2 903 | 2 922 | 2 925 | 2 954 | 2 947 |
| **Government** | 21 804 | 21 974 | 22 218 | 22 509 | 22 555 | 22 490 | 22 086 | 21 920 | 21 853 | 21 882 | 22 007 |
| Federal | 2 732 | 2 732 | 2 734 | 2 762 | 2 832 | 2 977 | 2 859 | 2 820 | 2 769 | 2 733 | 2 754 |
| Federal, excluding U.S. Postal Service | 1 957 | 1 963 | 1 965 | 2 014 | 2 129 | 2 318 | 2 228 | 2 209 | 2 175 | 2 140 | 2 157 |
| State | 5 032 | 5 075 | 5 122 | 5 177 | 5 169 | 5 137 | 5 078 | 5 055 | 5 046 | 5 064 | 5 103 |
| State, excluding education | 2 772 | 2 782 | 2 804 | 2 823 | 2 809 | 2 764 | 2 704 | 2 666 | 2 653 | 2 661 | 2 674 |
| Local | 14 041 | 14 167 | 14 362 | 14 571 | 14 554 | 14 376 | 14 150 | 14 045 | 14 037 | 14 084 | 14 149 |
| Local, excluding education | 6 185 | 6 254 | 6 376 | 6 487 | 6 475 | 6 363 | 6 278 | 6 267 | 6 260 | 6 283 | 6 320 |

## Table 2-2.  Women Employees on Nonfarm Payrolls, by Super Sector and Selected Component Groups, NAICS Basis, 2005–2015

(Thousands of people.)

| Industry | 2005 | 2006 | 2007 | 2008 | 2009 | 2010 | 2011 | 2012 | 2013 | 2014 | 2015 |
|---|---|---|---|---|---|---|---|---|---|---|---|
| **TOTAL NONFARM** | 64 997 | 65 821 | 67 134 | 67 452 | 65 617 | 65 087 | 65 444 | 66 374 | 67 430 | 68 569 | 70 006 |
| **Total Private** | 52 609 | 53 603 | 54 556 | 54 544 | 52 717 | 52 258 | 52 833 | 53 881 | 54 963 | 56 074 | 57 414 |
| **Goods-Producing** | 5 104 | 5 083 | 5 041 | 4 866 | 4 289 | 4 088 | 4 057 | 4 093 | 4 125 | 4 211 | 4 280 |
| Mining and logging | 79 | 82 | 93 | 101 | 98 | 98 | 105 | 113 | 116 | 119 | 114 |
| Construction | 890 | 944 | 947 | 916 | 801 | 723 | 711 | 724 | 746 | 780 | 811 |
| Manufacturing | 4 135 | 4 057 | 4 001 | 3 848 | 3 390 | 3 268 | 3 241 | 3 256 | 3 263 | 3 312 | 3 355 |
| **Private Service-Providing** | 47 505 | 48 520 | 49 515 | 49 678 | 48 428 | 48 169 | 48 777 | 49 789 | 50 838 | 51 863 | 53 133 |
| Trade, transportation, and utilities | 10 535 | 10 627 | 10 849 | 10 782 | 10 233 | 10 007 | 10 091 | 10 255 | 10 467 | 10 682 | 10 895 |
| Wholesale trade | 1 738 | 1 796 | 1 831 | 1 820 | 1 705 | 1 641 | 1 667 | 1 700 | 1 701 | 1 716 | 1 729 |
| Retail trade | 7 524 | 7 587 | 7 758 | 7 713 | 7 361 | 7 226 | 7 280 | 7 390 | 7 573 | 7 731 | 7 881 |
| Transportation and warehousing | 1 130 | 1 098 | 1 110 | 1 098 | 1 024 | 1 002 | 1 009 | 1 027 | 1 057 | 1 101 | 1 150 |
| Utilities | 143 | 146 | 150 | 151 | 143 | 139 | 135 | 137 | 136 | 134 | 134 |
| Information | 1 333 | 1 306 | 1 285 | 1 260 | 1 170 | 1 104 | 1 084 | 1 076 | 1 079 | 1 094 | 1 103 |
| Financial activities | 4 923 | 5 055 | 4 988 | 4 851 | 4 648 | 4 530 | 4 490 | 4 519 | 4 547 | 4 572 | 4 638 |
| Professional and business services | 7 574 | 7 779 | 8 007 | 7 946 | 7 472 | 7 454 | 7 686 | 7 933 | 8 248 | 8 500 | 8 753 |
| Education and health services | 13 661 | 14 037 | 14 478 | 14 904 | 15 218 | 15 435 | 15 637 | 15 964 | 16 202 | 16 469 | 16 969 |
| Leisure and hospitality | 6 708 | 6 903 | 7 054 | 7 056 | 6 861 | 6 819 | 6 964 | 7 190 | 7 421 | 7 636 | 7 840 |
| Other services | 2 772 | 2 814 | 2 854 | 2 880 | 2 824 | 2 820 | 2 823 | 2 852 | 2 874 | 2 912 | 2 936 |
| **Government** | 12 389 | 12 218 | 12 578 | 12 908 | 12 900 | 12 829 | 12 611 | 12 493 | 12 468 | 12 495 | 12 593 |
| Federal | 1 177 | 1 194 | 1 202 | 1 224 | 1 259 | 1 326 | 1 269 | 1 249 | 1 230 | 1 209 | 1 219 |
| State | 2 575 | 2 630 | 2 651 | 2 684 | 2 628 | 2 639 | 2 643 | 2 648 | 2 649 | 2 659 | 2 717 |
| Local | 8 637 | 8 395 | 8 725 | 9 000 | 9 014 | 8 864 | 8 700 | 8 596 | 8 589 | 8 627 | 8 657 |

## Table 2-3. Production Workers on Private Nonfarm Payrolls, by Super Sector, NAICS Basis, 2005–2015

(Thousands of people.)

| Industry | 2005 | 2006 | 2007 | 2008 | 2009 | 2010 | 2011 | 2012 | 2013 | 2014 | 2015 |
|---|---|---|---|---|---|---|---|---|---|---|---|
| TOTAL PRIVATE | 91 443 | 93 776 | 95 260 | 94 675 | 89 629 | 88 954 | 90 619 | 92 780 | 94 589 | 96 701 | 98 822 |
| Goods-Producing | 16 145 | 16 559 | 16 405 | 15 724 | 13 399 | 12 774 | 13 005 | 13 287 | 13 481 | 13 858 | 14 122 |
| Mining and logging | 473 | 519 | 547 | 574 | 510 | 525 | 594 | 641 | 636 | 653 | 598 |
| Construction | 5 611 | 5 903 | 5 883 | 5 521 | 4 567 | 4 172 | 4 184 | 4 246 | 4 423 | 4 640 | 4 855 |
| Manufacturing | 10 060 | 10 137 | 9 975 | 9 629 | 8 322 | 8 077 | 8 228 | 8 400 | 8 422 | 8 565 | 8 669 |
| Private Service-Providing | 75 298 | 77 217 | 78 855 | 78 951 | 76 230 | 76 180 | 77 614 | 79 493 | 81 109 | 82 843 | 84 700 |
| Trade, transportation, and utilities | 21 830 | 22 166 | 22 546 | 22 337 | 21 116 | 20 874 | 21 234 | 21 617 | 21 875 | 22 280 | 22 658 |
| Wholesale trade | 4 584 | 4 724 | 4 851 | 4 822 | 4 506 | 4 378 | 4 443 | 4 562 | 4 621 | 4 696 | 4 718 |
| Retail trade | 13 030 | 13 110 | 13 317 | 13 134 | 12 472 | 12 425 | 12 647 | 12 793 | 12 923 | 13 107 | 13 295 |
| Transportation and warehousing | 3 774 | 3 889 | 3 935 | 3 931 | 3 688 | 3 627 | 3 703 | 3 820 | 3 886 | 4 032 | 4 195 |
| Utilities | 443 | 443 | 444 | 450 | 451 | 444 | 441 | 443 | 445 | 446 | 449 |
| Information | 2 386 | 2 399 | 2 403 | 2 388 | 2 240 | 2 170 | 2 148 | 2 164 | 2 194 | 2 209 | 2 227 |
| Financial activities | 6 127 | 6 312 | 6 365 | 6 320 | 6 066 | 5 942 | 5 900 | 5 986 | 6 068 | 6 155 | 6 278 |
| Professional and business services | 13 854 | 14 446 | 14 784 | 14 585 | 13 520 | 13 699 | 14 251 | 14 802 | 15 305 | 15 766 | 16 165 |
| Education and health services | 15 401 | 15 832 | 16 318 | 16 842 | 17 240 | 17 531 | 17 818 | 18 230 | 18 505 | 18 827 | 19 359 |
| Leisure and hospitality | 11 263 | 11 568 | 11 861 | 11 873 | 11 560 | 11 507 | 11 772 | 12 154 | 12 589 | 12 969 | 13 332 |
| Other services | 4 438 | 4 494 | 4 578 | 4 606 | 4 488 | 4 458 | 4 491 | 4 541 | 4 573 | 4 637 | 4 681 |

## Table 2-4. Production Workers on Manufacturing Payrolls, by Industry, NAICS Basis, 2005–2015

(Thousands of people.)

| Industry | 2005 | 2006 | 2007 | 2008 | 2009 | 2010 | 2011 | 2012 | 2013 | 2014 | 2015 |
|---|---|---|---|---|---|---|---|---|---|---|---|
| Total Manufacturing | 10 060 | 10 137 | 9 975 | 9 629 | 8 322 | 8 077 | 8 228 | 8 400 | 8 422 | 8 565 | 8 669 |
| Durable Goods | 6 220 | 6 355 | 6 250 | 5 975 | 4 990 | 4 829 | 4 986 | 5 152 | 5 185 | 5 282 | 5 343 |
| Wood products | 454 | 451 | 407 | 358 | 278 | 269 | 269 | 272 | 283 | 298 | 303 |
| Nometallic mineral products | 387 | 391 | 384 | 363 | 303 | 284 | 278 | 273 | 275 | 280 | 295 |
| Primary metals | 363 | 363 | 358 | 348 | 273 | 275 | 301 | 317 | 306 | 310 | 306 |
| Fabricated metal products | 1 129 | 1 162 | 1 171 | 1 143 | 961 | 935 | 994 | 1 050 | 1 063 | 1 071 | 1 069 |
| Machinery | 749 | 770 | 774 | 772 | 641 | 616 | 662 | 700 | 699 | 716 | 712 |
| Computer and electronic products | 700 | 756 | 744 | 730 | 654 | 629 | 630 | 628 | 610 | 589 | 593 |
| Electrical equipment and appliances | 300 | 303 | 305 | 305 | 266 | 251 | 248 | 249 | 245 | 248 | 258 |
| Transportation equipment | 1 277 | 1 304 | 1 275 | 1 177 | 948 | 937 | 972 | 1 024 | 1 053 | 1 103 | 1 136 |
| Furniture and related products | 436 | 433 | 409 | 364 | 284 | 263 | 260 | 259 | 266 | 276 | 284 |
| Miscellaneous manufacturing | 424 | 423 | 425 | 416 | 382 | 370 | 373 | 380 | 386 | 390 | 386 |
| Nondurable Goods | 3 841 | 3 782 | 3 725 | 3 653 | 3 332 | 3 248 | 3 241 | 3 248 | 3 237 | 3 283 | 3 326 |
| Food manufacturing | 1 170 | 1 172 | 1 184 | 1 184 | 1 161 | 1 152 | 1 158 | 1 169 | 1 169 | 1 176 | 1 184 |
| Textile mills | 174 | 158 | 137 | 122 | 99 | 96 | 98 | 96 | 92 | 91 | 90 |
| Textile products mills | 143 | 135 | 123 | 115 | 98 | 92 | 89 | 85 | 83 | 86 | 88 |
| Apparel | 193 | 182 | 173 | 163 | 132 | 120 | 112 | 109 | 106 | 103 | 104 |
| Paper and paper products | 365 | 357 | 350 | 344 | 313 | 302 | 295 | 288 | 279 | 277 | 277 |
| Printing and related support | 447 | 447 | 443 | 424 | 369 | 342 | 327 | 316 | 310 | 312 | 309 |
| Petroleum and coal products | 75 | 72 | 73 | 77 | 70 | 70 | 70 | 72 | 70 | 72 | 75 |
| Chemicals | 510 | 508 | 504 | 512 | 479 | 474 | 480 | 491 | 490 | 497 | 508 |
| Plastics and rubber products | 620 | 608 | 592 | 572 | 476 | 472 | 482 | 487 | 497 | 518 | 530 |

## Table 2-5.  Total Employees on Manufacturing Payrolls, by Industry, NAICS Basis, 2005–2015

(Thousands of people.)

| Industry | 2005 | 2006 | 2007 | 2008 | 2009 | 2010 | 2011 | 2012 | 2013 | 2014 | 2015 |
|---|---|---|---|---|---|---|---|---|---|---|---|
| **Total Manufacturing** | 14 227 | 14 155 | 13 879 | 13 406 | 11 847 | 11 528 | 11 726 | 11 927 | 12 020 | 12 185 | 12 318 |
| **Durable Goods** | 8 956 | 8 981 | 8 808 | 8 463 | 7 284 | 7 064 | 7 273 | 7 470 | 7 548 | 7 674 | 7 756 |
| Wood products | 561 | 561 | 517 | 458 | 360 | 342 | 337 | 339 | 353 | 372 | 380 |
| Nometallic mineral products | 505 | 510 | 501 | 465 | 394 | 371 | 367 | 365 | 373 | 384 | 396 |
| Primary metals | 466 | 464 | 456 | 442 | 362 | 362 | 388 | 402 | 395 | 399 | 393 |
| Fabricated metal products | 1 522 | 1 553 | 1 563 | 1 528 | 1 312 | 1 282 | 1 347 | 1 410 | 1 432 | 1 454 | 1 459 |
| Machinery | 1 166 | 1 183 | 1 187 | 1 188 | 1 029 | 996 | 1 056 | 1 099 | 1 105 | 1 127 | 1 122 |
| Computer and electronic products | 1 316 | 1 308 | 1 273 | 1 244 | 1 137 | 1 095 | 1 104 | 1 089 | 1 066 | 1 049 | 1 050 |
| Electrical equipment and appliances | 434 | 433 | 429 | 424 | 374 | 360 | 366 | 373 | 374 | 378 | 384 |
| Transportation equipment | 1 772 | 1 769 | 1 712 | 1 608 | 1 348 | 1 333 | 1 382 | 1 461 | 1 509 | 1 559 | 1 599 |
| Furniture and related products | 566 | 558 | 529 | 478 | 384 | 357 | 353 | 351 | 360 | 370 | 381 |
| Miscellaneous manufacturing | 647 | 644 | 642 | 629 | 584 | 567 | 574 | 580 | 581 | 582 | 592 |
| **Nondurable Goods** | 5 271 | 5 174 | 5 071 | 4 943 | 4 564 | 4 464 | 4 453 | 4 457 | 4 472 | 4 512 | 4 562 |
| Food manufacturing | 1 478 | 1 479 | 1 484 | 1 481 | 1 456 | 1 451 | 1 459 | 1 469 | 1 474 | 1 484 | 1 505 |
| Beverage | 5 271 | 5 174 | 5 071 | 4 943 | 4 564 | 4 464 | 4 453 | 4 457 | 4 472 | 4 512 | 4 562 |
| Tobacco and tobacco products | 176 | 167 | 158 | 147 | 126 | 119 | 118 | 116 | 114 | 115 | 116 |
| Textile mills | 251 | 232 | 215 | 199 | 168 | 157 | 152 | 148 | 145 | 140 | 137 |
| Textile products mills | 40 | 37 | 34 | 33 | 29 | 28 | 29 | 30 | 30 | 29 | 30 |
| Apparel | 484 | 471 | 458 | 445 | 407 | 395 | 387 | 380 | 378 | 373 | 373 |
| Leather and allied products | 646 | 634 | 622 | 594 | 522 | 488 | 472 | 462 | 452 | 454 | 449 |
| Paper and paper products | 112 | 113 | 115 | 117 | 115 | 114 | 112 | 112 | 110 | 112 | 114 |
| Printing and related support | 872 | 866 | 861 | 847 | 804 | 787 | 784 | 783 | 793 | 803 | 810 |
| Petroleum and coal products | 802 | 786 | 757 | 729 | 625 | 625 | 635 | 645 | 659 | 674 | 687 |

## Table 2-6. Average Weekly Hours of All Employees on Private Nonfarm Payrolls by NAICS Super Sector, 2010–2015

(Hours per week, seasonally adjusted.)

| Year and month | Total private | Mining and logging | Construction | Manufacturing | Trade, transportation, and utilities | | | | Information | Financial activities | Professional and business services | Education and health services | Leisure and hospitality | Other services |
|---|---|---|---|---|---|---|---|---|---|---|---|---|---|---|
| | | | | | Total | Wholesale trade | Retail trade | Utilities | | | | | | |
| 2010 | 34.1 | 43.4 | 37.8 | 40.2 | 34.2 | 38.1 | 31.3 | 41.1 | 36.5 | 36.9 | 35.4 | 32.7 | 25.7 | 31.6 |
| 2011 | 34.3 | 44.5 | 38.3 | 40.5 | 34.6 | 38.6 | 31.6 | 41.8 | 36.6 | 37.3 | 35.7 | 32.7 | 25.9 | 31.7 |
| 2012 | 34.5 | 44.0 | 38.7 | 40.7 | 34.6 | 38.7 | 31.7 | 41.8 | 36.6 | 37.4 | 36.0 | 32.8 | 26.1 | 31.6 |
| 2013 | 34.4 | 44.0 | 39.0 | 40.8 | 34.5 | 38.7 | 31.4 | 42.2 | 36.6 | 37.1 | 36.1 | 32.7 | 26.0 | 31.7 |
| 2014 | 34.5 | 44.8 | 39.0 | 41.0 | 34.5 | 38.9 | 31.3 | 42.4 | 36.8 | 37.3 | 36.3 | 32.7 | 26.2 | 31.8 |
| 2015 | 34.5 | 44.0 | 39.1 | 40.8 | 34.6 | 38.9 | 31.4 | 42.5 | 36.3 | 37.6 | 36.2 | 32.8 | 26.3 | 31.9 |
| **2011** | | | | | | | | | | | | | | |
| January | 34.2 | 44.3 | 37.6 | 40.3 | 34.4 | 38.4 | 31.4 | 41.8 | 36.6 | 37.0 | 35.6 | 32.7 | 25.8 | 31.7 |
| February | 34.3 | 44.0 | 37.8 | 40.5 | 34.4 | 38.5 | 31.4 | 41.4 | 36.6 | 37.1 | 35.7 | 32.7 | 25.9 | 31.7 |
| March | 34.3 | 44.4 | 37.9 | 40.4 | 34.6 | 38.6 | 31.5 | 42.0 | 36.7 | 37.1 | 35.6 | 32.8 | 25.8 | 31.7 |
| April | 34.4 | 44.6 | 38.1 | 40.4 | 34.7 | 38.7 | 31.7 | 42.0 | 36.7 | 37.2 | 35.7 | 32.8 | 26.0 | 31.7 |
| May | 34.4 | 44.8 | 38.5 | 40.5 | 34.5 | 38.6 | 31.5 | 41.9 | 36.7 | 37.2 | 35.7 | 32.8 | 25.8 | 31.7 |
| June | 34.3 | 44.6 | 38.4 | 40.4 | 34.6 | 38.7 | 31.5 | 41.7 | 36.6 | 37.3 | 35.7 | 32.8 | 25.8 | 31.8 |
| July | 34.4 | 44.3 | 38.5 | 40.4 | 34.6 | 38.7 | 31.6 | 41.5 | 36.7 | 37.4 | 35.8 | 32.8 | 26.0 | 31.8 |
| August | 34.3 | 44.1 | 38.3 | 40.4 | 34.5 | 38.5 | 31.5 | 41.4 | 36.5 | 37.1 | 35.7 | 32.7 | 25.9 | 31.6 |
| September | 34.4 | 44.6 | 38.5 | 40.3 | 34.7 | 38.8 | 31.7 | 42.4 | 36.7 | 37.5 | 35.8 | 32.7 | 25.9 | 31.7 |
| October | 34.4 | 45.5 | 38.3 | 40.7 | 34.6 | 38.8 | 31.7 | 42.4 | 36.8 | 37.4 | 35.8 | 32.7 | 26.1 | 31.8 |
| November | 34.4 | 43.8 | 38.3 | 40.4 | 34.6 | 38.8 | 31.7 | 41.7 | 36.8 | 37.4 | 35.8 | 32.7 | 26.1 | 31.7 |
| December | 34.4 | 44.6 | 38.5 | 40.6 | 34.6 | 38.8 | 31.7 | 41.0 | 36.8 | 37.3 | 35.8 | 32.8 | 26.1 | 31.7 |
| **2012** | | | | | | | | | | | | | | |
| January | 34.5 | 45.3 | 38.6 | 40.8 | 34.7 | 38.8 | 31.8 | 41.4 | 36.8 | 37.3 | 35.8 | 32.7 | 26.2 | 31.7 |
| February | 34.5 | 44.6 | 38.7 | 40.8 | 34.7 | 38.8 | 31.9 | 41.2 | 36.8 | 37.3 | 35.9 | 32.8 | 26.0 | 31.7 |
| March | 34.4 | 44.1 | 38.6 | 40.7 | 34.6 | 38.7 | 31.8 | 41.3 | 36.7 | 37.3 | 35.8 | 32.8 | 26.1 | 31.7 |
| April | 34.4 | 44.3 | 38.7 | 40.9 | 34.6 | 38.7 | 31.7 | 41.8 | 36.6 | 37.2 | 35.9 | 32.7 | 26.0 | 31.7 |
| May | 34.4 | 43.7 | 38.5 | 40.6 | 34.5 | 38.6 | 31.6 | 41.6 | 36.6 | 37.0 | 35.9 | 32.7 | 26.0 | 31.5 |
| June | 34.4 | 44.0 | 38.6 | 40.7 | 34.6 | 38.6 | 31.7 | 41.6 | 36.6 | 37.1 | 35.9 | 32.8 | 26.1 | 31.6 |
| July | 34.4 | 44.2 | 38.5 | 40.8 | 34.5 | 38.6 | 31.5 | 42.1 | 36.5 | 37.1 | 36.0 | 32.7 | 26.0 | 31.6 |
| August | 34.4 | 43.6 | 38.6 | 40.6 | 34.5 | 38.5 | 31.5 | 41.8 | 36.5 | 37.1 | 36.0 | 32.8 | 26.0 | 31.5 |
| September | 34.4 | 43.6 | 38.7 | 40.7 | 34.6 | 38.7 | 31.6 | 41.8 | 36.5 | 37.3 | 36.1 | 32.7 | 26.1 | 31.6 |
| October | 34.4 | 43.5 | 38.8 | 40.6 | 34.5 | 38.5 | 31.5 | 41.7 | 36.3 | 37.2 | 35.8 | 32.8 | 26.0 | 31.6 |
| November | 34.4 | 43.0 | 38.9 | 40.6 | 34.6 | 38.5 | 31.6 | 43.7 | 36.4 | 37.2 | 36.0 | 32.7 | 26.0 | 31.5 |
| December | 34.5 | 43.4 | 39.1 | 40.7 | 34.6 | 38.7 | 31.5 | 42.2 | 36.4 | 37.3 | 36.1 | 32.8 | 26.1 | 31.6 |
| **2013** | | | | | | | | | | | | | | |
| January | 34.4 | 42.5 | 38.9 | 40.6 | 34.4 | 38.5 | 31.4 | 42.2 | 36.4 | 37.0 | 36.0 | 32.8 | 26.0 | 31.6 |
| February | 34.5 | 43.3 | 39.2 | 40.9 | 34.6 | 38.7 | 31.5 | 42.5 | 36.4 | 37.2 | 36.1 | 32.8 | 26.1 | 31.7 |
| March | 34.5 | 43.3 | 39.0 | 40.8 | 34.7 | 38.8 | 31.7 | 42.4 | 36.5 | 37.2 | 36.1 | 32.8 | 26.1 | 31.8 |
| April | 34.4 | 43.4 | 38.9 | 40.7 | 34.5 | 38.6 | 31.5 | 42.1 | 36.5 | 37.2 | 36.0 | 32.7 | 26.0 | 31.7 |
| May | 34.5 | 44.1 | 39.1 | 40.7 | 34.6 | 38.8 | 31.6 | 42.2 | 36.7 | 37.2 | 36.1 | 32.7 | 26.0 | 31.8 |
| June | 34.5 | 44.2 | 39.0 | 40.8 | 34.6 | 38.8 | 31.5 | 42.6 | 36.7 | 37.3 | 36.1 | 32.8 | 26.0 | 31.8 |
| July | 34.4 | 44.2 | 38.8 | 40.7 | 34.5 | 38.7 | 31.5 | 42.0 | 36.7 | 37.0 | 36.0 | 32.7 | 25.9 | 31.7 |
| August | 34.5 | 44.2 | 38.9 | 40.9 | 34.6 | 38.8 | 31.5 | 42.2 | 36.8 | 37.2 | 36.1 | 32.7 | 25.9 | 31.8 |
| September | 34.4 | 44.6 | 39.0 | 40.9 | 34.5 | 38.6 | 31.3 | 42.4 | 36.7 | 37.1 | 36.1 | 32.7 | 26.0 | 31.8 |
| October | 34.4 | 44.2 | 38.8 | 40.9 | 34.5 | 38.8 | 31.3 | 42.0 | 36.8 | 37.1 | 36.0 | 32.7 | 26.0 | 31.7 |
| November | 34.5 | 44.7 | 39.2 | 40.9 | 34.4 | 38.9 | 31.1 | 42.0 | 36.7 | 37.2 | 36.2 | 32.7 | 26.0 | 31.8 |
| December | 34.3 | 44.7 | 38.6 | 40.9 | 34.4 | 38.6 | 31.3 | 42.1 | 36.8 | 37.0 | 36.1 | 32.6 | 25.7 | 31.7 |
| **2014** | | | | | | | | | | | | | | |
| January | 34.4 | 44.1 | 38.7 | 40.7 | 34.4 | 38.7 | 31.2 | 42.3 | 36.7 | 37.1 | 36.1 | 32.7 | 26.0 | 31.7 |
| February | 34.3 | 45.0 | 37.8 | 40.7 | 34.3 | 38.7 | 31.0 | 42.3 | 36.8 | 37.2 | 36.1 | 32.6 | 26.0 | 31.7 |
| March | 34.6 | 45.7 | 39.1 | 41.0 | 34.5 | 38.9 | 31.3 | 42.4 | 36.9 | 37.2 | 36.4 | 32.7 | 26.2 | 31.9 |
| April | 34.5 | 44.7 | 39.1 | 40.9 | 34.6 | 38.8 | 31.5 | 42.2 | 36.8 | 37.1 | 36.2 | 32.7 | 26.2 | 31.8 |
| May | 34.5 | 44.6 | 39.0 | 41.1 | 34.4 | 38.9 | 31.2 | 42.4 | 36.7 | 37.3 | 36.3 | 32.7 | 26.1 | 31.8 |
| June | 34.5 | 45.0 | 39.1 | 41.1 | 34.5 | 38.9 | 31.3 | 42.3 | 36.6 | 37.2 | 36.3 | 32.7 | 26.1 | 31.7 |
| July | 34.5 | 44.6 | 39.3 | 40.9 | 34.5 | 38.9 | 31.3 | 42.5 | 36.7 | 37.2 | 36.2 | 32.7 | 26.2 | 31.7 |
| August | 34.5 | 45.0 | 39.1 | 41.0 | 34.5 | 38.9 | 31.3 | 42.4 | 36.6 | 37.2 | 36.2 | 32.8 | 26.2 | 31.8 |
| September | 34.5 | 44.5 | 39.0 | 40.9 | 34.5 | 39.0 | 31.3 | 42.2 | 36.6 | 37.3 | 36.2 | 32.8 | 26.2 | 31.8 |
| October | 34.5 | 44.9 | 38.8 | 40.9 | 34.6 | 38.8 | 31.4 | 42.6 | 36.7 | 37.3 | 36.2 | 32.8 | 26.2 | 31.8 |
| November | 34.6 | 44.8 | 39.0 | 41.1 | 34.6 | 38.9 | 31.4 | 42.6 | 36.6 | 37.3 | 36.3 | 32.8 | 26.2 | 31.8 |
| December | 34.6 | 44.9 | 39.2 | 40.9 | 34.6 | 38.8 | 31.4 | 42.2 | 36.5 | 37.4 | 36.3 | 32.8 | 26.2 | 31.8 |
| **2015** | | | | | | | | | | | | | | |
| January | 34.6 | 44.5 | 39.0 | 41.0 | 34.6 | 38.9 | 31.4 | 42.3 | 36.5 | 37.5 | 36.2 | 32.8 | 26.3 | 31.9 |
| February | 34.6 | 44.5 | 39.0 | 40.9 | 34.6 | 38.9 | 31.4 | 42.4 | 36.4 | 37.4 | 36.2 | 32.8 | 26.4 | 31.9 |
| March | 34.5 | 44.5 | 39.0 | 40.8 | 34.6 | 38.8 | 31.4 | 42.9 | 36.4 | 37.5 | 36.2 | 32.8 | 26.2 | 31.8 |
| April | 34.5 | 44.1 | 38.9 | 40.7 | 34.5 | 38.8 | 31.3 | 42.7 | 36.3 | 37.6 | 36.0 | 32.8 | 26.2 | 31.7 |
| May | 34.5 | 43.6 | 39.0 | 40.7 | 34.6 | 38.9 | 31.4 | 42.3 | 36.3 | 37.6 | 36.2 | 32.8 | 26.3 | 31.8 |
| June | 34.5 | 43.3 | 39.3 | 40.6 | 34.6 | 38.8 | 31.4 | 42.2 | 36.3 | 37.6 | 36.1 | 32.8 | 26.3 | 31.8 |
| July | 34.6 | 44.0 | 39.0 | 40.8 | 34.6 | 38.9 | 31.4 | 42.6 | 36.3 | 37.7 | 36.2 | 32.9 | 26.3 | 31.9 |
| August | 34.6 | 43.9 | 39.1 | 40.8 | 34.7 | 38.8 | 31.5 | 42.6 | 36.3 | 37.6 | 36.2 | 32.9 | 26.3 | 31.9 |
| September | 34.5 | 44.0 | 39.1 | 40.6 | 34.7 | 38.8 | 31.6 | 42.5 | 36.0 | 37.7 | 36.1 | 32.8 | 26.3 | 31.8 |
| October | 34.5 | 44.1 | 39.5 | 40.7 | 34.6 | 38.9 | 31.4 | 42.6 | 36.0 | 37.6 | 36.2 | 32.8 | 26.3 | 31.9 |
| November | 34.5 | 44.1 | 39.1 | 40.7 | 34.6 | 38.9 | 31.4 | 42.6 | 36.1 | 37.6 | 36.1 | 32.8 | 26.2 | 31.9 |
| December | 34.5 | 44.0 | 39.6 | 40.6 | 34.6 | 38.9 | 31.3 | 42.4 | 36.0 | 37.7 | 36.2 | 32.9 | 26.2 | 31.9 |

**Table 2-7.  Average Weekly Hours of Production Workers on Private Nonfarm Payrolls, by Super Sector, NAICS Basis, 2005–2015**

(Hours.)

| Industry | 2005 | 2006 | 2007 | 2008 | 2009 | 2010 | 2011 | 2012 | 2013 | 2014 | 2015 |
|---|---|---|---|---|---|---|---|---|---|---|---|
| **TOTAL PRIVATE** | 33.8 | 33.9 | 33.8 | 33.6 | 33.1 | 33.4 | 33.6 | 33.7 | 33.7 | 33.7 | 33.7 |
| **Goods-Producing** | 40.1 | 40.5 | 40.6 | 40.2 | 39.2 | 40.4 | 40.9 | 41.1 | 41.3 | 41.5 | 41.2 |
| Mining and logging | 45.6 | 45.6 | 45.9 | 45.1 | 43.2 | 44.6 | 46.7 | 46.6 | 45.9 | 47.3 | 45.8 |
| Construction | 38.6 | 39.0 | 39.0 | 38.5 | 37.6 | 38.4 | 39.0 | 39.3 | 39.6 | 39.6 | 39.6 |
| Manufacturing | 40.7 | 41.1 | 41.2 | 40.8 | 39.8 | 41.1 | 41.4 | 41.7 | 41.8 | 42.0 | 41.8 |
| **Private Service-Providing** | 32.4 | 32.4 | 32.4 | 32.3 | 32.1 | 32.2 | 32.4 | 32.5 | 32.4 | 32.4 | 32.4 |
| Trade, transportation, and utilities | 33.4 | 33.4 | 33.3 | 33.2 | 32.9 | 33.3 | 33.7 | 33.8 | 33.7 | 33.6 | 33.7 |
| Wholesale trade | 38.3 | 38.7 | 38.7 | 38.8 | 38.3 | 38.5 | 38.9 | 39.1 | 39.2 | 39.4 | 39.3 |
| Retail trade | 30.6 | 30.5 | 30.2 | 30.0 | 29.9 | 30.2 | 30.5 | 30.6 | 30.2 | 30.0 | 30.0 |
| Transportation and warehousing | 37.0 | 36.9 | 37.0 | 36.4 | 36.0 | 37.1 | 37.8 | 38.0 | 38.5 | 38.4 | 38.8 |
| Utilities | 41.1 | 41.4 | 42.4 | 42.7 | 42.0 | 42.0 | 42.1 | 41.1 | 41.7 | 42.3 | 42.4 |
| Information | 36.5 | 36.6 | 36.5 | 36.7 | 36.6 | 36.3 | 36.2 | 36.0 | 35.9 | 35.9 | 35.7 |
| Financial activities | 36.0 | 35.8 | 35.9 | 35.9 | 36.1 | 36.2 | 36.4 | 36.8 | 36.7 | 36.7 | 37.1 |
| Professional and business services | 34.2 | 34.6 | 34.8 | 34.8 | 34.7 | 35.1 | 35.2 | 35.3 | 35.4 | 35.6 | 35.5 |
| Education and health services | 32.6 | 32.5 | 32.5 | 32.4 | 32.2 | 32.0 | 32.2 | 32.3 | 32.1 | 32.0 | 32.1 |
| Leisure and hospitality | 25.7 | 25.7 | 25.5 | 25.2 | 24.8 | 24.8 | 24.8 | 25.0 | 25.0 | 25.1 | 25.1 |
| Other services | 30.9 | 30.9 | 30.9 | 30.8 | 30.5 | 30.7 | 30.8 | 30.7 | 30.8 | 30.7 | 30.7 |

## Table 2-8.  Employees on Total Nonfarm Payrolls, by State and Selected Territory, 1970–2015

(Thousands of people.)

| State | 1970 | 1971 | 1972 | 1973 | 1974 | 1975 | 1976 | 1977 | 1978 | 1979 | 1980 | 1981 | 1982 | 1983 | 1984 | 1985 |
|---|---|---|---|---|---|---|---|---|---|---|---|---|---|---|---|---|
| UNITED STATES | 71 006 | 71 335 | 73 798 | 76 912 | 78 389 | 77 069 | 79 502 | 82 593 | 86 826 | 89 933 | 90 533 | 91 297 | 89 689 | 90 295 | 94 548 | 97 532 |
| Alabama | 1 010 | 1 022 | 1 072 | 1 136 | 1 170 | 1 155 | 1 207 | 1 269 | 1 337 | 1 362 | 1 356 | 1 348 | 1 313 | 1 329 | 1 388 | 1 427 |
| Alaska | 93 | 98 | 104 | 110 | 128 | 162 | 172 | 163 | 164 | 167 | 169 | 186 | 200 | 214 | 226 | 231 |
| Arizona | 547 | 581 | 646 | 714 | 746 | 729 | 759 | 809 | 895 | 980 | 1 014 | 1 041 | 1 030 | 1 078 | 1 182 | 1 279 |
| Arkansas | 536 | 551 | 582 | 615 | 641 | 624 | 660 | 696 | 733 | 750 | 742 | 740 | 720 | 741 | 780 | 797 |
| California | 6 946 | 6 917 | 7 210 | 7 622 | 7 834 | 7 847 | 8 154 | 8 600 | 9 200 | 9 666 | 9 853 | 9 993 | 9 822 | 9 933 | 10 408 | 10 792 |
| Colorado | 750 | 787 | 869 | 936 | 960 | 964 | 1 003 | 1 058 | 1 150 | 1 218 | 1 251 | 1 295 | 1 317 | 1 327 | 1 402 | 1 419 |
| Connecticut | 1 198 | 1 164 | 1 190 | 1 239 | 1 264 | 1 223 | 1 240 | 1 282 | 1 346 | 1 398 | 1 427 | 1 438 | 1 429 | 1 444 | 1 517 | 1 558 |
| Delaware | 217 | 225 | 232 | 239 | 233 | 230 | 237 | 239 | 248 | 257 | 259 | 259 | 259 | 266 | 280 | 293 |
| District of Columbia | 567 | 567 | 572 | 574 | 580 | 577 | 576 | 579 | 596 | 613 | 616 | 611 | 598 | 597 | 614 | 629 |
| Florida | 2 152 | 2 276 | 2 513 | 2 779 | 2 864 | 2 746 | 2 784 | 2 933 | 3 181 | 3 381 | 3 576 | 3 736 | 3 762 | 3 905 | 4 204 | 4 410 |
| Georgia | 1 558 | 1 603 | 1 695 | 1 803 | 1 828 | 1 756 | 1 839 | 1 927 | 2 050 | 2 128 | 2 159 | 2 199 | 2 202 | 2 280 | 2 449 | 2 570 |
| Hawaii | 294 | 302 | 313 | 328 | 336 | 343 | 349 | 359 | 377 | 394 | 404 | 405 | 399 | 406 | 413 | 426 |
| Idaho | 208 | 217 | 237 | 252 | 267 | 273 | 291 | 307 | 331 | 338 | 330 | 328 | 312 | 318 | 331 | 336 |
| Illinois | 4 346 | 4 296 | 4 315 | 4 467 | 4 546 | 4 419 | 4 565 | 4 656 | 4 789 | 4 880 | 4 850 | 4 732 | 4 593 | 4 531 | 4 672 | 4 755 |
| Indiana | 1 849 | 1 841 | 1 922 | 2 028 | 2 031 | 1 942 | 2 024 | 2 114 | 2 206 | 2 236 | 2 130 | 2 115 | 2 028 | 2 030 | 2 122 | 2 169 |
| Iowa | 877 | 883 | 912 | 961 | 999 | 999 | 1 037 | 1 079 | 1 119 | 1 132 | 1 110 | 1 089 | 1 042 | 1 040 | 1 075 | 1 074 |
| Kansas | 679 | 678 | 718 | 763 | 790 | 801 | 835 | 871 | 913 | 947 | 945 | 950 | 921 | 922 | 961 | 968 |
| Kentucky | 910 | 932 | 988 | 1 039 | 1 066 | 1 058 | 1 103 | 1 148 | 1 210 | 1 245 | 1 210 | 1 196 | 1 161 | 1 152 | 1 214 | 1 250 |
| Louisiana | 1 034 | 1 056 | 1 129 | 1 176 | 1 221 | 1 250 | 1 314 | 1 365 | 1 464 | 1 517 | 1 579 | 1 631 | 1 607 | 1 565 | 1 602 | 1 591 |
| Maine | 332 | 332 | 344 | 355 | 362 | 357 | 375 | 388 | 406 | 416 | 418 | 419 | 416 | 425 | 446 | 458 |
| Maryland | 1 349 | 1 372 | 1 415 | 1 472 | 1 494 | 1 479 | 1 498 | 1 546 | 1 626 | 1 691 | 1 712 | 1 716 | 1 676 | 1 724 | 1 814 | 1 888 |
| Massachusetts | 2 244 | 2 211 | 2 252 | 2 333 | 2 354 | 2 273 | 2 324 | 2 416 | 2 526 | 2 604 | 2 654 | 2 672 | 2 642 | 2 697 | 2 856 | 2 931 |
| Michigan | 2 999 | 2 995 | 3 119 | 3 284 | 3 278 | 3 137 | 3 283 | 3 442 | 3 609 | 3 637 | 3 443 | 3 364 | 3 193 | 3 223 | 3 381 | 3 562 |
| Minnesota | 1 315 | 1 310 | 1 357 | 1 436 | 1 481 | 1 474 | 1 521 | 1 597 | 1 689 | 1 767 | 1 770 | 1 761 | 1 707 | 1 718 | 1 820 | 1 866 |
| Mississippi | 584 | 602 | 649 | 693 | 711 | 692 | 728 | 766 | 814 | 838 | 829 | 819 | 791 | 793 | 821 | 839 |
| Missouri | 1 668 | 1 661 | 1 700 | 1 771 | 1 789 | 1 741 | 1 798 | 1 862 | 1 953 | 2 011 | 1 970 | 1 957 | 1 923 | 1 937 | 2 033 | 2 095 |
| Montana | 199 | 205 | 215 | 224 | 234 | 238 | 251 | 265 | 280 | 284 | 280 | 282 | 274 | 276 | 281 | 279 |
| Nebraska | 484 | 491 | 517 | 541 | 562 | 558 | 572 | 594 | 610 | 631 | 628 | 623 | 610 | 611 | 635 | 650 |
| Nevada | 203 | 211 | 224 | 245 | 256 | 263 | 280 | 308 | 350 | 384 | 400 | 411 | 401 | 403 | 426 | 446 |
| New Hampshire | 259 | 260 | 279 | 298 | 300 | 293 | 313 | 337 | 360 | 379 | 385 | 395 | 394 | 410 | 442 | 466 |
| New Jersey | 2 606 | 2 608 | 2 673 | 2 760 | 2 783 | 2 700 | 2 754 | 2 837 | 2 962 | 3 027 | 3 060 | 3 099 | 3 093 | 3 165 | 3 329 | 3 414 |
| New Mexico | 293 | 306 | 328 | 346 | 360 | 370 | 390 | 415 | 444 | 461 | 465 | 476 | 474 | 480 | 503 | 520 |
| New York | 7 157 | 7 011 | 7 039 | 7 132 | 7 077 | 6 830 | 6 790 | 6 858 | 7 045 | 7 179 | 7 207 | 7 287 | 7 255 | 7 313 | 7 570 | 7 751 |
| North Carolina | 1 783 | 1 814 | 1 912 | 2 018 | 2 048 | 1 980 | 2 083 | 2 171 | 2 278 | 2 373 | 2 380 | 2 392 | 2 347 | 2 419 | 2 565 | 2 651 |
| North Dakota | 164 | 167 | 176 | 184 | 194 | 204 | 215 | 221 | 234 | 244 | 245 | 249 | 250 | 251 | 253 | 252 |
| Ohio | 3 881 | 3 840 | 3 938 | 4 113 | 4 169 | 4 016 | 4 095 | 4 230 | 4 395 | 4 485 | 4 367 | 4 318 | 4 124 | 4 093 | 4 260 | 4 373 |
| Oklahoma | 763 | 774 | 812 | 852 | 887 | 900 | 931 | 972 | 1 036 | 1 088 | 1 138 | 1 201 | 1 217 | 1 171 | 1 180 | 1 165 |
| Oregon | 711 | 729 | 775 | 816 | 838 | 837 | 879 | 937 | 1 009 | 1 056 | 1 045 | 1 019 | 961 | 967 | 1 007 | 1 030 |
| Pennsylvania | 4 352 | 4 291 | 4 400 | 4 507 | 4 515 | 4 436 | 4 513 | 4 565 | 4 716 | 4 806 | 4 753 | 4 729 | 4 580 | 4 524 | 4 655 | 4 730 |
| Rhode Island | 344 | 343 | 358 | 366 | 367 | 349 | 367 | 382 | 396 | 400 | 398 | 401 | 391 | 396 | 416 | 429 |
| South Carolina | 842 | 863 | 920 | 984 | 1 016 | 983 | 1 038 | 1 082 | 1 138 | 1 176 | 1 189 | 1 197 | 1 162 | 1 189 | 1 263 | 1 296 |
| South Dakota | 175 | 179 | 190 | 199 | 207 | 209 | 219 | 227 | 237 | 241 | 238 | 236 | 230 | 235 | 247 | 249 |
| Tennessee | 1 328 | 1 357 | 1 450 | 1 531 | 1 558 | 1 506 | 1 575 | 1 648 | 1 737 | 1 777 | 1 747 | 1 755 | 1 703 | 1 719 | 1 812 | 1 868 |
| Texas | 3 625 | 3 684 | 3 884 | 4 142 | 4 360 | 4 463 | 4 684 | 4 907 | 5 272 | 5 602 | 5 851 | 6 180 | 6 263 | 6 194 | 6 492 | 6 663 |
| Utah | 357 | 369 | 393 | 415 | 434 | 440 | 463 | 489 | 525 | 548 | 551 | 558 | 561 | 567 | 601 | 624 |
| Vermont | 148 | 148 | 154 | 161 | 163 | 162 | 168 | 178 | 191 | 198 | 200 | 204 | 203 | 206 | 215 | 225 |
| Virginia | 1 519 | 1 567 | 1 656 | 1 753 | 1 805 | 1 779 | 1 848 | 1 930 | 2 034 | 2 115 | 2 157 | 2 161 | 2 146 | 2 207 | 2 333 | 2 455 |
| Washington | 1 079 | 1 064 | 1 100 | 1 152 | 1 199 | 1 226 | 1 283 | 1 367 | 1 485 | 1 581 | 1 608 | 1 612 | 1 569 | 1 586 | 1 660 | 1 710 |
| West Virginia | 517 | 520 | 541 | 562 | 572 | 575 | 596 | 612 | 633 | 659 | 646 | 629 | 608 | 582 | 597 | 597 |
| Wisconsin | 1 530 | 1 525 | 1 581 | 1 661 | 1 703 | 1 677 | 1 726 | 1 799 | 1 887 | 1 960 | 1 938 | 1 923 | 1 867 | 1 867 | 1 949 | 1 983 |
| Wyoming | 108 | 111 | 117 | 126 | 137 | 146 | 157 | 171 | 187 | 201 | 210 | 224 | 218 | 203 | 204 | 207 |
| Puerto Rico | . . . | . . . | . . . | . . . | . . . | . . . | . . . | . . . | . . . | . . . | 693 | 680 | 642 | 646 | 684 | 692 |
| Virgin Islands | . . . | . . . | . . . | . . . | . . . | 33 | 31 | 32 | 34 | 36 | 37 | 38 | 37 | 36 | 37 | 37 |

. . . = Not available.

## Table 2-8. Employees on Total Nonfarm Payrolls, by State and Selected Territory, 1970–2015—*Continued*

(Thousands of people.)

| State | 1986 | 1987 | 1988 | 1989 | 1990 | 1991 | 1992 | 1993 | 1994 | 1995 | 1996 | 1997 | 1998 | 1999 |
|---|---|---|---|---|---|---|---|---|---|---|---|---|---|---|
| UNITED STATES | 99 500 | 102 116 | 105 378 | 108 051 | 109 527 | 108 427 | 108 802 | 110 935 | 114 398 | 117 407 | 119 836 | 122 951 | 126 157 | 129 240 |
| Alabama | 1 463 | 1 508 | 1 559 | 1 601 | 1 636 | 1 642 | 1 674 | 1 717 | 1 759 | 1 804 | 1 829 | 1 866 | 1 898 | 1 920 |
| Alaska | 221 | 210 | 214 | 227 | 237 | 242 | 246 | 252 | 258 | 261 | 263 | 268 | 274 | 278 |
| Arizona | 1 338 | 1 386 | 1 419 | 1 455 | 1 483 | 1 491 | 1 517 | 1 584 | 1 692 | 1 793 | 1 892 | 1 985 | 2 075 | 2 163 |
| Arkansas | 814 | 837 | 865 | 893 | 924 | 937 | 963 | 994 | 1 034 | 1 070 | 1 087 | 1 105 | 1 122 | 1 142 |
| California | 11 111 | 11 501 | 11 944 | 12 274 | 12 539 | 12 406 | 12 207 | 12 095 | 12 212 | 12 477 | 12 805 | 13 201 | 13 688 | 14 093 |
| Colorado | 1 408 | 1 413 | 1 436 | 1 482 | 1 521 | 1 545 | 1 597 | 1 671 | 1 756 | 1 835 | 1 901 | 1 980 | 2 058 | 2 133 |
| Connecticut | 1 598 | 1 638 | 1 667 | 1 666 | 1 620 | 1 557 | 1 526 | 1 531 | 1 544 | 1 562 | 1 583 | 1 608 | 1 644 | 1 669 |
| Delaware | 303 | 321 | 334 | 345 | 348 | 342 | 341 | 349 | 356 | 366 | 376 | 388 | 400 | 413 |
| District of Columbia | 640 | 656 | 674 | 681 | 686 | 677 | 674 | 670 | 659 | 643 | 623 | 619 | 614 | 627 |
| Florida | 4 599 | 4 848 | 5 067 | 5 261 | 5 363 | 5 274 | 5 337 | 5 550 | 5 777 | 5 973 | 6 159 | 6 395 | 6 611 | 6 801 |
| Georgia | 2 672 | 2 782 | 2 876 | 2 941 | 3 027 | 2 976 | 3 029 | 3 144 | 3 300 | 3 435 | 3 560 | 3 646 | 3 771 | 3 885 |
| Hawaii | 439 | 460 | 478 | 506 | 528 | 539 | 543 | 539 | 536 | 533 | 531 | 532 | 531 | 535 |
| Idaho | 328 | 333 | 349 | 366 | 385 | 398 | 415 | 433 | 459 | 475 | 489 | 506 | 521 | 539 |
| Illinois | 4 791 | 4 928 | 5 098 | 5 214 | 5 288 | 5 233 | 5 235 | 5 330 | 5 462 | 5 591 | 5 681 | 5 766 | 5 893 | 5 956 |
| Indiana | 2 222 | 2 305 | 2 396 | 2 479 | 2 522 | 2 508 | 2 555 | 2 628 | 2 714 | 2 788 | 2 817 | 2 861 | 2 920 | 2 973 |
| Iowa | 1 074 | 1 109 | 1 156 | 1 200 | 1 226 | 1 238 | 1 253 | 1 279 | 1 320 | 1 358 | 1 383 | 1 407 | 1 443 | 1 469 |
| Kansas | 985 | 1 005 | 1 035 | 1 064 | 1 092 | 1 097 | 1 116 | 1 135 | 1 167 | 1 200 | 1 228 | 1 270 | 1 314 | 1 328 |
| Kentucky | 1 274 | 1 328 | 1 382 | 1 433 | 1 460 | 1 464 | 1 498 | 1 537 | 1 587 | 1 632 | 1 661 | 1 701 | 1 742 | 1 785 |
| Louisiana | 1 519 | 1 484 | 1 512 | 1 539 | 1 588 | 1 611 | 1 625 | 1 657 | 1 720 | 1 770 | 1 808 | 1 848 | 1 887 | 1 894 |
| Maine | 477 | 501 | 527 | 542 | 535 | 514 | 512 | 519 | 532 | 538 | 542 | 554 | 569 | 586 |
| Maryland | 1 952 | 2 028 | 2 102 | 2 155 | 2 173 | 2 103 | 2 084 | 2 105 | 2 148 | 2 184 | 2 213 | 2 269 | 2 326 | 2 392 |
| Massachusetts | 2 992 | 3 071 | 3 138 | 3 118 | 2 988 | 2 825 | 2 799 | 2 845 | 2 908 | 2 982 | 3 042 | 3 117 | 3 187 | 3 250 |
| Michigan | 3 657 | 3 736 | 3 819 | 3 922 | 3 944 | 3 883 | 3 917 | 3 997 | 4 139 | 4 267 | 4 351 | 4 438 | 4 513 | 4 584 |
| Minnesota | 1 893 | 1 963 | 2 028 | 2 087 | 2 136 | 2 146 | 2 194 | 2 252 | 2 320 | 2 388 | 2 443 | 2 500 | 2 564 | 2 622 |
| Mississippi | 848 | 864 | 896 | 919 | 938 | 939 | 962 | 1 004 | 1 057 | 1 076 | 1 090 | 1 108 | 1 135 | 1 155 |
| Missouri | 2 143 | 2 198 | 2 259 | 2 315 | 2 345 | 2 309 | 2 334 | 2 394 | 2 471 | 2 521 | 2 568 | 2 640 | 2 684 | 2 727 |
| Montana | 275 | 274 | 283 | 291 | 297 | 304 | 317 | 326 | 340 | 352 | 362 | 367 | 376 | 384 |
| Nebraska | 653 | 667 | 688 | 708 | 731 | 741 | 752 | 770 | 799 | 820 | 839 | 858 | 880 | 896 |
| Nevada | 468 | 500 | 538 | 581 | 621 | 629 | 639 | 672 | 738 | 786 | 843 | 891 | 926 | 983 |
| New Hampshire | 490 | 513 | 529 | 529 | 508 | 482 | 487 | 502 | 523 | 540 | 554 | 570 | 589 | 606 |
| New Jersey | 3 488 | 3 576 | 3 651 | 3 690 | 3 635 | 3 498 | 3 456 | 3 491 | 3 550 | 3 597 | 3 635 | 3 720 | 3 801 | 3 901 |
| New Mexico | 526 | 529 | 548 | 562 | 580 | 585 | 602 | 626 | 657 | 682 | 695 | 709 | 720 | 730 |
| New York | 7 908 | 8 059 | 8 187 | 8 247 | 8 203 | 7 878 | 7 721 | 7 750 | 7 822 | 7 882 | 7 929 | 8 057 | 8 227 | 8 446 |
| North Carolina | 2 744 | 2 863 | 2 987 | 3 074 | 3 127 | 3 081 | 3 145 | 3 247 | 3 355 | 3 454 | 3 538 | 3 654 | 3 759 | 3 849 |
| North Dakota | 250 | 252 | 257 | 260 | 266 | 271 | 277 | 285 | 295 | 302 | 309 | 314 | 320 | 324 |
| Ohio | 4 472 | 4 583 | 4 701 | 4 818 | 4 882 | 4 819 | 4 848 | 4 918 | 5 076 | 5 221 | 5 296 | 5 393 | 5 482 | 5 564 |
| Oklahoma | 1 124 | 1 109 | 1 132 | 1 164 | 1 210 | 1 225 | 1 236 | 1 261 | 1 294 | 1 330 | 1 368 | 1 407 | 1 454 | 1 475 |
| Oregon | 1 059 | 1 100 | 1 153 | 1 206 | 1 256 | 1 254 | 1 277 | 1 318 | 1 372 | 1 428 | 1 485 | 1 537 | 1 562 | 1 586 |
| Pennsylvania | 4 791 | 4 915 | 5 042 | 5 139 | 5 173 | 5 086 | 5 078 | 5 126 | 5 195 | 5 256 | 5 309 | 5 409 | 5 497 | 5 588 |
| Rhode Island | 443 | 452 | 459 | 462 | 454 | 424 | 424 | 430 | 434 | 439 | 441 | 450 | 458 | 466 |
| South Carolina | 1 338 | 1 392 | 1 449 | 1 500 | 1 528 | 1 497 | 1 512 | 1 553 | 1 592 | 1 636 | 1 670 | 1 719 | 1 780 | 1 826 |
| South Dakota | 252 | 257 | 266 | 276 | 289 | 296 | 308 | 318 | 331 | 342 | 347 | 353 | 360 | 370 |
| Tennessee | 1 930 | 2 012 | 2 092 | 2 167 | 2 196 | 2 186 | 2 248 | 2 331 | 2 426 | 2 503 | 2 537 | 2 588 | 2 642 | 2 689 |
| Texas | 6 564 | 6 517 | 6 678 | 6 840 | 7 099 | 7 177 | 7 273 | 7 486 | 7 756 | 8 027 | 8 260 | 8 611 | 8 941 | 9 157 |
| Utah | 634 | 640 | 660 | 691 | 726 | 748 | 771 | 812 | 862 | 910 | 956 | 994 | 1 023 | 1 049 |
| Vermont | 234 | 246 | 256 | 262 | 258 | 249 | 251 | 257 | 264 | 270 | 275 | 279 | 285 | 292 |
| Virginia | 2 558 | 2 680 | 2 773 | 2 862 | 2 897 | 2 832 | 2 851 | 2 922 | 3 007 | 3 073 | 3 139 | 3 235 | 3 323 | 3 415 |
| Washington | 1 770 | 1 852 | 1 942 | 2 048 | 2 148 | 2 182 | 2 227 | 2 267 | 2 316 | 2 361 | 2 431 | 2 536 | 2 622 | 2 679 |
| West Virginia | 598 | 599 | 610 | 615 | 631 | 630 | 641 | 654 | 676 | 690 | 701 | 710 | 722 | 729 |
| Wisconsin | 2 024 | 2 090 | 2 169 | 2 236 | 2 291 | 2 302 | 2 358 | 2 412 | 2 490 | 2 558 | 2 600 | 2 655 | 2 717 | 2 783 |
| Wyoming | 196 | 183 | 189 | 193 | 199 | 203 | 206 | 210 | 217 | 219 | 221 | 225 | 228 | 233 |
| Puerto Rico | 728 | 764 | 818 | 837 | 846 | 838 | 858 | 872 | 898 | 930 | 973 | 989 | 997 | 1 011 |
| Virgin Islands | 38 | 40 | 42 | 42 | 43 | 44 | 45 | 49 | 45 | 42 | 41 | 42 | 42 | 41 |

## Table 2-8.  Employees on Total Nonfarm Payrolls, by State and Selected Territory, 1970–2015—*Continued*

(Thousands of people.)

| State | 2000 | 2001 | 2002 | 2003 | 2004 | 2005 | 2006 | 2007 | 2008 | 2009 | 2010 | 2011 | 2012 | 2013 | 2014 | 2015 |
|---|---|---|---|---|---|---|---|---|---|---|---|---|---|---|---|---|
| **UNITED STATES** | 132 024 | 132 087 | 130 649 | 130 347 | 131 787 | 134 051 | 136 453 | 137 999 | 137 242 | 131 313 | 130 361 | 131 932 | 134 175 | 136 381 | 138 958 | 141 865 |
| Alabama | 1 931 | 1 909 | 1 883 | 1 876 | 1 902 | 1 945 | 1 980 | 2 006 | 1 992 | 1 887 | 1 871 | 1 870 | 1 885 | 1 903 | 1 923 | 1 947 |
| Alaska | 283 | 288 | 294 | 298 | 303 | 309 | 314 | 317 | 321 | 320 | 324 | 330 | 335 | 336 | 338 | 339 |
| Arizona | 2 243 | 2 266 | 2 268 | 2 299 | 2 385 | 2 513 | 2 639 | 2 679 | 2 623 | 2 433 | 2 386 | 2 412 | 2 464 | 2 521 | 2 570 | 2 636 |
| Arkansas | 1 159 | 1 154 | 1 146 | 1 145 | 1 158 | 1 178 | 1 199 | 1 205 | 1 203 | 1 165 | 1 163 | 1 170 | 1 177 | 1 176 | 1 188 | 1 208 |
| California | 14 585 | 14 719 | 14 601 | 14 575 | 14 749 | 15 045 | 15 326 | 15 461 | 15 299 | 14 438 | 14 283 | 14 434 | 14 761 | 15 154 | 15 586 | 16 052 |
| Colorado | 2 214 | 2 227 | 2 184 | 2 153 | 2 180 | 2 226 | 2 279 | 2 331 | 2 350 | 2 246 | 2 222 | 2 259 | 2 313 | 2 382 | 2 465 | 2 541 |
| Connecticut | 1 693 | 1 681 | 1 665 | 1 645 | 1 650 | 1 662 | 1 681 | 1 698 | 1 699 | 1 627 | 1 608 | 1 624 | 1 638 | 1 650 | 1 662 | 1 674 |
| Delaware | 421 | 420 | 415 | 416 | 425 | 433 | 438 | 439 | 437 | 417 | 414 | 417 | 419 | 429 | 439 | 449 |
| District of Columbia | 650 | 654 | 664 | 666 | 674 | 682 | 688 | 694 | 704 | 702 | 712 | 726 | 735 | 748 | 754 | 766 |
| Florida | 7 054 | 7 144 | 7 152 | 7 233 | 7 481 | 7 781 | 7 983 | 7 998 | 7 715 | 7 232 | 7 173 | 7 252 | 7 397 | 7 583 | 7 825 | 8 093 |
| Georgia | 3 979 | 3 971 | 3 897 | 3 870 | 3 923 | 4 024 | 4 111 | 4 166 | 4 122 | 3 900 | 3 860 | 3 901 | 3 954 | 4 033 | 4 145 | 4 267 |
| Hawaii | 551 | 555 | 557 | 568 | 583 | 602 | 617 | 625 | 619 | 592 | 587 | 593 | 606 | 619 | 627 | 637 |
| Idaho | 560 | 568 | 568 | 572 | 588 | 611 | 638 | 655 | 649 | 610 | 604 | 611 | 622 | 638 | 655 | 674 |
| Illinois | 6 042 | 5 993 | 5 883 | 5 810 | 5 815 | 5 861 | 5 930 | 5 978 | 5 947 | 5 656 | 5 610 | 5 676 | 5 750 | 5 804 | 5 880 | 5 961 |
| Indiana | 3 004 | 2 937 | 2 907 | 2 902 | 2 934 | 2 960 | 2 979 | 2 992 | 2 963 | 2 791 | 2 799 | 2 845 | 2 902 | 2 938 | 2 980 | 3 034 |
| Iowa | 1 479 | 1 466 | 1 447 | 1 440 | 1 457 | 1 481 | 1 504 | 1 519 | 1 524 | 1 479 | 1 469 | 1 486 | 1 509 | 1 528 | 1 547 | 1 562 |
| Kansas | 1 346 | 1 349 | 1 336 | 1 313 | 1 325 | 1 334 | 1 355 | 1 381 | 1 392 | 1 345 | 1 330 | 1 340 | 1 357 | 1 372 | 1 391 | 1 400 |
| Kentucky | 1 817 | 1 795 | 1 778 | 1 773 | 1 788 | 1 814 | 1 836 | 1 856 | 1 841 | 1 759 | 1 759 | 1 783 | 1 811 | 1 830 | 1 857 | 1 884 |
| Louisiana | 1 918 | 1 915 | 1 896 | 1 906 | 1 918 | 1 892 | 1 853 | 1 916 | 1 938 | 1 902 | 1 886 | 1 903 | 1 927 | 1 954 | 1 985 | 1 989 |
| Maine | 604 | 608 | 607 | 607 | 612 | 612 | 615 | 618 | 617 | 596 | 593 | 595 | 598 | 602 | 605 | 610 |
| Maryland | 2 455 | 2 472 | 2 480 | 2 487 | 2 517 | 2 555 | 2 589 | 2 607 | 2 599 | 2 522 | 2 517 | 2 542 | 2 574 | 2 597 | 2 621 | 2 659 |
| Massachusetts | 3 338 | 3 350 | 3 272 | 3 214 | 3 213 | 3 231 | 3 267 | 3 305 | 3 318 | 3 211 | 3 222 | 3 260 | 3 311 | 3 367 | 3 434 | 3 493 |
| Michigan | 4 676 | 4 564 | 4 487 | 4 416 | 4 399 | 4 390 | 4 327 | 4 268 | 4 163 | 3 871 | 3 864 | 3 952 | 4 034 | 4 110 | 4 182 | 4 244 |
| Minnesota | 2 685 | 2 690 | 2 665 | 2 660 | 2 681 | 2 723 | 2 758 | 2 771 | 2 763 | 2 655 | 2 641 | 2 688 | 2 730 | 2 776 | 2 815 | 2 856 |
| Mississippi | 1 155 | 1 131 | 1 125 | 1 116 | 1 126 | 1 132 | 1 143 | 1 154 | 1 149 | 1 098 | 1 093 | 1 093 | 1 102 | 1 111 | 1 121 | 1 134 |
| Missouri | 2 749 | 2 731 | 2 700 | 2 682 | 2 696 | 2 737 | 2 777 | 2 798 | 2 793 | 2 690 | 2 658 | 2 667 | 2 685 | 2 711 | 2 739 | 2 785 |
| Montana | 391 | 391 | 396 | 400 | 411 | 420 | 434 | 444 | 445 | 429 | 428 | 431 | 440 | 449 | 453 | 461 |
| Nebraska | 913 | 920 | 911 | 914 | 921 | 934 | 946 | 962 | 970 | 950 | 945 | 953 | 969 | 980 | 993 | 1 006 |
| Nevada | 1 027 | 1 051 | 1 052 | 1 088 | 1 153 | 1 223 | 1 280 | 1 293 | 1 264 | 1 148 | 1 118 | 1 126 | 1 145 | 1 174 | 1 217 | 1 258 |
| New Hampshire | 622 | 627 | 618 | 618 | 627 | 637 | 643 | 648 | 650 | 628 | 625 | 628 | 634 | 640 | 647 | 656 |
| New Jersey | 3 995 | 3 997 | 3 984 | 3 977 | 3 998 | 4 038 | 4 070 | 4 077 | 4 048 | 3 894 | 3 848 | 3 847 | 3 890 | 3 935 | 3 968 | 4 022 |
| New Mexico | 745 | 757 | 766 | 776 | 790 | 809 | 832 | 844 | 847 | 812 | 803 | 802 | 804 | 811 | 819 | 826 |
| New York | 8 625 | 8 581 | 8 448 | 8 396 | 8 451 | 8 522 | 8 604 | 8 719 | 8 777 | 8 540 | 8 544 | 8 669 | 8 795 | 8 930 | 9 094 | 9 246 |
| North Carolina | 3 915 | 3 893 | 3 835 | 3 787 | 3 834 | 3 912 | 4 037 | 4 141 | 4 131 | 3 904 | 3 870 | 3 917 | 3 986 | 4 057 | 4 140 | 4 240 |
| North Dakota | 328 | 330 | 330 | 333 | 338 | 345 | 352 | 358 | 367 | 367 | 376 | 397 | 429 | 444 | 461 | 454 |
| Ohio | 5 625 | 5 543 | 5 445 | 5 398 | 5 408 | 5 427 | 5 435 | 5 427 | 5 362 | 5 073 | 5 036 | 5 108 | 5 202 | 5 267 | 5 344 | 5 421 |
| Oklahoma | 1 502 | 1 520 | 1 499 | 1 471 | 1 487 | 1 525 | 1 566 | 1 595 | 1 619 | 1 568 | 1 556 | 1 578 | 1 614 | 1 635 | 1 657 | 1 669 |
| Oregon | 1 618 | 1 605 | 1 585 | 1 574 | 1 606 | 1 654 | 1 703 | 1 731 | 1 718 | 1 612 | 1 602 | 1 620 | 1 640 | 1 674 | 1 722 | 1 779 |
| Pennsylvania | 5 693 | 5 684 | 5 642 | 5 613 | 5 645 | 5 703 | 5 757 | 5 799 | 5 800 | 5 617 | 5 622 | 5 686 | 5 726 | 5 741 | 5 789 | 5 836 |
| Rhode Island | 477 | 478 | 479 | 484 | 489 | 491 | 493 | 492 | 481 | 459 | 458 | 461 | 465 | 472 | 479 | 484 |
| South Carolina | 1 854 | 1 815 | 1 795 | 1 799 | 1 827 | 1 863 | 1 906 | 1 945 | 1 926 | 1 814 | 1 811 | 1 833 | 1 864 | 1 901 | 1 951 | 2 004 |
| South Dakota | 378 | 379 | 378 | 378 | 384 | 390 | 399 | 407 | 411 | 404 | 403 | 408 | 414 | 418 | 424 | 428 |
| Tennessee | 2 733 | 2 688 | 2 664 | 2 663 | 2 706 | 2 743 | 2 783 | 2 797 | 2 775 | 2 620 | 2 615 | 2 661 | 2 715 | 2 760 | 2 822 | 2 892 |
| Texas | 9 429 | 9 511 | 9 413 | 9 367 | 9 494 | 9 738 | 10 064 | 10 393 | 10 607 | 10 305 | 10 337 | 10 568 | 10 878 | 11 205 | 11 559 | 11 838 |
| Utah | 1 075 | 1 081 | 1 073 | 1 074 | 1 104 | 1 148 | 1 204 | 1 253 | 1 253 | 1 189 | 1 183 | 1 208 | 1 250 | 1 291 | 1 328 | 1 378 |
| Vermont | 299 | 302 | 299 | 299 | 303 | 306 | 308 | 308 | 307 | 297 | 298 | 301 | 305 | 307 | 310 | 312 |
| Virginia | 3 519 | 3 522 | 3 499 | 3 502 | 3 587 | 3 667 | 3 732 | 3 770 | 3 772 | 3 650 | 3 647 | 3 693 | 3 736 | 3 762 | 3 783 | 3 851 |
| Washington | 2 746 | 2 735 | 2 694 | 2 702 | 2 740 | 2 813 | 2 894 | 2 968 | 2 994 | 2 863 | 2 836 | 2 872 | 2 919 | 2 986 | 3 065 | 3 154 |
| West Virginia | 739 | 739 | 737 | 732 | 742 | 751 | 762 | 764 | 769 | 753 | 755 | 763 | 773 | 772 | 769 | 764 |
| Wisconsin | 2 832 | 2 812 | 2 780 | 2 772 | 2 802 | 2 836 | 2 859 | 2 876 | 2 868 | 2 741 | 2 725 | 2 752 | 2 781 | 2 809 | 2 852 | 2 889 |
| Wyoming | 239 | 245 | 248 | 250 | 255 | 264 | 277 | 289 | 298 | 285 | 282 | 286 | 289 | 289 | 293 | 290 |
| Puerto Rico | 1 025 | 1 009 | 1 005 | 1 024 | 1 050 | 1 051 | 1 045 | 1 032 | 1 014 | 965 | 932 | 924 | 940 | 926 | 910 | 900 |
| Virgin Islands | 42 | 44 | 43 | 42 | 43 | 44 | 46 | 46 | 46 | 44 | 44 | 44 | 40 | 39 | 38 | 38 |

## Table 2-9.  Employees on Total Private Payrolls, by State and Selected Territory, 2005–2015

(Thousands of people.)

| State | 2005 | 2006 | 2007 | 2008 | 2009 | 2010 | 2011 | 2012 | 2013 | 2014 | 2015 |
|---|---|---|---|---|---|---|---|---|---|---|---|
| UNITED STATES | 112 247 | 114 479 | 115 781 | 114 732 | 108 758 | 107 871 | 109 845 | 112 255 | 114 529 | 117 076 | 119 859 |
| Alabama | 1 582 | 1 609 | 1 629 | 1 608 | 1 503 | 1 484 | 1 488 | 1 507 | 1 525 | 1 544 | 1 570 |
| Alaska | 228 | 233 | 236 | 239 | 236 | 239 | 245 | 251 | 253 | 256 | 257 |
| Arizona | 2 110 | 2 231 | 2 258 | 2 190 | 2 010 | 1 970 | 2 004 | 2 054 | 2 111 | 2 160 | 2 228 |
| Arkansas | 974 | 991 | 994 | 989 | 948 | 945 | 953 | 960 | 961 | 974 | 996 |
| California | 12 625 | 12 873 | 12 966 | 12 780 | 11 958 | 11 834 | 12 029 | 12 385 | 12 780 | 13 172 | 13 593 |
| Colorado | 1 863 | 1 912 | 1 957 | 1 966 | 1 855 | 1 828 | 1 866 | 1 918 | 1 978 | 2 056 | 2 125 |
| Connecticut | 1 416 | 1 432 | 1 447 | 1 444 | 1 376 | 1 361 | 1 381 | 1 397 | 1 410 | 1 421 | 1 435 |
| Delaware | 373 | 377 | 377 | 374 | 353 | 350 | 353 | 356 | 365 | 374 | 383 |
| District of Columbia | 449 | 455 | 463 | 469 | 461 | 465 | 479 | 492 | 508 | 518 | 528 |
| Florida | 6 700 | 6 884 | 6 876 | 6 588 | 6 118 | 6 061 | 6 159 | 6 317 | 6 506 | 6 751 | 7 013 |
| Georgia | 3 358 | 3 431 | 3 474 | 3 411 | 3 191 | 3 161 | 3 213 | 3 268 | 3 351 | 3 467 | 3 588 |
| Hawaii | 482 | 496 | 503 | 494 | 466 | 462 | 469 | 481 | 494 | 501 | 510 |
| Idaho | 496 | 522 | 538 | 530 | 490 | 485 | 494 | 505 | 521 | 536 | 554 |
| Illinois | 5 015 | 5 085 | 5 129 | 5 092 | 4 798 | 4 757 | 4 838 | 4 918 | 4 974 | 5 052 | 5 130 |
| Indiana | 2 534 | 2 553 | 2 560 | 2 522 | 2 353 | 2 361 | 2 415 | 2 474 | 2 513 | 2 555 | 2 608 |
| Iowa | 1 235 | 1 257 | 1 269 | 1 272 | 1 224 | 1 216 | 1 233 | 1 255 | 1 274 | 1 292 | 1 307 |
| Kansas | 1 083 | 1 100 | 1 123 | 1 132 | 1 083 | 1 068 | 1 080 | 1 099 | 1 115 | 1 134 | 1 143 |
| Kentucky | 1 513 | 1 531 | 1 546 | 1 532 | 1 448 | 1 442 | 1 462 | 1 487 | 1 506 | 1 534 | 1 566 |
| Louisiana | 1 518 | 1 505 | 1 560 | 1 574 | 1 533 | 1 519 | 1 546 | 1 578 | 1 616 | 1 655 | 1 662 |
| Maine | 507 | 510 | 514 | 513 | 493 | 489 | 493 | 497 | 501 | 505 | 510 |
| Maryland | 2 089 | 2 117 | 2 129 | 2 111 | 2 028 | 2 015 | 2 037 | 2 069 | 2 093 | 2 118 | 2 157 |
| Massachusetts | 2 806 | 2 838 | 2 873 | 2 881 | 2 773 | 2 783 | 2 825 | 2 874 | 2 924 | 2 982 | 3 042 |
| Michigan | 3 716 | 3 662 | 3 612 | 3 512 | 3 224 | 3 228 | 3 335 | 3 425 | 3 511 | 3 586 | 3 649 |
| Minnesota | 2 308 | 2 342 | 2 357 | 2 344 | 2 237 | 2 224 | 2 277 | 2 317 | 2 361 | 2 394 | 2 435 |
| Mississippi | 891 | 903 | 910 | 901 | 848 | 844 | 847 | 856 | 866 | 877 | 890 |
| Missouri | 2 308 | 2 343 | 2 358 | 2 347 | 2 238 | 2 211 | 2 228 | 2 247 | 2 276 | 2 307 | 2 351 |
| Montana | 334 | 346 | 357 | 357 | 339 | 336 | 341 | 351 | 359 | 363 | 370 |
| Nebraska | 773 | 783 | 799 | 806 | 781 | 776 | 785 | 800 | 812 | 823 | 835 |
| Nevada | 1 080 | 1 130 | 1 137 | 1 102 | 991 | 964 | 976 | 995 | 1 023 | 1 064 | 1 103 |
| New Hampshire | 545 | 551 | 555 | 554 | 532 | 529 | 536 | 543 | 549 | 556 | 566 |
| New Jersey | 3 395 | 3 421 | 3 428 | 3 397 | 3 240 | 3 206 | 3 226 | 3 272 | 3 317 | 3 348 | 3 408 |
| New Mexico | 607 | 635 | 649 | 649 | 613 | 604 | 608 | 612 | 620 | 629 | 636 |
| New York | 7 033 | 7 118 | 7 218 | 7 262 | 7 016 | 7 033 | 7 187 | 7 336 | 7 487 | 7 659 | 7 808 |
| North Carolina | 3 241 | 3 350 | 3 439 | 3 410 | 3 180 | 3 149 | 3 203 | 3 274 | 3 341 | 3 425 | 3 519 |
| North Dakota | 270 | 277 | 283 | 291 | 289 | 296 | 317 | 350 | 365 | 381 | 373 |
| Ohio | 4 627 | 4 635 | 4 629 | 4 563 | 4 281 | 4 250 | 4 333 | 4 429 | 4 501 | 4 578 | 4 653 |
| Oklahoma | 1 204 | 1 236 | 1 261 | 1 281 | 1 219 | 1 208 | 1 234 | 1 267 | 1 287 | 1 308 | 1 317 |
| Oregon | 1 369 | 1 417 | 1 441 | 1 420 | 1 313 | 1 302 | 1 325 | 1 349 | 1 385 | 1 428 | 1 478 |
| Pennsylvania | 4 949 | 5 002 | 5 044 | 5 040 | 4 848 | 4 851 | 4 934 | 4 994 | 5 020 | 5 077 | 5 131 |
| Rhode Island | 426 | 428 | 427 | 418 | 397 | 396 | 400 | 405 | 411 | 418 | 424 |
| South Carolina | 1 527 | 1 566 | 1 599 | 1 571 | 1 459 | 1 456 | 1 484 | 1 513 | 1 548 | 1 595 | 1 644 |
| South Dakota | 315 | 323 | 331 | 335 | 326 | 325 | 330 | 337 | 340 | 346 | 350 |
| Tennessee | 2 333 | 2 369 | 2 379 | 2 350 | 2 194 | 2 185 | 2 236 | 2 293 | 2 337 | 2 398 | 2 468 |
| Texas | 8 057 | 8 360 | 8 662 | 8 831 | 8 487 | 8 481 | 8 747 | 9 084 | 9 396 | 9 731 | 9 985 |
| Utah | 946 | 999 | 1 046 | 1 041 | 974 | 965 | 988 | 1 027 | 1 065 | 1 097 | 1 144 |
| Vermont | 253 | 254 | 255 | 253 | 243 | 243 | 246 | 249 | 251 | 254 | 256 |
| Virginia | 3 005 | 3 057 | 3 086 | 3 077 | 2 949 | 2 940 | 2 980 | 3 022 | 3 050 | 3 073 | 3 140 |
| Washington | 2 286 | 2 364 | 2 435 | 2 448 | 2 313 | 2 286 | 2 329 | 2 378 | 2 443 | 2 515 | 2 592 |
| West Virginia | 608 | 617 | 619 | 621 | 603 | 601 | 611 | 620 | 618 | 617 | 612 |
| Wisconsin | 2 421 | 2 444 | 2 460 | 2 446 | 2 320 | 2 305 | 2 337 | 2 370 | 2 400 | 2 440 | 2 479 |
| Wyoming | 199 | 212 | 222 | 229 | 215 | 210 | 214 | 217 | 217 | 222 | 219 |
| Puerto Rico | 747 | 744 | 734 | 714 | 676 | 664 | 665 | 681 | 681 | 675 | 669 |
| Virgin Islands | 32 | 33 | 33 | 33 | 31 | 31 | 31 | 29 | 28 | 27 | 27 |

## Table 2-10.  Employees on Manufacturing Payrolls, by State and Selected Territory, NAICS Basis, 2005–2015

(Thousands of people.)

| State | 2005 | 2006 | 2007 | 2008 | 2009 | 2010 | 2011 | 2012 | 2013 | 2014 | 2015 |
|---|---|---|---|---|---|---|---|---|---|---|---|
| UNITED STATES | 14 227 | 14 155 | 13 879 | 13 406 | 11 847 | 11 528 | 11 726 | 11 927 | 12 020 | 12 185 | 12 318 |
| Alabama | 299 | 303 | 296 | 284 | 247 | 236 | 237 | 244 | 249 | 253 | 258 |
| Alaska | 13 | 13 | 13 | 13 | 13 | 13 | 14 | 14 | 14 | 14 | 14 |
| Arizona | 182 | 186 | 182 | 173 | 154 | 148 | 150 | 155 | 155 | 157 | 158 |
| Arkansas | 202 | 200 | 191 | 184 | 164 | 160 | 159 | 155 | 153 | 154 | 155 |
| California | 1 505 | 1 491 | 1 465 | 1 427 | 1 284 | 1 244 | 1 250 | 1 255 | 1 256 | 1 274 | 1 292 |
| Colorado | 148 | 147 | 145 | 142 | 128 | 124 | 128 | 131 | 133 | 137 | 141 |
| Connecticut | 195 | 193 | 190 | 187 | 171 | 165 | 165 | 164 | 162 | 159 | 159 |
| Delaware | 33 | 34 | 33 | 32 | 28 | 26 | 26 | 26 | 25 | 26 | 27 |
| District of Columbia | 2 | 2 | 2 | 2 | 1 | 1 | 1 | 1 | 1 | 1 | 1 |
| Florida | 416 | 416 | 399 | 371 | 324 | 309 | 313 | 317 | 322 | 332 | 343 |
| Georgia | 450 | 447 | 431 | 409 | 358 | 345 | 350 | 354 | 357 | 368 | 379 |
| Hawaii | 15 | 15 | 15 | 15 | 14 | 13 | 13 | 13 | 14 | 14 | 14 |
| Idaho | 64 | 66 | 66 | 63 | 55 | 53 | 55 | 57 | 60 | 60 | 62 |
| Illinois | 688 | 683 | 675 | 657 | 577 | 561 | 574 | 583 | 579 | 580 | 581 |
| Indiana | 571 | 565 | 550 | 521 | 442 | 447 | 464 | 482 | 492 | 508 | 519 |
| Iowa | 229 | 231 | 230 | 227 | 203 | 201 | 206 | 211 | 214 | 217 | 216 |
| Kansas | 179 | 182 | 185 | 185 | 165 | 158 | 159 | 161 | 161 | 162 | 161 |
| Kentucky | 262 | 261 | 256 | 245 | 213 | 209 | 213 | 223 | 229 | 235 | 241 |
| Louisiana | 152 | 153 | 157 | 153 | 142 | 138 | 140 | 142 | 145 | 148 | 144 |
| Maine | 61 | 60 | 59 | 59 | 52 | 51 | 51 | 51 | 50 | 50 | 51 |
| Maryland | 139 | 135 | 132 | 128 | 119 | 114 | 113 | 109 | 106 | 104 | 104 |
| Massachusetts | 305 | 300 | 295 | 286 | 259 | 253 | 253 | 252 | 251 | 250 | 250 |
| Michigan | 667 | 638 | 608 | 563 | 455 | 466 | 501 | 529 | 547 | 572 | 587 |
| Minnesota | 347 | 346 | 342 | 336 | 300 | 293 | 301 | 306 | 307 | 312 | 317 |
| Mississippi | 178 | 176 | 170 | 160 | 141 | 136 | 135 | 137 | 137 | 140 | 142 |
| Missouri | 312 | 310 | 304 | 292 | 257 | 246 | 250 | 252 | 253 | 256 | 261 |
| Montana | 20 | 20 | 21 | 20 | 17 | 17 | 17 | 18 | 18 | 19 | 19 |
| Nebraska | 101 | 102 | 101 | 101 | 93 | 92 | 93 | 95 | 97 | 97 | 97 |
| Nevada | 48 | 50 | 50 | 48 | 40 | 38 | 38 | 39 | 41 | 42 | 42 |
| New Hampshire | 80 | 78 | 78 | 76 | 68 | 66 | 67 | 66 | 66 | 66 | 67 |
| New Jersey | 328 | 321 | 308 | 295 | 261 | 252 | 247 | 241 | 239 | 239 | 238 |
| New Mexico | 36 | 38 | 37 | 35 | 30 | 29 | 30 | 30 | 29 | 28 | 28 |
| New York | 579 | 566 | 552 | 532 | 476 | 457 | 459 | 459 | 456 | 454 | 455 |
| North Carolina | 565 | 553 | 539 | 516 | 448 | 432 | 434 | 440 | 443 | 449 | 460 |
| North Dakota | 26 | 26 | 26 | 26 | 24 | 23 | 24 | 25 | 25 | 26 | 26 |
| Ohio | 812 | 796 | 771 | 739 | 629 | 621 | 639 | 656 | 663 | 675 | 687 |
| Oklahoma | 145 | 149 | 151 | 150 | 129 | 123 | 130 | 136 | 137 | 140 | 137 |
| Oregon | 204 | 207 | 204 | 195 | 167 | 164 | 168 | 172 | 175 | 180 | 186 |
| Pennsylvania | 679 | 670 | 659 | 644 | 574 | 560 | 565 | 567 | 565 | 568 | 568 |
| Rhode Island | 55 | 53 | 51 | 48 | 42 | 40 | 40 | 40 | 40 | 41 | 41 |
| South Carolina | 260 | 252 | 249 | 241 | 213 | 207 | 215 | 220 | 224 | 230 | 236 |
| South Dakota | 40 | 42 | 42 | 43 | 38 | 37 | 39 | 41 | 42 | 42 | 43 |
| Tennessee | 409 | 399 | 380 | 361 | 309 | 299 | 304 | 313 | 318 | 325 | 333 |
| Texas | 901 | 928 | 939 | 929 | 843 | 817 | 841 | 870 | 876 | 888 | 879 |
| Utah | 118 | 123 | 128 | 126 | 113 | 111 | 114 | 117 | 119 | 121 | 124 |
| Vermont | 37 | 36 | 36 | 35 | 31 | 31 | 31 | 32 | 32 | 31 | 31 |
| Virginia | 296 | 288 | 278 | 265 | 239 | 231 | 231 | 231 | 231 | 232 | 233 |
| Washington | 273 | 286 | 293 | 291 | 266 | 258 | 269 | 280 | 287 | 289 | 291 |
| West Virginia | 62 | 61 | 59 | 57 | 51 | 49 | 50 | 49 | 48 | 48 | 48 |
| Wisconsin | 505 | 506 | 501 | 493 | 436 | 431 | 445 | 456 | 458 | 465 | 469 |
| Wyoming | 10 | 10 | 10 | 10 | 9 | 9 | 9 | 9 | 10 | 10 | 10 |
| Puerto Rico | 115 | 110 | 107 | 101 | 92 | 87 | 84 | 82 | 77 | 75 | 74 |
| Virgin Islands | 260 | 252 | 249 | 241 | 213 | 207 | 215 | 220 | 224 | 230 | 236 |

## Table 2-11.  Employees on Government Payrolls, by State and Selected Territory, NAICS Basis, 2005–2015

(Thousands of people.)

| State | 2005 | 2006 | 2007 | 2008 | 2009 | 2010 | 2011 | 2012 | 2013 | 2014 | 2015 |
|---|---|---|---|---|---|---|---|---|---|---|---|
| UNITED STATES | 21 804 | 21 974 | 22 218 | 22 509 | 22 555 | 22 490 | 22 086 | 21 920 | 21 853 | 21 882 | 22 007 |
| Alabama | 363 | 370 | 377 | 384 | 384 | 387 | 382 | 378 | 378 | 378 | 377 |
| Alaska | 81 | 81 | 81 | 82 | 84 | 85 | 85 | 84 | 83 | 82 | 82 |
| Arizona | 403 | 409 | 421 | 432 | 423 | 416 | 408 | 410 | 410 | 410 | 409 |
| Arkansas | 204 | 208 | 211 | 214 | 217 | 218 | 217 | 216 | 215 | 213 | 213 |
| California | 2 420 | 2 452 | 2 495 | 2 519 | 2 480 | 2 448 | 2 405 | 2 376 | 2 374 | 2 414 | 2 459 |
| Colorado | 363 | 367 | 375 | 384 | 391 | 394 | 393 | 395 | 404 | 409 | 417 |
| Connecticut | 246 | 248 | 252 | 255 | 251 | 247 | 243 | 241 | 241 | 240 | 239 |
| Delaware | 60 | 61 | 62 | 63 | 63 | 64 | 64 | 64 | 64 | 65 | 65 |
| District of Columbia | 234 | 233 | 231 | 235 | 240 | 247 | 247 | 243 | 240 | 235 | 238 |
| Florida | 1 081 | 1 099 | 1 123 | 1 127 | 1 115 | 1 112 | 1 093 | 1 080 | 1 076 | 1 074 | 1 081 |
| Georgia | 667 | 680 | 693 | 711 | 709 | 699 | 687 | 686 | 682 | 678 | 679 |
| Hawaii | 120 | 121 | 122 | 125 | 126 | 125 | 125 | 126 | 125 | 126 | 127 |
| Idaho | 115 | 116 | 117 | 119 | 120 | 119 | 117 | 117 | 117 | 118 | 120 |
| Illinois | 846 | 846 | 849 | 856 | 858 | 854 | 838 | 832 | 830 | 827 | 830 |
| Indiana | 426 | 426 | 431 | 441 | 438 | 437 | 430 | 428 | 425 | 425 | 426 |
| Iowa | 245 | 247 | 250 | 253 | 255 | 253 | 253 | 254 | 255 | 255 | 255 |
| Kansas | 251 | 255 | 258 | 260 | 261 | 262 | 260 | 259 | 257 | 257 | 257 |
| Kentucky | 301 | 305 | 310 | 310 | 311 | 317 | 321 | 324 | 325 | 324 | 318 |
| Louisiana | 374 | 348 | 356 | 365 | 369 | 366 | 357 | 349 | 339 | 330 | 327 |
| Maine | 105 | 104 | 104 | 104 | 104 | 104 | 102 | 102 | 101 | 100 | 100 |
| Maryland | 466 | 471 | 478 | 488 | 494 | 502 | 505 | 505 | 504 | 503 | 503 |
| Massachusetts | 425 | 429 | 433 | 437 | 438 | 439 | 435 | 437 | 443 | 452 | 451 |
| Michigan | 674 | 665 | 656 | 650 | 647 | 636 | 617 | 609 | 599 | 596 | 594 |
| Minnesota | 415 | 416 | 415 | 419 | 417 | 417 | 411 | 413 | 415 | 421 | 421 |
| Mississippi | 241 | 239 | 244 | 248 | 250 | 249 | 246 | 246 | 245 | 244 | 244 |
| Missouri | 429 | 434 | 440 | 446 | 452 | 448 | 439 | 438 | 435 | 432 | 434 |
| Montana | 86 | 88 | 87 | 88 | 90 | 92 | 90 | 90 | 90 | 90 | 90 |
| Nebraska | 161 | 162 | 162 | 164 | 169 | 170 | 168 | 168 | 169 | 170 | 171 |
| Nevada | 143 | 149 | 156 | 161 | 157 | 154 | 150 | 149 | 151 | 153 | 155 |
| New Hampshire | 91 | 92 | 93 | 95 | 97 | 96 | 92 | 92 | 90 | 91 | 90 |
| New Jersey | 643 | 649 | 649 | 651 | 654 | 642 | 621 | 618 | 618 | 619 | 615 |
| New Mexico | 201 | 198 | 195 | 198 | 199 | 200 | 195 | 192 | 191 | 190 | 190 |
| New York | 1 489 | 1 485 | 1 501 | 1 516 | 1 524 | 1 511 | 1 482 | 1 459 | 1 443 | 1 435 | 1 439 |
| North Carolina | 671 | 687 | 703 | 721 | 724 | 721 | 713 | 713 | 716 | 715 | 721 |
| North Dakota | 75 | 76 | 76 | 76 | 78 | 80 | 79 | 79 | 80 | 80 | 81 |
| Ohio | 800 | 800 | 798 | 799 | 792 | 786 | 775 | 773 | 765 | 766 | 769 |
| Oklahoma | 321 | 330 | 334 | 337 | 348 | 349 | 344 | 347 | 349 | 348 | 352 |
| Oregon | 285 | 286 | 290 | 298 | 300 | 300 | 295 | 291 | 289 | 294 | 301 |
| Pennsylvania | 754 | 755 | 755 | 760 | 768 | 771 | 751 | 732 | 721 | 711 | 705 |
| Rhode Island | 65 | 65 | 64 | 64 | 62 | 62 | 61 | 60 | 60 | 60 | 60 |
| South Carolina | 336 | 340 | 346 | 356 | 355 | 355 | 348 | 352 | 353 | 356 | 360 |
| South Dakota | 75 | 75 | 76 | 76 | 78 | 79 | 78 | 78 | 77 | 78 | 78 |
| Tennessee | 410 | 414 | 419 | 425 | 426 | 431 | 426 | 422 | 423 | 424 | 424 |
| Texas | 1 681 | 1 703 | 1 731 | 1 776 | 1 818 | 1 857 | 1 821 | 1 794 | 1 809 | 1 828 | 1 853 |
| Utah | 202 | 205 | 207 | 212 | 215 | 218 | 220 | 223 | 225 | 230 | 234 |
| Vermont | 53 | 54 | 54 | 54 | 55 | 55 | 55 | 55 | 55 | 56 | 56 |
| Virginia | 662 | 675 | 683 | 695 | 702 | 707 | 713 | 714 | 713 | 711 | 712 |
| Washington | 527 | 530 | 534 | 546 | 550 | 550 | 544 | 541 | 543 | 551 | 562 |
| West Virginia | 143 | 145 | 145 | 148 | 150 | 153 | 151 | 154 | 154 | 152 | 152 |
| Wisconsin | 415 | 415 | 416 | 422 | 421 | 420 | 415 | 411 | 409 | 412 | 410 |
| Wyoming | 65 | 65 | 67 | 69 | 70 | 71 | 72 | 72 | 72 | 71 | 71 |
| Puerto Rico | 305 | 300 | 297 | 299 | 289 | 268 | 259 | 259 | 245 | 235 | 231 |
| Virgin Islands | 12 | 13 | 13 | 13 | 13 | 13 | 13 | 12 | 11 | 11 | 11 |

**EARNINGS**

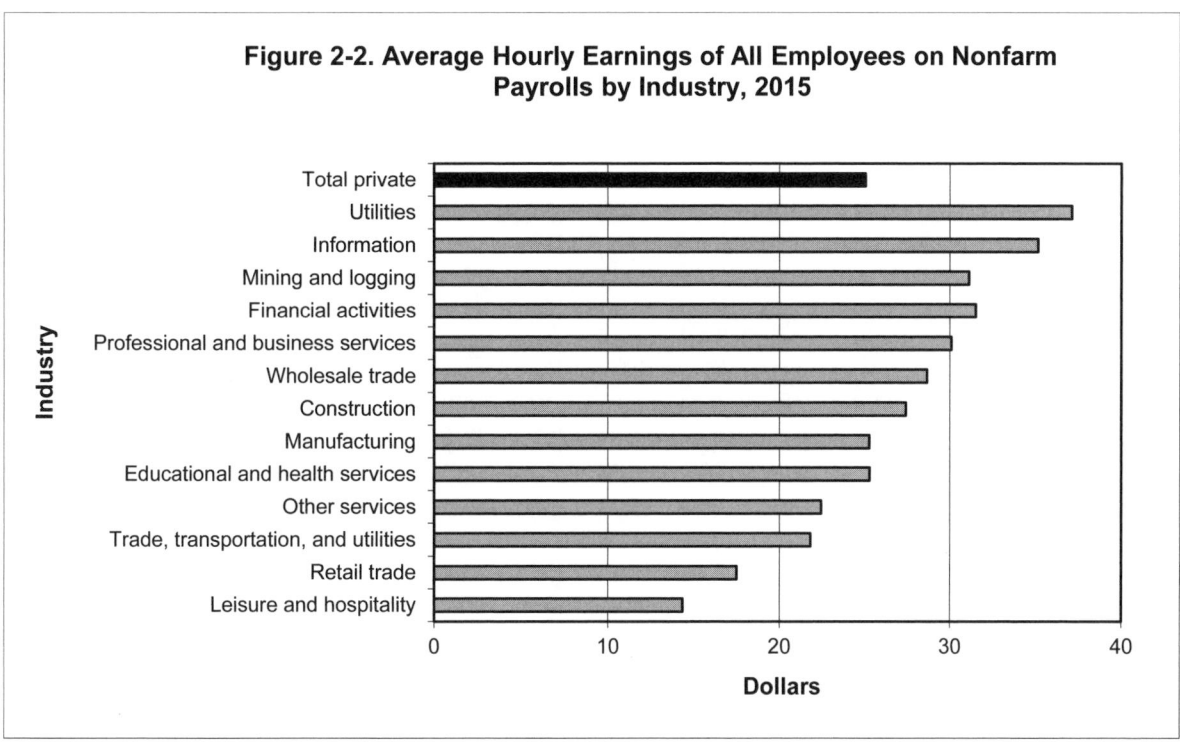

Figure 2-2. Average Hourly Earnings of All Employees on Nonfarm Payrolls by Industry, 2015

Workers in utilities had the highest average hourly earnings at $37.12 followed by those in information ($35.13), financial activities ($31.52), and mining and logging ($31.11). The average hourly earnings for all private employees were $25.03 in 2015. Earnings increased in all super sectors in 2015. (See Table 2-12.)

## OTHER HIGHLIGHTS

• Average hourly earnings for all employees also varied significantly by state and region in 2015. Earnings were highest in the District of Columbia ($38.29) Massachusetts ($30.44) followed by Washington ($29.63) and Connecticut ($29.15). Arkansas had the lowest average hourly earnings ($19.51) followed by Mississippi ($19.71) and New Mexico ($20.47). (See Table 2-13.)

• In 2015, average weekly earnings increased 2.3 percent for all employees on nonfarm payrolls. When adjusted for inflation, average weekly earnings increased 2.2 percent. Average weekly earnings of all employees on nonfarm payrolls ranged from $376.37 in leisure and hospitality to $1,579.27 in utilities. (See Table 2-15.)

• From 2014 to 2015, average weekly earnings increased the most in Nevada (5.4 percent), Delaware (5.2 percent), and Washington (4.8 percent). They declined in nine states and the District of Columbia in 2015. (See Table 2-17.)

## Table 2-12. Average Hourly Earnings of All Employees on Total Private Payrolls by NAICS Super Sector, 2010–2015

(Dollars, seasonally adjusted.)

| Year and month | Total private | Mining and logging | Construction | Manufacturing | Trade, transportation, and utilities | | | | Information | Financial activities | Professional and business services | Education and health services | Leisure and hospitality | Other services |
|---|---|---|---|---|---|---|---|---|---|---|---|---|---|---|
| | | | | | Total | Wholesale trade | Retail trade | Utilities | | | | | | |
| 2010 | 22.56 | 27.39 | 25.19 | 23.31 | 19.65 | 26.13 | 15.56 | 32.55 | 30.53 | 27.21 | 27.24 | 22.77 | 13.08 | 20.16 |
| 2011 | 23.03 | 28.10 | 25.41 | 23.69 | 20.04 | 26.38 | 15.86 | 33.62 | 31.59 | 27.91 | 27.76 | 23.44 | 13.23 | 20.50 |
| 2012 | 23.50 | 28.76 | 25.73 | 23.92 | 20.50 | 26.89 | 16.30 | 34.25 | 31.83 | 29.26 | 28.13 | 24.02 | 13.37 | 20.85 |
| 2013 | 23.96 | 29.72 | 26.12 | 24.35 | 20.96 | 27.64 | 16.63 | 35.17 | 32.91 | 30.15 | 28.55 | 24.44 | 13.50 | 21.40 |
| 2014 | 24.47 | 30.79 | 26.69 | 24.81 | 21.39 | 28.09 | 17.00 | 35.60 | 34.07 | 30.76 | 29.29 | 24.74 | 13.91 | 21.97 |
| 2015 | 25.03 | 31.11 | 27.37 | 25.25 | 21.83 | 28.65 | 17.51 | 37.12 | 35.13 | 31.52 | 30.09 | 25.27 | 14.32 | 22.48 |
| **2011** | | | | | | | | | | | | | | |
| January | 22.85 | 27.91 | 25.46 | 23.60 | 19.87 | 26.30 | 15.74 | 20.40 | 31.48 | 27.54 | 27.49 | 23.15 | 13.18 | 20.40 |
| February | 22.87 | 28.01 | 25.44 | 23.50 | 19.90 | 26.28 | 15.75 | 20.38 | 31.53 | 27.61 | 27.54 | 23.23 | 13.16 | 20.40 |
| March | 22.87 | 28.08 | 25.34 | 23.53 | 19.89 | 26.18 | 15.74 | 20.33 | 31.80 | 27.69 | 27.52 | 23.22 | 13.18 | 20.30 |
| April | 22.92 | 28.33 | 25.38 | 23.61 | 19.94 | 26.26 | 15.79 | 20.41 | 31.65 | 27.70 | 27.62 | 23.27 | 13.20 | 20.40 |
| May | 22.99 | 28.17 | 25.35 | 23.69 | 19.98 | 26.30 | 15.82 | 20.46 | 31.60 | 27.75 | 27.65 | 23.41 | 13.25 | 20.50 |
| June | 23.01 | 27.85 | 25.35 | 23.68 | 20.03 | 26.38 | 15.82 | 20.50 | 31.52 | 27.84 | 27.74 | 23.39 | 13.22 | 20.50 |
| July | 23.11 | 27.89 | 25.36 | 23.76 | 20.12 | 26.45 | 15.97 | 20.56 | 31.55 | 27.87 | 27.98 | 23.54 | 13.22 | 20.60 |
| August | 23.06 | 28.00 | 25.46 | 23.69 | 20.07 | 26.42 | 15.86 | 20.56 | 31.66 | 27.92 | 27.83 | 23.50 | 13.20 | 20.60 |
| September | 23.11 | 28.05 | 25.49 | 23.76 | 20.05 | 26.42 | 15.80 | 20.57 | 31.36 | 28.09 | 27.89 | 23.57 | 13.26 | 20.60 |
| October | 23.21 | 28.16 | 25.49 | 23.89 | 20.17 | 26.45 | 15.97 | 20.59 | 31.70 | 28.27 | 27.97 | 23.66 | 13.30 | 20.60 |
| November | 23.19 | 28.26 | 25.44 | 23.72 | 20.22 | 26.51 | 16.05 | 20.61 | 31.63 | 28.36 | 27.97 | 23.61 | 13.31 | 20.60 |
| December | 23.23 | 28.44 | 25.49 | 23.83 | 20.26 | 26.55 | 16.06 | 20.62 | 31.71 | 28.35 | 27.90 | 23.68 | 13.33 | 20.60 |
| **2012** | | | | | | | | | | | | | | |
| January | 23.25 | 28.03 | 25.50 | 23.87 | 20.22 | 26.51 | 16.04 | 20.62 | 31.64 | 28.60 | 27.84 | 23.84 | 13.33 | 20.62 |
| February | 23.28 | 28.62 | 25.55 | 23.85 | 20.24 | 26.54 | 16.08 | 20.62 | 31.63 | 28.70 | 27.91 | 23.81 | 13.34 | 20.62 |
| March | 23.36 | 28.67 | 25.66 | 23.86 | 20.29 | 26.65 | 16.10 | 20.70 | 31.64 | 28.92 | 28.00 | 23.96 | 13.35 | 20.70 |
| April | 23.39 | 28.83 | 25.64 | 23.93 | 20.35 | 26.67 | 16.15 | 20.72 | 31.73 | 29.00 | 27.96 | 23.95 | 13.37 | 20.72 |
| May | 23.40 | 28.53 | 25.70 | 23.82 | 20.40 | 26.72 | 16.21 | 20.78 | 31.82 | 29.17 | 28.03 | 23.89 | 13.33 | 20.78 |
| June | 23.46 | 28.76 | 25.71 | 23.91 | 20.50 | 26.80 | 16.35 | 20.79 | 31.81 | 29.12 | 28.06 | 24.00 | 13.38 | 20.79 |
| July | 23.52 | 28.99 | 25.74 | 23.95 | 20.55 | 26.84 | 16.36 | 20.86 | 31.90 | 29.17 | 28.12 | 24.02 | 13.41 | 20.86 |
| August | 23.49 | 28.71 | 25.76 | 23.90 | 20.54 | 26.88 | 16.35 | 20.91 | 31.58 | 29.26 | 28.05 | 24.03 | 13.39 | 20.91 |
| September | 23.58 | 28.90 | 25.87 | 23.95 | 20.59 | 26.96 | 16.41 | 20.96 | 31.78 | 29.43 | 28.20 | 24.12 | 13.40 | 20.96 |
| October | 23.57 | 28.58 | 25.84 | 23.93 | 20.60 | 27.07 | 16.42 | 20.98 | 31.76 | 29.53 | 28.19 | 24.10 | 13.37 | 20.98 |
| November | 23.64 | 28.79 | 25.94 | 23.99 | 20.64 | 27.17 | 16.37 | 21.00 | 31.87 | 29.67 | 28.25 | 24.21 | 13.40 | 21.00 |
| December | 23.73 | 29.19 | 25.95 | 24.08 | 20.78 | 27.43 | 16.52 | 21.09 | 32.22 | 29.77 | 28.35 | 24.26 | 13.38 | 21.09 |
| **2013** | | | | | | | | | | | | | | |
| January | 23.75 | 29.04 | 25.99 | 24.03 | 20.79 | 27.31 | 16.53 | 21.12 | 32.51 | 29.95 | 28.40 | 24.22 | 13.38 | 21.12 |
| February | 23.78 | 28.87 | 26.01 | 24.14 | 20.76 | 27.31 | 16.53 | 21.19 | 32.49 | 29.97 | 28.40 | 24.28 | 13.39 | 21.19 |
| March | 23.81 | 29.05 | 25.98 | 24.13 | 20.86 | 27.50 | 16.60 | 21.21 | 32.64 | 29.92 | 28.45 | 24.30 | 13.43 | 21.21 |
| April | 23.87 | 29.18 | 26.01 | 24.20 | 20.88 | 27.57 | 16.59 | 21.28 | 32.79 | 30.03 | 28.50 | 24.36 | 13.44 | 21.28 |
| May | 23.89 | 29.41 | 26.02 | 24.29 | 20.90 | 27.57 | 16.58 | 21.33 | 32.70 | 30.05 | 28.49 | 24.36 | 13.46 | 21.33 |
| June | 23.98 | 29.76 | 26.11 | 24.39 | 20.99 | 27.75 | 16.62 | 21.38 | 32.96 | 30.15 | 28.54 | 24.47 | 13.48 | 21.38 |
| July | 23.98 | 29.59 | 26.17 | 24.35 | 20.98 | 27.74 | 16.60 | 21.42 | 32.80 | 30.29 | 28.56 | 24.45 | 13.51 | 21.42 |
| August | 24.03 | 29.85 | 26.19 | 24.41 | 21.05 | 27.67 | 16.72 | 21.45 | 32.82 | 30.28 | 28.59 | 24.51 | 13.53 | 21.45 |
| September | 24.07 | 29.98 | 26.17 | 24.50 | 21.07 | 27.83 | 16.66 | 21.53 | 33.15 | 30.28 | 28.64 | 24.55 | 13.57 | 21.53 |
| October | 24.10 | 30.25 | 26.21 | 24.50 | 21.10 | 27.84 | 16.69 | 21.60 | 33.22 | 30.31 | 28.70 | 24.55 | 13.57 | 21.60 |
| November | 24.17 | 30.48 | 26.25 | 24.57 | 21.15 | 27.92 | 16.71 | 21.64 | 33.44 | 30.32 | 28.81 | 24.59 | 13.59 | 21.64 |
| December | 24.20 | 30.63 | 26.36 | 24.62 | 21.13 | 27.88 | 16.70 | 21.70 | 33.46 | 30.36 | 28.87 | 24.58 | 13.66 | 21.70 |
| **2014** | | | | | | | | | | | | | | |
| January | 24.23 | 30.65 | 26.38 | 24.64 | 21.19 | 27.94 | 16.75 | 21.77 | 33.43 | 30.39 | 28.94 | 24.60 | 13.69 | 21.77 |
| February | 24.33 | 30.76 | 26.70 | 24.71 | 21.27 | 27.94 | 16.84 | 21.80 | 33.45 | 30.47 | 29.10 | 24.63 | 13.77 | 21.80 |
| March | 24.33 | 30.72 | 26.46 | 24.73 | 21.31 | 28.02 | 16.89 | 21.74 | 33.68 | 30.60 | 29.08 | 24.60 | 13.75 | 21.74 |
| April | 24.34 | 30.72 | 26.54 | 24.69 | 21.35 | 28.08 | 16.96 | 21.86 | 33.91 | 30.56 | 29.11 | 24.63 | 13.77 | 21.86 |
| May | 24.40 | 30.90 | 26.58 | 24.72 | 21.40 | 28.06 | 17.00 | 21.87 | 33.93 | 30.57 | 29.21 | 24.67 | 13.83 | 21.87 |
| June | 24.47 | 30.99 | 26.69 | 24.85 | 21.38 | 28.01 | 17.01 | 21.95 | 34.08 | 30.75 | 29.28 | 24.70 | 13.90 | 21.95 |
| July | 24.48 | 30.80 | 26.68 | 24.84 | 21.39 | 28.01 | 17.04 | 22.00 | 34.21 | 30.77 | 29.34 | 24.71 | 13.93 | 22.00 |
| August | 24.55 | 30.84 | 26.72 | 24.88 | 21.47 | 28.20 | 17.08 | 22.05 | 34.25 | 30.86 | 29.40 | 24.80 | 13.98 | 22.05 |
| September | 24.56 | 30.84 | 26.82 | 24.83 | 21.44 | 28.11 | 17.06 | 22.06 | 34.41 | 30.91 | 29.41 | 24.81 | 14.03 | 22.06 |
| October | 24.58 | 30.86 | 26.85 | 24.91 | 21.44 | 28.11 | 17.10 | 22.09 | 34.22 | 30.92 | 29.44 | 24.84 | 14.09 | 22.09 |
| November | 24.68 | 30.87 | 26.92 | 24.94 | 21.52 | 28.24 | 17.16 | 22.16 | 34.51 | 31.12 | 29.57 | 24.96 | 14.11 | 22.16 |
| December | 24.61 | 30.73 | 26.85 | 24.87 | 21.47 | 28.20 | 17.11 | 22.16 | 34.49 | 31.03 | 29.45 | 24.90 | 14.09 | 22.16 |
| **2015** | | | | | | | | | | | | | | |
| January | 24.76 | 30.70 | 27.03 | 24.97 | 21.61 | 28.31 | 17.33 | 22.21 | 34.57 | 31.16 | 29.77 | 25.03 | 14.16 | 22.21 |
| February | 24.80 | 30.88 | 27.04 | 25.02 | 21.67 | 28.37 | 17.35 | 22.29 | 34.65 | 31.23 | 29.79 | 25.07 | 14.21 | 22.29 |
| March | 24.87 | 31.04 | 27.24 | 25.10 | 21.66 | 28.40 | 17.30 | 22.35 | 34.67 | 31.32 | 29.90 | 25.13 | 14.23 | 22.35 |
| April | 24.91 | 30.90 | 27.28 | 25.14 | 21.71 | 28.49 | 17.35 | 22.34 | 34.74 | 31.37 | 29.97 | 25.14 | 14.28 | 22.34 |
| May | 24.97 | 31.01 | 27.34 | 25.16 | 21.79 | 28.72 | 17.41 | 22.43 | 34.86 | 31.52 | 30.02 | 25.22 | 14.31 | 22.43 |
| June | 24.96 | 30.86 | 27.37 | 25.10 | 21.77 | 28.67 | 17.44 | 22.48 | 34.95 | 31.48 | 29.99 | 25.23 | 14.28 | 22.48 |
| July | 25.03 | 31.23 | 27.39 | 25.24 | 21.84 | 28.70 | 17.50 | 22.45 | 34.94 | 31.51 | 30.11 | 25.29 | 14.34 | 22.45 |
| August | 25.12 | 31.44 | 27.46 | 25.40 | 21.88 | 28.79 | 17.56 | 22.56 | 35.25 | 31.60 | 30.21 | 25.34 | 14.39 | 22.56 |
| September | 25.14 | 31.42 | 27.36 | 25.41 | 21.91 | 28.77 | 17.64 | 22.60 | 35.35 | 31.70 | 30.27 | 25.35 | 14.38 | 22.60 |
| October | 25.21 | 31.39 | 27.51 | 25.46 | 22.03 | 28.91 | 17.70 | 22.63 | 35.47 | 31.70 | 30.30 | 25.44 | 14.45 | 22.63 |
| November | 25.27 | 31.75 | 27.62 | 25.52 | 22.02 | 28.81 | 17.69 | 22.68 | 35.79 | 31.84 | 30.39 | 25.49 | 14.47 | 22.68 |
| December | 25.26 | 31.30 | 27.60 | 25.51 | 22.03 | 28.80 | 17.73 | 22.70 | 35.90 | 31.87 | 30.26 | 25.51 | 14.49 | 22.70 |

## Table 2-13.  Average Hourly Earnings of All Employees on Total Private Payrolls, by State, NAICS Basis, 2007–2015

(Dollars.)

| State | 2007 | 2008 | 2009 | 2010 | 2011 | 2012 | 2013 | 2014 | 2015 |
|---|---|---|---|---|---|---|---|---|---|
| UNITED STATES | 20.92 | 21.56 | 22.18 | 22.56 | 23.03 | 23.50 | 23.96 | 24.47 | 25.03 |
| Alabama | 19.37 | 19.56 | 19.68 | 19.86 | 20.14 | 20.21 | 20.18 | 20.73 | 21.02 |
| Alaska | 24.70 | 25.01 | 24.80 | 23.90 | 24.51 | 25.59 | 26.74 | 27.15 | 27.88 |
| Arizona | 19.83 | 20.69 | 22.03 | 22.16 | 22.56 | 22.60 | 23.00 | 22.90 | 23.13 |
| Arkansas | 16.27 | 17.21 | 17.97 | 18.08 | 18.36 | 18.57 | 19.28 | 19.54 | 19.51 |
| California | 24.68 | 24.71 | 25.47 | 26.35 | 26.89 | 26.88 | 27.23 | 27.51 | 28.04 |
| Colorado | 23.13 | 23.79 | 23.78 | 23.79 | 23.95 | 24.61 | 25.64 | 26.29 | 26.85 |
| Connecticut | 26.59 | 27.71 | 27.81 | 28.08 | 28.24 | 28.14 | 27.96 | 28.16 | 29.15 |
| Delaware | 21.98 | 22.73 | 22.30 | 22.72 | 22.32 | 22.01 | 22.12 | 21.70 | 22.63 |
| District of Columbia | 33.54 | 32.37 | 31.37 | 34.18 | 35.44 | 36.84 | 38.31 | 38.89 | 38.29 |
| Florida | 20.57 | 21.00 | 21.61 | 21.44 | 21.46 | 21.62 | 21.95 | 22.19 | 22.63 |
| Georgia | 20.44 | 20.77 | 21.08 | 21.57 | 21.83 | 21.75 | 22.47 | 23.34 | 23.84 |
| Hawaii | 20.68 | 20.80 | 21.11 | 21.65 | 22.16 | 22.72 | 23.74 | 24.33 | 24.63 |
| Idaho | 16.51 | 17.53 | 19.26 | 21.03 | 20.79 | 21.04 | 21.20 | 21.37 | 22.08 |
| Illinois | 22.94 | 22.67 | 23.05 | 23.15 | 23.58 | 24.32 | 24.82 | 25.40 | 25.98 |
| Indiana | 19.93 | 20.30 | 20.56 | 20.57 | 20.65 | 21.38 | 22.08 | 22.61 | 22.86 |
| Iowa | 18.01 | 18.35 | 20.01 | 20.38 | 20.22 | 20.87 | 21.56 | 21.88 | 22.55 |
| Kansas | 19.64 | 20.12 | 20.17 | 20.07 | 20.51 | 21.02 | 21.45 | 22.09 | 22.57 |
| Kentucky | 17.73 | 18.07 | 18.82 | 19.40 | 19.80 | 20.06 | 20.16 | 20.53 | 21.08 |
| Louisiana | 18.74 | 19.22 | 19.46 | 19.55 | 20.63 | 21.36 | 21.98 | 22.12 | 22.20 |
| Maine | 18.74 | 18.96 | 19.16 | 19.45 | 19.96 | 20.96 | 21.01 | 21.33 | 21.85 |
| Maryland | 24.04 | 24.56 | 25.42 | 26.17 | 25.80 | 25.95 | 26.66 | 27.35 | 27.31 |
| Massachusetts | 26.07 | 26.37 | 26.84 | 27.13 | 27.63 | 28.14 | 28.92 | 29.52 | 30.44 |
| Michigan | 21.55 | 21.61 | 21.89 | 22.26 | 22.35 | 22.45 | 22.94 | 23.58 | 24.06 |
| Minnesota | 23.13 | 23.23 | 23.41 | 23.85 | 24.54 | 24.95 | 25.64 | 25.79 | 26.06 |
| Mississippi | 16.46 | 16.89 | 17.87 | 18.05 | 18.13 | 18.83 | 19.43 | 19.39 | 19.71 |
| Missouri | 19.79 | 20.57 | 20.94 | 21.20 | 20.79 | 21.48 | 21.87 | 22.00 | 22.10 |
| Montana | 17.80 | 18.44 | 19.86 | 20.19 | 20.67 | 20.70 | 20.96 | 21.42 | 22.05 |
| Nebraska | 19.92 | 19.79 | 20.19 | 20.89 | 20.84 | 20.95 | 20.92 | 21.36 | 22.18 |
| Nevada | 19.64 | 19.75 | 19.56 | 19.13 | 19.35 | 19.83 | 20.21 | 20.95 | 21.95 |
| New Hampshire | 22.06 | 22.66 | 22.70 | 22.98 | 23.00 | 23.70 | 24.26 | 24.30 | 24.90 |
| New Jersey | 24.84 | 25.32 | 25.92 | 25.95 | 25.63 | 26.45 | 26.80 | 26.91 | 27.78 |
| New Mexico | 18.57 | 18.73 | 18.92 | 19.57 | 19.70 | 19.82 | 20.19 | 20.49 | 20.47 |
| New York | 25.27 | 25.49 | 25.71 | 26.08 | 26.48 | 27.18 | 27.81 | 28.16 | 28.79 |
| North Carolina | 19.26 | 19.92 | 20.61 | 20.63 | 20.91 | 21.71 | 21.68 | 21.85 | 22.30 |
| North Dakota | 18.34 | 18.75 | 19.21 | 20.19 | 21.45 | 22.77 | 23.88 | 24.87 | 25.28 |
| Ohio | 20.22 | 20.11 | 19.95 | 20.22 | 21.07 | 22.01 | 22.24 | 22.16 | 22.68 |
| Oklahoma | 17.33 | 17.42 | 18.06 | 19.18 | 20.35 | 20.90 | 21.21 | 21.52 | 21.79 |
| Oregon | 20.61 | 20.93 | 21.33 | 21.56 | 21.75 | 22.23 | 22.52 | 22.91 | 23.53 |
| Pennsylvania | 20.08 | 20.43 | 20.75 | 21.21 | 21.85 | 22.62 | 23.28 | 23.72 | 24.20 |
| Rhode Island | 22.17 | 22.50 | 22.52 | 22.67 | 23.73 | 25.00 | 25.42 | 25.10 | 24.94 |
| South Carolina | 18.76 | 18.80 | 19.18 | 19.89 | 20.58 | 20.09 | 20.52 | 21.05 | 21.42 |
| South Dakota | 16.47 | 16.53 | 17.94 | 18.55 | 19.05 | 19.42 | 19.62 | 20.17 | 20.98 |
| Tennessee | 19.01 | 19.40 | 19.52 | 19.94 | 20.20 | 20.13 | 20.29 | 20.75 | 20.90 |
| Texas | 21.07 | 21.30 | 21.39 | 21.36 | 21.97 | 22.21 | 22.91 | 23.86 | 24.46 |
| Utah | 21.41 | 21.10 | 22.48 | 24.31 | 23.11 | 22.28 | 23.00 | 23.59 | 24.17 |
| Vermont | 20.42 | 21.35 | 22.41 | 23.01 | 23.03 | 22.79 | 22.77 | 23.17 | 24.06 |
| Virginia | 22.46 | 22.31 | 22.58 | 23.55 | 24.66 | 24.98 | 25.23 | 25.34 | 26.14 |
| Washington | 24.18 | 25.21 | 26.30 | 26.94 | 27.25 | 27.32 | 27.69 | 28.44 | 29.63 |
| West Virginia | 17.03 | 17.69 | 18.07 | 18.64 | 18.93 | 19.55 | 20.34 | 20.52 | 20.74 |
| Wisconsin | 20.46 | 20.68 | 21.13 | 21.35 | 21.85 | 22.38 | 23.11 | 23.24 | 23.46 |
| Wyoming | 20.04 | 20.83 | 21.06 | 21.45 | 22.18 | 22.55 | 22.94 | 23.22 | 23.17 |

. . . = Not available.

**Table 2-14.  Average Hourly Earnings of Production Workers on Private Nonfarm Payrolls, by Super Sector, NAICS Basis, 2005–2015**

(Dollars.)

| Industry | 2005 | 2006 | 2007 | 2008 | 2009 | 2010 | 2011 | 2012 | 2013 | 2014 | 2015 |
|---|---|---|---|---|---|---|---|---|---|---|---|
| **TOTAL PRIVATE** | 16.12 | 16.75 | 17.42 | 18.06 | 18.61 | 19.05 | 19.44 | 19.74 | 20.13 | 20.61 | 21.04 |
| **Goods-Producing** | 17.60 | 18.02 | 18.67 | 19.33 | 19.90 | 20.28 | 20.67 | 20.94 | 21.24 | 21.59 | 21.96 |
| Mining and logging | 18.72 | 19.90 | 20.97 | 22.50 | 23.29 | 23.82 | 24.50 | 25.79 | 26.80 | 26.84 | 26.48 |
| Construction | 19.46 | 20.02 | 20.95 | 21.87 | 22.66 | 23.22 | 23.65 | 23.97 | 24.22 | 24.67 | 25.20 |
| Manufacturing | 16.56 | 16.81 | 17.26 | 17.75 | 18.24 | 18.61 | 18.93 | 19.08 | 19.30 | 19.56 | 19.91 |
| **Private Service-Providing** | 15.72 | 16.40 | 17.09 | 17.75 | 18.33 | 18.78 | 19.18 | 19.48 | 19.90 | 20.40 | 20.85 |
| Trade, transportation, and utilities | 14.92 | 15.39 | 15.78 | 16.16 | 16.48 | 16.82 | 17.15 | 17.43 | 17.74 | 18.27 | 18.67 |
| Wholesale trade | 18.16 | 18.91 | 19.59 | 20.13 | 20.84 | 21.54 | 21.97 | 22.24 | 22.62 | 23.24 | 23.63 |
| Retail trade | 12.36 | 12.57 | 12.75 | 12.87 | 13.01 | 13.25 | 13.51 | 13.82 | 14.02 | 14.40 | 14.82 |
| Transportation and warehousing | 16.70 | 17.27 | 17.72 | 18.41 | 18.81 | 19.16 | 19.49 | 19.54 | 19.81 | 20.51 | 20.77 |
| Utilities | 26.68 | 27.40 | 27.88 | 28.83 | 29.48 | 30.04 | 30.82 | 31.61 | 32.27 | 32.86 | 34.00 |
| Information | 22.06 | 23.23 | 23.96 | 24.78 | 25.45 | 25.87 | 26.62 | 27.04 | 27.98 | 28.70 | 29.04 |
| Financial activities | 17.98 | 18.83 | 19.67 | 20.32 | 20.90 | 21.55 | 21.93 | 22.82 | 23.87 | 24.71 | 25.35 |
| Professional and business services | 18.08 | 19.13 | 20.15 | 21.18 | 22.35 | 22.78 | 23.12 | 23.29 | 23.72 | 24.29 | 24.79 |
| Education and health services | 16.62 | 17.28 | 17.99 | 18.73 | 19.34 | 19.95 | 20.60 | 20.92 | 21.29 | 21.65 | 22.11 |
| Leisure and hospitality | 9.38 | 9.75 | 10.41 | 10.84 | 11.12 | 11.31 | 11.45 | 11.62 | 11.78 | 12.09 | 12.42 |
| Other services | 14.34 | 14.77 | 15.42 | 16.09 | 16.59 | 17.06 | 17.32 | 17.59 | 18.00 | 18.51 | 19.01 |

## Table 2-15.  Average Weekly Earnings of All Employees on Nonfarm Payrolls, by Industry, in Current and 1982–1984 Dollars, NAICS Basis, 2009–2015

(Dollars.)

| Industry | 2009 | 2010 | 2011 | 2012 | 2013 | 2014 | 2015 |
|---|---|---|---|---|---|---|---|
| **TOTAL PRIVATE** | | | | | | | |
| Current dollars | 750.09 | 769.66 | 791.07 | 809.83 | 825.37 | 845.00 | 864.59 |
| 1982–1984 dollars | 349.63 | 352.96 | 351.68 | 352.72 | 354.30 | 356.94 | 364.78 |
| **Goods-Producing** | | | | | | | |
| Current dollars | 915.87 | 952.07 | 976.37 | 994.38 | 1 016.09 | 1 041.52 | 1 057.29 |
| 1982–1984 dollars | 426.91 | 436.62 | 434.06 | 433.10 | 436.17 | 439.95 | 446.08 |
| Mining and logging | | | | | | | |
| Current dollars | 1 150.12 | 1 189.32 | 1 250.91 | 1 263.98 | 1 306.16 | 1 380.77 | 1 370.32 |
| 1982–1984 dollars | 536.09 | 545.42 | 556.11 | 550.53 | 560.69 | 583.25 | 578.15 |
| Construction | | | | | | | |
| Current dollars | 922.54 | 952.78 | 973.85 | 997.01 | 1 018.01 | 1 040.85 | 1 070.53 |
| 1982–1984 dollars | 430.01 | 436.94 | 432.94 | 434.25 | 436.99 | 439.67 | 451.67 |
| Manufacturing | | | | | | | |
| Current dollars | 898.44 | 937.34 | 958.84 | 973.96 | 994.30 | 1 016.42 | 1 029.94 |
| 1982–1984 dollars | 418.78 | 429.86 | 426.27 | 424.21 | 426.82 | 429.35 | 434.54 |
| **Private Service-Providing** | | | | | | | |
| Current dollars | 716.45 | 733.26 | 754.76 | 773.89 | 787.96 | 806.50 | 827.16 |
| 1982–1984 dollars | 333.95 | 336.27 | 335.54 | 337.07 | 338.24 | 340.67 | 348.99 |
| Trade, transportation, and utilities | | | | | | | |
| Current dollars | 659.78 | 672.58 | 692.51 | 709.33 | 723.31 | 738.22 | 756.24 |
| 1982–1984 dollars | 307.54 | 308.44 | 307.87 | 308.95 | 310.49 | 311.83 | 319.07 |
| Wholesale trade | | | | | | | |
| Current dollars | 963.44 | 994.71 | 1 019.05 | 1 041.41 | 1 070.25 | 1 092.30 | 1 114.33 |
| 1982–1984 dollars | 449.08 | 456.17 | 453.03 | 453.59 | 459.42 | 461.40 | 470.15 |
| Retail trade | | | | | | | |
| Current dollars | 481.18 | 487.66 | 500.75 | 515.81 | 522.26 | 532.57 | 549.91 |
| 1982–1984 dollars | 224.29 | 223.64 | 222.62 | 224.66 | 224.19 | 224.96 | 232.01 |
| Transportation and warehousing | | | | | | | |
| Current dollars | 780.53 | 803.81 | 834.65 | 844.50 | 864.67 | 882.79 | 891.50 |
| 1982–1984 dollars | 363.82 | 368.63 | 371.06 | 367.82 | 371.17 | 372.90 | 376.13 |
| Utilities | | | | | | | |
| Current dollars | 1 343.66 | 1 338.50 | 1 404.36 | 1 432.93 | 1 484.54 | 1 508.94 | 1 579.27 |
| 1982–1984 dollars | 626.31 | 613.83 | 624.33 | 624.11 | 637.26 | 637.39 | 666.31 |
| Information | | | | | | | |
| Current dollars | 1 073.27 | 1 114.65 | 1 156.56 | 1 166.45 | 1 206.05 | 1 252.44 | 1 274.45 |
| 1982–1984 dollars | 500.27 | 511.18 | 514.17 | 508.05 | 517.71 | 529.05 | 537.70 |
| Financial activities | | | | | | | |
| Current dollars | 971.73 | 1 004.14 | 1 039.70 | 1 093.00 | 1 119.71 | 1 146.22 | 1 185.79 |
| 1982–1984 dollars | 452.94 | 460.50 | 462.21 | 476.06 | 480.65 | 484.18 | 500.30 |
| Professional and business services | | | | | | | |
| Current dollars | 947.10 | 963.57 | 991.87 | 1 013.76 | 1 030.55 | 1 062.48 | 1 088.63 |
| 1982–1984 dollars | 441.46 | 441.89 | 440.95 | 441.54 | 442.38 | 448.80 | 459.30 |
| Education and health services | | | | | | | |
| Current dollars | 724.06 | 743.68 | 767.34 | 787.92 | 799.54 | 809.71 | 829.54 |
| 1982–1984 dollars | 337.50 | 341.05 | 341.13 | 343.18 | 343.21 | 342.03 | 349.99 |
| Leisure and hospitality | | | | | | | |
| Current dollars | 331.64 | 336.83 | 342.67 | 349.12 | 350.95 | 364.07 | 376.37 |
| 1982–1984 dollars | 154.58 | 154.47 | 152.34 | 152.06 | 150.65 | 153.79 | 158.79 |
| Other services | | | | | | | |
| Current dollars | 618.33 | 637.65 | 649.87 | 659.49 | 679.43 | 698.41 | 716.25 |
| 1982–1984 dollars | 288.22 | 292.42 | 288.91 | 287.24 | 291.65 | 295.02 | 302.19 |

## Table 2-16.  Average Weekly Earnings of Production Workers on Nonfarm Payrolls, by Industry, in Current and 1982–1984 Dollars, NAICS Basis, 2005–2015

(Dollars.)

| Industry | 2005 | 2006 | 2007 | 2008 | 2009 | 2010 | 2011 | 2012 | 2013 | 2014 | 2015 |
|---|---|---|---|---|---|---|---|---|---|---|---|
| **TOTAL PRIVATE** | | | | | | | | | | | |
| Current dollars | 544.00 | 567.06 | 589.18 | 607.42 | 615.96 | 636.19 | 652.89 | 665.65 | 677.73 | 694.91 | 709.13 |
| 1982–1984 dollars | 284.82 | 287.70 | 290.57 | 287.80 | 293.83 | 297.33 | 294.66 | 294.24 | 295.53 | 298.54 | 305.91 |
| **Goods-Producing** | | | | | | | | | | | |
| Current dollars | 705.31 | 730.16 | 757.50 | 776.63 | 779.68 | 818.96 | 844.89 | 861.39 | 877.09 | 895.09 | 905.52 |
| 1982–1984 dollars | 369.27 | 370.45 | 373.58 | 367.98 | 371.93 | 382.75 | 381.31 | 380.76 | 382.47 | 384.54 | 390.63 |
| Mining and logging | | | | | | | | | | | |
| Current dollars | 853.87 | 907.95 | 962.63 | 1 014.69 | 1 006.67 | 1 063.11 | 1 144.64 | 1 201.69 | 1 229.70 | 1 270.91 | 1 212.52 |
| 1982–1984 dollars | 447.05 | 460.65 | 474.75 | 480.77 | 480.21 | 496.86 | 516.59 | 531.18 | 536.23 | 545.99 | 523.07 |
| Construction | | | | | | | | | | | |
| Current dollars | 750.37 | 781.59 | 816.23 | 842.61 | 851.76 | 891.83 | 921.84 | 942.14 | 958.72 | 977.11 | 997.77 |
| 1982–1984 dollars | 392.86 | 396.54 | 402.55 | 399.24 | 406.32 | 416.81 | 416.04 | 416.45 | 418.06 | 419.77 | 430.43 |
| Manufacturing | | | | | | | | | | | |
| Current dollars | 673.30 | 690.88 | 711.53 | 724.46 | 726.12 | 765.18 | 784.29 | 794.63 | 807.37 | 822.03 | 832.42 |
| 1982–1984 dollars | 352.51 | 350.52 | 350.91 | 343.26 | 346.38 | 357.62 | 353.96 | 351.25 | 352.07 | 353.15 | 359.10 |
| **Private Service-Providing** | | | | | | | | | | | |
| Current dollars | 509.23 | 532.19 | 554.18 | 573.29 | 587.51 | 605.07 | 620.97 | 633.06 | 645.03 | 661.64 | 676.32 |
| 1982–1984 dollars | 266.61 | 270.01 | 273.31 | 271.63 | 280.26 | 282.79 | 280.25 | 279.83 | 281.27 | 284.25 | 291.76 |
| Trade, transportation, and utilities | | | | | | | | | | | |
| Current dollars | 498.46 | 514.37 | 525.91 | 536.11 | 541.88 | 559.63 | 577.71 | 588.86 | 597.40 | 613.95 | 628.51 |
| 1982–1984 dollars | 260.97 | 260.97 | 259.37 | 254.02 | 258.49 | 261.55 | 260.73 | 260.29 | 260.50 | 263.76 | 271.13 |
| Wholesale trade | | | | | | | | | | | |
| Current dollars | 685.00 | 718.50 | 748.94 | 769.62 | 784.49 | 816.50 | 845.44 | 860.70 | 875.79 | 897.73 | 911.41 |
| 1982–1984 dollars | 358.64 | 364.54 | 369.36 | 364.66 | 374.23 | 381.60 | 381.56 | 380.46 | 381.90 | 385.67 | 393.17 |
| Retail trade | | | | | | | | | | | |
| Current dollars | 377.58 | 383.12 | 385.00 | 386.21 | 388.57 | 400.07 | 412.09 | 422.10 | 423.07 | 431.82 | 445.25 |
| 1982–1984 dollars | 197.69 | 194.38 | 189.87 | 182.99 | 185.36 | 186.98 | 185.98 | 186.58 | 184.49 | 185.51 | 192.08 |
| Transportation and warehousing | | | | | | | | | | | |
| Current dollars | 618.55 | 636.80 | 654.95 | 670.22 | 677.56 | 710.85 | 737.00 | 742.23 | 762.06 | 788.77 | 805.24 |
| 1982–1984 dollars | 323.85 | 323.08 | 323.01 | 317.56 | 323.22 | 332.22 | 332.62 | 328.09 | 332.31 | 338.86 | 347.37 |
| Utilities | | | | | | | | | | | |
| Current dollars | 1 095.91 | 1 135.57 | 1 182.65 | 1 230.65 | 1 239.34 | 1 262.89 | 1 296.92 | 1 298.23 | 1 344.70 | 1 388.91 | 1 443.33 |
| 1982–1984 dollars | 573.77 | 576.14 | 583.26 | 583.10 | 591.20 | 590.23 | 585.32 | 573.86 | 586.38 | 596.69 | 622.63 |
| Information | | | | | | | | | | | |
| Current dollars | 805.11 | 850.64 | 874.45 | 908.78 | 931.08 | 939.85 | 964.85 | 973.52 | 1 003.65 | 1 030.17 | 1 037.71 |
| 1982–1984 dollars | 421.52 | 431.58 | 431.26 | 430.59 | 444.15 | 439.25 | 435.45 | 430.33 | 437.66 | 442.57 | 447.66 |
| Financial activities | | | | | | | | | | | |
| Current dollars | 646.48 | 673.63 | 706.52 | 729.64 | 754.90 | 780.19 | 798.68 | 840.04 | 875.04 | 907.98 | 939.90 |
| 1982–1984 dollars | 338.47 | 341.77 | 348.44 | 345.71 | 360.11 | 364.63 | 360.46 | 371.32 | 381.57 | 390.07 | 405.46 |
| Professional and business services | | | | | | | | | | | |
| Current dollars | 618.71 | 662.27 | 700.82 | 737.90 | 775.81 | 798.54 | 813.37 | 822.58 | 838.67 | 864.45 | 878.72 |
| 1982–1984 dollars | 323.93 | 336.01 | 345.63 | 349.63 | 370.09 | 373.21 | 367.09 | 363.61 | 365.71 | 371.37 | 379.07 |
| Education and health services | | | | | | | | | | | |
| Current dollars | 541.04 | 560.88 | 585.46 | 607.72 | 622.24 | 639.29 | 663.07 | 674.75 | 683.35 | 692.85 | 709.74 |
| 1982–1984 dollars | 283.27 | 284.57 | 288.74 | 287.95 | 296.83 | 298.78 | 299.25 | 298.26 | 297.98 | 297.65 | 306.17 |
| Leisure and hospitality | | | | | | | | | | | |
| Current dollars | 241.36 | 250.34 | 265.54 | 273.39 | 275.95 | 280.87 | 283.82 | 290.54 | 294.31 | 303.81 | 311.36 |
| 1982–1984 dollars | 126.37 | 127.01 | 130.96 | 129.54 | 131.64 | 131.27 | 128.09 | 128.43 | 128.34 | 130.52 | 134.32 |
| Other services | | | | | | | | | | | |
| Current dollars | 443.40 | 456.50 | 477.06 | 495.57 | 506.26 | 523.70 | 532.63 | 539.46 | 553.77 | 568.92 | 583.46 |
| 1982–1984 dollars | 232.15 | 231.61 | 235.27 | 234.81 | 241.50 | 244.76 | 240.38 | 238.46 | 241.48 | 244.41 | 251.70 |

**Table 2-17.  Average Weekly Earnings of All Employees on Total Private Payrolls, by State, NAICS Basis, 2007–2015**

(Dollars.)

| State | 2007 | 2008 | 2009 | 2010 | 2011 | 2012 | 2013 | 2014 | 2015 |
|---|---|---|---|---|---|---|---|---|---|
| UNITED STATES | 719.88 | 739.05 | 750.09 | 769.66 | 791.07 | 809.83 | 825.37 | 845.00 | 864.59 |
| Alabama | 708.94 | 704.16 | 684.86 | 697.09 | 710.94 | 727.56 | 728.50 | 735.92 | 746.21 |
| Alaska | 876.85 | 882.85 | 868.00 | 843.67 | 877.46 | 905.89 | 941.25 | 939.39 | 967.44 |
| Arizona | 698.02 | 720.01 | 766.64 | 780.03 | 789.60 | 791.00 | 800.40 | 790.05 | 802.61 |
| Arkansas | 571.08 | 605.79 | 621.76 | 630.99 | 642.60 | 648.09 | 672.87 | 681.95 | 673.10 |
| California | 851.46 | 845.08 | 860.89 | 895.90 | 925.02 | 924.67 | 936.71 | 949.10 | 970.18 |
| Colorado | 807.24 | 827.89 | 815.65 | 816.00 | 826.28 | 861.35 | 892.27 | 907.01 | 912.90 |
| Connecticut | 912.04 | 942.14 | 917.73 | 935.06 | 957.34 | 956.76 | 939.46 | 948.99 | 976.53 |
| Delaware | 753.91 | 768.27 | 729.21 | 736.13 | 738.79 | 726.33 | 718.90 | 713.93 | 751.32 |
| District of Columbia | 1 217.50 | 1 158.85 | 1 135.59 | 1 203.14 | 1 258.12 | 1 318.87 | 1 379.16 | 1 403.93 | 1 363.12 |
| Florida | 728.18 | 739.20 | 756.35 | 761.12 | 746.81 | 741.57 | 755.08 | 763.34 | 776.21 |
| Georgia | 727.66 | 733.18 | 729.37 | 748.48 | 757.50 | 761.25 | 790.94 | 821.57 | 836.78 |
| Hawaii | 674.17 | 678.08 | 686.08 | 710.12 | 740.14 | 770.21 | 788.17 | 817.49 | 820.18 |
| Idaho | 566.29 | 594.27 | 647.14 | 704.51 | 704.78 | 706.94 | 708.08 | 713.76 | 737.47 |
| Illinois | 789.14 | 777.58 | 792.92 | 796.36 | 815.87 | 843.90 | 856.29 | 873.76 | 891.11 |
| Indiana | 707.52 | 710.50 | 711.38 | 722.01 | 722.75 | 741.89 | 763.97 | 789.09 | 797.81 |
| Iowa | 615.94 | 620.23 | 666.33 | 694.96 | 687.48 | 715.84 | 743.82 | 767.99 | 782.49 |
| Kansas | 681.51 | 700.18 | 687.80 | 684.39 | 707.60 | 733.60 | 742.17 | 764.31 | 774.15 |
| Kentucky | 652.46 | 654.13 | 666.23 | 684.82 | 693.00 | 696.08 | 699.55 | 716.50 | 744.12 |
| Louisiana | 670.89 | 701.53 | 702.51 | 713.58 | 748.87 | 773.23 | 786.88 | 802.96 | 796.98 |
| Maine | 640.91 | 650.33 | 638.03 | 657.41 | 678.64 | 714.74 | 714.34 | 725.22 | 749.46 |
| Maryland | 836.59 | 852.23 | 876.99 | 892.40 | 887.52 | 882.30 | 903.77 | 932.64 | 936.73 |
| Massachusetts | 873.35 | 886.03 | 899.14 | 911.57 | 914.55 | 928.62 | 960.14 | 983.02 | 1 019.74 |
| Michigan | 752.10 | 739.06 | 728.94 | 750.16 | 764.37 | 767.79 | 784.55 | 811.15 | 827.66 |
| Minnesota | 779.48 | 775.88 | 763.17 | 787.05 | 817.18 | 838.32 | 861.50 | 876.86 | 886.04 |
| Mississippi | 587.62 | 601.28 | 632.60 | 648.00 | 652.68 | 670.35 | 687.82 | 694.16 | 685.91 |
| Missouri | 680.78 | 709.67 | 709.87 | 718.68 | 721.41 | 743.21 | 752.33 | 752.40 | 749.19 |
| Montana | 633.68 | 595.61 | 619.63 | 658.19 | 680.04 | 687.24 | 697.97 | 702.58 | 718.83 |
| Nebraska | 667.32 | 666.92 | 680.40 | 712.35 | 710.64 | 712.30 | 715.46 | 728.38 | 756.34 |
| Nevada | 732.57 | 730.75 | 700.25 | 659.99 | 665.64 | 674.22 | 677.04 | 699.73 | 737.52 |
| New Hampshire | 734.60 | 743.25 | 742.29 | 760.64 | 763.60 | 784.47 | 812.71 | 811.62 | 836.64 |
| New Jersey | 844.56 | 850.75 | 870.91 | 877.11 | 868.86 | 888.72 | 900.48 | 906.87 | 938.96 |
| New Mexico | 642.52 | 663.04 | 664.09 | 684.95 | 691.47 | 689.74 | 702.61 | 711.00 | 700.07 |
| New York | 861.71 | 869.21 | 866.43 | 884.11 | 902.97 | 924.12 | 939.98 | 948.99 | 970.22 |
| North Carolina | 670.25 | 683.26 | 696.62 | 703.48 | 717.21 | 749.00 | 747.96 | 758.20 | 769.35 |
| North Dakota | 605.22 | 607.50 | 614.72 | 660.21 | 731.45 | 799.23 | 850.13 | 890.35 | 887.33 |
| Ohio | 687.48 | 681.73 | 658.35 | 677.37 | 710.06 | 750.54 | 760.61 | 757.87 | 775.66 |
| Oklahoma | 606.55 | 618.41 | 633.91 | 682.81 | 720.39 | 739.86 | 742.35 | 757.50 | 756.11 |
| Oregon | 704.86 | 707.43 | 708.16 | 724.42 | 735.15 | 751.37 | 758.92 | 776.65 | 800.02 |
| Pennsylvania | 678.70 | 690.53 | 684.75 | 706.29 | 731.98 | 750.98 | 779.88 | 799.36 | 822.80 |
| Rhode Island | 742.70 | 767.25 | 763.43 | 768.51 | 783.09 | 827.50 | 836.32 | 828.30 | 825.51 |
| South Carolina | 675.36 | 669.28 | 665.55 | 692.17 | 716.18 | 705.16 | 716.15 | 726.23 | 743.27 |
| South Dakota | 543.51 | 543.84 | 597.40 | 626.99 | 645.80 | 673.87 | 676.89 | 693.85 | 713.32 |
| Tennessee | 671.05 | 682.88 | 687.10 | 703.88 | 711.04 | 712.60 | 716.24 | 732.48 | 735.68 |
| Texas | 769.06 | 771.06 | 752.93 | 766.82 | 808.50 | 808.44 | 831.63 | 870.89 | 883.01 |
| Utah | 747.21 | 730.06 | 804.78 | 863.01 | 808.85 | 784.26 | 805.00 | 830.37 | 841.12 |
| Vermont | 696.32 | 734.44 | 764.18 | 786.94 | 776.11 | 770.30 | 769.63 | 773.88 | 801.20 |
| Virginia | 790.59 | 780.85 | 781.27 | 833.67 | 872.96 | 874.30 | 870.44 | 879.30 | 917.51 |
| Washington | 851.14 | 872.27 | 902.09 | 918.65 | 940.13 | 942.54 | 949.77 | 972.65 | 1 019.27 |
| West Virginia | 599.46 | 622.69 | 621.61 | 650.54 | 653.09 | 672.52 | 701.73 | 714.10 | 719.68 |
| Wisconsin | 673.13 | 682.44 | 680.39 | 700.28 | 723.24 | 749.73 | 774.19 | 785.51 | 790.60 |
| Wyoming | 725.45 | 764.46 | 747.63 | 770.06 | 800.70 | 820.82 | 823.55 | 828.95 | 813.27 |

## NOTES AND DEFINITIONS

### QUARTERLY CENSUS OF EMPLOYMENT AND WAGES

The Quarterly Census of Employment and Wages (QCEW), often referred to as the ES-202 program, is a cooperative endeavor of the Bureau of Labor Statistics (BLS) and the State Employment Security Agencies (SESAs). Using quarterly data submitted by the agencies, BLS summarizes the employment and wage data for workers covered by state unemployment insurance laws and civilian workers covered by the Unemployment Compensation for Federal Employees (UCFE) program.

Since the introduction of 2001 data, the QCEW data have been coded according to the North American Classification System, either NAICS 2002, which was used for the data up through 2006; NAICS 2007, which was used for data from 2007 through 2010; or NAICS 2012 which was introduced with the release of first quarter data in 2011. As a result of the revision, approximately 8 percent of establishments, 11 percent of employment, and 6 percent of total wages were reclassified into different industries within private industry.

NAICS is the statistical classification standard underlying all establishment-based federal economic statistics classified by industry. Before 2001, QCEW data were coded according to the Standard Industrial Classification (SIC) system. Due to the differences in the classification systems, data coded according to NAICS are often not directly comparable to SIC coded data.

The QCEW data series is the most complete universe of employment and wage information by industry, county, and state. It includes 98 percent of all wage and salary civilian employment. These data serve as the basic source of benchmark information for employment by industry in the Current Employment Statistics (CES) survey, which is described in the first section of notes in this chapter. Therefore, the entire employment series is not presented here. The wage series is presented because the CES only provides earnings only for production and nonsupervisory employees. The QCEW is more comprehensive. BLS aggregates the data by industry and ownership; these aggregations are available at the national, state, county, and metropolitan statistical area (MSA) levels.

### Collection and Coverage

Employment data under the QCEW program represent the number of covered workers who worked during, or received pay for, the pay period including the 12th of the month. Excluded are members of the armed forces, the self-employed, proprietors, domestic workers, unpaid family workers, and railroad workers covered by the railroad unemployment insurance system. Wages represent total compensation paid during the calendar quarter, regardless of when services were performed. Included in wages are pay for vacation and other paid leave, bonuses, stock options, tips, the cash value of meals and lodging, and in some states, contributions to deferred compensation plans (such as 401(k) plans). The QCEW program does provide partial information on agricultural industries and employees in private households.

Data from the QCEW program serve as an important input to many BLS programs. The QCEW data are used as the benchmark source for employment by the Current Employment Statistics program and the Occupational employment statistics program. The UI administrative records collected under the QCEW program serve as a sampling frame for BLS establishment surveys.

In addition, data from the QCEW program serve as an input to other federal and state programs. The Bureau of Economic Analysis (BEA) of the Department of Commerce uses QCEW data as the base for developing the wage and salary component of personal income. The Employment and Training Administration (ETA) of the Department of Labor and the SESAs use QCEW data to administer the employment security program. The QCEW data accurately reflect the extent of coverage of the state UI laws and are used to measure UI revenues; national, state, and local area employment; and total and UI taxable wage trends.

### Sources of Additional Information

Additional information is available on the BLS Web site at <http://www.bls.gov/cew>.

**Table 2-18.  Employment and Average Annual Pay for Covered Workers,[1] by Industry, NAICS Basis, 2010–2015**

(Number, dollars.)

| Industry | 2010 | | 2011 | | 2012 | |
|---|---|---|---|---|---|---|
| | Employment | Average annual pay | Employment | Average annual pay | Employment | Average annual pay |
| **Total Private** | 106 201 232 | 46 455 | 108 184 795 | 47 815 | 110 645 869 | 49 200 |
| Natural resources and mining | 1 798 592 | 49 820 | 1 890 359 | 53 691 | 1 988 119 | 55 944 |
| Agriculture, forestry, fishing, and hunting | 1 146 962 | 26 636 | 1 160 311 | 27 543 | 1 189 986 | 28 619 |
| Construction | 5 489 499 | 49 597 | 5 473 045 | 50 693 | 5 586 553 | 52 298 |
| Manufacturing | 11 487 496 | 57 526 | 11 701 497 | 59 210 | 11 904 945 | 60 496 |
| Wholesale trade | 5 466 463 | 63 629 | 5 545 802 | 66 142 | 5 656 717 | 68 226 |
| Retail trade | 14 481 324 | 26 652 | 14 666 625 | 27 118 | 14 864 946 | 27 731 |
| Transportation and warehousing | 3 943 659 | 44 197 | 4 055 639 | 45 336 | 4 158 046 | 46 612 |
| Utilities | 551 287 | 86 791 | 549 921 | 90 609 | 549 681 | 93 722 |
| Information | 2 703 886 | 74 395 | 2 674 852 | 78 331 | 2 677 224 | 81 955 |
| Financial activities | 7 401 812 | 73 977 | 7 416 409 | 77 366 | 7 506 950 | 80 110 |
| Professional and business services | 16 712 011 | 60 145 | 17 298 233 | 61 902 | 17 887 637 | 64 487 |
| Education and health services | 18 656 160 | 43 604 | 19 035 334 | 44 383 | 19 405 016 | 45 285 |
| Leisure and hospitality | 13 006 814 | 19 387 | 13 294 603 | 19 772 | 13 739 315 | 20 218 |
| Other services | 4 349 563 | 29 370 | 4 408 735 | 29 916 | 4 548 785 | 30 090 |
| **Total Government** | 21 619 210 | 48 202 | 21 226 299 | 49 205 | 21 050 509 | 49 757 |
| Federal | 2 980 813 | 69 198 | 2 863 132 | 73 001 | 2 820 722 | 73 340 |
| State | 4 606 001 | 48 960 | 4 553 697 | 50 252 | 4 523 704 | 51 366 |
| Local | 14 032 396 | 43 493 | 13 809 471 | 43 926 | 13 706 083 | 44 373 |

[1]Includes workers covered by unemployment insurance (UI) and Unemployment Compensation for Federal Employees (UCFE) programs.

**Table 2-18.  Employment and Average Annual Pay for Covered Workers,[1] by Industry, NAICS Basis, 2010–2015**—*Continued*

(Number, dollars.)

| Industry | 2013 | | 2014 | | 2015 | |
|---|---|---|---|---|---|---|
| | Employment | Average annual pay | Employment | Average annual pay | Employment | Average annual pay |
| **Total Private** | 112 958 334 | 49 701 | 115 568 686 | 51 296 | 118 307 717 | 52 876 |
| Natural resources and mining | 2 023 732 | 57 070 | 2 073 041 | 59 660 | 2 001 103 | 58 461 |
| Agriculture, forestry, fishing, and hunting | 1 210 474 | 29 447 | 1 231 162 | 30 614 | 1 249 192 | 31 977 |
| Construction | 5 819 950 | 53 181 | 6 108 673 | 55 037 | 6 423 866 | 57 009 |
| Manufacturing | 11 994 922 | 61 102 | 12 156 537 | 62 976 | 12 291 676 | 64 305 |
| Wholesale trade | 5 739 082 | 68 580 | 5 815 992 | 71 043 | 5 874 282 | 73 363 |
| Retail trade | 15 073 504 | 28 008 | 15 343 711 | 28 742 | 15 642 116 | 29 742 |
| Transportation and warehousing | 4 246 329 | 47 444 | 4 391 274 | 48 708 | 4 600 012 | 49 931 |
| Utilities | 547 807 | 95 157 | 548 993 | 98 123 | 553 685 | 101 445 |
| Information | 2 703 250 | 86 787 | 2 732 191 | 90 823 | 2 754 109 | 95 098 |
| Financial activities | 7 616 922 | 80 731 | 7 674 037 | 85 267 | 7 828 679 | 87 915 |
| Professional and business services | 18 478 164 | 64 623 | 19 074 275 | 66 668 | 19 607 372 | 69 270 |
| Education and health services | 20 204 352 | 44 976 | 20 573 137 | 45 950 | 21 080 792 | 47 383 |
| Leisure and hospitality | 14 195 179 | 20 413 | 14 626 556 | 20 995 | 15 100 935 | 21 807 |
| Other services | 4 149 819 | 32 844 | 4 235 390 | 33 936 | 4 308 880 | 35 116 |
| **Total Government** | 21 010 100 | 50 380 | 21 044 923 | 51 733 | 21 183 982 | 53 309 |
| Federal | 2 770 831 | 72 903 | 2 729 603 | 75 797 | 2 756 434 | 77 900 |
| State | 4 525 213 | 52 544 | 4 545 441 | 54 179 | 4 566 622 | 55 878 |
| Local | 13 714 056 | 45 115 | 13 769 879 | 46 155 | 13 860 926 | 47 573 |

[1]Includes workers covered by unemployment insurance (UI) and Unemployment Compensation for Federal Employees (UCFE) programs.

## Table 2-19. Employment and Average Annual Pay for Covered Workers,[1] by State and Selected Territory, 2008–2015

(Number, dollars.)

| State | 2008 Employment | 2008 Average annual pay | 2009 Employment | 2009 Average annual pay | 2010 Employment | 2010 Average annual pay | 2011 Employment | 2011 Average annual pay |
|---|---|---|---|---|---|---|---|---|
| UNITED STATES | 134 805 659 | 45 563 | 128 607 842 | 45 559 | 127 820 442 | 46 751 | 129 411 095 | 48 043 |
| Alabama | 1 936 489 | 38 734 | 1 829 487 | 39 422 | 1 813 155 | 40 289 | 1 813 497 | 41 186 |
| Alaska | 315 285 | 45 805 | 313 802 | 47 103 | 316 691 | 48 230 | 322 084 | 49 383 |
| Arizona | 2 583 215 | 42 518 | 2 396 362 | 42 832 | 2 356 789 | 43 299 | 2 378 248 | 44 581 |
| Arkansas | 1 172 208 | 34 919 | 1 134 488 | 35 692 | 1 134 071 | 36 254 | 1 139 682 | 37 280 |
| California | 15 494 915 | 51 487 | 14 629 953 | 51 566 | 14 414 461 | 53 285 | 14 567 128 | 55 013 |
| Colorado | 2 310 865 | 46 614 | 2 201 427 | 46 861 | 2 176 986 | 47 868 | 2 213 059 | 49 082 |
| Connecticut | 1 687 902 | 58 395 | 1 615 356 | 57 771 | 1 595 713 | 59 465 | 1 612 292 | 61 145 |
| Delaware | 423 083 | 47 569 | 402 343 | 47 770 | 399 078 | 48 669 | 402 959 | 50 499 |
| District of Columbia | 685 069 | 76 518 | 681 875 | 77 483 | 693 274 | 80 200 | 707 359 | 81 529 |
| Florida | 7 666 374 | 40 568 | 7 182 815 | 40 970 | 7 109 630 | 41 581 | 7 195 232 | 42 313 |
| Georgia | 4 031 467 | 42 585 | 3 796 429 | 42 902 | 3 753 934 | 43 899 | 3 792 209 | 45 090 |
| Hawaii | 619 703 | 40 675 | 592 171 | 41 328 | 586 772 | 41 709 | 593 668 | 42 473 |
| Idaho | 653 108 | 33 897 | 613 814 | 34 124 | 605 571 | 34 900 | 607 504 | 35 626 |
| Illinois | 5 841 692 | 48 719 | 5 551 930 | 48 358 | 5 502 322 | 49 497 | 5 566 648 | 50 840 |
| Indiana | 2 872 442 | 38 403 | 2 705 331 | 38 270 | 2 709 831 | 39 256 | 2 755 826 | 40 248 |
| Iowa | 1 490 575 | 36 964 | 1 445 627 | 37 158 | 1 436 340 | 38 146 | 1 452 769 | 39 204 |
| Kansas | 1 366 878 | 38 178 | 1 317 029 | 38 154 | 1 297 779 | 38 936 | 1 303 799 | 39 989 |
| Kentucky | 1 791 017 | 37 434 | 1 710 677 | 37 996 | 1 712 178 | 38 720 | 1 734 503 | 39 646 |
| Louisiana | 1 890 007 | 40 381 | 1 849 303 | 40 579 | 1 832 357 | 41 461 | 1 848 399 | 42 375 |
| Maine | 602 074 | 36 317 | 581 796 | 36 617 | 577 790 | 37 338 | 579 838 | 38 020 |
| Maryland | 2 537 752 | 49 535 | 2 461 109 | 50 579 | 2 453 197 | 51 739 | 2 478 505 | 53 008 |
| Massachusetts | 3 245 983 | 56 746 | 3 135 497 | 56 267 | 3 149 169 | 57 770 | 3 189 753 | 59 671 |
| Michigan | 4 070 914 | 44 245 | 3 775 435 | 43 645 | 3 770 225 | 44 439 | 3 854 837 | 45 828 |
| Minnesota | 2 679 527 | 45 826 | 2 569 651 | 45 319 | 2 558 310 | 46 787 | 2 602 988 | 47 858 |
| Mississippi | 1 131 096 | 33 508 | 1 081 138 | 33 847 | 1 074 617 | 34 343 | 1 076 488 | 34 976 |
| Missouri | 2 715 183 | 40 361 | 2 607 595 | 40 022 | 2 573 703 | 40 679 | 2 585 009 | 41 461 |
| Montana | 437 591 | 33 305 | 421 566 | 33 762 | 419 231 | 34 595 | 422 726 | 35 791 |
| Nebraska | 922 929 | 36 243 | 901 470 | 36 644 | 896 936 | 37 324 | 901 584 | 38 269 |
| Nevada | 1 252 987 | 42 984 | 1 138 036 | 42 743 | 1 108 238 | 42 512 | 1 115 062 | 43 102 |
| New Hampshire | 628 763 | 44 912 | 605 004 | 44 932 | 600 697 | 45 957 | 605 853 | 47 281 |
| New Jersey | 3 934 789 | 55 280 | 3 771 296 | 55 168 | 3 735 703 | 56 382 | 3 734 660 | 57 546 |
| New Mexico | 825 736 | 37 910 | 791 509 | 38 529 | 781 694 | 39 264 | 781 226 | 40 032 |
| New York | 8 608 351 | 60 288 | 8 343 862 | 57 739 | 8 340 732 | 60 291 | 8 444 791 | 61 792 |
| North Carolina | 4 043 486 | 39 740 | 3 823 299 | 39 844 | 3 788 581 | 41 119 | 3 838 300 | 42 121 |
| North Dakota | 350 440 | 35 075 | 349 560 | 35 970 | 358 635 | 38 128 | 379 432 | 41 778 |
| Ohio | 5 235 972 | 40 784 | 4 943 970 | 40 900 | 4 908 571 | 41 788 | 4 968 724 | 42 972 |
| Oklahoma | 1 550 489 | 37 284 | 1 497 855 | 37 238 | 1 485 400 | 38 237 | 1 507 558 | 40 108 |
| Oregon | 1 713 764 | 40 500 | 1 607 915 | 40 757 | 1 598 173 | 41 675 | 1 616 634 | 43 090 |
| Pennsylvania | 5 658 771 | 44 381 | 5 468 176 | 44 829 | 5 472 171 | 45 733 | 5 535 283 | 47 035 |
| Rhode Island | 469 701 | 43 029 | 448 842 | 43 439 | 447 408 | 44 645 | 448 570 | 45 705 |
| South Carolina | 1 876 081 | 36 252 | 1 765 739 | 36 759 | 1 758 204 | 37 553 | 1 780 690 | 38 427 |
| South Dakota | 397 108 | 32 822 | 389 360 | 33 352 | 389 198 | 34 331 | 393 744 | 35 413 |
| Tennessee | 2 721 990 | 39 996 | 2 565 288 | 40 242 | 2 558 438 | 41 572 | 2 602 604 | 42 454 |
| Texas | 10 452 907 | 45 939 | 10 149 694 | 45 692 | 10 182 150 | 46 952 | 10 422 295 | 48 735 |
| Utah | 1 221 052 | 37 980 | 1 157 704 | 38 614 | 1 150 737 | 39 389 | 1 176 530 | 40 279 |
| Vermont | 302 627 | 38 328 | 292 406 | 38 778 | 293 058 | 39 434 | 295 512 | 40 293 |
| Virginia | 3 665 654 | 47 241 | 3 545 623 | 48 239 | 3 536 676 | 49 651 | 3 578 848 | 50 657 |
| Washington | 2 950 773 | 46 569 | 2 836 283 | 47 470 | 2 808 698 | 48 516 | 2 844 622 | 50 256 |
| West Virginia | 709 657 | 35 987 | 691 998 | 36 897 | 692 448 | 37 675 | 701 905 | 39 092 |
| Wisconsin | 2 772 889 | 39 119 | 2 644 190 | 39 131 | 2 633 572 | 39 966 | 2 664 920 | 41 003 |
| Wyoming | 286 333 | 41 487 | 274 758 | 40 709 | 271 151 | 41 963 | 274 743 | 43 394 |

[1] Includes workers covered by the unemployment insurance (UI) and Unemployment Compensation for Federal Employees (UCFE) programs.

**Table 2-19. Employment and Average Annual Pay for Covered Workers,[1] by State and Selected Territory, 2008–2015**—*Continued*

(Number, dollars.)

| State | 2012 | | 2013 | | 2014 | | 2015 | |
|---|---|---|---|---|---|---|---|---|
| | Employment | Average annual pay | Employment | Average annual pay | Employment | Average annual pay | Employment | Average annual pay |
| UNITED STATES | 131 696 378 | 49 289 | 133 968 434 | 49 808 | 136 613 609 | 51 364 | 139 491 699 | 52 942 |
| Alabama | 1 828 248 | 41 990 | 1 845 086 | 42 276 | 1 863 561 | 43 287 | 1 890 340 | 44 273 |
| Alaska | 327 378 | 50 614 | 328 716 | 51 566 | 330 105 | 53 418 | 331 681 | 54 755 |
| Arizona | 2 431 788 | 45 593 | 2 488 009 | 45 921 | 2 539 253 | 46 919 | 2 609 770 | 47 933 |
| Arkansas | 1 146 811 | 38 226 | 1 146 274 | 38 941 | 1 157 630 | 39 975 | 1 177 884 | 40 895 |
| California | 14 959 808 | 56 784 | 15 378 962 | 57 111 | 15 809 082 | 59 042 | 16 295 204 | 61 698 |
| Colorado | 2 266 503 | 50 563 | 2 335 803 | 50 873 | 2 417 735 | 52 724 | 2 494 450 | 54 182 |
| Connecticut | 1 627 748 | 62 085 | 1 640 333 | 62 357 | 1 653 573 | 63 919 | 1 662 825 | . . . |
| Delaware | 405 646 | 51 734 | 413 825 | 52 040 | 423 598 | 53 212 | 433 748 | 53 991 |
| District of Columbia | 714 930 | 82 783 | 724 270 | 83 054 | 729 349 | 85 877 | 743 596 | 88 159 |
| Florida | 7 341 002 | 43 211 | 7 518 448 | 43 649 | 7 755 371 | 44 803 | 8 039 635 | 46 260 |
| Georgia | 3 841 767 | 46 267 | 3 918 085 | 46 760 | 4 032 488 | 48 138 | 4 151 011 | 49 551 |
| Hawaii | 605 240 | 43 385 | 618 195 | 43 845 | 626 146 | 45 210 | 637 854 | 46 919 |
| Idaho | 614 463 | 36 152 | 630 328 | 36 836 | 646 305 | 37 982 | 664 792 | 38 857 |
| Illinois | 5 636 918 | 52 194 | 5 687 541 | 52 590 | 5 762 156 | 54 106 | 5 848 451 | 55 989 |
| Indiana | 2 812 347 | 41 240 | 2 849 311 | 41 660 | 2 890 758 | 42 553 | 2 941 991 | 43 903 |
| Iowa | 1 475 884 | 40 343 | 1 496 426 | 41 107 | 1 515 822 | 42 538 | 1 530 234 | 44 095 |
| Kansas | 1 320 285 | 41 118 | 1 336 948 | 41 548 | 1 357 090 | 42 716 | 1 367 329 | 43 878 |
| Kentucky | 1 761 043 | 40 451 | 1 779 777 | 40 793 | 1 807 068 | 41 941 | 1 835 550 | 43 365 |
| Louisiana | 1 871 037 | 43 300 | 1 893 823 | 44 008 | 1 923 745 | 45 336 | 1 930 688 | 45 928 |
| Maine | 583 196 | 38 606 | 586 525 | 39 279 | 590 377 | 40 442 | 595 889 | 41 791 |
| Maryland | 2 511 669 | 54 035 | 2 531 656 | 54 052 | 2 552 623 | 55 389 | 2 591 189 | 57 176 |
| Massachusetts | 3 242 273 | 60 898 | 3 295 647 | 61 790 | 3 360 035 | 64 103 | 3 428 020 | 66 692 |
| Michigan | 3 935 694 | 46 720 | 4 018 602 | 47 131 | 4 090 009 | 48 487 | 4 161 641 | 50 063 |
| Minnesota | 2 644 408 | 49 349 | 2 691 832 | 50 116 | 2 730 301 | 51 602 | 2 776 684 | 53 527 |
| Mississippi | 1 085 748 | 35 875 | 1 093 581 | 36 455 | 1 102 603 | 37 111 | 1 114 379 | 37 642 |
| Missouri | 2 607 420 | 42 695 | 2 637 273 | 43 066 | 2 667 996 | 44 258 | 2 715 579 | 45 565 |
| Montana | 430 315 | 37 096 | 436 867 | 37 575 | 440 198 | 38 878 | 448 688 | 40 056 |
| Nebraska | 920 295 | 39 268 | 932 768 | 39 965 | 946 110 | 41 185 | 959 176 | 42 854 |
| Nevada | 1 132 140 | 43 667 | 1 160 115 | 44 119 | 1 202 475 | 44 727 | 1 244 635 | 45 739 |
| New Hampshire | 612 419 | 48 272 | 618 781 | 48 963 | 626 566 | 51 165 | 636 806 | 52 553 |
| New Jersey | 3 768 935 | 58 644 | 3 812 940 | 59 467 | 3 841 854 | 60 597 | 3 889 975 | 62 365 |
| New Mexico | 785 455 | 40 698 | 791 804 | 40 809 | 798 912 | 41 925 | 806 762 | 42 555 |
| New York | 8 563 125 | 62 669 | 8 685 758 | 63 089 | 8 846 774 | 65 880 | 9 014 385 | 67 521 |
| North Carolina | 3 907 085 | 43 110 | 3 974 937 | 43 795 | 4 057 439 | 44 973 | 4 161 654 | 46 530 |
| North Dakota | 411 709 | 45 909 | 427 108 | 47 779 | 444 652 | 50 855 | 437 072 | 50 696 |
| Ohio | 5 048 166 | 44 244 | 5 110 011 | 44 671 | 5 183 462 | 46 000 | 5 257 971 | 47 146 |
| Oklahoma | 1 540 292 | 41 633 | 1 560 799 | 42 457 | 1 582 712 | 43 773 | 1 594 011 | 44 306 |
| Oregon | 1 642 434 | 44 258 | 1 678 726 | 45 019 | 1 725 906 | 46 529 | 1 787 398 | 48 328 |
| Pennsylvania | 5 578 414 | 48 397 | 5 596 841 | 49 077 | 5 644 443 | 50 567 | 5 691 613 | 52 187 |
| Rhode Island | 450 711 | 46 716 | 456 112 | 47 732 | 463 303 | 49 297 | 469 981 | 50 651 |
| South Carolina | 1 810 150 | 39 286 | 1 846 621 | 39 792 | 1 895 420 | 40 797 | 1 949 881 | 42 002 |
| South Dakota | 400 475 | 36 534 | 404 652 | 37 225 | 410 929 | 38 690 | 416 020 | 40 181 |
| Tennessee | 2 653 392 | 43 961 | 2 694 288 | 44 091 | 2 750 032 | 45 202 | 2 820 198 | 46 742 |
| Texas | 10 727 642 | 50 579 | 11 031 907 | 51 201 | 11 379 184 | 53 218 | 11 655 919 | 54 281 |
| Utah | 1 215 983 | 41 301 | 1 254 582 | 41 792 | 1 291 859 | 42 942 | 1 340 591 | 44 318 |
| Vermont | 299 519 | 40 967 | 301 586 | 42 043 | 304 472 | 43 025 | 307 058 | 44 234 |
| Virginia | 3 619 176 | 51 646 | 3 640 209 | 51 918 | 3 654 831 | 52 929 | 3 735 713 | 54 276 |
| Washington | 2 894 703 | 51 962 | 2 960 123 | 53 050 | 3 043 562 | 55 016 | 3 122 749 | 56 661 |
| West Virginia | 710 590 | 39 727 | 703 916 | 40 201 | 700 846 | 41 201 | 696 195 | 41 727 |
| Wisconsin | 2 695 404 | 41 966 | 2 721 960 | 42 777 | 2 758 496 | 43 829 | 2 794 170 | 45 365 |
| Wyoming | 278 595 | 44 580 | 279 748 | 44 972 | 284 394 | 46 492 | 282 667 | 46 306 |

[1]Includes workers covered by the unemployment insurance (UI) and Unemployment Compensation for Federal Employees (UCFE) programs.

## BUSINESS EMPLOYMENT DYNAMICS

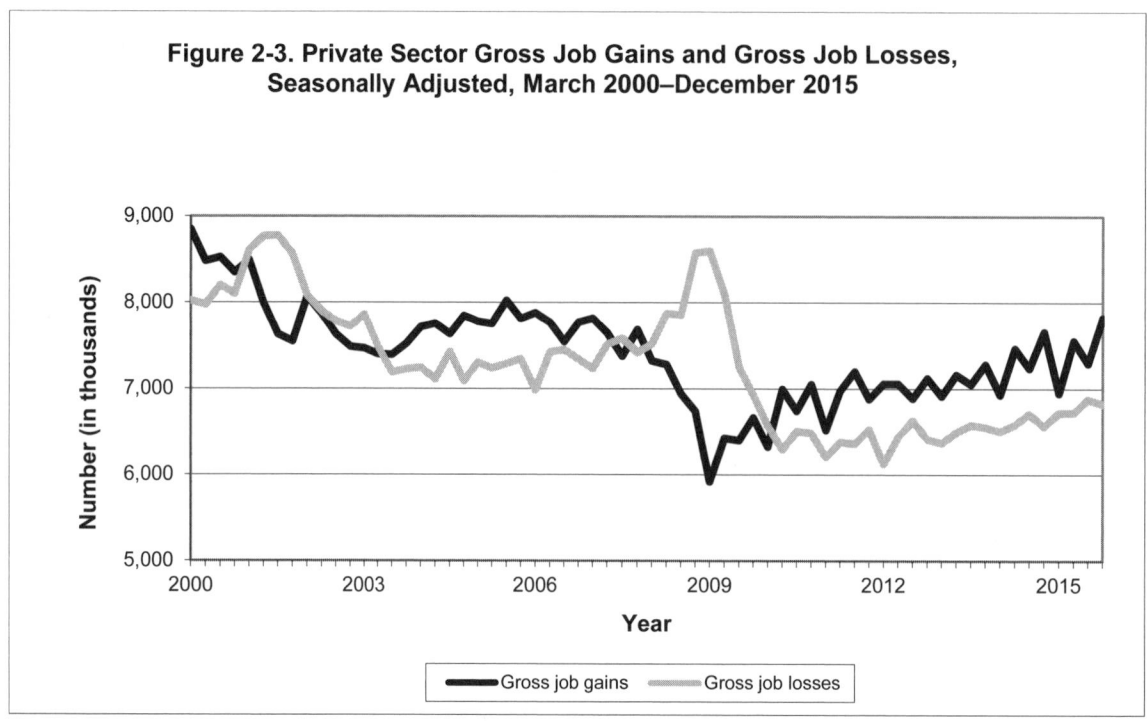

**Figure 2-3. Private Sector Gross Job Gains and Gross Job Losses, Seasonally Adjusted, March 2000–December 2015**

The change in the number of jobs is the net result of the gross increase in the number of jobs from expanding and opening establishments and the gross decrease in jobs from contracting and closing establishments. The net gain of 1.0 million jobs in the fourth quarter of 2015 resulted from 7.822 million gross job gains and 6.822 million gross job losses. There was a net gain of jobs in twenty-three consecutive quarters from June 2010 to December 2015. In contrast, there was a net loss in nine consecutive quarters from the first quarter of 2008 through the first quarter of 2010. (See Table 2-20.)

## OTHER HIGHLIGHTS

- Of the 6.8 million jobs that were lost in the fourth quarter of 2015, 81.4 percent resulted from contracting establishments while 18.6 percent were the result of establishments closing. (See Table 2-20.)

- The service-providing industries experienced a net job gain of 957,000 in the fourth quarter of 2015. Within the service-providing industry, professional and business services experienced the greatest net job gain at 278,000. (See Table 2-22.)

- In construction, gross job gains exceeded gross job losses by 109,000 in the fourth quarter of 2015—more than in any other goods-producing sector. (See Table 2-22.)

- Job gains exceeded job losses in 45 states and the District of Columbia in December 2015. In North Dakota, which has a low unemployment rate, job losses exceeded job gains by 4,846 while job gains exceeded job losses by 134,793 in California. (See Table 2-23.)

# NOTES AND DEFINITIONS

## BUSINESS EMPLOYMENT DYNAMICS (BED)

The Business Employment Dynamics (BED) data are a set of statistics generated from the federal-state cooperative program known as the Quarterly Census of Employment and Wages (QCEW), or the ES-202 program. These quarterly data series consist of gross job gains and gross job losses statistics from 1992 forward.

The Bureau of Labor Statistics (BLS) compiles the BED data from existing quarterly state unemployment insurance (UI) records. Most employers in the United States are required to file quarterly reports on the employment and wages of workers covered by UI laws and to pay quarterly UI taxes. The quarterly UI reports are sent by the State Workforce Agencies (SWAs) to BLS. These reports form the basis of the BLS establishment universe-sampling frame.

In the BED program, the quarterly UI records are linked across quarters to provide a longitudinal history for each establishment. The linkage process allows the tracking of net employment changes at the establishment level, which in turn allows estimations of jobs gained at opening and expanding establishments and of jobs lost at closing and contracting establishments. BLS publishes three different establishment-based employment measures for every given quarter. Each of these measures—the Current Employment Statistics (CES) survey, the QCEW program, and the BED data each make use of the quarterly UI employment reports. However, each measure has somewhat different types of universal coverage, estimation procedures, and publication products. (See the notes and corresponding tables for CES and QCEW in earlier sections of this chapter.)

## Concepts and Definitions

The BED data measure the net change in employment at the establishment level. These changes can come about in four different ways. A net increase in employment can come from either opening establishments or expanding establishments. A net decrease in employment can come from either closing establishments or contracting establishments.

*Gross job gains* include the sum of all jobs added at either opening or expanding establishments.

*Gross job losses* include the sum of all jobs lost in either closing or contracting establishments. The net change in employment is the difference between gross job gains and gross job losses.

*Openings* consist of establishments with positive third-month employment for the first time in the current quarter, with no links to the prior quarter, or with positive third-month employment in the current quarter, following zero employment in the previous quarter.

*Expansions* include establishments with positive employment in the third month in both the previous and current quarters, with a net increase in employment over this period.

*Closings* consist of establishments with positive third-month employment in the previous quarter, with no employment or zero employment reported in the current quarter.

*Contractions* include establishments with positive employment in the third month in both the previous and current quarters, with a net decrease in employment over this period.

## Sources of Additional Information

For additional information, see BLS news release 16-1538 "Business Employment Dynamics: Fourth Quarter 2015."

## Table 2-20.  Private Sector Gross Job Gains and Job Losses, Seasonally Adjusted, March 2000– December 2015

(Thousands of jobs.)

| Year and month | Net change[1] | Gross job gains | | | Gross job losses | | |
|---|---|---|---|---|---|---|---|
| | | Total | Expanding establishments | Opening establishments | Total | Contracting establishments | Closing establishments |
| **2000** | | | | | | | |
| March | 827 | 8 849 | 6 960 | 1 889 | 8 022 | 6 342 | 1 680 |
| June | 503 | 8 479 | 6 794 | 1 685 | 7 976 | 6 373 | 1 603 |
| September | 324 | 8 525 | 6 756 | 1 769 | 8 201 | 6 479 | 1 722 |
| December | 251 | 8 351 | 6 673 | 1 678 | 8 100 | 6 444 | 1 656 |
| **2001** | | | | | | | |
| March | -119 | 8 491 | 6 728 | 1 763 | 8 610 | 6 717 | 1 893 |
| June | -780 | 7 991 | 6 302 | 1 689 | 8 771 | 7 036 | 1 735 |
| September | -1 148 | 7 630 | 5 945 | 1 685 | 8 778 | 6 990 | 1 788 |
| December | -1 009 | 7 547 | 5 912 | 1 635 | 8 556 | 6 870 | 1 686 |
| **2002** | | | | | | | |
| March | -10 | 8 071 | 6 298 | 1 773 | 8 081 | 6 434 | 1 647 |
| June | -30 | 7 868 | 6 145 | 1 723 | 7 898 | 6 274 | 1 624 |
| September | -151 | 7 630 | 6 039 | 1 591 | 7 781 | 6 248 | 1 533 |
| December | -241 | 7 483 | 5 938 | 1 545 | 7 724 | 6 185 | 1 539 |
| **2003** | | | | | | | |
| March | -393 | 7 467 | 5 928 | 1 539 | 7 860 | 6 307 | 1 553 |
| June | -90 | 7 398 | 5 929 | 1 469 | 7 488 | 6 030 | 1 458 |
| September | 204 | 7 392 | 5 923 | 1 469 | 7 188 | 5 828 | 1 360 |
| December | 297 | 7 521 | 6 005 | 1 516 | 7 224 | 5 800 | 1 424 |
| **2004** | | | | | | | |
| March | 470 | 7 715 | 6 204 | 1 511 | 7 245 | 5 795 | 1 450 |
| June | 644 | 7 754 | 6 235 | 1 519 | 7 110 | 5 639 | 1 471 |
| September | 206 | 7 633 | 6 060 | 1 573 | 7 427 | 5 888 | 1 539 |
| December | 757 | 7 844 | 6 243 | 1 601 | 7 087 | 5 663 | 1 424 |
| **2005** | | | | | | | |
| March | 475 | 7 779 | 6 222 | 1 557 | 7 304 | 5 828 | 1 476 |
| June | 516 | 7 753 | 6 183 | 1 570 | 7 237 | 5 802 | 1 435 |
| September | 736 | 8 023 | 6 412 | 1 611 | 7 287 | 5 813 | 1 474 |
| December | 467 | 7 812 | 6 239 | 1 573 | 7 345 | 5 960 | 1 385 |
| **2006** | | | | | | | |
| March | 896 | 7 880 | 6 383 | 1 497 | 6 984 | 5 661 | 1 323 |
| June | 342 | 7 766 | 6 228 | 1 538 | 7 424 | 6 026 | 1 398 |
| September | 92 | 7 545 | 6 076 | 1 469 | 7 453 | 6 067 | 1 386 |
| December | 431 | 7 770 | 6 226 | 1 544 | 7 339 | 5 964 | 1 375 |
| **2007** | | | | | | | |
| March | 584 | 7 815 | 6 331 | 1 484 | 7 231 | 5 894 | 1 337 |
| June | 132 | 7 647 | 6 205 | 1 442 | 7 515 | 6 084 | 1 431 |
| September | -209 | 7 376 | 5 870 | 1 506 | 7 585 | 6 190 | 1 395 |
| December | 268 | 7 687 | 6 181 | 1 506 | 7 419 | 6 040 | 1 379 |
| **2008** | | | | | | | |
| March | -199 | 7 320 | 5 860 | 1 460 | 7 519 | 6 111 | 1 408 |
| June | -593 | 7 281 | 5 833 | 1 448 | 7 874 | 6 363 | 1 511 |
| September | -913 | 6 944 | 5 535 | 1 409 | 7 857 | 6 436 | 1 421 |
| December | -1 838 | 6 738 | 5 345 | 1 393 | 8 576 | 7 056 | 1 520 |
| **2009** | | | | | | | |
| March | -2 680 | 5 918 | 4 675 | 1 243 | 8 598 | 7 142 | 1 456 |
| June | -1 667 | 6 425 | 5 080 | 1 345 | 8 092 | 6 674 | 1 418 |
| September | -849 | 6 399 | 5 139 | 1 260 | 7 248 | 5 854 | 1 394 |
| December | -264 | 6 665 | 5 308 | 1 357 | 6 929 | 5 605 | 1 324 |
| **2010** | | | | | | | |
| March | -247 | 6 325 | 5 108 | 1 217 | 6 572 | 5 324 | 1 248 |
| June | 698 | 6 995 | 5 674 | 1 321 | 6 297 | 5 090 | 1 207 |
| September | 237 | 6 741 | 5 438 | 1 303 | 6 504 | 5 231 | 1 273 |
| December | 566 | 7 052 | 5 639 | 1 413 | 6 486 | 5 219 | 1 267 |
| **2011** | | | | | | | |
| March | 315 | 6 521 | 5 304 | 1 217 | 6 206 | 5 026 | 1 180 |
| June | 595 | 6 976 | 5 633 | 1 343 | 6 381 | 5 113 | 1 268 |
| September | 833 | 7 198 | 5 804 | 1 394 | 6 365 | 5 174 | 1 191 |
| December | 350 | 6 878 | 5 515 | 1 363 | 6 528 | 5 271 | 1 257 |
| **2012** | | | | | | | |
| March | 933 | 7 059 | 5 729 | 1 330 | 6 126 | 5 003 | 1 123 |
| June | 618 | 7 057 | 5 733 | 1 324 | 6 439 | 5 270 | 1 169 |
| September | 255 | 6 886 | 5 573 | 1 313 | 6 631 | 5 433 | 1 198 |
| December | 708 | 7 122 | 5 762 | 1 360 | 6 414 | 5 221 | 1 193 |
| **2013** | | | | | | | |
| March | 544 | 6 913 | 5 685 | 1 228 | 6 369 | 5 191 | 1 178 |
| June | 666 | 7 160 | 5 839 | 1 321 | 6 494 | 5 284 | 1 210 |
| September | 473 | 7 051 | 5 710 | 1 341 | 6 578 | 5 430 | 1 148 |
| December | 728 | 7 279 | 5 944 | 1 335 | 6 551 | 5 343 | 1 208 |
| **2014** | | | | | | | |
| March | 423 | 6 927 | 5 664 | 1 263 | 6 504 | 5 360 | 1 144 |
| June | 883 | 7 467 | 6 128 | 1 339 | 6 584 | 5 362 | 1 222 |
| September | 525 | 7 235 | 5 905 | 1 330 | 6 710 | 5 523 | 1 187 |
| December | 1 095 | 7 658 | 6 279 | 1 379 | 6 563 | 5 322 | 1 241 |
| **2015** | | | | | | | |
| March | 226 | 6 947 | 5 666 | 1 281 | 6 721 | 5 558 | 1 163 |
| June | 829 | 7 554 | 6 220 | 1 334 | 6 725 | 5 541 | 1 184 |
| September | 418 | 7 292 | 5 958 | 1 334 | 6 874 | 5 657 | 1 217 |
| December | 1 000 | 7 822 | 6 373 | 1 449 | 6 822 | 5 551 | 1 271 |

[1]Net change is the difference between total gross job gains and total gross job losses.

## Table 2-21. Private Sector Gross Job Gains and Job Losses, as a Percent of Employment,[1] Seasonally Adjusted, March 2000–December 2015

(Percent.)

| Year and month | Net change[2] | Gross job gains | | | Gross job losses | | |
|---|---|---|---|---|---|---|---|
| | | Total | Expanding establishments | Opening establishments | Total | Contracting establishments | Closing establishments |
| **2000** | | | | | | | |
| March | 0.8 | 8.1 | 6.4 | 1.7 | 7.3 | 5.8 | 1.5 |
| June | 0.4 | 7.7 | 6.2 | 1.5 | 7.3 | 5.8 | 1.5 |
| September | 0.2 | 7.7 | 6.1 | 1.6 | 7.5 | 5.9 | 1.6 |
| December | 0.2 | 7.5 | 6.0 | 1.5 | 7.3 | 5.8 | 1.5 |
| **2001** | | | | | | | |
| March | -0.1 | 7.7 | 6.1 | 1.6 | 7.8 | 6.1 | 1.7 |
| June | -0.8 | 7.2 | 5.7 | 1.5 | 8.0 | 6.4 | 1.6 |
| September | -1.1 | 6.9 | 5.4 | 1.5 | 8.0 | 6.4 | 1.6 |
| December | -1.0 | 7.0 | 5.5 | 1.5 | 8.0 | 6.4 | 1.6 |
| **2002** | | | | | | | |
| March | 0.0 | 7.5 | 5.9 | 1.6 | 7.5 | 6.0 | 1.5 |
| June | 0.0 | 7.3 | 5.7 | 1.6 | 7.3 | 5.8 | 1.5 |
| September | -0.1 | 7.1 | 5.6 | 1.5 | 7.2 | 5.8 | 1.4 |
| December | -0.3 | 6.9 | 5.5 | 1.4 | 7.2 | 5.8 | 1.4 |
| **2003** | | | | | | | |
| March | -0.5 | 6.9 | 5.5 | 1.4 | 7.4 | 5.9 | 1.5 |
| June | 0.0 | 7.0 | 5.6 | 1.4 | 7.0 | 5.6 | 1.4 |
| September | 0.1 | 6.9 | 5.5 | 1.4 | 6.8 | 5.5 | 1.3 |
| December | 0.3 | 7.0 | 5.6 | 1.4 | 6.7 | 5.4 | 1.3 |
| **2004** | | | | | | | |
| March | 0.5 | 7.2 | 5.8 | 1.4 | 6.7 | 5.4 | 1.3 |
| June | 0.6 | 7.2 | 5.8 | 1.4 | 6.6 | 5.2 | 1.4 |
| September | 0.3 | 7.1 | 5.6 | 1.5 | 6.8 | 5.4 | 1.4 |
| December | 0.7 | 7.2 | 5.7 | 1.5 | 6.5 | 5.2 | 1.3 |
| **2005** | | | | | | | |
| March | 0.5 | 7.1 | 5.7 | 1.4 | 6.6 | 5.3 | 1.3 |
| June | 0.4 | 7.0 | 5.6 | 1.4 | 6.6 | 5.3 | 1.3 |
| September | 0.8 | 7.3 | 5.8 | 1.5 | 6.5 | 5.2 | 1.3 |
| December | 0.4 | 7.0 | 5.6 | 1.4 | 6.6 | 5.4 | 1.2 |
| **2006** | | | | | | | |
| March | 0.8 | 7.0 | 5.7 | 1.3 | 6.2 | 5.0 | 1.2 |
| June | 0.4 | 6.9 | 5.5 | 1.4 | 6.5 | 5.3 | 1.2 |
| September | 0.1 | 6.7 | 5.4 | 1.3 | 6.6 | 5.4 | 1.2 |
| December | 0.4 | 6.9 | 5.5 | 1.4 | 6.5 | 5.3 | 1.2 |
| **2007** | | | | | | | |
| March | 0.5 | 6.9 | 5.6 | 1.3 | 6.4 | 5.2 | 1.2 |
| June | 0.1 | 6.7 | 5.4 | 1.3 | 6.6 | 5.3 | 1.3 |
| September | -0.2 | 6.4 | 5.1 | 1.3 | 6.6 | 5.4 | 1.2 |
| December | 0.2 | 6.7 | 5.4 | 1.3 | 6.5 | 5.3 | 1.2 |
| **2008** | | | | | | | |
| March | -0.1 | 6.4 | 5.1 | 1.3 | 6.5 | 5.3 | 1.2 |
| June | -0.5 | 6.4 | 5.1 | 1.3 | 6.9 | 5.6 | 1.3 |
| September | -0.9 | 6.1 | 4.9 | 1.2 | 7.0 | 5.7 | 1.3 |
| December | -1.7 | 6.0 | 4.8 | 1.2 | 7.7 | 6.3 | 1.4 |
| **2009** | | | | | | | |
| March | -2.4 | 5.4 | 4.3 | 1.1 | 7.8 | 6.5 | 1.3 |
| June | -1.5 | 6.0 | 4.7 | 1.3 | 7.5 | 6.2 | 1.3 |
| September | -0.8 | 6.0 | 4.8 | 1.2 | 6.8 | 5.5 | 1.3 |
| December | -0.3 | 6.3 | 5.0 | 1.3 | 6.6 | 5.3 | 1.3 |
| **2010** | | | | | | | |
| March | -0.2 | 6.0 | 4.8 | 1.2 | 6.2 | 5.0 | 1.2 |
| June | 0.7 | 6.6 | 5.4 | 1.2 | 5.9 | 4.8 | 1.1 |
| September | 0.2 | 6.3 | 5.1 | 1.2 | 6.1 | 4.9 | 1.2 |
| December | 0.5 | 6.6 | 5.3 | 1.3 | 6.1 | 4.9 | 1.2 |
| **2011** | | | | | | | |
| March | 0.2 | 6.0 | 4.9 | 1.1 | 5.8 | 4.7 | 1.1 |
| June | 0.5 | 6.4 | 5.2 | 1.2 | 5.9 | 4.7 | 1.2 |
| September | 0.8 | 6.7 | 5.4 | 1.3 | 5.9 | 4.8 | 1.1 |
| December | 0.4 | 6.4 | 5.1 | 1.3 | 6.0 | 4.8 | 1.2 |
| **2012** | | | | | | | |
| March | 0.8 | 6.4 | 5.2 | 1.2 | 5.6 | 4.6 | 1.0 |
| June | 0.5 | 6.4 | 5.2 | 1.2 | 5.9 | 4.8 | 1.1 |
| September | 0.2 | 6.2 | 5.0 | 1.2 | 6.0 | 4.9 | 1.1 |
| December | 0.6 | 6.4 | 5.2 | 1.2 | 5.8 | 4.7 | 1.1 |
| **2013** | | | | | | | |
| March | 0.5 | 6.2 | 5.1 | 1.1 | 5.7 | 4.6 | 1.1 |
| June | 0.6 | 6.4 | 5.2 | 1.2 | 5.8 | 4.7 | 1.1 |
| September | 0.5 | 6.3 | 5.1 | 1.2 | 5.8 | 4.8 | 1.0 |
| December | 0.6 | 6.4 | 5.2 | 1.2 | 5.8 | 4.7 | 1.1 |
| **2014** | | | | | | | |
| March | 0.4 | 6.1 | 5.0 | 1.1 | 5.7 | 4.7 | 1.0 |
| June | 0.7 | 6.5 | 5.3 | 1.2 | 5.8 | 4.7 | 1.1 |
| September | 0.5 | 6.3 | 5.1 | 1.2 | 5.8 | 4.8 | 1.0 |
| December | 0.9 | 6.6 | 5.4 | 1.2 | 5.7 | 4.6 | 1.1 |
| **2015** | | | | | | | |
| March | 0.2 | 5.9 | 4.8 | 1.1 | 5.7 | 4.7 | 1.0 |
| June | 0.7 | 6.4 | 5.3 | 1.1 | 5.7 | 4.7 | 1.0 |
| September | 0.3 | 6.1 | 5.0 | 1.1 | 5.8 | 4.8 | 1.0 |
| December | 0.8 | 6.6 | 5.4 | 1.2 | 5.8 | 4.7 | 1.1 |

[1]The rates measure gross job gains and job losses as a percentage of the average of the previous and current employment.
[2]Net change is the difference between total gross job gains and total gross job losses.

## Table 2-22.  Three-Month Private Sector Job Gains and Losses, by Industry, Seasonally Adjusted, December 2014–December 2015

(Thousands of jobs.)

| Industry | Gross job gains and job losses (3 months ended) | | | | | Gross job gains and losses as a percent of employment (3 months ended) | | | | |
|---|---|---|---|---|---|---|---|---|---|---|
| | December 2014 | March 2015 | June 2015 | September 2015 | December 2015 | December 2014 | March 2015 | June 2015 | September 2015 | December 2015 |
| **TOTAL PRIVATE**[1] | | | | | | | | | | |
| Gross job gains | 7 658 | 6 947 | 7 554 | 7 292 | 7 822 | 6.6 | 5.9 | 6.4 | 6.1 | 6.6 |
| Gross job losses | 6 563 | 6 721 | 6 725 | 6 874 | 6 822 | 5.7 | 5.7 | 5.7 | 5.8 | 5.8 |
| Net employment change | 1 095 | 226 | 829 | 418 | 1 000 | 0.9 | 0.2 | 0.7 | 0.3 | 0.8 |
| **Goods-Producing** | | | | | | | | | | |
| Gross job gains | 1 393 | 1 321 | 1 387 | 1 275 | 1 353 | 6.8 | 6.4 | 6.7 | 6.2 | 6.5 |
| Gross job losses | 1 269 | 1 298 | 1 331 | 1 302 | 1 310 | 6.2 | 6.3 | 6.4 | 6.3 | 6.3 |
| Net employment change | 124 | 23 | 56 | -27 | 43 | 0.6 | 0.1 | 0.3 | -0.1 | 0.2 |
| **Natural Resources and Mining** | | | | | | | | | | |
| Gross job gains | 280 | 284 | 263 | 243 | 245 | 13.4 | 13.5 | 13.0 | 12.3 | 12.6 |
| Gross job losses | 285 | 297 | 332 | 285 | 299 | 13.7 | 14.2 | 16.3 | 14.5 | 15.5 |
| Net employment change | -5 | -13 | -69 | -42 | -54 | -0.3 | -0.7 | -3.3 | -2.2 | -2.9 |
| **Construction** | | | | | | | | | | |
| Gross job gains | 669 | 652 | 693 | 643 | 696 | 10.8 | 10.3 | 10.9 | 10.0 | 10.7 |
| Gross job losses | 606 | 616 | 599 | 603 | 587 | 9.7 | 9.8 | 9.4 | 9.4 | 9.1 |
| Net employment change | 63 | 36 | 94 | 40 | 109 | 1.1 | 0.5 | 1.5 | 0.6 | 1.6 |
| **Manufacturing** | | | | | | | | | | |
| Gross job gains | 444 | 385 | 431 | 389 | 412 | 3.6 | 3.2 | 3.5 | 3.2 | 3.3 |
| Gross job losses | 378 | 385 | 400 | 414 | 424 | 3.1 | 3.1 | 3.2 | 3.4 | 3.5 |
| Net employment change | 66 | 0 | 31 | -25 | -12 | 0.5 | 0.1 | 0.3 | -0.2 | -0.2 |
| **Service-Providing**[1] | | | | | | | | | | |
| Gross job gains | 6 265 | 5 626 | 6 167 | 6 017 | 6 469 | 6.5 | 5.8 | 6.4 | 6.2 | 6.6 |
| Gross job losses | 5 294 | 5 423 | 5 394 | 5 572 | 5 512 | 5.5 | 5.6 | 5.5 | 5.8 | 5.6 |
| Net employment change | 971 | 203 | 773 | 445 | 957 | 1.0 | 0.2 | 0.9 | 0.4 | 1.0 |
| **Wholesale Trade** | | | | | | | | | | |
| Gross job gains | 293 | 262 | 284 | 269 | 294 | 5.0 | 4.5 | 4.8 | 4.5 | 5.0 |
| Gross job losses | 247 | 256 | 261 | 263 | 268 | 4.2 | 4.4 | 4.4 | 4.4 | 4.5 |
| Net employment change | 46 | 6 | 23 | 6 | 26 | 0.8 | 0.1 | 0.4 | 0.1 | 0.5 |
| **Retail Trade** | | | | | | | | | | |
| Gross job gains | 952 | 908 | 990 | 919 | 919 | 6.2 | 5.9 | 6.3 | 5.8 | 5.9 |
| Gross job losses | 842 | 873 | 825 | 930 | 916 | 5.4 | 5.6 | 5.2 | 5.9 | 5.8 |
| Net employment change | 110 | 35 | 165 | -11 | 3 | 0.8 | 0.3 | 1.1 | -0.1 | 0.1 |
| **Transportation and Warehousing** | | | | | | | | | | |
| Gross job gains | 330 | 228 | 257 | 264 | 343 | 7.3 | 5.0 | 5.6 | 5.7 | 7.3 |
| Gross job losses | 205 | 272 | 230 | 224 | 225 | 4.6 | 6.0 | 5.0 | 4.9 | 4.8 |
| Net employment change | 125 | -44 | 27 | 40 | 118 | 2.7 | -1.0 | 0.6 | 0.8 | 2.5 |
| **Utilities** | | | | | | | | | | |
| Gross job gains | 14 | 13 | 13 | 14 | 12 | 2.6 | 2.4 | 2.4 | 2.6 | 2.2 |
| Gross job losses | 12 | 11 | 12 | 12 | 11 | 2.2 | 2.0 | 2.2 | 2.2 | 2.0 |
| Net employment change | 2 | 2 | 1 | 2 | 1 | 0.4 | 0.4 | 0.2 | 0.4 | 0.2 |
| **Information** | | | | | | | | | | |
| Gross job gains | 145 | 124 | 147 | 143 | 161 | 5.3 | 4.5 | 5.4 | 5.2 | 5.8 |
| Gross job losses | 136 | 128 | 132 | 145 | 138 | 5.0 | 4.7 | 4.8 | 5.2 | 5.0 |
| Net employment change | 9 | -4 | 15 | -2 | 23 | 0.3 | -0.2 | 0.6 | 0.0 | 0.8 |
| **Financial Activities** | | | | | | | | | | |
| Gross job gains | 384 | 341 | 385 | 367 | 394 | 5.0 | 4.3 | 4.9 | 4.7 | 5.0 |
| Gross job losses | 344 | 330 | 332 | 345 | 352 | 4.4 | 4.2 | 4.2 | 4.4 | 4.5 |
| Net employment change | 40 | 11 | 53 | 22 | 42 | 0.6 | 0.1 | 0.7 | 0.3 | 0.5 |
| **Professional and Business Services** | | | | | | | | | | |
| Gross job gains | 1 570 | 1 253 | 1 438 | 1 401 | 1 588 | 8.1 | 6.5 | 7.3 | 7.1 | 8.0 |
| Gross job losses | 1 277 | 1 320 | 1 296 | 1 308 | 1 310 | 6.6 | 6.8 | 6.6 | 6.6 | 6.6 |
| Net employment change | 293 | -67 | 142 | 93 | 278 | 1.5 | -0.3 | 0.7 | 0.5 | 1.4 |
| **Education and Health Services** | | | | | | | | | | |
| Gross job gains | 930 | 855 | 933 | 961 | 1 002 | 4.5 | 4.1 | 4.4 | 4.5 | 4.7 |
| Gross job losses | 778 | 818 | 810 | 823 | 799 | 3.8 | 3.9 | 3.9 | 3.9 | 3.8 |
| Net employment change | 152 | 37 | 123 | 138 | 203 | 0.7 | 0.2 | 0.5 | 0.6 | 0.9 |
| **Leisure and Hospitality** | | | | | | | | | | |
| Gross job gains | 1 257 | 1 235 | 1 308 | 1 244 | 1 324 | 8.5 | 8.3 | 8.7 | 8.2 | 8.6 |
| Gross job losses | 1 146 | 1 112 | 1 197 | 1 209 | 1 180 | 7.7 | 7.4 | 7.9 | 8.1 | 7.7 |
| Net employment change | 111 | 123 | 111 | 35 | 144 | 0.8 | 0.9 | 0.8 | 0.1 | 0.9 |
| **Other Services** | | | | | | | | | | |
| Gross job gains | 284 | 276 | 301 | 280 | 289 | 7.2 | 7.0 | 7.5 | 7.0 | 7.1 |
| Gross job losses | 274 | 266 | 267 | 281 | 273 | 6.8 | 6.6 | 6.6 | 7.0 | 6.7 |
| Net employment change | 10 | 10 | 34 | -1 | 16 | 0.4 | 0.4 | 0.9 | 0.0 | 0.4 |

[1]Includes unclassified sector, not shown separately.

**Table 2-23.  Private Sector Gross Job Gains and Losses, by State and Selected Territory, Seasonally Adjusted, December 2014–December 2015**

(Number.)

| State | Gross job gains (3 months ended) | | | | | Gross job losses (3 months ended) | | | | |
|---|---|---|---|---|---|---|---|---|---|---|
| | December 2014 | March 2015 | June 2015 | September 2015 | December 2015 | December 2014 | March 2015 | September 2014 | December 2014 | December 2015 |
| UNITED STATES | 7 658 000 | 6 947 000 | 7 554 000 | 7 292 000 | 7 822 000 | 6 563 000 | 6 721 000 | 6 725 000 | 6 874 000 | 6 822 000 |
| Alabama | 90 302 | 84 986 | 89 888 | 88 051 | 96 278 | 79 390 | 83 133 | 81 281 | 86 070 | 82 503 |
| Alaska | 26 664 | 26 843 | 27 385 | 22 909 | 23 944 | 26 187 | 23 647 | 27 823 | 25 911 | 26 564 |
| Arizona | 151 389 | 130 192 | 131 338 | 150 336 | 154 963 | 114 098 | 126 022 | 125 809 | 119 366 | 122 506 |
| Arkansas | 63 560 | 52 074 | 57 124 | 58 978 | 62 235 | 48 759 | 55 318 | 51 031 | 50 906 | 50 080 |
| California | 1 009 991 | 938 495 | 934 842 | 955 474 | 1 068 393 | 876 809 | 853 530 | 897 517 | 811 020 | 933 600 |
| Colorado | 145 332 | 142 474 | 146 534 | 148 147 | 147 322 | 124 926 | 128 469 | 135 196 | 134 447 | 133 647 |
| Connecticut | 76 473 | 67 827 | 81 367 | 72 894 | 75 663 | 73 361 | 71 870 | 68 807 | 82 363 | 69 891 |
| Delaware | 25 677 | 20 948 | 27 972 | 22 481 | 27 012 | 19 694 | 26 759 | 20 802 | 22 614 | 22 998 |
| District of Columbia | 26 915 | 27 023 | 31 303 | 31 118 | 29 909 | 26 143 | 26 418 | 26 711 | 27 635 | 23 726 |
| Florida | 485 325 | 433 403 | 479 423 | 481 244 | 506 029 | 408 151 | 385 077 | 410 152 | 405 571 | 407 288 |
| Georgia | 238 116 | 215 750 | 232 741 | 226 362 | 247 039 | 191 800 | 195 401 | 200 532 | 208 499 | 202 852 |
| Hawaii | 26 591 | 25 524 | 25 438 | 25 807 | 29 858 | 22 314 | 24 417 | 25 488 | 24 416 | 23 585 |
| Idaho | 42 898 | 49 556 | 41 477 | 42 927 | 43 910 | 37 619 | 37 971 | 39 261 | 38 677 | 37 964 |
| Illinois | 311 522 | 289 355 | 309 794 | 277 165 | 323 308 | 274 821 | 287 323 | 263 025 | 287 722 | 285 139 |
| Indiana | 159 935 | 135 251 | 146 088 | 138 935 | 158 608 | 126 976 | 135 133 | 130 145 | 135 979 | 125 772 |
| Iowa | 78 199 | 75 990 | 77 630 | 73 194 | 77 425 | 72 224 | 68 787 | 76 474 | 77 479 | 72 893 |
| Kansas | 69 883 | 63 109 | 66 653 | 63 082 | 70 654 | 59 565 | 65 217 | 64 933 | 64 142 | 62 682 |
| Kentucky | 101 092 | 83 966 | 97 089 | 93 111 | 102 663 | 81 418 | 91 550 | 83 889 | 86 400 | 82 585 |
| Louisiana | 110 344 | 98 762 | 102 189 | 98 922 | 105 957 | 94 750 | 107 998 | 108 807 | 100 050 | 102 632 |
| Maine | 35 278 | 31 952 | 40 149 | 32 765 | 35 593 | 35 410 | 34 311 | 31 987 | 35 658 | 35 408 |
| Maryland | 138 559 | 122 791 | 147 032 | 134 789 | 142 178 | 126 916 | 128 633 | 122 825 | 132 518 | 125 070 |
| Massachusetts | 178 386 | 153 727 | 188 785 | 162 263 | 175 914 | 153 746 | 160 532 | 150 136 | 168 871 | 156 432 |
| Michigan | 220 069 | 186 698 | 219 556 | 195 118 | 218 548 | 186 438 | 185 816 | 187 213 | 204 087 | 192 282 |
| Minnesota | 136 923 | 132 507 | 147 427 | 131 516 | 146 558 | 128 935 | 124 085 | 122 494 | 141 927 | 139 112 |
| Mississippi | 60 007 | 48 649 | 55 359 | 54 075 | 62 207 | 46 688 | 55 261 | 51 607 | 51 187 | 48 431 |
| Missouri | 142 699 | 127 642 | 138 623 | 130 446 | 144 912 | 116 469 | 122 952 | 119 969 | 126 229 | 119 640 |
| Montana | 30 556 | 33 180 | 29 110 | 27 868 | 31 502 | 28 910 | 25 995 | 30 582 | 28 040 | 26 748 |
| Nebraska | 49 553 | 48 584 | 47 109 | 47 684 | 49 075 | 43 949 | 45 229 | 45 472 | 44 223 | 44 278 |
| Nevada | 70 287 | 67 468 | 66 653 | 67 838 | 75 894 | 56 851 | 57 353 | 62 062 | 58 211 | 57 714 |
| New Hampshire | 37 142 | 31 642 | 37 379 | 33 156 | 37 153 | 32 733 | 31 333 | 32 662 | 34 823 | 31 131 |
| New Jersey | 227 119 | 192 871 | 237 230 | 211 747 | 228 002 | 203 873 | 199 775 | 196 290 | 202 878 | 197 804 |
| New Mexico | 44 135 | 40 119 | 41 785 | 40 153 | 42 145 | 37 593 | 40 337 | 42 353 | 40 217 | 42 206 |
| New York | 492 207 | 452 751 | 510 517 | 478 685 | 499 754 | 438 941 | 447 485 | 442 513 | 465 778 | 448 260 |
| North Carolina | 224 428 | 201 554 | 222 540 | 215 149 | 231 306 | 183 831 | 195 257 | 186 438 | 196 782 | 192 146 |
| North Dakota | 32 877 | 27 400 | 24 976 | 25 618 | 24 097 | 25 770 | 33 253 | 41 954 | 30 853 | 28 943 |
| Ohio | 274 778 | 245 199 | 272 264 | 245 565 | 273 202 | 233 006 | 251 495 | 237 460 | 256 532 | 235 464 |
| Oklahoma | 85 458 | 72 454 | 75 658 | 75 238 | 79 209 | 69 618 | 78 715 | 82 570 | 76 608 | 81 183 |
| Oregon | 103 676 | 102 857 | 102 758 | 104 581 | 106 097 | 92 473 | 84 267 | 90 914 | 95 354 | 93 204 |
| Pennsylvania | 278 808 | 241 865 | 277 841 | 265 180 | 286 453 | 242 138 | 260 288 | 245 484 | 263 136 | 256 494 |
| Rhode Island | 26 349 | 21 815 | 27 189 | 23 866 | 27 116 | 22 897 | 23 924 | 24 003 | 23 613 | 23 503 |
| South Carolina | 107 723 | 89 525 | 103 461 | 99 083 | 114 551 | 78 630 | 88 343 | 88 733 | 92 986 | 86 340 |
| South Dakota | 21 338 | 21 738 | 21 381 | 20 412 | 22 952 | 19 835 | 19 475 | 20 354 | 21 112 | 20 368 |
| Tennessee | 147 613 | 122 997 | 142 377 | 140 614 | 153 458 | 114 067 | 123 505 | 114 804 | 123 495 | 113 930 |
| Texas | 621 191 | 558 120 | 580 476 | 584 743 | 600 717 | 482 093 | 554 065 | 542 136 | 542 464 | 541 352 |
| Utah | 77 688 | 81 508 | 77 194 | 78 335 | 81 518 | 63 747 | 64 830 | 68 853 | 67 127 | 67 774 |
| Vermont | 18 971 | 17 292 | 18 547 | 17 503 | 18 063 | 16 952 | 17 199 | 17 909 | 19 351 | 16 557 |
| Virginia | 170 860 | 179 773 | 194 303 | 210 997 | 195 211 | 163 277 | 166 667 | 161 279 | 178 620 | 170 622 |
| Washington | 175 377 | 172 884 | 185 623 | 170 134 | 176 144 | 156 237 | 145 606 | 150 744 | 174 709 | 157 999 |
| West Virginia | 37 372 | 33 488 | 35 119 | 32 371 | 36 485 | 34 173 | 38 029 | 37 109 | 37 289 | 35 357 |
| Wisconsin | 136 603 | 129 845 | 136 692 | 131 535 | 138 711 | 123 187 | 121 215 | 126 192 | 135 315 | 126 260 |
| Wyoming | 20 323 | 19 818 | 16 942 | 17 709 | 18 969 | 17 717 | 19 749 | 23 720 | 18 620 | 19 565 |
| Puerto Rico | 43 614 | 35 793 | 38 676 | 41 386 | 42 210 | 33 418 | 43 227 | 46 166 | 42 614 | 39 180 |
| Virgin Islands | 1 721 | 1 497 | 1 693 | 1 584 | 1 978 | 1 519 | 1 618 | 1 808 | 1 997 | 1 464 |

## Table 2-24. Private Sector Gross Job Gains and Losses as a Percent of Total Employment, by State and Selected Territory, Seasonally Adjusted, December 2014–December 2015

(Percent.)

| State | Gross job gains (3 months ended) | | | | | Gross job losses (3 months ended) | | | | |
|---|---|---|---|---|---|---|---|---|---|---|
| | December 2014 | March 2015 | June 2015 | September 2015 | December 2015 | December 2014 | March 2015 | June 2015 | September 2015 | December 2015 |
| UNITED STATES | 6.6 | 5.9 | 6.4 | 6.1 | 6.6 | 5.7 | 5.7 | 5.7 | 5.8 | 5.8 |
| Alabama | 6.0 | 5.6 | 5.9 | 5.8 | 6.2 | 5.2 | 5.4 | 5.3 | 5.6 | 5.3 |
| Alaska | 10.6 | 10.4 | 10.6 | 9.0 | 9.5 | 10.4 | 9.2 | 10.8 | 10.2 | 10.5 |
| Arizona | 7.0 | 6.0 | 5.9 | 6.8 | 6.9 | 5.3 | 5.7 | 5.7 | 5.4 | 5.4 |
| Arkansas | 6.6 | 5.4 | 5.9 | 6.1 | 6.3 | 5.1 | 5.7 | 5.3 | 5.2 | 5.1 |
| California | 7.4 | 6.8 | 6.8 | 6.9 | 7.6 | 6.4 | 6.2 | 6.5 | 5.8 | 6.7 |
| Colorado | 7.0 | 6.9 | 7.0 | 7.1 | 7.0 | 6.1 | 6.1 | 6.4 | 6.4 | 6.3 |
| Connecticut | 5.4 | 4.8 | 5.8 | 5.1 | 5.3 | 5.2 | 5.1 | 4.8 | 5.8 | 5.0 |
| Delaware | 7.0 | 5.7 | 7.6 | 6.1 | 7.2 | 5.4 | 7.3 | 5.6 | 6.1 | 6.2 |
| District of Columbia | 5.5 | 5.5 | 6.2 | 6.2 | 5.9 | 5.3 | 5.4 | 5.4 | 5.5 | 4.7 |
| Florida | 7.1 | 6.3 | 6.9 | 6.8 | 7.1 | 6.0 | 5.6 | 5.9 | 5.8 | 5.8 |
| Georgia | 6.9 | 6.2 | 6.7 | 6.5 | 6.9 | 5.5 | 5.6 | 5.7 | 5.9 | 5.7 |
| Hawaii | 5.2 | 4.9 | 4.9 | 5.1 | 5.7 | 4.4 | 4.8 | 5.0 | 4.8 | 4.6 |
| Idaho | 8.0 | 9.1 | 7.5 | 7.8 | 7.9 | 7.0 | 7.0 | 7.1 | 7.1 | 6.9 |
| Illinois | 6.2 | 5.8 | 6.2 | 5.4 | 6.4 | 5.5 | 5.7 | 5.2 | 5.7 | 5.6 |
| Indiana | 6.3 | 5.3 | 5.7 | 5.4 | 6.2 | 5.0 | 5.3 | 5.1 | 5.3 | 4.9 |
| Iowa | 6.1 | 5.9 | 6.1 | 5.6 | 6.0 | 5.6 | 5.4 | 5.9 | 6.0 | 5.6 |
| Kansas | 6.2 | 5.7 | 6.0 | 5.7 | 6.2 | 5.4 | 5.8 | 5.8 | 5.7 | 5.6 |
| Kentucky | 6.6 | 5.5 | 6.4 | 6.0 | 6.6 | 5.3 | 6.0 | 5.5 | 5.6 | 5.3 |
| Louisiana | 6.8 | 6.1 | 6.3 | 6.2 | 6.5 | 5.8 | 6.7 | 6.8 | 6.2 | 6.3 |
| Maine | 7.2 | 6.5 | 8.0 | 6.5 | 7.1 | 7.2 | 7.0 | 6.4 | 7.1 | 7.0 |
| Maryland | 6.7 | 5.9 | 7.0 | 6.5 | 6.7 | 6.2 | 6.2 | 5.9 | 6.3 | 5.9 |
| Massachusetts | 6.0 | 5.1 | 6.3 | 5.4 | 5.9 | 5.2 | 5.4 | 5.0 | 5.6 | 5.2 |
| Michigan | 6.2 | 5.2 | 6.1 | 5.4 | 6.1 | 5.2 | 5.1 | 5.2 | 5.7 | 5.3 |
| Minnesota | 5.8 | 5.6 | 6.1 | 5.4 | 6.1 | 5.4 | 5.2 | 5.2 | 5.9 | 5.8 |
| Mississippi | 6.9 | 5.5 | 6.3 | 6.2 | 7.1 | 5.4 | 6.4 | 5.9 | 5.8 | 5.4 |
| Missouri | 6.3 | 5.6 | 6.0 | 5.7 | 6.3 | 5.1 | 5.4 | 5.2 | 5.5 | 5.1 |
| Montana | 8.5 | 9.1 | 8.0 | 7.6 | 8.5 | 8.0 | 7.2 | 8.4 | 7.7 | 7.3 |
| Nebraska | 6.2 | 6.1 | 5.9 | 6.0 | 6.1 | 5.6 | 5.6 | 5.7 | 5.5 | 5.5 |
| Nevada | 6.6 | 6.3 | 6.2 | 6.2 | 6.8 | 5.3 | 5.3 | 5.7 | 5.3 | 5.2 |
| New Hampshire | 6.9 | 5.7 | 6.8 | 6.0 | 6.7 | 6.0 | 5.7 | 5.9 | 6.3 | 5.6 |
| New Jersey | 6.9 | 5.8 | 7.1 | 6.3 | 6.8 | 6.2 | 6.0 | 5.9 | 6.1 | 5.9 |
| New Mexico | 7.2 | 6.4 | 6.7 | 6.5 | 6.8 | 6.1 | 6.5 | 6.8 | 6.5 | 6.8 |
| New York | 6.6 | 5.9 | 6.7 | 6.3 | 6.5 | 5.8 | 5.9 | 5.8 | 6.0 | 5.9 |
| North Carolina | 6.5 | 5.9 | 6.4 | 6.1 | 6.6 | 5.4 | 5.7 | 5.4 | 5.6 | 5.5 |
| North Dakota | 8.7 | 7.1 | 6.7 | 7.1 | 6.7 | 6.7 | 8.7 | 11.3 | 8.5 | 8.1 |
| Ohio | 6.1 | 5.4 | 6.0 | 5.4 | 6.0 | 5.1 | 5.6 | 5.3 | 5.6 | 5.2 |
| Oklahoma | 6.7 | 5.7 | 6.0 | 6.0 | 6.3 | 5.5 | 6.1 | 6.5 | 6.1 | 6.5 |
| Oregon | 7.1 | 6.9 | 6.9 | 7.0 | 7.0 | 6.3 | 5.7 | 6.1 | 6.4 | 6.2 |
| Pennsylvania | 5.6 | 4.9 | 5.6 | 5.2 | 5.7 | 4.9 | 5.2 | 4.9 | 5.2 | 5.1 |
| Rhode Island | 6.4 | 5.3 | 6.6 | 5.8 | 6.6 | 5.6 | 5.8 | 5.8 | 5.7 | 5.7 |
| South Carolina | 6.8 | 5.7 | 6.5 | 6.2 | 7.1 | 5.0 | 5.5 | 5.6 | 5.8 | 5.3 |
| South Dakota | 6.3 | 6.3 | 6.3 | 5.9 | 6.6 | 5.8 | 5.7 | 5.9 | 6.1 | 5.9 |
| Tennessee | 6.2 | 5.2 | 5.9 | 5.8 | 6.3 | 4.8 | 5.2 | 4.8 | 5.1 | 4.6 |
| Texas | 6.4 | 5.8 | 6.0 | 5.9 | 6.0 | 5.0 | 5.7 | 5.5 | 5.5 | 5.5 |
| Utah | 7.2 | 7.3 | 6.9 | 7.0 | 7.2 | 5.8 | 5.9 | 6.1 | 5.9 | 6.0 |
| Vermont | 7.5 | 6.8 | 7.3 | 6.9 | 7.1 | 6.7 | 6.8 | 7.0 | 7.6 | 6.5 |
| Virginia | 5.8 | 6.0 | 6.4 | 6.9 | 6.4 | 5.5 | 5.6 | 5.4 | 5.9 | 5.5 |
| Washington | 6.9 | 6.7 | 7.2 | 6.5 | 6.7 | 6.1 | 5.6 | 5.8 | 6.7 | 6.0 |
| West Virginia | 6.6 | 6.0 | 6.3 | 5.8 | 6.6 | 6.0 | 6.7 | 6.6 | 6.8 | 6.4 |
| Wisconsin | 5.8 | 5.4 | 5.7 | 5.5 | 5.7 | 5.2 | 5.1 | 5.2 | 5.6 | 5.2 |
| Wyoming | 9.3 | 8.9 | 7.8 | 8.3 | 9.0 | 8.0 | 8.9 | 10.9 | 8.7 | 9.2 |
| Puerto Rico | 6.4 | 5.3 | 5.8 | 6.2 | 6.3 | 4.9 | 6.4 | 6.8 | 6.3 | 5.8 |
| Virgin Islands | 6.2 | 5.5 | 6.3 | 5.8 | 7.3 | 5.6 | 5.9 | 6.7 | 7.4 | 5.4 |

# CHAPTER 3: OCCUPATIONAL EMPLOYMENT AND WAGES

## HIGHLIGHTS

This chapter presents employment and wage statistics from the Bureau of Labor Statistics Occupational Employment Statistics (OES) program.

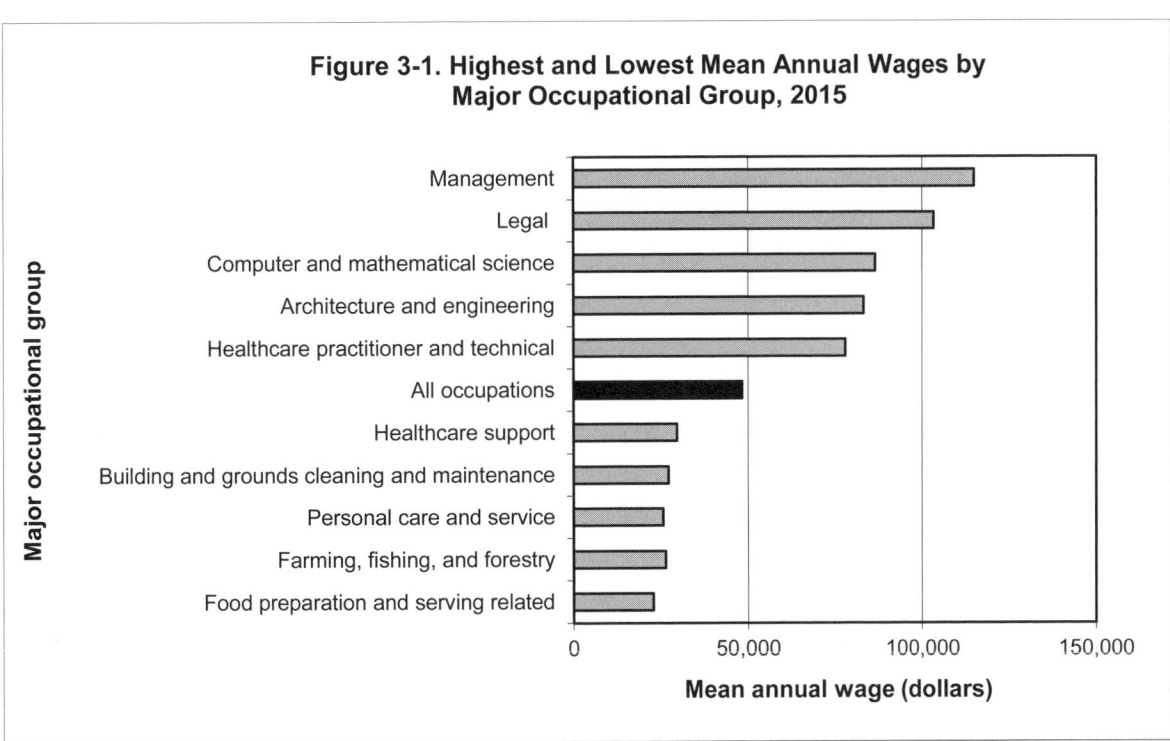

**Figure 3-1. Highest and Lowest Mean Annual Wages by Major Occupational Group, 2015**

Workers in management continued to have the highest mean annual wage ($115,020) followed by those in legal occupations ($103,460), and computer and mathematical science occupations ($86,170) in 2015. Meanwhile, workers in food preparation and serving related workers ($22,850) and personal care and services ($25,650) had the lowest mean annual wages. (See Table 3-1.)

## OTHER HIGHLIGHTS

- Within business and financial operations occupations, personal financial advisors had the highest salary at $118,050 while farm labor contractors had the lowest at $43,920. (See Table 3-2.)

- Most of the largest occupations were relatively low paying. Food preparation and serving related occupations, which employed over 12 million people, only had a mean annual wage of $22,580 in 2015. Likewise, office and administrative support occupations employed nearly 22 million people but only had a mean annual wage of $36,330 in 2015. Registered nurses were the largest occupation with an above-average wage ($71,000). (See Table 3-1)

- Healthcare occupations had employment of 12 million in May 2015, representing nearly 9 percent of total national employment. Nurse anesthetists, with an annual mean wage of $160,250; podiatrists ($136,180); and pharmacists ($119,270) were among the highest paying healthcare occupations not including physicians and dentists. (See Table 3-2.)

## NOTES AND DEFINITIONS

### Collection and Coverage

The Occupational Employment Statistics (OES) survey is a federal-state cooperative program conducted by the Bureau of Labor Statistics (BLS) and the State Workforce Agencies (SWAs). The OES program collects data on wage and salary workers in nonfarm establishments in order to produce employment and wage estimates for over 800 occupations. Data from self-employed persons are not collected and are not included in the estimates. BLS funds the survey and provides procedural and technical support, while the SWAs collect the necessary data.

Every six months, forms are mailed to two semiannual panels of around 200,000 taking three years to fully collect a sample of 1.2 million establishments. May 2015 estimates are based on responses from six semiannual panels collected over a 3-year period: May 2015, November 2014, May 2014, November 2013, May 2013, and November 2012.

### Scope of the Survey

Prior to 1996, the OES program collected only occupational employment data for selected industries in each year of the three-year survey cycle, and produced only industry-specific estimates of occupational employment. The 1996 survey round was the first year that the OES program began collecting occupational employment and wage data in every state. In addition, the program's three-year survey cycle was modified to collect data from all covered industries each year. In 1997, the OES program began producing estimates of cross-industry as well as industry-specific occupational employment and wages.

In 1999, the OES survey began using the Standard Occupational Classification (SOC) system. The SOC system is the first occupational classification system for federal agencies required by the Office of Management and Budget (OMB). The May 2012 estimates were the first estimates based on the 2010 Standard Occupational Classification (SOC) system. In addition to 22 major occupational groups and 821 detailed occupations, employment and wage estimates for 94 minor groups and 458 broad occupations are available for the first time.

In 2002, the OES survey switched from the Standard Industrial Classification System (SIC) to the North American Industry Classification System (NAICS). In 2008, the OES survey switched to the 2007 NAICS from the 2002 NAICS. The most significant revisions were in the information sector, particularly within the telecommunications area. The May 2012 OES estimates were the first to be produced using the 2012 North American Industry Classification System (NAICS). More information about NAICS can be found on the BLS Web site at <http://www.bls.gov/bls/naics.htm>.

### Concepts and Definitions

*Employment* is the estimate of total wage and salary employment in an occupation across the industries in which it was reported. The OES survey defines employment as the number of workers who can be classified as full-time or part-time employees, including workers on paid vacations or other types of leave; workers on unpaid short-term absences; employees who are salaried officers, executives, or staff members of incorporated firms; employees temporarily assigned to other units; and employees for whom the reporting unit is their permanent duty station regardless of whether that unit prepares their paycheck.

*Occupations* are classified based on work performed and required skills. Employees are assigned to an occupation based on the work they perform and not on their education or training. Employees who perform the duties of two or more occupations are reported as being in either the occupation that requires the highest level of skill or the occupation in which the most time is spent (if there is no measurable difference in skill requirements).

*Wages* are money that is paid or received for work or services performed in a specified period. Base rate, cost-of-living allowances, guaranteed pay, hazardous-duty pay, incentive pay (including commissions and production bonuses), tips, and on-call pay are included.

*Mean wage* refers to an average wage; an occupational mean wage estimate is calculated by summing the wages of all the employees in a given occupation and then dividing the total wages by the number of employees.

An *establishment* is defined as an economic unit that processes goods or provides services, such as a factory, store, or mine. The establishment is generally at a single physical location and is primarily engaged in one type of economic activity.

An *industry* is a group of establishments that produce similar products or provide similar services. A given industry, or even a particular establishment in that industry, might have employees in dozens of occupations. The North American Industry Classification System (NAICS) groups similar establishments into industries.

### Additional Information

For additional data including area data, see BLS news release USDL 16-0661, "Occupational Employment and Wages, May 2015," and special reports on the BLS Web site at <http://www.bls.gov/OES/>.

## Table 3-1.  Employment and Wages, by Major Occupational Group, May 2012–May 2015

(Number, percent, dollars.)

| Occupation | May 2012 | | | | May 2013 | | | |
|---|---|---|---|---|---|---|---|---|
| | Employment | | Mean hourly wage | Mean annual wage[1] | Employment | | Mean hourly wage | Mean annual wage[1] |
| | Number | Percent | | | Number | Percent | | |
| **All Occupations** | 130 287 700 | 100.0 | 22.01 | 45 790 | 132 588 810 | 100.0 | 22.33 | 46 440 |
| Management | 6 390 430 | 4.9 | 52.20 | 108 570 | 6 542 950 | 4.9 | 53.15 | 110 550 |
| Business and financial operations | 6 419 370 | 4.9 | 33.44 | 69 550 | 6 658 090 | 5.0 | 34.14 | 71 020 |
| Computer and mathematical sciences | 3 578 220 | 2.7 | 38.55 | 80 180 | 3 696 180 | 2.8 | 39.43 | 82 010 |
| Architecture and engineering | 2 356 530 | 1.8 | 37.98 | 79 000 | 2 380 840 | 1.8 | 38.51 | 80 100 |
| Life, physical, and social sciences | 1 104 100 | 0.8 | 32.87 | 68 360 | 1 135 030 | 0.9 | 33.37 | 69 400 |
| Community and social services | 1 882 080 | 1.4 | 21.27 | 44 240 | 1 901 730 | 1.4 | 21.50 | 44 710 |
| Legal | 1 023 020 | 0.8 | 47.39 | 98 570 | 1 041 700 | 0.8 | 47.89 | 99 620 |
| Education, training, and library | 8 374 910 | 6.4 | 24.62 | 51 210 | 8 400 640 | 6.3 | 24.76 | 51 500 |
| Arts, design, entertainment, sports, and media | 1 750 130 | 1.3 | 26.20 | 54 490 | 1 758 310 | 1.3 | 26.72 | 55 580 |
| Health care practitioner and technical | 7 649 930 | 5.9 | 35.35 | 73 540 | 7 755 810 | 5.8 | 35.93 | 74 740 |
| Health care support | 3 915 460 | 3.0 | 13.36 | 27 780 | 3 924 390 | 3.0 | 13.61 | 28 300 |
| Protective services | 3 207 790 | 2.5 | 20.70 | 43 050 | 3 257 690 | 2.5 | 20.92 | 43 510 |
| Food preparation and serving related | 11 546 880 | 8.9 | 10.28 | 21 380 | 11 914 590 | 9.0 | 10.38 | 21 580 |
| Building and grounds cleaning and maintenance | 4 246 260 | 3.3 | 12.34 | 25 670 | 4 291 410 | 3.2 | 12.51 | 26 010 |
| Personal care and services | 3 810 750 | 2.9 | 11.80 | 24 550 | 3 986 740 | 3.0 | 11.88 | 24 710 |
| Sales and related | 13 835 090 | 10.6 | 18.26 | 37 990 | 14 068 190 | 10.6 | 18.37 | 38 200 |
| Office and administrative support | 21 355 350 | 16.4 | 16.54 | 34 410 | 21 442 800 | 16.2 | 16.78 | 34 900 |
| Farming, fishing, and forestry | 427 670 | 0.3 | 11.65 | 24 230 | 435 250 | 0.3 | 11.70 | 24 330 |
| Construction and extraction | 4 978 290 | 3.8 | 21.61 | 44 960 | 5 088 030 | 3.8 | 21.94 | 45 630 |
| Installation, maintenance, and repair | 5 069 590 | 3.9 | 21.09 | 43 870 | 5 138 130 | 3.9 | 21.35 | 44 420 |
| Production | 8 594 170 | 6.6 | 16.59 | 34 500 | 8 765 180 | 6.6 | 16.79 | 34 930 |
| Transportation and material moving | 8 771 690 | 6.7 | 16.15 | 33 590 | 9 005 120 | 6.8 | 16.20 | 33 860 |

| Occupation | May 2014 | | | | May 2015 | | | |
|---|---|---|---|---|---|---|---|---|
| | Employment | | Mean hourly wage | Mean annual wage[1] | Employment | | Mean hourly wage | Mean annual wage[1] |
| | Number | Percent | | | Number | Percent | | |
| **All Occupations** | 135 128 260 | 100.0 | 22.71 | 47 230 | 137 896 660 | 100.0 | 23.23 | 48 320 |
| Management | 6 741 640 | 5.0 | 54.08 | 112 490 | 6 936 990 | 5.0 | 55.30 | 115 020 |
| Business and financial operations | 6 828 940 | 5.1 | 34.81 | 72 410 | 7 032 560 | 5.1 | 35.48 | 73 800 |
| Computer and mathematical sciences | 3 834 180 | 2.8 | 40.37 | 83 970 | 4 005 250 | 2.9 | 41.43 | 86 170 |
| Architecture and engineering | 2 418 020 | 1.8 | 39.19 | 81 520 | 2 475 390 | 1.8 | 39.89 | 82 980 |
| Life, physical, and social sciences | 1 144 440 | 0.8 | 33.69 | 70 070 | 1 146 110 | 0.8 | 34.24 | 71 220 |
| Community and social services | 1 930 750 | 1.4 | 21.79 | 45 310 | 1 972 140 | 1.4 | 22.19 | 46 160 |
| Legal | 1 052 900 | 0.8 | 48.61 | 101 110 | 1 062 370 | 0.8 | 49.74 | 103 460 |
| Education, training, and library | 8 435 780 | 6.2 | 25.10 | 52 210 | 8 542 670 | 6.2 | 25.48 | 53 000 |
| Arts, design, entertainment, sports, and media | 1 793 700 | 1.3 | 26.82 | 55 790 | 1 843 600 | 1.3 | 27.39 | 56 980 |
| Health care practitioner and technical | 7 854 380 | 5.8 | 36.54 | 76 010 | 8 021 800 | 5.8 | 37.40 | 77 800 |
| Health care support | 3 940 500 | 2.9 | 13.86 | 28 820 | 3 989 910 | 2.9 | 14.19 | 29 520 |
| Protective services | 3 297 180 | 2.4 | 21.14 | 43 980 | 3 351 620 | 2.4 | 21.45 | 44 610 |
| Food preparation and serving related | 12 277 720 | 9.1 | 10.57 | 21 980 | 12 577 080 | 9.1 | 10.98 | 22 850 |
| Building and grounds cleaning and maintenance | 4 371 450 | 3.2 | 12.68 | 26 370 | 4 407 050 | 3.2 | 13.02 | 27 080 |
| Personal care and services | 4 154 360 | 3.1 | 12.01 | 24 980 | 4 307 500 | 3.1 | 12.33 | 25 650 |
| Sales and related | 14 248 470 | 10.5 | 18.59 | 38 660 | 14 462 120 | 10.5 | 18.90 | 39 320 |
| Office and administrative support | 21 638 470 | 16.0 | 17.08 | 35 530 | 21 846 420 | 15.8 | 17.47 | 36 330 |
| Farming, fishing, and forestry | 447 130 | 0.3 | 12.09 | 25 160 | 454 230 | 0.3 | 12.67 | 26 360 |
| Construction and extraction | 5 290 270 | 3.9 | 22.40 | 46 600 | 5 477 820 | 4.0 | 22.88 | 47 580 |
| Installation, maintenance, and repair | 5 244 670 | 3.9 | 21.74 | 45 220 | 5 374 150 | 3.9 | 22.11 | 45 990 |
| Production | 8 934 050 | 6.6 | 17.06 | 35 490 | 9 073 290 | 6.6 | 17.41 | 36 220 |
| Transportation and material moving | 9 249 310 | 6.8 | 16.57 | 34 460 | 9 536 610 | 6.9 | 16.90 | 35 160 |

[1]The annual wage has been calculated by multiplying the hourly mean wage by a "year-round, full-time" hours figure of 2,080 hours; for occupations with no published hourly mean wage, the annual wage has been directly calculated from the reported survey data.

## Table 3-2. Employment and Wages, by Occupation, May 2015

(Number of people, dollars.)

| Occupation | May 2015 | | | |
| --- | --- | --- | --- | --- |
| | Employment | Mean hourly wage | Mean annual wage[1] | Median hourly wage |
| **All Occupations** | 137 896 660 | 23.23 | 48 320 | 17.40 |
| **Management Occupations** | | | | |
| Top executives | 2 439 900 | 59.71 | 124 210 | 48.53 |
| Chief executives | 238 940 | 89.35 | 185 850 | 84.19 |
| General and operations managers | 2 145 140 | 57.44 | 119 460 | 46.99 |
| Legislators | 55 820 | ([2]) | 42 530 | ([2]) |
| Advertising, marketing, promotions, public relations, and sales managers | 647 360 | 63.30 | 131 670 | 56.16 |
| Advertising and promotions managers | 29 340 | 54.62 | 113 610 | 46.10 |
| Marketing and sales managers | 557 640 | 64.40 | 133 950 | 57.35 |
| Marketing managers | 192 890 | 67.63 | 140 660 | 61.90 |
| Sales managers | 364 750 | 62.69 | 130 400 | 54.74 |
| Public relations and fundraising managers | 60 380 | 57.40 | 119 390 | 50.07 |
| Operations specialties managers | 1 663 790 | 58.12 | 120 900 | 52.05 |
| Administrative services managers | 270 080 | 45.60 | 94 840 | 41.40 |
| Computer and information systems managers | 341 250 | 67.79 | 141 000 | 63.27 |
| Financial managers | 531 120 | 64.58 | 134 330 | 56.73 |
| Industrial production managers | 169 390 | 49.87 | 103 720 | 45.17 |
| Purchasing managers | 72 600 | 54.87 | 114 130 | 51.98 |
| Transportation, storage, and distribution managers | 109 210 | 45.74 | 95 130 | 41.65 |
| Compensation and benefits managers | 15 930 | 58.48 | 121 630 | 53.57 |
| Human resources managers | 122 780 | 56.29 | 117 080 | 50.21 |
| Training and development managers | 31 430 | 53.69 | 111 680 | 49.35 |
| Other management occupations | 2 185 950 | 45.85 | 95 360 | 41.29 |
| Farmers, ranchers, and other agricultural managers | 4 370 | 33.60 | 69 880 | 30.85 |
| Construction managers | 239 640 | 46.88 | 97 510 | 42.02 |
| Education administrators | 449 430 | 43.74 | 90 970 | 41.01 |
| Education administrators, preschool and childcare center/program | 46 760 | 25.37 | 52 760 | 21.96 |
| Education administrators, elementary and secondary school | 235 110 | ([2]) | 92 940 | ([2]) |
| Education administrators, postsecondary | 135 690 | 49.33 | 102 610 | 42.59 |
| Education administrators, all other | 31 880 | 39.89 | 82 970 | 36.99 |
| Architectural and engineering managers | 179 770 | 68.10 | 141 650 | 63.85 |
| Food service managers | 201 370 | 25.79 | 53 640 | 23.41 |
| Funeral service managers | 8 300 | 40.61 | 84 470 | 34.08 |
| Gaming managers | 3 950 | 37.39 | 77 770 | 32.88 |
| Lodging managers | 35 480 | 27.79 | 57 810 | 23.91 |
| Medical and health services managers | 314 950 | 50.99 | 106 070 | 45.43 |
| Natural sciences managers | 53 450 | 65.66 | 136 570 | 57.77 |
| Postmasters and mail superintendents | 14 770 | 33.92 | 70 540 | 33.96 |
| Property, real estate, and community association managers | 174 410 | 32.81 | 68 240 | 26.63 |
| Social and community service managers | 119 770 | 33.38 | 69 430 | 30.54 |
| Emergency management directors | 9 840 | 35.46 | 73 750 | 32.37 |
| Managers, all other | 376 440 | 53.47 | 111 230 | 50.41 |
| **Business and Financial Operations Occupations** | | | | |
| Business operations specialists | 4 424 800 | 34.09 | 70 900 | 31.01 |
| Agents and business managers of artists, performers, and athletes | 13 230 | 46.06 | 95 810 | 30.26 |
| Buyers and purchasing agents | 414 900 | 30.85 | 64 170 | 28.66 |
| Buyers and purchasing agents, farm products | 12 160 | 29.94 | 62 280 | 27.05 |
| Wholesale and retail buyers, except farm products | 111 200 | 28.50 | 59 270 | 25.45 |
| Purchasing agents, except wholesale, retail, and farm products | 291 540 | 31.79 | 66 120 | 29.91 |
| Claims adjusters, appraisers, examiners, and investigators | 286 870 | 30.94 | 64 350 | 30.32 |
| Claims adjusters, examiners, and investigators | 271 600 | 30.91 | 64 300 | 30.28 |
| Insurance appraisers, auto damage | 15 270 | 31.39 | 65 300 | 30.78 |
| Compliance officers | 257 010 | 33.26 | 69 180 | 31.56 |
| Cost estimators | 216 270 | 31.16 | 64 810 | 29.03 |
| Human resources workers | 571 640 | 30.42 | 63 280 | 28.06 |
| Human resources specialists | 491 090 | 30.63 | 63 710 | 28.06 |
| Farm labor contractors | 1 230 | 21.11 | 43 920 | 14.86 |
| Labor relations specialists | 79 330 | 29.30 | 60 930 | 28.28 |
| Logisticians | 133 770 | 37.25 | 77 470 | 35.70 |
| Management analysts | 614 110 | 44.12 | 91 770 | 39.10 |
| Meeting, convention, and event planners | 87 400 | 24.62 | 51 200 | 22.52 |
| Fundraisers | 62 720 | 27.49 | 57 170 | 25.47 |
| Compensation, benefits, and job analysis specialists | 79 780 | 31.30 | 65 100 | 29.26 |
| Training and development specialists | 254 060 | 30.03 | 62 460 | 27.99 |
| Market research analysts and marketing specialists | 506 420 | 33.67 | 70 030 | 29.88 |
| Business operations specialists, all other | 926 610 | 35.33 | 73 480 | 32.77 |
| Financial specialists | 2 607 760 | 37.85 | 78 730 | 32.57 |
| Accountants and auditors | 1 226 910 | 36.19 | 75 280 | 32.30 |
| Appraisers and assessors of real estate | 60 290 | 28.08 | 58 400 | 24.93 |
| Budget analysts | 56 300 | 36.13 | 75 150 | 34.42 |
| Credit analysts | 70 840 | 38.33 | 79 720 | 33.50 |
| Financial analysts and advisors | 555 900 | 47.95 | 99 730 | 38.15 |
| Financial analysts | 268 360 | 45.83 | 95 320 | 38.61 |

[1]Annual wages have been calculated by multiplying the hourly mean wage by a "year-round, full-time" hours figure of 2,080 hours; for occupations with no published hourly mean wage, the annual wage has been directly calculated from the reported survey data.
[2]Wages for some occupations that do not generally entail year-round, full-time employment are reported as either hourly wages or annual salaries (depending on how employees are typically paid).

## Table 3-2.  Employment and Wages, by Occupation, May 2015—*Continued*

(Number of people, dollars.)

| Occupation | May 2015 | | | |
|---|---|---|---|---|
| | Employment | Mean hourly wage | Mean annual wage[1] | Median hourly wage |
| **Business and Financial Operations Occupations**—*Continued* | | | | |
| Personal financial advisors | 197 580 | 56.76 | 118 050 | 42.86 |
| Insurance underwriters | 89 960 | 34.93 | 72 650 | 31.27 |
| Financial examiners | 44 200 | 42.46 | 88 310 | 37.50 |
| Credit counselors and loan officers | 334 380 | 35.01 | 72 810 | 29.29 |
| Credit counselors | 30 510 | 23.70 | 49 310 | 21.08 |
| Loan officers | 303 870 | 36.14 | 75 170 | 30.49 |
| Tax examiners, collectors and preparers, and revenue agents | 131 700 | 24.24 | 50 410 | 21.56 |
| Tax examiners and collectors, and revenue agents | 59 640 | 27.54 | 57 280 | 24.73 |
| Tax preparers | 72 060 | 21.50 | 44 730 | 17.53 |
| Financial specialists, all other | 127 250 | 34.85 | 72 480 | 32.05 |
| **Computer and Mathematical Occupations** | | | | |
| Computer occupations | 3 853 860 | 41.39 | 86 090 | 39.15 |
| Computer and information research scientists | 25 510 | 55.57 | 115 580 | 53.18 |
| Computer and information analysts | 645 550 | 43.56 | 90 600 | 41.52 |
| Computer systems analysts | 556 660 | 43.36 | 90 180 | 41.25 |
| Information security analysts | 88 880 | 44.83 | 93 250 | 43.33 |
| Software developers and programmers | 1 554 960 | 47.08 | 97 930 | 45.23 |
| Computer programmers | 289 420 | 40.56 | 84 360 | 38.24 |
| Software developers, applications | 747 730 | 49.12 | 102 160 | 47.24 |
| Software developers, systems software | 390 750 | 52.29 | 108 760 | 50.76 |
| Web developers | 127 070 | 33.97 | 70 660 | 31.23 |
| Database and systems administrators and network architects | 634 850 | 42.02 | 87 400 | 39.80 |
| Database administrators | 113 770 | 40.51 | 84 250 | 39.29 |
| Network and computer systems administrators | 374 480 | 39.52 | 82 200 | 37.41 |
| Computer network architects | 146 600 | 49.57 | 103 100 | 48.19 |
| Computer support specialists | 769 630 | 26.92 | 55 980 | 24.75 |
| Computer user support specialists | 585 060 | 25.21 | 52 430 | 23.38 |
| Computer network support specialists | 184 570 | 32.33 | 67 260 | 29.93 |
| Computer occupations, all other | 223 370 | 41.98 | 87 310 | 40.98 |
| Mathematical science occupations | 151 380 | 42.33 | 88 040 | 39.12 |
| Actuaries | 19 770 | 53.15 | 110 560 | 46.67 |
| Mathematicians | 3 170 | 54.11 | 112 560 | 53.42 |
| Operations research analysts | 95 860 | 40.47 | 84 180 | 37.80 |
| Statisticians | 29 870 | 40.60 | 84 440 | 38.51 |
| Miscellaneous mathematical science occupations | 2 700 | 34.05 | 70 820 | 28.16 |
| Mathematical technicians | 820 | 25.79 | 53 630 | 22.40 |
| Mathematical science occupations, all other | 1 880 | 37.65 | 78 310 | 31.83 |
| **Architecture and Engineering Occupations** | | | | |
| Architects, surveyors, and cartographers | 168 660 | 35.85 | 74 580 | 33.23 |
| Architects, except naval | 113 550 | 38.64 | 80 370 | 35.60 |
| Architects, except landscape and naval | 93 720 | 39.83 | 82 850 | 36.59 |
| Landscape architects | 19 820 | 32.98 | 68 600 | 30.68 |
| Surveyors, cartographers, and photogrammetrists | 55 110 | 30.12 | 62 650 | 28.33 |
| Cartographers and photogrammetrists | 11 970 | 31.45 | 65 410 | 29.75 |
| Surveyors | 43 140 | 29.75 | 61 880 | 27.89 |
| Engineers | 1 610 480 | 45.79 | 95 240 | 43.30 |
| Aerospace engineers | 66 980 | 53.16 | 110 570 | 51.84 |
| Agricultural engineers | 2 330 | 37.73 | 78 490 | 36.10 |
| Biomedical engineers | 20 890 | 43.86 | 91 230 | 41.45 |
| Chemical engineers | 32 230 | 49.98 | 103 960 | 46.81 |
| Civil engineers | 275 210 | 42.28 | 87 940 | 39.53 |
| Computer hardware engineers | 75 870 | 55.27 | 114 970 | 53.72 |
| Electrical and electronics engineers | 313 970 | 47.85 | 99 520 | 45.78 |
| Electrical engineers | 178 580 | 46.80 | 97 340 | 44.71 |
| Electronics engineers, except computer | 135 390 | 49.23 | 102 390 | 47.24 |
| Environmental engineers | 52 600 | 42.33 | 88 040 | 40.65 |
| Industrial engineers, including health and safety | 272 470 | 41.86 | 87 070 | 40.18 |
| Health and safety engineers, except mining safety engineers and inspectors | 24 900 | 42.21 | 87 810 | 40.68 |
| Industrial engineers | 247 570 | 41.82 | 86 990 | 40.13 |
| Marine engineers and naval architects | 7 600 | 48.12 | 100 090 | 44.76 |
| Materials engineers | 27 040 | 45.53 | 94 690 | 43.90 |
| Mechanical engineers | 278 340 | 42.40 | 88 190 | 40.19 |
| Mining and geological engineers, including mining safety engineers | 8 000 | 51.87 | 107 880 | 45.21 |
| Nuclear engineers | 16 880 | 50.99 | 106 060 | 49.49 |
| Petroleum engineers | 34 600 | 71.92 | 149 590 | 62.49 |
| Engineers, all other | 125 460 | 47.19 | 98 150 | 46.11 |
| Drafters, engineering technicians, and mapping technicians | 696 250 | 27.24 | 56 650 | 26.03 |
| Drafters | 205 190 | 26.84 | 55 820 | 25.35 |
| Architectural and civil drafters | 95 280 | 25.71 | 53 470 | 24.38 |
| Electrical and electronics drafters | 29 200 | 30.24 | 62 890 | 28.62 |
| Mechanical drafters | 65 250 | 27.22 | 56 610 | 25.73 |
| Drafters, all other | 15 470 | 25.80 | 53 660 | 23.87 |
| Engineering technicians, except drafters | 437 440 | 28.12 | 58 490 | 27.14 |
| Aerospace engineering and operations technicians | 12 890 | 32.99 | 68 620 | 31.82 |
| Civil engineering technicians | 71 440 | 24.68 | 51 330 | 23.68 |
| Electrical and electronics engineering technicians | 139 080 | 29.74 | 61 870 | 29.39 |
| Electro-mechanical technicians | 14 720 | 27.08 | 56 320 | 25.65 |
| Environmental engineering technicians | 17 360 | 24.60 | 51 170 | 23.39 |

[1]Annual wages have been calculated by multiplying the hourly mean wage by a "year-round, full-time" hours figure of 2,080 hours; for occupations with no published hourly mean wage, the annual wage has been directly calculated from the reported survey data.

## Table 3-2.  Employment and Wages, by Occupation, May 2015—*Continued*

(Number of people, dollars.)

| Occupation | May 2015 | | | |
|---|---|---|---|---|
| | Employment | Mean hourly wage | Mean annual wage[1] | Median hourly wage |
| **Architecture and Engineering Occupations**—*Continued* | | | | |
| Industrial engineering technicians | 62 290 | 27.08 | 56 320 | 25.86 |
| Mechanical engineering technicians | 48 910 | 27.11 | 56 390 | 25.92 |
| Engineering technicians, except drafters, all other | 70 750 | 30.20 | 62 820 | 29.45 |
| Surveying and mapping technicians | 53 620 | 21.54 | 44 800 | 20.20 |
| **Life, Physical, and Social Science Occupations** | | | | |
| Life scientists | 281 440 | 39.39 | 81 920 | 34.66 |
| Agricultural and food scientists | 31 700 | 33.28 | 69 230 | 30.03 |
| Animal scientists | 2 430 | 34.53 | 71 830 | 29.03 |
| Food scientists and technologists | 14 660 | 34.63 | 72 030 | 31.65 |
| Soil and plant scientists | 14 610 | 31.72 | 65 980 | 28.87 |
| Biological scientists | 101 970 | 38.27 | 79 610 | 34.72 |
| Biochemists and biophysicists | 30 800 | 44.90 | 93 390 | 39.50 |
| Microbiologists | 21 210 | 36.65 | 76 230 | 32.47 |
| Zoologists and wildlife biologists | 17 910 | 30.88 | 64 230 | 28.69 |
| Biological scientists, all other | 32 050 | 37.11 | 77 190 | 36.13 |
| Conservation scientists and foresters | 28 790 | 30.22 | 62 860 | 28.95 |
| Conservation scientists | 20 200 | 30.67 | 63 800 | 29.38 |
| Foresters | 8 590 | 29.16 | 60 650 | 28.00 |
| Medical scientists | 109 900 | 44.66 | 92 900 | 38.97 |
| Epidemiologists | 5 460 | 36.97 | 76 900 | 33.39 |
| Medical scientists, except epidemiologists | 104 440 | 45.06 | 93 730 | 39.54 |
| Life scientists, all other | 9 070 | 38.40 | 79 870 | 33.92 |
| Physical scientists | 266 060 | 40.95 | 85 180 | 36.61 |
| Astronomers and physicists | 17 410 | 56.57 | 117 660 | 53.36 |
| Astronomers | 1 760 | 52.99 | 110 220 | 50.05 |
| Physicists | 15 650 | 56.97 | 118 500 | 53.65 |
| Atmospheric and space scientists | 10 370 | 43.37 | 90 210 | 43.18 |
| Chemists and materials scientists | 91 520 | 38.04 | 79 130 | 34.91 |
| Chemists | 84 720 | 37.43 | 77 860 | 34.26 |
| Materials scientists | 6 790 | 45.64 | 94 940 | 43.75 |
| Environmental scientists and geoscientists | 125 630 | 39.65 | 82 480 | 34.49 |
| Environmental scientists and specialists, including health | 87 250 | 35.55 | 73 930 | 32.43 |
| Geoscientists, except hydrologists and geographers | 31 800 | 50.83 | 105 720 | 43.13 |
| Hydrologists | 6 580 | 40.11 | 83 440 | 38.24 |
| Physical scientists, all other | 21 130 | 47.23 | 98 240 | 46.70 |
| Social scientists and related workers | 239 170 | 37.75 | 78 520 | 34.89 |
| Economists | 19 090 | 52.51 | 109 230 | 47.68 |
| Survey researchers | 13 650 | 28.53 | 59 340 | 25.92 |
| Psychologists | 118 990 | 37.47 | 77 950 | 34.89 |
| Clinical, counseling, and school psychologists | 105 600 | 36.56 | 76 040 | 33.93 |
| Industrial-organizational psychologists | 990 | 44.38 | 92 320 | 37.19 |
| Psychologists, all other | 12 400 | 44.73 | 93 050 | 45.47 |
| Sociologists | 2 620 | 39.47 | 82 100 | 35.46 |
| Urban and regional planners | 35 480 | 33.98 | 70 680 | 32.80 |
| Miscellaneous social scientists and related workers | 49 340 | 37.88 | 78 790 | 35.88 |
| Anthropologists and archeologists | 6 980 | 30.91 | 64 290 | 29.43 |
| Geographers | 1 280 | 36.02 | 74 920 | 35.70 |
| Historians | 3 010 | 29.38 | 61 120 | 26.83 |
| Political scientists | 3 910 | 49.62 | 103 210 | 47.95 |
| Social scientists and related workers, all other | 34 160 | 38.78 | 80 650 | 36.72 |
| Life, physical, and social science technicians | 359 440 | 22.90 | 47 640 | 20.91 |
| Agricultural and food science technicians | 20 260 | 18.75 | 39 000 | 17.54 |
| Biological technicians | 72 900 | 21.75 | 45 230 | 20.02 |
| Chemical technicians | 64 770 | 23.43 | 48 730 | 21.47 |
| Geological and petroleum technicians | 16 820 | 29.19 | 60 710 | 26.73 |
| Nuclear technicians | 6 500 | 37.91 | 78 850 | 38.59 |
| Social science research assistants | 28 060 | 22.00 | 45 760 | 20.42 |
| Miscellaneous life, physical, and social science technicians | 150 140 | 22.62 | 47 040 | 20.92 |
| Environmental science and protection technicians, including health | 34 250 | 22.38 | 46 540 | 20.69 |
| Forensic science technicians | 14 070 | 28.89 | 60 090 | 27.08 |
| Forest and conservation technicians | 29 810 | 18.40 | 38 260 | 17.04 |
| Life, physical, and social science technicians, all other | 72 020 | 23.25 | 48 360 | 21.78 |
| **Community and Social Service Occupations** | | | | |
| Counselors, social workers, and other community and social service specialists | 1 895 770 | 22.20 | 46 170 | 20.21 |
| Counselors | 628 820 | 23.46 | 48 790 | 21.71 |
| Substance abuse and behavioral disorder counselors | 87 090 | 20.64 | 42 920 | 19.22 |
| Educational, guidance, school, and vocational counselors | 253 460 | 27.16 | 56 490 | 25.80 |
| Marriage and family therapists | 32 070 | 25.73 | 53 520 | 23.37 |
| Mental health counselors | 128 200 | 21.67 | 45 080 | 20.13 |
| Rehabilitation counselors | 101 630 | 18.29 | 38 040 | 16.54 |
| Counselors, all other | 26 370 | 23.05 | 47 950 | 21.89 |
| Social workers | 619 300 | 23.88 | 49 670 | 22.07 |
| Child, family, and school social workers | 294 080 | 22.41 | 46 610 | 20.36 |
| Healthcare social workers | 155 590 | 25.97 | 54 020 | 25.18 |
| Mental health and substance abuse social workers | 110 070 | 22.69 | 47 190 | 20.28 |
| Social workers, all other | 59 570 | 27.87 | 57 970 | 28.15 |
| Miscellaneous community and social service specialists | 647 650 | 19.36 | 40 270 | 17.36 |
| Health educators | 57 570 | 27.26 | 56 690 | 24.98 |

[1]Annual wages have been calculated by multiplying the hourly mean wage by a "year-round, full-time" hours figure of 2,080 hours; for occupations with no published hourly mean wage, the annual wage has been directly calculated from the reported survey data.

## Table 3-2.  Employment and Wages, by Occupation, May 2015—*Continued*

(Number of people, dollars.)

| Occupation | May 2015 | | | |
| --- | --- | --- | --- | --- |
| | Employment | Mean hourly wage | Mean annual wage[1] | Median hourly wage |
| **Community and Social Service Occupations**—*Continued* | | | | |
| Probation officers and correctional treatment specialists ............... | 87 950 | 26.00 | 54 080 | 23.73 |
| Social and human service assistants ............... | 359 350 | 15.96 | 33 190 | 14.82 |
| Community health workers ............... | 48 130 | 19.30 | 40 150 | 17.45 |
| Community and social service specialists, all other ............... | 94 670 | 21.33 | 44 370 | 20.14 |
| Religious workers ............... | 76 370 | 22.12 | 46 020 | 19.98 |
| Clergy ............... | 48 250 | 23.15 | 48 150 | 21.27 |
| Directors, religious activities and education ............... | 20 280 | 21.71 | 45 160 | 18.65 |
| Religious workers, all other ............... | 7 840 | 16.90 | 35 160 | 13.82 |
| **Legal Occupations** | | | | |
| Lawyers, judges, and related workers ............... | 672 580 | 63.64 | 132 380 | 54.39 |
| Lawyers and judicial law clerks ............... | 622 590 | 64.76 | 134 710 | 54.94 |
| Lawyers ............... | 609 930 | 65.51 | 136 260 | 55.69 |
| Judicial law clerks ............... | 12 660 | 28.81 | 59 910 | 24.39 |
| Judges, magistrates, and other judicial workers ............... | 49 990 | 49.71 | 103 390 | 48.01 |
| Administrative law judges, adjudicators, and hearing officers ............... | 14 590 | 44.78 | 93 140 | 43.56 |
| Arbitrators, mediators, and conciliators ............... | 6 380 | 33.20 | 69 060 | 27.89 |
| Judges, magistrate judges, and magistrates ............... | 29 020 | 55.82 | 116 100 | 61.03 |
| Legal support workers ............... | 389 790 | 25.75 | 53 550 | 23.40 |
| Paralegals and legal assistants ............... | 271 930 | 25.19 | 52 390 | 23.47 |
| Miscellaneous legal support workers ............... | 117 850 | 27.04 | 56 250 | 23.23 |
| Court reporters ............... | 17 670 | 26.31 | 54 720 | 23.80 |
| Title examiners, abstractors, and searchers ............... | 54 620 | 23.96 | 49 840 | 21.33 |
| Legal support workers, all other ............... | 45 570 | 31.02 | 64 530 | 25.92 |
| **Education, Training, and Library Occupations** | | | | |
| Postsecondary teachers ............... | 1 531 350 | ( ² ) | 77 480 | ( ² ) |
| Business teachers, postsecondary ............... | 84 890 | ( ² ) | 92 220 | ( ² ) |
| Math and computer teachers, postsecondary ............... | 87 610 | ( ² ) | 80 140 | ( ² ) |
| Computer science teachers, postsecondary ............... | 33 760 | ( ² ) | 84 700 | ( ² ) |
| Mathematical science teachers, postsecondary ............... | 53 850 | ( ² ) | 77 290 | ( ² ) |
| Engineering and architecture teachers, postsecondary ............... | 44 610 | ( ² ) | 101 040 | ( ² ) |
| Architecture teachers, postsecondary ............... | 7 340 | ( ² ) | 84 880 | ( ² ) |
| Engineering teachers, postsecondary ............... | 37 270 | ( ² ) | 104 220 | ( ² ) |
| Life sciences teachers, postsecondary ............... | 62 990 | ( ² ) | 88 240 | ( ² ) |
| Agricultural sciences teachers, postsecondary ............... | 9 680 | ( ² ) | 95 280 | ( ² ) |
| Biological science teachers, postsecondary ............... | 51 640 | ( ² ) | 86 830 | ( ² ) |
| Forestry and conservation science teachers, postsecondary ............... | 1 660 | ( ² ) | 91 030 | ( ² ) |
| Physical sciences teachers, postsecondary ............... | 52 200 | ( ² ) | 89 840 | ( ² ) |
| Atmospheric, earth, marine, and space sciences teachers, postsecondary ............... | 10 890 | ( ² ) | 92 540 | ( ² ) |
| Chemistry teachers, postsecondary ............... | 21 460 | ( ² ) | 86 070 | ( ² ) |
| Environmental science teachers, postsecondary ............... | 5 540 | ( ² ) | 88 570 | ( ² ) |
| Physics teachers, postsecondary ............... | 14 310 | ( ² ) | 93 950 | ( ² ) |
| Social sciences teachers, postsecondary ............... | 116 420 | ( ² ) | 84 180 | ( ² ) |
| Anthropology and archeology teachers, postsecondary ............... | 6 000 | ( ² ) | 85 440 | ( ² ) |
| Area, ethnic, and cultural studies teachers, postsecondary ............... | 9 240 | ( ² ) | 81 700 | ( ² ) |
| Economics teachers, postsecondary ............... | 13 580 | ( ² ) | 106 980 | ( ² ) |
| Geography teachers, postsecondary ............... | 4 350 | ( ² ) | 79 690 | ( ² ) |
| Political science teachers, postsecondary ............... | 17 460 | ( ² ) | 88 680 | ( ² ) |
| Psychology teachers, postsecondary ............... | 38 380 | ( ² ) | 79 370 | ( ² ) |
| Sociology teachers, postsecondary ............... | 16 160 | ( ² ) | 76 750 | ( ² ) |
| Social sciences teachers, postsecondary, all other ............... | 11 250 | ( ² ) | 79 820 | ( ² ) |
| Health teachers, postsecondary ............... | 236 290 | ( ² ) | 104 470 | ( ² ) |
| Health specialties teachers, postsecondary ............... | 178 900 | ( ² ) | 114 510 | ( ² ) |
| Nursing instructors and teachers, postsecondary ............... | 57 390 | ( ² ) | 73 150 | ( ² ) |
| Education and library science teachers, postsecondary ............... | 65 160 | ( ² ) | 68 560 | ( ² ) |
| Education teachers, postsecondary ............... | 60 260 | ( ² ) | 68 200 | ( ² ) |
| Library science teachers, postsecondary ............... | 4 910 | ( ² ) | 73 030 | ( ² ) |
| Law, criminal justice, and social work teachers, postsecondary ............... | 42 720 | ( ² ) | 89 470 | ( ² ) |
| Criminal justice and law enforcement teachers, postsecondary ............... | 14 560 | ( ² ) | 64 460 | ( ² ) |
| Law teachers, postsecondary ............... | 16 430 | ( ² ) | 126 230 | ( ² ) |
| Social work teachers, postsecondary ............... | 11 740 | ( ² ) | 69 030 | ( ² ) |
| Arts, communications, and humanities teachers, postsecondary ............... | 280 710 | ( ² ) | 73 660 | ( ² ) |
| Art, drama, and music teachers, postsecondary ............... | 98 310 | ( ² ) | 76 710 | ( ² ) |
| Communications teachers, postsecondary ............... | 29 050 | ( ² ) | 70 290 | ( ² ) |
| English language and literature teachers, postsecondary ............... | 75 730 | ( ² ) | 71 210 | ( ² ) |
| Foreign language and literature teachers, postsecondary ............... | 30 120 | ( ² ) | 69 520 | ( ² ) |
| History teachers, postsecondary ............... | 23 680 | ( ² ) | 76 670 | ( ² ) |
| Philosophy and religion teachers, postsecondary ............... | 23 820 | ( ² ) | 75 140 | ( ² ) |
| Miscellaneous postsecondary teachers ............... | 457 750 | ( ² ) | 55 920 | ( ² ) |
| Graduate teaching assistants ............... | 125 100 | ( ² ) | 32 510 | ( ² ) |
| Home economics teachers, postsecondary ............... | 3 650 | ( ² ) | 69 090 | ( ² ) |
| Recreation and fitness studies teachers, postsecondary ............... | 17 980 | ( ² ) | 66 090 | ( ² ) |
| Vocational education teachers, postsecondary ............... | 119 800 | 26.09 | 54 260 | 23.79 |
| Postsecondary teachers, all other ............... | 191 220 | ( ² ) | 71 060 | ( ² ) |
| Preschool, primary, secondary, and special education school teachers ............... | 4 080 100 | ( ² ) | 56 370 | ( ² ) |

[1]Annual wages have been calculated by multiplying the hourly mean wage by a "year-round, full-time" hours figure of 2,080 hours; for occupations with no published hourly mean wage, the annual wage has been directly calculated from the reported survey data.
[2]Wages for some occupations that do not generally entail year-round, full-time employment are reported as either hourly wages or annual salaries (depending on how employees are typically paid).

## Table 3-2. Employment and Wages, by Occupation, May 2015—*Continued*

(Number of people, dollars.)

| Occupation | May 2015 | | | |
|---|---|---|---|---|
| | Employment | Mean hourly wage | Mean annual wage[1] | Median hourly wage |
| **Education, Training, and Library Occupations**—*Continued* | | | | |
| Preschool and kindergarten teachers | 528 330 | 18.79 | 39 090 | 16.51 |
| Preschool teachers, except special education | 370 190 | 15.62 | 32 500 | 13.74 |
| Kindergarten teachers, except special education | 158 150 | ([2]) | 54 510 | ([2]) |
| Elementary and middle school teachers | 2 027 280 | ([2]) | 58 060 | ([2]) |
| Elementary school teachers, except special education | 1 381 430 | ([2]) | 57 730 | ([2]) |
| Middle school teachers, except special and career/technical education | 632 760 | ([2]) | 58 760 | ([2]) |
| Career/technical education teachers, middle school | 13 090 | ([2]) | 58 480 | ([2]) |
| Secondary school teachers | 1 040 250 | ([2]) | 60 270 | ([2]) |
| Secondary school teachers, except special and career/technical education | 962 820 | ([2]) | 60 440 | ([2]) |
| Career/technical education teachers, secondary school | 77 430 | ([2]) | 58 170 | ([2]) |
| Special education teachers | 484 240 | ([2]) | 59 800 | ([2]) |
| Special education teachers, preschool | 29 230 | ([2]) | 58 210 | ([2]) |
| Special education teachers, kindergarten and elementary school | 195 780 | ([2]) | 58 640 | ([2]) |
| Special education teachers, middle school | 91 050 | ([2]) | 60 300 | ([2]) |
| Special education teachers, secondary school | 129 770 | ([2]) | 62 180 | ([2]) |
| Special education teachers, all other | 38 410 | ([2]) | 57 670 | ([2]) |
| Other teachers and instructors | 1 182 320 | 17.99 | 37 420 | 14.79 |
| Adult basic and secondary education and literacy teachers and instructors | 65 110 | 25.99 | 54 060 | 24.17 |
| Self-enrichment education teachers | 217 530 | 20.36 | 42 350 | 17.64 |
| Miscellaneous teachers and instructors | 899 670 | 16.84 | 35 020 | 13.92 |
| Substitute teachers | 626 750 | 14.25 | 29 630 | 12.90 |
| Teachers and instructors, all other, except substitute teachers | 272 920 | ([2]) | 47 410 | ([2]) |
| Librarians, curators, and archivists | 253 810 | 23.54 | 48 960 | 22.10 |
| Archivists, curators, and museum technicians | 28 080 | 24.88 | 51 750 | 22.46 |
| Archivists | 5 460 | 25.90 | 53 880 | 24.16 |
| Curators | 11 870 | 27.40 | 56 990 | 24.77 |
| Museum technicians and conservators | 10 750 | 21.58 | 44 880 | 19.40 |
| Librarians | 131 550 | 28.33 | 58 930 | 27.35 |
| Library technicians | 94 170 | 16.44 | 34 200 | 15.54 |
| Other education, training, and library occupations | 1 495 090 | ([2]) | 31 710 | ([2]) |
| Audio-visual and multimedia collections specialists | 10 170 | 23.18 | 48 220 | 22.06 |
| Farm and home management advisors | 8 760 | 24.91 | 51 820 | 23.65 |
| Instructional coordinators | 139 460 | 31.19 | 64 870 | 29.94 |
| Teacher assistants | 1 228 440 | ([2]) | 26 550 | ([2]) |
| Education, training, and library workers, all other | 108 270 | 21.34 | 44 380 | 19.41 |
| **Arts, Design, Entertainment, Sports, and Media Occupations** | | | | |
| Art and design workers | 559 820 | 25.11 | 52 240 | 21.13 |
| Artists and related workers | 90 150 | 37.30 | 77 580 | 32.51 |
| Art directors | 34 690 | 49.03 | 101 990 | 43.15 |
| Craft artists | 5 270 | 17.17 | 35 710 | 14.77 |
| Fine artists, including painters, sculptors, and illustrators | 12 240 | 26.04 | 54 170 | 22.34 |
| Multimedia artists and animators | 30 240 | 33.80 | 70 300 | 30.76 |
| Artists and related workers, all other | 7 700 | 29.87 | 62 130 | 28.10 |
| Designers | 469 670 | 22.78 | 47 370 | 19.49 |
| Commercial and industrial designers | 31 330 | 33.57 | 69 820 | 32.28 |
| Fashion designers | 19 040 | 35.18 | 73 180 | 30.61 |
| Floral designers | 44 350 | 12.98 | 27 010 | 12.02 |
| Graphic designers | 204 850 | 24.83 | 51 640 | 22.55 |
| Interior designers | 51 050 | 26.69 | 55 510 | 23.48 |
| Merchandise displayers and window trimmers | 100 540 | 14.32 | 29 790 | 12.92 |
| Set and exhibit designers | 11 930 | 26.40 | 54 920 | 23.81 |
| Designers, all other | 6 590 | 29.92 | 62 220 | 25.62 |
| Entertainers and performers, sports and related workers | 498 020 | 28.07 | 58 380 | 19.25 |
| Actors, producers, and directors | 155 210 | 41.28 | 85 850 | 29.08 |
| Actors | 50 570 | 37.47 | ([2]) | 18.80 |
| Producers and directors | 104 650 | 43.11 | 89 670 | 32.91 |
| Athletes, coaches, umpires, and related workers | 254 440 | ([2]) | 41 470 | ([2]) |
| Athletes and sports competitors | 11 710 | ([2]) | 80 490 | ([2]) |
| Coaches and scouts | 224 110 | ([2]) | 40 050 | ([2]) |
| Umpires, referees, and other sports officials | 18 620 | ([2]) | 33 990 | ([2]) |
| Dancers and choreographers | 15 160 | 20.39 | 42 410 | 16.85 |
| Dancers | 10 030 | 18.14 | ([2]) | 14.44 |
| Choreographers | 5 130 | 24.79 | 51 560 | 22.09 |
| Musicians, singers, and related workers | 58 630 | 31.70 | ([2]) | 24.08 |
| Music directors and composers | 21 540 | 28.38 | 59 040 | 23.95 |
| Musicians and singers | 37 090 | 33.62 | ([2]) | 24.20 |
| Entertainers and performers, sports and related workers, all other | 14 570 | 22.71 | ([2]) | 17.64 |
| Media and communication workers | 564 800 | 29.76 | 61 910 | 25.73 |
| Announcers | 38 380 | 21.72 | 45 170 | 14.46 |
| Radio and television announcers | 30 390 | 22.31 | 46 410 | 14.88 |
| Public address system and other announcers | 8 000 | 19.44 | 40 440 | 12.95 |
| News analysts, reporters and correspondents | 45 790 | 24.50 | 50 970 | 18.13 |
| Broadcast news analysts | 4 730 | 42.90 | 89 240 | 31.51 |
| Reporters and correspondents | 41 050 | 22.38 | 46 560 | 17.48 |
| Public relations specialists | 218 910 | 31.65 | 65 830 | 27.29 |
| Writers and editors | 189 840 | 32.74 | 68 090 | 29.24 |

[1]Annual wages have been calculated by multiplying the hourly mean wage by a "year-round, full-time" hours figure of 2,080 hours; for occupations with no published hourly mean wage, the annual wage has been directly calculated from the reported survey data.
[2]Wages for some occupations that do not generally entail year-round, full-time employment are reported as either hourly wages or annual salaries (depending on how employees are typically paid).

## Table 3-2.  Employment and Wages, by Occupation, May 2015—*Continued*

(Number of people, dollars.)

| Occupation | May 2015 | | | |
| --- | --- | --- | --- | --- |
| | Employment | Mean hourly wage | Mean annual wage[1] | Median hourly wage |
| **Arts, Design, Entertainment, Sports, and Media Occupations**—*Continued* | | | | |
| Editors ............................................................ | 96 690 | 31.21 | 64 910 | 26.93 |
| Technical writers ............................................... | 49 770 | 35.26 | 73 350 | 33.77 |
| Writers and authors ............................................ | 43 380 | 33.24 | 69 130 | 28.97 |
| Miscellaneous media and communication workers ........... | 71 890 | 23.82 | 49 550 | 21.39 |
| Interpreters and translators ................................... | 49 650 | 23.25 | 48 360 | 21.24 |
| | | | | |
| Media and communication workers, all other ................ | 22 240 | 25.10 | 52 200 | 21.74 |
| Media and communication equipment workers ............... | 220 950 | 25.59 | 53 220 | 20.91 |
| Broadcast and sound engineering technicians and radio operators ... | 105 500 | 23.14 | 48 140 | 20.13 |
| Audio and video equipment technicians ...................... | 62 460 | 22.42 | 46 630 | 19.92 |
| Broadcast technicians ......................................... | 28 270 | 21.18 | 44 050 | 18.02 |
| | | | | |
| Radio operators ............................................... | 940 | 22.69 | 47 200 | 24.06 |
| Sound engineering technicians ............................... | 13 840 | 30.45 | 63 340 | 25.64 |
| Photographers ................................................. | 50 070 | 19.37 | 40 280 | 15.24 |
| Television, video, and motion picture camera operators and editors ... | 47 710 | 34.37 | 71 500 | 26.80 |
| Camera operators, television, video, and motion picture ... | 20 060 | 28.54 | 59 360 | 23.60 |
| | | | | |
| Film and video editors ........................................ | 27 660 | 38.61 | 80 300 | 29.69 |
| Media and communication equipment workers, all other ... | 17 670 | 34.10 | 70 920 | 33.94 |
| **Healthcare Practitioners and Technical Occupations** | | | | |
| Health diagnosing and treating practitioners ............... | 4 960 900 | 46.65 | 97 030 | 36.90 |
| Chiropractors .................................................. | 32 080 | 37.68 | 78 370 | 30.98 |
| Dentists ........................................................ | 116 750 | 85.16 | 177 130 | 76.11 |
| Dentists, general .............................................. | 100 080 | 82.86 | 172 350 | 73.42 |
| Oral and maxillofacial surgeons ............................. | 5 000 | 112.45 | 233 900 | ([3]) |
| | | | | |
| Orthodontists .................................................. | 5 410 | 106.44 | 221 390 | ([3]) |
| Prosthodontists ................................................ | 710 | 77.41 | 161 020 | 57.57 |
| Dentists, all other specialists ................................ | 5 550 | 82.23 | 171 040 | 82.21 |
| Dietitians and nutritionists ................................... | 59 740 | 28.08 | 58 410 | 27.84 |
| Optometrists ................................................... | 35 300 | 55.65 | 115 750 | 49.95 |
| | | | | |
| Pharmacists .................................................... | 295 620 | 57.34 | 119 270 | 58.41 |
| Physicians and surgeons ...................................... | 642 720 | 97.33 | 202 450 | ([3]) |
| Anesthesiologists .............................................. | 29 220 | 124.09 | 258 100 | ([3]) |
| Family and general practitioners ............................. | 127 430 | 92.36 | 192 120 | 88.65 |
| Internists, general ............................................. | 48 920 | 94.48 | 196 520 | ([3]) |
| | | | | |
| Obstetricians and gynecologists ............................. | 20 090 | 106.92 | 222 400 | ([3]) |
| Pediatricians, general ......................................... | 28 660 | 88.07 | 183 180 | 81.87 |
| Psychiatrists ................................................... | 24 060 | 93.12 | 193 680 | ([3]) |
| Surgeons ....................................................... | 41 600 | 119.00 | 247 520 | ([3]) |
| Physicians and surgeons, all other .......................... | 322 740 | 95.05 | 197 700 | ([3]) |
| | | | | |
| Physician assistants .......................................... | 98 470 | 47.73 | 99 270 | 47.20 |
| Podiatrists ..................................................... | 9 500 | 65.47 | 136 180 | 57.37 |
| Therapists ..................................................... | 628 440 | 36.64 | 76 220 | 35.53 |
| Occupational therapists ....................................... | 114 660 | 39.27 | 81 690 | 38.54 |
| Physical therapists ............................................ | 209 690 | 41.25 | 85 790 | 40.40 |
| | | | | |
| Radiation therapists ........................................... | 16 930 | 40.61 | 84 460 | 38.57 |
| Recreational therapists ........................................ | 17 880 | 22.98 | 47 790 | 22.06 |
| Respiratory therapists ......................................... | 120 330 | 28.67 | 59 640 | 27.78 |
| Speech-language pathologists ................................ | 131 450 | 36.97 | 76 900 | 35.29 |
| Exercise physiologists ......................................... | 6 620 | 23.91 | 49 740 | 22.60 |
| Therapists, all other .......................................... | 10 890 | 28.46 | 59 210 | 26.93 |
| | | | | |
| Veterinarians ................................................... | 65 650 | 47.59 | 99 000 | 42.54 |
| Registered nurses ............................................. | 2 745 910 | 34.14 | 71 000 | 32.45 |
| Nurse anesthetists ............................................. | 39 410 | 77.04 | 160 250 | 75.55 |
| Nurse midwives ................................................ | 7 430 | 45.01 | 93 610 | 44.48 |
| Nurse practitioners ............................................ | 136 060 | 48.68 | 101 260 | 47.21 |
| | | | | |
| Audiologists .................................................... | 12 070 | 37.22 | 77 420 | 36.01 |
| Health diagnosing and treating practitioners, all other ... | 35 750 | 40.92 | 85 120 | 35.92 |
| Health technologists and technicians ........................ | 2 909 230 | 22.04 | 45 850 | 20.28 |
| Clinical laboratory technologists and technicians ........... | 320 550 | 24.91 | 51 810 | 24.30 |
| Medical and clinical laboratory technologists ............... | 162 950 | 29.74 | 61 860 | 29.09 |
| | | | | |
| Medical and clinical laboratory technicians ................. | 157 610 | 19.91 | 41 420 | 18.73 |
| Dental hygienists .............................................. | 200 550 | 34.96 | 72 720 | 34.77 |
| Diagnostic related technologists and technicians ........... | 361 430 | 29.84 | 62 080 | 29.04 |
| Cardiovascular technologists and technicians ............... | 51 400 | 26.97 | 56 100 | 26.38 |
| Diagnostic medical sonographers ............................ | 61 250 | 34.08 | 70 880 | 33.16 |
| | | | | |
| Nuclear medicine technologists .............................. | 19 740 | 36.06 | 74 990 | 35.27 |
| Radiologic technologists ...................................... | 195 590 | 28.13 | 58 520 | 27.25 |
| Magnetic resonance imaging technologists .................. | 33 460 | 32.86 | 68 340 | 32.56 |
| Emergency medical technicians and paramedics ............ | 236 890 | 17.04 | 35 430 | 15.38 |
| Health practitioner support technologists and technicians ... | 712 050 | 16.69 | 34 710 | 15.71 |
| | | | | |
| Dietetic technicians ........................................... | 28 950 | 14.03 | 29 170 | 12.52 |
| Pharmacy technicians ......................................... | 379 430 | 15.23 | 31 680 | 14.62 |
| Psychiatric technicians ........................................ | 58 450 | 17.44 | 36 280 | 14.97 |
| Respiratory therapy technicians .............................. | 10 000 | 23.90 | 49 720 | 23.31 |
| Surgical technologists ......................................... | 100 270 | 22.09 | 45 940 | 21.31 |

[1]Annual wages have been calculated by multiplying the hourly mean wage by a "year-round, full-time" hours figure of 2,080 hours; for occupations with no published hourly mean wage, the annual wage has been directly calculated from the reported survey data.
[3]Median hourly wage is equal to or greater than $90.00 per hour.

## Table 3-2. Employment and Wages, by Occupation, May 2015—*Continued*

(Number of people, dollars.)

| Occupation | May 2015 | | | |
|---|---|---|---|---|
| | Employment | Mean hourly wage | Mean annual wage[1] | Median hourly wage |
| **Healthcare Practitioners and Technical Occupations—***Continued* | | | | |
| Veterinary technologists and technicians ...... | 95 790 | 16.00 | 33 280 | 15.29 |
| Ophthalmic medical technicians ...... | 39 160 | 17.64 | 36 690 | 16.99 |
| Licensed practical and licensed vocational nurses ...... | 697 250 | 21.17 | 44 030 | 20.76 |
| Medical records and health information technicians ...... | 189 930 | 19.44 | 40 430 | 17.84 |
| Opticians, dispensing ...... | 73 520 | 17.70 | 36 820 | 16.75 |
| Miscellaneous health technologists and technicians ...... | 117 040 | 22.86 | 47 560 | 20.54 |
| Orthotists and prosthetists ...... | 7 100 | 33.63 | 69 960 | 30.98 |
| Hearing aid specialists ...... | 5 920 | 25.41 | 52 850 | 23.85 |
| Health technologists and technicians, all other ...... | 104 020 | 21.98 | 45 730 | 19.84 |
| Other healthcare practitioners and technical occupations ...... | 151 680 | 29.72 | 61 820 | 27.88 |
| Occupational health and safety specialists and technicians ...... | 86 270 | 32.68 | 67 970 | 31.69 |
| Occupational health and safety specialists ...... | 70 220 | 34.51 | 71 790 | 33.75 |
| Occupational health and safety technicians ...... | 16 050 | 24.65 | 51 270 | 23.11 |
| Miscellaneous health practitioners and technical workers ...... | 65 410 | 25.82 | 53 710 | 22.64 |
| Athletic trainers ...... | 23 450 | (2) | 46 940 | (2) |
| Genetic counselors ...... | 2 520 | 35.85 | 74 570 | 34.66 |
| Healthcare practitioners and technical workers, all other ...... | 39 440 | 27.12 | 56 400 | 23.21 |
| **Healthcare Support Occupations** | | | | |
| Nursing, psychiatric, and home health aides ...... | 2 363 400 | 12.26 | 25 500 | 11.56 |
| Nursing, psychiatric, and home health aides ...... | 2 363 400 | 12.26 | 25 500 | 11.56 |
| Home health aides ...... | 820 630 | 11.00 | 22 870 | 10.54 |
| Psychiatric aides ...... | 69 550 | 13.55 | 28 170 | 12.59 |
| Nursing assistants ...... | 1 420 570 | 12.89 | 26 820 | 12.36 |
| Orderlies ...... | 52 660 | 13.26 | 27 580 | 12.30 |
| Occupational therapy and physical therapist assistants and aides ...... | 174 800 | 22.50 | 46 790 | 22.46 |
| Occupational therapy assistants and aides ...... | 43 030 | 25.74 | 53 550 | 26.21 |
| Occupational therapy assistants ...... | 35 460 | 28.05 | 58 340 | 27.82 |
| Occupational therapy aides ...... | 7 570 | 14.95 | 31 090 | 13.37 |
| Physical therapist assistants and aides ...... | 131 770 | 21.44 | 44 590 | 20.66 |
| Physical therapist assistants ...... | 81 230 | 26.56 | 55 250 | 26.52 |
| Physical therapist aides ...... | 50 540 | 13.19 | 27 440 | 12.08 |
| Other healthcare support occupations ...... | 1 451 710 | 16.33 | 33 970 | 15.49 |
| Massage therapists ...... | 92 090 | 20.76 | 43 170 | 18.29 |
| Miscellaneous healthcare support occupations ...... | 1 359 620 | 16.03 | 33 340 | 15.36 |
| Dental assistants ...... | 323 110 | 17.75 | 36 920 | 17.30 |
| Medical assistants ...... | 601 240 | 15.34 | 31 910 | 14.71 |
| Medical equipment preparers ...... | 50 330 | 16.80 | 34 950 | 16.02 |
| Medical transcriptionists ...... | 57 830 | 17.17 | 35 720 | 16.77 |
| Pharmacy aides ...... | 38 040 | 13.20 | 27 460 | 11.75 |
| Veterinary assistants and laboratory animal caretakers ...... | 75 620 | 12.47 | 25 940 | 11.71 |
| Phlebotomists ...... | 118 160 | 15.76 | 32 770 | 15.21 |
| Healthcare support workers, all other ...... | 95 290 | 17.75 | 36 920 | 17.20 |
| **Protective Service Occupations** | | | | |
| Supervisors of protective service workers ...... | 270 660 | 33.91 | 70 530 | 31.76 |
| First-line supervisors of law enforcement workers ...... | 142 890 | 37.96 | 78 950 | 36.18 |
| First-line supervisors of correctional officers ...... | 42 520 | 30.18 | 62 770 | 28.71 |
| First-line supervisors of police and detectives ...... | 100 370 | 41.26 | 85 810 | 39.47 |
| First-line supervisors of fire fighting and prevention workers ...... | 58 110 | 36.05 | 74 970 | 34.72 |
| First-line supervisors of protective service workers, all other ...... | 69 660 | 23.82 | 49 540 | 22.55 |
| Fire fighting and prevention workers ...... | 332 730 | 23.89 | 49 690 | 22.72 |
| Firefighters ...... | 318 790 | 23.72 | 49 330 | 22.53 |
| Fire inspectors ...... | 13 940 | 27.89 | 58 020 | 26.34 |
| Fire inspectors and investigators ...... | 12 290 | 28.75 | 59 800 | 27.27 |
| Forest fire inspectors and prevention specialists ...... | 1 650 | 21.51 | 44 740 | 17.62 |
| Law enforcement workers ...... | 1 223 890 | 27.34 | 56 860 | 25.03 |
| Bailiffs, correctional officers, and jailers ...... | 445 520 | 21.78 | 45 310 | 19.51 |
| Bailiffs ...... | 17 730 | 21.59 | 44 900 | 20.03 |
| Correctional officers and jailers ...... | 427 790 | 21.79 | 45 320 | 19.49 |
| Detectives and criminal investigators ...... | 106 580 | 38.28 | 79 620 | 37.12 |
| Fish and game wardens ...... | 5 630 | 26.43 | 54 970 | 25.38 |
| Parking enforcement workers ...... | 8 710 | 18.40 | 38 280 | 17.56 |
| Police officers ...... | 657 460 | 29.46 | 61 270 | 28.04 |
| Police and sheriff's patrol officers ...... | 653 740 | 29.45 | 61 270 | 28.04 |
| Transit and railroad police ...... | 3 720 | 29.85 | 62 090 | 28.69 |
| Other protective service workers ...... | 1 524 340 | 13.97 | 29 050 | 11.95 |
| Animal control workers ...... | 13 180 | 16.98 | 35 330 | 16.08 |
| Private detectives and investigators ...... | 30 460 | 25.41 | 52 840 | 21.93 |
| Security guards and gaming surveillance officers ...... | 1 108 310 | 13.71 | 28 510 | 11.87 |
| Gaming surveillance officers and gaming investigators ...... | 10 650 | 16.29 | 33 880 | 14.99 |
| Security guards ...... | 1 097 660 | 13.68 | 28 460 | 11.84 |
| Miscellaneous protective service workers ...... | 372 390 | 13.71 | 28 510 | 11.67 |
| Crossing guards ...... | 68 640 | 13.33 | 27 730 | 12.07 |
| Lifeguards, ski patrol, and other recreational protective service workers ...... | 141 670 | 10.54 | 21 930 | 9.38 |
| Transportation security screeners ...... | 41 820 | 19.25 | 40 050 | 18.90 |
| Protective service workers, all other ...... | 120 270 | 15.72 | 32 690 | 13.77 |

[1]Annual wages have been calculated by multiplying the hourly mean wage by a "year-round, full-time" hours figure of 2,080 hours; for occupations with no published hourly mean wage, the annual wage has been directly calculated from the reported survey data.
[2]Wages for some occupations that do not generally entail year-round, full-time employment are reported as either hourly wages or annual salaries (depending on how employees are typically paid).

## Table 3-2. Employment and Wages, by Occupation, May 2015—*Continued*

(Number of people, dollars.)

| Occupation | May 2015 | | | |
| --- | --- | --- | --- | --- |
| | Employment | Mean hourly wage | Mean annual wage[1] | Median hourly wage |
| **Food Preparation and Serving Related Occupations** | | | | |
| Supervisors of food preparation and serving workers | 1 013 460 | 16.80 | 34 930 | 15.11 |
| Supervisors of food preparation and serving workers | 1 013 460 | 16.80 | 34 930 | 15.11 |
| Chefs and head cooks | 129 370 | 22.07 | 45 920 | 19.95 |
| First-line supervisors of food preparation and serving workers | 884 090 | 16.02 | 33 330 | 14.59 |
| Cooks and food preparation workers | 3 147 210 | 11.05 | 22 990 | 10.24 |
| Cooks | 2 284 470 | 11.23 | 23 350 | 10.44 |
| Cooks, fast food | 520 010 | 9.43 | 19 610 | 9.17 |
| Cooks, institution and cafeteria | 404 980 | 12.29 | 25 560 | 11.52 |
| Cooks, private household | 380 | 18.12 | 37 680 | 12.65 |
| Cooks, restaurant | 1 150 760 | 11.74 | 24 430 | 11.11 |
| Cooks, short order | 193 170 | 10.55 | 21 940 | 9.99 |
| Cooks, all other | 15 160 | 13.58 | 28 240 | 12.67 |
| Food preparation workers | 862 740 | 10.60 | 22 050 | 9.70 |
| Food and beverage serving workers | 7 054 960 | 10.30 | 21 430 | 9.19 |
| Bartenders | 589 150 | 11.59 | 24 110 | 9.39 |
| Fast food and counter workers | 3 703 110 | 9.53 | 19 820 | 9.11 |
| Combined food preparation and serving workers, including fast food | 3 216 460 | 9.47 | 19 710 | 9.09 |
| Counter attendants, cafeteria, food concession, and coffee shop | 486 650 | 9.90 | 20 590 | 9.24 |
| Waiters and waitresses | 2 505 630 | 11.07 | 23 020 | 9.25 |
| Food servers, nonrestaurant | 257 070 | 11.06 | 23 010 | 9.82 |
| Other food preparation and serving related workers | 1 361 450 | 10.01 | 20 830 | 9.27 |
| Dining room and cafeteria attendants and bartender helpers | 412 830 | 10.29 | 21 400 | 9.27 |
| Dishwashers | 505 000 | 9.79 | 20 360 | 9.30 |
| Hosts and hostesses, restaurant, lounge, and coffee shop | 391 150 | 9.87 | 20 530 | 9.22 |
| Food preparation and serving related workers, all other | 52 470 | 11.09 | 23 060 | 9.80 |
| **Building and Grounds Cleaning and Maintenance Occupations** | | | | |
| Supervisors of building and grounds cleaning and maintenance workers | 270 360 | 20.52 | 42 680 | 18.96 |
| First-line supervisors of building and grounds cleaning and maintenance workers | 270 360 | 20.52 | 42 680 | 18.96 |
| First-line supervisors of housekeeping and janitorial workers | 166 920 | 19.26 | 40 060 | 17.81 |
| First-line supervisors of landscaping, lawn service, and groundskeeping workers | 103 450 | 22.55 | 46 900 | 21.15 |
| Building cleaning and pest control workers | 3 159 840 | 12.23 | 25 440 | 10.93 |
| Building cleaning workers | 3 089 590 | 12.14 | 25 240 | 10.86 |
| Janitors and cleaners, except maids and housekeeping cleaners | 2 146 880 | 12.59 | 26 180 | 11.27 |
| Maids and housekeeping cleaners | 926 240 | 11.05 | 22 990 | 9.97 |
| Building cleaning workers, all other | 16 480 | 14.52 | 30 200 | 14.06 |
| Pest control workers | 70 250 | 16.39 | 34 080 | 15.46 |
| Grounds maintenance workers | 976 840 | 13.50 | 28 090 | 12.31 |
| Grounds maintenance workers | 976 840 | 13.50 | 28 090 | 12.31 |
| Landscaping and groundskeeping workers | 895 600 | 13.20 | 27 460 | 12.03 |
| Pesticide handlers, sprayers, and applicators, vegetation | 24 200 | 16.62 | 34 570 | 15.64 |
| Tree trimmers and pruners | 40 160 | 17.32 | 36 030 | 16.10 |
| Grounds maintenance workers, all other | 16 890 | 16.03 | 33 340 | 14.05 |
| **Personal Care and Service Occupations** | | | | |
| Supervisors of personal care and service workers | 208 040 | 19.17 | 39 870 | 17.71 |
| First-line supervisors of gaming workers | 30 340 | 22.57 | 46 940 | 22.19 |
| Gaming supervisors | 22 640 | 24.10 | 50 130 | 23.91 |
| Slot supervisors | 7 700 | 18.05 | 37 550 | 17.16 |
| First-line supervisors of personal service workers | 177 700 | 18.59 | 38 670 | 17.17 |
| Animal care and service workers | 185 780 | 11.66 | 24 260 | 10.22 |
| Animal trainers | 11 720 | 16.15 | 33 600 | 12.80 |
| Nonfarm animal caretakers | 174 060 | 11.36 | 23 630 | 10.10 |
| Entertainment attendants and related workers | 551 590 | 10.64 | 22 140 | 9.29 |
| Gaming services workers | 119 540 | 10.93 | 22 730 | 9.24 |
| Gaming dealers | 94 900 | 10.49 | 21 810 | 9.14 |
| Gaming and sports book writers and runners | 12 370 | 12.58 | 26 170 | 10.91 |
| Gaming service workers, all other | 12 280 | 12.68 | 26 380 | 11.56 |
| Motion picture projectionists | 5 620 | 11.80 | 24 540 | 10.33 |
| Ushers, lobby attendants, and ticket takers | 114 000 | 10.13 | 21 060 | 9.22 |
| Miscellaneous entertainment attendants and related workers | 312 430 | 10.70 | 22 260 | 9.33 |
| Amusement and recreation attendants | 273 870 | 10.27 | 21 360 | 9.27 |
| Costume attendants | 6 120 | 25.42 | 52 870 | 21.40 |
| Locker room, coatroom, and dressing room attendants | 17 430 | 11.53 | 23 990 | 10.11 |
| Entertainment attendants and related workers, all other | 15 010 | 11.59 | 24 110 | 10.92 |
| Funeral service workers | 64 470 | 18.01 | 37 460 | 14.79 |
| Embalmers | 3 710 | 19.95 | 41 490 | 19.43 |
| Funeral attendants | 35 290 | 12.42 | 25 840 | 11.43 |
| Morticians, undertakers, and funeral directors | 25 470 | 25.47 | 52 990 | 23.31 |
| Personal appearance workers | 504 640 | 13.67 | 28 420 | 11.17 |
| Barbers, hairdressers, hairstylists and cosmetologists | 362 360 | 13.84 | 28 790 | 11.40 |
| Barbers | 14 350 | 14.01 | 29 140 | 11.95 |
| Hairdressers, hairstylists, and cosmetologists | 348 010 | 13.83 | 28 770 | 11.38 |
| Miscellaneous personal appearance workers | 142 280 | 13.22 | 27 500 | 10.65 |
| Makeup artists, theatrical and performance | 3 060 | 32.00 | 66 560 | 25.59 |
| Manicurists and pedicurists | 83 840 | 11.36 | 23 630 | 10.01 |
| Shampooers | 15 190 | 9.78 | 20 350 | 9.27 |
| Skincare specialists | 40 190 | 16.97 | 35 300 | 14.47 |
| Baggage porters, bellhops, and concierges | 77 980 | 12.99 | 27 030 | 11.60 |
| Baggage porters and bellhops | 46 550 | 11.75 | 24 430 | 10.17 |

[1]Annual wages have been calculated by multiplying the hourly mean wage by a "year-round, full-time" hours figure of 2,080 hours; for occupations with no published hourly mean wage, the annual wage has been directly calculated from the reported survey data.

## Table 3-2. Employment and Wages, by Occupation, May 2015—*Continued*

(Number of people, dollars.)

| Occupation | May 2015 | | | |
|---|---|---|---|---|
| | Employment | Mean hourly wage | Mean annual wage[1] | Median hourly wage |
| **Personal Care and Service Occupations**—*Continued* | | | | |
| Concierges | 31 430 | 14.84 | 30 870 | 13.96 |
| Tour and travel guides | 38 740 | 13.29 | 27 640 | 11.85 |
| Tour and travel guides | 38 740 | 13.29 | 27 640 | 11.85 |
| Tour guides and escorts | 35 930 | 12.94 | 26 920 | 11.59 |
| Travel guides | 2 810 | 17.75 | 36 920 | 16.43 |
| Other personal care and service workers | 2 676 260 | 11.77 | 24 480 | 10.40 |
| Childcare workers | 573 440 | 10.72 | 22 310 | 9.77 |
| Personal care aides | 1 369 230 | 10.48 | 21 790 | 10.09 |
| Recreation and fitness workers | 573 920 | 15.66 | 32 560 | 12.76 |
| Fitness trainers and aerobics instructors | 237 760 | 19.70 | 40 970 | 17.39 |
| Recreation workers | 336 150 | 12.79 | 26 610 | 11.21 |
| Residential advisors | 102 540 | 13.05 | 27 140 | 12.01 |
| Personal care and service workers, all other | 57 140 | 11.99 | 24 950 | 10.73 |
| **Sales and Related Occupations** | | | | |
| Supervisors of sales workers | 1 441 700 | 24.10 | 50 120 | 19.87 |
| First-line supervisors of retail sales workers | 1 193 850 | 20.63 | 42 900 | 18.42 |
| First-line supervisors of non-retail sales workers | 247 850 | 40.82 | 84 910 | 34.76 |
| Retail sales workers | 8 799 250 | 11.77 | 24 490 | 9.84 |
| Cashiers | 3 501 210 | 10.10 | 21 010 | 9.29 |
| Gaming change persons and booth cashiers | 22 790 | 11.84 | 24 620 | 11.03 |
| Counter and rental clerks and parts salespersons | 685 520 | 14.32 | 29 790 | 12.58 |
| Counter and rental clerks | 447 050 | 13.57 | 28 210 | 11.75 |
| Parts salespersons | 238 470 | 15.74 | 32 750 | 14.25 |
| Retail salespersons | 4 612 510 | 12.67 | 26 340 | 10.47 |
| Sales representatives, services | 1 808 330 | 33.22 | 69 100 | 24.78 |
| Advertising sales agents | 149 770 | 29.66 | 61 690 | 23.31 |
| Insurance sales agents | 386 140 | 31.15 | 64 790 | 23.17 |
| Securities, commodities, and financial services sales agents | 319 280 | 49.45 | 102 860 | 34.40 |
| Travel agents | 66 560 | 18.63 | 38 750 | 17.15 |
| Sales representatives, services, all other | 886 580 | 29.98 | 62 360 | 24.86 |
| Sales representatives, wholesale and manufacturing | 1 743 560 | 34.17 | 71 080 | 28.41 |
| Sales representatives, wholesale and manufacturing, technical and scientific products | 334 010 | 42.87 | 89 170 | 36.63 |
| Sales representatives, wholesale and manufacturing, except technical and scientific products | 1 409 550 | 32.11 | 66 790 | 26.79 |
| Other sales and related workers | 669 270 | 22.97 | 47 780 | 14.84 |
| Models, demonstrators, and product promoters | 88 080 | 14.47 | 30 100 | 12.01 |
| Demonstrators and product promoters | 83 620 | 14.29 | 29 720 | 11.99 |
| Models | 4 460 | 17.91 | 37 240 | 13.23 |
| Real estate brokers and sales agents | 190 510 | 30.22 | 62 850 | 21.93 |
| Real estate brokers | 38 810 | 38.56 | 80 210 | 27.34 |
| Real estate sales agents | 151 700 | 28.08 | 58 410 | 20.85 |
| Sales engineers | 72 200 | 51.52 | 107 160 | 46.95 |
| Telemarketers | 226 730 | 12.73 | 26 470 | 11.31 |
| Miscellaneous sales and related workers | 91 760 | 18.93 | 39 370 | 15.35 |
| Door-to-door sales workers, news and street vendors, and related workers | 7 510 | 12.58 | 26 160 | 10.68 |
| Sales and related workers, all other | 84 240 | 19.49 | 40 540 | 15.98 |
| **Office and Administrative Support Occupations** | | | | |
| Supervisors of office and administrative support workers | 1 424 450 | 27.01 | 56 170 | 25.30 |
| First-line supervisors of office and administrative support workers | 1 424 450 | 27.01 | 56 170 | 25.30 |
| Communications equipment operators | 112 260 | 14.54 | 30 250 | 13.47 |
| Switchboard operators, including answering service | 100 500 | 13.94 | 28 990 | 13.19 |
| Telephone operators | 9 750 | 19.62 | 40 820 | 17.25 |
| Communications equipment operators, all other | 2 010 | 20.19 | 41 990 | 19.39 |
| Financial clerks | 3 179 250 | 17.63 | 36 680 | 16.74 |
| Bill and account collectors | 318 970 | 17.60 | 36 600 | 16.56 |
| Billing and posting clerks | 491 070 | 17.45 | 36 300 | 16.85 |
| Bookkeeping, accounting, and auditing clerks | 1 580 220 | 18.74 | 38 990 | 17.91 |
| Gaming cage workers | 17 650 | 13.36 | 27 780 | 12.43 |
| Payroll and timekeeping clerks | 166 700 | 20.26 | 42 130 | 19.71 |
| Procurement clerks | 71 470 | 19.72 | 41 010 | 19.52 |
| Tellers | 498 460 | 13.10 | 27 260 | 12.70 |
| Financial clerks, all other | 34 700 | 20.32 | 42 270 | 19.27 |
| Information and record clerks | 5 513 250 | 16.16 | 33 610 | 14.91 |
| Brokerage clerks | 57 490 | 24.83 | 51 640 | 23.16 |
| Correspondence clerks | 7 320 | 17.47 | 36 340 | 16.98 |
| Court, municipal, and license clerks | 130 190 | 18.38 | 38 230 | 17.23 |
| Credit authorizers, checkers, and clerks | 41 880 | 18.23 | 37 920 | 16.96 |
| Customer service representatives | 2 595 990 | 16.62 | 34 560 | 15.25 |
| Eligibility interviewers, government programs | 130 420 | 20.69 | 43 040 | 20.75 |
| File clerks | 140 560 | 14.38 | 29 900 | 13.39 |
| Hotel, motel, and resort desk clerks | 243 210 | 10.87 | 22 610 | 10.11 |
| Interviewers, except eligibility and loan | 184 050 | 15.83 | 32 930 | 15.10 |
| Library assistants, clerical | 100 090 | 12.78 | 26 580 | 11.77 |
| Loan interviewers and clerks | 216 380 | 18.85 | 39 210 | 18.13 |
| New accounts clerks | 48 970 | 17.22 | 35 820 | 16.77 |
| Order clerks | 185 890 | 16.38 | 34 080 | 15.54 |
| Human resources assistants, except payroll and timekeeping | 138 910 | 18.84 | 39 180 | 18.32 |

[1]Annual wages have been calculated by multiplying the hourly mean wage by a "year-round, full-time" hours figure of 2,080 hours; for occupations with no published hourly mean wage, the annual wage has been directly calculated from the reported survey data.

## Table 3-2.  Employment and Wages, by Occupation, May 2015—*Continued*

(Number of people, dollars.)

| Occupation | May 2015 | | | |
|---|---|---|---|---|
| | Employment | Mean hourly wage | Mean annual wage[1] | Median hourly wage |
| **Office and Administrative Support Occupations**—*Continued* | | | | |
| Receptionists and information clerks ............................................................. | 975 890 | 13.67 | 28 430 | 13.12 |
| Reservation and transportation ticket agents and travel clerks ...................... | 138 810 | 17.68 | 36 780 | 16.91 |
| Information and record clerks, all other ......................................................... | 177 210 | 18.64 | 38 770 | 18.26 |
| Material recording, scheduling, dispatching, and distributing workers .............. | 3 973 740 | 16.16 | 33 610 | 14.32 |
| Cargo and freight agents ............................................................................. | 81 120 | 21.38 | 44 470 | 20.13 |
| Couriers and messengers ............................................................................. | 73 180 | 14.01 | 29 130 | 13.12 |
| Dispatchers ................................................................................................ | 292 570 | 19.30 | 40 140 | 18.00 |
| Police, fire, and ambulance dispatchers ....................................................... | 95 630 | 19.23 | 40 000 | 18.27 |
| Dispatchers, except police, fire, and ambulance ........................................... | 196 940 | 19.33 | 40 210 | 17.86 |
| Meter readers, utilities ................................................................................ | 34 970 | 19.66 | 40 900 | 18.51 |
| Postal service workers ................................................................................ | 504 540 | 24.38 | 50 700 | 27.30 |
| Postal service clerks .................................................................................. | 78 660 | 23.60 | 49 090 | 27.30 |
| Postal service mail carriers ......................................................................... | 315 950 | 24.58 | 51 130 | 28.02 |
| Postal service mail sorters, processors, and processing machine operators ..... | 109 930 | 24.35 | 50 650 | 27.28 |
| Production, planning, and expediting clerks .................................................. | 309 110 | 23.18 | 48 210 | 22.19 |
| Shipping, receiving, and traffic clerks .......................................................... | 674 820 | 15.55 | 32 350 | 14.64 |
| Stock clerks and order fillers ....................................................................... | 1 934 060 | 12.47 | 25 940 | 11.17 |
| Weighers, measurers, checkers, and samplers, recordkeeping ...................... | 69 360 | 14.89 | 30 980 | 13.80 |
| Secretaries and administrative assistants .................................................... | 3 680 630 | 18.93 | 39 360 | 17.55 |
| Executive secretaries and executive administrative assistants ...................... | 666 490 | 26.66 | 55 460 | 25.66 |
| Legal secretaries ....................................................................................... | 202 660 | 22.34 | 46 470 | 20.77 |
| Medical secretaries .................................................................................... | 530 360 | 16.50 | 34 330 | 15.89 |
| Secretaries and administrative assistants, except legal, medical, and executive ...... | 2 281 120 | 16.92 | 35 200 | 16.31 |
| Other office and administrative support workers ............................................ | 3 962 840 | 15.77 | 32 800 | 14.67 |
| Computer operators .................................................................................... | 51 510 | 20.26 | 42 140 | 19.43 |
| Data entry and information processing workers ............................................. | 267 900 | 15.79 | 32 840 | 14.99 |
| Data entry keyers ....................................................................................... | 199 240 | 14.81 | 30 810 | 14.16 |
| Word processors and typists ....................................................................... | 68 660 | 18.61 | 38 710 | 18.08 |
| Desktop publishers ..................................................................................... | 13 240 | 21.10 | 43 900 | 19.15 |
| Insurance claims and policy processing clerks .............................................. | 262 910 | 19.02 | 39 560 | 18.04 |
| Mail clerks and mail machine operators, except postal service ...................... | 95 640 | 14.39 | 29 930 | 13.74 |
| Office clerks, general .................................................................................. | 2 944 420 | 15.33 | 31 890 | 14.22 |
| Office machine operators, except computer ................................................. | 63 290 | 14.90 | 30 980 | 13.95 |
| Proofreaders and copy markers ................................................................... | 10 810 | 18.12 | 37 690 | 17.13 |
| Statistical assistants .................................................................................. | 13 510 | 21.26 | 44 220 | 20.53 |
| Office and administrative support workers, all other ...................................... | 239 630 | 16.70 | 34 730 | 15.67 |
| **Farming, Fishing, and Forestry Occupations** | | | | |
| Supervisors of farming, fishing, and forestry workers .................................... | 19 060 | 23.22 | 48 290 | 21.80 |
| First-line supervisors of farming, fishing, and forestry workers ...................... | 19 060 | 23.22 | 48 290 | 21.80 |
| Agricultural workers ................................................................................... | 388 900 | 11.58 | 24 090 | 9.86 |
| Agricultural inspectors ................................................................................ | 14 670 | 21.06 | 43 810 | 20.86 |
| Animal breeders ......................................................................................... | 1 030 | 21.47 | 44 650 | 18.93 |
| Graders and sorters, agricultural products ................................................... | 35 290 | 11.18 | 23 260 | 10.14 |
| Miscellaneous agricultural workers .............................................................. | 337 920 | 11.18 | 23 260 | 9.65 |
| Agricultural equipment operators ................................................................ | 27 200 | 14.13 | 29 380 | 13.38 |
| Farmworkers and laborers, crop, nursery, and greenhouse ........................... | 272 170 | 10.64 | 22 130 | 9.51 |
| Farmworkers, farm, ranch, and aquacultural animals .................................... | 33 530 | 12.58 | 26 160 | 11.42 |
| Agricultural workers, all other ..................................................................... | 5 020 | 15.31 | 31 850 | 14.34 |
| Fishing and hunting workers ........................................................................ | 700 | 14.60 | 30 370 | 13.51 |
| Fishers and related fishing workers ............................................................. | 540 | 14.41 | 29 970 | 13.14 |
| Forest, conservation, and logging workers ................................................... | 45 570 | 17.53 | 36 470 | 16.90 |
| Forest and conservation workers ................................................................ | 6 870 | 14.36 | 29 860 | 12.59 |
| Logging workers ......................................................................................... | 38 700 | 18.10 | 37 640 | 17.41 |
| Fallers ....................................................................................................... | 5 840 | 20.07 | 41 750 | 17.50 |
| Logging equipment operators ..................................................................... | 27 290 | 17.76 | 36 930 | 17.45 |
| Log graders and scalers ............................................................................. | 2 740 | 17.99 | 37 420 | 17.36 |
| Logging workers, all other .......................................................................... | 2 830 | 17.41 | 36 210 | 17.13 |
| **Construction and Extraction Occupations** | | | | |
| Supervisors of construction and extraction workers ...................................... | 517 560 | 32.13 | 66 820 | 29.84 |
| Construction trades workers ....................................................................... | 4 076 800 | 22.25 | 46 290 | 19.72 |
| Boilermakers ............................................................................................. | 16 350 | 29.16 | 60 660 | 28.90 |
| Brickmasons, blockmasons, and stonemasons ............................................ | 74 570 | 24.13 | 50 200 | 22.32 |
| Brickmasons and blockmasons ................................................................... | 61 360 | 24.88 | 51 750 | 23.05 |
| Stonemasons ............................................................................................ | 13 210 | 20.66 | 42 970 | 18.57 |
| Carpenters ................................................................................................ | 639 190 | 22.49 | 46 780 | 20.24 |
| Carpet, floor, and tile installers and finishers .............................................. | 75 280 | 20.76 | 43 180 | 18.38 |
| Carpet installers ........................................................................................ | 25 810 | 20.77 | 43 210 | 17.89 |
| Floor layers, except carpet, wood, and hard tiles ......................................... | 9 830 | 20.44 | 42 520 | 17.80 |
| Floor sanders and finishers ......................................................................... | 4 700 | 18.35 | 38 160 | 17.76 |
| Tile and marble setters .............................................................................. | 34 940 | 21.16 | 44 010 | 18.94 |
| Cement masons, concrete finishers, and terrazzo workers ............................ | 166 610 | 20.27 | 42 150 | 18.16 |
| Cement masons and concrete finishers ....................................................... | 163 360 | 20.23 | 42 080 | 18.14 |
| Terrazzo workers and finishers ................................................................... | 3 250 | 22.14 | 46 050 | 19.57 |
| Construction laborers ................................................................................. | 887 580 | 17.57 | 36 550 | 15.34 |
| Construction equipment operators .............................................................. | 411 920 | 23.26 | 48 380 | 21.06 |
| Paving, surfacing, and tamping equipment operators .................................... | 53 110 | 20.68 | 43 020 | 18.40 |
| Pile-driver operators .................................................................................. | 3 670 | 26.51 | 55 150 | 23.77 |

[1]Annual wages have been calculated by multiplying the hourly mean wage by a "year-round, full-time" hours figure of 2,080 hours; for occupations with no published hourly mean wage, the annual wage has been directly calculated from the reported survey data.

## Table 3-2. Employment and Wages, by Occupation, May 2015—*Continued*

(Number of people, dollars.)

| Occupation | May 2015 | | | |
|---|---|---|---|---|
| | Employment | Mean hourly wage | Mean annual wage[1] | Median hourly wage |
| **Construction and Extraction Occupations** | | | | |
| Operating engineers and other construction equipment operators ............ | 355 140 | 23.61 | 49 110 | 21.44 |
| Drywall installers, ceiling tile installers, and tapers ............ | 106 000 | 22.48 | 46 760 | 19.46 |
| Drywall and ceiling tile installers ............ | 88 490 | 21.88 | 45 510 | 18.85 |
| Tapers ............ | 17 500 | 25.52 | 53 080 | 23.06 |
| Electricians ............ | 592 230 | 26.73 | 55 590 | 24.94 |
| Glaziers ............ | 44 230 | 21.84 | 45 420 | 18.96 |
| Insulation workers ............ | 55 180 | 21.51 | 44 740 | 18.57 |
| Insulation workers, floor, ceiling, and wall ............ | 25 850 | 18.66 | 38 810 | 16.85 |
| Insulation workers, mechanical ............ | 29 330 | 24.02 | 49 970 | 20.97 |
| Painters and paperhangers ............ | 216 340 | 19.47 | 40 490 | 17.57 |
| Painters, construction and maintenance ............ | 213 330 | 19.49 | 40 540 | 17.59 |
| Paperhangers ............ | 3 020 | 17.60 | 36 610 | 16.15 |
| Pipelayers, plumbers, pipefitters, and steamfitters ............ | 432 380 | 25.89 | 53 860 | 23.72 |
| Pipelayers ............ | 40 710 | 20.15 | 41 910 | 18.16 |
| Plumbers, pipefitters, and steamfitters ............ | 391 680 | 26.49 | 55 100 | 24.34 |
| Plasterers and stucco masons ............ | 22 420 | 20.22 | 42 070 | 17.94 |
| Reinforcing iron and rebar workers ............ | 20 060 | 25.98 | 54 030 | 23.08 |
| Roofers ............ | 109 720 | 19.54 | 40 630 | 17.65 |
| Sheet metal workers ............ | 135 570 | 23.95 | 49 810 | 21.99 |
| Structural iron and steel workers ............ | 64 280 | 26.32 | 54 750 | 24.28 |
| Solar photovoltaic installers ............ | 6 870 | 19.26 | 40 070 | 18.19 |
| Helpers, construction trades ............ | 228 710 | 14.37 | 29 890 | 13.64 |
| Helpers--brickmasons, blockmasons, stonemasons, and tile and marble setters ............ | 22 970 | 15.43 | 32 090 | 14.09 |
| Helpers--carpenters ............ | 37 820 | 14.04 | 29 200 | 13.41 |
| Helpers--electricians ............ | 71 610 | 14.42 | 30 000 | 13.81 |
| Helpers--painters, paperhangers, plasterers, and stucco masons ............ | 11 030 | 13.31 | 27 690 | 12.73 |
| Helpers--pipelayers, plumbers, pipefitters, and steamfitters ............ | 55 530 | 14.40 | 29 950 | 13.70 |
| Helpers--roofers ............ | 10 810 | 13.38 | 27 820 | 13.04 |
| Helpers, construction trades, all other ............ | 18 930 | 14.66 | 30 500 | 13.71 |
| Other construction and related workers ............ | 393 710 | 22.29 | 46 370 | 20.16 |
| Construction and building inspectors ............ | 91 480 | 28.86 | 60 030 | 27.57 |
| Elevator installers and repairers ............ | 21 000 | 37.19 | 77 350 | 38.88 |
| Fence erectors ............ | 21 160 | 16.75 | 34 840 | 15.60 |
| Hazardous materials removal workers ............ | 42 560 | 21.22 | 44 150 | 19.08 |
| Highway maintenance workers ............ | 142 300 | 18.36 | 38 200 | 17.75 |
| Rail-track laying and maintenance equipment operators ............ | 14 470 | 24.68 | 51 340 | 25.40 |
| Septic tank servicers and sewer pipe cleaners ............ | 27 080 | 18.21 | 37 880 | 17.00 |
| Miscellaneous construction and related workers ............ | 33 660 | 18.86 | 39 220 | 17.31 |
| Segmental pavers ............ | 1 240 | 15.30 | 31 820 | 14.77 |
| Construction and related workers, all other ............ | 32 420 | 18.99 | 39 500 | 17.45 |
| Extraction workers ............ | 261 040 | 22.58 | 46 970 | 20.52 |
| Derrick, rotary drill, and service unit operators, oil, gas, and mining ............ | 105 120 | 25.33 | 52 680 | 22.71 |
| Derrick operators, oil and gas ............ | 19 330 | 24.38 | 50 710 | 23.03 |
| Rotary drill operators, oil and gas ............ | 24 960 | 29.03 | 60 380 | 26.11 |
| Service unit operators, oil, gas, and mining ............ | 60 830 | 24.11 | 50 150 | 21.63 |
| Earth drillers, except oil and gas ............ | 19 490 | 24.92 | 51 840 | 21.27 |
| Explosives workers, ordnance handling experts, and blasters ............ | 7 540 | 25.28 | 52 580 | 24.14 |
| Mining machine operators ............ | 19 880 | 24.29 | 50 530 | 23.83 |
| Continuous mining machine operators ............ | 11 130 | 24.35 | 50 660 | 23.37 |
| Mine cutting and channeling machine operators ............ | 6 630 | 24.39 | 50 720 | 24.91 |
| Mining machine operators, all other ............ | 2 120 | 23.69 | 49 270 | 23.34 |
| Rock splitters, quarry ............ | 3 790 | 16.77 | 34 870 | 16.26 |
| Roof bolters, mining ............ | 5 220 | 26.68 | 55 500 | 26.42 |
| Roustabouts, oil and gas ............ | 71 790 | 18.61 | 38 700 | 17.56 |
| Helpers--extraction workers ............ | 22 820 | 17.83 | 37 080 | 17.19 |
| Extraction workers, all other ............ | 5 400 | 23.62 | 49 140 | 21.33 |
| **Installation, Maintenance, and Repair Occupations** | | | | |
| Supervisors of installation, maintenance, and repair workers ............ | 445 510 | 31.68 | 65 890 | 30.29 |
| Electrical and electronic equipment mechanics, installers, and repairers ............ | 585 270 | 24.22 | 50 380 | 23.30 |
| Computer, automated teller, and office machine repairers ............ | 106 100 | 18.75 | 38 990 | 17.71 |
| Radio and telecommunications equipment installers and repairers ............ | 233 260 | 26.16 | 54 420 | 26.15 |
| Radio, cellular, and tower equipment installers and repairers ............ | 14 160 | 25.45 | 52 940 | 24.84 |
| Telecommunications equipment installers and repairers, except line installers ............ | 219 100 | 26.21 | 54 510 | 26.24 |
| Miscellaneous electrical and electronic equipment mechanics, installers, and repairers ............ | 245 910 | 24.74 | 51 460 | 23.92 |
| Avionics technicians ............ | 17 340 | 28.94 | 60 200 | 28.15 |
| Electric motor, power tool, and related repairers ............ | 17 920 | 21.04 | 43 760 | 19.48 |
| Electrical and electronics installers and repairers, transportation equipment ............ | 14 210 | 28.41 | 59 080 | 28.36 |
| Electrical and electronics repairers, commercial and industrial equipment ............ | 69 290 | 27.25 | 56 670 | 26.77 |
| Electrical and electronics repairers, powerhouse, substation, and relay ............ | 23 070 | 34.83 | 72 450 | 35.49 |
| Electronic equipment installers and repairers, motor vehicles ............ | 12 470 | 16.10 | 33 500 | 15.08 |
| Electronic home entertainment equipment installers and repairers ............ | 26 890 | 19.07 | 39 670 | 18.17 |
| Security and fire alarm systems installers ............ | 64 730 | 21.57 | 44 860 | 20.87 |
| Vehicle and mobile equipment mechanics, installers, and repairers ............ | 1 554 340 | 20.67 | 42 990 | 19.31 |
| Aircraft mechanics and service technicians ............ | 124 040 | 28.92 | 60 160 | 28.06 |
| Automotive technicians and repairers ............ | 798 280 | 19.85 | 41 290 | 18.41 |
| Automotive body and related repairers ............ | 143 040 | 21.44 | 44 590 | 19.70 |

[1]Annual wages have been calculated by multiplying the hourly mean wage by a "year-round, full-time" hours figure of 2,080 hours; for occupations with no published hourly mean wage, the annual wage has been directly calculated from the reported survey data.

## Table 3-2.  Employment and Wages, by Occupation, May 2015—*Continued*

(Number of people, dollars.)

| Occupation | May 2015 | | | |
|---|---|---|---|---|
| | Employment | Mean hourly wage | Mean annual wage[1] | Median hourly wage |
| **Installation, Maintenance, and Repair Occupations**—*Continued* | | | | |
| Automotive glass installers and repairers | 17 160 | 16.93 | 35 210 | 16.27 |
| Automotive service technicians and mechanics | 638 080 | 19.58 | 40 720 | 18.20 |
| Bus and truck mechanics and diesel engine specialists | 251 750 | 22.17 | 46 110 | 21.40 |
| Heavy vehicle and mobile equipment service technicians and mechanics | 180 400 | 23.17 | 48 180 | 22.65 |
| Farm equipment mechanics and service technicians | 37 080 | 18.52 | 38 510 | 17.82 |
| Mobile heavy equipment mechanics, except engines | 121 900 | 24.08 | 50 080 | 23.45 |
| Rail car repairers | 21 410 | 26.02 | 54 130 | 26.72 |
| Small engine mechanics | 67 850 | 17.51 | 36 420 | 16.66 |
| Motorboat mechanics and service technicians | 20 440 | 18.99 | 39 500 | 18.41 |
| Motorcycle mechanics | 15 850 | 17.42 | 36 240 | 16.45 |
| Outdoor power equipment and other small engine mechanics | 31 560 | 16.60 | 34 520 | 15.72 |
| Miscellaneous vehicle and mobile equipment mechanics, installers, and repairers | 132 030 | 13.20 | 27 460 | 12.09 |
| Bicycle repairers | 12 560 | 13.41 | 27 900 | 13.20 |
| Recreational vehicle service technicians | 11 970 | 17.97 | 37 380 | 17.15 |
| Tire repairers and changers | 107 500 | 12.65 | 26 310 | 11.65 |
| Other installation, maintenance, and repair occupations | 2 789 020 | 20.95 | 43 570 | 19.39 |
| Control and valve installers and repairers | 60 440 | 24.55 | 51 060 | 22.79 |
| Mechanical door repairers | 17 930 | 19.18 | 39 900 | 18.34 |
| Control and valve installers and repairers, except mechanical door | 42 510 | 26.81 | 55 760 | 26.01 |
| Heating, air conditioning, and refrigeration mechanics and installers | 274 680 | 22.78 | 47 380 | 21.69 |
| Home appliance repairers | 33 990 | 18.66 | 38 820 | 17.40 |
| Industrial machinery installation, repair, and maintenance workers | 457 380 | 24.12 | 50 160 | 23.27 |
| Industrial machinery mechanics | 323 280 | 24.75 | 51 470 | 23.89 |
| Maintenance workers, machinery | 92 520 | 21.41 | 44 540 | 20.80 |
| Millwrights | 40 030 | 25.31 | 52 650 | 24.71 |
| Refractory materials repairers, except brickmasons | 1 550 | 23.52 | 48 920 | 22.62 |
| Line installers and repairers | 221 740 | 28.92 | 60 160 | 29.53 |
| Electrical power-line installers and repairers | 115 380 | 31.57 | 65 650 | 31.95 |
| Telecommunications line installers and repairers | 106 360 | 26.06 | 54 200 | 25.44 |
| Precision instrument and equipment repairers | 66 660 | 23.19 | 48 230 | 21.94 |
| Camera and photographic equipment repairers | 3 540 | 20.44 | 42 510 | 19.53 |
| Medical equipment repairers | 41 060 | 23.75 | 49 400 | 22.28 |
| Musical instrument repairers and tuners | 7 730 | 18.55 | 38 590 | 17.14 |
| Watch repairers | 2 200 | 17.84 | 37 110 | 16.71 |
| Precision instrument and equipment repairers, all other | 12 130 | 26.01 | 54 110 | 26.13 |
| Maintenance and repair workers, general | 1 314 560 | 18.73 | 38 950 | 17.61 |
| Wind turbine service technicians | 3 950 | 25.50 | 53 030 | 24.55 |
| Miscellaneous installation, maintenance, and repair workers | 355 620 | 17.81 | 37 050 | 15.98 |
| Coin, vending, and amusement machine servicers and repairers | 32 250 | 16.47 | 34 260 | 15.72 |
| Commercial divers | 3 450 | 26.27 | 54 640 | 24.26 |
| Fabric menders, except garment | 620 | 12.43 | 25 840 | 11.77 |
| Locksmiths and safe repairers | 17 800 | 19.84 | 41 270 | 18.83 |
| Manufactured building and mobile home installers | 3 650 | 15.94 | 33 150 | 14.45 |
| Riggers | 22 790 | 22.97 | 47 770 | 20.78 |
| Signal and track switch repairers | 8 190 | 30.12 | 62 650 | 30.69 |
| Helpers--installation, maintenance, and repair workers | 124 220 | 13.71 | 28 530 | 12.69 |
| Installation, maintenance, and repair workers, all other | 142 650 | 19.77 | 41 120 | 18.14 |
| **Production Occupations** | | | | |
| Supervisors of production workers | 603 080 | 28.81 | 59 930 | 27.09 |
| Assemblers and fabricators | 1 800 410 | 15.70 | 32 670 | 14.46 |
| Aircraft structure, surfaces, rigging, and systems assemblers | 42 810 | 24.54 | 51 040 | 23.55 |
| Electrical, electronics, and electromechanical assemblers | 273 030 | 16.14 | 33 570 | 15.07 |
| Coil winders, tapers, and finishers | 14 450 | 15.86 | 32 990 | 15.26 |
| Electrical and electronic equipment assemblers | 212 170 | 15.99 | 33 260 | 14.84 |
| Electromechanical equipment assemblers | 46 400 | 16.89 | 35 140 | 16.15 |
| Engine and other machine assemblers | 38 700 | 20.07 | 41 750 | 19.04 |
| Structural metal fabricators and fitters | 79 620 | 18.77 | 39 040 | 17.81 |
| Miscellaneous assemblers and fabricators | 1 366 250 | 15.04 | 31 280 | 13.87 |
| Fiberglass laminators and fabricators | 20 630 | 14.79 | 30 760 | 14.02 |
| Team assemblers | 1 115 510 | 15.17 | 31 560 | 13.98 |
| Timing device assemblers and adjusters | 1 190 | 19.96 | 41 510 | 17.76 |
| Assemblers and fabricators, all other | 228 930 | 14.39 | 29 920 | 13.28 |
| Food processing workers | 783 650 | 13.22 | 27 500 | 12.25 |
| Bakers | 176 610 | 12.63 | 26 270 | 11.62 |
| Butchers and other meat, poultry, and fish processing workers | 372 980 | 13.18 | 27 410 | 12.34 |
| Butchers and meat cutters | 137 350 | 14.88 | 30 940 | 14.01 |
| Meat, poultry, and fish cutters and trimmers | 155 390 | 11.93 | 24 810 | 11.48 |
| Slaughterers and meat packers | 80 250 | 12.70 | 26 420 | 12.33 |
| Miscellaneous food processing workers | 234 060 | 13.73 | 28 560 | 12.67 |
| Food and tobacco roasting, baking, and drying machine operators and tenders | 20 320 | 14.58 | 30 320 | 13.49 |
| Food batchmakers | 133 470 | 14.04 | 29 210 | 12.95 |
| Food cooking machine operators and tenders | 34 640 | 14.15 | 29 430 | 13.35 |
| Food processing workers, all other | 45 630 | 12.12 | 25 220 | 11.41 |
| Metal workers and plastic workers | 1 945 220 | 18.68 | 38 850 | 17.66 |
| Computer control programmers and operators | 172 260 | 19.54 | 40 650 | 18.48 |
| Computer-controlled machine tool operators, metal and plastic | 146 600 | 18.62 | 38 720 | 17.80 |
| Computer numerically controlled machine tool programmers, metal and plastic | 25 660 | 24.82 | 51 630 | 23.55 |

[1]Annual wages have been calculated by multiplying the hourly mean wage by a "year-round, full-time" hours figure of 2,080 hours; for occupations with no published hourly mean wage, the annual wage has been directly calculated from the reported survey data.

**Table 3-2. Employment and Wages, by Occupation, May 2015**—*Continued*

(Number of people, dollars.)

| Occupation | May 2015 | | | |
| --- | --- | --- | --- | --- |
| | Employment | Mean hourly wage | Mean annual wage[1] | Median hourly wage |
| **Production Occupations**—*Continued* | | | | |
| Forming machine setters, operators, and tenders, metal and plastic ........................... | 123 780 | 17.62 | 36 650 | 16.82 |
| Extruding and drawing machine setters, operators, and tenders, metal and plastic ..................... | 72 390 | 16.62 | 34 580 | 15.92 |
| Forging machine setters, operators, and tenders, metal and plastic ......................... | 19 650 | 17.75 | 36 910 | 16.86 |
| Rolling machine setters, operators, and tenders, metal and plastic ......................... | 31 740 | 19.81 | 41 200 | 19.51 |
| Machine tool cutting setters, operators, and tenders, metal and plastic ......................... | 342 970 | 16.60 | 34 530 | 15.79 |
| Cutting, punching, and press machine setters, operators, and tenders, metal and plastic ........... | 194 670 | 15.88 | 33 030 | 15.04 |
| Drilling and boring machine tool setters, operators, and tenders, metal and plastic ......................... | 14 840 | 18.11 | 37 660 | 17.06 |
| Grinding, lapping, polishing, and busgffing machine tool setters, operators, and tenders, metal and plastic ......................... | 73 570 | 16.62 | 34 560 | 15.79 |
| Lathe and turning machine tool setters, operators, and tenders, metal and plastic ..................... | 40 140 | 18.31 | 38 080 | 17.70 |
| Milling and planing machine setters, operators, and tenders, metal and plastic ......................... | 19 750 | 19.05 | 39 620 | 18.39 |
| Machinists ......................... | 399 040 | 20.25 | 42 120 | 19.49 |
| Metal furnace operators, tenders, pourers, and casters ......................... | 29 700 | 19.42 | 40 390 | 18.99 |
| Metal-refining furnace operators and tenders ......................... | 20 070 | 20.57 | 42 790 | 20.31 |
| Pourers and casters, metal ......................... | 9 630 | 17.01 | 35 390 | 16.28 |
| Model makers and patternmakers, metal and plastic ......................... | 10 400 | 21.93 | 45 620 | 21.13 |
| Model makers, metal and plastic ......................... | 6 380 | 23.18 | 48 210 | 22.11 |
| Patternmakers, metal and plastic ......................... | 4 020 | 19.95 | 41 500 | 19.69 |
| Molders and molding machine setters, operators, and tenders, metal and plastic ......................... | 148 410 | 15.25 | 31 720 | 14.24 |
| Foundry mold and coremakers ......................... | 12 860 | 16.31 | 33 930 | 15.71 |
| Molding, coremaking, and casting machine setters, operators, and tenders, metal and plastic ... | 135 550 | 15.15 | 31 510 | 14.11 |
| Multiple machine tool setters, operators, and tenders, metal and plastic ......................... | 105 570 | 17.01 | 35 380 | 16.32 |
| Tool and die makers ......................... | 74 510 | 24.58 | 51 130 | 24.18 |
| Welding, soldering, and brazing workers ......................... | 439 320 | 19.50 | 40 560 | 18.23 |
| Welders, cutters, solderers, and brazers ......................... | 386 240 | 19.70 | 40 970 | 18.34 |
| Welding, soldering, and brazing machine setters, operators, and tenders ......................... | 53 080 | 18.07 | 37 590 | 17.38 |
| Miscellaneous metal workers and plastic workers ......................... | 99 270 | 17.63 | 36 660 | 16.48 |
| Heat treating equipment setters, operators, and tenders, metal and plastic ......................... | 20 570 | 18.47 | 38 420 | 17.60 |
| Layout workers, metal and plastic ......................... | 10 660 | 22.32 | 46 430 | 21.41 |
| Plating and coating machine setters, operators, and tenders, metal and plastic ......................... | 35 640 | 15.83 | 32 930 | 14.69 |
| Tool grinders, filers, and sharpeners ......................... | 10 220 | 18.07 | 37 590 | 17.09 |
| Metal workers and plastic workers, all other ......................... | 22 190 | 17.26 | 35 910 | 15.86 |
| Printing workers ......................... | 256 040 | 17.52 | 36 440 | 16.64 |
| Printing workers ......................... | 256 040 | 17.52 | 36 440 | 16.64 |
| Prepress technicians and workers ......................... | 35 330 | 19.26 | 40 060 | 18.40 |
| Printing press operators ......................... | 168 330 | 17.80 | 37 020 | 16.94 |
| Print binding and finishing workers ......................... | 52 380 | 15.47 | 32 170 | 14.55 |
| Textile, apparel, and furnishings workers ......................... | 578 100 | 12.22 | 25 420 | 11.05 |
| Laundry and dry-cleaning workers ......................... | 201 620 | 10.90 | 22 660 | 10.01 |
| Pressers, textile, garment, and related materials ......................... | 48 340 | 10.40 | 21 640 | 9.84 |
| Sewing machine operators ......................... | 141 520 | 11.87 | 24 680 | 10.84 |
| Shoe and leather workers ......................... | 11 410 | 12.29 | 25 570 | 11.58 |
| Shoe and leather workers and repairers ......................... | 8 180 | 12.29 | 25 570 | 11.36 |
| Shoe machine operators and tenders ......................... | 3 230 | 12.29 | 25 560 | 12.11 |
| Tailors, dressmakers, and sewers ......................... | 26 900 | 13.31 | 27 690 | 12.08 |
| Sewers, hand ......................... | 6 920 | 12.01 | 24 980 | 11.37 |
| Tailors, dressmakers, and custom sewers ......................... | 19 980 | 13.76 | 28 630 | 12.42 |
| Textile machine setters, operators, and tenders ......................... | 76 630 | 13.29 | 27 640 | 12.83 |
| Textile bleaching and dyeing machine operators and tenders ......................... | 11 630 | 13.30 | 27 660 | 12.66 |
| Textile cutting machine setters, operators, and tenders ......................... | 14 680 | 12.96 | 26 950 | 12.26 |
| Textile knitting and weaving machine setters, operators, and tenders ......................... | 22 560 | 13.53 | 28 150 | 13.09 |
| Textile winding, twisting, and drawing out machine setters, operators, and tenders ......................... | 27 760 | 13.26 | 27 580 | 12.92 |
| Miscellaneous textile, apparel, and furnishings workers ......................... | 71 690 | 16.32 | 33 950 | 14.96 |
| Extruding and forming machine setters, operators, and tenders, synthetic and glass fibers ........ | 19 810 | 16.44 | 34 190 | 15.85 |
| Fabric and apparel patternmakers ......................... | 5 140 | 23.58 | 49 040 | 21.11 |
| Upholsterers ......................... | 30 180 | 16.13 | 33 550 | 15.39 |
| Textile, apparel, and furnishings workers, all other ......................... | 16 560 | 14.29 | 29 720 | 12.65 |
| Woodworkers ......................... | 243 350 | 15.05 | 31 300 | 14.18 |
| Cabinetmakers and bench carpenters ......................... | 93 650 | 16.34 | 33 980 | 15.52 |
| Furniture finishers ......................... | 16 480 | 14.87 | 30 920 | 14.04 |
| Model makers and patternmakers, wood ......................... | 2 180 | 19.16 | 39 840 | 17.18 |
| Model makers, wood ......................... | 1 160 | 18.43 | 38 330 | 16.15 |
| Patternmakers, wood ......................... | 1 030 | 19.98 | 41 550 | 18.46 |
| Woodworking machine setters, operators, and tenders ......................... | 124 150 | 14.00 | 29 130 | 13.37 |
| Sawing machine setters, operators, and tenders, wood ......................... | 48 600 | 14.04 | 29 190 | 13.37 |
| Woodworking machine setters, operators, and tenders, except sawing ......................... | 75 540 | 13.98 | 29 090 | 13.37 |
| Woodworkers, all other ......................... | 6 900 | 15.45 | 32 130 | 13.94 |
| Plant and system operators ......................... | 311 050 | 28.26 | 58 780 | 27.48 |
| Power plant operators, distributors, and dispatchers ......................... | 55 990 | 36.15 | 75 190 | 36.38 |
| Nuclear power reactor operators ......................... | 6 940 | 42.70 | 88 820 | 42.58 |
| Power distributors and dispatchers ......................... | 11 540 | 38.66 | 80 400 | 38.86 |
| Power plant operators ......................... | 37 510 | 34.17 | 71 070 | 34.58 |
| Stationary engineers and boiler operators ......................... | 34 630 | 29.08 | 60 480 | 28.14 |
| Water and wastewater treatment plant and system operators ......................... | 114 770 | 22.49 | 46 790 | 21.53 |
| Miscellaneous plant and system operators ......................... | 105 670 | 30.07 | 62 540 | 29.85 |
| Chemical plant and system operators ......................... | 35 020 | 28.40 | 59 070 | 28.52 |

[1]Annual wages have been calculated by multiplying the hourly mean wage by a "year-round, full-time" hours figure of 2,080 hours; for occupations with no published hourly mean wage, the annual wage has been directly calculated from the reported survey data.

## Table 3-2.  Employment and Wages, by Occupation, May 2015—*Continued*

(Number of people, dollars.)

| Occupation | May 2015 | | | |
|---|---|---|---|---|
| | Employment | Mean hourly wage | Mean annual wage[1] | Median hourly wage |
| **Production Occupations**—*Continued* | | | | |
| Gas plant operators ............................................................................ | 16 790 | 31.65 | 65 830 | 31.74 |
| Petroleum pump system operators, refinery operators, and gaugers ................. | 42 320 | 31.74 | 66 020 | 31.34 |
| Plant and system operators, all other ................................................... | 11 540 | 26.70 | 55 530 | 26.70 |
| Other production occupations ............................................................ | 2 552 380 | 16.31 | 33 930 | 14.71 |
| Chemical processing machine setters, operators, and tenders ...................... | 115 400 | 22.19 | 46 150 | 20.84 |
| Chemical equipment operators and tenders ............................................ | 67 650 | 23.87 | 49 640 | 22.70 |
| Separating, filtering, clarifying, precipitating, and still machine setters, operators, and tenders ... | 47 750 | 19.81 | 41 210 | 18.47 |
| Crushing, grinding, polishing, mixing, and blending workers ........................ | 188 510 | 17.01 | 35 370 | 16.09 |
| Crushing, grinding, and polishing machine setters, operators, and tenders .......... | 31 140 | 17.10 | 35 560 | 16.26 |
| Grinding and polishing workers, hand ................................................... | 28 110 | 14.60 | 30 370 | 13.76 |
| Mixing and blending machine setters, operators, and tenders ...................... | 129 270 | 17.51 | 36 410 | 16.63 |
| Cutting workers ............................................................................. | 79 070 | 15.56 | 32 370 | 14.89 |
| Cutters and trimmers, hand ............................................................... | 15 740 | 13.87 | 28 850 | 12.89 |
| Cutting and slicing machine setters, operators, and tenders ........................ | 63 330 | 15.98 | 33 250 | 15.48 |
| Extruding, forming, pressing, and compacting machine setters, operators, and tenders ............ | 71 430 | 16.36 | 34 030 | 15.46 |
| Furnace, kiln, oven, drier, and kettle operators and tenders ....................... | 19 650 | 17.77 | 36 970 | 17.00 |
| Inspectors, testers, sorters, samplers, and weighers ............................... | 508 590 | 18.95 | 39 410 | 17.31 |
| Jewelers and precious stone and metal workers ...................................... | 25 270 | 20.38 | 42 380 | 17.82 |
| Medical, dental, and ophthalmic laboratory technicians ............................ | 80 150 | 18.08 | 37 610 | 16.32 |
| Dental laboratory technicians ............................................................ | 37 520 | 19.48 | 40 520 | 17.88 |
| Medical appliance technicians ............................................................ | 14 640 | 18.76 | 39 020 | 16.77 |
| Ophthalmic laboratory technicians ...................................................... | 27 990 | 15.85 | 32 970 | 14.35 |
| Packaging and filling machine operators and tenders ................................. | 378 560 | 14.31 | 29 770 | 13.02 |
| Painting workers ........................................................................... | 156 550 | 17.84 | 37 110 | 16.51 |
| Coating, painting, and spraying machine setters, operators, and tenders ........... | 88 780 | 16.16 | 33 610 | 15.35 |
| Painters, transportation equipment ..................................................... | 51 760 | 21.60 | 44 920 | 19.79 |
| Painting, coating, and decorating workers ............................................ | 16 020 | 15.01 | 31 210 | 14.07 |
| Semiconductor processors ............................................................... | 24 230 | 18.08 | 37 600 | 17.01 |
| Photographic process workers and processing machine operators ................... | 23 940 | 14.77 | 30 720 | 12.78 |
| Miscellaneous production workers ...................................................... | 881 020 | 14.21 | 29 560 | 12.78 |
| Adhesive bonding machine operators and tenders .................................... | 17 400 | 16.23 | 33 750 | 15.25 |
| Cleaning, washing, and metal pickling equipment operators and tenders ........... | 17 420 | 14.38 | 29 910 | 13.41 |
| Cooling and freezing equipment operators and tenders .............................. | 7 970 | 15.14 | 31 490 | 13.76 |
| Etchers and engravers .................................................................... | 9 490 | 15.33 | 31 880 | 14.33 |
| Molders, shapers, and casters, except metal and plastic ........................... | 38 730 | 15.24 | 31 690 | 14.24 |
| Paper goods machine setters, operators, and tenders .............................. | 91 400 | 17.87 | 37 160 | 17.17 |
| Tire builders ............................................................................... | 17 710 | 19.34 | 40 230 | 18.81 |
| Helpers--production workers ............................................................. | 439 000 | 12.50 | 26 010 | 11.52 |
| Production workers, all other ............................................................ | 241 910 | 15.15 | 31 520 | 13.44 |
| **Transportation and Material Moving Occupations** | | | | |
| Supervisors of transportation and material moving workers ........................ | 386 340 | 26.10 | 54 290 | 24.66 |
| Aircraft cargo handling supervisors ..................................................... | 6 760 | 23.50 | 48 870 | 21.86 |
| First-line supervisors of helpers, laborers, and material movers, hand .............. | 176 030 | 23.88 | 49 670 | 22.58 |
| First-line supervisors of transportation and material-moving machine and vehicle operators ....... | 203 550 | 28.11 | 58 470 | 26.85 |
| Air transportation workers ............................................................... | 260 670 | (2) | 87 140 | (2) |
| Aircraft pilots and flight engineers ..................................................... | 121 110 | (2) | 119 360 | (2) |
| Airline pilots, copilots, and flight engineers ........................................... | 81 350 | (2) | 136 400 | (2) |
| Commercial pilots ......................................................................... | 39 760 | (2) | 84 510 | (2) |
| Air traffic controllers and airfield operations specialists ............................ | 31 050 | 49.32 | 102 580 | 48.05 |
| Air traffic controllers .................................................................... | 23 130 | 57.09 | 118 740 | 59.11 |
| Airfield operations specialists ........................................................... | 7 920 | 26.64 | 55 400 | 24.94 |
| Flight attendants .......................................................................... | 108 510 | (2) | 46 750 | (2) |
| Motor vehicle operators ................................................................. | 3 851 720 | 17.53 | 36 460 | 16.43 |
| Ambulance drivers and attendants, except emergency medical technicians .......... | 19 950 | 12.25 | 25 470 | 11.41 |
| Bus drivers ................................................................................. | 674 180 | 15.85 | 32 980 | 14.88 |
| Bus drivers, transit and intercity ........................................................ | 168 620 | 19.31 | 40 160 | 18.41 |
| Bus drivers, school or special client .................................................... | 505 560 | 14.70 | 30 580 | 14.18 |
| Driver/sales workers and truck drivers ................................................ | 2 922 450 | 18.28 | 38 030 | 17.23 |
| Driver/sales workers ..................................................................... | 417 660 | 13.41 | 27 890 | 10.79 |
| Heavy and tractor-trailer truck drivers ................................................ | 1 678 280 | 20.43 | 42 500 | 19.36 |
| Light truck or delivery services drivers ................................................ | 826 510 | 16.38 | 34 080 | 14.35 |
| Taxi drivers and chauffeurs .............................................................. | 180 960 | 12.53 | 26 070 | 11.30 |
| Motor vehicle operators, all other ...................................................... | 54 160 | 16.07 | 33 430 | 14.05 |
| Rail transportation workers .............................................................. | 122 010 | 27.52 | 57 230 | 26.88 |
| Locomotive engineers and operators ................................................... | 43 560 | 27.87 | 57 980 | 26.46 |
| Locomotive engineers .................................................................... | 37 490 | 28.54 | 59 360 | 27.04 |
| Locomotive firers .......................................................................... | 1 610 | 26.22 | 54 540 | 23.30 |
| Rail yard engineers, dinkey operators, and hostlers .................................. | 4 460 | 22.88 | 47 600 | 22.01 |
| Railroad brake, signal, and switch operators .......................................... | 18 970 | 25.96 | 53 990 | 25.97 |
| Railroad conductors and yardmasters .................................................. | 42 330 | 27.29 | 56 760 | 26.89 |
| Subway and streetcar operators ........................................................ | 12 600 | 29.12 | 60 580 | 29.98 |
| Rail transportation workers, all other ................................................... | 4 550 | 28.25 | 58 760 | 28.77 |
| Water transportation workers ........................................................... | 77 260 | 31.11 | 64 720 | 26.44 |
| Sailors and marine oilers ................................................................. | 30 570 | 20.63 | 42 910 | 19.84 |
| Ship and boat captains and operators .................................................. | 36 760 | 37.98 | 79 000 | 34.82 |

[1]Annual wages have been calculated by multiplying the hourly mean wage by a "year-round, full-time" hours figure of 2,080 hours; for occupations with no published hourly mean wage, the annual wage has been directly calculated from the reported survey data.
[2]Wages for some occupations that do not generally entail year-round, full-time employment are reported as either hourly wages or annual salaries (depending on how employees are typically paid).

## Table 3-2. Employment and Wages, by Occupation, May 2015—*Continued*

(Number of people, dollars.)

| Occupation | May 2015 | | | |
|---|---|---|---|---|
| | Employment | Mean hourly wage | Mean annual wage[1] | Median hourly wage |
| **Transportation and Material Moving Occupations**—*Continued* | | | | |
| Captains, mates, and pilots of water vessels ............................ | 33 110 | 39.98 | 83 150 | 36.91 |
| Motorboat operators ............................................................ | 3 650 | 19.88 | 41 350 | 17.69 |
| Ship engineers ................................................................... | 9 940 | 37.97 | 78 970 | 35.03 |
| Other transportation workers ............................................... | 343 230 | 14.14 | 29 410 | 11.00 |
| Bridge and lock tenders ...................................................... | 3 170 | 22.10 | 45 980 | 23.33 |
| Parking lot attendants ......................................................... | 144 150 | 10.83 | 22 520 | 9.92 |
| Automotive and watercraft service attendants ...................... | 109 710 | 11.27 | 23 440 | 10.36 |
| Traffic technicians ............................................................... | 6 750 | 22.92 | 47 660 | 21.12 |
| Transportation inspectors .................................................... | 25 860 | 34.72 | 72 220 | 34.05 |
| Transportation attendants, except flight attendants ............. | 15 680 | 14.68 | 30 540 | 12.47 |
| Transportation workers, all other ......................................... | 37 900 | 18.52 | 38 520 | 17.74 |
| Material moving workers ...................................................... | 4 495 380 | 13.81 | 28 710 | 12.22 |
| Conveyor operators and tenders .......................................... | 32 890 | 16.88 | 35 100 | 15.41 |
| Crane and tower operators .................................................. | 46 490 | 26.23 | 54 560 | 24.83 |
| Dredge, excavating, and loading machine operators ............ | 54 930 | 21.54 | 44 810 | 19.54 |
| Dredge operators ................................................................ | 1 850 | 21.18 | 44 040 | 19.26 |
| Excavating and loading machine and dragline operators ...... | 49 880 | 21.41 | 44 520 | 19.26 |
| Loading machine operators, underground mining .................. | 3 210 | 23.91 | 49 740 | 25.15 |
| Hoist and winch operators ................................................... | 2 880 | 24.37 | 50 680 | 20.30 |
| Industrial truck and tractor operators .................................. | 539 810 | 16.39 | 34 090 | 15.43 |
| Laborers and material movers, hand .................................... | 3 637 790 | 12.86 | 26 760 | 11.50 |
| Cleaners of vehicles and equipment .................................... | 336 960 | 11.51 | 23 940 | 10.25 |
| Laborers and freight, stock, and material movers, hand ....... | 2 487 680 | 13.39 | 27 840 | 12.02 |
| Machine feeders and offbearers .......................................... | 100 020 | 14.89 | 30 960 | 14.15 |
| Packers and packagers, hand .............................................. | 713 130 | 11.40 | 23 710 | 10.10 |
| Pumping station operators ................................................... | 30 350 | 23.35 | 48 570 | 22.69 |
| Gas compressor and gas pumping station operators ............ | 4 100 | 27.65 | 57 510 | 28.06 |
| Pump operators, except wellhead pumpers .......................... | 13 390 | 22.21 | 46 200 | 20.39 |
| Wellhead pumpers .............................................................. | 12 860 | 23.17 | 48 180 | 22.59 |
| Refuse and recyclable material collectors ............................ | 114 220 | 17.48 | 36 370 | 16.25 |
| Mine shuttle car operators .................................................. | 2 310 | 26.50 | 55 120 | 26.59 |
| Tank car, truck, and ship loaders ........................................ | 11 960 | 19.72 | 41 010 | 17.63 |
| Material moving workers, all other ....................................... | 21 740 | 17.82 | 37 060 | 14.60 |

[1]Annual wages have been calculated by multiplying the hourly mean wage by a "year-round, full-time" hours figure of 2,080 hours; for occupations with no published hourly mean wage, the annual wage has been directly calculated from the reported survey data.

# CHAPTER 4: LABOR FORCE AND EMPLOYMENT PROJECTIONS BY INDUSTRY AND OCCUPATION

## HIGHLIGHTS

Every two years, the Bureau of Labor Statistics (BLS) develops decade-long projections for industry output, employment, and occupations. This chapter presents the employment outlook for the 2014–2024 period. The projections are based on a set of explicit assumptions and an application of a model of economic relationships.

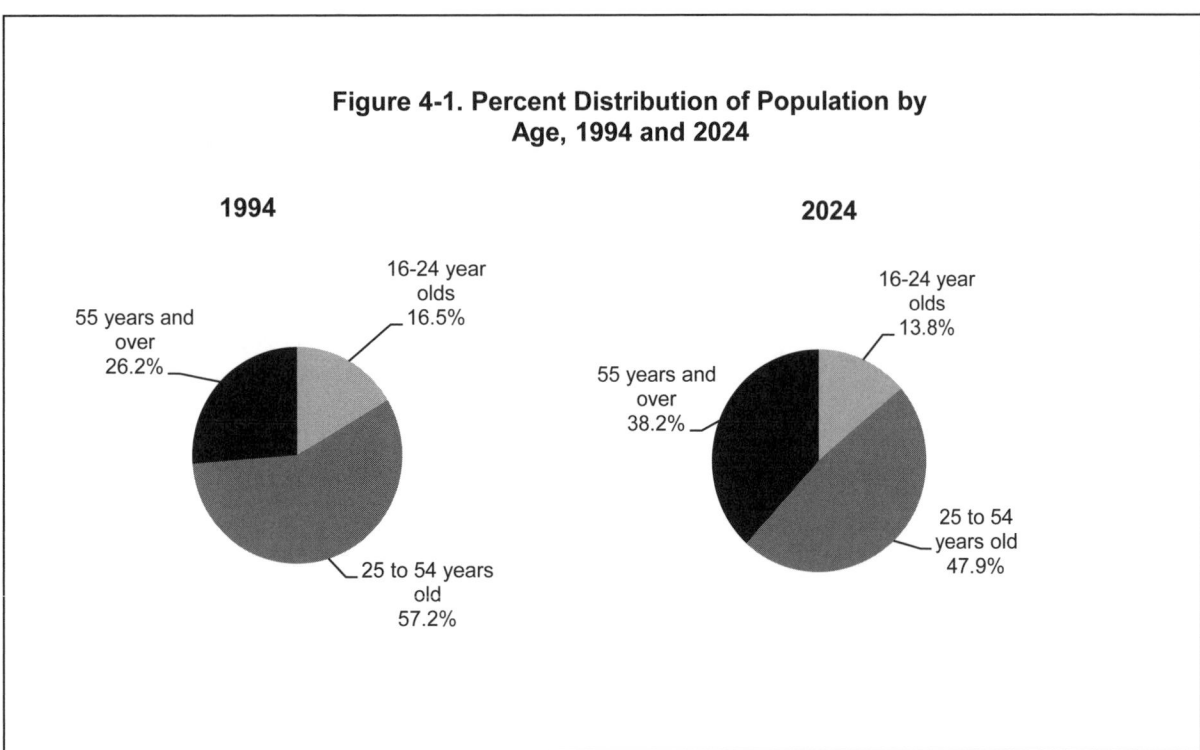

**Figure 4-1. Percent Distribution of Population by Age, 1994 and 2024**

**1994**

55 years and over 26.2%

16-24 year olds 16.5%

25 to 54 years old 57.2%

**2024**

55 years and over 38.2%

16-24 year olds 13.8%

25 to 54 years old 47.9%

From 2014 to 2024, the civilian non-institutional population is projected to grow at an annual rate of 0.8 percent. The number of Hispanics is expected to grow at a much faster rate than the general population, increasing at a rate of 2.5 percent per year. In contrast, the number of White non-Hispanics is expected to increase at a rate of 0.2 percent. (See Table 4-1.)

## OTHER HIGHLIGHTS

- It is projected that there will also be significant variation in growth rates by age group. While the number of persons 75 years and over is expected to increase by 3.4 percent, the number of those aged 45 to 54 is expected to decline 0.8 percent. (See Table 4.1.)

- The number of jobs in the healthcare and social assistance sector is projected to grow rapidly between 2014 and 2024. The number of personal care aids is projected to grow by 25.9 percent while the number of registered nurses is expected to grow by 16.0. Meanwhile, many of the occupations that are projected to decline are in the manufacturing sector. (See Table 4-3.)

- The labor force continues to age. The median age of the labor force was 37.7 in 1994, 40.3 in 2004, 41.9 in 2014, and is projected to be 42.4 in 2024. (See Table 4-7.)

## NOTES AND DEFINITIONS

The Bureau of Labor Statistics (BLS) develops long-term projections of likely employment patterns in the U.S. economy. Since the early 1970s, projections have been prepared on a 2-year cycle. The last projections were released in December 2015. The projections cover the future size and composition of the labor force, aggregate economic growth, detailed estimates of industry production, and industry and occupational employment. The resulting data serve a variety of users who need information about expected patterns of economic growth and the effects these patterns are expected to have on employment. For example, information about future employment opportunities by occupation is used by counselors, educators, and others helping people choose a career and by officials who plan education and training programs.

The labor force projections are a function of two components—projections of the population and projections of labor force participation rates. Population projections are provided by the Census Bureau for detailed age, sex, race, and ethnicity groupings. BLS extrapolates participation rates for these same categories by applying well-specified smoothing and time series techniques to historical time series for the detailed participation rates.

### Concepts and Definitions

*Economic dependency ratio.* This ratio is measured by estimating the number of persons in the total population (including all Armed Forces personnel overseas and children) who are *not* in the labor force per hundred of those who are.

*Employment.* In the employment projections survey, employment is defined as a count of jobs, not a count of individual workers.

*Employment change.* The numerical change in employment measures the projected number of job gains or losses.

*Employment change, percent.* The percent change in employment measures the projected rate of change of employment in an occupation. A rapidly growing occupation usually indicates favorable prospects for employment. However, even modest employment growth in a large occupation can result in many more job openings due to growth than can rapid employment growth in a small occupation.

*Job openings due to growth and replacement needs.* Estimates of the projected number of net entrants into an occupation. For occupations that require training, the data may be used to assess the minimum number of workers who will need to be trained. The number of openings due to growth is the positive employment change from 2014 to 2024. If employment declines, then there are no job openings due to growth. The number of openings due to replacement needs is the net number of workers leaving an occupation who will need to be replaced.

### On-the-Job Training Terms:

*Apprenticeship.* An apprenticeship is a formal relationship between a worker and sponsor that combines technical instruction and on-the-job training. The typical programs provides at least 2,000 hours of on-the-job training per year over a 3-to-5 year period and 144 hours of technical instruction. Apprenticeship programs are sponsored by individual employers, joint employer-and-labor groups, and employer associations.

*Internship/residency.* An internship or residency typically involves supervised training in a professional setting such as a classroom or hospital. Internships and/or residency programs are often required for certification or to obtain a license in fields such as architecture, counseling, medicine, and teaching. This does not include internships that are recommended for advancement.

*Moderate-term on-the-job training.* Skills needed for a worker to become fully qualified can be acquired during 1 to 12 months of combined on-the-job experience and informal training. Examples include heavy and tractor-trailer truck drivers and medical secretaries.

*Short-term on-the-job training.* Skills needed for a worker to become fully qualified can be acquired during a short demonstration of job duties or during 1 month or less of on-the-job experience or instruction. Examples include retail salespersons and waiters and waitresses.

*Long-term on-the-job training.* More than 12 months of on-the-job training or, alternatively, combined work experience and formal classroom instruction are needed for workers to develop the skills to become fully qualified. This category includes formal or informal apprenticeships that may last up to 5 years. Long-term on-the-job training also includes intensive occupation-specific, employer-sponsored programs that workers must complete. Such programs include those offered by fire and police academies and schools for air traffic controllers and flight attendants. Individuals undergoing training usually are considered to be employed in the occupation. Also included in this category is the development of some natural ability.

### Sources of Additional Information

A complete presentation of the projections, including analysis of results and additional tables and a comprehensive description of the methodology, can be found in the December 2015 edition of the *Monthly Labor Review* which is available on the BLS Web site at www.bls.gov/opub/mlr/mlrhome.htm. In addition, more information on employment projections can be found on the BLS Web site at <http://www.bls.gov/emp/>.

## Table 4-1.  Civilian Noninstitutional Population, by Age, Sex, Race, and Hispanic Origin, 1994, 2004, 2014, and Projected 2024

(Numbers in thousands, percent.)

| Age, sex, race, and Hispanic origin | Level | | | | Change | | |
|---|---|---|---|---|---|---|---|
| | 1994 | 2004 | 2014 | 2024 | 1994–2004 | 2004–2014 | 2014–2024 |
| **Both Sexes, 16 Years and Over** | 196 814 | 223 357 | 247 947 | 269 092 | 26 543 | 24 590 | 21 145 |
| 16 to 24 years | 32 549 | 36 419 | 38 712 | 37 245 | 3 870 | 2 293 | -1 467 |
| 16 to 19 years | 14 196 | 16 222 | 16 633 | 16 483 | 2 026 | 411 | -150 |
| 20 to 24 years | 18 353 | 20 197 | 22 079 | 20 762 | 1 844 | 1 882 | -1 317 |
| 25 to 54 years | 112 618 | 123 410 | 124 511 | 128 928 | 10 792 | 1 101 | 4 417 |
| 25 to 34 years | 41 306 | 38 939 | 42 131 | 45 369 | -2 367 | 3 192 | 3 238 |
| 35 to 44 years | 41 534 | 43 226 | 39 565 | 44 035 | 1 692 | -3 661 | 4 470 |
| 45 to 54 years | 29 778 | 41 245 | 42 815 | 39 524 | 11 467 | 1 570 | -3 291 |
| 55 years and over | 51 648 | 63 527 | 84 724 | 102 919 | 11 879 | 21 197 | 18 195 |
| 55 to 64 years | 20 635 | 28 919 | 39 764 | 40 981 | 8 284 | 10 845 | 1 217 |
| 65 to 74 years | 18 249 | 18 181 | 26 078 | 35 505 | -68 | 7 897 | 9 427 |
| 75 years and over | 12 763 | 16 429 | 18 882 | 26 433 | 3 666 | 2 453 | 7 551 |
| **Men, 16 Years and Over** | 94 355 | 107 710 | 119 748 | 130 726 | 13 355 | 12 038 | 10 978 |
| 16 to 24 years | 16 277 | 18 359 | 19 516 | 18 785 | 2 082 | 1 157 | -731 |
| 16 to 19 years | 7 203 | 8 234 | 8 449 | 8 356 | 1 031 | 215 | -93 |
| 20 to 24 years | 9 074 | 10 125 | 11 067 | 10 430 | 1 051 | 942 | -637 |
| 25 to 54 years | 55 349 | 60 773 | 61 149 | 64 136 | 5 424 | 376 | 2 987 |
| 25 to 34 years | 20 361 | 19 358 | 20 841 | 22 830 | -1 003 | 1 483 | 1 989 |
| 35 to 44 years | 20 443 | 21 255 | 19 388 | 21 921 | 812 | -1 867 | 2 533 |
| 45 to 54 years | 14 545 | 20 160 | 20 920 | 19 385 | 5 615 | 760 | -1 535 |
| 55 years and over | 22 728 | 28 578 | 39 083 | 47 804 | 5 850 | 10 505 | 8 721 |
| 55 to 64 years | 9 810 | 13 894 | 19 116 | 19 833 | 4 084 | 5 222 | 717 |
| 65 to 74 years | 8 109 | 8 294 | 12 184 | 16 591 | 185 | 3 890 | 4 407 |
| 75 years and over | 4 809 | 6 391 | 7 783 | 11 380 | 1 582 | 1 392 | 3 597 |
| **Women, 16 Years and Over** | 102 460 | 115 647 | 128 199 | 138 366 | 13 187 | 12 552 | 10 167 |
| 16 to 24 years | 16 272 | 18 061 | 19 197 | 18 460 | 1 789 | 1 136 | -737 |
| 16 to 19 years | 6 993 | 7 989 | 8 184 | 8 127 | 996 | 195 | -57 |
| 20 to 24 years | 9 279 | 10 072 | 11 012 | 10 332 | 793 | 940 | -680 |
| 25 to 54 years | 57 269 | 62 636 | 63 362 | 64 791 | 5 367 | 726 | 1 429 |
| 25 to 34 years | 20 945 | 19 581 | 21 290 | 22 539 | -1 364 | 1 709 | 1 249 |
| 35 to 44 years | 21 091 | 21 970 | 20 178 | 22 113 | 879 | -1 792 | 1 935 |
| 45 to 54 years | 15 233 | 21 085 | 21 894 | 20 139 | 5 852 | 809 | -1 755 |
| 55 years and over | 28 919 | 34 950 | 45 640 | 55 115 | 6 031 | 10 690 | 9 475 |
| 55 to 64 years | 10 825 | 15 025 | 20 648 | 21 148 | 4 200 | 5 623 | 500 |
| 65 to 74 years | 10 140 | 9 887 | 13 894 | 18 914 | -253 | 4 007 | 5 020 |
| 75 years and over | 7 955 | 10 038 | 11 098 | 15 053 | 2 083 | 1 060 | 3 955 |
| **White, 16 Years and Over** | 165 555 | 182 643 | 195 498 | 207 570 | 17 088 | 12 855 | 12 072 |
| Men | 80 059 | 89 044 | 95 513 | 101 957 | 8 985 | 6 469 | 6 444 |
| Women | 85 497 | 93 599 | 99 984 | 105 613 | 8 102 | 6 385 | 5 629 |
| **Black, 16 Years and Over** | 22 879 | 26 065 | 30 843 | 34 769 | 3 186 | 4 778 | 3 926 |
| Men | 10 258 | 11 656 | 13 997 | 15 950 | 1 398 | 2 341 | 1 953 |
| Women | 12 621 | 14 409 | 16 846 | 18 819 | 1 788 | 2 437 | 1 973 |
| **Asian, 16 Years and Over** | 8 383 | 9 519 | 13 785 | 17 143 | 1 136 | 4 266 | 3 358 |
| Men | 4 038 | 4 529 | 6 420 | 7 970 | 491 | 1 891 | 1 550 |
| Women | 4 345 | 4 990 | 7 365 | 9 173 | 645 | 2 375 | 1 808 |
| **All Other Groups,[1] 16 Years and Over** | . . . | 5 130 | 7 335 | 9 609 | . . . | 2 205 | 2 274 |
| Men | . . . | 2 481 | 3 676 | 4 849 | . . . | 1 195 | 1 173 |
| Women | . . . | 2 649 | 3 659 | 4 760 | . . . | 1 010 | 1 101 |
| **Hispanic,[2] 16 Years and Over** | 18 117 | 28 109 | 38 400 | 49 272 | 9 992 | 10 291 | 10 872 |
| Men | 9 104 | 14 417 | 19 244 | 24 938 | 5 314 | 4 827 | 5 694 |
| Women | 9 014 | 13 692 | 19 156 | 24 334 | 4 678 | 5 464 | 5 178 |
| **Non-Hispanic, 16 Years and Over** | 178 697 | 195 248 | 209 547 | 219 820 | 16 551 | 14 299 | 10 273 |
| Men | 85 252 | 93 293 | 100 504 | 105 788 | 8 042 | 7 211 | 5 284 |
| Women | 93 446 | 101 955 | 109 043 | 114 032 | 8 509 | 7 088 | 5 979 |
| **White Non-Hispanic, 16 Years and Over** | 149 473 | 156 555 | 161 193 | 163 739 | 7 082 | 4 638 | 2 546 |
| Men | 71 962 | 75 615 | 78 277 | 79 631 | 3 653 | 2 662 | 1 354 |
| Women | 77 511 | 80 940 | 82 916 | 84 108 | 3 429 | 1 976 | 1 192 |

[1]The "All other groups" category includes respondents who reported the racial categories of "American Indian and Alaska Native" or "Native Hawaiian and Other Pacific Islander," as well as those who reported two or more races. This category was not defined prior to 2003.
[2]May be of any race.
. . . = Not available.

## Table 4-1. Civilian Noninstitutional Population, by Age, Sex, Race, and Hispanic Origin, 1994, 2004, 2014, and Projected 2024—Continued

(Numbers in thousands, percent.)

| Age, sex, race, and Hispanic origin | Percent distribution | | | | Annual growth rate (percent) | | |
|---|---|---|---|---|---|---|---|
| | 1994 | 2004 | 2014 | 2024 | 1994–2004 | 2004–2014 | 2014–2024 |
| **Both Sexes, 16 Years and Over** | 100.0 | 100.0 | 100.0 | 100.0 | 1.3 | 1.0 | 0.8 |
| 16 to 24 years | 16.5 | 16.3 | 15.6 | 13.8 | 1.1 | 0.6 | -0.4 |
| 16 to 19 years | 7.2 | 7.3 | 6.7 | 6.1 | 1.3 | 0.3 | -0.1 |
| 20 to 24 years | 9.3 | 9.0 | 8.9 | 7.7 | 1.0 | 0.9 | -0.6 |
| 25 to 54 years | 57.2 | 55.3 | 50.2 | 47.9 | 0.9 | 0.1 | 0.3 |
| 25 to 34 years | 21.0 | 17.4 | 17.0 | 16.9 | -0.6 | 0.8 | 0.7 |
| 35 to 44 years | 21.1 | 19.4 | 16.0 | 16.4 | 0.4 | -0.9 | 1.1 |
| 45 to 54 years | 15.1 | 18.5 | 17.3 | 14.7 | 3.3 | 0.4 | -0.8 |
| 55 years and over | 26.2 | 28.4 | 34.2 | 38.2 | 2.1 | 2.9 | 2.0 |
| 55 to 64 years | 10.5 | 12.9 | 16.0 | 15.2 | 3.4 | 3.2 | 0.3 |
| 65 to 74 years | 9.3 | 8.1 | 10.5 | 13.2 | 0.0 | 3.7 | 3.1 |
| 75 years and over | 6.5 | 7.4 | 7.6 | 9.8 | 2.6 | 1.4 | 3.4 |
| **Men, 16 Years and Over** | 47.9 | 48.2 | 48.3 | 48.6 | 1.3 | 1.1 | 0.9 |
| 16 to 24 years | 8.3 | 8.2 | 7.9 | 7.0 | 1.2 | 0.6 | -0.4 |
| 16 to 19 years | 3.7 | 3.7 | 3.4 | 3.1 | 1.3 | 0.3 | -0.1 |
| 20 to 24 years | 4.6 | 4.5 | 4.5 | 3.9 | 1.1 | 0.9 | -0.6 |
| 25 to 54 years | 28.1 | 27.2 | 24.7 | 23.8 | 0.9 | 0.1 | 0.5 |
| 25 to 34 years | 10.3 | 8.7 | 8.4 | 8.5 | -0.5 | 0.7 | 0.9 |
| 35 to 44 years | 10.4 | 9.5 | 7.8 | 8.1 | 0.4 | -0.9 | 1.2 |
| 45 to 54 years | 7.4 | 9.0 | 8.4 | 7.2 | 3.3 | 0.4 | -0.8 |
| 55 years and over | 11.5 | 12.8 | 15.8 | 17.8 | 2.3 | 3.2 | 2.0 |
| 55 to 64 years | 5.0 | 6.2 | 7.7 | 7.4 | 3.5 | 3.2 | 0.4 |
| 65 to 74 years | 4.1 | 3.7 | 4.9 | 6.2 | 0.2 | 3.9 | 3.1 |
| 75 years and over | 2.4 | 2.9 | 3.1 | 4.2 | 2.9 | 2.0 | 3.9 |
| **Women, 16 Years and Over** | 52.1 | 51.8 | 51.7 | 51.4 | 1.2 | 1.0 | 0.8 |
| 16 to 24 years | 8.3 | 8.1 | 7.7 | 6.9 | 1.0 | 0.6 | -0.4 |
| 16 to 19 years | 3.6 | 3.6 | 3.3 | 3.0 | 1.3 | 0.2 | -0.1 |
| 20 to 24 years | 4.7 | 4.5 | 4.4 | 3.8 | 0.8 | 0.9 | -0.6 |
| 25 to 54 years | 29.1 | 28.0 | 25.6 | 24.1 | 0.9 | 0.1 | 0.2 |
| 25 to 34 years | 10.6 | 8.8 | 8.6 | 8.4 | -0.7 | 0.8 | 0.6 |
| 35 to 44 years | 10.7 | 9.8 | 8.1 | 8.2 | 0.4 | -0.8 | 0.9 |
| 45 to 54 years | 7.7 | 9.4 | 8.8 | 7.5 | 3.3 | 0.4 | -0.8 |
| 55 years and over | 14.7 | 15.6 | 18.4 | 20.5 | 1.9 | 2.7 | 1.9 |
| 55 to 64 years | 5.5 | 6.7 | 8.3 | 7.9 | 3.3 | 3.2 | 0.2 |
| 65 to 74 years | 5.2 | 4.4 | 5.6 | 7.0 | -0.3 | 3.5 | 3.1 |
| 75 years and over | 4.0 | 4.5 | 4.5 | 5.6 | 2.4 | 1.0 | 3.1 |
| **White, 16 Years and Over** | 84.1 | 81.8 | 78.8 | 77.1 | 1.0 | 0.7 | 0.6 |
| Men | 40.7 | 39.9 | 38.5 | 37.9 | 1.1 | 0.7 | 0.7 |
| Women | 43.4 | 41.9 | 40.3 | 39.2 | 0.9 | 0.7 | 0.5 |
| **Black, 16 Years and Over** | 11.6 | 11.7 | 12.4 | 12.9 | 1.3 | 1.7 | 1.2 |
| Men | 5.2 | 5.2 | 5.6 | 5.9 | 1.3 | 1.8 | 1.3 |
| Women | 6.4 | 6.5 | 6.8 | 7.0 | 1.3 | 1.6 | 1.1 |
| **Asian, 16 Years and Over** | 4.3 | 4.3 | 5.6 | 6.4 | 1.3 | 3.8 | 2.2 |
| Men | 2.1 | 2.0 | 2.6 | 3.0 | 1.2 | 3.6 | 2.2 |
| Women | 2.2 | 2.2 | 3.0 | 3.4 | 1.4 | 4.0 | 2.2 |
| **All Other Groups,[1] 16 Years and Over** | . . . | 2.1 | 3.0 | 3.6 | . . . | 3.6 | 2.7 |
| Men | . . . | 1.0 | 1.5 | 1.8 | . . . | 4.0 | 2.8 |
| Women | . . . | 1.1 | 1.5 | 1.8 | . . . | 3.3 | 2.7 |
| **Hispanic,[2] 16 Years and Over** | 9.2 | 12.6 | 15.5 | 18.3 | 4.5 | 3.2 | 2.5 |
| Men | 4.6 | 6.5 | 7.8 | 9.3 | 4.7 | 2.9 | 2.6 |
| Women | 4.6 | 6.1 | 7.7 | 9.0 | 4.3 | 3.4 | 2.4 |
| **Non-Hispanic, 16 Years and Over** | 90.8 | 87.4 | 84.5 | 81.7 | 0.9 | 0.7 | 0.5 |
| Men | 43.3 | 41.8 | 40.5 | 39.3 | 0.9 | 0.7 | 0.5 |
| Women | 47.5 | 45.6 | 44.0 | 42.7 | 0.9 | 0.7 | 0.5 |
| **White Non-Hispanic, 16 Years and Over** | 75.9 | 70.1 | 65.0 | 60.8 | 0.5 | 0.3 | 0.2 |
| Men | 36.6 | 33.9 | 31.6 | 29.6 | 0.5 | 0.3 | 0.2 |
| Women | 39.4 | 36.2 | 33.4 | 31.3 | 0.4 | 0.2 | 0.1 |

[1]The "All other groups" category includes respondents who reported the racial categories of "American Indian and Alaska Native" or "Native Hawaiian and Other Pacific Islander," as well as those who reported two or more races. This category was not defined prior to 2003.
[2]May be of any race.
. . . = Not available.

## Table 4-2.  Fastest-Growing Occupations, 2014 and Projected 2024

(Numbers in thousands, percent.)

| Occupation | Employment | | Change, 2014–2024 | | Mean annual wage, 2014 |
|---|---|---|---|---|---|
| | 2014 | 2024 | Number | Percent | |
| TOTAL, ALL OCCUPATIONS | 150 539.9 | 160 328.8 | 9 788.9 | 6.5 | 35 540 |
| Wind turbine service technicians | 4.4 | 9.2 | 4.8 | 108.0 | 48 800 |
| Occupational therapy assistants | 33.0 | 47.1 | 14.1 | 42.7 | 56 950 |
| Physical therapist assistants | 78.7 | 110.7 | 31.9 | 40.6 | 54 410 |
| Physical therapist aides | 50.0 | 69.5 | 19.5 | 39.0 | 24 650 |
| Home health aides | 913.5 | 1 261.9 | 348.4 | 38.1 | 21 380 |
| Commercial divers | 4.4 | 6.0 | 1.6 | 36.9 | 45 890 |
| Nurse practitioners | 126.9 | 171.7 | 44.7 | 35.2 | 95 350 |
| Physical therapists | 210.9 | 282.7 | 71.8 | 34.0 | 82 390 |
| Statisticians | 30.0 | 40.1 | 10.1 | 33.8 | 79 990 |
| Ambulance drivers and attendants, except emergency medical technicians | 19.6 | 26.1 | 6.5 | 33.0 | 24 080 |
| Occupational therapy aides | 8.8 | 11.6 | 2.7 | 30.6 | 26 550 |
| Physician assistants | 94.4 | 123.2 | 28.7 | 30.4 | 95 820 |
| Operations research analysts | 91.3 | 118.9 | 27.6 | 30.2 | 76 660 |
| Personal financial advisors | 249.4 | 323.2 | 73.9 | 29.6 | 81 060 |
| Cartographers and photogrammetrists | 12.3 | 15.9 | 3.6 | 29.3 | 60 930 |
| Genetic counselors | 2.4 | 3.1 | 0.7 | 28.8 | 67 500 |
| Interpreters and translators | 61.0 | 78.5 | 17.5 | 28.7 | 43 590 |
| Audiologists | 13.2 | 16.9 | 3.8 | 28.6 | 73 060 |
| Hearing aid specialists | 5.9 | 7.5 | 1.6 | 27.2 | 43 010 |
| Optometrists | 40.6 | 51.6 | 11.0 | 27.0 | 101 410 |
| Forensic science technicians | 14.4 | 18.2 | 3.8 | 26.6 | 55 360 |
| Web developers | 148.5 | 188.0 | 39.5 | 26.6 | 63 490 |
| Occupational therapists | 114.6 | 145.1 | 30.4 | 26.5 | 78 810 |
| Diagnostic medical sonographers | 60.7 | 76.7 | 16.0 | 26.4 | 67 530 |
| Personal care aides | 1 768.4 | 2 226.5 | 458.1 | 25.9 | 20 440 |
| Phlebotomists | 112.7 | 140.8 | 28.1 | 24.9 | 30 670 |
| Ophthalmic medical technicians | 37.0 | 46.1 | 9.1 | 24.7 | 35 230 |
| Nurse midwives | 5.3 | 6.6 | 1.3 | 24.6 | 96 970 |
| Solar photovoltaic installers | 5.9 | 7.4 | 1.4 | 24.3 | 40 020 |
| Emergency medical technicians and paramedics | 241.2 | 299.6 | 58.5 | 24.2 | 31 700 |

## Table 4-3.  Occupations with the Largest Job Growth, 2014–2024

(Numbers in thousands, percent.)

| Occupation | Employment | | Change, 2014–2024 | | Mean annual wage, 2014 |
|---|---|---|---|---|---|
| | 2014 | 2024 | Number | Percent | |
| **TOTAL, ALL OCCUPATIONS** ............................................ | 150 539.9 | 160 328.8 | 9 788.9 | 6.5 | 35 540 |
| Personal care aides ........................................................ | 1 768.4 | 2 226.5 | 458.1 | 25.9 | 20 440 |
| Registered nurses ........................................................... | 2 751.0 | 3 190.3 | 439.3 | 16.0 | 66 640 |
| Home health aides .......................................................... | 913.5 | 1 261.9 | 348.4 | 38.1 | 21 380 |
| Combined food preparation and serving workers, including fast food ...................................... | 3 159.7 | 3 503.2 | 343.5 | 10.9 | 18 410 |
| Retail salespersons ........................................................ | 4 624.9 | 4 939.1 | 314.2 | 6.8 | 21 390 |
| Nursing assistants .......................................................... | 1 492.1 | 1 754.1 | 262.0 | 17.6 | 25 100 |
| Customer service representatives ................................... | 2 581.8 | 2 834.8 | 252.9 | 9.8 | 31 200 |
| Cooks, restaurant ........................................................... | 1 109.7 | 1 268.7 | 158.9 | 14.3 | 22 490 |
| General and operations managers .................................. | 2 124.1 | 2 275.2 | 151.1 | 7.1 | 97 270 |
| Construction laborers ..................................................... | 1 159.1 | 1 306.5 | 147.4 | 12.7 | 31 090 |
| Accountants and auditors ............................................... | 1 332.7 | 1 475.1 | 142.4 | 10.7 | 65 940 |
| Medical assistants .......................................................... | 591.3 | 730.2 | 138.9 | 23.5 | 29 960 |
| Janitors and cleaners, except maids and housekeeping cleaners ............................................. | 2 360.6 | 2 496.9 | 136.3 | 5.8 | 22 840 |
| Software developers, applications ................................... | 718.4 | 853.7 | 135.3 | 18.8 | 95 510 |
| Laborers and freight, stock, and material movers, hand ....................................... | 2 441.3 | 2 566.4 | 125.1 | 5.1 | 24 430 |
| First-line supervisors of office and administrative support workers ..................................... | 1 466.1 | 1 587.3 | 121.2 | 8.3 | 50 780 |
| Computer systems analysts ............................................ | 567.8 | 686.3 | 118.6 | 20.9 | 82 710 |
| Licensed practical and licensed vocational nurses .......... | 719.9 | 837.2 | 117.3 | 16.3 | 42 490 |
| Maids and housekeeping cleaners .................................. | 1 457.7 | 1 569.4 | 111.7 | 7.7 | 20 120 |
| Medical secretaries ........................................................ | 527.6 | 635.8 | 108.2 | 20.5 | 32 240 |
| Management analysts ..................................................... | 758.0 | 861.4 | 103.4 | 13.6 | 80 880 |
| Heavy and tractor-trailer truck drivers ............................ | 1 797.7 | 1 896.4 | 98.8 | 5.5 | 39 520 |
| Receptionists and information clerks ............................... | 1 028.6 | 1 126.3 | 97.8 | 9.5 | 26 760 |
| Office clerks, general ...................................................... | 3 062.5 | 3 158.2 | 95.8 | 3.1 | 28 670 |
| Sales representatives, wholesale and manufacturing, except technical and scientific products | 1 453.1 | 1 546.5 | 93.4 | 6.4 | 55 020 |
| Stock clerks and order fillers ......................................... | 1 878.1 | 1 971.1 | 92.9 | 4.9 | 22 850 |
| Market research analysts and marketing specialists ........ | 495.5 | 587.8 | 92.3 | 18.6 | 61 290 |
| First-line supervisors of food preparation and serving workers ...................................... | 890.1 | 978.6 | 88.5 | 9.9 | 29 560 |
| Electricians ..................................................................... | 628.8 | 714.7 | 85.9 | 13.7 | 51 110 |
| Maintenance and repair workers, general ....................... | 1 374.7 | 1 458.1 | 83.5 | 6.1 | 36 170 |

## Table 4-4.  Fastest Declining Occupations, 2014 and Projected 2024

(Numbers in thousands, percent, dollars.)

| Occupation | 2014 | 2024 | Number | Percent | Median annual wage |
|---|---|---|---|---|---|
| **TOTAL, ALL OCCUPATIONS** ................................................ | 150 539.9 | 160 328.8 | 9 788.9 | 6.5 | 35 540 |
| Locomotive firers ................................................ | 1.7 | 0.5 | -1.2 | -69.9 | 46 740 |
| Electronic equipment installers and repairers, motor vehicles ................ | 11.5 | 5.8 | -5.8 | -50.0 | 31 020 |
| Telephone operators ................................................ | 13.1 | 7.5 | -5.5 | -42.4 | 35 140 |
| Postal service mail sorters, processors, and processing machine operators .......... | 117.6 | 78.0 | -39.7 | -33.7 | 54 520 |
| Switchboard operators, including answering service ............................ | 112.4 | 75.4 | -37.0 | -32.9 | 26 550 |
| Photographic process workers and processing machine operators ................. | 28.8 | 19.4 | -9.5 | -32.9 | 24 600 |
| Shoe machine operators and tenders ................................ | 3.5 | 2.5 | -1.1 | -30.5 | 24 750 |
| Manufactured building and mobile home installers ............................ | 4.0 | 2.8 | -1.2 | -30.0 | 29 600 |
| Foundry mold and coremakers ........................................ | 12.0 | 8.7 | -3.3 | -27.7 | 31 340 |
| Sewing machine operators ............................................ | 153.9 | 112.2 | -41.7 | -27.1 | 21 920 |
| Pourers and casters, metal ............................................ | 9.8 | 7.2 | -2.6 | -26.6 | 32 410 |
| Postal service clerks ................................................ | 69.6 | 51.3 | -18.3 | -26.2 | 55 590 |
| Postal service mail carriers ........................................... | 297.4 | 219.4 | -78.1 | -26.2 | 57 200 |
| Postmasters and mail superintendents ................................... | 17.3 | 12.8 | -4.6 | -26.2 | 65 800 |
| Fabric and apparel patternmakers ...................................... | 5.4 | 4.0 | -1.4 | -26.0 | 41 310 |
| Textile knitting and weaving machine setters, operators, and tenders ............. | 27.9 | 20.6 | -7.3 | -26.2 | 27 270 |
| Textile cutting machine setters, operators, and tenders ....................... | 14.3 | 10.6 | -3.7 | -25.7 | 25 590 |
| Watch repairers ................................................... | 2.7 | 2.0 | -0.7 | -25.7 | 35 450 |
| Molding, coremaking, and casting machine setters, operators, and tenders, metal and plastic ............ | 129.5 | 97.2 | -32.3 | -25.0 | 28 810 |
| Prepress technicians and workers ...................................... | 36.5 | 27.5 | -9.0 | -24.6 | 37 200 |
| Extruding and drawing machine setters, operators, and tenders, metal and plastic ........ | 73.4 | 55.5 | -17.9 | -24.4 | 32 610 |
| Textile bleaching and dyeing machine operators and tenders .................... | 11.7 | 8.9 | -2.8 | -23.9 | 24 930 |
| Patternmakers, metal and plastic ...................................... | 3.8 | 2.9 | -0.9 | -23.4 | 41 390 |
| Grinding, lapping, polishing, and buffing machine tool setters, operators, and tenders, metal and plastic ............ | 71.4 | 55.8 | -15.7 | -21.9 | 32 660 |
| Textile winding, twisting, and drawing out machine setters, operators, and tenders ....... | 26.0 | 20.3 | -5.6 | -21.7 | 26 250 |
| Model makers, metal and plastic ....................................... | 6.2 | 4.9 | -1.3 | -21.5 | 46 180 |
| Forging machine setters, operators, and tenders, metal and plastic ............... | 21.6 | 17.0 | -4.6 | -21.5 | 33 710 |
| Desktop publishers ................................................. | 14.8 | 11.7 | -3.1 | -21.0 | 38 200 |
| Parking enforcement workers ......................................... | 9.4 | 7.4 | -2.0 | -20.8 | 36 570 |
| Cutting, punching, and press machine setters, operators, and tenders, metal and plastic ...... | 192.2 | 152.7 | -39.5 | -20.6 | 30 680 |

## Table 4-5.  Economic Dependency Ratio, 1994, 2004, 2014, and Projected 2024

(Number.)

| Group | 1994 | 2004 | 2014 | 2024 |
|---|---|---|---|---|
| **TOTAL POPULATION** ................................................ | 96.4 | 96.7 | 102.6 | 108.1 |
| Under age 16 ..................................................... | 45.8 | 43.7 | 41.9 | 42.0 |
| Ages 16 to 64 ..................................................... | 29.6 | 33.0 | 37.6 | 36.9 |
| Ages 65 and older ................................................. | 22.2 | 21.0 | 24.0 | 30.1 |

## Table 4-6. Industries with the Largest Wage and Salary Employment Growth and Declines, 2014–2024

(Number in thousands, percent.)

| Industry | Sector | Employment 2014 | Employment 2024 | Change, 2014–2024 | Annual rate of change, 2014–2024 |
|---|---|---|---|---|---|
| **Largest Growth** | | | | | |
| Construction | Construction | 6 138.4 | 6 928.8 | 790.4 | 1.2 |
| Home health care services | Health care and social assistance | 1 262.2 | 2 022.6 | 760.4 | 4.8 |
| Nursing and residential care facilities | Health care and social assistance | 3 261.0 | 3 996.7 | 735.7 | 2.1 |
| Food services and drinking places | Leisure and hospitality | 10 717.0 | 11 375.0 | 658.0 | 0.6 |
| Offices of physicians | Health care and social assistance | 2 470.2 | 2 992.9 | 522.7 | 1.9 |
| Local government educational services compensation | State and local government | 7 791.2 | 8 217.6 | 426.4 | 0.5 |
| Employment services | Professional and business services | 3 421.0 | 3 845.8 | 424.8 | 1.2 |
| Computer systems design and related services | Professional and business services | 1 777.7 | 2 186.6 | 408.9 | 2.1 |
| Hospitals; private | Health care and social assistance | 4 784.3 | 5 179.2 | 394.9 | 0.8 |
| Offices of other health practitioners | Health care and social assistance | 784.2 | 1 136.5 | 352.3 | 3.8 |
| **Largest Declines** | | | | | |
| Postal Service | Federal government | 593.0 | 427.9 | -165.1 | -3.2 |
| Federal non-defense government compensation | Federal government | 1 514.8 | 1 404.3 | -110.5 | -0.8 |
| Newspaper, periodical, book, and directory publishers | Information | 412.3 | 309.0 | -103.3 | -2.8 |
| Wired telecommunications carriers | Information | 607.0 | 509.2 | -97.8 | -1.7 |
| Federal defense government compensation | Federal government | 522.2 | 440.0 | -82.2 | -1.7 |
| Printing and related support activities | Manufacturing | 452.7 | 371.3 | -81.4 | -2.0 |
| Apparel, leather, and allied manufacturing | Manufacturing | 168.5 | 91.7 | -76.8 | -5.9 |
| Crop production | Agriculture | 765.6 | 699.9 | -65.7 | -0.9 |
| Plastics product manufacturing | Manufacturing | 541.6 | 478.5 | -63.1 | -1.2 |
| Textile mills and textile product mills | Manufacturing | 232.1 | 174.2 | -57.9 | -2.8 |

## Table 4-7. Median Age of the Labor Force, by Sex, Race, and Ethnicity, 1994, 2004, 2014, and Projected 2024

(Number.)

| | 1994 | 2004 | 2014 | 2024 |
|---|---|---|---|---|
| **TOTAL** | 37.7 | 40.3 | 41.9 | 42.4 |
| **Sex** | | | | |
| Men | 37.7 | 40.1 | 41.8 | 42.0 |
| Women | 37.7 | 40.5 | 42.0 | 42.8 |
| **Race** | | | | |
| White | 37.7 | 40.8 | 42.6 | 43.0 |
| Black | 36.0 | 38.6 | 39.6 | 40.0 |
| Asian | 37.5 | 39.3 | 41.2 | 42.8 |
| **Ethnicity** | | | | |
| Hispanic origin[1] | 33.7 | 35.0 | 37.3 | 38.9 |
| White non-Hispanic | 38.5 | 41.8 | 44.1 | 44.4 |

[1] May be of any race.

## Table 4-8.  Employment and Output, by Industry, 2004, 2014, and Projected 2024

(Number, percent, dollars.)

| Industry | Employment | | | | | | | Output | | | | |
|---|---|---|---|---|---|---|---|---|---|---|---|---|
| | Number of jobs (thousands) | | | Change | | Average annual rate of change (percent) | | Billions of chained (2005) dollars | | | Average annual rate of change (percent) | |
| | 2004 | 2014 | 2024 | 2004–2014 | 2014–2024 | 2004–2014 | 2014–2024 | 2004 | 2014 | 2024 | 2004–2014 | 2014–2024 |
| **Total**[1,2] ............................ | 144 047 | 150 540 | 160 329 | 6 493 | 9 789 | 0.4 | 0.6 | 25 003 | 27 724 | 34 573 | 1.0 | 2.2 |
| **Nonagriculture Wage and Salary** ................ | 132 462 | 139 812 | 149 132 | 7 349 | 9 320 | 0.5 | 0.6 | 24 663 | 27 370 | 34 149 | 1.0 | 2.2 |
| **Mining** ................................ | 523 | 844 | 924 | 321 | 80 | 4.9 | 0.9 | 372 | 459 | 556 | 2.1 | 1.9 |
| Oil and gas extraction ................ | 123 | 198 | 219 | 74 | 22 | 4.8 | 1.0 | 207 | 266 | 317 | 2.6 | 1.7 |
| Mining, except oil and gas ................ | 205 | 207 | 203 | 2 | -4 | 0.1 | -0.2 | 108 | 102 | 121 | -0.5 | 1.7 |
| Coal mining ................ | 71 | 74 | 71 | 4 | -2.7 | 0.5 | -0.4 | 43 | 45 | 52 | 0.4 | 1.4 |
| Metal ore mining ................ | 28 | 44 | 44 | 17 | -0.5 | 4.8 | -0.1 | 25 | 22 | 25 | -1.7 | 1.4 |
| Nonmetallic mineral mining and quarrying ................ | 107 | 89 | 88 | -18 | -1 | -1.8 | -0.2 | 39 | 36 | 45 | -0.9 | 2.3 |
| Support activities for mining ................ | 195 | 438 | 502 | 244 | 63 | 8.5 | 1.4 | 57 | 94 | 124 | 5.1 | 2.9 |
| **Utilities** ................................ | 564 | 553 | 505 | -11 | -48 | -0.2 | -0.9 | 432 | 373 | 446 | -1.5 | 1.8 |
| Electric power generation, transmission and distribution ................ | 409 | 392 | 351 | -16 | -41 | -0.4 | -1.1 | 324 | 262 | 320 | -2.1 | 2.0 |
| Natural gas distribution ................ | 109 | 113 | 100 | 4 | -13 | 0.4 | -1.2 | 100 | 100 | 113 | 0.0 | 1.2 |
| Water, sewage and other systems ................ | 46.0 | 47.8 | 54.0 | 1.8 | 6.2 | 0.4 | 1.2 | 10.7 | 9.9 | 11.2 | -0.8 | 1.3 |
| **Construction** ................................ | 6 976 | 6 138 | 6 929 | -838 | 790 | -1.3 | 1.2 | 1 396 | 1 031 | 1 357 | -3.0 | 2.8 |
| **Manufacturing** ................................ | 14 316 | 12 188 | 11 374 | -2 128 | -814 | -1.6 | -0.7 | 5 096 | 5 446 | 6 587 | 0.7 | 1.9 |
| Food manufacturing ................ | 1 494 | 1 480 | 1 455 | -13 | -25 | -0.1 | -0.2 | 591 | 639 | 758 | 0.8 | 1.7 |
| Animal food manufacturing ................ | 50 | 55 | 53 | 5 | -2 | 1.0 | -0.4 | 42 | 51 | 64 | 2.0 | 2.2 |
| Grain and oilseed milling ................ | 60 | 58 | 54 | -2 | -4 | -0.4 | -0.7 | 77 | 98 | 116 | 2.5 | 1.7 |
| Sugar and confectionery product manufacturing ................ | 83 | 69 | 61 | -14 | -8 | -1.8 | -1.2 | 33 | 33 | 38 | 0.0 | 1.5 |
| Fruit and vegetable preserving and specialty food manufacturing .... | 181 | 169 | 163 | -12 | -6 | -0.7 | -0.4 | 70 | 71 | 81 | 0.2 | 1.3 |
| Dairy product manufacturing ................ | 131 | 134 | 132 | 2 | -1 | 0.2 | -0.1 | 76 | 83 | 102 | 0.8 | 2.1 |
| Animal slaughtering and processing ................ | 505 | 480 | 474 | -26 | -5 | -0.5 | -0.1 | 146 | 146 | 172 | 0.0 | 1.7 |
| Seafood product preparation and packaging ................ | 42 | 35 | 32 | -7 | -3 | -1.9 | -0.9 | 11 | 11 | 13 | -0.3 | 1.6 |
| Bakeries and tortilla manufacturing ................ | 285 | 294 | 289 | 9 | -5 | 0.3 | -0.2 | 62 | 63 | 73 | 0.1 | 1.5 |
| Other food manufacturing ................ | 156 | 187 | 196 | 31 | 9 | 1.8 | 0.5 | 77 | 87 | 103 | 1.3 | 1.7 |
| Beverage and tobacco product ................ | 195 | 209 | 210 | 14 | 1 | 0.7 | 0.1 | 149 | 158 | 169 | 0.6 | 0.7 |
| Beverage manufacturing ................ | 166 | 195 | 201 | 29 | 6 | 1.6 | 0.3 | 90 | 109 | 126 | 1.9 | 1.5 |
| Tobacco manufacturing ................ | 29 | 14 | 9 | -15 | -4 | -7.3 | -3.9 | 60 | 50 | 45 | -1.8 | -1.1 |
| Textile mills and textile product mills ................ | 420 | 232 | 174 | -188 | -58 | -5.8 | -2.8 | 82 | 50 | 51 | -4.8 | 0.2 |
| Apparel, leather, and allied manufacturing ................ | 320 | 168 | 92 | -151 | -77 | -6.2 | -5.9 | 39 | 28 | 28 | -3.5 | 0.0 |
| Wood product manufacturing ................ | 552 | 372 | 364 | -180 | -8 | -3.9 | -0.2 | 102 | 78 | 92 | -2.7 | 1.7 |
| Sawmills and wood preservation ................ | 119 | 91 | 90 | -28 | -1 | -2.6 | -0.1 | 25 | 20 | 23 | -2.4 | 1.8 |
| Veneer, plywood, and engineered wood product manufacturing ..... | 118 | 72 | 70 | -46 | -2 | -4.8 | -0.3 | 24 | 19 | 20 | -2.2 | 0.4 |
| Other wood product manufacturing ................ | 315 | 209 | 204 | -106 | -5 | -4.0 | -0.2 | 54 | 40 | 49 | -3.0 | 2.1 |
| Paper manufacturing ................ | 496 | 371 | 329 | -124 | -42 | -2.8 | -1.2 | 184 | 159 | 193 | -1.4 | 2.0 |
| Pulp, paper, and paperboard mills ................ | 146 | 104 | 83 | -42 | -21 | -3.3 | -2.2 | 86 | 75 | 90 | -1.4 | 1.9 |
| Converted paper product manufacturing ................ | 350 | 267 | 246 | -82 | -21 | -2.7 | -0.8 | 98 | 84 | 103 | -1.4 | 2.0 |
| Printing and related support activities ................ | 663 | 453 | 371 | -210 | -81 | -3.7 | -2.0 | 103 | 78 | 99 | -2.7 | 2.4 |
| Petroleum and coal products manufacturing ................ | 112 | 111 | 109 | -1 | -2 | -0.1 | -0.2 | 462 | 516 | 690 | 1.1 | 2.9 |
| Chemical manufacturing ................ | 887 | 804 | 744 | -83 | -60 | -1.0 | -0.8 | 717 | 711 | 858 | -0.1 | 1.9 |
| Basic chemical manufacturing ................ | 156 | 147 | 132 | -9 | -15 | -0.6 | -1.1 | 204 | 224 | 277 | 0.9 | 2.2 |
| Resin, synthetic rubber, and artificial synthetic fibers and filaments manufacturing ................ | 110 | 93 | 81 | -17 | -12 | -1.6 | -1.3 | 88 | 85 | 104 | -0.3 | 2.0 |
| Pesticide, fertilizer, and other agricultural chemical manufacturing .. | 42 | 36 | 32 | -5 | -5 | -1.3 | -1.3 | 33 | 38 | 45 | 1.5 | 1.7 |
| Pharmaceutical and medicine manufacturing ................ | 290 | 280 | 277 | -11 | -2 | -0.4 | -0.1 | 225 | 197 | 222 | -1.3 | 1.2 |
| Paint, coating, and adhesive manufacturing ................ | 68 | 60 | 55 | -8 | -5 | -1.2 | -0.9 | 41 | 33 | 40 | -2.2 | 1.9 |
| Soap, cleaning compound, and toilet preparation manufacturing ..... | 115 | 105 | 96 | -11 | -8 | -1.0 | -0.8 | 78 | 90 | 114 | 1.5 | 2.4 |
| Other chemical product and preparation manufacturing ................ | 107 | 83 | 70 | -23 | -13 | -2.4 | -1.7 | 48 | 43 | 54 | -1.2 | 2.3 |
| Plastics and rubber products manufacturing ................ | 805 | 675 | 590 | -130 | -84 | -1.7 | -1.3 | 222 | 194 | 233 | -1.3 | 1.8 |
| Plastics product manufacturing ................ | 633 | 542 | 478 | -91 | -63 | -1.5 | -1.2 | 180 | 157 | 192 | -1.3 | 2.0 |
| Rubber product manufacturing ................ | 172 | 133 | 112 | -39 | -21 | -2.5 | -1.7 | 42 | 37 | 41 | -1.1 | 1.0 |
| Nonmetallic mineral product manufacturing ................ | 506 | 386 | 352 | -120 | -33 | -2.7 | -0.9 | 123 | 108 | 128 | -1.3 | 1.8 |
| Clay product and refractory manufacturing ................ | 64 | 40 | 33 | -25 | -6 | -4.8 | -1.8 | 10 | 7 | 8 | -3.5 | 1.0 |
| Glass and glass product manufacturing ................ | 113 | 86 | 67 | -27 | -18 | -2.7 | -2.4 | 25 | 22 | 26 | -1.1 | 1.6 |
| Cement and concrete product manufacturing ................ | 235 | 174 | 170 | -61 | -4 | -3.0 | -0.2 | 62 | 54 | 68 | -1.5 | 2.5 |
| Lime, gypsum and other nonmetallic mineral product manufacturing ................ | 94 | 87 | 83 | -7 | -4 | -0.8 | -0.5 | 26 | 25 | 27 | -0.5 | 0.7 |
| Primary metal manufacturing ................ | 467 | 401 | 366 | -66 | -35 | -1.5 | -0.9 | 228 | 270 | 289 | 1.7 | 0.7 |
| Iron and steel mills and ferroalloy manufacturing ................ | 95 | 91 | 88 | -4 | -3 | -0.4 | -0.4 | 81 | 103 | 109 | 2.5 | 0.6 |
| Steel product manufacturing from purchased steel ................ | 61 | 60 | 62 | -1 | 2 | -0.1 | 0.3 | 23 | 26 | 28 | 1.2 | 0.8 |
| Alumina and aluminum production and processing ................ | 74 | 60 | 53 | -14 | -6 | -2.1 | -1.1 | 34 | 44 | 46 | 2.6 | 0.5 |
| Nonferrous metal (except aluminum) production and processing ..... | 71 | 62 | 57 | -9 | -5 | -1.4 | -0.9 | 55 | 62 | 66 | 1.2 | 0.7 |
| Foundries ................ | 165 | 127 | 105 | -38 | -22 | -2.6 | -1.9 | 38 | 35 | 39 | -0.9 | 1.2 |
| Fabricated metal product manufacturing ................ | 1 497 | 1 455 | 1 463 | -42 | 8 | -0.3 | 0.1 | 340 | 327 | 389 | -0.4 | 1.8 |
| Forging and stamping ................ | 110 | 100 | 95 | -9 | -5 | -0.9 | -0.5 | 29 | 35 | 41 | 1.9 | 1.5 |
| Cutlery and handtool manufacturing ................ | 58 | 38 | 34 | -21 | -4 | -4.3 | -1.1 | 12 | 10 | 13 | -1.3 | 2.6 |
| Architectural and structural metals manufacturing ................ | 389 | 362 | 373 | -27 | 12 | -0.7 | 0.3 | 79 | 87 | 107 | 1.0 | 2.1 |
| Boiler, tank, and shipping container manufacturing ................ | 92 | 99 | 102 | 6 | 4 | 0.7 | 0.4 | 33 | 37 | 42 | 1.2 | 1.4 |
| Hardware manufacturing ................ | 38 | 24 | 20 | -14 | -5 | -4.4 | -2.1 | 12 | 9 | 11 | -2.8 | 2.1 |
| Spring and wire product manufacturing ................ | 62 | 44 | 36 | -18 | -8 | -3.4 | -1.9 | 12 | 8 | 10 | -3.3 | 1.7 |

## Table 4-8. Employment and Output, by Industry, 2004, 2014, and Projected 2024—*Continued*

(Number, percent, dollars.)

| Industry | Employment Number of jobs (thousands) 2004 | 2014 | 2024 | Change 2004–2014 | 2014–2024 | Average annual rate of change (percent) 2004–2014 | 2014–2024 | Output Billions of chained (2005) dollars 2004 | 2014 | 2024 | Average annual rate of change (percent) 2004–2014 | 2014–2024 |
|---|---|---|---|---|---|---|---|---|---|---|---|---|
| **Manufacturing**—*Continued* | | | | | | | | | | | | |
| Machine shops; turned product; and screw, nut, and bolt manufacturing | 327 | 371 | 382 | 44 | 11 | 1.3 | 0.3 | 57 | 68 | 80 | 1.9 | 1.6 |
| Coating, engraving, heat treating, and allied activities | 143 | 139 | 138 | -5 | -0.5 | -0.3 | 0.0 | 24 | 26 | 32 | 0.9 | 2.2 |
| Other fabricated metal product manufacturing | 278 | 280 | 283 | 2 | 3 | 0.1 | 0.1 | 87 | 50 | 58 | -5.4 | 1.5 |
| Machinery manufacturing | 1 145 | 1 128 | 1 108 | -17 | -21 | -0.1 | -0.2 | 323 | 420 | 495 | 2.7 | 1.6 |
| Agriculture, construction, and mining machinery manufacturing | 195 | 255 | 269 | 60 | 14 | 2.7 | 0.5 | 71 | 112 | 138 | 4.6 | 2.1 |
| Industrial machinery manufacturing | 122 | 108 | 99 | -13 | -9 | -1.2 | -0.8 | 37 | 52 | 62 | 3.6 | 1.7 |
| Commercial and service industry machinery manufacturing | 115 | 88 | 76 | -27 | -11 | -2.7 | -1.3 | 24 | 28 | 32 | 1.7 | 1.3 |
| Ventilation, heating, air-conditioning, and commercial refrigeration equipment manufacturing | 153 | 128 | 122 | -24 | -6 | -1.7 | -0.5 | 41 | 45 | 55 | 0.9 | 2.0 |
| Metalworking machinery manufacturing | 202 | 182 | 171 | -20 | -11 | -1.0 | -0.6 | 27 | 34 | 38 | 2.5 | 1.0 |
| Engine, turbine, and power transmission equipment manufacturing | 93 | 103 | 106 | 10 | 3 | 1.0 | 0.3 | 44 | 49 | 55 | 1.1 | 1.0 |
| Other general purpose machinery manufacturing | 266 | 265 | 264 | -1 | -1 | 0.0 | 0.0 | 78 | 99 | 114 | 2.4 | 1.5 |
| Computer and electronic product manufacturing | 1 323 | 1 050 | 920 | -273 | -131 | -2.3 | -1.3 | 344 | 442 | 569 | 2.6 | 2.6 |
| Computer and peripheral equipment manufacturing | 210 | 163 | 136 | -47 | -27 | -2.5 | -1.8 | 42 | 74 | 105 | 5.8 | 3.5 |
| Communications equipment manufacturing | 143 | 94 | 70 | -50 | -24 | -4.2 | -2.9 | 69 | 61 | 74 | -1.3 | 2.1 |
| Audio and video equipment manufacturing | 32 | 19 | 15 | -14 | -4 | -5.3 | -2.6 | 9 | 7 | 9 | -2.6 | 2.3 |
| Semiconductor and other electronic component manufacturing | 454 | 368 | 333 | -86 | -35 | -2.1 | -1.0 | 100 | 144 | 182 | 3.6 | 2.4 |
| Navigational, measuring, electromedical, and control instruments manufacturing | 437 | 388 | 353 | -49 | -35 | -1.2 | -0.9 | 120 | 150 | 192 | 2.3 | 2.5 |
| Manufacturing and reproducing magnetic and optical media | 46 | 19 | 14 | -27 | -5 | -8.6 | -2.9 | 8 | 6 | 8 | -2.1 | 2.5 |
| Electrical equipment, appliance, and component manufacturing | 445 | 374 | 340 | -71 | -35 | -1.7 | -1.0 | 129 | 120 | 148 | -0.7 | 2.1 |
| Electric lighting equipment manufacturing | 64 | 46 | 40 | -18 | -7 | -3.3 | -1.6 | 13 | 12 | 16 | -0.7 | 2.8 |
| Household appliance manufacturing | 90 | 60 | 50 | -30 | -9 | -4.0 | -1.7 | 26 | 22 | 28 | -1.8 | 2.4 |
| Electrical equipment manufacturing | 154 | 144 | 136 | -10 | -8 | -0.7 | -0.5 | 40 | 37 | 43 | -0.9 | 1.7 |
| Other electrical equipment and component manufacturing | 137 | 125 | 114 | -12 | -11 | -0.9 | -1.0 | 50 | 49 | 61 | -0.1 | 2.2 |
| Transportation equipment manufacturing | 1 767 | 1 562 | 1 500 | -204 | -62 | -1.2 | -0.4 | 756 | 912 | 1 038 | 1.9 | 1.3 |
| Motor vehicle manufacturing | 256 | 199 | 192 | -57 | -7 | -2.5 | -0.4 | 277 | 308 | 346 | 1.1 | 1.2 |
| Motor vehicle body and trailer manufacturing | 165 | 141 | 137 | -24 | -4 | -1.6 | -0.3 | 36 | 40 | 44 | 1.1 | 1.1 |
| Motor vehicle parts manufacturing | 692 | 537 | 514 | -156 | -23 | -2.5 | -0.4 | 231 | 245 | 264 | 0.6 | 0.7 |
| Aerospace product and parts manufacturing | 442 | 488 | 464 | 47 | -24 | 1.0 | -0.5 | 156 | 233 | 284 | 4.1 | 2.0 |
| Railroad rolling stock manufacturing | 25 | 26 | 27 | 1 | 1 | 0.4 | 0.4 | 10 | 19 | 22 | 6.3 | 1.7 |
| Ship and boat building | 149 | 138 | 137 | -11 | -2 | -0.7 | -0.1 | 27 | 36 | 40 | 2.6 | 1.2 |
| Other transportation equipment manufacturing | 38 | 33 | 30 | -5 | -3 | -1.5 | -1.0 | 17 | 32 | 40 | 6.7 | 2.3 |
| Furniture and related product manufacturing | 574 | 373 | 356 | -201 | -17 | -4.2 | -0.5 | 91 | 67 | 80 | -3.1 | 1.9 |
| Household and institutional furniture and kitchen cabinet manufacturing | 386 | 235 | 228 | -151 | -8 | -4.8 | -0.3 | 53 | 35 | 44 | -3.9 | 2.2 |
| Office furniture (including fixtures) manufacturing | 135 | 104 | 98 | -31 | -6 | -2.6 | -0.6 | 29 | 22 | 25 | -2.6 | 1.4 |
| Other furniture related product manufacturing | 53 | 34 | 30 | -19 | -3.2 | -4.4 | -1.0 | 10 | 9 | 11 | -0.6 | 2.0 |
| Miscellaneous manufacturing | 651 | 583 | 531 | -68 | -52 | -1.1 | -0.9 | 136 | 187 | 260 | 3.3 | 3.3 |
| Medical equipment and supplies manufacturing | 296 | 308 | 312 | 11 | 4 | 0.4 | 0.1 | 63 | 109 | 151 | 5.6 | 3.3 |
| Other miscellaneous manufacturing | 354 | 275 | 219 | -79 | -56 | -2.5 | -2.2 | 73 | 78 | 109 | 0.6 | 3.4 |
| **Wholesale Trade** | 5 663 | 5 826 | 6 151 | 163 | 325 | 0.3 | 0.5 | 1 203 | 1 363 | 1 754 | 1.3 | 2.6 |
| **Retail Trade** | 15 058 | 15 364 | 16 129 | 306 | 765 | 0.2 | 0.5 | 1 319 | 1 427 | 1 893 | 0.8 | 2.9 |
| Motor vehicle and parts dealers | 1 902 | 1 861 | 2 017 | -41 | 156 | -0.2 | 0.8 | 233 | 242 | 318 | 0.4 | 2.7 |
| Food and beverage stores | 2 822 | 2 994 | 3 088 | 172 | 94 | 0.6 | 0.3 | 204 | 200 | 264 | -0.2 | 2.8 |
| General merchandise stores | 2 863 | 3 114 | 3 377 | 250 | 263 | 0.8 | 0.8 | 178 | 190 | 254 | 0.7 | 2.9 |
| Retail, except motor vehicle and parts dealers, food and beverage stores, and general merchandise stores | 7 471 | 7 396 | 7 647 | -76 | 251 | -0.1 | 0.3 | 704 | 797 | 1 061 | 1.3 | 2.9 |
| **Transportation and Warehousing** | 4 249 | 4 640 | 4 777 | 392 | 137 | 0.9 | 0.3 | 785 | 860 | 1 076 | 0.9 | 2.3 |
| Air transportation | 514 | 442 | 442 | -72 | 0.1 | -1.5 | 0.0 | 140 | 146 | 186 | 0.4 | 2.4 |
| Rail transportation | 226 | 235 | 229 | 10 | -6 | 0.4 | -0.3 | 61 | 67 | 82 | 0.9 | 2.1 |
| Water transportation | 56 | 67 | 75 | 11 | 8 | 1.8 | 1.1 | 43 | 50 | 62 | 1.7 | 2.1 |
| Truck transportation | 1 352 | 1 416 | 1 471 | 64 | 55 | 0.5 | 0.4 | 258 | 278 | 342 | 0.8 | 2.1 |
| Transit and ground passenger transportation | 385 | 465 | 482 | 80 | 16 | 1.9 | 0.3 | 37 | 51 | 61 | 3.3 | 1.9 |
| Pipeline transportation | 38 | 47 | 49 | 9 | 2 | 2.0 | 0.4 | 31 | 19 | 25 | -4.8 | 2.6 |
| Scenic and sightseeing transportation and support activities for transportation | 562 | 656 | 705 | 94 | 49 | 1.6 | 0.7 | 83 | 101 | 128 | 1.9 | 2.4 |
| Postal Service | 782 | 593 | 428 | -189 | -165 | -2.7 | -3.2 | 82 | 62 | 57 | -2.7 | -0.8 |
| Couriers and messengers | 557 | 574 | 559 | 18 | -16 | 0.3 | -0.3 | 78 | 73 | 93 | -0.7 | 2.5 |
| Warehousing and storage | 558 | 738 | 766 | 179.5 | 28 | 2.8 | 0.4 | 55 | 77 | 100 | 3.5 | 2.6 |
| **Information** | 3 118 | 2 740 | 2 713 | -379 | -27 | -1.3 | -0.1 | 1 101 | 1 535 | 2 040 | 3.4 | 2.9 |
| Publishing industries | 909 | 725 | 702 | -184 | -23 | -2.2 | -0.3 | 298 | 336 | 477 | 1.2 | 3.6 |
| Newspaper, periodical, book, and directory publishers | 673 | 412 | 309 | -261 | -103 | -4.8 | -2.8 | 178 | 142 | 173 | -2.3 | 2.0 |
| Software publishers | 236 | 312 | 393 | 77 | 81 | 2.9 | 2.3 | 121 | 195 | 308 | 4.9 | 4.7 |
| Motion picture, video, and sound recording industries | 385 | 376 | 415 | -9 | 39 | -0.2 | 1.0 | 147 | 141 | 183 | -0.4 | 2.6 |
| Broadcasting (except internet) | 325 | 286 | 267 | -39 | -19 | -1.3 | -0.7 | 111 | 150 | 196 | 3.0 | 2.7 |
| Radio and television broadcasting | 240 | 223 | 211 | -17 | -12 | -0.7 | -0.6 | 65 | 72 | 94 | 1.1 | 2.7 |
| Cable and other subscription programming | 86 | 63 | 56 | -23 | -7 | -3.0 | -1.1 | 46 | 78 | 102 | 5.3 | 2.8 |

**Table 4-8.  Employment and Output, by Industry, 2004, 2014, and Projected 2024**—*Continued*

(Number, percent, dollars.)

| Industry | Employment | | | | | | | Output | | | | |
|---|---|---|---|---|---|---|---|---|---|---|---|---|
| | Number of jobs (thousands) | | | Change | | Average annual rate of change (percent) | | Billions of chained (2005) dollars | | | Average annual rate of change (percent) | |
| | 2004 | 2014 | 2024 | 2004–2014 | 2014–2024 | 2004–2014 | 2014–2024 | 2004 | 2014 | 2024 | 2004–2014 | 2014–2024 |
| **Information**—*Continued* | | | | | | | | | | | | |
| Telecommunications ............................................... | 1 115 | 856 | 779 | -259 | -76 | -2.6 | -0.9 | 454 | 700 | 918 | 4.4 | 2.7 |
| Wired telecommunications carriers ................................. | 720 | 607 | 509 | -113 | -98 | -1.7 | -1.7 | 345 | 374 | 436 | 0.8 | 1.5 |
| Wireless telecommunications carriers (except satellite) .............. | 190 | 155 | 176 | -34 | 21 | -2.0 | 1.3 | 94 | 289 | 434 | 11.9 | 4.2 |
| Satellite, telecommunications resellers, and all other telecommunications .................................................. | 205 | 94 | 94 | -112 | 0.2 | -7.6 | 0.0 | 26 | 42 | 63 | 5.0 | 4.1 |
| Data processing, hosting, and related services ..................... | 267 | 279 | 298 | 12 | 19 | 0.5 | 0.7 | 70 | 134 | 171 | 6.7 | 2.5 |
| Other information services ........................................ | 117 | 218 | 251 | 101 | 33 | 6.4 | 1.4 | 25 | 76 | 98 | 11.6 | 2.6 |
| **Finance and Insurance** ............................................. | 6 020 | 5 933 | 6 340 | -86 | 407 | -0.1 | 0.7 | 1 710 | 1 815 | 2 367 | 0.6 | 2.7 |
| Monetary authorities, credit intermediation, and related activities ........ | 2 839 | 2 585 | 2 644 | -254 | 59 | -0.9 | 0.2 | 632 | 550 | 753 | -1.4 | 3.2 |
| Securities, commodity contracts, and other financial investments and related activities ................................................ | 809 | 878 | 1 074 | 68 | 197 | 0.8 | 2.0 | 362 | 403 | 561 | 1.1 | 3.4 |
| Insurance carriers and related activities .......................... | 2 368 | 2 467 | 2 617 | 100 | 150 | 0.4 | 0.6 | 633 | 761 | 914 | 1.9 | 1.9 |
| Insurance carriers ............................................. | 1 488 | 1 459 | 1 512 | -29 | 52 | -0.2 | 0.4 | 486 | 545 | 650 | 1.2 | 1.8 |
| Agencies, brokerages, and other insurance related activities .......... | 879 | 1 008 | 1 106 | 128 | 98 | 1.4 | 0.9 | 148 | 218 | 267 | 4.0 | 2.1 |
| Funds, trusts, and other financial vehicles ........................ | 4 | 4 | 4 | 0 | 1 | 0.0 | 1.7 | 79 | 107 | 142 | 3.0 | 2.9 |
| Real estate, rental, and leasing .................................. | 2 086 | 2 046 | 2 147 | -39 | 101 | -0.2 | 0.5 | 1 495 | 1 702 | 2 169 | 1.3 | 2.5 |
| Real estate ................................................... | 1 419 | 1 487 | 1 574 | 69 | 87 | 0.5 | 0.6 | 1 222 | 1 388 | 1 750 | 1.3 | 2.3 |
| Rental and leasing services and lessors of intangible assets ........... | 667 | 559 | 572 | -108 | 14 | -1.7 | 0.2 | 273 | 314 | 419 | 1.4 | 2.9 |
| Automotive equipment rental and leasing ......................... | 196 | 188 | 194 | -9 | 6 | -0.5 | 0.3 | 53 | 62 | 79 | 1.6 | 2.4 |
| Consumer goods rental and general rental centers ................. | 340 | 202 | 190 | -138 | -12 | -5.1 | -0.6 | 31 | 35 | 46 | 1.3 | 2.5 |
| Commercial and industrial machinery and equipment rental and leasing ...................................................... | 104 | 146 | 164 | 41 | 18 | 3.4 | 1.2 | 53 | 64 | 83 | 2.0 | 2.5 |
| Lessors of nonfinancial intangible assets (except copyrighted works) | 26 | 24 | 25 | -2 | 1 | -0.8 | 0.4 | 136 | 153 | 212 | 1.1 | 3.3 |
| **Professional, Scientific, and Technical Services** ........................ | 6 747 | 8 348 | 9 394 | 1 600 | 1 046 | 2.2 | 1.2 | 1 413 | 1 776 | 2 250 | 2.3 | 2.4 |
| Legal services ................................................... | 1 163 | 1 120 | 1 129 | -43 | 10 | -0.4 | 0.1 | 301 | 270 | 325 | -1.1 | 1.9 |
| Accounting, tax preparation, bookkeeping, and payroll services ......... | 806 | 958 | 1 010 | 152 | 52 | 1.7 | 0.5 | 140 | 134 | 168 | -0.4 | 2.2 |
| Architectural, engineering, and related services ..................... | 1 258 | 1 380 | 1 490 | 122 | 110 | 0.9 | 0.8 | 233 | 299 | 387 | 2.5 | 2.6 |
| Specialized design services ....................................... | 122 | 127 | 137 | 5 | 10 | 0.4 | 0.7 | 26 | 33 | 41 | 2.4 | 2.1 |
| Computer systems design and related services ...................... | 1 149 | 1 778 | 2 187 | 629 | 409 | 4.5 | 2.1 | 200 | 351 | 470 | 5.8 | 3.0 |
| Management, scientific, and technical consulting services ............. | 763 | 1 244 | 1 574 | 481 | 329 | 5.0 | 2.4 | 157 | 199 | 253 | 2.4 | 2.4 |
| Scientific research and development services ....................... | 550 | 635 | 674 | 85 | 39 | 1.4 | 0.6 | 161 | 215 | 258 | 2.9 | 1.8 |
| Advertising, public relations, and related services ................... | 429 | 476 | 486 | 46 | 11 | 1.0 | 0.2 | 101 | 172 | 222 | 5.5 | 2.6 |
| Other professional, scientific, and technical services ................. | 507 | 630 | 708 | 122 | 78 | 2.2 | 1.2 | 98 | 107 | 136 | 0.9 | 2.5 |
| Management of companies and enterprises ......................... | 1 724 | 2 169 | 2 258 | 445 | 89 | 2.3 | 0.4 | 318 | 486 | 604 | 4.3 | 2.2 |
| Administrative and support and waste management and remediation services ......................................................... | 7 923 | 8 579 | 9 333 | 656 | 754 | 0.8 | 0.8 | 590 | 774 | 979 | 2.8 | 2.4 |
| Administrative and support services ............................. | 7 595 | 8 194 | 8 928 | 599 | 734 | 0.8 | 0.9 | 520 | 691 | 877 | 2.9 | 2.4 |
| Office administrative services ................................. | 323 | 462 | 530 | 138 | 68 | 3.6 | 1.4 | 48 | 62 | 80 | 2.7 | 2.6 |
| Facilities support services ................................. | 116 | 131 | 163 | 16 | 32 | 1.3 | 2.2 | 18 | 34 | 42 | 6.3 | 2.3 |
| Employment services ................................... | 3 456 | 3 421 | 3 846 | -34 | 425 | -0.1 | 1.2 | 148 | 216 | 280 | 3.9 | 2.6 |
| Business support services ................................. | 758 | 884 | 973 | 126 | 90 | 1.6 | 1.0 | 67 | 76 | 96 | 1.3 | 2.3 |
| Travel arrangement and reservation services ................. | 226 | 196 | 169 | -31 | -27 | -1.5 | -1.5 | 33 | 46 | 58 | 3.4 | 2.3 |
| Investigation and security services ......................... | 724 | 859 | 898 | 135 | 39 | 1.7 | 0.4 | 41 | 51 | 64 | 2.1 | 2.3 |
| Services to buildings and dwellings ......................... | 1 694 | 1 940 | 2 026 | 246 | 86 | 1.4 | 0.4 | 123 | 162 | 204 | 2.8 | 2.3 |
| Other support services ................................... | 298 | 300 | 322 | 2 | 22 | 0.1 | 0.7 | 43 | 43 | 54 | 0.1 | 2.3 |
| Waste management and remediation services .................... | 329 | 386 | 406 | 57 | 20 | 1.6 | 0.5 | 70 | 84 | 103 | 1.8 | 2.1 |
| Education services; private ....................................... | 2 762 | 3 417 | 3 756 | 655 | 339 | 2.2 | 0.9 | 249 | 267 | 327 | 0.7 | 2.1 |
| Elementary and secondary schools; private ........................ | 824 | 929 | 980 | 105 | 51 | 1.2 | 0.5 | 39 | 33 | 37 | -1.6 | 1.2 |
| Junior colleges, colleges, universities, and professional schools; private ...................................................... | 1 462 | 1 777 | 1 997 | 315 | 220 | 2.0 | 1.2 | 156 | 168 | 209 | 0.7 | 2.2 |
| Other educational services; private ............................... | 476 | 711 | 779 | 235 | 68 | 4.1 | 0.9 | 54 | 65 | 80 | 1.9 | 2.1 |
| Health care and social assistance ................................. | 14 430 | 18 057 | 21 852 | 3 627.6 | 3 795 | 2.3 | 1.9 | 1 524 | 1 938 | 2 583 | 2.4 | 2.9 |
| Ambulatory health care services ................................... | 4 952 | 6 645 | 8 978 | 1 692 | 2 333 | 3.0 | 3.1 | 704 | 895 | 1 203 | 2.4 | 3.0 |
| Offices of physicians .......................................... | 2 048 | 2 470 | 2 993 | 422 | 523 | 1.9 | 1.9 | 343 | 431 | 590 | 2.3 | 3.2 |
| Offices of dentists ............................................ | 760 | 891 | 1 051 | 131 | 160 | 1.6 | 1.7 | 110 | 110 | 132 | 0.0 | 1.8 |
| Offices of other health practioners ............................... | 527 | 784 | 1 136 | 257 | 352 | 4.0 | 3.8 | 65 | 89 | 123 | 3.2 | 3.3 |
| Outpatient care centers ........................................ | 450 | 711 | 1 059 | 261 | 348 | 4.7 | 4.1 | 76 | 101 | 137 | 2.9 | 3.1 |
| Medical and diagnostic laboratories ............................. | 190 | 247 | 327 | 57 | 80 | 2.7 | 2.8 | 36 | 50 | 68 | 3.2 | 3.2 |
| Home health care services ..................................... | 777 | 1 262 | 2 023 | 486 | 760 | 5.0 | 4.8 | 45 | 74 | 102 | 5.0 | 3.2 |
| Other ambulatory health care services ............................ | 200 | 279 | 389 | 79 | 110 | 3.4 | 3.4 | 29 | 40 | 55 | 3.4 | 3.2 |
| Hospitals; private ................................................ | 4 285 | 4 784 | 5 179 | 500 | 395 | 1.1 | 0.8 | 519 | 682 | 921 | 2.8 | 3.0 |
| Nursing and residential care facilities .............................. | 2 818 | 3 261 | 3 997 | 442 | 736 | 1.5 | 2.1 | 168 | 202 | 260 | 1.8 | 2.6 |
| Social assistance ................................................ | 2 374 | 3 367 | 3 698 | 993 | 331 | 3.6 | 0.9 | 133 | 159 | 200 | 1.9 | 2.3 |
| Individual and family services .................................. | 1 102 | 2 032 | 2 319 | 931 | 286 | 6.3 | 1.3 | 55 | 78 | 100 | 3.5 | 2.4 |
| Community, and vocational rehabilitation services .................. | 508 | 482 | 463 | -26 | -18 | -0.5 | -0.4 | 34 | 37 | 47 | 0.7 | 2.5 |
| Child day care services ........................................ | 765 | 853 | 916 | 88 | 63 | 1.1 | 0.7 | 43 | 45 | 54 | 0.3 | 1.9 |
| Arts, entertainment, and recreation ................................ | 1 850 | 2 104 | 2 254 | 254 | 150 | 1.3 | 0.7 | 220 | 274 | 345 | 2.2 | 2.3 |
| Performing arts, spectator sports, and related industries ................ | 368 | 448 | 468 | 80 | 20 | 2.0 | 0.4 | 110 | 132 | 167 | 1.8 | 2.4 |
| Performing arts companies ...................................... | 116 | 112 | 116 | -4 | 3 | -0.3 | 0.3 | 20 | 23 | 29 | 1.5 | 2.4 |
| Spectator sports .............................................. | 120 | 142 | 148 | 22 | 6 | 1.7 | 0.4 | 36 | 39 | 50 | 0.9 | 2.5 |
| Promoters of events, and agents and managers .................... | 90 | 143 | 152 | 54 | 9 | 4.8 | 0.6 | 25 | 35 | 43 | 3.1 | 2.2 |
| Independent artists, writers, and performers ...................... | 42 | 50 | 52 | 8 | 2 | 1.9 | 0.5 | 29 | 35 | 44 | 1.9 | 2.4 |
| Museums, historical sites, and similar institutions .................... | 118 | 145 | 160 | 27 | 14 | 2.1 | 0.9 | 8 | 14 | 18 | 5.1 | 2.7 |
| Amusement, gambling, and recreation industries ..................... | 1 364 | 1 510 | 1 626 | 146 | 116 | 1.0 | 0.7 | 102 | 128 | 161 | 2.3 | 2.3 |
| Amusement parks and arcardes .................................. | 156 | 184 | 204 | 28 | 20 | 1.7 | 1.0 | 16 | 21 | 25 | 2.5 | 1.9 |
| Gambling industries (except casino hotels) ........................ | 139 | 132 | 141 | -7 | 9 | -0.5 | 0.6 | 22 | 30 | 36 | 3.1 | 1.9 |

## Table 4-8. Employment and Output, by Industry, 2004, 2014, and Projected 2024—*Continued*

(Number, percent, dollars.)

| Industry | Employment — Number of jobs (thousands) 2004 | 2014 | 2024 | Employment — Change 2004–2014 | 2014–2024 | Employment — Average annual rate of change (percent) 2004–2014 | 2014–2024 | Output — Billions of chained (2005) dollars 2004 | 2014 | 2024 | Output — Average annual rate of change (percent) 2004–2014 | 2014–2024 |
|---|---|---|---|---|---|---|---|---|---|---|---|---|
| **Professional, Scientific, and Technical Services**—*Continued* | | | | | | | | | | | | |
| Other amusement and recreation | 1 069 | 1 194 | 1 281 | 125 | 87 | 1.1 | 0.7 | 64 | 78 | 100 | 2.0 | 2.5 |
| Accommodation and food services | 10 643 | 12 606 | 13 397 | 1 963 | 791 | 1.7 | 0.6 | 723 | 777 | 956 | 0.7 | 2.1 |
| Accommodation | 1 790 | 1 889 | 2 022 | 100 | 133 | 0.5 | 0.7 | 194 | 197 | 247 | 0.2 | 2.3 |
| Food services and drinking places | 8 854 | 10 717 | 11 375 | 1 863 | 658 | 1.9 | 0.6 | 529 | 580 | 709 | 0.9 | 2.0 |
| Other services | 6 188 | 6 394 | 6 662 | 206 | 268 | 0.3 | 0.4 | 581 | 570 | 706 | -0.2 | 2.2 |
| Repair and maintenance | 1 229 | 1 240 | 1 342 | 12 | 102 | 0.1 | 0.8 | 204 | 195 | 234 | -0.5 | 1.9 |
| Automotive repair and maintenance | 891 | 868 | 953 | -22 | 84 | -0.3 | 0.9 | 128 | 118 | 137 | -0.8 | 1.5 |
| Electronic and precision equipment repair and maintenance | 101 | 101 | 102 | -0.2 | 1 | 0.0 | 0.1 | 20 | 23 | 29 | 1.3 | 2.3 |
| Commercial and industrial machinery and equipment (except automotive and electronic) repair and maintenance | 159 | 199 | 216 | 40 | 18 | 2.3 | 0.8 | 33 | 32 | 41 | -0.1 | 2.5 |
| Personal and household goods repair and maintenance | 78 | 72 | 71 | -6 | -2 | -0.8 | -0.2 | 24 | 22 | 28 | -1.0 | 2.6 |
| Personal and laundry services | 1 273 | 1 369 | 1 448 | 96 | 80 | 0.7 | 0.6 | 166 | 175 | 221 | 0.5 | 2.3 |
| Personal care services | 563 | 654 | 732 | 91 | 77 | 1.5 | 1.1 | 59 | 66 | 85 | 1.0 | 2.6 |
| Death care services | 137 | 133 | 135 | -3 | 2 | -0.3 | 0.1 | 21 | 26 | 28 | 1.9 | 0.7 |
| Drycleaning and laundry services | 352 | 299 | 282 | -53 | -17 | -1.6 | -0.6 | 29 | 27 | 34 | -0.7 | 2.6 |
| Other personal services | 221 | 282 | 299 | 61 | 18 | 2.5 | 0.6 | 57 | 57 | 74 | 0.0 | 2.6 |
| Religious, grantmaking, civic, professional, and similar organizations | 2 908 | 2 964 | 3 032 | 57 | 67 | 0.2 | 0.2 | 192 | 182 | 229 | -0.5 | 2.3 |
| Religious organizations | 1 689 | 1 702 | 1 748 | 13 | 46 | 0.1 | 0.3 | 76 | 70 | 91 | -0.8 | 2.6 |
| Grantmaking and giving services and social advocacy organizations | 303 | 391 | 419 | 88 | 28 | 2.6 | 0.7 | 38 | 47 | 61 | 2.1 | 2.6 |
| Civic, social, professional, and similar organizations | 915 | 871 | 865 | -44 | -6.2 | -0.5 | -0.1 | 78 | 66 | 78 | -1.7 | 1.8 |
| Private households | 779 | 821 | 840 | 42 | 19 | 0.5 | 0.2 | 18 | 18 | 22 | -0.4 | 2.1 |
| **Federal Government** | 2 730 | 2 729 | 2 346 | -1 | -383 | 0.0 | -1.5 | 933 | 1 037 | 1 025 | 1.1 | -0.1 |
| **Postal Service** | 782 | 593 | 428 | -189 | -165 | -2.7 | -3.2 | 82 | 62 | 57 | -2.7 | -0.8 |
| Federal electric utilities | 23 | 18 | 14 | -6 | -3 | -2.6 | -2.1 | 14 | 18 | 22 | 2.2 | 2.1 |
| Federal enterprises except the Postal Service and electric utilities | 88 | 81 | 59 | -7 | -22 | -0.9 | -3.1 | 7 | 19 | 25 | 10.2 | 2.7 |
| Federal defense government compensation | 473 | 522 | 440 | 49 | -82 | 1.0 | -1.7 | 210 | 220 | 212 | 0.5 | -0.4 |
| Federal defense government consumption of fixed capital | 0 | 0 | 0 | 0 | 0 | 0.0 | 0.0 | 118 | 155 | 149 | 2.7 | -0.4 |
| Federal defense government except compensation and consumption of fixed capital | 0 | 0 | 0 | 0 | 0 | 0.0 | 0.0 | 211 | 222 | 221 | 0.5 | 0.0 |
| Federal non-defense government compensation - except enterprises | 1 363 | 1 515 | 1 404 | 152 | -110 | 1.1 | -0.8 | 134 | 148 | 145 | 1.0 | -0.2 |
| Federal non-defense government consumption of fixed capital | 0 | 0 | 0 | 0 | 0 | 0.0 | 0.0 | 72 | 95 | 93 | 2.9 | -0.2 |
| Federal non-defense government except compensation and consumption of fixed capital | 0 | 0 | 0 | 0 | 0 | 0.0 | 0.0 | 86 | 101 | 104 | 1.5 | 0.3 |
| Federal government except enterprises | 1 836 | 2 037 | 1 844 | 201 | -193 | 1.0 | -1.0 | 831 | 940 | 923 | 1.2 | -0.2 |
| **State and Local Government** | 18 891 | 19 134 | 19 890 | 243 | 756 | 0.1 | 0.4 | 2 036 | 2 133 | 2 489 | 0.5 | 1.6 |
| Local government passenger transit | 250 | 278 | 322 | 28 | 44 | 1.1 | 1.5 | 12 | 14 | 17 | 1.3 | 1.9 |
| Local government enterprises except passenger transit | 1 252 | 1 323 | 1 410 | 70 | 86.7 | 0.5 | 0.6 | 177 | 205 | 242 | 1.5 | 1.7 |
| Local government hospitals - compensation | 656 | 644 | 631 | -12 | -13 | -0.2 | -0.2 | 61 | 65 | 72 | 0.6 | 1.2 |
| Local government educational services - compensation | 7 765 | 7 791 | 8 218 | 26 | 426 | 0.0 | 0.5 | 413 | 403 | 452 | -0.2 | 1.2 |
| Local government excluding enterprises, educational services, and hospitals - compensation | 3 986 | 4 038 | 4 150 | 52 | 112 | 0.1 | 0.3 | 304 | 313 | 351 | 0.3 | 1.2 |
| State government enterprises | 544 | 495 | 488 | -49 | -7 | -0.9 | -0.1 | 26 | 30 | 35 | 1.6 | 1.7 |
| State government hospitals - compensation | 348 | 347 | 334 | -0.5 | -13 | 0.0 | -0.4 | 44 | 42 | 47 | -0.6 | 1.2 |
| State government educational services - compensation | 2 238 | 2 409 | 2 514 | 171 | 105 | 0.7 | 0.4 | 116 | 134 | 150 | 1.4 | 1.2 |
| State government, other compensation | 1 852 | 1 809 | 1 824 | -44 | 15 | -0.2 | 0.1 | 165 | 162 | 182 | -0.1 | 1.2 |
| State and local government capital services | 0 | 0 | 0 | 0 | 0 | 0.0 | 0.0 | 142 | 174 | 195 | 2.0 | 1.2 |
| General state and local government except compensation and capital services | 0 | 0 | 0 | 0 | 0 | 0.0 | 0.0 | 577 | 592 | 743 | 0.3 | 2.3 |
| **Owner-Occupied Dwellings** | 0 | 0 | 0 | 0 | 0 | 0.0 | 0.0 | 1 175 | 1 318 | 1 649 | 1.2 | 2.3 |
| **Agriculture, Forestry, Fishing, and Hunting**[3] | 2 111 | 2 138 | 2 028 | 27 | -110 | 0.1 | -0.5 | 342 | 357 | 431 | 0.4 | 1.9 |
| Crop production | 849 | 1 091 | 1 019 | 242 | -71 | 2.5 | -0.7 | 165 | 149 | 181 | -1.0 | 1.9 |
| Animal production and aquaculture | 933 | 763 | 714 | -170 | -49 | -2.0 | -0.7 | 129 | 159 | 193 | 2.1 | 1.9 |
| Forestry | 24 | 21 | 24 | -4 | 3 | -1.6 | 1.2 | 8 | 6 | 7 | -3.0 | 1.9 |
| Logging | 99 | 72 | 64 | -27 | -8 | -3.2 | -1.1 | 16 | 12 | 15 | -2.6 | 1.8 |
| Fishing, hunting and trapping | 52 | 38 | 36 | -14 | -2 | -3.1 | -0.5 | 7 | 8 | 9 | 1.9 | 0.7 |
| Support activities for agriculture and forestry | 154 | 154 | 170 | -0.3 | 17 | 0.0 | 1.1 | 19 | 23 | 28 | 2.0 | 2.0 |
| **Nonagricultural Self-Employed Workers**[4] | 9 474 | 8 590 | 9 170 | -883 | 579 | -1.0 | 0.7 | . . . | . . . | . . . | . . . | . . . |

[3]Comparable estimate of output growth is not available.
[4]Workers who hold a secondary wage and salary job in agricultural production, forestry, fishing, and private household industries.
. . . = Not available.

## Table 4-9.  Civilian Labor Force: Entrants and Leavers, 2004, 2014, and Projected 2024

(Numbers in thousands, percent.)

| Characteristic | 2004 | 2004–2014 | | | 2014 | 2014–2024 | | | 2024 |
|---|---|---|---|---|---|---|---|---|---|
| | | Entrants | Leavers | Stayers | | Entrants | Leavers | Stayers | |
| **Both Sexes, 16 Years and Over** | 147 401 | 33 880 | 25 360 | 122 041 | 155 922 | 36 416 | 28 568 | 127 353 | 163 770 |
| 16 to 24 years | 78 980 | 17 851 | 13 949 | 65 031 | 82 882 | 19 664 | 16 023 | 66 859 | 86 524 |
| Women | 68 421 | 16 029 | 11 411 | 57 010 | 73 039 | 16 752 | 12 545 | 60 494 | 77 246 |
| White | 121 086 | 24 568 | 22 326 | 98 760 | 123 327 | 30 081 | 24 553 | 98 775 | 126 143 |
| Men | 65 994 | 13 323 | 12 637 | 53 357 | 66 680 | 16 616 | 13 114 | 53 566 | 67 849 |
| Women | 55 092 | 11 245 | 9 689 | 45 403 | 56 648 | 13 465 | 11 439 | 45 209 | 58 294 |
| Black | 16 638 | 4 947 | 2 712 | 13 926 | 18 873 | 4 834 | 3 022 | 15 851 | 20 772 |
| Men | 7 773 | 2 372 | 1 236 | 6 537 | 8 909 | 2 468 | 1 491 | 7 418 | 9 683 |
| Women | 8 865 | 2 575 | 1 476 | 7 389 | 9 964 | 2 366 | 1 531 | 8 433 | 11 089 |
| Asian | 6 271 | 2 985 | 601 | 5 671 | 8 760 | 3 005 | 823 | 7 937 | 10 792 |
| Men | 3 396 | 1 497 | 349 | 3 047 | 4 648 | 1 521 | 446 | 4 202 | 5 681 |
| Women | 2 876 | 1 488 | 252 | 2 624 | 4 112 | 1 484 | 377 | 3 735 | 5 111 |
| All other groups[1] | 3 406 | 1 893 | 257 | 3 149 | 4 961 | 2 032 | 930 | 4 031 | 6 063 |
| Men | 1 817 | 997 | 169 | 1 648 | 2 645 | 1 199 | 533 | 2 112 | 3 311 |
| Women | 1 589 | 896 | 88 | 1 501 | 2 316 | 833 | 397 | 1 919 | 2 752 |
| Hispanic origin[2] | 19 272 | 8 032 | 1 933 | 17 339 | 25 370 | 9 710 | 1 966 | 23 405 | 32 486 |
| Men | 11 587 | 4 289 | 1 225 | 10 362 | 14 651 | 5 553 | 1 205 | 13 446 | 18 522 |
| Women | 7 685 | 3 743 | 708 | 6 977 | 10 720 | 4 157 | 761 | 9 959 | 13 964 |
| Other than Hispanic origin | 128 129 | 25 848 | 23 427 | 104 702 | 130 552 | 26 706 | 26 602 | 103 950 | 131 284 |
| Men | 67 393 | 13 562 | 12 724 | 54 669 | 68 231 | 14 111 | 14 818 | 53 413 | 68 002 |
| Women | 60 736 | 12 286 | 10 703 | 50 033 | 62 319 | 12 595 | 11 784 | 50 535 | 63 282 |
| White Non-Hispanic | 103 202 | 17 990 | 20 531 | 91 066 | 100 661 | 18 099 | 19 676 | 80 986 | 97 622 |
| Men | 55 186 | 9 596 | 11 267 | 43 919 | 53 515 | 9 795 | 11 044 | 42 471 | 51 482 |
| Women | 48 017 | 8 394 | 9 264 | 47 147 | 47 147 | 8 304 | 8 632 | 38 515 | 46 140 |
| **SHARE, 16 YEARS AND OVER** | | | | | | | | | |
| **Total** | 100.0 | 100.0 | 100.0 | 100.0 | 100.0 | 100.0 | 100.0 | 100.0 | 100.0 |
| Men | 53.6 | 52.7 | 55.0 | 53.3 | 53.2 | 54.0 | 56.1 | 52.5 | 52.8 |
| Women | 46.4 | 47.3 | 45.0 | 46.7 | 46.8 | 46.0 | 43.9 | 47.5 | 47.2 |
| White | 82.1 | 72.5 | 88.0 | 80.9 | 79.1 | 82.6 | 85.9 | 77.6 | 77.0 |
| Men | 44.8 | 39.3 | 49.8 | 43.7 | 42.8 | 45.6 | 45.9 | 42.1 | 41.4 |
| Women | 37.4 | 33.2 | 38.2 | 37.2 | 36.3 | 37.0 | 40.0 | 35.5 | 35.6 |
| Black | 11.3 | 14.6 | 10.7 | 11.4 | 12.1 | 13.3 | 10.6 | 12.4 | 12.7 |
| Men | 5.3 | 7.0 | 4.9 | 5.4 | 5.7 | 6.8 | 5.2 | 5.8 | 5.9 |
| Women | 6.0 | 7.6 | 5.8 | 6.1 | 6.4 | 6.5 | 5.4 | 6.6 | 6.8 |
| Asian | 4.3 | 8.8 | 2.4 | 4.6 | 5.6 | 8.3 | 2.9 | 6.2 | 6.6 |
| Men | 2.3 | 4.4 | 1.4 | 2.5 | 3.0 | 4.2 | 1.6 | 3.3 | 3.5 |
| Women | 2.0 | 4.4 | 1.0 | 2.2 | 2.6 | 4.1 | 1.3 | 2.9 | 3.1 |
| All other groups[1] | 2.3 | 5.6 | 1.0 | 2.6 | 3.2 | 5.6 | 3.3 | 3.2 | 3.7 |
| Men | 1.2 | 2.9 | 0.7 | 1.4 | 1.7 | 3.3 | 1.9 | 1.7 | 2.0 |
| Women | 1.1 | 2.6 | 0.3 | 1.2 | 1.5 | 2.3 | 1.4 | 1.5 | 1.7 |
| Hispanic origin[2] | 13.1 | 23.7 | 7.6 | 14.2 | 16.3 | 26.7 | 6.9 | 18.4 | 19.8 |
| Men | 7.9 | 12.7 | 4.8 | 8.5 | 9.4 | 15.2 | 4.2 | 10.6 | 11.3 |
| Women | 5.2 | 11.0 | 2.8 | 5.7 | 6.9 | 11.4 | 2.7 | 7.8 | 8.5 |
| Other than Hispanic | 86.9 | 76.3 | 92.4 | 85.8 | 83.7 | 73.3 | 93.1 | 81.6 | 80.2 |
| Men | 45.7 | 40.0 | 50.2 | 44.8 | 43.8 | 38.7 | 51.9 | 41.9 | 41.5 |
| Women | 41.2 | 36.3 | 42.2 | 41.0 | 40.0 | 34.6 | 41.2 | 39.7 | 38.6 |
| White Non-Hispanic | 70.0 | 53.1 | 81.0 | 74.6 | 64.6 | 49.7 | 68.9 | 63.6 | 59.6 |
| Men | 37.4 | 28.3 | 44.4 | 36.0 | 34.3 | 26.9 | 38.7 | 33.3 | 31.4 |
| Women | 32.6 | 24.8 | 36.5 | 38.6 | 30.2 | 22.8 | 30.2 | 30.2 | 28.2 |

[1]The "All other groups" category includes those classified as of multiple racial origin and the race categories of American Indian and Alaska Native and Native Hawaiian and Other Pacific Islanders.
[2]May be of any race.

## Table 4-10.  Employment and Wages by Summary Education Assignment, 2014 and Projected 2014–2024

(Numbers in thousands, percent, dollars.)

| Education, work experience, and on-the-job training | 2014 Employment | | Employment changes, 2014–2024 (percent) | Median annual wage, 2014 |
|---|---|---|---|---|
| | Number | Percent distribution | | |
| **TOTAL, ALL OCCUPATIONS** | 150 540 | 100.0 | 6.5 | 35 540 |
| Doctoral or professional degree | 4 112 | 2.7 | 12.2 | 98 940 |
| Master's degree | 2 519 | 1.7 | 13.8 | 65 330 |
| Bachelor's degree | 31 849 | 21.2 | 8.2 | 69 260 |
| Associate's degree | 3 458 | 2.3 | 8.7 | 49 470 |
| Postsecondary nondegree award | 9 091 | 6.0 | 11.5 | 34 880 |
| Some college, no degree | 3 786 | 2.5 | 0.5 | 33 250 |
| High school diploma or equivalent | 54 927 | 36.5 | 3.9 | 35 540 |
| No formal educational credential | 40 799 | 27.1 | 6.9 | 20 730 |

# CHAPTER 5: PRODUCTIVITY AND COSTS

## HIGHLIGHTS

This chapter covers two kinds of productivity measures produced by the Bureau of Labor Statistics (BLS): output per hour (or labor productivity) and multifactor productivity. Multifactor productivity is designed to combine the joint influence of technological change, efficiency improvements, returns to scale, and other factors on economic growth.

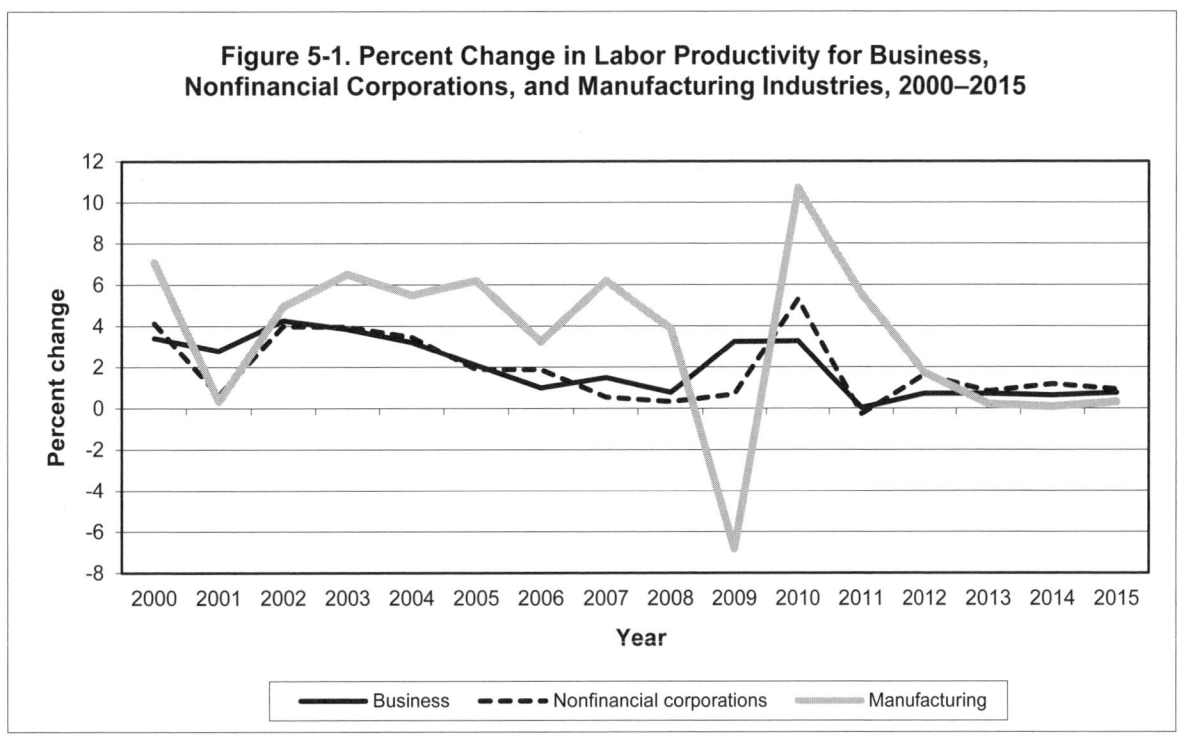

**Figure 5-1. Percent Change in Labor Productivity for Business, Nonfinancial Corporations, and Manufacturing Industries, 2000–2015**

In 2015, labor productivity increased slightly in all the major sectors. It increased 0.9 percent in nonfarm business and nonfinancial corporations, 0.8 percent in business and only 0.3 percent in manufacturing. (See Table 5-1.)

## OTHER HIGHLIGHTS

- Productivity increased in a majority of industries between 2007 and 2014, despite the fact that a long part of the period encompassed a severe recession. (See Table 5-2.)

- From 1987 through 2015, productivity grew on average 2.9 percent in wholesale trade, 2.8 percent in retail trade, 0.4 percent in food services and drinking places. (See Table 5-3.)

- The growth in productivity from 1987 to 2007 far exceeded the growth in productivity from 2007 to 2015 in all three industry groups (wholesale trade; retail trade; food services, and drinking places). Productivity increased in 45 out of 49 4-digit industries from 1987 to 2007 compared to 28 industries from 2007 to 2015. (See Table 5-3.)

- From 1987 to 2015, unit labor costs increased at an average annual rate of 3.1 percent in food services and drinking places, the greatest change within the three industry groups. Unit labor costs increased by 1.0 percent in wholesale trade and were unchanged in retail trade. (See Table 5-3.)

# NOTES AND DEFINITIONS

## PRODUCTIVITY AND COSTS

The Bureau of Labor Statistics (BLS) produces labor productivity and costs (LPC) measures for sectors of the U.S. economy. Productivity is a measure of economic efficiency that shows how effectively economic inputs are converted into output. The Major Sector Productivity program develops quarterly labor productivity measures for the major U.S. economic sectors including the business sector, the nonfarm business sector, nonfinancial corporations, and manufacturing, along with subsectors of durable and nondurable goods manufacturing. The Industry Productivity program develops annual labor productivity and unit labor cost measures for U.S. industries. In addition, the BLS produces multifactor productivity measures.

Quarterly labor productivity measures are available for business and nonfarm business sectors, nonfinancial corporations and Manufacturing sector. Annual labor productivity measures are available for selected 2-, 3-, 4-, 5-, and 6-digit NAICS industries.

## Concepts and Definitions

*Business sector output* is an annual-weighted index constructed after excluding from gross domestic product (GDP) the following outputs: General government, nonprofit institutions, paid employees of private households, and the rental value of owner-occupied dwellings. Corresponding exclusions also are made in labor inputs. The nonfarm business sector output also excludes the farm sector. Gross domestic product data are prepared by the Bureau of Economic Analysis of the U.S. Department of Commerce as part of the National Income and Product Accounts.

*Hourly compensation costs* are defined as the sum of wage and salary accruals and supplements to wages and salaries. Wage and salary accruals consist of the monetary remuneration of employees, including the compensation of corporate officers; commissions, tips, and bonuses; voluntary employee contributions to certain deferred compensation plans, such as 401(k) plans; employee gains from exercising nonqualified stock options; and receipts in kind that represent income. Supplements to wages and salaries consist of employer contributions for social insurance and employer payments (including payments in kind) to private pension and profit-sharing plans, group health and life insurance plans, privately administered workers' compensation plans. For employees (wage and salary workers), hourly compensation is measured relative to hours at work and includes payments made by employers for time not at work, such as vacation, holiday, and sick pay. Because compensation costs for the business and nonfarm business sectors would otherwise be severely understated, an estimate of the hourly compensation of proprietors of unincorporated businesses is made by assuming that their hourly compensation is equal to that of employees in the same sector.

Hours at work include paid time working, traveling between job sites, coffee breaks, and machine downtime. Hours at work, however, exclude hours for which employees are paid but not at work.

The *Nonfarm business sector* is a subset of the domestic economy and excludes the economic activities of the following: general government, private households, nonprofit organizations serving individuals, and farms.

*Nonfinancial corporations* are a subset of the domestic economy and excludes the economic activities of the following: general government, private households, nonprofit organizations serving individuals, and those corporations classified as offices of bank holding companies, offices of other holding companies, or offices in the finance and insurance sector.

*Nonlabor payments* include profits, consumption of fixed capital, taxes on production and imports less subsidies, net interest and miscellaneous payments, business current transfer payments, rental income of persons, and the current surplus of government enterprises.

*Output* is measured as an annual-weighted index of the changes in the various products or services (in real terms) provided for sale outside the industry. Real industry output is usually derived by deflating nominal sales or values of production using BLS price indexes, but for some industries it is measured by physical quantities of output. Industry output measures are constructed primarily using data from the economic censuses and annual surveys of the U.S. Census Bureau, U.S. Department of Commerce, together with information on price changes primarily from BLS. Output measures for some mining and utilities industries are based on physical quantity data from the Energy Information Administration, U.S. Department of Energy, while output measures for some transportation industries are based on physical quantity data from the Bureau of Transportation Statistics, U.S. Department of Transportation. Other data sources for some industries include the U.S. Geological Survey, U.S. Department of the Interior; the U.S. Postal Service; the Federal Deposit Insurance Corporation; and the Postal Rate Commission.

*Productivity* measures describe the relationship between industry output and the labor time involved in its production. They show the changes from period to period in the amount of goods and services produced per hour. Although the labor productivity measures relate output to hours of employees or all persons in an industry, they do not measure the specific contribution of labor or any other factor of production. Rather, they reflect the joint effects of many influences, including changes in technology; capital investment; utilization of capacity, energy, and materials; the use of purchased services inputs, including contract employment services; the organization of production; managerial skill; and the characteristics and effort of the workforce.

*Unit labor costs* show the growth in compensation relative to that of real output. These costs are calculated by dividing total labor compensation by real output. Changes in unit labor costs can be approximated by subtracting the change in productivity from the change in hourly compensation.

## Multifactor Productivity Concepts and Definitions

For the private business and private nonfarm business sectors, the growth rate of multifactor productivity is measured as the growth rate of output less the growth rate of combined inputs of labor and capital. Labor is measured by a weighted average of the number of hours worked classified by education, work experience, and gender. Capital services measure the flow of services from the stocks of equipment and software, structures, land, and inventories. For the manufacturing sector, multifactor productivity is the growth rate of output less the combined inputs of labor, capital, and intermediate purchases. Labor is measured by the number of hours worked. Capital services measure the flow of services from the stocks of equipment and software, structures, land, and inventories. Intermediate purchases are composed of materials, fuels, electricity, and purchased services.

*Sectoral output* is defined as gross output excluding intra-industry transactions. This measure defines output as deliveries to consumers outside the sector, in an effort to avoid the problem of double-counting that occurs when one establishment provides materials used by other establishments in the same industry.

*Value-added output* is defined as gross output (sales or receipts and other income, plus inventory change) minus intermediate inputs (goods and service inputs purchased from other domestic industries and foreign sources).

## Sources of Additional Information

Productivity concepts and methodology are described in Chapters 10 and 11 of the *BLS Handbook of Methods*. More information on productivity can be found in BLS news releases on the BLS Web site at <http://www.bls.gov/lpc/>. More information can be found in BLS new release USDL16-1654 "Productivity and Costs by Industry: Wholesale Trade, Retail Trade, and Food Services and Drinking Places Industries, 2015" as well as BLS new release 16-0988 "Productivity and Costs by Industry: Selected Service-Providing Industries, 2015."

## Table 5-1. Indexes of Productivity and Related Data, 1947–2015

(2009 = 100.)

| Year | Business | | | | | | | | | | | |
|------|----------|--------|-------|-------------------------------|-----------------------------------|--------------------|------------------------------|-------------------------------|------------|----------------|---------------------------------------------|-------------------------------------------|
| | Output per hour | Output | Hours | Hourly compen-sation | Real hourly compen-sation | Unit labor costs | Unit nonlabor payments | Implicit price deflator | Employment | Output per job | Compen-sation in current dollars | Nonlabor payments in current dollars |
| 1947 | 21.5 | 12.3 | 57.0 | 3.8 | 33.8 | 17.8 | 12.9 | 15.8 | 48.3 | 25.5 | 2.2 | 1.6 |
| 1948 | 22.5 | 12.9 | 57.5 | 4.2 | 33.9 | 18.6 | 14.2 | 16.8 | 48.8 | 26.5 | 2.4 | 1.8 |
| 1949 | 23.0 | 12.8 | 55.6 | 4.2 | 34.8 | 18.4 | 14.1 | 16.6 | 47.7 | 26.8 | 2.4 | 1.8 |
| 1950 | 24.9 | 14.0 | 56.4 | 4.5 | 36.8 | 18.2 | 14.8 | 16.8 | 48.2 | 29.1 | 2.6 | 2.1 |
| 1951 | 25.6 | 14.9 | 58.2 | 5.0 | 37.4 | 19.4 | 16.3 | 18.1 | 49.5 | 30.2 | 2.9 | 2.4 |
| 1952 | 26.4 | 15.4 | 58.3 | 5.3 | 38.9 | 20.0 | 16.0 | 18.3 | 49.7 | 31.0 | 3.1 | 2.5 |
| 1953 | 27.4 | 16.2 | 59.1 | 5.6 | 41.1 | 20.5 | 15.6 | 18.4 | 50.4 | 32.1 | 3.3 | 2.5 |
| 1954 | 28.0 | 16.0 | 57.1 | 5.8 | 42.1 | 20.7 | 15.6 | 18.5 | 49.2 | 32.5 | 3.3 | 2.5 |
| 1955 | 29.2 | 17.3 | 59.2 | 5.9 | 43.3 | 20.3 | 16.6 | 18.8 | 50.6 | 34.2 | 3.5 | 2.9 |
| 1956 | 29.3 | 17.6 | 60.1 | 6.3 | 45.5 | 21.6 | 16.3 | 19.4 | 51.6 | 34.1 | 3.8 | 2.9 |
| 1957 | 30.2 | 17.9 | 59.2 | 6.7 | 46.9 | 22.3 | 16.8 | 20.0 | 51.5 | 34.7 | 4.0 | 3.0 |
| 1958 | 31.1 | 17.6 | 56.6 | 7.0 | 47.6 | 22.6 | 17.2 | 20.4 | 49.6 | 35.5 | 4.0 | 3.0 |
| 1959 | 32.2 | 19.0 | 59.0 | 7.3 | 49.2 | 22.7 | 17.6 | 20.6 | 51.1 | 37.1 | 4.3 | 3.3 |
| 1960 | 32.7 | 19.3 | 59.0 | 7.6 | 50.4 | 23.3 | 17.4 | 20.8 | 51.4 | 37.6 | 4.5 | 3.4 |
| 1961 | 33.9 | 19.7 | 58.2 | 7.9 | 51.8 | 23.3 | 17.7 | 21.0 | 50.8 | 38.8 | 4.6 | 3.5 |
| 1962 | 35.5 | 21.0 | 59.2 | 8.3 | 53.6 | 23.3 | 18.2 | 21.2 | 51.5 | 40.8 | 4.9 | 3.8 |
| 1963 | 36.9 | 22.0 | 59.6 | 8.6 | 54.8 | 23.2 | 18.6 | 21.3 | 51.8 | 42.5 | 5.1 | 4.1 |
| 1964 | 38.1 | 23.4 | 61.3 | 8.9 | 56.1 | 23.3 | 19.1 | 21.5 | 52.7 | 44.3 | 5.5 | 4.5 |
| 1965 | 39.5 | 25.0 | 63.4 | 9.2 | 57.3 | 23.4 | 19.8 | 21.9 | 54.3 | 46.2 | 5.8 | 5.0 |
| 1966 | 41.1 | 26.7 | 65.1 | 9.8 | 59.5 | 23.9 | 20.3 | 22.4 | 55.9 | 47.9 | 6.4 | 5.4 |
| 1967 | 42.1 | 27.3 | 64.9 | 10.4 | 61.0 | 24.7 | 20.6 | 23.0 | 56.6 | 48.2 | 6.7 | 5.6 |
| 1968 | 43.5 | 28.7 | 65.9 | 11.2 | 63.1 | 25.7 | 21.4 | 23.9 | 57.7 | 49.7 | 7.4 | 6.1 |
| 1969 | 43.8 | 29.6 | 67.5 | 12.0 | 64.0 | 27.4 | 21.6 | 25.0 | 59.5 | 49.6 | 8.1 | 6.4 |
| 1970 | 44.6 | 29.5 | 66.2 | 12.9 | 65.1 | 28.9 | 22.2 | 26.1 | 59.4 | 49.8 | 8.5 | 6.5 |
| 1971 | 46.4 | 30.7 | 66.0 | 13.7 | 66.1 | 29.4 | 24.0 | 27.2 | 59.5 | 51.5 | 9.0 | 7.4 |
| 1972 | 48.0 | 32.7 | 68.1 | 14.5 | 68.0 | 30.3 | 25.1 | 28.1 | 61.2 | 53.3 | 9.9 | 8.2 |
| 1973 | 49.4 | 34.9 | 70.7 | 15.7 | 69.1 | 31.7 | 26.6 | 29.6 | 63.9 | 54.7 | 11.1 | 9.3 |
| 1974 | 48.5 | 34.4 | 70.8 | 17.1 | 68.1 | 35.3 | 28.6 | 32.5 | 64.8 | 53.0 | 12.1 | 9.8 |
| 1975 | 50.3 | 34.0 | 67.7 | 19.0 | 69.0 | 37.8 | 32.7 | 35.6 | 62.9 | 54.1 | 12.9 | 11.1 |
| 1976 | 51.9 | 36.3 | 70.0 | 20.5 | 70.5 | 39.5 | 34.8 | 37.5 | 64.8 | 56.0 | 14.3 | 12.6 |
| 1977 | 52.8 | 38.4 | 72.7 | 22.1 | 71.5 | 41.9 | 36.8 | 39.7 | 67.7 | 56.8 | 16.1 | 14.1 |
| 1978 | 53.4 | 40.8 | 76.4 | 24.0 | 72.4 | 44.9 | 39.2 | 42.5 | 71.4 | 57.2 | 18.3 | 16.0 |
| 1979 | 53.5 | 42.3 | 79.0 | 26.3 | 72.6 | 49.2 | 41.8 | 46.1 | 74.2 | 57.0 | 20.8 | 17.7 |
| 1980 | 53.5 | 41.9 | 78.3 | 29.1 | 72.3 | 54.5 | 44.2 | 50.2 | 74.3 | 56.3 | 22.8 | 18.5 |
| 1981 | 54.7 | 43.1 | 78.8 | 31.9 | 72.2 | 58.4 | 49.9 | 54.8 | 75.1 | 57.4 | 25.2 | 21.5 |
| 1982 | 54.2 | 41.8 | 77.1 | 34.2 | 73.1 | 63.1 | 50.9 | 58.0 | 73.9 | 56.6 | 26.4 | 21.3 |
| 1983 | 56.2 | 44.1 | 78.4 | 35.8 | 73.3 | 63.6 | 55.0 | 60.0 | 74.5 | 59.2 | 28.1 | 24.2 |
| 1984 | 57.8 | 48.0 | 83.0 | 37.4 | 73.5 | 64.7 | 57.7 | 61.7 | 78.3 | 61.3 | 31.0 | 27.7 |
| 1985 | 59.1 | 50.2 | 84.9 | 39.3 | 74.7 | 66.5 | 59.3 | 63.5 | 80.2 | 62.6 | 33.4 | 29.8 |
| 1986 | 60.8 | 52.0 | 85.6 | 41.5 | 77.5 | 68.3 | 58.9 | 64.3 | 81.5 | 63.8 | 35.5 | 30.6 |
| 1987 | 61.1 | 53.9 | 88.2 | 43.1 | 77.8 | 70.5 | 58.9 | 65.6 | 83.8 | 64.3 | 38.0 | 31.7 |
| 1988 | 62.0 | 56.2 | 90.6 | 45.3 | 79.0 | 73.1 | 60.2 | 67.7 | 86.3 | 65.1 | 41.1 | 33.8 |
| 1989 | 62.7 | 58.3 | 93.0 | 46.7 | 78.1 | 74.5 | 64.2 | 70.2 | 88.2 | 66.1 | 43.4 | 37.4 |
| 1990 | 64.1 | 59.3 | 92.4 | 49.7 | 79.2 | 77.6 | 65.4 | 72.5 | 88.8 | 66.8 | 46.0 | 38.8 |
| 1991 | 65.3 | 58.9 | 90.3 | 52.2 | 80.2 | 79.9 | 67.1 | 74.5 | 87.4 | 67.4 | 47.1 | 39.5 |
| 1992 | 68.2 | 61.4 | 90.1 | 55.3 | 82.8 | 81.0 | 68.4 | 75.7 | 86.9 | 70.7 | 49.8 | 42.0 |
| 1993 | 68.3 | 63.2 | 92.5 | 56.1 | 82.0 | 82.1 | 71.0 | 77.5 | 88.8 | 71.2 | 51.9 | 44.9 |
| 1994 | 68.8 | 66.2 | 96.2 | 56.6 | 81.1 | 82.2 | 74.2 | 78.9 | 91.8 | 72.2 | 54.5 | 49.1 |
| 1995 | 69.1 | 68.3 | 98.9 | 57.7 | 80.8 | 83.6 | 75.6 | 80.2 | 94.4 | 72.4 | 57.1 | 51.7 |
| 1996 | 71.2 | 71.5 | 100.5 | 60.1 | 81.9 | 84.5 | 77.3 | 81.5 | 96.5 | 74.1 | 60.4 | 55.3 |
| 1997 | 72.5 | 75.3 | 103.9 | 62.3 | 83.1 | 86.0 | 78.1 | 82.7 | 99.1 | 76.0 | 64.7 | 58.8 |
| 1998 | 74.7 | 79.2 | 105.9 | 66.0 | 86.8 | 88.3 | 75.9 | 83.1 | 101.1 | 78.3 | 69.9 | 60.1 |
| 1999 | 77.3 | 83.6 | 108.0 | 68.9 | 88.8 | 89.1 | 76.3 | 83.7 | 102.8 | 81.3 | 74.4 | 63.8 |
| 2000 | 80.0 | 87.3 | 109.2 | 73.9 | 92.1 | 92.4 | 75.3 | 85.3 | 104.5 | 83.5 | 80.7 | 65.8 |
| 2001 | 82.2 | 87.9 | 106.9 | 77.3 | 93.7 | 94.1 | 76.6 | 86.8 | 103.8 | 84.7 | 82.7 | 67.4 |
| 2002 | 85.7 | 89.5 | 104.4 | 79.0 | 94.3 | 92.2 | 80.7 | 87.4 | 101.5 | 88.1 | 82.5 | 72.2 |
| 2003 | 89.0 | 92.3 | 103.7 | 82.0 | 95.7 | 92.2 | 83.7 | 88.6 | 101.3 | 91.1 | 85.1 | 77.3 |
| 2004 | 91.9 | 96.5 | 105.0 | 85.8 | 97.5 | 93.4 | 86.8 | 90.7 | 102.7 | 94.0 | 90.1 | 83.7 |
| 2005 | 93.8 | 100.1 | 106.8 | 88.9 | 97.7 | 94.8 | 91.6 | 93.5 | 104.6 | 95.8 | 94.9 | 91.8 |
| 2006 | 94.7 | 103.3 | 109.1 | 92.4 | 98.3 | 97.6 | 93.9 | 96.0 | 106.6 | 96.9 | 100.8 | 97.0 |
| 2007 | 96.1 | 105.5 | 109.7 | 96.5 | 99.9 | 100.4 | 95.2 | 98.2 | 107.5 | 98.1 | 105.9 | 100.4 |
| 2008 | 96.9 | 104.2 | 107.6 | 99.0 | 98.7 | 102.2 | 96.3 | 99.8 | 106.0 | 98.4 | 106.6 | 100.4 |
| 2009 | 100.0 | 100.0 | 100.0 | 100.0 | 100.0 | 100.0 | 100.0 | 100.0 | 100.0 | 100.0 | 100.0 | 100.0 |
| 2010 | 103.3 | 103.2 | 99.9 | 101.8 | 100.2 | 98.6 | 104.7 | 101.1 | 98.8 | 104.4 | 101.7 | 108.0 |
| 2011 | 103.3 | 105.3 | 102.0 | 104.0 | 99.2 | 100.7 | 107.0 | 103.3 | 100.4 | 104.9 | 106.1 | 112.8 |
| 2012 | 104.0 | 108.4 | 104.2 | 106.8 | 99.8 | 102.7 | 108.9 | 105.3 | 102.4 | 105.9 | 111.4 | 118.0 |
| 2013 | 104.8 | 110.8 | 105.8 | 108.3 | 99.8 | 103.4 | 111.8 | 106.9 | 104.1 | 106.5 | 114.6 | 123.9 |
| 2014 | 105.4 | 114.1 | 108.2 | 111.1 | 100.7 | 105.4 | 112.9 | 108.5 | 106.3 | 107.4 | 120.3 | 128.8 |
| 2015 | 106.2 | 117.6 | 110.7 | 114.3 | 103.4 | 107.5 | 111.7 | 109.3 | 108.8 | 108.1 | 126.5 | 131.4 |

## Table 5-1. Indexes of Productivity and Related Data, 1947–2015—*Continued*

(2009 = 100.)

| Year | Nonfarm business | | | | | | | | | | | |
|---|---|---|---|---|---|---|---|---|---|---|---|---|
| | Output per hour | Output | Hours | Hourly compen-sation | Real hourly compen-sation | Unit labor costs | Unit nonlabor payments | Implicit price deflator | Employment | Output per job | Compen-sation in current dollars | Nonlabor payments in current dollars |
| 1947 | 24.9 | 12.1 | 48.4 | 4.1 | 36.2 | 16.5 | 12.2 | 14.7 | 40.5 | 24.9 | 2.0 | 1.5 |
| 1948 | 25.6 | 12.6 | 49.2 | 4.5 | 36.4 | 17.5 | 13.2 | 15.7 | 41.4 | 25.6 | 2.2 | 1.7 |
| 1949 | 26.4 | 12.5 | 47.3 | 4.6 | 37.9 | 17.5 | 13.6 | 15.8 | 40.2 | 26.4 | 2.2 | 1.7 |
| 1950 | 28.1 | 13.7 | 48.8 | 4.9 | 39.7 | 17.3 | 14.2 | 16.0 | 41.2 | 28.1 | 2.4 | 1.9 |
| 1951 | 28.9 | 14.8 | 51.1 | 5.3 | 39.9 | 18.4 | 15.2 | 17.1 | 43.0 | 28.9 | 2.7 | 2.2 |
| 1952 | 29.4 | 15.2 | 51.7 | 5.6 | 41.4 | 19.0 | 15.2 | 17.4 | 43.5 | 29.4 | 2.9 | 2.3 |
| 1953 | 30.1 | 16.0 | 53.0 | 5.9 | 43.3 | 19.6 | 15.2 | 17.8 | 44.8 | 30.1 | 3.1 | 2.4 |
| 1954 | 30.7 | 15.7 | 51.2 | 6.1 | 44.4 | 19.8 | 15.2 | 17.9 | 43.6 | 30.7 | 3.1 | 2.4 |
| 1955 | 32.0 | 17.1 | 53.2 | 6.3 | 46.2 | 19.7 | 16.1 | 18.2 | 44.9 | 32.0 | 3.4 | 2.8 |
| 1956 | 31.9 | 17.4 | 54.6 | 6.7 | 48.3 | 21.1 | 15.8 | 18.9 | 46.2 | 31.9 | 3.7 | 2.8 |
| 1957 | 32.7 | 17.7 | 54.3 | 7.1 | 49.4 | 21.7 | 16.4 | 19.5 | 46.5 | 32.7 | 3.9 | 2.9 |
| 1958 | 33.4 | 17.4 | 52.0 | 7.4 | 50.0 | 22.1 | 16.6 | 19.8 | 44.8 | 33.4 | 3.8 | 2.9 |
| 1959 | 34.6 | 18.8 | 54.4 | 7.7 | 51.5 | 22.1 | 17.2 | 20.1 | 46.5 | 34.6 | 4.2 | 3.2 |
| 1960 | 35.0 | 19.2 | 54.7 | 8.0 | 52.9 | 22.8 | 16.8 | 20.3 | 47.0 | 35.0 | 4.4 | 3.2 |
| 1961 | 36.2 | 19.6 | 54.1 | 8.3 | 54.1 | 22.8 | 17.2 | 20.5 | 46.6 | 36.2 | 4.5 | 3.4 |
| 1962 | 37.8 | 20.9 | 55.3 | 8.6 | 55.7 | 22.7 | 17.8 | 20.7 | 47.5 | 37.8 | 4.8 | 3.7 |
| 1963 | 39.1 | 21.9 | 55.9 | 8.9 | 56.8 | 22.7 | 18.2 | 20.8 | 48.0 | 39.1 | 5.0 | 4.0 |
| 1964 | 40.2 | 23.3 | 58.0 | 9.2 | 57.9 | 22.8 | 18.7 | 21.1 | 49.2 | 40.2 | 5.3 | 4.4 |
| 1965 | 41.5 | 25.0 | 60.2 | 9.5 | 58.8 | 22.8 | 19.4 | 21.4 | 50.9 | 41.5 | 5.7 | 4.8 |
| 1966 | 43.0 | 26.8 | 62.3 | 10.0 | 60.6 | 23.3 | 19.8 | 21.8 | 52.9 | 43.0 | 6.2 | 5.3 |
| 1967 | 43.8 | 27.3 | 62.3 | 10.6 | 62.2 | 24.2 | 20.2 | 22.5 | 53.8 | 43.8 | 6.6 | 5.5 |
| 1968 | 45.4 | 28.8 | 63.4 | 11.4 | 64.2 | 25.1 | 21.0 | 23.4 | 55.1 | 45.4 | 7.2 | 6.0 |
| 1969 | 45.5 | 29.7 | 65.2 | 12.2 | 65.0 | 26.8 | 21.1 | 24.4 | 57.0 | 45.5 | 8.0 | 6.3 |
| 1970 | 46.1 | 29.6 | 64.2 | 13.0 | 65.8 | 28.3 | 21.7 | 25.5 | 57.1 | 46.1 | 8.4 | 6.4 |
| 1971 | 47.9 | 30.7 | 64.1 | 13.8 | 66.9 | 28.9 | 23.5 | 26.6 | 57.2 | 47.9 | 8.9 | 7.2 |
| 1972 | 49.6 | 32.8 | 66.1 | 14.7 | 69.0 | 29.7 | 24.3 | 27.4 | 59.0 | 49.6 | 9.7 | 8.0 |
| 1973 | 51.1 | 35.2 | 68.8 | 15.8 | 69.9 | 31.0 | 24.8 | 28.4 | 61.6 | 51.1 | 10.9 | 8.7 |
| 1974 | 50.2 | 34.6 | 68.9 | 17.3 | 68.9 | 34.5 | 27.0 | 31.4 | 62.6 | 50.2 | 12.0 | 9.3 |
| 1975 | 51.6 | 34.1 | 66.0 | 19.2 | 69.8 | 37.2 | 31.3 | 34.7 | 60.8 | 51.6 | 12.7 | 10.7 |
| 1976 | 53.4 | 36.5 | 68.3 | 20.7 | 71.1 | 38.7 | 33.7 | 36.6 | 62.9 | 53.4 | 14.1 | 12.3 |
| 1977 | 54.3 | 38.6 | 71.0 | 22.4 | 72.2 | 41.2 | 35.8 | 38.9 | 65.7 | 54.3 | 15.9 | 13.8 |
| 1978 | 55.0 | 41.1 | 74.7 | 24.3 | 73.3 | 44.1 | 37.8 | 41.5 | 69.4 | 55.0 | 18.1 | 15.6 |
| 1979 | 54.9 | 42.5 | 77.4 | 26.6 | 73.3 | 48.5 | 40.1 | 45.0 | 72.3 | 54.9 | 20.6 | 17.1 |
| 1980 | 54.8 | 42.1 | 76.8 | 29.5 | 73.0 | 53.7 | 43.1 | 49.3 | 72.6 | 54.8 | 22.6 | 18.1 |
| 1981 | 55.7 | 43.1 | 77.3 | 32.3 | 73.1 | 58.0 | 48.4 | 54.0 | 73.4 | 55.7 | 25.0 | 20.8 |
| 1982 | 55.1 | 41.7 | 75.6 | 34.6 | 74.0 | 62.8 | 49.8 | 57.4 | 72.2 | 55.1 | 26.2 | 20.8 |
| 1983 | 57.6 | 44.4 | 77.1 | 36.2 | 74.2 | 62.9 | 54.1 | 59.2 | 72.9 | 57.6 | 27.9 | 24.0 |
| 1984 | 58.8 | 48.1 | 81.8 | 37.8 | 74.3 | 64.2 | 56.3 | 60.9 | 76.8 | 58.8 | 30.9 | 27.1 |
| 1985 | 59.8 | 50.2 | 84.0 | 39.6 | 75.3 | 66.3 | 58.3 | 62.9 | 79.0 | 59.8 | 33.2 | 29.2 |
| 1986 | 61.6 | 52.1 | 84.6 | 41.9 | 78.3 | 68.0 | 58.0 | 63.8 | 80.4 | 61.6 | 35.4 | 30.2 |
| 1987 | 61.9 | 54.0 | 87.2 | 43.5 | 78.6 | 70.2 | 57.9 | 65.1 | 82.7 | 61.9 | 37.9 | 31.2 |
| 1988 | 62.9 | 56.4 | 89.7 | 45.7 | 79.7 | 72.7 | 59.3 | 67.1 | 85.3 | 62.9 | 41.0 | 33.4 |
| 1989 | 63.5 | 58.5 | 92.1 | 47.0 | 78.6 | 74.1 | 63.1 | 69.5 | 87.2 | 63.5 | 43.3 | 36.9 |
| 1990 | 64.7 | 59.4 | 91.8 | 50.0 | 79.6 | 77.2 | 64.3 | 71.8 | 87.9 | 64.7 | 45.9 | 38.2 |
| 1991 | 65.9 | 59.0 | 89.6 | 52.5 | 80.6 | 79.6 | 66.3 | 74.1 | 86.4 | 65.9 | 47.0 | 39.2 |
| 1992 | 68.8 | 61.4 | 89.3 | 55.6 | 83.3 | 80.9 | 67.5 | 75.3 | 86.0 | 68.8 | 49.7 | 41.4 |
| 1993 | 68.8 | 63.3 | 92.0 | 56.3 | 82.3 | 81.8 | 70.4 | 77.0 | 88.0 | 68.8 | 51.8 | 44.6 |
| 1994 | 69.5 | 66.3 | 95.4 | 57.0 | 81.6 | 82.0 | 73.5 | 78.5 | 90.9 | 69.5 | 54.3 | 48.7 |
| 1995 | 70.0 | 68.6 | 98.0 | 58.1 | 81.3 | 83.1 | 75.3 | 79.8 | 93.5 | 70.0 | 56.9 | 51.6 |
| 1996 | 71.9 | 71.7 | 99.7 | 60.5 | 82.4 | 84.2 | 76.4 | 80.9 | 95.7 | 71.9 | 60.3 | 54.7 |
| 1997 | 73.0 | 75.4 | 103.2 | 62.6 | 83.5 | 85.7 | 77.5 | 82.3 | 98.4 | 73.0 | 64.6 | 58.5 |
| 1998 | 75.3 | 79.4 | 105.5 | 66.2 | 87.1 | 88.0 | 75.5 | 82.8 | 100.6 | 75.3 | 69.9 | 60.0 |
| 1999 | 77.7 | 83.8 | 107.8 | 69.0 | 88.9 | 88.8 | 76.3 | 83.6 | 102.5 | 77.7 | 74.4 | 63.9 |
| 2000 | 80.3 | 87.5 | 108.9 | 74.1 | 92.3 | 92.3 | 75.3 | 85.2 | 104.3 | 80.3 | 80.7 | 65.8 |
| 2001 | 82.5 | 88.1 | 106.8 | 77.4 | 93.7 | 93.8 | 76.6 | 86.6 | 103.7 | 82.5 | 82.6 | 67.5 |
| 2002 | 86.1 | 89.7 | 104.2 | 79.1 | 94.4 | 91.9 | 80.9 | 87.3 | 101.3 | 86.1 | 82.4 | 72.5 |
| 2003 | 89.2 | 92.5 | 103.6 | 82.1 | 95.7 | 92.0 | 83.5 | 88.5 | 101.3 | 89.2 | 85.1 | 77.2 |
| 2004 | 92.0 | 96.6 | 105.0 | 85.8 | 97.5 | 93.3 | 86.2 | 90.3 | 102.7 | 92.0 | 90.1 | 83.2 |
| 2005 | 93.9 | 100.2 | 106.8 | 88.9 | 97.7 | 94.7 | 91.5 | 93.4 | 104.5 | 93.9 | 95.0 | 91.7 |
| 2006 | 94.7 | 103.4 | 109.2 | 92.4 | 98.3 | 97.5 | 93.9 | 96.0 | 106.6 | 94.7 | 100.9 | 97.1 |
| 2007 | 96.3 | 105.8 | 109.9 | 96.4 | 99.7 | 100.1 | 94.9 | 97.9 | 107.6 | 96.3 | 105.9 | 100.4 |
| 2008 | 97.0 | 104.4 | 107.7 | 99.0 | 98.6 | 102.1 | 95.8 | 99.4 | 106.0 | 97.0 | 106.6 | 100.0 |
| 2009 | 100.0 | 100.0 | 100.0 | 100.0 | 100.0 | 100.0 | 100.0 | 100.0 | 100.0 | 100.0 | 100.0 | 100.0 |
| 2010 | 103.3 | 103.2 | 99.9 | 101.9 | 100.3 | 98.7 | 104.2 | 101.0 | 98.8 | 103.3 | 101.8 | 107.5 |
| 2011 | 103.4 | 105.5 | 102.0 | 104.1 | 99.4 | 100.7 | 105.7 | 102.8 | 100.4 | 103.4 | 106.2 | 111.5 |
| 2012 | 104.3 | 108.8 | 104.2 | 106.9 | 99.9 | 102.5 | 107.9 | 104.7 | 102.4 | 104.3 | 111.4 | 117.4 |
| 2013 | 104.7 | 110.9 | 106.0 | 108.2 | 99.6 | 103.3 | 110.5 | 106.3 | 104.2 | 104.7 | 114.6 | 122.5 |
| 2014 | 105.5 | 114.3 | 108.3 | 111.2 | 100.8 | 105.4 | 111.9 | 108.1 | 106.3 | 105.5 | 120.5 | 127.9 |
| 2015 | 106.5 | 117.8 | 110.6 | 114.5 | 103.6 | 107.5 | 111.5 | 109.2 | 108.7 | 106.5 | 126.7 | 131.3 |

## Table 5-1. Indexes of Productivity and Related Data, 1947–2015—*Continued*

(2009 = 100.)

| Year | Nonfinancial corporations | | | | | | | | | | | | |
|---|---|---|---|---|---|---|---|---|---|---|---|---|---|
| | Output per hour | Output | Hours | Hourly compensation | Real hourly compensation | Unit labor costs | Unit nonlabor costs | Unit profits | Implicit price deflator | Employment | Output per job | Compensation in current dollars | Nonlabor payments in current dollars |
| 1947 | 23.6 | 9.7 | 41.0 | 4.7 | 41.3 | 19.9 | 11.1 | 30.7 | 18.4 | 34.8 | 27.9 | 1.9 | 1.6 |
| 1948 | 25.2 | 10.4 | 41.4 | 5.2 | 42.0 | 20.5 | 11.7 | 36.6 | 19.6 | 35.3 | 29.5 | 2.1 | 1.9 |
| 1949 | 26.6 | 10.3 | 38.9 | 5.3 | 43.9 | 20.1 | 12.5 | 33.3 | 19.2 | 33.7 | 30.7 | 2.1 | 1.9 |
| 1950 | 28.5 | 11.7 | 40.9 | 5.6 | 45.8 | 19.8 | 12.0 | 37.6 | 19.3 | 35.0 | 33.4 | 2.3 | 2.2 |
| 1951 | 28.3 | 12.3 | 43.6 | 6.2 | 46.4 | 21.8 | 12.6 | 40.4 | 21.0 | 37.2 | 33.2 | 2.7 | 2.4 |
| 1952 | 28.9 | 12.8 | 44.2 | 6.5 | 48.1 | 22.5 | 13.1 | 36.4 | 21.2 | 37.7 | 33.9 | 2.9 | 2.5 |
| 1953 | 30.1 | 13.7 | 45.6 | 6.9 | 50.4 | 22.8 | 13.1 | 34.2 | 21.1 | 39.1 | 35.1 | 3.1 | 2.6 |
| 1954 | 31.4 | 13.6 | 43.3 | 7.1 | 51.8 | 22.6 | 13.4 | 33.3 | 21.0 | 37.5 | 36.3 | 3.1 | 2.5 |
| 1955 | 33.3 | 15.2 | 45.7 | 7.4 | 53.9 | 22.1 | 13.0 | 38.8 | 21.2 | 39.1 | 38.9 | 3.4 | 3.0 |
| 1956 | 33.5 | 15.8 | 47.0 | 7.8 | 56.4 | 23.4 | 13.9 | 36.4 | 21.9 | 40.5 | 38.9 | 3.7 | 3.1 |
| 1957 | 34.2 | 16.0 | 46.7 | 8.3 | 57.9 | 24.3 | 15.0 | 35.0 | 22.6 | 40.6 | 39.3 | 3.9 | 3.2 |
| 1958 | 34.9 | 15.4 | 44.0 | 8.6 | 58.5 | 24.7 | 16.4 | 31.7 | 23.0 | 38.5 | 39.9 | 3.8 | 3.1 |
| 1959 | 36.7 | 17.1 | 46.6 | 9.0 | 60.3 | 24.4 | 15.8 | 36.8 | 23.2 | 40.3 | 42.4 | 4.2 | 3.6 |
| 1960 | 37.3 | 17.7 | 47.4 | 9.3 | 61.6 | 25.0 | 16.2 | 33.9 | 23.3 | 41.2 | 42.9 | 4.4 | 3.7 |
| 1961 | 38.5 | 18.1 | 46.9 | 9.6 | 63.0 | 24.9 | 16.5 | 34.0 | 23.4 | 40.9 | 44.2 | 4.5 | 3.8 |
| 1962 | 40.2 | 19.6 | 48.8 | 10.0 | 64.8 | 24.8 | 16.3 | 36.5 | 23.5 | 42.3 | 46.4 | 4.9 | 4.2 |
| 1963 | 41.7 | 20.8 | 49.9 | 10.3 | 65.9 | 24.7 | 16.2 | 38.7 | 23.6 | 43.1 | 48.3 | 5.1 | 4.6 |
| 1964 | 42.4 | 22.3 | 52.6 | 10.5 | 66.3 | 24.8 | 16.2 | 40.1 | 23.8 | 44.8 | 49.8 | 5.5 | 5.0 |
| 1965 | 43.5 | 24.2 | 55.6 | 10.8 | 67.1 | 24.8 | 16.1 | 43.2 | 24.2 | 47.1 | 51.3 | 6.0 | 5.6 |
| 1966 | 44.3 | 26.0 | 58.5 | 11.4 | 68.9 | 25.7 | 16.2 | 43.2 | 24.7 | 49.8 | 52.2 | 6.7 | 6.0 |
| 1967 | 45.2 | 26.7 | 59.1 | 12.0 | 70.6 | 26.7 | 17.2 | 40.5 | 25.3 | 51.2 | 52.2 | 7.1 | 6.2 |
| 1968 | 46.8 | 28.4 | 60.8 | 12.9 | 72.6 | 27.6 | 18.3 | 40.6 | 26.2 | 53.0 | 53.7 | 7.8 | 6.9 |
| 1969 | 46.8 | 29.6 | 63.1 | 13.8 | 73.6 | 29.5 | 19.8 | 36.7 | 27.3 | 55.4 | 53.4 | 8.7 | 7.2 |
| 1970 | 47.1 | 29.3 | 62.2 | 14.7 | 74.3 | 31.2 | 22.3 | 30.2 | 28.5 | 55.5 | 52.8 | 9.2 | 7.2 |
| 1971 | 49.0 | 30.5 | 62.1 | 15.6 | 75.4 | 31.8 | 23.4 | 34.1 | 29.6 | 55.6 | 54.8 | 9.7 | 8.0 |
| 1972 | 50.0 | 32.8 | 65.5 | 16.4 | 76.9 | 32.8 | 23.4 | 37.3 | 30.5 | 58.4 | 56.1 | 10.8 | 8.9 |
| 1973 | 50.5 | 34.8 | 68.8 | 17.6 | 77.6 | 34.8 | 24.7 | 38.7 | 32.2 | 61.6 | 56.4 | 12.1 | 9.9 |
| 1974 | 49.5 | 34.2 | 69.1 | 19.2 | 76.3 | 38.8 | 28.4 | 35.3 | 35.3 | 62.8 | 54.5 | 13.3 | 10.4 |
| 1975 | 51.5 | 33.8 | 65.6 | 21.2 | 77.2 | 41.2 | 32.5 | 42.7 | 38.8 | 60.5 | 55.8 | 13.9 | 11.9 |
| 1976 | 53.2 | 36.5 | 68.7 | 22.8 | 78.5 | 42.9 | 32.2 | 50.4 | 40.5 | 63.1 | 57.8 | 15.7 | 13.5 |
| 1977 | 54.6 | 39.2 | 71.8 | 24.6 | 79.6 | 45.1 | 33.4 | 54.7 | 42.7 | 66.3 | 59.1 | 17.7 | 15.3 |
| 1978 | 55.3 | 41.8 | 75.5 | 26.9 | 81.1 | 48.6 | 34.9 | 58.2 | 45.5 | 70.1 | 59.6 | 20.3 | 17.1 |
| 1979 | 54.9 | 43.1 | 78.6 | 29.3 | 80.9 | 53.5 | 37.7 | 55.9 | 49.1 | 73.6 | 58.6 | 23.1 | 18.3 |
| 1980 | 54.7 | 42.7 | 78.0 | 32.3 | 80.2 | 59.1 | 44.3 | 50.5 | 53.8 | 73.9 | 57.8 | 25.2 | 19.6 |
| 1981 | 56.1 | 44.4 | 79.1 | 35.2 | 79.8 | 62.8 | 50.3 | 59.2 | 58.7 | 75.1 | 59.1 | 27.9 | 23.4 |
| 1982 | 56.4 | 43.4 | 77.0 | 37.6 | 80.3 | 66.6 | 55.8 | 55.2 | 62.2 | 73.4 | 59.1 | 28.9 | 24.2 |
| 1983 | 58.3 | 45.6 | 78.1 | 39.1 | 80.2 | 67.1 | 56.1 | 63.9 | 63.5 | 73.8 | 61.8 | 30.6 | 26.5 |
| 1984 | 59.7 | 49.6 | 83.1 | 40.8 | 80.4 | 68.4 | 55.8 | 75.0 | 65.4 | 78.1 | 63.5 | 34.0 | 30.2 |
| 1985 | 61.1 | 51.9 | 85.0 | 42.9 | 81.5 | 70.2 | 57.1 | 72.2 | 66.5 | 80.3 | 64.6 | 36.4 | 31.7 |
| 1986 | 62.5 | 53.3 | 85.3 | 45.3 | 84.6 | 72.5 | 60.1 | 59.8 | 67.5 | 81.5 | 65.4 | 38.6 | 32.0 |
| 1987 | 63.8 | 56.1 | 88.0 | 46.9 | 84.7 | 73.5 | 60.6 | 64.0 | 68.7 | 83.7 | 67.0 | 41.2 | 34.5 |
| 1988 | 65.6 | 59.5 | 90.7 | 49.2 | 85.8 | 75.0 | 61.7 | 68.4 | 70.4 | 86.5 | 68.8 | 44.6 | 37.9 |
| 1989 | 64.9 | 60.7 | 93.5 | 50.6 | 84.6 | 78.0 | 65.2 | 62.5 | 72.6 | 88.7 | 68.4 | 47.3 | 39.2 |
| 1990 | 65.6 | 61.6 | 93.9 | 53.1 | 84.5 | 81.0 | 68.2 | 58.9 | 74.9 | 90.2 | 68.2 | 49.8 | 40.5 |
| 1991 | 67.2 | 61.2 | 91.2 | 55.6 | 85.4 | 82.7 | 71.1 | 60.4 | 76.9 | 88.3 | 69.3 | 50.7 | 41.9 |
| 1992 | 68.9 | 63.1 | 91.5 | 58.5 | 87.6 | 84.8 | 69.7 | 62.6 | 78.0 | 88.3 | 71.4 | 53.5 | 42.9 |
| 1993 | 69.0 | 64.7 | 93.8 | 59.2 | 86.6 | 85.9 | 69.7 | 72.7 | 79.7 | 90.1 | 71.8 | 55.5 | 45.6 |
| 1994 | 70.2 | 68.6 | 97.8 | 60.0 | 86.0 | 85.5 | 70.0 | 86.8 | 81.1 | 93.4 | 73.5 | 58.7 | 51.2 |
| 1995 | 71.0 | 71.9 | 101.3 | 60.9 | 85.3 | 85.8 | 70.3 | 91.9 | 81.9 | 96.7 | 74.4 | 61.7 | 54.7 |
| 1996 | 73.9 | 76.2 | 103.1 | 63.3 | 86.2 | 85.7 | 69.5 | 98.5 | 82.2 | 99.2 | 76.8 | 65.3 | 58.8 |
| 1997 | 75.9 | 81.2 | 107.0 | 65.4 | 87.2 | 86.2 | 69.1 | 101.0 | 82.7 | 102.3 | 79.4 | 70.0 | 63.0 |
| 1998 | 78.5 | 85.9 | 109.4 | 69.2 | 91.0 | 88.1 | 69.3 | 90.1 | 82.7 | 104.8 | 81.9 | 75.7 | 64.2 |
| 1999 | 80.9 | 90.5 | 111.9 | 72.4 | 93.2 | 89.4 | 70.7 | 84.0 | 83.2 | 107.0 | 84.6 | 81.0 | 67.1 |
| 2000 | 84.3 | 95.5 | 113.3 | 77.7 | 96.7 | 92.1 | 73.2 | 70.4 | 84.2 | 109.1 | 87.5 | 88.0 | 69.1 |
| 2001 | 84.8 | 93.5 | 110.2 | 79.5 | 96.4 | 93.8 | 78.4 | 57.4 | 85.3 | 107.8 | 86.7 | 87.7 | 68.1 |
| 2002 | 88.2 | 94.3 | 106.9 | 81.0 | 96.7 | 91.9 | 79.0 | 69.7 | 85.7 | 104.7 | 90.0 | 86.6 | 72.1 |
| 2003 | 91.7 | 96.3 | 105.1 | 83.7 | 97.7 | 91.3 | 78.1 | 85.0 | 86.6 | 103.3 | 93.2 | 87.9 | 76.8 |
| 2004 | 94.9 | 100.6 | 106.1 | 86.7 | 98.5 | 91.4 | 77.6 | 103.3 | 88.5 | 104.2 | 96.6 | 92.0 | 84.6 |
| 2005 | 96.7 | 104.0 | 107.6 | 89.4 | 98.2 | 92.5 | 81.1 | 117.2 | 91.6 | 105.9 | 98.2 | 96.1 | 93.9 |
| 2006 | 98.5 | 108.0 | 109.6 | 92.1 | 98.0 | 93.5 | 83.2 | 131.2 | 94.4 | 107.6 | 100.4 | 101.0 | 103.2 |
| 2007 | 99.0 | 109.0 | 110.1 | 95.6 | 98.9 | 96.6 | 88.6 | 117.2 | 96.3 | 108.2 | 100.7 | 105.3 | 104.6 |
| 2008 | 99.3 | 107.6 | 108.4 | 98.4 | 98.0 | 99.0 | 94.3 | 105.7 | 98.3 | 106.8 | 100.8 | 106.6 | 104.6 |
| 2009 | 100.0 | 100.0 | 100.0 | 100.0 | 100.0 | 100.0 | 100.0 | 100.0 | 100.0 | 100.0 | 100.0 | 100.0 | 100.0 |
| 2010 | 105.3 | 105.5 | 100.2 | 101.5 | 99.9 | 96.4 | 96.8 | 131.2 | 100.0 | 99.0 | 106.6 | 101.7 | 111.1 |
| 2011 | 105.0 | 108.2 | 103.0 | 103.6 | 98.8 | 98.6 | 98.6 | 135.3 | 102.3 | 101.1 | 107.0 | 106.7 | 116.5 |
| 2012 | 106.7 | 112.6 | 105.5 | 106.5 | 99.6 | 99.8 | 98.2 | 144.9 | 103.8 | 105.5 | 108.7 | 112.3 | 123.4 |
| 2013 | 107.6 | 115.8 | 107.6 | 108.0 | 99.5 | 100.3 | 97.8 | 151.5 | 104.6 | 105.7 | 109.5 | 116.2 | 128.3 |
| 2014 | 108.9 | 120.3 | 110.5 | 110.7 | 100.3 | 101.6 | 97.5 | 155.1 | 105.5 | 108.4 | 111.0 | 122.3 | 133.7 |
| 2015 | 109.9 | 124.1 | 112.9 | 113.9 | 103.1 | 103.7 | 98.1 | 144.9 | 105.8 | 111.0 | 111.8 | 128.7 | 135.3 |

## Table 5-1.  Indexes of Productivity and Related Data, 1947–2015—*Continued*

(2009 = 100.)

| Year | Manufacturing | | | | | | | | | | | |
|---|---|---|---|---|---|---|---|---|---|---|---|---|
| | Output per hour | Output | Hours | Hourly compensation | Real hourly compensation | Unit labor costs | Unit nonlabor payments | Implicit price deflator | Employment | Output per job | Compensation in current dollars | Nonlabor payments in current dollars |
| 1947 | ... | ... | ... | ... | ... | ... | ... | ... | ... | ... | ... | ... |
| 1948 | ... | ... | ... | ... | ... | ... | ... | ... | ... | ... | ... | ... |
| 1949 | ... | ... | ... | ... | ... | ... | ... | ... | ... | ... | ... | ... |
| 1950 | ... | ... | ... | ... | ... | ... | ... | ... | ... | ... | ... | ... |
| 1951 | ... | ... | ... | ... | ... | ... | ... | ... | ... | ... | ... | ... |
| 1952 | ... | ... | ... | ... | ... | ... | ... | ... | ... | ... | ... | ... |
| 1953 | ... | ... | ... | ... | ... | ... | ... | ... | ... | ... | ... | ... |
| 1954 | ... | ... | ... | ... | ... | ... | ... | ... | ... | ... | ... | ... |
| 1955 | ... | ... | ... | ... | ... | ... | ... | ... | ... | ... | ... | ... |
| 1956 | ... | ... | ... | ... | ... | ... | ... | ... | ... | ... | ... | ... |
| 1957 | ... | ... | ... | ... | ... | ... | ... | ... | ... | ... | ... | ... |
| 1958 | ... | ... | ... | ... | ... | ... | ... | ... | ... | ... | ... | ... |
| 1959 | ... | ... | ... | ... | ... | ... | ... | ... | ... | ... | ... | ... |
| 1960 | ... | ... | ... | ... | ... | ... | ... | ... | ... | ... | ... | ... |
| 1961 | ... | ... | ... | ... | ... | ... | ... | ... | ... | ... | ... | ... |
| 1962 | ... | ... | ... | ... | ... | ... | ... | ... | ... | ... | ... | ... |
| 1963 | ... | ... | ... | ... | ... | ... | ... | ... | ... | ... | ... | ... |
| 1964 | ... | ... | ... | ... | ... | ... | ... | ... | ... | ... | ... | ... |
| 1965 | ... | ... | ... | ... | ... | ... | ... | ... | ... | ... | ... | ... |
| 1966 | ... | ... | ... | ... | ... | ... | ... | ... | ... | ... | ... | ... |
| 1967 | ... | ... | ... | ... | ... | ... | ... | ... | ... | ... | ... | ... |
| 1968 | ... | ... | ... | ... | ... | ... | ... | ... | ... | ... | ... | ... |
| 1969 | ... | ... | ... | ... | ... | ... | ... | ... | ... | ... | ... | ... |
| 1970 | ... | ... | ... | ... | ... | ... | ... | ... | ... | ... | ... | ... |
| 1971 | ... | ... | ... | ... | ... | ... | ... | ... | ... | ... | ... | ... |
| 1972 | ... | ... | ... | ... | ... | ... | ... | ... | ... | ... | ... | ... |
| 1973 | ... | ... | ... | ... | ... | ... | ... | ... | ... | ... | ... | ... |
| 1974 | ... | ... | ... | ... | ... | ... | ... | ... | ... | ... | ... | ... |
| 1975 | ... | ... | ... | ... | ... | ... | ... | ... | ... | ... | ... | ... |
| 1976 | ... | ... | ... | ... | ... | ... | ... | ... | ... | ... | ... | ... |
| 1977 | ... | ... | ... | ... | ... | ... | ... | ... | ... | ... | ... | ... |
| 1978 | ... | ... | ... | ... | ... | ... | ... | ... | ... | ... | ... | ... |
| 1979 | ... | ... | ... | ... | ... | ... | ... | ... | ... | ... | ... | ... |
| 1980 | ... | ... | ... | ... | ... | ... | ... | ... | ... | ... | ... | ... |
| 1981 | ... | ... | ... | ... | ... | ... | ... | ... | ... | ... | ... | ... |
| 1982 | ... | ... | ... | ... | ... | ... | ... | ... | ... | ... | ... | ... |
| 1983 | ... | ... | ... | ... | ... | ... | ... | ... | ... | ... | ... | ... |
| 1984 | ... | ... | ... | ... | ... | ... | ... | ... | ... | ... | ... | ... |
| 1985 | ... | ... | ... | ... | ... | ... | ... | ... | ... | ... | ... | ... |
| 1986 | ... | ... | ... | ... | ... | ... | ... | ... | ... | ... | ... | ... |
| 1987 | 48.1 | 71.6 | 148.7 | 44.4 | 80.3 | 92.4 | 64.7 | 72.5 | 147.3 | 48.6 | 66.1 | 46.3 |
| 1988 | 48.6 | 74.5 | 153.2 | 46.2 | 80.5 | 95.0 | 67.7 | 75.4 | 149.9 | 49.7 | 70.8 | 50.4 |
| 1989 | 48.8 | 75.2 | 154.2 | 47.7 | 79.8 | 97.9 | 71.0 | 78.6 | 150.8 | 49.9 | 73.6 | 53.4 |
| 1990 | 50.3 | 75.6 | 150.4 | 50.1 | 79.8 | 99.7 | 73.0 | 80.6 | 148.5 | 50.9 | 75.4 | 55.2 |
| 1991 | 51.6 | 74.3 | 144.1 | 52.9 | 81.2 | 102.5 | 72.3 | 80.8 | 143.3 | 51.9 | 76.2 | 53.7 |
| 1992 | 54.5 | 78.1 | 143.3 | 55.6 | 83.4 | 102.1 | 72.9 | 81.1 | 140.9 | 55.4 | 79.7 | 56.9 |
| 1993 | 55.7 | 80.9 | 145.2 | 56.4 | 82.4 | 101.1 | 73.9 | 81.6 | 141.0 | 57.4 | 81.8 | 59.9 |
| 1994 | 57.4 | 85.2 | 148.6 | 57.2 | 82.0 | 99.8 | 75.8 | 82.6 | 142.8 | 59.7 | 85.1 | 64.6 |
| 1995 | 59.2 | 88.6 | 149.6 | 58.3 | 81.6 | 98.5 | 79.3 | 84.7 | 144.9 | 61.1 | 87.2 | 70.2 |
| 1996 | 61.8 | 92.3 | 149.4 | 60.1 | 81.8 | 97.2 | 79.7 | 84.7 | 144.7 | 63.8 | 89.7 | 73.6 |
| 1997 | 64.8 | 98.5 | 152.0 | 62.1 | 82.9 | 95.9 | 79.2 | 83.9 | 146.0 | 67.5 | 94.5 | 78.1 |
| 1998 | 66.8 | 101.3 | 151.6 | 65.2 | 85.8 | 97.6 | 75.1 | 81.5 | 147.2 | 68.8 | 98.9 | 76.1 |
| 1999 | 70.0 | 105.4 | 150.6 | 68.2 | 87.8 | 97.4 | 74.9 | 81.3 | 144.9 | 72.7 | 102.7 | 79.0 |
| 2000 | 75.0 | 111.4 | 148.7 | 73.3 | 91.4 | 97.8 | 76.9 | 82.8 | 144.5 | 77.1 | 109.0 | 85.7 |
| 2001 | 75.2 | 104.5 | 138.9 | 75.6 | 91.6 | 100.5 | 74.7 | 82.0 | 137.8 | 75.8 | 105.0 | 78.1 |
| 2002 | 78.9 | 101.9 | 129.1 | 78.0 | 93.0 | 98.8 | 74.3 | 81.2 | 127.9 | 79.7 | 100.7 | 75.7 |
| 2003 | 84.1 | 103.3 | 122.8 | 82.2 | 95.9 | 97.7 | 76.7 | 82.7 | 121.9 | 84.7 | 100.9 | 79.2 |
| 2004 | 88.7 | 108.4 | 122.1 | 85.2 | 96.8 | 96.1 | 83.4 | 87.0 | 120.2 | 90.2 | 104.1 | 90.4 |
| 2005 | 94.2 | 113.7 | 120.7 | 88.4 | 97.2 | 93.9 | 92.0 | 92.6 | 119.6 | 95.1 | 106.8 | 104.7 |
| 2006 | 97.3 | 118.3 | 121.7 | 90.6 | 96.4 | 93.1 | 97.6 | 96.3 | 118.9 | 99.6 | 110.2 | 115.5 |
| 2007 | 103.3 | 123.5 | 119.6 | 94.2 | 97.5 | 91.2 | 103.4 | 99.9 | 116.8 | 105.7 | 112.6 | 127.7 |
| 2008 | 107.3 | 123.2 | 114.8 | 96.7 | 96.4 | 90.1 | 113.9 | 107.2 | 112.7 | 109.4 | 111.1 | 140.4 |
| 2009 | 100.0 | 100.0 | 100.0 | 100.0 | 100.0 | 100.0 | 100.0 | 100.0 | 100.0 | 100.0 | 100.0 | 100.0 |
| 2010 | 110.7 | 110.7 | 100.0 | 101.3 | 99.7 | 91.5 | 110.4 | 105.1 | 97.2 | 113.8 | 101.2 | 122.2 |
| 2011 | 116.8 | 119.2 | 102.1 | 103.0 | 98.3 | 88.2 | 124.2 | 114.0 | 98.5 | 121.0 | 105.1 | 148.1 |
| 2012 | 118.9 | 124.1 | 104.4 | 104.8 | 97.9 | 88.2 | 126.9 | 115.9 | 100.4 | 123.6 | 109.4 | 157.4 |
| 2013 | 119.1 | 125.3 | 105.2 | 105.0 | 96.8 | 88.2 | 127.2 | 116.2 | 101.0 | 124.1 | 110.5 | 159.4 |
| 2014 | 119.2 | 127.4 | 106.8 | 107.9 | 97.8 | 90.5 | 125.7 | 115.8 | 102.3 | 124.5 | 115.3 | 160.1 |
| 2015 | 119.6 | 128.8 | 107.7 | 110.7 | 100.2 | 92.5 | ... | ... | 103.5 | 124.5 | 119.2 | ... |

... = Not available.

**Table 5-2. Average Annual Percent Change in Output Per Hour and Related Series, Selected Industries, 1987–2014**

(Number, percent.)

| Industry | NAICS code | 2014 employment (thousands) | Average annual percent change, 1987–2014 | | | |
|---|---|---|---|---|---|---|
| | | | Labor productivity | Unit labor costs | Output | Hours worked |
| **Mining** | | | | | | |
| Mining | 21 | 861 | 0.0 | 4.2 | 1.1 | 1.1 |
| Oil and gas extraction | 211 | 202 | 1.0 | 4.5 | 1.1 | 0.1 |
| Mining, except oil and gas | 212 | 212 | 1.5 | 1.6 | 0.4 | -1.1 |
| Coal mining | 2121 | 76 | 1.6 | 1.2 | -0.5 | -2.0 |
| Metal ore mining | 2122 | 44 | 0.5 | 3.5 | 1.1 | 0.6 |
| Nonmetallic mineral mining and quarrying | 2123 | 92 | 1.5 | 1.8 | 0.8 | -0.7 |
| Support activities for mining | 213 | 448 | 2.4 | 2.4 | 5.9 | 3.4 |
| **Utilities** | | | | | | |
| Utilities | 22 | 552 | 2.4 | 1.4 | 1.5 | -0.8 |
| Power generation and supply | 2211 | 391 | 3.3 | 0.5 | 2.2 | -1.0 |
| Natural gas distribution | 2212 | 112 | 0.8 | 3.7 | -0.3 | -1.1 |
| Water, sewage and other systems | 2213 | 48 | -1.7 | 4.8 | 0.8 | 2.6 |
| **Transportation and Warehousing** | | | | | | |
| Air transportation | 481 | 423 | 3.2 | 0.4 | 2.6 | -0.6 |
| Line-haul railroads | 482111 | 187 | 3.7 | -0.4 | 2.1 | -1.5 |
| Truck transportation | 484 | 1 632 | 0.6 | 0.8 | 2.0 | 1.5 |
| General freight trucking | 4841 | 1 163 | 1.1 | 0.9 | 2.4 | 1.2 |
| General freight trucking, local | 48411 | 303 | 2.6 | 0.1 | 3.7 | 1.1 |
| General freight trucking, long-distance | 48412 | 860 | 1.2 | 0.3 | 2.3 | 1.0 |
| Used household and office goods moving | 48421 | 469 | -1.0 | 2.6 | -0.3 | 0.6 |
| Other specialized trucking, local | 48422 | 237 | -0.1 | 2.6 | 2.1 | 2.2 |
| Other specialized trucking, long distance | 48423 | 135 | 1.8 | 0.8 | 4.0 | 2.1 |
| Postal service | 491 | 593 | 0.6 | 3.2 | -0.6 | -1.3 |
| Couriers and messengers | 492 | 606 | -1.9 | 3.5 | 0.3 | 2.2 |
| Warehousing and storage | 493 | 753 | 2.6 | -0.5 | 5.9 | 3.2 |
| General warehousing and storage | 49311 | 647 | 3.9 | -1.4 | 7.4 | 3.3 |
| Refrigerated warehousing and storage | 49312 | 52 | 0.0 | 1.4 | 2.8 | 2.8 |
| **Information** | | | | | | |
| Publishing | 511 | 754 | 4.0 | 1.3 | 3.5 | -0.5 |
| Newspaper, book, and directory publishers | 5111 | 438 | -0.2 | 4.3 | -2.5 | -2.3 |
| Newspaper publishers | 51111 | 211 | -1.2 | 4.4 | -4.2 | -3.0 |
| Periodical publishers | 51112 | 111 | -0.4 | 4.9 | -1.5 | -1.1 |
| Book publishers | 51113 | 69 | 0.0 | 4.8 | -0.8 | -0.8 |
| Software publishers | 5112 | 316 | 12.3 | -6.4 | 18.8 | 5.8 |
| Motion picture and video exhibition | 51213 | 132 | 1.7 | 1.9 | 1.6 | -0.2 |
| Broadcasting, except Internet | 515 | 288 | 2.8 | 1.8 | 2.9 | 0.1 |
| Radio and television broadcasting | 5151 | 224 | 1.8 | 2.1 | 1.5 | -0.3 |
| Radio broadcasting | 51511 | 92 | 3.4 | 1.8 | 2.4 | -0.9 |
| Cable and other subscription programming | 5152 | 64 | 4.9 | 2.6 | 7.0 | 2.0 |
| Wired telecommunications carriers | 5171 | 608 | 3.6 | -1.1 | 2.8 | -0.8 |
| Wireless telecommunications carriers | 5172 | 150 | 11.2 | -6.3 | 19.4 | 7.4 |
| **Finance and Insurance** | | | | | | |
| Commercial banking | 52211 | 1 293 | 3.3 | 2.0 | 3.2 | -0.1 |
| **Real Estate and Rental and Leasing** | | | | | | |
| Passenger car rental | 532111 | 115 | 1.7 | 2.3 | 2.4 | 0.7 |
| Truck, trailer, and RV rental and leasing | 53212 | 66 | 2.5 | 0.9 | 2.4 | -0.1 |
| Video tape and disc rental | 53223 | 18 | 6.4 | -2.0 | -0.8 | -6.7 |
| **Professional and Technical Services** | | | | | | |
| Accounting and bookkeeping services | 54121 | 1 099 | 2.6 | 1.0 | 3.2 | 0.6 |
| Offices of certified public accountants | 541211 | 450 | 1.8 | 2.4 | 2.8 | 0.9 |
| Tax preparation services | 541213 | 131 | 0.8 | 1.7 | 2.4 | 1.6 |
| Other accounting services | 541219 | 339 | 4.7 | -2.3 | 4.8 | 0.1 |
| Architectural services | 54131 | 183 | 1.5 | 1.9 | 2.3 | 0.8 |
| Engineering services | 54133 | 948 | 1.1 | 3.0 | 2.8 | 1.7 |
| Advertising agencies | 54181 | 207 | 1.7 | 2.5 | 2.1 | 0.5 |
| Photography studios, portrait | 541921 | 60 | 0.6 | 2.1 | 1.0 | 0.4 |
| **Administrative and Waste Services** | | | | | | |
| Employment placement and executive search | 56131 | 303 | 3.9 | 0.3 | 5.1 | 1.2 |
| Travel arrangement and reservation services | 5615 | 215 | 6.7 | -1.6 | 3.6 | -2.9 |
| Travel agencies | 56151 | 97 | 5.7 | -1.0 | 4.2 | -1.4 |
| Janitorial services | 56172 | 1 323 | 2.0 | 1.4 | 3.6 | 1.6 |

**Table 5-2.  Average Annual Percent Change in Output Per Hour and Related Series, Selected Industries, 1987–2014**—*Continued*

(Number, percent.)

| Industry | NAICS code | 2014 employment (thousands) | Average annual percent change, 1987–2014 | | | |
|---|---|---|---|---|---|---|
| | | | Labor productivity | Unit labor costs | Output | Hours worked |
| **Health Care and Social Assistance** | | | | | | |
| Medical and diagnostic laboratories | 6215 | 262 | 2.2 | 0.3 | 5.3 | 3.0 |
| Medical laboratories | 621511 | 185 | 2.1 | 0.2 | 5.3 | 3.1 |
| Diagnostic imaging centers | 621512 | 77 | 2.4 | 0.7 | 5.4 | 2.9 |
| **Arts, Entertainment, and Recreation** | | | | | | |
| Amusement parks and arcades | 7131 | 190 | -4.3 | 6.7 | -1.7 | 2.7 |
| Amusement and theme parks | 71311 | 169 | -1.2 | 4.3 | 1.8 | 3.0 |
| Gambling industries | 7132 | 139 | 1.9 | 2.7 | 1.9 | 0.0 |
| Golf courses and country clubs | 71391 | 381 | -1.2 | 4.1 | 0.0 | 1.3 |
| Fitness and recreational sports centers | 71394 | 581 | 3.9 | -0.8 | 3.9 | 0.0 |
| Bowling centers | 71395 | 69 | 0.1 | 2.8 | -1.4 | -1.5 |
| **Accommodation and Food Services** | | | | | | |
| Accommodation and food services | 72 | 12 851 | 0.7 | 2.7 | 2.2 | 1.5 |
| Accommodation | 721 | 1 937 | 2.1 | 1.7 | 2.7 | 0.7 |
| Traveler accommodation | 7211 | 1 854 | 2.1 | 1.7 | 2.8 | 0.7 |
| Hotels and motels, except casino hotels | 72111 | 1 540 | 1.5 | 2.5 | 2.1 | 0.6 |
| Food services and drinking places | 722 | 10 914 | 0.4 | 3.1 | 2.0 | 1.6 |
| Special food services | 7223 | 766 | 1.0 | 1.3 | 2.3 | 1.3 |
| Drinking places, alcoholic beverages | 7224 | 376 | -0.5 | 3.3 | -0.8 | -0.3 |
| Restaurants and other eating places | 72251 | 9 772 | 0.4 | 3.3 | 2.2 | 1.8 |
| Full-service restaurants | 722511 | 5 084 | 0.5 | 3.7 | 2.2 | 1.7 |
| Limited-service eating places | 722513 | 4 688 | 0.3 | 2.8 | 2.1 | 1.8 |
| **Other Services** | | | | | | |
| Automotive repair and maintenance | 8111 | 1 113 | 0.9 | 2.3 | 1.3 | 0.4 |
| Reupholstery and furniture repair | 81142 | 21 | -0.5 | 3.6 | -2.7 | -2.2 |
| Personal care services | 8121 | 1 189 | 2.4 | 1.6 | 3.5 | 1.1 |
| Hair, nail, and skin care services | 81211 | 963 | 2.4 | 1.6 | 3.1 | 0.7 |
| Funeral homes and funeral services | 81221 | 114 | -0.9 | 4.6 | -0.4 | 0.5 |
| Drycleaning and laundry services | 8123 | 318 | 1.9 | 1.7 | 0.9 | -1.0 |
| Coin-operated laundries and drycleaners | 81231 | 43 | 2.9 | 1.8 | 0.6 | -2.3 |
| Drycleaning and laundry services | 81232 | 149 | 0.9 | 2.1 | -1.0 | -1.9 |
| Linen and uniform supply | 81233 | 126 | 1.8 | 1.4 | 2.7 | 0.8 |
| Photofinishing | 81292 | 12 | 2.5 | 1.8 | -4.4 | -6.7 |
| **Manufacturing** | | | | | | |
| Food | 311 | 1 510 | 1.2 | 1.5 | 1.4 | 0.2 |
| Beverages and tobacco products | 312 | 217 | 0.2 | 1.8 | -0.2 | -0.4 |
| Textile mills | 313 | 124 | 3.3 | -0.4 | -2.1 | -5.3 |
| Textile product mills | 314 | 121 | 1.0 | 2.2 | -1.7 | -2.7 |
| Apparel | 315 | 159 | -0.7 | 1.5 | -6.9 | -6.2 |
| Leather and allied products | 316 | 31 | 1.2 | 1.6 | -4.2 | -5.4 |
| Wood products | 321 | 392 | 1.4 | 1.5 | 0.0 | -1.5 |
| Paper | 322 | 375 | 2.1 | 1.0 | 0.1 | -1.9 |
| Printing and related support activities | 323 | 484 | 1.3 | 1.1 | -0.6 | -1.9 |
| Petroleum and coal products | 324 | 113 | 2.3 | 2.4 | 1.2 | -1.1 |
| Chemicals | 325 | 814 | 1.6 | 1.8 | 1.0 | -0.6 |
| Plastics and rubber products | 326 | 678 | 1.9 | 1.1 | 1.4 | -0.4 |
| Nometallic mineral products | 327 | 399 | 1.2 | 1.4 | 0.2 | -1.0 |
| Primary metals | 331 | 403 | 2.7 | 0.2 | 0.9 | -1.8 |
| Fabricated metal products | 332 | 1 496 | 1.2 | 1.5 | 1.1 | -0.1 |
| Machinery | 333 | 1 133 | 2.2 | 0.6 | 1.6 | -0.6 |
| Computer and electronic products | 334 | 1 054 | 9.9 | -6.1 | 7.4 | -2.3 |
| Electrical equipment and appliances | 335 | 380 | 2.2 | 1.1 | 0.0 | -2.1 |
| Transportation equipment | 336 | 1 573 | 3.2 | -0.6 | 2.1 | -1.1 |
| Furniture and related products | 337 | 400 | 1.4 | 1.4 | -0.3 | -1.7 |
| Miscellaneous manufacturing | 339 | 640 | 2.3 | 1.3 | 2.0 | -0.3 |

**Table 5-3. Average Annual Percent Change in Output Per Hour and Related Series, Wholesale Trade, Retail Trade, Food Service, and Drinking Places, 1987–2015**

(Number, percent.)

| Industry | NAICS code | 2015 employment (thousands) | Average annual percent change, 1987–2015 | | | |
|---|---|---|---|---|---|---|
| | | | Labor productivity | Unit labor costs | Output | Hours worked |
| **Wholesale Trade** | | | | | | |
| Wholesale trade ........................................................ | 42 | 6 015 | 2.9 | 1.0 | 3.2 | 0.3 |
| | | | | | | |
| Durable goods .......................................................... | 423 | 3 002 | 4.6 | -0.6 | 4.7 | 0.1 |
| Motor vehicles and parts ........................................... | 4231 | 336 | 3.7 | 0.1 | 3.4 | -0.3 |
| Furniture and furnishings ........................................... | 4232 | 109 | 2.0 | 2.2 | 1.7 | -0.3 |
| Lumber and construction supplies ............................... | 4233 | 214 | 1.1 | 1.5 | 1.4 | 0.4 |
| Commercial equipment .............................................. | 4234 | 627 | 12.3 | -7.1 | 12.4 | 0.1 |
| | | | | | | |
| Metals and minerals .................................................. | 4235 | 130 | -0.4 | 3.7 | -0.2 | 0.3 |
| Appliance and electric goods ..................................... | 4236 | 327 | 8.1 | -3.2 | 7.5 | -0.5 |
| Hardware and plumbing ............................................. | 4237 | 244 | 1.9 | 1.8 | 2.4 | 0.5 |
| Machinery and supplies ............................................. | 4238 | 701 | 1.8 | 2.2 | 1.9 | 0.1 |
| Miscellaneous durable goods ..................................... | 4239 | 315 | 1.0 | 2.7 | 1.6 | 0.5 |
| | | | | | | |
| Nondurable goods ..................................................... | 424 | 2 105 | 1.2 | 2.9 | 1.4 | 0.1 |
| Paper and paper products .......................................... | 4241 | 124 | 1.1 | 2.4 | 0.3 | -0.8 |
| Druggists' goods ....................................................... | 4242 | 199 | 2.8 | 3.9 | 4.0 | 1.1 |
| Apparel and piece goods ........................................... | 4243 | 157 | 2.2 | 1.3 | 1.9 | -0.3 |
| Grocery and related products ..................................... | 4244 | 777 | 1.0 | 2.7 | 1.6 | 0.6 |
| | | | | | | |
| Farm product raw materials ....................................... | 4245 | 78 | 1.2 | 4.2 | -0.4 | -1.6 |
| Chemicals ................................................................ | 4246 | 134 | 0.4 | 3.3 | 0.8 | 0.4 |
| Petroleum ................................................................ | 4247 | 102 | 2.2 | 2.6 | 0.8 | -1.4 |
| Alcoholic beverages .................................................. | 4248 | 190 | 0.2 | 3.1 | 1.9 | 1.8 |
| Miscellaneous nondurable goods ................................ | 4249 | 345 | 0.2 | 3.2 | -0.2 | -0.4 |
| Electronic markets and agents and brokers .................. | 425 | 909 | 1.2 | 1.3 | 3.4 | 2.2 |
| | | | | | | |
| **Retail Trade** | | | | | | |
| Retail trade .............................................................. | 44-45 | 16 508 | 2.8 | 0.0 | 3.3 | 0.5 |
| | | | | | | |
| Motor vehicle and parts dealers ................................. | 441 | 1 999 | 2.1 | 0.7 | 2.9 | 0.8 |
| Automobile dealers ................................................... | 4411 | 1 278 | 2.2 | 0.7 | 3.0 | 0.8 |
| Other motor vehicle dealers ....................................... | 4412 | 160 | 2.5 | 0.9 | 3.8 | 1.2 |
| Auto parts, accessories, and tire stores ...................... | 4413 | 562 | 1.0 | 1.4 | 1.8 | 0.8 |
| Furniture and home furnishings stores ........................ | 442 | 517 | 3.6 | -0.8 | 3.7 | 0.1 |
| | | | | | | |
| Furniture stores ........................................................ | 4421 | 238 | 3.2 | -0.6 | 3.2 | 0.0 |
| Home furnishings stores ............................................ | 4422 | 279 | 4.2 | -1.1 | 4.3 | 0.2 |
| Electronics and appliance stores ................................ | 443 | 544 | 10.9 | -7.4 | 11.9 | 0.8 |
| Building material and garden supply stores .................. | 444 | 1 274 | 2.6 | 0.0 | 3.2 | 0.6 |
| Building material and supplies dealers ........................ | 4441 | 1 109 | 2.5 | 0.2 | 3.2 | 0.7 |
| | | | | | | |
| Lawn and garden equipment and supplies stores .......... | 4442 | 166 | 3.4 | -0.9 | 3.3 | 0.0 |
| Food and beverage stores ......................................... | 445 | 3 163 | 0.4 | 2.5 | 0.4 | 0.0 |
| Grocery stores ......................................................... | 4451 | 2 742 | 0.3 | 2.7 | 0.4 | 0.2 |
| Specialty food stores ................................................ | 4452 | 254 | 0.3 | 2.2 | -0.3 | -0.6 |
| Beer, wine and liquor stores ...................................... | 4453 | 167 | 2.4 | 0.4 | 1.3 | -1.1 |
| | | | | | | |
| Health and personal care stores ................................ | 446 | 1 077 | 2.1 | 1.4 | 3.1 | 1.0 |
| Gasoline stations ...................................................... | 447 | 920 | 1.4 | 1.4 | 1.1 | -0.3 |
| Clothing and clothing accessories stores ..................... | 448 | 1 451 | 4.1 | -1.2 | 3.8 | -0.3 |
| Clothing stores ......................................................... | 4481 | 1 064 | 4.6 | -1.5 | 4.3 | -0.2 |
| Shoe stores ............................................................. | 4482 | 216 | 2.6 | -0.5 | 2.5 | -0.2 |
| | | | | | | |
| Jewelry, luggage, and leather goods stores ................. | 4483 | 172 | 3.4 | -0.2 | 2.7 | -0.7 |
| Sports, hobby, book, and music stores ........................ | 451 | 699 | 3.6 | -0.7 | 4.2 | 0.5 |
| Sporting goods and musical instrument stores .............. | 4511 | 606 | 4.2 | -1.2 | 5.0 | 0.9 |
| Book stores and news dealers .................................... | 4512 | 93 | 2.0 | 0.8 | 1.0 | -1.0 |
| General merchandise stores ....................................... | 452 | 3 153 | 3.1 | -0.8 | 4.5 | 1.3 |
| | | | | | | |
| Department stores ..................................................... | 4521 | 1 330 | 1.0 | 0.9 | 0.9 | -0.1 |
| Other general merchandise stores .............................. | 4529 | 1 824 | 5.1 | -2.2 | 7.8 | 2.6 |
| Miscellaneous store retailers ..................................... | 453 | 995 | 3.2 | -1.0 | 3.2 | 0.1 |
| Florists .................................................................... | 4531 | 85 | 2.5 | 0.0 | 0.0 | -2.4 |
| Office supplies, stationery and gift stores .................... | 4532 | 302 | 5.4 | -2.6 | 4.3 | -1.0 |
| | | | | | | |
| Used merchandise stores ........................................... | 4533 | 225 | 4.5 | -2.3 | 6.2 | 1.6 |
| Other miscellaneous store retailers ............................ | 4539 | 383 | 0.9 | 0.4 | 2.3 | 1.3 |
| Nonstore retailers ..................................................... | 454 | 714 | 8.1 | -4.1 | 8.7 | 0.6 |
| Electronic shopping and mail-order houses .................. | 4541 | 425 | 9.9 | -5.3 | 14.3 | 4.0 |
| Vending machine operators ........................................ | 4542 | 46 | -0.1 | 3.8 | -3.1 | -3.0 |
| Direct selling establishments ..................................... | 4543 | 244 | 2.3 | 0.5 | 0.7 | -1.6 |
| | | | | | | |
| **Food Services and Drinking Places** | | | | | | |
| Food services and drinking places .............................. | 722 | 11 298 | 0.4 | 3.1 | 2.1 | 1.7 |
| Special food services ................................................ | 7223 | 799 | 0.9 | 1.7 | 2.3 | 1.3 |
| Drinking places, alcoholic beverages .......................... | 7224 | 382 | -0.5 | 3.5 | -0.7 | -0.2 |
| Restaurants and other eating places ........................... | 7225 | 10 117 | 0.5 | 3.3 | 2.3 | 1.8 |

## Table 5-4.  Indexes of Multifactor Productivity and Related Measures, 1990–2015

(2009 =100.)

| Sector | 1990 | 1991 | 1992 | 1993 | 1994 | 1995 | 1996 | 1997 | 1998 | 1999 | 2000 | 2001 | 2002 |
|---|---|---|---|---|---|---|---|---|---|---|---|---|---|
| **PRIVATE BUSINESS** | | | | | | | | | | | | | |
| **Productivity** | | | | | | | | | | | | | |
| Output per hour of all persons | 63.5 | 64.7 | 67.6 | 67.7 | 68.3 | 68.6 | 70.7 | 72.0 | 74.3 | 77.0 | 79.7 | 82.2 | 85.7 |
| Output per unit of capital services | 115.9 | 112.1 | 114.2 | 114.2 | 115.7 | 114.6 | 114.7 | 114.7 | 113.9 | 113.0 | 111.2 | 107.2 | 105.9 |
| Multifactor productivity | 82.7 | 82.3 | 85.0 | 84.7 | 85.2 | 84.8 | 86.4 | 87.4 | 88.5 | 90.4 | 92.0 | 92.4 | 94.4 |
| Real value-added output | 58.7 | 58.3 | 60.8 | 62.6 | 65.7 | 67.8 | 71.0 | 74.8 | 78.7 | 83.1 | 86.8 | 87.5 | 89.1 |
| **Inputs** | | | | | | | | | | | | | |
| Labor input | 84.2 | 83.0 | 83.2 | 86.1 | 90.0 | 93.2 | 94.9 | 98.2 | 101.1 | 103.1 | 104.2 | 102.5 | 100.6 |
| Capital services | 50.6 | 52.0 | 53.3 | 54.9 | 56.8 | 59.2 | 61.9 | 65.2 | 69.1 | 73.5 | 78.0 | 81.6 | 84.1 |
| Combined input quantity | 70.9 | 70.9 | 71.6 | 73.9 | 77.1 | 80.0 | 82.2 | 85.6 | 88.9 | 91.9 | 94.4 | 94.6 | 94.4 |
| **PRIVATE NONFARM BUSINESS** | | | | | | | | | | | | | |
| **Productivity** | | | | | | | | | | | | | |
| Output per hour of all persons | 64.1 | 65.3 | 68.1 | 68.3 | 69.0 | 69.5 | 71.4 | 72.6 | 74.9 | 77.4 | 80.0 | 82.5 | 86.0 |
| Output per unit of capital services | 118.9 | 114.9 | 116.7 | 116.7 | 117.9 | 117.0 | 116.7 | 116.4 | 115.5 | 114.5 | 112.3 | 108.2 | 106.7 |
| Multifactor productivity | 83.6 | 83.3 | 85.9 | 85.6 | 86.1 | 85.9 | 87.3 | 88.1 | 89.2 | 90.9 | 92.4 | 92.9 | 94.8 |
| Real value-added output | 58.8 | 58.4 | 60.8 | 62.8 | 65.7 | 68.1 | 71.2 | 74.9 | 78.9 | 83.3 | 87.0 | 87.7 | 89.3 |
| **Inputs** | | | | | | | | | | | | | |
| Labor input | 83.7 | 82.4 | 82.5 | 85.6 | 89.2 | 92.4 | 94.2 | 97.7 | 100.6 | 102.9 | 104.0 | 102.4 | 100.4 |
| Capital services | 49.4 | 50.9 | 52.1 | 53.8 | 55.7 | 58.2 | 61.0 | 64.3 | 68.3 | 72.8 | 77.4 | 81.1 | 83.7 |
| Combined input quantity | 70.3 | 70.2 | 70.8 | 73.3 | 76.3 | 79.2 | 81.5 | 85.0 | 88.4 | 91.6 | 94.1 | 94.5 | 94.1 |
| **MANUFACTURING** | | | | | | | | | | | | | |
| **Productivity** | | | | | | | | | | | | | |
| Output per hour | 50.3 | 51.4 | 54.4 | 55.7 | 57.4 | 59.0 | 61.9 | 64.6 | 66.3 | 69.8 | 75.1 | 75.4 | 78.9 |
| Output per unit of capital services | 121.1 | 116.0 | 118.9 | 120.3 | 123.6 | 124.0 | 123.9 | 126.3 | 123.8 | 123.9 | 126.8 | 116.4 | 112.2 |
| Sector output | 75.6 | 74.3 | 78.1 | 80.9 | 85.2 | 88.6 | 92.3 | 98.5 | 101.3 | 105.4 | 111.4 | 104.5 | 101.9 |
| Combined inputs | 96.6 | 95.9 | 101.2 | 102.4 | 104.9 | 107.3 | 111.6 | 116.3 | 118.1 | 120.6 | 122.8 | 117.3 | 111.7 |
| Energy | 122.8 | 122.5 | 121.3 | 125.2 | 129.7 | 133.3 | 129.7 | 127.1 | 133.1 | 164.6 | 183.6 | 210.2 | 158.9 |
| Materials | 92.8 | 92.3 | 108.7 | 107.7 | 108.9 | 108.1 | 122.5 | 129.6 | 125.0 | 129.9 | 139.4 | 116.6 | 106.7 |
| Capital services | 62.4 | 64.0 | 65.7 | 67.3 | 69.0 | 71.4 | 74.4 | 78.0 | 81.8 | 85.1 | 87.9 | 89.8 | 90.9 |
| Purchased services | 94.4 | 93.8 | 100.8 | 101.3 | 105.2 | 110.4 | 109.8 | 114.2 | 119.7 | 120.5 | 118.0 | 121.3 | 119.7 |

| Sector | 2003 | 2004 | 2005 | 2006 | 2007 | 2008 | 2009 | 2010 | 2011 | 2012 | 2013 | 2014 | 2015 |
|---|---|---|---|---|---|---|---|---|---|---|---|---|---|
| **PRIVATE BUSINESS** | | | | | | | | | | | | | |
| **Productivity** | | | | | | | | | | | | | |
| Output per hour of all persons | 88.8 | 91.6 | 93.4 | 94.3 | 95.8 | 96.6 | 100.0 | 103.2 | 103.1 | 103.7 | 104.1 | 104.7 | 105.2 |
| Output per unit of capital services | 106.7 | 108.8 | 109.5 | 109.2 | 108.5 | 104.7 | 100.0 | 102.8 | 103.8 | 105.3 | 105.5 | 106.6 | 107.0 |
| Multifactor productivity | 96.6 | 99.1 | 100.6 | 100.9 | 101.4 | 100.2 | 100.0 | 102.9 | 103.0 | 103.6 | 103.8 | 104.6 | 104.8 |
| Real value-added output | 91.9 | 96.1 | 99.8 | 103.1 | 105.3 | 104.1 | 100.0 | 103.2 | 105.4 | 108.5 | 110.7 | 114.1 | 117.4 |
| **Inputs** | | | | | | | | | | | | | |
| Labor input | 100.7 | 102.3 | 104.2 | 106.9 | 108.0 | 106.6 | 100.0 | 100.3 | 102.9 | 105.8 | 107.7 | 110.4 | 113.5 |
| Capital services | 86.2 | 88.3 | 91.1 | 94.3 | 97.1 | 99.3 | 100.0 | 100.4 | 101.5 | 103.0 | 104.9 | 107.1 | 109.8 |
| Combined input quantity | 95.1 | 97.0 | 99.2 | 102.1 | 103.9 | 103.9 | 100.0 | 100.3 | 102.3 | 104.7 | 106.6 | 109.1 | 112.0 |
| **PRIVATE NONFARM BUSINESS** | | | | | | | | | | | | | |
| **Productivity** | | | | | | | | | | | | | |
| Output per hour of all persons | 89.1 | 91.7 | 93.5 | 94.3 | 95.9 | 96.7 | 100.0 | 103.2 | 103.2 | 104.0 | 103.9 | 104.6 | 105.2 |
| Output per unit of capital services | 107.2 | 109.4 | 110.1 | 109.9 | 109.2 | 105.1 | 100.0 | 102.8 | 104.1 | 105.9 | 105.8 | 106.9 | 107.1 |
| Multifactor productivity | 96.9 | 99.3 | 100.8 | 101.1 | 101.7 | 100.3 | 100.0 | 102.9 | 103.2 | 104.0 | 103.9 | 104.7 | 104.9 |
| Real value-added output | 92.1 | 96.2 | 99.9 | 103.2 | 105.6 | 104.3 | 100.0 | 103.2 | 105.5 | 108.8 | 110.8 | 114.2 | 117.4 |
| **Inputs** | | | | | | | | | | | | | |
| Labor input | 100.6 | 102.3 | 104.2 | 107.0 | 108.2 | 106.7 | 100.0 | 100.2 | 102.8 | 105.8 | 107.8 | 110.5 | 113.4 |
| Capital services | 85.9 | 88.0 | 90.7 | 93.9 | 96.7 | 99.2 | 100.0 | 100.4 | 101.4 | 102.8 | 104.7 | 106.8 | 109.6 |
| Combined input quantity | 95.0 | 96.9 | 99.1 | 102.1 | 103.9 | 103.9 | 100.0 | 100.3 | 102.3 | 104.6 | 106.6 | 109.1 | 111.9 |
| **MANUFACTURING** | | | | | | | | | | | | | |
| **Productivity** | | | | | | | | | | | | | |
| Output per hour | 84.0 | 88.6 | 93.8 | 97.1 | 102.9 | 107.0 | 100.0 | 110.2 | 116.2 | 118.2 | 118.2 | 118.2 | . . . |
| Output per unit of capital services | 113.0 | 118.3 | 123.0 | 126.1 | 128.9 | 124.8 | 100.0 | 109.8 | 117.0 | 120.2 | 119.1 | 118.1 | . . . |
| Sector output | 103.3 | 108.4 | 113.7 | 118.3 | 123.5 | 123.2 | 100.0 | 110.7 | 119.2 | 124.1 | 125.3 | 127.4 | . . . |
| Combined inputs | 107.4 | 110.2 | 114.7 | 117.0 | 120.9 | 120.5 | 100.0 | 106.7 | 116.5 | 124.7 | 125.7 | 129.0 | . . . |
| Energy | 139.3 | 132.1 | 141.3 | 130.5 | 139.1 | 137.7 | 100.0 | 97.3 | 105.7 | 111.4 | 111.1 | 109.4 | . . . |
| Materials | 99.8 | 116.7 | 129.9 | 138.8 | 149.9 | 154.7 | 100.0 | 121.5 | 149.7 | 168.5 | 166.9 | 172.3 | . . . |
| Capital services | 91.4 | 91.6 | 92.5 | 93.8 | 95.9 | 98.7 | 100.0 | 100.8 | 101.9 | 103.2 | 105.2 | 107.8 | . . . |
| Purchased services | 113.2 | 106.2 | 113.4 | 110.0 | 113.2 | 103.2 | 100.0 | 102.9 | 104.4 | 112.7 | 116.8 | 122.2 | . . . |

. . . = Not available.

# CHAPTER 6: COMPENSATION OF EMPLOYEES

## HIGHLIGHTS

This chapter discusses the Employment Cost Index (ECI), which covers changes in wages and salaries and benefits; the Employer Costs for Employee Compensation (ECEC); and employee participation in various benefit plans.

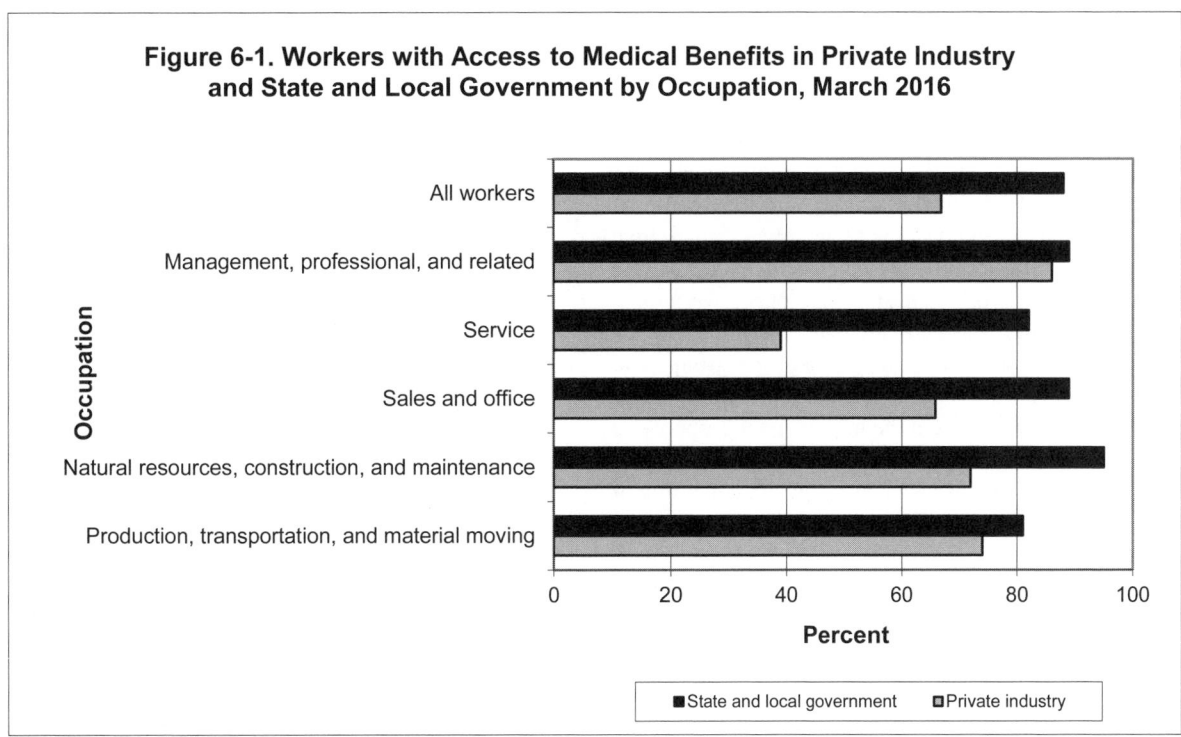

**Figure 6-1. Workers with Access to Medical Benefits in Private Industry and State and Local Government by Occupation, March 2016**

Among all industries in March 2015, state and local government workers were far more likely to have access to medical benefits than those in the private sector. Eighty-eight percent of state and local government workers had access to medical benefits compared with 67 percent of private industry workers. (See Table 6-10.)

## OTHER HIGHLIGHTS

- Employer compensation costs per hour worked increased to $32.27 in September 2016. Employer compensation costs per hour varied significantly by industry ranging from $13.95 in leisure and hospitality to $53.20 in information in September 2016. (See Table 6-5.)

- Total employer compensation costs per hour also varied among the different Census divisions, ranging from $25.28 in the East South Central states (Alabama, Kentucky, Mississippi, and Tennessee) to $39.12 in the Middle Atlantic states. (See Table 6-6.)

- Union workers were far more likely to have access to retirement and medical benefits than those that were not in a union. In March 2016, 91 percent of union workers in private industry had access to retirement benefits compared with only 64 percent of non-union workers. Similarly, 93 percent of union workers had access to medical care benefits compared with 65 percent of nonunion workers. (See Tables 6-9 and 6-10.)

# NOTES AND DEFINITIONS

## NATIONAL COMPENSATION SURVEY

The National Compensation Survey (NCS) is an establishment survey conducted by the Office of Compensation Levels and Trends (OCLT) at the Bureau of Labor Statistics (BLS). It provides data for the Employment Cost Index (ECI), the Employer Costs for Employee Compensation (ECEC), the occupational earnings series, and the employee benefits survey.

## EMPLOYMENT COST INDEX

The ECI is a measure of the change in the cost of labor, independent of the influence of employment shifts among occupations and industry categories. The total compensation series includes changes in wages and salaries and in employer costs for employee benefits. The ECI calculates indexes of total compensation, wages and salaries, and benefits separately for all civilian workers in the United States (as defined by the NCS), for private industry workers, and for workers in state and local government. For all of these categories, the ECI calculates the same indexes by occupational group, worker attribute, industry group, and establishment characteristic. Seasonally adjusted series are calculated as well. It was developed in the mid 1970s in response to the rapid acceleration of both wages and prices at that time. Monetary and fiscal policymakers needed a more accurate measure of the actual changes in employers' labor costs.

Beginning with estimates for March 2006, the following changes were introduced to the ECI:

- The Standard Industrial Classification (SIC) System was replaced by the North American Industry Classification System for classifying establishments by industry.

- The Occupational Classification System (OCS) Manual was replaced by the Standard Occupational Classification Manual for classifying occupations.

- Estimates were weighted to 2002 fixed employment counts until December 2013. For March 1995 through December 2005, ECI estimates were weighted on 1990 fixed employment counts.

- The ECI base was changed to December 2005=100. Prior to this, the base was June 1989=100, which was used from March 1990 through December 2005.

## Concepts and Definitions

*Compensation* is a term used to encompass the entire range of wages and benefits, both current and deferred, that employees receive in return for their work. In the Employment Cost Index (ECI), compensation includes the employer's cost of wages and salaries, plus the employer's cost of providing employee benefits.

*Lump-sum payments* are payments made to employees in lieu of a general wage rate increase. The payment may be a fixed amount as set forth in a labor agreement or an amount determined by a formula—for example, 2.5 percent of an employee's earnings during the prior year. Lump-sum payments are not incorporated into an employee's base pay rate or salary, but are considered as nonproduction bonuses in the Employment Cost Index and Employer Costs for Employee Compensation series.

*Wages and salaries* are defined as the hourly straight-time wage rate or, for workers not paid on an hourly basis, straight-time earnings divided by the corresponding hours. Straight-time wage and salary rates are total earnings before payroll deductions, excluding premium pay for overtime and for work on weekends and holidays, shift differentials, and nonproduction bonuses such as lump-sum payments provided in lieu of wage increases. Production bonuses, incentive earnings, commission payments, and cost-of-living adjustments are included in straight-time wage and salary rates.

*Benefits* covered by the ECI are: paid leave—vacations, holidays, sick leave, and personal leave; supplemental pay-premium pay for work in addition to the regular work schedule (such as overtime, weekends, and holidays), shift differentials, and nonproduction bonuses (such as referral bonuses and attendance bonuses); insurance benefits—life, health, short-term disability, and long-term disability; retirement and savings benefits—defined benefit and defined contribution plans; and legally required benefits—Social Security, Medicare, federal and state unemployment insurance, and workers' compensation.

## Sources of Additional Information

Additional information on ECI methodology and more tables are available in Chapter 8 of the *BLS Handbook of Methods* and BLS new releases. The BLS publication *Compensation and Working Conditions* contains articles on all aspects of the NCS. All of these resources are on the BLS Web site at <http://www.bls.gov/ncs/ect/>.

## Table 6-1. Employment Cost Index, Private Industry Workers, Total Compensation[1] and Wages and Salaries, by Selected Industry and Occupation, 2001–2016

(December 2005 = 100.)

| Characteristic and year | Total compensation | | | | | Wages and salaries | | | | |
|---|---|---|---|---|---|---|---|---|---|---|
| | Indexes | | | | Percent change for 12 months (ended December) | Indexes | | | | Percent change for 12 months (ended December) |
| | March | June | September | December | | March | June | September | December | |
| **WORKERS BY INDUSTRY** | | | | | | | | | | |
| **Total Private** | | | | | | | | | | |
| 2001 | 85.0 | 85.8 | 86.7 | 87.3 | 4.1 | 87.6 | 88.4 | 89.2 | 89.9 | 3.8 |
| 2002 | 88.2 | 89.2 | 89.7 | 90.0 | 3.1 | 90.7 | 91.6 | 92.0 | 92.2 | 2.6 |
| 2003 | 91.4 | 92.3 | 93.2 | 93.6 | 4.0 | 93.3 | 94.0 | 94.8 | 95.1 | 3.1 |
| 2004 | 94.9 | 95.9 | 96.7 | 97.2 | 3.8 | 95.7 | 96.5 | 97.3 | 97.6 | 2.6 |
| 2005 | 98.2 | 98.9 | 99.5 | 100.0 | 2.9 | 98.3 | 98.9 | 99.5 | 100.0 | 2.5 |
| 2006 | 100.8 | 101.7 | 102.5 | 103.2 | 3.2 | 100.7 | 101.7 | 102.5 | 103.2 | 3.2 |
| 2007 | 104.0 | 104.9 | 105.7 | 106.3 | 3.0 | 104.3 | 105.1 | 106.0 | 106.6 | 3.3 |
| 2008 | 107.3 | 108.0 | 108.7 | 108.9 | 2.4 | 107.6 | 108.4 | 109.1 | 109.4 | 2.6 |
| 2009 | 109.3 | 109.6 | 110.0 | 110.2 | 1.2 | 109.8 | 110.1 | 110.6 | 110.8 | 1.3 |
| 2010 | 111.1 | 111.7 | 112.2 | 112.5 | 2.1 | 111.4 | 111.9 | 112.4 | 112.8 | 1.8 |
| 2011 | 113.3 | 114.3 | 114.6 | 115.0 | 2.2 | 113.2 | 113.8 | 114.3 | 114.6 | 1.6 |
| 2012 | 115.7 | 116.4 | 116.8 | 117.1 | 1.8 | 115.3 | 115.9 | 116.4 | 116.6 | 1.7 |
| 2013 | 117.9 | 118.6 | 119.0 | 119.4 | 2.0 | 117.3 | 118.1 | 118.5 | 119.0 | 2.1 |
| 2014 | 119.9 | 121.0 | 121.7 | 122.2 | 2.3 | 119.3 | 120.3 | 121.2 | 121.6 | 2.2 |
| 2015 | 123.2 | 123.3 | 124.0 | 124.5 | 1.9 | 122.6 | 122.9 | 123.7 | 124.2 | 2.1 |
| 2016 | 125.4 | 126.2 | 126.8 | . . . | . . . | 125.1 | 126.1 | 126.7 | . . . | . . . |
| **Goods-Producing[2]** | | | | | | | | | | |
| 2001 | 83.9 | 84.7 | 85.3 | 86.0 | 3.6 | 87.9 | 88.8 | 89.3 | 90.0 | 3.6 |
| 2002 | 87.0 | 87.7 | 88.2 | 89.0 | 3.5 | 90.7 | 91.4 | 91.9 | 92.6 | 2.9 |
| 2003 | 90.5 | 91.5 | 92.1 | 92.6 | 4.0 | 93.3 | 94.1 | 94.6 | 94.9 | 2.5 |
| 2004 | 94.5 | 95.4 | 96.5 | 96.9 | 4.6 | 95.6 | 96.2 | 97.2 | 97.2 | 2.4 |
| 2005 | 98.0 | 99.0 | 99.8 | 100.0 | 3.2 | 97.9 | 98.7 | 99.5 | 100.0 | 2.9 |
| 2006 | 100.3 | 101.3 | 102.0 | 102.5 | 2.5 | 100.7 | 101.8 | 102.3 | 102.9 | 2.9 |
| 2007 | 102.9 | 103.9 | 104.4 | 105.0 | 2.4 | 103.9 | 104.7 | 105.4 | 106.0 | 3.0 |
| 2008 | 106.1 | 106.8 | 107.2 | 107.5 | 2.4 | 107.1 | 108.0 | 108.6 | 109.0 | 2.8 |
| 2009 | 107.9 | 108.2 | 108.4 | 108.6 | 1.0 | 109.2 | 109.5 | 109.8 | 110.0 | 0.9 |
| 2010 | 109.7 | 110.3 | 111.0 | 111.1 | 2.3 | 110.5 | 110.9 | 111.5 | 111.6 | 1.5 |
| 2011 | 112.0 | 113.2 | 113.4 | 113.8 | 2.4 | 112.2 | 112.7 | 113.2 | 113.5 | 1.7 |
| 2012 | 114.1 | 114.7 | 115.3 | 115.6 | 1.6 | 114.0 | 114.5 | 115.1 | 115.4 | 1.7 |
| 2013 | 116.4 | 117.0 | 117.5 | 117.7 | 1.8 | 116.1 | 116.8 | 117.4 | 117.6 | 1.9 |
| 2014 | 118.5 | 119.1 | 119.9 | 120.3 | 2.2 | 118.2 | 119.0 | 119.6 | 120.1 | 2.1 |
| 2015 | 121.0 | 121.9 | 122.5 | 123.2 | 2.4 | 120.8 | 121.8 | 122.5 | 123.2 | 2.6 |
| 2016 | 123.8 | 124.7 | 125.2 | . . . | . . . | 123.9 | 124.9 | 125.5 | . . . | . . . |
| **Service-Providing[3]** | | | | | | | | | | |
| 2001 | 85.4 | 86.2 | 87.1 | 87.8 | 4.4 | 87.4 | 88.3 | 89.2 | 89.8 | 3.8 |
| 2002 | 88.7 | 89.7 | 90.2 | 90.4 | 3.0 | 90.7 | 91.7 | 92.0 | 92.1 | 2.6 |
| 2003 | 91.7 | 92.5 | 93.6 | 94.0 | 4.0 | 93.3 | 93.9 | 94.9 | 95.2 | 3.4 |
| 2004 | 95.1 | 96.1 | 96.8 | 97.3 | 3.5 | 95.8 | 96.6 | 97.3 | 97.7 | 2.6 |
| 2005 | 98.3 | 98.9 | 99.5 | 100.0 | 2.8 | 98.4 | 99.0 | 99.5 | 100.0 | 2.4 |
| 2006 | 101.0 | 101.8 | 102.7 | 103.4 | 3.4 | 100.8 | 101.7 | 102.6 | 103.3 | 3.3 |
| 2007 | 104.3 | 105.2 | 106.1 | 106.7 | 3.2 | 104.4 | 105.3 | 106.1 | 106.8 | 3.4 |
| 2008 | 107.7 | 108.5 | 109.1 | 109.4 | 2.5 | 107.7 | 108.6 | 109.3 | 109.6 | 2.6 |
| 2009 | 109.8 | 110.1 | 110.5 | 110.8 | 1.3 | 110.0 | 110.3 | 110.8 | 111.1 | 1.4 |
| 2010 | 111.6 | 112.1 | 112.6 | 113.0 | 2.0 | 111.7 | 112.3 | 112.7 | 113.1 | 1.8 |
| 2011 | 113.8 | 114.6 | 115.0 | 115.3 | 2.0 | 113.5 | 114.1 | 114.6 | 114.9 | 1.6 |
| 2012 | 116.3 | 117.0 | 117.3 | 117.6 | 2.0 | 115.6 | 116.3 | 116.7 | 117.0 | 1.8 |
| 2013 | 118.4 | 119.1 | 119.6 | 120.0 | 2.0 | 117.7 | 118.4 | 118.9 | 119.4 | 2.1 |
| 2014 | 120.4 | 121.6 | 122.3 | 122.8 | 2.3 | 119.7 | 120.7 | 121.6 | 122.1 | 2.3 |
| 2015 | 123.8 | 123.8 | 124.5 | 124.9 | 1.7 | 123.1 | 123.3 | 124.1 | 124.5 | 2.0 |
| 2016 | 125.9 | 126.7 | 127.3 | . . . | . . . | 125.5 | 126.5 | 127.1 | . . . | . . . |

[1]Includes wages, salaries, and employer costs for employee benefits.
[2]Includes mining, construction, and manufacturing.
[3]Includes the following industries: wholesale trade; retail trade; transportation and warehousing; utilities; information; finance and insurance; real estate and rental and leasing; professional, scientific, and technical services; management of companies and enterprises; administrative and support and waste management and remediation services; education services; health care and social assistance; arts, entertainment, and recreation; accommodation and food services; and other services, except public administration.
. . . = Not available.

## Table 6-1. Employment Cost Index, Private Industry Workers, Total Compensation[1] and Wages and Salaries, by Selected Industry and Occupation, 2001–2016—*Continued*

(December 2005 = 100.)

| Characteristic and year | Total compensation | | | | | Wages and salaries | | | | |
|---|---|---|---|---|---|---|---|---|---|---|
| | Indexes | | | | Percent change for 12 months (ended December) | Indexes | | | | Percent change for 12 months (ended December) |
| | March | June | September | December | | March | June | September | December | |
| **WORKERS BY OCCUPATION** | | | | | | | | | | |
| **Management, Professional, and Related** | | | | | | | | | | |
| 2001 | 85.0 | 86.0 | 86.8 | 87.4 | 4.5 | 87.3 | 88.3 | 89.1 | 89.8 | 4.1 |
| 2002 | 88.3 | 89.2 | 89.5 | 89.7 | 2.6 | 90.8 | 92.2 | 92.4 | 92.1 | 2.6 |
| 2003 | 91.6 | 92.3 | 93.3 | 93.8 | 4.6 | 94.8 | 95.5 | 96.4 | 96.7 | 5.0 |
| 2004 | 94.9 | 95.7 | 96.5 | 97.1 | 3.5 | 96.8 | 97.5 | 98.1 | 98.5 | 1.9 |
| 2005 | 98.5 | 99.1 | 99.6 | 100.0 | 3.0 | 99.2 | 99.7 | 99.5 | 100.0 | 1.5 |
| 2006 | 101.1 | 101.9 | 102.9 | 103.5 | 3.5 | 101.3 | 102.2 | 102.8 | 103.1 | 3.1 |
| 2007 | 104.6 | 105.5 | 106.4 | 106.8 | 3.2 | 104.7 | 105.5 | 106.3 | 106.6 | 3.4 |
| 2008 | 108.1 | 108.9 | 109.6 | 109.9 | 2.9 | 108.2 | 109.0 | 109.7 | 110.0 | 3.2 |
| 2009 | 110.4 | 110.5 | 110.6 | 110.7 | 0.7 | 110.3 | 110.3 | 110.4 | 110.8 | 0.7 |
| 2010 | 111.8 | 112.2 | 112.7 | 113.0 | 2.1 | 112.0 | 112.6 | 112.8 | 113.2 | 2.2 |
| 2011 | 114.1 | 114.8 | 115.1 | 115.4 | 2.1 | 113.9 | 114.4 | 114.9 | 115.0 | 1.6 |
| 2012 | 116.4 | 117.1 | 117.4 | 117.7 | 2.0 | 115.7 | 116.7 | 116.7 | 116.9 | 1.7 |
| 2013 | 118.5 | 119.4 | 119.9 | 120.2 | 2.1 | 117.9 | 119.3 | 119.4 | 119.8 | 2.5 |
| 2014 | 120.7 | 122.0 | 122.7 | 123.0 | 2.3 | 120.2 | 121.7 | 122.8 | 122.7 | 2.4 |
| 2015 | 123.8 | 124.2 | 124.9 | 125.3 | 1.9 | 123.4 | 124.2 | 125.7 | 126.2 | 2.9 |
| 2016 | 126.0 | 126.5 | 127.1 | . . . | . . . | 127.1 | 127.3 | 128.4 | . . . | . . . |
| **Management, Business, and Financial** | | | | | | | | | | |
| 2001 | 86.1 | 87.1 | 87.8 | 88.5 | 4.4 | 87.3 | 88.3 | 89.1 | 89.8 | 4.1 |
| 2002 | 89.5 | 90.7 | 90.7 | 90.6 | 2.4 | 90.8 | 92.2 | 92.4 | 92.1 | 2.6 |
| 2003 | 93.3 | 93.9 | 94.9 | 95.4 | 5.3 | 94.8 | 95.5 | 96.4 | 96.7 | 5.0 |
| 2004 | 95.9 | 96.8 | 97.3 | 97.9 | 2.6 | 96.8 | 97.5 | 98.1 | 98.5 | 1.9 |
| 2005 | 99.1 | 99.6 | 99.7 | 100.0 | 2.1 | 99.2 | 99.7 | 99.5 | 100.0 | 1.5 |
| 2006 | 101.3 | 102.0 | 102.7 | 103.1 | 3.1 | 101.3 | 102.2 | 102.8 | 103.1 | 3.1 |
| 2007 | 104.3 | 105.1 | 106.0 | 106.3 | 3.1 | 104.7 | 105.5 | 106.3 | 106.6 | 3.4 |
| 2008 | 108.0 | 108.7 | 109.3 | 109.5 | 3.0 | 108.2 | 109.0 | 109.7 | 110.0 | 3.2 |
| 2009 | 109.6 | 109.7 | 109.7 | 109.9 | 0.4 | 110.3 | 110.3 | 110.4 | 110.8 | 0.7 |
| 2010 | 111.3 | 111.7 | 112.0 | 112.3 | 2.2 | 112.0 | 112.6 | 112.8 | 113.2 | 2.2 |
| 2011 | 113.6 | 114.5 | 114.8 | 115.0 | 2.4 | 113.9 | 114.4 | 114.9 | 115.0 | 1.6 |
| 2012 | 116.0 | 116.9 | 116.9 | 117.1 | 1.8 | 115.7 | 116.7 | 116.7 | 116.9 | 1.7 |
| 2013 | 118.0 | 119.3 | 119.6 | 119.9 | 2.4 | 117.9 | 119.3 | 119.4 | 119.8 | 2.5 |
| 2014 | 120.3 | 122.1 | 123.0 | 123.0 | 2.6 | 120.2 | 121.7 | 122.8 | 122.7 | 2.4 |
| 2015 | 123.9 | 124.2 | 125.4 | 125.7 | 2.2 | 123.4 | 124.2 | 125.7 | 126.2 | 2.9 |
| 2016 | 126.5 | 126.8 | 127.7 | . . . | . . . | 127.1 | 127.3 | 128.4 | . . . | . . . |
| **Professional and Related** | | | | | | | | | | |
| 2001 | 84.1 | 85.0 | 86.0 | 86.5 | 4.7 | 86.9 | 87.8 | 88.7 | 89.3 | 4.1 |
| 2002 | 87.3 | 87.9 | 88.5 | 89.1 | 3.0 | 90.1 | 90.5 | 91.0 | 91.4 | 2.4 |
| 2003 | 90.3 | 91.0 | 92.0 | 92.6 | 3.9 | 92.1 | 92.7 | 93.6 | 94.2 | 3.1 |
| 2004 | 94.1 | 94.8 | 95.8 | 96.5 | 4.2 | 95.3 | 95.7 | 96.7 | 97.2 | 3.2 |
| 2005 | 98.0 | 98.8 | 99.5 | 100.0 | 3.6 | 98.2 | 98.8 | 99.6 | 100.0 | 2.9 |
| 2006 | 101.0 | 101.8 | 103.1 | 103.9 | 3.9 | 100.9 | 101.8 | 103.1 | 104.0 | 4.0 |
| 2007 | 104.9 | 105.9 | 106.7 | 107.3 | 3.3 | 105.1 | 106.0 | 107.0 | 107.6 | 3.5 |
| 2008 | 108.3 | 109.0 | 109.9 | 110.3 | 2.8 | 108.7 | 109.5 | 110.4 | 110.9 | 3.1 |
| 2009 | 111.0 | 111.1 | 111.4 | 111.4 | 1.0 | 111.6 | 111.8 | 112.1 | 112.1 | 1.1 |
| 2010 | 112.2 | 112.6 | 113.3 | 113.5 | 1.9 | 112.8 | 113.2 | 113.9 | 114.1 | 1.8 |
| 2011 | 114.6 | 115.1 | 115.4 | 115.7 | 1.9 | 114.8 | 115.2 | 115.6 | 115.9 | 1.6 |
| 2012 | 116.8 | 117.3 | 117.7 | 118.2 | 2.2 | 116.7 | 117.2 | 117.7 | 118.2 | 2.0 |
| 2013 | 118.9 | 119.5 | 120.2 | 120.5 | 1.9 | 118.8 | 119.5 | 120.2 | 120.5 | 1.9 |
| 2014 | 121.0 | 121.9 | 122.5 | 122.9 | 2.0 | 120.9 | 121.7 | 122.3 | 122.8 | 1.9 |
| 2015 | 123.7 | 124.1 | 124.5 | 124.9 | 1.6 | 123.4 | 124.2 | 124.7 | 125.2 | 2.0 |
| 2016 | 125.7 | 126.2 | 126.7 | . . . | . . . | 126.0 | 126.6 | 127.2 | . . . | . . . |

[1]Includes wages, salaries, and employer costs for employee benefits.
[2]Includes mining, construction, and manufacturing.
[3]Includes the following industries: wholesale trade; retail trade; transportation and warehousing; utilities; information; finance and insurance; real estate and rental and leasing; professional, scientific, and technical services; management of companies and enterprises; administrative and support and waste management and remediation services; education services; health care and social assistance; arts, entertainment, and recreation; accommodation and food services; and other services, except public administration.
. . . = Not available.

## Table 6-1.  Employment Cost Index, Private Industry Workers, Total Compensation¹ and Wages and Salaries, by Selected Industry and Occupation, 2001–2016—*Continued*

(December 2005 = 100.)

| Characteristic and year | Total compensation | | | | | Wages and salaries | | | | |
|---|---|---|---|---|---|---|---|---|---|---|
| | Indexes | | | | Percent change for 12 months (ended December) | Indexes | | | | Percent change for 12 months (ended December) |
| | March | June | September | December | | March | June | September | December | |
| **Office and Administrative Support** | | | | | | | | | | |
| 2001 | 84.3 | 85.0 | 86.4 | 86.6 | 4.6 | 87.0 | 87.7 | 88.8 | 89.4 | 4.2 |
| 2002 | 87.4 | 88.5 | 89.3 | 89.7 | 3.8 | 90.7 | 91.3 | 91.8 | 92.4 | 3.4 |
| 2003 | 90.8 | 92.0 | 92.8 | 93.3 | 3.8 | 93.1 | 93.9 | 94.4 | 94.7 | 2.5 |
| 2004 | 94.8 | 96.1 | 96.5 | 97.1 | 4.2 | 95.6 | 96.4 | 97.1 | 97.6 | 3.1 |
| 2005 | 97.9 | 98.9 | 99.5 | 100.0 | 2.9 | 98.2 | 99.0 | 99.4 | 100.0 | 2.5 |
| 2006 | 100.8 | 102.1 | 103.0 | 103.6 | 3.4 | 100.9 | 101.9 | 102.6 | 103.3 | 3.3 |
| 2007 | 104.0 | 105.0 | 105.9 | 106.7 | 3.2 | 104.5 | 105.4 | 106.0 | 106.7 | 3.3 |
| 2008 | 107.6 | 108.3 | 109.0 | 109.6 | 2.7 | 107.7 | 108.5 | 109.2 | 109.7 | 2.8 |
| 2009 | 109.9 | 110.3 | 110.8 | 111.2 | 1.8 | 110.6 | 111.1 | 111.4 | 111.8 | 1.9 |
| 2010 | 112.2 | 112.7 | 113.1 | 113.3 | 2.2 | 112.2 | 112.6 | 113.3 | 113.6 | 1.6 |
| 2011 | 113.8 | 114.9 | 115.5 | 115.8 | 2.2 | 114.4 | 114.8 | 115.4 | 115.7 | 1.8 |
| 2012 | 116.3 | 117.0 | 117.7 | 117.8 | 1.9 | 116.4 | 117.0 | 117.4 | 117.7 | 1.7 |
| 2013 | 118.6 | 119.1 | 119.9 | 120.1 | 2.0 | 118.6 | 119.3 | 119.7 | 120.1 | 2.0 |
| 2014 | 120.8 | 122.0 | 122.8 | 123.2 | 2.2 | 120.8 | 121.5 | 122.0 | 122.5 | 2.0 |
| 2015 | 123.6 | 124.1 | 124.6 | 124.9 | 2.3 | 123.3 | 124.2 | 124.8 | 125.6 | 2.5 |
| 2016 | 125.7 | 126.6 | 127.1 | . . . | . . . | 127.1 | 128.0 | 128.7 | . . . | . . . |
| **Natural Resources, Construction, and Maintenance** | | | | | | | | | | |
| 2001 | 84.3 | 85.0 | 86.4 | 86.6 | 4.0 | 87.6 | 88.4 | 89.9 | 90.0 | 3.8 |
| 2002 | 87.4 | 88.5 | 89.3 | 89.7 | 3.6 | 90.5 | 91.7 | 92.3 | 92.6 | 2.9 |
| 2003 | 90.8 | 92.0 | 92.8 | 93.3 | 4.0 | 93.2 | 94.1 | 94.8 | 95.2 | 2.8 |
| 2004 | 94.8 | 96.1 | 96.5 | 97.1 | 4.1 | 95.8 | 96.7 | 97.1 | 97.5 | 2.4 |
| 2005 | 97.9 | 98.9 | 99.5 | 100.0 | 3.0 | 97.8 | 98.7 | 99.4 | 100.0 | 2.6 |
| 2006 | 100.8 | 102.1 | 103.0 | 103.6 | 3.6 | 100.7 | 101.8 | 102.8 | 103.4 | 3.4 |
| 2007 | 104.0 | 105.0 | 105.9 | 106.7 | 3.0 | 104.2 | 105.1 | 106.2 | 107.1 | 3.6 |
| 2008 | 107.6 | 108.3 | 109.0 | 109.6 | 2.7 | 108.1 | 109.0 | 109.8 | 110.5 | 3.2 |
| 2009 | 109.9 | 110.3 | 110.8 | 111.2 | 1.5 | 110.6 | 111.0 | 111.6 | 112.0 | 1.4 |
| 2010 | 112.2 | 112.7 | 113.1 | 113.3 | 1.9 | 112.5 | 112.8 | 113.1 | 113.3 | 1.2 |
| 2011 | 113.8 | 114.9 | 115.5 | 115.8 | 2.2 | 113.7 | 114.4 | 115.2 | 115.4 | 1.9 |
| 2012 | 116.3 | 117.0 | 117.7 | 117.8 | 1.7 | 115.6 | 116.0 | 116.6 | 116.7 | 1.1 |
| 2013 | 118.6 | 119.1 | 119.9 | 120.1 | 2.0 | 117.2 | 117.6 | 118.5 | 118.8 | 1.8 |
| 2014 | 120.8 | 122.0 | 122.8 | 123.2 | 2.6 | 119.3 | 120.0 | 120.9 | 121.4 | 2.2 |
| 2015 | 123.6 | 124.1 | 124.6 | 124.9 | 1.4 | 121.7 | 122.7 | 123.2 | 123.5 | 1.7 |
| 2016 | 125.7 | 126.6 | 127.1 | . . . | . . . | 124.3 | 125.5 | 126.0 | . . . | . . . |
| **Construction, Extraction, Farming, Fishing, and Forestry** | | | | | | | | | | |
| 2001 | 84.2 | 85.1 | 86.2 | 86.4 | 3.8 | 87.8 | 88.9 | 89.8 | 90.0 | 3.6 |
| 2002 | 87.3 | 88.1 | 88.8 | 89.5 | 3.6 | 90.6 | 91.3 | 91.9 | 92.4 | 2.7 |
| 2003 | 90.3 | 91.6 | 92.5 | 93.1 | 4.0 | 92.7 | 93.7 | 94.6 | 94.9 | 2.7 |
| 2004 | 94.7 | 95.8 | 96.4 | 97.2 | 4.4 | 95.8 | 96.6 | 96.9 | 97.5 | 2.7 |
| 2005 | 97.7 | 98.7 | 99.5 | 100.0 | 2.9 | 97.8 | 98.5 | 99.3 | 100.0 | 2.6 |
| 2006 | 100.7 | 102.2 | 103.1 | 103.7 | 3.7 | 100.7 | 102.0 | 103.0 | 103.7 | 3.7 |
| 2007 | 104.4 | 105.7 | 106.5 | 107.4 | 3.6 | 104.7 | 105.8 | 106.7 | 107.8 | 4.0 |
| 2008 | 108.6 | 109.7 | 110.3 | 110.8 | 3.2 | 109.2 | 110.1 | 110.8 | 111.5 | 3.4 |
| 2009 | 110.9 | 111.5 | 112.0 | 112.4 | 1.4 | 111.4 | 111.7 | 112.3 | 112.7 | 1.1 |
| 2010 | 113.1 | 113.6 | 114.3 | 114.4 | 1.8 | 112.9 | 113.3 | 113.9 | 114.0 | 1.2 |
| 2011 | 114.8 | 115.5 | 116.0 | 116.5 | 1.8 | 114.5 | 114.9 | 115.4 | 115.7 | 1.5 |
| 2012 | 116.6 | 117.1 | 117.8 | 117.9 | 1.2 | 115.7 | 116.0 | 116.8 | 116.7 | 0.9 |
| 2013 | 118.6 | 118.9 | 119.9 | 120.3 | 2.0 | 117.1 | 117.3 | 118.2 | 118.5 | 1.5 |
| 2014 | 120.7 | 121.4 | 122.1 | 122.9 | 2.2 | 118.7 | 119.6 | 120.3 | 121.1 | 2.2 |
| 2015 | 123.1 | 124.0 | 124.6 | 125.1 | 1.8 | 121.2 | 122.0 | 122.6 | 123.1 | 1.7 |
| 2016 | 125.8 | 127.1 | 127.3 | . . . | . . . | 124.0 | 125.5 | 125.6 | . . . | . . . |

¹Includes wages, salaries, and employer costs for employee benefits.
²Includes mining, construction, and manufacturing.
³Includes the following industries: wholesale trade; retail trade; transportation and warehousing; utilities; information; finance and insurance; real estate and rental and leasing; professional, scientific, and technical services; management of companies and enterprises; administrative and support and waste management and remediation services; education services; health care and social assistance; arts, entertainment, and recreation; accommodation and food services; and other services, except public administration.
. . . = Not available.

## Table 6-1. Employment Cost Index, Private Industry Workers, Total Compensation[1] and Wages and Salaries, by Selected Industry and Occupation, 2001–2016—*Continued*

(December 2005 = 100.)

| Characteristic and year | Total compensation | | | | | Wages and salaries | | | | |
|---|---|---|---|---|---|---|---|---|---|---|
| | Indexes | | | | Percent change for 12 months (ended December) | Indexes | | | | Percent change for 12 months (ended December) |
| | March | June | September | December | | March | June | September | December | |
| **Installation, Maintenance, and Repair** | | | | | | | | | | |
| 2001 | 84.4 | 84.9 | 86.8 | 86.8 | 4.1 | 87.4 | 87.9 | 90.1 | 90.1 | 4.3 |
| 2002 | 87.4 | 89.1 | 90.0 | 90.1 | 3.8 | 90.4 | 92.2 | 92.9 | 92.9 | 3.1 |
| 2003 | 91.4 | 92.5 | 93.1 | 93.6 | 3.9 | 93.8 | 94.6 | 95.1 | 95.5 | 2.8 |
| 2004 | 95.0 | 96.3 | 96.7 | 97.0 | 3.6 | 95.9 | 96.8 | 97.3 | 97.4 | 2.0 |
| 2005 | 98.1 | 99.3 | 99.6 | 100.0 | 3.1 | 97.8 | 99.1 | 99.5 | 100.0 | 2.7 |
| 2006 | 100.9 | 102.1 | 103.0 | 103.4 | 3.4 | 0.7 | 101.6 | 102.6 | 103.0 | 3.0 |
| 2007 | 103.5 | 104.1 | 105.2 | 105.8 | 2.3 | 3.7 | 104.2 | 105.6 | 106.1 | 3.0 |
| 2008 | 106.3 | 106.6 | 107.4 | 108.1 | 2.2 | 6.8 | 107.6 | 108.5 | 109.3 | 3.0 |
| 2009 | 108.6 | 108.9 | 109.4 | 109.8 | 1.6 | 9.7 | 110.2 | 110.7 | 111.2 | 1.7 |
| 2010 | 111.1 | 111.5 | 111.6 | 111.9 | 1.9 | 12.1 | 112.1 | 112.1 | 112.5 | 1.2 |
| 2011 | 112.6 | 114.2 | 114.9 | 115.0 | 2.8 | 12.7 | 113.9 | 115.0 | 115.0 | 2.2 |
| 2012 | 116.1 | 116.8 | 117.5 | 117.8 | 2.4 | 15.5 | 115.9 | 116.4 | 116.7 | 1.5 |
| 2013 | 118.6 | 119.3 | 119.9 | 119.9 | 1.8 | 17.5 | 118.0 | 119.0 | 119.2 | 2.1 |
| 2014 | 121.0 | 122.6 | 123.5 | 123.5 | 3.0 | 20.1 | 120.6 | 121.6 | 121.7 | 2.1 |
| 2015 | 124.1 | 124.2 | 124.6 | 124.8 | 1.1 | 22.3 | 123.4 | 123.9 | 124.1 | 2.0 |
| 2016 | 125.6 | 126.1 | 126.9 | . . . | . . . | 24.8 | 125.5 | 126.4 | . . . | . . . |
| **Production, Transportation, and Material Moving** | | | | | | | | | | |
| 2001 | 85.3 | 85.8 | 86.7 | 87.4 | 3.6 | 88.7 | 89.4 | 90.2 | 91.0 | 3.9 |
| 2002 | 88.4 | 89.1 | 89.7 | 90.3 | 3.3 | 91.9 | 92.4 | 92.8 | 93.3 | 2.5 |
| 2003 | 91.5 | 92.4 | 93.2 | 93.6 | 3.7 | 94.0 | 94.6 | 95.1 | 95.4 | 2.3 |
| 2004 | 95.5 | 96.5 | 97.4 | 97.8 | 4.5 | 96.0 | 96.7 | 97.6 | 97.8 | 2.5 |
| 2005 | 98.5 | 99.0 | 99.7 | 100.0 | 2.2 | 98.3 | 98.9 | 99.6 | 100.0 | 2.2 |
| 2006 | 100.4 | 101.1 | 101.7 | 102.3 | 2.3 | 100.6 | 101.2 | 101.8 | 102.4 | 2.4 |
| 2007 | 102.5 | 103.3 | 103.9 | 104.5 | 2.2 | 103.1 | 103.8 | 104.5 | 105.0 | 2.5 |
| 2008 | 105.5 | 106.0 | 106.6 | 106.9 | 2.3 | 106.0 | 106.8 | 107.5 | 107.8 | 2.7 |
| 2009 | 107.7 | 108.1 | 108.6 | 108.9 | 1.9 | 108.3 | 108.8 | 109.4 | 109.6 | 1.7 |
| 2010 | 109.9 | 110.5 | 111.3 | 111.5 | 2.4 | 109.8 | 110.3 | 111.1 | 111.3 | 1.6 |
| 2011 | 112.2 | 113.5 | 113.8 | 114.2 | 2.4 | 111.6 | 112.0 | 112.5 | 112.8 | 1.3 |
| 2012 | 114.5 | 115.1 | 115.7 | 116.0 | 1.6 | 113.7 | 114.0 | 114.7 | 115.1 | 2.0 |
| 2013 | 116.7 | 117.2 | 117.5 | 118.0 | 1.7 | 115.8 | 116.2 | 116.7 | 117.2 | 1.8 |
| 2014 | 118.9 | 119.5 | 120.3 | 120.6 | 2.2 | . . . | . . . | . . . | . . . | . . . |
| 2015 | 121.7 | 122.5 | 123.1 | 123.7 | 2.6 | 118.0 | 118.7 | 119.6 | 119.9 | 2.3 |
| 2016 | 124.7 | 125.6 | 126.4 | . . . | . . . | 123.9 | 124.9 | 125.9 | . . . | . . . |
| **Production** | | | | | | | | | | |
| 2001 | 84.9 | 85.2 | 86.0 | 86.7 | 3.2 | 88.4 | 89.1 | 89.7 | 90.5 | 3.7 |
| 2002 | 87.7 | 88.3 | 88.8 | 89.4 | 3.1 | 91.3 | 91.8 | 92.3 | 92.8 | 2.5 |
| 2003 | 91.0 | 91.7 | 92.5 | 93.0 | 4.0 | 93.6 | 94.1 | 94.8 | 95.1 | 2.5 |
| 2004 | 95.3 | 96.4 | 97.4 | 97.7 | 5.1 | 95.6 | 96.5 | 97.4 | 97.5 | 2.5 |
| 2005 | 98.6 | 99.1 | 99.6 | 100.0 | 2.4 | 98.3 | 98.9 | 99.5 | 100.0 | 2.6 |
| 2006 | 100.4 | 101.0 | 101.6 | 102.0 | 2.0 | 100.7 | 101.2 | 101.7 | 102.2 | 2.2 |
| 2007 | 102.1 | 102.8 | 103.2 | 104.0 | 2.0 | 103.1 | 103.6 | 104.2 | 104.6 | 2.3 |
| 2008 | 104.8 | 105.2 | 105.8 | 106.1 | 2.0 | 105.6 | 106.4 | 107.2 | 107.4 | 2.7 |
| 2009 | 107.1 | 107.6 | 108.0 | 108.2 | 2.0 | 108.1 | 108.5 | 109.0 | 109.3 | 1.8 |
| 2010 | 109.5 | 110.0 | 110.7 | 110.8 | 2.4 | 109.6 | 110.0 | 110.5 | 110.5 | 1.1 |
| 2011 | 111.7 | 113.2 | 113.4 | 113.8 | 2.7 | 111.1 | 111.5 | 112.0 | 112.3 | 1.6 |
| 2012 | 113.8 | 114.4 | 114.8 | 115.0 | 1.1 | 113.2 | 113.5 | 113.9 | 114.2 | 1.7 |
| 2013 | 115.7 | 116.1 | 116.3 | 116.7 | 1.5 | 115.0 | 115.5 | 116.0 | 116.4 | 1.9 |
| 2014 | 117.8 | 118.1 | 118.8 | 119.4 | 2.3 | 117.4 | 117.8 | 118.6 | 119.1 | 2.3 |
| 2015 | 120.4 | 121.0 | 121.7 | 122.5 | 2.6 | 119.9 | 120.5 | 121.2 | 122.0 | 2.4 |
| 2016 | 123.4 | 124.2 | 125.0 | . . . | . . . | 123.0 | 123.9 | 124.8 | . . . | . . . |

[1] Includes wages, salaries, and employer costs for employee benefits.
[2] Includes mining, construction, and manufacturing.
[3] Includes the following industries: wholesale trade; retail trade; transportation and warehousing; utilities; information; finance and insurance; real estate and rental and leasing; professional, scientific, and technical services; management of companies and enterprises; administrative and support and waste management and remediation services; education services; health care and social assistance; arts, entertainment, and recreation; accommodation and food services; and other services, except public administration.
. . . = Not available.

## Table 6-1. Employment Cost Index, Private Industry Workers, Total Compensation[1] and Wages and Salaries, by Selected Industry and Occupation, 2001–2016—*Continued*

(December 2005 = 100.)

| Characteristic and year | Total compensation | | | | | Wages and salaries | | | | |
|---|---|---|---|---|---|---|---|---|---|---|
| | Indexes | | | | Percent change for 12 months (ended December) | Indexes | | | | Percent change for 12 months (ended December) |
| | March | June | September | December | | March | June | September | December | |
| **Transportation and Material Moving** | | | | | | | | | | |
| 2001 | 85.8 | 86.7 | 87.7 | 88.5 | 4.2 | 89.0 | 89.9 | 90.8 | 91.6 | 4.1 |
| 2002 | 89.5 | 90.2 | 90.9 | 91.4 | 3.3 | 92.6 | 93.1 | 93.6 | 94.0 | 2.6 |
| 2003 | 92.4 | 93.4 | 94.0 | 94.4 | 3.3 | 94.7 | 95.3 | 95.6 | 95.8 | 1.9 |
| 2004 | 95.7 | 96.7 | 97.5 | 97.9 | 3.7 | 96.4 | 97.1 | 97.9 | 98.2 | 2.5 |
| 2005 | 98.3 | 99.0 | 99.8 | 100.0 | 2.1 | 98.5 | 98.9 | 99.7 | 100.0 | 1.8 |
| 2006 | 100.4 | 101.2 | 102.0 | 102.6 | 2.6 | 0.4 | 101.2 | 102.0 | 102.6 | 2.6 |
| 2007 | 103.1 | 104.1 | 104.9 | 105.3 | 2.6 | 3.2 | 104.1 | 105.0 | 105.4 | 2.7 |
| 2008 | 106.4 | 107.2 | 107.7 | 107.9 | 2.5 | 6.5 | 107.4 | 108.0 | 108.3 | 2.8 |
| 2009 | 108.4 | 108.9 | 109.6 | 109.7 | 1.7 | 8.5 | 109.2 | 109.9 | 110.1 | 1.7 |
| 2010 | 110.4 | 111.2 | 112.2 | 112.5 | 2.6 | 10.2 | 110.8 | 111.8 | 112.2 | 1.9 |
| 2011 | 113.0 | 114.0 | 114.4 | 114.9 | 2.1 | 12.2 | 112.8 | 113.2 | 113.6 | 1.2 |
| 2012 | 115.5 | 116.0 | 117.0 | 117.6 | 2.3 | 14.4 | 114.8 | 115.7 | 116.3 | 2.4 |
| 2013 | 118.2 | 118.6 | 119.2 | 119.7 | 1.8 | 16.9 | 117.0 | 117.7 | 118.2 | 1.6 |
| 2014 | 120.4 | 121.4 | 122.3 | 122.4 | 2.3 | 18.9 | 119.9 | 121.0 | 120.9 | 2.3 |
| 2015 | 123.5 | 124.4 | 125.1 | 125.3 | 2.4 | 21.9 | 122.8 | 123.4 | 123.8 | 2.4 |
| 2016 | 126.6 | 127.5 | 128.4 | . . . | . . . | 25.1 | 126.3 | 127.2 | . . . | . . . |
| **Service** | | | | | | | | | | |
| 2001 | 87.1 | 87.7 | 88.2 | 89.4 | 3.8 | 89.7 | 90.2 | 90.6 | 91.7 | 3.4 |
| 2002 | 90.2 | 90.6 | 91.5 | 92.0 | 2.9 | 92.5 | 92.8 | 93.4 | 93.9 | 2.4 |
| 2003 | 93.0 | 93.4 | 94.4 | 95.0 | 3.3 | 94.5 | 94.8 | 95.6 | 96.1 | 2.3 |
| 2004 | 95.9 | 96.7 | 97.2 | 97.7 | 2.8 | 96.4 | 96.9 | 97.4 | 97.9 | 1.9 |
| 2005 | 98.5 | 99.0 | 99.5 | 100.0 | 2.4 | 98.6 | 99.0 | 99.6 | 100.0 | 2.1 |
| 2006 | 0.8 | 101.5 | 102.3 | 103.1 | 3.1 | 100.6 | 101.3 | 102.0 | 102.9 | 2.9 |
| 2007 | 4.5 | 105.2 | 106.4 | 107.0 | 3.8 | 104.6 | 105.3 | 106.5 | 107.1 | 4.1 |
| 2008 | 7.8 | 108.7 | 109.4 | 109.8 | 2.6 | 107.9 | 108.8 | 109.7 | 110.1 | 2.8 |
| 2009 | 10.7 | 110.9 | 111.7 | 111.8 | 1.8 | 111.0 | 111.2 | 112.1 | 112.3 | 2.0 |
| 2010 | 12.4 | 112.7 | 113.3 | 113.5 | 1.5 | 112.6 | 112.7 | 113.3 | 113.5 | 1.1 |
| 2011 | 14.5 | 114.7 | 115.0 | 115.4 | 1.7 | 114.2 | 114.2 | 114.6 | 115.1 | 1.4 |
| 2012 | 16.0 | 116.4 | 116.8 | 117.4 | 1.7 | 115.4 | 115.8 | 116.2 | 116.8 | 1.5 |
| 2013 | 17.9 | 118.3 | 118.4 | 119.0 | 1.4 | 117.2 | 117.6 | 117.6 | 118.3 | 1.3 |
| 2014 | 19.2 | 119.6 | 120.5 | 121.1 | 1.8 | 118.5 | 119.0 | 120.1 | 120.7 | 2.0 |
| 2015 | 22.0 | 122.1 | 122.6 | 123.2 | 1.7 | 121.6 | 121.6 | 122.2 | 122.8 | 1.7 |
| 2016 | 24.4 | 125.5 | 126.5 | . . . | . . . | 124.0 | 125.2 | 126.4 | . . . | . . . |

[1]Includes wages, salaries, and employer costs for employee benefits.
[2]Includes mining, construction, and manufacturing.
[3]Includes the following industries: wholesale trade; retail trade; transportation and warehousing; utilities; information; finance and insurance; real estate and rental and leasing; professional, scientific, and technical services; management of companies and enterprises; administrative and support and waste management and remediation services; education services; health care and social assistance; arts, entertainment, and recreation; accommodation and food services; and other services, except public administration.
. . . = Not available.

## Table 6-2. Employment Cost Index, Private Industry Workers, Total Compensation[1] and Wages and Salaries, by Bargaining Status and Selected Industry, 2001–2016

(December 2005 = 100.)

| Characteristic and year | Total compensation | | | | | Wages and salaries | | | | |
|---|---|---|---|---|---|---|---|---|---|---|
| | Indexes | | | | Percent change for 12 months (ended December) | Indexes | | | | Percent change for 12 months (ended December) |
| | March | June | September | December | | March | June | September | December | |
| **WORKERS BY BARGAINING STATUS AND INDUSTRY** | | | | | | | | | | |
| **Union Workers** | | | | | | | | | | |
| 2001 | 82.0 | 82.9 | 83.7 | 84.8 | 4.2 | 86.5 | 87.4 | 88.3 | 89.6 | 4.3 |
| 2002 | 85.7 | 86.5 | 87.5 | 88.2 | 4.0 | 90.2 | 91.1 | 91.9 | 92.6 | 3.3 |
| 2003 | 89.5 | 90.7 | 91.6 | 92.3 | 4.6 | 93.0 | 93.8 | 94.4 | 94.9 | 2.5 |
| 2004 | 94.5 | 95.9 | 96.7 | 97.3 | 5.4 | 95.6 | 96.4 | 97.1 | 97.6 | 2.8 |
| 2005 | 97.9 | 98.8 | 99.6 | 100.0 | 2.8 | 97.9 | 98.7 | 99.5 | 100.0 | 2.5 |
| 2006 | 100.5 | 101.8 | 102.4 | 103.0 | 3.0 | 100.3 | 101.2 | 101.7 | 102.3 | 2.3 |
| 2007 | 102.7 | 103.9 | 104.4 | 105.1 | 2.0 | 102.8 | 103.7 | 104.4 | 104.7 | 2.3 |
| 2008 | 105.9 | 106.7 | 107.4 | 108.0 | 2.8 | 105.5 | 106.7 | 107.4 | 108.1 | 3.2 |
| 2009 | 109.1 | 109.8 | 110.5 | 111.1 | 2.9 | 108.8 | 109.6 | 110.2 | 110.9 | 2.6 |
| 2010 | 112.8 | 113.7 | 114.6 | 114.8 | 3.3 | 111.5 | 112.1 | 112.7 | 112.9 | 1.8 |
| 2011 | 115.6 | 117.1 | 117.4 | 117.9 | 2.7 | 113.6 | 114.0 | 114.6 | 114.9 | 1.8 |
| 2012 | 118.3 | 119.3 | 120.2 | 120.5 | 2.2 | 115.6 | 116.2 | 116.9 | 117.4 | 2.2 |
| 2013 | 121.5 | 122.1 | 122.5 | 122.6 | 1.7 | 118.4 | 119.0 | 119.6 | 119.8 | 2.0 |
| 2014 | 123.5 | 125.0 | 125.8 | 126.7 | 3.3 | 120.5 | 121.2 | 122.1 | 123.1 | 2.8 |
| 2015 | 127.4 | 127.5 | 128.0 | 128.7 | 1.6 | 123.7 | 124.5 | 124.8 | 125.5 | 1.9 |
| 2016 | 129.6 | 130.0 | 130.4 | . . . | . . . | 126.4 | 126.8 | 127.2 | . . . | . . . |
| **Union Workers, Goods-Producing[2]** | | | | | | | | | | |
| 2001 | 81.9 | 82.7 | 83.4 | 84.0 | 2.9 | 87.2 | 88.2 | 88.9 | 89.5 | 3.5 |
| 2002 | 84.8 | 85.5 | 86.4 | 87.1 | 3.7 | 90.0 | 90.9 | 91.7 | 92.4 | 3.2 |
| 2003 | 88.9 | 90.2 | 90.9 | 91.7 | 5.3 | 92.9 | 94.0 | 94.5 | 95.0 | 2.8 |
| 2004 | 94.6 | 95.9 | 96.7 | 97.2 | 6.0 | 95.4 | 96.3 | 96.9 | 97.1 | 2.2 |
| 2005 | 97.7 | 98.8 | 99.6 | 100.0 | 2.9 | 97.5 | 98.5 | 99.2 | 100.0 | 3.0 |
| 2006 | 99.9 | 101.2 | 101.8 | 102.2 | 2.2 | 100.5 | 101.6 | 101.9 | 102.3 | 2.3 |
| 2007 | 1.5 | 102.8 | 103.1 | 104.0 | 1.8 | 102.7 | 103.6 | 104.3 | 104.3 | 2.0 |
| 2008 | 4.6 | 105.6 | 106.2 | 106.9 | 2.8 | 105.2 | 106.4 | 107.1 | 107.7 | 3.3 |
| 2009 | 8.0 | 108.9 | 109.5 | 110.0 | 2.9 | 108.2 | 108.8 | 109.5 | 109.8 | 1.9 |
| 2010 | 11.9 | 112.6 | 113.8 | 113.9 | 3.5 | 110.2 | 110.7 | 111.1 | 111.2 | 1.3 |
| 2011 | 14.3 | 116.4 | 116.3 | 116.9 | 2.6 | 111.7 | 112.1 | 112.8 | 112.9 | 1.5 |
| 2012 | 15.8 | 116.6 | 117.7 | 118.0 | 0.9 | 113.5 | 113.8 | 114.4 | 115.0 | 1.9 |
| 2013 | 18.6 | 118.8 | 119.2 | 119.6 | 1.4 | 115.7 | 115.9 | 116.8 | 117.0 | 1.7 |
| 2014 | 20.6 | 120.9 | 121.9 | 122.4 | 2.3 | 117.7 | 118.2 | 119.0 | 119.5 | 2.1 |
| 2015 | 23.0 | 123.9 | 124.5 | 125.4 | 2.5 | 119.9 | 120.7 | 121.2 | 121.9 | 2.0 |
| 2016 | 25.9 | 126.8 | 127.1 | . . . | . . . | 122.3 | 123.3 | 123.7 | . . . | . . . |
| **Union Workers, Manufacturing** | | | | | | | | | | |
| 2001 | 81.1 | 81.4 | 82.0 | 83.0 | 2.7 | 87.3 | 88.1 | 88.8 | 89.7 | 3.7 |
| 2002 | 84.1 | 84.7 | 85.4 | 86.5 | 4.2 | 90.3 | 90.8 | 91.6 | 92.5 | 3.1 |
| 2003 | 88.6 | 89.5 | 90.1 | 91.0 | 5.2 | 93.3 | 94.2 | 94.5 | 95.0 | 2.7 |
| 2004 | 95.6 | 96.7 | 97.5 | 97.8 | 7.5 | 95.5 | 96.2 | 97.0 | 97.1 | 2.2 |
| 2005 | 98.3 | 99.1 | 99.7 | 100.0 | 2.2 | 97.6 | 98.3 | 99.0 | 100.0 | 3.0 |
| 2006 | 99.3 | 100.1 | 100.5 | 100.8 | 0.8 | 100.6 | 101.2 | 101.4 | 101.7 | 1.7 |
| 2007 | 99.2 | 100.0 | 100.0 | 101.0 | 0.2 | 102.0 | 102.5 | 102.9 | 102.6 | 0.9 |
| 2008 | 101.4 | 101.7 | 102.1 | 102.8 | 1.8 | 103.4 | 104.4 | 104.9 | 105.5 | 2.8 |
| 2009 | 104.4 | 104.8 | 105.3 | 105.8 | 2.9 | 106.0 | 106.4 | 107.0 | 107.3 | 1.7 |
| 2010 | 108.6 | 109.1 | 110.5 | 110.5 | 4.4 | 107.8 | 108.2 | 108.6 | 108.7 | 1.3 |
| 2011 | 110.9 | 113.8 | 113.2 | 113.8 | 3.0 | 109.4 | 109.8 | 110.6 | 110.7 | 1.8 |
| 2012 | 112.1 | 112.8 | 113.6 | 113.7 | -0.1 | 111.5 | 111.8 | 112.1 | 112.5 | 1.6 |
| 2013 | 113.9 | 114.1 | 113.8 | 114.2 | 0.4 | 113.5 | 113.9 | 114.4 | 114.8 | 2.0 |
| 2014 | 115.4 | 115.9 | 116.8 | 117.4 | 2.8 | 115.6 | 116.2 | 116.7 | 116.9 | 1.8 |
| 2015 | 118.1 | 118.6 | 119.3 | 120.4 | 2.6 | 117.8 | 118.5 | 118.8 | 119.6 | 2.3 |
| 2016 | 121.1 | 121.7 | 121.9 | . . . | . . . | 120.2 | 120.8 | 121.4 | . . . | . . . |
| **Union Workers, Service-Providing[3]** | | | | | | | | | | |
| 2001 | 82.0 | 83.0 | 84.0 | 85.5 | 5.2 | 85.9 | 86.8 | 87.8 | 89.6 | 4.9 |
| 2002 | 86.4 | 87.3 | 88.4 | 89.1 | 4.2 | 90.3 | 91.2 | 92.0 | 92.7 | 3.5 |
| 2003 | 90.1 | 91.1 | 92.3 | 92.8 | 4.2 | 93.1 | 93.6 | 94.4 | 94.8 | 2.3 |
| 2004 | 94.4 | 95.8 | 96.6 | 97.3 | 4.8 | 95.7 | 96.5 | 97.3 | 98.0 | 3.4 |
| 2005 | 98.1 | 98.8 | 99.6 | 100.0 | 2.8 | 98.2 | 99.0 | 99.7 | 100.0 | 2.0 |
| 2006 | 101.0 | 102.2 | 102.9 | 103.6 | 3.6 | 100.1 | 100.9 | 101.6 | 102.2 | 2.2 |
| 2007 | 103.7 | 104.7 | 105.4 | 106.0 | 2.3 | 102.9 | 103.8 | 104.6 | 104.9 | 2.6 |
| 2008 | 107.0 | 107.5 | 108.3 | 108.8 | 2.6 | 105.8 | 106.9 | 107.7 | 108.3 | 3.2 |
| 2009 | 109.9 | 110.6 | 111.3 | 111.9 | 2.8 | 109.2 | 110.1 | 110.8 | 111.6 | 3.0 |
| 2010 | 113.4 | 114.5 | 115.3 | 115.5 | 3.2 | 112.4 | 113.1 | 113.8 | 114.2 | 2.3 |
| 2011 | 116.8 | 117.7 | 118.3 | 118.8 | 2.9 | 115.0 | 115.3 | 115.8 | 116.3 | 1.8 |
| 2012 | 120.4 | 121.5 | 122.2 | 122.6 | 3.2 | 117.0 | 117.9 | 118.7 | 119.1 | 2.4 |
| 2013 | 123.9 | 124.9 | 125.2 | 125.2 | 2.1 | 120.4 | 121.3 | 121.7 | 121.8 | 2.3 |
| 2014 | 126.0 | 128.3 | 129.0 | 130.0 | 3.8 | 122.6 | 123.4 | 124.4 | 125.6 | 3.1 |
| 2015 | 130.8 | 130.4 | 130.8 | 131.4 | 1.1 | 126.3 | 127.2 | 127.3 | 128.0 | 1.9 |
| 2016 | 132.7 | 132.7 | 133.2 | . . . | . . . | 129.1 | 129.2 | 129.8 | . . . | . . . |

[1]Includes wages, salaries, and employer costs for employee benefits.
[2]Includes mining, construction, and manufacturing.
[3]Includes the following industries: wholesale trade; retail trade; transportation and warehousing; utilities; information; finance and insurance; real estate and rental and leasing; professional, scientific, and technical services; management of companies and enterprises; administrative and support and waste management and remediation services; education services; health care and social assistance; arts, entertainment, and recreation; accommodation and food services; and other services, except public administration.
. . . = Not available.

**Table 6-2. Employment Cost Index, Private Industry Workers, Total Compensation[1] and Wages and Salaries, by Bargaining Status and Selected Industry, 2001–2016**—*Continued*

(December 2005 = 100.)

| Characteristic and year | Total compensation | | | | | Wages and salaries | | | | |
|---|---|---|---|---|---|---|---|---|---|---|
| | Indexes | | | | Percent change for 12 months (ended December) | Indexes | | | | Percent change for 12 months (ended December) |
| | March | June | September | December | | March | June | September | December | |
| **Nonunion Workers** | | | | | | | | | | |
| 2001 | 85.5 | 86.3 | 87.2 | 87.8 | 4.2 | 87.7 | 88.6 | 89.3 | 89.9 | 3.7 |
| 2002 | 88.7 | 89.6 | 90.0 | 90.3 | 2.8 | 90.8 | 91.7 | 92.0 | 92.2 | 2.6 |
| 2003 | 91.8 | 92.5 | 93.5 | 93.9 | 4.0 | 93.3 | 94.0 | 94.9 | 95.1 | 3.1 |
| 2004 | 95.0 | 95.9 | 96.7 | 97.2 | 3.5 | 95.8 | 96.5 | 97.3 | 97.6 | 2.6 |
| 2005 | 98.3 | 98.9 | 99.5 | 100.0 | 2.9 | 98.3 | 98.9 | 99.5 | 100.0 | 2.5 |
| 2006 | 100.9 | 101.7 | 102.6 | 103.2 | 3.2 | 100.8 | 101.8 | 102.7 | 103.3 | 3.3 |
| 2007 | 104.2 | 105.1 | 105.9 | 106.5 | 3.2 | 104.5 | 105.3 | 106.2 | 106.9 | 3.5 |
| 2008 | 107.5 | 108.3 | 108.9 | 109.1 | 2.4 | 107.9 | 108.7 | 109.4 | 109.6 | 2.5 |
| 2009 | 109.4 | 109.6 | 109.9 | 110.1 | 0.9 | 110.0 | 110.2 | 110.6 | 110.9 | 1.2 |
| 2010 | 110.9 | 111.4 | 111.8 | 112.1 | 1.8 | 111.4 | 111.9 | 112.4 | 112.7 | 1.6 |
| 2011 | 113.0 | 113.8 | 114.2 | 114.5 | 2.1 | 113.2 | 113.8 | 114.3 | 114.6 | 1.7 |
| 2012 | 115.3 | 116.0 | 116.3 | 116.6 | 1.8 | 115.2 | 115.9 | 116.3 | 116.5 | 1.7 |
| 2013 | 117.3 | 118.0 | 118.5 | 119.0 | 2.1 | 117.2 | 117.9 | 118.4 | 118.9 | 2.1 |
| 2014 | 119.4 | 120.4 | 121.1 | 121.5 | 2.1 | 119.2 | 120.2 | 121.0 | 121.5 | 2.2 |
| 2015 | 122.5 | 122.7 | 123.4 | 123.8 | 1.9 | 122.4 | 122.7 | 123.6 | 124.0 | 2.1 |
| 2016 | 124.7 | 125.7 | 126.3 | . . . | . . . | 125.0 | 126.0 | 126.6 | . . . | . . . |
| **Nonunion, Goods-Producing[2]** | | | | | | | | | | |
| 2001 | 84.7 | 85.5 | 86.0 | 86.7 | 3.8 | 87.7 | 88.6 | 89.3 | 89.9 | 3.7 |
| 2002 | 87.8 | 88.5 | 88.8 | 89.7 | 3.5 | 90.8 | 91.7 | 92.0 | 92.2 | 2.6 |
| 2003 | 91.1 | 91.9 | 92.6 | 92.9 | 3.6 | 93.3 | 94.0 | 94.9 | 95.1 | 3.1 |
| 2004 | 94.5 | 95.2 | 96.4 | 96.8 | 4.2 | 95.8 | 96.5 | 97.3 | 97.6 | 2.6 |
| 2005 | 98.1 | 99.0 | 99.9 | 100.0 | 3.3 | 98.3 | 98.9 | 99.5 | 100.0 | 2.5 |
| 2006 | 100.5 | 101.4 | 102.0 | 102.5 | 2.5 | 100.8 | 101.8 | 102.7 | 103.3 | 3.3 |
| 2007 | 103.3 | 104.2 | 104.8 | 105.4 | 2.8 | 104.5 | 105.3 | 106.2 | 106.9 | 3.5 |
| 2008 | 106.5 | 107.1 | 107.6 | 107.7 | 2.2 | 107.9 | 108.7 | 109.4 | 109.6 | 2.5 |
| 2009 | 107.9 | 108.0 | 108.0 | 108.2 | 0.5 | 110.0 | 110.2 | 110.6 | 110.9 | 1.2 |
| 2010 | 109.1 | 109.5 | 110.1 | 110.2 | 1.8 | 111.4 | 111.9 | 112.4 | 112.7 | 1.6 |
| 2011 | 111.3 | 112.2 | 112.5 | 112.9 | 2.5 | 113.2 | 113.8 | 114.3 | 114.6 | 1.7 |
| 2012 | 113.5 | 114.1 | 114.6 | 114.9 | 1.8 | 115.2 | 115.9 | 116.3 | 116.5 | 1.7 |
| 2013 | 115.7 | 116.4 | 116.9 | 117.2 | 2.0 | 117.2 | 117.9 | 118.4 | 118.9 | 2.1 |
| 2014 | 117.9 | 118.6 | 119.2 | 119.7 | 2.1 | 119.2 | 120.2 | 121.0 | 121.5 | 2.2 |
| 2015 | 120.4 | 121.3 | 121.8 | 122.5 | 2.3 | 122.4 | 122.7 | 123.6 | 124.0 | 2.1 |
| 2016 | 123.2 | 124.1 | 124.6 | . . . | . . . | 125.0 | 126.0 | 126.6 | . . . | . . . |
| **Nonunion Workers, Manufacturing** | | | | | | | | | | |
| 2001 | 84.5 | 85.3 | 85.8 | 86.3 | 3.6 | 88.5 | 89.4 | 89.8 | 90.3 | 3.4 |
| 2002 | 87.6 | 88.4 | 88.7 | 89.4 | 3.6 | 91.4 | 92.0 | 92.4 | 92.9 | 2.9 |
| 2003 | 91.2 | 91.9 | 92.6 | 92.8 | 3.8 | 93.9 | 94.5 | 94.9 | 95.2 | 2.5 |
| 2004 | 94.4 | 95.3 | 96.4 | 96.6 | 4.1 | 95.8 | 96.5 | 97.5 | 97.5 | 2.4 |
| 2005 | 98.2 | 99.1 | 99.8 | 100.0 | 3.5 | 98.4 | 99.0 | 99.8 | 100.0 | 2.6 |
| 2006 | 100.3 | 101.3 | 101.7 | 102.1 | 2.1 | 100.7 | 101.8 | 102.0 | 102.5 | 2.5 |
| 2007 | 102.8 | 103.7 | 104.1 | 104.6 | 2.4 | 103.6 | 104.2 | 104.9 | 105.5 | 2.9 |
| 2008 | 105.6 | 106.2 | 106.6 | 106.8 | 2.1 | 106.6 | 107.3 | 108.0 | 108.2 | 2.6 |
| 2009 | 107.1 | 107.3 | 107.3 | 107.5 | 0.7 | 108.6 | 108.9 | 109.1 | 109.3 | 1.0 |
| 2010 | 108.5 | 109.2 | 109.9 | 110.0 | 2.3 | 109.8 | 110.5 | 111.1 | 111.2 | 1.7 |
| 2011 | 111.6 | 112.5 | 112.8 | 113.0 | 2.7 | 112.1 | 112.6 | 113.0 | 113.3 | 1.9 |
| 2012 | 113.9 | 114.4 | 115.0 | 115.3 | 2.0 | 114.1 | 114.6 | 115.2 | 115.4 | 1.9 |
| 2013 | 116.3 | 117.0 | 117.5 | 117.8 | 2.2 | 116.2 | 117.1 | 117.5 | 117.8 | 2.1 |
| 2014 | 118.8 | 119.5 | 120.1 | 120.6 | 2.4 | 118.7 | 119.6 | 120.0 | 120.5 | 2.3 |
| 2015 | 121.6 | 122.5 | 122.9 | 123.5 | 2.4 | 121.5 | 122.5 | 123.2 | 123.8 | 2.7 |
| 2016 | 124.4 | 125.3 | 126.0 | . . . | . . . | 124.8 | 125.9 | 126.6 | . . . | . . . |
| **Nonunion, Service-Providing[3]** | | | | | | | | | | |
| 2001 | 85.7 | 86.5 | 87.5 | 88.0 | 4.1 | 87.6 | 88.5 | 89.3 | 89.9 | 3.8 |
| 2002 | 88.9 | 89.9 | 90.4 | 90.5 | 2.8 | 90.8 | 91.7 | 92.0 | 92.1 | 2.4 |
| 2003 | 91.9 | 92.7 | 93.7 | 94.1 | 4.0 | 93.3 | 94.0 | 94.9 | 95.2 | 3.4 |
| 2004 | 95.2 | 96.1 | 96.9 | 97.3 | 3.4 | 95.8 | 96.6 | 97.3 | 97.7 | 2.6 |
| 2005 | 98.3 | 98.9 | 99.4 | 100.0 | 2.8 | 98.4 | 99.0 | 99.5 | 100.0 | 2.4 |
| 2006 | 101.0 | 101.8 | 102.7 | 103.4 | 3.4 | 100.8 | 101.7 | 102.7 | 103.4 | 3.4 |
| 2007 | 104.4 | 105.3 | 106.2 | 106.8 | 3.3 | 104.6 | 105.4 | 106.3 | 107.0 | 3.5 |
| 2008 | 107.7 | 108.6 | 109.2 | 109.4 | 2.4 | 107.9 | 108.8 | 109.4 | 109.7 | 2.5 |
| 2009 | 109.8 | 110.0 | 110.4 | 110.6 | 1.1 | 110.1 | 110.3 | 110.8 | 111.0 | 1.2 |
| 2010 | 111.3 | 111.9 | 112.3 | 112.7 | 1.9 | 111.6 | 112.2 | 112.6 | 113.0 | 1.8 |
| 2011 | 113.5 | 114.3 | 114.7 | 115.0 | 2.0 | 113.4 | 114.0 | 114.5 | 114.8 | 1.6 |
| 2012 | 115.8 | 116.5 | 116.8 | 117.1 | 1.8 | 115.5 | 116.2 | 116.5 | 116.8 | 1.7 |
| 2013 | 117.8 | 118.5 | 119.0 | 119.4 | 2.0 | 117.4 | 118.2 | 118.6 | 119.2 | 2.1 |
| 2014 | 119.8 | 120.9 | 121.6 | 122.0 | 2.2 | 119.4 | 120.5 | 121.3 | 121.7 | 2.1 |
| 2015 | 123.1 | 123.1 | 123.9 | 124.2 | 1.8 | 122.8 | 122.9 | 123.8 | 124.2 | 2.1 |
| 2016 | 125.2 | 126.1 | 126.7 | . . . | . . . | 125.1 | 126.2 | 126.8 | . . . | . . . |

[1]Includes wages, salaries, and employer costs for employee benefits.
[2]Includes mining, construction, and manufacturing.
[3]Includes the following industries: wholesale trade; retail trade; transportation and warehousing; utilities; information; finance and insurance; real estate and rental and leasing; professional, scientific, and technical services; management of companies and enterprises; administrative and support and waste management and remediation services; education services; health care and social assistance; arts, entertainment, and recreation; accommodation and food services; and other services, except public administration.
. . . = Not available.

## Table 6-3. Employment Cost Index, Private Industry Workers, Total Compensation[1] and Wages and Salaries, by Region, and Metropolitan Area Status, 2001–2016

(December 2005 = 100.)

| Geography type and year | Total compensation | | | | | Wages and salaries | | | | |
|---|---|---|---|---|---|---|---|---|---|---|
| | Indexes | | | | Percent change for 12 months (ended December) | Indexes | | | | Percent change for 12 months (ended December) |
| | March | June | September | December | | March | June | September | December | |
| **CENSUS REGIONS AND DIVISIONS** | | | | | | | | | | |
| **Northeast** | | | | | | | | | | |
| 2001 | 84.3 | 85.3 | 86.2 | 86.7 | 3.8 | 86.8 | 87.8 | 88.6 | 89.2 | 3.8 |
| 2002 | 87.7 | 88.6 | 88.9 | 89.3 | 3.0 | 90.2 | 91.0 | 91.1 | 91.5 | 2.6 |
| 2003 | 90.6 | 91.4 | 92.4 | 92.9 | 4.0 | 92.4 | 93.2 | 94.1 | 94.5 | 3.3 |
| 2004 | 94.2 | 95.5 | 96.3 | 96.6 | 4.0 | 95.3 | 96.3 | 97.1 | 97.2 | 2.9 |
| 2005 | 97.6 | 98.5 | 99.2 | 100.0 | 3.5 | 97.8 | 98.6 | 99.2 | 100.0 | 2.9 |
| 2006 | 100.9 | 101.8 | 102.5 | 103.3 | 3.3 | 100.8 | 101.7 | 102.5 | 103.1 | 3.1 |
| 2007 | 104.0 | 105.1 | 106.2 | 106.8 | 3.4 | 104.0 | 105.0 | 106.1 | 106.6 | 3.4 |
| 2008 | 107.4 | 108.1 | 108.7 | 109.5 | 2.5 | 107.5 | 108.2 | 108.7 | 109.6 | 2.8 |
| 2009 | 109.8 | 110.2 | 110.7 | 111.0 | 1.4 | 109.9 | 110.3 | 110.8 | 111.1 | 1.4 |
| 2010 | 111.8 | 112.7 | 113.1 | 113.6 | 2.3 | 111.7 | 112.6 | 112.9 | 113.4 | 2.1 |
| 2011 | 114.4 | 115.3 | 115.7 | 116.1 | 2.2 | 113.7 | 114.6 | 114.9 | 115.3 | 1.7 |
| 2012 | 116.5 | 117.1 | 117.6 | 117.8 | 1.5 | 115.8 | 116.4 | 116.7 | 117.0 | 1.5 |
| 2013 | 118.7 | 119.4 | 119.7 | 120.1 | 2.0 | 117.6 | 118.4 | 118.7 | 119.1 | 1.8 |
| 2014 | 120.5 | 121.8 | 122.7 | 123.2 | 2.6 | 119.4 | 120.6 | 121.7 | 122.2 | 2.6 |
| 2015 | 125.3 | 124.3 | 125.1 | 125.6 | 1.9 | 124.7 | 123.2 | 124.2 | 124.7 | 2.0 |
| 2016 | 127.3 | 127.7 | 128.2 | . . . | . . . | 126.9 | 127.2 | 127.7 | . . . | . . . |
| **New England** | | | | | | | | | | |
| 2006 | 100.7 | 101.4 | 102.1 | 103.1 | 3.1 | 100.7 | 101.5 | 102.3 | 103.1 | 3.1 |
| 2007 | 103.6 | 104.8 | 105.4 | 106.1 | 2.9 | 103.6 | 104.8 | 105.7 | 106.3 | 3.1 |
| 2008 | 106.7 | 107.1 | 107.8 | 109.5 | 3.2 | 107.1 | 107.6 | 108.3 | 110.3 | 3.8 |
| 2009 | 109.9 | 110.2 | 111.2 | 111.5 | 1.8 | 110.5 | 110.6 | 111.7 | 112.1 | 1.6 |
| 2010 | 112.3 | 113.1 | 113.4 | 114.1 | 2.3 | 112.6 | 113.4 | 113.5 | 114.3 | 2.0 |
| 2011 | 114.8 | 116.0 | 116.2 | 116.3 | 1.9 | 114.5 | 115.9 | 116.0 | 116.0 | 1.5 |
| 2012 | 116.9 | 117.4 | 118.0 | 118.5 | 1.9 | 116.6 | 117.2 | 117.8 | 118.2 | 1.9 |
| 2013 | 118.9 | 120.0 | 120.5 | 121.6 | 2.6 | 118.6 | 119.8 | 120.5 | 121.8 | 3.0 |
| 2014 | 121.5 | 123.4 | 125.2 | 124.8 | 2.6 | 121.4 | 123.5 | 126.0 | 125.3 | 2.9 |
| 2015 | 130.6 | 125.3 | 127.6 | 127.7 | 2.3 | 133.1 | 125.5 | 128.5 | 128.4 | 2.5 |
| 2016 | 131.2 | 131.3 | 130.2 | . . . | . . . | 132.9 | 132.8 | 131.1 | . . . | . . . |
| **Middle Atlantic** | | | | | | | | | | |
| 2006 | 100.9 | 101.9 | 102.6 | 103.3 | 3.3 | 100.8 | 101.7 | 102.5 | 103.1 | 3.1 |
| 2007 | 104.2 | 105.3 | 106.5 | 107.1 | 3.7 | 104.2 | 105.1 | 106.4 | 106.7 | 3.5 |
| 2008 | 107.8 | 108.6 | 109.1 | 109.5 | 2.2 | 107.6 | 108.4 | 109.0 | 109.4 | 2.5 |
| 2009 | 109.8 | 110.2 | 110.6 | 110.8 | 1.2 | 109.7 | 110.1 | 110.4 | 110.7 | 1.2 |
| 2010 | 111.6 | 112.5 | 113.0 | 113.4 | 2.3 | 111.3 | 112.3 | 112.7 | 113.1 | 2.2 |
| 2011 | 114.3 | 115.1 | 115.5 | 116.0 | 2.3 | 113.4 | 114.0 | 114.5 | 115.0 | 1.7 |
| 2012 | 116.4 | 117.0 | 117.4 | 117.6 | 1.4 | 115.4 | 116.1 | 116.4 | 116.5 | 1.3 |
| 2013 | 118.6 | 119.2 | 119.5 | 119.6 | 1.7 | 117.3 | 117.9 | 118.0 | 118.1 | 1.4 |
| 2014 | 120.1 | 121.2 | 121.8 | 122.6 | 2.5 | 118.6 | 119.4 | 120.1 | 120.9 | 2.4 |
| 2015 | 123.4 | 123.9 | 124.2 | 124.8 | 1.8 | 121.6 | 122.3 | 122.6 | 123.3 | 2.0 |
| 2016 | 125.9 | 126.3 | 127.4 | . . . | . . . | 124.6 | 125.2 | 126.3 | . . . | . . . |
| **South** | | | | | | | | | | |
| 2001 | 86.4 | 87.2 | 88.1 | 88.7 | 4.2 | 88.9 | 89.7 | 90.5 | 91.0 | 3.6 |
| 2002 | 89.5 | 90.5 | 91.2 | 91.2 | 2.8 | 91.8 | 92.7 | 93.3 | 93.2 | 2.4 |
| 2003 | 92.0 | 92.7 | 93.6 | 93.9 | 3.0 | 93.5 | 94.1 | 94.9 | 95.0 | 1.9 |
| 2004 | 95.2 | 96.2 | 97.1 | 97.7 | 4.0 | 95.8 | 96.7 | 97.5 | 98.0 | 3.2 |
| 2005 | 98.9 | 99.3 | 99.7 | 100.0 | 2.4 | 98.9 | 99.3 | 99.7 | 100.0 | 2.0 |
| 2006 | 101.0 | 101.6 | 102.8 | 103.5 | 3.5 | 101.0 | 101.6 | 102.9 | 103.6 | 3.6 |
| 2007 | 104.3 | 105.3 | 106.1 | 106.7 | 3.1 | 104.6 | 105.6 | 106.5 | 107.0 | 3.3 |
| 2008 | 107.8 | 108.5 | 109.1 | 109.3 | 2.4 | 108.1 | 109.1 | 109.8 | 110.0 | 2.8 |
| 2009 | 109.8 | 110.1 | 110.6 | 110.7 | 1.3 | 110.4 | 110.7 | 111.3 | 111.5 | 1.4 |
| 2010 | 111.5 | 112.0 | 112.5 | 112.8 | 1.9 | 111.9 | 112.4 | 112.9 | 113.4 | 1.7 |
| 2011 | 113.4 | 114.3 | 114.7 | 115.0 | 2.0 | 113.7 | 114.4 | 115.0 | 115.2 | 1.6 |
| 2012 | 116.0 | 116.8 | 117.2 | 117.7 | 2.3 | 116.0 | 116.7 | 117.3 | 117.8 | 2.3 |
| 2013 | 118.6 | 119.3 | 119.7 | 120.1 | 2.0 | 118.7 | 119.3 | 119.7 | 120.2 | 2.0 |
| 2014 | 120.6 | 121.7 | 122.3 | 122.7 | 2.2 | 120.7 | 121.7 | 122.4 | 122.8 | 2.2 |
| 2015 | 123.2 | 123.9 | 124.3 | 124.6 | 1.5 | 123.3 | 124.2 | 124.7 | 125.0 | 1.8 |
| 2016 | 125.1 | 125.9 | 126.2 | . . . | . . . | 125.4 | 126.5 | 126.8 | . . . | . . . |

[1]Includes wages, salaries, and employer costs for employee benefits.
. . . = Not available.

## Table 6-3. Employment Cost Index, Private Industry Workers, Total Compensation[1] and Wages and Salaries, by Region, and Metropolitan Area Status, 2001–2016—*Continued*

(December 2005 = 100.)

| Geography type and year | Total compensation | | | | | Wages and salaries | | | | |
|---|---|---|---|---|---|---|---|---|---|---|
| | Indexes | | | | Percent change for 12 months (ended December) | Indexes | | | | Percent change for 12 months (ended December) |
| | March | June | September | December | | March | June | September | December | |
| **South Atlantic** | | | | | | | | | | |
| 2006 | 101.2 | 101.9 | 103.1 | 103.8 | 3.8 | 101.3 | 101.9 | 103.2 | 103.9 | 3.9 |
| 2007 | 104.9 | 106.0 | 106.8 | 107.3 | 3.4 | 105.0 | 106.1 | 106.9 | 107.5 | 3.5 |
| 2008 | 108.5 | 109.1 | 109.7 | 109.8 | 2.3 | 108.6 | 109.5 | 110.2 | 110.3 | 2.6 |
| 2009 | 110.3 | 110.7 | 111.3 | 111.5 | 1.5 | 110.8 | 111.3 | 111.9 | 112.2 | 1.7 |
| 2010 | 112.2 | 112.6 | 113.0 | 113.3 | 1.6 | 112.5 | 112.9 | 113.3 | 113.7 | 1.3 |
| 2011 | 113.8 | 114.6 | 115.1 | 115.4 | 1.9 | 114.0 | 114.6 | 115.4 | 115.6 | 1.7 |
| 2012 | 116.4 | 117.3 | 117.8 | 118.3 | 2.5 | 116.4 | 117.3 | 118.0 | 118.5 | 2.5 |
| 2013 | 119.1 | 119.8 | 120.2 | 120.6 | 1.9 | 119.2 | 120.0 | 120.2 | 120.7 | 1.9 |
| 2014 | 121.3 | 122.4 | 122.9 | 123.4 | 2.3 | 121.3 | 122.3 | 122.9 | 123.4 | 2.2 |
| 2015 | 124.2 | 124.6 | 125.3 | 125.6 | 1.8 | 124.1 | 124.7 | 125.6 | 126.0 | 2.1 |
| 2016 | 126.0 | 127.4 | 127.4 | . . . | . . . | 126.4 | 128.0 | 127.9 | . . . | . . . |
| **East South Central** | | | | | | | | | | |
| 2006 | 100.7 | 100.9 | 101.5 | 102.3 | 2.3 | 100.7 | 101.5 | 102.1 | 103.1 | 3.1 |
| 2007 | 103.3 | 103.8 | 104.8 | 105.4 | 3.0 | 104.2 | 104.5 | 105.6 | 106.3 | 3.1 |
| 2008 | 106.5 | 107.2 | 108.0 | 108.0 | 2.5 | 107.2 | 107.9 | 109.0 | 109.0 | 2.5 |
| 2009 | 108.5 | 108.7 | 109.2 | 109.3 | 1.2 | 109.2 | 109.5 | 110.1 | 110.2 | 1.1 |
| 2010 | 110.0 | 110.8 | 111.0 | 110.9 | 1.5 | 110.8 | 111.4 | 111.6 | 111.5 | 1.2 |
| 2011 | 112.1 | 112.7 | 113.0 | 113.2 | 2.1 | 112.6 | 112.9 | 113.4 | 113.5 | 1.8 |
| 2012 | 114.0 | 115.1 | 115.3 | 115.8 | 2.3 | 114.1 | 114.8 | 114.9 | 115.4 | 1.7 |
| 2013 | 116.8 | 116.9 | 117.5 | 117.8 | 1.7 | 116.3 | 116.4 | 116.8 | 117.3 | 1.6 |
| 2014 | 118.4 | 119.1 | 119.3 | 119.8 | 1.7 | 117.8 | 118.5 | 118.8 | 119.4 | 1.8 |
| 2015 | 120.7 | 121.3 | 121.7 | 122.4 | 2.2 | 120.2 | 121.2 | 121.7 | 122.5 | 2.6 |
| 2016 | 123.1 | 124.7 | 125.1 | . . . | . . . | 123.0 | 124.7 | 125.2 | . . . | . . . |
| **West South Central** | | | | | | | | | | |
| 2006 | 100.7 | 101.4 | 102.7 | 103.4 | 3.4 | 100.6 | 101.2 | 102.7 | 103.4 | 3.4 |
| 2007 | 103.7 | 104.8 | 105.6 | 106.1 | 2.6 | 104.1 | 105.3 | 106.1 | 106.6 | 3.1 |
| 2008 | 107.3 | 108.2 | 108.7 | 109.0 | 2.7 | 107.8 | 108.8 | 109.4 | 109.8 | 3.0 |
| 2009 | 109.4 | 109.5 | 109.9 | 109.9 | 0.8 | 110.1 | 110.2 | 110.8 | 110.9 | 1.0 |
| 2010 | 110.8 | 111.4 | 112.2 | 112.7 | 2.5 | 111.3 | 111.9 | 112.8 | 113.5 | 2.3 |
| 2011 | 113.2 | 114.4 | 114.7 | 115.0 | 2.0 | 113.7 | 114.5 | 115.0 | 115.2 | 1.5 |
| 2012 | 116.2 | 116.8 | 117.0 | 117.6 | 2.3 | 116.1 | 116.6 | 117.1 | 117.7 | 2.2 |
| 2013 | 118.5 | 119.3 | 119.8 | 120.2 | 2.2 | 118.7 | 119.5 | 120.0 | 120.6 | 2.5 |
| 2014 | 120.3 | 121.7 | 122.4 | 122.6 | 2.0 | 120.8 | 121.9 | 122.9 | 123.1 | 2.1 |
| 2015 | 122.6 | 123.7 | 123.6 | 123.6 | 0.8 | 123.2 | 124.5 | 124.4 | 124.3 | 1.0 |
| 2016 | 124.1 | 123.9 | 124.6 | . . . | . . . | 124.8 | 124.5 | 125.5 | . . . | . . . |
| **Midwest** | | | | | | | | | | |
| 2001 | 84.8 | 85.4 | 86.1 | 86.7 | 3.5 | 86.8 | 87.6 | 88.3 | 88.9 | 3.3 |
| 2002 | 88.0 | 88.7 | 89.0 | 89.5 | 3.2 | 90.3 | 91.0 | 91.3 | 91.7 | 3.1 |
| 2003 | 92.1 | 92.8 | 93.6 | 94.0 | 5.0 | 94.2 | 94.7 | 95.2 | 95.5 | 4.1 |
| 2004 | 95.0 | 95.9 | 96.6 | 96.9 | 3.1 | 95.6 | 96.1 | 96.9 | 97.1 | 1.7 |
| 2005 | 97.8 | 98.4 | 99.5 | 100.0 | 3.2 | 97.8 | 98.2 | 99.4 | 100.0 | 3.0 |
| 2006 | 100.7 | 101.7 | 102.3 | 102.8 | 2.8 | 0.4 | 101.4 | 102.0 | 102.6 | 2.6 |
| 2007 | 103.3 | 104.2 | 104.6 | 105.3 | 2.4 | 3.6 | 104.4 | 105.0 | 105.6 | 2.9 |
| 2008 | 106.0 | 107.0 | 107.4 | 107.6 | 2.2 | 6.3 | 107.5 | 107.9 | 108.0 | 2.3 |
| 2009 | 107.9 | 108.1 | 108.4 | 108.6 | 0.9 | 8.4 | 108.6 | 108.9 | 109.2 | 1.1 |
| 2010 | 109.9 | 110.4 | 111.0 | 111.3 | 2.5 | 9.9 | 110.4 | 110.9 | 111.2 | 1.8 |
| 2011 | 112.2 | 113.3 | 113.6 | 113.9 | 2.3 | 11.8 | 112.2 | 112.7 | 112.9 | 1.5 |
| 2012 | 114.7 | 115.3 | 115.6 | 115.9 | 1.8 | 13.8 | 114.3 | 114.7 | 115.0 | 1.9 |
| 2013 | 116.4 | 117.0 | 117.4 | 117.8 | 1.6 | 15.5 | 116.0 | 116.6 | 117.1 | 1.8 |
| 2014 | 118.4 | 119.5 | 120.0 | 120.3 | 2.1 | 17.4 | 118.3 | 118.9 | 119.1 | 1.7 |
| 2015 | 121.2 | 121.4 | 122.1 | 122.5 | 1.8 | 19.8 | 120.6 | 121.4 | 121.8 | 2.3 |
| 2016 | 123.4 | 124.5 | 125.3 | . . . | . . . | 22.5 | 123.9 | 124.8 | . . . | . . . |
| **East North Central** | | | | | | | | | | |
| 2006 | 100.7 | 101.7 | 102.3 | 102.8 | 2.8 | 100.3 | 101.4 | 101.9 | 102.5 | 2.5 |
| 2007 | 103.2 | 104.1 | 104.4 | 105.0 | 2.1 | 103.6 | 104.4 | 104.7 | 105.3 | 2.7 |
| 2008 | 105.5 | 106.5 | 106.9 | 107.0 | 1.9 | 105.8 | 107.0 | 107.3 | 107.4 | 2.0 |
| 2009 | 107.0 | 107.3 | 107.5 | 107.8 | 0.7 | 107.5 | 107.7 | 108.0 | 108.3 | 0.8 |
| 2010 | 109.2 | 109.8 | 110.3 | 110.5 | 2.5 | 109.1 | 109.7 | 110.1 | 110.3 | 1.8 |
| 2011 | 111.6 | 112.7 | 113.1 | 113.2 | 2.4 | 110.9 | 111.3 | 111.8 | 111.9 | 1.5 |
| 2012 | 113.9 | 114.5 | 114.6 | 114.8 | 1.4 | 112.7 | 113.1 | 113.4 | 113.5 | 1.4 |
| 2013 | 115.4 | 116.0 | 116.4 | 116.7 | 1.7 | 114.1 | 114.7 | 115.3 | 115.7 | 1.9 |
| 2014 | 117.3 | 118.4 | 118.8 | 119.1 | 2.1 | 116.0 | 116.8 | 117.2 | 117.5 | 1.6 |
| 2015 | 120.2 | 120.4 | 120.8 | 121.1 | 1.7 | 118.4 | 119.4 | 119.8 | 120.1 | 2.2 |
| 2016 | 121.9 | 123.0 | 123.6 | . . . | . . . | 120.8 | 122.1 | 122.8 | . . . | . . . |

[1]Includes wages, salaries, and employer costs for employee benefits.

. . . = Not available.

## Table 6-3. Employment Cost Index, Private Industry Workers, Total Compensation[1] and Wages and Salaries, by Region, and Metropolitan Area Status, 2001–2016—Continued

(December 2005 = 100.)

| Geography type and year | Total compensation | | | | | Wages and salaries | | | | |
|---|---|---|---|---|---|---|---|---|---|---|
| | Indexes | | | | Percent change for 12 months (ended December) | Indexes | | | | Percent change for 12 months (ended December) |
| | March | June | September | December | | March | June | September | December | |
| **West North Central** | | | | | | | | | | |
| 2006 | 100.6 | 101.5 | 102.4 | 102.7 | 2.7 | 100.6 | 101.5 | 102.4 | 102.7 | 2.7 |
| 2007 | 103.5 | 104.3 | 105.3 | 105.9 | 3.1 | 103.8 | 104.5 | 105.6 | 106.3 | 3.5 |
| 2008 | 107.3 | 108.4 | 108.8 | 109.0 | 2.9 | 107.9 | 108.9 | 109.5 | 109.7 | 3.2 |
| 2009 | 109.9 | 110.2 | 110.6 | 110.7 | 1.6 | 110.7 | 110.8 | 111.2 | 111.4 | 1.5 |
| 2010 | 111.6 | 112.0 | 112.8 | 113.2 | 2.3 | 111.9 | 112.4 | 113.1 | 113.5 | 1.9 |
| 2011 | 113.9 | 114.8 | 115.0 | 115.6 | 2.1 | 114.0 | 114.5 | 114.9 | 115.4 | 1.7 |
| 2012 | 116.9 | 117.5 | 118.2 | 118.7 | 2.7 | 116.5 | 117.1 | 118.0 | 118.5 | 2.7 |
| 2013 | 119.1 | 119.4 | 119.9 | 120.6 | 1.6 | 119.0 | 119.2 | 119.8 | 120.7 | 1.9 |
| 2014 | 121.0 | 122.3 | 123.0 | 123.3 | 2.2 | 120.7 | 122.0 | 122.8 | 123.1 | 2.0 |
| 2015 | 123.7 | 123.8 | 125.3 | 125.8 | 2.0 | 123.1 | 123.5 | 125.3 | 125.8 | 2.2 |
| 2016 | 126.9 | 128.4 | 129.5 | . . . | . . . | 126.5 | 128.2 | 129.4 | . . . | . . . |
| **West** | | | | | | | | | | |
| 2001 | 84.1 | 85.0 | 85.9 | 86.0 | 5.2 | 87.4 | 88.3 | 89.2 | 90.2 | 4.8 |
| 2002 | 87.4 | 88.5 | 89.1 | 89.0 | 3.3 | 90.4 | 91.5 | 92.0 | 92.4 | 2.4 |
| 2003 | 90.9 | 92.0 | 93.2 | 93.0 | 4.5 | 93.0 | 93.9 | 95.1 | 95.5 | 3.4 |
| 2004 | 95.3 | 96.2 | 96.9 | 97.0 | 3.8 | 96.4 | 97.0 | 97.7 | 98.0 | 2.6 |
| 2005 | 98.4 | 99.3 | 99.7 | 100.0 | 2.7 | 98.4 | 99.3 | 99.6 | 100.0 | 2.0 |
| 2006 | 100.6 | 101.8 | 102.5 | 103.0 | 3.0 | 100.7 | 102.1 | 102.7 | 103.2 | 3.2 |
| 2007 | 104.2 | 104.9 | 105.7 | 106.0 | 3.4 | 104.8 | 105.4 | 106.2 | 107.0 | 3.7 |
| 2008 | 107.8 | 108.4 | 109.3 | 109.0 | 2.7 | 108.3 | 108.9 | 109.9 | 110.1 | 2.9 |
| 2009 | 109.9 | 110.0 | 110.3 | 110.0 | 1.1 | 110.5 | 110.8 | 111.2 | 111.6 | 1.4 |
| 2010 | 111.3 | 111.7 | 112.3 | 112.0 | 1.7 | 112.0 | 112.4 | 112.9 | 113.0 | 1.3 |
| 2011 | 113.5 | 114.3 | 114.6 | 115.0 | 2.3 | 113.6 | 114.1 | 114.5 | 114.9 | 1.7 |
| 2012 | 115.7 | 116.3 | 116.8 | 116.0 | 1.5 | 115.4 | 116.1 | 116.5 | 116.4 | 1.3 |
| 2013 | 117.6 | 118.5 | 119.2 | 119.0 | 2.4 | 117.1 | 118.1 | 118.8 | 119.2 | 2.4 |
| 2014 | 120.1 | 120.9 | 121.9 | 122.0 | 2.4 | 119.5 | 120.4 | 121.5 | 122.2 | 2.5 |
| 2015 | 123.1 | 123.8 | 124.6 | 125.0 | 2.3 | 122.6 | 123.4 | 124.4 | 125.2 | 2.5 |
| 2016 | 126.2 | 127.2 | 127.9 | . . . | . . . | 125.8 | 127.0 | 127.9 | . . . | . . . |
| **Mountain** | | | | | | | | | | |
| 2006 | 101.0 | 101.8 | 102.7 | 103.1 | 3.1 | 100.6 | 101.7 | 102.8 | 103.2 | 3.2 |
| 2007 | 105.2 | 105.2 | 106.6 | 107.5 | 4.3 | 105.3 | 105.5 | 106.7 | 107.8 | 4.5 |
| 2008 | 108.4 | 109.4 | 110.3 | 110.4 | 2.7 | 108.9 | 109.9 | 110.8 | 111.0 | 3.0 |
| 2009 | 110.5 | 110.6 | 110.9 | 111.0 | 0.5 | 111.1 | 111.4 | 111.9 | 111.9 | 0.8 |
| 2010 | 111.3 | 112.3 | 113.0 | 112.8 | 1.6 | 112.3 | 113.2 | 114.1 | 113.7 | 1.6 |
| 2011 | 113.4 | 113.9 | 114.8 | 115.3 | 2.2 | 113.7 | 114.1 | 115.0 | 115.2 | 1.3 |
| 2012 | 115.4 | 116.0 | 116.5 | 115.7 | 0.3 | 115.2 | 115.7 | 116.3 | 115.2 | 0.0 |
| 2013 | 116.6 | 118.1 | 118.7 | 119.2 | 3.0 | 116.0 | 117.8 | 118.3 | 118.8 | 3.1 |
| 2014 | 119.5 | 119.8 | 120.1 | 120.6 | 1.2 | 119.0 | 120.5 | 120.8 | 121.5 | 2.3 |
| 2015 | 121.9 | 122.5 | 123.4 | 124.0 | 2.8 | 122.5 | 123.0 | 124.1 | 124.9 | 2.8 |
| 2016 | 124.1 | 125.4 | 125.8 | . . . | . . . | 124.4 | 125.9 | 126.4 | . . . | . . . |
| **Pacific** | | | | | | | | | | |
| 2006 | 100.5 | 101.8 | 102.5 | 103.0 | 3.0 | 100.8 | 102.2 | 102.7 | 103.3 | 3.3 |
| 2007 | 103.9 | 104.8 | 105.4 | 106.1 | 3.0 | 104.6 | 105.3 | 106.0 | 106.8 | 3.4 |
| 2008 | 107.6 | 108.1 | 108.9 | 109.1 | 2.8 | 108.1 | 108.6 | 109.6 | 109.8 | 2.8 |
| 2009 | 109.7 | 109.9 | 110.1 | 110.5 | 1.3 | 110.3 | 110.6 | 110.9 | 111.5 | 1.5 |
| 2010 | 111.4 | 111.5 | 112.0 | 112.4 | 1.7 | 112.0 | 112.1 | 112.4 | 112.8 | 1.2 |
| 2011 | 113.6 | 114.5 | 114.6 | 115.1 | 2.4 | 113.6 | 114.1 | 114.4 | 114.9 | 1.9 |
| 2012 | 115.9 | 116.5 | 117.0 | 117.4 | 2.0 | 115.5 | 116.3 | 116.7 | 117.0 | 1.8 |
| 2013 | 118.1 | 118.7 | 119.5 | 119.9 | 2.1 | 117.6 | 118.3 | 119.1 | 119.5 | 2.1 |
| 2014 | 120.5 | 121.4 | 122.7 | 123.3 | 2.8 | 119.8 | 120.5 | 121.8 | 122.5 | 2.5 |
| 2015 | 123.7 | 124.4 | 125.2 | 125.9 | 2.1 | 122.7 | 123.7 | 124.6 | 125.4 | 2.4 |
| 2016 | 127.1 | 128.0 | 128.8 | . . . | . . . | 126.5 | 127.5 | 128.6 | . . . | . . . |

[1] Includes wages, salaries, and employer costs for employee benefits.

. . . = Not available.

## Table 6-4.  Employment Cost Index, Benefits, by Industry and Occupation, 2002–2016

(December 2005 = 100.)

| Characteristic and year | Indexes | | | | Percent change for 3 months (ended December) |
|---|---|---|---|---|---|
| | March | June | September | December | |
| **Civilian Workers**[1] | | | | | |
| 2002 | 81.5 | 82.5 | 83.5 | 84.6 | 1.3 |
| 2003 | 86.3 | 87.5 | 88.9 | 90.0 | 1.2 |
| 2004 | 92.1 | 93.7 | 94.8 | 95.9 | 1.2 |
| 2005 | 97.5 | 98.4 | 99.4 | 100.2 | 0.8 |
| 2006 | 100.8 | 101.7 | 102.7 | 103.7 | 1.0 |
| 2007 | 104.0 | 105.2 | 106.0 | 107.0 | 0.9 |
| 2008 | 107.5 | 108.1 | 108.8 | 109.3 | 0.5 |
| 2009 | 109.6 | 109.9 | 110.4 | 110.9 | 0.5 |
| 2010 | 112.0 | 112.7 | 113.5 | 114.1 | 0.5 |
| 2011 | 115.4 | 116.8 | 117.1 | 117.7 | 0.5 |
| 2012 | 118.5 | 119.3 | 119.9 | 120.5 | 0.5 |
| 2013 | 121.3 | 121.9 | 122.6 | 123.2 | 0.5 |
| 2014 | 123.8 | 125.1 | 125.7 | 126.4 | 0.6 |
| 2015 | 127.1 | 127.2 | 127.9 | 128.7 | 0.6 |
| 2016 | 129.3 | 129.9 | 130.8 | . . . | . . . |
| **Total Private** | | | | | |
| 2002 | 82.3 | 83.3 | 84.1 | 85.0 | 1.1 |
| 2003 | 87.0 | 88.1 | 89.4 | 90.5 | 1.2 |
| 2004 | 92.9 | 94.4 | 95.4 | 96.5 | 1.2 |
| 2005 | 98.0 | 98.8 | 99.7 | 100.3 | 0.6 |
| 2006 | 100.8 | 101.6 | 102.5 | 103.4 | 0.9 |
| 2007 | 103.1 | 104.2 | 105.0 | 105.9 | 0.9 |
| 2008 | 106.4 | 106.9 | 107.5 | 107.9 | 0.4 |
| 2009 | 108.1 | 108.2 | 108.6 | 109.1 | 0.5 |
| 2010 | 110.3 | 110.9 | 111.6 | 112.1 | 0.4 |
| 2011 | 113.6 | 115.2 | 115.4 | 116.1 | 0.6 |
| 2012 | 116.8 | 117.5 | 118.0 | 118.5 | 0.4 |
| 2013 | 119.1 | 119.7 | 120.3 | 120.8 | 0.4 |
| 2014 | 121.2 | 122.6 | 123.2 | 123.8 | 0.5 |
| 2015 | 124.4 | 124.2 | 124.8 | 125.3 | 0.4 |
| 2016 | 125.9 | 126.4 | 127.0 | . . . | . . . |
| **State and Local Government Workers** | | | | | |
| 2002 | 78.8 | 79.9 | 81.4 | 82.9 | 1.8 |
| 2003 | 84.1 | 85.4 | 86.9 | 88.0 | 1.3 |
| 2004 | 89.5 | 91.1 | 92.5 | 93.9 | 1.5 |
| 2005 | 95.6 | 96.8 | 98.4 | 99.9 | 1.5 |
| 2006 | 100.8 | 102.0 | 103.5 | 105.1 | 1.5 |
| 2007 | 107.1 | 108.7 | 109.7 | 110.9 | 1.1 |
| 2008 | 111.4 | 112.4 | 113.3 | 114.1 | 0.7 |
| 2009 | 115.3 | 116.2 | 116.8 | 117.7 | 0.8 |
| 2010 | 118.1 | 119.1 | 120.2 | 121.2 | 0.8 |
| 2011 | 122.0 | 122.5 | 123.2 | 123.7 | 0.4 |
| 2012 | 124.7 | 125.8 | 127.1 | 127.9 | 0.6 |
| 2013 | 129.1 | 129.9 | 130.9 | 132.1 | 0.9 |
| 2014 | 133.0 | 134.2 | 134.8 | 135.8 | 0.7 |
| 2015 | 136.7 | 137.8 | 138.9 | 140.6 | 1.2 |
| 2016 | 141.4 | 142.3 | 144.0 | . . . | . . . |
| **WORKERS BY OCCUPATION** | | | | | |
| **Management, Professional, and Related** | | | | | |
| 2002 | 82.7 | 83.7 | 84.2 | 85.2 | 1.2 |
| 2003 | 87.1 | 88.0 | 89.5 | 90.7 | 1.3 |
| 2004 | 91.9 | 93.4 | 94.5 | 95.9 | 1.5 |
| 2005 | 97.9 | 98.8 | 99.8 | 100.4 | 0.6 |
| 2006 | 101.0 | 101.7 | 102.8 | 103.8 | 1.0 |
| 2007 | 103.5 | 104.8 | 105.5 | 106.4 | 0.9 |
| 2008 | 107.1 | 107.8 | 108.5 | 109.0 | 0.5 |
| 2009 | 108.5 | 108.7 | 108.9 | 109.2 | 0.3 |
| 2010 | 110.0 | 110.3 | 110.9 | 111.7 | 0.7 |
| 2011 | 113.2 | 114.6 | 114.7 | 115.6 | 0.8 |
| 2012 | 116.6 | 117.1 | 117.7 | 118.3 | 0.5 |
| 2013 | 118.5 | 119.3 | 120.2 | 120.6 | 0.3 |
| 2014 | 120.9 | 122.4 | 123.1 | 123.8 | 0.6 |
| 2015 | 124.5 | 123.9 | 124.3 | 124.9 | 0.5 |
| 2016 | 124.9 | 125.2 | 125.8 | . . . | . . . |

[1]Includes workers in the private nonfarm economy, except those in private households, and workers in the public sector, except those in the federal government.
. . . = Not available.

## Table 6-4. Employment Cost Index, Benefits, by Industry and Occupation, 2002–2016—Continued

(December 2005 = 100.)

| Characteristic and year | Indexes | | | | Percent change for 3 months (ended December) |
|---|---|---|---|---|---|
| | March | June | September | December | |
| **Sales and Office** | | | | | |
| 2002 | 81.8 | 83.2 | 84.2 | 85.1 | 1.1 |
| 2003 | 86.6 | 88.0 | 89.3 | 90.4 | 1.2 |
| 2004 | 92.5 | 94.2 | 95.2 | 96.1 | 0.9 |
| 2005 | 97.5 | 98.4 | 99.3 | 100.2 | 0.9 |
| 2006 | 100.7 | 101.5 | 102.1 | 103.0 | 0.9 |
| 2007 | 103.3 | 104.2 | 105.2 | 106.1 | 0.9 |
| 2008 | 106.5 | 106.9 | 107.6 | 108.0 | 0.4 |
| 2009 | 108.0 | 108.0 | 108.6 | 108.9 | 0.3 |
| 2010 | 110.1 | 110.9 | 111.6 | 112.1 | 0.4 |
| 2011 | 113.3 | 114.9 | 115.3 | 115.8 | 0.4 |
| 2012 | 116.6 | 117.4 | 117.4 | 117.9 | 0.4 |
| 2013 | 118.9 | 119.4 | 120.1 | 120.7 | 0.5 |
| 2014 | 121.2 | 122.6 | 123.0 | 123.6 | 0.5 |
| 2015 | 123.7 | 124.0 | 124.7 | 125.3 | 0.5 |
| 2016 | 126.7 | 127.5 | 128.3 | . . . | . . . |
| **Natural Resources, Construction, and Maintenance** | | | | | |
| 2002 | 81.2 | 82.1 | 83.3 | 84.6 | 1.6 |
| 2003 | 86.0 | 87.6 | 88.7 | 90.3 | 1.8 |
| 2004 | 92.9 | 94.5 | 95.4 | 96.9 | 1.6 |
| 2005 | 98.0 | 98.9 | 99.7 | 100.4 | 0.7 |
| 2006 | 101.1 | 102.4 | 103.4 | 104.4 | 1.0 |
| 2007 | 103.5 | 104.5 | 105.2 | 106.3 | 1.0 |
| 2008 | 106.6 | 106.7 | 107.4 | 108.0 | 0.6 |
| 2009 | 108.3 | 108.5 | 109.1 | 109.8 | 0.6 |
| 2010 | 111.6 | 112.1 | 112.8 | 113.5 | 0.6 |
| 2011 | 114.2 | 115.6 | 116.1 | 117.1 | 0.9 |
| 2012 | 117.9 | 118.8 | 119.8 | 120.6 | 0.7 |
| 2013 | 121.6 | 121.9 | 122.6 | 123.2 | 0.5 |
| 2014 | 124.0 | 126.0 | 126.7 | 127.5 | 0.6 |
| 2015 | 127.6 | 126.9 | 127.6 | 128.2 | 0.5 |
| 2016 | 128.5 | 128.9 | 129.4 | . . . | . . . |
| **Production, Transportation, and Material Moving** | | | | | |
| 2002 | 81.8 | 82.7 | 83.7 | 84.8 | 1.3 |
| 2003 | 86.7 | 88.1 | 89.4 | 90.4 | 1.1 |
| 2004 | 94.4 | 96.0 | 97.1 | 98.0 | 0.9 |
| 2005 | 98.7 | 99.2 | 99.9 | 100.1 | 0.2 |
| 2006 | 100.0 | 100.8 | 101.6 | 102.3 | 0.7 |
| 2007 | 101.1 | 102.3 | 102.7 | 103.9 | 1.2 |
| 2008 | 104.4 | 104.4 | 104.8 | 105.3 | 0.5 |
| 2009 | 106.4 | 106.7 | 107.1 | 107.5 | 0.4 |
| 2010 | 109.9 | 110.7 | 111.7 | 112.2 | 0.4 |
| 2011 | 113.5 | 116.4 | 116.3 | 117.1 | 0.7 |
| 2012 | 116.1 | 117.0 | 117.6 | 118.1 | 0.4 |
| 2013 | 118.7 | 119.0 | 119.1 | 119.7 | 0.5 |
| 2014 | 120.5 | 120.9 | 121.6 | 122.3 | 0.6 |
| 2015 | 123.5 | 124.2 | 124.9 | 125.6 | 0.6 |
| 2016 | 126.3 | 126.7 | 127.4 | . . . | . . . |
| **Service** | | | | | |
| 2002 | 83.5 | 84.4 | 86.0 | 86.8 | 0.9 |
| 2003 | 88.5 | 89.4 | 90.8 | 92.0 | 1.3 |
| 2004 | 94.3 | 95.9 | 96.7 | 97.3 | 0.6 |
| 2005 | 98.0 | 98.8 | 99.5 | 100.3 | 0.8 |
| 2006 | 101.3 | 102.1 | 103.0 | 103.9 | 0.9 |
| 2007 | 104.0 | 105.0 | 106.0 | 107.0 | 0.9 |
| 2008 | 107.4 | 108.3 | 108.7 | 109.2 | 0.5 |
| 2009 | 109.5 | 109.8 | 110.4 | 110.9 | 0.5 |
| 2010 | 111.5 | 112.3 | 113.3 | 113.8 | 0.4 |
| 2011 | 115.2 | 115.9 | 116.0 | 116.7 | 0.6 |
| 2012 | 117.8 | 118.2 | 118.8 | 119.4 | 0.5 |
| 2013 | 119.7 | 120.4 | 120.8 | 121.1 | 0.2 |
| 2014 | 120.9 | 121.1 | 121.7 | 122.3 | 0.5 |
| 2015 | 122.9 | 123.4 | 123.9 | 124.4 | 0.4 |
| 2016 | 125.2 | 126.1 | 126.7 | . . . | . . . |

. . . = Not available.

## Table 6-4.  Employment Cost Index, Benefits, by Industry and Occupation, 2002–2016—*Continued*

(December 2005 = 100.)

| Characteristic and year | Indexes | | | | Percent change for 3 months (ended December) |
|---|---|---|---|---|---|
| | March | June | September | December | |
| **WORKERS BY INDUSTRY** | | | | | |
| **Goods-Producing Industries**[2] | | | | | |
| 2002 | 79.9 | 80.6 | 81.2 | 82.5 | 1.6 |
| 2003 | 85.2 | 86.5 | 87.5 | 88.4 | 1.0 |
| 2004 | 92.4 | 93.8 | 95.0 | 96.5 | 1.6 |
| 2005 | 98.3 | 99.5 | 100.3 | 100.2 | -0.1 |
| 2006 | 99.4 | 100.3 | 101.3 | 102.0 | 0.7 |
| 2007 | 100.9 | 102.1 | 102.4 | 103.4 | 1.0 |
| 2008 | 104.0 | 104.3 | 104.6 | 105.0 | 0.4 |
| 2009 | 105.4 | 105.5 | 105.6 | 106.2 | 0.6 |
| 2010 | 108.4 | 108.9 | 110.0 | 110.2 | 0.2 |
| 2011 | 111.7 | 114.1 | 113.8 | 114.5 | 0.6 |
| 2012 | 114.2 | 114.9 | 115.7 | 116.1 | 0.3 |
| 2013 | 117.0 | 117.3 | 117.6 | 118.1 | 0.4 |
| 2014 | 119.2 | 119.4 | 120.3 | 120.8 | 0.4 |
| 2015 | 121.4 | 122.1 | 122.4 | 123.2 | 0.7 |
| 2016 | 123.5 | 124.2 | 124.6 | . . . | . . . |
| **Manufacturing** | | | | | |
| 2002 | 78.8 | 79.7 | 80.3 | 81.5 | 1.5 |
| 2003 | 84.7 | 85.7 | 86.8 | 87.5 | 0.8 |
| 2004 | 92.7 | 94.1 | 95.4 | 96.1 | 0.7 |
| 2005 | 98.2 | 99.4 | 100.1 | 100.1 | 0.0 |
| 2006 | 98.6 | 99.6 | 100.7 | 101.1 | 0.4 |
| 2007 | 99.4 | 100.8 | 100.9 | 101.9 | 1.0 |
| 2008 | 2.2 | 102.0 | 102.4 | 102.8 | 0.4 |
| 2009 | 3.4 | 103.4 | 103.4 | 104.0 | 0.6 |
| 2010 | 6.6 | 107.4 | 108.7 | 108.9 | 0.2 |
| 2011 | 11.0 | 113.9 | 113.4 | 114.0 | 0.5 |
| 2012 | 13.2 | 113.9 | 114.8 | 115.1 | 0.3 |
| 2013 | 15.7 | 116.0 | 116.4 | 116.7 | 0.3 |
| 2014 | 18.1 | 118.2 | 119.3 | 119.9 | 0.5 |
| 2015 | 20.8 | 121.4 | 121.6 | 122.6 | 0.8 |
| 2016 | 23.1 | 123.6 | 124.1 | . . . | . . . |
| **Service-Providing**[3] | | | | | |
| 2002 | 83.2 | 84.4 | 85.2 | 86.0 | 0.7 |
| 2003 | 87.7 | 88.8 | 90.2 | 91.4 | 2.0 |
| 2004 | 93.0 | 94.6 | 95.5 | 96.5 | 1.8 |
| 2005 | 97.9 | 98.6 | 99.4 | 100.3 | 1.5 |
| 2006 | 101.3 | 102.2 | 103.0 | 104.0 | 1.0 |
| 2007 | 104.0 | 105.1 | 106.0 | 106.9 | 0.0 |
| 2008 | 107.4 | 108.0 | 108.7 | 109.1 | 0.5 |
| 2009 | 109.2 | 109.3 | 109.9 | 110.2 | 0.1 |
| 2010 | 111.1 | 111.7 | 112.3 | 112.9 | 0.8 |
| 2011 | 114.4 | 115.7 | 116.0 | 116.7 | 1.3 |
| 2012 | 117.8 | 118.5 | 118.9 | 119.4 | 0.9 |
| 2013 | 119.9 | 120.6 | 121.4 | 121.8 | 0.4 |
| 2014 | 122.1 | 123.8 | 124.4 | 125.0 | 0.2 |
| 2015 | 125.7 | 125.2 | 125.8 | 126.2 | 0.6 |
| 2016 | 126.9 | 127.3 | 128.1 | . . . | 0.6 |

[2]Includes mining, construction, and manufacturing.
[3]Includes the following industries: wholesale trade; retail trade; transportation and warehousing; utilities; information; finance and insurance; real estate and rental and leasing; professional, scientific, and technical services; management of companies and enterprises; administrative and support and waste management and remediation services; education services; health care and social assistance; arts, entertainment, and recreation; accommodation and food services; and other services, except public administration.
. . . = Not available.

## NOTES AND DEFINITIONS

### EMPLOYER COSTS FOR EMPLOYEE COMPENSATION (ECEC)

The ECEC series measures the average cost to employers for wages and salaries, and for benefits, per employee hour worked. The series provides quarterly data on employer costs per hour worked for total compensation, wages and salaries, total benefits, and the following benefits: paid leave—vacations, holidays, sick leave, and personal leave; supplemental pay—premium pay for work in addition to the regular work schedule (such as overtime, weekend, and holiday work) and for shift differentials, and non-production bonuses (such as yearend, referral, and attend-ance bonuses); insurance benefits—life, health, short-term disability, and long-term disability insurance; retirement and savings benefits—defined benefit and defined contribution plans; and legally required benefits—Social Security, Medicare, federal and state unemployment insurance, and workers' compensation. Cost data are presented both in dollar amounts and as percentages of total compensation. The ECEC uses current employment weights to reflect the composition of today's labor force.

Differences in the estimates for the state and local government and private industry sectors stem from factors such as variation in work activities and in occupational structures. Manufacturing and sales, for example, make up a large part of private industry work activities but are rare in state and local government. In contrast, professional and administrative support occupations (including teachers) account for two-thirds of the state and local government workforce but less than one-half of private industry.

The cost levels for September 2016 were collected from a probability sample of 28,400 occupational observations selected from a sample of about 86,800 establishments in private industry and approximately 8,800 occupational from a sample of about 1,500 establishments in state and local governments.

ECEC includes the civilian economy, which includes data from both private industry and state and local government. Excluded from private industry are the self-employed and farm and private household workers. Federal government workers are excluded from the public sector. The private industry series and the state and local government series provide data for the two sectors separately.

### Sources of Additional Information

Additional information may be obtained from BLS news release 16-2255 "Employer Costs for Employee Compensation—September 2016," and Chapter 8 of *the Handbook of Methods*.

## Table 6-5. Employer Compensation Costs Per Hour Worked for Employee Compensation and Costs as a Percent of Total Compensation: Private Industry Workers, by Major Industry Group, September 2016

(Dollars, percent of total cost.)

| Compensation component | All workers Cost | All workers Percent | All goods-producing[1] Cost | All goods-producing[1] Percent | Construction Cost | Construction Percent | Manufacturing Cost | Manufacturing Percent | All service-providing[2] Cost | All service-providing[2] Percent | Trade, transportation, and utilities Cost | Trade, transportation, and utilities Percent |
|---|---|---|---|---|---|---|---|---|---|---|---|---|
| TOTAL COMPENSATION | 32.27 | 100.0 | 38.99 | 100.0 | 38.34 | 100.0 | 39.22 | 100.0 | 30.87 | 100.0 | 26.80 | 100.0 |
| Wages and Salaries | 22.52 | 69.8 | 25.90 | 66.4 | 26.65 | 69.5 | 25.53 | 65.1 | 21.82 | 70.7 | 18.83 | 70.3 |
| Total Benefits | 9.75 | 30.2 | 13.09 | 33.6 | 11.69 | 30.5 | 13.69 | 34.9 | 9.06 | 29.3 | 7.97 | 29.7 |
| Paid leave | 2.21 | 6.9 | 2.52 | 6.5 | 1.67 | 4.4 | 2.96 | 7.5 | 2.15 | 7.0 | 1.68 | 6.3 |
| Vacation | 1.15 | 3.6 | 1.31 | 3.4 | 0.88 | 2.3 | 1.53 | 3.9 | 1.11 | 3.6 | 0.89 | 3.3 |
| Holiday | 0.67 | 2.1 | 0.87 | 2.2 | 0.57 | 1.5 | 1.03 | 2.6 | 0.63 | 2.0 | 0.49 | 1.8 |
| Sick | 0.27 | 0.8 | 0.24 | 0.6 | 0.13 | 0.3 | 0.30 | 0.8 | 0.27 | 0.9 | 0.21 | 0.8 |
| Personal | 0.13 | 0.4 | 0.10 | 0.3 | 0.09 | 0.2 | 0.11 | 0.3 | 0.13 | 0.4 | 0.09 | 0.3 |
| Supplemental pay | 1.16 | 3.6 | 1.50 | 3.8 | 1.02 | 2.7 | 1.68 | 4.3 | 1.09 | 3.5 | 0.72 | 2.7 |
| Overtime and premium pay[3] | 0.27 | 0.8 | 0.58 | 1.5 | 0.61 | 1.6 | 0.53 | 1.4 | 0.20 | 0.7 | 0.28 | 1.0 |
| Shift differentials | 0.06 | 0.2 | 0.08 | 0.2 | 0.02 | (4) | 0.12 | 0.3 | 0.05 | 0.2 | 0.02 | 0.1 |
| Nonproduction bonuses | 0.83 | 2.6 | 0.84 | 2.2 | 0.39 | 1.0 | 1.03 | 2.6 | 0.83 | 2.7 | 0.42 | 1.6 |
| Insurance | 2.59 | 8.0 | 3.65 | 9.4 | 3.02 | 7.9 | 3.97 | 10.1 | 2.37 | 7.7 | 2.27 | 8.5 |
| Life insurance | 0.04 | 0.1 | 0.06 | 0.2 | 0.04 | 0.1 | 0.07 | 0.2 | 0.04 | 0.1 | 0.03 | 0.1 |
| Health insurance | 2.44 | 7.6 | 3.46 | 8.9 | 2.89 | 7.5 | 3.75 | 9.6 | 2.23 | 7.2 | 2.14 | 8.0 |
| Short-term disability | 0.06 | 0.2 | 0.08 | 0.2 | 0.04 | 0.1 | 0.09 | 0.2 | 0.05 | 0.2 | 0.04 | 0.2 |
| Long-term disability | 0.05 | 0.1 | 0.05 | 0.1 | 0.04 | 0.1 | 0.06 | 0.2 | 0.04 | 0.1 | 0.05 | 0.2 |
| Retirement and savings | 1.25 | 3.9 | 2.12 | 5.4 | 2.04 | 5.3 | 2.13 | 5.4 | 1.06 | 3.4 | 1.04 | 3.9 |
| Defined benefit plans | 0.54 | 1.7 | 1.17 | 3.0 | 1.27 | 3.3 | 1.09 | 2.8 | 0.41 | 1.3 | 0.49 | 1.8 |
| Defined contribution plans | 0.70 | 2.2 | 0.95 | 2.4 | 0.78 | 2.0 | 1.03 | 2.6 | 0.65 | 2.1 | 0.56 | 2.1 |
| Legally required benefits | 2.54 | 7.9 | 3.29 | 8.4 | 3.94 | 10.3 | 2.95 | 7.5 | 2.39 | 7.7 | 2.27 | 8.5 |
| Social Security and Medicare | 1.87 | 5.8 | 2.19 | 5.6 | 2.20 | 5.7 | 2.18 | 5.6 | 1.80 | 5.8 | 1.56 | 5.8 |
| Social Security[6] | 1.49 | 4.6 | 1.76 | 4.5 | 1.77 | 4.6 | 1.75 | 4.5 | 1.44 | 4.7 | 1.25 | 4.7 |
| Medicare | 0.38 | 1.2 | 0.43 | 1.1 | 0.42 | 1.1 | 0.43 | 1.1 | 0.36 | 1.2 | 0.31 | 1.1 |
| Federal unemployment insurance | 0.04 | 0.1 | 0.03 | 0.1 | 0.03 | 0.1 | 0.03 | 0.1 | 0.04 | 0.1 | 0.04 | 0.1 |
| State unemployment insurance | 0.18 | 0.6 | 0.24 | 0.6 | 0.33 | 0.9 | 0.19 | 0.5 | 0.17 | 0.6 | 0.15 | 0.6 |
| Workers' compensation | 0.46 | 1.4 | 0.84 | 2.2 | 1.38 | 3.6 | 0.55 | 1.4 | 0.38 | 1.2 | 0.52 | 2.0 |

Service-providing[2]

| Compensation component | Information Cost | Information Percent | Financial activities Cost | Financial activities Percent | Professional and business services Cost | Professional and business services Percent | Education and health services Cost | Education and health services Percent | Leisure and hospitality Cost | Leisure and hospitality Percent | Other services Cost | Other services Percent |
|---|---|---|---|---|---|---|---|---|---|---|---|---|
| TOTAL COMPENSATION | 53.20 | 100.0 | 46.89 | 100.0 | 39.64 | 100.0 | 33.25 | 100.0 | 13.95 | 100.0 | 26.37 | 100.0 |
| Wages and Salaries | 35.35 | 66.5 | 30.84 | 65.8 | 28.33 | 71.5 | 23.49 | 70.6 | 10.99 | 78.8 | 19.18 | 72.7 |
| Total Benefits | 17.85 | 33.5 | 16.05 | 34.2 | 11.31 | 28.5 | 9.76 | 29.4 | 2.96 | 21.2 | 7.19 | 27.3 |
| Paid leave | 4.83 | 9.1 | 3.96 | 8.5 | 2.83 | 7.1 | 2.57 | 7.7 | 0.41 | 2.9 | 1.60 | 6.1 |
| Vacation | 2.49 | 4.7 | 2.07 | 4.4 | 1.50 | 3.8 | 1.28 | 3.9 | 0.21 | 1.5 | 0.76 | 2.9 |
| Holiday | 1.29 | 2.4 | 1.13 | 2.4 | 0.85 | 2.1 | 0.75 | 2.3 | 0.11 | 0.8 | 0.54 | 2.1 |
| Sick | 0.56 | 1.1 | 0.52 | 1.1 | 0.31 | 0.8 | 0.36 | 1.1 | 0.05 | 0.4 | 0.20 | 0.7 |
| Personal | 0.48 | 0.9 | 0.24 | 0.5 | 0.16 | 0.4 | 0.16 | 0.5 | 0.03 | 0.2 | 0.10 | 0.4 |
| Supplemental pay | 2.39 | 4.5 | 3.42 | 7.3 | 1.95 | 4.9 | 0.64 | 1.9 | 0.13 | 0.9 | 0.33 | 1.2 |
| Overtime and premium pay[3] | 0.30 | 0.6 | 0.19 | 0.4 | 0.24 | 0.6 | 0.18 | 0.6 | 0.07 | 0.5 | 0.14 | 0.5 |
| Shift differentials | 0.04 | 0.1 | (5) | (4) | (5) | (4) | 0.18 | 0.6 | (5) | (4) | 0.02 | 0.0 |
| Nonproduction bonuses | 2.04 | 3.8 | 3.22 | 6.9 | 1.70 | 4.3 | 0.27 | 0.8 | 0.05 | 0.4 | 0.17 | 0.6 |
| Insurance | 4.99 | 9.4 | 3.89 | 8.3 | 2.41 | 6.1 | 2.90 | 8.7 | 0.73 | 5.2 | 2.01 | 7.6 |
| Life insurance | 0.07 | 0.1 | 0.06 | 0.1 | 0.05 | 0.1 | 0.04 | 0.1 | (5) | (4) | 0.03 | 0.1 |
| Health insurance | 4.58 | 8.6 | 3.64 | 7.8 | 2.25 | 5.7 | 2.76 | 8.3 | 0.71 | 5.1 | 1.93 | 7.3 |
| Short-term disability | 0.25 | 0.5 | 0.13 | 0.3 | 0.06 | 0.2 | 0.05 | 0.1 | (5) | (4) | 0.03 | 0.1 |
| Long-term disability | 0.08 | 0.2 | 0.06 | 0.1 | 0.06 | 0.1 | 0.05 | 0.2 | (5) | (4) | 0.02 | 0.1 |
| Retirement and savings | 2.17 | 4.1 | 1.86 | 4.0 | 1.22 | 3.1 | 1.19 | 3.6 | 0.20 | 1.4 | 1.06 | 4.0 |
| Defined benefit plans | 0.67 | 1.3 | 0.57 | 1.2 | 0.49 | 1.2 | 0.38 | 1.2 | 0.09 | 0.7 | 0.57 | 2.2 |
| Defined contribution plans | 1.50 | 2.8 | 1.29 | 2.7 | 0.73 | 1.8 | 0.80 | 2.4 | 0.11 | 0.8 | 0.48 | 1.8 |
| Legally required benefits | 3.48 | 6.5 | 2.92 | 6.2 | 2.91 | 7.3 | 2.47 | 7.4 | 1.49 | 10.7 | 2.20 | 8.3 |
| Social Security and Medicare | 2.98 | 5.6 | 2.50 | 5.3 | 2.27 | 5.7 | 1.97 | 5.9 | 0.97 | 7.0 | 1.58 | 6.0 |
| Social Security[6] | 2.37 | 4.5 | 1.95 | 4.2 | 1.79 | 4.5 | 1.58 | 4.8 | 0.79 | 5.7 | 1.28 | 4.8 |
| Medicare | 0.61 | 1.1 | 0.55 | 1.2 | 0.48 | 1.2 | 0.39 | 1.2 | 0.19 | 1.3 | 0.31 | 1.2 |
| Federal unemployment insurance | 0.03 | 0.1 | 0.04 | 0.1 | 0.04 | 0.1 | 0.03 | 0.1 | 0.05 | 0.4 | 0.03 | 0.1 |
| State unemployment insurance | 0.19 | 0.3 | 0.17 | 0.4 | 0.22 | 0.5 | 0.17 | 0.5 | 0.16 | 1.1 | 0.17 | 0.6 |
| Workers' compensation | 0.28 | 0.5 | 0.21 | 0.4 | 0.39 | 1.0 | 0.31 | 0.9 | 0.31 | 2.2 | 0.42 | 1.6 |

*Note:* Individual items may not sum to totals due to rounding.

[1] Includes mining, construction, and manufacturing. The agriculture, forestry, farming, and hunting sector is excluded.
[2] Includes utilities; wholesale trade; retail trade; transportation and warehousing; information; finance and insurance; real estate and rental and leasing; professional and technical services; management of companies and enterprises; administrative and waste services; education services; health care and social assistance; arts, entertainment, and recreation; accommodation and food services; and other services, except public administration.
[3] Includes premium pay for work in addition to the regular work schedule (such as overtime, weekends, and holidays).
[4] Less than 0.05 percent.
[5] Cost per hour worked is $0.01 or less.
[6] Comprises the Old Age, Survivors, and Disability Insurance (OASDI) program.

## Table 6-6. Employer Compensation Costs Per Hour Worked for Employee Compensation and Costs as a Percent of Total Compensation: Private Industry Workers, by Census Region and Area, September 2016

(Dollars, percent of total costs.)

| Compensation component | Census region and division[1] | | | | | |
|---|---|---|---|---|---|---|
| | Northeast | | Northeast divisions | | | |
| | | | New England | | Middle Atlantic | |
| | Cost | Percent | Cost | Percent | Cost | Percent |
| TOTAL COMPENSATION ................... | 39.06 | 100.0 | 38.92 | 100.0 | 39.12 | 100.0 |
| Wages and Salaries .............................. | 26.13 | 66.9 | 27.33 | 70.2 | 25.72 | 65.8 |
| Total Benefits ........................................ | 12.93 | 33.1 | 11.59 | 29.8 | 13.39 | 34.2 |
| Paid leave ............................................. | 2.85 | 7.3 | 2.86 | 7.3 | 2.85 | 7.3 |
| Vacation .......................................... | 1.46 | 3.7 | 1.50 | 3.8 | 1.44 | 3.7 |
| Holiday ............................................. | 0.84 | 2.1 | 0.85 | 2.2 | 0.83 | 2.1 |
| Sick .................................................. | 0.37 | 0.9 | 0.34 | 0.9 | 0.38 | 1.0 |
| Personal .......................................... | 0.19 | 0.5 | 0.17 | 0.4 | 0.20 | 0.5 |
| Supplemental pay ................................. | 2.44 | 6.2 | 1.10 | 2.8 | 2.90 | 7.4 |
| Overtime and premium pay[2] ........... | 0.25 | 0.6 | 0.25 | 0.6 | 0.25 | 0.6 |
| Shift differentials ............................. | 0.08 | 0.2 | 0.09 | 0.2 | 0.07 | 0.2 |
| Nonproduction bonuses .................. | 2.11 | 5.4 | 0.76 | 1.9 | 2.58 | 6.6 |
| Insurance ............................................. | 3.21 | 8.2 | 3.22 | 8.3 | 3.21 | 8.2 |
| Life insurance ................................. | 0.05 | 0.1 | 0.04 | 0.1 | 0.05 | 0.1 |
| Health insurance ............................. | 3.02 | 7.7 | 3.03 | 7.8 | 3.02 | 7.7 |
| Short-term disability ........................ | 0.09 | 0.2 | 0.09 | 0.2 | 0.09 | 0.2 |
| Long-term disability ......................... | 0.05 | 0.1 | 0.06 | 0.2 | 0.05 | 0.1 |
| Retirement and savings ....................... | 1.42 | 3.6 | 1.53 | 3.9 | 1.38 | 3.5 |
| Defined benefit plans ...................... | 0.63 | 1.6 | 0.61 | 1.6 | 0.63 | 1.6 |
| Defined contribution plans ............... | 0.79 | 2.0 | 0.92 | 2.4 | 0.75 | 1.9 |
| Legally required benefits ..................... | 3.01 | 7.7 | 2.88 | 7.4 | 3.06 | 7.8 |
| Social Security and Medicare ........... | 2.14 | 5.5 | 2.19 | 5.6 | 2.13 | 5.4 |
| Social Security .............................. | 1.69 | 4.3 | 1.74 | 4.5 | 1.67 | 4.3 |
| Medicare ....................................... | 0.46 | 1.2 | 0.45 | 1.2 | 0.46 | 1.2 |
| Federal unemployment insurance ..... | 0.03 | 0.1 | 0.04 | 0.1 | 0.02 | 0.1 |
| State unemployment insurance ........ | 0.30 | 0.8 | 0.26 | 0.7 | 0.31 | 0.8 |
| Workers' compensation .................... | 0.54 | 1.4 | 0.39 | 1.0 | 0.59 | 1.5 |

| Compensation component | Census region and division[1] | | | | | | | |
|---|---|---|---|---|---|---|---|---|
| | South | | South divisions | | | | | |
| | | | South Atlantic | | East South Central | | West South Central | |
| | Cost | Percent | Cost | Percent | Cost | Percent | Cost | Percent |
| TOTAL COMPENSATION ................... | 29.46 | 100.0 | 30.43 | 100.0 | 25.28 | 100.0 | 29.91 | 100.0 |
| Wages and Salaries .............................. | 20.96 | 71.1 | 21.52 | 70.7 | 17.87 | 70.7 | 21.55 | 72.0 |
| Total Benefits ........................................ | 8.50 | 28.9 | 8.91 | 29.3 | 7.41 | 29.3 | 8.37 | 28.0 |
| Paid leave ............................................. | 1.99 | 6.8 | 2.16 | 7.1 | 1.65 | 6.5 | 1.89 | 6.3 |
| Vacation .......................................... | 1.02 | 3.4 | 1.12 | 3.7 | 0.83 | 3.3 | 0.94 | 3.2 |
| Holiday ............................................. | 0.62 | 2.1 | 0.64 | 2.1 | 0.55 | 2.2 | 0.61 | 2.0 |
| Sick .................................................. | 0.23 | 0.8 | 0.26 | 0.9 | 0.18 | 0.7 | 0.22 | 0.7 |
| Personal .......................................... | 0.13 | 0.4 | 0.14 | 0.5 | 0.09 | 0.3 | 0.12 | 0.4 |
| Supplemental pay ................................. | 0.90 | 3.1 | 0.83 | 2.7 | 0.70 | 2.8 | 1.12 | 3.7 |
| Overtime and premium pay[2] ........... | 0.31 | 1.0 | 0.24 | 0.8 | 0.31 | 1.2 | 0.41 | 1.4 |
| Shift differentials ............................. | 0.06 | 0.2 | 0.07 | 0.2 | 0.04 | 0.2 | 0.05 | 0.2 |
| Nonproduction bonuses .................. | 0.53 | 1.8 | 0.51 | 1.7 | 0.35 | 1.4 | 0.66 | 2.2 |
| Insurance ............................................. | 2.25 | 7.6 | 2.38 | 7.8 | 2.24 | 8.9 | 2.04 | 6.8 |
| Life insurance ................................. | 0.05 | 0.2 | 0.05 | 0.2 | 0.04 | 0.2 | 0.04 | 0.1 |
| Health insurance ............................. | 2.11 | 7.2 | 2.23 | 7.3 | 2.13 | 8.4 | 1.92 | 6.4 |
| Short-term disability ........................ | 0.05 | 0.2 | 0.06 | 0.2 | 0.04 | 0.2 | 0.04 | 0.1 |
| Long-term disability ......................... | 0.04 | 0.1 | 0.05 | 0.2 | 0.04 | 0.2 | 0.04 | 0.1 |
| Retirement and savings ....................... | 1.12 | 3.8 | 1.25 | 4.1 | 0.86 | 3.4 | 1.03 | 3.5 |
| Defined benefit plans ...................... | 0.49 | 1.7 | 0.56 | 1.8 | 0.38 | 1.5 | 0.42 | 1.4 |
| Defined contribution plans ............... | 0.63 | 2.1 | 0.68 | 2.2 | 0.49 | 1.9 | 0.62 | 2.1 |
| Legally required benefits ..................... | 2.24 | 7.6 | 2.29 | 7.5 | 1.96 | 7.7 | 2.29 | 7.7 |
| Social Security and Medicare ........... | 1.75 | 5.9 | 1.80 | 5.9 | 1.52 | 6.0 | 1.78 | 5.9 |
| Social Security .............................. | 1.40 | 4.8 | 1.44 | 4.7 | 1.23 | 4.8 | 1.42 | 4.8 |
| Medicare ....................................... | 0.35 | 1.2 | 0.36 | 1.2 | 0.29 | 1.2 | 0.36 | 1.2 |
| Federal unemployment insurance ..... | 0.02 | 0.1 | 0.03 | 0.1 | 0.02 | 0.1 | 0.02 | 0.1 |
| State unemployment insurance ........ | 0.11 | 0.4 | 0.11 | 0.4 | 0.09 | 0.3 | 0.11 | 0.4 |
| Workers' compensation .................... | 0.36 | 1.2 | 0.36 | 1.2 | 0.33 | 1.3 | 0.38 | 1.3 |

*Note:* Individual items may not sum to totals due to rounding.

[1] The states that comprise the Census divisions are: New England—Connecticut, Maine, Massachusetts, New Hampshire, Rhode Island, and Vermont; Middle Atlantic—New Jersey, New York, and Pennsylvania; South Atlantic—Delaware, District of Columbia, Florida, Georgia, Maryland, North Carolina, South Carolina, Virginia, and West Virginia; East South Central—Alabama, Kentucky, Mississippi, and Tennessee; West South Central—Arkansas, Louisiana, Oklahoma, and Texas; East North Central—Illinois, Indiana, Michigan, Ohio, and Wisconsin; West North Central—Iowa, Kansas, Minnesota, Missouri, Nebraska, North Dakota, and South Dakota; Mountain—Arizona, Colorado, Idaho, Montana, Nevada, New Mexico, Utah, and Wyoming; and Pacific—Alaska, California, Hawaii, Oregon, and Washington.
[2] Comprises the Old-Age, Survivors, and Disability Insurance (OASDI) program.

**Table 6-6.  Employer Compensation Costs Per Hour Worked for Employee Compensation and Costs as a Percent of Total Compensation: Private Industry Workers, by Census Region and Area, September 2016**—*Continued*

(Dollars, percent of total costs.)

| Compensation component | Census region and division[1] | | | | | |
|---|---|---|---|---|---|---|
| | Midwest | | Midwest divisions | | | |
| | | | East North Central | | West North Central | |
| | Cost | Percent | Cost | Percent | Cost | Percent |
| TOTAL COMPENSATION ................... | 29.90 | 100.0 | 30.06 | 100.0 | 29.55 | 100.0 |
| Wages and Salaries ........................... | 20.81 | 69.6 | 20.89 | 69.5 | 20.65 | 69.9 |
| Total Benefits ...................................... | 9.09 | 30.4 | 9.17 | 30.5 | 8.91 | 30.1 |
| Paid leave ......................................... | 2.03 | 6.8 | 2.05 | 6.8 | 1.99 | 6.7 |
| Vacation ......................................... | 1.11 | 3.7 | 1.12 | 3.7 | 1.09 | 3.7 |
| Holiday ........................................... | 0.60 | 2.0 | 0.61 | 2.0 | 0.59 | 2.0 |
| Sick ................................................ | 0.22 | 0.7 | 0.21 | 0.7 | 0.22 | 0.8 |
| Personal ......................................... | 0.10 | 0.3 | 0.10 | 0.3 | 0.09 | 0.3 |
| Supplemental pay .............................. | 0.83 | 2.8 | 0.85 | 2.8 | 0.79 | 2.7 |
| Overtime and premium pay[2] ........... | 0.27 | 0.9 | 0.28 | 0.9 | 0.23 | 0.8 |
| Shift differentials ........................... | 0.06 | 0.2 | 0.06 | 0.2 | 0.07 | 0.2 |
| Nonproduction bonuses ................... | 0.50 | 1.7 | 0.51 | 1.7 | 0.49 | 1.7 |
| Insurance ........................................... | 2.64 | 8.8 | 2.69 | 9.0 | 2.54 | 8.6 |
| Life insurance ................................ | 0.04 | 0.1 | 0.04 | 0.1 | 0.04 | 0.1 |
| Health insurance ........................... | 2.49 | 8.3 | 2.54 | 8.4 | 2.40 | 8.1 |
| Short-term disability ...................... | 0.06 | 0.2 | 0.07 | 0.2 | 0.06 | 0.2 |
| Long-term disability ....................... | 0.05 | 0.2 | 0.05 | 0.2 | 0.05 | 0.2 |
| Retirement and savings ..................... | 1.19 | 4.0 | 1.17 | 3.9 | 1.23 | 4.2 |
| Defined benefit plans ..................... | 0.47 | 1.6 | 0.52 | 1.7 | 0.37 | 1.3 |
| Defined contribution plans ............. | 0.72 | 2.4 | 0.65 | 2.2 | 0.86 | 2.9 |
| Legally required benefits .................... | 2.39 | 8.0 | 2.41 | 8.0 | 2.36 | 8.0 |
| Social Security and Medicare ......... | 1.77 | 5.9 | 1.77 | 5.9 | 1.77 | 6.0 |
| Social Security ........................... | 1.43 | 4.8 | 1.43 | 4.8 | 1.43 | 4.8 |
| Medicare ..................................... | 0.34 | 1.2 | 0.34 | 1.1 | 0.34 | 1.2 |
| Federal unemployment insurance ..... | 0.04 | 0.1 | 0.04 | 0.1 | 0.03 | 0.1 |
| State unemployment insurance ......... | 0.18 | 0.6 | 0.19 | 0.6 | 0.14 | 0.5 |
| Workers' compensation .................... | 0.41 | 1.4 | 0.41 | 1.3 | 0.41 | 1.4 |

| Compensation component | Census region and division[1] | | | | | |
|---|---|---|---|---|---|---|
| | West | | West divisions | | | |
| | | | Mountain | | Pacific | |
| | Cost | Percent | Cost | Percent | Cost | Percent |
| TOTAL COMPENSATION ................... | 33.61 | 100.0 | 29.15 | 100.0 | 35.79 | 100.0 |
| Wages and Salaries ........................... | 23.83 | 70.9 | 21.13 | 72.5 | 25.15 | 70.3 |
| Total Benefits ...................................... | 9.78 | 29.1 | 8.02 | 27.5 | 10.64 | 29.7 |
| Paid leave ......................................... | 2.22 | 6.6 | 1.81 | 6.2 | 2.41 | 6.7 |
| Vacation ......................................... | 1.13 | 3.4 | 0.94 | 3.2 | 1.22 | 3.4 |
| Holiday ........................................... | 0.69 | 2.1 | 0.54 | 1.9 | 0.77 | 2.1 |
| Sick ................................................ | 0.29 | 0.9 | 0.22 | 0.8 | 0.32 | 0.9 |
| Personal ......................................... | 0.10 | 0.3 | 0.11 | 0.4 | 0.10 | 0.3 |
| Supplemental pay .............................. | 0.86 | 2.6 | 0.75 | 2.6 | 0.91 | 2.6 |
| Overtime and premium pay[2] ........... | 0.22 | 0.7 | 0.21 | 0.7 | 0.23 | 0.6 |
| Shift differentials ........................... | 0.03 | 0.1 | 0.03 | 0.1 | 0.03 | 0.1 |
| Nonproduction bonuses ................... | 0.60 | 1.8 | 0.50 | 1.7 | 0.65 | 1.8 |
| Insurance ........................................... | 2.54 | 7.5 | 2.13 | 7.3 | 2.74 | 7.6 |
| Life insurance ................................ | 0.04 | 0.1 | 0.04 | 0.1 | 0.04 | 0.1 |
| Health insurance ........................... | 2.43 | 7.2 | 2.01 | 6.9 | 2.63 | 7.4 |
| Short-term disability ...................... | 0.03 | 0.1 | 0.04 | 0.1 | 0.03 | 0.1 |
| Long-term disability ....................... | 0.04 | 0.1 | 0.04 | 0.2 | 0.04 | 0.1 |
| Retirement and savings ..................... | 1.36 | 4.1 | 0.99 | 3.4 | 1.55 | 4.3 |
| Defined benefit plans ..................... | 0.65 | 1.9 | 0.30 | 1.0 | 0.81 | 2.3 |
| Defined contribution plans ............. | 0.72 | 2.1 | 0.68 | 2.3 | 0.73 | 2.0 |
| Legally required benefits .................... | 2.80 | 8.3 | 2.34 | 8.0 | 3.03 | 8.5 |
| Social Security and Medicare ......... | 1.94 | 5.8 | 1.75 | 6.0 | 2.02 | 5.7 |
| Social Security ........................... | 1.55 | 4.6 | 1.41 | 4.8 | 1.61 | 4.5 |
| Medicare ..................................... | 0.39 | 1.2 | 0.34 | 1.2 | 0.41 | 1.2 |
| Federal unemployment insurance ..... | 0.06 | 0.2 | 0.03 | 0.1 | 0.08 | 0.2 |
| State unemployment insurance ......... | 0.21 | 0.6 | 0.16 | 0.5 | 0.24 | 0.7 |
| Workers' compensation .................... | 0.59 | 1.8 | 0.40 | 1.4 | 0.69 | 1.9 |

*Note:* Individual items may not sum to totals due to rounding.

[1]The states that comprise the Census divisions are: New England—Connecticut, Maine, Massachusetts, New Hampshire, Rhode Island, and Vermont; Middle Atlantic—New Jersey, New York, and Pennsylvania; South Atlantic—Delaware, District of Columbia, Florida, Georgia, Maryland, North Carolina, South Carolina, Virginia, and West Virginia; East South Central—Alabama, Kentucky, Mississippi, and Tennessee; West South Central—Arkansas, Louisiana, Oklahoma, and Texas; East North Central—Illinois, Indiana, Michigan, Ohio, and Wisconsin; West North Central—Iowa, Kansas, Minnesota, Missouri, Nebraska, North Dakota, and South Dakota; Mountain—Arizona, Colorado, Idaho, Montana, Nevada, New Mexico, Utah, and Wyoming; and Pacific—Alaska, California, Hawaii, Oregon, and Washington.
[2]Comprises the Old-Age, Survivors, and Disability Insurance (OASDI) program.

**Table 6-7. Employer Compensation Costs Per Hour Worked for Employee Compensation and Costs as a Percent of Total Compensation: State and Local Government, by Major Occupational and Industry Group, September 2016**

(Dollars, percent of total compensation.)

| Characteristic | Total compensation | Wages and salaries | Benefit costs | | | | | |
|---|---|---|---|---|---|---|---|---|
| | | | Total | Paid leave | Supplemental pay | Insurance | Retirement and savings | Legally required benefits |
| **COSTS PER HOUR WORKED** | | | | | | | | |
| **State and Local Government Workers** | 45.93 | 29.06 | 16.87 | 3.28 | 0.38 | 5.55 | 4.98 | 2.67 |
| **Occupational Group** | | | | | | | | |
| Management, professional, and related | 55.25 | 36.43 | 18.83 | 3.56 | 0.28 | 6.03 | 5.94 | 3.03 |
| Professional and related | 54.18 | 35.93 | 18.25 | 3.18 | 0.27 | 6.03 | 5.89 | 2.89 |
| Teachers[1] | 62.39 | 42.76 | 19.62 | 2.81 | 0.17 | 6.50 | 6.99 | 3.15 |
| Primary, secondary, and special education school teachers | 62.91 | 42.44 | 20.47 | 2.68 | 0.20 | 7.18 | 7.45 | 2.97 |
| Sales and office | 32.05 | 18.83 | 13.22 | 2.78 | 0.22 | 5.15 | 3.09 | 1.97 |
| Office and administrative support | 32.22 | 18.88 | 13.34 | 2.81 | 0.22 | 5.21 | 3.13 | 1.97 |
| Service | 35.16 | 20.23 | 14.93 | 3.04 | 0.64 | 4.71 | 4.32 | 2.23 |
| **Industry Group** | | | | | | | | |
| Education and health services | 48.00 | 31.57 | 16.44 | 2.89 | 0.25 | 5.73 | 4.98 | 2.58 |
| Education services | 49.27 | 32.68 | 16.59 | 2.77 | 0.18 | 5.80 | 5.26 | 2.58 |
| Elementary and secondary schools | 48.22 | 31.91 | 16.31 | 2.42 | 0.19 | 5.96 | 5.30 | 2.45 |
| Junior colleges, colleges, and universities | 53.05 | 35.49 | 17.56 | 4.03 | 0.15 | 5.18 | 5.17 | 3.03 |
| Health care and social assistance | 40.08 | 24.61 | 15.47 | 3.65 | 0.64 | 5.35 | 3.21 | 2.62 |
| Hospitals | 42.52 | 26.26 | 16.26 | 3.90 | 0.79 | 5.68 | 3.23 | 2.66 |
| Public administration | 43.84 | 25.79 | 18.05 | 4.02 | 0.61 | 5.41 | 5.22 | 2.80 |
| **PERCENT OF TOTAL COMPENSATION** | | | | | | | | |
| **State and Local Government Workers** | 100.0 | 63.3 | 36.7 | 7.1 | 0.8 | 12.1 | 10.9 | 5.8 |
| **Occupational Group** | | | | | | | | |
| Management, professional, and related | 100.0 | 65.9 | 34.1 | 6.4 | 0.5 | 10.9 | 10.7 | 5.5 |
| Professional and related | 100.0 | 66.3 | 33.7 | 5.9 | 0.5 | 11.1 | 10.9 | 5.3 |
| Teachers[1] | 100.0 | 68.5 | 31.5 | 4.5 | 0.3 | 10.4 | 11.2 | 5.0 |
| Primary, secondary, and special education school teachers | 100.0 | 67.5 | 32.5 | 4.3 | 0.3 | 11.4 | 11.8 | 4.7 |
| Sales and office | 100.0 | 58.8 | 41.2 | 8.7 | 0.7 | 16.1 | 9.7 | 6.2 |
| Office and administrative support | 100.0 | 58.6 | 41.4 | 8.7 | 0.7 | 16.2 | 9.7 | 6.1 |
| Service | 100.0 | 57.5 | 42.5 | 8.6 | 1.8 | 13.4 | 12.3 | 6.3 |
| **Industry Group** | | | | | | | | |
| Education and health services | 100.0 | 65.8 | 34.2 | 6.0 | 0.5 | 11.9 | 10.4 | 5.4 |
| Education services | 100.0 | 66.3 | 33.7 | 5.6 | 0.4 | 11.8 | 10.7 | 5.2 |
| Elementary and secondary schools | 100.0 | 66.2 | 33.8 | 5.0 | 0.4 | 12.4 | 11.0 | 5.1 |
| Junior colleges, colleges, and universities | 100.0 | 66.9 | 33.1 | 7.6 | 0.3 | 9.8 | 9.7 | 5.7 |
| Health care and social assistance | 100.0 | 61.4 | 38.6 | 9.1 | 1.6 | 13.3 | 8.0 | 6.5 |
| Hospitals | 100.0 | 61.8 | 38.2 | 9.2 | 1.9 | 13.4 | 7.6 | 6.3 |
| Public administration | 100.0 | 58.8 | 41.2 | 9.2 | 1.4 | 12.3 | 11.9 | 6.4 |

*Note:* Individual items may not sum to totals due to rounding.

[1] Includes postsecondary teachers; primary, secondary, and special education teachers; and other teachers and instructors.

## Table 6-8. Employer Costs Per Hour Worked for Employee Compensation and Costs as a Percent of Total Compensation: Private Industry Workers, by Establishment Employment Size, September 2016

(Dollars, percent.)

| Compensation component | 1–99 workers | | | | | | 100 workers or more | | | | | |
|---|---|---|---|---|---|---|---|---|---|---|---|---|
| | 1–99 workers | | 1–49 workers | | 50–99 workers | | 100 workers or more | | 100–499 workers | | 500 workers or more | |
| | Cost | Percent | Cost | Percent | Cost | Percent | Cost | Percent | Cost | Percent | Cost | Percent |
| TOTAL COMPENSATION | 27.01 | 100.0 | 26.71 | 100.0 | 27.97 | 100.0 | 38.60 | 100.0 | 32.62 | 100.0 | 47.73 | 100.0 |
| Wages and Salaries | 19.70 | 72.9 | 19.69 | 73.7 | 19.73 | 70.5 | 25.91 | 67.1 | 22.51 | 69.0 | 31.12 | 65.2 |
| Total Benefits | 7.31 | 27.1 | 7.02 | 26.3 | 8.24 | 29.5 | 12.68 | 32.9 | 10.11 | 31.0 | 16.61 | 34.8 |
| Paid leave | 1.53 | 5.6 | 1.47 | 5.5 | 1.69 | 6.0 | 3.04 | 7.9 | 2.34 | 7.2 | 4.10 | 8.6 |
| Vacation | 0.78 | 2.9 | 0.75 | 2.8 | 0.88 | 3.2 | 1.59 | 4.1 | 1.23 | 3.8 | 2.13 | 4.5 |
| Holiday | 0.49 | 1.8 | 0.48 | 1.8 | 0.52 | 1.9 | 0.89 | 2.3 | 0.71 | 2.2 | 1.17 | 2.5 |
| Sick | 0.18 | 0.7 | 0.17 | 0.6 | 0.19 | 0.7 | 0.38 | 1.0 | 0.26 | 0.8 | 0.54 | 1.1 |
| Personal | 0.08 | 0.3 | 0.08 | 0.3 | 0.09 | 0.3 | 0.18 | 0.5 | 0.14 | 0.4 | 0.24 | 0.5 |
| Supplemental pay | 1.02 | 3.8 | 0.93 | 3.5 | 1.28 | 4.6 | 1.33 | 3.4 | 0.95 | 2.9 | 1.90 | 4.0 |
| Overtime and premium pay[1] | 0.21 | 0.8 | 0.19 | 0.7 | 0.25 | 0.9 | 0.34 | 0.9 | 0.32 | 1.0 | 0.38 | 0.8 |
| Shift differentials | ([2]) | ([3]) | ([2]) | ([3]) | 0.03 | 0.1 | 0.11 | 0.3 | 0.06 | 0.2 | 0.19 | 0.4 |
| Nonproduction bonuses | 0.80 | 3.0 | 0.74 | 2.8 | 1.00 | 3.6 | 0.87 | 2.3 | 0.57 | 1.7 | 1.33 | 2.8 |
| Insurance | 1.77 | 6.5 | 1.68 | 6.3 | 2.05 | 7.3 | 3.58 | 9.3 | 2.93 | 9.0 | 4.57 | 9.6 |
| Life insurance | 0.03 | 0.1 | 0.03 | 0.1 | 0.04 | 0.1 | 0.06 | 0.1 | 0.05 | 0.1 | 0.07 | 0.1 |
| Health insurance | 1.68 | 6.2 | 1.59 | 6.0 | 1.94 | 7.0 | 3.37 | 8.7 | 2.77 | 8.5 | 4.28 | 9.0 |
| Short-term disability | 0.03 | 0.1 | 0.03 | 0.1 | 0.04 | 0.1 | 0.09 | 0.2 | 0.07 | 0.2 | 0.12 | 0.3 |
| Long-term disability | 0.03 | 0.1 | 0.02 | 0.1 | 0.03 | 0.1 | 0.07 | 0.2 | 0.05 | 0.1 | 0.10 | 0.2 |
| Retirement and savings | 0.69 | 2.6 | 0.62 | 2.3 | 0.91 | 3.3 | 1.91 | 5.0 | 1.32 | 4.0 | 2.82 | 5.9 |
| Defined benefit plans | 0.25 | 0.9 | 0.21 | 0.8 | 0.38 | 1.4 | 0.89 | 2.3 | 0.57 | 1.8 | 1.39 | 2.9 |
| Defined contribution plans | 0.44 | 1.6 | 0.41 | 1.5 | 0.53 | 1.9 | 1.02 | 2.6 | 0.75 | 2.3 | 1.43 | 3.0 |
| Legally required benefits | 2.31 | 8.6 | 2.31 | 8.7 | 2.31 | 8.3 | 2.83 | 7.3 | 2.56 | 7.9 | 3.23 | 6.8 |
| Social Security and Medicare | 1.61 | 6.0 | 1.61 | 6.0 | 1.63 | 5.8 | 2.18 | 5.6 | 1.88 | 5.8 | 2.63 | 5.5 |
| Social Security[4] | 1.29 | 4.8 | 1.28 | 4.8 | 1.30 | 4.6 | 1.74 | 4.5 | 1.51 | 4.6 | 2.09 | 4.4 |
| Medicare | 0.33 | 1.2 | 0.32 | 1.2 | 0.33 | 1.2 | 0.44 | 1.1 | 0.37 | 1.1 | 0.53 | 1.1 |
| Federal unemployment insurance | 0.04 | 0.2 | 0.04 | 0.2 | 0.04 | 0.1 | 0.03 | 0.1 | 0.04 | 0.1 | 0.03 | 0.1 |
| State unemployment insurance | 0.18 | 0.7 | 0.19 | 0.7 | 0.18 | 0.6 | 0.18 | 0.5 | 0.20 | 0.6 | 0.16 | 0.3 |
| Workers' compensation | 0.48 | 1.8 | 0.48 | 1.8 | 0.47 | 1.7 | 0.44 | 1.1 | 0.45 | 1.4 | 0.42 | 0.9 |

[1]Includes premium pay for work in addition to the regular work schedule (such as overtime, weekends, and holidays).
[2]Cost per hour worked is $0.01 or less.
[3]Less than .05 percent.
[4]Comprises the Old-Age, Survivors, and Disability Insurance (OASDI) program.

## NOTES AND DEFINITIONS

### EMPLOYEE BENEFITS SURVEY

The Employee Benefits Survey provides data on the incidence and provisions of selected employee benefit plans.

### Coverage

Data in this section are from the National Compensation Survey (NCS), conducted by the Bureau of Labor Statistics (BLS). This release contains March 2016 data on employer-provided benefits offered to civilian, private industry, and state and local government workers in the United States. Excluded are federal government workers, the military, agricultural workers, private household workers, and the self-employed.

### Definitions

*Access* to a benefit is determined on an occupational basis within an establishment. An employee is considered to have access to a benefit if it is available for his or her use.

*Participation* refers to the proportion of employees covered by a benefit. There will be cases where employees with access to a plan will not participate. For example, some employees may decline to participate in a health insurance plan if there is an employee cost involved.

A *private establishment* is an economic unit that produces goods or services, a central administrative office, or an auxiliary unit providing support services to a company. For private industries, the establishment is usually at a single physical location. For state and local governments, an establishment is defined as an agency or entity such as a school district, college, university, hospital, nursing home, administrative body, court, police department, fire department, health or social service operation, highway maintenance operation, urban transit operation, or other governmental unit. It provides services under the authority of a specific state or local government organization within a defined geographic area or jurisdiction.

*Take-up rates* are the percentage of workers with access to a plan who participate in the plan. They are computed by using the number of workers participating in a plan divided by the number of workers with access to the plan, times 100 and rounded to the nearest one percent. Since the computation of take-up rates is based on the number of workers collected, rather the rounded percentage estimates, the take-up rates in the tables may not equal the ratio of participation to access estimates.

An employee is considered to be a *union worker* when all the following conditions are met: 1.) a labor organization is recognized as the bargaining agent for all workers in the occupation. 2.) wage and salary rates are determined through collective bargaining or negotiations. 3.) settlement terms, which must include earnings provisions and may include benefit provisions, are embodied in a signed, mutually binding collective bargaining agreement

### Sources of Additional Information

For more information, see Bureau of Labor Statistics (BLS) news release 16-1493 "Employee Benefits in the United States in the United States–March 2016" which is available on the BLS Web site at <http://www.bls.gov/ncs/ebs/>.

## Table 6-9.  Retirement Benefits:[1] Access, Participation, and Take-Up Rates,[2] March 2016

(Percent.)

| Characteristic | Civilian[3] | | | Private industry | | | State and local government | | |
|---|---|---|---|---|---|---|---|---|---|
| | Access | Participation | Take-up rate | Access | Participation | Take-up rate | Access | Participation | Take-up rate |
| **ALL WORKERS** .................................................. | 69 | 54 | 78 | 66 | 49 | 75 | 90 | 81 | 90 |
| **Worker Characteristics** | | | | | | | | | |
| Management, professional, and related ..................................... | 84 | 72 | 86 | 81 | 69 | 85 | 92 | 81 | 89 |
| Management, business, and financial ..................................... | 86 | 76 | 88 | 85 | 75 | 88 | - | - | - |
| Professional and related ................................................ | 83 | 70 | 85 | 79 | 65 | 83 | 92 | 81 | 89 |
| Teachers .................................................................. | 84 | 73 | 87 | - | - | - | 91 | 80 | 88 |
| Primary, secondary, and special education school teachers .......................................................... | 94 | 83 | 88 | - | - | - | 99 | 88 | 89 |
| Registered nurses .................................................... | 88 | 72 | 81 | - | - | - | - | - | - |
| Service ..................................................................... | 47 | 31 | 65 | 41 | 23 | 56 | 86 | 78 | 90 |
| Protective service ........................................................ | 78 | 62 | 79 | 60 | 31 | 52 | 92 | 85 | 92 |
| Sales and office ............................................................ | 71 | 52 | 74 | 69 | 50 | 72 | 91 | 82 | 90 |
| Sales and related ........................................................ | 66 | 41 | 61 | 66 | 41 | 61 | - | - | - |
| Office and administrative support ......................................... | 74 | 59 | 80 | 72 | 56 | 78 | 92 | 83 | 90 |
| Natural resources, construction, and maintenance .................... | 65 | 53 | 81 | 62 | 49 | 79 | 97 | 91 | 94 |
| Construction, extraction, farming, fishing, and forestry .......... | 62 | 50 | 82 | 57 | 45 | 79 | - | - | - |
| Installation, maintenance, and repair ................................... | 69 | 55 | 80 | 67 | 52 | 78 | - | - | - |
| Production, transportation, and material moving ...................... | 71 | 54 | 76 | 70 | 53 | 75 | 85 | 78 | 91 |
| Production ................................................................ | 74 | 56 | 76 | 74 | 56 | 75 | - | - | - |
| Transportation and material moving .................................... | 68 | 52 | 76 | 67 | 50 | 74 | - | - | - |
| Full-time workers ............................................................ | 80 | 65 | 81 | 77 | 60 | 78 | 99 | 89 | 90 |
| Part-time workers ........................................................... | 37 | 22 | 59 | 37 | 21 | 56 | 40 | 34 | 85 |
| Union workers .............................................................. | 94 | 84 | 90 | 91 | 81 | 90 | 97 | 87 | 89 |
| Nonunion workers .......................................................... | 65 | 49 | 75 | 64 | 46 | 73 | 84 | 76 | 90 |
| **Average Wage Within the Following Percentiles**[4] | | | | | | | | | |
| Lowest 25 percent ......................................................... | 44 | 24 | 56 | 42 | 22 | 52 | 76 | 68 | 89 |
| Lowest 10 percent ...................................................... | 33 | 15 | 45 | 33 | 14 | 42 | 63 | 55 | 87 |
| Second 25 percent ......................................................... | 71 | 52 | 74 | 65 | 45 | 69 | 93 | 84 | 90 |
| Third 25 percent ........................................................... | 81 | 68 | 84 | 78 | 64 | 82 | 95 | 86 | 91 |
| Highest 25 percent ........................................................ | 89 | 79 | 89 | 87 | 76 | 88 | 98 | 87 | 89 |
| Highest 10 percent ..................................................... | 90 | 80 | 89 | 88 | 79 | 90 | 97 | 84 | 86 |
| **Establishment Characteristics** | | | | | | | | | |
| Goods-producing industries ............................................... | 75 | 60 | 81 | 74 | 60 | 80 | - | - | - |
| Service-providing industries .............................................. | 69 | 53 | 77 | 64 | 47 | 74 | 90 | 81 | 90 |
| Education and health services .......................................... | 79 | 65 | 83 | 72 | 56 | 79 | 92 | 81 | 88 |
| Educational services .................................................. | 87 | 77 | 88 | 72 | 64 | 88 | 92 | 81 | 88 |
| Elementary and secondary schools ............................... | 89 | 80 | 89 | - | - | - | 92 | 82 | 89 |
| Junior colleges, colleges, and universities .................... | 88 | 77 | 87 | 88 | 77 | 88 | 89 | 77 | 86 |
| Health care and social assistance ................................. | 73 | 57 | 78 | 71 | 55 | 77 | 91 | 79 | 87 |
| Hospitals .............................................................. | 91 | 78 | 85 | - | - | - | 94 | 79 | 84 |
| Public administration .................................................... | 91 | 83 | 92 | - | - | - | 91 | 83 | 92 |
| **Number of Workers** | | | | | | | | | |
| 1 to 99 workers ............................................................ | 53 | 38 | 71 | 52 | 36 | 70 | 80 | 72 | 91 |
| 1 to 49 workers .......................................................... | 48 | 34 | 71 | 47 | 33 | 70 | 73 | 66 | 91 |
| 50 to 99 workers ........................................................ | 67 | 48 | 72 | 65 | 46 | 70 | 90 | 81 | 90 |
| 100 workers or more ..................................................... | 86 | 70 | 82 | 83 | 66 | 79 | 92 | 82 | 90 |
| 100 to 499 workers ..................................................... | 81 | 62 | 77 | 80 | 59 | 74 | 88 | 81 | 92 |
| 500 workers or more .................................................... | 91 | 78 | 86 | 90 | 76 | 85 | 93 | 83 | 89 |
| **Geographic Areas**[5] | | | | | | | | | |
| Northeast ................................................................... | 71 | 58 | 82 | 68 | 55 | 80 | 91 | 82 | 90 |
| New England ............................................................ | 72 | 59 | 81 | 70 | 55 | 78 | 85 | 81 | 95 |
| Middle Atlantic .......................................................... | 71 | 58 | 82 | 68 | 55 | 81 | 93 | 82 | 88 |
| South ....................................................................... | 70 | 52 | 74 | 66 | 47 | 71 | 92 | 82 | 89 |
| South Atlantic ........................................................... | 70 | 54 | 76 | 67 | 49 | 73 | 90 | 81 | 89 |
| East South Central ..................................................... | 73 | 51 | 70 | 68 | 44 | 65 | 95 | 83 | 87 |
| West South Central ..................................................... | 68 | 50 | 74 | 64 | 45 | 70 | 92 | 83 | 91 |
| Midwest .................................................................... | 73 | 57 | 78 | 70 | 53 | 76 | 87 | 77 | 89 |
| East North Central ...................................................... | 72 | 56 | 78 | 70 | 53 | 76 | 85 | 78 | 91 |
| West North Central ..................................................... | 75 | 58 | 77 | 72 | 54 | 75 | 91 | 77 | 85 |
| West ........................................................................ | 63 | 50 | 80 | 59 | 45 | 77 | 91 | 83 | 91 |
| Mountain .................................................................. | 66 | 50 | 76 | 62 | 46 | 74 | 88 | 77 | 88 |
| Pacific ..................................................................... | 62 | 51 | 81 | 57 | 45 | 78 | 92 | 86 | 93 |

[1] Includes defined benefit pension plans and defined contribution retirement plans. Workers are considered as having access or as participating if they have access to or participate in at least one of these plan types.
[2] The take-up rate is an estimate of the percentage of workers with access to a plan who participate in the plan, rounded for presentation.
[3] Includes workers in the private nonfarm economy except those in private households, and workers in the public sector, except the federal government.
[4] The percentile groupings are based on the average wage for each occupation surveyed, which may include workers both above and below the threshold.
[5] The states that comprise the Census divisions are: New England—Connecticut, Maine, Massachusetts, New Hampshire, Rhode Island, and Vermont; Middle Atlantic—New Jersey, New York, and Pennsylvania; South Atlantic—Delaware, District of Columbia, Florida, Georgia, Maryland, North Carolina, South Carolina, Virginia, and West Virginia; East South Central—Alabama, Kentucky, Mississippi, and Tennessee; West South Central—Arkansas, Louisiana, Oklahoma, and Texas; East North Central—Illinois, Indiana, Michigan, Ohio, and Wisconsin; West North Central—Iowa, Kansas, Minnesota, Missouri, Nebraska, North Dakota, and South Dakota; Mountain—Arizona, Colorado, Idaho, Montana, Nevada, New Mexico, Utah, and Wyoming; and Pacific—Alaska, California, Hawaii, Oregon, and Washington.
- = No workers in this area or data does not meet standards of reliability or precision.

## Table 6-10. Medical Care Benefits: Access, Participation, and Take-Up Rates,[1] March 2016

(Percent.)

| Characteristic | Civilian[2] | | | Private industry | | | State and local government | | |
|---|---|---|---|---|---|---|---|---|---|
| | Access | Participation | Take-up rate | Access | Participation | Take-up rate | Access | Participation | Take-up rate |
| **ALL WORKERS** .................................... | 70 | 52 | 75 | 67 | 49 | 73 | 88 | 73 | 83 |
| **Worker Characteristics** | | | | | | | | | |
| Management, professional, and related ...................................... | 87 | 68 | 78 | 86 | 66 | 77 | 89 | 73 | 82 |
| Management, business, and financial ...................................... | 94 | 73 | 78 | 94 | 73 | 77 | - | - | - |
| Professional and related ...................................... | 84 | 66 | 78 | 82 | 62 | 76 | 89 | 72 | 82 |
| Teachers ...................................... | 81 | 66 | 81 | - | - | - | 88 | 72 | 82 |
| Primary, secondary, and special education school teachers ...................................... | 94 | 76 | 81 | - | - | - | 98 | 80 | 82 |
| Registered nurses ...................................... | 88 | 63 | 72 | - | - | - | - | - | - |
| Service ...................................... | 45 | 29 | 65 | 39 | 23 | 58 | 82 | 69 | 84 |
| Protective service ...................................... | 68 | 52 | 77 | 40 | 20 | 51 | 90 | 76 | 85 |
| Sales and office ...................................... | 68 | 49 | 73 | 66 | 47 | 71 | 89 | 75 | 83 |
| Sales and related ...................................... | 55 | 37 | 68 | 55 | 37 | 67 | - | - | - |
| Office and administrative support ...................................... | 76 | 57 | 75 | 74 | 54 | 73 | 90 | 75 | 83 |
| Natural resources, construction, and maintenance ................... | 74 | 60 | 81 | 72 | 58 | 80 | 95 | 81 | 85 |
| Construction, extraction, farming, fishing, and forestry .......... | 68 | 56 | 82 | 65 | 53 | 82 | - | - | - |
| Installation, maintenance, and repair ...................................... | 80 | 64 | 79 | 79 | 62 | 79 | - | - | - |
| Production, transportation, and material moving ...................... | 74 | 55 | 75 | 74 | 55 | 74 | 81 | 68 | 85 |
| Production ...................................... | 80 | 61 | 75 | 80 | 61 | 75 | - | - | - |
| Transportation and material moving ...................................... | 69 | 51 | 74 | 68 | 49 | 73 | - | - | - |
| Full-time workers ...................................... | 88 | 66 | 76 | 86 | 63 | 74 | 99 | 82 | 83 |
| Part-time workers ...................................... | 19 | 12 | 61 | 19 | 11 | 59 | 24 | 17 | 71 |
| Union workers ...................................... | 94 | 79 | 84 | 93 | 78 | 85 | 95 | 79 | 84 |
| Nonunion workers ...................................... | 66 | 48 | 72 | 65 | 46 | 71 | 81 | 67 | 82 |
| **Average Wage Within the Following Percentiles**[3] | | | | | | | | | |
| Lowest 25 percent ...................................... | 36 | 22 | 61 | 33 | 19 | 57 | 70 | 57 | 81 |
| Lowest 10 percent ...................................... | 22 | 11 | 49 | 22 | 11 | 48 | 56 | 45 | 80 |
| Second 25 percent ...................................... | 75 | 54 | 73 | 71 | 50 | 70 | 91 | 77 | 84 |
| Third 25 percent ...................................... | 87 | 68 | 79 | 85 | 65 | 77 | 94 | 78 | 83 |
| Highest 25 percent ...................................... | 93 | 74 | 79 | 92 | 72 | 78 | 97 | 80 | 82 |
| Highest 10 percent ...................................... | 94 | 74 | 79 | 93 | 72 | 78 | 96 | 80 | 83 |
| **Establishment Characteristics** | | | | | | | | | |
| Goods-producing industries ...................................... | 84 | 66 | 79 | 84 | 66 | 79 | - | - | - |
| Service-providing industries ...................................... | 68 | 50 | 74 | 64 | 46 | 71 | 88 | 72 | 83 |
| Education and health services ...................................... | 79 | 59 | 75 | 74 | 52 | 70 | 88 | 72 | 81 |
| Educational services ...................................... | 85 | 69 | 80 | 76 | 57 | 75 | 88 | 72 | 82 |
| Elementary and secondary schools ...................................... | 87 | 70 | 80 | - | - | - | 88 | 72 | 81 |
| Junior colleges, colleges, and universities ...................... | 88 | 71 | 80 | 90 | 68 | 76 | 87 | 72 | 83 |
| Health care and social assistance ...................................... | 75 | 53 | 70 | 73 | 51 | 70 | 90 | 70 | 77 |
| Hospitals ...................................... | 91 | 69 | 76 | - | - | - | 94 | 73 | 78 |
| Public administration ...................................... | 88 | 76 | 86 | - | - | - | 88 | 76 | 86 |
| **Number of Workers** | | | | | | | | | |
| 1 to 99 workers ...................................... | 56 | 40 | 71 | 55 | 39 | 70 | 76 | 63 | 83 |
| 1 to 49 workers ...................................... | 52 | 37 | 70 | 52 | 36 | 69 | 69 | 57 | 84 |
| 50 to 99 workers ...................................... | 67 | 49 | 73 | 66 | 47 | 72 | 88 | 72 | 82 |
| 100 workers or more ...................................... | 84 | 65 | 77 | 82 | 62 | 75 | 89 | 74 | 83 |
| 100 to 499 workers ...................................... | 79 | 59 | 75 | 79 | 58 | 74 | 85 | 70 | 82 |
| 500 workers or more ...................................... | 89 | 71 | 79 | 88 | 68 | 77 | 91 | 75 | 83 |
| **Geographic Areas**[4] | | | | | | | | | |
| Northeast ...................................... | 71 | 53 | 75 | 68 | 50 | 73 | 88 | 74 | 84 |
| New England ...................................... | 69 | 50 | 73 | 66 | 46 | 71 | 87 | 70 | 81 |
| Middle Atlantic ...................................... | 71 | 54 | 76 | 69 | 51 | 74 | 88 | 75 | 85 |
| South ...................................... | 71 | 53 | 74 | 68 | 48 | 71 | 91 | 76 | 84 |
| South Atlantic ...................................... | 71 | 52 | 73 | 67 | 48 | 71 | 90 | 74 | 83 |
| East South Central ...................................... | 75 | 56 | 74 | 71 | 49 | 69 | 95 | 85 | 90 |
| West South Central ...................................... | 70 | 52 | 74 | 67 | 49 | 73 | 90 | 74 | 82 |
| Midwest ...................................... | 71 | 51 | 72 | 69 | 49 | 71 | 82 | 63 | 78 |
| East North Central ...................................... | 70 | 51 | 72 | 69 | 49 | 71 | 79 | 62 | 78 |
| West North Central ...................................... | 71 | 52 | 73 | 69 | 49 | 72 | 86 | 66 | 77 |
| West ...................................... | 69 | 53 | 78 | 65 | 50 | 76 | 89 | 75 | 84 |
| Mountain ...................................... | 68 | 51 | 75 | 65 | 48 | 74 | 87 | 73 | 85 |
| Pacific ...................................... | 69 | 55 | 79 | 66 | 51 | 78 | 90 | 75 | 84 |

[1] The take-up rate is an estimate of the percentage of workers with access to a plan who participate in the plan, rounded for presentation.
[2] Includes workers in the private nonfarm economy except those in private households, and workers in the public sector, except the federal government.
[3] The percentile groupings are based on the average wage for each occupation surveyed, which may include workers both above and below the threshold.
[4] The states that comprise the Census divisions are: New England—Connecticut, Maine, Massachusetts, New Hampshire, Rhode Island, and Vermont; Middle Atlantic—New Jersey, New York, and Pennsylvania; South Atlantic—Delaware, District of Columbia, Florida, Georgia, Maryland, North Carolina, South Carolina, Virginia, and West Virginia; East South Central—Alabama, Kentucky, Mississippi, and Tennessee; West South Central—Arkansas, Louisiana, Oklahoma, and Texas; East North Central—Illinois, Indiana, Michigan, Ohio, and Wisconsin; West North Central—Iowa, Kansas, Minnesota, Missouri, Nebraska, North Dakota, and South Dakota; Mountain—Arizona, Colorado, Idaho, Montana, Nevada, New Mexico, Utah, and Wyoming; and Pacific—Alaska, California, Hawaii, Oregon, and Washington.
- = No workers in this area or data does not meet standards of reliability or precision.

## Table 6-11.  Medical Plans: Share of Premiums Paid by Employer and Employee for Single Coverage, March 2016

(Percent.)

| Characteristic | Civilian[1] | | Private industry | | State and local government | |
|---|---|---|---|---|---|---|
| | Employer share of premium | Employee share of premium | Employer share of premium | Employee share of premium | Employer share of premium | Employee share of premium |
| **ALL WORKERS** | 81 | 19 | 79 | 21 | 87 | 13 |
| **Worker Characteristics** | | | | | | |
| Management, professional, and related | 82 | 18 | 80 | 20 | 87 | 13 |
| Management, business, and financial | 81 | 19 | 80 | 20 | - | - |
| Professional and related | 83 | 17 | 80 | 20 | 87 | 13 |
| Teachers | 86 | 14 | - | - | 87 | 13 |
| Primary, secondary, and special education school teachers | 85 | 15 | - | - | 86 | 14 |
| Registered nurses | 81 | 19 | - | - | - | - |
| Service | 82 | 18 | 80 | 20 | 88 | 12 |
| Protective service | 87 | 13 | 83 | 17 | 88 | 12 |
| Sales and office | 79 | 21 | 77 | 23 | 88 | 12 |
| Sales and related | 75 | 25 | 75 | 25 | - | - |
| Office and administrative support | 80 | 20 | 78 | 22 | 88 | 12 |
| Natural resources, construction, and maintenance | 81 | 19 | 80 | 20 | 86 | 14 |
| Construction, extraction, farming, fishing, and forestry | 82 | 18 | 81 | 19 | - | - |
| Installation, maintenance, and repair | 80 | 20 | 79 | 21 | - | - |
| Production, transportation, and material moving | 80 | 20 | 80 | 20 | 84 | 16 |
| Production | 79 | 21 | 79 | 21 | - | - |
| Transportation and material moving | 81 | 19 | 81 | 19 | - | - |
| Full-time workers | 81 | 19 | 79 | 21 | 87 | 13 |
| Part-time workers | 78 | 22 | 77 | 23 | 85 | 15 |
| Union workers | 87 | 13 | 87 | 13 | 87 | 13 |
| Nonunion workers | 79 | 21 | 78 | 22 | 87 | 13 |
| **Average Wage Within the Following Percentiles[2]** | | | | | | |
| Lowest 25 percent | 77 | 23 | 76 | 24 | 87 | 13 |
| Lowest 10 percent | 75 | 25 | 75 | 25 | 88 | 12 |
| Second 25 percent | 80 | 20 | 78 | 22 | 88 | 12 |
| Third 25 percent | 82 | 18 | 80 | 20 | 88 | 12 |
| Highest 25 percent | 82 | 18 | 81 | 19 | 86 | 14 |
| Highest 10 percent | 82 | 18 | 81 | 19 | 87 | 13 |
| **Establishment Characteristics** | | | | | | |
| Goods-producing industries | 80 | 20 | 80 | 20 | - | - |
| Service-providing industries | 81 | 19 | 79 | 21 | 87 | 13 |
| Education and health services | 82 | 18 | 79 | 21 | 87 | 13 |
| Educational services | 85 | 15 | 80 | 20 | 86 | 14 |
| Elementary and secondary schools | 86 | 14 | - | - | 86 | 14 |
| Junior colleges, colleges, and universities | 85 | 15 | 80 | 20 | 88 | 12 |
| Health care and social assistance | 80 | 20 | 79 | 21 | 88 | 12 |
| Hospitals | 81 | 19 | - | - | 88 | 12 |
| Public administration | 87 | 13 | - | - | 87 | 13 |
| **Number of Workers** | | | | | | |
| 1 to 99 workers | 80 | 20 | 79 | 21 | 91 | 9 |
| 1 to 49 workers | 81 | 19 | 80 | 20 | 91 | 9 |
| 50 to 99 workers | 78 | 22 | 77 | 23 | 91 | 9 |
| 100 workers or more | 81 | 19 | 79 | 21 | 87 | 13 |
| 100 to 499 workers | 79 | 21 | 78 | 22 | 86 | 14 |
| 500 workers or more | 83 | 17 | 80 | 20 | 87 | 13 |
| **Geographic Areas[3]** | | | | | | |
| Northeast | 82 | 18 | 81 | 19 | 85 | 15 |
| New England | 79 | 21 | 79 | 21 | 82 | 18 |
| Middle Atlantic | 83 | 17 | 82 | 18 | 87 | 13 |
| South | 80 | 20 | 78 | 22 | 87 | 13 |
| South Atlantic | 79 | 21 | 77 | 23 | 88 | 12 |
| East South Central | 80 | 20 | 78 | 22 | 87 | 13 |
| West South Central | 79 | 21 | 78 | 22 | 85 | 15 |
| Midwest | 80 | 20 | 78 | 22 | 87 | 13 |
| East North Central | 79 | 21 | 78 | 22 | 86 | 14 |
| West North Central | 81 | 19 | 79 | 21 | 89 | 11 |
| West | 83 | 17 | 82 | 18 | 88 | 12 |
| Mountain | 81 | 19 | 80 | 20 | 89 | 11 |
| Pacific | 83 | 17 | 82 | 18 | 88 | 12 |

[1]Includes workers in the private nonfarm economy except those in private households, and workers in the public sector, except the federal government.
[2]The percentile groupings are based on the average wage for each occupation surveyed, which may include workers both above and below the threshold.
[3]The states that comprise the Census divisions are: New England—Connecticut, Maine, Massachusetts, New Hampshire, Rhode Island, and Vermont; Middle Atlantic—New Jersey, New York, and Pennsylvania; South Atlantic—Delaware, District of Columbia, Florida, Georgia, Maryland, North Carolina, South Carolina, Virginia, and West Virginia; East South Central—Alabama, Kentucky, Mississippi, and Tennessee; West South Central—Arkansas, Louisiana, Oklahoma, and Texas; East North Central—Illinois, Indiana, Michigan, Ohio, and Wisconsin; West North Central—Iowa, Kansas, Minnesota, Missouri, Nebraska, North Dakota, and South Dakota; Mountain—Arizona, Colorado, Idaho, Montana, Nevada, New Mexico, Utah, and Wyoming; and Pacific—Alaska, California, Hawaii, Oregon, and Washington.
- = No workers in this area or data does not meet standards of reliability or precision.

## Table 6-12.  Medical Plans: Share of Premiums Paid by Employer and Employee for Family Coverage, March 2016

(Percent.)

| Characteristic | Civilian[1] | | Private industry | | State and local government | |
|---|---|---|---|---|---|---|
| | Employer share of premium | Employee share of premium | Employer share of premium | Employee share of premium | Employer share of premium | Employee share of premium |
| **ALL WORKERS** ........................................ | 68 | 32 | 68 | 32 | 71 | 29 |
| **Worker Characteristics** | | | | | | |
| Management, professional, and related ................................... | 69 | 31 | 69 | 31 | 69 | 31 |
| Management, business, and financial .......................... | 71 | 29 | 70 | 30 | - | - |
| Professional and related ........................... | 68 | 32 | 68 | 32 | 68 | 32 |
| Teachers ........................................ | 66 | 34 | - | - | 67 | 33 |
| Primary, secondary, and special education school teachers ........................... | 65 | 35 | - | - | 66 | 34 |
| Registered nurses ........................... | 69 | 31 | - | - | - | - |
| Service ........................................ | 67 | 33 | 64 | 36 | 74 | 26 |
| Protective service ........................... | 77 | 23 | 72 | 28 | 78 | 22 |
| Sales and office ........................... | 66 | 34 | 65 | 35 | 73 | 27 |
| Sales and related ........................... | 63 | 37 | 63 | 37 | - | - |
| Office and administrative support ........... | 67 | 33 | 66 | 34 | 73 | 27 |
| Natural resources, construction, and maintenance ................... | 69 | 31 | 69 | 31 | 74 | 26 |
| Construction, extraction, farming, fishing, and forestry ........... | 69 | 31 | 68 | 32 | - | - |
| Installation, maintenance, and repair ........... | 70 | 30 | 69 | 31 | - | - |
| Production, transportation, and material moving ................... | 71 | 29 | 71 | 29 | 67 | 33 |
| Production ........................... | 71 | 29 | 71 | 29 | - | - |
| Transportation and material moving ................... | 70 | 30 | 71 | 29 | - | - |
| | | | | | | |
| Full-time workers ........................... | 69 | 31 | 68 | 32 | 71 | 29 |
| Part-time workers ........................... | 64 | 36 | 63 | 37 | 70 | 30 |
| | | | | | | |
| Union workers ........................... | 80 | 20 | 83 | 17 | 78 | 22 |
| Nonunion workers ........................... | 65 | 35 | 65 | 35 | 64 | 36 |
| **Average Wage Within the Following Percentiles[2]** | | | | | | |
| Lowest 25 percent ........................... | 61 | 39 | 62 | 38 | 65 | 35 |
| Lowest 10 percent ........................... | 61 | 39 | 62 | 38 | 58 | 42 |
| Second 25 percent ........................... | 66 | 34 | 64 | 36 | 73 | 27 |
| Third 25 percent ........................... | 70 | 30 | 68 | 32 | 71 | 29 |
| Highest 25 percent ........................... | 72 | 28 | 72 | 28 | 73 | 27 |
| Highest 10 percent ........................... | 73 | 27 | 73 | 27 | 77 | 23 |
| **Establishment Characteristics** | | | | | | |
| Goods-producing industries ........................... | 72 | 28 | 72 | 28 | - | - |
| Service-providing industries ........................... | 68 | 32 | 67 | 33 | 71 | 29 |
| Education and health services ........................... | 65 | 35 | 64 | 36 | 67 | 33 |
| Educational services ........................... | 66 | 34 | 66 | 34 | 66 | 34 |
| Elementary and secondary schools ........................... | 64 | 36 | - | - | 64 | 36 |
| Junior colleges, colleges, and universities ........................... | 70 | 30 | 71 | 29 | 70 | 30 |
| Health care and social assistance ........................... | 65 | 35 | 64 | 36 | 74 | 26 |
| Hospitals ........................... | 72 | 28 | - | - | 73 | 27 |
| Public administration ........................... | 77 | 23 | - | - | 77 | 23 |
| **Number of Workers** | | | | | | |
| 1 to 99 workers ........................... | 64 | 36 | 64 | 36 | 73 | 27 |
| 1 to 49 workers ........................... | 65 | 35 | 64 | 36 | 74 | 26 |
| 50 to 99 workers ........................... | 64 | 36 | 63 | 37 | 71 | 29 |
| 100 workers or more ........................... | 71 | 29 | 71 | 29 | 70 | 30 |
| 100 to 499 workers ........................... | 68 | 32 | 67 | 33 | 70 | 30 |
| 500 workers or more ........................... | 73 | 27 | 75 | 25 | 71 | 29 |
| **Geographic Areas[3]** | | | | | | |
| Northeast ........................... | 75 | 25 | 73 | 27 | 82 | 18 |
| New England ........................... | 73 | 27 | 71 | 29 | 79 | 21 |
| Middle Atlantic ........................... | 76 | 24 | 74 | 26 | 84 | 16 |
| South ........................... | 63 | 37 | 63 | 37 | 60 | 40 |
| South Atlantic ........................... | 66 | 34 | 65 | 35 | 68 | 32 |
| | | | | | | |
| East South Central ........................... | 61 | 39 | 65 | 35 | 49 | 51 |
| West South Central ........................... | 59 | 41 | 60 | 40 | 55 | 45 |
| Midwest ........................... | 70 | 30 | 69 | 31 | 76 | 24 |
| East North Central ........................... | 71 | 29 | 70 | 30 | 78 | 22 |
| West North Central ........................... | 68 | 32 | 67 | 33 | 74 | 26 |
| | | | | | | |
| West ........................... | 70 | 30 | 69 | 31 | 75 | 25 |
| Mountain ........................... | 68 | 32 | 68 | 32 | 67 | 33 |
| Pacific ........................... | 71 | 29 | 69 | 31 | 78 | 22 |

[1]Includes workers in the private nonfarm economy except those in private households, and workers in the public sector, except the federal government.
[2]The percentile groupings are based on the average wage for each occupation surveyed, which may include workers both above and below the threshold.
[3]The states that comprise the Census divisions are: New England—Connecticut, Maine, Massachusetts, New Hampshire, Rhode Island, and Vermont; Middle Atlantic—New Jersey, New York, and Pennsylvania; South Atlantic—Delaware, District of Columbia, Florida, Georgia, Maryland, North Carolina, South Carolina, Virginia, and West Virginia; East South Central—Alabama, Kentucky, Mississippi, and Tennessee; West South Central—Arkansas, Louisiana, Oklahoma, and Texas; East North Central—Illinois, Indiana, Michigan, Ohio, and Wisconsin; West North Central—Iowa, Kansas, Minnesota, Missouri, Nebraska, North Dakota, and South Dakota; Mountain—Arizona, Colorado, Idaho, Montana, Nevada, New Mexico, Utah, and Wyoming; and Pacific—Alaska, California, Hawaii, Oregon, and Washington.
- = No workers in this area or data does not meet standards of reliability or precision.

## Table 6-13.  Life Insurance Benefits: Access, Participation, and Take-Up Rates, National Compensation Survey, March 2016

(Percent.)

| Characteristic | Civilian[1] | | | Private industry | | | State and local government | | |
|---|---|---|---|---|---|---|---|---|---|
| | Access | Participation | Take-up rates[2] | Access | Participation | Take-up rates[2] | Access | Participation | Take-up rates[2] |
| **ALL WORKERS** | 59 | 57 | 98 | 55 | 54 | 98 | 80 | 78 | 98 |
| **Worker Characteristics** | | | | | | | | | |
| Management, professional, and related | 77 | 76 | 99 | 75 | 75 | 99 | 80 | 78 | 98 |
| Management, business, and financial | 83 | 83 | 99 | 83 | 83 | 99 | - | - | - |
| Professional and related | 74 | 73 | 98 | 71 | 71 | 99 | 79 | 77 | 98 |
| Teachers | 73 | 71 | 98 | - | - | - | 79 | 77 | 98 |
| Primary, secondary, and special education school teachers | 82 | 81 | 98 | - | - | - | 86 | 84 | 98 |
| Registered nurses | 77 | 77 | 99 | - | - | - | - | - | - |
| Service | 34 | 32 | 95 | 27 | 25 | 94 | 77 | 76 | 98 |
| Protective service | 71 | 69 | 97 | 50 | 47 | 95 | 86 | 85 | 98 |
| Sales and office | 56 | 55 | 98 | 54 | 52 | 98 | 81 | 80 | 98 |
| Sales and related | 42 | 40 | 96 | 41 | 40 | 96 | - | - | - |
| Office and administrative support | 64 | 63 | 98 | 62 | 61 | 98 | 82 | 80 | 98 |
| Natural resources, construction, and maintenance | 58 | 56 | 97 | 54 | 53 | 97 | 93 | 91 | 99 |
| Construction, extraction, farming, fishing, and forestry | 51 | 49 | 97 | 46 | 44 | 97 | - | - | - |
| Installation, maintenance, and repair | 65 | 63 | 97 | 62 | 61 | 97 | - | - | - |
| Production, transportation, and material moving | 63 | 60 | 97 | 62 | 60 | 97 | 77 | 74 | 97 |
| Production | 68 | 66 | 98 | 68 | 66 | 98 | - | - | - |
| Transportation and material moving | 58 | 55 | 96 | 56 | 54 | 95 | - | - | - |
| Full-time workers | 74 | 73 | 98 | 71 | 70 | 98 | 90 | 88 | 98 |
| Part-time workers | 12 | 11 | 89 | 12 | 10 | 88 | 22 | 21 | 96 |
| Union workers | 85 | 83 | 97 | 84 | 80 | 96 | 86 | 85 | 98 |
| Nonunion workers | 54 | 53 | 98 | 52 | 51 | 98 | 74 | 72 | 97 |
| **Average Wage Within the Following Percentiles[3]** | | | | | | | | | |
| Lowest 25 percent | 24 | 22 | 92 | 21 | 19 | 91 | 64 | 62 | 98 |
| Lowest 10 percent | 14 | 12 | 86 | 13 | 11 | 83 | 50 | 49 | 97 |
| Second 25 percent | 61 | 60 | 98 | 57 | 55 | 97 | 84 | 83 | 98 |
| Third 25 percent | 75 | 74 | 98 | 71 | 70 | 98 | 84 | 83 | 98 |
| Highest 25 percent | 84 | 83 | 99 | 82 | 82 | 99 | 89 | 87 | 97 |
| Highest 10 percent | 86 | 85 | 99 | 85 | 85 | 99 | 89 | 85 | 96 |
| **Establishment Characteristics** | | | | | | | | | |
| Goods-producing industries | 70 | 68 | 98 | 70 | 68 | 98 | - | - | - |
| Service-providing industries | 57 | 55 | 98 | 52 | 51 | 97 | 80 | 78 | 98 |
| Education and health services | 69 | 68 | 99 | 62 | 62 | 99 | 80 | 78 | 98 |
| Educational services | 77 | 75 | 98 | 67 | 66 | 98 | 79 | 78 | 98 |
| Elementary and secondary schools | 76 | 74 | 98 | - | - | - | 78 | 76 | 98 |
| Junior colleges, colleges, and universities | 85 | 83 | 98 | 87 | 86 | 98 | 84 | 81 | 97 |
| Health care and social assistance | 63 | 63 | 99 | 62 | 61 | 99 | 83 | 79 | 95 |
| Hospitals | 90 | 89 | 99 | - | - | - | 91 | 87 | 96 |
| Public administration | 82 | 81 | 98 | - | - | - | 82 | 81 | 98 |
| **Number of Workers** | | | | | | | | | |
| 1 to 99 workers | 41 | 39 | 97 | 40 | 39 | 97 | 64 | 62 | 96 |
| 1 to 49 workers | 36 | 35 | 98 | 35 | 34 | 98 | 64 | 62 | 97 |
| 50 to 99 workers | 55 | 52 | 95 | 54 | 52 | 95 | 64 | 62 | 96 |
| 100 workers or more | 76 | 74 | 98 | 74 | 72 | 98 | 82 | 80 | 98 |
| 100 to 499 workers | 68 | 66 | 98 | 67 | 65 | 98 | 75 | 73 | 98 |
| 500 workers or more | 85 | 83 | 98 | 85 | 84 | 99 | 85 | 83 | 98 |
| **Geographic Areas[4]** | | | | | | | | | |
| Northeast | 59 | 58 | 98 | 56 | 55 | 98 | 81 | 79 | 98 |
| New England | 58 | 56 | 97 | 56 | 54 | 98 | 71 | 66 | 92 |
| Middle Atlantic | 60 | 59 | 99 | 56 | 55 | 98 | 85 | 84 | 99 |
| South | 61 | 59 | 97 | 57 | 55 | 97 | 82 | 80 | 97 |
| South Atlantic | 60 | 59 | 98 | 56 | 55 | 98 | 83 | 81 | 98 |
| East South Central | 62 | 59 | 96 | 56 | 53 | 96 | 89 | 85 | 96 |
| West South Central | 62 | 60 | 96 | 60 | 57 | 96 | 76 | 75 | 98 |
| Midwest | 62 | 60 | 98 | 59 | 57 | 98 | 79 | 77 | 98 |
| East North Central | 61 | 59 | 97 | 58 | 56 | 98 | 79 | 76 | 97 |
| West North Central | 64 | 63 | 98 | 61 | 59 | 98 | 79 | 79 | 100 |
| West | 51 | 50 | 98 | 48 | 47 | 98 | 76 | 75 | 99 |
| Mountain | 54 | 53 | 98 | 50 | 49 | 98 | 80 | 79 | 99 |
| Pacific | 50 | 49 | 98 | 46 | 45 | 98 | 75 | 73 | 98 |

[1]Includes workers in the private nonfarm economy except those in private households, and workers in the public sector, except the federal government.
[2]The take-up rate is an estimate of the percentage of workers with access to a plan who participate in the plan, rounded for presentation.
[3]The percentile groupings are based on the average wage for each occupation surveyed, which may include workers both above and below the threshold.
[4]The states that comprise the Census divisions are: New England—Connecticut, Maine, Massachusetts, New Hampshire, Rhode Island, and Vermont; Middle Atlantic—New Jersey, New York, and Pennsylvania; South Atlantic—Delaware, District of Columbia, Florida, Georgia, Maryland, North Carolina, South Carolina, Virginia, and West Virginia; East South Central—Alabama, Kentucky, Mississippi, and Tennessee; West South Central—Arkansas, Louisiana, Oklahoma, and Texas; East North Central—Illinois, Indiana, Michigan, Ohio, and Wisconsin; West North Central—Iowa, Kansas, Minnesota, Missouri, Nebraska, North Dakota, and South Dakota; Mountain—Arizona, Colorado, Idaho, Montana, Nevada, New Mexico, Utah, and Wyoming; and Pacific—Alaska, California, Hawaii, Oregon, and Washington.
- = No workers in this area or data does not meet standards of reliability or precision.

## Table 6-14.  Life Insurance Plans: Employee Contribution Requirement, Civilian Workers,[1] March 2016

(Percent.)

| Characteristic | Employee contribution required | Employee contribution not required |
|---|---|---|
| **ALL WORKERS** ................................................................... | 6 | 94 |
| **Worker Characteristics** | | |
| Management, professional, and related ............................... | 5 | 95 |
| Management, business, and financial ............................... | 4 | 96 |
| Professional and related ............................................... | 6 | 94 |
| Teachers ...................................................................... | 9 | 91 |
| Primary, secondary, and special education school teachers .................. | 9 | 91 |
| Registered nurses ...................................................... | 4 | 96 |
| Service ................................................................................ | 9 | 91 |
| Sales and office .................................................................... | 6 | 94 |
| Sales and related ........................................................... | 9 | 91 |
| Office and administrative support .................................... | 4 | 96 |
| Natural resources, construction, and maintenance ............. | 5 | 95 |
| Construction, extraction, farming, fishing, and forestry ...... | 4 | 96 |
| Installation, maintenance, and repair ............................. | 5 | 95 |
| Production, transportation, and material moving ................. | 5 | 95 |
| Transportation and material moving ............................... | 5 | 95 |
| Full-time workers ................................................................. | 6 | 94 |
| Part-time workers ................................................................ | 5 | 95 |
| Union workers ..................................................................... | 5 | 95 |
| Nonunion workers ................................................................ | 6 | 94 |
| **Average Wage Within the Following Percentiles**[2] | | |
| Lowest 25 percent ............................................................... | 9 | 91 |
| Lowest 10 percent ........................................................... | 6 | 94 |
| Second 25 percent ............................................................... | 5 | 95 |
| Third 25 percent .................................................................. | 5 | 95 |
| Highest 25 percent ............................................................... | 5 | 95 |
| Highest 10 percent ........................................................... | 5 | 95 |
| **Establishment Characteristics** | | |
| Service-providing industries ................................................. | 6 | 94 |
| Education and health services ......................................... | 6 | 94 |
| Educational services ..................................................... | 9 | 91 |
| Elementary and secondary schools ............................. | 9 | 91 |
| Health care and social assistance ................................. | 3 | 97 |
| Hospitals ................................................................. | 4 | 96 |
| Public administration ......................................................... | 10 | 90 |
| **Number of Workers** | | |
| 1 to 99 workers .................................................................. | 7 | 93 |
| 1 to 49 workers ............................................................... | 8 | 92 |
| 50 to 99 workers ............................................................. | 5 | 95 |
| 100 workers or more ............................................................ | 5 | 95 |
| 100 to 499 workers .......................................................... | 5 | 95 |
| 500 workers or more ........................................................ | 5 | 95 |
| **Geographic Areas**[3] | | |
| Northeast ........................................................................... | 6 | 94 |
| New England .................................................................. | 11 | 89 |
| Middle Atlantic ................................................................ | 5 | 95 |
| South ................................................................................. | 7 | 93 |
| South Atlantic ................................................................. | 6 | 94 |
| West South Central ......................................................... | 5 | 95 |
| Midwest ............................................................................. | 5 | 95 |
| East North Central .......................................................... | 6 | 94 |
| West North Central ......................................................... | 3 | 97 |
| West .................................................................................. | 4 | 96 |
| Mountain ........................................................................ | 5 | 95 |
| Pacific ............................................................................ | 3 | 97 |

[1]Includes workers in the private nonfarm economy except those in private households, and workers in the public sector, except the federal government.
[2]The percentile groupings are based on the average wage for each occupation surveyed, which may include workers both above and below the threshold.
[3]The states that comprise the Census divisions are: New England—Connecticut, Maine, Massachusetts, New Hampshire, Rhode Island, and Vermont; Middle Atlantic—New Jersey, New York, and Pennsylvania; South Atlantic—Delaware, District of Columbia, Florida, Georgia, Maryland, North Carolina, South Carolina, Virginia, and West Virginia; East South Central—Alabama, Kentucky, Mississippi, and Tennessee; West South Central—Arkansas, Louisiana, Oklahoma, and Texas; East North Central—Illinois, Indiana, Michigan, Ohio, and Wisconsin; West North Central—Iowa, Kansas, Minnesota, Missouri, Nebraska, North Dakota, and South Dakota; Mountain—Arizona, Colorado, Idaho, Montana, Nevada, New Mexico, Utah, and Wyoming; and Pacific—Alaska, California, Hawaii, Oregon, and Washington.

## Table 6-15. Access to Paid Sick Leave, Vacation, and Holidays, March 2016

(Percent.)

| Characteristic | Civilian[1] | | | Private industry | | | State and local government | | |
|---|---|---|---|---|---|---|---|---|---|
| | Paid sick leave | Paid vacation | Paid holidays | Paid sick leave | Paid vacation | Paid holidays | Paid sick leave | Paid vacation | Paid holidays |
| **ALL WORKERS** | 68 | 73 | 75 | 64 | 76 | 77 | 90 | 59 | 67 |
| **Worker Characteristics** | | | | | | | | | |
| Management, professional, and related | 84 | 76 | 81 | 82 | 88 | 89 | 91 | 42 | 55 |
| Management, business, and financial | 89 | 95 | 96 | 89 | 97 | 97 | - | - | - |
| Professional and related | 82 | 68 | 74 | 78 | 83 | 85 | 91 | 35 | 49 |
| Teachers | 83 | 16 | 35 | - | - | - | 89 | 10 | 30 |
| Primary, secondary, and special education school teachers | 93 | 16 | 31 | - | - | - | 96 | 9 | 26 |
| Registered nurses | 79 | 88 | 89 | - | - | - | - | - | - |
| Service | 48 | 55 | 54 | 42 | 52 | 50 | 86 | 76 | 78 |
| Protective service | 72 | 76 | 77 | 47 | 58 | 64 | 90 | 89 | 87 |
| Sales and office | 70 | 80 | 81 | 69 | 79 | 81 | 91 | 85 | 86 |
| Sales and related | 60 | 72 | 73 | 60 | 72 | 73 | - | - | - |
| Office and administrative support | 77 | 85 | 86 | 75 | 85 | 86 | 92 | 86 | 87 |
| Natural resources, construction, and maintenance | 60 | 79 | 81 | 56 | 77 | 79 | 96 | 97 | 96 |
| Construction, extraction, farming, fishing, and forestry | 48 | 67 | 69 | 42 | 63 | 66 | - | - | - |
| Installation, maintenance, and repair | 72 | 90 | 92 | 69 | 90 | 91 | - | - | - |
| Production, transportation, and material moving | 61 | 80 | 82 | 59 | 81 | 83 | 89 | 64 | 74 |
| Production | 58 | 87 | 90 | 57 | 87 | 89 | - | - | - |
| Transportation and material moving | 63 | 74 | 76 | 61 | 75 | 76 | - | - | - |
| Full-time workers | 80 | 87 | 88 | 76 | 91 | 90 | 98 | 66 | 74 |
| Part-time workers | 31 | 35 | 39 | 30 | 36 | 40 | 43 | 21 | 28 |
| Union workers | 86 | 74 | 79 | 76 | 88 | 89 | 97 | 57 | 69 |
| Nonunion workers | 65 | 73 | 75 | 63 | 75 | 76 | 84 | 61 | 66 |
| **Average Wage Within the Following Percentiles[2]** | | | | | | | | | |
| Lowest 25 percent | 41 | 51 | 53 | 39 | 50 | 52 | 77 | 57 | 64 |
| Lowest 10 percent | 28 | 40 | 40 | 27 | 41 | 40 | 65 | 43 | 49 |
| Second 25 percent | 70 | 82 | 83 | 65 | 81 | 82 | 94 | 84 | 87 |
| Third 25 percent | 79 | 87 | 88 | 75 | 88 | 89 | 93 | 65 | 74 |
| Highest 25 percent | 87 | 79 | 83 | 84 | 91 | 92 | 97 | 35 | 48 |
| Highest 10 percent | 90 | 79 | 83 | 87 | 92 | 93 | 98 | 33 | 45 |
| **Establishment Characteristics** | | | | | | | | | |
| Goods-producing industries | 63 | 87 | 89 | 63 | 87 | 89 | - | - | - |
| Service-providing industries | 68 | 71 | 73 | 64 | 74 | 74 | 90 | 59 | 67 |
| Education and health services | 79 | 66 | 73 | 73 | 79 | 83 | 91 | 42 | 55 |
| Educational services | 87 | 40 | 53 | 75 | 56 | 65 | 91 | 35 | 49 |
| Elementary and secondary schools | 90 | 28 | 42 | - | - | - | 91 | 26 | 41 |
| Junior colleges, colleges, and universities | 87 | 67 | 79 | 83 | 73 | 81 | 90 | 63 | 78 |
| Health care and social assistance | 74 | 83 | 86 | 73 | 83 | 86 | 91 | 89 | 91 |
| Hospitals | 84 | 93 | 94 | - | - | - | 93 | 93 | 93 |
| Public administration | 89 | 88 | 88 | - | - | - | 89 | 88 | 88 |
| **Number of Workers** | | | | | | | | | |
| 1 to 99 workers | 56 | 68 | 69 | 55 | 68 | 69 | 81 | 66 | 71 |
| 1 to 49 workers | 54 | 67 | 68 | 53 | 67 | 68 | 74 | 68 | 69 |
| 50 to 99 workers | 62 | 72 | 73 | 60 | 72 | 73 | 90 | 65 | 73 |
| 100 workers or more | 79 | 79 | 82 | 75 | 85 | 87 | 91 | 58 | 67 |
| 100 to 499 workers | 74 | 80 | 82 | 72 | 83 | 85 | 88 | 60 | 63 |
| 500 workers or more | 85 | 77 | 81 | 80 | 89 | 89 | 92 | 58 | 68 |
| **Geographic Areas[3]** | | | | | | | | | |
| Northeast | 70 | 73 | 74 | 67 | 76 | 76 | 90 | 55 | 60 |
| New England | 68 | 69 | 70 | 65 | 73 | 73 | 89 | 47 | 52 |
| Middle Atlantic | 71 | 75 | 76 | 68 | 77 | 78 | 91 | 58 | 63 |
| South | 66 | 76 | 78 | 62 | 78 | 79 | 91 | 61 | 69 |
| South Atlantic | 66 | 76 | 79 | 61 | 78 | 79 | 92 | 65 | 77 |
| East South Central | 68 | 78 | 78 | 62 | 81 | 79 | 93 | 63 | 72 |
| West South Central | 66 | 74 | 75 | 63 | 78 | 79 | 88 | 52 | 53 |
| Midwest | 64 | 74 | 75 | 60 | 77 | 76 | 87 | 55 | 67 |
| East North Central | 63 | 74 | 75 | 60 | 77 | 76 | 86 | 53 | 66 |
| West North Central | 65 | 73 | 74 | 60 | 76 | 75 | 90 | 58 | 69 |
| West | 71 | 70 | 74 | 68 | 71 | 74 | 91 | 64 | 70 |
| Mountain | 61 | 69 | 71 | 58 | 71 | 73 | 83 | 53 | 58 |
| Pacific | 76 | 70 | 75 | 73 | 71 | 75 | 94 | 68 | 74 |

[1]Includes workers in the private nonfarm economy except those in private households, and workers in the public sector, except the federal government.
[2]The percentile groupings are based on the average wage for each occupation surveyed, which may include workers both above and below the threshold.
[3]The states that comprise the Census divisions are: New England—Connecticut, Maine, Massachusetts, New Hampshire, Rhode Island, and Vermont; Middle Atlantic—New Jersey, New York, and Pennsylvania; South Atlantic—Delaware, District of Columbia, Florida, Georgia, Maryland, North Carolina, South Carolina, Virginia, and West Virginia; East South Central—Alabama, Kentucky, Mississippi, and Tennessee; West South Central—Arkansas, Louisiana, Oklahoma, and Texas; East North Central—Illinois, Indiana, Michigan, Ohio, and Wisconsin; West North Central—Iowa, Kansas, Minnesota, Missouri, Nebraska, North Dakota, and South Dakota; Mountain—Arizona, Colorado, Idaho, Montana, Nevada, New Mexico, Utah, and Wyoming; and Pacific—Alaska, California, Hawaii, Oregon, and Washington.
- = No workers in this area or data does not meet standards of reliability or precision.

## Table 6-16. Quality of Life Benefits:[1] Access for Civilian Workers, March 2016

(Percent.)

| Characteristic | Childcare[2] | Flexible workplace | Subsidized commuting | Wellness programs | Employee assistance programs |
|---|---|---|---|---|---|
| ALL WORKERS ..................... | 11 | 6 | 7 | 41 | 54 |
| **Worker Characteristics** | | | | | |
| Management, professional, and related ..................... | 18 | 12 | 12 | 55 | 69 |
| Management, business, and financial ..................... | 18 | 19 | 14 | 57 | 70 |
| Professional and related ..................... | 18 | 9 | 11 | 55 | 68 |
| Teachers ..................... | 14 | 3 | 7 | 49 | 66 |
| Primary, secondary, and special education school teachers ..................... | 11 | - | 4 | 47 | 67 |
| Registered nurses ..................... | 23 | 4 | 10 | 71 | 83 |
| Service ..................... | 8 | 1 | 5 | 26 | 39 |
| Protective service ..................... | 11 | 4 | 8 | 43 | 62 |
| Sales and office ..................... | 9 | 6 | 6 | 42 | 56 |
| Sales and related ..................... | 4 | 4 | 3 | 38 | 53 |
| Office and administrative support ..................... | 12 | 7 | 8 | 45 | 58 |
| Natural resources, construction, and maintenance ..................... | 7 | 1 | 4 | 30 | 39 |
| Construction, extraction, farming, fishing, and forestry ........... | 4 | 1 | 3 | 22 | 29 |
| Installation, maintenance, and repair ..................... | 11 | 2 | 4 | 38 | 50 |
| Production, transportation, and material moving ..................... | 4 | 3 | 2 | 38 | 51 |
| Production ..................... | 7 | 3 | 1 | 42 | 50 |
| Transportation and material moving ..................... | 2 | 3 | 2 | 35 | 52 |
| Full-time workers ..................... | 13 | 8 | 8 | 47 | 60 |
| Part-time workers ..................... | 5 | 2 | 3 | 25 | 37 |
| Union workers ..................... | 17 | 2 | 10 | 54 | 78 |
| Nonunion workers ..................... | 10 | 7 | 6 | 39 | 50 |
| **Average Wage Within the Following Percentiles[3]** | | | | | |
| Lowest 25 percent ..................... | 4 | 1 | 2 | 24 | 35 |
| Lowest 10 percent ..................... | 2 | 1 | 2 | 16 | 28 |
| Second 25 percent ..................... | 8 | 3 | 5 | 39 | 53 |
| Third 25 percent ..................... | 13 | 7 | 9 | 49 | 61 |
| Highest 25 percent ..................... | 19 | 15 | 13 | 58 | 72 |
| Highest 10 percent ..................... | 22 | 19 | 15 | 62 | 77 |
| **Establishment Characteristics** | | | | | |
| Goods-producing industries ..................... | 8 | 6 | 3 | 43 | 50 |
| Service-providing industries ..................... | 11 | 6 | 8 | 41 | 55 |
| Education and health services ..................... | 16 | 4 | 8 | 51 | 68 |
| Educational services ..................... | 14 | 5 | 10 | 51 | 71 |
| Elementary and secondary schools ..................... | 9 | 2 | 4 | 46 | 68 |
| Junior colleges, colleges, and universities ..................... | 29 | - | 22 | 68 | 82 |
| Health care and social assistance ..................... | 17 | 3 | 7 | 51 | 65 |
| Hospitals ..................... | 35 | 3 | 16 | 83 | 94 |
| Public administration ..................... | 16 | 5 | 17 | 55 | 77 |
| **Number of Workers** | | | | | |
| 1 to 99 workers ..................... | 5 | 4 | 3 | 22 | 32 |
| 1 to 49 workers ..................... | 4 | 5 | 3 | 19 | 27 |
| 50 to 99 workers ..................... | 7 | 4 | 4 | 31 | 45 |
| 100 workers or more ..................... | 16 | 8 | 10 | 60 | 76 |
| 100 to 499 workers ..................... | 10 | 7 | 6 | 52 | 67 |
| 500 workers or more ..................... | 24 | 9 | 15 | 68 | 85 |
| **Geographic Areas[4]** | | | | | |
| Northeast ..................... | 15 | 8 | 9 | 40 | 56 |
| New England ..................... | 16 | 10 | 11 | 40 | 57 |
| Middle Atlantic ..................... | 15 | 8 | 9 | 40 | 56 |
| South ..................... | 10 | 6 | 5 | 44 | 55 |
| South Atlantic ..................... | 11 | 7 | 5 | 47 | 59 |
| East South Central ..................... | - | 5 | 1 | 37 | 50 |
| West South Central ..................... | 9 | 6 | 5 | 44 | 51 |
| Midwest ..................... | 9 | 6 | 5 | 40 | 53 |
| East North Central ..................... | 9 | 6 | 6 | 39 | 52 |
| West North Central ..................... | 8 | 6 | 5 | 43 | 56 |
| West ..................... | 10 | 5 | 10 | 39 | 53 |
| Mountain ..................... | 11 | 6 | 9 | 36 | 49 |
| Pacific ..................... | 10 | 5 | 10 | 41 | 54 |

[1]Includes workers in the private nonfarm economy except those in private households, and workers in the public sector, except the federal government.
[2]A workplace program that provides for either the full or partial cost of caring for an employee's children in a nursery, day care center, or a baby sitter in facilities either on or off the employer's premises.
[3]The categories are based on the average wage for each occupation surveyed, which may include workers with earnings both above and below the threshold.
[4]The states that comprise the Census divisions are: New England—Connecticut, Maine, Massachusetts, New Hampshire, Rhode Island, and Vermont; Middle Atlantic—New Jersey, New York, and Pennsylvania; South Atlantic—Delaware, District of Columbia, Florida, Georgia, Maryland, North Carolina, South Carolina, Virginia, and West Virginia; East South Central—Alabama, Kentucky, Mississippi, and Tennessee; West South Central—Arkansas, Louisiana, Oklahoma, and Texas; East North Central—Illinois, Indiana, Michigan, Ohio, and Wisconsin; West North Central—Iowa, Kansas, Minnesota, Missouri, Nebraska, North Dakota, and South Dakota; Mountain—Arizona, Colorado, Idaho, Montana, Nevada, New Mexico, Utah, and Wyoming; and Pacific—Alaska, California, Hawaii, Oregon, and Washington.
- = No workers in this area or data does not meet standards of reliability or precision.

## Table 6-17  Financial Benefits: Access for Civilian Workers, March 2016

(Percent.)

| Characteristic | Health savings account | Section 125 cafeteria benefits | | | Savings plans with no employer contribution[1] | Financial planning |
| | | Flexible benefits | Dependent care flexible spending account | Healthcare flexible spending account | | |
| --- | --- | --- | --- | --- | --- | --- |
| **ALL WORKERS** | 25 | 19 | 40 | 43 | 23 | 20 |
| **Worker Characteristics** | | | | | | |
| Management, professional, and related | 36 | 28 | 58 | 62 | 33 | 27 |
| Management, business, and financial | 46 | 29 | 62 | 65 | 27 | 30 |
| Professional and related | 32 | 28 | 56 | 61 | 36 | 27 |
| Teachers | 23 | 32 | 50 | 58 | 53 | 21 |
| Primary, secondary, and special education school teachers | 20 | 34 | 50 | 59 | 55 | 20 |
| Registered nurses | 32 | 35 | 70 | 73 | 31 | 32 |
| Service | 10 | 10 | 23 | 24 | 17 | 12 |
| Protective service | 19 | 22 | 44 | 47 | 38 | 21 |
| Sales and office | 29 | 17 | 38 | 41 | 19 | 23 |
| Sales and related | 25 | 10 | 30 | 31 | 10 | 21 |
| Office and administrative support | 31 | 21 | 43 | 46 | 24 | 25 |
| Natural resources, construction, and maintenance | 18 | 13 | 28 | 31 | 20 | 16 |
| Construction, extraction, farming, fishing, and forestry | 13 | 9 | 17 | 21 | 19 | 10 |
| Installation, maintenance, and repair | 23 | 17 | 38 | 41 | 21 | 21 |
| Production, transportation, and material moving | 21 | 18 | 38 | 39 | 19 | 15 |
| Production | 25 | 19 | 39 | 40 | 18 | 17 |
| Transportation and material moving | 18 | 16 | 37 | 38 | 21 | 13 |
| Full-time workers | 31 | 23 | 47 | 51 | 26 | 23 |
| Part-time workers | 9 | 6 | 18 | 18 | 13 | 11 |
| Union workers | 23 | 22 | 54 | 58 | 45 | 25 |
| Nonunion workers | 25 | 18 | 38 | 40 | 19 | 19 |
| **Average Wage Within Following Percentiles:[2]** | | | | | | |
| Lowest 25 percent | 10 | 7 | 18 | 18 | 12 | 11 |
| Lowest 10 percent | 4 | 4 | 11 | 11 | 8 | 6 |
| Second 25 percent | 25 | 19 | 38 | 41 | 22 | 19 |
| Third 25 percent | 31 | 24 | 49 | 52 | 28 | 25 |
| Highest 25 percent | 38 | 29 | 61 | 65 | 33 | 29 |
| Highest 10 percent | 42 | 29 | 65 | 69 | 33 | 31 |
| **Establishment Characteristics** | | | | | | |
| Goods-producing industries | 26 | 17 | 39 | 40 | 16 | 20 |
| Service-providing industries | 25 | 19 | 40 | 43 | 24 | 20 |
| Education and health services | 26 | 28 | 50 | 56 | 37 | 22 |
| Educational services | 28 | 33 | 55 | 62 | 55 | 23 |
| Elementary and secondary schools | 22 | 34 | 50 | 57 | 55 | 19 |
| Junior colleges, colleges, and universities | 46 | 35 | 71 | 78 | 63 | 34 |
| Health care and social assistance | 25 | 24 | 46 | 51 | 24 | 22 |
| Hospitals | 35 | 45 | 77 | 83 | 37 | 41 |
| Public administration | 25 | 32 | 58 | 60 | 63 | 30 |
| **Number of Workers** | | | | | | |
| 1 to 99 workers | 16 | 9 | 21 | 23 | 14 | 10 |
| 1 to 49 workers | 15 | 7 | 19 | 20 | 12 | 9 |
| 50 to 99 workers | 20 | 15 | 30 | 33 | 19 | 14 |
| 100 workers or more | 34 | 28 | 58 | 61 | 32 | 30 |
| 100 to 499 workers | 33 | 21 | 48 | 50 | 23 | 26 |
| 500 workers or more | 35 | 35 | 69 | 74 | 41 | 33 |
| **Geographic Areas[3]** | | | | | | |
| Northeast | 21 | 14 | 38 | 42 | 26 | 21 |
| New England | 22 | 13 | 42 | 47 | 24 | 20 |
| Middle Atlantic | 21 | 14 | 37 | 41 | 27 | 21 |
| South | 24 | 23 | 41 | 43 | 23 | 21 |
| South Atlantic | 25 | 21 | 40 | 43 | 23 | 22 |
| East South Central | 29 | 25 | 33 | 36 | 24 | 18 |
| West South Central | 22 | 24 | 45 | 46 | 23 | 20 |
| Midwest | 28 | 20 | 42 | 44 | 23 | 20 |
| East North Central | 27 | 17 | 41 | 42 | 24 | 19 |
| West North Central | 31 | 26 | 45 | 49 | 21 | 21 |
| West | 26 | 15 | 38 | 41 | 20 | 20 |
| Mountain | 26 | 13 | 36 | 38 | 17 | 21 |
| Pacific | 26 | 16 | 39 | 42 | 22 | 19 |

[1]Savings plans established by the employer on behalf of the employee, but with no employer contribution. These are cash or deferred arrangement plans or individual retirement accounts used to fund savings and retirement plans authorized by section 401(k), 403(b), or 457 of the Internal Revenue Code. The employees' contributions can be pre- and post-tax. Employees may authorize a payroll deduction by the employer to fund the established plan.

[2]Surveyed occupations are classified into wage categories based on the average wage for the occupation, which may include workers with earnings both above and below the threshold. The categories were formed using percentile estimates generated using ECEC data for March 2016.

[3]The states that comprise the Census divisions are: New England—Connecticut, Maine, Massachusetts, New Hampshire, Rhode Island, and Vermont; Middle Atlantic—New Jersey, New York, and Pennsylvania; South Atlantic—Delaware, District of Columbia, Florida, Georgia, Maryland, North Carolina, South Carolina, Virginia, and West Virginia; East South Central—Alabama, Kentucky, Mississippi, and Tennessee; West South Central—Arkansas, Louisiana, Oklahoma, and Texas; East North Central—Illinois, Indiana, Michigan, Ohio, and Wisconsin; West North Central—Iowa, Kansas, Minnesota, Missouri, Nebraska, North Dakota, and South Dakota; Mountain—Arizona, Colorado, Idaho, Montana, Nevada, New Mexico, Utah, and Wyoming; and Pacific—Alaska, California, Hawaii, Oregon, and Washington.

- = No workers in this area or data does not meet standards of reliability or precision.

## Table 6-18  Nonproduction Bonuses: Access for Civilian Workers,[1] March 2016

(Percent.)

| Characteristic | All nonproduction bonuses[2] | Cash-profit sharing bonus | Employee recognition bonus | End-of-year bonus | Holiday bonus | Payment in lieu of benefits bonus | Longevity bonus | Referral bonus | Other bonus[3] |
|---|---|---|---|---|---|---|---|---|---|
| **ALL WORKERS** | 38 | 6 | 3 | 9 | 6 | 5 | 2 | 5 | 12 |
| **Worker Characteristics** | | | | | | | | | |
| Management, professional, and related | 43 | 5 | 5 | 10 | 4 | 9 | 2 | 6 | 13 |
| Management, business, and financial | 52 | 8 | 6 | 16 | 5 | 7 | 2 | 7 | 15 |
| Professional and related | 40 | 4 | 4 | 8 | 4 | 9 | 3 | 6 | 13 |
| Teachers | 25 | - | 2 | 1 | (4) | 12 | 2 | (4) | 10 |
| Primary, secondary, and special education school teachers | 29 | - | 2 | 1 | - | 15 | 2 | - | 12 |
| Registered nurses | 46 | 2 | 7 | - | 3 | 9 | 3 | 15 | 16 |
| Service | 24 | 1 | 2 | 5 | 6 | 4 | 3 | 4 | 7 |
| Protective service | 32 | 1 | 5 | 1 | 2 | 10 | 7 | - | 13 |
| Sales and office | 40 | 9 | 3 | 11 | 5 | 4 | 1 | 5 | 12 |
| Sales and related | 33 | 11 | 1 | 8 | 5 | 2 | 1 | 3 | 13 |
| Office and administrative support | 44 | 7 | 4 | 12 | 6 | 5 | 2 | 7 | 12 |
| Natural resources, construction, and maintenance | 39 | 6 | 2 | 11 | 9 | 4 | 2 | 4 | 11 |
| Construction, extraction, farming, fishing, and forestry | 32 | 2 | 1 | 12 | 9 | 2 | 2 | 1 | 7 |
| Installation, maintenance, and repair | 44 | 9 | 3 | 11 | 9 | 6 | 2 | 6 | 14 |
| Production, transportation, and material moving | 40 | 7 | 2 | 9 | 6 | 4 | 1 | 4 | 15 |
| Production | 43 | 10 | 2 | 10 | 7 | 3 | 1 | 4 | 16 |
| Transportation and material moving | 36 | 5 | 1 | 7 | 6 | 4 | 1 | 4 | 13 |
| Full-time workers | 43 | 6 | 4 | 11 | 6 | 7 | 2 | 5 | 14 |
| Part-time workers | 20 | 3 | 1 | 4 | 5 | 1 | 1 | 4 | 5 |
| Union workers | 36 | 5 | 5 | 2 | 1 | 15 | 3 | 4 | 15 |
| Nonunion workers | 38 | 6 | 3 | 10 | 6 | 4 | 2 | 5 | 11 |
| **Average Wage Within the Following Percentiles[5]** | | | | | | | | | |
| Lowest 25 percent | 24 | 3 | 1 | 5 | 6 | 1 | 2 | 4 | 7 |
| Lowest 10 percent | 17 | 1 | 1 | 5 | 6 | 1 | 1 | 2 | 4 |
| Second 25 percent | 39 | 5 | 2 | 9 | 7 | 4 | 2 | 5 | 12 |
| Third 25 percent | 45 | 6 | 3 | 12 | 5 | 7 | 2 | 5 | 14 |
| Highest 25 percent | 47 | 8 | 6 | 11 | 4 | 10 | 2 | 6 | 15 |
| Highest 10 percent | 49 | 8 | 6 | 12 | 3 | 11 | 2 | 7 | 16 |
| **Establishment Characteristics** | | | | | | | | | |
| Goods-producing industries | 47 | 10 | 3 | 13 | 9 | 4 | 1 | 3 | 15 |
| Service-providing industries | 36 | 5 | 3 | 8 | 5 | 5 | 2 | 5 | 11 |
| Education and health services | 32 | 1 | 3 | 5 | 5 | 9 | 3 | 6 | 10 |
| Educational services | 25 | - | 2 | 1 | (4) | 12 | 3 | (4) | 9 |
| Elementary and secondary schools | 26 | - | 1 | 1 | (4) | 14 | 3 | - | 10 |
| Junior colleges, colleges, and universities | 23 | - | 5 | 1 | 1 | 10 | 2 | 1 | 8 |
| Health care and social assistance | 37 | 1 | 3 | 8 | 8 | 6 | 4 | 11 | 10 |
| Hospitals | 42 | 3 | 4 | 5 | 2 | 10 | 3 | 16 | 15 |
| Public administration | 42 | 1 | 6 | 1 | 2 | 18 | 9 | - | 16 |
| **Number of Workers** | | | | | | | | | |
| 1 to 99 workers | 34 | 3 | 1 | 12 | 9 | 3 | 1 | 3 | 6 |
| 1 to 49 workers | 34 | 3 | 1 | 13 | 9 | 2 | 1 | 2 | 6 |
| 50 to 99 workers | 35 | 4 | 2 | 10 | 6 | 4 | 2 | 5 | 8 |
| 100 workers or more | 41 | 8 | 5 | 6 | 3 | 8 | 3 | 7 | 17 |
| 100 to 499 workers | 40 | 8 | 4 | 6 | 4 | 6 | 2 | 8 | 16 |
| 500 workers or more | 41 | 7 | 5 | 5 | 1 | 10 | 3 | 6 | 17 |
| **Geographic Areas[6]** | | | | | | | | | |
| Northeast | 38 | 4 | 2 | 12 | 3 | 8 | 2 | 5 | 11 |
| New England | 36 | 5 | 3 | 12 | 2 | 8 | 2 | 4 | 9 |
| Middle Atlantic | 38 | 3 | 2 | 12 | 3 | 8 | 1 | 5 | 12 |
| South | 41 | 5 | 4 | 9 | 8 | 3 | 2 | 5 | 15 |
| South Atlantic | 42 | 5 | 5 | 9 | 8 | 3 | 3 | 6 | 16 |
| East South Central | 37 | 5 | - | 9 | 8 | 2 | 2 | 5 | 13 |
| West South Central | 41 | 6 | 3 | 10 | 9 | 3 | 2 | 5 | 14 |
| Midwest | 36 | 7 | 2 | 8 | 5 | 5 | 2 | 5 | 11 |
| East North Central | 37 | 7 | 3 | 9 | 6 | 5 | 2 | 5 | 10 |
| West North Central | 34 | 7 | 2 | 8 | 2 | 5 | 3 | 5 | 11 |
| West | 33 | 5 | 3 | 7 | 5 | 7 | - | 5 | 8 |
| Mountain | 34 | 5 | 2 | 10 | 6 | 3 | 1 | 3 | 10 |
| Pacific | 32 | 5 | 4 | 5 | 4 | 9 | - | 5 | 8 |

[1]Includes workers in the private nonfarm economy except those in private households, and workers in the public sector, except the federal government.
[2]The sum of the individual components may be greater than the total because some employees may have access to more than one type of stock option.
[3]Includes all other bonuses provided to employees and not published separately.
[4]Less than 0.5.
[5]The categories are based on the average wage for each occupation surveyed, which may include workers with earnings both above and below the threshold.
[6]The states that comprise the Census divisions are: New England—Connecticut, Maine, Massachusetts, New Hampshire, Rhode Island, and Vermont; Middle Atlantic—New Jersey, New York, and Pennsylvania; South Atlantic—Delaware, District of Columbia, Florida, Georgia, Maryland, North Carolina, South Carolina, Virginia, and West Virginia; East South Central—Alabama, Kentucky, Mississippi, and Tennessee; West South Central—Arkansas, Louisiana, Oklahoma, and Texas; East North Central—Illinois, Indiana, Michigan, Ohio, and Wisconsin; West North Central—Iowa, Kansas, Minnesota, Missouri, Nebraska, North Dakota, and South Dakota; Mountain—Arizona, Colorado, Idaho, Montana, Nevada, New Mexico, Utah, and Wyoming; and Pacific—Alaska, California, Hawaii, Oregon, and Washington.

## Table 6-19  Unmarried Domestic Partner Benefits: Access[1] for Civilian Workers,[2] March 2016

(Percent.)

| Characteristic | Defined benefit retirement survivor benefits | | Healthcare benefits | |
|---|---|---|---|---|
| | Same sex | Opposite sex | Same sex | Opposite sex |
| **ALL WORKERS** | 16 | 16 | 38 | 34 |
| **Worker Characteristics** | | | | |
| Management, professional, and related | 26 | 26 | 52 | 46 |
| Management, business, and financial | 24 | 24 | 59 | 54 |
| Professional and related | 27 | 26 | 49 | 42 |
| Teachers | 43 | 41 | 35 | 29 |
| Primary, secondary, and special education school teachers | 51 | 49 | 33 | 29 |
| Registered nurses | 21 | 22 | 45 | 38 |
| Service | 10 | 10 | 23 | 20 |
| Protective service | 28 | 28 | 34 | 27 |
| Sales and office | 13 | 13 | 41 | 37 |
| Sales and related | 6 | 6 | 35 | 31 |
| Office and administrative support | 18 | 18 | 44 | 41 |
| Natural resources, construction, and maintenance | 13 | 11 | 29 | 25 |
| Construction, extraction, farming, fishing, and forestry | 11 | 11 | 19 | 20 |
| Installation, maintenance, and repair | 15 | 11 | 38 | 29 |
| Production, transportation, and material moving | 11 | 11 | 33 | 30 |
| Production | 9 | 8 | 31 | 29 |
| Transportation and material moving | 14 | 14 | 35 | 30 |
| Full-time workers | 20 | 19 | 45 | 40 |
| Part-time workers | 6 | 6 | 17 | 16 |
| Union workers | 43 | 39 | 56 | 45 |
| Nonunion workers | 12 | 12 | 35 | 32 |
| **Average Wage Within the Following Percentiles[3]** | | | | |
| Lowest 25 percent | 5 | 6 | 19 | 18 |
| Lowest 10 percent | 2 | 2 | 9 | 9 |
| Second 25 percent | 13 | 13 | 36 | 33 |
| Third 25 percent | 20 | 19 | 45 | 39 |
| Highest 25 percent | 30 | 28 | 58 | 50 |
| Highest 10 percent | 32 | 30 | 67 | 59 |
| **Establishment Characteristics** | | | | |
| Goods-producing industries | 10 | 9 | 35 | 32 |
| Service-providing industries | 17 | 17 | 39 | 34 |
| Education and health services | 26 | 25 | 40 | 35 |
| Educational services | 44 | 43 | 38 | 31 |
| Elementary and secondary schools | 48 | 47 | 30 | 26 |
| Junior colleges, colleges, and universities | 40 | 39 | 57 | 44 |
| Health care and social assistance | 13 | 14 | 42 | 37 |
| Hospitals | 23 | 24 | 52 | 42 |
| Public administration | 49 | 48 | 40 | 33 |
| **Number of Workers** | | | | |
| 1 to 99 workers | 6 | 6 | 25 | 24 |
| 1 to 49 workers | 5 | 6 | 24 | 23 |
| 50 to 99 workers | 9 | 8 | 30 | 29 |
| 100 workers or more | 26 | 25 | 50 | 43 |
| 100 to 499 workers | 16 | 16 | 46 | 42 |
| 500 workers or more | 37 | 35 | 55 | 44 |
| **Geographic Areas[4]** | | | | |
| Northeast | 20 | 20 | 45 | 39 |
| New England | 15 | 15 | 41 | 36 |
| Middle Atlantic | 22 | 22 | 46 | 40 |
| South | 17 | 16 | 30 | 28 |
| South Atlantic | 16 | 16 | 32 | 28 |
| East South Central | 20 | 19 | 28 | 26 |
| West South Central | 15 | 15 | 29 | 28 |
| Midwest | 9 | 8 | 28 | 22 |
| East North Central | 7 | 6 | 28 | 21 |
| West North Central | 13 | 12 | 28 | 25 |
| West | 21 | 20 | 56 | 53 |
| Mountain | 14 | 14 | 43 | 38 |
| Pacific | 23 | 23 | 62 | 59 |

[1]The percentage of workers with access to the benefit reflects both the availability of the benefit and the employer's policy on providing the benefit to unmarried domestic partners.

[2]Includes workers in the private nonfarm economy except those in private households, and workers in the public sector, except the federal government.

[3]The categories are based on the average wage for each occupation surveyed, which may include workers with earnings both above and below the threshold.

[4]The states that comprise the Census divisions are: New England—Connecticut, Maine, Massachusetts, New Hampshire, Rhode Island, and Vermont; Middle Atlantic—New Jersey, New York, and Pennsylvania; South Atlantic—Delaware, District of Columbia, Florida, Georgia, Maryland, North Carolina, South Carolina, Virginia, and West Virginia; East South Central—Alabama, Kentucky, Mississippi, and Tennessee; West South Central—Arkansas, Louisiana, Oklahoma, and Texas; East North Central—Illinois, Indiana, Michigan, Ohio, and Wisconsin; West North Central—Iowa, Kansas, Minnesota, Missouri, Nebraska, North Dakota, and South Dakota; Mountain—Arizona, Colorado, Idaho, Montana, Nevada, New Mexico, Utah, and Wyoming; and Pacific—Alaska, California, Hawaii, Oregon, and Washington.

# CHAPTER 7: RECENT TRENDS IN THE LABOR MARKET

## HIGHLIGHTS

This chapter contains information on local area unemployment statistics, movement of work, job openings, hires, and separations.

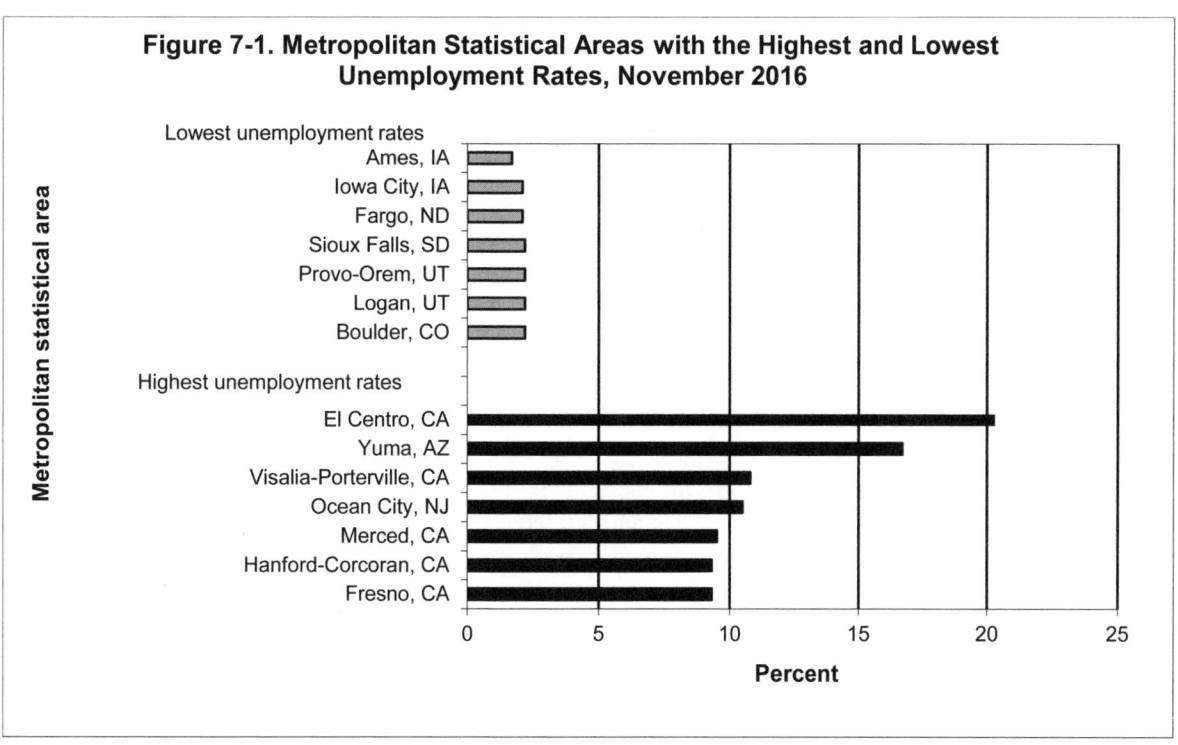

**Figure 7-1. Metropolitan Statistical Areas with the Highest and Lowest Unemployment Rates, November 2016**

In November 2016, El Centro, CA again had the highest unemployment rate at 20.3 percent of all metropolitan areas listed in Table 7-3 followed by Yuma, AZ at 16.7 percent. Ames, IA had the lowest unemployment rate at 1.7 percent. (See Table 7-3.)

## OTHER HIGHLIGHTS

- From October 2015 to October 2016, the number of job openings increased only slightly from 5.42 million to 5.45 million. The number of job openings during this period were highest in education and health services (109,000) and retail trade (90,000). Meanwhile, job opening declined in professional and business services (-169,000), accommodation and food services (-87,000), leisure and hospitality (-67,000), and state and local government (-4,000). (See Table 7-4.)

- The total number of hires increased from nearly 5.125 million in in January 2016 to nearly 5.160 million in October 2016. (See Table 7-5.)

- In October 2016, there were over 1.6 million layoffs and discharges. The number of layoffs and discharges declined drastically in early 2016 then increased in August before declining again in September. Layoffs and discharges were highest in construction followed by retail trade. (See Table 7-8.)

# NOTES AND DEFINITIONS

## LOCAL AREA UNEMPLOYMENT STATISTICS

### Collection and Coverage

The LAUS program provides monthly and annual average estimates for labor force, employment, unemployment, and the unemployment rate for some 7,500 areas. The areas include census regions and divisions, states, metropolitan areas, metropolitan divisions, micropolitan areas, combined areas, small labor market areas, counties and county equivalents, cities with a population of 25,000 and over, and all cities and towns in New England regardless of population.

The labor force and unemployment data are based on the same concepts and definitions as those used for the official national estimates obtained from the Current Population Survey (CPS), a sample survey of households that is conducted for the Bureau of Labor Statistics (BLS) by the U.S. Census Bureau. More information on the CPS can be found in Chapter 1. The LAUS program measures employment and unemployment on a place-of-residence basis. The universe for each is the civilian noninstitutional population 16 years of age and over.

The estimates presented in this chapter are based on sample surveys, administrative data, and modeling and, thus, are subject to sampling and other types of errors. Sampling error is a measure of sampling variability—that is, variation that occurs by chance because a sample rather than the entire population is surveyed. Survey data also are subject to nonsampling errors, such as those which can be introduced into the data collection and processing operations. Estimates not directly derived from sample surveys are subject to additional errors resulting from the specific estimation processes used.

### Concepts and Definitions

*Employed* persons are those who did any work at all for pay or profit in the reference week (the week including the 12th of the month) or worked 15 hours or more without pay in a family business or farm, plus those not working who had a job from which they were temporarily absent, whether or not paid, for such reasons as labor management dispute, illness, or vacation.

The *employment-population ratio* is the proportion of the civilian noninstitutional population 16 years of age and over that is employed.

The *labor force* is the sum of employed and unemployed persons.

*Unemployed* persons are those who were not employed during the reference week (based on the definition above), had actively looked for a job sometime in the 4-week period ending with the reference week, and were currently available for work; persons on layoff expecting recall need not be looking for work to be counted as unemployed.

The *unemployment rate* is the number of unemployed expressed as a percent of the labor force.

### Sources of Additional Information

For more extensive information on Local Area Unemployment Statistics, please see http://www.bls.gov/lau/.

**Table 7-1.  Employees on Nonfarm Payrolls by State and Selected Metropolitan Areas, October 2015–November 2016**

(Number in thousands, percent.)

| State and area | October 2015 | October 2016 | November 2015 | November 2016 | Change from November 2015 to November 2016 Number | Change from November 2015 to November 2016 Percent |
|---|---|---|---|---|---|---|
| **Alabama** | 1 957.9 | 1 981.4 | 1 971.2 | 1 990.2 | 19.0 | 1.0 |
| Anniston-Oxford-Jacksonville | 46.2 | 46.3 | 46.0 | 46.7 | 0.7 | 1.5 |
| Auburn-Opelika | 62.1 | 64.1 | 62.2 | 64.4 | 2.2 | 3.5 |
| Birmingham-Hoover | 517.1 | 522.2 | 522.0 | 526.2 | 4.2 | 0.8 |
| Daphne-Fairhope-Foley | 69.9 | 71.5 | 69.8 | 71.3 | 1.5 | 2.1 |
| Decatur | 53.7 | 54.0 | 54.1 | 54.4 | 0.3 | 0.6 |
| Dothan | 56.9 | 57.3 | 57.3 | 57.3 | 0.0 | 0.0 |
| Florence-Muscle Shoals | 56.4 | 56.8 | 56.9 | 57.0 | 0.1 | 0.2 |
| Gadsden | 37.8 | 38.1 | 38.1 | 38.4 | 0.3 | 0.8 |
| Huntsville | 221.7 | 224.7 | 223.5 | 226.2 | 2.7 | 1.2 |
| Mobile | 176.9 | 179.0 | 178.5 | 179.1 | 0.6 | 0.3 |
| Montgomery | 170.5 | 172.9 | 172.0 | 173.2 | 1.2 | 0.7 |
| Tuscaloosa | 106.1 | 107.9 | 106.9 | 107.5 | 0.6 | 0.6 |
| **Alaska** | 332.9 | 329.2 | 325.2 | 322.4 | -2.8 | -0.9 |
| Anchorage | 181.3 | 179.2 | 179.0 | 177.0 | -2.0 | -1.1 |
| Fairbanks | 38.3 | 38.1 | 37.8 | 37.1 | -0.7 | -1.9 |
| **Arizona** | 2 683.8 | 2 730.1 | 2 717.0 | 2 746.9 | 29.9 | 1.1 |
| Flagstaff | 67.6 | 68.0 | 66.6 | 66.9 | 0.3 | 0.5 |
| Lake Havasu-City-Kingman | 47.8 | 47.8 | 47.5 | 48.1 | 0.6 | 1.3 |
| Phoenix-Mesa-Scottsdale | 1 952.5 | 1 987.8 | 1 979.0 | 2 000.5 | 21.5 | 1.1 |
| Prescott | 62.7 | 65.8 | 63.0 | 65.5 | 2.5 | 4.0 |
| Sierra Vista-Douglas | 34.1 | 34.2 | 34.3 | 34.1 | -0.2 | -0.6 |
| Tucson | 373.6 | 380.6 | 379.4 | 385.0 | 5.6 | 1.5 |
| Yuma | 53.6 | 54.2 | 54.6 | 54.6 | 0.0 | 0.0 |
| **Arkansas** | 1 226.1 | 1 237.7 | 1 228.2 | 1 236.9 | 8.7 | 0.7 |
| Fayetteville-Springdale-Rogers | 241.0 | 244.9 | 242.5 | 246.0 | 3.5 | 1.4 |
| Fort Smith | 114.5 | 115.0 | 114.3 | 114.4 | 0.1 | 0.1 |
| Hot Springs | 37.5 | 38.0 | 37.4 | 37.9 | 0.5 | 1.3 |
| Jonesboro | 55.3 | 56.9 | 55.5 | 56.8 | 1.3 | 2.3 |
| Little Rock-North Little Rock-Conway | 355.2 | 357.5 | 356.3 | 357.9 | 1.6 | 0.4 |
| Pine Bluff | 34.1 | 33.5 | 34.2 | 33.5 | -0.7 | -2.0 |
| **California** | 16 290.8 | 16 661.4 | 16 376.2 | 16 755.1 | 378.9 | 2.3 |
| Bakersfield | 261.0 | 264.9 | 263.1 | 268.0 | 4.9 | 1.9 |
| Chico | 79.6 | 80.9 | 79.2 | 81.5 | 2.3 | 2.9 |
| El Centro | 52.3 | 53.8 | 53.6 | 54.9 | 1.3 | 2.4 |
| Fresno | 332.7 | 336.7 | 332.4 | 338.5 | 6.1 | 1.8 |
| Hanford-Corcoran | 39.1 | 38.5 | 38.7 | 38.7 | 0.0 | 0.0 |
| Los Angeles-Long Beach-Anaheim | 5 895.1 | 6 000.7 | 5 928.5 | 6 032.1 | 103.6 | 1.7 |
| Madera | 36.4 | 38.5 | 36.5 | 38.1 | 1.6 | 4.4 |
| Merced | 65.8 | 66.8 | 64.9 | 66.2 | 1.3 | 2.0 |
| Modesto | 167.5 | 174.2 | 168.6 | 174.8 | 6.2 | 3.7 |
| Napa | 73.4 | 75.8 | 72.6 | 75.1 | 2.5 | 3.4 |
| Oxnard-Thousand Oaks-Ventura | 297.4 | 301.4 | 299.5 | 302.7 | 3.2 | 1.1 |
| Redding | 64.8 | 64.7 | 64.5 | 64.5 | 0.0 | 0.0 |
| Riverside-San Bernardino-Ontario | 1 369.6 | 1 396.6 | 1 384.9 | 1 419.0 | 34.1 | 2.5 |
| Sacramento—Roseville—Arden-Arcade | 927.7 | 951.7 | 930.0 | 956.2 | 26.2 | 2.8 |
| Salinas | 136.6 | 136.1 | 137.5 | 137.1 | -0.4 | -0.3 |
| San Diego-Carlsbad | 1 402.2 | 1 433.0 | 1 414.2 | 1 445.1 | 30.9 | 2.2 |
| San Francisco-Oakland-Hayward | 2 296.7 | 2 352.9 | 2 304.1 | 2 360.7 | 56.6 | 2.5 |
| San Jose-Sunnyvale-Santa Clara | 1 059.6 | 1 095.3 | 1 066.5 | 1 101.8 | 35.3 | 3.3 |
| San Luis Obispo-Paso Robles-Arroyo | 115.7 | 118.5 | 116.5 | 118.8 | 2.3 | 2.0 |
| Grande Santa Cruz-Watsonville | 99.0 | 102.4 | 98.8 | 102.5 | 3.7 | 3.7 |
| Santa Maria-Santa Barbara | 183.2 | 187.4 | 184.1 | 188.0 | 3.9 | 2.1 |
| Santa Rosa | 199.8 | 203.9 | 200.2 | 203.1 | 2.9 | 1.4 |
| Stockton-Lodi | 223.6 | 227.7 | 223.9 | 226.7 | 2.8 | 1.3 |
| Vallejo-Fairfield | 134.9 | 137.8 | 135.9 | 138.9 | 3.0 | 2.2 |
| Visalia-Porterville | 119.4 | 122.5 | 120.8 | 123.0 | 2.2 | 1.8 |
| Yuba City | 42.0 | 41.8 | 41.9 | 42.3 | 0.4 | 1.0 |
| **Colorado** | 2 564.5 | 2 634.6 | 2 570.3 | 2 625.5 | 55.2 | 2.1 |
| Boulder | 184.2 | 189.0 | 183.2 | 190.2 | 7.0 | 3.8 |
| Colorado Springs | 275.7 | 280.0 | 275.1 | 280.7 | 5.6 | 2.0 |
| Denver-Aurora-Lakewood | 1 410.3 | 1 463.3 | 1 414.8 | 1 458.2 | 43.4 | 3.1 |
| Fort Collins | 158.7 | 162.4 | 158.7 | 162.1 | 3.4 | 2.1 |
| Grand Junction | 62.3 | 63.1 | 62.7 | 62.9 | 0.2 | 0.3 |
| Greeley | 101.9 | 105.0 | 101.7 | 104.5 | 2.8 | 2.8 |
| Pueblo | 61.6 | 62.7 | 61.8 | 63.1 | 1.3 | 2.1 |

**Table 7-1. Employees on Nonfarm Payrolls by State and Selected Metropolitan Areas, October 2015–November 2016**—*Continued*

(Number in thousands, percent.)

| State and area | October | | November | | Change from November 2015 to November 2016 | |
|---|---|---|---|---|---|---|
| | 2015 | 2016 | 2015 | 2016 | Number | Percent |
| **Connecticut** | 1 687.7 | 1 692.0 | 1 700.2 | 1 701.1 | 0.9 | 0.1 |
| Bridgeport-Stamford-Norwalk | 412.0 | 411.1 | 415.5 | 412.0 | -3.5 | -0.8 |
| Danbury | 78.3 | 78.8 | 79.1 | 79.4 | 0.3 | 0.4 |
| Hartford-West Hartford-East Hartford | 574.5 | 580.2 | 578.3 | 580.4 | 2.1 | 0.4 |
| New Haven | 282.8 | 283.9 | 285.0 | 286.7 | 1.7 | 0.6 |
| Norwich-New London-Westerly | 129.1 | 128.6 | 129.5 | 128.9 | -0.6 | -0.5 |
| Waterbury | 66.4 | 67.4 | 67.5 | 68.0 | 0.5 | 0.7 |
| **Delaware** | 454.4 | 461.0 | 458.6 | 464.1 | 5.5 | 1.2 |
| Dover | 69.5 | 71.2 | 69.7 | 70.8 | 1.1 | 1.6 |
| Salisbury | 155.6 | 158.5 | 151.7 | 156.0 | 4.3 | 2.8 |
| **District of Columbia** | 772.0 | 787.0 | 773.3 | 787.7 | 14.4 | 1.9 |
| Washington-Arlington-Alexandria | 3 206.6 | 3 279.2 | 3 219.5 | 3 285.0 | 65.5 | 2.0 |
| **Florida** | 8 182.0 | 8 441.0 | 8 268.1 | 8 532.9 | 264.8 | 3.2 |
| Cape Coral-Fort Myers | 248.1 | 256.3 | 253.6 | 260.9 | 7.3 | 2.9 |
| Crestview-Fort Walton Beach-Destin | 106.3 | 107.6 | 106.1 | 107.1 | 1.0 | 0.9 |
| Deltona-Daytona Beach-Ormond Beach | 189.8 | 198.9 | 191.7 | 200.2 | 8.5 | 4.4 |
| Gainesville | 138.6 | 139.4 | 139.0 | 139.9 | 0.9 | 0.6 |
| Homosassa Springs | 33.1 | 33.1 | 33.1 | 33.3 | 0.2 | 0.6 |
| Jacksonville | 655.3 | 680.6 | 662.7 | 686.4 | 23.7 | 3.6 |
| Lakeland-Winter Haven | 210.4 | 213.5 | 212.2 | 215.5 | 3.3 | 1.6 |
| Miami-Fort Lauderdale-West Palm Beach | 2 532.3 | 2 586.6 | 2 564.1 | 2 626.0 | 61.9 | 2.4 |
| Naples-Immokalee-Marco Island | 134.2 | 138.4 | 138.6 | 141.9 | 3.3 | 2.4 |
| North Port-Sarasota-Bradenton | 284.0 | 294.8 | 287.6 | 297.2 | 9.6 | 3.3 |
| Ocala | 98.5 | 99.6 | 98.9 | 101.0 | 2.1 | 2.1 |
| Orlando-Kissimmee-Sanford | 1 173.7 | 1 222.6 | 1 185.4 | 1 238.5 | 53.1 | 4.5 |
| Palm Bay-Melbourne-Titusville | 202.4 | 206.2 | 204.3 | 207.7 | 3.4 | 1.7 |
| Panama City | 81.8 | 82.7 | 80.9 | 82.5 | 1.6 | 2.0 |
| Pensacola-Ferry Pass-Brent | 168.6 | 172.2 | 169.5 | 173.0 | 3.5 | 2.1 |
| Port St Lucie | 139.0 | 141.0 | 141.1 | 143.1 | 2.0 | 1.4 |
| Punta Gorda | 45.7 | 46.8 | 46.7 | 47.7 | 1.0 | 2.1 |
| Sebastian-Vero Beach | 48.6 | 49.4 | 49.6 | 50.5 | 0.9 | 1.8 |
| Sebring | 25.0 | 25.9 | 25.2 | 26.0 | 0.8 | 3.2 |
| Tallahassee | 175.4 | 178.8 | 176.2 | 179.2 | 3.0 | 1.7 |
| Tampa-St Petersburg-Clearwater | 1 264.0 | 1 298.3 | 1 276.2 | 1 309.6 | 33.4 | 2.6 |
| The Villages | 26.5 | 27.4 | 26.8 | 27.6 | 0.8 | 3.0 |
| **Georgia** | 4 334.4 | 4 430.7 | 4 362.4 | 4 462.1 | 99.7 | 2.3 |
| Albany | 62.1 | 63.5 | 62.7 | 63.7 | 1.0 | 1.6 |
| Athens-Clarke County | 93.4 | 96.7 | 94.2 | 97.5 | 3.3 | 3.5 |
| Atlanta-Sandy Springs-Roswell | 2 623.2 | 2 692.7 | 2 643.7 | 2 711.9 | 68.2 | 2.6 |
| Augusta-Richmond County | 229.1 | 231.3 | 228.6 | 234.2 | 5.6 | 2.4 |
| Brunswick | 42.6 | 43.0 | 42.7 | 42.9 | 0.2 | 0.5 |
| Columbus | 122.2 | 123.0 | 122.6 | 123.9 | 1.3 | 1.1 |
| Dalton | 68.6 | 68.1 | 68.4 | 68.3 | -0.1 | -0.1 |
| Gainesville | 85.6 | 87.5 | 86.2 | 87.7 | 1.5 | 1.7 |
| Hinesville | 19.9 | 19.7 | 19.9 | 19.9 | 0.0 | 0.0 |
| Macon | 103.2 | 104.7 | 104.3 | 105.5 | 1.2 | 1.2 |
| Rome | 40.5 | 41.0 | 40.7 | 41.2 | 0.5 | 1.2 |
| Savannah | 174.4 | 180.0 | 175.3 | 182.5 | 7.2 | 4.1 |
| Valdosta | 55.8 | 56.4 | 56.3 | 56.7 | 0.4 | 0.7 |
| Warner Robins | 70.7 | 70.8 | 70.9 | 71.0 | 0.1 | 0.1 |
| **Hawaii** | 642.5 | 656.7 | 645.9 | 661.5 | 15.6 | 2.4 |
| Kahului-Wailuku-Lahaina | 73.6 | 75.6 | 74.0 | 76.2 | 2.2 | 3.0 |
| Urban Honolulu | 473.8 | 483.5 | 475.5 | 486.9 | 11.4 | 2.4 |
| **Idaho** | 689.5 | 705.2 | 687.4 | 703.8 | 16.4 | 2.4 |
| Boise City | 297.1 | 306.6 | 295.8 | 308.3 | 12.5 | 4.2 |
| Coeur d'Alene | 60.8 | 62.4 | 59.9 | 61.2 | 1.3 | 2.2 |
| Idaho Falls | 63.4 | 64.4 | 63.4 | 64.1 | 0.7 | 1.1 |
| Lewiston | 27.9 | 29.0 | 28.0 | 29.1 | 1.1 | 3.9 |
| Pocatello | 36.0 | 36.4 | 36.4 | 36.4 | 0.0 | 0.0 |
| **Illinois** | 6 059.3 | 6 091.2 | 6 052.9 | 6 095.7 | 42.8 | 0.7 |
| Bloomington | 96.4 | 95.0 | 96.2 | 95.0 | -1.2 | -1.2 |
| Carbondale-Marion | 59.5 | 57.0 | 59.6 | 57.2 | -2.4 | -4.0 |
| Champaign-Urbana | 112.0 | 113.6 | 111.7 | 113.8 | 2.1 | 1.9 |
| Chicago-Naperville-Elgin | 4 659.6 | 4 701.6 | 4 660.1 | 4 698.0 | 37.9 | 0.8 |
| Danville | 29.4 | 29.5 | 29.6 | 29.5 | -0.1 | -0.3 |

## Table 7-1. Employees on Nonfarm Payrolls by State and Selected Metropolitan Areas, October 2015–November 2016—*Continued*

(Number in thousands, percent.)

| State and area | October | | November | | Change from November 2015 to November 2016 | |
| --- | --- | --- | --- | --- | --- | --- |
| | 2015 | 2016 | 2015 | 2016 | Number | Percent |
| **Illinois**— *Continued* | | | | | | |
| Davenport-Moline-Rock Island | 182.8 | 180.9 | 182.8 | 181.1 | -1.7 | -0.9 |
| Decatur | 52.4 | 51.5 | 52.6 | 51.6 | -1.0 | -1.9 |
| Kankakee | 45.5 | 46.1 | 45.9 | 46.4 | 0.5 | 1.1 |
| Peoria | 179.3 | 177.6 | 180.0 | 176.7 | -3.3 | -1.8 |
| Rockford | 153.8 | 155.9 | 154.2 | 155.3 | 1.1 | 0.7 |
| Springfield | 115.0 | 116.1 | 115.3 | 116.5 | 1.2 | 1.0 |
| **Indiana** | 3 082.2 | 3 110.2 | 3 086.8 | 3 126.1 | 39.3 | 1.3 |
| Bloomington | 77.2 | 77.3 | 77.9 | 77.3 | -0.6 | -0.8 |
| Columbus | 53.0 | 53.8 | 53.6 | 54.0 | 0.4 | 0.7 |
| Elkhart-Goshen | 130.4 | 127.5 | 129.1 | 127.3 | -1.8 | -1.4 |
| Evansville | 158.7 | 157.2 | 159.4 | 157.8 | -1.6 | -1.0 |
| Fort Wayne | 221.9 | 225.6 | 222.4 | 225.5 | 3.1 | 1.4 |
| Indianapolis-Carmel-Anderson | 1 029.2 | 1 045.4 | 1 034.9 | 1 056.5 | 21.6 | 2.1 |
| Kokomo | 40.7 | 41.4 | 41.0 | 41.4 | 0.4 | 1.0 |
| Lafayette-West Lafayette | 104.1 | 106.7 | 104.4 | 106.2 | 1.8 | 1.7 |
| Michigan City-La Porte | 41.9 | 41.9 | 41.9 | 41.9 | 0.0 | 0.0 |
| Muncie | 52.8 | 52.3 | 52.8 | 52.4 | -0.4 | -0.8 |
| South Bend-Mishawaka | 143.1 | 143.2 | 144.0 | 143.8 | -0.2 | -0.1 |
| Terre Haute | 71.7 | 72.2 | 71.9 | 72.5 | 0.6 | 0.8 |
| **Iowa** | 1 583.1 | 1 601.2 | 1 590.3 | 1 600.1 | 9.8 | 0.6 |
| Ames | 55.1 | 55.7 | 55.1 | 55.9 | 0.8 | 1.5 |
| Cedar Rapids | 144.3 | 145.9 | 145.0 | 146.3 | 1.3 | 0.9 |
| Des Moines-West Des Moines | 351.9 | 356.3 | 352.4 | 356.3 | 3.9 | 1.1 |
| Dubuque | 61.1 | 61.6 | 61.3 | 62.0 | 0.7 | 1.1 |
| Iowa City | 100.4 | 102.8 | 100.8 | 102.9 | 2.1 | 2.1 |
| Sioux City | 89.1 | 88.8 | 89.4 | 88.9 | -0.5 | -0.6 |
| Waterloo-Cedar Falls | 92.4 | 91.7 | 92.5 | 91.2 | -1.3 | -1.4 |
| **Kansas** | 1 416.8 | 1 412.3 | 1 415.6 | 1 411.7 | -3.9 | -0.3 |
| Lawrence | 54.9 | 55.1 | 54.9 | 54.2 | -0.7 | -1.3 |
| Manhattan | 47.8 | 46.8 | 47.8 | 46.6 | -1.2 | -2.5 |
| Topeka | 112.3 | 111.1 | 111.6 | 110.8 | -0.8 | -0.7 |
| Wichita | 299.9 | 302.0 | 300.7 | 303.0 | 2.3 | 0.8 |
| **Kentucky** | 1 908.6 | 1 921.1 | 1 920.4 | 1 936.0 | 15.6 | 0.8 |
| Bowling Green | 73.1 | 74.6 | 73.6 | 75.0 | 1.4 | 1.9 |
| Elizabethtown-Fort Knox | 56.4 | 57.8 | 56.8 | 58.4 | 1.6 | 2.8 |
| Lexington-Fayette | 277.4 | 276.1 | 277.2 | 279.1 | 1.9 | 0.7 |
| Louisville/Jefferson County | 650.7 | 660.1 | 658.8 | 669.7 | 10.9 | 1.7 |
| Owensboro | 53.3 | 54.5 | 53.3 | 54.9 | 1.6 | 3.0 |
| **Louisiana** | 1 994.3 | 1 987.6 | 1 998.0 | 1 991.8 | -6.2 | -0.3 |
| Alexandria | 64.0 | 64.0 | 64.4 | 63.9 | -0.5 | -0.8 |
| Baton Rouge | 407.4 | 421.8 | 410.3 | 420.8 | 10.5 | 2.6 |
| Hammond | 44.0 | 44.2 | 44.2 | 44.2 | 0.0 | 0.0 |
| Houma-Thibodaux | 95.7 | 93.6 | 94.8 | 92.7 | -2.1 | -2.2 |
| Lafayette | 212.5 | 205.7 | 212.3 | 205.1 | -7.2 | -3.4 |
| Lake Charles | 103.9 | 106.6 | 104.5 | 106.6 | 2.1 | 2.0 |
| Monroe | 79.6 | 80.0 | 79.4 | 80.0 | 0.6 | 0.8 |
| New Orleans-Metairie | 575.3 | 576.3 | 575.0 | 578.8 | 3.8 | 0.7 |
| Shreveport-Bossier City | 183.4 | 182.3 | 184.3 | 182.9 | -1.4 | -0.8 |
| **Maine** | 620.1 | 619.8 | 612.8 | 615.2 | 2.4 | 0.4 |
| Bangor | 67.9 | 68.2 | 67.6 | 67.3 | -0.3 | -0.4 |
| Lewiston-Auburn | 51.4 | 52.3 | 51.2 | 52.4 | 1.2 | 2.3 |
| Portland-South Portland | 200.1 | 203.2 | 198.1 | 202.0 | 3.9 | 2.0 |
| **Maryland** | 2 695.6 | 2 723.8 | 2 698.3 | 2 728.5 | 30.2 | 1.1 |
| Baltimore-Columbia-Towson | 1 382.9 | 1 405.3 | 1 382.6 | 1 406.2 | 23.6 | 1.7 |
| California-Lexington Park | 44.8 | 45.2 | 45.0 | 45.2 | 0.2 | 0.4 |
| Cumberland | 39.4 | 39.5 | 39.3 | 39.7 | 0.4 | 1.0 |
| Hagerstown-Martinsburg | 104.5 | 106.4 | 105.1 | 107.7 | 2.6 | 2.5 |
| **Massachusetts** | 3 542.8 | 3 613.1 | 3 539.3 | 3 610.0 | 70.7 | 2.0 |
| Barnstable Town | 105.3 | 107.0 | 101.6 | 103.8 | 2.2 | 2.2 |
| Boston-Cambridge-Nashua | 2 680.5 | 2 727.3 | 2 684.7 | 2 732.2 | 47.5 | 1.8 |
| Leominster-Gardner | 51.2 | 52.5 | 51.7 | 52.8 | 1.1 | 2.1 |
| New Bedford | 68.2 | 67.9 | 67.7 | 67.8 | 0.1 | 0.1 |
| Pittsfield | 42.4 | 42.6 | 42.5 | 42.6 | 0.1 | 0.2 |
| Springfield | 333.2 | 338.3 | 332.4 | 338.3 | 5.9 | 1.8 |
| Worcester | 281.7 | 287.9 | 281.7 | 287.9 | 6.2 | 2.2 |

**Table 7-1. Employees on Nonfarm Payrolls by State and Selected Metropolitan Areas, October 2015–November 2016**—*Continued*

(Number in thousands, percent.)

| State and area | October | | November | | Change from November 2015 to November 2016 | |
|---|---|---|---|---|---|---|
| | 2015 | 2016 | 2015 | 2016 | Number | Percent |
| **Michigan** | 4 314.9 | 4 407.0 | 4 317.2 | 4 400.0 | 82.8 | 1.9 |
| Ann Arbor | 220.3 | 230.9 | 219.9 | 232.3 | 12.4 | 5.6 |
| Battle Creek | 59.5 | 60.2 | 59.4 | 60.0 | 0.6 | 1.0 |
| Bay City | 37.2 | 36.8 | 37.0 | 36.7 | -0.3 | -0.8 |
| Detroit-Warren-Dearborn | 1 955.4 | 1 998.1 | 1 965.1 | 1 999.5 | 34.4 | 1.8 |
| Flint | 140.9 | 142.3 | 141.3 | 142.9 | 1.6 | 1.1 |
| Grand Rapids-Wyoming | 538.7 | 551.0 | 538.9 | 551.9 | 13.0 | 2.4 |
| Jackson | 55.7 | 55.6 | 55.8 | 55.7 | -0.1 | -0.2 |
| Kalamazoo-Portage | 145.6 | 150.4 | 146.4 | 150.1 | 3.7 | 2.5 |
| Lansing-East Lansing | 231.8 | 236.0 | 231.8 | 236.3 | 4.5 | 1.9 |
| Midland | 38.2 | 38.5 | 38.3 | 38.3 | 0.0 | 0.0 |
| Monroe | 44.1 | 44.5 | 43.7 | 44.2 | 0.5 | 1.1 |
| Muskegon | 63.7 | 65.8 | 63.9 | 65.4 | 1.5 | 2.3 |
| Niles-Benton Harbor | 63.0 | 63.5 | 62.3 | 62.7 | 0.4 | 0.6 |
| Saginaw | 89.8 | 91.3 | 90.8 | 91.3 | 0.5 | 0.6 |
| **Minnesota** | 2 891.8 | 2 924.7 | 2 886.6 | 2 918.3 | 31.7 | 1.1 |
| Duluth | 135.5 | 135.8 | 134.7 | 135.3 | 0.6 | 0.4 |
| Mankato-North Mankato | 57.6 | 57.8 | 57.2 | 57.4 | 0.2 | 0.3 |
| Minneapolis-St Paul-Bloomington | 1 955.7 | 1 983.7 | 1 953.9 | 1 981.0 | 27.1 | 1.4 |
| Rochester | 117.2 | 120.4 | 117.0 | 120.1 | 3.1 | 2.6 |
| St. Cloud | 109.9 | 111.5 | 109.5 | 111.5 | 2.0 | 1.8 |
| **Mississippi** | 1 148.2 | 1 146.2 | 1 148.1 | 1 145.4 | -2.7 | -0.2 |
| Gulfport-Biloxi-Pascagoula | 154.3 | 153.3 | 153.9 | 153.4 | -0.5 | -0.3 |
| Hattiesburg | 63.3 | 64.8 | 64.1 | 64.8 | 0.7 | 1.1 |
| Jackson | 277.9 | 278.9 | 277.3 | 278.4 | 1.1 | 0.4 |
| **Missouri** | 2 814.8 | 2 864.7 | 2 809.6 | 2 867.1 | 57.5 | 2.0 |
| Cape Girardeau | 44.3 | 44.1 | 44.9 | 44.4 | -0.5 | -1.1 |
| Columbia | 101.5 | 103.3 | 102.2 | 103.4 | 1.2 | 1.2 |
| Jefferson City | 76.8 | 77.4 | 76.5 | 77.3 | 0.8 | 1.0 |
| Joplin | 81.7 | 80.8 | 82.4 | 81.3 | -1.1 | -1.3 |
| Kansas City | 1 053.8 | 1 065.6 | 1 055.0 | 1 064.6 | 9.6 | 0.9 |
| St. Joseph | 62.8 | 63.1 | 63.2 | 63.3 | 0.1 | 0.2 |
| St. Louis | 1 365.9 | 1 398.2 | 1 359.1 | 1 400.6 | 41.5 | 3.1 |
| Springfield | 209.2 | 215.9 | 211.2 | 215.8 | 4.6 | 2.2 |
| **Montana** | 465.2 | 468.6 | 460.5 | 465.7 | 5.2 | 1.1 |
| Billings | 85.7 | 86.5 | 85.6 | 86.1 | 0.5 | 0.6 |
| Great Falls | 36.3 | 36.3 | 36.2 | 36.3 | 0.1 | 0.3 |
| Missoula | 60.8 | 61.7 | 60.0 | 61.2 | 1.2 | 2.0 |
| **Nebraska** | 1 022.1 | 1 026.0 | 1 021.3 | 1 032.2 | 10.9 | 1.1 |
| Grand Island | 42.3 | 42.5 | 42.2 | 42.4 | 0.2 | 0.5 |
| Lincoln | 189.6 | 190.6 | 189.4 | 191.5 | 2.1 | 1.1 |
| Omaha-Council Bluffs | 497.5 | 500.7 | 498.3 | 504.9 | 6.6 | 1.3 |
| **Nevada** | 1 281.7 | 1 305.9 | 1 276.9 | 1 311.5 | 34.6 | 2.7 |
| Carson City | 28.1 | 28.2 | 28.0 | 28.3 | 0.3 | 1.1 |
| Las Vegas-Henderson-Paradise | 934.3 | 947.5 | 932.0 | 951.1 | 19.1 | 2.0 |
| Reno | 215.9 | 223.1 | 215.8 | 224.7 | 8.9 | 4.1 |
| **New Hampshire** | 664.0 | 676.9 | 663.3 | 677.5 | 14.2 | 2.1 |
| Dover-Durham | 53.6 | 53.8 | 53.5 | 53.7 | 0.2 | 0.4 |
| Manchester | 110.5 | 111.6 | 110.8 | 112.1 | 1.3 | 1.2 |
| Portsmouth | 90.3 | 91.5 | 89.5 | 90.9 | 1.4 | 1.6 |
| **New Jersey** | 4 074.8 | 4 100.5 | 4 095.4 | 4 117.5 | 22.1 | 0.5 |
| Atlantic City-Hammonton | 129.3 | 127.9 | 129.0 | 127.8 | -1.2 | -0.9 |
| Ocean City | 41.6 | 42.8 | 38.1 | 39.0 | 0.9 | 2.4 |
| Trenton | 264.6 | 267.8 | 267.4 | 272.7 | 5.3 | 2.0 |
| Vineland-Bridgeton | 58.1 | 57.7 | 58.2 | 58.7 | 0.5 | 0.9 |
| **New Mexico** | 831.6 | 827.8 | 834.4 | 832.1 | -2.3 | -0.3 |
| Albuquerque | 383.5 | 385.0 | 387.2 | 386.7 | -0.5 | -0.1 |
| Farmington | 51.7 | 51.8 | 51.5 | 51.8 | 0.3 | 0.6 |
| Las Cruces | 71.8 | 72.5 | 71.9 | 72.7 | 0.8 | 1.1 |
| Santa Fe | 62.9 | 63.4 | 62.9 | 63.4 | 0.5 | 0.8 |
| **New York** | 9 372.8 | 9 478.9 | 9 398.9 | 9 503.4 | 104.5 | 1.1 |
| Albany-Schenectady-Troy | 462.5 | 462.2 | 463.6 | 464.1 | 0.5 | 0.1 |
| Binghamton | 104.9 | 103.4 | 105.1 | 103.9 | -1.2 | -1.1 |
| Buffalo-Cheektowaga-Niagara Falls | 564.5 | 568.5 | 563.0 | 566.7 | 3.7 | 0.7 |
| Elmira | 39.0 | 38.6 | 38.9 | 38.9 | 0.0 | 0.0 |
| Glens Falls | 56.6 | 56.8 | 54.8 | 55.4 | 0.6 | 1.1 |

## Table 7-1.  Employees on Nonfarm Payrolls by State and Selected Metropolitan Areas, October 2015–November 2016—*Continued*

(Number in thousands, percent.)

| State and area | October | | November | | Change from November 2015 to November 2016 | |
|---|---|---|---|---|---|---|
| | 2015 | 2016 | 2015 | 2016 | Number | Percent |
| **New York**—*Continued* | | | | | | |
| Ithaca ................................................. | 72.0 | 74.2 | 72.0 | 74.3 | 2.3 | 3.2 |
| Kingston ............................................. | 62.2 | 63.3 | 62.0 | 62.9 | 0.9 | 1.5 |
| New York-Newark-Jersey City ............. | 9 467.2 | 9 601.4 | 9 522.4 | 9 639.7 | 117.3 | 1.2 |
| Rochester ........................................... | 534.1 | 534.1 | 531.3 | 534.1 | 2.8 | 0.5 |
| Syracuse ............................................ | 321.8 | 321.3 | 322.5 | 321.7 | -0.8 | -0.2 |
| Utica-Rome ........................................ | 129.2 | 128.1 | 128.8 | 127.5 | -1.3 | -1.0 |
| Watertown-Fort Drum ......................... | 42.9 | 43.7 | 42.7 | 42.9 | 0.2 | 0.5 |
| **North Carolina** .............................. | 4 298.7 | 4 379.3 | 4 318.5 | 4 401.2 | 82.7 | 1.9 |
| Asheville ............................................ | 184.7 | 189.4 | 185.8 | 189.9 | 4.1 | 2.2 |
| Burlington ........................................... | 60.0 | 60.4 | 60.4 | 60.8 | 0.4 | 0.7 |
| Charlotte-Concord-Gastonia .............. | 1 121.6 | 1 147.1 | 1 128.0 | 1 149.9 | 21.9 | 1.9 |
| Durham-Chapel Hill ............................ | 297.5 | 305.8 | 299.2 | 307.9 | 8.7 | 2.9 |
| Fayetteville ......................................... | 128.6 | 129.5 | 129.7 | 131.4 | 1.7 | 1.3 |
| Goldsboro .......................................... | 42.5 | 42.4 | 42.9 | 42.3 | -0.6 | -1.4 |
| Greensboro-High Point ....................... | 359.9 | 367.2 | 362.4 | 369.7 | 7.3 | 2.0 |
| Greenville ........................................... | 78.6 | 78.1 | 79.1 | 78.8 | -0.3 | -0.4 |
| Hickory-Lenoir-Morganton .................. | 147.8 | 147.5 | 148.2 | 147.8 | -0.4 | -0.3 |
| Jacksonville ....................................... | 49.4 | 49.7 | 49.7 | 50.1 | 0.4 | 0.8 |
| New Bern ........................................... | 44.6 | 45.0 | 44.7 | 45.1 | 0.4 | 0.9 |
| Raleigh ............................................... | 590.1 | 604.7 | 595.9 | 608.0 | 12.1 | 2.0 |
| Rocky Mount ....................................... | 58.4 | 57.7 | 59.0 | 58.4 | -0.6 | -1.0 |
| Wilmington ......................................... | 121.0 | 122.7 | 120.8 | 122.0 | 1.2 | 1.0 |
| Winston-Salem ................................... | 258.8 | 261.5 | 258.9 | 260.9 | 2.0 | 0.8 |
| **North Dakota** ................................ | 456.3 | 448.5 | 453.2 | 446.1 | -7.1 | -1.6 |
| Bismarck ............................................ | 75.9 | 76.0 | 75.4 | 75.1 | -0.3 | -0.4 |
| Fargo .................................................. | 141.9 | 143.5 | 142.1 | 143.8 | 1.7 | 1.2 |
| Grand Forks ....................................... | 58.4 | 58.2 | 58.3 | 58.2 | -0.1 | -0.2 |
| **Ohio** ............................................... | 5 497.2 | 5 547.8 | 5 502.7 | 5 552.7 | 50.0 | 0.9 |
| Akron .................................................. | 346.0 | 348.9 | 346.6 | 349.3 | 2.7 | 0.8 |
| Canton-Massillon ............................... | 172.7 | 175.3 | 173.4 | 175.1 | 1.7 | 1.0 |
| Cincinnati ........................................... | 1 070.1 | 1 091.2 | 1 073.2 | 1 090.2 | 17.0 | 1.6 |
| Cleveland-Elyria ................................ | 1 056.9 | 1 066.4 | 1 058.0 | 1 065.9 | 7.9 | 0.7 |
| Columbus ........................................... | 1 057.0 | 1 070.4 | 1 060.0 | 1 079.2 | 19.2 | 1.8 |
| Dayton ................................................ | 383.7 | 388.9 | 385.4 | 390.2 | 4.8 | 1.2 |
| Lima ................................................... | 53.3 | 54.5 | 53.4 | 54.8 | 1.4 | 2.6 |
| Mansfield ............................................ | 52.8 | 52.4 | 52.8 | 52.3 | -0.5 | -0.9 |
| Springfield .......................................... | 51.1 | 51.1 | 51.2 | 51.0 | -0.2 | -0.4 |
| Toledo ................................................ | 309.1 | 314.0 | 309.5 | 315.4 | 5.9 | 1.9 |
| Weirton-Steubenville .......................... | 44.1 | 44.2 | 44.0 | 43.6 | -0.4 | -0.9 |
| Youngstown-Warren-Boardman .......... | 227.2 | 227.2 | 228.9 | 227.7 | -1.2 | -0.5 |
| **Oklahoma** ...................................... | 1 678.5 | 1 668.4 | 1 682.0 | 1 666.7 | -15.3 | -0.9 |
| Lawton ............................................... | 46.5 | 46.6 | 46.6 | 47.0 | 0.4 | 0.9 |
| Oklahoma City .................................... | 636.5 | 635.8 | 640.0 | 634.1 | -5.9 | -0.9 |
| Tulsa .................................................. | 448.2 | 449.6 | 449.6 | 449.4 | -0.2 | 0.0 |
| **Oregon** ........................................... | 1 810.1 | 1 869.6 | 1 818.0 | 1 871.5 | 53.5 | 2.9 |
| Albany ................................................ | 41.8 | 42.9 | 41.8 | 43.1 | 1.3 | 3.1 |
| Bend-Redmond ................................... | 75.4 | 79.2 | 75.2 | 78.7 | 3.5 | 4.7 |
| Corvallis ............................................. | 41.9 | 41.7 | 41.8 | 42.0 | 0.2 | 0.5 |
| Eugene ............................................... | 154.4 | 156.9 | 155.4 | 158.1 | 2.7 | 1.7 |
| Grants Pass ....................................... | 25.1 | 25.8 | 25.0 | 25.6 | 0.6 | 2.4 |
| Medford .............................................. | 83.6 | 86.3 | 84.4 | 86.4 | 2.0 | 2.4 |
| Portland-Vancouver-Hillsboro ............ | 1 127.8 | 1 159.0 | 1 133.0 | 1 162.5 | 29.5 | 2.6 |
| Salem ................................................. | 159.4 | 165.9 | 159.3 | 165.6 | 6.3 | 4.0 |
| **Pennsylvania** ................................ | 5 922.2 | 5 950.6 | 5 916.7 | 5 954.6 | 37.9 | 0.6 |
| Allentown-Bethlehem-Easton .............. | 361.9 | 359.7 | 360.7 | 357.3 | -3.4 | -0.9 |
| Altoona ............................................... | 61.0 | 62.5 | 61.4 | 62.3 | 0.9 | 1.5 |
| Bloomsburg-Berwick .......................... | 42.8 | 43.7 | 43.0 | 43.5 | 0.5 | 1.2 |
| Chambersburg-Waynesboro ............... | 60.5 | 62.5 | 60.5 | 62.6 | 2.1 | 3.5 |
| East Stroudsburg ............................... | 56.6 | 57.4 | 56.8 | 57.2 | 0.4 | 0.7 |
| Erie .................................................... | 132.0 | 130.4 | 131.9 | 130.5 | -1.4 | -1.1 |
| Gettysburg ......................................... | 34.4 | 35.1 | 34.4 | 34.8 | 0.4 | 1.2 |
| Harrisburg-Carlisle ............................ | 336.3 | 338.3 | 336.9 | 338.6 | 1.7 | 0.5 |
| Johnstown .......................................... | 57.6 | 56.8 | 57.4 | 56.6 | -0.8 | -1.4 |
| Lancaster ........................................... | 248.0 | 248.3 | 247.4 | 247.4 | 0.0 | 0.0 |

## Table 7-1.  Employees on Nonfarm Payrolls by State and Selected Metropolitan Areas, October 2015–November 2016—*Continued*

(Number in thousands, percent.)

| State and area | October 2015 | October 2016 | November 2015 | November 2016 | Change from November 2015 to November 2016 Number | Change from November 2015 to November 2016 Percent |
|---|---|---|---|---|---|---|
| **Pennsylvania**—*Continued* | | | | | | |
| Lebanon | 51.5 | 52.1 | 51.7 | 52.2 | 0.5 | 1.0 |
| Philadelphia-Camden-Wilmington | 2 860.8 | 2 905.0 | 2 875.4 | 2 919.0 | 43.6 | 1.5 |
| Pittsburgh | 1 175.4 | 1 176.1 | 1 171.3 | 1 179.7 | 8.4 | 0.7 |
| Reading | 179.2 | 181.1 | 180.1 | 181.8 | 1.7 | 0.9 |
| Scranton—Wilkes-Barre—Hazleton | 262.0 | 260.7 | 262.2 | 261.6 | -0.6 | -0.2 |
| State College | 79.9 | 80.7 | 79.6 | 81.2 | 1.6 | 2.0 |
| Williamsport | 55.4 | 54.7 | 55.3 | 54.8 | -0.5 | -0.9 |
| York-Hanover | 184.0 | 186.6 | 184.5 | 187.0 | 2.5 | 1.4 |
| **Rhode Island** | 491.6 | 498.7 | 491.4 | 497.1 | 5.7 | 1.2 |
| Providence-Warwick | 583.5 | 592.9 | 584.5 | 590.8 | 6.3 | 1.1 |
| **South Carolina** | 2 027.0 | 2 067.0 | 2 034.8 | 2 080.2 | 45.4 | 2.2 |
| Charleston-North Charleston | 336.2 | 346.6 | 338.9 | 349.7 | 10.8 | 3.2 |
| Columbia | 389.8 | 397.6 | 393.7 | 399.1 | 5.4 | 1.4 |
| Florence | 87.0 | 87.3 | 87.7 | 88.1 | 0.4 | 0.5 |
| Greenville-Anderson-Mauldin | 408.7 | 414.1 | 408.5 | 415.6 | 7.1 | 1.7 |
| Hilton Head Island-Bluffton-Beaufort | 75.4 | 76.5 | 75.2 | 76.3 | 1.1 | 1.5 |
| Myrtle Beach-Conway-North Myrtle Beach | 154.9 | 155.9 | 153.8 | 155.6 | 1.8 | 1.2 |
| Spartanburg | 145.1 | 147.6 | 146.0 | 148.0 | 2.0 | 1.4 |
| Sumter | 39.3 | 39.3 | 39.3 | 39.4 | 0.1 | 0.3 |
| **South Dakota** | 432.2 | 442.1 | 429.8 | 439.7 | 9.9 | 2.3 |
| Rapid City | 66.8 | 68.7 | 65.2 | 66.8 | 1.6 | 2.5 |
| Sioux Falls | 152.4 | 158.1 | 152.7 | 159.0 | 6.3 | 4.1 |
| Tennessee | 2 938.2 | 3 005.1 | 2 962.2 | 3 018.3 | 56.1 | 1.9 |
| Chattanooga | 249.9 | 253.4 | 250.8 | 254.1 | 3.3 | 1.3 |
| Clarksville | 89.7 | 91.3 | 90.3 | 91.9 | 1.6 | 1.8 |
| Cleveland | 48.1 | 48.8 | 49.8 | 53.5 | 3.7 | 7.4 |
| Jackson | 67.4 | 67.8 | 67.4 | 68.2 | 0.8 | 1.2 |
| Johnson City | 80.2 | 81.0 | 80.2 | 81.1 | 0.9 | 1.1 |
| Kingsport-Bristol-Bristol | 122.8 | 122.7 | 123.6 | 123.1 | -0.5 | -0.4 |
| Knoxville | 392.4 | 400.8 | 395.3 | 400.8 | 5.5 | 1.4 |
| Memphis | 630.7 | 640.0 | 635.1 | 643.0 | 7.9 | 1.2 |
| Morristown | 45.9 | 46.9 | 45.8 | 46.9 | 1.1 | 2.4 |
| Nashville-Davidson—Murfreesboro—Franklin | 929.8 | 955.1 | 936.3 | 959.8 | 23.5 | 2.5 |
| **Texas** | 11 949.1 | 12 157.4 | 11 998.1 | 12 210.7 | 212.6 | 1.8 |
| Abilene | 68.5 | 69.6 | 69.0 | 69.8 | 0.8 | 1.2 |
| Amarillo | 119.8 | 120.5 | 120.3 | 120.6 | 0.3 | 0.2 |
| Austin-Round Rock | 977.1 | 999.4 | 985.5 | 1 005.0 | 19.5 | 2.0 |
| Beaumont-Port Arthur | 168.0 | 168.3 | 168.4 | 167.8 | -0.6 | -0.4 |
| Brownsville-Harlingen | 139.7 | 143.4 | 140.5 | 144.7 | 4.2 | 3.0 |
| College Station-Bryan | 112.5 | 116.1 | 113.6 | 116.8 | 3.2 | 2.8 |
| Corpus Christi | 195.8 | 197.6 | 196.8 | 198.3 | 1.5 | 0.8 |
| Dallas-Fort Worth-Arlington | 3 451.7 | 3 569.5 | 3 475.3 | 3 590.1 | 114.8 | 3.3 |
| El Paso | 306.6 | 313.3 | 308.5 | 315.6 | 7.1 | 2.3 |
| Houston-The Woodlands-Sugar Land | 3 009.4 | 3 025.8 | 3 015.4 | 3 031.5 | 16.1 | 0.5 |
| Killeen-Temple | 140.6 | 142.9 | 141.4 | 143.7 | 2.3 | 1.6 |
| Laredo | 102.6 | 104.9 | 103.6 | 105.4 | 1.8 | 1.7 |
| Longview | 100.6 | 101.4 | 101.2 | 101.1 | -0.1 | -0.1 |
| Lubbock | 142.1 | 144.0 | 142.9 | 145.0 | 2.1 | 1.5 |
| McAllen-Edinburg-Mission | 249.5 | 257.1 | 250.7 | 259.8 | 9.1 | 3.6 |
| Midland | 90.4 | 90.9 | 91.5 | 91.9 | 0.4 | 0.4 |
| Odessa | 73.7 | 73.2 | 73.9 | 73.5 | -0.4 | -0.5 |
| San Angelo | 49.3 | 50.2 | 49.6 | 51.0 | 1.4 | 2.8 |
| San Antonio-New Braunfels | 993.4 | 1 008.3 | 996.9 | 1 012.7 | 15.8 | 1.6 |
| Sherman-Denison | 46.4 | 46.9 | 47.0 | 47.6 | 0.6 | 1.3 |
| Texarkana | 60.8 | 60.5 | 61.2 | 60.9 | -0.3 | -0.5 |
| Tyler | 102.4 | 103.9 | 102.8 | 103.8 | 1.0 | 1.0 |
| Victoria | 44.7 | 45.9 | 45.3 | 46.3 | 1.0 | 2.2 |
| Waco | 115.7 | 118.4 | 116.8 | 119.0 | 2.2 | 1.9 |
| Wichita Falls | 58.7 | 58.3 | 58.8 | 58.4 | -0.4 | -0.7 |
| **Utah** | 1 401.8 | 1 444.1 | 1 405.6 | 1 447.7 | 42.1 | 3.0 |
| Logan | 60.5 | 62.4 | 60.8 | 62.6 | 1.8 | 3.0 |
| Ogden-Clearfield | 244.2 | 252.8 | 244.5 | 253.0 | 8.5 | 3.5 |
| Provo-Orem | 231.4 | 238.5 | 231.7 | 239.8 | 8.1 | 3.5 |
| St. George | 59.4 | 62.2 | 59.4 | 62.1 | 2.7 | 4.5 |
| Salt Lake City | 686.0 | 709.6 | 688.9 | 713.3 | 24.4 | 3.5 |

**Table 7-1.  Employees on Nonfarm Payrolls by State and Selected Metropolitan Areas, October 2015–November 2016**—*Continued*

(Number in thousands, percent.)

| State and area | October 2015 | October 2016 | November 2015 | November 2016 | Change from November 2015 to November 2016 Number | Change from November 2015 to November 2016 Percent |
|---|---|---|---|---|---|---|
| **Vermont** .............................................. | 317.9 | 319.4 | 318.1 | 318.1 | 0.0 | 0.0 |
| Burlington-South Burlington ............................. | 127.5 | 128.7 | 127.4 | 128.5 | 1.1 | 0.9 |
| **Virginia** ............................................. | 3 901.0 | 3 966.1 | 3 927.6 | 3 965.5 | 37.9 | 1.0 |
| Blacksburg-Christiansburg-Radford ................. | 79.1 | 79.4 | 78.9 | 78.6 | -0.3 | -0.4 |
| Charlottesville ....................................... | 113.7 | 118.1 | 115.3 | 119.1 | 3.8 | 3.3 |
| Harrisonburg ......................................... | 65.7 | 65.9 | 65.8 | 65.9 | 0.1 | 0.2 |
| Lynchburg ............................................ | 105.1 | 104.3 | 105.4 | 104.7 | -0.7 | -0.7 |
| Richmond ............................................. | 666.9 | 678.2 | 671.3 | 677.1 | 5.8 | 0.9 |
| Roanoke .............................................. | 162.6 | 164.6 | 164.3 | 164.8 | 0.5 | 0.3 |
| Staunton-Waynesboro ............................... | 49.6 | 48.9 | 49.7 | 49.2 | -0.5 | -1.0 |
| Virginia Beach-Norfolk-Newport News .............. | 769.7 | 773.5 | 772.0 | 770.4 | -1.6 | -0.2 |
| Winchester ........................................... | 62.5 | 63.9 | 62.8 | 64.4 | 1.6 | 2.5 |
| **Washington** ........................................ | 3 196.3 | 3 302.6 | 3 205.2 | 3 303.0 | 97.8 | 3.1 |
| Bellingham ........................................... | 88.3 | 91.1 | 88.1 | 90.8 | 2.7 | 3.1 |
| Bremerton-Silverdale ................................ | 89.4 | 90.3 | 89.4 | 90.6 | 1.2 | 1.3 |
| Kennewick-Richland .................................. | 108.8 | 110.6 | 108.5 | 110.9 | 2.4 | 2.2 |
| Longview ............................................. | 39.6 | 41.0 | 39.6 | 40.7 | 1.1 | 2.8 |
| Mount Vernon-Anacortes ............................ | 49.0 | 50.5 | 48.9 | 50.1 | 1.2 | 2.5 |
| Olympia-Tumwate .................................... | 110.3 | 112.9 | 111.1 | 112.3 | 1.2 | 1.1 |
| Seattle-Tacoma-Bellevue ............................ | 1 913.2 | 1 984.4 | 1 922.1 | 1 989.1 | 67.0 | 3.5 |
| Spokane-Spokane Valley ............................. | 238.8 | 248.5 | 239.3 | 248.0 | 8.7 | 3.6 |
| Walla Walla .......................................... | 27.6 | 27.8 | 27.8 | 27.6 | -0.2 | -0.7 |
| Wenatchee ........................................... | 44.5 | 44.8 | 43.7 | 44.7 | 1.0 | 2.3 |
| Yakima ............................................... | 84.0 | 84.7 | 83.4 | 84.9 | 1.5 | 1.8 |
| **West Virginia** ..................................... | 771.0 | 771.1 | 770.3 | 781.3 | 11.0 | 1.4 |
| Beckley .............................................. | 47.4 | 46.7 | 46.7 | 47.0 | 0.3 | 0.6 |
| Charleston ........................................... | 123.4 | 122.7 | 123.7 | 124.0 | 0.3 | 0.2 |
| Huntington-Ashland .................................. | 142.8 | 143.4 | 142.3 | 143.9 | 1.6 | 1.1 |
| Morgantown .......................................... | 73.3 | 73.8 | 73.4 | 74.4 | 1.0 | 1.4 |
| Parkersburg-Vienna .................................. | 42.5 | 41.8 | 42.7 | 42.5 | -0.2 | -0.5 |
| Wheeling ............................................. | 68.8 | 68.3 | 69.1 | 68.9 | -0.2 | -0.3 |
| **Wisconsin** ......................................... | 2 938.8 | 2 968.7 | 2 932.9 | 2 966.8 | 33.9 | 1.2 |
| Appleton ............................................. | 124.4 | 125.4 | 125.1 | 125.5 | 0.4 | 0.3 |
| Eau Claire ........................................... | 86.3 | 86.8 | 86.8 | 87.5 | 0.7 | 0.8 |
| Fond du Lac .......................................... | 48.8 | 49.1 | 48.8 | 49.0 | 0.2 | 0.4 |
| Green Bay ............................................ | 175.5 | 178.2 | 175.5 | 177.9 | 2.4 | 1.4 |
| Janesville-Beloit ..................................... | 67.8 | 70.8 | 68.1 | 71.1 | 3.0 | 4.4 |
| La Crosse-Onalaska .................................. | 79.1 | 79.5 | 79.2 | 80.5 | 1.3 | 1.6 |
| Madison .............................................. | 396.2 | 399.8 | 399.0 | 399.7 | 0.7 | 0.2 |
| Milwaukee-Waukesha-West Allis ..................... | 867.9 | 865.4 | 866.2 | 864.2 | -2.0 | -0.2 |
| Oshkosh-Neenah ..................................... | 95.9 | 96.0 | 96.0 | 95.9 | -0.1 | -0.1 |
| Racine ............................................... | 77.3 | 77.4 | 77.0 | 77.4 | 0.4 | 0.5 |
| Sheboygan ........................................... | 61.4 | 61.8 | 61.0 | 61.5 | 0.5 | 0.8 |
| Wausau .............................................. | 73.3 | 73.7 | 73.4 | 74.2 | 0.8 | 1.1 |
| **Wyoming** .......................................... | 291.6 | 281.5 | 285.4 | 276.6 | -8.8 | -3.1 |
| Casper ............................................... | 41.8 | 39.6 | 41.2 | 38.8 | -2.4 | -5.8 |
| Cheyenne ............................................ | 47.6 | 46.0 | 47.4 | 46.0 | -1.4 | -3.0 |

**Table 7-2. Civilian Labor Force by State and Selected Metropolitan Areas, October 2015–November 2016**

(Number in thousands, percent.)

| State and area | October | | November | |
| --- | --- | --- | --- | --- |
| | 2015 | 2016 | 2015 | 2016 |
| **Alabama** | 2 148 602 | 2 212 421 | 2 149 027 | 2 199 462 |
| Anniston-Oxford-Jacksonville | 45 909 | 46 809 | 45 843 | 46 528 |
| Auburn-Opelika | 71 801 | 75 401 | 72 064 | 75 154 |
| Birmingham-Hoover | 530 791 | 545 798 | 534 456 | 545 389 |
| Daphne-Fairhope-Foley | 87 205 | 90 591 | 86 533 | 89 339 |
| Decatur | 68 893 | 70 537 | 68 835 | 70 073 |
| | | | | |
| Dothan | 62 249 | 63 904 | 61 916 | 63 006 |
| Florence-Muscle Shoals | 66 490 | 67 512 | 66 413 | 67 347 |
| Gadsden | 43 476 | 44 605 | 43 537 | 44 477 |
| Huntsville | 209 965 | 216 207 | 210 774 | 215 928 |
| Mobile | 182 532 | 187 806 | 183 329 | 187 046 |
| | | | | |
| Montgomery | 168 702 | 173 417 | 169 531 | 172 550 |
| Tuscaloosa | 112 572 | 117 024 | 113 249 | 116 148 |
| | | | | |
| **Alaska** | 361 078 | 355 355 | 360 156 | 354 457 |
| Anchorage | 203 415 | 200 193 | 205 540 | 203 215 |
| Fairbanks | 46 545 | 45 879 | 46 740 | 46 002 |
| | | | | |
| **Arizona** | 3 171 338 | 3 259 112 | 3 174 476 | 3 262 399 |
| Flagstaff | 73 948 | 75 617 | 72 584 | 74 505 |
| Lake Havasu-City-Kingman | 79 137 | 79 754 | 77 978 | 79 928 |
| Phoenix-Mesa-Scottsdale | 2 183 950 | 2 246 378 | 2 189 591 | 2 253 682 |
| Prescott | 98 427 | 104 049 | 97 919 | 103 174 |
| Sierra Vista-Douglas | 49 212 | 50 016 | 49 130 | 49 502 |
| | | | | |
| Tucson | 466 218 | 479 287 | 467 914 | 482 669 |
| Yuma | 92 291 | 94 897 | 91 879 | 91 253 |
| | | | | |
| **Arkansas** | 1 335 461 | 1 348 643 | 1 331 955 | 1 338 918 |
| Fayetteville-Springdale-Rogers | 257 197 | 262 899 | 256 931 | 261 762 |
| Fort Smith | 121 602 | 121 899 | 121 025 | 120 829 |
| Hot Springs | 39 705 | 40 264 | 39 392 | 39 908 |
| Jonesboro | 61 354 | 63 147 | 61 415 | 62 654 |
| Little Rock-North Little Rock-Conway | 348 912 | 353 658 | 347 734 | 350 245 |
| Pine Bluff | 36 564 | 36 059 | 36 489 | 35 672 |
| | | | | |
| **California** | 18 995 347 | 19 465 194 | 18 995 979 | 358 018 |
| Bakersfield | 396 572 | 404 032 | 393 078 | 399 263 |
| Chico | 102 822 | 104 762 | 102 273 | 104 069 |
| El Centro | 79 643 | 81 861 | 79 817 | 78 405 |
| Fresno | 442 475 | 448 707 | 440 584 | 445 842 |
| Hanford-Corcoran | 57 660 | 57 972 | 57 732 | 57 912 |
| | | | | |
| Los Angeles-Long Beach-Anaheim | 6 595 274 | 6 782 855 | 6 600 183 | 6 742 604 |
| Madera | 59 502 | 61 205 | 59 075 | 60 171 |
| Merced | 116 258 | 118 318 | 115 104 | 115 368 |
| Modesto | 240 557 | 247 704 | 241 127 | 246 315 |
| Napa | 76 444 | 78 810 | 74 026 | 76 248 |
| | | | | |
| Oxnard-Thousand Oaks-Ventura | 428 582 | 435 558 | 429 330 | 432 872 |
| Redding | 75 346 | 75 568 | 74 402 | 74 446 |
| Riverside-San Bernardino-Ontario | 1 968 126 | 2 007 586 | 1 977 876 | 2 013 676 |
| Sacramento—Roseville—Arden-Arcade | 1 059 804 | 1 087 083 | 1 058 509 | 1 082 736 |
| Salinas | 225 931 | 226 048 | 222 966 | 221 527 |
| | | | | |
| San Diego-Carlsbad | 1 564 233 | 1 599 872 | 1 570 065 | 1 597 644 |
| San Francisco-Oakland-Hayward | 2 517 869 | 2 584 034 | 2 516 938 | 2 570 628 |
| San Jose-Sunnyvale-Santa Clara | 1 053 517 | 1 090 117 | 1 056 007 | 1 087 652 |
| San Luis Obispo-Paso Robles-Arroyo | 143 159 | 146 441 | 143 182 | 145 316 |
| Grande Santa Cruz-Watsonville | 143 253 | 148 348 | 142 750 | 146 601 |
| | | | | |
| Santa Maria-Santa Barbara | 220 179 | 225 010 | 220 881 | 223 978 |
| Santa Rosa | 261 053 | 265 958 | 259 387 | 262 033 |
| Stockton-Lodi | 318 292 | 322 682 | 316 308 | 317 557 |
| Vallejo-Fairfield | 207 533 | 212 117 | 208 371 | 211 975 |
| Visalia-Porterville | 198 778 | 203 983 | 198 531 | 201 239 |
| Yuba City | 72 372 | 72 890 | 72 147 | 72 560 |
| | | | | |
| **Colorado** | 2 833 658 | 2 921 197 | 2 825 155 | 2 906 905 |
| Boulder | 179 043 | 183 856 | 177 291 | 183 979 |
| Colorado Springs | 321 506 | 326 693 | 319 058 | 326 344 |
| Denver-Aurora-Lakewood | 1 511 722 | 1 567 333 | 1 505 753 | 1 557 705 |
| Fort Collins | 182 915 | 188 155 | 181 832 | 187 528 |
| Grand Junction | 72 250 | 73 405 | 72 279 | 73 191 |
| | | | | |
| Greeley | 148 555 | 154 514 | 147 923 | 153 937 |
| Pueblo | 72 186 | 73 990 | 72 082 | 74 165 |

**Table 7-2.  Civilian Labor Force by State and Selected Metropolitan Areas, October 2015–November 2016**—*Continued*

(Number in thousands, percent.)

| State and area | October | | November | |
|---|---|---|---|---|
| | 2015 | 2016 | 2015 | 2016 |
| **Connecticut** ........................................ | 1 882 726 | 1 896 776 | 1 883 525 | 1 888 141 |
| Bridgeport-Stamford-Norwalk .......................... | 461 602 | 464 089 | 463 400 | 463 601 |
| Danbury ................................................ | 105 715 | 106 612 | 105 834 | 106 603 |
| Hartford-West Hartford-East Hartford .............. | 616 370 | 622 724 | 615 873 | 617 876 |
| New Haven ............................................. | 322 536 | 324 221 | 322 924 | 323 930 |
| Norwich-New London-Westerly ........................ | 141 782 | 141 550 | 141 766 | 140 631 |
| Waterbury ............................................. | 110 185 | 111 081 | 110 536 | 110 579 |
| **Delaware** ............................................ | 471 473 | 472 868 | 473 250 | 470 765 |
| Dover .................................................. | 77 859 | 78 455 | 78 077 | 77 988 |
| Salisbury .............................................. | 184 437 | 185 691 | 181 119 | 183 337 |
| **District of Columbia** ............................... | 390 409 | 399 323 | 391 291 | 399 220 |
| Washington-Arlington-Alexandria ...................... | 3 291 298 | 3 335 541 | 3 293 304 | 3 335 937 |
| **Florida** ............................................. | 9 698 746 | 9 885 370 | 9 685 448 | 9 895 824 |
| Cape Coral-Fort Myers .................................. | 320 685 | 329 147 | 323 393 | 331 456 |
| Crestview-Fort Walton Beach-Destin ................ | 118 788 | 120 021 | 117 109 | 118 266 |
| Deltona-Daytona Beach-Ormond Beach .......... | 283 268 | 294 107 | 282 218 | 293 183 |
| Gainesville ............................................ | 139 211 | 139 657 | 138 013 | 138 588 |
| Homosassa Springs .................................... | 47 923 | 47 789 | 47 386 | 47 482 |
| Jacksonville .......................................... | 726 991 | 749 161 | 724 995 | 747 596 |
| Lakeland-Winter Haven ................................ | 280 501 | 283 713 | 279 324 | 283 504 |
| Miami-Fort Lauderdale-West Palm Beach ........ | 3 031 755 | 3 068 012 | 3 034 541 | 3 081 768 |
| Naples-Immokalee-Marco Island ...................... | 159 852 | 163 739 | 163 383 | 166 609 |
| North Port-Sarasota-Bradenton ...................... | 342 688 | 353 158 | 342 633 | 352 649 |
| Ocala .................................................. | 131 087 | 132 133 | 130 029 | 132 473 |
| Orlando-Kissimmee-Sanford ........................... | 1 231 822 | 1 272 174 | 1 227 226 | 1 273 890 |
| Palm Bay-Melbourne-Titusville ....................... | 256 644 | 259 741 | 255 758 | 258 729 |
| Panama City ........................................... | 92 768 | 93 152 | 91 051 | 92 430 |
| Pensacola-Ferry Pass-Brent ........................... | 213 421 | 217 489 | 211 963 | 216 178 |
| Port St Lucie ......................................... | 201 668 | 204 038 | 202 288 | 204 865 |
| Punta Gorda .......................................... | 67 308 | 68 716 | 67 503 | 68 790 |
| Sebastian-Vero Beach ................................. | 60 934 | 61 511 | 61 497 | 62 267 |
| Sebring ............................................... | 35 074 | 36 021 | 35 051 | 35 951 |
| Tallahassee ........................................... | 187 821 | 190 710 | 185 939 | 189 034 |
| Tampa-St Petersburg-Clearwater ..................... | 1 450 859 | 1 480 341 | 1 446 958 | 1 479 026 |
| The Villages .......................................... | 28 673 | 29 570 | 28 524 | 29 544 |
| **Georgia** ............................................. | 4 772 874 | 4 957 282 | 4 782 554 | 4 965 450 |
| Albany ................................................ | 65 534 | 68 042 | 66 228 | 68 369 |
| Athens-Clarke County ................................. | 94 376 | 99 135 | 94 907 | 100 342 |
| Atlanta-Sandy Springs-Roswell ....................... | 2 842 017 | 2 958 894 | 2 846 032 | 2 960 745 |
| Augusta-Richmond County ............................. | 255 042 | 260 291 | 252 739 | 260 556 |
| Brunswick ............................................. | 50 154 | 51 717 | 50 111 | 51 353 |
| Columbus ............................................. | 123 771 | 126 557 | 123 539 | 126 619 |
| Dalton ................................................ | 60 429 | 61 206 | 60 130 | 61 038 |
| Gainesville ........................................... | 92 804 | 96 974 | 93 224 | 96 780 |
| Hinesville ............................................ | 31 828 | 32 511 | 31 887 | 32 665 |
| Macon ................................................ | 103 166 | 106 567 | 103 534 | 106 357 |
| Rome .................................................. | 42 598 | 43 758 | 42 535 | 43 728 |
| Savannah .............................................. | 176 049 | 184 477 | 175 893 | 185 720 |
| Valdosta .............................................. | 62 637 | 64 290 | 63 110 | 64 773 |
| Warner Robins ........................................ | 80 489 | 82 798 | 80 057 | 81 794 |
| **Hawaii** ............................................. | 676 437 | 694 859 | 681 609 | 699 397 |
| Kahului-Wailuku-Lahaina ............................. | 83 930 | 86 360 | 84 486 | 86 689 |
| Urban Honolulu ....................................... | 469 705 | 481 988 | 472 881 | 485 414 |
| **Idaho** .............................................. | 803 823 | 811 990 | 800 840 | 810 473 |
| Boise City ............................................ | 323 008 | 328 443 | 325 525 | 333 382 |
| Coeur d'Alene ........................................ | 71 770 | 72 620 | 72 045 | 72 456 |
| Idaho Falls ........................................... | 65 683 | 65 728 | 66 060 | 65 872 |
| Lewiston .............................................. | 30 331 | 30 981 | 30 692 | 31 363 |
| Pocatello ............................................. | 43 068 | 42 785 | 43 138 | 42 475 |
| **Illinois** ........................................... | 6 529 418 | 6 560 737 | 6 541 640 | 6 548 171 |
| Bloomington .......................................... | 99 733 | 98 370 | 100 319 | 98 296 |
| Carbondale-Marion .................................... | 62 223 | 59 497 | 62 772 | 59 728 |
| Champaign-Urbana .................................... | 122 445 | 123 721 | 122 867 | 123 780 |
| Chicago-Naperville-Elgin ............................. | 4 887 598 | 4 930 903 | 4 887 867 | 4 916 464 |
| Danville .............................................. | 35 803 | 35 487 | 36 015 | 35 565 |

**Table 7-2.   Civilian Labor Force by State and Selected Metropolitan Areas, October 2015–November 2016**—*Continued*

(Number in thousands, percent.)

| State and area | October | | November | |
| --- | --- | --- | --- | --- |
| | 2015 | 2016 | 2015 | 2016 |
| **Illinois**— *Continued* | | | | |
| Davenport-Moline-Rock Island | 191 543 | 189 685 | 192 124 | 188 268 |
| Decatur | 51 146 | 49 973 | 51 544 | 50 033 |
| Kankakee | 55 873 | 55 890 | 56 568 | 56 104 |
| Peoria | 187 111 | 183 817 | 188 694 | 183 245 |
| Rockford | 169 869 | 170 303 | 171 425 | 170 074 |
| Springfield | 112 764 | 112 701 | 113 603 | 113 411 |
| **Indiana** | 3 283 775 | 3 333 493 | 3 286 144 | 3 331 984 |
| Bloomington | 78 032 | 78 472 | 77 958 | 78 024 |
| Columbus | 44 444 | 45 196 | 44 651 | 45 288 |
| Elkhart-Goshen | 106 084 | 104 566 | 104 843 | 104 116 |
| Evansville | 157 805 | 158 333 | 158 273 | 158 179 |
| Fort Wayne | 212 378 | 216 667 | 212 165 | 215 685 |
| Indianapolis-Carmel-Anderson | 1 012 738 | 1 033 011 | 1 013 317 | 1 037 979 |
| Kokomo | 36 965 | 37 853 | 37 130 | 37 635 |
| Lafayette-West Lafayette | 109 632 | 112 799 | 109 951 | 111 981 |
| Michigan City-La Porte | 48 171 | 48 506 | 48 047 | 48 400 |
| Muncie | 55 379 | 55 387 | 55 249 | 55 218 |
| South Bend-Mishawaka | 157 769 | 158 540 | 157 910 | 158 910 |
| Terre Haute | 77 755 | 78 193 | 77 875 | 78 307 |
| **Iowa** | 1 706 137 | 1 724 281 | 1 704 515 | 1 702 400 |
| Ames | 59 106 | 60 138 | 59 092 | 59 621 |
| Cedar Rapids | 144 111 | 146 405 | 144 966 | 145 125 |
| Des Moines-West Des Moines | 338 744 | 345 055 | 339 781 | 341 415 |
| Dubuque | 56 084 | 56 929 | 56 419 | 56 551 |
| Iowa City | 97 195 | 99 915 | 97 393 | 98 830 |
| Sioux City | 93 408 | 93 343 | 93 593 | 92 613 |
| Waterloo-Cedar Falls | 91 448 | 91 663 | 91 590 | 90 112 |
| **Kansas** | 1 504 437 | 1 491 585 | 1 507 632 | 1 490 940 |
| Lawrence | 66 442 | 66 373 | 66 781 | 65 760 |
| Manhattan | 52 908 | 51 779 | 53 234 | 51 797 |
| Topeka | 120 460 | 118 635 | 120 206 | 118 624 |
| Wichita | 312 175 | 312 909 | 313 671 | 314 406 |
| **Kentucky** | 1 938 168 | 2 005 229 | 1 953 308 | 2 003 531 |
| Bowling Green | 75 223 | 78 280 | 76 048 | 78 129 |
| Elizabethtown-Fort Knox | 63 201 | 65 980 | 63 654 | 65 973 |
| Lexington-Fayette | 255 980 | 260 918 | 257 062 | 262 325 |
| Louisville/Jefferson County | 619 931 | 641 753 | 625 566 | 644 166 |
| Owensboro | 52 146 | 54 724 | 52 531 | 54 459 |
| **Louisiana** | 2 150 874 | 2 120 158 | 2 136 802 | 2 109 694 |
| Alexandria | 66 599 | 65 484 | 66 400 | 65 240 |
| Baton Rouge | 422 810 | 430 402 | 422 058 | 426 367 |
| Hammond | 53 716 | 52 960 | 53 465 | 52 820 |
| Houma-Thibodaux | 98 218 | 95 031 | 96 893 | 93 915 |
| Lafayette | 225 790 | 216 087 | 223 882 | 214 549 |
| Lake Charles | 103 261 | 103 781 | 102 935 | 103 286 |
| Monroe | 82 012 | 80 934 | 81 150 | 80 574 |
| New Orleans-Metairie | 602 814 | 592 924 | 596 877 | 591 362 |
| Shreveport-Bossier City | 194 385 | 189 988 | 193 369 | 189 493 |
| **Maine** | 678 333 | 695 637 | 670 780 | 690 904 |
| Bangor | 70 558 | 72 066 | 70 091 | 71 446 |
| Lewiston-Auburn | 54 839 | 56 725 | 54 870 | 56 953 |
| Portland-South Portland | 196 482 | 203 003 | 195 180 | 203 182 |
| **Maryland** | 3 162 575 | 3 193 565 | 3 156 822 | 3 195 320 |
| Baltimore-Columbia-Towson | 1 476 835 | 1 491 024 | 1 472 598 | 1 492 793 |
| California-Lexington Park | 54 501 | 54 615 | 54 516 | 54 535 |
| Cumberland | 44 140 | 44 167 | 44 013 | 43 972 |
| Hagerstown-Martinsburg | 128 426 | 130 698 | 127 948 | 130 388 |
| **Massachusetts** | 3 557 973 | 3 584 829 | 3 562 821 | 3 579 700 |
| Barnstable Town | 121 674 | 122 091 | 118 882 | 118 818 |
| Boston-Cambridge-Nashua | 2 620 948 | 2 646 900 | 2 629 115 | 2 650 297 |
| Leominster-Gardner | 75 440 | 76 005 | 75 846 | 76 047 |
| New Bedford | 83 266 | 82 638 | 83 286 | 82 119 |
| Pittsfield | 43 256 | 42 957 | 43 431 | 42 844 |
| Springfield | 363 382 | 365 520 | 363 356 | 364 602 |
| Worcester | 343 557 | 347 573 | 343 800 | 346 763 |

## Table 7-2. Civilian Labor Force by State and Selected Metropolitan Areas, October 2015–November 2016—*Continued*

(Number in thousands, percent.)

| State and area | October | | November | |
|---|---|---|---|---|
| | 2015 | 2016 | 2015 | 2016 |
| **Michigan** | 4 754 223 | 4 859 681 | 4 747 157 | 4 863 763 |
| Ann Arbor | 192 346 | 200 166 | 193 420 | 202 157 |
| Battle Creek | 64 157 | 64 841 | 64 584 | 65 186 |
| Bay City | 52 209 | 52 065 | 52 680 | 52 496 |
| Detroit-Warren-Dearborn | 2 010 141 | 2 078 753 | 1 991 684 | 2 070 642 |
| Flint | 180 939 | 182 897 | 182 895 | 184 675 |
| | | | | |
| Grand Rapids-Wyoming | 556 512 | 566 501 | 559 921 | 571 048 |
| Jackson | 71 792 | 71 960 | 72 385 | 72 719 |
| Kalamazoo-Portage | 165 347 | 169 653 | 166 827 | 170 437 |
| Lansing-East Lansing | 244 429 | 248 058 | 245 983 | 250 018 |
| Midland | 41 224 | 41 413 | 41 684 | 41 776 |
| | | | | |
| Monroe | 77 344 | 78 902 | 77 546 | 78 550 |
| Muskegon | 76 296 | 78 323 | 77 152 | 78 592 |
| Niles-Benton Harbor | 74 003 | 74 496 | 74 047 | 74 492 |
| Saginaw | 88 614 | 89 828 | 90 240 | 90 507 |
| | | | | |
| **Minnesota** | 3 015 656 | 2 975 087 | 3 016 922 | 2 970 004 |
| Duluth | 141 609 | 139 246 | 142 085 | 139 440 |
| Mankato-North Mankato | 60 664 | 59 251 | 60 159 | 58 880 |
| Minneapolis-St Paul-Bloomington | 1 934 844 | 1 920 606 | 1 941 290 | 1 917 634 |
| Rochester | 118 796 | 118 443 | 118 727 | 118 370 |
| St. Cloud | 111 827 | 110 599 | 111 612 | 110 628 |
| | | | | |
| **Mississippi** | 1 283 181 | 1 293 029 | 1 285 356 | 1 286 099 |
| Gulfport-Biloxi-Pascagoula | 164 762 | 164 425 | 165 142 | 163 864 |
| Hattiesburg | 67 508 | 69 184 | 68 471 | 68 953 |
| Jackson | 270 279 | 272 349 | 270 787 | 270 965 |
| | | | | |
| **Missouri** | 3 116 491 | 3 147 988 | 3 112 765 | 3 120 209 |
| Cape Girardeau | 49 174 | 49 004 | 49 672 | 48 726 |
| Columbia | 102 223 | 103 329 | 102 761 | 102 793 |
| Jefferson City | 76 535 | 76 666 | 76 496 | 76 010 |
| Joplin | 88 058 | 86 956 | 88 358 | 86 582 |
| Kansas City | 1 117 777 | 1 124 881 | 1 118 495 | 1 117 555 |
| St. Joseph | 65 892 | 65 744 | 66 245 | 65 399 |
| | | | | |
| St. Louis | 1 487 365 | 1 512 527 | 1 481 282 | 1 501 577 |
| Springfield | 233 221 | 238 756 | 234 941 | 236 248 |
| | | | | |
| **Montana** | 522 181 | 523 083 | 520 839 | 521 654 |
| Billings | 88 598 | 89 191 | 88 791 | 89 026 |
| Great Falls | 38 883 | 38 631 | 38 944 | 38 683 |
| Missoula | 62 228 | 62 788 | 62 087 | 62 522 |
| | | | | |
| **Nebraska** | 1 015 740 | 1 013 857 | 1 014 674 | 1 013 261 |
| Grand Island | 43 534 | 43 489 | 43 529 | 43 213 |
| Lincoln | 180 425 | 180 127 | 180 000 | 180 251 |
| Omaha-Council Bluffs | 481 617 | 482 182 | 482 257 | 484 002 |
| | | | | |
| **Nevada** | 1 432 183 | 1 429 371 | 1 429 441 | 1 432 478 |
| Carson City | 24 799 | 24 547 | 24 784 | 24 587 |
| Las Vegas-Henderson-Paradise | 1 053 684 | 1 049 919 | 1 050 704 | 1 050 578 |
| Reno | 231 994 | 234 856 | 232 206 | 236 146 |
| | | | | |
| **New Hampshire** | 738 395 | 749 104 | 739 341 | 750 229 |
| Dover-Durham | 82 379 | 83 381 | 82 463 | 83 424 |
| Manchester | 115 011 | 116 754 | 115 575 | 117 513 |
| Portsmouth | 73 613 | 75 231 | 73 357 | 74 978 |
| | | | | |
| **New Jersey** | 4 537 695 | 4 535 670 | 4 544 725 | 4 512 278 |
| Atlantic City-Hammonton | 124 651 | 122 424 | 124 117 | 120 754 |
| Ocean City | 46 199 | 46 507 | 44 502 | 44 131 |
| Trenton | 200 165 | 199 953 | 201 338 | 201 330 |
| Vineland-Bridgeton | 67 058 | 65 788 | 67 324 | 66 118 |
| | | | | |
| **New Mexico** | 918 660 | 928 168 | 922 421 | 933 817 |
| Albuquerque | 413 897 | 420 426 | 418 025 | 424 567 |
| Farmington | 55 820 | 57 230 | 55 119 | 56 883 |
| Las Cruces | 93 301 | 94 606 | 93 627 | 95 298 |
| Santa Fe | 72 143 | 73 244 | 72 289 | 73 870 |
| | | | | |
| **New York** | 9 668 199 | 9 627 220 | 9 673 441 | 9 586 850 |
| Albany-Schenectady-Troy | 447 343 | 443 122 | 446 998 | 441 417 |
| Binghamton | 109 869 | 107 614 | 110 190 | 107 281 |
| Buffalo-Cheektowaga-Niagara Falls | 549 533 | 549 447 | 547 958 | 543 849 |
| Elmira | 37 614 | 37 062 | 37 587 | 36 932 |
| Glens Falls | 60 893 | 60 517 | 59 693 | 59 580 |

## Table 7-2.  Civilian Labor Force by State and Selected Metropolitan Areas, October 2015–November 2016—*Continued*

(Number in thousands, percent.)

| State and area | October | | November | |
|---|---|---|---|---|
| | 2015 | 2016 | 2015 | 2016 |
| **New York**—*Continued* | | | | |
| Ithaca | 55 693 | 56 880 | 55 615 | 56 491 |
| Kingston | 88 774 | 89 455 | 88 457 | 88 620 |
| New York-Newark-Jersey City | 68 742 | 10 044 033 | 10 095 383 | 10 189 |
| Rochester | 524 257 | 521 051 | 520 328 | 516 692 |
| Syracuse | 312 022 | 309 120 | 311 900 | 306 959 |
| Utica-Rome | 131 767 | 129 670 | 131 106 | 128 398 |
| Watertown-Fort Drum | 46 035 | 46 532 | 46 013 | 45 734 |
| **North Carolina** | 4 786 211 | 4 896 136 | 4 784 064 | 4 895 846 |
| Asheville | 220 046 | 226 940 | 220 553 | 227 455 |
| Burlington | 77 268 | 78 770 | 77 392 | 78 911 |
| Charlotte-Concord-Gastonia | 1 243 420 | 1 278 265 | 1 242 208 | 1 278 197 |
| Durham-Chapel Hill | 281 140 | 290 333 | 281 254 | 291 769 |
| Fayetteville | 145 884 | 147 881 | 146 308 | 149 165 |
| Goldsboro | 54 188 | 54 918 | 54 304 | 54 109 |
| Greensboro-High Point | 366 508 | 375 496 | 366 792 | 376 956 |
| Greenville | 87 479 | 87 940 | 87 504 | 87 953 |
| Hickory-Lenoir-Morganton | 167 312 | 167 903 | 166 940 | 168 117 |
| Jacksonville | 63 980 | 64 792 | 64 159 | 65 237 |
| New Bern | 51 375 | 52 231 | 51 299 | 52 178 |
| Raleigh | 661 146 | 682 238 | 662 717 | 684 726 |
| Rocky Mount | 67 849 | 67 870 | 68 208 | 68 039 |
| Wilmington | 139 600 | 142 134 | 139 087 | 141 359 |
| Winston-Salem | 317 638 | 323 505 | 316 555 | 322 905 |
| **North Dakota** | 412 906 | 428 537 | 409 616 | 427 210 |
| Bismarck | 67 663 | 72 040 | 67 109 | 71 537 |
| Fargo | 132 300 | 138 412 | 132 142 | 139 360 |
| Grand Forks | 55 781 | 57 571 | 55 501 | 57 630 |
| **Ohio** | 5 703 746 | 5 716 228 | 5 705 880 | 5 694 313 |
| Akron | 362 676 | 362 794 | 363 116 | 360 675 |
| Canton-Massillon | 199 837 | 200 095 | 200 952 | 198 856 |
| Cincinnati | 1 070 481 | 1 087 278 | 1 072 041 | 1 078 539 |
| Cleveland-Elyria | 1 013 298 | 1 024 214 | 1 014 692 | 1 021 358 |
| Columbus | 1 046 516 | 1 047 164 | 1 047 424 | 1 048 785 |
| Dayton | 382 594 | 383 649 | 383 968 | 382 218 |
| Lima | 48 271 | 48 939 | 48 464 | 48 881 |
| Mansfield | 53 435 | 52 232 | 53 494 | 52 073 |
| Springfield | 64 163 | 63 656 | 64 317 | 63 458 |
| Toledo | 302 168 | 303 891 | 302 302 | 303 156 |
| Weirton-Steubenville | 52 792 | 53 022 | 52 686 | 51 864 |
| Youngstown-Warren-Boardman | 250 668 | 249 099 | 252 108 | 247 848 |
| **Oklahoma** | 1 854 140 | 1 830 272 | 1 858 307 | 1 846 198 |
| Lawton | 53 452 | 52 529 | 53 501 | 53 486 |
| Oklahoma City | 675 948 | 665 429 | 678 368 | 669 994 |
| Tulsa | 480 984 | 475 298 | 481 192 | 479 292 |
| Oregon | 1 995 937 | 2 092 225 | 2 000 046 | 2 068 907 |
| Albany | 55 121 | 57 420 | 55 380 | 56 915 |
| Bend-Redmond | 85 599 | 91 361 | 85 597 | 90 102 |
| Corvallis | 45 867 | 47 336 | 46 177 | 47 481 |
| Eugene | 174 021 | 180 721 | 175 099 | 179 836 |
| Grants Pass | 33 716 | 34 584 | 33 695 | 34 320 |
| Medford | 99 323 | 103 697 | 100 207 | 102 673 |
| Portland-Vancouver-Hillsboro | 1 237 579 | 1 296 512 | 1 246 766 | 1 290 648 |
| Salem | 192 516 | 203 573 | 192 191 | 200 410 |
| **Pennsylvania** | 6 415 244 | 6 503 839 | 6 418 087 | 6 473 055 |
| Allentown-Bethlehem-Easton | 429 487 | 430 274 | 428 434 | 425 562 |
| Altoona | 60 075 | 61 890 | 60 480 | 61 285 |
| Bloomsburg-Berwick | 43 083 | 43 959 | 43 244 | 43 449 |
| Chambersburg-Waynesboro | 77 437 | 79 724 | 77 066 | 78 987 |
| East Stroudsburg | 80 142 | 81 575 | 80 362 | 80 923 |
| Erie | 134 597 | 135 338 | 134 823 | 134 548 |
| Gettysburg | 54 894 | 55 840 | 54 691 | 54 954 |
| Harrisburg-Carlisle | 292 196 | 295 840 | 292 434 | 294 187 |
| Johnstown | 61 984 | 62 056 | 61 997 | 61 585 |
| Lancaster | 276 220 | 277 288 | 274 448 | 273 308 |

**Table 7-2.  Civilian Labor Force by State and Selected Metropolitan Areas, October 2015–November 2016**—*Continued*

(Number in thousands, percent.)

| State and area | October | | November | |
|---|---|---|---|---|
| | 2015 | 2016 | 2015 | 2016 |
| **Pennsylvania**—*Continued* | | | | |
| Lebanon | 69 957 | 70 791 | 69 880 | 70 070 |
| Philadelphia-Camden-Wilmington | 3 063 452 | 3 107 778 | 3 074 123 | 3 102 393 |
| Pittsburgh | 1 211 182 | 1 223 353 | 1 209 998 | 1 221 740 |
| Reading | 213 661 | 217 065 | 214 065 | 215 806 |
| Scranton—Wilkes-Barre—Hazleton | 278 635 | 279 482 | 279 069 | 278 742 |
| State College | 80 536 | 81 802 | 80 304 | 81 567 |
| Williamsport | 60 144 | 59 811 | 60 106 | 59 460 |
| York-Hanover | 232 699 | 236 945 | 233 175 | 235 927 |
| **Rhode Island** | 553 739 | 553 866 | 555 755 | 554 972 |
| Providence-Warwick | 679 100 | 680 179 | 681 587 | 680 747 |
| **South Carolina** | 2 261 830 | 2 297 226 | 2 248 867 | 2 282 714 |
| Charleston-North Charleston | 361 566 | 372 182 | 361 175 | 371 154 |
| Columbia | 397 930 | 404 917 | 397 444 | 401 918 |
| Florence | 95 397 | 95 099 | 94 954 | 94 591 |
| Greenville-Anderson-Mauldin | 418 675 | 424 641 | 415 489 | 421 777 |
| Hilton Head Island-Bluffton-Beaufort | 83 258 | 84 482 | 82 409 | 83 237 |
| Myrtle Beach-Conway-North Myrtle Beach | 182 484 | 183 165 | 180 811 | 181 814 |
| Spartanburg | 151 548 | 154 135 | 151 258 | 152 985 |
| Sumter | 44 452 | 44 403 | 44 090 | 43 952 |
| **South Dakota** | 453 231 | 456 087 | 453 046 | 455 133 |
| Rapid City | 71 787 | 73 052 | 70 680 | 71 567 |
| Sioux Falls | 146 307 | 150 707 | 147 232 | 151 620 |
| Tennessee | 3 061 405 | 3 174 393 | 3 065 810 | 3 171 510 |
| Chattanooga | 253 461 | 262 820 | 253 147 | 261 863 |
| Clarksville | 108 705 | 112 655 | 108 979 | 112 539 |
| Cleveland | 56 980 | 58 934 | 58 444 | 63 231 |
| Jackson | 61 550 | 63 101 | 61 561 | 63 156 |
| Johnson City | 88 632 | 91 494 | 88 610 | 91 361 |
| Kingsport-Bristol-Bristol | 136 956 | 138 697 | 137 105 | 138 389 |
| Knoxville | 405 204 | 422 616 | 406 492 | 420 628 |
| Memphis | 611 841 | 629 239 | 614 070 | 628 502 |
| Morristown | 49 900 | 52 112 | 49 833 | 51 789 |
| Nashville-Davidson—Murfreesboro—Franklin | 937 745 | 981 304 | 939 524 | 980 830 |
| **Texas** | 13 114 424 | 13 334 552 | 13 147 382 | 3 391 218 |
| Abilene | 74 871 | 76 007 | 75 003 | 76 208 |
| Amarillo | 130 484 | 131 110 | 130 358 | 131 493 |
| Austin-Round Rock | 1 080 815 | 1 105 764 | 1 087 165 | 1 112 370 |
| Beaumont-Port Arthur | 176 550 | 176 866 | 176 997 | 177 105 |
| Brownsville-Harlingen | 162 958 | 166 357 | 163 705 | 168 006 |
| College Station-Bryan | 123 473 | 127 033 | 124 155 | 127 816 |
| Corpus Christi | 208 420 | 211 323 | 209 164 | 212 574 |
| Dallas-Fort Worth-Arlington | 3 610 389 | 3 727 510 | 3 626 424 | 3 750 323 |
| El Paso | 346 594 | 353 736 | 347 606 | 355 862 |
| Houston-The Woodlands-Sugar Land | 3 258 399 | 3 297 332 | 3 262 891 | 3 304 933 |
| Killeen-Temple | 170 698 | 173 294 | 171 183 | 174 310 |
| Laredo | 112 811 | 115 351 | 113 910 | 115 952 |
| Longview | 100 331 | 101 742 | 100 891 | 101 560 |
| Lubbock | 154 462 | 155 925 | 154 380 | 156 919 |
| McAllen-Edinburg-Mission | 329 705 | 335 128 | 331 482 | 339 520 |
| Midland | 88 879 | 89 529 | 89 437 | 90 267 |
| Odessa | 78 174 | 78 290 | 78 302 | 78 474 |
| San Angelo | 54 964 | 56 041 | 55 089 | 56 512 |
| San Antonio-New Braunfels | 1 105 544 | 1 122 915 | 1 106 382 | 1 127 776 |
| Sherman-Denison | 60 595 | 61 374 | 61 066 | 62 003 |
| Texarkana | 64 787 | 64 902 | 64 821 | 64 880 |
| Tyler | 103 052 | 104 797 | 103 301 | 104 894 |
| Victoria | 49 239 | 50 595 | 49 473 | 50 945 |
| Waco | 118 731 | 121 367 | 119 215 | 121 749 |
| Wichita Falls | 64 732 | 64 203 | 64 669 | 64 338 |
| **Utah** | 1 473 640 | 1 513 098 | 1 473 182 | 1 518 680 |
| Logan | 68 045 | 69 893 | 67 777 | 69 604 |
| Ogden-Clearfield | 308 978 | 317 931 | 308 554 | 318 472 |
| Provo-Orem | 275 419 | 282 885 | 275 250 | 284 758 |
| St. George | 65 279 | 68 081 | 65 317 | 67 885 |
| Salt Lake City | 620 384 | 637 635 | 622 729 | 643 033 |

**Table 7-2. Civilian Labor Force by State and Selected Metropolitan Areas, October 2015–November 2016**—*Continued*

(Number in thousands, percent.)

| State and area | October | | November | |
|---|---|---|---|---|
| | 2015 | 2016 | 2015 | 2016 |
| **Vermont** | 343 193 | 343 808 | 343 291 | 344 578 |
| Burlington-South Burlington | 125 515 | 126 382 | 125 161 | 126 569 |
| | | | | |
| **Virginia** | 4 221 613 | 4 243 656 | 4 220 907 | 4 233 406 |
| Blacksburg-Christiansburg-Radford | 92 034 | 91 871 | 91 129 | 90 732 |
| Charlottesville | 115 256 | 117 760 | 116 744 | 118 881 |
| Harrisonburg | 63 596 | 63 196 | 63 111 | 62 937 |
| Lynchburg | 122 533 | 120 840 | 122 260 | 120 874 |
| Richmond | 666 730 | 671 669 | 668 189 | 668 427 |
| | | | | |
| Roanoke | 157 990 | 158 492 | 158 490 | 158 076 |
| Staunton-Waynesboro | 58 063 | 57 152 | 57 949 | 57 102 |
| Virginia Beach-Norfolk-Newport News | 832 766 | 830 588 | 832 172 | 825 125 |
| Winchester | 69 086 | 70 347 | 68 913 | 70 090 |
| | | | | |
| **Washington** | 3 561 952 | 3 687 724 | 3 560 884 | 3 677 831 |
| Bellingham | 102 540 | 106 216 | 103 525 | 106 871 |
| Bremerton-Silverdale | 115 900 | 118 493 | 117 535 | 120 097 |
| Kennewick-Richland | 130 748 | 134 696 | 130 432 | 134 094 |
| Longview | 44 355 | 45 992 | 44 991 | 46 305 |
| Mount Vernon-Anacortes | 57 160 | 59 107 | 57 316 | 58 819 |
| | | | | |
| Olympia-Tumwate | 125 995 | 129 780 | 128 576 | 130 766 |
| Seattle-Tacoma-Bellevue | 1 972 909 | 2 049 771 | 1 976 496 | 2 050 956 |
| Spokane-Spokane Valley | 250 908 | 261 444 | 254 703 | 263 824 |
| Walla Walla | 30 686 | 31 032 | 30 947 | 30 995 |
| Wenatchee | 65 800 | 66 609 | 61 211 | 62 832 |
| Yakima | 128 715 | 131 487 | 119 569 | 122 167 |
| | | | | |
| **West Virginia** | 785 475 | 800 924 | 779 570 | 786 681 |
| Beckley | 46 704 | 46 909 | 45 976 | 45 857 |
| Charleston | 98 296 | 99 258 | 97 896 | 97 689 |
| Huntington-Ashland | 147 619 | 150 634 | 146 912 | 148 146 |
| Morgantown | 67 176 | 68 939 | 66 702 | 67 581 |
| Parkersburg-Vienna | 39 714 | 39 756 | 39 654 | 39 290 |
| Wheeling | 66 132 | 66 047 | 66 276 | 65 512 |
| | | | | |
| **Wisconsin** | 3 104 566 | 3 134 747 | 3 105 431 | 3 132 986 |
| Appleton | 129 619 | 131 071 | 130 373 | 131 389 |
| Eau Claire | 91 551 | 92 616 | 91 841 | 93 391 |
| Fond du Lac | 57 589 | 57 979 | 57 680 | 58 004 |
| Green Bay | 170 857 | 173 956 | 171 383 | 173 737 |
| Janesville-Beloit | 83 692 | 86 885 | 84 181 | 87 352 |
| | | | | |
| La Crosse-Onalaska | 78 155 | 78 690 | 78 556 | 79 315 |
| Madison | 379 617 | 385 176 | 382 347 | 385 138 |
| Milwaukee-Waukesha-West Allis | 827 282 | 827 416 | 826 928 | 825 215 |
| Oshkosh-Neenah | 91 870 | 92 241 | 92 224 | 92 329 |
| Racine | 98 868 | 99 053 | 98 799 | 98 966 |
| | | | | |
| Sheboygan | 61 038 | 61 762 | 61 059 | 61 923 |
| Wausau | 74 117 | 74 983 | 74 340 | 75 479 |
| | | | | |
| **Wyoming** | 304 839 | 303 050 | 304 589 | 303 355 |
| Casper | 42 224 | 41 425 | 42 383 | 41 481 |
| Cheyenne | 48 659 | 48 079 | 49 396 | 49 051 |

## Table 7-3.  Unemployment Number and Rate by State and Selected Metropolitan Area October 2015–November 2016

(Number, rate.)

| State and area | October 2015 | October 2016 | November 2015 | November 2016 | October Number | October Percent | November 2015 | November 2016 |
|---|---|---|---|---|---|---|---|---|
| **Alabama** | 124 703 | 132 466 | 122 654 | 123 462 | 5.8 | 6.0 | 5.7 | 5.6 |
| Anniston-Oxford-Jacksonville | 3 144 | 3 066 | 3 069 | 2 886 | 6.8 | 6.6 | 6.7 | 6.2 |
| Auburn-Opelika | 3 395 | 3 822 | 3 467 | 3 518 | 4.7 | 5.1 | 4.8 | 4.7 |
| Birmingham-Hoover | 28 268 | 30 949 | 28 009 | 28 440 | 5.3 | 5.7 | 5.2 | 5.2 |
| Daphne-Fairhope-Foley | 4 600 | 4 997 | 4 553 | 4 626 | 5.3 | 5.5 | 5.3 | 5.2 |
| Decatur | 4 073 | 4 116 | 3 973 | 3 809 | 5.9 | 5.8 | 5.8 | 5.4 |
| Dothan | 3 645 | 3 786 | 3 537 | 3 526 | 5.9 | 5.9 | 5.7 | 5.6 |
| Florence-Muscle Shoals | 4 463 | 4 238 | 4 361 | 4 126 | 6.7 | 6.3 | 6.6 | 6.1 |
| Gadsden | 2 552 | 2 731 | 2 518 | 2 506 | 5.9 | 6.1 | 5.8 | 5.6 |
| Huntsville | 10 883 | 11 347 | 10 551 | 10 632 | 5.2 | 5.2 | 5.0 | 4.9 |
| Mobile | 12 387 | 12 896 | 12 068 | 12 521 | 6.8 | 6.9 | 6.6 | 6.7 |
| Montgomery | 9 648 | 9 986 | 9 370 | 9 242 | 5.7 | 5.8 | 5.5 | 5.4 |
| Tuscaloosa | 5 867 | 6 716 | 5 975 | 6 273 | 5.2 | 5.7 | 5.3 | 5.4 |
| **Alaska** | 22 367 | 22 607 | 23 410 | 23 297 | 6.2 | 6.4 | 6.5 | 6.6 |
| Anchorage | 10 878 | 11 448 | 11 506 | 11 846 | 5.3 | 5.7 | 5.6 | 5.8 |
| Fairbanks | 2 482 | 2 477 | 2 634 | 2 643 | 5.3 | 5.4 | 5.6 | 5.7 |
| **Arizona** | 189 172 | 169 790 | 179 006 | 154 488 | 6.0 | 5.2 | 5.6 | 4.7 |
| Flagstaff | 4 551 | 4 306 | 4 493 | 4 068 | 6.2 | 5.7 | 6.2 | 5.5 |
| Lake Havasu-City-Kingman | 6 045 | 5 021 | 5 834 | 4 673 | 7.6 | 6.3 | 7.5 | 5.8 |
| Phoenix-Mesa-Scottsdale | 111 589 | 100 796 | 106 671 | 92 754 | 5.1 | 4.5 | 4.9 | 4.1 |
| Prescott | 5 157 | 4 658 | 5 029 | 4 406 | 5.2 | 4.5 | 5.1 | 4.3 |
| Sierra Vista-Douglas | 3 467 | 2 959 | 3 332 | 2 724 | 7.0 | 5.9 | 6.8 | 5.5 |
| Tucson | 25 360 | 22 817 | 24 288 | 20 990 | 5.4 | 4.8 | 5.2 | 4.3 |
| Yuma | 20 625 | 18 429 | 17 725 | 15 239 | 22.3 | 19.4 | 19.3 | 16.7 |
| **Arkansas** | 57 984 | 46 439 | 57 334 | 47 192 | 4.3 | 3.4 | 4.3 | 3.5 |
| Fayetteville-Springdale-Rogers | 8 035 | 6 677 | 7 688 | 6 723 | 3.1 | 2.5 | 3.0 | 2.6 |
| Fort Smith | 5 950 | 5 174 | 5 900 | 5 126 | 4.9 | 4.2 | 4.9 | 4.2 |
| Hot Springs | 1 977 | 1 591 | 1 917 | 1 605 | 5.0 | 4.0 | 4.9 | 4.0 |
| Jonesboro | 2 385 | 1 828 | 2 405 | 1 841 | 3.9 | 2.9 | 3.9 | 2.9 |
| Little Rock-North Little Rock-Conway | 13 752 | 10 992 | 13 243 | 11 151 | 3.9 | 3.1 | 3.8 | 3.2 |
| Pine Bluff | 2 123 | 1 695 | 2 133 | 1 680 | 5.8 | 4.7 | 5.8 | 4.7 |
| **California** | 1 094 641 | 1 030 568 | 1 101 576 | 976 424 | 5.8 | 5.3 | 5.8 | 5.0 |
| Bakersfield | 35 686 | 36 614 | 37 499 | 36 652 | 9.0 | 9.1 | 9.5 | 9.2 |
| Chico | 6 485 | 6 238 | 6 939 | 6 175 | 6.3 | 6.0 | 6.8 | 5.9 |
| El Centro | 19 479 | 19 843 | 18 371 | 15 887 | 24.5 | 24.2 | 23.0 | 20.3 |
| Fresno | 41 140 | 40 899 | 44 154 | 41 638 | 9.3 | 9.1 | 10.0 | 9.3 |
| Hanford-Corcoran | 5 513 | 5 189 | 5 982 | 5 380 | 9.6 | 9.0 | 10.4 | 9.3 |
| Los Angeles-Long Beach-Anaheim | 370 412 | 328 460 | 360 349 | 306 431 | 5.6 | 4.8 | 5.5 | 4.5 |
| Madera | 5 562 | 5 146 | 6 171 | 5 398 | 9.3 | 8.4 | 10.4 | 9.0 |
| Merced | 10 640 | 10 113 | 12 870 | 10 908 | 9.2 | 8.5 | 11.2 | 9.5 |
| Modesto | 20 577 | 19 358 | 21 797 | 19 438 | 8.6 | 7.8 | 9.0 | 7.9 |
| Napa | 3 271 | 2 988 | 3 687 | 3 170 | 4.3 | 3.8 | 5.0 | 4.2 |
| Oxnard-Thousand Oaks-Ventura | 23 732 | 23 250 | 24 172 | 21 836 | 5.5 | 5.3 | 5.6 | 5.0 |
| Redding | 5 180 | 4 821 | 5 409 | 4 800 | 6.9 | 6.4 | 7.3 | 6.4 |
| Riverside-San Bernardino-Ontario | 125 351 | 121 788 | 122 138 | 110 828 | 6.4 | 6.1 | 6.2 | 5.5 |
| Sacramento—Roseville—Arden-Arcade | 58 890 | 56 483 | 59 256 | 53 183 | 5.6 | 5.2 | 5.6 | 4.9 |
| Salinas | 13 198 | 12 298 | 17 031 | 14 562 | 5.8 | 5.4 | 7.6 | 6.6 |
| San Diego-Carlsbad | 79 225 | 75 827 | 77 914 | 69 491 | 5.1 | 4.7 | 5.0 | 4.3 |
| San Francisco-Oakland-Hayward | 102 805 | 99 843 | 101 472 | 91 531 | 4.1 | 3.9 | 4.0 | 3.6 |
| San Jose-Sunnyvale-Santa Clara | 43 020 | 41 956 | 42 889 | 38 693 | 4.1 | 3.8 | 4.1 | 3.6 |
| San Luis Obispo-Paso Robles-Arroyo | 6 299 | 6 004 | 6 458 | 5 574 | 4.4 | 4.1 | 4.5 | 3.8 |
| Grande Santa Cruz-Watsonville | 8 373 | 7 893 | 10 275 | 8 978 | 5.8 | 5.3 | 7.2 | 6.1 |
| Santa Maria-Santa Barbara | 10 810 | 10 346 | 11 745 | 10 432 | 4.9 | 4.6 | 5.3 | 4.7 |
| Santa Rosa | 10 993 | 10 253 | 11 246 | 9 729 | 4.2 | 3.9 | 4.3 | 3.7 |
| Stockton-Lodi | 25 695 | 24 397 | 27 385 | 24 693 | 8.1 | 7.6 | 8.7 | 7.8 |
| Vallejo-Fairfield | 11 818 | 11 325 | 12 005 | 10 831 | 5.7 | 5.3 | 5.8 | 5.1 |
| Visalia-Porterville | 21 374 | 22 008 | 22 394 | 21 819 | 10.8 | 10.8 | 11.3 | 10.8 |
| Yuba City | 6 250 | 5 961 | 7 074 | 6 372 | 8.6 | 8.2 | 9.8 | 8.8 |
| **Colorado** | 90 094 | 89 450 | 93 177 | 80 686 | 3.2 | 3.1 | 3.3 | 2.8 |
| Boulder | 4 679 | 4 615 | 4 722 | 4 004 | 2.6 | 2.5 | 2.7 | 2.2 |
| Colorado Springs | 11 917 | 11 525 | 12 378 | 10 369 | 3.7 | 3.5 | 3.9 | 3.2 |
| Denver-Aurora-Lakewood | 45 722 | 45 760 | 46 515 | 40 710 | 3.0 | 2.9 | 3.1 | 2.6 |
| Fort Collins | 4 920 | 4 955 | 5 045 | 4 339 | 2.7 | 2.6 | 2.8 | 2.3 |
| Grand Junction | 3 293 | 3 330 | 3 550 | 3 138 | 4.6 | 4.5 | 4.9 | 4.3 |
| Greeley | 4 769 | 4 647 | 4 912 | 4 073 | 3.2 | 3.0 | 3.3 | 2.6 |
| Pueblo | 3 220 | 3 248 | 3 415 | 3 181 | 4.5 | 4.4 | 4.7 | 4.3 |

## Table 7-3.  Unemployment Number and Rate by State and Selected Metropolitan Area October 2015–November 2016—*Continued*

(Number, rate.)

| State and area | October 2015 | October 2016 | November 2015 | November 2016 | October Number | October Percent | November 2015 | November 2016 |
|---|---|---|---|---|---|---|---|---|
| **Connecticut** | 95 007 | 85 417 | 94 823 | 70 502 | 5.0 | 4.5 | 5.0 | 3.7 |
| Bridgeport-Stamford-Norwalk | 22 881 | 20 744 | 22 744 | 17 256 | 5.0 | 4.5 | 4.9 | 3.7 |
| Danbury | 4 271 | 3 847 | 4 242 | 3 161 | 4.0 | 3.6 | 4.0 | 3.0 |
| Hartford-West Hartford-East Hartford | 31 051 | 27 786 | 30 949 | 22 825 | 5.0 | 4.5 | 5.0 | 3.7 |
| New Haven | 16 613 | 14 768 | 16 507 | 12 101 | 5.2 | 4.6 | 5.1 | 3.7 |
| Norwich-New London-Westerly | 7 500 | 6 576 | 7 644 | 5 557 | 5.3 | 4.6 | 5.4 | 4.0 |
| Waterbury | 6 969 | 6 293 | 6 967 | 5 223 | 6.3 | 5.7 | 6.3 | 4.7 |
| **Delaware** | 22 355 | 19 973 | 20 503 | 18 312 | 4.7 | 4.2 | 4.3 | 3.9 |
| Dover | 4 035 | 3 568 | 3 517 | 3 167 | 5.2 | 4.5 | 4.5 | 4.1 |
| Salisbury | 10 562 | 9 386 | 11 753 | 10 258 | 5.7 | 5.1 | 6.5 | 5.6 |
| **District of Columbia** | 25 983 | 24 583 | 25 845 | 23 374 | 6.7 | 6.2 | 6.6 | 5.9 |
| Washington-Arlington-Alexandria | 139 006 | 130 502 | 133 738 | 123 908 | 4.2 | 3.9 | 4.1 | 3.7 |
| **Florida** | 495 501 | 485 967 | 480 189 | 479 154 | 5.1 | 4.9 | 5.0 | 4.8 |
| Cape Coral-Fort Myers | 15 325 | 15 389 | 14 870 | 15 146 | 4.8 | 4.7 | 4.6 | 4.6 |
| Crestview-Fort Walton Beach-Destin | 5 044 | 5 043 | 5 001 | 5 016 | 4.2 | 4.2 | 4.3 | 4.2 |
| Deltona-Daytona Beach-Ormond Beach | 15 258 | 15 238 | 14 936 | 15 377 | 5.4 | 5.2 | 5.3 | 5.2 |
| Gainesville | 5 814 | 6 168 | 5 823 | 6 097 | 4.2 | 4.4 | 4.2 | 4.4 |
| Homosassa Springs | 3 252 | 3 222 | 3 190 | 3 234 | 6.8 | 6.7 | 6.7 | 6.8 |
| Jacksonville | 35 186 | 34 820 | 34 457 | 34 910 | 4.8 | 4.6 | 4.8 | 4.7 |
| Lakeland-Winter Haven | 16 432 | 16 312 | 15 954 | 16 244 | 5.9 | 5.7 | 5.7 | 5.7 |
| Miami-Fort Lauderdale-West Palm Beach | 161 753 | 154 016 | 154 221 | 149 443 | 5.3 | 5.0 | 5.1 | 4.8 |
| Naples-Immokalee-Marco Island | 8 428 | 8 500 | 7 886 | 8 163 | 5.3 | 5.2 | 4.8 | 4.9 |
| North Port-Sarasota-Bradenton | 16 458 | 16 546 | 15 766 | 16 183 | 4.8 | 4.7 | 4.6 | 4.6 |
| Ocala | 7 809 | 7 946 | 7 645 | 7 905 | 6.0 | 6.0 | 5.9 | 6.0 |
| Orlando-Kissimmee-Sanford | 57 788 | 56 887 | 56 605 | 56 446 | 4.7 | 4.5 | 4.6 | 4.4 |
| Palm Bay-Melbourne-Titusville | 14 125 | 13 564 | 13 849 | 13 506 | 5.5 | 5.2 | 5.4 | 5.2 |
| Panama City | 4 529 | 4 490 | 4 704 | 4 606 | 4.9 | 4.8 | 5.2 | 5.0 |
| Pensacola-Ferry Pass-Brent | 10 471 | 10 658 | 10 435 | 10 639 | 4.9 | 4.9 | 4.9 | 4.9 |
| Port St Lucie | 11 073 | 11 240 | 10 788 | 11 061 | 5.5 | 5.5 | 5.3 | 5.4 |
| Punta Gorda | 3 848 | 3 779 | 3 654 | 3 696 | 5.7 | 5.5 | 5.4 | 5.4 |
| Sebastian-Vero Beach | 4 066 | 3 981 | 3 822 | 3 839 | 6.7 | 6.5 | 6.2 | 6.2 |
| Sebring | 2 481 | 2 446 | 2 420 | 2 442 | 7.1 | 6.8 | 6.9 | 6.8 |
| Tallahassee | 8 944 | 9 049 | 8 939 | 8 991 | 4.8 | 4.7 | 4.8 | 4.8 |
| Tampa-St Petersburg-Clearwater | 69 608 | 69 188 | 67 911 | 68 933 | 4.8 | 4.7 | 4.7 | 4.7 |
| The Villages | 2 040 | 2 090 | 1 962 | 2 076 | 7.1 | 7.1 | 6.9 | 7.0 |
| **Georgia** | 265 087 | 264 694 | 248 130 | 249 870 | 5.6 | 5.3 | 5.2 | 5.0 |
| Albany | 4 309 | 4 196 | 4 097 | 3 993 | 6.6 | 6.2 | 6.2 | 5.8 |
| Athens-Clarke County | 4 874 | 4 878 | 4 474 | 5 142 | 5.2 | 4.9 | 4.7 | 5.1 |
| Atlanta-Sandy Springs-Roswell | 150 163 | 148 204 | 140 694 | 142 204 | 5.3 | 5.0 | 4.9 | 4.8 |
| Augusta-Richmond County | 15 653 | 15 010 | 14 557 | 13 245 | 6.1 | 5.8 | 5.8 | 5.1 |
| Brunswick | 2 912 | 3 039 | 2 688 | 2 684 | 5.8 | 5.9 | 5.4 | 5.2 |
| Columbus | 8 045 | 7 952 | 7 810 | 7 639 | 6.5 | 6.3 | 6.3 | 6.0 |
| Dalton | 3 748 | 3 761 | 3 593 | 3 611 | 6.2 | 6.1 | 6.0 | 5.9 |
| Gainesville | 4 197 | 4 434 | 3 860 | 3 949 | 4.5 | 4.6 | 4.1 | 4.1 |
| Hinesville | 1 877 | 1 906 | 1 766 | 1 824 | 5.9 | 5.9 | 5.5 | 5.6 |
| Macon | 6 323 | 6 488 | 5 805 | 5 764 | 6.1 | 6.1 | 5.6 | 5.4 |
| Rome | 2 654 | 2 528 | 2 456 | 2 387 | 6.2 | 5.8 | 5.8 | 5.5 |
| Savannah | 9 196 | 9 317 | 8 518 | 8 737 | 5.2 | 5.1 | 4.8 | 4.7 |
| Valdosta | 3 492 | 3 358 | 3 272 | 3 251 | 5.6 | 5.2 | 5.2 | 5.0 |
| Warner Robins | 5 137 | 5 714 | 4 361 | 4 407 | 6.4 | 6.9 | 5.4 | 5.4 |
| **Hawaii** | 22 709 | 21 475 | 22 815 | 19 704 | 3.4 | 3.1 | 3.3 | 2.8 |
| Kahului-Wailuku-Lahaina | 2 947 | 2 849 | 2 946 | 2 584 | 3.5 | 3.3 | 3.5 | 3.0 |
| Urban Honolulu | 14 835 | 14 028 | 14 820 | 12 865 | 3.2 | 2.9 | 3.1 | 2.7 |
| **Idaho** | 28 286 | 26 795 | 31 218 | 30 413 | 3.5 | 3.3 | 3.9 | 3.8 |
| Boise City | 11 453 | 11 124 | 12 375 | 12 389 | 3.5 | 3.4 | 3.8 | 3.7 |
| Coeur d'Alene | 3 189 | 2 947 | 3 486 | 3 317 | 4.4 | 4.1 | 4.8 | 4.6 |
| Idaho Falls | 1 903 | 1 787 | 2 119 | 2 048 | 2.9 | 2.7 | 3.2 | 3.1 |
| Lewiston | 1 081 | 1 106 | 1 154 | 1 166 | 3.6 | 3.6 | 3.8 | 3.7 |
| Pocatello | 1 410 | 1 352 | 1 512 | 1 474 | 3.3 | 3.2 | 3.5 | 3.5 |
| **Illinois** | 366 098 | 363 545 | 379 763 | 345 614 | 5.6 | 5.5 | 5.8 | 5.3 |
| Bloomington | 5 005 | 4 697 | 5 355 | 4 480 | 5.0 | 4.8 | 5.3 | 4.6 |
| Carbondale-Marion | 3 730 | 3 248 | 3 988 | 3 109 | 6.0 | 5.5 | 6.2 | 5.2 |
| Champaign-Urbana | 6 537 | 5 902 | 6 959 | 5 612 | 5.3 | 4.8 | 5.7 | 4.5 |
| Chicago-Naperville-Elgin | 259 280 | 272 050 | 266 114 | 259 181 | 5.3 | 5.5 | 5.4 | 5.3 |
| Danville | 2 581 | 2 352 | 2 768 | 2 282 | 7.2 | 6.6 | 7.7 | 6.4 |

## Table 7-3. Unemployment Number and Rate by State and Selected Metropolitan Area October 2015–November 2016—*Continued*

(Number, rate.)

| State and area | October 2015 | October 2016 | November 2015 | November 2016 | October Number | October Percent | November 2015 | November 2016 |
|---|---|---|---|---|---|---|---|---|
| **Illinois**— *Continued* | | | | | | | | |
| Davenport-Moline-Rock Island | 10 970 | 10 352 | 10 947 | 9 120 | 5.7 | 5.5 | 5.7 | 4.8 |
| Decatur | 3 566 | 3 063 | 3 775 | 2 936 | 7.0 | 6.1 | 7.3 | 5.9 |
| Kankakee | 3 746 | 3 225 | 4 014 | 3 134 | 6.7 | 5.8 | 7.1 | 5.6 |
| Peoria | 12 825 | 10 902 | 13 255 | 10 542 | 6.9 | 5.9 | 7.0 | 5.8 |
| Rockford | 12 047 | 10 280 | 12 613 | 9 838 | 7.1 | 6.0 | 7.4 | 5.8 |
| Springfield | 5 993 | 5 057 | 6 370 | 4 883 | 5.3 | 4.5 | 5.6 | 4.3 |
| **Indiana** | 139 610 | 128 762 | 147 181 | 130 119 | 4.3 | 3.9 | 4.5 | 3.9 |
| Bloomington | 3 545 | 3 140 | 3 716 | 3 137 | 4.5 | 4.0 | 4.8 | 4.0 |
| Columbus | 1 391 | 1 302 | 1 488 | 1 330 | 3.1 | 2.9 | 3.3 | 2.9 |
| Elkhart-Goshen | 3 700 | 3 380 | 3 923 | 3 423 | 3.5 | 3.2 | 3.7 | 3.3 |
| Evansville | 6 114 | 6 053 | 6 573 | 6 111 | 3.9 | 3.8 | 4.2 | 3.9 |
| Fort Wayne | 8 430 | 7 604 | 8 909 | 7 797 | 4.0 | 3.5 | 4.2 | 3.6 |
| Indianapolis-Carmel-Anderson | 40 786 | 37 221 | 42 687 | 37 539 | 4.0 | 3.6 | 4.2 | 3.6 |
| Kokomo | 1 668 | 1 669 | 1 736 | 1 556 | 4.5 | 4.4 | 4.7 | 4.1 |
| Lafayette-West Lafayette | 4 141 | 3 921 | 4 533 | 3 907 | 3.8 | 3.5 | 4.1 | 3.5 |
| Michigan City-La Porte | 2 606 | 2 392 | 2 769 | 2 451 | 5.4 | 4.9 | 5.8 | 5.1 |
| Muncie | 2 712 | 2 531 | 2 885 | 2 537 | 4.9 | 4.6 | 5.2 | 4.6 |
| South Bend-Mishawaka | 6 651 | 6 605 | 6 929 | 6 686 | 4.2 | 4.2 | 4.4 | 4.2 |
| Terre Haute | 4 082 | 3 513 | 4 306 | 3 607 | 5.2 | 4.5 | 5.5 | 4.6 |
| **Iowa** | 53 403 | 59 476 | 53 601 | 52 164 | 3.1 | 3.4 | 3.1 | 3.1 |
| Ames | 1 219 | 1 299 | 1 116 | 999 | 2.1 | 2.2 | 1.9 | 1.7 |
| Cedar Rapids | 4 614 | 5 103 | 4 707 | 4 438 | 3.2 | 3.5 | 3.2 | 3.1 |
| Des Moines-West Des Moines | 10 099 | 11 315 | 10 120 | 9 841 | 3.0 | 3.3 | 3.0 | 2.9 |
| Dubuque | 1 632 | 1 747 | 1 664 | 1 497 | 2.9 | 3.1 | 2.9 | 2.6 |
| Iowa City | 2 273 | 2 622 | 2 158 | 2 096 | 2.3 | 2.6 | 2.2 | 2.1 |
| Sioux City | 2 767 | 3 051 | 2 844 | 2 883 | 3.0 | 3.3 | 3.0 | 3.1 |
| Waterloo-Cedar Falls | 3 269 | 3 863 | 3 397 | 3 481 | 3.6 | 4.2 | 3.7 | 3.9 |
| **Kansas** | 55 675 | 59 325 | 54 119 | 56 416 | 3.7 | 4.0 | 3.6 | 3.8 |
| Lawrence | 2 024 | 2 185 | 2 012 | 2 160 | 3.0 | 3.3 | 3.0 | 3.3 |
| Manhattan | 1 352 | 1 587 | 1 398 | 1 607 | 2.6 | 3.1 | 2.6 | 3.1 |
| Topeka | 4 452 | 4 621 | 4 357 | 4 445 | 3.7 | 3.9 | 3.6 | 3.7 |
| Wichita | 13 241 | 14 042 | 12 673 | 13 322 | 4.2 | 4.5 | 4.0 | 4.2 |
| **Kentucky** | 93 529 | 93 107 | 103 215 | 80 319 | 4.8 | 4.6 | 5.3 | 4.0 |
| Bowling Green | 3 200 | 2 879 | 3 566 | 2 550 | 4.3 | 3.7 | 4.7 | 3.3 |
| Elizabethtown-Fort Knox | 2 956 | 2 850 | 3 201 | 2 479 | 4.7 | 4.3 | 5.0 | 3.8 |
| Lexington-Fayette | 9 248 | 9 063 | 10 300 | 7 799 | 3.6 | 3.5 | 4.0 | 3.0 |
| Louisville/Jefferson County | 26 397 | 25 376 | 28 337 | 22 667 | 4.3 | 4.0 | 4.5 | 3.5 |
| Owensboro | 2 244 | 2 410 | 2 530 | 2 030 | 4.3 | 4.4 | 4.8 | 3.7 |
| **Louisiana** | 126 997 | 124 268 | 115 730 | 116 864 | 5.9 | 5.9 | 5.4 | 5.5 |
| Alexandria | 4 016 | 4 000 | 3 632 | 3 826 | 6.0 | 6.1 | 5.5 | 5.9 |
| Baton Rouge | 20 946 | 21 506 | 19 103 | 20 186 | 5.0 | 5.0 | 4.5 | 4.7 |
| Hammond | 3 506 | 3 405 | 3 252 | 3 239 | 6.5 | 6.4 | 6.1 | 6.1 |
| Houma-Thibodaux | 5 646 | 6 003 | 5 236 | 5 592 | 5.7 | 6.3 | 5.4 | 6.0 |
| Lafayette | 14 464 | 14 517 | 13 338 | 13 534 | 6.4 | 6.7 | 6.0 | 6.3 |
| Lake Charles | 5 023 | 4 900 | 4 580 | 4 660 | 4.9 | 4.7 | 4.4 | 4.5 |
| Monroe | 5 017 | 4 797 | 4 516 | 4 592 | 6.1 | 5.9 | 5.6 | 5.7 |
| New Orleans-Metairie | 33 855 | 32 003 | 30 465 | 29 858 | 5.6 | 5.4 | 5.1 | 5.0 |
| Shreveport-Bossier City | 12 652 | 12 134 | 11 390 | 11 371 | 6.5 | 6.4 | 5.9 | 6.0 |
| **Maine** | 24 059 | 23 836 | 26 173 | 26 581 | 3.5 | 3.4 | 3.9 | 3.8 |
| Bangor | 2 493 | 2 488 | 2 641 | 2 688 | 3.5 | 3.5 | 3.8 | 3.8 |
| Lewiston-Auburn | 1 870 | 1 802 | 1 982 | 1 986 | 3.4 | 3.2 | 3.6 | 3.5 |
| Portland-South Portland | 5 776 | 5 726 | 6 158 | 6 338 | 2.9 | 2.8 | 3.2 | 3.1 |
| **Maryland** | 156 868 | 133 569 | 153 069 | 129 607 | 5.0 | 4.2 | 4.8 | 4.1 |
| Baltimore-Columbia-Towson | 75 972 | 64 542 | 73 421 | 62 496 | 5.1 | 4.3 | 5.0 | 4.2 |
| California-Lexington Park | 2 595 | 2 106 | 2 516 | 1 997 | 4.8 | 3.9 | 4.6 | 3.7 |
| Cumberland | 2 693 | 2 388 | 2 779 | 2 259 | 6.1 | 5.4 | 6.3 | 5.1 |
| Hagerstown-Martinsburg | 6 141 | 5 675 | 5 951 | 5 312 | 4.8 | 4.3 | 4.7 | 4.1 |
| **Massachusetts** | 158 980 | 97 923 | 160 734 | 91 520 | 4.5 | 2.7 | 4.5 | 2.6 |
| Barnstable Town | 5 852 | 3 434 | 6 705 | 3 687 | 4.8 | 2.8 | 5.6 | 3.1 |
| Boston-Cambridge-Nashua | 107 258 | 67 844 | 107 387 | 63 405 | 4.1 | 2.6 | 4.1 | 2.4 |
| Leominster-Gardner | 4 006 | 2 401 | 3 999 | 2 216 | 5.3 | 3.2 | 5.3 | 2.9 |
| New Bedford | 5 327 | 3 309 | 5 428 | 3 059 | 6.4 | 4.0 | 6.5 | 3.7 |
| Pittsfield | 2 174 | 1 320 | 2 301 | 1 295 | 5.0 | 3.1 | 5.3 | 3.0 |
| Springfield | 18 946 | 12 470 | 19 167 | 11 472 | 5.2 | 3.4 | 5.3 | 3.1 |
| Worcester | 16 352 | 10 685 | 16 315 | 9 718 | 4.8 | 3.1 | 4.7 | 2.8 |

## Table 7-3. Unemployment Number and Rate by State and Selected Metropolitan Area October 2015–November 2016—*Continued*

(Number, rate.)

| State and area | October 2015 | October 2016 | November 2015 | November 2016 | October Number | October Percent | November 2015 | November 2016 |
|---|---|---|---|---|---|---|---|---|
| **Michigan** | 223 097 | 224 780 | 201 429 | 217 820 | 4.7 | 4.6 | 4.2 | 4.5 |
| Ann Arbor | 5 741 | 6 920 | 5 148 | 6 085 | 3.0 | 3.5 | 2.7 | 3.0 |
| Battle Creek | 2 479 | 2 746 | 2 419 | 2 682 | 3.9 | 4.2 | 3.7 | 4.1 |
| Bay City | 2 089 | 2 298 | 2 094 | 2 328 | 4.0 | 4.4 | 4.0 | 4.4 |
| Detroit-Warren-Dearborn | 122 750 | 111 689 | 101 235 | 105 123 | 6.1 | 5.4 | 5.1 | 5.1 |
| Flint | 8 154 | 8 916 | 8 059 | 8 729 | 4.5 | 4.9 | 4.4 | 4.7 |
| Grand Rapids-Wyoming | 15 777 | 18 166 | 15 495 | 17 883 | 2.8 | 3.2 | 2.8 | 3.1 |
| Jackson | 2 898 | 3 185 | 2 776 | 3 096 | 4.0 | 4.4 | 3.8 | 4.3 |
| Kalamazoo-Portage | 5 792 | 6 516 | 5 681 | 6 539 | 3.5 | 3.8 | 3.4 | 3.8 |
| Lansing-East Lansing | 7 923 | 8 936 | 7 630 | 8 573 | 3.2 | 3.6 | 3.1 | 3.4 |
| Midland | 1 469 | 1 666 | 1 472 | 1 703 | 3.6 | 4.0 | 3.5 | 4.1 |
| Monroe | 2 799 | 3 623 | 2 518 | 2 789 | 3.6 | 4.6 | 3.2 | 3.6 |
| Muskegon | 3 363 | 3 661 | 3 339 | 3 634 | 4.4 | 4.7 | 4.3 | 4.6 |
| Niles-Benton Harbor | 2 824 | 3 229 | 2 817 | 3 263 | 3.8 | 4.3 | 3.8 | 4.4 |
| Saginaw | 3 648 | 3 990 | 3 673 | 4 022 | 4.1 | 4.4 | 4.1 | 4.4 |
| **Minnesota** | 90 896 | 96 172 | 93 799 | 96 182 | 3.0 | 3.2 | 3.1 | 3.2 |
| Duluth | 6 254 | 6 381 | 7 164 | 6 756 | 4.4 | 4.6 | 5.0 | 4.8 |
| Mankato-North Mankato | 1 445 | 1 509 | 1 297 | 1 439 | 2.4 | 2.5 | 2.2 | 2.4 |
| Minneapolis-St Paul-Bloomington | 56 678 | 59 997 | 55 693 | 57 774 | 2.9 | 3.1 | 2.9 | 3.0 |
| Rochester | 2 930 | 3 153 | 2 899 | 3 110 | 2.5 | 2.7 | 2.4 | 2.6 |
| St. Cloud | 3 180 | 3 414 | 3 369 | 3 432 | 2.8 | 3.1 | 3.0 | 3.1 |
| **Mississippi** | 79 922 | 73 712 | 79 139 | 67 345 | 6.2 | 5.7 | 6.2 | 5.2 |
| Gulfport-Biloxi-Pascagoula | 10 585 | 9 783 | 10 482 | 9 036 | 6.4 | 5.9 | 6.3 | 5.5 |
| Hattiesburg | 3 856 | 3 597 | 3 720 | 3 247 | 5.7 | 5.2 | 5.4 | 4.7 |
| Jackson | 14 321 | 13 398 | 14 003 | 12 105 | 5.3 | 4.9 | 5.2 | 4.5 |
| **Missouri** | 125 554 | 129 406 | 122 172 | 116 508 | 4.0 | 4.1 | 3.9 | 3.7 |
| Cape Girardeau | 1 933 | 2 129 | 1 915 | 1 910 | 3.9 | 4.3 | 3.9 | 3.9 |
| Columbia | 2 784 | 2 803 | 2 775 | 2 656 | 2.7 | 2.7 | 2.7 | 2.6 |
| Jefferson City | 2 453 | 2 442 | 2 501 | 2 268 | 3.2 | 3.2 | 3.3 | 3.0 |
| Joplin | 3 127 | 3 450 | 2 936 | 3 161 | 3.6 | 4.0 | 3.3 | 3.7 |
| Kansas City | 44 719 | 46 278 | 42 602 | 42 281 | 4.0 | 4.1 | 3.8 | 3.8 |
| St. Joseph | 2 519 | 2 472 | 2 357 | 2 322 | 3.8 | 3.8 | 3.6 | 3.6 |
| St. Louis | 65 415 | 64 190 | 65 261 | 56 994 | 4.4 | 4.2 | 4.4 | 3.8 |
| Springfield | 8 361 | 8 507 | 8 161 | 7 756 | 3.6 | 3.6 | 3.5 | 3.3 |
| **Montana** | 19 326 | 20 185 | 21 331 | 19 533 | 3.7 | 3.9 | 4.1 | 3.7 |
| Billings | 2 724 | 2 997 | 2 777 | 2 754 | 3.1 | 3.4 | 3.1 | 3.1 |
| Great Falls | 1 468 | 1 435 | 1 576 | 1 324 | 3.8 | 3.7 | 4.0 | 3.4 |
| Missoula | 2 080 | 2 131 | 2 266 | 2 053 | 3.3 | 3.4 | 3.6 | 3.3 |
| **Nebraska** | 27 346 | 31 261 | 25 840 | 28 563 | 2.7 | 3.1 | 2.5 | 2.8 |
| Grand Island | 1 296 | 1 425 | 1 302 | 1 305 | 3.0 | 3.3 | 3.0 | 3.0 |
| Lincoln | 4 303 | 5 033 | 3 937 | 4 458 | 2.4 | 2.8 | 2.2 | 2.5 |
| Omaha-Council Bluffs | 13 934 | 15 485 | 13 264 | 14 099 | 2.9 | 3.2 | 2.8 | 2.9 |
| **Nevada** | 89 743 | 75 706 | 88 199 | 71 394 | 6.3 | 5.3 | 6.2 | 5.0 |
| Carson City | 1 644 | 1 345 | 1 663 | 1 298 | 6.6 | 5.5 | 6.7 | 5.3 |
| Las Vegas-Henderson-Paradise | 67 149 | 57 372 | 65 662 | 54 073 | 6.4 | 5.5 | 6.2 | 5.1 |
| Reno | 12 944 | 10 518 | 12 833 | 9 915 | 5.6 | 4.5 | 5.5 | 4.2 |
| **New Hampshire** | 21 514 | 17 455 | 22 365 | 18 658 | 2.9 | 2.3 | 3.0 | 2.5 |
| Dover-Durham | 2 167 | 1 790 | 2 240 | 1 903 | 2.6 | 2.1 | 2.7 | 2.3 |
| Manchester | 3 325 | 2 688 | 3 415 | 2 837 | 2.9 | 2.3 | 3.0 | 2.4 |
| Portsmouth | 1 828 | 1 657 | 1 936 | 1 778 | 2.5 | 2.2 | 2.6 | 2.4 |
| **New Jersey** | 216 593 | 221 123 | 205 875 | 186 758 | 4.8 | 4.9 | 4.5 | 4.1 |
| Atlantic City-Hammonton | 9 417 | 9 153 | 9 204 | 8 543 | 7.6 | 7.5 | 7.4 | 7.1 |
| Ocean City | 3 879 | 3 823 | 5 046 | 4 622 | 8.4 | 8.2 | 11.3 | 10.5 |
| Trenton | 8 271 | 8 552 | 7 672 | 7 014 | 4.1 | 4.3 | 3.8 | 3.5 |
| Vineland-Bridgeton | 4 702 | 4 563 | 4 742 | 4 071 | 7.0 | 6.9 | 7.0 | 6.2 |
| **New Mexico** | 58 327 | 60 303 | 58 430 | 59 648 | 6.3 | 6.5 | 6.3 | 6.4 |
| Albuquerque | 25 003 | 25 437 | 24 464 | 24 831 | 6.0 | 6.1 | 5.9 | 5.8 |
| Farmington | 3 853 | 4 695 | 3 907 | 4 522 | 6.9 | 8.2 | 7.1 | 7.9 |
| Las Cruces | 6 344 | 6 197 | 6 505 | 6 352 | 6.8 | 6.6 | 6.9 | 6.7 |
| Santa Fe | 3 864 | 3 814 | 3 767 | 3 727 | 5.4 | 5.2 | 5.2 | 5.0 |
| **New York** | 457 318 | 476 060 | 462 578 | 450 246 | 4.7 | 4.9 | 4.8 | 4.7 |
| Albany-Schenectady-Troy | 18 317 | 17 763 | 18 159 | 17 026 | 4.1 | 4.0 | 4.1 | 3.9 |
| Binghamton | 5 705 | 5 503 | 5 809 | 5 342 | 5.2 | 5.1 | 5.3 | 5.0 |
| Buffalo-Cheektowaga-Niagara Falls | 26 747 | 26 903 | 27 273 | 26 520 | 4.9 | 4.9 | 5.0 | 4.9 |
| Elmira | 2 045 | 1 977 | 2 028 | 1 888 | 5.4 | 5.3 | 5.4 | 5.1 |
| Glens Falls | 2 690 | 2 643 | 3 016 | 2 951 | 4.4 | 4.4 | 5.1 | 5.0 |

## Table 7-3. Unemployment Number and Rate by State and Selected Metropolitan Area October 2015–November 2016—*Continued*

(Number, rate.)

| State and area | October 2015 | October 2016 | November 2015 | November 2016 | October Number | October Percent | November 2015 | November 2016 |
|---|---|---|---|---|---|---|---|---|
| **New York**—*Continued* | | | | | | | | |
| Ithaca | 1 996 | 2 020 | 2 056 | 1 946 | 3.6 | 3.6 | 3.7 | 3.4 |
| Kingston | 3 801 | 3 749 | 3 781 | 3 663 | 4.3 | 4.2 | 4.3 | 4.1 |
| New York-Newark-Jersey City | 473 411 | 498 897 | 465 362 | 446 892 | 4.7 | 5.0 | 4.6 | 4.5 |
| Rochester | 23 746 | 23 937 | 24 039 | 23 334 | 4.5 | 4.6 | 4.6 | 4.5 |
| Syracuse | 14 723 | 14 318 | 15 032 | 14 167 | 4.7 | 4.6 | 4.8 | 4.6 |
| Utica-Rome | 6 274 | 5 951 | 6 491 | 6 025 | 4.8 | 4.6 | 5.0 | 4.7 |
| Watertown-Fort Drum | 2 565 | 2 629 | 2 921 | 2 873 | 5.6 | 5.6 | 6.3 | 6.3 |
| **North Carolina** | 260 600 | 236 626 | 259 937 | 234 214 | 5.4 | 4.8 | 5.4 | 4.8 |
| Asheville | 9 448 | 8 505 | 9 442 | 8 833 | 4.3 | 3.7 | 4.3 | 3.9 |
| Burlington | 3 943 | 3 457 | 3 924 | 3 482 | 5.1 | 4.4 | 5.1 | 4.4 |
| Charlotte-Concord-Gastonia | 64 660 | 57 212 | 63 493 | 57 479 | 5.2 | 4.5 | 5.1 | 4.5 |
| Durham-Chapel Hill | 13 555 | 11 996 | 13 327 | 12 203 | 4.8 | 4.1 | 4.7 | 4.2 |
| Fayetteville | 10 450 | 9 276 | 10 363 | 9 127 | 7.2 | 6.3 | 7.1 | 6.1 |
| Goldsboro | 3 136 | 3 793 | 3 114 | 3 070 | 5.8 | 6.9 | 5.7 | 5.7 |
| Greensboro-High Point | 20 683 | 17 758 | 20 481 | 18 011 | 5.6 | 4.7 | 5.6 | 4.8 |
| Greenville | 5 118 | 5 146 | 4 998 | 4 528 | 5.9 | 5.9 | 5.7 | 5.1 |
| Hickory-Lenoir-Morganton | 8 982 | 7 687 | 8 949 | 7 886 | 5.4 | 4.6 | 5.4 | 4.7 |
| Jacksonville | 3 746 | 3 349 | 3 843 | 3 500 | 5.9 | 5.2 | 6.0 | 5.4 |
| New Bern | 2 957 | 2 768 | 2 980 | 2 701 | 5.8 | 5.3 | 5.8 | 5.2 |
| Raleigh | 30 529 | 27 382 | 30 021 | 27 703 | 4.6 | 4.0 | 4.5 | 4.0 |
| Rocky Mount | 5 060 | 4 971 | 5 115 | 4 614 | 7.5 | 7.3 | 7.5 | 6.8 |
| Wilmington | 7 265 | 6 359 | 7 470 | 6 422 | 5.2 | 4.5 | 5.4 | 4.5 |
| Winston-Salem | 16 534 | 14 253 | 16 392 | 14 610 | 5.2 | 4.4 | 5.2 | 4.5 |
| **North Dakota** | 7 962 | 9 356 | 9 475 | 10 861 | 1.9 | 2.2 | 2.3 | 2.5 |
| Bismarck | 1 122 | 1 424 | 1 400 | 1 715 | 1.7 | 2.0 | 2.1 | 2.4 |
| Fargo | 2 250 | 2 562 | 2 511 | 2 896 | 1.7 | 1.9 | 1.9 | 2.1 |
| Grand Forks | 1 063 | 1 220 | 1 246 | 1 406 | 1.9 | 2.1 | 2.2 | 2.4 |
| **Ohio** | 243 005 | 264 799 | 256 462 | 250 344 | 4.3 | 4.6 | 4.5 | 4.4 |
| Akron | 15 794 | 17 003 | 16 829 | 16 259 | 4.4 | 4.7 | 4.6 | 4.5 |
| Canton-Massillon | 9 817 | 10 136 | 10 702 | 9 741 | 4.9 | 5.1 | 5.3 | 4.9 |
| Cincinnati | 43 713 | 44 463 | 46 128 | 41 459 | 4.1 | 4.1 | 4.3 | 3.8 |
| Cleveland-Elyria | 38 981 | 51 428 | 39 171 | 45 917 | 3.8 | 5.0 | 3.9 | 4.5 |
| Columbus | 39 485 | 40 923 | 41 087 | 38 763 | 3.8 | 3.9 | 3.9 | 3.7 |
| Dayton | 16 453 | 17 219 | 17 356 | 16 207 | 4.3 | 4.5 | 4.5 | 4.2 |
| Lima | 2 060 | 2 280 | 2 197 | 2 196 | 4.3 | 4.7 | 4.5 | 4.5 |
| Mansfield | 2 669 | 2 704 | 2 912 | 2 637 | 5.0 | 5.2 | 5.4 | 5.1 |
| Springfield | 2 860 | 3 018 | 3 124 | 2 987 | 4.5 | 4.7 | 4.9 | 4.7 |
| Toledo | 13 327 | 14 276 | 14 055 | 13 541 | 4.4 | 4.7 | 4.6 | 4.5 |
| Weirton-Steubenville | 3 427 | 3 508 | 3 655 | 3 331 | 6.5 | 6.6 | 6.9 | 6.4 |
| Youngstown-Warren-Boardman | 13 494 | 14 826 | 14 264 | 14 060 | 5.4 | 6.0 | 5.7 | 5.7 |
| **Oklahoma** | 77 457 | 90 080 | 75 774 | 85 936 | 4.2 | 4.9 | 4.1 | 4.7 |
| Lawton | 2 228 | 2 500 | 2 160 | 2 373 | 4.2 | 4.8 | 4.0 | 4.4 |
| Oklahoma City | 24 184 | 28 836 | 23 535 | 27 440 | 3.6 | 4.3 | 3.5 | 4.1 |
| Tulsa | 20 590 | 24 366 | 19 818 | 23 226 | 4.3 | 5.1 | 4.1 | 4.8 |
| Oregon | 105 083 | 100 550 | 106 183 | 92 379 | 5.3 | 4.8 | 5.3 | 4.5 |
| Albany | 3 617 | 3 224 | 3 752 | 2 987 | 6.6 | 5.6 | 6.8 | 5.2 |
| Bend-Redmond | 4 635 | 4 306 | 4 777 | 4 060 | 5.4 | 4.7 | 5.6 | 4.5 |
| Corvallis | 1 805 | 1 784 | 1 745 | 1 634 | 3.9 | 3.8 | 3.8 | 3.4 |
| Eugene | 9 672 | 9 439 | 9 609 | 8 663 | 5.6 | 5.2 | 5.5 | 4.8 |
| Grants Pass | 2 444 | 2 229 | 2 544 | 2 034 | 7.2 | 6.4 | 7.6 | 5.9 |
| Medford | 6 003 | 5 648 | 6 203 | 5 215 | 6.0 | 5.4 | 6.2 | 5.1 |
| Portland-Vancouver-Hillsboro | 60 941 | 60 672 | 60 426 | 55 265 | 4.9 | 4.7 | 4.8 | 4.3 |
| Salem | 10 624 | 10 011 | 10 763 | 9 163 | 5.5 | 4.9 | 5.6 | 4.6 |
| **Pennsylvania** | 284 564 | 350 172 | 279 299 | 317 913 | 4.4 | 5.4 | 4.4 | 4.9 |
| Allentown-Bethlehem-Easton | 19 088 | 22 951 | 18 241 | 20 553 | 4.4 | 5.3 | 4.3 | 4.8 |
| Altoona | 2 530 | 3 200 | 2 578 | 2 924 | 4.2 | 5.2 | 4.3 | 4.8 |
| Bloomsburg-Berwick | 1 799 | 2 114 | 1 835 | 1 919 | 4.2 | 4.8 | 4.2 | 4.4 |
| Chambersburg-Waynesboro | 3 331 | 4 069 | 3 248 | 3 650 | 4.3 | 5.1 | 4.2 | 4.6 |
| East Stroudsburg | 4 348 | 5 172 | 4 214 | 4 672 | 5.4 | 6.3 | 5.2 | 5.8 |
| Erie | 6 140 | 8 680 | 6 337 | 7 972 | 4.6 | 6.4 | 4.7 | 5.9 |
| Gettysburg | 1 783 | 2 156 | 1 764 | 1 952 | 3.2 | 3.9 | 3.2 | 3.6 |
| Harrisburg-Carlisle | 10 658 | 13 427 | 10 193 | 12 080 | 3.6 | 4.5 | 3.5 | 4.1 |
| Johnstown | 3 214 | 3 958 | 3 276 | 3 724 | 5.2 | 6.4 | 5.3 | 6.0 |
| Lancaster | 9 233 | 11 652 | 9 066 | 10 306 | 3.3 | 4.2 | 3.3 | 3.8 |

## Table 7-3. Unemployment Number and Rate by State and Selected Metropolitan Area October 2015–November 2016—*Continued*

(Number, rate.)

| State and area | October 2015 | October 2016 | November 2015 | November 2016 | October Number | October Percent | November 2015 | November 2016 |
|---|---|---|---|---|---|---|---|---|
| **Pennsylvania**—*Continued* | | | | | | | | |
| Lebanon | 2 586 | 3 198 | 2 567 | 2 874 | 3.7 | 4.5 | 3.7 | 4.1 |
| Philadelphia-Camden-Wilmington | 142 631 | 159 863 | 135 299 | 141 600 | 4.7 | 5.1 | 4.4 | 4.6 |
| Pittsburgh | 54 238 | 67 643 | 54 013 | 62 504 | 4.5 | 5.5 | 4.5 | 5.1 |
| Reading | 8 621 | 10 791 | 8 423 | 9 772 | 4.0 | 5.0 | 3.9 | 4.5 |
| Scranton—Wilkes-Barre—Hazleton | 14 145 | 16 690 | 13 820 | 15 091 | 5.1 | 6.0 | 5.0 | 5.4 |
| State College | 2 504 | 3 311 | 2 573 | 2 850 | 3.1 | 4.0 | 3.2 | 3.5 |
| Williamsport | 3 177 | 3 686 | 3 202 | 3 329 | 5.3 | 6.2 | 5.3 | 5.6 |
| York-Hanover | 8 936 | 10 877 | 8 676 | 9 768 | 3.8 | 4.6 | 3.7 | 4.1 |
| **Rhode Island** | 28 373 | 26 619 | 29 115 | 25 568 | 5.1 | 4.8 | 5.2 | 4.6 |
| Providence-Warwick | 34 707 | 30 256 | 35 365 | 28 819 | 5.1 | 4.4 | 5.2 | 4.2 |
| **South Carolina** | 127 480 | 105 657 | 119 592 | 91 583 | 5.6 | 4.6 | 5.3 | 4.0 |
| Charleston-North Charleston | 17 449 | 14 544 | 16 286 | 12 466 | 4.8 | 3.9 | 4.5 | 3.4 |
| Columbia | 21 406 | 17 437 | 19 590 | 15 256 | 5.4 | 4.3 | 4.9 | 3.8 |
| Florence | 6 186 | 4 895 | 5 785 | 4 266 | 6.5 | 5.1 | 6.1 | 4.5 |
| Greenville-Anderson-Mauldin | 20 115 | 17 323 | 19 241 | 15 130 | 4.8 | 4.1 | 4.6 | 3.6 |
| Hilton Head Island-Bluffton-Beaufort | 4 089 | 3 763 | 3 844 | 3 123 | 4.9 | 4.5 | 4.7 | 3.8 |
| Myrtle Beach-Conway-North Myrtle Beach | 11 875 | 9 935 | 12 275 | 9 538 | 6.5 | 5.4 | 6.8 | 5.2 |
| Spartanburg | 8 058 | 6 780 | 7 713 | 5 915 | 5.3 | 4.4 | 5.1 | 3.9 |
| Sumter | 2 946 | 2 417 | 2 766 | 2 156 | 6.6 | 5.4 | 6.3 | 4.9 |
| **South Dakota** | 11 320 | 10 771 | 12 651 | 11 914 | 2.5 | 2.4 | 2.8 | 2.6 |
| Rapid City | 1 917 | 1 870 | 2 178 | 2 077 | 2.7 | 2.6 | 3.1 | 2.9 |
| Sioux Falls | 3 038 | 2 902 | 3 351 | 3 265 | 2.1 | 1.9 | 2.3 | 2.2 |
| Tennessee | 163 038 | 153 667 | 163 260 | 145 596 | 5.3 | 4.8 | 5.3 | 4.6 |
| Chattanooga | 13 122 | 13 344 | 12 838 | 12 451 | 5.2 | 5.1 | 5.1 | 4.8 |
| Clarksville | 6 230 | 5 948 | 6 283 | 5 477 | 5.7 | 5.3 | 5.8 | 4.9 |
| Cleveland | 2 824 | 2 749 | 2 830 | 2 605 | 5.0 | 4.7 | 4.8 | 4.1 |
| Jackson | 3 459 | 3 164 | 3 506 | 3 021 | 5.6 | 5.0 | 5.7 | 4.8 |
| Johnson City | 5 028 | 4 857 | 5 014 | 4 661 | 5.7 | 5.3 | 5.7 | 5.1 |
| Kingsport-Bristol-Bristol | 7 310 | 7 280 | 7 138 | 6 930 | 5.3 | 5.2 | 5.2 | 5.0 |
| Knoxville | 19 884 | 19 277 | 19 940 | 18 340 | 4.9 | 4.6 | 4.9 | 4.4 |
| Memphis | 37 403 | 33 990 | 37 007 | 31 789 | 6.1 | 5.4 | 6.0 | 5.1 |
| Morristown | 2 859 | 2 640 | 2 901 | 2 513 | 5.7 | 5.1 | 5.8 | 4.9 |
| Nashville-Davidson—Murfreesboro—Franklin | 40 361 | 37 354 | 40 168 | 35 465 | 4.3 | 3.8 | 4.3 | 3.6 |
| **Texas** | 582 556 | 584 597 | 583 304 | 566 893 | 4.4 | 4.4 | 4.4 | 4.2 |
| Abilene | 2 875 | 2 870 | 2 840 | 2 737 | 3.8 | 3.8 | 3.8 | 3.6 |
| Amarillo | 4 056 | 4 138 | 3 958 | 3 957 | 3.1 | 3.2 | 3.0 | 3.0 |
| Austin-Round Rock | 35 653 | 35 338 | 34 851 | 33 706 | 3.3 | 3.2 | 3.2 | 3.0 |
| Beaumont-Port Arthur | 11 820 | 11 067 | 12 118 | 11 416 | 6.7 | 6.3 | 6.8 | 6.4 |
| Brownsville-Harlingen | 10 907 | 10 972 | 11 363 | 11 124 | 6.7 | 6.6 | 6.9 | 6.6 |
| College Station-Bryan | 4 212 | 4 288 | 4 176 | 4 072 | 3.4 | 3.4 | 3.4 | 3.2 |
| Corpus Christi | 10 980 | 11 927 | 11 299 | 11 814 | 5.3 | 5.6 | 5.4 | 5.6 |
| Dallas-Fort Worth-Arlington | 142 921 | 135 729 | 140 460 | 130 432 | 4.0 | 3.6 | 3.9 | 3.5 |
| El Paso | 17 656 | 16 977 | 17 343 | 16 213 | 5.1 | 4.8 | 5.0 | 4.6 |
| Houston-The Woodlands-Sugar Land | 154 263 | 166 966 | 156 652 | 162 121 | 4.7 | 5.1 | 4.8 | 4.9 |
| Killeen-Temple | 7 874 | 7 519 | 7 698 | 7 239 | 4.6 | 4.3 | 4.5 | 4.2 |
| Laredo | 5 313 | 5 088 | 5 325 | 4 826 | 4.7 | 4.4 | 4.7 | 4.2 |
| Longview | 5 213 | 5 814 | 5 173 | 5 603 | 5.2 | 5.7 | 5.1 | 5.5 |
| Lubbock | 5 189 | 5 046 | 5 053 | 4 778 | 3.4 | 3.2 | 3.3 | 3.0 |
| McAllen-Edinburg-Mission | 24 492 | 22 582 | 26 259 | 23 968 | 7.4 | 6.7 | 7.9 | 7.1 |
| Midland | 3 362 | 3 509 | 3 358 | 3 285 | 3.8 | 3.9 | 3.8 | 3.6 |
| Odessa | 4 086 | 4 438 | 4 128 | 4 128 | 5.2 | 5.7 | 5.3 | 5.3 |
| San Angelo | 2 295 | 2 330 | 2 310 | 2 209 | 4.2 | 4.2 | 4.2 | 3.9 |
| San Antonio-New Braunfels | 41 693 | 41 264 | 41 129 | 39 437 | 3.8 | 3.7 | 3.7 | 3.5 |
| Sherman-Denison | 2 358 | 2 189 | 2 333 | 2 112 | 3.9 | 3.6 | 3.8 | 3.4 |
| Texarkana | 3 016 | 2 895 | 2 951 | 2 778 | 4.7 | 4.5 | 4.6 | 4.3 |
| Tyler | 4 634 | 4 631 | 4 587 | 4 393 | 4.5 | 4.4 | 4.4 | 4.2 |
| Victoria | 2 192 | 2 488 | 2 161 | 2 406 | 4.5 | 4.9 | 4.4 | 4.7 |
| Waco | 4 761 | 4 753 | 4 667 | 4 512 | 4.0 | 3.9 | 3.9 | 3.7 |
| Wichita Falls | 2 871 | 2 640 | 2 826 | 2 524 | 4.4 | 4.1 | 4.4 | 3.9 |
| **Utah** | 47 435 | 47 130 | 44 259 | 38 810 | 3.2 | 3.1 | 3.0 | 2.6 |
| Logan | 1 827 | 1 830 | 1 731 | 1 565 | 2.7 | 2.6 | 2.6 | 2.2 |
| Ogden-Clearfield | 10 227 | 10 096 | 9 336 | 8 215 | 3.3 | 3.2 | 3.0 | 2.6 |
| Provo-Orem | 7 966 | 8 006 | 7 188 | 6 393 | 2.9 | 2.8 | 2.6 | 2.2 |
| St. George | 2 306 | 2 253 | 2 193 | 1 836 | 3.5 | 3.3 | 3.4 | 2.7 |
| Salt Lake City | 18 942 | 18 805 | 17 583 | 15 411 | 3.1 | 2.9 | 2.8 | 2.4 |

## Table 7-3.  Unemployment Number and Rate by State and Selected Metropolitan Area October 2015–November 2016—*Continued*

(Number, rate.)

| State and area | October 2015 | October 2016 | November 2015 | November 2016 | October Number | October Percent | November 2015 | November 2016 |
|---|---|---|---|---|---|---|---|---|
| **Vermont** | 10 460 | 9 128 | 11 648 | 9 926 | 3.0 | 2.7 | 3.4 | 2.9 |
| Burlington-South Burlington | 3 107 | 2 822 | 3 347 | 2 919 | 2.5 | 2.2 | 2.7 | 2.3 |
| **Virginia** | 169 890 | 172 991 | 164 809 | 168 373 | 4.0 | 4.1 | 3.9 | 4.0 |
| Blacksburg-Christiansburg-Radford | 3 861 | 4 184 | 3 587 | 3 945 | 4.2 | 4.6 | 3.9 | 4.3 |
| Charlottesville | 4 129 | 4 226 | 3 838 | 4 000 | 3.6 | 3.6 | 3.3 | 3.4 |
| Harrisonburg | 2 608 | 2 635 | 2 443 | 2 390 | 4.1 | 4.2 | 3.9 | 3.8 |
| Lynchburg | 5 363 | 5 528 | 5 156 | 5 374 | 4.4 | 4.6 | 4.2 | 4.4 |
| Richmond | 27 558 | 27 655 | 26 904 | 27 320 | 4.1 | 4.1 | 4.0 | 4.1 |
| Roanoke | 6 247 | 6 378 | 6 009 | 6 224 | 4.0 | 4.0 | 3.8 | 3.9 |
| Staunton-Waynesboro | 2 268 | 2 370 | 2 201 | 2 259 | 3.9 | 4.1 | 3.8 | 4.0 |
| Virginia Beach-Norfolk-Newport News | 37 539 | 38 021 | 37 102 | 37 614 | 4.5 | 4.6 | 4.5 | 4.6 |
| Winchester | 2 547 | 2 578 | 2 485 | 2 419 | 3.7 | 3.7 | 3.6 | 3.5 |
| **Washington** | 189 562 | 186 221 | 202 545 | 190 343 | 5.3 | 5.0 | 5.7 | 5.2 |
| Bellingham | 5 629 | 6 263 | 5 781 | 6 043 | 5.5 | 5.9 | 5.6 | 5.7 |
| Bremerton-Silverdale | 5 860 | 6 823 | 5 904 | 6 616 | 5.1 | 5.8 | 5.0 | 5.5 |
| Kennewick-Richland | 7 578 | 8 259 | 8 700 | 8 906 | 5.8 | 6.1 | 6.7 | 6.6 |
| Longview | 3 097 | 3 290 | 3 136 | 3 183 | 7.0 | 7.2 | 7.0 | 6.9 |
| Mount Vernon-Anacortes | 3 428 | 3 793 | 3 677 | 3 807 | 6.0 | 6.4 | 6.4 | 6.5 |
| Olympia-Tumwate | 6 844 | 7 495 | 7 033 | 7 265 | 5.4 | 5.8 | 5.5 | 5.6 |
| Seattle-Tacoma-Bellevue | 97 907 | 86 750 | 104 146 | 88 876 | 5.0 | 4.2 | 5.3 | 4.3 |
| Spokane-Spokane Valley | 14 741 | 15 490 | 15 111 | 15 251 | 5.9 | 5.9 | 5.9 | 5.8 |
| Walla Walla | 1 438 | 1 577 | 1 603 | 1 636 | 4.7 | 5.1 | 5.2 | 5.3 |
| Wenatchee | 3 063 | 3 416 | 3 542 | 3 750 | 4.7 | 5.1 | 5.8 | 6.0 |
| Yakima | 7 945 | 8 309 | 9 819 | 10 118 | 6.2 | 6.3 | 8.2 | 8.3 |
| **West Virginia** | 43 716 | 44 649 | 44 556 | 40 461 | 5.6 | 5.6 | 5.7 | 5.1 |
| Beckley | 3 065 | 3 068 | 3 219 | 2 872 | 6.6 | 6.5 | 7.0 | 6.3 |
| Charleston | 5 408 | 5 606 | 5 469 | 5 027 | 5.5 | 5.6 | 5.6 | 5.1 |
| Huntington-Ashland | 7 766 | 8 518 | 8 148 | 7 645 | 5.3 | 5.7 | 5.5 | 5.2 |
| Morgantown | 2 696 | 2 898 | 2 698 | 2 458 | 4.0 | 4.2 | 4.0 | 3.6 |
| Parkersburg-Vienna | 2 134 | 2 187 | 2 183 | 2 025 | 5.4 | 5.5 | 5.5 | 5.2 |
| Wheeling | 3 710 | 3 954 | 3 942 | 3 722 | 5.6 | 6.0 | 5.9 | 5.7 |
| **Wisconsin** | 122 057 | 110 281 | 129 459 | 112 449 | 3.9 | 3.5 | 4.2 | 3.6 |
| Appleton | 4 241 | 4 000 | 4 551 | 4 073 | 3.3 | 3.1 | 3.5 | 3.1 |
| Eau Claire | 3 141 | 2 860 | 3 361 | 2 922 | 3.4 | 3.1 | 3.7 | 3.1 |
| Fond du Lac | 1 939 | 1 688 | 2 053 | 1 703 | 3.4 | 2.9 | 3.6 | 2.9 |
| Green Bay | 6 117 | 5 636 | 6 588 | 5 733 | 3.6 | 3.2 | 3.8 | 3.3 |
| Janesville-Beloit | 3 763 | 3 351 | 3 878 | 3 341 | 4.5 | 3.9 | 4.6 | 3.8 |
| La Crosse-Onalaska | 2 567 | 2 450 | 2 856 | 2 454 | 3.3 | 3.1 | 3.6 | 3.1 |
| Madison | 11 140 | 10 518 | 11 877 | 10 462 | 2.9 | 2.7 | 3.1 | 2.7 |
| Milwaukee-Waukesha-West Allis | 37 076 | 33 097 | 37 951 | 33 024 | 4.5 | 4.0 | 4.6 | 4.0 |
| Oshkosh-Neenah | 3 384 | 3 019 | 3 554 | 3 084 | 3.7 | 3.3 | 3.9 | 3.3 |
| Racine | 4 877 | 4 316 | 5 002 | 4 339 | 4.9 | 4.4 | 5.1 | 4.4 |
| Sheboygan | 2 006 | 1 956 | 2 160 | 1 985 | 3.3 | 3.2 | 3.5 | 3.2 |
| Wausau | 2 517 | 2 296 | 2 722 | 2 347 | 3.4 | 3.1 | 3.7 | 3.1 |
| **Wyoming** | 11 948 | 13 932 | 13 291 | 13 808 | 3.9 | 4.6 | 4.4 | 4.6 |
| Casper | 2 029 | 2 592 | 2 192 | 2 488 | 4.8 | 6.3 | 5.2 | 6.0 |
| Cheyenne | 1 749 | 1 817 | 1 833 | 1 712 | 3.6 | 3.8 | 3.7 | 3.5 |

# NOTES AND DEFINITIONS

## JOB OPENINGS AND LABOR TURNOVER SURVEY

Data from a sample of approximately 16,000 businesses for the Job Openings and Labor Turnover Survey (JOLTS) are collected and compiled monthly from a sample of business establishments by the Bureau of Labor Statistics (BLS). Each month, data are collected in a survey of business establishments for total employment, job openings, hires, quits, layoffs and discharges, and other separations. Data collection methods include computer-assisted telephone interviewing, touchtone data entry, fax, and mail.

## Concepts and Definitions

The JOLTS program covers all private nonfarm establishments such as factories, offices, and stores, as well as federal, state, and local government entities in the 50 states and the District of Columbia.

*Employment* includes persons on the payroll who worked or received pay for the pay period that includes the 12th day of the reference month. Full-time, part-time, permanent, short-term, seasonal, salaried, and hourly employees are included, as are employees on paid vacations or other paid leave. Proprietors or partners of unincorporated businesses, unpaid family workers, or persons on leave without pay or on strike for the entire pay period, are not counted as employed. Employees of temporary help agencies, employee leasing companies, outside contractors, and consultants are counted by their employer of record, not by the establishment where they are working.

*Job openings* information is submitted by establishments for the last business day of the reference month. A job opening requires that: 1) a specific position exists and there is work available for that position, 2) work could start within 30 days regardless of whether a suitable candidate is found, and 3) the employer is actively recruiting from outside the establishment to fill the position. Included are full-time, part-time, permanent, short-term, and seasonal openings. Active recruiting means that the establishment is taking steps to fill a position by advertising in newspapers or on the Internet, posting help-wanted signs, accepting applications, or using other similar methods.

Jobs to be filled only by internal transfers, promotions, demotions, or recall from layoffs are excluded. Also excluded are jobs with start dates more than 30 days in the future, jobs for which employees have been hired but have not yet reported for work, and jobs to be filled by employees of temporary help agencies, employee leasing companies, outside contractors, or consultants. The job openings rate is computed by dividing the number of job openings by the sum of employment and job openings and multiplying that quotient by 100.

*Hires* are the total number of additions to the payroll occurring at any time during the reference month, including both new and rehired employees, full-time and part-time, permanent, short-term

and seasonal employees, employees recalled to the location after a layoff lasting more than 7 days, on-call or intermittent employees who returned to work after having been formally separated, and transfers from other locations. The hires count does not include transfers or promotions within the reporting site, employees returning from strike, employees of temporary help agencies or employee leasing companies, outside contractors, or consultants. The hires rate is computed by dividing the number of hires by employment and multiplying that quotient by 100.

*Separations* are the total number of terminations of employment occurring at any time during the reference month, and are reported by type of separation—quits, layoffs and discharges, and other separations. Quits are voluntary separations by employees (except for retirements, which are reported as other separations). Layoffs and discharges are involuntary separations initiated by the employer and include layoffs with no intent to rehire, formal layoffs lasting or expected to last more than 7 days, discharges resulting from mergers, downsizing, or closings, firings or other discharges for cause, terminations of permanent or short-term employees, and terminations of seasonal employees. Other separations include retirements, transfers to other locations, deaths, and separations due to disability. Separations do not include transfers within the same location or employees on strike.

The separations rate is computed by dividing the number of separations by employment and multiplying that quotient by 100. The quits, layoffs and discharges, and other separations rates are computed similarly, dividing the number by employment and multiplying by 100.

The JOLTS annual level estimates for hires, quits, layoffs and discharges, other separations, and total separations are the sum of the 12 published monthly levels. The annual rate estimates are computed by dividing the annual level by the Current Employment Statistics (CES) annual average employment level, and multiplying that quotient by 100. This figure will be approximately equal to the sum of the 12 monthly rates.

Annual estimates are not calculated for job openings because job openings are a stock, or point-in-time, measurement for the last business day of each month. Only jobs still open on the last day of the month are counted. For the same reason job openings cannot be cumulated throughout each month, annual figures for job openings cannot be created by summing the monthly estimates. Hires and separations are flow measures and are cumulated over the month with a total reported for the month. Therefore, the annual figures can be created by summing the monthly estimates.

## Sources of Additional Information

For more extensive information see the Job Openings and Labor Turnover Survey (JOLTS) page on the BLS Web site at <http://www.bls.gov/jlt/>.

## Table 7-4.  Job Openings Levels and Rates, by Industry, 2005–October 2016

(Seasonally adjusted, levels in thousands, rates per 100.)

| Year and month | Level | | | | | | | | | | | |
|---|---|---|---|---|---|---|---|---|---|---|---|---|
| | Total nonfarm[1] | Total private[1] | Construc-tion | Manufac-turing | Trade, transpor-tation, and utilities[2] | Retail trade | Profes-sional and business services | Education and health services | Leisure and hospitality[3] | Accommo-dation and food services | Govern-ment[4] | State and local govern-ment |
| **2005** | | | | | | | | | | | | |
| January ................................ | 3 670 | 3 358 | 138 | 296 | 628 | 413 | 653 | 607 | 493 | 430 | 312 | 279 |
| February .............................. | 3 845 | 3 489 | 139 | 279 | 695 | 424 | 741 | 619 | 543 | 482 | 356 | 314 |
| March ................................... | 3 831 | 3 467 | 147 | 271 | 682 | 454 | 756 | 658 | 474 | 413 | 364 | 312 |
| April ..................................... | 4 243 | 3 865 | 176 | 314 | 731 | 464 | 815 | 651 | 588 | 513 | 378 | 333 |
| May ...................................... | 3 884 | 3 506 | 158 | 280 | 692 | 429 | 790 | 684 | 491 | 428 | 378 | 323 |
| June ..................................... | 4 022 | 3 648 | 144 | 289 | 682 | 418 | 829 | 666 | 498 | 424 | 374 | 328 |
| July ...................................... | 4 319 | 3 910 | 182 | 348 | 716 | 425 | 835 | 698 | 546 | 456 | 409 | 359 |
| August ................................. | 4 073 | 3 686 | 155 | 306 | 700 | 446 | 817 | 667 | 479 | 414 | 387 | 334 |
| September ........................... | 4 237 | 3 833 | 160 | 341 | 701 | 425 | 827 | 685 | 466 | 418 | 404 | 354 |
| October ................................ | 4 277 | 3 898 | 179 | 284 | 759 | 462 | 884 | 663 | 473 | 415 | 379 | 341 |
| November ............................ | 4 220 | 3 863 | 155 | 323 | 763 | 525 | 867 | 666 | 551 | 489 | 357 | 317 |
| December ............................ | 4 064 | 3 666 | 123 | 303 | 661 | 431 | 824 | 664 | 530 | 470 | 399 | 344 |
| **2006** | | | | | | | | | | | | |
| January ................................ | 4 298 | 3 928 | 138 | 329 | 635 | 374 | 892 | 716 | 555 | 483 | 370 | 330 |
| February .............................. | 4 229 | 3 841 | 130 | 369 | 706 | 414 | 763 | 743 | 580 | 522 | 389 | 339 |
| March ................................... | 4 493 | 4 063 | 199 | 361 | 723 | 419 | 756 | 743 | 593 | 535 | 430 | 379 |
| April ..................................... | 4 680 | 4 243 | 231 | 396 | 767 | 414 | 708 | 760 | 646 | 572 | 437 | 381 |
| May ...................................... | 4 389 | 3 976 | 197 | 320 | 781 | 439 | 763 | 707 | 563 | 509 | 413 | 365 |
| June ..................................... | 4 349 | 3 930 | 228 | 366 | 699 | 404 | 705 | 735 | 527 | 468 | 419 | 368 |
| July ...................................... | 4 154 | 3 652 | 245 | 344 | 695 | 377 | 605 | 641 | 545 | 480 | 502 | 436 |
| August ................................. | 4 560 | 4 078 | 217 | 347 | 755 | 453 | 743 | 778 | 540 | 490 | 482 | 418 |
| September ........................... | 4 516 | 4 048 | 177 | 361 | 842 | 444 | 689 | 771 | 557 | 458 | 468 | 431 |
| October ................................ | 4 472 | 4 066 | 158 | 359 | 800 | 445 | 705 | 792 | 600 | 503 | 406 | 371 |
| November ............................ | 4 341 | 3 917 | 104 | 289 | 726 | 432 | 750 | 778 | 647 | 564 | 423 | 384 |
| December ............................ | 4 278 | 3 876 | 91 | 315 | 797 | 497 | 692 | 763 | 584 | 520 | 402 | 367 |
| **2007** | | | | | | | | | | | | |
| January ................................ | 4 630 | 4 194 | 256 | 365 | 870 | 464 | 798 | 744 | 549 | 472 | 436 | 396 |
| February .............................. | 4 465 | 4 033 | 273 | 349 | 729 | 441 | 719 | 713 | 563 | 489 | 432 | 387 |
| March ................................... | 4 666 | 4 210 | 209 | 362 | 821 | 434 | 805 | 744 | 594 | 522 | 455 | 396 |
| April ..................................... | 4 824 | 4 379 | 219 | 387 | 902 | 420 | 870 | 774 | 562 | 481 | 445 | 391 |
| May ...................................... | 4 550 | 4 117 | 210 | 367 | 735 | 374 | 758 | 796 | 599 | 529 | 433 | 389 |
| June ..................................... | 4 608 | 4 163 | 170 | 371 | 798 | 450 | 772 | 822 | 595 | 525 | 445 | 404 |
| July ...................................... | 4 490 | 4 038 | 207 | 387 | 816 | 445 | 692 | 694 | 595 | 535 | 452 | 405 |
| August ................................. | 4 555 | 4 079 | 164 | 334 | 793 | 401 | 745 | 794 | 636 | 577 | 475 | 413 |
| September ........................... | 4 523 | 4 072 | 121 | 323 | 792 | 410 | 757 | 866 | 636 | 573 | 451 | 399 |
| October ................................ | 4 300 | 3 881 | 126 | 298 | 728 | 360 | 767 | 742 | 615 | 551 | 418 | 376 |
| November ............................ | 4 156 | 3 730 | 87 | 270 | 716 | 427 | 742 | 760 | 630 | 534 | 426 | 377 |
| December ............................ | 4 123 | 3 713 | 96 | 266 | 724 | 393 | 778 | 755 | 580 | 539 | 410 | 359 |
| **2008** | | | | | | | | | | | | |
| January ................................ | 4 260 | 3 858 | 132 | 293 | 752 | 379 | 755 | 722 | 578 | 522 | 402 | 364 |
| February .............................. | 4 042 | 3 619 | 112 | 270 | 670 | 362 | 754 | 802 | 557 | 480 | 423 | 371 |
| March ................................... | 4 001 | 3 574 | 100 | 248 | 628 | 386 | 762 | 792 | 547 | 476 | 426 | 367 |
| April ..................................... | 4 098 | 3 703 | 119 | 300 | 652 | 394 | 763 | 750 | 542 | 485 | 395 | 359 |
| May ...................................... | 3 960 | 3 486 | 170 | 291 | 619 | 380 | 633 | 743 | 533 | 469 | 474 | 412 |
| June ..................................... | 3 767 | 3 335 | 117 | 248 | 543 | 301 | 739 | 729 | 487 | 437 | 432 | 375 |
| July ...................................... | 3 821 | 3 412 | 121 | 256 | 626 | 382 | 662 | 751 | 451 | 402 | 409 | 349 |
| August ................................. | 3 665 | 3 245 | 84 | 272 | 584 | 360 | 642 | 700 | 397 | 335 | 420 | 336 |
| September ........................... | 3 264 | 2 854 | 120 | 214 | 488 | 267 | 629 | 610 | 406 | 365 | 410 | 353 |
| October ................................ | 3 292 | 2 910 | 68 | 238 | 556 | 372 | 580 | 652 | 384 | 340 | 382 | 322 |
| November ............................ | 2 956 | 2 594 | 45 | 147 | 478 | 354 | 533 | 631 | 326 | 291 | 362 | 336 |
| December ............................ | 2 830 | 2 545 | 47 | 139 | 413 | 287 | 564 | 633 | 313 | 277 | 285 | 259 |
| **2009** | | | | | | | | | | | | |
| January ................................ | 2 767 | 2 387 | 42 | 113 | 448 | 325 | 553 | 599 | 234 | 207 | 380 | 300 |
| February .............................. | 2 791 | 2 441 | 63 | 130 | 429 | 305 | 533 | 562 | 308 | 285 | 351 | 279 |
| March ................................... | 2 491 | 2 131 | 46 | 114 | 392 | 255 | 425 | 508 | 269 | 246 | 359 | 248 |
| April ..................................... | 2 357 | 1 977 | 25 | 104 | 336 | 208 | 415 | 521 | 274 | 252 | 379 | 294 |
| May ...................................... | 2 427 | 2 135 | 41 | 101 | 450 | 314 | 408 | 534 | 264 | 242 | 293 | 253 |
| June ..................................... | 2 428 | 2 101 | 54 | 99 | 415 | 262 | 405 | 541 | 261 | 245 | 327 | 275 |
| July ...................................... | 2 196 | 1 917 | 57 | 109 | 272 | 157 | 439 | 538 | 220 | 204 | 279 | 223 |
| August ................................. | 2 306 | 1 989 | 62 | 133 | 410 | 233 | 346 | 549 | 198 | 178 | 317 | 284 |
| September ........................... | 2 478 | 2 208 | 66 | 131 | 412 | 281 | 441 | 557 | 289 | 263 | 271 | 216 |
| October ................................ | 2 400 | 1 996 | 57 | 146 | 296 | 188 | 376 | 539 | 247 | 222 | 404 | 279 |
| November ............................ | 2 350 | 2 010 | 48 | 128 | 321 | 228 | 425 | 520 | 262 | 237 | 340 | 246 |
| December ............................ | 2 407 | 2 090 | 54 | 154 | 355 | 249 | 436 | 544 | 256 | 239 | 317 | 244 |
| **2010** | | | | | | | | | | | | |
| January ................................ | 2 636 | 2 251 | 50 | 138 | 368 | 236 | 399 | 590 | 262 | 246 | 385 | 248 |
| February .............................. | 2 578 | 2 230 | 63 | 152 | 431 | 285 | 395 | 537 | 244 | 223 | 348 | 219 |
| March ................................... | 2 666 | 2 251 | 77 | 146 | 497 | 342 | 429 | 521 | 225 | 196 | 416 | 251 |
| April ..................................... | 3 220 | 2 571 | 103 | 189 | 434 | 267 | 505 | 532 | 266 | 240 | 648 | 269 |
| May ...................................... | 2 891 | 2 511 | 84 | 196 | 428 | 259 | 587 | 514 | 287 | 242 | 380 | 244 |
| June ..................................... | 2 664 | 2 357 | 81 | 216 | 417 | 258 | 487 | 485 | 282 | 232 | 307 | 222 |
| July ...................................... | 2 965 | 2 645 | 118 | 223 | 410 | 247 | 556 | 536 | 306 | 263 | 320 | 245 |
| August ................................. | 2 920 | 2 588 | 52 | 190 | 404 | 240 | 615 | 475 | 344 | 306 | 332 | 243 |
| September ........................... | 2 767 | 2 457 | 73 | 196 | 419 | 220 | 574 | 513 | 281 | 246 | 309 | 232 |
| October ................................ | 3 033 | 2 685 | 65 | 204 | 436 | 258 | 609 | 616 | 301 | 271 | 348 | 284 |
| November ............................ | 2 914 | 2 617 | 67 | 196 | 402 | 262 | 659 | 540 | 291 | 262 | 298 | 220 |
| December ............................ | 2 857 | 2 469 | 31 | 168 | 445 | 290 | 597 | 544 | 302 | 261 | 388 | 302 |

[1]Includes natural resources and mining, information, financial activities, and other services, not shown separately.
[2]Includes wholesale trade and transportation, warehousing, and utilities, not shown separately.
[3]Includes arts, entertainment, and recreation, not shown separately.
[4]Includes federal government, not shown separately.

## Table 7-4. Job Openings Levels and Rates, by Industry, 2005–October 2016—*Continued*

(Seasonally adjusted, levels in thousands, rates per 100.)

| Year and month | Rate | | | | | | | | | | | |
|---|---|---|---|---|---|---|---|---|---|---|---|---|
| | Total[1] | Total private[1] | Construction | Manufac-turing | Trade, transpor-tation, and utilities[2] | Retail trade | Profes-sional and business services | Education and health services | Leisure and hospitality[3] | Accommo-dation and food services | Govern-ment[4] | State and local govern-ment |
| **2005** | | | | | | | | | | | | |
| January | 2.7 | 2.9 | 1.9 | 2.0 | 2.4 | 2.7 | 3.8 | 3.4 | 3.7 | 3.8 | 1.4 | 1.4 |
| February | 2.8 | 3.0 | 1.9 | 1.9 | 2.6 | 2.7 | 4.2 | 3.4 | 4.1 | 4.3 | 1.6 | 1.6 |
| March | 2.8 | 3.0 | 2.0 | 1.9 | 2.6 | 2.9 | 4.3 | 3.6 | 3.6 | 3.7 | 1.6 | 1.6 |
| April | 3.1 | 3.3 | 2.4 | 2.2 | 2.7 | 3.0 | 4.6 | 3.6 | 4.4 | 4.5 | 1.7 | 1.7 |
| May | 2.8 | 3.0 | 2.1 | 1.9 | 2.6 | 2.7 | 4.5 | 3.7 | 3.7 | 3.8 | 1.7 | 1.7 |
| June | 2.9 | 3.1 | 1.9 | 2.0 | 2.6 | 2.7 | 4.7 | 3.6 | 3.7 | 3.7 | 1.7 | 1.7 |
| July | 3.1 | 3.4 | 2.4 | 2.4 | 2.7 | 2.7 | 4.7 | 3.8 | 4.1 | 4.0 | 1.8 | 1.8 |
| August | 2.9 | 3.2 | 2.1 | 2.1 | 2.6 | 2.8 | 4.6 | 3.6 | 3.6 | 3.6 | 1.7 | 1.7 |
| September | 3.1 | 3.3 | 2.1 | 2.3 | 2.6 | 2.7 | 4.6 | 3.7 | 3.5 | 3.7 | 1.8 | 1.8 |
| October | 3.1 | 3.3 | 2.3 | 2.0 | 2.8 | 2.9 | 4.9 | 3.6 | 3.6 | 3.7 | 1.7 | 1.8 |
| November | 3.0 | 3.3 | 2.0 | 2.2 | 2.8 | 3.3 | 4.8 | 3.6 | 4.1 | 4.3 | 1.6 | 1.6 |
| December | 2.9 | 3.1 | 1.6 | 2.1 | 2.5 | 2.7 | 4.6 | 3.6 | 3.9 | 4.1 | 1.8 | 1.8 |
| **2006** | | | | | | | | | | | | |
| January | 3.1 | 3.3 | 1.8 | 2.3 | 2.4 | 2.4 | 4.9 | 3.8 | 4.1 | 4.2 | 1.7 | 1.7 |
| February | 3.0 | 3.3 | 1.7 | 2.5 | 2.6 | 2.6 | 4.2 | 4.0 | 4.3 | 4.5 | 1.7 | 1.7 |
| March | 3.2 | 3.4 | 2.5 | 2.5 | 2.7 | 2.7 | 4.2 | 4.0 | 4.3 | 4.6 | 1.9 | 1.9 |
| April | 3.3 | 3.6 | 2.9 | 2.7 | 2.8 | 2.6 | 3.9 | 4.0 | 4.7 | 4.9 | 2.0 | 1.9 |
| May | 3.1 | 3.4 | 2.5 | 2.2 | 2.9 | 2.8 | 4.2 | 3.8 | 4.1 | 4.4 | 1.8 | 1.9 |
| June | 3.1 | 3.3 | 2.9 | 2.5 | 2.6 | 2.6 | 3.9 | 3.9 | 3.9 | 4.0 | 1.9 | 1.9 |
| July | 3.0 | 3.1 | 3.1 | 2.4 | 2.6 | 2.4 | 3.3 | 3.4 | 4.0 | 4.1 | 2.2 | 2.2 |
| August | 3.2 | 3.4 | 2.7 | 2.4 | 2.8 | 2.9 | 4.0 | 4.1 | 3.9 | 4.2 | 2.1 | 2.1 |
| September | 3.2 | 3.4 | 2.2 | 2.5 | 3.1 | 2.8 | 3.8 | 4.1 | 4.1 | 3.9 | 2.1 | 2.2 |
| October | 3.2 | 3.4 | 2.0 | 2.5 | 2.9 | 2.8 | 3.8 | 4.2 | 4.4 | 4.3 | 1.8 | 1.9 |
| November | 3.1 | 3.3 | 1.3 | 2.0 | 2.7 | 2.7 | 4.1 | 4.1 | 4.7 | 4.8 | 1.9 | 1.9 |
| December | 3.0 | 3.3 | 1.2 | 2.2 | 2.9 | 3.1 | 3.7 | 4.0 | 4.2 | 4.4 | 1.8 | 1.9 |
| **2007** | | | | | | | | | | | | |
| January | 3.3 | 3.5 | 3.2 | 2.5 | 3.2 | 2.9 | 4.3 | 3.9 | 4.0 | 4.0 | 1.9 | 2.0 |
| February | 3.1 | 3.4 | 3.5 | 2.4 | 2.7 | 2.8 | 3.9 | 3.7 | 4.0 | 4.1 | 1.9 | 2.0 |
| March | 3.3 | 3.5 | 2.6 | 2.5 | 3.0 | 2.7 | 4.3 | 3.9 | 4.3 | 4.4 | 2.0 | 2.0 |
| April | 3.4 | 3.6 | 2.8 | 2.7 | 3.3 | 2.6 | 4.6 | 4.0 | 4.0 | 4.0 | 2.0 | 2.0 |
| May | 3.2 | 3.4 | 2.7 | 2.6 | 2.7 | 2.3 | 4.1 | 4.1 | 4.3 | 4.4 | 1.9 | 2.0 |
| June | 3.2 | 3.5 | 2.2 | 2.6 | 2.9 | 2.8 | 4.1 | 4.2 | 4.2 | 4.4 | 2.0 | 2.0 |
| July | 3.1 | 3.4 | 2.6 | 2.7 | 3.0 | 2.8 | 3.7 | 3.6 | 4.2 | 4.5 | 2.0 | 2.0 |
| August | 3.2 | 3.4 | 2.1 | 2.4 | 2.9 | 2.5 | 4.0 | 4.1 | 4.5 | 4.8 | 2.1 | 2.1 |
| September | 3.2 | 3.4 | 1.6 | 2.3 | 2.9 | 2.6 | 4.0 | 4.4 | 4.5 | 4.7 | 2.0 | 2.0 |
| October | 3.0 | 3.2 | 1.6 | 2.1 | 2.7 | 2.3 | 4.1 | 3.8 | 4.4 | 4.6 | 1.8 | 1.9 |
| November | 2.9 | 3.1 | 1.1 | 1.9 | 2.6 | 2.7 | 4.0 | 3.9 | 4.4 | 4.4 | 1.9 | 1.9 |
| December | 2.9 | 3.1 | 1.3 | 1.9 | 2.6 | 2.5 | 4.1 | 3.8 | 4.1 | 4.5 | 1.8 | 1.8 |
| **2008** | | | | | | | | | | | | |
| January | 3.0 | 3.2 | 1.7 | 2.1 | 2.7 | 2.4 | 4.0 | 3.7 | 4.1 | 4.3 | 1.8 | 1.8 |
| February | 2.8 | 3.0 | 1.5 | 1.9 | 2.5 | 2.3 | 4.0 | 4.0 | 3.9 | 4.0 | 1.9 | 1.9 |
| March | 2.8 | 3.0 | 1.3 | 1.8 | 2.3 | 2.4 | 4.1 | 4.0 | 3.9 | 4.0 | 1.9 | 1.8 |
| April | 2.9 | 3.1 | 1.6 | 2.2 | 2.4 | 2.5 | 4.1 | 3.8 | 3.9 | 4.0 | 1.7 | 1.8 |
| May | 2.8 | 2.9 | 2.3 | 2.1 | 2.3 | 2.4 | 3.4 | 3.7 | 3.8 | 3.9 | 2.1 | 2.0 |
| June | 2.7 | 2.8 | 1.6 | 1.8 | 2.0 | 1.9 | 4.0 | 3.7 | 3.5 | 3.7 | 1.9 | 1.9 |
| July | 2.7 | 2.9 | 1.7 | 1.9 | 2.3 | 2.4 | 3.6 | 3.7 | 3.2 | 3.4 | 1.8 | 1.7 |
| August | 2.6 | 2.8 | 1.2 | 2.0 | 2.2 | 2.3 | 3.5 | 3.5 | 2.9 | 2.8 | 1.8 | 1.7 |
| September | 2.3 | 2.4 | 1.7 | 1.6 | 1.8 | 1.7 | 3.4 | 3.1 | 2.9 | 3.1 | 1.8 | 1.8 |
| October | 2.4 | 2.5 | 1.0 | 1.8 | 2.1 | 2.4 | 3.2 | 3.3 | 2.8 | 2.9 | 1.7 | 1.6 |
| November | 2.1 | 2.2 | 0.7 | 1.1 | 1.8 | 2.3 | 3.0 | 3.1 | 2.4 | 2.5 | 1.6 | 1.7 |
| December | 2.1 | 2.2 | 0.7 | 1.1 | 1.6 | 1.9 | 3.2 | 3.2 | 2.3 | 2.4 | 1.2 | 1.3 |
| **2009** | | | | | | | | | | | | |
| January | 2.0 | 2.1 | 0.6 | 0.9 | 1.7 | 2.2 | 3.1 | 3.0 | 1.7 | 1.8 | 1.7 | 1.5 |
| February | 2.1 | 2.2 | 1.0 | 1.0 | 1.7 | 2.0 | 3.1 | 2.8 | 2.3 | 2.5 | 1.5 | 1.4 |
| March | 1.8 | 1.9 | 0.7 | 0.9 | 1.5 | 1.7 | 2.5 | 2.5 | 2.0 | 2.2 | 1.6 | 1.2 |
| April | 1.8 | 1.8 | 0.4 | 0.9 | 1.3 | 1.4 | 2.4 | 2.6 | 2.1 | 2.2 | 1.6 | 1.5 |
| May | 1.8 | 1.9 | 0.7 | 0.8 | 1.8 | 2.1 | 2.4 | 2.7 | 2.0 | 2.1 | 1.3 | 1.3 |
| June | 1.8 | 1.9 | 0.9 | 0.8 | 1.6 | 1.8 | 2.4 | 2.7 | 2.0 | 2.1 | 1.4 | 1.4 |
| July | 1.7 | 1.7 | 1.0 | 0.9 | 1.1 | 1.1 | 2.6 | 2.7 | 1.7 | 1.8 | 1.2 | 1.1 |
| August | 1.7 | 1.8 | 1.0 | 1.1 | 1.6 | 1.6 | 2.1 | 2.7 | 1.5 | 1.6 | 1.4 | 1.4 |
| September | 1.9 | 2.0 | 1.1 | 1.1 | 1.6 | 1.9 | 2.6 | 2.8 | 2.2 | 2.3 | 1.2 | 1.1 |
| October | 1.8 | 1.8 | 1.0 | 1.3 | 1.2 | 1.3 | 2.2 | 2.7 | 1.9 | 2.0 | 1.8 | 1.4 |
| November | 1.8 | 1.8 | 0.8 | 1.1 | 1.3 | 1.6 | 2.5 | 2.6 | 2.0 | 2.1 | 1.5 | 1.2 |
| December | 1.8 | 1.9 | 1.0 | 1.3 | 1.4 | 1.7 | 2.6 | 2.7 | 1.9 | 2.1 | 1.4 | 1.2 |
| **2010** | | | | | | | | | | | | |
| January | 2.0 | 2.1 | 0.9 | 1.2 | 1.5 | 1.6 | 2.4 | 2.9 | 2.0 | 2.2 | 1.7 | 1.2 |
| February | 1.9 | 2.0 | 1.1 | 1.3 | 1.7 | 1.9 | 2.3 | 2.6 | 1.8 | 2.0 | 1.5 | 1.1 |
| March | 2.0 | 2.1 | 1.4 | 1.3 | 2.0 | 2.3 | 2.5 | 2.6 | 1.7 | 1.7 | 1.8 | 1.3 |
| April | 2.4 | 2.3 | 1.8 | 1.6 | 1.7 | 1.8 | 3.0 | 2.6 | 2.0 | 2.1 | 2.8 | 1.4 |
| May | 2.2 | 2.3 | 1.5 | 1.7 | 1.7 | 1.8 | 3.4 | 2.5 | 2.2 | 2.1 | 1.6 | 1.2 |
| June | 2.0 | 2.1 | 1.5 | 1.8 | 1.7 | 1.8 | 2.8 | 2.4 | 2.1 | 2.0 | 1.3 | 1.1 |
| July | 2.2 | 2.4 | 2.1 | 1.9 | 1.6 | 1.7 | 3.2 | 2.6 | 2.3 | 2.3 | 1.4 | 1.2 |
| August | 2.2 | 2.3 | 0.9 | 1.6 | 1.6 | 1.6 | 3.5 | 2.3 | 2.6 | 2.7 | 1.5 | 1.2 |
| September | 2.1 | 2.2 | 1.3 | 1.7 | 1.7 | 1.5 | 3.3 | 2.5 | 2.1 | 2.1 | 1.4 | 1.2 |
| October | 2.3 | 2.4 | 1.2 | 1.7 | 1.7 | 1.7 | 3.5 | 3.0 | 2.2 | 2.4 | 1.5 | 1.4 |
| November | 2.2 | 2.4 | 1.2 | 1.7 | 1.6 | 1.8 | 3.7 | 2.6 | 2.2 | 2.3 | 1.3 | 1.1 |
| December | 2.1 | 2.2 | 0.6 | 1.4 | 1.8 | 2.0 | 3.4 | 2.6 | 2.2 | 2.3 | 1.7 | 1.5 |

[1]Includes natural resources and mining, information, financial activities, and other services, not shown separately.
[2]Includes wholesale trade and transportation, warehousing, and utilities, not shown separately.
[3]Includes arts, entertainment, and recreation, not shown separately.
[4]Includes federal government, not shown separately.

## Table 7-4. Job Openings Levels and Rates, by Industry, 2005–October 2016—*Continued*

(Seasonally adjusted, levels in thousands, rates per 100.)

| Year and month | Total nonfarm[1] | Total private[1] | Construction | Manufacturing | Trade, transportation, and utilities[2] | Retail trade | Professional and business services | Education and health services | Leisure and hospitality[3] | Accommodation and food services | Government[4] | State and local government |
|---|---|---|---|---|---|---|---|---|---|---|---|---|
| **2011** | | | | | | | | | | | | |
| January | 2 939 | 2 611 | 62 | 228 | 510 | 288 | 474 | 531 | 320 | 286 | 328 | 267 |
| February | 3 056 | 2 754 | 44 | 207 | 518 | 270 | 598 | 549 | 407 | 353 | 302 | 248 |
| March | 3 130 | 2 797 | 66 | 220 | 513 | 272 | 603 | 567 | 374 | 331 | 333 | 272 |
| April | 3 287 | 2 948 | 121 | 247 | 577 | 326 | 578 | 600 | 317 | 284 | 339 | 290 |
| May | 3 114 | 2 826 | 120 | 239 | 534 | 311 | 592 | 580 | 328 | 292 | 289 | 241 |
| June | 3 224 | 2 877 | 65 | 222 | 546 | 353 | 624 | 607 | 360 | 303 | 347 | 297 |
| July | 3 475 | 3 161 | 88 | 258 | 599 | 340 | 770 | 622 | 321 | 249 | 314 | 251 |
| August | 3 168 | 2 839 | 98 | 233 | 509 | 328 | 598 | 615 | 372 | 333 | 330 | 284 |
| September | 3 495 | 3 108 | 83 | 244 | 577 | 325 | 743 | 600 | 419 | 361 | 387 | 336 |
| October | 3 421 | 3 059 | 76 | 242 | 600 | 345 | 617 | 633 | 407 | 356 | 362 | 297 |
| November | 3 153 | 2 820 | 62 | 210 | 550 | 324 | 541 | 639 | 414 | 361 | 333 | 287 |
| December | 3 369 | 3 023 | 43 | 218 | 548 | 334 | 776 | 612 | 418 | 385 | 346 | 297 |
| **2012** | | | | | | | | | | | | |
| January | 3 664 | 3 320 | 79 | 254 | 626 | 352 | 770 | 672 | 448 | 381 | 344 | 289 |
| February | 3 501 | 3 115 | 57 | 248 | 610 | 359 | 640 | 688 | 404 | 347 | 386 | 324 |
| March | 3 852 | 3 441 | 93 | 316 | 615 | 376 | 820 | 694 | 423 | 375 | 411 | 329 |
| April | 3 663 | 3 287 | 123 | 273 | 579 | 330 | 627 | 695 | 468 | 388 | 376 | 299 |
| May | 3 706 | 3 337 | 83 | 317 | 593 | 350 | 695 | 705 | 450 | 394 | 369 | 311 |
| June | 3 792 | 3 417 | 98 | 323 | 570 | 321 | 738 | 746 | 464 | 414 | 376 | 304 |
| July | 3 694 | 3 331 | 81 | 302 | 590 | 329 | 705 | 698 | 467 | 409 | 363 | 313 |
| August | 3 655 | 3 241 | 116 | 263 | 598 | 365 | 751 | 623 | 426 | 373 | 413 | 329 |
| September | 3 533 | 3 170 | 83 | 255 | 605 | 361 | 620 | 718 | 373 | 322 | 364 | 293 |
| October | 3 713 | 3 338 | 103 | 272 | 619 | 386 | 653 | 706 | 445 | 397 | 374 | 301 |
| November | 3 556 | 3 212 | 69 | 221 | 670 | 464 | 621 | 697 | 484 | 430 | 344 | 290 |
| December | 3 576 | 3 198 | 68 | 235 | 633 | 395 | 610 | 703 | 485 | 420 | 378 | 314 |
| **2013** | | | | | | | | | | | | |
| January | 3 712 | 3 308 | 113 | 263 | 699 | 402 | 668 | 592 | 463 | 410 | 404 | 331 |
| February | 3 972 | 3 550 | 112 | 281 | 631 | 399 | 754 | 690 | 491 | 435 | 422 | 355 |
| March | 3 901 | 3 505 | 108 | 271 | 648 | 415 | 709 | 709 | 495 | 435 | 396 | 337 |
| April | 3 962 | 3 525 | 138 | 261 | 724 | 440 | 684 | 728 | 470 | 419 | 437 | 360 |
| May | 3 886 | 3 463 | 122 | 243 | 739 | 483 | 645 | 677 | 463 | 420 | 423 | 375 |
| June | 3 913 | 3 534 | 139 | 215 | 810 | 576 | 637 | 682 | 489 | 444 | 379 | 335 |
| July | 3 915 | 3 541 | 116 | 262 | 758 | 474 | 602 | 684 | 523 | 474 | 374 | 324 |
| August | 3 921 | 3 535 | 128 | 285 | 725 | 445 | 683 | 707 | 544 | 469 | 386 | 346 |
| September | 3 985 | 3 606 | 116 | 264 | 785 | 487 | 714 | 663 | 544 | 481 | 379 | 331 |
| October | 4 104 | 3 711 | 130 | 315 | 700 | 449 | 792 | 670 | 538 | 454 | 394 | 348 |
| November | 3 878 | 3 515 | 103 | 246 | 727 | 448 | 718 | 678 | 563 | 480 | 363 | 315 |
| December | 3 742 | 3 413 | 84 | 254 | 696 | 440 | 692 | 614 | 573 | 493 | 329 | 285 |
| **2014** | | | | | | | | | | | | |
| January | 3 884 | 3 510 | 123 | 256 | 708 | 403 | 617 | 703 | 592 | 497 | 374 | 328 |
| February | 4 098 | 3 695 | 105 | 263 | 702 | 452 | 805 | 717 | 597 | 528 | 403 | 344 |
| March | 4 202 | 3 758 | 128 | 273 | 774 | 503 | 737 | 729 | 618 | 557 | 444 | 367 |
| April | 4 575 | 4 126 | 129 | 303 | 868 | 533 | 824 | 735 | 677 | 588 | 449 | 385 |
| May | 4 603 | 4 149 | 148 | 310 | 759 | 440 | 836 | 814 | 739 | 656 | 454 | 390 |
| June | 4 690 | 4 186 | 171 | 322 | 787 | 456 | 852 | 813 | 703 | 631 | 504 | 435 |
| July | 4 680 | 4 219 | 157 | 320 | 833 | 459 | 867 | 863 | 595 | 524 | 460 | 407 |
| August | 4 952 | 4 493 | 147 | 311 | 857 | 519 | 933 | 900 | 697 | 623 | 459 | 387 |
| September | 4 658 | 4 180 | 108 | 297 | 814 | 486 | 872 | 874 | 661 | 605 | 478 | 414 |
| October | 4 896 | 4 478 | 147 | 284 | 853 | 501 | 927 | 923 | 713 | 656 | 418 | 361 |
| November | 4 721 | 4 280 | 105 | 299 | 833 | 513 | 1 056 | 803 | 621 | 573 | 441 | 385 |
| December | 4 815 | 4 355 | 100 | 281 | 836 | 553 | 994 | 935 | 665 | 587 | 460 | 395 |
| **2015** | | | | | | | | | | | | |
| January | 4 972 | 4 456 | 137 | 306 | 845 | 469 | 890 | 903 | 756 | 689 | 516 | 447 |
| February | 5 131 | 4 595 | 152 | 300 | 883 | 539 | 920 | 952 | 745 | 680 | 536 | 443 |
| March | 5 180 | 4 660 | 177 | 311 | 877 | 519 | 1 062 | 877 | 745 | 644 | 520 | 435 |
| April | 5 580 | 5 083 | 170 | 337 | 978 | 538 | 1 116 | 1 056 | 726 | 659 | 496 | 418 |
| May | 5 386 | 4 852 | 177 | 330 | 942 | 539 | 1 134 | 977 | 717 | 646 | 534 | 459 |
| June | 5 168 | 4 718 | 156 | 284 | 898 | 534 | 1 143 | 1 015 | 691 | 630 | 450 | 385 |
| July | 5 788 | 5 243 | 151 | 366 | 1 037 | 604 | 1 125 | 1 133 | 743 | 678 | 546 | 477 |
| August | 5 308 | 4 824 | 151 | 321 | 920 | 561 | 1 054 | 1 018 | 707 | 661 | 483 | 418 |
| September | 5 360 | 4 880 | 104 | 312 | 954 | 623 | 1 111 | 1 080 | 706 | 656 | 480 | 424 |
| October | 5 422 | 4 938 | 129 | 311 | 931 | 563 | 1 149 | 1 050 | 737 | 676 | 484 | 423 |
| November | 5 198 | 4 725 | 101 | 238 | 861 | 527 | 1 126 | 1 113 | 732 | 668 | 473 | 401 |
| December | 5 281 | 4 786 | 124 | 317 | 822 | 538 | 1 034 | 1 075 | 710 | 648 | 495 | 415 |
| **2016** | | | | | | | | | | | | |
| January | 5 604 | 5 137 | 157 | 336 | 979 | 602 | 1 088 | 1 129 | 745 | 677 | 467 | 387 |
| February | 5 608 | 5 132 | 201 | 320 | 1 026 | 649 | 1 101 | 1 047 | 751 | 682 | 475 | 387 |
| March | 5 670 | 5 175 | 215 | 337 | 975 | 605 | 1 145 | 1 042 | 781 | 701 | 494 | 404 |
| April | 5 845 | 5 311 | 193 | 397 | 1 060 | 589 | 961 | 1 112 | 793 | 717 | 534 | 449 |
| May | 5 514 | 4 986 | 193 | 350 | 970 | 605 | 1 032 | 1 073 | 791 | 704 | 528 | 435 |
| June | 5 643 | 5 115 | 187 | 361 | 986 | 588 | 1 104 | 1 127 | 741 | 651 | 527 | 441 |
| July | 5 831 | 5 284 | 225 | 379 | 1 046 | 623 | 1 212 | 1 073 | 747 | 653 | 546 | 457 |
| August | 5 453 | 4 941 | 192 | 326 | 997 | 628 | 1 022 | 1 041 | 749 | 675 | 511 | 424 |
| September | 5 631 | 5 112 | 221 | 328 | 1 020 | 663 | 1 113 | 1 072 | 710 | 642 | 519 | 419 |
| October | 5 451 | 4 951 | 193 | 320 | 1 024 | 653 | 980 | 1 159 | 670 | 589 | 501 | 419 |

[1]Includes natural resources and mining, information, financial activities, and other services, not shown separately.
[2]Includes wholesale trade and transportation, warehousing, and utilities, not shown separately.
[3]Includes arts, entertainment, and recreation, not shown separately.
[4]Includes federal government, not shown separately.

## Table 7-4. Job Openings Levels and Rates, by Industry, 2005–October 2016—*Continued*

(Seasonally adjusted, levels in thousands, rates per 100.)

| Year and month | Rate | | | | | | | | | | | |
|---|---|---|---|---|---|---|---|---|---|---|---|---|
| | Total[1] | Total private[1] | Construction | Manufacturing | Trade, transportation, and utilities[2] | Retail trade | Professional and business services | Education and health services | Leisure and hospitality[3] | Accommodation and food services | Government[4] | State and local government |
| **2011** | | | | | | | | | | | | |
| January | 2.2 | 2.3 | 1.1 | 1.9 | 2.0 | 1.9 | 2.7 | 2.6 | 2.4 | 2.5 | 1.5 | 1.4 |
| February | 2.3 | 2.5 | 0.8 | 1.7 | 2.0 | 1.8 | 3.4 | 2.7 | 3.0 | 3.0 | 1.3 | 1.3 |
| March | 2.3 | 2.5 | 1.2 | 1.9 | 2.0 | 1.8 | 3.4 | 2.7 | 2.7 | 2.8 | 1.5 | 1.4 |
| April | 2.4 | 2.6 | 2.2 | 2.1 | 2.3 | 2.2 | 3.2 | 2.9 | 2.3 | 2.4 | 1.5 | 1.5 |
| May | 2.3 | 2.5 | 2.1 | 2.0 | 2.1 | 2.1 | 3.3 | 2.8 | 2.4 | 2.5 | 1.3 | 1.2 |
| June | 2.4 | 2.6 | 1.2 | 1.9 | 2.1 | 2.3 | 3.5 | 2.9 | 2.6 | 2.6 | 1.5 | 1.5 |
| July | 2.6 | 2.8 | 1.6 | 2.2 | 2.3 | 2.3 | 4.3 | 3.0 | 2.3 | 2.1 | 1.4 | 1.3 |
| August | 2.3 | 2.5 | 1.7 | 1.9 | 2.0 | 2.2 | 3.3 | 2.9 | 2.7 | 2.8 | 1.5 | 1.5 |
| September | 2.6 | 2.7 | 1.5 | 2.0 | 2.2 | 2.2 | 4.1 | 2.9 | 3.0 | 3.0 | 1.7 | 1.7 |
| October | 2.5 | 2.7 | 1.3 | 2.0 | 2.3 | 2.3 | 3.4 | 3.0 | 2.9 | 3.0 | 1.6 | 1.5 |
| November | 2.3 | 2.5 | 1.1 | 1.8 | 2.1 | 2.1 | 3.0 | 3.0 | 3.0 | 3.0 | 1.5 | 1.5 |
| December | 2.5 | 2.7 | 0.8 | 1.8 | 2.1 | 2.2 | 4.2 | 2.9 | 3.0 | 3.2 | 1.6 | 1.5 |
| **2012** | | | | | | | | | | | | |
| January | 2.7 | 2.9 | 1.4 | 2.1 | 2.4 | 2.3 | 4.2 | 3.2 | 3.2 | 3.2 | 1.5 | 1.5 |
| February | 2.6 | 2.7 | 1.0 | 2.0 | 2.3 | 2.4 | 3.5 | 3.2 | 2.9 | 2.9 | 1.7 | 1.7 |
| March | 2.8 | 3.0 | 1.6 | 2.6 | 2.4 | 2.5 | 4.4 | 3.2 | 3.0 | 3.1 | 1.8 | 1.7 |
| April | 2.7 | 2.9 | 2.1 | 2.2 | 2.2 | 2.2 | 3.4 | 3.2 | 3.3 | 3.2 | 1.7 | 1.5 |
| May | 2.7 | 2.9 | 1.5 | 2.6 | 2.3 | 2.3 | 3.7 | 3.3 | 3.2 | 3.2 | 1.7 | 1.6 |
| June | 2.8 | 3.0 | 1.7 | 2.6 | 2.2 | 2.1 | 4.0 | 3.5 | 3.3 | 3.4 | 1.7 | 1.6 |
| July | 2.7 | 2.9 | 1.4 | 2.5 | 2.3 | 2.2 | 3.8 | 3.3 | 3.3 | 3.4 | 1.6 | 1.6 |
| August | 2.6 | 2.8 | 2.0 | 2.2 | 2.3 | 2.4 | 4.0 | 2.9 | 3.0 | 3.1 | 1.9 | 1.7 |
| September | 2.6 | 2.7 | 1.4 | 2.1 | 2.3 | 2.4 | 3.3 | 3.3 | 2.6 | 2.6 | 1.6 | 1.5 |
| October | 2.7 | 2.9 | 1.8 | 2.2 | 2.4 | 2.5 | 3.5 | 3.3 | 3.1 | 3.2 | 1.7 | 1.6 |
| November | 2.6 | 2.8 | 1.2 | 1.8 | 2.5 | 3.0 | 3.3 | 3.2 | 3.4 | 3.5 | 1.5 | 1.5 |
| December | 2.6 | 2.7 | 1.2 | 1.9 | 2.4 | 2.6 | 3.3 | 3.2 | 3.4 | 3.4 | 1.7 | 1.6 |
| **2013** | | | | | | | | | | | | |
| January | 2.7 | 2.8 | 1.9 | 2.1 | 2.7 | 2.6 | 3.5 | 2.8 | 3.2 | 3.3 | 1.8 | 1.7 |
| February | 2.8 | 3.0 | 1.9 | 2.3 | 2.4 | 2.6 | 4.0 | 3.2 | 3.4 | 3.5 | 1.9 | 1.8 |
| March | 2.8 | 3.0 | 1.8 | 2.2 | 2.5 | 2.7 | 3.7 | 3.3 | 3.4 | 3.5 | 1.8 | 1.7 |
| April | 2.8 | 3.0 | 2.3 | 2.1 | 2.7 | 2.9 | 3.6 | 3.3 | 3.2 | 3.3 | 2.0 | 1.9 |
| May | 2.8 | 2.9 | 2.1 | 2.0 | 2.8 | 3.1 | 3.4 | 3.1 | 3.2 | 3.3 | 1.9 | 1.9 |
| June | 2.8 | 3.0 | 2.3 | 1.8 | 3.0 | 3.7 | 3.3 | 3.1 | 3.3 | 3.5 | 1.7 | 1.7 |
| July | 2.8 | 3.0 | 1.9 | 2.1 | 2.8 | 3.0 | 3.1 | 3.1 | 3.5 | 3.7 | 1.7 | 1.7 |
| August | 2.8 | 3.0 | 2.1 | 2.3 | 2.7 | 2.9 | 3.5 | 3.2 | 3.7 | 3.7 | 1.7 | 1.8 |
| September | 2.8 | 3.0 | 1.9 | 2.2 | 2.9 | 3.1 | 3.7 | 3.0 | 3.7 | 3.8 | 1.7 | 1.7 |
| October | 2.9 | 3.1 | 2.2 | 2.5 | 2.6 | 2.9 | 4.1 | 3.1 | 3.6 | 3.6 | 1.8 | 1.8 |
| November | 2.7 | 3.0 | 1.7 | 2.0 | 2.7 | 2.9 | 3.7 | 3.1 | 3.8 | 3.7 | 1.6 | 1.6 |
| December | 2.7 | 2.9 | 1.4 | 2.1 | 2.6 | 2.8 | 3.6 | 2.8 | 3.8 | 3.8 | 1.5 | 1.5 |
| **2014** | | | | | | | | | | | | |
| January | 2.7 | 2.9 | 2.0 | 2.1 | 2.6 | 2.6 | 3.2 | 3.2 | 3.9 | 3.9 | 1.7 | 1.7 |
| February | 2.9 | 3.1 | 1.7 | 2.1 | 2.6 | 2.9 | 4.1 | 3.3 | 4.0 | 4.1 | 1.8 | 1.8 |
| March | 3.0 | 3.1 | 2.1 | 2.2 | 2.9 | 3.2 | 3.8 | 3.3 | 4.1 | 4.3 | 2.0 | 1.9 |
| April | 3.2 | 3.4 | 2.1 | 2.4 | 3.2 | 3.4 | 4.2 | 3.3 | 4.4 | 4.5 | 2.0 | 2.0 |
| May | 3.2 | 3.4 | 2.4 | 2.5 | 2.8 | 2.8 | 4.2 | 3.7 | 4.8 | 5.0 | 2.0 | 2.0 |
| June | 3.3 | 3.5 | 2.7 | 2.6 | 2.9 | 2.9 | 4.3 | 3.7 | 4.6 | 4.8 | 2.3 | 2.2 |
| July | 3.3 | 3.5 | 2.5 | 2.6 | 3.1 | 2.9 | 4.3 | 3.9 | 3.9 | 4.0 | 2.1 | 2.1 |
| August | 3.4 | 3.7 | 2.3 | 2.5 | 3.1 | 3.3 | 4.6 | 4.0 | 4.5 | 4.7 | 2.1 | 2.0 |
| September | 3.2 | 3.4 | 1.7 | 2.4 | 3.0 | 3.1 | 4.3 | 3.9 | 4.3 | 4.6 | 2.1 | 2.1 |
| October | 3.4 | 3.7 | 2.3 | 2.3 | 3.1 | 3.1 | 4.6 | 4.1 | 4.6 | 4.9 | 1.9 | 1.8 |
| November | 3.3 | 3.5 | 1.6 | 2.4 | 3.0 | 3.2 | 5.2 | 3.6 | 4.0 | 4.3 | 2.0 | 2.0 |
| December | 3.3 | 3.5 | 1.6 | 2.2 | 3.0 | 3.5 | 4.9 | 4.1 | 4.3 | 4.4 | 2.1 | 2.0 |
| **2015** | | | | | | | | | | | | |
| January | 3.4 | 3.6 | 2.1 | 2.4 | 3.1 | 2.9 | 4.4 | 4.0 | 4.8 | 5.1 | 2.3 | 2.3 |
| February | 3.5 | 3.7 | 2.3 | 2.4 | 3.2 | 3.4 | 4.5 | 4.2 | 4.7 | 5.0 | 2.4 | 2.3 |
| March | 3.5 | 3.8 | 2.7 | 2.5 | 3.2 | 3.2 | 5.2 | 3.9 | 4.7 | 4.8 | 2.3 | 2.2 |
| April | 3.8 | 4.1 | 2.6 | 2.7 | 3.5 | 3.3 | 5.4 | 4.6 | 4.6 | 4.9 | 2.2 | 2.1 |
| May | 3.7 | 3.9 | 2.7 | 2.6 | 3.4 | 3.3 | 5.5 | 4.3 | 4.5 | 4.8 | 2.4 | 2.3 |
| June | 3.5 | 3.8 | 2.4 | 2.3 | 3.2 | 3.3 | 5.5 | 4.4 | 4.4 | 4.6 | 2.0 | 2.0 |
| July | 3.9 | 4.2 | 2.3 | 2.9 | 3.7 | 3.7 | 5.4 | 4.9 | 4.7 | 5.0 | 2.4 | 2.4 |
| August | 3.6 | 3.9 | 2.3 | 2.5 | 3.3 | 3.5 | 5.1 | 4.4 | 4.5 | 4.8 | 2.1 | 2.1 |
| September | 3.6 | 3.9 | 1.6 | 2.5 | 3.4 | 3.8 | 5.3 | 4.6 | 4.4 | 4.8 | 2.1 | 2.2 |
| October | 3.7 | 3.9 | 1.9 | 2.5 | 3.3 | 3.5 | 5.5 | 4.5 | 4.6 | 4.9 | 2.1 | 2.1 |
| November | 3.5 | 3.8 | 1.5 | 1.9 | 3.1 | 3.2 | 5.4 | 4.7 | 4.6 | 4.8 | 2.1 | 2.0 |
| December | 3.6 | 3.8 | 1.8 | 2.5 | 2.9 | 3.3 | 4.9 | 4.6 | 4.4 | 4.7 | 2.2 | 2.1 |
| **2016** | | | | | | | | | | | | |
| January | 3.8 | 4.1 | 2.3 | 2.6 | 3.5 | 3.7 | 5.2 | 4.8 | 4.6 | 4.9 | 2.1 | 2.0 |
| February | 3.8 | 4.1 | 2.9 | 2.5 | 3.6 | 3.9 | 5.2 | 4.4 | 4.6 | 4.9 | 2.1 | 2.0 |
| March | 3.8 | 4.1 | 3.1 | 2.7 | 3.5 | 3.7 | 5.4 | 4.4 | 4.8 | 5.0 | 2.2 | 2.0 |
| April | 3.9 | 4.2 | 2.8 | 3.1 | 3.7 | 3.6 | 4.6 | 4.7 | 4.9 | 5.1 | 2.4 | 2.3 |
| May | 3.7 | 3.9 | 2.8 | 2.8 | 3.4 | 3.7 | 4.9 | 4.5 | 4.9 | 5.1 | 2.3 | 2.2 |
| June | 3.8 | 4.0 | 2.7 | 2.8 | 3.5 | 3.6 | 5.2 | 4.7 | 4.6 | 4.7 | 2.3 | 2.2 |
| July | 3.9 | 4.1 | 3.3 | 3.0 | 3.7 | 3.8 | 5.6 | 4.5 | 4.6 | 4.7 | 2.4 | 2.3 |
| August | 3.6 | 3.9 | 2.8 | 2.6 | 3.5 | 3.8 | 4.8 | 4.4 | 4.6 | 4.8 | 2.3 | 2.1 |
| September | 3.7 | 4.0 | 3.2 | 2.6 | 3.6 | 4.0 | 5.2 | 4.5 | 4.4 | 4.6 | 2.3 | 2.1 |
| October | 3.6 | 3.9 | 2.8 | 2.5 | 3.6 | 3.9 | 4.6 | 4.8 | 4.1 | 4.2 | 2.2 | 2.1 |

[1] Includes natural resources and mining, information, financial activities, and other services, not shown separately.
[2] Includes wholesale trade and transportation, warehousing, and utilities, not shown separately.
[3] Includes arts, entertainment, and recreation, not shown separately.
[4] Includes federal government, not shown separately.

## Table 7-5. Hires Levels[1] and Rates,[2] by Industry, 2005–October 2016

(Seasonally adjusted, levels in thousands, rates per 100.)

| Year and month | Level[3] | | | | | | | | | | | |
|---|---|---|---|---|---|---|---|---|---|---|---|---|
| | Total[4] | Total private[4] | Construction | Manufacturing | Trade, transportation, and utilities[5] | Retail trade | Professional and business services | Education and health services | Leisure and hospitality[6] | Accommodation and food services | Government[7] | State and local government |
| **2005** | | | | | | | | | | | | |
| January | 5 207 | 4 876 | 455 | 358 | 1 103 | 761 | 974 | 494 | 904 | 767 | 331 | 293 |
| February | 5 273 | 4 960 | 493 | 367 | 1 132 | 768 | 1 069 | 498 | 853 | 731 | 314 | 278 |
| March | 5 216 | 4 910 | 439 | 369 | 1 155 | 823 | 1 018 | 522 | 872 | 753 | 306 | 268 |
| April | 5 270 | 4 959 | 507 | 370 | 1 128 | 785 | 1 007 | 522 | 875 | 738 | 312 | 278 |
| May | 5 298 | 4 988 | 499 | 361 | 1 147 | 796 | 1 011 | 513 | 870 | 741 | 309 | 271 |
| June | 5 332 | 5 036 | 474 | 348 | 1 152 | 802 | 1 099 | 511 | 928 | 777 | 296 | 260 |
| July | 5 275 | 4 922 | 416 | 377 | 1 128 | 803 | 1 041 | 503 | 916 | 776 | 352 | 318 |
| August | 5 410 | 5 103 | 523 | 373 | 1 144 | 814 | 1 077 | 515 | 911 | 776 | 308 | 269 |
| September | 5 427 | 5 110 | 527 | 387 | 1 113 | 776 | 1 053 | 543 | 936 | 775 | 318 | 273 |
| October | 4 988 | 4 676 | 492 | 370 | 1 061 | 726 | 863 | 499 | 873 | 754 | 312 | 277 |
| November | 5 308 | 4 967 | 490 | 376 | 1 123 | 716 | 944 | 512 | 944 | 826 | 340 | 296 |
| December | 5 103 | 4 780 | 475 | 372 | 1 097 | 735 | 897 | 510 | 903 | 784 | 323 | 277 |
| **2006** | | | | | | | | | | | | |
| January | 5 196 | 4 884 | 479 | 376 | 1 089 | 764 | 977 | 494 | 944 | 831 | 312 | 265 |
| February | 5 329 | 4 988 | 467 | 370 | 1 156 | 807 | 898 | 500 | 1 018 | 903 | 341 | 290 |
| March | 5 372 | 5 005 | 489 | 421 | 1 121 | 789 | 923 | 495 | 979 | 855 | 366 | 311 |
| April | 5 113 | 4 772 | 452 | 360 | 1 122 | 783 | 871 | 512 | 865 | 743 | 341 | 279 |
| May | 5 489 | 5 126 | 475 | 384 | 1 159 | 785 | 1 167 | 583 | 851 | 733 | 362 | 301 |
| June | 5 278 | 4 926 | 411 | 406 | 1 200 | 853 | 953 | 507 | 898 | 769 | 352 | 295 |
| July | 5 372 | 5 006 | 436 | 388 | 1 132 | 780 | 997 | 551 | 946 | 794 | 366 | 303 |
| August | 5 208 | 4 839 | 417 | 375 | 1 153 | 770 | 941 | 525 | 897 | 769 | 369 | 303 |
| September | 5 214 | 4 800 | 395 | 353 | 1 099 | 766 | 997 | 539 | 859 | 763 | 414 | 340 |
| October | 5 179 | 4 869 | 394 | 347 | 1 103 | 771 | 957 | 543 | 929 | 787 | 310 | 277 |
| November | 5 528 | 5 184 | 467 | 364 | 1 135 | 799 | 1 125 | 535 | 1 004 | 865 | 344 | 295 |
| December | 5 223 | 4 902 | 438 | 374 | 1 086 | 760 | 948 | 535 | 972 | 844 | 321 | 277 |
| **2007** | | | | | | | | | | | | |
| January | 5 245 | 4 883 | 419 | 380 | 1 134 | 808 | 972 | 541 | 919 | 780 | 362 | 297 |
| February | 5 202 | 4 832 | 318 | 400 | 1 120 | 792 | 987 | 523 | 960 | 819 | 370 | 303 |
| March | 5 380 | 5 012 | 466 | 377 | 1 132 | 778 | 992 | 544 | 916 | 783 | 368 | 288 |
| April | 5 158 | 4 776 | 382 | 361 | 1 076 | 725 | 904 | 542 | 964 | 829 | 383 | 304 |
| May | 5 268 | 4 893 | 404 | 370 | 1 102 | 766 | 962 | 552 | 920 | 787 | 375 | 293 |
| June | 5 187 | 4 814 | 429 | 378 | 1 071 | 717 | 885 | 557 | 934 | 799 | 373 | 296 |
| July | 5 075 | 4 725 | 401 | 367 | 1 048 | 716 | 921 | 509 | 915 | 793 | 350 | 261 |
| August | 5 106 | 4 719 | 405 | 367 | 1 040 | 734 | 921 | 542 | 905 | 783 | 388 | 300 |
| September | 5 145 | 4 755 | 389 | 367 | 1 077 | 759 | 922 | 543 | 911 | 769 | 390 | 303 |
| October | 5 227 | 4 908 | 402 | 392 | 1 119 | 775 | 973 | 548 | 934 | 799 | 319 | 290 |
| November | 5 162 | 4 830 | 374 | 388 | 1 127 | 818 | 973 | 561 | 902 | 760 | 332 | 286 |
| December | 4 968 | 4 615 | 371 | 344 | 1 014 | 746 | 927 | 501 | 905 | 770 | 354 | 305 |
| **2008** | | | | | | | | | | | | |
| January | 4 868 | 4 554 | 376 | 339 | 1 018 | 702 | 869 | 563 | 865 | 731 | 315 | 280 |
| February | 4 943 | 4 620 | 378 | 322 | 1 023 | 709 | 845 | 580 | 952 | 806 | 323 | 278 |
| March | 4 766 | 4 439 | 397 | 315 | 983 | 681 | 816 | 571 | 840 | 710 | 327 | 293 |
| April | 4 875 | 4 568 | 382 | 330 | 1 002 | 676 | 914 | 579 | 846 | 731 | 308 | 276 |
| May | 4 602 | 4 297 | 351 | 317 | 888 | 607 | 807 | 552 | 873 | 734 | 306 | 281 |
| June | 4 751 | 4 447 | 385 | 306 | 998 | 689 | 941 | 516 | 804 | 702 | 304 | 280 |
| July | 4 471 | 4 183 | 353 | 263 | 970 | 676 | 788 | 538 | 799 | 689 | 289 | 263 |
| August | 4 522 | 4 239 | 400 | 279 | 962 | 664 | 801 | 535 | 774 | 671 | 283 | 260 |
| September | 4 316 | 4 040 | 330 | 292 | 892 | 623 | 768 | 502 | 775 | 676 | 276 | 255 |
| October | 4 454 | 4 162 | 377 | 302 | 921 | 629 | 781 | 548 | 789 | 666 | 292 | 267 |
| November | 3 954 | 3 688 | 336 | 239 | 790 | 566 | 734 | 497 | 685 | 598 | 267 | 239 |
| December | 4 218 | 3 951 | 340 | 263 | 880 | 622 | 832 | 507 | 705 | 593 | 266 | 241 |
| **2009** | | | | | | | | | | | | |
| January | 4 158 | 3 832 | 353 | 210 | 829 | 547 | 751 | 525 | 688 | 582 | 326 | 289 |
| February | 4 011 | 3 753 | 330 | 238 | 770 | 530 | 734 | 530 | 698 | 603 | 257 | 232 |
| March | 3 730 | 3 489 | 311 | 231 | 807 | 532 | 607 | 488 | 633 | 559 | 241 | 217 |
| April | 3 853 | 3 483 | 326 | 212 | 789 | 563 | 669 | 477 | 631 | 546 | 370 | 223 |
| May | 3 793 | 3 541 | 332 | 196 | 810 | 550 | 668 | 472 | 677 | 588 | 253 | 232 |
| June | 3 675 | 3 415 | 256 | 201 | 715 | 497 | 634 | 499 | 643 | 544 | 260 | 231 |
| July | 3 854 | 3 617 | 324 | 245 | 725 | 489 | 692 | 510 | 654 | 521 | 237 | 201 |
| August | 3 744 | 3 466 | 253 | 244 | 764 | 530 | 618 | 535 | 650 | 535 | 277 | 254 |
| September | 3 859 | 3 626 | 319 | 268 | 819 | 545 | 684 | 523 | 621 | 516 | 233 | 213 |
| October | 3 767 | 3 450 | 309 | 237 | 712 | 489 | 695 | 506 | 607 | 504 | 316 | 275 |
| November | 3 992 | 3 718 | 316 | 240 | 787 | 513 | 839 | 489 | 669 | 554 | 274 | 240 |
| December | 3 806 | 3 565 | 341 | 234 | 761 | 523 | 671 | 495 | 620 | 529 | 241 | 216 |
| **2010** | | | | | | | | | | | | |
| January | 3 880 | 3 596 | 315 | 274 | 771 | 542 | 737 | 449 | 641 | 542 | 284 | 236 |
| February | 3 781 | 3 510 | 273 | 256 | 777 | 542 | 735 | 468 | 602 | 523 | 272 | 227 |
| March | 4 182 | 3 849 | 409 | 250 | 895 | 648 | 733 | 516 | 658 | 553 | 333 | 245 |
| April | 4 082 | 3 756 | 368 | 273 | 785 | 538 | 778 | 479 | 666 | 544 | 326 | 223 |
| May | 4 376 | 3 646 | 306 | 248 | 775 | 529 | 785 | 466 | 648 | 537 | 730 | 238 |
| June | 4 064 | 3 781 | 273 | 256 | 840 | 568 | 833 | 505 | 650 | 525 | 283 | 228 |
| July | 4 116 | 3 843 | 344 | 271 | 850 | 580 | 797 | 526 | 672 | 544 | 272 | 230 |
| August | 3 910 | 3 656 | 326 | 260 | 758 | 539 | 783 | 466 | 652 | 536 | 254 | 212 |
| September | 3 978 | 3 736 | 319 | 262 | 835 | 570 | 754 | 504 | 666 | 556 | 242 | 211 |
| October | 4 061 | 3 762 | 353 | 271 | 793 | 560 | 765 | 500 | 651 | 551 | 299 | 267 |
| November | 4 101 | 3 804 | 341 | 287 | 813 | 559 | 804 | 522 | 625 | 533 | 296 | 269 |
| December | 4 155 | 3 880 | 374 | 265 | 773 | 490 | 911 | 491 | 635 | 533 | 274 | 246 |

[1]Hires are the number of hires during the entire month.
[2]The hires rate is the number of hires during the entire month as a percent of total employment.
[3]Detail will not necessarily add to totals because of the independent seasonal adjustment of the various series.
[4]Includes natural resources and mining, information, financial activities, and other services, not shown separately.
[5]Includes wholesale trade and transportation, warehousing, and utilities, not shown separately.
[6]Includes arts, entertainment, and recreation, not shown separately.
[7]Includes federal government, not shown separately.
. . . = Not available.

## Table 7-5. Hires Levels[1] and Rates,[2] by Industry, 2005–October 2016—*Continued*

(Seasonally adjusted, levels in thousands, rates per 100.)

| Year and month | Rate | | | | | | | | | | | |
|---|---|---|---|---|---|---|---|---|---|---|---|---|
| | Total[4] | Total private[4] | Construction | Manufacturing | Trade, transportation, and utilities[5] | Retail trade | Professional and business services | Education and health services | Leisure and hospitality[6] | Accommodation and food services | Government[7] | State and local government |
| **2005** | | | | | | | | | | | | |
| January | 3.9 | 4.4 | 6.4 | 2.5 | 4.3 | 5.0 | 5.9 | 2.8 | 7.1 | 7.1 | 1.5 | 1.5 |
| February | 4.0 | 4.5 | 6.9 | 2.6 | 4.4 | 5.1 | 6.4 | 2.8 | 6.7 | 6.7 | 1.4 | 1.5 |
| March | 3.9 | 4.4 | 6.1 | 2.6 | 4.5 | 5.4 | 6.1 | 3.0 | 6.9 | 6.9 | 1.4 | 1.4 |
| April | 3.9 | 4.4 | 7.0 | 2.6 | 4.4 | 5.2 | 6.0 | 3.0 | 6.8 | 6.8 | 1.4 | 1.5 |
| May | 4.0 | 4.5 | 6.8 | 2.5 | 4.4 | 5.2 | 6.0 | 2.9 | 6.8 | 6.8 | 1.4 | 1.4 |
| June | 4.0 | 4.5 | 6.5 | 2.4 | 4.4 | 5.2 | 6.5 | 2.9 | 7.2 | 7.1 | 1.4 | 1.4 |
| July | 3.9 | 4.4 | 5.7 | 2.7 | 4.3 | 5.2 | 6.1 | 2.8 | 7.1 | 7.1 | 1.6 | 1.7 |
| August | 4.0 | 4.5 | 7.1 | 2.6 | 4.4 | 5.3 | 6.3 | 2.9 | 7.1 | 7.1 | 1.4 | 1.4 |
| September | 4.0 | 4.5 | 7.1 | 2.7 | 4.3 | 5.1 | 6.1 | 3.1 | 7.3 | 7.1 | 1.5 | 1.4 |
| October | 3.7 | 4.1 | 6.6 | 2.6 | 4.1 | 4.7 | 5.0 | 2.8 | 6.8 | 6.9 | 1.4 | 1.4 |
| November | 3.9 | 4.4 | 6.5 | 2.6 | 4.3 | 4.7 | 5.5 | 2.9 | 7.3 | 7.5 | 1.6 | 1.5 |
| December | 3.8 | 4.2 | 6.3 | 2.6 | 4.2 | 4.8 | 5.2 | 2.8 | 7.0 | 7.1 | 1.5 | 1.4 |
| **2006** | | | | | | | | | | | | |
| January | 3.8 | 4.3 | 6.3 | 2.6 | 4.2 | 5.0 | 5.6 | 2.8 | 7.3 | 7.5 | 1.4 | 1.4 |
| February | 3.9 | 4.4 | 6.1 | 2.6 | 4.4 | 5.3 | 5.2 | 2.8 | 7.8 | 8.2 | 1.6 | 1.5 |
| March | 3.9 | 4.4 | 6.4 | 3.0 | 4.3 | 5.1 | 5.3 | 2.7 | 7.5 | 7.7 | 1.7 | 1.6 |
| April | 3.8 | 4.2 | 5.9 | 2.5 | 4.3 | 5.1 | 5.0 | 2.8 | 6.6 | 6.7 | 1.6 | 1.5 |
| May | 4.0 | 4.5 | 6.2 | 2.7 | 4.4 | 5.1 | 6.7 | 3.2 | 6.5 | 6.6 | 1.7 | 1.6 |
| June | 3.9 | 4.3 | 5.3 | 2.9 | 4.6 | 5.6 | 5.4 | 2.8 | 6.9 | 6.9 | 1.6 | 1.5 |
| July | 3.9 | 4.4 | 5.7 | 2.7 | 4.3 | 5.1 | 5.7 | 3.0 | 7.2 | 7.1 | 1.7 | 1.6 |
| August | 3.8 | 4.2 | 5.4 | 2.6 | 4.4 | 5.0 | 5.3 | 2.9 | 6.8 | 6.9 | 1.7 | 1.6 |
| September | 3.8 | 4.2 | 5.1 | 2.5 | 4.2 | 5.0 | 5.6 | 3.0 | 6.5 | 6.8 | 1.9 | 1.8 |
| October | 3.8 | 4.2 | 5.1 | 2.5 | 4.2 | 5.0 | 5.4 | 3.0 | 7.0 | 7.0 | 1.4 | 1.4 |
| November | 4.0 | 4.5 | 6.1 | 2.6 | 4.3 | 5.2 | 6.3 | 2.9 | 7.6 | 7.7 | 1.6 | 1.5 |
| December | 3.8 | 4.3 | 5.7 | 2.7 | 4.1 | 4.9 | 5.3 | 2.9 | 7.3 | 7.4 | 1.5 | 1.4 |
| **2007** | | | | | | | | | | | | |
| January | 3.8 | 4.2 | 5.4 | 2.7 | 4.3 | 5.2 | 5.5 | 2.9 | 6.9 | 6.9 | 1.6 | 1.5 |
| February | 3.8 | 4.2 | 4.2 | 2.9 | 4.2 | 5.1 | 5.5 | 2.8 | 7.2 | 7.2 | 1.7 | 1.6 |
| March | 3.9 | 4.3 | 6.1 | 2.7 | 4.3 | 5.0 | 5.5 | 2.9 | 6.9 | 6.9 | 1.7 | 1.5 |
| April | 3.7 | 4.1 | 5.0 | 2.6 | 4.0 | 4.7 | 5.0 | 2.9 | 7.2 | 7.3 | 1.7 | 1.6 |
| May | 3.8 | 4.2 | 5.3 | 2.7 | 4.1 | 4.9 | 5.4 | 3.0 | 6.9 | 6.9 | 1.7 | 1.5 |
| June | 3.8 | 4.2 | 5.6 | 2.7 | 4.0 | 4.6 | 4.9 | 3.0 | 7.0 | 7.0 | 1.7 | 1.5 |
| July | 3.7 | 4.1 | 5.2 | 2.6 | 3.9 | 4.6 | 5.1 | 2.7 | 6.8 | 6.9 | 1.6 | 1.3 |
| August | 3.7 | 4.1 | 5.3 | 2.7 | 3.9 | 4.7 | 5.1 | 2.9 | 6.7 | 6.8 | 1.7 | 1.5 |
| September | 3.7 | 4.1 | 5.1 | 2.7 | 4.0 | 4.9 | 5.1 | 2.9 | 6.8 | 6.7 | 1.8 | 1.5 |
| October | 3.8 | 4.2 | 5.3 | 2.8 | 4.2 | 5.0 | 5.4 | 2.9 | 6.9 | 6.9 | 1.4 | 1.5 |
| November | 3.7 | 4.2 | 5.0 | 2.8 | 4.2 | 5.2 | 5.4 | 3.0 | 6.7 | 6.6 | 1.5 | 1.5 |
| December | 3.6 | 4.0 | 5.0 | 2.5 | 3.8 | 4.8 | 5.1 | 2.6 | 6.7 | 6.7 | 1.6 | 1.6 |
| **2008** | | | | | | | | | | | | |
| January | 3.5 | 3.9 | 5.0 | 2.5 | 3.8 | 4.5 | 4.8 | 3.0 | 6.4 | 6.3 | 1.4 | 1.4 |
| February | 3.6 | 4.0 | 5.1 | 2.3 | 3.8 | 4.6 | 4.7 | 3.0 | 7.0 | 7.0 | 1.4 | 1.4 |
| March | 3.4 | 3.8 | 5.4 | 2.3 | 3.7 | 4.4 | 4.5 | 3.0 | 6.2 | 6.2 | 1.5 | 1.5 |
| April | 3.5 | 4.0 | 5.2 | 2.4 | 3.8 | 4.4 | 5.1 | 3.0 | 6.3 | 6.3 | 1.4 | 1.4 |
| May | 3.3 | 3.7 | 4.8 | 2.3 | 3.4 | 3.9 | 4.5 | 2.9 | 6.5 | 6.4 | 1.4 | 1.4 |
| June | 3.5 | 3.9 | 5.3 | 2.3 | 3.8 | 4.5 | 5.3 | 2.7 | 6.0 | 6.1 | 1.3 | 1.4 |
| July | 3.3 | 3.6 | 4.9 | 2.0 | 3.7 | 4.4 | 4.4 | 2.8 | 5.9 | 6.0 | 1.3 | 1.3 |
| August | 3.3 | 3.7 | 5.6 | 2.1 | 3.7 | 4.4 | 4.5 | 2.8 | 5.8 | 5.9 | 1.3 | 1.3 |
| September | 3.2 | 3.5 | 4.7 | 2.2 | 3.4 | 4.1 | 4.3 | 2.6 | 5.8 | 5.9 | 1.2 | 1.3 |
| October | 3.3 | 3.7 | 5.4 | 2.3 | 3.5 | 4.2 | 4.5 | 2.8 | 5.9 | 5.8 | 1.3 | 1.3 |
| November | 2.9 | 3.3 | 4.9 | 1.8 | 3.1 | 3.8 | 4.2 | 2.6 | 5.1 | 5.3 | 1.2 | 1.2 |
| December | 3.1 | 3.5 | 5.1 | 2.0 | 3.4 | 4.2 | 4.8 | 2.6 | 5.3 | 5.2 | 1.2 | 1.2 |
| **2009** | | | | | | | | | | | | |
| January | 3.1 | 3.4 | 5.4 | 1.7 | 3.3 | 3.7 | 4.4 | 2.7 | 5.2 | 5.2 | 1.4 | 1.5 |
| February | 3.0 | 3.4 | 5.1 | 1.9 | 3.0 | 3.6 | 4.3 | 2.7 | 5.3 | 5.4 | 1.1 | 1.2 |
| March | 2.8 | 3.2 | 4.9 | 1.9 | 3.2 | 3.6 | 3.6 | 2.5 | 4.8 | 5.0 | 1.1 | 1.1 |
| April | 2.9 | 3.2 | 5.3 | 1.8 | 3.2 | 3.9 | 4.0 | 2.4 | 4.8 | 4.9 | 1.6 | 1.1 |
| May | 2.9 | 3.3 | 5.4 | 1.7 | 3.2 | 3.8 | 4.0 | 2.4 | 5.2 | 5.3 | 1.1 | 1.2 |
| June | 2.8 | 3.1 | 4.3 | 1.7 | 2.9 | 3.4 | 3.9 | 2.5 | 4.9 | 4.9 | 1.2 | 1.2 |
| July | 2.9 | 3.3 | 5.5 | 2.1 | 2.9 | 3.4 | 4.2 | 2.6 | 5.0 | 4.7 | 1.1 | 1.0 |
| August | 2.9 | 3.2 | 4.3 | 2.1 | 3.1 | 3.7 | 3.8 | 2.7 | 5.0 | 4.8 | 1.2 | 1.3 |
| September | 3.0 | 3.4 | 5.5 | 2.3 | 3.3 | 3.8 | 4.2 | 2.7 | 4.8 | 4.6 | 1.0 | 1.1 |
| October | 2.9 | 3.2 | 5.4 | 2.1 | 2.9 | 3.4 | 4.2 | 2.6 | 4.7 | 4.5 | 1.4 | 1.4 |
| November | 3.1 | 3.5 | 5.5 | 2.1 | 3.2 | 3.6 | 5.1 | 2.5 | 5.2 | 5.0 | 1.2 | 1.2 |
| December | 2.9 | 3.3 | 6.0 | 2.0 | 3.1 | 3.7 | 4.1 | 2.5 | 4.8 | 4.8 | 1.1 | 1.1 |
| **2010** | | | | | | | | | | | | |
| January | 3.0 | 3.4 | 5.6 | 2.4 | 3.3 | 3.8 | 4.5 | 2.3 | 5.0 | 4.9 | 1.3 | 1.2 |
| February | 2.9 | 3.3 | 5.0 | 2.2 | 3.0 | 3.8 | 4.4 | 2.4 | 4.7 | 4.7 | 1.2 | 1.2 |
| March | 3.2 | 3.6 | 7.4 | 2.2 | 3.2 | 4.5 | 4.4 | 2.6 | 5.1 | 5.0 | 1.5 | 1.2 |
| April | 3.1 | 3.5 | 6.6 | 2.4 | 3.2 | 3.7 | 4.7 | 2.4 | 5.1 | 4.9 | 1.4 | 1.1 |
| May | 3.3 | 3.4 | 5.5 | 2.2 | 3.2 | 3.7 | 4.7 | 2.3 | 5.0 | 4.8 | 3.2 | 1.2 |
| June | 3.1 | 3.5 | 5.0 | 2.2 | 2.9 | 3.9 | 5.0 | 2.5 | 5.0 | 4.7 | 1.2 | 1.2 |
| July | 3.2 | 3.6 | 6.2 | 2.3 | 2.9 | 4.0 | 4.8 | 2.6 | 5.1 | 4.9 | 1.2 | 1.2 |
| August | 3.0 | 3.4 | 5.9 | 2.3 | 3.1 | 3.7 | 4.7 | 2.3 | 5.0 | 4.8 | 1.1 | 1.1 |
| September | 3.1 | 3.5 | 5.8 | 2.3 | 3.3 | 3.9 | 4.5 | 2.5 | 5.1 | 5.0 | 1.1 | 1.1 |
| October | 3.1 | 3.5 | 6.4 | 2.3 | 2.9 | 3.9 | 4.5 | 2.5 | 5.0 | 4.9 | 1.3 | 1.4 |
| November | 3.1 | 3.5 | 6.2 | 2.5 | 3.2 | 3.9 | 4.7 | 2.6 | 4.8 | 4.8 | 1.3 | 1.4 |
| December | 3.2 | 3.6 | 6.8 | 2.3 | 3.1 | 3.4 | 5.4 | 2.4 | 4.8 | 4.7 | 1.2 | 1.3 |

[1]Hires are the number of hires during the entire month.
[2]The hires rate is the number of hires during the entire month as a percent of total employment.
[3]Detail will not necessarily add to totals because of the independent seasonal adjustment of the various series.
[4]Includes natural resources and mining, information, financial activities, and other services, not shown separately.
[5]Includes wholesale trade and transportation, warehousing, and utilities, not shown separately.
[6]Includes arts, entertainment, and recreation, not shown separately.
[7]Includes federal government, not shown separately.
. . . = Not available.

## Table 7-5.  Hires Levels[1] and Rates,[2] by Industry, 2005–October 2016—*Continued*

(Seasonally adjusted, levels in thousands, rates per 100.)

| Year and month | Level[3] | | | | | | | | | | | |
| --- | --- | --- | --- | --- | --- | --- | --- | --- | --- | --- | --- | --- |
| | Total[4] | Total private[4] | Construction | Manufacturing | Trade, transportation, and utilities[5] | Retail trade | Professional and business services | Education and health services | Leisure and hospitality[6] | Accommodation and food services | Government[7] | State and local government |
| **2011** | | | | | | | | | | | | |
| January | 3 910 | 3 642 | 279 | 264 | 807 | 573 | 826 | 448 | 619 | 524 | 267 | 238 |
| February | 4 061 | 3 840 | 345 | 264 | 865 | 574 | 849 | 470 | 647 | 547 | 221 | 191 |
| March | 4 291 | 4 044 | 377 | 270 | 850 | 582 | 919 | 462 | 752 | 627 | 247 | 219 |
| April | 4 218 | 3 946 | 369 | 260 | 842 | 586 | 883 | 492 | 692 | 582 | 272 | 248 |
| May | 4 116 | 3 869 | 375 | 252 | 834 | 565 | 876 | 467 | 654 | 539 | 248 | 218 |
| June | 4 297 | 4 005 | 374 | 255 | 864 | 588 | 829 | 514 | 728 | 609 | 292 | 269 |
| July | 4 139 | 3 911 | 345 | 261 | 824 | 581 | 830 | 484 | 726 | 608 | 228 | 199 |
| August | 4 168 | 3 927 | 330 | 258 | 798 | 533 | 878 | 503 | 727 | 599 | 241 | 215 |
| September | 4 320 | 4 043 | 376 | 236 | 835 | 581 | 901 | 490 | 745 | 610 | 276 | 248 |
| October | 4 239 | 3 972 | 329 | 239 | 841 | 556 | 874 | 490 | 729 | 595 | 266 | 237 |
| November | 4 244 | 3 976 | 312 | 228 | 828 | 563 | 864 | 512 | 784 | 625 | 267 | 241 |
| December | 4 234 | 3 933 | 313 | 264 | 809 | 506 | 865 | 507 | 730 | 611 | 300 | 270 |
| **2012** | | | | | | | | | | | | |
| January | 4 291 | 4 015 | 330 | 259 | 851 | 572 | 826 | 524 | 782 | 626 | 276 | 257 |
| February | 4 470 | 4 180 | 337 | 257 | 847 | 572 | 981 | 568 | 758 | 601 | 289 | 259 |
| March | 4 454 | 4 166 | 303 | 263 | 871 | 577 | 912 | 526 | 830 | 677 | 287 | 256 |
| April | 4 290 | 4 005 | 293 | 256 | 869 | 574 | 855 | 487 | 751 | 611 | 284 | 252 |
| May | 4 440 | 4 154 | 327 | 261 | 873 | 573 | 926 | 542 | 749 | 622 | 287 | 255 |
| June | 4 435 | 4 139 | 352 | 272 | 874 | 575 | 958 | 518 | 727 | 614 | 296 | 263 |
| July | 4 256 | 3 970 | 361 | 245 | 844 | 569 | 863 | 502 | 742 | 625 | 287 | 265 |
| August | 4 421 | 4 116 | 330 | 231 | 921 | 607 | 855 | 501 | 789 | 651 | 306 | 268 |
| September | 4 240 | 3 961 | 353 | 219 | 848 | 585 | 843 | 509 | 729 | 630 | 280 | 243 |
| October | 4 314 | 4 049 | 319 | 241 | 900 | 600 | 859 | 507 | 757 | 638 | 264 | 230 |
| November | 4 400 | 4 121 | 395 | 234 | 872 | 592 | 882 | 486 | 732 | 615 | 279 | 255 |
| December | 4 345 | 4 049 | 301 | 228 | 876 | 580 | 862 | 543 | 779 | 643 | 296 | 256 |
| **2013** | | | | | | | | | | | | |
| January | 4 433 | 4 150 | 332 | 239 | 894 | 603 | 889 | 521 | 793 | 672 | 283 | 247 |
| February | 4 557 | 4 248 | 383 | 245 | 934 | 651 | 840 | 526 | 796 | 677 | 309 | 260 |
| March | 4 275 | 4 000 | 357 | 205 | 810 | 557 | 833 | 531 | 787 | 664 | 274 | 247 |
| April | 4 503 | 4 213 | 291 | 241 | 877 | 608 | 905 | 558 | 863 | 733 | 289 | 252 |
| May | 4 551 | 4 271 | 329 | 255 | 894 | 627 | 909 | 561 | 800 | 663 | 280 | 257 |
| June | 4 411 | 4 146 | 329 | 227 | 863 | 606 | 957 | 474 | 808 | 666 | 266 | 236 |
| July | 4 524 | 4 255 | 310 | 232 | 902 | 626 | 970 | 549 | 791 | 668 | 269 | 242 |
| August | 4 694 | 4 399 | 302 | 268 | 984 | 695 | 1 007 | 579 | 771 | 651 | 294 | 267 |
| September | 4 692 | 4 395 | 315 | 258 | 987 | 676 | 967 | 542 | 820 | 678 | 297 | 267 |
| October | 4 457 | 4 175 | 335 | 226 | 968 | 686 | 854 | 517 | 810 | 673 | 283 | 251 |
| November | 4 600 | 4 301 | 306 | 250 | 1 012 | 709 | 981 | 529 | 778 | 650 | 298 | 267 |
| December | 4 488 | 4 218 | 270 | 251 | 982 | 726 | 929 | 531 | 780 | 646 | 270 | 241 |
| **2014** | | | | | | | | | | | | |
| January | 4 640 | 4 350 | 294 | 248 | 955 | 633 | 977 | 567 | 835 | 700 | 289 | 260 |
| February | 4 700 | 4 402 | 276 | 239 | 1 033 | 730 | 988 | 532 | 872 | 736 | 297 | 266 |
| March | 4 768 | 4 451 | 267 | 252 | 1 021 | 711 | 997 | 577 | 832 | 703 | 318 | 284 |
| April | 4 763 | 4 457 | 297 | 253 | 1 059 | 744 | 959 | 571 | 850 | 700 | 305 | 274 |
| May | 4 755 | 4 464 | 320 | 240 | 1 074 | 751 | 939 | 538 | 880 | 729 | 290 | 260 |
| June | 4 839 | 4 524 | 275 | 273 | 1 093 | 748 | 972 | 554 | 892 | 742 | 315 | 279 |
| July | 4 991 | 4 718 | 389 | 268 | 1 091 | 761 | 1 010 | 579 | 874 | 719 | 274 | 245 |
| August | 4 787 | 4 507 | 333 | 247 | 1 030 | 701 | 1 031 | 520 | 837 | 693 | 281 | 251 |
| September | 5 092 | 4 742 | 294 | 280 | 1 047 | 718 | 1 118 | 639 | 888 | 741 | 349 | 316 |
| October | 5 103 | 4 790 | 319 | 280 | 1 141 | 774 | 1 056 | 608 | 916 | 757 | 313 | 281 |
| November | 5 026 | 4 718 | 316 | 274 | 1 111 | 765 | 986 | 570 | 924 | 770 | 308 | 269 |
| December | 5 186 | 4 866 | 394 | 279 | 1 101 | 765 | 1 040 | 598 | 940 | 790 | 320 | 286 |
| **2015** | | | | | | | | | | | | |
| January | 5 052 | 4 723 | 369 | 255 | 1 089 | 770 | 1 006 | 582 | 907 | 758 | 329 | 290 |
| February | 5 091 | 4 759 | 336 | 260 | 1 061 | 731 | 1 049 | 617 | 932 | 777 | 332 | 295 |
| March | 5 110 | 4 783 | 314 | 259 | 1 117 | 770 | 1 056 | 590 | 938 | 778 | 328 | 290 |
| April | 5 071 | 4 730 | 335 | 254 | 1 040 | 720 | 1 066 | 594 | 929 | 788 | 341 | 302 |
| May | 5 111 | 4 775 | 320 | 248 | 1 095 | 766 | 1 071 | 604 | 949 | 789 | 336 | 293 |
| June | 5 147 | 4 823 | 322 | 268 | 1 126 | 774 | 1 039 | 594 | 932 | 783 | 324 | 290 |
| July | 5 084 | 4 710 | 301 | 264 | 1 109 | 773 | 1 003 | 603 | 925 | 805 | 374 | 329 |
| August | 5 060 | 4 705 | 322 | 265 | 1 070 | 751 | 972 | 605 | 988 | 843 | 355 | 314 |
| September | 5 131 | 4 806 | 324 | 279 | 1 060 | 744 | 1 058 | 610 | 961 | 820 | 325 | 292 |
| October | 5 212 | 4 856 | 314 | 264 | 1 057 | 748 | 1 058 | 644 | 991 | 820 | 356 | 316 |
| November | 5 253 | 4 904 | 340 | 278 | 1 085 | 766 | 1 056 | 661 | 992 | 861 | 349 | 304 |
| December | 5 401 | 5 042 | 322 | 274 | 1 087 | 760 | 1 175 | 641 | 1 024 | 873 | 359 | 314 |
| **2016** | | | | | | | | | | | | |
| January | 5 125 | 4 789 | 305 | 274 | 1 062 | 765 | 1 080 | 579 | 967 | 810 | 335 | 295 |
| February | 5 510 | 5 154 | 341 | 276 | 1 182 | 856 | 1 110 | 651 | 1 062 | 909 | 357 | 313 |
| March | 5 290 | 4 912 | 346 | 251 | 1 094 | 769 | 1 071 | 615 | 1 001 | 852 | 379 | 339 |
| April | 5 085 | 4 734 | 339 | 269 | 1 031 | 714 | 1 031 | 605 | 959 | 832 | 351 | 315 |
| May | 5 047 | 4 695 | 325 | 268 | 1 019 | 710 | 987 | 644 | 986 | 840 | 352 | 311 |
| June | 5 172 | 4 814 | 281 | 281 | 1 038 | 719 | 1 003 | 654 | 1 024 | 844 | 358 | 320 |
| July | 5 258 | 4 889 | 328 | 276 | 1 059 | 750 | 1 162 | 626 | 1 001 | 840 | 368 | 328 |
| August | 5 268 | 4 888 | 337 | 274 | 1 091 | 752 | 1 072 | 634 | 1 005 | 831 | 380 | 339 |
| September | 5 121 | 4 757 | 314 | 279 | 1 097 | 769 | 1 080 | 616 | 909 | 790 | 365 | 325 |
| October | 5 160 | 4 804 | 331 | 274 | 1 083 | 739 | 1 043 | 646 | 972 | 824 | 356 | 314 |

[1]Hires are the number of hires during the entire month.
[2]The hires rate is the number of hires during the entire month as a percent of total employment.
[3]Detail will not necessarily add to totals because of the independent seasonal adjustment of the various series.
[4]Includes natural resources and mining, information, financial activities, and other services, not shown separately.
[5]Includes wholesale trade and transportation, warehousing, and utilities, not shown separately.
[6]Includes arts, entertainment, and recreation, not shown separately.
[7]Includes federal government, not shown separately.
. . . = Not available.

## Table 7-5. Hires Levels[1] and Rates,[2] by Industry, 2005–October 2016—*Continued*

(Seasonally adjusted, levels in thousands, rates per 100.)

| Year and month | Rate | | | | | | | | | | | |
|---|---|---|---|---|---|---|---|---|---|---|---|---|
| | Total[4] | Total private[4] | Construc-tion | Manufac-turing | Trade, transpor-tation, and utilities[5] | Retail trade | Profes-sional and business services | Education and health services | Leisure and hospitality[6] | Accommo-dation and food services | Govern-ment[7] | State and local govern-ment |
| **2011** | | | | | | | | | | | | |
| January | 3.0 | 3.4 | 5.1 | 2.3 | 3.3 | 3.9 | 4.8 | 2.2 | 4.7 | 4.7 | 1.2 | 1.2 |
| February | 3.1 | 3.5 | 6.3 | 2.3 | 3.5 | 3.9 | 5.0 | 2.3 | 4.9 | 4.8 | 1.0 | 1.0 |
| March | 3.3 | 3.7 | 6.9 | 2.3 | 3.4 | 4.0 | 5.3 | 2.3 | 5.7 | 5.5 | 1.1 | 1.1 |
| April | 3.2 | 3.6 | 6.7 | 2.2 | 3.4 | 4.0 | 5.1 | 2.4 | 5.2 | 5.1 | 1.2 | 1.3 |
| May | 3.1 | 3.5 | 6.8 | 2.2 | 3.3 | 3.9 | 5.1 | 2.3 | 4.9 | 4.7 | 1.1 | 1.1 |
| June | 3.3 | 3.6 | 6.8 | 2.2 | 3.4 | 4.0 | 4.8 | 2.5 | 5.5 | 5.3 | 1.3 | 1.4 |
| July | 3.1 | 3.6 | 6.2 | 2.2 | 3.3 | 4.0 | 4.8 | 2.4 | 5.4 | 5.3 | 1.0 | 1.0 |
| August | 3.2 | 3.6 | 5.9 | 2.2 | 3.2 | 3.6 | 5.1 | 2.5 | 5.4 | 5.2 | 1.1 | 1.1 |
| September | 3.3 | 3.7 | 6.7 | 2.0 | 3.3 | 3.9 | 5.2 | 2.4 | 5.6 | 5.3 | 1.3 | 1.3 |
| October | 3.2 | 3.6 | 5.9 | 2.0 | 3.3 | 3.8 | 5.0 | 2.4 | 5.4 | 5.2 | 1.2 | 1.2 |
| November | 3.2 | 3.6 | 5.6 | 1.9 | 3.3 | 3.8 | 4.9 | 2.5 | 5.8 | 5.4 | 1.2 | 1.3 |
| December | 3.2 | 3.5 | 5.6 | 2.2 | 3.2 | 3.4 | 4.9 | 2.5 | 5.4 | 5.3 | 1.4 | 1.4 |
| **2012** | | | | | | | | | | | | |
| January | 3.2 | 3.6 | 5.9 | 2.2 | 3.4 | 3.9 | 4.7 | 2.5 | 5.7 | 5.4 | 1.3 | 1.3 |
| February | 3.3 | 3.7 | 6.0 | 2.2 | 3.3 | 3.9 | 5.5 | 2.8 | 5.6 | 5.1 | 1.3 | 1.4 |
| March | 3.3 | 3.7 | 5.4 | 2.2 | 3.4 | 3.9 | 5.1 | 2.5 | 6.1 | 5.8 | 1.3 | 1.3 |
| April | 3.2 | 3.6 | 5.2 | 2.2 | 3.4 | 3.9 | 4.8 | 2.4 | 5.5 | 5.2 | 1.3 | 1.3 |
| May | 3.3 | 3.7 | 5.8 | 2.2 | 3.4 | 3.9 | 5.2 | 2.6 | 5.5 | 5.3 | 1.3 | 1.3 |
| June | 3.3 | 3.7 | 6.3 | 2.3 | 3.4 | 3.9 | 5.3 | 2.5 | 5.3 | 5.2 | 1.4 | 1.4 |
| July | 3.2 | 3.5 | 6.4 | 2.0 | 3.3 | 3.8 | 4.8 | 2.4 | 5.4 | 5.3 | 1.3 | 1.4 |
| August | 3.3 | 3.7 | 5.8 | 1.9 | 3.6 | 4.1 | 4.8 | 2.4 | 5.7 | 5.5 | 1.4 | 1.4 |
| September | 3.2 | 3.5 | 6.2 | 1.8 | 3.3 | 3.9 | 4.7 | 2.4 | 5.3 | 5.3 | 1.3 | 1.3 |
| October | 3.2 | 3.6 | 5.6 | 2.0 | 3.5 | 4.0 | 4.7 | 2.4 | 5.5 | 5.4 | 1.2 | 1.2 |
| November | 3.3 | 3.6 | 7.0 | 2.0 | 3.4 | 4.0 | 4.9 | 2.3 | 5.3 | 5.2 | 1.3 | 1.3 |
| December | 3.2 | 3.6 | 5.3 | 1.9 | 3.4 | 3.9 | 4.7 | 2.6 | 5.6 | 5.4 | 1.4 | 1.3 |
| **2013** | | | | | | | | | | | | |
| January | 3.3 | 3.7 | 5.8 | 2.0 | 3.5 | 4.0 | 4.9 | 2.5 | 5.7 | 5.6 | 1.3 | 1.3 |
| February | 3.4 | 3.7 | 6.6 | 2.0 | 3.6 | 4.4 | 4.6 | 2.5 | 5.7 | 5.6 | 1.4 | 1.4 |
| March | 3.1 | 3.5 | 6.1 | 1.7 | 3.2 | 3.7 | 4.5 | 2.5 | 5.6 | 5.5 | 1.3 | 1.3 |
| April | 3.3 | 3.7 | 5.0 | 2.0 | 3.4 | 4.1 | 4.9 | 2.6 | 6.1 | 6.0 | 1.3 | 1.3 |
| May | 3.3 | 3.7 | 5.7 | 2.1 | 3.5 | 4.2 | 4.9 | 2.7 | 5.6 | 5.4 | 1.3 | 1.3 |
| June | 3.2 | 3.6 | 5.6 | 1.9 | 3.3 | 4.0 | 5.2 | 2.2 | 5.7 | 5.5 | 1.2 | 1.2 |
| July | 3.3 | 3.7 | 5.3 | 1.9 | 3.5 | 4.2 | 5.2 | 2.6 | 5.5 | 5.4 | 1.2 | 1.3 |
| August | 3.4 | 3.8 | 5.1 | 2.2 | 3.8 | 4.6 | 5.4 | 2.7 | 5.4 | 5.3 | 1.3 | 1.4 |
| September | 3.4 | 3.8 | 5.3 | 2.1 | 3.8 | 4.5 | 5.2 | 2.6 | 5.7 | 5.5 | 1.4 | 1.4 |
| October | 3.3 | 3.6 | 5.6 | 1.9 | 3.7 | 4.5 | 4.6 | 2.4 | 5.6 | 5.5 | 1.3 | 1.3 |
| November | 3.3 | 3.7 | 5.1 | 2.1 | 3.9 | 4.7 | 5.2 | 2.5 | 5.4 | 5.2 | 1.4 | 1.4 |
| December | 3.3 | 3.6 | 4.5 | 2.1 | 3.8 | 4.8 | 5.0 | 2.5 | 5.4 | 5.2 | 1.2 | 1.3 |
| **2014** | | | | | | | | | | | | |
| January | 3.4 | 3.8 | 4.9 | 2.0 | 3.7 | 4.1 | 5.2 | 2.7 | 5.8 | 5.6 | 1.3 | 1.4 |
| February | 3.4 | 3.8 | 4.6 | 2.0 | 4.0 | 4.8 | 5.2 | 2.5 | 6.0 | 5.9 | 1.4 | 1.4 |
| March | 3.5 | 3.8 | 4.4 | 2.1 | 3.9 | 4.7 | 5.3 | 2.7 | 5.7 | 5.6 | 1.5 | 1.5 |
| April | 3.4 | 3.8 | 4.9 | 2.1 | 4.0 | 4.9 | 5.1 | 2.7 | 5.8 | 5.6 | 1.4 | 1.4 |
| May | 3.4 | 3.8 | 5.2 | 2.0 | 4.1 | 4.9 | 4.9 | 2.5 | 6.0 | 5.8 | 1.3 | 1.4 |
| June | 3.5 | 3.9 | 4.5 | 2.2 | 4.1 | 4.9 | 5.1 | 2.6 | 6.1 | 5.9 | 1.4 | 1.5 |
| July | 3.6 | 4.0 | 6.3 | 2.2 | 4.1 | 5.0 | 5.3 | 2.7 | 5.9 | 5.7 | 1.3 | 1.3 |
| August | 3.4 | 3.8 | 5.4 | 2.0 | 3.9 | 4.6 | 5.4 | 2.4 | 5.7 | 5.5 | 1.3 | 1.3 |
| September | 3.6 | 4.0 | 4.7 | 2.3 | 4.0 | 4.7 | 5.8 | 3.0 | 6.0 | 5.9 | 1.6 | 1.6 |
| October | 3.7 | 4.1 | 5.1 | 2.3 | 4.3 | 5.0 | 5.5 | 2.8 | 6.2 | 6.0 | 1.4 | 1.5 |
| November | 3.6 | 4.0 | 5.0 | 2.2 | 4.2 | 4.9 | 5.1 | 2.6 | 6.2 | 6.0 | 1.4 | 1.4 |
| December | 3.7 | 4.1 | 6.2 | 2.3 | 4.1 | 4.9 | 5.4 | 2.8 | 6.3 | 6.2 | 1.5 | 1.5 |
| **2015** | | | | | | | | | | | | |
| January | 3.6 | 4.0 | 5.8 | 2.1 | 4.1 | 5.0 | 5.2 | 2.7 | 6.1 | 5.9 | 1.5 | 1.5 |
| February | 3.6 | 4.0 | 5.3 | 2.1 | 4.0 | 4.7 | 5.4 | 2.8 | 6.2 | 6.0 | 1.5 | 1.5 |
| March | 3.6 | 4.0 | 4.9 | 2.1 | 4.2 | 4.9 | 5.4 | 2.7 | 6.3 | 6.1 | 1.5 | 1.5 |
| April | 3.6 | 4.0 | 5.2 | 2.1 | 3.9 | 4.6 | 5.5 | 2.7 | 6.2 | 6.1 | 1.6 | 1.6 |
| May | 3.6 | 4.0 | 5.0 | 2.0 | 4.1 | 4.9 | 5.5 | 2.7 | 6.3 | 6.1 | 1.5 | 1.5 |
| June | 3.6 | 4.0 | 5.0 | 2.2 | 4.2 | 5.0 | 5.3 | 2.7 | 6.2 | 6.1 | 1.5 | 1.5 |
| July | 3.6 | 3.9 | 4.7 | 2.1 | 4.1 | 4.9 | 5.1 | 2.7 | 6.1 | 6.2 | 1.7 | 1.7 |
| August | 3.6 | 3.9 | 5.0 | 2.1 | 4.0 | 4.8 | 4.9 | 2.7 | 6.5 | 6.5 | 1.6 | 1.6 |
| September | 3.6 | 4.0 | 5.0 | 2.3 | 3.9 | 4.7 | 5.3 | 2.7 | 6.3 | 6.3 | 1.5 | 1.5 |
| October | 3.7 | 4.0 | 4.8 | 2.1 | 3.9 | 4.8 | 5.3 | 2.9 | 6.5 | 6.3 | 1.6 | 1.6 |
| November | 3.7 | 4.1 | 5.2 | 2.3 | 4.0 | 4.9 | 5.3 | 3.0 | 6.5 | 6.6 | 1.6 | 1.6 |
| December | 3.8 | 4.2 | 4.9 | 2.2 | 4.0 | 4.8 | 5.9 | 2.9 | 6.7 | 6.6 | 1.6 | 1.6 |
| **2016** | | | | | | | | | | | | |
| January | 3.6 | 3.9 | 4.6 | 2.2 | 3.9 | 4.8 | 5.4 | 2.6 | 6.3 | 6.1 | 1.5 | 1.5 |
| February | 3.8 | 4.2 | 5.1 | 2.2 | 4.3 | 5.4 | 5.5 | 2.9 | 6.9 | 6.9 | 1.6 | 1.6 |
| March | 3.7 | 4.0 | 5.2 | 2.0 | 4.0 | 4.8 | 5.3 | 2.7 | 6.5 | 6.4 | 1.7 | 1.8 |
| April | 3.5 | 3.9 | 5.1 | 2.2 | 3.8 | 4.5 | 5.1 | 2.7 | 6.2 | 6.3 | 1.6 | 1.6 |
| May | 3.5 | 3.9 | 4.9 | 2.2 | 3.7 | 4.5 | 4.9 | 2.8 | 6.4 | 6.3 | 1.6 | 1.6 |
| June | 3.6 | 3.9 | 4.2 | 2.3 | 3.8 | 4.5 | 5.0 | 2.9 | 6.6 | 6.4 | 1.6 | 1.7 |
| July | 3.6 | 4.0 | 4.9 | 2.2 | 3.9 | 4.7 | 5.7 | 2.8 | 6.4 | 6.3 | 1.7 | 1.7 |
| August | 3.6 | 4.0 | 5.1 | 2.2 | 4.0 | 4.7 | 5.3 | 2.8 | 6.5 | 6.2 | 1.7 | 1.7 |
| September | 3.5 | 3.9 | 4.7 | 2.3 | 4.0 | 4.8 | 5.3 | 2.7 | 5.8 | 5.9 | 1.6 | 1.7 |
| October | 3.6 | 3.9 | 4.9 | 2.2 | 4.0 | 4.6 | 5.1 | 2.8 | 6.2 | 6.2 | 1.6 | 1.6 |

[1] Hires are the number of hires during the entire month.
[2] The hires rate is the number of hires during the entire month as a percent of total employment.
[3] Detail will not necessarily add to totals because of the independent seasonal adjustment of the various series.
[4] Includes natural resources and mining, information, financial activities, and other services, not shown separately.
[5] Includes wholesale trade and transportation, warehousing, and utilities, not shown separately.
[6] Includes arts, entertainment, and recreation, not shown separately.
[7] Includes federal government, not shown separately.
. . . = Not available.

## Table 7-6.  Separations Levels[1] and Rates,[2] by Industry, 2005–October 2016

(Seasonally adjusted, levels in thousands, rates per 100.)

| Year and month | Total[4] | Total private[4] | Construction | Manufacturing | Trade, transportation, and utilities[5] | Retail trade | Professional and business services | Education and health services | Leisure and hospitality[6] | Accommodation and food services | Government[7] | State and local government |
|---|---|---|---|---|---|---|---|---|---|---|---|---|
| **2005** | | | | | | | | | | | | |
| January | 5 177 | 4 898 | 493 | 386 | 1 084 | 728 | 970 | 469 | 892 | 764 | 279 | 246 |
| February | 5 006 | 4 700 | 449 | 352 | 1 052 | 710 | 1 024 | 480 | 806 | 685 | 306 | 270 |
| March | 5 071 | 4 752 | 394 | 385 | 1 137 | 842 | 1 011 | 495 | 824 | 714 | 319 | 284 |
| April | 4 970 | 4 666 | 419 | 376 | 1 068 | 739 | 981 | 486 | 790 | 671 | 304 | 266 |
| May | 5 105 | 4 815 | 461 | 375 | 1 097 | 763 | 913 | 474 | 889 | 765 | 290 | 262 |
| June | 5 074 | 4 767 | 427 | 367 | 1 094 | 773 | 1 027 | 465 | 904 | 754 | 306 | 262 |
| July | 4 917 | 4 653 | 394 | 379 | 1 066 | 758 | 966 | 446 | 863 | 756 | 264 | 226 |
| August | 5 220 | 4 916 | 471 | 389 | 1 101 | 793 | 1 023 | 488 | 879 | 757 | 304 | 269 |
| September | 5 305 | 4 973 | 499 | 383 | 1 138 | 815 | 974 | 490 | 948 | 786 | 332 | 290 |
| October | 4 960 | 4 634 | 454 | 367 | 1 055 | 722 | 854 | 470 | 923 | 781 | 326 | 289 |
| November | 4 949 | 4 635 | 442 | 389 | 1 075 | 716 | 834 | 461 | 912 | 799 | 315 | 276 |
| December | 4 945 | 4 639 | 482 | 371 | 1 116 | 752 | 839 | 478 | 877 | 750 | 306 | 253 |
| **2006** | | | | | | | | | | | | |
| January | 5 043 | 4 714 | 452 | 364 | 1 055 | 756 | 959 | 449 | 929 | 810 | 330 | 287 |
| February | 4 983 | 4 666 | 423 | 379 | 1 093 | 782 | 856 | 438 | 963 | 855 | 318 | 271 |
| March | 5 037 | 4 695 | 431 | 427 | 1 081 | 782 | 882 | 450 | 907 | 790 | 342 | 286 |
| April | 5 012 | 4 686 | 414 | 340 | 1 127 | 814 | 885 | 488 | 823 | 716 | 326 | 269 |
| May | 5 417 | 5 057 | 464 | 438 | 1 195 | 841 | 1 016 | 576 | 871 | 751 | 361 | 303 |
| June | 5 136 | 4 785 | 395 | 382 | 1 158 | 845 | 874 | 515 | 901 | 780 | 351 | 288 |
| July | 5 183 | 4 856 | 425 | 408 | 1 097 | 766 | 937 | 526 | 871 | 748 | 327 | 270 |
| August | 5 001 | 4 659 | 387 | 388 | 1 117 | 750 | 866 | 486 | 860 | 733 | 342 | 270 |
| September | 5 007 | 4 684 | 395 | 376 | 1 062 | 749 | 1 012 | 450 | 850 | 738 | 323 | 249 |
| October | 5 171 | 4 843 | 434 | 374 | 1 071 | 740 | 969 | 494 | 897 | 768 | 328 | 288 |
| November | 5 291 | 4 956 | 481 | 414 | 1 097 | 792 | 1 026 | 477 | 945 | 813 | 335 | 281 |
| December | 5 108 | 4 781 | 419 | 426 | 1 069 | 757 | 937 | 500 | 937 | 813 | 326 | 275 |
| **2007** | | | | | | | | | | | | |
| January | 5 144 | 4 812 | 412 | 410 | 1 100 | 758 | 941 | 516 | 895 | 763 | 332 | 284 |
| February | 5 094 | 4 761 | 419 | 423 | 1 059 | 756 | 967 | 483 | 936 | 797 | 333 | 267 |
| March | 5 123 | 4 790 | 352 | 414 | 1 055 | 727 | 1 008 | 489 | 901 | 762 | 333 | 255 |
| April | 5 138 | 4 788 | 416 | 384 | 1 065 | 733 | 920 | 484 | 933 | 794 | 349 | 275 |
| May | 5 080 | 4 719 | 407 | 412 | 1 089 | 771 | 841 | 519 | 901 | 773 | 361 | 280 |
| June | 5 065 | 4 704 | 414 | 387 | 1 046 | 731 | 851 | 510 | 945 | 805 | 362 | 271 |
| July | 5 118 | 4 721 | 413 | 383 | 1 043 | 714 | 909 | 489 | 894 | 790 | 397 | 305 |
| August | 5 105 | 4 763 | 430 | 395 | 1 043 | 736 | 901 | 501 | 882 | 762 | 342 | 265 |
| September | 5 031 | 4 702 | 423 | 391 | 1 054 | 755 | 935 | 462 | 861 | 731 | 328 | 241 |
| October | 5 129 | 4 821 | 414 | 406 | 1 105 | 763 | 951 | 494 | 901 | 779 | 308 | 268 |
| November | 5 031 | 4 730 | 425 | 409 | 1 064 | 761 | 931 | 527 | 896 | 757 | 301 | 263 |
| December | 4 926 | 4 612 | 409 | 378 | 1 063 | 761 | 892 | 459 | 895 | 762 | 314 | 277 |
| **2008** | | | | | | | | | | | | |
| January | 5 005 | 4 715 | 416 | 371 | 1 072 | 726 | 903 | 522 | 895 | 756 | 290 | 247 |
| February | 5 010 | 4 723 | 404 | 364 | 1 052 | 732 | 908 | 530 | 959 | 811 | 287 | 252 |
| March | 4 762 | 4 475 | 416 | 359 | 979 | 685 | 871 | 512 | 842 | 710 | 287 | 261 |
| April | 5 121 | 4 824 | 482 | 387 | 1 085 | 750 | 955 | 519 | 843 | 724 | 297 | 269 |
| May | 4 728 | 4 457 | 400 | 360 | 980 | 683 | 792 | 513 | 897 | 747 | 272 | 249 |
| June | 4 900 | 4 626 | 446 | 376 | 1 050 | 739 | 929 | 476 | 826 | 723 | 274 | 252 |
| July | 4 713 | 4 467 | 405 | 330 | 1 040 | 715 | 871 | 485 | 807 | 704 | 246 | 228 |
| August | 4 815 | 4 526 | 431 | 326 | 1 055 | 722 | 880 | 501 | 805 | 695 | 290 | 266 |
| September | 4 751 | 4 463 | 400 | 373 | 1 022 | 697 | 849 | 466 | 825 | 707 | 288 | 269 |
| October | 4 895 | 4 599 | 451 | 399 | 1 036 | 692 | 905 | 513 | 803 | 695 | 296 | 269 |
| November | 4 605 | 4 340 | 467 | 375 | 968 | 673 | 886 | 451 | 731 | 643 | 265 | 241 |
| December | 4 814 | 4 542 | 420 | 426 | 1 059 | 708 | 954 | 470 | 736 | 623 | 271 | 245 |
| **2009** | | | | | | | | | | | | |
| January | 4 974 | 4 676 | 477 | 479 | 1 012 | 644 | 903 | 504 | 728 | 621 | 298 | 275 |
| February | 4 674 | 4 399 | 439 | 420 | 887 | 576 | 897 | 500 | 728 | 626 | 274 | 259 |
| March | 4 536 | 4 281 | 453 | 418 | 969 | 624 | 754 | 469 | 695 | 606 | 255 | 235 |
| April | 4 655 | 4 390 | 495 | 389 | 972 | 662 | 844 | 468 | 700 | 593 | 265 | 244 |
| May | 4 146 | 3 837 | 398 | 377 | 859 | 568 | 694 | 403 | 645 | 569 | 309 | 227 |
| June | 4 192 | 3 882 | 365 | 349 | 768 | 516 | 721 | 489 | 684 | 557 | 310 | 235 |
| July | 4 297 | 4 006 | 430 | 307 | 834 | 539 | 748 | 494 | 670 | 542 | 291 | 267 |
| August | 4 060 | 3 797 | 347 | 284 | 813 | 552 | 677 | 504 | 696 | 578 | 263 | 239 |
| September | 4 084 | 3 781 | 387 | 300 | 914 | 602 | 671 | 484 | 609 | 539 | 303 | 284 |
| October | 3 951 | 3 691 | 375 | 284 | 809 | 546 | 696 | 452 | 639 | 521 | 260 | 227 |
| November | 3 873 | 3 603 | 328 | 258 | 790 | 503 | 750 | 454 | 665 | 551 | 270 | 235 |
| December | 3 989 | 3 700 | 362 | 255 | 867 | 554 | 672 | 468 | 643 | 536 | 290 | 256 |
| **2010** | | | | | | | | | | | | |
| January | 3 894 | 3 620 | 396 | 284 | 726 | 481 | 680 | 450 | 663 | 552 | 274 | 255 |
| February | 3 830 | 3 539 | 345 | 270 | 764 | 516 | 703 | 449 | 602 | 527 | 292 | 261 |
| March | 3 949 | 3 663 | 354 | 255 | 836 | 614 | 743 | 445 | 633 | 527 | 286 | 252 |
| April | 3 892 | 3 600 | 375 | 246 | 774 | 549 | 718 | 466 | 618 | 519 | 291 | 250 |
| May | 3 831 | 3 532 | 349 | 214 | 748 | 518 | 733 | 422 | 633 | 532 | 299 | 239 |
| June | 4 223 | 3 676 | 295 | 235 | 804 | 565 | 733 | 506 | 649 | 515 | 548 | 272 |
| July | 4 278 | 3 840 | 354 | 258 | 825 | 566 | 810 | 501 | 688 | 543 | 438 | 252 |
| August | 4 009 | 3 591 | 329 | 260 | 769 | 553 | 740 | 441 | 631 | 519 | 418 | 271 |
| September | 4 026 | 3 632 | 340 | 247 | 801 | 553 | 740 | 495 | 620 | 513 | 394 | 286 |
| October | 3 784 | 3 522 | 337 | 266 | 741 | 525 | 705 | 420 | 649 | 531 | 262 | 223 |
| November | 3 843 | 3 532 | 323 | 254 | 791 | 553 | 687 | 468 | 610 | 508 | 310 | 282 |
| December | 4 026 | 3 731 | 390 | 254 | 761 | 496 | 857 | 470 | 593 | 489 | 295 | 273 |

[1]Total separations are the number of separations during the entire month.
[2]The total separations rate is the number of total separations during the entire month as a percent of total employment.
[3]Detail will not necessarily add to totals because of the independent seasonal adjustment of the various series.
[4]Includes natural resources and mining, information, financial activities, and other services, not shown separately.
[5]Includes wholesale trade and transportation, warehousing, and utilities, not shown separately.
[6]Includes arts, entertainment, and recreation, not shown separately.
[7]Includes federal government, not shown separately.

## Table 7-6. Separations Levels[1] and Rates,[2] by Industry, 2005–October 2016—*Continued*

(Seasonally adjusted, levels in thousands, rates per 100.)

| Year and month | Rate | | | | | | | | | | | |
|---|---|---|---|---|---|---|---|---|---|---|---|---|
| | Total[4] | Total private[4] | Construction | Manufacturing | Trade, transportation, and utilities[5] | Retail trade | Professional and business services | Education and health services | Leisure and hospitality[6] | Accommodation and food services | Government[7] | State and local government |
| **2005** | | | | | | | | | | | | |
| January | 3.9 | 4.4 | 6.9 | 2.7 | 4.2 | 4.8 | 5.8 | 2.7 | 7.0 | 7.1 | 1.3 | 1.3 |
| February | 3.8 | 4.2 | 6.3 | 2.5 | 4.1 | 4.7 | 6.1 | 2.7 | 6.3 | 6.3 | 1.4 | 1.4 |
| March | 3.8 | 4.3 | 5.5 | 2.7 | 4.4 | 5.5 | 6.0 | 2.8 | 6.5 | 6.6 | 1.5 | 1.5 |
| April | 3.7 | 4.2 | 5.8 | 2.6 | 4.1 | 4.9 | 5.8 | 2.8 | 6.2 | 6.1 | 1.4 | 1.4 |
| May | 3.8 | 4.3 | 6.3 | 2.6 | 4.2 | 5.0 | 5.4 | 2.7 | 6.9 | 7.0 | 1.3 | 1.4 |
| June | 3.8 | 4.2 | 5.8 | 2.6 | 4.2 | 5.1 | 6.1 | 2.6 | 7.0 | 6.9 | 1.4 | 1.4 |
| July | 3.7 | 4.1 | 5.4 | 2.7 | 4.1 | 4.9 | 5.7 | 2.5 | 6.7 | 6.9 | 1.2 | 1.2 |
| August | 3.9 | 4.4 | 6.4 | 2.7 | 4.2 | 5.2 | 6.0 | 2.8 | 6.8 | 6.9 | 1.4 | 1.4 |
| September | 3.9 | 4.4 | 6.7 | 2.7 | 4.4 | 5.3 | 5.7 | 2.8 | 7.4 | 7.2 | 1.5 | 1.5 |
| October | 3.7 | 4.1 | 6.1 | 2.6 | 4.0 | 4.7 | 5.0 | 2.6 | 7.2 | 7.1 | 1.5 | 1.5 |
| November | 3.7 | 4.1 | 5.9 | 2.7 | 4.1 | 4.7 | 4.8 | 2.6 | 7.1 | 7.3 | 1.4 | 1.4 |
| December | 3.7 | 4.1 | 6.4 | 2.6 | 4.3 | 4.9 | 4.9 | 2.7 | 6.8 | 6.8 | 1.4 | 1.3 |
| **2006** | | | | | | | | | | | | |
| January | 3.7 | 4.1 | 6.0 | 2.6 | 4.0 | 4.9 | 5.5 | 2.5 | 7.2 | 7.3 | 1.5 | 1.5 |
| February | 3.7 | 4.1 | 5.5 | 2.7 | 4.2 | 5.1 | 4.9 | 2.4 | 7.4 | 7.7 | 1.5 | 1.4 |
| March | 3.7 | 4.1 | 5.6 | 3.0 | 4.1 | 5.1 | 5.1 | 2.5 | 7.0 | 7.1 | 1.6 | 1.5 |
| April | 3.7 | 4.1 | 5.4 | 2.4 | 4.3 | 5.3 | 5.1 | 2.7 | 6.3 | 6.4 | 1.5 | 1.4 |
| May | 4.0 | 4.4 | 6.0 | 3.1 | 4.6 | 5.5 | 5.8 | 3.2 | 6.7 | 6.7 | 1.6 | 1.6 |
| June | 3.8 | 4.2 | 5.1 | 2.7 | 4.4 | 5.5 | 5.0 | 2.8 | 6.9 | 7.0 | 1.6 | 1.5 |
| July | 3.8 | 4.2 | 5.5 | 2.9 | 4.2 | 5.0 | 5.3 | 2.9 | 6.6 | 6.7 | 1.5 | 1.4 |
| August | 3.7 | 4.1 | 5.0 | 2.7 | 4.3 | 4.9 | 4.9 | 2.7 | 6.5 | 6.5 | 1.6 | 1.4 |
| September | 3.7 | 4.1 | 5.1 | 2.7 | 4.0 | 4.9 | 5.7 | 2.5 | 6.5 | 6.6 | 1.5 | 1.3 |
| October | 3.8 | 4.2 | 5.6 | 2.7 | 4.1 | 4.8 | 5.5 | 2.7 | 6.8 | 6.8 | 1.5 | 1.5 |
| November | 3.9 | 4.3 | 6.3 | 2.9 | 4.2 | 5.1 | 5.8 | 2.6 | 7.1 | 7.2 | 1.5 | 1.5 |
| December | 3.7 | 4.2 | 5.5 | 3.0 | 4.0 | 4.9 | 5.3 | 2.7 | 7.0 | 7.2 | 1.5 | 1.4 |
| **2007** | | | | | | | | | | | | |
| January | 3.7 | 4.2 | 5.3 | 2.9 | 4.2 | 4.9 | 5.3 | 2.8 | 6.7 | 6.7 | 1.5 | 1.5 |
| February | 3.7 | 4.1 | 5.5 | 3.0 | 4.0 | 4.9 | 5.4 | 2.6 | 7.0 | 7.0 | 1.5 | 1.4 |
| March | 3.7 | 4.1 | 4.6 | 3.0 | 4.0 | 4.7 | 5.6 | 2.6 | 6.7 | 6.7 | 1.5 | 1.3 |
| April | 3.7 | 4.1 | 5.4 | 2.8 | 4.0 | 4.7 | 5.1 | 2.6 | 7.0 | 7.0 | 1.6 | 1.4 |
| May | 3.7 | 4.1 | 5.3 | 3.0 | 4.1 | 5.0 | 4.7 | 2.8 | 6.7 | 6.8 | 1.6 | 1.4 |
| June | 3.7 | 4.1 | 5.4 | 2.8 | 3.9 | 4.7 | 4.7 | 2.7 | 7.0 | 7.0 | 1.6 | 1.4 |
| July | 3.7 | 4.1 | 5.4 | 2.8 | 3.9 | 4.6 | 5.1 | 2.6 | 6.7 | 6.9 | 1.8 | 1.6 |
| August | 3.7 | 4.1 | 5.6 | 2.9 | 3.9 | 4.7 | 5.0 | 2.7 | 6.6 | 6.7 | 1.5 | 1.4 |
| September | 3.6 | 4.1 | 5.6 | 2.8 | 4.0 | 4.9 | 5.2 | 2.5 | 6.4 | 6.4 | 1.5 | 1.2 |
| October | 3.7 | 4.2 | 5.5 | 2.9 | 4.1 | 4.9 | 5.3 | 2.6 | 6.7 | 6.8 | 1.4 | 1.4 |
| November | 3.6 | 4.1 | 5.6 | 3.0 | 4.0 | 4.9 | 5.2 | 2.8 | 6.6 | 6.6 | 1.3 | 1.3 |
| December | 3.6 | 4.0 | 5.5 | 2.7 | 4.0 | 4.9 | 4.9 | 2.4 | 6.6 | 6.6 | 1.4 | 1.4 |
| **2008** | | | | | | | | | | | | |
| January | 3.6 | 4.1 | 5.6 | 2.7 | 4.0 | 4.7 | 5.0 | 2.8 | 6.6 | 6.5 | 1.3 | 1.3 |
| February | 3.6 | 4.1 | 5.4 | 2.7 | 3.9 | 4.7 | 5.0 | 2.8 | 7.1 | 7.0 | 1.3 | 1.3 |
| March | 3.4 | 3.9 | 5.6 | 2.6 | 3.7 | 4.4 | 4.9 | 2.7 | 6.2 | 6.2 | 1.3 | 1.3 |
| April | 3.7 | 4.2 | 6.6 | 2.8 | 4.1 | 4.9 | 5.3 | 2.7 | 6.2 | 6.3 | 1.3 | 1.4 |
| May | 3.4 | 3.9 | 5.5 | 2.7 | 3.7 | 4.4 | 4.4 | 2.7 | 6.6 | 6.5 | 1.2 | 1.3 |
| June | 3.6 | 4.0 | 6.2 | 2.8 | 4.0 | 4.8 | 5.2 | 2.5 | 6.1 | 6.3 | 1.2 | 1.3 |
| July | 3.4 | 3.9 | 5.7 | 2.5 | 3.9 | 4.7 | 4.9 | 2.5 | 6.0 | 6.1 | 1.1 | 1.2 |
| August | 3.5 | 3.9 | 6.1 | 2.4 | 4.0 | 4.7 | 5.0 | 2.6 | 6.0 | 6.1 | 1.3 | 1.3 |
| September | 3.5 | 3.9 | 5.7 | 2.8 | 3.9 | 4.6 | 4.8 | 2.4 | 6.2 | 6.2 | 1.3 | 1.4 |
| October | 3.6 | 4.0 | 6.5 | 3.0 | 4.0 | 4.6 | 5.2 | 2.7 | 6.0 | 6.1 | 1.3 | 1.4 |
| November | 3.4 | 3.8 | 6.8 | 2.9 | 3.8 | 4.5 | 5.1 | 2.3 | 5.5 | 5.7 | 1.2 | 1.2 |
| December | 3.6 | 4.0 | 6.3 | 3.3 | 4.1 | 4.8 | 5.5 | 2.4 | 5.6 | 5.5 | 1.2 | 1.2 |
| **2009** | | | | | | | | | | | | |
| January | 3.7 | 4.2 | 7.3 | 3.8 | 4.0 | 4.4 | 5.3 | 2.6 | 5.5 | 5.5 | 1.3 | 1.4 |
| February | 3.5 | 4.0 | 6.8 | 3.4 | 3.5 | 3.9 | 5.3 | 2.6 | 5.5 | 5.6 | 1.2 | 1.3 |
| March | 3.4 | 3.9 | 7.2 | 3.4 | 3.9 | 4.3 | 4.5 | 2.4 | 5.3 | 5.4 | 1.1 | 1.2 |
| April | 3.5 | 4.0 | 8.0 | 3.2 | 3.9 | 4.6 | 5.1 | 2.4 | 5.4 | 5.3 | 1.2 | 1.2 |
| May | 3.2 | 3.5 | 6.5 | 3.2 | 3.4 | 3.9 | 4.2 | 2.1 | 4.9 | 5.1 | 1.4 | 1.1 |
| June | 3.2 | 3.6 | 6.1 | 3.0 | 3.1 | 3.6 | 4.4 | 2.5 | 5.2 | 5.0 | 1.4 | 1.2 |
| July | 3.3 | 3.7 | 7.2 | 2.6 | 3.4 | 3.7 | 4.6 | 2.5 | 5.1 | 4.9 | 1.3 | 1.4 |
| August | 3.1 | 3.5 | 5.9 | 2.4 | 3.3 | 3.8 | 4.1 | 2.6 | 5.3 | 5.2 | 1.2 | 1.2 |
| September | 3.1 | 3.5 | 6.7 | 2.6 | 3.7 | 4.2 | 4.1 | 2.5 | 4.7 | 4.9 | 1.3 | 1.4 |
| October | 3.0 | 3.4 | 6.6 | 2.5 | 3.3 | 3.8 | 4.2 | 2.3 | 4.9 | 4.7 | 1.2 | 1.2 |
| November | 3.0 | 3.4 | 5.8 | 2.2 | 3.2 | 3.5 | 4.6 | 2.3 | 5.1 | 5.0 | 1.2 | 1.2 |
| December | 3.1 | 3.4 | 6.4 | 2.2 | 3.5 | 3.9 | 4.1 | 2.4 | 5.0 | 4.8 | 1.3 | 1.3 |
| **2010** | | | | | | | | | | | | |
| January | 3.0 | 3.4 | 7.1 | 2.5 | 3.0 | 3.3 | 4.1 | 2.3 | 5.1 | 5.0 | 1.2 | 1.3 |
| February | 3.0 | 3.3 | 6.3 | 2.4 | 3.1 | 3.6 | 4.2 | 2.3 | 4.7 | 4.8 | 1.3 | 1.3 |
| March | 3.0 | 3.4 | 6.4 | 2.2 | 3.4 | 4.3 | 4.5 | 2.2 | 4.9 | 4.8 | 1.3 | 1.3 |
| April | 3.0 | 3.3 | 6.7 | 2.1 | 3.1 | 3.8 | 4.3 | 2.3 | 4.8 | 4.7 | 1.3 | 1.3 |
| May | 2.9 | 3.3 | 6.3 | 1.9 | 3.0 | 3.6 | 4.4 | 2.1 | 4.9 | 4.8 | 1.3 | 1.2 |
| June | 3.2 | 3.4 | 5.3 | 2.0 | 3.3 | 3.9 | 4.4 | 2.5 | 5.0 | 4.6 | 2.4 | 1.4 |
| July | 3.3 | 3.6 | 6.4 | 2.2 | 3.3 | 3.9 | 4.8 | 2.5 | 5.3 | 4.9 | 1.9 | 1.3 |
| August | 3.1 | 3.3 | 6.0 | 2.3 | 3.1 | 3.8 | 4.4 | 2.2 | 4.8 | 4.6 | 1.9 | 1.4 |
| September | 3.1 | 3.4 | 6.2 | 2.1 | 3.2 | 3.8 | 4.4 | 2.5 | 4.7 | 4.6 | 1.8 | 1.5 |
| October | 2.9 | 3.3 | 6.1 | 2.3 | 3.0 | 3.6 | 4.2 | 2.1 | 4.9 | 4.7 | 1.2 | 1.1 |
| November | 2.9 | 3.3 | 5.9 | 2.2 | 3.2 | 3.8 | 4.1 | 2.3 | 4.6 | 4.5 | 1.4 | 1.5 |
| December | 3.1 | 3.4 | 7.1 | 2.2 | 3.1 | 3.4 | 5.0 | 2.3 | 4.5 | 4.3 | 1.3 | 1.4 |

[1]Total separations are the number of separations during the entire month.
[2]The total separations rate is the number of total separations during the entire month as a percent of total employment.
[3]Detail will not necessarily add to totals because of the independent seasonal adjustment of the various series.
[4]Includes natural resources and mining, information, financial activities, and other services, not shown separately.
[5]Includes wholesale trade and transportation, warehousing, and utilities, not shown separately.
[6]Includes arts, entertainment, and recreation, not shown separately.
[7]Includes federal government, not shown separately.

## Table 7-6.  Separations Levels[1] and Rates,[2] by Industry, 2005–October 2016—*Continued*

(Seasonally adjusted, levels in thousands, rates per 100.)

| Year and month | Level[3] | | | | | | | | | | | |
| --- | --- | --- | --- | --- | --- | --- | --- | --- | --- | --- | --- | --- |
| | Total[4] | Total private[4] | Construction | Manufacturing | Trade, transportation, and utilities[5] | Retail trade | Professional and business services | Education and health services | Leisure and hospitality[6] | Accommodation and food services | Government[7] | State and local government |
| **2011** | | | | | | | | | | | | |
| January | 3 908 | 3 638 | 314 | 241 | 784 | 519 | 789 | 451 | 634 | 524 | 270 | 243 |
| February | 3 838 | 3 570 | 317 | 236 | 772 | 528 | 792 | 462 | 601 | 513 | 268 | 242 |
| March | 3 980 | 3 710 | 342 | 255 | 792 | 566 | 827 | 436 | 685 | 569 | 270 | 246 |
| April | 3 924 | 3 621 | 382 | 236 | 725 | 519 | 834 | 427 | 631 | 534 | 303 | 273 |
| May | 4 035 | 3 738 | 348 | 245 | 805 | 559 | 826 | 442 | 683 | 552 | 297 | 269 |
| June | 4 094 | 3 824 | 388 | 239 | 789 | 547 | 799 | 500 | 684 | 577 | 270 | 238 |
| July | 4 082 | 3 773 | 331 | 241 | 787 | 543 | 821 | 446 | 707 | 599 | 309 | 280 |
| August | 4 120 | 3 816 | 345 | 237 | 788 | 543 | 827 | 478 | 708 | 583 | 304 | 264 |
| September | 4 115 | 3 832 | 342 | 227 | 812 | 569 | 835 | 419 | 731 | 584 | 284 | 251 |
| October | 4 011 | 3 749 | 313 | 227 | 805 | 539 | 840 | 446 | 667 | 550 | 263 | 233 |
| November | 4 001 | 3 704 | 317 | 230 | 770 | 525 | 806 | 466 | 704 | 554 | 297 | 262 |
| December | 3 994 | 3 677 | 287 | 230 | 812 | 512 | 802 | 463 | 684 | 562 | 317 | 283 |
| **2012** | | | | | | | | | | | | |
| January | 4 031 | 3 750 | 308 | 231 | 816 | 542 | 728 | 508 | 721 | 587 | 282 | 258 |
| February | 4 174 | 3 876 | 336 | 240 | 796 | 567 | 911 | 487 | 714 | 563 | 298 | 265 |
| March | 4 130 | 3 845 | 294 | 229 | 819 | 561 | 878 | 470 | 756 | 618 | 284 | 257 |
| April | 4 247 | 3 931 | 313 | 242 | 853 | 568 | 811 | 476 | 742 | 596 | 316 | 284 |
| May | 4 331 | 4 032 | 352 | 245 | 817 | 568 | 898 | 493 | 758 | 626 | 299 | 268 |
| June | 4 374 | 4 080 | 354 | 259 | 868 | 587 | 901 | 550 | 714 | 611 | 293 | 262 |
| July | 4 145 | 3 852 | 352 | 224 | 844 | 572 | 825 | 463 | 712 | 606 | 293 | 261 |
| August | 4 352 | 4 058 | 334 | 236 | 906 | 614 | 827 | 495 | 730 | 616 | 294 | 260 |
| September | 4 061 | 3 795 | 345 | 220 | 833 | 569 | 826 | 432 | 678 | 570 | 266 | 231 |
| October | 4 177 | 3 872 | 286 | 233 | 847 | 565 | 829 | 480 | 738 | 623 | 305 | 269 |
| November | 4 145 | 3 853 | 383 | 229 | 777 | 507 | 830 | 468 | 685 | 574 | 292 | 254 |
| December | 4 069 | 3 780 | 254 | 219 | 898 | 614 | 812 | 470 | 704 | 577 | 289 | 247 |
| **2013** | | | | | | | | | | | | |
| January | 4 328 | 4 033 | 329 | 227 | 887 | 597 | 831 | 535 | 745 | 635 | 295 | 259 |
| February | 4 163 | 3 868 | 331 | 229 | 871 | 609 | 749 | 511 | 740 | 637 | 295 | 250 |
| March | 4 106 | 3 812 | 341 | 208 | 811 | 562 | 769 | 484 | 748 | 638 | 294 | 252 |
| April | 4 357 | 4 064 | 307 | 240 | 855 | 604 | 855 | 519 | 823 | 692 | 293 | 258 |
| May | 4 358 | 4 065 | 302 | 263 | 851 | 586 | 848 | 543 | 759 | 630 | 293 | 253 |
| June | 4 278 | 3 977 | 314 | 227 | 798 | 565 | 914 | 510 | 746 | 625 | 301 | 266 |
| July | 4 374 | 4 093 | 298 | 252 | 876 | 578 | 893 | 526 | 751 | 626 | 280 | 246 |
| August | 4 514 | 4 239 | 288 | 240 | 915 | 651 | 975 | 528 | 741 | 628 | 275 | 238 |
| September | 4 504 | 4 221 | 289 | 233 | 905 | 644 | 934 | 524 | 824 | 672 | 283 | 251 |
| October | 4 262 | 3 958 | 296 | 208 | 922 | 640 | 846 | 493 | 763 | 642 | 304 | 261 |
| November | 4 265 | 3 987 | 279 | 213 | 946 | 682 | 931 | 477 | 728 | 602 | 279 | 247 |
| December | 4 383 | 4 087 | 278 | 240 | 922 | 661 | 919 | 520 | 759 | 638 | 296 | 262 |
| **2014** | | | | | | | | | | | | |
| January | 4 476 | 4 180 | 239 | 246 | 971 | 670 | 915 | 565 | 790 | 665 | 296 | 260 |
| February | 4 465 | 4 179 | 250 | 223 | 981 | 706 | 926 | 504 | 863 | 727 | 286 | 252 |
| March | 4 446 | 4 138 | 232 | 245 | 977 | 694 | 946 | 529 | 767 | 639 | 308 | 275 |
| April | 4 499 | 4 220 | 260 | 240 | 1 005 | 725 | 912 | 565 | 803 | 666 | 278 | 246 |
| May | 4 562 | 4 268 | 294 | 239 | 1 030 | 731 | 901 | 490 | 824 | 687 | 294 | 265 |
| June | 4 543 | 4 258 | 262 | 246 | 1 005 | 706 | 911 | 536 | 851 | 714 | 285 | 252 |
| July | 4 756 | 4 482 | 337 | 246 | 1 051 | 726 | 947 | 523 | 870 | 711 | 273 | 248 |
| August | 4 634 | 4 333 | 304 | 228 | 994 | 686 | 980 | 487 | 829 | 669 | 301 | 275 |
| September | 4 830 | 4 528 | 269 | 255 | 991 | 692 | 1 068 | 572 | 877 | 723 | 302 | 269 |
| October | 4 914 | 4 603 | 294 | 259 | 1 075 | 746 | 1 073 | 566 | 876 | 731 | 311 | 278 |
| November | 4 654 | 4 365 | 295 | 227 | 1 048 | 728 | 924 | 509 | 884 | 731 | 289 | 254 |
| December | 4 840 | 4 528 | 347 | 260 | 1 080 | 772 | 926 | 535 | 904 | 766 | 312 | 281 |
| **2015** | | | | | | | | | | | | |
| January | 4 883 | 4 561 | 316 | 249 | 1 091 | 764 | 999 | 540 | 868 | 716 | 321 | 281 |
| February | 4 740 | 4 420 | 304 | 259 | 954 | 660 | 1 010 | 550 | 873 | 722 | 320 | 286 |
| March | 4 985 | 4 654 | 335 | 260 | 1 082 | 752 | 1 021 | 543 | 922 | 776 | 331 | 295 |
| April | 4 887 | 4 558 | 299 | 259 | 1 018 | 712 | 1 027 | 531 | 929 | 794 | 329 | 293 |
| May | 4 869 | 4 548 | 292 | 245 | 1 060 | 736 | 989 | 557 | 896 | 767 | 321 | 281 |
| June | 4 937 | 4 599 | 343 | 268 | 1 064 | 739 | 969 | 553 | 881 | 741 | 338 | 302 |
| July | 4 794 | 4 458 | 274 | 253 | 1 071 | 739 | 940 | 541 | 873 | 767 | 336 | 294 |
| August | 4 951 | 4 624 | 321 | 273 | 1 049 | 752 | 930 | 559 | 961 | 819 | 327 | 290 |
| September | 4 956 | 4 633 | 316 | 272 | 1 022 | 718 | 1 012 | 542 | 938 | 799 | 323 | 288 |
| October | 4 912 | 4 544 | 275 | 271 | 1 003 | 706 | 1 002 | 558 | 935 | 767 | 369 | 325 |
| November | 4 958 | 4 616 | 292 | 267 | 1 040 | 744 | 1 020 | 600 | 939 | 809 | 342 | 300 |
| December | 5 128 | 4 774 | 283 | 263 | 1 074 | 762 | 1 095 | 578 | 1 003 | 862 | 354 | 314 |
| **2016** | | | | | | | | | | | | |
| January | 4 977 | 4 631 | 279 | 266 | 1 052 | 725 | 1 053 | 557 | 907 | 750 | 346 | 304 |
| February | 5 159 | 4 812 | 325 | 304 | 1 052 | 751 | 1 072 | 552 | 1 011 | 879 | 348 | 308 |
| March | 5 096 | 4 747 | 334 | 288 | 1 043 | 747 | 1 042 | 557 | 972 | 828 | 349 | 310 |
| April | 5 015 | 4 660 | 354 | 279 | 1 012 | 702 | 1 004 | 570 | 950 | 819 | 355 | 317 |
| May | 4 978 | 4 642 | 338 | 294 | 1 010 | 706 | 966 | 593 | 969 | 815 | 335 | 303 |
| June | 4 964 | 4 612 | 293 | 264 | 1 047 | 711 | 943 | 618 | 950 | 795 | 352 | 317 |
| July | 4 991 | 4 665 | 294 | 263 | 1 068 | 750 | 1 045 | 584 | 944 | 804 | 326 | 289 |
| August | 5 052 | 4 696 | 327 | 268 | 1 009 | 707 | 1 008 | 595 | 988 | 795 | 357 | 320 |
| September | 4 936 | 4 578 | 296 | 278 | 1 039 | 722 | 1 009 | 560 | 928 | 781 | 357 | 320 |
| October | 4 966 | 4 631 | 311 | 269 | 1 046 | 736 | 1 016 | 591 | 965 | 815 | 334 | 302 |

[1]Total separations are the number of separations during the entire month.
[2]The total separations rate is the number of total separations during the entire month as a percent of total employment.
[3]Detail will not necessarily add to totals because of the independent seasonal adjustment of the various series.
[4]Includes natural resources and mining, information, financial activities, and other services, not shown separately.
[5]Includes wholesale trade and transportation, warehousing, and utilities, not shown separately.
[6]Includes arts, entertainment, and recreation, not shown separately.
[7]Includes federal government, not shown separately.

## Table 7-6.  Separations Levels[1] and Rates,[2] by Industry, 2005–October 2016—*Continued*

(Seasonally adjusted, levels in thousands, rates per 100.)

| Year and month | Rate | | | | | | | | | | | |
|---|---|---|---|---|---|---|---|---|---|---|---|---|
| | Total[4] | Total private[4] | Construction | Manufacturing | Trade, transportation, and utilities[5] | Retail trade | Professional and business services | Education and health services | Leisure and hospitality[6] | Accommodation and food services | Government[7] | State and local government |
| **2011** | | | | | | | | | | | | |
| January | 3.0 | 3.3 | 5.8 | 2.1 | 3.2 | 3.6 | 4.6 | 2.2 | 4.8 | 4.7 | 1.2 | 1.3 |
| February | 2.9 | 3.3 | 5.8 | 2.0 | 3.1 | 3.6 | 4.6 | 2.3 | 4.6 | 4.5 | 1.2 | 1.3 |
| March | 3.0 | 3.4 | 6.2 | 2.2 | 3.2 | 3.9 | 4.8 | 2.2 | 5.2 | 5.0 | 1.2 | 1.3 |
| April | 3.0 | 3.3 | 7.0 | 2.0 | 2.9 | 3.5 | 4.8 | 2.1 | 4.7 | 4.7 | 1.4 | 1.4 |
| May | 3.1 | 3.4 | 6.3 | 2.1 | 3.2 | 3.8 | 4.8 | 2.2 | 5.1 | 4.8 | 1.3 | 1.4 |
| June | 3.1 | 3.5 | 7.0 | 2.0 | 3.1 | 3.7 | 4.6 | 2.5 | 5.1 | 5.1 | 1.2 | 1.2 |
| July | 3.1 | 3.4 | 6.0 | 2.0 | 3.1 | 3.7 | 4.7 | 2.2 | 5.3 | 5.2 | 1.4 | 1.5 |
| August | 3.1 | 3.5 | 6.2 | 2.0 | 3.1 | 3.7 | 4.8 | 2.3 | 5.3 | 5.1 | 1.4 | 1.4 |
| September | 3.1 | 3.5 | 6.1 | 1.9 | 3.2 | 3.9 | 4.8 | 2.1 | 5.4 | 5.1 | 1.3 | 1.3 |
| October | 3.0 | 3.4 | 5.6 | 1.9 | 3.2 | 3.7 | 4.8 | 2.2 | 5.0 | 4.8 | 1.2 | 1.2 |
| November | 3.0 | 3.3 | 5.7 | 2.0 | 3.1 | 3.6 | 4.6 | 2.3 | 5.2 | 4.8 | 1.4 | 1.4 |
| December | 3.0 | 3.3 | 5.1 | 1.9 | 3.2 | 3.5 | 4.6 | 2.3 | 5.1 | 4.8 | 1.4 | 1.5 |
| **2012** | | | | | | | | | | | | |
| January | 3.0 | 3.4 | 5.5 | 2.0 | 3.2 | 3.7 | 4.1 | 2.5 | 5.3 | 5.0 | 1.3 | 1.3 |
| February | 3.1 | 3.5 | 6.0 | 2.0 | 3.1 | 3.8 | 5.1 | 2.4 | 5.2 | 4.8 | 1.4 | 1.4 |
| March | 3.1 | 3.4 | 5.2 | 1.9 | 3.2 | 3.8 | 4.9 | 2.3 | 5.5 | 5.3 | 1.3 | 1.4 |
| April | 3.2 | 3.5 | 5.6 | 2.0 | 3.4 | 3.8 | 4.5 | 2.3 | 5.4 | 5.1 | 1.4 | 1.5 |
| May | 3.2 | 3.6 | 6.3 | 2.1 | 3.2 | 3.8 | 5.0 | 2.4 | 5.5 | 5.3 | 1.4 | 1.4 |
| June | 3.3 | 3.6 | 6.3 | 2.2 | 3.4 | 4.0 | 5.0 | 2.7 | 5.2 | 5.2 | 1.3 | 1.4 |
| July | 3.1 | 3.4 | 6.3 | 1.9 | 3.3 | 3.9 | 4.6 | 2.2 | 5.2 | 5.1 | 1.3 | 1.4 |
| August | 3.2 | 3.6 | 5.9 | 2.0 | 3.6 | 4.1 | 4.6 | 2.4 | 5.3 | 5.2 | 1.3 | 1.4 |
| September | 3.0 | 3.4 | 6.1 | 1.8 | 3.3 | 3.8 | 4.6 | 2.1 | 4.9 | 4.8 | 1.2 | 1.2 |
| October | 3.1 | 3.4 | 5.0 | 2.0 | 3.3 | 3.8 | 4.6 | 2.3 | 5.3 | 5.2 | 1.4 | 1.4 |
| November | 3.1 | 3.4 | 6.7 | 1.9 | 3.0 | 3.4 | 4.6 | 2.2 | 4.9 | 4.8 | 1.3 | 1.3 |
| December | 3.0 | 3.3 | 4.4 | 1.8 | 3.5 | 4.1 | 4.5 | 2.2 | 5.0 | 4.8 | 1.3 | 1.3 |
| **2013** | | | | | | | | | | | | |
| January | 3.2 | 3.6 | 5.7 | 1.9 | 3.5 | 4.0 | 4.6 | 2.6 | 5.3 | 5.3 | 1.3 | 1.4 |
| February | 3.1 | 3.4 | 5.7 | 1.9 | 3.4 | 4.1 | 4.1 | 2.4 | 5.3 | 5.3 | 1.3 | 1.3 |
| March | 3.0 | 3.3 | 5.9 | 1.7 | 3.2 | 3.8 | 4.2 | 2.3 | 5.3 | 5.3 | 1.3 | 1.3 |
| April | 3.2 | 3.6 | 5.3 | 2.0 | 3.3 | 4.0 | 4.6 | 2.5 | 5.8 | 5.7 | 1.3 | 1.4 |
| May | 3.2 | 3.6 | 5.2 | 2.2 | 3.3 | 3.9 | 4.6 | 2.6 | 5.3 | 5.2 | 1.3 | 1.3 |
| June | 3.1 | 3.5 | 5.4 | 1.9 | 3.1 | 3.8 | 4.9 | 2.4 | 5.2 | 5.1 | 1.4 | 1.4 |
| July | 3.2 | 3.6 | 5.1 | 2.1 | 3.4 | 3.8 | 4.8 | 2.5 | 5.3 | 5.1 | 1.3 | 1.3 |
| August | 3.3 | 3.7 | 4.9 | 2.0 | 3.5 | 4.3 | 5.2 | 2.5 | 5.2 | 5.1 | 1.3 | 1.2 |
| September | 3.3 | 3.7 | 4.9 | 1.9 | 3.5 | 4.2 | 5.0 | 2.5 | 5.7 | 5.5 | 1.3 | 1.3 |
| October | 3.1 | 3.4 | 5.0 | 1.7 | 3.5 | 4.2 | 4.5 | 2.3 | 5.3 | 5.2 | 1.4 | 1.4 |
| November | 3.1 | 3.5 | 4.7 | 1.8 | 3.6 | 4.5 | 5.0 | 2.2 | 5.0 | 4.9 | 1.3 | 1.3 |
| December | 3.2 | 3.5 | 4.7 | 2.0 | 3.5 | 4.3 | 4.9 | 2.5 | 5.3 | 5.1 | 1.4 | 1.4 |
| **2014** | | | | | | | | | | | | |
| January | 3.3 | 3.6 | 4.0 | 2.0 | 3.7 | 4.4 | 4.9 | 2.7 | 5.4 | 5.4 | 1.4 | 1.4 |
| February | 3.2 | 3.6 | 4.1 | 1.8 | 3.8 | 4.6 | 4.9 | 2.4 | 5.9 | 5.9 | 1.3 | 1.3 |
| March | 3.2 | 3.6 | 3.8 | 2.0 | 3.7 | 4.5 | 5.0 | 2.5 | 5.3 | 5.1 | 1.4 | 1.4 |
| April | 3.3 | 3.6 | 4.3 | 2.0 | 3.8 | 4.7 | 4.8 | 2.7 | 5.5 | 5.3 | 1.3 | 1.3 |
| May | 3.3 | 3.7 | 4.8 | 2.0 | 3.9 | 4.8 | 4.7 | 2.3 | 5.6 | 5.5 | 1.3 | 1.4 |
| June | 3.3 | 3.6 | 4.3 | 2.0 | 3.8 | 4.6 | 4.8 | 2.5 | 5.8 | 5.7 | 1.3 | 1.3 |
| July | 3.4 | 3.8 | 5.5 | 2.0 | 4.0 | 4.7 | 5.0 | 2.4 | 5.9 | 5.6 | 1.2 | 1.3 |
| August | 3.3 | 3.7 | 4.9 | 1.9 | 3.8 | 4.5 | 5.1 | 2.3 | 5.6 | 5.3 | 1.4 | 1.4 |
| September | 3.5 | 3.8 | 4.3 | 2.1 | 3.7 | 4.5 | 5.6 | 2.7 | 5.9 | 5.7 | 1.4 | 1.4 |
| October | 3.5 | 3.9 | 4.7 | 2.1 | 4.1 | 4.8 | 5.6 | 2.6 | 5.9 | 5.8 | 1.4 | 1.4 |
| November | 3.3 | 3.7 | 4.7 | 1.9 | 3.9 | 4.7 | 4.8 | 2.4 | 6.0 | 5.7 | 1.3 | 1.3 |
| December | 3.4 | 3.8 | 5.5 | 2.1 | 4.1 | 5.0 | 4.8 | 2.5 | 6.1 | 6.0 | 1.4 | 1.5 |
| **2015** | | | | | | | | | | | | |
| January | 3.5 | 3.8 | 5.0 | 2.0 | 4.1 | 4.9 | 5.2 | 2.5 | 5.8 | 5.6 | 1.5 | 1.5 |
| February | 3.4 | 3.7 | 4.8 | 2.1 | 3.6 | 4.2 | 5.2 | 2.5 | 5.8 | 5.6 | 1.5 | 1.5 |
| March | 3.5 | 3.9 | 5.3 | 2.1 | 4.0 | 4.8 | 5.3 | 2.5 | 6.1 | 6.0 | 1.5 | 1.5 |
| April | 3.5 | 3.8 | 4.7 | 2.1 | 3.8 | 4.6 | 5.3 | 2.4 | 6.2 | 6.2 | 1.5 | 1.5 |
| May | 3.4 | 3.8 | 4.5 | 2.0 | 3.9 | 4.7 | 5.1 | 2.5 | 5.9 | 5.9 | 1.5 | 1.5 |
| June | 3.5 | 3.8 | 5.3 | 2.2 | 4.0 | 4.7 | 4.9 | 2.5 | 5.8 | 5.7 | 1.5 | 1.6 |
| July | 3.4 | 3.7 | 4.3 | 2.0 | 4.0 | 4.7 | 4.8 | 2.5 | 5.8 | 5.9 | 1.5 | 1.5 |
| August | 3.5 | 3.9 | 5.0 | 2.2 | 3.9 | 4.8 | 4.7 | 2.5 | 6.3 | 6.3 | 1.5 | 1.5 |
| September | 3.5 | 3.9 | 4.9 | 2.2 | 3.8 | 4.6 | 5.1 | 2.4 | 6.2 | 6.1 | 1.5 | 1.5 |
| October | 3.4 | 3.8 | 4.2 | 2.2 | 3.7 | 4.5 | 5.0 | 2.5 | 6.1 | 5.9 | 1.7 | 1.7 |
| November | 3.5 | 3.8 | 4.5 | 2.2 | 3.8 | 4.7 | 5.1 | 2.7 | 6.1 | 6.2 | 1.6 | 1.6 |
| December | 3.6 | 3.9 | 4.3 | 2.1 | 4.0 | 4.8 | 5.5 | 2.6 | 6.5 | 6.6 | 1.6 | 1.6 |
| **2016** | | | | | | | | | | | | |
| January | 3.5 | 3.8 | 4.2 | 2.2 | 3.9 | 4.6 | 5.3 | 2.5 | 5.9 | 5.7 | 1.6 | 1.6 |
| February | 3.6 | 4.0 | 4.9 | 2.5 | 3.9 | 4.7 | 5.4 | 2.5 | 6.6 | 6.7 | 1.6 | 1.6 |
| March | 3.5 | 3.9 | 5.0 | 2.3 | 3.8 | 4.7 | 5.2 | 2.5 | 6.3 | 6.3 | 1.6 | 1.6 |
| April | 3.5 | 3.8 | 5.3 | 2.3 | 3.7 | 4.4 | 5.0 | 2.5 | 6.2 | 6.2 | 1.6 | 1.6 |
| May | 3.5 | 3.8 | 5.1 | 2.4 | 3.7 | 4.4 | 4.8 | 2.6 | 6.3 | 6.2 | 1.5 | 1.6 |
| June | 3.4 | 3.8 | 4.4 | 2.1 | 3.8 | 4.5 | 4.7 | 2.7 | 6.1 | 6.0 | 1.6 | 1.6 |
| July | 3.5 | 3.8 | 4.4 | 2.1 | 3.9 | 4.7 | 5.2 | 2.6 | 6.1 | 6.1 | 1.5 | 1.5 |
| August | 3.5 | 3.8 | 4.9 | 2.2 | 3.7 | 4.4 | 5.0 | 2.6 | 6.4 | 6.0 | 1.6 | 1.6 |
| September | 3.4 | 3.7 | 4.4 | 2.3 | 3.8 | 4.5 | 5.0 | 2.5 | 6.0 | 5.9 | 1.6 | 1.7 |
| October | 3.4 | 3.8 | 4.6 | 2.2 | 3.8 | 4.6 | 5.0 | 2.6 | 6.2 | 6.1 | 1.5 | 1.6 |

[1]Total separations are the number of separations during the entire month.
[2]The total separations rate is the number of total separations during the entire month as a percent of total employment.
[3]Detail will not necessarily add to totals because of the independent seasonal adjustment of the various series.
[4]Includes natural resources and mining, information, financial activities, and other services, not shown separately.
[5]Includes wholesale trade and transportation, warehousing, and utilities, not shown separately.
[6]Includes arts, entertainment, and recreation, not shown separately.
[7]Includes federal government, not shown separately.

## Table 7-7.  Quits Levels[1] and Rates,[2] by Industry, 2005–October 2016

(Seasonally adjusted, levels in thousands, rates per 100.)

| Year and month | Level[3] | | | | | | | | | | | |
|---|---|---|---|---|---|---|---|---|---|---|---|---|
| | Total[4] | Total private[4] | Construction | Manufacturing | Trade, transportation, and utilities[5] | Retail trade | Professional and business services | Education and health services | Leisure and hospitality[6] | Accommodation and food services | Government[7] | State and local government |
| **2005** | | | | | | | | | | | | |
| January | 2 844 | 2 706 | 190 | 188 | 644 | 456 | 490 | 289 | 573 | 519 | 138 | 127 |
| February | 2 660 | 2 519 | 174 | 183 | 576 | 424 | 493 | 297 | 512 | 459 | 141 | 126 |
| March | 2 841 | 2 689 | 198 | 203 | 664 | 495 | 503 | 316 | 513 | 457 | 152 | 139 |
| April | 2 801 | 2 665 | 160 | 189 | 620 | 467 | 524 | 315 | 515 | 458 | 137 | 124 |
| May | 2 882 | 2 744 | 195 | 183 | 656 | 515 | 512 | 296 | 561 | 505 | 138 | 127 |
| June | 2 821 | 2 675 | 171 | 206 | 662 | 491 | 467 | 304 | 529 | 477 | 146 | 133 |
| July | 2 794 | 2 674 | 181 | 202 | 620 | 463 | 414 | 298 | 597 | 542 | 120 | 104 |
| August | 2 966 | 2 818 | 191 | 197 | 683 | 503 | 467 | 309 | 597 | 549 | 148 | 135 |
| September | 3 053 | 2 895 | 240 | 208 | 642 | 471 | 510 | 314 | 633 | 585 | 158 | 140 |
| October | 2 967 | 2 795 | 224 | 203 | 640 | 478 | 426 | 304 | 673 | 595 | 171 | 152 |
| November | 2 920 | 2 758 | 211 | 197 | 662 | 487 | 404 | 309 | 644 | 596 | 161 | 143 |
| December | 2 805 | 2 657 | 242 | 188 | 663 | 493 | 424 | 298 | 575 | 523 | 148 | 127 |
| **2006** | | | | | | | | | | | | |
| January | 2 954 | 2 791 | 210 | 190 | 650 | 495 | 477 | 278 | 657 | 597 | 163 | 146 |
| February | 2 975 | 2 818 | 200 | 206 | 671 | 506 | 454 | 304 | 677 | 629 | 157 | 137 |
| March | 3 004 | 2 844 | 198 | 195 | 689 | 521 | 495 | 290 | 646 | 585 | 160 | 137 |
| April | 2 789 | 2 631 | 206 | 179 | 682 | 500 | 482 | 291 | 517 | 464 | 158 | 131 |
| May | 3 056 | 2 869 | 199 | 236 | 684 | 497 | 498 | 329 | 620 | 568 | 187 | 161 |
| June | 3 050 | 2 873 | 202 | 186 | 649 | 481 | 475 | 334 | 680 | 623 | 177 | 144 |
| July | 2 977 | 2 818 | 177 | 216 | 679 | 510 | 463 | 325 | 584 | 541 | 158 | 137 |
| August | 3 003 | 2 830 | 168 | 204 | 701 | 488 | 499 | 323 | 590 | 541 | 173 | 147 |
| September | 2 940 | 2 777 | 160 | 171 | 653 | 483 | 565 | 295 | 601 | 557 | 163 | 126 |
| October | 2 931 | 2 773 | 167 | 201 | 653 | 482 | 486 | 315 | 613 | 559 | 158 | 140 |
| November | 3 069 | 2 902 | 161 | 238 | 715 | 531 | 555 | 320 | 611 | 557 | 167 | 142 |
| December | 3 046 | 2 876 | 160 | 247 | 666 | 471 | 536 | 343 | 662 | 606 | 170 | 148 |
| **2007** | | | | | | | | | | | | |
| January | 2 988 | 2 816 | 159 | 235 | 645 | 471 | 538 | 308 | 607 | 570 | 173 | 154 |
| February | 2 993 | 2 843 | 146 | 213 | 694 | 507 | 531 | 321 | 652 | 599 | 150 | 128 |
| March | 2 989 | 2 810 | 141 | 227 | 639 | 454 | 521 | 310 | 635 | 576 | 180 | 147 |
| April | 2 901 | 2 726 | 162 | 205 | 634 | 460 | 468 | 313 | 630 | 586 | 175 | 149 |
| May | 3 008 | 2 825 | 162 | 227 | 689 | 494 | 462 | 336 | 595 | 551 | 183 | 152 |
| June | 2 841 | 2 672 | 138 | 201 | 654 | 472 | 445 | 293 | 619 | 570 | 169 | 138 |
| July | 2 947 | 2 775 | 200 | 185 | 587 | 439 | 498 | 324 | 642 | 588 | 171 | 137 |
| August | 2 950 | 2 793 | 172 | 210 | 597 | 439 | 480 | 325 | 624 | 563 | 157 | 133 |
| September | 2 643 | 2 480 | 145 | 186 | 599 | 434 | 451 | 266 | 498 | 445 | 163 | 127 |
| October | 2 884 | 2 727 | 159 | 197 | 633 | 466 | 470 | 295 | 638 | 588 | 157 | 141 |
| November | 2 777 | 2 623 | 164 | 191 | 562 | 418 | 462 | 317 | 670 | 612 | 154 | 141 |
| December | 2 792 | 2 651 | 156 | 210 | 652 | 492 | 432 | 294 | 625 | 564 | 141 | 129 |
| **2008** | | | | | | | | | | | | |
| January | 2 831 | 2 687 | 148 | 200 | 646 | 472 | 439 | 319 | 600 | 538 | 144 | 129 |
| February | 2 789 | 2 642 | 159 | 189 | 606 | 422 | 487 | 312 | 603 | 549 | 148 | 135 |
| March | 2 575 | 2 443 | 112 | 183 | 575 | 415 | 402 | 307 | 594 | 547 | 132 | 124 |
| April | 2 882 | 2 730 | 185 | 179 | 590 | 417 | 538 | 332 | 583 | 533 | 153 | 142 |
| May | 2 602 | 2 471 | 135 | 167 | 568 | 398 | 453 | 275 | 594 | 542 | 131 | 124 |
| June | 2 662 | 2 530 | 150 | 160 | 567 | 411 | 466 | 289 | 582 | 534 | 132 | 125 |
| July | 2 550 | 2 431 | 152 | 143 | 558 | 401 | 449 | 297 | 556 | 503 | 120 | 114 |
| August | 2 416 | 2 270 | 149 | 137 | 550 | 411 | 369 | 281 | 507 | 466 | 145 | 136 |
| September | 2 446 | 2 312 | 110 | 146 | 554 | 406 | 404 | 279 | 538 | 492 | 134 | 127 |
| October | 2 412 | 2 279 | 108 | 144 | 523 | 364 | 427 | 295 | 525 | 487 | 133 | 125 |
| November | 2 063 | 1 952 | 89 | 125 | 481 | 364 | 356 | 254 | 454 | 422 | 112 | 107 |
| December | 2 104 | 1 977 | 83 | 102 | 517 | 381 | 385 | 247 | 443 | 413 | 127 | 120 |
| **2009** | | | | | | | | | | | | |
| January | 2 043 | 1 938 | 77 | 109 | 481 | 360 | 362 | 257 | 436 | 407 | 105 | 98 |
| February | 1 906 | 1 803 | 91 | 98 | 381 | 285 | 312 | 264 | 422 | 388 | 104 | 100 |
| March | 1 794 | 1 693 | 85 | 86 | 427 | 309 | 268 | 246 | 383 | 350 | 101 | 97 |
| April | 1 734 | 1 635 | 71 | 82 | 348 | 245 | 274 | 231 | 395 | 357 | 99 | 95 |
| May | 1 740 | 1 640 | 77 | 85 | 377 | 277 | 295 | 240 | 370 | 332 | 99 | 89 |
| June | 1 782 | 1 684 | 75 | 92 | 381 | 290 | 272 | 264 | 388 | 339 | 98 | 91 |
| July | 1 726 | 1 624 | 68 | 87 | 390 | 281 | 255 | 242 | 369 | 331 | 103 | 99 |
| August | 1 676 | 1 572 | 58 | 77 | 391 | 292 | 237 | 241 | 375 | 341 | 104 | 94 |
| September | 1 639 | 1 541 | 73 | 91 | 370 | 265 | 250 | 261 | 318 | 306 | 98 | 93 |
| October | 1 671 | 1 574 | 61 | 77 | 377 | 279 | 275 | 256 | 351 | 319 | 97 | 92 |
| November | 1 784 | 1 680 | 94 | 70 | 408 | 276 | 284 | 261 | 387 | 349 | 105 | 96 |
| December | 1 697 | 1 589 | 87 | 72 | 399 | 299 | 256 | 263 | 356 | 324 | 108 | 98 |
| **2010** | | | | | | | | | | | | |
| January | 1 668 | 1 569 | 96 | 81 | 323 | 236 | 263 | 241 | 395 | 341 | 99 | 95 |
| February | 1 724 | 1 602 | 77 | 104 | 398 | 307 | 286 | 237 | 363 | 332 | 121 | 112 |
| March | 1 793 | 1 684 | 77 | 85 | 402 | 301 | 302 | 245 | 374 | 344 | 109 | 101 |
| April | 1 914 | 1 812 | 69 | 91 | 427 | 323 | 351 | 282 | 373 | 335 | 101 | 92 |
| May | 1 790 | 1 700 | 57 | 87 | 418 | 316 | 307 | 240 | 377 | 343 | 90 | 78 |
| June | 1 940 | 1 806 | 62 | 95 | 413 | 312 | 353 | 277 | 357 | 327 | 133 | 107 |
| July | 1 848 | 1 740 | 73 | 92 | 433 | 330 | 339 | 238 | 356 | 328 | 108 | 88 |
| August | 1 904 | 1 792 | 87 | 105 | 399 | 294 | 373 | 238 | 376 | 340 | 112 | 97 |
| September | 1 921 | 1 799 | 83 | 96 | 441 | 342 | 341 | 250 | 370 | 329 | 122 | 110 |
| October | 1 852 | 1 748 | 76 | 104 | 384 | 302 | 362 | 251 | 383 | 334 | 104 | 95 |
| November | 1 778 | 1 668 | 59 | 96 | 431 | 328 | 296 | 265 | 341 | 300 | 111 | 103 |
| December | 1 937 | 1 830 | 92 | 102 | 397 | 294 | 392 | 251 | 381 | 340 | 107 | 100 |

[1]Quits are the number of quits during the entire month.
[2]The quits rate is the number of quits during the entire month as a percent of total employment.
[3]Detail will not necessarily add to totals because of the independent seasonal adjustment of the various series.
[4]Includes natural resources and mining, information, financial activities, and other services, not shown separately.
[5]Includes wholesale trade and transportation, warehousing, and utilities, not shown separately.
[6]Includes arts, entertainment, and recreation, not shown separately.
[7]Includes federal government, not shown separately.

## Table 7-7. Quits Levels[1] and Rates,[2] by Industry, 2005–October 2016—*Continued*

(Seasonally adjusted, levels in thousands, rates per 100.)

| Year and month | Rate | | | | | | | | | | | |
|---|---|---|---|---|---|---|---|---|---|---|---|---|
| | Total[4] | Total private[4] | Construction | Manufacturing | Trade, transportation, and utilities[5] | Retail trade | Professional and business services | Education and health services | Leisure and hospitality[6] | Accommodation and food services | Government[7] | State and local government |
| **2005** | | | | | | | | | | | | |
| January | 2.1 | 2.4 | 2.7 | 1.3 | 2.5 | 3.0 | 2.9 | 1.7 | 4.5 | 4.8 | 0.6 | 0.7 |
| February | 2.0 | 2.3 | 2.4 | 1.3 | 2.2 | 2.8 | 3.0 | 1.7 | 4.0 | 4.2 | 0.6 | 0.7 |
| March | 2.1 | 2.4 | 2.8 | 1.4 | 2.6 | 3.3 | 3.0 | 1.8 | 4.0 | 4.2 | 0.7 | 0.7 |
| April | 2.1 | 2.4 | 2.2 | 1.3 | 2.4 | 3.1 | 3.1 | 1.8 | 4.0 | 4.2 | 0.6 | 0.7 |
| May | 2.2 | 2.5 | 2.7 | 1.3 | 2.5 | 3.4 | 3.0 | 1.7 | 4.4 | 4.6 | 0.6 | 0.7 |
| June | 2.1 | 2.4 | 2.3 | 1.4 | 2.5 | 3.2 | 2.8 | 1.7 | 4.1 | 4.4 | 0.7 | 0.7 |
| July | 2.1 | 2.4 | 2.5 | 1.4 | 2.4 | 3.0 | 2.4 | 1.7 | 4.6 | 4.9 | 0.5 | 0.5 |
| August | 2.2 | 2.5 | 2.6 | 1.4 | 2.6 | 3.3 | 2.7 | 1.7 | 4.6 | 5.0 | 0.7 | 0.7 |
| September | 2.3 | 2.6 | 3.2 | 1.5 | 2.5 | 3.1 | 3.0 | 1.8 | 4.9 | 5.3 | 0.7 | 0.7 |
| October | 2.2 | 2.5 | 3.0 | 1.4 | 2.5 | 3.1 | 2.5 | 1.7 | 5.2 | 5.4 | 0.8 | 0.8 |
| November | 2.2 | 2.4 | 2.8 | 1.4 | 2.5 | 3.2 | 2.3 | 1.7 | 5.0 | 5.4 | 0.7 | 0.8 |
| December | 2.1 | 2.3 | 3.2 | 1.3 | 2.5 | 3.2 | 2.5 | 1.7 | 4.5 | 4.8 | 0.7 | 0.7 |
| **2006** | | | | | | | | | | | | |
| January | 2.2 | 2.5 | 2.8 | 1.3 | 2.5 | 3.2 | 2.8 | 1.6 | 5.1 | 5.4 | 0.7 | 0.8 |
| February | 2.2 | 2.5 | 2.6 | 1.5 | 2.6 | 3.3 | 2.6 | 1.7 | 5.2 | 5.7 | 0.7 | 0.7 |
| March | 2.2 | 2.5 | 2.6 | 1.4 | 2.6 | 3.4 | 2.8 | 1.6 | 5.0 | 5.3 | 0.7 | 0.7 |
| April | 2.0 | 2.3 | 2.7 | 1.3 | 2.6 | 3.3 | 2.8 | 1.6 | 4.0 | 4.2 | 0.7 | 0.7 |
| May | 2.2 | 2.5 | 2.6 | 1.7 | 2.6 | 3.2 | 2.8 | 1.8 | 4.7 | 5.1 | 0.9 | 0.8 |
| June | 2.2 | 2.5 | 2.6 | 1.3 | 2.5 | 3.1 | 2.7 | 1.8 | 5.2 | 5.6 | 0.8 | 0.7 |
| July | 2.2 | 2.5 | 2.3 | 1.5 | 2.6 | 3.3 | 2.6 | 1.8 | 4.4 | 4.8 | 0.7 | 0.7 |
| August | 2.2 | 2.5 | 2.2 | 1.4 | 2.7 | 3.2 | 2.8 | 1.8 | 4.5 | 4.8 | 0.8 | 0.8 |
| September | 2.1 | 2.4 | 2.1 | 1.2 | 2.5 | 3.1 | 3.2 | 1.6 | 4.6 | 5.0 | 0.7 | 0.6 |
| October | 2.1 | 2.4 | 2.2 | 1.4 | 2.5 | 3.1 | 2.7 | 1.7 | 4.7 | 5.0 | 0.7 | 0.7 |
| November | 2.2 | 2.5 | 2.1 | 1.7 | 2.7 | 3.4 | 3.1 | 1.7 | 4.6 | 4.9 | 0.8 | 0.7 |
| December | 2.2 | 2.5 | 2.1 | 1.8 | 2.5 | 3.1 | 3.0 | 1.9 | 5.0 | 5.3 | 0.8 | 0.8 |
| **2007** | | | | | | | | | | | | |
| January | 2.2 | 2.4 | 2.1 | 1.7 | 2.4 | 3.0 | 3.0 | 1.7 | 4.6 | 5.0 | 0.8 | 0.8 |
| February | 2.2 | 2.5 | 1.9 | 1.5 | 2.6 | 3.3 | 3.0 | 1.7 | 4.9 | 5.3 | 0.7 | 0.7 |
| March | 2.2 | 2.4 | 1.8 | 1.6 | 2.4 | 2.9 | 2.9 | 1.7 | 4.8 | 5.1 | 0.8 | 0.8 |
| April | 2.1 | 2.4 | 2.1 | 1.5 | 2.4 | 3.0 | 2.6 | 1.7 | 4.7 | 5.1 | 0.8 | 0.8 |
| May | 2.2 | 2.4 | 2.1 | 1.6 | 2.6 | 3.2 | 2.6 | 1.8 | 4.4 | 4.8 | 0.8 | 0.8 |
| June | 2.1 | 2.3 | 1.8 | 1.4 | 2.5 | 3.0 | 2.5 | 1.6 | 4.6 | 5.0 | 0.8 | 0.7 |
| July | 2.1 | 2.4 | 2.6 | 1.3 | 2.2 | 2.8 | 2.8 | 1.7 | 4.8 | 5.1 | 0.8 | 0.7 |
| August | 2.1 | 2.4 | 2.3 | 1.5 | 2.2 | 2.8 | 2.7 | 1.7 | 4.7 | 4.9 | 0.7 | 0.7 |
| September | 1.9 | 2.1 | 1.9 | 1.3 | 2.2 | 2.8 | 2.5 | 1.4 | 3.7 | 3.9 | 0.7 | 0.7 |
| October | 2.1 | 2.4 | 2.1 | 1.4 | 2.4 | 3.0 | 2.6 | 1.6 | 4.7 | 5.1 | 0.7 | 0.7 |
| November | 2.0 | 2.3 | 2.2 | 1.4 | 2.1 | 2.7 | 2.6 | 1.7 | 5.0 | 5.3 | 0.7 | 0.7 |
| December | 2.0 | 2.3 | 2.1 | 1.5 | 2.4 | 3.2 | 2.4 | 1.6 | 4.6 | 4.9 | 0.6 | 0.7 |
| **2008** | | | | | | | | | | | | |
| January | 2.0 | 2.3 | 2.0 | 1.5 | 2.4 | 3.0 | 2.4 | 1.7 | 4.4 | 4.7 | 0.6 | 0.7 |
| February | 2.0 | 2.3 | 2.1 | 1.4 | 2.3 | 2.7 | 2.7 | 1.6 | 4.5 | 4.8 | 0.7 | 0.7 |
| March | 1.9 | 2.1 | 1.5 | 1.3 | 2.2 | 2.7 | 2.2 | 1.6 | 4.4 | 4.7 | 0.6 | 0.6 |
| April | 2.1 | 2.4 | 2.5 | 1.3 | 2.2 | 2.7 | 3.0 | 1.7 | 4.3 | 4.6 | 0.7 | 0.7 |
| May | 1.9 | 2.1 | 1.9 | 1.2 | 2.1 | 2.6 | 2.5 | 1.4 | 4.4 | 4.7 | 0.6 | 0.6 |
| June | 1.9 | 2.2 | 2.1 | 1.2 | 2.1 | 2.7 | 2.6 | 1.5 | 4.3 | 4.6 | 0.6 | 0.6 |
| July | 1.9 | 2.1 | 2.1 | 1.1 | 2.1 | 2.6 | 2.5 | 1.5 | 4.1 | 4.4 | 0.5 | 0.6 |
| August | 1.8 | 2.0 | 2.1 | 1.0 | 2.1 | 2.7 | 2.1 | 1.5 | 3.8 | 4.1 | 0.6 | 0.7 |
| September | 1.8 | 2.0 | 1.6 | 1.1 | 2.1 | 2.7 | 2.3 | 1.4 | 4.0 | 4.3 | 0.6 | 0.6 |
| October | 1.8 | 2.0 | 1.6 | 1.1 | 2.0 | 2.4 | 2.4 | 1.5 | 3.9 | 4.3 | 0.6 | 0.6 |
| November | 1.5 | 1.7 | 1.3 | 1.0 | 1.9 | 2.4 | 2.1 | 1.3 | 3.4 | 3.7 | 0.5 | 0.5 |
| December | 1.6 | 1.8 | 1.2 | 0.8 | 2.0 | 2.6 | 2.2 | 1.3 | 3.3 | 3.7 | 0.6 | 0.6 |
| **2009** | | | | | | | | | | | | |
| January | 1.5 | 1.7 | 1.2 | 0.9 | 1.9 | 2.4 | 2.1 | 1.3 | 3.3 | 3.6 | 0.5 | 0.5 |
| February | 1.4 | 1.6 | 1.4 | 0.8 | 1.5 | 1.9 | 1.8 | 1.4 | 3.2 | 3.4 | 0.5 | 0.5 |
| March | 1.4 | 1.5 | 1.4 | 0.7 | 1.7 | 2.1 | 1.6 | 1.3 | 2.9 | 3.1 | 0.4 | 0.5 |
| April | 1.3 | 1.5 | 1.1 | 0.7 | 1.4 | 1.7 | 1.7 | 1.2 | 3.0 | 3.2 | 0.4 | 0.5 |
| May | 1.3 | 1.5 | 1.3 | 0.7 | 1.5 | 1.9 | 1.8 | 1.2 | 2.8 | 3.0 | 0.4 | 0.4 |
| June | 1.4 | 1.6 | 1.3 | 0.8 | 1.5 | 2.0 | 1.7 | 1.3 | 3.0 | 3.0 | 0.4 | 0.5 |
| July | 1.3 | 1.5 | 1.2 | 0.7 | 1.6 | 1.9 | 1.6 | 1.2 | 2.8 | 3.0 | 0.5 | 0.5 |
| August | 1.3 | 1.5 | 1.0 | 0.7 | 1.6 | 2.0 | 1.4 | 1.2 | 2.9 | 3.1 | 0.5 | 0.5 |
| September | 1.3 | 1.4 | 1.3 | 0.8 | 1.5 | 1.8 | 1.5 | 1.3 | 2.4 | 2.8 | 0.4 | 0.5 |
| October | 1.3 | 1.5 | 1.1 | 0.7 | 1.5 | 1.9 | 1.7 | 1.3 | 2.7 | 2.9 | 0.4 | 0.5 |
| November | 1.4 | 1.6 | 1.6 | 0.6 | 1.7 | 1.9 | 1.7 | 1.3 | 3.0 | 3.1 | 0.5 | 0.5 |
| December | 1.3 | 1.5 | 1.5 | 0.6 | 1.6 | 2.1 | 1.6 | 1.3 | 2.7 | 2.9 | 0.5 | 0.5 |
| **2010** | | | | | | | | | | | | |
| January | 1.3 | 1.5 | 1.7 | 0.7 | 1.3 | 1.6 | 1.6 | 1.2 | 3.1 | 3.1 | 0.4 | 0.5 |
| February | 1.3 | 1.5 | 1.4 | 0.9 | 1.6 | 2.1 | 1.7 | 1.2 | 2.8 | 3.0 | 0.5 | 0.6 |
| March | 1.4 | 1.6 | 1.4 | 0.7 | 1.6 | 2.1 | 1.8 | 1.2 | 2.9 | 3.1 | 0.5 | 0.5 |
| April | 1.5 | 1.7 | 1.2 | 0.8 | 1.7 | 2.2 | 2.1 | 1.4 | 2.9 | 3.0 | 0.4 | 0.5 |
| May | 1.4 | 1.6 | 1.0 | 0.8 | 1.7 | 2.2 | 1.8 | 1.2 | 2.9 | 3.1 | 0.4 | 0.4 |
| June | 1.5 | 1.7 | 1.1 | 0.8 | 1.7 | 2.2 | 2.1 | 1.4 | 2.7 | 2.9 | 0.6 | 0.5 |
| July | 1.4 | 1.6 | 1.3 | 0.8 | 1.8 | 2.3 | 2.0 | 1.2 | 2.7 | 2.9 | 0.5 | 0.4 |
| August | 1.5 | 1.7 | 1.6 | 0.9 | 1.6 | 2.0 | 2.2 | 1.2 | 2.9 | 3.0 | 0.5 | 0.5 |
| September | 1.5 | 1.7 | 1.5 | 0.8 | 1.8 | 2.4 | 2.0 | 1.2 | 2.8 | 2.9 | 0.5 | 0.6 |
| October | 1.4 | 1.6 | 1.4 | 0.9 | 1.6 | 2.1 | 2.1 | 1.2 | 2.9 | 3.0 | 0.5 | 0.5 |
| November | 1.4 | 1.5 | 1.1 | 0.8 | 1.7 | 2.3 | 1.7 | 1.3 | 2.6 | 2.7 | 0.5 | 0.5 |
| December | 1.5 | 1.7 | 1.7 | 0.9 | 1.6 | 2.0 | 2.3 | 1.2 | 2.9 | 3.0 | 0.5 | 0.5 |

[1]Quits are the number of quits during the entire month.
[2]The quits rate is the number of quits during the entire month as a percent of total employment.
[3]Detail will not necessarily add to totals because of the independent seasonal adjustment of the various series.
[4]Includes natural resources and mining, information, financial activities, and other services, not shown separately.
[5]Includes wholesale trade and transportation, warehousing, and utilities, not shown separately.
[6]Includes arts, entertainment, and recreation, not shown separately.
[7]Includes federal government, not shown separately.

## Table 7-7.  Quits Levels[1] and Rates,[2] by Industry, 2005–October 2016—*Continued*

(Seasonally adjusted, levels in thousands, rates per 100.)

| Year and month | Level[3] | | | | | | | | | | | |
|---|---|---|---|---|---|---|---|---|---|---|---|---|
| | Total[4] | Total private[4] | Construction | Manufacturing | Trade, transportation, and utilities[5] | Retail trade | Professional and business services | Education and health services | Leisure and hospitality[6] | Accommodation and food services | Government[7] | State and local government |
| **2011** | | | | | | | | | | | | |
| January | 1 825 | 1 709 | 63 | 100 | 372 | 261 | 371 | 236 | 371 | 336 | 116 | 107 |
| February | 1 872 | 1 760 | 59 | 95 | 426 | 301 | 391 | 246 | 362 | 325 | 112 | 105 |
| March | 1 967 | 1 863 | 71 | 110 | 452 | 346 | 389 | 256 | 399 | 358 | 104 | 96 |
| April | 1 925 | 1 820 | 104 | 104 | 416 | 318 | 359 | 253 | 394 | 353 | 105 | 96 |
| May | 2 037 | 1 915 | 87 | 107 | 496 | 372 | 366 | 257 | 393 | 354 | 122 | 114 |
| June | 1 949 | 1 846 | 75 | 107 | 446 | 344 | 350 | 251 | 416 | 377 | 103 | 93 |
| July | 1 981 | 1 851 | 71 | 105 | 419 | 315 | 382 | 229 | 403 | 359 | 130 | 122 |
| August | 2 087 | 1 963 | 69 | 99 | 439 | 328 | 391 | 273 | 442 | 396 | 124 | 114 |
| September | 2 046 | 1 933 | 82 | 95 | 455 | 339 | 390 | 253 | 424 | 369 | 113 | 102 |
| October | 1 953 | 1 845 | 77 | 112 | 451 | 327 | 353 | 247 | 377 | 339 | 107 | 97 |
| November | 1 949 | 1 829 | 118 | 115 | 413 | 293 | 367 | 251 | 369 | 328 | 120 | 110 |
| December | 1 955 | 1 819 | 73 | 106 | 444 | 328 | 348 | 260 | 397 | 344 | 136 | 126 |
| **2012** | | | | | | | | | | | | |
| January | 1 994 | 1 866 | 65 | 103 | 439 | 315 | 359 | 278 | 398 | 358 | 128 | 117 |
| February | 2 083 | 1 953 | 78 | 107 | 468 | 355 | 392 | 303 | 411 | 362 | 130 | 117 |
| March | 2 162 | 2 032 | 90 | 105 | 469 | 338 | 402 | 280 | 477 | 432 | 130 | 119 |
| April | 2 103 | 1 968 | 72 | 111 | 480 | 346 | 366 | 273 | 432 | 391 | 134 | 122 |
| May | 2 185 | 2 049 | 80 | 115 | 457 | 331 | 405 | 282 | 469 | 418 | 137 | 124 |
| June | 2 189 | 2 061 | 90 | 112 | 488 | 349 | 370 | 277 | 461 | 414 | 128 | 119 |
| July | 2 114 | 1 991 | 82 | 104 | 493 | 349 | 340 | 273 | 446 | 401 | 123 | 113 |
| August | 2 174 | 2 048 | 75 | 111 | 496 | 351 | 346 | 280 | 429 | 384 | 126 | 116 |
| September | 1 973 | 1 859 | 72 | 107 | 452 | 334 | 348 | 247 | 397 | 362 | 114 | 104 |
| October | 2 032 | 1 896 | 101 | 100 | 460 | 326 | 320 | 262 | 425 | 384 | 136 | 126 |
| November | 2 056 | 1 922 | 100 | 107 | 451 | 324 | 346 | 287 | 414 | 375 | 134 | 122 |
| December | 2 102 | 1 968 | 78 | 108 | 455 | 333 | 417 | 271 | 439 | 401 | 134 | 123 |
| **2013** | | | | | | | | | | | | |
| January | 2 316 | 2 184 | 130 | 106 | 512 | 373 | 363 | 326 | 484 | 438 | 132 | 122 |
| February | 2 257 | 2 127 | 117 | 106 | 511 | 371 | 353 | 299 | 500 | 445 | 131 | 119 |
| March | 2 078 | 1 950 | 94 | 95 | 443 | 321 | 350 | 291 | 462 | 409 | 128 | 116 |
| April | 2 298 | 2 152 | 100 | 116 | 499 | 363 | 413 | 297 | 498 | 453 | 146 | 135 |
| May | 2 253 | 2 122 | 97 | 117 | 457 | 330 | 421 | 295 | 472 | 426 | 131 | 120 |
| June | 2 247 | 2 111 | 102 | 106 | 457 | 331 | 481 | 295 | 443 | 395 | 137 | 125 |
| July | 2 369 | 2 236 | 103 | 117 | 475 | 355 | 493 | 308 | 463 | 412 | 132 | 121 |
| August | 2 384 | 2 260 | 97 | 103 | 548 | 424 | 451 | 305 | 445 | 402 | 123 | 111 |
| September | 2 396 | 2 277 | 96 | 115 | 536 | 404 | 481 | 314 | 475 | 430 | 118 | 108 |
| October | 2 399 | 2 266 | 90 | 110 | 536 | 400 | 466 | 318 | 524 | 477 | 133 | 120 |
| November | 2 378 | 2 252 | 81 | 114 | 555 | 407 | 503 | 283 | 502 | 446 | 126 | 116 |
| December | 2 309 | 2 178 | 83 | 116 | 500 | 365 | 485 | 321 | 462 | 411 | 130 | 118 |
| **2014** | | | | | | | | | | | | |
| January | 2 360 | 2 231 | 94 | 112 | 541 | 413 | 474 | 300 | 483 | 432 | 130 | 120 |
| February | 2 421 | 2 291 | 93 | 113 | 564 | 424 | 439 | 308 | 553 | 510 | 131 | 121 |
| March | 2 419 | 2 285 | 89 | 127 | 562 | 410 | 506 | 275 | 503 | 454 | 134 | 123 |
| April | 2 442 | 2 308 | 117 | 110 | 560 | 413 | 445 | 317 | 514 | 464 | 135 | 123 |
| May | 2 516 | 2 381 | 120 | 123 | 615 | 450 | 437 | 316 | 499 | 452 | 135 | 124 |
| June | 2 467 | 2 338 | 110 | 109 | 582 | 432 | 421 | 332 | 541 | 490 | 129 | 118 |
| July | 2 578 | 2 439 | 109 | 131 | 594 | 440 | 457 | 340 | 529 | 479 | 139 | 130 |
| August | 2 543 | 2 393 | 124 | 116 | 555 | 404 | 449 | 290 | 551 | 497 | 150 | 143 |
| September | 2 787 | 2 626 | 113 | 130 | 577 | 411 | 567 | 344 | 583 | 525 | 161 | 149 |
| October | 2 767 | 2 612 | 109 | 134 | 611 | 449 | 533 | 361 | 592 | 532 | 155 | 144 |
| November | 2 662 | 2 526 | 87 | 108 | 643 | 462 | 459 | 344 | 619 | 564 | 136 | 124 |
| December | 2 655 | 2 510 | 130 | 137 | 639 | 456 | 430 | 335 | 601 | 553 | 145 | 134 |
| **2015** | | | | | | | | | | | | |
| January | 2 770 | 2 627 | 115 | 137 | 614 | 452 | 560 | 363 | 573 | 518 | 143 | 130 |
| February | 2 703 | 2 554 | 121 | 131 | 575 | 422 | 521 | 380 | 564 | 513 | 149 | 138 |
| March | 2 722 | 2 561 | 116 | 127 | 637 | 479 | 478 | 362 | 600 | 558 | 161 | 149 |
| April | 2 681 | 2 531 | 118 | 139 | 601 | 438 | 510 | 354 | 532 | 482 | 151 | 139 |
| May | 2 758 | 2 609 | 115 | 128 | 629 | 448 | 503 | 366 | 575 | 519 | 149 | 137 |
| June | 2 746 | 2 575 | 108 | 138 | 620 | 458 | 498 | 354 | 582 | 528 | 171 | 159 |
| July | 2 724 | 2 566 | 108 | 127 | 610 | 438 | 468 | 356 | 609 | 556 | 158 | 144 |
| August | 2 855 | 2 696 | 112 | 142 | 611 | 441 | 525 | 372 | 631 | 566 | 159 | 148 |
| September | 2 748 | 2 601 | 133 | 144 | 620 | 446 | 486 | 342 | 608 | 552 | 147 | 134 |
| October | 2 797 | 2 631 | 87 | 147 | 646 | 470 | 531 | 364 | 588 | 532 | 166 | 152 |
| November | 2 862 | 2 705 | 129 | 145 | 627 | 471 | 522 | 408 | 636 | 583 | 157 | 143 |
| December | 3 088 | 2 922 | 137 | 133 | 719 | 518 | 614 | 385 | 671 | 611 | 166 | 153 |
| **2016** | | | | | | | | | | | | |
| January | 2 851 | 2 684 | 86 | 147 | 637 | 462 | 550 | 343 | 636 | 572 | 167 | 154 |
| February | 2 955 | 2 793 | 111 | 154 | 618 | 446 | 577 | 379 | 683 | 606 | 162 | 149 |
| March | 2 948 | 2 780 | 158 | 142 | 656 | 492 | 545 | 386 | 644 | 588 | 168 | 154 |
| April | 2 909 | 2 738 | 118 | 139 | 624 | 447 | 558 | 382 | 645 | 582 | 171 | 157 |
| May | 2 942 | 2 775 | 120 | 142 | 623 | 462 | 547 | 405 | 678 | 612 | 168 | 156 |
| June | 2 979 | 2 785 | 110 | 136 | 649 | 459 | 542 | 410 | 645 | 587 | 194 | 181 |
| July | 2 977 | 2 807 | 128 | 143 | 653 | 467 | 565 | 398 | 635 | 573 | 170 | 156 |
| August | 3 009 | 2 847 | 137 | 140 | 651 | 475 | 598 | 375 | 639 | 576 | 162 | 149 |
| September | 3 052 | 2 867 | 124 | 150 | 654 | 462 | 597 | 411 | 671 | 599 | 185 | 172 |
| October | 3 023 | 2 861 | 128 | 155 | 675 | 492 | 588 | 396 | 668 | 600 | 163 | 151 |

[1]Quits are the number of quits during the entire month.
[2]The quits rate is the number of quits during the entire month as a percent of total employment.
[3]Detail will not necessarily add to totals because of the independent seasonal adjustment of the various series.
[4]Includes natural resources and mining, information, financial activities, and other services, not shown separately.
[5]Includes wholesale trade and transportation, warehousing, and utilities, not shown separately.
[6]Includes arts, entertainment, and recreation, not shown separately.
[7]Includes federal government, not shown separately.

## Table 7-7. Quits Levels[1] and Rates,[2] by Industry, 2005–October 2016—*Continued*

(Seasonally adjusted, levels in thousands, rates per 100.)

| Year and month | Rate | | | | | | | | | | | |
|---|---|---|---|---|---|---|---|---|---|---|---|---|
| | Total[4] | Total private[4] | Construction | Manufacturing | Trade, transportation, and utilities[5] | Retail trade | Professional and business services | Education and health services | Leisure and hospitality[6] | Accommodation and food services | Government[7] | State and local government |
| **2011** | | | | | | | | | | | | |
| January | 1.4 | 1.6 | 1.2 | 0.9 | 1.5 | 1.8 | 2.2 | 1.2 | 2.8 | 3.0 | 0.5 | 0.6 |
| February | 1.4 | 1.6 | 1.1 | 0.8 | 1.7 | 2.1 | 2.3 | 1.2 | 2.7 | 2.9 | 0.5 | 0.5 |
| March | 1.5 | 1.7 | 1.3 | 0.9 | 1.8 | 2.4 | 2.3 | 1.3 | 3.0 | 3.2 | 0.5 | 0.5 |
| April | 1.5 | 1.7 | 1.9 | 0.9 | 1.7 | 2.2 | 2.1 | 1.2 | 3.0 | 3.1 | 0.5 | 0.5 |
| May | 1.5 | 1.7 | 1.6 | 0.9 | 2.0 | 2.5 | 2.1 | 1.3 | 3.0 | 3.1 | 0.6 | 0.6 |
| June | 1.5 | 1.7 | 1.4 | 0.9 | 1.8 | 2.3 | 2.0 | 1.2 | 3.1 | 3.3 | 0.5 | 0.5 |
| July | 1.5 | 1.7 | 1.3 | 0.9 | 1.7 | 2.1 | 2.2 | 1.1 | 3.0 | 3.1 | 0.6 | 0.6 |
| August | 1.6 | 1.8 | 1.2 | 0.8 | 1.7 | 2.2 | 2.3 | 1.3 | 3.3 | 3.5 | 0.6 | 0.6 |
| September | 1.5 | 1.8 | 1.5 | 0.8 | 1.8 | 2.3 | 2.2 | 1.2 | 3.2 | 3.2 | 0.5 | 0.5 |
| October | 1.5 | 1.7 | 1.4 | 0.9 | 1.8 | 2.2 | 2.0 | 1.2 | 2.8 | 2.9 | 0.5 | 0.5 |
| November | 1.5 | 1.7 | 2.1 | 1.0 | 1.6 | 2.0 | 2.1 | 1.2 | 2.7 | 2.8 | 0.5 | 0.6 |
| December | 1.5 | 1.6 | 1.3 | 0.9 | 1.8 | 2.2 | 2.0 | 1.3 | 2.9 | 3.0 | 0.6 | 0.7 |
| **2012** | | | | | | | | | | | | |
| January | 1.5 | 1.7 | 1.2 | 0.9 | 1.7 | 2.1 | 2.0 | 1.4 | 2.9 | 3.1 | 0.6 | 0.6 |
| February | 1.6 | 1.7 | 1.4 | 0.9 | 1.8 | 2.4 | 2.2 | 1.5 | 3.0 | 3.1 | 0.6 | 0.6 |
| March | 1.6 | 1.8 | 1.6 | 0.9 | 1.8 | 2.3 | 2.3 | 1.4 | 3.5 | 3.7 | 0.6 | 0.6 |
| April | 1.6 | 1.8 | 1.3 | 0.9 | 1.9 | 2.3 | 2.1 | 1.3 | 3.2 | 3.3 | 0.6 | 0.6 |
| May | 1.6 | 1.8 | 1.4 | 1.0 | 1.8 | 2.2 | 2.3 | 1.4 | 3.4 | 3.6 | 0.6 | 0.7 |
| June | 1.6 | 1.8 | 1.6 | 0.9 | 1.9 | 2.4 | 2.1 | 1.3 | 3.4 | 3.5 | 0.6 | 0.6 |
| July | 1.6 | 1.8 | 1.5 | 0.9 | 1.9 | 2.4 | 1.9 | 1.3 | 3.2 | 3.4 | 0.6 | 0.6 |
| August | 1.6 | 1.8 | 1.3 | 0.9 | 1.9 | 2.4 | 1.9 | 1.3 | 3.1 | 3.2 | 0.6 | 0.6 |
| September | 1.5 | 1.7 | 1.3 | 0.9 | 1.8 | 2.3 | 1.9 | 1.2 | 2.9 | 3.0 | 0.5 | 0.5 |
| October | 1.5 | 1.7 | 1.8 | 0.8 | 1.8 | 2.2 | 1.8 | 1.3 | 3.1 | 3.2 | 0.6 | 0.7 |
| November | 1.5 | 1.7 | 1.8 | 0.9 | 1.8 | 2.2 | 1.9 | 1.4 | 3.0 | 3.1 | 0.6 | 0.6 |
| December | 1.6 | 1.7 | 1.4 | 0.9 | 1.8 | 2.2 | 2.3 | 1.3 | 3.1 | 3.3 | 0.6 | 0.6 |
| **2013** | | | | | | | | | | | | |
| January | 1.7 | 1.9 | 2.3 | 0.9 | 2.0 | 2.5 | 2.0 | 1.6 | 3.5 | 3.6 | 0.6 | 0.6 |
| February | 1.7 | 1.9 | 2.0 | 0.9 | 2.0 | 2.5 | 1.9 | 1.4 | 3.6 | 3.7 | 0.6 | 0.6 |
| March | 1.5 | 1.7 | 1.6 | 0.8 | 1.7 | 2.1 | 1.9 | 1.4 | 3.3 | 3.4 | 0.6 | 0.6 |
| April | 1.7 | 1.9 | 1.7 | 1.0 | 1.9 | 2.4 | 2.2 | 1.4 | 3.5 | 3.7 | 0.7 | 0.7 |
| May | 1.7 | 1.9 | 1.7 | 1.0 | 1.8 | 2.2 | 2.3 | 1.4 | 3.3 | 3.5 | 0.6 | 0.6 |
| June | 1.6 | 1.8 | 1.7 | 0.9 | 1.8 | 2.2 | 2.6 | 1.4 | 3.1 | 3.2 | 0.6 | 0.7 |
| July | 1.7 | 2.0 | 1.8 | 1.0 | 1.8 | 2.4 | 2.7 | 1.5 | 3.2 | 3.4 | 0.6 | 0.6 |
| August | 1.7 | 2.0 | 1.6 | 0.9 | 2.1 | 2.8 | 2.4 | 1.4 | 3.1 | 3.3 | 0.6 | 0.6 |
| September | 1.8 | 2.0 | 1.6 | 1.0 | 2.1 | 2.7 | 2.6 | 1.5 | 3.3 | 3.5 | 0.5 | 0.6 |
| October | 1.8 | 2.0 | 1.5 | 0.9 | 2.1 | 2.6 | 2.5 | 1.5 | 3.6 | 3.9 | 0.6 | 0.6 |
| November | 1.7 | 2.0 | 1.4 | 0.9 | 2.1 | 2.7 | 2.7 | 1.3 | 3.5 | 3.6 | 0.6 | 0.6 |
| December | 1.7 | 1.9 | 1.4 | 1.0 | 1.9 | 2.4 | 2.6 | 1.5 | 3.2 | 3.3 | 0.6 | 0.6 |
| **2014** | | | | | | | | | | | | |
| January | 1.7 | 1.9 | 1.6 | 0.9 | 2.1 | 2.7 | 2.5 | 1.4 | 3.3 | 3.5 | 0.6 | 0.6 |
| February | 1.8 | 2.0 | 1.5 | 0.9 | 2.2 | 2.8 | 2.3 | 1.4 | 3.8 | 4.1 | 0.6 | 0.6 |
| March | 1.8 | 2.0 | 1.5 | 1.0 | 2.1 | 2.7 | 2.7 | 1.3 | 3.5 | 3.6 | 0.6 | 0.6 |
| April | 1.8 | 2.0 | 1.9 | 0.9 | 2.1 | 2.7 | 2.3 | 1.5 | 3.5 | 3.7 | 0.6 | 0.6 |
| May | 1.8 | 2.0 | 2.0 | 1.0 | 2.3 | 2.9 | 2.3 | 1.5 | 3.4 | 3.6 | 0.6 | 0.7 |
| June | 1.8 | 2.0 | 1.8 | 0.9 | 2.2 | 2.8 | 2.2 | 1.6 | 3.7 | 3.9 | 0.6 | 0.6 |
| July | 1.9 | 2.1 | 1.8 | 1.1 | 2.3 | 2.9 | 2.4 | 1.6 | 3.6 | 3.8 | 0.6 | 0.7 |
| August | 1.8 | 2.0 | 2.0 | 0.9 | 2.1 | 2.6 | 2.3 | 1.4 | 3.7 | 3.9 | 0.7 | 0.7 |
| September | 2.0 | 2.2 | 1.8 | 1.1 | 2.2 | 2.7 | 3.0 | 1.6 | 3.9 | 4.1 | 0.7 | 0.8 |
| October | 2.0 | 2.2 | 1.7 | 1.1 | 2.3 | 2.9 | 2.8 | 1.7 | 4.0 | 4.2 | 0.7 | 0.7 |
| November | 1.9 | 2.1 | 1.4 | 0.9 | 2.4 | 3.0 | 2.4 | 1.6 | 4.2 | 4.4 | 0.6 | 0.6 |
| December | 1.9 | 2.1 | 2.1 | 1.1 | 2.4 | 2.9 | 2.2 | 1.5 | 4.0 | 4.3 | 0.7 | 0.7 |
| **2015** | | | | | | | | | | | | |
| January | 2.0 | 2.2 | 1.8 | 1.1 | 2.3 | 2.9 | 2.9 | 1.7 | 3.8 | 4.0 | 0.7 | 0.7 |
| February | 1.9 | 2.1 | 1.9 | 1.1 | 2.2 | 2.7 | 2.7 | 1.7 | 3.8 | 4.0 | 0.7 | 0.7 |
| March | 1.9 | 2.2 | 1.8 | 1.0 | 2.4 | 3.1 | 2.5 | 1.7 | 4.0 | 4.3 | 0.7 | 0.8 |
| April | 1.9 | 2.1 | 1.8 | 1.1 | 2.2 | 2.8 | 2.6 | 1.6 | 3.5 | 3.7 | 0.7 | 0.7 |
| May | 1.9 | 2.2 | 1.8 | 1.0 | 2.3 | 2.9 | 2.6 | 1.7 | 3.8 | 4.0 | 0.7 | 0.7 |
| June | 1.9 | 2.2 | 1.7 | 1.1 | 2.3 | 2.9 | 2.5 | 1.6 | 3.9 | 4.1 | 0.8 | 0.8 |
| July | 1.9 | 2.1 | 1.7 | 1.0 | 2.3 | 2.8 | 2.4 | 1.6 | 4.0 | 4.3 | 0.7 | 0.7 |
| August | 2.0 | 2.2 | 1.7 | 1.2 | 2.3 | 2.8 | 2.7 | 1.7 | 4.2 | 4.4 | 0.7 | 0.8 |
| September | 1.9 | 2.2 | 2.1 | 1.2 | 2.3 | 2.8 | 2.5 | 1.5 | 4.0 | 4.2 | 0.7 | 0.7 |
| October | 2.0 | 2.2 | 1.3 | 1.2 | 2.4 | 3.0 | 2.7 | 1.6 | 3.9 | 4.1 | 0.8 | 0.8 |
| November | 2.0 | 2.2 | 2.0 | 1.2 | 2.3 | 3.0 | 2.6 | 1.8 | 4.2 | 4.4 | 0.7 | 0.7 |
| December | 2.2 | 2.4 | 2.1 | 1.1 | 2.7 | 3.3 | 3.1 | 1.7 | 4.4 | 4.6 | 0.8 | 0.8 |
| **2016** | | | | | | | | | | | | |
| January | 2.0 | 2.2 | 1.3 | 1.2 | 2.3 | 2.9 | 2.8 | 1.5 | 4.1 | 4.3 | 0.8 | 0.8 |
| February | 2.1 | 2.3 | 1.7 | 1.2 | 2.3 | 2.8 | 2.9 | 1.7 | 4.4 | 4.6 | 0.7 | 0.8 |
| March | 2.1 | 2.3 | 2.4 | 1.2 | 2.4 | 3.1 | 2.7 | 1.7 | 4.2 | 4.4 | 0.8 | 0.8 |
| April | 2.0 | 2.2 | 1.8 | 1.1 | 2.3 | 2.8 | 2.8 | 1.7 | 4.2 | 4.4 | 0.8 | 0.8 |
| May | 2.0 | 2.3 | 1.8 | 1.2 | 2.3 | 2.9 | 2.7 | 1.8 | 4.4 | 4.6 | 0.8 | 0.8 |
| June | 2.1 | 2.3 | 1.7 | 1.1 | 2.4 | 2.9 | 2.7 | 1.8 | 4.2 | 4.4 | 0.9 | 0.9 |
| July | 2.1 | 2.3 | 1.9 | 1.2 | 2.4 | 2.9 | 2.8 | 1.8 | 4.1 | 4.3 | 0.8 | 0.8 |
| August | 2.1 | 2.3 | 2.1 | 1.1 | 2.4 | 3.0 | 2.9 | 1.6 | 4.1 | 4.3 | 0.7 | 0.8 |
| September | 2.1 | 2.3 | 1.9 | 1.2 | 2.4 | 2.9 | 2.9 | 1.8 | 4.3 | 4.5 | 0.8 | 0.9 |
| October | 2.1 | 2.3 | 1.9 | 1.3 | 2.5 | 3.1 | 2.9 | 1.7 | 4.3 | 4.5 | 0.7 | 0.8 |

[1]Quits are the number of quits during the entire month.
[2]The quits rate is the number of quits during the entire month as a percent of total employment.
[3]Detail will not necessarily add to totals because of the independent seasonal adjustment of the various series.
[4]Includes natural resources and mining, information, financial activities, and other services, not shown separately.
[5]Includes wholesale trade and transportation, warehousing, and utilities, not shown separately.
[6]Includes arts, entertainment, and recreation, not shown separately.
[7]Includes federal government, not shown separately.

## Table 7-8. Layoffs and Discharges Levels[1] and Rates,[2] by Industry, 2005–October 2016

(Not seasonally adjusted, levels in thousands, rates per 100.)

| Year and month | Level | | | | | | | | | | | | |
|---|---|---|---|---|---|---|---|---|---|---|---|---|---|
| | Total | Total private | Mining and logging | Construc-tion | Manufac-turing | Durable goods | Non-durable goods | Trade, transpor-tation, and utilities | Whole-sale trade | Retail trade | Transpor-tation, ware-housing, and utilities | Infor-mation | Financial activities |
| 2009 | 26 444 | 24 916 | 186 | 3 743 | 2 812 | 1 822 | 994 | 4 920 | 990 | 2 861 | 1 070 | 380 | 1 277 |
| 2010 | 21 827 | 19 775 | 95 | 3 157 | 1 678 | 959 | 720 | 3 674 | 734 | 2 320 | 620 | 294 | 778 |
| 2011 | 20 801 | 19 466 | 83 | 2 868 | 1 330 | 742 | 587 | 3 396 | 585 | 2 154 | 657 | 277 | 659 |
| 2012 | 20 872 | 19 686 | 143 | 2 766 | 1 252 | 778 | 473 | 3 570 | 638 | 2 249 | 685 | 276 | 625 |
| 2013 | 19 889 | 18 725 | 137 | 2 325 | 1 191 | 743 | 444 | 3 552 | 518 | 2 320 | 713 | 307 | 716 |
| 2014 | 20 418 | 19 347 | 144 | 2 049 | 1 163 | 679 | 483 | 3 965 | 616 | 2 516 | 834 | 305 | 650 |
| 2015 | 20 942 | 19 624 | 240 | 2 065 | 1 229 | 764 | 466 | 3 824 | 564 | 2 429 | 832 | 300 | 710 |
| **2005** | | | | | | | | | | | | | |
| January | 2 478 | 2 414 | 10 | 409 | 213 | 141 | 72 | 574 | 73 | 422 | 79 | 41 | 117 |
| February | 1 589 | 1 539 | 6 | 246 | 120 | 78 | 42 | 380 | 53 | 257 | 71 | 13 | 72 |
| March | 1 590 | 1 537 | 5 | 160 | 135 | 79 | 56 | 313 | 40 | 219 | 54 | 22 | 60 |
| April | 1 724 | 1 665 | 7 | 207 | 163 | 112 | 51 | 327 | 72 | 194 | 62 | 17 | 82 |
| May | 1 577 | 1 469 | 4 | 197 | 135 | 93 | 42 | 334 | 85 | 180 | 69 | 20 | 62 |
| June | 1 845 | 1 687 | 4 | 179 | 129 | 83 | 46 | 333 | 47 | 206 | 79 | 15 | 33 |
| July | 1 895 | 1 770 | 7 | 183 | 131 | 85 | 47 | 355 | 58 | 230 | 67 | 22 | 60 |
| August | 2 044 | 1 866 | 7 | 251 | 152 | 101 | 51 | 322 | 47 | 220 | 55 | 17 | 55 |
| September | 2 010 | 1 843 | 8 | 229 | 134 | 73 | 61 | 377 | 34 | 260 | 84 | 19 | 73 |
| October | 1 827 | 1 740 | 7 | 232 | 134 | 77 | 58 | 345 | 72 | 200 | 72 | 19 | 83 |
| November | 1 656 | 1 584 | 4 | 236 | 156 | 74 | 82 | 349 | 78 | 184 | 87 | 22 | 64 |
| December | 1 916 | 1 825 | 9 | 286 | 148 | 82 | 66 | 488 | 73 | 278 | 137 | 21 | 64 |
| **2006** | | | | | | | | | | | | | |
| January | 2 103 | 2 021 | 5 | 312 | 171 | 84 | 87 | 515 | 47 | 382 | 86 | 17 | 89 |
| February | 1 356 | 1 306 | 6 | 183 | 116 | 63 | 53 | 328 | 60 | 234 | 34 | 18 | 57 |
| March | 1 358 | 1 296 | 8 | 182 | 172 | 88 | 83 | 236 | 37 | 160 | 39 | 15 | 77 |
| April | 1 648 | 1 589 | 10 | 147 | 138 | 63 | 74 | 301 | 53 | 217 | 30 | 32 | 80 |
| May | 1 627 | 1 512 | 3 | 171 | 150 | 86 | 63 | 319 | 47 | 214 | 58 | 12 | 48 |
| June | 1 612 | 1 413 | 3 | 126 | 145 | 75 | 69 | 352 | 50 | 248 | 54 | 17 | 54 |
| July | 1 821 | 1 675 | 4 | 203 | 146 | 92 | 54 | 312 | 66 | 188 | 58 | 22 | 73 |
| August | 1 742 | 1 589 | 6 | 200 | 156 | 92 | 63 | 310 | 58 | 191 | 61 | 18 | 77 |
| September | 1 789 | 1 610 | 11 | 191 | 172 | 102 | 69 | 293 | 54 | 178 | 61 | 17 | 64 |
| October | 1 998 | 1 906 | 5 | 254 | 151 | 92 | 59 | 321 | 60 | 199 | 63 | 30 | 82 |
| November | 1 872 | 1 797 | 6 | 331 | 151 | 97 | 53 | 301 | 46 | 201 | 54 | 23 | 66 |
| December | 1 930 | 1 848 | 7 | 312 | 159 | 94 | 65 | 446 | 44 | 333 | 69 | 26 | 93 |
| **2007** | | | | | | | | | | | | | |
| January | 2 187 | 2 108 | 10 | 319 | 184 | 113 | 70 | 545 | 63 | 380 | 102 | 53 | 93 |
| February | 1 412 | 1 364 | 7 | 223 | 151 | 97 | 55 | 277 | 35 | 204 | 38 | 28 | 63 |
| March | 1 487 | 1 438 | 6 | 159 | 142 | 91 | 51 | 259 | 43 | 161 | 54 | 20 | 97 |
| April | 1 735 | 1 676 | 6 | 212 | 157 | 100 | 57 | 303 | 61 | 183 | 58 | 18 | 74 |
| May | 1 523 | 1 412 | 6 | 176 | 131 | 77 | 54 | 295 | 51 | 205 | 39 | 22 | 71 |
| June | 1 755 | 1 584 | 4 | 201 | 134 | 84 | 50 | 275 | 51 | 177 | 47 | 21 | 64 |
| July | 1 827 | 1 615 | 7 | 178 | 169 | 104 | 65 | 363 | 93 | 208 | 61 | 32 | 103 |
| August | 1 960 | 1 778 | 9 | 244 | 161 | 98 | 63 | 343 | 67 | 227 | 49 | 26 | 100 |
| September | 2 135 | 1 991 | 7 | 255 | 178 | 109 | 69 | 339 | 66 | 230 | 43 | 19 | 96 |
| October | 2 079 | 1 998 | 8 | 270 | 202 | 126 | 76 | 395 | 84 | 247 | 64 | 18 | 106 |
| November | 1 914 | 1 857 | 11 | 268 | 187 | 113 | 74 | 405 | 68 | 266 | 71 | 15 | 74 |
| December | 1 983 | 1 887 | 10 | 297 | 151 | 84 | 67 | 430 | 78 | 295 | 56 | 18 | 104 |
| **2008** | | | | | | | | | | | | | |
| January | 2 303 | 2 225 | 12 | 352 | 177 | 121 | 56 | 539 | 99 | 363 | 77 | 40 | 124 |
| February | 1 546 | 1 510 | 11 | 209 | 138 | 77 | 62 | 334 | 59 | 235 | 40 | 20 | 61 |
| March | 1 518 | 1 464 | 6 | 239 | 125 | 78 | 47 | 263 | 61 | 157 | 45 | 31 | 73 |
| April | 1 706 | 1 656 | 10 | 231 | 185 | 111 | 74 | 316 | 73 | 189 | 54 | 19 | 94 |
| May | 1 623 | 1 520 | 5 | 201 | 144 | 89 | 56 | 303 | 55 | 203 | 45 | 16 | 65 |
| June | 1 839 | 1 685 | 5 | 208 | 165 | 100 | 65 | 372 | 76 | 248 | 48 | 30 | 74 |
| July | 1 939 | 1 822 | 9 | 228 | 156 | 109 | 47 | 389 | 54 | 248 | 87 | 21 | 112 |
| August | 2 238 | 2 073 | 5 | 261 | 170 | 122 | 48 | 391 | 77 | 241 | 74 | 18 | 115 |
| September | 2 016 | 1 868 | 6 | 276 | 196 | 122 | 73 | 344 | 64 | 209 | 71 | 36 | 81 |
| October | 2 289 | 2 211 | 11 | 356 | 235 | 141 | 93 | 434 | 98 | 273 | 63 | 41 | 84 |
| November | 2 224 | 2 161 | 15 | 407 | 235 | 149 | 86 | 392 | 79 | 239 | 74 | 42 | 74 |
| December | 2 728 | 2 639 | 18 | 412 | 320 | 213 | 106 | 622 | 127 | 394 | 100 | 40 | 90 |
| **2009** | | | | | | | | | | | | | |
| January | 3 209 | 3 096 | 18 | 523 | 432 | 313 | 119 | 652 | 134 | 407 | 110 | 60 | 208 |
| February | 2 037 | 1 985 | 16 | 303 | 285 | 195 | 90 | 398 | 87 | 240 | 72 | 35 | 113 |
| March | 2 015 | 1 958 | 23 | 298 | 276 | 204 | 72 | 377 | 83 | 205 | 89 | 33 | 102 |
| April | 2 351 | 2 280 | 15 | 355 | 286 | 210 | 76 | 433 | 93 | 269 | 71 | 40 | 106 |
| May | 1 905 | 1 730 | 13 | 259 | 235 | 157 | 77 | 347 | 88 | 199 | 60 | 24 | 93 |
| June | 1 997 | 1 750 | 11 | 209 | 192 | 126 | 65 | 314 | 71 | 175 | 68 | 28 | 93 |
| July | 2 335 | 2 149 | 16 | 328 | 192 | 106 | 86 | 356 | 82 | 193 | 82 | 32 | 121 |
| August | 2 265 | 2 061 | 8 | 272 | 188 | 94 | 94 | 328 | 79 | 187 | 62 | 19 | 115 |
| September | 2 161 | 1 964 | 12 | 303 | 179 | 102 | 77 | 404 | 64 | 244 | 97 | 15 | 73 |
| October | 2 134 | 2 047 | 15 | 340 | 213 | 121 | 92 | 339 | 65 | 208 | 67 | 25 | 118 |
| November | 1 858 | 1 784 | 12 | 262 | 184 | 106 | 77 | 327 | 64 | 187 | 76 | 28 | 44 |
| December | 2 290 | 2 180 | 19 | 340 | 168 | 101 | 67 | 579 | 80 | 309 | 190 | 44 | 83 |
| **2010** | | | | | | | | | | | | | |
| January | 2 343 | 2 244 | 12 | 375 | 223 | 168 | 54 | 527 | 83 | 378 | 66 | 51 | 113 |
| February | 1 429 | 1 378 | 8 | 220 | 140 | 81 | 59 | 257 | 65 | 153 | 39 | 21 | 51 |
| March | 1 484 | 1 420 | 7 | 200 | 128 | 75 | 53 | 312 | 54 | 229 | 29 | 21 | 54 |
| April | 1 521 | 1 448 | 7 | 249 | 129 | 63 | 65 | 242 | 55 | 149 | 38 | 16 | 63 |
| May | 1 584 | 1 424 | 8 | 234 | 96 | 59 | 36 | 226 | 56 | 129 | 42 | 25 | 70 |
| June | 1 907 | 1 469 | 4 | 166 | 105 | 51 | 55 | 296 | 45 | 194 | 56 | 22 | 42 |
| July | 2 091 | 1 787 | 6 | 251 | 135 | 73 | 62 | 310 | 80 | 183 | 48 | 25 | 72 |
| August | 1 935 | 1 626 | 6 | 225 | 147 | 75 | 72 | 253 | 49 | 170 | 34 | 22 | 54 |
| September | 1 830 | 1 589 | 7 | 238 | 136 | 82 | 54 | 254 | 71 | 143 | 40 | 18 | 48 |
| October | 1 771 | 1 675 | 7 | 263 | 161 | 89 | 72 | 287 | 55 | 170 | 62 | 20 | 95 |
| November | 1 762 | 1 668 | 9 | 297 | 149 | 77 | 72 | 284 | 58 | 181 | 45 | 24 | 57 |
| December | 2 046 | 1 934 | 14 | 393 | 129 | 74 | 56 | 413 | 63 | 230 | 119 | 33 | 69 |

[1]Layoffs and discharges are the number of layoffs and discharges during the entire month.
[2]The layoffs and discharges rate is the number of layoffs and discharges during the entire month as a percent of total employment.

## Table 7-8. Layoffs and Discharges Levels[1] and Rates,[2] by Industry, 2005–October 2016
### —Continued

(Not seasonally adjusted, levels in thousands, rates per 100.)

| Year and month | Level | | | | | | | | | | | | |
|---|---|---|---|---|---|---|---|---|---|---|---|---|---|
| | Finance and insurance | Real estate and rental and leasing | Professional and business services | Education and health services | Educational services | Health care and social assistance | Leisure and hospitality | Arts, entertainment, and recreation | Accommodation and food services | Other services | Government | Federal | State and local government |
| 2009 | 699 | 578 | 4 954 | 2 232 | 2 232 | 1 777 | 3 265 | 817 | 2 449 | 1 145 | 1 527 | 217 | 1 311 |
| 2010 | 462 | 318 | 4 319 | 2 122 | 2 122 | 1 715 | 2 807 | 790 | 2 016 | 855 | 2 049 | 738 | 1 312 |
| 2011 | 355 | 304 | 4 821 | 1 873 | 1 873 | 1 500 | 3 109 | 925 | 2 186 | 1 048 | 1 337 | 134 | 1 202 |
| 2012 | 339 | 286 | 5 022 | 1 952 | 1 952 | 1 560 | 3 091 | 896 | 2 193 | 998 | 1 185 | 128 | 1 060 |
| 2013 | 406 | 309 | 4 665 | 1 929 | 1 929 | 1 519 | 3 042 | 881 | 2 161 | 865 | 1 163 | 150 | 1 014 |
| 2014 | 411 | 240 | 5 120 | 2 022 | 2 022 | 1 630 | 3 154 | 989 | 2 163 | 777 | 1 070 | 130 | 940 |
| 2015 | 415 | 295 | 5 078 | 1 706 | 1 706 | 1 341 | 3 523 | 996 | 2 529 | 944 | 1 317 | 144 | 1 172 |
| **2005** | | | | | | | | | | | | | |
| January | 70 | 46 | 518 | 148 | 16 | 132 | 304 | 57 | 247 | 81 | 64 | 10 | 54 |
| February | 28 | 44 | 343 | 121 | 11 | 111 | 182 | 36 | 146 | 54 | 51 | 8 | 42 |
| March | 34 | 25 | 407 | 144 | 17 | 128 | 232 | 31 | 201 | 57 | 53 | 9 | 44 |
| April | 50 | 32 | 437 | 148 | 23 | 126 | 232 | 58 | 174 | 44 | 60 | 10 | 50 |
| May | 36 | 26 | 271 | 142 | 32 | 111 | 216 | 40 | 176 | 87 | 108 | 9 | 100 |
| June | 21 | 12 | 471 | 157 | 29 | 127 | 319 | 54 | 266 | 49 | 158 | 18 | 140 |
| July | 33 | 27 | 579 | 143 | 31 | 113 | 234 | 35 | 199 | 55 | 125 | 14 | 111 |
| August | 44 | 12 | 476 | 168 | 23 | 145 | 252 | 89 | 163 | 167 | 177 | 14 | 163 |
| September | 26 | 47 | 352 | 129 | 33 | 96 | 447 | 236 | 210 | 75 | 167 | 15 | 152 |
| October | 35 | 48 | 416 | 119 | 17 | 102 | 333 | 96 | 238 | 52 | 87 | 8 | 78 |
| November | 21 | 43 | 344 | 97 | 12 | 84 | 270 | 91 | 179 | 43 | 72 | 10 | 61 |
| December | 27 | 37 | 417 | 122 | 37 | 86 | 219 | 56 | 163 | 51 | 91 | 27 | 64 |
| **2006** | | | | | | | | | | | | | |
| January | 50 | 39 | 421 | 143 | 23 | 120 | 281 | 46 | 236 | 67 | 82 | 12 | 70 |
| February | 36 | 21 | 288 | 88 | 8 | 80 | 174 | 32 | 142 | 50 | 50 | 9 | 41 |
| March | 35 | 42 | 279 | 116 | 20 | 96 | 186 | 34 | 152 | 27 | 62 | 11 | 51 |
| April | 43 | 36 | 351 | 147 | 25 | 123 | 242 | 48 | 194 | 142 | 58 | 11 | 47 |
| May | 26 | 22 | 361 | 232 | 50 | 182 | 167 | 40 | 127 | 50 | 115 | 12 | 103 |
| June | 29 | 26 | 290 | 185 | 53 | 131 | 178 | 35 | 143 | 64 | 198 | 19 | 180 |
| July | 31 | 42 | 437 | 180 | 41 | 140 | 236 | 51 | 185 | 62 | 146 | 17 | 129 |
| August | 43 | 33 | 315 | 148 | 26 | 122 | 256 | 89 | 167 | 103 | 153 | 32 | 122 |
| September | 37 | 27 | 357 | 118 | 23 | 95 | 318 | 134 | 184 | 70 | 179 | 25 | 155 |
| October | 41 | 41 | 464 | 123 | 22 | 101 | 386 | 117 | 269 | 90 | 92 | 10 | 82 |
| November | 24 | 42 | 414 | 91 | 13 | 78 | 356 | 105 | 251 | 59 | 75 | 9 | 66 |
| December | 61 | 32 | 416 | 108 | 26 | 82 | 225 | 51 | 174 | 56 | 82 | 16 | 66 |
| **2007** | | | | | | | | | | | | | |
| January | 46 | 47 | 417 | 150 | 36 | 113 | 277 | 79 | 198 | 60 | 79 | 15 | 64 |
| February | 30 | 33 | 308 | 102 | 22 | 80 | 181 | 48 | 133 | 25 | 48 | 12 | 36 |
| March | 47 | 49 | 388 | 134 | 18 | 116 | 189 | 51 | 139 | 46 | 48 | 15 | 34 |
| April | 43 | 31 | 428 | 135 | 31 | 104 | 246 | 85 | 161 | 97 | 59 | 15 | 44 |
| May | 28 | 43 | 290 | 163 | 39 | 124 | 224 | 51 | 172 | 35 | 111 | 17 | 95 |
| June | 44 | 20 | 307 | 234 | 83 | 152 | 272 | 53 | 219 | 70 | 171 | 27 | 144 |
| July | 61 | 42 | 365 | 139 | 21 | 118 | 184 | 28 | 156 | 75 | 212 | 29 | 183 |
| August | 72 | 28 | 339 | 186 | 60 | 126 | 246 | 60 | 186 | 124 | 182 | 28 | 154 |
| September | 53 | 44 | 386 | 162 | 19 | 143 | 453 | 141 | 313 | 94 | 144 | 31 | 113 |
| October | 64 | 42 | 469 | 132 | 15 | 118 | 348 | 115 | 233 | 51 | 81 | 11 | 69 |
| November | 22 | 52 | 459 | 127 | 24 | 103 | 244 | 107 | 137 | 67 | 57 | 9 | 48 |
| December | 59 | 46 | 488 | 108 | 24 | 84 | 227 | 58 | 169 | 54 | 96 | 20 | 76 |
| **2008** | | | | | | | | | | | | | |
| January | 76 | 47 | 501 | 172 | 25 | 147 | 250 | 67 | 183 | 60 | 78 | 18 | 60 |
| February | 38 | 23 | 321 | 136 | 14 | 121 | 229 | 51 | 178 | 50 | 36 | 6 | 30 |
| March | 53 | 20 | 347 | 149 | 12 | 137 | 178 | 58 | 120 | 53 | 54 | 6 | 48 |
| April | 64 | 29 | 426 | 129 | 27 | 101 | 199 | 61 | 139 | 47 | 51 | 9 | 42 |
| May | 32 | 34 | 263 | 212 | 38 | 174 | 214 | 63 | 151 | 97 | 103 | 5 | 97 |
| June | 53 | 21 | 379 | 205 | 56 | 149 | 196 | 33 | 163 | 52 | 154 | 9 | 144 |
| July | 66 | 46 | 395 | 216 | 53 | 163 | 195 | 29 | 166 | 102 | 116 | 7 | 110 |
| August | 74 | 42 | 417 | 214 | 50 | 164 | 309 | 78 | 230 | 173 | 166 | 7 | 159 |
| September | 43 | 37 | 360 | 144 | 21 | 123 | 353 | 121 | 232 | 73 | 148 | 7 | 141 |
| October | 38 | 46 | 442 | 144 | 25 | 119 | 388 | 117 | 271 | 77 | 78 | 10 | 69 |
| November | 31 | 43 | 520 | 112 | 22 | 89 | 309 | 75 | 234 | 54 | 63 | 5 | 58 |
| December | 52 | 38 | 616 | 177 | 31 | 146 | 265 | 68 | 197 | 79 | 89 | 15 | 74 |
| **2009** | | | | | | | | | | | | | |
| January | 122 | 86 | 594 | 189 | 25 | 164 | 290 | 64 | 226 | 129 | 114 | 10 | 104 |
| February | 66 | 48 | 451 | 144 | 17 | 127 | 184 | 35 | 150 | 55 | 52 | 4 | 48 |
| March | 56 | 46 | 396 | 144 | 14 | 131 | 231 | 39 | 192 | 78 | 57 | 6 | 51 |
| April | 67 | 39 | 547 | 183 | 26 | 157 | 244 | 64 | 180 | 72 | 70 | 11 | 60 |
| May | 67 | 26 | 322 | 148 | 51 | 97 | 209 | 24 | 184 | 81 | 176 | 63 | 113 |
| June | 55 | 38 | 348 | 221 | 62 | 160 | 232 | 44 | 188 | 103 | 247 | 62 | 185 |
| July | 73 | 48 | 431 | 308 | 99 | 209 | 226 | 51 | 176 | 139 | 185 | 9 | 177 |
| August | 51 | 64 | 375 | 262 | 71 | 191 | 335 | 97 | 237 | 159 | 204 | 8 | 196 |
| September | 29 | 44 | 348 | 175 | 31 | 144 | 340 | 103 | 237 | 116 | 196 | 9 | 187 |
| October | 50 | 68 | 382 | 142 | 20 | 122 | 396 | 135 | 261 | 79 | 86 | 9 | 78 |
| November | 22 | 22 | 416 | 134 | 12 | 122 | 323 | 102 | 221 | 54 | 74 | 17 | 57 |
| December | 43 | 41 | 458 | 157 | 22 | 135 | 255 | 65 | 189 | 76 | 110 | 13 | 96 |
| **2010** | | | | | | | | | | | | | |
| January | 46 | 67 | 443 | 161 | 20 | 140 | 258 | 47 | 211 | 81 | 98 | 7 | 91 |
| February | 29 | 22 | 312 | 142 | 11 | 132 | 137 | 19 | 118 | 90 | 51 | 8 | 43 |
| March | 33 | 21 | 338 | 128 | 14 | 114 | 186 | 56 | 130 | 47 | 64 | 11 | 53 |
| April | 37 | 26 | 367 | 143 | 17 | 126 | 188 | 62 | 126 | 44 | 72 | 18 | 55 |
| May | 42 | 28 | 348 | 165 | 39 | 126 | 187 | 44 | 143 | 64 | 161 | 38 | 123 |
| June | 25 | 17 | 299 | 243 | 73 | 170 | 225 | 58 | 167 | 68 | 438 | 240 | 198 |
| July | 35 | 37 | 397 | 299 | 71 | 227 | 222 | 61 | 161 | 71 | 304 | 153 | 150 |
| August | 40 | 15 | 300 | 217 | 63 | 154 | 248 | 87 | 161 | 153 | 309 | 127 | 182 |
| September | 39 | 8 | 320 | 208 | 40 | 168 | 300 | 122 | 177 | 61 | 241 | 90 | 151 |
| October | 61 | 34 | 306 | 116 | 12 | 104 | 341 | 102 | 238 | 78 | 96 | 25 | 70 |
| November | 29 | 28 | 351 | 135 | 17 | 118 | 293 | 85 | 208 | 69 | 94 | 11 | 83 |
| December | 46 | 23 | 501 | 166 | 25 | 141 | 178 | 50 | 127 | 38 | 112 | 8 | 104 |

[1] Layoffs and discharges are the number of layoffs and discharges during the entire month.
[2] The layoffs and discharges rate is the number of layoffs and discharges during the entire month as a percent of total employment.

## Table 7-8.  Layoffs and Discharges Levels[1] and Rates,[2] by Industry, 2005–October 2016
### —Continued

(Not seasonally adjusted, levels in thousands, rates per 100.)

| Year and month | Rate | | | | | | | | | | | | |
|---|---|---|---|---|---|---|---|---|---|---|---|---|---|
| | Total | Total private | Mining and logging | Construc-tion | Manufac-turing | Durable goods | Non-durable goods | Trade, transpor-tation, and utilities | Whole-sale trade | Retail trade | Transpor-tation, ware-housing, and utilities | Infor-mation | Financial activities |
| 2009 | 20.2 | 22.9 | 26.8 | 62.2 | 23.7 | 25.0 | 21.8 | 19.8 | 17.7 | 19.7 | 22.3 | 13.6 | 16.3 |
| 2010 | 16.8 | 18.3 | 13.5 | 57.2 | 14.6 | 13.6 | 16.1 | 14.9 | 13.5 | 16.1 | 13.1 | 10.9 | 10.1 |
| 2011 | 15.8 | 17.7 | 10.5 | 51.8 | 11.3 | 10.2 | 13.2 | 13.5 | 10.6 | 14.7 | 13.5 | 10.3 | 8.6 |
| 2012 | 15.6 | 17.5 | 16.9 | 49.0 | 10.5 | 10.4 | 10.6 | 14.0 | 11.3 | 15.2 | 13.8 | 10.3 | 8.0 |
| 2013 | 14.6 | 16.3 | 15.9 | 39.7 | 9.9 | 9.8 | 9.9 | 13.7 | 9.0 | 15.4 | 14.1 | 11.3 | 9.1 |
| 2014 | 14.7 | 16.5 | 16.1 | 33.4 | 9.5 | 8.8 | 10.7 | 15.0 | 10.6 | 16.4 | 16.1 | 11.1 | 8.1 |
| 2015 | 14.8 | 16.4 | 29.3 | 32.0 | 10.0 | 9.9 | 10.2 | 14.2 | 9.6 | 15.5 | 15.4 | 10.9 | 8.7 |
| **2005** | | | | | | | | | | | | | |
| January | 1.9 | 2.2 | 1.8 | 6.1 | 1.5 | 1.6 | 1.4 | 2.2 | 1.3 | 2.8 | 1.6 | 1.4 | 1.4 |
| February | 1.2 | 1.4 | 1.0 | 3.7 | 0.8 | 0.9 | 0.8 | 1.5 | 0.9 | 1.7 | 1.5 | 0.4 | 0.9 |
| March | 1.2 | 1.4 | 0.9 | 2.3 | 1.0 | 0.9 | 1.1 | 1.2 | 0.7 | 1.5 | 1.1 | 0.7 | 0.7 |
| April | 1.3 | 1.5 | 1.2 | 2.9 | 1.1 | 1.2 | 1.0 | 1.3 | 1.3 | 1.3 | 1.3 | 0.6 | 1.0 |
| May | 1.2 | 1.3 | 0.7 | 2.7 | 0.9 | 1.0 | 0.8 | 1.3 | 1.5 | 1.2 | 1.4 | 0.6 | 0.8 |
| June | 1.4 | 1.5 | 0.6 | 2.4 | 0.9 | 0.9 | 0.9 | 1.3 | 0.8 | 1.3 | 1.6 | 0.5 | 0.4 |
| July | 1.4 | 1.6 | 1.0 | 2.4 | 0.9 | 0.9 | 0.9 | 1.4 | 1.0 | 1.5 | 1.4 | 0.7 | 0.7 |
| August | 1.5 | 1.6 | 1.0 | 3.3 | 1.1 | 1.1 | 1.0 | 1.2 | 0.8 | 1.4 | 1.1 | 0.6 | 0.7 |
| September | 1.5 | 1.6 | 1.3 | 3.0 | 0.9 | 0.8 | 1.2 | 1.5 | 0.6 | 1.7 | 1.7 | 0.6 | 0.9 |
| October | 1.3 | 1.5 | 1.1 | 3.0 | 0.9 | 0.9 | 1.1 | 1.3 | 1.2 | 1.3 | 1.4 | 0.6 | 1.0 |
| November | 1.2 | 1.4 | 0.6 | 3.1 | 1.1 | 0.8 | 1.6 | 1.3 | 1.3 | 1.2 | 1.8 | 0.7 | 0.8 |
| December | 1.4 | 1.6 | 1.4 | 3.8 | 1.0 | 0.9 | 1.3 | 1.8 | 1.3 | 1.7 | 2.7 | 0.7 | 0.8 |
| **2006** | | | | | | | | | | | | | |
| January | 1.6 | 1.8 | 0.8 | 4.3 | 1.2 | 0.9 | 1.7 | 2.0 | 0.8 | 2.5 | 1.7 | 0.6 | 1.1 |
| February | 1.0 | 1.2 | 1.0 | 2.5 | 0.8 | 0.7 | 1.0 | 1.3 | 1.0 | 1.6 | 0.7 | 0.6 | 0.7 |
| March | 1.0 | 1.1 | 1.2 | 2.5 | 1.2 | 1.0 | 1.6 | 0.9 | 0.6 | 1.1 | 0.8 | 0.5 | 0.9 |
| April | 1.2 | 1.4 | 1.4 | 1.9 | 1.0 | 0.7 | 1.4 | 1.2 | 0.9 | 1.4 | 0.6 | 1.0 | 1.0 |
| May | 1.2 | 1.3 | 0.4 | 2.2 | 1.1 | 1.0 | 1.2 | 1.2 | 0.8 | 1.4 | 1.2 | 0.4 | 0.6 |
| June | 1.2 | 1.2 | 0.4 | 1.6 | 1.0 | 0.8 | 1.3 | 1.3 | 0.8 | 1.6 | 1.1 | 0.5 | 0.6 |
| July | 1.3 | 1.5 | 0.6 | 2.5 | 1.0 | 1.0 | 1.0 | 1.2 | 1.1 | 1.2 | 1.2 | 0.7 | 0.9 |
| August | 1.3 | 1.4 | 0.9 | 2.5 | 1.1 | 1.0 | 1.2 | 1.2 | 1.0 | 1.2 | 1.2 | 0.6 | 0.9 |
| September | 1.3 | 1.4 | 1.5 | 2.4 | 1.2 | 1.1 | 1.3 | 1.1 | 0.9 | 1.2 | 1.2 | 0.6 | 0.8 |
| October | 1.4 | 1.7 | 0.7 | 3.2 | 1.1 | 1.0 | 1.1 | 1.2 | 1.0 | 1.3 | 1.2 | 1.0 | 1.0 |
| November | 1.4 | 1.6 | 0.8 | 4.3 | 1.1 | 1.1 | 1.0 | 1.1 | 0.8 | 1.3 | 1.1 | 0.8 | 0.8 |
| December | 1.4 | 1.6 | 1.0 | 4.1 | 1.1 | 1.0 | 1.3 | 1.6 | 0.7 | 2.1 | 1.4 | 0.8 | 1.1 |
| **2007** | | | | | | | | | | | | | |
| January | 1.6 | 1.9 | 1.5 | 4.4 | 1.3 | 1.3 | 1.4 | 2.1 | 1.1 | 2.5 | 2.0 | 1.7 | 1.1 |
| February | 1.0 | 1.2 | 1.0 | 3.1 | 1.1 | 1.1 | 1.1 | 1.1 | 0.6 | 1.3 | 0.8 | 0.9 | 0.8 |
| March | 1.1 | 1.3 | 0.8 | 2.2 | 1.0 | 1.0 | 1.0 | 1.0 | 0.7 | 1.1 | 1.1 | 0.6 | 1.2 |
| April | 1.3 | 1.5 | 0.9 | 2.8 | 1.1 | 1.1 | 1.1 | 1.1 | 1.0 | 1.2 | 1.2 | 0.6 | 0.9 |
| May | 1.1 | 1.2 | 0.8 | 2.3 | 0.9 | 0.9 | 1.1 | 1.1 | 0.8 | 1.3 | 0.8 | 0.7 | 0.9 |
| June | 1.3 | 1.4 | 0.5 | 2.5 | 1.0 | 1.0 | 1.0 | 1.0 | 0.8 | 1.1 | 0.9 | 0.7 | 0.8 |
| July | 1.3 | 1.4 | 0.9 | 2.2 | 1.2 | 1.2 | 1.3 | 1.4 | 1.5 | 1.3 | 1.2 | 1.1 | 1.2 |
| August | 1.4 | 1.5 | 1.2 | 3.1 | 1.2 | 1.1 | 1.2 | 1.3 | 1.1 | 1.5 | 1.0 | 0.9 | 1.2 |
| September | 1.5 | 1.7 | 1.0 | 3.2 | 1.3 | 1.2 | 1.3 | 1.3 | 1.1 | 1.5 | 0.8 | 0.6 | 1.2 |
| October | 1.5 | 1.7 | 1.0 | 3.5 | 1.5 | 1.4 | 1.5 | 1.5 | 1.4 | 1.6 | 1.2 | 0.6 | 1.3 |
| November | 1.4 | 1.6 | 1.5 | 3.5 | 1.4 | 1.3 | 1.5 | 1.5 | 1.1 | 1.7 | 1.4 | 0.5 | 0.9 |
| December | 1.4 | 1.6 | 1.3 | 4.0 | 1.1 | 1.0 | 1.3 | 1.6 | 1.3 | 1.8 | 1.1 | 0.6 | 1.3 |
| **2008** | | | | | | | | | | | | | |
| January | 1.7 | 2.0 | 1.6 | 5.0 | 1.3 | 1.4 | 1.1 | 2.0 | 1.6 | 2.3 | 1.5 | 1.3 | 1.5 |
| February | 1.1 | 1.3 | 1.5 | 3.0 | 1.0 | 0.9 | 1.2 | 1.3 | 1.0 | 1.5 | 0.8 | 0.7 | 0.7 |
| March | 1.1 | 1.3 | 0.8 | 3.4 | 0.9 | 0.9 | 0.9 | 1.0 | 1.0 | 1.0 | 0.9 | 1.0 | 0.9 |
| April | 1.2 | 1.4 | 1.3 | 3.2 | 1.4 | 1.3 | 1.5 | 1.2 | 1.2 | 1.2 | 1.1 | 0.6 | 1.1 |
| May | 1.2 | 1.3 | 0.6 | 2.7 | 1.1 | 1.0 | 1.1 | 1.1 | 0.9 | 1.3 | 0.9 | 0.5 | 0.8 |
| June | 1.3 | 1.5 | 0.7 | 2.8 | 1.2 | 1.2 | 1.3 | 1.4 | 1.3 | 1.6 | 0.9 | 1.0 | 0.9 |
| July | 1.4 | 1.6 | 1.2 | 3.1 | 1.2 | 1.2 | 1.3 | 0.9 | 1.5 | 0.9 | 1.7 | 0.7 | 1.4 |
| August | 1.6 | 1.8 | 0.6 | 3.5 | 1.3 | 1.4 | 1.0 | 1.5 | 1.3 | 1.6 | 1.5 | 0.6 | 1.4 |
| September | 1.5 | 1.6 | 0.7 | 3.8 | 1.5 | 1.5 | 1.5 | 1.3 | 1.1 | 1.4 | 1.4 | 1.2 | 1.0 |
| October | 1.7 | 1.9 | 1.3 | 4.9 | 1.8 | 1.7 | 1.9 | 1.7 | 1.7 | 1.8 | 1.2 | 1.4 | 1.0 |
| November | 1.6 | 1.9 | 2.0 | 5.9 | 1.8 | 1.8 | 1.8 | 1.5 | 1.3 | 1.6 | 1.5 | 1.4 | 0.9 |
| December | 2.0 | 2.3 | 2.3 | 6.2 | 2.5 | 2.6 | 2.2 | 2.4 | 2.2 | 2.6 | 2.0 | 1.4 | 1.1 |
| **2009** | | | | | | | | | | | | | |
| January | 2.4 | 2.8 | 2.4 | 8.5 | 3.5 | 4.0 | 2.6 | 2.6 | 2.4 | 2.8 | 2.2 | 2.1 | 2.6 |
| February | 1.5 | 1.8 | 2.2 | 5.1 | 2.3 | 2.6 | 1.9 | 1.6 | 1.5 | 1.7 | 1.5 | 1.2 | 1.4 |
| March | 1.5 | 1.8 | 3.2 | 5.0 | 2.3 | 2.7 | 1.6 | 1.5 | 1.5 | 1.4 | 1.8 | 1.1 | 1.3 |
| April | 1.8 | 2.1 | 2.1 | 5.9 | 2.4 | 2.8 | 1.7 | 1.7 | 1.6 | 1.9 | 1.5 | 1.4 | 1.4 |
| May | 1.4 | 1.6 | 1.8 | 4.2 | 2.0 | 2.2 | 1.7 | 1.4 | 1.6 | 1.4 | 1.2 | 0.9 | 1.2 |
| June | 1.5 | 1.6 | 1.6 | 3.4 | 1.6 | 1.8 | 1.4 | 1.3 | 1.3 | 1.2 | 1.4 | 1.0 | 1.2 |
| July | 1.8 | 2.0 | 2.2 | 5.3 | 1.6 | 1.5 | 1.9 | 1.4 | 1.5 | 1.3 | 1.7 | 1.1 | 1.5 |
| August | 1.7 | 1.9 | 1.2 | 4.4 | 1.6 | 1.3 | 2.1 | 1.3 | 1.4 | 1.3 | 1.3 | 0.7 | 1.5 |
| September | 1.7 | 1.8 | 1.8 | 5.0 | 1.5 | 1.4 | 1.7 | 1.6 | 1.2 | 1.7 | 2.0 | 0.5 | 0.9 |
| October | 1.6 | 1.9 | 2.2 | 5.7 | 1.8 | 1.7 | 2.0 | 1.4 | 1.2 | 1.4 | 1.4 | 0.9 | 1.5 |
| November | 1.4 | 1.6 | 1.7 | 4.5 | 1.6 | 1.5 | 1.7 | 1.3 | 1.2 | 1.3 | 1.6 | 1.0 | 0.6 |
| December | 1.8 | 2.0 | 2.8 | 6.1 | 1.5 | 1.4 | 1.5 | 2.3 | 1.5 | 2.1 | 4.0 | 1.6 | 1.1 |
| **2010** | | | | | | | | | | | | | |
| January | 1.8 | 2.1 | 1.8 | 7.2 | 2.0 | 2.4 | 1.2 | 2.2 | 1.5 | 2.6 | 1.4 | 1.9 | 1.5 |
| February | 1.1 | 1.3 | 1.1 | 4.3 | 1.2 | 1.2 | 1.3 | 1.1 | 1.2 | 1.1 | 0.9 | 0.8 | 0.7 |
| March | 1.1 | 1.3 | 1.0 | 3.8 | 1.1 | 1.1 | 1.2 | 1.3 | 1.0 | 1.6 | 0.6 | 0.8 | 0.7 |
| April | 1.2 | 1.4 | 1.1 | 4.6 | 1.1 | 0.9 | 1.5 | 1.0 | 1.0 | 1.0 | 0.8 | 0.6 | 0.8 |
| May | 1.2 | 1.3 | 1.2 | 4.2 | 0.8 | 0.8 | 0.8 | 0.9 | 1.0 | 0.9 | 0.9 | 0.9 | 0.9 |
| June | 1.5 | 1.4 | 0.6 | 2.9 | 0.9 | 0.7 | 1.2 | 1.2 | 0.8 | 1.3 | 1.2 | 0.8 | 0.5 |
| July | 1.6 | 1.6 | 0.9 | 4.3 | 1.2 | 1.0 | 1.4 | 1.3 | 1.5 | 1.3 | 1.0 | 0.9 | 0.9 |
| August | 1.5 | 1.5 | 0.9 | 3.9 | 1.3 | 1.1 | 1.6 | 1.0 | 0.9 | 1.2 | 0.7 | 0.8 | 0.7 |
| September | 1.4 | 1.5 | 1.0 | 4.2 | 1.2 | 1.1 | 1.2 | 1.0 | 1.3 | 1.0 | 0.8 | 0.7 | 0.6 |
| October | 1.3 | 1.5 | 0.9 | 4.6 | 1.4 | 1.2 | 1.6 | 1.2 | 1.0 | 1.2 | 1.3 | 0.8 | 1.2 |
| November | 1.3 | 1.5 | 1.2 | 5.3 | 1.3 | 1.1 | 1.6 | 1.1 | 1.1 | 1.2 | 0.9 | 0.9 | 0.7 |
| December | 1.6 | 1.8 | 1.9 | 7.3 | 1.1 | 1.0 | 1.2 | 1.6 | 1.2 | 1.5 | 2.4 | 1.2 | 0.9 |

[1]Layoffs and discharges are the number of layoffs and discharges during the entire month.
[2]The layoffs and discharges rate is the number of layoffs and discharges during the entire month as a percent of total employment.

### Table 7-8. Layoffs and Discharges Levels[1] and Rates,[2] by Industry, 2005–October 2016 —Continued

(Not seasonally adjusted, levels in thousands, rates per 100.)

| Year and month | Finance and insurance | Real estate and rental and leasing | Professional and business services | Education and health services | Educational services | Health care and social assistance | Leisure and hospitality | Arts, entertainment, and recreation | Accommodation and food services | Other services | Government | Federal | State and local government |
|---|---|---|---|---|---|---|---|---|---|---|---|---|---|
| | | | | | | | Rate | | | | | | |
| 2009 | 12.0 | 29.0 | 29.9 | 11.4 | 14.7 | 10.8 | 25.0 | 42.6 | 21.9 | 21.3 | 6.8 | 7.7 | 6.6 |
| 2010 | 8.0 | 16.4 | 25.8 | 10.7 | 12.9 | 10.2 | 21.5 | 41.3 | 18.1 | 16.0 | 9.1 | 24.8 | 6.7 |
| 2011 | 6.2 | 15.8 | 27.8 | 9.3 | 11.5 | 8.8 | 23.3 | 48.2 | 19.1 | 19.6 | 6.1 | 4.7 | 6.3 |
| 2012 | 5.8 | 14.6 | 28.0 | 9.4 | 11.7 | 9.0 | 22.5 | 45.5 | 18.6 | 18.4 | 5.4 | 4.5 | 5.5 |
| 2013 | 6.9 | 15.5 | 25.2 | 9.1 | 12.1 | 8.6 | 21.3 | 43.4 | 17.7 | 15.8 | 5.3 | 5.4 | 5.3 |
| 2014 | 6.9 | 11.7 | 26.8 | 9.4 | 11.5 | 9.0 | 21.4 | 47.0 | 17.2 | 13.9 | 4.9 | 4.8 | 4.9 |
| 2015 | 6.9 | 14.1 | 25.8 | 7.7 | 10.6 | 7.2 | 23.3 | 46.0 | 19.5 | 16.8 | 6.0 | 5.2 | 6.1 |
| **2005** | | | | | | | | | | | | | |
| January | 1.2 | 2.2 | 3.2 | 0.9 | 0.6 | 0.9 | 2.5 | 3.5 | 2.4 | 1.5 | 0.3 | 0.4 | 0.3 |
| February | 0.5 | 2.1 | 2.1 | 0.7 | 0.4 | 0.8 | 1.5 | 2.2 | 1.4 | 1.0 | 0.2 | 0.3 | 0.2 |
| March | 0.6 | 1.2 | 2.5 | 0.8 | 0.6 | 0.9 | 1.9 | 1.8 | 1.9 | 1.1 | 0.2 | 0.3 | 0.2 |
| April | 0.8 | 1.5 | 2.6 | 0.8 | 0.8 | 0.9 | 1.8 | 3.2 | 1.6 | 0.8 | 0.3 | 0.4 | 0.3 |
| May | 0.6 | 1.2 | 1.6 | 0.8 | 1.1 | 0.7 | 1.7 | 2.1 | 1.6 | 1.6 | 0.5 | 0.3 | 0.5 |
| June | 0.3 | 0.5 | 2.8 | 0.9 | 1.1 | 0.9 | 2.4 | 2.5 | 2.4 | 0.9 | 0.7 | 0.6 | 0.7 |
| July | 0.5 | 1.2 | 3.4 | 0.8 | 1.2 | 0.8 | 1.7 | 1.6 | 1.8 | 1.0 | 0.6 | 0.5 | 0.6 |
| August | 0.7 | 0.5 | 2.8 | 1.0 | 0.9 | 1.0 | 1.9 | 4.1 | 1.4 | 3.1 | 0.9 | 0.5 | 0.9 |
| September | 0.4 | 2.2 | 2.0 | 0.7 | 1.2 | 0.6 | 3.4 | 11.9 | 1.9 | 1.4 | 0.8 | 0.6 | 0.8 |
| October | 0.6 | 2.3 | 2.4 | 0.7 | 0.6 | 0.7 | 2.6 | 5.2 | 2.2 | 1.0 | 0.4 | 0.3 | 0.4 |
| November | 0.3 | 2.0 | 2.0 | 0.5 | 0.4 | 0.6 | 2.1 | 5.2 | 1.6 | 0.8 | 0.3 | 0.4 | 0.3 |
| December | 0.4 | 1.7 | 2.4 | 0.7 | 1.2 | 0.6 | 1.7 | 3.2 | 1.5 | 1.0 | 0.4 | 1.0 | 0.3 |
| **2006** | | | | | | | | | | | | | |
| January | 0.8 | 1.8 | 2.5 | 0.8 | 0.8 | 0.8 | 2.3 | 2.7 | 2.2 | 1.2 | 0.4 | 0.5 | 0.4 |
| February | 0.6 | 1.0 | 1.7 | 0.5 | 0.3 | 0.5 | 1.4 | 1.9 | 1.3 | 0.9 | 0.2 | 0.3 | 0.2 |
| March | 0.6 | 2.0 | 1.6 | 0.6 | 0.7 | 0.6 | 1.5 | 1.9 | 1.4 | 0.5 | 0.3 | 0.4 | 0.3 |
| April | 0.7 | 1.7 | 2.0 | 0.8 | 0.8 | 0.8 | 1.9 | 2.6 | 1.7 | 2.6 | 0.3 | 0.4 | 0.2 |
| May | 0.4 | 1.0 | 2.1 | 1.3 | 1.7 | 1.2 | 1.3 | 2.0 | 1.1 | 0.9 | 0.5 | 0.4 | 0.5 |
| June | 0.5 | 1.2 | 1.6 | 1.0 | 2.0 | 0.9 | 1.3 | 1.6 | 1.2 | 1.2 | 0.9 | 0.7 | 0.9 |
| July | 0.5 | 1.9 | 2.5 | 1.0 | 1.6 | 0.9 | 1.7 | 2.3 | 1.6 | 1.1 | 0.7 | 0.6 | 0.7 |
| August | 0.7 | 1.5 | 1.8 | 0.8 | 1.0 | 0.8 | 1.9 | 4.0 | 1.4 | 1.9 | 0.7 | 1.2 | 0.7 |
| September | 0.6 | 1.2 | 2.0 | 0.6 | 0.8 | 0.6 | 2.4 | 6.7 | 1.6 | 1.3 | 0.8 | 0.9 | 0.8 |
| October | 0.7 | 1.9 | 2.6 | 0.7 | 0.7 | 0.7 | 2.9 | 6.2 | 2.4 | 1.7 | 0.4 | 0.4 | 0.4 |
| November | 0.4 | 1.9 | 2.3 | 0.5 | 0.4 | 0.5 | 2.7 | 5.8 | 2.2 | 1.1 | 0.3 | 0.3 | 0.3 |
| December | 1.0 | 1.5 | 2.3 | 0.6 | 0.9 | 0.5 | 1.7 | 2.8 | 1.6 | 1.0 | 0.4 | 0.6 | 0.3 |
| **2007** | | | | | | | | | | | | | |
| January | 0.7 | 2.2 | 2.4 | 0.8 | 1.3 | 0.7 | 2.2 | 4.5 | 1.8 | 1.1 | 0.4 | 0.6 | 0.3 |
| February | 0.5 | 1.5 | 1.8 | 0.5 | 0.7 | 0.5 | 1.4 | 2.7 | 1.2 | 0.5 | 0.2 | 0.4 | 0.2 |
| March | 0.8 | 2.3 | 2.2 | 0.7 | 0.6 | 0.7 | 1.5 | 2.8 | 1.2 | 0.8 | 0.2 | 0.5 | 0.2 |
| April | 0.7 | 1.4 | 2.4 | 0.7 | 1.0 | 0.7 | 1.9 | 4.5 | 1.4 | 1.8 | 0.3 | 0.5 | 0.2 |
| May | 0.4 | 2.0 | 1.6 | 0.9 | 1.3 | 0.8 | 1.6 | 2.5 | 1.5 | 0.6 | 0.5 | 0.6 | 0.5 |
| June | 0.7 | 0.9 | 1.7 | 1.3 | 3.0 | 1.0 | 1.9 | 2.4 | 1.9 | 1.3 | 0.8 | 1.0 | 0.7 |
| July | 1.0 | 1.9 | 2.0 | 0.8 | 0.8 | 0.8 | 1.3 | 1.2 | 1.3 | 1.3 | 1.0 | 1.0 | 1.0 |
| August | 1.2 | 1.3 | 1.9 | 1.0 | 2.3 | 0.8 | 1.7 | 2.7 | 1.6 | 2.2 | 0.9 | 1.0 | 0.8 |
| September | 0.9 | 2.0 | 2.1 | 0.9 | 0.7 | 0.9 | 3.3 | 6.9 | 2.7 | 1.7 | 0.7 | 1.1 | 0.6 |
| October | 1.0 | 1.9 | 2.6 | 0.7 | 0.5 | 0.7 | 2.6 | 5.9 | 2.0 | 0.9 | 0.4 | 0.4 | 0.3 |
| November | 0.4 | 2.4 | 2.5 | 0.7 | 0.8 | 0.6 | 1.8 | 5.8 | 1.2 | 1.2 | 0.3 | 0.3 | 0.2 |
| December | 1.0 | 2.1 | 2.7 | 0.6 | 0.8 | 0.5 | 1.7 | 3.1 | 1.5 | 1.0 | 0.4 | 0.7 | 0.4 |
| **2008** | | | | | | | | | | | | | |
| January | 1.3 | 2.2 | 2.8 | 0.9 | 0.9 | 0.9 | 1.9 | 3.8 | 1.6 | 1.1 | 0.3 | 0.7 | 0.3 |
| February | 0.6 | 1.1 | 1.8 | 0.7 | 0.5 | 0.8 | 1.8 | 2.9 | 1.6 | 0.9 | 0.2 | 0.2 | 0.1 |
| March | 0.9 | 1.0 | 2.0 | 0.8 | 0.4 | 0.9 | 1.4 | 3.2 | 1.1 | 1.0 | 0.2 | 0.2 | 0.2 |
| April | 1.1 | 1.4 | 2.4 | 0.7 | 0.9 | 0.6 | 1.5 | 3.1 | 1.2 | 0.8 | 0.2 | 0.3 | 0.2 |
| May | 0.5 | 1.6 | 1.5 | 1.1 | 1.3 | 1.1 | 1.6 | 3.0 | 1.3 | 1.8 | 0.4 | 0.2 | 0.5 |
| June | 0.9 | 1.0 | 2.1 | 1.1 | 1.9 | 0.9 | 1.4 | 1.5 | 1.4 | 0.9 | 0.7 | 0.3 | 0.7 |
| July | 1.1 | 2.1 | 2.2 | 1.1 | 1.9 | 1.0 | 1.4 | 1.3 | 1.4 | 1.8 | 0.5 | 0.2 | 0.6 |
| August | 1.2 | 1.9 | 2.3 | 1.1 | 1.8 | 1.0 | 2.2 | 3.5 | 1.9 | 3.1 | 0.8 | 0.3 | 0.9 |
| September | 0.7 | 1.8 | 2.0 | 0.7 | 0.7 | 0.8 | 2.6 | 6.0 | 2.0 | 1.3 | 0.7 | 0.3 | 0.7 |
| October | 0.6 | 2.2 | 2.5 | 0.7 | 0.8 | 0.7 | 2.9 | 6.1 | 2.4 | 1.4 | 0.3 | 0.3 | 0.3 |
| November | 0.5 | 2.1 | 3.0 | 0.6 | 0.7 | 0.5 | 2.4 | 4.2 | 2.1 | 1.0 | 0.3 | 0.2 | 0.3 |
| December | 0.9 | 1.8 | 3.6 | 0.9 | 1.0 | 0.9 | 2.0 | 3.8 | 1.8 | 1.5 | 0.4 | 0.6 | 0.4 |
| **2009** | | | | | | | | | | | | | |
| January | 2.0 | 4.2 | 3.5 | 1.0 | 0.8 | 1.0 | 2.3 | 3.7 | 2.1 | 2.4 | 0.5 | 0.4 | 0.5 |
| February | 1.1 | 2.4 | 2.7 | 0.7 | 0.5 | 0.8 | 1.5 | 2.0 | 1.4 | 1.0 | 0.2 | 0.2 | 0.2 |
| March | 0.9 | 2.3 | 2.4 | 0.7 | 0.4 | 0.8 | 1.8 | 2.2 | 1.7 | 1.5 | 0.2 | 0.2 | 0.3 |
| April | 1.1 | 2.0 | 3.3 | 0.9 | 0.8 | 1.0 | 1.9 | 3.4 | 1.6 | 1.3 | 0.3 | 0.4 | 0.3 |
| May | 1.1 | 1.3 | 1.9 | 0.8 | 1.6 | 0.6 | 1.6 | 1.2 | 1.6 | 1.5 | 0.8 | 2.2 | 0.6 |
| June | 0.9 | 1.9 | 2.1 | 1.1 | 2.1 | 1.0 | 1.7 | 2.1 | 1.6 | 1.9 | 1.1 | 2.2 | 0.9 |
| July | 1.3 | 2.4 | 2.6 | 1.6 | 3.5 | 1.3 | 1.6 | 2.3 | 1.5 | 2.6 | 0.9 | 0.3 | 1.0 |
| August | 0.9 | 3.2 | 2.3 | 1.4 | 2.6 | 1.2 | 2.4 | 4.5 | 2.1 | 2.9 | 1.0 | 0.3 | 1.1 |
| September | 0.5 | 2.2 | 2.1 | 0.9 | 1.0 | 0.9 | 2.6 | 5.2 | 2.1 | 2.2 | 0.9 | 0.3 | 1.0 |
| October | 0.9 | 3.4 | 2.3 | 0.7 | 0.6 | 0.7 | 3.1 | 7.3 | 2.3 | 1.5 | 0.4 | 0.3 | 0.4 |
| November | 0.4 | 1.1 | 2.5 | 0.7 | 0.4 | 0.7 | 2.5 | 5.8 | 2.0 | 1.0 | 0.3 | 0.6 | 0.3 |
| December | 0.7 | 2.1 | 2.8 | 0.8 | 0.7 | 0.8 | 2.0 | 3.7 | 1.7 | 1.4 | 0.5 | 0.5 | 0.5 |
| **2010** | | | | | | | | | | | | | |
| January | 0.8 | 3.5 | 2.7 | 0.8 | 0.7 | 0.8 | 2.1 | 2.8 | 2.0 | 1.5 | 0.4 | 0.2 | 0.5 |
| February | 0.5 | 1.2 | 1.9 | 0.7 | 0.3 | 0.8 | 1.1 | 1.1 | 1.1 | 1.7 | 0.2 | 0.3 | 0.2 |
| March | 0.6 | 1.1 | 2.1 | 0.6 | 0.4 | 0.7 | 1.5 | 3.2 | 1.2 | 0.9 | 0.3 | 0.4 | 0.3 |
| April | 0.7 | 1.3 | 2.2 | 0.7 | 0.5 | 0.8 | 1.5 | 3.3 | 1.1 | 0.8 | 0.3 | 0.6 | 0.3 |
| May | 0.7 | 1.4 | 2.1 | 0.8 | 1.2 | 0.8 | 1.4 | 2.2 | 1.3 | 1.2 | 0.7 | 1.1 | 0.6 |
| June | 0.4 | 0.9 | 1.8 | 1.2 | 2.5 | 1.0 | 1.7 | 2.7 | 1.5 | 1.3 | 1.9 | 7.5 | 1.0 |
| July | 0.6 | 1.9 | 2.4 | 1.5 | 2.5 | 1.4 | 1.6 | 2.7 | 1.4 | 1.3 | 1.4 | 5.0 | 0.8 |
| August | 0.7 | 0.7 | 1.8 | 1.1 | 2.2 | 0.9 | 1.8 | 4.0 | 1.4 | 2.8 | 1.5 | 4.3 | 1.0 |
| September | 0.7 | 0.4 | 1.9 | 1.0 | 1.3 | 1.0 | 2.2 | 6.1 | 1.6 | 1.1 | 1.1 | 3.1 | 0.8 |
| October | 1.1 | 1.8 | 1.8 | 0.6 | 0.4 | 0.6 | 2.6 | 5.5 | 2.1 | 1.5 | 0.4 | 0.9 | 0.4 |
| November | 0.5 | 1.5 | 2.1 | 0.7 | 0.5 | 0.7 | 2.3 | 4.8 | 1.9 | 1.3 | 0.4 | 0.4 | 0.4 |
| December | 0.8 | 1.2 | 2.9 | 0.8 | 0.7 | 0.8 | 1.4 | 2.9 | 1.1 | 0.7 | 0.5 | 0.3 | 0.5 |

[1]Layoffs and discharges are the number of layoffs and discharges during the entire month.
[2]The layoffs and discharges rate is the number of layoffs and discharges during the entire month as a percent of total employment.

## Table 7-8.  Layoffs and Discharges Levels[1] and Rates,[2] by Industry, 2005–October 2016
### —Continued

(Not seasonally adjusted, levels in thousands, rates per 100.)

| Year and month | Total | Total private | Mining and logging | Construction | Manufacturing | Durable goods | Nondurable goods | Trade, transportation, and utilities | Wholesale trade | Retail trade | Transportation, warehousing, and utilities | Information | Financial activities |
|---|---|---|---|---|---|---|---|---|---|---|---|---|---|
| **2011** | | | | | | | | | | | | | |
| January | 2 161 | 2 085 | 11 | 319 | 145 | 79 | 66 | 559 | 56 | 399 | 105 | 35 | 110 |
| February | 1 295 | 1 249 | 4 | 217 | 112 | 63 | 49 | 247 | 46 | 173 | 28 | 18 | 46 |
| March | 1 369 | 1 315 | 3 | 210 | 107 | 63 | 43 | 234 | 44 | 153 | 37 | 34 | 36 |
| April | 1 516 | 1 446 | 8 | 228 | 103 | 49 | 54 | 204 | 33 | 139 | 33 | 17 | 38 |
| May | 1 583 | 1 443 | 6 | 207 | 106 | 59 | 48 | 208 | 60 | 123 | 24 | 21 | 37 |
| June | 1 742 | 1 586 | 6 | 223 | 99 | 55 | 44 | 250 | 59 | 148 | 42 | 18 | 57 |
| July | 1 781 | 1 610 | 6 | 236 | 105 | 62 | 43 | 266 | 48 | 162 | 56 | 26 | 47 |
| August | 1 889 | 1 701 | 7 | 253 | 127 | 71 | 56 | 248 | 36 | 164 | 48 | 18 | 55 |
| September | 1 876 | 1 711 | 7 | 242 | 113 | 64 | 48 | 240 | 48 | 149 | 44 | 18 | 59 |
| October | 1 825 | 1 734 | 5 | 246 | 105 | 60 | 45 | 249 | 46 | 138 | 65 | 22 | 64 |
| November | 1 753 | 1 690 | 8 | 222 | 108 | 60 | 48 | 271 | 47 | 178 | 46 | 25 | 57 |
| December | 1 966 | 1 861 | 12 | 277 | 107 | 62 | 44 | 429 | 69 | 214 | 146 | 27 | 50 |
| **2012** | | | | | | | | | | | | | |
| January | 2 076 | 2 003 | 17 | 304 | 121 | 68 | 53 | 500 | 82 | 334 | 84 | 33 | 58 |
| February | 1 377 | 1 325 | 12 | 218 | 98 | 60 | 37 | 224 | 35 | 156 | 32 | 22 | 36 |
| March | 1 332 | 1 279 | 12 | 159 | 84 | 48 | 36 | 234 | 55 | 142 | 38 | 22 | 41 |
| April | 1 697 | 1 636 | 11 | 197 | 96 | 55 | 41 | 250 | 55 | 148 | 47 | 24 | 58 |
| May | 1 725 | 1 598 | 12 | 217 | 97 | 56 | 42 | 253 | 42 | 170 | 41 | 21 | 53 |
| June | 1 762 | 1 610 | 9 | 188 | 119 | 77 | 42 | 257 | 38 | 162 | 58 | 16 | 46 |
| July | 1 642 | 1 514 | 6 | 248 | 96 | 59 | 37 | 250 | 44 | 151 | 55 | 18 | 49 |
| August | 2 003 | 1 830 | 10 | 231 | 112 | 75 | 38 | 318 | 60 | 203 | 54 | 29 | 64 |
| September | 1 884 | 1 750 | 9 | 262 | 101 | 67 | 33 | 263 | 64 | 143 | 56 | 17 | 35 |
| October | 1 865 | 1 770 | 12 | 205 | 132 | 78 | 54 | 280 | 60 | 165 | 55 | 18 | 69 |
| November | 1 771 | 1 705 | 10 | 330 | 110 | 70 | 40 | 231 | 52 | 134 | 45 | 19 | 70 |
| December | 1 818 | 1 738 | 20 | 232 | 95 | 61 | 34 | 494 | 72 | 305 | 116 | 20 | 49 |
| **2013** | | | | | | | | | | | | | |
| January | 1 986 | 1 915 | 18 | 245 | 118 | 77 | 41 | 488 | 54 | 328 | 106 | 29 | 86 |
| February | 1 239 | 1 187 | 12 | 179 | 92 | 61 | 31 | 234 | 37 | 159 | 39 | 18 | 43 |
| March | 1 355 | 1 288 | 7 | 195 | 80 | 56 | 24 | 244 | 29 | 166 | 50 | 12 | 42 |
| April | 1 605 | 1 552 | 12 | 166 | 90 | 64 | 26 | 246 | 32 | 169 | 45 | 26 | 47 |
| May | 1 630 | 1 520 | 8 | 158 | 103 | 69 | 34 | 286 | 44 | 187 | 54 | 23 | 55 |
| June | 1 611 | 1 446 | 7 | 148 | 92 | 57 | 35 | 229 | 30 | 159 | 39 | 36 | 46 |
| July | 1 607 | 1 497 | 10 | 180 | 98 | 60 | 38 | 305 | 80 | 160 | 65 | 24 | 60 |
| August | 1 912 | 1 776 | 9 | 166 | 126 | 74 | 52 | 255 | 34 | 157 | 64 | 37 | 69 |
| September | 1 941 | 1 799 | 11 | 176 | 107 | 62 | 44 | 240 | 49 | 142 | 49 | 33 | 87 |
| October | 1 601 | 1 509 | 17 | 224 | 94 | 55 | 39 | 269 | 48 | 159 | 63 | 18 | 72 |
| November | 1 487 | 1 426 | 9 | 228 | 84 | 45 | 39 | 286 | 40 | 198 | 48 | 18 | 52 |
| December | 1 929 | 1 833 | 19 | 256 | 101 | 59 | 42 | 474 | 48 | 332 | 94 | 28 | 61 |
| **2014** | | | | | | | | | | | | | |
| January | 2 157 | 2 072 | 13 | 182 | 119 | 79 | 40 | 631 | 53 | 387 | 191 | 34 | 86 |
| February | 1 278 | 1 236 | 11 | 125 | 73 | 47 | 25 | 262 | 37 | 181 | 44 | 20 | 39 |
| March | 1 320 | 1 257 | 13 | 110 | 72 | 40 | 31 | 248 | 33 | 164 | 51 | 36 | 58 |
| April | 1 604 | 1 555 | 9 | 113 | 96 | 64 | 32 | 303 | 47 | 209 | 46 | 28 | 65 |
| May | 1 567 | 1 462 | 12 | 132 | 80 | 45 | 34 | 278 | 42 | 184 | 52 | 20 | 57 |
| June | 1 652 | 1 507 | 9 | 105 | 102 | 56 | 46 | 274 | 57 | 173 | 44 | 22 | 51 |
| July | 1 745 | 1 644 | 7 | 215 | 80 | 55 | 25 | 326 | 82 | 177 | 66 | 36 | 46 |
| August | 1 847 | 1 729 | 9 | 152 | 101 | 58 | 43 | 302 | 69 | 182 | 51 | 20 | 85 |
| September | 1 833 | 1 716 | 12 | 144 | 118 | 65 | 53 | 253 | 46 | 155 | 52 | 26 | 33 |
| October | 1 830 | 1 755 | 12 | 186 | 114 | 58 | 56 | 316 | 56 | 187 | 74 | 25 | 47 |
| November | 1 626 | 1 552 | 15 | 237 | 110 | 67 | 43 | 285 | 50 | 181 | 54 | 19 | 45 |
| December | 1 961 | 1 865 | 20 | 279 | 111 | 59 | 52 | 424 | 48 | 287 | 88 | 22 | 61 |
| **2015** | | | | | | | | | | | | | |
| January | 2 175 | 2 074 | 30 | 259 | 99 | 57 | 43 | 651 | 61 | 412 | 178 | 40 | 75 |
| February | 1 297 | 1 246 | 27 | 152 | 94 | 63 | 31 | 236 | 49 | 145 | 42 | 18 | 30 |
| March | 1 543 | 1 482 | 31 | 160 | 89 | 55 | 35 | 301 | 64 | 169 | 68 | 23 | 54 |
| April | 1 697 | 1 634 | 25 | 131 | 85 | 53 | 31 | 277 | 30 | 193 | 54 | 21 | 77 |
| May | 1 624 | 1 492 | 15 | 122 | 77 | 47 | 30 | 284 | 26 | 187 | 71 | 23 | 47 |
| June | 1 730 | 1 566 | 9 | 167 | 103 | 60 | 43 | 308 | 72 | 184 | 53 | 27 | 62 |
| July | 1 625 | 1 490 | 16 | 138 | 98 | 67 | 31 | 330 | 68 | 198 | 63 | 23 | 59 |
| August | 1 910 | 1 750 | 16 | 182 | 125 | 89 | 36 | 297 | 39 | 203 | 55 | 23 | 81 |
| September | 2 056 | 1 911 | 15 | 172 | 122 | 74 | 48 | 248 | 25 | 162 | 61 | 25 | 64 |
| October | 1 817 | 1 706 | 18 | 200 | 117 | 63 | 54 | 250 | 46 | 154 | 51 | 30 | 48 |
| November | 1 624 | 1 546 | 12 | 192 | 108 | 69 | 39 | 273 | 45 | 172 | 56 | 29 | 53 |
| December | 1 844 | 1 727 | 26 | 190 | 112 | 67 | 45 | 369 | 39 | 250 | 80 | 18 | 60 |
| **2016** | | | | | | | | | | | | | |
| January | 2 114 | 1 996 | 21 | 238 | 105 | 67 | 37 | 579 | 48 | 364 | 167 | 38 | 77 |
| February | 1 406 | 1 352 | 27 | 173 | 113 | 83 | 30 | 266 | 42 | 181 | 43 | 17 | 46 |
| March | 1 461 | 1 396 | 21 | 133 | 101 | 63 | 38 | 241 | 44 | 147 | 50 | 21 | 64 |
| April | 1 560 | 1 492 | 20 | 176 | 102 | 58 | 43 | 247 | 49 | 158 | 40 | 30 | 60 |
| May | 1 601 | 1 469 | 10 | 173 | 114 | 80 | 33 | 270 | 59 | 154 | 58 | 28 | 43 |
| June | 1 561 | 1 419 | 11 | 124 | 104 | 67 | 38 | 269 | 37 | 166 | 67 | 24 | 47 |
| July | 1 591 | 1 476 | 8 | 137 | 88 | 62 | 26 | 311 | 40 | 203 | 68 | 32 | 45 |
| August | 1 891 | 1 689 | 13 | 164 | 127 | 85 | 42 | 248 | 48 | 158 | 42 | 22 | 63 |
| September | 1 683 | 1 527 | 8 | 146 | 113 | 65 | 48 | 245 | 33 | 167 | 45 | 19 | 49 |
| October | 1 634 | 1 528 | 13 | 190 | 100 | 53 | 47 | 235 | 35 | 141 | 58 | 19 | 53 |

[1]Layoffs and discharges are the number of layoffs and discharges during the entire month.
[2]The layoffs and discharges rate is the number of layoffs and discharges during the entire month as a percent of total employment.

## Table 7-8. Layoffs and Discharges Levels[1] and Rates,[2] by Industry, 2005–October 2016
### —Continued

(Not seasonally adjusted, levels in thousands, rates per 100.)

| Year and month | Finance and insurance | Real estate and rental and leasing | Professional and business services | Education and health services | Educational services | Health care and social assistance | Leisure and hospitality | Arts, entertainment, and recreation | Accommodation and food services | Other services | Government | Federal | State and local government |
|---|---|---|---|---|---|---|---|---|---|---|---|---|---|
| **2011** | | | | | | | | | | | | | |
| January | 51 | 59 | 440 | 142 | 20 | 122 | 247 | 61 | 186 | 76 | 76 | 11 | 65 |
| February | 25 | 21 | 294 | 113 | 20 | 93 | 131 | 22 | 109 | 67 | 45 | 5 | 40 |
| March | 25 | 11 | 334 | 104 | 14 | 90 | 206 | 54 | 152 | 46 | 54 | 6 | 48 |
| April | 14 | 25 | 473 | 113 | 15 | 98 | 180 | 58 | 122 | 82 | 70 | 9 | 60 |
| May | 26 | 11 | 403 | 157 | 40 | 117 | 223 | 62 | 161 | 76 | 139 | 7 | 132 |
| June | 29 | 28 | 382 | 257 | 66 | 191 | 213 | 34 | 179 | 82 | 157 | 10 | 147 |
| July | 26 | 21 | 359 | 222 | 68 | 154 | 227 | 33 | 194 | 116 | 171 | 8 | 163 |
| August | 30 | 25 | 378 | 212 | 37 | 175 | 283 | 93 | 191 | 119 | 188 | 27 | 161 |
| September | 39 | 21 | 380 | 135 | 29 | 106 | 398 | 180 | 218 | 118 | 165 | 20 | 145 |
| October | 24 | 40 | 406 | 133 | 19 | 114 | 385 | 120 | 264 | 119 | 91 | 13 | 79 |
| November | 32 | 26 | 388 | 147 | 19 | 127 | 382 | 155 | 228 | 81 | 64 | 11 | 53 |
| December | 33 | 17 | 488 | 141 | 22 | 119 | 255 | 56 | 199 | 75 | 106 | 10 | 96 |
| **2012** | | | | | | | | | | | | | |
| January | 30 | 27 | 385 | 184 | 41 | 144 | 321 | 77 | 244 | 80 | 73 | 9 | 65 |
| February | 19 | 16 | 401 | 99 | 10 | 89 | 159 | 43 | 116 | 57 | 52 | 6 | 46 |
| March | 20 | 22 | 362 | 117 | 12 | 105 | 196 | 68 | 128 | 51 | 53 | 6 | 47 |
| April | 38 | 20 | 470 | 157 | 20 | 137 | 255 | 124 | 131 | 118 | 61 | 7 | 54 |
| May | 29 | 23 | 443 | 194 | 54 | 139 | 221 | 54 | 167 | 87 | 127 | 7 | 120 |
| June | 21 | 25 | 446 | 283 | 77 | 206 | 191 | 26 | 165 | 55 | 152 | 9 | 143 |
| July | 24 | 25 | 380 | 209 | 61 | 148 | 198 | 30 | 167 | 60 | 129 | 7 | 122 |
| August | 38 | 27 | 451 | 194 | 36 | 158 | 321 | 78 | 242 | 99 | 173 | 19 | 154 |
| September | 22 | 13 | 436 | 143 | 20 | 123 | 363 | 148 | 216 | 120 | 135 | 21 | 114 |
| October | 37 | 32 | 426 | 159 | 26 | 133 | 363 | 105 | 258 | 106 | 94 | 20 | 74 |
| November | 44 | 26 | 424 | 111 | 13 | 98 | 304 | 105 | 200 | 95 | 66 | 13 | 54 |
| December | 22 | 27 | 402 | 142 | 32 | 111 | 223 | 71 | 152 | 61 | 80 | 17 | 64 |
| **2013** | | | | | | | | | | | | | |
| January | 38 | 48 | 501 | 152 | 22 | 130 | 232 | 51 | 180 | 47 | 70 | 9 | 62 |
| February | 30 | 13 | 306 | 132 | 16 | 116 | 133 | 21 | 112 | 39 | 52 | 15 | 37 |
| March | 25 | 17 | 327 | 117 | 17 | 100 | 187 | 41 | 146 | 77 | 67 | 16 | 52 |
| April | 31 | 17 | 459 | 150 | 19 | 132 | 261 | 107 | 154 | 93 | 53 | 13 | 39 |
| May | 30 | 25 | 394 | 195 | 39 | 156 | 209 | 54 | 155 | 87 | 110 | 11 | 99 |
| June | 18 | 28 | 383 | 205 | 64 | 141 | 217 | 31 | 186 | 84 | 165 | 10 | 156 |
| July | 36 | 24 | 320 | 199 | 54 | 144 | 213 | 35 | 178 | 88 | 110 | 8 | 102 |
| August | 41 | 29 | 485 | 220 | 70 | 149 | 315 | 76 | 239 | 94 | 137 | 12 | 125 |
| September | 49 | 38 | 412 | 170 | 41 | 130 | 488 | 218 | 269 | 77 | 142 | 12 | 130 |
| October | 38 | 34 | 333 | 131 | 17 | 114 | 290 | 99 | 192 | 61 | 92 | 20 | 72 |
| November | 31 | 21 | 339 | 124 | 17 | 107 | 232 | 97 | 135 | 54 | 61 | 11 | 50 |
| December | 38 | 23 | 419 | 145 | 31 | 114 | 265 | 55 | 209 | 65 | 95 | 11 | 84 |
| **2014** | | | | | | | | | | | | | |
| January | 59 | 27 | 435 | 223 | 39 | 185 | 286 | 60 | 226 | 63 | 85 | 23 | 62 |
| February | 20 | 20 | 368 | 112 | 13 | 99 | 167 | 43 | 124 | 58 | 42 | 7 | 35 |
| March | 43 | 15 | 350 | 163 | 23 | 140 | 174 | 58 | 116 | 35 | 62 | 10 | 52 |
| April | 40 | 25 | 475 | 180 | 17 | 163 | 250 | 113 | 138 | 36 | 49 | 10 | 39 |
| May | 17 | 39 | 405 | 157 | 37 | 120 | 263 | 59 | 204 | 58 | 105 | 7 | 98 |
| June | 29 | 22 | 437 | 210 | 67 | 142 | 231 | 34 | 197 | 67 | 145 | 10 | 135 |
| July | 25 | 21 | 399 | 187 | 52 | 135 | 247 | 51 | 196 | 101 | 101 | 5 | 96 |
| August | 41 | 44 | 500 | 182 | 48 | 134 | 280 | 117 | 163 | 97 | 119 | 10 | 109 |
| September | 19 | 14 | 452 | 186 | 38 | 148 | 426 | 204 | 222 | 67 | 117 | 15 | 102 |
| October | 35 | 12 | 484 | 155 | 16 | 138 | 347 | 121 | 226 | 69 | 75 | 13 | 61 |
| November | 26 | 20 | 390 | 104 | 11 | 93 | 277 | 131 | 146 | 69 | 74 | 11 | 63 |
| December | 49 | 12 | 487 | 147 | 24 | 124 | 263 | 69 | 194 | 50 | 96 | 7 | 89 |
| **2015** | | | | | | | | | | | | | |
| January | 35 | 40 | 462 | 133 | 25 | 108 | 254 | 76 | 178 | 70 | 101 | 32 | 69 |
| February | 14 | 17 | 370 | 96 | 10 | 86 | 165 | 46 | 119 | 58 | 51 | 8 | 43 |
| March | 38 | 16 | 432 | 117 | 14 | 103 | 213 | 75 | 138 | 60 | 61 | 12 | 49 |
| April | 50 | 27 | 500 | 113 | 16 | 97 | 350 | 110 | 241 | 56 | 63 | 11 | 52 |
| May | 29 | 18 | 420 | 166 | 44 | 122 | 278 | 45 | 233 | 60 | 132 | 11 | 120 |
| June | 30 | 31 | 392 | 192 | 85 | 107 | 212 | 35 | 177 | 92 | 164 | 10 | 155 |
| July | 39 | 20 | 386 | 164 | 33 | 130 | 186 | 23 | 163 | 89 | 135 | 10 | 124 |
| August | 51 | 30 | 349 | 174 | 58 | 117 | 379 | 86 | 293 | 124 | 160 | 10 | 149 |
| September | 35 | 29 | 487 | 166 | 23 | 143 | 474 | 177 | 297 | 138 | 145 | 9 | 136 |
| October | 28 | 20 | 407 | 128 | 22 | 106 | 422 | 158 | 264 | 86 | 111 | 13 | 98 |
| November | 26 | 27 | 415 | 115 | 18 | 97 | 296 | 100 | 196 | 53 | 78 | 11 | 68 |
| December | 40 | 20 | 458 | 142 | 18 | 125 | 294 | 65 | 230 | 58 | 116 | 7 | 109 |
| **2016** | | | | | | | | | | | | | |
| January | 50 | 28 | 502 | 158 | 22 | 135 | 228 | 80 | 148 | 50 | 118 | 35 | 83 |
| February | 29 | 17 | 378 | 95 | 17 | 79 | 188 | 25 | 163 | 49 | 53 | 4 | 49 |
| March | 47 | 16 | 413 | 117 | 19 | 97 | 219 | 66 | 153 | 67 | 65 | 11 | 54 |
| April | 32 | 28 | 428 | 128 | 27 | 101 | 243 | 79 | 165 | 58 | 67 | 10 | 57 |
| May | 29 | 14 | 346 | 177 | 44 | 133 | 230 | 55 | 175 | 77 | 132 | 8 | 124 |
| June | 24 | 23 | 312 | 235 | 85 | 150 | 218 | 45 | 173 | 74 | 142 | 9 | 133 |
| July | 22 | 24 | 383 | 174 | 55 | 119 | 237 | 35 | 201 | 61 | 116 | 8 | 107 |
| August | 42 | 21 | 362 | 213 | 41 | 171 | 392 | 152 | 241 | 85 | 202 | 11 | 190 |
| September | 26 | 23 | 369 | 114 | 15 | 99 | 350 | 150 | 200 | 114 | 155 | 13 | 142 |
| October | 19 | 35 | 365 | 147 | 15 | 132 | 350 | 116 | 234 | 56 | 105 | 11 | 94 |

[1]Layoffs and discharges are the number of layoffs and discharges during the entire month.
[2]The layoffs and discharges rate is the number of layoffs and discharges during the entire month as a percent of total employment.

## Table 7-8.  Layoffs and Discharges Levels[1] and Rates,[2] by Industry, 2005–October 2016
### —Continued

(Not seasonally adjusted, levels in thousands, rates per 100.)

| Year and month | Total | Total private | Mining and logging | Construction | Manufacturing | Durable goods | Non-durable goods | Trade, transportation, and utilities | Whole-sale trade | Retail trade | Transportation, ware-housing, and utilities | Infor-mation | Financial activities |
|---|---|---|---|---|---|---|---|---|---|---|---|---|---|
| **2011** | | | | | | | | | | | | | |
| January | 1.7 | 2.0 | 1.6 | 6.3 | 1.3 | 1.1 | 1.5 | 2.3 | 1.0 | 2.8 | 2.2 | 1.3 | 1.4 |
| February | 1.0 | 1.2 | 0.5 | 4.3 | 1.0 | 0.9 | 1.1 | 1.0 | 0.8 | 1.2 | 0.6 | 0.7 | 0.6 |
| March | 1.0 | 1.2 | 0.4 | 4.1 | 0.9 | 0.9 | 1.0 | 1.0 | 0.8 | 1.1 | 0.8 | 1.3 | 0.5 |
| April | 1.2 | 1.3 | 1.1 | 4.3 | 0.9 | 0.7 | 1.2 | 0.8 | 0.6 | 1.0 | 0.7 | 0.6 | 0.5 |
| May | 1.2 | 1.3 | 0.8 | 3.7 | 0.9 | 0.8 | 1.1 | 0.8 | 1.1 | 0.8 | 0.5 | 0.8 | 0.5 |
| June | 1.3 | 1.4 | 0.7 | 3.9 | 0.8 | 0.8 | 1.0 | 1.0 | 1.1 | 1.0 | 0.9 | 0.7 | 0.7 |
| July | 1.4 | 1.5 | 0.7 | 4.1 | 0.9 | 0.9 | 0.9 | 1.1 | 0.9 | 1.1 | 1.2 | 1.0 | 0.6 |
| August | 1.4 | 1.5 | 0.8 | 4.3 | 1.1 | 1.0 | 1.2 | 1.0 | 0.6 | 1.1 | 1.0 | 0.7 | 0.7 |
| September | 1.4 | 1.5 | 0.9 | 4.2 | 1.0 | 0.9 | 1.1 | 1.0 | 0.9 | 1.0 | 0.9 | 0.7 | 0.8 |
| October | 1.4 | 1.6 | 0.6 | 4.2 | 0.9 | 0.8 | 1.0 | 1.0 | 0.8 | 0.9 | 1.3 | 0.8 | 0.8 |
| November | 1.3 | 1.5 | 1.0 | 3.9 | 0.9 | 0.8 | 1.1 | 1.1 | 0.8 | 1.2 | 0.9 | 0.9 | 0.7 |
| December | 1.5 | 1.7 | 1.4 | 5.0 | 0.9 | 0.8 | 1.0 | 1.7 | 1.2 | 1.4 | 2.9 | 1.0 | 0.6 |
| **2012** | | | | | | | | | | | | | |
| January | 1.6 | 1.8 | 2.0 | 5.8 | 1.0 | 0.9 | 1.2 | 2.0 | 1.5 | 2.3 | 1.7 | 1.3 | 0.8 |
| February | 1.0 | 1.2 | 1.4 | 4.2 | 0.8 | 0.8 | 0.9 | 0.9 | 0.6 | 1.1 | 0.7 | 0.8 | 0.5 |
| March | 1.0 | 1.2 | 1.4 | 3.0 | 0.7 | 0.6 | 0.8 | 0.9 | 1.0 | 1.0 | 0.8 | 0.8 | 0.5 |
| April | 1.3 | 1.5 | 1.3 | 3.6 | 0.8 | 0.7 | 0.9 | 1.0 | 1.0 | 1.0 | 1.0 | 0.9 | 0.7 |
| May | 1.3 | 1.4 | 1.4 | 3.8 | 0.8 | 0.7 | 0.9 | 1.0 | 0.7 | 1.2 | 0.8 | 0.8 | 0.7 |
| June | 1.3 | 1.4 | 1.0 | 3.2 | 1.0 | 1.0 | 0.9 | 1.0 | 0.7 | 1.1 | 1.2 | 0.6 | 0.6 |
| July | 1.2 | 1.3 | 0.7 | 4.2 | 0.8 | 0.8 | 0.8 | 1.0 | 0.8 | 1.0 | 1.1 | 0.7 | 0.6 |
| August | 1.5 | 1.6 | 1.2 | 3.9 | 0.9 | 1.0 | 0.8 | 1.2 | 1.1 | 1.4 | 1.1 | 1.1 | 0.8 |
| September | 1.4 | 1.5 | 1.1 | 4.5 | 0.8 | 0.9 | 0.7 | 1.0 | 1.1 | 1.0 | 1.1 | 0.6 | 0.5 |
| October | 1.4 | 1.6 | 1.4 | 3.5 | 1.1 | 1.0 | 1.2 | 1.1 | 1.1 | 1.1 | 1.1 | 0.7 | 0.9 |
| November | 1.3 | 1.5 | 1.2 | 5.7 | 0.9 | 0.9 | 0.9 | 0.9 | 0.9 | 0.9 | 0.9 | 0.7 | 0.9 |
| December | 1.3 | 1.5 | 2.3 | 4.1 | 0.8 | 0.8 | 0.8 | 1.9 | 1.3 | 2.0 | 2.2 | 0.7 | 0.6 |
| **2013** | | | | | | | | | | | | | |
| January | 1.5 | 1.7 | 2.1 | 4.6 | 1.0 | 1.0 | 0.9 | 1.9 | 1.0 | 2.2 | 2.1 | 1.1 | 1.1 |
| February | 0.9 | 1.1 | 1.4 | 3.3 | 0.8 | 0.8 | 0.7 | 0.9 | 0.6 | 1.1 | 0.8 | 0.7 | 0.5 |
| March | 1.0 | 1.1 | 0.8 | 3.5 | 0.7 | 0.8 | 0.5 | 1.0 | 0.5 | 1.1 | 1.0 | 0.4 | 0.5 |
| April | 1.2 | 1.4 | 1.5 | 2.9 | 0.8 | 0.9 | 0.6 | 1.0 | 0.6 | 1.1 | 0.9 | 1.0 | 0.6 |
| May | 1.2 | 1.3 | 1.0 | 2.7 | 0.9 | 0.9 | 0.8 | 1.1 | 0.8 | 1.3 | 1.1 | 0.9 | 0.7 |
| June | 1.2 | 1.3 | 0.8 | 2.5 | 0.8 | 0.7 | 0.8 | 0.9 | 0.5 | 1.1 | 0.8 | 1.3 | 0.6 |
| July | 1.2 | 1.3 | 1.2 | 2.9 | 0.8 | 0.8 | 0.8 | 1.2 | 1.4 | 1.1 | 1.3 | 0.9 | 0.8 |
| August | 1.4 | 1.5 | 1.0 | 2.7 | 1.0 | 1.0 | 1.1 | 1.0 | 0.6 | 1.0 | 1.3 | 1.4 | 0.9 |
| September | 1.4 | 1.6 | 1.3 | 2.9 | 0.9 | 0.8 | 1.0 | 0.9 | 0.8 | 0.9 | 1.0 | 1.2 | 1.1 |
| October | 1.2 | 1.3 | 1.9 | 3.6 | 0.8 | 0.7 | 0.9 | 1.0 | 0.8 | 1.0 | 1.2 | 0.7 | 0.9 |
| November | 1.1 | 1.2 | 1.1 | 3.8 | 0.7 | 0.6 | 0.9 | 1.1 | 0.7 | 1.3 | 0.9 | 0.7 | 0.7 |
| December | 1.4 | 1.6 | 2.2 | 4.4 | 0.8 | 0.8 | 0.9 | 1.8 | 0.8 | 2.1 | 1.8 | 1.0 | 0.8 |
| **2014** | | | | | | | | | | | | | |
| January | 1.6 | 1.8 | 1.6 | 3.2 | 1.0 | 1.0 | 0.9 | 2.4 | 0.9 | 2.5 | 3.8 | 1.3 | 1.1 |
| February | 0.9 | 1.1 | 1.3 | 2.2 | 0.6 | 0.6 | 0.6 | 1.0 | 0.6 | 1.2 | 0.9 | 0.7 | 0.5 |
| March | 1.0 | 1.1 | 1.5 | 1.9 | 0.6 | 0.5 | 0.7 | 1.0 | 0.6 | 1.1 | 1.0 | 1.3 | 0.7 |
| April | 1.2 | 1.3 | 1.0 | 1.9 | 0.8 | 0.8 | 0.7 | 1.2 | 0.8 | 1.4 | 0.9 | 1.0 | 0.8 |
| May | 1.1 | 1.2 | 1.3 | 2.1 | 0.7 | 0.6 | 0.8 | 1.1 | 0.7 | 1.2 | 1.0 | 0.7 | 0.7 |
| June | 1.2 | 1.3 | 1.0 | 1.7 | 0.8 | 0.7 | 1.0 | 1.0 | 1.0 | 1.1 | 0.8 | 0.8 | 0.6 |
| July | 1.3 | 1.4 | 0.8 | 3.3 | 0.7 | 0.7 | 0.6 | 1.2 | 1.4 | 1.2 | 1.3 | 1.3 | 0.6 |
| August | 1.3 | 1.5 | 1.0 | 2.3 | 0.8 | 0.7 | 0.9 | 1.1 | 1.2 | 1.2 | 1.0 | 0.7 | 1.1 |
| September | 1.3 | 1.5 | 1.3 | 2.2 | 1.0 | 0.8 | 1.2 | 1.0 | 0.8 | 1.0 | 1.0 | 0.9 | 0.4 |
| October | 1.3 | 1.5 | 1.3 | 2.9 | 0.9 | 0.8 | 1.2 | 1.2 | 1.0 | 1.2 | 1.4 | 0.9 | 0.6 |
| November | 1.2 | 1.3 | 1.6 | 3.7 | 0.9 | 0.9 | 0.9 | 1.1 | 0.9 | 1.1 | 1.0 | 0.7 | 0.6 |
| December | 1.4 | 1.6 | 2.2 | 4.5 | 0.9 | 0.8 | 1.2 | 1.5 | 0.8 | 1.8 | 1.6 | 0.8 | 0.8 |
| **2015** | | | | | | | | | | | | | |
| January | 1.6 | 1.8 | 3.5 | 4.4 | 0.8 | 0.7 | 0.9 | 2.5 | 1.0 | 2.7 | 3.3 | 1.5 | 0.9 |
| February | 0.9 | 1.1 | 3.2 | 2.6 | 0.8 | 0.8 | 0.7 | 0.9 | 0.8 | 1.0 | 0.8 | 0.7 | 0.4 |
| March | 1.1 | 1.3 | 3.7 | 2.6 | 0.7 | 0.7 | 0.8 | 1.1 | 1.1 | 1.1 | 1.3 | 0.8 | 0.7 |
| April | 1.2 | 1.4 | 3.0 | 2.1 | 0.7 | 0.7 | 0.7 | 1.0 | 0.5 | 1.3 | 1.0 | 0.8 | 1.0 |
| May | 1.1 | 1.2 | 1.8 | 1.9 | 0.6 | 0.6 | 0.7 | 1.1 | 0.4 | 1.2 | 1.3 | 0.8 | 0.6 |
| June | 1.2 | 1.3 | 1.1 | 2.5 | 0.8 | 0.8 | 0.9 | 1.1 | 1.2 | 1.2 | 1.0 | 1.0 | 0.8 |
| July | 1.1 | 1.2 | 2.0 | 2.1 | 0.8 | 0.9 | 0.7 | 1.2 | 1.2 | 1.3 | 1.2 | 0.8 | 0.7 |
| August | 1.3 | 1.4 | 2.0 | 2.7 | 1.0 | 1.1 | 0.8 | 1.1 | 0.7 | 1.3 | 1.0 | 0.8 | 1.0 |
| September | 1.4 | 1.6 | 1.9 | 2.6 | 1.0 | 1.0 | 1.0 | 0.9 | 0.4 | 1.0 | 1.1 | 0.9 | 0.8 |
| October | 1.3 | 1.4 | 2.2 | 3.0 | 1.0 | 0.8 | 1.2 | 0.9 | 0.8 | 1.0 | 0.9 | 1.1 | 0.6 |
| November | 1.1 | 1.3 | 1.5 | 2.9 | 0.9 | 0.9 | 0.8 | 1.0 | 0.8 | 1.1 | 1.0 | 1.1 | 0.6 |
| December | 1.3 | 1.4 | 3.4 | 2.9 | 0.9 | 0.9 | 1.0 | 1.3 | 0.7 | 1.5 | 1.4 | 0.6 | 0.7 |
| **2016** | | | | | | | | | | | | | |
| January | 1.5 | 1.7 | 2.9 | 3.8 | 0.9 | 0.9 | 0.8 | 2.1 | 0.8 | 2.3 | 3.1 | 1.4 | 0.9 |
| February | 1.0 | 1.1 | 3.7 | 2.8 | 0.9 | 1.1 | 0.7 | 1.0 | 0.7 | 1.2 | 0.8 | 0.6 | 0.6 |
| March | 1.0 | 1.2 | 2.9 | 2.1 | 0.8 | 0.8 | 0.8 | 0.9 | 0.8 | 0.9 | 0.9 | 0.7 | 0.8 |
| April | 1.1 | 1.2 | 2.9 | 2.7 | 0.8 | 0.8 | 1.0 | 0.9 | 0.8 | 1.0 | 0.7 | 1.1 | 0.7 |
| May | 1.1 | 1.2 | 1.4 | 2.6 | 0.9 | 1.0 | 0.7 | 1.0 | 1.0 | 1.0 | 1.1 | 1.0 | 0.5 |
| June | 1.1 | 1.2 | 1.6 | 1.8 | 0.8 | 0.9 | 0.8 | 1.0 | 0.6 | 1.0 | 1.2 | 0.8 | 0.6 |
| July | 1.1 | 1.2 | 1.1 | 2.0 | 0.7 | 0.8 | 0.6 | 1.1 | 0.7 | 1.3 | 1.3 | 1.2 | 0.5 |
| August | 1.3 | 1.4 | 1.9 | 2.4 | 1.0 | 1.1 | 0.9 | 0.9 | 0.8 | 1.0 | 0.8 | 0.8 | 0.7 |
| September | 1.2 | 1.2 | 1.1 | 2.1 | 0.9 | 0.8 | 1.0 | 0.9 | 0.6 | 1.1 | 0.8 | 0.7 | 0.6 |
| October | 1.1 | 1.2 | 1.9 | 2.8 | 0.8 | 0.7 | 1.0 | 0.9 | 0.6 | 0.9 | 1.1 | 0.7 | 0.6 |

[1]Layoffs and discharges are the number of layoffs and discharges during the entire month.
[2]The layoffs and discharges rate is the number of layoffs and discharges during the entire month as a percent of total employment.

## Table 7-8.  Layoffs and Discharges Levels[1] and Rates,[2] by Industry, 2005–October 2016
### —Continued

(Not seasonally adjusted, levels in thousands, rates per 100.)

| Year and month | Finance and insurance | Real estate and rental and leasing | Professional and business services | Education and health services | Educational services | Health care and social assistance | Leisure and hospitality | Arts, entertainment, and recreation | Accommodation and food services | Other services | Government | Federal | State and local government |
|---|---|---|---|---|---|---|---|---|---|---|---|---|---|
| **2011** | | | | | | | | | | | | | |
| January | 0.9 | 3.2 | 2.6 | 0.7 | 0.6 | 0.7 | 2.0 | 3.6 | 1.7 | 1.5 | 0.3 | 0.4 | 0.3 |
| February | 0.4 | 1.1 | 1.7 | 0.6 | 0.6 | 0.5 | 1.0 | 1.3 | 1.0 | 1.3 | 0.2 | 0.2 | 0.2 |
| March | 0.4 | 0.6 | 2.0 | 0.5 | 0.4 | 0.5 | 1.6 | 3.1 | 1.4 | 0.9 | 0.2 | 0.2 | 0.2 |
| April | 0.2 | 1.3 | 2.7 | 0.6 | 0.4 | 0.6 | 1.4 | 3.1 | 1.1 | 1.5 | 0.3 | 0.3 | 0.3 |
| May | 0.5 | 0.6 | 2.3 | 0.8 | 1.2 | 0.7 | 1.6 | 3.1 | 1.4 | 1.4 | 0.6 | 0.3 | 0.7 |
| June | 0.5 | 1.4 | 2.2 | 1.3 | 2.2 | 1.1 | 1.5 | 1.6 | 1.5 | 1.5 | 0.7 | 0.3 | 0.8 |
| July | 0.5 | 1.1 | 2.1 | 1.1 | 2.3 | 0.9 | 1.6 | 1.5 | 1.6 | 2.1 | 0.8 | 0.3 | 0.9 |
| August | 0.5 | 1.3 | 2.2 | 1.1 | 1.3 | 1.0 | 2.0 | 4.2 | 1.6 | 2.2 | 0.9 | 0.9 | 0.9 |
| September | 0.7 | 1.1 | 2.2 | 0.7 | 0.9 | 0.6 | 2.9 | 9.0 | 1.9 | 2.2 | 0.8 | 0.7 | 0.8 |
| October | 0.4 | 2.1 | 2.3 | 0.6 | 0.6 | 0.7 | 2.9 | 6.4 | 2.3 | 2.2 | 0.4 | 0.4 | 0.4 |
| November | 0.6 | 1.3 | 2.2 | 0.7 | 0.6 | 0.7 | 2.9 | 8.7 | 2.0 | 1.5 | 0.3 | 0.4 | 0.3 |
| December | 0.6 | 0.9 | 2.8 | 0.7 | 0.6 | 0.7 | 1.9 | 3.2 | 1.7 | 1.4 | 0.5 | 0.3 | 0.5 |
| **2012** | | | | | | | | | | | | | |
| January | 0.5 | 1.4 | 2.2 | 0.9 | 1.3 | 0.8 | 2.5 | 4.5 | 2.2 | 1.5 | 0.3 | 0.3 | 0.3 |
| February | 0.3 | 0.9 | 2.3 | 0.5 | 0.3 | 0.5 | 1.2 | 2.5 | 1.0 | 1.1 | 0.2 | 0.2 | 0.2 |
| March | 0.3 | 1.1 | 2.1 | 0.6 | 0.3 | 0.6 | 1.5 | 3.7 | 1.1 | 0.9 | 0.2 | 0.2 | 0.2 |
| April | 0.7 | 1.0 | 2.6 | 0.8 | 0.6 | 0.8 | 1.9 | 6.5 | 1.1 | 2.2 | 0.3 | 0.2 | 0.3 |
| May | 0.5 | 1.2 | 2.5 | 0.9 | 1.6 | 0.8 | 1.6 | 2.7 | 1.4 | 1.6 | 0.6 | 0.2 | 0.6 |
| June | 0.4 | 1.3 | 2.5 | 1.4 | 2.5 | 1.2 | 1.3 | 1.2 | 1.4 | 1.0 | 0.7 | 0.3 | 0.8 |
| July | 0.4 | 1.3 | 2.1 | 1.0 | 2.0 | 0.8 | 1.4 | 1.3 | 1.4 | 1.1 | 0.6 | 0.2 | 0.7 |
| August | 0.6 | 1.3 | 2.5 | 0.9 | 1.2 | 0.9 | 2.2 | 3.5 | 2.0 | 1.8 | 0.8 | 0.7 | 0.9 |
| September | 0.4 | 0.7 | 2.4 | 0.7 | 0.6 | 0.7 | 2.6 | 7.2 | 1.8 | 2.2 | 0.6 | 0.7 | 0.6 |
| October | 0.6 | 1.6 | 2.3 | 0.8 | 0.8 | 0.8 | 2.6 | 5.4 | 2.2 | 2.0 | 0.4 | 0.7 | 0.4 |
| November | 0.8 | 1.3 | 2.3 | 0.5 | 0.4 | 0.6 | 2.2 | 5.7 | 1.7 | 1.7 | 0.3 | 0.5 | 0.3 |
| December | 0.4 | 1.4 | 2.2 | 0.7 | 0.9 | 0.6 | 1.6 | 3.9 | 1.3 | 1.1 | 0.4 | 0.6 | 0.3 |
| **2013** | | | | | | | | | | | | | |
| January | 0.7 | 2.5 | 2.8 | 0.7 | 0.7 | 0.7 | 1.7 | 2.9 | 1.6 | 0.9 | 0.3 | 0.3 | 0.3 |
| February | 0.5 | 0.7 | 1.7 | 0.6 | 0.5 | 0.7 | 1.0 | 1.2 | 1.0 | 0.7 | 0.2 | 0.5 | 0.2 |
| March | 0.4 | 0.9 | 1.8 | 0.6 | 0.5 | 0.6 | 1.4 | 2.2 | 1.2 | 1.4 | 0.3 | 0.6 | 0.3 |
| April | 0.5 | 0.8 | 2.5 | 0.7 | 0.5 | 0.7 | 1.9 | 5.4 | 1.3 | 1.7 | 0.2 | 0.5 | 0.2 |
| May | 0.5 | 1.2 | 2.1 | 0.9 | 1.1 | 0.9 | 1.4 | 2.6 | 1.3 | 1.6 | 0.5 | 0.4 | 0.5 |
| June | 0.3 | 1.4 | 2.1 | 1.0 | 2.0 | 0.8 | 1.5 | 1.3 | 1.5 | 1.5 | 0.8 | 0.4 | 0.8 |
| July | 0.6 | 1.2 | 1.7 | 1.0 | 1.8 | 0.8 | 1.4 | 1.5 | 1.4 | 1.6 | 0.5 | 0.3 | 0.6 |
| August | 0.7 | 1.4 | 2.6 | 1.1 | 2.3 | 0.8 | 2.1 | 3.3 | 1.9 | 1.7 | 0.7 | 0.4 | 0.7 |
| September | 0.8 | 1.9 | 2.2 | 0.8 | 1.2 | 0.7 | 3.4 | 10.5 | 2.2 | 1.4 | 0.7 | 0.4 | 0.7 |
| October | 0.6 | 1.7 | 1.8 | 0.6 | 0.5 | 0.6 | 2.0 | 4.9 | 1.6 | 1.1 | 0.4 | 0.7 | 0.4 |
| November | 0.5 | 1.1 | 1.8 | 0.6 | 0.5 | 0.6 | 1.6 | 5.1 | 1.1 | 1.0 | 0.3 | 0.4 | 0.3 |
| December | 0.6 | 1.1 | 2.2 | 0.7 | 0.9 | 0.6 | 1.9 | 2.9 | 1.7 | 1.2 | 0.4 | 0.4 | 0.4 |
| **2014** | | | | | | | | | | | | | |
| January | 1.0 | 1.4 | 2.4 | 1.1 | 1.2 | 1.0 | 2.1 | 3.2 | 1.9 | 1.1 | 0.4 | 0.9 | 0.3 |
| February | 0.3 | 1.0 | 2.0 | 0.5 | 0.4 | 0.6 | 1.2 | 2.3 | 1.0 | 1.1 | 0.2 | 0.2 | 0.2 |
| March | 0.7 | 0.7 | 1.9 | 0.8 | 0.7 | 0.8 | 1.2 | 3.0 | 0.9 | 0.6 | 0.3 | 0.4 | 0.3 |
| April | 0.7 | 1.2 | 2.5 | 0.8 | 0.5 | 0.9 | 1.7 | 5.5 | 1.1 | 0.6 | 0.2 | 0.4 | 0.2 |
| May | 0.3 | 1.9 | 2.1 | 0.7 | 1.1 | 0.7 | 1.8 | 2.7 | 1.6 | 1.0 | 0.5 | 0.2 | 0.5 |
| June | 0.5 | 1.0 | 2.3 | 1.0 | 2.1 | 0.8 | 1.5 | 1.4 | 1.5 | 1.2 | 0.7 | 0.4 | 0.7 |
| July | 0.4 | 1.0 | 2.1 | 0.9 | 1.7 | 0.8 | 1.6 | 2.1 | 1.5 | 1.8 | 0.5 | 0.2 | 0.5 |
| August | 0.7 | 2.1 | 2.6 | 0.9 | 1.6 | 0.7 | 1.8 | 5.0 | 1.3 | 1.7 | 0.6 | 0.4 | 0.6 |
| September | 0.3 | 0.7 | 2.3 | 0.9 | 1.1 | 0.8 | 2.9 | 9.5 | 1.7 | 1.2 | 0.5 | 0.6 | 0.5 |
| October | 0.6 | 0.6 | 2.5 | 0.7 | 0.5 | 0.8 | 2.3 | 5.8 | 1.8 | 1.2 | 0.3 | 0.5 | 0.3 |
| November | 0.4 | 1.0 | 2.0 | 0.5 | 0.3 | 0.5 | 1.9 | 6.6 | 1.2 | 1.2 | 0.3 | 0.4 | 0.3 |
| December | 0.8 | 0.6 | 2.5 | 0.7 | 0.7 | 0.7 | 1.8 | 3.5 | 1.5 | 0.9 | 0.4 | 0.3 | 0.5 |
| **2015** | | | | | | | | | | | | | |
| January | 0.6 | 2.0 | 2.4 | 0.6 | 0.8 | 0.6 | 1.8 | 4.0 | 1.4 | 1.3 | 0.5 | 1.2 | 0.4 |
| February | 0.2 | 0.8 | 1.9 | 0.4 | 0.3 | 0.5 | 1.1 | 2.4 | 1.0 | 1.0 | 0.2 | 0.3 | 0.2 |
| March | 0.6 | 0.8 | 2.2 | 0.5 | 0.4 | 0.6 | 1.5 | 3.8 | 1.1 | 1.1 | 0.3 | 0.5 | 0.2 |
| April | 0.8 | 1.3 | 2.6 | 0.5 | 0.5 | 0.5 | 2.3 | 5.2 | 1.9 | 1.0 | 0.3 | 0.4 | 0.3 |
| May | 0.5 | 0.9 | 2.1 | 0.8 | 1.2 | 0.7 | 1.8 | 2.0 | 1.8 | 1.1 | 0.6 | 0.4 | 0.6 |
| June | 0.5 | 1.5 | 2.0 | 0.9 | 2.6 | 0.6 | 1.3 | 1.4 | 1.3 | 1.6 | 0.7 | 0.3 | 0.8 |
| July | 0.6 | 1.0 | 1.9 | 0.8 | 1.1 | 0.7 | 1.2 | 0.9 | 1.2 | 1.6 | 0.6 | 0.4 | 0.7 |
| August | 0.8 | 1.4 | 1.8 | 0.8 | 1.8 | 0.6 | 2.4 | 3.5 | 2.2 | 2.2 | 0.8 | 0.4 | 0.8 |
| September | 0.6 | 1.4 | 2.5 | 0.8 | 0.7 | 0.8 | 3.1 | 7.9 | 2.3 | 2.5 | 0.7 | 0.3 | 0.7 |
| October | 0.5 | 1.0 | 2.0 | 0.6 | 0.6 | 0.6 | 2.8 | 7.4 | 2.0 | 1.5 | 0.5 | 0.5 | 0.5 |
| November | 0.4 | 1.3 | 2.1 | 0.5 | 0.5 | 0.5 | 2.0 | 4.9 | 1.5 | 0.9 | 0.3 | 0.4 | 0.3 |
| December | 0.7 | 1.0 | 2.3 | 0.6 | 0.5 | 0.7 | 2.0 | 3.2 | 1.8 | 1.0 | 0.5 | 0.3 | 0.6 |
| **2016** | | | | | | | | | | | | | |
| January | 0.8 | 1.3 | 2.5 | 0.7 | 0.7 | 0.7 | 1.6 | 4.1 | 1.2 | 0.9 | 0.5 | 1.3 | 0.4 |
| February | 0.5 | 0.8 | 1.9 | 0.4 | 0.5 | 0.4 | 1.3 | 1.3 | 1.3 | 0.9 | 0.2 | 0.2 | 0.2 |
| March | 0.8 | 0.8 | 2.1 | 0.5 | 0.5 | 0.5 | 1.5 | 3.2 | 1.2 | 1.2 | 0.3 | 0.4 | 0.3 |
| April | 0.5 | 1.3 | 2.1 | 0.6 | 0.7 | 0.5 | 1.6 | 3.6 | 1.2 | 1.0 | 0.3 | 0.4 | 0.3 |
| May | 0.5 | 0.7 | 1.7 | 0.8 | 1.2 | 0.7 | 1.5 | 2.4 | 1.3 | 1.4 | 0.6 | 0.3 | 0.6 |
| June | 0.4 | 1.0 | 1.5 | 1.0 | 2.6 | 0.8 | 1.3 | 1.8 | 1.3 | 1.3 | 0.6 | 0.3 | 0.7 |
| July | 0.3 | 1.1 | 1.9 | 0.8 | 1.7 | 0.6 | 1.5 | 1.4 | 1.5 | 1.1 | 0.6 | 0.3 | 0.6 |
| August | 0.7 | 0.9 | 1.8 | 0.9 | 1.3 | 0.9 | 2.4 | 6.0 | 1.8 | 1.5 | 1.0 | 0.4 | 1.0 |
| September | 0.4 | 1.1 | 1.8 | 0.5 | 0.4 | 0.5 | 2.2 | 6.5 | 1.5 | 2.0 | 0.7 | 0.5 | 0.7 |
| October | 0.3 | 1.6 | 1.8 | 0.6 | 0.4 | 0.7 | 2.3 | 5.3 | 1.8 | 1.0 | 0.5 | 0.4 | 0.5 |

[1]Layoffs and discharges are the number of layoffs and discharges during the entire month.
[2]The layoffs and discharges rate is the number of layoffs and discharges during the entire month as a percent of total employment.

# CHAPTER 8: LABOR-MANAGEMENT RELATIONS

## HIGHLIGHTS

This chapter contains information on historical trends in union membership, earnings, and work stoppages.

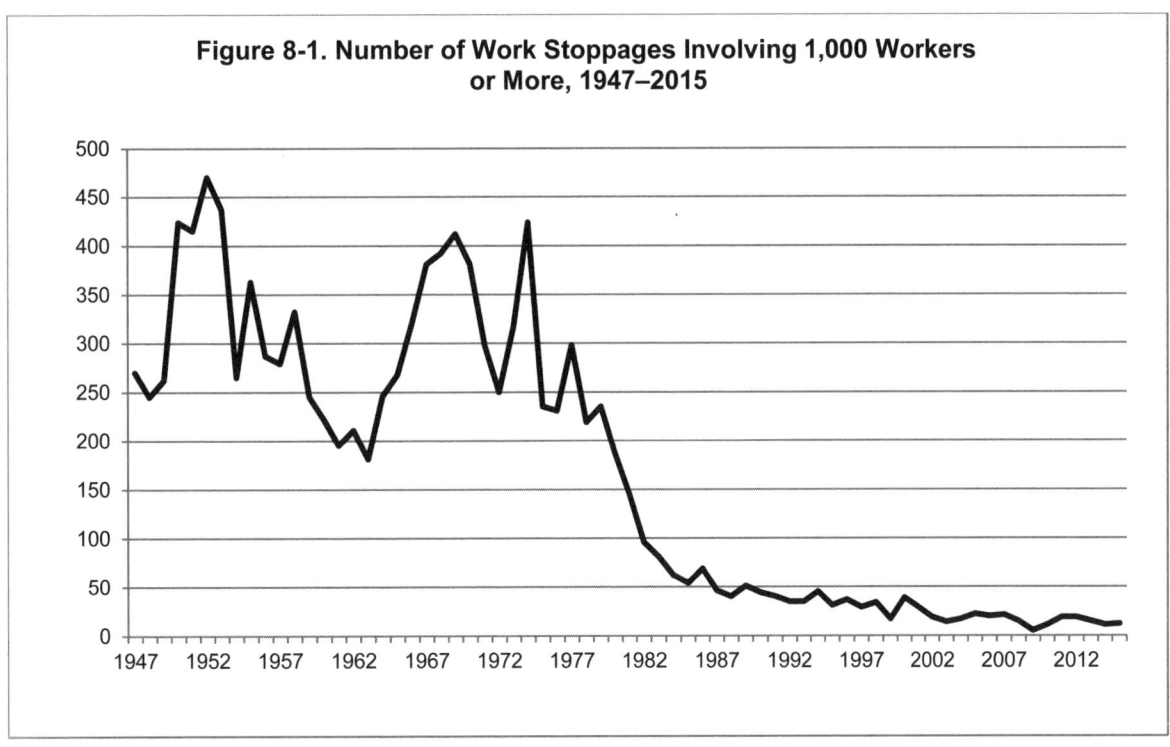

**Figure 8-1. Number of Work Stoppages Involving 1,000 Workers or More, 1947–2015**

The number of work stoppages has declined dramatically since 1947. The number of work stoppages involving 1,000 employees or more has declined from a high of 470 in 1952 to only 12 in 2015. (See Table 8-1.)

## OTHER HIGHLIGHTS

- Union membership was higher for men (11.5 percent) than for women (10.6 percent) in 2015. According to race, Black workers had the highest rate of union membership at 13.6 percent, followed by White workers at 10.8 percent, Asians at 9.8 percent, and Hispanics at 9.4 percent. (See Table 8-2.)

- In 2015, the percentage of workers belonging to a union remained steady at 11.1 percent. The number of workers in unions has declined from 17.7 million workers in 1983 to nearly 14.8 million workers in 2015. (See Tables 8-2 and 8-5.)

- Workers in the public sector were far more likely to be in a union than those in the private sector (35.2 percent compared with 6.7 percent). In the private sector, workers in utilities had the highest unionization rate at 21.4 percent while those in agriculture and related industries had the lowest rate at 1.2 percent. (See Table 8-3.)

- New York continued to have the highest rate of union representation in 2015 at 26.0 percent followed by Alaska and Hawaii at 21.7 percent and Washington (18.0 percent). Union membership and representation is typically lower in southern states. South Carolina had the lowest rate of union representation at 2.9 percent followed by North Carolina at 4.1 percent. (See Table 8-6.)

# NOTES AND DEFINITIONS

## WORK STOPPAGES

### Collection and Coverage

Data on work stoppages measure the number and duration of major strikes or lockouts (involving 1,000 workers or more) during the year, the number of workers involved in these stoppages, and the amount of time lost due to these stoppages.

Information on work stoppages is obtained from reports issued by the Federal Mediation and Conciliation Service, state labor market information offices, Bureau of Labor Statistics (BLS) Strike Reports from the Office of Employment and Unemployment Statistics, and media sources such as the *Daily Labor Report* and the *Wall Street Journal*. One or both parties involved in the work stoppage (employer and/or union) is contacted to verify the duration of the stoppage and number of workers idled by the stoppage.

### Concepts and Definitions

*Days of idleness* is calculated by taking the number of workers involved in the strike or lockout and multiplying it by the number of days workers are off the job. The number of working days lost for every major work stoppage is based on a 5-day workweek (Monday through Friday), excluding federal holidays.

*Major work stoppage* includes both worker-initiated strikes and employer-initiated lockouts involving 1,000 workers or more. BLS does not distinguish between lockouts and strikes in its statistics.

*Workers involved* consists of workers directly involved in the stoppage. This category does not measure the indirect or secondary effect of stoppages on other establishments whose employees are idle from material shortages or lack of service.

### Sources of Additional Information

Additional information is available in BLS news release USDL 16-0272, "Major Work Stoppages in 2015". More information on measures and methods used to calculate the information in this chapter can be found on the BLS Web site at www.bls.gov/opub/hom/pdf/homch8.pdf

## UNION MEMBERSHIP

### Collection and Coverage

The estimates of union membership are obtained from the Current Population Survey (CPS), which provides basic information on the labor force, employment, and unemployment. The survey is conducted monthly for the Bureau of Labor Statistics by the U.S. Census Bureau from a scientifically selected national sample of about 60,000 households. The union membership and earnings data are tabulated from one-quarter of the CPS monthly sample and are limited to wage and salary workers. All self-employed workers are excluded. The data in these tables are annual averages.

Beginning in January of each year, data reflect revised population controls used in the CPS.

### Concepts and Definitions

*Full-time workers* are workers who usually work 35 hours or more per week at their sole or principal job.

*Part-time workers* are workers who usually work fewer than 35 hours per week at their sole or principal job.

*Wage and salary workers* are workers who receive wages, salaries, commissions, tips, payment in kind, or piece rates. The group includes employees in both the private and public sectors, but, for the purposes of the union membership and earnings series, excludes all self-employed persons, regardless of whether or not their businesses are incorporated.

*Hispanic or Latino ethnicity* refers to persons who identified themselves in the enumeration process as being Spanish, Hispanic, or Latino. Persons whose ethnicity is identified as Hispanic or Latino may be of any race.

*Union members* are members of a labor union or an employee association similar to a union.

*Represented by unions* refers to union members, as well as to workers who have no union affiliation but whose jobs are covered by a union contract.

*Median earnings* is the amount which divides a given earnings distribution into two equal groups, one having earnings above the median and the other having earnings below the median. The estimating procedure places each reported or calculated weekly earnings value into $50-wide intervals which are centered around multiples of $50. The actual value is estimated through the linear interpolation of the interval in which the median lies.

*Usual weekly earnings* represent earnings before taxes and other deductions and include any overtime pay, commissions, or tips usually received (at the main job in the case of multiple jobholders). Prior to 1994, respondents were asked how much they usually earned per week. Since January 1994, respondents have been asked to identify the easiest way for them to report earnings (hourly, weekly, biweekly, twice monthly, monthly, annually, other) and how much they usually earn in the reported time period. Earnings reported on a basis other than weekly are converted to a weekly equivalent. The term "usual" is as perceived by the respondent. If the respondent asks for a definition of "usual," interviewers are instructed to define the term as more than half of the weeks worked during the past 4 or 5 months.

### Sources of Additional Information

For additional information see BLS news release USDL 16-0158, "Union Members–2015."

# Table 8-1. Work Stoppages Involving 1,000 Workers or More, 1947–2015

(Number, percent.)

| Year | Stoppages beginning during the year | | Days idle during the year[1] | |
|---|---|---|---|---|
| | Number | Workers involved (thousands)[2] | Number (thousands) | Percent of estimated total working time[3] |
| 1947 | 270 | 1 629 | 25 720 | . . . |
| 1948 | 245 | 1 435 | 26 127 | 0.22 |
| 1949 | 262 | 2 537 | 43 420 | 0.38 |
| 1950 | 424 | 1 698 | 30 390 | 0.26 |
| 1951 | 415 | 1 462 | 15 070 | 0.12 |
| 1952 | 470 | 2 746 | 48 820 | 0.38 |
| 1953 | 437 | 1 623 | 18 130 | 0.14 |
| 1954 | 265 | 1 075 | 16 630 | 0.13 |
| 1955 | 363 | 2 055 | 21 180 | 0.16 |
| 1956 | 287 | 1 370 | 26 840 | 0.20 |
| 1957 | 279 | 887 | 10 340 | 0.07 |
| 1958 | 332 | 1 587 | 17 900 | 0.13 |
| 1959 | 245 | 1 381 | 60 850 | 0.43 |
| 1960 | 222 | 896 | 13 260 | 0.09 |
| 1961 | 195 | 1 031 | 10 140 | 0.07 |
| 1962 | 211 | 793 | 11 760 | 0.08 |
| 1963 | 181 | 512 | 10 020 | 0.07 |
| 1964 | 246 | 1 183 | 16 220 | 0.11 |
| 1965 | 268 | 999 | 15 140 | 0.10 |
| 1966 | 321 | 1 300 | 16 000 | 0.10 |
| 1967 | 381 | 2 192 | 31 320 | 0.18 |
| 1968 | 392 | 1 855 | 35 367 | 0.20 |
| 1969 | 412 | 1 576 | 29 397 | 0.16 |
| 1970 | 381 | 2 468 | 52 761 | 0.29 |
| 1971 | 298 | 2 516 | 35 538 | 0.19 |
| 1972 | 250 | 975 | 16 764 | 0.09 |
| 1973 | 317 | 1 400 | 16 260 | 0.08 |
| 1974 | 424 | 1 796 | 31 809 | 0.16 |
| 1975 | 235 | 965 | 17 563 | 0.09 |
| 1976 | 231 | 1 519 | 23 962 | 0.12 |
| 1977 | 298 | 1 212 | 21 258 | 0.10 |
| 1978 | 219 | 1 006 | 23 774 | 0.11 |
| 1979 | 235 | 1 021 | 20 409 | 0.09 |
| 1980 | 187 | 795 | 20 844 | 0.09 |
| 1981 | 145 | 729 | 16 908 | 0.07 |
| 1982 | 96 | 656 | 9 061 | 0.04 |
| 1983 | 81 | 909 | 17 461 | 0.08 |
| 1984 | 62 | 376 | 8 499 | 0.04 |
| 1985 | 54 | 324 | 7 079 | 0.03 |
| 1986 | 69 | 533 | 11 861 | 0.05 |
| 1987 | 46 | 174 | 4 481 | 0.02 |
| 1988 | 40 | 118 | 4 381 | 0.02 |
| 1989 | 51 | 452 | 16 996 | 0.07 |
| 1990 | 44 | 185 | 5 926 | 0.02 |
| 1991 | 40 | 392 | 4 584 | 0.02 |
| 1992 | 35 | 364 | 3 989 | 0.01 |
| 1993 | 35 | 182 | 3 981 | 0.01 |
| 1994 | 45 | 322 | 5 021 | 0.02 |
| 1995 | 31 | 192 | 5 771 | 0.02 |
| 1996 | 37 | 273 | 4 889 | 0.02 |
| 1997 | 29 | 339 | 4 497 | 0.01 |
| 1998 | 34 | 387 | 5 116 | 0.02 |
| 1999 | 17 | 73 | 1 996 | 0.01 |
| 2000 | 39 | 394 | 20 419 | 0.06 |
| 2001 | 29 | 99 | 1 151 | ($^4$) |
| 2002 | 19 | 46 | 660 | ($^4$) |
| 2003 | 14 | 129 | 4 091 | 0.01 |
| 2004 | 17 | 171 | 3 344 | 0.01 |
| 2005 | 22 | 100 | 1 736 | 0.01 |
| 2006 | 20 | 70 | 2 688 | 0.01 |
| 2007 | 21 | 189 | 1 265 | ($^4$) |
| 2008 | 15 | 72 | 1 954 | 0.01 |
| 2009 | 5 | 13 | 124 | ($^4$) |
| 2010 | 11 | 45 | 302 | ($^4$) |
| 2011 | 19 | 113 | 1 020 | ($^4$) |
| 2012 | 19 | 148 | 1 131 | ($^4$) |
| 2013 | 15 | 55 | 290 | ($^4$) |
| 2014 | 11 | 34 | 200 | ($^4$) |
| 2015 | 12 | 47 | 740 | ($^4$) |

[1]Days idle include all stoppages in effect during the reference period. For work stoppages that are still ongoing at the end of the calendar year, only those days of idleness during the calendar year are counted.
[2]Workers are counted more than once if involved in more than one stoppage during the reference period.
[3]Agricultural and government workers are included in the calculation of estimated working time; private household, forestry, and fishery workers are excluded.
[4]Less than 0.005 percent.
. . . = Not available.

## Table 8-2. Union Affiliation of Employed Wage and Salary Workers, by Selected Characteristics, 2010–2015

(Numbers in thousands, percent.)

| Characteristic | 2010 Total employed | 2010 Member of union[1] Total | 2010 Member of union[1] Percent of employed | 2010 Represented by union[2] Total | 2010 Represented by union[2] Percent of employed | 2011 Total employed | 2011 Member of union[1] Total | 2011 Member of union[1] Percent of employed | 2011 Represented by union[2] Total | 2011 Represented by union[2] Percent of employed | 2012 Total employed | 2012 Member of union[1] Total | 2012 Member of union[1] Percent of employed | 2012 Represented by union[2] Total | 2012 Represented by union[2] Percent of employed |
|---|---|---|---|---|---|---|---|---|---|---|---|---|---|---|---|
| **SEX AND AGE** | | | | | | | | | | | | | | | |
| Both Sexes, 16 Years and Over .... | 124 073 | 14 715 | 11.9 | 16 290 | 13.1 | 125 187 | 14 764 | 11.8 | 16 290 | 13.0 | 127 577 | 14 366 | 11.3 | 15 922 | 12.5 |
| 16 to 24 years ............................ | 16 638 | 722 | 4.3 | 836 | 5.0 | 16 910 | 737 | 4.4 | 845 | 5.0 | 17 417 | 731 | 4.2 | 869 | 5.0 |
| 25 years and over ........................ | 107 435 | 13 993 | 13.0 | 15 453 | 14.4 | 108 278 | 14 027 | 13.0 | 15 444 | 14.3 | 110 160 | 13 635 | 12.4 | 15 053 | 13.7 |
| 25 to 34 years ......................... | 28 363 | 2 860 | 10.1 | 3 179 | 11.2 | 28 682 | 2 829 | 9.9 | 3 155 | 11.0 | 28 875 | 2 755 | 9.5 | 3 083 | 10.7 |
| 35 to 44 years ......................... | 27 356 | 3 512 | 12.8 | 3 888 | 14.2 | 27 231 | 3 470 | 12.7 | 3 804 | 14.0 | 27 442 | 3 424 | 12.5 | 3 746 | 13.6 |
| 45 to 54 years ......................... | 28 860 | 4 340 | 15.0 | 4 774 | 16.5 | 28 693 | 4 286 | 14.9 | 4 707 | 16.4 | 28 765 | 4 032 | 14.0 | 4 437 | 15.4 |
| 55 to 64 years ......................... | 18 199 | 2 849 | 15.7 | 3 126 | 17.2 | 18 751 | 2 949 | 15.7 | 3 219 | 17.2 | 19 694 | 2 932 | 14.9 | 3 233 | 16.4 |
| 65 years and over ..................... | 4 657 | 432 | 9.3 | 486 | 10.4 | 4 920 | 494 | 10.0 | 559 | 11.4 | 5 385 | 491 | 9.1 | 554 | 10.3 |
| **Men, 16 Years and Over** ............. | 63 531 | 7 994 | 12.6 | 8 761 | 13.8 | 64 686 | 8 006 | 12.4 | 8 731 | 13.5 | 65 898 | 7 895 | 12.0 | 8 611 | 13.1 |
| 16 to 24 years ............................ | 8 291 | 419 | 5.0 | 476 | 5.7 | 8 636 | 435 | 5.0 | 486 | 5.6 | 8 830 | 448 | 5.1 | 521 | 5.9 |
| 25 years and over ........................ | 55 240 | 7 575 | 13.7 | 8 286 | 15.0 | 56 050 | 7 571 | 13.5 | 8 246 | 14.7 | 57 067 | 7 448 | 13.1 | 8 090 | 14.2 |
| 25 to 34 years ......................... | 15 148 | 1 603 | 10.6 | 1 759 | 11.6 | 15 465 | 1 541 | 10.0 | 1 706 | 11.0 | 15 465 | 1 546 | 10.0 | 1 688 | 10.9 |
| 35 to 44 years ......................... | 14 430 | 1 966 | 13.6 | 2 151 | 14.9 | 14 412 | 1 946 | 13.5 | 2 114 | 14.7 | 14 481 | 1 919 | 13.3 | 2 085 | 14.4 |
| 45 to 54 years ......................... | 14 423 | 2 349 | 16.3 | 2 554 | 17.7 | 14 415 | 2 327 | 16.1 | 2 513 | 17.4 | 14 601 | 2 214 | 15.2 | 2 385 | 16.3 |
| 55 to 64 years ......................... | 8 895 | 1 430 | 16.1 | 1 566 | 17.6 | 9 212 | 1 497 | 16.2 | 1 623 | 17.6 | 9 728 | 1 521 | 15.6 | 1 655 | 17.0 |
| 65 years and over ..................... | 2 343 | 227 | 9.7 | 256 | 10.9 | 2 547 | 260 | 10.2 | 290 | 11.4 | 2 792 | 248 | 8.9 | 277 | 9.9 |
| **Women, 16 Years and Over** ......... | 60 542 | 6 722 | 11.1 | 7 528 | 12.4 | 60 502 | 6 758 | 11.2 | 7 558 | 12.5 | 61 679 | 6 470 | 10.5 | 7 311 | 11.9 |
| 16 to 24 years ............................ | 8 347 | 303 | 3.6 | 361 | 4.3 | 8 274 | 302 | 3.6 | 360 | 4.3 | 8 586 | 283 | 3.3 | 347 | 4.0 |
| 25 years and over ........................ | 52 195 | 6 418 | 12.3 | 7 167 | 13.7 | 52 228 | 6 456 | 12.4 | 7 199 | 13.8 | 53 093 | 6 187 | 11.7 | 6 964 | 13.1 |
| 25 to 34 years ......................... | 13 215 | 1 257 | 9.5 | 1 420 | 10.7 | 13 218 | 1 288 | 9.7 | 1 449 | 11.0 | 13 410 | 1 209 | 9.0 | 1 396 | 10.4 |
| 35 to 44 years ......................... | 12 926 | 1 546 | 12.0 | 1 737 | 13.4 | 12 819 | 1 524 | 11.9 | 1 690 | 13.2 | 12 961 | 1 505 | 11.6 | 1 661 | 12.8 |
| 45 to 54 years ......................... | 14 437 | 1 991 | 13.8 | 2 219 | 15.4 | 14 278 | 1 959 | 13.7 | 2 195 | 15.4 | 14 164 | 1 819 | 12.8 | 2 052 | 14.5 |
| 55 to 64 years ......................... | 9 303 | 1 419 | 15.3 | 1 560 | 16.8 | 9 540 | 1 452 | 15.2 | 1 596 | 16.7 | 9 966 | 1 411 | 14.2 | 1 579 | 15.8 |
| 65 years and over ..................... | 2 314 | 205 | 8.8 | 230 | 10.0 | 2 373 | 233 | 9.8 | 269 | 11.3 | 2 593 | 244 | 9.4 | 277 | 10.7 |
| **RACE, HISPANIC ORIGIN, AND SEX** | | | | | | | | | | | | | | | |
| **White, 16 Years and Over**[3] ........... | 101 042 | 11 865 | 11.7 | 13 111 | 13.0 | 101 768 | 11 853 | 11.6 | 13 061 | 12.8 | 101 851 | 11 306 | 11.1 | 12 517 | 12.3 |
| Men .................................................. | 52 565 | 6 588 | 12.5 | 7 208 | 13.7 | 53 418 | 6 568 | 12.3 | 7 156 | 13.4 | 53 542 | 6 359 | 11.9 | 6 933 | 12.9 |
| Women .............................................. | 48 477 | 5 277 | 10.9 | 5 903 | 12.2 | 48 351 | 5 285 | 10.9 | 5 905 | 12.2 | 48 309 | 4 947 | 10.2 | 5 584 | 11.6 |
| **Black, 16 Years and Over**[3] ........... | 14 195 | 1 896 | 13.4 | 2 115 | 14.9 | 14 249 | 1 927 | 13.5 | 2 140 | 15.0 | 14 975 | 2 009 | 13.4 | 2 220 | 14.8 |
| Men .................................................. | 6 347 | 938 | 14.8 | 1 031 | 16.2 | 6 440 | 940 | 14.6 | 1 020 | 15.8 | 6 753 | 999 | 14.8 | 1 078 | 16.0 |
| Women .............................................. | 7 848 | 958 | 12.2 | 1 085 | 13.8 | 7 808 | 987 | 12.6 | 1 119 | 14.3 | 8 222 | 1 009 | 12.3 | 1 142 | 13.9 |
| **Asian, 16 Years and Over**[3] ........... | 5 900 | 645 | 10.9 | 713 | 12.1 | 6 153 | 623 | 10.1 | 690 | 11.2 | 6 953 | 668 | 9.6 | 758 | 10.9 |
| Men .................................................. | 3 112 | 292 | 9.4 | 325 | 10.4 | 3 269 | 296 | 9.1 | 331 | 10.1 | 3 650 | 323 | 8.9 | 369 | 10.1 |
| Women .............................................. | 2 787 | 353 | 12.6 | 388 | 13.9 | 2 884 | 327 | 11.4 | 359 | 12.4 | 3 303 | 345 | 10.4 | 388 | 11.8 |
| **Hispanic, 16 Years and Over**[4] ....... | 18 263 | 1 820 | 10.0 | 2 021 | 11.1 | 18 733 | 1 826 | 9.7 | 2 015 | 10.8 | 20 144 | 1 982 | 9.8 | 2 197 | 10.9 |
| Men .................................................. | 10 646 | 1 090 | 10.2 | 1 196 | 11.2 | 10 980 | 1 078 | 9.8 | 1 186 | 10.8 | 11 415 | 1 148 | 10.1 | 1 266 | 11.1 |
| Women .............................................. | 7 616 | 730 | 9.6 | 825 | 10.8 | 7 754 | 748 | 9.6 | 829 | 10.7 | 8 730 | 834 | 9.6 | 931 | 10.7 |
| **FULL- OR PART-TIME STATUS**[5] | | | | | | | | | | | | | | | |
| Full-time workers ............................ | 99 531 | 13 125 | 13.2 | 14 498 | 14.6 | 100 457 | 13 177 | 13.1 | 14 487 | 14.4 | 102 749 | 12 847 | 12.5 | 14 173 | 13.8 |
| Part-time workers ............................ | 24 351 | 1 560 | 6.4 | 1 760 | 7.2 | 24 502 | 1 557 | 6.4 | 1 769 | 7.2 | 24 614 | 1 483 | 6.0 | 1 710 | 6.9 |

[1]Data refer to members of a labor union or to an employee association similar to a union.

[2]Data refer to members of a labor union or to an employee association similar to a union, as well as to workers who report no union affiliation but whose jobs are covered by a union or an employee association contract.

[3]Beginning in 2003, persons who selected this race group only; persons who selected more than one race group are not included. Prior to 2003, persons who reported more than one race group were included in the group they identified as their main race. Additionally, estimates for the above race groups (White, Black, and Asian) do not sum to totals because data are not presented for all races.

[4]May be of any race.

[5]The distinction between full- and part-time workers is based on hours usually worked. Data will not sum to totals because full- or part-time status on the principal job is not identifiable for a small number of multiple job holders.

## Table 8-2. Union Affiliation of Employed Wage and Salary Workers, by Selected Characteristics, 2010–2015
### —Continued

(Numbers in thousands, percent.)

| Characteristic | 2013 | | | | | 2014 | | | | | 2015 | | | | |
|---|---|---|---|---|---|---|---|---|---|---|---|---|---|---|---|
| | Total employed | Member of union[1] | | Represented by union[2] | | Total employed | Member of union[1] | | Represented by union[2] | | Total employed | Member of union[1] | | Represented by union[2] | |
| | | Total | Percent of employed | Total | Percent of employed | | Total | Percent of employed | Total | Percent of employed | | Total | Percent of employed | Total | Percent of employed |
| **SEX AND AGE** | | | | | | | | | | | | | | | |
| **Both Sexes, 16 Years and Over** .... | 129 110 | 14 528 | 11.3 | 16 028 | 12.4 | 131 431 | 14 576 | 11.1 | 16 152 | 12.3 | 133 743 | 14 795 | 11.1 | 16 441 | 12.3 |
| 16 to 24 years ................................. | 17 647 | 745 | 4.2 | 854 | 4.8 | 18 019 | 804 | 4.5 | 956 | 5.3 | 18 311 | 800 | 4.4 | 967 | 5.3 |
| 25 years and over ........................... | 111 463 | 13 783 | 12.4 | 15 174 | 13.6 | 113 412 | 13 772 | 12.1 | 15 196 | 13.4 | 115 431 | 13 995 | 12.1 | 15 474 | 13.4 |
| 25 to 34 years ............................. | 29 404 | 2 886 | 9.8 | 3 228 | 11.0 | 30 158 | 2 879 | 9.5 | 3 205 | 10.6 | 30 870 | 2 985 | 9.7 | 3 363 | 10.9 |
| 35 to 44 years ............................. | 27 631 | 3 458 | 12.5 | 3 790 | 13.7 | 27 948 | 3 460 | 12.4 | 3 823 | 13.7 | 28 101 | 3 457 | 12.3 | 3 785 | 13.5 |
| 45 to 54 years ............................. | 28 498 | 3 990 | 14.0 | 4 377 | 15.4 | 28 540 | 3 927 | 13.8 | 4 286 | 15.0 | 28 764 | 3 909 | 13.6 | 4 306 | 15.0 |
| 55 to 64 years ............................. | 20 207 | 2 899 | 14.3 | 3 176 | 15.7 | 20 781 | 2 924 | 14.1 | 3 229 | 15.5 | 21 288 | 3 035 | 14.3 | 3 329 | 15.6 |
| 65 years and over ........................ | 5 723 | 549 | 9.6 | 603 | 10.5 | 5 985 | 582 | 9.7 | 653 | 10.9 | 6 408 | 610 | 9.5 | 691 | 10.8 |
| **Men, 16 Years and Over** .............. | 66 794 | 7 955 | 11.9 | 8 688 | 13.0 | 68 048 | 7 939 | 11.7 | 8 717 | 12.8 | 69 298 | 7 963 | 11.5 | 8 760 | 12.6 |
| 16 to 24 years ................................. | 8 918 | 434 | 4.9 | 488 | 5.5 | 9 141 | 462 | 5.1 | 540 | 5.9 | 9 250 | 485 | 5.2 | 563 | 6.1 |
| 25 years and over ........................... | 57 876 | 7 522 | 13.0 | 8 200 | 14.2 | 58 907 | 7 476 | 12.7 | 8 177 | 13.9 | 60 048 | 7 478 | 12.5 | 8 197 | 13.7 |
| 25 to 34 years ............................. | 15 755 | 1 635 | 10.4 | 1 807 | 11.5 | 16 172 | 1 611 | 10.0 | 1 773 | 11.0 | 16 550 | 1 639 | 9.9 | 1 825 | 11.0 |
| 35 to 44 years ............................. | 14 667 | 1 940 | 13.2 | 2 104 | 14.3 | 14 769 | 1 913 | 13.0 | 2 108 | 14.3 | 14 844 | 1 857 | 12.5 | 2 023 | 13.6 |
| 45 to 54 years ............................. | 14 466 | 2 157 | 14.9 | 2 347 | 16.2 | 14 508 | 2 085 | 14.4 | 2 256 | 15.6 | 14 696 | 2 079 | 14.1 | 2 281 | 15.5 |
| 55 to 64 years ............................. | 10 033 | 1 513 | 15.1 | 1 640 | 16.3 | 10 419 | 1 553 | 14.9 | 1 689 | 16.2 | 10 698 | 1 588 | 14.8 | 1 717 | 16.0 |
| 65 years and over ........................ | 2 954 | 277 | 9.4 | 302 | 10.2 | 3 040 | 315 | 10.4 | 351 | 11.5 | 3 259 | 315 | 9.7 | 352 | 10.8 |
| **Women, 16 Years and Over** .......... | 62 316 | 6 573 | 10.5 | 7 340 | 11.8 | 63 383 | 6 638 | 10.5 | 7 434 | 11.7 | 64 445 | 6 833 | 10.6 | 7 681 | 11.9 |
| 16 to 24 years ................................. | 8 729 | 311 | 3.6 | 366 | 4.2 | 8 879 | 342 | 3.8 | 416 | 4.7 | 9 061 | 315 | 3.5 | 405 | 4.5 |
| 25 years and over ........................... | 53 587 | 6 261 | 11.7 | 6 974 | 13.0 | 54 505 | 6 296 | 11.6 | 7 019 | 12.9 | 55 384 | 6 518 | 11.8 | 7 277 | 13.1 |
| 25 to 34 years ............................. | 13 649 | 1 251 | 9.2 | 1 420 | 10.4 | 13 985 | 1 268 | 9.1 | 1 431 | 10.2 | 14 320 | 1 346 | 9.4 | 1 538 | 10.7 |
| 35 to 44 years ............................. | 12 964 | 1 518 | 11.7 | 1 686 | 13.0 | 13 180 | 1 548 | 11.7 | 1 715 | 13.0 | 13 257 | 1 600 | 12.1 | 1 762 | 13.3 |
| 45 to 54 years ............................. | 14 032 | 1 834 | 13.1 | 2 030 | 14.5 | 14 032 | 1 842 | 13.1 | 2 030 | 14.5 | 14 068 | 1 830 | 13.0 | 2 025 | 14.4 |
| 55 to 64 years ............................. | 10 175 | 1 386 | 13.6 | 1 536 | 15.1 | 10 362 | 1 371 | 13.2 | 1 541 | 14.9 | 10 590 | 1 447 | 13.7 | 1 613 | 15.2 |
| 65 years and over ........................ | 2 768 | 273 | 9.8 | 302 | 10.9 | 2 946 | 267 | 9.1 | 302 | 10.2 | 3 149 | 294 | 9.3 | 339 | 10.8 |
| **RACE, HISPANIC ORIGIN, AND SEX** | | | | | | | | | | | | | | | |
| **White, 16 Years and Over**[3] ........... | 102 670 | 11 324 | 11.0 | 12 507 | 12.2 | 104 065 | 11 274 | 10.8 | 12 503 | 12.0 | 104 991 | 11 301 | 10.8 | 12 627 | 12.0 |
| Men ................................................. | 54 017 | 6 320 | 11.7 | 6 897 | 12.8 | 54 747 | 6 295 | 11.5 | 6 900 | 12.6 | 55 402 | 6 222 | 11.2 | 6 875 | 12.4 |
| Women ............................................ | 48 653 | 5 004 | 10.3 | 5 609 | 11.5 | 49 318 | 4 979 | 10.1 | 5 602 | 11.4 | 49 590 | 5 079 | 10.2 | 5 752 | 11.6 |
| **Black, 16 Years and Over**[3] ........... | 15 274 | 2 081 | 13.6 | 2 294 | 15.0 | 15 830 | 2 097 | 13.2 | 2 303 | 14.6 | 16 552 | 2 246 | 13.6 | 2 427 | 14.7 |
| Men ................................................. | 6 965 | 1 031 | 14.8 | 1 129 | 16.2 | 7 243 | 1 047 | 14.5 | 1 147 | 15.8 | 7 558 | 1 097 | 14.5 | 1 174 | 15.5 |
| Women ............................................ | 8 310 | 1 049 | 12.6 | 1 165 | 14.0 | 8 586 | 1 050 | 12.2 | 1 156 | 13.5 | 8 995 | 1 149 | 12.8 | 1 253 | 13.9 |
| **Asian, 16 Years and Over**[3] ........... | 7 271 | 683 | 9.4 | 758 | 10.4 | 7 476 | 779 | 10.4 | 866 | 11.6 | 7 883 | 770 | 9.8 | 860 | 10.9 |
| Men ................................................. | 3 786 | 338 | 8.9 | 380 | 10.0 | 3 921 | 361 | 9.2 | 416 | 10.6 | 4 113 | 367 | 8.9 | 416 | 10.1 |
| Women ............................................ | 3 485 | 346 | 9.9 | 377 | 10.8 | 3 555 | 418 | 11.8 | 450 | 12.6 | 3 770 | 403 | 10.7 | 444 | 11.8 |
| **Hispanic, 16 Years and Over**[4] ....... | 20 730 | 1 952 | 9.4 | 2 141 | 10.3 | 21 571 | 1 978 | 9.2 | 2 220 | 10.3 | 22 351 | 2 104 | 9.4 | 2 365 | 10.6 |
| Men ................................................. | 11 903 | 1 121 | 9.4 | 1 218 | 10.2 | 12 339 | 1 155 | 9.4 | 1 286 | 10.4 | 12 670 | 1 211 | 9.6 | 1 346 | 10.6 |
| Women ............................................ | 8 827 | 831 | 9.4 | 923 | 10.5 | 9 232 | 823 | 8.9 | 933 | 10.1 | 9 681 | 892 | 9.2 | 1 019 | 10.5 |
| **FULL- OR PART-TIME STATUS**[5] | | | | | | | | | | | | | | | |
| Full-time workers ............................. | 104 262 | 13 020 | 12.5 | 14 341 | 13.8 | 106 526 | 13 132 | 12.3 | 14 491 | 13.6 | 109 080 | 13 340 | 12.2 | 14 768 | 13.5 |
| Part-time workers ............................. | 24 664 | 1 483 | 6.0 | 1 662 | 6.7 | 24 707 | 1 424 | 5.8 | 1 636 | 6.6 | 24 445 | 1 431 | 5.9 | 1 646 | 6.7 |

[1]Data refer to members of a labor union or to an employee association similar to a union.

[2]Data refer to members of a labor union or to an employee association similar to a union, as well as to workers who report no union affiliation but whose jobs are covered by a union or an employee association contract.

[3]Beginning in 2003, persons who selected this race group only; persons who selected more than one race group are not included. Prior to 2003, persons who reported more than one race group were included in the group they identified as their main race. Additionally, estimates for the above race groups (White, Black, and Asian) do not sum to totals because data are not presented for all races.

[4]May be of any race.

[5]The distinction between full- and part-time workers is based on hours usually worked. Data will not sum to totals because full- or part-time status on the principal job is not identifiable for a small number of multiple job holders.

## Table 8-3. Union Affiliation of Wage and Salary Workers, by Occupation and Industry, 2014–2015

(Thousands of people, percent.)

| Occupation and industry | 2014 | | | | | 2015 | | | | |
|---|---|---|---|---|---|---|---|---|---|---|
| | Total employed | Member of union[1] | | Represented by union[2] | | Total employed | Member of union[1] | | Represented by union[2] | |
| | | Total | Percent of employed | Total | Percent of employed | | Total | Percent of employed | Total | Percent of employed |
| **OCCUPATION** | | | | | | | | | | |
| Management, professional, and related ....................... | 48 890 | 5 835 | 11.9 | 6 612 | 13.5 | 50 939 | 6 132 | 12.0 | 6 983 | 13.7 |
| Management, business, and financial operations ............... | 18 717 | 870 | 4.6 | 1 016 | 5.4 | 19 636 | 871 | 4.4 | 1 057 | 5.4 |
| Management ......................................... | 12 550 | 562 | 4.5 | 653 | 5.2 | 13 213 | 581 | 4.4 | 701 | 5.3 |
| Business and financial operations ..................... | 6 168 | 308 | 5.0 | 362 | 5.9 | 6 423 | 290 | 4.5 | 356 | 5.5 |
| Professional and related ................................... | 30 173 | 4 965 | 16.5 | 5 597 | 18.5 | 31 302 | 5 261 | 16.8 | 5 926 | 18.9 |
| Computer and mathematical ........................ | 4 057 | 169 | 4.2 | 223 | 5.5 | 4 195 | 162 | 3.9 | 221 | 5.3 |
| Architecture and engineering ....................... | 2 635 | 160 | 6.1 | 190 | 7.2 | 2 777 | 190 | 6.8 | 219 | 7.9 |
| Life, physical, and social science ................... | 1 232 | 122 | 9.9 | 149 | 12.1 | 1 309 | 109 | 8.3 | 139 | 10.6 |
| Community and social service ...................... | 2 373 | 358 | 15.1 | 396 | 16.7 | 2 517 | 386 | 15.3 | 412 | 16.4 |
| Legal ................................................ | 1 440 | 86 | 6.0 | 107 | 7.5 | 1 475 | 83 | 5.6 | 100 | 6.8 |
| Education, training, and library ..................... | 8 437 | 2 976 | 35.3 | 3 279 | 38.9 | 8 766 | 3 112 | 35.5 | 3 466 | 39.5 |
| Arts, design, entertainment, sports, and media .............. | 2 071 | 117 | 5.6 | 137 | 6.6 | 2 120 | 161 | 7.6 | 187 | 8.8 |
| Health care practitioner and technical ............... | 7 928 | 977 | 12.3 | 1 115 | 14.1 | 8 142 | 1 059 | 13.0 | 1 183 | 14.5 |
| Services ................................................... | 23 481 | 2 498 | 10.6 | 2 740 | 11.7 | 23 503 | 2 492 | 10.6 | 2 759 | 11.7 |
| Health care support ................................... | 3 326 | 305 | 9.2 | 346 | 10.4 | 3 305 | 279 | 8.4 | 314 | 9.5 |
| Protective service .................................... | 3 128 | 1 103 | 35.3 | 1 166 | 37.3 | 3 092 | 1 123 | 36.3 | 1 189 | 38.5 |
| Food preparation and serving related ............... | 8 021 | 338 | 4.2 | 389 | 4.9 | 8 016 | 329 | 4.1 | 381 | 4.8 |
| Building and grounds cleaning and maintenance .............. | 4 916 | 504 | 10.2 | 560 | 11.4 | 4 868 | 473 | 9.7 | 537 | 11.0 |
| Personal care and service ........................... | 4 090 | 248 | 6.1 | 279 | 6.8 | 4 222 | 288 | 6.8 | 338 | 8.0 |
| Sales and office ........................................... | 30 903 | 2 023 | 6.5 | 2 277 | 7.4 | 30 931 | 2 055 | 6.6 | 2 311 | 7.5 |
| Sales and related ..................................... | 13 529 | 415 | 3.1 | 499 | 3.7 | 13 574 | 441 | 3.3 | 505 | 3.7 |
| Office and administrative support .................... | 17 374 | 1 608 | 9.3 | 1 778 | 10.2 | 17 357 | 1 614 | 9.3 | 1 806 | 10.4 |
| Natural resources, construction, and maintenance ............... | 11 627 | 1 782 | 15.3 | 1 909 | 16.4 | 11 694 | 1 751 | 15.0 | 1 868 | 16.0 |
| Farming, fishing, and forestry ....................... | 935 | 24 | 2.5 | 30 | 3.2 | 971 | 18 | 1.9 | 25 | 2.5 |
| Construction and extraction .......................... | 6 196 | 1 104 | 17.8 | 1 167 | 18.8 | 6 193 | 1 067 | 17.2 | 1 133 | 18.3 |
| Installation, maintenance, and repair ................ | 4 496 | 655 | 14.6 | 711 | 15.8 | 4 530 | 666 | 14.7 | 710 | 15.7 |
| Production, transportation, and material moving ............... | 16 530 | 2 438 | 14.8 | 2 614 | 15.8 | 16 676 | 2 365 | 14.2 | 2 521 | 15.1 |
| Production ............................................. | 8 098 | 1 066 | 13.2 | 1 150 | 14.2 | 8 180 | 1 031 | 12.6 | 1 098 | 13.4 |
| Transportation and material moving .................. | 8 432 | 1 372 | 16.3 | 1 464 | 17.4 | 8 496 | 1 334 | 15.7 | 1 422 | 16.7 |
| **INDUSTRY** | | | | | | | | | | |
| Private sector ............................................. | 111 228 | 7 359 | 6.6 | 8 224 | 7.4 | 113 152 | 7 554 | 6.7 | 8 411 | 7.4 |
| Agriculture and related industries ...................... | 1 199 | 14 | 1.1 | 19 | 1.6 | 1 269 | 15 | 1.2 | 22 | 1.7 |
| Nonagricultural industries .............................. | 110 028 | 7 345 | 6.7 | 8 205 | 7.5 | 111 882 | 7 539 | 6.7 | 8 389 | 7.5 |
| Mining ................................................ | 1 040 | 50 | 4.8 | 61 | 5.9 | 866 | 47 | 5.4 | 57 | 6.5 |
| Construction .......................................... | 6 968 | 968 | 13.9 | 1 023 | 14.7 | 7 109 | 940 | 13.2 | 992 | 14.0 |
| Manufacturing ........................................ | 14 471 | 1 409 | 9.7 | 1 517 | 10.5 | 14 547 | 1 369 | 9.4 | 1 462 | 10.0 |
| Durable goods ..................................... | 9 111 | 876 | 9.6 | 944 | 10.4 | 9 288 | 874 | 9.4 | 933 | 10.0 |
| Nondurable goods ................................. | 5 359 | 534 | 10.0 | 572 | 10.7 | 5 258 | 494 | 9.4 | 529 | 10.1 |
| Wholesale and retail trade ........................... | 18 372 | 769 | 4.2 | 892 | 4.9 | 18 798 | 871 | 4.6 | 962 | 5.1 |
| Wholesale trade ................................... | 3 232 | 107 | 3.3 | 129 | 4.0 | 3 346 | 126 | 3.8 | 139 | 4.2 |
| Retail trade ........................................ | 15 141 | 662 | 4.4 | 763 | 5.0 | 15 452 | 745 | 4.8 | 823 | 5.3 |
| Transportation and utilities ........................... | 5 750 | 1 153 | 20.1 | 1 217 | 21.2 | 5 722 | 1 106 | 19.3 | 1 159 | 20.3 |
| Transportation and warehousing .................... | 4 814 | 945 | 19.6 | 996 | 20.7 | 4 765 | 901 | 18.9 | 946 | 19.8 |
| Utilities ............................................ | 935 | 209 | 22.3 | 221 | 23.7 | 957 | 205 | 21.4 | 213 | 22.3 |
| Information[3] ......................................... | 2 681 | 231 | 8.6 | 255 | 9.5 | 2 525 | 217 | 8.6 | 249 | 9.9 |
| Publishing, except Internet ......................... | 581 | 21 | 3.6 | 22 | 3.8 | 495 | 19 | 3.9 | 22 | 4.4 |
| Motion pictures and sound recording ............... | 347 | 25 | 7.3 | 29 | 8.2 | 314 | 37 | 11.7 | 40 | 12.8 |
| Broadcasting, except Internet ...................... | 569 | 40 | 7.0 | 43 | 7.6 | 561 | 37 | 6.7 | 48 | 8.5 |
| Telecommunications ............................... | 915 | 135 | 14.8 | 151 | 16.5 | 883 | 118 | 13.3 | 131 | 14.8 |
| Financial activities ................................... | 8 481 | 169 | 2.0 | 200 | 2.4 | 8 781 | 208 | 2.4 | 242 | 2.8 |
| Finance and insurance ............................. | 6 409 | 92 | 1.4 | 112 | 1.8 | 6 550 | 103 | 1.6 | 129 | 2.0 |
| Finance ......................................... | 4 039 | 53 | 1.3 | 63 | 1.6 | 4 126 | 53 | 1.3 | 70 | 1.7 |
| Insurance ....................................... | 2 370 | 39 | 1.6 | 49 | 2.1 | 2 424 | 51 | 2.1 | 59 | 2.4 |
| Real estate and rental and leasing ................. | 2 071 | 77 | 3.7 | 88 | 4.2 | 2 231 | 105 | 4.7 | 113 | 5.1 |
| Professional and business services ................... | 13 300 | 309 | 2.3 | 389 | 2.9 | 13 738 | 348 | 2.5 | 458 | 3.3 |
| Professional and technical services ................ | 8 045 | 109 | 1.4 | 157 | 2.0 | 8 327 | 142 | 1.7 | 218 | 2.6 |
| Management, administrative, and waste services ....... | 5 254 | 199 | 3.8 | 232 | 4.4 | 5 411 | 206 | 3.8 | 240 | 4.4 |
| Education and health services ........................ | 21 147 | 1 728 | 8.2 | 2 003 | 9.5 | 21 572 | 1 867 | 8.7 | 2 132 | 9.9 |
| Education services ................................. | 4 338 | 508 | 11.7 | 599 | 13.8 | 4 551 | 625 | 13.7 | 720 | 15.8 |
| Health care and social assistance ................. | 16 809 | 1 220 | 7.3 | 1 404 | 8.4 | 17 021 | 1 242 | 7.3 | 1 412 | 8.3 |
| Leisure and hospitality ............................... | 11 997 | 387 | 3.2 | 454 | 3.8 | 12 357 | 389 | 3.1 | 449 | 3.6 |
| Arts, entertainment, and recreation ................ | 2 166 | 140 | 6.5 | 158 | 7.3 | 2 250 | 144 | 6.4 | 158 | 7.0 |
| Accommodation and food services ................. | 9 831 | 247 | 2.5 | 296 | 3.0 | 10 107 | 245 | 2.4 | 291 | 2.9 |
| Accommodation ................................. | 1 455 | 130 | 8.9 | 143 | 9.8 | 1 575 | 116 | 7.4 | 127 | 8.0 |
| Food services and drinking places .............. | 8 377 | 117 | 1.4 | 153 | 1.8 | 8 532 | 129 | 1.5 | 165 | 1.9 |
| Other services[3] .................................... | 5 821 | 171 | 2.9 | 193 | 3.3 | 5 867 | 177 | 3.0 | 227 | 3.9 |
| Other services, except private households ................ | 5 026 | 157 | 3.1 | 178 | 3.5 | 5 055 | 166 | 3.3 | 205 | 4.1 |
| Public sector ............................................. | 20 203 | 7 218 | 35.7 | 7 927 | 39.2 | 20 591 | 7 241 | 35.2 | 8 031 | 39.0 |
| Federal government ................................... | 3 408 | 939 | 27.5 | 1 078 | 31.6 | 3 591 | 979 | 27.3 | 1 160 | 32.3 |
| State government ..................................... | 6 264 | 1 867 | 29.8 | 2 056 | 32.8 | 6 875 | 2 079 | 30.2 | 2 312 | 33.6 |
| Local government .................................... | 10 532 | 4 412 | 41.9 | 4 793 | 45.5 | 10 126 | 4 183 | 41.3 | 4 559 | 45.0 |

*Note:* Updated population controls are introduced annually with the release of January data. Data refer to the sole or principal job of full- and part-time workers. Excluded are all self-employed workers, regardless of whether or not their businesses are incorporated.

[1]Data refer to members of a labor union or an employee association similar to a union.
[2]Data refer to members of a labor union or an employee association similar to a union, as well as to workers who report no union affiliation but whose jobs are covered by a union or an employee association contract.
[3]Includes other industries, not shown separately.

## Table 8-4. Median Weekly Earnings of Full-Time Wage and Salary Workers, by Union Affiliation, Occupation, and Industry, 2014–2015

(Dollars.)

| Occupation and industry | 2014 | | | | 2015 | | | |
|---|---|---|---|---|---|---|---|---|
| | Total | Member of union[1] | Represented by union[2] | Non-union | Total | Member of union[1] | Represented by union[2] | Non-union |
| **OCCUPATION** | | | | | | | | |
| Management, professional, and related | 1 137 | 1 132 | 1 129 | 1 139 | 1 158 | 1 152 | 1 148 | 1 160 |
| Management, business, and financial operations | 1 227 | 1 246 | 1 243 | 1 226 | 1 258 | 1 273 | 1 291 | 1 257 |
| Management | 1 295 | 1 333 | 1 333 | 1 292 | 1 351 | 1 386 | 1 380 | 1 349 |
| Business and financial operations | 1 107 | 1 135 | 1 131 | 1 104 | 1 137 | 1 108 | 1 132 | 1 138 |
| Professional and related | 1 078 | 1 117 | 1 112 | 1 068 | 1 112 | 1 140 | 1 132 | 1 103 |
| Computer and mathematical | 1 368 | 1 288 | 1 277 | 1 373 | 1 428 | 1 388 | 1 327 | 1 434 |
| Architecture and engineering | 1 377 | 1 416 | 1 424 | 1 370 | 1 424 | 1 393 | 1 399 | 1 427 |
| Life, physical, and social science | 1 168 | 1 271 | 1 276 | 1 141 | 1 206 | 1 249 | 1 266 | 1 187 |
| Community and social service | 858 | 1 017 | 1 010 | 822 | 889 | 1 014 | 1 008 | 855 |
| Legal | 1 271 | 1 208 | 1 333 | 1 270 | 1 391 | 1 551 | 1 547 | 1 373 |
| Education, training, and library | 953 | 1 077 | 1 069 | 851 | 956 | 1 095 | 1 074 | 860 |
| Arts, design, entertainment, sports, and media | 956 | 1 130 | 1 110 | 946 | 1 001 | 1 228 | 1 212 | 984 |
| Health care practitioner and technical | 1 033 | 1 128 | 1 115 | 1 020 | 1 041 | 1 211 | 1 194 | 1 014 |
| Services | 505 | 762 | 751 | 482 | 509 | 753 | 742 | 489 |
| Health care support | 498 | 569 | 558 | 493 | 498 | 544 | 546 | 495 |
| Protective service | 833 | 1 107 | 1 093 | 687 | 796 | 1 031 | 1 029 | 687 |
| Food preparation and serving related | 439 | 535 | 525 | 433 | 441 | 515 | 512 | 436 |
| Building and grounds cleaning and maintenance | 480 | 644 | 633 | 456 | 486 | 648 | 628 | 469 |
| Personal care and service | 487 | 591 | 583 | 480 | 498 | 515 | 521 | 496 |
| Sales and office | 666 | 788 | 788 | 654 | 673 | 810 | 801 | 662 |
| Sales and related | 705 | 728 | 724 | 704 | 716 | 702 | 710 | 716 |
| Office and administrative support | 651 | 801 | 801 | 632 | 656 | 831 | 821 | 639 |
| Natural resources, construction, and maintenance | 756 | 1 076 | 1 062 | 705 | 761 | 1 070 | 1 052 | 711 |
| Farming, fishing, and forestry | 429 | (3) | (3) | 423 | 464 | (3) | (3) | 460 |
| Construction and extraction | 756 | 1 095 | 1 078 | 697 | 749 | 1 082 | 1 064 | 695 |
| Installation, maintenance, and repair | 821 | 1 064 | 1 057 | 782 | 839 | 1 066 | 1 051 | 799 |
| Production, transportation, and material moving | 642 | 838 | 830 | 614 | 656 | 850 | 842 | 622 |
| Production | 646 | 825 | 824 | 620 | 663 | 824 | 826 | 635 |
| Transportation and material moving | 637 | 850 | 836 | 608 | 646 | 876 | 859 | 610 |
| **INDUSTRY** | | | | | | | | |
| Private sector | 763 | 907 | 900 | 753 | 776 | 917 | 912 | 765 |
| Agriculture and related industries | 502 | (3) | (3) | 501 | 522 | (3) | (3) | 519 |
| Nonagricultural industries | 767 | 907 | 901 | 756 | 781 | 918 | 913 | 769 |
| Mining | 1 136 | 1 150 | 1 176 | 1 130 | 1 162 | (3) | 1 170 | 1 162 |
| Construction | 775 | 1 123 | 1 108 | 724 | 784 | 1 099 | 1 093 | 743 |
| Manufacturing | 812 | 861 | 854 | 807 | 839 | 876 | 868 | 833 |
| Durable goods | 840 | 888 | 886 | 833 | 872 | 889 | 881 | 871 |
| Nondurable goods | 765 | 808 | 795 | 761 | 776 | 849 | 841 | 768 |
| Wholesale and retail trade | 641 | 669 | 670 | 638 | 653 | 673 | 671 | 652 |
| Wholesale trade | 818 | 772 | 773 | 821 | 841 | 876 | 863 | 840 |
| Retail trade | 602 | 641 | 643 | 600 | 610 | 621 | 622 | 609 |
| Transportation and utilities | 826 | 1 011 | 1 009 | 785 | 843 | 1 007 | 1 003 | 803 |
| Transportation and warehousing | 780 | 947 | 947 | 748 | 790 | 980 | 977 | 754 |
| Utilities | 1 156 | 1 275 | 1 283 | 1 078 | 1 133 | 1 194 | 1 188 | 1 116 |
| Information[4] | 1 040 | 1 115 | 1 090 | 1 029 | 1 102 | 1 260 | 1 242 | 1 077 |
| Publishing, except Internet | 1 068 | (3) | (3) | 1 081 | 1 098 | (3) | (3) | 1 102 |
| Motion pictures and sound recording | 1 021 | (3) | (3) | 993 | 996 | (3) | (3) | 935 |
| Broadcasting, except Internet | 902 | (3) | (3) | 879 | 980 | (3) | (3) | 968 |
| Telecommunications | 1 145 | 1 143 | 1 114 | 1 151 | 1 162 | 1 212 | 1 208 | 1 148 |
| Financial activities | 941 | 879 | 884 | 942 | 964 | 915 | 924 | 964 |
| Finance and insurance | 989 | 880 | 893 | 991 | 1 024 | 983 | 1 004 | 1 024 |
| Finance | 1 012 | 862 | 889 | 1 014 | 1 061 | 923 | 1 082 | 1 060 |
| Insurance | 959 | (3) | (3) | 960 | 973 | 988 | 981 | 973 |
| Real estate and rental and leasing | 768 | 876 | 869 | 762 | 782 | 891 | 893 | 772 |
| Professional and business services | 915 | 805 | 851 | 918 | 951 | 874 | 906 | 953 |
| Professional and technical services | 1 199 | 1 081 | 1 145 | 1 203 | 1 256 | 1 297 | 1 268 | 1 255 |
| Management, administrative, and waste services | 580 | 743 | 735 | 575 | 605 | 684 | 672 | 603 |
| Education and health services | 777 | 926 | 925 | 763 | 787 | 962 | 946 | 768 |
| Education services | 902 | 967 | 978 | 879 | 918 | 1 025 | 1 015 | 896 |
| Health care and social assistance | 750 | 893 | 886 | 740 | 754 | 916 | 904 | 742 |
| Leisure and hospitality | 505 | 636 | 624 | 500 | 515 | 606 | 592 | 511 |
| Arts, entertainment, and recreation | 650 | 688 | 683 | 642 | 657 | 672 | 680 | 655 |
| Accommodation and food services | 481 | 602 | 591 | 478 | 492 | 579 | 558 | 489 |
| Accommodation | 544 | 639 | 639 | 522 | 546 | 645 | 639 | 532 |
| Food services and drinking places | 465 | 496 | 485 | 465 | 480 | 492 | 490 | 480 |
| Other services[4] | 644 | 871 | 843 | 636 | 684 | 903 | 879 | 677 |
| Other services, except private households | 671 | 887 | 865 | 662 | 710 | 916 | 900 | 703 |
| Public sector | 927 | 1 014 | 1 014 | 850 | 944 | 1 029 | 1 023 | 878 |
| Federal government | 1 103 | 1 050 | 1 072 | 1 136 | 1 113 | 1 058 | 1 064 | 1 159 |
| State government | 886 | 967 | 966 | 821 | 909 | 988 | 982 | 867 |
| Local government | 899 | 1 026 | 1 020 | 780 | 914 | 1 043 | 1 033 | 783 |

*Note:* Updated population controls are introduced annually with the release of January data. Data refer to the sole or principal job of full- and part-time workers. Excluded are all self-employed workers, regardless of whether or not their businesses are incorporated.

[1]Data refer to members of a labor union or an employee association similar to a union.
[2]Data refer to members of a labor union or an employee association similar to a union, as well as to workers who report no union affiliation but whose jobs are covered by a union or an employee association contract.
[3]Data not shown where base is less than 50,000.
[4]Includes other industries, not shown separately.

## Table 8-5. Union or Employee Association Members Among Wage and Salary Employees, 1977–2015

(Numbers in thousands, percent.)

| Year | Total wage and salary employment | Union or employee association member | Union or association members as a percent of total wage and salary employment |
|---|---|---|---|
| 1977 | 81 334 | 19 335 | 23.8 |
| 1978 | 84 968 | 19 548 | 23.0 |
| 1979 | 87 117 | 20 986 | 24.1 |
| 1980 | 87 480 | 20 095 | 23.0 |
| 1983[1] | 88 290 | 17 717 | 20.1 |
| 1984 | 92 194 | 17 340 | 18.8 |
| 1985 | 94 521 | 16 996 | 18.0 |
| 1986 | 96 903 | 16 975 | 17.5 |
| 1987 | 99 303 | 16 913 | 17.0 |
| 1988 | 101 407 | 17 002 | 16.8 |
| 1989 | 103 480 | 16 980 | 16.4 |
| 1990 | 103 905 | 16 740 | 16.1 |
| 1991 | 102 786 | 16 568 | 16.1 |
| 1992 | 103 688 | 16 390 | 15.8 |
| 1993 | 105 087 | 16 598 | 15.8 |
| 1994[2] | 107 989 | 16 748 | 15.5 |
| 1995 | 110 038 | 16 360 | 14.9 |
| 1996 | 111 960 | 16 269 | 14.5 |
| 1997 | 114 533 | 16 110 | 14.1 |
| 1998 | 116 730 | 16 211 | 13.9 |
| 1999 | 118 963 | 16 477 | 13.9 |
| 2000 | 120 786 | 16 258 | 13.5 |
| 2001 | 122 482 | 16 387 | 13.4 |
| 2002 | 121 826 | 16 145 | 13.3 |
| 2003 | 122 358 | 15 776 | 12.9 |
| 2004 | 123 554 | 15 472 | 12.5 |
| 2005 | 125 889 | 15 685 | 12.5 |
| 2006 | 128 237 | 15 359 | 12.0 |
| 2007 | 129 767 | 15 670 | 12.1 |
| 2008 | 129 377 | 16 098 | 12.4 |
| 2009 | 124 490 | 15 327 | 12.3 |
| 2010 | 124 073 | 14 715 | 11.9 |
| 2011 | 125 187 | 14 764 | 13.0 |
| 2012 | 127 577 | 14 366 | 11.3 |
| 2013 | 129 110 | 14 528 | 11.3 |
| 2014 | 131 431 | 14 576 | 11.1 |
| 2015 | 133 743 | 14 795 | 11.1 |

[1]Annual average data beginning in 1983 are not directly comparable with the data for 1977–1980.
[2]Data beginning in 1994 are not strictly comparable with data for 1993 and earlier years because of the introduction of a major redesign of the Current Population Survey questionnaire and collection methodology and the introduction of 1990 census–based population controls.
. . . = Not available.

## Table 8-6. Union Affiliation of Employed Wage and Salary Workers, by State, 2014–2015

(Numbers in thousands, percent.)

| State | 2014 | | | | | 2015 | | | | |
|-------|------|--|--|--|--|------|--|--|--|--|
| | Total employed | Member of union[1] | | Represented by union[2] | | Total employed | Member of union[1] | | Represented by union[2] | |
| | | Total | Percent of employed | Total | Percent of employed | | Total | Percent of employed | Total | Percent of employed |
| UNITED STATES | 131 431 | 14 576 | 11.1 | 16 152 | 12.3 | 133 743 | 14 795 | 11.1 | 16 441 | 12.3 |
| Alabama | 1 887 | 204 | 10.8 | 228 | 12.1 | 1 863 | 190 | 10.2 | 204 | 11.0 |
| Alaska | 307 | 70 | 22.8 | 75 | 24.4 | 304 | 60 | 19.6 | 66 | 21.7 |
| Arizona | 2 593 | 138 | 5.3 | 173 | 6.7 | 2 661 | 138 | 5.2 | 163 | 6.1 |
| Arkansas | 1 108 | 52 | 4.7 | 60 | 5.4 | 1 155 | 58 | 5.1 | 74 | 6.4 |
| California | 15 135 | 2 472 | 16.3 | 2 652 | 17.5 | 15 657 | 2 486 | 15.9 | 2 689 | 17.2 |
| Colorado | 2 328 | 221 | 9.5 | 250 | 10.7 | 2 310 | 194 | 8.4 | 215 | 9.3 |
| Connecticut | 1 564 | 231 | 14.8 | 245 | 15.7 | 1 587 | 269 | 17.0 | 277 | 17.4 |
| Delaware | 384 | 38 | 9.9 | 43 | 11.3 | 412 | 38 | 9.2 | 43 | 10.4 |
| District of Columbia | 325 | 28 | 8.6 | 35 | 10.7 | 334 | 35 | 10.4 | 40 | 12.1 |
| Florida | 8 042 | 455 | 5.7 | 561 | 7.0 | 7 994 | 546 | 6.8 | 671 | 8.4 |
| Georgia | 3 926 | 170 | 4.3 | 193 | 4.9 | 4 016 | 162 | 4.0 | 206 | 5.1 |
| Hawaii | 572 | 124 | 21.8 | 131 | 22.9 | 583 | 119 | 20.4 | 126 | 21.7 |
| Idaho | 641 | 34 | 5.3 | 43 | 6.7 | 679 | 46 | 6.8 | 50 | 7.3 |
| Illinois | 5 500 | 831 | 15.1 | 880 | 16.0 | 5 566 | 847 | 15.2 | 892 | 16.0 |
| Indiana | 2 802 | 299 | 10.7 | 335 | 12.0 | 2 828 | 283 | 10.0 | 319 | 11.3 |
| Iowa | 1 459 | 156 | 10.7 | 184 | 12.6 | 1 435 | 138 | 9.6 | 174 | 12.2 |
| Kansas | 1 287 | 95 | 7.4 | 116 | 9.0 | 1 255 | 110 | 8.7 | 136 | 10.8 |
| Kentucky | 1 714 | 189 | 11.0 | 219 | 12.8 | 1 705 | 187 | 11.0 | 207 | 12.1 |
| Louisiana | 1 834 | 96 | 5.2 | 118 | 6.4 | 1 847 | 107 | 5.8 | 126 | 6.8 |
| Maine | 566 | 62 | 11.0 | 71 | 12.5 | 549 | 64 | 11.6 | 75 | 13.6 |
| Maryland | 2 612 | 310 | 11.9 | 347 | 13.3 | 2 757 | 287 | 10.4 | 337 | 12.2 |
| Massachusetts | 3 036 | 415 | 13.7 | 445 | 14.7 | 3 103 | 402 | 12.9 | 441 | 14.2 |
| Michigan | 4 028 | 585 | 14.5 | 631 | 15.7 | 4 083 | 621 | 15.2 | 672 | 16.5 |
| Minnesota | 2 538 | 360 | 14.2 | 380 | 15.0 | 2 565 | 363 | 14.2 | 385 | 15.0 |
| Mississippi | 1 028 | 38 | 3.7 | 46 | 4.5 | 1 103 | 60 | 5.4 | 75 | 6.8 |
| Missouri | 2 559 | 214 | 8.4 | 249 | 9.7 | 2 615 | 230 | 8.8 | 257 | 9.8 |
| Montana | 414 | 52 | 12.7 | 57 | 13.8 | 427 | 52 | 12.2 | 59 | 13.9 |
| Nebraska | 877 | 64 | 7.3 | 79 | 9.0 | 882 | 68 | 7.7 | 80 | 9.0 |
| Nevada | 1 173 | 169 | 14.4 | 192 | 16.4 | 1 232 | 177 | 14.3 | 203 | 16.5 |
| New Hampshire | 626 | 62 | 9.9 | 72 | 11.5 | 641 | 62 | 9.7 | 73 | 11.4 |
| New Jersey | 3 860 | 635 | 16.5 | 664 | 17.2 | 3 880 | 596 | 15.4 | 644 | 16.6 |
| New Mexico | 763 | 43 | 5.7 | 56 | 7.4 | 782 | 49 | 6.2 | 61 | 7.9 |
| New York | 8 060 | 1 980 | 24.6 | 2 081 | 25.8 | 8 249 | 2 038 | 24.7 | 2 141 | 26.0 |
| North Carolina | 3 936 | 76 | 1.9 | 126 | 3.2 | 4 089 | 123 | 3.0 | 167 | 4.1 |
| North Dakota | 353 | 18 | 5.0 | 24 | 6.9 | 352 | 19 | 5.4 | 24 | 6.8 |
| Ohio | 4 958 | 615 | 12.4 | 688 | 13.9 | 4 914 | 606 | 12.3 | 670 | 13.6 |
| Oklahoma | 1 465 | 89 | 6.0 | 106 | 7.2 | 1 567 | 88 | 5.6 | 116 | 7.4 |
| Oregon | 1 554 | 243 | 15.6 | 264 | 17.0 | 1 586 | 235 | 14.8 | 256 | 16.2 |
| Pennsylvania | 5 525 | 703 | 12.7 | 754 | 13.7 | 5 601 | 747 | 13.3 | 804 | 14.4 |
| Rhode Island | 453 | 68 | 15.1 | 72 | 15.8 | 483 | 68 | 14.2 | 72 | 14.9 |
| South Carolina | 1 884 | 41 | 2.2 | 61 | 3.2 | 1 960 | 41 | 2.1 | 57 | 2.9 |
| South Dakota | 363 | 18 | 4.9 | 22 | 6.0 | 382 | 22 | 5.9 | 26 | 6.9 |
| Tennessee | 2 514 | 127 | 5.0 | 141 | 5.6 | 2 693 | 146 | 5.4 | 175 | 6.5 |
| Texas | 11 205 | 543 | 4.8 | 700 | 6.2 | 11 177 | 503 | 4.5 | 626 | 5.6 |
| Utah | 1 236 | 46 | 3.7 | 57 | 4.6 | 1 274 | 50 | 3.9 | 67 | 5.2 |
| Vermont | 286 | 32 | 11.1 | 37 | 13.1 | 284 | 36 | 12.6 | 42 | 14.7 |
| Virginia | 3 665 | 179 | 4.9 | 228 | 6.2 | 3 736 | 202 | 5.4 | 258 | 6.9 |
| Washington | 2 914 | 491 | 16.8 | 536 | 18.4 | 2 977 | 500 | 16.8 | 536 | 18.0 |
| West Virginia | 687 | 73 | 10.6 | 80 | 11.6 | 665 | 83 | 12.4 | 91 | 13.7 |
| Wisconsin | 2 626 | 306 | 11.7 | 327 | 12.5 | 2 682 | 223 | 8.3 | 253 | 9.4 |
| Wyoming | 255 | 17 | 6.7 | 19 | 7.5 | 261 | 19 | 7.1 | 22 | 8.2 |

Note: Updated population controls are introduced annually with the release of January data. Data refer to the sole or principal job of full- and part-time workers. Excluded are all self-employed workers, regardless of whether or not their businesses are incorporated.

[1]Data refer to members of a labor union or an employee association similar to a union.
[2]Data refer to members of a labor union or an employee association similar to a union, as well as to workers who report no union affiliation but whose jobs are covered by a union or an employee association contract.

# CHAPTER 9: PRICES

## HIGHLIGHTS

This chapter examines the movement of prices, which is one of the most important indicators of the state of the economy. Several indexes are covered: the Producer Price Index (PPI), which gives information about prices received by producers; the Consumer Price Index (CPI), which gives information about prices paid by consumers; and the Import Price Index (MPI) and the Export Price Index (XPI), which give information about prices involved in various foreign trade, export, and import price indexes.

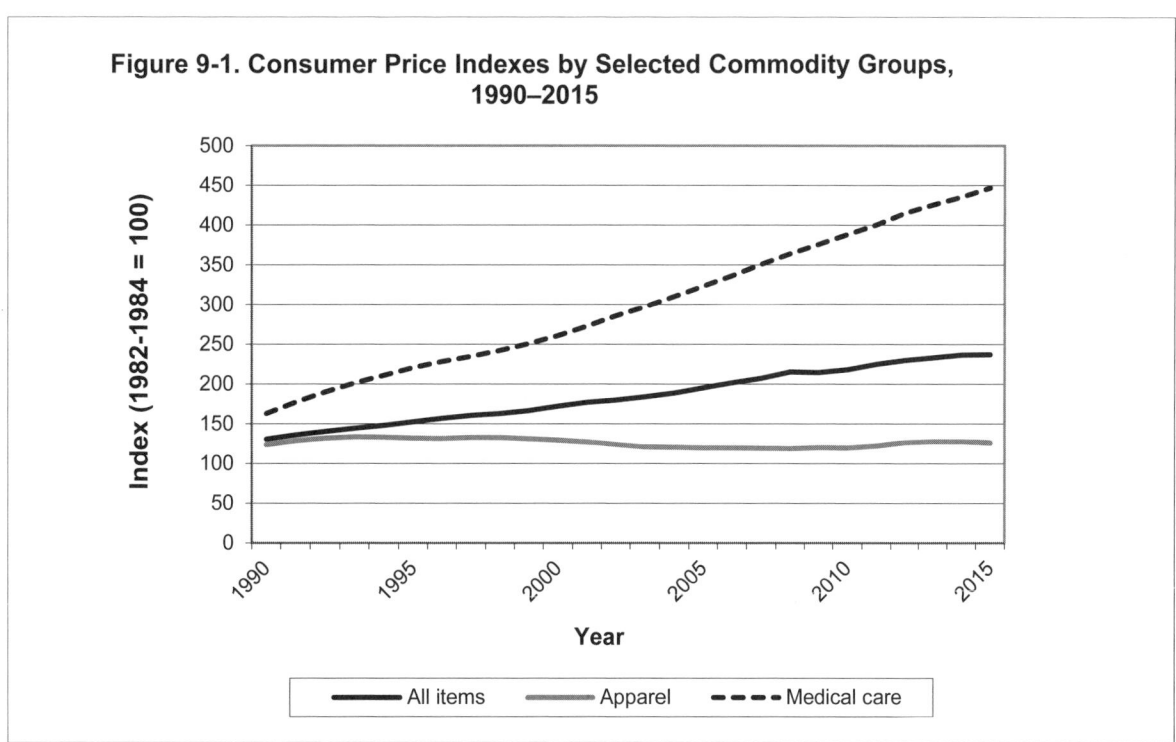

**Figure 9-1. Consumer Price Indexes by Selected Commodity Groups, 1990–2015**

The CPI-U increased slightly in 2015. It rose for all major groups listed in Table 9-2 except for apparel and transportation. The CPI for medical care continued to grow at a faster than average rate. In 2015, the CPI for medical care increased 2.6 percent while the CPI for all items only grew 0.1 percent. (See Table 9-2.)

## OTHER HIGHLIGHTS

- The PPI for all items decreased 7.3 percent after increasing the previous five years. (See Table 9-1.)

- From 2000 to 2015, the producer price index increased 43.5 percent. Chemicals and related products grew the fastest at 76.2 percent followed by farm products at 74.7 percent. (See Table 9-1.)

- The CPI-W decreased for only the second time since 1955 in 2015 dropping from 232.8 in 2014 to 231.8 in 2015. Previously, 2009 was the only other year in which the CPI-W experienced a decline. (See Table 9-5.)

- In 2015, the CPI for San Francisco-Oakland-San Jose grew the fastest at 2.6 percent while the CPI for Detroit-Ann Arbor-Flint declined the most at 1.4 percent. (See Table 9-8.)

# NOTES AND DEFINITIONS

## PRODUCER PRICE INDEX

### Coverage

The *Producer Price Index (PPI)* measures average changes in prices received by domestic producers of goods and services. PPIs measure price change from the perspective of the seller. This contrasts with other measures, such as the Consumer Price Index (CPI). CPIs measure price change from the purchaser's perspective. Sellers' and purchasers' prices can differ due to government subsidies, sales and excise taxes, and distribution costs.

The PPI is the oldest continuous series of the federal government. When first published in 1902, it covered the years from 1890 through 1901 and was named the Wholesale Price Index (WPI). It was renamed the Producer Price Index in 1978. Many major commodity-based indexes are available from the early 1900s. Indexes for the major stage-of-processing categories are available from 1947 to present. Most manufacturing and mining industry indexes, however, are available only since the early 1980s; most indexes for services began being introduced in the mid 2000s.

Over 25,000 establishments provide approximately 100,000 price quotations per month today. Establishments report selling prices on the Tuesday that includes the 13th of each month and they usually respond by mail or fax. Over 10,000 PPIs for individual products and groups of products are released each month.

PPIs are typically organized into one of three main structures: (1) industry classification, (2) commodity classification, and (3) commodity-based final demand-intermediate demand (FD-ID) system. The PPI publishes approximately 535 industry price indexes in combination with over 4,000 specific product line and product category sub-indexes, as well as, roughly 500 indexes for groupings of industries. The commodity classification structure of the PPI organizes products and services by similarity or material composition, regardless of the industry classification of the producing establishment. Commodity-based FD-ID price indexes regroup commodity indexes for goods, services, and construction at the subproduct class (six-digit) level, according to the type of buyer and the amount of physical processing or assembling the products have undergone.

The PPI is widely used in many aspects of business and government. It is commonly used as an economic indicator, a deflator of other economic series, and as a basis for contract escalation.

A PPI may go out of publication if there is not cooperation from a minimum number of establishments or if in any given month, the index does not have actual prices from a minimum number of reporting units.

### Sources of Additional Information

For more information on the underlying concepts and methodology of the Producer Price Index, see Chapter 14 in the *BLS Handbook of Methods,* which is available on the BLS Web site at http://www.bls.gov/opub/hom/.

## Table 9-1. Producer Price Indexes, by Commodity Group, 1913–2015

(1982 = 100.)

| Year | All commodities | Farm products | Processed foods and feeds | Industrial commodities Total | Textile products and apparel | Hides, leather, and related products | Fuels and related products and power | Chemicals and related products | Rubber and plastics products | Lumber and wood products | Pulp, paper, and allied products | Metals and metal products | Machinery and equipment | Furniture and household durables | Nonmetallic mineral products | Transportation equipment | Miscellaneous products |
|---|---|---|---|---|---|---|---|---|---|---|---|---|---|---|---|---|---|
| 1913 | 12.0 | 18.0 | ... | 11.9 | ... | ... | ... | ... | ... | ... | ... | ... | ... | ... | ... | ... | ... |
| 1914 | 11.8 | 17.9 | ... | 11.3 | ... | ... | ... | ... | ... | ... | ... | ... | ... | ... | ... | ... | ... |
| 1915 | 12.0 | 18.0 | ... | 11.6 | ... | ... | ... | ... | ... | ... | ... | ... | ... | ... | ... | ... | ... |
| 1916 | 14.7 | 21.3 | ... | 15.0 | ... | ... | ... | ... | ... | ... | ... | ... | ... | ... | ... | ... | ... |
| 1917 | 20.2 | 32.6 | ... | 19.5 | ... | ... | ... | ... | ... | ... | ... | ... | ... | ... | ... | ... | ... |
| 1918 | 22.6 | 37.4 | ... | 21.1 | ... | ... | ... | ... | ... | ... | ... | ... | ... | ... | ... | ... | ... |
| 1919 | 23.9 | 39.8 | ... | 22.0 | ... | ... | ... | ... | ... | ... | ... | ... | ... | ... | ... | ... | ... |
| 1920 | 26.6 | 38.0 | ... | 27.4 | ... | ... | ... | ... | ... | ... | ... | ... | ... | ... | ... | ... | ... |
| 1921 | 16.8 | 22.3 | ... | 17.8 | ... | ... | ... | ... | ... | ... | ... | ... | ... | ... | ... | ... | ... |
| 1922 | 16.7 | 23.7 | ... | 17.4 | ... | ... | ... | ... | ... | ... | ... | ... | ... | ... | ... | ... | ... |
| 1923 | 17.3 | 24.9 | ... | 17.8 | ... | ... | ... | ... | ... | ... | ... | ... | ... | ... | ... | ... | ... |
| 1924 | 16.9 | 25.2 | ... | 17.0 | ... | ... | ... | ... | ... | ... | ... | ... | ... | ... | ... | ... | ... |
| 1925 | 17.8 | 27.7 | ... | 17.5 | ... | ... | ... | ... | ... | ... | ... | ... | ... | ... | ... | ... | ... |
| 1926 | 17.2 | 25.3 | ... | 17.0 | ... | 17.1 | 10.3 | ... | 47.1 | 9.3 | ... | 13.7 | ... | 28.6 | 16.4 | ... | ... |
| 1927 | 16.5 | 25.1 | ... | 16.0 | ... | 18.4 | 9.1 | ... | 35.7 | 8.8 | ... | 12.9 | ... | 27.9 | 15.7 | ... | ... |
| 1928 | 16.7 | 26.7 | ... | 15.8 | ... | 20.7 | 8.7 | ... | 28.3 | 8.5 | ... | 12.9 | ... | 27.2 | 16.2 | ... | ... |
| 1929 | 16.4 | 26.4 | ... | 15.6 | ... | 18.6 | 8.6 | ... | 24.6 | 8.8 | ... | 13.3 | ... | 27.0 | 16.0 | ... | ... |
| 1930 | 14.9 | 22.4 | ... | 14.5 | ... | 17.1 | 8.1 | ... | 21.5 | 8.0 | ... | 12.0 | ... | 26.5 | 15.9 | ... | ... |
| 1931 | 12.6 | 16.4 | ... | 12.8 | ... | 14.7 | 7.0 | ... | 18.3 | 6.5 | ... | 10.8 | ... | 24.4 | 14.9 | ... | ... |
| 1932 | 11.2 | 12.2 | ... | 11.9 | ... | 12.5 | 7.3 | ... | 15.9 | 5.6 | ... | 9.9 | ... | 21.5 | 13.9 | ... | ... |
| 1933 | 11.4 | 13.0 | ... | 12.1 | ... | 13.8 | 6.9 | 16.2 | 16.7 | 6.7 | ... | 10.2 | ... | 21.6 | 14.7 | ... | ... |
| 1934 | 12.9 | 16.5 | ... | 13.3 | ... | 14.8 | 7.6 | 17.0 | 19.5 | 7.8 | ... | 11.2 | ... | 23.4 | 15.7 | ... | ... |
| 1935 | 13.8 | 19.8 | ... | 13.3 | ... | 15.3 | 7.6 | 17.7 | 19.6 | 7.5 | ... | 11.2 | ... | 23.2 | 15.7 | ... | ... |
| 1936 | 13.9 | 20.4 | ... | 13.5 | ... | 16.3 | 7.9 | 17.8 | 21.1 | 7.9 | ... | 11.4 | ... | 23.6 | 15.8 | ... | ... |
| 1937 | 14.9 | 21.8 | ... | 14.5 | ... | 17.9 | 8.0 | 18.6 | 24.9 | 9.3 | ... | 13.1 | ... | 26.1 | 16.1 | ... | ... |
| 1938 | 13.5 | 17.3 | ... | 13.9 | ... | 15.8 | 7.9 | 17.7 | 24.4 | 8.5 | ... | 12.6 | ... | 25.5 | 15.6 | ... | ... |
| 1939 | 13.3 | 16.5 | ... | 13.9 | ... | 16.3 | 7.5 | 17.6 | 25.4 | 8.7 | ... | 12.5 | 14.8 | 25.4 | 15.3 | ... | ... |
| 1940 | 13.5 | 17.1 | ... | 14.1 | ... | 17.2 | 7.4 | 17.9 | 23.7 | 9.6 | ... | 12.5 | 14.9 | 26.0 | 15.3 | ... | ... |
| 1941 | 15.1 | 20.8 | ... | 15.1 | ... | 18.4 | 7.9 | 19.5 | 25.5 | 11.5 | ... | 12.8 | 15.1 | 27.6 | 15.7 | ... | ... |
| 1942 | 17.0 | 26.7 | ... | 16.2 | ... | 20.1 | 8.1 | 21.7 | 29.7 | 12.5 | ... | 13.0 | 15.4 | 29.9 | 16.3 | ... | ... |
| 1943 | 17.8 | 30.9 | ... | 16.5 | ... | 20.1 | 8.3 | 21.9 | 30.5 | 13.2 | ... | 12.9 | 15.2 | 29.7 | 16.4 | ... | ... |
| 1944 | 17.9 | 31.2 | ... | 16.7 | ... | 19.9 | 8.6 | 22.2 | 30.1 | 14.3 | ... | 12.9 | 15.1 | 30.5 | 16.7 | ... | ... |
| 1945 | 18.2 | 32.4 | ... | 17.0 | ... | 20.1 | 8.7 | 22.3 | 29.2 | 14.5 | ... | 13.1 | 15.1 | 30.5 | 17.4 | ... | ... |
| 1946 | 20.8 | 37.5 | ... | 18.6 | ... | 23.3 | 9.3 | 24.1 | 29.3 | 16.6 | ... | 14.7 | 16.6 | 32.4 | 18.5 | ... | ... |
| 1947 | 25.6 | 45.1 | 33.0 | 22.7 | 50.6 | 31.7 | 11.1 | 32.1 | 29.2 | 25.8 | 25.1 | 18.2 | 19.3 | 37.2 | 20.7 | ... | 26.6 |
| 1948 | 27.7 | 48.5 | 35.3 | 24.6 | 52.8 | 32.1 | 13.1 | 32.8 | 30.2 | 29.5 | 26.2 | 20.7 | 20.9 | 39.4 | 22.4 | ... | 27.7 |
| 1949 | 26.3 | 41.9 | 32.1 | 24.1 | 48.3 | 30.4 | 12.4 | 30.0 | 29.2 | 27.3 | 25.1 | 20.9 | 21.9 | 40.1 | 23.0 | ... | 28.2 |
| 1950 | 27.3 | 44.0 | 33.2 | 25.0 | 50.2 | 32.9 | 12.6 | 30.4 | 35.6 | 31.4 | 25.7 | 22.0 | 22.6 | 40.9 | 23.5 | ... | 28.6 |
| 1951 | 30.4 | 51.2 | 36.9 | 27.6 | 56.0 | 37.7 | 13.0 | 34.8 | 43.7 | 34.1 | 30.5 | 24.5 | 25.3 | 44.4 | 25.0 | ... | 30.3 |
| 1952 | 29.6 | 48.4 | 36.4 | 26.9 | 50.5 | 30.5 | 13.0 | 33.0 | 39.6 | 33.2 | 29.7 | 24.5 | 25.3 | 43.5 | 25.0 | ... | 30.2 |
| 1953 | 29.2 | 43.8 | 34.8 | 27.2 | 49.3 | 31.0 | 13.4 | 33.4 | 36.9 | 33.1 | 29.6 | 25.3 | 25.9 | 44.4 | 26.0 | ... | 31.0 |
| 1954 | 29.3 | 43.2 | 35.4 | 27.2 | 48.2 | 29.5 | 13.2 | 33.8 | 37.5 | 32.5 | 29.6 | 25.5 | 26.3 | 44.9 | 26.6 | ... | 31.3 |
| 1955 | 29.3 | 40.5 | 33.8 | 27.8 | 48.2 | 29.4 | 13.2 | 33.7 | 42.4 | 34.1 | 30.4 | 27.2 | 27.2 | 45.1 | 27.3 | ... | 31.3 |
| 1956 | 30.3 | 40.0 | 33.8 | 29.1 | 48.2 | 31.2 | 13.6 | 33.9 | 43.0 | 34.6 | 32.4 | 29.6 | 29.3 | 46.3 | 28.5 | ... | 31.7 |
| 1957 | 31.2 | 41.1 | 34.8 | 29.9 | 48.3 | 31.2 | 14.3 | 34.6 | 42.8 | 32.8 | 33.0 | 30.2 | 31.4 | 47.5 | 29.6 | ... | 32.6 |
| 1958 | 31.6 | 42.9 | 36.5 | 30.0 | 47.4 | 31.6 | 13.7 | 34.9 | 42.8 | 32.5 | 33.4 | 30.0 | 32.1 | 47.9 | 29.9 | ... | 33.3 |
| 1959 | 31.7 | 40.2 | 35.6 | 30.5 | 48.1 | 35.9 | 13.7 | 34.8 | 42.6 | 34.7 | 33.7 | 30.6 | 32.8 | 48.0 | 30.3 | ... | 33.4 |
| 1960 | 31.7 | 40.1 | 35.6 | 30.5 | 48.6 | 34.6 | 13.9 | 34.8 | 42.7 | 33.5 | 34.0 | 30.6 | 33.0 | 47.8 | 30.4 | ... | 33.6 |
| 1961 | 31.6 | 39.7 | 36.2 | 30.4 | 47.8 | 34.9 | 14.0 | 34.5 | 41.1 | 32.0 | 33.0 | 30.5 | 33.0 | 47.5 | 30.5 | ... | 33.7 |
| 1962 | 31.7 | 40.4 | 36.5 | 30.4 | 48.2 | 35.3 | 14.0 | 33.9 | 39.9 | 32.2 | 33.4 | 30.2 | 33.0 | 47.2 | 30.5 | ... | 33.9 |
| 1963 | 31.6 | 39.6 | 36.8 | 30.3 | 48.2 | 34.3 | 13.9 | 33.5 | 40.1 | 32.8 | 33.1 | 30.3 | 33.1 | 46.9 | 30.3 | ... | 34.2 |
| 1964 | 31.6 | 39.0 | 36.7 | 30.5 | 48.5 | 34.4 | 13.5 | 33.6 | 39.6 | 33.5 | 33.0 | 31.1 | 33.3 | 47.1 | 30.4 | ... | 34.4 |

. . . = Not available.

## Table 9-1. Producer Price Indexes, by Commodity Group, 1913–2015—*Continued*

(1982 = 100.)

| Year | All com-modities | Farm products | Processed foods and feeds | Industrial commodities Total | Textile products and apparel | Hides, leather, and related products | Fuels and related products and power | Chemi-cals and related products | Rubber and plastics products | Lumber and wood products | Pulp, paper, and allied products | Metals and metal products | Machin-ery and equip-ment | Furniture and house-hold durables | Non-metallic mineral products | Trans-porta-tion equip-ment | Miscel-laneous products |
|---|---|---|---|---|---|---|---|---|---|---|---|---|---|---|---|---|---|
| 1965 ................. | 32.3 | 40.7 | 38.0 | 30.9 | 48.8 | 35.9 | 13.8 | 33.9 | 39.7 | 33.7 | 33.3 | 32.0 | 33.7 | 46.8 | 30.4 | . . . | 34.7 |
| 1966 ................. | 33.3 | 43.7 | 40.2 | 31.5 | 48.9 | 39.4 | 14.1 | 34.0 | 40.5 | 35.2 | 34.2 | 32.8 | 34.7 | 47.4 | 30.7 | . . . | 35.3 |
| 1967 ................. | 33.4 | 41.3 | 39.8 | 32.0 | 48.9 | 38.1 | 14.4 | 34.2 | 41.4 | 35.1 | 34.6 | 33.2 | 35.9 | 48.3 | 31.2 | . . . | 36.2 |
| 1968 ................. | 34.2 | 42.3 | 40.6 | 32.8 | 50.7 | 39.3 | 14.3 | 34.1 | 42.8 | 39.8 | 35.0 | 34.0 | 37.0 | 49.7 | 32.4 | . . . | 37.0 |
| 1969 ................. | 35.6 | 45.0 | 42.7 | 33.9 | 51.8 | 41.5 | 14.6 | 34.2 | 43.6 | 44.0 | 36.0 | 36.0 | 38.2 | 50.7 | 33.6 | 40.4 | 38.1 |
| 1970 ................. | 36.9 | 45.8 | 44.6 | 35.2 | 52.4 | 42.0 | 15.3 | 35.0 | 44.9 | 39.9 | 37.5 | 38.7 | 40.0 | 51.9 | 35.3 | 41.9 | 39.8 |
| 1971 ................. | 38.1 | 46.6 | 45.5 | 36.5 | 53.3 | 43.4 | 16.6 | 35.6 | 45.2 | 44.7 | 38.1 | 39.4 | 41.4 | 53.1 | 38.2 | 44.2 | 40.8 |
| 1972 ................. | 39.8 | 51.6 | 48.0 | 37.8 | 55.5 | 50.0 | 17.1 | 35.6 | 45.3 | 50.7 | 39.3 | 40.9 | 42.3 | 53.8 | 39.4 | 45.5 | 41.5 |
| 1973 ................. | 45.0 | 72.7 | 58.9 | 40.3 | 60.5 | 54.5 | 19.4 | 37.6 | 46.6 | 62.2 | 42.3 | 44.0 | 43.7 | 55.7 | 40.7 | 46.1 | 43.3 |
| 1974 ................. | 53.5 | 77.4 | 68.0 | 49.2 | 68.0 | 55.2 | 30.1 | 50.2 | 56.4 | 64.5 | 52.5 | 57.0 | 50.0 | 61.8 | 47.8 | 50.3 | 48.1 |
| 1975 ................. | 58.4 | 77.0 | 72.6 | 54.9 | 67.4 | 56.5 | 35.4 | 62.0 | 62.2 | 62.1 | 59.0 | 61.5 | 57.9 | 67.5 | 54.4 | 56.7 | 53.4 |
| 1976 ................. | 61.1 | 78.8 | 70.8 | 58.4 | 72.4 | 63.9 | 38.3 | 64.0 | 66.0 | 72.2 | 62.1 | 65.0 | 61.3 | 70.3 | 58.2 | 60.5 | 55.6 |
| 1977 ................. | 64.9 | 79.4 | 74.0 | 62.5 | 75.3 | 68.3 | 43.6 | 65.9 | 69.4 | 83.0 | 64.6 | 69.3 | 65.2 | 73.2 | 62.6 | 64.6 | 59.4 |
| 1978 ................. | 69.9 | 87.7 | 80.6 | 67.0 | 78.1 | 76.1 | 46.5 | 68.0 | 72.4 | 96.9 | 67.7 | 75.3 | 70.3 | 77.5 | 69.6 | 69.5 | 66.7 |
| 1979 ................. | 78.7 | 99.6 | 88.5 | 75.7 | 82.5 | 96.1 | 58.9 | 76.0 | 80.5 | 105.5 | 75.9 | 86.0 | 76.7 | 82.8 | 77.6 | 75.3 | 75.5 |
| 1980 ................. | 89.8 | 102.9 | 95.9 | 88.0 | 89.7 | 94.7 | 82.8 | 89.0 | 90.1 | 101.5 | 86.3 | 95.0 | 86.0 | 90.7 | 88.4 | 82.9 | 93.6 |
| 1981 ................. | 98.0 | 105.2 | 98.9 | 97.4 | 97.6 | 99.3 | 100.2 | 98.4 | 96.4 | 102.8 | 94.8 | 99.6 | 94.4 | 95.9 | 96.7 | 94.3 | 96.1 |
| 1982 ................. | 100.0 | 100.0 | 100.0 | 100.0 | 100.0 | 100.0 | 100.0 | 100.0 | 100.0 | 100.0 | 100.0 | 100.0 | 100.0 | 100.0 | 100.0 | 100.0 | 100.0 |
| 1983 ................. | 101.3 | 102.4 | 101.8 | 101.1 | 100.3 | 103.2 | 95.9 | 100.3 | 100.8 | 107.9 | 103.3 | 101.8 | 102.7 | 103.4 | 101.6 | 102.8 | 104.8 |
| 1984 ................. | 103.7 | 105.5 | 105.4 | 103.3 | 102.7 | 109.0 | 94.8 | 102.9 | 102.3 | 108.0 | 110.3 | 104.8 | 105.1 | 105.7 | 105.4 | 105.2 | 107.0 |
| 1985 ................. | 103.2 | 95.1 | 103.5 | 103.7 | 102.9 | 108.9 | 91.4 | 103.7 | 101.9 | 106.6 | 113.3 | 104.4 | 107.2 | 107.1 | 108.6 | 107.9 | 109.4 |
| 1986 ................. | 100.2 | 92.9 | 105.4 | 100.0 | 103.2 | 113.0 | 69.8 | 102.6 | 101.9 | 107.2 | 116.1 | 103.2 | 108.8 | 108.2 | 110.0 | 110.5 | 111.6 |
| 1987 ................. | 102.8 | 95.5 | 107.9 | 102.6 | 105.1 | 120.4 | 70.2 | 106.4 | 103.0 | 112.8 | 121.8 | 107.1 | 110.4 | 109.9 | 110.0 | 112.5 | 114.9 |
| 1988 ................. | 106.9 | 104.9 | 112.7 | 106.3 | 109.2 | 131.4 | 66.7 | 116.3 | 109.3 | 118.9 | 130.4 | 118.7 | 113.2 | 111.1 | 111.2 | 114.3 | 120.2 |
| 1989 ................. | 112.2 | 110.9 | 117.8 | 111.6 | 112.3 | 136.3 | 72.9 | 123.0 | 112.6 | 126.7 | 137.8 | 124.1 | 117.4 | 116.9 | 112.6 | 117.7 | 126.5 |
| 1990 ................. | 116.3 | 112.2 | 121.9 | 115.8 | 115.0 | 141.7 | 82.3 | 123.6 | 113.6 | 129.7 | 141.2 | 122.9 | 120.7 | 119.2 | 114.7 | 121.5 | 134.2 |
| 1991 ................. | 116.5 | 105.7 | 121.9 | 116.5 | 116.3 | 138.9 | 81.2 | 125.6 | 115.1 | 132.1 | 142.9 | 120.2 | 123.0 | 121.2 | 117.2 | 126.4 | 140.8 |
| 1992 ................. | 117.2 | 103.6 | 122.1 | 117.4 | 117.8 | 140.4 | 80.4 | 125.9 | 115.1 | 146.6 | 145.2 | 119.2 | 123.4 | 122.2 | 117.3 | 130.4 | 145.3 |
| 1993 ................. | 118.9 | 107.1 | 124.0 | 119.0 | 118.0 | 143.7 | 80.0 | 128.2 | 116.0 | 174.0 | 147.3 | 119.2 | 124.0 | 123.7 | 120.0 | 133.7 | 145.4 |
| 1994 ................. | 120.4 | 106.3 | 125.5 | 120.7 | 118.3 | 148.5 | 77.8 | 132.1 | 117.6 | 180.0 | 152.5 | 124.8 | 125.1 | 126.1 | 124.2 | 137.2 | 141.9 |
| 1995 ................. | 124.7 | 107.4 | 127.0 | 125.5 | 120.8 | 153.7 | 78.0 | 142.5 | 124.3 | 178.1 | 172.2 | 134.5 | 126.6 | 128.2 | 129.0 | 139.7 | 145.4 |
| 1996 ................. | 127.7 | 122.4 | 133.3 | 127.3 | 122.4 | 150.5 | 85.8 | 142.1 | 123.8 | 176.1 | 168.7 | 131.0 | 126.5 | 130.4 | 131.0 | 141.7 | 147.7 |
| 1997 ................. | 127.6 | 112.9 | 134.0 | 127.7 | 122.6 | 154.2 | 86.1 | 143.6 | 123.2 | 183.8 | 167.9 | 131.8 | 125.9 | 130.8 | 133.2 | 141.6 | 150.9 |
| 1998 ................. | 124.4 | 104.6 | 131.6 | 124.8 | 122.9 | 148.0 | 75.3 | 143.9 | 122.6 | 179.1 | 171.7 | 127.8 | 124.9 | 131.3 | 135.4 | 141.2 | 156.0 |
| 1999 ................. | 125.5 | 98.4 | 131.1 | 126.5 | 121.1 | 146.0 | 80.5 | 144.2 | 122.5 | 183.6 | 174.1 | 124.6 | 124.3 | 131.7 | 138.9 | 141.8 | 166.6 |
| 2000 ................. | 132.7 | 99.5 | 133.1 | 134.8 | 121.4 | 151.5 | 103.5 | 151.0 | 125.5 | 178.2 | 183.7 | 128.1 | 124.0 | 132.6 | 142.5 | 143.8 | 170.8 |
| 2001 ................. | 134.2 | 103.8 | 137.3 | 135.7 | 121.3 | 158.4 | 105.3 | 151.8 | 127.2 | 174.4 | 184.8 | 125.4 | 123.7 | 133.2 | 144.3 | 145.2 | 181.3 |
| 2002 ................. | 131.1 | 99.0 | 136.2 | 132.4 | 119.9 | 157.6 | 93.2 | 151.9 | 126.8 | 173.3 | 185.9 | 125.9 | 122.9 | 133.5 | 146.2 | 144.6 | 182.4 |
| 2003 ................. | 138.1 | 111.5 | 143.4 | 139.1 | 119.8 | 162.3 | 112.9 | 161.8 | 130.1 | 177.4 | 190.0 | 129.2 | 121.9 | 133.9 | 148.2 | 145.7 | 179.6 |
| 2004 ................. | 146.7 | 123.3 | 151.2 | 147.6 | 121.0 | 164.5 | 126.9 | 174.4 | 133.8 | 195.6 | 195.7 | 149.6 | 122.1 | 135.1 | 153.2 | 148.6 | 183.2 |
| 2005 ................. | 157.4 | 118.5 | 153.1 | 160.2 | 122.8 | 165.4 | 156.4 | 192.0 | 143.8 | 196.5 | 202.6 | 160.8 | 123.7 | 139.4 | 164.2 | 151.0 | 195.1 |
| 2006 ................. | 164.7 | 117.0 | 153.8 | 168.8 | 124.5 | 168.4 | 166.7 | 205.8 | 153.8 | 194.4 | 209.8 | 181.6 | 126.2 | 142.6 | 179.9 | 152.6 | 205.6 |
| 2007 ................. | 172.6 | 143.4 | 165.1 | 175.1 | 125.8 | 173.6 | 177.6 | 214.8 | 155.0 | 192.4 | 216.9 | 193.5 | 127.3 | 144.7 | 186.2 | 155.0 | 210.3 |
| 2008 ................. | 189.6 | 161.3 | 180.5 | 192.3 | 128.9 | 173.1 | 214.6 | 245.5 | 165.9 | 191.3 | 226.8 | 213.0 | 129.7 | 148.9 | 197.1 | 158.6 | 216.6 |
| 2009 ................. | 172.9 | 134.6 | 176.2 | 174.8 | 129.5 | 157.0 | 158.7 | 229.4 | 165.2 | 182.8 | 225.6 | 186.8 | 131.3 | 153.1 | 202.4 | 162.2 | 217.5 |
| 2010 ................. | 184.7 | 151.0 | 182.3 | 187.0 | 131.7 | 181.4 | 185.8 | 246.6 | 170.7 | 192.7 | 236.9 | 207.6 | 131.1 | 153.2 | 201.8 | 163.4 | 221.5 |
| 2011 ................. | 201.0 | 186.7 | 197.5 | 202.0 | 141.7 | 199.9 | 215.9 | 275.1 | 182.7 | 194.7 | 245.1 | 225.9 | 132.7 | 156.4 | 205.0 | 166.1 | 229.2 |
| 2012 ................. | 202.2 | 192.5 | 205.2 | 202.1 | 142.2 | 202.3 | 212.1 | 276.6 | 186.9 | 201.6 | 244.2 | 219.9 | 134.2 | 160.6 | 211.0 | 169.8 | 235.6 |
| 2013 ................. | 203.4 | 195.3 | 208.3 | 203.0 | 143.4 | 217.9 | 211.8 | 279.2 | 189.0 | 214.9 | 248.8 | 213.5 | 135.2 | 161.1 | 216.9 | 171.8 | 239.5 |
| 2014 ................. | 205.3 | 197.4 | 216.5 | 204.1 | 145.5 | 229.1 | 209.8 | 280.9 | 190.2 | 224.2 | 250.5 | 215.0 | 136.2 | 163.2 | 223.7 | 174.1 | 243.0 |
| 2015 ................. | 190.4 | 173.8 | 209.1 | 188.8 | 144.1 | 210.4 | 160.5 | 266.0 | 187.0 | 221.9 | 248.8 | 200.3 | 136.9 | 164.7 | 228.9 | 176.5 | 247.4 |

. . . = Not available.

# NOTES AND DEFINITIONS

## CONSUMER PRICE INDEX

The Consumer Price Index (CPI) is a measure of the average change over time in the prices of consumer items—goods and services that people buy for day-to-day living. The CPI is a complex construct that combines economic theory with sampling and other statistical techniques and uses data from several surveys to produce a timely and precise measure of average price change for the consumption sector of the American economy.

The Bureau of Labor Statistics (BLS) publishes CPIs for the following population groups: (1) the CPI for Urban Wage Earners and Clerical Workers (CPI-W), which covers households of wage earners and clerical workers that comprise approximately 32 percent of the total population and (2) the CPI for All Urban Consumers (CPI-U) and the Chained CPI for All Urban Consumers (C-CPI-U), which cover approximately 87 percent of the total population and include in addition to wage earners and clerical worker households, groups such as professional, managerial, and technical workers, the self-employed, short-term workers, the unemployed, and retirees and others not in the labor force. BLS began publishing the CPI-U in January 1978, but did not begin publishing the C-CPI-U until August 2002 with data beginning in January 2000. The CPI-W is much older than either the CPI-U or C-CPI-U.

The CPIs are based on prices of food, clothing, shelter, and fuels, transportation fares, charges for doctors' and dentists' services, drugs, and other goods and services that people buy for day-to-day living. Prices are collected each month in 87 urban areas across the country from about 23,000 retail and service establishments. Data on rents are collected from about 50,000 landlords or tenants. All taxes directly associated with the purchase and use of items are included in the index.

Various indexes have been devised to measure different aspects of inflation. The CPI measures inflation as experienced by consumers in their day-to-day living expenses; the Producer Price Index (PPI), as described earlier in this chapter, measures inflation at earlier stages of the production process; the Employment Cost Index (ECI), as described in Chapter 6, measures it in the labor market; the BLS International Price Program measures it for imports and exports; and the Gross Domestic Product Deflator (GDP Deflator) measures inflation experienced by both consumers themselves as well as governments and other institutions providing goods and services to consumers. Finally, there are specialized measures, such as measures of interest rates. The CPI is generally the best measure for adjusting payments to consumers when the intent is to allow consumers to purchase at today's prices, a market basket of goods and services equivalent to one that they could purchase in an earlier period.

The CPI does have some limitation, however. The CPI may not be applicable to all population groups. For example, the CPI-U is designed to measure inflation for the U.S. urban population and thus may not accurately reflect the experience of people living in rural areas. In addition, the CPI does not produce official estimates for the rate of inflation experienced by subgroups of the population, such as the elderly or the poor.

The Consumer Price Index Research Series Using Current Methods (CPI-U-RS), shown in Table 9-10 provides estimates for the period since 1977 of what the CPI would have been had the most current methods been in effect. Each time there are new methods introduced into the CPI, the CPI-U-RS is revised from 1978 forward.

The CPI-U-RS provides an annual inflation series that adjusts only for specified changes in BLS methodology. It does not incorporate all possible research results on past inflation.

### Sources of Additional Information

An extensive description of the methodology is available in the updated version of Chapter 17 in the *BLS Handbook of Methods*. Additional detailed data can be found in the *Consumer Price Index Detailed Report* and in special reports. These resources can be found on the BLS Web site at <http://www.bls.gov>.

### Table 9-2. Consumer Price Indexes, All Urban Consumers (CPI-U): U.S. City Average, Major Groups, 1957–2015

(1982–1984 = 100, unless otherwise specified.)

| Year | All items | Food and beverages | Housing | Apparel | Transportation | Medical care | Recreation[1] | Education and communication[1] | Other goods and services |
|---|---|---|---|---|---|---|---|---|---|
| 1957 | 28.1 | . . . | . . . | 44.5 | 27.7 | 19.7 | . . . | . . . | . . . |
| 1958 | 28.9 | . . . | . . . | 44.6 | 28.6 | 20.6 | . . . | . . . | . . . |
| 1959 | 29.1 | . . . | . . . | 45.0 | 29.8 | 21.5 | . . . | . . . | . . . |
| 1960 | 29.6 | . . . | . . . | 45.7 | 29.8 | 22.3 | . . . | . . . | . . . |
| 1961 | 29.9 | . . . | . . . | 46.1 | 30.1 | 22.9 | . . . | . . . | . . . |
| 1962 | 30.2 | . . . | . . . | 46.3 | 30.8 | 23.5 | . . . | . . . | . . . |
| 1963 | 30.6 | . . . | . . . | 46.9 | 30.9 | 24.1 | . . . | . . . | . . . |
| 1964 | 31.0 | . . . | . . . | 47.3 | 31.4 | 24.6 | . . . | . . . | . . . |
| 1965 | 31.5 | . . . | . . . | 47.8 | 31.9 | 25.2 | . . . | . . . | . . . |
| 1966 | 32.4 | . . . | . . . | 49.0 | 32.3 | 26.3 | . . . | . . . | . . . |
| 1967 | 33.4 | 35.0 | 30.8 | 51.0 | 33.3 | 28.2 | . . . | . . . | 35.1 |
| 1968 | 34.8 | 36.2 | 32.0 | 53.7 | 34.3 | 29.9 | . . . | . . . | 36.9 |
| 1969 | 36.7 | 38.1 | 34.0 | 56.8 | 35.7 | 31.9 | . . . | . . . | 38.7 |
| 1970 | 38.8 | 40.1 | 36.4 | 59.2 | 37.5 | 34.0 | . . . | . . . | 40.9 |
| 1971 | 40.5 | 41.4 | 38.0 | 61.1 | 39.5 | 36.1 | . . . | . . . | 42.9 |
| 1972 | 41.8 | 43.1 | 39.4 | 62.3 | 39.9 | 37.3 | . . . | . . . | 44.7 |
| 1973 | 44.4 | 48.8 | 41.2 | 64.6 | 41.2 | 38.8 | . . . | . . . | 46.4 |
| 1974 | 49.3 | 55.5 | 45.8 | 69.4 | 45.8 | 42.4 | . . . | . . . | 49.8 |
| 1975 | 53.8 | 60.2 | 50.7 | 72.5 | 50.1 | 47.5 | . . . | . . . | 53.9 |
| 1976 | 56.9 | 62.1 | 53.8 | 75.2 | 55.1 | 52.0 | . . . | . . . | 57.0 |
| 1977 | 60.6 | 65.8 | 57.4 | 78.6 | 59.0 | 57.0 | . . . | . . . | 60.4 |
| 1978 | 65.2 | 72.2 | 62.4 | 81.4 | 61.7 | 61.8 | . . . | . . . | 64.3 |
| 1979 | 72.6 | 79.9 | 70.1 | 84.9 | 70.5 | 67.5 | . . . | . . . | 68.9 |
| 1980 | 82.4 | 86.7 | 81.1 | 90.9 | 83.1 | 74.9 | . . . | . . . | 75.2 |
| 1981 | 90.9 | 93.5 | 90.4 | 95.3 | 93.2 | 82.9 | . . . | . . . | 82.6 |
| 1982 | 96.5 | 97.3 | 96.9 | 97.8 | 97.0 | 92.5 | . . . | . . . | 91.1 |
| 1983 | 99.6 | 99.5 | 99.5 | 100.2 | 99.3 | 100.6 | . . . | . . . | 101.1 |
| 1984 | 103.9 | 103.2 | 103.6 | 102.1 | 103.7 | 106.8 | . . . | . . . | 107.9 |
| 1985 | 107.6 | 105.6 | 107.7 | 105.0 | 106.4 | 113.5 | . . . | . . . | 114.5 |
| 1986 | 109.6 | 109.1 | 110.9 | 105.9 | 102.3 | 122.0 | . . . | . . . | 121.4 |
| 1987 | 113.6 | 113.5 | 114.2 | 110.6 | 105.4 | 130.1 | . . . | . . . | 128.5 |
| 1988 | 118.3 | 118.2 | 118.5 | 115.4 | 108.7 | 138.6 | . . . | . . . | 137.0 |
| 1989 | 124.0 | 124.9 | 123.0 | 118.6 | 114.1 | 149.3 | . . . | . . . | 147.7 |
| 1990 | 130.7 | 132.1 | 128.5 | 124.1 | 120.5 | 162.8 | . . . | . . . | 159.0 |
| 1991 | 136.2 | 136.8 | 133.6 | 128.7 | 123.8 | 177.0 | . . . | . . . | 171.6 |
| 1992 | 140.3 | 138.7 | 137.5 | 131.9 | 126.5 | 190.1 | . . . | . . . | 183.3 |
| 1993 | 144.5 | 141.6 | 141.2 | 133.7 | 130.4 | 201.4 | 90.7 | 85.5 | 192.9 |
| 1994 | 148.2 | 144.9 | 144.8 | 133.4 | 134.3 | 211.0 | 92.7 | 88.8 | 198.5 |
| 1995 | 152.4 | 148.9 | 148.5 | 132.0 | 139.1 | 220.5 | 94.5 | 92.2 | 206.9 |
| 1996 | 156.9 | 153.7 | 152.8 | 131.7 | 143.0 | 228.2 | 97.4 | 95.3 | 215.4 |
| 1997 | 160.5 | 157.7 | 156.8 | 132.9 | 144.3 | 234.6 | 99.6 | 98.4 | 224.8 |
| 1998 | 163.0 | 161.1 | 160.4 | 133.0 | 141.6 | 242.1 | 101.1 | 100.3 | 237.7 |
| 1999 | 166.6 | 164.6 | 163.9 | 131.3 | 144.4 | 250.6 | 102.0 | 101.2 | 258.3 |
| 2000 | 172.2 | 168.4 | 169.6 | 129.6 | 153.3 | 260.8 | 103.3 | 102.5 | 271.1 |
| 2001 | 177.1 | 173.6 | 176.4 | 127.3 | 154.3 | 272.8 | 104.9 | 105.2 | 282.6 |
| 2002 | 179.9 | 176.8 | 180.3 | 124.0 | 152.9 | 285.6 | 106.2 | 107.9 | 293.2 |
| 2003 | 184.0 | 180.5 | 184.8 | 120.9 | 157.6 | 297.1 | 107.5 | 109.8 | 298.7 |
| 2004 | 188.9 | 186.6 | 189.5 | 120.4 | 163.1 | 310.1 | 108.6 | 111.6 | 304.7 |
| 2005 | 195.3 | 191.2 | 195.7 | 119.5 | 173.9 | 323.2 | 109.4 | 113.7 | 313.4 |
| 2006 | 201.6 | 195.7 | 203.2 | 119.5 | 180.9 | 336.2 | 110.9 | 116.8 | 321.7 |
| 2007 | 207.3 | 203.3 | 209.6 | 119.0 | 184.7 | 351.1 | 111.4 | 119.6 | 333.3 |
| 2008 | 215.3 | 214.2 | 216.3 | 118.9 | 195.5 | 364.1 | 113.3 | 123.6 | 345.4 |
| 2009 | 214.5 | 218.2 | 217.1 | 120.1 | 179.3 | 375.6 | 114.3 | 127.4 | 368.6 |
| 2010 | 218.1 | 220.0 | 216.3 | 119.5 | 193.4 | 388.4 | 113.3 | 129.9 | 381.3 |
| 2011 | 224.9 | 227.9 | 219.1 | 122.1 | 212.4 | 400.3 | 113.4 | 131.5 | 387.2 |
| 2012 | 229.6 | 233.7 | 222.7 | 126.3 | 217.3 | 414.9 | 114.7 | 133.8 | 394.4 |
| 2013 | 233.0 | 237.0 | 227.4 | 127.4 | 217.4 | 425.1 | 115.3 | 135.9 | 401.0 |
| 2014 | 236.7 | 242.4 | 233.2 | 127.5 | 215.9 | 435.3 | 115.5 | 137.5 | 408.1 |
| 2015 | 237.0 | 246.8 | 238.1 | 125.9 | 199.1 | 446.8 | 115.9 | 138.2 | 414.9 |

[1]December 1997 = 100.
. . . = Not available.

## Table 9-3. Consumer Price Indexes, All Urban Consumers (CPI-U): U.S. City Average, Commodity, Service, and Special Groups, 1957–2015

(1982–1984 = 100, unless otherwise specified.)

| Year | All items less food | All items less shelter | All items less medical care | All items less energy | All items less food and energy | Commodities | Commodities less food and beverages | Commodities less food and energy | Energy commodities | Nondurables | Nondurables less food | Nondurables less food and apparel |
|---|---|---|---|---|---|---|---|---|---|---|---|---|
| 1957 | 28.0 | 29.7 | 28.7 | 28.9 | 28.9 | 32.6 | . . . | 37.4 | 21.6 | 30.9 | 32.9 | 28.5 |
| 1958 | 28.6 | 30.6 | 29.5 | 29.7 | 29.6 | 33.3 | . . . | 37.9 | 21.3 | 31.7 | 33.1 | 28.8 |
| 1959 | 29.2 | 30.8 | 29.8 | 29.9 | 30.2 | 33.3 | . . . | 38.4 | 21.5 | 31.5 | 33.5 | 29.2 |
| 1960 | 29.7 | 31.3 | 30.2 | 30.4 | 30.6 | 33.6 | . . . | 38.5 | 21.9 | 32.0 | 34.1 | 29.7 |
| 1961 | 30.0 | 31.7 | 30.5 | 30.7 | 31.0 | 33.8 | . . . | 38.6 | 21.9 | 32.2 | 34.3 | 29.8 |
| 1962 | 30.3 | 32.0 | 30.8 | 31.1 | 31.4 | 34.1 | . . . | 38.9 | 22.0 | 32.5 | 34.5 | 30.1 |
| 1963 | 30.7 | 32.4 | 31.1 | 31.5 | 31.8 | 34.4 | . . . | 39.2 | 22.1 | 32.9 | 34.8 | 30.4 |
| 1964 | 31.1 | 32.8 | 31.5 | 32.0 | 32.3 | 34.8 | . . . | 39.6 | 21.9 | 33.2 | 35.1 | 30.6 |
| 1965 | 31.6 | 33.3 | 32.0 | 32.5 | 32.7 | 35.2 | . . . | 39.8 | 22.6 | 33.8 | 35.6 | 31.2 |
| 1966 | 32.3 | 34.3 | 33.0 | 33.5 | 33.5 | 36.1 | . . . | 40.3 | 23.2 | 35.1 | 36.4 | 31.8 |
| 1967 | 33.4 | 35.2 | 33.7 | 34.4 | 34.7 | 36.8 | 38.3 | 41.3 | 23.9 | 35.7 | 37.6 | 32.6 |
| 1968 | 34.9 | 36.7 | 35.1 | 35.9 | 36.3 | 38.1 | 39.7 | 42.9 | 24.4 | 37.1 | 39.1 | 33.7 |
| 1969 | 36.8 | 38.4 | 37.0 | 38.0 | 38.4 | 39.9 | 41.4 | 44.7 | 25.2 | 38.9 | 40.9 | 34.9 |
| 1970 | 39.0 | 40.3 | 39.2 | 40.3 | 40.8 | 41.7 | 43.1 | 46.7 | 25.6 | 40.8 | 42.5 | 36.3 |
| 1971 | 40.8 | 42.0 | 40.8 | 42.0 | 42.7 | 43.2 | 44.7 | 48.5 | 26.1 | 42.1 | 44.0 | 37.6 |
| 1972 | 42.0 | 43.3 | 42.1 | 43.4 | 44.0 | 44.5 | 45.8 | 49.7 | 26.4 | 43.5 | 45.0 | 38.6 |
| 1973 | 43.7 | 46.2 | 44.8 | 46.1 | 45.6 | 47.8 | 47.3 | 51.1 | 29.1 | 47.5 | 46.9 | 40.3 |
| 1974 | 48.0 | 51.4 | 49.8 | 50.6 | 49.4 | 53.5 | 52.4 | 55.0 | 40.4 | 54.0 | 52.9 | 46.9 |
| 1975 | 52.5 | 56.0 | 54.3 | 55.1 | 53.9 | 58.2 | 57.3 | 60.1 | 43.4 | 58.3 | 57.0 | 51.5 |
| 1976 | 56.0 | 59.3 | 57.2 | 58.2 | 57.4 | 60.7 | 60.2 | 63.2 | 45.4 | 60.5 | 59.5 | 54.1 |
| 1977 | 59.6 | 63.1 | 60.8 | 61.9 | 61.0 | 64.2 | 63.6 | 66.5 | 48.7 | 64.0 | 62.5 | 57.2 |
| 1978 | 63.9 | 67.4 | 65.4 | 66.7 | 65.5 | 68.8 | 67.3 | 70.5 | 51.0 | 68.6 | 65.5 | 60.4 |
| 1979 | 71.2 | 74.2 | 72.9 | 73.4 | 71.9 | 76.6 | 75.2 | 76.4 | 68.7 | 77.2 | 74.6 | 71.2 |
| 1980 | 81.5 | 82.9 | 82.8 | 81.9 | 80.8 | 86.0 | 85.7 | 83.5 | 95.2 | 87.6 | 88.4 | 87.1 |
| 1981 | 90.4 | 91.0 | 91.4 | 90.1 | 89.2 | 93.2 | 93.1 | 90.0 | 107.6 | 95.2 | 96.7 | 96.8 |
| 1982 | 96.3 | 96.2 | 96.8 | 96.1 | 95.8 | 97.0 | 96.9 | 95.3 | 102.9 | 97.8 | 98.3 | 98.2 |
| 1983 | 99.7 | 99.8 | 99.6 | 99.6 | 99.6 | 99.8 | 100.0 | 100.2 | 99.0 | 99.7 | 100.0 | 100.0 |
| 1984 | 104.0 | 103.9 | 103.7 | 104.3 | 104.6 | 103.2 | 103.1 | 104.4 | 98.1 | 102.5 | 101.7 | 101.8 |
| 1985 | 108.0 | 107.0 | 107.2 | 108.4 | 109.1 | 105.4 | 105.2 | 107.1 | 98.2 | 104.8 | 104.1 | 104.1 |
| 1986 | 109.8 | 108.0 | 108.8 | 112.6 | 113.5 | 104.4 | 101.4 | 108.6 | 77.2 | 103.5 | 98.5 | 96.9 |
| 1987 | 113.6 | 111.6 | 112.6 | 117.2 | 118.2 | 107.7 | 104.0 | 111.8 | 80.2 | 107.5 | 101.8 | 100.3 |
| 1988 | 118.3 | 115.9 | 117.0 | 122.3 | 123.4 | 111.5 | 107.3 | 115.8 | 80.8 | 111.8 | 105.8 | 104.0 |
| 1989 | 123.7 | 121.6 | 122.4 | 128.1 | 129.0 | 116.7 | 111.6 | 119.6 | 87.9 | 118.2 | 111.7 | 111.3 |
| 1990 | 130.3 | 128.2 | 128.8 | 134.7 | 135.5 | 122.8 | 117.0 | 123.6 | 101.2 | 126.0 | 119.9 | 120.9 |
| 1991 | 136.1 | 133.5 | 133.8 | 140.9 | 142.1 | 126.6 | 120.4 | 128.8 | 99.1 | 130.3 | 124.5 | 125.7 |
| 1992 | 140.8 | 137.3 | 137.5 | 145.4 | 147.3 | 129.1 | 123.2 | 132.5 | 98.3 | 132.8 | 127.6 | 128.9 |
| 1993 | 145.1 | 141.4 | 141.2 | 150.0 | 152.2 | 131.5 | 125.3 | 135.2 | 97.3 | 135.1 | 129.3 | 130.7 |
| 1994 | 149.0 | 144.8 | 144.7 | 154.1 | 156.5 | 133.8 | 126.9 | 137.1 | 97.6 | 136.8 | 129.7 | 131.6 |
| 1995 | 153.1 | 148.6 | 148.6 | 158.7 | 161.2 | 136.4 | 128.9 | 139.3 | 98.8 | 139.3 | 130.9 | 134.1 |
| 1996 | 157.5 | 152.8 | 152.8 | 163.1 | 165.6 | 139.9 | 131.5 | 141.3 | 105.7 | 143.5 | 134.5 | 139.5 |
| 1997 | 161.1 | 155.9 | 156.3 | 167.1 | 169.5 | 141.8 | 132.2 | 142.3 | 105.7 | 146.4 | 136.3 | 141.8 |
| 1998 | 163.4 | 157.2 | 158.6 | 170.9 | 173.4 | 141.9 | 130.5 | 143.2 | 92.1 | 146.9 | 134.6 | 139.2 |
| 1999 | 167.0 | 160.2 | 162.0 | 174.4 | 177.0 | 144.4 | 132.5 | 144.1 | 100.0 | 151.2 | 139.4 | 147.5 |
| 2000 | 173.0 | 165.7 | 167.3 | 178.6 | 181.3 | 149.2 | 137.7 | 144.9 | 129.5 | 158.2 | 149.1 | 162.9 |
| 2001 | 177.8 | 169.7 | 171.9 | 183.5 | 186.1 | 150.7 | 137.2 | 145.3 | 125.2 | 160.6 | 149.1 | 164.1 |
| 2002 | 180.5 | 170.8 | 174.3 | 187.7 | 190.5 | 149.7 | 134.2 | 143.7 | 117.1 | 161.1 | 147.4 | 163.3 |
| 2003 | 184.7 | 174.6 | 178.1 | 190.6 | 193.2 | 151.2 | 134.5 | 140.9 | 136.7 | 165.3 | 151.9 | 172.1 |
| 2004 | 189.4 | 179.3 | 182.7 | 194.4 | 196.6 | 154.7 | 136.7 | 139.6 | 161.2 | 172.2 | 159.3 | 183.8 |
| 2005 | 196.0 | 186.1 | 188.7 | 198.7 | 200.9 | 160.2 | 142.5 | 140.3 | 197.4 | 180.2 | 170.1 | 201.2 |
| 2006 | 202.7 | 191.9 | 194.7 | 203.7 | 205.9 | 164.0 | 145.9 | 140.6 | 223.0 | 186.7 | 178.2 | 213.9 |
| 2007 | 208.1 | 196.6 | 200.1 | 208.9 | 210.7 | 167.5 | 147.5 | 140.1 | 241.0 | 193.5 | 184.0 | 223.4 |
| 2008 | 215.5 | 205.5 | 207.8 | 214.8 | 215.6 | 174.8 | 153.0 | 140.2 | 284.4 | 205.9 | 197.3 | 244.4 |
| 2009 | 214.0 | 203.3 | 206.6 | 218.4 | 219.2 | 169.7 | 144.4 | 142.0 | 205.3 | 198.5 | 181.5 | 218.7 |
| 2010 | 217.8 | 208.6 | 209.7 | 220.5 | 221.3 | 174.6 | 150.4 | 143.6 | 242.6 | 205.3 | 191.9 | 235.6 |
| 2011 | 224.5 | 217.0 | 216.3 | 224.8 | 225.0 | 183.9 | 159.9 | 145.5 | 306.4 | 219.0 | 209.6 | 262.1 |
| 2012 | 229.0 | 221.4 | 220.6 | 229.7 | 229.8 | 187.6 | 162.7 | 147.3 | 316.0 | 224.6 | 215.0 | 268.2 |
| 2013 | 232.3 | 223.8 | 223.6 | 233.6 | 233.8 | 187.7 | 161.5 | 147.3 | 307.4 | 225.3 | 213.6 | 265.4 |
| 2014 | 235.8 | 226.2 | 227.1 | 238.0 | 237.9 | 187.9 | 159.6 | 146.8 | 296.9 | 226.7 | 211.7 | 262.3 |
| 2015 | 235.4 | 223.3 | 226.9 | 242.3 | 242.2 | 181.7 | 149.2 | 146.1 | 216.7 | 217.6 | 192.3 | 232.7 |

. . . = Not available.

**Table 9-3. Consumer Price Indexes, All Urban Consumers (CPI-U): U.S. City Average, Commodity, Service, and Special Groups, 1957–2015**—*Continued*

(1982–1984 = 100, unless otherwise specified.)

| Year | Total services[1] | Rent of shelter[2] | Gasoline, all types | Transportation services | Medical care services | Other services | Services less medical care | Energy | Services less energy |
|------|------|------|------|------|------|------|------|------|------|
| 1957 | 21.8 | . . . | 23.8 | 24.1 | 17.0 | . . . | 22.8 | 21.5 | 21.9 |
| 1958 | 22.6 | . . . | 23.5 | 25.6 | 17.9 | . . . | 23.6 | 21.5 | 22.7 |
| 1959 | 23.3 | . . . | 23.7 | 26.5 | 18.7 | . . . | 24.2 | 21.9 | 23.4 |
| 1960 | 24.1 | . . . | 24.4 | 27.2 | 19.5 | . . . | 25.0 | 22.4 | 24.2 |
| 1961 | 24.5 | . . . | 24.1 | 27.8 | 20.2 | . . . | 25.4 | 22.5 | 24.7 |
| 1962 | 25.0 | . . . | 24.3 | 28.3 | 20.9 | . . . | 25.9 | 22.6 | 25.2 |
| 1963 | 25.5 | . . . | 24.2 | 28.6 | 21.5 | . . . | 26.3 | 22.6 | 25.7 |
| 1964 | 26.0 | . . . | 24.1 | 29.2 | 22.0 | . . . | 26.8 | 22.5 | 26.2 |
| 1965 | 26.6 | . . . | 25.1 | 30.3 | 22.7 | . . . | 27.4 | 22.9 | 26.9 |
| 1966 | 27.6 | . . . | 25.6 | 31.6 | 23.9 | . . . | 28.3 | 23.3 | 28.0 |
| 1967 | 28.8 | . . . | 26.4 | 32.6 | 26.0 | 36.0 | 29.3 | 23.8 | 29.3 |
| 1968 | 30.3 | . . . | 26.8 | 33.9 | 27.9 | 38.1 | 30.8 | 24.2 | 30.9 |
| 1969 | 32.4 | . . . | 27.7 | 36.3 | 30.2 | 40.0 | 32.9 | 24.8 | 33.2 |
| 1970 | 35.0 | . . . | 27.9 | 40.2 | 32.3 | 42.2 | 35.6 | 25.5 | 36.0 |
| 1971 | 37.0 | . . . | 28.1 | 43.4 | 34.7 | 44.4 | 37.5 | 26.5 | 38.0 |
| 1972 | 38.4 | . . . | 28.4 | 44.4 | 35.9 | 45.6 | 38.9 | 27.2 | 39.4 |
| 1973 | 40.1 | . . . | 31.2 | 44.7 | 37.5 | 47.7 | 40.6 | 29.4 | 41.1 |
| 1974 | 43.8 | . . . | 42.2 | 46.3 | 41.4 | 51.3 | 44.3 | 38.1 | 44.8 |
| 1975 | 48.0 | . . . | 45.1 | 49.8 | 46.6 | 55.1 | 48.3 | 42.1 | 48.8 |
| 1976 | 52.0 | . . . | 47.0 | 56.9 | 51.3 | 58.4 | 52.2 | 45.1 | 52.7 |
| 1977 | 56.0 | . . . | 49.7 | 61.5 | 56.4 | 62.1 | 55.9 | 49.4 | 56.5 |
| 1978 | 60.8 | . . . | 51.8 | 64.4 | 61.2 | 66.4 | 60.7 | 52.5 | 61.3 |
| 1979 | 67.5 | . . . | 70.2 | 69.5 | 67.2 | 71.9 | 67.5 | 65.7 | 68.2 |
| 1980 | 77.9 | . . . | 97.5 | 79.2 | 74.8 | 78.7 | 78.2 | 86.0 | 78.5 |
| 1981 | 88.1 | . . . | 108.5 | 88.6 | 82.8 | 86.1 | 88.7 | 97.7 | 88.7 |
| 1982 | 96.0 | . . . | 102.8 | 96.1 | 92.6 | 93.5 | 96.4 | 99.2 | 96.3 |
| 1983 | 99.4 | 102.7 | 99.4 | 99.1 | 100.7 | 100.0 | 99.2 | 99.9 | 99.2 |
| 1984 | 104.6 | 107.7 | 97.8 | 104.8 | 106.7 | 106.5 | 104.4 | 100.9 | 104.5 |
| 1985 | 109.9 | 113.9 | 98.6 | 110.0 | 113.2 | 113.0 | 109.6 | 101.6 | 110.2 |
| 1986 | 115.4 | 120.2 | 77.0 | 116.3 | 121.9 | 119.4 | 114.6 | 88.2 | 116.5 |
| 1987 | 120.2 | 125.9 | 80.1 | 121.9 | 130.0 | 125.7 | 119.1 | 88.6 | 122.0 |
| 1988 | 125.7 | 132.0 | 80.8 | 128.0 | 138.3 | 132.6 | 124.3 | 89.3 | 127.9 |
| 1989 | 131.9 | 138.0 | 88.5 | 135.6 | 148.9 | 140.9 | 130.1 | 94.3 | 134.4 |
| 1990 | 139.2 | 145.5 | 101.0 | 144.2 | 162.7 | 150.2 | 136.8 | 102.1 | 142.3 |
| 1991 | 146.3 | 152.1 | 99.2 | 151.2 | 177.1 | 159.8 | 143.3 | 102.5 | 149.8 |
| 1992 | 152.0 | 157.3 | 99.0 | 155.7 | 190.5 | 168.5 | 148.4 | 103.0 | 155.9 |
| 1993 | 157.9 | 162.0 | 97.7 | 162.9 | 202.9 | 177.0 | 153.6 | 104.2 | 161.9 |
| 1994 | 163.1 | 167.0 | 98.2 | 168.6 | 213.4 | 185.4 | 158.4 | 104.6 | 167.6 |
| 1995 | 168.7 | 172.4 | 99.8 | 175.9 | 224.2 | 193.3 | 163.5 | 105.2 | 173.7 |
| 1996 | 174.1 | 178.0 | 105.9 | 180.5 | 232.4 | 201.4 | 168.7 | 110.1 | 179.4 |
| 1997 | 179.4 | 183.4 | 105.8 | 185.0 | 239.1 | 209.6 | 173.9 | 111.5 | 185.0 |
| 1998 | 184.2 | 189.6 | 91.6 | 187.9 | 246.8 | 216.9 | 178.4 | 102.9 | 190.6 |
| 1999 | 188.8 | 195.0 | 100.1 | 190.7 | 255.1 | 223.1 | 182.7 | 106.6 | 195.7 |
| 2000 | 195.3 | 201.3 | 128.6 | 196.1 | 266.0 | 229.9 | 188.9 | 124.6 | 202.1 |
| 2001 | 203.4 | 208.9 | 124.0 | 201.9 | 278.8 | 238.0 | 196.6 | 129.3 | 209.6 |
| 2002 | 209.8 | 216.7 | 116.0 | 209.1 | 292.9 | 246.4 | 202.5 | 121.7 | 217.5 |
| 2003 | 216.5 | 221.9 | 135.1 | 216.3 | 306.0 | 254.4 | 208.7 | 136.5 | 223.8 |
| 2004 | 222.8 | 227.9 | 159.7 | 220.6 | 321.3 | 261.3 | 214.5 | 151.4 | 230.2 |
| 2005 | 230.1 | 233.7 | 194.7 | 225.7 | 336.7 | 268.4 | 221.2 | 177.1 | 236.6 |
| 2006 | 238.9 | 241.9 | 219.9 | 230.8 | 350.6 | 277.5 | 229.6 | 196.9 | 244.7 |
| 2007 | 246.8 | 250.8 | 238.0 | 233.7 | 369.3 | 285.6 | 236.8 | 207.7 | 253.1 |
| 2008 | 255.5 | 257.2 | 277.5 | 244.1 | 384.9 | 295.8 | 245.0 | 236.7 | 261.0 |
| 2009 | 259.2 | 259.9 | 201.6 | 251.0 | 397.3 | 304.0 | 248.1 | 193.1 | 265.9 |
| 2010 | 261.3 | 258.8 | 238.6 | 259.8 | 411.2 | 309.6 | 249.6 | 211.4 | 268.3 |
| 2011 | 265.8 | 262.2 | 301.7 | 268.0 | 423.8 | 314.4 | 253.6 | 243.9 | 273.1 |
| 2012 | 271.4 | 267.8 | 311.5 | 272.9 | 440.3 | 322.3 | 258.5 | 246.1 | 279.7 |
| 2013 | 277.9 | 274.0 | 302.6 | 280.0 | 454.0 | 328.7 | 264.5 | 244.4 | 286.4 |
| 2014 | 285.1 | 281.8 | 290.9 | 285.3 | 464.8 | 334.4 | 271.5 | 243.6 | 293.5 |
| 2015 | 291.7 | 290.4 | 212.0 | 291.0 | 476.2 | 339.4 | 277.7 | 202.9 | 301.1 |

[1]Includes tenants, household insurance, water, sewer, trash, and household operations services, not shown separately.
[2]December 1982 = 100.
. . . = Not available.

## Table 9-4. Consumer Price Indexes, All Urban Consumers (CPI-U): U.S. City Average, Selected Groups and Purchasing Power of the Consumer Dollar, 1913–2015

(1982–1984 = 100, unless otherwise specified.)

| Year | All items | Food | Rent of primary residence | Owners' equivalent of primary residence[1] | Apparel | Purchasing power of the consumer dollar |
|---|---|---|---|---|---|---|
| 1913 | 9.9 | 10.0 | 21.0 | . . . | 14.9 | 1 007.7 |
| 1914 | 10.0 | 10.2 | 21.0 | . . . | 15.0 | 994.2 |
| 1915 | 10.1 | 10.0 | 21.1 | . . . | 15.3 | 984.3 |
| 1916 | 10.9 | 11.3 | 21.3 | . . . | 16.8 | 915.2 |
| 1917 | 12.8 | 14.5 | 21.2 | . . . | 20.2 | 779.3 |
| 1918 | 15.1 | 16.7 | 21.5 | . . . | 27.3 | 663.5 |
| 1919 | 17.3 | 18.6 | 23.3 | . . . | 36.2 | 577.9 |
| 1920 | 20.0 | 21.0 | 27.4 | . . . | 43.1 | 498.9 |
| 1921 | 17.9 | 15.9 | 31.5 | . . . | 33.2 | 558.5 |
| 1922 | 16.8 | 14.9 | 32.4 | . . . | 27.0 | 596.2 |
| 1923 | 17.1 | 15.4 | 33.2 | . . . | 27.1 | 585.7 |
| 1924 | 17.1 | 15.2 | 34.4 | . . . | 26.8 | 584.5 |
| 1925 | 17.5 | 16.5 | 34.6 | . . . | 26.3 | 570.1 |
| 1926 | 17.7 | 17.0 | 34.2 | . . . | 25.9 | 564.7 |
| 1927 | 17.4 | 16.4 | 33.7 | . . . | 25.3 | 575.5 |
| 1928 | 17.1 | 16.3 | 32.9 | . . . | 25.0 | 583.3 |
| 1929 | 17.1 | 16.5 | 32.1 | . . . | 24.7 | 583.3 |
| 1930 | 16.7 | 15.6 | 31.2 | . . . | 24.2 | 598.6 |
| 1931 | 15.2 | 12.9 | 29.6 | . . . | 22.0 | 656.3 |
| 1932 | 13.7 | 10.7 | 26.5 | . . . | 19.5 | 731.7 |
| 1933 | 13.0 | 10.4 | 22.9 | . . . | 18.8 | 771.2 |
| 1934 | 13.4 | 11.6 | 21.4 | . . . | 20.6 | 746.4 |
| 1935 | 13.7 | 12.4 | 21.4 | . . . | 20.8 | 728.1 |
| 1936 | 13.9 | 12.6 | 21.9 | . . . | 21.0 | 721.3 |
| 1937 | 14.4 | 13.1 | 22.9 | . . . | 22.0 | 696.1 |
| 1938 | 14.1 | 12.1 | 23.7 | . . . | 21.9 | 709.3 |
| 1939 | 13.9 | 11.8 | 23.7 | . . . | 21.6 | 719.5 |
| 1940 | 14.0 | 12.0 | 23.7 | . . . | 21.8 | 712.6 |
| 1941 | 14.7 | 13.1 | 24.2 | . . . | 22.8 | 678.8 |
| 1942 | 16.3 | 15.4 | 24.7 | . . . | 26.7 | 613.2 |
| 1943 | 17.3 | 17.1 | 24.7 | . . . | 27.8 | 577.9 |
| 1944 | 17.6 | 16.9 | 24.8 | . . . | 29.8 | 568.0 |
| 1945 | 18.0 | 17.3 | 24.8 | . . . | 31.4 | 555.2 |
| 1946 | 19.5 | 19.8 | 25.0 | . . . | 34.4 | 511.5 |
| 1947 | 22.3 | 24.1 | 25.8 | . . . | 39.9 | 447.4 |
| 1948 | 24.1 | 26.1 | 27.5 | . . . | 42.5 | 415.1 |
| 1949 | 23.8 | 25.0 | 28.7 | . . . | 40.8 | 419.3 |
| 1950 | 24.1 | 25.4 | 29.7 | . . . | 40.3 | 415.1 |
| 1951 | 26.0 | 28.2 | 30.9 | . . . | 43.9 | 384.6 |
| 1952 | 26.5 | 28.7 | 32.2 | . . . | 43.5 | 376.5 |
| 1953 | 26.7 | 28.3 | 33.9 | . . . | 43.1 | 373.5 |
| 1954 | 26.9 | 28.2 | 35.1 | . . . | 43.1 | 371.7 |
| 1955 | 26.8 | 27.8 | 35.6 | . . . | 42.9 | 373.2 |
| 1956 | 27.2 | 28.0 | 36.3 | . . . | 43.7 | 367.8 |
| 1957 | 28.1 | 28.9 | 37.0 | . . . | 44.5 | 354.9 |
| 1958 | 28.9 | 30.2 | 37.6 | . . . | 44.6 | 345.7 |
| 1959 | 29.1 | 29.7 | 38.2 | . . . | 45.0 | 342.7 |
| 1960 | 29.6 | 30.0 | 38.7 | . . . | 45.7 | 337.3 |
| 1961 | 29.9 | 30.4 | 39.2 | . . . | 46.1 | 334.0 |
| 1962 | 30.2 | 30.6 | 39.7 | . . . | 46.3 | 330.4 |
| 1963 | 30.6 | 31.1 | 40.1 | . . . | 46.9 | 326.5 |
| 1964 | 31.0 | 31.5 | 40.5 | . . . | 47.3 | 322.0 |
| 1965 | 31.5 | 32.2 | 40.9 | . . . | 47.8 | 316.6 |
| 1966 | 32.4 | 33.8 | 41.5 | . . . | 49.0 | 308.0 |
| 1967 | 33.4 | 34.1 | 42.2 | . . . | 51.0 | 299.3 |
| 1968 | 34.8 | 35.3 | 43.3 | . . . | 53.7 | 287.3 |
| 1969 | 36.7 | 37.1 | 44.7 | . . . | 56.8 | 272.6 |
| 1970 | 38.8 | 39.2 | 46.5 | . . . | 59.2 | 257.4 |
| 1971 | 40.5 | 40.4 | 48.7 | . . . | 61.1 | 246.6 |
| 1972 | 41.8 | 42.1 | 50.4 | . . . | 62.3 | 239.1 |
| 1973 | 44.4 | 48.2 | 52.5 | . . . | 64.6 | 225.1 |
| 1974 | 49.3 | 55.1 | 55.2 | . . . | 69.4 | 202.9 |
| 1975 | 53.8 | 59.8 | 58.0 | . . . | 72.5 | 185.9 |
| 1976 | 56.9 | 61.6 | 61.1 | . . . | 75.2 | 175.7 |
| 1977 | 60.6 | 65.5 | 64.8 | . . . | 78.6 | 164.9 |
| 1978 | 65.2 | 72.0 | 69.3 | . . . | 81.4 | 153.2 |
| 1979 | 72.6 | 79.9 | 74.3 | . . . | 84.9 | 138.0 |

[1]December 1982 = 100.
. . . = Not available.

**Table 9-4.  Consumer Price Indexes, All Urban Consumers (CPI-U): U.S. City Average, Selected Groups and Purchasing Power of the Consumer Dollar, 1913–2015**—*Continued*

(1982–1984 = 100, unless otherwise specified.)

| Year | All items | Food | Rent of primary residence | Owners' equivalent of primary residence[1] | Apparel | Purchasing power of the consumer dollar |
|---|---|---|---|---|---|---|
| 1980 | 82.4 | 86.8 | 80.9 | . . . | 90.9 | 121.5 |
| 1981 | 90.9 | 93.6 | 87.9 | . . . | 95.3 | 109.8 |
| 1982 | 96.5 | 97.4 | 94.6 | . . . | 97.8 | 103.5 |
| 1983 | 99.6 | 99.4 | 100.1 | 102.5 | 100.2 | 100.3 |
| 1984 | 103.9 | 103.2 | 105.3 | 107.3 | 102.1 | 96.1 |
| 1985 | 107.6 | 105.6 | 111.8 | 113.2 | 105.0 | 92.8 |
| 1986 | 109.6 | 109.0 | 118.3 | 119.4 | 105.9 | 91.3 |
| 1987 | 113.6 | 113.5 | 123.1 | 124.8 | 110.6 | 88.0 |
| 1988 | 118.3 | 118.2 | 127.8 | 131.1 | 115.4 | 84.6 |
| 1989 | 124.0 | 125.1 | 132.8 | 137.4 | 118.6 | 80.7 |
| 1990 | 130.7 | 132.4 | 138.4 | 144.8 | 124.1 | 76.6 |
| 1991 | 136.2 | 136.3 | 143.3 | 150.4 | 128.7 | 73.4 |
| 1992 | 140.3 | 137.9 | 146.9 | 155.5 | 131.9 | 71.3 |
| 1993 | 144.5 | 140.9 | 150.3 | 160.5 | 133.7 | 69.2 |
| 1994 | 148.2 | 144.3 | 154.0 | 165.8 | 133.4 | 67.5 |
| 1995 | 152.4 | 148.4 | 157.8 | 171.3 | 132.0 | 65.6 |
| 1996 | 156.9 | 153.3 | 162.0 | 176.8 | 131.7 | 63.8 |
| 1997 | 160.5 | 157.3 | 166.7 | 181.9 | 132.9 | 62.3 |
| 1998 | 163.0 | 160.7 | 172.1 | 187.8 | 133.0 | 61.4 |
| 1999 | 166.6 | 164.1 | 177.5 | 192.9 | 131.3 | 60.0 |
| 2000 | 172.2 | 167.8 | 183.9 | 198.7 | 129.6 | 58.1 |
| 2001 | 177.1 | 173.1 | 192.1 | 206.3 | 127.3 | 56.5 |
| 2002 | 179.9 | 176.2 | 199.7 | 214.7 | 124.0 | 55.6 |
| 2003 | 184.0 | 180.0 | 205.5 | 219.9 | 120.9 | 54.4 |
| 2004 | 188.9 | 186.2 | 211.0 | 224.9 | 120.4 | 53.0 |
| 2005 | 195.3 | 190.7 | 217.3 | 230.2 | 119.5 | 51.2 |
| 2006 | 201.6 | 195.2 | 225.1 | 238.2 | 119.5 | 49.6 |
| 2007 | 207.3 | 202.9 | 234.7 | 246.2 | 119.0 | 48.2 |
| 2008 | 215.3 | 214.1 | 243.3 | 252.4 | 118.9 | 46.5 |
| 2009 | 214.5 | 218.0 | 248.8 | 256.6 | 120.1 | 46.6 |
| 2010 | 218.1 | 219.6 | 249.4 | 256.6 | 119.5 | 45.9 |
| 2011 | 224.9 | 227.8 | 253.6 | 259.6 | 122.1 | 44.5 |
| 2012 | 229.6 | 233.8 | 260.4 | 264.8 | 126.3 | 43.6 |
| 2013 | 233.0 | 237.0 | 267.7 | 270.7 | 127.4 | 42.9 |
| 2014 | 236.7 | 242.7 | 276.2 | 277.8 | 127.5 | 42.2 |
| 2015 | 237.0 | 247.2 | 286.0 | 285.9 | 125.9 | 42.2 |

[1]December 1982 = 100.
. . . = Not available.

**Table 9-5.  Consumer Price Indexes, Urban Wage Earners and Clerical Workers (CPI-W): U.S. City Average, Major Groups, 1913–2015**

(1982–1984 = 100, unless otherwise specified.)

| Year | All items | Food and beverages | Housing | Apparel | Transportation | Medical care | Recreation[1] | Education and communication[1] | Other goods and services |
|------|-----------|--------------------|---------|---------|----------------|--------------|---------------|-------------------------------|--------------------------|
| 1913 | 10.0 | ... | ... | 15.0 | ... | ... | ... | ... | ... |
| 1914 | 10.1 | ... | ... | 15.1 | ... | ... | ... | ... | ... |
| 1915 | 10.2 | ... | ... | 15.4 | ... | ... | ... | ... | ... |
| 1916 | 11.0 | ... | ... | 16.9 | ... | ... | ... | ... | ... |
| 1917 | 12.9 | ... | ... | 20.3 | ... | ... | ... | ... | ... |
| 1918 | 15.1 | ... | ... | 27.5 | ... | ... | ... | ... | ... |
| 1919 | 17.4 | ... | ... | 36.4 | ... | ... | ... | ... | ... |
| 1920 | 20.1 | ... | ... | 43.3 | ... | ... | ... | ... | ... |
| 1921 | 18.0 | ... | ... | 33.4 | ... | ... | ... | ... | ... |
| 1922 | 16.9 | ... | ... | 27.2 | ... | ... | ... | ... | ... |
| 1923 | 17.2 | ... | ... | 27.2 | ... | ... | ... | ... | ... |
| 1924 | 17.2 | ... | ... | 26.9 | ... | ... | ... | ... | ... |
| 1925 | 17.6 | ... | ... | 26.4 | ... | ... | ... | ... | ... |
| 1926 | 17.8 | ... | ... | 26.0 | ... | ... | ... | ... | ... |
| 1927 | 17.5 | ... | ... | 25.5 | ... | ... | ... | ... | ... |
| 1928 | 17.2 | ... | ... | 25.1 | ... | ... | ... | ... | ... |
| 1929 | 17.2 | ... | ... | 24.8 | ... | ... | ... | ... | ... |
| 1930 | 16.8 | ... | ... | 24.3 | ... | ... | ... | ... | ... |
| 1931 | 15.3 | ... | ... | 22.1 | ... | ... | ... | ... | ... |
| 1932 | 13.7 | ... | ... | 19.6 | ... | ... | ... | ... | ... |
| 1933 | 13.0 | ... | ... | 18.9 | ... | ... | ... | ... | ... |
| 1934 | 13.5 | ... | ... | 20.7 | ... | ... | ... | ... | ... |
| 1935 | 13.8 | ... | ... | 20.9 | 14.1 | 10.2 | ... | ... | ... |
| 1936 | 13.9 | ... | ... | 21.1 | 14.2 | 10.3 | ... | ... | ... |
| 1937 | 14.4 | ... | ... | 22.1 | 14.5 | 10.4 | ... | ... | ... |
| 1938 | 14.2 | ... | ... | 22.0 | 14.6 | 10.4 | ... | ... | ... |
| 1939 | 14.0 | ... | ... | 21.7 | 14.2 | 10.4 | ... | ... | ... |
| 1940 | 14.1 | ... | ... | 21.9 | 14.1 | 10.4 | ... | ... | ... |
| 1941 | 14.8 | ... | ... | 23.0 | 14.6 | 10.5 | ... | ... | ... |
| 1942 | 16.4 | ... | ... | 26.8 | 15.9 | 10.8 | ... | ... | ... |
| 1943 | 17.4 | ... | ... | 28.0 | 15.8 | 11.3 | ... | ... | ... |
| 1944 | 17.7 | ... | ... | 30.0 | 15.8 | 11.6 | ... | ... | ... |
| 1945 | 18.1 | ... | ... | 31.5 | 15.8 | 11.9 | ... | ... | ... |
| 1946 | 19.6 | ... | ... | 34.6 | 16.6 | 12.6 | ... | ... | ... |
| 1947 | 22.5 | ... | ... | 40.1 | 18.4 | 13.6 | ... | ... | ... |
| 1948 | 24.2 | ... | ... | 42.7 | 20.4 | 14.5 | ... | ... | ... |
| 1949 | 24.0 | ... | ... | 41.0 | 22.0 | 14.9 | ... | ... | ... |
| 1950 | 24.2 | ... | ... | 40.5 | 22.6 | 15.2 | ... | ... | ... |
| 1951 | 26.1 | ... | ... | 44.1 | 24.0 | 15.9 | ... | ... | ... |
| 1952 | 26.7 | ... | ... | 43.7 | 25.6 | 16.8 | ... | ... | ... |
| 1953 | 26.9 | ... | ... | 43.3 | 26.3 | 17.4 | ... | ... | ... |
| 1954 | 27.0 | ... | ... | 43.3 | 25.9 | 17.9 | ... | ... | ... |
| 1955 | 26.9 | ... | ... | 43.1 | 25.6 | 18.3 | ... | ... | ... |
| 1956 | 27.3 | ... | ... | 44.0 | 26.1 | 19.0 | ... | ... | ... |
| 1957 | 28.3 | ... | ... | 44.7 | 27.6 | 19.8 | ... | ... | ... |
| 1958 | 29.1 | ... | ... | 44.8 | 28.4 | 20.7 | ... | ... | ... |
| 1959 | 29.3 | ... | ... | 45.2 | 29.6 | 21.6 | ... | ... | ... |
| 1960 | 29.8 | ... | ... | 45.9 | 29.6 | 22.4 | ... | ... | ... |
| 1961 | 30.1 | ... | ... | 46.3 | 30.0 | 23.0 | ... | ... | ... |
| 1962 | 30.4 | ... | ... | 46.6 | 30.6 | 23.6 | ... | ... | ... |
| 1963 | 30.8 | ... | ... | 47.1 | 30.8 | 24.2 | ... | ... | ... |
| 1964 | 31.2 | ... | ... | 47.5 | 31.2 | 24.7 | ... | ... | ... |
| 1965 | 31.7 | ... | ... | 48.0 | 31.7 | 25.3 | ... | ... | ... |
| 1966 | 32.6 | ... | ... | 49.2 | 32.2 | 26.4 | ... | ... | ... |
| 1967 | 33.6 | 35.0 | 31.1 | 51.2 | 33.1 | 28.3 | ... | ... | 35.4 |
| 1968 | 35.0 | 36.2 | 32.3 | 54.0 | 34.1 | 30.0 | ... | ... | 37.2 |
| 1969 | 36.9 | 38.0 | 34.3 | 57.1 | 35.5 | 32.1 | ... | ... | 39.1 |
| 1970 | 39.0 | 40.1 | 36.7 | 59.5 | 37.3 | 34.1 | ... | ... | 41.3 |
| 1971 | 40.7 | 41.3 | 38.3 | 61.4 | 39.2 | 36.3 | ... | ... | 43.3 |
| 1972 | 42.1 | 43.1 | 39.8 | 62.7 | 39.7 | 37.5 | ... | ... | 45.1 |
| 1973 | 44.7 | 48.8 | 41.5 | 65.0 | 41.0 | 39.0 | ... | ... | 46.9 |
| 1974 | 49.6 | 55.5 | 46.2 | 69.8 | 45.5 | 42.6 | ... | ... | 50.2 |
| 1975 | 54.1 | 60.2 | 51.1 | 72.9 | 49.8 | 47.7 | ... | ... | 54.4 |
| 1976 | 57.2 | 62.0 | 54.2 | 75.6 | 54.7 | 52.3 | ... | ... | 57.6 |
| 1977 | 60.9 | 65.7 | 57.9 | 79.0 | 58.6 | 57.3 | ... | ... | 60.9 |
| 1978 | 65.6 | 72.1 | 62.9 | 81.7 | 61.5 | 62.1 | ... | ... | 64.8 |
| 1979 | 73.1 | 79.9 | 70.7 | 85.2 | 70.4 | 68.0 | ... | ... | 69.4 |

[1]December 1997 = 100.

. . . = Not available.

**Table 9-5. Consumer Price Indexes, Urban Wage Earners and Clerical Workers (CPI-W): U.S. City Average, Major Groups, 1913–2015**—*Continued*

(1982–1984 = 100, unless otherwise specified.)

| Year | All items | Food and beverages | Housing | Apparel | Transportation | Medical care | Recreation[1] | Education and communication[1] | Other goods and services |
|---|---|---|---|---|---|---|---|---|---|
| 1980 | 82.9 | 86.9 | 81.7 | 90.9 | 82.9 | 75.6 | . . . | . . . | 75.6 |
| 1981 | 91.4 | 93.6 | 91.1 | 95.6 | 93.0 | 83.5 | . . . | . . . | 82.5 |
| 1982 | 96.9 | 97.3 | 97.7 | 97.8 | 97.0 | 92.5 | . . . | . . . | 90.9 |
| 1983 | 99.8 | 99.5 | 100.0 | 100.2 | 99.2 | 100.5 | . . . | . . . | 101.3 |
| 1984 | 103.3 | 103.2 | 102.2 | 102.0 | 103.8 | 106.9 | . . . | . . . | 107.9 |
| 1985 | 106.9 | 105.5 | 106.6 | 105.0 | 106.4 | 113.6 | . . . | . . . | 114.2 |
| 1986 | 108.6 | 108.9 | 109.7 | 105.8 | 101.7 | 122.0 | . . . | . . . | 120.9 |
| 1987 | 112.5 | 113.3 | 112.8 | 110.4 | 105.1 | 130.2 | . . . | . . . | 127.8 |
| 1988 | 117.0 | 117.9 | 116.8 | 114.9 | 108.3 | 139.0 | . . . | . . . | 136.5 |
| 1989 | 122.6 | 124.6 | 121.2 | 117.9 | 113.9 | 149.6 | . . . | . . . | 147.4 |
| 1990 | 129.0 | 131.8 | 126.4 | 123.1 | 120.1 | 162.7 | . . . | . . . | 158.9 |
| 1991 | 134.3 | 136.5 | 131.2 | 127.4 | 123.1 | 176.5 | . . . | . . . | 171.7 |
| 1992 | 138.2 | 138.3 | 135.0 | 130.7 | 125.8 | 189.6 | . . . | . . . | 183.3 |
| 1993 | 142.1 | 141.2 | 138.5 | 132.4 | 129.4 | 200.9 | 91.2 | 86.0 | 192.2 |
| 1994 | 145.6 | 144.4 | 142.0 | 132.2 | 133.4 | 210.4 | 93.0 | 89.1 | 196.4 |
| 1995 | 149.8 | 148.3 | 145.4 | 130.9 | 138.8 | 219.8 | 94.7 | 92.3 | 204.2 |
| 1996 | 154.1 | 153.2 | 149.6 | 130.9 | 142.8 | 227.6 | 97.5 | 95.4 | 212.2 |
| 1997 | 157.6 | 157.2 | 153.4 | 132.1 | 143.6 | 234.0 | 99.7 | 98.5 | 221.6 |
| 1998 | 159.7 | 160.4 | 156.7 | 131.6 | 140.5 | 241.4 | 100.9 | 100.4 | 236.1 |
| 1999 | 163.2 | 163.8 | 160.0 | 130.1 | 143.4 | 249.7 | 101.3 | 101.5 | 261.9 |
| 2000 | 168.9 | 167.7 | 165.4 | 128.3 | 152.8 | 259.9 | 102.4 | 102.7 | 276.5 |
| 2001 | 173.5 | 173.0 | 172.1 | 126.1 | 153.6 | 271.8 | 103.6 | 105.3 | 289.5 |
| 2002 | 175.9 | 176.1 | 175.7 | 123.1 | 151.8 | 284.6 | 104.6 | 107.6 | 302.0 |
| 2003 | 179.8 | 179.9 | 180.4 | 120.0 | 156.3 | 296.3 | 105.5 | 109.0 | 307.0 |
| 2004 | 184.5 | 186.2 | 185.0 | 120.0 | 161.5 | 309.5 | 106.3 | 110.0 | 312.6 |
| 2005 | 191.0 | 190.5 | 191.2 | 119.1 | 173.0 | 322.8 | 106.8 | 111.4 | 322.2 |
| 2006 | 197.1 | 194.9 | 198.5 | 119.1 | 180.3 | 335.7 | 108.2 | 113.9 | 330.9 |
| 2007 | 202.8 | 202.5 | 204.8 | 118.5 | 184.3 | 350.9 | 108.6 | 116.3 | 344.0 |
| 2008 | 211.1 | 213.5 | 211.8 | 118.7 | 195.7 | 364.2 | 110.1 | 119.8 | 357.9 |
| 2009 | 209.6 | 217.5 | 213.1 | 119.8 | 176.7 | 376.1 | 111.0 | 123.0 | 391.6 |
| 2010 | 214.0 | 219.2 | 212.9 | 118.7 | 192.6 | 389.8 | 109.8 | 124.9 | 409.3 |
| 2011 | 221.6 | 227.3 | 215.8 | 121.3 | 213.3 | 402.2 | 109.9 | 125.5 | 416.9 |
| 2012 | 226.2 | 233.1 | 219.3 | 125.8 | 218.7 | 417.8 | 111.1 | 127.3 | 424.7 |
| 2013 | 229.3 | 236.3 | 224.0 | 126.8 | 218.3 | 428.3 | 111.7 | 128.7 | 432.6 |
| 2014 | 232.8 | 241.9 | 229.9 | 126.6 | 216.4 | 438.3 | 111.8 | 129.7 | 440.9 |
| 2015 | 231.8 | 246.3 | 234.5 | 125.3 | 197.8 | 449.6 | 111.8 | 129.5 | 449.5 |

[1]December 1997 = 100.
. . . = Not available.

## Table 9-6. Consumer Price Indexes, All Urban Consumers (CPI-U): U.S. City Average, by Expenditure Category, 1990–2015

(1982–1984 = 100, unless otherwise specified.)

| Expenditure category | 1990 | 1991 | 1992 | 1993 | 1994 | 1995 | 1996 | 1997 | 1998 | 1999 | 2000 | 2001 | 2002 |
|---|---|---|---|---|---|---|---|---|---|---|---|---|---|
| **ALL ITEMS** | 130.7 | 136.2 | 140.3 | 144.5 | 148.2 | 152.4 | 156.9 | 160.5 | 163.0 | 166.6 | 172.2 | 177.1 | 179.9 |
| **Food and Beverages** | 132.1 | 136.8 | 138.7 | 141.6 | 144.9 | 148.9 | 153.7 | 157.7 | 161.1 | 164.6 | 168.4 | 173.6 | 176.8 |
| Food | 132.4 | 136.3 | 137.9 | 140.9 | 144.3 | 148.4 | 153.3 | 157.3 | 160.7 | 164.1 | 167.8 | 173.1 | 176.2 |
| Food at home | 132.3 | 135.8 | 136.8 | 140.1 | 144.1 | 148.8 | 154.3 | 158.1 | 161.1 | 164.2 | 167.9 | 173.4 | 175.6 |
| Cereals and bakery product | 140.0 | 145.8 | 151.5 | 156.6 | 163.0 | 167.5 | 174.0 | 177.6 | 181.1 | 185.0 | 188.3 | 193.8 | 198.0 |
| Meats, poultry, fish, and eggs | 130.0 | 132.6 | 130.9 | 135.5 | 137.2 | 138.8 | 144.8 | 148.5 | 147.3 | 147.9 | 154.5 | 161.3 | 162.1 |
| Dairy and related product | 126.5 | 125.1 | 128.5 | 129.4 | 131.7 | 132.8 | 142.1 | 145.5 | 150.8 | 159.6 | 160.7 | 167.1 | 168.1 |
| Fruits and vegetables | 149.0 | 155.8 | 155.4 | 159.0 | 165.0 | 177.7 | 183.9 | 187.5 | 198.2 | 203.1 | 204.6 | 212.2 | 220.9 |
| Nonalcoholic beverages and beverage materials | 113.5 | 114.1 | 114.3 | 114.6 | 123.2 | 131.7 | 128.6 | 133.4 | 133.0 | 134.3 | 137.8 | 139.2 | 139.2 |
| Other food at home | 123.4 | 127.3 | 128.8 | 130.5 | 135.6 | 140.8 | 142.9 | 147.3 | 150.8 | 153.5 | 155.6 | 159.6 | 160.8 |
| Sugar and sweets | 124.7 | 129.3 | 133.1 | 133.4 | 135.2 | 137.5 | 143.7 | 147.8 | 150.2 | 152.3 | 154.0 | 155.7 | 159.0 |
| Fats and oils | 126.3 | 131.7 | 129.8 | 130.0 | 133.5 | 137.3 | 140.5 | 141.7 | 146.9 | 148.3 | 147.4 | 155.7 | 155.4 |
| Other food | 131.2 | 137.1 | 140.1 | 143.7 | 147.5 | 151.1 | 156.2 | 161.2 | 165.5 | 168.9 | 172.2 | 176.0 | 177.1 |
| Other miscellaneous food[1] | . . . | . . . | . . . | . . . | . . . | . . . | . . . | . . . | 102.6 | 104.9 | 107.5 | 108.9 | 109.2 |
| Food away from home | 133.4 | 137.9 | 140.7 | 143.2 | 145.7 | 149.0 | 152.7 | 157.0 | 161.1 | 165.1 | 169.0 | 173.9 | 178.3 |
| Other food away from home[1] | . . . | . . . | . . . | . . . | . . . | . . . | . . . | . . . | 101.6 | 105.2 | 109.0 | 113.4 | 117.7 |
| Alcoholic beverages | 129.3 | 142.8 | 147.3 | 149.6 | 151.5 | 153.9 | 158.5 | 162.8 | 165.7 | 169.7 | 174.7 | 179.3 | 183.6 |
| **Housing** | 128.5 | 133.6 | 137.5 | 141.2 | 144.8 | 148.5 | 152.8 | 156.8 | 160.4 | 163.9 | 169.6 | 176.4 | 180.3 |
| Shelter | 140.0 | 146.3 | 151.2 | 155.7 | 160.5 | 165.7 | 171.0 | 176.3 | 182.1 | 187.3 | 193.4 | 200.6 | 208.1 |
| Rent of primary residence | 138.4 | 143.3 | 146.9 | 150.3 | 154.0 | 157.8 | 162.0 | 166.7 | 172.1 | 177.5 | 183.9 | 192.1 | 199.7 |
| Lodging away from home[1] | . . . | . . . | . . . | . . . | . . . | . . . | . . . | . . . | 109.0 | 112.3 | 117.5 | 118.6 | 118.3 |
| Owners' equivalent rent of primary residence[2] | 144.8 | 150.4 | 155.5 | 160.5 | 165.8 | 171.3 | 176.8 | 181.9 | 187.8 | 192.9 | 198.7 | 206.3 | 214.7 |
| Tenants' and household insurance[1] | . . . | . . . | . . . | . . . | . . . | . . . | . . . | . . . | 99.8 | 101.3 | 103.7 | 106.2 | 108.7 |
| Fuels and utilities | 111.6 | 115.3 | 117.8 | 121.3 | 122.8 | 123.7 | 127.5 | 130.8 | 128.5 | 128.8 | 137.9 | 150.2 | 143.6 |
| Household energy | 104.5 | 106.7 | 108.1 | 111.2 | 111.7 | 111.5 | 115.2 | 117.9 | 113.7 | 113.5 | 122.8 | 135.4 | 127.2 |
| Fuel oil and other fuels | 99.3 | 94.6 | 90.7 | 90.3 | 88.8 | 88.1 | 99.2 | 99.8 | 90.0 | 91.4 | 129.7 | 129.3 | 115.5 |
| Energy services | 109.3 | 112.6 | 114.8 | 118.5 | 119.2 | 119.2 | 122.1 | 125.1 | 121.2 | 120.9 | 128.0 | 142.4 | 134.4 |
| Water, sewer, and trash collection services[1] | . . . | . . . | . . . | . . . | . . . | . . . | . . . | . . . | 101.6 | 104.0 | 106.5 | 109.6 | 113.0 |
| Household furnishings and operations | 113.3 | 116.0 | 118.0 | 119.3 | 121.0 | 123.0 | 124.7 | 125.4 | 126.6 | 126.7 | 128.2 | 129.1 | 128.3 |
| Household operations[1] | . . . | . . . | . . . | . . . | . . . | . . . | . . . | . . . | 101.5 | 104.5 | 110.5 | 115.6 | 119.0 |
| **Apparel** | 124.1 | 128.7 | 131.9 | 133.7 | 133.4 | 132.0 | 131.7 | 132.9 | 133.0 | 131.3 | 129.6 | 127.3 | 124.0 |
| Men's and boys' apparel | 120.4 | 124.2 | 126.5 | 127.5 | 126.4 | 126.2 | 127.7 | 130.1 | 131.8 | 131.1 | 129.7 | 125.7 | 121.7 |
| Women's and girls' apparel | 122.6 | 127.6 | 130.4 | 132.6 | 130.9 | 126.9 | 124.7 | 126.1 | 126.0 | 123.3 | 121.5 | 119.3 | 115.8 |
| Infants' and toddlers' apparel | 125.8 | 128.9 | 129.3 | 127.1 | 128.1 | 127.2 | 129.7 | 129.0 | 126.1 | 129.0 | 130.6 | 129.2 | 126.4 |
| Footwear | 117.4 | 120.9 | 125.0 | 125.9 | 126.0 | 125.4 | 126.6 | 127.6 | 128.0 | 125.7 | 123.8 | 123.0 | 121.4 |
| **Transportation** | 120.5 | 123.8 | 126.5 | 130.4 | 134.3 | 139.1 | 143.0 | 144.3 | 141.6 | 144.4 | 153.3 | 154.3 | 152.9 |
| Private transportation | 118.8 | 121.9 | 124.6 | 127.5 | 131.4 | 136.3 | 140.0 | 141.0 | 137.9 | 140.5 | 149.1 | 150.0 | 148.8 |
| New and used motor vehicles[1] | . . . | . . . | . . . | 91.8 | 95.5 | 99.4 | 101.0 | 100.5 | 100.1 | 100.1 | 100.8 | 101.3 | 99.2 |
| New vehicles | 121.4 | 126.0 | 129.2 | 132.7 | 137.6 | 141.0 | 143.7 | 144.3 | 143.4 | 142.9 | 142.8 | 142.1 | 140.0 |
| Used cars and trucks | 117.6 | 118.1 | 123.2 | 133.9 | 141.7 | 156.5 | 157.0 | 151.1 | 150.6 | 152.0 | 155.8 | 158.7 | 152.0 |
| Motor fuel | 101.2 | 99.4 | 99.0 | 98.0 | 98.5 | 100.0 | 106.3 | 106.2 | 92.2 | 100.7 | 129.3 | 124.7 | 116.6 |
| Gasoline (all types) | 101.0 | 99.2 | 99.0 | 97.7 | 98.2 | 99.8 | 105.9 | 105.8 | 91.6 | 100.1 | 128.6 | 124.0 | 116.0 |
| Motor vehicle parts and equipment | 100.9 | 102.2 | 103.1 | 101.6 | 101.4 | 102.1 | 102.2 | 101.9 | 101.1 | 100.5 | 101.5 | 104.8 | 106.9 |
| Motor vehicle maintenance and repair | 130.1 | 136.0 | 141.3 | 145.9 | 150.2 | 154.0 | 158.4 | 162.7 | 167.1 | 171.9 | 177.3 | 183.5 | 190.2 |
| Public transportation | 142.6 | 148.9 | 151.4 | 167.0 | 172.0 | 175.9 | 181.9 | 186.7 | 190.3 | 197.7 | 209.6 | 210.6 | 207.4 |
| **Medical Care** | 162.8 | 177.0 | 190.1 | 201.4 | 211.0 | 220.5 | 228.2 | 234.6 | 242.1 | 250.6 | 260.8 | 272.8 | 285.6 |
| Medical care commodities | 163.4 | 176.8 | 188.1 | 195.0 | 200.7 | 204.5 | 210.4 | 215.3 | 221.8 | 230.7 | 238.1 | 247.6 | 256.4 |
| Medical care services | 162.7 | 177.1 | 190.5 | 202.9 | 213.4 | 224.2 | 232.4 | 239.1 | 246.8 | 255.1 | 266.0 | 278.8 | 292.9 |
| Professional services | 156.1 | 165.7 | 175.8 | 184.7 | 192.5 | 201.0 | 208.3 | 215.4 | 222.2 | 229.2 | 237.7 | 246.5 | 253.9 |
| Hospital and related services | 178.0 | 196.1 | 214.0 | 231.9 | 245.6 | 257.8 | 269.5 | 278.4 | 287.5 | 299.5 | 317.3 | 338.3 | 367.8 |
| **Recreation[1]** | . . . | . . . | . . . | 90.7 | 92.7 | 94.5 | 97.4 | 99.6 | 101.1 | 102.0 | 103.3 | 104.9 | 106.2 |
| Video and audio[1] | . . . | . . . | . . . | 96.5 | 95.4 | 95.1 | 96.6 | 99.4 | 101.1 | 100.7 | 101.0 | 101.5 | 102.8 |
| **Education and Communication[1]** | . . . | . . . | . . . | 85.5 | 88.8 | 92.2 | 95.3 | 98.4 | 100.3 | 101.2 | 102.5 | 105.2 | 107.9 |
| Education[1] | . . . | . . . | . . . | 78.4 | 83.3 | 88.0 | 92.7 | 97.3 | 102.1 | 107.0 | 112.5 | 118.5 | 126.0 |
| Educational books and supplies | 171.3 | 180.3 | 190.3 | 197.6 | 205.5 | 214.4 | 226.9 | 238.4 | 250.8 | 261.7 | 279.9 | 295.9 | 317.6 |
| Tuition, other school fees, and childcare | 175.7 | 191.4 | 208.5 | 225.3 | 239.8 | 253.8 | 267.1 | 280.4 | 294.2 | 308.4 | 324.0 | 341.1 | 362.1 |
| Communication[1] | . . . | . . . | . . . | 96.7 | 97.6 | 98.8 | 99.6 | 100.3 | 98.7 | 96.0 | 93.6 | 93.3 | 92.3 |
| Information and information processing[1] | . . . | . . . | . . . | 97.7 | 98.6 | 98.7 | 99.5 | 100.4 | 98.5 | 95.5 | 92.8 | 92.3 | 90.8 |
| Telephone services[1] | . . . | . . . | . . . | . . . | . . . | . . . | . . . | . . . | 100.7 | 100.1 | 98.5 | 99.3 | 99.7 |
| Information technology, hardware, and services[3] | 93.5 | 88.6 | 83.7 | 78.8 | 72.0 | 63.8 | 57.2 | 50.1 | 39.9 | 30.5 | 25.9 | 21.3 | 18.3 |
| Personal computers and peripheral equipment[1] | . . . | . . . | . . . | . . . | . . . | . . . | . . . | . . . | 875.1 | 598.7 | 459.9 | 330.1 | 248.4 |
| **Other Goods and Services** | 159.0 | 171.6 | 183.3 | 192.9 | 198.5 | 206.9 | 215.4 | 224.8 | 237.7 | 258.3 | 271.1 | 282.6 | 293.2 |
| Tobacco and smoking product | 181.5 | 202.7 | 219.8 | 228.4 | 220.0 | 225.7 | 232.8 | 243.7 | 274.8 | 355.8 | 394.9 | 425.2 | 461.5 |
| Personal care | 130.4 | 134.9 | 138.3 | 141.5 | 144.6 | 147.1 | 150.1 | 152.7 | 156.7 | 161.1 | 165.6 | 170.5 | 174.7 |
| Personal care product | 128.2 | 132.8 | 136.5 | 139.0 | 141.5 | 143.1 | 144.3 | 144.2 | 148.3 | 151.8 | 153.7 | 155.1 | 154.7 |
| Personal care services | 132.8 | 137.0 | 140.0 | 144.0 | 147.9 | 151.5 | 156.6 | 162.4 | 166.0 | 171.4 | 178.1 | 184.3 | 188.4 |
| Miscellaneous personal services | 158.4 | 168.8 | 177.5 | 186.1 | 195.9 | 205.9 | 215.6 | 226.1 | 234.7 | 243.0 | 252.3 | 263.1 | 274.4 |

[1]December 1997 = 100.
[2]December 1982 = 100.
[3]December 1988 = 100.
. . . = Not available.

**Table 9-6. Consumer Price Indexes, All Urban Consumers (CPI-U): U.S. City Average, by Expenditure Category, 1990–2015**—*Continued*

(1982–1984 = 100, unless otherwise specified.)

| Expenditure category | 2003 | 2004 | 2005 | 2006 | 2007 | 2008 | 2009 | 2010 | 2011 | 2012 | 2013 | 2014 | 2015 |
|---|---|---|---|---|---|---|---|---|---|---|---|---|---|
| **ALL ITEMS** | 184.0 | 188.9 | 195.3 | 201.6 | 207.3 | 215.3 | 214.5 | 218.1 | 224.9 | 229.6 | 233.0 | 236.7 | 237.0 |
| **Food and Beverages** | 180.5 | 186.6 | 191.2 | 195.7 | 203.3 | 214.2 | 218.2 | 220.0 | 227.9 | 233.7 | 237.0 | 242.4 | 246.8 |
| Food | 180.0 | 186.2 | 190.7 | 195.2 | 202.9 | 214.1 | 218.0 | 219.6 | 227.8 | 233.8 | 237.0 | 242.7 | 247.2 |
| Food at home | 179.4 | 186.2 | 189.8 | 193.1 | 201.2 | 214.1 | 215.1 | 215.8 | 226.2 | 231.8 | 233.9 | 239.5 | 242.3 |
| Cereals and bakery product | 202.8 | 206.0 | 209.0 | 212.8 | 222.1 | 244.9 | 252.6 | 250.4 | 260.3 | 267.7 | 270.4 | 271.1 | 274.1 |
| Meats, poultry, fish, and eggs | 169.3 | 181.7 | 184.7 | 186.6 | 195.6 | 204.7 | 203.8 | 207.7 | 223.2 | 231.0 | 236.0 | 253.0 | 260.3 |
| Dairy and related product | 167.9 | 180.2 | 182.4 | 181.4 | 194.8 | 210.4 | 197.0 | 199.2 | 212.7 | 217.3 | 217.6 | 225.3 | 222.4 |
| Fruits and vegetables | 225.9 | 232.7 | 241.4 | 252.9 | 262.6 | 278.9 | 272.9 | 273.5 | 284.7 | 282.8 | 290.0 | 294.4 | 293.8 |
| Nonalcoholic beverages and beverage materials | 139.8 | 140.4 | 144.4 | 147.4 | 153.4 | 160.0 | 163.0 | 161.6 | 166.8 | 168.6 | 166.9 | 166.0 | 167.9 |
| Other food at home | 162.6 | 164.9 | 167.0 | 169.6 | 173.3 | 184.2 | 191.2 | 191.1 | 197.4 | 204.8 | 204.8 | 206.2 | 209.3 |
| Sugar and sweets | 162.0 | 163.2 | 165.2 | 171.5 | 176.8 | 186.6 | 196.9 | 201.2 | 207.8 | 214.7 | 211.0 | 209.3 | 216.1 |
| Fats and oils | 157.4 | 167.8 | 167.7 | 168.0 | 172.9 | 196.8 | 201.2 | 200.6 | 219.2 | 232.6 | 229.3 | 229.7 | 227.3 |
| Other food | 178.8 | 179.7 | 182.5 | 185.0 | 188.2 | 198.1 | 205.5 | 204.6 | 209.3 | 216.6 | 217.7 | 219.9 | 223.4 |
| Other miscellaneous food[1] | 110.3 | 110.4 | 111.3 | 113.9 | 115.1 | 119.9 | 122.4 | 121.7 | 124.0 | 128.3 | 129.2 | 130.4 | 131.8 |
| Food away from home | 182.1 | 187.5 | 193.4 | 199.4 | 206.7 | 215.8 | 223.3 | 226.1 | 231.4 | 238.0 | 243.1 | 249.0 | 256.1 |
| Other food away from home[1] | 121.3 | 125.3 | 131.3 | 136.6 | 144.1 | 150.6 | 155.9 | 159.3 | 162.8 | 166.5 | 169.6 | 173.8 | 179.6 |
| Alcoholic beverages | 187.2 | 192.1 | 195.9 | 200.7 | 207.0 | 214.5 | 220.8 | 223.3 | 226.7 | 230.8 | 234.6 | 237.3 | 239.5 |
| **Housing** | 184.8 | 189.5 | 195.7 | 203.2 | 209.6 | 216.3 | 217.1 | 216.3 | 219.1 | 222.7 | 227.4 | 233.2 | 238.1 |
| Shelter | 213.1 | 218.8 | 224.4 | 232.1 | 240.6 | 246.7 | 249.4 | 248.4 | 251.6 | 257.1 | 263.1 | 270.5 | 278.8 |
| Rent of primary residence | 205.5 | 211.0 | 217.3 | 225.1 | 234.7 | 243.3 | 248.8 | 249.4 | 253.6 | 260.4 | 267.7 | 276.2 | 286.0 |
| Lodging away from home[1] | 119.3 | 125.9 | 130.3 | 136.0 | 142.8 | 143.7 | 134.2 | 133.7 | 137.4 | 140.5 | 142.4 | 148.5 | 153.0 |
| Owners' equivalent rent of primary residence[2] | 219.9 | 224.9 | 230.2 | 238.2 | 246.2 | 252.4 | 256.6 | 256.6 | 259.6 | 264.8 | 270.7 | 277.8 | 285.9 |
| Tenants' and household insurance[1] | 114.8 | 116.2 | 117.6 | 116.5 | 117.0 | 118.8 | 121.5 | 125.7 | 127.4 | 131.3 | 135.4 | 141.9 | 146.4 |
| Fuels and utilities | 154.5 | 161.9 | 179.0 | 194.7 | 200.6 | 220.0 | 210.7 | 214.2 | 220.4 | 219.0 | 225.2 | 236.6 | 230.1 |
| Household energy | 138.2 | 144.4 | 161.6 | 177.1 | 181.7 | 200.8 | 188.1 | 189.3 | 193.6 | 189.3 | 193.8 | 202.2 | 194.7 |
| Fuel oil and other fuels | 139.5 | 160.5 | 208.6 | 234.9 | 251.5 | 334.4 | 239.8 | 275.1 | 337.1 | 335.9 | 332.0 | 338.9 | 256.2 |
| Energy services | 145.0 | 150.6 | 166.5 | 182.1 | 186.3 | 202.2 | 193.6 | 192.9 | 194.4 | 189.7 | 194.8 | 203.4 | 198.7 |
| Water, sewer, and trash collection services[1] | 117.2 | 124.0 | 130.3 | 136.8 | 143.7 | 152.1 | 161.1 | 170.9 | 179.6 | 189.3 | 197.6 | 204.9 | 214.0 |
| Household furnishings and operations | 126.1 | 125.5 | 126.1 | 127.0 | 126.9 | 127.8 | 128.7 | 125.5 | 124.9 | 125.7 | 124.8 | 123.1 | 122.6 |
| Household operations[1] | 121.8 | 125.0 | 130.3 | 136.6 | 140.6 | 147.5 | 150.3 | 150.3 | 151.8 | 155.2 | 157.6 | 161.6 | 166.9 |
| **Apparel** | 120.9 | 120.4 | 119.5 | 119.5 | 119.0 | 118.9 | 120.1 | 119.5 | 122.1 | 126.3 | 127.4 | 127.5 | 125.9 |
| Men's and boys' apparel | 118.0 | 117.5 | 116.1 | 114.1 | 112.4 | 113.0 | 113.6 | 111.9 | 114.7 | 119.5 | 121.6 | 120.6 | 119.6 |
| Women's and girls' apparel | 113.1 | 113.0 | 110.8 | 110.7 | 110.3 | 107.5 | 108.1 | 107.1 | 109.2 | 113.0 | 113.3 | 114.4 | 111.2 |
| Infants' and toddlers' apparel | 122.1 | 118.5 | 116.7 | 116.5 | 113.9 | 113.8 | 114.5 | 114.2 | 113.6 | 119.7 | 116.5 | 117.6 | 119.7 |
| Footwear | 119.6 | 119.3 | 122.6 | 123.5 | 122.4 | 124.2 | 126.9 | 128.0 | 128.5 | 131.8 | 135.0 | 135.5 | 136.8 |
| **Transportation** | 157.6 | 163.1 | 173.9 | 180.9 | 184.7 | 195.5 | 179.3 | 193.4 | 212.4 | 217.3 | 217.4 | 215.9 | 199.1 |
| Private transportation | 153.6 | 159.4 | 170.2 | 177.0 | 180.8 | 191.0 | 174.8 | 188.7 | 207.6 | 212.8 | 212.4 | 211.0 | 193.7 |
| New and used motor vehicles[1] | 96.5 | 94.2 | 95.6 | 95.6 | 94.3 | 93.3 | 93.5 | 97.1 | 99.8 | 100.6 | 100.9 | 100.8 | 100.8 |
| New vehicles | 137.9 | 137.1 | 137.9 | 137.6 | 136.3 | 134.2 | 135.6 | 138.0 | 141.9 | 144.2 | 145.8 | 146.3 | 147.1 |
| Used cars and trucks | 142.9 | 133.3 | 139.4 | 140.0 | 135.7 | 134.0 | 127.0 | 143.1 | 149.0 | 150.3 | 149.9 | 149.1 | 147.1 |
| Motor fuel | 135.8 | 160.4 | 195.7 | 221.0 | 239.1 | 279.7 | 202.0 | 239.2 | 302.6 | 312.7 | 303.9 | 292.4 | 213.1 |
| Gasoline (all types) | 135.1 | 159.7 | 194.7 | 219.9 | 238.0 | 277.5 | 201.6 | 238.6 | 301.7 | 311.5 | 302.6 | 290.9 | 212.0 |
| Motor vehicle parts and equipment | 107.8 | 108.7 | 111.9 | 117.3 | 121.6 | 128.7 | 134.1 | 137.0 | 143.9 | 148.6 | 146.4 | 144.8 | 144.2 |
| Motor vehicle maintenance and repair | 195.6 | 200.2 | 206.9 | 215.6 | 223.0 | 233.9 | 243.3 | 248.0 | 253.1 | 257.6 | 261.6 | 266.0 | 270.7 |
| Public transportation | 209.3 | 209.1 | 217.3 | 226.6 | 230.0 | 250.5 | 236.3 | 251.4 | 269.4 | 271.4 | 278.9 | 276.4 | 268.7 |
| **Medical Care** | 297.1 | 310.1 | 323.2 | 336.2 | 351.1 | 364.1 | 375.6 | 388.4 | 400.3 | 414.9 | 425.1 | 435.3 | 446.8 |
| Medical care commodities | 262.8 | 269.3 | 276.0 | 285.9 | 290.0 | 296.0 | 305.1 | 314.7 | 324.1 | 333.6 | 335.1 | 343.4 | 354.6 |
| Medical care services | 306.0 | 321.3 | 336.7 | 350.6 | 369.3 | 384.9 | 397.3 | 411.2 | 423.8 | 440.3 | 454.0 | 464.8 | 476.2 |
| Professional services | 261.2 | 271.5 | 281.7 | 289.3 | 300.8 | 311.0 | 319.4 | 328.2 | 335.7 | 342.0 | 349.5 | 355.2 | 361.5 |
| Hospital and related services | 394.8 | 417.9 | 439.9 | 468.1 | 498.9 | 534.0 | 567.9 | 607.7 | 641.5 | 672.1 | 701.3 | 733.8 | 761.9 |
| **Recreation[1]** | 107.5 | 108.6 | 109.4 | 110.9 | 111.4 | 113.3 | 114.3 | 113.3 | 113.4 | 114.7 | 115.3 | 115.5 | 115.9 |
| Video and audio[1] | 103.6 | 104.2 | 104.2 | 104.6 | 102.9 | 102.6 | 101.3 | 99.1 | 98.4 | 99.4 | 99.7 | 99.8 | 99.6 |
| **Education and Communication[1]** | 109.8 | 111.6 | 113.7 | 116.8 | 119.6 | 123.6 | 127.4 | 129.9 | 131.5 | 133.8 | 135.9 | 137.5 | 138.2 |
| Education[1] | 134.4 | 143.7 | 152.7 | 162.1 | 171.4 | 181.3 | 190.9 | 199.3 | 207.8 | 216.3 | 224.5 | 231.9 | 240.5 |
| Educational books and supplies | 335.4 | 351.0 | 365.6 | 388.9 | 420.4 | 450.2 | 482.1 | 505.6 | 529.5 | 562.6 | 594.7 | 615.4 | 648.2 |
| Tuition, other school fees, and childcare | 386.7 | 414.3 | 440.9 | 468.1 | 494.1 | 522.1 | 549.0 | 573.2 | 597.2 | 621.0 | 643.7 | 664.8 | 688.8 |
| Communication[1] | 89.7 | 86.7 | 84.7 | 84.1 | 83.4 | 84.2 | 85.0 | 84.7 | 83.3 | 83.1 | 82.6 | 82.1 | 80.2 |
| Information and information processing[1] | 87.8 | 84.6 | 82.6 | 81.7 | 80.7 | 81.4 | 81.9 | 81.5 | 80.0 | 79.5 | 78.9 | 78.2 | 76.4 |
| Telephone services[1] | 98.3 | 95.8 | 94.9 | 95.8 | 98.2 | 100.5 | 102.4 | 102.4 | 101.2 | 101.7 | 101.6 | 101.1 | 99.3 |
| Information technology, hardware, and services[3] | 16.1 | 14.8 | 13.6 | 12.5 | 10.6 | 10.1 | 9.7 | 9.4 | 9.0 | 8.7 | 8.5 | 8.4 | 8.1 |
| Personal computers and peripheral equipment[1] | 196.9 | 171.2 | 143.2 | 120.9 | 108.4 | 94.9 | 82.3 | 76.4 | 68.9 | 62.3 | 56.8 | 52.6 | 47.9 |
| **Other Goods and Services** | 298.7 | 304.7 | 313.4 | 321.7 | 333.3 | 345.4 | 368.6 | 381.3 | 387.2 | 394.4 | 401.0 | 408.1 | 414.9 |
| Tobacco and smoking product | 469.0 | 478.0 | 502.8 | 519.9 | 554.2 | 588.7 | 730.3 | 807.3 | 834.8 | 853.5 | 876.8 | 903.3 | 930.8 |
| Personal care | 178.0 | 181.7 | 185.6 | 190.2 | 195.6 | 201.3 | 204.6 | 206.6 | 208.6 | 212.1 | 215.0 | 218.0 | 220.8 |
| Personal care product | 153.5 | 153.9 | 154.4 | 155.8 | 158.3 | 159.3 | 162.6 | 161.1 | 160.5 | 162.2 | 161.8 | 163.4 | 163.3 |
| Personal care services | 193.2 | 197.6 | 203.9 | 209.7 | 216.6 | 223.7 | 227.6 | 229.6 | 230.8 | 234.2 | 238.8 | 242.0 | 247.2 |
| Miscellaneous personal services | 283.5 | 293.9 | 303.0 | 313.6 | 325.0 | 338.9 | 344.5 | 354.1 | 362.9 | 372.7 | 381.9 | 389.7 | 399.3 |

[1]December 1997 = 100.
[2]December 1982 = 100.
[3]December 1988 = 100.

**Table 9-7.  Relative Importance of Components in the Consumer Price Index: U.S. City Average, Selected Groups, December 1997–December 2015**

(Percent distribution.)

| Index and year | All items | Food and beverages | Housing | Apparel | Transportation | Medical care | Recreation | Education and communication | Other goods and services |
|---|---|---|---|---|---|---|---|---|---|
| **ALL URBAN CONSUMERS (CPI-U)** | | | | | | | | | |
| December 1997 | 100.0 | 16.3 | 39.6 | 4.9 | 17.6 | 5.6 | 6.1 | 5.5 | 4.3 |
| December 1998 | 100.0 | 16.4 | 39.8 | 4.8 | 17.0 | 5.7 | 6.1 | 5.5 | 4.6 |
| December 1999 | 100.0 | 16.3 | 39.6 | 4.7 | 17.5 | 5.8 | 6.0 | 5.4 | 4.7 |
| December 2000 | 100.0 | 16.2 | 40.0 | 4.4 | 17.6 | 5.8 | 5.9 | 5.3 | 4.8 |
| December 2001[1] | 100.0 | 16.4 | 40.5 | 4.2 | 16.6 | 6.0 | 5.9 | 5.4 | 4.9 |
| December 2001[2] | 100.0 | 15.7 | 40.9 | 4.4 | 17.1 | 5.8 | 6.0 | 5.8 | 4.3 |
| December 2002 | 100.0 | 15.6 | 40.9 | 4.2 | 17.3 | 6.0 | 5.9 | 5.8 | 4.4 |
| December 2003 | 100.0 | 15.4 | 42.1 | 4.0 | 16.9 | 6.1 | 5.9 | 5.9 | 3.8 |
| December 2004 | 100.0 | 15.3 | 42.0 | 3.8 | 17.4 | 6.1 | 5.7 | 5.8 | 3.8 |
| December 2005 | 100.0 | 15.1 | 42.2 | 3.7 | 17.7 | 6.2 | 5.6 | 5.8 | 3.7 |
| December 2006 | 100.0 | 15.0 | 42.7 | 3.7 | 17.2 | 6.3 | 5.6 | 6.0 | 3.5 |
| December 2007 | 100.0 | 14.9 | 42.4 | 3.7 | 17.7 | 6.2 | 5.6 | 6.1 | 3.3 |
| December 2008 | 100.0 | 15.8 | 43.4 | 3.7 | 15.3 | 6.4 | 5.7 | 6.3 | 3.4 |
| December 2009 | 100.0 | 14.8 | 42.0 | 3.7 | 16.7 | 6.5 | 6.4 | 6.4 | 3.5 |
| December 2010 | 100.0 | 14.8 | 42.0 | 3.7 | 16.7 | 6.5 | 6.4 | 3.0 | 3.5 |
| December 2011 | 100.0 | 15.3 | 41.0 | 3.6 | 16.9 | 7.1 | 6.0 | 6.8 | 3.4 |
| December 2012 | 100.0 | 15.3 | 41.0 | 3.6 | 16.8 | 7.2 | 6.0 | 6.8 | 3.4 |
| December 2013 | 100.0 | 15.2 | 41.3 | 3.5 | 16.7 | 7.2 | 5.9 | 6.8 | 3.4 |
| December 2014 | 100.0 | 15.3 | 42.2 | 3.3 | 15.3 | 7.7 | 5.8 | 7.1 | 3.4 |
| December 2015 | 100.0 | 15.3 | 42.7 | 3.3 | 14.6 | 7.9 | 5.7 | 7.1 | 3.4 |
| **URBAN WAGE EARNERS AND WORKERS (CPI-W)** | | | | | | | | | |
| December 1997 | 100.0 | 17.9 | 36.5 | 5.3 | 19.8 | 4.6 | 6.0 | 5.4 | 4.5 |
| December 1998 | 100.0 | 18.0 | 36.7 | 5.2 | 19.2 | 4.7 | 5.9 | 5.4 | 5.0 |
| December 1999 | 100.0 | 17.9 | 36.5 | 5.0 | 19.7 | 4.7 | 5.8 | 5.3 | 5.1 |
| December 2000 | 100.0 | 17.8 | 36.8 | 4.8 | 19.9 | 4.7 | 5.7 | 5.2 | 5.2 |
| December 2001[1] | 100.0 | 18.0 | 37.3 | 4.6 | 18.8 | 4.9 | 5.7 | 5.3 | 5.4 |
| December 2001[2] | 100.0 | 17.2 | 38.1 | 4.8 | 19.4 | 4.6 | 5.6 | 5.6 | 4.5 |
| December 2002 | 100.0 | 17.1 | 38.1 | 4.6 | 19.7 | 4.7 | 5.6 | 5.6 | 4.6 |
| December 2003 | 100.0 | 17.2 | 39.1 | 4.4 | 19.1 | 5.0 | 5.7 | 5.6 | 3.9 |
| December 2004 | 100.0 | 17.0 | 39.0 | 4.2 | 19.8 | 5.0 | 5.5 | 5.5 | 3.9 |
| December 2005 | 100.0 | 16.8 | 39.2 | 4.0 | 20.1 | 5.1 | 5.4 | 5.4 | 3.9 |
| December 2006 | 100.0 | 16.5 | 40.5 | 4.0 | 19.5 | 5.2 | 5.0 | 5.6 | 3.7 |
| December 2007 | 100.0 | 15.9 | 40.0 | 4.0 | 20.1 | 5.2 | 5.3 | 6.0 | 3.5 |
| December 2008 | 100.0 | 16.9 | 41.3 | 4.0 | 17.1 | 5.4 | 5.5 | 6.2 | 3.7 |
| December 2009 | 100.0 | 16.4 | 39.8 | 3.8 | 18.6 | 5.3 | 6.0 | 6.2 | 3.9 |
| December 2010 | 100.0 | 16.4 | 39.8 | 3.8 | 18.6 | 5.3 | 6.0 | 6.2 | 3.9 |
| December 2011 | 100.0 | 15.9 | 39.8 | 3.6 | 19.0 | 5.7 | 5.6 | 6.8 | 3.5 |
| December 2012 | 100.0 | 15.9 | 39.9 | 3.6 | 19.0 | 5.8 | 5.5 | 6.8 | 3.5 |
| December 2013 | 100.0 | 15.9 | 40.2 | 3.6 | 18.8 | 5.8 | 5.5 | 6.7 | 3.5 |
| December 2014 | 100.0 | 16.0 | 40.5 | 3.6 | 18.0 | 6.3 | 5.1 | 6.9 | 3.6 |
| December 2015 | 100.0 | 16.1 | 41.1 | 3.5 | 17.1 | 6.5 | 5.1 | 6.9 | 3.7 |

[1]1993–1995 weights.
[2]1999–2000 weights.

## Table 9-8.  Consumer Price Indexes, All Urban Consumers (CPI-U), All Items: Selected Metropolitan Statistical Areas, Selected Years, 1985–2015

(1982–1984 = 100, unless otherwise specified.)

| Area | 1985 | 1990 | 1991 | 1992 | 1993 | 1994 | 1995 | 1996 | 1997 | 1998 | 1999 | 2000 | 2001 |
|---|---|---|---|---|---|---|---|---|---|---|---|---|---|
| **NORTHEAST** | | | | | | | | | | | | | |
| Boston-Brockton-Nashua, MA-NH-ME-CT ............ | 109.4 | 138.9 | 145.0 | 148.6 | 152.9 | 154.9 | 158.6 | 163.3 | 167.9 | 171.7 | 176.0 | 183.6 | 191.5 |
| New York-Northern New Jersey-Long Island, NY-NJ-CT-PA ............ | 108.7 | 138.5 | 144.8 | 150.0 | 154.5 | 158.2 | 162.2 | 166.9 | 170.8 | 173.6 | 177.0 | 182.5 | 187.1 |
| Philadelphia-Wilmington-Atlantic City, PA-NJ-DE-MD ............ | 108.8 | 135.8 | 142.2 | 146.6 | 150.2 | 154.6 | 158.7 | 162.8 | 166.5 | 168.2 | 171.9 | 176.5 | 181.3 |
| Pittsburgh, PA ............ | 106.9 | 126.2 | 131.3 | 136.0 | 139.9 | 144.6 | 149.2 | 153.2 | 157.0 | 159.2 | 162.5 | 168.0 | 172.5 |
| **NORTH CENTRAL** | | | | | | | | | | | | | |
| Chicago-Gary-Kenosha, IL-IN-WI ............ | 107.7 | 131.7 | 137.0 | 141.1 | 145.4 | 148.6 | 153.3 | 157.4 | 161.7 | 165.0 | 168.4 | 173.8 | 178.3 |
| Cincinnati-Hamilton, OH-KY-IN ............ | 106.6 | 126.5 | 131.4 | 134.1 | 137.8 | 142.4 | 146.2 | 149.6 | 152.1 | 155.1 | 159.2 | 164.8 | 167.9 |
| Cleveland-Akron, OH ............ | 107.8 | 129.0 | 134.2 | 136.8 | 140.3 | 144.4 | 147.9 | 152.0 | 156.1 | 159.8 | 162.5 | 168.0 | 172.9 |
| Detroit-Ann Arbor-Flint, MI ............ | 106.8 | 128.6 | 133.1 | 135.9 | 139.6 | 144.0 | 148.6 | 152.5 | 156.3 | 159.8 | 163.9 | 169.8 | 174.4 |
| Kansas City, MO-KS ............ | 107.7 | 126.0 | 131.2 | 134.3 | 138.1 | 141.3 | 145.3 | 151.6 | 155.8 | 157.8 | 160.1 | 166.6 | 172.2 |
| Milwaukee-Racine, WI ............ | 107.0 | 126.2 | 132.2 | 137.1 | 142.1 | 147.0 | 151.0 | 154.7 | 157.7 | 160.3 | 163.7 | 168.6 | 171.7 |
| Minneapolis-St. Paul, MN-WI ............ | 107.0 | 127.0 | 130.4 | 135.0 | 139.2 | 143.6 | 147.0 | 151.9 | 155.4 | 158.3 | 163.3 | 170.1 | 176.5 |
| St. Louis, MO-IL ............ | 107.1 | 128.1 | 132.1 | 134.7 | 137.5 | 141.3 | 145.2 | 149.6 | 152.9 | 154.5 | 157.6 | 163.1 | 167.3 |
| **SOUTH** | | | | | | | | | | | | | |
| Atlanta, GA ............ | 108.9 | 131.7 | 135.9 | 138.5 | 143.4 | 146.7 | 150.9 | 156.0 | 158.9 | 161.2 | 164.8 | 170.6 | 176.2 |
| Dallas-Fort Worth, TX ............ | 108.2 | 125.1 | 130.8 | 133.9 | 137.3 | 141.2 | 144.9 | 148.8 | 151.4 | 153.6 | 158.0 | 164.7 | 170.4 |
| Houston-Galveston-Brazoria, TX ............ | 104.9 | 120.6 | 125.1 | 129.1 | 133.4 | 137.9 | 139.8 | 142.7 | 145.4 | 146.8 | 148.7 | 154.2 | 158.8 |
| Miami-Fort Lauderdale, FL ............ | 106.5 | 128.0 | 132.3 | 134.5 | 139.1 | 143.6 | 148.9 | 153.7 | 158.4 | 160.5 | 162.4 | 167.8 | 173.0 |
| Tampa-St. Petersburg-Clearwater, FL[1] ............ | . . . | 111.7 | 116.4 | 119.2 | 124.0 | 126.5 | 129.7 | 131.6 | 134.0 | 137.5 | 140.6 | 145.7 | 148.8 |
| Washington-Baltimore, DC-MD-VA-WV[2] ............ | . . . | . . . | . . . | . . . | . . . | . . . | . . . | . . . | 100.8 | 102.1 | 104.2 | 107.6 | 110.4 |
| **WEST** | | | | | | | | | | | | | |
| Anchorage, AK ............ | 105.8 | 118.6 | 124.0 | 128.2 | 132.2 | 135.0 | 138.9 | 142.7 | 144.8 | 146.9 | 148.4 | 150.9 | 155.2 |
| Denver-Boulder-Greeley, CO ............ | 107.1 | 120.9 | 125.6 | 130.3 | 135.8 | 141.8 | 147.9 | 153.1 | 158.1 | 161.9 | 166.6 | 173.2 | 181.3 |
| Honolulu, HI ............ | 106.8 | 138.1 | 148.0 | 155.1 | 160.1 | 164.5 | 168.1 | 170.7 | 171.9 | 171.5 | 173.3 | 176.3 | 178.4 |
| Los Angeles-Riverside-Orange County, CA ............ | 108.4 | 135.9 | 141.4 | 146.5 | 150.3 | 152.3 | 154.6 | 157.5 | 160.0 | 162.3 | 166.1 | 171.6 | 177.3 |
| Phoenix-Mesa, AZ ............ | . . . | . . . | . . . | . . . | . . . | . . . | . . . | . . . | . . . | . . . | . . . | . . . | . . . |
| Portland-Salem, OR-WA ............ | 106.7 | 127.4 | 133.9 | 139.8 | 144.7 | 148.9 | 153.2 | 158.6 | 164.0 | 167.1 | 172.6 | 178.0 | 182.4 |
| San Diego, CA ............ | 110.4 | 138.4 | 143.4 | 147.4 | 150.6 | 154.5 | 156.8 | 160.9 | 163.7 | 166.9 | 172.8 | 182.8 | 191.2 |
| San Francisco-Oakland-San Jose, CA ............ | 108.4 | 132.1 | 137.9 | 142.5 | 146.3 | 148.7 | 151.6 | 155.1 | 160.4 | 165.5 | 172.5 | 180.2 | 189.9 |
| Seattle-Tacoma-Bremerton, WA ............ | 105.6 | 126.8 | 134.1 | 139.0 | 142.9 | 147.8 | 152.3 | 157.5 | 163.0 | 167.7 | 172.8 | 179.2 | 185.7 |

| Area | 2002 | 2003 | 2004 | 2005 | 2006 | 2007 | 2008 | 2009 | 2010 | 2011 | 2012 | 2013 | 2014 | 2015 |
|---|---|---|---|---|---|---|---|---|---|---|---|---|---|---|
| **NORTHEAST** | | | | | | | | | | | | | | |
| Boston-Brockton-Nashua, MA-NH-ME-CT ..... | 196.5 | 203.9 | 209.5 | 216.4 | 223.1 | 227.4 | 235.4 | 233.8 | 237.4 | 243.9 | 247.7 | 251.1 | 255.2 | 256.7 |
| New York-Northern New Jersey-Long Island, NY-NJ-CT-PA ............ | 191.9 | 197.8 | 204.8 | 212.7 | 220.7 | 226.9 | 235.8 | 236.8 | 240.9 | 247.7 | 252.6 | 256.8 | 260.2 | 260.6 |
| Philadelphia-Wilmington-Atlantic City, PA-NJ-DE-MD ............ | 184.9 | 188.8 | 196.5 | 204.2 | 212.1 | 216.7 | 224.1 | 223.3 | 227.7 | 233.8 | 238.1 | 240.9 | 244.1 | 243.9 |
| Pittsburgh, PA ............ | 174.0 | 177.5 | 183.0 | 189.8 | 195.7 | 201.5 | 211.3 | 212.1 | 215.4 | 225.1 | 232.9 | 235.9 | 239.0 | 240.6 |
| **NORTH CENTRAL** | | | | | | | | | | | | | | |
| Chicago-Gary-Kenosha, IL-IN-WI ............ | 181.2 | 184.5 | 188.6 | 194.3 | 198.3 | 204.8 | 212.5 | 210.0 | 212.9 | 218.7 | 222.0 | 224.5 | 228.5 | 227.8 |
| Cincinnati-Hamilton, OH-KY-IN ............ | 170.0 | 173.4 | 176.5 | 181.6 | 186.6 | 193.9 | 201.5 | 200.6 | 204.7 | 211.1 | 216.3 | 220.0 | 224.1 | 223.3 |
| Cleveland-Akron, OH ............ | 173.3 | 176.2 | 181.6 | 187.9 | 191.1 | 196.0 | 203.0 | 200.5 | 204.6 | 211.0 | 214.7 | 217.5 | 220.6 | 220.5 |
| Detroit-Ann Arbor-Flint, MI ............ | 178.9 | 182.5 | 185.4 | 190.8 | 196.6 | 200.1 | 204.7 | 203.5 | 205.1 | 211.8 | 216.1 | 219.5 | 221.8 | 218.7 |
| Kansas City, MO-KS ............ | 174.0 | 177.0 | 180.7 | 185.3 | 190.1 | 194.5 | 201.2 | 201.0 | 205.4 | 213.5 | 218.5 | 221.6 | 222.7 | 222.3 |
| Milwaukee-Racine, WI ............ | 174.0 | 177.7 | 180.2 | 185.2 | 189.9 | 194.1 | 203.0 | 203.0 | 209.6 | 216.9 | 221.1 | 225.1 | 227.8 | 226.6 |
| Minneapolis-St. Paul, MN-WI ............ | 179.6 | 182.7 | 187.9 | 193.1 | 196.2 | 201.2 | 209.0 | 207.9 | 211.7 | 219.3 | 224.5 | 228.8 | 232.0 | 230.6 |
| St. Louis, MO-IL ............ | 169.1 | 173.4 | 180.3 | 186.2 | 189.5 | 193.2 | 198.7 | 198.5 | 203.2 | 209.8 | 214.8 | 218.0 | 220.2 | 219.3 |
| **SOUTH** | | | | | | | | | | | | | | |
| Atlanta, GA ............ | 178.2 | 180.8 | 183.2 | 188.9 | 193.8 | 200.0 | 206.5 | 201.0 | 203.5 | 209.1 | 212.8 | 216.3 | 221.0 | 221.6 |
| Dallas-Fort Worth, TX ............ | 172.7 | 176.2 | 178.7 | 184.7 | 190.1 | 193.2 | 201.8 | 200.5 | 201.6 | 207.9 | 212.2 | 216.0 | 218.4 | 217.5 |
| Houston-Galveston-Brazoria, TX ............ | 159.2 | 163.7 | 169.5 | 175.6 | 180.6 | 183.8 | 190.0 | 190.5 | 194.2 | 200.5 | 204.2 | 207.6 | 213.4 | 213.0 |
| Miami-Fort Lauderdale, FL ............ | 175.5 | 180.6 | 185.6 | 194.3 | 203.9 | 212.4 | 222.1 | 221.4 | 223.1 | 230.9 | 235.2 | 238.2 | 243.1 | 245.4 |
| Tampa-St. Petersburg-Clearwater, FL[1] ........ | 153.9 | 158.1 | 162.0 | 168.5 | 175.2 | 184.3 | 190.1 | 189.9 | 193.5 | 198.9 | 203.6 | 206.8 | 210.8 | 211.6 |
| Washington-Baltimore, DC-MD-VA-WV[2] ....... | 113.0 | 116.2 | 119.5 | 124.3 | 128.8 | 133.5 | 139.5 | 139.8 | 142.2 | 147.0 | 150.2 | 152.5 | 154.8 | 155.4 |
| **WEST** | | | | | | | | | | | | | | |
| Anchorage, AK ............ | 158.2 | 162.5 | 166.7 | 171.8 | 177.3 | 181.2 | 189.5 | 191.7 | 195.1 | 201.4 | 205.9 | 212.4 | 215.8 | 216.9 |
| Denver-Boulder-Greeley, CO ............ | 184.8 | 186.8 | 187.0 | 190.9 | 197.7 | 202.0 | 209.9 | 208.5 | 212.4 | 220.3 | 224.6 | 230.8 | 237.2 | 240.0 |
| Honolulu, HI ............ | 180.3 | 184.5 | 190.6 | 197.8 | 209.4 | 219.5 | 228.9 | 230.0 | 234.9 | 243.6 | 249.5 | 253.9 | 257.6 | 260.2 |
| Los Angeles-Riverside-Orange County, CA ... | 182.2 | 187.0 | 193.2 | 201.8 | 210.4 | 217.3 | 225.0 | 223.2 | 225.9 | 231.9 | 236.6 | 239.2 | 242.4 | 244.6 |
| Phoenix-Mesa, AZ ............ | 101.2 | 103.3 | 105.2 | 108.3 | 111.5 | 115.3 | 119.3 | 117.6 | 118.2 | 121.5 | 124.2 | 125.8 | 127.8 | 128.0 |
| Portland-Salem, OR-WA ............ | 183.8 | 186.3 | 191.1 | 196.0 | 201.1 | 208.6 | 215.4 | 215.6 | 218.3 | 224.6 | 229.8 | 235.5 | 241.2 | 244.2 |
| San Diego, CA ............ | 197.9 | 205.3 | 212.8 | 220.6 | 228.1 | 233.3 | 242.3 | 242.3 | 245.5 | 252.9 | 257.0 | 260.3 | 265.1 | 269.4 |
| San Francisco-Oakland-San Jose, CA ......... | 193.0 | 196.4 | 198.8 | 202.7 | 209.2 | 216.0 | 222.8 | 224.4 | 227.5 | 233.4 | 239.7 | 245.0 | 252.0 | 258.6 |
| Seattle-Tacoma-Bremerton, WA ............ | 189.3 | 192.3 | 194.7 | 200.2 | 207.6 | 215.7 | 224.7 | 226.0 | 226.7 | 232.8 | 238.7 | 241.6 | 246.0 | 249.4 |

[1]1987 = 100.
[2]November 1996 = 100.
. . . = Not available.

**Table 9-9. Consumer Price Index Research Series, Using Current Methods (CPI-U-RS), by Month and Annual Average, 1977–2015**

(December 1977 = 100.)

| Year | January | February | March | April | May | June | July | August | September | October | November | December | Annual average |
|---|---|---|---|---|---|---|---|---|---|---|---|---|---|
| 1977 | . . . | . . . | . . . | . . . | . . . | . . . | . . . | . . . | . . . | . . . | . . . | 100.0 | . . . |
| 1978 | 100.5 | 101.1 | 101.8 | 102.7 | 103.6 | 104.5 | 105.0 | 105.5 | 106.1 | 106.7 | 107.3 | 107.8 | 104.4 |
| 1979 | 108.7 | 109.7 | 110.7 | 111.8 | 113.0 | 114.1 | 115.1 | 116.0 | 117.1 | 117.9 | 118.5 | 119.5 | 114.3 |
| 1980 | 120.9 | 122.4 | 123.8 | 124.7 | 125.7 | 126.7 | 127.6 | 128.6 | 130.0 | 130.7 | 131.5 | 132.4 | 127.1 |
| 1981 | 133.6 | 135.3 | 136.3 | 137.1 | 137.9 | 138.7 | 139.7 | 140.7 | 141.8 | 142.4 | 142.9 | 143.4 | 139.2 |
| 1982 | 144.2 | 144.7 | 144.9 | 145.1 | 146.1 | 147.5 | 148.5 | 148.8 | 149.5 | 150.2 | 150.5 | 150.7 | 147.6 |
| 1983 | 151.1 | 151.2 | 151.2 | 152.4 | 153.2 | 153.7 | 154.3 | 154.8 | 155.6 | 156.0 | 156.2 | 156.4 | 153.8 |
| 1984 | 157.2 | 158.0 | 158.3 | 159.1 | 159.5 | 160.0 | 160.5 | 161.1 | 161.9 | 162.2 | 162.2 | 162.4 | 160.2 |
| 1985 | 162.6 | 163.3 | 164.0 | 164.6 | 165.3 | 165.7 | 166.0 | 166.4 | 166.9 | 167.3 | 167.9 | 168.3 | 165.7 |
| 1986 | 168.8 | 168.3 | 167.5 | 167.1 | 167.6 | 168.4 | 168.4 | 168.7 | 169.6 | 169.7 | 169.8 | 169.9 | 168.7 |
| 1987 | 170.9 | 171.5 | 172.3 | 173.1 | 173.6 | 174.3 | 174.6 | 175.5 | 176.4 | 176.7 | 176.9 | 176.8 | 174.4 |
| 1988 | 177.3 | 177.5 | 178.3 | 179.2 | 179.7 | 180.4 | 181.1 | 181.9 | 183.0 | 183.5 | 183.6 | 183.7 | 180.8 |
| 1989 | 184.5 | 185.2 | 186.2 | 187.5 | 188.4 | 188.8 | 189.3 | 189.5 | 190.1 | 190.9 | 191.2 | 191.4 | 188.6 |
| 1990 | 193.3 | 194.2 | 195.2 | 195.5 | 195.8 | 196.8 | 197.6 | 199.3 | 200.9 | 202.1 | 202.3 | 202.3 | 197.9 |
| 1991 | 203.2 | 203.4 | 203.6 | 203.8 | 204.4 | 204.8 | 205.0 | 205.6 | 206.4 | 206.6 | 207.0 | 207.1 | 205.1 |
| 1992 | 207.5 | 208.1 | 208.9 | 209.3 | 209.6 | 210.1 | 210.4 | 210.9 | 211.5 | 212.1 | 212.4 | 212.3 | 210.3 |
| 1993 | 212.9 | 213.6 | 214.3 | 214.9 | 215.3 | 215.5 | 215.6 | 216.1 | 216.3 | 217.1 | 217.2 | 217.1 | 215.5 |
| 1994 | 217.4 | 218.0 | 218.7 | 219.0 | 219.2 | 219.8 | 220.3 | 221.1 | 221.4 | 221.6 | 221.8 | 221.7 | 220.0 |
| 1995 | 222.5 | 223.2 | 223.9 | 224.7 | 225.1 | 225.5 | 225.6 | 226.0 | 226.5 | 227.0 | 226.9 | 226.8 | 225.3 |
| 1996 | 227.8 | 228.7 | 229.8 | 230.6 | 231.1 | 231.3 | 231.7 | 231.9 | 232.7 | 233.3 | 233.7 | 233.7 | 231.4 |
| 1997 | 234.4 | 235.1 | 235.6 | 235.8 | 235.8 | 236.1 | 236.3 | 236.7 | 237.4 | 237.9 | 237.8 | 237.4 | 236.4 |
| 1998 | 237.8 | 238.1 | 238.6 | 239.0 | 239.4 | 239.6 | 239.8 | 240.2 | 240.4 | 240.9 | 240.9 | 240.7 | 239.6 |
| 1999 | 241.3 | 241.7 | 242.4 | 244.1 | 244.0 | 244.1 | 244.8 | 245.5 | 246.6 | 247.2 | 247.2 | 247.3 | 244.7 |
| 2000 | 248.1 | 249.5 | 251.5 | 251.7 | 251.9 | 253.3 | 253.8 | 253.9 | 255.2 | 255.6 | 255.8 | 255.6 | 253.0 |
| 2001 | 257.2 | 258.3 | 258.9 | 259.9 | 261.0 | 261.5 | 260.7 | 260.8 | 261.9 | 261.0 | 260.5 | 259.5 | 260.1 |
| 2002 | 260.2 | 261.2 | 262.6 | 264.1 | 264.1 | 264.3 | 264.6 | 265.4 | 265.9 | 266.4 | 266.4 | 265.8 | 264.3 |
| 2003 | 266.9 | 269.0 | 270.6 | 270.0 | 269.6 | 269.9 | 270.2 | 271.2 | 272.0 | 271.8 | 271.0 | 270.7 | 270.2 |
| 2004 | 272.1 | 273.6 | 275.4 | 276.2 | 277.8 | 278.7 | 278.3 | 278.4 | 278.9 | 280.5 | 280.6 | 279.6 | 277.5 |
| 2005 | 280.1 | 281.7 | 283.9 | 285.9 | 285.6 | 285.7 | 287.0 | 288.5 | 292.0 | 292.6 | 290.3 | 290.3 | 286.9 |
| 2006 | 291.3 | 291.9 | 293.6 | 296.0 | 297.4 | 298.1 | 298.9 | 299.6 | 298.1 | 296.5 | 296.0 | 296.5 | 296.2 |
| 2007 | 297.4 | 299.0 | 301.7 | 303.6 | 305.5 | 306.1 | 306.0 | 305.4 | 306.3 | 306.9 | 308.8 | 308.6 | 304.6 |
| 2008 | 310.1 | 311.0 | 313.7 | 315.6 | 318.2 | 321.5 | 323.1 | 321.9 | 321.4 | 318.2 | 312.1 | 308.8 | 316.3 |
| 2009 | 310.2 | 311.7 | 312.5 | 313.3 | 314.2 | 316.9 | 316.4 | 317.1 | 317.3 | 317.6 | 317.8 | 317.2 | 315.2 |
| 2010 | 318.3 | 318.4 | 319.7 | 320.3 | 320.5 | 320.2 | 320.3 | 320.7 | 320.9 | 321.3 | 321.4 | 322.0 | 320.3 |
| 2011 | 323.5 | 325.1 | 328.3 | 330.4 | 332.0 | 331.6 | 331.9 | 332.8 | 333.3 | 332.6 | 332.3 | 331.5 | 330.4 |
| 2012 | 333.0 | 334.5 | 337.0 | 338.0 | 337.6 | 337.1 | 336.6 | 338.4 | 340.0 | 339.8 | 338.2 | 337.3 | 337.3 |
| 2013 | 338.3 | 341.1 | 342.0 | 341.6 | 342.2 | 343.0 | 343.2 | 343.6 | 344.0 | 343.1 | 342.4 | 342.4 | 342.2 |
| 2014 | 343.6 | 344.9 | 347.1 | 348.3 | 349.5 | 350.1 | 350.0 | 349.4 | 349.7 | 348.8 | 346.9 | 345.0 | 347.8 |
| 2015 | 343.3 | 344.8 | 346.9 | 347.6 | 349.4 | 350.6 | 350.6 | 350.1 | 349.6 | 349.4 | 348.7 | 347.5 | 348.2 |

. . . = Not available.

# NOTES AND DEFINITIONS

## IMPORT AND EXPORT PRICE INDEXES

### Collection and Coverage

The International Price Program (IPP) at the Bureau of Labor Statistics (BLS) produces Import/Export Price Indexes (MXP) which contain data on changes in the prices of goods and services traded between the U.S. and the rest of the world. Price indexes are available for nearly all merchandise categories. Military goods, works of art, used items, charity donations, railroad equipment, items leased for less than a year, rebuilt and repaired items, and selected exports are not included in the IPP program.

The (IPP) selects sample establishments based upon their relative trade value in imports and exports during the course of a year. After an establishment is selected for inclusion, a BLS field economist visits the establishment to enlist cooperation and to select the exact items that will be priced on a monthly basis. All information provided by the establishment is protected under BLS confidentiality rules.

The MXP are primarily used to deflate foreign trade statistics produced by the U.S. government. The MXP are also a valuable input into the processes of measuring inflation, formulating fiscal and monetary policy, forecasting future prices, conducting elasticity studies, measuring U.S. industrial competitiveness, analyzing exchange rates, negotiating trade contracts, and analyzing import prices by locality of origin. The IPP collects prices as close as possible to the first day of each reference month.

The formula used to calculate the MXP is a modified form of the Laspeyres index. A Laspeyres index uses fixed base period quantities to aggregate prices. This means that the quality of goods and services is fixed; new goods do not appear, and the prices of goods that disappear must be observable. Because these implications are not consistent with the actually workings of the economy, adjustments must be made to the index. All MXP data are not seasonally adjusted.

Items are classified by end use for the Bureau of Economic Analysis System, by industry according to the North American Industry Classification System (NAICS), and product category according to the Harmonized System (HS). While classification by end use and product category are self-explanatory, a couple of notes are in order for classifying items by industry. In the NAICS tables, for both imports and exports, items are classified by output industry, not input industry. As an example, NAICS import index 326 (plastics and rubber products) includes outputs such as manufactured plastic rather than inputs such as petroleum. The NAICS classification structure also matches the classification system used by the PPI to produce the NAICS primary products indexes.

Although import and export transaction prices are used to calculate the MXP, the IPP does not publish price information. For this reason, the MXP cannot be used to measure differences in price levels among different products and services or among different localities of origin.

### Sources of Additional Information

Concepts and methodology are described in Chapter 15 of the *BLS Handbook of Methods* and in monthly BLS press releases. These resources are available on the BLS Web site at <http://www.bls.gov>.

## Table 9-10. U.S. Export Price Indexes for Selected Categories of Goods, by End Use, 2004–2015

(2000 = 100, unless otherwise indicated.)

| Commodity | 2004 | | | | 2005 | | | | 2006 | | | |
|---|---|---|---|---|---|---|---|---|---|---|---|---|
| | March | June | September | December | March | June | September | December | March | June | September | December |
| **ALL COMMODITIES** | 103.0 | 103.4 | 103.8 | 104.8 | 106.4 | 106.7 | 107.5 | 107.7 | 108.8 | 111.2 | 111.7 | 112.5 |
| **Foods, Feeds, and Beverages** | 130.5 | 129.1 | 118.7 | 116.9 | 120.9 | 125.2 | 122.8 | 121.9 | 121.7 | 125.6 | 128.8 | 138.7 |
| Agricultural foods, feeds, and beverages excluding distilled beverages | 132.4 | 131.1 | 119.3 | 116.6 | 120.7 | 125.6 | 122.6 | 121.7 | 121.5 | 125.7 | 129.1 | 140.5 |
| Nonagricultural foods (fish, distilled beverages) | 112.1 | 110.7 | 113.0 | 118.4 | 121.8 | 120.1 | 123.6 | 123.6 | 123.2 | 125.0 | 126.0 | 123.5 |
| **Industrial Supplies and Materials** | 108.1 | 109.9 | 114.0 | 118.0 | 122.3 | 122.3 | 127.4 | 127.9 | 131.3 | 138.8 | 139.5 | 139.4 |
| Industrial supplies and materials, durable | 110.3 | 111.8 | 116.0 | 120.2 | 122.6 | 122.7 | 123.4 | 129.1 | 135.7 | 146.2 | 146.9 | 150.1 |
| Industrial supplies and materials, nondurable | 107.0 | 108.9 | 112.9 | 116.9 | 122.2 | 122.1 | 129.8 | 127.4 | 129.0 | 134.9 | 135.7 | 133.9 |
| Agricultural industrial supplies and materials | 117.2 | 110.7 | 109.4 | 109.5 | 115.6 | 115.8 | 116.4 | 117.4 | 116.8 | 117.3 | 118.1 | 123.9 |
| Fuels and lubricants | 108.9 | 114.9 | 121.5 | 125.4 | 143.8 | 148.8 | 184.8 | 163.4 | 173.5 | 196.3 | 191.1 | 183.5 |
| Nonagricultural supplies and materials excluding fuels and building materials | 108.1 | 110.0 | 114.4 | 118.9 | 121.4 | 120.6 | 122.2 | 125.7 | 128.5 | 134.7 | 136.3 | 136.8 |
| Selected building materials | 102.3 | 103.4 | 104.0 | 104.4 | 105.3 | 106.2 | 105.7 | 106.5 | 108.5 | 109.8 | 110.0 | 111.5 |
| **Capital Goods** | 98.0 | 97.8 | 97.8 | 98.2 | 98.4 | 98.4 | 97.6 | 97.7 | 98.2 | 98.4 | 98.5 | 98.8 |
| Electrical generating equipment | 102.0 | 102.0 | 102.4 | 103.6 | 103.9 | 103.4 | 102.6 | 103.6 | 104.4 | 104.8 | 105.1 | 106.2 |
| Nonelectrical machinery | 94.5 | 94.1 | 93.9 | 93.9 | 93.9 | 93.7 | 92.7 | 92.5 | 92.7 | 92.7 | 92.6 | 92.6 |
| Transportation equipment excluding motor vehicles[1] | 106.6 | 107.2 | 108.3 | 109.5 | 111.1 | 111.8 | 112.6 | 113.8 | 116.0 | 117.1 | 117.7 | 119.1 |
| **Automotive Vehicles, Parts, and Engines** | 101.9 | 102.3 | 102.5 | 102.9 | 103.3 | 103.4 | 103.7 | 103.9 | 104.4 | 104.9 | 105.2 | 105.5 |
| **Consumer Goods, Excluding Automotives** | 100.2 | 100.4 | 101.0 | 101.2 | 101.6 | 101.5 | 101.9 | 101.9 | 102.3 | 103.5 | 104.0 | 104.0 |
| Nondurables, manufactured | 99.9 | 100.0 | 101.0 | 101.0 | 101.5 | 101.2 | 101.5 | 101.6 | 102.4 | 103.3 | 103.8 | 104.0 |
| Durables, manufactured | 100.1 | 100.7 | 100.9 | 101.1 | 101.5 | 101.5 | 101.8 | 101.5 | 101.3 | 102.4 | 103.1 | 102.8 |
| **Agricultural Commodities** | 129.7 | 127.4 | 117.6 | 115.4 | 119.9 | 123.9 | 121.5 | 121.0 | 120.7 | 124.1 | 127.1 | 137.3 |
| **Nonagricultural Commodities** | 100.9 | 101.5 | 102.8 | 104.1 | 105.4 | 105.4 | 106.5 | 106.8 | 108.0 | 110.3 | 110.6 | 110.7 |

| Commodity | 2007 | | | | 2008 | | | | 2009 | | | |
|---|---|---|---|---|---|---|---|---|---|---|---|---|
| | March | June | September | December | March | June | September | December | March | June | September | December |
| **ALL COMMODITIES** | 114.7 | 116.0 | 116.7 | 119.3 | 123.8 | 126.1 | 124.9 | 115.8 | 115.5 | 117.8 | 117.9 | 119.7 |
| **Foods, Feeds, and Beverages** | 146.9 | 148.6 | 157.8 | 171.1 | 196.9 | 198.0 | 190.4 | 155.1 | 156.7 | 174.8 | 158.2 | 165.1 |
| Agricultural foods, feeds, and beverages excluding distilled beverages | 149.2 | 151.0 | 160.8 | 175.2 | 202.6 | 204.0 | 195.6 | 156.6 | 158.3 | 178.6 | 160.7 | 167.9 |
| Nonagricultural foods (fish, distilled beverages) | 128.0 | 128.5 | 133.0 | 136.1 | 148.3 | 146.1 | 145.5 | 143.5 | 144.4 | 141.5 | 137.3 | 140.9 |
| **Industrial Supplies and Materials** | 145.5 | 149.0 | 148.8 | 154.1 | 165.5 | 173.2 | 169.4 | 139.6 | 136.5 | 140.4 | 143.9 | 150.1 |
| Industrial supplies and materials, durable | 160.2 | 160.9 | 155.5 | 159.2 | 172.7 | 172.9 | 167.1 | 141.5 | 143.4 | 144.0 | 150.7 | 157.7 |
| Industrial supplies and materials, nondurable | 137.6 | 142.8 | 145.5 | 151.9 | 162.0 | 174.2 | 171.6 | 139.1 | 133.1 | 139.0 | 140.5 | 146.2 |
| Agricultural industrial supplies and materials | 127.3 | 128.7 | 140.0 | 144.7 | 159.3 | 158.0 | 157.4 | 126.1 | 122.9 | 131.0 | 142.2 | 152.5 |
| Fuels and lubricants | 188.8 | 201.1 | 200.9 | 222.8 | 249.5 | 297.2 | 267.2 | 166.8 | 146.9 | 175.2 | 171.9 | 189.6 |
| Nonagricultural supplies and materials excluding fuels and building materials | 143.5 | 146.1 | 145.0 | 148.5 | 158.2 | 161.6 | 160.8 | 138.8 | 138.2 | 138.5 | 142.7 | 147.3 |
| Selected building materials | 112.7 | 113.9 | 114.4 | 113.7 | 114.2 | 113.8 | 115.4 | 115.1 | 114.0 | 113.0 | 114.0 | 113.5 |
| **Capital Goods** | 99.2 | 99.6 | 99.9 | 100.6 | 101.2 | 102.0 | 101.8 | 101.5 | 102.3 | 103.1 | 103.5 | 103.3 |
| Electrical generating equipment | 106.0 | 106.5 | 106.7 | 107.5 | 108.6 | 108.9 | 109.5 | 109.0 | 106.8 | 107.2 | 107.4 | 109.3 |
| Nonelectrical machinery | 92.8 | 92.9 | 93.1 | 93.6 | 93.7 | 94.2 | 93.9 | 93.3 | 93.8 | 94.4 | 94.9 | 94.5 |
| Transportation equipment excluding motor vehicles[1] | 121.1 | 122.3 | 123.4 | 125.0 | 128.1 | 130.3 | 130.7 | 131.5 | 135.1 | 137.3 | 137.2 | 136.5 |
| **Automotive Vehicles, Parts, and Engines** | 105.9 | 106.1 | 106.3 | 106.7 | 107.1 | 107.4 | 107.9 | 108.0 | 108.2 | 108.0 | 108.0 | 108.2 |
| **Consumer Goods, Excluding Automotives** | 104.8 | 105.8 | 106.2 | 107.3 | 108.0 | 108.2 | 109.3 | 109.0 | 108.5 | 108.4 | 109.2 | 109.4 |
| Nondurables, manufactured | 105.0 | 106.7 | 107.0 | 108.2 | 109.3 | 110.1 | 109.0 | 107.2 | 107.1 | 108.5 | 109.4 | 110.0 |
| Durables, manufactured | 103.4 | 103.7 | 104.2 | 105.2 | 105.4 | 105.2 | 108.7 | 109.7 | 109.9 | 108.1 | 109.5 | 109.2 |
| **Agricultural Commodities** | 145.0 | 146.7 | 156.8 | 169.3 | 194.3 | 195.2 | 188.3 | 150.8 | 151.6 | 169.7 | 156.9 | 164.7 |
| **Nonagricultural Commodities** | 112.6 | 113.8 | 113.8 | 115.7 | 118.8 | 121.2 | 120.4 | 113.2 | 112.9 | 114.1 | 115.1 | 116.5 |

[1]December 2001 = 100.

## Table 9-10.  U.S. Export Price Indexes for Selected Categories of Goods, by End Use, 2004–2015—*Continued*

(2000 = 100, unless otherwise indicated.)

| Commodity | 2010 | | | | 2011 | | | | 2012 | | | |
|---|---|---|---|---|---|---|---|---|---|---|---|---|
| | March | June | September | December | March | June | September | December | March | June | September | December |
| **ALL COMMODITIES** | 121.2 | 122.2 | 123.7 | 127.5 | 132.7 | 134.5 | 135.3 | 132.1 | 134.1 | 131.7 | 134.5 | 133.6 |
| **Foods, Feeds, and Beverages** | 163.4 | 164.5 | 174.6 | 191.1 | 206.9 | 210.6 | 213.8 | 199.0 | 206.0 | 205.8 | 231.6 | 229.3 |
| Agricultural foods, feeds, and beverages excluding distilled beverages | 165.7 | 166.7 | 177.6 | 194.6 | 212.1 | 214.6 | 217.3 | 201.2 | 208.6 | 208.0 | 235.9 | 233.8 |
| Nonagricultural foods (fish, distilled beverages) | 145.9 | 147.2 | 149.4 | 161.1 | 157.9 | 174.6 | 184.6 | 183.8 | 186.2 | 190.1 | 193.0 | 187.9 |
| **Industrial Supplies and Materials** | 155.1 | 159.8 | 162.6 | 172.6 | 188.3 | 191.8 | 192.8 | 184.6 | 188.2 | 178.4 | 183.6 | 180.6 |
| Industrial supplies and materials, durable | 160.4 | 165.5 | 167.0 | 174.8 | 186.1 | 190.3 | 196.6 | 188.2 | 191.1 | 183.5 | 183.4 | 186.1 |
| Industrial supplies and materials, nondurable | 152.6 | 157.2 | 160.8 | 172.2 | 190.4 | 193.6 | 191.7 | 183.4 | 187.4 | 176.3 | 184.5 | 178.4 |
| Agricultural industrial supplies and materials | 155.7 | 162.5 | 173.2 | 223.0 | 258.9 | 234.8 | 212.5 | 200.7 | 201.4 | 189.2 | 201.2 | 196.3 |
| Fuels and lubricants | 197.0 | 208.0 | 213.1 | 233.9 | 276.4 | 284.0 | 284.6 | 270.6 | 280.4 | 248.3 | 272.9 | 253.8 |
| Nonagricultural supplies and materials excluding fuels and building materials | 152.2 | 155.8 | 158.0 | 164.4 | 173.8 | 178.5 | 181.2 | 173.8 | 176.3 | 171.0 | 171.6 | 172.4 |
| Selected building materials | 116.0 | 118.7 | 117.1 | 116.2 | 116.3 | 116.2 | 115.8 | 115.6 | 117.2 | 118.1 | 118.8 | 117.9 |
| **Capital Goods** | 103.8 | 103.5 | 103.5 | 103.9 | 104.0 | 104.6 | 104.6 | 104.6 | 105.9 | 105.8 | 105.6 | 105.7 |
| Electrical generating equipment | 109.8 | 109.3 | 108.7 | 109.8 | 111.1 | 113.6 | 114.1 | 112.8 | 113.1 | 114.3 | 113.9 | 114.3 |
| Nonelectrical machinery | 94.7 | 94.3 | 94.3 | 94.4 | 93.9 | 94.2 | 94.2 | 94.3 | 95.3 | 95.0 | 94.8 | 94.9 |
| Transportation equipment excluding motor vehicles[1] | 139.1 | 139.5 | 140.1 | 141.6 | 144.5 | 145.3 | 144.9 | 145.6 | 148.6 | 149.1 | 149.2 | 149.0 |
| **Automotive Vehicles, Parts, and Engines** | 108.6 | 108.5 | 108.7 | 109.1 | 109.7 | 110.3 | 111.4 | 111.9 | 112.5 | 112.9 | 112.9 | 112.9 |
| **Consumer Goods, Excluding Automotives** | 110.2 | 110.4 | 111.8 | 112.7 | 113.9 | 116.3 | 117.4 | 116.6 | 116.8 | 117.0 | 116.7 | 116.4 |
| Nondurables, manufactured | 111.9 | 111.5 | 112.9 | 114.0 | 113.4 | 114.1 | 114.7 | 113.9 | 114.9 | 114.9 | 115.3 | 115.6 |
| Durables, manufactured | 107.7 | 108.2 | 109.9 | 110.9 | 112.9 | 112.7 | 113.6 | 113.3 | 114.3 | 114.9 | 114.9 | 113.9 |
| **Agricultural Commodities** | 163.3 | 165.3 | 176.1 | 198.5 | 218.8 | 217.2 | 216.0 | 200.5 | 206.9 | 204.5 | 229.9 | 227.4 |
| **Nonagricultural Commodities** | 118.1 | 119.1 | 120.0 | 122.4 | 126.5 | 128.6 | 129.5 | 127.3 | 128.9 | 126.5 | 127.6 | 126.9 |

| Commodity | 2013 | | | | 2014 | | | | 2015 | | | |
|---|---|---|---|---|---|---|---|---|---|---|---|---|
| | March | June | September | December | March | June | September | December | March | June | September | December |
| **ALL COMMODITIES** | 134.4 | 132.8 | 132.4 | 132.3 | 134.9 | 133.0 | 131.9 | 128.3 | 125.9 | 125.3 | 122.3 | 119.8 |
| **Foods, Feeds, and Beverages** | 225.5 | 223.8 | 215.2 | 213.2 | 220.9 | 222.5 | 210.0 | 204.1 | 193.6 | 184.6 | 179.6 | 177.2 |
| Agricultural foods, feeds, and beverages excluding distilled beverages | 229.4 | 228.8 | 218.8 | 216.2 | 224.7 | 226.5 | 212.4 | 206.1 | 192.9 | 185.8 | 180.4 | 177.5 |
| Nonagricultural foods (fish, distilled beverages) | 191.2 | 178.3 | 184.3 | 189.6 | 187.6 | 185.7 | 192.5 | 190.1 | 210.0 | 179.3 | 177.8 | 182.2 |
| **Industrial Supplies and Materials** | 183.1 | 177.6 | 178.4 | 178.0 | 185.9 | 177.0 | 175.3 | 162.6 | 155.6 | 155.8 | 145.7 | 137.4 |
| Industrial supplies and materials, durable | 182.8 | 175.5 | 172.5 | 170.8 | 171.6 | 170.3 | 170.2 | 165.0 | 160.8 | 159.6 | 152.8 | 147.7 |
| Industrial supplies and materials, nondurable | 184.1 | 179.5 | 182.5 | 182.9 | 194.5 | 181.5 | 179.0 | 162.1 | 153.7 | 154.5 | 142.7 | 132.7 |
| Agricultural industrial supplies and materials | 205.1 | 203.8 | 202.1 | 199.6 | 210.0 | 198.8 | 185.6 | 182.5 | 188.1 | 180.4 | 174.7 | 169.9 |
| Fuels and lubricants | 264.5 | 250.7 | 261.4 | 265.3 | 294.4 | 257.1 | 250.5 | 204.2 | 183.6 | 186.3 | 157.9 | 136.9 |
| Nonagricultural supplies and materials excluding fuels and building materials | 172.4 | 168.2 | 166.4 | 164.8 | 167.0 | 165.8 | 166.4 | 161.6 | 157.8 | 157.7 | 152.3 | 146.9 |
| Selected building materials | 120.7 | 122.5 | 125.1 | 126.5 | 128.8 | 125.7 | 121.6 | 121.3 | 119.2 | 115.8 | 112.9 | 114.5 |
| **Capital Goods** | 106.7 | 106.5 | 106.5 | 106.5 | 107.1 | 107.5 | 107.3 | 107.4 | 107.8 | 107.5 | 107.4 | 106.9 |
| Electrical generating equipment | 114.9 | 114.5 | 115.1 | 114.6 | 115.2 | 115.9 | 116.0 | 115.4 | 114.8 | 114.3 | 113.3 | 112.3 |
| Nonelectrical machinery | 95.6 | 95.4 | 95.4 | 95.3 | 95.5 | 95.7 | 95.5 | 95.4 | 95.6 | 95.1 | 94.9 | 94.5 |
| Transportation equipment excluding motor vehicles[1] | 151.6 | 151.6 | 151.9 | 152.0 | 155.7 | 156.3 | 156.6 | 158.4 | 160.6 | 161.4 | 162.2 | 161.9 |
| **Automotive Vehicles, Parts, and Engines** | 113.5 | 113.4 | 113.3 | 113.6 | 113.5 | 114.1 | 114.0 | 114.1 | 113.9 | 114.0 | 113.8 | 113.5 |
| **Consumer Goods, Excluding Automotives** | 115.8 | 115.2 | 114.5 | 115.0 | 114.8 | 115.0 | 115.2 | 114.3 | 112.9 | 113.0 | 112.0 | 111.5 |
| Nondurables, manufactured | 115.0 | 114.9 | 113.9 | 114.2 | 111.0 | 111.0 | 112.2 | 111.6 | 108.8 | 108.8 | 107.7 | 107.2 |
| Durables, manufactured | 112.3 | 111.5 | 111.7 | 111.8 | 112.2 | 112.3 | 111.6 | 111.1 | 110.9 | 111.1 | 110.1 | 109.5 |
| **Agricultural Commodities** | 224.9 | 224.2 | 215.4 | 212.8 | 221.7 | 221.4 | 207.5 | 201.8 | 191.4 | 184.3 | 178.9 | 175.7 |
| **Nonagricultural Commodities** | 127.9 | 126.2 | 126.4 | 126.4 | 128.6 | 126.6 | 126.3 | 122.9 | 121.1 | 120.9 | 118.0 | 115.6 |

[1]December 2001 = 100.

## Table 9-11. U.S. Import Price Indexes for Selected Categories of Goods, by End Use, 2004–2015

(2000 = 100, unless otherwise indicated.)

| Commodity | 2004 | | | | 2005 | | | | 2006 | | | |
|---|---|---|---|---|---|---|---|---|---|---|---|---|
| | March | June | September | December | March | June | September | December | March | June | September | December |
| **ALL COMMODITIES** | 100.2 | 101.7 | 104.1 | 104.0 | 107.8 | 109.2 | 114.4 | 112.3 | 112.7 | 117.3 | 116.2 | 115.1 |
| **Foods, Feeds, and Beverages** | 105.9 | 106.9 | 108.7 | 111.5 | 115.9 | 114.1 | 114.2 | 117.5 | 117.0 | 118.0 | 120.9 | 122.6 |
| Agricultural foods, feeds, and beverages, excluding distilled beverages | 113.0 | 114.3 | 116.4 | 120.7 | 125.7 | 123.5 | 122.6 | 127.2 | 125.4 | 126.8 | 130.4 | 133.7 |
| Nonagricultural foods (fish and distilled beverages) | 90.1 | 90.3 | 91.4 | 91.0 | 94.0 | 93.1 | 95.6 | 95.9 | 98.3 | 98.5 | 99.8 | 97.9 |
| **Industrial Supplies and Materials** | 112.7 | 119.3 | 128.5 | 126.4 | 139.8 | 145.5 | 167.2 | 158.6 | 160.4 | 178.1 | 172.2 | 166.6 |
| Fuels and lubricants | 120.2 | 130.9 | 146.2 | 141.0 | 165.6 | 178.0 | 222.1 | 202.4 | 201.5 | 230.2 | 216.3 | 204.3 |
| Paper and paper base stocks | 95.6 | 99.0 | 101.1 | 101.3 | 103.8 | 103.8 | 104.3 | 106.1 | 107.7 | 111.3 | 113.1 | 112.8 |
| Materials associated with nondurable supplies and materials | 105.4 | 106.0 | 108.0 | 109.8 | 113.0 | 113.5 | 117.3 | 117.8 | 119.3 | 120.6 | 121.8 | 123.0 |
| Selected building materials | 118.4 | 120.5 | 125.6 | 115.6 | 122.7 | 118.1 | 117.6 | 116.9 | 118.0 | 117.2 | 115.8 | 110.6 |
| Unfinished metals related to durable goods | 114.9 | 124.4 | 133.1 | 138.5 | 140.4 | 139.9 | 138.2 | 145.8 | 161.1 | 193.2 | 194.4 | 195.9 |
| Finished metals related to durable goods | 104.8 | 108.1 | 112.4 | 114.7 | 115.9 | 116.6 | 117.3 | 117.6 | 119.2 | 125.3 | 128.4 | 128.9 |
| Nonmetals related to durable goods | 99.3 | 98.7 | 98.8 | 99.7 | 100.8 | 100.9 | 100.7 | 100.5 | 100.8 | 101.1 | 101.3 | 101.7 |
| **Industrial Supplies and Materials, Durable** | 108.5 | 112.8 | 117.8 | 118.0 | 120.8 | 119.7 | 119.1 | 121.4 | 127.2 | 139.1 | 139.8 | 139.2 |
| **Industrial Supplies and Materials, Excluding Fuels[1]** | 116.5 | 119.8 | 124.1 | 124.8 | 128.0 | 127.5 | 128.5 | 130.3 | 134.9 | 143.7 | 144.7 | 144.7 |
| **Industrial Supplies and Materials, Excluding Petroleum** | 107.9 | 112.5 | 114.4 | 118.8 | 119.9 | 120.2 | 126.8 | 132.2 | 128.1 | 133.9 | 135.1 | 138.3 |
| **Industrial Supplies and Materials, Nondurable, Excluding Petroleum** | 107.1 | 112.0 | 110.2 | 119.7 | 118.7 | 120.7 | 135.4 | 144.3 | 128.3 | 126.7 | 128.5 | 136.3 |
| **Capital Goods** | 93.1 | 92.2 | 92.0 | 92.2 | 92.3 | 92.3 | 91.5 | 91.0 | 91.1 | 91.2 | 91.3 | 91.5 |
| Electric generating equipment | 97.8 | 97.0 | 97.4 | 98.0 | 98.8 | 98.8 | 99.0 | 99.3 | 100.1 | 102.1 | 102.7 | 103.0 |
| Nonelectrical machinery | 91.2 | 90.1 | 89.8 | 89.9 | 89.8 | 89.8 | 88.7 | 88.1 | 88.0 | 87.8 | 87.8 | 87.9 |
| Transportation equipment, excluding motor vehicles[1] | 103.5 | 104.0 | 103.9 | 104.5 | 105.6 | 106.0 | 106.4 | 106.1 | 107.0 | 107.9 | 108.3 | 109.1 |
| **Automotive Parts and Accessories** | 99.6 | 100.1 | 100.2 | 101.5 | 101.8 | 102.0 | 102.1 | 101.8 | 101.6 | 102.7 | 103.2 | 103.0 |
| **Consumer Goods, Excluding Automotive** | 98.7 | 98.5 | 98.4 | 99.0 | 99.9 | 99.9 | 99.7 | 99.6 | 99.6 | 99.8 | 100.5 | 101.0 |
| Nondurables, manufactured | 101.3 | 100.9 | 100.8 | 101.4 | 102.8 | 102.8 | 103.1 | 102.7 | 102.8 | 102.6 | 103.0 | 103.4 |
| Nonmanufactured consumer goods | 96.4 | 96.8 | 97.9 | 98.2 | 100.3 | 101.8 | 100.6 | 101.2 | 98.2 | 98.6 | 100.5 | 101.8 |
| **All Imports, Excluding Fuels** | 102.4 | 102.7 | 103.4 | 104.0 | 105.0 | 104.9 | 104.8 | 105.1 | 105.7 | 107.2 | 107.8 | 108.1 |
| **All Imports, Excluding Petroleum** | 99.1 | 99.7 | 100.1 | 101.3 | 102.0 | 102.0 | 102.8 | 103.7 | 103.0 | 104.2 | 104.8 | 105.7 |

| Commodity | 2007 | | | | 2008 | | | | 2009 | | | |
|---|---|---|---|---|---|---|---|---|---|---|---|---|
| | March | June | September | December | March | June | September | December | March | June | September | December |
| **ALL COMMODITIES** | 115.9 | 120.0 | 121.8 | 127.3 | 133.5 | 145.5 | 137.8 | 114.5 | 113.6 | 120.0 | 121.3 | 124.4 |
| **Foods, Feeds, and Beverages** | 124.6 | 127.8 | 131.8 | 134.4 | 141.8 | 147.7 | 147.9 | 142.3 | 137.0 | 139.8 | 140.6 | 143.7 |
| Agricultural foods, feeds, and beverages, excluding distilled beverages | 135.1 | 139.5 | 144.4 | 148.3 | 157.3 | 165.1 | 165.1 | 159.4 | 151.3 | 155.5 | 156.8 | 160.8 |
| Nonagricultural foods (fish and distilled beverages) | 101.3 | 101.5 | 103.5 | 103.0 | 106.8 | 108.4 | 109.1 | 103.8 | 104.8 | 104.4 | 104.1 | 104.9 |
| **Industrial Supplies and Materials** | 169.8 | 185.6 | 190.7 | 211.3 | 234.5 | 283.0 | 248.9 | 150.4 | 149.3 | 177.3 | 183.0 | 196.2 |
| Fuels and lubricants | 209.6 | 238.2 | 250.0 | 290.3 | 329.0 | 423.7 | 346.3 | 153.9 | 162.3 | 222.1 | 228.5 | 249.7 |
| Paper and paper base stocks | 111.5 | 110.8 | 111.2 | 109.2 | 114.1 | 117.3 | 119.9 | 113.2 | 106.6 | 101.8 | 99.1 | 103.1 |
| Materials associated with nondurable supplies and materials | 124.0 | 125.4 | 128.2 | 135.3 | 147.8 | 152.9 | 162.4 | 148.5 | 136.7 | 137.5 | 134.8 | 140.6 |
| Selected building materials | 111.4 | 113.1 | 116.9 | 116.0 | 114.1 | 119.2 | 122.7 | 118.1 | 116.2 | 116.0 | 118.9 | 120.9 |
| Unfinished metals related to durable goods | 202.9 | 219.7 | 209.1 | 217.2 | 241.5 | 273.2 | 255.4 | 185.7 | 171.6 | 178.3 | 204.0 | 221.5 |
| Finished metals related to durable goods | 125.4 | 133.7 | 134.8 | 135.0 | 145.8 | 158.7 | 159.9 | 140.8 | 132.7 | 133.2 | 137.1 | 140.4 |
| Nonmetals related to durable goods | 101.8 | 101.6 | 102.5 | 103.8 | 105.2 | 107.6 | 111.4 | 109.0 | 105.2 | 103.0 | 104.3 | 105.4 |
| **Industrial Supplies and Materials, Durable** | 141.0 | 148.4 | 146.3 | 149.1 | 158.9 | 173.5 | 169.7 | 141.8 | 134.7 | 136.0 | 145.7 | 152.5 |
| **Industrial Supplies and Materials, Excluding Fuels[1]** | 146.2 | 151.6 | 151.2 | 155.4 | 166.8 | 178.8 | 179.5 | 155.1 | 145.5 | 146.5 | 151.7 | 158.6 |
| **Industrial Supplies and Materials, Excluding Petroleum** | 139.3 | 144.6 | 141.0 | 147.5 | 159.4 | 173.7 | 167.4 | 146.0 | 133.1 | 132.1 | 134.4 | 145.2 |
| **Industrial Supplies and Materials, Nondurable, Excluding Petroleum** | 136.3 | 139.1 | 133.6 | 144.5 | 159.3 | 173.0 | 163.5 | 150.8 | 131.0 | 127.4 | 121.0 | 136.3 |
| **Capital Goods** | 91.1 | 91.3 | 91.9 | 92.2 | 92.2 | 93.2 | 93.3 | 92.7 | 91.8 | 91.9 | 91.9 | 91.9 |
| Electric generating equipment | 104.3 | 105.7 | 106.5 | 107.9 | 109.3 | 112.0 | 112.9 | 111.4 | 109.4 | 110.0 | 110.3 | 111.3 |
| Nonelectrical machinery | 87.2 | 87.2 | 87.7 | 87.7 | 87.5 | 88.2 | 88.2 | 87.5 | 86.6 | 86.5 | 86.5 | 86.4 |
| Transportation equipment, excluding motor vehicles[1] | 110.1 | 111.0 | 113.4 | 114.7 | 115.3 | 117.7 | 118.2 | 120.2 | 120.6 | 122.4 | 123.2 | 122.6 |
| **Automotive Parts and Accessories** | 103.5 | 103.3 | 103.6 | 104.8 | 106.2 | 106.7 | 107.4 | 108.8 | 108.9 | 108.5 | 109.2 | 110.0 |
| **Consumer Goods, Excluding Automotive** | 101.3 | 101.4 | 102.1 | 102.6 | 104.0 | 104.9 | 105.1 | 104.4 | 103.9 | 104.3 | 104.1 | 104.3 |
| Nondurables, manufactured | 104.1 | 104.3 | 105.0 | 105.5 | 107.5 | 107.9 | 108.2 | 108.2 | 108.0 | 108.1 | 107.8 | 107.9 |
| Nonmanufactured consumer goods | 102.2 | 102.6 | 103.4 | 103.8 | 104.3 | 106.6 | 106.6 | 103.6 | 101.2 | 101.4 | 101.2 | 102.1 |
| **All Imports, Excluding Fuels** | 108.4 | 109.5 | 110.1 | 111.4 | 113.9 | 116.5 | 116.8 | 112.7 | 110.7 | 111.2 | 111.9 | 113.0 |
| **All Imports, Excluding Petroleum** | 105.9 | 107.1 | 107.1 | 108.9 | 111.6 | 114.9 | 114.0 | 109.9 | 107.3 | 107.4 | 107.9 | 109.7 |

[1]December 2001 = 100.

## Table 9-11. U.S. Import Price Indexes for Selected Categories of Goods, by End Use, 2004–2015—*Continued*

(2000 = 100, unless otherwise indicated.)

| Commodity | 2010 | | | | 2011 | | | | 2012 | | | |
|---|---|---|---|---|---|---|---|---|---|---|---|---|
| | March | June | September | December | March | June | September | December | March | June | September | December |
| **ALL COMMODITIES** | 126.3 | 125.2 | 125.7 | 131.0 | 139.3 | 142.2 | 141.7 | 142.2 | 144.2 | 138.7 | 140.8 | 139.4 |
| **Foods, Feeds, and Beverages** | 147.4 | 148.7 | 153.3 | 162.7 | 174.9 | 174.8 | 174.7 | 172.4 | 174.4 | 171.8 | 171.6 | 169.1 |
| Agricultural foods, feeds, and beverages, excluding distilled beverages | 165.8 | 166.1 | 171.1 | 182.6 | 198.9 | 197.0 | 196.5 | 194.0 | 196.3 | 193.4 | 194.4 | 190.7 |
| Nonagricultural foods (fish and distilled beverages) | 105.6 | 109.2 | 113.0 | 117.4 | 120.7 | 124.5 | 125.3 | 123.7 | 124.7 | 122.9 | 120.1 | 120.4 |
| **Industrial Supplies and Materials** | 205.0 | 199.5 | 200.1 | 222.6 | 256.3 | 266.1 | 262.5 | 263.6 | 272.0 | 245.5 | 255.8 | 249.3 |
| Fuels and lubricants | 262.4 | 245.8 | 247.1 | 285.2 | 343.7 | 359.0 | 348.2 | 356.3 | 371.0 | 317.7 | 343.1 | 328.2 |
| Paper and paper base stocks | 107.6 | 115.5 | 117.5 | 117.5 | 116.3 | 119.4 | 117.1 | 114.8 | 114.0 | 114.1 | 112.6 | 111.5 |
| Materials associated with nondurable supplies and materials | 144.6 | 146.2 | 147.7 | 157.0 | 165.8 | 173.0 | 175.9 | 175.1 | 177.7 | 183.3 | 176.0 | 175.6 |
| Selected building materials | 127.6 | 131.9 | 124.6 | 127.0 | 131.5 | 129.3 | 131.2 | 130.7 | 134.4 | 138.1 | 141.3 | 143.6 |
| Unfinished metals related to durable goods | 233.4 | 244.6 | 244.2 | 266.0 | 290.2 | 297.0 | 304.9 | 277.8 | 283.9 | 263.5 | 257.1 | 263.8 |
| Finished metals related to durable goods | 142.4 | 146.5 | 147.7 | 152.7 | 157.4 | 161.1 | 165.6 | 162.1 | 163.9 | 161.8 | 161.6 | 161.7 |
| Nonmetals related to durable goods | 107.1 | 107.2 | 107.7 | 108.7 | 112.1 | 114.3 | 116.3 | 115.2 | 115.4 | 115.0 | 114.2 | 114.4 |
| **Industrial Supplies and Materials, Durable** | 158.4 | 163.7 | 162.5 | 171.2 | 181.4 | 184.7 | 189.3 | 179.9 | 183.4 | 176.7 | 174.9 | 177.4 |
| **Industrial Supplies and Materials, Excluding Fuels**[1] | 164.3 | 168.9 | 168.9 | 178.0 | 187.8 | 192.8 | 196.6 | 190.0 | 192.9 | 191.1 | 187.1 | 188.4 |
| **Industrial Supplies and Materials, Excluding Petroleum** | 149.7 | 151.6 | 151.0 | 159.4 | 168.4 | 172.5 | 174.5 | 167.8 | 167.6 | 165.3 | 163.1 | 167.8 |
| **Industrial Supplies and Materials, Nondurable, Excluding Petroleum** | 139.4 | 137.5 | 137.5 | 145.5 | 153.1 | 158.2 | 157.4 | 153.5 | 149.5 | 151.7 | 149.1 | 155.9 |
| **Capital Goods** | 91.4 | 91.5 | 91.8 | 92.0 | 92.6 | 92.7 | 92.9 | 93.1 | 93.5 | 93.2 | 93.4 | 93.2 |
| Electric generating equipment | 111.0 | 111.4 | 112.7 | 113.7 | 115.6 | 117.1 | 118.4 | 118.4 | 118.9 | 118.8 | 119.5 | 119.7 |
| Nonelectrical machinery | 85.9 | 86.0 | 86.1 | 86.2 | 86.5 | 86.4 | 86.4 | 86.4 | 86.6 | 86.2 | 86.4 | 86.0 |
| Transportation equipment, excluding motor vehicles[1] | 121.5 | 121.3 | 121.6 | 121.9 | 124.8 | 126.1 | 126.4 | 130.0 | 133.1 | 133.8 | 133.8 | 134.8 |
| **Automotive Parts and Accessories** | 109.9 | 110.2 | 111.5 | 112.0 | 113.7 | 115.7 | 116.6 | 117.0 | 117.6 | 118.3 | 118.9 | 118.6 |
| **Consumer Goods, Excluding Automotive** | 104.5 | 104.4 | 104.2 | 104.2 | 104.7 | 105.8 | 106.6 | 107.7 | 107.6 | 107.6 | 107.3 | 107.6 |
| Nondurables, manufactured | 109.0 | 109.3 | 110.0 | 110.4 | 110.3 | 111.6 | 112.8 | 114.4 | 114.5 | 114.8 | 114.7 | 115.3 |
| Nonmanufactured consumer goods | 102.5 | 102.4 | 103.0 | 103.7 | 107.8 | 111.8 | 114.9 | 119.3 | 118.0 | 119.3 | 115.5 | 115.3 |
| **All Imports, Excluding Fuels** | 113.7 | 114.4 | 114.7 | 116.4 | 118.7 | 120.1 | 120.9 | 120.4 | 121.1 | 120.8 | 120.4 | 120.4 |
| **All Imports, Excluding Petroleum** | 110.3 | 110.7 | 111.0 | 112.6 | 115.0 | 116.4 | 117.0 | 116.4 | 116.7 | 116.3 | 116.0 | 116.5 |

| Commodity | 2013 | | | | 2014 | | | | 2015 | | | |
|---|---|---|---|---|---|---|---|---|---|---|---|---|
| | March | June | September | December | March | June | September | December | March | June | September | December |
| **ALL COMMODITIES** | 141.2 | 138.8 | 139.8 | 137.8 | 140.5 | 140.5 | 137.9 | 130.1 | 125.3 | 126.6 | 121.9 | 119.3 |
| **Foods, Feeds, and Beverages** | 173.7 | 172.2 | 174.9 | 175.9 | 182.1 | 176.6 | 180.1 | 182.1 | 178.0 | 175.5 | 174.7 | 172.4 |
| Agricultural foods, feeds, and beverages, excluding distilled beverages | 194.5 | 190.0 | 191.1 | 192.1 | 198.9 | 193.6 | 197.4 | 201.5 | 196.0 | 195.0 | 193.5 | 190.1 |
| Nonagricultural foods (fish and distilled beverages) | 126.4 | 131.9 | 138.1 | 138.9 | 143.9 | 138.0 | 140.7 | 137.9 | 137.2 | 131.1 | 132.1 | 132.3 |
| **Industrial Supplies and Materials** | 257.7 | 247.2 | 253.2 | 242.3 | 254.8 | 254.7 | 241.4 | 199.4 | 175.9 | 185.9 | 160.2 | 148.2 |
| Fuels and lubricants | 346.5 | 329.9 | 347.3 | 324.3 | 349.8 | 350.3 | 320.0 | 230.0 | 183.0 | 209.7 | 157.5 | 135.7 |
| Paper and paper base stocks | 112.7 | 113.2 | 113.3 | 113.9 | 112.7 | 113.6 | 113.2 | 112.8 | 111.6 | 110.3 | 109.9 | 108.4 |
| Materials associated with nondurable supplies and materials | 175.0 | 173.4 | 168.3 | 168.0 | 171.4 | 169.8 | 168.3 | 167.9 | 161.2 | 161.1 | 156.4 | 151.8 |
| Selected building materials | 148.9 | 143.6 | 141.5 | 142.4 | 143.0 | 141.6 | 142.5 | 140.6 | 138.3 | 136.6 | 133.2 | 134.3 |
| Unfinished metals related to durable goods | 263.7 | 243.6 | 238.9 | 235.6 | 239.2 | 239.6 | 242.3 | 228.9 | 214.8 | 207.1 | 189.8 | 177.1 |
| Finished metals related to durable goods | 160.6 | 158.3 | 156.1 | 155.8 | 157.4 | 157.9 | 158.5 | 156.9 | 154.1 | 152.7 | 149.0 | 145.5 |
| Nonmetals related to durable goods | 114.4 | 113.7 | 112.2 | 112.3 | 111.5 | 112.0 | 112.3 | 111.5 | 110.2 | 109.8 | 109.1 | 108.4 |
| **Industrial Supplies and Materials, Durable** | 178.0 | 170.1 | 167.3 | 166.8 | 168.0 | 168.2 | 169.3 | 164.1 | 158.4 | 155.2 | 148.2 | 143.5 |
| **Industrial Supplies and Materials, Excluding Fuels**[1] | 188.6 | 182.9 | 179.2 | 178.5 | 180.6 | 180.2 | 180.4 | 176.9 | 170.5 | 168.4 | 162.0 | 157.2 |
| **Industrial Supplies and Materials, Excluding Petroleum** | 167.1 | 163.4 | 157.3 | 160.1 | 167.4 | 161.6 | 160.3 | 158.2 | 150.8 | 148.4 | 143.2 | 138.4 |
| **Industrial Supplies and Materials, Nondurable, Excluding Petroleum** | 153.9 | 154.8 | 145.3 | 151.7 | 165.8 | 153.2 | 149.1 | 150.5 | 141.3 | 139.8 | 136.7 | 131.8 |
| **Capital Goods** | 93.0 | 92.6 | 92.4 | 92.5 | 92.3 | 92.6 | 92.4 | 92.1 | 91.4 | 90.9 | 90.4 | 89.8 |
| Electric generating equipment | 119.5 | 119.5 | 119.5 | 119.3 | 119.0 | 120.0 | 120.4 | 120.1 | 119.2 | 118.2 | 117.7 | 116.6 |
| Nonelectrical machinery | 85.8 | 85.3 | 85.1 | 85.2 | 85.0 | 85.2 | 84.9 | 84.6 | 83.9 | 83.4 | 82.9 | 82.3 |
| Transportation equipment, excluding motor vehicles[1] | 135.8 | 135.8 | 136.0 | 136.0 | 136.2 | 135.8 | 136.7 | 136.8 | 136.8 | 137.0 | 136.9 | 137.0 |
| **Automotive Parts and Accessories** | 118.6 | 117.1 | 115.6 | 115.5 | 115.8 | 116.1 | 115.6 | 115.4 | 113.2 | 112.0 | 111.5 | 111.0 |
| **Consumer Goods, Excluding Automotive** | 107.7 | 107.6 | 107.3 | 107.2 | 108.1 | 108.4 | 108.3 | 107.9 | 107.5 | 107.4 | 107.2 | 107.2 |
| Nondurables, manufactured | 115.8 | 116.0 | 116.1 | 116.3 | 117.9 | 118.5 | 118.8 | 119.1 | 119.1 | 119.1 | 119.2 | 119.3 |
| Nonmanufactured consumer goods | 116.4 | 116.4 | 116.4 | 117.1 | 120.4 | 121.3 | 121.1 | 119.1 | 118.1 | 118.4 | 116.7 | 120.3 |
| **All Imports, Excluding Fuels** | 120.6 | 119.6 | 119.0 | 119.0 | 119.7 | 119.6 | 119.5 | 119.0 | 117.5 | 116.9 | 115.9 | 114.9 |
| **All Imports, Excluding Petroleum** | 116.5 | 115.7 | 114.8 | 115.2 | 116.5 | 115.8 | 115.6 | 115.1 | 113.5 | 112.8 | 111.9 | 110.8 |

[1]December 2001 = 100.

# CHAPTER 10: VOLUNTEERING IN THE UNITED STATES

## HIGHLIGHTS

This chapter includes information on volunteering that was collected through a supplement to the September 2015 Current Population Survey (CPS). The supplement was sponsored by the Corporation for National and Community Service. For more information about the CPS, please see Chapter 1.

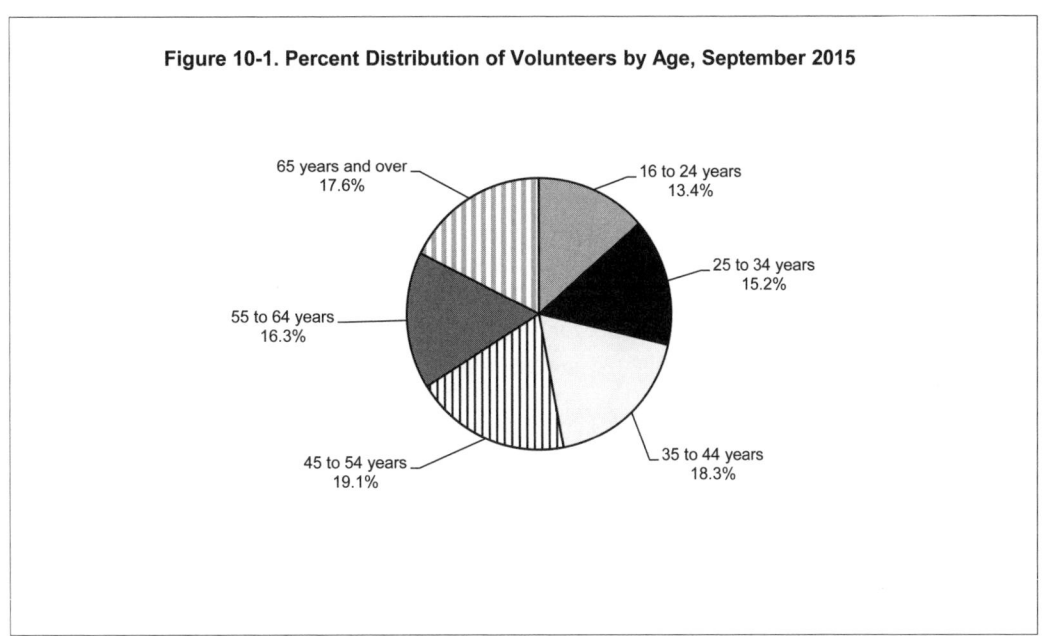

Figure 10-1. Percent Distribution of Volunteers by Age, September 2015

Nearly 63 million people in the United States volunteered through or for an organization at some point from September 2014 through September 2015. Those age 45 to 54 years old made up the largest group of volunteers followed by those in the 35 to 44 age group. Sixteen to 24 year olds made up the smallest volunteer group at 13.4 percent. (See Table 10-1).

## OTHER HIGHLIGHTS

- Across all age groups, educational levels, and other major demographic characteristics, women volunteered at a higher rate than men (27.8 percent compared with 21.8 percent). (See Table 10-1.)

- Individuals with higher levels of education were more likely to volunteer than were those with less education. Among persons age 25 and over, 38.8 percent of college graduates with a bachelor's degree and higher volunteered, compared with 26.5 percent of persons with some college or an associate's degree, 15.6 percent of high school graduates, and 8.1 percent of those with less than a high school diploma. (See Table 10-2.)

- In 2015, the organization for which the volunteer worked the most hours during the year—was most frequently religious (33.1 percent of all volunteers), followed by educational or youth service related (25.2 percent). Another 14.6 percent of volunteers performed activities mainly for social or community service organizations. (See Table 10-5.)

## NOTES AND DEFINITIONS

### Collection and Coverage

The data in this release were collected through a supplement to the September 2015 Current Population Survey (CPS). The CPS—a monthly survey of about 60,000 eligible households conducted by the U.S. Census Bureau for the Bureau of Labor Statistics—focuses on obtaining information on employment and unemployment among the nation's civilian noninstitutional population age 16 and over. More information on the CPS is available in Chapter 1 of this *Handbook.*

In the September supplement, questions on volunteer activities were asked of all households. Self-response was considered important for the volunteer supplement because research indicated that self-respondents could more easily answer questions on the characteristics of the volunteer activity. About two-thirds of responses were self-reports. The survey was introduced as follows: "This month, we are interested in volunteer activities, that is, activities for which people are not paid, except perhaps expenses. We only want you to include volunteer activities that you did through or for an organization, even if you only did them once in a while."

Following this introduction, respondents were asked the first supplement question: "Since September 1st of last year, have you done any volunteer activities through or for an organization?"

If respondents did not answer "yes" to the first question, they were asked the following question: "Sometimes people don't think of activities they do infrequently or activities they do for children's schools or youth organizations as volunteer activities. Since September 1st of last year, have you done any of these types of volunteer activities?"

Respondents were considered volunteers if they answered "yes" to either of these questions. This method has been used since the supplement was first administered in 2002. Respondents classified as volunteers were asked further questions about the number and type of organizations for which they volunteered, total hours spent volunteering, how they became involved with the main organization for which they volunteered, the type of activities they performed for the main organization, and what their main

activity was. The reference period for the questions on volunteering was about one year, from September 1, 2014, through the survey reference week in September 2015. The reference period for other characteristics—such as labor force status, educational attainment, and marital status—refer to the survey reference week in September 2015. It is possible that these characteristics were different at the time volunteer activities were performed.

### Concepts and Definitions

*Volunteers* are persons who performed unpaid volunteer activities at any point during the survey reference year. The count of volunteers only includes persons who volunteered through or for an organization; the figures do not include persons who volunteered in a more informal manner. For example, a woman who taught acting to children through a local theater would be considered a volunteer. However, a woman who, on her own, organized softball games for the children in her neighborhood would not be counted as a volunteer for the purpose of this survey.

*Organizations* are associations, societies, or groups of people who share a common interest. Examples include churches, youth groups, and civic organizations. For the purpose of this study, organizations are grouped into eight major categories, including religious, youth, and social or community service organizations.

The *main organization* is the organization for which the volunteer worked the most hours during the year. If a respondent volunteered for only one organization, it was considered the main organization, even if exact hours were not obtained.

*Activities* are the specific tasks the volunteer did for an organization. Examples include tutoring, fundraising, and serving food. The activity categories were modified in 2005, thus creating a break in the comparability of activities between 2005 and prior years.

### Sources of Additional Information

Additional information on volunteering can be found in the BLS news release "Volunteering in the United States—2015" 16-0363 at http://www.bls.gov/cps/.

## Table 10-1.  Volunteers by Selected Characteristics, September 2011–September 2015

(Number in thousands, percent.)

| Characteristic | September 2011 | | September 2012 | | September 2013 | | September 2014 | | September 2015 | |
|---|---|---|---|---|---|---|---|---|---|---|
| | Number | Percent of Population | Number | Percent of Population | Number | Percent of Population | Number | Percent of Population | Number | Percent of Population |
| **Sex** | | | | | | | | | | |
| Total, both sexes ................................ | 64 252 | 26.8 | 64 513 | 26.5 | 62 615 | 25.4 | 62 757 | 25.3 | 62 623 | 24.9 |
| Men ................................................. | 27 354 | 23.5 | 27 238 | 23.2 | 26 404 | 22.2 | 26 375 | 22.0 | 26 498 | 21.8 |
| Women ............................................. | 36 898 | 29.9 | 37 274 | 29.5 | 36 211 | 28.4 | 36 381 | 28.3 | 36 126 | 27.8 |
| **Age** | | | | | | | | | | |
| Total, 16 years and over ..................... | 64 252 | 26.8 | 64 513 | 26.5 | 62 615 | 25.4 | 62 757 | 25.3 | 62 623 | 24.9 |
| 16 to 24 years .................................. | 8 578 | 22.5 | 8 776 | 22.6 | 8 466 | 21.8 | 8 469 | 21.9 | 8 415 | 21.8 |
| 25 to 34 years .................................. | 9 691 | 23.3 | 9 513 | 23.2 | 9 118 | 21.9 | 9 291 | 22.0 | 9 548 | 22.3 |
| 35 to 44 years .................................. | 12 566 | 31.8 | 12 527 | 31.6 | 12 098 | 30.6 | 11 783 | 29.8 | 11 490 | 28.9 |
| 45 to 54 years .................................. | 13 420 | 30.6 | 12 777 | 29.3 | 12 184 | 28.2 | 12 204 | 28.5 | 11 933 | 28.0 |
| 55 to 64 years .................................. | 10 449 | 28.1 | 10 619 | 27.6 | 10 191 | 26.0 | 10 331 | 25.9 | 10 213 | 25.1 |
| 65 years and over ............................. | 9 547 | 24.0 | 10 301 | 24.4 | 10 558 | 24.1 | 10 679 | 23.6 | 11 024 | 23.5 |
| **Race and Hispanic or Latino Ethnicity** | | | | | | | | | | |
| White ............................................... | 54 432 | 28.2 | 53 778 | 27.8 | 52 685 | 27.1 | 52 201 | 26.7 | 51 986 | 26.4 |
| Black or African American ................... | 5 934 | 20.3 | 6 316 | 21.1 | 5 637 | 18.5 | 6 094 | 19.7 | 6 086 | 19.3 |
| Asian .............................................. | 2 304 | 20.0 | 2 524 | 19.6 | 2 525 | 19.0 | 2 513 | 18.2 | 2 596 | 17.9 |
| Hispanic or Latino ethnicity ............... | 5 151 | 14.9 | 5 635 | 15.2 | 5 838 | 15.5 | 5 982 | 15.5 | 6 165 | 15.5 |
| **Educational Attainment**[1] | | | | | | | | | | |
| Less than a high school diploma ........ | 2 461 | 9.8 | 2 177 | 8.8 | 2 204 | 9.0 | 2 100 | 8.8 | 1 900 | 8.1 |
| High school graduates, no college[2] ..... | 11 049 | 18.2 | 10 527 | 17.3 | 10 138 | 16.7 | 10 075 | 16.4 | 9 576 | 15.6 |
| Some college or associate degree ...... | 15 946 | 29.5 | 15 832 | 28.7 | 15 562 | 27.7 | 15 494 | 27.3 | 15 102 | 26.5 |
| Bachelor's degree and higher[3] ........... | 26 218 | 42.4 | 27 202 | 42.2 | 26 244 | 39.8 | 26 619 | 39.4 | 27 629 | 38.8 |
| **Employment Status** | | | | | | | | | | |
| Civilian labor force ............................. | 45 249 | 29.1 | 44 974 | 28.7 | 43 162 | 27.5 | 42 780 | 27.3 | 42 563 | 27.0 |
| Employed ......................................... | 41 881 | 29.6 | 42 083 | 29.1 | 40 401 | 27.7 | 40 497 | 27.5 | 40 701 | 27.2 |
| Full-time[4] ..................................... | 32 517 | 28.7 | 32 568 | 28.1 | 31 524 | 26.8 | 31 557 | 26.5 | 32 085 | 26.3 |
| Part-time[5] .................................... | 9 363 | 33.3 | 9 515 | 33.4 | 8 877 | 31.7 | 8 940 | 31.7 | 8 616 | 31.1 |
| Unemployed ..................................... | 3 368 | 23.8 | 2 891 | 23.8 | 2 761 | 24.1 | 2 283 | 24.0 | 1 861 | 23.3 |
| Not in the labor force ........................ | 19 003 | 22.5 | 19 539 | 22.4 | 19 452 | 21.9 | 19 977 | 21.8 | 20 060 | 21.4 |

[1]Data refer to persons 25 years and over.
[2]Includes persons with a high school diploma or equivalent.
[3]Includes persons with bachelor's, master's, professional, and doctoral degrees.
[4]Usually work 35 hours or more a week at all jobs.
[5]Usually work less than 35 hours a week at all jobs.

## Table 10-2. Volunteers by Selected Characteristics, September 2015

(Number in thousands, percent.)

| Characteristic | Total, both sexes | | | Men | | | Women | | |
|---|---|---|---|---|---|---|---|---|---|
| | Civilian noninstitutional population | Volunteers | | Civilian noninstitutional population | Volunteers | | Civilian noninstitutional population | Volunteers | |
| | | Number | Percent of population | | Number | Percent of population | | Number | Percent of population |
| **Age** | | | | | | | | | |
| Total, 16 years and over ........ | 251 325 | 62 623 | 24.9 | 121 365 | 26 498 | 21.8 | 129 960 | 36 126 | 27.8 |
| 16 to 24 years ....................... | 38 525 | 8 415 | 21.8 | 19 409 | 3 702 | 19.1 | 19 115 | 4 714 | 24.7 |
| 16 to 19 years .................... | 16 612 | 4 382 | 26.4 | 8 425 | 2 089 | 24.8 | 8 187 | 2 293 | 28.0 |
| 20 to 24 years .................... | 21 913 | 4 033 | 18.4 | 10 984 | 1 613 | 14.7 | 10 928 | 2 421 | 22.2 |
| 25 years and over ................... | 212 801 | 54 208 | 25.5 | 101 956 | 22 796 | 22.4 | 110 844 | 31 412 | 28.3 |
| 25 to 34 years .................... | 42 901 | 9 548 | 22.3 | 21 211 | 3 836 | 18.1 | 21 690 | 5 712 | 26.3 |
| 35 to 44 years .................... | 39 719 | 11 490 | 28.9 | 19 454 | 4 768 | 24.5 | 20 265 | 6 723 | 33.2 |
| 45 to 54 years .................... | 42 588 | 11 933 | 28.0 | 20 816 | 5 127 | 24.6 | 21 772 | 6 806 | 31.3 |
| 55 to 64 years .................... | 40 763 | 10 213 | 25.1 | 19 602 | 4 384 | 22.4 | 21 161 | 5 829 | 27.5 |
| 65 years and over ............... | 46 830 | 11 024 | 23.5 | 20 872 | 4 681 | 22.4 | 25 957 | 6 343 | 24.4 |
| **Race and Hispanic or Latino Ethnicity** | | | | | | | | | |
| White ....................................... | 197 152 | 51 986 | 26.4 | 96 294 | 22 222 | 23.1 | 100 858 | 29 764 | 29.5 |
| Black or African American ...... | 31 479 | 6 086 | 19.3 | 14 315 | 2 378 | 16.6 | 17 164 | 3 708 | 21.6 |
| Asian ...................................... | 14 466 | 2 596 | 17.9 | 6 734 | 1 037 | 15.4 | 7 732 | 1 558 | 20.2 |
| Hispanic or Latino ethnicity .... | 39 828 | 6 165 | 15.5 | 19 849 | 2 583 | 13.0 | 19 979 | 3 582 | 17.9 |
| **Educational Attainment[1]** | | | | | | | | | |
| Less than a high school diploma ......... | 23 528 | 1 900 | 8.1 | 11 802 | 781 | 6.6 | 11 726 | 1 120 | 9.5 |
| High school graduates, no college[2] ..... | 61 199 | 9 576 | 15.6 | 30 074 | 4 097 | 13.6 | 31 125 | 5 479 | 17.6 |
| Some college or associate degree ..... | 56 948 | 15 102 | 26.5 | 26 155 | 6 043 | 23.1 | 30 793 | 9 059 | 29.4 |
| Bachelor's degree and higher[3] ........... | 71 126 | 27 629 | 38.8 | 33 925 | 11 875 | 35.0 | 37 201 | 15 755 | 42.4 |
| **Marital Status** | | | | | | | | | |
| Single, never married ........... | 76 268 | 15 143 | 19.9 | 40 226 | 6 672 | 16.6 | 36 042 | 8 471 | 23.5 |
| Married, spouse present ......... | 124 783 | 37 348 | 29.9 | 62 869 | 16 825 | 26.8 | 61 914 | 20 523 | 33.1 |
| Other marital status[4] ............ | 50 274 | 10 132 | 20.2 | 18 270 | 3 000 | 16.4 | 32 005 | 7 132 | 22.3 |
| **Presence of Own Children Under 18 Years[5]** | | | | | | | | | |
| Without own children under 18 ........ | 184 577 | 41 738 | 22.6 | 91 802 | 18 263 | 19.9 | 92 775 | 23 475 | 25.3 |
| With own children under 18 ...... | 66 748 | 20 885 | 31.3 | 29 563 | 8 235 | 27.9 | 37 185 | 12 651 | 34.0 |
| **Employment Status** | | | | | | | | | |
| Civilian labor force ................. | 157 627 | 42 563 | 27.0 | 83 920 | 19 700 | 23.5 | 73 708 | 22 862 | 31.0 |
| Employed ............................... | 149 639 | 40 701 | 27.2 | 79 812 | 18 934 | 23.7 | 69 826 | 21 767 | 31.2 |
| Full-time[6] ......................... | 121 914 | 32 085 | 26.3 | 69 954 | 16 535 | 23.6 | 51 959 | 15 549 | 29.9 |
| Part-time[7] ........................ | 27 725 | 8 616 | 31.1 | 9 858 | 2 399 | 24.3 | 17 867 | 6 218 | 34.8 |
| Unemployed ....................... | 7 989 | 1 861 | 23.3 | 4 107 | 766 | 18.7 | 3 882 | 1 095 | 28.2 |
| Not in the labor force ............. | 93 698 | 20 060 | 21.4 | 37 446 | 6 797 | 18.2 | 56 252 | 13 263 | 23.6 |

[1]Data refer to persons 25 years and over.
[2]Includes persons with a high school diploma or equivalent.
[3]Includes persons with bachelor's, master's, professional, and doctoral degrees.
[4]Includes divorced, separated, and widowed persons.
[5]Own children include sons, daughters, stepchildren, and adopted children.
[6]Usually work 35 hours or more a week at all jobs.
[7]Usually work less than 35 hours or more a week at all jobs.

## Table 10-3.  Volunteers by Number of Organizations for Which Volunteer Activities Were Performed and Selected Characteristics, September 2015

(Number in thousands, percent.)

| Characteristic | Total volunteers (thousands) | Percent distribution of the number of organizations for which volunteer activities were performed | | | | | | |
|---|---|---|---|---|---|---|---|---|
| | | Total | One | Two | Three | Four | Five or more | Not reporting number of organizations |
| **Sex** | | | | | | | | |
| Total, both sexes ............................. | 62 623 | 100.0 | 72.0 | 18.3 | 6.4 | 2.0 | 1.2 | 0.2 |
| Men ....................................................... | 26 498 | 100.0 | 73.2 | 17.8 | 6.0 | 1.7 | 1.1 | 0.2 |
| Women ................................................. | 36 126 | 100.0 | 71.1 | 18.6 | 6.7 | 2.1 | 1.2 | 0.2 |
| **Age** | | | | | | | | |
| Total, 16 years and over ................. | 62 623 | 100.0 | 72.0 | 18.3 | 6.4 | 2.0 | 1.2 | 0.2 |
| 16 to 24 years ................................. | 8 415 | 100.0 | 77.7 | 14.7 | 5.3 | 1.2 | 0.7 | 0.3 |
| 16 to 19 years ............................. | 4 382 | 100.0 | 75.3 | 16.1 | 6.0 | 1.6 | 0.6 | 0.4 |
| 20 to 24 years ............................. | 4 033 | 100.0 | 80.4 | 13.1 | 4.5 | 0.8 | 0.9 | 0.2 |
| 25 years and over .......................... | 54 208 | 100.0 | 71.1 | 18.8 | 6.5 | 2.1 | 1.2 | 0.2 |
| 25 to 34 years ............................. | 9 548 | 100.0 | 76.5 | 17.5 | 4.3 | 1.1 | 0.5 | 0.1 |
| 35 to 44 years ............................. | 11 490 | 100.0 | 70.0 | 19.9 | 6.5 | 2.2 | 1.1 | 0.2 |
| 45 to 54 years ............................. | 11 933 | 100.0 | 68.0 | 20.3 | 7.7 | 2.1 | 1.5 | 0.4 |
| 55 to 64 years ............................. | 10 213 | 100.0 | 70.4 | 18.7 | 7.4 | 2.1 | 1.1 | 0.2 |
| 65 years and over ........................ | 11 024 | 100.0 | 71.6 | 17.3 | 6.4 | 2.7 | 1.8 | 0.1 |
| **Race and Hispanic or Latino Ethnicity** | | | | | | | | |
| White ................................................... | 51 986 | 100.0 | 70.5 | 19.1 | 6.8 | 2.1 | 1.2 | 0.3 |
| Black or African American ................. | 6 086 | 100.0 | 81.2 | 13.4 | 3.6 | 1.1 | 0.6 | 0.1 |
| Asian ................................................... | 2 596 | 100.0 | 79.5 | 14.2 | 3.3 | 1.9 | 0.8 | 0.2 |
| Hispanic or Latino ethnicity ............... | 6 165 | 100.0 | 82.4 | 13.0 | 3.2 | 0.5 | 0.6 | 0.2 |
| **Educational Attainment[1]** | | | | | | | | |
| Less than a high school diploma ....... | 1 900 | 100.0 | 90.4 | 7.6 | 1.7 | 0.2 | ... | ... |
| High school graduates, no college[2] ... | 9 576 | 100.0 | 81.1 | 14.1 | 3.1 | 1.0 | 0.5 | 0.2 |
| Some college or associate degree ..... | 15 102 | 100.0 | 75.9 | 16.8 | 5.1 | 1.3 | 0.7 | 0.2 |
| Bachelor's degree and higher[3] .......... | 27 629 | 100.0 | 63.7 | 22.4 | 8.9 | 3.0 | 1.9 | 0.2 |
| **Marital Status** | | | | | | | | |
| Single, never married ........................ | 15 143 | 100.0 | 76.6 | 15.7 | 5.3 | 1.3 | 0.8 | 0.3 |
| Married, spouse present .................... | 37 348 | 100.0 | 70.0 | 19.6 | 6.9 | 2.1 | 1.2 | 0.2 |
| Other marital status[4] ......................... | 10 132 | 100.0 | 72.6 | 17.0 | 6.1 | 2.4 | 1.6 | 0.2 |
| **Presence of Own Children Under 18 Years[5]** | | | | | | | | |
| Men | | | | | | | | |
| Without own children under 18 .......... | 18 263 | 100.0 | 74.8 | 16.7 | 5.8 | 1.5 | 1.0 | 0.2 |
| With own children under 18 ............... | 8 235 | 100.0 | 69.8 | 20.2 | 6.3 | 2.3 | 1.2 | 0.2 |
| Women | | | | | | | | |
| Without own children under 18 .......... | 23 475 | 100.0 | 72.7 | 17.3 | 6.4 | 2.1 | 1.3 | 0.3 |
| With own children under 18 ............... | 12 651 | 100.0 | 68.1 | 21.1 | 7.2 | 2.2 | 1.2 | 0.2 |
| **Employment Status** | | | | | | | | |
| Civilian labor force ............................. | 42 563 | 100.0 | 71.2 | 19.1 | 6.4 | 1.9 | 1.1 | 0.3 |
| Employed ............................................ | 40 701 | 100.0 | 70.9 | 19.3 | 6.5 | 1.9 | 1.1 | 0.3 |
| Full-time[6] ......................................... | 32 085 | 100.0 | 71.3 | 19.0 | 6.3 | 2.0 | 1.1 | 0.3 |
| Part-time[7] ........................................ | 8 616 | 100.0 | 69.7 | 20.2 | 7.3 | 1.6 | 1.2 | 0.1 |
| Unemployed ........................................ | 1 861 | 100.0 | 77.0 | 16.5 | 4.9 | 0.8 | 0.8 | ... |
| Not in the labor force ......................... | 20 060 | 100.0 | 73.7 | 16.4 | 6.2 | 2.2 | 1.3 | 0.2 |

[1]Data refer to persons 25 years and over.
[2]Includes persons with a high school diploma or equivalent.
[3]Includes persons with bachelor's, master's, professional, and doctoral degrees.
[4]Includes divorced, separated, and widowed persons.
[5]Own children include sons, daughters, stepchildren, and adopted children.
[6]Usually work 35 hours or more a week at all jobs.
[7]Usually work less than 35 hours or more a week at all jobs.
. . . = Not available.

## Table 10-4.  Volunteers by Annual Hours of Volunteer Activities and Selected Characteristics, September 2015

(Number in thousands, percent.)

| Year | Total volunteers (thousands) | Percent distribution of total annual hours spent volunteering at all organizations | | | | | | | Median annual hours |
|---|---|---|---|---|---|---|---|---|---|
| | | Total | 1 to 14 hour(s) | 15 to 49 hours | 50 to 99 hours | 100 to 499 hours | 500 hours and over | Not reporting annual hours | |
| **Sex** | | | | | | | | | |
| Total, both sexes ............................... | 62 623 | 100.0 | 21.1 | 24.7 | 15.1 | 27.4 | 5.9 | 5.9 | 52 |
| Men ....................................................... | 26 498 | 100.0 | 20.4 | 24.1 | 15.2 | 28.2 | 6.4 | 5.8 | 52 |
| Women .................................................. | 36 126 | 100.0 | 21.7 | 25.1 | 15.0 | 26.9 | 5.5 | 5.9 | 50 |
| **Age** | | | | | | | | | |
| Total, 16 years and over ..................... | 62 623 | 100.0 | 21.1 | 24.7 | 15.1 | 27.4 | 5.9 | 5.9 | 52 |
| 16 to 24 years ................................... | 8 415 | 100.0 | 24.9 | 29.0 | 14.6 | 20.3 | 3.7 | 7.6 | 36 |
| 16 to 19 years ............................... | 4 382 | 100.0 | 23.9 | 30.1 | 16.2 | 20.3 | 2.5 | 7.1 | 36 |
| 20 to 24 years ............................... | 4 033 | 100.0 | 26.0 | 27.7 | 12.9 | 20.2 | 5.0 | 8.2 | 36 |
| 25 years and over .............................. | 54 208 | 100.0 | 20.5 | 24.0 | 15.1 | 28.5 | 6.2 | 5.6 | 52 |
| 25 to 34 years ............................... | 9 548 | 100.0 | 27.7 | 25.8 | 14.2 | 21.2 | 4.6 | 6.4 | 36 |
| 35 to 44 years ............................... | 11 490 | 100.0 | 23.0 | 26.3 | 15.8 | 25.9 | 4.5 | 4.4 | 48 |
| 45 to 54 years ............................... | 11 933 | 100.0 | 20.5 | 24.5 | 15.7 | 28.4 | 5.6 | 5.4 | 52 |
| 55 to 64 years ............................... | 10 213 | 100.0 | 18.7 | 24.3 | 14.8 | 29.9 | 6.8 | 5.4 | 56 |
| 65 years and over .......................... | 11 024 | 100.0 | 13.5 | 19.2 | 14.9 | 36.5 | 9.4 | 6.5 | 94 |
| **Race and Hispanic or Latino Ethnicity** | | | | | | | | | |
| White ..................................................... | 51 986 | 100.0 | 20.8 | 24.9 | 15.4 | 27.5 | 5.8 | 5.5 | 52 |
| Black or African American .................... | 6 086 | 100.0 | 20.7 | 22.0 | 14.1 | 28.6 | 6.4 | 8.4 | 52 |
| Asian ..................................................... | 2 596 | 100.0 | 25.8 | 26.5 | 11.7 | 24.6 | 4.5 | 6.9 | 40 |
| Hispanic or Latino ethnicity ................. | 6 165 | 100.0 | 22.4 | 24.6 | 12.8 | 27.6 | 5.8 | 6.8 | 48 |
| **Educational Attainment[1]** | | | | | | | | | |
| Less than a high school diploma ......... | 1 900 | 100.0 | 22.4 | 22.0 | 13.3 | 28.4 | 5.5 | 8.4 | 52 |
| High school graduates, no college[2] ... | 9 576 | 100.0 | 21.5 | 23.2 | 13.9 | 27.2 | 7.1 | 7.1 | 52 |
| Some college or associate degree ....... | 15 102 | 100.0 | 21.8 | 23.4 | 14.0 | 29.1 | 6.4 | 5.4 | 52 |
| Bachelor's degree and higher[3] .......... | 27 629 | 100.0 | 19.4 | 24.8 | 16.3 | 28.7 | 5.8 | 5.0 | 52 |
| **Marital Status** | | | | | | | | | |
| Single, never married .......................... | 15 143 | 100.0 | 25.5 | 27.0 | 14.3 | 20.9 | 4.5 | 7.7 | 36 |
| Married, spouse present ...................... | 37 348 | 100.0 | 19.5 | 24.2 | 15.4 | 29.8 | 6.1 | 5.0 | 52 |
| Other marital status[4] ......................... | 10 132 | 100.0 | 20.8 | 22.7 | 14.8 | 28.4 | 6.8 | 6.5 | 52 |
| **Presence of Own Children Under 18 Years[5]** | | | | | | | | | |
| Men | | | | | | | | | |
| Without own children under 18 ............ | 18 263 | 100.0 | 19.4 | 23.9 | 15.2 | 27.5 | 7.1 | 6.8 | 52 |
| With own children under 18 ................. | 8 235 | 100.0 | 22.6 | 24.5 | 15.1 | 29.7 | 4.6 | 3.5 | 50 |
| Women | | | | | | | | | |
| Without own children under 18 ............ | 23 475 | 100.0 | 20.0 | 24.0 | 14.9 | 28.0 | 6.3 | 6.8 | 52 |
| With own children under 18 ................. | 12 651 | 100.0 | 24.8 | 27.2 | 15.1 | 24.7 | 3.9 | 4.4 | 40 |
| **Employment Status** | | | | | | | | | |
| Civilian labor force .............................. | 42 563 | 100.0 | 22.9 | 26.0 | 15.2 | 25.9 | 4.5 | 5.5 | 48 |
| Employed .............................................. | 40 701 | 100.0 | 22.9 | 26.2 | 15.2 | 25.8 | 4.3 | 5.5 | 48 |
| Full-time[6] ........................................ | 32 085 | 100.0 | 23.3 | 26.4 | 15.4 | 25.4 | 4.1 | 5.4 | 48 |
| Part-time[7] ........................................ | 8 616 | 100.0 | 21.4 | 25.7 | 14.5 | 27.5 | 5.0 | 5.8 | 49 |
| Unemployed ......................................... | 1 861 | 100.0 | 23.4 | 21.7 | 14.2 | 26.6 | 8.1 | 6.0 | 52 |
| Not in the labor force .......................... | 20 060 | 100.0 | 17.3 | 21.8 | 14.8 | 30.7 | 8.8 | 6.6 | 66 |

[1]Data refer to persons 25 years and over.
[2]Includes persons with a high school diploma or equivalent.
[3]Includes persons with bachelor's, master's, professional, and doctoral degrees.
[4]Includes divorced, separated, and widowed persons.
[5]Own children include sons, daughters, stepchildren, and adopted children.
[6]Usually work 35 hours or more a week at all jobs.
[7]Usually work less than 35 hours or more a week at all jobs.

## Table 10-5.  Volunteers by Type of Main Organization for Which Volunteer Activities Were Performed and Selected Characteristics, September 2015

(Numbers in thousands, percent.)

| Year | Total volunteers (thousands) | Percent distribution of volunteers by type of main organization | | | | | | | | | | |
|---|---|---|---|---|---|---|---|---|---|---|---|---|
| | | Total | Civic, political, profess-ional, or inter-national | Educa-tional or youth service | Environ-mental or animal care | Hospital or other health | Public safety | Religious | Social or community service | Sport, hobby, cultural, or arts | Other | Not determined |
| **Sex** | | | | | | | | | | | | |
| Total, both sexes ............................. | 62 623 | 100.0 | 4.8 | 25.2 | 2.9 | 6.6 | 1.1 | 33.1 | 14.6 | 3.7 | 5.2 | 2.8 |
| Men ................................................ | 26 498 | 100.0 | 5.9 | 23.9 | 2.7 | 5.3 | 1.7 | 32.6 | 15.6 | 4.0 | 5.6 | 2.8 |
| Women ............................................ | 36 126 | 100.0 | 4.0 | 26.2 | 3.0 | 7.6 | 0.6 | 33.5 | 14.0 | 3.4 | 4.8 | 2.8 |
| **Age** | | | | | | | | | | | | |
| Total, 16 years and over .................. | 62 623 | 100.0 | 4.8 | 25.2 | 2.9 | 6.6 | 1.1 | 33.1 | 14.6 | 3.7 | 5.2 | 2.8 |
| 16 to 24 years ................................. | 8 415 | 100.0 | 3.8 | 30.6 | 3.9 | 8.5 | 1.2 | 25.4 | 14.4 | 3.3 | 4.9 | 4.0 |
| 16 to 19 years ............................. | 4 382 | 100.0 | 3.8 | 33.6 | 4.1 | 7.2 | 0.8 | 28.6 | 11.9 | 2.8 | 4.1 | 3.1 |
| 20 to 24 years ............................. | 4 033 | 100.0 | 3.7 | 27.3 | 3.6 | 9.9 | 1.7 | 22.0 | 17.1 | 3.7 | 5.9 | 5.0 |
| 25 years and over .......................... | 54 208 | 100.0 | 5.0 | 24.4 | 2.7 | 6.3 | 1.0 | 34.3 | 14.7 | 3.7 | 5.2 | 2.6 |
| 25 to 34 years ............................. | 9 548 | 100.0 | 4.0 | 28.6 | 3.6 | 8.0 | 1.7 | 28.2 | 14.7 | 2.5 | 5.8 | 2.9 |
| 35 to 44 years ............................. | 11 490 | 100.0 | 4.4 | 37.6 | 1.8 | 5.1 | 1.0 | 27.7 | 11.7 | 4.0 | 4.4 | 2.5 |
| 45 to 54 years ............................. | 11 933 | 100.0 | 4.6 | 29.4 | 2.6 | 5.4 | 0.9 | 33.4 | 13.7 | 3.4 | 3.6 | 2.9 |
| 55 to 64 years ............................. | 10 213 | 100.0 | 5.3 | 16.2 | 3.4 | 6.3 | 0.9 | 39.5 | 16.2 | 4.0 | 5.7 | 2.5 |
| 65 years and over ........................ | 11 024 | 100.0 | 6.6 | 9.3 | 2.4 | 7.3 | 0.9 | 42.7 | 17.3 | 4.5 | 6.8 | 2.3 |
| **Race and Hispanic or Latino Ethnicity** | | | | | | | | | | | | |
| White ............................................... | 51 986 | 100.0 | 5.0 | 24.8 | 3.1 | 6.7 | 1.2 | 32.6 | 14.7 | 3.8 | 5.4 | 2.7 |
| Black or African American ................ | 6 086 | 100.0 | 3.4 | 25.6 | 1.0 | 5.9 | 0.6 | 41.2 | 12.7 | 1.8 | 3.8 | 4.0 |
| Asian ............................................... | 2 596 | 100.0 | 3.9 | 32.1 | 1.2 | 8.3 | 0.6 | 29.1 | 13.4 | 3.1 | 4.7 | 3.5 |
| Hispanic or Latino ethnicity .............. | 6 165 | 100.0 | 4.2 | 31.3 | 1.6 | 5.6 | 0.7 | 37.3 | 10.5 | 2.3 | 3.4 | 3.2 |
| **Educational Attainment[1]** | | | | | | | | | | | | |
| Less than a high school diploma ....... | 1 900 | 100.0 | 2.3 | 19.9 | 1.0 | 2.7 | 1.1 | 52.7 | 12.1 | 1.6 | 3.7 | 2.9 |
| High school graduates, no college[2] .. | 9 576 | 100.0 | 4.5 | 21.7 | 2.1 | 5.1 | 2.2 | 40.3 | 13.8 | 3.4 | 4.8 | 2.2 |
| Some college or associate degree .... | 15 102 | 100.0 | 5.1 | 23.3 | 2.4 | 5.9 | 1.2 | 36.3 | 15.3 | 3.1 | 4.9 | 2.4 |
| Bachelor's degree and higher[3] ........ | 27 629 | 100.0 | 5.3 | 26.3 | 3.2 | 7.2 | 0.6 | 29.9 | 14.8 | 4.3 | 5.6 | 2.9 |
| **Marital Status** | | | | | | | | | | | | |
| Single, never married ....................... | 15 143 | 100.0 | 4.7 | 27.0 | 4.6 | 8.2 | 1.2 | 23.5 | 16.4 | 4.3 | 5.9 | 4.2 |
| Married, spouse present ................... | 37 348 | 100.0 | 4.7 | 26.2 | 2.2 | 5.7 | 1.1 | 37.6 | 12.6 | 3.4 | 4.2 | 2.3 |
| Other marital status[4] ....................... | 10 132 | 100.0 | 5.4 | 18.9 | 2.8 | 7.8 | 0.8 | 31.2 | 19.5 | 3.5 | 7.4 | 2.8 |
| **Presence of Own Children Under 18 Years[5]** | | | | | | | | | | | | |
| Men | | | | | | | | | | | | |
| Without own children under 18 ........ | 18 263 | 100.0 | 6.3 | 18.1 | 3.4 | 6.0 | 1.5 | 33.7 | 17.4 | 4.2 | 6.4 | 3.1 |
| With own children under 18 .............. | 8 235 | 100.0 | 5.0 | 36.8 | 1.1 | 3.7 | 2.2 | 30.3 | 11.4 | 3.5 | 3.8 | 2.2 |
| Women | | | | | | | | | | | | |
| Without own children under 18 ........ | 23 475 | 100.0 | 4.7 | 16.1 | 3.9 | 9.0 | 0.7 | 36.1 | 16.7 | 4.1 | 5.6 | 3.3 |
| With own children under 18 .............. | 12 651 | 100.0 | 2.9 | 45.1 | 1.4 | 5.1 | 0.4 | 28.8 | 9.0 | 2.2 | 3.4 | 1.9 |
| **Employment Status** | | | | | | | | | | | | |
| Civilian labor force ............................ | 42 563 | 100.0 | 5.0 | 27.3 | 2.9 | 6.5 | 1.2 | 30.8 | 14.8 | 3.7 | 5.1 | 2.8 |
| Employed ......................................... | 40 701 | 100.0 | 5.0 | 27.0 | 2.9 | 6.6 | 1.3 | 30.8 | 14.8 | 3.8 | 5.1 | 2.8 |
| Full-time[6] ................................... | 32 085 | 100.0 | 5.2 | 27.0 | 2.9 | 6.6 | 1.4 | 30.2 | 15.3 | 3.7 | 5.0 | 2.9 |
| Part-time[7] .................................. | 8 616 | 100.0 | 4.6 | 27.1 | 2.9 | 6.3 | 0.9 | 33.1 | 12.8 | 4.1 | 5.6 | 2.4 |
| Unemployed ..................................... | 1 861 | 100.0 | 3.2 | 32.2 | 4.2 | 4.1 | 0.2 | 29.3 | 15.1 | 2.8 | 5.7 | 3.4 |
| Not in the labor force ........................ | 20 060 | 100.0 | 4.6 | 21.0 | 2.7 | 7.0 | 0.7 | 38.1 | 14.3 | 3.5 | 5.2 | 2.9 |

[1]Data refer to persons 25 years and over.
[2]Includes persons with a high school diploma or equivalent.
[3]Includes persons with bachelor's, master's, professional, and doctoral degrees.
[4]Includes divorced, separated, and widowed persons.
[5]Own children include sons, daughters, stepchildren, and adopted children.
[6]Usually work 35 hours or more a week at all jobs.
[7]Usually work less than 35 hours or more a week at all jobs.

## Table 10-6. Main Volunteer Activity for Main Organization for Which Activities Were Performed and Selected Characteristics, September 2015

(Number in thousands, percent.)

| Characteristic | Total volunteers (thousands) | Percent distribution of the number of organizations for which volunteer activities were performed | | | | | | |
|---|---|---|---|---|---|---|---|---|
| | | Coach or referee sports teams | Teach or tutor | Mentor youth | Be an usher, greeter, minister | Collect, prepare, distribute, or serve food | Collect, make, or distribute clothing, crafts or goods other than food | Fundraise or sell items to raise money |
| **Sex** | | | | | | | | |
| Total, both sexes ............................. | 62 623 | 5.5 | 9.2 | 6.7 | 4.2 | 11.3 | 3.5 | 9.0 |
| Men .................................................. | 26 498 | 9.3 | 7.2 | 6.5 | 5.3 | 9.2 | 2.4 | 7.6 |
| Women .............................................. | 36 126 | 2.7 | 10.6 | 6.8 | 3.5 | 12.9 | 4.4 | 9.9 |
| **Age** | | | | | | | | |
| Total, 16 years and over ..................... | 62 623 | 5.5 | 9.2 | 6.7 | 4.2 | 11.3 | 3.5 | 9.0 |
| 16 to 24 years .................................. | 8 415 | 5.8 | 9.0 | 8.5 | 3.1 | 9.7 | 2.8 | 8.7 |
| 16 to 19 years .............................. | 4 382 | 4.8 | 8.5 | 8.9 | 3.4 | 9.6 | 3.4 | 7.6 |
| 20 to 24 years .............................. | 4 033 | 6.8 | 9.7 | 8.1 | 2.8 | 9.8 | 2.2 | 9.9 |
| 25 years and over ............................. | 54 208 | 5.5 | 9.2 | 6.4 | 4.4 | 11.6 | 3.6 | 9.0 |
| 25 to 34 years .............................. | 9 548 | 5.9 | 11.0 | 8.8 | 2.8 | 8.6 | 3.0 | 8.5 |
| 35 to 44 years .............................. | 11 490 | 10.3 | 11.5 | 9.0 | 3.1 | 9.8 | 3.1 | 10.0 |
| 45 to 54 years .............................. | 11 933 | 6.7 | 8.3 | 7.5 | 4.0 | 11.7 | 2.8 | 10.4 |
| 55 to 64 years .............................. | 10 213 | 3.0 | 8.7 | 3.9 | 5.8 | 13.1 | 4.2 | 9.2 |
| 65 years and over .......................... | 11 024 | 1.0 | 6.6 | 2.8 | 6.2 | 14.7 | 5.0 | 6.7 |
| **Race and Hispanic or Latino Ethnicity** | | | | | | | | |
| White ................................................ | 51 986 | 5.6 | 9.2 | 6.3 | 3.9 | 11.0 | 3.4 | 9.5 |
| Black or African American ................... | 6 086 | 5.2 | 9.1 | 9.7 | 7.3 | 14.9 | 4.0 | 5.9 |
| Asian ................................................ | 2 596 | 3.0 | 11.1 | 6.7 | 3.4 | 11.9 | 3.6 | 6.7 |
| Hispanic or Latino ethnicity ................ | 6 165 | 6.2 | 9.5 | 7.6 | 5.0 | 10.2 | 3.9 | 7.2 |
| **Educational Attainment[1]** | | | | | | | | |
| Less than a high school diploma ........ | 1 900 | 3.1 | 8.6 | 3.2 | 5.9 | 20.6 | 4.9 | 5.3 |
| High school graduates, no college[2] .... | 9 576 | 5.9 | 6.3 | 4.8 | 4.9 | 16.6 | 4.4 | 8.9 |
| Some college or associate degree ....... | 15 102 | 5.6 | 8.2 | 6.3 | 5.0 | 12.8 | 4.2 | 8.7 |
| Bachelor's degree and higher[3] .......... | 27 629 | 5.4 | 10.8 | 7.3 | 3.8 | 8.6 | 3.0 | 9.5 |
| **Marital Status** | | | | | | | | |
| Single, never married ....................... | 15 143 | 5.5 | 8.5 | 8.1 | 3.0 | 10.4 | 3.3 | 8.1 |
| Married, spouse present ..................... | 37 348 | 6.0 | 10.1 | 6.7 | 4.8 | 10.7 | 3.2 | 9.4 |
| Other marital status[4] ........................ | 10 132 | 3.8 | 6.8 | 4.7 | 3.9 | 15.2 | 4.8 | 8.7 |
| **Presence of Own Children Under 18 Years[5]** | | | | | | | | |
| Men | | | | | | | | |
| Without own children under 18 .......... | 18 263 | 5.5 | 6.9 | 5.9 | 5.6 | 10.2 | 2.5 | 7.5 |
| With own children under 18 ............... | 8 235 | 18.0 | 8.1 | 7.7 | 4.4 | 7.0 | 2.1 | 8.0 |
| Women | | | | | | | | |
| Without own children under 18 .......... | 23 475 | 1.6 | 8.9 | 5.2 | 4.0 | 14.1 | 4.8 | 8.8 |
| With own children under 18 ............... | 12 651 | 4.7 | 13.7 | 9.8 | 2.5 | 10.6 | 3.5 | 12.2 |
| **Employment Status** | | | | | | | | |
| Civilian labor force ............................. | 42 563 | 7.0 | 9.1 | 7.4 | 3.9 | 10.4 | 3.0 | 9.6 |
| Employed .......................................... | 40 701 | 7.1 | 9.2 | 7.4 | 3.9 | 10.4 | 2.9 | 9.8 |
| Full-time[6] .................................... | 32 085 | 8.1 | 8.5 | 7.6 | 4.0 | 10.0 | 2.9 | 10.2 |
| Part-time[7] ................................... | 8 616 | 3.2 | 11.9 | 6.8 | 3.3 | 11.7 | 2.9 | 8.2 |
| Unemployed ...................................... | 1 861 | 5.6 | 6.8 | 7.5 | 3.9 | 12.1 | 4.4 | 5.6 |
| Not in the labor force ........................ | 20 060 | 2.3 | 9.2 | 5.2 | 5.0 | 13.2 | 4.6 | 7.7 |

[1] Data refer to persons 25 years and over.
[2] Includes persons with a high school diploma or equivalent.
[3] Includes persons with bachelor's, master's, professional, and doctoral degrees.
[4] Includes divorced, separated, and widowed persons.
[5] Own children include sons, daughters, stepchildren, and adopted children.
[6] Usually work 35 hours or more a week at all jobs.
[7] Usually work less than 35 hours or more a week at all jobs.

**Table 10-6.  Main Volunteer Activity for Main Organization for Which Activities Were Performed and Selected Characteristics, September 2015—Continued**

(Number in thousands, percent.)

| Characteristic | Percent distribution of the number of organizations for which volunteer activities were performed | | | | | | |
|---|---|---|---|---|---|---|---|
| | Provide counseling, medical, EMS, or protective services | Provide general office services | Provide professional or management assistance | Engage in music, performance, or other artistic activities | Engage in general labor | Other | Equal time among all |
| **Sex** | | | | | | | |
| Total, both sexes .......................................... | 3.0 | 4.4 | 7.2 | 4.0 | 8.8 | 15.3 | 8.0 |
| Men ................................................................ | 3.3 | 2.5 | 8.5 | 3.0 | 9.0 | 12.3 | 14.8 |
| Women ........................................................... | 2.8 | 5.7 | 6.2 | 4.1 | 6.1 | 15.6 | 8.7 |
| **Age** | | | | | | | |
| Total, 16 years and over .............................. | 3.0 | 4.4 | 7.2 | 4.0 | 8.8 | 15.3 | 8.0 |
| 16 to 24 years ............................................ | 2.7 | 3.6 | 1.5 | 5.5 | 13.5 | 16.6 | 9.0 |
| 16 to 19 years ........................................ | 2.3 | 3.4 | 0.9 | 6.0 | 9.0 | 15.8 | 15.6 |
| 20 to 24 years ........................................ | 3.1 | 3.9 | 2.1 | 4.0 | 11.1 | 17.6 | 8.9 |
| 25 years and over ...................................... | 3.1 | 4.5 | 8.1 | 3.8 | 8.0 | 15.1 | 7.8 |
| 25 to 34 years ........................................ | 4.4 | 3.9 | 5.3 | 3.6 | 8.9 | 18.6 | 6.8 |
| 35 to 44 years ........................................ | 2.5 | 3.8 | 6.8 | 2.9 | 7.5 | 12.2 | 7.4 |
| 45 to 54 years ........................................ | 2.5 | 3.6 | 8.3 | 3.6 | 9.2 | 13.6 | 7.8 |
| 55 to 64 years ........................................ | 3.1 | 5.1 | 10.5 | 4.4 | 6.4 | 13.7 | 8.9 |
| 65 years and over ................................... | 3.1 | 6.1 | 9.4 | 4.4 | 7.9 | 17.8 | 8.3 |
| **Race and Hispanic or Latino Ethnicity** | | | | | | | |
| White ............................................................. | 3.1 | 4.4 | 7.6 | 3.8 | 8.9 | 15.3 | 7.9 |
| Black or African American ............................ | 1.6 | 4.2 | 3.8 | 4.7 | 6.4 | 14.1 | 9.1 |
| Asian ............................................................. | 5.0 | 5.8 | 6.6 | 4.9 | 6.9 | 18.0 | 6.3 |
| Hispanic or Latino ethnicity ......................... | 3.0 | 4.7 | 2.9 | 2.5 | 9.8 | 18.4 | 8.8 |
| **Educational Attainment[1]** | | | | | | | |
| Less than a high school diploma ................... | 3.7 | 2.8 | 0.8 | 1.3 | 10.9 | 19.4 | 9.5 |
| High school graduates, no college[2] ............ | 2.5 | 5.2 | 3.7 | 3.7 | 10.2 | 15.4 | 7.5 |
| Some college or associate degree ................ | 3.1 | 5.0 | 5.0 | 4.1 | 8.8 | 15.2 | 8.1 |
| Bachelor's degree and higher[3] ................... | 3.3 | 4.1 | 11.8 | 3.7 | 6.6 | 14.6 | 7.7 |
| **Marital Status** | | | | | | | |
| Single, never married ................................... | 3.2 | 4.3 | 4.1 | 4.4 | 11.2 | 18.3 | 7.5 |
| Married, spouse present ............................... | 2.9 | 4.2 | 8.5 | 3.9 | 7.8 | 13.6 | 8.3 |
| Other marital status[4] ................................. | 3.2 | 5.2 | 6.9 | 3.8 | 8.5 | 17.1 | 7.5 |
| **Presence of Own Children Under 18 Years[5]** | | | | | | | |
| Men | | | | | | | |
| Without own children under 18 ..................... | 3.2 | 2.9 | 8.9 | 4.3 | 13.2 | 16.1 | 7.2 |
| With own children under 18 .......................... | 3.4 | 1.7 | 7.7 | 2.8 | 10.4 | 11.9 | 6.8 |
| Women | | | | | | | |
| Without own children under 18 ..................... | 3.3 | 6.2 | 6.7 | 4.8 | 6.4 | 16.7 | 8.6 |
| With own children under 18 .......................... | 2.1 | 4.8 | 5.2 | 2.8 | 5.6 | 13.6 | 8.9 |
| **Employment Status** | | | | | | | |
| Civilian labor force ....................................... | 3.3 | 3.5 | 8.0 | 3.7 | 8.8 | 14.4 | 7.8 |
| Employed ...................................................... | 3.3 | 3.4 | 8.2 | 3.7 | 8.8 | 14.2 | 7.7 |
| Full-time[6] .............................................. | 3.4 | 3.3 | 8.7 | 3.3 | 8.6 | 13.9 | 7.4 |
| Part-time[7] .............................................. | 3.2 | 3.9 | 6.2 | 5.1 | 9.3 | 15.5 | 8.9 |
| Unemployed .................................................. | 2.8 | 5.4 | 5.2 | 3.3 | 9.6 | 19.4 | 8.3 |
| Not in the labor force .................................... | 2.4 | 6.1 | 5.4 | 4.6 | 8.6 | 17.0 | 8.5 |

[1]Data refer to persons 25 years and over.
[2]Includes persons with a high school diploma or equivalent.
[3]Includes persons with bachelor's, master's, professional, and doctoral degrees.
[4]Includes divorced, separated, and widowed persons.
[5]Own children include sons, daughters, stepchildren, and adopted children.
[6]Usually work 35 hours or more a week at all jobs.
[7]Usually work less than 35 hours or more a week at all jobs.

## Table 10-7. Volunteers by How They Became Involved With Main Organization for Which Activities Were Performed and Selected Characteristics, September 2015

(Number in thousands, percent.)

| Characteristic | Total volunteers (thousands) | Percent distribution of the number of organizations for which volunteer activities were performed | | | | | | | | |
|---|---|---|---|---|---|---|---|---|---|---|
| | | Total | Approached the organization | Was asked by | | | | | Other | Not reporting how became involved |
| | | | | Total | Boss or employer | Relative, friend, or co-worker | Someone in the organization | Someone else | | |
| **Sex** | | | | | | | | | | |
| Total, both sexes ............................ | 62 623 | 100.0 | 41.6 | 41.2 | 1.5 | 14.5 | 23.7 | 1.4 | 13.4 | 3.8 |
| Men ................................ | 26 498 | 100.0 | 40.9 | 42.1 | 1.4 | 15.4 | 23.6 | 1.6 | 13.1 | 3.9 |
| Women ................................ | 36 126 | 100.0 | 42.0 | 40.5 | 1.5 | 13.8 | 23.8 | 1.3 | 13.6 | 3.8 |
| **Age** | | | | | | | | | | |
| Total, 16 years and over .................... | 62 623 | 100.0 | 41.6 | 41.2 | 1.5 | 14.5 | 23.7 | 1.4 | 13.4 | 3.8 |
| 16 to 24 years ............................ | 8 415 | 100.0 | 40.6 | 38.6 | 0.8 | 15.8 | 19.4 | 2.4 | 15.7 | 5.0 |
| 16 to 19 years ......................... | 4 382 | 100.0 | 41.1 | 40.5 | 0.3 | 16.0 | 21.3 | 2.7 | 14.0 | 4.4 |
| 20 to 24 years ......................... | 4 033 | 100.0 | 40.1 | 36.6 | 1.4 | 15.7 | 17.3 | 2.1 | 17.7 | 5.6 |
| 25 years and over ........................ | 54 208 | 100.0 | 41.7 | 41.6 | 1.6 | 14.2 | 24.4 | 1.2 | 13.1 | 3.6 |
| 25 to 34 years ......................... | 9 548 | 100.0 | 44.1 | 39.3 | 2.7 | 16.0 | 19.2 | 1.3 | 12.7 | 3.9 |
| 35 to 44 years ......................... | 11 490 | 100.0 | 41.2 | 43.6 | 1.7 | 12.6 | 28.1 | 1.2 | 12.1 | 3.1 |
| 45 to 54 years ......................... | 11 933 | 100.0 | 39.6 | 42.7 | 1.7 | 13.4 | 26.4 | 0.9 | 13.9 | 3.8 |
| 55 to 64 years ......................... | 10 213 | 100.0 | 41.2 | 41.7 | 1.3 | 15.2 | 23.4 | 1.5 | 13.6 | 3.4 |
| 65 years and over ..................... | 11 024 | 100.0 | 42.9 | 40.1 | 0.5 | 14.4 | 23.7 | 1.2 | 13.0 | 4.0 |
| **Race and Hispanic or Latino Ethnicity** | | | | | | | | | | |
| White ................................ | 51 986 | 100.0 | 41.3 | 41.8 | 1.4 | 14.8 | 24.0 | 1.5 | 13.2 | 3.7 |
| Black or African American ................. | 6 086 | 100.0 | 42.7 | 37.5 | 1.7 | 12.3 | 22.3 | 1.0 | 14.8 | 5.1 |
| Asian ................................ | 2 596 | 100.0 | 42.8 | 40.1 | 1.8 | 14.0 | 22.8 | 1.2 | 12.5 | 4.5 |
| Hispanic or Latino ethnicity ............... | 6 165 | 100.0 | 46.1 | 38.2 | 1.6 | 13.1 | 21.3 | 2.1 | 11.9 | 3.9 |
| **Educational Attainment**[1] | | | | | | | | | | |
| Less than a high school diploma ......... | 1 900 | 100.0 | 41.1 | 40.9 | 0.8 | 13.0 | 25.3 | 1.8 | 13.2 | 4.8 |
| High school graduates, no college[2] ...... | 9 576 | 100.0 | 40.9 | 41.9 | 1.1 | 15.2 | 24.2 | 1.3 | 13.6 | 3.6 |
| Some college or associate degree ......... | 15 102 | 100.0 | 41.5 | 41.8 | 1.7 | 14.5 | 24.4 | 1.1 | 13.4 | 3.3 |
| Bachelor's degree and higher[3] ........... | 27 629 | 100.0 | 42.1 | 41.4 | 1.7 | 13.8 | 24.4 | 1.3 | 12.7 | 3.8 |
| **Marital Status** | | | | | | | | | | |
| Single, never married ..................... | 15 143 | 100.0 | 41.0 | 38.8 | 1.8 | 16.1 | 18.9 | 1.9 | 15.1 | 5.1 |
| Married, spouse present ................... | 37 348 | 100.0 | 41.9 | 42.7 | 1.3 | 13.8 | 26.1 | 1.3 | 12.2 | 3.3 |
| Other marital status[4] .................... | 10 132 | 100.0 | 41.4 | 39.2 | 1.4 | 14.3 | 22.1 | 1.1 | 15.4 | 4.0 |
| **Presence of Own Children Under 18 Years**[5] | | | | | | | | | | |
| Men | | | | | | | | | | |
| Without own children under 18 ........... | 18 263 | 100.0 | 40.9 | 41.0 | 1.2 | 16.1 | 21.7 | 1.8 | 13.8 | 4.2 |
| With own children under 18 ............... | 8 235 | 100.0 | 40.8 | 44.5 | 1.8 | 13.7 | 27.8 | 1.1 | 11.7 | 3.0 |
| Women | | | | | | | | | | |
| Without own children under 18 ........... | 23 475 | 100.0 | 42.4 | 38.7 | 1.5 | 15.1 | 20.6 | 1.3 | 14.4 | 4.5 |
| With own children under 18 ............... | 12 651 | 100.0 | 41.3 | 43.9 | 1.5 | 11.3 | 29.7 | 1.3 | 12.3 | 2.5 |
| **Employment Status** | | | | | | | | | | |
| Civilian labor force ....................... | 42 563 | 100.0 | 40.8 | 41.8 | 1.9 | 14.6 | 23.7 | 1.3 | 13.7 | 3.8 |
| Employed ................................ | 40 701 | 100.0 | 40.6 | 42.2 | 2.0 | 14.6 | 24.1 | 1.3 | 13.4 | 3.8 |
| Full-time[6] ............................ | 32 085 | 100.0 | 39.9 | 42.8 | 2.3 | 15.0 | 24.0 | 1.3 | 13.4 | 3.9 |
| Part-time[7] ............................ | 8 616 | 100.0 | 43.1 | 39.9 | 0.7 | 13.2 | 24.2 | 1.5 | 13.5 | 3.5 |
| Unemployed ............................ | 1 861 | 100.0 | 44.7 | 33.3 | 1.2 | 14.1 | 16.2 | 1.8 | 18.1 | 3.9 |
| Not in the labor force ..................... | 20 060 | 100.0 | 43.2 | 40.0 | 0.4 | 14.1 | 23.7 | 1.5 | 12.9 | 3.9 |

[1]Data refer to persons 25 years and over.
[2]Includes persons with a high school diploma or equivalent.
[3]Includes persons with bachelor's, master's, professional, and doctoral degrees.
[4]Includes divorced, separated, and widowed persons.
[5]Own children include sons, daughters, stepchildren, and adopted children.
[6]Usually work 35 hours or more a week at all jobs.
[7]Usually work less than 35 hours or more a week at all jobs.

# CHAPTER 11: CONSUMER EXPENDITURES

## HIGHLIGHTS

The principal objective of the Consumer Expenditure (CE) Survey is to collect information about the buying habits of American households. The survey breaks down expenditures for different demographic categories, such as income, age, family size, and geographic location. These data are used in a variety of government, business, and academic research projects and provide important weights for the periodic revisions of the Consumer Price Index (CPI).

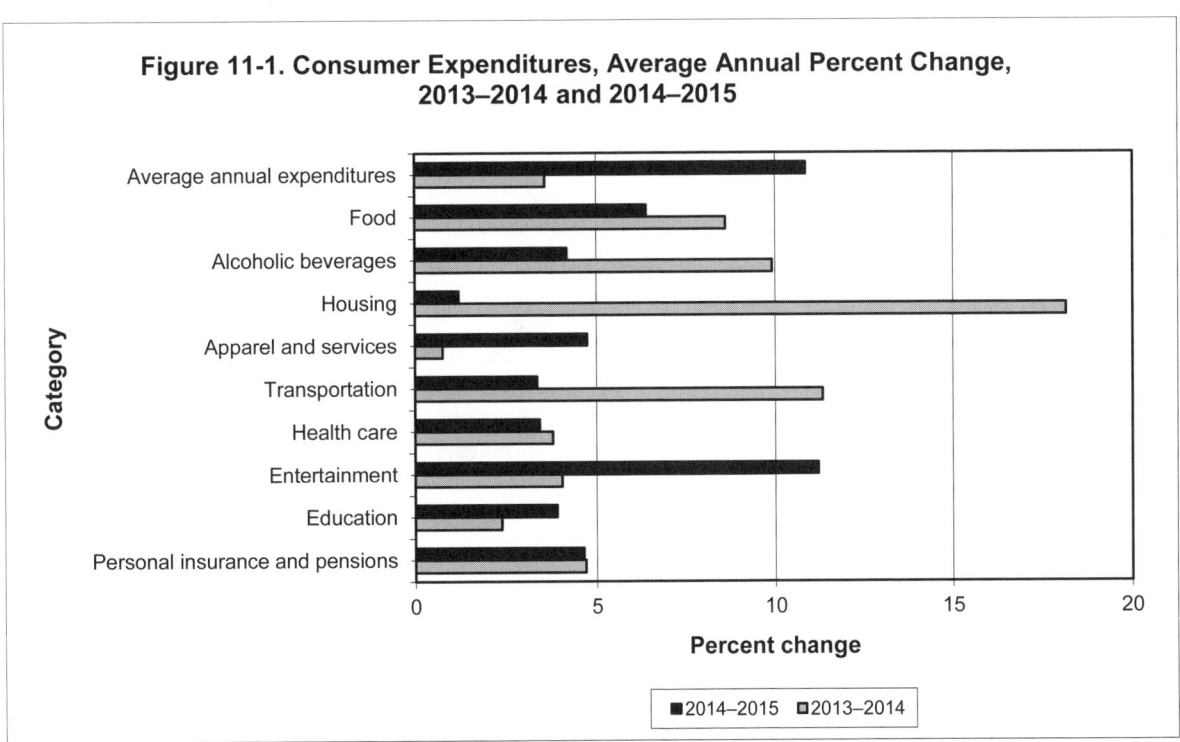

Figure 11-1. Consumer Expenditures, Average Annual Percent Change, 2013–2014 and 2014–2015

Average annual expenditures increased for the second straight year in 2015 after decreasing for in 2013. Even tobacco and smoking supplies experienced an increase in average annual expenditures after decreasing for five consecutive years. (See Table 11-1.)

## OTHER HIGHLIGHTS

- Average annual consumer expenditures varied substantially by age group. Older age groups typically spend more in health care while those in younger age groups spent more on education. In 2015, persons 65 years and older had $5,756 in annual expenditures for health care while those under 30 years of age had less than $2,000 in annual expenditures. (See Table 11-10.)

- As educational attainment increased, so did average annual expenditures. Those with less than a high school diploma had average annual expenditures of $26,766 while those with a master's, professional, or doctoral degree had average annual expenditures of $87,927. (See Table 11-13.)

- Homeowners had far higher average annual expenditures than renters ($65,656 compared with $39,937). Meanwhile, those in urban areas had higher expenditures than those in rural areas ($57,059 compared with $45,031). (See Table 11-14.)

## NOTES AND DEFINITIONS

### Purpose, Collection, and Coverage

The buying habits of American consumers change over time because of changes in relative prices, real income, family size and composition, and other determinants of tastes and preferences. The introduction of new products into the marketplace and the emergence of new concepts in retailing also influence consumer buying habits. Data from the Consumer Expenditure Survey (CE), the only national survey that relates family expenditures to demographic characteristics, are of great importance to researchers. The survey data are also used to revise the Consumer Price Index market baskets and item samples.

Until the 1970s, the Bureau of Labor Statistics (BLS) conducted surveys of consumer expenditures approximately once every 10 years. The last such survey was conducted in 1972–1973. In late 1979, in a significant departure from previous methodology, BLS initiated a survey to be conducted on a continuous basis with rotating panels of respondents.

The current CE is similar to its 1972–1973 predecessor in that it consists of two separate components. Each component has its own questionnaire and sample: (1) the Interview Survey, in which an interviewer visits each consumer unit every three months for a twelve-month period; and (2) the Diary Survey, a record-keeping survey completed by other consumer units for two consecutive one-week periods. The Census Bureau, under contract to BLS, collects the data for both components of the survey. Beginning in 1999, the sample was increased from 5,000 to 7,500 households.

In 2003, the survey modified the questions on race and Hispanic origin to comply with the new standards for maintaining, collecting, and presenting federal data on race and ethnicity for federal statistical agencies. Beginning with the data collected in 2003, the CE tables use data collected from the new race and ethnicity questions. A number of new classifications were made with publication of the 2003 data.

Beginning with the publication of the 2004 tables, the CE has been implementing multiple imputations of income data. Prior to 2004, the CE only published income data collected from complete income reporters. The introduction of multiply imputed income data affects the published CE tables in several ways, because income data are now published for all consumer units (instead of for complete reporters only). The most obvious result of this change is seen on the tables showing expenditures categorized by income before taxes, including income by quintile. Starting with the 2004 data, columns describing income, expenditures, and characteristics for "total complete reporting" and "incomplete reporting of income" no longer appear in these tables, and the column entitled "all consumer units" appears on all income tables. Due to the implementation of income imputation, data for

2004 are not strictly comparable to those of prior years, especially for the income tables. Averages for demographic characteristics and annual expenditures will change due to differences between the incomplete and complete income reporters in these categories. Furthermore, certain expenditures (such as personal insurance and pensions) are computed using income data. As a result of imputation, average annual values for these expenditures may be substantially different in the 2004 CE tables than in tables for previous years. The regular flow of data resulting from this design substantially enhances the usefulness of the survey by providing more timely information on consumption patterns within different kinds of consumer units.

The Quarterly *Interview Survey* is designed to collect data on the types of expenditures that respondents can be expected to recall after a period of three months or longer. These include relatively large expenditures (such as those for property, travel, automobiles, and major appliances) and expenditures that occur on a regular basis (such as those for rent, utilities, insurance premiums, and clothing). The interview also obtains "global estimates" for food and other selected items. The survey collects data for approximately 95 percent of total expenditures. Each sample household is interviewed once per quarter, for five consecutive quarters.

The *Diary Survey* is designed to collect data on expenditures for frequently purchased items that are more difficult to recall over longer periods of time. Respondents complete a diary of expenses for two consecutive 1-week periods. Expenditures for tobacco, drugs (including nonprescription drugs), and personal care supplies and services are also collected in the Diary Survey.

Participants in both surveys record dollar amounts for goods and services purchased during the reporting period, regardless of whether payment was made at the time of purchase. Excluded from both surveys are business-related expenditures and expenditures for which the family is reimbursed. Information is collected on demographic and family characteristics at the initial interview for each survey.

The tables in this chapter present integrated data from the Diary Survey and the Interview Survey and provide a complete accounting of consumer expenditures and income, which neither survey component is designed to do alone. Data for some expenditure items are only collected in one of the surveys. For example, the Diary Survey does not collect data for expenditures on overnight travel or information on reimbursements, while the Interview Survey records these purchases. Examples of expenditures for which reimbursements are netted out include those for medical care, auto repair, and construction, repairs, alterations, and maintenance of property.

For items unique to one survey or the other, the choice of which survey to use as the source of data is obvious. However, there is considerable overlap in coverage between the two surveys. Integrating the data thus presents the problem of determining the appropriate survey component. When data are available from both survey sources, the more reliable of the two (as determined by statistical methods) is selected. As a result, some items are selected from the Interview Survey and others are selected from the Diary Survey.

## Data Included in This Edition

Data for single characteristics are for calendar year 2015 and data for two cross-classified characteristics are for an average of calendar years 2014 and 2015. Income values from the survey are derived from "complete income reporters" only. Complete income reporters are defined as consumer units that provide values for at least one of the major sources of their income: wages and salaries, self-employment income, retirement income, dividends and interest, and welfare benefits. Some consumer units are defined as complete income reporters, even though they may not have provided a full accounting of all income from all sources.

Consumer units are classified by quintiles of income before taxes, age of reference person, size of consumer unit, region, composition of consumer unit, number of earners in consumer unit, housing tenure, race, type of area (urban or rural), and occupation.

## Concepts and Definitions

A *consumer unit* comprises either (1) all members of a particular household related by blood, marriage, adoption, or other legal arrangements; (2) a person living alone, sharing a household with others, living as a roomer in a private home or lodging house or in permanent living quarters in a hotel or motel, but who is financially independent; or (3) two or more persons living together who pool their income to make joint expenditure decisions. Financial independence is determined by the three major expense categories: housing, food, and other living expenses. To be considered financially independent, at least two of the three major expense categories have to be provided by the respondent.

The terms "family," "household," and "consumer unit" are used interchangeably in descriptions of the CE.

An *earner* is a consumer unit member, 14 years of age or older, who reported having worked at least 1 week during the 12 months prior to the interview date.

The *education of reference person* refers to the number of years of formal education of the reference person, on the basis of the highest grade completed. If enrolled at time of the interview, the interviewer records the grade currently attended. Persons not reporting the extent of their education are classified under no school or not reported.

The *householder* or *reference person* is the first member of the consumer unit mentioned by the respondent as owner or renter of the premises at the time of the initial interview.

*Housing tenure* refers to the family's principal place of residence during the survey. "Owner" includes families living in their own homes, cooperatives or condominium apartments, or townhouses. "Renter" includes families paying rent, as well as families living rent-free in lieu of wages.

*Quintiles of income before taxes* refers to the ranking of complete income reporters in ascending order, according to the level of total before-tax income reported by the consumer unit. The ranking is then divided into five equal groups. Incomplete income reporters are not ranked and are shown separately.

*Total expenditures* include the transaction costs, including excise and sales taxes of goods and services acquired during the interview period. Estimates include expenditures for gifts and contributions and payments for pensions and personal insurance.

## Sources of Additional Information

More extensive descriptions and tables can be found in an updated version of Chapter 16 in the *BLS Handbook of Methods* and in an anthology of articles relating to consumer expenditures. These resources can be found on the BLS Web site at <http://www.bls.gov>.

## Table 11-1. Consumer Expenditures, Annual Average of All Consumer Units, 2005–2015

(Number, dollar, percent.)

| Item | 2005 | 2006 | 2007 | 2008 | 2009 | 2010 | 2011 | 2012 | 2013 | 2014 | 2015 |
|---|---|---|---|---|---|---|---|---|---|---|---|
| **NUMBER OF CONSUMER UNITS (THOUSANDS)** | 117 356 | 118 843 | 120 171 | 120 770 | 120 847 | 121 107 | 122 287 | 124 416 | 125 670 | 127 006 | 128 437 |
| **CONSUMER UNIT CHARACTERISTICS** | | | | | | | | | | | |
| **Income Before Taxes** | 58 712 | 60 533 | 63 091 | 63 563 | 62 857 | 62 481 | 63 685 | 65 596 | 63 784 | 66 877 | 69 627 |
| **Age of Reference Person** | 48.6 | 48.7 | 48.8 | 49.1 | 49.0 | 49.0 | 50.0 | . . . | 50.1 | 50.3 | 50.5 |
| **Average Number in Consumer Unit** | | | | | | | | | | | |
| All persons | 2.5 | 2.5 | 2.5 | 2.5 | 2.5 | 2.5 | 2.5 | 2.5 | 2.5 | 2.5 | 2.5 |
| Children under 18 years | 0.6 | 0.6 | 0.6 | 0.6 | 0.6 | 0.6 | 0.6 | 0.6 | 0.6 | 0.6 | 0.6 |
| Persons 65 years and over | 0.3 | 0.3 | 0.3 | 0.3 | 0.3 | 0.3 | 0.3 | 0.3 | 0.3 | 0.4 | 0.4 |
| Earners | 1.3 | 1.3 | 1.3 | 1.3 | 1.3 | 1.3 | 1.3 | 1.3 | 1.3 | 1.3 | 1.3 |
| Vehicles | 2.0 | 1.9 | 1.9 | 2.0 | 2.0 | 1.9 | 1.9 | 1.9 | 1.9 | 1.9 | 1.9 |
| **Percent Homeowner** | 67 | 67 | 67 | 66 | 66 | 66 | 65 | 64 | 64 | 63 | 62 |
| With mortgage | 43 | 43 | 43 | 42 | 41 | 41 | 40 | 39 | 37 | 37 | 35 |
| Without mortgage | 25 | 24 | 23 | 24 | 25 | 25 | 25 | 26 | 26 | 26 | 27 |
| **AVERAGE ANNUAL EXPENDITURES** | 46 409 | 48 398 | 49 638 | 50 486 | 49 067 | 48 109 | 49 705 | 51 442 | 51 100 | 53 495 | 55 978 |
| **Food** | 5 931 | 6 111 | 6 133 | 6 443 | 6 372 | 6 129 | 6 458 | 6 599 | 6 602 | 6 759 | 7 023 |
| Food at home | 3 297 | 3 417 | 3 465 | 3 744 | 3 753 | 3 624 | 3 838 | 3 921 | 3 977 | 3 971 | 4 015 |
| Cereals and bakery products | 445 | 446 | 460 | 507 | 506 | 502 | 531 | 538 | 544 | 519 | 518 |
| Meats, poultry, fish, and eggs | 764 | 797 | 777 | 846 | 841 | 784 | 832 | 852 | 856 | 892 | 896 |
| Dairy products | 378 | 368 | 387 | 430 | 406 | 380 | 407 | 419 | 414 | 423 | 413 |
| Fruits and vegetables | 552 | 592 | 600 | 657 | 656 | 679 | 715 | 731 | 751 | 756 | 769 |
| Other food at home | 1 158 | 1 212 | 1 241 | 1 305 | 1 343 | 1 278 | 1 353 | 1 380 | 1 412 | 1 382 | 1 419 |
| Food away from home | 2 634 | 2 694 | 2 668 | 2 698 | 2 619 | 2 505 | 2 620 | 2 678 | 2 625 | 2 787 | 3 008 |
| **Alcoholic Beverages** | 426 | 497 | 457 | 444 | 435 | 412 | 456 | 451 | 445 | 463 | 515 |
| **Housing** | 15 167 | 16 366 | 16 920 | 17 109 | 16 895 | 16 557 | 16 803 | 16 887 | 17 148 | 17 798 | 18 409 |
| Shelter | 8 805 | 9 673 | 10 023 | 10 183 | 10 075 | 9 812 | 9 825 | 9 891 | 10 080 | 10 491 | 10 742 |
| Owned dwellings | 5 958 | 6 516 | 6 730 | 6 760 | 6 543 | 6 277 | 6 148 | 6 056 | 6 108 | 6 149 | 6 210 |
| Rented dwellings | 2 345 | 2 590 | 2 602 | 2 724 | 2 860 | 2 900 | 3 029 | 3 186 | 3 324 | 3 631 | 3 802 |
| Other lodging | 502 | 567 | 691 | 698 | 672 | 635 | 648 | 649 | 649 | 710 | 730 |
| Utilities, fuels, and public services | 3 183 | 3 397 | 3 477 | 3 649 | 3 645 | 3 660 | 3 727 | 3 648 | 3 737 | 3 921 | 3 885 |
| Household operations | 801 | 948 | 984 | 998 | 1 011 | 1 007 | 1 122 | 1 159 | 1 144 | 1 174 | 1 309 |
| Housekeeping supplies | 611 | 640 | 639 | 654 | 659 | 612 | 615 | 610 | 645 | 632 | 655 |
| Household furnishings and equipment | 1 767 | 1 708 | 1 797 | 1 624 | 1 506 | 1 467 | 1 514 | 1 580 | 1 542 | 1 581 | 1 818 |
| **Apparel and Services** | 1 886 | 1 874 | 1 881 | 1 801 | 1 725 | 1 700 | 1 740 | 1 736 | 1 604 | 1 786 | 1 846 |
| **Transportation** | 8 344 | 8 508 | 8 758 | 8 604 | 7 658 | 7 677 | 8 293 | 8 998 | 9 004 | 9 073 | 9 503 |
| Vehicle purchases (net outlay) | 3 544 | 3 421 | 3 244 | 2 755 | 2 657 | 2 588 | 2 669 | 3 210 | 3 271 | 3 301 | 3 997 |
| Gasoline and motor oil | 2 013 | 2 227 | 2 384 | 2 715 | 1 986 | 2 132 | 2 655 | 2 756 | 2 611 | 2 468 | 2 090 |
| Other vehicle expenses | 2 339 | 2 355 | 2 592 | 2 621 | 2 536 | 2 464 | 2 454 | 2 490 | 2 584 | 2 723 | 2 756 |
| Public and other transportation | 448 | 505 | 538 | 513 | 479 | 493 | 516 | 542 | 537 | 581 | 661 |
| **Health Care** | 2 664 | 2 766 | 2 853 | 2 976 | 3 126 | 3 157 | 3 313 | 3 556 | 3 631 | 4 290 | 4 342 |
| Health insurance | 1 361 | 1 465 | 1 545 | 1 653 | 1 785 | 1 831 | 1 922 | 2 061 | 2 229 | 2 868 | 2 977 |
| Medical services | 677 | 670 | 709 | 727 | 736 | 722 | 768 | 839 | 796 | 790 | 791 |
| Drugs | 521 | 514 | 481 | 482 | 486 | 485 | 489 | 515 | 470 | 486 | 425 |
| Medical supplies | 105 | 117 | 118 | 114 | 119 | 119 | 134 | 142 | 135 | 146 | 149 |
| **Entertainment** | 2 388 | 2 376 | 2 698 | 2 835 | 2 693 | 2 504 | 2 572 | 2 605 | 2 482 | 2 728 | 2 842 |
| **Personal Care Products and Services** | 541 | 585 | 588 | 616 | 596 | 582 | 634 | 628 | 608 | 645 | 683 |
| **Reading** | 126 | 117 | 118 | 116 | 110 | 100 | 115 | 109 | 102 | 103 | 114 |
| **Education** | 940 | 888 | 945 | 1 046 | 1 068 | 1 074 | 1 051 | 1 207 | 1 138 | 1 236 | 1 315 |
| **Tobacco Products and Smoking Supplies** | 319 | 327 | 323 | 317 | 380 | 362 | 351 | 332 | 330 | 319 | 349 |
| **Miscellaneous** | 808 | 846 | 808 | 840 | 816 | 849 | 775 | 829 | 645 | 782 | 871 |
| **Cash Contributions** | 1 663 | 1 869 | 1 821 | 1 737 | 1 723 | 1 633 | 1 721 | 1 913 | 1 834 | 1 788 | 1 819 |
| **Personal Insurance and Pensions** | 5 204 | 5 270 | 5 336 | 5 605 | 5 471 | 5 373 | 5 424 | 5 591 | 5 528 | 5 726 | 6 349 |
| Life and other personal insurance | 381 | 322 | 309 | 317 | 309 | 318 | 317 | 353 | 319 | 327 | 333 |
| Pensions and Social Security | 4 823 | 4 948 | 5 027 | 5 288 | 5 162 | 5 054 | 5 106 | 5 238 | 5 209 | 5 399 | 6 016 |

## Table 11-2.  Consumer Expenditures, Deciles of Income, 2015

(Number, dollar, percent.)

| Item | All consumer units | Lowest 10 percent | Second 10 percent | Third 10 percent | Fourth 10 percent | Fifth 10 percent | Sixth 10 percent | Seventh 10 percent | Eighth 10 percent | Ninth 10 percent | Highest 10 percent |
|---|---|---|---|---|---|---|---|---|---|---|---|
| NUMBER OF CONSUMER UNITS (THOUSANDS) .. | 128 437 | 12 886 | 12 787 | 12 800 | 12 762 | 12 853 | 12 847 | 12 862 | 12 867 | 12 897 | 12 876 |
| **CONSUMER UNIT CHARACTERISTICS** | | | | | | | | | | | |
| Income Before Taxes ............................ | 69 627 | 6 063 | 15 806 | 23 902 | 32 797 | 43 280 | 55 934 | 70 812 | 90 810 | 120 634 | 235 160 |
| Income After Taxes ............................... | 60 448 | 6 350 | 16 522 | 24 461 | 33 006 | 41 678 | 51 938 | 64 275 | 80 472 | 103 181 | 181 774 |
| Age of Reference Person ...................... | 50.5 | 48.1 | 58.4 | 55.0 | 52.3 | 50.3 | 48.3 | 48.2 | 47.5 | 48.0 | 49.4 |
| **Average Number in Consumer Unit** | | | | | | | | | | | |
| All persons ...................................... | 2.5 | 1.6 | 1.7 | 2.0 | 2.4 | 2.5 | 2.6 | 2.8 | 2.9 | 3.0 | 3.1 |
| Children under 18 years ...................... | 0.6 | 0.3 | 0.4 | 0.5 | 0.6 | 0.6 | 0.6 | 0.7 | 0.7 | 0.7 | 0.8 |
| Persons 65 years and over ................... | 0.4 | 0.3 | 0.5 | 0.5 | 0.5 | 0.4 | 0.3 | 0.3 | 0.2 | 0.2 | 0.2 |
| Earners ............................................. | 1.3 | 0.5 | 0.5 | 0.7 | 1.0 | 1.3 | 1.4 | 1.7 | 1.8 | 2.0 | 2.1 |
| Vehicles ............................................. | 1.9 | 0.8 | 1.0 | 1.3 | 1.7 | 1.8 | 2.0 | 2.3 | 2.5 | 2.7 | 2.8 |
| **Percent Distribution** | | | | | | | | | | | |
| Male ................................................. | 47 | 39 | 35 | 42 | 43 | 47 | 49 | 50 | 54 | 55 | 56 |
| Female .............................................. | 53 | 61 | 65 | 58 | 57 | 53 | 51 | 50 | 46 | 45 | 44 |
| **Percent Homeowner** ........................ | 62 | 31 | 46 | 52 | 55 | 58 | 63 | 71 | 75 | 84 | 89 |
| With mortgage .................................... | 35 | 10 | 12 | 15 | 20 | 28 | 36 | 47 | 56 | 63 | 66 |
| Without mortgage ................................ | 27 | 21 | 34 | 37 | 34 | 30 | 26 | 23 | 20 | 21 | 23 |
| **AVERAGE ANNUAL EXPENDITURES** .................... | 55 978 | 23 705 | 25 244 | 32 545 | 37 586 | 42 227 | 49 599 | 58 398 | 68 942 | 87 860 | 133 180 |
| **Food** ................................................. | 7 023 | 3 860 | 3 674 | 4 554 | 5 489 | 5 312 | 6 287 | 7 512 | 8 817 | 10 537 | 14 160 |
| Food at home ..................................... | 4 015 | 2 566 | 2 432 | 2 918 | 3 623 | 3 245 | 3 645 | 4 246 | 4 844 | 5 526 | 7 092 |
| Cereals and bakery products ............... | 518 | 345 | 322 | 384 | 481 | 427 | 473 | 530 | 666 | 683 | 868 |
| Meats, poultry, fish, and eggs ............. | 896 | 604 | 577 | 674 | 878 | 746 | 785 | 1 000 | 1 016 | 1 216 | 1 460 |
| Dairy products .................................... | 413 | 252 | 247 | 296 | 361 | 328 | 395 | 425 | 498 | 579 | 744 |
| Fruits and vegetables .......................... | 769 | 499 | 467 | 532 | 710 | 600 | 685 | 808 | 919 | 1 045 | 1 420 |
| Other food at home ............................. | 1 419 | 866 | 819 | 1 032 | 1 193 | 1 144 | 1 306 | 1 483 | 1 745 | 2 003 | 2 601 |
| Food away from home .......................... | 3 008 | 1 294 | 1 241 | 1 636 | 1 867 | 2 067 | 2 641 | 3 266 | 3 973 | 5 010 | 7 068 |
| **Alcoholic Beverages** .......................... | 515 | 226 | 164 | 235 | 271 | 317 | 457 | 461 | 694 | 875 | 1 447 |
| **Housing** ............................................. | 18 409 | 9 322 | 10 463 | 12 407 | 13 258 | 14 991 | 16 628 | 18 978 | 21 837 | 26 286 | 39 776 |
| Shelter .............................................. | 10 742 | 5 727 | 6 341 | 7 215 | 7 426 | 8 531 | 9 439 | 10 898 | 12 674 | 15 200 | 23 882 |
| Owned dwellings ................................ | 6 210 | 1 529 | 2 107 | 2 767 | 3 045 | 3 869 | 4 858 | 6 653 | 8 306 | 11 281 | 17 598 |
| Rented dwellings ................................ | 3 802 | 4 043 | 4 024 | 4 140 | 4 103 | 4 329 | 4 205 | 3 715 | 3 604 | 2 632 | 3 235 |
| Other lodging ..................................... | 730 | 155 | 209 | 308 | 279 | 334 | 376 | 530 | 763 | 1 287 | 3 048 |
| Utilities, fuels, and public services ........ | 3 885 | 2 126 | 2 532 | 3 056 | 3 367 | 3 629 | 3 907 | 4 299 | 4 608 | 5 252 | 6 055 |
| Household operations .......................... | 1 309 | 451 | 474 | 697 | 731 | 870 | 1 142 | 1 246 | 1 446 | 2 186 | 3 828 |
| Housekeeping supplies ........................ | 655 | 356 | 400 | 479 | 554 | 538 | 589 | 626 | 777 | 957 | 1 268 |
| Household furnishings and equipment ...... | 1 818 | 661 | 717 | 960 | 1 180 | 1 422 | 1 552 | 1 910 | 2 332 | 2 691 | 4 743 |
| **Apparel and Services** .......................... | 1 846 | 745 | 807 | 1 001 | 1 276 | 1 198 | 1 408 | 1 781 | 2 186 | 2 606 | 5 443 |
| **Transportation** .................................. | 9 503 | 3 616 | 3 504 | 5 389 | 6 459 | 8 081 | 9 558 | 10 795 | 11 865 | 16 492 | 19 178 |
| Vehicle purchases (net outlay) .............. | 3 997 | 1 170 | 1 101 | 1 881 | 2 641 | 3 482 | 3 949 | 4 828 | 5 162 | 7 528 | 8 178 |
| Gasoline and motor oil ......................... | 2 090 | 901 | 978 | 1 341 | 1 725 | 1 993 | 2 228 | 2 493 | 2 771 | 3 185 | 3 267 |
| Other vehicle expenses ........................ | 2 756 | 1 346 | 1 194 | 1 859 | 1 860 | 2 232 | 2 845 | 2 972 | 3 259 | 4 712 | 5 260 |
| Public and other transportation .............. | 661 | 199 | 230 | 309 | 234 | 374 | 536 | 502 | 673 | 1 067 | 2 473 |
| **Health Care** ....................................... | 4 342 | 1 508 | 2 356 | 3 237 | 3 610 | 3 719 | 4 211 | 5 073 | 5 581 | 6 407 | 7 691 |
| Health insurance ................................ | 2 977 | 1 040 | 1 559 | 2 148 | 2 476 | 2 637 | 2 935 | 3 604 | 3 879 | 4 369 | 5 107 |
| Medical services ................................. | 791 | 239 | 412 | 594 | 628 | 575 | 716 | 864 | 1 014 | 1 228 | 1 636 |
| Drugs ................................................ | 425 | 174 | 275 | 392 | 390 | 383 | 441 | 439 | 519 | 591 | 641 |
| Medical supplies ................................. | 149 | 54 | 109 | 104 | 115 | 124 | 120 | 167 | 169 | 218 | 307 |
| **Entertainment** ................................... | 2 842 | 1 179 | 1 361 | 1 530 | 1 947 | 2 042 | 2 395 | 2 731 | 3 372 | 4 598 | 7 240 |
| **Personal Care Products and Services** ........ | 683 | 323 | 290 | 424 | 481 | 500 | 547 | 732 | 861 | 1 092 | 1 569 |
| **Reading** ............................................. | 114 | 31 | 42 | 77 | 87 | 110 | 104 | 131 | 138 | 161 | 259 |
| **Education** .......................................... | 1 315 | 1 019 | 356 | 579 | 409 | 507 | 722 | 825 | 1 147 | 2 237 | 5 323 |
| **Tobacco Products and Smoking Supplies** ........ | 349 | 296 | 320 | 329 | 390 | 380 | 371 | 354 | 390 | 382 | 281 |
| **Miscellaneous** ................................... | 871 | 469 | 409 | 469 | 631 | 583 | 764 | 885 | 1 078 | 1 338 | 2 075 |
| **Cash Contributions** ............................ | 1 819 | 696 | 729 | 1 015 | 1 093 | 1 233 | 1 438 | 1 833 | 1 948 | 2 725 | 5 454 |
| **Personal Insurance and Pensions** .......... | 6 349 | 414 | 771 | 1 298 | 2 184 | 3 252 | 4 709 | 6 306 | 9 028 | 12 124 | 23 283 |
| Life and other personal insurance ......... | 333 | 54 | 116 | 105 | 159 | 185 | 201 | 306 | 505 | 515 | 1 177 |
| Pensions and Social Security ................ | 6 016 | 359 | 655 | 1 193 | 2 025 | 3 067 | 4 508 | 6 000 | 8 523 | 11 609 | 22 106 |

## Table 11-3.  Consumer Expenditures, Averages by Income Before Taxes, 2015

(Number, dollar, percent.)

| Item | All consumer units | Less than $15,000 | $15,000 to $29,999 | $30,000 to $39,999 | $40,000 to $49,999 | $50,000 to $69,999 | $70,000 to $99,999 | $100,000 to $149,999 | $150,000 to $199,999 | $200,000 and over |
|---|---|---|---|---|---|---|---|---|---|---|
| NUMBER OF CONSUMER UNITS (THOUSANDS) ........... | 128 437 | 17 946 | 23 162 | 12 536 | 10 914 | 18 112 | 18 168 | 15 616 | 6 020 | 5 964 |
| **CONSUMER UNIT CHARACTERISTICS** | | | | | | | | | | |
| **Income Before Taxes** .............. | 69 627 | 8 169 | 22 263 | 34 746 | 44 568 | 59 293 | 83 413 | 119 828 | 170 277 | 314 010 |
| **Income After Taxes** ................. | 60 448 | 8 538 | 22 937 | 34 718 | 42 659 | 54 841 | 74 441 | 102 542 | 139 555 | 233 299 |
| **Age of Reference Person** ......... | 50.5 | 51.3 | 55.9 | 51.7 | 49.9 | 48.5 | 47.6 | 48.0 | 49.2 | 49.6 |
| **Average Number in Consumer Unit** | | | | | | | | | | |
| All persons ........................... | 2.5 | 1.6 | 2.0 | 2.4 | 2.5 | 2.6 | 2.9 | 3.0 | 3.1 | 3.2 |
| Children under 18 years ............. | 0.6 | 0.3 | 0.5 | 0.6 | 0.6 | 0.7 | 0.7 | 0.7 | 0.8 | 0.9 |
| Persons 65 years and over ......... | 0.4 | 0.4 | 0.5 | 0.5 | 0.4 | 0.3 | 0.3 | 0.2 | 0.2 | 0.2 |
| Earners ............................... | 1.3 | 0.5 | 0.7 | 1.0 | 1.3 | 1.5 | 1.8 | 1.9 | 2.1 | 2.1 |
| Vehicles ............................. | 1.9 | 0.8 | 1.3 | 1.7 | 1.9 | 2.1 | 2.4 | 2.7 | 2.8 | 2.8 |
| **Percent Distribution** | | | | | | | | | | |
| Male ................................. | 47 | 37 | 40 | 43 | 48 | 49 | 52 | 56 | 55 | 56 |
| Female ............................... | 53 | 63 | 60 | 57 | 52 | 51 | 48 | 44 | 45 | 44 |
| **Percent Homeowner** ............. | 62 | 34 | 52 | 54 | 58 | 65 | 74 | 84 | 87 | 90 |
| With mortgage ....................... | 35 | 10 | 14 | 22 | 29 | 39 | 52 | 64 | 66 | 66 |
| Without mortgage .................... | 27 | 24 | 37 | 32 | 30 | 25 | 22 | 21 | 21 | 24 |
| **AVERAGE ANNUAL EXPENDITURES** ............... | 55 978 | 23 479 | 30 974 | 38 634 | 42 529 | 51 394 | 66 008 | 86 140 | 113 272 | 158 731 |
| **Food** ............... | 7 023 | 3 751 | 4 394 | 5 550 | 5 219 | 6 595 | 8 506 | 10 349 | 13 433 | 15 210 |
| Food at home ........................ | 4 015 | 2 523 | 2 843 | 3 588 | 3 152 | 3 864 | 4 611 | 5 539 | 6 858 | 7 360 |
| Cereals and bakery products ........ | 518 | 338 | 380 | 460 | 427 | 493 | 615 | 691 | 852 | 879 |
| Meats, poultry, fish, and eggs ..... | 896 | 603 | 652 | 889 | 706 | 843 | 1 013 | 1 209 | 1 469 | 1 494 |
| Dairy products ...................... | 413 | 248 | 288 | 354 | 333 | 412 | 461 | 581 | 716 | 777 |
| Fruits and vegetables ............... | 769 | 482 | 532 | 701 | 585 | 724 | 888 | 1 050 | 1 411 | 1 428 |
| Other food at home ................. | 1 419 | 850 | 992 | 1 185 | 1 101 | 1 391 | 1 633 | 2 008 | 2 410 | 2 782 |
| Food away from home ................. | 3 008 | 1 228 | 1 551 | 1 961 | 2 067 | 2 731 | 3 895 | 4 810 | 6 575 | 7 850 |
| **Alcoholic Beverages** .............. | 515 | 204 | 210 | 280 | 369 | 410 | 605 | 893 | 1 188 | 1 777 |
| **Housing** ............... | 18 409 | 9 507 | 11 821 | 13 714 | 15 082 | 17 213 | 20 871 | 26 032 | 33 244 | 47 927 |
| Shelter ............................. | 10 742 | 5 875 | 6 840 | 7 772 | 8 603 | 9 798 | 12 105 | 14 992 | 19 390 | 29 557 |
| Owned dwellings .................... | 6 210 | 1 680 | 2 566 | 3 217 | 3 896 | 5 289 | 7 763 | 11 114 | 14 378 | 21 500 |
| Rented dwellings ................... | 3 802 | 4 019 | 4 017 | 4 254 | 4 370 | 4 101 | 3 650 | 2 665 | 3 001 | 3 669 |
| Other lodging ...................... | 730 | 177 | 257 | 302 | 337 | 408 | 692 | 1 213 | 2 011 | 4 388 |
| Utilities, fuels, and public services ... | 3 885 | 2 191 | 2 953 | 3 447 | 3 618 | 4 041 | 4 489 | 5 172 | 5 813 | 6 382 |
| Household operations ................ | 1 309 | 439 | 633 | 735 | 915 | 1 164 | 1 371 | 2 107 | 2 712 | 5 213 |
| Housekeeping supplies ............... | 655 | 346 | 475 | 571 | 515 | 575 | 763 | 957 | 1 356 | 1 139 |
| Household furnishings and equipment ... | 1 818 | 656 | 920 | 1 188 | 1 432 | 1 635 | 2 143 | 2 803 | 3 973 | 5 635 |
| **Apparel and Services** ............... | 1 846 | 725 | 995 | 1 279 | 1 157 | 1 450 | 2 132 | 2 551 | 4 245 | 6 957 |
| **Transportation** ............... | 9 503 | 3 407 | 5 069 | 6 494 | 8 221 | 9 809 | 11 857 | 15 745 | 16 835 | 22 003 |
| Vehicle purchases (net outlay) ...... | 3 997 | 1 048 | 1 864 | 2 421 | 3 652 | 4 155 | 5 289 | 7 217 | 6 715 | 9 509 |
| Gasoline and motor oil .............. | 2 090 | 896 | 1 291 | 1 757 | 2 003 | 2 315 | 2 661 | 3 126 | 3 201 | 3 378 |
| Other vehicle expenses ............. | 2 756 | 1 271 | 1 631 | 2 050 | 2 197 | 2 827 | 3 278 | 4 364 | 5 276 | 5 659 |
| Public and other transportation ..... | 661 | 193 | 283 | 266 | 369 | 513 | 629 | 1 039 | 1 643 | 3 458 |
| **Health Care** ............... | 4 342 | 1 724 | 3 019 | 3 587 | 3 761 | 4 444 | 5 436 | 6 308 | 7 351 | 8 185 |
| Health insurance ................... | 2 977 | 1 156 | 2 029 | 2 469 | 2 664 | 3 115 | 3 792 | 4 291 | 4 665 | 5 740 |
| Medical services ................... | 791 | 312 | 518 | 609 | 583 | 755 | 983 | 1 210 | 1 701 | 1 573 |
| Drugs ............................... | 425 | 199 | 364 | 369 | 393 | 447 | 484 | 587 | 682 | 584 |
| Medical supplies ................... | 149 | 57 | 108 | 138 | 120 | 127 | 177 | 220 | 304 | 288 |
| **Entertainment** ............... | 2 842 | 1 146 | 1 590 | 1 934 | 2 091 | 2 431 | 3 213 | 4 442 | 6 588 | 8 273 |
| **Personal Care Products and Services** ............... | 683 | 302 | 393 | 523 | 443 | 604 | 842 | 1 082 | 1 443 | 1 681 |
| **Reading** ............... | 114 | 34 | 63 | 102 | 117 | 101 | 134 | 166 | 209 | 315 |
| **Education** ............... | 1 315 | 799 | 495 | 423 | 586 | 709 | 1 057 | 2 077 | 4 512 | 6 664 |
| **Tobacco Products and Smoking Supplies** ............... | 349 | 306 | 331 | 384 | 384 | 382 | 354 | 389 | 334 | 215 |
| **Miscellaneous** ............... | 871 | 399 | 481 | 666 | 648 | 720 | 1 018 | 1 366 | 1 728 | 2 486 |
| **Cash Contributions** ............... | 1 819 | 698 | 929 | 1 161 | 1 207 | 1 432 | 2 002 | 2 723 | 3 594 | 7 597 |
| **Personal Insurance and Pensions** ............... | 6 349 | 477 | 1 182 | 2 537 | 3 244 | 5 093 | 7 982 | 12 018 | 18 566 | 29 440 |
| Life and other personal insurance ... | 333 | 73 | 109 | 169 | 194 | 222 | 459 | 499 | 1 016 | 1 413 |
| Pensions and Social Security ........ | 6 016 | 404 | 1 073 | 2 368 | 3 050 | 4 871 | 7 522 | 11 519 | 17 550 | 28 027 |

## Table 11-4.  Consumer Expenditures, Averages by Higher Income Before Taxes, Third Quarter 2014 through Second Quarter 2015

(Number, dollar, percent.)

| Item | All consumer units | Less than $70,000 | $70,000 to $79,999 | $80,000 to $99,999 | $100,000 and over | $100,000 to $119,999 | $120,000 to $149,999 | $150,000 and over |
|---|---|---|---|---|---|---|---|---|
| **NUMBER OF CONSUMER UNITS (THOUSANDS)** | 127 783 | 83 242 | 7 058 | 10 557 | 26 925 | 8 543 | 6 768 | 11 614 |
| **CONSUMER UNIT CHARACTERISTICS** | | | | | | | | |
| Income Before Taxes | 68 662 | 31 858 | 74 838 | 89 235 | 172 758 | 108 638 | 132 961 | 243 115 |
| Income After Taxes | 59 633 | 30 963 | 67 487 | 79 211 | 138 534 | 93 207 | 113 028 | 186 739 |
| Age of Reference Person | 50.4 | 51.4 | 48.4 | 47.9 | 48.7 | 48.5 | 48.3 | 49.0 |
| **Average Number in Consumer Unit** | | | | | | | | |
| All persons | 2.5 | 2.2 | 2.8 | 2.9 | 3.1 | 2.9 | 3.2 | 3.2 |
| Children under 18 years | 0.6 | 0.5 | 0.7 | 0.7 | 0.8 | 0.7 | 0.8 | 0.8 |
| Persons 65 years and over | 0.4 | 0.4 | 0.3 | 0.3 | 0.2 | 0.2 | 0.2 | 0.2 |
| Earners | 1.3 | 0.9 | 1.7 | 1.8 | 2.0 | 1.9 | 2.0 | 2.1 |
| Vehicles | 1.9 | 1.5 | 2.2 | 2.5 | 2.8 | 2.6 | 2.8 | 2.9 |
| **Percent Distribution** | | | | | | | | |
| Male | 47 | 44 | 53 | 53 | 55 | 54 | 57 | 55 |
| Female | 53 | 56 | 47 | 47 | 45 | 46 | 43 | 45 |
| **Percent Homeowner** | 62 | 52 | 72 | 76 | 86 | 82 | 87 | 89 |
| With mortgage | 36 | 23 | 49 | 55 | 65 | 60 | 67 | 67 |
| Without mortgage | 27 | 29 | 23 | 22 | 21 | 21 | 20 | 22 |
| **AVERAGE ANNUAL EXPENDITURES** | 54 992 | 36 477 | 59 759 | 68 776 | 105 922 | 79 531 | 93 106 | 132 975 |
| **Food** | 6 887 | 5 021 | 7 624 | 8 559 | 11 954 | 9 937 | 10 671 | 14 259 |
| Food at home | 3 983 | 3 207 | 4 261 | 4 749 | 6 079 | 5 309 | 5 719 | 6 882 |
| Cereals and bakery products | 514 | 419 | 524 | 641 | 766 | 673 | 739 | 853 |
| Meats, poultry, fish, and eggs | 907 | 752 | 1 025 | 1 024 | 1 326 | 1 204 | 1 159 | 1 522 |
| Dairy products | 419 | 341 | 431 | 487 | 638 | 540 | 633 | 714 |
| Fruits and vegetables | 750 | 595 | 799 | 908 | 1 170 | 991 | 1 091 | 1 355 |
| Other food at home | 1 393 | 1 101 | 1 482 | 1 688 | 2 179 | 1 902 | 2 098 | 2 438 |
| Food away from home | 2 904 | 1 814 | 3 362 | 3 810 | 5 875 | 4 628 | 4 951 | 7 376 |
| **Alcoholic Beverages** | 478 | 251 | 558 | 642 | 1 112 | 843 | 777 | 1 519 |
| **Housing** | 18 128 | 13 108 | 19 177 | 21 464 | 32 099 | 24 233 | 28 529 | 39 977 |
| Shelter | 10 604 | 7 613 | 11 060 | 12 399 | 19 030 | 14 045 | 16 288 | 24 295 |
| Owned dwellings | 6 131 | 3 272 | 6 671 | 8 142 | 14 039 | 9 893 | 12 375 | 18 058 |
| Rented dwellings | 3 748 | 4 048 | 3 798 | 3 437 | 2 930 | 3 107 | 2 511 | 3 044 |
| Other lodging | 725 | 293 | 592 | 820 | 2 061 | 1 045 | 1 402 | 3 193 |
| Utilities, fuels, and public services | 3 893 | 3 194 | 4 432 | 4 649 | 5 618 | 5 016 | 5 442 | 6 163 |
| Household operations | 1 263 | 713 | 1 159 | 1 470 | 2 909 | 1 787 | 2 372 | 4 047 |
| Housekeeping supplies | 643 | 493 | 703 | 859 | 1 017 | 848 | 1 008 | 1 152 |
| Household furnishings and equipment | 1 724 | 1 095 | 1 822 | 2 087 | 3 525 | 2 538 | 3 419 | 4 320 |
| **Apparel and Services** | 1 885 | 1 204 | 1 811 | 2 315 | 3 906 | 2 469 | 3 125 | 5 464 |
| **Transportation** | 9 315 | 6 353 | 11 155 | 12 550 | 16 750 | 14 148 | 15 941 | 19 144 |
| Vehicle purchases (net outlay) | 3 723 | 2 408 | 4 496 | 5 422 | 6 922 | 5 968 | 6 796 | 7 698 |
| Gasoline and motor oil | 2 275 | 1 747 | 2 710 | 3 032 | 3 497 | 3 281 | 3 602 | 3 596 |
| Other vehicle expenses | 2 674 | 1 867 | 3 247 | 3 387 | 4 767 | 4 006 | 4 462 | 5 512 |
| Public and other transportation | 642 | 331 | 702 | 710 | 1 563 | 893 | 1 081 | 2 338 |
| **Health Care** | 4 379 | 3 239 | 5 143 | 5 727 | 7 178 | 6 021 | 6 864 | 8 213 |
| Health insurance | 2 972 | 2 193 | 3 622 | 3 844 | 4 866 | 4 119 | 4 534 | 5 609 |
| Medical services | 799 | 555 | 923 | 1 099 | 1 402 | 1 104 | 1 453 | 1 591 |
| Drugs | 460 | 380 | 430 | 593 | 665 | 595 | 638 | 732 |
| Medical supplies | 149 | 112 | 167 | 191 | 246 | 203 | 239 | 282 |
| **Entertainment** | 2 782 | 1 773 | 2 869 | 3 545 | 5 611 | 4 407 | 4 677 | 7 054 |
| **Personal Care Products and Services** | 676 | 454 | 781 | 820 | 1 289 | 1 010 | 1 255 | 1 516 |
| **Reading** | 121 | 86 | 125 | 157 | 214 | 159 | 199 | 264 |
| **Education** | 1 362 | 730 | 771 | 1 300 | 3 497 | 1 744 | 2 641 | 5 288 |
| **Tobacco Products and Smoking Supplies** | 339 | 334 | 391 | 383 | 319 | 401 | 338 | 249 |
| **Miscellaneous** | 832 | 544 | 871 | 969 | 1 662 | 1 101 | 1 548 | 2 143 |
| **Cash Contributions** | 1 761 | 1 104 | 1 777 | 1 961 | 3 711 | 2 391 | 3 001 | 5 095 |
| **Personal Insurance and Pensions** | 6 048 | 2 276 | 6 706 | 8 384 | 16 619 | 10 669 | 13 540 | 22 791 |
| Life and other personal insurance | 315 | 153 | 320 | 415 | 774 | 482 | 628 | 1 075 |
| Pensions and Social Security | 5 733 | 2 123 | 6 385 | 7 969 | 15 845 | 10 187 | 12 912 | 21 716 |

## Table 11-5. Consumer Expenditures, Averages by Quintiles of Income Before Taxes, 2015

(Number, dollar, percent.)

| Item | All consumer units | Lowest 20 percent | Second 20 percent | Third 20 percent | Fourth 20 percent | Highest 20 percent |
|---|---|---|---|---|---|---|
| **NUMBER OF CONSUMER UNITS (THOUSANDS)** | 128 437 | 25 672 | 25 562 | 25 700 | 25 730 | 25 773 |
| **CONSUMER UNIT CHARACTERISTICS** | | | | | | |
| **Income Before Taxes** | 69 627 | 10 916 | 28 343 | 49 606 | 80 813 | 177 851 |
| **Income After Taxes** | 60 448 | 11 416 | 28 727 | 46 807 | 72 375 | 142 446 |
| **Age of Reference Person** | 50.5 | 53.3 | 53.6 | 49.3 | 47.9 | 48.7 |
| **Average Number in Consumer Unit** | | | | | | |
| All persons | 2.5 | 1.7 | 2.2 | 2.5 | 2.9 | 3.1 |
| Children under 18 years | 0.6 | 0.3 | 0.5 | 0.6 | 0.7 | 0.8 |
| Persons 65 years and over | 0.4 | 0.4 | 0.5 | 0.4 | 0.3 | 0.2 |
| Earners | 1.3 | 0.5 | 0.8 | 1.3 | 1.8 | 2.0 |
| Vehicles | 1.9 | 0.9 | 1.5 | 1.9 | 2.4 | 2.7 |
| **Percent Distribution** | | | | | | |
| Male | 47 | 37 | 43 | 48 | 52 | 56 |
| Female | 53 | 63 | 57 | 52 | 48 | 44 |
| **Percent Homeowner** | 62 | 38 | 53 | 60 | 73 | 87 |
| With mortgage | 35 | 11 | 18 | 32 | 52 | 65 |
| Without mortgage | 27 | 27 | 36 | 28 | 22 | 22 |
| **AVERAGE ANNUAL EXPENDITURES** | 55 978 | 24 470 | 35 063 | 45 912 | 63 671 | 110 508 |
| **Food** | 7 023 | 3 767 | 5 022 | 5 799 | 8 165 | 12 350 |
| Food at home | 4 015 | 2 499 | 3 271 | 3 445 | 4 545 | 6 310 |
| Cereals and bakery products | 518 | 333 | 432 | 450 | 598 | 776 |
| Meats, poultry, fish, and eggs | 896 | 590 | 776 | 766 | 1 008 | 1 338 |
| Dairy products | 413 | 249 | 329 | 362 | 462 | 662 |
| Fruits and vegetables | 769 | 483 | 621 | 643 | 863 | 1 233 |
| Other food at home | 1 419 | 843 | 1 112 | 1 225 | 1 614 | 2 302 |
| Food away from home | 3 008 | 1 268 | 1 751 | 2 354 | 3 620 | 6 040 |
| **Alcoholic Beverages** | 515 | 195 | 253 | 387 | 578 | 1 161 |
| **Housing** | 18 409 | 9 890 | 12 832 | 15 809 | 20 408 | 33 027 |
| Shelter | 10 742 | 6 033 | 7 320 | 8 985 | 11 786 | 19 537 |
| Owned dwellings | 6 210 | 1 817 | 2 906 | 4 363 | 7 480 | 14 437 |
| Rented dwellings | 3 802 | 4 034 | 4 121 | 4 267 | 3 660 | 2 933 |
| Other lodging | 730 | 182 | 293 | 355 | 647 | 2 167 |
| Utilities, fuels, and public services | 3 885 | 2 328 | 3 211 | 3 768 | 4 454 | 5 653 |
| Household operations | 1 309 | 462 | 714 | 1 006 | 1 346 | 3 006 |
| Housekeeping supplies | 655 | 378 | 517 | 563 | 701 | 1 113 |
| Household furnishings and equipment | 1 818 | 689 | 1 070 | 1 487 | 2 121 | 3 717 |
| **Apparel and Services** | 1 846 | 776 | 1 139 | 1 303 | 1 984 | 4 025 |
| **Transportation** | 9 503 | 3 559 | 5 923 | 8 820 | 11 330 | 17 834 |
| Vehicle purchases (net outlay) | 3 997 | 1 136 | 2 260 | 3 716 | 4 995 | 7 853 |
| Gasoline and motor oil | 2 090 | 939 | 1 532 | 2 110 | 2 632 | 3 226 |
| Other vehicle expenses | 2 756 | 1 270 | 1 859 | 2 538 | 3 115 | 4 985 |
| Public and other transportation | 661 | 214 | 271 | 455 | 587 | 1 769 |
| **Health Care** | 4 342 | 1 930 | 3 423 | 3 965 | 5 327 | 7 048 |
| Health insurance | 2 977 | 1 299 | 2 312 | 2 786 | 3 742 | 4 738 |
| Medical services | 791 | 326 | 611 | 645 | 939 | 1 432 |
| Drugs | 425 | 224 | 391 | 412 | 479 | 616 |
| Medical supplies | 149 | 81 | 109 | 122 | 168 | 263 |
| **Entertainment** | 2 842 | 1 270 | 1 738 | 2 219 | 3 051 | 5 919 |
| **Personal Care Products and Services** | 683 | 307 | 453 | 524 | 797 | 1 331 |
| **Reading** | 114 | 37 | 82 | 107 | 134 | 210 |
| **Education** | 1 315 | 689 | 494 | 614 | 986 | 3 779 |
| **Tobacco Products and Smoking Supplies** | 349 | 308 | 360 | 376 | 372 | 332 |
| **Miscellaneous** | 871 | 439 | 550 | 674 | 982 | 1 706 |
| **Cash Contributions** | 1 819 | 712 | 1 054 | 1 335 | 1 890 | 4 089 |
| **Personal Insurance and Pensions** | 6 349 | 592 | 1 740 | 3 980 | 7 667 | 17 699 |
| Life and other personal insurance | 333 | 85 | 132 | 193 | 405 | 846 |
| Pensions and Social Security | 6 016 | 507 | 1 609 | 3 787 | 7 261 | 16 853 |

## Table 11-6. Consumer Expenditures, Averages by Occupation of Reference Person, 2015

(Number, dollar, percent.)

| Item | All consumer units | Self-employed workers | Wage and salary earners | | | | | | Retired | All others, including those not reporting |
|---|---|---|---|---|---|---|---|---|---|---|
| | | | Total wage and salary earners | Managers and professional workers | Technical sales and clerical workers | Service workers | Construction workers and mechanics | Operators, fabricators, and laborers | | |
| **NUMBER OF CONSUMER UNITS (THOUSANDS)** .......... | 128 437 | 7 953 | 77 591 | 31 036 | 20 214 | 15 256 | 3 455 | 7 630 | 24 986 | 17 908 |
| **CONSUMER UNIT CHARACTERISTICS** | | | | | | | | | | |
| **Income Before Taxes** ............... | 69 627 | 110 918 | 82 008 | 111 909 | 67 902 | 53 779 | 63 869 | 62 406 | 38 947 | 40 449 |
| **Income After Taxes** ............... | 60 448 | 89 622 | 70 312 | 92 371 | 59 765 | 49 413 | 57 436 | 56 149 | 37 048 | 37 401 |
| **Age of Reference Person** ............... | 50.5 | 50.5 | 43.9 | 44.4 | 42.9 | 43.7 | 44.5 | 44.7 | 73.5 | 47.0 |
| **Average Number in Consumer Unit** | | | | | | | | | | |
| All persons ............... | 2.5 | 2.7 | 2.6 | 2.6 | 2.5 | 2.7 | 2.7 | 2.7 | 1.7 | 3.0 |
| Children under 18 years ............... | 0.6 | 0.7 | 0.7 | 0.7 | 0.7 | 0.7 | 0.7 | 0.7 | 0.1 | 1.0 |
| Persons 65 years and over ............... | 0.4 | 0.3 | 0.1 | 0.1 | 0.1 | 0.2 | 0.1 | 0.1 | 1.2 | 0.0 |
| Earners ............... | 1.3 | 1.8 | 1.7 | 1.7 | 1.7 | 1.7 | 1.8 | 1.8 | 0.2 | 1.0 |
| Vehicles ............... | 1.9 | 2.2 | 2.0 | 2.1 | 1.9 | 1.7 | 2.3 | 2.1 | 1.7 | 2.0 |
| **Percent Distribution** | | | | | | | | | | |
| Male ............... | 47 | 60 | 50 | 48 | 43 | 44 | 90 | 74 | 46 | 29 |
| Female ............... | 53 | 40 | 50 | 52 | 57 | 56 | 10 | 26 | 54 | 71 |
| **Percent Homeowner** ............... | 62 | 72 | 59 | 69 | 55 | 47 | 60 | 57 | 79 | 48 |
| With mortgage ............... | 35 | 44 | 42 | 53 | 39 | 29 | 39 | 37 | 19 | 24 |
| Without mortgage ............... | 27 | 29 | 17 | 16 | 16 | 19 | 21 | 20 | 59 | 24 |
| **AVERAGE ANNUAL EXPENDITURES** ............... | 55 978 | 78 132 | 61 634 | 78 813 | 54 270 | 46 337 | 49 941 | 48 287 | 42 478 | 40 759 |
| **Food** ............... | 7 023 | 8 382 | 7 645 | 9 502 | 6 999 | 5 989 | 6 547 | 6 142 | 5 265 | 6 301 |
| Food at home ............... | 4 015 | 4 648 | 4 155 | 4 873 | 3 989 | 3 446 | 3 863 | 3 454 | 3 334 | 4 094 |
| Cereals and bakery products ............... | 518 | 609 | 526 | 609 | 511 | 474 | 453 | 393 | 452 | 534 |
| Meats, poultry, fish, and eggs ............... | 896 | 1 051 | 918 | 981 | 931 | 789 | 988 | 873 | 711 | 990 |
| Dairy products ............... | 413 | 502 | 420 | 515 | 386 | 338 | 365 | 346 | 357 | 419 |
| Fruits and vegetables ............... | 769 | 892 | 801 | 969 | 755 | 665 | 753 | 578 | 655 | 742 |
| Other food at home ............... | 1 419 | 1 595 | 1 491 | 1 800 | 1 405 | 1 181 | 1 305 | 1 263 | 1 158 | 1 409 |
| Food away from home ............... | 3 008 | 3 734 | 3 490 | 4 629 | 3 009 | 2 543 | 2 684 | 2 687 | 1 930 | 2 207 |
| **Alcoholic Beverages** ............... | 515 | 725 | 603 | 840 | 474 | 408 | 567 | 437 | 367 | 274 |
| **Housing** ............... | 18 409 | 23 419 | 19 960 | 24 919 | 18 047 | 15 918 | 15 403 | 15 189 | 14 947 | 14 318 |
| Shelter ............... | 10 742 | 14 233 | 11 800 | 14 760 | 10 715 | 9 525 | 8 902 | 8 492 | 8 169 | 8 200 |
| Owned dwellings ............... | 6 210 | 9 396 | 6 764 | 9 528 | 5 689 | 4 112 | 4 897 | 4 519 | 5 146 | 3 878 |
| Rented dwellings ............... | 3 802 | 3 565 | 4 284 | 4 000 | 4 491 | 5 046 | 3 619 | 3 675 | 2 265 | 3 962 |
| Other lodging ............... | 730 | 1 272 | 751 | 1 232 | 535 | 367 | 385 | 297 | 758 | 360 |
| Utilities, fuels, and public services ............... | 3 885 | 4 388 | 4 034 | 4 469 | 3 837 | 3 573 | 3 843 | 3 796 | 3 551 | 3 481 |
| Household operations ............... | 1 309 | 1 591 | 1 509 | 2 210 | 1 207 | 947 | 871 | 876 | 1 052 | 676 |
| Housekeeping supplies ............... | 655 | 779 | 641 | 788 | 552 | 479 | 467 | 735 | 732 | 557 |
| Household furnishings and equipment ............... | 1 818 | 2 428 | 1 976 | 2 691 | 1 736 | 1 395 | 1 320 | 1 290 | 1 443 | 1 404 |
| **Apparel and Services** ............... | 1 846 | 3 958 | 1 979 | 2 570 | 1 696 | 1 675 | 1 199 | 1 440 | 1 031 | 1 518 |
| **Transportation** ............... | 9 503 | 11 643 | 10 865 | 12 860 | 10 118 | 8 545 | 10 818 | 9 438 | 6 838 | 6 401 |
| Vehicle purchases (net outlay) ............... | 3 997 | 4 302 | 4 741 | 5 669 | 4 445 | 3 579 | 5 011 | 3 956 | 2 614 | 2 566 |
| Gasoline and motor oil ............... | 2 090 | 2 497 | 2 364 | 2 500 | 2 271 | 2 098 | 2 687 | 2 445 | 1 420 | 1 653 |
| Other vehicle expenses ............... | 2 756 | 3 788 | 3 028 | 3 556 | 2 875 | 2 385 | 2 769 | 2 732 | 2 278 | 1 811 |
| Public and other transportation ............... | 661 | 1 056 | 731 | 1 135 | 527 | 484 | 351 | 306 | 526 | 370 |
| **Health Care** ............... | 4 342 | 5 871 | 4 001 | 5 067 | 3 600 | 2 955 | 3 208 | 3 197 | 5 811 | 3 092 |
| Health insurance ............... | 2 977 | 3 965 | 2 792 | 3 495 | 2 555 | 2 083 | 2 180 | 2 250 | 3 939 | 2 002 |
| Medical services ............... | 791 | 1 150 | 738 | 966 | 644 | 528 | 601 | 542 | 977 | 603 |
| Drugs ............... | 425 | 559 | 341 | 433 | 296 | 255 | 321 | 285 | 676 | 375 |
| Medical supplies ............... | 149 | 197 | 130 | 173 | 105 | 90 | 106 | 119 | 219 | 112 |
| **Entertainment** ............... | 2 842 | 3 967 | 2 998 | 4 081 | 2 400 | 2 173 | 1 952 | 2 398 | 2 525 | 2 121 |
| **Personal Care Products and Services** ............... | 683 | 856 | 745 | 1 010 | 641 | 541 | 460 | 530 | 568 | 503 |
| **Reading** ............... | 114 | 113 | 106 | 167 | 66 | 69 | 53 | 70 | 171 | 68 |
| **Education** ............... | 1 315 | 1 916 | 1 639 | 2 372 | 1 207 | 985 | 1 560 | 1 150 | 214 | 1 180 |
| **Tobacco Products and Smoking Supplies** ............... | 349 | 353 | 347 | 252 | 392 | 367 | 516 | 492 | 225 | 534 |
| **Miscellaneous** ............... | 871 | 1 528 | 914 | 1 126 | 765 | 822 | 724 | 706 | 788 | 515 |
| **Cash Contributions** ............... | 1 819 | 2 948 | 1 797 | 2 640 | 1 361 | 1 138 | 1 167 | 1 129 | 2 140 | 961 |
| **Personal Insurance and Pensions** ............... | 6 349 | 12 452 | 8 035 | 11 407 | 6 503 | 4 752 | 5 769 | 5 969 | 1 588 | 2 972 |
| Life and other personal insurance ............... | 333 | 858 | 313 | 464 | 234 | 176 | 204 | 232 | 353 | 157 |
| Pensions and Social Security ............... | 6 016 | 11 595 | 7 722 | 10 943 | 6 269 | 4 575 | 5 565 | 5 737 | 1 235 | 2 816 |

## Table 11-7. Consumer Expenditures, Averages by Number of Earners, 2015

(Number, dollar, percent.)

| Item | All consumer units | Single consumer | | Consumer units of two or more persons | | | |
|---|---|---|---|---|---|---|---|
| | | No earner | One earner | No earner | One earner | Two earners | Three or more earners |
| **NUMBER OF CONSUMER UNITS (THOUSANDS)** | 128 437 | 16 018 | 21 459 | 13 198 | 26 013 | 40 675 | 11 075 |
| **CONSUMER UNIT CHARACTERISTICS** | | | | | | | |
| **Income Before Taxes** | 69 627 | 18 958 | 47 887 | 33 542 | 63 614 | 103 808 | 116 617 |
| **Income After Taxes** | 60 448 | 18 057 | 39 602 | 32 671 | 57 900 | 87 563 | 101 653 |
| **Age of Reference Person** | 50.5 | 67.5 | 44.0 | 66.2 | 48.7 | 44.1 | 48.0 |
| **Average Number in Consumer Unit** | | | | | | | |
| All persons | 2.5 | 1.0 | 1.0 | 2.3 | 3.0 | 3.0 | 4.3 |
| Children under 18 years | 0.6 | X | X | 0.3 | 1.1 | 0.8 | 1.0 |
| Persons 65 years and over | 0.4 | 0.7 | 0.1 | 1.3 | 0.3 | 0.1 | 0.2 |
| Earners | 1.3 | X | 1.0 | X | 1.0 | 2.0 | 3.3 |
| Vehicles | 1.9 | 0.9 | 1.2 | 1.8 | 1.9 | 2.3 | 3.1 |
| **Percent Distribution** | | | | | | | |
| Male | 47 | 38 | 53 | 48 | 42 | 51 | 45 |
| Female | 53 | 62 | 47 | 52 | 58 | 49 | 55 |
| **Percent Homeowner** | 62 | 54 | 41 | 75 | 61 | 70 | 75 |
| With mortgage | 35 | 11 | 25 | 19 | 34 | 51 | 53 |
| Without mortgage | 27 | 43 | 16 | 56 | 27 | 18 | 21 |
| **AVERAGE ANNUAL EXPENDITURES** | 55 978 | 25 975 | 39 117 | 43 102 | 56 354 | 73 178 | 84 242 |
| **Food** | 7 023 | 3 272 | 4 516 | 5 956 | 7 530 | 8 940 | 10 774 |
| Food at home | 4 015 | 2 143 | 2 215 | 3 947 | 4 585 | 4 871 | 6 005 |
| Cereals and bakery products | 518 | 289 | 249 | 540 | 601 | 628 | 768 |
| Meats, poultry, fish, and eggs | 896 | 459 | 458 | 906 | 1 046 | 1 073 | 1 413 |
| Dairy products | 413 | 222 | 212 | 399 | 485 | 504 | 611 |
| Fruits and vegetables | 769 | 438 | 432 | 759 | 846 | 932 | 1 173 |
| Other food at home | 1 419 | 736 | 865 | 1 343 | 1 606 | 1 735 | 2 040 |
| Food away from home | 3 008 | 1 129 | 2 301 | 2 009 | 2 945 | 4 069 | 4 770 |
| **Alcoholic Beverages** | 515 | 170 | 556 | 334 | 428 | 715 | 647 |
| **Housing** | 18 409 | 10 767 | 13 607 | 14 639 | 19 380 | 23 283 | 23 148 |
| Shelter | 10 742 | 6 589 | 9 174 | 7 489 | 11 001 | 13 535 | 12 800 |
| Owned dwellings | 6 210 | 2 882 | 3 648 | 4 739 | 6 209 | 8 771 | 8 337 |
| Rented dwellings | 3 802 | 3 437 | 5 088 | 2 045 | 3 945 | 3 812 | 3 562 |
| Other lodging | 730 | 270 | 438 | 705 | 847 | 952 | 901 |
| Utilities, fuels, and public services | 3 885 | 2 291 | 2 391 | 3 901 | 4 227 | 4 575 | 5 730 |
| Household operations | 1 309 | 654 | 647 | 1 019 | 1 367 | 1 982 | 1 272 |
| Housekeeping supplies | 655 | 429 | 336 | 757 | 728 | 761 | 934 |
| Household furnishings and equipment | 1 818 | 805 | 1 059 | 1 472 | 2 058 | 2 429 | 2 412 |
| **Apparel and Services** | 1 846 | 707 | 1 142 | 902 | 2 006 | 2 607 | 2 995 |
| **Transportation** | 9 503 | 3 379 | 6 141 | 7 021 | 9 334 | 12 515 | 17 302 |
| Vehicle purchases (net outlay) | 3 997 | 1 112 | 2 402 | 2 962 | 3 623 | 5 433 | 8 097 |
| Gasoline and motor oil | 2 090 | 706 | 1 368 | 1 523 | 2 157 | 2 733 | 3 645 |
| Other vehicle expenses | 2 756 | 1 295 | 1 883 | 2 105 | 2 842 | 3 481 | 4 604 |
| Public and other transportation | 661 | 266 | 488 | 432 | 712 | 868 | 956 |
| **Health Care** | 4 342 | 2 937 | 2 415 | 6 139 | 4 517 | 4 947 | 5 322 |
| Health insurance | 2 977 | 1 906 | 1 691 | 4 113 | 3 109 | 3 462 | 3 577 |
| Medical services | 791 | 496 | 442 | 1 105 | 774 | 908 | 1 135 |
| Drugs | 425 | 395 | 204 | 697 | 481 | 424 | 433 |
| Medical supplies | 149 | 140 | 78 | 225 | 152 | 154 | 177 |
| **Entertainment** | 2 842 | 1 448 | 1 907 | 2 801 | 2 833 | 3 687 | 3 675 |
| **Personal Care Products and Services** | 683 | 355 | 463 | 531 | 717 | 883 | 969 |
| **Reading** | 114 | 91 | 72 | 179 | 111 | 123 | 116 |
| **Education** | 1 315 | 482 | 923 | 403 | 1 048 | 1 785 | 3 270 |
| **Tobacco Products and Smoking Supplies** | 349 | 236 | 265 | 317 | 383 | 358 | 608 |
| **Miscellaneous** | 871 | 543 | 790 | 768 | 846 | 1 011 | 1 171 |
| **Cash Contributions** | 1 819 | 1 154 | 1 584 | 2 148 | 1 849 | 2 018 | 2 036 |
| **Personal Insurance and Pensions** | 6 349 | 435 | 4 735 | 964 | 5 373 | 10 304 | 12 209 |
| Life and other personal insurance | 333 | 116 | 135 | 418 | 307 | 465 | 504 |
| Pensions and Social Security | 6 016 | 319 | 4 600 | 546 | 5 066 | 9 840 | 11 706 |

X = Not applicable.

## Table 11-8.  Consumer Expenditures, Averages by Size of Consumer Unit, 2015

(Number, dollar, percent.)

| Item | All consumer units | One person | Two or more persons | | | | |
|---|---|---|---|---|---|---|---|
| | | | Total | Two persons | Three persons | Four persons | Five or more persons |
| **NUMBER OF CONSUMER UNITS (THOUSANDS)** ............................ | 128 437 | 37 477 | 90 961 | 42 943 | 19 562 | 16 338 | 12 117 |
| **CONSUMER UNIT CHARACTERISTICS** | | | | | | | |
| **Income Before Taxes** ................................................................ | 69 627 | 35 522 | 83 678 | 74 527 | 88 483 | 95 886 | 91 889 |
| **Income After Taxes** ................................................................... | 60 448 | 30 393 | 72 831 | 64 222 | 75 995 | 83 706 | 83 573 |
| **Age of Reference Person** ......................................................... | 50.5 | 54.0 | 49.1 | 55.0 | 45.5 | 42.8 | 42.4 |
| **Average Number in Consumer Unit** | | | | | | | |
| All persons ................................................................................ | 2.5 | 1.0 | 3.1 | 2.0 | 3.0 | 4.0 | 5.7 |
| Children under 18 years ............................................................. | 0.6 | X | 0.8 | 0.1 | 0.7 | 1.5 | 2.8 |
| Persons 65 years and over ........................................................ | 0.4 | 0.3 | 0.4 | 0.6 | 0.2 | 0.1 | 0.2 |
| Earners ...................................................................................... | 1.3 | 0.6 | 1.6 | 1.2 | 1.8 | 2.0 | 2.2 |
| Vehicles ..................................................................................... | 1.9 | 1.0 | 2.2 | 2.1 | 2.2 | 2.4 | 2.5 |
| **Percent Distribution** | | | | | | | |
| Male .......................................................................................... | 47 | 47 | 47 | 50 | 46 | 45 | 40 |
| Female ...................................................................................... | 53 | 53 | 53 | 50 | 54 | 55 | 60 |
| **Percent Homeowner** ................................................................ | 62 | 47 | 69 | 72 | 66 | 68 | 64 |
| With mortgage ........................................................................... | 35 | 19 | 42 | 34 | 47 | 52 | 48 |
| Without mortgage ...................................................................... | 27 | 28 | 27 | 37 | 19 | 16 | 16 |
| **AVERAGE ANNUAL EXPENDITURES** ..................................... | 55 978 | 33 508 | 65 228 | 58 668 | 67 702 | 75 276 | 70 972 |
| **Food** ........................................................................................ | 7 023 | 3 989 | 8 268 | 7 085 | 8 526 | 9 771 | 10 015 |
| Food at home ............................................................................ | 4 015 | 2 185 | 4 766 | 3 964 | 4 929 | 5 624 | 6 180 |
| Cereals and bakery products ................................................. | 518 | 266 | 621 | 506 | 628 | 741 | 858 |
| Meats, poultry, fish, and eggs .............................................. | 896 | 459 | 1 075 | 884 | 1 094 | 1 274 | 1 450 |
| Dairy products ....................................................................... | 273 | 143 | 326 | 280 | 328 | 401 | 384 |
| Fruits and vegetables ........................................................... | 769 | 435 | 906 | 752 | 950 | 1 077 | 1 151 |
| Other food at home ............................................................... | 1 419 | 810 | 1 670 | 1 414 | 1 763 | 1 917 | 2 096 |
| Food away from home .............................................................. | 3 008 | 1 805 | 3 502 | 3 121 | 3 597 | 4 148 | 3 835 |
| **Alcoholic Beverages** ............................................................... | 515 | 393 | 565 | 648 | 569 | 511 | 343 |
| **Housing** .................................................................................. | 18 409 | 12 393 | 20 886 | 19 059 | 21 268 | 24 044 | 22 504 |
| Shelter ...................................................................................... | 10 742 | 8 069 | 11 843 | 10 903 | 12 026 | 13 615 | 12 495 |
| Owned dwellings .................................................................... | 6 210 | 3 321 | 7 400 | 6 699 | 7 405 | 8 999 | 7 723 |
| Rented dwellings .................................................................... | 3 802 | 4 382 | 3 563 | 3 111 | 3 943 | 3 865 | 4 146 |
| Other lodging ......................................................................... | 730 | 366 | 880 | 1 093 | 678 | 751 | 626 |
| Utilities, fuels, and public services ......................................... | 3 885 | 2 348 | 4 518 | 4 062 | 4 580 | 5 026 | 5 353 |
| Household operations ............................................................... | 1 309 | 650 | 1 580 | 1 156 | 1 796 | 2 371 | 1 667 |
| Housekeeping supplies ............................................................ | 655 | 375 | 769 | 754 | 764 | 749 | 857 |
| Household furnishings and equipment ...................................... | 1 818 | 951 | 2 175 | 2 184 | 2 103 | 2 283 | 2 131 |
| **Apparel and Services** ............................................................. | 1 846 | 957 | 2 211 | 1 596 | 2 230 | 3 390 | 2 766 |
| **Transportation** ........................................................................ | 9 503 | 4 960 | 11 374 | 9 669 | 12 216 | 13 687 | 12 951 |
| Vehicle purchases (net outlay) ................................................. | 3 997 | 1 851 | 4 881 | 3 877 | 5 407 | 6 238 | 5 763 |
| Gasoline and motor oil .............................................................. | 2 090 | 1 085 | 2 503 | 2 085 | 2 589 | 3 043 | 3 121 |
| Other vehicle expenses ............................................................ | 2 756 | 1 632 | 3 218 | 2 896 | 3 474 | 3 672 | 3 353 |
| Public and other transportation ................................................ | 661 | 393 | 771 | 812 | 746 | 735 | 714 |
| **Health Care** ............................................................................ | 4 342 | 2 638 | 5 044 | 5 406 | 4 728 | 4 943 | 4 406 |
| Health insurance ...................................................................... | 2 977 | 1 783 | 3 469 | 3 713 | 3 318 | 3 374 | 2 979 |
| Medical services ....................................................................... | 791 | 465 | 926 | 933 | 831 | 1 026 | 918 |
| Drugs ........................................................................................ | 425 | 285 | 482 | 571 | 438 | 395 | 356 |
| Medical supplies ....................................................................... | 149 | 105 | 167 | 190 | 141 | 148 | 154 |
| **Entertainment** ........................................................................ | 2 842 | 1 711 | 3 307 | 3 312 | 3 219 | 3 468 | 3 229 |
| **Personal Care Products and Services** ................................... | 683 | 417 | 792 | 729 | 839 | 887 | 814 |
| **Reading** .................................................................................. | 114 | 80 | 128 | 151 | 101 | 124 | 94 |
| **Education** ............................................................................... | 1 315 | 735 | 1 554 | 991 | 2 102 | 2 074 | 1 963 |
| **Tobacco Products and Smoking Supplies** ............................ | 349 | 253 | 389 | 321 | 449 | 449 | 455 |
| **Miscellaneous** ........................................................................ | 871 | 685 | 948 | 870 | 1 003 | 998 | 1 069 |
| **Cash Contributions** ................................................................ | 1 819 | 1 400 | 1 991 | 2 238 | 1 791 | 1 517 | 2 076 |
| **Personal Insurance and Pensions** ........................................ | 6 349 | 2 897 | 7 771 | 6 594 | 8 662 | 9 413 | 8 288 |
| Life and other personal insurance ............................................ | 333 | 127 | 418 | 404 | 438 | 408 | 443 |
| Pensions and Social Security .................................................... | 6 016 | 2 770 | 7 353 | 6 190 | 8 223 | 9 005 | 7 844 |

X = Not applicable.

## Table 11-9.  Consumer Expenditures, Averages by Composition of Consumer Unit, 2015

(Number, dollar, percent.)

| Item | All consumer unit | Husband and wife consumer units | | | | | | Other husband and wife consumer units | One parent, at least one child under 18 years | Single person and other consumer units |
| | | Total | Husband and wife only | Husband and wife with children | | | | | | |
| | | | | Total | Oldest child under 6 years | Oldest child 6 to 17 years | Oldest child 18 years or over | | | |
| NUMBER OF CONSUMER UNITS (THOUSANDS) ......... | 128 437 | 62 003 | 28 007 | 29 300 | 5 313 | 14 374 | 9 613 | 4 697 | 7 400 | 59 034 |
| **CONSUMER UNIT CHARACTERISTICS** | | | | | | | | | | |
| Income Before Taxes ............................................... | 69 627 | 96 764 | 84 390 | 107 586 | 99 362 | 110 541 | 107 713 | 103 044 | 41 092 | 44 701 |
| Income After Taxes ................................................. | 60 448 | 83 075 | 72 346 | 91 894 | 85 078 | 93 490 | 93 275 | 92 030 | 39 241 | 39 342 |
| Age of Reference Person ........................................ | 50.5 | 51.3 | 59.3 | 43.7 | 32.9 | 41.5 | 53.0 | 51.2 | 39.0 | 51.0 |
| **Average Number in Consumer Unit** | | | | | | | | | | |
| All persons ............................................................ | 2.5 | 3.2 | 2.0 | 4.0 | 3.5 | 4.2 | 3.9 | 5.0 | 2.9 | 2.0 |
| Children under 18 years ........................................ | 0.6 | 0.8 | . . . | 1.5 | 1.5 | 2.2 | 0.6 | 1.4 | 1.7 | 0.0 |
| Persons 65 years and over .................................... | 0.4 | 0.4 | 0.8 | 0.1 | . . . | ( [1] ) | 0.2 | 0.6 | ( [1] ) | 0.0 |
| Earners .................................................................. | 1.3 | 1.6 | 1.1 | 2.0 | 1.7 | 1.8 | 2.5 | 2.4 | 1.0 | 1.0 |
| Vehicles ................................................................. | 1.9 | 2.5 | 2.4 | 2.5 | 2.0 | 2.4 | 3.0 | 2.9 | 1.2 | 1.0 |
| **Percent Distribution** | | | | | | | | | | |
| Male ...................................................................... | 47 | 54 | 57 | 53 | 56 | 51 | 54 | 44 | 16 | 44 |
| Female ................................................................... | 53 | 46 | 43 | 47 | 44 | 49 | 46 | 56 | 84 | 56 |
| **Percent Homeowner** ............................................... | 62 | 79 | 84 | 74 | 64 | 73 | 82 | 75 | 37 | 48 |
| With mortgage ....................................................... | 35 | 49 | 39 | 58 | 57 | 61 | 56 | 49 | 27 | 22 |
| Without mortgage .................................................. | 27 | 30 | 46 | 16 | 7 | 13 | 26 | 26 | 10 | 26 |
| **AVERAGE ANNUAL EXPENDITURES** ......................... | 55 978 | 73 344 | 65 534 | 80 741 | 74 838 | 81 612 | 82 782 | 74 292 | 45 745 | 38 899 |
| **Food** ....................................................................... | 7 023 | 9 142 | 7 733 | 10 555 | 8 961 | 10 766 | 11 143 | 9 069 | 6 112 | 4 850 |
| Food at home ......................................................... | 4 015 | 5 169 | 4 273 | 6 003 | 5 059 | 6 139 | 6 328 | 5 481 | 3 786 | 2 797 |
| Cereals and bakery products .............................. | 518 | 667 | 532 | 789 | 647 | 828 | 809 | 729 | 537 | 355 |
| Meats, poultry, fish, and eggs ........................... | 896 | 1 147 | 939 | 1 336 | 980 | 1 379 | 1 474 | 1 241 | 851 | 630 |
| Dairy products .................................................... | 413 | 540 | 436 | 637 | 591 | 658 | 630 | 570 | 387 | 279 |
| Fruits and vegetables ........................................ | 769 | 1 000 | 838 | 1 145 | 1 023 | 1 129 | 1 242 | 1 098 | 656 | 532 |
| Other food at home ........................................... | 1 419 | 1 815 | 1 530 | 2 095 | 1 819 | 2 146 | 2 174 | 1 843 | 1 356 | 1 001 |
| Food away from home ........................................... | 3 008 | 3 974 | 3 460 | 4 552 | 3 902 | 4 627 | 4 814 | 3 587 | 2 326 | 2 053 |
| **Alcoholic Beverages** .............................................. | 515 | 620 | 701 | 564 | 591 | 531 | 603 | 486 | 249 | 434 |
| **Housing** ................................................................... | 18 409 | 22 901 | 20 508 | 25 198 | 27 153 | 26 132 | 22 737 | 22 846 | 16 829 | 13 869 |
| Shelter .................................................................. | 10 742 | 12 925 | 11 554 | 14 334 | 14 755 | 15 324 | 12 622 | 12 305 | 9 837 | 8 564 |
| Owned dwellings ................................................ | 6 210 | 9 017 | 8 098 | 10 063 | 9 519 | 10 943 | 9 049 | 7 964 | 3 898 | 3 552 |
| Rented dwellings ............................................... | 3 802 | 2 783 | 2 013 | 3 414 | 4 794 | 3 442 | 2 609 | 3 433 | 5 560 | 4 652 |
| Other lodging ..................................................... | 730 | 1 125 | 1 442 | 857 | 442 | 939 | 964 | 908 | 379 | 359 |
| Utilities, fuels, and public services ...................... | 3 885 | 4 814 | 4 374 | 5 092 | 4 067 | 5 147 | 5 577 | 5 705 | 3 717 | 2 930 |
| Household operations ............................................ | 1 309 | 1 811 | 1 239 | 2 417 | 5 191 | 2 270 | 1 103 | 1 438 | 1 562 | 749 |
| Housekeeping supplies ......................................... | 655 | 893 | 890 | 904 | 797 | 884 | 997 | 846 | 418 | 426 |
| Household furnishings and equipment ................... | 1 818 | 2 459 | 2 450 | 2 451 | 2 342 | 2 508 | 2 438 | 2 553 | 1 296 | 1 200 |
| **Apparel and Services** ............................................. | 1 846 | 2 287 | 1 650 | 2 913 | 2 931 | 2 987 | 2 802 | 2 307 | 1 806 | 1 377 |
| **Transportation** ....................................................... | 9 503 | 12 691 | 10 852 | 14 196 | 12 997 | 13 628 | 15 747 | 14 268 | 7 983 | 6 334 |
| Vehicle purchases (net outlay) ............................. | 3 997 | 5 494 | 4 382 | 6 441 | 6 309 | 6 140 | 6 963 | 6 214 | 3 499 | 2 487 |
| Gasoline and motor oil .......................................... | 2 090 | 2 735 | 2 260 | 3 085 | 2 629 | 3 030 | 3 420 | 3 388 | 1 753 | 1 453 |
| Other vehicle expenses ........................................ | 2 756 | 3 560 | 3 254 | 3 819 | 3 420 | 3 491 | 4 571 | 3 771 | 2 356 | 1 950 |
| Public and other transportation ............................ | 661 | 901 | 956 | 851 | 639 | 966 | 792 | 896 | 374 | 444 |
| **Health Care** ............................................................ | 4 342 | 6 077 | 6 692 | 5 529 | 4 778 | 5 435 | 6 083 | 5 833 | 2 371 | 2 765 |
| Health insurance ................................................... | 2 977 | 4 160 | 4 566 | 3 783 | 3 395 | 3 702 | 4 119 | 4 084 | 1 622 | 1 905 |
| Medical services ................................................... | 791 | 1 149 | 1 186 | 1 138 | 957 | 1 143 | 1 231 | 1 002 | 473 | 455 |
| Drugs ..................................................................... | 425 | 566 | 699 | 437 | 303 | 416 | 543 | 587 | 195 | 303 |
| Medical supplies ................................................... | 149 | 201 | 242 | 170 | 123 | 174 | 190 | 161 | 81 | 101 |
| **Entertainment** ........................................................ | 2 842 | 3 807 | 3 811 | 3 897 | 2 998 | 4 325 | 3 751 | 3 263 | 2 144 | 1 906 |
| **Personal Care Products and Services** ......................... | 683 | 875 | 811 | 928 | 815 | 967 | 931 | 928 | 641 | 483 |
| **Reading** .................................................................. | 114 | 152 | 183 | 134 | 91 | 143 | 147 | 79 | 57 | 80 |
| **Education** ................................................................ | 1 315 | 1 794 | 957 | 2 533 | 924 | 2 194 | 3 927 | 2 177 | 1 108 | 837 |
| **Tobacco Products and Smoking Supplies** .................. | 349 | 341 | 270 | 346 | 228 | 340 | 420 | 726 | 232 | 373 |
| **Miscellaneous** ........................................................ | 871 | 1 032 | 961 | 1 091 | 1 062 | 1 026 | 1 204 | 1 087 | 849 | 704 |
| **Cash Contributions** ................................................ | 1 819 | 2 419 | 2 823 | 2 150 | 1 303 | 2 372 | 2 285 | 1 690 | 1 294 | 1 254 |
| **Personal Insurance and Pensions** ............................. | 6 349 | 9 206 | 7 582 | 10 706 | 10 006 | 10 766 | 11 003 | 9 532 | 4 071 | 3 633 |
| Life and other personal insurance ........................ | 333 | 545 | 535 | 548 | 356 | 589 | 593 | 590 | 167 | 131 |
| Pensions and Social Security ............................... | 6 016 | 8 661 | 7 048 | 10 158 | 9 650 | 10 177 | 10 410 | 8 942 | 3 904 | 3 503 |

[1]Value is too small to display.

. . . = Not available.

## Table 11-10. Consumer Expenditures, Averages by Selected Age of Reference Person, 2015

(Number, dollar, percent.)

| Item | All consumer units | Under 30 years | 30 years and older | Under 50 | 50 years and older | Under 55 years | 55 years and older | Under 65 years | 65 years and older |
|---|---|---|---|---|---|---|---|---|---|
| **NUMBER OF CONSUMER UNITS (THOUSANDS)** ........ | 128 437 | 17 840 | 110 598 | 61 793 | 66 644 | 74 389 | 54 048 | 98 478 | 29 960 |
| **CONSUMER UNIT CHARACTERISTICS** | | | | | | | | | |
| Income Before Taxes ..................................................... | 69 627 | 46 130 | 73 417 | 73 626 | 65 918 | 77 065 | 59 389 | 76 624 | 46 627 |
| Income After Taxes ....................................................... | 60 448 | 41 781 | 63 459 | 63 843 | 57 301 | 66 347 | 52 330 | 65 769 | 42 959 |
| Age of Reference Person ............................................. | 50.5 | 24.7 | 54.7 | 35.3 | 64.7 | 38.2 | 67.6 | 43.3 | 74.3 |
| **Average Number in Consumer Unit** | | | | | | | | | |
| All persons ............................................................... | 2.5 | 2.2 | 2.5 | 2.9 | 2.1 | 2.9 | 1.9 | 2.7 | 1.7 |
| Children under 18 years ........................................ | 0.6 | 0.6 | 0.6 | 1.0 | 0.2 | 0.9 | 0.1 | 0.8 | 0.1 |
| Persons 65 years and over .................................... | 0.4 | ( [1] ) | 0.4 | ( [1] ) | 0.7 | ( [1] ) | 0.8 | 0.1 | 1.4 |
| Earners ..................................................................... | 1.3 | 1.4 | 1.3 | 1.6 | 1.0 | 1.6 | 0.9 | 1.5 | 0.5 |
| Vehicles ................................................................... | 1.9 | 1.4 | 2.0 | 1.8 | 2.0 | 1.9 | 1.9 | 1.9 | 1.7 |
| **Percent Distribution** | | | | | | | | | |
| Male ......................................................................... | 47 | 47 | 47 | 47 | 47 | 47 | 47 | 47 | 46 |
| Female ..................................................................... | 53 | 53 | 53 | 53 | 53 | 53 | 53 | 53 | 54 |
| **Percent Homeowner** .................................................. | 62 | 23 | 69 | 48 | 76 | 52 | 77 | 57 | 79 |
| With mortgage ......................................................... | 35 | 17 | 38 | 38 | 33 | 40 | 30 | 40 | 22 |
| Without mortgage .................................................... | 27 | 6 | 30 | 10 | 43 | 12 | 47 | 18 | 57 |
| **AVERAGE ANNUAL EXPENDITURES** ......................... | 55 978 | 40 761 | 58 463 | 57 421 | 54 630 | 59 594 | 50 989 | 59 395 | 44 664 |
| **Food** ........................................................................... | 7 023 | 5 520 | 7 278 | 7 541 | 6 526 | 7 626 | 6 183 | 7 469 | 5 506 |
| Food at home ............................................................. | 4 015 | 2 830 | 4 217 | 4 120 | 3 913 | 4 194 | 3 764 | 4 196 | 3 398 |
| Cereals and bakery products ................................. | 518 | 373 | 543 | 529 | 507 | 535 | 494 | 532 | 470 |
| Meats, poultry, fish, and eggs ............................... | 896 | 649 | 938 | 926 | 867 | 952 | 818 | 949 | 715 |
| Dairy products ........................................................ | 413 | 284 | 435 | 423 | 403 | 429 | 391 | 428 | 360 |
| Fruits and vegetables ............................................ | 769 | 519 | 811 | 786 | 752 | 797 | 730 | 795 | 678 |
| Other food at home ................................................ | 1 419 | 1 004 | 1 490 | 1 456 | 1 384 | 1 482 | 1 332 | 1 491 | 1 174 |
| Food away from home ................................................ | 3 008 | 2 690 | 3 061 | 3 420 | 2 613 | 3 432 | 2 419 | 3 274 | 2 108 |
| **Alcoholic Beverages** ................................................ | 515 | 420 | 531 | 552 | 480 | 556 | 459 | 560 | 362 |
| **Housing** ...................................................................... | 18 409 | 14 280 | 19 080 | 19 453 | 17 445 | 19 638 | 16 718 | 19 285 | 15 529 |
| Shelter ........................................................................ | 10 742 | 9 119 | 11 004 | 11 741 | 9 816 | 11 778 | 9 317 | 11 403 | 8 570 |
| Owned dwellings ................................................... | 6 210 | 2 202 | 6 857 | 5 966 | 6 436 | 6 299 | 6 088 | 6 439 | 5 457 |
| Rented dwellings ................................................... | 3 802 | 6 658 | 3 341 | 5 257 | 2 453 | 4 876 | 2 323 | 4 284 | 2 218 |
| Other lodging ......................................................... | 730 | 259 | 806 | 518 | 927 | 603 | 906 | 680 | 895 |
| Utilities, fuels, and public services ......................... | 3 885 | 2 524 | 4 105 | 3 732 | 4 027 | 3 894 | 3 873 | 3 964 | 3 624 |
| Household operations ................................................. | 1 309 | 897 | 1 375 | 1 568 | 1 068 | 1 501 | 1 044 | 1 365 | 1 122 |
| Housekeeping supplies ............................................. | 655 | 367 | 704 | 579 | 727 | 598 | 733 | 635 | 722 |
| Household furnishings and equipment ..................... | 1 818 | 1 373 | 1 893 | 1 833 | 1 807 | 1 867 | 1 752 | 1 917 | 1 492 |
| **Apparel and Services** ................................................ | 1 846 | 1 540 | 1 898 | 2 095 | 1 610 | 2 236 | 1 304 | 2 079 | 1 060 |
| **Transportation** ........................................................... | 9 503 | 7 693 | 9 798 | 10 111 | 8 943 | 10 402 | 8 266 | 10 310 | 6 846 |
| Vehicle purchases (net outlay) ................................. | 3 997 | 3 435 | 4 088 | 4 514 | 3 518 | 4 548 | 3 238 | 4 432 | 2 567 |
| Gasoline and motor oil ............................................... | 2 090 | 1 762 | 2 142 | 2 274 | 1 918 | 2 333 | 1 754 | 2 286 | 1 445 |
| Other vehicle expenses ............................................. | 2 756 | 2 005 | 2 881 | 2 653 | 2 856 | 2 841 | 2 639 | 2 903 | 2 268 |
| Public and other transportation ................................ | 661 | 491 | 688 | 670 | 651 | 679 | 635 | 689 | 566 |
| **Health Care** ............................................................... | 4 342 | 1 708 | 4 768 | 3 287 | 5 322 | 3 523 | 5 469 | 3 912 | 5 756 |
| Health insurance ........................................................ | 2 977 | 1 191 | 3 265 | 2 306 | 3 600 | 2 460 | 3 689 | 2 699 | 3 893 |
| Medical services ........................................................ | 791 | 307 | 869 | 616 | 954 | 659 | 974 | 738 | 967 |
| Drugs .......................................................................... | 425 | 144 | 470 | 257 | 581 | 290 | 610 | 350 | 672 |
| Medical supplies ........................................................ | 149 | 66 | 162 | 108 | 187 | 114 | 196 | 126 | 224 |
| **Entertainment** ........................................................... | 2 842 | 1 887 | 2 998 | 2 735 | 2 942 | 2 836 | 2 850 | 2 956 | 2 464 |
| **Personal Care Products and Services** ......................... | 683 | 484 | 715 | 698 | 667 | 715 | 637 | 715 | 573 |
| **Reading** ..................................................................... | 114 | 65 | 122 | 84 | 143 | 90 | 148 | 96 | 175 |
| **Education** ................................................................... | 1 315 | 1 925 | 1 216 | 1 447 | 1 192 | 1 787 | 664 | 1 634 | 263 |
| **Tobacco Products and Smoking Supplies** ................. | 349 | 291 | 359 | 377 | 323 | 389 | 295 | 392 | 209 |
| **Miscellaneous** ........................................................... | 871 | 362 | 953 | 804 | 934 | 867 | 877 | 862 | 900 |
| **Cash Contributions** .................................................. | 1 819 | 534 | 2 026 | 1 382 | 2 223 | 1 550 | 2 188 | 1 676 | 2 287 |
| **Personal Insurance and Pensions** ............................. | 6 349 | 4 054 | 6 719 | 6 854 | 5 880 | 7 379 | 4 931 | 7 449 | 2 733 |
| Life and other personal insurance ............................ | 333 | 51 | 378 | 229 | 429 | 285 | 399 | 333 | 332 |
| Pensions and Social Security .................................... | 6 016 | 4 003 | 6 340 | 6 625 | 5 451 | 7 094 | 4 532 | 7 116 | 2 401 |

[1]Value is too small to display.

## Table 11-11.  Consumer Expenditures, Averages by Race of Reference Person, 2015

(Number, dollar, percent.)

| Item | All consumer units | White, Asian, and other races | | | Black |
| --- | --- | --- | --- | --- | --- |
| | | Total | White and other races | Asian | |
| NUMBER OF CONSUMER UNITS (THOUSANDS) ................................. | 128 437 | 111 771 | 106 176 | 5 595 | 16 667 |
| **CONSUMER UNIT CHARACTERISTICS** | | | | | |
| **Income Before Taxes** ................................................ | 69 627 | 72 781 | 71 750 | 92 364 | 48 469 |
| **Income After Taxes** .................................................. | 60 448 | 62 867 | 62 091 | 77 591 | 44 229 |
| **Age of Reference Person** ......................................... | 50.5 | 51.0 | 51.3 | 44.2 | 47.9 |
| **Average Number in Consumer Unit** | | | | | |
| All persons ................................................................ | 2.5 | 2.5 | 2.5 | 2.8 | 2.4 |
| Children under 18 years ............................................ | 0.6 | 0.6 | 0.6 | 0.7 | 0.6 |
| Persons 65 years and over ....................................... | 0.4 | 0.4 | 0.4 | 0.3 | 0.3 |
| Earners .................................................................... | 1.3 | 1.3 | 1.3 | 1.5 | 1.2 |
| Vehicles ................................................................... | 1.9 | 2.0 | 2.0 | 1.5 | 1.2 |
| **Percent Distribution** | | | | | |
| Male ......................................................................... | 47 | 49 | 48 | 56 | 36 |
| Female ..................................................................... | 53 | 51 | 52 | 44 | 64 |
| **Percent Homeowner** ................................................ | 62 | 65 | 66 | 54 | 41 |
| With mortgage .......................................................... | 35 | 37 | 37 | 33 | 25 |
| Without mortgage ..................................................... | 27 | 29 | 29 | 20 | 16 |
| **AVERAGE ANNUAL EXPENDITURES** ....................... | 55 978 | 58 281 | 57 997 | 63 672 | 40 372 |
| **Food** ........................................................................ | 7 023 | 7 365 | 7 302 | 8 515 | 4 644 |
| Food at home ........................................................... | 4 015 | 4 190 | 4 180 | 4 375 | 2 792 |
| Cereals and bakery products ............................... | 518 | 538 | 536 | 574 | 376 |
| Meats, poultry, fish, and eggs ............................. | 896 | 916 | 913 | 977 | 752 |
| Dairy products ...................................................... | 413 | 439 | 441 | 403 | 230 |
| Fruits and vegetables .......................................... | 769 | 806 | 789 | 1 117 | 510 |
| Other food at home ............................................. | 1 419 | 1 491 | 1 501 | 1 303 | 923 |
| Food away from home .............................................. | 3 008 | 3 175 | 3 122 | 4 140 | 1 851 |
| **Alcoholic Beverages** .............................................. | 515 | 561 | 573 | 362 | 193 |
| **Housing** .................................................................. | 18 409 | 18 883 | 18 711 | 22 170 | 15 213 |
| Shelter ..................................................................... | 10 742 | 10 998 | 10 795 | 14 856 | 9 024 |
| Owned dwellings .................................................. | 6 210 | 6 618 | 6 525 | 8 386 | 3 476 |
| Rented dwellings .................................................. | 3 802 | 3 595 | 3 485 | 5 694 | 5 189 |
| Other lodging ....................................................... | 730 | 786 | 786 | 776 | 358 |
| Utilities, fuels, and public services .......................... | 3 885 | 3 916 | 3 934 | 3 567 | 3 678 |
| Household operations ............................................... | 1 309 | 1 383 | 1 371 | 1 612 | 811 |
| Housekeeping supplies ............................................ | 655 | 687 | 697 | 505 | 429 |
| Household furnishings and equipment ...................... | 1 818 | 1 898 | 1 913 | 1 631 | 1 271 |
| **Apparel and Services** ............................................. | 1 846 | 1 903 | 1 889 | 2 149 | 1 453 |
| **Transportation** ....................................................... | 9 503 | 9 810 | 9 790 | 10 174 | 7 436 |
| Vehicle purchases (net outlay) ................................. | 3 997 | 4 136 | 4 158 | 3 723 | 3 065 |
| Gasoline and motor oil ............................................. | 2 090 | 2 149 | 2 151 | 2 097 | 1 694 |
| Other vehicle expenses ........................................... | 2 756 | 2 831 | 2 822 | 3 003 | 2 244 |
| Public and other transportation ............................... | 661 | 695 | 660 | 1 351 | 432 |
| **Health Care** ........................................................... | 4 342 | 4 645 | 4 686 | 3 876 | 2 305 |
| Health insurance ..................................................... | 2 977 | 3 154 | 3 173 | 2 777 | 1 795 |
| Medical services ...................................................... | 791 | 874 | 884 | 677 | 238 |
| Drugs ....................................................................... | 425 | 458 | 466 | 311 | 196 |
| Medical supplies ...................................................... | 149 | 160 | 162 | 111 | 76 |
| **Entertainment** ........................................................ | 2 842 | 3 039 | 3 075 | 2 371 | 1 500 |
| **Personal Care Products and Services** ................... | 683 | 698 | 698 | 696 | 574 |
| **Reading** .................................................................. | 114 | 124 | 125 | 97 | 48 |
| **Education** ............................................................... | 1 315 | 1 399 | 1 347 | 2 380 | 747 |
| **Tobacco Products and Smoking Supplies** ............. | 349 | 363 | 374 | 146 | 260 |
| **Miscellaneous** ....................................................... | 871 | 922 | 932 | 718 | 530 |
| **Cash Contributions** ............................................... | 1 819 | 1 892 | 1 926 | 1 245 | 1 328 |
| **Personal Insurance and Pensions** ........................ | 6 349 | 6 678 | 6 567 | 8 773 | 4 142 |
| Life and other personal insurance ........................... | 333 | 346 | 346 | 334 | 247 |
| Pensions and Social Security ................................... | 6 016 | 6 332 | 6 221 | 8 440 | 3 895 |

## Table 11-12.  Consumer Expenditures, Averages by Hispanic Origin of Reference Person, 2015

(Number, dollar, percent.)

| Item | All consumer units | Hispanic[1] | Not Hispanic | | |
|---|---|---|---|---|---|
| | | | Total | White, Asian, and other races | Black |
| NUMBER OF CONSUMER UNITS (THOUSANDS) ...................................... | 128 437 | 16 728 | 111 710 | 95 409 | 16 301 |
| **CONSUMER UNIT CHARACTERISTICS** | | | | | |
| **Income Before Taxes** ........................................................................ | 69 627 | 54 746 | 71 855 | 75 864 | 48 387 |
| **Income After Taxes** .......................................................................... | 60 448 | 50 628 | 61 919 | 64 951 | 44 169 |
| **Age of Reference Person** ................................................................ | 50.5 | 43.9 | 51.5 | 52.2 | 47.9 |
| **Average Number in Consumer Unit** | | | | | |
| All persons ......................................................................................... | 2.5 | 3.1 | 2.4 | 2.4 | 2.4 |
| Children under 18 years ..................................................................... | 0.6 | 1.0 | 0.5 | 0.5 | 0.6 |
| Persons 65 years and over ................................................................ | 0.4 | 0.2 | 0.4 | 0.4 | 0.3 |
| Earners .............................................................................................. | 1.3 | 1.6 | 1.2 | 1.3 | 1.2 |
| Vehicles ............................................................................................. | 1.9 | 1.7 | 1.9 | 2.0 | 1.3 |
| **Percent Distribution** | | | | | |
| Male ................................................................................................... | 47 | 45 | 47 | 49 | 36 |
| Female ............................................................................................... | 53 | 55 | 53 | 51 | 64 |
| **Percent Homeowner** ......................................................................... | 62 | 45 | 65 | 69 | 41 |
| With mortgage .................................................................................... | 35 | 30 | 36 | 38 | 25 |
| Without mortgage ............................................................................... | 27 | 15 | 29 | 31 | 16 |
| **AVERAGE ANNUAL EXPENDITURES** ............................................. | 55 978 | 47 663 | 57 223 | 60 072 | 40 421 |
| **Food** ................................................................................................. | 7 023 | 6 929 | 7 037 | 7 437 | 4 632 |
| Food at home ..................................................................................... | 4 015 | 4 182 | 3 990 | 4 190 | 2 785 |
| Cereals and bakery products .......................................................... | 518 | 526 | 517 | 541 | 372 |
| Meats, poultry, fish, and eggs ........................................................ | 896 | 1 080 | 868 | 888 | 752 |
| Dairy products ................................................................................. | 413 | 396 | 415 | 446 | 229 |
| Fruits and vegetables ..................................................................... | 769 | 857 | 756 | 796 | 510 |
| Other food at home ......................................................................... | 1 419 | 1 323 | 1 434 | 1 519 | 922 |
| Food away from home ........................................................................ | 3 008 | 2 747 | 3 047 | 3 247 | 1 847 |
| **Alcoholic Beverages** ........................................................................ | 515 | 354 | 539 | 596 | 195 |
| **Housing** ........................................................................................... | 18 409 | 16 855 | 18 641 | 19 222 | 15 228 |
| Shelter ................................................................................................ | 10 742 | 10 257 | 10 815 | 11 120 | 9 030 |
| Owned dwellings ............................................................................. | 6 210 | 4 256 | 6 503 | 7 015 | 3 501 |
| Rented dwellings ............................................................................. | 3 802 | 5 695 | 3 519 | 3 237 | 5 169 |
| Other lodging .................................................................................. | 730 | 305 | 794 | 868 | 359 |
| Utilities, fuels, and public services ..................................................... | 3 885 | 3 567 | 3 933 | 3 974 | 3 694 |
| Household operations ......................................................................... | 1 309 | 1 000 | 1 355 | 1 451 | 793 |
| Housekeeping supplies ....................................................................... | 655 | 575 | 666 | 706 | 429 |
| Household furnishings and equipment ................................................ | 1 818 | 1 457 | 1 872 | 1 971 | 1 282 |
| **Apparel and Services** ....................................................................... | 1 846 | 2 035 | 1 818 | 1 881 | 1 444 |
| **Transportation** ................................................................................. | 9 503 | 9 101 | 9 563 | 9 915 | 7 501 |
| Vehicle purchases (net outlay) ........................................................... | 3 997 | 3 718 | 4 039 | 4 198 | 3 106 |
| Gasoline and motor oil ....................................................................... | 2 090 | 2 208 | 2 072 | 2 134 | 1 707 |
| Other vehicle expenses ...................................................................... | 2 756 | 2 700 | 2 764 | 2 849 | 2 262 |
| Public and other transportation .......................................................... | 661 | 475 | 688 | 733 | 426 |
| **Health Care** ..................................................................................... | 4 342 | 2 632 | 4 598 | 4 987 | 2 318 |
| Health insurance ................................................................................ | 2 977 | 1 868 | 3 143 | 3 373 | 1 800 |
| Medical services ................................................................................. | 791 | 454 | 842 | 944 | 242 |
| Drugs .................................................................................................. | 425 | 224 | 455 | 498 | 198 |
| Medical supplies ................................................................................ | 149 | 85 | 158 | 172 | 77 |
| **Entertainment** .................................................................................. | 2 842 | 1 771 | 3 002 | 3 256 | 1 499 |
| **Personal Care Products and Services** ............................................ | 683 | 604 | 694 | 714 | 575 |
| **Reading** ........................................................................................... | 114 | 48 | 124 | 137 | 48 |
| **Education** ......................................................................................... | 1 315 | 825 | 1 388 | 1 500 | 732 |
| **Tobacco Products and Smoking Supplies** ..................................... | 349 | 154 | 379 | 398 | 264 |
| **Miscellaneous** ................................................................................. | 871 | 619 | 909 | 973 | 531 |
| **Cash Contributions** ......................................................................... | 1 819 | 923 | 1 953 | 2 059 | 1 332 |
| **Personal Insurance and Pensions** ................................................. | 6 349 | 4 814 | 6 579 | 6 998 | 4 122 |
| Life and other personal insurance ...................................................... | 333 | 157 | 359 | 379 | 242 |
| Pensions and Social Security .............................................................. | 6 016 | 4 657 | 6 219 | 6 619 | 3 881 |

[1]May be of any race.

## Table 11-13. Consumer Expenditures, Averages by Education of Reference Person, 2015

(Number, dollar, percent.)

| Item | All consumer units | Less than a college graduate | | | | | College graduate or more | | |
| --- | --- | --- | --- | --- | --- | --- | --- | --- | --- |
| | | Total | Less than a high school graduate | High school graduate | High school graduate with some college | Associate's degree | Total | Bachelor's degree | Master's, professional, or doctoral degree |
| **NUMBER OF CONSUMER UNITS (THOUSANDS)** ........ | 128 437 | 76 988 | 9 382 | 25 760 | 28 263 | 13 582 | 51 450 | 30 405 | 21 044 |
| **CONSUMER UNIT CHARACTERISTICS** | | | | | | | | | |
| **Income Before Taxes** ..................................... | 69 627 | 46 470 | 26 359 | 40 082 | 51 118 | 62 806 | 104 277 | 90 594 | 124 046 |
| **Income After Taxes** ...................................... | 60 448 | 42 915 | 26 197 | 37 842 | 46 632 | 56 351 | 86 684 | 76 721 | 101 080 |
| **Age of Reference Person** ............................. | 50.5 | 51.4 | 56.0 | 53.6 | 48.8 | 49.5 | 49.2 | 48.0 | 51.0 |
| **Average Number in Consumer Unit** | | | | | | | | | |
| All persons ................................................... | 2.5 | 2.4 | 2.2 | 2.3 | 2.4 | 2.5 | 2.6 | 2.5 | 2.6 |
| Children under 18 years .............................. | 0.6 | 0.6 | 0.7 | 0.6 | 0.6 | 0.6 | 0.6 | 0.6 | 0.6 |
| Persons 65 years and over ......................... | 0.4 | 0.4 | 0.5 | 0.4 | 0.4 | 0.3 | 0.3 | 0.3 | 0.4 |
| Earners ........................................................ | 1.3 | 1.1 | 0.7 | 1.0 | 1.2 | 1.4 | 1.5 | 1.5 | 1.5 |
| Vehicles ....................................................... | 1.9 | 1.7 | 1.0 | 1.6 | 1.9 | 2.2 | 2.1 | 2.1 | 2.1 |
| **Percent Distribution** | | | | | | | | | |
| Male ............................................................. | 47 | 44 | 41 | 45 | 44 | 45 | 51 | 51 | 52 |
| Female ......................................................... | 53 | 56 | 59 | 55 | 56 | 55 | 49 | 49 | 48 |
| **Percent Homeowner** ..................................... | 62 | 56 | 44 | 56 | 55 | 66 | 71 | 68 | 77 |
| With mortgage .............................................. | 35 | 27 | 13 | 22 | 31 | 39 | 48 | 45 | 51 |
| Without mortgage ......................................... | 27 | 29 | 31 | 35 | 24 | 27 | 24 | 23 | 25 |
| **AVERAGE ANNUAL EXPENDITURES** ........................ | 55 978 | 41 715 | 26 766 | 36 381 | 45 991 | 53 144 | 76 988 | 69 373 | 87 927 |
| **Food** ............................................................... | 7 023 | 5 568 | 4 278 | 4 959 | 5 988 | 6 688 | 9 051 | 8 405 | 9 951 |
| Food at home ............................................... | 4 015 | 3 422 | 3 126 | 3 123 | 3 590 | 3 835 | 4 834 | 4 564 | 5 207 |
| Cereals and bakery products ..................... | 518 | 448 | 392 | 423 | 463 | 503 | 614 | 576 | 665 |
| Meats, poultry, fish, and eggs .................. | 896 | 813 | 770 | 747 | 862 | 868 | 1 009 | 987 | 1 040 |
| Dairy products ............................................ | 413 | 339 | 299 | 303 | 358 | 397 | 514 | 484 | 555 |
| Fruits and vegetables ................................ | 769 | 614 | 595 | 551 | 649 | 678 | 981 | 903 | 1 089 |
| Other food at home .................................... | 1 419 | 1 206 | 1 069 | 1 100 | 1 259 | 1 389 | 1 716 | 1 614 | 1 857 |
| Food away from home ................................. | 3 008 | 2 147 | 1 152 | 1 835 | 2 398 | 2 853 | 4 217 | 3 841 | 4 744 |
| **Alcoholic Beverages** .................................... | 515 | 324 | 163 | 271 | 383 | 409 | 782 | 659 | 951 |
| **Housing** ......................................................... | 18 409 | 14 140 | 10 429 | 12 831 | 15 118 | 17 139 | 24 750 | 22 231 | 28 379 |
| Shelter ......................................................... | 10 742 | 7 977 | 6 265 | 7 156 | 8 613 | 9 395 | 14 879 | 13 286 | 17 182 |
| Owned dwellings ........................................ | 6 210 | 3 910 | 1 953 | 3 275 | 4 383 | 5 483 | 9 652 | 8 250 | 11 677 |
| Rented dwellings ........................................ | 3 802 | 3 729 | 4 196 | 3 665 | 3 794 | 3 392 | 3 911 | 4 012 | 3 766 |
| Other lodging .............................................. | 730 | 338 | 116 | 216 | 436 | 520 | 1 316 | 1 024 | 1 739 |
| Utilities, fuels, and public services ............ | 3 885 | 3 544 | 2 594 | 3 418 | 3 643 | 4 232 | 4 396 | 4 183 | 4 704 |
| Household operations ................................. | 1 309 | 796 | 390 | 668 | 910 | 1 082 | 2 074 | 1 680 | 2 643 |
| Housekeeping supplies ............................... | 655 | 530 | 450 | 462 | 563 | 641 | 826 | 747 | 935 |
| Household furnishings and equipment ........ | 1 818 | 1 294 | 730 | 1 127 | 1 389 | 1 790 | 2 574 | 2 335 | 2 915 |
| **Apparel and Services** .................................. | 1 846 | 1 234 | 846 | 959 | 1 452 | 1 561 | 2 704 | 2 576 | 2 890 |
| **Transportation** ............................................. | 9 503 | 7 723 | 4 127 | 6 766 | 8 788 | 9 796 | 12 153 | 11 605 | 12 948 |
| Vehicle purchases (net outlay) .................. | 3 997 | 3 259 | 1 478 | 2 896 | 3 800 | 4 054 | 5 101 | 4 934 | 5 342 |
| Gasoline and motor oil ............................... | 2 090 | 1 887 | 1 178 | 1 747 | 2 021 | 2 366 | 2 392 | 2 383 | 2 405 |
| Other vehicle expenses .............................. | 2 756 | 2 286 | 1 255 | 1 919 | 2 651 | 2 923 | 3 447 | 3 385 | 3 541 |
| Public and other transportation .................. | 661 | 290 | 216 | 204 | 317 | 453 | 1 213 | 903 | 1 660 |
| **Health Care** ................................................... | 4 342 | 3 434 | 2 358 | 3 203 | 3 600 | 4 269 | 5 696 | 5 097 | 6 560 |
| Health insurance ......................................... | 2 977 | 2 374 | 1 351 | 2 306 | 2 507 | 2 935 | 3 880 | 3 565 | 4 334 |
| Medical services ......................................... | 791 | 588 | 628 | 451 | 611 | 772 | 1 096 | 894 | 1 388 |
| Drugs ........................................................... | 425 | 361 | 327 | 335 | 371 | 414 | 516 | 474 | 575 |
| Medical supplies ......................................... | 149 | 111 | 52 | 112 | 111 | 148 | 204 | 164 | 262 |
| **Entertainment** ............................................... | 2 842 | 2 112 | 1 103 | 1 725 | 2 359 | 3 017 | 3 906 | 3 398 | 4 628 |
| **Personal Care Products and Services** ........................... | 683 | 501 | 308 | 414 | 566 | 658 | 944 | 858 | 1 065 |
| **Reading** ......................................................... | 114 | 72 | 39 | 65 | 83 | 84 | 175 | 143 | 219 |
| **Education** ....................................................... | 1 315 | 539 | 199 | 198 | 846 | 784 | 2 472 | 2 160 | 2 923 |
| **Tobacco Products and Smoking Supplies** ................... | 349 | 458 | 332 | 499 | 484 | 414 | 186 | 227 | 127 |
| **Miscellaneous** .............................................. | 871 | 723 | 309 | 580 | 836 | 1 044 | 1 091 | 1 093 | 1 090 |
| **Cash Contributions** ..................................... | 1 819 | 1 107 | 646 | 839 | 1 269 | 1 595 | 2 884 | 2 165 | 3 922 |
| **Personal Insurance and Pensions** .............. | 6 349 | 3 778 | 1 627 | 3 073 | 4 217 | 5 688 | 10 195 | 8 755 | 12 275 |
| Life and other personal insurance .............. | 333 | 191 | 100 | 164 | 217 | 250 | 545 | 499 | 612 |
| Pensions and Social Security ..................... | 6 016 | 3 587 | 1 527 | 2 909 | 4 000 | 5 438 | 9 650 | 8 256 | 11 663 |

## Table 11-14.  Consumer Expenditures, Averages by Housing Tenure and Type of Area, 2015

(Number, dollar, percent.)

| Item | All consumer units | Housing tenure | | | | Type of area | | | |
|---|---|---|---|---|---|---|---|---|---|
| | | Homeowner | | | Renter | Urban | | | Rural |
| | | Total | Homeowner with mortgage | Homeowner without mortgage | | Total | Central city | Other urban | |
| **NUMBER OF CONSUMER UNITS (THOUSANDS)** ........... | 128 437 | 80 049 | 45 453 | 34 596 | 48 388 | 116 906 | 45 975 | 70 930 | 11 532 |
| **CONSUMER UNIT CHARACTERISTICS** | | | | | | | | | |
| Income Before Taxes ................................................. | 69 627 | 85 254 | 101 721 | 63 619 | 43 774 | 71 578 | 62 517 | 77 451 | 49 841 |
| Income After Taxes ..................................................... | 60 448 | 72 938 | 86 235 | 55 468 | 39 786 | 61 904 | 54 649 | 66 606 | 45 689 |
| Age of Reference Person ............................................ | 50.5 | 55.1 | 49.2 | 63.0 | 42.9 | 50.0 | 48.0 | 51.3 | 55.7 |
| **Average Number in Consumer Unit** | | | | | | | | | |
| All persons ................................................................ | 2.5 | 2.6 | 2.9 | 2.2 | 2.3 | 2.5 | 2.4 | 2.5 | 2.5 |
| Children under 18 years .......................................... | 0.6 | 0.6 | 0.8 | 0.3 | 0.6 | 0.6 | 0.6 | 0.6 | 0.6 |
| Persons 65 years and over ..................................... | 0.4 | 0.5 | 0.2 | 0.8 | 0.2 | 0.3 | 0.3 | 0.4 | 0.5 |
| Earners .................................................................... | 1.3 | 1.4 | 1.7 | 1.0 | 1.2 | 1.3 | 1.3 | 1.3 | 1.1 |
| Vehicles ................................................................... | 1.9 | 2.3 | 2.5 | 2.1 | 1.2 | 1.8 | 1.5 | 2.1 | 2.4 |
| **Percent Distribution** | | | | | | | | | |
| Male ........................................................................ | 47 | 49 | 50 | 48 | 44 | 47 | 45 | 48 | 48 |
| Female ..................................................................... | 53 | 51 | 50 | 52 | 56 | 53 | 55 | 52 | 52 |
| **Percent Homeowner** ................................................. | 62 | 100 | 100 | 100 | X | 61 | 48 | 69 | 79 |
| With mortgage .......................................................... | 35 | 57 | 100 | X | X | 36 | 28 | 41 | 30 |
| Without mortgage ..................................................... | 27 | 43 | X | 100 | X | 25 | 20 | 28 | 49 |
| **AVERAGE ANNUAL EXPENDITURES** ........................ | 55 978 | 65 656 | 75 486 | 52 198 | 39 937 | 57 059 | 50 175 | 61 494 | 45 031 |
| **Food** ............................................................................ | 7 023 | 8 000 | 8 622 | 6 899 | 5 392 | 7 133 | 6 438 | 7 573 | 5 909 |
| Food at home ............................................................. | 4 015 | 4 569 | 4 767 | 4 200 | 3 089 | 4 043 | 3 596 | 4 325 | 3 731 |
| Cereals and bakery products ................................. | 518 | 592 | 613 | 552 | 394 | 524 | 460 | 565 | 455 |
| Meats, poultry, fish, and eggs .............................. | 896 | 1 003 | 1 048 | 917 | 717 | 897 | 827 | 942 | 879 |
| Dairy products ........................................................ | 413 | 474 | 489 | 445 | 310 | 413 | 358 | 449 | 406 |
| Fruits and vegetables ............................................ | 769 | 866 | 899 | 803 | 606 | 781 | 711 | 826 | 640 |
| Other food at home ................................................ | 1 419 | 1 634 | 1 717 | 1 483 | 1 061 | 1 426 | 1 239 | 1 544 | 1 351 |
| Food away from home ................................................ | 3 008 | 3 431 | 3 856 | 2 699 | 2 303 | 3 090 | 2 842 | 3 248 | 2 178 |
| **Alcoholic Beverages** ................................................ | 515 | 591 | 679 | 431 | 389 | 536 | 505 | 556 | 299 |
| **Housing** ..................................................................... | 18 409 | 20 353 | 24 964 | 14 269 | 15 187 | 19 035 | 17 605 | 19 958 | 12 063 |
| Shelter ....................................................................... | 10 742 | 11 018 | 14 691 | 6 193 | 10 286 | 11 284 | 10 882 | 11 546 | 5 245 |
| Owned dwellings ..................................................... | 6 210 | 9 920 | 13 512 | 5 202 | 72 | 6 456 | 4 955 | 7 429 | 3 713 |
| Rented dwellings .................................................... | 3 802 | 116 | 106 | 128 | 9 901 | 4 069 | 5 260 | 3 296 | 1 099 |
| Other lodging ......................................................... | 730 | 982 | 1 073 | 863 | 313 | 759 | 666 | 820 | 433 |
| Utilities, fuels, and public services .......................... | 3 885 | 4 634 | 4 981 | 4 177 | 2 647 | 3 885 | 3 429 | 4 180 | 3 887 |
| Household operations ................................................ | 1 309 | 1 605 | 1 931 | 1 174 | 819 | 1 367 | 1 195 | 1 478 | 719 |
| Housekeeping supplies .............................................. | 655 | 804 | 802 | 809 | 404 | 651 | 561 | 708 | 692 |
| Household furnishings and equipment ....................... | 1 818 | 2 292 | 2 559 | 1 917 | 1 031 | 1 848 | 1 538 | 2 047 | 1 520 |
| **Apparel and Services** ............................................... | 1 846 | 2 165 | 2 555 | 1 477 | 1 314 | 1 915 | 1 714 | 2 041 | 1 151 |
| **Transportation** ......................................................... | 9 503 | 11 332 | 12 812 | 9 419 | 6 474 | 9 425 | 7 723 | 10 524 | 10 294 |
| Vehicle purchases (net outlay) ................................. | 3 997 | 4 947 | 5 808 | 3 816 | 2 425 | 3 866 | 2 971 | 4 446 | 5 324 |
| Gasoline and motor oil .............................................. | 2 090 | 2 408 | 2 725 | 1 992 | 1 563 | 2 068 | 1 714 | 2 297 | 2 313 |
| Other vehicle expenses ............................................ | 2 756 | 3 203 | 3 479 | 2 872 | 2 012 | 2 790 | 2 329 | 3 086 | 2 404 |
| Public and other transportation ................................ | 661 | 773 | 800 | 738 | 474 | 701 | 709 | 696 | 253 |
| **Health Care** .............................................................. | 4 342 | 5 534 | 5 375 | 5 749 | 2 369 | 4 313 | 3 590 | 4 780 | 4 641 |
| Health insurance ....................................................... | 2 977 | 3 778 | 3 676 | 3 913 | 1 652 | 2 968 | 2 463 | 3 295 | 3 073 |
| Medical services ....................................................... | 791 | 1 034 | 1 038 | 1 028 | 390 | 777 | 669 | 847 | 937 |
| Drugs ........................................................................ | 425 | 530 | 487 | 591 | 249 | 419 | 327 | 479 | 478 |
| Medical supplies ....................................................... | 149 | 192 | 173 | 217 | 77 | 148 | 131 | 159 | 152 |
| **Entertainment** ........................................................... | 2 842 | 3 541 | 3 854 | 3 097 | 1 683 | 2 850 | 2 286 | 3 214 | 2 756 |
| **Personal Care Products and Services** ......................... | 683 | 793 | 890 | 642 | 498 | 705 | 628 | 754 | 452 |
| **Reading** .................................................................... | 114 | 139 | 134 | 153 | 73 | 119 | 109 | 125 | 66 |
| **Education** .................................................................. | 1 315 | 1 482 | 1 799 | 1 060 | 1 038 | 1 396 | 1 332 | 1 437 | 494 |
| **Tobacco Products and Smoking Supplies** .................... | 349 | 333 | 330 | 338 | 376 | 330 | 300 | 349 | 549 |
| **Miscellaneous** ........................................................... | 871 | 1 027 | 1 111 | 917 | 613 | 873 | 723 | 970 | 852 |
| **Cash Contributions** ................................................. | 1 819 | 2 366 | 2 313 | 2 435 | 913 | 1 859 | 1 552 | 2 058 | 1 409 |
| **Personal Insurance and Pensions** ........................... | 6 349 | 8 000 | 10 048 | 5 309 | 3 617 | 6 571 | 5 669 | 7 156 | 4 094 |
| Life and other personal insurance ............................ | 333 | 466 | 543 | 364 | 113 | 338 | 288 | 370 | 279 |
| Pensions and Social Security ................................... | 6 016 | 7 534 | 9 504 | 4 946 | 3 504 | 6 233 | 5 380 | 6 786 | 3 815 |

X = Not applicable.

## Table 11-15.  Consumer Expenditures, Averages by Selected Cities,  2015

(Number, dollar, percent.)

| Item | Washington, D.C. | Philadelphia | New York | Miami | Dallas-Fort Worth | Chicago | Detroit | Minneapolis-St. Paul | San Fransisco | Phoenix |
|---|---|---|---|---|---|---|---|---|---|---|
| **NUMBER OF CONSUMER UNITS (THOUSANDS)** | 2 267 | 2 894 | 8 418 | 1 871 | 2 716 | 3 791 | 1 836 | 1 592 | 2 336 | 1 591 |
| **CONSUMER UNIT CHARACTERISTICS** | | | | | | | | | | |
| **Income Before Taxes** | 115 258 | 78 350 | 87 198 | 53 517 | 76 434 | 85 418 | 79 443 | 87 576 | 101 998 | 72 130 |
| **Age of Reference Person** | 50.0 | 52.0 | 52.0 | 53.0 | 47.0 | 50.0 | 50.0 | 50.0 | 50.0 | 48.0 |
| **Average Number in Consumer Unit** | | | | | | | | | | |
| All persons | 2.7 | 2.3 | 2.5 | 2.3 | 2.6 | 2.6 | 2.6 | 2.4 | 2.6 | 3.0 |
| Children under 18 years | 0.6 | 0.5 | 0.6 | 0.5 | 0.7 | 0.6 | 0.6 | 0.6 | 0.6 | 1.0 |
| Persons 65 years and over | 0.3 | 0.4 | 0.4 | 0.4 | 0.3 | 0.3 | 0.3 | 0.3 | 0.3 | 0.0 |
| Earners | 1.6 | 1.3 | 1.3 | 1.2 | 1.4 | 1.4 | 1.3 | 1.4 | 1.4 | 1.0 |
| Vehicles | 1.9 | 1.6 | 1.3 | 1.4 | 1.8 | 1.7 | 2.1 | 2.4 | 1.8 | 2.0 |
| **Percent Homeowner** | 65.0 | 65.0 | 53.0 | 55.0 | 59.0 | 63.0 | 69.0 | 69.0 | 50.0 | 58.0 |
| **AVERAGE ANNUAL EXPENDITURES** | 81 293 | 60 480 | 62 872 | 48 967 | 63 976 | 63 697 | 60 485 | 69 967 | 71 433 | 55 118 |
| **Food** | 7 840 | 6 788 | 6 943 | 6 755 | 8 240 | 7 926 | 7 356 | 7 843 | 8 612 | 7 167 |
| Food at home | 4 114 | 4 065 | 4 055 | 4 112 | 4 241 | 4 586 | 4 132 | 4 427 | 4 114 | 4 370 |
| Cereals and bakery products | 513 | 545 | 564 | 505 | 525 | 595 | 521 | 549 | 489 | 552 |
| Meats, poultry, fish, and eggs | 882 | 959 | 946 | 1 135 | 927 | 1 043 | 993 | 772 | 945 | 918 |
| Dairy products | 426 | 419 | 439 | 408 | 407 | 453 | 431 | 448 | 427 | 444 |
| Fruits and vegetables | 863 | 838 | 879 | 881 | 850 | 917 | 786 | 865 | 955 | 799 |
| Other food at home | 1 430 | 1 305 | 1 228 | 1 184 | 1 532 | 1 578 | 1 400 | 1 792 | 1 298 | 1 656 |
| Food away from home | 3 726 | 2 722 | 2 888 | 2 643 | 3 999 | 3 339 | 3 225 | 3 416 | 4 498 | 2 798 |
| **Alcoholic Beverages** | 650 | 654 | 488 | 510 | 678 | 630 | 515 | 774 | 1 005 | 611 |
| **Housing** | 29 753 | 21 195 | 24 879 | 17 750 | 20 976 | 21 964 | 18 356 | 22 526 | 26 483 | 18 328 |
| Shelter | 19 813 | 12 805 | 16 835 | 11 878 | 11 415 | 14 063 | 10 308 | 14 219 | 18 724 | 10 908 |
| Owned dwellings | 12 123 | 7 924 | 9 478 | 5 633 | 6 206 | 8 918 | 6 358 | 8 819 | 8 947 | 5 963 |
| Rented dwellings | 6 056 | 3 736 | 6 481 | 5 726 | 4 502 | 4 230 | 2 665 | 4 045 | 8 743 | 4 057 |
| Other lodging | 1 635 | 1 145 | 876 | 520 | 708 | 914 | 1 285 | 1 355 | 1 034 | 889 |
| Utilities, fuels, and public services | 4 537 | 4 673 | 4 318 | 3 362 | 4 557 | 3 894 | 4 305 | 3 702 | 3 493 | 4 217 |
| Household operations | 2 534 | 1 238 | 1 823 | 944 | 1 605 | 1 378 | 1 384 | 1 340 | 2 171 | 1 250 |
| Housekeeping supplies | 648 | 759 | 564 | 709 | 813 | 661 | 668 | 819 | 581 | 519 |
| Household furnishings and equipment | 2 220 | 1 720 | 1 339 | 858 | 2 585 | 1 968 | 1 691 | 2 446 | 1 514 | 1 434 |
| **Apparel and Services** | 2 286 | 2 293 | 2 089 | 2 302 | 2 198 | 2 283 | 2 165 | 1 973 | 2 366 | 1 848 |
| **Transportation** | 12 744 | 9 588 | 8 002 | 8 884 | 11 306 | 9 908 | 11 357 | 11 652 | 9 911 | 8 981 |
| Vehicle purchases (net outlay) | 5 498 | 3 236 | 1 903 | 2 538 | 5 082 | 3 910 | 2 926 | 5 003 | 2 677 | 3 290 |
| Gasoline and motor oil | 2 386 | 2 070 | 1 796 | 2 282 | 2 606 | 2 276 | 2 643 | 2 502 | 2 219 | 2 352 |
| Other vehicle expenses | 3 464 | 3 408 | 2 909 | 3 494 | 3 073 | 2 783 | 5 009 | 3 340 | 3 411 | 2 676 |
| Public and other transportation | 1 396 | 875 | 1 394 | 569 | 546 | 939 | 780 | 807 | 1 603 | 663 |
| **Health Care** | 5 556 | 4 901 | 4 146 | 2 929 | 4 935 | 4 843 | 4 334 | 5 672 | 4 685 | 4 474 |
| **Entertainment** | 3 192 | 2 814 | 2 576 | 1 755 | 3 221 | 3 138 | 3 596 | 3 715 | 3 318 | 2 756 |
| **Personal Care Products and Services** | 816 | 676 | 766 | 636 | 790 | 806 | 788 | 924 | 845 | 712 |
| **Reading** | 239 | 124 | 99 | 50 | 127 | 124 | 132 | 204 | 147 | 116 |
| **Education** | 2 243 | 2 387 | 2 483 | 504 | 935 | 1 795 | 1 412 | 2 337 | 1 806 | 1 546 |
| **Tobacco Products and Smoking Supplies** | 249 | 399 | 222 | 202 | 328 | 334 | 375 | 320 | 133 | 278 |
| **Miscellaneous** | 1 014 | 712 | 869 | 449 | 926 | 957 | 900 | 759 | 780 | 468 |
| **Cash Contributions** | 4 180 | 1 575 | 1 768 | 1 101 | 1 938 | 1 632 | 1 943 | 3 081 | 2 262 | 1 414 |
| **Personal Insurance and Pensions** | 10 532 | 6 373 | 7 543 | 5 139 | 7 377 | 7 357 | 7 254 | 8 189 | 9 079 | 6 418 |
| Life and other personal insurance | 719 | 305 | 411 | 242 | 390 | 425 | 408 | 471 | 419 | 253 |
| Pensions and Social Security | 9 814 | 6 069 | 7 132 | 4 898 | 6 987 | 6 932 | 6 846 | 7 718 | 8 661 | 6 164 |

## Table 11-16. Consumer Expenditures, Averages by Region of Residence, 2015

(Number, dollar, percent.)

| Item | All consumer units | Region[1] | | | |
|---|---|---|---|---|---|
| | | Northeast | South | Midwest | West |
| **NUMBER OF CONSUMER UNITS (THOUSANDS)** .......... | 128 437 | 23 426 | 27 674 | 49 104 | 28 233 |
| **CONSUMER UNIT CHARACTERISTICS** | | | | | |
| **Income Before Taxes** ........................................ | 69 627 | 79 482 | 67 760 | 61 792 | 76 905 |
| **Income After Taxes** ........................................... | 60 448 | 67 179 | 59 178 | 54 700 | 66 105 |
| **Age of Reference Person** ................................. | 50.5 | 51.8 | 50.7 | 50.7 | 49.1 |
| **Average Number in Consumer Unit** | | | | | |
| All persons ......................................................... | 2.5 | 2.4 | 2.4 | 2.4 | 2.7 |
| Children under 18 years ...................................... | 0.6 | 0.5 | 0.6 | 0.6 | 0.7 |
| Persons 65 years and over ................................. | 0.4 | 0.4 | 0.3 | 0.4 | 0.3 |
| Earners ............................................................... | 1.3 | 1.3 | 1.3 | 1.2 | 1.4 |
| Vehicles .............................................................. | 1.9 | 1.6 | 2.0 | 1.9 | 2.0 |
| **Percent Distribution** | | | | | |
| Male .................................................................... | 47 | 48 | 48 | 46 | 47 |
| Female ................................................................ | 53 | 52 | 52 | 54 | 53 |
| **Percent Homeowner** ......................................... | 62 | 61 | 65 | 65 | 56 |
| With mortgage ..................................................... | 35 | 32 | 38 | 35 | 37 |
| Without mortgage ................................................ | 27 | 28 | 27 | 31 | 20 |
| **AVERAGE ANNUAL EXPENDITURES** ............................ | 55 978 | 58 976 | 55 071 | 52 020 | 61 244 |
| **Food** ................................................................... | 7 023 | 6 882 | 7 090 | 6 613 | 7 776 |
| Food at home ...................................................... | 4 015 | 3 939 | 4 152 | 3 756 | 4 387 |
| Cereals and bakery products ......................... | 518 | 542 | 533 | 481 | 546 |
| Meats, poultry, fish, and eggs ....................... | 896 | 879 | 946 | 869 | 907 |
| Dairy products ............................................... | 413 | 426 | 439 | 365 | 458 |
| Fruits and vegetables .................................... | 769 | 823 | 757 | 690 | 870 |
| Other food at home ....................................... | 1 419 | 1 268 | 1 478 | 1 351 | 1 607 |
| Food away from home ......................................... | 3 008 | 2 943 | 2 938 | 2 857 | 3 389 |
| **Alcoholic Beverages** ........................................ | 515 | 562 | 523 | 421 | 630 |
| **Housing** ............................................................. | 18 409 | 20 817 | 17 370 | 16 518 | 20 716 |
| Shelter ................................................................ | 10 742 | 12 814 | 9 886 | 8 939 | 12 999 |
| Owned dwellings ........................................... | 6 210 | 7 684 | 6 115 | 5 224 | 6 796 |
| Rented dwellings ........................................... | 3 802 | 4 277 | 3 076 | 3 032 | 5 460 |
| Other lodging ................................................. | 730 | 853 | 695 | 683 | 744 |
| Utilities, fuels, and public services .................... | 3 885 | 4 210 | 3 775 | 3 954 | 3 604 |
| Household operations .......................................... | 1 309 | 1 575 | 1 121 | 1 176 | 1 503 |
| Housekeeping supplies ....................................... | 655 | 594 | 702 | 662 | 648 |
| Household furnishings and equipment ................. | 1 818 | 1 624 | 1 887 | 1 789 | 1 962 |
| **Apparel and Services** ....................................... | 1 846 | 1 792 | 1 716 | 1 656 | 2 343 |
| **Transportation** ................................................. | 9 503 | 9 026 | 9 597 | 9 598 | 9 640 |
| Vehicle purchases (net outlay) ........................... | 3 997 | 3 570 | 3 996 | 4 527 | 3 431 |
| Gasoline and motor oil ........................................ | 2 090 | 1 827 | 2 058 | 2 123 | 2 279 |
| Other vehicle expenses ...................................... | 2 756 | 2 656 | 2 965 | 2 495 | 3 086 |
| Public and other transportation .......................... | 661 | 972 | 578 | 453 | 844 |
| **Health Care** ...................................................... | 4 342 | 4 328 | 4 616 | 4 264 | 4 221 |
| Health insurance ................................................. | 2 977 | 3 112 | 3 022 | 2 971 | 2 834 |
| Medical services ................................................. | 791 | 682 | 982 | 714 | 830 |
| Drugs .................................................................. | 425 | 398 | 458 | 436 | 395 |
| Medical supplies ................................................. | 149 | 136 | 155 | 144 | 162 |
| **Entertainment** ................................................... | 2 842 | 2 754 | 2 859 | 2 682 | 3 177 |
| **Personal Care Products and Services** ............................ | 683 | 699 | 673 | 615 | 794 |
| **Reading** ............................................................. | 114 | 130 | 117 | 89 | 142 |
| **Education** ........................................................... | 1 315 | 2 021 | 1 343 | 973 | 1 295 |
| **Tobacco Products and Smoking Supplies** ..................... | 349 | 318 | 418 | 388 | 240 |
| **Miscellaneous** ................................................... | 871 | 877 | 926 | 698 | 1 113 |
| **Cash Contributions** .......................................... | 1 819 | 1 667 | 1 563 | 1 896 | 2 059 |
| **Personal Insurance and Pensions** ................................. | 6 349 | 7 103 | 6 260 | 5 608 | 7 098 |
| Life and other personal insurance ...................... | 333 | 409 | 323 | 291 | 353 |
| Pensions and Social Security .............................. | 6 016 | 6 694 | 5 937 | 5 317 | 6 746 |

[1]The states that comprise the Census regions are: Northeast—Connecticut, Maine, Massachusetts, New Hampshire, New Jersey, New York, Pennsylvania, Rhode Island, and Vermont; South—Alabama, Arkansas, Delaware, District of Columbia, Florida, Georgia, Kentucky, Louisiana, Maryland, Mississippi, North Carolina, Oklahoma, South Carolina, Tennessee, Texas, Virginia, and West Virginia; Midwest—Illinois, Indiana, Iowa, Kansas, Michigan, Minnesota, Missouri, Nebraska, North Dakota, Ohio, South Dakota, and Wisconsin; and West—Alaska, Arizona, California, Colorado, Hawaii, Idaho, Montana, Nevada, New Mexico, Oregon, Utah, Washington, and Wyoming.

## Table 11-17.  Consumer Expenditures, Averages for Single Men by Income Before Taxes, 2014–2015

(Number, dollar, percent.)

| Item | All single men | Complete reporting of income | | | | | | |
|---|---|---|---|---|---|---|---|---|
| | | Less than $5,000 | $5,000 to $9,999 | $10,000 to $14,999 | $15,000 to $19,999 | $20,000 to $29,999 | $30,000 to $39,999 | $40,000 and over |
| **NUMBER OF CONSUMER UNITS (THOUSANDS)** | 17 887 | 1 749 | 1 196 | 2 028 | 1 952 | 2 774 | 1 770 | 6 419 |
| **CONSUMER UNIT CHARACTERISTICS** | | | | | | | | |
| **Income Before Taxes** | 39 383 | 2 422 | 8 014 | 12 693 | 17 350 | 24 658 | 34 553 | 78 130 |
| **Income After Taxes** | 33 442 | 2 589 | 8 167 | 12 227 | 17 005 | 22 468 | 31 224 | 63 614 |
| **Age of Reference Person** | 49.1 | 42.3 | 42.5 | 52.3 | 56.9 | 53.1 | 48.7 | 47.1 |
| **Average Number in Consumer Unit** | | | | | | | | |
| All persons | 1.0 | 1.0 | 1.0 | 1.0 | 1.0 | 1.0 | 1.0 | 1.0 |
| Persons 65 years and over | 0.2 | 0.1 | 0.2 | 0.3 | 0.4 | 0.4 | 0.2 | 0.1 |
| Earners | 0.7 | 0.4 | 0.5 | 0.3 | 0.4 | 0.6 | 0.8 | 0.9 |
| Vehicles | 1.2 | 0.7 | 0.7 | 0.7 | 1.1 | 1.3 | 1.3 | 1.6 |
| **Percent Homeowner** | 43 | 26 | 22 | 32 | 40 | 44 | 42 | 56 |
| With mortgage | 20 | 7 | 5 | 5 | 9 | 13 | 18 | 37 |
| Without mortgage | 23 | 19 | 17 | 27 | 31 | 31 | 24 | 19 |
| **AVERAGE ANNUAL EXPENDITURES** | 33 479 | 17 340 | 17 656 | 18 268 | 21 854 | 28 996 | 30 147 | 51 732 |
| **Food** | 4 059 | 3 301 | 2 734 | 2 799 | 2 991 | 3 477 | 3 673 | 5 453 |
| Food at home | 2 023 | 1 758 | 1 412 | 1 785 | 1 686 | 1 831 | 2 010 | 2 425 |
| Cereals and bakery products | 257 | 231 | 203 | 239 | 257 | 235 | 246 | 288 |
| Meats, poultry, fish, and eggs | 451 | 455 | 298 | 441 | 361 | 418 | 492 | 504 |
| Dairy products | 203 | 153 | 157 | 186 | 179 | 181 | 197 | 243 |
| Fruits and vegetables | 372 | 337 | 228 | 330 | 313 | 325 | 345 | 457 |
| Other food at home | 741 | 582 | 526 | 589 | 576 | 672 | 730 | 933 |
| Food away from home | 2 035 | 1 543 | 1 322 | 1 014 | 1 305 | 1 646 | 1 662 | 3 028 |
| **Alcoholic Beverages** | 515 | 326 | 242 | 244 | 247 | 378 | 281 | 880 |
| **Housing** | 12 092 | 6 880 | 6 963 | 7 478 | 8 566 | 10 837 | 11 156 | 17 761 |
| Shelter | 8 154 | 4 691 | 4 880 | 4 916 | 5 556 | 7 120 | 7 375 | 12 182 |
| Owned dwellings | 3 292 | 1 167 | 936 | 1 059 | 1 499 | 2 424 | 2 456 | 6 167 |
| Rented dwellings | 4 502 | 3 366 | 3 781 | 3 748 | 3 970 | 4 497 | 4 625 | 5 315 |
| Other lodging | 359 | 158 | 163 | 109 | 87 | 199 | 294 | 700 |
| Utilities, fuels, and public services | 2 287 | 1 456 | 1 267 | 1 784 | 2 033 | 2 369 | 2 350 | 2 886 |
| Household operations | 516 | 179 | 206 | 267 | 299 | 474 | 448 | 845 |
| Housekeeping supplies | 282 | 195 | 98 | 147 | 181 | 291 | 335 | 378 |
| Household furnishings and equipment | 853 | 358 | 513 | 363 | 497 | 582 | 649 | 1 468 |
| **Apparel and Services** | 730 | 509 | 554 | 462 | 585 | 690 | 410 | 1 046 |
| **Transportation** | 5 170 | 1 898 | 2 412 | 2 708 | 3 779 | 4 759 | 4 750 | 8 043 |
| Vehicle purchases (net outlay) | 1 855 | 456 | 702 | 774 | 1 349 | 1 552 | 1 442 | 3 191 |
| Gasoline and motor oil | 1 414 | 706 | 818 | 875 | 1 039 | 1 291 | 1 613 | 2 002 |
| Other vehicle expenses | 1 559 | 543 | 727 | 943 | 1 215 | 1 612 | 1 468 | 2 268 |
| Public and other transportation | 342 | 193 | 165 | 116 | 176 | 304 | 228 | 583 |
| **Health Care** | 2 249 | 773 | 837 | 1 009 | 1 848 | 2 487 | 2 504 | 3 247 |
| Health insurance | 1 510 | 541 | 610 | 659 | 1 312 | 1 587 | 1 691 | 2 187 |
| Medical services | 412 | 148 | 85 | 140 | 197 | 440 | 515 | 657 |
| Drugs | 253 | 77 | 92 | 186 | 265 | 386 | 227 | 292 |
| Medical supplies | 74 | [1]7 | [1]50 | 24 | 75 | 74 | 71 | 111 |
| **Entertainment** | 1 652 | 765 | 899 | 803 | 920 | 1 366 | 1 442 | 2 685 |
| **Personal Care Products and Services** | 230 | 138 | 119 | 122 | 159 | 217 | 208 | 337 |
| **Reading** | 82 | 48 | 16 | 36 | 49 | 66 | 70 | 135 |
| **Education** | 933 | 1 626 | 1 610 | 1 214 | 622 | 844 | 458 | 793 |
| **Tobacco Products and Smoking Supplies** | 331 | 267 | 268 | 326 | 334 | 345 | 386 | 338 |
| **Miscellaneous** | 639 | 351 | 238 | 262 | 256 | 734 | 769 | 946 |
| **Cash Contributions** | 1 551 | 296 | 472 | 430 | 763 | 1 157 | 1 362 | 2 912 |
| **Personal Insurance and Pensions** | 3 245 | 161 | 290 | 376 | 735 | 1 641 | 2 677 | 7 157 |
| Life and other personal insurance | 123 | [1]23 | 16 | 47 | 94 | 71 | 216 | 199 |
| Pensions and Social Security | 3 122 | 138 | 273 | 329 | 642 | 1 569 | 2 460 | 6 957 |

[1]Data are likely to have large sampling errors.

## Table 11-18.  Consumer Expenditures, Averages for Single Women by Age Before Taxes, 2014–2015

| Item | All single women | Under 25 years | 25-34 years | 35-44 years | 45-54 years | 55-64 years | 65 years and over |
|---|---|---|---|---|---|---|---|
| **NUMBER OF CONSUMER UNITS (THOUSANDS)** | 19 804 | 1 895 | 2 059 | 1 284 | 2 100 | 3 994 | 8 471 |
| **CONSUMER UNIT CHARACTERISTICS** | | | | | | | |
| **Income Before Taxes** | 30 056 | 12 747 | 38 404 | 42 379 | 39 685 | 35 952 | 24 865 |
| **Income After Taxes** | 26 372 | 11 826 | 32 629 | 35 254 | 31 496 | 30 916 | 23 348 |
| **Age of Reference Person** | 58 | 21 | 29 | 40 | 50 | 60 | 77 |
| **Average Number in Consumer Unit** | | | | | | | |
| All persons | 1.0 | 1.0 | 1.0 | 1.0 | 1.0 | 1.0 | 1.0 |
| Persons 65 years and over | 0.4 | X | X | X | X | X | 1.0 |
| Earners | 0.5 | 0.7 | 0.9 | 0.8 | 0.8 | 0.6 | 0.2 |
| Vehicles | 0.9 | 0.5 | 0.9 | 0.9 | 1.1 | 1.0 | 0.9 |
| **Percent Homeowner** | 52 | 3 | 20 | 41 | 50 | 60 | 69 |
| With mortgage | 21 | 1 | 16 | 32 | 35 | 33 | 16 |
| Without mortgage | 31 | 1 | 4 | 10 | 15 | 27 | 53 |
| **AVERAGE ANNUAL EXPENDITURES** | 32 092 | 21 502 | 35 445 | 37 717 | 37 797 | 35 139 | 29 814 |
| **Food** | 3 590 | 2 759 | 3 984 | 4 455 | 4 316 | 3 590 | 3 312 |
| Food at home | 2 253 | 1 198 | 2 220 | 2 391 | 2 741 | 2 369 | 2 256 |
| Cereals and bakery products | 286 | 185 | 255 | 269 | 310 | 277 | 316 |
| Meats, poultry, fish, and eggs | 427 | 199 | 412 | 483 | 486 | 457 | 436 |
| Dairy products | 243 | 128 | 241 | 243 | 248 | 266 | 255 |
| Fruits and vegetables | 456 | 239 | 480 | 546 | 520 | 455 | 462 |
| Other food at home | 840 | 447 | 832 | 849 | 1 177 | 915 | 786 |
| Food away from home | 1 336 | 1 562 | 1 764 | 2 064 | 1 575 | 1 221 | 1 056 |
| **Alcoholic Beverages** | 213 | 208 | 399 | 387 | 253 | 206 | 131 |
| **Housing** | 12 657 | 8 088 | 13 662 | 14 948 | 14 315 | 13 760 | 12 150 |
| Shelter | 8 013 | 6 295 | 9 758 | 10 072 | 9 402 | 8 664 | 7 010 |
| Owned dwellings | 3 649 | 663 | 1 810 | 4 179 | 4 637 | 4 913 | 3 842 |
| Rented dwellings | 3 997 | 5 415 | 7 740 | 5 549 | 4 207 | 3 175 | 2 870 |
| Other lodging | 368 | 217 | 208 | 344 | 559 | 576 | 298 |
| Utilities, fuels, and public services | 2 499 | 719 | 2 048 | 2 636 | 2 830 | 2 907 | 2 711 |
| Household operations | 759 | 216 | 557 | 720 | 674 | 697 | 986 |
| Housekeeping supplies | 445 | 218 | 309 | 459 | 382 | 443 | 543 |
| Household furnishings and equipment | 941 | 640 | 990 | 1 061 | 1 027 | 1 048 | 901 |
| **Apparel and Services** | 1 020 | 987 | 1 311 | 1 581 | 1 156 | 1 063 | 804 |
| **Transportation** | 4 396 | 2 875 | 5 904 | 5 251 | 5 879 | 5 382 | 3 386 |
| Vehicle purchases (net outlay) | 1 438 | [1]1 215 | 2 090 | [1]1 546 | 2 188 | 2 053 | 838 |
| Gasoline and motor oil | 993 | 753 | 1 324 | 1 277 | 1 301 | 1 201 | 748 |
| Other vehicle expenses | 1 579 | 622 | 1 912 | 1 811 | 1 997 | 1 729 | 1 484 |
| Public and other transportation | 385 | 285 | 578 | 617 | 394 | 400 | 316 |
| **Health Care** | 2 857 | 544 | 1 759 | 1 981 | 2 370 | 2 911 | 3 867 |
| Health insurance | 1 843 | 239 | 1 200 | 1 157 | 1 541 | 1 854 | 2 531 |
| Medical services | 540 | 179 | 293 | 533 | 409 | 596 | 689 |
| Drugs | 348 | 90 | 170 | 195 | 332 | 326 | 486 |
| Medical supplies | 125 | 35 | 96 | 97 | 88 | 135 | 161 |
| **Entertainment** | 1 677 | 783 | 1 521 | 1 847 | 1 944 | 2 092 | 1 609 |
| **Personal Care Products and Services** | 572 | 345 | 679 | 842 | 698 | 549 | 528 |
| **Reading** | 84 | 28 | 77 | 69 | 59 | 83 | 107 |
| **Education** | 718 | 3 654 | 1 287 | 840 | 606 | 373 | 95 |
| **Tobacco Products and Smoking Supplies** | 167 | 54 | 179 | 208 | 279 | 261 | 113 |
| **Miscellaneous** | 650 | 66 | 636 | 545 | 1 181 | 623 | 681 |
| **Cash Contributions** | 1 266 | 224 | 539 | 756 | 779 | 1 022 | 1 989 |
| **Personal Insurance and Pensions** | 2 225 | 886 | 3 506 | 4 007 | 3 962 | 3 225 | 1 042 |
| Life and other personal insurance | 142 | 6 | 70 | 130 | 163 | 164 | 175 |
| Pensions and Social Security | 2 084 | 880 | 3 436 | 3 877 | 3 798 | 3 061 | 866 |

[1]Data are likely to have large sampling errors.
X = Not applicable.

## Table 11-19. Consumer Expenditures, Averages for Age Groups by Income Before Taxes: Reference Person Under 25 Years of Age, 2014–2015

(Number, dollar, percent.)

| Item | Total | Complete reporting of income | | | | | | |
|---|---|---|---|---|---|---|---|---|
| | | Less than $5,000 | $5,000 to $9,999 | $10,000 to $14,999 | $15,000 to $19,999 | $20,000 to $29,999 | $30,000 to $39,999 | $40,000 and over |
| **NUMBER OF CONSUMER UNITS (THOUSANDS)** | 8 049 | 1 416 | 1 063 | 875 | 663 | 1 023 | 782 | 2 226 |
| **CONSUMER UNIT CHARACTERISTICS** | | | | | | | | |
| Income Before Taxes | 30 744 | 2 331 | 7 462 | 12 359 | 17 198 | 24 796 | 34 718 | 72 538 |
| Income After Taxes | 28 986 | 2 540 | 7 918 | 12 853 | 18 083 | 25 553 | 34 588 | 65 071 |
| Age of Reference Person | 21.5 | 20.5 | 20.9 | 21.2 | 21.4 | 21.8 | 22.2 | 22.1 |
| **Average Number in Consumer Unit** | | | | | | | | |
| All persons | 2.0 | 1.3 | 1.3 | 1.5 | 1.9 | 2.1 | 2.6 | 2.9 |
| Children under 18 years | 0.4 | 0.1 | 0.2 | 0.3 | 0.4 | 0.5 | 0.6 | 0.5 |
| Earners | 1.3 | 0.7 | 0.8 | 0.8 | 1.1 | 1.3 | 1.6 | 2.1 |
| Vehicles | 1.1 | 0.5 | 0.5 | 0.5 | 0.7 | 1.0 | 1.4 | 2.0 |
| **Percent Distribution** | | | | | | | | |
| Male | 46 | 41 | 48 | 53 | 41 | 49 | 49 | 46 |
| Female | 54 | 59 | 52 | 47 | 59 | 51 | 51 | 54 |
| **Percent Homeowner** | 12 | 1 | 3 | 2 | 7 | 8 | 15 | 31 |
| With mortgage | 7 | ($^1$) | ($^1$) | 1 | 2 | 5 | 6 | 20 |
| Without mortgage | 5 | 1 | 2 | 1 | 5 | 3 | 9 | 11 |
| **AVERAGE ANNUAL EXPENDITURES** | 32 476 | 19 615 | 17 377 | 23 690 | 25 206 | 28 701 | 34 693 | 53 341 |
| **Food** | 4 648 | 3 041 | 2 824 | 3 881 | 3 840 | 4 070 | 5 367 | 6 560 |
| Food at home | 2 519 | 1 410 | 1 363 | 1 997 | 2 254 | 2 200 | 3 143 | 3 603 |
| Cereals and bakery products | 351 | 203 | 221 | 288 | 319 | 321 | 414 | 484 |
| Meats, poultry, fish, and eggs | 572 | 282 | 254 | 426 | 501 | 501 | 825 | 824 |
| Dairy products | 253 | 131 | 129 | 221 | 208 | 214 | 321 | 369 |
| Fruits and vegetables | 455 | 266 | 242 | 406 | 448 | 338 | 543 | 658 |
| Other food at home | 888 | 529 | 516 | 656 | 778 | 825 | 1 040 | 1 268 |
| Food away from home | 2 128 | 1 631 | 1 460 | 1 884 | 1 586 | 1 871 | 2 224 | 2 957 |
| **Alcoholic Beverages** | 276 | 184 | 190 | 204 | 292 | 182 | 281 | 416 |
| **Housing** | 11 374 | 7 528 | 6 685 | 8 350 | 9 037 | 11 054 | 12 407 | 17 653 |
| Shelter | 7 665 | 5 857 | 4 893 | 5 945 | 6 263 | 7 436 | 7 861 | 11 268 |
| Owned dwellings | 1 126 | 720 | 276 | 277 | 329 | 497 | 810 | 2 763 |
| Rented dwellings | 6 313 | 4 933 | 4 420 | 5 192 | 5 826 | 6 872 | 6 875 | 8 226 |
| Other lodging | 225 | $^2$204 | $^2$198 | 475 | $^2$109 | $^2$68 | $^2$176 | 278 |
| Utilities, fuels, and public services | 1 992 | 718 | 860 | 1 280 | 1 545 | 2 056 | 2 597 | 3 514 |
| Household operations | 459 | 187 | 226 | 242 | 290 | 545 | 593 | 792 |
| Housekeeping supplies | 249 | 188 | 122 | 214 | 129 | 179 | 366 | 359 |
| Household furnishings and equipment | 1 009 | 579 | 584 | 668 | 809 | 837 | 990 | 1 720 |
| **Apparel and Services** | 1 282 | 784 | 566 | 1 172 | 875 | 1 398 | 1 656 | 1 763 |
| **Transportation** | 6 181 | 2 111 | 2 404 | 3 172 | 5 341 | 4 969 | 7 131 | 12 030 |
| Vehicle purchases (net outlay) | 2 814 | $^2$912 | $^2$883 | $^2$1175 | 2 696 | 1 863 | 2 960 | 6 011 |
| Gasoline and motor oil | 1 555 | 625 | 854 | 1 029 | 1 163 | 1 475 | 2 070 | 2 660 |
| Other vehicle expenses | 1 495 | 374 | 478 | 705 | 1 252 | 1 359 | 1 739 | 2 855 |
| Public and other transportation | 317 | 201 | 189 | 263 | 231 | 272 | 363 | 504 |
| **Health Care** | 1 047 | 310 | 237 | 463 | 651 | 699 | 1 063 | 2 396 |
| Health insurance | 678 | 134 | 102 | 240 | 232 | 479 | 672 | 1 700 |
| Medical services | 207 | 72 | 77 | 62 | 314 | 99 | 201 | 434 |
| Drugs | 110 | 78 | 22 | 133 | 58 | 73 | 127 | 185 |
| Medical supplies | 51 | $^2$26 | $^2$36 | $^2$27 | $^2$48 | 47 | 63 | 79 |
| **Entertainment** | 1 320 | 702 | 807 | 859 | 932 | 1 331 | 1 574 | 2 094 |
| **Personal Care Products and Services** | 353 | 216 | 148 | 264 | 295 | 328 | 387 | 559 |
| **Reading** | 41 | 18 | 15 | 53 | 23 | 55 | 45 | 60 |
| **Education** | 2 761 | 4 305 | 2 836 | 4 228 | 2 316 | 2 128 | 898 | 2 246 |
| **Tobacco Products and Smoking Supplies** | 238 | 99 | 85 | 171 | 198 | 279 | 405 | 359 |
| **Miscellaneous** | 197 | 81 | 80 | 68 | 86 | 206 | 170 | 414 |
| **Cash Contributions** | 356 | 82 | 112 | 127 | 295 | 306 | 459 | 740 |
| **Personal Insurance and Pensions** | 2 402 | 154 | 388 | 679 | 1 023 | 1 696 | 2 849 | 6 051 |
| Life and other personal insurance | 27 | $^2$2 | $^2$6 | $^2$10 | $^2$6 | $^2$24 | $^2$27 | 69 |
| Pensions and Social Security | 2 375 | 152 | 383 | 668 | 1 017 | 1 672 | 2 822 | 5 982 |

$^1$Value is too small to display.
$^2$Data are likely to have large sampling errors.

## Table 11-20. Consumer Expenditures, Averages for Age Groups by Income Before Taxes: Reference Person 25 to 34 Years of Age, 2014–2015

(Number, dollar, percent.)

| Item | Total | Complete reporting of income | | | | | | | | |
|---|---|---|---|---|---|---|---|---|---|---|
| | | Les than $5,000 | $5,000 to $9,999 | $10,000 to $14,999 | $15,000 to $19,999 | $20,000 to $29,999 | $30,000 to $39,999 | $40,000 to $49,999 | $50,000 to $69,999 | $70,000 or more |
| NUMBER OF CONSUMER UNITS (THOUSANDS) | 20 809 | 686 | 644 | 818 | 1 073 | 2 478 | 2 297 | 2 243 | 3 641 | 6 930 |
| **CONSUMER UNIT CHARACTERISTICS** | | | | | | | | | | |
| Income Before Taxes | 62 912 | 2 635 | 7 936 | 13 008 | 17 370 | 24 998 | 34 717 | 44 429 | 59 155 | 117 779 |
| Income After Taxes | 56 052 | 2 798 | 8 734 | 14 591 | 19 739 | 27 009 | 34 875 | 42 279 | 53 907 | 99 219 |
| Age of Reference Person | 29.7 | 29.0 | 28.7 | 29.6 | 29.0 | 29.2 | 29.4 | 29.3 | 29.6 | 30.3 |
| **Average Number in Consumer Unit** | | | | | | | | | | |
| All persons | 2.7 | 2.1 | 2.5 | 2.3 | 2.5 | 2.6 | 2.7 | 2.7 | 2.8 | 3.0 |
| Children under 18 years | 1.0 | 0.8 | 1.3 | 1.0 | 1.1 | 1.1 | 1.1 | 1.0 | 0.9 | 1.0 |
| Earners | 1.5 | 0.7 | 0.7 | 0.8 | 1.0 | 1.2 | 1.3 | 1.4 | 1.6 | 1.9 |
| Vehicles | 1.6 | 1.0 | 0.8 | 0.9 | 1.0 | 1.1 | 1.4 | 1.6 | 1.9 | 2.1 |
| **Percent Distribution** | | | | | | | | | | |
| Male | 49 | 45 | 26 | 36 | 36 | 40 | 45 | 50 | 55 | 55 |
| Female | 51 | 55 | 74 | 64 | 64 | 60 | 55 | 50 | 45 | 45 |
| **Percent Homeowner** | 39 | 12 | 16 | 12 | 15 | 15 | 25 | 33 | 44 | 62 |
| With mortgage | 32 | 5 | 7 | 7 | 6 | 8 | 18 | 27 | 37 | 57 |
| Without mortgage | 7 | 7 | 9 | 5 | 9 | 7 | 7 | 5 | 7 | 6 |
| **AVERAGE ANNUAL EXPENDITURES** | 50 829 | 26 401 | 22 659 | 25 331 | 28 096 | 32 329 | 35 483 | 42 344 | 50 250 | 76 818 |
| **Food** | 6 633 | 4 518 | 3 861 | 4 339 | 4 378 | 4 999 | 5 179 | 5 627 | 6 397 | 9 086 |
| Food at home | 3 624 | 2 482 | 3 002 | 3 274 | 2 715 | 3 110 | 3 254 | 3 154 | 3 321 | 4 539 |
| Cereals and bakery products | 461 | 325 | 372 | 463 | 377 | 386 | 431 | 388 | 409 | 575 |
| Meats, poultry, fish, and eggs | 802 | 517 | 671 | 715 | 579 | 856 | 755 | 716 | 698 | 961 |
| Dairy products | 388 | 286 | 354 | 319 | 279 | 305 | 334 | 356 | 381 | 483 |
| Fruits and vegetables | 698 | 486 | 538 | 611 | 546 | 559 | 641 | 632 | 608 | 891 |
| Other food at home | 1 274 | 869 | 1 068 | 1 165 | 934 | 1 004 | 1 092 | 1 061 | 1 225 | 1 629 |
| Food away from home | 3 009 | 2 036 | 859 | 1 066 | 1 663 | 1 889 | 1 925 | 2 473 | 3 077 | 4 547 |
| **Alcoholic Beverages** | 536 | 267 | 74 | 131 | 240 | 349 | 251 | 443 | 534 | 871 |
| **Housing** | 17 833 | 9 902 | 9 737 | 10 438 | 11 393 | 12 488 | 13 347 | 15 135 | 17 436 | 25 681 |
| Shelter | 10 890 | 6 436 | 5 600 | 6 695 | 7 006 | 7 694 | 8 254 | 9 486 | 10 584 | 15 550 |
| Owned dwellings | 4 283 | 715 | 734 | 758 | 602 | 874 | 1 668 | 2 553 | 4 133 | 8 677 |
| Rented dwellings | 6 235 | 5 571 | 4 788 | 5 868 | 6 302 | 6 678 | 6 417 | 6 752 | 6 209 | 6 096 |
| Other lodging | 371 | [1]150 | [1]78 | [1]68 | [1]102 | 142 | 168 | 182 | 241 | 777 |
| Utilities, fuels, and public services | 3 300 | 2 072 | 2 157 | 2 333 | 2 445 | 2 737 | 2 868 | 3 053 | 3 457 | 4 116 |
| Household operations | 1 567 | 409 | 643 | 569 | 503 | 716 | 871 | 981 | 1 357 | 2 884 |
| Housekeeping supplies | 502 | 323 | 240 | 306 | 406 | 396 | 424 | 400 | 514 | 658 |
| Household furnishings and equipment | 1 574 | 662 | 1 096 | 536 | 1 033 | 944 | 929 | 1 215 | 1 524 | 2 473 |
| **Apparel and Services** | 1 889 | 1 574 | 1 273 | 1 051 | 1 016 | 1 417 | 1 311 | 1 399 | 1 513 | 2 880 |
| **Transportation** | 9 360 | 4 866 | 3 658 | 4 690 | 5 006 | 5 930 | 6 508 | 8 443 | 10 237 | 13 549 |
| Vehicle purchases (net outlay) | 4 087 | [1]2 084 | [1]1 502 | 2 013 | 2 111 | 2 550 | 2 083 | 3 536 | 4 663 | 6 166 |
| Gasoline and motor oil | 2 303 | 1 442 | 1 205 | 1 351 | 1 426 | 1 648 | 2 202 | 2 152 | 2 507 | 2 949 |
| Other vehicle expenses | 2 401 | 1 039 | 753 | 1 100 | 1 160 | 1 449 | 1 983 | 2 413 | 2 689 | 3 340 |
| Public and other transportation | 569 | 300 | 199 | 227 | 310 | 284 | 240 | 342 | 379 | 1 094 |
| **Health Care** | 2 731 | 1 094 | 663 | 592 | 872 | 1 318 | 1 825 | 2 414 | 3 077 | 4 348 |
| Health insurance | 1 965 | 746 | 504 | 350 | 554 | 844 | 1 332 | 1 701 | 2 301 | 3 149 |
| Medical services | 484 | 259 | 89 | 108 | 206 | 240 | 321 | 474 | 498 | 768 |
| Drugs | 203 | 63 | 57 | 99 | 89 | 184 | 124 | 180 | 187 | 305 |
| Medical supplies | 80 | [1]27 | [1]13 | [1]35 | [1]23 | 50 | 48 | 59 | 91 | 126 |
| **Entertainment** | 2 445 | 1 058 | 1 000 | 1 143 | 1 023 | 1 301 | 1 750 | 2 077 | 2 357 | 3 865 |
| **Personal Care Products and Services** | 573 | 319 | 169 | 316 | 340 | 452 | 473 | 389 | 540 | 844 |
| **Reading** | 86 | 53 | 17 | 30 | 55 | 47 | 91 | 94 | 74 | 122 |
| **Education** | 1 106 | [1]1 457 | [1]979 | 1 026 | 1 430 | 894 | 681 | 863 | 849 | 1 472 |
| **Tobacco Products and Smoking Supplies** | 322 | 418 | 424 | 388 | 262 | 403 | 366 | 275 | 312 | 281 |
| **Miscellaneous** | 601 | 510 | 203 | 133 | 376 | 261 | 319 | 606 | 547 | 978 |
| **Cash Contributions** | 964 | 269 | 267 | 312 | 537 | 659 | 583 | 753 | 1 035 | 1 506 |
| **Personal Insurance and Pensions** | 5 750 | 95 | 335 | 741 | 1 168 | 1 811 | 2 797 | 3 828 | 5 342 | 11 337 |
| Life and other personal insurance | 130 | [1]4 | [1]3 | [1]36 | [1]19 | 34 | 51 | 101 | 97 | 271 |
| Pensions and Social Security | 5 620 | 91 | 332 | 705 | 1 149 | 1 777 | 2 746 | 3 726 | 5 245 | 11 067 |

[1]Data are likely to have large sampling errors.

## Table 11-21. Consumer Expenditures, Averages for Age Groups by Income Before Taxes: Reference Person 35 to 44 Years of Age, 2014–2015

(Number, dollar, percent.)

| Item | Total | Complete reporting of income | | | | | | | | |
|---|---|---|---|---|---|---|---|---|---|---|
| | | Less than $5,000 | $5,000 to $9,999 | $10,000 to $14,999 | $15,000 to $19,999 | $20,000 to $29,999 | $30,000 to $39,999 | $40,000 to $49,999 | $50,000 to $69,999 | $70,000 and over |
| NUMBER OF CONSUMER UNITS (THOUSANDS) ............. | 21 624 | 679 | 481 | 787 | 843 | 1 774 | 1 964 | 1 755 | 3 406 | 9 936 |
| **CONSUMER UNIT CHARACTERISTICS** | | | | | | | | | | |
| Income Before Taxes ......................................... | 84 725 | 2 769 | 8 155 | 12 574 | 17 607 | 24 921 | 34 963 | 44 634 | 59 538 | 141 667 |
| Income After Taxes ........................................... | 72 891 | 3 056 | 8 856 | 14 349 | 19 880 | 27 781 | 36 049 | 43 352 | 55 386 | 116 449 |
| Age of Reference Person ................................... | 39.6 | 39.7 | 39.1 | 39.4 | 39.9 | 39.6 | 39.5 | 39.3 | 39.4 | 39.7 |
| **Average Number in Consumer Unit** | | | | | | | | | | |
| All persons .................................................... | 3.3 | 2.2 | 2.5 | 2.6 | 2.8 | 3.1 | 3.1 | 3.1 | 3.4 | 3.6 |
| Children under 18 years .............................. | 1.4 | 0.8 | 1.1 | 1.1 | 1.2 | 1.4 | 1.3 | 1.3 | 1.4 | 1.5 |
| Persons 65 years and over .......................... | ([1]) | ([1]) | ([1]) | ([1]) | [2]0.1 | [2]0.1 | ([1]) | ([1]) | ([1]) | ([1]) |
| Earners ......................................................... | 1.6 | 0.7 | 0.7 | 0.8 | 1.0 | 1.2 | 1.4 | 1.5 | 1.7 | 1.9 |
| Vehicles ........................................................ | 1.9 | 0.9 | 0.8 | 0.9 | 1.0 | 1.2 | 1.5 | 1.7 | 2.0 | 2.4 |
| **Percent Distribution** | | | | | | | | | | |
| Male .............................................................. | 46 | 44 | 27 | 28 | 40 | 35 | 42 | 47 | 47 | 52 |
| Female .......................................................... | 54 | 56 | 73 | 72 | 60 | 65 | 58 | 53 | 53 | 48 |
| **Percent Homeowner** ...................................... | 58 | 27 | 27 | 31 | 30 | 30 | 38 | 45 | 56 | 77 |
| With mortgage .............................................. | 47 | 15 | 11 | 12 | 16 | 15 | 26 | 32 | 46 | 69 |
| Without mortgage ......................................... | 11 | 12 | 16 | 19 | 15 | 15 | 12 | 13 | 10 | 8 |
| **AVERAGE ANNUAL EXPENDITURES** ................. | 63 901 | 29 454 | 24 714 | 24 390 | 28 164 | 32 782 | 39 966 | 43 947 | 52 146 | 91 959 |
| **Food** | 8 451 | 4 904 | 3 944 | 4 287 | 5 182 | 4 695 | 6 414 | 6 046 | 7 023 | 11 417 |
| Food at home ................................................ | 4 808 | 3 604 | 2 758 | 3 055 | 3 347 | 3 182 | 4 227 | 3 868 | 4 203 | 5 991 |
| Cereals and bakery products ................... | 632 | 472 | 288 | 461 | 396 | 411 | 510 | 531 | 541 | 800 |
| Meats, poultry, fish, and eggs ................. | 1 080 | 1 024 | 587 | 844 | 790 | 764 | 1 048 | 932 | 989 | 1 265 |
| Dairy products ......................................... | 505 | 353 | 287 | 251 | 318 | 328 | 402 | 411 | 452 | 643 |
| Fruits and vegetables ............................. | 935 | 720 | 529 | 532 | 598 | 548 | 847 | 718 | 818 | 1 185 |
| Other food at home ................................. | 1 657 | 1 035 | 1 065 | 966 | 1 245 | 1 131 | 1 420 | 1 276 | 1 402 | 2 098 |
| Food away from home ................................... | 3 643 | 1 300 | 1 187 | 1 232 | 1 835 | 1 513 | 2 186 | 2 178 | 2 820 | 5 426 |
| **Alcoholic Beverages** ................................... | 600 | 195 | [2]197 | 187 | 213 | 218 | 260 | 271 | 436 | 953 |
| **Housing** | 21 720 | 11 050 | 11 063 | 11 059 | 11 098 | 12 664 | 14 391 | 15 601 | 18 426 | 29 965 |
| Shelter ......................................................... | 13 061 | 7 200 | 6 939 | 6 577 | 6 541 | 7 787 | 8 532 | 9 485 | 10 916 | 18 027 |
| Owned dwellings ..................................... | 7 724 | 1 871 | 1 797 | 1 477 | 1 571 | 1 795 | 2 598 | 3 693 | 5 349 | 13 026 |
| Rented dwellings ..................................... | 4 729 | 5 205 | 5 057 | 5 014 | 4 863 | 5 883 | 5 698 | 5 590 | 5 248 | 3 918 |
| Other lodging ........................................... | 608 | [2]125 | [2]85 | [2]86 | [2]107 | [1]108 | 236 | 202 | 318 | 1 083 |
| Utilities, fuels, and public services ............. | 4 300 | 2 632 | 2 812 | 2 902 | 2 958 | 3 256 | 3 489 | 3 703 | 4 333 | 5 151 |
| Household operations ................................... | 1 848 | 537 | 640 | 405 | 494 | 473 | 750 | 866 | 1 120 | 3 110 |
| Housekeeping supplies ................................ | 639 | 250 | 268 | 364 | 366 | 430 | 490 | 548 | 543 | 835 |
| Household furnishings and equipment ......... | 1 873 | 430 | 405 | 811 | 739 | 719 | 1 130 | 999 | 1 514 | 2 842 |
| **Apparel and Services** .................................. | 2 417 | 1 420 | 1 018 | 923 | 1 399 | 1 206 | 2 033 | 1 706 | 1 556 | 3 438 |
| **Transportation** | 10 730 | 5 925 | 3 411 | 3 740 | 4 165 | 6 986 | 7 323 | 8 447 | 9 882 | 14 538 |
| Vehicle purchases (net outlay) .................... | 4 281 | [2]2 603 | [2]1 017 | [2]1 260 | [2]1 393 | 2 994 | 2 915 | 3 347 | 4 090 | 5 769 |
| Gasoline and motor oil ................................. | 2 757 | 1 418 | 1 266 | 1 366 | 1 466 | 1 884 | 2 181 | 2 500 | 2 800 | 3 440 |
| Other vehicle expenses ................................ | 2 956 | 1 618 | 911 | 1 000 | 1 080 | 1 819 | 1 984 | 2 250 | 2 585 | 4 088 |
| Public and other transportation ................... | 735 | 286 | 217 | 114 | 226 | 289 | 243 | 349 | 408 | 1 241 |
| **Health Care** | 3 958 | 1 284 | 763 | 859 | 1 122 | 1 327 | 2 096 | 2 687 | 3 452 | 6 014 |
| Health insurance .......................................... | 2 697 | 936 | 459 | 531 | 616 | 925 | 1 381 | 1 887 | 2 398 | 4 096 |
| Medical services .......................................... | 805 | 161 | [2]149 | 170 | 251 | 202 | 390 | 470 | 670 | 1 273 |
| Drugs ........................................................... | 332 | 137 | 120 | 130 | 187 | 153 | 251 | 250 | 300 | 455 |
| Medical supplies .......................................... | 124 | [2]49 | [2]35 | [2]28 | 67 | 48 | 75 | 79 | 85 | 190 |
| **Entertainment** ............................................. | 3 290 | 1 307 | 1 132 | 1 105 | 1 302 | 1 459 | 1 759 | 1 865 | 2 388 | 5 046 |
| **Personal Care Products and Services** ............. | 780 | 403 | 354 | 510 | 362 | 420 | 568 | 464 | 609 | 1 103 |
| **Reading** .................................................... | 95 | 16 | 30 | 26 | 50 | 37 | 59 | 56 | 78 | 142 |
| **Education** .................................................. | 1 218 | 807 | 859 | 333 | 212 | 550 | 510 | 734 | 626 | 1 966 |
| **Tobacco Products and Smoking Supplies** ......... | 350 | 360 | 442 | 318 | 408 | 440 | 338 | 455 | 366 | 305 |
| **Miscellaneous** ............................................ | 1 007 | 1 083 | 943 | 139 | 1 170 | 326 | 561 | 673 | 587 | 1 469 |
| **Cash Contributions** ..................................... | 1 612 | 555 | 261 | 290 | 401 | 667 | 732 | 1 013 | 1 244 | 2 532 |
| **Personal Insurance and Pensions** ................. | 7 675 | 144 | 297 | 615 | 1 079 | 1 788 | 2 924 | 3 929 | 5 471 | 13 072 |
| Life and other personal insurance ............... | 326 | [2]25 | [2]29 | [2]20 | [2]29 | 45 | 73 | 162 | 193 | 586 |
| Pensions and Social Security ....................... | 7 349 | 119 | 268 | 595 | 1 050 | 1 743 | 2 851 | 3 766 | 5 278 | 12 487 |

[1]Value too small to dispaly.
[2]Data are likely to have large sampling errors.

## Table 11-22.  Consumer Expenditures, Averages for Age Groups by Income Before Taxes: Reference Person 45 to 54 Years of Age, 2014–2015

(Number, dollar, percent.)

| Item | Total | Complete reporting of income | | | | | | | | |
|---|---|---|---|---|---|---|---|---|---|---|
| | | Less than $5,000 | $5,000 to $9,999 | $10,000 to $14,999 | $15,000 to $19,999 | $20,000 to $29,999 | $30,000 to $39,999 | $40,000 to $49,999 | $50,000 to $69,999 | $70,000 and over |
| NUMBER OF CONSUMER UNITS (THOUSANDS) | 23 903 | 852 | 612 | 946 | 825 | 1 807 | 1 798 | 1 698 | 3 359 | 12 006 |
| **CONSUMER UNIT CHARACTERISTICS** | | | | | | | | | | |
| Income Before Taxes | 91 582 | 785 | 8 076 | 12 807 | 17 707 | 25 162 | 34 759 | 44 694 | 59 343 | 147 720 |
| Income After Taxes | 77 125 | 912 | 8 609 | 13 475 | 18 964 | 26 180 | 34 559 | 42 402 | 54 141 | 120 419 |
| Age of Reference Person | 49.7 | 49.8 | 49.7 | 50.2 | 50.0 | 50.0 | 49.8 | 49.6 | 49.5 | 49.6 |
| **Average Number in Consumer Unit** | | | | | | | | | | |
| All persons | 2.8 | 1.8 | 2.1 | 1.8 | 2.2 | 2.3 | 2.6 | 2.7 | 2.7 | 3.2 |
| Children under 18 years | 0.7 | 0.3 | 0.5 | 0.3 | 0.6 | 0.6 | 0.6 | 0.6 | 0.6 | 0.8 |
| Persons 65 years and over | (1) | (1) | (1) | (1) | 20.1 | 0.1 | 0.1 | (1) | (1) | (1) |
| Earners | 1.7 | 0.5 | 0.6 | 0.6 | 0.8 | 1.1 | 1.4 | 1.7 | 1.7 | 2.2 |
| Vehicles | 2.3 | 0.9 | 1.0 | 0.9 | 1.2 | 1.5 | 1.7 | 1.8 | 2.2 | 2.9 |
| **Percent Distribution** | | | | | | | | | | |
| Male | 48 | 44 | 33 | 37 | 38 | 43 | 39 | 45 | 48 | 53 |
| Female | 52 | 56 | 67 | 63 | 62 | 57 | 61 | 55 | 52 | 47 |
| **Percent Homeowner** | 70 | 37 | 35 | 38 | 39 | 48 | 53 | 59 | 68 | 87 |
| With mortgage | 50 | 19 | 16 | 19 | 20 | 22 | 32 | 38 | 47 | 68 |
| Without mortgage | 20 | 18 | 19 | 19 | 19 | 26 | 22 | 21 | 21 | 18 |
| **AVERAGE ANNUAL EXPENDITURES** | 67 708 | 23 330 | 23 945 | 23 749 | 27 167 | 30 492 | 37 657 | 42 884 | 51 774 | 97 481 |
| **Food** | 8 218 | 3 701 | 4 272 | 3 148 | 4 113 | 4 764 | 5 141 | 5 755 | 6 486 | 11 258 |
| Food at home | 4 679 | 2 634 | 3 098 | 2 429 | 2 903 | 3 207 | 3 123 | 3 609 | 3 959 | 6 023 |
| Cereals and bakery products | 594 | 366 | 372 | 295 | 353 | 365 | 389 | 469 | 514 | 768 |
| Meats, poultry, fish, and eggs | 1 097 | 696 | 797 | 631 | 856 | 899 | 741 | 903 | 942 | 1 351 |
| Dairy products | 475 | 224 | 307 | 232 | 315 | 320 | 308 | 375 | 404 | 615 |
| Fruits and vegetables | 852 | 434 | 574 | 411 | 484 | 579 | 587 | 631 | 708 | 1 109 |
| Other food at home | 1 662 | 913 | 1 048 | 861 | 896 | 1 045 | 1 099 | 1 230 | 1 391 | 2 181 |
| Food away from home | 3 540 | 1 068 | 1 173 | 719 | 1 210 | 1 557 | 2 017 | 2 147 | 2 527 | 5 235 |
| **Alcoholic Beverages** | 553 | 242 | 1382 | 161 | 156 | 186 | 297 | 282 | 307 | 848 |
| **Housing** | 21 009 | 9 928 | 9 690 | 9 686 | 11 283 | 11 795 | 13 986 | 15 546 | 16 825 | 28 313 |
| Shelter | 12 471 | 5 903 | 6 127 | 5 660 | 6 813 | 6 661 | 8 064 | 8 887 | 9 819 | 16 969 |
| Owned dwellings | 8 323 | 2 105 | 1 906 | 1 886 | 1 958 | 2 442 | 3 336 | 4 227 | 5 698 | 12 982 |
| Rented dwellings | 3 211 | 3 692 | 4 171 | 3 714 | 4 770 | 4 083 | 4 466 | 4 330 | 3 667 | 2 376 |
| Other lodging | 937 | 2105 | 249 | 260 | 285 | 135 | 263 | 331 | 455 | 1 610 |
| Utilities, fuels, and public services | 4 640 | 2 806 | 2 410 | 2 558 | 2 952 | 3 324 | 3 901 | 3 973 | 4 263 | 5 672 |
| Household operations | 1 159 | 388 | 352 | 509 | 482 | 440 | 519 | 596 | 702 | 1 764 |
| Housekeeping supplies | 741 | 294 | 294 | 405 | 362 | 468 | 415 | 488 | 618 | 1 012 |
| Household furnishings and equipment | 1 998 | 538 | 508 | 554 | 673 | 902 | 1 086 | 1 602 | 1 423 | 2 896 |
| **Apparel and Services** | 2 422 | 647 | 601 | 639 | 1 122 | 1 053 | 1 152 | 1 527 | 1 389 | 3 702 |
| **Transportation** | 11 554 | 3 466 | 4 763 | 5 167 | 3 829 | 5 127 | 6 343 | 7 823 | 10 400 | 16 120 |
| Vehicle purchases (net outlay) | 4 548 | 2949 | 22 585 | 21 374 | 2503 | 1 266 | 2 417 | 2 744 | 4 232 | 6 587 |
| Gasoline and motor oil | 2 826 | 1 131 | 1 128 | 1 165 | 1 485 | 1 803 | 2 031 | 2 368 | 2 763 | 3 612 |
| Other vehicle expenses | 3 466 | 1 193 | 846 | 2 522 | 1 703 | 1 894 | 1 558 | 2 338 | 3 013 | 4 778 |
| Public and other transportation | 714 | 193 | 203 | 107 | 138 | 164 | 337 | 374 | 393 | 1 142 |
| **Health Care** | 4 575 | 1 402 | 1 173 | 1 429 | 1 559 | 2 372 | 2 626 | 2 953 | 4 139 | 6 404 |
| Health insurance | 3 070 | 772 | 746 | 822 | 923 | 1 485 | 1 796 | 1 956 | 2 781 | 4 345 |
| Medical services | 882 | 208 | 214 | 276 | 250 | 509 | 385 | 570 | 800 | 1 252 |
| Drugs | 467 | 335 | 171 | 307 | 319 | 323 | 345 | 349 | 433 | 581 |
| Medical supplies | 156 | 286 | 242 | 224 | 67 | 55 | 101 | 79 | 125 | 226 |
| **Entertainment** | 3 247 | 1 257 | 1 389 | 1 123 | 1 676 | 1 328 | 1 629 | 1 951 | 2 327 | 4 738 |
| **Personal Care Products and Services** | 807 | 217 | 330 | 302 | 321 | 338 | 409 | 481 | 544 | 1 201 |
| **Reading** | 109 | 231 | 220 | 36 | 35 | 21 | 43 | 41 | 83 | 171 |
| **Education** | 2 425 | 2501 | 2205 | 280 | 263 | 200 | 754 | 609 | 991 | 4 235 |
| **Tobacco Products and Smoking Supplies** | 437 | 469 | 352 | 481 | 560 | 470 | 474 | 501 | 486 | 394 |
| **Miscellaneous** | 1 068 | 675 | 183 | 318 | 414 | 288 | 1 034 | 518 | 1 159 | 1 421 |
| **Cash Contributions** | 2 234 | 560 | 239 | 484 | 832 | 680 | 729 | 927 | 1 166 | 3 631 |
| **Personal Insurance and Pensions** | 9 049 | 233 | 348 | 494 | 1 003 | 1 871 | 3 040 | 3 969 | 5 472 | 15 045 |
| Life and other personal insurance | 444 | 294 | 286 | 248 | 86 | 87 | 137 | 150 | 193 | 754 |
| Pensions and Social Security | 8 605 | 139 | 262 | 446 | 917 | 1 784 | 2 903 | 3 819 | 5 279 | 14 291 |

1Value too small to display.
2Data are likely to have large sampling errors.

## Table 11-23. Consumer Expenditures, Averages for Age Groups by Income Before Taxes: Reference Person 55 to 64 Years of Age, 2014–2015

(Number, dollar, percent.)

| Item | | Complete reporting of income | | | | | | | | |
|---|---|---|---|---|---|---|---|---|---|---|
| | Total | Less than $5,000 | $5,000 to $9,999 | $10,000 to $14,999 | $15,000 to $19,999 | $20,000 to $29,999 | $30,000 to $39,999 | $40,000 to $49,999 | $50,000 to $69,999 | $70,000 and over |
| **NUMBER OF CONSUMER UNITS (THOUSANDS)** | 23 794 | 1 317 | 846 | 1 414 | 1 185 | 2 320 | 2 109 | 1 927 | 3 370 | 9 306 |
| **CONSUMER UNIT CHARACTERISTICS** | | | | | | | | | | |
| **Income Before Taxes** | 75 228 | 2 244 | 8 010 | 12 712 | 17 436 | 24 878 | 34 814 | 44 633 | 59 257 | 142 356 |
| **Income After Taxes** | 63 815 | 2 267 | 8 388 | 12 369 | 17 614 | 23 796 | 33 334 | 41 699 | 53 578 | 116 436 |
| **Age of Reference Person** | 59.3 | 59.1 | 59.4 | 59.6 | 59.7 | 59.6 | 59.8 | 59.5 | 59.3 | 59.0 |
| **Average Number in Consumer Unit** | | | | | | | | | | |
| All persons | 2.2 | 1.4 | 1.7 | 1.5 | 1.7 | 1.8 | 1.9 | 2.2 | 2.2 | 2.6 |
| Children under 18 years | 0.2 | 0.1 | 0.2 | 0.1 | 0.2 | 0.2 | 0.2 | 0.3 | 0.2 | 0.2 |
| Persons 65 years and over | 0.1 | (1) | 20.1 | 20.1 | 0.1 | 0.1 | 0.1 | 0.1 | 0.1 | 0.1 |
| Earners | 1.3 | 0.3 | 0.4 | 0.4 | 0.6 | 0.8 | 1.0 | 1.3 | 1.4 | 2.0 |
| Vehicles | 2.1 | 1.0 | 1.1 | 0.9 | 1.2 | 1.6 | 1.7 | 2.0 | 2.3 | 2.8 |
| **Percent Distribution** | | | | | | | | | | |
| Male | 48 | 45 | 37 | 41 | 51 | 45 | 42 | 44 | 48 | 54 |
| Female | 52 | 55 | 63 | 59 | 49 | 55 | 58 | 56 | 52 | 46 |
| **Percent Homeowner** | 76 | 49 | 46 | 47 | 53 | 65 | 68 | 77 | 83 | 92 |
| With mortgage | 41 | 16 | 19 | 14 | 18 | 28 | 36 | 38 | 48 | 57 |
| Without mortgage | 35 | 34 | 27 | 32 | 34 | 37 | 31 | 39 | 35 | 35 |
| **AVERAGE ANNUAL EXPENDITURES** | 57 409 | 23 997 | 24 348 | 21 842 | 27 458 | 33 948 | 36 520 | 42 074 | 51 067 | 90 055 |
| **Food** | 6 897 | 4 232 | 3 521 | 3 408 | 3 612 | 4 613 | 4 818 | 5 039 | 6 386 | 9 997 |
| Food at home | 4 155 | 3 033 | 2 691 | 2 586 | 2 418 | 3 300 | 3 232 | 3 275 | 4 056 | 5 481 |
| Cereals and bakery products | 513 | 387 | 293 | 342 | 299 | 442 | 421 | 434 | 498 | 654 |
| Meats, poultry, fish, and eggs | 932 | 760 | 647 | 628 | 497 | 729 | 809 | 681 | 876 | 1 223 |
| Dairy products | 429 | 269 | 233 | 272 | 297 | 325 | 329 | 369 | 460 | 550 |
| Fruits and vegetables | 785 | 583 | 453 | 395 | 461 | 608 | 605 | 578 | 736 | 1 073 |
| Other food at home | 1 497 | 1 034 | 1 066 | 948 | 864 | 1 196 | 1 069 | 1 212 | 1 487 | 1 980 |
| Food away from home | 2 742 | 1 200 | 830 | 822 | 1 194 | 1 313 | 1 585 | 1 765 | 2 329 | 4 516 |
| **Alcoholic Beverages** | 516 | 226 | 134 | 97 | 195 | 194 | 282 | 283 | 384 | 910 |
| **Housing** | 18 027 | 9 489 | 10 791 | 8 982 | 10 550 | 11 735 | 13 120 | 14 289 | 16 286 | 26 251 |
| Shelter | 10 140 | 5 128 | 6 499 | 5 101 | 6 160 | 6 495 | 7 418 | 7 852 | 8 849 | 14 919 |
| Owned dwellings | 6 919 | 2 177 | 2 962 | 1 865 | 2 593 | 3 275 | 4 228 | 4 991 | 6 136 | 11 469 |
| Rented dwellings | 2 209 | 2 822 | 3 360 | 3 077 | 3 360 | 2 947 | 2 911 | 2 385 | 2 254 | 1 344 |
| Other lodging | 1 012 | 129 | 2178 | 158 | 207 | 274 | 279 | 476 | 459 | 2 106 |
| Utilities, fuels, and public services | 4 247 | 2 708 | 2 798 | 2 593 | 2 884 | 3 293 | 3 538 | 3 848 | 4 298 | 5 483 |
| Household operations | 950 | 384 | 467 | 390 | 479 | 510 | 502 | 675 | 811 | 1 536 |
| Housekeeping supplies | 764 | 447 | 351 | 389 | 399 | 552 | 613 | 539 | 652 | 1 102 |
| Household furnishings and equipment | 1 927 | 822 | 676 | 509 | 628 | 886 | 1 049 | 1 375 | 1 676 | 3 211 |
| **Apparel and Services** | 1 692 | 851 | 559 | 498 | 811 | 992 | 1 036 | 1 084 | 1 623 | 2 634 |
| **Transportation** | 9 621 | 3 764 | 3 330 | 3 615 | 5 051 | 6 988 | 5 491 | 8 447 | 9 023 | 14 530 |
| Vehicle purchases (net outlay) | 3 567 | 21 188 | 2830 | 1 191 | 21 886 | 2 876 | 1 510 | 3 703 | 2 647 | 5 671 |
| Gasoline and motor oil | 2 356 | 1 093 | 1 030 | 1 050 | 1 350 | 1 770 | 1 929 | 2 186 | 2 478 | 3 216 |
| Other vehicle expenses | 3 023 | 1 317 | 1 236 | 1 213 | 1 508 | 2 085 | 1 877 | 2 137 | 3 313 | 4 429 |
| Public and other transportation | 675 | 167 | 233 | 161 | 307 | 257 | 175 | 421 | 585 | 1 215 |
| **Health Care** | 5 059 | 2 083 | 2 096 | 1 912 | 2 435 | 3 346 | 3 809 | 4 278 | 5 209 | 7 371 |
| Health insurance | 3 342 | 1 398 | 1 296 | 1 191 | 1 578 | 2 222 | 2 691 | 2 915 | 3 373 | 4 859 |
| Medical services | 952 | 315 | 429 | 327 | 375 | 550 | 472 | 685 | 1 039 | 1 491 |
| Drugs | 603 | 303 | 246 | 324 | 411 | 489 | 509 | 508 | 641 | 792 |
| Medical supplies | 162 | 67 | 125 | 70 | 71 | 84 | 137 | 170 | 156 | 228 |
| **Entertainment** | 3 080 | 1 236 | 1 194 | 1 116 | 1 599 | 1 842 | 2 056 | 2 027 | 2 650 | 4 876 |
| **Personal Care Products and Services** | 695 | 344 | 298 | 195 | 311 | 368 | 399 | 476 | 617 | 1 119 |
| **Reading** | 131 | 54 | 53 | 61 | 54 | 75 | 80 | 94 | 84 | 217 |
| **Education** | 1 098 | 2108 | 267 | 274 | 2266 | 161 | 364 | 135 | 829 | 2 289 |
| **Tobacco Products and Smoking Supplies** | 405 | 380 | 440 | 451 | 457 | 510 | 559 | 432 | 425 | 317 |
| **Miscellaneous** | 821 | 287 | 591 | 505 | 512 | 466 | 590 | 726 | 791 | 1 176 |
| **Cash Contributions** | 1 989 | 550 | 999 | 476 | 791 | 833 | 1 280 | 1 190 | 1 486 | 3 462 |
| **Personal Insurance and Pensions** | 7 377 | 392 | 277 | 451 | 812 | 1 825 | 2 638 | 3 574 | 5 274 | 14 905 |
| Life and other personal insurance | 508 | 146 | 75 | 105 | 231 | 154 | 379 | 257 | 338 | 926 |
| Pensions and Social Security | 6 869 | 246 | 202 | 346 | 581 | 1 671 | 2 259 | 3 317 | 4 937 | 13 979 |

1Value is too small to display.
2Data are likely to have large sampling errors.

## Table 11-24. Consumer Expenditures, Averages for Age Groups by Income Before Taxes: Reference Person 65 Years of Age and Over, 2014–2015

(Number, dollar, percent.)

| Item | Total | Less than $5,000 | $5,000 to $9,999 | $10,000 to $14,999 | $15,000 to $19,999 | $20,000 to $29,999 | $30,000 to $39,999 | $40,000 to $49,999 | $50,000 to $69,999 | $70,000 and over |
|---|---|---|---|---|---|---|---|---|---|---|
| | | | | | | Complete reporting of income | | | | |
| NUMBER OF CONSUMER UNITS (THOUSANDS) | 29 554 | 975 | 1 023 | 3 207 | 3 702 | 5 468 | 3 890 | 2 681 | 3 519 | 5 089 |
| **CONSUMER UNIT CHARACTERISTICS** | | | | | | | | | | |
| Income Before Taxes | 45 964 | 2 416 | 8 614 | 12 944 | 17 405 | 24 862 | 34 553 | 44 741 | 58 775 | 126 590 |
| Income After Taxes | 42 509 | 2 455 | 8 617 | 13 073 | 17 547 | 24 916 | 34 376 | 43 670 | 56 394 | 108 616 |
| Age of Reference Person | 74.2 | 74.7 | 76.2 | 76.5 | 76.7 | 75.4 | 74.1 | 73.0 | 72.5 | 71.2 |
| **Average Number in Consumer Unit** | | | | | | | | | | |
| All persons | 1.8 | 1.4 | 1.2 | 1.2 | 1.3 | 1.6 | 1.9 | 2.0 | 2.1 | 2.3 |
| Children under 18 years | 0.1 | ¹0.1 | (²) | (²) | (²) | (²) | 0.1 | 0.1 | 0.1 | 0.1 |
| Persons 65 years and over | 1.4 | 1.2 | 1.1 | 1.1 | 1.1 | 1.4 | 1.6 | 1.5 | 1.5 | 1.5 |
| Earners | 0.5 | 0.2 | 0.1 | 0.1 | 0.1 | 0.2 | 0.4 | 0.6 | 0.8 | 1.2 |
| Vehicles | 1.7 | 0.9 | 0.8 | 0.8 | 1.2 | 1.6 | 1.9 | 2.1 | 2.2 | 2.6 |
| **Percent Distribution** | | | | | | | | | | |
| Male | 46 | 38 | 34 | 29 | 34 | 44 | 48 | 52 | 51 | 61 |
| Female | 54 | 62 | 66 | 71 | 66 | 56 | 52 | 48 | 49 | 39 |
| **Percent Homeowner** | 80 | 56 | 57 | 59 | 73 | 80 | 85 | 85 | 89 | 93 |
| With mortgage | 22 | 13 | 12 | 12 | 16 | 17 | 21 | 27 | 27 | 40 |
| Without mortgage | 57 | 43 | 45 | 47 | 57 | 64 | 64 | 58 | 61 | 53 |
| AVERAGE ANNUAL EXPENDITURES | 44 178 | 24 555 | 21 278 | 22 072 | 26 803 | 33 843 | 41 039 | 44 919 | 51 732 | 86 534 |
| **Food** | 5 486 | 3 660 | 2 819 | 3 199 | 3 516 | 4 383 | 5 422 | 5 606 | 6 476 | 9 547 |
| Food at home | 3 398 | 2 579 | 1 829 | 2 334 | 2 412 | 2 854 | 3 601 | 3 467 | 4 093 | 5 105 |
| Cereals and bakery products | 469 | 334 | 307 | 319 | 359 | 407 | 495 | 491 | 555 | 666 |
| Meats, poultry, fish, and eggs | 720 | 607 | 360 | 574 | 521 | 575 | 798 | 694 | 873 | 1 049 |
| Dairy products | 368 | 286 | 217 | 255 | 266 | 315 | 359 | 384 | 455 | 547 |
| Fruits and vegetables | 681 | 571 | 365 | 445 | 458 | 575 | 692 | 721 | 821 | 1 051 |
| Other food at home | 1 160 | 781 | 580 | 741 | 808 | 982 | 1 257 | 1 177 | 1 388 | 1 792 |
| Food away from home | 2 088 | 1 080 | 990 | 865 | 1 103 | 1 529 | 1 821 | 2 139 | 2 384 | 4 442 |
| **Alcoholic Beverages** | 358 | 351 | 83 | 157 | 145 | 171 | 250 | 408 | 339 | 945 |
| **Housing** | 15 180 | 10 030 | 8 643 | 9 549 | 10 787 | 12 634 | 13 969 | 15 356 | 16 771 | 26 627 |
| Shelter | 8 307 | 5 908 | 5 079 | 5 709 | 6 006 | 6 913 | 7 324 | 8 114 | 8 706 | 14 803 |
| Owned dwellings | 5 469 | 2 930 | 2 432 | 2 550 | 3 224 | 4 346 | 5 061 | 5 484 | 6 472 | 10 855 |
| Rented dwellings | 2 056 | 2 770 | 2 491 | 2 952 | 2 502 | 2 145 | 1 714 | 1 973 | 1 546 | 1 505 |
| Other lodging | 782 | 208 | 156 | 206 | 280 | 421 | 550 | 657 | 688 | 2 443 |
| Utilities, fuels, and public services | 3 677 | 2 648 | 2 291 | 2 342 | 2 896 | 3 349 | 3 759 | 4 054 | 4 215 | 5 284 |
| Household operations | 1 086 | 439 | 379 | 559 | 702 | 866 | 811 | 963 | 1 366 | 2 281 |
| Housekeeping supplies | 687 | 372 | 411 | 405 | 451 | 563 | 746 | 686 | 766 | 1 157 |
| Household furnishings and equipment | 1 423 | 663 | 483 | 535 | 733 | 944 | 1 329 | 1 540 | 1 718 | 3 103 |
| **Apparel and Services** | 1 081 | 376 | 465 | 477 | 611 | 686 | 1 050 | 1 135 | 1 346 | 2 244 |
| **Transportation** | 6 895 | 3 071 | 2 362 | 2 141 | 3 427 | 5 072 | 6 337 | 7 514 | 8 383 | 15 007 |
| Vehicle purchases (net outlay) | 2 410 | ¹812 | ¹140 | ¹279 | 861 | 1 446 | 1 770 | 2 946 | 3 018 | 6 465 |
| Gasoline and motor oil | 1 598 | 777 | 819 | 700 | 994 | 1 336 | 1 724 | 1 899 | 2 100 | 2 598 |
| Other vehicle expenses | 2 337 | 1 242 | 1 301 | 1 013 | 1 301 | 1 989 | 2 383 | 2 181 | 2 530 | 4 550 |
| Public and other transportation | 550 | 241 | 102 | 150 | 271 | 301 | 460 | 487 | 734 | 1 395 |
| **Health Care** | 5 796 | 3 086 | 3 018 | 3 004 | 4 052 | 5 439 | 6 109 | 6 339 | 7 532 | 8 551 |
| Health insurance | 3 921 | 2 134 | 2 181 | 2 016 | 2 803 | 3 721 | 4 305 | 4 501 | 4 963 | 5 522 |
| Medical services | 957 | 489 | 480 | 542 | 577 | 903 | 854 | 896 | 1 335 | 1 589 |
| Drugs | 698 | 402 | 259 | 375 | 493 | 654 | 723 | 736 | 933 | 1 039 |
| Medical supplies | 219 | 61 | 98 | 71 | 179 | 160 | 227 | 206 | 302 | 401 |
| **Entertainment** | 2 440 | 1 351 | 1 236 | 1 009 | 1 529 | 1 588 | 2 349 | 2 487 | 2 907 | 5 068 |
| **Personal Care Products and Services** | 591 | 324 | 262 | 331 | 346 | 479 | 614 | 602 | 646 | 1 100 |
| **Reading** | 176 | 74 | 40 | 48 | 93 | 126 | 185 | 202 | 209 | 365 |
| **Education** | 243 | ¹60 | ¹31 | 62 | 70 | 129 | 202 | 205 | 154 | 795 |
| **Tobacco Products and Smoking Supplies** | 219 | 189 | 149 | 136 | 190 | 190 | 215 | 210 | 257 | 325 |
| **Miscellaneous** | 826 | 842 | 273 | 195 | 469 | 615 | 758 | 943 | 852 | 1 783 |
| **Cash Contributions** | 2 386 | 772 | 886 | 1 198 | 1 005 | 1 703 | 2 031 | 2 273 | 2 883 | 5 474 |
| **Personal Insurance and Pensions** | 2 501 | 370 | 1 011 | 566 | 565 | 629 | 1 549 | 1 638 | 2 976 | 8 703 |
| Life and other personal insurance | 327 | 158 | 65 | 149 | 156 | 197 | 305 | 359 | 413 | 726 |
| Pensions and Social Security | 2 174 | 212 | 946 | 417 | 408 | 432 | 1 244 | 1 279 | 2 563 | 7 976 |

¹Data are likely to have large sampling errors.
²Value too small to display.

# CHAPTER 12: AMERICAN TIME USE SURVEY

## HIGHLIGHTS

This chapter presents data from the American Time Use Survey (ATUS). The survey was introduced in the sixth edition of the *Handbook of U.S. Labor Statistics*. Its purpose is to collect data on the activities people do during the day and the amount of time they spend on each one.

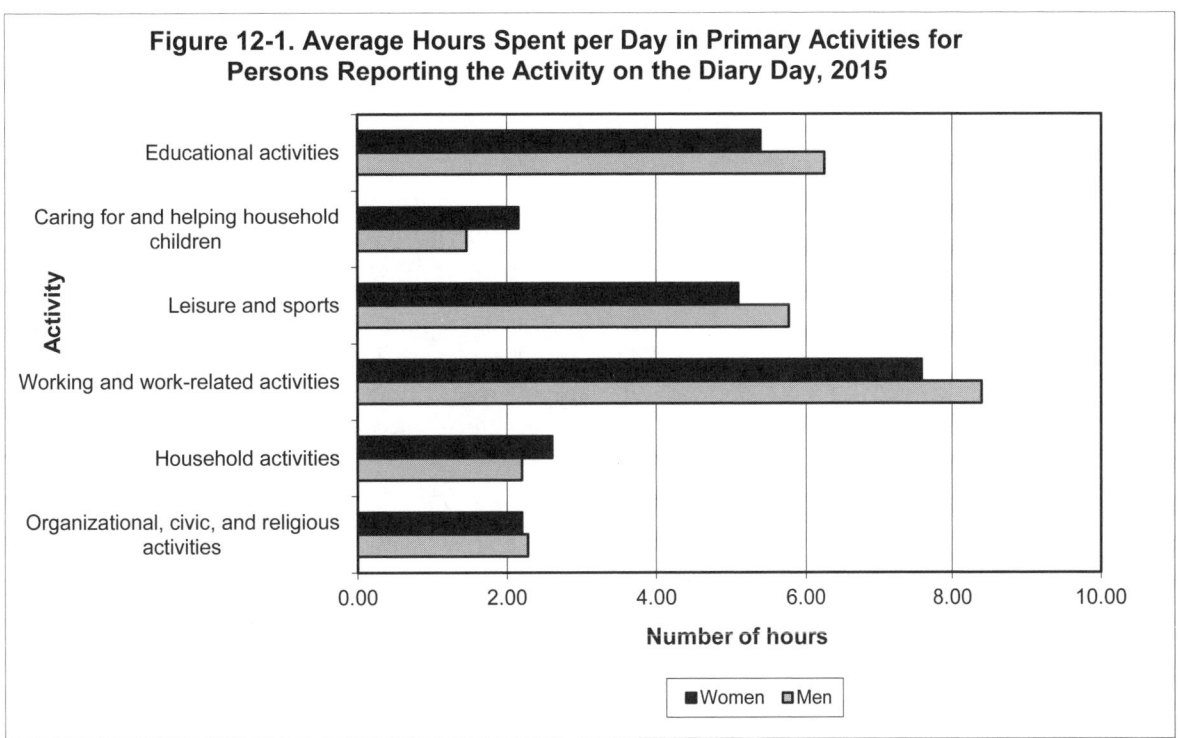

**Figure 12-1. Average Hours Spent per Day in Primary Activities for Persons Reporting the Activity on the Diary Day, 2015**

Men typically worked longer hours than women in 2015. This partly reflects women's greater likelihood of working part-time. Men also spent more time on leisure and sports while women spent more time on household activities and caring for and helping household children. (See Table 12-1).

## OTHER HIGHLIGHTS

- Employed persons worked an average of 7.6 hours on the days they worked. More hours were worked, on average, on weekdays than on weekend days—8.0 hours compared with 5.6 hours. (See Table 12-3.)

- Watching TV was the leisure activity that occupied the most time (2.8 hours per day), accounting for more than half of leisure time, on average, for those age 15 and over. Socializing, such as visiting with friends or attending or hosting social events, was the next most common leisure activity, accounting for 41 minutes per day. (See Table 12-1.)

- Multiple jobholders were more likely to work on an average day than were single jobholders—80.4 percent compared with 66.9 percent. Multiple jobholders also were more likely to work at home than were single jobholders—36.1 percent compared with 22.7 percent. (See Table 12-5.)

- On the days they worked, 39.2 percent of employed people age 25 and over with a bachelor's degree or higher did some work at home, compared with only 7.2 percent of those with less than a high school diploma. (See Table 12-5.)

# NOTES AND DEFINITIONS

## Survey Methodology

While the Bureau of Labor Statistics (BLS) has long produced statistics about the labor market, including information about employment, hours, and earnings, the American Time Use Survey (ATUS) marks the first time that a federal statistical agency has produced estimates on how Americans spend another critical resource—their time. Data collection for the ATUS began in January 2003. Sample cases for the survey are selected monthly, and interviews are conducted continuously throughout the year. In 2015, approximately 10,900 individuals were interviewed.

ATUS sample households are chosen from the households that have completed their eighth (final) interview for the Current Population Survey (CPS), the nation's monthly household labor force survey. (See Chapter 1 of this *Handbook* for a description of the CPS.) ATUS sample households are selected to ensure that estimates will be representative of the nation.

An individual age 15 years or older is randomly chosen from each sample household. This "designated person" takes part in a one-time telephone interview about his or her activities on the previous day (the "diary day").

All ATUS interviews are conducted using Computer Assisted Telephone Interviewing. Procedures are in place to collect information from the small number of households that did not provide a telephone number during the CPS interview.

ATUS designated persons are preassigned a day of the week about which to report. Preassignment is designed to reduce variability in response rates across the week and to allow oversampling of weekend days so that accurate weekend day measures can be developed. Interviews occur on the day following the assigned day. For example, a person assigned to report about a Monday would be contacted on the following Tuesday. Ten percent of designated persons are assigned to report about each of the five weekdays. Twenty five percent are assigned to report about each weekend day. Households are called for up to 8 consecutive weeks (for example, 8 Tuesdays) in order to secure an interview.

## Concepts and Definitions

Average day reflects an average distribution across all persons in the reference population and all days of the week. Average day measures for the entire population provide a mechanism for seeing the overall distribution of time allocation for society as a whole. The ATUS collects data about daily activities from all segments of the population age 15 and over, including persons who are employed and not employed. Many activities are not typically done on a daily basis, and some activities are only done by a subset of the population.

*Average hours per day refers to time spent* in a 24-hour day (between 4 a.m. on the diary day and 4 a.m. on the interview day) doing a specified activity.

*Average hours per day, persons reporting the activity on the diary day* is computed using responses only from those engaged in the particular activity on the diary day.

*Average hours per day, population* is computed using all responses from the sample population, including those from respondents who did not do the particular activity on their diary day. These estimates reflect the total number of respondents engaged in an activity and the total amount of time they spent on the activity.

*Diary day* the day about which the designated person reports. For example, the diary day of a designated person interviewed on Tuesday would be Monday.

*Household children refers to* children under 18 years of age who reside in the household of the ATUS respondent. The children may be related to the respondent (such as their own children, grandchildren, nieces, nephews, brothers, or sisters) or not related (such as foster children or children of roommates). For secondary childcare calculations, respondents are asked about care of household children under 13 years of age.

## Earnings

*Usual weekly earnings* represent the earnings of full-time wage and salary workers before taxes and other deductions and include any overtime pay, commissions, or tips usually received (at the main job in the case of multiple jobholders). Usual weekly earnings are only updated in ATUS for about a third of employed respondents—if the respondent changed jobs or employment status or if the CPS weekly earnings value was imputed. This means that the earnings information could be out of date because the CPS interview was done 2 to 5 months prior to the ATUS interview. Respondents are asked to identify the easiest way for them to report earnings (hourly, weekly, biweekly, twice monthly, annually, or other) and how much they usually earn in the reported time period. Earnings reported on a basis other than weekly are converted to a weekly equivalent. The term "usual" is as perceived by the respondent. If the respondent asks for a definition of usual, interviewers are instructed to define the term as more than half the weeks worked during the past 4 or 5 months.

*Weekly earnings ranges* refers to The ranges used represent approximately 25 percent of full-time wage and salary workers. For example, 25 percent of full-time wage and salary workers with one job only had weekly earnings of $500 or less. These dollar values vary from year to year.

## Employment Status

*Employed* persons are those who, at any time during the seven days prior to the interview: 1) did any work at all as paid employees, worked in their own business professions, or on their own farms, or usually worked 15 hours or more an unpaid workers in family-operated enterprises; and 2) all those who were not working but had jobs or businesses from which they were temporarily absent due to illness, bad weather, vacation, childcare problems, labor-management disputes, maternity or paternity leave, job training, or other family or personal reasons, whether or not they were paid for the time off or were seeking other jobs.

*Employed full time* workers are those who usually work 35 hours or more per week at all jobs combined.

*Employed part time* workers are those who usually work fewer than 35 hours per week at all jobs combined.

*Not employed includes* persons are not employed if they do not meet the conditions for employment. Not employed workers include those classified as unemployed as well as those classified as not in the labor force (using CPS definitions).

The numbers of employed and not employed persons in this report do not correspond to published totals from the CPS. While the information on employment from the ATUS is useful for assessing work in the context of other daily activities, the employment data are not intended for analysis of current employment trends. Compared to the CPS and other estimates of employment, the ATUS estimates are based on a much smaller sample and are only available with a substantial lag.

## Major Activity Category Definitions

*Caring for and helping household members refers to* time spent doing activities to care for or help any child (under age 18) or adult in the household, regardless of relationship to the respondent or the physical or mental health status of the person being helped, is classified here. Caring for and helping activities for household children and adults are coded separately in subcategories.

*Caring for and helping non-household members* includes time spent caring for and helping any child or adult who is not part of the respondent's household, regardless of the relationship to the respondent or the physical or mental health status of the person being helped, is classified in this category.

*Eating and drinking* includes all time spent eating or drinking (except when identified by the respondent as part of a work or volunteer activity), whether alone, with others, at home, at a place of purchase, in transit, or somewhere else, is classified in this category.

*Educational activities* include taking classes (including Internet and other distance-learning courses), doing research and homework, and taking care of administrative tasks, such as registering for classes or obtaining a school ID. For high school students, before- and after-school extracurricular activities (except sports) also are classified as educational activities.

*Household activities* are those done by respondents to maintain their households. These include housework, cooking, yard care, pet care, vehicle maintenance and repair, and home maintenance, repair, decoration, and renovation. Food preparation is always classified as a household activity.

*Leisure and sports* includes sports, exercise, and recreation; socializing and communicating; and other leisure activities, such as watching television, reading or attending entertainment events.

*Organizational, civic, and religious activities* captures time spent volunteering for or through an organization, performing civic obligations, and participating in religious and spiritual activities.

*Other activities, not elsewhere classified* includes security procedures related to traveling, traveling not associated with a specific activity category, ambiguous activities that could not be coded, or missing activities that were considered too private to report.

*Personal care activities* consist of sleeping, bathing, dressing, health-related self-care, and personal or private activities. Receiving unpaid personal care from others (for example, "my sister put polish on my nails") is also captured in this category.

*Primary activity* is the main activity of a respondent at a specified time.

*Purchasing goods and service* includes the purchase of consumer goods as well as the purchase or use of professional and personal care services, household services, and government services. Most purchases and rentals of consumer goods, regardless of mode or place of purchase or rental are classified in this category.

*Secondary activity* is an activity done at the same time as a primary activity. With the exception of the care of children under age 13, information on secondary activities is not systematically collected in the ATUS.

*Telephone calls, mail, and email* captures telephone communication and handling household or personal mail and email. Telephone and Internet purchases are classified in purchasing goods and services.

*Working and work-related activities refers to time* spent working, doing activities as part of one's job, engaging in income-generating activities (not as part of one's job), and job search activities. "Working" includes hours spent doing the specific tasks required of one's main or other job, regardless of location or time of day. Travel time related to working and work-related activities includes time spent commuting to and from one's job, as well as time spent traveling for work-related activities, generating income, and job searching.

## Sources of Additional Information

Additional information, including expanded definitions and estimation methodology, is available from BLS news release USDL 16-1250 "American Time Use Survey—2015 Results" which is available on the BLS Web site at <http://www.bls.gov/tus/>.

## Table 12-1.  Average Hours Per Day Spent in Primary Activities[1] for the Total Population and for Persons Reporting the Activity on the Diary Day, by Activity Category and Sex, 2014 and 2015 Annual Averages

(Hours, percent.)

| Activity | Hours per day, total population | | | Percent of population reporting the activity on the diary day | | | Hours per day for persons reporting the activity on the diary day | | |
|---|---|---|---|---|---|---|---|---|---|
| | Both sexes | Men | Women | Both sexes | Men | Women | Both sexes | Men | Women |
| **2014** | | | | | | | | | |
| **All Activities**[2] | 24.00 | 24.00 | 24.00 | X | X | X | X | X | X |
| Personal care activities | 9.58 | 9.32 | 9.82 | 100.0 | 99.9 | 100.0 | 9.58 | 9.33 | 9.82 |
| Sleeping | 8.80 | 8.69 | 8.90 | 99.9 | 99.9 | 100.0 | 8.80 | 8.70 | 8.90 |
| Eating and drinking | 1.17 | 1.21 | 1.14 | 95.6 | 95.4 | 95.8 | 1.23 | 1.27 | 1.19 |
| Household activities | 1.77 | 1.38 | 2.14 | 74.4 | 65.1 | 83.1 | 2.38 | 2.11 | 2.57 |
| Housework | 0.55 | 0.27 | 0.82 | 34.8 | 20.0 | 48.7 | 1.59 | 1.35 | 1.68 |
| Food preparation and cleanup | 0.59 | 0.34 | 0.82 | 56.3 | 42.8 | 68.9 | 1.04 | 0.79 | 1.19 |
| Lawn and garden care | 0.19 | 0.25 | 0.12 | 9.3 | 10.8 | 7.9 | 2.02 | 2.37 | 1.56 |
| Household management | 0.12 | 0.10 | 0.13 | 16.8 | 13.9 | 19.4 | 0.69 | 0.72 | 0.67 |
| Purchasing goods and services | 0.74 | 0.60 | 0.87 | 42.9 | 38.6 | 47.0 | 1.71 | 1.54 | 1.84 |
| Consumer goods purchases | 0.36 | 0.27 | 0.44 | 38.7 | 34.7 | 42.4 | 0.93 | 0.77 | 1.04 |
| Professional and personal care services | 0.09 | 0.06 | 0.12 | 8.0 | 5.5 | 10.3 | 1.12 | 1.13 | 1.12 |
| Caring for and helping household members | 0.54 | 0.35 | 0.72 | 25.7 | 20.5 | 30.5 | 2.10 | 1.70 | 2.35 |
| Caring for and helping household children | 0.41 | 0.26 | 0.55 | 21.1 | 16.3 | 25.6 | 1.95 | 1.58 | 2.17 |
| Caring for and helping non-household members | 0.18 | 0.15 | 0.21 | 10.8 | 8.8 | 12.6 | 1.69 | 1.74 | 1.66 |
| Caring for and helping non-household adults | 0.06 | 0.07 | 0.06 | 6.6 | 6.0 | 7.1 | 0.95 | 1.15 | 0.79 |
| Working and work-related activities | 3.59 | 4.29 | 2.94 | 44.0 | 49.9 | 38.5 | 8.16 | 8.60 | 7.64 |
| Working | 3.25 | 3.87 | 2.68 | 42.0 | 47.6 | 36.8 | 7.73 | 8.12 | 7.27 |
| Educational activities | 0.42 | 0.40 | 0.44 | 8.0 | 7.5 | 8.5 | 5.27 | 5.35 | 5.21 |
| Attending class | 0.23 | 0.24 | 0.23 | 4.9 | 4.7 | 5.0 | 4.83 | 5.08 | 4.62 |
| Homework and research | 0.15 | 0.12 | 0.18 | 5.4 | 4.9 | 6.0 | 2.77 | 2.55 | 2.93 |
| Organizational, civic, and religious activities | 0.32 | 0.27 | 0.37 | 14.5 | 11.6 | 17.2 | 2.24 | 2.36 | 2.17 |
| Religious and spiritual activities | 0.14 | 0.11 | 0.17 | 9.1 | 6.8 | 11.2 | 1.57 | 1.66 | 1.52 |
| Volunteering (organizational and civic activities) | 0.14 | 0.12 | 0.16 | 6.5 | 5.6 | 7.4 | 2.14 | 2.20 | 2.10 |
| Leisure and sports | 5.30 | 5.71 | 4.93 | 95.7 | 95.8 | 95.7 | 5.54 | 5.96 | 5.15 |
| Socializing and communicating | 0.71 | 0.69 | 0.73 | 37.5 | 34.7 | 40.1 | 1.89 | 1.99 | 1.82 |
| Watching television | 2.82 | 3.05 | 2.61 | 79.9 | 80.4 | 79.4 | 3.53 | 3.80 | 3.29 |
| Participating in sports, exercise, and recreation | 0.29 | 0.38 | 0.21 | 19.1 | 21.5 | 16.8 | 1.54 | 1.78 | 1.25 |
| Telephone calls, mail, and e-mail | 0.14 | 0.10 | 0.19 | 20.2 | 15.1 | 25.0 | 0.71 | 0.65 | 0.75 |
| Other activities n.e.c. | 0.23 | 0.22 | 0.24 | 15.5 | 13.7 | 17.2 | 1.48 | 1.62 | 1.37 |
| **2015** | | | | | | | | | |
| **All Activities**[2] | 24.00 | 24.00 | 24.00 | X | X | X | X | X | X |
| Personal care activities | 9.64 | 9.43 | 9.85 | 100.0 | 99.9 | 100.0 | 9.65 | 9.44 | 9.85 |
| Sleeping | 8.83 | 8.77 | 8.90 | 99.9 | 99.9 | 100.0 | 8.84 | 8.78 | 8.90 |
| Eating and drinking | 1.18 | 1.24 | 1.13 | 95.0 | 95.1 | 95.0 | 1.24 | 1.30 | 1.19 |
| Household activities | 1.84 | 1.43 | 2.23 | 76.4 | 67.0 | 85.2 | 2.41 | 2.13 | 2.61 |
| Housework | 0.57 | 0.26 | 0.86 | 36.3 | 21.5 | 50.1 | 1.58 | 1.23 | 1.71 |
| Food preparation and cleanup | 0.60 | 0.35 | 0.83 | 56.9 | 42.7 | 70.2 | 1.05 | 0.82 | 1.19 |
| Lawn and garden care | 0.20 | 0.28 | 0.12 | 9.8 | 12.1 | 7.7 | 2.00 | 2.30 | 1.57 |
| Household management | 0.13 | 0.10 | 0.16 | 18.4 | 15.2 | 21.4 | 0.72 | 0.68 | 0.75 |
| Purchasing goods and services | 0.75 | 0.60 | 0.88 | 44.0 | 40.0 | 47.7 | 1.70 | 1.50 | 1.86 |
| Consumer goods purchases | 0.36 | 0.28 | 0.44 | 40.4 | 36.6 | 43.9 | 0.90 | 0.77 | 0.99 |
| Professional and personal care services | 0.08 | 0.05 | 0.11 | 7.8 | 5.5 | 10.0 | 1.06 | 0.91 | 1.13 |
| Caring for and helping household members | 0.51 | 0.31 | 0.70 | 25.0 | 19.4 | 30.1 | 2.06 | 1.61 | 2.32 |
| Caring for and helping household children | 0.40 | 0.23 | 0.55 | 20.7 | 15.6 | 25.6 | 1.91 | 1.46 | 2.16 |
| Caring for and helping non-household members | 0.19 | 0.16 | 0.21 | 11.2 | 9.5 | 12.8 | 1.66 | 1.68 | 1.65 |
| Caring for and helping non-household adults | 0.07 | 0.07 | 0.07 | 7.1 | 6.4 | 7.7 | 0.96 | 1.03 | 0.90 |
| Working and work-related activities | 3.53 | 4.18 | 2.92 | 43.9 | 49.8 | 38.5 | 8.03 | 8.40 | 7.58 |
| Working | 3.19 | 3.78 | 2.64 | 42.1 | 47.8 | 36.7 | 7.57 | 7.89 | 7.19 |
| Educational activities | 0.46 | 0.48 | 0.45 | 8.0 | 7.6 | 8.3 | 5.79 | 6.26 | 5.39 |
| Attending class | 0.25 | 0.26 | 0.23 | 5.0 | 5.1 | 4.9 | 4.94 | 5.13 | 4.76 |
| Homework and research | 0.17 | 0.17 | 0.17 | 5.7 | 5.4 | 5.9 | 2.99 | 3.08 | 2.92 |
| Organizational, civic, and religious activities | 0.33 | 0.29 | 0.37 | 15.0 | 12.8 | 16.9 | 2.23 | 2.28 | 2.20 |
| Religious and spiritual activities | 0.15 | 0.12 | 0.17 | 9.9 | 8.1 | 11.5 | 1.52 | 1.54 | 1.50 |
| Volunteering (organizational and civic activities) | 0.15 | 0.13 | 0.16 | 6.5 | 6.0 | 7.0 | 2.23 | 2.21 | 2.25 |
| Leisure and sports | 5.21 | 5.58 | 4.86 | 96.1 | 96.6 | 95.6 | 5.42 | 5.77 | 5.09 |
| Socializing and communicating | 0.68 | 0.64 | 0.72 | 38.1 | 36.2 | 39.9 | 1.78 | 1.77 | 1.80 |
| Watching television | 2.78 | 3.02 | 2.56 | 79.9 | 81.5 | 78.3 | 3.48 | 3.70 | 3.26 |
| Participating in sports, exercise, and recreation | 0.31 | 0.39 | 0.22 | 20.4 | 22.9 | 18.1 | 1.50 | 1.71 | 1.24 |
| Telephone calls, mail, and e-mail | 0.16 | 0.12 | 0.20 | 21.4 | 16.7 | 25.7 | 0.75 | 0.71 | 0.78 |
| Other activities n.e.c. | 0.19 | 0.19 | 0.20 | 13.9 | 12.3 | 15.4 | 1.40 | 1.54 | 1.30 |

*Note:* Data refer to respondents age 15 years and over, unless otherwise specified.

n.e.c. = Not elsewhere classified.

[1]A primary activity is designated by a respondent as his or her main activity. Other activities done simultaneously are not included.
[2]All major activity categories include related travel time.
X = Not applicable.

## Table 12-2. Average Hours Per Day Spent in Primary Activities[1] for the Total Population, by Age, Sex, Race, Hispanic Origin, and Educational Attainment, 2015 Annual Averages

(Hours.)

| Characteristic | Personal care activities | Eating and drinking | Household activities | Purchasing goods and services | Caring for and helping household members | Caring for and helping non-household members | Working and work-related activities | Educational activities | Organizational, civic, and religious activities | Leisure activities | Telephone calls, mail, and e-mail | Other activities n.e.c. |
|---|---|---|---|---|---|---|---|---|---|---|---|---|
| **Both Sexes, 15 Years and Over** | 9.64 | 1.18 | 1.84 | 0.75 | 0.51 | 0.19 | 3.53 | 0.46 | 0.33 | 5.21 | 0.16 | 0.19 |
| 15 to 19 years | 10.70 | 1.13 | 0.64 | 0.56 | 0.15 | 0.11 | 1.01 | 3.20 | 0.23 | 5.81 | 0.26 | 0.22 |
| 20 to 24 years | 10.11 | 1.06 | 1.16 | 0.59 | 0.44 | 0.14 | 3.98 | 1.33 | 0.18 | 4.72 | 0.11 | 0.17 |
| 25 to 34 years | 9.64 | 1.15 | 1.65 | 0.65 | 1.06 | 0.11 | 4.71 | 0.29 | 0.20 | 4.25 | 0.10 | 0.18 |
| 35 to 44 years | 9.42 | 1.14 | 1.85 | 0.75 | 1.17 | 0.14 | 4.90 | 0.09 | 0.27 | 4.00 | 0.09 | 0.19 |
| 45 to 54 years | 9.16 | 1.15 | 2.04 | 0.82 | 0.38 | 0.24 | 4.79 | 0.08 | 0.36 | 4.70 | 0.12 | 0.17 |
| 55 to 64 years | 9.37 | 1.19 | 2.18 | 0.79 | 0.12 | 0.28 | 3.67 | 0.05 | 0.40 | 5.57 | 0.18 | 0.20 |
| 65 to 74 years | 9.63 | 1.35 | 2.45 | 0.91 | 0.12 | 0.28 | 1.37 | 0.02 | 0.58 | 6.84 | 0.26 | 0.20 |
| 75 years and over | 10.10 | 1.35 | 2.30 | 0.84 | 0.11 | 0.16 | 0.23 | * | 0.50 | 7.82 | 0.30 | 0.29 |
| **Men, 15 Years and Over** | 9.43 | 1.24 | 1.43 | 0.60 | 0.31 | 0.16 | 4.18 | 0.48 | 0.29 | 5.58 | 0.12 | 0.19 |
| 15 to 19 years | 10.57 | 1.10 | 0.48 | 0.43 | 0.07 | 0.08 | 1.02 | 3.22 | 0.20 | 6.38 | 0.23 | 0.22 |
| 20 to 24 years | 9.90 | 1.10 | 1.07 | 0.48 | 0.08 | 0.21 | 4.08 | 1.49 | 0.20 | 5.10 | 0.13 | 0.16 |
| 25 to 34 years | 9.40 | 1.20 | 1.26 | 0.48 | 0.53 | 0.10 | 5.63 | 0.24 | 0.19 | 4.69 | 0.09 | 0.19 |
| 35 to 44 years | 9.31 | 1.20 | 1.29 | 0.58 | 0.76 | 0.12 | 5.91 | 0.06 | 0.25 | 4.30 | 0.07 | 0.16 |
| 45 to 54 years | 8.86 | 1.22 | 1.48 | 0.66 | 0.32 | 0.15 | 5.75 | 0.07 | 0.31 | 4.96 | 0.08 | 0.15 |
| 55 to 64 years | 9.09 | 1.26 | 1.82 | 0.67 | 0.12 | 0.25 | 4.10 | * | 0.34 | 6.00 | 0.11 | 0.21 |
| 65 to 74 years | 9.49 | 1.44 | 2.01 | 0.73 | 0.09 | 0.23 | 1.75 | * | 0.50 | 7.41 | 0.14 | 0.18 |
| 75 years and over | 9.82 | 1.49 | 1.91 | 0.79 | 0.09 | 0.16 | 0.41 | * | 0.44 | 8.31 | 0.23 | 0.35 |
| **Women, 15 Years and Over** | 9.85 | 1.13 | 2.23 | 0.88 | 0.70 | 0.21 | 2.92 | 0.45 | 0.37 | 4.86 | 0.20 | 0.20 |
| 15 to 19 years | 10.84 | 1.15 | 0.80 | 0.69 | 0.24 | 0.13 | 0.99 | 3.18 | 0.25 | 5.22 | 0.29 | 0.22 |
| 20 to 24 years | 10.33 | 1.01 | 1.25 | 0.70 | 0.81 | 0.07 | 3.89 | 1.17 | 0.16 | 4.33 | 0.09 | 0.18 |
| 25 to 34 years | 9.88 | 1.11 | 2.04 | 0.82 | 1.58 | 0.12 | 3.81 | 0.34 | 0.21 | 3.82 | 0.11 | 0.17 |
| 35 to 44 years | 9.53 | 1.08 | 2.38 | 0.92 | 1.56 | 0.16 | 3.92 | 0.12 | 0.29 | 3.71 | 0.12 | 0.22 |
| 45 to 54 years | 9.45 | 1.09 | 2.56 | 0.97 | 0.43 | 0.33 | 3.87 | 0.10 | 0.40 | 4.45 | 0.16 | 0.18 |
| 55 to 64 years | 9.62 | 1.13 | 2.51 | 0.91 | 0.12 | 0.30 | 3.27 | 0.07 | 0.47 | 5.17 | 0.24 | 0.19 |
| 65 to 74 years | 9.75 | 1.28 | 2.83 | 1.05 | 0.15 | 0.32 | 1.04 | * | 0.64 | 6.35 | 0.36 | 0.21 |
| 75 years and over | 10.30 | 1.25 | 2.59 | 0.87 | 0.12 | 0.16 | 0.11 | * | 0.54 | 7.46 | 0.34 | 0.25 |
| **White, 15 Years and Over** | 9.58 | 1.22 | 1.94 | 0.76 | 0.51 | 0.19 | 3.58 | 0.42 | 0.31 | 5.15 | 0.16 | 0.19 |
| Men | 9.38 | 1.28 | 1.53 | 0.61 | 0.32 | 0.16 | 4.30 | 0.41 | 0.28 | 5.43 | 0.11 | 0.19 |
| Women | 9.77 | 1.17 | 2.33 | 0.89 | 0.70 | 0.22 | 2.89 | 0.42 | 0.35 | 4.87 | 0.20 | 0.20 |
| **Black, 15 Years and Over** | 10.03 | 0.84 | 1.29 | 0.69 | 0.40 | 0.19 | 3.13 | 0.47 | 0.52 | 6.01 | 0.20 | 0.22 |
| Men | 9.72 | 0.88 | 0.90 | 0.54 | 0.16 | 0.18 | 3.52 | 0.48 | 0.49 | 6.78 | 0.17 | 0.18 |
| Women | 10.29 | 0.80 | 1.62 | 0.82 | 0.59 | 0.21 | 2.81 | 0.46 | 0.55 | 5.38 | 0.23 | 0.25 |
| **Asian, 15 Years and Over** | 9.76 | 1.46 | 1.68 | 0.71 | 0.78 | 0.15 | 3.50 | 1.04 | 0.23 | 4.38 | 0.14 | 0.17 |
| Men | 9.60 | 1.46 | 1.07 | 0.58 | 0.44 | 0.18 | 3.73 | * | 0.10 | 5.24 | 0.08 | 0.19 |
| Women | 9.91 | 1.46 | 2.27 | 0.84 | 1.10 | 0.12 | 3.29 | 0.74 | 0.35 | 3.56 | 0.20 | 0.15 |
| **Hispanic,[3] 15 Years and Over** | 9.97 | 1.15 | 1.83 | 0.74 | 0.67 | 0.16 | 3.75 | 0.70 | 0.25 | 4.49 | 0.11 | 0.19 |
| Men | 9.93 | 1.14 | 1.11 | 0.61 | 0.39 | 0.14 | 4.62 | 0.66 | 0.22 | 4.90 | 0.08 | 0.20 |
| Women | 10.01 | 1.15 | 2.54 | 0.86 | 0.95 | 0.17 | 2.89 | 0.74 | 0.29 | 4.09 | 0.14 | 0.17 |
| **Marital Status and Sex** | | | | | | | | | | | | |
| Married, spouse present | 9.34 | 1.27 | 2.16 | 0.79 | 0.72 | 0.20 | 3.86 | 0.09 | 0.38 | 4.87 | 0.13 | 0.20 |
| Men | 9.11 | 1.34 | 1.61 | 0.63 | 0.47 | 0.16 | 4.74 | 0.07 | 0.34 | 5.24 | 0.08 | 0.20 |
| Women | 9.57 | 1.20 | 2.72 | 0.94 | 0.97 | 0.23 | 2.96 | 0.11 | 0.43 | 4.49 | 0.18 | 0.21 |
| Other marital statuses | 9.97 | 1.09 | 1.51 | 0.71 | 0.30 | 0.18 | 3.18 | 0.85 | 0.28 | 5.56 | 0.20 | 0.19 |
| Men | 9.79 | 1.12 | 1.22 | 0.56 | 0.13 | 0.16 | 3.53 | 0.95 | 0.24 | 5.96 | 0.16 | 0.18 |
| Women | 10.11 | 1.07 | 1.75 | 0.83 | 0.44 | 0.19 | 2.88 | 0.78 | 0.32 | 5.22 | 0.23 | 0.19 |
| **Educational Attainment, 25 Years and Over** | | | | | | | | | | | | |
| Less than a high school diploma | 10.07 | 1.10 | 2.11 | 0.70 | 0.55 | 0.21 | 2.76 | * | 0.36 | 5.84 | 0.09 | 0.19 |
| High school graduate, no college[4] | 9.67 | 1.12 | 2.15 | 0.73 | 0.42 | 0.23 | 3.21 | 0.04 | 0.30 | 5.81 | 0.14 | 0.18 |
| Some college or associate degree | 9.44 | 1.15 | 2.10 | 0.80 | 0.56 | 0.19 | 3.72 | 0.18 | 0.33 | 5.14 | 0.19 | 0.21 |
| Bachelor's degree and higher[5] | 9.20 | 1.34 | 1.85 | 0.84 | 0.67 | 0.18 | 4.46 | 0.13 | 0.43 | 4.53 | 0.17 | 0.20 |

*Note:* 0.00 = Estimates are approximately zero.

[1] A primary activity is designated by a respondent as his or her main activity. Other activities done simultaneously are not included.
[2] All major activity categories include related travel time.
[3] May be of any race.
[4] Includes persons with a high school diploma or equivalent.
[5] Includes persons with bachelor's, master's, professional, and doctoral degrees.
* = Figure does not meet standards of reliability or quality.

## Table 12-3. Average Hours Worked Per Day by Employed Persons on Weekdays and Weekends, by Selected Characteristics, 2015 Annual Averages

(Number, percent.)

| Characteristic | Total employed (thousands) | Employed persons who worked on an average day | | | Employed persons who worked on an average weekday | | | Employed persons who worked on an average Saturday, Sunday, or holiday[1] | | |
|---|---|---|---|---|---|---|---|---|---|---|
| | | Number (thousands) | Percent of employed | Hours per day[2] | Number[3] (thousands) | Percent of employed | Hours per day[2] | Number[4] (thousands) | Percent of employed | Hours per day[2] |
| **Both Sexes[5]** | 156 867 | 106 765 | 68.1 | 7.60 | 130 024 | 82.9 | 7.95 | 52 717 | 33.6 | 5.57 |
| Full-time worker | 122 640 | 88 594 | 72.2 | 8.06 | 108 195 | 88.2 | 8.46 | 41 988 | 34.2 | 5.62 |
| Part-time worker | 34 227 | 18 170 | 53.1 | 5.31 | 21 617 | 63.2 | 5.29 | 10 783 | 31.5 | 5.42 |
| **Men[5]** | 83 072 | 58 601 | 70.5 | 7.91 | 71 045 | 85.5 | 8.34 | 29 918 | 36.0 | 5.56 |
| Full-time worker | 70 174 | 51 953 | 74.0 | 8.22 | 63 129 | 90.0 | 8.70 | 25 658 | 36.6 | 5.49 |
| Part-time worker | 12 898 | 6 648 | 51.5 | 5.50 | 7 788 | 60.4 | 5.38 | 4 292 | 33.3 | 5.96 |
| **Women[5]** | 73 795 | 48 164 | 65.3 | 7.21 | 58 990 | 79.9 | 7.47 | 22 775 | 30.9 | 5.59 |
| Full-time worker | 52 466 | 36 641 | 69.8 | 7.84 | 45 075 | 85.9 | 8.14 | 16 301 | 31.1 | 5.82 |
| Part-time worker | 21 329 | 11 522 | 54.0 | 5.20 | 13 823 | 64.8 | 5.24 | 6 481 | 30.4 | 5.04 |
| **Multiple Job Holding Status** | | | | | | | | | | |
| Single job holder | 142 925 | 95 558 | 66.9 | 7.57 | 117 455 | 82.2 | 7.90 | 44 605 | 31.2 | 5.60 |
| Multiple job holder | 13 942 | 11 206 | 80.4 | 7.77 | 12 574 | 90.2 | 8.43 | 8 074 | 57.9 | 5.40 |
| **Educational Attainment, 25 Years and Over** | | | | | | | | | | |
| Less than a high school diploma | 10 736 | 7 272 | 67.7 | 7.95 | 9 210 | 85.8 | 8.09 | 2 907 | 27.1 | 6.92 |
| High school graduate, no college[6] | 34 366 | 22 892 | 66.6 | 7.85 | 27 760 | 80.8 | 8.05 | 10 356 | 30.1 | 6.50 |
| Some college or associate degree | 33 456 | 22 706 | 67.9 | 7.78 | 28 023 | 83.8 | 8.04 | 10 374 | 31.0 | 6.17 |
| Bachelor's degree or higher[7] | 56 632 | 40 506 | 71.5 | 7.43 | 49 442 | 87.3 | 8.04 | 19 662 | 34.7 | 3.84 |

Note: Data refer to persons age 15 years and over, unless otherwise specified.

[1]Holidays are New Year's Day, Easter, Memorial Day, the Fourth of July, Labor Day, Thanksgiving Day, and Christmas Day.
[2]Includes work at main and other job(s) and excludes travel related to work.
[3]Number was derived by multiplying the "total employed" by the percentage of employed persons who worked on an average weekday.
[4]Number was derived by multiplying the "total employed" by the percentage of employed persons who worked on an average Saturday, Sunday, or holiday.
[5]Includes workers whose hours vary.
[6]Includes persons with a high school diploma or equivalent.
[7]Includes persons with bachelor's, master's, professional, and doctoral degrees.

## Table 12-4. Average Hours Worked Per Day at Main Job Only by Employed Persons on Weekdays and Weekend Days, by Selected Characteristics, 2015 Annual Averages

(Number, percent.)

| Characteristic | Total employed (thousands) | Worked on an average day | | | Worked on an average weekday | | | Worked on an average Saturday, Sunday, or holiday[1] | | |
|---|---|---|---|---|---|---|---|---|---|---|
| | | Number (thousands) | Percent | Hours per day[2] | Number[3] (thousands) | Percent | Hours per day[2] | Number[4] (thousands) | Percent | Hours per day[2] |
| **Class of Worker** | | | | | | | | | | |
| Wage and salary workers | 144 820 | 96 599 | 66.7 | 7.62 | 119 217 | 82.3 | 7.94 | 44 801 | 30.9 | 5.63 |
| Self-employed workers[5] | 11 788 | 8 370 | 71.0 | 6.59 | 9 693 | 82.2 | 7.00 | 4 672 | 39.6 | 4.22 |
| **Occupation** | | | | | | | | | | |
| Management, business, and financial operations | 26 128 | 19 026 | 72.8 | 7.52 | 23 737 | 90.8 | 8.02 | 7 618 | 29.2 | 3.74 |
| Professional and related | 39 491 | 26 921 | 68.2 | 7.22 | 33 051 | 83.7 | 7.76 | 12 644 | 32.0 | 3.95 |
| Services | 25 733 | 15 666 | 60.9 | 7.19 | 18 405 | 71.5 | 7.24 | 9 433 | 36.7 | 6.98 |
| Sales and related | 15 679 | 10 191 | 65.0 | 7.76 | 12 091 | 77.1 | 8.03 | 6 217 | 39.6 | 6.69 |
| Office and administrative support | 18 230 | 12 220 | 67.0 | 7.52 | 15 134 | 83.0 | 7.62 | 3 993 | 21.9 | 6.47 |
| Farming, fishing, and forestry | 1 132 | * | * | 8.22 | * | * | 8.47 | * | * | 7.14 |
| Construction and extraction | 7 456 | 5 019 | 67.3 | 8.18 | 6 596 | 88.5 | 8.40 | 1 610 | 21.6 | 6.26 |
| Installation, maintenance, and repair | 4 442 | 3 184 | 71.7 | 8.00 | 3 787 | 85.2 | 8.33 | . . . | . . . | 5.86 |
| Production | 8 695 | 5 686 | 65.4 | 8.13 | 7 473 | 85.9 | 8.42 | 2 112 | 24.3 | 6.08 |
| Transportation and material moving | 9 881 | 6 409 | 64.9 | 8.05 | 7 702 | 77.9 | 8.36 | 3 550 | 35.9 | 6.55 |
| **Earnings of Full-Time Wage and Salary Earners[6]** | | | | | | | | | | |
| $0 to $560 | 25 605 | 17 152 | 67.0 | 8.01 | 20 767 | 81.1 | 8.11 | 8 551 | 33.4 | 7.45 |
| $561 to $870 | 25 388 | 17 296 | 68.1 | 8.18 | 22 056 | 86.9 | 8.38 | 6 141 | 24.2 | 6.50 |
| $871 to $1,380 | 25 045 | 17 586 | 70.2 | 8.17 | 21 992 | 87.8 | 8.48 | 6 785 | 27.1 | 5.70 |
| $1,381 and higher | 25 450 | 18 618 | 73.2 | 7.93 | 23 570 | 92.6 | 8.55 | 7 819 | 30.7 | 3.85 |

Note: Data refer to persons age 15 years and over, unless otherwise specified.

[1]Holidays are New Year's Day, Easter, Memorial Day, the Fourth of July, Labor Day, Thanksgiving Day, and Christmas Day.
[2]Includes work at main job only and excludes travel related to work.
[3]Number was derived by multiplying the "total employed" by the percentage of employed persons who worked on an average weekday.
[4]Number was derived by multiplying the "total employed" by the percentage of employed persons who worked on an average Saturday, Sunday, or holiday.
[5]Includes self-employed workers whose businesses are unincorporated. Self-employed workers whose businesses are incorporated are classified as wage and salary workers.
[6]These values are based on usual weekly earnings. Each earnings range represents approximately 25 percent of full-time wage and salary workers who held only one job.
* = Figure does not meet standards for reliability or quality.

### Table 12-5. Average Hours Worked Per Day at All Jobs by Employed Persons at Workplaces or at Home, by Selected Characteristics, 2015 Annual Averages

(Number, percent.)

| Characteristic | Total employed (thousands) | Employed persons who reported working on an average day[1] | | | | | | | | |
|---|---|---|---|---|---|---|---|---|---|---|
| | | Number (thousands) | Percent | Average hours of work | Location of work[2] | | | | | |
| | | | | | Persons who reported working at their workplaces on an average day | | | Persons who reported working at home on an average day[3] | | |
| | | | | | Number (thousands) | Percent | Average hours of work at workplace | Number (thousands) | Percent | Average hours of work at home |
| **Full- and Part-Time Status and Sex** | | | | | | | | | | |
| Both sexes[4] ............................... | 156 867 | 106 765 | 68.1 | 7.60 | 87 625 | 82.1 | 7.96 | 25 703 | 24.1 | 3.22 |
| Full-time worker ....................... | 122 640 | 88 594 | 72.2 | 8.06 | 74 245 | 83.8 | 8.33 | 21 459 | 24.2 | 3.33 |
| Part-time worker ...................... | 34 227 | 18 170 | 53.1 | 5.31 | 13 380 | 73.6 | 5.93 | 4 244 | 23.4 | 2.67 |
| Men[4] ....................................... | 83 072 | 58 601 | 70.5 | 7.91 | 48 421 | 82.6 | 8.22 | 14 033 | 23.9 | 3.31 |
| Full-time worker ....................... | 70 174 | 51 953 | 74.0 | 8.22 | 43 718 | 84.1 | 8.47 | 12 535 | 24.1 | 3.24 |
| Part-time worker ...................... | 12 898 | 6 648 | 51.5 | 5.50 | 4 703 | 70.7 | 5.88 | 1 498 | 22.5 | 3.84 |
| Women[4] ................................... | 73 795 | 48 164 | 65.3 | 7.21 | 39 204 | 81.4 | 7.64 | 11 670 | 24.2 | 3.11 |
| Full-time worker ....................... | 52 466 | 36 641 | 69.8 | 7.84 | 30 527 | 83.3 | 8.11 | 8 924 | 24.4 | 3.44 |
| Part-time worker ...................... | 21 329 | 11 522 | 54.0 | 5.20 | 8 677 | 75.3 | 5.96 | 2 746 | 23.8 | 2.03 |
| | | | | | | | | | | |
| **Multiple Job Holding Status** | | | | | | | | | | |
| Single job holder ...................... | 142 925 | 95 558 | 66.9 | 7.57 | 79 143 | 82.8 | 7.95 | 21 660 | 22.7 | 3.28 |
| Multiple job holder ................... | 13 942 | 11 206 | 80.4 | 7.77 | 8 482 | 75.7 | 8.06 | 4 043 | 36.1 | 2.88 |
| | | | | | | | | | | |
| **Educational Attainment, 25 Years and Over** | | | | | | | | | | |
| Less than a high school diploma ............... | 10 736 | 7 272 | 67.7 | 7.95 | 6 800 | 93.5 | 7.98 | 527 | 7.2 | * |
| High school graduate, no college[5] ........... | 34 366 | 22 892 | 66.6 | 7.85 | 19 714 | 86.1 | 8.05 | 3 198 | 14.0 | 3.95 |
| Some college or associate degree .......... | 33 456 | 22 706 | 67.9 | 7.78 | 19 379 | 85.3 | 8.02 | 4 486 | 19.8 | 3.58 |
| Bachelor's degree or higher[6] ................... | 56 632 | 40 506 | 71.5 | 7.43 | 30 012 | 74.1 | 8.06 | 15 870 | 39.2 | 3.02 |

*Note:* Data refer to persons age 15 years and over, unless otherwise specified.

[1]Includes work at main and other job(s) and excludes travel related to work.
[2]Respondents may have worked at more than one location.
[3]"Working at home" includes any time the respondent reported doing activities that were identified as "part of one's job"; this category is not restricted to persons whose usual workplace is their home.
[4]Includes workers whose hours vary.
[5]Includes persons with a high school diploma or equivalent.
[6]Includes persons with bachelor's, master's, professional, and doctoral degrees.
* = Figure does not meet standards for reliability or quality.

## Table 12-6.  Average Hours Worked Per Day at Main Job Only by Employed Persons at Workplaces or at Home, by Selected Characteristics, 2015 Annual Averages

(Number, percent.)

| Characteristic | Total employed (thousands) | Employed persons who reported working on an average day[1] | | | | | | | | |
| | | Number (thousands) | Percent | Hours of work | Location of work[2] | | | | | |
| | | | | | Persons who reported working at their workplaces on an average day | | | Persons who reported working at home on an average day[3] | | |
| | | | | | Number (thousands) | Percent | Hours of work at workplace | Number (thousands) | Percent | Hours of work at home |
| **Class of Worker** | | | | | | | | | | |
| Wage and salary worker ............................ | 144 820 | 96 599 | 66.7 | 7.62 | 82 095 | 85.0 | 7.93 | 19 449 | 20.1 | 3.08 |
| Self-employed worker[3] .............................. | 11 788 | 8 370 | 71.0 | 6.59 | 4 655 | 55.6 | 7.47 | 4 296 | 51.3 | 4.23 |
| **Occupation[4]** | | | | | | | | | | |
| Management, business, and financial operations ..... | 26 128 | 19 026 | 72.8 | 7.52 | 13 900 | 73.1 | 8.20 | 7 190 | 37.8 | 3.61 |
| Professional and related ........................... | 39 491 | 26 921 | 68.2 | 7.22 | 19 717 | 73.2 | 7.90 | 9 311 | 34.6 | 2.94 |
| Services ............................................ | 25 733 | 15 666 | 60.9 | 7.19 | 14 196 | 90.6 | 7.36 | 1 647 | 10.5 | 3.25 |
| Sales and related .................................. | 15 679 | 10 191 | 65.0 | 7.76 | 8 877 | 87.1 | 7.89 | 2 255 | 22.1 | 3.70 |
| Office and administrative support ............... | 18 230 | 12 220 | 67.0 | 7.52 | 10 940 | 89.5 | 7.73 | 1 367 | 11.2 | 4.08 |
| Farming, fishing, and forestry .................. | 1 132 | * | * | 8.22 | * | * | 8.28 | * | * | * |
| Construction and extraction ..................... | 7 456 | 5 019 | 67.3 | 8.18 | 4 661 | 92.9 | 8.13 | 815 | 16.2 | * |
| Installation, maintenance, and repair ......... | 4 442 | 3 184 | 71.7 | 8.00 | 2 908 | 91.3 | 8.39 | 305 | 9.6 | * |
| Production ......................................... | 8 695 | 5 686 | 65.4 | 8.13 | 5 391 | 94.8 | 8.31 | 314 | 5.5 | * |
| Transportation and material moving ......... | 9 881 | 6 409 | 64.9 | 8.05 | 5 605 | 87.4 | 8.08 | 492 | 7.7 | * |
| **Earnings of Full-Time Wage and Salary Earners[5]** | | | | | | | | | | |
| $0 to $560 ........................................ | 25 605 | 17 152 | 67.0 | 8.01 | 16 013 | 93.4 | 8.14 | 1 441 | 8.4 | 3.11 |
| $561 to $870 ..................................... | 25 388 | 17 296 | 68.1 | 8.18 | 15 823 | 91.5 | 8.34 | 2 269 | 13.1 | 2.61 |
| $871 to $1,380 .................................. | 25 045 | 17 586 | 70.2 | 8.17 | 15 036 | 85.5 | 8.46 | 3 751 | 21.3 | 2.80 |
| $1,381 and higher ............................... | 25 450 | 18 618 | 73.2 | 7.93 | 14 394 | 77.3 | 8.47 | 6 619 | 35.5 | 3.45 |

Note: Data refer to persons age 15 years and over, unless otherwise specified.

[1]Individuals may have worked at more than one location.
[2]Working at home includes any time persons did work at home and is not restricted to persons whose usual workplace is their home.
[3]Includes self-employed workers whose businesses are unincorporated. Self-employed workers whose businesses are incorporated are classified as wage and salary workers.
[4]These values were generated using the 2010 Census occupational classification system which was introduced with the 2011 estimates. Estimates are not strictly comparable to those from earlier years.
[5]These values are based on usual weekly earnings. Each earnings range covers approximately 25 percent of full-time wage and salary workers.
* = Figure does not meet standards for reliability or quality.

**Table 12-7.  Average Hours Per Day Spent by Persons Age 18 Years and Over Caring for Household Children Under 18 Years, by Sex of Respondent, Age of Youngest Household Child, and Day, 2011–2015 Combined Annual Averages**

(Number.)

| Activity | Hours per day caring for household children | | | | | | | | |
| --- | --- | --- | --- | --- | --- | --- | --- | --- | --- |
| | Total | | | Weekdays | | | Weekends and holidays | | |
| | Both sexes | Men | Women | Both sexes | Men | Women | Both sexes | Men | Women |
| **Persons in Households with Children Under 18 Years** | | | | | | | | | |
| Caring for household children as a primary activity | 1.35 | 0.91 | 1.73 | 1.43 | 0.90 | 1.87 | 1.17 | 0.91 | 1.38 |
| Physical care | 0.42 | 0.22 | 0.58 | 0.44 | 0.23 | 0.62 | 0.36 | 0.21 | 0.49 |
| Education-related activities | 0.11 | 0.07 | 0.15 | 0.14 | 0.08 | 0.19 | 0.04 | 0.03 | 0.05 |
| Reading to/with children | 0.04 | 0.02 | 0.05 | 0.04 | 0.02 | 0.05 | 0.03 | 0.02 | 0.04 |
| Talking to/with children | 0.05 | 0.03 | 0.07 | 0.06 | 0.03 | 0.07 | 0.03 | 0.02 | 0.05 |
| Playing/doing hobbies with children | 0.30 | 0.26 | 0.34 | 0.28 | 0.22 | 0.32 | 0.37 | 0.35 | 0.38 |
| Looking after children | 0.08 | 0.07 | 0.09 | 0.07 | 0.06 | 0.09 | 0.09 | 0.09 | 0.10 |
| Attending children's events | 0.06 | 0.05 | 0.07 | 0.04 | 0.03 | 0.05 | 0.09 | 0.08 | 0.10 |
| Travel related to care of household children | 0.18 | 0.12 | 0.23 | 0.22 | 0.14 | 0.29 | 0.09 | 0.08 | 0.10 |
| Other childcare activities | 0.11 | 0.07 | 0.15 | 0.14 | 0.08 | 0.19 | 0.05 | 0.04 | 0.06 |
| **Persons in Households with Youngest Child 6 to 17 Years** | | | | | | | | | |
| Caring for household children as a primary activity | 0.82 | 0.57 | 1.03 | 0.90 | 0.60 | 1.15 | 0.63 | 0.51 | 0.74 |
| Physical care | 0.14 | 0.07 | 0.20 | 0.16 | 0.09 | 0.22 | 0.10 | 0.05 | 0.14 |
| Education-related activities | 0.13 | 0.08 | 0.17 | 0.17 | 0.10 | 0.22 | 0.05 | 0.04 | 0.06 |
| Reading to/with children | 0.02 | 0.01 | 0.02 | 0.02 | 0.01 | 0.02 | 0.01 | 0.01 | 0.02 |
| Talking to/with children | 0.06 | 0.04 | 0.08 | 0.07 | 0.04 | 0.09 | 0.04 | 0.02 | 0.05 |
| Playing/doing hobbies with children | 0.07 | 0.08 | 0.06 | 0.06 | 0.06 | 0.05 | 0.11 | 0.13 | 0.09 |
| Looking after children | 0.05 | 0.04 | 0.06 | 0.05 | 0.04 | 0.06 | 0.06 | 0.05 | 0.06 |
| Attending children's events | 0.08 | 0.06 | 0.09 | 0.06 | 0.05 | 0.07 | 0.13 | 0.10 | 0.15 |
| Travel related to care of household children | 0.17 | 0.12 | 0.21 | 0.20 | 0.14 | 0.26 | 0.09 | 0.07 | 0.10 |
| Other childcare activities | 0.10 | 0.06 | 0.13 | 0.11 | 0.07 | 0.16 | 0.05 | 0.04 | 0.06 |
| **Persons in Households with Youngest Child Under 6 Years** | | | | | | | | | |
| Caring for household children as a primary activity | 2.02 | 1.34 | 2.56 | 2.10 | 1.30 | 2.74 | 1.82 | 1.44 | 2.13 |
| Physical care | 0.76 | 0.41 | 1.04 | 0.79 | 0.41 | 1.10 | 0.69 | 0.41 | 0.91 |
| Education-related activities | 0.09 | 0.05 | 0.12 | 0.12 | 0.06 | 0.16 | 0.03 | 0.02 | 0.04 |
| Reading to/with children | 0.06 | 0.04 | 0.08 | 0.06 | 0.04 | 0.08 | 0.05 | 0.04 | 0.06 |
| Talking to/with children | 0.04 | 0.02 | 0.05 | 0.04 | 0.02 | 0.06 | 0.03 | 0.02 | 0.04 |
| Playing/doing hobbies with children | 0.59 | 0.49 | 0.67 | 0.55 | 0.42 | 0.65 | 0.69 | 0.64 | 0.73 |
| Looking after children | 0.11 | 0.09 | 0.13 | 0.10 | 0.07 | 0.12 | 0.14 | 0.14 | 0.14 |
| Attending children's events | 0.03 | 0.03 | 0.03 | 0.02 | 0.02 | 0.03 | 0.05 | 0.06 | 0.04 |
| Travel related to care of household children | 0.20 | 0.13 | 0.25 | 0.24 | 0.15 | 0.32 | 0.09 | 0.08 | 0.10 |
| Other childcare activities | 0.13 | 0.08 | 0.18 | 0.17 | 0.10 | 0.23 | 0.05 | 0.03 | 0.07 |

*Note:* Universe includes respondents age 18 years and over living in households with children under 18 years of age, whether or not they provided childcare.

# CHAPTER 13: INCOME IN THE UNITED STATES (CENSUS BUREAU)

## HIGHLIGHTS

This chapter presents data on income and earnings in the United States collected by the Census Bureau. Income, as distinguished from earnings, includes income from pensions, investments, and other sources and is measured as real income in 2015 dollars.

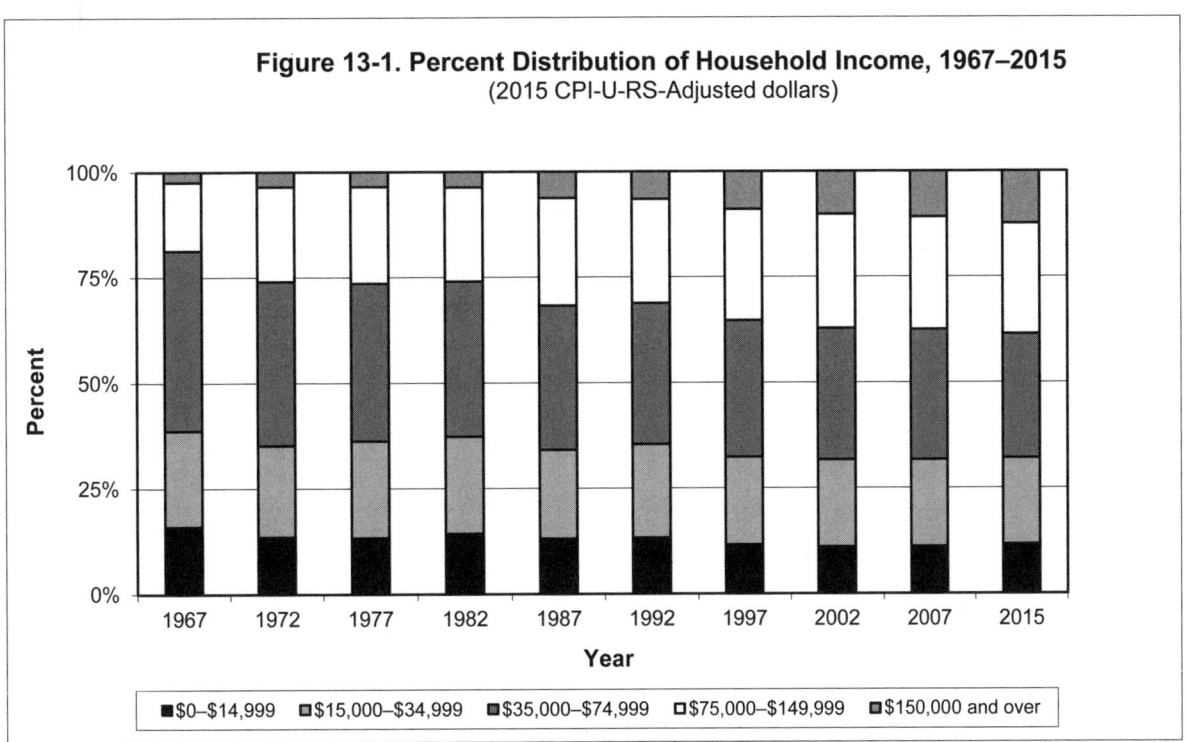

**Figure 13-1. Percent Distribution of Household Income, 1967–2015**
(2015 CPI-U-RS-Adjusted dollars)

In 2015, 12.3 percent of households had an income above $150,000—the highest percentage ever. The number of households with income above $200,000 increased from 5.6 percent in 2014 to 6.1 percent in 2015. From 2010 to 2012, this percentage remained steady at 4.8. The percentage of households with and income above $200,000 grew to 5.7 in 2013 before declining slightly to 5.6 in 2014. (See Table 13-2.)

## OTHER HIGHLIGHTS

- Median income varied by race and ethnic origin. In 2015, Asians had the highest median income at $77,166 followed non-Hispanic Whites ($62,950), Hispanics ($45,148), and Blacks ($36,898). (See Table 13-1.)

- Real median income increased in all four regions listed on Table 13-1. The West experienced the highest increase at 6.4 percent, followed by the Midwest at 5.1 percent, 4.9 percent in the Northeast, and 2.9 percent in the South. (See Table 13-1.)

- Median household income increased in 2015 to $56,516. This was only the second time since 2008 that median household income as increased. It varied significantly by state. Median household income was the highest in New Hampshire ($75,675) followed by Alaska ($75,112) and Maryland ($73,594). (See Table 13-5.)

- Mississippi continued to have the lowest family income at $50,069 in 2015 followed by Arkansas at $52,449. The District of Columbia had the highest median family income at $94,846 followed by Maryland ($91,567) and Connecticut ($91,388). (See Table 13-7.)

# NOTES AND DEFINITIONS

## Collection and Coverage

The data in tables 13-1 through 13-5 are from the Annual Social and Economic Supplement (ASEC) to the Current Population Survey (CPS). The CPS ASEC provides timely estimates of household income and individual earnings, as well as the distribution of that income. The population represented is the civilian noninstitutionalized population living in the United States. Members of the Armed Forces living off post or with their families on post are included if at least one civilian adult lives in the household, hence, the CPS ASEC universe is slightly larger than the CPS universe which does not include persons who are on active duty in the armed forces.

The data in Tables 13-6 and 13-7 come from the American Community Survey (ACS). The ACS is an annual survey that covers the same type of information that had been collected every 10 years from the decennial census long form questionnaire. The ACS eliminated the need for a separate long form in the 2010 Census. The CPS ASEC and ACS surveys differ in the length and detail of its questionnaire, the number of households interviewed, the methodology used to collect and process the data, and, consequently, in the income and poverty estimates produced.

The sample size of the ACS is much larger (approximately 3.54 million in 2013) compared to the sample size of the CPS ASEC (100,000). Although it is smaller, the CPS ASEC is a high quality source of information due to its detailed questionnaire and experienced interviewing staff. Another notable difference between the two surveys is that the ACS is a mandatory whereas the CPS ASEC is voluntary.

## Concepts and Definitions

The *Gini index of income inequality* (also known as the Gini ratio, Gini coefficient, or index of income concentration) is a statistical measure that summarizes the dispersion of income across an entire income distribution. Values range from 0 to 1. A Gini value of 1 indicates "perfect" inequality; that is, one household has all the income and the rest have none. A value of zero indicates "perfect" equality, a situation in which all households have equal income.

*Equivalence-adjusted income inequality* is another way to measure income inequality. Equivalence adjusted income takes into consideration the number of people living in the household and how these people share resources and take advantage of economies of scale. For example, the household-income-based distribution treats income of $30,000 for a single-person household and a family household similarly, while the equivalence-adjusted income of $30,000 for a single-person household would be more than twice the equivalence-adjusted income of $30,000 for a family household with two adults and two children. The equivalence adjustment used here is based on a three-parameter scale that reflects:

1. On average, children consume less than adults.

2. As family size increases, expenses do not increase at the same rate.

3. The increase in expenses is larger for a first child of a single-parent family than the first child of a two-adult family.

## Additional Information

Additional information is available in the Census publication "Income and Poverty in the United States: 2015," on the Census Bureau Web site at <http://www.census.gov/hhes/www/income/income.html>.

## Table 13-1.  Income and Earnings Summary Measures, by Selected Characteristics, 2014 and 2015

(Numbers in thousands, dollars, percent; income in 2015 dollars.)

| Characteristic | 2014 | | | 2015 | | | Percent change in real median income (2015 less 2014) | |
|---|---|---|---|---|---|---|---|---|
| | Number | Median income (dollars) | | Number | Median income (dollars) | | Estimate | Margin of error [1] (+/-) |
| | | Estimate | Margin of error [1] (+/-) | | Estimate | Margin of error [1] (+/-) | | |
| **ALL HOUSEHOLDS** ............................................ | 124 587 | 53 718 | 645 | 125 819 | 56 516 | 528 | 5.2 | 1.60 |
| **Type of Households** | | | | | | | | |
| Family households ............................................ | 81 716 | 68 504 | 815 | 82 184 | 72 165 | 608 | 5.3 | 1.46 |
| Married-couple ............................................ | 60 010 | 81 118 | 677 | 60 251 | 84 626 | 983 | 4.3 | 1.32 |
| Female householder, no husband present .................. | 15 544 | 36 192 | 682 | 15 622 | 37 797 | 995 | 4.4 | 3.17 |
| Male householder, no wife present ........................ | 6 162 | 53 746 | 1 644 | 6 310 | 55 861 | 1 595 | 3.9 | 4.37 |
| Nonfamily households ....................................... | 42 871 | 32 084 | 466 | 43 635 | 33 805 | 776 | 5.4 | 2.82 |
| Female householder ....................................... | 22 728 | 26 703 | 523 | 23 093 | 29 022 | 822 | 8.7 | 3.74 |
| Male householder ......................................... | 20 143 | 39 226 | 1 118 | 20 542 | 40 762 | 745 | 3.9 | 3.51 |
| **Race[2] and Hispanic Origin of Householder** | | | | | | | | |
| White ............................................ | 98 679 | 56 932 | 585 | 99 313 | 60 109 | 627 | 5.6 | 1.58 |
| White, not Hispanic ............................. | 84 228 | 60 325 | 606 | 84 445 | 62 950 | 892 | 4.4 | 1.76 |
| Black ............................................ | 16 437 | 35 439 | 759 | 16 539 | 36 898 | 845 | 4.1 | 2.96 |
| Asian ............................................ | 6 040 | 74 382 | 3 470 | 6 328 | 77 166 | 2 791 | 3.7 | 5.47 |
| Hispanic (any race) ............................. | 16 239 | 42 540 | 849 | 16 667 | 45 148 | 1 012 | 6.1 | 2.97 |
| **Age of Householder** | | | | | | | | |
| Under 65 years ................................... | 94 640 | 60 531 | 443 | 94 820 | 63 344 | 822 | 4.6 | 1.53 |
| 15 to 24 years ................................. | 6 370 | 34 645 | 1 297 | 6 361 | 36 108 | 1 333 | 4.2 | 5.41 |
| 25 to 34 years ................................. | 20 075 | 54 305 | 1 316 | 20 047 | 57 366 | 1 121 | 5.6 | 2.98 |
| 35 to 44 years ................................. | 21 121 | 66 770 | 1 025 | 21 222 | 71 417 | 958 | 7.0 | 2.01 |
| 45 to 54 years ................................. | 23 566 | 70 913 | 1 365 | 23 294 | 73 857 | 1 867 | 4.2 | 3.23 |
| 55 to 64 years ................................. | 23 509 | 60 649 | 1 126 | 23 896 | 62 802 | 1 471 | 3.5 | 2.84 |
| 65 years and older ............................... | 29 946 | 36 938 | 585 | 30 998 | 38 515 | 772 | 4.3 | 2.75 |
| **Nativity of Householder** | | | | | | | | |
| Native born ...................................... | 106 191 | 54 741 | 713 | 107 081 | 57 173 | 558 | 4.4 | 1.68 |
| Foreign born ..................................... | 18 396 | 49 649 | 1 142 | 18 738 | 52 295 | 1 126 | 5.3 | 3.23 |
| Naturalized citizen ............................ | 9 735 | 59 329 | 2 239 | 9 856 | 61 982 | 1 325 | 4.5 | 4.55 |
| Not a citizen .................................. | 8 661 | 40 842 | 780 | 8 881 | 45 137 | 1 722 | 10.5 | 4.39 |
| **Region** | | | | | | | | |
| Northeast ........................................ | 22 179 | 59 278 | 2 266 | 22 347 | 62 182 | 1 342 | 4.9 | 4.15 |
| Midwest .......................................... | 27 459 | 54 330 | 1 367 | 27 455 | 57 082 | 1 336 | 5.1 | 3.30 |
| South ............................................ | 47 040 | 49 712 | 838 | 47 822 | 51 174 | 622 | 2.9 | 2.04 |
| West ............................................. | 27 909 | 57 754 | 1 320 | 28 195 | 61 442 | 945 | 6.4 | 2.84 |
| **Residence** | | | | | | | | |
| Inside metropolitan statistical areas ............ | 104 009 | 55 920 | 582 | 107 615 | 59 258 | 780 | N | N |
| Inside principal cities ........................ | 40 578 | 47 905 | 974 | 42 615 | 51 378 | 646 | N | N |
| Outside principal cities ....................... | 63 431 | 61 671 | 626 | 65 000 | 64 144 | 952 | N | N |
| Outside metropolitan statistical areas ........... | 20 578 | 45 534 | 859 | 18 204 | 44 657 | 1 543 | N | N |
| **Earnings of Year-Round Full-Time Workers** | | | | | | | | |
| Men with earnings ................................ | 62 455 | 50 441 | 218 | 63 887 | 51 212 | 225 | 1.5 | 0.60 |
| Women with earnings ............................. | 46 226 | 39 667 | 719 | 47 211 | 40 742 | 241 | 2.7 | 1.86 |
| Female-to-male earnings ratio .................... | X | 0.79 | 0.01 | X | 0.80 | 0.005 | 1.2 | 1.80 |

[1] A margin of error is a measure of an estimate's variability. The larger the margin of error in relation to the size of the estimate, the less reliable the estimate.
[2] Federal surveys now give respondents the option of reporting more than one race. Therefore, there are two basic ways of defining a race group. A group such as Asian may be defined as those who reported Asian and no other race (the race-alone or single-race concept) or as those who reported Asian regardless of whether they also reported another race (the race-alone-or-in-combination concept). This table shows data using the race-alone concept. The use of the single-race population does not imply that it is the preferred method of presenting or analyzing data; the Census Bureau uses a variety of approaches. Information on people who reported more than one race, such as White and American Indian and Alaska Native or Asian and Black or African American, is available from Census 2010 through American FactFinder. About 2.9 percent of respondents reported more than one race in Census 2010.
X = Not applicable.
N = Not comparable.

## Table 13-2. Households, by Total Money Income, Race, and Hispanic Origin of Householder, 1967–2015

(Numbers in thousands, percent, dollars; income in 2015 CPI-U-RS adjusted dollars.)

| Race and Hispanic origin of householder and year | Number | Percent distribution | | | | | | | | | | Median income (dollars) | | Mean income (dollars) | |
|---|---|---|---|---|---|---|---|---|---|---|---|---|---|---|---|
| | | Total | Under $15,000 | $15,000 to $24,999 | $25,000 to $34,999 | $35,000 to $49,999 | $50,000 to $74,999 | $75,000 to $99,999 | $100,000 to $149,999 | $150,000 to $199,000 | $200,000 and over | Value | Standard error | Value | Standard error |
| **All Races** | | | | | | | | | | | | | | | |
| 1967[1] | 60 813 | 100.0 | 16.0 | 11.3 | 11.4 | 19.5 | 23.2 | 10.5 | 5.7 | 1.4 | 1.0 | 44 335 | 161 | 49 586 | 161 |
| 1968 | 62 214 | 100.0 | 14.7 | 10.9 | 10.9 | 18.7 | 24.3 | 11.7 | 6.5 | 1.3 | 0.9 | 46 245 | 167 | 52 320 | 167 |
| 1969 | 63 401 | 100.0 | 14.4 | 10.5 | 10.7 | 17.2 | 24.5 | 12.4 | 7.7 | 1.5 | 1.1 | 47 965 | 177 | 54 568 | 172 |
| 1970 | 64 778 | 100.0 | 14.5 | 10.6 | 10.9 | 17.1 | 23.7 | 12.5 | 7.8 | 1.7 | 1.1 | 47 593 | 174 | 54 497 | 174 |
| 1971[2] | 66 676 | 100.0 | 14.5 | 11.0 | 11.2 | 16.7 | 23.6 | 12.5 | 7.8 | 1.6 | 1.1 | 47 130 | 183 | 54 203 | 172 |
| 1972[3] | 68 251 | 100.0 | 13.6 | 11.1 | 10.5 | 15.8 | 22.9 | 13.5 | 9.1 | 2.1 | 1.4 | 49 148 | 188 | 57 202 | 177 |
| 1973 | 69 859 | 100.0 | 13.2 | 11.5 | 10.0 | 15.5 | 22.6 | 13.7 | 9.7 | 2.2 | 1.6 | 50 141 | 191 | 57 987 | 176 |
| 1974[4,5] | 71 163 | 100.0 | 13.2 | 11.4 | 11.0 | 16.3 | 22.5 | 13.3 | 9.0 | 2.1 | 1.2 | 48 553 | 186 | 56 779 | 178 |
| 1975[5] | 72 867 | 100.0 | 13.7 | 12.3 | 11.1 | 16.1 | 22.4 | 12.7 | 8.7 | 1.9 | 1.2 | 47 281 | 192 | 55 211 | 172 |
| 1976[6] | 74 142 | 100.0 | 13.3 | 12.1 | 11.1 | 15.6 | 22.2 | 13.4 | 9.0 | 2.0 | 1.2 | 48 066 | 178 | 56 538 | 174 |
| 1977 | 76 030 | 100.0 | 13.3 | 12.1 | 10.8 | 15.5 | 21.8 | 13.5 | 9.5 | 2.2 | 1.4 | 48 370 | 182 | 57 380 | 175 |
| 1978 | 77 330 | 100.0 | 12.9 | 11.5 | 10.9 | 14.5 | 22.1 | 13.6 | 10.4 | 2.5 | 1.5 | 50 242 | 203 | 59 134 | 227 |
| 1979[7] | 80 776 | 100.0 | 13.1 | 11.2 | 10.9 | 15.0 | 21.3 | 14.0 | 10.3 | 2.7 | 1.6 | 50 146 | 238 | 59 569 | 225 |
| 1980 | 82 368 | 100.0 | 13.5 | 11.5 | 11.2 | 15.3 | 21.5 | 13.2 | 9.9 | 2.5 | 1.4 | 48 518 | 249 | 57 704 | 211 |
| 1981 | 83 527 | 100.0 | 13.7 | 11.7 | 11.7 | 15.0 | 21.1 | 13.1 | 10.0 | 2.3 | 1.4 | 47 712 | 250 | 57 000 | 208 |
| 1982 | 83 918 | 100.0 | 14.2 | 11.7 | 11.2 | 15.8 | 20.6 | 12.4 | 9.9 | 2.5 | 1.6 | 47 585 | 215 | 57 347 | 212 |
| 1983 | 85 407 | 100.0 | 14.0 | 11.8 | 11.3 | 15.6 | 20.3 | 12.6 | 10.0 | 2.7 | 1.7 | 47 283 | 215 | 57 507 | 215 |
| 1984[8] | 86 789 | 100.0 | 13.4 | 11.7 | 11.2 | 14.9 | 20.2 | 12.9 | 10.7 | 3.0 | 1.9 | 48 720 | 222 | 59 694 | 220 |
| 1985[9] | 88 458 | 100.0 | 13.6 | 11.0 | 10.9 | 14.8 | 20.4 | 12.9 | 11.3 | 3.1 | 2.1 | 49 631 | 269 | 61 079 | 242 |
| 1986 | 89 479 | 100.0 | 13.4 | 10.8 | 10.3 | 14.5 | 20.0 | 13.2 | 11.9 | 3.6 | 2.4 | 51 388 | 266 | 63 487 | 258 |
| 1987[10] | 91 124 | 100.0 | 13.1 | 10.7 | 10.2 | 14.4 | 19.7 | 13.2 | 12.3 | 3.6 | 2.6 | 52 032 | 246 | 64 708 | 266 |
| 1988 | 92 830 | 100.0 | 12.7 | 10.5 | 10.6 | 14.0 | 19.7 | 13.5 | 12.4 | 3.8 | 2.8 | 52 432 | 256 | 65 513 | 293 |
| 1989 | 93 347 | 100.0 | 12.1 | 10.7 | 9.9 | 14.6 | 19.6 | 13.5 | 12.6 | 4.0 | 3.0 | 53 367 | 294 | 67 425 | 294 |
| 1990 | 94 312 | 100.0 | 12.4 | 10.8 | 9.9 | 14.9 | 20.0 | 13.2 | 12.2 | 3.8 | 2.9 | 52 684 | 269 | 65 810 | 278 |
| 1991 | 95 669 | 100.0 | 12.8 | 11.1 | 10.5 | 14.7 | 19.4 | 12.8 | 12.1 | 3.8 | 2.6 | 51 145 | 246 | 64 380 | 265 |
| 1992[11] | 96 426 | 100.0 | 13.2 | 11.7 | 10.5 | 14.5 | 18.9 | 13.1 | 11.7 | 3.8 | 2.7 | 50 725 | 240 | 64 309 | 270 |
| 1993[12] | 97 107 | 100.0 | 13.1 | 11.5 | 10.6 | 14.6 | 18.6 | 12.6 | 12.0 | 4.0 | 3.1 | 50 478 | 236 | 66 938 | 362 |
| 1994[13] | 98 990 | 100.0 | 12.7 | 11.7 | 10.6 | 14.1 | 18.6 | 12.5 | 12.1 | 4.2 | 3.4 | 51 065 | 233 | 68 268 | 367 |
| 1995[14] | 99 627 | 100.0 | 11.8 | 11.6 | 10.3 | 14.3 | 18.9 | 12.8 | 12.6 | 4.2 | 3.5 | 52 664 | 304 | 69 451 | 380 |
| 1996 | 101 018 | 100.0 | 11.7 | 11.3 | 10.2 | 14.3 | 18.0 | 13.6 | 12.6 | 4.7 | 3.6 | 53 407 | 269 | 70 909 | 397 |
| 1997 | 102 528 | 100.0 | 11.6 | 10.7 | 10.1 | 13.7 | 18.7 | 13.0 | 13.4 | 4.8 | 4.1 | 54 506 | 252 | 73 193 | 409 |
| 1998 | 103 874 | 100.0 | 11.0 | 10.4 | 9.7 | 13.7 | 18.5 | 13.0 | 14.1 | 5.1 | 4.5 | 56 510 | 334 | 75 359 | 407 |
| 1999[15] | 106 434 | 100.0 | 10.2 | 10.3 | 9.7 | 13.7 | 18.0 | 13.1 | 14.3 | 5.4 | 5.1 | 57 909 | 270 | 77 889 | 404 |
| 2000[16] | 108 209 | 100.0 | 10.4 | 10.1 | 9.8 | 13.5 | 18.0 | 13.1 | 14.3 | 5.7 | 5.0 | 57 790 | 182 | 78 634 | 310 |
| 2001 | 109 297 | 100.0 | 10.7 | 10.3 | 10.1 | 13.6 | 17.8 | 12.7 | 14.4 | 5.2 | 5.2 | 56 531 | 173 | 77 924 | 311 |
| 2002 | 111 278 | 100.0 | 11.0 | 10.4 | 10.3 | 13.3 | 17.8 | 12.9 | 14.2 | 5.3 | 4.8 | 55 871 | 183 | 76 217 | 286 |
| 2003 | 112 000 | 100.0 | 11.4 | 10.5 | 10.0 | 13.2 | 17.7 | 12.6 | 14.1 | 5.4 | 4.9 | 55 823 | 242 | 76 118 | 278 |
| 2004[17] | 113 343 | 100.0 | 11.3 | 10.4 | 10.5 | 13.3 | 17.6 | 12.8 | 13.7 | 5.6 | 4.8 | 55 629 | 246 | 75 871 | 286 |
| 2005 | 114 384 | 100.0 | 11.4 | 10.6 | 9.7 | 13.7 | 17.8 | 12.6 | 13.6 | 5.4 | 5.1 | 56 224 | 188 | 76 878 | 290 |
| 2006 | 116 011 | 100.0 | 10.9 | 10.3 | 9.6 | 14.3 | 17.6 | 12.5 | 13.9 | 5.7 | 5.3 | 56 663 | 243 | 78 257 | 302 |
| 2007 | 116 783 | 100.0 | 11.1 | 10.4 | 10.2 | 12.9 | 17.9 | 12.3 | 14.4 | 5.6 | 5.2 | 57 423 | 160 | 77 286 | 270 |
| 2008 | 117 181 | 100.0 | 11.6 | 10.7 | 10.3 | 13.8 | 17.2 | 12.5 | 13.6 | 5.5 | 4.8 | 55 376 | 151 | 75 325 | 266 |
| 2009[18] | 117 538 | 100.0 | 11.6 | 10.8 | 10.5 | 13.8 | 17.3 | 12.4 | 13.3 | 5.4 | 4.9 | 54 988 | 235 | 75 093 | 268 |
| 2010[19] | 119 927 | 100.0 | 12.4 | 11.3 | 10.6 | 13.1 | 17.2 | 12.2 | 13.0 | 5.4 | 4.8 | 53 568 | 353 | 73 262 | 391 |
| 2011 | 121 084 | 100.0 | 12.7 | 11.0 | 10.9 | 13.6 | 17.5 | 11.4 | 12.7 | 5.4 | 4.8 | 52 751 | 265 | 73 431 | 388 |
| 2012 | 122 459 | 100.0 | 12.7 | 11.4 | 10.4 | 13.5 | 17.4 | 11.8 | 12.8 | 5.2 | 4.8 | 52 666 | 216 | 73 577 | 435 |
| 2013[20] | 123 931 | 100.0 | 12.5 | 11.2 | 9.8 | 13.1 | 17.1 | 11.9 | 12.9 | 5.9 | 5.7 | 54 525 | 665 | 76 513 | 676 |
| 2014 | 124 587 | 100.0 | 12.6 | 10.9 | 10.1 | 13.1 | 17.0 | 11.5 | 13.4 | 5.7 | 5.6 | 53 718 | 392 | 75 825 | 447 |
| 2015 | 125 819 | 100.0 | 11.6 | 10.5 | 10.0 | 12.7 | 16.7 | 12.1 | 14.1 | 6.2 | 6.1 | 56 516 | 321 | 79 263 | 403 |

[1]Implementation of a new Curent Population Survey (CPS) Annual Social and Economic Supplements (ASEC) processing system.
[2]Introduction of 1970 census sample design and population controls.
[3]Full implementation of 1970 census–based sample design.
[4]Implementation of a new CPS ASEC processing system. Questionnaire expanded to ask 11 income questions.
[5]Some of these estimates were derived using Pareto interpolation and may differ from published data that were derived using linear interpolation.
[6]First-year medians were derived using both Pareto and linear interpolation. Before this year, all medians were derived using linear interpolation.
[7]Implementation of 1980 census population controls. Questionnaire expanded to show 27 possible values from a list of 51 possible sources of income.
[8]Implementation of Hispanic population weighting controls and introduction of 1980 census–based sample design.
[9]Recording of amounts for earnings from longest job increased to $299,999. Full implementation of 1980 census–based sample design.
[10]Implementation of a new CPS ASEC processing system.
[11]Implementation of 1990 census population controls.
[12]Data collection method changed from paper and pencil to computer-assisted interviewing. In addition, the 1994 ASEC was revised to allow for the coding of different income amounts on selected questionnaire items. Limits either increased or decreased in the following categories: earnings limits increased to $999,999, Social Security limits increased to $49,999, Supplemental Security Income and public assistance limits increased to $24,999, veterans' benefits limits increased to $99,999, and child support and alimony limits decreased to $49,999.
[13]Introduction of 1990 census sample design.
[14]Full implementation of 1990 census–based sample design and metropolitan definitions, 7,000 household sample reduction, and revised editing of responses on race.
[15]Implementation of the 2000 census–based population controls.
[16]Implementation of a 28,000 household sample expansion.
[17]Data revised to reflect a correction to the weights in the 2005 ASEC.
[18]Median income is calculated using $2,500 intervals. Beginning with 2009 income data, the Census Bureau expanded the upper income intervals used to calculate medians to $250,000 or more.
[19]Implementation of 2010 census-based population controls.
[20]Data are based on the CPS ASEC sample of 68,000 addresses. The 2014 CPS ASEC included redesigned questions for income and health insurance coverage.

## Table 13-2. Households, by Total Money Income, Race, and Hispanic Origin of Householder, 1967–2015
### —Continued

(Numbers in thousands, percent, dollars; income in 2015 CPI-U-RS adjusted dollars.)

| Race and Hispanic origin of householder and year | Number | Percent distribution | | | | | | | | | | Median income (dollars) | | Mean income (dollars) | |
|---|---|---|---|---|---|---|---|---|---|---|---|---|---|---|---|
| | | Total | Under $15,000 | $15,000 to $24,999 | $25,000 to $34,999 | $35,000 to $49,999 | $50,000 to $74,999 | $75,000 to $99,999 | $100,000 to $149,999 | $150,000 to $199,000 | $200,000 and over | Value | Standard error | Value | Standard error |
| **White[21]** | | | | | | | | | | | | | | | |
| 1967[1] | 54 188 | 100.0 | 14.0 | 10.0 | 11.0 | 19.0 | 24.0 | 11.0 | 6.0 | 1.0 | 1.0 | 46 181 | 167 | 51 339 | 174 |
| 1968 | 55 394 | 100.0 | 13.0 | 10.0 | 10.0 | 18.0 | 25.0 | 12.0 | 6.0 | 1.0 | 1.0 | 48 095 | 179 | 54 139 | 179 |
| 1969 | 56 248 | 100.0 | 13.0 | 9.0 | 10.0 | 17.0 | 25.0 | 13.0 | 8.0 | 1.0 | 1.0 | 50 000 | 183 | 56 527 | 188 |
| 1970 | 57 575 | 100.0 | 13.0 | 10.0 | 10.0 | 17.0 | 24.0 | 13.0 | 8.0 | 1.0 | 1.0 | 49 514 | 191 | 56 339 | 185 |
| 1971[2] | 59 463 | 100.0 | 13.0 | 10.0 | 10.0 | 16.0 | 24.0 | 13.0 | 8.0 | 1.0 | 1.0 | 49 240 | 188 | 56 102 | 183 |
| 1972[3] | 60 618 | 100.0 | 12.0 | 10.0 | 10.0 | 15.0 | 23.0 | 14.0 | 9.0 | 2.0 | 1.0 | 51 502 | 197 | 59 359 | 192 |
| 1973 | 61 965 | 100.0 | 11.0 | 10.0 | 9.0 | 15.0 | 23.0 | 14.0 | 10.0 | 2.0 | 1.0 | 52 489 | 200 | 60 160 | 191 |
| 1974[4,5] | 62 984 | 100.0 | 11.0 | 10.0 | 10.0 | 16.0 | 23.0 | 13.0 | 9.0 | 2.0 | 1.0 | 50 719 | 191 | 58 814 | 191 |
| 1975[5] | 64 392 | 100.0 | 12.0 | 11.0 | 10.0 | 16.0 | 23.0 | 13.0 | 9.0 | 2.0 | 1.0 | 49 388 | 180 | 57 185 | 188 |
| 1976[6] | 65 353 | 100.0 | 11.0 | 11.0 | 10.0 | 15.0 | 22.0 | 14.0 | 9.0 | 2.0 | 1.0 | 50 293 | 208 | 58 645 | 189 |
| 1977 | 66 934 | 100.0 | 11.0 | 11.0 | 10.0 | 15.0 | 22.0 | 14.0 | 10.0 | 2.0 | 1.0 | 50 807 | 214 | 59 553 | 192 |
| 1978 | 68 028 | 100.0 | 11.0 | 11.0 | 10.0 | 14.0 | 22.0 | 14.0 | 10.0 | 2.0 | 1.0 | 52 170 | 230 | 61 255 | 247 |
| 1979[7] | 70 766 | 100.0 | 11.0 | 10.0 | 10.0 | 15.0 | 22.0 | 14.0 | 10.0 | 2.0 | 1.0 | 52 517 | 250 | 61 846 | 246 |
| 1980 | 71 872 | 100.0 | 11.0 | 10.0 | 11.0 | 15.0 | 22.0 | 13.0 | 10.0 | 2.0 | 1.0 | 51 127 | 263 | 59 963 | 230 |
| 1981 | 72 845 | 100.0 | 12.0 | 11.0 | 11.0 | 15.0 | 21.0 | 13.0 | 10.0 | 2.0 | 1.0 | 50 354 | 232 | 59 321 | 225 |
| 1982 | 73 182 | 100.0 | 12.0 | 11.0 | 11.0 | 16.0 | 21.0 | 13.0 | 10.0 | 2.0 | 1.0 | 49 759 | 226 | 59 642 | 233 |
| 1983 | 74 376 | 100.0 | 12.0 | 11.0 | 11.0 | 15.0 | 21.0 | 13.0 | 10.0 | 2.0 | 1.0 | 49 529 | 224 | 59 825 | 233 |
| 1984[8] | 75 328 | 100.0 | 11.0 | 11.0 | 11.0 | 15.0 | 20.0 | 13.0 | 11.0 | 3.0 | 2.0 | 51 338 | 258 | 62 085 | 241 |
| 1985[9] | 76 576 | 100.0 | 11.0 | 10.0 | 10.0 | 14.0 | 21.0 | 13.0 | 12.0 | 3.0 | 2.0 | 52 281 | 279 | 63 513 | 267 |
| 1986 | 77 284 | 100.0 | 11.0 | 10.0 | 10.0 | 14.0 | 20.0 | 13.0 | 12.0 | 3.0 | 2.0 | 53 964 | 262 | 66 055 | 282 |
| 1987[10] | 78 519 | 100.0 | 11.0 | 10.0 | 10.0 | 14.0 | 20.0 | 13.0 | 13.0 | 3.0 | 2.0 | 54 759 | 275 | 67 396 | 291 |
| 1988 | 79 734 | 100.0 | 10.0 | 9.0 | 10.0 | 14.0 | 20.0 | 14.0 | 13.0 | 4.0 | 3.0 | 55 365 | 327 | 68 229 | 321 |
| 1989 | 80 163 | 100.0 | 10.0 | 10.0 | 9.0 | 14.0 | 20.0 | 14.0 | 13.0 | 4.0 | 3.0 | 56 072 | 273 | 70 152 | 325 |
| 1990 | 80 968 | 100.0 | 10.0 | 10.0 | 9.0 | 15.0 | 20.0 | 13.0 | 12.0 | 4.0 | 3.0 | 54 887 | 251 | 68 386 | 306 |
| 1991 | 81 675 | 100.0 | 10.0 | 10.0 | 10.0 | 14.0 | 19.0 | 13.0 | 12.0 | 4.0 | 2.0 | 53 533 | 259 | 67 021 | 292 |
| 1992[11] | 81 795 | 100.0 | 11.0 | 11.0 | 10.0 | 14.0 | 19.0 | 13.0 | 12.0 | 4.0 | 3.0 | 53 268 | 258 | 67 135 | 299 |
| 1993[12] | 82 387 | 100.0 | 11.0 | 11.0 | 10.0 | 14.0 | 19.0 | 13.0 | 12.0 | 4.0 | 3.0 | 53 195 | 310 | 69 859 | 403 |
| 1994[13] | 83 737 | 100.0 | 10.0 | 11.0 | 10.0 | 14.0 | 19.0 | 13.0 | 12.0 | 4.0 | 3.0 | 53 795 | 302 | 71 195 | 414 |
| 1995[14] | 84 511 | 100.0 | 10.0 | 11.0 | 10.0 | 14.0 | 19.0 | 13.0 | 13.0 | 4.0 | 3.0 | 55 213 | 289 | 72 136 | 418 |
| 1996 | 85 059 | 100.0 | 10.0 | 11.0 | 10.0 | 14.0 | 18.0 | 14.0 | 13.0 | 5.0 | 3.0 | 55 854 | 289 | 73 639 | 436 |
| 1997 | 86 106 | 100.0 | 10.0 | 10.0 | 9.0 | 13.0 | 19.0 | 13.0 | 14.0 | 5.0 | 4.0 | 57 337 | 363 | 76 360 | 465 |
| 1998 | 87 212 | 100.0 | 9.0 | 9.0 | 9.0 | 13.0 | 18.0 | 13.0 | 14.0 | 5.0 | 4.0 | 59 387 | 298 | 78 686 | 463 |
| 1999[15] | 88 893 | 100.0 | 8.0 | 10.0 | 9.0 | 13.0 | 18.0 | 13.0 | 15.0 | 5.0 | 5.0 | 60 158 | 304 | 80 626 | 456 |
| 2000[16] | 90 030 | 100.0 | 9.0 | 9.0 | 9.0 | 13.0 | 18.0 | 13.0 | 15.0 | 6.0 | 5.0 | 60 371 | 267 | 81 457 | 349 |
| 2001 | 90 682 | 100.0 | 9.0 | 9.0 | 9.0 | 13.0 | 18.0 | 13.0 | 15.0 | 5.0 | 5.0 | 59 527 | 279 | 80 915 | 348 |
| **White Alone[22]** | | | | | | | | | | | | | | | |
| 2002 | 91 645 | 100.0 | 9.6 | 10.0 | 10.1 | 13.0 | 18.0 | 13.5 | 15.0 | 5.6 | 5.1 | 59 398 | 241 | 79 265 | 323 |
| 2003 | 91 962 | 100.0 | 9.9 | 10.2 | 9.9 | 13.3 | 17.9 | 13.0 | 14.8 | 5.8 | 5.3 | 58 804 | 231 | 79 366 | 318 |
| 2004[17] | 92 880 | 100.0 | 9.8 | 10.1 | 10.2 | 13.1 | 17.9 | 13.3 | 14.5 | 5.9 | 5.2 | 58 545 | 230 | 78 937 | 325 |
| 2005 | 93 588 | 100.0 | 9.8 | 10.2 | 9.5 | 13.8 | 18.1 | 13.2 | 14.2 | 5.8 | 5.5 | 58 928 | 257 | 80 056 | 331 |
| 2006 | 94 705 | 100.0 | 9.4 | 9.9 | 9.4 | 14.1 | 17.8 | 13.1 | 14.6 | 6.0 | 5.6 | 59 569 | 173 | 81 239 | 339 |
| 2007 | 95 112 | 100.0 | 9.5 | 10.2 | 10.0 | 12.8 | 18.2 | 12.7 | 15.1 | 5.9 | 5.6 | 59 575 | 176 | 80 398 | 306 |
| 2008 | 95 297 | 100.0 | 10.1 | 10.4 | 10.0 | 13.5 | 17.6 | 13.0 | 14.3 | 5.8 | 5.2 | 57 588 | 167 | 78 371 | 302 |
| 2009[18] | 95 489 | 100.0 | 9.9 | 10.5 | 10.2 | 13.8 | 17.8 | 12.9 | 14.0 | 5.7 | 5.2 | 57 291 | 170 | 77 930 | 300 |
| 2010[19] | 96 306 | 100.0 | 10.6 | 11.0 | 10.4 | 13.2 | 17.5 | 12.7 | 13.8 | 5.7 | 5.2 | 56 213 | 275 | 76 545 | 440 |
| 2011 | 96 964 | 100.0 | 10.8 | 10.5 | 10.7 | 13.7 | 18.0 | 11.9 | 13.3 | 5.8 | 5.2 | 55 027 | 237 | 76 735 | 445 |
| 2012 | 97 705 | 100.0 | 10.8 | 11.0 | 10.3 | 13.4 | 17.8 | 12.4 | 13.5 | 5.6 | 5.2 | 55 442 | 396 | 76 821 | 479 |
| 2013[20] | 98 807 | 100.0 | 10.8 | 10.9 | 9.6 | 12.9 | 17.5 | 12.6 | 13.4 | 6.3 | 6.0 | 57 740 | 526 | 79 190 | 771 |
| 2014[20] | 98 679 | 100.0 | 10.9 | 10.5 | 9.8 | 13.1 | 17.5 | 12.1 | 14.0 | 6.0 | 6.1 | 56 931 | 355 | 78 981 | 524 |
| 2015[20] | 99 313 | 100.0 | 9.9 | 10.1 | 9.9 | 12.7 | 16.9 | 12.6 | 15.0 | 6.6 | 6.4 | 60 109 | 381 | 82 226 | 470 |

[1]Implementation of a new Curent Population Survey (CPS) Annual Social and Economic Supplements (ASEC) processing system.
[2]Introduction of 1970 census sample design and population controls.
[3]Full implementation of 1970 census–based sample design.
[4]Implementation of a new CPS ASEC processing system. Questionnaire expanded to ask 11 income questions.
[5]Some of these estimates were derived using Pareto interpolation and may differ from published data that were derived using linear interpolation.
[6]First-year medians were derived using both Pareto and linear interpolation. Before this year, all medians were derived using linear interpolation.
[7]Implementation of 1980 census population controls. Questionnaire expanded to show 27 possible values from a list of 51 possible sources of income.
[8]Implementation of Hispanic population weighting controls and introduction of 1980 census–based sample design.
[9]Recording of amounts for earnings from longest job increased to $299,999. Full implementation of 1980 census–based sample design.
[10]Implementation of a new CPS ASEC processing system.
[11]Implementation of 1990 census population controls.
[12]Data collection method changed from paper and pencil to computer-assisted interviewing. In addition, the 1994 ASEC was revised to allow for the coding of different income amounts on selected questionnaire items. Limits either increased or decreased in the following categories: earnings limits increased to $999,999, Social Security limits increased to $49,999, Supplemental Security Income and public assistance limits increased to $24,999, veterans' benefits limits increased to $99,999, and child support and alimony limits decreased to $49,999.
[13]Introduction of 1990 census sample design.
[14]Full implementation of 1990 census–based sample design and metropolitan definitions, 7,000 household sample reduction, and revised editing of responses on race.
[15]Implementation of the 2000 census–based population controls.
[16]Implementation of a 28,000 household sample expansion.
[17]Data revised to reflect a correction to the weights in the 2005 ASEC.
[18]Median income is calculated using $2,500 intervals. Beginning with 2009 income data, the Census Bureau expanded the upper income intervals used to calculate medians to $250,000 or more.
[19]Implementation of 2010 census-based population controls.
[20]Data are based on the CPS ASEC sample of 68,000 addresses. The 2014 CPS ASEC included redesigned questions for income and health insurance coverage.
[21]For 2001 and earlier years, the CPS allowed respondents to report only one race group.
[22]Beginning with the 2003 CPS, respondents were allowed to choose one or more races. White alone refers to people who reported White and did not report any other race category. The use of this single-race population does not imply that it is the preferred method of presenting or analyzing the data; the Census Bureau uses a variety of approaches. Information on people who reported more than one race, such as White and American Indian and Alaska Native or Asian and Black or African American, is available from Census 2010 through American FactFinder. About 2.9 percent of respondents reported more than one race in Census 2010.

## Table 13-2. Households, by Total Money Income, Race, and Hispanic Origin of Householder, 1967–2015 —Continued

(Numbers in thousands, percent, dollars; income in 2015 CPI-U-RS adjusted dollars.)

| Race and Hispanic origin of householder and year | Number | Percent distribution | | | | | | | | | | Median income (dollars) | | Mean income (dollars) | |
|---|---|---|---|---|---|---|---|---|---|---|---|---|---|---|---|
| | | Total | Under $15,000 | $15,000 to $24,999 | $25,000 to $34,999 | $35,000 to $49,999 | $50,000 to $74,999 | $75,000 to $99,999 | $100,000 to $149,999 | $150,000 to $199,000 | $200,000 and over | Value | Standard error | Value | Standard error |
| **White, Not Hispanic[21]** | | | | | | | | | | | | | | | |
| 1972[3] | 58 005 | 100.0 | 12.0 | 10.0 | 9.0 | 15.0 | 24.0 | 14.0 | 10.0 | 2.0 | 1.0 | 52 236 | 248 | 60 047 | 268 |
| 1973 | 59 236 | 100.0 | 11.0 | 10.0 | 9.0 | 15.0 | 23.0 | 14.0 | 10.0 | 2.0 | 1.0 | 52 951 | 248 | 60 832 | 257 |
| 1974[4,5] | 60 164 | 100.0 | 11.0 | 10.0 | 10.0 | 16.0 | 23.0 | 14.0 | 9.0 | 2.0 | 1.0 | 51 152 | 251 | 59 477 | 260 |
| 1975[5] | 61 533 | 100.0 | 12.0 | 11.0 | 10.0 | 16.0 | 23.0 | 13.0 | 9.0 | 2.0 | 1.0 | 49 761 | 264 | 57 885 | 280 |
| 1976[6] | 62 365 | 100.0 | 11.0 | 11.0 | 10.0 | 15.0 | 22.0 | 14.0 | 9.0 | 2.0 | 1.0 | 51 318 | 299 | 59 398 | 265 |
| 1977 | 63 721 | 100.0 | 11.0 | 11.0 | 10.0 | 15.0 | 22.0 | 14.0 | 10.0 | 2.0 | 1.0 | 51 814 | 292 | 60 290 | 285 |
| 1978 | 64 836 | 100.0 | 11.0 | 10.0 | 10.0 | 14.0 | 22.0 | 14.0 | 11.0 | 2.0 | 1.0 | 53 153 | 280 | 61 978 | 267 |
| 1979[7] | 67 203 | 100.0 | 11.0 | 10.0 | 10.0 | 14.0 | 22.0 | 14.0 | 11.0 | 3.0 | 1.0 | 53 256 | 295 | 62 561 | 274 |
| 1980 | 68 106 | 100.0 | 11.0 | 10.0 | 10.0 | 15.0 | 22.0 | 14.0 | 10.0 | 2.0 | 1.0 | 52 033 | 108 | 60 751 | 274 |
| 1981 | 68 996 | 100.0 | 11.0 | 11.0 | 11.0 | 15.0 | 21.0 | 13.0 | 10.0 | 2.0 | 1.0 | 51 081 | 260 | 60 068 | 250 |
| 1982 | 69 214 | 100.0 | 12.0 | 10.0 | 10.0 | 16.0 | 21.0 | 13.0 | 10.0 | 2.0 | 1.0 | 50 594 | 254 | 60 519 | 259 |
| 1983 | 69 648 | 100.0 | 11.0 | 11.0 | 11.0 | 15.0 | 21.0 | 13.0 | 10.0 | 3.0 | 2.0 | 50 802 | 256 | 61 396 | 262 |
| 1984[8] | 70 586 | 100.0 | 11.0 | 10.0 | 10.0 | 15.0 | 21.0 | 13.0 | 11.0 | 3.0 | 2.0 | 52 404 | 291 | 63 164 | 282 |
| 1985[9] | 71 540 | 100.0 | 11.0 | 10.0 | 10.0 | 14.0 | 21.0 | 13.0 | 12.0 | 3.0 | 2.0 | 53 457 | 273 | 64 749 | 294 |
| 1986 | 72 067 | 100.0 | 11.0 | 9.0 | 9.0 | 14.0 | 20.0 | 14.0 | 12.0 | 4.0 | 2.0 | 55 190 | 285 | 67 366 | 309 |
| 1987[10] | 73 120 | 100.0 | 10.0 | 9.0 | 10.0 | 14.0 | 20.0 | 14.0 | 13.0 | 4.0 | 2.0 | 56 264 | 313 | 68 714 | 319 |
| 1988 | 74 067 | 100.0 | 10.0 | 9.0 | 10.0 | 13.0 | 20.0 | 14.0 | 13.0 | 4.0 | 3.0 | 56 891 | 335 | 69 622 | 327 |
| 1989 | 74 495 | 100.0 | 9.0 | 10.0 | 9.0 | 14.0 | 20.0 | 14.0 | 13.0 | 4.0 | 3.0 | 57 278 | 280 | 71 557 | 350 |
| 1990 | 75 035 | 100.0 | 10.0 | 9.0 | 9.0 | 14.0 | 20.0 | 14.0 | 13.0 | 4.0 | 3.0 | 56 142 | 262 | 69 901 | 316 |
| 1991 | 75 625 | 100.0 | 10.0 | 10.0 | 10.0 | 14.0 | 20.0 | 13.0 | 13.0 | 4.0 | 3.0 | 54 812 | 270 | 68 459 | 305 |
| 1992[11] | 75 107 | 100.0 | 10.0 | 10.0 | 10.0 | 14.0 | 19.0 | 14.0 | 13.0 | 4.0 | 3.0 | 55 056 | 341 | 68 841 | 318 |
| 1993[12] | 75 697 | 100.0 | 10.0 | 10.0 | 10.0 | 14.0 | 19.0 | 13.0 | 13.0 | 4.0 | 3.0 | 55 153 | 323 | 71 700 | 428 |
| 1994[13] | 77 004 | 100.0 | 10.0 | 10.0 | 10.0 | 14.0 | 19.0 | 13.0 | 13.0 | 4.0 | 3.0 | 55 531 | 294 | 73 008 | 433 |
| 1995[14] | 76 932 | 100.0 | 9.0 | 10.0 | 9.0 | 14.0 | 19.0 | 13.0 | 13.0 | 4.0 | 4.0 | 57 392 | 299 | 74 489 | 446 |
| 1996 | 77 240 | 100.0 | 9.0 | 10.0 | 9.0 | 14.0 | 18.0 | 14.0 | 13.0 | 5.0 | 4.0 | 58 298 | 400 | 75 867 | . . . |
| 1997 | 77 936 | 100.0 | 9.0 | 9.0 | 9.0 | 13.0 | 19.0 | 13.0 | 14.0 | 5.0 | 4.0 | 59 698 | 312 | 78 807 | . . . |
| 1998 | 78 577 | 100.0 | 8.0 | 9.0 | 9.0 | 13.0 | 18.0 | 13.0 | 15.0 | 5.0 | 5.0 | 61 604 | 354 | 81 206 | 496 |
| 1999[15] | 79 819 | 100.0 | 8.0 | 9.0 | 9.0 | 13.0 | 18.0 | 13.0 | 15.0 | 5.0 | 5.0 | 62 762 | 397 | 83 270 | 493 |
| 2000[16] | 80 527 | 100.0 | 8.0 | 9.0 | 9.0 | 13.0 | 18.0 | 13.0 | 15.0 | 6.0 | 5.0 | 62 718 | 252 | 83 935 | 377 |
| 2001 | 80 818 | 100.0 | 9.0 | 9.0 | 9.0 | 13.0 | 17.0 | 13.0 | 15.0 | 5.0 | 6.0 | 61 918 | 257 | 83 499 | 378 |
| **White Alone, Not Hispanic[22]** | | | | | | | | | | | | | | | |
| 2002 | 81 166 | 100.0 | 9.2 | 9.6 | 9.6 | 12.6 | 18.0 | 13.8 | 15.8 | 6.0 | 5.5 | 61 788 | 242 | 81 833 | 348 |
| 2003 | 81 148 | 100.0 | 9.4 | 9.7 | 9.4 | 12.8 | 17.9 | 13.3 | 15.6 | 6.2 | 5.7 | 61 569 | 298 | 82 330 | 349 |
| 2004[17] | 81 628 | 100.0 | 9.3 | 9.7 | 9.7 | 12.7 | 17.7 | 13.6 | 15.2 | 6.3 | 5.6 | 61 371 | 281 | 81 884 | 356 |
| 2005 | 82 003 | 100.0 | 9.3 | 9.7 | 9.2 | 13.2 | 18.0 | 13.6 | 15.0 | 6.2 | 5.9 | 61 635 | 209 | 83 261 | 368 |
| 2006 | 82 675 | 100.0 | 8.9 | 9.4 | 9.1 | 13.6 | 17.7 | 13.4 | 15.4 | 6.4 | 6.2 | 61 626 | 221 | 84 340 | 373 |
| 2007 | 82 765 | 100.0 | 8.9 | 9.7 | 9.5 | 12.4 | 18.0 | 13.0 | 16.0 | 6.4 | 6.2 | 62 781 | 282 | 83 657 | 337 |
| 2008 | 82 884 | 100.0 | 9.4 | 9.9 | 9.6 | 12.9 | 17.7 | 13.5 | 15.1 | 6.2 | 0.0 | 61 130 | 248 | 81 575 | 334 |
| 2009[18] | 83 158 | 100.0 | 9.3 | 9.9 | 9.7 | 13.6 | 17.8 | 13.2 | 14.8 | 6.2 | 5.6 | 60 163 | 308 | 80 908 | 330 |
| 2010[19] | 83 314 | 100.0 | 9.8 | 10.5 | 9.8 | 12.8 | 17.5 | 13.1 | 14.6 | 6.1 | 5.7 | 59 204 | 485 | 79 721 | 500 |
| 2011 | 83 573 | 100.0 | 10.1 | 10.1 | 10.2 | 13.2 | 18.0 | 12.3 | 14.1 | 6.3 | 5.7 | 58 397 | 346 | 80 161 | 504 |
| 2012 | 83 792 | 100.0 | 10.0 | 10.4 | 9.8 | 13.0 | 17.9 | 12.8 | 14.3 | 6.0 | 5.7 | 58 851 | 371 | 80 359 | 532 |
| 2013[20] | 84 432 | 100.0 | 10.1 | 10.3 | 8.8 | 12.5 | 17.8 | 13.0 | 14.2 | 6.8 | 6.5 | 61 387 | 542 | 82 652 | 863 |
| 2014 | 84 228 | 100.0 | 10.4 | 10.0 | 9.4 | 12.6 | 17.4 | 12.3 | 14.8 | 6.5 | 6.7 | 60 325 | 368 | 82 560 | 580 |
| 2015 | 84 445 | 100.0 | 9.3 | 9.6 | 9.4 | 12.2 | 16.7 | 13.0 | 15.9 | 7.1 | 6.9 | 62 950 | 542 | 85 585 | 531 |

[3]Full implementation of 1970 census–based sample design.
[4]Implementation of a new CPS ASEC processing system. Questionnaire expanded to ask 11 income questions.
[5]Some of these estimates were derived using Pareto interpolation and may differ from published data that were derived using linear interpolation.
[6]First-year medians were derived using both Pareto and linear interpolation. Before this year, all medians were derived using linear interpolation.
[7]Implementation of 1980 census population controls. Questionnaire expanded to show 27 possible values from a list of 51 possible sources of income.
[8]Implementation of Hispanic population weighting controls and introduction of 1980 census–based sample design.
[9]Recording of amounts for earnings from longest job increased to $299,999. Full implementation of 1980 census–based sample design.
[10]Implementation of a new CPS ASEC processing system.
[11]Implementation of 1990 census population controls.
[12]Data collection method changed from paper and pencil to computer-assisted interviewing. In addition, the 1994 ASEC was revised to allow for the coding of different income amounts on selected questionnaire items. Limits either increased or decreased in the following categories: earnings limits increased to $999,999, Social Security limits increased to $49,999, Supplemental Security Income and public assistance limits increased to $24,999, veterans' benefits limits increased to $99,999, and child support and alimony limits decreased to $49,999.
[13]Introduction of 1990 census sample design.
[14]Full implementation of 1990 census–based sample design and metropolitan definitions, 7,000 household sample reduction, and revised editing of responses on race.
[15]Implementation of the 2000 census–based population controls.
[16]Implementation of a 28,000 household sample expansion.
[17]Data revised to reflect a correction to the weights in the 2005 ASEC.
[18]Median income is calculated using $2,500 intervals. Beginning with 2009 income data, the Census Bureau expanded the upper income intervals used to calculate medians to $250,000 or more.
[19]Implementation of 2010 census-based population controls.
[20]Data are based on the CPS ASEC sample of 68,000 addresses. The 2014 CPS ASEC included redesigned questions for income and health insurance coverage.
[21]For 2001 and earlier years, the CPS allowed respondents to report only one race group.
[22]Beginning with the 2003 CPS, respondents were allowed to choose one or more races. White alone refers to people who reported White and did not report any other race category. The use of this single-race population does not imply that it is the preferred method of presenting or analyzing the data; the Census Bureau uses a variety of approaches. Information on people who reported more than one race, such as White and American Indian and Alaska Native or Asian and Black or African American, is available from Census 2010 through American FactFinder. About 2.9 percent of respondents reported more than one race in Census 2010.
. . . = Not available.

## Table 13-2. Households, by Total Money Income, Race, and Hispanic Origin of Householder, 1967–2015
### —Continued

(Numbers in thousands, percent, dollars; income in 2015 CPI-U-RS adjusted dollars.)

| Race and Hispanic origin of householder and year | Number | Percent distribution | | | | | | | | | | Median income (dollars) | | Mean income (dollars) | |
| --- | --- | --- | --- | --- | --- | --- | --- | --- | --- | --- | --- | --- | --- | --- | --- |
| | | Total | Under $15,000 | $15,000 to $24,999 | $25,000 to $34,999 | $35,000 to $49,999 | $50,000 to $74,999 | $75,000 to $99,999 | $100,000 to $149,999 | $150,000 to $199,000 | $200,000 and over | Value | Standard error | Value | Standard error |
| **Black**[21] | | | | | | | | | | | | | | | |
| 1967[1] | 5 728 | 100.0 | 29.0 | 18.0 | 15.0 | 16.0 | 12.0 | 4.0 | 2.0 | - | - | 26 813 | 446 | 32 220 | 360 |
| 1968 | 5 870 | 100.0 | 26.0 | 18.0 | 15.0 | 17.0 | 14.0 | 5.0 | 2.0 | - | ... | 28 361 | 412 | 34 541 | 364 |
| 1969 | 6 053 | 100.0 | 25.0 | 17.0 | 15.0 | 17.0 | 16.0 | 5.0 | 2.0 | - | - | 30 223 | 445 | 35 979 | 383 |
| 1970 | 6 180 | 100.0 | 26.0 | 16.0 | 14.0 | 16.0 | 15.0 | 6.0 | 3.0 | - | - | 30 137 | 414 | 36 799 | 397 |
| 1971[2] | 6 578 | 100.0 | 26.0 | 16.0 | 14.0 | 16.0 | 15.0 | 6.0 | 2.0 | - | - | 29 086 | 433 | 36 042 | 370 |
| 1972[3] | 6 809 | 100.0 | 25.0 | 17.0 | 13.0 | 16.0 | 15.0 | 7.0 | 3.0 | - | - | 30 062 | 451 | 37 974 | 405 |
| 1973 | 7 040 | 100.0 | 24.0 | 18.0 | 12.0 | 16.0 | 17.0 | 6.0 | 3.0 | - | - | 30 897 | 481 | 38 368 | 381 |
| 1974[4,5] | 7 263 | 100.0 | 25.0 | 16.0 | 15.0 | 16.0 | 16.0 | 7.0 | 3.0 | - | - | 30 163 | 364 | 37 513 | 334 |
| 1975[5] | 7 489 | 100.0 | 26.0 | 17.0 | 12.0 | 16.0 | 15.0 | 6.0 | 3.0 | - | ... | 29 649 | 436 | 37 009 | 328 |
| 1976[6] | 7 776 | 100.0 | 25.0 | 17.0 | 13.0 | 15.0 | 16.0 | 7.0 | 3.0 | - | - | 29 906 | 371 | 38 209 | 341 |
| 1977 | 7 977 | 100.0 | 25.0 | 18.0 | 13.0 | 15.0 | 15.0 | 6.0 | 4.0 | - | - | 29 981 | 402 | 38 415 | 342 |
| 1978 | 8 066 | 100.0 | 26.0 | 15.0 | 13.0 | 14.0 | 16.0 | 7.0 | 5.0 | - | - | 31 352 | 663 | 40 067 | 523 |
| 1979[7] | 8 586 | 100.0 | 25.0 | 17.0 | 13.0 | 14.0 | 15.0 | 8.0 | 4.0 | - | - | 30 833 | 563 | 39 563 | 487 |
| 1980 | 8 847 | 100.0 | 27.0 | 17.0 | 12.0 | 14.0 | 15.0 | 7.0 | 4.0 | - | - | 29 455 | 555 | 38 228 | 471 |
| 1981 | 8 961 | 100.0 | 29.0 | 16.0 | 13.0 | 14.0 | 15.0 | 7.0 | 4.0 | - | - | 28 256 | 475 | 37 119 | 450 |
| 1982 | 8 916 | 100.0 | 28.0 | 16.0 | 12.0 | 14.0 | 15.0 | 7.0 | 3.0 | - | - | 28 201 | 452 | 37 106 | 464 |
| 1983 | 9 236 | 100.0 | 29.0 | 16.0 | 13.0 | 14.0 | 14.0 | 7.0 | 4.0 | - | - | 28 107 | 527 | 37 383 | 461 |
| 1984[8] | 9 480 | 100.0 | 27.0 | 16.0 | 13.0 | 14.0 | 14.0 | 7.0 | 5.0 | - | - | 29 246 | 562 | 39 005 | 480 |
| 1985[9] | 9 797 | 100.0 | 27.0 | 15.0 | 12.0 | 14.0 | 15.0 | 8.0 | 5.0 | 1.0 | - | 31 105 | 605 | 40 584 | 527 |
| 1986 | 9 922 | 100.0 | 27.0 | 14.0 | 12.0 | 14.0 | 15.0 | 8.0 | 5.0 | 1.0 | - | 31 090 | 610 | 41 711 | 567 |
| 1987[10] | 10 192 | 100.0 | 28.0 | 14.0 | 11.0 | 15.0 | 14.0 | 8.0 | 5.0 | 1.0 | - | 31 254 | 598 | 42 201 | 580 |
| 1988 | 10 561 | 100.0 | 27.0 | 14.0 | 11.0 | 14.0 | 14.0 | 8.0 | 6.0 | 1.0 | - | 31 562 | 658 | 43 238 | 631 |
| 1989 | 10 486 | 100.0 | 26.0 | 14.0 | 11.0 | 14.0 | 15.0 | 8.0 | 7.0 | 1.0 | - | 33 347 | 679 | 44 250 | 601 |
| 1990 | 10 671 | 100.0 | 26.0 | 14.0 | 11.0 | 14.0 | 16.0 | 8.0 | 6.0 | 1.0 | - | 32 822 | 749 | 43 609 | 589 |
| 1991 | 11 083 | 100.0 | 28.0 | 14.0 | 11.0 | 14.0 | 16.0 | 8.0 | 5.0 | 1.0 | - | 31 892 | 670 | 42 467 | 555 |
| 1992[11] | 11 269 | 100.0 | 28.0 | 15.0 | 10.0 | 14.0 | 15.0 | 8.0 | 5.0 | 1.0 | - | 31 018 | 633 | 42 090 | 571 |
| 1993[12] | 11 281 | 100.0 | 27.0 | 14.0 | 12.0 | 14.0 | 14.0 | 7.0 | 6.0 | 1.0 | - | 31 525 | 623 | 43 945 | 729 |
| 1994[13] | 11 655 | 100.0 | 25.0 | 14.0 | 12.0 | 14.0 | 15.0 | 8.0 | 6.0 | 2.0 | 1.0 | 33 242 | 618 | 46 256 | 664 |
| 1995[14] | 11 577 | 100.0 | 23.0 | 15.0 | 11.0 | 15.0 | 16.0 | 8.0 | 7.0 | 1.0 | 1.0 | 34 569 | 590 | 46 929 | 803 |
| 1996 | 12 109 | 100.0 | 23.0 | 14.0 | 12.0 | 14.0 | 15.0 | 10.0 | 6.0 | 1.0 | 1.0 | 35 294 | 694 | 48 788 | 953 |
| 1997 | 12 474 | 100.0 | 22.0 | 13.0 | 12.0 | 14.0 | 16.0 | 9.0 | 7.0 | 2.0 | 1.0 | 36 854 | 634 | 48 496 | 696 |
| 1998 | 12 579 | 100.0 | 22.0 | 14.0 | 11.0 | 14.0 | 16.0 | 9.0 | 8.0 | 2.0 | 1.0 | 36 799 | 576 | 49 556 | 662 |
| 1999[15] | 12 838 | 100.0 | 19.0 | 13.0 | 11.0 | 14.0 | 16.0 | 10.0 | 8.0 | 3.0 | 1.0 | 39 669 | 739 | 54 667 | 785 |
| 2000[16] | 13 174 | 100.0 | 19.0 | 13.0 | 12.0 | 14.0 | 17.0 | 9.0 | 8.0 | 3.0 | 1.0 | 40 783 | 540 | 53 858 | 546 |
| 2001 | 13 315 | 100.0 | 20.0 | 13.0 | 12.0 | 15.0 | 17.0 | 10.0 | 8.0 | 2.0 | 1.0 | 39 407 | 464 | 52 482 | 554 |
| **Black Alone**[23] | | | | | | | | | | | | | | | |
| 2002 | 13 465 | 100.0 | 20.7 | 13.8 | 12.3 | 15.4 | 15.9 | 9.5 | 8.1 | 2.5 | 1.9 | 38 240 | 515 | 52 712 | 609 |
| 2003 | 13 629 | 100.0 | 21.3 | 13.5 | 12.2 | 14.0 | 16.9 | 9.3 | 8.7 | 2.5 | 1.5 | 38 203 | 497 | 51 716 | 554 |
| 2004[17] | 13 809 | 100.0 | 21.6 | 12.7 | 12.9 | 15.3 | 15.5 | 10.0 | 7.9 | 2.4 | 1.6 | 37 762 | 393 | 50 985 | 552 |
| 2005 | 14 002 | 100.0 | 21.6 | 14.7 | 11.2 | 15.0 | 15.9 | 9.2 | 8.1 | 2.8 | 1.5 | 37 451 | 365 | 51 525 | 559 |
| 2006 | 14 354 | 100.0 | 20.8 | 13.9 | 11.3 | 16.2 | 15.8 | 9.2 | 8.4 | 2.4 | 2.0 | 37 581 | 283 | 53 049 | 656 |
| 2007 | 14 551 | 100.0 | 21.2 | 13.2 | 12.3 | 14.0 | 16.6 | 9.6 | 8.8 | 2.7 | 1.7 | 38 771 | 543 | 53 306 | 594 |
| 2008 | 14 595 | 100.0 | 21.2 | 13.4 | 12.6 | 16.0 | 15.7 | 9.0 | 8.0 | 2.6 | 1.5 | 37 669 | 485 | 51 226 | 548 |
| 2009[18] | 14 730 | 100.0 | 21.6 | 13.9 | 13.3 | 14.8 | 15.3 | 9.6 | 7.6 | 2.4 | 1.5 | 35 995 | 435 | 50 867 | 580 |
| 2010[19] | 15 265 | 100.0 | 23.9 | 14.0 | 12.4 | 14.3 | 15.0 | 9.3 | 7.3 | 2.4 | 1.4 | 34 922 | 542 | 48 873 | 681 |
| 2011 | 15 583 | 100.0 | 24.4 | 14.5 | 12.3 | 13.4 | 15.3 | 8.5 | 7.4 | 2.5 | 1.7 | 33 965 | 536 | 49 801 | 846 |
| 2012 | 15 872 | 100.0 | 23.6 | 15.2 | 11.7 | 14.3 | 15.0 | 8.6 | 7.7 | 2.2 | 1.6 | 34 398 | 816 | 49 280 | 777 |
| 2013[20] | 16 009 | 100.0 | 22.9 | 14.0 | 12.4 | 14.7 | 15.1 | 7.6 | 8.4 | 2.9 | 2.0 | 35 943 | 872 | 51 339 | 1 206 |
| 2014[20] | 16 437 | 100.0 | 22.4 | 14.4 | 12.7 | 14.4 | 15.1 | 8.2 | 8.1 | 2.7 | 2.0 | 35 439 | 462 | 51 289 | 692 |
| 2015[20] | 16 539 | 100.0 | 21.7 | 14.2 | 11.9 | 13.6 | 15.9 | 8.9 | 8.8 | 2.8 | 2.3 | 36 898 | 513 | 54 352 | 861 |

[1]Implementation of a new Curent Population Survey (CPS) Annual Social and Economic Supplements (ASEC) processing system.
[2]Introduction of 1970 census sample design and population controls.
[3]Full implementation of 1970 census–based sample design.
[4]Implementation of a new CPS ASEC processing system. Questionnaire expanded to ask 11 income questions.
[5]Some of these estimates were derived using Pareto interpolation and may differ from published data that were derived using linear interpolation.
[6]First-year medians were derived using both Pareto and linear interpolation. Before this year, all medians were derived using linear interpolation.
[7]Implementation of 1980 census population controls. Questionnaire expanded to show 27 possible values from a list of 51 possible sources of income.
[8]Implementation of Hispanic population weighting controls and introduction of 1980 census–based sample design.
[9]Recording of amounts for earnings from longest job increased to $299,999. Full implementation of 1980 census–based sample design.
[10]Implementation of a new CPS ASEC processing system.
[11]Implementation of 1990 census population controls.
[12]Data collection method changed from paper and pencil to computer-assisted interviewing. In addition, the 1994 ASEC was revised to allow for the coding of different income amounts on selected questionnaire items. Limits either increased or decreased in the following categories: earnings limits increased to $999,999, Social Security limits increased to $49,999, Supplemental Security Income and public assistance limits increased to $24,999, veterans' benefits limits increased to $99,999, and child support and alimony limits decreased to $49,999.
[13]Introduction of 1990 census sample design.
[14]Full implementation of 1990 census–based sample design and metropolitan definitions, 7,000 household sample reduction, and revised editing of responses on race.
[15]Implementation of the 2000 census–based population controls.
[16]Implementation of a 28,000 household sample expansion.
[17]Data revised to reflect a correction to the weights in the 2005 ASEC.
[18]Median income is calculated using $2,500 intervals. Beginning with 2009 income data, the Census Bureau expanded the upper income intervals used to calculate medians to $250,000 or more.
[19]Implementation of 2010 census-based population controls.
[20]Data are based on the CPS ASEC sample of 68,000 addresses. The 2014 CPS ASEC included redesigned questions for income and health insurance coverage.
[21]For 2001 and earlier years, the CPS allowed respondents to report only one race group.
[23]Black alone refers to persons who reported Black and did not report any other race category.
. . . = Not available.
- = Quantity zero.

## Table 13-2. Households, by Total Money Income, Race, and Hispanic Origin of Householder, 1967–2015
### —Continued

(Numbers in thousands, percent, dollars; income in 2015 CPI-U-RS adjusted dollars.)

| Race and Hispanic origin of householder and year | Number | Percent distribution | | | | | | | | | | Median income (dollars) | | Mean income (dollars) | |
|---|---|---|---|---|---|---|---|---|---|---|---|---|---|---|---|
| | | Total | Under $15,000 | $15,000 to $24,999 | $25,000 to $34,999 | $35,000 to $49,999 | $50,000 to $74,999 | $75,000 to $99,999 | $100,000 to $149,999 | $150,000 to $199,000 | $200,000 and over | Value | Standard error | Value | Standard error |
| **Black Alone or in Combination** | | | | | | | | | | | | | | | |
| 2002 | 13 778 | 100.0 | 20.6 | 13.7 | 12.2 | 15.4 | 15.9 | 9.4 | 8.2 | 2.6 | 2.0 | 38 439 | 506 | 53 138 | 619 |
| 2003 | 13 969 | 100.0 | 21.2 | 13.5 | 12.3 | 13.9 | 16.8 | 9.5 | 8.6 | 2.5 | 1.5 | 38 259 | 481 | 51 954 | 550 |
| 2004[17] | 14 151 | 100.0 | 21.4 | 12.7 | 12.9 | 15.2 | 15.7 | 10.0 | 8.0 | 2.5 | 1.6 | 37 938 | 348 | 51 143 | 543 |
| 2005 | 14 399 | 100.0 | 21.5 | 14.7 | 11.2 | 15.0 | 15.9 | 9.2 | 8.2 | 2.8 | 1.5 | 37 568 | 358 | 51 856 | 564 |
| 2006 | 14 709 | 100.0 | 20.7 | 13.8 | 11.2 | 16.3 | 16.0 | 9.1 | 8.5 | 2.5 | 2.0 | 37 773 | 280 | 53 480 | 656 |
| 2007 | 14 976 | 100.0 | 21.2 | 13.2 | 12.1 | 14.1 | 16.6 | 9.5 | 8.9 | 2.8 | 1.7 | 38 971 | 532 | 53 534 | 585 |
| 2008 | 15 056 | 100.0 | 21.1 | 13.4 | 12.6 | 16.0 | 15.7 | 9.0 | 8.0 | 2.7 | 1.5 | 37 809 | 483 | 51 387 | 537 |
| 2009[18] | 15 212 | 100.0 | 21.5 | 13.8 | 13.3 | 14.7 | 15.3 | 9.6 | 7.6 | 2.5 | 1.6 | 36 179 | 462 | 51 125 | 570 |
| 2010[19] | 15 909 | 100.0 | 23.6 | 14.1 | 12.5 | 14.2 | 14.8 | 9.3 | 7.4 | 2.5 | 1.5 | 34 957 | 511 | 49 462 | 682 |
| 2011 | 16 165 | 100.0 | 24.3 | 14.5 | 12.3 | 13.4 | 15.3 | 8.4 | 7.5 | 2.6 | 1.8 | 34 110 | 583 | 50 065 | 815 |
| 2012 | 16 559 | 100.0 | 23.5 | 15.0 | 11.7 | 14.3 | 15.0 | 8.6 | 8.0 | 2.3 | 1.6 | 34 808 | 824 | 49 716 | 762 |
| 2013[20] | 16 723 | 100.0 | 22.3 | 14.0 | 12.5 | 14.9 | 15.2 | 7.4 | 8.7 | 3.0 | 2.0 | 36 391 | 792 | 52 580 | 1 346 |
| 2014 | 17 198 | 100.0 | 22.2 | 14.4 | 12.6 | 14.5 | 15.1 | 8.3 | 8.2 | 2.8 | 2.1 | 35 694 | 473 | 51 680 | 694 |
| 2015 | 17 322 | 100.0 | 21.5 | 14.1 | 11.8 | 13.5 | 16.0 | 9.0 | 8.8 | 2.8 | 2.4 | 37 211 | 546 | 54 805 | 867 |
| **Asian and Pacific Islander[21]** | | | | | | | | | | | | | | | |
| 1987[10] | . . . | 100.0 | 10.7 | 11.0 | 7.8 | 10.8 | 18.9 | 13.0 | 17.3 | 7.0 | 3.4 | 64 267 | 2 389 | . . . | . . . |
| 1988 | 1 913 | 100.0 | 8.6 | 10.5 | 9.1 | 11.5 | 18.6 | 14.7 | 15.6 | 7.1 | 4.3 | 62 071 | 2 551 | 77 603 | 2 318 |
| 1989 | 1 988 | 100.0 | 8.7 | 8.0 | 7.5 | 12.5 | 19.9 | 15.2 | 16.8 | 5.0 | 6.0 | 66 576 | 1 800 | 82 764 | 2 408 |
| 1990 | 1 958 | 100.0 | 9.3 | 8.2 | 7.8 | 12.4 | 18.5 | 14.0 | 18.0 | 6.0 | 5.0 | 67 574 | 2 002 | 81 567 | 2 309 |
| 1991 | 2 094 | 100.0 | 10.9 | 8.2 | 9.3 | 12.4 | 17.9 | 14.1 | 15.4 | 7.0 | 4.0 | 61 809 | 1 994 | 78 476 | 2 313 |
| 1992[11] | 2 262 | 100.0 | 10.8 | 9.4 | 8.8 | 11.2 | 19.0 | 13.4 | 16.0 | 6.0 | 4.0 | 62 516 | 1 804 | 77 482 | 2 130 |
| 1993[12] | 2 233 | 100.0 | 13.0 | 8.9 | 9.1 | 11.6 | 15.0 | 13.9 | 17.0 | 6.0 | 4.0 | 61 889 | 3 044 | 81 090 | 3 265 |
| 1994[13] | 2 040 | 100.0 | 10.5 | 9.9 | 7.3 | 12.7 | 17.3 | 14.0 | 16.3 | 6.0 | 5.0 | 63 998 | 2 425 | 83 096 | 2 961 |
| 1995[14] | 2 777 | 100.0 | 11.0 | 9.9 | 6.4 | 12.1 | 19.2 | 14.2 | 15.5 | 5.0 | 6.0 | 62 697 | 1 573 | 85 257 | 3 439 |
| 1996 | 2 998 | 100.0 | 11.0 | 7.5 | 8.0 | 11.7 | 18.7 | 12.5 | 17.9 | 7.0 | 4.0 | 65 045 | 2 331 | 84 992 | 3 048 |
| 1997 | 3 125 | 100.0 | 10.4 | 7.9 | 7.3 | 10.7 | 19.1 | 14.5 | 16.0 | 7.0 | 5.0 | 66 572 | 1 851 | 86 641 | 2 685 |
| 1998 | 3 308 | 100.0 | 9.8 | 7.7 | 7.4 | 12.3 | 18.0 | 11.7 | 18.0 | 7.0 | 6.3 | 67 698 | 1 884 | 87 397 | 2 524 |
| 1999[15] | 3 742 | 100.0 | 9.5 | 7.1 | 6.8 | 11.8 | 16.0 | 13.2 | 16.0 | 9.0 | 9.0 | 72 431 | 2 553 | 95 779 | 2 428 |
| 2000[16] | 3 963 | 100.0 | 8.1 | 6.8 | 7.4 | 10.9 | 15.8 | 14.4 | 18.1 | 9.0 | 8.0 | 76 649 | 1 307 | 100 074 | 2 077 |
| 2001 | 4 071 | 100.0 | 9.4 | 6.9 | 7.9 | 11.5 | 16.7 | 13.0 | 17.0 | 8.0 | 8.0 | 71 720 | 1 712 | 97 827 | 2 309 |
| **Asian Alone[24]** | | | | | | | | | | | | | | | |
| 2002 | 3 917 | 100.0 | 9.0 | 7.2 | 8.3 | 11.6 | 17.4 | 12.8 | 17.6 | 8.4 | 7.7 | 69 332 | 1 213 | 92 283 | 1 800 |
| 2003 | 4 040 | 100.0 | 12.1 | 8.4 | 5.6 | 9.3 | 16.7 | 13.9 | 17.6 | 8.6 | 7.9 | 71 778 | 1 410 | 90 172 | 1 597 |
| 2004[17] | 4 123 | 100.0 | 9.2 | 6.9 | 7.9 | 9.6 | 17.9 | 13.4 | 17.7 | 9.2 | 8.3 | 72 155 | 1 533 | 96 012 | 1 857 |
| 2005 | 4 273 | 100.0 | 10.1 | 7.5 | 6.5 | 9.3 | 17.6 | 12.6 | 18.6 | 8.2 | 9.7 | 74 148 | 864 | 97 210 | 1 715 |
| 2006 | 4 454 | 100.0 | 8.9 | 6.9 | 7.2 | 10.1 | 16.9 | 12.7 | 17.7 | 10.3 | 9.3 | 75 515 | 1 968 | 103 793 | 2 234 |
| 2007 | 4 494 | 100.0 | 9.2 | 7.4 | 7.6 | 9.3 | 16.5 | 12.7 | 19.3 | 9.2 | 8.9 | 75 565 | 1 583 | 97 187 | 1 715 |
| 2008 | 4 573 | 100.0 | 10.9 | 7.6 | 7.5 | 11.5 | 14.1 | 12.9 | 17.4 | 9.7 | 8.5 | 72 257 | 1 526 | 94 877 | 1 655 |
| 2009[18] | 4 687 | 100.0 | 10.8 | 6.9 | 8.2 | 9.9 | 15.9 | 12.6 | 16.9 | 8.9 | 9.9 | 72 323 | 1 400 | 100 318 | 2 038 |
| 2010[19] | 5 212 | 100.0 | 10.1 | 8.4 | 7.8 | 9.5 | 17.7 | 11.7 | 16.5 | 9.9 | 8.4 | 69 856 | 1 712 | 91 952 | 1 844 |
| 2011 | 5 374 | 100.0 | 9.9 | 8.6 | 8.3 | 10.8 | 17.0 | 12.6 | 17.7 | 7.5 | 7.8 | 68 638 | 1 651 | 90 258 | 2 185 |
| 2012 | 5 560 | 100.0 | 10.3 | 7.1 | 7.4 | 10.6 | 17.4 | 12.4 | 16.9 | 8.8 | 9.1 | 70 854 | 1 591 | 94 354 | 1 895 |
| 2013[20] | 5 818 | 100.0 | 10.4 | 7.9 | 5.2 | 10.4 | 16.8 | 12.4 | 16.9 | 8.5 | 11.5 | 73 652 | 3 421 | 102 984 | 4 544 |
| 2014 | 6 040 | 100.0 | 10.3 | 7.0 | 7.7 | 9.7 | 15.6 | 11.8 | 18.4 | 9.7 | 9.8 | 74 382 | 2 109 | 97 674 | 1 922 |
| 2015 | 6 328 | 100.0 | 9.7 | 6.7 | 6.2 | 10.2 | 15.5 | 12.2 | 16.8 | 10.5 | 12.1 | 77 166 | 1 697 | 105 417 | 2 227 |
| **Asian Alone or in Combination** | | | | | | | | | | | | | | | |
| 2002 | 4 079 | 100.0 | 9.2 | 7.1 | 8.3 | 11.5 | 17.7 | 12.8 | 17.4 | 8.4 | 7.5 | 68 882 | 1 042 | 91 531 | 1 740 |
| 2003 | 4 235 | 100.0 | 11.9 | 8.4 | 5.9 | 9.3 | 16.9 | 13.9 | 17.5 | 8.5 | 7.7 | 71 215 | 1 588 | 89 450 | 1 539 |
| 2004[17] | 4 346 | 100.0 | 9.2 | 6.9 | 7.8 | 9.6 | 18.1 | 13.5 | 17.6 | 9.2 | 8.1 | 72 086 | 1 453 | 95 527 | 1 803 |
| 2005 | 4 500 | 100.0 | 10.0 | 7.5 | 6.4 | 9.5 | 17.5 | 12.6 | 18.7 | 8.1 | 9.7 | 74 092 | 885 | 97 089 | 1 694 |
| 2006 | 4 664 | 100.0 | 8.8 | 6.8 | 7.1 | 10.3 | 17.1 | 12.9 | 17.7 | 10.3 | 9.0 | 75 118 | 1 901 | 102 894 | 2 154 |
| 2007 | 4 715 | 100.0 | 9.2 | 7.3 | 7.6 | 9.5 | 16.4 | 12.9 | 18.9 | 9.4 | 8.8 | 75 305 | 1 584 | 96 665 | 1 653 |
| 2008 | 4 805 | 100.0 | 10.7 | 7.6 | 7.5 | 11.7 | 14.1 | 13.0 | 17.5 | 9.4 | 8.6 | 72 180 | 1 556 | 95 029 | 1 637 |
| 2009[18] | 4 940 | 100.0 | 10.9 | 6.9 | 8.2 | 10.3 | 15.7 | 12.5 | 16.8 | 8.9 | 9.8 | 71 886 | 1 585 | 99 544 | 1 955 |
| 2010[19] | 5 550 | 100.0 | 9.9 | 8.4 | 8.1 | 9.9 | 17.6 | 11.8 | 16.4 | 9.6 | 8.3 | 69 061 | 1 593 | 91 005 | 1 748 |
| 2011 | 5 705 | 100.0 | 10.0 | 8.7 | 8.2 | 10.8 | 16.8 | 12.6 | 17.6 | 7.4 | 8.0 | 68 497 | 1 648 | 90 407 | 2 164 |
| 2012 | 5 872 | 100.0 | 10.2 | 7.1 | 7.4 | 10.7 | 17.7 | 12.3 | 16.7 | 8.7 | 9.2 | 70 385 | 1 793 | 94 666 | 1 955 |
| 2013[20] | 6 160 | 100.0 | 10.3 | 7.8 | 5.5 | 10.7 | 16.5 | 12.7 | 16.8 | 8.6 | 11.2 | 73 743 | 3 248 | 102 850 | 4 298 |
| 2014[20] | 6 333 | 100.0 | 10.0 | 6.9 | 7.7 | 9.7 | 15.7 | 12.2 | 18.4 | 9.5 | 9.8 | 74 915 | 1 983 | 98 255 | 1 929 |
| 2015[20] | 6 640 | 100.0 | 9.9 | 6.9 | 6.1 | 10.3 | 15.5 | 12.2 | 16.7 | 10.5 | 12.0 | 76 761 | 1 399 | 105 132 | 2 199 |

[10]Implementation of a new CPS ASEC processing system.
[11]Implementation of 1990 census population controls.
[12]Data collection method changed from paper and pencil to computer-assisted interviewing. In addition, the 1994 ASEC was revised to allow for the coding of different income amounts on selected questionnaire items. Limits either increased or decreased in the following categories: earnings limits increased to $999,999, Social Security limits increased to $49,999, Supplemental Security Income and public assistance limits increased to $24,999, veterans' benefits limits increased to $99,999, and child support and alimony limits decreased to $49,999.
[13]Introduction of 1990 census sample design.
[14]Full implementation of 1990 census–based sample design and metropolitan definitions, 7,000 household sample reduction, and revised editing of responses on race.
[15]Implementation of the 2000 census–based population controls.
[16]Implementation of a 28,000 household sample expansion.
[17]Data revised to reflect a correction to the weights in the 2005 ASEC.
[18]Median income is calculated using $2,500 intervals. Beginning with 2009 income data, the Census Bureau expanded the upper income intervals used to calculate medians to $250,000 or more.
[19]Implementation of 2010 census-based population controls.
[20]Data are based on the CPS ASEC sample of 68,000 addresses. The 2014 CPS ASEC included redesigned questions for income and health insurance coverage.
[21]For 2001 and earlier years, the CPS allowed respondents to report only one race group.
[24]Asian alone refers to persons who reported Asian and did not report any other race category.
. . . = Not available.

## Table 13-2. Households, by Total Money Income, Race, and Hispanic Origin of Householder, 1967–2015
### —Continued

(Numbers in thousands, percent, dollars; income in 2015 CPI-U-RS adjusted dollars.)

| Race and Hispanic origin of householder and year | Number | Percent distribution | | | | | | | | | | Median income (dollars) | | Mean income (dollars) | |
|---|---|---|---|---|---|---|---|---|---|---|---|---|---|---|---|
| | | Total | Under $15,000 | $15,000 to $24,999 | $25,000 to $34,999 | $35,000 to $49,999 | $50,000 to $74,999 | $75,000 to $99,999 | $100,000 to $149,999 | $150,000 to $199,000 | $200,000 and over | Value | Standard error | Value | Standard error |
| **Hispanic[25]** | | | | | | | | | | | | | | | |
| 1972[3] | 2 655 | 100.0 | 13.5 | 17.0 | 14.3 | 21.3 | 20.7 | 8.3 | 3.7 | 0.7 | 0.5 | 38 910 | 760 | 44 724 | 76 |
| 1973 | 2 722 | 100.0 | 13.9 | 15.8 | 14.7 | 19.3 | 22.3 | 8.5 | 4.6 | 0.6 | 0.3 | 38 846 | 882 | 45 132 | 735 |
| 1974[4,5] | 2 897 | 100.0 | 14.8 | 16.2 | 14.9 | 18.8 | 21.3 | 8.4 | 4.3 | 0.8 | 0.4 | 38 619 | 846 | 44 737 | 728 |
| 1975[5] | 2 948 | 100.0 | 17.7 | 16.9 | 15.0 | 18.2 | 20.0 | 7.6 | 3.4 | 0.6 | 0.5 | 35 521 | 785 | 42 169 | 749 |
| 1976[6] | 3 081 | 100.0 | 18.0 | 16.9 | 13.6 | 18.4 | 19.7 | 8.6 | 4.1 | 0.6 | 0.2 | 36 256 | 773 | 42 845 | 697 |
| 1977 | 3 304 | 100.0 | 16.0 | 15.5 | 14.3 | 19.1 | 20.2 | 8.9 | 4.8 | 1.0 | 0.3 | 37 946 | 666 | 44 781 | 691 |
| 1978 | 3 291 | 100.0 | 15.5 | 14.7 | 14.1 | 17.6 | 21.4 | 9.9 | 5.4 | 1.1 | 0.3 | 39 366 | 954 | 46 500 | 941 |
| 1979[7] | 3 684 | 100.0 | 15.9 | 14.2 | 14.4 | 17.2 | 20.5 | 9.9 | 6.1 | 1.2 | 0.7 | 39 731 | 1 145 | 48 072 | 966 |
| 1980 | 3 906 | 100.0 | 17.5 | 15.6 | 13.6 | 17.8 | 18.8 | 9.6 | 5.3 | 1.2 | 0.5 | 37 398 | 1 014 | 45 680 | 910 |
| 1981 | 3 980 | 100.0 | 16.8 | 15.1 | 13.8 | 17.7 | 19.7 | 9.8 | 5.7 | 0.9 | 0.5 | 38 272 | 1 048 | 45 959 | 878 |
| 1982 | 4 085 | 100.0 | 19.5 | 16.4 | 13.2 | 17.7 | 17.4 | 8.9 | 5.2 | 1.0 | 0.6 | 35 806 | 946 | 44 190 | 896 |
| 1983 | 4 326 | 100.0 | 20.5 | 15.6 | 13.1 | 17.4 | 17.8 | 8.8 | 5.5 | 1.0 | 0.4 | 36 011 | 912 | 43 851 | 842 |
| 1984[8] | 4 883 | 100.0 | 19.3 | 15.2 | 14.0 | 15.2 | 18.8 | 9.7 | 5.9 | 1.3 | 0.5 | 36 933 | 926 | 45 925 | 895 |
| 1985[9] | 5 213 | 100.0 | 19.2 | 16.0 | 12.7 | 16.0 | 18.7 | 8.9 | 6.7 | 1.1 | 0.6 | 36 701 | 857 | 45 859 | 746 |
| 1986 | 5 418 | 100.0 | 18.2 | 16.0 | 12.6 | 15.9 | 17.9 | 9.7 | 7.5 | 1.6 | 0.6 | 37 879 | 987 | 47 830 | 786 |
| 1987[10] | 5 642 | 100.0 | 18.7 | 14.9 | 12.4 | 16.9 | 17.5 | 10.0 | 6.5 | 1.8 | 1.3 | 38 605 | 839 | 49 487 | 916 |
| 1988 | 5 910 | 100.0 | 18.5 | 13.4 | 13.5 | 16.0 | 18.6 | 10.0 | 6.9 | 1.9 | 1.2 | 39 209 | 994 | 50 060 | 1 061 |
| 1989 | 5 933 | 100.0 | 17.3 | 13.7 | 12.1 | 16.5 | 18.3 | 11.2 | 7.5 | 2.0 | 1.3 | 40 471 | 785 | 51 680 | 888 |
| 1990 | 6 220 | 100.0 | 17.3 | 15.5 | 12.0 | 16.9 | 19.0 | 9.7 | 6.9 | 1.7 | 1.1 | 39 289 | 806 | 49 216 | 811 |
| 1991 | 6 379 | 100.0 | 17.4 | 14.8 | 13.5 | 16.6 | 18.1 | 9.4 | 7.1 | 2.0 | 1.0 | 38 523 | 801 | 49 016 | 784 |
| 1992[11] | 7 153 | 100.0 | 18.8 | 15.3 | 13.7 | 16.8 | 16.9 | 9.3 | 6.5 | 1.9 | 0.9 | 37 415 | 773 | 47 721 | 750 |
| 1993[12] | 7 362 | 100.0 | 18.6 | 15.6 | 13.5 | 17.0 | 17.2 | 8.7 | 6.7 | 1.5 | 1.2 | 36 979 | 743 | 48 944 | 1 029 |
| 1994[13] | 7 735 | 100.0 | 19.2 | 15.8 | 12.7 | 15.9 | 17.0 | 9.1 | 7.0 | 2.0 | 1.3 | 37 069 | 688 | 49 986 | 1 247 |
| 1995[14] | 7 939 | 100.0 | 19.2 | 16.8 | 13.5 | 16.1 | 16.0 | 9.2 | 6.5 | 1.6 | 1.1 | 35 330 | 770 | 48 221 | 1 082 |
| 1996 | 8 225 | 100.0 | 17.2 | 16.0 | 14.0 | 16.2 | 16.7 | 9.5 | 7.0 | 2.1 | 1.3 | 37 477 | 727 | 51 169 | 1 184 |
| 1997 | 8 590 | 100.0 | 17.9 | 14.0 | 13.4 | 15.9 | 18.5 | 9.1 | 7.5 | 2.1 | 1.7 | 39 221 | 700 | 52 853 | 1 066 |
| 1998 | 9 060 | 100.0 | 16.2 | 14.1 | 12.4 | 16.8 | 17.8 | 10.1 | 8.5 | 2.2 | 1.8 | 41 171 | 793 | 55 631 | 1 183 |
| 1999[15] | 9 579 | 100.0 | 13.1 | 13.9 | 13.0 | 17.2 | 18.3 | 10.6 | 9.7 | 2.3 | 2.0 | 43 751 | 636 | 57 474 | 1 020 |
| 2000[16] | 10 034 | 100.0 | 12.3 | 13.4 | 12.1 | 16.7 | 19.5 | 11.5 | 9.5 | 2.7 | 2.1 | 45 649 | 658 | 60 526 | 871 |
| 2001 | 10 499 | 100.0 | 12.8 | 13.5 | 12.8 | 16.4 | 18.5 | 11.3 | 9.5 | 3.0 | 2.0 | 44 934 | 570 | 59 416 | 751 |
| 2002 | 11 339 | 100.0 | 13.1 | 13.0 | 13.8 | 16.4 | 18.6 | 11.0 | 9.2 | 2.7 | 2.1 | 43 611 | 635 | 59 136 | 790 |
| 2003 | 11 693 | 100.0 | 13.6 | 13.6 | 13.5 | 16.9 | 18.0 | 10.7 | 9.1 | 2.5 | 2.2 | 42 522 | 592 | 57 305 | 634 |
| 2004[17] | 12 178 | 100.0 | 13.5 | 13.2 | 14.2 | 15.9 | 19.3 | 10.3 | 8.7 | 2.8 | 2.1 | 43 002 | 602 | 57 565 | 704 |
| 2005 | 12 519 | 100.0 | 13.9 | 13.7 | 12.1 | 17.3 | 18.7 | 10.4 | 8.9 | 2.7 | 2.2 | 43 652 | 433 | 57 210 | 575 |
| 2006 | 12 973 | 100.0 | 13.6 | 13.3 | 11.3 | 17.7 | 18.6 | 10.9 | 9.4 | 3.3 | 2.0 | 44 414 | 594 | 59 454 | 682 |
| 2007 | 13 339 | 100.0 | 13.9 | 12.9 | 13.5 | 15.4 | 19.0 | 11.1 | 9.3 | 2.9 | 2.0 | 44 215 | 594 | 58 103 | 612 |
| 2008 | 13 425 | 100.0 | 15.1 | 13.6 | 13.1 | 17.1 | 17.0 | 9.8 | 9.3 | 3.2 | 1.9 | 41 737 | 535 | 56 773 | 588 |
| 2009[18] | 13 298 | 100.0 | 14.7 | 13.9 | 13.5 | 15.7 | 17.6 | 10.5 | 9.1 | 2.9 | 2.2 | 42 022 | 555 | 57 697 | 633 |
| 2010[19] | 14 435 | 100.0 | 15.8 | 13.9 | 14.1 | 14.8 | 17.6 | 10.2 | 8.6 | 3.2 | 1.8 | 40 909 | 633 | 55 871 | 717 |
| 2011 | 14 939 | 100.0 | 15.8 | 13.7 | 14.0 | 16.6 | 17.3 | 9.1 | 8.4 | 3.0 | 1.9 | 40 705 | 576 | 55 172 | 626 |
| 2012 | 15 589 | 100.0 | 16.4 | 14.4 | 13.1 | 15.8 | 17.4 | 9.7 | 8.4 | 2.8 | 2.0 | 40 265 | 551 | 55 148 | 721 |
| 2013[20] | 16 088 | 100.0 | 15.3 | 14.7 | 14.4 | 15.1 | 15.7 | 10.0 | 8.8 | 3.2 | 2.9 | 40 383 | 1 209 | 58 627 | 1 732 |
| 2014[20] | 16 239 | 100.0 | 14.6 | 14.1 | 12.4 | 15.6 | 18.0 | 10.7 | 9.7 | 2.8 | 2.2 | 42 540 | 517 | 57 600 | 657 |
| 2015[20] | 16 667 | 100.0 | 13.6 | 13.0 | 12.7 | 15.1 | 18.1 | 10.8 | 9.7 | 3.7 | 3.2 | 45 148 | 615 | 63 612 | 837 |

3Full implementation of 1970 census–based sample design.
4Implementation of a new CPS ASEC processing system. Questionnaire expanded to ask 11 income questions.
5Some of these estimates were derived using Pareto interpolation and may differ from published data that were derived using linear interpolation.
6First-year medians were derived using both Pareto and linear interpolation. Before this year, all medians were derived using linear interpolation.
7Implementation of 1980 census population controls. Questionnaire expanded to show 27 possible values from a list of 51 possible sources of income.
8Implementation of Hispanic population weighting controls and introduction of 1980 census–based sample design.
9Recording of amounts for earnings from longest job increased to $299,999. Full implementation of 1980 census–based sample design.
10Implementation of a new CPS ASEC processing system.
11Implementation of 1990 census population controls.
12Data collection method changed from paper and pencil to computer-assisted interviewing. In addition, the 1994 ASEC was revised to allow for the coding of different income amounts on selected questionnaire items. Limits either increased or decreased in the following categories: earnings limits increased to $999,999, Social Security limits increased to $49,999, Supplemental Security Income and public assistance limits increased to $24,999, veterans' benefits limits increased to $99,999, and child support and alimony limits decreased to $49,999.
13Introduction of 1990 census sample design.
14Full implementation of 1990 census–based sample design and metropolitan definitions, 7,000 household sample reduction, and revised editing of responses on race.
15Implementation of the 2000 census–based population controls.
16Implementation of a 28,000 household sample expansion.
17Data revised to reflect a correction to the weights in the 2005 ASEC.
18Median income is calculated using $2,500 intervals. Beginning with 2009 income data, the Census Bureau expanded the upper income intervals used to calculate medians to $250,000 or more.
19Implementation of 2010 census-based population controls.
20Data are based on the CPS ASEC sample of 68,000 addresses. The 2014 CPS ASEC included redesigned questions for income and health insurance coverage.
25Because Hispanics may be of any race, data in this report for Hispanics overlap with data for racial groups. Hispanic origin was reported by 15.0 percent of White householders who reported only one race, 4.3 percent of Black householders who reported only one race, and 2.4 percent of Asian householders who reported only one race. Data users should exercise caution when interpreting aggregate results for the Hispanic population and for race groups, because these populations consist of many distinct groups that differ in socioeconomic characteristics, culture, and recentness of immigration. Data were first collected for Hispanics in 1972.

## Table 13-3.  Income Deficit or Surplus of Families and Unrelated Individuals by Poverty Status, 2015

(Numbers of families and unrelated individuals in thousands, deficits and surpluses in dollars.)

| Characteristic | Total | Size of deficit or surplus | | | | | | | | Average deficit or surplus (dollars) | | Deficit or surplus per capita (dollars) | |
|---|---|---|---|---|---|---|---|---|---|---|---|---|---|
| | | Under $1,000 | $1,000 to $2,499 | $2,500 to $4,999 | $5,000 to $7,499 | $7,500 to $9,999 | $10,000 to $12,499 | $12,500 to $14,499 | $15,000 or more | Estimate | 90 percent confidence interval[1] (+/-) | Estimate | 90 percent confidence interval[1] (+/-) |
| **Below Poverty Threshold, Deficit** | | | | | | | | | | | | | |
| All families ............... | 8 589 | 482 | 836 | 1 304 | 1 184 | 886 | 806 | 840 | 2 251 | 10 118 | 178 | 2 907 | 54 |
| Married-couple families ............... | 3 245 | 242 | 376 | 556 | 410 | 339 | 239 | 350 | 732 | 9 456 | 303 | 2 501 | 83 |
| Families with a female householder, no husband present ............... | 4 404 | 180 | 339 | 603 | 637 | 448 | 484 | 423 | 1 290 | 10 759 | 236 | 3 219 | 73 |
| Families with a male householder, no wife present ............... | 939 | 60 | 121 | 145 | 138 | 99 | 82 | 66 | 230 | 9 402 | 611 | 3 041 | 180 |
| Unrelated individuals ............... | 12 671 | 1 312 | 1 985 | 2 347 | 1 209 | 897 | 4 921 | – | – | 6 873 | 110 | 6 873 | 110 |
| **Above Poverty Threshold, Surplus** | | | | | | | | | | | | | |
| All families ............... | 73 610 | 621 | 903 | 1 568 | 1 659 | 1 851 | 1 909 | 1 805 | 63 295 | 82 483 | 938 | 26 603 | 333 |
| Married-couple families ............... | 57 013 | 307 | 456 | 725 | 920 | 1 057 | 1 139 | 1 141 | 51 267 | 92 683 | 1 162 | 29 509 | 397 |
| Families with a female householder, no husband present ............... | 11 225 | 242 | 341 | 672 | 543 | 568 | 574 | 475 | 7 811 | 42 299 | 1 212 | 14 057 | 434 |
| Families with a male householder, no wife present ............... | 5 372 | 72 | 106 | 171 | 196 | 226 | 196 | 189 | 4 217 | 58 203 | 2 792 | 20 326 | 1 059 |
| Unrelated individuals ............... | 46 317 | 1 064 | 1 426 | 3 171 | 2 469 | 2 963 | 2 252 | 2 834 | 30 139 | 37 608 | 780 | 37 608 | 780 |

[1]A 90 percent confidence interval is a measure of an estimate's variability. The larger the confidence interval in relation to the size of the estimate, the less reliable the estimate.
– = Quantity represents or rounds to zero.

## Table 13-4.  Income Distribution Measures Using Money Income and Equivalence-Adjusted Income, 2014 and 2015

(Percent distribution.)

| Measure | 2014 | | | | 2015 | | | | Percent change (2014–2015) | | | |
|---|---|---|---|---|---|---|---|---|---|---|---|---|
| | Money income | | Equivalence-adjusted income | | Money income | | Equivalence-adjusted income | | Money income | | Equivalence-adjusted income | |
| | Estimate | 90 percent confidence interval[1] (+/-) | Estimate | 90 percent confidence interval[1] (+/-) | Estimate | 90 percent confidence interval[1] (+/-) | Estimate | 90 percent confidence interval[1] (+/-) | Estimate | 90 percent confidence interval[1] (+/-) | Estimate | 90 percent confidence interval[1] (+/-) |
| **Shares of Aggregate Income by Percentile** | | | | | | | | | | | | |
| Lowest quintile ............... | 3.1 | 0.05 | 3.3 | 0.05 | 3.1 | 0.05 | 3.4 | 0.06 | 1.0 | 2.31 | 3.0 | 2.37 |
| Second quintile ............... | 8.2 | 0.08 | 9.0 | 0.08 | 8.2 | 0.09 | 9.0 | 0.09 | 0.0 | 1.46 | 0.6 | 1.31 |
| Middle quintile ............... | 14.3 | 0.11 | 14.8 | 0.11 | 14.3 | 0.12 | 14.8 | 0.11 | 0.5 | 1.12 | 0.4 | 1.05 |
| Fourth quintile ............... | 23.2 | 0.15 | 22.9 | 0.14 | 23.2 | 0.15 | 22.9 | 0.14 | 0.1 | 0.89 | -0.1 | 0.86 |
| Highest quintile ............... | 51.2 | 0.33 | 50.0 | 0.32 | 51.1 | 0.32 | 49.8 | 0.33 | -0.4 | 0.88 | -0.4 | 0.92 |
| Top 5 percent ............... | 21.9 | 0.39 | 21.8 | 0.39 | 22.1 | 0.38 | 21.8 | 0.38 | 0.9 | 2.53 | 0.4 | 2.55 |
| **Summary Measures** | | | | | | | | | | | | |
| Gini index of income inequality ............... | 0.480 | 0.003 | 0.464 | 0.003 | 0.479 | 0.003 | 0.462 | 0.004 | -0.30 | 0.98 | -0.50 | 1.03 |

[1]A 90-percent confidence interval is a measure of an estimate's variability. The larger the confidence interval in relation to the size of the estimate, the less reliable the estimate.
– = Quantity represents or rounds to zero.

## Table 13-5.   Median Household Income by State, 2005 to 2015

(Income in 2015 CPI-U-RS adjusted dollars.)

| State | 2005 | 2006 | 2007 | 2008 | 2009 | 2010 | 2011 | 2012 | 2013 | 2014 | 2015 |
|---|---|---|---|---|---|---|---|---|---|---|---|
| UNITED STATES | 56 224 | 56 663 | 57 423 | 55 376 | 54 988 | 53 568 | 52 751 | 52 666 | 54 525 | 53 718 | 56 516 |
| Alabama | 45 088 | 44 615 | 48 254 | 48 962 | 44 166 | 44 499 | 44 884 | 44 869 | 48 150 | 42 327 | 44 509 |
| Alaska | 67 833 | 66 323 | 72 010 | 70 443 | 68 054 | 62 887 | 60 525 | 65 705 | 73 743 | 67 707 | 75 112 |
| Arizona | 54 912 | 54 848 | 53 973 | 51 645 | 50 528 | 50 981 | 51 240 | 48 564 | 53 533 | 49 311 | 52 248 |
| Arkansas | 44 490 | 43 563 | 46 634 | 43 578 | 40 363 | 41 948 | 43 527 | 40 279 | 40 066 | 44 974 | 42 798 |
| California | 62 813 | 65 031 | 63 712 | 62 764 | 62 011 | 59 011 | 56 242 | 58 863 | 61 860 | 60 557 | 63 636 |
| Colorado | 61 228 | 65 475 | 69 893 | 67 089 | 61 786 | 65 480 | 61 788 | 59 105 | 69 103 | 61 010 | 66 596 |
| Connecticut | 68 979 | 73 359 | 73 322 | 71 205 | 71 641 | 71 747 | 68 939 | 66 323 | 70 506 | 70 242 | 72 889 |
| Delaware | 62 182 | 61 644 | 62 403 | 55 815 | 57 570 | 60 023 | 57 605 | 50 555 | 55 039 | 57 588 | 57 756 |
| District of Columbia | 54 606 | 56 987 | 58 052 | 61 196 | 58 705 | 61 887 | 58 228 | 67 354 | 61 110 | 68 356 | 70 071 |
| Florida | 52 175 | 53 695 | 52 349 | 49 381 | 50 408 | 47 904 | 47 535 | 47 560 | 49 383 | 46 193 | 48 825 |
| Georgia | 55 739 | 58 007 | 55 603 | 50 889 | 47 878 | 47 960 | 48 450 | 49 676 | 47 816 | 49 612 | 50 768 |
| Hawaii | 72 317 | 71 086 | 73 186 | 67 726 | 61 475 | 64 725 | 62 228 | 58 081 | 65 361 | 71 305 | 64 514 |
| Idaho | 53 615 | 54 326 | 56 224 | 52 202 | 51 675 | 58 405 | 50 016 | 49 471 | 49 317 | 53 499 | 51 624 |
| Illinois | 58 739 | 57 216 | 60 022 | 58 625 | 58 405 | 55 147 | 55 365 | 53 410 | 54 883 | 54 979 | 60 413 |
| Indiana | 51 504 | 53 379 | 54 245 | 51 212 | 48 944 | 50 158 | 46 839 | 47 650 | 50 322 | 48 115 | 51 983 |
| Iowa | 56 435 | 56 575 | 55 909 | 55 199 | 56 031 | 53 286 | 52 925 | 55 169 | 61 211 | 57 876 | 60 855 |
| Kansas | 51 007 | 53 549 | 55 439 | 52 706 | 49 399 | 50 066 | 48 633 | 51 619 | 48 658 | 53 505 | 54 865 |
| Kentucky | 44 540 | 46 417 | 45 099 | 45 298 | 47 131 | 44 684 | 42 003 | 42 414 | 45 666 | 42 835 | 42 387 |
| Louisiana | 45 192 | 42 894 | 47 226 | 43 553 | 50 190 | 42 723 | 42 848 | 40 348 | 47 239 | 42 455 | 45 922 |
| Maine | 53 308 | 53 655 | 54 749 | 51 991 | 52 475 | 52 106 | 52 370 | 50 747 | 55 921 | 51 769 | 50 756 |
| Maryland | 73 441 | 74 845 | 75 024 | 70 136 | 70 906 | 69 793 | 72 587 | 74 157 | 70 569 | 76 253 | 73 594 |
| Massachusetts | 67 986 | 65 044 | 66 831 | 66 403 | 65 589 | 66 242 | 66 724 | 65 713 | 63 625 | 63 224 | 67 861 |
| Michigan | 55 747 | 57 187 | 56 437 | 54 809 | 50 809 | 50 307 | 51 512 | 51 631 | 57 559 | 52 065 | 54 203 |
| Minnesota | 65 799 | 66 079 | 66 368 | 60 464 | 61 962 | 56 878 | 60 935 | 63 792 | 65 452 | 67 321 | 68 730 |
| Mississippi | 39 899 | 40 831 | 42 615 | 40 122 | 38 751 | 41 484 | 43 304 | 37 825 | 32 905 | 35 562 | 40 037 |
| Missouri | 52 171 | 52 405 | 52 590 | 50 681 | 53 875 | 49 808 | 48 240 | 51 372 | 47 115 | 56 695 | 59 196 |
| Montana | 45 285 | 48 321 | 49 904 | 47 227 | 44 671 | 44 876 | 42 447 | 46 545 | 43 958 | 51 161 | 51 395 |
| Nebraska | 58 162 | 56 597 | 56 213 | 55 844 | 54 787 | 57 077 | 58 612 | 53 883 | 58 633 | 56 935 | 60 474 |
| Nevada | 58 509 | 61 460 | 61 796 | 60 265 | 56 819 | 55 660 | 49 577 | 48 863 | 52 755 | 49 932 | 52 008 |
| New Hampshire | 69 159 | 72 849 | 77 249 | 72 850 | 70 845 | 72 437 | 69 429 | 70 011 | 70 311 | 73 481 | 75 675 |
| New Jersey | 76 907 | 80 007 | 69 169 | 71 892 | 71 559 | 68 453 | 65 696 | 68 847 | 64 872 | 65 318 | 68 357 |
| New Mexico | 47 269 | 47 055 | 50 705 | 46 348 | 48 101 | 49 065 | 44 244 | 44 827 | 40 870 | 46 740 | 45 119 |
| New York | 57 256 | 56 688 | 55 950 | 55 550 | 55 473 | 54 117 | 53 364 | 49 221 | 50 842 | 54 372 | 58 005 |
| North Carolina | 51 042 | 46 784 | 49 741 | 47 260 | 46 293 | 47 648 | 47 641 | 42 896 | 47 149 | 46 838 | 50 797 |
| North Dakota | 51 207 | 48 253 | 53 962 | 54 636 | 55 318 | 55 449 | 59 397 | 57 568 | 60 189 | 60 800 | 57 415 |
| Ohio | 53 648 | 53 958 | 56 127 | 51 667 | 50 682 | 49 883 | 47 053 | 45 809 | 51 638 | 49 701 | 53 301 |
| Oklahoma | 45 688 | 45 656 | 49 402 | 50 761 | 50 681 | 46 858 | 51 065 | 49 971 | 46 971 | 47 253 | 47 077 |
| Oregon | 53 594 | 55 358 | 57 427 | 56 944 | 54 238 | 55 010 | 54 302 | 53 448 | 49 858 | 58 943 | 60 834 |
| Pennsylvania | 56 193 | 56 987 | 55 370 | 56 586 | 53 215 | 52 522 | 52 599 | 53 581 | 56 123 | 55 236 | 60 389 |
| Rhode Island | 60 057 | 63 170 | 61 970 | 58 611 | 57 040 | 56 120 | 51 675 | 57 877 | 57 311 | 58 700 | 55 701 |
| South Carolina | 48 826 | 46 572 | 50 542 | 46 406 | 45 404 | 45 330 | 42 243 | 45 836 | 44 327 | 44 981 | 46 360 |
| South Dakota | 52 371 | 53 402 | 53 062 | 56 804 | 50 624 | 49 302 | 49 767 | 51 012 | 54 350 | 53 114 | 55 065 |
| Tennessee | 47 826 | 47 837 | 47 092 | 43 706 | 44 759 | 41 953 | 44 557 | 44 384 | 44 121 | 43 766 | 47 330 |
| Texas | 50 272 | 50 910 | 52 645 | 51 179 | 52 445 | 51 383 | 51 689 | 53 604 | 52 307 | 53 937 | 56 473 |
| Utah | 66 525 | 64 218 | 61 191 | 68 844 | 64 615 | 61 640 | 58 483 | 60 226 | 62 117 | 63 456 | 66 258 |
| Vermont | 61 538 | 61 107 | 54 173 | 55 820 | 57 795 | 60 800 | 54 656 | 57 378 | 66 662 | 60 778 | 59 494 |
| Virginia | 63 006 | 67 147 | 67 629 | 68 236 | 66 835 | 65 625 | 65 989 | 66 721 | 67 063 | 66 231 | 61 486 |
| Washington | 61 467 | 64 330 | 66 393 | 62 342 | 66 715 | 61 055 | 59 913 | 64 197 | 65 043 | 59 136 | 67 243 |
| West Virginia | 44 232 | 45 164 | 48 116 | 41 826 | 44 729 | 46 503 | 44 074 | 44 960 | 43 824 | 39 597 | 42 824 |
| Wisconsin | 54 190 | 60 767 | 58 617 | 56 364 | 56 601 | 54 737 | 54 863 | 54 794 | 52 633 | 58 147 | 55 425 |
| Wyoming | 54 273 | 55 299 | 55 721 | 58 716 | 57 963 | 56 748 | 57 446 | 59 371 | 68 623 | 55 754 | 60 925 |

## Table 13-6. Median Family Income in the Past Twelve Months, by the Number of Earners and State, 2015

(Income in 2015 inflation-adjusted dollars.)

| State | Total | No earners | 1 earner | 2 earners | 3 or more earners |
|---|---|---|---|---|---|
| UNITED STATES | 68 260 | 35 114 | 48 410 | 88 747 | 108 075 |
| Alabama | 57 160 | 30 758 | 42 934 | 80 253 | 99 315 |
| Alaska | 86 376 | 45 301 | 61 550 | 102 158 | 131 499 |
| Arizona | 61 042 | 39 862 | 46 196 | 82 227 | 97 938 |
| Arkansas | 52 449 | 30 174 | 38 776 | 72 250 | 90 475 |
| California | 73 581 | 33 429 | 51 763 | 95 777 | 106 216 |
| Colorado | 78 384 | 43 187 | 55 162 | 95 362 | 114 871 |
| Connecticut | 91 388 | 39 948 | 62 145 | 112 263 | 137 440 |
| Delaware | 74 931 | 44 666 | 51 059 | 95 047 | 122 719 |
| District of Columbia | 94 846 | 16 595 | 51 260 | 150 012 | 123 144 |
| Florida | 59 339 | 37 912 | 44 021 | 78 985 | 94 185 |
| Georgia | 61 250 | 31 653 | 42 735 | 82 653 | 98 832 |
| Hawaii | 83 823 | 43 822 | 60 296 | 96 082 | 132 571 |
| Idaho | 60 081 | 39 046 | 46 196 | 72 166 | 88 336 |
| Illinois | 73 884 | 36 943 | 50 133 | 95 607 | 110 188 |
| Indiana | 63 165 | 35 462 | 45 834 | 81 490 | 101 470 |
| Iowa | 69 382 | 40 830 | 46 560 | 82 265 | 102 077 |
| Kansas | 69 401 | 39 647 | 46 998 | 85 063 | 105 763 |
| Kentucky | 56 187 | 27 906 | 42 058 | 79 472 | 98 589 |
| Louisiana | 58 964 | 25 979 | 42 527 | 85 190 | 104 022 |
| Maine | 64 651 | 33 890 | 48 234 | 80 642 | 105 448 |
| Maryland | 91 567 | 40 028 | 62 611 | 112 801 | 133 141 |
| Massachusetts | 90 590 | 35 899 | 60 341 | 113 059 | 131 620 |
| Michigan | 63 893 | 38 234 | 46 501 | 85 008 | 106 801 |
| Minnesota | 79 893 | 44 025 | 52 127 | 95 532 | 117 801 |
| Mississippi | 50 069 | 23 833 | 36 589 | 74 158 | 96 029 |
| Missouri | 62 989 | 36 066 | 44 433 | 81 392 | 102 596 |
| Montana | 64 061 | 36 296 | 47 081 | 79 216 | 103 589 |
| Nebraska | 71 039 | 37 957 | 46 485 | 85 671 | 104 710 |
| Nevada | 63 206 | 36 254 | 46 471 | 80 720 | 96 617 |
| New Hampshire | 85 873 | 43 182 | 61 580 | 101 687 | 128 054 |
| New Jersey | 90 245 | 38 762 | 62 149 | 114 521 | 133 776 |
| New Mexico | 56 207 | 31 916 | 42 567 | 76 250 | 92 887 |
| New York | 73 854 | 30 818 | 50 768 | 99 266 | 119 474 |
| North Carolina | 60 074 | 33 333 | 42 411 | 81 011 | 94 398 |
| North Dakota | 79 642 | 37 146 | 52 856 | 91 221 | 122 203 |
| Ohio | 65 176 | 35 407 | 45 666 | 85 109 | 108 936 |
| Oklahoma | 60 215 | 33 054 | 43 438 | 77 325 | 99 958 |
| Oregon | 66 287 | 40 685 | 49 706 | 84 416 | 101 525 |
| Pennsylvania | 70 194 | 34 819 | 50 501 | 90 036 | 111 303 |
| Rhode Island | 76 623 | 33 882 | 49 691 | 98 658 | 116 181 |
| South Carolina | 59 282 | 34 978 | 42 717 | 77 494 | 95 412 |
| South Dakota | 67 643 | 37 821 | 41 719 | 80 297 | 100 184 |
| Tennessee | 57 830 | 30 518 | 42 731 | 76 556 | 96 415 |
| Texas | 65 316 | 30 877 | 46 127 | 85 735 | 99 897 |
| Utah | 71 594 | 42 729 | 55 932 | 78 183 | 107 146 |
| Vermont | 75 595 | 37 280 | 53 447 | 90 469 | 105 868 |
| Virginia | 80 403 | 40 332 | 55 753 | 100 824 | 119 772 |
| Washington | 76 954 | 44 103 | 58 417 | 96 054 | 117 063 |
| West Virginia | 53 463 | 29 841 | 44 835 | 78 668 | 99 507 |
| Wisconsin | 70 870 | 38 936 | 47 804 | 85 897 | 106 459 |
| Wyoming | 75 540 | 42 204 | 59 227 | 88 193 | 106 872 |

## Table 13-7.  Median Family Income in the Past Twelve Months, by Size of Family and State, 2015

(Income in 2015 inflation-adjusted dollars.)

| State | Total | 2-person families | 3-person families | 4-person families | 5-person families | 6-person families | 7-or-more-person families |
|---|---|---|---|---|---|---|---|
| UNITED STATES | 68 260 | 61 288 | 70 029 | 82 508 | 76 235 | 71 703 | 73 873 |
| Alabama | 57 160 | 52 310 | 59 615 | 70 056 | 64 363 | 58 616 | 58 252 |
| Alaska | 86 376 | 84 219 | 85 861 | 96 612 | 94 362 | 72 260 | 69 493 |
| Arizona | 61 042 | 57 953 | 61 452 | 71 154 | 61 670 | 63 514 | 58 956 |
| Arkansas | 52 449 | 47 997 | 54 488 | 66 645 | 58 696 | 53 649 | 49 433 |
| California | 73 581 | 69 370 | 74 224 | 83 012 | 71 727 | 70 512 | 80 974 |
| Colorado | 78 384 | 71 140 | 80 481 | 93 932 | 82 442 | 83 159 | 85 033 |
| Connecticut | 91 388 | 79 965 | 90 723 | 111 996 | 118 416 | 110 170 | 100 324 |
| Delaware | 74 931 | 67 193 | 76 892 | 92 642 | 88 056 | 92 074 | 78 272 |
| District of Columbia | 94 846 | 97 812 | 91 521 | 112 064 | 65 676 | 47 197 | 106 210 |
| Florida | 59 339 | 54 655 | 59 881 | 71 480 | 62 990 | 64 207 | 68 501 |
| Georgia | 61 250 | 55 600 | 61 705 | 72 290 | 67 237 | 62 535 | 70 324 |
| Hawaii | 83 823 | 72 738 | 84 039 | 96 837 | 100 443 | 101 345 | 147 731 |
| Idaho | 60 081 | 54 840 | 56 527 | 70 308 | 68 329 | 71 691 | 79 073 |
| Illinois | 73 884 | 65 659 | 75 454 | 90 080 | 84 092 | 76 047 | 77 764 |
| Indiana | 63 165 | 56 841 | 65 324 | 76 600 | 75 434 | 65 097 | 71 331 |
| Iowa | 69 382 | 62 966 | 70 105 | 82 481 | 81 538 | 77 775 | 66 703 |
| Kansas | 69 401 | 62 538 | 72 072 | 82 487 | 76 495 | 71 097 | 73 750 |
| Kentucky | 56 187 | 50 882 | 56 977 | 71 955 | 66 434 | 60 777 | 51 859 |
| Louisiana | 58 964 | 52 419 | 58 564 | 71 061 | 71 292 | 62 201 | 64 663 |
| Maine | 64 651 | 59 646 | 66 847 | 80 929 | 82 126 | 74 110 | 83 267 |
| Maryland | 91 567 | 80 492 | 91 663 | 111 281 | 106 600 | 95 006 | 100 523 |
| Massachusetts | 90 590 | 75 462 | 92 587 | 112 235 | 115 940 | 109 489 | 111 033 |
| Michigan | 63 893 | 56 651 | 67 342 | 81 951 | 77 423 | 67 171 | 61 619 |
| Minnesota | 79 893 | 70 006 | 83 974 | 100 494 | 93 479 | 82 488 | 79 149 |
| Mississippi | 50 069 | 46 130 | 49 983 | 60 420 | 54 097 | 47 369 | 56 927 |
| Missouri | 62 989 | 56 574 | 64 447 | 80 161 | 73 286 | 80 111 | 65 778 |
| Montana | 64 061 | 57 621 | 64 161 | 78 933 | 74 287 | 70 618 | 68 277 |
| Nebraska | 71 039 | 65 341 | 71 043 | 82 676 | 82 257 | 75 847 | 69 456 |
| Nevada | 63 206 | 60 841 | 61 211 | 72 010 | 65 463 | 70 149 | 73 244 |
| New Hampshire | 85 873 | 74 428 | 88 077 | 107 348 | 105 112 | 109 146 | 126 721 |
| New Jersey | 90 245 | 74 367 | 92 489 | 113 455 | 105 008 | 105 311 | 90 817 |
| New Mexico | 56 207 | 56 985 | 51 800 | 59 505 | 58 735 | 53 119 | 48 569 |
| New York | 73 854 | 65 233 | 74 925 | 90 852 | 85 375 | 79 244 | 83 830 |
| North Carolina | 60 074 | 55 028 | 63 717 | 71 923 | 62 433 | 58 356 | 58 936 |
| North Dakota | 79 642 | 70 214 | 80 155 | 95 271 | 101 839 | 94 319 | 118 520 |
| Ohio | 65 176 | 57 216 | 67 509 | 82 005 | 81 591 | 73 394 | 68 456 |
| Oklahoma | 60 215 | 55 828 | 60 621 | 68 201 | 67 805 | 64 362 | 61 324 |
| Oregon | 66 287 | 60 786 | 69 994 | 79 171 | 77 341 | 61 552 | 66 809 |
| Pennsylvania | 70 194 | 60 508 | 74 083 | 89 690 | 84 338 | 83 510 | 72 706 |
| Rhode Island | 76 623 | 67 452 | 76 119 | 99 216 | 83 865 | 85 621 | 72 801 |
| South Carolina | 59 282 | 54 905 | 60 687 | 70 981 | 65 728 | 60 072 | 53 301 |
| South Dakota | 67 643 | 62 891 | 65 706 | 80 494 | 82 747 | 70 116 | 56 543 |
| Tennessee | 57 830 | 53 216 | 59 294 | 68 298 | 62 750 | 61 942 | 58 984 |
| Texas | 65 316 | 60 935 | 64 894 | 75 885 | 68 551 | 64 592 | 62 577 |
| Utah | 71 594 | 62 119 | 70 162 | 78 717 | 81 386 | 86 091 | 90 222 |
| Vermont | 75 595 | 66 365 | 79 413 | 91 793 | 90 672 | 62 773 | 59 844 |
| Virginia | 80 403 | 70 976 | 81 369 | 96 513 | 94 374 | 84 151 | 91 691 |
| Washington | 76 954 | 71 557 | 78 760 | 91 572 | 80 508 | 75 172 | 76 585 |
| West Virginia | 53 463 | 47 723 | 56 074 | 70 510 | 62 179 | 68 669 | 67 435 |
| Wisconsin | 70 870 | 62 130 | 75 230 | 88 133 | 85 105 | 75 763 | 68 267 |
| Wyoming | 75 540 | 71 074 | 79 220 | 81 839 | 73 455 | 86 884 | 80 866 |

# CHAPTER 14: OCCUPATIONAL SAFETY AND HEALTH

## HIGHLIGHTS

This chapter includes data on work-related illnesses and injuries and fatal work injuries from the Injuries, Illnesses, and Fatalities (IIF) program. Data are classified by industry and selected worker characteristics.

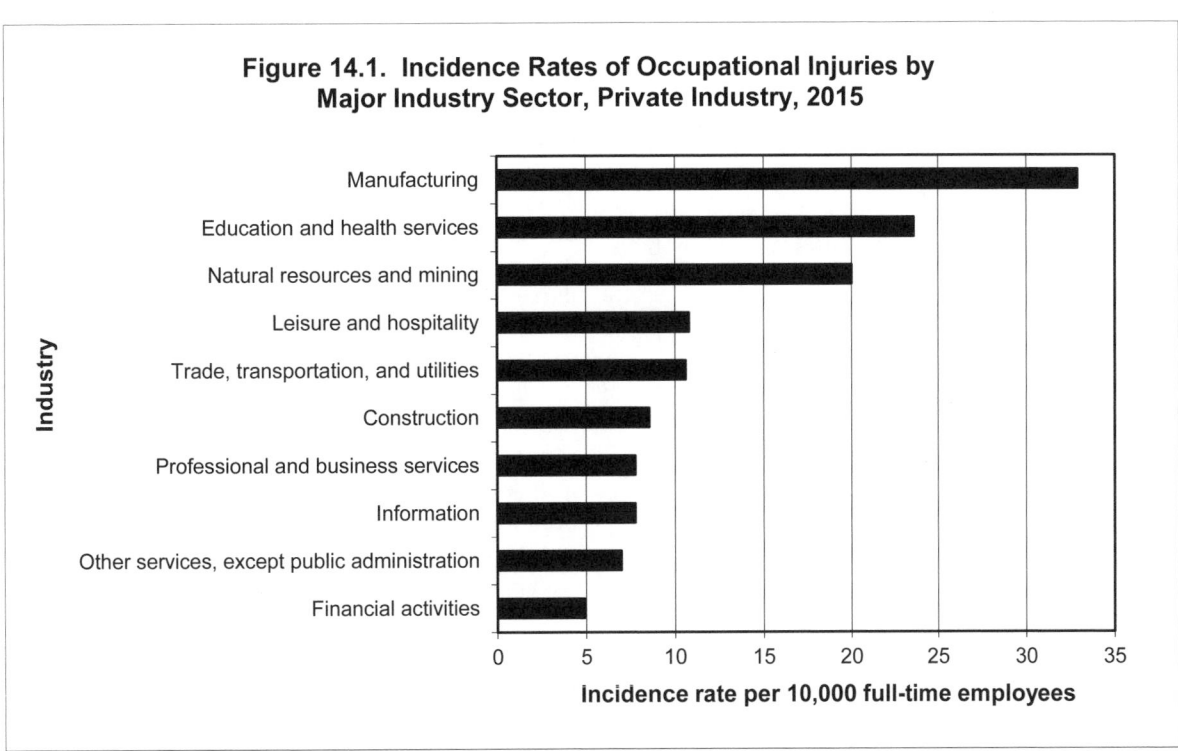

**Figure 14.1. Incidence Rates of Occupational Injuries by Major Industry Sector, Private Industry, 2015**

The incidence rate of occupational injuries was 14.6 per 10,000 full-time workers in private industry in 2015. Workers in manufacturing had the highest rate at 32.9 per 10,000 workers followed by workers in education and health services at 23.6 per 10,000 full-time workers. Those in financial activities had the lowest rate at 4.9 per 10,000 full-time workers. (Table 14-3.)

## OTHER HIGHLIGHTS

- In 2015, the nonfatal occupational injuries and illnesses rate for all workers in private industry declined to 3.0 cases per 100 full-time workers. It has declined throughout the past decade with the exception of 2012. Among industries, education and health services had the highest incidence rate at 4.0 per 100 full-time workers while the financial activities sector had the lowest rate at 1.1 per 100 full-time workers. (See Table 14-1.)

- Workers aged 45 to 54 years had the highest number of nonfatal occupational injuries and illnesses involving days away from work in 2015 followed by those age 35 to 44 years. (See Table 14-5.)

- Men were far more likely to be killed on the job than women accounting for over 92 percent of fatalities. (See Table 14-10.)

- Workers age 65 years and older incurred 650 fatal injuries, the second-largest number for the group since the national census began in 1992, but a decrease from the 2014 figure of 684. (See Table 14-10.)

## NOTES AND DEFINITIONS

### Collection and Coverage

The Injuries, Illnesses, and Fatalities (IIF) program at the Bureau of Labor Statistics (BLS) provides annual reports on the number of workplace injuries, illnesses, and fatalities. BLS has reported annually on the number of work-related injuries, illnesses, and fatalities since 1972 after the Occupational Safety and Health Act of 1970 was passed.

### Nonfatal Occupational Injuries and Illnesses

The Survey of Occupational Injuries and Illnesses is a federal-state program in which employer's reports are collected annually from over 176,000 private industry establishments and processed by state agencies cooperating with the BLS. Summary information on the number of injuries and illnesses is copied by these employers directly from their recordkeeping logs to the survey questionnaire. The questionnaire also asks for the number of employee hours worked (needed in the calculation of incidence rates) as well as its average employment (needed to verify the unit's employment-size class).

Occupational injury and illness data for coal, metal, and non-metal mining and for railroad activities were provided by the Department of Labor's Mine Safety and Health Administration and the Department of Transportation's Federal Railroad Administration. The survey excludes all work-related fatalities as well as nonfatal work injuries and illnesses to the self employed; to workers on farms with 10 or fewer employees; to private household workers; and, nationally, to federal, state, and local government workers.

Injuries and illnesses logged by employers conform with definitions and recordkeeping guidelines set by the Occupational Safety and Health Administration, U.S. Department of Labor. Under those guidelines, nonfatal cases are recordable if they are occupational illnesses or if they are occupational injuries which involve lost worktime, medical treatment other than first aid, restriction of work or motion, loss of consciousness, or transfer to another job. Employers keep counts of injuries separate from illnesses and also identify for each whether a case involved any days away from work or days of restricted work activity, or both, beyond the day of injury or onset of illness.

Occupational injuries, such as sprains, cuts, and fractures, account for the vast majority of all cases that employers log and report to the BLS survey. Occupational illnesses are new cases recognized, diagnosed, and reported during the year. Overwhelmingly, those reported are easier to directly relate to workplace activity (e.g., contact dermatitis or carpal tunnel syndrome) than are long-term latent illnesses, such as cancers. The latter illnesses are believed to be under recorded and, thus, understated in the BLS survey.

### Concepts and Definitions

*Days away from work* are cases that involve days away from work, days of restricted work activity, or both.

The data are presented in the form of *incidence rates*, defined as the number of injuries and illnesses or cases of days away from work per 100 full-time employees. The formula is (N/EH) x 200,000, where N = number of injuries and illnesses or days away from work, EH = total hours worked by all employees during the calendar year, and 200,000 represents the base for 100 full-time equivalent workers (working 40 hours per week, 50 weeks per year).

*Median days away from work* is a measure used to summarize the varying lengths of absences from work among the cases with days away from work. The median is the point at which half of the cases involved more days away from work and half involved less days away from work.

*Occupational illness* is an abnormal condition or disorder (other than one resulting from an occupational injury) caused by exposure to environmental factors associated with employment. It includes acute and chronic illnesses and diseases that may have been caused by inhalation, absorption, ingestion, or direct contact. Long-term latent illnesses can be difficult to relate to the workplace and are believed to be understated in this survey.

*Occupational injury* is any injury—such as a cut, fracture, sprain, or amputation—that results from a work accident or from exposure to an incident in the work environment

### Fatal Occupational Injuries

The Bureau of Labor Statistics (BLS) Census of Fatal Occupational Injuries (CFOI) produces comprehensive, accurate, and timely counts of fatal work injuries. CFOI is a federal-state cooperative program that has been implemented in all 50 states and the District of Columbia since 1992. To compile counts that are as complete as possible, the census uses multiple sources to identify, verify, and profile fatal worker injuries. Information about each workplace fatality—occupation and other worker characteristics, equipment involved, and circumstances of the event—is obtained by cross referencing the source records, such as death certificates, workers' compensation reports, and federal and state agency administrative reports. To ensure that fatalities are work-related, cases are substantiated with two or more independent source documents, or a source document and a follow-up questionnaire.

Data compiled by the CFOI program are issued annually for the preceding calendar year. These data are used by safety and health policy analysts and researchers to help prevent fatal work injuries by:

- Informing workers of life threatening hazards associated with various jobs;

- Promoting safer work practices through enhanced job safety training;

- Assessing and improving workplace safety standards; and

- Identifying new areas of safety research.

The National Safety Council has adopted the Census of Fatal Occupational Injuries figure, beginning with the 1992 data year, as the authoritative count for work related deaths in the United States.

## Sources of Additional Information

For more extensive definitions and description of collection methods see Chapter 9 in the *BLS Handbook of Methods* and BLS news release USDL 16-2130, "Nonfatal Occupational Injuries and Illnesses Requiring Days Away from Work, 2015", USDL 16-2056, "Employee Reported Workplace Injuries and Illnesses 2015", and USDL 16-2304 "National Census of Fatal Occupational Injuries in 2015" available on the BLS Web site at <http://www.bls.gov/iif/>.

## Table 14-1.  Incidence Rates[1] of Nonfatal Occupational Injuries and Illnesses, by Major Industry Sector, Employment Size, and Ownership, 2015

(Rate per 100 full-time workers.)

| Industry sector | All establishments | Establishment employment size (workers) | | | | |
|---|---|---|---|---|---|---|
| | | 1 to 10 | 11 to 49 | 50 to 249 | 250 to 999 | 1,000 or more |
| **ALL INDUSTRIES INCLUDING STATE AND LOCAL GOVERNMENT**[2] | 3.3 | 1.5 | 2.9 | 3.9 | 3.7 | 4.0 |
| **Private Industry**[2] | 3.0 | 1.4 | 2.8 | 3.7 | 3.3 | 3.3 |
| **Goods Producing**[2] | 3.7 | 2.6 | 4.0 | 4.2 | 3.2 | 3.2 |
| Natural resources and mining[2,3] | 3.7 | 1.6 | 3.6 | 4.3 | 3.6 | 3.3 |
| Construction | 3.5 | 3.0 | 4.1 | 3.5 | 2.5 | 1.3 |
| Manufacturing | 3.8 | 1.9 | 4.0 | 4.5 | 3.3 | 3.3 |
| **Service Providing** | 2.9 | 1.2 | 2.5 | 3.6 | 3.3 | 3.4 |
| Trade, transportation, and utilities[4] | 3.6 | 1.7 | 3.1 | 4.2 | 4.6 | 4.0 |
| Information | 1.3 | 0.2 | 1.3 | 2.1 | 1.1 | 0.8 |
| Financial activities | 1.1 | 1.1 | 1.3 | 1.3 | 1.0 | 0.6 |
| Professional and business services | 1.4 | 0.8 | 1.8 | 1.7 | 1.3 | 0.8 |
| Education and health services | 4.0 | 1.3 | 2.5 | 4.9 | 4.8 | 5.0 |
| Leisure and hospitality | 3.5 | 1.3 | 2.8 | 4.3 | 5.4 | 5.0 |
| Other services, except public administration | 2.3 | 1.2 | 2.7 | 3.5 | 2.8 | 2.0 |
| **State and Local Government**[2] | 5.1 | 3.5 | 4.5 | 4.9 | 5.6 | 5.2 |
| State government[2] | 3.7 | 1.6 | 2.6 | 3.2 | 5.2 | 3.5 |
| Local government[2] | 5.6 | 4.4 | 5.1 | 5.2 | 5.7 | 6.0 |

[1]The incidence rates represent the number of injuries and illnesses per 100 full-time workers and were calculated as: (N/EH) x 200,000 (where N = number of injuries and illnesses; EH = total hours worked by all employees during the calendar year; 200,000 = base for 100 equivalent full-time workers working 40 hours per week, 50 weeks per year).
[2]Excludes farms with fewer than 11 employees.
[3]Data for mining include establishments not goverened by the Mine and Safety and Health Administration rules and reporting such as those in oil and gas extraction and related support activities.
[4]Data for employers in railroad transportation are provided to the Bureau of Labor Statistics (BLS) by the Federal Reserve Administration, U.S. Department of Transportation.
* = Figure does not meet standards of reliability or quality.

## Table 14-2.  Number of Cases and Incidence Rate[1] of Nonfatal Occupational Injuries and Illnesses for Industries with 100,000 or More Cases, 2015

(Number, rate per 100 full-time workers.)

| Industry[2] | NAICS Code[3] | Total cases (thousands) | Incidence rate |
|---|---|---|---|
| **ALL INDUSTRIES INCLUDING STATE AND LOCAL GOVERNMENT**[4] | | 3 658.5 | 3.3 |
| Elementary and secondary schools (local government) | 6 111 | 259.5 | 4.8 |
| General medical and surgical hospitals (private industry) | 6 221 | 214.1 | 6.0 |
| Restaurants and other eating places (private industry) | 72 251 | 185.2 | 3.0 |
| Nursing and residential care facilities (private industry) | 623 | 171.9 | 6.8 |
| Specialty trade contractors (private industry) | 238 | 138.0 | 3.7 |
| Ambulatory health care services (private industry) | 621 | 130.0 | 2.4 |
| General merchandise stores (private industry) | 452 | 103.3 | 4.5 |

[1]The incidence rates represent the number of injuries and illnesses per 100 full-time workers and were calculated as: (N/EH) x 200,000 (where N = number of injuries and illnesses; EH = total hours worked by all employees during the calendar year; 200,000 = base for 100 equivalent full-time workers working 40 hours per week, 50 weeks per year).
[2]Totals include data for industries not shown separately.
[3]North American Industry Classification System—United States, 2012.
[4]Excludes farms with fewer than 11 employees.

**Table 14-3.   Incidence Rates[1] of Nonfatal Occupational Injuries and Illnesses, by Major Industry Sector, Category of Illness, and Ownership, 2015**

(Incidence rate per 10,000 full-time workers.)

| Industry sector | Total cases | Skin diseases or disorders | Respiratory conditions | Poisonings | Hearing loss | All other illnesses |
|---|---|---|---|---|---|---|
| ALL INDUSTRIES INCLUDING STATE AND LOCAL GOVERNMENT[2] | 16.9 | 2.6 | 1.5 | 0.2 | 1.8 | 10.9 |
| Private Industry[2] | 14.6 | 2.3 | 1.3 | 0.2 | 1.8 | 9.2 |
| Goods Producing[2] | 24.6 | 3.3 | 1.3 | 0.2 | 6.9 | 12.9 |
| Natural resources and mining[2,3] | 20.0 | 5.3 | 3.0 | 0.9 | 1.6 | 9.1 |
| Construction | 8.6 | 2.3 | 0.8 | 0.2 | 0.1 | 5.2 |
| Manufacturing | 32.9 | 3.4 | 1.3 | 0.2 | 10.9 | 17.1 |
| Service Providing | 12.0 | 2.0 | 1.2 | 0.2 | 0.4 | 8.2 |
| Trade, transportation, and utilities[4] | 10.6 | 1.3 | 0.7 | 0.1 | 1.1 | 7.3 |
| Information | 7.8 | 0.8 | 0.3 | * | 0.7 | 6.0 |
| Financial activities | 4.9 | 0.5 | 0.4 | * | * | 4.0 |
| Professional and business services | 7.8 | 2.1 | 0.8 | 0.2 | 0.1 | 4.6 |
| Education and health services | 23.6 | 3.7 | 3.0 | 0.1 | 0.1 | 16.7 |
| Leisure and hospitality | 10.8 | 2.4 | 1.2 | 0.3 | 0.1 | 6.8 |
| Other services, except public administration | 7.0 | 1.6 | 0.7 | * | 0.1 | 4.0 |
| State and Local Government[2] | 32.0 | 4.3 | 3.4 | 0.5 | 1.8 | 21.9 |
| State government[2] | 31.4 | 4.1 | 3.5 | 0.4 | 1.7 | 21.7 |
| Local government[2] | 32.2 | 4.4 | 3.4 | 0.6 | 1.8 | 22.0 |

[1]The incidence rates represent the number of injuries and illnesses per 100 full-time workers and were calculated as: (N/EH) x 200,000 (where N = number of injuries and illnesses; EH = total hours worked by all employees during the calendar year; 200,000 = base for 100 equivalent full-time workers working 40 hours per week, 50 weeks per year).
[2]Excludes farms with fewer than 11 employees.
[3]Data for mining include establishments not goverened by the Mine and Safety and Health Administration rules and reporting such as those in oil and gas extraction and related support activities.
[4]Data for employers in railroad transportation are provided to the Bureau of Labor Statistics (BLS) by the Federal Reserve Administration, U.S. Department of Transportation.
* = Figure does not meet standards of reliability or quality.

**Table 14-4.   Number of Cases of Nonfatal Occupational Injuries and Illnesses, by Major Industry Sector, Category of Illness, and Ownership, 2015**

(Number of illnesses in thousands.)

| Industry sector | Total cases | Skin diseases or disorders | Respiratory conditions | Poisonings | Hearing loss | All other illnesses |
|---|---|---|---|---|---|---|
| ALL INDUSTRIES INCLUDING STATE AND LOCAL GOVERNMENT[1] | 187.9 | 28.3 | 17.2 | 2.5 | 19.5 | 120.4 |
| Private Industry[1] | 140.5 | 21.9 | 12.1 | 1.7 | 16.8 | 88.0 |
| Goods Producing[1] | 49.7 | 6.6 | 2.7 | 0.5 | 13.8 | 26.0 |
| Natural resources and mining[1,2] | 3.8 | 1.0 | 0.6 | 0.2 | 0.3 | 1.7 |
| Construction | 5.1 | 1.4 | 0.5 | 0.1 | 0.1 | 3.1 |
| Manufacturing | 40.8 | 4.2 | 1.7 | 0.2 | 13.5 | 21.2 |
| Service Providing | 90.9 | 15.4 | 9.3 | 1.2 | 3.0 | 61.9 |
| Trade, transportation, and utilities[3] | 23.7 | 3.0 | 1.6 | 0.3 | 2.4 | 16.3 |
| Information | 1.9 | 0.2 | 0.1 | * | 0.2 | 1.5 |
| Financial activities | 3.6 | 0.3 | 0.3 | * | * | 2.9 |
| Professional and business services | 11.8 | 3.1 | 1.3 | 0.2 | 0.1 | 7.0 |
| Education and health services | 37.3 | 5.8 | 4.7 | 0.2 | 0.1 | 26.4 |
| Leisure and hospitality | 10.4 | 2.4 | 1.2 | 0.3 | 0.1 | 6.5 |
| Other services, except public administration | 2.2 | 0.5 | 0.2 | * | (4) | 1.2 |
| State and Local Government[1] | 47.4 | 6.4 | 5.1 | 0.8 | 2.7 | 32.4 |
| State government[1] | 12.5 | 1.6 | 1.4 | 0.1 | 0.7 | 8.7 |
| Local government[1] | 34.8 | 4.8 | 3.7 | 0.6 | 2.0 | 23.7 |

[1]Excludes farms with fewer than 11 employees.
[2]Data for mining include establishments not goverened by the Mine and Safety and Health Administration rules and reporting such as those in oil and gas extraction and related support activities.
[3]Data for employers in railroad transportation are provided to the Bureau of Labor Statistics (BLS) by the Federal Reserve Administration, U.S. Department of Transportation.
[4]Data too small to be displayed.
* = Figure does not meet standards of reliability or quality.

## Table 14-5.  Number, Incidence Rate,[1] and Median Days Away From Work[2,3] by Selected Worker Characteristics, 2015

(Number, rate.)

| Characteristic | Total private, state, and local government[4,5,6] | | | Private industry[4,5,6] | | |
|---|---|---|---|---|---|---|
| | Number | Incidence rate | Median days away from work | Number | Incidence rate | Median days away from work |
| **TOTAL CASES** .................................... | 1 153 490 | 104.0 | 8 | 902 160 | 94.0 | 8 |
| **Sex** | | | | | | |
| Men .......................................................... | 702 400 | 114.0 | 10 | 556 370 | 101.0 | 9 |
| Women ...................................................... | 445 970 | 92.0 | 7 | 341 130 | 85.0 | 7 |
| **Age** | | | | | | |
| 14 to 15 years .......................................... | 140 | * | 4 | 130 | * | 3 |
| 16 to 19 years .......................................... | 24 910 | 111.0 | 4 | 23 560 | 109.0 | 4 |
| 20 to 24 years .......................................... | 93 940 | 98.0 | 4 | 86 590 | 98.0 | 4 |
| 25 to 34 years .......................................... | 233 940 | 93.0 | 6 | 190 500 | 85.0 | 6 |
| 35 to 44 years .......................................... | 245 450 | 103.0 | 9 | 187 950 | 91.0 | 9 |
| 45 to 54 years .......................................... | 280 100 | 113.0 | 12 | 210 200 | 100.0 | 12 |
| 55 to 64 years .......................................... | 207 250 | 116.0 | 13 | 152 590 | 101.0 | 14 |
| 65 years and over ..................................... | 43 390 | 89.0 | 14 | 33 850 | 81.0 | 17 |
| **Length of Service with Employer** | | | | | | |
| Less than 3 months ................................. | 111 110 | * | 6 | 103 010 | * | 6 |
| 3 to 11 months ......................................... | 200 000 | * | 6 | 183 470 | * | 7 |
| 1 to 5 years .............................................. | 352 170 | * | 7 | 293 100 | * | 7 |
| More than 5 years ..................................... | 465 720 | * | 12 | 306 050 | * | 13 |
| **Race and Hispanic Origin** | | | | | | |
| White only ................................................. | 434 250 | * | 7 | 347 200 | * | 7 |
| Black only ................................................. | 91 190 | * | 8 | 73 590 | * | 8 |
| Hispanic only[7] .......................................... | 142 170 | * | 7 | 125 360 | * | 7 |
| Asian only ................................................. | 16 190 | * | 7 | 14 530 | * | 7 |
| Native Hawaiian or Pacific Islander only ......... | 3 050 | * | 9 | 2 490 | * | 7 |
| American Indian or Alaskan Native only ......... | 4 830 | * | 4 | 4 040 | * | 4 |
| Hispanic[5] and other race ........................... | 630 | * | 5 | 460 | * | 5 |
| Multiple races .......................................... | 1 240 | * | 2 | 1 130 | * | 2 |
| Not reported ............................................. | 459 960 | * | 10 | 333 370 | * | 10 |

| Characteristic | State government[5,6] | | | Local government[5,6] | | |
|---|---|---|---|---|---|---|
| | Number | Incidence rate | Median days away from work | Number | Incidence rate | Median days away from work |
| **TOTAL CASES** ................................. | 59 590 | 149.2 | 11 | 191 750 | 177.5 | 9 |
| **Sex** | | | | | | |
| Men .......................................................... | 31 420 | 188.0 | 12 | 114 600 | 237.9 | 10 |
| Women ...................................................... | 28 060 | 121.1 | 9 | 76 780 | 128.7 | 8 |
| **Age** | | | | | | |
| 14 to 15 years .......................................... | * | * | * | * | * | * |
| 16 to 19 years .......................................... | 360 | 138.4 | 4 | 1 000 | 128.3 | 4 |
| 20 to 24 years .......................................... | 2 160 | 93.3 | 6 | 5 200 | 112.3 | 5 |
| 25 to 34 years .......................................... | 10 280 | 132.3 | 8 | 33 170 | 158.1 | 6 |
| 35 to 44 years .......................................... | 13 560 | 150.8 | 10 | 43 940 | 176.1 | 9 |
| 45 to 54 years .......................................... | 17 740 | 180.0 | 13 | 52 170 | 188.5 | 10 |
| 55 to 64 years .......................................... | 12 720 | 158.3 | 14 | 41 940 | 205.5 | 11 |
| 65 years and over ..................................... | 1 710 | 85.1 | 12 | 7 830 | 158.5 | 8 |
| **Length of Service with Employer** | | | | | | |
| Less than 3 months ................................. | 2 230 | * | 5 | 5 870 | * | 5 |
| 3 to 11 months ......................................... | 4 130 | * | 5 | 12 390 | * | 6 |
| 1 to 5 years .............................................. | 13 690 | * | 9 | 45 380 | * | 7 |
| More than 5 years ..................................... | 37 570 | * | 13 | 122 100 | * | 10 |
| **Race and Hispanic Origin** | | | | | | |
| White only ................................................. | 17 350 | * | 10 | 69 700 | * | 7 |
| Black only ................................................. | 6 380 | * | 9 | 11 230 | * | 10 |
| Hispanic only[7] .......................................... | 2 030 | * | 18 | 14 770 | * | 9 |
| Asian only ................................................. | 500 | * | 7 | 1 160 | * | 5 |
| Native Hawaiian or Pacific Islander only ......... | 130 | * | 22 | 430 | * | 30 |
| American Indian or Alaskan Native only ......... | 230 | * | 7 | 570 | * | 7 |
| Hispanic[5] and other race ........................... | 40 | * | 6 | 130 | * | 5 |
| Multiple races .......................................... | 40 | * | 5 | 70 | * | 43 |
| Not reported ............................................. | 32 900 | * | 11 | 93 690 | * | 10 |

[1]The incidence rates represent the number of injuries and illnesses per 10,000 full-time workers and were calculated as (N/EH) x 20,000,000, where N = number of injuries and illnesses EH = total hours worked by all employees during the calendar year 20,000,000 = base for 10,000 equivalent full-time workers (40 hours per week, 50 weeks per year).
[2]Median days away from work is the measure used to summarize the varying lengths of absences from work among the cases with days away from work.
[3]Days-away-from-work cases include those that resulted in days away from work, some of which also included job transfer or restriction.
[4]Excludes farms with fewer than 11 employees.
[5]Data for Mining (Sector 21 in the North American Industry Classification System-United States, 2012) include establishments not governed by the Mine Safety and Health Administration rules and reporting, such as those in Oil and Gas Extraction and related support activities.
[6]Data for employers in rail transportation are provided to BLS by the Federal Railroad Administration, U.S. Department of Transportation.
[7]May be of any race.
* = Figure does not meet standards of reliability or quality.

**Table 14-6.  Number, Median Days Away from Work,[1] and Incidence Rate[2] for Nonfatal Occupational Injuries and Illnesses Involving Days Away from Work[3] by Ownership, Industry, and Muscoskeletal Disorders[4] and Event or Exposure, 2015**

(Number, rate.)

| Characteristic | Number | Median days away from work | Musco-skeletal disorders | Incidence rate | Event or exposure leading to injury or illness (incidence rate) | |
|---|---|---|---|---|---|---|
| | | | | | Contacts with objects | Falls, slips, and trips |
| **TOTAL** | 1 153 490 | 8 | 32.2 | 104.0 | 24.3 | 27.9 |
| **Total Private Industry[5,6,7]** | 902 160 | 8 | 29.8 | 93.9 | 24.2 | 24.8 |
| Total goods producing | 226 320 | 10 | 33.1 | 112.1 | 39.2 | 26.8 |
| Natural resources and mining[5,6] | 23 830 | 8 | 26.9 | 126.8 | 38.4 | 35.8 |
| Agriculture, forestry, fishing, and hunting[5] | 18 660 | 6 | 39.6 | 189.0 | 53.5 | 54.4 |
| Mining[6] | 5 160 | 29 | 12.9 | 57.9 | 21.7 | 15.2 |
| Construction | 79 890 | 13 | 34.6 | 134.8 | 44.8 | 40.3 |
| Manufacturing | 122 610 | 9 | 33.4 | 99.0 | 36.7 | 19.0 |
| Total service providing | 675 840 | 8 | 28.9 | 89.1 | 20.1 | 24.3 |
| Trade, transportation and utilities[7] | 279 150 | 11 | 44.5 | 124.5 | 33.1 | 30.8 |
| Wholesale trade | 60 340 | 9 | 38.4 | 106.5 | 31.8 | 24.1 |
| Retail trade | 123 770 | 7 | 36.2 | 105.3 | 32.0 | 26.6 |
| Transportation and warehousing | 90 990 | 20 | 76.4 | 204.3 | 40.1 | 51.4 |
| Utilities | 4 060 | 19 | 27.7 | 73.4 | 12.3 | 22.0 |
| Information | 14 050 | 18 | 21.3 | 56.3 | 9.1 | 15.7 |
| Financial activities | 30 110 | 7 | 11.7 | 41.3 | 7.5 | 15.3 |
| Real estate and rental and leasing | 20 630 | 7 | 34.5 | 111.0 | 26.8 | 31.5 |
| Professional and business services | 67 320 | 7 | 11.3 | 44.5 | 9.4 | 14.6 |
| Professional, scientific, and technical services | 18 030 | 5 | 5.6 | 22.8 | 3.4 | 7.1 |
| Management of companies and enterprises | 5 700 | 8 | 7.0 | 26.6 | 5.1 | 11.2 |
| Administrative and support and waste management and remediation services | 43 590 | 9 | 21.9 | 85.7 | 20.6 | 27.5 |
| Education and health services | 168 940 | 6 | 39.3 | 106.8 | 13.4 | 29.2 |
| Educational services | 10 530 | 5 | 12.8 | 56.3 | 10.5 | 18.8 |
| Health care and social assistance | 158 410 | 6 | 42.9 | 113.6 | 13.8 | 30.6 |
| Leisure and hospitality | 92 670 | 6 | 20.3 | 96.2 | 29.7 | 27.6 |
| Arts, entertainment, and recreation | 14 110 | 6 | 28.8 | 105.8 | 24.6 | 30.9 |
| Accommodation and food services | 78 560 | 6 | 19.0 | 94.7 | 30.5 | 27.1 |
| Other services | 23 600 | 6 | 22.0 | 75.9 | 21.9 | 17.9 |
| **Total State Government[5,6,7]** | 59 590 | 11 | 41.0 | 149.2 | 17.8 | 38.3 |
| Total service providing | 57 960 | 11 | 40.5 | 147.8 | 17.3 | 37.9 |
| Education and health services | 25 980 | 10 | 36.8 | 127.2 | 14.4 | 30.5 |
| Educational services | 7 520 | 10 | 17.3 | 50.5 | 7.1 | 18.6 |
| Health care and social assistance | 18 460 | 10 | 89.4 | 334.4 | 34.0 | 62.5 |
| Public administration | 27 500 | 12 | 40.7 | 157.5 | 17.1 | 45.5 |
| Justice, public order, and safety activities | 18 620 | 13 | 67.2 | 261.6 | 26.2 | 67.3 |
| **Total Local Government[5,6,7]** | 91 750 | 9 | 50.2 | 177.5 | 28.4 | 51.1 |
| Total goods producing | 3 250 | 20 | 112.7 | 320.9 | 69.1 | 102.8 |
| Construction | 3 250 | 20 | 113.2 | 322.0 | 69.2 | 103.0 |
| Total service providing | 88 490 | 9 | 49.6 | 176.1 | 28.0 | 50.6 |
| Trade, transportation and utilities | 14 920 | 17 | 123.5 | 315.2 | 49.6 | 55.1 |
| Transportation and warehousing | 9 790 | 19 | 148.0 | 391.0 | 60.1 | 48.9 |
| Utilities | 5 130 | 10 | 96.8 | 232.1 | 38.0 | 62.8 |
| Education and health services | 80 810 | 8 | 34.2 | 124.7 | 21.2 | 43.1 |
| Educational services | 69 800 | 8 | 31.0 | 121.7 | 21.7 | 43.8 |
| Health care and social assistance | 11 010 | 7 | 58.8 | 148.5 | 16.7 | 37.3 |
| Public administration | 84 380 | 9 | 66.8 | 248.2 | 34.7 | 63.6 |
| Justice, public order, and safety activities | 38 200 | 10 | 103.6 | 414.0 | 56.2 | 93.6 |

[1]Median days away from work is the measure used to summarize the varying lengths of absences from work among the cases with days away from work.

[2]The incidence rates represent the number of injuries and illnesses per 10,000 full-time workers and were calculated as (N/EH) x 20,000,000, where N = number of injuries and illnesses EH = total hours worked by all employees during the calendar year 20,000,000 = base for 10,000 equivalent full-time workers (40 hours per week, 50 weeks per year).

[3]Days-away-from-work cases include those that resulted in days away from work, some of which also included job transfer or restriction.

[4]Musculoskeletal disorders include cases in which the nature of the injury or illness is pinched nerve; herniated disc; meniscus tear; sprains, strains, tears; hernia (traumatic and nontraumatic); pain, swelling, and numbness; carpal or tarsal tunnel syndrome; Raynaud's syndrome or phenomenon; musculoskeletal system and connective tissue diseases and disorders, and when the event or exposure leading to the injury or illness is overexertion and bodily reaction, unspecified; overexertion involving outside sources; repetitive motion involving microtasks; other and multiple exertions or bodily reactions; and rubbed, abraded, or jarred by vibration.

[5]Excludes farms with fewer than 11 employees.

[6]Data for Mining (Sector 21 in the North American Industry Classification System-United States, 2012) include establishments not governed by the Mine Safety and Health Administration rules and reporting, such as those in Oil and Gas Extraction and related support activities.

[7]Data for employers in rail transportation are provided to BLS by the Federal Railroad Administration, U.S. Department of Transportation.

**Table 14-6. Number, Median Days Away from Work,[1] and Incidence Rate[2] for Nonfatal Occupational Injuries and Illnesses Involving Days Away from Work[3] by Ownership, Industry, and Muscoskeletal Disorders[4] and Event or Exposure, 2015—*Continued***

(Number, rate.)

| Characteristic | Event or exposure leading to injury or illness (incidence rate) | | | | | |
|---|---|---|---|---|---|---|
| | Overexertion in lifting/lowering | Repetitive motion | Exposure to harmful substances or environments | Transportation incidents | Fires and explosions | Violence and other injuries by persons or animals |
| **TOTAL** | 10.2 | 2.2 | 4.7 | 6.9 | 0.2 | 6.8 |
| **Total Private Industry[5,6,7]** | 9.8 | 2.2 | 4.2 | 5.9 | 0.1 | 4.0 |
| Total goods producing | 9.9 | 4.0 | 5.2 | 4.9 | 0.3 | 1.5 |
| Natural resources and mining[5,6] | 8.4 | 2.1 | 7.0 | 6.9 | 0.8 | 8.1 |
| Agriculture, forestry, fishing, and hunting[5] | 11.2 | 3.8 | 10.9 | 10.9 | 0.9 | 15.0 |
| Mining[6] | 5.3 | * | 2.5 | 2.9 | 0.7 | 0.5 |
| Construction | 10.6 | 1.2 | 4.7 | 6.9 | 0.2 | 1.3 |
| Manufacturing | 9.7 | 5.7 | 5.2 | 2.9 | 0.2 | 0.5 |
| Total service providing | 9.8 | 1.7 | 3.9 | 5.9 | 0.1 | 4.7 |
| Trade, transportation and utilities[7] | 17.3 | 2.0 | 3.1 | 9.9 | 0.2 | 1.6 |
| Wholesale trade | 14.7 | 1.9 | 2.6 | 7.9 | 0.2 | 0.8 |
| Retail trade | 16.1 | 1.9 | 3.2 | 4.9 | 0.1 | 1.7 |
| Transportation and warehousing | 25.2 | 2.3 | 3.6 | 26.9 | 0.1 | 2.6 |
| Utilities | 5.1 | 3.0 | 2.1 | 5.9 | 1.4 | 1.1 |
| Information | 3.0 | 2.0 | 1.8 | 5.9 | * | 1.2 |
| Financial activities | 4.8 | 2.3 | 1.5 | 3.9 | * | 1.1 |
| Real estate and rental and leasing | 17.0 | 2.1 | 4.4 | 8.9 | * | 3.0 |
| Professional and business services | 3.6 | 1.0 | 1.7 | 4.9 | * | 2.8 |
| Professional, scientific, and technical services | 1.6 | 0.5 | 1.1 | 1.9 | * | 3.2 |
| Management of companies and enterprises | 2.5 | 0.7 | 1.1 | 1.9 | * | 0.2 |
| Administrative and support and waste management and remediation services | 7.1 | 2.0 | 3.0 | 8.9 | 0.1 | 3.1 |
| Education and health services | 10.9 | 1.7 | 4.8 | 4.9 | 0.1 | 13.7 |
| Educational services | 3.4 | 0.9 | 1.3 | 1.9 | * | 10.8 |
| Health care and social assistance | 11.9 | 1.8 | 5.2 | 5.9 | 0.1 | 14.0 |
| Leisure and hospitality | 6.9 | 1.8 | 10.5 | 2.9 | 0.1 | 3.7 |
| Arts, entertainment, and recreation | 8.5 | 2.5 | 6.4 | 3.9 | 0.1 | 8.4 |
| Accommodation and food services | 6.7 | 1.6 | 11.1 | 2.9 | 0.1 | 2.9 |
| Other services | 6.5 | 1.7 | 3.4 | 5.9 | 0.3 | 4.6 |
| **Total State Government[5,6,7]** | 8.4 | 2.3 | 6.5 | 11.9 | 0.1 | 31.2 |
| Total service providing | 8.2 | 2.3 | 6.4 | 10.9 | 0.1 | 31.7 |
| Education and health services | 9.1 | 1.8 | 3.4 | 4.9 | * | 35.6 |
| Educational services | 5.4 | 1.2 | 2.5 | 2.9 | * | 1.4 |
| Health care and social assistance | 19.2 | 3.5 | 5.9 | 12.9 | * | 127.7 |
| Public administration | 6.5 | 2.6 | 9.6 | 10.9 | 0.2 | 29.0 |
| Justice, public order, and safety activities | 10.5 | 2.5 | 11.4 | 14.9 | * | 66.6 |
| **Total Local Government[5,6,7]** | 14.4 | 2.1 | 8.2 | 12.9 | 0.5 | 23.0 |
| Total goods producing | 35.9 | 5.8 | 5.6 | 25.9 | * | * |
| Construction | 36.0 | 5.8 | 5.6 | 25.9 | * | * |
| Total service providing | 14.1 | 2.1 | 8.2 | 12.9 | 0.5 | 23.2 |
| Trade, transportation and utilities | 26.3 | 8.9 | 13.9 | 44.9 | * | 24.6 |
| Transportation and warehousing | 15.0 | 9.1 | 12.9 | 80.9 | * | 35.1 |
| Utilities | 39.3 | 8.8 | 15.1 | 4.9 | * | 12.8 |
| Education and health services | 10.7 | 1.1 | 4.6 | 3.9 | * | 15.4 |
| Educational services | 10.1 | 0.9 | 4.2 | 4.9 | * | 14.8 |
| Health care and social assistance | 15.9 | 2.7 | 7.4 | 3.9 | * | 20.1 |
| Public administration | 17.5 | 2.8 | 13.7 | 20.9 | 1.4 | 39.4 |
| Justice, public order, and safety activities | 20.8 | 2.4 | 26.1 | 32.9 | 2.1 | 85.2 |

[1]Median days away from work is the measure used to summarize the varying lengths of absences from work among the cases with days away from work.
[2]The incidence rates represent the number of injuries and illnesses per 10,000 full-time workers and were calculated as (N/EH) x 20,000,000, where N = number of injuries and illnesses EH = total hours worked by all employees during the calendar year 20,000,000 = base for 10,000 equivalent full-time workers (40 hours per week, 50 weeks per year).
[3]Days-away-from-work cases include those that resulted in days away from work, some of which also included job transfer or restriction.
[4]Muscoskeletal disorders include cases in which the nature of the injury or illness is pinched nerve; herniated disc; meniscus tear; sprains, strains, tears; hernia (traumatic and nontraumatic); pain, swelling, and numbness; carpal or tarsal tunnel syndrome; Raynaud's syndrome or phenomenon; musculoskeletal system and connective tissue diseases and disorders, and when the event or exposure leading to the injury or illness is overexertion and bodily reaction, unspecified; overexertion involving outside sources; repetitive motion involving microtasks; other and multiple exertions or bodily reactions; and rubbed, abraded, or jarred by vibration.
[5]Excludes farms with fewer than 11 employees.
[6]Data for Mining (Sector 21 in the North American Industry Classification System-United States, 2012) include establishments not governed by the Mine Safety and Health Administration rules and reporting, such as those in Oil and Gas Extraction and related support activities.
[7]Data for employers in rail transportation are provided to BLS by the Federal Railroad Administration, U.S. Department of Transportation.
* = Figure does not meet standards of reliability or quality.

**Table 14-7.  Incidence Rates[1] for Nonfatal Occupational Injuries and Illnesses Involving Days Away from Work[2] Per 10,000 Full-Time Workers by Selected Worker Occupation, 2015**

(Rate.)

| Occupation[3] | Nature of injury and illness[4] | | | | | | |
|---|---|---|---|---|---|---|---|
| | Total incidence rate | Sprains, strains, and tears | Fractures | Cuts, lacerations, punctures | Bruises, contusions | Heat burns | Chemical burns |
| TOTAL ................................................ | 104.0 | 38.0 | 8.9 | 9.6 | 9.1 | 1.6 | 0.3 |
| Police and sheriffs patrol officers ............................. | 497.7 | 187.5 | 27.2 | 28.6 | 45.4 | 4.3 | ... |
| Correctional officers and jailers ................................. | 420.2 | 138.8 | 22.3 | 28.3 | 44.8 | 0.7 | 0.6 |
| Firefighters ................................................................ | 397.5 | 212.7 | 8.8 | 15.7 | 15.1 | 8.6 | ... |
| Nursing assistants .................................................... | 348.5 | 187.1 | 10.8 | 5.9 | 31.6 | 0.5 | ... |
| Heating, air conditioning, and refrigeration mechanics and installers ....................................................... | 319.5 | 93.1 | 32.5 | 56.8 | 29.0 | 5.4 | 3.1 |
| Light truck or delivery services drivers ....................... | 314.0 | 144.8 | 20.4 | 14.7 | 23.0 | 1.2 | ... |
| Emergency medical technicians and paramedics ....... | 313.5 | 177.7 | 7.6 | 5.4 | 18.1 | 1.5 | ... |
| Heavy and tractor-trailer truck drivers ....................... | 307.5 | 132.9 | 36.1 | 12.6 | 26.0 | 0.9 | 1.1 |
| Laborers and freight, stock, and material ................... | 297.8 | 119.9 | 23.5 | 30.9 | 29.2 | 1.3 | 0.9 |
| Food preparation workers ......................................... | 290.8 | 68.7 | 14.8 | 94.5 | 27.1 | 24.5 | 0.9 |
| Sheet metal workers ................................................. | 289.9 | 117.0 | 15.6 | 86.5 | 11.2 | ... | ... |
| Nonfarm animal caretakers ....................................... | 278.0 | 103.0 | 6.4 | 81.2 | 5.1 | ... | ... |
| Janitors and cleaners, except maids and housekeeping cleaners ......................................... | 277.4 | 113.1 | 23.3 | 20.0 | 26.5 | 1.6 | 2.0 |
| Construction laborers ................................................ | 265.3 | 72.2 | 38.1 | 46.1 | 18.7 | 1.8 | 1.8 |
| Maintenance and repair workers, general .................. | 262.4 | 92.9 | 23.7 | 31.6 | 13.9 | 3.3 | 2.6 |
| Maids and housekeeping cleaners ............................ | 255.6 | 106.2 | 14.6 | 12.1 | 29.8 | 0.3 | 1.7 |
| Bus and truck mechanics and diesel engine specialists ............................................................ | 246.0 | 93.6 | 23.8 | 24.6 | 21.6 | 1.2 | ... |
| Painters, construction and maintenance .................... | 235.9 | 82.6 | 67.9 | 28.1 | 17.0 | ... | ... |
| Taxi drivers and chauffeurs ...................................... | 213.6 | 104.2 | 14.4 | 5.7 | 10.1 | ... | ... |
| Automotive service technicians and mechanics ......... | 207.2 | 66.5 | 16.2 | 34.0 | 8.2 | 4.0 | 0.9 |
| Food servers, nonrestaurant ..................................... | 201.0 | 63.7 | 11.6 | 34.5 | 21.8 | 11.6 | ... |
| Landscaping and groundskeeping workers ............... | 194.1 | 72.2 | 21.1 | 25.7 | 7.1 | 0.5 | 0.3 |
| Plumbers, pipefitters, and steamfitters ...................... | 193.7 | 58.2 | 20.8 | 26.0 | 6.1 | 2.1 | 3.6 |
| Teacher assistants ................................................... | 185.9 | 54.3 | 12.7 | 4.2 | 29.9 | ... | ... |
| Bus drivers, school or special client ......................... | 185.8 | 93.5 | 10.3 | 2.2 | 17.7 | ... | ... |
| Cooks, institution and cafeteria ................................ | 184.9 | 54.5 | 8.1 | 26.2 | 21.1 | 19.2 | 0.8 |
| Chefs and head cooks .............................................. | 182.7 | 42.0 | 5.3 | 39.5 | 11.7 | 28.5 | ... |
| Counter attendants, cafeteria, food concession, and coffee shop carpenters ...................................... | 182.6 | 62.2 | 24.0 | 19.1 | 8.3 | 25.2 | ... |
| Carpenters ............................................................... | 179.6 | 42.2 | 26.4 | 50.8 | 5.3 | ... | ... |
| Laundry and dry-cleaning workers ............................ | 175.5 | 63.9 | 6.7 | 5.4 | 18.6 | 5.8 | 1.4 |
| Telecommunications equipment installers and repairers, except line installers ........................... | 175.3 | 93.7 | 9.1 | 12.8 | 10.2 | ... | ... |
| Welders, cutters, solderers, and brazers .................. | 163.9 | 41.7 | 19.5 | 28.3 | 7.2 | 4.1 | ... |
| Reservation and transportation ticket agents and travel clerks ....................................................... | 158.0 | 98.1 | 6.7 | 3.3 | 13.0 | ... | ... |
| First-line supervisors of housekeeping and janitorial workers ............................................................... | 156.8 | 47.5 | 8.7 | 12.7 | 9.1 | 19.5 | ... |
| First-Line supervisors of helpers, laborers, and material movers, hand ....................................... | 155.7 | 65.4 | 15.4 | 2.6 | 14.6 | 1.5 | ... |
| Stock clerks and order fillers ................................... | 154.4 | 75.3 | 8.2 | 12.0 | 19.5 | 0.2 | ... |
| Dining room and cafeteria attendants and bartender helpers ............................................................... | 151.4 | 37.1 | 9.1 | 30.3 | 26.7 | 7.2 | ... |
| Personal care aides ................................................. | 149.4 | 67.2 | 9.4 | 3.4 | 13.3 | 1.2 | ... |
| Dishwashers ............................................................. | 145.6 | 29.5 | 7.0 | 53.4 | 9.2 | 5.0 | 1.6 |
| Medical and clinical laboratory technicians ............... | 144.5 | 61.6 | 7.0 | 5.5 | 10.2 | ... | ... |

[1]The incidence rates represent the number of injuries and illnesses per 10,000 full-time workers and were calculated as (N/EH) x 20,000,000, where N = number of injuries and illnesses EH = total hours worked by all employees during the calendar year 20,000,000 = base for 10,000 equivalent full-time workers (40 hours per week, 50 weeks per year).
[2]Days-away-from-work cases include those that resulted in days away from work, some of which also included job transfer or restriction.
[3]These occupations have at least 0.1 percent of full-time equivalent employment.
[4]Data shown in columns correspond to Nature codes based on the Occupational Injury and Illness Classification System 2.01 developed by the Bureau of Labor Statistics (BLS).
[5]Includes nonclassifiable responses.
... = Data not available.

**Table 14-7. Incidence Rates[1] for Nonfatal Occupational Injuries and Illnesses Involving Days Away from Work[2] Per 10,000 Full-Time Workers by Selected Worker Occupation, 2015—***Continued*

(Rate.)

| Occupation[3] | Nature of injury and illness[4] | | | | | |
|---|---|---|---|---|---|---|
| | Amputations | Carpel tunnel syndrome | Tendonitis | Multiple traumatic injuries and disorders | Soreness, pain | All other natures[5] |
| TOTAL ................................................ | 0.5 | 0.5 | 0.2 | 2.8 | 16.6 | 15.8 |
| Police and sheriffs patrol officers ............................... | ... | 0.8 | ... | 25.5 | 87.0 | 91.1 |
| Correctional officers and jailers ................................ | ... | 1.6 | ... | 21.8 | 94.0 | 67.0 |
| Firefighters ............................................................... | ... | ... | ... | 6.1 | 52.0 | 78.4 |
| Nursing assistants ................................................... | ... | ... | 0.4 | 6.9 | 72.9 | 32.3 |
| Heating, air conditioning, and refrigeration mechanics and installers ....................................... | 1.8 | 1.3 | ... | 5.8 | 39.6 | 50.9 |
| Light truck or delivery services drivers ...................... | 0.6 | ... | 1.0 | 9.1 | 48.7 | 50.1 |
| Emergency medical technicians and paramedics ....... | ... | ... | 1.0 | 3.7 | 55.0 | 43.0 |
| Heavy and tractor-trailer truck drivers ...................... | 1.8 | 0.4 | 0.3 | 11.2 | 46.9 | 37.1 |
| Laborers and freight, stock, and material .................. | 2.2 | 0.8 | 0.4 | 6.4 | 41.5 | 40.7 |
| Food preparation workers ......................................... | 1.9 | 1.1 | 0.5 | 3.5 | 30.9 | 22.4 |
| Sheet metal workers ................................................ | ... | ... | ... | 9.0 | 11.0 | 38.5 |
| Nonfarm animal caretakers ...................................... | ... | ... | ... | ... | 29.1 | 50.2 |
| Janitors and cleaners, except maids and housekeeping cleaners ......................................... | 0.3 | 0.7 | 0.4 | 5.0 | 42.9 | 41.6 |
| Construction laborers ............................................... | 1.2 | 0.3 | 0.2 | 5.4 | 34.7 | 44.7 |
| Maintenance and repair workers, general .................. | 2.3 | 0.7 | 0.2 | 5.0 | 38.8 | 47.3 |
| Maids and housekeeping cleaners ............................ | ... | 1.0 | 1.3 | 6.3 | 50.1 | 32.1 |
| Bus and truck mechanics and diesel engine specialists ........................................................... | ... | ... | ... | 6.3 | 36.7 | 37.1 |
| Painters, construction and maintenance .................... | ... | ... | ... | 2.1 | 19.8 | 17.3 |
| Taxi drivers and chauffeurs ...................................... | ... | ... | ... | 13.9 | 45.2 | 19.9 |
| Automotive service technicians and mechanics ......... | 6.4 | 0.6 | ... | 1.3 | 27.9 | 41.0 |
| Food servers, nonrestaurant ..................................... | ... | ... | ... | 6.9 | 27.1 | 23.4 |
| Landscaping and groundskeeping workers ............... | 1.4 | 0.4 | ... | 3.6 | 24.2 | 37.5 |
| Plumbers, pipefitters, and steamfitters ...................... | 1.8 | ... | 0.6 | 2.1 | 37.7 | 34.7 |
| Teacher assistants ................................................... | ... | ... | ... | 5.6 | 55.4 | 23.6 |
| Bus drivers, school or special client .......................... | ... | ... | ... | 6.5 | 41.8 | 13.2 |
| Cooks, institution and cafeteria ................................ | ... | ... | ... | 2.6 | 41.2 | 10.4 |
| Chefs and head cooks .............................................. | ... | ... | ... | 23.6 | 12.0 | 11.5 |
| Counter attendants, cafeteria, food concession, and coffee shop carpenters ................................. | ... | ... | ... | 2.6 | 17.5 | 22.9 |
| Carpenters ............................................................... | 0.6 | 0.4 | ... | 3.0 | 33.8 | 16.9 |
| Laundry and dry-cleaning workers ............................ | ... | 1.2 | ... | 7.1 | 41.7 | 23.5 |
| Telecommunications equipment installers and repairers, except line installers .......................... | ... | ... | ... | 4.7 | 23.1 | 21.6 |
| Welders, cutters, solderers, and brazers .................. | 1.0 | 0.5 | 0.6 | 1.7 | 20.0 | 39.3 |
| Reservation and transportation ticket agents and travel clerks ................................................... | ... | ... | ... | 3.4 | 11.9 | 21.4 |
| First-line supervisors of housekeeping and janitorial workers ............................................. | ... | ... | ... | 3.1 | 40.9 | 14.5 |
| First-Line supervisors of helpers, laborers, and material movers, hand ....................................... | 2.3 | ... | ... | 4.7 | 24.8 | 24.2 |
| Stock clerks and order fillers .................................... | 0.4 | 0.5 | 0.3 | 2.6 | 18.7 | 16.5 |
| Dining room and cafeteria attendants and bartender helpers ............................................. | ... | ... | ... | 3.5 | 18.4 | 18.3 |
| Personal care aides ................................................. | ... | ... | ... | 4.1 | 32.8 | 17.8 |
| Dishwashers ............................................................ | ... | ... | ... | 3.7 | 10.8 | 24.8 |
| Medical and clinical laboratory technicians ............... | ... | 1.4 | 2.7 | 3.5 | 22.1 | 30.1 |

[1]The incidence rates represent the number of injuries and illnesses per 10,000 full-time workers and were calculated as (N/EH) x 20,000,000, where N = number of injuries and illnesses EH = total hours worked by all employees during the calendar year 20,000,000 = base for 10,000 equivalent full-time workers (40 hours per week, 50 weeks per year).
[2]Days-away-from-work cases include those that resulted in days away from work, some of which also included job transfer or restriction.
[3]These occupations have at least 0.1 percent of full-time equivalent employment.
[4]Data shown in columns correspond to Nature codes based on the Occupational Injury and Illness Classification System 2.01 developed by the Bureau of Labor Statistics (BLS).
[5]Includes nonclassifiable responses.
... = Data not available.

**Table 14-8.  Incidence Rates[1] for Nonfatal Occupational Injuries and Illnesses Involving Days Away from Work[2] Per 10,000 Full-Time Workers by Selected Occupation[3] and Events or Exposure,[4] 2015**

(Rate.)

| Occupation | Total incidence rate | Contact with objects | Falls, slips, and trips | Overexertion and bodily reaction | | | Exposure to harmful substances or environments |
|---|---|---|---|---|---|---|---|
| | | | | Total | Overexertion in lifting | Repetitive motion | |
| **TOTAL** | 104.0 | 24.3 | 27.9 | 33.9 | 10.2 | 2.2 | 4.7 |
| Police and sheriffs patrol officers | 497.7 | 42.4 | 108.8 | 98.8 | 10.5 | 2.0 | 23.8 |
| Correctional officers and jailers | 420.2 | 50.5 | 100.4 | 93.9 | 13.1 | 2.5 | 18.1 |
| Firefighters | 397.5 | 53.4 | 102.8 | 189.3 | 44.6 | ... | 28.8 |
| Nursing assistants | 348.5 | 31.0 | 64.7 | 186.3 | 42.5 | 1.7 | 5.6 |
| Heating, air conditioning, and refrigeration mechanics and installers | 319.5 | 111.8 | 88.7 | 87.7 | 21.3 | 3.3 | 18.1 |
| Light truck or delivery services drivers | 314.0 | 42.3 | 82.8 | 144.4 | 47.7 | 2.0 | 4.2 |
| Emergency medical technicians and paramedics | 313.5 | 33.9 | 40.3 | 193.7 | 95.0 | 1.9 | 8.2 |
| Heavy and tractor-trailer truck drivers | 307.5 | 52.1 | 101.1 | 97.0 | 21.4 | 1.8 | 4.3 |
| Laborers and freight, stock, and material | 297.8 | 102.9 | 55.8 | 115.3 | 49.5 | 5.0 | 5.2 |
| Food preparation workers | 290.8 | 133.1 | 71.0 | 54.5 | 26.7 | 5.5 | 29.3 |
| Sheet metal workers | 289.9 | 124.5 | 27.5 | 107.6 | 28.6 | ... | 2.5 |
| Nonfarm animal caretakers | 278.0 | 22.7 | 27.5 | 116.5 | 19.2 | 2.3 | 6.5 |
| Janitors and cleaners, except maids and housekeeping cleaners | 277.4 | 62.0 | 79.8 | 106.9 | 36.8 | 3.3 | 19.0 |
| Construction laborers | 265.3 | 102.8 | 59.3 | 70.4 | 20.6 | 2.0 | 14.0 |
| Maintenance and repair workers, general | 262.4 | 75.1 | 69.6 | 92.7 | 28.2 | 2.8 | 14.8 |
| Maids and housekeeping cleaners | 255.6 | 49.1 | 83.3 | 103.0 | 27.8 | 5.3 | 12.0 |
| Bus and truck mechanics and diesel engine specialists | 246.0 | 83.9 | 42.9 | 95.1 | 25.3 | 2.0 | 7.9 |
| Painters, construction and maintenance | 235.9 | 65.3 | 116.8 | 49.0 | 13.6 | 4.2 | 2.4 |
| Taxi drivers and chauffeurs | 213.6 | 10.7 | 54.9 | 71.8 | 44.3 | ... | 1.2 |
| Automotive service technicians and mechanics | 207.2 | 90.4 | 20.0 | 79.4 | 29.7 | 2.7 | 5.9 |
| Food servers, nonrestaurant | 201.0 | 66.3 | 66.0 | 50.3 | 18.9 | 1.1 | 14.5 |
| Landscaping and groundskeeping workers | 194.1 | 63.1 | 44.6 | 54.9 | 19.4 | 1.5 | 9.4 |
| Plumbers, pipefitters, and steamfitters | 193.7 | 56.1 | 44.4 | 72.1 | 15.3 | 2.7 | 12.1 |
| Teacher assistants | 185.9 | 23.9 | 64.9 | 35.3 | 9.6 | ... | 0.5 |
| Bus drivers, school or special client | 185.8 | 14.2 | 60.4 | 43.9 | 5.7 | 1.3 | 1.8 |
| Cooks, institution and cafeteria | 184.9 | 49.8 | 55.8 | 53.2 | 21.7 | 2.0 | 22.0 |
| Chefs and head cooks | 182.7 | 60.5 | 43.8 | 44.6 | 15.0 | ... | 28.4 |
| Counter attendants, cafeteria, food concession, and coffee shop carpenters | 182.6 | 35.3 | 66.2 | 51.5 | 17.4 | 6.6 | 27.2 |
| Carpenters | 179.6 | 80.2 | 49.7 | 41.3 | 14.5 | 2.0 | 3.2 |
| Laundry and dry-cleaning workers | 175.5 | 37.5 | 43.4 | 75.7 | 16.8 | 4.7 | 17.0 |
| Telecommunications equipment installers and repairers, except line installers | 175.3 | 26.2 | 45.9 | 75.2 | 8.7 | 1.8 | 6.9 |
| Welders, cutters, solderers, and brazers | 163.9 | 77.1 | 35.6 | 36.2 | 13.6 | 2.3 | 11.8 |
| Reservation and transportation ticket agents and travel clerks | 158.0 | 26.8 | 42.5 | 81.3 | 41.6 | 2.3 | 1.8 |
| First-line supervisors of housekeeping and janitorial workers | 156.8 | 33.0 | 38.3 | 50.0 | 18.0 | 2.0 | 3.2 |
| First-Line supervisors of helpers, laborers, and material movers, hand | 155.7 | 43.6 | 37.5 | 63.5 | 19.7 | ... | 2.8 |
| Stock clerks and order fillers | 154.4 | 44.7 | 25.9 | 75.1 | 38.2 | 5.1 | 2.3 |
| Dining room and cafeteria attendants and bartender helpers | 151.4 | 65.5 | 34.8 | 37.9 | 16.1 | 1.5 | 11.2 |
| Personal care aides | 149.4 | 11.8 | 36.0 | 56.1 | 18.5 | 0.7 | 3.0 |
| Dishwashers | 145.6 | 79.9 | 25.0 | 24.5 | 10.0 | 1.9 | 14.2 |
| Medical and clinical laboratory technicians | 144.5 | 19.4 | 42.8 | 62.3 | 8.9 | 17.1 | 12.7 |

[1]The incidence rates represent the number of injuries and illnesses per 10,000 full-time workers and were calculated as (N/EH) x 20,000,000, where N = number of injuries and illnesses EH = total hours worked by all employees during the calendar year 20,000,000 = base for 10,000 equivalent full-time workers (40 hours per week, 50 weeks per year).
[2]Days-away-from-work cases include those that resulted in days away from work, some of which also included job transfer or restriction.
[3]These occupations have at least 0.1 percent of full-time equivalent employment.
[4]Data shown in columns correspond to Event codes based on the Occupational Injury and Illness Classification System 2.01 developed by the Bureau of Labor Statistics (BLS).
[5]Includes nonclassifiable responses.
... = Data not available.

**Table 14-8. Incidence Rates[1] for Nonfatal Occupational Injuries and Illnesses Involving Days Away from Work[2] Per 10,000 Full-Time Workers by Selected Occupation[3] and Events or Exposure,[4] 2015**—*Continued*

(Rate.)

| Occupation | Transportation incidents | | | Violence and other injuries by persons or animal | | | | All other events[5] |
|---|---|---|---|---|---|---|---|---|
| | Total | Roadway incidents | Fire explosions | Total | Intentional injury by other person | Injury by person unintentional or intent unknown | Animal and insect related | |
| TOTAL | 5.7 | 4.0 | 0.2 | 6.8 | 3.1 | 2.3 | 1.3 | 0.5 |
| Police and sheriffs patrol officers | 78.4 | 66.1 | 0.8 | 140.4 | 51.2 | 76.1 | 12.8 | 4.4 |
| Correctional officers and jailers | 6.6 | 3.1 | ... | 147.5 | 72.3 | 71.0 | 1.2 | 3.3 |
| Firefighters | 6.1 | 4.4 | 10.0 | 4.6 | ... | 2.3 | 2.2 | 2.6 |
| Nursing assistants | 2.8 | 2.6 | ... | 56.3 | 34.5 | 17.0 | 4.6 | 1.8 |
| Heating, air conditioning, and refrigeration mechanics and installers | 8.2 | 7.5 | ... | 1.2 | ... | ... | 1.1 | 3.5 |
| Light truck or delivery services drivers | 36.7 | 30.3 | ... | 2.7 | 0.4 | ... | 2.2 | 0.9 |
| Emergency medical technicians and paramedics | 21.2 | 18.8 | ... | 15.5 | 6.3 | 8.8 | ... | ... |
| Heavy and tractor-trailer truck drivers | 48.0 | 40.7 | 0.7 | 2.3 | 0.3 | 0.1 | 1.8 | 2.0 |
| Laborers and freight, stock, and material | 14.6 | 2.5 | 0.5 | 1.9 | 0.3 | 0.3 | 1.2 | 1.6 |
| Food preparation workers | 1.0 | ... | ... | 0.5 | ... | 0.3 | ... | 1.2 |
| Sheet metal workers | ... | ... | ... | ... | ... | ... | ... | ... |
| Nonfarm animal caretakers | ... | ... | ... | 102.8 | ... | ... | 102.5 | ... |
| Janitors and cleaners, except maids and housekeeping cleaners | 4.8 | 2.8 | 0.2 | 2.9 | 0.6 | 0.2 | 2.1 | 1.8 |
| Construction laborers | 16.0 | 6.8 | 0.4 | 1.6 | ... | ... | 1.4 | 0.8 |
| Maintenance and repair workers, general | 7.3 | 4.6 | ... | 1.6 | 0.3 | ... | 1.2 | 1.1 |
| Maids and housekeeping cleaners | 3.8 | 3.4 | ... | 3.4 | 0.7 | 0.3 | 2.4 | 1.0 |
| Bus and truck mechanics and diesel engine specialists | 11.4 | 5.2 | 0.8 | 3.6 | ... | ... | 2.7 | ... |
| Painters, construction and maintenance | ... | ... | ... | 1.5 | ... | ... | ... | ... |
| Taxi drivers and chauffeurs | 66.3 | 62.6 | ... | 8.8 | 2.9 | ... | 5.2 | ... |
| Automotive service technicians and mechanics | 8.8 | 3.8 | 1.5 | 0.5 | ... | ... | 0.4 | 0.7 |
| Food servers, nonrestaurant | ... | ... | ... | 1.5 | 0.9 | ... | ... | ... |
| Landscaping and groundskeeping workers | 13.1 | 6.5 | ... | 8.2 | 0.3 | ... | 7.8 | 0.9 |
| Plumbers, pipefitters, and steamfitters | 5.1 | 4.6 | ... | 1.1 | ... | ... | 1.1 | 2.8 |
| Teacher assistants | 2.8 | 2.5 | ... | 56.6 | 34.0 | 21.6 | 0.2 | 1.9 |
| Bus drivers, school or special client | 58.5 | 50.2 | ... | 6.8 | 4.2 | 1.6 | 1.1 | ... |
| Cooks, institution and cafeteria | 0.9 | ... | ... | 1.7 | 1.5 | ... | ... | 1.3 |
| Chefs and head cooks | 1.4 | ... | 3.5 | ... | ... | ... | ... | ... |
| Counter attendants, cafeteria, food concession, and coffee shop carpenters | 1.4 | ... | ... | 1.0 | ... | 1.0 | ... | ... |
| Carpenters | 2.3 | 1.2 | ... | 0.6 | ... | ... | 0.6 | 1.9 |
| Laundry and dry-cleaning workers | ... | ... | ... | 1.6 | ... | ... | 1.6 | ... |
| Telecommunications equipment installers and repairers, except line installers | 13.4 | 12.1 | ... | 7.6 | ... | ... | 7.3 | ... |
| Welders, cutters, solderers, and brazers | 1.4 | ... | 1.2 | ... | ... | ... | ... | 0.5 |
| Reservation and transportation ticket agents and travel clerks | ... | ... | ... | 3.9 | ... | 1.5 | 1.7 | ... |
| First-line supervisors of housekeeping and janitorial workers | 21.8 | 2.1 | ... | 10.3 | ... | ... | 9.4 | ... |
| First-Line supervisors of helpers, laborers, and material movers, hand | 8.1 | 1.1 | ... | ... | ... | ... | ... | ... |
| Stock clerks and order fillers | 4.4 | 0.6 | ... | 1.6 | 0.8 | 0.2 | 0.6 | 0.4 |
| Dining room and cafeteria attendants and bartender helpers | ... | ... | ... | 1.2 | 0.8 | ... | ... | ... |
| Personal care aides | 9.2 | 7.7 | ... | 32.9 | 21.2 | 9.8 | 1.6 | 0.5 |
| Dishwashers | 1.6 | ... | ... | ... | ... | ... | ... | ... |
| Medical and clinical laboratory technicians | 2.8 | 2.6 | ... | 3.2 | ... | 1.8 | ... | ... |

[1]The incidence rates represent the number of injuries and illnesses per 10,000 full-time workers and were calculated as (N/EH) x 20,000,000, where N = number of injuries and illnesses EH = total hours worked by all employees during the calendar year 20,000,000 = base for 10,000 equivalent full-time workers (40 hours per week, 50 weeks per year).
[2]Days-away-from-work cases include those that resulted in days away from work, some of which also included job transfer or restriction.
[3]These occupations have at least 0.1 percent of full-time equivalent employment.
[4]Data shown in columns correspond to Event codes based on the Occupational Injury and Illness Classification System 2.01 developed by the Bureau of Labor Statistics (BLS).
[5]Includes nonclassifiable responses.
... = Data not available.

**Table 14-9. Number, Incidence Rate,[1] and Median Days Away From Work[2,3] by Selected Worker Occupation and Ownership, 2015**

(Number, rate.)

| Characteristic | Total private, state, and local government[4,5,6] | | | Private industry[4,5,6] | | |
|---|---|---|---|---|---|---|
| | Number | Incidence rate | Median days away from work | Number | Incidence rate | Median days away from work |
| TOTAL ........................................ | 1 153 490 | 104.0 | 8 | 902 160 | 93.9 | 8 |
| Police and sheriffs patrol officers ........................................ | 29 670 | 497.7 | 8 | 200 | 401.1 | 16 |
| Correctional officers and jailers ............................. | 16 080 | 420.2 | 11 | 610 | 345.4 | 7 |
| Firefighters ..................................................... | 13 280 | 397.5 | 11 | 200 | 143.0 | 14 |
| Nursing assistants .......................................... | 37 370 | 348.5 | 6 | 32 320 | 327.8 | 5 |
| Heating, air conditioning, and refrigeration mechanics and installers | 7 880 | 319.5 | 9 | 7 420 | 318.7 | 8 |
| Light truck or delivery services drivers ............................. | 24 780 | 314.0 | 14 | 23 330 | 298.0 | 15 |
| Emergency medical technicians and paramedics .............. | 6 670 | 313.5 | 9 | 4 160 | 291.0 | 8 |
| Heavy and tractor-trailer truck drivers ......................... | 49 260 | 307.5 | 22 | 47 350 | 298.7 | 21 |
| Laborers and freight, stock, and material ........................... | 59 010 | 297.8 | 9 | 56 550 | 289.4 | 9 |
| Food preparation workers ........................................ | 15 860 | 290.8 | 6 | 14 310 | 277.0 | 6 |
| Sheet metal workers ........................................ | 3 360 | 289.9 | 7 | 3 340 | 289.5 | 7 |
| Nonfarm animal caretakers ........................................ | 3 320 | 278.0 | 3 | 3 080 | 264.6 | 3 |
| Janitors and cleaners, except maids and housekeeping cleaners ........................................ | 42 740 | 277.4 | 10 | 20 200 | 172.0 | 9 |
| Construction laborers ........................................ | 19 960 | 265.3 | 11 | 18 530 | 256.0 | 11 |
| Maintenance and repair workers, general ......................... | 30 020 | 262.4 | 9 | 22 820 | 240.2 | 8 |
| Maids and housekeeping cleaners ........................... | 17 440 | 255.6 | 7 | 16 390 | 248.6 | 7 |
| Bus and truck mechanics and diesel engine specialists ...... | 5 870 | 246.0 | 18 | 4 080 | 199.6 | 18 |
| Painters, construction and maintenance .......................... | 4 140 | 235.9 | 9 | 3 490 | 208.8 | 10 |
| Taxi drivers and chauffeurs .......................................... | 3 100 | 213.6 | 11 | 2 990 | 213.6 | 11 |
| Automotive service technicians and mechanics ................. | 11 920 | 207.2 | 8 | 11 450 | 206.3 | 7 |
| Food servers, nonrestaurant .......................................... | 3 360 | 201.0 | 5 | 2 700 | 165.3 | 5 |
| Landscaping and groundskeeping workers ....................... | 14 180 | 194.1 | 7 | 10 100 | 157.2 | 7 |
| Plumbers, pipefitters, and steamfitters ......................... | 6 860 | 193.7 | 22 | 6 410 | 190.0 | 23 |
| Teacher assistants ........................................ | 15 590 | 185.9 | 5 | 2 840 | 156.5 | 5 |
| Bus drivers, school or special client ........................... | 6 680 | 185.8 | 13 | 3 130 | 176.4 | 12 |
| Cooks, institution and cafeteria ........................... | 5 450 | 184.9 | 8 | 2 970 | 161.6 | 5 |
| Chefs and head cooks ........................................ | 2 180 | 182.7 | 5 | 2 120 | 181.9 | 5 |
| Counter attendants, cafeteria, food concession, and coffee shop carpenters ........................................ | 4 400 | 182.6 | 13 | 3 130 | 137.2 | 19 |
| Carpenters ........................................ | 9 990 | 179.6 | 12 | 9 710 | 178.2 | 12 |
| Laundry and dry-cleaning workers ........................... | 2 770 | 175.5 | 11 | 2 600 | 169.4 | 10 |
| Telecommunications equipment installers and repairers, except line installers ........................................ | 3 510 | 175.3 | 20 | 3 490 | 177.5 | 20 |
| Welders, cutters, solderers, and brazers ........................ | 5 950 | 163.9 | 7 | 5 800 | 160.4 | 7 |
| Reservation and transportation ticket agents and travel clerks ........................................ | 1 810 | 158.0 | 13 | 1 780 | 156.6 | 13 |
| First-line supervisors of housekeeping and janitorial workers ........................................ | 2 350 | 156.8 | 7 | 1 560 | 130.2 | 4 |
| First-Line supervisors of helpers, laborers, and material movers, hand ........................................ | 2 650 | 155.7 | 10 | 2 340 | 140.2 | 8 |
| Stock clerks and order fillers ........................... | 21 420 | 154.4 | 8 | 21 160 | 154.7 | 8 |
| Dining room and cafeteria attendants and bartender helpers ........................................ | 3 450 | 151.4 | 5 | 2 800 | 130.2 | 5 |
| Personal care aides ........................................ | 14 640 | 149.4 | 8 | 12 800 | 132.0 | 8 |
| Dishwashers ........................................ | 4 600 | 145.6 | 6 | 4 510 | 144.3 | 6 |
| Medical and clinical laboratory technicians ....................... | 1 830 | 144.5 | 8 | 1 640 | 143.8 | 8 |

[1]The incidence rates represent the number of injuries and illnesses per 10,000 full-time workers and were calculated as (N/EH) x 20,000,000, where N = number of injuries and illnesses EH = total hours worked by all employees during the calendar year 20,000,000 = base for 10,000 equivalent full-time workers (40 hours per week, 50 weeks per year).
[2]Median days away from work is the measure used to summarize the varying lengths of absences from work among the cases with days away from work.
[3]Days-away-from-work cases include those that resulted in days away from work, some of which also included job transfer or restriction.
[4]Excludes farms with fewer than 11 employees.
[5]Data for Mining (Sector 21 in the North American Industry Classification System-United States, 2012) include establishments not governed by the Mine Safety and Health Administration rules and reporting, such as those in Oil and Gas Extraction and related support activities.
[6]Data for employers in rail transportation are provided to BLS by the Federal Railroad Administration, U.S. Department of Transportation.

## Table 14-9. Number, Incidence Rate,[1] and Median Days Away From Work[2,3] by Selected Worker Occupation and Ownership, 2015—*Continued*

(Number, rate.)

| Characteristic | State government[5,6] | | | Local government[5,6] | | |
|---|---|---|---|---|---|---|
| | Number | Incidence rate | Median days away from work | Number | Incidence rate | Median days away from work |
| **TOTAL** ............................................ | 59 590 | 149.2 | 11 | 191 750 | 177.5 | 9 |
| Police and sheriffs patrol officers ........................................ | 2 790 | 393.9 | 13 | 26 680 | 530.2 | 7 |
| Correctional officers and jailers ........................................ | 10 790 | 457.5 | 14 | 4 680 | 333.0 | 5 |
| Firefighters ........................................ | 690 | 624.4 | 4 | 12 390 | 422.2 | 12 |
| Nursing assistants ........................................ | 2 220 | 737.9 | 8 | 2 830 | 494.5 | 6 |
| Heating, air conditioning, and refrigeration mechanics and installers | 180 | 368.5 | 9 | 280 | 303.8 | 16 |
| Light truck or delivery services drivers ........................ | 60 | * | 14 | 1 390 | 1 975.9 | 8 |
| Emergency medical technicians and paramedics ............. | * | * | * | 2 | 500.0 | 10 |
| Heavy and tractor-trailer truck drivers ........................ | 110 | * | 16 | 1 790 | 896.5 | 30 |
| Laborers and freight, stock, and material ........................ | 240 | 296.0 | 9 | 2 210 | 957.6 | 8 |
| Food preparation workers ........................ | 310 | 853.1 | 10 | 1 240 | 490.5 | 6 |
| Sheet metal workers ........................ | 20 | * | 43 | * | * | * |
| Nonfarm animal caretakers ........................ | 60 | * | 24 | 170 | * | 3 |
| Janitors and cleaners, except maids and housekeeping cleaners ........................ | 2 400 | 405.7 | 15 | 20 140 | 657.4 | 10 |
| Construction laborers ........................ | 130 | * | 25 | 1 310 | 485.8 | 7 |
| Maintenance and repair workers, general ........................ | 1 400 | 320.3 | 10 | 5 810 | 390.4 | 10 |
| Maids and housekeeping cleaners ........................ | 340 | 687.5 | 6 | 710 | 365.9 | 6 |
| Bus and truck mechanics and diesel engine specialists ...... | 350 | 863.1 | 22 | 1 430 | 486.3 | 15 |
| Painters, construction and maintenance ........................ | 120 | * | 6 | 540 | 834.2 | 9 |
| Taxi drivers and chauffeurs ........................ | 20 | * | 14 | 90 | 215.6 | 14 |
| Automotive service technicians and mechanics ................ | 180 | 310.6 | 10 | 290 | 193.1 | 10 |
| Food servers, nonrestaurant ........................ | 370 | * | 13 | 290 | 547.7 | 3 |
| Landscaping and groundskeeping workers ........................ | 710 | 557.1 | 7 | 3 370 | 451.0 | 7 |
| Plumbers, pipefitters, and steamfitters ........................ | 120 | 295.5 | 13 | 330 | 246.4 | 9 |
| Teacher assistants ........................ | 120 | 53.7 | 9 | 12 630 | 207.7 | 5 |
| Bus drivers, school or special client ........................ | * | * | * | 3 | 530.0 | 13 |
| Cooks, institution and cafeteria ........................ | 500 | 576.5 | 20 | 1 980 | 210.2 | 12 |
| Chefs and head cooks ........................ | 50 | * | 180 | * | * | * |
| Counter attendants, cafeteria, food concession, and coffee shop carpenters ........................ | 60 | * | 12 | 1 200 | 1 505.8 | 7 |
| Carpenters ........................ | 140 | 378.4 | 10 | 140 | 155.2 | 21 |
| Laundry and dry-cleaning workers ........................ | 100 | * | 85 | 80 | 275.5 | 15 |
| Telecommunications equipment installers and repairers, except line installers | * | * | * | * | * | * |
| Welders, cutters, solderers, and brazers ........................ | 30 | * | 5 | 120 | * | 6 |
| Reservation and transportation ticket agents and travel clerks ........................ | * | * | * | * | 20.0 | * |
| First-line supervisors of housekeeping and janitorial workers ........................ | 130 | 216.2 | 10 | 650 | 284.0 | 20 |
| First-Line supervisors of helpers, laborers, and material movers, hand ........................ | 120 | * | 25 | 200 | 721.5 | 34 |
| Stock clerks and order fillers ........................ | 150 | 132.4 | 7 | 120 | 96.9 | 26 |
| Dining room and cafeteria attendants and bartender helpers ........................ | 60 | * | 7 | 590 | 619.0 | 6 |
| Personal care aides ........................ | 1 180 | 894.1 | 9 | 660 | 698.4 | 13 |
| Dishwashers ........................ | * | * | * | 90 | * | 4 |
| Medical and clinical laboratory technicians ........................ | 110 | 182.0 | 15 | 80 | 108.8 | 4 |

[1] The incidence rates represent the number of injuries and illnesses per 10,000 full-time workers and were calculated as (N/EH) x 20,000,000, where N = number of injuries and illnesses EH = total hours worked by all employees during the calendar year 20,000,000 = base for 10,000 equivalent full-time workers (40 hours per week, 50 weeks per year).
[2] Median days away from work is the measure used to summarize the varying lengths of absences from work among the cases with days away from work.
[3] Days-away-from-work cases include those that resulted in days away from work, some of which also included job transfer or restriction.
[4] Excludes farms with fewer than 11 employees.
[5] Data for Mining (Sector 21 in the North American Industry Classification System-United States, 2012) include establishments not governed by the Mine Safety and Health Administration rules and reporting, such as those in Oil and Gas Extraction and related support activities.
[6] Data for employers in rail transportation are provided to BLS by the Federal Railroad Administration, U.S. Department of Transportation.
* = Figure does not meet standards of reliability or quality.

**Table 14-10.  Fatal Occupational Injuries Counts and Rates by Selected Demographic Characteristics 2014–2015**

(Number, rate.)

| Characteristic | Counts | | Rates[1] | |
|---|---|---|---|---|
| | 2014 | 2015 | 2014 | 2015 |
| TOTAL[2] ....................................................... | 4 821 | 4 836 | 3.4 | 3.4 |
| **Employee Status** | | | | |
| Wage and salary workers[3] ............................ | 3 728 | 3 751 | 2.8 | 2.8 |
| Self-employed[4] ............................................ | 1 093 | 1 085 | 13.6 | 13.1 |
| **Sex** | | | | |
| Men ............................................................... | 4 454 | 4 492 | 5.6 | 5.5 |
| Women .......................................................... | 367 | 344 | 0.6 | 0.6 |
| **Age** | | | | |
| Under 16 years ............................................. | 8 | 12 | . . . | . . . |
| 16 to 17 years ............................................. | 14 | 12 | . . . | . . . |
| 18 to 19 years ............................................. | 42 | 50 | 2.0 | 2.1 |
| 20 to 24 years ............................................. | 292 | 329 | 2.3 | 2.7 |
| 25 to 34 years ............................................. | 753 | 758 | 2.4 | 2.3 |
| 35 to 44 years ............................................. | 860 | 864 | 2.8 | 2.7 |
| 45 to 54 years ............................................. | 1 161 | 1 130 | 3.6 | 3.5 |
| 55 to 64 years ............................................. | 1 007 | 1 031 | 4.3 | 4.3 |
| 65 years and over ........................................ | 684 | 650 | 10.7 | 9.4 |
| **Race and Hispanic Origin** | | | | |
| White ............................................................. | 3 332 | 3 241 | 3.6 | 3.5 |
| Black ............................................................. | 475 | 495 | 3.2 | 3.2 |
| Hispanic[5] ..................................................... | 804 | 903 | 3.7 | 4.0 |
| American Indian or Alaskan Native ............... | 34 | 36 | . . . | . . . |
| Asian ............................................................. | 137 | 114 | 1.8 | 1.4 |
| Native Hawaiian or Pacific Islander .............. | 5 | 9 | . . . | . . . |
| Multiple races ............................................... | 20 | 12 | . . . | . . . |
| Other or not reported ................................... | 14 | 26 | . . . | . . . |

[1]Fatal injury rates are per 100,000 full-time equivalent workers (FTEs).
[2]The Census of Fatal Occupational Injuries (CFOI) has published data on fatal occupational injuries for the United States since 1992. During this time, the classification systems and definitions of many data elements have changed
[3]May include volunteers and other workers receiving compensation.
[4]Includes self-employed workers, owners of unincorporated businesses and farms, paid and unpaid family workers, and members of partnerships; may also include owners of incorporated businesses.
[5]May be of any race. The race categories shown exclude data for Hispanics and Latinos.
. . . = Not available.

## Table 14-11.  Fatal Occupational Injuries Counts and Rates for Selected Occupations, 2014–2015

(Number, rate.)

| Occupation | Counts | | Rates[1] | |
|---|---|---|---|---|
| | 2014 | 2015 | 2014 | 2015 |
| TOTAL[2] ......................................................................... | 4 821 | 4 836 | 3.4 | 3.4 |
| OCCUPATION (SOC)[3] | | | | |
| Management .................................................................. | 440 | 379 | 2.5 | 2.1 |
| Business and financial operations ................................ | 28 | 31 | 0.4 | 0.4 |
| Computer and mathematical ......................................... | 16 | 8 | 0.4 | . . . |
| Architecture and engineering ....................................... | 35 | 37 | 1.2 | 1.2 |
| Life, physical, and social science ................................. | 18 | 11 | 1.3 | . . . |
| Community and social services  ................................... | 33 | 28 | 1.1 | 1.0 |
| Legal ............................................................................ | 7 | 12 | . . . | . . . |
| Education, training, and library .................................... | 27 | 19 | 0.4 | 0.3 |
| Arts, design, entertainment, sports, and media  .......... | 47 | 65 | 1.6 | 2.4 |
| Health care practitioners and technical ........................ | 53 | 74 | 0.7 | 0.9 |
| Health care support ..................................................... | 14 | 23 | . . . | 0.7 |
| Protective service ........................................................ | 213 | 213 | 6.1 | 6.2 |
| Fire fighting and prevention workers ........................ | 26 | 30 | . . . | . . . |
| Law enforcement workers ......................................... | 106 | 102 | . . . | . . . |
| Food preparation and serving related .......................... | 55 | 56 | 0.9 | 0.9 |
| Building and grounds cleaning and maintenance .......... | 252 | 289 | 5.1 | 5.8 |
| Building cleaning and pest control workers .............. | 56 | 59 | . . . | . . . |
| Grounds maintenance workers .................................. | 158 | 183 | 13.1 | 15.0 |
| Personal care and service  .......................................... | 63 | 51 | 1.4 | 1.1 |
| Sales and related ........................................................ | 239 | 228 | 1.7 | 1.6 |
| Supervisors, sales workers ...................................... | 124 | 101 | . . . | . . . |
| Retail sales workers ................................................. | 78 | 82 | . . . | . . . |
| Office and administrative support  ............................... | 100 | 86 | 0.6 | 0.5 |
| Farming, fishing, and forestry ..................................... | 259 | 284 | 24.7 | 25.3 |
| Agricultural workers ................................................. | 148 | 180 | . . . | . . . |
| Fishing and hunting workers ..................................... | 22 | 25 | . . . | . . . |
| Forest, conservation, and logging workers .............. | 78 | 69 | . . . | . . . |
| Construction and extraction  ........................................ | 902 | 924 | 12.1 | 12.5 |
| Supervisors, construction and extraction workers ....... | 130 | 123 | 17.4 | 16.1 |
| Construction trades workers ........................................ | 625 | 694 | . . . | . . . |
| Extraction workers ...................................................... | 88 | 45 | . . . | . . . |
| Installation, maintenance, and repair .......................... | 406 | 392 | 8.1 | 7.6 |
| Vehicle and mobile equipment mechanics, installers, and repairers ... | 128 | 129 | . . . | . . . |
| Production .................................................................... | 212 | 250 | 2.5 | 3.0 |
| Transportation and material moving ............................. | 1 346 | 1 301 | 15.4 | 14.7 |
| Air transportation workers .......................................... | 84 | 57 | . . . | . . . |
| Motor vehicle operators .............................................. | 979 | 978 | . . . | . . . |
| Material moving ........................................................... | 224 | 206 | . . . | . . . |
| Military ......................................................................... | 56 | 73 | . . . | . . . |

*Note:* Data for all years are final. Totals for major categories may include subcategories not shown separately.

[1] Fatal injury rates are per 100,000 full-time equivalent workers (FTEs).
[2] The Census of Fatal Occupational Injuries (CFOI) has published data on fatal occupational injuries for the United States since 1992. During this time, the classification systems and definitions of many data elements have changed.
[3] CFOI has used several versions of the Standard Occupation Classification (SOC) system since 2003 to define occupation.
. . . = Not available.

## Table 14-12.  Fatal Occupational Injury Counts and Rates by State of Incident, 2014–2015

(Number, rate.)

| State | Counts | | Rates[1] | |
|---|---|---|---|---|
| | 2014 | 2015 | 2014 | 2015 |
| **Total** | 4 821 | 4 836 | 3.4 | 3.4 |
| Alabama | 75 | 70 | 4.0 | 3.7 |
| Alaska | 30 | 14 | 7.8 | 4.1 |
| Arizona | 88 | 69 | 3.1 | 2.4 |
| Arkansas | 67 | 74 | 5.7 | 5.8 |
| California | 344 | 388 | 2.0 | 2.2 |
| Colorado | 84 | 75 | 3.3 | 2.9 |
| Connecticut | 35 | 44 | 2.1 | 2.6 |
| Delaware | 12 | 8 | 2.8 | 1.9 |
| District of Columbia | 11 | 8 | 3.1 | 2.4 |
| Florida | 228 | 272 | 2.7 | 3.1 |
| Georgia | 152 | 180 | 3.6 | 4.3 |
| Hawaii | 31 | 18 | 5.0 | 2.6 |
| Idaho | 34 | 36 | 4.7 | 4.8 |
| Illinois | 164 | 172 | 2.9 | 2.9 |
| Indiana | 130 | 115 | 4.4 | 3.9 |
| Iowa | 91 | 60 | 6.0 | 3.9 |
| Kansas | 73 | 60 | 5.5 | 4.4 |
| Kentucky | 82 | 99 | 4.5 | 5.5 |
| Louisiana | 120 | 112 | 6.3 | 5.8 |
| Maine | 19 | 15 | 2.9 | 2.5 |
| Maryland | 74 | 69 | 2.6 | 2.4 |
| Massachusetts | 55 | 69 | 1.7 | 2.1 |
| Michigan | 143 | 134 | 3.3 | 3.1 |
| Minnesota | 62 | 74 | 2.3 | 2.7 |
| Mississippi | 75 | 77 | 7.1 | 6.8 |
| Missouri | 106 | 117 | 3.9 | 4.3 |
| Montana | 28 | 36 | 4.9 | 7.5 |
| Nebraska | 55 | 50 | 5.8 | 5.4 |
| Nevada | 40 | 44 | 3.1 | 3.5 |
| New Hampshire | 17 | 18 | 2.6 | 2.7 |
| New Jersey | 87 | 97 | 2.1 | 2.3 |
| New Mexico | 53 | 35 | 6.7 | 4.1 |
| New York (including NYC) | 241 | 236 | 2.8 | 2.7 |
| New York City | 79 | 74 | 2.2 | 2.0 |
| North Carolina | 137 | 150 | 3.1 | 3.4 |
| North Dakota | 38 | 47 | 9.8 | 12.5 |
| Ohio | 185 | 202 | 3.6 | 3.9 |
| Oklahoma | 98 | 91 | 6.2 | 5.5 |
| Oregon | 69 | 44 | 3.9 | 2.6 |
| Pennsylvania | 179 | 173 | 3.1 | 3.0 |
| Rhode Island | 10 | 6 | 2.1 | 1.2 |
| South Carolina | 64 | 117 | 3.3 | 5.6 |
| South Dakota | 29 | 21 | 7.2 | 4.9 |
| Tennessee | 127 | 112 | 4.8 | 3.7 |
| Texas | 531 | 527 | 4.5 | 4.5 |
| Utah | 54 | 42 | 4.2 | 3.2 |
| Vermont | 10 | 9 | 3.2 | 2.9 |
| Virginia | 116 | 106 | 2.8 | 2.8 |
| Washington | 88 | 70 | 2.7 | 2.1 |
| West Virginia | 38 | 35 | 5.2 | 5.0 |
| Wisconsin | 99 | 104 | 3.5 | 3.6 |
| Wyoming | 37 | 34 | 13.1 | 12.0 |

[1]Fatal injury rates are per 100,000 full-time equivalent workers (FTEs).

# INDEX